THE STATESMAN'S YEAR-BOOK
1988–1989

Man hat behauptet, die Welt werde durch Zahlen regiert:
das aber weiss ich, dass die Zahlen uns belehren, ob sie gut
oder schlecht regiert werde. GOETHE

Editors

THE
STATESMAN'S
YEAR-BOOK

STATISTICAL AND HISTORICAL ANNUAL
OF THE STATES OF THE WORLD
FOR THE YEAR

1988–1989

EDITED BY

JOHN PAXTON

ST. MARTIN'S PRESS
NEW YORK

First published in 1864
125th edition 1988

For information, write:
ST. MARTIN'S PRESS, INC.
175 Fifth Ave., New York, N.Y.10010

Typeset in Great Britain by
MB GRAPHIC (TYPESETTING) SERVICES
Dunstable, Bedfordshire

Printed in Great Britain by
RICHARD CLAY (THE CHAUCER PRESS) LTD
Bungay, Suffolk

Library of Congress Catalog Card No. 4–3776

ISBN 0–312–02094–5

This edition published in the United States of America in 1988

PREFACE

THE STATESMAN'S YEAR-BOOK made its first appearance in the year when, in America, Lincoln was elected President of the Union for the second time, when Jefferson Davis was President of the Confederate States and Archduke Maximilian was precariously perched on the Mexican throne. In Britain Palmerston was presiding over his second ministry and income tax was ninepence in the pound. Now in its 125th year this essential book of reference is still unrivalled.

The continuity of THE STATESMAN'S YEAR-BOOK over this long period is in the first place guaranteed by the continuity of its publishing house. Alexander Macmillan, who, together with brother David, founded Macmillans in 1843, was still alive and took the liveliest interest in the new venture, and 125 years later the fifth generation of the Macmillan family is at the head of the firm. There are other aspects of continuity including that THE STATESMAN'S YEAR-BOOK has had the same printers for most of its life and there have only been five editors over this long period.

The history of THE STATESMAN'S YEAR-BOOK shows fascinating evidence of the development from a comparatively modest handbook of 685 pages, catering mainly for a British public, not altogether devoid of insular prejudices, into a world-wide book of reference of over 1600 closely packed pages.

The authenticity and reliability of the facts and figures published in THE STATESMAN'S YEAR-BOOK is guaranteed by the contributors. These contributors are, with few exceptions, all government departments of the world's states. The central and provincial statistical offices, the political and administrative departments of state, the secretariats of international and national corporations and institutions, the diplomatic representatives and executive authorities which determine and administer the policies of the world today contribute their share in making THE STATESMAN'S YEAR-BOOK a book of reference unique in its comprehensiveness as well as its trustworthiness. The editor would once again like to thank all these faithful correspondents.

To celebrate this anniversary THE STATESMAN'S YEAR-BOOK HISTORICAL COMPANION is being published. These 125 years have seen global wars, the end of empires, great constitutional and political change. From 1864 these changes have been recorded in THE STATESMAN'S YEAR-BOOK. However, because of lack of space not all this information is retained in the annual volumes and as a celebration it was decided to bring much of this historical data back into one volume.

The editor would also like to remind readers that THE STATESMAN'S YEAR-BOOK WORLD GAZETTEER, now in its third edition, is also available.

J.P.

THE STATESMAN'S YEAR-BOOK OFFICE,
THE MACMILLAN PRESS LTD,
LITTLE ESSEX STREET,
LONDON, WC2R 3LF

WEIGHTS AND MEASURES

On 1 Jan. 1960 following an agreement between the standards laboratories of Great Britain, Canada, Australia, New Zealand, South Africa and the USA, an international yard and an international pound (avoirdupois) came into existence. 1 yard = 91·44 centimetres; 1 lb. = 453·59237 grammes.

The abbreviation 'm' signifies 'million(s)' and tonnes implies metric tons.

LENGTH		DRY MEASURE	
Centimetre	0·394 inch	Litre	0·91 quart
Metre	1·094 yards	Hectolitre	2·75 bushels
Kilometre	0·621 mile		
		WEIGHT—AVOIRDUPOIS	
LIQUID MEASURE		Gramme	15·42 grains
Litre	1·75 pints	Kilogramme	2·205 pounds
Hectolitre	22 gallons	Quintal (= 100 kg)	220·46 pounds
		Tonne (= 1,000 kg)	{ 0·984 long ton / 1·102 short tons
SURFACE MEASURE		**WEIGHT—TROY**	
Square metre	10·76 sq. feet	Gramme	15·43 grains
Hectare	2·47 acres	Kilogramme	{ 32·15 ounces / 2·68 pounds
Square kilometre	0·386 sq. mile		

BRITISH WEIGHTS AND MEASURES

LENGTH		WEIGHT	
1 foot	0·305 metre	1 ounce (= 437·2 grains)	28·350 grammes
1 yard	0·914 metre	1 lb. (= 7,000 grains)	453·6 grammes
1 mile (= 1,760 yds)	1·609 kilometres	1 cwt. (= 112 lb.)	50·802 kilogrammes
		1 long ton (= 2,240 lb.)	1·016 tonnes
		1 short ton (= 2,000 lb.)	0·907 tonne
SURFACE MEASURE		**LIQUID MEASURE**	
1 sq. foot	9·290 sq. decimetres		
1 sq. yard	0·836 sq. metre	1 pint	0·568 litre
1 acre	0·405 hectare	1 gallon	4·546 litres
1 sq. mile	2·590 sq. kilometres	1 quarter	2·909 hectolitres

CONVERSION OF UNITS

To convert from	To	Multiply by
acre	hectare	0·4047
barrel (oil)	cu. metre	0·159
bushel (imperial)	litre	36·37
bushel (US)	litre	35·24
carat	gramme	0·2
cu. foot	cu. metre	0·028 317
cu. metre	cu. foot	35·315
foot	metre	0·3048
gigawatt-hour	kilowatt-hour	1,000,000
hectare	acre	2·471
hundredweight (long)	kilogramme	50·802
hundredweight (short)	kilogramme	45·359
inch	millimetre	25·4
kilogramme	pound	2·2046
kilometre	mile (statute)	0·621 37
megawatt	kilowatt	1,000
metre	foot	3·2808
mile (nautical)	kilometre	1·852
mile (statute)	kilometre	1·6093
millimetre	inch	0·03937
ounce (troy)	gramme	31·103
pound	kilogramme	0·453 59
register ton	cu. metre	2·832
sq. kilometre	sq. mile	0·3861
sq. mile	sq. kilometre	2·590
per sq. mile	per sq. kilometre	0·3861
ton (long)	tonne (metric)	1·016
ton (short)	tonne (metric)	0·9072

CONTENTS

Part I: International Organizations

Part II: Countries of the World A–Z

WHEAT

Countries	Area (1,000 hectares)					Production (1,000 tonnes)				
	Average 1979-81	1980	1984	1985	1986	Average 1979-81	1980	1984	1985	1986
Afghánistán	2,220	2,192	2,321	2,313	2,100	2,754	2,750	2,850	2,750	2,500
Algeria	1,943	2,071	1,657	1,668	1,550	1,270	1,511	1,200	1,478	1,445
Argentina	5,245	5,023	5,900	5,382	4,900	8,060	7,780	13,220	8,700	8,900
Australia[1]	11,440	11,283	12,078	11,727	11,170	14,468	10,856	18,666	16,127	17,356
Bulgaria[1,2]	986	968	1,126	1,067	1,000	3,881	3,847	4,836	3,068	4,000*
Canada	11,386	11,098	13,158	13,729	14,217	20,430	19,292	21,199	24,252	31,850
Chile[1]	513	546	471	506	569	882	966	988	1,165	1,626
China[1]	28,930	29,231	29,577	29,219	29,617	59,196	55,213	87,817	85,812	89,002
Czechoslovakia[2]	1,121	1,189	1,201	1,209	1,205	4,482	5,386	6,170	6,023	5,305
Egypt[1]	577	557	495	498	507	1,844	1,796	1,815	1,872	1,929
France	4,473	4,582	5,105	4,805	4,877	22,362	23,683	32,977	28,890	26,587
Germany, Fed. Rep. of[2]	1,642	1,668	1,634	1,624	1,648	8,177	8,156	10,223	9,866	10,406
Greece	1,022	1,012	874	875	880	2,770	2,970	2,308	1,789	2,200
Hungary[1,3]	1,187	1,276	1,361	1,358	1,318	4,800	6,077	7,392	6,578	5,803
India	22,364	22,172	24,672	23,565	23,074	34,550	31,830*	45,476	44,069	46,885
Iran	5,894	5,500*	5,800	6,209	6,458	6,100	5,700*	5,500	6,661	7,128
Iraq	1,215	1,500*	493	1,540	1,100	854	1,300	471	1,406	1,100*
Italy	3,373	3,408	3,274	3,032	3,133	8,989	9,156	10,057	8,516	9,070
Japan[1]	188	191	232	234	246	571	583	741	874	876
Mexico	723	739	1,033	1,224	1,206	2,754	2,785	4,505	5,207	4,772
Morocco	1,673	1,715	1,856	1,894	2,223	1,500	1,811	1,989	2,358	3,809
Pakistan[1]	6,865	6,912	7,343	7,259	7,403	10,760	10,805	10,882	11,703	13,923
Poland[1]	1,525	1,609	1,706	1,885	2,025*	4,189	4,175	6,010	6,461	7,390*
Romania[1]	2,154	2,244	2,360	2,366	2,450	5,471	6,427	7,580	5,666	7,900*
S. Africa, Republic of	1,770	1,620*	1,919	1,913	1,925*	1,965	1,470	2,332	1,680	2,034
Spain[2]	2,628	2,699	2,306	2,043	2,096	4,510	6,040	6,052	5,329	4,292
Turkey[2]	9,265	8,915	9,026	9,275	10,000	17,058	16,554	17,235	17,032	19,000
USSR[1]	59,463	61,475	51,061	50,265	48,803	89,859	98,182	68,600	78,100	92,300
UK	1,434	1,441	1,939	1,902	1,999	8,116	8,470	14,970	12,046	13,874
USA	28,898	28,727	27,085	26,197	24,560	66,229	64,619	70,618	65,999	56,792
Yugoslavia[2]	1,475	1,516	1,458	1,348	1,346	4,624	5,091	5,595	4,859	4,776
World total	235,226	236,873	231,600	230,719	228,945	443,516	446,107	516,457	506,034	535,842

* Unofficial figures.   [1] Sown area.   [2] Includes spelt.   [3] Field crops and other crops.

RYE

Countries	Area (1,000 hectares)					Production (1,000 tonnes)				
	Average 1979–81	1980	1984	1985	1986	Average 1979–81	1980	1984	1985	1986
Argentina	199	210	157	115	90	169	155	140	105	94
Austria	105	109	94	88	83*	327	383	381	339	284
Belgium	12	11	8	6	8*	43	42	38	25	36*
Bulgaria¹	21	20	26	32	25*	29	28	37	49	35*
Canada	364	310	370	372	341	638	455	664	598	670
China	733	700	700	600	650	1,167	1,000	1,400	1,000	1,000
Czechoslovakia²	171	177	192	179	155	534	570	710	620	547
Denmark	59	56	122	126	121	221	199	608	565	546
Finland	44	53	44	31	27	88	124	92	72	71
France	121	130	102	87	80	368	408	349	297	226
German Demo. Rep.	671	678	718	690	680	1,848	1,917	2,510	2,505	2,403
Germany, Fed. Rep. of	532	547	439	438	425	1,980	2,098	1,931	1,877	1,818
Hungary¹,³	72	73	75	85	89	117	141	193	166	171
Netherlands	10	10	6	5	4	39	39	25	19	19
Poland¹	2,970	3,039	3,545	3,083	2,830*	6,166	6,566	9,540	7,600	7,179*
Portugal	166	206	130	123	118	128	138	103	97	93
Romania¹	33	35*	30	30*	30	38	40*	47*	45*	47
Spain	219	217	231	214	223	239	284	315	295	230
Sweden	58	67	62	45	36*	197	223	246	157	159
Turkey	441	443	250	240	235*	558	525	360	360	350
USSR¹	7,557	8,645	9,420	9,520	8,751	9,309	10,205	14,000	15,700	15,000
USA	295	273	397	290	274	474	419	825	524	495
Yugoslavia	56	55	47	45	42	78	79	81	77	74
World total	15,078	16,223	17,324	16,629	15,492	24,978	26,257	34,825	33,354	31,791

* Unofficial figures. ¹ Sown area. ² Includes mixture of wheat and rye. ³ Field crops and other crops.

BARLEY

Countries	Area (1,000 hectares)					Production (1,000 tonnes)				
	Average 1979–81	1980	1984	1985	1986	Average 1979–81	1980	1984	1985	1986
Australia [1]	2,539	2,452	3,518	3,301	2,277	3,278	2,682	5,554	4,913	3,530
Austria	370	374	329	334	333	1,288	1,514	1,517	1,521	1,292
Belgium	173	171	152	131	142*	844	865	935	723	679*
Bulgaria [1]	425	426	315	260	300*	1,439	1,375	1,279	800	1,050*
Canada	4,631	4,634	4,566	4,773	4,952	11,199	11,394	10,296	12,443	15,026
China	1,295	1,239	1,201	1,021	1,101	3,133	2,700	3,300	2,701	2,701
Czechoslovakia	972	911	777	789	821	3,524	3,575	3,672	3,538	3,530
Denmark	1,580	1,577	1,181	1,094	1,088	6,250	6,044	6,072	5,251	5,134
Finland	579	533	562	646	589	1,421	1,534	1,715	1,854	1,714
France	2,670	2,581	2,107	2,255	2,091	10,997	11,423	11,543	11,440	10,063
German Demo. Rep.	959	969	866	882	896	3,592	3,979	4,138	4,366	4,295
Germany, Fed. Rep. of	2,011	2,002	2,060	1,949	1,947	8,566	8,826	10,284	9,690	9,377
Greece	344	331	364	310	290	838	950	890	606	750
Hungary	265	246	269	279	253	848	929	1,220	1,046	854
India	1,802	1,771	1,386	1,253	1,379	2,020	1,624	1,834	1,556	1,952
Iran	1,394	1,300	1,400	1,800	2,200	1,409	1,100	1,500	2,000	2,500
Ireland	349	332	304	298	283	1,603	1,247	1,770	1,494	1,330*
Italy	324	329	434	468	466	914	947	1,618	1,630	1,548
Japan [1]	120	122	117	113	107	392	385	396	378	344
Korea, South [1]	386	331	338	237	190*	1,059	811	804	571	453*
Morocco	2,190	2,150	2,126	2,383	2,472	1,712	2,210	1,405	2,541	3,563
Poland [1]	1,362	1,322	1,054	1,242	1,335*	3,563	3,420	3,555	4,086	4,639*
Romania [1]	833	809	672	680	685	2,360	2,466	2,448	1,850	2,200*
Spain	3,520	3,575	4,023	4,246	4,334	6,571	8,705	10,789	10,698	7,331
Sweden	678	648	643	670	672*	2,323	2,172	2,733	2,309	2,292*
Syria	1,220	1,210	1,289	1,386	1,548	1,129	1,587	304	740	1,116
Turkey	2,855	2,800	3,250	3,350	3,500	5,480	5,300	6,500	6,500	7,000
USSR [1]	33,456	31,583	30,426	29,058	30,052	42,502	43,450	41,800	46,500	51,400
UK	2,333	2,330	1,979	1,966	1,922	10,058	10,320	11,064	9,740	10,012
USA	3,214	2,944	4,545	4,696	4,859	8,838	7,859	13,046	12,876	13,292
World total	81,125	78,242	78,039	78,967	79,645	156,878	159,319	171,828	176,435	180,441

* Unofficial figures. [1] Sown area. [2] Field crops and other crops.

OATS

Countries	Area (1,000 hectares)					Production (1,000 tonnes)				
	Average 1979–81	1980	1984	1985	1986	Average 1979–81	1980	1984	1985	1986
Argentina	353	350	384	333	400*	431	433	610	400	560*
Australia	1,201	1,093	1,041	1,056	1,255	1,386	1,128	1,367	1,339	1,580
Austria	93	92	77	75	73	298	316	292	284	270
Belgium	39	38	27	29*	21*	152	136	118	123*	84*
Canada	1,501	1,515	1,406	1,411	1,555	2,993	2,911	2,670	2,997	3,906
Chile	84	92	96	85	64	151	173	163	170	124
China	400	400	300	300	300	600	500	500	490	500
Czechoslovakia [2]	132	121	129	121	115	418	421	479	473	419
Denmark	40	40	34	42	25	166	159	158	168	111
Finland	444	448	419	411	403	1,183	1,258	1,321	1,218	1,175
France	525	534	444	433	315	1,850	1,927	1,875	1,770	1,096
German Demo. Rep.	154	155	161	178	163	571	582	700	746	666
Germany, Fed.Rep.of	700	691	555	692	605	2,777	2,658	2,507	3,278	2,687
Ireland	25	26	25	23	21	95	90	141	106	90
Italy	223	226	190	184	184	433	450	141	387	397
Netherlands	20	18	12	11	6	106	94	58	58	40
Norway	108	112	123	127	131*	424	428	601	518	450*
Poland [1]	1,082	997	934	995	938*	2,387	2,245	2,604	2,682	2,300*
Spain	453	458	479	459	384	527	680	788	680	422
Sweden	461	452	428	445	433	1,635	1,567	1,904	1,668	1,478
Turkey	199	197	172	167	185	350	355	316	314	350
USSR [1]	12,160	11,770	12,806	12,664	13,393	14,372	15,544	19,200	20,500	21,400
UK	142	148	106	134	95	587	600	517	614	470
USA	3,743	3,501	3,304	3,309	2,780	7,234	6,652	6,875	7,559	5,582
Yugoslavia	199	194	153	151	152	296	294	256	252	260
World total	25,691	24,853	25,399	25,366	25,563	42,563	42,760	47,887	50,148	47,769

* Unofficial figures. [1] Sown area. [2] Includes spelt. [3] Field crops and other crops.

MAIZE

Countries	Area (1,000 hectares)					Production (1,000 tonnes)				
	Average 1979–81	1980	1984	1985	1986	Average 1979–81	1980	1984	1985	1986
Argentina	2,895	2,490	3,014	3,190	3,351	9,333	6,400	9,500	11,530	12,400
Austria	190	193	207	208	217	1,338	1,293	1,542	1,727	1,740
Brazil	11,430	11,451	12,018	11,802	12,465	19,265	20,372	21,164	22,020	20,510
Bulgaria	605	585	542	435	550*	2,626	2,256	2,994	1,350	2,750*
Canada	1,038	958	1,192	1,197	1,087	5,901	5,753	7,024	7,472	6,694
China	19,986	20,385	18,589	17,756	19,219	60,720	62,715	73,600	64,056	65,560
Egypt	800	800	830	900	761*	3,159	3,231	3,170	3,982*	3,801*
France	1,774	1,757	1,743	1,887	1,855	9,641	9,358	10,493	12,409	10,792
Greece	157	172	230	221	230	1,165	1,279	2,091	1,948	2,070
Hungary	1,270	1,253	1,133	1,082	1,149	7,022	6,673	6,686	6,818	7,214
India	5,887	6,005	5,800	5,879	5,900	6,486	6,957	8,442	6,890	8,000
Indonesia	2,761	2,735	3,086	2,440	3,047	4,035	3,991	5,288	4,330	5,767
Italy	956	942	961	917	866	6,590	6,377	6,672	6,309	6,560
Kenya	1,273	939	985	1,400	1,398	1,714	1,620	1,440	2,520	2,650
Malawi	1,120	1,100	1,156	1,210	1,192*	1,268	1,165	1,398	1,355	1,374
Mexico	6,836	6,955	6,972	7,498	6,818	11,866	12,383	12,910	13,957	12,154
Nigeria	443	1,710	562	562	800	591	1,550	1,058	1,196	1,800
Philippines	3,267	3,319	3,315	3,545	3,629*	3,174	3,176	3,439	3,922	4,155*
Portugal	333	377	271	261	272	486	489	521	570	607
Romania	3,309	3,288	3,090	3,090	4,250	11,823	11,153	13,274	15,238	20,000*
S. Africa, Republic of	4,900	6,000	3,953	3,887	4,150*	11,207	10,790	4,393	7,658	8,077
Spain	450	455	440	526	519	2,227	2,314	2,529	3,414	3,451
Tanzania	1,350	1,300	1,750	1,718*	1,905*	1,642	750	1,939	2,093*	2,210*
Thailand	1,408	1,335	1,660	1,861	1,789	3,103	2,998	4,226	4,934	4,197
Turkey	583	583	550	567	695	1,263	1,240	1,500	1,900	2,300
USSR [1]	3,063	2,977	3,919	4,482	5,169	9,076	9,454	13,600	14,400	12,500
USA	29,661	29,555	29,103	30,442	28,800	192,084	168,787	194,928	225,478	209,632
Yugoslavia	2,250	2,202	2,331	2,401	2,376	9,736	9,317	11,312	9,896	12,502
Zimbabwe	1,097	1,146	1,356	1,428	1,350	1,829	1,539	1,283	2,960	2,546*
World total	126,059	128,014	126,808	128,958	131,475	421,750	395,949	452,753	488,325	480,609

* Unofficial figures.   [1] For dry grain only.

RICE (Paddy)

Countries	Area (1,000 hectares)					Production (1,000 tonnes)				
	Average 1979–81	1980	1984	1985	1986	Average 1979–81	1980	1984	1985	1986
Bangladesh	10,310	10,309	10,223	10,368	10,320	20,125	20,821	21,930	23,012	24,247
Brazil	5,932	6,243	5,351	4,760	5,590	8,533	9,776	9,027	9,019	10,399
Burma	4,684	4,801	4,601	4,830	4,800	12,637	13,100	14,255	15,219	15,000
Cambodia	1,186	1,356*	1,700	1,750	1,700	1,160	1,470*	1,970	2,100	2,000
China	34,323	34,517	33,765	32,634	32,948	145,665	142,993	181,193	171,417	177,000
Colombia	424	416	364	386	333	1,843	1,798	1,696	1,798	1,632
Egypt	416	408	414	308	412*	2,376	2,384	2,236	2,310	2,450*
India	40,091	40,152	41,159	40,912	41,000	74,557	80,312	87,553	96,306	90,000
Indonesia	9,063	9,005	9,764	9,902	9,871	29,570	29,652	38,136	39,033	39,275
Iran	444	300	485	447	453	1,359	1,212	1,600	1,523	1,569
Italy	176	176	180	186	188	989	968	1,009	1,123	1,082
Japan	2,384	2,377	2,315	2,342	2,303	13,320	12,189	14,848	14,578	14,559
Korea, North	793	800	830	840	880	4,970	4,960	5,570	5,800	6,000
Korea, South	1,230	1,233	1,231	1,237	1,236	6,780	5,311	7,790	7,855	7,790
Madagascar	1,182	1,178	1,198	1,181	1,168*	2,055	2,109	2,131	2,178	2,138*
Malaysia	658	718	620	656	645	2,053	2,070	1,572	1,953	1,860*
Mexico	153	132	153	279	151	528	456	484	809	523
Nepal	1,275	1,270	1,377	1,391	1,200	2,361	2,464	2,709	2,804	2,350
Nigeria	517	550*	670*	700*	700*	1,027	1,090*	1,300*	1,430*	1,416
Pakistan	1,981	1,935	1,999	1,848	2,041	4,884	4,679	4,973	4,437	5,241
Philippines	3,513	3,637	3,222	3,403	3,471	7,893	7,836	8,200	9,097	9,350
Sri Lanka	819	824	888	867	837	2,093	2,137	2,414	2,661	2,594
Thailand	8,953	9,099	9,630	9,833	9,970	16,967	17,368	19,905	20,264	19,100
USSR	637	666	688	671	617	2,558	2,791	2,720	2,570	2,600
USA	1,345	1,340	1,134	1,009	963	6,968	6,629	6,296	6,120	6,097
Vietnam	5,558	5,544	5,675	5,704	5,668	11,663	11,679	15,506	15,875	16,197
World total	143,767	144,529	145,697	144,468	145,358	396,388	399,112	470,284	474,728	475,533

* Unofficial figures.

MILLET

Countries	Area (1,000 hectares)					Production (1,000 tonnes)				
	Average 1979–81	1980	1984	1985	1986	Average 1979–81	1980	1984	1985	1986
Argentina	203	182	114	123	200	245	188	136	140	240
Australia	26	19	37	30	30	26	14	43	26	30*
Burkina Faso	803	800	723	974	1,054	390	330	372	587	687
Cameroon	503	450	373	500	500	402	400	207	443	400
Chad	790	1,150*	688	950*	1,078*	409	600	254	526*	624*
China	3,981	3,874	3,798	3,320	2,964	5,790	5,448	7,026	5,983	6,102
Egypt	172	172	153	142	168	641	635	561	547*	600
Ethiopia	226	233	235	230	230	203	205	190	200	200
Ghana	182	240*	220*	135*	200*	117	66	106	80	130*
India	17,845	18,158	16,220	16,212	16,250*	9,189	9,337	9,771	7,503	8,500
Kenya	80	81	29	56	60	84	130	10	60	65
Korea, North	418	420	425	435	437	447	450	500	535	545
Korea, South	3	3	2	4	2	4	4	2	5	3
Mali	1,077	1,400	1,297	1,400	1,500	801	750	876	1,100*	1,264*
Nepal	122	120	134	151	140	121	122	124	138	138
Niger	3,011	3,072	3,030	3,160	3,239	1,311	1,364	771	1,435	1,383
Nigeria	2,882	5,030*	4,000	4,000	4,000	2,732	3,130*	3,200*	3,600*	3,780*
Pakistan	509	406	606	561	455	255	215	284	258	263
Senegal	1,062	1,115	1,003	1,336	1,211*	603	540	471	950	703*
Sudan	1,094	1,300	1,313	1,725	1,485	458	450	158	428	544
Tanzania	450	220	330	341*	332*	355	160	267	300*	273*
Togo	121	170	59	66	70	44	128	76	74	70
Uganda	297	279	332	312	350	473	459	223	210	350
USSR	2,794	2,907	2,640	2,808	2,474	1,759	1,873	1,890	2,890	2,800
Zimbabwe [1]	353	380	250	250	250	153	180	120	224*	141*
World total	40,090	43,261	39,048	40,287	39,941	27,754	27,887	28,389	29,111	30,800

* Unofficial figures. [1] On farms and estates.

SORGHUM

Countries	Area (1,000 hectares)					Production (1,000 tonnes)				
	Average 1979–81	1980	1984	1985	1986	Average 1979–81	1980	1984	1985	1986
Argentina	1,866	1,279	2,392	1,965	1,400	5,641	2,960	6,930	6,200	4,200
Australia	548	519	730	723	724	1,084	922	1,885	1,369	1,285
Burkina Faso	1,051	850	965	1,077	1,210	620	559	594	798	1,012
China	2,828	2,696	2,458	1,951	1,877	7,034	6,785	7,747	5,680	6,538
Colombia	220	206	238	192	227	488	431	590	499	600
Ethiopia [1,2]	1,048	1,014	900	900	910	1,419	1,642	515	1,000	1,100
France	75	74	58	44	48	332	321	262	206	187
India	16,361	15,809	15,939	15,789	16,000*	11,380	10,431	11,402	10,123	10,500
Mexico	1,491	1,579	1,622	1,836	1,619	4,991	4,812	5,009	6,550	6,000
Niger	822	768	1,098	1,140	1,109	347	368	236	328	360
Nigeria	3,047	6,000*	4,500	4,600	4,600	3,545	3,800*	4,608	4,991	5,000
S. Africa, Republic of	377	450	283	315	300	539	695	477	604	450*
Sudan	3,163	3,000	3,355	5,408	4,896	2,361	2,200	1,097	3,542	3,605
Thailand	220	234	266	274	278	237	237	374	404	394
Uganda	175	167	206	186	200	312	299	164	148	300
USA	5,273	5,068	6,214	6,792	5,627	19,157	14,712	22,004	28,456	23,919
Venezuela	227	265	239	250	338*	365	403	472	481	660*
Yemen Arab Republic	684	791	687	690	690	631	692	276	281	391
World total	44,044	44,905	46,460	48,797	46,807	64,515	55,703	68,842	76,302	71,445

* Unofficial figures. [1] Includes teff. [2] Unspecified millet and sorghum.

CENTRIFUGAL RAW SUGAR
(in 1,000 tonnes)

Countries	Average 1979–81	1981	1982	1983	1984	1985	1986
Argentina	1,584	1,624	1,623*	1,625	1,545	1,174	1,145*
Australia [1]	3,243	3,435	3,500	3,171	3,548	3,350	3,350
Barbados [2]	113	94	89	85	100	100	113*
Brazil	7,991	8,393*	9,314*	9,576*	9,332*	8,274*	8,500*
Canada	118	140*	122*	132	113	54	112
China	3,809	4,191	4,649	4,910	5,352*	6,241	5,960*
Colombia	1,192	1,225*	1,318*	1,379	1,178	1,429	1,277*
Cuba	7,510	7,926	8,279	7,460	8,331*	8,101*	7,347*
Czechoslovakia	808	747*	885	792	844*	939*	862
Dominican Rep.	1,142	1,108	1,255	1,219	1,156	905	830*
Egypt	666	677*	754	782*	780	902*	959*
France	4,720	5,576	4,800	3,875	4,305	4,324	3,728*
Fiji [1]	446	470	487	276	480	341	502*
German Demo. Rep.	675	747*	876*	692*	778*	805*	730*
Germany, Fed. Rep.of	3,261	3,702	3,586	2,725	3,151	3,441	3,478
Guyana	294	306	288	248	238	265	249
India [3]	5,380	5,596	9,190	8,948	6,430	6,650	7,600
Indonesia [4]	1,286	1,247	1,629	1,643	1,500	1,767	1,860*
Italy	1,956	2,207	1,290	1,352	1,385*	1,352*	1,870
Jamaica	238	205*	202	198	193	206	204*
Mauritius [4]	615	609	729	640	610	684	748*
Mexico	2,796	2,586*	2,873*	3,108*	3,297*	3,489*	3,949*
Pakistan [3]	734	925	1,414	1,246	1,258	1,430	1,210
Peru	571	493*	614	455*	620*	757*	620*
Philippines	2,289	2,394	2,527	2,540	2,335	1,718	1,500
Poland	1,530	1,872	2,011	2,140	1,878	1,857	1,886*
Puerto Rico	156	137	102	90	87	98	87*
S. Africa, Rep. of	2,011	2,218	2,304	1,495	2,560	2,280	2,050*
Spain	934	1,111	1,242	1,356	1,166	976	1,071*
Sweden	350	374	389	298	392	347*	386*
Thailand	1,534	1,641	2,930	2,268*	2,350*	2,572	2,586
Trinidad	117	94	79	77	70	81	95*
Turkey	1,178	1,521*	1,860*	1,770*	1,655*	1,398*	1,413*
USSR	7,017	6,200*	7,400	8,760*	8,685*	8,260*	8,350*
UK	1,215	1,187	1,544	1,185	1,400	1,317*	1,413*
USA [5]	5,342	5,644	5,262	5,107	5,363	5,473	5,881
World total	88,609	92,778	102,422	97,929	99,976	99,052	100,090

[1] 94° net titre.
[2] Includes the sugar equivalent of fancy molasses.
[3] Includes sugar (raw value) refined from gur.
[4] Tel quel.
[5] Includes Hawaii.
* Unofficial figures.

WORLD ESTIMATED CRUDE OIL PRODUCTION [1]
(in 1,000 tonnes)

	1960	1970	1986	1987
North America				
USA	384,080	533,677	477,254	460,500
Canada	27,480	69,954	84,161	87,500
Caribbean Area				
Venezuela	148,690	193,209	91,260	90,200
Trinidad	6,075	7,225	8,676	8,300
Colombia	8,100	11,071	15,607	19,000
Cuba	—	—	939	1,000
Other Latin America				
Mexico	14,125	21,877	137,500	143,500
Argentina	9,160	19,969	21,977	21,250
Brazil	390	8,009	28,880	28,625
Ecuador	2,680	191	13,964	8,500
Peru	450	3,450	8,758	8,000
Bolivia	990	1,128	816	800
Chile		1,620	1,565	1,400
Middle East				
Saudi Arabia	61,090	176,851	251,305	209,500
Iran	52,065	191,663	93,370	112,500
Iraq	47,480	76,600	82,665	101,200
Kuwait	81,860	137,397	71,615	61,000
Abu Dhabi	—	33,288	45,885	51,100
Qatar	8,210	17,257	16,050	15,000
Syria	—	4,350	9,660	12,000
Turkey	350	3,461	2,392	2,300
Bahrain	2,250	3,834	2,075	2,000
Sharjah	—	—	3,125	3,100
Oman	—	—	27,540	28,250
Dubai	—	—	16,820	18,200
Africa				
Nigeria	880	53,420	72,805	64,000
Libya	—	159,201	49,725	46,500
Egypt	—	—	40,900	45,000
Algeria	8,630	47,253	27,918	29,500
Gabon	850	5,460	8,295	7,900
Angola	70	5,066	14,100	16,500
Tunisia	—	4,151	5,195	5,000
Congo	—	—	5,606	5,300
Zaïre	—	—	1,061	1,400
Côte d'Ivoire	—	—	1,350	1,200

[1] Excluding small scale production in Afghánistán, Bangladesh and Mongolia; including other small producers not specified here.

WORLD ESTIMATED CRUDE OIL PRODUCTION
(contd.)

(in 1,000 tonnes)

	1960	1970	1986	1987
Western Europe				
UK	90	84	126,987	122,000
Norway	—	—	44,609	50,000
Germany, Fed. Rep. of	5,560	7,536	4,030	3,800
Austria	2,440	2,798	1,116	1,000
Spain	—	156	1,858	1,600
Netherlands	1,920	1,919	4,981	4,600
France	2,260	2,308	2,950	3,300
Italy	1,990	1,408	2,548	3,300
Denmark	—	—	3,622	4,500
Far East				
Indonesia	20,560	42,102	65,956	64,100
Australia	—	8,292	24,185	27,000
Brunei	4,690	6,916	7,393	7,750
India	440	6,809	31,146	30,500
Malaysia	—	—	24,350	23,500
Burma	530	750	850	750
Japan	510	750	631	600
Pakistan	360	486	2,010	2,400
Thailand	—	—	1,425	1,800
New Zealand	—	—	1,180	1,225
USSR and Eastern Europe				
USSR	148,000	352,667	615,000	625,000
Romania	11,500	13,377	10,740	10,500
Yugoslavia	1,040	2,854	4,131	4,150
Albania	600	1,199	3,000	3,000
Hungary	1,215	1,937	1,997	2,000
Poland	195	424	192	190
German Dem. Rep.	—	60	60	60
Bulgaria	200	334	280	280
Czechoslovakia	140	203	139	150
China	5,000	20,000	130,650	133,000
World total	1,090,080	2,336,153	2,150,698	2,907,315

PERCENTAGE CHANGES IN CONSUMER PRICES

	1982	1983	1984	1985	1986	1987
Australia	11·1	10·1	3·9	6·8	9·1	8·5
Austria	5·4	3·3	5·6	3·2	1·7	1·4
Belgium	8·7	7·7	6·3	4·9	1·3	1·6
Canada	10·8	5·9	4·3	4·0	4·2	4·4
Denmark	10·1	6·9	6·3	4·7	3·6	4·0
Finland	9·6	8·3	7·1	5·9	3·6	3·7
France	11·8	9·6	7·4	5·8	2·7	3·1
Germany, Fed. Rep. of	5·3	3·3	2·4	2·2	−0·2	0·2
Greece	21·0	20·2	18·5	19·3	23·0	16·4
Iceland	49·1	86·5	30·9	31·9	22·2	...
Ireland	17·1	10·5	8·6	5·4	3·8	3·2
Italy	16·6	14·6	10·8	8·6	6·1	4·6
Japan	2·7	1·9	2·2	2·1	0·4	−0·2
Luxembourg	9·4	8·7	5·6	4·1	0·3	−0·1
Netherlands	6·0	2·8	3·3	2·3	0·2	−0·5
New Zealand	7·8	7·4	6·2	15·4	13·2	15·7
Norway	11·3	8·4	6·2	5·7	7·2	8·7
Portugal	22·4	25·5	29·3	19·3	11·7	...
Spain	14·4	12·2	11·3	8·8	8·8	5·3
Sweden	8·6	8·9	8·0	7·4	4·3	4·2
Switzerland	5·6	3·0	3·0	3·4	0·7	1·5
Turkey	32·7	28·8	45·6	45·0	34·6	38·9
UK	8·6	4·6	5·0	6·1	3·4	4·2
USA	6·1	3·2	4·3	3·6	1·9	3·7

The increase in overall consumer price inflation in OECD countries in 1987 was significant only in the USA and UK. In Japan, Italy and most of the smaller countries there were continued declines in the annual inflation rate. Inflation was below 2% in Japan, the Federal Republic of Germany, Austria, Belgium, Luxembourg, the Netherlands and Switzerland.

Source: OECD

TERRITORIAL SEA LIMITS (IN MILES)

State	Territorial Sea	Jurisdiction over fisheries (measured from the baseline of the territorial sea)
Albania	15 (1976)	—
Algeria	12 (1963)	—
Angola	20 (1975)	200 (1975)
Antigua and Barbuda	12 (1982)	200 (1982) [1]
Argentina	200 (1967)	
Australia	3 (1973)	200 (1979)
Bahamas	3 (1878)	200 (1977)
Bahrain	3	—
Bangladesh	12 (1974)	200 (1974) [1]
Barbados	12 (1977)	200 (1979) [1]
Belgium	3	up to median line (1978)
Belize	3 (1878)	—
Benin	200 (1976)	—
Brazil	200 (1970)	—
Brunei Darussalam	12 (1983)	200 (1983) (or median line)
Bulgaria	12 (1951)	200 (1987) [1]
Burma	12 (1968)	200 (1977) [1]
Cambodia	12 (1969)	200 (1979) [1]
Cameroon	50 (1974)	—
Canada	12 (1970)	200 (1977)
Cape Verde	12 (1977)	200 (1977) [1]
Chile	12 (1986)	200 (1947–52) [1]
China	12 (1958)	—
Colombia	12 (1970)	200 (1978) [1]
Comoros	12 (1976)	200 (1976) [1]
Congo	200 (1977)	
Costa Rica	12 (1972)	200 (1975) [1]
Côte d'Ivoire	12 (1977)	200 (1977) [1]
Cuba	12 (1977)	200 (1977) [1]
Cyprus	12 (1964)	—
Denmark (including Faroe Islands and Greenland)	3 (1966)	200 (1977)
Djibouti	12 (1971)	200 (1979) [1]
Dominica	12 (1981)	200 (1981) [1]
Dominican Republic	6 (1967)	200 (1977) [1]
Ecuador	200 (1966)	—
Egypt	12 (1958)	—
El Salvador	200 (1950)	—
Equatorial Guinea	12 (1970)	200 (1984) [1]
Ethiopia	12 (1953)	—
Fiji	12 (1978)	200 (1981) [1]
Finland	4 (1956)	12 (1975) (or agreed boundary)
France	12 (1971)	200 (1977) [1] (except Mediterranean)
Gabon	12 (1986)	200 (1986) [1]
Gambia	12 (1969)	200 (1978)
German Democratic Republic	12 (1985)	up to median line (1978)
Germany, Federal Republic of	3 [2]	200 (1977)
Ghana	12 (1986)	200 (1986) [1]
Greece	6 (1936)	—
Grenada	12 (1978)	200 (1978) [1]
Guatemala	12 (1934)	200 (1976) [1]
Guinea	12 (1980)	200 (1980) [1]
Guinea-Bissau	12 (1978)	200 (1978) [1]

[1] Economic zone.   [2] 3–16 miles in North Sea (German Bight); area defined by coordinates.

TERRITORIAL SEA LIMITS (IN MILES)—*contd.*

State	Territorial Sea	Jurisdiction over fisheries (measured from the baseline of the territorial sea)
Guyana	12 (1977)	200 (1977) [9]
Haiti	12 (1972)	200 (1977) [1]
Honduras	12 (1965)	200 (1951) [1]
Iceland	12 (1979)	200 (1979) [1]
India	12 (1967)	200 (1977) [1]
Indonesia	12 (1957) [2]	200 (1980) [1, 7]
Iran	12 (1959)	[8]
Iraq	12 (1958)	—
Ireland	3 (1959)	200 (1977)
Israel	6 (1956)	—
Italy	12 (1974)	—
Jamaica	12 (1971)	—
Japan	12 (1977)	200 (1977)
Jordan	3 (1943)	—
Kenya	12 (1969)	200 (1979) [1]
Kiribati	12 (1983)	200 (1983) [1]
Korea (North)	12	200 (1977) [1]
Korea (South)	12 (1978)	12
Kuwait	12 (1967)	—
Lebanon	12 (1983)	—
Liberia	200 (1976)	—
Libya	12 (1959)	—
Madagascar	12 (1985)	200 (1985) [1]
Malaysia	12 (1969)	200 (1980) [1]
Maldive, Republic of	12 (1975)	(1976) [1, 3]
Malta	12 (1978)	25 (1978)
Mauritania	70 (1978)	200 (1978) [1]
Mauritius	12 (1970)	200 (1977) [1]
Mexico	12 (1969)	200 (1976) [1]
Monaco	12 (1973)	—
Morocco	12 (1973) [4]	200 (1981) [1]
Mozambique	12 (1976)	200 (1976) [1]
Namibia	6 (1963)	12 (1963)
Nauru	12 (1971)	200 (1978)
Netherlands	12 (1985)	200 (1977)
New Zealand	12 (1977)	200 (1978) [1]
Nicaragua	(1979) [5]	200 (1979) [5]
Nigeria	30 (1971)	200 (1978) [1]
Norway	4 (1812)	200 (1977) [1]
Oman	12 (1977)	200 (1981) [1]
Pakistan	12 (1966)	200 (1976) [1]
Panama	200 (1967)	—
Papua New Guinea	12 (1978)	200 (1978) (offshore waters)
Peru	(1947) [5]	200 (1947) [5]
Philippines	[6]	200 (1978) [1]

[1] Economic zone.

[2] The territorial sea of Indonesia is measured by straight lines surrounding the archipelago.

[3] Territorial limits and economic zone defined by geographical co-ordinates.

[4] Limits with opposite or adjacent states to be fixed by agreement, failing which median line principle to apply.

[5] Sovereignty and jurisdiction over the sea, its soil and subsoil up to 200 miles (1947).

[6] The territorial sea of the Philippines is determined by straight base-lines joining appropriate points of the outermost islands forming the Philippine archipelago in accordance with Treaties of 1898, 1900 and 1930 (1961).

[7] 200 mile exclusive fisheries zone established 1985.

[8] Outer limits of the superjacent waters of the continental shelf. Median line in the Sea of Oman (1973).

[9] The Guyana Maritime Boundaries Act 1977 empowers the President to declare a 200 mile economic zone. In Jan. 1988 no such zone had been declared.

TERRITORIAL SEA LIMITS (IN MILES)—*contd.*

State	*Territorial Sea*	*Jurisdiction over fisheries (measured from the baseline of the territorial sea)*
Poland	12 (1978)	up to median line (1978)
Portugal	12 (1977)	200 (1977) [2]
Qatar	3	[1]
Romania	12 (1951)	200 (1986) [2]
St Christopher (St Kitts)—Nevis	12 (1984)	200 (1984) [2]
St Lucia	12 (1984)	200 (1984) [2]
St Vincent and the Grenadines	12 (1983)	200 (1983) [2]
São Tomé and Principe	12 (1978)	200 (1978) [2]
Saudi Arabia	12 (1958)	[6]
Senegal	12 (1985)	200 (1985) [2]
Seychelles	12 (1977)	200 (1977) [2]
Sierra Leone	200 (1971)	—
Singapore	3 (1878)	
Solomon Islands	12	200 (1986)
Somalia	200 (1972)	—
South Africa, Republic of	12 (1977)	200 (1977)
Spain	12 (1977)	200 (1978) [2] (except Mediterranean)
Sri Lanka	12 (1971)	200 (1977) [2]
Sudan	12 (1960)	—
Suriname	12 (1978)	200 (1978) [2]
Sweden	12 (1980)	200 (1978)
Syria	35 (1981)	—
Tanzania	50 (1973)	—
Thailand	12 (1966)	200 (1980) [2]
Togo	30 (1977)	200 (1977) [2]
Tonga	[3]	—
Trinidad and Tobago	12 (1969)	200 (1986) [2]
Tunisia	12 (1973)	—
Turkey	[7]	12 (1964) 200 (1986) [2] (Black Sea)
Tuvalu	12 (1984)	200 (1984) [2]
USSR	12 (1909)	200 (1984) [2]
United Arab Emirates	3 [4]	[5]
UK	3 (1878)	200 (1977)
USA	3 (1793)	200 (1983) [2]
Uruguay	200 (1969)	
Vanuatu	12 (1978–82)	200 (1978–82) [2]
Venezuela	12 (1956)	200 (1978) [2]
Vietnam	12 (1977)	200 (1977) [2]
Western Samoa	12 (1971)	200 (1980) [2]
Yemen, People's Dem. Rep. of	12 (1970)	200 (1978) [2]
Yemen, Republic of	12 (1967)	—
Yugoslavia	12 (1979)	—
Zaïre	12 (1974)	—

[1] Limited by agreement by the outer limits of the superjacent waters of the continental shelf or by a median line (1974).

[2] Economic zone.

[3] Territorial limits defined by geographical co-ordinates (173–177° W. and 15–23° 30′ S.) (1887).

[4] Sharjah, 12 miles.

[5] Limits to be defined by agreement, failing which median line to apply (1980).

[6] Outer limits of the superjacent waters of the continental shelf.

[7] 6 Aegean (1964), 12 Black and Mediterranean.

The table above, reproduced from a survey prepared by the FAO of the UN shows: *(a)* the territorial sea limit, and *(b)* jurisdiction over fisheries.

Books of Reference

Booth, K., *Law, Force and Diplomacy at Sea.* London, 1985

Buzan, B., *Seabed Politics.* New York, 1976

Janis, M. W., *Sea Power and the Law of the Sea.* Lexington, 1977

Luard, E., *The Control of the Sea-Bed.* London, 1974

Moore, G., *Coastal State Requirements for Foreign Fishing. FAO Legislative Study No. 21.* Rev. 2. Rome, 1985

Sangar, C., *Ordering the Oceans: The Making of the Law of the Sea.* Univ. of Toronto Press, 1987

CHRONOLOGY

1987

April   3   Finland. Government resigns; followed on 30th by a Conservative-
              led coalition under H. Holkeri; Foreign Minister, K. Sorsa.

         6–8 Lebanon. End of the Amal siege of Chatila refugee camp.

         7–8 Paraguay. State of Siege (imposed in 1947) officially ended at
              midnight.

         12–13 Fiji. General election returned a Labour Party government under
              Timoci Bavadra, with a cabinet mainly of Indian descent.

         13   Macao. Agreement by China and Portugal, ensuring the ultimate
              reversion of Macao to China.

         15–19 Argentina. Army rebellion, arising from the trial of officers on
              charges of violating human rights; rebellion quashed.

         24   Republic of South Africa. Supreme Court quashed most of the
              government's restrictions on reporting unrest; also, on 28th
              quashed a police prohibition of campaigning to free detainees.

         29   Malaysia. Dato Rais bin Yatim resigned as Foreign Minister.

May   5   Republic of South Africa. Kwa Ndebele voted to proceed to the
              status of an 'independent' republic such as Transkei.

         6   Iran–Iraq. Attacks on US and Soviet ships lead to foreign inter-
              vention in the Gulf war.

         9–12 Malta. General election returned a Nationalist Party government
              under E. Fenech Adami.

         13   Zambia. Finance Minister, K. Musokotwane replaced by Gibson
              Chigaga.

         13–29 Argentina. Parliament approved a bill to end officers' trials for
              human rights violation (finally upheld on 23 June by the
              Supreme Court, as applying to all but the most senior officers).

         14   Fiji. Lieut.-Col. Sitiveni Rabuka overthrew the government; sworn
              in as chairman of a Council of Ministers on 17th; formed an
              Advisory Council on 22nd.

         15   Uganda. Currency devalued by 76·6%.
              Yugoslavia. Lazar Mosjov became President of the collective state
              presidency.

         18   Colombia. Luis Fernando Alarcon became the new Finance
              Minister.

         19   Malaysia. Datuk Haji Abu Hassan Omar became the new Foreign
              Minister.

June   1   Kenya. Zachary Onyonka became the new Foreign Minister.

         1–2 Barbados. Prime Minister Errol Barrow died; succeeded by
              Erskine Sandiford.

         1   Lebanon. Prime Minister Rashid Karami killed by a bomb;
              succeeded by Selim Hoss as acting Prime Minister.

         3   Canada. Agreement between central and state governments,
              redefining federalism and recognizing Quebec as a 'distinct
              society' within the federation.
              Sir Lanka. First Indian attempts to send relief supplies to the
              North; successful from 4th, regular from 24th.

CHRONOLOGY—*contd.*

CHRONOLOGY—*contd.*

CHRONOLOGY—*contd.*

1987

Dec   6   Fiji. Rabuka resigned as head of state; he appointed Ratu Mara Prime Minister and Ratu Sir Penaia Ganilau (former Governor-General) as President.

8   USA–USSR. Treaty to eliminate both nations' intermediate-range land-based nuclear missiles within three years.
Gibraltar. Sir Joshua Hassan resigned as Chief Minister; he was replaced by Adolfo Cánepa on 11 Nov.

9   Israeli-occupied territories. Beginning of violent unrest.

13   Belgium. A general election leaves no party with a clear majority.

16   South Korea. Roh Tae Woo was elected President.

17   Czechoslovakia. Gustav Husak resigned as General Secretary of the Communist Party; he was replaced by Milos Jakes.

21   Nigeria. Bolagi Akinyemi dismissed as Foreign Minister; replaced by Maj.-Gen. Ike Nwachukwu.

22   Zimbabwe. Zanu PF and Zapu agreed to merge, to create a one-party state.

28   Libya–Tunisia. Diplomatic relations resumed.

1988

Jan.   3   Israel. Deportation orders were served on nine Palestinians from the occupied territories; unrest increased.

13   Taiwan. President Chiang Ching-Kuo died; succeeded by Lee Teng-hui.

17   Haiti. Presidential election (postponed from Nov.). Official estimates of a 70% turn-out were challenged by figures down to 10%. Leslie Manigat was elected.

18   Sri Lanka. Ronnie de Mell resigned as Finance Minister; he was replaced by Naina Marikkar.

19   Nicaragua. The State of Emergency was lifted.

23   Zanzibar. The President dismissed the government and took command of the army.

25   Suriname. Return to civilian government; Ramsewak Shankar was installed as President.
North Korea. The USA having imposed sanctions, North Korea broke off diplomatic relations.

Feb.   8   Panama. Gen. Manuel Noriega, Commander of the Defence Forces, ordered the recall of ambassadors to the USA and the UN, after a US federal grand jury charged him with drug offences; he had called for the removal of US forces from Panama.

9   South Yemen–Egypt. Diplomatic relations resumed (broken off in 1979).

9–10   Bophuthatswana. Attempted military *coup* quashed by South African forces.

19   Brazil. Heavy rains and storms culminate in mud-slides, with severe damage and loss of life, in Rio.

21   Cyprus. Final ballot of the presidential election; George Vassiliou was elected.

CHRONOLOGY—*contd.*

1988

Feb. 24 Republic of South Africa. Seventeen anti-apartheid organizations banned from activity.

26 Panama. Gen. Manuel Noriega overthrew President Delvalle and appointed Manuel Solis Palma as head of state.

28 USSR. Azerbaijanis murdered Armenians living in Sumgait; unrest arose from Armenian claims to the Nagorny Karabakh region of Azerbaijan.

29 Senegal. A State of Emergency was proclaimed when riots followed the re-election of President Diouf.

March 3 Turks and Caicos Islands. General elections marked the end of direct rule from the UK (since July 1986). The People's Democratic Movement won 11 of 13 seats.

4 Panama. The USA froze Panamanian assets as part of a programme of economic sanctions. Panama's banks closed. A State of Emergency was proclaimed on 18th.

5–6 Tibet. Nationalist riots in Lhasa.

10 Vietnam. Prime Minister Pham Hung died.

20 El Salvador. General election; the Arena party won a majority in the Legislative Assembly.

23 Nicaragua. The government signed a cease-fire agreement with the Contra rebels.

24 Gibraltar. General election; a Labour government elected, under Joe Bossano.

ADDENDA

NEPÁL. In March 1988 the Cabinet was composed as follows: *Prime Minister, Defence and Royal Palace Affairs:* Marich Man Singh Shrestha. *Foreign Affairs:* Shailendra Kumar Upadhyaya. *Local Supply:* Dil Bahadur Shrestha. *Communications:* Hari Bahadur Basnyet. *Land Reform and Management:* Padma Sundar Lawate. *Panchayat and Local Development:* Pashupati Rana. *Industry:* Bala Ram Ghartimagar. *Water Resources:* Yadav Prasad Pant. *Commerce, Labour and Social Services:* Parshu Narayan Chaudhary. *Housing and Physical Planning:* Prakash Chandra Lohani. *Health:* Shushila Thapa. *Education:* Keshar Bahadur Bista. *Finance:* Bharat Bahadur Pradhan. *Tourism:* Mohammad Mohashin. There were 6 Ministers of State.

GIBRALTAR. At the General election held in March 1988, the Gibraltar Labour Party won 8 seats (with 58% of the poll), Association for the Advancement of Civil Rights 7 seats (29%). There was a 76% turn-out.
Joe Bassano was sworn in as Chief Minister on 25 March 1988.

BANGLADESH. At the General election held on 3 March 1988, the ruling Jatiya Party won 259 seats, the Combined Opposition Alliance, 15, Independents, 22, others 4. A 23-member cabinet was appointed on 27 March, with Moumoud Ahmed as Prime Minister.

FRANCE. President Mitterand achieved 34% of the vote in the first round of the Presidential elections held on 24 April 1988.

THAILAND. General elections will take place on 24 July 1988.

CZECHOSLOVAKIA. *UK Ambassador:* P. L. O'Keeffe.

DENMARK. General elections will be held on 10 May 1988.

PANAMA. US-backed sanctions that had closed banks since 4 March 1988 and brought the economy to a halt caused the President to reshuffle the cabinet on 25 April. *Foreign Affairs:* Jorge Abadía. *Finance:* Gustavo González.

PART I

INTERNATIONAL ORGANIZATIONS

PART III

INTERNATIONAL
ORGANIZATIONS

THE UNITED NATIONS

The United Nations is an association of states which have pledged themselves, through signing the Charter, to maintain international peace and security and to co-operate in establishing political, economic and social conditions under which this task can be securely achieved. Nothing contained in the Charter authorizes the organization to intervene in matters which are essentially within the domestic jurisdiction of any state.

The United Nations Charter originated from proposals agreed upon at discussions held at Dumbarton Oaks (Washington, D.C.) between the USSR, US and UK from 21 Aug. to 28 Sept., and between US, UK and China from 29 Sept. to 7 Oct. 1944. These proposals were laid before the United Nations Conference on International Organization, held at San Francisco from 25 April to 26 June 1945, and (after amendments had been made to the original proposals) the Charter of the United Nations was signed on 26 June 1945 by the delegates of 50 countries. Ratification of all the signatures had been received by 31 Dec. 1945. (For the complete text of the Charter see THE STATESMAN'S YEAR-BOOK, 1946, pp. xxi–xxxii.)

The United Nations formally came into existence on 24 Oct. 1945, with the deposit of the requisite number of ratifications of the Charter with the US Department of State. The official languages of the United Nations are Arabic, Chinese, English, French, Russian and Spanish.

The headquarters of the United Nations is in New York City, USA.

Flag: UN emblem in white centred on a light blue ground.

Membership. Membership is open to all peace-loving states whose admission will be effected by the General Assembly upon recommendation of the Security Council. The table on pp. 7–8 shows the 159 member states of the United Nations.

The Principal Organs of the United Nations are: 1. The General Assembly. 2. The Security Council. 3. The Economic and Social Council. 4 The Trusteeship Council. 5. The International Court of Justice. 6. The Secretariat.

1. **The General Assembly** consists of all the members of the United Nations. Each member has only 1 vote. The General Assembly meets regularly once a year, commencing on the third Tuesday in Sept.; the session normally lasts until mid-December and is resumed for some weeks in the new year if this is required. Special sessions may be convoked by the Secretary-General if requested by the Security Council, by a majority of the members of the United Nations or by 1 member concurred with by the majority of the members. The Assembly also meets in emergency special session. The General Assembly elects its President for each session.

The first regular session was held in London from 10 Jan. to 14 Feb. and in New York from 23 Oct. to 16 Dec. 1946.

Special sessions have been held on Palestine (1947, 1948), Tunisia (1961), Financial Situation of UN (1963), South West Africa, Peace-Keeping, Postponement of Outer Space Conference (1967), Raw Materials and Development (1974), New International Economic Order (1975), Peace-keeping force in the Lebanon, Namibia, Disarmament (1978, 1982), Economic Issues (1980); Emergency Special sessions were held on Suez, Hungary (1956), Lebanon-Jordan-United Arab Republic dispute (1958), Congo (1960), Middle East (1967), Afghánistán, Palestine (1980, resumed 1982), Namibia (1981), Economic Situation in Africa (1986) and Namibia (1986).

The work of the General Assembly is divided between 7 Main Committees, on which every member state is represented. These are: First committee (disarmament and related international security matters); special political committee; second committee (economic and financial matters); third committee (social, humanitarian and cultural matters); fourth committee (decolonisation matters); fifth committee (administrative and budgetary matters); sixth committee (legal matters).

In addition there is a General Committee charged with the task of co-ordinating the proceedings of the Assembly and its Committees; and a Credentials Committee which verifies the credentials of the delegates. The General Committee consists of 29 members, comprising the President of the General Assembly, its 17 Vice-Presidents and the Chairmen of the 7 Main Committees. The Credentials Committee consists of 9 members, elected at the beginning of each session of the General Assembly. The Assembly has 2 standing committees—an Advisory Committee on Administrative and Budgetary Questions, and a Committee on Contributions. The General Assembly establishes subsidiary and *ad hoc* bodies when necessary to deal with specific matters. These include: Special Committee on Peace-keeping Operations (33 members), Commission on Human Rights (43 members), Committee on the peaceful uses of outer space (53 members), Conciliation Commission for Palestine (3 members), Conference on Disarmament (40 members), International Law Commission (34 members), Scientific Committee on the effects of atomic radiation (20 members), Special Committee on the implementation of the declaration on the granting of independence to colonial countries and peoples (24 members), Special Committee on the policies of Apartheid of the Government of the Republic of South Africa (18 members) and UN Commission on International Trade Law (36 members).

The General Assembly may discuss any matters within the scope of the Charter, and, with the exception of any situation or dispute on the agenda of the Security Council, may make recommendations on any such questions or matters. For decisions on important questions a two-thirds majority is required, on other questions a simple majority of members present and voting. In addition, the Assembly at its fifth session, in 1950, decided that if the Security Council, because of lack of unanimity of the permanent members, fails to exercise its primary responsibility for the maintenance of international peace and security in any case where there appears to be a threat to the peace, breach of the peace or act of aggression, the General Assembly shall consider the matter immediately with a view to making appropriate recommendations to members for collective measures, including in the case of a breach of the peace or act of aggression the use of armed force when necessary, to maintain or restore international peace and security.

The General Assembly receives and considers reports from the other organs of the United Nations, including the Security Council. The Secretary-General makes an annual report to it on the work of the Organization.

2. **The Security Council** consists of 15 members, each of which has 1 vote. There are 5 permanent and 10 non-permanent members elected for a 2-year term by a two-thirds majority of the General Assembly.

Retiring members are not eligible for immediate re-election. Any other member of the United Nations may be invited to participate without vote in the discussion of questions specially affecting its interests.

The Security Council bears the primary responsibility for the maintenance of peace and security. It is also responsible for the functions of the UN in trust territories classed as 'strategic areas'. Decisions on procedural questions are made by an affirmative vote of 9 members. On all other matters the affirmative vote of 9 members must include the concurring votes of all permanent members (in practice, however, an abstention by a permanent member is not considered a veto), subject to the provision that when the Security Council is considering methods for the peaceful settlement of a dispute, parties to the dispute abstain from voting.

For the maintenance of international peace and security the Security Council can, in accordance with special agreements to be concluded, call on armed forces, assistance and facilities of the member states. It is assisted by a Military Staff Committee consisting of the Chiefs of Staff of the permanent members of the Security Council or their representatives.

The Presidency of the Security Council is held for 1 month in rotation by the member states in the English alphabetical order of their names.

The Security Council functions continuously. Its members are permanently represented at the seat of the organization, but it may meet at any place that will best facilitate its work.

The Council has 2 standing committees of Experts and on the Admission of New Members. In addition, from time to time, it establishes *ad hoc* committees and commissions such as the Truce Supervision Organization in Palestine.

Permanent Members: China, France, USSR, UK, USA.

Non-Permanent Members: Argentina, Federal Republic of Germany, Italy, Japan, Zambia (until 31 Dec. 1988); Algeria, Brazil, Nepál, Senegal, Yugoslavia (until 31 Dec. 1989).

3. **The Economic and Social Council** is responsible under the General Assembly for carrying out the functions of the United Nations with regard to international economic, social, cultural, educational, health and related matters.

By Nov. 1977, 15 'specialized' inter-governmental agencies working in these fields had been brought into relationship with the United Nations. The Economic and Social Council may also make arrangements for consultation with international non-governmental organizations and, after consultation with the member concerned, with national organizations; by 1983 over 600 non-governmental organizations had been granted consultative status.

The Economic and Social Council consists of 54 Member States elected by a two-thirds majority of the General Assembly. Forty-two are elected each year for a 18-year term. Retiring members are eligible for immediate re-election. Each member has 1 vote. Decisions are made by a majority of the members present and voting.

The Council nominally holds 2 sessions a year, and special sessions may be held if required. The President is elected for 1 year and is eligible for immediate re-election.

The Economic and Social Council has the following commissions:

Regional Economic Commissions: ECE (Economic Commission for Europe. Geneva); ESCAP (Economic and Social Commission for Asia and the Pacific. Bangkok); ECLAC (Economic Commission for Latin America and the Caribbean. Santiago, Chile); ECA (Economic Commission for Africa. Addis Ababa). ESCWA (Economic Commission for Western Asia. Baghdad). These Commissions have been established to enable the nations of the major regions of the world to co-operate on common problems and also to produce economic information.

Six functional commissions, including: (1) a Statistical Commission with sub-commission on Statistical Sampling. (2) Commission on Human Rights; with sub-commission on Prevention of Discrimination and Protection of Minorities; (3) Social Development Commission; (4) Commission on the Status of Women; (5) Commission on Narcotic Drugs; (6) Population Commission.

The Economic and Social Council has the following standing committees: The Economic Committee, Social Committee, Co-ordination Committee, Committee on Non-Governmental Organizations, Interim Committee on Programme of Conferences, Committee for Industrial Development, Advisory Committee on the Application of Science and Technology to Development, Committee on Housing, Building and Planning.

Other special bodies are the International Narcotics Control Board, the Interim Co-ordinating Committee for International Commodity Arrangements and the Administrative Committee on Co-ordination to ensure (1) the most effective implementation of the agreements entered into between the United Nations and the specialized agencies and (2) co-ordination of activities.

Membership: Australia, Belgium, Byelorussia, Djibouti, Egypt, Gabon, German Democratic Republic, Iraq, Italy, Jamaica, Mozambique, Pakistan, Panama, Peru, Philippines, Sierra Leone, Syria, United States (until 31 Dec. 1988). Belize, Bolivia, Bulgaria, Canada, China, Denmark, Iran, Norway, Oman, Poland, Rwanda, Somalia, Sri Lanka, Sudan, USSR, United Kingdom, Uruguay, Zaïre (until 31 Dec. 1989). Colombia, Cuba, France, Federal Republic of Germany, Ghana, Greece, Guinea, India, Ireland, Japan, Lesotho, Liberia, Libya, Portugal, Saudi Arabia, Trinidad and Tobago, Venezuela, Yugoslavia (until 31 Dec. 1990).

4. The Trusteeship Council. The Charter provides for an international trusteeship system to safeguard the interests of the inhabitants of territories which are not yet fully self-governing and which may be placed thereunder by individual trusteeship agreements. These are called trust territories.

All of the original 11 trust territories except one, the Pacific Islands (Micronesia), administered by the USA, have become independent or joined independent countries. The Trusteeship Council consists of the 1 member administering trust territories: USA; the permanent members of the Security Council that are not administering trust territories: China, France, USSR and UK. Decisions of the Council are made by a majority of the members present and voting, each member having 1 vote. The Council holds one regular session each year, and special sessions if required.

5. The International Court of Justice was created by an international treaty, the Statute of the Court, which forms an integral part of the United Nations Charter. All members of the United Nations are *ipso facto* parties to the Statute of the Court.

The Court is composed of independent judges, elected regardless of their nationality, who possess the qualifications required in their countries for appointment to the highest judicial offices, or are jurisconsults of recognized competence in international law. There are 15 judges, no 2 of whom may be nationals of the same state. They are elected by the Security Council and the General Assembly of the United Nations sitting independently. Candidates are chosen from a list of persons nominated by the national groups in the Permanent Court of Arbitration established by the Hague Conventions of 1899 and 1907. In the case of members of the United Nations not represented in the Permanent Court of Arbitration, candidates are nominated by national groups appointed for the purpose by their governments. The judges are elected for a 9-year term and are eligible for immediate re-election. When engaged on business of the Court, they enjoy diplomatic privileges and immunities.

The Court elects its own President and Vice-President for 3 years and remains permanently in session, except for judicial vacations. The full court of 15 judges normally sits, but a quorum of 9 judges is sufficient to constitute the Court. It may form chambers of 3 or more judges for dealing with a particular case or particular categories of cases. Nagendra Singh (India) and Kéba Mbaye (Senegal) are, respectively, President and Vice-President of the Court until 1991.

Competence and Jurisdiction. Only states may be parties in cases before the Court, which is open to the states parties to its Statute. The conditions under which the Court will be open to other states are laid down by the Security Council. The Court exercises its jurisdiction in all cases which the parties refer to it and in all matters provided for in the Charter, or in treaties and conventions in force. Disputes concerning the jurisdiction of the Court are settled by the Court's own decision.

The Court may apply in its decision: *(a)* international conventions; *(b)* international custom; *(c)* the general principles of law recognized by civilized nations; and *(d)* as subsidiary means for the determination of the rules of law, judicial decisions and the teachings of highly qualified publicists. If the parties agree, the Court may decide a case *ex aequo et bono.* The Court may also give advisory opinions on legal questions to the General Assembly, the Security Council, certain other organs of the UN and a number of international organizations.

Procedure. The official languages of the Court are French and English. All questions are decided by a majority of the judges present. If the votes are equal, the President has a casting vote. The judgment is final and without appeal, but a revision may be applied for within 10 years from the date of the judgment on the ground of a new decisive factor. No court fees are paid by parties to the Statute.

Judges. The judges of the Court, elected by the Security Council and the General Assembly, are as follows: (1) To serve until 5 Feb. 1991: Nagendra Singh (India), José Maria Ruda (Argentina), Sir Robert Jennings (UK), Gilbert Guillaume (France), Kéba Mbaye (Senegal). (2) To serve until 5 Feb. 1994: Taslim Olawale Elias (Nigeria), Manfred Lachs (Poland), Jens Evensen (Norway), Shigeru Oda (Japan), Ni Zhengyu (China). (3) To serve until 5 Feb. 1997: Roberto Ago (Italy), Mohamed Shahabuddeen (Guyana), Stephen Schwebel (USA), Mohammed Bedjaoui (Algeria), Nikolai K. Tarasov (USSR).

If there is no judge on the bench of the nationality of a party to a case, that party has the right to choose a person to sit as judge for that case. Such judges take part in the decision on terms of complete equality with their colleagues.

The Court has its seat at The Hague, but may sit elsewhere whenever it considers this desirable. The expenses of the Court are borne by the UN.

Registrar: Santiago Torres Bernárdez (Spain).

6. **The Secretariat** is composed of the Secretary-General, who is the chief administrative officer of the organization, and an international staff appointed by him under regulations established by the General Assembly. However, the Secretary-General, the High Commissioner for Refugees and the Managing Director of the Fund are appointed by the General Assembly. The first Secretary-General was Trygve Lie (Norway), 1946–53; the second, Dag Hammarskjöld (Sweden), 1953–61; the third, U. Thant (Burma), 1961–71; the fourth, Kurt Waldheim (Austria), 1972–81.

The Secretary-General acts as chief administrative officer in all meetings of the General Assembly, the Security Council, the Economic and Social Council and the Trusteeship Council.

The financial year coincides with the calendar year; accountancy is in US$. Budget for 1986–87, $1,711,801,200.

Secretary-General: Javier Perez de Cuellar (Peru), re-appointed 1 Jan. 1986 for a 5-year term.

The Secretary-General is assisted by Under-Secretaries-General and Assistant Secretaries-General.

MEMBER STATES OF THE UN

(as in 1986 with percentage scale of contribution)

Afghánistán	0·01	1946	Byelorussia [1]	0·34	1945
Albania	0·01	1955	Cambodia	0·01	1955
Algeria	0·14	1962	Cameroon	0·01	1960
Angola	0·01	1976	Canada [1]	3·06	1945
Antigua and Barbuda	0·01	1981	Cape Verde	0·01	1975
Argentina [1]	0·62	1945	Central African Rep.	0·01	1960
Australia [1]	1·66	1945	Chad	0·01	1960
Austria	0·74	1955	Chile [1]	0·07	1945
Bahamas	0·01	1973	China [1]	0·79	1945
Bahrain	0·02	1971	Colombia [1]	0·13	1945
Bangladesh	0·02	1974	Comoros	0·01	1975
Barbados	0·01	1966	Congo	0·01	1960
Belgium [1]	1·18	1945	Costa Rica [1]	0·02	1945
Belize	0·01	1981	Côte d'Ivoire	0·02	1960
Benin	0·01	1960	Cuba [1]	0·09	1945
Bhután	0·01	1971	Cyprus	0·02	1960
Bolivia [1]	0·01	1945	Czechoslovakia [1]	0·70	1945
Botswana	0·01	1966	Denmark [1]	0·72	1945
Brazil [1]	1·40	1945	Djibouti	0·01	1977
Brunei Darussalam	0·04	1984	Dominica	0·01	1978
Bulgaria	0·16	1955	Dominican Republic [1]	0·03	1945
Burkina Faso	0·01	1960	Ecuador [1]	0·03	1945
Burma	0·01	1948	Egypt [1]	0·07	1945
Burundi	0·01	1962	El Salvador [1]	0·01	1945

Equatorial Guinea	0·01	1968	Oman	0·02	1971
Ethiopia [1]	0·01	1945	Pakistan	0·06	1947
Fiji	0·01	1970	Panama [1]	0·02	1945
Finland	0·50	1955	Papua New Guinea	0·01	1975
France [1]	6·37	1945	Paraguay [1]	0·02	1945
Gabon	0·03	1960	Peru [1]	0·07	1945
Gambia	0·01	1965	Philippines [1]	0·10	1945
German Democratic Rep.	1·33	1973	Poland [1]	0·64	1945
Germany, Federal Rep. of	8·26	1973	Portugal	0·18	1955
Ghana	0·01	1957	Qatar	0·04	1971
Greece [1]	0·44	1945	Romania	0·19	1955
Grenada	0·01	1974	Rwanda	0·01	1962
Guatemala [1]	0·02	1945	St Christopher and Nevis	0·01	1983
Guinea	0·01	1958	St Lucia	0·01	1979
Guinea-Bissau	0·01	1974	St Vincent and the		
Guyana	0·01	1966	Grenadines	0·01	1980
Haiti [1]	0·01	1945	Samoa, Western	0·01	1976
Honduras [1]	0·01	1945	São Tomé and Principe	0·01	1975
Hungary	0·22	1955	Saudi Arabia [1]	0·97	1945
Iceland	0·03	1946	Senegal	0·01	1960
India [1]	0·35	1945	Seychelles	0·01	1976
Indonesia	0·14	1950	Sierra Leone	0·01	1961
Iran [1]	0·63	1945	Singapore	0·10	1965
Iraq [1]	0·12	1945	Solomon Islands	0·01	1978
Ireland	0·18	1955	Somalia	0·01	1960
Israel	0·22	1949	South Africa [1]	0·44	1945
Italy	3·79	1955	Spain	2·03	1955
Jamaica	0·02	1962	Sri Lanka	0·01	1955
Japan	10·84	1956	Sudan	0·01	1956
Jordan	0·01	1955	Suriname	0·01	1975
Kenya	0·01	1963	Swaziland	0·01	1968
Kuwait	0·29	1963	Sweden	1·25	1946
Laos People's Dem. Rep.	0·01	1955	Syrian Arab Rep.[1]	0·04	1945
Lebanon [1]	0·01	1945	Tanzania	0·01	1961
Lesotho	0·01	1966	Thailand	0·09	1946
Liberia [1]	0·01	1945	Togo	0·01	1960
Libyan Arab Jamahiriya	0·26	1955	Trinidad and Tobago	0·04	1962
Luxembourg [1]	0·05	1945	Tunisia	0·03	1956
Madagascar	0·01	1960	Turkey [1]	0·34	1945
Malawi	0·01	1964	Uganda	0·01	1962
Malaysia	0·10	1957	Ukrainian Soviet		
Maldives	0·01	1965	Socialist Rep.[1]	1·28	1945
Mali	0·01	1960	USSR [1]	10·20	1945
Malta	0·01	1964	United Arab Emirates	0·18	1971
Mauritania	0·01	1961	UK [1]	4·86	1945
Mauritius	0·01	1968	USA [1]	25·00	1945
Mexico [1]	0·89	1945	Uruguay [1]	0·04	1945
Mongolia	0·01	1961	Vanuatu	0·01	1981
Morocco	0·05	1956	Venezuela [1]	0·60	1945
Mozambique	0·01	1975	Vietnam	0·01	1977
Nepál	0·01	1955	Yemen Arab Republic	0·01	1947
Netherlands [1]	1·74	1945	Yemen, P.D.R.	0·01	1967
New Zealand [1]	0·24	1945	Yugoslavia [1]	0·46	1945
Nicaragua [1]	0·01	1945	Zaïre	0·01	1960
Niger	0·01	1960	Zambia	0·01	1964
Nigeria	0·19	1960	Zimbabwe	0·02	1980
Norway [1]	0·54	1945			

[1] Original member.

Books of Reference

Yearbook of the United Nations. New York, 1947 ff. Annual
United Nations Chronicle. Quarterly
Monthly Bulletin of Statistics
General Assembly: Official-Records: Resolutions
Reports of the Secretary-General of the United Nations on the Work of the Organization.
   1946 ff.

Documents of the United Nations Conference on International Organization, San Francisco, 1945. 16 vols.

Charter of the United Nations and Statute of the International Court of Justice. Text in English, French, Chinese, Russian and Spanish.

Repertory of Practice of UN's Organs. 5 vols. New York, 1955

Official Records of the Security Council, the Economic and Social Council, Trusteeship Council and the Disarmament Commission

Demographic Yearbook, 1948 ff. New York, 1969

Everyone's United Nations. New York. 10th ed., 1986

Statistical Yearbook. New York, 1947 ff.

United Nations Handbook 1987. New Zealand Ministry of Foreign Affairs, Wellington, 1987

Yearbook of International Statistics. New York, 1950 ff.

World Economic Survey. New York, 1947 ff.

Economic Survey of Asia and the Far East. New York, 1946 ff.

Economic Survey of Latin America. New York, 1948 ff.

Economic Survey of Europe. New York, 1948 ff.

Economic Survey of Africa. New York, 1960 ff.

Foote, W., *Dag Hammarskjöld—Servant of Peace.* London, 1962

Forsythe, D., *United Nations Peacemaking: The Conciliation Commission for Palestine.* Johns Hopkins Univ. Press, 1973

Humana, C., *World Human Rights Guide.* 2nd ed. London, 1986

Lie, Trygve, *In the Cause of Peace.* London, 1954

Luard, E., *A History of the United Nations.* Vol. 1. London, 1982

Osmanczyk, E., *Encyclopaedia of the United Nations.* London, 1985

Peterson, M. J., *The General Assembly in World Politics.* Winchester, Mass, 1986

Thant, U., *Towards World Peace.* New York, 1964

Walters, F. P., *A History of the League of Nations.* 2 vols. London, 1952

Williams, D., *The Specialised Agencies of the United Nations.* London, 1987

Witthauer, K., *Die Bevölkerung der Erde: Verteilung und Dynamik.* Gotha, 1958.— *Distribution and Dynamics Relating to World Population.* Gotha, 1969

United Nations Information Centre. 20 Buckingham Gate, London SW1E 6LB

UNITED NATIONS SYSTEM

The bulk of the work of the UN, measured in terms of money and personnel, is aimed at achieving the pledge made in Article 55 of the Charter to 'promote higher standards of living, full employment and conditions of economic and social progress and development'.

In addition to the 18 independent specialized agencies, there are some 14 major United Nations programmes and funds devoted to achieving economic and social progress in the developing countries.

Total contributions to the funds and programmes of the UN and specialized agencies for development activities amounted to $1,100m. (not including contributions to the World Bank group) in 1987. The highest total contributions in 1988 went to the UN Development Programme (UNDP – $1,000m.) the UN Children's Fund (UNICEF – $290m.) and the UN Fund for Population Activities (UNFPA – $167m.). The World Food Programme, which provides food aid to support development projects and emergency relief operations, provided aid worth $900m. in 1983, making it the largest single source of development assistance in the UN system, apart from the World Bank.

The *United Nations Development Programme* (UNDP) is the world's largest agency for multilateral technical and pre-investment co-operation. It is the funding source for most of the technical assistance provided by the United Nations system, and UNDP is active in almost 150 countries and territories and in virtually every economic and social sector. UNDP assistance is provided only at the request of Governments and in response to their priority needs, integrated into over-all national and regional plans.

There are more than 5,000 UNDP-supported projects currently in operation at the national, regional, inter-regional and global levels, all aimed at helping developing countries make better use of their assets, improve living standards and expand productivity. The volume of such work was $1,200m. in 1983.

UNICEF, established in 1946 to deliver post-war relief to children, now concentrates its assistance on development activities aimed at improving the quality of life for children and mothers in developing countries. During 1983, UNICEF was working in over 110 countries with a child population of some 1,300m., concentrating on basic services for children and maternal health care, nutrition, water supply and sanitation and education. *The State of the World's Children Report: 1984*, published by UNICEF, has helped to spread acceptance by local and national leaders of a strategy for child health and nutrition which UNICEF estimates could save the lives of 7m. children. UNICEF has focused on popularising four primary health care techniques which are low in cost and produce results in a relatively short time. These include: oral rehydration therapy to fight the effects of diarrhoeal infections, which kill some 4m. children each year; expanded immunization against the 6 most common childhood diseases; child growth monitoring, and promotion of breast-feeding. The World Health Organization and UNICEF work closely together, providing training, equipment and the services of health care professionals. UNICEF is the world's largest supplier of vaccines and the 'cold chain' equipment needed to deliver them, as well as oral rehydration salts.

Executive Director: James P. Grant (USA).

The UN Population Fund (UNFPA) carries out programmes in over 130 countries and territories. The Fund's aims are to build up capacity to respond to needs in population and family planning; to promote awareness of population problems in both developed and developing countries and possible strategies to deal with them; to assist developing countries at their request in dealing with population problems. More than 25% of international population assistance to developing countries is channeled through UNFPA.

Executive Director: Dr Nafis Sadik (Philippines).

An International Conference on Population was convened by the United Nations in 1984 in Mexico City to review the World Population Plan of Action adopted by the 1974 population conference, and make recommendations for its future implementation.

Humanitarian relief to refugees and victims of natural and man-made disasters is also an important function of the UN system. Among the organizations involved in such relief activities are the Office of the UN Disaster Relief Co-ordinator (UNDRO), the Office of the UN High Commissioner for Refugees (UNHCR) and the UN Relief and Works Agency for Palestine Refugees in the Near East (UNRWA).

UNRWA was created by the General Assembly in 1949 as a temporary, non-political agency to provide relief to the nearly 750,000 people who became refugees as a result of the disturbances during and after the creation of the State of Israel in the former British Mandate territory of Palestine. 'Palestine refugees', as defined by UNRWA's mandate, are persons or descendants of persons whose normal residence was Palestine for at least 2 years prior to the 1948 conflict and who, as a result of the conflict, lost their homes and means of livelihood. UNRWA has also been called upon to assist persons displaced as a result of renewed hostilities in the Middle East in 1967. The situation of Palestine refugees in south Lebanon was of special concern to the Agency in 1984 which has carried out an emergency relief programme in that area for Palestine refugees affected in the aftermath of the Israeli invasion of Lebanon in 1982.

Over 2m. refugees are registered with the Agency which provides education, health care, supplementary feeding and relief services. Education and basic health care account for over 80% of the Agency's budget, which is financed by voluntary contributions from Governments. In 1986 its operating budget amounted to $230m., while cash contributions were expected to total only $194m.

Commissioner-General: Giorgio Giacomelli.

The *Office of the United Nations High Commissioner for Refugees* (UNHCR) was established by the UN General Assembly with effect from 1 Jan. 1951, originally for three years. Since 1954, its mandate has been renewed for successive five-year periods.

The work of UNHCR is of a purely humanitarian and non-political character.

The main functions of the Office are to provide international protection for refugees and to seek permanent solutions to their problems through voluntary repatriation, local integration into the country of first asylum or resettlement in other countries. UNHCR may also be called upon to provide emergency relief and ongoing material assistance where necessary.

UNHCR concerns itself with refugees who have been determined to come within its mandate under the Statute, and with persons in analogous circumstances whom it assists under the terms of the good offices resolutions adopted by the General Assembly.

The High Commissioner is elected by the General Assembly and follows policy directives given by the General Assembly or the Economic and Social Council.

International protection is the primary function of UNHCR. Its main objective is to promote and safeguard the rights and interests of refugees. In so doing UNHCR devotes special attention to promoting a generous policy of asylum on the part of Governments and seeks to improve the status of refugees in their country of residence. It also helps them to cease being refugees through the acquisition of the nationality of their country of residence when voluntary repatriation is not possible. UNHCR pursues its objectives in the field of protection by encouraging the conclusion of intergovernmental legal instruments in favour of refugees, by supervising the implementation of their provisions and by encouraging Governments to adopt legislation and administrative procedures for the benefit of refugees.

UNHCR also provides material assistance to refugees, largely in camps and settlements, and seeks to promote their self-sufficiency leading to the attainment of durable solutions for their plight. Since 1951 UNHCR has assisted and found solutions for an estimated 30 million refugees and displaced persons.

In 1987 a number of major movements occurred in Africa and there were repatriations from the Sudan to Ethiopia and Uganda and from the Central African Republic to Chad and some voluntary return for Ethiopians from Somalia and Djibouti. Afghans, estimated at 3m. in Pakistan and 2m. in Iran, remained the largest single problem. Resettlement remained the main durable solution for south-east Asian refugees in camps. Voluntary repatriation of 9,000 refugees in Central America (mainly Guatemalans, Nicaraguans and Salvadorans) took place. More restrictive measures and regulations were imposed for refugees in European and North American countries.

In Oct. 1987 the Executive Committee of the High Commissioner's Programme approved a revised financial target of US$349m. for UNHCR general programmes in 1986 and also approved the figure of US$378m. for projected requirements in 1988.

For its work on behalf of refugees around the world, UNHCR was awarded the Nobel Peace Prize in 1955 and again in 1981.

Headquarters: Palais des Nations, 1211, Geneva 10, Switzerland.
UK Office: 36 Westminster Palace Gardens, London, SW1P 1RR.

High Commissioner: Jean-Pierre Hocké (Swiss).

UN funds and programmes participating in the 1984 pledging conference for development activities:
UN Development Programme; Special Measures Fund for the Least Developed Countries; UN Development Programme Energy Account; UN Capital Development Fund; UN Special Fund for Land-Locked Developing Countries; UN Revolving Fund for National Resources Exploration; Special Voluntary Fund for the UN Volunteers; UN Financing System for Science and Technology for Development; UN Trust Fund for Sudano-Sahelian Activities; UN Children's Fund; UN Fund for Population Activities; UN Industrial Development Fund; UN Trust Fund for African Development Activities; Voluntary Fund for the UN Decade for Women; UN Trust Fund for the International Research and Training Institute for the Advancement of Women; UN Centre for Human Settlements (Habitat): UN Habitat and Human Settlements Foundation; UN Trust Fund for the Transport and Communications Decade in Africa; Trust Fund for the UN Centre on Transnational Corporations; UN Institute for Training and Research; UN Fund for Drug

Abuse Control; UN Trust Fund for Social Defence; UN Development Programme Study Programme; Fund of the UN Environment Programme.

SPECIALIZED AGENCIES OF THE UN

INTERNATIONAL ATOMIC ENERGY AGENCY (IAEA)

Origin. The International Atomic Energy Agency came into existence on 29 July 1957. Its statute had been approved on 26 Oct. 1956, at an international conference held at UN Headquarters, New York. A relationship agreement links it with the United Nations. The IAEA had 113 member states in 1986.

Functions. (1) To accelerate and enlarge the contribution of atomic energy to peace, health and prosperity throughout the world, and (2) to ensure that assistance provided by it or at its request or under its supervision or control is not used in such a way as to further any military purpose. In addition, under the terms of the Non-Proliferation Treaty, to verify states' obligation to prevent diversion of nuclear energy from peaceful uses to nuclear weapons or other nuclear explosive devices.

The IAEA gives advice and technical assistance to developing countries on nuclear power development, on nuclear safety, on radioactive waste management, on legal aspects of the use of atomic energy, and on prospecting for and exploiting nuclear raw materials; in addition it promotes the use of radiation and isotopes in agriculture, industry, medicine and hydrology through expert services, training courses and fellowships, grants of equipment and supplies, research contracts, scientific meetings and publications. During 1986, 937 scientists and technicians received training through fellowships and 'scientific visits'. In addition, 71 training courses and study tours were attended by 970 participants from developing countries. The IAEA has research laboratories in Austria and Monaco. At Trieste, the International Centre for Theoretical Physics was established in 1964 which is now operated jointly by UNESCO and IAEA.

In Dec. 1986, a total of 164 safeguards agreements were in force with 96 states. Safeguards are the technical means applied by the IAEA to verify that nuclear equipment or materials are used exclusively for peaceful purposes. IAEA safeguards cover more than 95% of the civilian nuclear installations outside the 5 nuclear-weapon states (China, France, UK, USA and USSR). Four of the five nuclear-weapon states have opened all (UK, USA) or some (France, USSR) of their civilian nuclear plants to IAEA safeguards inspection. The IAEA is also holding negotiations on a safeguards agreement with China, the fifth and last nuclear-weapon state not yet involved in its inspection system. Installations in non-nuclear weapon states under safeguards or containing safeguarded material at 31 Dec. 1986 were 178 power reactors, 176 research reactors and critical assemblies, 6 conversion plants, 36 fuel fabrication plants, 6 reprocessing plants, 6 enrichment plants, and 493 other installations.

Organization. The Statute provides for an annual General Conference, a Board of Governors of 35 members and a Secretariat headed by a Director-General.

Headquarters: Vienna International Centre, PO Box 100, A-1400 Vienna, Austria.

Director-General: Hans Blix (Sweden).

INTERNATIONAL LABOUR ORGANISATION (ILO)

Origin. The ILO, established in 1919 as an autonomous part of the League of Nations, is an intergovernmental agency with a tripartite structure, in which representatives of governments, employers and workers participate. It seeks through international action to improve labour conditions, raise living standards and promote productive employment. In 1946 the ILO was recognized by the United Nations as a specialized agency. In 1969 it was awarded the Nobel Peace Prize. In 1987 it numbered 150 members.

Functions. One of the ILO's principal functions is the formulation of international standards in the form of International Labour Conventions and Recommendations. Member countries are required to submit Conventions to their competent national authorities with a view to ratification. If a country ratifies a Convention it agrees to bring its laws into line with its terms and to report periodically how these regulations are being applied. More than 5,200 ratifications of 166 Conventions had been deposited by mid-1987. Machinery is available to ascertain whether Conventions thus ratified are effectively applied.

Recommendations do not require ratification, but member states are obliged to consider them with a view to giving effect to their provisions by legislation or other action. By the end of 1987 the International Labour Conference had adopted 174 recommendations.

Organization. The ILO consists of the International Labour Conference, the Governing Body and the International Labour Office.

The Conference is the supreme deliberative organ of the ILO; it meets annually at Geneva. National delegations are composed of 2 government delegates, 1 employers' delegate and 1 workers' delegate.

The Governing Body, elected by the Conference, is the executive council. It is composed of 28 government members, 14 workers' members and 14 employers' members.

Ten governments hold permanent seats on the Governing Board because of their industrial importance, namely, Brazil, China, Federal Republic of Germany, France, India, Italy, Japan, USA, USSR and UK. The remaining 18 government seats were, at the end of 1987, held by Algeria, Angola, Argentina, Burkina Faso, Canada, Ethiopia, Finland, Ghana, Hungary, Indonesia, Iraq, Jamaica, Mongolia, Nicaragua, Pakistan, Ukraine, Venezuela, Zimbabwe.

The Office serves as secretariat, operational headquarters, research centre and publishing house.

The ILO budget for 1988–89 amounted to US$324m.

Activities. In addition to its research and advisory activities, the ILO extends technical co-operation to governments under its regular budget and under the UN Development Programme and Funds-in-Trust in the fields of employment promotion, human resources development (including vocational and management training), development of social institutions, small-scale industries, rural development, social security, industrial safety and hygiene, productivity, etc. Technical co-operation also includes expert missions and a fellowship programme. Over $100m. was spent on technical co-operation in 1986. Projects were in progress in some 115 countries and about 900 experts involved.

Major emphasis is being given to the ILO's World Employment Programme, launched in 1969 with the purpose of stimulating national and international efforts to increase the volume of productive employment, and so to counter the problem of rising unemployment in developing countries. Employment strategy missions were carried out under the Programme in Colombia, the Dominican Republic, Egypt, Iran, Kenya, Sri Lanka, Sudan and the Philippines. The work of these missions was complemented by an ILO programme of research designed to provide policy-makers with the information to promote employment. A World Employment Conference was held in June 1976.

The International Labour Conference (Geneva, June 1987) held a first discussion on proposed new standards concerning employment and social security, and concerning safety and health in the construction industry. At its Maritime Session (Geneva, Sept.-Oct. 1987) the Conference adopted a Convention and a Recommendation on seafarers' welfare, a Convention on social security protection, a Convention on health protection and medical care and a revised Convention and Recommendation on repatriation.

In 1960 the ILO established in Geneva the International Institute for Labour Studies. The Institute specializes in advanced education and research on social and labour policy. It brings together for group study experienced persons from all parts of the world—government administrators, trade-union officials, industrial experts, management, university and other specialists.

A training institution was opened by the ILO in Turin, Italy, in 1965—the International Centre for Advanced Technical and Vocational Training. The Centre provides opportunities for technical, vocational and management training for individuals who have advanced beyond the facilities available in their own countries. Courses are geared particularly to the needs of developing countries.

Headquarters: International Labour Office, CH-1211 Geneva 22, Switzerland.
Director-General: Francis Blanchard (France).
Chairman of the Governing Body: Victor Russomano (Brazil).
London Branch Office: 96/98 Marsham St., SW1P 4LY.

The ILO has regional offices in Addis Ababa (for Africa), Bangkok (for Asia and the Pacific), Lima (for Latin America and the Caribbean) and Geneva (for Arab States).

Publications: Regular periodicals in English, French and Spanish include the *International Labour Review, Legislative Series, Bulletin of Labour Statistics, Year Book of Labour Statistics, Official Bulletin* and *Labour Education. Women at Work* and the *Social and Labour Bulletin* are issued in English and French.

New volumes published in 1987 included: *Adjustment and Economic Performance in Developing Countries: A Synthesis. The Cost of Occupational Accidents and Diseases. Economically Active Population, Estimates and Projections: 1950–2025* (Vols. I-VI). *Employers and the Environmental Challenge. Ethanol, Employment and Development: Lessons from Brazil. Improve Your Business. Indirect Remuneration: An International Overview. Job Evaluation. Management Consulting: A Guide to the Profession. A Manager's Guide to International Labour Standards. New Cargo-Handling Techniques: Implications for Port Employment and Skills. Safety and Health in Coal Mines: An ILO Code of Practice. Social and Economic Effects of Petroleum Development in Non-OPEC Developing Countries: Synthesis Report. Trade, Employment and Industrialisation in Singapore. Workers' Participation: A Voice in Decisions, 1981-85.*

FOOD AND AGRICULTURE ORGANIZATION OF THE UNITED NATIONS (FAO)

Origin. The UN Conference on Food and Agriculture in May 1943, at Hot Springs, Virginia, set up an Interim Commission in Washington in July 1943 to plan the Organization, which came into being on 16 Oct. 1945.

Aims and Activities. The aims of FAO are to raise levels of nutrition and standards of living; to improve the production and distribution of all food and agricultural products from farms, forests and fisheries; to improve the living conditions of rural populations; and, by these means, to eliminate hunger.

In carrying out these aims, FAO promotes investment in agriculture, better soil and water management, improved yields of crops and livestock, and the transfer of technology to, and the development of agricultural research in, developing countries. FAO promotes the conservation of natural resources and the rational use of fertilizers and pesticides. The Organization combats animal diseases, promotes the development of marine and inland fisheries, and encourages the rational use of forest resources. Technical assistance is provided in all these fields and others such as nutrition, agricultural engineering, agrarian reform, development communications, remote sensing for natural resources, and the prevention of food losses.

Special FAO programmes help countries prepare for, and provide relief in the event of, emergency food situations, in particular through the setting up of food reserves. Since the early 1980s, Africa has needed special emphasis and FAO created a special task force for that continent. The Agricultural Rehabitation Plan for Africa, begun in 1985, channelled some US$190m. to projects in 25 countries during its two years of operation. The Global Information and Early Warning System provides current information on the world food situation and identifies countries threatened by shortages to guide potential donors.

The Organization also has a major rôle in the collection, analysis and dissemination of information on natural resources and agricultural production.

FAO sponsors the World Food Programme (WFP) with the UN; WFP uses food commodities, cash and services contributed by member States of the UN to back programmes of social and economic development, as well as for relief in emergency situations.

Finance and Administration. The FAO Conference, composed of all member states, meets every other year to determine the policy and approve the budget and work programme of FAO. The Council, consisting of 49 member nations elected by the Conference, serves as FAO's governing body between Sessions of the Conference. At its 24th Session in Nov. 1987, the Conference approved a Regular Programme budget for the two years 1988–89 of US$492m., an increase of about 0·25% in real terms over the previous period. However, the slide in the value of the US dollar was a contributing factor, together with other international financial conditions, in reducing considerably the funds available to FAO by the end of the previous biennium. The Regular Programme, which is financed by contributions from member governments, covers the cost of the Organization's secretariat, its Technical Co-operation Programme and part of the cost of several Special Action Programmes.

FAO provides advice and assistance in the field through its Field Programmes, funded largely from external sources, such as the UN Development Programme (UNDP) and trust funds provided by governments. Funds available from UNDP have declined – from US$167m. in 1980 to around US$125m. in 1986. The drop has been partially offset by increases in trust funds and in funds available through the Technical Co-operation Programme funded from FAO's own Regular Programme budget. Trust fund delivery in 1986 was expected to be about US$150m. Delivery under the Technical Co-operation Programme in 1986 was about US$35m., compared with US$21m. in 1984. Total Field Programme delivery in 1986 exceeded US$315m., still well below 1981 delivery in real terms.

Headquarters: Via delle Terme di Caracalla, Rome, Italy.
Director-General: Dr Edouard Saouma (Lebanon).

FAO publications include: FAO Books in Print 1980–81: The State of Food and Agriculture (annual), 1974 ff.; *The FAO World Food Report* (annual), 1983 ff.; *Animal Health Yearbook* (annual), 1957 ff.; *Production Yearbook* (annual), 1947 ff.; *Trade Yearbook* (annual), 1947 ff.; *FAO Commodity Review* (annual), 1961 ff.; *Yearbook of Forest Products Statistics* (annual), 1947 ff.; *Yearbook of Fishery Statistics* (in two volumes). *Ceres* (bi-monthly). *Food and Nutrition* (bi-annual), *FAO Fertilizer Yearbook, FAO Plant Protection Bulletin* (quarterly), *World Animal Review* (quarterly).

UNITED NATIONS EDUCATIONAL, SCIENTIFIC AND CULTURAL ORGANIZATION (UNESCO)

Origin. A Conference for the establishment of an Educational, Scientific and Cultural Organization of the United Nations was convened by the Government of the UK in association with the Government of France, and met in London, 1–16 Nov. 1945. UNESCO came into being on 4 Nov. 1946.

Functions. The purpose of UNESCO is to contribute to peace and security by promoting collaboration among the nations through education, science and culture in order to further universal respect for justice, for the rule of law and for the human rights and fundamental freedoms which are affirmed for the peoples of the world, without distinction of race, sex, language or religion, by the Charter of the United Nations.

Activities. The education programme has four main objectives: the extension of education; the improvement of education; and life-long education for living in a world community.

To train teachers specialized in the techniques of fundamental education UNESCO is helping to establish regional and national training centres. A centre for Latin America was opened in Mexico in 1951, one for the Arab States was set up in Egypt in 1953. UNESCO seeks to promote the progressive application of the right to free and compulsory education for all and to improve the quality of education everywhere.

In the natural sciences, UNESCO seeks to promote international scientific co-operation, such as the International Hydrological Programme which began in

1966. It encourages scientific research designed to improve the living conditions of mankind. Science co-operation offices have been set up in Montevideo, Cairo, New Delhi, Nairobi and Jakarta.

In the field of communication, UNESCO endeavours, by disseminating information, carrying out research and providing advice, to increase the scope and quality of press, film and radio services throughout the world.

In the cultural field, UNESCO assists member states in studying and preserving both the physical and the non-physical heritage of each society.

In the social sciences UNESCO helps in the development of research and teaching facilities and focuses on questions concerning Peace, Human Rights, Philosophy, Youth and Development Studies.

Organization. The organs of UNESCO are a General Conference (composed of representatives from each member state), an Executive Board (consisting of 51 government representatives elected by the General Conference) and a Secretariat. UNESCO had 158 members in 1986.

National commissions act as liaison groups between UNESCO and the educational, scientific and cultural life of their own countries.

Budget for 1986–87: $289,338,980.

Headquarters: UNESCO House, 7 Place de Fontenoy, Paris.
Director-General: Federico Mayor (Spain).

Periodicals. Museum (quarterly, English and French); *International Social Science Journal* (quarterly, English and French); *Impact of Science on Society* (quarterly, English and French); *Unesco Courier* (monthly, English, French and Spanish); *Prospects* (quarterly, English, French and Spanish); *Copyright Bulletin* (twice-yearly, English and French); *Unesco News* (English and French); *Nature and Resources* (quarterly, English, French and Spanish).

Hajnal, P. I., *Guide to UNESCO.* London and New York, 1983

WORLD HEALTH ORGANIZATION (WHO)

Origin. An International Conference, convened by the UN Economic and Social Council, to consider a single health organization resulted in the adoption on 22 July 1946 of the constitution of the World Health Organization. This constitution came into force on 7 April 1948.

Structure. The principal organs of WHO are the World Health Assembly, the Executive Board and the Secretariat. Each of the 166 member states and 1 Associate Member (1986) has the right to be represented at the Assembly, which meets annually usually in Geneva, Switzerland. The 31-member Executive Board is composed of technically qualified health experts designated by as many member states elected by the Assembly. The Secretariat consists of technical and administrative staff headed by a Director-General. Health activities in member countries are carried out through regional organizations which have been established in Africa (regional office, Brazzaville), South-East Asia (New Delhi), Europe (Copenhagen), Eastern Mediterranean (Alexandria) and Western Pacific (Manila). The Pan American Sanitary Bureau in Washington serves as the Regional Office of WHO for the Americas.

Functions. WHO's objective, as stated in the first article of the Constitution is 'the attainment by all peoples of the highest possible level of health'. As the directing and co-ordinating authority on international health it establishes and maintains collaboration with the UN, specialized agencies, government health administrations, professional and other groups concerned with health. The Constitution also directs WHO to assist governments to strengthen their health services, to stimulate and advance work to eradicate diseases, to promote maternal and child health, mental health, medical research and the prevention of accidents; to improve standards of teaching and training in the health professions, and of nutrition, housing, sanitation, working conditions and other aspects of environment health. The Organization also is empowered to propose conventions, agreements and regulations and make recommendations about international health matters; to revise the international nomenclature of diseases, causes of death and public health practices; to develop, establish and promote international standards concerning foods, biological, pharmaceutical and similar substances.

Methods of work. Co-operation in country projects is undertaken only on the request of the government concerned, through the 6 regional offices of the Organization. Worldwide technical services are made available by headquarters. Expert committees whose members are chosen from the 54 advisory panels of experts meet to advise the Director-General on a given subject. Scientific groups and consultative meetings are called for similar purposes. To further the education of health personnel of all categories, seminars, technical conferences and training courses are organized and advisors, consultants and lecturers are provided. WHO awards fellowships for study to nationals of member countries.

Activities. The main thrust of WHO's activities in recent years has been towards promoting national, regional and global strategies for the attainment of the main social target of the Member States for the coming years: 'Health for All by the Year 2000', or the attainment by all citizens of the world of a level of health that will permit them to lead a socially and economically productive life.

Almost all countries indicated a high level of political commitment to this goal, and guiding principles for formulating corresponding strategies and plans of action were prepared.

The 40th World Health Assembly, meeting in May 1987, approved an effective working budget of US$633·98m for 1988-89. This represented a slight decrease over the 1986-87 budget in real terms, the increase of about US$90m. in nominal terms being due to the rate of exchange of the US$1 and other cost increases due mainly to inflation.

AIDS. The Assembly urged Member States to co-operate with one another and share in full openness with WHO all information on AIDS and related infections. It also appealed to countries to make voluntary contributions in cash and kind for the implementation of the global strategy for the prevention and control of AIDS.

Health Manpower Imbalance. In a resolution, the Assembly asked countries to take urgent measures to adjust the production of health manpower in order to bring the supply and distribution into line with expected future demand for services. It had been noted that while there was a shortage of certain categories of health workers in many countries, an increasing number of Member States had an oversupply of health professionals such as physicians and dentists, leading to their under-utilization, unemployment and migration to other countries.

Fortieth Anniversary of WHO. In 1988, 40 years will have elapsed since the WHO was founded. All governments were invited to take the greatest possible advantage of the anniversary to focus the attention of people in all walks of life – from ordinary citizens to the highest political leaders – upon past achievements, and present and future aspirations of the Organization through appropriate events, celebrations and information dissemination.

Maternal Health and Safe Motherhood. Noting that extremely high levels of maternal mortality and morbidity prevail in many developing countries, constituting in some cases 50% of all deaths in women of childbearing age, the Assembly urged Member States to give high priority to health and nutrition programmes directed towards girls from infancy to adolescence.

Diarrhoeal Diseases Control. The Assembly noted 'with appreciation' the reduction in deaths due to diarrhoea as a result of progress made by national diarrhoeal diseases control programmes and requested WHO to increase collaboration with Member States in this area.

Technical Discussions. The topic of the Technical Discussions in 1987 was Economic Support for National Health for All Strategies. The main conclusion drawn was that health is a shared responsibility which rests upon the individual, the community and the government and that the collective commitment of all concerned is required in order to secure adequate economic support for health for all strategies.

Traditional Medicine. The Assembly urged countries to ensure quality control of drugs derived from traditional plant remedies by using modern techniques and applying suitable standards and good manufacturing practices.

World Health Day. World Health Day, 7 April 1987, was devoted to the theme Immunization – A Chance for Every Child. The theme chosen for World Health Day 1988 (WHO's 40th Anniversary) is Health for All – All for Health.

Headquarters: 1211 Geneva 27. *Regional Offices:* Alexandria, Brazzaville, Copenhagen, Manila, New Delhi, Washington.
  Director-General: Dr Halfdan T. Mahler (Denmark).

Basic Documents. 36th ed., 1986 (Arabic, Chinese, English, French, Russian, Spanish)
Handbook of Resolutions and Decisions. Vol. I, 1973, Vol. II, 1985 and Vol. III, 1 ed., 1987 (Arabic, English, French, Russian, Spanish)
World Health Forum (from 1980, quarterly: Arabic, Chinese, English, French, Russian and Spanish)
Bulletin of WHO (quarterly, 1947–51; 6 issues a year from 1978; bilingual English/French)
International Digest of Health Legislation (quarterly, from 1948; English and French)
World Health, the Magazine of WHO. 1957 ff. (10 issues a year; English, French, German, Portuguese, Russian and Spanish; and 4 issues a year. Arabic and Persian)
WHO Technical Report Series, 1950 ff. (Arabic, Chinese, English, French, Russian, Spanish)
Public Health Papers, 1959 ff. (Arabic, English, French, Russian, Spanish)
World Health Statistics Annual (from 1952; English, French and Russian)
World Health Statistics Quarterly (monthly, 1947–76 then quarterly; bilingual English/French)
Weekly Epidemiological Record (from 1926; bilingual English/French)
Publications of the WHO, 1947–57; catalogue: 1947–79 (1980); 1980–85 (1985), 1986
World Directories:
Medical Schools, 1987; Schools of Public Health and Postgraduate Training Programmes in Public Health (1985); Schools for Medical Assistants, 1973 (1976); *Auxiliary Sanitarians 1973* (1978); *Dental Auxiliaries 1973* (1977); *Medical Lab. Technicians and Assistants, 1973* (1977)
The International Pharmacopoeia. 3rd. ed., 3 vols, 1979, 1981, 1987 (English, French and Spanish)
Manual of the International Statistical Classification of Diseases, Injuries and Causes of Death. 9th rev. (1977; English, French, Russian, Spanish)
IARC Monographs on the Evaluation of Carcinogenic Risk of Chemicals to Humans. 1967 ff. (English)
International Histological Classification of Tumours. Books and slides, from 1967, No. 25, 1980 (English, French, Russian and Spanish)
Report on the World Health Situation. 1959 ff. (Arabic, Chinese, English, French, Russian, Spanish); Seventh report (1987)
The Work of WHO, 1984–85: Biennial Report of the Director-General (1986) (Arabic, Chinese, English, French, Russian, Spanish)
International Health Regulations (1969). 3rd annotated ed., 1983 (Arabic, English, French, Russian, Spanish)

INTERNATIONAL MONETARY FUND (IMF)

The International Monetary Fund was established on 27 Dec. 1945 as an independent international organization and began operations on 1 March 1947; its relationship with the UN is defined in an agreement of mutual co-operation which came into force on 15 Nov. 1947. The first amendment to the Fund's articles creating the special drawing right (SDR) took effect on 28 July 1969 and the second amendment took effect on 1 April 1978.

The capital resources of the Fund come from SDRs and currencies that the members pay under quotas calculated for them when they join the Fund. Members' quotas in the Fund, in 1987, amounted to SDR 89,988m. and are closely related to (*i*) subscription to the Fund, (*ii*) their drawing rights on the Fund under both regular and special facilities, (*iii*) their voting power, and (*iv*) their share of any allocations of SDRs. Every Fund member is required to subscribe to the Fund an amount equal to its quota. An amount not exceeding 25% of the quota has to be paid in reserve assets, the balance in the member's own currency.

The Fund is authorized under its Articles of Agreement to supplement its resources by borrowing. In Jan. 1962, a 4-year agreement was concluded with 10 industrial members (Belgium, Canada, France, Federal Republic of Germany, Italy, Japan, Netherlands, Sweden, UK, USA) who undertook to lend the Fund up to $6,000m. in their own currencies, if this should be needed to forestall or cope with an impairment of the international monetary system. Switzerland subsequently joined the group. These arrangements, known as the General Arrangements to Borrow (GAB), have been extended several times and the most recent 5-year renewal was to end in Oct. 1985. In early 1983 agreement was reached to increase the credit arrangements under the GAB to SDR 17,000m.; to permit use of GAB resources in transactions with Fund members that are not GAB participants; to authorize Swiss participation; and to permit borrowing arrangements with non-participating members to be associated with the GAB. Saudi Arabia and the Fund have entered into such an arrangement under which the Fund will be able to borrow up to SDR 1,500m. to assist in financing purchases by any member for the same purpose and under the same circumstances as in the GAB. The changes became effective by 26 Dec. 1983. The GAB have been used to finance drawings made by the UK in 1964, 1965, 1968, 1969, and 1977, by France in 1969 and 1970, and by the USA in 1978. The Fund has also borrowed from member countries and official institutions for two oil facilities and a supplementary financing facility. More recently, it has borrowed from the Saudi Arabian Monetary Agency (SAMA) and has concluded an SDR 3,000m. borrowing arrangement with Japan.

Purposes: To promote international monetary co-operation, the expansion of international trade and exchange rate stability; to assist in the removal of exchange restrictions and the establishment of a multilateral system of payments; and to alleviate any serious disequilibrium in members' international balance of payments by making the financial resources of the Fund available to them, usually subject to conditions to ensure the revolving nature of Fund resources.

Activities. Each member of the Fund undertakes a broad obligation to collaborate with the Fund and other members to ensure the existence of orderly exchange arrangements and to promote a system of stable exchange rates. In addition, members are subject to certain obligations relating to domestic and external policies that can affect the balance of payments and the exchange rate. The Fund makes its resources available, under proper safeguards, to its members to meet short-term or medium-term payments difficulties. The first allocation of special drawing rights was made on 1 Jan. 1970 with five SDR allocations since then. SDRs in existence now total SDR 21,400m. To further enhance its balance of payments assistance to its members the Fund established a compensatory financing facility on 27 Feb. 1963, temporary oil facilities in 1974 and 1975, a trust fund in 1976, and an extended facility for medium-term assistance to members with special balance of payments problems on 13 Sept. 1974 with additional financing now provided through a policy of enlarged access. In March 1986, it established the structural adjustment facility (SAF) to provide assistance to low-income countries.

The Committee on Reform of the International Monetary System and Related Issues, generally known as the Committee of Twenty, held its first session at the 1972 annual meeting, with the mandate to advise and report to the Board of Governors on all aspects of the international monetary system, including proposals for any amendments of the Articles of Agreement. The Committee of Twenty disbanded after submitting its final report in 1974. An Interim Committee of the Board of Governors on the International Monetary System and a Joint Ministerial Committee of the Boards of Governors of the World Bank and the Fund on the Transfer of Real Resources to Developing Countries (Development Committee) were established and held their initial meetings in Jan. 1975 and since then have met on a semi-annual basis. Details of the reform of the international monetary system were incorporated in the second amendment of the Fund's Articles of Agreement, effective April 1978. In order to oversee the compliance of members with their obligations under the Articles of Agreement, the Fund is required to exercise firm surveillance over their exchange rate policies.

Organization. The highest authority in the Fund is exercised by the Board of Governors on which each member government is represented. Normally the Governors meet once a year, although the Governors may take votes by mail or other means between annual meetings. The Board of Governors has delegated many of its powers to the executive directors in Washington, of whom there are 22, of which 6 are appointed by individual members and the other 16 elected by groups of countries. Each appointed director has voting power proportionate to the quota of the government he represents, while each elected director casts all the votes of the countries which elected him. The 6 appointed executive directors represent the US, UK, France, Federal Republic of Germany, Japan and Saudi Arabia.

The managing director is selected by the executive directors; he presides as chairman at their meetings, but may not vote except in case of a tie. His term is for 5 years, but may be extended or terminated at the discretion of the executive directors. He is responsible for the ordinary business of the Fund, under general control of the executive directors, and supervises a staff of about 1,700.

Headquarters: 700 19th St. NW, Washington, D.C., 20431. Offices in Paris and Geneva.

Managing Director: Michel Camdessus (France).

Publications. *Summary Proceedings of Annual Meetings of the Board of Governors.— Annual Report of the Executive Board.—Selected Decisions of the International Monetary Fund and Selected Documents.—Financial Statement* (quarterly).*—International Financial Statistics* (monthly).*—IMF Survey* (bi-weekly).*—Balance of Payments Statistics.* Washington, monthly.*—IMF Staff Papers* (four times a year). Washington, from Feb. 1950.*—IMF Occasional Papers.—IMF Pamphlets.—Annual Report on Exchange Arrangements and Exchange Restrictions.* Washington, 1950 ff.*—Finance and Development.* Washington, from June 1964 (quarterly).*—Direction of Trade Statistics.* Washington (monthly). *IMF World Economic and Financial Surveys.* Washington. *Government Finance Statistics Yearbook. The International Monetary Fund, 1945–65: Twenty Years of International Monetary Co-operation.* 3 vols. Washington D.C. 1969

de Vries, M. G., *The International Monetary Fund, 1966–1971: The System Under Stress.* 2 vols. Washington D.C. 1976.*—The International Monetary Fund 1972–1978: Co-operation on Trial.* 3 vols. Washington D.C., 1985

INTERNATIONAL BANK FOR RECONSTRUCTION AND DEVELOPMENT (IBRD)

Conceived at the Bretton Woods Conference, July 1944, the 'World Bank' began operations in June 1946. Its purpose is to provide funds and technical assistance to facilitate economic development in its poorer member countries.

The Bank obtains its funds from the following sources: Capital paid in by member countries; sales of its own securities; sales of parts of its loans; repayments; and net earnings. The subscribed capital of the Bank amounted to $85,231m. at 30 June 1987. On 4 Jan. 1980, the Board of Governors adopted a resolution that increased the authorized capital stock of the Bank by 331,500 shares. This represented an increase of approximately $40,000m. The resolution provides that the paid-in portion of the shares authorized to be subscribed under it will be 7·5%, compared with the 10% paid-in portion of existing capital stock. Outstanding market-based borrowings had reached $79,420m. by 30 June 1987. The Bank is self-supporting. Its net earnings for year ending 30 June 1987 amounted to $1,113m.

By 30 June 1986 the Bank had made 2,818 loans totalling $140,286m. in 102 of its 150 member countries. Lending was for the following purposes: Agriculture and rural development, $29,119·2m.; Development Finance Companies, $13,961·6m.; education, $4,955·1m.; energy, $32,097·1m.; industry, $8,547·6m.; non-project, $9,622·4m.; population, health and nutrition, $742·1m.; small-scale enterprizes, $3,397·8m.; telecommunications, $2,507·2m.; tourism, $363·6m.; transportation, $22,980·4m.; urban development, $5,080·2m.; water supply and sewerage, $6,638·8m., and technical assistance, $273·7m. In order to eliminate wasteful overlapping of development assistance and to ensure that the funds available are used to the best possible effect, the Bank has organized consortia or consultative groups of aidgiving nations for the following countries: Bangladesh, Bolivia, Burma, Colombia, Côte d'Ivoire, Egypt, Ethiopia, Ghana, Guinea, Guinea-Bissau, India, Kenya, Korea, Madagascar, Malawi, Mauritania, Mauritius, Morocco, Nepál, Nigeria, Pakistan, Peru, the Philippines, Senegal, Somalia, Sri Lanka, Sudan, Tanzania, Thailand, Togo, Tunisia, Uganda, Zaïre, Zambia and the Caribbean Group for Co-operation in Economic Development. The Bank furnishes a wide variety of technical assistance. It acts as executing agency for a number of pre-investment surveys financed by the UN Development Programme. Resident missions have been established in 38 developing member countries as well as 3 regional missions in East and West Africa and Thailand primarily to assist in the preparation of projects. The Bank helps member countries to identify and prepare projects for the development of agriculture, education and water supply by drawing on the expertise of the FAO, WHO, UNIDO and UNESCO through its co-operative agreements with these organizations. The Bank maintains a staff college, the Economic Development Institute in Washington, D.C., for senior officials of the member countries.

Headquarters: 1818 H St., NW, Washington, D.C., 20433, USA. *European office:* 66 avenue d'Iéna, 75116 Paris, France. *London office:* New Zealand House, Haymarket, SW1Y 4TE, England. *Tōkyō office:* Kokusai Building, 1-1, Marunouchi 3-chome, Chiyoda-ku, Tōkyō 100, Japan.

President: Barber B. Conable, Jr., (USA).

Publications. Annual Reports. 1946 ff.—*Summary Proceedings of Annual Meetings.* 1947 ff.—*The World Bank Group.* 1971.—*The World Bank Atlas.* 1967 ff.—*Catalog of Publications,* 1986.—*World Development Report.* 1978 ff.
Payer, C., *The World Bank: A Critical Analysis.* London, 1982

INTERNATIONAL DEVELOPMENT ASSOCIATION (IDA)

A lending agency which came into existence on 24 Sept. 1960. Administered by the World Bank, IDA is open to all members of the Bank.

IDA concentrates its assistance on those countries with an annual *per capita* gross national product of less than $790 (1983 rate). Its resources consist mostly of subscriptions, general replenishments from its more industrialized and developed members, special contributions, and transfers from the net earnings of the Bank. IDA credits are made to Governments only. It had committed over $43,307·7m. for 1,699 development projects in 83 countries, by 30 June 1987.

INTERNATIONAL FINANCE CORPORATION (IFC)

The Corporation, an affiliate of the World Bank, was established in July 1956. Paid-in capital at 30 June 1987 was $721·9m., subscribed by 132 member countries. In addition, it has accumulated earnings of $337·6m. IFC supplements the activities of the World Bank by encouraging the growth of productive private enterprises in less developed member countries. Chiefly, IFC makes investments in the form of subscriptions to the share capital of privately owned companies, or long-term loans, or both. The Corporation will help finance new ventures, and it will also assist established enterprises to expand, improve or diversify their operations.

At 30 June 1986 IFC had approved investments amounting to $9,230m., in 92 countries. The total amount of loans and equity which IFC had sold or agreed to sell to other investors as of that date was $3,826m.

President: Barber B. Conable, Jr., (USA).
Executive Vice-President: Sir William Ryrie (UK).

Publications. Annual Reports. 1956 ff.—*IFC Basic Information.* 1986

INTERNATIONAL CIVIL AVIATION ORGANIZATION (ICAO)

Origin. The Convention providing for the establishment of the International Civil Aviation Organization was drawn up by the International Civil Aviation

Conference held in Chicago from 1 Nov. to 7 Dec. 1944. A Provisional International Civil Aviation Organization (PICAO) operated for 20 months until the formal establishment of ICAO on 4 April 1947.

The Convention on International Civil Aviation superseded the provisions of the Paris Convention of 1919, which established the International Commission for Air Navigation (ICAN), and the Pan American Convention on Air Navigation drawn up at Havana in 1928.

Functions. It assists international civil aviation by establishing technical standards for safety and efficiency of air navigation and promoting simpler procedures at borders; develops regional plans for ground facilities and services needed for international flying; disseminates air-transport statistics and prepares studies on aviation economics; fosters the development of air law conventions. As part of the UN Development Programme it provides technical assistance to States in developing civil aviation programmes.

Organization. The principal organs of ICAO are an Assembly, consisting of all members of the Organization, and a Council, which is composed of 33 states elected by the Assembly, for 3 years, and meets in virtually continuous session. In electing these states, the Assembly must give adequate representation to: (1) states of major importance in air transport; (2) states which make the largest contribution to the provision of facilities for the international civil air navigation; (3) those states not otherwise included whose election will ensure that all major geographical areas of the world are represented. The main subsidiary bodies are: the Air Navigation Commission, composed of 15 members appointed by the Council; Air Transport Committee, open to council members; and the Legal Committee, on which all members of ICAO may be represented. There are 157 members. Budget for 1987: US$30,816,000.

Headquarters: 1000 Sherbrooke St. West, Montreal, Quebec, Canada H3A 2R2.
President: Dr Assad Kotaite (Lebanon).
Secretary-General: Yves Lambert (France).

Annual Report of the Council. (English, French, Russian, Spanish)
ICAO Bulletin (Monthly)

UNIVERSAL POSTAL UNION (UPU)

Origin. The UPU was established on 1 July 1875, when the Universal Postal Convention adopted by the Postal Congress of Berne on 9 Oct. 1874 came into force. The UPU was known at first as the General Postal Union, its name being changed at the Congress of Paris in 1878. In 1980 there were 158 member countries.

Functions. The aim of the UPU is to assure the organization and perfection of the various postal services and to promote, in this field, the development of international collaboration. To this end, the members of UPU are united in a single postal territory for the reciprocal exchange of correspondence.

Organization. The UPU is composed of a Universal Postal Congress which usually meets every 5 years, a permanent Executive Council consisting of 40 members, a consultative Committee, which consists of 35 members elected on a geographical basis by each Congress, and an International Bureau, which functions as the permanent secretariat.

Since 1 July 1948 the Union has been governed by the revised Convention adopted by the twelfth Congress in Paris on 5 July 1947.
Budget for 1981: US$9·5m.

Headquarters: Weltpoststrasse 4, 3000, Berne 15, Switzerland.
Director-General: Mohamed Ibrahim Sobhi (Egypt).

Publications. Documents of the Lausanne Congress 1974. Bern, 1975.—*Universal Postal Convention: Paris, 5 July, 1948.* (Cmd. 7435).—*The Postal Union* (monthly, Arabic, Chinese, English, French, German, Spanish, Russian).—*The UPU: Its Foundation and Development.* Bern, 1959.

INTERNATIONAL TELECOMMUNICATION UNION (ITU)

Origin. In 1932, at Madrid, the Union decided to merge the Telegraph Convention adopted in 1865 and the Radiotelegraph Convention adopted in 1906 into a single International Telecommunication Convention within annex, the Telegraph and Radio Regulations. It also decided to change its name to International Telecommunication Union to better reflect all its new responsibilities. The ITU has been governed since 1 Jan. 1983 by the revised International Telecommunication Convention adopted in Nairobi in 1982.

Functions. (1) to maintain and extend international co-operation for the improvement and rational use of telecommunications of all kinds, as well as to promote and to offer technical assistance to developing countries in the field of telecommunications; (2) to promote the development of technical facilities and their most efficient operation with a view to improving the efficiency of telecommunication services, increasing their usefulness and making them, so far as possible, generally available to the public; (3) to harmonize the actions of nations in the attainment of those ends.

Organization. The ITU consists of the Plenipotentiary Conference, Administrative Conferences, the Administrative Council of 41 members, and of 4 permanent organs (the General Secretariat, the International Frequency Registration Board, and 2 international consultative committees, one for radio and one for telephone and telegraph).

Budget for 1988: Sw.Frs.106,011,000.

Headquarters: Place des Nations, Geneva, Switzerland.
Secretary-General: Richard E. Butler (Australia).

WORLD METEOROLOGICAL ORGANIZATION (WMO)

Origin. A Conference of Directors of the International Meteorological Organization (set up in 1873), meeting in Washington in 1947, adopted a Convention creating the World Meteorological Organization. The WMO Convention became effective on 23 March 1950, and WMO was formally established on 19 March 1951, when the first session of its Congress was convened in Paris. An agreement to bring WMO into relationship with the United Nations was approved by this Congress and came into force on 21 Dec. 1951 with its approval by the General Assembly of the United Nations.

Functions. (1) To facilitate world-wide co-operation in the establishment of networks of stations for the making of meteorological observations as well as hydrological or other geophysical observations related to meteorology, and to promote the establishment and maintenance of meteorological centres charged with the provision of meteorological and related services; (2) to promote the establishment and maintenance of systems for the rapid exchange of meteorological and related information; (3) to promote standardization of meteorological and related observations and to ensure the uniform publication of observations and statistics; (4) to further the application of meteorology to aviation, shipping, water problems, agriculture and other human activities; (5) to promote activities in operational hydrology and to further close co-operation between meteorological and hydrological services; and (6) to encourage research and training in meteorology and, as appropriate, to assist in co-ordinating the international aspects of such research and training.

Organization. WMO is an inter-governmental organization of 155 member states and 5 member territories responsible for the operation of their own meteorological services. Constituent bodies of WMO are the World Meteorological Congress which meets every 4 years, the executive council composed of 36 members elected in their personal capacity and including the President and 3 Vice-Presidents of the Organization, 6 regional associations of members and 8 technical commissions established by the Congress. A permanent secretariat is maintained in Geneva.

Budget for 1988–91: Sw.Frs.170m.

Headquarters: Case postale 5, CH-1211, Geneva 20, Switzerland.
Secretary-General: G. O. P. Obasi (Nigeria).
Publications. *WMO Bulletin.* 1952 ff.—*Meteorological Services of the World.* 1985.
—*Publications of the World Meteorological Organization, 1951–1986.*

INTERNATIONAL MARITIME ORGANIZATION (IMO)

Origin. The International Maritime Organization, until 1982 known as Inter-Governmental Maritime Consultative Organization (IMCO), was established as a specialized agency of the UN by a convention drawn up at the UN Maritime Conference held at Geneva in Feb./March 1948. The Convention became effective on 17 March 1958 when it had been ratified by 21 countries, including 7 with at least 1 m. gross tons of shipping each. The International Maritime Organization started operations in Jan. 1959.

Functions. To facilitate co-operation among governments on technical matters affecting merchant shipping, especially concerning safety at sea; to prevent and control marine pollution caused by ships; to facilitate international maritime traffic. The International Maritime Organization is responsible for convening international maritime conferences and for drafting international maritime conventions. It also provides technical assistance to countries wishing to develop their maritime activities.

Organization. The International Maritime Organization had 131 members (and 1 associate member) in 1987. The Assembly, composed of all member states, normally meets every 2 years. The Council of 32 member states acts as governing body between Assembly sessions. The Maritime Safety Committee deals with all technical questions relating to maritime safety. It has established several sub-committees to deal with specific problems and like the Marine Environment Protection Committee, Legal Committee, Facilitation Committee and Committee on Technical Co-operation is open to all International Maritime Organization members. The Secretariat is composed of international civil servants.

The International Maritime Organization is depositary authority for the International Convention for the Safety of Life at Sea, 1960, and the Regulations for Preventing Collisions at Sea, 1948 and 1960; the International Convention for the Prevention of Pollution of the Sea by Oil, 1954, as amended in 1962 and 1969; the Convention on Facilitation of International Maritime Traffic, 1965; the International Convention on Load Lines, 1966; the International Convention on Tonnage Measurement of Ships, 1969; the International Convention relating to Intervention on the High Seas in cases of Oil Pollution Casualties, 1969; the International Convention on Civil Liability for Oil Pollution Damage, 1969; Convention on International Compensation Fund for Oil Pollution Damage, 1971; Special Trade Passenger Ships Agreement, 1971; Convention on International Regulations for Preventing Collisions at Sea, 1972; the International Convention for Safe Containers, 1972; the International Convention on Prevention of Pollution from Ships, 1973 as modified by the Protocol of 1978; the International Convention for the Safety of Life at Sea, 1974; Athens Convention relating to the Carriage of Passengers and their Luggage by Sea, 1974; Convention on the International Maritime Satellite Organization, 1976; Convention on Limitation of Maritime Claims, 1976; Torremolinos International Convention for the Safety of Fishing Vessels, 1977; International Convention on Standards of Training, Certification and Watchkeeping for Seafarers, 1978; International Convention on Maritime Search and Rescue, 1979.

Headquarters: 4 Albert Embankment, London SE1 7SR.
Secretary-General: C. P. Srivastava (India).
Assistant General Secretaries: T. A. Mensah (Ghana), Y. Sasamura (Japan).
IMO News

GENERAL AGREEMENT ON TARIFFS AND TRADE (GATT)

Origin. The General Agreement on Tariffs and Trade was negotiated in 1947 and entered into force on 1 Jan. 1948. Its 23 original signatories were members of a Preparatory Committee appointed by the UN Economic and Social Council to draft the charter for a proposed International Trade Organization. Since this charter was never ratified, the General Agreement, intended as an interim arrangement, has instead remained as the only international instrument laying down trade rules accepted by countries responsible for most of the world's trade. In Oct. 1987 there were 95 contracting parties, with one country acceding provisionally, and a further 29 countries applying GATT rules on a *de facto* basis.

Functions. GATT functions both as a multilateral treaty that lays down a common code of conduct in international trade and trade relations and as a forum for negotiation and consultation to overcome trade problems and reduce trade barriers. Key provisions of the Agreement guarantee most-favoured-nation treatment (exceptions being granted to customs unions and free trade areas, and for certain preferences in favour of developing countries); require that protection be given to domestic industry only through tariffs (apart from specified exceptions); provide for negotiations to reduce tariffs (which are then 'bound' against subsequent increase) and other trade distortions; and lay down principles (particularly in Part IV of the Agreement, added in 1965) to assist the trade of developing countries. The Agreement also provides for consultation on, and settlement of, disputes, for 'waivers' (the grant of authorization, when warranted, to derogate from specific GATT obligations) and for emergency action in defined circumstances.

Seven 'rounds' of multilateral trade negotiations, including the Kennedy Round of 1964–67, have been completed in GATT. The latest in this series, the Tōkyō Round, although held in Geneva, was so called because it was launched at a Ministerial meeting in the Japanese capital in Sept. 1973.

Ninety-nine countries participated in the Tōkyō Round. In Nov. 1979, the negotiations were concluded with agreements covering: an improved legal framework for the conduct of world trade (which includes recognition of tariff and non-tariff treatment in favour of and among developing countries as a permanent legal feature of the world trading system); non-tariff measures (subsidies and countervailing duties; technical barriers to trade; government procurement; customs valuation; import licensing procedures; and a revision of the 1967 GATT anti-dumping code); bovine meat; dairy products; tropical products; and an agreement on free trade in civil aircraft. The agreements contain provisions for special and more favourable treatment for developing countries.

Participating countries also agreed to reduce tariffs on thousands of industrial and agricultural products, for the most part over a period of 7 years ending on 1 Jan. 1987. As a result of these concessions, industrialized countries have reduced the average level of their import duties on manufactures by about 34%, a cut comparable to that achieved in the Kennedy Round.

The agreements providing an improved framework for the conduct of world trade took effect in Nov. 1979. The other agreements took effect on 1 Jan. 1980, except for those covering government procurement and customs valuation, which took effect on 1 Jan. 1981, and the concessions on tropical products which began as early as 1977. Committees were established to supervise implementation of each of the Tōkyō Round agreements.

On 20 Sept. 1986, agreement was reached to launch the Uruguay Round of multilateral trade negotiations. In Oct. 1987, there were 105 states participating in the negotiations.

The Declaration is divided into two sections. The first covers negotiations on trade in goods. Its objectives are to bring about further liberalization and expansion of world trade; to strengthen the role of GATT and improve the multilateral trading system; to increase the responsiveness of GATT to the evolving international economic environment; and to encourage co-operation in strengthening the inter-relationship between trade and other economic policies affecting growth and development.

In the area of trade in goods, Ministers committed themselves to a 'standstill' on new trade measures inconsistent with their GATT obligations and to a 'rollback' programme aimed at phasing out existing inconsistent measures. Negotiations are being undertaken in the following areas: tariffs, non-tariff measures, tropical products, natural resource-based products, textiles and clothing, agriculture, subsidies, safeguards, trade-related aspects of intellectual property rights, including trade in counterfeit goods, and trade-related investment measures. Participants are reviewing certain GATT Articles, attempting to improve and strengthen the dispute settlement procedure, and negotiations aimed at improving, clarifying or expanding the agreements reached during the Tōkyō Round. One part of the negotiation is devoted to the functioning of the GATT system itself.

The second part of the Declaration covers a negotiation on trade in services.

To assist the trade of developing countries, GATT established in 1964 the International Trade Centre (since 1968 operated jointly with the UN Conference on Trade and Development) to provide information and training on export markets and marketing techniques. Other GATT action in favour of developing countries includes training courses on trade policy questions, organization of seminars and briefings, and technical assistance to delegations in the form of data and background documentation.

Budget for 1987: Sw. Frs. 61,122,300.

Headquarters: Centre William Rappard, 154 rue de Lausanne, 1211 Geneva 21, Switzerland.

Director-General: Arthur Dunkel (Switzerland).

Publications. *Basic Instruments and Selected Documents.* 4 vols. and 33 supplements 1952–86.—*International Trade* [i.e., annual review], 1952 ff. Annually from 1953.—*GATT, What It Is, What It Does.*—*GATT Activities,* 1960 ff. Annually from 1972.—*GATT Focus.* From Feb. 1981 (10 issues a year).—*GATT Studies in International Trade.* 1971 ff. (irregular series).—*The Tokyo Round of Multilateral Trade Negotiations.* Report of the Director-General, 2 vols., 1979.—*Textile and Clothing in the World Economy,* 1984.—*The World Markets for Dairy Products.* Annually from 1981.—*The International Markets for Meat.* Annually from 1981

Casadio, G. P., *Transatlantic Trade: USA–EEC Confrontation in the GATT Negotiations.* Farnborough, 1973

Dam, K. W., *The GATT: Law and International Economic Organization.* Chicago and London, 1970

Golt, S., *The GATT Negotiations, 1973–75: A Guide to the Issues.* London, 1974

Hudec, R. E., *The GATT Legal System and World Trade Diplomacy.* New York, 1975

Long, O., *Law and its Limitations in the GATT Multilateral Trade System.* Dordrecht, 1985

WORLD INTELLECTUAL PROPERTY ORGANIZATION (WIPO)

Origin. The Convention establishing WIPO was signed at Stockholm in 1967 by 51 countries, and entered into force in April 1970. In Dec. 1974 WIPO became a specialized agency of the UN. *Inter alia* it took over the functions of the United International Bureaux for the Protection of Intellectual Property, also known as BIRPI (the French acronym of that name), which were established in 1893 to administer the affairs of the two principal international intellectual property treaties – the Paris Convention for the Protection of Industrial Property of 1883 and the Berne Convention for the Protection of Literary and Artistic Works of 1886.

Functions. WIPO is responsible for the promotion of the protection of intellectual property throughout the world. Intellectual property comprises two main branches: industrial property (chiefly, patent and other rights in technological inventions, rights in trademarks, industrial designs, appellations of origin, etc.) and copyright and neighbouring rights (chiefly in literary, musical and artistic works, in films and records, etc.). WIPO administers various international treaties, of which the most important are the Paris Convention for the Protection of Industrial Property and the Berne Convention for the Protection of Literary and Artistic Works. WIPO also carries out a substantial programme of activities in promoting creative intellectual activity and in facilitating the transfer of technology, especially to and among developing countries.

Membership of WIPO is open to any State which is a member of at least one of the Unions created by the Paris Convention and the Berne Convention and to other States which are members of the organizations of the United Nations system, are party to the Statute of the International Court of Justice, or are invited to join by the General Assembly of WIPO. Membership of the Unions is open to any State.

The number of member states of WIPO was 117 on 31 Dec. 1987; in addition, 14 States are party to treaties administered by WIPO but have not yet become members of WIPO.

Organization. The bodies of WIPO are: The *General Assembly* consisting of all member states of WIPO which are members of any of the Unions. Among its other functions, the General Assembly appoints and gives instructions to the Director General, reviews and approves his reports and adopts the biennial budget of expenses common to the Unions. The *Conference,* consisting of all States members of WIPO whether or not they are members of any of the Unions. Among its functions, the Conference adopts its biennial budget and establishes the biennial programme of legal-technical assistance. The *Co-ordination Committee,* consisting of the States members of WIPO which are members of the Executive Committees of the Paris or Berne Unions.

In addition, the Paris and Berne Unions have Assemblies and Executive Committees, with functions similar to those of the WIPO bodies in respect of the biennial budgets and programmes of the Unions.

The *WIPO Permanent Committees for Development Co-operation Related to Industrial Property* and *Related to Copyright and Neighbouring Rights* plan and review activities in the said fields; the *WIPO Permanent Committee on Industrial Property Information* is responsible for intergovernmental co-operation in industrial property documentation and information matters such as the standardization and exchange of patent documents.

WIPO has an international staff of around 300. The working languages of the Organization are: English, French and Spanish, with, to a lesser extent, Arabic and Russian.

Headquarters: 34, chemin des Colombettes, 1211 Geneva 20, Switzerland.
Director-General: Dr Arpad Bogsch (USA).

Periodicals. Industrial Property (monthly, in English and French).—*Copyright* (monthly, in English and French).—*Les Marques internationales* (monthly, in French).—*International Designs Bulletin* (monthly, in English and French)—*Newsletter* (irregular, in Arabic, English, French, Portuguese, Russian and Spanish)—*PCT Gazette* (fortnightly, in English and French)—*Les appellations d'origine* (irregular, in French)—*Intellectual Property in Asia and the Pacific* (quarterly, in English). The Organization also produces a large selection of publications related to intellectual property.

INTERNATIONAL FUND FOR AGRICULTURAL DEVELOPMENT (IFAD)

The establishment of IFAD was one of the major actions proposed by the 1974 World Food Conference. The agreement for IFAD entered into force on 30 Nov. 1977 following attainment of initial pledges of $1,000m. and the agency began its operations the following month. IFAD's purpose is to mobilise additional funds for agricultural and rural development in developing countries through projects and programmes directly benefiting the poorest rural population. In line with the Fund's focus on the rural poor, its resources are being made available in highly concessional loans.

Organization. The Governing Council, consisting of the entire membership, directs the Fund's operations. The chief executive is the President, who is also the Chairman of the 18-member Executive Board.

President: Idriss Jafairy (Algeria).
Headquarters: 107 Via del Serafico, Rome, Italy.

THE COMMONWEALTH

The Commonwealth is a free association of sovereign independent states, numbering 48 at the beginning of 1988. There is no charter, treaty or constitution; the association is expressed in co-operation, consultation and mutual assistance for which the Commonwealth Secretariat is the central co-ordinating body.

The Commonwealth was first defined by the Imperial Conference of 1926 as a group of 'autonomous communities within the British Empire, equal in status, in no way subordinate one to another in any aspect of their domestic or foreign affairs, though united by a common allegiance to the Crown, and freely associated as members of the British Commonwealth of Nations'. The basis of the association changed from one owing allegiance to a common Crown, and the modern Commonwealth was born in 1949 when the member countries accepted India's intention of becoming a republic at the same time continuing 'her full membership of the Commonwealth of Nations and her acceptance of the King as the symbol of the free association of its independent member nations and as such the Head of the Commonwealth'. There are now (1988) 17 Queen's realms, 26 republics, and 5 indigenous monarchies in the Commonwealth. All acknowledge the Queen symbolically as Head of the Commonwealth.

The Queen's legal title rests on the statute of 12 and 13 Will. III, c. 3, by which the succession to the Crown of Great Britain and Ireland was settled on the Princess Sophia of Hanover and the 'heirs of her body being Protestants'. By proclamation of 17 July 1917 the royal family became known as the House and Family of Windsor. On 8 Feb. 1960 the Queen issued a declaration varying her confirmatory declaration of 9 April 1952 to the effect that while the Queen and her children should continue to be known as the House of Windsor, her descendants, other than descendants entitled to the style of Royal Highness and the title of Prince or Princess, and female descendants who marry and their descendants should bear the name of Mountbatten-Windsor. The Royal Style and Titles of Queen Elizabeth are: In *Antigua and Barbuda* 'Elizabeth the Second, by the Grace of God, Queen of Antigua and Barbuda and of Her other Realms and Territories, Head of the Commonwealth'. In *Australia*: 'Elizabeth the Second, by the Grace of God Queen of Australia and Her other Realms and Territories, Head of the Commonwealth'. In the *Bahamas*: 'Elizabeth the Second, by the Grace of God, Queen of the Commonwealth of the Bahamas and of Her other Realms and Territories, Head of the Commonwealth'. In *Barbados*: 'Elizabeth the Second, by the Grace of God, Queen of Barbados and of Her other Realms and Territories, Head of the Commonwealth'. In *Belize*: 'Elizabeth the Second, by the Grace of God, Queen of Belize and of Her Other Realms and Territories, Head of the Commonwealth'. In *Canada*: 'Elizabeth the Second, by the Grace of God of the United Kingdom, Canada and Her other Realms and Territories Queen, Head of the Commonwealth, Defender of the Faith'. In *Grenada*: 'Elizabeth the Second, by the Grace of God, Queen of the United Kingdom of Great Britain and Northern Ireland and of Grenada and Her other Realms and Territories, Head of the Commonwealth'. In *Jamaica*: 'Elizabeth the Second, by the Grace of God of Jamaica and of Her other Realms and Territories Queen, Head of the Commonwealth'. In *Mauritius*: 'Elizabeth the Second, Queen of Mauritius and of Her other Realms and Territories, Head of the Commonwealth'. In *New Zealand*: 'Elizabeth the Second, by the Grace of God Queen of New Zealand and Her Other Realms and Territories, Head of the Commonwealth, Defender of the Faith'. In *Papua New Guinea*: 'Elizabeth the Second, Queen of Papua New Guinea and Her other Realms and Territories, Head of the Commonwealth'. In *Saint Christopher and Nevis:* 'Elizabeth the Second, by the Grace of God, Queen of Saint Christopher and Nevis and Her other Realms and Territories, Head of the Commonwealth'. In *Saint Lucia*: 'Elizabeth the Second, by the Grace of God, Queen of Saint Lucia and of Her other Realms and Territories, Head of Commonwealth'. In *Saint Vincent and the Grenadines*: 'Elizabeth the Second, by the Grace of God, Queen of Saint Vincent and the Grenadines and of Her other Realms and Territories, Head of the Commonwealth'. In *Solomon Islands*: 'Elizabeth the Second by the Grace of God Queen of Solomon Islands and of Her other Realms and Territories, Head of the Commonwealth'. In *Tuvalu*: 'Elizabeth the Second by the Grace of God Queen of Tuvalu and of Her other Realms and Territories, Head of the Commonwealth'. In the *United Kingdom*: 'Elizabeth the Second, by the Grace of God of the United Kingdom of Great Britain and Northern Ireland and of Her other Realms and Territories Queen, Head of the Commonwealth, Defender of the Faith'.

A number of territories, formerly under British jurisdiction or mandate did not join the Commonwealth: Egypt, Iraq, Transjordan, Burma, Palestine, Sudan, British Somaliland, South Cameroons, and Aden. Two countries, the Republic of South Africa in 1961 and Pakistan in 1972, have left the Commonwealth. Fiji's membership lapsed with the emergence of the Republic in 1987.

Nauru and Tuvalu are special members, with the right to participate in all functional Commonwealth meetings and activities but not to attend meetings of Commonwealth Heads of Government.

Member States. The following are the member countries, with their dates of independence, and, where appropriate, the date on which they became republics: *United Kingdom*; *Canada* 1 July 1867[1]; *Australia* 1 Jan. 1901[1]; *New Zealand* 26 Sept. 1907[1]; *India* 15 Aug. 1947 (Republic on 26 Jan. 1950); *Sri Lanka* 4 Feb. 1948 (Republic on 22 May 1972); *Ghana* 6 March 1957 (Republic on 1 July 1960); *Malaysia* 31 Aug. 1957 as Federation of Malaya, 16 Sept. 1963 as Federation of Malaysia; *Cyprus* 16 Aug. 1960 (Republic on independence; joined Commonwealth on 13 March 1961); *Nigeria* 1 Oct. 1960 (Republic on 1 Oct. 1963); *Sierra Leone* 27 April 1961 (Republic on 19 April 1971); *Tanzania*–Tanganyika 9 Dec. 1961 (Republic on 9 Dec. 1962), Zanzibar 10 Dec. 1963 (Republic on 12 Jan. 1964), United Republic of Tanganyika and Zanzibar 26 April 1964; renamed United Republic of Tanzania 29 Oct. 1964; *Western Samoa* 1 Jan. 1962 (joined Commonwealth on 28 Aug. 1970); *Jamaica* 6 Aug. 1962; *Trinidad and Tobago* 31 Aug. 1962 (Republic on 1 Aug. 1976); *Uganda* 9 Oct. 1962 (Republic 8 Sept. 1967, second republic 25 Jan. 1971); *Kenya* 12 Dec. 1963 (Republic on 12 Dec. 1964); *Malaŵi* 6 July 1964 (Republic on 6 July 1966); *Malta* 21 Sept. 1964 (Republic on 13 Dec. 1974); *Zambia* 24 Oct. 1964 (Republic on independence); *The Gambia* 18 Feb. 1965 (Republic on 24 April 1970); *Maldives* 26 July 1965 (Republic on independence, joined Commonwealth on 9 July 1982); *Singapore* 16 Sept. 1963 as a state in the Federation of Malaysia, 9 Aug. 1965 as an independent state and republic not part of Malaysia; *Guyana* 26 May 1966 (Republic on 23 Feb. 1970); *Botswana* 30 Sept. 1966 (Republic on independence); *Lesotho* 4 Oct. 1966; *Barbados* 30 Nov. 1966; *Nauru* 31 Jan. 1968 (Republic on independence); *Mauritius* 12 March 1968; *Swaziland* 6 Sept. 1968; *Tonga* 4 June 1970; *Bangladesh* seceded from Pakistan as Republic 16 Dec. 1971, recognized by United Kingdom 4 Feb. 1972 (joined Commonwealth on 18 April 1972); *Bahamas* 10 July 1973; *Grenada* 7 Feb. 1974; *Papua New Guinea* 16 Sept. 1975; *Seychelles* 29 June 1976 (Republic on independence); *Solomon Islands* 7 July 1978; *Tuvalu* 1 Oct. 1978; *Dominica* 3 Nov. 1978 (Republic on independence); *Saint Lucia* 22 Feb. 1979; *Kiribati* 12 July 1979 (Republic on independence); *Saint Vincent and the Grenadines* 27 Oct. 1979; *Zimbabwe* 18 April 1980 (Republic on independence); *Vanuatu* 30 July 1980 (Republic on independence); *Belize* 21 Sept. 1981; *Antigua* and *Barbuda* 1 Nov. 1981; *Saint Christopher and Nevis* 19 Sept. 1983; *Brunei*[2] 1 Jan 1984.

[1] These are the effective dates of independence, given legal effect by the Statute of Westminster 1931.

[2] Brunei was a sovereign state in treaty relationship with Britain, whereby Britain was responsible for the conduct of external affairs and had a consultative responsibility for defence. It had never been a dependent territory, and in 1971 had ceased to be a protected state. A Treaty of Friendship and Co-operation was signed on 7 Jan. 1979, becoming effective on 1 Jan. 1984 when Brunei assumed her full international responsibilities and Britain gave up her consultative commitment over defence matters.

Dependent Territories and Associated States. There are 15 British dependent territories, 7 Australian external territories, 2 New Zealand dependent territories and 2 New Zealand associated states. A dependent territory is a territory belonging by settlement, conquest or annexation to the British, Australian or New Zealand Crown.

United Kingdom dependent territories administered through the Foreign and Commonwealth Office comprise, in the Far East: Hong Kong; in the Indian Ocean: British Indian Ocean Territory; in the Mediterranean: Gibraltar; in the Atlantic Ocean: Bermuda, Falkland Islands, South Georgia and the South Sandwich Islands, British Antarctic Territory, St Helena, St Helena Dependencies (Ascension and Tristan da Cunha); in the Caribbean: Montserrat, British Virgin Islands,

Cayman Islands, Turks and Caicos Islands, Anguilla; in the Western Pacific: Pitcairn Group of Islands. The Australian external territories are: Coral Sea Islands Territory, Cocos (Keeling) Islands, Christmas Island, Heard Island and McDonald Islands, Norfolk Island, Australian Antarctic Territory and the Territory of Ashmore and Cartier Islands. The New Zealand dependent territories are: Tokelau and Ross Dependency. The New Zealand associated states are: Cook Islands and Niue.

While constitutional responsibility to Parliament for the government of the British dependent territories rests with the Secretary of State for Foreign and Commonwealth Affairs, the administration of the territories is carried out by the Governments of the territories themselves.

British Government Department. With effect from 17 Oct. 1968, the Secretary of State for Foreign and Commonwealth Affairs is responsible for the conduct of relations with members of the Commonwealth as well as with foreign countries, and for the administration of British dependent territories.

Commonwealth Secretariat. The Commonwealth Secretariat is an international body at the service of all 48 member countries. It provides the central organization for joint consultation and co-operation in many fields. It was established in 1965 by Commonwealth Heads of Government and has observer status at the UN General Assembly.

The Secretariat disseminates information on matters of common concern, organizes and services meetings and conferences, co-ordinates many Commonwealth activities, and provides expert technical assistance for economic and social development through the multilateral Commonwealth Fund for Technical Cooperation. The Secretariat is organized in divisions and sections which correspond to its main areas of operation: International affairs, economic affairs, food production and rural development, youth, education, information, applied studies in government, science and technology, law and health. Within this structure the Secretariat organizes the biennial meetings of Commonwealth Heads of Government, annual meetings of Finance Ministers of member countries, and regular meetings of Ministers of Education, Law, Health, and others as appropriate.

To emphasize the multilateral nature of the association, meetings are held in different cities and regions within the Commonwealth. Heads of Government decided that the Secretariat should work from London as it has the widest range of communications of any Commonwealth city, as well as the largest assembly of diplomatic missions.

The Commonwealth Secretary-General, who has access to Heads of Government, is the head of the Secretariat which is staffed by officers from member countries and financed by contributions from member governments.

Commonwealth Day is observed throughout the Commonwealth on the second Monday in March.

Headquarters: Marlborough House, Pall Mall, London, SW1Y 5HX.
Secretary-General: Shridath S. Ramphal (Guyana).

Books of Reference

The Commonwealth Year-Book, HMSO, Annual
The Cambridge History of the British Empire. 8 vols. CUP, 1929 ff.
Burns, Sir Alan, *In Defence of Colonies.* London, 1957
Chadwick, J., *The Unofficial Commonwealth.* London, 1982
Dale, W., *The Modern Commonwealth.* London, 1983
Garner, J., *The Commonwealth Office, 1925–1968.* London, 1978
Hailey, Lord, *An African Survey.* Rev. ed. Oxford, 1957.—*Native Administration in the British African Territories.* 5 vols. HMSO, 1951 ff.
Hall, H. D., *Commonwealth: A History of the British Commonwealth.* London and New York, 1971
Judd, D., and Slinn, P., *The Evolution of the Modern Commonwealth.* London, 1982
Keeton, G. W. (ed.), *The British Commonwealth: Its Laws and Constitutions.* 9 vols. London, 1951 ff.
McIntyre, W. D., *The Commonwealth of Nations: Origins and Impact 1869–1971.* Univ. of Minnesota Press and OUP, 1978

Mansbergh, N., *The Commonwealth Experience*. 2 vols. London, 1982

Maxwell, W. H. and L. F., *A Legal Bibliography of the British Commonwealth of Nations*. 2nd ed. London, 1956

Moore, R. J., *Making the New Commonwealth*. Oxford, 1987

Papadopoulos, A. N., *Multilateral Diplomacy within the Commonwealth: A Decade of Expansion*. The Hague, 1982

Smith, A., and Sanger, C., *Stitches in Time: The Commonwealth in World Politics*. New York, 1983

Wade, E. C. S., and Phillips, G. G., *Constitutional Law: An Outline of the Law and Practice of the Constitution, Including Central and Local Government and the Constitutional Relations of the British Commonwealth and Empire*. 8th ed. London, 1970

WORLD COUNCIL OF CHURCHES

The World Council of Churches was formally constituted on 23 Aug. 1948, at Amsterdam, by an assembly representing 147 churches from 44 countries. By 1988 the member churches numbered over 300, from more than 100 countries.

The basis of membership (1975) states: 'The World Council of Churches is a fellowship of Churches which confess the Lord Jesus Christ as God and Saviour according to the Scriptures and therefore seek to fulfil together their common calling to the glory of the one God, Father, Son and Holy Spirit.' Membership is open to Churches which express their agreement with this basis and satisfy such criteria as the Assembly or Central Committee may prescribe. Today 305 Churches of Protestant, Anglican, Orthodox, Old Catholic and Pentecostal confessions belong to this fellowship.

The World Council was founded by the coming together of several diverse Christian movements. These included the overseas mission groups gathered from 1921 in the International Missionary Council, the Faith and Order Movement founded by American Episcopal Bishop Charles Brent, and the Life and Work Movement led by Swedish Lutheran Archbishop Nathan Söderblom.

On 13 May 1938 at Utrecht a provisional committee was appointed to prepare for the formation of a World Council of Churches. It was under the chairmanship of William Temple, then Archbishop of York.

Assembly. The governing body of the World Council, consisting of delegates specially appointed by the member Churches. It meets every 7 or 8 years to frame policy and to consider some main theme. The Assembly has no legislative powers and depends for the implementation of its decisions upon the action of the member Churches. Assemblies have been held in Amsterdam (1948), Evanston (1954), New Delhi (1961), Uppsala (1968), and Nairobi (1975) and most recently in Vancouver, Canada in 1983 under the theme 'Jesus Christ – the Life of the World'. In between assemblies, a 150-member Central Committee meets annually to carry out the assembly mandate, with a smaller 22-member Executive Committee meeting twice a year.

Presidents: Dr Marga Bührig (Switzerland), Most Rev. W. P. K. Makhulu (Botswana), Dame R. Nita Barrow (Barbados), Bishop Johannes Hempel (German Democratic Republic), Dr Lois Wilson (Canada), Metropolitan Paulos Mar Gregorios (India), Patriarch Ignatios IV (Syria).

WCC programmes are organized from headquarters in Geneva, Switzerland, by a staff of 300 and a range of supervisory committees drawn from member churches. The 3 programme units are:

(i) Faith and Witness includes the Commission on Faith and Order, World Mission and Evangelism, Church and Society and the sub-unit on Dialogue with People of Living Faiths.

(ii) Justice and Service which includes Inter-Church Aid, Refugee and World Service (channelling over $35m. from member churches to areas of need); the Commission on the Churches' Participation in Development; the Commission of the Churches on International Affairs, the Programme to Combat Racism and the Christian Medical Commission.

(iii) Education and Renewal includes sections dealing with renewal and congregational life, women, youth, church-related education, biblical studies, family ministry and the Programme on Theological Education.

A General Secretariat with a Communication Department, finance and central services co-ordinates the work of these 3 units.

Since 1975 the WCC has held several major world conferences on such diverse themes as 'Faith, Science and the Future', 'Your Kingdom Come', 'Family Power and Social Change', 'Strategies for Churches Combating Racism in the 1980's', 'The Community of Women and Men in the Church', 'Giving an Account of the Hope that is in Us' and 'Called to be Neighbours'.

Officers of the Central and Executive Committees: *Moderator:* Rev. Dr Heinz J. Held (Federal Republic of Germany). *Vice-moderators:* Dr Sylvia Ross Talbot (USA), Metropolitan Chrysostomos of Myra (Turkey). *General Secretary:* The Rev. Dr Emilio Castro.

Office: PO Box 66, 150 route de Ferney, 1211 Geneva 20, Switzerland.

Books of Reference

Official Reports: The First [. . . *etc.*] *Assembly* (London, 1948, 1955, 1962, Geneva, 1968, 1975, 1983)
Directory of Christian Councils. 1985
New Delhi to Uppsala 1961–68. Geneva, 1968
Uppsala to Nairobi 1968–75. Geneva, 1975
Nairobi to Vancouver. Geneva, 1983
Official Reports of the Faith and Order Conferences at Lausanne 1927, Edinburgh 1937, Lund 1952, Montreal 1963, Meeting of Faith and Order Commission, Louvain 1971, Accra 1974, Bangalore 1978, Vancouver 1983
Official Reports of the Life and Work Conferences at Stockholm 1925 and Oxford 1937; World Conference on Church and Society 1966
Minutes of the Central Committee. Geneva, 1949 to date
Howell, L., *Acting in Faith: The World Council of Churches since 1975.* London, 1982
Hudson, D., *The World Council of Churches in International Affairs.* Leighton Buzzard, 1977
Potter, P., *Life in all its Fullness.* Geneva, 1981
van der Bent, A. J., *What in the World is the World Council of Churches?* Geneva, 1978.—*Handbook of Member Churches of the World Council of Churches.* Geneva, 1985
Visser 't Hooft, W. A., *The Genesis and Formation of the World Council of Churches.* Geneva, 1982

INTERNATIONAL TRADE UNIONISM

There are three main international trade union confederations *(i)* the International Confederation of Free Trade Unions (ICFTU) which has in membership most of the national trade union confederations in the Western industrialized countries as well as democratic organizations in Asia, Africa, and Latin America; *(ii)* the World Federation of Trade Unions (WFTU) which draws its support mainly from Eastern Europe, but which also has affiliates in France and in several developing countries; and *(iii)* the World Confederation of Labour (WCL) which has affiliates in Western Europe, Latin America and a small number of African and Asian countries. In addition, national trade unions are frequently members of international trade union federations, set up to protect the interests of working people in particular industries or trades, which are associated with the international confederations. The International Trade Secretariats (ITS) are associated with the ICFTU; Trade Union Internationals (TUI) with the WFTU; and the International Trade Federations (ITF) with the WCL.

Coldrick, A. P., and Jones, P., *International Directory of the Trade Union Movement.* London, 1979

History. The international trade union structure in 1988 was shaped mainly by developments since 1945. In that year the WFTU was set up with world-wide membership. Attempts by trade unions in Eastern Europe to turn the WFTU into an organization voicing unquestioning support for the policies of the USSR led most of the affiliates in the Western European countries to break away from the WFTU and to form the ICFTU in 1949.

EUROPEAN TRADE UNION CONFEDERATION. In Feb. 1973 the European Trade Union Confederation was formed by trade unionists in 15 Western European countries to deal with questions of interest to European working people arising inside and outside the EEC. All the founding organizations were ICFTU affiliates but subsequently they accepted into membership European WCL affiliates, the Irish Congress of Trade Unions and the Italian Communist and Socialist trade union centre (CGIL) and other national organizations. The ETUC Congress meets every 3 years and the Executive Committee 6 times a year. The membership was (June 1987) about 43m. from 35 centres in 21 countries.

General Secretary: Mathias Hinterscheid.
Headquarters: Rue Montagne aux Herbes Potagères 37, 1000 Brussels.

INTERNATIONAL CONFEDERATION OF FREE TRADE UNIONS. The first congress of ICFTU was held in London in Dec. 1949. The constitution as amended provides for co-operation with the United Nations and the International Labour Organization and for regional organizations to promote free trade unionism, especially in less-developed countries.

Organization. The Congress meets every 4 years. It elects the Executive Board of 37 members nominated on an area basis for a 4-year period; the Board meets at least twice a year. Various committees cover policy *vis-à-vis* such problems as those connected with nuclear energy and also the administration of the International Solidarity Fund. There are joint ICFTU–ITS committees for co-ordinating activities.

Headquarters: 37–41, rue Montagne aux Herbes Potagères, Brussels 1000, Belgium.

General Secretary: John Vanderveken.

Regional organizations exist in America, offices in Mexico City and Caracas; Asia, offices in New Delhi and Singapore; and Africa.

Membership. The ICFTU had Dec. 1977, 141 affiliated organizations in 97 countries, which together represent about 87m. workers. The 10 largest groups were the American Federation of Labor and Congress of Industrial Organizations (12·8m.), the British Trades Union Congress (9·6m.), the Federal German Deutscher Gewerkschaftsbund (7·8m.), the Confederazione Italiana Sindacati Lavoratori (3m.), the Swedish Landsorganisationen (2·1m.), the Indian National Trade Union Congress (4·3m.), Japanese Confederation of Labour, Rengo (4·5m.), Polish NSZZ Solidarnosc (5m.), Argentinian Confederacion General de Trabajo (5m.), Indian Hind Mazdoor Sabha (2·1m.).

Publications (in 4 languages). *Free Labour World* (bi-monthly); *Economic and Social Bulletin* (bi-monthly).

THE WORLD FEDERATION OF TRADE UNIONS. The WFTU formally came into existence on 3 Oct. 1945, representing trade-union organizations in more than 50 countries of the world, both Communist and non-Communist, excluding Federal Republic of Germany and Japan, as well as a number of lesser and colonial territories. Representation from the USA was limited to the Congress of Industrial Organizations, as the American Federation of Labor declined to participate.

In Jan. 1949 the British, USA and Netherlands trade unions withdrew from WFTU, which had come under complete Communist control; and by June 1951 all non-Communist trade-unions, and the Yugoslavian Federation, had left WFTU.

Organization. The Congress meets every 4 years. In between, the General Council, of 134 members (including deputies), is the governing body, meeting (in theory) at least once a year. The Bureau controls the activities of WFTU between meetings of the General Council; it consists of the President, the General Secretary and members from different continents, the total number being decided at each Congress. The Bureau is elected by the General Council.

General Secretary: I. Zakaria (Sudan).

Membership. A total membership of 206m. from 90 national centres is claimed. The biggest groups are the Soviet All-Union Central Council of Trade Unions (107m.), the German Democratic Republic Free German Trade Union Federation (8m.), the Czechoslovak Central Council of Trade Unions (6m.), the Romanian General Confederation of Labour (6·4m.), the Hungarian Central Council of Trade Unions (4·5m.) and the French Confederation of Labour (CGT, 2m.).

Publications. *World Trade Union Movement* (monthly, in 9 languages); *Trade Union Press* (fortnightly, in 6 languages).

WORLD CONFEDERATION OF LABOUR. The first congress of the International Federation of Christian Trade Unions (IFCTU), as the WCL was then called, met in 1920; but a large proportion of its 3·4m. members were in Italy and Germany, where affiliated unions were suppressed by the Fascist and Nazi régimes, and in 1940 IFCTU went out of existence. It was reconstituted in 1945, and declined to merge with WFTU and, later, with ICFTU. The policy of IFCTU was based on the papal encyclicals *Rerum novarum* (1891) and *Quadragesimo anno* (1931), but in 1968, when the Federation became the WCL, it was broadened to include other concepts. The WCL now has Protestant, Buddhist and Moslem members as well as its mainly Roman Catholic members.

Organization. The WCL is organized on a federative basis which leaves wide discretion to its autonomous constituent unions. Its governing body is the Congress, which meets every 4 years. The Congress appoints (or re-appoints) the Secretary-General at each 4-yearly meeting. The General Council which meets at least once a year, is composed of the members of the Confederal Board (at least 22 members, elected by the Congress) and representatives of national confederations, international trade federations, and trade union organizations where there is no confederation affiliated to the WCL. The Confederal Board is responsible for the general leadership of the WCL, in accordance with the decisions and directives of the Council and Congress. Headquarters: 71 rue Joseph II, Brussels 1040, Belgium.

Secretary-General: Jan Kulakowski.

There are regional organizations in Latin America (office in Caracas), Africa (office in Banjul, Gambia) and Asia (office in Manila) There is also a liaison centre in Montreal.

Membership. A total membership of 14m. in about 90 countries is claimed. The biggest group is the Confederation of Christian Trade Unions of Belgium (1·1m.).

Publication. *Labour Press and Information* (11 each year, in 5 languages).

ORGANISATION FOR ECONOMIC CO-OPERATION AND DEVELOPMENT (OECD)

History and Membership. On 30 Sept. 1961 the Organisation for European Economic Co-operation (OEEC), after a history of 13 years (*see* THE STATESMAN'S YEAR-BOOK, 1961, p. 32), was replaced by the Organisation for Economic Co-operation and Development. The change of title marks the Organisation's altered status and functions: with the accession of Canada and USA as full members it ceased to be a purely European body; while at the same time it added development aid to the list of its other activities. The member countries are now Australia,

Austria, Belgium, Canada, Denmark, Federal Republic of Germany, Finland, France, Greece, Iceland, Ireland, Italy, Japan, Luxembourg, the Netherlands, New Zealand, Norway, Portugal, Spain, Sweden, Switzerland, Turkey, UK and USA. Yugoslavia participates in the Organisation's activities with a special status. The Commission of the European Communities generally takes part in OECD's work.

Objectives. To promote economic and social welfare throughout the OECD area by assisting its member governments in the formulation of policies designed to this end and by co-ordinating these policies; and to stimulate and harmonize its members' efforts in favour of developing countries.

Organs. The supreme body of the Organisation is the Council composed of one representative for each member country. It meets either at Heads of Delegations level (about once a week) under the Chairmanship of the Secretary-General, or at Ministerial level (usually once a year) under the Chairmanship of a Minister of a country elected annually to assume these functions. Decisions and Recommendations are adopted by mutual agreement of all members of the Council.

The Council is assisted by an Executive Committee composed of 14 members of the Council designated annually by the latter. The major part of the Organisation's work is, however, prepared and carried out in numerous specialized committees and working parties and sub-groups, of which there exist over 200. Thus, the Organisation comprises Committees for Economic Policy; Economic and Development Review; Development Assistance (DAC); North-South Economics Issues; Commodities; Trade; Capital Movements and Invisible Transactions; Financial Markets; Fiscal Affairs; Restrictive Business Practices; Consumer Policy; Maritime Transport; International Investment and Multinational Enterprises; Tourism; Energy Policy; Industry; Steel; Scientific and Technological Policy; Information, Computer and Communications Policy; Road Transport Research; Education; Manpower and Social Affairs; Environment; Urban Affairs; Control of Chemicals; Agriculture; Fisheries, etc.

Four autonomous or semi-autonomous bodies also belong to the Organisation: the International Energy Agency (IEA); the Nuclear Energy Agency (NEA); the Development Centre and the Centre for Educational Research and Innovation (CERI). Each one of these bodies has its own governing committee.

The Council, the committees and the other bodies are serviced by an international Secretariat headed by the Secretary-General of the Organisation.

All member countries have established permanent Delegations to OECD, each headed by an Ambassador.

Chairman of the Council (ministerial): A minister from the country elected (annually) to assume this function.

Chairman of the Council (official level): The Secretary-General.

Secretary-General: Jean-Claude Paye (France).

Deputy Secretaries-General: Jacob M. Myerson (USA), Pierre Vinde (Sweden).

Executive Director of the International Energy Agency: Helga Steeg (Federal Republic of Germany).

Headquarters: 2, rue André Pascal, 75775 Paris Cedex 16, France.

OECD publishes numerous reports and statistical papers. Regular features include:
Activities of OECD. Annual
News from OECD. Monthly
Main Economic Indicators. Monthly
The OECD Observer. Bi-monthly
The OECD Economic Outlook. Semi-annual
OEEC/OECD Economic Surveys of Member Countries.
OECD Employment Outlook. Annual
Geographical Distribution of Financial Flows to Developing Countries. Annual
Development Co-operation Report. Annual
Tourism Policy and International Tourism in OECD Member Countries.
Maritime Transport. Annual
Energy Policies and Programmes of the IEA Member Countries.

NORTH ATLANTIC TREATY ORGANIZATION (NATO)

Western perceptions of the political situation in Europe following World War II gave rise, in 1947, to 2 major US initiatives – the Truman Doctrine and the Marshall Plan. These policies were designed to increase the ability of Western European countries to resist outside pressure and to assist them in bringing about their economic recovery. By 1948, on the initiative of the Foreign Secretary of the UK Ernest Bevin, 5 Western European nations had also entered into a treaty of mutual assistance in which they pledged themselves to come to each other's aid in the event of armed aggression against them (Brussels Treaty, 17 March 1948). The idea of a single mutual defence system involving North America as well as the European signatories of the Brussels Treaty was put forward by the Canadian Secretary of State for External Affairs in April 1948. It led, via the Vandenberg Resolution which enabled the US constitutionally to participate, to the creation of the Atlantic Alliance.

On 4 April 1949 the foreign ministers of Belgium, Canada, Denmark, France, Iceland, Italy, Luxembourg, the Netherlands, Norway, Portugal, the UK and the USA met in Washington and signed a treaty, the main clauses of which read as follows:

Article 1. The parties undertake, as set forth in the Charter of the United Nations, to settle any international disputes in which they may be involved by peaceful means in such a manner that international peace and security and justice are not endangered, and to refrain in their international relations from the threat or use of force in any manner inconsistent with the purposes of the United Nations.

Article 2. The parties will contribute toward the further development of peaceful and friendly international relations by strengthening their free institutions, by bringing about a better understanding of the principles upon which these institutions are founded, and by promoting conditions of stability and well-being. They will seek to eliminate conflict in their international economic policies and will encourage economic collaboration between any or all of them.

Article 3. In order more effectively to achieve the objectives of this treaty, the parties, separately and jointly by means of continuous and effective self-help and mutual aid, will maintain and develop their individual and collective capacity to resist armed attack.

Article 4. The parties will consult together whenever, in the opinion of any of them, the territorial integrity, political independence or security of any of the parties is threatened.

Article 5. The parties agree that an armed attack against one or more of them in Europe or North America shall be considered an attack against them all and consequently they agree that, if such an armed attack occurs, each of them, in exercise of the right of individual or collective self-defence recognized by article 51 of the Charter of the United Nations, will assist the party or parties so attacked by taking forthwith, individually and in concert with the other parties, such action as it deems necessary, including the use of armed force, to restore and maintain the security of the North Atlantic area. Any such armed attack and all measures taken as a result thereof shall immediately be reported to the Security Council. Such measures shall be terminated when the Security Council has taken the measures necessary to restore and maintain international peace and security.

Article 6. For the purpose of Article 5 an armed attack on one or more of the parties is deemed to include an armed attack *(i)* on the territory of any of the parties in Europe or North America, on the Algerian Departments of France, on the territory of Turkey or on the islands under the jurisdiction of any of the parties in the North Atlantic area north of the Tropic of Cancer; *(ii)* on the forces, vessels or aircraft of any of the parties, when in or over these territories or any other area in Europe in which occupation forces of any of the parties were stationed on the date when the treaty entered into force or the Mediterranean Sea or the North Atlantic area north of the Tropic of Cancer.

Article 8. Each party declares that none of the international engagements now in force between it and any other of the parties or any third state is in conflict with the provisions of this treaty, and undertakes not to enter into any international engagement in conflict with this treaty.

Article 10. The parties may, by unanimous agreement, invite any other European state in a position to further the principles of this treaty and to contribute to the security of the North Atlantic area to accede to this treaty. Any state so invited may become a party to the treaty by depositing its instrument of accession with the government of the United States of America. The government of the United States of America will inform each of the parties of the deposit of each such instrument of accession.

Article 12. After the treaty has been in force for 10 years, or at any time thereafter, the parties shall, if any of them so requests, consult together for the purpose of reviewing the treaty, having regard for the factors then affecting peace and security in the North Atlantic area, including the development of universal as well as regional arrangements under the Charter of the United Nations for the maintenance of international peace and security.

Article 13. After the treaty has been in force for 20 years, any party may cease to be a party one year after its notice of denunciation has been given to the government of the United States of America, which will inform the governments of the other parties of the deposit of each notice of denunciation.

The treaty came into force on 24 Aug. 1949. Greece and Turkey were admitted as parties to the treaty in 1952, the Federal Republic of Germany in 1955 and Spain in 1982.

NATO is an organization of sovereign states equal in status. Decisions taken are expressions of the collective will of member governments arrived at by common consent.

The North Atlantic Council is composed of representatives of the 16 member countries. At Ministerial Meetings of the Council, member nations are represented by Ministers of Foreign Affairs. These meetings are held twice a year. The Council also meets on occasion at the level of Heads of State and Government. In permanent session, at the level of Ambassadors, the Council meets at least once a week.

The Defence Planning Committee is composed of representatives of all member countries except France. Like the Council, it meets both in permanent session at the level of Ambassadors and twice a year at Ministerial level. At Ministerial Meetings member nations are represented by Defence Ministers.

The Council and Defence Planning Committee are chaired by the Secretary General of NATO at whatever level they meet. Opening sessions of Ministerial Meetings of the Council are presided over by the President, an honorary position held annually by the Foreign Minister of one of the member nations.

Nuclear matters are discussed by the Nuclear Planning Group in which 15 countries now participate. It meets regularly at the level of Permanent Representatives (Ambassadors) and twice a year at the level of Ministers of Defence.

The Permanent Representatives of member countries are supported by the National Delegations located at NATO Headquarters. The Delegations are composed of advisors and officials qualified to represent their countries on the various committees created by the Council. The Committees are supported by the International Staff responsible to the Secretary General.

Headquarters: 1110 Brussels, Belgium.
Secretary-General: Lord Carrington (UK).
Flag: Dark blue with a white compass rose of 4 points in the centre.

The *Military Committee* is responsible for making recommendations to the Council and the Defence Planning Committee on military matters and for supplying guidance to the Allied Commanders. Composed of the Chiefs-of-Staff of all member countries except France and Iceland (which has no military forces), the Committee is assisted by an International Military Staff. It meets at Chiefs-of-Staff level at least twice a year but remains in permanent session at the level of national military representatives. Liaison between the Military Committee and the French High Command is effected through the French Mission to the Military Committee. The permanent chairman of the Military Committee is elected by the Chiefs-of-Staff for a period of 2–3 years. The present chairman is Gen. Wolfgang Altenburg (Federal Republic of Germany), appointed Oct. 1986.

The area covered by the North Atlantic Treaty is divided among three commands: The Atlantic Ocean Command, the European Command and the Channel Command. Defence plans for the North American area are developed by the Canada–US Regional Planning Group.

The NATO commanders are responsible for the development of defence plans for their respective areas, for the determination of force requirements and for the deployment and exercise of the forces under their command.

The *Allied Command Europe* (ACE) covers the area extending from the North Cape to the Mediterranean and from the Atlantic to the eastern border of Turkey. Responsibilities relating to the defence of Portugal and the UK are included but these come within the purview of more than one NATO Command. The European area, which is subdivided into a number of subordinate commands, is under the Supreme Allied Commander Europe (SACEUR) whose Headquarters, near Mons in Belgium, are known as SHAPE (Supreme Headquarters Allied Powers Europe).

SACEUR has also under his orders the ACE Mobile Force, composed of both land and air force units from different member countries, which can be ready for action at very short notice in any threatened area. The present SACEUR is Gen. John R. Galvin (USA).

Under the Supreme Allied Commander Atlantic (SACLANT) the *Atlantic Command* extends from the North Pole to the Tropic of Cancer and from the coastal waters of North America to those of Europe and Africa, but excludes the Channel and the British Isles. SACLANT, who would have the primary task in wartime of ensuring the security of the sea lanes in the whole Atlantic area, is an operational rather than an administrative commander. Under his direct command is the Standing Naval Force Atlantic (STANAVFORLANT) which is a permanent international squadron of ships drawn from NATO navies which normally operate in the Atlantic.

The present SACLANT, whose Headquarters are in Norfolk (USA), is Admiral Lee Baggett, Jr. (US), appointed Nov. 1985.

The *Channel Command* covers the English Channel and the southern North Sea. Under the Allied Commander-in-Chief Channel (CINCHAN) its mission is to control and protect merchant shipping in the area, co-operating with SACEUR in the air defence of the Channel. The forces earmarked to the Command in emergency are predominantly naval but include maritime air forces. CINCHAN also has under his command the NATO Standing Naval Force Channel (STANAVFORCHAN) which is a permanent force comprizing mine counter-measure ships of different NATO countries. The present CINCHAN, with Head-quarters at Northwood (UK), is Vice-Admiral Sir Julian Oswald (UK), appointed May 1987.

The *Canada–US Regional Planning Group*, which covers the North American area, develops and recommends to the Military Committee plans for the defence of this area. It meets alternately in Washington and Ottawa.

Books of Reference

The NATO Information Service publishes documentation, reference material and information brochures including: *The NATO Handbook; NATO: Facts and Figures; The NATO Review* (periodical); economic and scientific publications.

De Staercke, A., *Nato's Anxious Birth: The Prophetic Vision of the 1940's.* London, 1985
Hanning, H., *NATO–Our Guarantee for Peace.* London, 1986
Henderson, N., *The Birth of NATO.* London, 1982
Hill-Norton, P., *No Soft Options: The Politico-Military Realities of NATO.* London, 1980
Kaplan, L. S., and Clawson, R. W., *NATO After Thirty Years.* Wilmington, 1981
Vigeveno, G., *The Bomb and European Security.* London, 1983
Williams, G. and A. Lee, *The European Defence Initiative.* London, 1986

WESTERN EUROPEAN UNION

On 17 March 1948 a 50-year treaty 'for collaboration in economic, social and cultural matters and for collective self-defence' was signed in Brussels by the Foreign Ministers of the UK, France, the Netherlands, Belgium and Luxembourg. (*See* THE STATESMAN'S YEAR-BOOK, 1954, pp. 32 f.)

On 20 Dec. 1950 the functions of the Western Union defence organization were transferred to the North Atlantic Treaty command, but it was decided that the reorganization of the military machinery should not affect the right of the Western

Union Defence Ministers and the Chiefs of Staff to meet as they please to consider matters of mutual concern to the Brussels Treaty powers.

After the breakdown of the European Defence Community on 30 Aug. 1954 a conference was held in London from 28 Sept. to 3 Oct. 1954, attended by Belgium, Canada, France, the Federal Republic of Germany, Italy, Luxembourg, the Netherlands, the UK and the USA, at which it was decided to invite the Federal Republic of Germany and Italy to accede to the Brussels Treaty, to end the occupation of Western Germany and to invite the latter to accede to the North Atlantic Treaty; the Federal Republic agreed that it would voluntarily limit its arms production, and provision was made for the setting up of an agency to control the armaments of the 7 Brussels Treaty powers; the UK undertook not to withdraw from the Continent her 4 divisions and the Tactical Air Force assigned to the Supreme Allied Commander against the wishes of a majority, *i.e.*, 4 of the Brussels Treaty powers, except in the event of an acute overseas emergency.

At a Conference of Ministers held in Paris from 20 to 23 Oct. 1954 these decisions were embodied in 4 Protocols modifying the Brussels Treaty which were signed in Paris on 23 Oct. 1954 and came into force on 6 May 1955.

The *Council of WEU* consists of the Foreign Ministers of the 7 powers or their representatives; it is so organized as to be able to exercise its functions continuously. An *Assembly,* composed of representatives of the Brussels Treaty powers to the Consultative Assembly of the Council of Europe, meets twice a year, usually in Paris. An *Agency for the Control of Armaments* and a *Standing Armaments Committee* have been set up in Paris. The social and cultural activities were transferred to the Council of Europe on 1 June 1960.

At a meeting of the Foreign, and Defence, Ministers of Western European Union held in Rome on 26–27 Oct. 1984, the Council adopted the 'Rome Declaration' and a document on the institutional reform of Western European Union. Member Governments support the reactivation of the Organization as a means of strengthening the European contribution to the North Atlantic Alliance and improving defence co-operation among the countries of Western Europe.

The Foreign Affairs and Defence Ministers meet twice a year. They met in Bonn, 22–23 April 1985, in Rome on 14 Nov. 1985, Venice on 29–30 April 1986, Luxembourg on 28 April 1987 and The Hague on 26–27 Oct. 1987.

Secretariat-General: 9 Grosvenor Place, London, SW1X 7HL.
Secretary-General: Alfred Cahen.

COUNCIL OF EUROPE

In 1948 the 'Congress of Europe', bringing together at The Hague nearly 1,000 influential Europeans from 26 countries, called for the creation of a united Europe, including a European Assembly. This proposal, examined first by the Ministerial Council of the Brussels Treaty Organization, then by a conference of ambassadors, was at the origin of the Council of Europe, which is, with its 21 member States, the widest organization bringing together all European democracies. The Statute of the Council was signed at London on 5 May 1949 and came into force 2 months later. The founder members were Belgium, Denmark, France, Ireland, Italy, Luxembourg, the Netherlands, Norway, Sweden and the UK. Turkey and Greece joined in 1949, Iceland in 1950, the Federal Republic of Germany in 1951 (having been an associate since 1950), Austria in 1956, Cyprus in 1961, Switzerland in 1963, Malta in 1965, Portugal in 1976, Spain in 1977 and Liechtenstein in 1978.

Membership is limited to European States which 'accept the principles of the rule of law and of the enjoyment by all persons within [their] jurisdiction of human rights and fundamental freedoms'. The Statute provides for both withdrawal (Art. 7) and suspension (Arts. 8 and 9). Greece withdrew from the Council in Dec. 1969 and rejoined in Nov. 1974.

Structure. Under the Statute two organs were set up: an inter-governmental *Committee of [Foreign] Ministers* with powers of decision and of recommendation to governments, and an inter-parliamentary deliberative body, the *Parliamentary Assembly* (referred to in the Statute as the *Consultative Assembly*)—both of which are served by the Secretariat. In addition, a large number of committees of experts have been established, two of them, the Council for Cultural Co-operation and the Committee on Legal Co-operation, having a measure of autonomy; on municipal matters the Committee of Ministers receives recommendations from the Conference of Local and Regional Authorities of Europe.

The Committee of Ministers meets usually twice a year, their deputies 12 times a year.

The Parliamentary Assembly normally consists of 170 parliamentarians elected or appointed by their national parliaments (Austria 6, Belgium 7, Cyprus 3, Denmark 5, France 18, Federal Republic of Germany 18, Greece 7, Iceland 3, Ireland 4, Italy 18, Liechtenstein 2, Luxembourg 3, Malta 3, Netherlands 7, Norway 5, Portugal 7, Spain 12, Sweden 6, Switzerland 6, Turkey 12, UK 18); it meets 3 times a year for approximately a week. The work of the Assembly is prepared by parliamentary committees.

The *Joint Committee* acts as an organ of co-ordination and liaison between representatives of the Committee of Ministers and members of the Parliamentary Assembly and gives members an opportunity to exchange views on matters of important European interest.

The European Convention on Human Rights, signed in 1950, set up special machinery to guarantee internationally fundamental rights and freedoms. The *European Commission of Human Rights* investigates alleged violations of the Convention submitted to it either by States or, in most cases, by individuals. Its findings can then be examined by the *European Court of Human Rights* (set up in 1959), whose obligatory jurisdiction has been recognized by 19 States, or by the Committee of Ministers, empowered to take binding decisions by two-thirds majority vote.

In 1956 the Resettlement Fund for National Refugees and Over-Population was created, the Governor of the Fund is responsible to the governments collectively. With 19 member countries, the main purpose of the Fund is to give financial aid, particularly in the spheres of housing, vocational training, regional planning and regional development. Since its foundation, the total amount of loans thus granted comes to over US$5,300m. at 31 Dec. 1987.

In 1970 the Council set up a European Youth Centre at Strasbourg, where young people can discuss their own approach to international co-operation. More recently, a European Youth Foundation was created, and which provides money to subsidize activities by European Youth Organizations in their own countries.

Aims and Achievements. Art. 1 of the Statute states that the Council's aim is 'to achieve a greater unity between its members for the purpose of safeguarding and realising the ideals and principles which are their common heritage and facilitating their economic and social progress'; 'this aim shall be pursued . . . by discussion of questions of common concern and by agreements and common action'. The only limitation is provided by Art. 1 *(d)*, which excludes 'matters relating to national defence'.

Although without legislative powers, the Assembly acts as the power-house of the Council, initiating European action in key areas by making recommendations to the Committee of Ministers. As the widest parliamentary forum in Western Europe, the Assembly also acts as the conscience of the area by voicing its opinions on important current issues. These are embodied in resolutions. The Ministers' rôle is to translate the Assembly's recommendations into action, particularly as regards lowering the barriers between the European countries, harmonizing their legislation or introducing where possible common European laws, abolishing discrimination on grounds of nationality and undertaking certain tasks on a joint European basis.

In May 1976 the first plan of intergovernmental co-operation to be undertaken by the Council of Europe was adopted by the Committee of Ministers. The third one, adopted in Nov. 1986, will run until Dec. 1991. The plan takes account of political developments and progress achieved, and covers 9 key areas: human rights, the media, social and socio-economic questions, education, culture and sport, youth, public health, environment and regional planning, local and regional government, and legal co-operation.

Some 125 Conventions and Agreements have been concluded covering such matters as social security, cultural affairs, conservation of European wild life and natural habitats, protection of archaeological heritage, extradition, medical treatment, equivalence of degrees and diplomas, the protection of television broadcasts, adoption of children and transportation of animals. Treaties in the legal field include the adoption of the European Convention on the Suppression of Terrorism, the European Convention on the Legal Status of Migrant Workers and the Transfer of Sentenced Persons. The Committee of Ministers adopted a European Convention for the protection of individuals with regard to the automatic processing of personal data (1981), a Convention on the transfer of sentenced persons (1983), a Convention on the compensation of victims of violent crimes (1983) and a Convention on spectator violence and misbehaviour at sport events and in particular at football matches (1985). The European Social Charter of 1965 sets out the social and economic rights which all member governments agree to guarantee to their citizens.

The official languages are English and French.

Chairman of the Committee of Ministers: (held in rotation).
President of the Parliamentary Assembly: Louis Jung (France).
President of the European Court of Human Rights: Rolv Ryssdal (Norway).
President of the European Commission of Human Rights: Carl Aage Nørgaard (Denmark).
Secretary-General: Marcelino Oreja (Spain).
Headquarters: Palais de l'Europe, 67006, Strasbourg, Cedex, France.
Flag: Dark blue with a ring of 12 gold stars in the centre.

The Information Department, Council of Europe, BP 431, R6-67006 Strasbourg-Cedex.
European Yearbook. The Hague, from 1955
Forum. Strasbourg, from 1978, 4 times a year
Yearbook on the Convention on Human Rights. Strasbourg, from 1958
Cook, C., and Paxton, J., *European Political Facts, 1918–84.* London, 1986

EUROPEAN COMMUNITIES

In May 1950 Belgium, France, the Federal Republic of Germany, Italy, Luxembourg and the Netherlands started negotiations with the aim of ensuring continual peace by a merging of their essential interests. The negotiations culminated in the signing in 1951 of the Treaty of Paris creating the European Coal and Steel Community (ECSC). After it was found impossible to create European Communities covering Defence and Foreign Affairs, two more communities with the aims of gradually integrating the economies of the 6 nations and of moving towards closer political unity, the European Economic Community (EEC) and the European Atomic Energy Community (EAEC or Euratom) were created in 1957 by the signing of the Treaties of Rome.

On 30 June 1970 membership negotiations began between the Six and the UK, Denmark, Ireland and Norway. On 22 Jan. 1972 those 4 countries signed a Treaty of Accession, although this was rejected by Norway in a referendum in Nov. 1972. On 1 Jan. 1973 the UK, Denmark and Ireland became full members. On 28 May 1979 the Greek Treaty of Accession was signed, and Greece joined the Community on 1 Jan. 1981. Negotiations with Spain and Portugal culminated in the signature of Treaties of Accession on 12 June 1985; they joined the Community on 1 Jan. 1986, although existing Community Legislation will only apply after a transitional period. In Dec. 1985 the Treaties were amended again by the Single Act of Luxembourg. Turkey applied for membership in April 1987.

The institutional arrangements of the Communities provide an independent executive with powers of proposal (the Commission), various consultative bodies, and a decision-making body drawn from the Governments (the Council). Until

1967 the 3 Communities were completely distinct, although they shared some non-decision-making bodies: from that date the executives were merged in the European Commission, and the decision-taking bodies in the Council. The institutions and organs of the Communities are as follows:

The *Commission* consists of 17 members appointed by the member states to serve for 4 years; the President and Vice-Presidents are appointed initially for 2 years, but are generally re-appointed for the rest of their term. The Commission acts independently of any country in the interests of the Community as a whole, with as its mandate the implementation and guardianship of the Treaties. In this it has the right of initiative (putting proposals to the Council for action); and execution (once the Council has decided); and can take the other institutions or individual countries before the Court of Justice (see below) should any of these renege upon its responsibilities.

President: Jacques Delors.
Address: 200 rue de la Loi, 1049, Brussels, Belgium.

The *Council of Ministers* consists of foreign ministers from the 12 national governments and represents the national as opposed to the Community interests. It is the body which takes decisions under the Treaties. Although legally most of its decisions should be made by majority, it has since 1966 sought unanimity wherever possible, using majority votes only rarely. Specialist Councils (*e.g.* the Agriculture Council) meet to discuss matters related to individual policies. Since 1974 the Heads of State and Government have met 3 times a year as the *European Council* to discuss Community, and also Foreign Policy, affairs. The Foreign Ministers also meet in Political Co-operation to discuss Foreign Policy matters. The Presidency of the Council is held for a 6-month term in the following order: Belgium, Denmark, Federal Republic of Germany, Greece, Spain, France, Ireland, Italy, Luxembourg, Netherlands, Portugal, UK.

Address: 170 rue de la Loi, 1048, Brussels.

The *European Parliament* consists of 518 members, directly elected from all Member States. France, the Federal Republic of Germany, Italy and the UK return 81 members each, Spain 60, the Netherlands 25, Belgium, Greece and Portugal 24, Denmark 16, Ireland 15 and Luxembourg 6. Party representation in Parliament was as follows: Socialists, 172; European People's Party (Christian Democratic Group), 119; European Democrats (formerly European Conservatives), 63; Communists and Allies, 46; Liberal, Democratic and Reform Group 41; European Democratic Alliance, 34; the 'Rainbow' group (a group of mixed tendencies), 20; the European Right, 16; Independents, 7. The Parliament has a right to be consulted on a wide range of legislative proposals, and forms one arm of the Community's Budgetary Authority.

President: Lord Plumb.
Address: Centre européen du Kirchberg, Luxembourg.

The *Economic and Social Committee* has an advisory role and consists of 189 representatives, employers, trade unions, consumers, etc. The *Consultative Committee*, of 96 members, performs a similar role for the ECSC.

President: Alphonse Margot.
Address: 2, rue Ravenstein, 1000 Brussels.

The *European Court of Justice* is composed of 13 judges and 6 advocates-general, is responsible for the adjudication of disputes arising out of the application of the treaties, and its findings are enforceable in all member countries.

President: Lord Mackenzie Stuart.
Address: Palais de la Cour de Justice, Kirchberg, Luxembourg.

The *Court of Auditors* was established by a Treaty signed on 22 July 1975 which took effect on 1 June 1977. It consists of 12 members, and replaced the former *Audit Board*. It audits all income and current and past expenditure of the European Communities.

President: Marcel Mart.
Address: 29 Rue Aldringen, Luxembourg.
Annual Report of the Court of Auditors, from 1977

The *European Investment Bank* (EIB) was created by the EEC Treaty to which its statute is annexed. Its governing body is the Board of Governors consisting of ministers designated by member states. Its main task is to contribute to the balanced development of the common market in the interest of the Community by financing projects: developing less-developed regions; for modernizing or converting undertakings; or developing new activities, or those of common interest to several member states.

Address: 100, Boulevard Konrad Adenauer, Plateau du Kirchberg, Luxembourg.

Annual Report of the European Investment Bank

Community Law. Provisions of the Treaties and secondary legislation may be either directly applicable in Member States or only applicable after Member States have enacted their own implementing legislation. Secondary legislation consists of: regulations, which are of general application and binding in their entirety and directly applicable in all member states; directives which are binding upon each Member State as to the result to be achieved within a given time, but leave the national authority the choice of form and method of achieving this result; decisions, which are binding in their entirety on their addressees. In addition the Council and Commission can issue recommendations and opinions, which have no binding force.

The Community's Legislative Process starts with a proposal from the Commission (either at the suggestion of its services or in pursuit of its declared political aims) to the Council. The Council generally seeks the views of the European Parliament on the proposal, and the Parliament adopts a formal Opinion, after consideration of the matter by its specialist Committees. The Council may also (and in some cases is obliged to) consult the Economic and Social Committee, which similarly delivers an opinion. When these opinions have been received, the Council will decide. Most decisions are taken on a majority basis, but will take account of reserves expressed by individual member states. The text eventually approved may differ substantially from the original Commission proposal.

Community Finances. The general budget of the European Communities for 1987, in ECUm. (1 ECU at Nov. 1987 = UK£0·69 or US$1·19) was:

Receipts		Expenditure	
Agricultural levies	3,377	Agriculture	24,131
Import duties	9,761	Social	2,746
VAT	22,755	Regional and transport	3,565
Miscellaneous	906	Industry, energy,	
		research	934
	36,795	Development aid	1,088
		Administration and	
		miscellaneous	4,331
			36,795

The resources of the Community (the levies and duties mentioned above, and up to a 1·4% VAT charge) have been surrendered to it by Treaty. The Budget is made by the Council and the Parliament acting jointly as the Budgetary Authority. The Parliament has control, within a certain margin, of non-obligatory expenditure (*i.e.*, expenditure where the amount to be spent is not set out in the legislation concerned), and can also reject the Budget totally as in 1980 and 1985. Otherwise, the Council decides. ECSC operations are partly funded by a turnover levy (1987: 0·31%) on the coal and steel industries of the Community, partly from the general budget. The ECSC operating budget for 1986 was ECU408m.

THE EUROPEAN COAL AND STEEL COMMUNITY. The ECSC was the first of the 3 Communities, coming into existence on 10 Aug. 1952 following the signature of the Treaty of Paris on 18 April 1951. Its aim was to contribute towards economic expansion, growth of employment and a rising standard of living in Member States, through common action in the coal and steel sector, in a Community open to other nations. Since 1957 it has had the same membership as the other Communities.

The Common Market for Coal and Steel. This first aim of the ECSC was achieved for coal, iron ore and scrap in Feb. 1953, for steel in May 1953 and for special steels in Aug. 1954. The Common External Tariff on ECSC products is between 4-8%. Rules for fair competition within the Common Market, based on non-discrimination by nationality and the free movement of goods, have been established. The ECSC also gives readaptation and retraining grants to former workers in these industries, and makes capital grants for new industrial investment in former coal and steel areas.

The Commission has to approve take-overs and mergers of coal or steel undertakings, and has the power in the case of crisis (and with the approval of the Council) to set production quotas and minimum prices by product, with fines for non-observance. This power was first used in 1980.

THE EUROPEAN ECONOMIC COMMUNITY (EEC) or COMMON MARKET

Based on the Treaty of Rome of 25 March 1957 the EEC came into being on 1 Jan. 1958 with the same original members as the ECSC. The Treaty guarantees certain rights to the citizens of all Member States (*e.g.,* the outlawing of economic discrimination by nationality, and equal pay for equal work as between men and women) and sets out certain other areas where secondary legislation is to fill in the details. The most important policy areas are as follows:

Freedom of movement for persons, goods and capital. Under the Treaty individuals or companies from one Member State may establish themselves in another country (for the purposes of economic activity) or sell goods or services there on the same basis as nationals of that country. With a few exceptions, restrictions on the movement of capital have also been ended.

Customs Union and External Trade Relations. Goods or Services originating in one Member State have free circulation within the EEC, which implies common arrangements for trade with the rest of the world. Member States can no longer make bilateral trade agreements with third countries: this power has been ceded to the Community. The Customs Union was achieved in July 1968, with the abolition of internal customs tariffs (or equivalents) and quantitative restrictions, and the establishment of the Common External Tariff. Denmark, Ireland and the UK adopted these from July 1977; Greece from Jan. 1986.

Following the 1973 accessions the Community made a series of agreements with the member states of EFTA to form an industrial free trade zone and to start the liberalization of agricultural trade. Association agreements which could lead to accession or customs union have been made with Cyprus, Malta and Turkey; and commercial, industrial, technical and financial aid agreements with Algeria, Egypt, Israel, Jordan, Lebanon, Morocco, Syria and Tunisia. In 1976 Canada signed a framework agreement for co-operation in industrial trade, science and natural resources.

In the *Development Aid* sector, the Community has an agreement (the Lomé Convention, originally signed in 1975 but renewed and enlarged in 1979 and 1984) with some 60 African, Caribbean and Pacific countries which removes customs duties without reciprocal arrangements for most of their imports to the Community, and under which ECU8,760m. of aid was granted between 1986–90. An economic and commercial agreement has also been signed with ASEAN.

The Common Agricultural Policy (CAP). The objectives set out in the Treaty are to increase agricultural productivity, to ensure a fair standard of living for the agricultural community, to stabilise markets, to assure supplies, and to ensure reasonable consumer prices. In Dec. 1960 the Council laid down the fundamental principles on which the CAP is based: a single market, which calls for common prices, stable currency parities and the harmonising of health and veterinary legislation; Community preference, which protects the single Community market from imports; common financing, through the European Agricultural Guidance and Guarantee Fund (EAGGF), which seeks to improve agriculture through its

Guidance section, and to stabilise markets against world price fluctuations through market intervention, with levies and refunds on exports. At present common market organizations cover over 95% of EEC agricultural production. Greece is bringing its agricultural prices into line with the Community over a period of up to 7 years.

Following the disappearance of stable currency parities, artificial currency levels have been applied in the CAP. This factor, together with over-production due to high producer prices, means that the CAP consumes about two-thirds of the Communities' budget.

The European Monetary System (EMS), whose immediate objective is to create a zone of monetary stability in Europe by closer monetary co-operation, began operating in March 1979. All Member States (except Greece, the UK, Spain and Portugal 1986) limit fluctuations in the exchange rates of their currencies against a central rate denominated in ECU.

Competition. The Competition (anti-trust) law of the Community is based on 2 principles: that businesses should not seek to nullify the creation of the common market by the erection of artificial national (or other) barriers to the free movement of goods; and against the abuse of dominant positions in any market. These two principles have led among other things to the outlawing of prohibitions on exports to other Member States, of price-fixing agreements and of refusal to supply; and to the refusal by the Commission to allow mergers or take-overs by dominant under-takings in specific cases. Increasingly heavy fines are imposed on offenders.

THE EUROPEAN ATOMIC ENERGY COMMUNITY (EURATOM)

Like the EEC, Euratom came into being on 1 Jan. 1958 following a Treaty signed in Rome on 25 March 1957, and it had the same Member States as the EEC. Its task is to promote common efforts between its members in the development of nuclear energy for peaceful purposes, and for this purpose it has monopoly powers of acquisition of fissile materials for civil purposes. It is in no way concerned with military uses of nuclear power; indeed, its members are forbidden under the Treaty to use nuclear materials obtained through Euratom for such purposes.

The execution of the Treaty now rests with the European Commission, which is advised by the Scientific and Technical Committee (28 members). Major decisions rest with the Council. Euratom has 1 substantial research institute of its own, at Ispra, in Italy; it does other work in co-operation with research institutes in the Member States, or in joint and international undertakings.

A common market for nuclear materials and equipment came into force, and external tariffs were suspended, in Jan. 1959. Although the Court of Justice has confirmed that Member States have ceded to Euratom the right to make supply contracts with outside suppliers (*e.g.* Australia, Canada or the USA), Euratom has generally been growing less effective in recent years, and most major new nuclear energy projects within the Member States have been undertaken outside its framework.

European Community Delegation to the US: 2111 M Street NW (Suite 707), Washington DC 20037.
Head of Delegation: Sir Roy Denman.
US Delegation to the European Community: 40 Boulevard du Régent, 1000 Brussels.
Head of Delegation: George S. Vest.
European Community Delegation to the United Nations: 1 Dag Hammarskjöld Plaza, 245 East 47th Street, New York NY 10017.
Head of Delegation: Jean-Pierre Derisbourg.

Books of Reference

Official Journal of the European Communities.—General Report on the Activities of the European Communities (annual, from 1967).—*The Agricultural Situation in the Community.* (annual).—*The Social Situation in the Community.* (annual).—*Report on Competition Policy in the European Community.* (annual).—*Basic Statistics of the Community* (annual).—

Bulletin of the European Community (monthly).—*Register of Current Community Legal Instruments.* 1983
Europe (monthly), obtainable from the Information Office of the European Commission, 8 Storey's Gate, London, SW1P 3AT
Arbuthnott, H. and Edwards, G., (eds.), *A Common Man's Guide to the Common Market.* London, 1979
Cook, C., and Francis, M., *The First European Elections.* London, 1979
Drew, J., *Doing Business with the European Community.* London, 1979
Fennell, R., *The Common Agricultural Policy of the European Community.* London, 1979
Fitzmaurice, J., *The European Parliament.* London, 1982
Hallstein, W., *Europe in the Making.* London, 1973
Lodge, J., *The European Community: Bibliographical Excursions.* London, 1983
Mayre, R., *Postwar Europe.* London, 1983
Morris, B., *et al The European Community: A Practical Guide for Business and Government.* London, 1982
Palmer, D. M., *Sources of Information on the European Communities.* London, 1979
Parry, A., and Dinnage, J., *EEC Law.* London, 1982
Paxton, J., *The Developing Common Market.* London, 1976.—*A Dictionary of the European Communities.* 2nd ed. London, 1982
Twitchett, C. C., *Harmonisation in the EEC.* London, 1981
Wallace, W., and Herreman, I. (eds.), *A Community of Twelve?* Bruges, 1978
Walsh, A. E., and Paxton, J., *Competition Policy.* London, 1975

EUROPEAN FREE TRADE ASSOCIATION (EFTA)

The European Free Trade Association has 6 member countries: Austria, Finland (an associate member from 1961–1985), Iceland, Norway, Sweden and Switzerland. The Stockholm Convention establishing the Association entered into force on 3 May 1960 and Finland became associated on 27 March 1961. Iceland joined EFTA on 1 March 1970 and was immediately granted duty-free entry for industrial goods exported to EFTA countries, while being given 10 years to abolish her own existing protective duties. The UK and Denmark, both founder members, left EFTA on 31 Dec. 1972 to join the EEC as did Portugal, also a founder member, on 31 Dec. 1985.

When the Association was created it had three objectives: to achieve free trade in industrial products between member countries, to assist in the creation of a single market embracing the countries of Western Europe, and to contribute to the expansion of world trade in general.

The first objective was achieved on 31 Dec. 1966, when virtually all inter-EFTA tariffs were removed. This was 3 years earlier than originally planned. Finland removed her remaining EFTA tariffs a year later on 31 Dec. 1967 and Iceland removed her tariffs on 31 Dec. 1979.

The fulfilment of the second aim was secured in 1972. On 22 Jan. 1972 the UK and Denmark signed the Treaty of Accession to the EEC whereby they became members of the enlarged Community from 1 Jan. 1973. On 22 July 1972, 5 other EFTA countries, Austria, Iceland, Portugal, Sweden and Switzerland signed Free Trade Agreements with the enlarged EEC. A similar agreement negotiated with Finland was signed on 5 Oct. 1973. Norway, whose intention of joining the EEC was reversed following a referendum, signed a similar agreement on 14 May 1973. Through these agreements virtually complete free trade in industrial goods was achieved in 16 Western European countries from July 1977. The agreements now also apply to trade between the EFTA countries and the 3 countries which joined the EEC at later dates: Greece (1 Jan. 1981) and Spain and Portugal (1 Jan. 1986).

The third objective was to contribute to the expansion of world trade. In 1959 trade between the countries now in EFTA amounted to US$705·6m. and total exports from these countries were US$6,562m. In 1986 the respective figures were US$19,322m. and US$133,021m. More than half EFTA trade is with the EEC.

EFTA tariff treatment applies to those industrial products which are of EFTA origin, and these are traded freely between member countries. Each EFTA country remains free, however, to impose its own rates of duty on products entering from outside EFTA or the EEC.

Generally, agricultural products do not come under the provisions for free trade, but bilateral agreements have been negotiated to increase trade in these products.

The operation of the Convention is the responsibility of a Council assisted by a small secretariat. Each EFTA country holds the chairmanship of the Council for 6 months.

Secretary-General: Georg Reisch (Austria).
Headquarters: 9–11 rue de Varembé, 1211 Geneva 20, Switzerland.

Convention Establishing the European Free Trade Association
EFTA Bulletin (Four issues a year)
EFTA What it is, What it does
The European Free Trade Association

THE WARSAW PACT

On 14 May 1955 the USSR, Albania, Bulgaria, Czechoslovakia, the German Democratic Republic, Hungary, Poland and Romania signed, in Warsaw, a 20-year treaty of friendship and collaboration, after the USSR had (on 7 May) annulled the 20-year treaties of alliance with the UK (1942) and France (1944).

The main provisions of the treaty are as follows:

Article 4. In case of armed aggression in Europe against one or several States party to the pact by a State or group of States, each State member of the pact ... will afford to the State or States which are the object of such aggression immediate assistance ... with all means which appear necessary, including the use of armed force ... These measures will cease as soon as the Security Council takes measures necessary for establishing and preserving international peace and security.

Article 5. The contracting Powers agree to set up a joint command of their armed forces to be allotted by agreement between the Powers, at the disposal of this command and used on the basis of jointly established principles. They will also take over agreed measures necessary to strengthen their defences.

Article 9. The present treaty is open to other States, irrespective of their social or Government regime, who declare their readiness to abide by the terms of the treaty in order to safeguard peace and security of the peoples.

Article 11. In the event of a system of collective security being set up in Europe and a pact to this effect being signed—to which each party to this treaty will direct its efforts—the present treaty will lapse from the day such a collective security treaty comes into force.

It is estimated (1981) that the armed forces of the Warsaw Pact countries total 4·82m., including 3·71m. Russians, compared with 4·99m. NATO forces.

Marshal Grechko was from July 1960 to April 1967 C.-in-C. of the united Armed Forces, with headquarters in Moscow. He was succeeded by Marshal I. I. Yakubovsky in 1967 and by Marshal V. G. Kulikov in Jan. 1977.

In 1962 Albania was no longer invited to the Warsaw Pact meetings without being formally expelled.

Two Soviet divisions are stationed in Poland, 20 divisions in German Democratic Republic, 4 divisions in Hungary and 5 in Czechoslovakia.

Clawson, R. W. and Kaplan, L. S. (eds.), *The Warsaw Pact: Political Purpose and Military Means.* Wilmington, 1982
Lewis, W. J., *The Warsaw Pact: Doctrine and Strategy.* Maidenhead, 1982

COUNCIL FOR MUTUAL ECONOMIC ASSISTANCE [1]

Membership. Founder members were USSR, Bulgaria, Czechoslovakia, Hungary, Poland and Romania. Later admissions were Albania (1949; ceased participation 1961), German Democratic Republic (1950), Mongolia (1962), Cuba (1972), Vietnam (1978). In 1964 Yugoslavia concluded an agreement with CMEA whereby Yugoslavia would participate in the work of some CMEA bodies (at present 21). Afghánistán, Angola, Ethiopia, Laos, Mexico, Mozambique, Nicaragua and the People's Democratic Republic of Yemen attend CMEA sessions as observers.

External relations. There are co-operation agreements with Finland, Iraq, Mexico and Nicaragua. Talks on formal official links with the European Communities began in Sept. 1986.

The Charter. The charter consists of a preamble and 18 articles. Extracts (in the language of the official English version) are as follows:

Article 1. Aims and Principles: 1 'The purpose of the Council is to promote, by uniting and co-ordinating the efforts of the member countries, the further extension and improvement of co-operation and the development of socialist economic integration, the planned development of their national economies, the acceleration of economic and technical progress in these countries, higher level of industrialization of the less industrialized countries, a continuous increase in labour productivity, a gradual approximation and equalization of economic development levels and a steady improvement in the wellbeing of the peoples. 2 The Council is based on the principles of the sovereign equality of all member countries.'

Article 2. Membership 'open to other countries which subscribe to the purposes and principles of the Council'.

Article 3. Functions and Powers to (a) 'organize all-round . . . co-operation of member countries in the most rational use of natural resources and acceleration of the development of their productive forces'; (b) 'foster the improvement of the international socialist division of labour by co-ordinating national economic development plans, and the specialization and co-operation of production in member countries'; (c) to assist in . . . carrying out joint measures for the development of industry and agriculture . . . transport . . . principal capital investments . . . [and] trade'.

Article 4. Recommendations and Decisions '. . . shall be adopted only with the consent of the interested member countries.'

The Structure. The supreme authority is the 'Session' of all members held (usually annually) in members' capitals in rotation under the chairmanship of the head of the delegation of the host country; all members must be present, and decisions must be unanimous. Delegations are usually led by prime ministers.

The *Executive Committee* is made up of 1 representative from each member state of deputy premier rank. It meets at least once every 3 months.

The administrative organ is the *Secretariat.*

Headquarters: Prospekt Kalinina, 56, Moscow, G-205.
Secretary: V. V. Sychev (appointed 1983).

There is a *Committee for Co-operation in the Field of Planning* and a *Committee for Scientific and Technical Co-operation* set up in 1971 and a *Committee for Material and Technical Supply* set up in 1974. There are *Permanent Commissions* on: Statistics, Foreign Trade, Currency and Finance, Electricity, Peaceful Uses of Atomic Energy, Geology, Coal Industry, Oil and Gas Industry, Chemical Industry, Iron and Steel Industry, Non-Ferrous Metals Industry, Engineering Industry, Radio Engineering and Electronics Industries, Light Industry, Food Industry, Agriculture, Construction, Transport, Posts and Telecommunications, Standardization, Civil Aviation, Public Health.

There are 7 *Standing Conferences:* for Legal Problems; of Ministers of Internal

---

[1] Abbreviations and Foreign Names. CMEA is the official abbreviation. Other unofficial abbreviations are COMECON and CEMA. The working language of the organization is Russian. The Russian form is *Sovet Ekonomicheskoi Vzaimopomoshchi* (SEV).

Trade; of Chiefs of Water Resources Authorities; of Chiefs of Patent Authorities; of Chiefs of Pricing Authorities; of Chiefs of Labour Authorities, and of Representatives of Freight and Shipping Organizations.

There are 3 semi-autonomous bodies within CMEA: The Institute of Standardization, The Bureau for the Co-ordination of Ship Freighting and The International Institute of Economic Problems of the World Socialist System.

In 1988 there were over 20 technical and economic agencies associated with CMEA.

Also associated with CMEA are:

The **International Bank for Economic Co-operation** was founded in 1963 with a capital of 300m. roubles and started operating on 1 Jan. 1964. It undertakes multilateral settlements in 'transferable roubles' (*i.e.*, used for intra-CMEA clearing accounts only) and advances credits to finance trading and other operations. The transferable rouble is a unit of account: gold content 0·987412 gramme.

The **International Investments Bank** was founded in 1970 and went into operation on 1 Jan. 1971 with a capital of 1,713m. roubles (70% transferable and 30% convertible or in gold).

Banking and Sources of Finance in Comecon. London, 1978
Charter of the Council for Mutual Economic Assistance. Moscow, 1980
Comecon Foreign Trade Data. London, biennial, from 1979
Council for Mutual Economic Assistance: Thirty Years. Moscow, 1979
Comprehensive Programme for the Further Extension and Improvement of Co-operation and the Development of Socialist Economic Integration by the CMEA-member Countries. Moscow, 1971 (The official English-language version. This document also frequently referred to as the *Complex Programme,* etc.)
Ekonomicheskoe Sotrudnichestvo Stran-Chlenov SEV. Moscow, monthly
Multilateral Economic Co-operation of Socialist States: A Collection of Documents. Moscow, 1977
Statistical Year Book of CMEA Member Countries. Moscow, annual
Survey of CMEA Activities. Moscow, annual
Marrese, M., and Vanous, J., *Soviet Subsidization of Trade with Eastern Europe.* Berkeley, 1983
Nagy, L., *The Socialist Collective Agreement.* Budapest, 1984
Saunders, C. T. (ed.), *Regional Integration in East and West.* London, 1983
Schiavone, G., *The Institutions of Comecon.* London, 1981
Sobell, V., *The Red Market: Industrial Co-operation and Specialisation in Comecon.* Aldershot, 1984
Wallace, W. V. and Clarke, A. R., *Comecon, Trade and the West.* London, 1986

COLOMBO PLAN

History: Founded in 1950 to promote the development of newly independent Asian member countries, the Colombo Plan has grown from its modest beginning as a group of seven Commonwealth nations into an international organization of 26 countries.

Originally the Plan was conceived for a period of six years. Its life has since been extended from time to time, generally at five-year intervals. The Consultative Committee, the Plan's highest deliberative body, at its meeting in Jakarta in 1980, gave the Plan an indefinite span of life; its need and relevance will henceforth be examined only if considered necessary.

The Plan is multilateral in approach but bilateral in operation: multilateral in that it takes cognizance of the problems of development of member countries in the Asia and Pacific region and endeavours to deal with them in a co-ordinated way; bilateral because negotiations for assistance are made direct between a donor and a recipient country.

Aims: The aims of the Colombo Plan are: *(a)* to promote interest in and support for the economic and social development in Asia and the Pacific; *(b)* to keep under review economic and social progress in the region and help accelerate development through co-operative effort; and *(c)* to facilitate development assistance to and within the region.

Member Countries: Afghánistán, Australia, Bangladesh, Bhután, Burma, Cambodia, Canada, Fiji, India, Indonesia, Iran, Japan, Republic of Korea, Lao People's Democratic Republic, Malaysia, Maldives, Nepál, New Zealand, Pakistan, Papua New Guinea, Philippines, Singapore, Sri Lanka, Thailand, UK and USA.

Development Assistance: Colombo Plan aid covers all fields of socio-economic development and amounted to US$5,015·7m. in 1986. It takes three principal forms:

(i) *Capital Aid* including grants and loans for national projects mainly from the six developed member countries of the Plan.
    The total amount of capital aid and technical co-operation assistance provided by the developed donors under the plan in 1986 was as follows:

	US$1m.
Japan	2,695·6
USA	1,224·0
UK	433·8
Australia	383·6
Canada	269·9
New Zealand	8·8
Total	5,015·7

(ii) *Technical Co-operation:* Assistance is provided in the form of services of experts and volunteers, fellowships, and equipment for training and research.
    During 1986, 21,135 students and trainees received training, 10,306 experts and 2,488 volunteers were sent out. Total disbursements on technical co-operation by the developed member countries in 1986 amounted to $746·3m.

(iii) *Technical Co-operation Among Developing Countries (TCDC):* The promotion of TCDC is a major objective of the Plan. Under TCDC programmes in 1986, 2,874 students and trainees received training and 107 experts were sent out. TCDC expenditures during 1986 amounted to $20·5m.

Structure: There are four organs which give focus to the Plan:

Consultative Committee: The Committee is the highest deliberative body of the Plan and consists of Ministers of member Governments who meet once in two years. The Ministerial meeting is preceded by a meeting of senior officials who are directly concerned with the operation of the Plan in various countries.

Colombo Plan Council: The Council is also a deliberative body which meets several times a year in Colombo, where most member countries have resident diplomatic missions, to review the economic and social development of the Asia-Pacific region and promote co-operation among member countries.

Colombo Plan Bureau: Its functions include servicing the meetings of the Colombo Plan Council and the Consultative Committee, carrying out research, and dissemination of statistical and other information relating to activities under the Plan. Since 1973 the Bureau has been operating a Drug Advisory Programme to assist national and regional efforts to eliminate the causes and ameliorate the effects of drug abuse.

Colombo Plan Staff College: The Colombo Plan Staff College for Technician Education, established in 1975, transferred from Singapore to the Philippines in 1987. The College helps member countries in developing their systems of technician education, mainly through training courses, seminars and consultancies. It is separately financed by most Colombo Plan member countries and functions under the guidance of its own Governing Board consisting of the heads of member countries' diplomatic missions resident in Singapore.

Headquarters: Colombo Plan Bureau, 12 Melbourne Avenue, PO Box 596, Colombo 4, Sri Lanka.

The Colombo Plan (Cmd. 8080). HMSO, 1950; reprinted 1952.—*Annual Report.* HMSO 1952 to 1971 followed by Colombo Plan Bureau, Sri Lanka, 1971–86

Reports of the Council for Technical Co-operation. HMSO annually until 1966–67 followed by the Colombo Plan Bureau, Sri Lanka, 1967–68 to date

ASSOCIATION OF SOUTH EAST ASIAN NATIONS (ASEAN)

History and Membership. The Association of South East Asian Nations is a regional organization formed by the governments of Indonesia, Malaysia, the Philippines, Singapore and Thailand through the Bangkok Declaration which was signed by the Foreign Ministers of ASEAN countries on 8 Aug. 1967. Brunei joined in 1984.

Objectives. The main objectives are to accelerate economic growth, social progress and cultural development, to promote active collaboration and mutual assistance in matters of common interest, to ensure the stability of the South East Asian region and to maintain close co-operation with existing international and regional organizations with similar aims. Principal projects concern economic co-operation and development, with the intensification of intra-ASEAN trade and trade between the region and the rest of the world; joint research and technological programmes; co-operation in transportation and communications; promotion of tourism and South East Asian studies; including cultural, scientific, educational and administrative exchanges.

Organs. The highest authority in ASEAN are the Heads of Government of the Member Countries who meet as and when necessary to give directions to ASEAN. The highest policy-making body is the Meeting of Foreign Ministers, commonly known as the Annual Ministerial Meeting, which convenes in each of the ASEAN member countries on a rotational basis in alphabetical order. The Standing Committee, comprising the Foreign Minister of the country hosting the Ministerial Meeting in that particular year and the accredited ambassadors of the other member countries, carries out the work of the Association in between the Ministerial Meetings and handles the routine matters to ensure continuity and to make decisions based on the guidelines or policies set by the Ministerial Meetings and submit for the consideration of the Foreign Ministers all reports and recommendations of the various ASEAN committees. There are five economic committees under the ASEAN Economic Ministers and three non-economic committees that recommend and draw up programmes for ASEAN co-operation. These committees are responsible for the operation and implementation of ASEAN projects in their respective fields. Each ASEAN capital has an ASEAN National Secretariat. The central secretariat for ASEAN is located in Jakarta, Indonesia, and is headed by the Secretary General, a post that revolves among the member states in alphabetical order every 3 years. Bureau directors and other officers of the ASEAN Secretariat remain in office for 3 years.

Secretary-General: Roderick Yong (Brunei Darussalam).

Books of Reference

Broinowski, A., *Understanding ASEAN.* London, 1982
Wawn, B., *The Economies of the ASEAN Countries.* London, 1982
Wong, J., *ASEAN Economics in Perspective.* London, 1979

ORGANIZATION OF AMERICAN STATES

On 14 April 1890 representatives of the American republics, meeting in Washington at the First International Conference of American States, established an 'International Union of American Republics' and, as its central office, a 'Commercial Bureau of American Republics', which later became the Pan American Union. This international organization's object was to foster mutual understanding and co-operation among the nations of the western hemisphere. Since that time, successive inter-American conferences have greatly broadened the scope of work of the organization.

This led to the adoption on 30 April 1948 by the Ninth International Conference of American States, at Bogotá, Colombia, of the Charter of the Organization of American States. This co-ordinated the work of all the former independent official entities in the inter-American system and defined their mutual relationships. The purposes of the OAS are to achieve an order of peace and justice, promote American solidarity, strengthen collaboration among the member states and defend their sovereignty, territorial integrity and independence. The OAS is a regional organization of the United Nations for the maintenance of peace and security.

Membership is on a basis of absolute equality. Each country has one vote in the Council of the Organization and its organs. The member countries were (1980): Antigua and Barbuda, Argentina, Bahamas, Barbados, Bolivia, Brazil, Chile, Colombia, Costa Rica, Cuba, Commonwealth of Dominica, Dominican Republic, Ecuador, El Salvador, Grenada, Guatemala, Haiti, Honduras, Jamaica, Mexico, Nicaragua, Panama, Paraguay, Peru, Saint Christopher (Kitts) and Nevis, Saint Lucia, Saint Vincent and the Grenadines, Suriname, Trinidad and Tobago, USA, Uruguay, Venezuela.

The OAS has been concerned increasingly in recent years with programmes to promote Latin American economic and social development. The OAS provides specialized training for thousands of Latin Americans each year in a wide variety of development-related fields. It also carries out several missions projects each year in response to requests from member governments.

On 27 Feb. 1967 the Third Special Inter-American Conference in Buenos Aires approved the Protocol of Amendment to the Charter of the OAS, which contained new standards for inter-American co-operation and a number of structural changes in the Organization.

On 14 April 1967 the Declaration of the Presidents of America, signed in Punta del Este, Uruguay, expressed the commitment of the American chiefs of state to promote Latin American economic integration; to join in efforts to increase substantially Latin American foreign-trade earnings; to modernize the living conditions of the rural population and raise agricultural productivity; and to expand programmes in education, science, technology and health.

On 22 Feb. 1968, in the Resolution of Maracay, the Inter-American Cultural Council launched new regional programmes for educational development and for scientific and technological development.

On 27 Feb. 1970, by ratification of more than the mandatory two-thirds of the OAS member states, the Protocol of Buenos Aires, modifying the 1948 Charter, entered into effect.

Under the amended Charter, the OAS accomplishes its purposes by means of:

(a) The *General Assembly*, which meets annually in various countries of the member states.

(b) The *Meeting of Consultation of Ministers of Foreign Affairs*, held to consider problems of an urgent nature and of common interest.

(c) Three councils of equal rank: the *Permanent Council*, which replaces the old OAS Council; the *Inter-American Economic and Social Council*; and the *Inter-American Council for Education, Science and Culture*. Functions are to direct and co-ordinate work in the areas of their competence and render the governments such specialized services as they may request. Each council is composed of 1 representative from each member state, appointed by his government.

(d) The *Inter-American Juridical Committee* which acts as an advisory body to the OAS on juridical matters and promotes the development and codification of international law. Eleven jurists, elected every 4 years by the General Assembly, represent all the American States.

(e) The *Inter-American Commission on Human Rights* which oversees the observance and protection of human rights. Seven members represent all the OAS member states.

(f) The *General Secretariat* is the central and permanent organ of the OAS.

(g) The *Specialized Conferences*, meeting to deal with special technical matters or to develop specific aspects of inter-American co-operation.

(h) The *Specialized Organizations*, inter-governmental organizations established by multilateral agreements to discharge specific functions in their respective fields of action, such as women's affairs, agriculture, child welfare, Indian affairs, geography and history, and health.

Secretary-General: João Clemente Baena Soares (Brazil).

Assistant Secretary-General: Valerie T. McComie (Barbados).

The Secretary-General and the Assistant Secretary-General are elected by the General Assembly for 5-year terms. The General Assembly approves the annual budget for the Organization, which is financed by quotas contributed by the member governments.

General Secretariat: Washington, D.C., 20006, USA.
Flag: Light blue with the OAS seal in colour in the centre.

Books of Reference

Publications of the OAS General Secretariat include:

Charter of the Organization of American States. 1948.—*As Amended by the Protocol of Buenos Aires in 1967*
Americas. Illustrated bi-monthly, from 1949 (Spanish and English edition)
Organization of American States, a Handbook. Rev. ed. 1977
Organization of American States. Directory. Quarterly, from 1951
Report on the Tenth Inter-American Conference, Caracas 1954. 1955
Inter-American Review of Bibliography. Quarterly, from 1951
Annual Report of the Secretary-General
Status of Inter-American Treaties and Conventions. Annual
The Alliance for Progress: The Charter of Punta del Este. 1962
The Americas in the 1980s: An Agenda for the Decade Ahead. 1982

Publications on Latin America (*see also* the bibliographical notes appended to each country):

Revenue, Expenditure and Public Debts of the Latin American Republics. Division of Financial Information, US Department of Commerce. Annual
Boundaries of the Latin American Republics: An Annotated List of Documents, 1493–1943. Department of State, Office of the Geographer. Washington, 1944
Burgin, M. (ed.), *Handbook of Latin American Studies.* Gainesville, Fla., 1935 ff.
Hirschman, Albert O., *Latin American Issues:* [11] *Essays and Comments.* New York, 1961
Plaza, G., *The Organization of American States: Instrument for Hemispheric Development.* Washington, 1969.—*Latin America Today and Tomorrow.* Washington, 1971
Steward, J. H. (ed.), *Handbook of the South American Indian.* 7 vols. Washington, 1946–59
Thomas, A. V. W. and A. J., *The Organization of American States.* Southern Methodist Univ. Press, 1963

LATIN AMERICAN ECONOMIC GROUPINGS

Latin American Integration Association (LAIA) took over the Latin American Free Trade Area (LAFTA) on 1 Jan. 1981. Members: Argentina, Bolivia, Brazil, Chile, Colombia, Ecuador, Mexico, Paraguay, Peru, Uruguay and Venezuela. The permanent secretariat is at Montevideo.

Central American Common Market (ODECA). On 13 Dec. 1960, at Managua, El Salvador, Guatemala, Honduras and Nicaragua concluded a general treaty on Central American integration; a protocol on the equalization of import duties and charges; and an agreement establishing the Central American Bank for Economic Integration. Costa Rica acceded in 1962 and in Sept. 1963 ratified the charter of the Banco Centroamericano de Integración Económica (in Tegucigalpa), whose capital was increased to $600m. in 1982.

The San Salvador Charter, signed on 14 Dec. 1962, expanded these provisions, envisaging permanent political, economic, educational, defence, etc., councils. The permanent secretariat is at Guatemala City.

The Andean Group (Grupo Andino). On 26 May 1969 an agreement was signed by Bolivia, Chile, Colombia, Ecuador and Peru creating the Andean Group. Venezuela was initially actively involved but did not sign the agreement until 1973. Chile withdrew from the Group in 1977. Under the Cartagena Agreement of 1975 the development of an integrated petrochemical industry in each of the member countries was established.

Sistema Económico Latinoamericano (SELA) was created by 25 Latin American and Caribbean countries (Suriname joined in 1979) meeting at Panama, 17 Oct. 1975. The System provides member countries with permanent institutional machinery for joint consultation, co-ordination, co-operation and promotion in economic and social matters at both intraregional and extraregional level.

Urupabol. A tripartite commission for economic co-operation, trade and integration between Bolivia, Paraguay and Uruguay was constituted formally on 29 May 1981. This organization had existed informally since 1963 when the members started rotating a seat on the Inter-American Development Bank among themselves. By late 1981 both Paraguay and Uruguay had ratified membership of the new commission.

Britain and Latin America. Latin America Bureau, London (annual)
British Bulletin of Publications on Latin America, the Caribbean, Portugal and Spain. London, from June 1949 (half-yearly)
Hispanic and Luso–Brazilian Councils, Portuguese and Spanish Dictionaries. London, 1971
Instruments of Economic Integration in Latin America and the Caribbean. New York, 1975
Libre Comercio. Revista oficial de la Associación de Empresarios participantes de la ALALC. Montevideo, from June 1964 (monthly)
Committee on Latin America (COLA), *Latin American Serials.* 3 vols. London, 1969, 1973, 1977
Brooks, J. (ed.), *The South American Handbook.* Bath (Annual)
Loveman, B., and Davies, T. M., *The Politics of Antipolitics: The Military in Latin America.* Univ. of Nebraska Press, 1978
Morawetz, D., *The Andean Group: A Case Study in Economic Integration Among Developing Countries.* MIT Press, 1974
UN Economic Commission for Latin America. *The Latin America Economy.* Washington (annual)

CARIBBEAN COMMUNITY
(CARICOM)

Establishment and Functions. The Treaty establishing the Caribbean Community, including the Caribbean Common Market, and the Agreement establishing the Common External Tariff for the Caribbean Common Market, was signed by the Prime Ministers of Barbados, Guyana, Jamaica and Trinidad and Tobago at Chaguaramas, Trinidad, on 4 July 1973, and entered into force on 1 Aug. 1973. Six less developed countries of CARIFTA signed the Treaty of Chaguaramas on 17 April 1974. They were Belize, Dominica, Grenada, Saint Lucia, St Vincent and Montserrat, and the Treaty came into effect for those countries on 1 May 1974. Antigua acceded to membership on 4 July 1974 and on 26 July the Associated State of St Kitts–Nevis–Anguilla signed the Treaty of Chaguaramas in Kingston, Jamaica, and became a member of the Caribbean Community. Bahamas became a member of the Community but not of the Common Market on 4 July 1983.

The Caribbean Community has 3 areas of activity: *(i)* economic co-operation through the Caribbean Common Market; *(ii)* co-ordination of foreign policy; *(iii)* functional co-operation in areas such as health, education and culture, youth and sports, science and technology, and tax administration.

The Caribbean Common Market provides for the establishment of a Common External Tariff, a common protective policy and the progressive co-ordination of external trade policies; the adoption of a scheme for the harmonization of fiscal incentives to industry; double taxation arrangements among member countries; the co-ordination of economic policies and development planning; and a special regime for the less developed countries of the community.

Membership: Antigua and Barbuda, Bahamas, Barbados, Belize, Dominica, Grenada, Guyana, Jamaica, Montserrat, St Kitts–Nevis, Saint Lucia, St Vincent and the Grenadines, and Trinidad and Tobago.

Structure: The *Heads of Government Conference* is the principal organ of the Community, and its primary responsibility is to determine the policy of the Community. It is the final authority of the Community and the Common Market, and for the conclusion of treaties and relationships between the Community and international organizations and States. It is responsible for financial arrangements for meeting the expenses of the Community.

The *Common Market Council* is the principal organ of the Common Market and consists of a Minister of Government designated by each member state. Decisions in both the Conference and the Council are in the main taken on the basis of unanimity.

The *Secretariat*, successor to the Commonwealth Caribbean Regional Secretariat, is the principal administrative organ of the Community and of the Common Market. The Secretary-General is appointed by the Conference on the recommendation of the Council for a term not exceeding 5 years and may be reappointed. The Secretary-General shall act in that capacity in all meetings of the Conference, the Council, and of the institutions of the Community.

Institutions of the Community, established by the Heads of Government Conference, are: Conference of Ministers responsible for Health; Standing Committees of Ministers responsible for Education, Industry, Labour, Foreign Affairs, Finance, Agriculture, Energy, Mines and Natural Resources, Industry, Science and Technology, and Transport, respectively.

Associate Institutions: Caribbean Development Bank; Caribbean Examinations Council; Council of Legal Education; University of the West Indies; University of Guyana; Caribbean Meteorological Organization.

Secretary-General: Roderick Rainford.
Deputy Secretary-General: Louis Wiltshire.
Headquarters: Bank of Guyana Building, PO Box 10827, Georgetown, Guyana.

The language of the Community is English.

Books of Reference

CARICOM Perspective. (3 times a year). *CARICOM Bibliography* (Bi-annual)
The Caribbean Community in the 1980's. Caribbean Community Secretariat, 1982
Axline, A. W., *Caribbean Integration: The Politics of Regionalism.* London and New York, 1979
Payne, A. J., *The Politics of the Caribbean Community 1961–79.* Manchester Univ. Press, 1980

SOUTH PACIFIC FORUM

The South Pacific Forum held its first meeting of Heads of Government in New Zealand in 1971. Membership: Australia, Cook Islands, Fiji, Kiribati, Nauru, New Zealand, Niue, Papua New Guinea, Solomon Islands, Tonga, Tuvalu, Vanuatu and Western Samoa. The Federated States of Micronesia have observer status.

In 1985 the Forum adopted a Treaty for a nuclear-free zone in the Pacific.

THE LEAGUE OF ARAB STATES

Origin. The formation of the League of Arab States in 1945 was largely inspired by the Arab awakening of the 19th century. This movement sought to re-create and reintegrate the Arab community which, though for 400 years a part of the Ottoman Empire, had preserved its identity as a separate national group held together by memories of a common past, a common religion and a common language, as well as by the consciousness of being part of a common cultural heritage. The leaders of the Arab movement in the 19th century and of the Arab revolt against Turkey in the First World War sought to achieve these aims through secession from the Ottoman Empire into a united and independent Arab state comprising all the Arab countries in Asia. However the 1919 peace settlement divided the Arab world in Asia (with the exception of Saudi Arabia and the Yemen) into British and French spheres of influence and established in them a number of separate states and administrations (Syria, Lebanon, Iraq, Jordan and Palestine) under temporary mandatory control.

By 1943, however, 7 of these countries had substantially achieved their independence. An Arab conference therefore met in Alexandria in the autumn of 1944; it formulated the 'Alexandria Protocol', which delineated the outlines of the Arab League. It was found that neither a unitary state nor a federation could be achieved, but only a league of sovereign states. A covenant, establishing such a league, was signed in Cairo on 22 March 1945 by the representatives of Egypt, Iraq, Saudi Arabia, Syria, Lebanon, Jordan and Yemen. There were (1980) 21 members of the League: Algeria, Bahrain, Djibouti, Iraq, Jordan, Kuwait, Lebanon, Libya, Mauritania, Morocco, Oman, Palestine L.O., Qatar, Saudi Arabia, Somalia, Sudan, Syria, Tunisia, United Arab Emirates, P.D.R. of Yemen and Yemen Arab Republic.

In the Charter's Special Annex on Palestine, the signatories considered the special circumstances of Palestine and decided that until the country can effectively exercise its independence, the Council of the League should take charge in the selection of an Arab representative from Palestine to take part in its work.

Egypt's membership of the League was suspended, in accordance with a resolution passed at the Baghdad summit, in March 1979, at which time it was also agreed that the League secretariat should be moved from Cairo to Tunis. This action was taken in response to the signing of a bilateral peace treaty between Egypt and Israel.

Organization. The machinery of the League consists of a Council, a number of Special Committees and a Permanent Secretariat. On the Council each state has one vote. The Council may meet in any of the League capitals. Its functions include mediation in any dispute between any of the League states or a League state and a country outside the League. The Council has a Political Committee consisting of the Foreign Ministers of the Arab states. There are also 22 specialized agencies.

The Permanent Secretariat of the League, under a Secretary-General (who enjoys, along with his senior colleagues, full diplomatic status), has its seat in Tunisia.

The League considers itself a regional organization within the framework of the United Nations at which its secretary-general is an observer.

Secretary-General: Chedli Klibi (Tunisia).

Flag: Dark green with the seal of the Arab League in white in the centre.

Arab Common Market. The Arab Common Market came into operation on 1 Jan. 1965. The agreement, reached on 13 Aug. 1964 and open to all the Arab League states, has been signed by Iraq, Jordan, Syria and Egypt. The agreement provides for the abolition of customs duties on agricultural products and natural resources within 5 years, by reducing tariffs at an annual rate of 20%. Customs duties on industrial products are to be reduced by 10% annually. The agreement also provides for the free movement of capital and labour between member countries, the establishment of common external tariffs, the co-ordination of economical development and the framing of a common foreign economic policy.

Books of Reference

Arab Maritime Data, 1979–80. London, 1979
Gomaa, A. M., *The Foundation of the League of Arab States.* London, 1977

ORGANIZATION OF THE PETROLEUM EXPORTING COUNTRIES

Aims. The Organization was founded in Baghdad, Iraq, in 1960 with the following founder members, Iran, Iraq, Kuwait, Saudi Arabia and Venezuela. The principal aims are unifying the petroleum policies of member countries and determining the best means for safeguarding their interests, individually and collectively; to devise ways and means of ensuring the stabilization of prices in international oil markets with a view to eliminating harmful and unnecessary fluctuations; and to secure a steady income for the producing countries, an efficient, economic and regular supply of petroleum to consuming nations, and a fair return on their capital to those investing in the petroleum industry.

Membership (1986). Algeria, Ecuador, Gabon, Indonesia, Iran, Iraq, Kuwait, Libya, Nigeria, Qatar, Saudi Arabia, United Arab Emirates and Venezuela. Membership is open to any other country having substantial net exports of crude petroleum, which has fundamentally similar interests to those of member countries.

OPEC Fund for International Development: The Fund was established in 1976 to provide financial aid to developing countries, other than OPEC members, on advantageous terms.

Deputy Secretary-General: Dr Fadhil J. Al-Chalabi (Iraq).

Headquarters: Obere Donaustrasse 93, A–1020 Vienna, Austria.

Flag: Light blue with the Opec logo in white in the centre.

Books of Reference

OPEC publications include: *Annual Statistical Bulletin. Annual Report. OPEC Bulletin* (monthly). *OPEC Review* (quarterly).
Ahrari, M. E., *Opec: The Failing Giant.* Univ. Press of Kentucky, 1986
Al-Chalabi, Dr F., *OPEC and the International Oil Industry: A Changing Structure.* OUP, 1980
El Mallakh, R., *OPEC: Twenty Years and Beyond.* London, 1982
Griffin, J., and Teece, D. J., *OPEC Behaviour and World Oil Prices.* London and Boston, 1982

ORGANIZATION OF AFRICAN UNITY

On 25 May 1963 the heads of state or government of 32 African countries, at a conference in Addis Ababa, signed a charter establishing an 'Organization of African Unity' *(Organisation de l'Unité Africaine).*

Its chief objects are the furtherance of African unity and solidarity; the co-ordination of the political, economic, cultural, health, scientific and defence policies and the elimination of colonialism in Africa.

The organs of the Organization are: (1) the assembly of the heads of state and government; (2) the council of ministers; (3) the general secretariat; (4) a commission of mediation, conciliation and arbitration. Arabic, French and English are recognized as working languages.

Chairman: Abdou Diouf (Senegal).
Secretary-General a.i.: Ide Oumarou (Niger).
Headquarters: Addis Ababa.
Flag: Horizontally green, white, green, with the white fimbriated yellow, and the seal of the OAU in the centre.

DANUBE COMMISSION

The Danube Commission was constituted in 1949 based on the Convention regarding the regime of navigation on the Danube, which was signed in Belgrade on 18 Aug. 1948. The Belgrade Convention reaffirmed that navigation on the Danube from Ulm to the Black Sea, with access to the sea through the Sulina arm and the Sulina Canal, is equally free and open to the nationals, merchant shipping and merchandise of all states as to harbour and navigation fees as well as conditions of merchant navigation.

The Danube Commission is composed of representatives from the countries on the Danube (1 for each of these countries), namely, Austria, Bulgaria, Hungary, Romania, Czechoslovakia, USSR and Yugoslavia. Since 1957, representatives of the Ministry of Transport from the Federal Republic of Germany have attended the meetings of the Commission as guests of the Secretariat.

The functions of the Danube Commission are to check that the provisions of the Convention are carried out, to establish a uniform buoying system on all the Danube's navigable waterways and to establish the basic regulations for navigation on the river. The Commission co-ordinates the regulations for river, customs and sanitation control as well as the hydrometeorological service and collects statistical data concerning navigation on the Danube.

The Danube Commission enjoys legal status. It has its own seal and flag. The members of the Commission and elected officers enjoy diplomatic immunity. The Commission's official buildings, archives and documents are inviolable. French and Russian are the official languages of the Commission.

Since 1954 the headquarters of the Commission have been in Budapest.

Flag: Blue, with a red strip fimbriated white along the bottom edge, and the initials of the Commission within a wreath in the canton—Latin letters on obverse Cyrillic on reverse.

Books of Reference

Danube Commission's publications include: *Summary Records and Documents Adopted by the Sessions of the Danube Commission. Rules of Procedure of the Danube Commission. Basic Regulations for Navigation on the Danube. Reports on the Maintenance of the Navigability of the Danube. Guidebook for Sailors. Hydrological Yearbooks. Statistical Yearbooks. Mileage Chart of the Danube. Ice Control on the Danube. Collection of Internal Laws Concerning Navigation on the Danube. Collection of International Agreements Relating to Navigation on the Danube. Radio-Codes for Navigation on the Danube.*

PART II

COUNTRIES OF THE WORLD

A—Z

AFGHÁNISTÁN

Jamhuria Afghanistan

Capital: Kábul
Population: 8–10m. (1986)
GNP per capita: US$250 (1985)

HISTORY. A military *coup* on 17 July 1973 overthrew the monarchy of King Záhir Shàh. The *coup* was led by the King's cousin and brother-in-law Mohammad Daoud who declared a Republic. King Záhir abdicated on 24 Aug. 1973. President Daoud was killed in a military *coup* in April 1978 which led to the establishment of a pro-Soviet government of the People's Democratic Party of Afghánistán (PDPA).

AREA AND POPULATION. Afghánistán is bounded north by the USSR, east and south by Pakistan and west by Iran.

The area is 251,773 sq. miles (652,090 sq. km). Population, according to the (1979) census, is 15,551,358, of which some 2·5m. are nomadic tribes. Estimate (1986) 8–10m. Approximately 3m. Afghans have sought refuge in Pakistan, over 1m. in Iran and several hundred thousand have been killed since 1979. Infant mortality rates are as high as 200 per 1,000 live births in some areas. The population of Kábul is over 2m. There are no current reliable population figures for other cities and major towns.

Census (1979), Kábul 913,164; Kandahár, 178,409; Herát, 140,323; Mazár-i-Sharif, 103,372; Jalálábád, 53,915; Kunduz, 53,251; Baghlan, 39,228; Maimana, 38,251; Pul-i-Khumri, 31,101; Ghazni, 30,425; Charikar, 22,424; Shiberghan, 18,955; Gardez, 9,550; Faizabad, 9,098; Qala-i-nau, 5,340; Uiback, 4,938; Meterlam, 3,987; Cheghcherán, 2,974.

The main ethnic group are the Pathans. Other ethnic groups include the Tajiks, the Hazaras, the Turkomans and the Uzbeks.

CLIMATE. The climate is arid, with a big annual range of temperature and very little rain, apart from the period Jan. to April. Winters are very cold, with considerable snowfall, which may last the year round on mountain summits. Kábul. Jan. 27°F (–2·8°C), July 76°F (24·4°C). Annual rainfall 13″ (338 mm).

CONSTITUTION AND GOVERNMENT. In Dec. 1979 Soviet troops invaded Afghánistán and Hafizullah Amin was deposed and replaced by Babrak Karmal. The pretext for the airlift of combat troops to Kábul was the Treaty of Friendship signed in Dec. 1978 between USSR and Afghánistán. In May 1986 Karmal was replaced as General Secretary of the PDPA by Dr Sayid Mohammed Najibullah who was elected President in Sept. 1987 at a special session of the Revolutionary Council. In early 1988 there were some 115,000 Soviet troops in Afghánistán but plans for their withdrawal were announced in Feb. 1988.

A new Constitution was approved in Nov. 1987. The PDPA remains the leading political force in the country. It is governed by a 63-65 strong Central Committee, which elects a Political Bureau, currently of 13 full, and 4 alternate, members to decide policy in association with the 14-member Presidium of the Revolutionary Council. At that time, the name of the country was changed from the Democratic Republic of Afghánistán to the Republic of Afghánistán.

Ministers in Jan. 1988:
Prime Minister: Sultan Ali Kishtmand. *Finance:* Mohammad Kabir. *Foreign Affairs:* Abdul Wakil. *Interior:* Sayed Mohammad Gulabzoi. *Defence:* Lieut.-Gen. Mohammad Rafi. *Education:* Abdul Samad Qayyumi. *Commerce:* Mohammad Khan Jalalar.

National flag: Three equal horizontal stripes of red, black and green, with the national arms in the canton.

The official languages are Pushtu and Dari (Persian).

Local Government: There are 29 provinces each administered by an appointed governor.

DEFENCE. Conscription is for a period of 4 years, with reserve liability continuing for 3 years beginning 2 years from the end of the initial conscription period.

Army. The Army is organized in 3 armoured and 11 infantry divisions, 1 mechanized infantry brigade, 1 artillery brigade, 2 mountain infantry and 3 commando regiments. Equipment includes 50 T-34, 300 T-54/-55 and 100 T-62 battle tanks. Strength was (1987) about 45,000, but most units of the Army, effectively under Soviet control, are well below strength, largely as a result of desertions.

Air Force. The Air Force, which is Russian-equipped, has about 180 combat aircraft and 5,000 officers and men. Nominal strength comprises 3 squadrons of Su-17 attack aircraft, 3 squadrons of MiG-21 interceptors (about 40 aircraft), 3 squadrons of MiG-17s and 3 squadrons of MiG-23s, a helicopter attack force of at least 30 Mi-24s, a transport wing with 10 An-12s, 12 twin-turboprop An-26s, about 10 piston-engined An-2s, 30 Mi-8 and 10 Mi-4 helicopters and 2 turboprop Il-18s, and Yak-18, Aero L-39 and MiG-15UTI trainers. The main fighter station is Bagram, with facilities for the largest jet airliners and bombers. There is a fighter-bomber station at Shindand, a training station at Mazár-i-Sharif and an air academy at Sherpur. Large numbers of SA-2 and SA-3 surface-to-air missiles are operational in Afghánistán. Strong Soviet forces in Afghánistán in 1987 included MiG-21, MiG-23, MiG-27, Su-17 and Su-25 attack aircraft, and large numbers of Mi-6, Mi-8 assault helicopters and Mi-24 helicopter gunships.

Police and Militia. In addition to the Army and Air Force there are a number of paramilitary units, including a 30,000-strong gendarmerie, secret police and 'Defence of the Revolution' forces.

INTERNATIONAL RELATIONS

Membership. Afghánistán is a member of UN and of the Colombo Plan.

ECONOMY

Planning. A 5-year plan was adopted in 1986 to cover period 1986–1991. Emphasis is on reconstruction of agriculture and irrigation systems as well as exploitation of natural gas resources.

Budget. In 1983–84 the budget envisaged expenditure of Afs. 49,941m. and revenue of Afs. 34,120m.

Currency. The monetary system is on the silver standard. The unit is the *afgháni*, weighing 10 grammes of silver 0·900 fine, which is subdivided into 100 *puls*. Rates of exchange are fixed (1988) Afs. 99·25 = £1; Afs. 50·60 = US$1.

Banking. The Afghán State Bank *(Da Afghánistán Bank)* is the largest of the 3 main banks and also undertakes the functions of a central bank, holding the exclusive right of note issue. Total assets of the 3 main banks were: Da Afghánistán Bánk (1981), Afs. 22,839m.; Pashtany Tejaraty Bánk (1981), Afs. 6,997m.; Bánk-i-Milli (1981), Afs. 3,087m.

Weights and Measures. Weights and measures used in Kábul are: Weights: 1 *khurd* = 0·244 lb.; 1 *pao* = 0·974 lb.; 1 *charak* = 3·896 lb.; 1 *sere* = 16 lb.; 1 *kharwár* = 1,280 lb. or 16 maunds of 80 lb. each. Long measure: 1 yard or *gaz* = 40 in. The metric system is in increasingly common use. Square measures: 1 *jaríb* = 60 × 60 kábuli yd or ½ acre; 1 *kulbá* = 40 jaríbs (area in which 2½ kharwárs of seed can be sown); 1 jaríb yd = 29 in. Local weights and measures are in use in the provinces.

ENERGY AND NATURAL RESOURCES

Electricity. Hydro-electric plants have been constructed at Sarobi, Nangarhár, Naghlu, Mahipár, Pul-i-Khumri and Kandahár. Production (1986) 1,390m. kwh. Supply 220 volts; 50 Hz.

Natural gas. Production (1985) 2,400m. cu. metres. Natural gas is found in northern Afghánistán around Shiberghan and Sar-i-Pol; over 2,000m. cu. metres, about 95% of production, is piped to the USSR annually.

Minerals. Mineral resources are scattered and little developed. Coal is mined at Karkar in Pul-i-Khumri, Ishpushta near Doshi, north of Kábul and Dar-i-Suf south of Mazar (total production, 1983–84, 145,300 tonnes). Rich, but as yet unexploited, deposits of iron ore exist in the Hajigak hills about 100 miles west of Kábul; beryllium has been found in the Kunar valley and barite in Bamian province. Other deposits include gold; silver (now unexploited, in the Panjshir valley); lapis lazuli (in the Panjshir valley and Badakhshán); asbestos; mica; sulphur (near Maimana); chrome (in the Logar valley and near Herát); and copper (in the north).

Agriculture. Although the greater part of Afghánistán is more or less mountainous and a good deal of the country is too dry and rocky for successful cultivation, there are many fertile plains and valleys, which, with the assistance of irrigation from small rivers or wells, yield very satisfactory crops of fruit, vegetables and cereals. It is estimated that there are 14m. hectares of cultivable land in the country, of which only 6% of the total land was being cultivated in 1982–83 (5·34m. hectares of this being irrigated land). Before 1979 Afghánistán was virtually self-supporting in foodstuffs (including wheat in 1973), apart from sugar. The USSR now provides wheat, sugar and other foodstuffs.

The castor-oil plant, madder and the asafœtida plant abound.

Fruit forms a staple food (with bread) of many people throughout the year, both in the fresh and preserved state, and in the latter condition is exported in great quantities. The fat-tailed sheep furnish the principal meat diet, and the grease of the tail is a substitute for butter. Wool and skins provide material for warm apparel and one of the more important articles of export. Persian lambskins (Karakuls) are one of the chief exports.

Production, 1986, in 1,000 tonnes: Seed cotton, 66; wheat, 2,500; barley, 300; maize, 750; rice, 454.

Livestock (1986): Cattle, 3·75m.; horses, donkeys and mules, 1·69m.; sheep, 20m.; goats, 3m.; chickens, 7m.

INDUSTRY AND TRADE

Industry. At Kábul there are factories for the manufacture of cotton and woollen textiles, leather, boots, marble-ware, furniture, glass, bicycles, prefabricated houses and plastics. A large machine shop has been constructed and equipped by the USSR, with a capability of manufacturing motor spares. There is a wool factory and there are several cotton-ginning plants; a small cotton factory at Jabal-us-Seráj and a larger one at Pul-i-Khumri; a cotton-seed oil extraction plant at Lashkargah; a cotton textile factory at Gulbahar, and a cotton plant at Balkh.

An ordnance factory manufactures arms and ammunition, boots and clothing, etc. for the Army. There is a beet sugar plant at Baghlan (equipped with Soviet machinery) and a fruit-canning factory in Kandahár.

Industries include cement, coalmining, cotton textiles, small vehicle assembly plants, fruit canning, carpet making, leather tanning, footwear manufacture, sugar manufacture, preparation of hides and skins, and building. Most of these are relatively small and, with the exception of hides and skins, carpets and fruits, do not meet domestic requirements.

Commerce. Trade is supervised by the Government through the Ministries of Commerce and Finance and the Da Afghánistán Bánk. The Association of Afghán Chambers of Commerce works in close liaison with the Ministry of Commerce. The Government monopoly controls the import of petrol and oil, sugar, cigarettes and tobacco, motor vehicles and consignment goods from bilateral trading countries. The principal surface routes for imports to Afghánistán are *via* the Soviet rail system and the border posts at Torghundi and Hairatan; and from Karachi *via* the border post at Torkham.

In the year ended March 1985 Afghán imports totalled US$964·7m. and exports US$670·5m. Main export commodities were karakul skins (US$13·5m.), raw cotton (US$12·5m.), dried fruit and nuts (US$141m.), fresh fruit (US$53·3m.) and natural gas (US$302·4m.). Main items imported were petroleum products (US$164m.), textiles (US$122·5m.). Over 50% of trade is with the USSR.

Total trade between Afghánistán and UK (in £1,000 sterling, British Department of Trade returns):

	1983	1984	1985	1986	1987
Imports to UK	19,837	20,776	52,061	11,913	11,289
Exports and re-exports from UK	10,310	11,892	13,882	11,444	10,735

Tourism. Owing to internal political instability there has been negligible tourism since 1979.

COMMUNICATIONS

Roads. There were in 1978 over 2,812 km of asphalted road and 15,940 km of other roads. The Americans asphalted the Kandahár–Chaman and Kábul–Torkham roads. The Russians constructed a road and tunnel through the Salang pass (over 11,000 ft) which was opened in Sept. 1964 and cut 120 miles off the old road from Kábul to the north; they continued this road to Kunduz and Sherkhan Bandar (Qizil Qala) on the Oxus. In addition, the Americans in 1966 completed the road between Kábul and Kandahár and the Russians constructed a concrete road between Kandahár and Herát. In 1968 the Americans completed an asphalt road from Herát to the Iranian frontier at Islam Qala. With Soviet assistance a metalled road from Pul-i-Khumri to Mazár-i-Sharif was completed in 1969 and Mazár-i-Sharif to Shiberghán in 1971. A Soviet-built road and rail bridge across the Oxus (Amu Darya) River was opened in May 1982. There are about 90,000 cars and commercial vehicles registered in Kábul. All roads, particularly outside the towns, are in a very poor state of repair as a result of the war.

Railways. There are no railways in the country, but the Oxus bridge opened in 1982, brought Soviet Railways' track into the country. A 200 km line of 1,520 mm gauge has been authorized from Termez to Pul-i-Khumri.

Aviation. On 29 June 1956 Afghánistán signed an agreement with the USA for the development of civil aviation, including the construction of the international airport at Kandahár, comprising a loan of $5m. and a grant of $9·56m. Kábul airport has been expanded with Russian assistance. New runways at Kábul and Kandahár airports have been completed. Provincial all-weather airports have been constructed at Herát, Qunduz, Jalálábád and Mazár-i-Sharif.

Bakhtar Afghan Airlines (the domestic national airline) began operations on 8 Feb. 1968 and regularly serves the main internal airfields, which, from 1985 was merged with Ariana Afghan Airlines (a national airline) operating regular services to New Delhi, Prague, Tashkent and Moscow.

Shipping. There are practically no navigable rivers in Afghánistán, and timber is the only article of commerce conveyed by water, floated down the Kunar and Kábul rivers from Chitral on rafts. A port has been built at Qizil Qala on the Oxus; barge traffic is increasing on the Oxus. Three river ports on the Amu Darya have been built at Sherkhan Bandar, Tashguzar and Hairatan, linked by road to Kábul.

Post and Broadcasting. Telephones, installed in most of the large towns, numbered 31,200 in 1978. There is telegraphic communication between all the larger towns and with other parts of the world. Kábul Radio broadcasts in Pushtu, Persian, Urdu, English, French, Russian and German. The first TV colour transmissions in Kábul began in mid-1978. An agreement was signed in 1981 under which the USSR undertook to assist with the development of communications. In 1978 there were 823,000 radio receivers and in 1982 12,000 television receivers.

Newspapers. In 1983 there were 3 daily newspapers with a circulation of 67,000.

JUSTICE, RELIGION, EDUCATION AND WELFARE

Justice. A Supreme Court was established in June 1978. If no provision exists in the Constitution or in the general laws of the State, the courts follow the Hanafi jurisprudence of Islamic law.

Religion. The predominant religion is Islam, mostly of the Sunni sect, though there is a minority of about 1m. Shiah Moslems.

Education. There are elementary schools throughout the country, but secondary schools exist only in Kábul and provincial capitals. Both elementary and secondary education are free. In 1982 there were 1·1m. pupils (35,364 teachers) in primary education and 124,000 pupils (6,170 teachers) in secondary education. There are 3 teacher-training institutions in Kábul and 11 elsewhere; UNESCO is supporting an expansion programme. Technical, art, commercial and medical schools exist for higher education. Kábul University was founded in 1932 and has 9 faculties (medicine, science, agriculture, engineering, law and political science, letters, economics, theology, pharmacology). The University of Nangarhar in Jalálábád was founded in 1963. A Polytechnic in Kábul was completed in 1968. In 1982 there were 13,115 students in higher education, 4,427 in teacher-training schools and 1,230 in technical schools.

Health. In 1982 there were 1,215 doctors and 6,875 hospital beds. Two-thirds of the doctors and half the beds were in Kábul.

DIPLOMATIC REPRESENTATIVES

Of Afghánistán in Great Britain (31 Prince's Gate, London, SW7 1QQ)
Chargé d'Affaires: Ahmad Sarwar.

Of Great Britain in Afghánistán (Karte Parwan, Kábul)
Chargé d'Affaires: I. W. Mackley.

Of Afghánistán in the USA (2341 Wyoming Ave., NW, Washington, D.C., 20008)
Chargé d'Affaires: Ruhullah Elfari.

Of the USA in Afghánistán (Wazir Akbar Khan Mina, Kábul)
Chargé d'Affaires: J. D. Glassman.

Of Afghánistán to the United Nations
Ambassador: Shah Mohd Dost.

Books of Reference

Arnold, A., *Afghanistan: The Soviet Invasion in Perspective.* Oxford and Stanford, 1981.—*Afghanistan's Two-Party Communism.* Oxford and Santa Barbara, 1983
Bradsher, H. S., *Afghanistan and the Soviet Union.* Duke Univ. Press, 1983
Chaliand, G., *Rapport sur la résistance afghane.* Paris, 1981.—*Report from Afghanistan.* New York, 1982
Gilbertson, G. W., *Pakkhto Idiom Dictionary.* 2 vols. London, 1932
Giradet, E. R., *Afghanistan: The Soviet War.* London, 1985
Gregorian, V., *The Emergence of Modern Afghanistan.* Stanford, 1970
Griffiths, J. C., *Afghanistan: Key to a Continent.* London, 1981
Hammond, T. T., *Red Star over Afghanistan.* Boulder and London, 1984
Hanifi, M. J., *Historical and Cultural Dictionary of Afghanistan.* Metuchen, 1976
Hyman, A., *Afghanistan under Soviet Domination 1964–83.* London, 1984
Male, B., *Revolutionary Afghanistan.* London, 1982
Misra, K. P., *Afghanistan in Crisis.* London, 1981
Newell, N. P. and Newell, R. S., *The Struggle for Afghanistan.* Cornell Univ. Press, 1981
Sykes, P. M., *A History of Afghanistan.* 2 vols. New York, 1975

ALBANIA

Republika Popullore
Socialiste e Shqipërisë

Capital: Tirana
Population: 3·08m. (1987)
GNP per capita: US$930 (1986)

HISTORY. For the history of Albania before the Second World War *see* The Statesman's Year-Book 1985–86, p. 66. During the years 1939–44 the country was overrun by Italians and Germans. The official Albanian date of the liberation is 29 Nov. 1944.

On 10 Nov. 1945 the British, US and USSR Governments recognized a Provisional Government under Gen. Enver Hoxha, on the understanding that it would hold free elections. The elections of 2 Dec. 1945 resulted in a Communist-controlled assembly, which on 11 Jan. 1946 proclaimed Albania a republic.

In 1946 Great Britain and the USA broke off relations with Albania and vetoed its admission to the UN. Albania was finally admitted in 1955.

Because of Albania's Stalinist and pro-Chinese attitudes diplomatic relations with USSR were broken off in 1961. In 1977 Albania terminated its special relationship with China. Since the death of Enver Hoxha on 11 April 1985 Albania has been moving out of its diplomatic isolation.

AREA AND POPULATION. Albania is bounded north and east by Yugoslavia, south by Greece and west by the Adriatic. The area of the country is 28,748 sq. km (11,101 sq. miles). By the peace treaty Italy restored the island of Sazan (Saseno) to Albania. At the census of 1982 the population was, 2,786,100. Population in 1987, 3·08m (34% urban; density 107 per sq. km). The capital is Tirana (1983 population (in 1,000), 206); other large towns are Durrës (Durrsi, Durazzo) (72), Shkodër (Shkodra, Scutari) (71), Elbasan (70), Vlorë (Vlona, Vlonë, Vlora, Valona) (61), Korçë (Korça, Koritza) (57), Fier (37), Berat (37), Lushnjë (24), Kavajë (23) and Gjirokastër (Argyrocastro) (21).

Ethnic minorities (mainly Greeks) numbered some 200,000 in 1987.

Vital statistics, 1985 (per 1,000): Births, 26·5; deaths, 5·8; marriages, 9; divorces (1982), 0·8; natural increase, 21 per thousand. Growth rate, 1980–85, 2·1%. Life expectancy in 1987 was 72 years.

The country is administratively divided into 26 districts (*rreth*, pl. *rrethët*) (*see* map in The Statesman's Year-Book, 1962. N.B. The district of Ersekë has been renamed Kolonjë). Districts are subdivided into 3,315 *lokaliteteve*.

Districts	Area (sq. km)	Population (in 1,000) (1982)	Districts	Area (sq. km)	Population (in 1,000) (1982)
Berat	1,026	154·0	Lushnjë	712	115·4
Dibrë	1,569	134·8	Mat	1,028	67·0
Durrës	859	217·0	Mirditë	698	45·0
Elbasan	1,466	208·0	Permet	930	36·4
Fier	1,191	212·0	Pogradec	725	62·0
Gjirokastër	1,137	60·3	Pukë	969	45·0
Gramsh	695	38·0	Sarandë	1,097	76·7
Kolonjë	805	22·3	Shkodër	2,528	206·2
Korçë	2,181	199·0	Skrapar	775	42·0
Krujë	607	93·0	Tepelenë	817	45·2
Kukës	1,564	86·0	Tirana	1,222	310·0
Lezhë	479	53·0	Tropojë	1,043	39·8
Librazhd	1,013	63·0	Vlorë	1,609	155·0

Districts are named after their capitals; exceptions: Tropojë, capital—Bajram Curri; Mat—Burrel; Mirditë—Rrëshen; Skrapar—Çorovodë; Dibrë—Peshkopi; Kolonjë—Ersekë.

The Albanian language is divided into two dialects—Gheg, north of the river Shkumbi, and Tosk in the south. Many places therefore have two forms of name: Vlonë (Gheg), Vlorë (Tosk), etc., and many are known also by an Italian name, *e.g.*, Valona. Since 1945 the official language has been based on Tosk.

CLIMATE. Mediterranean-type, with rainfall mainly in winter, but thunderstorms are frequent and severe in the great heat of the plains in summer. Winters in the highlands can be severe, with much snow. Tirana. Jan. 44°F (6·8°C), July 75°F (23·9°C). Annual rainfall 54″ (1,353 mm). Shkodër. Jan. 39°F (3·9°C), July 77°F (25°C). Annual rainfall 57″ (1,425 mm).

CONSTITUTION AND GOVERNMENT. The political structure derived from the Constitution of 14 March 1946 as amended in 1950, 1955, 1960 and 1963. In Dec. 1976 a new Constitution was adopted, by which Albania became a 'Socialist People's Republic'. The supreme legislative body is the single-chamber People's Assembly of 250 deputies, which meets twice a year, and delegates its day-to-day functions to a Presidium. Election to the People's Assembly is by universal suffrage (at 18) every 4 years.

In the elections of 1 Feb. 1987 a 100% turnout of the electorate of 1,830,653 was claimed to vote for the 250 candidates (66 women) on the single list of the Democratic Front. (There was 1 vote against).

The Government consists of a prime minister (Chairman of the Council of Ministers), 4 deputy prime ministers and 17 ministers. Effective rule is exercised by the Albanian Labour (*i.e.*, Communist) Party, founded 8 Nov. 1941, whose governing body is the Politburo.

In 1981 the Party had 122,600 full members and candidates (in 1979 37·5% workers, 29% farmers, 27% women).

Titular Head of State: Chairman of the Presidium of the People's Assembly: Ramiz Alia, elected Nov. 1982. In March 1988 the chief Party and Government posts were filled as follows: Full members of the Politburo: *First Secretary of the Central Committee of the Party:* Ramiz Alia, Adil Çarçani *(Prime Minister)*, Foto Çami, Prokop Murra *(Minister of Defence)*, Hekuran Isai[1] *(Minister of the Interior)*, Besnik Bekteshi[1], Pali Miska, Manush Myftiu[1], Rita Marko, Muho Asllani, Hajredin Celiku; Simon Stefani, Ms. Lenka Çuko. Candidate members: Llambi Gegprifti *(Minister of Industry)*, Qirjako Mihali, Pirro Kondi, Kico Mustaqi, Vangel Cerava[1].

Ministers not in the Politburo include: *Foreign Affairs:* Reiz Malile. *Foreign Trade:* Shane Korbeci. *Agriculture:* Themie Thomai. *Chairman, State Planning Commission:* Niko Gjyzari. *Finance:* Andrea Nako. *Education:* Skender Gjinush. *Health:* Ahmet Kamberi.

[1] Deputy Prime Minister.

Local Government is carried out by People's Councils at village, *lokalitet*, town and district level. Councillors are elected for 3 years.

National flag: Red, with a black double-headed eagle and a red, gold-edged 5-pointed star above it. *Mercantile flag:* Red, black, red (horizontal) with a red yellow-edged star in the centre.

National anthem: Rreth Flamurit te per bashkuar (The flag that united us in the struggle).

DEFENCE. Albania withdrew from the Warsaw Pact in 1968 in protest against the invasion of Czechoslovakia. The Constitution precludes the stationing of foreign troops in Albania. Conscription is for 2 years.

Army. The Army consists of 1 tank brigade, 4 infantry brigades and 3 artillery regiments. Equipment includes 70 T-34, 15 T-54 and 15 T-59 main battle tanks. Strength is 31,500 (including 20,000 conscripts) and reserves number 155,000. There are also paramilitary internal security forces (5,000 men) and frontier guards (7,000).

Navy. The Navy consists of 3 submarines, 2 fleet minesweepers, 2 patrol vessels, 4 inshore minesweepers, 32 very fast (hydro foil) torpedo boats, 6 fast gunboats, 9 minesweeping boats, 1 degaussing ship, 4 small oilers, 1 diving tender, 1 torpedo recovery craft, 4 tugs and 12 small auxiliaries and service tenders. Navy personnel in 1988 totalled 3,200 officers and ratings, including 400 coastal defence guards. Service for ratings is 3 years. There are naval bases at Durrës and Vlorë.

Air Force. The Air Force, controlled by the Army, has about 7,200 officers and men, and in 1987 operated 80 combat aircraft received before relations with China were broken. The force included 20 Chinese-built F-7s and 30 F-6s, and 3 ground attack squadrons of F-2s and F-4s. Transport and training types include 3 Il-14s, 10 An-2s, Mi-4 helicopters, Yak-18s and MiG-15UTIs. Personnel in 1986: 7,200.

INTERNATIONAL RELATIONS

Membership. Albania is a member of UN.

ECONOMY

Planning. For the first six 5-year plans *see* THE STATESMAN'S Year-Book, 1985–86. The seventh 5-year plan (1981–85) was the first to be completed without foreign aid (Economic self-reliance is now stated to be a revolutionary principle). Increases over 1980 (and targets): Social product, 18% (32%); national income, 16% (34%); agriculture, 13% (31%). Targets of the eighth 5-year plan (1986–90): Social production, 30–32%; national income, 34–36%; industry, 29–31%; agriculture, 34–36%.

Budget. Budget figures for 1985: Revenue, 9,250m. leks; expenditure, 9,200m. leks (1984 expenditure: Economy 5,062m. leks; social, 2,401m. leks; administration 144m. leks). Defence expenditure (1986) 998m. leks.

Currency. The monetary unit is the *lek* of 100 *qintars*. It replaced the gold franc *(franc ar)* in July 1947. In Aug. 1965 a new *lek* was introduced: 10 old *leks* = 1 new *lek*. There are 5, 10, 20 and 50 *qintar* coins and a 1 *lek* coin; notes are for 1, 3, 5, 10, 25, 50 and 100 *leks*. Exchange rates, Feb. 1988: US$1 = 5·51 *leks*; £1 = 9·97.

Banking. The Albanian State Bank was founded in 1925 with Italian aid. In 1970 savings deposits amounted to 572m. leks. In 1970 the Agricultural Bank was set up as a credit institution for agricultural co-operatives.

Weights and Measures. The metric system is in force.

ENERGY AND NATURAL RESOURCES

Electricity. Albania is rich in hydro-electric potential. Electric power production in 1985 was 4,700m. kwh., of which 53m. was from thermal plants. 2,000m. kwh. were exported in 1984 to Yugoslavia, Bulgaria, Romania and Greece.

Oil. Oil reserves are some 20m. tonnes. Output in 1987: Crude, 3m. tonnes; refined (1973), 1,596,000 tonnes. Refining capacity in 1970 was over 1m. tonnes. Oil is produced chiefly at Qytet Stalin which a pipeline connects to the port of Vlorë. Natural gas is extracted. Reserves: 8,000m. cu. metres; 1985 production, 420m. cu. metres.

Minerals. The mineral wealth of Albania is considerable and includes coal (not bituminous), oil, chrome and ferro-nickel ores but it is only recently being developed. Chromium ore output was some 1·5m. tonnes in 1986. Reserves are about 20m. tonnes. Salt is extracted near Vlorë and bitumen mined at Selenicë. Production in tonnes (1984): Copper ore, 168,000; nickel ore, 6,000; brown coal, 1·78m.; phosphate, 18,000; nitrogenous fertilizer, 75,000; cement, 1·1m.

Agriculture. The country for the greater part is rugged, wild and mountainous, the exceptions being along the Adriatic littoral and the Korçë (Koritza) Basin, which are fertile. In 1983 arable land comprised 709,800 hectares, 55% of which was irrigated.

Land is held by the State (largely forests and non-agricultural), state farms (50 in 1982 averaging 3,000 hectares of arable land) and co-operatives (500 in 1983 averaging 1,100 hectares). Co-operatives are divided into 'advanced' and 'ordinary'. There is a pension scheme for collective farmers. In 1982 there were 31 machine and tractor stations. Tractors in 1980 numbered 17,300 (in 15-h.p. units).

Production of the main crops in 1986 was (in 1,000 tonnes): Wheat, 540; sugarbeet, 320; maize, 410; potatoes, 136; fruit, 198; grapes, 83; oats, 30; sorghum, 36; seed cotton, 16; barley, 36; sunflower seeds, 55; wine, 23; rice, 14; tobacco, 20.

Livestock, 1986: Cattle, 610,000; sheep, 1·23m.; goats, 700,000; pigs, 220,000; horses and mules, 64,000; poultry, 5m.

Forestry. 35% of the territory of Albania is forest land, mainly oak, elm, pine and birch. Some 40,000 hectares per annum are afforested or improved.

Fisheries. The catch in 1984 was 4,000 tonnes.

INDUSTRY AND TRADE

Industry. All industry is nationalized down to the smallest workshop. Output is small, and the principal industries are agricultural product processing, textiles, oil products and cement. Chemical and engineering industries are being built up. The metallurgical combine at Elbasan is being extended.

Labour. In 1978, 583,600 persons worked in the socialist sector of the national economy. In 1976, 46% of wage-earners were women.

Minimum wages may not fall below one-third of maximum. Hours of labour: 8-hour day, 6-day week and 12 days yearly paid holiday. Retirement age is 60 for men and 55 for women.

Commerce. Yugoslavia is Albania's main trading partner: in Nov. 1985 a 5-year agreement provided for a 20% increase in trade. Trade links with China were re-established in 1983, and a 5-year agreement was signed in Dec. 1985. Trade is conducted with the Comecon countries Bulgaria, Czechoslovakia, North Korea, Poland, and Vietnam; and also with Italy, France and India. The establishment of joint companies with, and the acceptance of credits from, capitalist firms is forbidden.

Exports which in 1983 were (estimate) US$500m. included crude oil, bitumen, chrome, nickel, copper, tobacco, fruit and vegetables.

Total trade between Albania and UK (British Department of Trade returns, in £1,000 sterling):

	1983	1984	1985	1986	1987
Imports to UK	60	1,097	212	129	91
Exports and re-exports from UK	240	4,481	5,252	2,887	2,565

COMMUNICATIONS

Roads. There were, in 1981, 21,000 km of roads suitable for motor traffic. The mountain districts of the north are still mostly inaccessible for wheeled vehicles, and communications are still by means of pack ponies or donkeys. Motor vehicles in 1970: Cars, 3,500; lorries and buses, 11,000. Road traffic carried 8·6m. passengers in 1970; goods carried, 34m. tonnes. There are no private cars.

Railways. Total length, in 1987 was 378 km. They comprise the lines from Durrës to Tirana, Vlorë, Ballsh, Pogradec, Shkodër and across the Yugoslav border to Titograd. This cross-border line, opened in 1986, is the country's first international rail link. A line from Pogradec to Korcë is under construction.

Aviation. There are regular scheduled flights from Tirana (Rinas Airport) to Belgrade, Bucharest, Budapest, East Berlin and Zurich. Olympic Airways operate a weekly flight from Athens to Tirana.

Shipping. In 1986 there were 20 ships totalling 56,133 GRT. The main ports are the Enver Hoxha Port of Durrës, Vlorë and Sarandë. A ferry service from Trieste to Durrës opened in Nov. 1983.

Post and Broadcasting. Number of post and telegraph offices (1970), 292; telephones (1963), 10,150. There are 17 broadcasting stations, including Tirana and Korçë. Radio Tirana operates a foreign service in 18 languages. Radio receiving sets (1983), 210,000; television sets, 20,500. Regular television broadcasting began in 1971. There were 7 TV stations in 1984.

Cinemas and Theatres. In 1975 there were 410 cinemas (including mobile) and in 1973 27 theatres with an attendance of 1·6m. 14 full-length films were produced in 1980.

Newspapers and Books. In 1978 there were 30 newspapers with an annual circulation of 57m. The Party paper is *Zëri i Popullit* (Voice of the People) (daily circulation, 105,000). 1,043 book titles were published in 1981.

JUSTICE, RELIGION, EDUCATION AND WELFARE

Justice is administered by People's Courts. Minor crimes are tried by tribunals. Judges of the Supreme Court are elected by the People's Assembly for 4-year terms. The Office of the Procurator-General oversees the administration of justice. In 1983 an Investigator's Office was set up, separate from the Ministry of the Interior and answerable to the People's Assembly.

Religion. Albania is constitutionally an atheist state. In 1967 the Government closed all mosques and churches. For details of the situation before 1967 *see* THE STATESMAN'S YEAR-BOOK, 1969–70. The population had been 70% Moslem.

Education. Primary education is free and compulsory in 8-year schools from 7 to 15 years. Secondary education is available in 12-year (general), technical-professional or lower vocational schools. Periods of productive work and military service are intermingled with full-time education. There were, in 1979–80, 2,541 kindergartens with 83,697 pupils and 3,920 teachers and in 1984–85, 721,057 primary and secondary school children with 35,846 teachers. In 1979–80 there were 116 technical–professional schools with 69,700 pupils and (in 1969–70) 36 institutes of higher education with 36,525 students and 941 teachers, including the Enver Hoxha University of Tirana (founded 1957), a polytechnic, an agricultural college, a medical school, 5 teachers' training colleges and an institute of science. In 1985–86 there were 820 teachers and some 12,000 students at Tirana University. An Albanian Academy was founded in 1972.

Health. Medical services are free, though medicines are charged for. In 1986 there were 797 hospitals and 3,307 outpatient clinics. In 1983 there were 4,967 doctors and dentists, and 17,600 hospital beds. In 1986 there were 710 maternity hospitals or hospital sections and 256 dental clinics.

DIPLOMATIC REPRESENTATIVE

Of Albania to the United Nations
Ambassador: Bashkim Pitarka.

Books of Reference

Vjetari Statistikor (Statistical Yearbook). Tirana, irregular, 1959–72
35 vjet Shqipëri socialiste (statistical handbook). Tirana, 1979
History of the Labour Party of Albania 1966–1980. Tirana, 1981
Portrait of Albania. Tirana, 1982
Bertolino, J., *Albanie: la Citadelle de Staline.* Paris, 1979
Duro, I., and Hysa, R., *Albanian-English Dictionary.* Tirana, 1981
Dwyer, J. D., *Albania.* [Bibliography] Oxford and Santa Barbara, 1986
Fischer, B. J., *King Zog and the Struggle for Stability in Albania.* Boulder, 1984
Halliday, J., (ed.), *The Artful Albanian: The Memoirs of Enver Hoxha.* London, 1986
Hetzer, A., and Roman, V. S. *Albania: A Bibliographic Research Survey.* Munich, 1983
Hoxha, E., *Speeches, Conversations and Articles, 1969–1970.* Tirana, 1980.—*The Khrushchevites: Memoirs.* Tirana, 1980.—*The Anglo-American Threat to Albania.* Tirana, 1982.—*Selected works.* Tirana, 1982.

Lendvai, P., *Das einsame Albanien*. Zurich, 1985

Logoreci, A., *The Albanians: Europe's Forgotten Survivors*. London, 1977

Marmullaku, R., *Albania and the Albanians*. London, 1975

Martin, N., *La Forteresse Albanaise: un Communisme National*. Paris, 1979

Pollo, S. and Arben, P., *The History of Albania*. London, 1981

Prifti, P. R., *Socialist Albania since 1944*. Cambridge, Mass., 1978

Russ, W., *Der Entwicklungsweg Albaniens*. Meisenheim-am-Glan, 1979

Schnytzer, A., *Stalinist Economic Strategy in Practice: The Case of Albania*. OUP, 1982

Tönnes, B., *Sonderfall Albanien: Enver Hoxhas 'Eigener Weg und die Historischen Ursprünge seiner Ideologie*. Munich, 1980

ALGERIA

Capital: Algiers
Population: 22·6m. (1986)
GNP per capita: US$2,430 (1984)

al-Jumhuriya al-Jazairiya ad-Dimuqratiya ash-Shabiya

HISTORY. On 1 Nov. 1954 the National Liberation Front (FLN) went over to open warfare against the French administration and armed forces. For details of history 1958–62 see p. 76 THE STATESMAN'S YEAR-BOOK, 1982–83. A cease-fire agreement was reached on 18 March 1962, and Gen. de Gaulle declared Algeria independent on 3 July 1962; the Republic was declared on 25 Sept. 1962.

The Government was overthrown by a junta of army officers which, on 19 June 1965, established a Revolutionary Council under Col. Houari Boumédienne.

AREA AND POPULATION. Algeria is bounded west by Morocco and Western Sahara, south-west by Mauritania and Mali, south-east by Niger, east by Libya and Tunisia, and north by the Mediterranean Sea. It has an area of 2,381,741 sq. km (919,595 sq. miles). Population (census 1977) 17,422,000; estimate (1986) 22·6m.

The 31 departments were as follows in 1984; 17 additional departments were created in 1984:

Departments	Area (sq. km)	Population (1984)	Departments	Area (sq. km)	Population (1984)
Adrar	422,498	161,936	Médéa	8,704	575,305
al-Jazair (Algiers)	786	2,442,303	Mostaganem	7,024	896,767
Annaba (Bône)	3,489	650,096	M'Sila	19,825	540,013
Batna	14,882	691,079	Ouahran (Oran)	1,820	889,800
Béchar	306,000	184,069	Ouargla	559,234	261,760
Béjaia (Bougie)	3,442	659,040	Oum el Bouaghi	8,123	464,806
Biskra	109,728	662,778	Saida	106,777	450,594
al-Boulaida (Blida)	3,704	1,126,303	Sétif	10,350	1,176,673
Bouira	4,517	454,805	Sidi-Bel-Abbès	11,648	604,773
Qacentina (Constantine)	3,562	809,245	Skikda	4,748	597,530
Djelfa	22,905	403,500	Tamanrasset	556,000	62,680
al-Asnam (Orléansville)	8,677	1,040,563	Tébessa	16,575	439,638
Guelma	8,624	633,733	Tiaret	23,456	731,542
Jijel	3,705	604,319	Tizi-Ouzou	3,756	1,028,864
Laghouat	112,052	391,817	Tlemcen	9,284	678,025
Mascara	5,846	526,644			

The chief towns (1983) are as follows: Algiers, 1,721,607; Oran, 663,504; Constantine, 448,578; Annaba, 348,322; Blida, 191,314; Sétif, 186,978; Sidi-Bel-Abbès, 186,978; Tlemcen, 146,089; Skikda, 141,159; Bejaia, 124,122; Batna, 122,788; al Asnam, 118,996; Tizi-Ouzou, 100,749; Médéa, 84,292.

CLIMATE. Coastal areas have a warm temperate climate, with most rain in winter, which is mild, while summers are hot and dry. Inland, conditions become more arid beyond the Atlas Mountains. Algiers. Jan. 54°F (12·2°C), July 76°F (24·4°C). Annual rainfall 30″ (762 mm). Biskra. Jan. 52°F (11·1°C), July 93°F (33·9°C). Annual rainfall 6″ (158 mm). Oran. Jan. 54°F (12·2°C), July 76°F (24·4°C). Annual rainfall 15″ (376 mm).

CONSTITUTION AND GOVERNMENT. A Constitution was approved by referendum in Nov. 1976. It provides for a single Party, the *Front de Libération Nationale,* working in parallel with state organs. On 16 Jan. 1986 the revised

National Charter was approved by referendum by 98% of voters. The original charter formally established Algeria as a one-party state in 1976.

The President of the Republic is Head of State, Head of the Armed Forces, and Head of Government. He is nominated by the FLN Congress and elected by universal suffrage for 5-year terms (renewable).

President of the Republic, General Secretary of the FLN, Minister of Defence: Bendjedid Chadli (sworn in 9 Feb. 1979, re-elected on 12 Jan. 1984).

The President appoints a Prime Minister and other Ministers, and presides over meetings of the Council of Ministers.

The Council of Ministers, as in Feb. 1988, consisted of:

Prime Minister: Abdelhamid Brahimi.

Foreign Affairs: Ahmed Taleb Ibrahimi. *Interior:* M'hamed Yala. *Finance:* Abdel Aziz Khellef. *Justice:* Boualem Baki. *Agriculture and Fisheries:* Mohamed Rouighi. *Information:* Bachir Rouis. *Posts and Telecommunications:* Boualem Bessaieh. *Transport:* Rachid Beyelles. *Energy, Chemical and Petrochemical Industries:* Belkacem Nabi. *Heavy Industry:* Salim Saadi. *Light Industry:* Zitouni Messaoudi. *Hydraulics, Environment and Forests:* (Vacant). *Trade:* Mustefa Ben Amar. *Education:* Mohamed Cherif Kherroubi. *Higher Education:* Rafik Abdelhak Brerhi. *Technical Education:* Mohamed Nabi. *Youth and Sports:* Kamal Bouchama. *Public Health:* Kasdi Merbah. *Social Security:* Z'hor Hounissi. *Veterans:* Djelloul Bakhti Nemiche. *Public Works:* Ahmed Benfreha. *Town Planning and Housing:* Abderrahmane Belayat. *Religious Affairs:* Abderrahmane Chibane. *Culture and Tourism:* Abdelmadjid Meziane. *Labour:* Mouloud Oumeziane.

Legislative power is held by the National People's Assembly, whose 261 members are elected for a 5-year term by universal suffrage from the single list of the FLN who nominate 3 candidates for each single-member seat.

National flag: Vertically green and white, a red crescent and star over all in centre.

The official language is Arabic, French being the principal foreign language. Arabic is spoken by 83·5% of the population and Berber by 16·1%.

DEFENCE. Conscription is for a period of 6 months at the age of 19.

Army. The Army had a strength of 150,000 in 1988, organized in 2 armoured, 5 mechanized and 9 motorized brigades; 28 infantry, 4 paratroop, 5 artillery, 5 air defence and 4 engineer battalions; and 12 companies of desert troops. Equipment includes 95 T-34, 375 T-54/-55, 325 T-62 and 100 T-72 main battle tanks.

Navy. The Navy, largely supplied from the USSR, consists of 2 diesel powered patrol submarines, 3 frigates, 4 missile-armed corvettes, 2 fleet minesweepers, 8 patrol vessels, 11 fast missile boats, 6 fast gunboats, 2 logistic landing ships, 1 landing vessel, 1 diving tender, 2 training craft, 1 torpedo recovery vessel, 1 degaussing ship, 1 survey ship, 12 fishery protection craft and 19 coastguard cutters (16 Italian-built). Naval personnel in 1988 totalled 6,500 officers, cadets and ratings.

There are naval bases at Algiers, Annaba and Mers el Kebir.

Air Force. Five MiG-15 jet-fighters were delivered in 1962 as the nucleus of an Algerian Air Force. Since then many more aircraft of Soviet design have followed, and the Air Force now has about 360 combat aircraft and 12,000 personnel. Training and technical assistance have been given by Egypt and the Soviet Union. There are 8 squadrons of MiG-21s, 3 squadrons of MiG-23 variable-geometry interceptors and fighter-bombers, 3 squadrons of Su-7 and Su-20 variable-geometry attack aircraft, 2 squadrons with MiG-25 fighter and reconnaissance aircraft, more than 40 Mi-24 assault helicopters and gunships, 17 C-130H Hercules, 2 F.27 and 6 An-12 transports, an Il-18 and a variety of smaller transports, a wing of 4 Mi-6, 30 Mi-8, about 30 Mi-4, 5 Puma, 6 Alouette III and 6 Hughes 269 helicopters, and training units equipped with CM.170 Magister armed jet counter-insurgency/trainers (20), 3 Beech Queen Air twin-engine/instrument trainers, MiG-15UTIs and MiG-17s, and two-seat versions of operational types. Surface-to-air missile units have Soviet-built 'Guidelines', 'Goas', 'Gainfuls' and 'Gaskins'.

INTERNATIONAL RELATIONS

Membership. Algeria is a member of UN, OAU, the Arab League and Opec.

ECONOMY

Planning. The fourth development plan (1985–89) envisages expenditure of DA 550,000m. primarily on housing, agriculture and water resources.

Budget. The budget (including the development budget of DA 54,800m.) was DA 117,000m. for 1985.

Currency. The Algerian currency is the *dinar* (DA). There are in circulation banknotes of DA 5, 10, 50 and 100 and coins of 1, 2, 5, 20 and 50 centimes and DA 1, 5 and 10. In March 1988, £1 = 9·24 DA; US$1 = 5·21 DA.

Banking. The Banque Centrale d'Algérie is the government emission bank. Other banks operating in Algeria are Banque National d'Algérie, Crédit Populaire d'Algérie, Banque Extérieure d'Algérie, Caisse Algérienne de Développement, Banque Algérienne de Développement, Banque de l'Agriculture et du Développement.

Weights and Measures. The metric system is in use.

ENERGY AND NATURAL RESOURCES

Electricity. Production (1986) 12,410m. kwh. Supply 127 and 220 volts; 50 Hz.

Oil. Two large oilfields went into production in 1957 around Edjélé and Hassi Messaoud and in 1959 at El Gassi. In 1960 about 200 wells were productive. Natural gas was discovered at Djebel Berga in 1954 and at Hassi-R'Mel in 1956. Oil pipelines from Edjélé to Skirra (Tunisia) and from Hassi Messaoud to Béjaia, and a gas pipeline from Hassi Messaoud *via* Hassi-R'Mel to Mostaganem–Oran–Algiers, have been completed. Oil production in 1987, 29·5m. tonnes.

Gas. Production of natural gas in 1985 was 50,000m. cu. metres.

Minerals. Algeria possesses deposits of iron, zinc, lead, mercury, silver, copper and antimony. Kaolin, marble and onyx, salt and coal are also found. Mineral output in 1982 (1,000 tonnes): Iron ore, 3,900; zinc, 12·9; copper, 0·9; lead, 3·6; phosphates (1980), 1,025; barite, 100; clay, 58; sulphur, 10; coal, 7.

Agriculture. The greater part of Algeria is of limited value for agricultural purposes. In the northern portion the mountains are generally better adapted to grazing and forestry than agriculture, and a large portion of the native population is quite poor. In spite of the many excellent roads built by the Government, a considerable area of the mountainous region is without adequate means of communication and is accessible only with difficulty. There were an estimated 7·5m. hectares of agricultural land in 1978–79, of which 6·8m. hectares were arable; 200,000 hectares under vine and 31·7m. hectares pastures and brushlands.

The chief crops in 1986 were (in 1,000 tonnes): Wheat, 1,445; barley, 1,100; dates, 190; potatoes, 850; oranges, 220; mandarins and tangerines, 105; watermelons, 350; wine, 180; tomatoes, 275; olives, 140; onions, 152; oats, 80.

Livestock, 1986: 120,000 horses, 635,000 mules and asses, 1·75m. cattle, 1,557,000 sheep, 3·09m. goats and 130,000 camels.

Forestry. The greater part of the state forests are mere brushwood, but there are very large areas covered with cork-oak trees, Aleppo pine, evergreen oak and cedar. The dwarf-palm is grown on the plains, alfa on the table-land. Timber is cut for firewood, also for industrial purposes, for railway sleepers, telegraph poles, etc., and for bark for tanning. Considerable portions of the forest area are also leased for tillage, or for pasturage for cattle and sheep.

Fisheries. There are extensive fisheries for sardines, anchovies, sprats, tunny fish, etc., and also shellfish. Fish taken in 1982 amounted to 64,500 tonnes.

INDUSTRY AND TRADE

Industry. In 1981, 10·5m. tonnes of petroleum products were refined. Production of cement (1981) 4·45m. tonnes, crude steel (1982) 842,000 tonnes.

Labour. In 1984 the economically active population was estimated at 3·7% of whom 40% were in the agricultural sector.

Trade Unions. The *Union Générale des Travailleurs Algériens* had in 1982 about 1m. members in 8 affiliated groups, while the *Union Nationale des Paysans Algériens* had 700,000.

Commerce. The foreign trade of Algeria was as follows (in DA 1m.):

	1980	1981	1982	1983
Imports	41,545	49,782	49,384	49,782
Exports	52,418	62,837	60,478	60,722

In 1986 imports came chiefly from France, Federal Republic of Germany and Italy. Exports went mainly to Federal Republic of Germany and France.

Total trade between Algeria and UK (British Department of Trade returns, in £1,000 sterling):

	1983	1984	1985	1986	1987
Imports to UK	157,645	274,155	251,462	140,860	172,927
Exports and re-exports from UK	233,425	272,438	176,596	129,624	73,115

Tourism. In 1986, there were 596,000 visitors.

COMMUNICATIONS

Roads. There were in 1986, 78,410 km of national highway including 45,070 km of concrete or bituminous roads. Motor vehicles in 1980 included 472,483 passenger cars and 283,966 commercial vehicles.

Railways. In 1984 there were 3,761 km of which 2,649 km is of standard gauge (298 km electrified) and 1,112 km of 1,055mm gauge railway open for traffic. In 1984 the railways carried 11m. tonnes of freight and 35·7m. passengers.

Aviation. There are 5 international airports as well as another 65 airfields controlled by government and 135 owned by petroleum companies. Air Algeria serves the main Algerian cities, and an international network. Algeria is also served by Swissair, Royal Air Maroc and United Arab Airline. In 1980 the airports handled 2·84m. passengers and 22,479 tonnes of freight.

Shipping. In 1982, 69·4m. tonnes of goods were handled at Algerian ports.

A state shipping line, Compagnie Nationale Algérienne de Navigation, was formed in Jan. 1964.

Post and Broadcasting. There were, in 1980, 1,534 post offices; number of telephones (1982), 606,869, of which 186,312 were in Algiers and 48,428 in Oran. In 1982 *Radiodiffusion Télévision Algérienne* broadcast in Arabic, French and Kabyle (Berber) from 16 radio stations to (1984) 3·5m. radio receivers and from 16 television stations to about (1984) 1·33m. receivers.

Newspapers (1986). There were 4 daily newspapers, with a combined circulation of 480,000.

JUSTICE, RELIGION, EDUCATION AND WELFARE

Justice. There are appeal courts at Algiers, Constantine and Oran; and in the *arrondissements* are 17 courts of first instance. There are also commercial courts and justices of the peace with extensive powers. Criminal justice is organized as in France. The Supreme Court is at the same time Council of State and High Court of Appeal.

Religion. The overwhelming part of the population are Sunni Moslems. There are about 150,000 Christians, mainly Roman Catholic.

Education. In 1982 there were 9,263 state primary schools with 88,481 teachers and 4·6m. pupils; 1,128 secondary schools with 38,845 teachers and 1,029,884 pupils; and 71 technical and teacher-training colleges with 1,168 teachers and 12,903 students in technical education and 1,124 teachers and 13,315 students in teacher-training.

In 1981 there were 72,200 students in higher education including universities at Algiers (with 17,086 students), Oran (9,000), Constantine (8,340), Annaba (6,126), Sétif (5,800) and Boumedes. There are also Universities of Science and Technology at Algiers (11,500) and Oran (5,800) and university centres at Tlemcen, Tizi-Ouzou, Batna, Tiaret, Constantine, Mostaganem, Sidi-Bel-Abbès and Boulaida.

Health. There were in 1980, 182 general and specialized hospitals with together 45,160 beds; there were 6,081 doctors, 1,183 dentists, 778 pharmacists. There were also 1,422 dispensaries and consulting rooms, 747 health centres and 175 specializing centres for tuberculosis, venereal disease and trachoma.

DIPLOMATIC REPRESENTATIVES

Of Algeria in Great Britain (54 Holland Park, London, W11 3RS)
Ambassador: Ahmed Laïdi.

Of Great Britain in Algeria (Résidence Cassiopée, 7 Chemin des Glycines, Algiers)
Ambassador: P. H. C. Eyers, CMG, LVO.

Of Algeria in the USA (2118 Kalorama Rd., NW, Washington, D.C., 20008)
Ambassador: Mohamed Sahnoun.

Of the USA in Algeria (4 Chemin Cheich Bachir Brahimi, Algiers)
Ambassador: L. Craig Johnstone.

Of Algeria to the United Nations
Ambassador: Hocine Djoudi.

Books of Reference

Statistical Information: The Service de Statisque Générale publishes the annual *Statistique Générale de l'Algérie, Documents statistiques sur le commerce de l'Algérie* (from 1902).

Horne, A., *A Savage War of Peace: Algeria 1954–1962.* London, 1977
Knapp, W., *North West Africa: A Political and Economic Survey.* OUP, 1977
Lawless, R. I., *Algeria.* [Bibliography] Oxford and Santa Barbara, 1981
Ottaway, D., *Algeria: The Politics of a Socialist Revolution.* Berkeley, 1970

ANDORRA

Capital: Andorre-la-Vieille
Population: 42,712 (1984)

Principat d'Andorra

HISTORY. The political status of Andorra was regulated by the *Paréage* of 1278 which placed Andorra under the joint suzerainty of the Comte de Foix and of the Bishop of Urgel. The rights vested in the house of Foix passed by marriage to that of Bearn and, on the accession of Henri IV, to the French crown.

AREA AND POPULATION. The co-principality of Andorra is situated in the eastern Pyrenees on the French–Spanish border. The country consists of gorges, narrow valleys and defiles, surrounded by high mountain peaks varying between 1,880 and 3,000 metres. Its maximum length is 30 km and its width 20 km; it has an area of 465 sq. km (180 sq. miles) and a population of (1984) 42,712, scattered in 7 villages.

Catalan is the official language and was spoken by 30% of the population in 1985 but 58% spoke Spanish and 7% French.

CLIMATE. Les Escaldes. Jan. 36°F (2·3°C), July 67°F (19·3°C). Annual rainfall 32" (808 mm).

CONSTITUTION AND GOVERNMENT. Sovereignty is exercised jointly by the President of the French Republic and the Bishop of Urgel. The co-princes are represented in Andorra by the *'Viguier français'* and the *'Viguier Episcopal'*. Each co-prince has set up a Permanent Delegation for Andorran affairs; the Prefect of the Eastern Pyrenees is the French Permanent Delegate.

The valleys pay every second year a due of 960 francs to France and 460 pesetas to the bishop.

A 'General Council of the Valleys' submits motions and proposals to the Permanent Delegations. Its 28 members are elected for 4 years; half of the council is renewed every 2 years. The council nominates a First Syndic *(Syndic Procureur Général)* and a Second Syndic from outside its members.

In Jan. 1982 an Executive Council was appointed, following elections held in Dec. 1981, and legislative and executive powers were separated.

First Syndic: Francesc Cerqueda-Pascuet.

Head of Government: Josef Pintat Solans (from 3 Jan. 1986).

Finance: Bonaventura Riberaygua Miquel. *Education and Culture:* Roc Rossell Dolcet. *Tourism and Sports:* Josep Miño Guitart. *Public Works:* Merce Sansa Reñe. *Agriculture, Commerce and Industry:* Luis Molne Armengol. *Labour and Social Welfare:* Maestre Campderros.

National flag: Three vertical strips of blue, yellow, red, with the arms of Andorra in the centre.

ECONOMY

Budget. In 1983 revenue was envisaged at 3,720m. pesetas and expenditure at 3,683m. pesetas.

Currency. French and Spanish currency are both in use.

ENERGY AND NATURAL RESOURCES

Electricity. Production (1986) 140m. kwh. Andorra imported another 200m. kwh from Spain.

Agriculture. In 1981, 472 tonnes of potatoes and 264 tonnes of tobacco were produced.

Livestock (1982): 9,000 sheep, 1,115 cattle, 217 horses.

TRADE. Total trade between Andorra and UK (British Department of Trade returns, in £1,000 sterling):

	1985	1986	1987
Imports to UK	198	40	200
Exports and re-exports from UK	10,413	13,174	10,976

Tourism. Tourism is the main industry, and over 6m. people visited Andorra in 1982.

COMMUNICATIONS

Roads. A good road connects the Spanish and French frontiers by way of Sant Julià, Andorre-la-Vieille, les Escaldes, Encamp, Canillo and Soldeu: it crosses the Col d'Envalira (2,400 metres). Another road connects Andorre-la-Vieille with La Massana and Ordino. Motor vehicles (1983) 24,789.

Aviation. The nearest airports are at Seo de Urgel, Barcelona and Perpignan.

Post and Broadcasting. Number of telephones (1982) 17,719. Number of receivers (1977), radio, 7,000; TV, 3,000.

JUSTICE, RELIGION, EDUCATION AND WELFARE

Justice. Judicial power is exercised in civil matters in the first instance, according to the plaintiff's choice, by either the *Bayle Français* or the *Bayle Episcopal*, who are nominated by the respective co-princes. The judge of appeal is nominated alternately for 5 years by each co-prince; the third instance *(Tercera Sala)* is either the supreme court of Andorra at Perpignan or the supreme court of the Bishop at Urgel.

Criminal justice is administered by the *Corts* consisting of the 2 Viguiers, the judge of appeal, 2 *rahonadors* elected by the general council of the valleys, a general attorney and an attorney nominated for 5 years alternatively by each of the co-princes. The accused may be assisted by a barrister.

Religion. The prevailing religious denomination is Roman Catholic.

Education. In 1985–86 there were 1,911 pupils at infant schools, 3,490 at primary schools, 3,113 at secondary schools, 170 at technical schools and 46 at special schools.

Health. In 1981 there were 42 doctors and 113 hospital beds.

Books of Reference

Brutails, *La Coutume d'Andorre.* Paris, 1904
Corts Peyret, J., *Geografia e Historia de Andorra.* Barcelona, 1945
Llobet, S., *El medio y la vida en Andorra.* Barcelona, 1947
Riberaygua-Argelich, B., *Les Valls d'Andorra.* Barcelona, 1946
Vidally Guitart, J. M., *Institutiones politicas y sociales de Andorra.* Madrid, 1949

ANGOLA

Capital: Luanda
Population: 8·96m. (1986)
GNP per capita: US$500 (1985)

República Popular de Angola

HISTORY. The first Europeans to arrive in Angola were the Portuguese in 1482, and the first settlers arrived there in 1491. Luanda was founded in 1575. Apart from a brief period of Dutch occupation from 1641 to 1648, Angola remained a Portuguese colony until 11 June 1951, when it became an Overseas Province of Portugal. On 11 Nov. 1975 Angola became fully independent as the People's Republic of Angola.

AREA AND POPULATION. Angola is bounded by Congo on the north, Zaïre on the north and north-east, Zambia on the east, South West Africa/Namibia on the south and the Atlantic ocean on the west. The area is 1,246,700 sq. km (481,351 sq. miles) including the 7,107 sq. km province of Cabinda, an enclave of territory separated by 30 km of Zaïre. The population at census, 1970, was 5,646,166, of whom 14% urban. Estimate (1986) 8·96m. (30% urban), of whom 38% speak Umbundu, 27% Kimbundu, 13% Lunda and 11% Kikongo. Portuguese remains the official language. There were (1980) about 38,000 Cubans and 30,000 Europeans (mostly Portuguese) in Angola. Refugees living in Angola totalled 91,400 (1987) mainly Namibians.

The most important towns (with 1970 populations) are Luanda, the capital (480,613; 1984, 960,000), Huambo (61,885), Lobito (59,258), Benguela (40,996), Lubango (31,674; 1984, 105,000), Malange (31,559) and Namibe (formerly Moçâmedes, 23,145; 1981, 100,000).

CLIMATE. The climate is tropical, with low rainfall in the west but increasing inland. Temperatures are constant over the year and most rain falls in March and April. Luanda. Jan. 78°F (25·6°C), July 69°F (20·6°C). Annual rainfall 13″ (323 mm). Lobito. Jan. 77°F (25°C), July 68°F (20°C). Annual rainfall 14″ (353 mm).

CONSTITUTION AND GOVERNMENT. Under the Constitution adopted at independence, the sole legal party is the *Movimento Popular de Libertação de Angola – Partido do Trabalho.* The supreme organ of state is the unicameral National People's Assembly, whose members were first elected in Aug. 1980 for a 3-year term. In 1987 the Assembly had 206 members. There is an executive President elected for renewable terms of 5 years, who appoints a Council of Ministers to assist him.

Substantial parts of the country are, however, under the control of the anti-government forces of the *União Nacional para a Independência Total de Angola* (UNITA).

The Council of Ministers in Dec. 1987 was as follows:

President: José Eduardo dos Santos (re-elected 9 Dec. 1985).
Ministers of State: (Vacant) *(Economic and Social Sphere),* Pedro de Castro Van-Dunen *(Productive Sphere),* Kundi Payama *(Inspection and Control).*
Agriculture: Evaristo Domingos Kimba. *Construction:* João Garcia. *Defence:* Col. Pedro Maria Tonha. *Education:* Augusto Lopes Teixeira. *Energy and Petroleum:* (held by Minister of State for Productive Sphere). *Finance:* Augusto Teixeira de Matos. *Fisheries:* Emilio Jose Guerra de Carvalho. *Foreign Affairs:* Afonso Van-Dunen Mbinda. *Foreign Trade:* Ismael Gaspar Martins. *Health:* António Ferreira Neto. *Industry:* Lieut.-Col. Henrique de Carvalho dos Santos. *Interior:* Manuel Alexandre Duarte Rodrigues. *Internal Trade:* Adriano Pereira

dos Santos Júnior. *Justice:* Fernando Jose Franca Dias Van-Dunen. *Labour and Social Security:* Diogo Jorge de Jesus. *Planning:* António Henriques da Silva. *State Security:* (vacant). *Transport and Communications:* Manuel Bernardo de Sousa. *Governor of National Bank:* Antonio Inacio.

There are also 6 Secretaries of State.

Flag: Horizontally red over black, with a star and an arc of cogwheel crossed by a machete, all yellow over all in the centre.

Local government: Angola is divided into 18 provinces divided into 139 districts – (Cabinda, Zaïre, Uíge, Luanda, Cuanza Norte, Cuanza Sul, Malange, Lunda Norte, Lunda Sul, Benguela, Huambo, Bié, Moxico, Cuando-Cubango, Namibe, Huíla, Cunene and Bengo) each under a Provincial Commissioner, appointed by the President and an elected legislative of from 55 to 85 members.

DEFENCE. Conscription is for a period of 2 years.

Army. The Army has 5 motorized infantry, 19 infantry, and 4 air defence brigades; 10 tank and 6 artillery battalions; and 10 SAM batteries. Total strength (1988) 49,500. Equipment includes Soviet T-34, T-54/55, T-62 and PT-76 tanks.

Navy. Twenty Portuguese naval craft were transferred on independence in 1975 and 9 vessels were acquired from the Soviet Navy in 1977-79, when 8 merchant ships were taken over from local trade for naval use. There are 6 fast missile boats, 4 fast torpedo boats, 4 patrol craft, 9 coastal patrol boats, 9 landing craft, 1 survey ship and 10 auxiliary vessels. Naval personnel in 1988 totalled 1,250.

Air Force. The Angolan People's Air Force (FAPA) was formed in 1976. The combat force has been expanded since 1983 with Soviet assistance. It included (1987) 70 MiG-21, 50 MiG-23 and 30 Su-22 fighters, plus 25 Mi-24 and 6 Gazelle gunships. (The MiG-17 is being withdrawn from service.) There are 10 An-2, 30 An-26, 12 Islander, 4 Turbo-Porter, 8 Aviocar and 2 F.27 transports, 1 F.27MPA maritime surveillance aircraft, 4 PC-9,12 PC-7 and 3 MiG-15UTI trainers, and 40 Mi-8, 15 Mi-17, 6 Dauphin and 40 Alouette III helicopters. Personnel (1988) 2,000.

INTERNATIONAL RELATIONS

Membership. Angola is a member of UN, OAU and is an ACP state of the EEC.

ECONOMY

Budget. The 1986 budget includes 90,400m. kwanza for capital and current expenditure and revenue at 78,500m. kwanza.

Currency. The currency is the *kwanza* divided into 100 *lwei*. Coins are of 50 *lwei*, 1, 2, 5, 10 and 20 *kwanza*; notes are of 20, 50, 100, 500 and 1,000 *kwanza*. In March 1988, £1 = 52·77 *kwanza*; US$1 = 29·92 *kwanza*.

Banking. All banking was nationalized in 1975. The *Banco Nacional de Angola* is the central bank and bank of issue, while the *Banco Popular de Angola* handles all commercial activities throughout the country.

Weights and Measures. The metric system is in force.

ENERGY AND NATURAL RESOURCES

Electricity. Production (1986) totalled 851m. kwh, mainly hydro-electricity. In Nov. 1984 an agreement was signed with Brazil and USSR to construct a hydroelectric plant at Kapanda on the river Kwanza, 250 miles south of Luanda.

Oil. Total production (1987) about 16·5m. tonnes.

Minerals. Production of diamonds during 1983 totalled 1,034,000 carats (1978, 650,000). Production (1983) of salt, 55,000 tonnes. There has been no production of iron ore since 1975, but the mines at Kassinga were restarted in 1985. Phosphate mining commenced in the north in 1981. Manganese and copper deposits exist.

Agriculture. The principal cash crops (with 1986 production, in 1,000 tonnes): Sugar-cane (250), coffee (35), bananas (280), palm oil (40), palm kernels (12), seed cotton (33); others include tobacco, citrus fruit and sisal. Food crops comprise cassava (1,970), maize (230), sweet potatoes (180) and beans (40).

Livestock (1986): 3·38m. cattle, 255,000 sheep, 965,000 goats, 470,000 pigs.

Forestry. Mahogany and other hardwoods are exported, chiefly from the tropical rain forests of the north, especially Cabinda. Production (1984) 9m. cu. metres.

Fisheries. Total catch (1983) 112,414 tonnes.

COMMERCE. Imports and exports for 3 calendar years in 1m. Kwanza.

	1982	1983	1984 [1]	1985 [1]
Imports	25,946	20,197	19,448	41,240
Exports	48,736	54,508	60,112	59,280

[1] Provisional.

The chief imports are textiles, transport equipment, foodstuffs, pig-iron and steel; chief exports are crude oil, coffee, diamonds, sisal, fish, maize, palm-oil. In 1983, crude petroleum represented 85% of exports, petroleum products, 5·6%, coffee 3·9% and diamonds 5·6%. In 1984 Portugal provided 17% of imports, the USA 11%, France 11% and Brazil 10%, while 42% of exports went to the USA%, 19% (all diamonds) to the Bahamas and 9% to the UK.

Total trade between Angola and UK (British Department of Trade returns, in £1,000 sterling):

	1984	1985	1986	1987
Imports to UK	158,636	150,639	43,147	2,312
Exports and re-exports from UK	35,581	43,187	30,896	29,573

COMMUNICATIONS

Roads. There were, in 1974, 72,323 km of roads, and in 1982, 148,000 cars and 43,600 commercial vehicles.

Railways. The length of railways open for traffic in 1984 was 2,952 km comprising 2,798 km of 1,067 mm gauge and 154 km of 600 mm gauge. The Benguela Railway runs from Lobito to the Zaïre border at Dilolo where it connects with the National Railways of Zaïre. Other lines link Luanda with Malange; Gunza with Gabela; and Namibe with Menongue. In 1981 Angola's railways carried 7·6m. passengers and 725,000 tonnes of freight.

Aviation. Luanda has international air links to Lisbon, Rome, Paris, Moscow, Budapest, Brazzaville, Saõ Tomé, Lusaka, Maputo, Sal (Cape Verde Islands), Havana, Kinshasa, Libreville, Berlin, Tripoli, Lagos, Algiers, Niamey, Sofia, Malta, Rio de Janeiro and São Paulo.

Shipping. In 1975, 2·85m. tonnes were discharged and 16m. tonnes loaded in Angolan ports. In 1982 there were 56 merchant vessels (over 100 GRT) totalling 90,428 GRT.

Post and Broadcasting. Angola is connected by cable with east, west and south African telegraph systems. There were, in 1973, 1,808 km of telegraph lines, 77 telephone stations (with 29,796 instruments in 1978), 162 telegraph stations and 31 wireless stations.

Rádio Nacional de Angola is the largest of the 18 stations operating on medium- and short-waves. *Rádio Nacional* transmits 3 programmes as well as operating 2 regional stations. Number of radio receivers (1984) 230,000 and television receivers 21,000.

Cinemas. There were, in 1972, 47 cinemas with seating capacity of 35,142.

Newspaper. The national daily newspaper is *Jornal de Angola*, with a circulation of 50,000 in 1984.

JUSTICE, RELIGION, EDUCATION AND WELFARE

Justice. The Supreme Court and Court of Appeal are in Luanda.

Religion. Article 7 of the Constitution of the People's Republic of Angola states that: 'The People's Republic of Angola is a secular state, where there is a complete separation of religious institutions from the state. All religions will be respected.

In 1980 55% of the population were Roman Catholic, 9% Protestant and 34% animist.

Education. In 1983 there were 2·4m. pupils in primary schools, 153,000 in secondary schools and 4,746 students in higher education. The *Universidade de Angola* (founded 1963) at Luanda with faculties at Huambo and Lubango, had 3,500 students in 1982.

Health. In 1980 there were 436 doctors and 20,700 hospital beds and in 1973, 87 pharmacists, 284 midwives and 3,115 nursing personnel.

DIPLOMATIC REPRESENTATIVES

Of Angola in Great Britain (87 Jermyn St., London, SW1)
Ambassador: Elísio de Figueiredo (accredited 28 Nov. 1984).

Of Great Britain in Angola (Rua Diogo Cão, 4, Luanda)
Ambassador: M. J. C. Glaze.

Of Angola to the United Nations
Ambassador: Elísio de Figueiredo.

Books of Reference

Anuário Estatistico de Angola. Luanda, from 1897
Araújo, A. Correia de, *Aspectos do desenvolvimento económico e social de Angola.* Lisbon, 1964
Bender, G. J., *Angola under the Portuguese: Myth and Reality.* London, 1979
Bhagavan, M. R., *Angola's Political Economy 1975–1985.* Uppsala, 1986
Davidson, B., *In the Eye of the Storm.* London, 1972
Dias, G. de Sousa, *Os portugueses em Angola.* Lisbon, 1959
Klinghoffer, A. J., *The Angolan War.* Boulder, 1980
Marcrum, J., *The Angolan Revolution.* (2 vols.) MIT Press, 1969 and 1978
Pélissier, R., *Les guerres grises.* Montamets, 1980.—*La Colonie du Minotaure.* Montamets, 1980.—*Le naufrage des coravelles.* Montamets, 1980
Somerville, K., *Angola: Politics, Economics and Society.* London and Boulder, 1986
Wheeler, D. L., and Pélissier, R., *Angola.* London, 1971
Wolfers, M., and Bergerol., *Angola in the Frontline.* London, 1983
Zirka, A. K., *Angola Libre?* Paris, 1975

ANGUILLA

HISTORY. Anguilla was probably given its name by the Spaniards because of its eel-like shape. After British settlements in the 17th century, the territory was administered as part of the Leeward Islands. From 1825 it became more closely associated with St Kitts and ultimately incorporated in the colony of St Kitts-Nevis-Anguilla. Opposition to this association grew and finally in 1967 the island seceded unilaterally. Following direct intervention by the UK in 1969 Anguilla became *de facto* a separate dependency of Britain; and this was formalized on 19 Dec. 1980 under the Anguilla Act 1980. A new Constitution came into effect in April 1982.

AREA AND POPULATION. Anguilla is the most northerly of the Leeward Islands, some 70 miles (112 km) to the north-west of St Kitts and 5 miles (8 km) to the north of St Martin/St Maarten. The territory also comprises the island of Sombrero (on which there is an important lighthouse) and several other off-shore islets or cays. The total area of the territory is about 60 sq. miles (155 sq. km). Census population (1984) was 7,000. The capital is The Valley.

CONSTITUTION AND GOVERNMENT. The House of Assembly consists of a Speaker, 7 elected members, 2 nominated members and 2 official members.

Executive power is vested in the Governor who is appointed by HM The Queen. Apart from his special responsibilities (External Affairs, Defence, Internal Security, including the Police, and the Public Service) and his reserve powers in respect of legislation, the Governor discharges his executive powers on the advice of an Executive Council comprising a Chief Minister, 3 Ministers and 2 official members: Attorney-General and Permanent Secretary, Finance.

Governor: G. O. Whittaker, OBE.
Chief Minister: Emile Gumbs.

ECONOMY

Budget. In 1986, the budget was: Expenditure EC$15·44m.; revenue EC$17·55m. Anguilla finances its recurrent budget but aid for capital projects comes from UK and other donors.

Currency. The currency is the Eastern Caribbean *dollar.*

ENERGY AND NATURAL RESOURCES

Electricity. Production (1988) 4m. kwh.

Agriculture. Because of low rainfall agriculture potential is limited. Main crops are pigeon peas, corn and sweet potatoes. Livestock consists of sheep, goats, cattle and poultry.

Fisheries. Fishing is a thriving industry with exports to neighbouring islands.

INDUSTRY AND TRADE

Trade. Total trade between Anguilla and UK (British Department of Trade returns, in £1,000 sterling):

	1985	1986	1987
Imports to UK	165	60	188
Exports and re-exports from UK	1,754	1,136	1,328

Tourism. There are a few hotels of international standing and others are under construction. There are also several locally-owned hotels, guest houses and apartments.

COMMUNICATIONS

Roads. There are about 43 miles of tarred roads and 25 miles of secondary roads.

Aviation. There is a 3,600 ft surfaced runway at Wallblake Airport. Apart from regular air taxi and charter flights WINAIR (subsidiary of ALM) provides daily scheduled services between Juliana International Airport, St Martin and Anguilla. WINAIR, LIAT and American Eagle operate direct flights from San Juan, Puerto Rico. Air BVI flies from Tortola and St Thomas to Anguilla.

Shipping. The main seaports are Road Bay and Blowing Point, the latter serving passenger and cargo traffic to and from St Martin.

Post and Telecommunications. There is a modern internal telephone service with (1986–87) 1,825 exchange lines; and international telegraph, telex and telephone services, all operated by Cable & Wireless.

Newspapers. In 1988 there was 1 daily newspaper.

RELIGION, EDUCATION AND WELFARE

Religion. There were in 1988 Anglicans, Roman Catholics, Methodists, Seventh Day Adventists and Baptists.

Education. There are 6 government primary schools and 1 secondary school. Tertiary education is provided at regional universities and similar institutions.

Health. There is a 24-bed cottage hospital, clinics and a modern dental clinic. There were (1987) 4 doctors and 1 dentist.

Book of Reference

Petty, C. L., *Anguilla: Where there's a Will, there's a Way.* Anguilla, 1984

ANTIGUA AND BARBUDA

Capital: St John's
Population: 81,500 (1986)
GNP per capita: US$ 1,990 (1984)

HISTORY. Antigua was discovered by Colombus in 1493 and named by him after a church in Seville (Spain). It was first colonized by English settlers in 1632; nearby Barbuda was colonized in 1661 from Antigua. Formed part of the Leeward Islands Federation from 1871 until 30 June 1956, when Antigua became a separate Crown Colony, which was part of the West Indies Federation from 3 Jan. 1958 until 31 May 1962. It became an Associated State of the UK on 27 Feb. 1967 and obtained independence on 1 Nov. 1981.

AREA AND POPULATION. Antigua and Barbuda comprises 3 islands of the Lesser Antilles situated in the Eastern Caribbean with a total land area of 442 sq. km (171 sq. miles); it consists of Antigua (280 sq. km), Barbuda, 40 km to the north (161 sq. km) and uninhabited Redonda, 40 km to the southwest (1 sq. km).

The population at the Census of 7 April 1970 was 65,525. In 1986 the estimated population was 81,500 of whom 1,500 lived in Barbuda. The chief towns are St John's, the capital on Antigua (30,000 inhabitants in 1982) and Codrington, the only settlement on Barbuda.

CLIMATE. A tropical climate, but drier than most West Indies islands. The hot season is from May to Nov., when rainfall is greater. Mean annual rainfall is 40″ (1,000 mm).

CONSTITUTION AND GOVERNMENT. H.M. Queen Elizabeth, as Head of State, is represented by a Governor-General appointed by her on the advice of the Prime Minister. There is a bicameral legislature, comprising a 17-member Senate appointed by the Governor-General and a 17-member House of Representatives elected by universal suffrage for a 5-year term. The Governor-General appoints a Prime Minister and, on the latter's advice, other members of the Cabinet.

Governor-General: Sir Wilfred Ebenezer Jacobs, KCVO, OBE, QC.

Prime Minister and Finance: Right Hon. Vere C. Bird, Sen., PC.
Deputy Prime Minister, Foreign Affairs, Economic Development, Tourism and Energy: Lester Bryant Bird.

At the general elections held on 17 April 1984, the ruling Antigua Labour Party won all 16 seats on Antigua and there was one independent (representing Barbuda).

Flag: Red, with a triangle based on the top edge, divided horizontally black, blue, white, with a rising sun in gold on the black portion.

DEFENCE. The defence force has a strength of about 700. A coastguard service has been formed.

INTERNATIONAL RELATIONS

Membership. Antigua and Barbuda is a member of UN, the Commonwealth, CARICOM and is an ACP state of the EEC.

ECONOMY

Budget. The budget for 1987 envisaged revenue at EC$181·1m. and expenditure of EC$187m.

Currency. The Eastern Caribbean $. In March 1988, £1 = EC$4·79; US$1 = EC$2·70.

Banking. Barclays Bank International, Royal Bank of Canada, Canadian Imperial Bank of Commerce, the Virgin Islands National Bank, the Antilles International Trust Co. and the Bank of Nova Scotia have branches at St John's. There is also the Antigua Co-operative Bank and a government savings bank.

ENERGY AND NATURAL RESOURCES

Electricity. Production (1986) 63·8m. kwh.

Agriculture. Cotton and fruits are the main crops. Production (1986) of fruits, 9,000 tonnes. There were 70,000 tonnes of cotton produced in 1985.

Livestock (1986): Cattle, 18,000; pigs, 4,000; sheep, 13,000; goats, 13,000.

Fisheries. Catch (1983) 1,013 tonnes.

INDUSTRY AND TRADE

Industry. An oil refinery was opened in 1982. Manufactures include toilet tissue, stoves, refrigerators, blenders, fans, garments and rum (molasses imported from Guyana).

Labour. In 1985 the workforce numbered 32,254, and there was 21% unemployment.

Commerce. Imports in 1984 amounted to EC$356·1m. and exports to EC$47·5m. of which the major amount came from bunkering provided to ships. The main trading partners were the USA, the UK and Canada.

Total trade between Antigua and Barbuda and UK (British Department of Trade returns, in £1,000 sterling):

	1985	1986	1987
Imports to UK	1,877	2,069	4,271
Exports and re-exports from UK	28,798	17,774	19,334

Tourism. There were 149,000 tourists (excluding cruise passengers) in 1986.

COMMUNICATIONS

Roads. There are 600 miles of roads (150 miles main road). In 1985 there were 10,000 passenger cars and 15,000 commercial vehicles.

Aviation. There is an international airport (V. C. Bird) on Antigua, and a small airstrip at Codrington on Barbuda.

Shipping. The main harbour is the St John's deep water harbour. There are 2 tugs for the berthing of ships and all modern and efficient general cargo handling equipment. The harbour can also accommodate 3 large cruise ships simultaneously.

Post and Broadcasting. In 1983 there were 10,470 telephones. In 1983 there were 20,000 radios and 17,000 television sets.

RELIGION, EDUCATION AND WELFARE.

Religion. The vast majority of the population are Christian, preponderantly Anglican.

Education. In 1985 there were 10,551 pupils and 436 teachers in 48 primary schools, and 5,106 pupils and 304 teachers in (1983) 16 secondary schools.

Health. There is a general hospital (Holberton) with 215 beds, a mental hospital with 200 beds, a geriatric unit with 150 beds, 4 health centres and 16 dispensaries.

DIPLOMATIC REPRESENTATIVES

Of Antigua and Barbuda in Great Britain (15 Thayer St., London, W1M 5DL)
High Commissioner: James A. E. Thomas.

Of Great Britain in Antigua and Barbuda (38 St Mary's St., St John's)
High Commissioner: K. F. X. Burns, CMG.

Of Antigua and Barbuda in the USA (3400 International Dr., NW, Washington, D.C., 20008)
Ambassador: Paul A. Russo.

Of the USA in Antigua and Barbuda
Chargé d'Affaires: Robert DuBose (resides in Bridgetown).

Of Antigua and Barbuda to the United Nations
Ambassador: Lloydstone Jacobs.

Book of Reference

Dyde, B., *Antigua and Barbuda: The Heart of the Caribbean.* London, 1986

ARGENTINA

República Argentina

Capital: Buenos Aires
Population: 31·06m. (1986)
GNP per capita: US$2,470 (1984)

HISTORY. In 1515 Juan Díaz de Solis discovered the Río de La Plata. In 1534 Pedro de Mendoza was sent by the King of Spain to take charge of the 'Gobernación y Capitanía de las tierras del Rio de La Plata', and in Feb. 1536 he founded the city of the 'Puerto de Santa María del Buen Aire'. In 1810 the population rose against Spanish rule, and in 1816 Argentina proclaimed its independence. Civil wars and anarchy followed until, in 1853, stable government was established.

Military leaders supported by the Navy and Air Force staged a *coup d'état* on 24 March 1976, and The Junta of Commanders in Chief deposed Isobel Perón and her Government elected in 1972. The Commander in Chief of the Army, Lieut-Gen. Videla, was appointed President. The previous Constitution remained in force in so far as it was consistent with the statutes and objectives of the Junta. Return to civilian rule took place on 10 Dec. 1983. For details of earlier history and Constitutions *see* THE STATESMAN'S YEAR-BOOK, 1982–83 and 1985–86.

AREA AND POPULATION. The Argentine Republic is bounded in the north by Bolivia, in the north-east by Paraguay, in the east by Brazil, Uruguay and the Atlantic Ocean and the west by Chile. The republic consists of 22 provinces, 1 federal district and the National Territories of Tierra del Fuego, the Antarctic and the South Atlantic Islands (census of 1980) as follows:

Provinces	Area: sq. km. 1960	Population: census, 1980	Capital	Population census, 1980 (1,000)
Litoral				
Federal Capital	200	2,922,829	Buenos Aires	2,908
Buenos Aires	307,571	10,865,408	La Plata	455
Corrientes	88,199	661,454	Corrientes	180
Entre Ríos	78,781	908,313	Paraná	160
Chaco	99,633	701,392	Resistencia	218
Santa Fé	133,007	2,465,546	Santa Fé	287
Formosa	72,066	295,887	Formosa	95
Misiones	29,801	588,977	Posadas	140
Norte				
Jujuy	53,219	410,008	San Salvador de Jujuy	124
Salta	154,775	662,870	Salta	260
Santiago del Estero	135,254	594,920	Santiago del Estero	148
Tucumán	22,524	972,655	San Miguel de Tucuman	393
Centro				
Córdoba	168,766	2,407,754	Córdoba	969
La Pampa	143,440	208,260	Santa Rosa	52
San Luis	76,748	214,416	San Luis	71
Andina				
Catamarca	100,967	207,717	Catamarca	78
La Rioja	89,680	164,217	La Rioja	67
Mendoza	148,827	1,196,228	Mendoza	118
San Juan	89,651	465,976	San Juan	118
Neuquén	94,078	243,850	Neuquén	90

	Area: sq. km.	Population: census, 1980		Population census, 1980
Provinces	1960		Capital	(1,000)
Patagonia				
Chubut	224,686	263,116	Rawson	13
Rio Negro	203,013	383,354	Viedma	24
Santa Cruz	243,943	114,941	Rio Gallegos	43
Tierra del Fuego [1]	21,263	29,392	Ushuaia	11

[1] The total area is 2,780,092 sq. km excluding the claimed 'Antarctic Sector' and the population at the 1980 Census was 27,947,446; estimate (1986) 31·06m. In 1980, 95% spoke the national language, Spanish, while 3% spoke Italian, 1% Guarani and 1% other languages. In 1983, 83% lived in urban areas and 17% rural, while 98% were white and 2% mestizo (mixed).

The official census including the 'Antarctic Sector', and stated to comprise the 'Malvinas' (Falklands), South Orcadas (Orkneys), South Georgias, South Sandwich Islands and the 'sovereign territories of Argentina in the Antarctic': population 3,300.

The principal metropolitan areas (1980 Census) are Buenos Aires (9,927,404), Córdoba (982,018), Rosario (954,606), Mendoza (596,796), La Plata (560,341), San Miguel de Tucumán (496,914), Mar del Plata (407,024), and San Juan (290,479). The suburbs of Buenos Aires, outside the Federal District, include San Justo (946,715), Morón (596,769), Lomas de Zamora (508,620), General Sarmiento (499,648), Lanus (465,891), Quilmes (441,780), General San Martín (384,306), Caseros (340,343), Almirante Brown (332,548), Avellaneda (330,654), Vicente López (289,815), San Isidro (287,048), Merlo (282,828), Tigre (205,926), Berazategui (200,926), and Esteban Echeverría (187,969).

Other large cities (1980 Census) are Rosario (875,664), Mar del Plata (407,024), Bahía Blanca (220,765), Guaymallén (157,334), Godoy Cruz (141,553), Rio Cuarto (110,254), Comodoro Rivadavia (98,985), San Nicolás (96,313) and Concordia (93,618).

CLIMATE. The climate is warm temperate over the pampas, where rainfall occurs at all seasons, but diminishes towards the west. In the north and west, the climate is more arid, with high summer temperatures, while in the extreme south conditions are also dry, but much cooler. Buenos Aires. Jan. 74°F (23·3°C), July 50°F (10°C). Annual rainfall 37" (950 mm). Bahia Blanca. Jan. 74°F (23·3°C), July 48°F (8·9°C). Annual rainfall 21" (523 mm). Mendoza. Jan. 75°F (23·9°C), July 47°F (8·3°C). Annual rainfall 8" (190 mm). Rosario. Jan. 76°F (24·4°C), July 51°F (10·6°C). Annual rainfall 35" (869 mm). San Juan. Jan. 78°F (25·6°C), July 50°F (10°C). Annual rainfall 4" (89 mm). San Miguel de Tucuman. Jan. 79°F (26·1°C), July 56°F (13·3°C). Annual rainfall 38" (970 mm). Ushuaia. Jan. 50°F (10°C), July 34°F (1·1°C). Annual rainfall 19" (475 mm).

CONSTITUTION AND GOVERNMENT. Presidential, congressional and municipal elections took place on 30 Oct. 1983 and a return to civilian rule took place on 10 Dec. 1983. With the return to constitutional rule the Constitution of 1853 (as amended up to 1898) is again in effect. The President and Vice-President are elected by a 600-member electoral college (directly elected by popular vote) for 6-year terms; both must be Roman Catholics of Argentine birth. The President is Commander-in-Chief of the Armed Services, and appoints to all civil and judicial offices.

The following is a list of Presidents from 1973 onwards:

Gen. Juan Domingo Perón. 12 Oct. 1973–1 July 1974.

Maria Estela (Isabel) Martinez Perón. 1 July 1974 (a.i. from 29 June 1974)–23 March 1976. (Deposed.)

Gen. Jorge Rafael Videla. 29 March 1976–29 March 1981.

Gen. Roberto Viola, 29 March–22 Dec. 1981.

Gen. Leopoldo Fortunato Galtieri, 22 Dec. 1981–17 June 1982.

Gen. Reynaldo Benito Antonio Bignone, 1 July 1982–10 Dec. 1983.

The National Congress consists of a Senate and a House of Deputies: The Senate comprises 46 members, 2 nominated by each provincial legislature and 2 from the Federal District for 9 years (one-third retiring every 3 years). The House of Deputies comprises 254 members directly elected by universal suffrage (at age 18).

In the General Election held on 3 Nov. 1985, the *Unión Cívica Radical* won 130 seats in the House of Deputies, the *Movimiento Justicialista Nacional* (Peronists) 103 seats and others 21 seats. Mid-term elections are due in Sept. 1988.

President of the Republic: Dr Raúl Alfonsín (sworn in 10 Dec. 1983).

Vice-President: Dr Víctor Martínez.
The Cabinet in Jan. 1987 was composed as follows:
Foreign Affairs: Dante Caputto. *Interior:* Dr Antonio Tróccoli. *Treasury and Finance:* Juan Sourrouille. *Labour:* Hugo Barrionuevo. *Defence:* Horacio Jaunarena. *Education and Justice:* Julio Rajneri. *Public Health and Environment:* Conrado Storani. *Public Works:* Pedro Trucco. *Agriculture and Fisheries:* Ernesto Figueras.
National flag: Three horizontal stripes of light blue, white and light blue, with the gold Sun of May in the centre.

National anthem: Oid, mortales, el grito sagrado Libertad (words by V. López y Planes, 1813; tune by J. Blas Parera).

Local Government. In Oct. 1983 the governors were elected by the people.

DEFENCE

Army. There are 5 military districts. The Army is organized in 4 army corps; it consists of 2 armoured, 3 motorized infantry and 1 mechanized, 1 airborne, 2 mountain and 1 jungle brigades; 15 artillery, 1 aviation and 5 air defence battalions. The Army has over 80 fixed-wing aircraft and helicopters.

In 1988 the Army was 45,000 strong, of whom 25,000 were conscripts.

The trained reserve numbers about 250,000, of whom 200,000 belong to the National Guard and 50,000 to the Territorial Guard.

Navy. Principal ships of the Argentine Navy: [3]

Com- pleted	Name	Standard displace- ment Tons	Aircraft	Guns	Shaft horse- power	Speed Knots
		Aircraft Carrier [1]				
1945	Veinticinco de Mayo [2]	15,892	{18 fixed-wing / 4 helicopters}	9 40mm	40,000	24·0

[1] The aircraft carrier *Independence,* ex-*Warrior,* purchased from the UK in 1958 was withdrawn from service in 1971.

[2] Ex-*Karel Doorman,* purchased from the Netherlands in 1968, ex-*Venerable,* purchased from UK in 1948.

[3] The cruiser *General Belgrano, ex-Phoenix,* purchased from the USA in 1951 was sunk by the British fleet submarine *Conqueror* in May 1982. Sister ship *Nueve de Julio* (ex-USS *Bloise*) was withdrawn from service in 1980. The cruiser *La Argentina* was stricken from the list in 1975.

There are 2 modern German-built diesel powered submarines, 2 older German-built smaller diesel-driven submarines, 4 modern German-built destroyers, 2 modern British-built destroyers (Type 42), 3 modern German-designed medium frigates, 3 modern French-built small frigates, 2 old training frigates, 4 coastal minesweepers, 2 minehunters, 4 patrol vessels (armed ocean tugs), 2 fast patrol vessels, 6 patrol craft, 3 survey ships, 2 survey launches, 2 training ships, 3 transports, 2 oilers, 2 tank landing ships, 12 minor landing craft, 2 polar ships, 20 ancillary vessels and service craft and 10 tugs.

The new construction programme includes 4 diesel-powered patrol submarines (one building and three projected), and 3 frigates.

The diesel-powered submarine *Sante Fe,* ex-USS *Catfish,* was damaged and beached during the Falklands invasion in April 1982, and was later sunk in deep water.

The active personnel of the Navy in 1988 comprised 24,000 officers and ratings, and 5,000 conscripts. The Marine Corps numbered 4,500.

The *Prefectura Naval Argentina* (PNA) for Coast Guard and rescue duties comprises five new 910-ton corvettes with helicopter and hangar, an ex-whaler of 700 tons, 7 patrol vessels, 40 coastal patrol craft and a training ship.

The Naval Aviation Service has some 100 fixed-wing aircraft and helicopters with 3,000 personnel, in 6 wings. Aircraft include 14 Super Entendard fighters, 24 A-4Q Skyhawk attack bombers, 13 Aermacchi M.B. 326 and 5 M.B.339A light jet armed trainers, 7 Lockheed Electra maritime surveillance aircraft and 6 S-2E ship-based Tracker anti-submarine aircraft, and a dozen types of training, transport and general purpose aircraft, plus 2 types of helicopters. A variable mix of Super Entendards, Skyhawks, Trackers and Sea King and Alouette helicopters operated from the aircraft carrier.

Air Force. The Air Force, founded on 10 Aug. 1912 and autonomous since 4 Jan. 1945, is organized into Air Operations, Air Regions, Materiel and Personnel Commands. Air Operations Command, responsible for all operational flying, is made up of air brigades, each with 1 to 4 squadrons, usually operating from a single base. No. I Air Brigade is a military air transport service, with responsibility also for LADE (state airline) operations into areas of Argentina not served by civilian companies. Its equipment includes 6 C-130E/H Hercules and 10 F.27 Friendship/ Troopship turboprop transports, 2 KC-130H Hercules tanker/transports, 5 twin-turbofan F.28 Fellowship freighters, 7 Twin Otters, 15 Guarani IIs, the Presidential Boeing 707-320B and 707-320C, 4 more 707s, 2 VIP Fellowships, and many older or smaller types. No. II Air Brigade has 4 Canberra twin-jet bombers and 2 Canberra trainers; a photographic squadron with Guarani IIs and Learjets. No. III Air Brigade has 2 squadrons of IA 58 Pucara twin-turboprop COIN aircraft. No. IV Air Brigade comprises 2 ground attack squadrons equipped with about 30 Paris light jet combat and liaison aircraft. No. V Air Brigade comprises 2 squadrons with a total of about 30 A-4P Skyhawk strike aircraft. No. VI Air Brigade has 40 Dagger (Israeli-built Mirage III) fighters, equipping 2 squadrons. No. VII Air Brigade has 2 COIN, general-purpose, and search and rescue squadrons with 12 armed Hughes 500M, 5 Lama, 5 Sikorsky S-58T/S-61, 8 Bell 212 and 6 Bell UH-1 helicopters. No. VIII Air Brigade has 1 squadron with 14 Mirage IIIE fighter-bombers and 2 Mirage IIID trainers. No. X Air Brigade has 2 squadrons of Mirage IIIC fighters. There is a flying school at Córdoba, equipped with piston-engined T-34 Mentors and Paris jets. There were (1988) about 13,000 personnel and 143 combat aircraft.

INTERNATIONAL RELATIONS

Membership. Argentina is a member of UN, OAS and LAIA (formerly LAFTA).

ECONOMY

Budget. The financial year commences on 1 Nov. Budget receipts in 1985 6,517m. australes and expenditure 8,811m. australes.

Currency. The monetary system is on a gold-exchange standard, the unit for foreign transactions being, nominally, the *peso oro* (gold peso) and for domestic transactions, the *Austral* (paper peso), legal tender for all domestic debts.

The gold peso weighs 1·6129 grammes of gold 0·900 fine; it is divided into 100 *centavos*, but gold is not in circulation. Circulation consists chiefly of paper notes (issued since 1897) ranging from 100 *australes* down to 10 *cents*. The coins actually circulating, 1985, were steel-nickel, 5, 1 and ½ *cents*. In March 1988, US$1 = 4·60 *austral*; £1 = 10·77 *austral*.

Banking. In 1984 there were 35 government banks, 141 private banks and 33 foreign banks. The total foreign debt at 31 Dec. 1984 was US$48m.

Weights and Measures. Since 1 Jan. 1887 the use of the metric system has been compulsory.

ENERGY AND NATURAL RESOURCES

Electricity. Electric power production (1986) was 42,790m. kwh. Supply 220 volts; 50 Hz.

Oil. Crude oil production (1987) 21·25m. tonnes. The oil industry aims at achieving self-sufficiency.

Gas. Natural gas production (1983) 13,500,000m. cu. metres. New offshore fields were reported in 1988.

Minerals. Argentina produced 600,000 tonnes of washed coal in 1983. Gold, silver and copper are worked in Catamarca, where there are also 2 tin-mines, and gold and copper in San Juan, La Rioja and the south-western territories. Iron ore (90,000 tonnes in 1983), tungsten, beryllium, mica, uranium (30 tonnes in 1983), lead (32,000 tonnes in 1983), barites, zinc (43,500 tonnes in 1972), tin (1·8m. tonnes in 1972), manganese and limestone are produced.

Agriculture. Argentina has an area of about 670,251,000 acres, of which about 41% is pasture land, 32% woodland and 11% (73·73m. acres) cultivated.

Livestock (1986): Cattle 53m.; sheep, 29,243,000; pigs, 4m.; horses, 3m. The Province of Buenos Aires has 38% of the cattle. Wool production, 1983, was 126,000 tonnes.

Wheat production (1986) 8·9m. tonnes from 4·9m. hectares.

Argentina's meat exports are calculated in terms of actual weight; not 'carcase weight', as is the international practice. In 1983, 84·16m. tons of meat were exported.

Cotton, potatoes, vine, tobacco, citrus fruit, olives, rice, soya, and yerba maté (Paraguayan tea) are also cultivated. There are 36 cane-sugar mills and 1 beet-sugar factory; cane-sugar production, 1986, 14m. tonnes. Potato harvest, 1985, amounted to 2·1m. tonnes. The area under tobacco, 1986, was 50,000 hectares; output 66,000 tonnes.

Sunflower seed (production (1986) 4·2m. tonnes), first grown by Russian immigrants in 1900, now furnishes the country's most popular edible oil. There are more than 10m. olive trees. 205,000 tonnes of groundnuts were produced in 1986 (mainly in Córdoba). Argentina is the world's largest source of tannin.

Fisheries. Fish landings in 1983 amounted to 550,000 tonnes.

INDUSTRY AND TRADE

Industry. Production (1983 in tonnes) Paper, 873,000; steel, 2·95m.; sulphuric acid (1979), 279,066; cement (1979), 6·7m. Motor vehicles produced (1981) totalled, 172,350; television receivers, 262,000.

Commerce. Import values include charges for carriage, insurance and freight; export values are on a f.o.b. basis. Real values of foreign trade (in US$1m.), exclusive of coin and bullion:

	1979	1980	1981	1982	1983	1984 [1]
Imports	6,300	10,541	9,430	5,337	4,504	4,585
Exports	7,750	8,021	9,146	7,625	7,836	8,107

[1] Provisional.

Total trade between Argentina and UK (British Department of Trade returns, in £1,000 sterling):

	1983	1984	1985	1986	1987
Imports to UK	194	65	2,032	28,635	64,595
Exports and re-exports from UK	4,472	5,232	3,815	10,115	10,267

Tourism. In 1986, 1·6m. tourists visited Argentina.

COMMUNICATIONS

Roads. In 1983 there were 220,093 km of national and provincial highways. The 4 main roads constituting Argentina's portion of the Pan-American Highway were opened to traffic in 1942. In 1985 there were 5·08m. cars and commercial vehicles.

Railways. The system based on the 1949 amalgamation of 18 government, British and French-owned railways, comprises 7 railways with a total route-km in 1985 of

33,807 km (210 km electrified) on metre, 1,435 mm and 1,676 mm gauges. In 1984 railways carried 17·6m. tonnes of freight and 345m. passengers.

Aviation. There were (1985) 10 international airports. Commercial airlines flew a total of 75m. km in 1984, with 47,500 tonnes and 4·3m. passengers.

Shipping. The merchant fleet, 31 Dec. 1976 (registered with Lloyd's), consisted of 1,869,662 GRT; traffic during 1971: vessels of 13·27m. GRT entered ports; 14m. tonnes of goods were unloaded and 10·6m. tonnes were loaded.

Post and Broadcasting. In 1949 the telephone service was nationalized; instruments numbered 3,250,000 in 1984. There were (1984) 122 radio stations and 4 television channels in Buenos Aires. In 1984 there were 8m. radio receivers and 6·5m. television receivers.

Cinemas (1972). Cinemas numbered 1,650, with seating capacity of 611,400.

Newspapers (1984). Daily newspapers numbered 297. Buenos Aires had (1984) 11 daily newspapers with a circulation of 2·5m.

JUSTICE, RELIGION, EDUCATION AND WELFARE

Justice. Justice is administered by federal and provincial courts. The former deal only with cases of a national character, or in which different provinces or inhabitants of different provinces are parties. The chief federal court is the Supreme Court, with 5 judges at Buenos Aires. Other federal courts are the appeal courts, at Buenos Aires, Bahía Blanca, La Plata, Córdoba, Mendoza, Tucumán and Resistencia. Each province has its own judicial system, with a Supreme Court (generally so designated) and several minor chambers. Trial by jury is established by the Constitution for criminal cases, but never practised, except occasionally in the provinces of Buenos Aires and Córdoba.

The death penalty was re-introduced in 1976 for the killing of government, military police and judicial officials, and for participation in terrorist activities.

The police force is centralized under the Federal Security Council.

Religion. The Roman Catholic religion is supported by the State and membership was 26m. in 1986. There are several Protestant denominations with a total congregation (1983) of 500,000. The Jewish congregation numbered 300,000 in 1983.

Education. In 1982 the primary schools had 225,000 teachers and 4,382,000 pupils; secondary schools had 192,000 teachers and 1,426,000 pupils.

There are National Universities at Buenos Aires (2), Córdoba (2), La Plata, Tucumán, Santa Fé (Litoral), Rosario, Corrientes (Nordeste,), Mendoza (Cuyo), Bahía Blanca (Sur), Catamarca, Tandil, Neuquén (Comahue), San Salvador de Jujuy, Salta, Santa Rosa (La Pampa), Mar del Plata, Comodoro Rivadavia (Patagonia), Río Cuarto, Entre Ríos, Resistencia, San Juan and Santiago del Estero. There are also private universities in Buenos Aires (6), Mendoza (3), Córdoba, Comodoro Rivadavia, La Plata, Morón, Tucumán, Salta, Santa Fé and Santiago del Estero. In 1981 universities had 525,688 students and 54,039 lecturers.

Health. Free medical attention is obtainable from public hospitals. Many trade unions provide medical, dental and maternity services for their members and dependants. A Ministry of Social Welfare was set up in 1966. In 1971 there were 2,864 hospitals with 133,847 beds and in 1975 there were 48,693 doctors.

DIPLOMATIC REPRESENTATIVES

Diplomatic links with Argentina were broken by Great Britain in April 1982 following the invasion of the Falkland Islands.

Of Argentina in the USA (1600 New Hampshire Ave., NW, Washington, D.C., 20009)
Ambassador: Dr Enrique J. Candiotti.

Of the USA in Argentina (4300 Colombia, Palermo, Buenos Aires)
Ambassador: Theodore Gildred.

Of Argentina to the United Nations
Ambassador: Dr Marcelo E. R. Delpech.

Books of Reference

Boletin del comercio exterio Argentino y estadisticas económicas retrospectivas. Annual
Anuario de comercio exterior de la República Argentina. Annual
Economic Review, Banco de la Nación. Buenos Aires
Sintesis Estadistica Mensual. Dirección General de Estadistica. Buenos Aires, 1947 ff.
Boletin Internacional de Bibliografia Argentina. Ministry of Foreign Relations. Buenos
    Aires. Monthly
Geografia de la República Argentino. Ed. by the Sociedad Argentina de Estudios Geográficos.
    7 vols. Buenos Aires. 1945–53
Bridges, E. L., *Uttermost Part of the Earth [Tierra del Fuego].* New York, 1949
Crawley, E., *A House Divided: Argentina 1880–1980.* London, 1984
Ferns, H. S., *Britain and Argentina in the 19th Century.* OUP, 1960.—*The Argentine Republic
    1516–1971.* Newton Abbot, 1973
Graham-Yooll, A., *The Forgotten Colony: A History of the English-Speaking Communities in
    Argentina.* London, 1981
Rock, D., *Argentina 1516–1982.* London, 1986
Santillán, Diego A. de (ed.), *Gran Enciclopedia Argentina.* 9 vols. 1956–64
Simpson, J., and Bennett, J., *The Disappeared: Voices from a Secret War.* London, 1985
Wynia, G. W., *Argentina.* Hoddesdon, 1986

AUSTRALIA

Capital: Canberra
Population: 15·97m. (1986)
GNP per capita: US$11,172 (1984)

HISTORY. On 1 Jan. 1901 the former British colonies of New South Wales, Victoria, Queensland, South Australia, Western Australia and Tasmania were federated under the name of the 'Commonwealth of Australia', the designation of 'colonies' being at the same time changed into that of 'states'—except in the case of Northern Territory, which was transferred from South Australia to the Commonwealth as a 'territory' on 1 Jan. 1911.

In 1911 the Commonwealth acquired from the State of New South Wales the Canberra site for the Australian capital. Building began in 1923 and Parliament was opened at Canberra on 9 May 1927 by HRH the Duke of York (afterwards King George VI). A further area at Jervis Bay was acquired in 1915.

Territories under the administration of Australia in Jan. 1987, but not included in it, comprise Norfolk Island, the territory of Ashmore and Cartier Islands, and the Australian Antarctic Territory (acquired 24 Aug. 1936), comprising all the islands and territory, other than Adélie Land, situated south of 60° S. lat. and between 160° and 45° E. long. The Coral Sea Islands became an External Territory in 1969.

The British Government transferred sovereignty in the Heard Island and McDonald Islands to the Australian Government on 26 Dec. 1947. Cocos (Keeling) Islands on 23 Nov. 1955 and Christmas Island on 1 Oct. 1958 were also transferred to Australian jurisdiction.

AREA AND POPULATION. Australia, including Tasmania but excluding external territories, covers a land area of 7,682,300 sq. km, extending from Cape York (10° 41′ S) in the north some 3,680 km to Tasmania (43° 39′ S), and from Cape Byron (153° 39′ E) in the east some 4,000 km west to Western Australia (113° 9′ E). Growth in Census population has been:

1891	3,177,502	1933	6,629,839	1966	11,599,498
1901	3,774,310	1947	7,579,358	1971	12,755,638
1911	4,455,005	1954	8,986,530	1976	13,915,500
1921	5,435,734	1961	10,508,186	1981	15,053,600

Area and resident population (estimate), 31 Dec. 1983:

States and Territories (capitals in brackets)	Area (sq. km)	Males	Females	Total	Per 100 sq. km
New South Wales (Sydney)	801,600	2,679,200	2,699,100	5,378,300	671
Victoria (Melbourne)	227,600	2,011,800	2,041,600	4,053,400	1,781
Queensland (Brisbane)	1,727,200	1,249,500	1,238,500	2,488,000	144
South Australia (Adelaide)	984,000	667,300	679,700	1,347,000	137
Western Australia (Perth)	2,525,500	693,800	679,900	1,373,700	54
Tasmania (Hobart)	67,800	215,900	218,700	434,700	641
Northern Territory (Darwin)	1,346,200	72,400	64,400	136,800	10
Aust. Cap. Terr. (Canberra)	2,400	120,000	120,000	240,100	10,004
Total	7,682,300	7,710,000	7,741,900	15,451,900	201

Resident population (estimate) in State capitals and other major cities, 30 June 1986:

Statistical division	State	Population	Statistical district	State	Population
Sydney	NSW	3,430,600	Newcastle	NSW	429,300
Melbourne	Vic.	2,942,000	Canberra [1]	ACT	285,800
Brisbane	Qld.	1,171,300	Wollongong	NSW	237,600
Adelaide	SA	993,100	Gold Coast [2]	Qld.	219,300
Perth	WA	1,025,300	Geelong	Vic.	148,300
Hobart	Tas.	180,300	Townsville	Qld.	103,700
Darwin	NT	68,500			

[1] Includes Queanbeyan (20,450).   [2] Includes Tweed Heads.

95

At 30 June 1984 the age-group distribution was: under 15, 3,730,100; 15-44, 7,289,600; 45-64, 2,968,900; 65 and over, 1,567,400.

Australians born overseas (30 June 1984), 3·28m., of whom 1·2m. came from the UK and Ireland; 1·2m. from continental Europe; 481,400 from Asia and 183,400 from New Zealand.

At the 1981 census there were 144,665 Aboriginal Australians and 15,232 Torres Straits Islanders.

Vital statistics for 1986:

States and Territories	Marriages	Divorces	Births	Deaths	Infant deaths
New South Wales	41,319	11,661	84,018	42,167	759
Victoria	29,390	9,670	60,416	30,175	517
Queensland	18,030	7,042	40,165	17,861	351
South Australia	9,878	3,776	19,742	10,328	146
Western Australia	10,379	4,001	24,187	9,307	214
Tasmania	3,302	1,245	6,913	3,454	79
Northern Territory	759	381	3,307	661	53
Aust. Cap. Terr.	1,856	1,641	4,526	1,028	35
Total	114,913	39,417	234,274	114,981	2,154
Rate [1]	7·2	2·5	14·7	7·2	9·2 [2]

[1] Resident (estimate).   [2] Per 1,000 live births registered.

Overseas arrivals and departures:

	1984–85	1985–86	1986–87
Arrivals	2·68m.	2·94m.	3·32m.
Long term and permanent	163,260	186,400	205,750
of whom, settlers	77,510	77,510	113,540
Departures	2·63m.	2·81m.	3·19m.
Long term and permanent	95,250	92,460	102,100
of whom, Australian residents leaving for good	51,710	49,690	49,360

Australian Bureau of Statistics, *Australian Demographic Statistics.* Quarterly. Canberra, June 1979 to date

National Population Inquiry, Population and Australia: Recent Demographic Trends and their Implications. Canberra, 1978

CLIMATE. Over most of the continent, four seasons may be recognised. Spring is from Sept. to Nov., Summer from Dec. to Feb., Autumn from March to May and Winter from June to Aug., but because of its great size there are climates that range from tropical monsoon to cool temperate, with large areas of desert as well. In Northern Australia there are only two seasons, the wet one lasting from Nov. to March, but rainfall amounts diminish markedly from the coast to the interior. Central and southern Queensland are subtropical, north and central New South Wales are warm temperate, as are parts of Victoria, Western Australia and Tasmania, where most rain falls in winter. Canberra. Jan. 68°F (20°C), July 42°F (5·6°C). Annual rainfall 23″ (629 mm). Adelaide. Jan. 73°F (22·8°C), July 52°F (11·1°C). Annual rainfall 21″ (528 mm). Brisbane. Jan. 77°F (25°C), July 58°F (14·4°C). Annual rainfall 45″ (1,153 mm). Darwin. Jan. 83°F (28·3°C), July 77°F (25°C). Annual rainfall 59″ (1,536 mm). Hobart. Jan. 62°F (16·7°C), July 46°F (7·8°C). Annual rainfall 24″ (629 mm). Melbourne. Jan. 67°F (19·4°C), July 49°F (9·4°C). Annual rainfall 26″ (659 mm). Perth. Jan. 74°F (23·3°C), July 55°F (12·8°C). Annual rainfall 35″ (873 mm). Sydney. Jan. 71°F (21·7°C), July 53°F (11·7°C). Annual rainfall 47″ (1,215 mm).

CONSTITUTION AND GOVERNMENT. *Federal Government:* Under the Australian Constitution legislative power in Australia is vested in a Federal Parliament, consisting of the Queen, represented by a Governor-General, a Senate and a House of Representatives. Under the terms of the constitution there must be a session of parliament at least once a year.

The Senate comprises 64 Senators (10 for each State voting as one electorate and as from Aug. 1974, 2 Senators respectively for the Australian Capital Territory and the Northern Territory). Senators representing the States are chosen for 6 years. The terms of Senators representing the Territories expire at the close of the day next preceding the polling day for the general elections of the House of Representatives. In general, the Senate is renewed to the extent of one-half every 3 years, but in case of disagreement with the House of Representatives, it, together with the House of Representatives, may be dissolved, and an entirely new Senate elected. The House of Representatives consists, as nearly as practicable, of twice as many Members as there are Senators, the numbers chosen in the several States being in proportion to population as shown by the latest statistics, but not less than 5 for any original State. The numerical size of the House after the election in 1980 was 125, including the Members for Northern Territory and the Australian Capital Territory. The Northern Territory has been represented by 1 Member in the House of Representatives since 1922, and the Australian Capital Territory by 1 Member since 1949 and 2 Members since May 1974. The Member for the Australian Capital Territory was given full voting rights as from the Parliament elected in Nov. 1966. The Member for the Northern Territory was given full voting rights in 1968. The House of Representatives continues for 3 years from the date of its first meeting, unless sooner dissolved.

Every Senator or Member of the House of Representatives must be a subject of the Queen, be of full age, possess electoral qualifications and have resided for 3 years within Australia. The franchise for both Houses is the same and is based on universal (males and females aged 18 years) suffrage. Compulsory voting was introduced in 1925. If a Member of a State Parliament wishes to be a candidate in a federal election, he must first resign his State seat.

Executive power in Australia is vested in the Governor-General advised by an Executive Council. The Governor-General presides over the Council, and its members hold office at his pleasure. All Ministers of State, who are members of the party or parties commanding a majority in the lower House, are members of the Executive Council under summons. A record of proceedings of meetings is kept by the Secretary to the Council. At Executive Council meetings the decisions of the Cabinet are (where necessary) given legal form, appointments made, resignations accepted, proclamations, regulations and the like made.

The policy of a ministry is, in practice, determined by the Ministers of State meeting without the Governor-General under the chairmanship of the Prime Minister. This group is known as the Cabinet. There are 11 Standing Committees of the Cabinet comprising varying numbers of Cabinet and non-Cabinet Ministers. In Labour Governments all Ministers have been members of Cabinet. In Liberal and National Country Party government, only the senior ministers. Cabinet meetings are private and deliberative and records of meetings are not made public. The Cabinet does not form part of the legal mechanisms of Government; the decisions it takes have, in themselves, no legal effect. The Cabinet substantially controls, in ordinary circumstances, not only the general legislative programme of Parliament but the whole course of Parliamentary proceedings. In effect, though not in form, the Cabinet, by reason of the fact that all Ministers are members of the Executive Council, is also the dominant element in the executive government of the country.

The legislative powers of the Federal Parliament embrace trade and commerce, shipping, etc.; taxation, finance, banking, currency, bills of exchange, bankruptcy, insurance; defence; external affairs, naturalization and aliens, quarantine, immigration and emigration; the people of any race for whom it is deemed necessary to make special laws; postal, telegraph and like services; census and statistics; weights and measures; astronomical and meteorological observations; copyrights; railways; conciliation and arbitration in disputes extending beyond the limits of any one State; social services; marriage, divorce etc.; service and execution of the civil and criminal process; recognition of the laws, Acts and records, and judicial proceedings of the States. The Senate may not originate or amend money bills; and disagreement with the House of Representatives may result in dissolution and, in the last resort, a joint sitting of the two Houses. No religion may be established by the Commonwealth. The Federal Parliament has limited and enumerated powers, the several State parliaments retaining the residuary power of government over their respective territories. If a State law is inconsistent with a Commonwealth law, the latter prevails.

The Constitution also provides for the admission or creation of new States. Proposed laws for the alteration of the Constitution must be submitted to the electors, and they can be enacted only if approved by a majority of the States and by a majority of all the electors voting.

The Australia Acts 1986 removed residual powers of the British government to intervene in the government of Australia or the individual states.

The 35th Parliament was elected in July 1987.

House of Representatives (following July 1987 elections): Australian Labor Party, 86 seats; Liberal Party, 43; National Party, 19.

Senate: Australian Labor Party, 32; Liberal Party, 28; Australian Democratic Party, 7; National Party, 6; others, 3.

Governor-General: The Rt Hon. Sir Ninian Stephen, AK, GCMG, GCVO, KBE.

The following is a list of Governors-General of the Commonwealth:

Earl of Hopetoun	1901–02	HRH the Duke of Gloucester	1945–47
Lord Tennyson	1902–04	Sir William McKell	1947–53
Lord Northcote	1904–08	Viscount Slim	1953–60
Earl of Dudley	1908–11	Viscount Dunrossil	1960–61
Lord Denman	1911–14	Viscount De L'Isle	1961–65
Viscount Novar	1914–20	Lord Casey	1965–69
Lord Forster	1920–25	Sir Paul Hasluck	1969–74
Lord Stonehaven	1925–31	Sir John Kerr	1974–77
Sir Isaac Isaacs	1931–36	Sir Zelman Cowen	1977–82
Earl Gowrie	1936–45	Sir Ninian Stephen	1982–

National flag: The British Blue Ensign with a large star of 7 points beneath the Union Flag, and in the fly 5 stars of the Southern Cross, all in white.

The cabinet of the Labour administration in Feb. 1988 was composed as follows:

Prime Minister: Robert Hawke.
Deputy Prime Minister and Attorney-General: Lionel Bowen.
Industry, Technology and Commerce: John Button.
Community Services and Health: Neil Blewett.
Industrial Relations: Ralph Willis.
Treasurer: Paul Keating.
Immigration, Local Government and Ethnic Affairs: Clyde Holding.
Finance: Peter Walsh.
Foreign Affairs and Trade: Bill Hayden.
Special Minister of State: Susan Ryan.
Transport and Communications: Gareth Evans.
Employment, Education and Training: John Dawkins.
Primary Industry and Energy: John Kerin.
Administrative Services: Stewart West.
Defence: Kim Beazley.
Social Security: Brian Howe.
Arts, Sport, Environment, Tourism and Territories: Graham Richardson.
Science and Small Business: Barry Jones.
Aboriginal Affairs: Gerry Hand.
Veterans' Affairs: Ben Humphries.
Consumer Affairs: Peter Staples.

The Acts of the Parliament of the Commonwealth of Australia Passed from 1901 to 1973. 12 vols. Annual volumes, 1974 to date
The Australian Constitution Annotated. Attorney-General's Department, Canberra, 1980
Parliamentary Handbook of the Commonwealth of Australia. Canberra, 1915 to date

Commonwealth of Australia Directory [1921–1958 The Federal Guide; 1961–72 *Common-wealth Directory;* 1973–75 *Australian Government Directory*]. Prime Minister's Department. Canberra, 1924 to date

Crisp, L. F., *Australian National Government.* 3rd ed. Melbourne and London, 1975

Hughes, C. A., and Graham, B. D., *A Handbook of Australian Government and Politics.* Canberra, 1968

Odgers, J. R., *Australian Senate Practice.* 5th ed. Canberra, 1976

Paton, Sir George (ed.), *The Commonwealth of Australia: its Laws and Constitution.* London, 1952

Pettifer, J. A., *House of Representatives Practice.* Canberra, 1981

Sawer, G., *Australian Federal Politics and Law 1901–1929, 1929–1949.* 2 vols. Melbourne, 1974.—*Australian Government To-day.* 11th ed. Melbourne, 1973

Wynes, W. A., *Executive and Judicial Powers in Australia.* 5th ed. Sydney, 1976

State Government: In each of the 6 States (New South Wales, Victoria, Queensland, South Australia, Western Australia, Tasmania) there is a State government whose constitution, powers and laws continue, subject to changes embodied in the Australian Constitution and subsequent alterations and agreements, as they were before federation. The system of government is basically the same as that described above for the Commonwealth—*i.e.*, the Sovereign, her representative (in this case a Governor), an upper and lower house of Parliament (except in Queensland, where the upper house was abolished in 1922), a cabinet led by the Premier and an Executive Council. Among the more important functions of the State governments are those relating to education, health, hospitals and charities, law, order and public safety, business undertakings such as railways and tramways, and public utilities such as water supply and sewerage. In the domains of education, hospitals, justice, the police, penal establishments, and railway and tramway operation, State government activity predominates. Care of the public health and recreative activities are shared with local government authorities and the Federal Government, social services other than those referred to above are now primarily the concern of the Federal Government, and the operation of public utilities is shared with local and semi-government authorities.

Administration of Territories. Since 1911, responsibility for administration and development of the Australian Capital Territory has been vested in Federal Ministers and Departments.

The ACT House of Assembly has been accorded the forms of a legislature, but continues to perform an advisory function for the Minister for the Capital Territory.

On 1 July 1978 the Northern Territory of Australia became a self-governing Territory with expenditure responsibilities and revenue-raising powers broadly approximating those of a State, although the Territory is not a State under the Constitution.

Local Government. The system of municipal government is broadly the same throughout Australia, although local government legislation is a State matter.

Each State is sub-divided into areas known variously as municipalities, cities, boroughs, towns, shires or district councils, totalling about 900. Within these areas the management of road, street and bridge construction, health, sanitary and garbage services, water supply and sewerage, and electric light and gas undertakings, hospitals, fire brigades, tramways and omnibus services and harbours is generally part of the functions of elected aldermen and councillors. The scope of their duties, however, differs considerably, for in all States the State Government, either directly or through semi-government authorities, also carries out some or all of these types of services.

In some instances, *e.g.*, in New South Wales, a number of local government authorities combine to conduct a public undertaking such as the supply of water or electricity.

DEFENCE. The Minister for Defence has responsibility under legislation for the control and administration of the Defence Force. The Chief of Defence Force Staff is vested with command of the Defence Force. He is the principal military adviser to the Minister. The Secretary, Department of Defence is the Permanent Head of the Department. He is the principal civilian adviser to the Minister and has statutory responsibility for financial administration of the Defence outlay. The Chief of Defence Force Staff and the Secretary are jointly responsible for the administration of the Defence Force except with respect to matters falling within the command of the Defence Force or any other matter specified by the Minister.

The Chief of Naval Staff, the Chief of the General Staff and the Chief of the Air Staff command the Navy, Army and Air Force respectively. They have delegated authority from the Chief of Defence Force Staff and the Secretary to administer matters relating to their particular Service.

The structure of Defence is characterized by 3 organizational types: *(i)* A Central Office comprising 5 groups of functional orientated Divisions: Strategic Policy and Force Development; Supply and Support; Manpower and Financial Services; Management and Infrastructure Services; and, Defence Science and Technology; *(ii)* the 3 Armed Services of the Defence Force, each having a Service Office element in addition to the command structure; and *(iii)* a small number of outrider organizations concerned with such specialist fields as intelligence and natural disasters.

Defence Support. The Department of Defence Support purchases goods and services for defence purposes; provides technical expertise and other assistance to the defence industry; involves Australian industry in defence equipment to the maximum practical extent; administers the Australian Offsets Program so as to stimulate technological advancement and broaden the capabilities of strategic industries; within overall defence policies helps the capacity, efficiency and capability of Australian industry to design and export defence materiel; manages the Government's munitions and aircraft factories, and dockyards; markets defence and allied products and services to help maintain strategic industries.

The Department employs approximately 15,000 people (under the Public Service Act, the Supply and Development Act and the Naval Defence Act) in five states. This workforce includes some 2,100 professional and technical staff, 4,200 tradesmen and 1,500 apprentices.

Army. Overall organization and financial control of the Australian Army is vested in the Chief of General Staff. Under the Defence Force Re-organisation Act, which received the Royal Assent on 9 Sept. 1975, the Military Board, which was previously the controlling body of the Army, was abolished. The Act became effective on 1 Feb. 1976. A functional command structure, Headquarters Field Force Command, Headquarters Logistic Command, and Headquarters Training Command, with Headquarters in military districts, was introduced in 1973.

The strength of the Army was 32,000 in 1988. The field force organization emphasises the combat element and high-priority logistic units to meet the requirements for limited war and tropical warfare with light air-portable formations. The Field Force is organized in divisions; 6 battalions organized in 3 brigades each with combat and logistic support. The Army Aviation Corps has 13 N22 Missionmaster 14 Turbo-Porter transports, and 47 JetRanger helicopters.

The effective strength of the Army Reserve in 1988 was 26,112.

Staff and command training is carried out at the Command and Staff College, Queenscliff, Victoria, and the Land Warfare Centre, Canungra, Queensland.

In Jan. 1986 the Australian Defence Force Academy, Canberra, accepted its first officer cadets for the 3 Services. Cadets will study at the academy for degrees in arts, science and engineering. During semester breaks they will carry out military training with their particular Services.

At the end of 3 years at the academy, army officer cadets will undertake a year of military training at the Royal Military College, Duntroon. This will culminate with commissioning as a lieutenant.

From 1986 the Royal Military College have taken officer cadets for commissioning who previously would have attended the Officer Cadet School, Portsea, and the Women's Officer Cadet School, Sydney.

Navy. The Chief of Naval Staff is assisted by the Deputy Chief of Naval Staff with the Chief of Naval Personnel, the Chief of Naval Operational Requirements and Plans, the Chief of Naval Material and the Chief of Naval Engineering. On 1 Feb. 1976 the Naval Board was abolished. The command, operation and administration of the Fleet is by the Flag Officer Commanding HM Australian Fleet while materiel support of the fleet is by the Flag Officer Naval Support Command.

There are 6 UK-built Oberon class diesel-driven patrol submarines, four commissioned 1967–69 and two in 1977–78; 3 US-built guided missile destroyers, commissioned 1965–67; 4 US-built guided missile frigates, commissioned 1980–84; 5 frigates; 1 destroyer parent ship, 1 fleet replenishment ship, 1 training ship (ex-liner), 3 survey ships; 3 minehunters; 1 landing ship; 20 patrol boats; 6 landing craft; 1 amphibious heavy lift ship; 85 auxiliaries and service craft, and 7 tugs. Two frigates are being built.

The Fleet Air Arm lately operated 32 Sea King, Wessex, Iroquois, Squirrel and Bell 206B helicopters and 2 HS748 fixed wing aircraft.

The serving strength in 1988 totalled 14,800 personnel including women.

The main training establishments are in Victoria, Sydney, Nowra and Jervis Bay.

Navy estimates 1984–85, $A1,240,743,000; 1985–86, $A1,394,000,000, 1986–87, $A1,671,600.

Air Force. Command of the Royal Australian Air Force is vested in the Chief of the Air Staff (CAS) assisted by the Deputy Chief of the Air Staff, Chief of Air Force Operations and Plans, Chief of Air Force Materiel, Chief of Air Force Personnel, Chief of Air Force Technical Services, Director-General Supply—Air Force and Assistant Secretary Resources Planning.

The CAS administers and controls RAAF units through two commands: Operational Command and Support Command. Operational Command is responsible to the CAS for the command of operational units and the conduct of their operations within Australia and overseas. Support Command is responsible to the CAS for training of personnel, and the supply and maintenance of service equipment.

Flying establishment comprises 16 squadrons, of which 2 are equipped with 24 F-111 strike/reconnaissance aircraft. Of the others, 1 is equipped with missile-armed Mirage III-O Mach 2 fighters, 3 with F-18 Hornet interceptors, 2 with Orion maritime reconnaissance aircraft. There are eight transport squadrons, 2 with Hercules turboprop transports, 1 with Caribou STOL transports, 1 with a mix of Ecureuil and Iroquois helicopters, 1 with Boeing Vertol CH-47C medium lift helicopters, 1 with Iroquois helicopters, and a special transport squadron equipped with BAC One-Eleven, Mystère 20 and HS 748 aircraft. There is also one squadron operating B707 aircraft. Training aircraft include piston-engined Airtrainers, built in New Zealand, Aermacchi MB 326H jets for pilot training, and HS 748 aircraft for navigator training. A training unit has F-18 Hornets for crew conversion.

Training for commissioned rank is carried out at the RAAF Academy and Officers' Training School, both located at Point Cook, Victoria. Other major training activities which lead to commissioned rank include basic aircrew training and technical and commercial cadet schemes. Basic ground training to tradesman level is conducted at RAAF technical training schools. Higher command and staff training is, in the main, carried out at the RAAF Staff College, Fairbairn, ACT.

Personnel (1988) 22,800. There is also an Australian Air Force Reserve.

Long, G. (ed.), *Australia in the War of 1939–45.* 22 vols. Canberra, 1952 ff.

O'Neil, R., and Horner, D. M., *Australian Defence Policy for the 1980s.* Univ. of Queensland Press, 1983

INTERNATIONAL RELATIONS

Membership. Australia is a member of the UN, the Commonwealth, OECD, Colombo Plan, the South Pacific Commission and the South Pacific Bureau for Economic Co-operation.

ECONOMY

Financial relations with the States. Since 1942 the Federal Government alone has levied taxes on incomes. In return for vacating this field of taxation, the State Governments are reimbursed by grants from the Federal Government out of revenue received. Payments to the States represent about one-third of Federal Government outlays, and in turn the payments State Governments receive from the Federal Government account for nearly half of their revenues.

The Financial Agreement of 1927 established the Australian Loan Council which represents the Federal and six State Governments, and co-ordinates domestic and overseas borrowings by these governments, including annual borrowing programmes. The Federal Government acts as a central borrowing agency in raising loans to finance the major part of those programmes. The Loan Council in 1984 agreed upon arrangements for the co-ordination of borrowings by semi-government and local authorities and government-owned companies.

Budget. In 1929, under a financial agreement between the Federal Government and States, approved by a referendum, the Federal Government took over all State debts existing on 30 June 1927 and agreed to pay $A15·17m. a year for 58 years towards the interest charges thereon, and to make substantial contributions towards a sinking fund on State debt. The Sinking Fund arrangements were revised under an amendment to the agreement in 1976.

Receipts, Financing Transactions and Outlays of the Federal Government for years ending 30 June (in $A1m.):

Receipts:	1984–85	1985–86	1986–87	1987–88 [1]
Income tax	35,334	39,435	45,968	50,195
Gross PAYE	24,476	27,575	30,657	32,655
Companies	5,505	6,089	6,701	7,675
Sales tax	4,966	5,728	6,348	7,110
Excise				
Oil and LP gas and products	6,409	6,900	6,728	6,987
Other	4,352	2,306	2,557	2,700
Customs	2,987	3,339	3,228	3,280
Total taxation	*52,422*	*58,399*	*65,685*	*71,243*
Interest from States				
and Northern Territory	2,227	2,331	2,427	2,497
Interest from non-Budget				
authorities	782	819	782	772
Rent, Dividends, etc.	1,373	2,347	2,934	3,199
Total non-tax receipts	*4,571*	*5,793*	*6,498*	*6,876*
Total Receipts	56,994	64,193	72,184	78,119
Outlays:				
Defence	5,941	6,673	7,209	7,404
Forces manpower	1,749	1,948	2,008	2,078
Equipment, stores, etc.	2,609	2,620	2,903	2,765
Education	4,519	4,915	5,216	5,685
Universities	1,250	1,375	1,427	1,547
Schools and pre-schools	1,654	1,761	1,823	1,976
Student assistance	353	422	498	613
Health	6,114	6,870	7,499	8,213
Medical services and				
benefits	2,547	2,939	3,242	3,527
Hospital services				
and benefits	1,415	1,549	1,561	1,686
Pharmaceutical services				
and benefits	656	724	871	999
Nursing home and				
domicillary benefits	1,093	1,167	1,298	1,443

Outlays (continued)	1984–85	1985–86	1986–87	1987–88 [1]
Social Security and				
Welfare	17,833	19,144	20,533	22,599
Aged	5,795	6,063	6,479	7,255
Veterans and				
dependants	2,323	2,575	2,754	3,127
Handicapped	1,710	1,946	2,218	2,506
Widows and				
single parents	1,956	2,162	2,319	2,521
Families	1,681	1,749	1,634	1,797
Unemployed and				
sick	3,449	3,622	4,008	4,156
Housing	1,328	1,406	1,545	1,259
Assistance to				
States and Northern				
Territory	954	1,033	1,191	991
Urban and Regional				
Development n.e.s.				
environment, sewerage				
and sanitation	33	11	62	54
Culture and Recreation	757	903	949	1,032
Transport and Communication	1,900	1,795	1,669	1,662
Industry, assistance and				
development	1,221	1,425	1,180	1,224
Labour and employment	1,133	1,041	1,031	1,040
Public Services	4,426	4,809	5,314	5,793
Administration	1,976	2,178	2,496	2,723
Foreign affairs and				
overseas aid	1,280	1,325	1,302	1,392
Payments to or for States,				
NT and local governments	12,658	13,587	14,437	14,869
Total outlay	*63,714*	*69,918*	*74,899*	*78,146*

[1] Estimate.

The following table shows Government securities on issue on account of the Commonwealth Government and States, at 30 June 1985:

Repayable in Australian currency	Total ($A1m.)
Treasury bonds	21,288·6
Australian savings bonds	3,914·7
Treasury notes	2,894·7
Total (including other categories)	28,718·7
Repayable in foreign currency	
(Australian currency equivalent)	9,845·2

Debt per head of population at 30 June 1984 was $A3,019, while the annual interest charge amounted to $A329 per head.

Australian National Accounts. Australian Bureau of Statistics. 1953–54 to date
Public Authority Finance: Commonwealth Government Finance, Australia. Australian Bureau of Statistics, 1962–63 to date
Public Authority Finance: State and Local Government Finance, Australia. Australian Bureau of Statistics, 1971–72 to date
Public Authority Finance: Government Financial Estimates. Australian Bureau of Statistics, 1975–76 to date
National Income and Expenditure. Australian Bureau of Statistics. Canberra, 1946 to date
Treasury Information Bulletin (and Supplements). Canberra Treasury Dept., 1956 to date (quarterly)
Hagger, A. J., *A Guide to Australian Economic and Social Statistics.* Sydney, 1983

Currency. On 14 Feb. 1966 Australia adopted a system of decimal currency. The currency unit, the *dollar* ($) is divided into 100 *cents*. The transition period ended on 31 July 1967. Decimal notes are issued in denominations of $2, 5, 10, 20, 50 and 100. Coins are issued in denominations of 1, 2, 5, 10, 20 and 50 cents and $1.

Australian notes, issued by the note-issue department of the Reserve Bank, are legal tender throughout Australia. The total value of notes in circulation on 30 June 1984 was $A7,205m., of which $A6,418m. was held by the public. In March 1988, US$1 = 1·39 *dollars*; £1 = 2·46 *dollars*.

Banking. The banking system in Australia comprises:

(a) The Reserve Bank of Australia. This is the central bank which in addition to its central banking business (including the note-issue department) provides special finance through the rural credits department for the processing, manufacture and marketing of primary produce.

The Reserve Bank's functions and responsibilities derive from the Reserve Bank Act 1959 and the Banking Act 1959, and the Financial Corporations Act 1974.

(b) Four major trading banks: (i) The Commonwealth Bank of Australia; (ii) 3 private trading banks: The Australia and New Zealand Banking Group Ltd, Westpac Banking Corporation and the National Commercial Banking Corporation of Australia Ltd.

(c) Other trading banks: (i) 3 State Government banks—The State Bank of New South Wales, The State Bank of South Australia, and the Rural and Industries Bank of Western Australia; (ii) one joint stock bank—The Bank of Queensland Ltd, formerly The Brisbane Permanent Building and Banking Co. Ltd, which has specialized business in one district only; (iii) The Australian Bank Ltd; (iv) branches of 17 overseas banks—the restrictions on foreign banks operating in Australia, and on foreign investment in the merchant banks, were lifted in 1984–85.

(d) The Commonwealth Development Bank of Australia.

(e) The Australian Resources Development Bank Ltd opened on 29 March 1968, to assist Australian enterprises in developing Australia's natural resources, through direct loans and equity investment or by re-financing loans made by trading banks. The bank is jointly owned by the 4 major Australian trading banks.

(f) The Primary Industry Bank of Australia Ltd commenced operations on 22 Sept. 1978. The equity capital of the bank consists of eight shares. Seven shares are held by the Australian Government and the major trading banks while the eighth share is held equally by the 4 State banks. The main objective of the bank is to facilitate the provision of loans to primary producers on longer terms than are otherwise generally available. The role of the bank is restricted to re-financing loans made by banks and other financial institutions.

(g) Savings banks, of which the leader is the Commonwealth Savings Bank (the main source of housing loans). Total deposits, all savings banks, (at 30 June 1985), $38,878m.; (1986), $42,614m.; (1987), $52,495m.

For history of the Reserve Bank see THE STATESMAN'S YEAR-BOOK 1986–87, p. 104.

Reserve Bank, 30 June 1987, total liabilities $26,541m., of which notes on issue, $9,801m.; deposits by trading banks, $3,472m.; deposits by Commonwealth Government, $2,090m.; assets $26,541m. of which gold and foreign exchange (including IMF Special Drawing Rights), $17,120m., treasury notes $1,657m., other Commonwealth Government securities $6,638m.

At 30 June 1984, 11 savings banks were operating in Australia. These are the 4 major savings banks being wholly owned subsidiaries of the trading banks; the Bank of New Zealand Saving Bank Ltd; the Bank of Queensland Saving Bank Ltd; the State Bank of Victoria and the Savings Bank of South Australia; the Rural and Industries Bank of Western Australia, and 2 Trustee Savings Banks in Tasmania. At 30 June 1984 these savings banks had 5,592 branches and 10,533 agencies throughout Australia.

The following table is a summary of banking business (in $A1m.) in the several States of the Commonwealth:

Particulars	NSW	Vic.	Q'ld	SA	WA	Tas.	Australia (including A.C.T. and N.T.)
All trading banks:[1]							
Fixed deposits	10,961	5,876	4,013	1,225	2,052	344	24,891
Current deposits	5,686	3,295	2,055	752	1,027	231	13,494
Advances	13,148	6,388	4,879	2,840	2,966	445	31,743
Savings bank deposits [2]	9,532	12,916	4,709	3,327	2,214	1,103	34,328

[1] Weekly averages for June 1984. [2] At June 1984.

Treasury Information Bulletin. Department of the Treasury. Canberra, 1956 to date (quarterly)

Weights and Measures. Conversion to the metric system is in progress.

ENERGY AND NATURAL RESOURCES

Electricity. Production 1985–86, 124,369m. kwh. Supply 240 and 250 volts; 50 Hz.

Minerals. Production:

	1983–84	1984–85	1985–86
Copper (1,000 tonnes)	254	259	241
Lead (1,000 tonnes)	442	480	469
Zinc (1,000 tonnes)	650	736	687
Tin (1,000 tonnes)	8·7	6·4	7·4
Coal	104,600	118,400	128,000
Lignite	33·2	38·5	35·5
Iron Ore	76,300	91,700	97,700
Gold (kg. refined)	30,661	40,501	56,928
Crude Oil (m. bbls.)	169	194	199

Agriculture. In 1983, of a total Australian area of 768m. hectares, 641·5m. hectares (83·5%) were Crown lands; private lands formed the remainder, of which 126·7m. hectares (16·5%) were alienated or in the process of alienation.

Area and production of the principal crops in 1984–85:

Crops	Total area (1,000 hectares)	Total production (1,000 tonnes)
Wheat (grain)	12,039	18,635
Oats (grain)	1,060	1,395
Barley (grain)	3,503	5,559
Hay (cereal)	238	808
Potatoes (ordinary)	38	...
Sugar-cane (for crushing)	306	25,448
Vineyards	63	837
Fruit	90	...
Rice	118	777

The following summary shows the production and gross value of the most important items or classes of production, classified by States:

1984–85	NSW	Vic.	Q'ld	SA	WA	Tas.	Aust.[1]
Area of crops (1,000 hectares)	5,708	2,660	3,010	2,893	6,721	99	20,997
Production of wheat (1,000 tonnes)	5,813	2,660	1,540	2,038	6,580	4	18,635
Total wool production (1,000 tonnes)	275·1	170·2	67·9	109	170·3	21·9	815·1
All meat (tonnes, carcase weight)	628,508	618,269	653,738	219,916	216,545	60,280	2,085,863
Total Agriculture (value $A1m.)	4,406·9	3,273·4	3,157·8	1,660·3	2,678·4	382·2	15,650·5

[1] Includes Northern Territory and Australian Capital Territory.

Livestock (in 1,000) at 31 March 1986:

	NSW	Vic.	Q'ld	SA	WA	Tas.	N. Terr.	ACT	Australia
Cattle	5,409	3,720	9,662	914	1,690	570	1,458	13	23,436
Sheep	58,001	26,892	14,311	17,938	33,213	5,083	1	122	155,561
Pigs	798	432	585	414	278	45	3	—	2,553

Forestry. At 31 March 1981 there were 741,000 hectares of coniferous plantations.

INDUSTRY AND TRADE

Industry. Statistics of the manufacturing industries in Australia in 1984–85: Number of establishments, 27,647; workers employed, 1,018,700; salaries and wages paid, $A18,779·9m.; value-added, $A38,253·5m. (excludes small single-establishment enterprises employing less than 4 persons).

Manufacturing by sector, 1984–85:

Sector	Employment	Value Added ($Am.)
Food, beverages and tobacco	167,800	6,847·7
Meat products	44,500	1,311·5
Textiles	33,000	1,014·5
Clothing and footwear	74,300	1,667·2
Wood and products	45,000	1,465·7
Printing and allied	78,700	3,019·3
Chemical, petroleum and coal products	55,100	3,397·6
Basic metals and products	76,900	4,022·5
Fabricated metal	92,900	2,901·2
Transport equipment	119,800	3,816·6
Other machinery	127,000	4,383·0

Labour. The majority of wage and salary earners in Australia have their minimum wages and conditions of work prescribed in awards of industrial arbitration authorities established under federal and State legislation. However, in some States, some conditions of work (*e.g.*, normal weekly hours of work, long-service leave, annual leave) are set down in State legislation. In May 1985 it was estimated that the average weekly earnings of adult males (other than managerial, professional and higher supervisory staff) in full-time private and government employment was $A413·90 and average weekly hours 39.

Employees in all States are covered by workers' compensation legislation and by certain industrial award provisions relating to work injuries.

During 1986 industrial disputes involving stoppages of work of 10 man-days or more accounted for 1,390,700 working days lost. In these disputes 675,900 workers were involved.

The following table shows estimates (in 1,000) of the civilian population, by labour force status. The estimates are derived by the ABS from the population survey which is based on a sample of dwellings, carried out by personal interview, covering about two-thirds of 1% of the population.

	May 1984	May 1985	May 1986	May 1987
In the labour force	7,127·5	7,238·6	7,536·7	7,719·0
Employed	6,490·5	6,631·8	6,944·5	7,084·0
Unemployed	637·0	606·7	592·2	635·0
Not in the labour force	4,622·3	4,704·0	4,624·1	4,721·9
Civilian population aged 15 years and over	11,744·8	11,942·6	12,160·9	12,440·9

The following table shows population survey estimates (in 1,000) of employed persons in Australia classified by industry:

Industry [1]	Financial Year 1985–86	1986–87
Agriculture, forestry and logging, fishing and hunting	435·4	421·3
Mining	106·7	101·7
Manufacturing	1,139·3	1,134·7
Food, beverages and tobacco	176·3	175·5
Metal products	191·3	185·4
Other manufacturing	771·7	773·8
Electricity, gas and water	143·4	132·7
Construction	474·6	497·3
Wholesale and retail trade	1,380·9	1,405·0
Transport and storage	375·0	389·0
Communication	143·2	139·9
Finance, property and business services	689·0	722·8
Public administration and defence	328·5	332·5
Community services	1,179·5	1,238·9
Recreation, personal and other services	452·8	477·7
Total employed	6,848·0	6,993·7

[1] Australian Standard Industrial Classification.

The following table shows the number of unemployed persons (from the population survey), job vacancies (from the ABS Job Vacancies survey) and the number of persons in receipt of unemployment benefit:

	May 1984	May 1985	May 1986	May 1987
Persons unemployed	637,000	606,700	592,200	635,000
Job Vacancies	34,800 [2]	56,600	54,400	53,800
Unemployment benefit recipients [1]	584,500	561,400	569,966	561,698

[1] Data relates to the month of June   [2] Not strictly comparable with earlier surveys.

Trade Unions. At the end of June 1985 there were 323 trade unions reporting in Australia with an estimated membership of 3,154,200. About 57% of wage and salary earners were estimated to be members of unions. In 1985 there were 35 unions with fewer than 100 members and 10 unions with 80,000 or more members. Many of the larger trade unions are affiliated with central labour organizations, the oldest and by far the largest being the Australian Council of Trade Unions formed in 1927.

Labour Statistics. Australian Bureau of Statistics. Canberra, 1982
Isaac, J. E., and Ford, G. W., *Australian Industrial Relations.* Melbourne, 1971
Portus, J. H., *The Development of Australian Trade Union Law.* Melbourne, 1958
Rawson, D. W., *A Handbook of Australian Trade Unions and Employees' Associations.* Canberra, 1977

Commerce. Throughout Australia there are uniform customs duties, and trade between the States is free.

Value of the total imports and exports for years ending 30 June, in $A1,000:

	Imports	Exports (excluding ships' and aircraft stores)		
		Australian produce	Re-exports	Total
1981–82	23,004,930	18,816,343	758,863	19,575,206
1982–83	21,806,179	20,757,048	1,303,258	22,060,306
1983–84 [1]	24,062,896	23,550,377	1,254,866	24,805,243

[1] Preliminary, subject to revision.

The Australian customs tariff provides for preferences to goods produced in and shipped from certain specified countries such as UK, Canada, New Zealand and Ireland. Preferences occur as a result of reciprocal trade agreements between Australia and these countries.

Australia also has bilateral agreements with a number of other countries guaranteeing reciprocal treatment in matters of trade.

The Australia–New Zealand free-trade agreement came into force on 1 Jan. 1966 in certain scheduled goods.

In addition, Australia is a signatory to the multilateral General Agreement on Tariffs and Trade (GATT).

Principal commodities exported and imported from Australia (in $A1,000):

Exports	1985–86 $m.	Exports	1985–86 $m.
Live animals, chiefly for food	279·7	Greasy and fleece-washed wool	2,292·1
Beef and veal	1,319·1	Sheep's or lambs' wool, n.e.s.	
Mutton and lamb	211·0	(excl. wool tops)	523·9
Other meat and meat prep.	173·1	Crude fertilizers, minerals	
Milk and cream	188·1	(excl. fuels)	152·4
Cheese and curd	165·5	Iron ore and conc.	1,937·0
Crustaceans and molluscs	413·2	Uranium ores and conc.	295·9
Wheat	2,939·4	Nickel matte, ores and conc. etc	364·4
Barley, unmilled	536·7	Alumina	1,377·5
Sorghum	177·6	Zinc ores and conc.	240·8
Cereal and flour prep.	122·4	Mineral sands (excl. monazite)	219·6
Vegetables and fruit	373·0	Other ores and conc. of base metal,	
Raw sugar, bulk	613·2	n.e.s.	290·7
Feeding-stuff for animals	150·0	Coal	5,213·0
Cattle hides	177·5	Petroleum oils, crude	1,152·5
Other hides, skins and furskins, raw	218·8	Petroleum prod. refined	1,110·2
Pulpwood	248·8	Gas, natural and manuf.	462·4
Cotton	382·4	Medicinal and pharm. prod.	147·1

Exports (continued)	1985–86 $m.
Artificial resins and plastic materials	132·6
Other chemicals and related prod. n.e.s.	311·1
Textiles	220·9
Non-metallic mineral manuf. n.e.s.	150·2
Iron or steel ingots	160·3
Iron or steel universals, plates and sheets	236·2
Other iron and steel	184·6
Copper	193·2
Nickel	124·0
Aluminium and aluminium alloys, unworked	906·8
Aluminium and aluminium alloys, worked	153·6
Lead and lead alloys, unworked	281·1
Zinc and zinc alloys, unworked	213·3
Manuf. of metal, n.e.s.	192·3
Internal combustion piston engines and parts	176·0
Mach. specialized for particular industries	242·2

Exports	1985–86 $m.
General industrial mach. and equip. and parts	179·5
Office mach. and ADP equip.	218·5
Elec. mach. apparatus and appliances, n.e.s.	183·2
Parts and accessories, n.e.s. for road vehicles	157·8
Aircraft and associated equip. and parts	167·1
Professional instruments and apparatus, n.e.s.	162·0
Photo. and cinematographic supplies	159·4
Misc. manuf. articles, n.e.s.	228·5
Special transactions and commodities, n.e.s.	114·7
Gold, non-monetary (excl. gold ores and conc.)	771·0
Items for which details are not separately available	449·5
Other	1,681·4
Total	32,820·0

Imports	1985–86 $m.
Fish, crustaceans and molluscs and prep.	333·4
Vegetables and fruit	262·9
Coffee, tea, cocoa, spices and manuf.	418·8
Other food and live animals, chiefly for food	403·3
Beverages and tobacco	297·6
Wood, simply worked, and railway sleepers	327·4
Crude fertilizers, minerals (excl. coal, petroleum and prec. stones)	259·9
Other crude materials, inedible (excl. fuels)	435·4
Petroleum oils, crude	587·5
Petroleum prod. refined	1,218·1
Organo-inorganic and heterocyclic compounds	282·6
Other organic chemicals	483·2
Inorganic chemicals	248·8
Medicinal and pharm. prod.	393·0
Condensation, polycondensation and polyaddition prod.	257·5
Polymerization and copolymerization prod.	342·1
Chemical materials and prod. n.e.s.	411·5
Other chemicals and related prod. n.e.s.	606·0
Rubber manuf. n.e.s.	449·6
Paper and paperboard	716·8
Textile yarn (incl. wool tops)	438·4
Cotton fabrics, woven	329·4
Woven m.m.f. fabrics	301·1
Other textiles	609·5
Non-metallic mineral manuf. n.e.s.	653·8
Iron or steel universals, plates and sheets	205·8
Iron or steel tubes, pipes and fittings	177·9
Other iron and steel	225·2
Manuf. of metal, n.e.s.	928·8
Other manuf. goods classified chiefly by material	583·9

Imports	1985–86 $m.
Internal combustion piston engines and parts	543·3
Rotating elec. plant and parts, n.e.s.	246·9
Agricultural mach. (excl. tractors) and parts	155·9
Tractors	222·4
Civil engineering plant and equip. and parts	588·7
Other mach. specialized for particular industries	1,085·2
Metal working mach.	385·0
Pumps and compressors (excl. for liquids)	349·0
Non-elec. parts and accessories of mach. n.e.s.	568·4
Other general industrial mach. and equip. n.e.s. and parts	936·4
Office mach.	321·5
ADP mach.	1,350·6
Parts and accessories for office and ADP mach.	501·5
Gramophones, dictating mach. etc.	318·2
Telecom. equip. and parts, n.e.s.	865·8
Other telecom. recording and reproducing equip.	282·4
Elec. switches, fuses, etc. and parts	393·7
Household equip. n.e.s.	380·4
Other elec. mach. apparatus and appliances, n.e.s. and parts	1,068·4
Passenger motor cars	1,541·3
Motor vehicles for the transport of goods	1,173·0
Parts and accessories, n.e.s. for road motor vehicles	712·4
Motor cycles, motor scooters, etc.	180·1
Aircraft and associated equip. and parts	359·4
Ships, boats and floating structures	195·8
Furniture and parts	237·7
Clothing	567·9
Footwear	207·6

Imports (continued)	1985–86 $m.	Imports	1985–86 $m.
Measuring, checking, etc. instruments, n.e.s. and parts	670·1	Musical instruments, parts and accessories	297·5
Photo and cinematographic supplies	255·0	Other misc. manuf. articles, n.e.s.	434·1
Other photo apparatus, equip., optical goods, watches	380·4	Special transactions and commodities, n.e.s.	1,235·5
Printed matter	537·2	Other	1,249·5
Articles of artificial resins, plastics, etc.	300·0	Total	34,667·2
Perambulators, toys, games and sporting goods	379·8		

Total trade in ($A1m.) with the more important countries, according to origin (imports) and consignment (exports):

	1984–85		1985–86	
From or to	Imports	Exports	Imports	Exports
Belgium–Luxembourg	216·2	216·7	287·1	259·8
Canada	606·4	298·4	691·1	460·4
China–excl. Taiwan Province	375·3	1,061·8	435·0	1,498·0
Egypt, Arab Republic of	...	499·4	...	560·9
France	558·9	669·8	776·1	710·3
Germany, Fed. Republic of	1,811·6	722·1	2,718·4	885·8
Hong Kong	656·8	839·4	676·5	722·4
India	169·1	238·2	170·7	428·6
Indonesia	363·1	431·1	209·3	526·5
Iran	...	453·2	...	305·3
Italy	882·1	581·3	1,094·7	688·4
Japan	6,608·6	7,985·9	8,248·3	9,358·4
Korea, Rep. of	474·0	1,157·9	556·7	1,322·0
Kuwait	339·3	118·3	297·0	132·3
Malaysia	318·4	603·8	325·4	516·3
Netherlands	350·7	457·3	430·7	432·3
New Zealand	1,104·2	1,541·6	1,454·5	1,507·6
Pakistan	...	160·5	...	126·8
Papua New Guinea	114·1	516·2	170·9	558·0
Saudi Arabia	638·1	468·9	470·8	493·6
Singapore, Republic of	711·8	782·0	745·2	725·8
Sweden	483·5	48·8	657·9	91·2
Switzerland	276·4	...	428·5	...
Taiwan	1,052·3	846·4	1,161·1	1,064·1
USSR	...	834·4	...	969·7
UK	1,961·6	923·0	2,516·0	1,151·2
USA	6,425·9	3,457·8	7,284·8	3,253·6

Overseas Trade. Australian Bureau of Statistics. Canberra, 1906 to date

Total trade between UK and Australia (British Department of Trade returns, in £1,000 sterling):

	1983	1984	1985	1986	1987
Imports to UK	552,642	612,087	736,986	643,238	673,837
Exports and re-exports from UK	940,279	1,186,521	1,373,184	1,227,647	1,223,613

Tourism. During 1986, 1·43m. overseas visitors arrived in Australia intending to stay for less than 12 months.

Australian Bureau of Statistics, Canberra: *Rural Industries.* 1962–63 to date.—*Manufacturing Establishments: Details of Operations.* 1968–69 to date.—*Non-rural Primary Industries.* 1967–68 and 1968–69.—*Value of Production.* 1964–65 to 1968–69.—*Manufacturing Industry.* 1963–64 to 1967–68.—*Manufacturing Commodities.* 1963–64 and 1964–65.— *Building and Construction.* 1964–65 to date
Quarterly Review of Agricultural Economics. Bureau of Agricultural Economics. Canberra, 1948 to date
Developments in Australian Manufacturing Industry. Department of Trade. Melbourne, 1954–55 to date (annual)
The Australian Mineral Industry Review. Department of National Development—Bureau of Mineral Resources, Geology and Geophysics. Canberra, 1948 to date
Australian Economy. Department of the Treasury. Canberra, 1956 to date
Australasian Institute of Mining and Metallurgy. *Proceedings: New Series.* Melbourne, 1912 to date

COMMUNICATIONS

Roads. The length of roads in Australia for general traffic (1985) is 804,753 km, of which 266,686 is sealed, 200,862 of gravel, crushed stone or other improved surface, and 337,179 of cleared or formed surface only.

At 30 June 1984, 8,832,800 motor vehicles, including 6,636,200 cars and station wagons, 1,798,200 utilities, panel-vans, truck type vehicles and buses and 398,400 motor cycles, were registered in Australia. New motor vehicle registration figures for 1984–85 include 510,893 cars and station wagons, 100,089 utilities and panel-vans, 63,848 truck type vehicles and buses and 45,879 motor cycles.

Railways. Government railways for the year ended 30 June 1984:

System	Route-km open [4]	Revenue train-km run, 1,000	Passenger journeys, 1,000	Goods and livestock, carried, 1,000 tonnes	Gross earnings, $A1,000	Working expenses, $A1,000
State:						
New South Wales	9,884	61,659	202,253	46,594	823,055	1,234,053
Victoria	5,783	30,702	84,599	10,486	305,283	717,447
Queensland	10,381	33,303	37,652	53,150	717,956	725,059
South Australia [3]	130	3,697	69,680	...	50,277	126,127
Western Australia	5,623	10,333	8,665	19,870	228,339	246,552
Australian National [1] [2]	7,450	10,238	357	12,083	227,063	325,170

[1] The Australian National Railways operates services of the former Commonwealth Railways, the non-metropolitan South Australian Railways and the Tasmanian Railways.

[2] Excludes Adelaide metropolitan rail passenger services and the Tasmanian Region.

[3] The South Australian State Transport Authority operates services in the Adelaide metropolitan area.

[4] Inter system traffic is included in the total for each system over which it passes.

The State railway gauges are: New South Wales, 1,435 mm; Victoria, 1,600 mm (325 km 1,435 mm); Queensland, 1,067 mm (111 km 1,435 mm); South Australia, 1,600 mm for 2,533 km, 1,824 km 1,435 mm and the rest 1,067 mm; West Australia, 137 km, 1,435 mm and the rest 1,067 mm, and Tasmania, 1,067 mm. Of the Australian National Railways, the gauge of the Trans-Australian and Australian Capital Territory is 1,435 mm, and for the Central Australia 1,067 mm for 869 km and 1,435 mm for 350 km. Under various Commonwealth–State standardization agreements, all the State capitals are now linked by 1,435 mm gauge track. The Central Australia railway extends as far north as Alice Springs (now standard gauge on new alignment from Tarcoola to Alice Springs).

Aviation. All civil flying in Australia and its Territories is subject to legislative control by the Australian Government. In some cases intrastate air services are also subject to legislative control by the relevant State Government. The administration of the Air Navigation Act and Regulations and other Commonwealth aviation legislation is a function of the Commonwealth Department of Aviation under the Minister for Aviation.

All Australian-owned airlines, except Qantas Airways, operate regular internal air services. During 1984–85 hours flown numbered 250,779; paying passengers carried numbered 11,359,700; weight of goods carried was 153,181 tonnes, and gross weight of mail was 18,467 tonnes.

During 1983 hours flown by Australian regular overseas services which are operated by or on behalf of Qantas numbered 89,952; km flown, 71m.; paying passengers, 2,449,596; freight, 90,357 tonnes; mail, 4,744 tonnes.

Expenditure by the Aviation Portfolio on air transport for the year 1983–84 was $A448·8m. Aviation related expenditure by other Australian Government Departments for the same period was $A71·6m.

At 30 June 1984 there were 441 licensed aerodromes and 71 governmental aerodromes in Australia.

Shipping. As at 30 June 1983 the Australian merchant marine (vessels of 150 tons gross and over) consisted of 74 coastal vessels of 1,146,505 tons gross and 30 overseas vessels of 924,037 tons gross.

Entrances and clearances of vessels (with cargo and in ballast) engaged in overseas trade:

	Entrances		Clearances	
	No.	DWT	No.	DWT
1982–83	9,998	315,465,880	9,914	316,847,814
1983–84	6,131	263,614,000	6,026	267,264,000

The following summary shows shipping activity by States, 1983–84:

Particulars	NSW	Vic.	Q'ld	SA	WA	Tas.	N.T.	Aust.
Overseas vessel arrivals								
Calls	2,607	1,903	2,142	853	2,621	469	268	10,863
DWT (1,000 tonnes)	78,331	43,407	71,325	19,651	133,714	12,591	7,839	366,859
Overseas cargo:								
Discharged 1,000 gross weight tonnes	6,324	4,321	2,413	2,326	4,928		476 1,208	22,859
Overseas vessel departures								
Calls	2,599	1,865	2,132	846	2,599	470	268	10,779
DWT (1,000 tonnes)	79,663	42,283	72,950	19,487	135,124	12,556	7,906	369,968
Overseas cargo Loaded 1,000 gross weight tonnes	37,475	7,236	40,506	5,264	94,651		5,026 4,742	197,048

Post and Broadcasting. Business, year ended 30 June 1985. Postal services revenue, \$A1,211·3m., of which mail services earned \$A1,080·5m.; expenditure \$A1,186·8m., of which labour cost \$A911·8m.

At 30 June 1985, there were 6,187,947 telephone services. Telecommunications revenue, \$A4,764·8m., of which telephone calls earned \$A2,640·4m.; expenditure, \$A4,379·7m., of which marketing and operations cost \$A890·1m. and interest \$A898·9m.

The National Broadcasting and Television Service is provided by the Australian Broadcasting Corporation, which at 30 June 1983 operated 95 medium-wave, 25 frequency modulation and 6 high-frequency radio stations, and 10 high-frequency radio stations for overseas services. In addition, 130 medium-wave, and 7 frequency modulation, commercial broadcasting stations plus 38 public radio stations (both MW and FM) were operating.

Television services are provided in each State, the Northern Territory and the Australian Capital Territory by the ABC and by commercial television stations. There were 272 national stations (including translators) and 50 commercial television stations in 1983.

The Overseas Telecommunications Commission (OTC), established by the Overseas Telecommunications Act 1946, is responsible for the establishment, maintenance, operation and development of all public telecommunications' services between Australia and other countries, between Australia and its external territories and with ships at sea.

Cinemas (1971). There were 976 cinemas including 241 drive-in cinemas, with a total seating capacity of about 478,000.

Newspapers (1981). There was 1 national newspaper (average daily circulation 126,000) and 14 metropolitan daily newspapers in Australia with a combined daily circulation of 3·6m. Of these, 3 papers published in Melbourne accounted for 1·3m. and 4 published in Sydney for 1·2m.

Australian Transport. Sydney, Institute of Transport, 1937 to date (quarterly)

JUSTICE, RELIGION, EDUCATION AND WELFARE

Justice. The judicial power of the Commonwealth of Australia is vested in the High Court of Australia (the Federal Supreme Court), in the Federal courts created by the Federal Parliament (the Federal Court of Australia and the Family Court of Australia) and in the State courts invested by Parliament with Federal jurisdiction.

High Court. The High Court consists of a Chief Justice and 6 other Justices, appointed by the Governor-General in Council. The Constitution confers on the High Court original jurisdiction, *inter alia*, in all matters arising under treaties or affecting consuls or other foreign representatives, matters between the States of the Commonwealth, matters to which the Commonwealth is a party and matters between residents of different States. Federal Parliament may make laws conferring original jurisdiction on the High Court, *inter alia*, in matters arising under the Constitution or under any laws made by the Parliament. It has in fact conferred jurisdiction on the High Court in matters arising under the Constitution and in matters arising under certain laws made by Parliament.

The High Court may hear and determine appeals from its own Justices exercising original jurisdiction, from any other Federal Court, from a Court exercising Federal jurisdiction and from the Supreme Courts of the States. It also has jurisdiction to hear and determine appeals from the Supreme Courts of the Territories. The right of appeal from the High Court to the Privy Council was abolished in 1986.

Other Federal Courts. Since 1924, 4 other Federal courts have been created to exercise special Federal jurisdiction, *i.e.* the Federal Court of Australia, the Family Court of Australia, the Australian Industrial Court and the Federal Court of Bankruptcy. The Federal Court of Australia was created by the Federal Court of Australia Act 1976 and began to exercise jurisdiction on 1 Feb. 1977. It exercises such original jurisdiction as is invested in it by laws made by the Federal Parliament including jurisdiction formerly exercised by the Australian Industrial Court and the Federal Court of Bankruptcy, and in some matters previously invested in either the High Court or State and Territory Supreme Courts. The Federal Court also acts as a court of appeal from State and Territory courts in relation to Federal matters. Appeal from the Federal Court to the High Court will be by way of special leave only. The State Supreme Courts have also been invested with Federal jurisdiction in bankruptcy.

State Courts. The general Federal jurisdiction of the State courts extends, subject to certain restrictions and exceptions, to all matters in which the High Court has jurisdiction or in which jurisdiction may be conferred upon it.

Industrial Tribunals. The major Federal industrial tribunal in Australia is the Australian Conciliation and Arbitration Commission, constituted by presidential members (with the status of judges) and commissioners. The Commission's functions include settling industrial disputes, making awards, determining the standard hours of work, wage fixation, etc. Questions of law, the judicial interpretation of awards, imposition of penalties, etc., in relation to industrial matters, are now dealt with by the Federal Court.

Australian Digest of Reported Decisions of the Australian Courts and of Australian Appeals to the Privy Council. 2nd ed. Sydney, Law Book Co. 1963—Supplements 1964 ff.
Baalman, J., *Outline of Law in Australia.* 4th ed. Sydney, 1979
Bates, N., *Introduction to Legal Studies.* 3rd ed. Melbourne, 1980
Benjafield, D. G., and Whitmore, H., *Principles of Australian Administrative Law.* 3rd ed. Sydney, 1966
Cowen, Z., *Federal Jurisdiction in Australia.* 2nd ed. Melbourne, 1978
Fleming, J. G., *The Law of Torts.* 5th ed. Sydney, 1977
Gunn, J. A. L., *Australian Income Tax Law and Practice.* 9th ed. by F. C. Bock and E. F. Mannix, Sydney, 1969, and *Butterworth's Taxation Service* to date
Howard, C., *Criminal Law.* 3rd ed. Sydney, 1975
Mills, C. P., and Sorrell, G. H., *Federal Industrial Law. (Nolan and Cohen.)* 5th ed. Sydney, 1975
O'Connell, D. P. (ed.), *International Law in Australia.* Sydney, 1966
Paterson, W. E., and Ednie, H. H., *Australian Company Law.* 2nd ed. Sydney, 1976, and *Butterworth's Company Service* to date
Sawer, G., *The Australian and the Law.* Melbourne, 1976
Twyford, J., *The Layman and the Law in Australia.* 2nd ed. Sydney, 1980
Wynes, A., *Legislative, Executive and Judicial Powers in Australia.* 5th ed. Sydney, 1976
Yorston, R. K., and Fortescue, E. E., *Australian Mercantile Law.* 14th ed. Sydney, 1971

Religion. Under the Constitution the Commonwealth cannot make any law to establish any religion, to impose any religious observance or to prohibit the free exercise of any religion, nor can it require a religious test as qualification for office or public trust under the Commonwealth. The figures in the table refer to those religions with the largest number of adherents at the census of 1981. The census question on religion was not obligatory, however.

Religion	Persons	Religion	Persons
Christian		Non-Christian	
Baptist	190,259	Hebrew	62,126
Brethren	21,489	Muslim	76,792
Catholic [1]	3,786,505	Other	23,577
Churches of Christ	89,424		
Church of England	3,810,469	Total Non-Christian	197,568
Congregational	23,017		
Jehovah's Witness	51,815	Indefinite	73,551
Orthodox	421,281	No religion	1,576,718
Lutheran	199,760	No reply	1,595,195
Methodist, inc. Wesley	490,767		
Presbyterian	637,818	Grand Total	14,576,330
Salvation Army	71,570		
Seventh-day Adventist	712,609		
Protestant (undefined)	220,679		
Other (including Christian undefined)	250,188		
Total Christian	11,133,298		

[1] Includes 'Catholic' and 'Roman Catholic'.

Education. The Governments of the Australian States and the Northern Territory have the major responsibility for education, including the administration and substantial funding of primary, secondary, and technical and further education. In most States, a single Education Department is responsible for these three levels, but in New South Wales and South Australia there is a separate department responsible solely for technical and further education and in Victoria, a Technical and Further Education Board. Furthermore, in New South Wales an Education Commission advises the Minister on primary, secondary and post-secondary education.

The Australian Government is directly responsible for education services in the Australian Capital Territory, administered through an education authority, and for services to Norfolk Island, Christmas Island and the Cocos (Keeling) Islands. The Australian Government provides supplementary finance to the States and is responsible for the total funding of universities and colleges of advanced education. It also has special responsibilities for student assistance, education programmes for Aboriginal people and children from non-English-speaking backgrounds, and for international relations in education.

The Australian Constitution empowers the Federal Government to make grants to the States and to place conditions upon such grants. There are two national Education Commissions which advise the Federal Government on the financial needs of educational institutions. The Commonwealth Schools Commission, established in 1973, advises on financial assistance to the States for schools. The Commonwealth Tertiary Education Commission advises on providing the States with total funding for universities and colleges of advanced education, and supplementary assistance for their institutions of technical and further education.

In 1984 legislation was passed to reactivate the national Curriculum Development Centre (CDC) within the framework of the Commonwealth Schools Commission. The CDC's functions are to concentrate on co-ordination and dissemination and on sponsoring the development of materials through contract arrangements with other agencies.

School attendance is compulsory between the ages of 6 and 15 years (16 years in Tasmania), at either a government school or a recognized non-government educational institution. Many Australian children attend pre-schools for a year before entering school (usually in sessions of 2-3 hours, for 2-5 days per week). Government schools are usually co-educational and comprehensive. Non-government schools have been traditionally single-sex, particularly in secondary schools, but there is a trend towards co-education. Tuition is free at government schools, but fees are normally charged at non-government schools.

The following is a summary at July 1986 of primary and secondary school education:

	Schools		Teachers [1]		Pupils [2]	
States and Territories	Govern-ment	Non-govern-ment	Govern-ment schools	Non-govern-ment schools	Govern-ment schools	Non-govern-ment schools
New South Wales	2,233	848	47,123	16,194	755,257	270,718
Victoria	2,114	733	40,723	15,907	546,136	250,396
Queensland	1,313	381	23,906	6,689	374,329	116,831
South Australia	711	178	14,187	3,340	192,489	52,788
Western Australia	730	233	12,706	3,661	207,436	60,255
Tasmania	255	69	4,985	1,115	66,050	17,459
Northern Territory	137	18	1,882	331	26,288	4,952
Aust. Cap. Terr.	96	36	2,822	1,152	39,816	20,189
	7,589	2,496	148,334	48,388	2,207,801	793,588

[1] Full-time teachers plus the full-time equivalent of part-time teaching.
[2] Full-time pupils only.

In post-secondary education, tuition fees were abolished in 1974 and student allowances are provided for full-time students subject to a means test. Universities are autonomous institutions, as are the substantial majority of colleges of advanced education. While both offer degree courses, colleges also offer diploma and associate diploma courses; these tend to be vocational or of applied learning.

Students enrolled at university (1985) 175,476 as follows:

Type of Course		Type of Enrolment	
Doctorate	7,805	Full-time internal	107,427
Master	16,749	Part-time internal	51,562
Bachelor	137,490	External	16,487
Non-degree	13,432		

University teaching staff, full-time and full-time equivalent in 1985, 10,539.
Other advanced education (1985) 195,231 students enrolled and 11,039 staff.
Type of institution and enrollment:

College of advanced education	184,335
Institute of advanced education within a university	2,960
Technical and further education institution	5,275
Other Commonwealth institution	312
Other institution	2,349
Full-time internal	97,360
Part-time internal	68,759
External	29,112

Teacher education usually takes place in colleges of advanced education, though a substantial number of secondary teachers and a few primary teachers receive their pre-service education in a university. Government school teachers are recruited by the State and Northern Territory departments of education, and in the Australian Capital Territory by the ACT Schools Authority and the Public Service Board. Non-government schools recruit their own teachers.

The Australian Government provides assistance for students. The Secondary Allowances Scheme aims to help parents with a limited income to keep their children at school for the final 2 years of secondary education. The Assistance for Isolated Children Scheme provides special support to families whose children are isolated from schooling or are handicapped. The Adult Secondary Education Assistance Scheme provides assistance for mature-age students undertaking a full-time one-year matriculation level programme or a two-year programme if studies beyond the tenth year in the Australian secondary school system have not previously been undertaken. The Tertiary Education Assistance Scheme is a means-tested scheme to assist students enrolled for full-time study in approved courses at post-secondary institutions. Allowances are also available for post-graduate study and overseas study. Aboriginal students are eligible for assistance under the Aboriginal Secondary Grants Scheme and the Aboriginal Study Grants Scheme. The States also offer various schemes of assistance, principally at the primary and secondary levels.

National bodies with a co-ordinating, planning or funding rôle include: the Australian Education Council, comprising the Federal and State Ministers of Education, the Conference of Directors-General of Education and an advisory body, the National Aboriginal Education Committee.

Total expenditure on education in Australia (public and private sectors) in 1983–84 was estimated at $A10,805m.

Austin, A. G., *Australian Education 1788–1900*. Melbourne, 1961
Australian Education Directory. Canberra, 1983
Directory of Higher Education Courses 1982. Canberra, 1982
Primary and Secondary Schooling in Australia. Canberra, 1977
Schools Commission, *Triennium 1982–84. Report for 1982*. Canberra, 1981
Tertiary Education Commission, *Report for 1982–84, Triennium Vol. 2: Recommendations for 1982*. Canberra, 1981

Social Security and Welfare. All Commonwealth Government social security pensions, benefits and allowances are financed from the Commonwealth Government's general revenue. In addition, assistance is provided for welfare services.

Expenditure on main programmes, 1984–85: Age pensions, $A5,638·9m.; invalid, $A1,469·7m.; family allowances, $A1,504·95m.; single parents, $A1,066·2m.; widows' pensions, $A889·4m.

The following summarizes the rates and conditions of the major benefits provided at June 1985.

Age and invalid pensions—age pensions are payable to men 65 years of age or more and women 60 years of age or more who have lived in Australia for a specified period and, unless permanently blind, also satisfy an income test. Persons over 16 years of age who are permanently blind or permanently incapacitated for work to the extent of at least 85% may receive an invalid pension. There is no residence qualification for an invalid pension if the permanent incapacity or blindness occurred within Australia or during temporary absence from Australia. An income test must be satisfied for an invalid pension unless permanently blind. The maximum rates are $A89.40 a week in the case of the 'standard' rate pension, and in the case of the 'married' rate pension, $A149.10 a week ($A74.55 each). Additional amounts are paid to pensioners with dependent children. Supplementary assistance of up to $A10 a week for 'standard' rate pension and $A5 for each 'married' rate person may be paid to a pensioner paying rent or private lodging subject to an income test. Remote area allowance is payable to pensioners living in income tax zone A, except for those aged 70 or more receiving the special rate of age pension. Supplementary assistance, additional pension for children, mother's/guardian's allowance and remote area allowance are not taxable.

Wife's pension—payable to the wife of an age or invalid pensioner if she is not eligible for a pension in her own right. The maximum rate and the income test are identical to those for age and invalid pensioners.

Spouse carer's pension—payable to the husband of an age or invalid pensioner who is providing constant care and attention at home for his wife if he is not eligible for pension in his own right. The maximum rate and the income test are identical to those for age and invalid pensions.

Widow's pension—widows, divorcees, certain deserted wives, women who have been the dependant of a man for 3 years immediately prior to his death and women whose husbands have been convicted of an offence and have been imprisoned for not less than 6 months may, if they satisfy a residence requirement and an income test, receive a widow's pension. Such women may be paid a pension of up to $A89.40 a week. If they have any dependent children they also receive a mother's/guardian's allowance of $A8 a week plus an additional allowance of $A12 for each child. Persons who pay private rent may also receive supplementary assistance of up to $A10 a week subject to an income test. Pensions are subject to income tax, but not mother's allowances, additional pension for children, supplementary assistance, or remote area allowance.

Supporting parents benefit—sole parents who have custody, care and control of any dependent children may, if they satisfy a residence requirement and an income test, receive supporting parents benefit. It is payable at the same rate as the widow's pension and is subject to the same income test. Mother's/guardian's allowance, additional pension for each dependent child, supplementary assistance and remote area allowance are also payable.

Sheltered employment allowance—is payable to disabled persons under age— pension age engaged in approved sheltered employment who are qualified to receive invalid pension. The rates of payment and allowances and income test are the same as invalid pension.

Rehabilitation allowance—persons undertaking a rehabilitation programme with the Commonwealth Rehabilitation Service who are eligible for a social security pension or benefit are eligible to receive a non taxable rehabilitation allowance during treatment or training and for up to 6 months thereafter. The allowance is equivalent to the invalid pension and is subject to the same income test.

Family Allowance—is paid without income test to assist families with children under 16 years or dependent full-time students aged 16 years to under 25 years. It is not subject to income tax. Monthly rates payable are: first child, $A22.80; second child, $A32.55; third child, $A39; fourth child, $A39 and $A45.55 for each subsequent child. For each child or eligible student in an approved institution, the rate is $A39 per month.

Family income supplement—payable subject to an income test to families with one or more children eligible for family allowances so long as they are not in receipt of any Commonwealth pension, benefit or allowance which provides additional payment for dependent children. The maximum rate per child is $A12 a week and this is not taxable.

Handicapped child's allowance—payable to parents or guardians of severely physically or mentally handicapped children in the family home and needing constant care and attention. The allowance is $A85 per month and is free of an income test but is subject to a residence qualification similar to that for family allowance. It may also be paid, subject to an income test, in cases where the child is handicapped but not severely, and requires marginally less care and attention.

Double orphan's pension—the guardian of a child under 16 years of age or of a full-time student under 25, both of whose parents are dead, or one of whose parents is dead and the whereabouts of the other parent unknown, and for refugee children where both parents are outside Australia, may receive double orphan's pension of $A55.70 a month per child. The payment is not subject to an income test nor is it taxable.

Unemployment and sickness benefits—are paid, subject to an income test, to persons between the ages of 16 and age pension age who are unemployed, able and willing to work and making efforts to obtain work, or temporarily unable to work because of sickness or injury. The maximum weekly rates of benefit are for unemployment benefits $A45 (single, under 18 years), $A78.60 (single 18 and over without dependents), $A89.40 (single, 18 and over with dependents), $A149.10 (married); and for sickness benefits $A45 (single, under 18), $A89.40 (single, 18 and over), $A149.10 (married). To be granted benefit a person must have resided in Australia for at least 12 months preceding his claim or intend to remain in Australia permanently. For unemployment benefit purposes unemployment must not be due to industrial action by that person or by members of a union to which that person is a member.

Service Pension is a Social-Welfare type payment paid by the Department of Veterans' Affairs, similar to the age and invalid pensions provided by the Department of Social Security. Male Veterans who have reached the age of 60 years or are permanently unemployable, and who served in a theatre of war, are eligible for service pension subject to an income test. Female Veterans who served abroad or embarked for service abroad, and who have reached the age of 55 or are permanently unemployable, are also eligible. Wives of service pensioners are also eligible provided that they do not receive a pension from the Department of Social Security.

Disability pension is a compensatory payment in respect of incapacity attributable to war service. It is paid at a rate commensurate with the degree of incapacity suffered from service-related disabilities and is free of any income test. A separate allowance may be paid to dependents.

In addition to cash benefits, welfare services are provided either directly or through State and Local government authorities and voluntary agencies, for people with special needs.

Medicare. On 1 Feb. 1984 the Commonwealth Government introduced the new universal health scheme known as Medicare. This covers: Automatic entitlement under a single public health fund to medical and optometrical benefits of 85% of the Medical Benefits Schedule fee, with a maximum patient payment for any service of $A10 where the Schedule fee is charged; access without direct charge to public hospital accommodation and to inpatient and outpatient treatment by doctors appointed by the hospital; the restoration of funds for community health to approximately the same real level as 1975; the reduction in charges for private treatment in shared wards of public hospitals to $A80 per day, and increases in the daily bed subsidy payable to private hospital to an average of $A30.

The Medicare programme is financed in part by a 1% levy on taxable incomes, with low income cut-off points. The tax rebate formerly paid for basic health insurance contributions ceased from 30 June 1983. In addition, the Commonwealth's annual contribution to the Health Benefits Reinsurance Trust Fund was reduced from $A100m. to $A20m. from 1 July 1983. Under the provisions of the National Health Act, the Commonwealth Government subsidises registered health insurance organizations by contributing to the Reinsurance Trust Fund for payments of benefits to patients with hospital treatment in excess of 35 days.

Medicare benefits are available to all persons ordinarily resident in Australia with the exception of members of foreign diplomatic missions and their dependants; visitors staying more than 6 months.

Medical Benefits. The Health Insurance Act provides for a Medical Benefits Schedule which lists medical services and the Schedule (standard) fee applicable in each State in respect of each medical service. Schedule fees are set and updated by an independent fees tribunal appointed by the Government. The fees so determined are to apply for Medicare benefits purposes.

DIPLOMATIC REPRESENTATIVES

Of Australia in Great Britain (Australia House, Strand, London, WC2B 4LA)
High Commissioner: (Vacant).

Of Great Britain in Australia (Commonwealth Ave., Canberra)
High Commissioner: A. J. Coles.

Of Australia in the USA (1601 Massachusetts Ave., NW, Washington, D.C., 20036)
Ambassador: F. Rawdon Dalrymple.

Of the USA in Australia (Moonah Pl., Canberra)
Ambassador: Laurence W. Lane, Jr.

Of Australia to the United Nations
Ambassador: Richard A. Woolcott.

Books of Reference

Statistical Information: The Australian Bureau of Statistics (Cameron Offices, Belconnen, A.C.T., 2616) was established in 1906. All the activities of the Bureau are covered by the Census and Statistics Act, which confers authority to collect information and contains secrecy provisions to ensure that individual particulars obtained are not divulged. Under the provisions of the Statistics (Arrangements with States) Act which became law on 12 May 1956, the statistical services of all the States have been integrated with the Australian Bureau. An outline of the development of statistics in Australia is published in the *Official Year Book,* No. 51, 1965. *Australian Statistician:* Dr R. J. Cameron.

The principal publications of the Bureau are:

Official Year Book of Australia. 1907 to date
Pocket Year Book Australia. 1913 to date
Monthly Summary of Statistics Australia. Oct. 1937 to date
Digest of Current Economic Statistics Australia. Aug. 1959 to date
Catalogue of Publications, 1976 to date

Other Official Publications

Atlas of Australian Resources. Dept. of Resources and Energy, Division of National Mapping
Climatological Atlas of Australia. Bureau of Meteorology. Melbourne, 1940
Norfolk Island—Annual Report. Dept. of Territories and Local Government
Cocos (Keeling) Islands—Annual Report. Dept. of Territories and Local Government
Christmas Island—Annual Report. Dept. of Territories and Local Government
Australian Books: Select List of Works About or Published in Australia. National Library of Australia, Canberra, 1934 to date
Australian National Bibliography. Canberra, 1936 to date
Historical Records of Australia. 34 vols. National Library, Canberra, 1914–25
Australia Handbook. Dept. of Administrative Services. Australian Information Services
Annual Report. Dept. of Foreign Affairs, Canberra, 1932 to date
Australian Foreign Affairs Record. Dept. of Foreign Affairs, Canberra, 1936 to date
Australian Treaty List. Dept. of Foreign Affairs, Canberra, consolidated volume from Federation to 1970 with supplements to date
Coxon, H., *Australian Official Publications.* Oxford, 1981
Documents on Australian Foreign Policy 1937–49. Vols. I–VI. Dept. of Foreign Affairs, Canberra, 1975–83
Diplomatic List. Dept. of Foreign Affairs, Canberra. 1949 to date
Consular and Trade Representatives. Dept. of Foreign Affairs, Canberra. 1936 to date

Non-Official Publications

Australian Encyclopædia. 12 vols. Sydney, 1983
Australian Quarterly: A Quarterly Review of Australian Affairs. Sydney, 1929 to date
Ball, D., and Langtry, J. O., *Civil Defence and Australia's Security in a Nuclear Age.* Sydney, 1984
Blainey, G., *The Tyranny of Distance: How Distance Shaped Australia's History.* Melbourne, 1982
Caves, P. E. and Krause, L. B., *The Australian Economy: A View from the North.* Sydney, 1984
Clark, M., *A Short History of Australia.* Melbourne, 1981
Deery, S. and Plowman, D., *Australian Industrial Relations.* Sydney, 1985
Dixson, M., *The Real Matilda: Women and Identity in Australia 1788 to the Present.* Melbourne, 1984
Gilbert, A. D., and Inglis, K. S. (eds.), *Australians: A Historical Library.* 5 vols. CUP, 1988
Howard, C., *Australia's Constitution.* Melbourne, 1985
Hurst, J., *Hawke P. M.* Sydney, 1983
Inglis, K., *This is the ABC: The Australian Broadcasting Commission.* Melbourne, 1983
Jupp, J., *Party Politics: Australia, 1966–1981.* Sydney, 1982
Kepars, I., *Australia.* [Bibliography] Oxford and Santa Barbara, 1984
Lucy, R., *The Australian Form of Government.* Melbourne, 1985
Moore, D., and Hall, R., *Australia: Image of a Nation.* London, 1983
Serle, P., *Dictionary of Australian Biography.* 2 vols. Sydney, 1949
Solomon, D., *Australia's Government and Parliament.* Melbourne, 1981
Spann, R. N., *Government Administration in Australia.* Sydney, 1979
Who's Who in Australia. Melbourne, 1906 to date
Wilson, R. K., *Australia's Resources and their Development.* Univ. of Sydney, 1980

National Library: The National Library, Canberra, A.C.T. *Director-General:* Harrison Bryan.

AUSTRALIAN TERRITORIES

AUSTRALIAN CAPITAL TERRITORY

HISTORY. The area, now the Australian Capital Territory, was first visited by white men in 1820 and settlement commenced in 1824. Until its selection as the seat of government it was a quiet pastoral and agricultural community.

AREA AND POPULATION. The area of the Australian Capital Territory is 2,432 sq. km (including Jervis Bay area). The population (estimate) at 30 June 1986 was 264,400. Previous census population:

	Males	Females	Total		Males	Females	Total
1911	992	722	1,714	1966	49,991	46,041	96,032
1921	1,567	1,005	2,572	1971	73,589	70,474	144,063
1933	4,805	4,142	8,947	1976	100,103	95,519	197,622
1947	9,092	7,813	16,905	1981	110,415	111,194	221,609
1954	16,229	14,086	30,315	1986	132,100	132,300	264,400
1961	30,858	27,970	58,828				

(Figures before 1961 exclude particulars of full-blood Aborigines.)

CONSTITUTION AND GOVERNMENT. The Constitution of Australia provided (Sec. 125) that the seat of government should be selected by parliament and that it should be within New South Wales, distance not less than 160 km from Sydney. The present area was surrendered by New South Wales and accepted by the Australian Government from 1 Jan. 1911. In 1915 an additional 73 sq. km at Jervis Bay was transferred from New South Wales to the Commonwealth. In 1911 an international competition was held for the city plan. The plan chosen was that of W. Burley Griffin, of Chicago. Construction was delayed by the First World War, and it was not until 1927 that, with the transfer of parliament and certain departments, Canberra became in fact the seat of government. Most Australian Government departments now have their headquarters in Canberra.

The general administration lies with the A.C.T. Administration, responsible to the Federal Minister for the Arts, Sport, Environment, Tourism and Territories. The Administration provides all municipal and Territorial services except police and courts (responsibility of the Federal Attorney-General).

The Australian Capital Territory Representation (House of Representatives) Act, 1973, provided for the representation of residents of the Territory by 2 elected members in the House of Representatives. The Senate (Representation of Territories) Act 1973 provided for the election of 2 Senators from the Territory. Elections took place on 1 Dec. 1984.

FINANCE. In 1987–88 the A.C.T. was given its own budget for the first time. The Territory is treated equitably with the States regarding local revenue raising, expenditure and assistance by the Commonwealth government.

PRODUCTION. Outside Canberra the Territory is mainly reserved for forestry and nature conservation (Namadgi National Park is 94,000 hectares). A considerable amount of reafforestation (mostly pine) has been undertaken, the total area of commercial plantations at 30 June 1987 being 16,060 hectares. Farming is mainly in grazing: Livestock (1986), 13,181 cattle, 119,393 sheep, over 1,000 horses. There is no secondary industry of any importance.

EDUCATION. In July 1986 there were 96 government schools comprising 67 primary schools, 24 secondary schools and colleges, 1 combined primary/secondary school and 4 special schools. Non-government schools numbered 36 of which there were 23 primary schools, 5 secondary schools and 8 schools with both primary and secondary enrolments. Students enrolled full-time in government schools in 1986 numbered 22,003 and 17,369 in primary and secondary school levels respectively. Enrolments at non-government schools comprised 10,451 primary school students and 9,317 secondary school students. Pre-school education is provided at 73 centres with a total enrolment of 4,356 (1986). The Canberra, Woden and Bruce Colleges of Technical and Further Education with a total enrolment of about 24,100 in 1986 provide trade, post-trade certificate, associate diploma, craft and leisure courses.

The Canberra School of Music, opened in 1965, had 483 students in 1986. The Canberra School of Arts had 589 students in 1986. In 1987 two amalgamations were announced: Canberra, Woden and Bruce Colleges of T.A.F.E., to form the A.C.T. Institute of T.A.F.E.; the Schools of Art and Music to form the Canberra Institute of the Arts.

The Canberra College of Advanced Education commenced operation in 1970. Enrolments (1986) 5,964. The Australian National University is situated in Canberra. Enrolments (1986) 6,349.

Books of Reference

A.C.T. Statistical Summary. Australian Bureau of Statistics. From 1960
Tomorrow's Canberra. National Capital Development Commission, 1970
Wigmore, L., *Canberra: A History of Australia's National Capital.* 2nd ed. Canberra, 1971

NORTHERN TERRITORY

HISTORY. The Northern Territory, after forming part of New South Wales, was annexed on 6 July 1863 to South Australia and in 1901 entered the Commonwealth as a corporate part of South Australia. The Commonwealth Constitution Act of 1900 made provision for the surrender to the Commonwealth of any territory by any state, and under this provision an agreement was entered into on 7 Dec. 1907 for the transfer of the Northern Territory to the Commonwealth, and it formally passed under the control of the Commonwealth Government on 1 Jan. 1911. For details of Constitutional development until 1978 *see* THE STATESMAN'S YEAR-BOOK 1980–81 pp. 123–24. The Commonwealth Government retained responsibility until Self-Government was granted on 1 July 1978.

AREA AND POPULATION. The Northern Territory is bounded by the 26th parallel of S. lat. and 129° and 138° E. long. Its total area is 1,346, 200 sq. km. The coastline is about 6,200 km in length, and the Territory includes adjacent islands between 129° and 138° E. long. The greater part of the interior consists of a tableland rising gradually from the coast to a height of about 700 metres. On this tableland there are large areas of excellent pasturage. The southern part of the Territory is generally sandy and has a small rainfall, but water may be obtained by means of sub-artesian bores.

The total population of the Territory (1986) is 154,000. The capital, seat of Government and principal port is Darwin, on the north coast; population 66,131 in June 1986. Other main centres include Katherine (5,691), 330 km south of Darwin; Alice Springs (22,759), in Central Australia; Tennant Creek (3,503), a rich mining centre 500 km north of Alice Springs; Nhulunbuy (3,515), a bauxite mining centre on the Gove Peninsula in eastern Arnhem Land; and Jabiru, a model town built to serve the rich Uranium Province in eastern Arnhem Land with a planned population of 6,000 (actual, 1986, 1,410). Palmerston is a Darwin satellite town (5,700); Yulara (estimate, 500) is a resort village serving Uluru National Park and Ayers Rock. There also are a number of large self-contained Aboriginal communities. Aboriginals were 29,087 at the 1981 Census. On 31 July 1984, 26,692,400 hectares were designated Aboriginal Land under the Aboriginal Land Rights (N.T.) Act 1976.

Vital statistics for 1983: Births, 3,127; deaths, 727; marriages, 776; divorces, 371.

CONSTITUTION AND GOVERNMENT. The Northern Territory (Self-Government) Act 1978 established the Northern Territory as a body politic as from 1 July 1978, with Ministers having control over and responsibility for Territory finances and the administration of the functions of government as specified by the Federal Government. Regulations have been made conferring executive authority for the bulk of administrative functions. At 31 Dec. 1979 the only important powers retained by the Commonwealth related to rights in respect of Aboriginal land, some significant National Parks and the mining of uranium and other substances prescribed in the Atomic Energy Act. Proposed laws passed by the Legislative Assembly require the assent of the Administrator, who may assent, with-hold assent, return them with recommended amendments or reserve them for the Governor-General's pleasure. The Governor-General may disallow any law assented to by the Administrator within 6 months of the Administrator's assent.

The Northern Territory has federal representation, electing 1 member to the House of Representatives and 2 members to the Senate.

FINANCE. Budgets since the introduction of self-government in 1978 in $A1m.:

	1980–81	1981–82	1982–83	1983–84	1984–85 [1]
Revenue	656	744	850	972·8	1,095·7
Expenditure	656	746	851	970·4	1,081·3

[1] Estimate.

The revenue available in 1984–85 comprised $A945·7m. in payments to the Northern Territory from the Commonwealth, as established by agreement at the time of self-government, together with $A150m. raised by the Northern Territory which included $A52·9m. through state-like taxes.

Expenditure during 1984–85 included $A189m. for education; $A86m. for lands and housing; $A116·2m. for health; $A71·9m. for law, order and public safety; $A38·8m. for local government and $A371·9m. for economic services.

ENERGY AND NATURAL RESOURCES

Oil and Gas. Significant oil and gas reserves have been discovered in the Amadeus Basin. In 1981 the Territory's first petroleum leases were granted at Mereenie. There are estimated recoverable reserves of 28m. bbls of oil. Estimated gas reserves at Mereenie are 23,000m. cu. metres. A pipeline has been constructed from Palm Valley to carry natural gas 150 km to Alice Springs where it is providing fuel for the local power station. Proven reserves are 1,400m. cu. metres of gas.

Minerals. The most important natural resources are minerals and the mining industry, by far the largest commercial industry in the Territory. Gross value of output, $A915m. in 1986, of which 45% was for uranium oxide.

At present there are five major mining organizations extracting bauxite, manganese, uranium, gold and copper; in addition, one firm is producing uranium oxide from stockpiled ore. Zinc, lead and silver are also mined, and rock, sand and gravel are produced as construction materials.

Gove Peninsula bauxite reserves are estimated at 250m. tonnes with an average alumina content of 50%. Alumina is exported to Europe, the USA, Africa and Asia. More than half the bauxite goes to Japan as does a large quantity of manganese ore.

Copper, gold and bismuth are mined in the Tennant Creek area. Warrego Mine has a proven copper/gold ore resource of 4·8m. tonnes and Gecko Mine has a proven ore resource of 3·3m. tonnes. Nobles Nob has been producing gold since 1938 and currently mills 8,000 tonnes of ore per month.

Agriculture. Cattle and buffalo production, valued at $A109m. in 1986, constitutes the largest farming industry in the Northern Territory. Many buffalo are exported live to Indonesia. Value of cattle and buffalo exports, 1986, about $20m.

The USA is the largest importer of Territory beef, followed by Japan, Taiwan, Saudi Arabia and Hong Kong.

There are 243 pastoral stations in the Northern Territory which produce cattle for Australian and overseas markets. They vary from small stations of 383 sq. km. to huge properties like Wave Hill Station which runs cattle over 12,380 sq. km.

General agriculture is conducted on a small scale. Fruit, vegetables, eggs, dairy produce, poultry and cereals are produced. Properties in the Katherine and Douglas-Daly districts produce the Territory's four main crops – sorghum, maize, mung beans and peanuts. Area under crops, 1986, 8,000 hectares.

Forestry. A forest development programme which commenced in 1970 has continued the multiple use management of Northern Territory forested areas; this included a softwood programme of 400 hectares per year, the introduction of additional suitable tree species in both arid and higher rainfall areas, conservation and management of native forests for production and recreational purposes, survey and assessment of resources, fire control activities and the creation of training opportunities for Aboriginals in forestry and allied saw-milling activities.

Local production of sawn timber is mainly of Cypress pine.

Fisheries. The total value (ex-vessel) of commercial fish products landed in the Northern Territory in 1986 was $A30.3m. Of this, prawns contributed $A24.98m. and barramundi $A1.8m. Mud crabs, reef fish, and shark made up most of the remainder.

INDUSTRY AND TRADE. In 1983–84 value added in the manufacturing industry, from 113 factories (with 4 or more persons employed) was $A108m. 2,402 persons were employed in these factories. In 1984, 75 trade unions had 20,300 members.

Tourism. Tourism is the second most important industry (after mining), contributing about $A300m. to the economy in 1985–86, when there were 651,000 visitors.

National Parks and Reserves. About 43,000 sq. km have been set aside as wildlife sanctuaries under the Wildlife Conservation and Control Ordinance. They are controlled by the Chief Inspector of Wildlife who is an officer of the Department of the Northern Territory. 236,000 sq. km of Aboriginal reserves are also wild-life protected areas.

The Conservation Commission of the Northern Territory administers some 53 national parks and reserves covering an area of over 5,800 sq. km. The Commission is responsible under the National Parks and Gardens Ordinance for the care, control and management of these reserves, and its functions include the preservation and protection of natural and historical features and the encouragement of public use and enjoyment of land set aside in such reserves.

COMMUNICATIONS

Roads. There are now (1986) 6,300 km of sealed road and 5,705 km of gravel and crushed stone road within the Northern Territory. They include three major interstate links: the Stuart Highway from Darwin to the South Australian border, the Barkly Highway, Tennant Creek to Mt. Isa, 444 km of which is in the Northern Territory, and the Victoria Highway, Katherine to the Western Australian border, a distance of 468 km. In addition to this there are 4,849 km of formed roads and 4,176 km of unformed roads or tracks, totalling approximately 21,029 km of roads. In 1984–85 registrations of new motor vehicles included 4,504 cars, 2,248 utilities etc., 294 trucks, 82 buses and 1,092 motor cycles.

Railways. Alice Springs is linked to the Trans-continental network by a new standard (1,435 mm) gauge railway to Tarcoola (831 km), opened in 1980. This replaced the largely narrow gauge line to Port Augusta. The standard gauge railway is to be extended to Darwin, providing Australia with its first north-south rail link.

Aviation. Ansett and Australian Airlines operate daily services between the Territory and southern states. In addition, intra-Territory services are provided by Ansett NT and smaller commuter operators. In all, 45 general charter companies operate throughout the Territory, using fixed wing aircraft, helicopters or both. Qantas currently operates three international flights out of Darwin each week and Garuda provide 2 services weekly to Bali and Jakarta. Royal Brunei provide a twice-weekly to Bali and Jakarta. Royal Brunei provide a twice-weekly service linking Darwin and Bandar Seri Begawan with connections to Hong Kong etc. Merpati Nusantara provide a twice-weekly service to Koepang.

Shipping. Regular freight shipping services connect Darwin with Western Australia, the eastern States and overseas. Passenger vessels also call at Darwin at irregular intervals.

The Port of Darwin is 997 km in extent; it is equipped to handle bulk, container and roll-on-roll-off traffic. There is a cyclone shelter for fishing vessels.

The ports of Melville Bay (Gove) and Milner Bay (Groote Eylandt) are connected with Darwin, the eastern States and overseas by regular shipping freight services.

The inland and coastal communities around the coast are provided with regular freight barge services from Darwin. Some of these communities also receive a barge freight-transhipment service out of a Brisbane vessel which calls at Melville and Milner Bays.

Radio and Television. In 1984 there were 8,658 radio-communication stations, 8 radio broadcasting stations and 5 television stations.

EDUCATION AND WELFARE

Education. There were (1986) about 35,000 pre-school, primary and secondary students enrolled in about 160 Government and non-Government schools. The proportion of migrant and Aboriginal students in the Territory is high with the latter comprising about 30% of total school enrolments. Schools range from single classrooms and transportable units catering for the needs of small Aboriginal communities and pastoral properties to urban high schools for over 1,000 pupils. Bilingual programmes operate in Aboriginal communities where traditional Aboriginal culture prevails. Secondary education extends from years 8 to 12. Technical and Further Education courses are conducted by the Darwin Institute of Technology, the NT Open College, the Alice Springs College of TAFE, Katherine Rural College, and Bachelor College which is primarily an Aboriginal teacher training institution. Advanced education courses, including a range of degree courses, are conducted by the Darwin Institute of Technology. In Jan. 1987, the University College of the Northern Territory began operation with an enrolment of over 250 students, including a number from South East Asian countries. The college awards arts and science degrees of the University of Queensland.

Health. In 1984 there were 5 hospitals with 650 beds. Community health services are provided from urban and rural Health Centres including mobile units. Remote communities are served by the Aerial Medical Service and by resident Aboriginal health workers.

Books of Reference

The Northern Territory: Annual Report. Dept. of Territories, Canberra, from 1911. Dept. of the Interior, Canberra, from 1966–67. Dept. of Northern Territory, from 1972
Australian Territories, Dept. of Territories, Canberra, 1960 to 1973. Dept. of Special Minister of State, Canberra, 1973–75. Department of Administrative Services, 1976
Northern Territory Statistical Summary. Australian Bureau of Statistics, Canberra, from 1960
Donovan, P. F., *A Land Full of Possibilities: A History of South Australia's Northern Territory 1863–1911.* 1981.—*At the Other End of Australia: The Commonwealth and the Northern Territory 1911–1978.* Univ. of Queensland Press, 1984
Heatley, A., *The Government of the Northern Territory.* Univ. of Queensland Press, 1979
Mills, C. M., *A Bibliography of the Northern Territory.* Canberra, 1977
Powell, A., *Far Country: A Short History of the Northern Territory.* Melbourne Univ. Press, 1982

AUSTRALIAN EXTERNAL TERRITORIES

AUSTRALIAN ANTARCTIC TERRITORY. An Imperial Order in Council of 7 Feb. 1933 placed under Australian authority all the islands and territories other than Adélie Land situated south of 60° S. lat. and lying between 160° E. long. and 45° E. long. The Order came into force with a Proclamation issued by the Governor-General on 24 Aug. 1936 after the passage of the Australian Antarctic Territory Acceptance Act 1933. The boundaries of Adélie Land were definitively fixed by a French Decree of 1 April 1938 as the islands and territories south of 60° S. lat. lying between 136° E. long. and 142° E. long. The Australian Antarctic Territory Act 1954 declared that the laws in force in the Australian Capital Territory are, so far as they are applicable and are not inconsistent with any ordinance made under the Act, in force in the Australian Antarctic Territory.

In 1968 responsibility for the administration of this Act was transferred from the Minister for External Affairs to the Minister for Supply; in 1972 responsibility was transferred to the Minister for Science.

On 13 Feb. 1954 the Australian National Antarctic Research Expeditions (ANARE) established a station on MacRobertson Land at lat. 67° 37′ S. and long. 62° 52′ E. The station was named Mawson in honour of the late Sir Douglas Mawson. Meteorological and other scientific research is conducted at Mawson, which is the centre for coastal and inland survey expeditions.

A second Australian scientific research station was established on the coast of Princess Elizabeth Land on 13 Jan. 1957 at lat. 68° 34′ S. and long. 77° 58′ E. The station was named Davis in honour of Capt. John King Davis, Mawson's second-in-command on 2 expeditions. The station was temporarily closed down in Jan. 1965 and re-opened in Feb. 1969.

In Feb. 1959 the Australian Government accepted from the US Government custody of Wilkes Station, which was established by the US on 16 Jan. 1957 on the Budd Coast of Wilkes Land, at lat. 66° 15′ S. and long. 110° 32′ E. The station was named in honour of Lieut. Charles Wilkes, who commanded the 1838–40 US expedition to the area, and was closed in Feb. 1969. Operations were then transferred to the new station, Casey. Construction commenced on Casey station in Jan. 1965 and was continued, mainly during summer visits, until Feb. 1969, when it was opened. The station, specially designed to withstand blizzard winds and prevent inundation by snow, is situated 2·4 km south of Wilkes at lat. 66° 17′ S. and long. 110° 32′ E. The Antarctic Division has also operated a station, since March 1948, at Macquarie Island, about 1,370 km south-east of Hobart. Macquarie Island is a dependency of the State of Tasmania.

On 1 Dec. 1959 Australia signed the Antarctic Treaty with Argentina, Belgium, Chile, France, Japan, New Zealand, Norway, South Africa, the USSR, the UK and the USA. Poland, Czechoslovakia, German Democratic Republic, Netherlands, Romania, Brazil, Denmark, Bulgaria, Federal Republic of Germany, Italy, India, People's Republic of China, Spain, Papua New Guinea, Peru, Hungary and Uruguay have subsequently acceded to the Treaty. Poland became a full member of the Antarctic Treaty in 1977 and the Federal Republic of Germany in 1981 and India and Brazil in 1983. The Treaty reserves the Antarctic area south of 60° S. lat. for peaceful purposes, provides for international co-operation in scientific investigation and research, and preserves, for the duration of the Treaty, the *status quo* with regard to territorial sovereignty, rights and claims. The Treaty entered into force on 23 June 1961.

COCOS (KEELING) ISLANDS. The Cocos (Keeling) Islands are 2 separate atolls comprising some 27 small coral islands with a total area of about 14·2 sq. km, and are situated in the Indian Ocean at 12° 05′ S. lat. and 96° 53′ E. long. They lie 2,768 km north-west of Perth and 3,685 km west of Darwin, while Colombo is 2,255 km to the north-west of the group.

The main islands in this Australian Territory are West Island (the largest, about 10 km from north to south) on which is an airport and an animal quarantine station, and most of the European community; Home Island, occupied by the Cocos Malay community; Direction, South and Horsburgh Islands, and North Keeling Island, 24 km to the north of the group.

Although the islands were discovered in 1609 by Capt. William Keeling of the East India Company, they remained uninhabited until 1826, when the first settlement was established on the main atoll by an Englishman, Alexander Hare, with a group of followers, predominantly of Malay origin. Hare left the islands in 1831, by which time a second settlement had been formed on the main atoll by John Clunies-Ross, a Scottish seaman and adventurer, who began commercial development of the islands' coconut palms.

In 1857 the islands were annexed to the Crown; in 1878 responsibility was transferred from the Colonial Office to the Government of Ceylon, and in 1886 to the Government of the Straits Settlement. By indenture in 1886 Queen Victoria granted all land in the islands to George Clunies-Ross and his heirs in perpetuity (with certain rights reserved to the Crown). In 1903 the islands were incorporated in the Settlement of Singapore and in 1942–46 temporarily placed under the Governor of Ceylon. In 1946 a Resident Administrator, responsible to the Governor of Singapore, was appointed.

On 23 Nov. 1955 the Cocos Islands were placed under the authority of the Australian Government as the Territory of Cocos (Keeling) Islands. An Administrator, appointed by the Governor-General, is the Government's representative in the Territory and is responsible to the Minister for Territories and Local Government. The Cocos (Keeling) Islands Council, established as the elected body of the Cocos Malay community in July 1979, advises the Administrator on all issues affecting the Territory.

In 1978 the Australian Government purchased the Clunies-Ross family's entire interests in the islands, except for the family residence. A Cocos Malay co-operative has been established to take over the running of the Clunies-Ross copra plantation (118 tonnes of copra were exported in 1985–86) and to engage in other business with the Commonwealth in the Territory, including construction projects.

The population of the Territory at 30 June 1986 was 616, distributed between Home Island (414) and West Island (202).

The islands are low-lying, flat and thickly covered by coconut palms, and surround a lagoon in which ships drawing up to 7 metres may be anchored, but which is extremely difficult for navigation.

An equable and pleasant climate, affected for much of the year by the south-east trade winds. Temperatures range over the year from 68° F (20° C) to 88° F (31·1° C) and rainfall averages 80″ (2,000 mm) a year.

The Cocos (Keeling) Islands Act 1955 is the basis of the Territory's administrative, legislative and judicial systems. Under section 8 of this Act, those laws which were in force in the Territory immediately before the transfer continued in force there.

The *Singapore Ordinances Application Ordinance* 1979 repealed all those contained Ordinances and re-applied the provisions of 95 Ordinances of Singapore. These Ordinances can be amended, repealed or substituted by Ordinances made by the Governor-General.

Administrator: C. M. Stuart.

CHRISTMAS ISLAND is an isolated peak in the Indian Ocean, lat. 10° 25′ 22″ S., long. 105° 39′ 59″ E. It lies 360 km S., 8° E. of Java Head, and 417 km N. 79° E. from Cocos Islands, 1,310 km from Singapore and 2,623 km from Fremantle. Area about 135 sq. km. The climate is tropical with temperatures varying little over the year at 27° C. The wet season lasts from Nov. to April with an annual total of about 2,673 mm. The island was formally annexed by the UK on 6 June 1888, placed under the administration of the Governor of the Straits Settlements in 1889, and incorporated with the Settlement of Singapore in 1900. Sovereignty was transferred to the Australian Government on 1 Oct. 1958. The population (estimate, 1986), 2,000 (Chinese, Malays, and Europeans; there is no indigenous population).

The legislative, judicial and administrative systems are regulated by the Christmas Island Act, 1958–73. They are the responsibility of the Commonwealth Government and operated by an Administrator. The laws of Singapore which were in force before the transfer have been continued but can be amended, repealed or substituted by ordinances made by the Governor-General. The first Island Assembly was elected in Sept. 1985.

Extraction and export of rock phosphate dust was the island's only industry until 1987. In Dec. 1948 Australia and New Zealand bought the lease rights of the Christmas Island Phosphate Co. and set up the Christmas Island Phosphate Commission (CIPC), which conducted the mining operation until mid-1981. The Phosphate Mining Co. of Christmas Island Ltd (PMCI) acted as managing agents for the CIPC until the Commission was wound up and then mined in its own right. The Commonwealth Government appointed liquidators on 11 Nov. 1987, with a view to ending all mining.

The Commonwealth Government also announced a programme of retraining and redevelopment ($A2·5m.).

There is direct radio communication with Australia and Singapore. Regular air charter flights commenced in 1974 to South-east Asia.

In 1987 there were about 437 primary and secondary pupils at the Christmas Island Area School. From April 1986 PMCI provided English-language and trade-skills courses for employees; the company also provided medical care. In 1984 the Christmas Island Services Corporation was formed, to be the future provider of local services, under the Assembly's direction.

Administrator: T. F. Paterson.

NORFOLK ISLAND. 29° 02′ S. lat. 167° 57′ E. long., area 3,455 hectares, population, (June 1986), 1,977. The island was formerly part of the colony of New South Wales and then of Van Diemen's Land. It was a penal colony 1788–1814 and 1825–55. In 1856 it received all 194 descendants of the *Bounty* mutineers from Pitcairn Island. It has been a distinct settlement since 1856, under the jurisdiction of the state of New South Wales; and finally by the passage of the Norfolk Island Act 1913, it was accepted as a Territory of the Australian Government. The Norfolk Island Act 1957 is the basis of the Territory's legislative, administrative and judicial systems. An Administrator, appointed by the Governor-General and responsible to the Minister for Territories and Local Government, is the senior government representative in the Territory.

The Norfolk Island Act 1979 equips Norfolk Island with responsible legislative and executive government to enable it to run its own affairs to the greatest practicable extent. Wide powers are exercised by the Norfolk Island Legislative Assembly and by an Executive Council, comprising the executive members of the Legislative Assembly who have ministerial-type responsibilities. The Act preserves the Commonwealth's responsibility for Norfolk Island as a Territory under its authority, indicating Parliament's intention that consideration would be given to an extension of the powers of the Legislative Assembly and the political and administrative institutions of Norfolk Island within 5 years. Some powers were transferred in 1985 and further transfers are being considered.

The island's Supreme Court sits as required and a Court of Petty Sessions exercises both civil and criminal jurisdiction.

The Territory Administration is financed from local revenue which for 1985–86 totalled $A5,140,000; expenditure, $A5,388,000.

Public revenue is derived mainly from tourism, the sale of postage stamps, customs duties, liquor sales and company registration and licence fees. Residents are not liable for income tax on earnings within the Territory, nor are death and personal stamp duties levied.

An estimated 29,000 visitors travelled to Norfolk during 1985–86. Descendants of the *Bounty* mutineer families constitute the 'original' settlers and are known locally as 'Islanders', while later settlers, mostly from Australia, New Zealand and UK, are identified as 'mainlanders'. Over the years the Islanders have preserved their own lifestyle and customs, and their language remains a mixture of West Country English, Gaelic and Tahitian.

The Administration subsidises a public hospital and dispensary, and health services, together with free dental services for children, are provided by qualified government officers.

Norfolk Island's public school is staffed by the New South Wales Department of Education and follows the State's education system. A bursary scheme is available to help students continue education on the mainland or in New Zealand.

The island has a local automatic telephone exchange and an international telephone connection by way of the ANZCAN submarine cable system. A local radio broadcasting service is operated by the Norfolk Island Administration and the Island also has access to ABC-TV and ABC-FM radio programs transmitted from the mainland *via* satellite. Regular air and sea services operate to the island.

Administrator: Commodore J. A. Matthew, CVO, MBE.

HEARD AND McDONALD ISLANDS. These islands, about 2,500 miles south-west of Fremantle, were transferred from UK to Australian control as from 26 Dec. 1947. Heard Island is about 43 km long and 21 km wide; Shag Island is about 8 km north of Heard. The total area is 412 sq. km (159 sq. miles). The McDonald Islands are 42 km to the west of Heard.

TERRITORY OF ASHMORE AND CARTIER ISLANDS. By Imperial Order in Council of 23 July 1931, Ashmore Islands (known as Middle, East and West Islands) and Cartier Island, situated in the Indian Ocean, some 320 km off the north-west coast of Australia (area, 5 sq. km), were placed under the authority of the Commonwealth.

Under the Ashmore and Cartier Islands Acceptance Act, 1933, the islands were accepted by the Commonwealth under the name of the Territory of Ashmore and Cartier Islands, and the effective date was proclaimed by the Governor-General to be 10 May 1934. It was the intention that the Territory should be administered by the State of Western Australia, but owing to administrative difficulties the Territory was annexed to and deemed to form part of the Northern Territory of Australia (by amendment to the Act in 1938) with relevant laws of the Northern Territory, applying to the Territory of Ashmore and Cartier Islands. Responsibility for the administration of Ashmore and Cartier Islands rests with the Minister for the Arts, Sport, the Environment, Tourism and Territories.

On 16 Aug. 1983 a national nature reserve was declared over Ashmore Reef and the area so declared is now known as Ashmore Reef National Nature Reserve.

The islands are uninhabited but Indonesian fishing boats, which have traditionally plied the area, fish within the Territory and land to collect water in accordance with an agreement between the governments of Australia and Indonesia.

Periodic visits are made to the islands by ships of the Royal Australian Navy, and aircraft of the Royal Australian Air Force make aerial surveys of the islands and neighbouring waters.

TERRITORY OF CORAL SEA ISLANDS. The Coral Sea Islands became a Territory of the Commonwealth of Australia under the Coral Sea Islands Act 1969. It comprises scattered reefs and islands over a sea area of about 1m. sq. km. The Territory is uninhabited apart from a manned meteorological station on Willis Island.

NEW SOUTH WALES

HISTORY. New South Wales became a British possession in 1770; the first settlement was established at Port Jackson in 1788; a partially elective Council was established in 1843, and responsible government in 1856. New South Wales federated with the other Australian states to form the Commonwealth of Australia in 1901.

AREA AND POPULATION. New South Wales is situated between the 28th and 38th parallels of S. lat. and 141st and 154th meridians of E. long., and comprises 309,433 sq. miles (801,428 sq. km), inclusive of Lord Howe Island, 6 sq. miles (17 sq. km), but exclusive of the Australian Capital Territory (911 sq. miles, 2,359 sq. km) and 28 sq. miles (73 sq. km) at Jervis Bay.

Lord Howe Island, 31° 33′ 4″ S., 159° 4′ 26″ E., which is part of New South Wales, is situated about 702 km north-east of Sydney; area, 1,654 hectares, of which only about 120 hectares are arable; resident population, estimate (30 June 1986), 300. The Island, which was discovered in 1788, is of volcanic origin. Mount Gower, the highest point, reaches a height of 866 metres.

The Lord Howe Island Board manages the affairs of the Island and supervises the Kentia palm-seed industry.

Census population of New South Wales (including full-blood Aboriginals from 1966):

	Males	Females	Persons	Population per sq. km	Average annual increase % since previous census
1901	710,264	645,091	1,355,355	2	1·86
1911	857,698	789,036	1,646,734	2	1·97
1921	1,071,501	1,028,870	2,100,371	3	2·46
1933	1,318,471	1,282,376	2,600,847	3	1·76
1947	1,492,211	1,492,627	2,984,838	4	0·99
1954	1,720,860	1,702,669	3,423,529	4	1·98
1961	1,972,909	1,944,104	3,917,013	5	1·94
1966	2,126,652	2,111,249	4,237,901	5	1·58
1971	2,307,210	2,293,970	4,601,180	6	1·66
1976	2,380,172	2,396,931	4,777,103	6	0·75
1981	2,548,984	2,577,233	5,126,217	6	1·42
1986	2,684,570	2,717,311	5,401,881	7	1·05

At 30 June 1985 the resident population (estimate) of New South Wales was 5,474,300 (1984, 5,412,000). Sydney (Statistical Division), 3,430,550 (3,392,700); Newcastle (Statistical Subdivision), 429,250 (424,650); Wollongong (Statistical Subdivision), 237,600 (236,850). Population of principal country municipalities: Albury, 40,400 (39,800); Armidale, 20,000 (19,800); Bathurst, 26,250 (25,700); Broken Hill, 26,650 (26,950); Casino, 10,650 (10,600); Dubbo, 31,850 (31,200); Goulburn, 22,800 (22,650); Grafton, 17,500 (17,450); Hastings, 43,500 (41,900); Lake Macquarie, 165,300 (162,800); Lismore, 38,750 (37,950); Greater Lithgow, 21,750 (21,450); Orange, 32,800 (32,450); Queanbeyan, 22,550 (21,650); Shellharbour, 47,350 (46,700); Shoalhaven, 61,700 (59,100); Tamworth, 33,900 (33,650); Greater Taree, 36,850 (35,950); Wagga Wagga, 50,900 (50,100).

Vital statistics for calendar years:

	Live births	Marriages	Divorces	Deaths (excluding still-births)	Infantile mortality per 1,000 live births
1984	77,994	33,938	13,203	39,302	9·2
1985	87,786	41,183	11,871	44,264	9·8
1986	84,531	41,319	11,661	42,167	9·0

The annual rates per 1,000 of mean resident population (estimate) in 1986 were: Births, 15·2; deaths, 7·6; marriages, 6·7.

CONSTITUTION AND GOVERNMENT. Within the State there are three levels of government: the Commonwealth Government, with authority derived from a written constitution; the State Government with residual powers; the local government authorities with powers based upon a State Act of Parliament, operating within incorporated areas extending over almost 90% of the State.

The Constitution of New South Wales is drawn from several diverse sources; certain Imperial statutes such as the Commonwealth of Australia Constitution Act (1900); the Australian States Constitution Act (1907); an element of inherited English law; amendments to the Commonwealth of Australia Constitution Act; the (State) Constitution Act; the Australia Acts of 1986; the Constitution (Amendment) Act 1987 and certain other State Statutes; numerous legal decisions; and a large amount of English and local convention.

The Parliament of New South Wales may legislate for the peace, welfare and good government of the State in all matters not specifically reserved to the Commonwealth Government.

The State Legislature consists of the Sovereign, represented by the Governor, and two Houses of Parliament, the Legislative Council (upper house) and the Legislative Assembly (lower house).

Australian citizens aged 18 and over, and other British subjects who were enrolled prior to 25 Jan. 1984, men and women aged 18 years and over, are entitled to the franchise. Voting is compulsory. The optional preferential method of voting is used for both houses.

The Legislative Council has 45 members elected for a term of office equivalent to three terms of the Legislative Assembly, with 15 members retiring at the same time as the Legislative Assembly elections. The whole State constitutes a single electoral district. In Sept. 1987, the Council consisted of the following parties: Labor, 24; Liberal, 11; National Party, 6; Australian Democrats, 1; Independents, 3.

The President of the Legislative Council has an annual salary (1987) of $A71,200; the Leader of the Opposition members, the Chairman of Committees and the Deputy Leader of the Government members (if not a Minister), $A53,074 each; the Deputy Leader of the Opposition members and Government and Opposition Whips, $A48,839 each. The President is paid an annual expense allowance of $A11,908; the Leader of the Opposition members, the Chairman of Committees, the Deputy Leader of the Government members (if not a Minister) and the Deputy Leader of the Opposition members (when a leader of a party), $A6,545 each; the Deputy Leader of the Opposition members (when not a leader of a party) and Government and Opposition Whips, $A2,625 each. Other members who are not Ministers receive an annual salary of $A43,620. All members receive an annual electoral allowance of $A15,343. Special expenses allowances ($A6,454, $A8,042 or $A9,706) are paid to members who are not Ministers and reside in outlying electorates.

The Legislative Assembly has 99 members elected in single seat electoral districts for a maximum period of 4 years. The Legislative Assembly, elected on 24 March 1984, consisted in Sept. 1987 of the following parties: Labor, 55; Liberal, 23; National Party, 16; Independents, 4; Illeway Workers Party, 1.

The Speaker of the Legislative Assembly and the Leader of the Opposition members receive a salary of (1987) $A71,200 each; the Chairman of Committees, Deputy Leader of the Opposition members and Leader of the National Party, $A53,074 each; Government and Opposition Whips, $A49,878 each. The Speaker and the Leader of the Opposition members also receive an expense allowance of $A11,908 each; the Chairman of Committees, Deputy Leader of the Opposition members and Leader of the National Party, $A6,545 each; Government and Opposition Whips, and Deputy Leader of the National Party, $A3,090 each. Members who are not Ministers receive an annual salary of $A43,620. All members receive an annual electoral allowance ranging from $A15,343 to $A27,221 according to the location of their constituencies. Special expenses allowances ($A6,454, $A8,042 or $A9,706) are paid to members who are not Ministers and represent outlying electorates.

Executive power is vested in the Governor, who is appointed by the Crown, and an Executive Council consisting of members of the Cabinet. Ministers receive the following annual salaries (1987): Premier, $A89,088; Deputy Premier, $A80,257; the Leader of the Government members in the Legislative Council, $A81,155; Deputy Leader of Government members in the Legislative Council, $A77,325; other Ministers, $A75,808. Ministers also receive an expense allowance (Premier, $A25,488; Deputy Premier, $A12,743; other Ministers, $A11,908 each). Ministers also receive an electoral allowance ranging from $A15,343 to $A27,221 to members of the Legislative Assembly, according to the location of their electorate; and $A15,343 to each member of the Legislative Council. A special expenses allowance of $A9,706 is paid to Ministers who represent or reside in outlying electorates.

Governor: Air Marshal Sir James Anthony Rowland, AC, KBE, DFC, AFC (sworn in 20 Jan. 1981).

The Labor Party Cabinet, in June 1987, was as follows:

Premier, Minister for State Development and Minister for Ethnic Affairs: The Hon. B. J. Unsworth, MP.

Deputy Premier and Minister for Transport: The Hon. R. J. Mulock, LLB, MP. *Minister for Housing and Minister for the Arts:* The Hon. F. J. Walker, QC, MP. *Minister for Public Works and Ports and Minister for Roads:* The Hon. L. J. Brereton, MP. *Minister for Industrial Relations and Minister for Employment:* The

Hon. P. D. Hills, MP. *Minister for Health and Minister for the Drug Offensive:* The Hon. P. T. Anderson, MP. *Treasurer:* The Hon. K. G. Booth, MP. *Attorney-General and Minister Assisting the Premier:* The Hon. T. W. Sheahan, BA, LLB, MP. *Minister for Industry and Small Business and Minister for Energy and Technology:* The Hon. P. F. Cox, MP. *Minister for Agriculture, Minister for Lands, Minister for Forests and Vice-President of the Executive Council:* The Hon. J. R. Hallam, MLC. *Minister for Education:* The Hon. R. M. Cavalier, MP. *Minister for Sport and Recreation, Minister for Racing and Minister for Tourism:* The Hon. M. A. Cleary, MP. *Minister for Police and Emergency Services:* The Hon. G. Paciullo, MP. *Minister for Local Government and Minister for Water Resources:* The Hon. J. A. Crosio, MP. *Minister for Finance, Minister for Co-operative Societies and Assistant Minister for Education:* The Hon. R. J. Debus, BA, LLB, MP. *Minister for Corrective Services and Assistant Minister for Transport:* The Hon. J. E. Akister, MP. *Minister for Planning and Environment and Minister for Heritage:* The Hon. R. J. Carr, MP. *Minister for Youth and Community Services and Assistant Minister for Ethnic Affairs:* The Hon. J. J. Aquilina, MP. *Minister for Mineral Resources and Minister for Aboriginal Affairs:* The Hon. K. G. Gabb, LLB, MP. *Minister for Consumer Affairs and Assistant Minister for Health:* The Hon. D. M. Grusovin, MLC.

Agent-General in London: The Hon. K. J. Stewart (66 Strand, WC2N 5LZ).

Local Government. A system of local government extends over most of the State, including the whole of the Eastern and Central land divisions and almost three-quarters of the sparsely populated Western division. At 1 Sept. 1987 there were 64 municipalities, and 111 corporate bodies called shires. A number of the municipalities and shires have combined to form 42 county councils, which administer electricity or water supply undertakings or render other services of common benefit.

ECONOMY

Budget. State Consolidated Fund: statement of receipts and expenditure (in $A1m.) for financial years ending 30 June:

	1983–84	1984–85	1985–86	1986–87
Receipts: Recurrent	6,812	7,348	8,220	10,664
Capital	595	654	659	1,517
Total Receipts	7,407	8,002	8,879	12,181
Expenditure: Recurrent	6,955	7,511	8,305	10,461
Capital	486	491	573	1,540
Total Expenditure	7,441	8,002	8,879	12,181
Surplus/deficit	– 34	—	—	—

State Government receipts (in $A1m.) for 1986–87 included receipts from loan raisings, 250; Commonwealth general revenue grant, 3,977; and state taxation, 4,481. Expenditure included capital works and services, 1,540; education, 2,484; health, 2,667; and public debt charges, 736.

Public Debt. In terms of the financial agreement between the Commonwealth and State Governments, the Commonwealth Government has assumed responsibility for debts of the Australian States, and contributes towards the interest thereon and sinking funds established for redemption of the debts. Loans for the States are raised by the Commonwealth Government in accordance with decisions of the Australian Loan Council.

The public debt in terms of the financial agreement of New South Wales at 30 June 1987 was $A6,043m. Interest liability for this debt in 1986–87 amounted to $A694m. Contributions to the sinking fund for New South Wales debt, $A68m., includes $A17m. contributed by the Commonwealth Government. The net cost of securities redeemed in the year was $A71m. Statutory authorities also raise finance in their own right.

Banking. There were 28 trading banks operating in New South Wales at 30 June

1987, including the Commonwealth Bank of Australia and the State Bank of New South Wales (Government banks). The trading bank business is transacted chiefly by the Commonwealth Bank of Australia, the State Bank of New South Wales and 3 private banks. Seventeen of the 24 private banks operating in New South Wales have their head offices in Sydney, with the remaining 7 banks having their head offices in other States of Australia. At 30 June 1987 the 28 banks operated 1,872 branches and 398 agencies in New South Wales.

The weekly average amount of deposits held in New South Wales by the 28 banks was $A24,003·1m. in June 1987, consisting of $A18,396·9m. bearing interest and $A5,606·3m. not bearing interest. Bank advances, overdrafts, bills discounted, etc., amounted to $A26,615·5m. A statement of other assets and liabilities of the banks in New South Wales is of little significance, as banking business is conducted on an Australia-wide basis.

Savings bank deposits at the end of June 1987 amounted to $A17,362·6m., representing $A3,111 per head of population.

ENERGY AND NATURAL RESOURCES

Minerals. New South Wales contains extensive mineral deposits. The most important minerals mined are: Coal (which accounts for 76% of the value of the State's mineral production); silver–lead–zinc (9%); construction materials (sand, gravel, stone, etc., 10%); and mineral sands (rutile, zircon, etc., 1%). At 30 June 1986, there were 516 mining establishments with an average employment of 26,649. During 1985–86, wages and salaries paid were $A894m., and value added was $A2,155m. Mine production of coal and metallic minerals (gross content) is shown below:

	1982–83	1983–84	1984–85	1985–86
Antimony (tonnes)	769	718	1,409	1,264
Cadmium (tonnes)	1,424	1,339	1,735	1,216
Coal (1,000 tonnes)	66,297	66,823	70,034	77,186
Cobalt (tonnes)	92	60	66	55
Copper (tonnes)	26,878	25,541	23,038	26,733
Gold (kg)	606	966	1,464	1,015
Lead (tonnes)	237,437	213,154	251,595	233,270
Silver (kg)	322,390	304,314	355,827	367,751
Sulphur (tonnes)	298,850	220,203	248,681	253,800
Tin (tonnes)	1,576	1,388	1,306	1,280
Titanium dioxide (tonnes)	47,612	41,392	41,283	47,240
Zinc (tonnes)	374,783	330,940	385,075	355,443
Zircon (tonnes)	55,588	59,181	47,113	53,607

The value of output in mining and quarrying in 1985–86 was $A3,031m.

Land settlement. The total area of land alienated from the Crown at 30 June 1987 was 310,337 sq. km; land resumed or reverted to the Crown during 1986–87 was 140 sq. km. During 1986–87, 4,152 sq. km were alienated.

Agriculture. The area under cultivation in New South Wales during 3 years (ended 31 March) and the principal crops (in tonnes) produced were as follows:

	1984	1985	1986
Area of crops (hectares)	6,942,321	5,963,038	5,989,601
Value (farm) of all crops	$A2,176m.	$A1,851m.	$A1,786m.

	1984		1985		1986	
Principal crops	Hectares	Production	Hectares	Production	Hectares	Production
Wheat { Grain	3,999,275	8,960,784	3,602,630	5,804,702	3,662,593	5,915,526
Wheat { Hay	22,462	84,290	13,440	39,008	15,708	48,566
Barley { Grain	554,154	941,131	604,815	914,974	546,224	821,394
Barley { Hay	2,001	6,044	1,535	2,631	1,451	3,381
Oats { Grain	812,578	1,120,377	311,687	401,787	429,070	538,324
Oats { Hay	60,734	212,570	21,591	56,500	27,317	76,767
Grain Sorghum	177,414	489,480	205,896	318,587	160,076	299,266
Potatoes	6,807	129,564	6,601	109,258	5,901	108,568
Lucerne (hay)	79,579	413,083	64,691	310,726	68,933	336,230
Rice	114,627	610,551	117,780	845,119	102,994	702,073
Cotton	104,523	292,444	131,237	534,039	135,820	541,751
Oilseeds	123,606	98,578	201,731	184,964	207,109	208,079

In 1985–86, 15,341 hectares of sugar-cane were cut for crushing, the production being 1,398,183 tonnes. The total area under grapes was 13,161 (including 841 not bearing) hectares; the production of table grapes was 7,750 tonnes; of wine, 137,812 tonnes; of dried vine fruits, 12,169 tonnes.

In 1985–86, 5,164 hectares of banana plantations; production from 4,567 hectares, 60,867 tonnes; there were 30,884 hectares of orchard fruit.

At 31 March 1986 the State had 58m. sheep and lambs, 5,409,264 cattle and 797,911 pigs. The production of shorn and crutched wool in 1985–86 was 258·8m. kg (greasy). In the year ended 30 June 1987 production of butter was 829 tonnes; cheese, 13,363 tonnes, and bacon and ham, 26,062 tonnes.

Forestry. The estimated area of Crown and private lands is 15m. hectares. The total area of State forests amounts to 3·3m. hectares, and 223,000 hectares have been set apart as timber reserves.

In 1985–86, 3,505,000 cu. metres of timber (excluding firewood) were produced, including 1,275,000 cu. metres of forest hardwoood and 1,284,000 cu. metres of pulpwoods.

INDUSTRY AND TRADE

Industry. Approximately 20% of employed persons in New South Wales are employed in manufacturing industries.

A very wide range of manufacturing activities is undertaken in the Sydney area, and there are large iron and steel works and associated metal fabrication works in operation in proximity to the coalfields at Newcastle and Port Kembla.

The following table shows a summary of manufacturing industries' statistics for 1984–85:

Industry	Establishments[1] No.	Employment[2] Males (No.)	Females (No.)	Wages and salaries[3] ($A1m.)	Value added ($A1m.)
Food, beverages and tobacco	972	35,796	15,971	997·7	2,175·1
Textiles	210	5,495	3,959	176·5	328·6
Clothing and footwear	790	4,617	16,847	279·6	476·7
Wood, wood products and furniture	1,365	19,517	3,758	365·8	718·5
Paper, paper products, printing and publishing	1,251	24,258	11,752	722·5	1,514·1
Chemical, petroleum and coal products	400	17,651	8,224	602·8	1,629·6
Non-metallic mineral products	556	11,623	1,480	274·7	603·9
Basic metal products	194	36,790	2,900	908·6	1,856·5
Fabricated metal products	1,661	28,990	6,574	628·4	1,118·9
Transport equipment	421	29,591	2,837	640·0	1,022·4
Other machinery and equipment	1,553	40,264	14,492	1,014·3	1,900·0
Miscellaneous manufacturing	843	14,329	7,090	375·4	715·5
Total manufacturing	10,218	268,921	95,884	6,998·3	14,059·8

[1] Operating at 30 June 1985. Excludes single-establishment manufacturing enterprises with less than 4 persons employed.
[2] Persons employed—average over whole year, including working proprietors.
[3] Excludes drawings of working proprietors.

Some of the principal articles manufactured in 1986–87 were:

Article	Quantity	Article	Quantity
Flour (1,000 tonnes)	548	Ready mixed concrete (1,000 cu. metres)	4,492
Woven fabric (1,000 sq. metres)	84,769	Clay bricks (1m.)[1]	699
Raw steel (1,000 tonnes)	5,080	Electricity (1m. kwh.)[1]	47,960

[1] Includes the Australian Capital Territory.

During 1985–86 the value of all building jobs commenced in New South Wales was $A5,410m. (of which jobs valued at $A1,191m. were being built for government ownership), jobs completed were valued at $A4,723m. ($A841m. for government ownership), and jobs under construction at the end of the period were valued at $A4,928m. ($A1,807m. for government ownership).

Labour. Two systems of industrial arbitration and conciliation for the adjustment of industrial relations between employers and employees are in operation—the

State system which operates within the territorial limits of the State, and the Commonwealth system, which applies to industrial disputes extending beyond State borders.

The industrial tribunals are authorized to fix minimum rates of wages and other conditions of employment. Their awards may be enforced by law, as may be industrial agreements between employers and organizations of employees, when registered.

The principal State tribunal is the Industrial Commission of New South Wales. The Commission is empowered to exercise all the arbitration and conciliation powers conferred on subsidiary tribunals, and has in addition authority to determine any widely defined 'industrial matter', to adjudicate in case of illegal strikes and lockouts, etc., to investigate union ballots when irregularities are alleged and to hear appeals from subsidiary tribunals. Subsidiary tribunals are Conciliation Committees for various industries, each having an equal number representing employers and employees and a Conciliation Commissioner as chairman.

The chief industrial tribunals of the Commonwealth are the Industrial Division of the Federal Court of Australia, composed of judges, and the Australian Conciliation and Arbitration Commission, composed of presidential members, and commissioners.

Most State awards and agreements prescribe a basic wage. However, since 1974, the State Industrial Commission has also specified a minimum wage in line with Commonwealth awards. For May 1987, average weekly earnings were $A500·90 for full-time adult males and $A396·80 for full-time adult females.

The standard working week is still regarded as 40 hours for employees under both Commonwealth and State awards. However, some awards prescribe less than 40 hours per week and, since early 1981, a campaign by trade unions has resulted in the extension of shorter working hours to more industries. Overtime is permitted under prescribed conditions.

Trade Unions. Registration of trade unions is effected under the New South Wales Trade Union Act 1881, which follows substantially the Trade Union Acts of 1871 and 1876 of England. Registration confers a quasi-corporate existence with power to hold property, to sue and be sued, etc., and the various classes of employees covered by the union are required to be prescribed by the constitution of the union. For the purpose of bringing an industry under the review of the State industrial tribunals, or participating in proceedings relating to disputes before Commonwealth tribunals, employees and employers must be registered as industrial unions, under State or Commonwealth industrial legislation respectively. At 30 June 1986, there were 182 trade unions with a total membership of 1,148,200. Approximately 58% (estimate) of wage and salary earners were members of trade unions.

Commerce. The external commerce of New South Wales, exclusive of interstate trade, is included in the statement of the commerce of Australia (*see* pp. 107–9). The overseas commerce of New South Wales is given in $A1,000 ending 30 June:

	Imports	Exports		Imports	Exports
1981–82	9,235,716	4,188,394	1984–85	12,707,157	6,717,850
1982–83	8,610,870	4,963,957	1985–86	15,130,137	7,329,298
1983–84	10,027,696	5,240,042	1986–87	16,195,265	8,355,713

The main exports from New South Wales of Australian produce in 1986–87 were coal (26·3%), wool (11·1%), cereals (6·9%), meat (5·6%), non-ferrous metals (3·7%), iron and steel (3·4%), metalliferous ores and metal scrap (2·2%). Principal imports were office machines (13·2%), chemicals (9·9%), electrical machinery, apparatus and appliances (5·2%), road vehicles (4·9%), telecommunications equipment (4·6%), textiles (4·4%), petroleum and petroleum products (3·3%).

Principal destinations of all exports from New South Wales in 1986–87 were Japan (29·4%), EEC countries (13·7%), USA (7·6%), Republic of Korea (7·3%), New Zealand (5·9%), ASEAN countries (5·4%), Taiwan (5·1%). Major sources of supply were EEC countries (24·6%), USA (22·5%), Japan (21%), New Zealand (4·2%), Taiwan (4%), ASEAN countries (4%).

COMMUNICATIONS

Roads. At 31 Dec. 1985 there were 195,129 km of roads and streets open for general traffic in New South Wales (excluding unincorporated and Lord Howe Island), comprising 75,259 km bitumen or concrete, 63,999 km gravel, crushed stone or other improved surface, 34,584 km earth formed and 21,287 km natural surface.

The principal bus services in Sydney and Newcastle are operated by the State Government.

The number of registered motor vehicles (excluding tractors and trailers) at 30 June 1987 was 3,023,025, including 1,898,556 cars, 367,990 station wagons, 179,919 utilities, 211,850 panel vans, 201,066 trucks, 51,691 buses and 111,953 motor cycles.

Railways. At 30 June 1986, 9,909 km of government railway were open. The revenue (including supplements) in 1985–86 was $A1,430m.; the expenditure from revenue, $A1,430m.; the number of passengers carried, 218·6m. and 54m. tonnes of freight carried. Also open for traffic are 325 km of Victorian Government railways which extend over the border; 68 km of private railways (mainly in mining districts) and 53 km of Commonwealth Government-owned track.

Aviation. Sydney is the major airport in New South Wales and Australia's principal international air terminal. During the year ended 31 Dec. 1986 scheduled aircraft movements at Sydney totalled 107,081. Passengers totalled 6,538,616 on domestic services and 3,010,000 on international services. Freight handled on domestic and international services was 67,831 tonnes and 128,000 tonnes respectively.

Shipping. Arrivals of vessels engaged in overseas trade in the ports of New South Wales in 1985–86 numbered 2,955 and clearances numbered 2,912. The revenue tonnage of cargo discharged and loaded was 8m. and 46·7m. respectively. Sydney Harbour is the principal port of Australia. The number of overseas vessels which entered in 1985–86 was 1,379.

JUSTICE, RELIGION, EDUCATION AND WELFARE

Justice. Legal processes may be conducted in Local Courts presided over by magistrates or in higher courts (District Court or Supreme Court) presided over by judges. There is also an appellate jurisdiction. Persons charged with the more serious crimes must be tried before a higher court.

Children's Courts have been established with the object of removing children as far as possible from the atmosphere of a public court. There are also a number of tribunals exercising special jurisdiction, *e.g.*, the Industrial Commission and the Compensation Court.

At 30 June 1987 there were 4,156 persons (3,944 males; 212 females) in prison custody in New South Wales.

Religion. There is no established church in New South Wales, and freedom of worship is accorded to all.

The following table shows the statistics of the religious denominations in New South Wales at the census in 1986, and of ministers of religion registered for the celebration of marriages in 1986:

Denomination	Ministers	Adherents	Denomination	Ministers	Adherents
Church of England	991	1,519,806	Other Christian	1,507	288,865
Roman Catholic	1,667	1,529,176	Muslim	10	57,551
Presbyterian	199	227,663	Hebrew	29	28,236
Uniting Church	600	327,360	Other Non-Christian	34	57,079
Orthodox	69	165,659	Others	...	1,101,409 [1]
Baptist	407	67,187			
Lutheran	42	31,890	Total	5,555	5,401,881

[1] Comprises 539,467 'no religion' and 561,942 'religion not stated' or 'inadequately described' (this is not a compulsory question in the census schedule).

Education. The State Government maintains a system of primary and secondary education, and attendance at school is compulsory from 6 to 15 years of age. In all government schools education is free. Non-government schools are subject to government inspection.

In July 1986 there were 2,233 government schools, comprising 1,674 primary schools, 65 combined primary and secondary schools, 377 secondary schools and 117 special-purpose schools. Total enrolment was 755,257 students, comprising 435,454 receiving primary instruction and 319,803 receiving secondary instruction. There were 47,123 teachers (including the full-time equivalent of part-time teachers) in 1986.

In July 1986 there were 848 non-government schools with 16,194 teachers (including the full-time equivalent of part-time teachers) and 270,793 students. This included 604 Roman Catholic schools with 11,959 teachers and 212,116 students and 36 Anglican schools with 1,469 teachers and 20,236 students.

The University of Sydney, founded in 1850, had 18,070 students in 1986. There are 7 colleges providing residential facilities at the university. The University of New England at Armidale, previously affiliated with the University of Sydney, was incorporated in 1954, and in 1986 had 9,561 students.

The University of New South Wales was established in 1949. Enrolments in 1986 numbered 18,989. There are 7 colleges providing residential facilities at the university. The University of Newcastle, previously affiliated with the University of New South Wales, was granted autonomy from 1965, and in 1986 had 5,418 students. The University of Wollongong, also previously associated with the University of New South Wales, became autonomous in 1975, and in 1986 had 5,310 students. Macquarie University in Sydney, established in 1964, had 11,585 students in 1986.

Advanced education courses at colleges of advanced education and other institutions provide tertiary training with a vocational emphasis. In 1986 there were 57,580 students (including 30,203 part-time and external students) enrolled in these courses.

Post-school technical and further education is provided at State technical and further education colleges. Enrolments in 1986 totalled 402,572 (85% being part-time).

State Government expenditure (including capital expenditure and federal grants) on education in 1985–86 was $A3,787m.

Social Welfare. The Commonwealth Government makes provision for social benefits, such as age and invalid pensions, widows' pensions, supporting parents' benefits, family allowances, and unemployment, sickness and special benefits.

The number of age and invalid pensions (including wives' and carers' pensions) current in New South Wales on 30 June 1987 was: Age, 487,855; invalid, 127,552. Expenditure for the year ended 30 June 1987 was $A2,316m. for age pensions and $A651m. for invalid pensions.

In addition there were 53,726 widows' pensions current in New South Wales at 30 June 1987. Expenditure on widows' pensions totalled $A340m. in 1986–87. Supporting parents' benefits at 30 June 1987 numbered 66,379; expenditure in 1986–87 was $A525m.

Under the Family Allowance scheme, which commenced in 1976, payments to families and approved institutions for children under 16 years and full-time students under 18 years (under 25 in special circumstances) during 1986–87 amounted to $A497m. The scheme covered 1,402,413 children and students at 30 June 1987.

Unemployment, sickness and special benefits commenced in 1945. During the year 1986–87 claims totalling $A1,566m. were paid in New South Wales. At 30 June 1987 unemployment benefit was being paid to 203,339 persons, sickness benefits to 30,945 persons and special benefits to 8,329 persons.

Direct State Government social welfare services are limited, for the most part, to the assistance of persons not eligible for Commonwealth Government pensions or benefits and the provision of certain forms of assistance not available from the Commonwealth Government. The State also subsidizes many approved services for needy persons.

Books of Reference

Statistical Information: The NSW Government Statistician's Office was established in 1886, and in 1957 was integrated with the Commonwealth Bureau of Census and Statistics (now called the Australian Bureau of Statistics). *Deputy Commonwealth Statistician:* John Wilson. Its principal publications are:

New South Wales Year Book (1886/87–1900/01 under the title *Wealth and Progress of New South Wales*): latest issue, 1986
   Regional Statistics: latest issue, 1987
   New South Wales Pocket Year Book. Published since 1913; latest issue, 1987
   Monthly Summary of Statistics. Published since May 1931
   New South Wales in Brief. 1987

New South Wales Dept. of Industrial Development and Decentralisation, *New South Wales Handbook for Industrialists.* Sydney, 1983
State Planning Authority, *Sydney Region 1970–2000 A.D.: Outline Plan.* Sydney, 1968
New South Wales Planning and Environment Commission, *Review: Sydney Region Outline Plan.* Sydney, 1980
New South Wales Government Information Service, *New South Wales Government Directory.* 5th ed. Sydney, 1987

State Library: The State Library of NSW, Macquarie St., Sydney. *State Librarian:* Alison Crook, BA (Hons), MBA, Dip Lib, Dip Ed, ALAA, AAIM.

QUEENSLAND

AREA AND POPULATION. Queensland comprises the whole north-eastern portion of the Australian continent, including the adjacent islands in the Pacific Ocean and in the Gulf of Carpentaria. Estimated area 1,727,000 sq. km.

The increase in the population as shown by the censuses since 1901 has been as follows:

Year	Males	Census counts Females	Total	Intercensal increase Numerical	Rate per annum %
1901	277,003	221,126	498,129	—	—
1911	329,506	276,307	605,813	107,684	1·98
1921	398,969	357,003	755,972	150,159	2·24
1933	497,217	450,317	947,534	191,562	1·86
1947	567,471	538,944	1,106,415	158,881	1·11
1954	676,252	642,007	1,318,259	211,844	2·53
1961	774,579	744,249	1,518,828	200,569	2·04
1966	849,390 [1]	824,934 [1]	1,674,324 [1]	144,857	1·84
1971	921,665 [1]	905,400 [1]	1,827,065 [1]	152,741 [1]	1·76 [1]
1976	1,024,611 [1]	1,012,586 [1]	2,037,197 [1]	210,132 [1]	2·20 [1]
1981	1,153,404 [1]	1,141,719 [1]	2,295,123 [1]	257,926 [1]	2·41 [1]
1986	1,295,630 [1]	1,291,685 [1]	2,587,315 [1]	292,192 [1]	2·43 [1]

[1] Including Aboriginals.

Since the 1981 census, official population estimates are according to place of usual residence and are referred to as estimated resident population. Estimated resident populations at the census dates of 1971, 1976, 1981 and 1986 were 1,851,500; 2,092,400; 2,345,200; and 2,592,600 respectively.

Statistics on birthplaces from the 1986 census are as follows: Australia, 2,162,995 (83·6%); UK and Ireland, 158,949 (6·1%); other countries, 229,760 (8·9%); at sea and not stated, 35,611 (1·4%).

Vital statistics (including Aboriginals) for calendar years:

	Total births	Marriages	Divorces	Deaths
1984	40,446	19,039	8,056	17,405
1985	40,437	17,810	6,816	18,629
1986	40,371	18,030	7,042	17,861

The annual rates per 1,000 population in 1986 were: Marriages, 7; births, 15·6; deaths, 6·9. The infant death rate was 8·7 per 1,000 births.

Brisbane, the capital, had on 30 June 1986 (estimate) a resident population of 1,171,340 (Statistical Division). The resident populations of the other major centres (Statistical Districts) at the same date were: Gold Coast-Tweed, 193,890; Townsville, 103,660; Sunshine Coast, 90,330; Cairns, 69,500; Rockhampton, 57,020; Mackay, 49,140 and Bundaberg, 42,550. Other cities included Toowoomba, 75,060; Gladstone, 25,500; Mount Isa, 24,190; and Maryborough, 22,220.

CONSTITUTION AND GOVERNMENT. Queensland, formerly a portion of New South Wales, was formed into a separate colony in 1859, and responsible government was conferred. The power of making laws and imposing taxes is vested in a Parliament of one House—the Legislative Assembly, which comprises 89 members, returned from 4 electoral zones for 3 years, elected for single-member constituencies at compulsory ballot. Members are entitled to $A45,177 per annum, with individual electorate allowances for travelling, postage, etc., of from $A11,552 to $A29,790.

At the general election of 1 Nov. 1986 there were 1,563,294 persons registered as qualified to vote under the Elections Act 1983. This Act provides franchise for all males and females, 18 years of age and over, qualified by 6 months' residence in Australia and 3 months in the electoral district.

The Legislative Assembly, following the elections of 1 Nov. 1986, was composed of the following parties: National, 49; Liberal, 10; Australian Labor, 30; total, 89.

Governor of Queensland: Sir Walter Benjamin Campbell, QC (assumed office 22 July 1985).

The Executive Council of Ministers, at 9 Dec. 1987 consisted of the following members:

Premier and Treasurer and Minister for the Arts: Michael John Ahern.

Deputy Premier, Minister for Public Works, Main Roads and Expo and Minister for Police: William Angus Manson Gunn. *Transport:* Ivan James Gibbs. *Land Management:* William Hamline Glasson. *Finance and Minister Assisting the Premier and Treasurer:* Brian Douglas Austin. *Employment, Training and Industrial Affairs:* Vincent Patrick Lester. *Mines and Energy:* Martin James Tenni. *Primary Industries:* Neville John Harper. *Environment, Conservation and Tourism:* Geoffrey Hugh Muntz. *Family Services and Welfare Housing:* Peter Richard McKechnie. *Northern Development, Community Services and Ethnic Affairs:* Robert Carl Katter. *Water Resources and Maritime Services:* Donald McConnell Neal. *Justice and Attorney-General:* Paul John Clauson. *Industry, Small Business, Communications and Technology:* Robert Edward Borbidge. *Local Government and Racing:* James Henry Randell. *Corrective Services and Administrative Services:* Theo Russell Cooper. *Health:* Leisha Teresa Harvey. *Education, Youth and Sport:* Brian George Littleproud.

Each Minister has a salary of $A73,885, the Premier receives $A93,712, the Deputy Premier, $A80,450, and the Leader of the Opposition, $A63,839.

Agent-General in London: J. F. S. Brown (392–3 Strand, WC2R 0LZ).

Local Government. Provision is made for local government by the subdivision of the State into cities, towns and shires. These are under the management of aldermen or councillors, who are elected by all persons 18 years and over. Local Authorities are charged with the control of all matters of a parochial nature, such as sewerage, cleansing and sanitary services, health services, domestic water supplies, and roads and bridges within their allotted areas. In addition to Government grants and subsidies, Local Authority revenue is derived from general rates, paid by landowners on the unimproved capital value of land, and by charging for some specific services.

For the year ended 30 June 1986, the receipts and expenditure (including loans) for the 134 Local Authorities were $A1,739m. and $A1,733m. respectively and their rateable values amounted to $A14,211m.

ECONOMY

Budget. Revenue and expenditure of the Consolidated Revenue Fund of Queensland during 5 years ending 30 June (in $A1,000):

	1982–83	1983–84	1984–85	1985–86	1986–87
Revenue	3,690,187	4,212,842	4,681,674	5,190,941	5,649,027
Expenditure	3,690,956	4,211,919	4,682,431	5,190,727	5,648,701

Total receipts of the Queensland Government Authorities in 1985–86 were $A7,812·1m., of which Taxation and Federal Government grants amounted to $A4,845·5m. Expenditure from these funds included: Education, $A1,863·1m.; fuel and energy, $A571·5m.; transport and communications, $A999·3m.; health, $A967m.

Revenue and expenditure of Commonwealth Government departments on account of Queensland are not included.

Debt. The gross public debt of the State at 30 June 1987 was $A2,477·5m.

Banking. The major national trading and savings banks dominate banking operations in Queensland. The Bank of Queensland, which is a privately owned bank with its head office in Queensland, and several licensed foreign banks also provide trading and savings bank facilities. In June 1987 the average of weekly deposits held in trading banks in Queensland amounted to $A7,949·8m. while the average of advances owing to the banks was $A7,136·7m. The total depositors' balances held in savings banks in Queensland at 30 June 1987 was $A5,813·3m.

ENERGY AND NATURAL RESOURCES

Electricity. During 1986–87, 97·8% of the State's generation of 21,134m. kwh was derived from coal-fuelled steam power stations. The hydro-electric stations located in north Queensland provided 2% of the State's electricity needs with the remainder being produced by gas turbine and internal combustion generation using light fuel oil and natural gas.

Minerals. Principal minerals produced during 1985–86 were: Copper, 168,549 tonnes; coal, 63,997,000 tonnes; lead, 208,000 tonnes; zinc, 230,000 tonnes; silver, 570,281 kg; tin, 1,227 tonnes; gold, 10,936 kg; bauxite, 7,169,000 tonnes; mineral sands concentrates, 379,000 tonnes; nickel, 28,250 tonnes; liquid petroleum, 1,741,000 kilolitres. Value of output, at the mine, was $A4,192m. The chief mines are Mount Isa (copper, silver, lead, zinc), Weipa (bauxite), Mount Morgan and Kidston (gold), Moreton and Bowen Basin (coal), Greenvale (nickel), Cooper-Eromanga Basin (petroleum) and North Stradbroke Island (mineral sands).

Land Settlement. At 30 June 1986, of the 172·7m. hectares of the State, 122·9m. hectares was Crown leasehold, 20·4m. hectares was in process of freeholding and the remaining 29·4m. hectares was roads, reserves, freehold, mining tenures and vacant land.

In the western portion of the State water is comparatively easily found by sinking artesian bores. At 30 June 1985, 3,552 such bores had been drilled, of which 2,453 were flowing.

Agriculture. Livestock on farms and stations at 31 March 1986 numbered 9·66m. cattle, 14·31m. sheep and 585,000 pigs. The wool production (greasy) was, in 1985–86, 66m. kg, valued at $A220m. The total area under crops during 1985–86 was 3·2m. hectares.

| | Area (hectares) | | Yield (tonnes) | |
Crop	1984–85	1985–86	1984–85	1985–86
Sugar-cane, crushed	297,765	288,325	23,909,855	23,003,451
Wheat	921,007	972,727	1,579,146	1,690,960
Maize	81,151	63,222	206,890	175,777
Sorghum	514,027	569,460	1,043,189	1,109,312
Barley	328,787	342,637	704,310	809,850
Oats	12,365	21,259	14,311	26,064
Potatoes	6,033	5,521	117,194	113,248
Pumpkins	3,875	3,698	32,574	33,009
Tomatoes	3,457	4,338	77,089	85,194
Peanuts	29,145	28,363	40,981	41,336
Tobacco	2,932	2,766	7,000	6,495
Apples [1]	3,227	3,050	33,892	26,753
Grapes [2]	1,341	1,284	5,132	5,390
Citrus [1]	1,692	1,716	43,587	47,036
Bananas [2]	2,800	3,043	72,856	61,795
Pineapples [2]	3,754	3,795	124,344	131,473
Green fodder [3]	337,730	442,657	...	...
Hay (all kinds)	36,521	42,399	213,067	242,703
Cotton (raw)	51,895	41,230	51,932	51,039

[1] Area of trees 6 years and over.   [2] Bearing area only.
[3] Excluding lucerne and other pastures.

Forestry. A considerable area consists of natural forest, eucalyptus, pine and cabinet woods being the timbers mostly in evidence; a large quantity of ornamental woods is utilized by cabinet makers. The amount of timber processed, including plantation and imported, in 1985–86 was (in cu. metres): Conifers, 619,183; hardwoods, structural timbers and cabinet woods, 665,692.

INDUSTRY AND TRADE

Industry. The 1970s created a milestone in the State's industrial progress when the value added in production by the manufacturing sector exceeded the value of production in the agriculture, forestry, fishing and hunting sector. In 1984–85, there were 3,392 establishments, with four or more workers, employing 87,593 males and 22,347 females, and producing goods and services worth $A12,921m. The value added was $A4,385m. The manufacturing establishments contributing most to the overall production during 1984–85 were those predominantly engaged in the processing of food, beverages and tobacco.

The gross value of Queensland agricultural commodity production (in $A1,000) during 1985–86, amounted to 3,135,382, which included crops, 1,670,977; livestock disposals, 1,056,712; livestock products, 407,693.

Labour. Of the total population of 2·6m., 1,109,200 were in employment in Aug. 1987, 132,600 in manufacturing. Industrial wages and conditions are controlled partly by Federal and partly by State authorities. A State Industrial Commission is empowered to determine all industrial matters in relation to employers and employees, to fix minimum wage-rates and other conditions of employment. An Industrial Court hears appeals and decides points of industrial law. The Federal Court of Australia and the Conciliation and Arbitration Commission are superior within their jurisdictions. In Queensland most employees (64%) work under State awards; 24% under Federal awards.

Rates of wages for each occupation are prescribed by these courts. The minimum weighted average award rate of pay for adult male wage and salary earners was $A351·60 and for adult females $A323·40, at 30 June 1987, while for the June quarter 1987, average weekly earnings were $A475·90 for full-time adult males and $A372·70 for full-time adult females. (Average earnings include award, over-award and overtime payments.) A standard working week of either 38 or 40 hours is prescribed for most awards.

Trade Unions. Unions both of employees and employers must be registered with the State or Australian Commission. There were 69 employees' and 40 employers' unions registered with the State Commission at 31 Dec. 1986, the former comprising 379,331 and the latter 36,867 members.

Commerce. The overseas commerce of Queensland is included in the statement of the commerce of Australia (*see* pp. 107–9).

Total value of the direct overseas imports and exports of Queensland (in $A1,000) f.o.b. port of shipment for both imports and exports:

	1981–82	1982–83	1983–84	1984–85	1985–86	1986–87
Imports	2,179,752	1,994,608	2,086,861	2,319,651	2,649,953	2,501,990
Exports	4,414,452 [1]	4,470,870 [1]	5,473,718 [1]	6,602,512 [1]	7,737,046 [1]	7,799,966 [1]

[1] State of origin.

In 1986–87 interstate exports totalled $A2,530·8m. and imports $A6,014·1m. The chief exports overseas are minerals including alumina, coal, meat (preserved or frozen), sugar, wool, cereal grains, copper and lead, and manufactured goods. Principal overseas imports are machinery, motor vehicles, mineral fuels (including lubricants, etc.), chemicals and manufactured goods classified by material. Chief sources of imports in 1986–87 were Japan ($A583·9m.), USA ($A479·4m.), UK ($A137·4m.), EEC, excluding UK ($A273·4m.); exports went chiefly to Japan ($A2,730·3m.), USA ($A736·1m.), UK ($A431·2m.), EEC, excluding UK ($A1,044m.).

COMMUNICATIONS

Roads. At 30 June 1986 there were 167,681 km of roads; of these, 150,188 km were formed roads, of which 54,524 km were surfaced with sealed pavement.

At 30 June 1986 motor vehicles registered in Queensland totalled 1,567,350, comprising 1,105,047 cars and station wagons, 214,598 utilities, 87,277 panel vans, 9,576 buses, 72,395 trucks and 78,457 motor cycles.

Railways. Practically all the railways are owned by the State Government. Total length of line at 30 June 1986 was 10,225 km, of which 1,236 km electrified. In 1985–86, 41·5m. passengers and 73·6m. tonnes of goods and livestock were carried.

Aviation. Queensland is well served with a network of air services, with overseas and interstate connexions. Subsidiary companies provide planes for taxi and charter work, and the Flying Doctor Service operates throughout western Queensland.

Shipping. In 1985–86, cargo discharged was 3·2m. revenue tonnes and cargo loaded was 60·7m. revenue tonnes.

Broadcasting. At 30 June 1986, 64 broadcasting and 43 television stations were in operation throughout Queensland.

JUSTICE, RELIGION, EDUCATION AND WELFARE

Justice. Justice is administered by a Supreme Court, District Court, Magistrates' Court and Children's Court. The Supreme Court comprises a Chief Justice, a senior puisne judge, 17 puisne judges and 2 masters; the District Court, 24 district court judges of whom 1 is chairman. Stipendiary magistrates preside over the Lower Courts, except in the smaller centres, where justices of the peace officiate. A parole board may recommend prisoners for release.

The total number of persons convicted of serious offences by the Supreme and District Courts in 1985–86 was 2,559; summary convictions and proven offences in lower courts numbered 129,811. There were, at 30 June 1986, 5 prisons, 2 prison farms conducted on the honour system and 1 prison for criminally-insane patients, with 2,126 male and 79 female prisoners. The total police force was 5,145 at 30 June 1986.

Religion. There is no State Church. Membership, census 1986: Anglican, 640,867; Catholic, 628,906; Uniting Church, 255,287; Presbyterian, 120,239; Lutheran,

56,910; Baptist, 39,099; other Christian, 211,316; Buddhist, 5,769; Muslim, 3,731; Hebrew, 2,631; all others (including not stated and no religion), 622,560.

Education. Education in Queensland ranges from pre-school level through to tertiary level. In addition, child care, kindergarten and adult education facilities are available. Education is compulsory between the ages of 6 and 15 years and is provided free in government schools. Expenditure on education by State and local government authorities for 1984–85 was $A1,645m.

At July 1986, pre-school education and child care was provided at 1,302 centres with 4,228 staff and 71,455 children.

Primary and secondary education comprises 12 years of full-time formal schooling and is provided by both the government and non-government sectors. At July 1986, the State administered 984 primary, 85 primary/secondary, and 161 secondary schools with 229,877 primary students and 139,553 secondary students. In addition, 83 special schools provided educational programmes for 4,899 children. State education programmes were provided by 24,059 teachers. Non-government enrolments at July 1986 were 58,525 primary students and 58,242 secondary students at 236 primary, 66 primary/secondary and 78 secondary schools. Educational programmes were provided at 5 non-government special schools for 94 children. Educational programmes at non-government schools were provided by 7,563 teachers.

Post-secondary education in Queensland involves technical and further education, advanced education and university education. In 1985, enrolments in TAFE courses totalled 184,234, while 29,518 students were enrolled in advanced education courses. At 30 April 1985 there were 23,996 university students.

Social Welfare. Public hospitals are maintained by State and Federal Government endowment, supplemented by fees from patients not in standard wards. Welfare institutions providing shelter and social care for the aged, the handicapped, and children, are maintained or assisted by the State. A maternal and child welfare service is provided throughout the State. Age, invalid, widows', disability and war service pensions, family allowances, and unemployment and sickness benefits are paid by the Federal Government. Age pensioners in the State at 30 June 1986 numbered 207,328; invalid pensioners, 39,144; disability and service pensioners, 149,755 (including dependants).

There were 23,377 widows' pensions current at 30 June 1986, and at the same date family allowances were being paid to 354,935 families in respect of 701,525 children under 16 years or students aged 16 or more but under 25. In addition, family allowances were paid to 2,541 children and students in institutions.

Housing. In 1986–87, 22,498 dwelling units in new residential buildings valued at $A1,166m. were approved for construction. This total comprised 17,448 houses and 5,050 dwelling units in new other residential buildings comprising flats, semi-detached units, home units, villa units, town houses, etc. In 1986–87, 21,600 dwelling units in new residential buildings were completed and 6,630 were being built at 30 June 1987. The Queensland Housing Commission, financed by Federal and State Government loans, builds dwellings for sale and for rental. Building and co-operative housing societies are assisted by Federal and State Government loans.

Books of Reference

Statistical Information: The Statistical Office (313 Adelaide St., Brisbane) was set up in 1859. *Deputy Commonwealth Statistician:* D. N. Allen. *A Queensland Official Year Book* was issued in 1901, the annual *ABC of Queensland Statistics* from 1905 to 1936 with exception of 1918 and 1922. Present publications include: *Queensland Year Book.* Annual, from 1937 (omitting 1942, 1943, 1944, 1987).—*Queensland Pocket Year Book.* Annual from 1950.—*Monthly Summary of Queensland Statistics.* From Jan. 1961
Australian Sugar Year Book. Brisbane, from 1941
Endean, R., *Australia's Great Barrier Reef.* Brisbane, 1982
Johnston, W. R., *A Bibliography of Queensland History.* Brisbane, 1981.—*The Call of the Land: A History of Queensland to the Present Day.* Brisbane, 1982
Johnston, W. R., and Zerner, M., *Guide to the History of Queensland.* Brisbane, 1985
Queensland State Public Relations Bureau, *Queensland Resources Atlas,* Brisbane, 1980

Queensland Department of Commercial and Industrial Development, *Resources and Industry of Far North Queensland,* Brisbane, 1980

State Library: The State Library of Queensland, William St., Brisbane. *State Librarian:* S. L. Ryan.

SOUTH AUSTRALIA

AREA AND POPULATION. The total area of South Australia is 380,070 sq. miles (984,377 sq. km). The settled part is divided into counties and hundreds. There are 49 counties proclaimed, covering 23m. hectares, of which 19m. hectares are occupied. Outside this area there are extensive pastoral districts, covering 76m. hectares, 43m. of which are under pastoral leases.

Census population (exclusive of full-blood Aboriginals before 1966):

	Males	Females	Total		Males	Females	Total
1901	180,485	177,861	358,346	1966	550,196	544,788	1,094,984
1911	207,358	201,200	408,558	1971	586,051	587,656	1,173,707
1921	248,267	246,893	495,160	1976	620,162	624,594	1,244,756
1933	290,962	289,987	580,949	1981	635,696	649,337	1,285,033
1947	320,031	326,042	646,073	1986	665,960	679,985	1,345,945
1961	490,225	479,115	969,340				

The number of Aboriginals (as reported on Census schedules) in the State at the Census of 30 June 1986 was 13,298.

Vital statistics for calendar years:

	Live Births	Marriages	Divorces	Deaths
1984	20,052	10,643	4,114	10,099
1985	19,790	10,148	4,216	10,496
1986	19,741	9,878	3,776	10,328

The infant mortality rate in 1986 was 7·40 per 1,000 live births.

The Adelaide Statistical Division had 993,130 inhabitants at 30 June 1986 in 22 cities and 8 municipalities and other districts. Cities outside this area (with populations at the 1986 Census) are Whyalla (27,102), Mount Gambier (18,729), Port Augusta (15,621), Port Pirie (14,597) and Port Lincoln (11,943).

CONSTITUTION AND GOVERNMENT. South Australia was formed into a British province by letters patent of Feb. 1836, and a partially elective Legislative Council was established in 1851. The present Constitution bears date 24 Oct. 1856. It vests the legislative power in an elected Parliament, consisting of a Legislative Council and a House of Assembly. The former is composed of 22 members. Every 4 years half the members retire, and the resulting vacancies are filled at a general election on the basis of proportional representation with the State as one multi-member electorate. The qualifications of an elector are, to be an Australian citizen, or a British subject who on 25 Jan. 1984 was enrolled on a Commonwealth electoral roll and/or at some time between 26 Oct. 1983 and 25 Jan. 1984 inclusive was enrolled on an electoral roll for a South Australian Assembly district or a Commonwealth electoral roll in any State. The person must be of at least 18 years of age and have lived continuously in Australia for at least 6 months, in South Australia for at least 3 months and in the sub-division for which he is enrolled at least 1 month. War service may substitute for residential qualifications in some cases. By the Constitution Act Amendment Act, 1894, the franchise was extended to women, who voted for the first time at the general election of 25 April 1896. The qualifications for election as a member of both Houses are the same as for an elector. Certain persons are ineligible for election to either House.

The House of Assembly consists of 47 members elected for 4 years, representing single electorates. Election of members of both Houses takes place by preferential secret ballot. Voting is compulsory for those on the Electoral Roll.

The House of Assembly, elected on 7 Dec. 1985, consists of the following members: Liberal Party of Australia, 16; Australian Labor Party, 27; National

Party of Australia, 1; Independent, 3. The Legislative Council consists of 9 Liberal Party of Australia, 11 Labor and 2 Australian Democrat members.

Each member of Parliament receives $A41,378 per annum with allowances of $A11,920–38,680 according to location of electorate, a free pass over government railways and superannuation rights. Electors enrolled (Aug. 1987) numbered 947,469.

The executive power is vested in a Governor appointed by the Crown and an Executive Council, consisting of the Governor and the Ministers of the Crown. The Governor has the power to dissolve the House of Assembly but not the Legislative Council unless that Chamber has twice consecutively with an election intervening defeated the same or substantially the same Bill passed in the House of Assembly by an absolute majority.

Governor: Lieut.-Gen. Sir Donald Dunstan, KBE, CB.

The South Australian Labor Ministry, in Sept. 1987 was as follows:

Premier, Treasurer and Minister for the Arts: John Charles Bannon, MP.

Deputy Premier, Minister of Environment and Planning, Chief Secretary, Minister of Emergency Services and Minister of Water Resources: Donald Jack Hopgood, MP. *Attorney-General, Minister of Consumer Affairs, Minister of Corporate Affairs and Minister of Ethnic Affairs:* Christopher John Sumner, MLC. *Minister of Lands, Minister of Forests, Minister of Marine and Minister of Repatriation:* Roy Kitto Abbott, MP. *Minister of Health and Minister of Community Welfare:* John Robert Cornwall, MLC. *Minister of State Development and Technology and Minister of Employment and Further Education:* Lynn Maurice Ferguson Arnold, MP. *Minister of Transport:* Gavin Francis Keneally, MP. *Minister of Mines and Energy:* Ronald George Payne, MP. *Minister of Education, Minister of Children's Services and Minister of Aboriginal Affairs:* Gregory John Crafter, MP. *Minister of Housing and Construction and Minister of Public Works:* Terence Henry Hemmings, MP. *Minister of Labour, Minister of Correctional Services and Minister Assisting the Treasurer:* Frank Trevor Blevins, MLC. *Minister of Tourism, Minister of Local Government, Minister of Youth Affairs and Minister Assisting the Minister for the Arts:* Barbara Jean Wiese, MLC. *Minister of Agriculture, Minister of Fisheries and Minister of Recreation and Sport:* Milton Kym Mayes, MP.

Ministers are jointly and individually responsible to the legislature for all their official acts, as in the UK.

Agent-General in London: G. Walls (50 Strand, WC2N 5LW).

Local Government. The closely settled part of the State (mainly near the sea-coast and the River Murray) is incorporated into local government areas, and subdivided into district councils (rural areas only), municipal corporations (mainly metropolitan, but including larger country towns) and cities (more densely populated areas with a qualification of 15,000 residents in the Adelaide metropolitan area, and 10,000 in the country). The main functions of councils are the construction and maintenance of roads and bridges, sport and recreational facilities and garbage collection and disposal.

The number and area of the sub-divisions, together with expenditure (in $A1,000) for the year ended 30 June 1986, were:

	No.	Area (1,000 hectares)	Roads and bridges	Recreation and culture	All other	Total expenditure
Adelaide statistical division	30	189·4	54,365	61,269	179,149	294,783
Other municipal corporations and district councils	95	15,199·5	47,593	20,450	87,066	155,109
Total	125	15,388·8	101,958	81,719	266,215	449,892

ECONOMY

Budget. Recurrent revenue and expenditure (in $A1,000) for years ended 30 June:

	1982	1983	1984	1985	1986	1987
Revenue	1,705,499	1,923,808	2,160,679	2,639,937	2,966,345	3,217,176
Expenditure	1,766,772	2,032,765	2,190,399	2,626,240	2,955,350	3,214,926

Banking. Deregulation of the Australian Banking System has seen an additional 7 trading banks operating since June 1985. In June 1987 the average weekly balance of deposits held by all 13 trading banks was $A3,783·8m. The average weekly balance of loans, advances and bills discounted was $A4,625m.

The 7 savings banks on 30 June 1987 had deposits amounting to $A3,389·9m. or $A2,458 per head of population.

NATURAL RESOURCES

Minerals. The value of minerals produced in 1985–86 was $A1,099·2m. The principal minerals produced are opals, natural gas, iron ore, copper, gypsum, salt, talc, clays, limestone, dolomite and sub-bituminous coal.

Agriculture. Of the total area of South Australia (984,377 sq. km), 258,335 sq. km were alienated, 496,207 sq. km were held under lease and 229,835 sq. km were unoccupied. Area used for agricultural purposes, at 31 March 1986, was 606,620 sq. km.

Soil Conservation. Under the direction of special officers in the Department of Agriculture, determined efforts are made to deal with the problems of erosion and soil conservation. Included in the programme are the planting of cereal rye, perennial rye and other grasses to check sand drifts; contour-furrowing and contour banking; contour planting with vines and fruit trees and several water-diversion schemes.

Irrigation. For the year ended 31 March 1984, 88,721 hectares were under irrigated culture, being used as follows: Vineyards, 18,213; orchards, 12,806; vegetables, 6,480, and other crops and pasture, 51,222. Most of these areas are along the river Murray.

Gross value of agricultural production (in $A1,000), 1985–86: Crops, 916,462; livestock slaughtering, 251,596; livestock products, 429,932. Total gross value, 1,597,990; local value (*i.e.* less marketing costs), 1,427,041.

Chief crops	1984–85		1985–86	
	Hectares	Tonnes	Hectares	Tonnes
Wheat	1,377,589	2,030,939	1,442,513	1,943,711
Barley	1,121,921	1,836,387	1,169,111	1,709,329
Oats	127,846	132,316	108,499	110,228
Hay	161,092	507,332	152,933	487,396
Vines	...	259,094,000 [1]	...	211,770,000 [1]

[1] Litres of wine.

Fruit culture is extensively carried on, and in 1985–86, 276,819 tonnes of fresh fruit were produced. Other products, in addition to all kinds of root crops and vegetables, are grass seeds and oil seeds. Livestock, March 1986: 914,462 cattle, 17,938,370 sheep and 413,128 pigs. In 1985–86, 112,250 tonnes of wool and 364m. litres of milk were produced.

INDUSTRY AND TRADE

Industry. The turnover for manufacturing industries for 1984–85 was $A7,847m.

Industry sub-division	Establish-ments (No.)	Persons employed (No.)	Wages and salaries ($A1m.)	Turnover ($A1m.)	Value added ($A1m.)
Food, beverages and tobacco	349	15,284	248	1,695	529
Textiles, clothing and footwear	124	7,011	99	383	163
Wood, wood products and furniture	329	7,519	116	527	224
Paper, paper products, printing and publishing	213	7,311	125	522	279
Chemical, petroleum and coal products	47	2,499	55	346	139
Non-metallic mineral products	139	3,254	66	407	182
Basic metal products	38	7,270	160	809	287
Fabricated metal products	336	6,942	106	494	214
Transport equipment	125	16,162	310	1,395	490
Other machinery and equipment	317	12,538	215	817	396
Miscellaneous manufacturing	179	6,415	104	451	192
Total	2,196	92,205	1,604	7,847	3,095

Practically all forms of secondary industry are to be found, the most important being, motor vehicle manufacture, saw-milling and the manufacture of household appliances, basic iron and steel, meat and meat products, and wine and brandy.

Labour. Two systems of industrial arbitration and conciliation for the adjustment of industrial relations between employers and employees are in operation—the State system, which operates when industrial disputes are confined to the territorial limits of the State, and the Federal system, which applies when disputes involve other parts of Australia as well as South Australia.

The industrial tribunals are authorized to fix minimum rates of wages and other conditions of employment, and their awards may be enforced by law. Industrial agreements between employers and organizations of employees, when registered, may be enforced in the same manner as awards. In March 1987 the minimum wage under State awards was $A182.40.

Commerce. The commerce of South Australia, exclusive of inter-state trade, is comprised in the statement of the commerce of Australia given under the heading of the Commonwealth, see pp. 107–9.

Overseas imports and exports in $A1m. (year ending 30 June):

	1982–83	1983–84	1984–85	1985–86	1986–87
Imports	1,244·2	1,318·7	1,603·2	1,737·5	1,503·8
Exports	1,227·1	1,635·8	1,921·4	1,987·3	2,058·5

Principal exports in 1986–87 were (in $A1m.): Wheat, 331·7; wool, 282·1; barley, 181·7; petroleum and petroleum products, 159; meat, 135·8; iron and steel, 103·2.

Principal imports in 1986–87 were (in $A1m.): Machinery, 406·8; transport equipment (including motor vehicles), 241·9; petrol and products, 147·4.

In 1986–87 the leading suppliers of imports were (in $A1m.): Japan (571·2), USA (197·6), Saudi Arabia (98), Federal Republic of Germany (74·3); main exports went to Japan (300·6), USA (191·7), China (148·8), USSR (142·2), New Zealand (140·1), Saudi Arabia, (132·9).

Tourism. In June 1987 there were 309 hotels and motels with 8,497 rooms; 192 caravan parks had a total of 21,775 sites.

COMMUNICATIONS

Roads. At 30 June 1986, of the roads customarily used by the public, there were 2,527 km of national roads, 10,000 km of arterial roads and 89,473 km of local roads, totalling 102,000 km. Lengths of road classified by surface were as follows: Sealed, 22,382 km; unsealed, 79,618 km. Costs of construction and maintenance are shared by the State and Commonwealth governments and by the councils of the local areas. Motor vehicles registered at 30 June 1987 included 543,784 cars, 110,435 station wagons, 147,981 commercial vehicles and 32,667 cycles.

Railways. At 30 June 1986, Australian National Railways operated 5,438 km of railway in country areas. The State Transport Authority operated 153 km of railway in the metropolitan area of Adelaide. All public freight and non-metropolitan passenger services are operated by Australian National.

Aviation. For the year ended 30 June 1986 there were 1,980,063 passengers and 17,111 tonnes of freight handled by 23,537 aircraft movements at Adelaide, South Australia's principal airport (including Adelaide International). On 30 June 1986 there were 7 government and 29 licensed aerodromes.

Shipping. There are several good harbours, of which Port Adelaide is the principal one. In 1985–86, 891 vessels conducting overseas trade entered South Australia with 1,701,640 import tonnes of cargo and left with 5,779,505 export tonnes.

Post and Broadcasting. At 30 June 1986, there were 562 post offices. Telephone services connected totalled 618,338 on 30 June 1986. There were 31 radio and 51 television stations at 30 June 1987.

JUSTICE, RELIGION, EDUCATION AND WELFARE

Justice. There is a Supreme Court, which incorporates admiralty, civil, criminal, land and valuation, and testamentary jurisdiction; district criminal courts, which have jurisdiction in many indictable offences; local courts and courts of summary jurisdiction. Circuit courts are held at several places. In the year ended 31 Dec. 1985, 2,923 criminal matters were proven in higher courts. During the year 1985 there were 706 sequestrations and schemes under the Bankruptcy Act. There were 2,425 prisoners received under sentence in 1985 with an average prison population of 580.

Religion. At the Census of 1986 the religious distribution of the population (as reported on Census schedules) was as follows: Anglican, 242,722; Catholic, 267,137; Uniting Church, 176,980; Lutheran, 64,851; Orthodox, 37,149; Baptist, 21,415; Presbyterian, 18,566; other Christians, 108,048; non-Christian, 13,843; indefinite, 5,458; no religion, 227,564; not stated, 162,212.

Education. Education is secular and is compulsory for children 6–15 years of age. Primary and secondary education at government schools is free. In 1986 there were 711 government schools, comprising 518 primary, 69 primary and secondary, 101 secondary schools and 23 special schools. There were 192,489 full-time students. The Department of Technical and Further Education is responsible for technical, adult and vocational education. In 1986 there were 22 colleges of technical and further education, among the facilities are an adult migrant education service, a centre for performing arts and schools of music, maritime and external studies. Tertiary education, including teacher education, is provided by the 2 universities and 3 colleges of advanced education. There were 178 non-government schools and colleges, most of which are associated with religious denominations (52,788 students). In 1986 there were 408 pre-school centres with an enrolment of 25,710 pre-school children.

Social Welfare. Age, invalidity, war, etc., pensions are paid by the Commonwealth Government. The number of pensioners in South Australia at 30 June 1986 was: Disability and service, 78,401; age, 133,750; invalid, 28,184. There are schemes for family allowances, widows, supporting parents, unemployment and sickness and hospital and pharmaceutical benefits.

Books of Reference

Statistical Information: The State branch of the Australian Bureau of Statistics is in Capita Centre, 10–20 Pulteney St., Adelaide (GPO Box 2272). *Deputy Commonwealth Statistician:* G. C. Sims. Although the first printed statistical publication was the *Statistics of South Australia, 1854* with the title altered to *Statistical Register* in 1859, there is a written volume for each year back to 1838. These contain simple records of trade, demography, production, etc. and were prepared only for the use of the Colonial Office; one copy was retained in the State.

The publications of the State branch include the *South Australian Year Book*, the *Pocket Year Book of South Australia* and a *Monthly Summary of Statistics*, a quarterly bulletin of building activity, a quarterly bulletin of tourist accommodation and approximately 40 special bulletins issued each year as particulars of various sections of statistics become available.

South Australia: Premier's Department, Adelaide, 1980
Douglas, J., *South Australia from Space.* Adelaide, 1980
Finlayson, H. H., *The Red Centre: Man and Beast in the Heart of Australia.* 2nd ed. Sydney, 1952
Gibbs, R. M., *A History of South Australia: From Colonial Days to the Present.* Adelaide, 1984
Whitelock, D., *Adelaide, 1836–1976: A History of Difference.* Univ. of Queensland Press, 1977

State Library: The State Library of S.A., North Terrace, Adelaide. *State Librarian:* E. M. Miller, MA (Hons), Dip. NZLS, ANZLA, ALAA.

TASMANIA

HISTORY. Abel Janzoon Tasman discovered Van Diemen's Land (Tasmania) on 24 Nov. 1642. The island became a British settlement in 1803 as a dependency of New South Wales; in 1825 its connexion with New South Wales was terminated; in 1851 a partially elective Legislative Council was established, and in 1856 responsible government came into operation. On 1 Jan. 1901 Tasmania was federated with the other Australian states into the Commonwealth of Australia.

AREA AND POPULATION. Tasmania is an island separated from the mainland by the Bass Strait with an area (including islands) of 68,331 sq. km, or 6·83m. hectares, of which 6,441,000 hectares form the area of the main island. The population at 10 consecutive censuses was:

	Population	Increase % per annum		Population	Increase % per annum
1921	213,780	1·12	1966	371,436	1·18
1933	227,599	0·52	1971	398,100 [1]	0·99
1947	257,078	0·87	1976	412,300 [1]	0·70 [2]
1954	308,752	2·65	1981	427,200 [1]	0·72 [2]
1961	350,340	1·82	1986	436,353	...

[1] Resident population.   [2] Not comparable with previous censuses.

At the census of 30 June 1986, 5·32% were born in the UK and Ireland, 2·68% in other European countries and 88·61% in Australia. The last full-blooded Tasmanian Aboriginal died in 1876.

Vital statistics for calendar years:

	Marriages	Divorces	Births	Deaths	Natural increase
1984	3,704	1,185	7,098	3,548	3,549
1985	3,520	1,169	7,215	3,658	3,557
1986	3,302	1,245	...	...	...

The largest cities and towns (with populations at the 1986 Census) are Hobart (175,082), Launceston (88,486), Devonport (1981, 21,424) and Burnie (20,585).

CONSTITUTION AND GOVERNMENT. Parliament consists of the Governor, the Legislative Council and the House of Assembly. The Council has 19 members, elected by adults with 6 months' residence. Members sit for 6 years, 3 retiring annually and 4 every sixth year. There is no power to dissolve the Council. Vacancies are filled by by-elections. The House of Assembly has 35 members; the maximum term for the House of Assembly is 4 years. Members of both Houses are paid a basic salary of $A38,248 (Oct. 1987), plus an electorate allowance, according to the division represented. The annual allowance payable is calculated as a percentage of basic salary. The amounts vary from $A5,659 (11%) to $A13,205 (35%). Women received the right to vote in 1903. Proportional representation was adopted in 1907, the method now being the single transferable vote in 7-member constituencies. Casual vacancies in the House of Assembly are determined by a transfer of the preference of the vacating member's ballot papers to consenting candidates who were unsuccessful at the last general election.

A Minister must have a seat in one of the two Houses; all present Ministers are members of the House of Assembly.

In addition to the salary paid to Ministers as members of either House, the following allowances are payable: Premier, in conjunction with a ministerial office, $A47,160; Deputy Premier, in conjunction with a ministerial office, $A32,069; other Ministers, $A26,410. The Leader of the Opposition in the House of Assembly receives an allowance of $A26,410. The holders of some other offices receive allowances ranging from $A2,264 to $A12,576.

An election in Feb. 1986 resulted in the Liberal Party retaining government. The composition of the new House of Assembly was Liberal, 18 seats, Labor, 14 and 3 Independents.

The Legislative Council is predominantly independent without formal party allegiance; 1 member is Labor-endorsed.

Governor: Sir Phillip Bennett, AO, KBE, DSO.

The Liberal Party Cabinet was composed as follows in July 1987:

Premier, Treasurer, Minister for State Development and Small Business and for Energy: R. T. Gray.
Deputy Premier, Tourism, Licensing, Police and Emergency Services, Road Safety, Gaming: G. A. Pearsall. *Attorney-General, Lands, Parks and Wildlife, Sport and Recreation:* J. M. Bennett. *Employment and Training, Housing, Labour and Industry, Consumer Affairs:* R. J. Beswick. *Main Roads, Local Government, Water Resources, Racing:* I. M. Braid. *Public Administration, Primary Industry, Transport:* N. C. K. Evers. *Health, Community Welfare and the Elderly, Ethnic Affairs:* F. R. Groom. *Forests, Mines, Sea Fisheries:* R. J. Groom. *Construction, Administrative Services, Environment, Inland Fisheries:* P. C. L. Hodgman. *Education and the Arts, Industrial Relations, Deregulation, Technology:* P. E. Rae.

Local Government. For the purposes of local government, the State is divided into 47 municipal areas comprising the cities of Hobart, Launceston, Glenorchy and Devonport and 43 municipalities. The number of municipalities was reduced from 45 in May 1985 because of the amalgamation of 2 municipalities with the City of Launceston. The cities and municipalities are managed by elected aldermen and councillors, respectively, with reference to local matters such as sanitation and health services, domestic water supplies and roads and bridges within each particular area. The chief source of revenue is rates (based on assessed annual value) levied on owners of property.

Tasmanian Islands. Three inhabited Tasmanian islands (Bruny, King and Flinders) are organized as municipalities. Nearly 1,600 km south-east lies Macquarie Island, part of the State, and used only as an Australian research base and meteorological station.

ECONOMY
Budget. The revenue is derived chiefly from taxation (pay-roll, motor, lottery and land tax, business franchises and stamp duties), and from grants and reimbursements from the Commonwealth Government. Customs, excise, sales and income tax are levied by the Commonwealth Government, which makes grants to Tasmania for both revenue and capital purposes. Commonwealth Government grants

to Tasmania in 1986–87 totalled $A852m. These included General Purpose Revenue Funds, $A448m.; Specific Purpose Grants, $A303m.; Capital Grants, $A30m.; and Health Grants, $A70m.

Specific Purpose Grants are mainly used to provide essential services such as hospitals, housing, roads and educational services, while General Purpose Revenue Funds have been paid since 1942 to compensate the State for the loss of income tax to the federal government.

Consolidated Revenue Fund receipts and expenditure, in $A1,000, for financial years ending 30 June:

	1981–82	1982–83	1983–84	1984–85	1985–86	1986–87
Revenue	683,231	764,990	853,107	953,209	1,024,697	1,107,870
Expenditure	717,628	772,735	855,006	952,922	1,036,954	1,106,608

The public debt at current exchange rates amounted to $A1,256m. at 30 June 1987.

In 1986–87 State taxation revenue amounted to $A277m., of which pay-roll tax provided $A83·7m.; motor tax, $A18·6m.; stamp duties, $A58·4m.; business franchises, $A56·1m., and lottery tax, $A10·6m.

Banking. Trading bank activity in Tasmania is divided between 3 private banks and the Commonwealth Trading Bank. For the month of June 1986 liabilities represented by depositors' balances averaged $A778m. and assets represented by advances, $A656m. The 6 savings banks operating in Tasmania are the Commonwealth Savings Bank, 2 trustee savings banks and 3 private savings banks operated by trading banks. At 30 June 1985 total savings bank deposits were $A1,256m.

ENERGY AND NATURAL RESOURCES

Electricity. Tasmania has good supplies of hydro-electric power because of assured rainfall and high level water storages (natural and artificial). The Hydro-Electric Commission, Tasmania's sole commercial supplier of electricity, has been surveying water power resources of the State for many years and it is estimated that about 3m. kw. can be economically developed. With the addition of the Reece Dam, 2,055,800 kw. of generating plant was in commission in 1985–86. In 1985–86 the peak loading was 1,319,400 kw. The Pieman River Power Development, comprising 3 stations, was scheduled for completion in 1986. The Gordon River Power Development Stage 2 (the Gordon-below-Franklin scheme) was halted by a High Court decision.

Minerals. The assayed content of principal metallic minerals contained in locally produced concentrates for 1984–85 was (in tonnes): Zinc, 94,621; iron pellets, 1,504,000; copper, 26,500; lead, 35,995; tin, 3,474; gold, 2,182 kg; silver, 106,484 kg. Coal production, 453,288 tonnes.

Primary Industries. The estimated gross value of recorded production from agriculture in 1985–86 was (in $A1m.): Livestock products, 147·3; livestock slaughterings and other disposals, 95·1; crops, 147·8; total gross value, 390·2. Estimated gross value of fisheries was $A59m.

Agriculture. The area occupied by the 5,315 holdings in 1985–86 totalled 2,087,105 hectares, of which 1,004,861 were devoted to crops and sown pasture. The following table shows the area and production, in tonnes, of the principal crops:

	1983–84		1984–85		1985–86	
	Hectares	Production	Hectares	Production	Hectares	Production
Wheat	1,142	2,841	2,456	4,389	1,837	4,014
Barley	15,059	34,119	12,352	29,700	12,209	27,722
Oats	13,978	24,729	9,851	15,855	10,264	16,530
Green peas	7,639	33,243	7,042	31,400	6,622	27,908
Potatoes	5,203	213,090	5,209	203,472	4,832	193,485
Hay	66,255	283,493	51,667	212,543	56,664	261,455
Hops (bearing) (dry)	896	1,902	...	...	...	...

Livestock at 31 March 1986: Sheep, 5·1m.; cattle, 570,300; pigs, 44,900.

Wool produced during 1985–86 was 24,994 tonnes, valued at $A83·7m. In 1985–86 butter production was 6,159 tonnes; cheese, 16,647 tonnes.

Forestry. Indigenous forests cover a considerable part of the State, and the sawmilling and woodchipping industries are very important. Production of sawn timber in 1985–86 was 311,600 cu. metres. 858,900 cu. metres of logs were used for milling in 1985–86 and a further 3,595,900 cu. metres were used for chipping, grinding or flaking. Newsprint and paper are produced from native hardwoods, principally eucalypts.

INDUSTRY AND TRADE

Industry. The most important manufactures for export are refined metals, newsprint and other paper manufactures, pigments, woollen goods, fruit pulp, confectionery, butter, cheese, preserved and dried vegetables, sawn timber, and processed fish products. The electrolytic-zinc works at Risdon near Hobart treat large quantities of local and imported ore, and produce zinc, sulphuric acid, superphosphate, sulphate of ammonia, cadmium and other by-products. At George Town, large-scale plants produce refined aluminium and manganese alloys. During 1985–86, 3,615,200 tonnes (green weight) of woodchips were produced. In 1984–85 the average employment in manufacturing establishments employing 4 or more persons was 24,494; wages and salaries (excluding proprietors' drawings), $A443m.; turnover, $A2,423m.; value added, $A938m.; and number operating at 30 June 1985, 575.

Labour. The Commonwealth Industrial Court (judicial powers) and Commonwealth Conciliation and Arbitration Commission (arbitral powers) have jurisdiction over federal unions, *i.e.*, with interstate membership. Most Tasmanian employees are covered by federal awards.

State Industrial Boards, established for the various trades by resolution of Parliament or proclamation of the Governor, cover most of the remaining employees. Each Board consists of a Chairman appointed by the Governor with equal representation of employers and employees. The Boards have authority over minimum rates for wages or piecework, number of working hours for which the wage is payable, conditions of apprenticeship, annual leave and adjustment of wage and piecework rates. Industrial Boards follow to a large extent the wage rates fixed by the Conciliation and Arbitration Commission.

Commerce. Trade by sea and air in $A1m. for years ending 30 June:

	1980–81	1981–82	1982–83	1983–84	1984–85
Imports	1,207·1	1,258·5	1,339·1	1,461·7	1,895·3
Exports	1,540·2	1,574·6	1,728·9	1,907·2	2,093·1

In 1985–86 exports by sea and air comprised $A1,256m. to other Australian states and $A902·9m. to overseas countries. The principal countries of destination (with values in $A1m.) for overseas exports were: Japan, 325·6; USA, 98·7; Malaysia, 63·5; Indonesia, 45·9; and China (excluding Taiwan), 44·9. In 1984–85 imports totalled $A1,462m.; comprising $A1,259m. from other Australian states and $A203m. from overseas countries. The principal countries of origin (with values in $A1m.) for overseas imports were: Japan, 51·7; USA, 159·6; New Zealand, 23·9; Canada, 23·3; Taiwan 11·4; China, 1·4 and Malaysia, 1·1.

The main commodities by value (with values in $A1m.) exported during 1985–86 were: Ores and concentrates (mainly iron, copper, lead, tin and tungsten), 201; refined zinc, 198; timber, 97; vegetables (including preserved), 168; and greasy wool, 70. Other main exports, for which details are not available for separate publication were woodchips, newsprint, printing and writing papers, refined aluminium, ferro-alloys and chocolate confectionery. The main imports in 1983–84 (with values in $A1m.) were: Petroleum products, 295; ores and concentrates, 135; new motor vehicles, 127; and machinery, clothing and wood-pulp.

Tourism. In 1984 (estimate) 274,344 adult visitors spent at least one night in Tasmania.

COMMUNICATIONS

Roads. The total road length at 30 June 1983 was 22,210 km, consisting of a classified road system of 3,967 km maintained by the State Department of Main Roads, and the remainder maintained by local government authorities, the Forestry Commission and the Hydro-Electric Commission. Motor vehicles registered at 30 June 1986 comprised 205,500 cars and station wagons, 59,800 other vehicles and 6,300 motor cycles.

Railways. There is an 851-km network of 1,067-mm gauge lines linking Hobart and Launceston with coastal and country areas, formerly operated by Tasmanian Government Railways, but since 1 July 1975 worked by the Australian National Railways Commission. A private railway of 134 km, operated by the Emu Bay Railway Co. Ltd, connects Burnie with the mining settlements on the west coast.

Aviation. Regular daily passenger and freight air services connect the south, north and north-west of the State with the mainland of Australia. In 1985 there was a total of 32,763 scheduled aircraft movements at Tasmanian airports; a total of 1·17m. passengers and 42,714 tonnes of freight, including mail, was carried.

Shipping. In 1982–83 overseas vessels made a total of 438 calls to Tasmanian ports discharging 362,716 revenue tonnes of cargo; departures numbered 421 with total cargo of 4,815,555 revenue tonnes.

For posts and telegraphs, see p. 111.

JUSTICE, RELIGION, EDUCATION AND WELFARE

Justice. The Supreme Court of Tasmania, with civil, criminal, ecclesiastical, admiralty and matrimonial jurisdiction, established by Royal Charter on 13 Oct. 1823, is a superior court of record, with both original and appellate jurisdiction, and consists of a Chief Justice and 6 puisne judges. There are also inferior civil courts with limited jurisdiction, licensing courts, mining courts, courts of petty sessions and coroners' courts.

During the year 1986, 23,608 offences were finalized in the lower courts, 1,824 in the higher courts and 4,341 in the children's courts. The total police force on 30 Sept. 1987 was 1,013. There was 1 gaol, with 665 prisoners received into it in 1985–86.

Religion. There is no State Church. At the census of 1986 the following numbers of adherents of the principal religions were recorded:

Anglican Church	154,748	Other religions	33,625
Roman Catholic	80,479	No religion	47,852
Methodist ⎱ Uniting Church ⎰	36,724	Not stated [1]	61,742
Presbyterian	12,084	Total	435,346
Baptist	8,092		

Education. Education is controlled by the State and is free, secular and compulsory between the ages of 6 and 16. At 1 July 1986 government schools had a total enrolment of 66,050 pupils, including 28,473 at secondary level; private schools had a total enrolment of 17,459 pupils, including 8,327 at secondary level.

Technical and further education is conducted at technical and community colleges in the major centres throughout the state. In 1984 there were 20,166 students enrolled in the Division of Technical and Further Education, 19,515 students in the Division of Adult Education. Teaching staff was made up of 518 full-time and 2,641 part-time teachers.

Tertiary education is offered at the University of Tasmania in Hobart, the Tasmanian State Institute of Technology and the Australian Maritime College, in Launceston. The University (established 1890) had (1987) 3,457 full-time and 1,725 part-time students, and 363 full-time teachers. There were 1,468 full-time and 1,456 part-time students enrolled in advanced education courses in 1985.

Social Welfare. Old Age, Invalid, War Service and Widows' Pensions are paid by the Commonwealth Government. The number of pensioners in Tasmania on 30

June 1986 was: Age, 38,627; invalid, 7,835; war (disability), 16,783; widows, 4,897. Benefit payments totalled $A366·9m. (including payments to wives).

Books of Reference

Statistical Information: The State Government Statistical Office (Commonwealth Government Centre, Hobart), established in 1877, became in 1924 the Tasmanian Office of the Australian Bureau of Statistics, but continues to serve State statistical needs as required.
Deputy Commonwealth Statistician and Government Statistician of Tasmania: G. D. Cocking.
Main publications: *Annual Statistical Bulletins (e.g., Demography, Courts, Agricultural Industry, Finance, Manufacturing Establishments* etc.).—*Pocket Year Book of Tasmania.* Annual (from 1913).—*Tasmanian Year Book.* Annual (from 1967).—*Monthly Summary of Statistics* (from July 1945).

Tasmanian Development Authority, *Tasmanian Manufacturers Directory.* Hobart, 1985
Angus, M., *The World of Olegas Truchanas.* Hobart, 1975
Green, F. C. (ed.), *A Century of Responsible Government.* Hobart, 1956
Phillips, D., *Making more Adequate Provisions: State Education in Tasmania 1839–1985.* Hobart, 1985
Robson, L., *A History of Tasmania. Volume 1: Van Diemen's Land from the Earliest Times to 1855.* Melbourne, 1983
Townsley, W. A., *The Government of Tasmania.* Brisbane, 1976

State Library: The State Library of Tasmania, Hobart. *State Librarian:* D. W. Dunstan.

VICTORIA

AREA AND POPULATION. The State has an area of 227,600 sq. km, and a resident population (estimate) of 4,164,720 at 30 June 1986.

The resident population (estimate) of the Melbourne Statistical Division at 30 June 1986 was 2,942,600 or 71% of the population of the State. The resident population (estimate) of each statistical district in Victoria at 30 June 1986 was: Ballarat, 78,290; Bendigo, 64,790; Geelong, 148,270; Morwell, 18,090; Shepparton-Mooroopna, 39,540.

The census count (exclusive of full-blood aboriginals prior to 1971) was:

Date of census enumeration	Males	Population Females	Total	On previous census Numerical increase	Increase %
5 April 1891	598,222	541,866	1,140,088	278,522	32·33
31 March 1901	603,720	597,350	1,201,070	60,982	5·35
3 April 1911	655,591	659,960	1,315,551	114,481	9·53
4 April 1921	754,724	776,556	1,531,280	215,729	16·40
30 June 1933	903,244	917,017	1,820,261	288,981	18·87
30 June 1947	1,013,867	1,040,834	2,054,701	234,440	12·88
30 June 1954	1,231,099	1,221,242	2,452,341	397,640	19·35
30 June 1961	1,474,395	1,455,718	2,930,113	477,772	19·48
30 June 1966	1,614,240	1,605,977	3,220,217	290,104	9·90
30 June 1971	1,750,061	1,752,290	3,502,351	282,134	8·76
30 June 1976	1,814,783	1,832,192	3,646,975	144,624	4·13
30 June 1981	1,901,411	1,931,032	3,832,443	185,468	5·09
30 June 1986	1,991,469	2,028,009	4,019,478	187,035	4·88

The count for the Melbourne Statistical Division (S.D.) on 30 June 1986 was 2,832,893. The count for the Geelong S.D. was 139,792; Ballarat S.D., 75,210; Bendigo S.D., 62,380; Shepparton-Mooroopna S.D., 37,086; and the Victorian component of Albury-Wodonga S.D., 35,183. Other urban centres: Warrnambool, 22,706; Traralgon, 19,233; Morwell, 16,387; Wangaratta, 16,598; Mildura, 18,382; Sale, 13,559; Horsham, 12,174; Colac, 9,532; Hamilton, 9,969; Bairnsdale, 10,328; Portland, 10,934; Swan Hill, 8,831; Ararat, 8,015; Benalla, 8,490; Maryborough, 7,705; Castlemaine, 6,603.

Vital statistics for calendar years:

	Births	Marriages	Divorces	Deaths
1984	59,485	28,931	10,501	29,532
1985	61,555	29,810	9,688	31,353
1986	60,162	29,390	9,670	30,175

The annual rates per 1,000 of the mean resident population (estimate) in 1986 were: Marriages, 7·1; births, 14·5; deaths, 7·2; divorces, 2·3.

CONSTITUTION AND GOVERNMENT. Victoria, formerly a portion of New South Wales, was, in 1851, proclaimed a separate colony, with a partially elective Legislative Council. In 1855 responsible government was conferred, the legislative power being vested in a parliament of two Houses, the Legislative Council and the Legislative Assembly. At present the Council consists of 44 members who are elected for 2 terms of the Assembly, one-half retiring at each election. The Assembly consists of 88 members, elected for 3 years from the date of its first meeting unless sooner dissolved by the Governor. Members and electors of both Houses must be aged 18 years and Australian citizens or those British subjects previously enrolled as electors, according to the Constitution (Qualification of Electors) Act 1982. No property qualification is required, but judges, members of the Commonwealth Parliament and undischarged bankrupts may not be members of either House. Single voting (one elector one vote) and compulsory preferential voting apply to Council and Assembly elections. Enrolment for Council and Assembly electors is compulsory. The Council may not initiate or amend money bills, but may suggest amendments in such bills other than amendments which would increase any charge. A bill shall not become law unless passed by both Houses.

Private members of both Houses receive salaries of $A45,043 per annum, additional allowances rising from $A12,709 to $A18,413.

Members holding the following offices receive the salaries and allowances specified: The President of the Council, $A78,825 salary and $A4,955 expense allowance; the Speaker of the Assembly, $A78,825 salary and $A4,955 expense allowance; the Chairman of Committees of the Council, $A59,457 salary and $A1,802 expense allowance; the Chairman of Committees of the Assembly, $A59,457 salary and $A1,802 expense allowance; the Leader of the Opposition in the Assembly, $A78,825 salary and $A8,108 expense allowance; the Deputy Leader of the Opposition in the Assembly, $A59,457 salary and $A2,703 expense allowance; the Leader of the Third Party, $A59,457 salary and $A2,703 expense allowance; a member of either House who is the Parliamentary Secretary of the Cabinet, $A59,457 salary and $A2,703 expense allowance; the Government Whip in the Assembly, $A53,151 salary; the Whip of any recognized Party which consists of at least 12 members of Parliament, of which Party no member is a responsible Minister, $A49,998 salary. Members receive electorate allowances and allowances for attending Parliament and Parliamentary Committees

The Legislative Assembly, elected on 2 March 1985, is composed as follows: Labor Party, 47; Liberal Party, 31; National Party, 10.

Governor: Dr Davis McCaughey.

In the exercise of the executive power the Governor is advised by a Cabinet of responsible Ministers. Section 50 of the Constitution Act 1975 provides that the number of Ministers shall not at any one time exceed 18, of whom not more than 6 may sit in the Legislative Council. No Minister may hold office for more than 3 months unless he or she is or becomes a member of the Council or the Assembly.

Responsible Ministers receive the following amounts: The Premier, $A90,086 salary and $A18,918 expense allowance; the Deputy Premier, $A83,330 salary and $A9,459 expense allowance; 16 other Ministers, $A78,825 salary and $A8,108 expense allowance. The President, Speaker, Chairman of Committees in the Assembly and in the Council, Parliamentary Secretary of the Cabinet, Leader and Deputy Leader of the Opposition in the Assembly, Leader of the Opposition in the Council and Leader in the Assembly of the Third Party, also receive a travelling allowance when travelling on official business. Members of Committees receive attendance fees and certain travelling expenses when on Committee duties.

The Labor Party Government (first appointed 8 April 1982) was as follows on 6 Oct. 1986:

Premier: John Cain, MP.

Deputy Premier, Minister for Industry, Technology and Resources: R. C. Fordham, MP. *Agriculture and Rural Affairs:* E. H. Walker, MLC. *Health:* D. R. White, MLC. *Education:* I. R. Cathie, MP. *Labour:* S. M. Crabb, MP. *Community Services:* C. J. Hogg, MLC. *Treasurer:* R. A. Jolly, MP. *Attorney-General, Planning and Environment:* J. H. Kennan, MLC. *Conservation, Forests and Lands:* J. E. Kirner, MLC. *Arts, Police and Emergency Services:* C. R. T. Matthews, MP. *Water Resources, Property and Services:* A. McCutcheon, MP. *Transport:* T. W. Roper, MP. *Local Government:* J. L. Simmonds, MP. *Consumer Affairs, and Ethnic Affairs:* P. C. Spyker, MP. *Sport and Recreation:* N. B. Trezise, MP. *Public Works and Minister assisting the Minister for Labour:* R. W. Walsh, MP. *Housing:* F. N. Wilkes, MP. *Parliamentary Secretary of the Cabinet:* Dr K. A. Coghill, MP.

Agent-General in London: K. A. Finnen (Victoria House, Melbourne Place, Strand, London, WC28 4LG).

Local Government. With the exception of Yallourn Works area (26·9 sq. km) and the unincorporated areas—French Island (154 sq. km), Lady Julia Percy Island (1·3 sq. km), the Bass Strait Islands and part of Gippsland Lakes (312·8 sq. km) and Tower Hill Lake Reserve (5 sq. km), the State is divided (at 30 June 1987) into 210 municipal districts, namely 67 cities, 5 towns, 6 boroughs and 132 shires. The constitution of cities, towns, boroughs and shires is based on statutory requirements concerning population, rate revenue and net annual value of rateable property.

ECONOMY

Budget. The receipts and payments (in $A1m.) of the Consolidated Fund in the years shown (ended 30 June) were:

	1982–83	1983–84	1984–85	1985–86
Receipts	7,203	7,781	8,827	9,659
Payments	7,209	7,752	8,828	9,686

The Consolidated Fund is divided into two sectors: the Current Account and the Works and Services (capital account).

Total receipts for 1985–86 of the Current Account sector were 7,865. Principal receipt items were: State taxation, 3,095; Commonwealth tax sharing, 2,248; other Commonwealth payments, 821 and public authorities, 410.

The Works and Services sector contributed 1,793. Principal receipt items were: Commonwealth payments, 646; loan raisings, 360 and the State Development Account (an investment account receiving deposits from various State Authorities), 89.

Of total Consolidated Fund payments during 1985–86 7,894 was paid through the Current Account sector. Principal payment items were: Debt charges, 702; education, 2,503; health, 1,612 and transport, 1,633.

The remaining 1,763 paid through the Works and Services sector was appropriated into the Works and Services Account, from which the Victorian Government makes its capital expenditure. Principal payment items were: Education, 249; housing, 239; transport, 739 and water resources, 53.

The public debt of Victoria at 30 June 1985 was 4,385. Victoria had other liabilities due to the Commonwealth Government of 1,336 largely being advances for housing.

Banking. The State Bank of Victoria, the largest bank in the State, joined with the State Banks of New South Wales, South Australia and Western Australia to form the State Banks Association in Feb. 1984. The Bank provides a full range of domestic and international banking services for both business and personal customers and is the largest supplier of housing finance in Victoria, with approvals for owner-occupied dwellings totalling $A853m. in the year to June 1985.

There are 4 major trading banks in Victoria (Commonwealth Bank of Australia, Australia and New Zealand Banking Group Ltd, Westpac Banking Corporation and National Australia Bank) with a total of 1,201 branches and 236 agencies between them at 30 June 1985, and 4 other trading banks. Private savings banks had 1,049 branches and 483 agencies at 30 June 1984. On 30 June 1986 there were 8·8m. operative accounts (excluding school bank accounts) in savings banks in Victoria. The total credit due to depositors amounted to $A16,586m., made up of State Savings Bank, $A8,059·8m.; Commonwealth Savings Bank, $A2,635m.; private savings banks, $A5,891·3m.

The weekly average of deposits and advances of trading banks operating in Victoria during June 1986 were as follows: Deposits, not bearing interest, $A3,145·5m.; deposits, bearing interest, $A9,961·6m.; total deposits, $A13,107·1m.; loans, advances, and bills discounted, $A12,684·9m. The weekly average of debits to customers' accounts (excluding debits to Federal and State Government accounts at City branches in State capitals) for the same period totalled $A26,514m.

ENERGY AND NATURAL RESOURCES

Electricity. All electricity in this State for public supply is generated by the largest electricity supply authority in Australia, the State Electricity Commission of Victoria. Through its network of 116,000 km of power lines the SEC supplies more than 1,424,000 customers. Another 277,800 customers take SEC power from 11 metropolitan councils which buy in bulk and distribute electricity through their own systems.

Electricity demand has almost doubled in 10 years and is now over 25,000 megawatt/hours a year. Generating capacity at 30 June 1985 was 6,603 megawatts compared with 3,863 in 1973. This includes capacity within Victoria and that available from New South Wales.

About 80% of the power generated for the state system is supplied by brown-coal fired generating stations, Yallourn, Morwell, Hazelwood and Loy Yang, located in the La Trobe Valley on one of the largest single brown coal deposits in the world 140 to 180 km east of Melbourne in Central Gippsland.

There are 2 other thermal stations and 3 hydro-electric stations in north east Victoria. Victoria is also entitled to approximately 30% of the output of the Snowy Mountains hydro-electric scheme and half the output of the Hume hydro-electric station, both of which are in New South Wales.

Oil and Natural Gas. Crude oil in commercially recoverable quantities was first discovered by the Esso/BHP partnership in 1967 in 2 large fields offshore in East Gippsland in Bass Strait between 65 and 80 km from land. These fields, Halibut and Kingfish, with 10 other fields since discovered—Marlin, Snapper, Barracouta, Mackerel, Tuna, Cobia, Flounder, Fortescue, Bream and Seahorse have been assessed as containing initial recoverable reserves of more than 2,930m. bbls of treated crude oil.

Gippsland crude now supplies approximately 72% of Australia's refinery requirements, and during 1984 a total of 159m. bbls were produced. Depletion of production from the 2 major fields, Kingfish and Halibut and the smaller Barracouta field, is now expected to occur in the late-1980s.

Natural gas was discovered offshore in East Gippsland in 1965. The initial recoverable reserves of treated gas are 220,400m. cu. metres. Reserves are sufficient for at least 30 years. Following an extensive development and distribution programme, natural gas was first connected to homes and industry in Victoria in April 1969. All gas consumers in Melbourne, Geelong, Ballarat, Bendigo, Shepparton, Euroa, Benalla, Wangaratta, Wodonga, Albury and a number of towns near Melbourne, in the La Trobe Valley and in East Gippsland, are now using natural gas. At 30 June 1985 a total of 1,013,455 consumers were being supplied with it. During the period 1 July 1982 to 30 June 1983 a total volume of 5,646m. cu. metres of gas was consumed in Victoria, including commercial sales and plant usage.

Natural gas and crude oil are conveyed from the producing fields to a large treatment plant at Longford in East Gippsland from where both hydrocarbons are distributed by a network of transmission lines to tank farms and city gate distribution points.

The crude oil is then distributed to refineries in Victoria by pipeline and to other States by seagoing tankers. Natural gas is distributed to residential and industrial consumers through a network of approximately 20,289 km of mains.

Liquefied petroleum gas is now being produced after extraction of the propane and butane fractions from the untreated oil and gas.

Brown Coal. Major deposits of brown coal are located in the Central Gippsland region and comprise approximately 94% of the total resources in Victoria. The resource is estimated to be 202,000 megatonnes, of which about 31,000 megatonnes are regarded as readily accessible reserves. It is young and soft with a water content of 60% to 70%. In the La Trobe Valley section of the region, the thick brown coal seams underlie an area from 10 to 30 km wide extending over approximately 70 kilometres from Yallourn in the west to the south of Sale in the east. It can be won continuously in large quantities and at low cost by specialized mechanical plant.

About 54% of the resources occur in areas where the overburden over the uppermost seam is less than 30·5 metres while 95% is in areas with less than 91·4 metres of overburden. The current primary use of these reserves is to fuel the major base load electricity generating stations located at Morwell and Yallourn.

Land Settlement. Of the total area of Victoria (22·76m. hectares), 13,973,915 hectares on 30 June 1984 were either alienated or in process of alienation. The remainder (8,786,085) constituted Crown land as follows: Perpetual leases, grazing and other leases and licences, 2,160,352; reservations including forest and timber reserves, water, catchment and drainage purposes, national parks, wildlife reserves, water frontages and other reserves, plus unoccupied and unreserved including areas set aside for roads, 6,625,733. Establishments with agricultural activity at 31 March 1985 numbered 45,884.

Minerals. The recorded production of certain metals and minerals raised in Victoria for the year 1985–86 was: Gold, 1,271,669 grammes, value $A17,901,000; coal, brown, 35m. tonnes, value $A245·7m.

Agriculture. The following table shows the area under the principal crops and the produce of each for 3 seasons (in 1,000 units):

Season	Total crop area Hectares	Wheat Hectares	Wheat Tonnes	Oats Hectares	Oats Tonnes	Barley Hectares	Barley Tonnes	Potatoes Hectares	Potatoes Tonnes	Hay Hectares	Hay Tonnes
1983–84	2,655	1,614	3,862	324	495	403	759	13	362	718	3,032
1984–85	2,569	1,523	2,666	228	343	486	638	15	379	387	1,516
1985–86	2,528	1,508	2,250	212	300	389	476	14	367	425	1,648

In 1985–86 there were 20,025 hectares of vines, yielding 68,782 tonnes of grapes for wine-making and 290,652 tonnes of grapes for drying or for table use. The area cut for green feed and silage covered 90,738 hectares, and orchards and vegetables, including potatoes and onions, occupied 47,776 hectares.

At March 1986 there were in the State 3·7m. head of cattle, 26,892,261 sheep and 431,680 pigs. In 1985–86, 655,132 tonnes of fresh meat was produced. The wool produced in the season 1985–86 amounted to 171m. kg, valued at $A542m. The quantity of butter produced in 1985–86 was 90·9m. kg.

The gross value of Victorian primary production (rural and non-rural) in 1985–86 was $A3,413m.

INDUSTRY AND TRADE

Industry. From the 1975–76 Census of Manufacturing Establishments onwards only a limited range of data—employment and wages and salaries—has been collected from single-establishment manufacturing enterprises with less than 4 persons employed. This procedure significantly reduces the statistical reporting obligations of small businesses. Data in respect of the larger manufacturers provides reliable information for the evaluation of trends in the manufacturing sector of the economy. From 1983–84, the classification of census units to industry is based on the 1983 edition of the Australian Standard Industrial Classification. The following data relates to manufacturing establishments owned by multi-establishment enterprises, and single-establishment manufacturing enterprises with 4 or more persons employed.

The total number of manufacturing establishments in Victoria in 1984–85 (figures for 1983–84 in brackets) was 8,499 (8,404). Persons employed, including working proprietors, on the last pay day in June were males 250,513 (249,139) and females 106,174 (104,109). Salaries and wages paid were $A6,551m. ($A6,059m.), excluding drawings of working proprietors. The cost of purchases, transfers in, and selected expenses was $A20,782m. ($A18,405m.) and sales, transfers out and other operating revenue were $A33,463m. ($A30,081m.).

The preceding figures exclude gas and electricity producing and distributing establishments. In terms of persons employed the most important manufacturing activities were: Transport equipment, 54,549 (52,441); food, beverages and tobacco, 49,651 (49,883); other machinery and equipment, 42,834 (42,133); clothing and footwear, 42,816 (42,436).

Trade Unions. There were 177 trade unions with a total membership of 858,500 operating in Victoria in June 1985.

Commerce. The commerce of Victoria, exclusive of inter-state trade, is included in the statement of the commerce of Australia, *see* pp. 107–9.

The total value of the overseas imports and exports of Victoria, including bullion and specie but excluding inter-state trade, was as follows (in $A1,000):

	1980–81	1981–82	1982–83	1983–84	1984–85	1985–86[1]
Imports	5,929,278	7,175,776	6,989,815	8,185,717	10,084,483	12,409,575
Exports[2]	3,989,429	4,177,187	4,321,674	5,059,996	6,382,293	6,810,680

[1] Preliminary.   [2] Includes re-exports.

The chief exports in 1985–86 were: Petroleum products and gases; textile fibres and their wastes; cereals and cereal preparations; dairy products; meat and meat preparations; road vehicles, and power generating machinery.

COMMUNICATIONS

Roads. At 30 June 1984 there were 157,311 km of road open for general traffic consisting of 64,728 km of bituminous seal, etc., 47,397 km of waterbound macadam, gravel, etc., 23,415 km formed, but not paved, and 21,771 km not formed. The number of registered motor vehicles (other than tractors) at 30 June 1985 was 2,437,700.

Railways. All the railways are the property of the State and are under the management of the State Transport Authority and the Metropolitan Transit Authority, responsible to the Victorian Government.

At 30 June 1985, 5,760 km of government railway were open. During the year 1984–85 the gross revenue amounted to $A360,357,000 and the total working expenses to $A887,888,000. 11,859,000 tonnes of freight and 13,000 tonnes of livestock were carried.

Aviation. During the year ended 31 Dec. 1984 there were 57,488 aircraft movements at Melbourne (Tullamarine) airport. Passengers totalled 4·7m. on domestic flights (international, 1,043,546). Freight handled, 91,160 tonnes, domestic flights (international, 54,547).

JUSTICE, RELIGION, EDUCATION AND WELFARE

Justice. There is a Supreme Court with a Chief Justice and 21 puisne judges. There are a county court, magistrates' courts, a court of licensing, and a bankruptcy court, etc.

Criminal matters proven for 1985 in the children's court were 13,504; magistrates' courts, 70,802; and higher (judges') courts, 2,795 (excluding driving and traffic offences).

There are 12 gaols in Victoria. At 30 June 1987 there were 1,956 persons confined in these prisons.

Religion. There is no State Church in Victoria, and no State assistance has been given to religion since 1875. At the date of the 1986 census the following were the enumerated numbers of each of the principal religions: Catholic,[1] 1,104,044; Church of England, 715,414; Uniting, 280,262 (including Methodist); Orthodox, 177,565; Presbyterian, 138,000; Protestant (undefined), 87,557; other Christian, 90,756; Moslem, 37,965; Hebrew, 32,387; no religion, 557,939; no reply, 574,712; other groups, 222,877.

[1] So described on individual census schedules.

Education. Education establishments in Victoria consist of 4 universities, established under special Acts and opened in 1855, 1961, 1967 and 1977; Colleges of Advanced Education; government schools (primary, primary-secondary, high and secondary technical, and further education colleges), and non-government schools.

The University of Melbourne, founded in 1853, had, in 1986, 16,099 students and 1,387 academic staff.

Monash University, founded in 1958 in an eastern suburb of Melbourne, had, in 1986, 13,839 students and 1,122 teaching and research staff.

La Trobe University, founded in 1964 in a northern suburb of Melbourne, had 9,927 students and 609 academic staff in 1986.

Deakin University (1974) near Melbourne had 7,068 students and 261 academic staff in 1986.

Primary education of children of the ages of 6 to 15 years inclusive is free, secular and compulsory. On 1 July 1986 there were 1,602 government primary schools, 82 special schools, 23 combined primary-secondary schools and 407 secondary schools (including both junior technical schools and high schools). There were 19,114 teaching staff (FTE or full-time equivalent units) with an enrolment of 302,404 pupils in primary and special grades, and 21,609 teaching staff (FTE) with an enrolment of 243,732 pupils in secondary grades. In 1985 there were 204,603 students (excluding adult education programmes) enrolled in technical and further education schools and colleges.

Non-government Schools. There were at 1 July 1986, 734 non-government schools, excluding commercial colleges, with 15,907 teaching staff (FTE) and 250,396 pupils enrolled. Of these schools, 503 were Roman Catholic.

Social Services. Victoria was the first State of Australia to make a statutory provision for the payment of Age Pensions. The Act providing for the payment of such pensions came into operation on 18 Jan. 1901, and continued until 1 July 1909, when the Australian Invalid and Old Age Pension Act came into force. The Social Services Consolidation Act, which came into operation on 1 July 1947, repealed the various legislative enactments relating to age (previously old-age) and invalid pensions, maternity allowances, child endowment, and unemployment, and sickness benefits and while following in general the Acts repealed, considerably liberalized many of their provisions: it has since been amended. On 30 June 1986 there were 349,667 aged and 75,954 invalid pensioners in Victoria, and the amount paid in pensions, including payments to wives of invalid pensioners, during 1985–86 was $A1,966·5m.

The number of disability pensions (members of the forces and their dependants) payable in Victoria on 30 June 1986 was 100,245, and the number of service pensions was 97,517. The amount paid in war and service pensions by the Federal Government during 1985–86 was $A638m.

Under the Australian Unemployment and Sickness Benefit Act 1944, there were 102,155 persons receiving benefits at June 1986 (excluding migrants in accommodation centres) and the amount paid in benefits totalled $A680·3m. in the year ended 30 June 1986.

The number of widows' pensions in force in Victoria at 30 June 1986 was 42,308, and the total amount paid in allowances during the year was $A248·6m.

The number of family allowances in force in Victoria at 30 June 1986 was 1,084,467 (including students). In addition (in 1986), endowment was being paid in respect of 1,518 children who were being maintained in approved institutions. The total amount paid in endowment in Victoria during the year ended 30 June 1986 was $A401·4m.

State Housing. The various State housing authorities were consolidated under the control of the Ministry of Housing early in 1973. These authorities then included the Housing Commission, the Government Employee Housing Authority and the Co-operative Housing registry.

The Housing Act 1983, proclaimed in Dec. 1983, abolished the Housing Commission and the Home Finance Trust, replacing these bodies by a Body Corporate under the name of the Director of Housing.

The Commonwealth State Housing Agreement (CSHA) came into effect as of 1 July 1984. This Agreement established the framework for the provision of Commonwealth funds to the States to support all forms of tenure. The agreement expires on 30 June 1994.

Since the inception in 1938 of the Housing Commission, public housing stock has been provided both through the Commission and the Director of Housing. As at 30 June 1986, public rental housing stock consisted of 51,007 units, of which 64% were located within the Melbourne metropolitan area. 3,096 of these units were produced/acquired during 1985–86. At 30 June 1986 the waiting list for public rental housing was 32,644. The Housing Advisory Council was abolished at this time.

Rental charges for the year ended 30 June 1986 were $A168·8m., against which $A55m. was allowed in rent rebates to tenants on low incomes, including pensioners.

Books of Reference

Statistical Information: Australian Bureau of Statistics (The Rialto Building, 525 Collins Street, Melbourne, 3000). *Deputy Commonwealth Statistician:* Erle Bourke.

Victorian Year Book. (Annually since 1873)
Victorian Pocket Year Book. (Annually since 1956)
Victorian Statistical Register. (Annually from 1854 to 1916)
Monthly Summary of Statistics (from Jan. 1960)

Historical Records of Victoria. Victorian Government Printing Office, Melbourne (From 1981)

Victoria: The First Century. Official History of Victoria. Melbourne, 1934
Victorian Municipal Directory. Melbourne, (From 1866). Melbourne, Arnall and Jackson
Broome, R., *The Victorians: Arriving.* New South Wales, 1984
Christie, M. F., *Aborigines in Colonial Victoria, 1835–86.* Sydney Univ. Press, 1979
Dingle, T., *The Victorians: Settling.* New South Wales, 1984
Dunstan, D., *Governing the Metropolis: Politics, Technology, and Social Change in a Victorian City: Melbourne 1850–1891.* Melbourne Univ. Press, 1984
Grant, J., and Serle, G., *The Melbourne Scene 1803–1956.* Melbourne Univ. Press, 1956
Pratt, A., *The Centenary History of Victoria.* Melbourne, 1934
Priestley, S., *The Victorians: Making Their Mark.* Melbourne, 1984

State Library: The State Library of Victoria, 328 Swanston St., Melbourne, 3000. *State Librarian:* W. Horton, BA, ALAA.

WESTERN AUSTRALIA

HISTORY. In 1791 Vancouver, in the *Discovery*, took formal possession of the country about King George Sound. In 1826 the Government of New South Wales sent 20 convicts and a detachment of soldiers to King George Sound and formed a settlement then called Frederickstown. In 1827 Captain (afterwards Sir) James Stirling surveyed the coast from King George Sound to the Swan River, and in May 1829 Captain (afterwards Sir) Charles Fremantle took possession of the territory. In June 1829 Captain Stirling, newly appointed Lieut.-Governor, founded the colony now known as the State of Western Australia. On 1 Jan. 1901 Western

Australia became one of the 6 federated States within the Commonwealth of Australia.

AREA AND POPULATION. Western Australia lies between 113° 09′ and 129° E. long. and 13° 44′ and 35° 08′ S. lat.; its area is 2,525,500 sq. km.

The population at each census from 1947 was as follows [1]:

	Males	Females	Total		Males	Females	Total
1947	258,076	244,404	502,480	1971	539,332	514,502	1,053,834
1954	330,358	309,413	639,771	1976	599,959	578,383	1,178,342
1961	375,452	361,177	736,629	1981	659,249	642,807	1,300,056
1966	432,569	415,531	848,100	1986	726,299	714,308	1,440,607

[1] 1961 and earlier exclude full-blood Aboriginals; from 1966 figures refer to total population (*i.e.*, including Aboriginals). Figures from 1971 are based on estimated resident population.

The population at the 1986 census was 1,406,949 (709,569 males and 699,360 females). Of these 1,020,362 were born in Australia. Married persons numbered 617,382 (308,974 males and 308,408 females); widowers, 10,787; widows, 49,776; divorced, 23,505 males and 28,268 females; never married, 348,343 males and 294,771 females. The number of males under 21 was 247,826 and of females 235,620.

Perth, the capital, had an estimated resident population of 1,025,340 at June 1986. Of this, the area administered by the City of Perth had a population of 82,900 while the population in the area for which the City of Fremantle is responsible (which includes the chief port of the State) was 24,010.

Principal local government areas outside the metropolitan area, with population at 30 June 1986 (estimate): Bunbury, 24,960; Geraldton, 20,360; Mandurah, 18,030; Roebourne, 16,970; Port Hedland, 14,500; Albany, 14,120; Boulder, 12,820; Kalgoorlie, 10,930.

Vital statistics for calendar years [1]:

	Births	Ex-nuptial births	Marriages	Divorces	Deaths
1983	23,046	3,642	10,519	3,822	8,359
1984	21,625	3,489	9,920	4,069	8,503
1985	23,109	3,886	10,398	4,039	8,836
1986 [2]	24,236	4,481	10,379	9,307	4,001

[1] Figures prior to 1984 are on State of registration basis; those from 1984 are on State of usual residence basis.   [2] Provisional.

CONSTITUTION AND GOVERNMENT. In 1870 partially representative government was instituted, and in 1890 the administration was vested in the Governor, a Legislative Council and a Legislative Assembly. The Legislative Council was, in the first instance, nominated by the Governor, but it was provided that in the event of the population of the colony reaching 60,000, it should be elective. In 1893 this limit of population being reached, the Colonial Parliament amended the Constitution accordingly.

The Legislative Council consists of 34 members, 2 members representing each of the 17 electoral provinces. Each member is elected for a term of 6 years, one-half of the members retiring every 3 years.

There are 57 members of the Legislative Assembly, each member representing one of the 57 electoral districts of the State. Members are elected for the duration of the Parliament, normally 3 years. The qualifications applying to candidates and electors are identical for the Legislative Council and the Legislative Assembly. A candidate must have resided in Western Australia for a minimum of 12 months, be at least 18 years of age and free from legal incapacity, be an Australian citizen, and be enrolled, or qualified for enrolment, as an elector. A judge of the Supreme Court, the Sheriff of Western Australia, an undischarged bankrupt or a debtor against whose estate there is a subsisting order in bankruptcy may not be elected to Parliament. No person may hold office as a member of the Legislative Assembly and the Legislative Council at the same time. An elector must be at least 18 years of age, be an Australian citizen free from legal incapacity, must have resided in the

Commonwealth of Australia for 6 and in Western Australia for 3 months continuously and in the electoral district for which he claims enrolment for a continuous period of 1 month immediately preceding the date of his claim. Enrolment is compulsory for all qualified persons except Aboriginal natives of Australia, who are entitled but not required to enrol. Voting at elections is on the preferential system and is compulsory for all enrolled persons.

Ordinary members of the legislature are paid a salary of $A46,477 a year, with an additional electorate allowance, ranging from $A14,000 to $A31,928 according to location of electorate. Members are entitled to free travel on Western Australian government railway, bus and ferry services, and, by arrangement, once every year on government railways in other States. All members of Parliament contribute to superannuation benefits.

The Premier receives a salary, including an electorate allowance, of $A110,397, the Deputy Premier $A98,462, the Leader of the Government in the Legislative Council $A95,021, and all other Ministers $A88,689—105,710 according to location of electorate.

The Legislative Assembly, elected on 18 Feb. 1986, is composed as follows: Australian Labor Party, 32; Liberal Party, 19; National Party of Australia, 6. The Legislative Council, one-half of which was elected on the same day, is composed of 16 Australian Labor Party, 14 Liberal Party, 4 National Party of Australia.

Governor: Gordon Reid, AC.

The Australian Labor Party Cabinet was, at 30 June 1987:

Premier, Treasurer, Minister for Public Sector Management, Women's Interests: Brian Thomas Burke, MLA.

Deputy Premier, Industry and Technology, Defence Liaison, Communications, Parliamentary and Electoral Reform: Hon. Malcolm John Bryce, MLA. *Attorney-General, Budget Management, Corrective Services, Leader of the Government in the Legislative Council:* Hon. Joseph Max Berinson, MLC. *Community Services, The Family, Youth, The Aged, Minister assisting the Minister for Women's Interests, Deputy Leader of the Government in the Legislative Council:* Hon. Elsie Kay Hallahan, MLC. *Local Government, Regional Development:* Hon. Jeffrey Phillip Carr, MLA. *Education, Planning, Intergovernmental Relations, Leader of the House in the Legislative Assembly:* Hon. Robert John Pearce, MLA. *Conservation and Land Management, Environment:* Hon. Barry James Hodge, MLA. *Minerals and Energy, Economic Development, The Arts:* Hon. David Charles Parker, MLA. *Agriculture, The South West, Fisheries:* Hon. Julian Fletcher Grill, MLA. *Housing, Lands:* Hon. Keith James Wilson, MLA. *Works and Services, Labour, Productivity and Employment, Minister assisting the Treasurer, Minister assisting the Minister for Public Sector Management:* Hon. Peter M'Callum Dowding, MLA. *Health, Consumer Affairs, Minister assisting the Minister for Economic Development:* Hon. Ian Frederick Taylor, MLA. *Tourism, Racing and Gaming:* Hon. Pamela Anne Beggs, MLA. *Transport, Small Business:* Hon. Gavan John Troy, MLA. *Water Resources, The North West, Aboriginal Affairs:* Hon. Ernest Francis Bridge, MLA. *Police and Emergency Services, Multicultural and Ethnic Affairs:* Hon. Gordon Leslie Hill, MLA. *Sport and Recreation, Parliamentary Secretary of the Cabinet:* Hon. Graham John Edwards, MLC.

Agent-General in London: R. Davies (Western Australia House, 115 Strand, WC2R 0AJ).

Local Government. The only unincorporated area in mainland Western Australia is King's Park, a public reserve of about 403 hectares in Perth. Including the lord-mayoralty of Perth there were 15 cities, 11 towns and 113 shires at 30 June 1987. The executive body in each of these districts is normally an elective council, presided over by a mayor (city and town) or a president (shire), but in certain circumstances it may be a commissioner appointed by the Governor. Their functions include road construction and repair, the provision of parks and recreation grounds, the administration of building controls and local services such as health and library services. Finance is derived largely from rates levied on property owners as well as charges for services and government grants (mainly for road construction).

ECONOMY

Budget. The revenue and expenditure (in $A) of Western Australia in years ended 30 June, are given as follows:

	1984	1985	1986	1987[1]
Revenue	2,660,758,263	2,843,079,541	3,099,411,391	3,278,800,000
Expenditure	2,659,761,394	2,842,267,768	3,099,044,981	3,278,800,000

[1] Estimates.

Main items of revenue in 1985–86: Railways ($A227,221,860), taxation ($A727,838,654), lands, timber and mining ($A258,868,239), public utilities other than railways ($A13,595,483), from Federal funds ($A1,425,700,590). Western Australia had a net loan liability of $A1,589,828,314 on 30 June 1986, the charge for the year being $A194,870,988.

Banking. There are 20 trading banks in Western Australia including the Commonwealth Trading Bank and The Rural and Industries Bank of Western Australia. In June 1987, the average of customers' balances was $A5,365m. and average advances $A4,951m.

At 30 June 1987, the 9 savings banks held deposits of $A3,975·3m., in 2,618,596 accounts.

ENERGY AND NATURAL RESOURCES

Minerals. The mining industry has been for many years of considerable significance in the Western Australian economy. Until the mid-1960s the major mineral produced was gold. However, in recent years gold has been displaced by iron ore in terms of value, and has at various times fallen behind nickel concentrates, bauxite, oil, mineral sands and salt.

The total ex-mine value of minerals from mining and quarrying in the State in 1985–86 was $A4,204·1m. Principal minerals produced in 1985–86 were: Iron ore, 93m. tonnes, value $A1,795m.; crude oil, 1·77m. kilolitres; gold bullion, 56·9m. grammes, value $A704·4m.; bauxite, 19·4m. tonnes; black coal, 3·8m. tonnes, value $A126·8m.; salt, 4·7m. tonnes, value $A88·6m.; tin concentrates, 679 tonnes; nickel concentrates, 455,000 tonnes; natural gas, 2,928m. kilolitres; diamonds, 17·5m. carats, value $A147·6m.; copper concentrates, 15,000 tonnes and zinc concentrates, 14,000 tonnes.

Agriculture.

	1984–85		1985–86	
	Area	Production	Area	Production
Crop	1,000 hectares	1,000 tonnes	1,000 hectares	1,000 tonnes
Wheat	4,652	6,580	4,148	4,362
Oats	351	460	288	338
Barley	965	1,431	826	1,024
Hay	225	746	201	633
Potatoes	2	70	2	68
Cauliflower	1	26	1	17

	1984–85		1985–86	
	No. Trees	Production	No. Trees	Production
Crop	(1,000)	Tonnes	(1,000)	Tonnes
Apples	737	59,128	721	46,678
Pears	114	7,592	126	6,403
Oranges	200	7,970	190	6,773

Irrigation has been established by the Government along the south-western coastal plain and in the north of the State. Reservoirs with an aggregate capacity of 6,207m. cu. metres provided irrigation water for 20,402 hectares in 6 districts during 1985–86.

Livestock at 31 March 1986 included 1,690,000 cattle, 33,213,000 sheep and 278,000 pigs.

The wool clip in 1985–86 was 170,800 tonnes; the overseas exports for 1985–86, greasy wool, 134,134 tonnes; degreased wool, 19,853 tonnes.

Forestry. The area of State forests and timber reserves at 30 June 1986 was 2,016,621 hectares; 1985–86 production of sawn timber was 328,976 cu. metres, principally Jarrah and Karri hardwoods.

Fisheries. The catch of fish, crustaceans and molluscs in Western Australia in 1985–86 totalled 30,765 tonnes for a gross value of $A138·7m. Of this, rock lobsters, with a total catch of 7,231 tonnes accounted for $A89·1m.

Value of Agricultural Commodities Produced. The estimated gross values of Western Australian agricultural commodities during 1985–86 were: Crops and pastures, $A1,185·56m.; livestock slaughterings and other disposals, $A372m.; livestock products, $A656·59m.

INDUSTRY AND TRADE

Industry. Perhaps the most significant change in Western Australian manufacturing came when the basis for an integrated industrial complex was established with the opening of a large oil refinery at Kwinana in 1954. Two of the plants in the Kwinana complex are directly concerned with metals processing. An alumina refinery commenced operations in 1964 and a nickel refinery commenced operations in 1970. Major mineral processing plants outside Kwinana also contribute to Western Australia's manufacturing industry. A plant at Australind, near Bunbury, which extracts titanium dioxide from ilmenite has been in operation since 1963. A nickel smelter commenced operations at Kalgoorlie in 1973 and another alumina refinery, at Pinjarra, began operating in 1972. In addition, two new alumina refineries are now in operation, one at Wagerup and the other at Worsley.

Besides providing for heavy industry directly associated with minerals processing, the mining development of recent years, especially on the North West Shelf, has also given impetus to other manufacturing activity, particularly to industries associated with the provision of capital equipment and other manufactured goods for the major mining projects.

The following table shows manufacturing industry statistics for 1984–85 [1]:

Industry sub-division	Number of establishments operating at 30 June	Persons employed [2]	Wages and salaries $Am.	Turnover $Am.	Value added $Am.
Food, beverages and tobacco	369	11,990	195·3	1,494·3	453·7
Textiles	38	987	14·8	75·1	31·4
Clothing and footwear	60	1,452	17·8	50·3	29·7
Wood, wood products and furniture	417	7,863	106·7	479·2	224·1
Paper, paper products, printing and publishing	221	7,091	120·6	402·8	214·3
Chemical, petroleum and coal products	69	3,029	62·9	516·7	169·2
Non-metallic mineral products	199	4,462	86·1	459·0	197·7
Basic metal products	40	6,081	162·7	1,836·5	578·2
Fabricated metal products	395	6,731	112·1	531·9	194·4
Transport equipment	150	4,802	92·0	251·7	126·4
Other machinery and equipment	325	7,146	126·0	485·7	210·9
Miscellaneous manufacturing	168	2,608	40·6	205·5	83·1
Total	2,451	64,242	1,137·6	6,788·5	2,513·2

[1] Excludes single establishment enterprises with less than 4 persons employed.
[2] Annual average. Includes working proprietors.

Labour. A Court of Arbitration was established in Western Australia in 1901 under the provisions of the 'Industrial Conciliation and Arbitration Act 1900'. The Court of Arbitration was replaced, with effect from 1 Feb. 1964, by the Western Australian Industrial Appeal Court and The Western Australian Industrial Commission, authorities constituted in terms of the *Industrial Arbitration Act 1912*. These authorities continue to operate under the provisions of the *Industrial Arbitration Act 1979* which was proclaimed on 1 March 1980.

The Western Australian Industrial Appeal Court consists of 3 Judges, one of whom is the Presiding Judge. The members are nominated by the Chief Justice of Western Australia. An appeal lies to the Court from decisions of the President of the Western Australian Industrial Commission, the Full Bench or the Commission in Court Session but only on the ground that the decision is erroneous in law or is in excess of jurisdiction.

The Western Australian Industrial Commission consists of a President, a Chief Industrial Commissioner, a Senior Commissioner, and 'such number of other Commissioners as may, from time to time, be necessary'. There were 5 'other Commissioners' at 1 Jan. 1985. A person shall not be appointed as President unless he is qualified to be a Judge, and on appointment he is entitled to the status of a Puisne Judge. The President or a Commissioner sitting or acting alone constitutes the Commission and may exercise the appropriate powers of the Commission.

The Commission can inquire into any industrial matter and make an award, order or declaration relating to such matter. 'Industrial matter' means any matter affecting or relating to the work, privileges, rights, or duties of employers or employees in any industry and includes any matter relating to the wages, salaries, allowances, or other remuneration of employees or the prices to be paid in respect of their employment; the hours of employment, sex, age, qualification or status of employees and the mode, terms and conditions of employment including conditions which are to take effect after the termination of employment. The Commission may also make inquiries where industrial action has occurred or is likely to occur.

The Commission in Court Session is constituted by not less than 3 Commissioners sitting or acting together, and may make General Orders, hear matters referred by the Commission, and hear appeals from decisions of Boards of Reference.

The Full Bench is constituted by not less than 3 members of the Commission, 1 of whom is the President, and may hear matters referred by the Commission on questions of law, and appeals from decisions of the Commission and Industrial Magistrates.

The following table shows details of the number of industrial awards, unions and members registered with The Western Australian Industrial Commission.

At 30 June	1983	1984	1985	1986	1987
Awards in force	488	491	630	608	592
Employee organizations:					
Number	66	67	70	72	69
Membership	176,065	174,330	185,061	176,769	189,770
Employer organizations:					
Number	14	14	15	15	15
Membership	2,138	2,144	2,535	3,561	2,690

Commerce. The external commerce of Western Australia, exclusive of interstate trade, is comprised in the statement of the commerce of Australia, *see* pp. 107–9.

The total value of imports and exports, including interstate trade, but excluding interstate value of horses, in 5 years (30 June) is, in $A1m., as follows:

	1981–82	1982–83	1983–84	1984–85	1985–86
Imports	5,676·2	5,683·8	5,574·4	6,446·5	6,880·0
Exports	4,796·1	5,922·3 [1]	6,464·5 [1]	7,577·4 [1]	8,139·2 [1]

[1] Including ships' stores.

Selected overseas exports (in $A) for 1985–86: Iron ore and concentrates, 1,866,722,547; wheat, 989,144,430; wool, 614,210,941; petroleum and petroleum products, 180,133,708; gold bullion, 458,728,144; live sheep and lambs, 84,418,281; beef and veal, 76,709,491; rock lobster tails, 84,231,876; salt, 93,362,590; mutton and lamb, 41,765,960; barley, 128,989,211; prawns, 38,240,577; zirconium, 50,568,499; rutile, 33,144,067; ilmenite and leucoxene, 45,149,450; hides and skins (including fur skins), 30,566,567; whole rock lobsters, 30,336,214; fruit and nuts (fresh or dried), 12,808,601; oats, 10,705,506.

Selected overseas imports (in $A) for 1985–86: Petroleum and petroleum products, 339,935,836; machinery, 525,437,080; transport equipment,

309,443,938; iron and steel, 59,823,212; chemicals, 132,584,130; food, 75,142,787; crude fertilizer, 29,658,434; rubber manufactures, 48,604,525; paper and paperboard, 39,610,754.

The chief countries exporting to Western Australia in 1985–86 were (in $A): Japan, 439,353,956; USA, 344,450,239; UK, 152,900,196; Singapore, 126,833,367; Federal Republic of Germany, 122,835,855; Qatar, 89,118,942; Italy, 65,216,812. Western Australia's exports in 1985–86 (in $A) went chiefly to: Japan, 2,129,282,722; USA, 807,616,181; China, People's Republic of, 364,552,590; USSR, 346,295,534; Republic of Korea, 233,403,564; Federal Republic of Germany, 208,168,118; Egypt, 201,443,585.

Tourism. In 1985–86, 175,000 international visitors contributed $A146m. to the economy; 383,800 interstate tourists contributed $215m.; 5,260,000 intrastate tourists contributed $A952m.

COMMUNICATIONS

Roads. At 30 June 1986 there were 119,941 km of prepared and formed roads in Western Australia, 39,877 km of bituminous surface, 37,272 km other constructed surfaces and 42,792 km formed but not metalled or otherwise prepared. In addition, there are 20,216 km of roads unprepared except for clearing which are used for general traffic.

New motor vehicles registered in Western Australia during the year ended 30 June 1987 were 46,145.

Railways. At 30 June 1986 the State had 5,553 km of State government railway and 731 km of Federal line, the latter being the western portion of the Trans-Australian line (Kalgoorlie–Port Pirie), which links the State railway system to those of the other States of the Commonwealth. At 30 June 1985, mining companies operated 1,285 km of private railways for the transport of ore to ports on the north-west coast. In 1985–86 state railways carried 21m. tonnes and 380,000 passengers. Perth suburban lines, controlled by a separate authority, carried 9·7m. passengers.

Aviation. An extensive system of regular air services operates in Western Australia for the transport of passengers, freight and mail. During the year ended 31 Dec. 1985, Perth Airport handled 20,111 aircraft movements and 1,693,437 passengers on domestic and international services.

Shipping. In 1985–86, the number of overseas direct vessels through the major ports was: Port of Fremantle, 988 entered, 976 cleared; Dampier, 462 entered, 463 cleared; Port Hedland, 449 entered, 434 cleared; Port Walcott, 96 entered, 100 cleared. The gross weight (in tonnes) of overseas cargo through those ports was: Port of Fremantle, 2,812,654 discharged, 6,991,747 loaded; Dampier, 216,618 discharged, 37,967,979 loaded; Port Hedland, 143,520 discharged, 29,360,869 loaded; Port Walcott, nil discharged, 14,007,971 loaded.

Post and Broadcasting. Postal, telephone and telegraph facilities are afforded at 411 offices. Telephone services connected totalled 575,862 at 30 June 1986.

There were 55 radio broadcasting and 87 television stations, including translator stations, in operation at 30 June 1986.

JUSTICE, RELIGION, EDUCATION AND WELFARE

Justice. In Western Australia justice is administered by a Supreme Court, consisting of a Chief Justice, 8 puisne judges and 2 masters at 30 June 1987; a District Court comprising a chief judge and 12 other judges and Magistrates' Courts exercising both civil and criminal jurisdiction. The lower courts are presided over by justices of the peace, except in the more important centres, where the court is constituted by a stipendiary magistrate. Juvenile offenders may be dealt with either by the Children's (Suspended Proceedings) Panel or by the Children's Court. The Panel is comprised of 1 representative from the Department for Community Services and 1 from the Police Department. It is empowered to deal with certain offences involving first offenders under the age of 16 years who have pleaded guilty. Other young offenders are dealt with by the Children's Court, which is presided over by a Magistrate.

Offences against law	1981	1982	1983–84	1984–85	1985–86
Charges	122,176	...	109,580 [1]	115,739 [1]	...
Lower Court convictions [2]	116,930	...	101,241 [1]	105,025 [1]	...
Higher Court convictions	1,759	1,857	2,581	3,369	4,142

[1] Excludes Perth and East Perth Lower Courts.
[2] Includes convictions for traffic offences: 55,325 in 1981; 42,654 in 1983–84; 43,851 in 1984–85. In addition, small fines were imposed for minor traffic offences as follows: 1981, 348,452; 1982, 358,395; 1983, 348,009; 1984, 373,662; 1985, 416,774; 1986, 401,415.

Persons in prison at 30 June 1987 numbered 1,565 males and 83 females.

Religion. There is no State Church, and freedom of worship is accorded to all. At the census, 30 June 1986, the principal denominations were: Anglican, 371,302; Catholic, 347,695; Uniting, 82,876; Presbyterian, 31,641; Baptist, 16,869; Orthodox, 16,722; other Christian, 110,922; Buddhist, 7,178; all other, including not stated and no religion, 421,724.

Education. School attendance is compulsory from the age of 6 until the end of the year in which the child attains 15 years. Pre-school education is provided by a kindergarten system partly financed from government subsidy. In 1986 there were 728 government primary and secondary schools providing free education to 207,426 students and 233 non-government primary and secondary schools providing education, for which fees are charged, to 60,255 students.

Technical education is available at a number of technical colleges, schools and centres, which are staffed and controlled by the Education Department.

Tertiary Education at 30 April 1986:

	Teaching Staff [1]	Students Enrolled
University of Western Australia	661	9,512
Murdoch University	227	4,624
Western Australian Institute of Technology	735	12,586
Western Australian College of Advanced Education	504	10,651

[1] Comprises full-time teaching staff and part-time staff on the basis of equivalent full-time staff.

State Government expenditure from consolidated revenue on education during the year ended 30 June 1987, amounted to $A844,900,889.

Social Welfare. At 30 June 1987 there were 44 general hospitals and 8 nursing homes maintained wholly by public funds and 43 general hospitals and 9 nursing homes partly assisted therefrom. In addition, there are numerous private hospitals.

The Health Department of Western Australia Psychiatric Services comprises 3 approved hospitals, 10 outpatient clinics for adults, 10 general rehabilitation units, 7 psychiatric extended care units and 1 rehabilitation hostel. Specifically for children are: 3 outpatient clinics and 3 residential units. The Authority for the Intellectually Handicapped comprises 24 hostels and 20 group homes.

The Department for Community Services is responsible for the provision of welfare and community services throughout the State. There were 10 directorates in the Department on 30 June 1986. Six were regionally based, 3 in the Perth metropolitan area and 3 were in the country. These are concerned with direct service delivery, which is provided through 20 divisional and 35 district offices.

Direct services provided to the community include emergency financial assistance, family and substitute care, and counselling and psychological services. The Department supervises children's Day Care Centres. There is a 24-hour emergency welfare service provided through the Crisis Care Unit. Specialist units work in the areas of child abuse, adoptions, youth activities and Family Court counselling.

The Department provides residential facilities for the temporary accommodation, care and training of children and is also responsible for young offenders recommended for detention or remand by a Court.

Age, invalid, widows', disability and service pensions, and unemployment benefits are paid by the Federal Government. The number of pensioners in Western

Australia at 30 June 1986 was: Age, 103,085; invalid, 25,769; widows, 12,817; disability, 35,223 and service, 36,423. There were 55,089 recipients of unemployment benefits at 30 June 1986.

During 1985–86 the department provided emergency assistance in 102,734 cases. This assistance, valued at $A4,504,000, was in the form of cash, vouchers to purchase goods and services, and payment on behalf of individuals.

Housing. In 1985–86, 12,620 new houses and 4,217 new other dwellings were completed in Western Australia. Of these, the State Housing Commission provided 1,026 new dwelling units for sale and for rental.

The value of dwellings completed during this period was $A773·9m. Additions and alterations valued at $A10,000 or more to dwellings, were valued at $A60·5m.

Books of Reference

Statistical Information: The State Government Statistician's Office was established in 1897 and now functions as the Western Australian Office of the Australian Bureau of Statistics (Merlin Centre, 30 Terrace Road, Perth). *Deputy Commonwealth Statistician and Government Statistician:* B. N. Pink. Its principal publications are: *Western Australian Year Book* (new series, from 1957). *Western Australian Pocket Year Book* (from 1919). *Monthly Summary of Statistics* (from 1958)

Battye, J. S., *Western Australia: A History from its Discovery to the Inauguration of the Commonwealth.* Oxford, 1924.—*The Cyclopedia of Western Australia.* Adelaide, Vol. 1 (1912), Vol. 2 (1913)
Crowley, F. K., *Australia's Western Third: A History of Western Australia from the First Settlements to Modern Times.* (Rev. ed.). Melbourne, 1970
Kimberly, W. B., *History of Western Australia: A Narrative of Her Past.* Melbourne, 1897
Stannage, C. T. (ed.) *A New History of Western Australia.* Perth, 1980
Stephenson, G., and Hepburn, J. A., *Plan for the Metropolitan Region: Perth and Fremantle.* Perth, 1955

State Library: Alexander Library Building, Perth. *State Librarian:* R. C. Sharman, BA, FLAA.

AUSTRIA

Republik Österreich

Capital: Vienna
Population: 7·57m. (1986)
GNP per capita: US$12,297 (1986)

HISTORY. On 27 April 1945 a provisional government restored the Republic of Austria and was recognized by the Allied Control Council on 20 Oct. 1945.

AREA AND POPULATION. For the boundaries of Austria according to the Treaty of St Germain, signed in Sept. 1919, *see* THE STATESMAN'S YEAR-BOOK, 1920, pp. 674–75. The population at census, 12 May 1981, was 7,555,338.

Federal Provinces	Area sq. km	Population (1986)	Percentage of population	Population per sq. km
Vienna (Wien)	415	1,481,399	19·6	3,570
Lower Austria (Niederösterreich)	19,172	1,424,911	18·8	74
Burgenland	3,965	267,279	3·5	67
Upper Austria (Oberösterreich)	11,980	1,290,497	17·1	108
Salzburg	7,154	459,886	6·1	64
Styria (Steiermark)	16,387	1,182,599	15·6	72
Carinthia (Kärnten)	9,534	541,526	7·2	57
Tirol	12,647	605,774	8·0	48
Vorarlberg	2,601	311,732	4·1	120
Total	83,855 [1]	7,565,603	100·0	90

[1] 32,376 sq. miles.

Vital statistics for calendar years:

	Live births	Still births	Deaths [1]	Marriages	Divorces
1983	90,118	481	93,041	56,171	14,692
1984	89,234	409	88,466	45,823	14,869
1985	87,440	407	89,578	44,867	15,460
1986	86,964	385	87,071	45,821	14,679

[1] Excluding still births.

The populations of the principal towns (excluding Vienna), according to the census of 12 May 1981 (area, 1 Jan. 1987) were as follows:

Graz	243,166	Steyr	38,942	Feldkirch	23,745	Mödling	19,276
Linz	199,910	Dornbirn	38,641	Baden	23,140	Lustenau	17,401
Salzburg	139,426	Wiener		Krems a.d.D.	23,056	Braunau	
Innsbruck	117,287	Neustadt	35,006	Klosterneu-		am Inn	16,318
Klagenfurt	87,321	Leoben	31,989	burg	22,975	Ternitz	16,104
Villach	52,692	Wolfsberg	28,097	Amstetten	21,989	Hallein	15,377
Wels	51,060	Kapfenberg	25,716	Traun	21,464	Bruck an	
St Pölten	50,419	Bregenz	24,561	Leonding	19,389	der Mur	15,068

CLIMATE. Climate ranges from cool temperate to mountain type according to situation. Winters are cold, with considerable snowfall, but summers are very warm. The wettest months are May to August.

Vienna, Jan. 28°F (–2°C), July 67°F (19·5°C). Annual rainfall 25·6" (640 mm). Graz, Jan. 28°F (–2°C), July 67°F (19·5°C). Annual rainfall 34" (849 mm). Innsbruck, Jan. 27°F (–2·7°C), July 66°F (18·8°C). Annual rainfall 34·7" (868 mm). Salzburg, Jan. 28°F (–2·0°C), July 65°F (18·3°C). Annual rainfall 50·6" (1,266 mm).

CONSTITUTION AND GOVERNMENT. Austria recovered its sovereignty and independence on 27 July 1955 by the coming into force of the Austrian State Treaty between the UK, the USA, the USSR and France on the one part and the Republic of Austria on the other part (signed on 15 May).

On 12 March 1938 Austria was forcibly absorbed in the German Reich until it was liberated by the American, British, French and Soviet armies in spring 1945. Already in the Moscow Declaration of Oct. 1943, UK, the USA and the USSR had resolved upon the re-establishment of a free and independent Austria.

On 27 April 1945 Dr Karl Renner set up a provisional government which restored the Republic of Austria in the spirit of the Constitution of 1920–29, and was recognized by the Four-Power Allied Control Council on 20 Oct. 1945. The last occupation forces left Austria in Oct. 1955.

President of the Republic: Dr Kurt Waldheim, elected on 8 June 1986.

On 23 Nov. 1986 the elections were held for the National Assembly, which returned 80 Socialists, 77 People's Party, 18 Freedom Party, Ecology Party, 8.

The Coalition government between the Socialist Party and the People's Party, which was formed in Oct. 1987 was composed as follows:

Chancellor: Dr Franz Vranitzky.

Vice Chancellor and Foreign Affairs: Dr Alois Mock. *Finance:* Ferdinand Lacina. *Social Affairs:* Alfred Dallinger. *Interior:* Karl Blecha. *State Industry:* Dr Rudolf Streicher. *Education:* Dr Hilde Hawlicek. *Women's Affairs:* Johanna Dohnal. *Chancellery:* Dr Franz Löschnak, Dr Heinrich Neisser, Dr Johannes Ditz. *Defence:* Dr Robert Lichal. *Agriculture:* Josef Riegler. *Science:* Dr Hans Tuppy. *Trade:* Robert Graf. *Youth and Environment:* Dr Marilies Flemming. *Justice:* Dr Egmont Foregger.

The Federal Council *(Bundesrat)* which represents the federal provinces has 63 members and (1987) the Socialist Party had 30 members and the People's Party 33. The *Nationalrat* and *Bundesrat* together form the National Assembly.

National flag: Three horizontal stripes of red, white, red.

National anthem: Land der Berge, Land am Strome (words by Paula Preradovic; tune by W. A. Mozart).

The official language is German.

Local Government. The Republic of Austria comprises 9 Federal States (Vienna, Lower Austria, Upper Austria, Salzburg, Styria, Carinthia, Tirol, Vorarlberg, Burgenland). There is in every province an elected Provincial Assembly.

Every community has a Council, which chooses one of its number to be head of the Community (burgomaster) and a committee for the administration and execution of its resolutions.

DEFENCE. Conscription is for a 6-month period, with liability for 60 days reservist refresher training spread over 15 years.

Army. The Army consists of an alert force *(Bereitschafts truppe)*, mainly the 1st Armoured Division organized in 3 armoured infantry brigades; a mobile militia, comprising 8 motorized infantry brigades; and a stationary militia, comprising 26 regiments and security companies. The country is divided into 2 corps areas, I (Graz) and II (Salzburg). Strength was (1988) 50,000 (25,000 conscripts).

Army Aviation. *(Heeresfliegerkräfte):* The Army Air Division comprises 10 squadrons with about 4,700 personnel and 166 aircraft, organized in three Aviation Regiments each of which including air defence battalions. About 30 SAAB105 Oe strike/trainer aircraft equip a surveillance wing of one squadron responsible for defence of Austrian airspace and a fighter-bomber wing of two squadrons. Helicopters equip six squadrons for transport/support, communications, observation, search and rescue duties. Types in service include Alouette III, armed Kiowa, JetRanger and Agusta-Bell AB.204s and AB.212s. Fixed-wing transports comprise two Skyvans and 11 Turbo-Porters.

INTERNATIONAL RELATIONS

Membership. Austria is a member of UN, OECD and EFTA.

ECONOMY

Budget. The budget for calendar years provided revenue and expenditure (ordinary and extraordinary) as follows (in 1m. schilling):

	1981	1982	1983	1984	1985	1986	1987[1]
Revenue	287,791	300,955	316,673	344,901	372,895	391,321	398,456
Expenditure	339,456	372,774	407,791	435,136	464,673	498,033	509,582

[1] Provisional.

External debt. The budgetary external debt was (1986) 124,605m. schilling.

Currency. The Austrian unit of currency is the *schilling* of 100 *groschen*. The rate of exchange in March 1988, £1 = 21·03 *schilling*, US$1 = 11·85 *schilling*.

Banking. The National Bank of Austria, opened on 2 Jan. 1923, was taken over by the German Reichsbank on 17 March 1938. It was re-established on 3 July 1945. At 31 Dec. 1987 foreign exchange amounted to 75,428m. and note circulation to 98,387m. schilling.

Principal banks with total assets (in 1m. schilling 1986): Creditanstalt, 372,469; Girozentrale Und Bank der Österreichischen Sparkassen, 265,737; Österreichische National Bank, 220,238; Österreichische Länderbank, 197,692; Zentralsparkasse Und Kommerzialbank, 191,037; Österreichische Kontrollbank, 184,265; Bank Für Arbeit Und Wirtschaft, 176,763; Genossenschaftliche Zentralbank, 160,117; Österreichische Postsparkasse, 155,079; Die Erste Osterreichische Spar-Casse-Bank, 130,489; Österreichische Volksbanken, 55,144; Österreichische Investitionskredit, 42,600; Bank Für Oberösterreich Und Salzburg, 38,101; Österreichisches Creditinstitut, 36,865.

Weights and Measures. The metric system of weights and measures is in use.

ENERGY AND NATURAL RESOURCES

Electricity. Electric energy produced (1m. kwh.): 1986, 44,653; 1985, 44,534; 1984, 42,382; 1983, 42,625. Supply 220 volts; 50 Hz.

Oil. The commercial production of petroleum began in the early 1930s. Production of crude oil (in tonnes): 1960, 2,448,391; 1971, 2,798,237; 1983, 1,268,573; 1984, 1,205,430; 1985, 1,146,958; 1986, 1,115,924.

Minerals. The mineral production (in tonnes) was as follows:

	1985	1986		1985	1986
Lignite	3,081,071	2,968,978	Pig-iron	3,703,992	3,348,600
Iron ore	3,270,000	3,120,000	Raw steel	4,660,426	4,291,895
Lead and zinc ore [1]	643,255	400,246	Rolled steel	3,759,595	3,461,545
Raw magnesite [1]	1,255,043	1,084,360	Tungsten ore	538,306	489,006

[1] Including recovery from slag.

Austria is one of the world's largest sources of high-grade graphite. Production, which averaged 20,000 tonnes yearly from 1929 to 1944, dropped to 246 in 1946, but rose to 102,237 in 1964, and fell again to 23,992 in 1970, 37,199 in 1980, 23,807 in 1981, 24,451 in 1982, 40,418 in 1983, 43,789 in 1984, 30,764 in 1985 and 36,167 in 1986.

Agriculture. In 1986 the total area sown amounted to 1,418,120 hectares.

The chief products (area in hectares, yield in tonnes) were as follows:

	1984		1985		1986	
	Area	Yield	Area	Yield	Area	Yield
Wheat	315,126	1,501,005	319,837	1,562,770	324,415	1,414,599
Rye	93,525	380,722	88,131	338,700	83,406	283,601
Barley	328,579	1,516,981	344,079	1,521,408	332,685	1,292,450
Oats	77,457	292,024	75,247	283,893	73,362	269,919
Potatoes	41,322	1,138,097	37,719	1,042,196	34,854	982,405

Production of raw sugar in 1949, 66,700; 1955, 219,300; 1960, 308,000; refined sugar: 1970, 298,000; 1980, 419,800; 1981, 446,900; 1982, 563,472; 1983, 354,479; 1984, 426,544; 1985, 430,730; 1986, 282,576 tonnes.

Livestock (1986): Cattle, 2,637,224; pigs, 3,800,510; sheep, 255,708; goats, 30,694; horses, 43,567; poultry, 14,197,751.

Forestry. Forested area 41% of which 75% coniferous. Felled timber, in cu. metres: 1960, 10,015,925; 1970, 11,122,896; 1980, 12,732,507; 1985, 11,625,732; 1986, 12,130,950.

INDUSTRY AND TRADE

Industry. On 26 July 1946 the Austrian parliament passed a government bill, nationalizing some 70 industrial concerns. As from 17 Sept. 1946 ownership of the 3 largest commercial banks, most oil-producing and refining companies and the principal firms in the following industries devolved upon the Austrian state: River navigation; coal extraction; non-ferrous mining and refining; iron-ore mining; pig-iron and steel production; manufacture of iron and steel products, including structural material, machinery, railroad equipment and repairs, and shipbuilding; electrical machinery and appliances. Six companies supplying electric power were nationalized in accordance with a law of 26 March 1947.

In 1986, 9,291 industrial establishments (including 2,124 sawmills) employed 561,587 persons, producing a value of 632m. schillings.

Commerce. Imports and exports are as follows (excluding coined gold):

	Imports			Exports		
	1984	1985	1986	1984	1985	1986
Quantity (1,000 tonnes)	37,657	39,238	38,910	18,198	18,279	18,050
Value (1m. sch.)	392,094	430,469	407,954	314,504	353,962	342,479

The total trade between Austria and UK (British Department of Trade returns, in £1,000 sterling):

	1983	1984	1985	1986	1987
Imports to UK	438,445	529,620	630,586	705,732	781,986
Exports and re-exports from UK	273,702	320,901	381,047	403,000	463,187

Tourism. Tourism is an important industry. In 1986, 20,637 hotels and boarding-houses had a total of 665,156 beds available; 15,092,283 foreigners visited Austria; of these 772,650 came from the UK and 509,472 from the USA.

COMMUNICATIONS

Roads. On 31 Dec. 1986 federal roads had a total length of 10,240 km, 1,303 km autobahn; provincial roads, 23,464 km. On 31 Dec. 1986 there were registered 3,873,574 motor vehicles, including 2,609,390 passenger cars, 212,463 lorries, 369,924 tractors and 278,310 trailers.

Railways. Austrian railways have been nationalized since before the First World War. Length of route (Dec. 1986), 5,772 km, of which 3,134 km were electrified. Nineteen private railways have a total length of 563 km. Passengers in 1986 numbered 173m., and 64m. tonnes of freight were carried.

Aviation. Austria has 6 airports in Vienna (Schwechat), Linz, Salzburg, Graz, Klagenfurt and Innsbruck. In 1986, 89,235 commercial aircraft arrived and departed at Austrian airports.

Shipping. Austria has no sea frontiers, but the Danube is an important waterway. Goods traffic (in tonnes): 6,622,486 in 1982; 6,533,730 in 1983; 8,093,854 in 1984; 7,619,115 in 1985; 7,708,311 in 1986. Ore and metal, coal and coke and iron ore comprise in bulk more than two-thirds of these cargoes. The Danube Steam-ship Co. (DDSG) is the main Austrian shipping company.

Post and Broadcasting. All postal, telegraph and telephone services are run by the State. In 1986 there were 2,818,000 telephones.

The 'Österreichische Rundfunk' transmits 2 national and 9 regional program-mes. In the local area of Vienna there is an additional special service in English and French; there is also a 24 hour foreign service (short wave). All broadcasting is financed by licence payments and advertisements. There were 2·6m. registered listeners in Jan. 1986. Television was inaugurated in summer 1955 and 2 programmes are transmitted, both in colour.

Cinemas (1986). There were 479 cinemas.

Newspapers (1986). There were 33 daily newspapers (6 of them in Vienna) with a combined circulation of 2·7m.

JUSTICE, RELIGION, EDUCATION AND WELFARE

Justice. The Supreme Court of Justice *(Oberster Gerichtshof)* in Vienna is the highest court in the land. Besides there are 4 higher provincial courts *(Oberlandesgerichte)*, 20 provincial and district courts *(Landes- und Kreisgerichte)* and 205 local courts *(Bezirksgerichte)*.

Religion. In 1981 there were 6,372,645 Roman Catholics (84·3%), 423,162 Protestants (5·6%), 118,866 others (1·6%), 452,039 without religious allegiance (6%) and 79,017 (1%) unknown. The Roman Catholic Church has 2 archbishoprics and 7 bishoprics.

Education (1986–87). There were in Austria 5,138 elementary and special schools with 68,587 teachers and 658,178 pupils. Of all kinds of secondary schools there were 1,523 with 532,070 pupils.

There were also 112 commercial academies with 37,289 students and 4,645 teachers. There were 248 schools of technical and industrial training (including schools of hotel management and catering) with 5,999 teachers and 62,103 pupils; 49 higher schools of women's professions (secondary level) with 14,176 pupils; 9 training colleges of social workers with 647 pupils. 143 trade schools had 19,987 pupils.

Austria has 12 universities and 6 colleges of arts maintained by the State: Universities at Vienna (2,819 teachers, 58,696 students), Graz (1,163 teachers, 22,086 students), Innsbruck (1,283 teachers, 18,771 students) and Salzburg (501 teachers, 9,443 students). There are also technical universities at Vienna (1,069 teachers, 14,828 students) and Graz (567 teachers, 8,024 students), a mining university at Leoben (201 teachers, 1,760 students), an agricultural university at Vienna (232 teachers, 4,985 students), a veterinary university at Vienna (187 teachers, 2,304 students), a commercial university at Vienna (259 teachers, 16,187 students), a university for social and economic sciences at Linz (366 teachers, 8,646 students) and a university for educational science at Klagenfurt (147 teachers, 2,763 students). There is an academy of fine arts at Vienna (152 teachers, 471 students), a college of applied arts at Vienna (213 teachers, 953 students), 3 colleges of music and dramatic art at Vienna (480 teachers, 2,153 students), 'Mozarteum' Salzburg (317 teachers, 1,284 students) and Graz (278 teachers, 1,084 students); the college for industrial design at Linz (118 teachers, 383 students).

Health. In 1986 there were 21,676 doctors, 332 hospitals and 83,021 hospital beds.

DIPLOMATIC REPRESENTATIVES

Of Austria in Great Britain (18 Belgrave Mews West, London, SW1X 8HU)
Ambassador: Dr Walter F. Magrutsch (accredited 11 Feb. 1988).

Of Great Britain in Austria (Reisnerstrasse 40, 1030 Vienna)
Ambassador: R. J. O'Neill, CMG (accredited 5 Sept. 1986).

Of Austria in the USA (2343 Massachusetts Ave., NW, Washington, D.C., 20008)
Ambassador: Dr Friedrich Hoess.

Of the USA in Austria (Boltzmanngasse, 16, A-1091 Vienna)
Ambassador: Henry A. Grunwald.

Of Austria to the United Nations
Ambassador: Dr Peter Hohenfellner.

Books of Reference

Statistical Information: The Austrian Central Statistical Office was founded in 1829. *Address:* Hintere Zollamtsstrasze, 2b, 1033 Vienna. *Main publications:*
Statistisches Handbuch für die Republik Österreich. New Series from 1950. Annually
Statistische Nachrichten. Monthly
Beiträge zur österreichischen Statistik (850 vols.)
Ergebnisse der Volkszählung vom 12 Mai 1981 (26 vols.)
Ergebnisse der Häuser- und Wohnungszählung vom 12 Mai 1981 (14 vols.)
Statistik in Österreich 1918–1938. [Bibliography] Vienna, 1985
Veröffentlichungen des Österr. Statist Zentralamfes 1945–1985. [Bibliography] Vienna, 1986

Bobek, H. (ed.), *Atlas der Republik Österreich.* 3 vols. Vienna, 1961 ff.
Salt, D., *Austria.* [Bibliography] Oxford and Santa Barbara, 1986
Sotriffer, K., *Greater Austria: 100 Years of Intellectual and Social Life from 1800 to the Present Time.* Vienna, 1982
Waldheim, K., *In the Eye of the Storm.* London, 1985

National Library: Österreichische Nationalbibliothek, Vienna. *Director General:* Magda Strebl.

THE COMMONWEALTH OF THE BAHAMAS

Capital: Nassau
Population: 235,000 (1986)
GNP per capita: US$7,950 (1984)

HISTORY. The Bahamas were discovered by Columbus in 1492 but the Spanish did not make a permanent settlement. British settlers arrived in the 17th century and it was occupied by Britain, except for a short period in the 18th century, until it gained independence. Internal self-government with cabinet responsibility was introduced on 7 Jan. 1964 and full independence achieved on 10 July 1973.

AREA AND POPULATION. The Commonwealth of the Bahamas consists of 700 islands and more than 1,000 cays off the south-east coast of Florida. They are the surface protuberances of two oceanic banks, the Little Bahama Bank and the Great Bahama Bank. Land area, 5,353 sq. miles (13,864 sq. km).

The areas and populations of the major islands are as follows:

	Sq. km	1980		Sq. km	1980
Grand Bahama	1,373	33,102	San Salvador	163 ⎫	825
Abaco	1,681	7,271	Rum Cay	78 ⎭	
Bimini Islands	23	1,411	Long Island	448	3,404
Berry Islands	31	509	Ragged Island	23	164
New Providence	207	135,437	Crooked Island	238	518
Andros	5,957	8,307	Long Cay	23	33
Eleuthera	518	10,631	Acklins Island	389	618
Cat Island	388	2,215	Mayaguana	110	464
Exuma Islands	290	3,670	Inagua Islands	1,671	924

The capital is Nassau on New Providence Island (135,437 inhabitants in 1980). About 15% of the population are of British extraction, the rest being of African and mixed descent.

Vital statistics, 1984: Births, 5,177; deaths, 1,150 (excluding still-births); marriages, 1,720.

CLIMATE. Winters are mild and summers pleasantly warm. Most rain falls in May, June, Sept. and Oct., and thunderstorms are frequent in summer. Rainfall amounts vary over the islands from 30″ (750 mm) to 60″ (1,500 mm). Nassau. Jan. 71°F (21·7°C), July 81°F (27·2°C). Annual rainfall 47″ (1,179 mm).

CONSTITUTION AND GOVERNMENT. The Commonwealth of the Bahamas is a free and democratic sovereign state. Executive power rests with Her Majesty the Queen, who appoints a Governor-General to represent her, advised by a Cabinet whom he appoints. There is a bicameral legislature. The Senate comprises 16 members all appointed by the Governor-General, 9 on the advice of the Prime Minister, 4 on the advice of the Leader of the Opposition, and 3 after consultation with both of them. The House of Assembly consists of 49 members elected from single-member constituencies for a maximum term of 5 years. At the general election of 19 June 1987, the Progressive Liberal Party obtained 31 seats, the Free National Movement 16 seats and 2 independents.

Independence from Britain took place on 10 July 1973.

Governor-General: Sir Gerald Cash, GCMG, KCVO, OBE.

The Cabinet in Jan. 1988 was composed as follows:

Prime Minister, Finance: Rt. Hon. Sir Lynden O. Pindling, KCMG.
Foreign Affairs and Tourism: Clement T. Maynard. *Youth, Sports and Community Affairs:* Peter Bethel. *Housing:* George Mackey. *Works and Utilities, Housing and National Insurance:* Darrell E. Rolle. *Attorney-General and*

Education: Senator Paul L. Adderley. *Employment:* Alfred T. Maycock. *Transport and Local Government:* Philip M. Bethel. *Health:* Norman R. Gay. *Agriculture:* Ervin Knowles.

National flag: Three horizontal stripes of aquamarine, gold, aquamarine, with a black triangle on the hoist.

INTERNATIONAL RELATIONS

Membership. The Commonwealth of the Bahamas is a member of UN, OAS, the Commonwealth, CARICOM and an ACP state of the EEC.

ECONOMY

Budget (in B$):

	1984	1985	1986
Revenue	350,875,000	423,000,000	458,242,095
Expenditure	383,092,000	486,858,000	529,368,000

The main sources of revenue were customs duties and receipts from fees, post office and public utilities.

Currency. A decimal system of currency was introduced in 1966. Bahamian $1.77 = £1 sterling (March 1988). Notes: $0.50, 1, 3, 5, 10, 20, 50, 100; coins: 1, 5, 10, 15, 25, 50 cents, $1, 2, 5. Sterling currency has been withdrawn. American currency is generally accepted.

Bank of England and Canadian notes are not accepted, except at the banks from travellers from the UK.

Banking. The Central Bank of the Bahamas was established in June 1974 with assets (Dec. 1985) of B$224·19m. and capital and reserves of B$48·57m. On 30 Sept. 1985 there were 375 institutions licensed to carry on banking and/or trust business under the Banks and Trust Companies Regulations Act. There were 19 designated institutions by the Exchange Control Department as authorized dealers and agents. Among these were the Royal Bank of Canada, the Bank of Nova Scotia, the Bank of Montreal, Chase Manhattan Bank, Barclays Bank, the Canadian Imperial Bank of Commerce and Citibank. While the majority of banks are located in Nassau, there are branches on several of the other islands. The Bahamas Development Bank was established in 1974 and began operations in Jan. 1978; at Dec. 1985 it had total assets of B$12·07m. and paid-up capital of B$6m.

The post office savings bank, 31 Dec. 1983, had deposits of B$2·6m.

Weights and Measures. The UK (Imperial) system is in force.

ENERGY AND NATURAL RESOURCES

Electricity. Total units generated in New Providence/Paradise Island and Family Islands (1985), 789·3m. mwh. Supply 115 volts; 60 Hz.

Agriculture. In 1985 crop diversification continued to be a major area of emphasis. Orchards established in the early 1980's were in full production, with an estimated 2,500 acres of fruit crops, mainly citrus, for export. 12,528 tons of fruit and vegetables were exported in 1985. Pigeon peas, Irish potatoes and peanuts were the main field crops on which increased emphasis was placed and cassava and sweet potatoes the most important root crops. Poultry production in 1985 was estimated at 15·2m. lb of broilers valued at B$15·5m. An estimated 4·2m. dozen eggs valued at B$4·3m. were produced in 1985. Production of sheep, goats and pigs declined in 1985: 133 sheep, 122 goats and 3,871 pigs were slaughtered. Beef production increased, with 19 beef cattle slaughtered.

Total agricultural production including fisheries was valued at B$34m. in 1985. Production, 1986 (in 1,000 tonnes): Sugar-cane, 232; vegetables, 28; fruit, 13.

Livestock (1986): Cattle, 5,000; sheep, 40,000; goats, 18,000; pigs, 20,000; poultry, 1m.

Forestry. Production of cascarilla bark and pulp-wood in 1976 was B$1·8m., all of which was exported.

Fisheries. Crawfish exports were valued at B$12m. in 1982.

INDUSTRY AND TRADE

Industry. Tourism is the major industry. Several light industries have been established on Grand Bahama and New Providence in response to special encouragement legislation; these include garment manufacturing, ice, furniture, purified water, plastic containers, perfumes, industrial gases, jewellery and others. Larger industrial activities in the Bahamas include manufacture of alcoholic beverages, pharmaceuticals, aragonite mining and solar salt production. Two industrial sites, one in New Providence and the other in Grand Bahama, have been developed as part of the industrialization programme.

Trade Unions. In 1986 there were 36 unions, the largest is the Bahamas Hotel Catering and Allied Workers' Union (5,000 members) and the Bahamas Public Services Union (over 4,000 members).

Commerce. The principal exports in 1980 were hormones, rum, salt, crawfish, cement, aragonite and plywood.

The principal imports in 1977 were: Food, drink and tobacco, raw materials and articles mainly unmanufactured, articles wholly or mainly manufactured, animals not for food.

Imports and exports (excluding bullion and specie) for 6 calendar years in B$:

	Imports	Exports		Imports	Exports
1977	2,787,943	2,597,352	1980	5,506,577	4,836,366
1978	2,482,235	2,117,938	1981	4,203,000	3,515,000
1979	3,985,034	3,495,043	1982	3,051,000	2,444,000

Total trade between Bahamas and UK, in £1,000 sterling (British Department of Trade returns):

	1983	1984	1985	1986	1987
Imports to UK	24,013	38,478	70,763	10,266	15,943
Exports and re-exports from UK	17,815	220,356	94,059	95,816	27,063

Tourism. Tourism is the most important industry in the Bahamas. In 1986 there were 3,002,000 foreign arrivals in the Bahamas.

COMMUNICATIONS

Roads. There are 240 miles of paved roads in New Providence, and approximately 885 miles in Grand Bahama and the Family Islands. In 1985, 85,105 motor vehicles were registered. There are no railroads.

Aviation. Nassau international airport is located on the island of New Providence, about 10 miles from the city of Nassau. There is another international airport at Freeport. Scheduled flights—Air Canada: 3 times weekly from Toronto and once weekly from Montreal to Nassau; twice weekly from Toronto to Freeport and once weekly from Montreal to Freeport. Delta: twice daily from New York to Nassau; once daily from Boston and Newark. Eastern Airlines: 3 flights daily from New York, 3 times daily from Miami, once daily from Fort Lauderdale, twice weekly from Baltimore, Washington and Philadelphia, once daily from Boston and Newark, once daily from New York *via* Miami and Fort Lauderdale to Nassau; 3 times daily from Miami, once daily from Baltimore and Philadelphia to Freeport: Lufthansa: 3 times weekly from Frankfurt and Mexico and once weekly from Merida to Nassau. Air Jamaica: once daily from Chicago, Kingston and Montego Bay to Nassau. American Airlines: once daily from New York to Nassau and 4 times weekly from New York to Freeport. British Airways: 4 times weekly from London and Bermuda, twice weekly from Kingston and Panama and once weekly from Mexico City, all to Nassau; once weekly from London, Bermuda, Kingston and Panama to Freeport. There are numerous domestic schedules to the Family Islands and Florida. There are 55 airstrips on the various Family Islands and numerous water alighting areas. During 1985, 1·07m. passengers landed at Nassau and 54,565 aircraft arrivals. At Freeport in 1985, 485,936 passengers landed from 32,043 aircraft arrivals.

Shipping. In 1980, 678 cruise liners cleared Nassau carrying 499,527 passengers; 653 cargo vessels discharged 268,477 tons of cargo at Nassau. There are indirect cargo services with UK and Canada *via* the USA and passenger services with the USA only.

Telecommunications. New Providence and most of the other major islands have modern automatic telephone systems in operation, interconnected by an extensive multi-channel radio network, while local distribution within the islands is by over-head and underground cables. The total number of telephones in use at 31 Dec. 1986 was approximately 105,000. International telecommunications service is provided by a submarine cable system to Florida, USA, and international operator assisted and direct dialling telephone services are available to all major countries. There is an automatic Telex system and a packet switching system for data transmission, and land mobile and marine telephone services. The Bahamas Broadcasting Corporation operates radio broadcasting stations on AM and FM in New Providence and Grand Bahama and a TV station in New Providence.

Cinemas (1986). There are 4 cinemas.

Newspapers (1986). There are 2 daily and 1 weekly newspapers in Nassau.

JUSTICE, EDUCATION AND WELFARE

Justice (1977). 9,655 cases (traffic, 3,550; criminal, 3,218; civil, 1,880; domestic, 1,007) were dealt with in the magistrates' court, and civil, 816; divorce, 256 in the Supreme Court. The strength of the police force (1973) was 932 officers and other ranks.

Education. Education is under the jurisdiction of the Ministry of Education and Culture. In 1985–86 there were 226 schools, and of these, 188 are fully maintained by Government and 38 are independent schools. Total school enrolment, 60,744. There are 38 government-owned schools in New Providence and 150 on the Family Islands. 25 independent schools are located on New Providence and 13 on the Family Islands. 292 students attended 5 special schools, 3 on New Providence and 2 on Grand Bahama; total staff, 49. Free education is available in ministry schools in New Providence and the Family Islands. Courses lead to the Bahamas Junior Certificate and the General Certificate of Education (GCE). Independent schools provide education at primary, secondary and higher levels.

The College of the Bahamas, officially opened in 1975, is the only publicly-funded tertiary level institution. It offers a wide range of programmes leading to the associate degree, advanced level GCE (London), college diplomas and certificates. Degree programmes in education are offered in conjunction with the University of the West Indies and the University of Miami.

The Hotel Training College offers a wide range of subjects up to middle management level in aspects of hotel work. Enrolment in this institution includes Bahamian as well as regional and international students. Several schools of continuing education offer secretarial and academic courses. The Government-operated Princess Margaret Hospital offers a nursing course at two levels.

Health. In 1984 there was a government general hospital (454 beds) and a psychiatric/geriatric rehabilitation centre (417 beds) in Nassau, and a hospital in Freeport (74 beds). The Family Islands, comprising 19 health districts, had 12 health centres, 35 main clinics and 50 satellite clinics. There was 1 private hospital (24 beds) in Nassau.

DIPLOMATIC REPRESENTATIVES

Of the Bahamas in Great Britain (10 Chesterfield St., London, W1X 8AH)
High Commissioner: Richard C. Demeritte (accredited 24 Oct. 1984).

Of Great Britain in the Bahamas (Bitco Bldg., East St., Nassau)
High Commissioner: Colin Mays.

Of the Bahamas in the USA (600 New Hampshire Ave., NW, Washington, D.C., 20037)
Ambassador: Margaret MacDonald.

Of the USA in the Bahamas (Queen St., Nassau)
Ambassador: Carol Boyd Hallett.

Of the Bahamas to the United Nations
Ambassador: Dr Davidson L. Hepburn.

Books of Reference

Bahamas Handbook and Businessman's Annual (Annual)
Albury, P., *The Story of the Bahamas.* London, 1975.—*Paradise Island Story.* London, 1984
Barrett, P. J. H., *Grand Bahama.* London, 1982
Craton, M. A., *A History of the Bahamas.* London, 1962
Hughes, C. A., *Race and Politics in the Bahamas.* Univ. of Queensland Press, 1981
Hunte, G., *The Bahamas.* London, 1975
Stevenson, C. St. J., *The Bahamas Reference Annual.* Annual

Library: Nassau Public Library.

BAHRAIN

Dawlat al Bahrayn

Capital: Manama
Population: 416,275 (1987)
GNP per capita: US$11,708 (1985)

HISTORY. Treaties with Britain of 1882 and 1892 were replaced by a treaty of friendship which was signed on 15 Aug. 1971. Under the earlier treaties Britain had been responsible for Bahrain's defence and foreign relations. On the same day the State of Bahrain declared its independence.

AREA AND POPULATION. The State of Bahrain forms an archipelago of about 33 small islands in the Arabian Gulf, between the Qatar peninsula and the mainland of Saudi Arabia. The total area is about 265·5 sq. miles (687·75 sq. km). Bahrain ('Two Seas'), is 30 miles long and 10 miles wide (578 sq. km). It is connected by a causeway nearly 1·5 miles long, carrying a motor road, with the second largest island, Muharraq, 4 miles long and 1 mile wide, to the north-east, and by a causeway with Sitra, an island 3 miles long and 1 mile wide, to the east. In Nov. 1986 a causeway linking Bahrain with Saudi Arabia was officially opened. Other islands are Umm Al-Nassan, 3 miles by 2 miles, and Jidda, 1 mile by 0·5 mile, both to the west; Nabih Saleh, to the east; the Hawar group of 16 small islands off Qatar, to the south-east, and several islets, some uninhabited. From Sitra oil pipelines and a causeway carrying a road extend out to sea for 3 miles to a deep-water anchorage. The islands are low-lying, the highest ground being a hill in the centre of Bahrain, 450 ft. (122·4 metres) high.

The population in 1981 (census) was 350,798. Estimate (1987) 416,275. The majority of the people are Moslem arabs.

Arabic is the official language. English is widely used in business.

Manama, the capital of the state and the commercial centre, is situated at the northern end of the largest island and extends for 1·5 miles along the shore. It has a population 1987, of 121,986 (1981 census, 108,684). Other towns are Muharraq, 1987, 61,853 (46,061); Jidhafs, 33,693 (7,232); Rifa'a, 28,150 (22,408); Isa Town (21,275) and Hidd (7,111).

CLIMATE. The climate is pleasantly warm between Dec. and March but from June to Sept. the conditions are very hot and humid. The period June to Nov. is virtually rainless. Bahrain. Jan. 66°F (19°C), July 97°F (36°C). Annual rainfall 5·2″ (130 mm).

CONSTITUTION AND GOVERNMENT. A Constitution was ratified in June 1973 providing for a National Assembly of 30 members, popularly elected for a 4-year term, together with all members of the Cabinet (appointed by the Amir). Elections took place in Dec. 1973, but in Aug. 1975 the Amir dissolved the Assembly and has since ruled through the Cabinet alone.

Reigning Amir: The ruling family is the Al Khalifa, an Arab dynasty, who have been in power since 1782. The present Amir, HH Shaikh Isa bin Sulman Al-Khalifa (born 1933) succeeded on 2 Nov. 1961. *Crown Prince and Minister of Defence:* Shaikh Hamad bin Isa Al-Khalifa.

In Oct. 1987 the cabinet was composed as follows:
Prime Minister: Shaikh Khalifa bin Sulman Al-Khalifa.
Defence: Shaikh Hamad bin Isa Al-Khalifa. *Transport:* Ibrahim Mohammed Hassan Homaidan. *Housing:* Shaikh Khalid bin Abdulla Al-Khalifa. *Information:* Tariq Abdulrahman Almoayed. *Education:* Dr Ali Fakhro. *Health:* Jawad Salim Al-Arrayed. *Justice and Islamic Affairs:* Shaikh Abdullah bin Khalid Al-Khalifa. *Labour and Social Affairs:* Shaikh Khalifa bin Sulman bin Mohammed Al-Khalifa. *Works, Power and Water:* Majid Jawad Al Jishi. *Interior:* Shaikh

Mohammed bin Khalifa Al-Khalifa. *Foreign Affairs:* Shaikh Mohammed bin Mubarak Al-Khalifa. *Finance and National Economy:* Ibrahim Abdul-Karim. *Development and Industry:* Yousuf Ahmed Al-Shirawi. *Commerce and Agriculture:* Habib Ahmed Kassim. *Acting Minister of State for Cabinet Affairs:* Yousuf Ahmed Al-Shirawi. *Minister of State for Legal Affairs:* Dr Hussain Al Baharna.

Flag: Red, with white serrated vertical strip on hoist.

DEFENCE

Army. The Army consists of 1 infantry battalion, 1 armoured car squadron, 1 artillery and 2 mortar batteries with a personnel strength of 2,300 (1988). Equipment included 8 Saladin armoured cars and 8 Ferret scout cars.

Navy. The Naval force consists of 4 fast missile craft and 2 fast gunboats; personnel (1988) 300. There is also a Coast Guard with 20 coastal patrol craft and 4 other vessels. Coast Guard personnel number 250.

Air Force. An independent Air Force was created in 1985 as the successor to the Air Wing of the Army (Bahrain Defence Force). A fighter squadron operates 12 F-5E/F Tiger IIs, while 12 F-16s are on order for delivery in 1989–90. Three MBB BO 105 helicopters are also in use. Police and security forces both also operate helicopters.

INTERNATIONAL RELATIONS

Membership. Bahrain is a member of UN, the Arab League, the Gulf Co-operation Council and OAPEC.

ECONOMY

Budget. The revenue of the State is derived from oil royalties and from customs duties, which are 10% *ad valorem* for luxury goods and 5% for essential goods. The exceptions are motor vehicles (20%); tobacco (30%); alcoholic beverages (100%); fresh fruit and vegetables (7%). Total revenues in 1987, BD 560m. (of which oil BD 346m.) and expenditure BD 560m.

On 2 Jan. 1958 Manama was declared a free transit port and the former 2% transit duty was abolished, but storage charges are levied.

Currency. The Bahrain *dinar* is divided into 1,000 *fils*. The Bahrain currency board issues notes of 20, 10, 5 and 1 *dinars*, and 500 *fils*, and coins of 100, 50, 25, 10, 5 and 1 *fils*. £1 = BD 0·669 in March 1988; US$1 = BD 0·377.

Banking. The Bahrain Monetary Agency has central banking powers. Since Nov. 1984 it has been responsible for licensing and monitoring the activities of money changers. There were (1986) 19 full commercial banks (including Bahrain Islamic Bank), 6 of which are locally incorporated and the rest branches of foreign banks. Total assets at 31 Dec. 1986, BD 2,085m. Two types of offshore banking units were operating in 1985: Locally incorporated banks (including 4 Islamic) with headquarters in Bahrain, and branches of foreign banks. Total assets at 31 Dec. 1986 US$55,700m. There are 15 investment banks (3 Islamic), with assets of US$1,750m. in Dec. 1985. The state-owned Housing Bank provides financing for construction, development of real estate and reclamation of land.

Weights and Measures. The metric system of weights and measures is officially in use.

ENERGY AND NATURAL RESOURCES

Electricity. Production (1986) 2,891·2m. kwh. Supply 230 volts; 50 Hz.

Oil. In 1931 oil was discovered. Operations were conducted by the Bahrain Petroleum Co., registered in Canada but owned by US interests, under a concession granted by the Shaikh. Production of crude oil in 1987 was 2m. tonnes. A large oil refinery on Bahrain Island, besides treating crude oil produced locally, also processes oil from Saudi Arabia transported by pipeline.

In 1975 the Bahrain Government assumed a direct 60% interest in the Bahrain oilfield and related crude oil facilities of BAPCO.

Bahrain's oil reserves will be exhausted by the end of the century.

Gas. There is an abundant supply of natural gas with known reserves of 7·1m. cu. ft. in 1986. Production, 1986, 204,972m. cu. ft. Bahrain's gas reserves are 100% government-owned.

Water. Water is obtained from artesian wells and desalination plants and there is a piped supply to Manama, Muharraq, Isa Town, Rifa'a and most villages.

Agriculture. The 6-year agricultural plan, commissioned in 1982, aimed to increase food production from 6–16% of total domestic requirements and to improve conservation of natural water and irrigation techniques.

There are about 900 farms and small holdings (average 2·5 hectares) operated by about 2,500 farmers who produce a wide variety of fruits (45,000 tonnes in 1986) and vegetables (30,000 tonnes in 1986). The major crop is alfalfa for animal fodder. Ninety tonnes of dates a year are processed and a new processing plant produced a further 300 tonnes in 1986.

Over 30 poultry farms produced about 3,000 tonnes of domestic poultry in 1986. 85% of egg requirements are met by domestic production of 61·2m. eggs a year, and 51% of broiler needs.

Livestock (1986): Cattle, 6,000; camels, 1,000; sheep, 7,000; goats, 15,000; poultry 1m.

Fisheries. The government operates a fleet of 2 large and 5 smaller trawlers. In 1985 total landings weighed 7,762 tonnes with a value of BD6·1m.

INDUSTRY AND TRADE

Industry. Bahrain is being developed as a major manufacturing state, the first important enterprise being the Aluminium Bahrain (ALBA), a company whose original shareholders included the Bahrain Government and British, Swedish, Federal German and US interests. In 1975, the government acquired a majority shareholding in the enterprise. The aluminium smelter operation is the largest non-oil industry in the Gulf. Ancillary industries developed around aluminium smelting include the production of aluminium powder. The Gulf Aluminium Rolling Mill Company (GARMCO), a joint venture between Bahrain, Saudi Arabia, Kuwait, Iraq, Oman and Qatar, was inaugurated in Feb. 1986. The Arab Shipbuilding and Repair Yard (ASRY), commissioned in 1977, is now in service. The dry dock can handle up to 50 tankers (500,000 DWT each) annually. A US$207m. iron ore pelletizing plant was inaugurated in Dec. 1984 and a US$400m. petrochemical complex started operations in 1985.

In addition to the traditional minor industries such as boat-building, weaving, pottery, etc., other modern industries have developed, which include electronics assembly and the production of building materials, furniture, syringes and other medical items, matches, asbestos pipes and plastics, foodstuffs and textiles.

The pearling industry for which Bahrain used to be famous has considerably declined.

Employment. Total work force (estimate 1986) 172,500, of which 41·5% Bahraini.

Commerce. In 1986 total imports were BD916·8m. and total exports were BD885·6m. Refined petroleum accounted for almost 86% of exports; crude oil accounted for 47% of merchandise imports.

The major non-oil imports in 1985 were machinery and transport, BD246·2m.; classified manufactured goods, including Alumina, BD133·2m.; chemicals, BD60·4m.; food and live animals, BD82·2m., and miscellaneous manufactured articles, BD79·6m. The chief sources of supply (in BD1m.) were USA (119·6); UK (105); Japan (98·6); Federal Republic of Germany (42·1), and Australia (36·5).

The chief non-oil exports in 1985 were classified manufactured goods, including aluminium, BD96·6m., and machinery and transport, BD30m. The main markets (in BD1m.) were Saudi Arabia (26); Japan (16); UAE (15·5); China (8·3), and India (7·3).

Import of arms and ammunition and telecommunication equipment is subject to special permission; the sale of alcoholic liquor is restricted and the import of cultured pearls is forbidden.

Total trade between Bahrain and UK (British Department of Trade returns, in £1,000 sterling):

	1983	1984	1985	1986	1987
Imports to UK	37,488	28,240	45,219	19,732	60,687
Exports and re-exports from UK	150,264	138,614	161,560	130,991	125,189

Tourism. More than 165,000 tourists from the Gulf area arrived in 1985.

COMMUNICATIONS

Roads. The 25 km causeway links Bahrain with Saudi Arabia. In 1986 there were 109,982 registered vehicles.

Aviation. The airport, situated at Muharraq, can take the largest aircraft and is considered one of the most modern and efficient in the Middle East, used by 2,110,132 passengers in 1986. British Airways, Gulf Air, Middle East Airlines, Pakistan International Airways, Qantas, Kuwait Airways, Air India International, Singapore Airlines, UTA, Saudi Arabian Airlines, KLM, Air Lanka, Cathay Pacific Airways, Iraqi Airways, Korean Airways, Philippine Airlines, Thai Airways International, Trans-Mediterranean Airways, Egyptair, Alia, Cyprus Airways, Ethiopia Airlines and Sudan Airways also operate to and from Bahrain. Bahrain International Airport is the Arabian Gulf's main air communication centre.

Shipping. Bahrain's traditional position as the entrepôt of the Southern Gulf has been supplemented by the development of Mina Sulman—the new modern harbour—as a free transit and industrial area. Local and international companies have developed industries in this area, which is also used as a storage centre for firms selling elsewhere in the Gulf. The facilities offered by Mina Sulman include engineering and ship repairing yards; the Basrec slipway is probably the largest between Rotterdam and Hong Kong.

Post and Broadcasting. There were, at Dec. 1986, 73,522 telephones. There is a state-operated radio and television station and in 1983 there were 150,500 radio and 120,000 television receivers. There were 3 public service satellite stations in 1987.

Cinemas. There were 6 cinemas in 1986.

Newspapers. In 1986 there were several Arabic newspapers, and 1 English language newspaper 6 days a week, published in Manama.

JUSTICE, RELIGION, EDUCATION AND WELFARE

Justice. Criminal law is codified, based on English jurisprudence.

Religion. Islam is the State religion. In 1981 85% of the population were Moslem and 7·3% Christian. There are also Jews, Bahai, Hindu and Parsee minorities.

Education. Government schools provide free education from primary to technical college level. There were, in 1986, 139 schools for boys and girls with 4,931 teachers and 85,867 pupils. In 1984, 5 boys' general and commercial schools had 2,177 pupils; 3 boys' industrial schools at secondary level, had 1,306 pupils. In addition there were 7 private schools. The Men's Teacher Training College (established 1966) and the Women's Teacher Training College (established 1967) give 2-year courses. In 1985–86, 1,670 Bahrainis were in higher education abroad. The Gulf Technical College opened in Bahrain in Sept. 1968 and Bahrain University in 1978. In 1985–86, 8,288 adult education centres were open throughout Bahrain.

Health. There is a free medical service for all residents of Bahrain. In 1986, there were 4 government hospitals and 18 health centres, an American mission hospital, an oil company hospital, a military hospital and an international hospital.

Social Security. In Oct. 1976, pensions, sickness and industrial injury benefits, unemployment, maternity and family allowances were established.

DIPLOMATIC REPRESENTATIVES

Of Bahrain in Great Britain (98 Gloucester Rd., London, SW7 4AU)
Ambassador: Sulman Abdul Wahab Al Sabbagh (accredited 19 Dec. 1984).

Of Great Britain in Bahrain (21 Government Ave., P.O. Box 114, Manama)
Ambassador: J. A. Shepherd.

Of Bahrain in the USA (3502 International Dr., NW, Washington D.C., 20008)
Ambassador: Ghazi Mohammed Al-Gosaibi.

Of the USA in Bahrain (Shaikh Isa Road, P.O. Box 26431, Manama)
Ambassador: Dr Sam H. Zakhem.

Of Bahrain to the United Nations
Ambassador: Karim Ebrahim Al-Shakar.

Books of Reference

Bahrain Business Directory. Manama (annual)
Statistical and General Information: Ministry of Information, PO Box 253, Manama
Statistical Abstract. Central Statistics Organisation (annual)

Belgrave, J. H. D., *Welcome to Bahrain.* 9th ed. Manama, 1975
Rumaihi, M. G., *Bahrain: Social and Political Change since the First World War.* New York and London, 1976
Unwin, P. T. H., *Bahrain.* [Bibliography]. London and Santa Barbara, 1984

BANGLADESH

Capital: Dhaka
Population: 104·1m. (1987)
GNP per capita: US$140 (1986)

People's Republic of Bangladesh

HISTORY. The state was formerly the Eastern Province of Pakistan. In Dec. 1970 Sheikh Mujibur Rahman's Awami League Party gained 167 seats out of 300 at the Pakistan general election and immediately made known their wish for greater independence for the then Eastern Province. Martial law was imposed following disturbances in Dhaka, and civil war developed in March 1971. The war ended in Dec. 1971 and Bangladesh was proclaimed an independent state.

AREA AND POPULATION. Bangladesh is bounded west and north-west by West Bengal (India), north by Assam and Meghalaya (India), east by Assam, Tripura (India) and Burma, south by the Bay of Bengal. The area is 55,598 sq. miles (143,999 sq. km). Bangladesh's population (1981 census), 87,120,000. An adjustment for underenumeration produced a revised census figure of 89,912,000, of whom 14·09m. were urban and 46·3m. were male. Population estimate, 1987, 104·1m. In 1984 the birth-rate was 33·6 per 1,000 population; death-rate, 11·88; infant mortality 121 per 1,000 live births. Life expectancy (1983) 53·9 years (60·3 in urban areas). The capital is Dhaka (population, 1981, 3,440,147) and its ports are Chittagong (1,391,877) and Khulna (646,359). Other large cities are Rajshahi (253,740) and Barisal (142,098). There are 21 regions divided into 64 districts:

		Area (sq. km)	Population 1981			Area (sq. km)	Population 1981
Dinajpur	(3 districts)	6,566	3,198,000	Kushtia	(3)	3,440	2,292,000
Rangpur	(5)	9,593	6,510,000	Jessore	(4)	6,573	4,020,000
Bogra	(2)	3,888	2,728,000	Khulna	(3)	12,168	4,329,000
Rajshahi	(4)	9,456	5,270,000	Barisal	(4)	7,299	4,667,000
Pabna	(2)	4,732	3,424,000	Patuakhali	(2)	4,095	1,843,000
Rajshahi division		34,238	21,132,000	Khulna division		33,575	17,151,000
Tangail	(1)	3,403	2,444,000	Sylhet	(4)	12,718	5,656,000
Mymensingh	(3)	9,668	6,568,000	Comilla	(3)	6,599	6,881,000
Jamalpur	(2)	3,349	2,452,000	Noakhali	(3)	5,460	3,816,000
Dhaka	(6)	7,470	10,014,000	Chittagong	(2)	7,457	5,491,000
Faridpur	(5)	6,882	4,764,000	Chittagong Hill Tracts	(2)	8,679	580,000
Dhaka division		30,772	26,242,000	Bandarban	(1)	4,501	171,000
				Chittagong division		45,414	22,595,000

The official language is Bangla.

CLIMATE. A tropical monsoon climate with heat, extreme humidity and heavy rainfall in the monsoon season, from June to Sept. The short winter season is mild and dry. Rainfall varies between 50″ (1,250 mm) in the west to 100″ (2,500 mm) in the south-east and up to 200″ (5,000 mm) in the north-east. Dhaka. Jan. 66°F (19°C), July 84°F (28·9°C). Annual rainfall 81″ (2,025 mm). Chittagong. Jan. 66°F (19°C), July 81°F (27·2°C). Annual rainfall 108″ (2,831 mm).

CONSTITUTION AND GOVERNMENT. Bangladesh is a republic. The Constitution came into force on 16 Dec. 1972 and provided for a parliamentary democracy.

For developments between Jan. 1975 and March 1982, see THE STATESMAN'S YEAR-BOOK, 1986–87, pp. 186–187.

On 23 March 1982 there was a bloodless military *coup*, by which Lieut.-Gen. Hossain Mohammad Ershad became chief martial law administrator. President Sattar was deposed. The Constitution was suspended and parliament ceased to function. Assanuddin Chowdhury was sworn in as civilian president on 27 March. Lieut-Gen. Ershad assumed the presidency on 11 Dec. 1983. He was re-elected on 15 Oct. 1986.

Martial law ended on 10 Nov. 1986. The Constitution (Seventh Amendment) Act restored the constitution but protected the legality of President Ershad's decrees under martial law.

Parliament has one chamber of 300 members directly elected every 5 years by citizens over 18. There are 30 seats reserved for women members elected by Parliament.

In Jan. 1986 a National Executive Committee was formed and the National Party launched, composed of government supporters. The Party won the election of 3 March 1988, but there was a low turn-out and the result was disputed.

President, Minister for Defence, Information: Lieut.-Gen. Hossain Mohammad Ershad.

The Council of Ministers was as follows in Feb. 1988:

Prime Minister, Posts and Telecommunications: Mizanur Rahman Choudhury.

Deputy Prime Ministers: Moudud Ahmed *(Industries)*, Abdul Matin *(Home Affairs). Relief:* Maj.-Gen. Shamsul Huq. *Commerce:* Maj.-Gen. Abdul Munim Shah. *Local Authorities:* Moazzem Hussain Anisul. *Flood Control and Irrigation:* Islam Mahmood. *Land:* Sirajul Hussain Khan. *Energy, Mineral Resources:* Anwar Hussain. *Foreign Affairs:* Humayun Rasheed Choudhury. *Health, Family Planning:* Salahuddin Qader Chowdhury. *Ports, Shipping:* Mayeedul Islam. *Fisheries, Livestock:* Mirza Ruhul Amin. *Religious Affairs:* Maulana Abdul Mannan. *Textiles:* Sunil Gupta. *Labour, Manpower:* Anwar Zahid. *Finance:* (Vacant). *Planning:* Air Vice Marshal A. K. Khandakar. *Education:* Mahbubur Rahman. *Jute:* Zafar Imam. *Communication:* Matiur Rahman. *Agriculture:* M. Mahbubuzzaman.

National flag: Bottle green with a red disc in the centre.

National anthem: Amar Sonar Bangla, ami tomay bhalobashi (My golden Bengal, I love you). Words by Rabindranath Tagore.

DEFENCE

Army. There are 5 infantry divisional headquarters, with 13 infantry brigades, and 2 armoured and 6 artillery regiments, and 6 engineer battalions. Strength (1988) 90,000, with an additional 55,000 paramilitary volunteers, including an armed police reserve and the Bangladesh Rifles. Equipment includes 30 Soviet T-54 and 20 Chinese Type-59 tanks.

Navy. Naval bases are at Chittagong (handed over by India on 14 Feb. 1972), Kaptai, Khulna and Dacca.

The fleet comprises 3 former British frigates (*Ali Hyder, ex*-HMS *Jaguar,* and *Abu Bakr, ex*-HMS *Lynx,* each 2,520 tons full load, transferred in July 1978 and March 1982, respectively, and *Umar Farooq, ex*-HMS *Llandaff,* 2,408 tons full load, transferred in Dec 1976); 8 new Chinese-built 390-ton fast attack craft, 4 Chinese-built fast missile craft, 4 Chinese-built fast torpedo boats, 2 *ex*-Yugoslav 200-ton patrol vessels, 8 *ex*-Chinese 155-ton fast gunboats, 2 *ex*-Indian 150-ton patrol craft, 1 British-built 140-ton patrol craft, 5 indigenously built 70-ton river gunboats, 1 oiler, 1 repair vessel, 12 auxiliaries and 1 training ship of 710 tons.

The manpower of the Navy in 1988 was 7,500, comprising 600 officers and 6,900 ratings.

Air Force. Deliveries, from the Soviet Union and China successively, have built up a current strength of about 30 J-6 (MiG-19) fighter-bombers; 1 An-24 and 4 An-26

turboprop transports; about 20 Mi-8, Bell 212, Bell 206L and Alouette III helicopters; 10 Chinese CJ-6 piston-engined primary trainers, FT-2 (MiG-15UTI) jet
advanced trainers, 12 Magister armed jet trainers and some light aircraft. Personnel
strength, (1988) 4,000.

INTERNATIONAL RELATIONS

Membership. Bangladesh is a member of the Commonwealth, the Asian Development Bank, the Organisation for South Asian Regional Co-operation, the UN and
all its related agencies, the Colombo Plan and the Islamic Conference.

External Debt. Estimated debt, June 1985, US$6,000m. Most of this was in loans
from the Western aid group through the World Bank.

Treaties. Bangladesh signed an economic and technical co-operation agreement
with China on 4 Jan. 1977. The amended constitution of 1977 states that Bangladesh seeks fraternal relations with Moslem countries based on Islamic solidarity.

ECONOMY

Planning. The third 5-year development plan, 1985–90, envisages an annual
growth rate of 5·4%, and an industrial growth rate of 10·1% annually; of industrial
development funds, 55% is for the private sector. Agriculture receives 30% of total
plan expenditure, and the plan aims at self-sufficiency in food by 1990.

Budget. Details were as follows for the financial year 1984–85 (Tk.1m.):

Revenue receipts	34,650	Expenditure	26,433
Customs duties	11,600	Defence	3,573
Income and		Education	3,381
corporation tax	3,690	General	
Excise duties	6,750	administration	5,131
Sales tax	3,900	Interest on	
Non-tax revenue	7,120	domestic and	
		foreign debt	3,185

Money supply (April 1987) stood at Tk.47,097m.

Currency. A new currency, the *Taka*, was floated in 1976 (Tk.54 = £1 and
Tk.31·43 = US$1 in March 1988).

Banking. The former private banking system, except for foreign banks, has been
nationalized. In April 1987 the Bangladesh Bank had Tk.21,909m. notes in
circulation; Tk.7,602m. deposits; Tk.25,297m. foreign liabilities, Tk.68,053m.
assets. The scheduled banks had Tk.111,884m. deposits, Tk.19,446m. assets and
Tk.19,367m. borrowings from the Bangladesh Bank.

Weights and Measures. The metric system was introduced from July 1982, but
imperial measures are still in use. Weight is in the *seer* (1 *seer* = 2 lb.); the *maund*
(1 *maund* = 40 *seers*) and the ton.

ENERGY AND NATURAL RESOURCES

Electricity. Electric power is generated and distributed by the Bangladesh Power
Development Board and the Rural Electrification Board. Installed capacity, April
1987, 1,607 mw.; electricity generated, at Feb. 1986, 359·21m. kwh.; consumption, 248·83m. kwh.

Oil. Supplies have been located in the Bay of Bengal. Drilling is in progress.

Gas. Natural gas from Titas and other sites is piped to Dhaka; reserves are considered sufficient for 200 years. Production, 1985–86, 104,974m. cu. ft. Consumption, 1985–86, 99,657m. cu. ft.

Water. India and Bangladesh are working towards agreement on sharing the
water of the river Ganges. The flow will be monitored daily at the Farakka barrage
and two other points.

Minerals. Coal has been found at Jamalpur (about 700m. tons). Other minerals include salt, limestone, white clay, glass sand. The Rajshahi area has known reserves of deep-lying coal.

Agriculture. Agriculture contributed 45·7% of GDP in 1986–87 and employs about 80% of the economically active population. The land area is 35·7m. acres, of which 7m. is not available for cultivation, 5·2m. is forest, 1·1m. is (1986–87) fallow and 32·4m. is cropped (26·2m. under rice, 1·4m. wheat and 1·9m. jute). Cultivable waste is about 721,000 acres. About 5·1m. acres (1985) is irrigated; 2·2m. by tubewells and another 1·68m. by power pump. Rice is the most important food crop; production in 1986–87, 15·4m. tons. Other crops (1,000 tons): Sugar-cane, 6,787; wheat, 1,074; tobacco, 52 (1986); tea, 35 (1986); potatoes, 1,052; bananas, 706 (1986); sweet potatoes, 539.

Fertilizers used (1985), 1·16m. tonnes, of which 802m. tonnes was urea.

Livestock in 1986 (1,000): Poultry, 91,000; cattle, 23,200; goats, 10,722; sheep, 1,110; buffalo, 1,860. Livestock products in 1986 (tonnes): beef and veal, 130,000; cow and buffalo milk, 977,000; goats' milk, 528,000; eggs, 83,800.

Bangladesh produces about 70% of the world production of raw jute which is the principal foreign exchange earner. Production, 1986, 907,000 tonnes.

Forestry. The total area under forests (1977) is 9,283 sq. miles, of which 5,105 sq. miles are Reserved Forests. The output of roundwood timber in 1980 (1,000 cu. metres): sawlogs, veneer logs and sleepers, 555; pulpwood, 63; fuel wood, 9,754.

Fisheries. Being bounded on the south by the Bay of Bengal and having numerous rivers, streams, khals and bils, the state is pre-eminently a fish-producing area and possesses great possibilities for the manufacture of various oils and fish products. Fish production, 1980–81, 640,000 tons, of which 517,000 was from inland water.

INDUSTRY AND TRADE

Industry. Out of the existing industries, the textile-mills, sugar factories, match factories, glass works, hosiery factories, a paper-mill, jute-mills, aluminium works and a cement factory, with a capacity of 2m. tons per annum, are the most prominent. New government policy in 1982 aimed to restore public-sector jute and textile mills to private ownership and encourage the private sector. Arms and ammunition, atomic energy, forestry, air transport, communications and electrical industries would remain in the public sector.

In April 1987, 69 jute mills had 25,000 working looms; they employed 187,000 workers; monthly production 45,000 tons, valued at Tk.724m.

Refinery distillation capacity, 1·68m. tonnes. There is a steel mill at Chittagong with a capacity of 250,000 ingot-tons per annum. There is also a newsprint factory, 4 fertilizer factories, a shipyard, a dockyard and a liquified natural gas plant. Large-scale industry employs about 7% of the active population and provided 5·8% (1986–87) of the GDP. Production, 1985–86: jute goods, 437,000 tonnes (value Tk.7,864m.); cotton yarn, 96·3m. lb.; cotton cloth, 65·9m. yd.; cement, 288,000 tonnes; steel ingots, 99,853 tonnes; steel billets, 45,916 tonnes, newsprint, 47,863 tonnes; diesel engines valued at Tk.233·6m.; bicycles at Tk.14·3m. and motor cycles at Tk.398·8m.

Labour. In 1983–84, the total employed were 27,972,000; agriculture, forestry and fisheries, 16,389,000; trade, hotels and restaurants, 3,271,000; personal service, 3,250,000; manufacturing, 2,108,000. In 1985–86 an agricultural worker earned Tk.27·38 per day, a skilled mason Tk.52·32.

Commerce. The main export commodities are jute goods, hide, skins, leather and tea. In 1985–86 exports were valued at Tk.27,396·20m., of which Tk.5,503·5m. was from food and live animals (mainly fish, but Tk.997·3m. from tea); inedible crude materials except fuels, Tk.3,660·6m., of which Tk.3,437·89 from jute; manufactured goods, Tk.17,320·4m. (mainly jute goods). Principal imports (Tk.62,929·62m.) are machinery and transport equipment (Tk.11,449m.); manufactured goods (Tk.14,900·66m.); minerals, fuels and lubricants (Tk.12,161·3m.).

Sources of imports: Tk.9,070·8m. from Singapore (mainly petroleum); Tk.8,233·2m. from Japan (machinery and vehicles); Tk.5,088·2m. from USA (foodstuffs). Of exports, Tk.6,408·5m. worth went to USA (clothing, jute products); Tk.5,450·6m. to EC countries; Tk.1,946·36m. to Japan; Tk.1,272·2m. to Singapore.

Total trade between Bangladesh and UK (British Department of Trade returns, in £1,000 sterling):

	1984	1985	1986	1987
Imports to UK	46,506	35,348	34,117	35,454
Exports and re-exports from UK	51,591	69,420	48,218	54,382

Tourism. In 1986 there were 129,070 visitors to Bangladesh of whom 60,574 were from India. Foreign exchange earnings, Tk.446·4m.

COMMUNICATIONS

Roads. The State is backward in the matter of road communications, but there are some 2,700 miles of paved and 1,500 miles of unpaved road.

Railways. In 1984 there were 2,892 km of railways, comprising 979 km of 1,676 mm gauge and 1,913 km of metre gauge. In 1985–86 the railways carried 2·5m. tons of freight and 82m. passengers. Passenger earnings, Tk.631m.; goods, Tk.721m.

Aviation. Bangladesh Biman (Bangladesh Airways) has domestic flights from Dhaka and international services to Calcutta, Kathmandu, Bombay, Dubai, Abu Dhabi, Jeddah, Bangkok, Singapore, London, Doha, Kuwait, Amsterdam, Rome, Karachi, Kuala Lumpur, Dahrain, Tripoli, Athens and Muscat. In 1986 Zia International Airport handled 1·2m. passengers, Chittagong, 166,942, Osmani, 112,676, Jessore, 77,235. Total, including small aerodromes, 1·6m.

Shipping. Navigable channels provide 5,000 miles of cheap water routes. There are 3 principal waterways, the Padma, Brahmaputra and Meghna. These are freely used by inland steam vessels, which serve areas where railways cannot be economically constructed. The Bangladesh Shipping Corporation owns 24 ships including a 93,000-ton oil tanker *(Banglar Noor)* and has the capacity to carry 20% of imports and 12% of exports. In 1985–86 the port of Chittagong handled 5·9m. tons of imports and 334,000 tons of exports; Chalna, 1·56m. tons of imports and 762,000 tons of exports. Vessels entered (all ports) 1,794 and cleared, 1,765.

Post and Broadcasting. There were 122,190 telephones in 1982. Dhaka and Islamabad were linked by telephone in Oct. 1976 and a second telephone circuit was agreed on 11 April 1977. International communications are by satellite, Chittagong being linked to the Indian Ocean Intelsat IV satellite.

Newspapers. In Nov. 1981 there were 53 daily newspapers, 200 weeklies, 34 fortnightlies, 194 monthlies and 43 quarterly periodicals. Most papers are published in Dhaka. The Government has set up a paper *(Dainik Barta-at Rajshahi)* to stimulate a regional press. Most papers are privately owned. There is a Press Institute.

JUSTICE, RELIGION, EDUCATION AND WELFARE

Justice. The amended constitution in 1977 set up a Supreme Judicial Council to establish a code of conduct for Supreme Court and High Court judges, who may be removed from office by the President on the Council's recommendation.

Religion. Islam is the official religion, about 80% of the people being Muslim and the rest Hindus, Buddhists and Christians.

Education. At the 1981 census 19·7% of the population was literate (male 25·8%, female 13·2%). The compulsory primary education scheme has been replaced by model primary education. The Government has dissolved the District School Boards and taken over school administration.

In 1984–85 there were 42,200 primary schools (8·5m. pupils), 9,360 secondary schools (2·5m.) and (1983–84) 657 intermediate and degree colleges. Of these, there were 123 government colleges, of which 113 gave degrees and 10 were intermediate; degree colleges had 126,060 students and 4,764 faculty; intermediate, 2,936 students and 194. There were 534 non-government colleges (256 degree-giving). They had 287,781 students and 9,033 teachers. There were 6 universities: in 1982–83 Dhaka had 12,394 students (and 893 faculty); Rajshahi 10,198 (463); Chittagong 5,420 (427); Jahangirnagar 1,284 (164); Engineering University 3,015 (300); Agricultural, 3,771 (379). There are 10 teacher-training colleges, 49 primary training institutes and 57 vocational institutes.

Health. In 1984 there were 452 government hospitals, 1 mental and 12 tuberculosis and chest hospitals, 11 medical colleges and nursing training centres which train about 1,200 nurses annually. There were 21,370 beds. Voluntary agencies ran 164 hospitals with 4,771 beds.

DIPLOMATIC REPRESENTATIVES

Of Bangladesh in Great Britain (28 Queen's Gate, London, SW7)
High Commissioner: Maj.-Gen. K. M. Safiullah.

Of Great Britain in Bangladesh (Abu Bakr Hse., Plot 7, Road 84, Gulshan, Dhaka, 12)
High Commissioner: T. G. Streeton, CMG, MBE.

Of Bangladesh in the USA (2201 Wisconsin Ave., NW, Washington, D.C., 20007)
Ambassador: A. Z. M. Obaidullah Khan.

Of the USA in Bangladesh (Adamjee Court Bldg., Motijheel, Dhaka)
Ambassador: Willard A. DePree.

Of Bangladesh to the United Nations
Ambassador: Justice B. A. Siddiky.

Books of Reference

Bangladesh Planning Commission, *The First Five Year Plan—The Second Five Year Plan.*
Ministry of Finance. *Bangladesh Economic Survey.* 1979–80
Abdullah, T., and Zeidenstein, S., *Village Women of Bangladesh: Prospects for Change.* Oxford, 1981
Baxter, C., *Bangladesh: A New Nation in an Old Setting.* Boulder, 1986
Chen, L. C. (ed.), *Disaster in Bangladesh, Health Crisis in a Developing Nation.* OUP, 1973
Chowdhury, R., *The Genesis of Bangladesh.* London, 1972
Dutt, K., *Bangladesh Economy: An Analytical Study.* New Delhi, 1973
Franda, M., *Bangladesh: The First Decade.* New Delhi, 1982
Hartmann, B., and Boyce, J., *A Quiet Violence: View from a Bangladesh Village.* London, 1983
Kamal, K. A., *Sheikh Mujibur Rahman.* 2nd ed. Dhaka, 1970
Kashyap, S. C. (ed.), *Bangla Desh: Background and Perspectives.* New Delhi, 1971
Khan, A. R., *The Economy of Bangladesh.* London, 1972
de Lucia, R. J., and Jacoby, H. D., *Energy Planning for Developing Countries: A Study of Bangladesh.* John Hopkins Univ. Press, 1982
Mascarenhas, A., *The Rape of Bangladesh.* London, 1971
de Vylder, S., *Agriculture in Chains. Bangladesh: A Case Study in Contradictions and Constraints.* London, 1982
O'Donnell, C. P., *Bangladesh: Biography of a Muslim Nation.* Boulder, 1986
Rahman, M., *Bangladesh Today: An Indictment and a Lament.* London, 1978
Robinson, E. A. G., and Griffin, K. (ed.), *The Economic Development of Bangladesh.* London, 1974

BARBADOS

Capital: Bridgetown
Population: 253,055 (1985)
GNP per capita: US$4,560 (1984)

HISTORY. Barbados was occupied by the British in 1627 and during its colonial history never changed hands. Full internal self-government was attained in 1961. Barbados became an independent sovereign state within the Commonwealth on 30 Nov. 1966.

AREA AND POPULATION. Barbados lies to the east of the Windward Islands. Area 166 sq. miles (430 sq. km). In 1980 the census population was 248,983. Estimate (1985) 253,055. Bridgetown is the principal city: Population, 7,466.

CLIMATE. An equable climate in winter, but the wet season, from June to Nov., is more humid. Rainfall varies from 50" (1,250 mm) on the coast to 75" (1,875 mm) in the higher interior. Bridgetown. Jan. 76°F (24·4°C), July 80°F (26·7°C). Annual rainfall 51" (1,275 mm).

CONSTITUTION AND GOVERNMENT. The Legislature consists of the Governor-General, a Senate and a House of Assembly. The Senate comprises 21 members appointed by the Governor-General, 12 being appointed on the advice of the Prime Minister, 2 on the advice of the leader of the opposition and 7 in the Governor-General's discretion. The House of Assembly comprises 27 members elected every 5 years. In 1963 the voting age was reduced to 18.

The Privy Council is appointed by the Governor-General after consultation with the Prime Minister. It consists of 12 members and the Governor-General as chairman. It advises the Governor-General in the exercise of the royal prerogative of mercy and in the exercise of his disciplinary powers over members of the public and police services.

In the general election of May 1986 the Democratic Labour Party gained 24 seats and the Barbados Labour Party 3 seats.

Governor-General: Sir Hugh Springer, GCMG, CBE.

The Cabinet, in June 1987, was composed as follows:

Prime Minister, Minister of Economic Affairs, Education and Culture: Erskine Sandiford.

Deputy Prime Minister, Transport, Works and Communications: Philip Greaves. *Attorney-General, Legal Affairs:* Maurice King. *Trade, Industry and Commerce:* Evelyn Greaves. *Agriculture, Food and Fisheries:* Warwick Franklin. *Tourism and Sports:* Wesley Hall. *Finance:* Dr Richard Haynes. *Health:* Branford Taitt. *Foreign Affairs:* J. Cameron Tudor. *Employment, Labour Relations and Community Development:* Keith Simmons. *Housing and Lands:* Harold Blackman. There were two Ministers of State.

National flag: Three vertical strips of blue, gold, blue, with a black trident in the centre.

INTERNATIONAL RELATIONS

Membership. Barbados is a member of UN, OAS, Caricom, the Commonwealth and an ACP state of the EEC.

ECONOMY

Budget. The budget for 1986–87 envisaged capital expenditure of BD$188,503,768 and current expenditure of BD$700,283,943.

Currency. The monetary unit is the *Barbados dollar* (BD$) divided into 100 *cents*. In March 1988, £1 = BD$3.57; US$1 = 2.11.

Banking. Eight main commercial banks operate in Barbados including Barclays Bank International, the Royal Bank of Canada, Canadian Imperial Bank of Commerce, the Bank of Nova Scotia, Chase Manhattan Bank, Caribbean Commercial Bank, The Barbados National Bank, Bank of Credit and Commerce International.

Barbados is headquarters for the Caribbean Development Bank. The Barbados Development Bank opened on 15 April 1969 and Barbados became a member of the Inter-American Development Bank on 19 March 1969.

NATURAL RESOURCES

Electricity. Production (1986) 390m. kwh. Supply 150 volts; 50 Hz.

Oil. Crude oil production (1986) 23,484,000 US gallons.

Gas. Output of gas (1986) 933m. cu. ft.

Agriculture. Of the total area of 106,240 acres, about 54,932 acres are arable land. The land is intensely cultivated. In 1986, 15,000 hectares of sugar-cane were harvested. Cotton was successfully replanted in 1983 and 91 bales were harvested from 300 acres in 1985. The agricultural sector accounted for 7·1% (provisional) of GDP in 1985 (1946, 45%; 1967, 24%). In 1985, 6·9% of the total labour force were employed in agriculture. In 1986, 113,000 tonnes of sugar were produced. There are 6 sugar factories and 2 rum refineries in production. In 1986, 3,000 tonnes of yams and 2,000 tonnes of sweet potatoes were produced. Hot peppers, eggplants, watermelons, breadfruit and red ginger lilies are also grown for export.

Livestock (1986): Cattle, 18,000; sheep, 55,000; goats, 33,000; pigs, 49,000; poultry, 1m.

Fisheries. There are about 651 (1985) powered boats and many men and women are employed during the flying-fish season. Large numbers of these boats are laid up from July to Oct. The fish catch in 1984 was 5,774 tonnes.

INDUSTRY AND TRADE

Industry. Industrial establishments operating in Barbados in 1985 numbered approximately 300 and ranged from the manufacture of processed food to small specialized products such as garment manufacturing, furniture and household appliances, electrical components, plastic products and electronic parts.

Commerce. Total trade for calendar years in BD$1,000:

	1982	1983	1984	1985	1986
Domestic Imports [1]	1,106,589	1,257,961	1,324,623	1,221,595	1,181,075
Domestic Exports [1]	374,061	581,579	583,667	496,471	420,614

[1] Exclusive of bullion and specie.

In 1986 the principal imports (BD$1m.) were: Machinery and transport equipment, 428·5; manufactured goods, 295·3; food and live animals, 149·7; lubricants, mineral fuels, etc., 110·3; chemicals, 104·4; crude minerals, 31·4; beverages and tobacco, 25·2; animal and vegetable oils and fats, 9·9. In 1986 the principal domestic exports (BD$1m.) were: Electronic components, 214·7; sugar, 48·7; clothing, 35·5.

Total trade between Barbados and UK (British Department of Trade returns, in £1,000 sterling):

	1983	1984	1985	1986	1987
Imports from UK	11,899	22,509	13,512	11,661	23,320
Exports and re-exports to UK	31,938	30,654	36,856	38,338	33,067

Tourism. In 1986, 369,770 tourists visited Barbados spending in 1985, BD$618·1m. The industry employs over 10,000 people.

COMMUNICATIONS

Roads. There are 1,020 miles of road open to traffic, of which 840 miles are all-weather roads. From Jan. to Dec. 1985 there were 30,908 private cars, 1,871 hired cars and taxis, 444 buses and 10,988 other vehicles including motorcycles and bicycles.

Aviation. There is an international airport at Seawell, Christ Church, Barbados, served by British Airways, BWIA, Leeward Islands Air Transport, PANAM, American Airlines, Wardair, Air Martinique Cruziero (SC), Air Canada, Caribbean Airways and Eastern Airlines, Cubana Airlines, Venezuelan Airlines.

Shipping. A deep-water harbour opened in 1961 at Bridgetown provides 8 berths for ships 500–600 ft in length, including one specially designed for bulk sugar loading. The number of merchant vessels entering in 1986 was 1,961 of 6,452,000 net tons.

Post and Telephone. There is a general post office in Bridgetown and 16 branches on the island. In 1985 there were 86,785 telephones in service.

Cinemas. There were (1985) 3 cinemas and 2 drive-in cinemas for 600 cars.

Newspapers. In 1984 there were 2 daily newspapers with a total circulation of 39,000.

JUSTICE, RELIGION, EDUCATION AND WELFARE

Justice. Justice is administered by the Supreme Court and by magistrates' courts. All have both civil and criminal jurisdiction. There is a Chief Justice and 3 puisne judges of the Supreme Court and 8 magistrates.

Religion. The majority (about 70%) of the population are Anglicans, the remainder mainly Methodists, Moravians and Roman Catholics.

Education. In 1984–85 children in 105 government primary schools numbered 29,392; in 21 secondary schools, 21,501; in 5 vocational centres, 967; in 15 assisted private approved secondary schools, 4,227. There are 23 independent primary schools with 3,547 pupils and a number of independent schools for which no accurate figures are available. Education is free in all government-owned and maintained institutions from primary to university level.

In 1963 Erdiston College became one of the constituent Colleges of the University of the West Indies Institute of Education. The College of Arts and Sciences of the University of the West Indies in Barbados was opened in Sept. 1963 and Cave Hill campus in 1967. In 1984–85, 186 students attended Erdiston College and 1,617 students attended the Cave Hill campus. The Barbados Community College for higher education at pre-university level was opened in 1969; in 1984–85, 1,806 students (full- and part-time) were enrolled.

Health. In 1984 there were 2,143 hospital beds and 213 doctors.

DIPLOMATIC REPRESENTATIVES

Of Barbados in Great Britain (1 Great Russell St., London, WC1B 3NH)
High Commissioner: Vernon Smith.

Of Great Britain in Barbados (147/9 Roebuck St., Bridgetown)
High Commissioner: Kevin Burns, CMG.

Of Barbados in the USA (2144 Wyoming Ave., NW, Washington, D.C. 20008)
Ambassador: Sir William Douglas, KCMG.

Of the USA in Barbados (PO Box 302, Bridgetown)
Ambassador: Paul A. Russo.

Of Barbados to the United Nations
Ambassador: Dame Nita Barrow.

Books of Reference

Statistical Information: The Barbados Statistical Service (NIS Bldg, Fairchild St, St Michael) produces selected monthly statistics and annual abstracts. *Director:* Eric Straughn.
Dann, G., *The Quality of Life in Barbados.* London, 1984.
Hoyos, F. A., *Barbados: A History from the Amerindians to Independence.* London, 1978.—*Barbados: A Visitor's Guide.* London, 1983
Potter, R. B., and Dann, G. M. S., *Barbados* [Bibliography]. Oxford and Santa Barbara, 1987
Worrell, D., *The Economy of Barbados 1946–1980.* Bridgetown, 1982
Library: The Barbados Public Library, Bridgetown. *Acting Chief Librarian:* Edwin Igill.

BELGIUM

Capital: Brussels
Population: 9·86m. (1986)
GNP per capita: US$7,870 (1984)

Royaume de Belgique—
Koninkrijk België

HISTORY. The kingdom of Belgium formed itself into an independent state in 1830, having from 1815 been part of the Netherlands. The secession was decreed on 4 Oct. 1830 by a provisional government, established in consequence of a revolution which broke out at Brussels, on 25 Aug. 1830. A National Congress elected Prince Leopold of Saxe-Coburg King of the Belgians on 4 June 1831; he ascended the throne 21 July 1831.

By the Treaty of London, 15 Nov. 1831, the neutrality of Belgium was guaranteed by Austria, Russia, Great Britain and Prussia. It was not until after the signing of the Treaty of London, 19 April 1839, which established peace between King Leopold I and the King of the Netherlands, that all the states of Europe recognized the kingdom of Belgium. In the Treaty of Versailles (28 June 1919) it is stated that as the treaties of 1839 'no longer conform to the requirements of the situation', these are abrogated and will be replaced by other treaties.

AREA AND POPULATION. Belgium is bounded north by the Netherlands, north-west by the North Sea, west and south by France, east by Federal Republic of Germany and Luxembourg. Belgium has an area of 30,518 sq. km (11,778 sq. miles). The Belgian exclave of Baarle-Hertog in the Netherlands has an area of 7 sq. km, and a population (1 Jan. 1986) of 1,101 males and 1,030 females.

By an agreement, 23 Sept. 1956, the frontier with Germany was slightly readjusted.

Census	Population	Increase % per annum	Census	Population	Increase % per annum
1900	6,693,548	1·03	1947	8,512,195	0·36
1910	7,423,784	1·09	1961	9,189,741	0·52
1920	7,405,569	0·06	1970	9,650,944	0·55
1930	8,092,004	0·84			

Provinces	Provincial capitals	Area (hectares)	1970 [1]	Estimated population (31 Dec.) 1984	1985	1986
Antwerp (Anvers)	Antwerp	286,726	1,533,249	1,581,480	1,582,786	1,585,163
Brabant	Brussels	335,811	2,176,373	2,217,445	2,218,349	2,219,272
Flanders { West	Bruges	313,439	1,054,429	1,088,655	1,090,387	1,328,931
Flanders { East	Ghent	298,167	1,310,117	1,330,422	1,328,805	1,032,696
Hainaut	Mons	378,669	1,317,453	1,282,119	1,277,939	1,274,034
Liège	Liège	386,213	1,008,905	992,383	991,535	991,089
Limbourg	Hasselt	242,231	652,547	729,620	731,875	734,382
Luxembourg	Arlon	444,114	217,310	224,375	224,988	225,563
Namur	Namur	366,501	380,561	411,222	412,231	413,621
Total		3,051,871	9,650,944	9,857,721	9,858,895	9,864,751

[1] Census.

In 1986 there were 4,816,234 males and 5,048,517 females.
Foreigners numbered 853,244 on 1 Jan. 1987.
Vital statistics for calendar years:

	Births	Deaths	Marriages	Divorces	Immigration	Emigration
1983	117,395	114,814	59,652	17,238	43,657	61,339
1984	115,790	110,577	58,989	18,768	47,002	56,447
1985	114,283	112,691	57,630	18,530	47,042	54,021
1986	117,271	111,671	56,657	18,434	48,959	53,793

	1983	1984	1985	1986
Of the total births				
excluding still-born	117,395	115,790	114,283	117,271
Boys	60,440	59,353	58,695	60,569
Girls	56,955	56,437	55,588	56,702

The most important towns, with estimated population on 1 Jan. 1987:

Brussels and suburbs [1]	973,499	St Niklass (St Nicolas)	68,082
Antwerp (Antwerpen) [2]	479,748	Tournai (Doornik)	66,998
Ghent (Gent)	233,856	Hasselt	65,563
Charleroi	209,395	Seraing	61,731
Liège (Luik)	200,891	Genk	61,391
Brugge (Bruges)	117,755	Mouscron (Moeskroen)	53,713
Namur (Namen)	102,670	Verviers	53,499
Mons (Bergen)	89,697	Roeselare (Roulers)	51,963
Leuven (Louvain)	84,583	Turnhout	37,462
Aalst (Alost)	77,113	Herstal	36,049
La Louvière	76,340	Lokeren	34,256
Kortrijk (Courtrai)	76,216	Vilvoorde (Vilvorde)	32,885
Mechelen (Malines)	75,808	Lier (Lierre)	30,867
Oostende (Ostende)	68,318		

[1] The suburbs comprise 18 distinct communes, viz., Anderlecht, Etterbeek, Forest, Ixelles, Jette, Koekelberg, Molenbeek St Jean, St Gilles, St Josse-ten-Noode, Schaerbeek, Uccle, Woluwe-St Lambert, Auderghem, Watermael-Boitsfort, Woluwe-St Pierre, Berchem Ste Agathe, Evere and Ganshoren.
[2] Including Berchem, Borgerhout, Deurne, Hoboken, Merksem and Wilrijk.

CLIMATE. Cool temperate climate, influenced by the sea, giving mild winters and cool summers. Brussels. Jan. 36°F (2·2°C), July 64°F (17·8°C). Annual rainfall 33″ (825 mm). Ostend. Jan. 38°F (3·3°C), July 62°F (16·7°C). Annual rainfall 31″ (775 mm).

KING. Baudouin, born 7 Sept. 1930, succeeded his father, Leopold III, on 17 July 1951, when he took the oath on the constitution before the two Chambers: married on 15 Dec. 1960 to Fabiola de Mora y Aragón, daughter of the Conde de Mora and Marqués de Casa Riera.

Brother and Sister of the King. (1) Josephine Charlotte, Princess of Belgium, born 11 Oct. 1927; married to Prince Jean of Luxembourg, 9 April 1953; (2) Albert, Prince of Liège, born 6 June 1934; married to Paola Ruffo di Calabria, 2 July 1959; *offspring:* Prince Philippe, born 15 April 1960; Princess Astrid, born 5 June 1962; married to Archduke Lorenz of Austria, 22 Sept. 1984; Prince Laurent, born 19 Oct. 1963. *Half-brother and half-sisters of the King.* Prince Alexandre, born 18 July 1942; Princess Marie Christine, born 6 Feb. 1951; Princess María-Esmeralda, born 30 Sept. 1956.

Aunt of the King. Princess Marie-José, born 4 Aug. 1906, married to Prince Umberto (King Umberto II of Italy in 1946) on 8 Jan. 1930.

BELGIAN SOVEREIGNS

Leopold I	1831–65	Leopold III	1934–44, 1950–51
Leopold II	1865–1909	Regency	1944–50
Albert	1909–34	Baudouin	1951–

CONSTITUTION AND GOVERNMENT. According to the constitution of 1831, Belgium is a constitutional, representative and hereditary monarchy. The legislative power is vested in the King, the Senate and the Chamber of Representatives. The royal succession is in direct male line in the order of primogeniture. By marriage without the King's consent, however, the right of succession is forfeited, but may be restored by the King with the consent of the two Chambers. No act of the King can have effect unless countersigned by one of his Ministers, who thus becomes responsible for it. The King convokes, prorogues and dissolves the

Chambers. In default of male heirs, the King may nominate his successor with the consent of the Chambers. If the successor be under 18 years of age the two Chambers meet together for the purpose of nominating a regent during the minority.

National flag: Three vertical strips of black, yellow, red.

National anthem: Après des siècles d'esclavage (La Brabançonne; words by Jenneval, 1830; tune by F. van Campenhout, 1930).

French, Dutch and German are official languages.

Those sections of the Belgian Constitution which regulate the organization of the legislative power were revised in Oct. 1921. For both Senate and Chamber all elections are held on the principle of universal suffrage.

The Senate consists of members elected for 4 years, partly directly and partly indirectly. The number elected directly is equal to half the number of members of the Chamber of Representatives. The constituent body is similar to that which elects deputies to the Chamber; the minimum age of electors is 18 years, and the minimum length of residence required is 6 months. Women were given the suffrage at parliamentary elections on 24 March 1948. In the direct elections of members of both the Senate and Chamber of Representatives the principle of proportional representation was introduced by law of 29 Dec. 1899.

Senators are elected indirectly by the provincial councils, on the basis of 1 for 200,000 inhabitants. Every addition of 125,000 inhabitants gives the right to 1 senator more. Each provincial council elects at least 3 senators. There are at present 51 provincial senators. No one, during 2 years preceding the election, must have been a member of the council appointing him. Senators are elected by the Senate itself in the proportion of half the preceding category. The senators belonging to these two latter categories are also elected by the method of proportional representation. All senators must be at least 40 years of age. They receive 900,000 francs per annum. Sons of the King, or failing these, Belgian princes of the reigning branch of the royal family, are by right senators at the age of 18, but have no voice in the deliberations till the age of 25 years; this prerogative is hardly ever used.

The members of the Chamber of Representatives are elected by the electoral body. Their number, at present 212 (law of 3 April 1965), is proportional to the population, and cannot exceed one for every 40,000 inhabitants. They sit for 4 years. Deputies must be not less than 25 years of age, and resident in Belgium.

Each deputy has an annual allowance of 900,000 francs. Senators and deputies have also free railway passes.

The Senate and Chamber meet annually in October and must sit for at least 40 days; but the King has the power of convoking extraordinary sessions and of dissolving them either simultaneously or separately. In the latter case a new election must take place within 40 days and a meeting of the chambers within 2 months.

An adjournment cannot be made for a period exceeding 1 month without the consent of the Chambers.

After the revision of the Constitution by the laws of 24 Dec. 1970 and 28 July 1971 establishing three regions and two cultural councils, legislation on 'preparatory regionalization' was enacted in July 1974. Further revisions of the functions of the Cultural Councils took place on 8 and 9 Aug. 1980. The Cultural Councils became Community Councils with greater authority and the Regional Councils became competent on economic matters.

On 19 Oct. 1987 the government of Wilfried Martens resigned and on 21 Oct. a caretaker government was formed which was to serve until general elections had taken place. Elections were held on 13 Dec. but the results were inconclusive and at the time of going to press no new government had been formed.

A 4-party coalition government was as follows in Oct. 1987:

Prime Minister: Wilfried Martens (CVP).

Deputy Prime Ministers: Jean Gol, PRL (*Justice and Institutional Reform*);

Guy Verhofstadt, PVV *(Budget, Scientific Policy and Research)*; Philippe Maystadt, PSC *(Economic Affairs). Foreign Affairs:* Léo Tindemanns (CVP). *Finance:* Mark Eyskens (CVP). *Public Works:* Louis Olivier (PRL). *Communications and Foreign Trade:* Herman De Croo (PVV). *Employment and Labour:* Michel Hansenne (PSC). *Education (Dutch-language):* Daniel Coens (CVP). *Interior:* J. Michel (PSC). *Social Affairs and Institutional Reform:* Jean-Luc Dehaene (CVP). *Defence:* François-Xavier de Donnéa (PRL). *Middle Classes:* Jacky Buchmann (PVV). *Education (French):* André Damseaux (PRL).

There are thirteen Secretaries of State.

Local Government. Belgium has 9 provinces and since the so-called 'Amalgamation Law' of 30 Dec. 1975, 589 communes (instead of 2,359). They have a large measure of autonomous government. According to the law of 9 June 1982, all Belgians over 18 years of age, who are recorded in the registers of population of the commune have the right to vote in the communal elections. Proportional representation is applied to the communal elections, and communal councils are to be renewed every 6 years. In each commune there is a college composed of the burgomaster as the president and a certain number of aldermen.

DEFENCE. Belgium is a full member of NATO since 1949 and of the Eurogroup since 1968. The need to extend European armaments co-operation led to the formation of the Independent European Program Group (IEPG) in 1976. Its members include Belgium.

According to the Law of 30 April 1962, the Belgian Armed Forces are recruited by annual calls to the colours and by voluntary enlistments.

Military service is 10 months for conscripts serving in the Federal Republic of Germany and 12 months for those serving in Belgium, 13 months for voluntary reserve officers and 15 for the paracommando regiment. Duration of military obligation is 8 years for most soldiers called for compulsory service.

The Medical Service has a strength of 5,785 personnel. Beside the medical units and detachments in the Armed Forces, the medical service manages 6 military hospitals and a central pharmacy.

Army. The Army comprises as major units 1 armoured and 3 mechanized brigades (2 of which are deployed as the Belgian divisions in the Belgian corps area in the Federal Republic of Germany) and 1 paracommando regiment. There are also 3 reconnaissance battalions. Total strength (1987) 67,400. *Gendarmerie,* 15,900.

Equipment includes nearly 334 LEOPARD Main Battle Tanks, 135 SCORPION Light Tanks, 150 SCIMITAR Armoured Fighting Vehicles, 1,150 Armoured Personnel Carriers and 80 JPK 90mm Self-Propelled Anti-Tank Guns; Artillery Battalions are equipped with 155mm and 203mm Self-Propelled Howitzers, LANCE Surface-to-Surface Missiles, HAWK Surface-to-Air Missiles and GEPARD Armoured Vehicles with 35mm Anti-Aircraft Guns.

Other equipment in use: MILAN Anti-Tank Guided Weapon, STRIKER Armoured Fighting Vehicle with SWINGFIRE Anti-Tank Guided Weapon, Islander aircraft, Alouette II helicopters, Epervier Remotely Piloted Vehicle.

Navy. The naval forces include 4 frigates (Navy designed and built) completed in 1978, 6 ocean minehunters, 2 command and logistic support ships, 4 coastal minehunters, 5 coastal minesweepers, 13 inshore minesweepers, 2 research ships, 1 ammunition transport, 6 tugs and 2 service craft. Ten tripartite minehunters are being built (with a further 5 on option). Naval personnel in 1987 totalled 4,490 officers and ratings.

The naval air arm comprises 3 Alouette III general utility helicopters.

Air Force. The Air Force has a strength of more than 20,000 personnel and more than 270 aircraft in 14 operational squadrons and support units. There are 5 flying wings. The all-weather fighter wing consists of 2 squadrons of F-16s. One fighter-bomber wing has 2 squadrons of F-16s; 2 others operate Mirage 5s, organized as 3 squadrons of Mirage 5Bs and Mirage 5BD two-seat trainers, and 1 squadron of Mirage 5BR photo-reconnaissance aircraft. The transport wing consists of 1 squadron equipped with 12 C-130H Hercules turboprop transports, and 1 squadron flying 2 Boeing 727s, 3 HS 748 twin-turboprop transports, 5 Swearingen Merlin III light turboprop transports and 2 light twin-jet Falcons. Other types in service include Sea King Mk 48 search and rescue helicopters, SIAI-Marchetti SF.260M and Alpha Jet training aircraft. Two surface-to-air missile groups, stationed in Germany, are equipped with Nike Hercules missiles. Aircraft on order include 44 more F-16s with deliveries scheduled to start early in 1988.

INTERNATIONAL RELATIONS

Membership. Belgium is a member of UN, European Communities, Benelux Economic Union, Council of Europe, Nato, OECD and WEU.

ECONOMY

Budget. Revenue and expenditure for calendar years (in 1 m. francs):

	1982	1983	1984	1985	1986	1987
Receipts						
Current	1,153,105	1,210,518	1,310,921	1,382,786	1,408,727	1,449,000
Capital	253,843	338,596	373,447	391,763	204,415	...
Total	1,406,948	1,549,114	1,684,368	1,774,549	1,614,142	...
Expenditure						
Current	1,506,161	1,611,881	1,710,302	1,841,481	1,840,903	1,817,600
Capital	169,199	216,147	166,317	170,839	173,352	160,000
Total	1,675,360	1,828,028	1,876,619	2,012,320	2,014,255	1,977,600

On 31 Dec. 1986 the Belgian public debt consisted of (in 1m. francs): Internal debt consolidated, 2,775,100; short and middle terms, 1,528,700; at sight, 94,000. External debt, 1,020,400.

Currency. The *franc*, containing 0·01826 gramme of fine gold, is the unit of currency.

No gold has been minted since 1882 (save only 5m. francs struck in 1914). Note circulation 31 Dec. 1986, 394,700m. francs.

The official rate of exchange in March 1988 was US$1 = 35·28 francs; £1 = 62·50 francs.

Banking. The bank of issue in Belgium is the National Bank, instituted in 1850. It is the cashier of the State, and is authorized to carry on the usual banking operations. The articles of association of the National Bank of Belgium were modified on 13 Sept. 1948 so as to strengthen public control.

The savings banks are mainly operated by the *Caisse Générale d'Epargne et de Retraite* and by the private savings banks. *The Caisse Générale d'Epargne et de Retraite* (CGER), a state institution, consists of 2 parts: *the Caisse d'Epargne* which performs the whole range of banking activities and a further unit which embodies the funds engaged in social security and insurance activities; the CGER operates under the authority of the Minister of Finance. The *Commission bancaire* (bank commission) supervises the financial situation and the activities of the Caisse d'Epargne. It co-operates with the Belgian postal service, thus obviating any need of a postal-savings system. The savings deposits and savings bonds of the Caisse d'Epargne amounted to 697,337m. francs on 31 Dec. 1986. The private savings banks, whose liabilities expressed in savings accounts and bonds amounted to 946,287m. francs on 31 Dec. 1986, are controlled by the 'Commission bancaire'.

Weights and Measures. The metric system is in force.

ENERGY AND NATURAL RESOURCES

Electricity. The production of electricity (1m. kwh.) amounted to 51,015 in 1980; 48,179 in 1981; 47,936 in 1982; 49,912 in 1983; 51,850 in 1984; 54,184 in 1985; 57,505 in 1986. Supply 127 and 220 volts; 50 Hz.

Gas. Production of gas (in 1 m. cu. metres): 675 in 1980; 690 in 1981; 594 in 1982; 623 in 1983; 717 in 1984; 716 in 1985; 636 in 1986.

Minerals. Output (in tonnes) for 5 calendar years:

	1982	1983	1984	1985	1986
Coal	6,538,874	6,097,428	6,297,563	6,211,471	5,589,208
Briquettes	49,836	45,265	44,682	...	...
Coke	5,216,692	5,105,675	5,925,767	5,963,729	5,130,229
Cast iron	7,831,469	8,033,206	8,968,470	8,719,040	8,047,635
Wrought steel	9,995,850	10,157,031	11,303,381	10,687,461	9,764,551
Finished steel	7,364,139	7,056,770	8,138,190	8,072,766	7,359,316

Agriculture. Of the total area of 3,051,871 hectares, there were, in 1986, 1,382,914 hectares under cultivation, of which 349,609 were under cereals, 31,172 vegetables, 125,659 industrial plants, 148,639 root crops, 661,155 pastures and meadows.

Chief crops	Area in hectares			Produce in tonnes		
	1984	1985	1986	1984	1985	1986
Wheat	176,994	179,883	181,412	1,248,588	1,149,592	1,256,924
Barley	135,801	118,243	127,893	873,480	685,369	793,069
Oats	18,783	20,931	13,543	91,848	93,562	59,317
Rye	7,049	5,159	4,476	32,214	22,546	19,337
Potatoes	36,036	40,940	39,990	1,332,226	1,521,706	1,400,721
Beet (sugar)	117,001	117,865	112,763	5,763,454	5,952,187	5,886,234
Beet (fodder)	15,082	14,752	13,898	1,409,010	1,355,302	1,315,591
Tobacco	521	534	548	1,782	1,863	1,957

In 1986 there were 24,355 horses, 3,060,077 cattle, 176,566 sheep, 8,037 goats and 5,585,454 pigs.

Forestry. In 1970 the forest area covered 19·7% of the land surface. In 1970, 2·85 cu. metres of timber were felled.

Fisheries. The total quantity of fish landed amounted to 34,050 tons valued at 3,295m. francs in 1986. The fishing fleet had a total tonnage of 22,846 gross tons at 31 Dec. 1986.

INDUSTRY AND TRADE

Industry. In 1985 there were 13 sugar factories, output 145,279 tonnes of raw sugar; 3 sugar refineries, output 219,570 tonnes; 9 distilleries, output 88,504 hectolitres of potable and industrial alcohol; 132 breweries, output 13,930,884 hectolitres of beer; margarine factories, output 171,755 tonnes.

Six trusts control the greater part of Belgian industry: the Société Générale (founded in 1822) owns about 40% of coal, 50% of steel, 65% of non-ferrous metals and 35% of electricity; Brufina-Confinindus operates in steel, coal, electricity and heavy engineering; the Groupe Solvay rules the chemical industry; the Groupe Copée has interests in steel and coal; Empain controls tramways and electrical equipment; the Banque Lambert owns petroleum firms and their accessories.

Commerce. By the convention concluded at Brussels on 25 July 1921 between Belgium and Luxembourg and ratified on 5 March 1922 an economic union was formed by the two countries, and the customs frontier between them was abolished on 1 May 1922. Dissolved in Aug. 1940, the union was re-established on 1 May 1945. On 14 March 1947, in execution of an agreement signed in London on 5 Sept. 1944, there was concluded a customs union between Belgium and Luxembourg, on the one hand, and the Netherlands, on the other. The union came into force on 1 Jan. 1948, and is now known as the Benelux Economic Union. A joint tariff has been adopted and import duties are no longer levied at the Netherlands frontier, but import licences may still be required. A full economic union of the three countries came into operation on 1 Nov. 1960.

Benelux information is supplied by the Secretariat General of the Benelux Economic Union, Rue de la Régence, 39, 1000 Brussels. It publishes *Benelux. Bulletin Trimestriel de Statistique; Statistisch Kwartaalbericht* (1955 ff.).

Trade by selected countries (in 1,000 Belgian francs):

	Imports from			Exports to		
	1983	1984	1985	1983	1984	1985
France	396,327,868	467,319,104	498,946,005	482,962,732	552,404,053	600,636,737
USA	180,684,980	192,387,281	187,924,213	136,381,246	181,389,766	200,789,652
UK	243,584,424	279,911,478	295,653,660	261,183,269	296,366,695	309,864,652
Netherlands	511,840,493	600,549,793	614,602,338	377,544,382	416,593,502	451,005,568
German Dem. Rep.	6,581,325	7,645,774	9,425,453	5,470,610	4,190,421	3,790,007
Germany, Fed. Rep.	582,294,115	636,514,989	695,513,488	560,475,111	589,671,742	588,661,598
Argentina	10,693,659	16,013,614	11,867,259	2,771,822	2,250,301	2,032,665
Italy	103,566,527	114,354,583	118,169,483	123,775,439	153,807,487	172,280,290
Switzerland	79,771,840	77,857,390	77,349,479	75,462,491	80,353,780	76,325,828
Zaïre	20,131,220	29,461,682	32,604,538	8,905,660	12,474,415	13,989,196
Denmark	14,390,835	15,746,617	16,909,563	26,002,238	27,322,164	34,469,832
USSR	71,359,209	108,166,623	74,000,531	34,024,691	31,638,834	37,305,363
India	13,249,850	10,924,242	11,609,454	29,395,789	38,026,426	41,809,451
Rep. of S. Africa	15,880,722	16,869,599	20,687,570	11,305,781	14,327,206	10,824,906
Canada	15,727,033	18,619,131	18,772,444	11,351,857	17,000,443	21,847,569
Brazil	16,997,391	24,197,028	29,597,678	4,055,784	4,326,998	3,970,743
Australia	7,837,604	9,388,174	9,825,578	5,740,808	9,265,495	10,632,024

Imports and exports for 6 calendar years (in 1,000 Belgian francs):

	Imports	Exports		Imports	Exports
1981	2,309,761,017	2,062,315,689	1984	3,195,768,712	2,992,116,161
1982	2,653,362,108	2,393,152,616	1985	3,317,811,996	3,167,691,043
1983	2,820,864,806	2,651,340,902	1986	3,061,850,000	3,066,578,000

The total trade between Belgium and Luxembourg and UK was as follows (British Department of Trade returns, in £1,000 sterling):

	1983	1984	1985	1986	1987
Imports to UK	3,133,905	3,691,794	4,016,889	4,083,883	4,362,463
Exports and re-exports from UK	2,572,673	3,051,722	3,347,596	3,832,605	3,857,717

Principal Belgian-Luxembourg exports to UK in 1983 [1] (tonnes; francs): Textiles (128,698; 20,567m.); metals (534,473; 19,869m.); chemical and pharmaceutical products (536,421; 20,929m.); precious stones and manufactures thereof (362; 46,600m.).

Principal Belgian-Luxembourg imports from the UK in 1983[1] (tonnes; francs): Machinery and electrical apparatus (39,024; 19,047m.); vehicles, chiefly motor cars, and aircraft (102,808; 19,490m.); textiles (40,499; 7,444m.); precious stones (191; 66,681m.); base metals and manufactures thereof (270,320; 10,985m.).

[1] Provisional.

Tourism. In 1986 receipts totalled 101·4m. francs.

COMMUNICATIONS

Roads. The total length of the roads in Belgium on 31 Dec. 1986 was as follows: State roads (including 1,549 km of motorway), 14,259 km; provincial roads, 1,375 km; communal roads, 115,006 km. The majority of roads are metalled. Number of motor vehicles in Belgium, 1 Aug. 1987, 4,158,127, including 3,497,818 passenger cars, 16,095 buses, 296,415 lorries, 31,627 non-agricultural tractors, 146,550 agricultural tractors, 131,095 motor cycles and 38,527 special vehicles.

Railways. The main Belgian lines were a State enterprise from their inception in 1834. In 1926 the *Société Nationale des Chemins de Fer Belges (SNCB)* was formed to take over the railways. The State is sole holder of the ordinary shares of SNCB, which carry the majority vote at General Meetings. The length of railway operated on 31 Dec. 1986 was 3,618 km. Revenue (1986), 52,379m. francs; expenditure, 56,046m. francs. In 1986, 63·3m. tonnes of freight and 139·1m. passengers were carried.

The *Société Nationale des Chemins de Vicinaux (SNCV)* operates electrified light railways around Charleroi (97 km) and from De Panne to Knokke (68 km). There is also a metro and tramway in Brussels, and tramways in Antwerp and Ghent.

Aviation. The national Belgian airline SABENA (*Société anonyme belge d'exploitation de la navigation aérienne*) was set up in 1923. Its capital is 750m. francs. In addition to its European network, SABENA operates different routes to North and South America, to North, Central and South Africa and to the Near, the Middle and the Far East. In 1985 its airfleet comprised 24 aircraft. In 1985 SABENA flew 53m. km, carrying 2,188,707 revenue passengers, 581m. ton-km of freight and 18·25m. ton-km of mail.

Shipping.[1] On 1 Jan. 1987 the Belgian merchant fleet was composed of 96 vessels of 2,270,010 tons. There were 51 shipping companies, of which the most important were the Compagnie Maritime Belge, with 15 ships, and the Belcan, SA, with 4 ships.

[1] Belgian shipping returns are given in the official 'Moorsom tons', which may be converted into net tons by deducting 19·85% from the Moorsom total.

The navigation at the port of Antwerp in 1986 was as follows: Number of vessels entered, 16,201; tonnage, 125,507,686. Number of vessels cleared, 16,032; tonnage, 124,752,746.

The total length of navigable waterways (rivers and canals) was 1,569·5 km in 1986.

Post and Broadcasting. On 31 Dec. 1986 there were 1,863 post offices. The gross revenue of the post office in the year 1986 amounted to 30,603m. francs.

In 1986 there were 3,227,160 telephone subscribers, 3,798 mobile telephone subscribers, 31,533 subscribers to the paging service and 27,570 telex subscribers. As to data transmission, there were 50,226 modems connected to subscriber lines, 23,141 data transmission lines and 1,792 telegraph type lines.

Radio-Television belge de la Communauté française (RTBF) and *Belgische Radio en Televisie* (BRT) are public institutions broadcasting in French and Dutch respectively.

BRT has 5 radio programmes: BRT 1 is for service and information, documentary programmes, radio drama and light music; BRT 2 is for regional entertainments from each of the Flemish provinces. Both stations broadcast on medium-wave and on FM (stereo). BRT 3, on FM (stereo) is the cultural station; Studio Brussels (medium-wave and FM) gives local information and light music for 10 hours daily to Dutch-speaking residents; the International Service (short-and medium-wave) aims at reaching the Fleming dwelling abroad and at presenting a picture of Flemish cultural life.

RTBF has 5 radio programmes: Radio I (medium-wave) for information; Radio II (FM stereo) for entertainment and local information; Radio III (FM stereo) for classical music; Radio 21 (FM stereo) a young people's popular music and news programme; *Radio quatre internationale* (short-wave) which broadcasts to Africa.

Each body has 2 television channels, one general and one mainly for sport, special events, cultural events, feature films; broadcasting is by PAL standards. Commercial advertising is not allowed on radio or television, which are financed by the Flemish and French Community Councils. In 1985 the Flemish community had 2·77m. radio receivers and 1·7m. television sets of which 76·5% were colour sets; the French-speaking community had 1·7m. radio receivers and 1·2m. television sets of which 72% were colour sets; 83·2% of the Flemish and 89% of the French-speaking households were connected to a television cable-network. Number of receivers (1986), radio, 4,515,973; TV, 2,984,119.

Cinemas (1986). There were 433 cinemas, with a seating capacity of 109,755.

Newspapers (1986). There are 39 daily newspapers (some of them only regional or local editions of larger dailies), of which 23 are in French, 15 in Dutch and 1 in German.

JUSTICE, RELIGION, EDUCATION AND WELFARE

Justice. Judges are appointed for life. There is a court of cassation, 5 courts of appeal, and assize courts for political and criminal cases. There are 27 judicial districts, each with a court of first instance. In each of the 222 cantons is a justice and judge of the peace. There are, besides, various special tribunals. There is trial by jury in assize courts.

Religion. Of the inhabitants professing a religion the majority are Roman Catholic, but no inquiry as to the profession of faith is now made at the censuses. There are, however, statistics concerning the clergy, and according to these there were in 1986: Roman Catholic higher clergy, 131; inferior clergy, 5,856; Protestant pastors, 77; Anglican Church, 9 chaplains; Jews (rabbis and ministers), 24. The State does not interfere in any way with the internal affairs of any church. There is full religious liberty, and part of the income of the ministers of all denominations is paid by the State.

There are 8 Roman Catholic dioceses subdivided into 260 deaneries.

Estimated number of Protestants, 24,000; of Jews, 35,000.

The Protestant (Evangelical) Church is under a synod. There is also a Central Jewish Consistory, a Central Committee of the Anglican Church and a Free Protestant Church.

Education. On 8 Nov. 1962/2 Aug. 1963 a linguistic frontier was fixed between the Dutch-speaking, French-speaking and German-speaking parts of Belgium. In the north, Dutch is recognized as the official language, in the south, French, and along the eastern border, German. The city and *arrondissement* of Brussels are bilingual. The percentage of the population in the Flemish, French, German and bilingual regions was 57·6, 31·8, 0·7, 9·9 on 1 Jan. 1986. (*See* map in THE STATESMAN'S YEAR-BOOK, 1967–68.)

Higher Education (1985–86). Higher education is given in state universities: Ghent (13,237 students), Liège (9,978 students), Mons (1,881 students), the Polytechnic Faculty in Mons (624 students), the Antwerp State University Centre (2,205 students), the Gembloux Faculty of Agronomical Sciences (929 students), the Royal Military School in Brussels (775 students) and in the private universities: Catholic University of Louvain (40,106 students), the Free University of Brussels (20,745), University Institution Antwerp (1,808 students), St Ignatius Antwerp (3,576 students), Our Lady of Peace in Namur (3,930 students), Catholic University Faculty in Mons (871 students), St Louis in Brussels (1,156 students), St Aloysius in Brussels (790 students), the Limbourg University Centre (860 students) and the Protestant Faculty of Theology in Brussels (127 students). The total number of students in university colleges, faculties and institutes was 103,598.

There are 5 royal academies of fine arts and 5 royal conservatoires at Brussels, Liège, Ghent, Antwerp and Mons.

Secondary Education. 2,165 (1985–86) middle schools had a total of 103,846 pupils in the general classes and 157,783 in the technical classes in the traditional system and 594,075 pupils in the new system.

Elementary Education. There were 4,734 (1985–86) primary schools, with 758,260 pupils and 4,240 (1985–86) infant schools, with 393,741 pupils.

Normal Schools. Under the French and German linguistic systems there were 27 (1985–86) schools for training secondary teachers (2,317 students) in 1985–86; 42 (1985–86) for training elementary teachers (2,382 students) in 1985–86, 26 technical normal schools in 1985–86 with 943 students and 17 normal infant schools with 1,184 students in 1985–86.

Health. In 1986 there were 29,776 physicians (including 454,dentists), 5,760 other dentists and 10,792 pharmacists. Hospital beds numbered 90,720 on 1 Jan. 1986.

Social Security. Social security is based on the law of Dec. 1944. It applies to all workers subject to an employment contract, and is administered by the Central National Office of Social Security (ONSS), which collects from employers and employees all contributions referring to family allowances, health insurance, old age insurance, holidays and unemployment. These sums are distributed by the Central Office to the various institutions concerned with these benefits. Insurance against unemployment is organized through a common fund, which also undertakes to re-train the unemployed for another employment while providing for their families. Since 1944 further laws have increased allowances, made fresh provisions for hous-ing (1945), injuries while working, professional illnesses, etc. (1948).

Apart from private charity, the poor are assisted by the communes through the agency of the *Centre Public d'Aide Sociale* in French-speaking parts of the country and *Openbaar Centrum voor Maatschappelijk Welzijn* in Dutch-speaking areas. Provisions of a national character have been made for looking after war orphans and men disabled in the war. Certain other establishments, either state or provin-cial, provide for the needs of the deaf-mutes and the blind, and of children who are placed under the control of the courts. Provision is also made for repressing begging and providing shelter for the homeless.

DIPLOMATIC REPRESENTATIVES

Of Belgium in Great Britain (103 Eaton Sq., London, SW1W 9AB)
Ambassador: Jean-Paul Van Bellinghen (accredited 24 Feb. 1984).

Of Great Britain in Belgium (Britannia Hse., rue Joseph II 28, 1040 Brussels)
Ambassador: Peter Charles Petrie, CMG.

Of Belgium in the USA (3330 Garfield St., NW, Washington, D.C., 20008)
Ambassador: Herman Dehennin.

Of the USA in Belgium (Blvd. du Régent 27, 1000 Brussels)
Ambassador: Geoffrey Swaebe.

Of Belgium to the United Nations
Ambassador: (Vacant).

Books of Reference

Statistical Information: The Institut National de Statistique (44 rue de Louvain, Brussels) was set up on 24 Jan. 1831, under the designation of Bureau de Statistique Générale; after several changes, it received its present name on 2 May 1946. *Director-General (in charge):* L. Diels. *Main publications:*

Statistiques du commerce extérieur (monthly)
Bulletin de Statistique. Monthly
Annuaire Statistique de la Belgique (from 1870).—*Annuaire statistique de poche* (from 1965)
Statistiques Agricoles. Monthly

Annuaire administratif et judiciaire de Belgique. Annual. Brussels
L'économie belge. Ministère des Affaires Economiques. Annual (from 1947)
Guide des Ministères: Revue de l'Administration Belge. Brussels, Annual

BELIZE

Capital: Belmopan
Population: 171,000 (1986)
GNP per capita: US$1,200 (1985)

HISTORY. The early settlement of the territory was probably effected by British woodcutters about 1638; from that date to 1798, in spite of armed opposition from the Spaniards, settlers held their own and prospered. In 1780 the Home Government appointed a superintendent, and in 1862 the settlement was declared a colony, subordinate to Jamaica. It became an independent colony in 1884. Self-government was attained in 1964. Independence was achieved on 21 Sept. 1981.

AREA AND POPULATION. Belize is bounded north by Mexico, west and south by Guatemala and east by the Caribbean sea. Area, 22,963 sq. km. There are 6 districts:

	Sq. km	Population census, 1980		Sq. km	Population census, 1980
Corozal	1,860	22,902	Cayo	5,338	22,337
Belize	4,204	50,801	Stann Creek	2,176	14,181
Orange Walk	4,737	22,870	Toledo	4,649	11,762

Total population (census, 1980) 145,353. Estimate (1986) 171,000. In 1986 the birth rate per 1,000 was 36·1 and the death rate 4·1; infantile mortality 20·4 per 1,000 births; there were 1,025 marriages.

English is the official language. Spanish is spoken by 31·6% of the population. The main ethnic groups are Creole (African descent), Mestizo (Spanish-Maya) and Garifuna (Caribs).

Main city, Belize City; population, census 1980, 39,771. Estimate (1986) 47,000. Following the severe hurricane which struck the territory on 31 Oct. 1961 the capital Belmopan (population, 1986, 3,500) has been moved to a new site 50 miles inland; construction began in Jan. 1967 and it became the seat of government on 3 Aug. 1970. *See* map in the 1978–79 edition of THE STATESMAN'S YEAR-BOOK.

CLIMATE. A tropical climate with high rainfall and small annual range of temperature. The driest months are Feb. and March. Belize. Jan. 74°F (23·3°C), July 81°F (27·2°C). Annual rainfall 76″ (1,890 mm).

CONSTITUTION AND GOVERNMENT. Having achieved self-government in Jan. 1964 delays occurred in achieving independence because of the outstanding territorial claim by Guatemala. Attempts to reach agreement on the claim finally failed prior to independence being granted, but guarantees were given by Britain that a military force would remain.

The Constitution, which came into force on 21 Sept. 1981, provided for a National Assembly, with a 5-year term, comprising a 28-member House of Representatives elected by universal adult suffrage, and a Senate consisting of 5 members appointed by the Governor-General on the advice of the Prime Minister, 2 on the advice of the Leader of the Opposition and 1 on the advice of the Belize Advisory Council.

At the general election in Dec. 1984 the United Democratic Party won 21 seats in the House of Representatives and the People's United Party 7.

Governor-General: Dame Elmira Minita Gordon, GCMG, GCVO.

The cabinet in Jan. 1987 was composed as follows:

Prime Minister and Minister of Finance and Defence: The Rt Hon. Manuel Amadeo Esquivel, PC.

Deputy Prime Minister and Minister of Home Affairs: Curl Thompson. *Attorney-General and Minister of Foreign Affairs and Economic Development:* Dean Barrow. *Agriculture:* Dean Lindo. *Labour and Social Services:* Philip Goldson. *Natural Resources:* Charles Wagner. *Health:* Israel Alpuche. *Electricity,*

Communication and Transport: Derek Aikman. *Works and Housing:* Hubert Elrington. *Commerce, Industry and Tourism:* Edwardo Juan. *Education, Youth, Sports and Culture:* Elodio Aragon.

Flag: Blue with red band along the top and bottom edges. In the centre a white disc containing the coat of arms surrounded by a green garland.

DEFENCE. The Belize Defence Force consists of 3 rifle company battalions. There is an Air Wing which operates two twin-engined BN-2B Defenders for maritime patrol and transport duties. There is also a Maritime wing of the Belize Defence Force. It operates 2 armed 65 ft. patrol vessels utilized for anti-smuggling and coast guard duties. British Forces Belize number about 1,600, including a detachment of the Royal Air Force which deploys Harrier V/STOL ground attack/reconnaissance aircraft. Total personnel (1988) 600.

INTERNATIONAL RELATIONS

Membership. Belize is a member of UN, the Commonwealth, CARICOM and is an ACP state of EEC.

ECONOMY

Budget. In 1987–88 revenue was $B121m. and expenditure $B130m.
Public external debt, 31 Dec. 1986, US$104·2m.

Currency. There are notes of $B100, 20, 10, 5 and 1, and a subsidiary mixed metal coinage of 1-, 5-, 10-, 25- and 50-cent pieces. In March 1988, £1 = $B3·55 and US$1 = $B2.

Banking. A Central Bank was established in 1981. There were (1987) 4 commercial banks with a total of 14 branches: Belize Bank of Commerce and Industry Ltd, Barclays Bank PLC, Bank of Nova Scotia and the locally incorporated Atlantic Bank. The Development Finance Corporation provides long-term credit for development of agriculture and industry. There were (1985) 7 government savings banks, 26 credit unions and 17 insurance companies. Amendments to the Banking Ordinance permit offshore banking.

ENERGY AND NATURAL RESOURCES

Electricity. Production (1986) 74·4m. kwh. Supply 110 and 220 volts; 60 Hz.

Oil. Several oil companies were (1986) exploring for oil both off-shore and on-shore. Oil was discovered in the north in 1981 but not in commercial quantities.

Agriculture. In 1986 agriculture provided 65% of total foreign exchange earnings and employed 30% of the total labour force. The main agricultural export is sugar, followed by citrus fruit, chiefly grapefruit and oranges processed into oil, squash and concentrates. Citrus production, 1986, 1,265,000 boxes of oranges, 650,000 boxes of grapefruit. Sugar-cane production in 1986 was 854,000 tonnes. Bananas are the third export crop; production, 1986, 671,000 boxes. [Ed. note: Box of grapefruit, 80 lb., oranges, 90 lb., bananas, 42 lb.]. Cacao is becoming increasingly important as an export crop. Mangoes are also grown commercially; production, 1986, 1,000 tonnes. Main cultivated food crops (with production, 1986) are maize (18,000 tonnes), rice (4,000 tonnes) and red kidney beans. Belize is self-sufficient in fresh beef and pork, poultry and eggs. A dairy plant (daily milk processing capacity 400 gallons) began operations in 1986. Beekeeping co-operatives produced 618,000 lbs of honey in 1986.

Livestock (1986): Cattle, 50,000; sheep, 3,000; pigs, 20,000; poultry, 1m.

Forestry. 2,964 sq. miles, 49% of the total land area, are under forests which include mahogany, cedar, Santa Maria, pine and rosewood, and many secondary hardwoods of known or probable market value, as well as woods suitable for pulp production. Exports of forest produce in 1986 amounted to $B1m.

Fisheries. There are 5 registered fishing co-operatives. Food and game fish are plentiful, and domestic consumption is heavy. Main export markets for scale fish are in the USA, Mexico and Jamaica. Fish products exported in 1986 to the USA were valued at $B10·8m. Turtles—Hawksbill, Loggerhead and Green—are plentiful but as yet are not exported. There were 758 fishing vessels in 1987.

INDUSTRY AND TRADE

Industry. In 1986 production of the major commodities was: Sugar, 93,300 tons; molasses, 25,000 tons; cigarettes, 76m.; beer, 650,000 gallons; batteries, 6,000; wheat flour, 6m. lb.; rum, 4·5m. gallons; fertilizer, 4,000 tons; garments, 2·8m.; citrus concentrates, 1·1m. gallons. The labour market alternates between full employment, often accompanied by local shortages in the citrus and sugar-cane harvesting (Jan.–July), and under-employment during the wet season (Aug.–Dec.), aggravated by the seasonal nature of the major industries.

Trade Unions. There are more than 10 accredited unions with an estimated membership of 5,000.

Commerce. In 1986 total imports amounted to $B244·6m. Total exports, $B181·7m. The principal domestic exports were timber ($B1m.), sugar ($B62m.), fish products ($B10·8m.), garments ($B32·4m.), bananas ($B8·8m.), citrus products ($B23·2m.), molasses ($B1m.) and honey ($B400,000).

Total trade between Belize and UK (British Department of Trade returns, in £1,000 sterling):

	1983	1984	1985	1986	1987
Imports to UK	11,565	15,911	15,050	17,954	22,757
Exports and re-exports from UK	8,726	11,501	8,329	8,232	7,543

Tourism. Tourists totalled 93,440 in 1986 spending (1985) $B23·5m.

COMMUNICATIONS

Roads. There are four major highways and all principal towns and villages are linked by road to Belmopan and Belize City. In 1986, there were 11,000 licensed vehicles.

Aviation. Belize International Airport is 14 km from Belize City. Three airlines maintain international services to and from the USA, Central America and Mexico. In 1986, 356,600 passengers arrived and departed on international flights. Domestic air services provide connections to all main towns and 3 of the main offshore islands.

Shipping. The main port is Belize City, with a modern deep water port able to handle containerized shipping. Registered shipping (1981), 55 sailing vessels, 1,348 net tons, and 323 motor vessels, 745,197 net tons. The second largest port, Commerce Bight just south of Dangriga, can accommodate medium-sized vessels.

Post and Broadcasting. Number of telephones (1985), 8,800. The Belize Telecommunication Authority has instituted a country-wide fully automatic telephone dialling facility. There are 6 post offices and 45 rural sub-post offices.

Belize National Radio Network broadcasts daily, with 80% of its programmes in English and the remainder in Spanish.

Cinemas (1985). There were 10 cinemas with seating capacity of 10,000.

Newspapers. There were 5 weekly newspapers and 2 monthly magazines in 1987.

JUSTICE, RELIGION, EDUCATION AND WELFARE

Justice. Each of the 6 judicial districts has summary jurisdiction courts (criminal) and district courts (civil), both of which are presided over by magistrates. There is a Supreme Court and a Court of Appeal. There is a Director of Public Prosecutions, a Chief Justice and 2 Puisne Judges.

Religion. In 1986 about 62% of the population was Roman Catholic and 28% Protestant, including Anglican, Methodist, Seventh Day Adventist, Mennonite,

Nazarene, Jehovah's Witness, Pentecostal and Baptist. There was a small group of Bahai.

Education. Education is compulsory for children between 6-14 years and primary education is free. In 1986, 225 primary schools had a total enrolment of 39,190 pupils with 1,571 teachers; 24 secondary schools, 6,853 pupils with 499 teachers; 5 other technical schools, 834 students with 64 teachers. The School of Education offers courses for primary school teachers. The 2-year course leads to a teachers' diploma. The University College of Belize opened in 1986. There is 1 government-maintained special school for mentally handicapped and physically handicapped children. The University of the West Indies maintains an extra-mural department in Belize City.

Health. In 1986 there were 7 government hospitals (1 in Belmopan, 1 in Belize City and 1 in each of the other 5 districts) and an infirmary for geriatric and chronically ill patients, with 75 doctors and 583 hospital beds. Medical services in rural areas are provided by health care centres and mobile clinics.

DIPLOMATIC REPRESENTATIVES

Of Belize in Great Britain (15 Thayer St., London, W1M 5DL)
High Commissioner: Sir Edney Cain, OBE.

Of Great Britain in Belize (P.O. Box 91, Belmopan)
High Commissioner: P. A. B. Thomson, CVO.

Of Belize in the USA (3400 International Dr., NW, Washington, D.C., 20008)
Ambassador: Edward A. Laing.

Of the USA in Belize (Gabourel Lane and Hutson St., Belize City)
Ambassador: Richard G. Rick, Jr.

Of Belize to the United Nations
Ambassador: Kenneth E. Tillett.

Books of Reference

Abstract of Statistics 1981. Government Printer, Belize City, 1982
Bianchi, W. J., *Belize: The Controversy Between Guatemala and Great Britain.* New York, 1959
Dobson, D., *A History of Belize.* Belize, 1973
Grant, C. H., *The Making of Modern Belize.* CUP, 1976
Setzekorn, W. D., *Formerly British Honduras: A Profile of the New Nation of Belize.* Ohio Univ. Press, 1981
Woodward, R. L., Jr, *Belize.* [Bibliography] Oxford and Santa Barbara, 1980

BENIN

Capital: Porto Novo
Population: 4·15m. (1987)
GNP per capita: US$250 (1983)

République Populaire du Bénin

HISTORY. The territory of the present State was occupied by France in 1892 and was constituted a division of French West Africa in 1904 under the name of Dahomey. It became an independent republic within the French Community on 4 Dec. 1958, and acquired full independence on 1 Aug. 1960.

In the sixth *coup* since independence, Maj. Mathieu (now Ahmed) Kerekou came to power on 26 Oct. 1972 and proclaimed a Marxist–Leninist state, whose name was altered from Dahomey to Benin on 1 Dec. 1975.

AREA AND POPULATION. Benin is bounded east by Nigeria, north by Niger and Burkina Faso, west by Togo and south by the Gulf of Guinea. The area is 112,622 sq. km, and the population, census 1979, 3,338,240. Estimate (1987) 4,153,000. In 1979, 48% of the inhabitants were male, 14·2% urban and 49% were under 15 years of age. The seat of government is Porto-Novo (208,258 inhabitants in 1982); the chief port and business centre is Cotonou (487,020 in 1982); other important towns (1982) are Parakou (65,945), Natitingou (50,800, 1979), Abomey (54,418), Kandi (53,000) and Ouidah.

The areas, populations and capitals of the 6 provinces are as follows:

Province	Sq. km	Census 1979	Estimate 1985	Capital
Atakora	31,200	479,604	568,000	Natitingou
Borgou	51,000	490,669	577,000	Parakou
Zou	18,700	570,433	670,000	Abomey
Mono	3,800	477,378	560,000	Lokossa
Atlantique	3,200	686,258	824,000	Cotonou
Ouémé	4,700	626,868	738,000	Porto-Novo

French is the official language, while 47% of the people speak Fon, 12% Adja, 10% Bariba, 9% Yoruba, 6% Fulani, 5% Somba and 5% Aizo.

CLIMATE. In coastal parts there is an equatorial climate, with a long rainy season from March to July and a short rainy season in Oct. and Nov. The dry season increases in length from the coast, with inland areas having rain only between May and Sept. Porto Novo. Jan. 82°F (27·8°C), July 78°F (25·6°C). Annual rainfall 52″ (1,300 mm). Cotonou. Jan. 81°F (27·2°C), July 77°F (25°C). Annual rainfall 53″ (1,325 mm).

CONSTITUTION AND GOVERNMENT. Under a *Loi fondamentale* adopted in Aug. 1977, the sole political party is the *Parti de la Révolution Populaire du Bénin;* its Congress held in Nov. 1985 elected a Central Committee of 45 members to direct Party policy and to appoint the 11-member Political Bureau.

There is a unicameral legislature, the National Revolutionary Assembly of 196 People's Commissioners elected on 10 June 1984 for 5 years from the sole list of the PRPB. The Assembly elects the President for a 5-year term, and he appoints and leads a National Executive Council composed in Feb. 1987 as follows:

President, Minister of National Defence: Brig.-Gen. Ahmed Kerekou (re-elected 31 July 1984).

Ministers-Delegate to the Presidency: Maj. Edouard Zodehougan *(Interior, Security and Territorial Administration),* Kifouli Salami *(Planning and Statistics).* *Rural Development and Co-operative Action:* Maj. Adolphe Biaou. *Equipment and Transport:* Giriguissou Gado. *Finance and Economy:* Hospice Antonio. *Commerce, Crafts and Tourism:* Soule Dankoro. *Nursery and Primary Education:*

Capt. Philippe Akpo. *Secondary and Higher Education:* Vincent Guezodje. *Culture, Youth and Sports:* Ousmane Batoko. *Labour and Social Affairs:* Lieut-Col. Nathaneal Mensah. *Public Health:* André Archade. *Information and Communications:* Ali Houdou. *Foreign Affairs and Co-operation:* Guy Laudry Hazoume. *Justice, Inspection and Parastatal Enterprises:* Didier Dassi.

National flag: Green with a red star in the canton.

Local Government. The 6 provinces, each governed by an appointed Prefect and a Provincial Revolutionary Council, are divided into 84 districts.

DEFENCE. National service is for a period of 18 months.

Army. The Army consists of 3 infantry, 1 para-commando, 1 engineer and 1 service battalion, 1 armoured reconnaissance squadron and 1 artillery battery. Strength (1988) 3,800, with an additional 2,000-strong paramilitary gendarmerie.

Navy. A naval force was formed in 1979 with 4 fast gunboats and 2 fast torpedo boats transferred from the USSR, constituting a somewhat over-ambitious flotilla for such a short coastline, but a fast patrol craft and a tug were recently added. Personnel in 1988, under 200.

Air Force. The Air Force had a strength of (1988) about 100 officers and men, 2 twin-turboprop An-26 and 2 C-47 transports, 1 Cessna Skymaster, 1 Aero Commander 500, 2 Broussard communications aircraft and 2 Ecureuil II helicopters. A twin-turbofan Corvette is operated by the Air Force on VIP missions for government agencies.

INTERNATIONAL RELATIONS

Membership. Benin is a member of UN, OAU and is an ACP state of EEC.

ECONOMY

Planning. A 10-year development plan (1981–90) envisages an expenditure of 958,800m. francs CFA.

Budget. The 1986 recurrent budget balanced at 57,028m. francs CFA and the investment budget at 49,849m. francs CFA.

Currency. The monetary unit is the *franc CFA (Communauté financière africaine)*, with a parity value of 50 *francs CFA* to 1 French *franc.* There are coins of 1, 2, 5, 10, 25, 50 and 100 *francs CFA*, and banknotes of 50, 100, 500, 1,000, 5,000 and 10,000 *francs CFA*. In March 1988, £1 = 507 *francs CFA*; US$1 = 286 *francs CFA*.

Banking. The *Banque Centrale des Etats de l'Afrique de l'Ouest* is the bank of issue and the central bank. The *Banque Commerciale du Bénin*, in Cotonou, conducts all government business.

ENERGY AND NATURAL RESOURCES

Electricity. *Société Béninoise d'Electricité et d'Eau*, produced 88m. kwh in 1984 from generating plants at Cotonou, Porto-Novo and Parakou. Major development of hydro-electric resources along the Mono river are being conducted jointly with Togo. Supply 220 volts; 50 Hz.

Oil. The Semé oilfield, located 10 miles offshore, was discovered in 1968. Production commenced in 1982 and reached 2·5m. bbls in 1984.

Agriculture. 90% of the population subsist by agriculture. The chief products, 1986 (in 1,000 tonnes) were: Cassava, 726; yams, 858; maize, 364; sorghum, 90; groundnuts, 67; beans, 44; rice, 9; and sweet potatoes, 34, while cash crops were palm kernels, 18, and palm oil, 38. Cotton cultivation has been successfully introduced in the north; coffee cultivation has given good results in the south.

Livestock (1986 in 1,000): Cattle (930), sheep (1,160), goats (1,100), pigs (600), poultry (22,000), horses (6), asses (1).

Forestry. There are about 16,000 sq. km of classified forest, mainly in the north. Roundwood production in 1984 was 4·23m. cu. metres.

Fisheries. Total catch in 1983 was 21,000 tonnes (80% from inland and lagoon waters).

INDUSTRY AND TRADE

Industry. Industrial plants are few, limited mainly to palm-oil processing and brewing. There is a sugar complex at Savé, a cement plant at Onigbolo and textile mills at Cotonou and Parakou. Production (1984) included 49,000 tonnes of sugar, 36,000 tonnes of palm oil and (1983) cement 315,000 tonnes.

Labour. In 1973 the small trade unions were amalgamated to form a single body, now named the *Union Nationale des Syndicats des Travaillers du Bénin*.

Commerce. Imports in 1983, US$113m.; exports, US$78m. The main exports are palm oil and kernels, cocoa, cotton and sugar. In 1984, 32% of exports were to Spain, 21% to Federal Republic of Germany and 16% to France, which provided the largest share (23%) of imports.

Total trade between Benin and UK (British Department of Trade returns, in £1,000 sterling):

	1983	1984	1985	1986	1987
Imports to UK	2,887	2,101	7,390	4,910	2,930
Exports and re-exports from UK	10,577	6,829	8,362	6,728	7,207

Tourism. There were 41,000 foreign tourists in 1980.

COMMUNICATIONS

Roads. There were 8,400 km of roads in 1984, 917 motor cars and 506 goods vehicles.

Railways. There are 579 km of metre-gauge railway. One line connects Cotonou with Parakou (438 km) and is being extended to Dosso (in Niger); the second runs from Cotonou *via* Porto-Novo to Pobé (107 km); and the third from Cotonou *via* Ouidah to Segboroué on the Togo frontier (34 km), continuing to Lomé. In 1981 1·9m. passengers and 419,000 tonnes of freight were carried.

Aviation. In 1981, 80,400 passengers and 9,763 tonnes of freight passed through Cotonou airport. There are other airports at Abomey, Natitingou, Kandi and Parakou.

Shipping. In 1983, 736,000 tonnes were unloaded and 64,400 tonnes loaded at the port of Cotonou. There were (1986) 15 vessels of 4,887 GRT registered in Benin.

Post and Broadcasting. There were, in 1985, 8,650 telephones. Telegraph lines connect Cotonou with Togo, Niger and Senegal. In 1984 there were 68,000 radios and 17,250 television receivers.

Cinemas. In 1976 there were 4 cinemas with a seating capacity of 4,400.

Newspapers. In 1984 there was 1 daily newspaper with a circulation of 12,000.

JUSTICE, RELIGION, EDUCATION AND WELFARE

Justice. The Supreme Court is at Cotonou. There are Magistrates Courts in Cotonou, Porto-Novo, Natitingou, Abomey, Kandi, Ouidah and Parakou, and a *tribunal de conciliation* in each district.

Religion. 61% of the population follow animist beliefs, chiefly Voodoo, about 22% are Christian, mainly Roman Catholic, and 15% Moslem.

Education. There were, in 1983, 428,185 pupils in primary schools, 117,724 in secondary schools and 6,369 students in technical schools. The University of Benin (Cotonou) had 6,302 students in 1983. Adult literacy (1980) 28%.

Health. In 1982 there were 6 hospitals, 31 health centres, 186 dispensaries and 65 maternity clinics with (1978, combined) 4,968 beds, and in 1979 there were 204 doctors, 13 dentists, 55 pharmacists and 1,294 midwives.

DIPLOMATIC REPRESENTATIVES

Of Benin in Great Britain
Ambassador: Souler Issoufou Idrissou (resides in Paris).

Of Great Britain in Benin
Ambassador: Sir Martin Ewans, KCMG (resides in Lagos).

Of Benin in the USA (2737 Cathedral Ave., NW, Washington, D.C., 20008)
Ambassador: (Vacant).

Of the USA in Benin (Rue Caporal Anani Bernard, Cotonou)
Ambassador: Walter E. Stadtler.

Of Benin to the United Nations
Ambassador: Simon Ifedé Ogouma.

BERMUDA

Capital: Hamilton
Population: 57,145 (1985)
GNP per capita: US$16,300 (1985)

HISTORY. The Spaniards visited the islands in 1515, but, according to a 17th-century French cartographer, they were discovered in 1503 by Juan Bermudez, after whom they were named. No settlement was made, and they were uninhabited until a party of colonists under Sir George Somers was wrecked there in 1609. A company was formed for the 'Plantation of the Somers' Islands', as they were called at first, and in 1684 the Crown took over the government.

AREA AND POPULATION. Bermuda consists of a group of some 150 small islands (about 20 inhabited), situated in the western Atlantic (32° 18' N. lat., 64° 46' W. long.); the nearest point of the mainland, about 570 miles distant, is Cape Hatteras, N.C., and 690 miles from New York.

The area is 20·59 sq. miles (53·3 sq. km), of which 2·3 sq. miles were leased in 1941 for 99 years to the US Government for naval and air bases. The civil population (*i.e.,* excluding British and American military, naval and air force personnel) in 1980 (Census) was 54,893. Estimate (1985) 57,145.

Chief town, Hamilton; population, about 3,000.

In 1985 there were 914 live births, 694 marriages and 421 deaths; infantile mortality rate (1984) was 7·1 per 1,000 live births.

CLIMATE. A pleasantly warm and humid climate, with up to 60″ (1,500 mm) of rain, spread evenly throughout the year. Hamilton. Jan. 63°F (17·2°C), July 79°F (26·1°C). Annual rainfall 59″ (1,463 mm).

CONSTITUTION AND GOVERNMENT. Bermuda is a colony with representative government. Under the constitution of 8 June 1968 the Governor, appointed by the Crown, is normally bound to accept the advice of the Cabinet in matters other than external affairs, defence, internal security and the police, for which he retains special responsibility. The Cabinet is appointed from among members of the bicameral legislature, on the recommendation of the Premier. The Senate, of whom one or two members may serve on Cabinet, consists of 11 members. As a result of a Constitutional Conference held in Feb. 1979, it was decided that 5 Senators would be appointed by the Governor on the recommendation of the Premier, 3 by the Governor on the recommendation of the Opposition Leader and 3 by the Governor in his own discretion. The 40 members of the House of Assembly are elected 2 from each of 20 constituencies under full universal, adult suffrage. A general election was held on 29 Oct. 1985. The United Bermuda Party won 31 seats, the Progressive Labour Party, 7 and the National Liberal Party, 2.

Governor: The Viscount Dunrossil, CMG.
Premier: John W. D. Swan.
Flag: The British Red Ensign with the badge of the Colony in the fly.

DEFENCE. The Bermuda Regiment had 734 men and women in 1987.

ECONOMY

Budget. Revenue and expenditure in $B for years ending 31 March:

	1983–84	1984–85	1985–86	1986–87	1987–88
Revenue	165,498,190	186,553,800	214,800,000	231,508,700	251,550,300
Expenditure	165,466,440	186,553,245	190,362,000	200,706,300	220,172,000

Expenditure in $B1,000 (excluding capital items) was earmarked as follows:

	1983–84	1984–85	1985–86	1986–87	1987–88
Education	24,068	30,589	25,585	27,853	30,187
Health and Social Services	41,855	37,113	434,100	491,600	553,300
Public Works	16,069	16,090	20,195	21,427	23,234
Police	13,933	13,953	15,970	17,204	19,025
Tourism	13,335	14,750	17,793	19,383	21,566
Marine and Ports Services	4,267	4,678	5,127	5,852	6,285
Public Transportation	936	953	93,200	77,800	3,431
Agriculture and Fisheries	5,827	6,266	5,719	6,126	6,716
Post Office	4,196	4,196	5,022	5,991	6,255

The estimated chief sources of revenue in 1987–88 were: Customs duties, $105m.; employment tax, $20·9m.; land tax, $11m.; hospital levy, $28m.; vehicle licenses, $7,655,000; stamp duties, $9m.; passenger taxes, $9·6m. Public debt, as at 31 March 1987, was nil.

Currency. Decimal currency based on a *Bermuda dollar* of 100 *cents* was introduced 6 Feb. 1970. In March 1988 £1 = 1.77 Bermuda dollars and US$1 = 1 Bermuda dollar. The Bermuda Monetary Authority issues notes in denominations of $100, $50, $20, $10, $5 and $1, and coins in values of 50c, 25c, 10c, 5c and 1c.

Banking. There are 3 banks, the Bank of Bermuda, Ltd, the Bank of N. T. Butterfield and Son, Ltd, and the Bermuda Commercial Bank, Ltd, with correspondent banks and representatives in either New York, London, Canada or Hong Kong.

Weights and Measures. Metric, except that US and Imperial measures are used in certain fields.

ENERGY AND NATURAL RESOURCES

Electricity. Production (1986) 378m. kwh. Supply 115 volts; 60 Hz.

Agriculture. The chief products are fresh vegetables, bananas and citrus fruit. In 1986, 603 acres were under cultivation. In 1987 6,859 persons were employed in agriculture, fishing and horticulture.

In 1986, total value of agricultural products was $B6,187,000.

Livestock (1986): Cattle, 1,000; pigs, 3,000; goats, 1,000; poultry (1982), 47,000.

INDUSTRY AND TRADE

Trade Unions. Legislation providing for trade unions was enacted in Oct. 1946, and there are 9 trade unions with a total membership (1983) of 7,622.

Commerce. Imports and exports in $B:

	1982	1983	1984	1985
Imports	348,000,000	377,732,000	414,094,688	402,491,252
Exports	17,000,000	22,762,000	40,544,514	23,053,764

The visible adverse balance of trade is more than compensated for by invisible exports, including tourism and off-shore insurance business.

Imports in 1985 from USA, $241m.; UK, $40m.; Canada, $25m.; Japan, $13,637,000; Hong Kong, $4,961,000; France, $6,665,000; Federal Republic of Germany, $4,818,000; New Zealand, $2,834,000; Denmark, $3,937,000; Netherlands, $2,894,000.

In 1985 the principal imports were food, drink and tobacco ($130·5m.); clothing ($29m.), electric appliances ($39m.), transport equipment ($24m.). The bulk of exports comprise sales of fuel to aircraft and ships, and re-exports of pharmaceuticals.

Total trade between Bermuda and UK, in £1,000 sterling (British Department of Trade returns):

	1983	1984	1985	1986	1987
Imports to UK	4,019	3,037	6,394	1,262	1,208
Exports and re-exports from UK	24,924	22,843	28,024	26,180	25,383

Tourism. In 1987, 613,628 tourists visited Bermuda including those arriving by air and cruise ship.

COMMUNICATIONS

Roads. In 1948 the railway service was discontinued and a government-operated bus service introduced.

Between 1908 and Aug. 1946 the use of motor vehicles, with the exception of ambulances, fire engines and other essential services, was prohibited. In 1986, out of 43,359 registered vehicles 17,240 were private cars.

Aviation. American Airlines, Pan American, Delta Airlines and Eastern Airlines maintain regular services between Bermuda and the USA. British Airways also have regular flights through Bermuda linking Bermuda with Baltimore and London. Air Canada Airlines call at Bermuda on their service between Toronto, Montreal and Halifax. United Airlines began a daily service between Bermuda and USA in May 1988.

Shipping. In 1986, there were 155 visits by cruise ships, 249 visits by cargo ships and 28 visits by oil and gas tankers.

Post and Broadcasting (1987). There are 15 post offices. The telephone company is privately owned and rented 52,670 telephones in 1987. Cables connect the islands with the USA, Halifax (N.S.) and Tortola, providing connexion with the world. Radio and television broadcasting is commercial.

Newspapers (1987). There is 1 daily newspaper with a circulation of 17,961 and 2 weeklies with a total circulation of 26,000.

JUSTICE, EDUCATION AND WELFARE

Justice. There are 3 magistrates' courts, 3 Supreme Courts and a court of appeal. The police had a strength of 463 men and women in 1987.

Education. Education is compulsory between the ages of 5 and 16, and government assistance is given by the payment of grants, and, where necessary, of school fees. In 1987, there were 18 primary schools, 14 secondary schools (of which 5 are private, including 2 denominational schools and one run by the US Armed Forces in Bermuda), 4 special schools at the primary and secondary levels which cater to 190 blind, deaf, speech impaired and multiple handicapped persons aged 14–21, and 11 pre-school nurseries. There were 2,371 students attending the Bermuda College in 1985. There is no university, but extra-mural courses are available from Queen's University in Canada and the University of Maryland in the USA.

Health. In 1987 there were 2 hospitals, 70 doctors, 20 dentists, 561 professional nurses and 31 pharmacists.

Books of Reference

Bermuda Report, 1980–84. Hamilton, 1986
Bermuda Historical Quarterly. 1944 ff.
Dyer, H. T., *The Next 20 Years: A Report of the Development Plans for Bermuda.* Hamilton, 1963
Hayward, S. J., Holt-Gomez, V., and Sterrer, W., *Bermuda's Delicate Balance: People and the Environment.* Hamilton, 1981
Warwick, J. B., (ed.), *Who's Who in Bermuda 1980–81.* Hamilton, 1982
Wilkinson, H. C., *Bermuda from Sail to Steam.* OUP, 1973
Zuill, W. S., *The Story of Bermuda and Her People.* London, 1973

National Library: The Bermuda Library, Hamilton. *Head Librarian:* Cyril O. Packwood.

BHUTÁN

Druk-yul

Capital: Thimphu
Population: 1·3m. (1986)
GNP per capita: US$140 (1984)

HISTORY. In 1774 the East India Company concluded a treaty with the ruler of Bhután. Under a treaty signed in Nov. 1865 the Bhután Government was granted an annual subsidy. By an amending treaty concluded in Jan. 1910 the British Government undertook to exercise no interference in the internal affairs of Bhután, and the Bhután Government agreed to be guided by the advice of the British Government in regard to its external relations.

The Government of India concluded a fresh treaty with Bhután on 8 Aug. 1949. Under this treaty the Government of Bhután continues to be guided by the Government of India in regard to its external relations, and the Government of India have undertaken not to interfere in the internal administration of Bhután. The subsidy paid to Bhután was increased to Rs 500,000, and the Government of India agreed to retrocede to Bhután an area of about 32 sq. miles in the territory known as Dewangiri, which was annexed in 1865.

AREA AND POPULATION. Bhután is situated in the eastern Himalayas, bordered north by China and on all other sides by India. Extreme length from east to west 190 miles: extreme breadth 90 miles. Area about 18,000 sq. miles (46,500 sq. km); population estimated at approximately 1,300,000 (1986). Hindus, of Nepálese origin, form 25%-30% of the population. Life expectancy (1985) was 46 years. The capital is at Thimphu (1987, 15,000 population).

CLIMATE. The climate is largely controlled by altitude. The mountainous north is cold, with perpetual snow on the summits, but the centre has a more moderate climate, though winters are cold, with rainfall under 40″ (1,000 mm). In the south, the climate is humid sub-tropical and rainfall approaches 200″ (5,000 mm).

KING. Jigme Singye Wangchuck, succeeded his father Jigme Dorji Wangchuck who died 21 July 1972.

GOVERNMENT. In 1907 the Tongsa Penlop (the governor of the province of Tongsa in central Bhután), Sir Ugyen Wangchuk, GCIE, KCSI, was elected as the first hereditary Maharaja of Bhután. The Bhutánese title is Druk Gyalpo, and his successor is now addressed as King of Bhután. From Oct. 1969 the absolute monarchy was changed to a form of 'democratic monarchy'. The National Assembly (*Tshogdu*) was reinstituted in 1953. It has 151 members and meets twice a year. Two-thirds are representatives of the people and are elected for a 3-year term. All Bhutánese over 25 years may be candidates. Ten monastic representatives are elected by the central and regional ecclesiastical bodies, while the remaining members are nominated by the King, and include members of the Council of Ministers (the Cabinet) and the Royal Advisory Council.

The official languages are Dzongkha, Lhotsam (Nepáli) and English.

National flag: Diagonally yellow over orange, over all in the centre a white dragon.

Local government: There are 18 districts, each under a district officer *(Dzongda)*.

DEFENCE

Army. There was (1988) an Army of about 5,000 men.

INTERNATIONAL RELATIONS

Membership. Bhután is a member of UN.

ECONOMY

Planning. The 6th 5-year plan (1987–92), allows for expenditure of N9,485m.

Budget. The budget for 1987–88 envisaged expenditure of N2,019m. and internal revenue of N411m.

Currency. Paper currency has been introduced, known as the *Ngultrum*. Cupro-nickel and bronze currency is known as *Chetrum* (100 *Chetrum* = 1 *Ngultrum*). Indian currency is also legal tender. In March 1988, £1 = N22·90; US$1 = N13·05.

Banking. The Bank of Bhután was established in 1968. The headquarters are at Phuntsholing with 21 branches throughout the country. The Royal Monetary Authority, Thimphu, was founded in 1982 to act as Bhután's central bank. Deposits (Dec. 1986) N583m.

ENERGY AND NATURAL RESOURCES

Electricity. Production (1986) 1,950m. kwh, and 23 towns and 93 villages had electricity.

Minerals. Large deposits of limestone, marble, dolomite, graphite, lead, copper, slate, coal, talc, gypsum, beryl, mica, pyrites and tufa have been found.

Agriculture. The area under cultivation in 1985 was some 775,000 hectares. The chief products (1986 production in 1,000 tonnes) are rice (63), millet (8), wheat (11), barley (5), maize (88), cardamom, potatoes (28), oranges (27), apples, hand-loom cloth, timber and yaks. Extensive and valuable forests abound.

Livestock (1986): Cattle, 325,000; yaks (1985), 31,271; pigs, 77,000; sheep and goats, 91,000; poultry (1985), 179,521.

INDUSTRY AND TRADE

Industry. In 1987 there were about 400 small-scale cottage and industrial units and also a cement plant, a fruit processing factory, a tea-chest ply veneer factory, a resin and turpentine factory, a salt iodization plant and 3 distilleries.

Commerce. Trade with India dominates but timber, cardamom and liquor are also exported to the Middle East, Singapore and Western Europe.

Total trade between Bhután and UK (British Department of Trade returns, in £1,000 sterling):

	1985	1986	1987
Imports to UK	...	...	14
Exports and re-exports from UK	109	76	411

Tourism. The country has been opened for controlled tourism since 1974 and this is the largest source of foreign exchange (1986, US$2·19m. net). In 1986, 2,486 tourists visited Bhután.

COMMUNICATIONS

Roads. In 1987 there were about 2,000 km of roads. In 1985, there were 3,633 vehicles, of which 716 were private cars and 1,761 buses, jeeps and trucks.

Aviation. (1987) There are 3 to 6 flights weekly by Druk-Air between Paro and Calcutta and a weekly return service from Paro to Dhaka.

Post and Broadcasting. A modern postal system was introduced in 1962. There are 54 general post offices and 30 branch post offices. In 1986 there were 1,086 km of telephone lines, 15 automatic exchanges and (1985) 1,890 telephones.

An international microwave link connects Thimphu to the Calcutta and Delhi satellite connexions. Thimphu and Phuntsholing are connected by telex to Delhi.

In 1985 there were 34 wireless stations for internal administrative communications, and 8 hydro-met stations, with an estimated 15,000 radio receivers. Bhután Broadcasting Service, Thimphu, broadcasts a daily programme in English, Sharchopkha, Dzongkha and Nepáli.

Newspapers. The only weekly newspaper, *Kuensel*, began publication in Aug.

1986 to replace the government weekly bulletin. It is published in 3 languages (English, Dzongkha and Nepáli). Total circulation (1987) about 10,700.

JUSTICE, RELIGION, EDUCATION AND WELFARE

Justice. The High Court consists of 8 judges (2 elected by the National Assembly for 5-year terms) appointed by the King. There is a Magistrate's Court in each district, under a *Thrimpon*, from which appeal is to the High Court at Thimphu.

Religion. In 1987 there were 1,160 monks in the Central Monastic Body (Thimphu and Punakha) and 2,120 in the District Monk Bodies. The monks are headed by an elected Je Khempo (Head Abbot). The majority of the people are Mahayana Buddhists of the Drukpa subsect of the Kagyud School which was first introduced from Tibet during the 12th century. Hindus of Nepálese origin represent approximately 25% of population.

Education. In 1987 there were 40,688 pupils and 1,398 teachers in primary schools, 11,276 pupils and 314 teachers in junior high schools, 4,277 pupils and 130 teachers in high schools and 604 pupils and 145 teachers in technical, vocational and tertiary-level schools. Many students receive higher technical training in India, as well as under the UN Development Programme, the Colombo Plan, etc., in Australia, the Federal Republic of Germany, New Zealand, Japan, Singapore, the USA and UK.

Health. There were (1985) 28 hospitals, 44 dispensaries, 65 basic health units, 4 indigenous dispensaries, 5 leprosy hospitals, 1 mobile hospital, 1 health school and 15 malaria eradication centres. In 1985 beds totalled 857 and there were 70 doctors.

DIPLOMATIC REPRESENTATIVE

Of Bhután to the United Nations
Ambassador: Dasho Jigmi Thinley.

The Government of Bhután is in diplomatic relations with Bangladesh and India at ambassadorial level with resident missions in Thimphu. Honorary Consuls have also been appointed in Singapore, South Korea and Hong Kong (the latter also responsible for Macao).

Books of Reference

Bhutan, Himalayan Kingdom. Bhután Government, Thimphu, 1979
Aris, M., *Bhutan: The Early History of an Himalayan Kingdom.* Warminster, 1979
Chakravarti, B., *A Cultural History of Bhutan.* 2nd rev. ed., 2 vols. Chitteranjan, 1981
Collister, P., *Bhutan and the British.* London, 1987
Das, N., *The Dragon Country.* New Delhi, 1973
Mehra, G. N., *Bhutan: Land of the Peaceful Dragon.* Rev. ed. New Delhi, 1985
Rahul, R., *Royal Bhutan.* New Delhi, 1983
Ronaldshay, the Earl of, *Lands of the Thunderbolt.* 2nd ed. London, 1931
Rose, L. E., *The Politics of Bhutan.* Cornell Univ. Press, 1977
Rustomji, N., *Bhutan: The Dragon Kingdom in Crisis.* OUP, 1978

BOLIVIA

República de Bolivia

Capital: Sucre
Seat of Government: La Paz
Population: 6·25m. (1984)
GNP per capita: US$400 (1985)

HISTORY. Until 1884, when Bolivia was defeated by Chile, she had a strip bordering on the Pacific which contains extensive nitrate beds and at that time the port of Cobija (which no longer exists). She lost this area to Chile; but in Sept. 1953 Chile declared Arica a free port and, although it is no longer a free port for Bolivian imports, Bolivia still has certain privileges.

AREA AND POPULATION. Bolivia is a landlocked state bounded north and east by Brazil, south by Paraguay and Argentina and west by Chile and Peru, with an area of some 424,165 sq. miles (1,098,581 sq. km).

The following table shows the area and population of the departments (the capitals of each are given in brackets):

Departments	Area (sq. km)	Census 1976	Census 1982 [1]	Per sq. km 1975
La Paz (La Paz)	133,985	1,456,078	1,913,184	12·50
Cochabamba (Cochabamba)	55,631	720,952	908,674	15·57
Potosí (Potosí)	118,218	657,743	823,485	7·98
Santa Cruz (Santa Cruz)	370,621	710,724	942,986	1·36
Chuquisaca (Sucre)	51,524	358,516	435,406	9·69
Tarija (Tarija)	37,623	186,704	246,691	5·95
Oruro (Oruro)	53,588	310,409	385,121	6·93
Beni (Trinidad)	213,564	168,367	217,700	0·99
Pando (Cobija)	63,827	34,493	42,594	0·55
Total	1,098,581	4,687,718	5,915,841	4·85

[1] Preliminary.

Total population (estimate 1984) 6,252,250.

Population (estimate 1982) of the principal towns: La Paz, 881,404; Santa Cruz, 376,917; Cochabamba, 281,962; Oruro, 132,213; Potosí, 103,182; Sucre, 79,941; Tarija, 54,001.

Spanish is the official and commercial language, but the majority of Indians speak Aymará (25·2%) or Quechua (34·4%).

CLIMATE. The very varied geography of Bolivia produces several different climates. The two most significant are the low-lying areas in the Amazon Basin, which are very warm and damp throughout the year, with heavy rainfall from Nov. to March, and the alti-plano, which is generally dry between May and Nov. with abundant sunshine, but the nights are cold in June and July, while the months from Dec. to March are the wettest. La Paz. Jan. 53°F (11·7°C), July 47°F (8·3°C). Annual rainfall 23″ (574 mm). Sucre. Jan. 55°F (13°C), July 49°F (9·4°C). Annual rainfall 27″ (675 mm).

CONSTITUTION AND GOVERNMENT. The Republic of Bolivia was proclaimed on 6 Aug. 1825; its first constitution was adopted on 19 Nov. 1826.

La Paz is the actual capital and seat of the Government, but Sucre is the legal capital and the seat of the judiciary.

The following is a list of presidents since 1966 and the date on which they took office:

Gen. René Barrientos Ortuño (Constitutional President killed in air accident), 6 Aug. 1966–27 April 1969.

Dr Luis Adolfo Siles Salinas (deposed), 27 April 1969–26 Sept. 1969.

Gen. Alfredo Ovando Candia, 26 Sept. 1969–6 Oct. 1970.

Gen. Juan José Torres, 7 Oct. 1970–21 Aug. 1971.

Gen. Hugo Banzer Suarez, 21 Aug. 1971–21 July 1978.

Gen. Juan Pereda Asbun, 21 July 1978–24 Nov. 1978.

Gen. David Padilla Arancibia, 24 Nov. 1978–8 Aug. 1979.

Dr Walter Guevara Arze (deposed), 8 Aug. 1979–1 Nov. 1979.

Dr Lydia Gueiler Tejada (deposed), 16 Nov. 1979–17 July 1980.

Maj.-Gen. Luis García Meza Tejada (resigned), 18 July 1980–4 Aug. 1981.

Military Junta, 4 Aug. 1981–4 Sept. 1981.

Gen. Celso Torrelio Villa, (resigned), 4 Sept. 1981–19 July 1982.

Brig.-Gen. Guido Vildoso Calderón, 21 July 1982–10 Oct. 1982.

Dr Hernan Siles Zuazo, 10 Oct. 1982–6 Aug. 1985.

Following elections in July 1979 which were inconclusive an interim President was chosen with the agreement of the three parties who had polled most votes. For details of political history 1970–78 *see* THE STATESMAN'S YEAR-BOOK, 1980–81 and for the period 1978–1980 *see* THE STATESMAN'S YEAR-BOOK, 1983–84.

The President and Vice-President are elected by universal suffrage for a four year term. The President appoints the members of his Cabinet from candidates nominated by the Senate. There is a bicameral legislature; the Senate comprises 27 members, 3 from each department, and the Chamber of Deputies 117 members, all elected for 4 years. Elections to the National Congress were held on 14 July 1985. The *Movimiento Nacionalista Revolucionario* gained 59 seats; *Alianza Democrática Nacionalista*, 51; *Movimiento de la Izquierda Revolucionaria*, 16; *Movimiento Nacionalista Revolucionario de Izquierda*, 8.

The Cabinet was composed as follows in Jan. 1988:

President: Dr Victor Paz Esstensoro (sworn in 6 Aug. 1985).

Foreign Affairs and Culture: Dr Guillermo Bedregal Gutierrez. *Interior, Migration and Justice:* Dr Juan Carlos Duran Saucedo. *National Defence:* Alfonso Revollo. *Finance:* Juan Cariaga. *Planning and Co-ordination:* Gonzalo Sanchez de Lozada. *Education:* Enrique Ipina. *Transport and Communications:* Andres Petricevich. *Industry and Commerce:* Fernando Moscoso. *Labour:* Dr Alfredo Franco Guachalla. *Health:* Dr Carlos Perez. *Minerals and Metallurgy:* Jaime Villalobos. *Agriculture:* Jose Guillermo Justiniano S. *Energy and Hydrocarbons:* Fernando Illanes. *Housing:* Franklin Anaya. *Information:* Hernan Antelo. *Aeronautics:* Jaime Zegada Hurtado. *Secretary-General:* Dr Walter Zuleta Roncali.

National flag: Three horizontal stripes of red, yellow, green, with the arms of Bolivia in the centre.

National anthem: Bolivianos, el hado propicio (words by I. de Sanjinés; tune by B. Vincenti).

Local Government: The republic is divided into 9 departments, established in Jan. 1826, with 98 provinces administered by sub-prefects, and 1,272 cantons administered by corregidores. The supreme authority in each department is vested in a prefect appointed by the President.

DEFENCE. Bolivia is divided into 8 military districts, with divisional headquarters in Viacha, Oruro, Villa Montes, Camiri, Roboré, Riberalta, Santa Cruz, Cochabamba; regional HQ are located at La Paz, Sucre, Tarija, Potosí, Trinidad and Cobija. There is selective conscription for 12 months at the age of 18 years.

Army. The Army consists of 11 infantry, 6 cavalry, 4 mechanized, 4 artillery, 1 ranger and 1 parachute regiments, and 2 armoured anti-tank and 7 engineer battalions. Equipment, 24 EE-9 Cascavel armoured cars. Strength (1988) 20,000.

Navy. A small Navy exists for river and lake patrol comprising 35 patrol craft operating in Lake Titicaca, Beni river systems and the Bolivia-Paraguay 6,000-mile river systems, 1 transport (a gift from Venezuela for use to and from Bolivian free zones in Argentina and Uruguay) and 2 hospital ships (one a gift from USA). There are two armed T-6 patrol aircraft and a Cessna light transport.

Personnel in 1988 totalled 4,000 officers and men including marines. Most training of officers and petty officers is carried out in Argentina. The junior ratings are almost entirely converted soldiers.

Air Force. The Air Force, established in 1923, has 5 combat-capable squadrons, four equipped with T-33 armed jet trainers, and one with armed T6s, SF.260s and Hughes 500 helicopters, for counter-insurgency operations. A search and rescue helicopter squadron has 9 Brazilian-assembled Gaviãos (Lamas) and 20 UH-1 Iroquois. Other types in service include Brazilian T-23 Uirapuru and American T-41 primary trainers and Swiss turboprop-powered Pilatus PC-7 basic trainers, 1 Electra four-turboprop transport, 6 Fokker F.27 and 4 Israeli-built Arava twin-turboprop light transports, 2 Convair transports, 2 C-130H/L-100-30 Hercules, 6 C-47 and about 30 Cessna single- and twin-engined light aircraft. Personnel strength (1987) about 4,000.

INTERNATIONAL RELATIONS

Membership. Bolivia is a member of UN, OAS, LAIA (formerly Lafta), the Andean Group and the Amazon Pact.

ECONOMY

Budget. Revenue and expenditures in 1m. *pesos bolivianos* balanced as follows: In 1982 there was a projected budget deficit of $b.110,959m.

Currency. On 1 Jan. 1987 the *boliviano* ($b. equal to 1m. *pesos*) was introduced. Exchange rates were $b.2·21 = US$1 and $b.3·92 = £1 in March 1988.

Banking. In 1986 the principal banks were Banco Central de Bolivia, Banco del Estado, Banco de Santa Cruz de la Sierra, Banco Agricola de Bolivia, Banco Boliviano Americano, Banco Hipotecario Nacional, Banco Mercantil, Banco Minero de Bolivia, Banco Nacional de Bolivia, Banco do Brasil, Banco de la Nacion Argentina, Banco Popular del Peru, Banco Industrial S.A., First National City Bank, Banco del Progress Nacional, Bank of America and Bank of Boston.

Weights and Measures. The metric system of weights and measures is used by the administration and prescribed by law, but the old Spanish system is also employed.

ENERGY AND NATURAL RESOURCES

Electricity. Electric power production is expanding. Installed capacity was estimated at 490,000 kw. in 1985. Estimated production from all sources (1986), 2,080m. kwh. Supply 110 volts in La Paz but 220 volts in most other cities; 60 Hz.

Oil and Gas. There are petroleum and natural gas deposits in the Santa Cruz-Camiri areas. A pipeline for crude oil connects Caranda (Santa Cruz) with the Pacific coast at Arica (Chile) and a natural gas pipeline to Argentina was inaugurated in May 1972. All production, refining and internal distribution is now in the hands of *Yacimientos Petroliferos Fiscales Bolivianos* (the State Petroleum Organization). Total production of crude oil in 1987 was estimated at 800,000 tonnes. Production of natural gas in 1981 was estimated at 175,478m. cu. ft.

Minerals. Mining is the most important industry, accounting for about 69% of the foreign-exchange earnings. About half the mineral mined is tin. Tin mines are at altitudes of from 12,000 to 18,000 ft, where few except native Indians can stand the conditions; transport is costly. Bolivian tin is extracted by shaft-mining, frequently very deep; the ore yields only 0·7% or less of tin and is very refractory; tin is exported in concentrates called *barrilla,* through Pacific ports for refining. Smelting capacity was increased in 1980 and it is planned to smelt all the ores from the State Mining Co. but complex ores still have to be exported for smelting. Tin production in 1984 was 17,875 tonnes.

The state industry is being run by the *Corporación Minera de Bolivia* (COMIBOL) employing about 23,000 in mining and administrative capacities.

Alluvial gold deposits in the Alto Beni region are being exploited. Production (1984) 1·1 tonne.

Foreign firms are seeking exploration rights for uranium and a small uranium processing plant was opened in Oct. 1980 at Cotaje (Potosí province). Large deposits of salt are found near Lake Poopó and in the south of Bolivia.

Agriculture. The extensive and still largely undeveloped region east of the Andes comprises about three-quarters of the entire area of the country, and since the agrarian reform of 1953 sugar-cane, rice and cotton have been grown in this *Oriente* in increasing abundance, reaching self-sufficiency in all these products. Output in 1,000 tonnes in 1986 was: Sugar-cane, 1,850; rice, 137; coffee, 19; maize, 457; potatoes, 697; wheat, 81; cotton (lint), 2; cocoa, 3. Cocaine is by far the largest crop grown.

Livestock: In 1986 there were 6m. head of cattle, mostly in the Santa Cruz and Beni departments; some are exported to Peru; horses, 311,000; asses, 600,000; pigs, 1·1m.; sheep, 9·5m.; goats, 1·2m.; poultry, 8m.

Forestry. Tropical forests with woods ranging from the 'iron tree' to the light *palo de balsa* are beginning to be exploited. In 1962 the Forestry Service announced proved reserves of 46·3m. hectares, plus a similar amount available for immediate development.

INDUSTRY AND TRADE

Industry. There are few industrial establishments and the country relies on imports for the supply of many consumer goods. However a new investment law passed in 1971 provides incentives and protection for new investment, both foreign and domestic, and for reinvestment in various fields including manufacturing industry, mining, agriculture, construction and tourism.

Commerce. The value of imports and exports in US$1,000 has been as follows:

	1980	1981	1982	1983	1984	1985
Imports	833,160	917,081	496,300	451,100	713,800	...
Exports	942,000	995,298	898,500	786,700	609,500	672,500

Chief exports in 1983 (in US$1m.): Natural gas, 378·2; tin, 207·9; silver, 58·3; zinc, 33·4; wolfram, 20; coffee, 12·9; sugar, 12·3.

Chief imports in 1983 (in US$1m.): Raw materials for industry, 211·3; capital goods for industry, 152·4; consumer goods, 52·3; transport equipment, 52·2; construction materials, 38·4.

Imports and exports (in US$1m.), by country, 1984:

Country	Imports	Exports	Country	Imports	Exports
Argentina	97·2	271·1	Japan	22·9	—
Brazil	154·6	14·7	Korea	125·5	—
Chile	16·2	—	Peru	—	14·8
Federal Republic			UK	24·9	24·6
of Germany	31·5	38·6	USA	116·1	145·1
France	—	23·9			

Total exports, 1984, of all minerals, in concentrates, ingots or solder, were valued at US$363·9m.

Bolivia having no seaport, imports and exports pass chiefly through the ports of Arica and Antofagasta in Chile, Mollendo-Matarani in Peru, through La Quiaca on the Bolivian-Argentine border and through river-ports on the rivers flowing into the Amazon.

Total trade between Bolivia and UK (British Department of Trade returns in £1,000 sterling):

	1983	1984	1985	1986	1987
Imports to UK	14,834	20,052	14,434	10,225	14,799
Exports and re-exports from UK	4,711	17,170	10,443	3,663	3,658

Tourism. There were 133,000 visitors in 1986.

COMMUNICATIONS

Roads. A highway, in poor condition, 497 km long, runs from Cochabamba to the lowland farming region of Santa Cruz. La Paz and Oruro are also connected by a metalled road. Of other main highways (unmetalled) there is one from La Paz through Guaqui into Peru, another from La Paz, *via* Oruro, Potosí, Tarija and Bermejo, into Argentina, with branches to Cochabamba, Sucre and Camiri, passable throughout the year except at the height of the rainy season, and others from Villazón to Villa Montes *via* Tarija, passable during the dry season. The total length of the road system is 41,000 km (1984). Motor vehicles in use in 1984, 168,600, including 43,677 cars.

Railways. In 1964 Bolivian National Railways (ENFE) was formed by the amalgamation of the Bolivian Government Railways, Bolivian Railway Co. and the Bolivian section of the Antofagasta (Chili) & Bolivia Railway. The Guaqui-La Paz Railway, formerly operated by Peru, became part of ENFE in 1973 and the privately-owned Marchacamarca Uncia mineral line was taken over in 1987. Access to the Pacific is by 3 routes: to Antofagasta and Arica in Chile, and to Mollendo in Peru *via* Guaqui, the Lake Titicaca train ferry to Puno (Peru), then rail to the coast. Construction began in 1978 of a 150-km line linking Puno with Desaguadero on the Bolivian border which would by-pass the train ferry, though gauge difference would still prevent through running to Peru. Current network totals 3,642 km of metre gauge, comprising unconnected Eastern (1,386 km) and Western (2,257 km) systems. In 1986 the railways carried 1·2m. passengers and 536,000 tonnes of freight.

Aviation. The 2 international airports are El Alto (8½ miles from La Paz) and Viru Viru (10 miles from Santa Cruz). The national airline is Lloyd Aéreo Boliviano. The airline runs regular services between La Paz and Lima, São Paulo, Buenos Aires, Miami, Caracas, Salta and Arica as well as many internal services. Eastern Airways runs regular flights between La Paz, Buenos Aires, Santiago and Asunción linking Bolivia to the USA. Lufthansa links Bolivia with Europe. Other airlines serving Bolivia are Aerolineas Argentinas, Cruzeiro, Aero Peru and Lan Chile.

Shipping. Traffic on Lake Titicaca between Guaqui and Puno is carried on by the steamers of the Peruvian Corporation. About 12,000 miles of rivers, in 4 main systems (Beni, Pilcomayo, Titicaca-Desaguadero, Mamoré), are open to navigation by light-draught vessels.

Post and Broadcasting. In Bolivia there were, in 1978, 458 post offices, of these, 205 provided telegraph and telephone services together with a further 245 offices for telegraph and telephone service only. There is telephone service in the cities of La Paz, Cochabamba, Oruro, Sucre, Potosí, Santa Cruz, Tarija, Camiri, Tupiza, Villazon, Riberalta and Trinidad with (1983), 204,747 telephones. There were (1987) about 85 radio stations, the majority of which are local and commercial. There is a commercial government television service. There are 4 private television stations and 1 University station (educational channel) in La Paz.

Cinemas. In 1986 there were 29 cinemas in La Paz and some 15 in other cities.

Newspapers. There were (1984) 7 daily newspapers in La Paz, 2 in Oruro, and 1 in Cochabamba. Several other towns have regular newspapers devoted to local news, but most of them appear only a few times a week. An economic monthly journal *Revista Economica* and 4 daily newspapers are produced in Santa Cruz.

JUSTICE, RELIGION, EDUCATION AND WELFARE

Justice. Justice is administered by the Supreme Court, superior district courts (of 5 or 7 judges) and courts of local justice. The Supreme Court, with headquarters at Sucre, is divided into two sections, civil and criminal, of 5 justices each, with the Chief Justice presiding over both. Members of the Supreme Court are chosen on a two-thirds vote of Congress.

Religion. The Roman Catholic is the recognized religion of the state; the free exercise of other forms of worship is permitted. The Catholic Church is under a cardinal (in Sucre), an archbishop (in La Paz), 6 bishops (Cochabamba, Santa Cruz, Oruro, Potosí, Riberalta and Tarija) and vicars apostolic (titular bishops resident in Cueva, Trinidad, San Ignacio de Velasco, Riberalta and Rurrenabaque).

By a law of 11 Oct. 1911 all marriages must be celebrated by the civil authorities. Divorce is permitted by a law enacted on 15 April 1932.

Education. Primary instruction is free and obligatory between the ages of 6 and 14 years. In 1981 there were 1·1m. pupils and 51,000 teachers in 10,662 primary and elementary schools.

At Sucre, Oruro, Potosí, Cochabamba, Santa Cruz, Tarija, Trinidad and La Paz are universities; La Paz is the most important of them while the San Francisco Xavier University at Sucre is one of the oldest in America, founded in 1624.

Health. In 1972 there were 2,143 doctors.

DIPLOMATIC REPRESENTATIVES

Of Bolivia in Great Britain (106 Eaton Sq., London, SW1W 9AD)
Ambassador: Eduardo Arauco Paz (accredited 15 Nov. 1985).

Of Great Britain in Bolivia (Avenida Arce 2732–2754, La Paz)
Ambassador: C. J. Sharkey, CMG, MBE.

Of Bolivia in the USA (3014 Massachusetts Ave, NW, Washington, D.C., 20008)
Ambassador: Fernando Illanes.

Of the USA in Bolivia (Banco Popular Del Peru Bldg, La Paz)
Ambassador: Edward M. Rowell.

Of Bolivia to the United Nations
Ambassador: Dr Jorge Gumucio Granier.

Books of Reference

Anuario Geográfico y Estadístico de la República de Bolivia
Anuario del Comercia Exterior de Bolivia
Boletín Mensual de Información Estadística
Dunkerley, J., *Rebellion in the Veins: Political Struggle in Bolivia 1952–1982.* London, 1984
Fifer, J. V., *Bolivia: Land, Location and Politics Since 1825.* CUP, 1972
Guillermo, L., *A History of the Bolivian Labour Movement 1848–1971.* CUP, 1977
Klein, H., *Bolivia: The Evolution of a Multi-Ethnic Society.* OUP, 1982
Yaegar, G. M., *Bolivia.* [Bibliography] Oxford and Santa Barbara, 1988

BOTSWANA

Capital: Gaborone
Population: 1·13m. (1986)
GNP per capita: US$920 (1983)

HISTORY. In 1885 the territory was declared to be within the British sphere; in 1889 it was included in the sphere of the British South Africa Company, but was never administered by the company; in 1890 a Resident Commissioner was appointed, and in 1895, on the annexation of the Crown Colony of British Bechuanaland to the Cape of Good Hope, the British Government was in favour of transferring the Protectorate to the BSA Company, but the three major chiefs of the Bakwena, the Bangwaketse and the Bamangwato went to England to protest against this proposal, and agreement was reached that their country should remain a British Protectorate if they ceded a strip of land on the eastern side of the country for railway construction. This railway was built in 1896–97.

On 30 Sept. 1966 the Bechuanaland Protectorate became an independent and sovereign member of the Commonwealth under the name of the Republic of Botswana.

AREA AND POPULATION. Botswana is bounded west and north by South-West Africa (Namibia), north-east by Zambia and Zimbabwe and east and south by the Republic of South Africa. Area about 222,000 sq. miles (582,000 sq. km); population, estimate 1986, was 1,127,880 (census, 1981, 941,027).

The main business centres (with estimated population, 1984) are Gaborone (96,000, 1986), Francistown (35,960), Selebi-Phikwe (32,480), Serowe (28,980), Kanye (23,400), Lobatse (22,030), Mochudi (21,280), Molepolole (23,810), Mahalapye (25,370), Maun (17,280), Palapye (11,750), Orapa (5,760), Jwaneng (7,410).

The seat of government is at Gaborone.

The official language is English; the national language is Setswana.

CLIMATE. Most of the country is sub-tropical, but there are arid areas in the south and west. In winter, days are warm and nights cold, with occasional frosts. Summer heat is tempered by prevailing north-east winds. Rainfall comes mainly in summer, from Oct. to April, while the rest of the year is almost completely dry with very high sunshine amounts. Gaborone. Jan. 79°F (26·1°C), July 55°F (12·8°C). Annual rainfall 21″ (538 mm).

CONSTITUTION AND GOVERNMENT. The Constitution of the republic is based on the Constitution which came into effect in March 1965, with some minor alterations.

The executive rests with the President of the Republic who is responsible to the National Assembly.

The National Assembly consists of 38 members, 34 elected by universal suffrage. The general election, held in Sept. 1984, returned 28 members of the Botswana Democratic Party, 5 Botswana National Front and 1 Botswana People's Party.

The President is an *ex-officio* member of the Assembly. If the President is already a member of the National Assembly, a by-election will be held in that constituency.

There is also a House of Chiefs to advise the Government. It consists of the Chiefs of the 8 tribes who were autonomous during the days of the British protectorate, and 4 members elected by and from among the sub-chiefs in 4 districts.

The first President of Botswana, who was re-elected 3 times, was Sir Seretse Khama, KBE, who died 13 July 1980.

President of the Republic: Dr Quett Ketumile Joni Masire (re-elected 1984).

In Sept. 1987 the Cabinet was as follows:

Vice President and Minister of Finance and Development Planning: P. S. Mmusi. *Presidential Affairs and Public Administration:* P. H. K. Kedikilwe.

External Affairs: Dr G. K. T. Chiepe. *Health:* J. L. T. Mothibamele. *Agriculture:* D. K. Kwelagobe. *Local Government and Lands:* P. Balopi. *Works and Communications:* C. Blackbeard. *Commerce and Industry:* M. P. K. Nwako. *Mineral Resources and Water Affairs:* A. M. Mogwe. *Education:* K. P. Morake. *Home Affairs:* E. M. K. Kgabo. *Assistant Minister of Finance and Development Planning:* O. I. Chilume. *Assistant Ministers of Local Government and Lands:* M. R. Tshipinare and C. J. Butale. *Assistant Minister of Agriculture:* G. Oteng. *Attorney-General:* Moleleki Mokama. *Speaker of the National Assembly:* J. G. Haskins.

National flag: Light blue with a horizontal black stripe, edged white, across the centre.

Local Government. Local government is carried out by 9 district councils and 4 town councils. Revenue is obtained mainly from sales taxes; from rates in the towns and from central government subventions in the districts.

DEFENCE

Army. A defence force has been created for border control and comprises 2 infantry battalions. Personnel (1988) 3,100.

Air Force. Equipment includes 5 Britten-Norman Defender armed light transports for border patrol, counter-insurgency and casualty evacuation duties, 5 Bulldog piston-engined basic trainers, 2 Skyvan turboprop passenger/cargo transports, 2 Trislander 3-engined transports, 2 Ecureuil helicopters and 2 Cessna 152 light aircraft. Personnel (1987) about 150.

INTERNATIONAL RELATIONS

Membership. Botswana is a member of UN, OAU, SADCC, the Non-Aligned Movement, the Commonwealth and is an ACP state of EEC.

ECONOMY

Planning. The Development Plan 1986–91 envisages a total capital expenditure of P1,200m.

Budget. The 1987–88 budget envisaged expenditure of P1,081m., revenue was expected to rise to P1,428m. The budget allowed for P5,000m. for drought relief.

Currency. The currency was formerly the South African Rand but in Aug. 1976 a new currency, the *pula*, was introduced (P2·97 = £1 sterling and P1·68 = US$1 in March 1988).

Banking. There were (1986) 3 commercial banks (Barclays Bank of Botswana Ltd, Standard Chartered Bank Botswana Ltd and Bank of Credit and Commerce (Botswana) Ltd) with 34 branches and sub-branches, and 44 agencies. The Bank of Botswana, established in 1976, is the central bank. The National Development Bank, founded in 1964, has 6 regional offices and agricultural, industrial and commercial development divisions. The government-owned Botswana Savings Bank operates through 64 post offices.

ENERGY AND NATURAL RESOURCES

Electricity. Production (1986) 533m. kwh. Supply 220 volts; 50 Hz.

Water. Surface water resources are about 18,000m. cu. metres a year. Nearly all flows into northern districts from Angola through the Okavango and Kwando river systems. The Zambezi, also in the north, provides irrigation in Chobe District. In the south-east, there are dams to exploit the ephemeral flow of the tributaries of the Limpopo. 80% of the land has no surface water, and must be served by boreholes.

Minerals. An important part of government revenue comes from the diamond mines at Orapa and Jwaneng and the nickel–copper complex at Selebi-Phikwe. An open-pit coalmine has been developed at Morupule. Mineral production 1985: Diamonds, 12·6m. carats (value P894,900,000); copper–nickel (1984), 51,845 tonnes (P71,661,000); coal (1984), 392,854 tonnes (P5,518,000).

Mineral resources in north-east Botswana are being investigated, including salt and soda ash on the Sua Pan of the Makgadikgadi Salt Pans, nickel–copper at Selkirk and Phoenix, copper south of Maun and close to Ghanzi, and coal at Mmamabula.

Agriculture. Cattle-rearing is the chief industry, and the country is more a pastoral than an agricultural one, crops depending entirely upon the rainfall. In 1986 the number of cattle was 2·72m.; goats, 1m.; sheep, 210,000; poultry, 1m. Beef exports (1984) P88,853,000; meat sold locally P2,760,000.

Production (1985, in 1,000 tonnes): Maize, 10; sorghum, 8; groundnuts, 2; millet, 1; wheat, 1; roots and tubers, 9; sunflower seeds, 1; pulses, 17; seed cotton, 3; vegetables, 16; fruit, 11.

Forestry. There are forest nurseries and plantations. Concessions have been granted to harvest 7,500 cu. metres in Kasane and Chobe Forest Reserves and up to 2,500 cu. metres in the Masame area.

WILDLIFE. About 17% of land is set aside for wildlife preservation. In 1986 there were 4 national parks, 6 game reserves, 3 game sanctuaries and 40 controlled hunting areas for photographic and game viewing safaris and recreational (safari) and subsistence hunting.

COMMERCE. In 1985 imports totalled P1,140m. and exports P1,358m. Of imports, 83% come from South Africa, 8% from Zimbabwe. Exports are mainly diamonds (to Switzerland), copper–nickel matte (to USA), beef and beef products (to EEC).

Botswana is a member of the South African customs union with Lesotho, the Republic of South Africa and Swaziland.

Total trade between Botswana and UK (British Department of Trade returns, in £1,000 sterling):

	1983	1984	1985	1986	1987
Imports to UK	21,713	14,913	20,998	16,652	11,836
Exports and re-exports from UK	3,250	9,015	6,680	8,629	10,275

TOURISM. There were 55,928 foreign tourists in 1984.

COMMUNICATIONS

Roads. On 31 Dec. 1985, 1,914 km of road were bitumen-surfaced, 1,255 km gravel and about 4,860 km earth. In 1979 there were 21,800 registered motor vehicles.

Railways. The main line from Mafikeng in Bophuthatswana to Bulawayo in Zimbabwe traverses Botswana. With two short branches the total is 708 km. These lines, formerly operated by National Railways of Zimbabwe, were taken over by the new Botswana Railways organization in 1987. In 1985–86 railways carried 1,328m. tonne-km and 241m. passenger-km.

Aviation. The Seretse Khama International Airport at Gaborone opened in 1984. Regular international flights are flown by Air Botswana, Air Zimbabwe, Royal Swazi Air and Air Zambia into Gaborone. Air Botswana carried an estimated 53,000 passengers, 420,000 kg of cargo and 94,656 kg of mail in 1984.

Post and Broadcasting. In 1986 there were 66 post offices and 72 agencies. Wireless communication has been established between headquarters at Gaborone and various district offices and police stations. There were 12,511 telephones installed in 1987.

Newspapers. In 1987 there was 1 daily newspaper, the bilingual (Setswana-English) *Daily News*, which is published by the Department of Information and Broadcasting; circulation, 36,000. There are 3 other privately-owned newspapers.

JUSTICE, RELIGION, EDUCATION AND WELFARE

Justice. The Botswana Court of Appeal was established in 1954. It has jurisdiction in respect of criminal and civil appeals emanating from the High Court of Botswana and has jurisdiction in all criminal and civil causes and proceedings. Subordinate courts and traditional courts are in each of the 12 administrative districts. The police force was 2,359 in 1985.

Religion. Freedom of worship is guaranteed under the Constitution. Christian denominations include the United Congregational Church of Southern Africa, the Catholic Church, Anglican, Lutheran, Dutch Reformed, Seventh Day Adventist, Assemblies of God, Methodist and Quaker groups. Non-Christian religions include Bahais, Moslems and Hindus.

Education (1985). Primary education has been free since 1980 and secondary education from Jan. 1988. There were 518 primary, 63 secondary schools, and 3 teacher training colleges. Primary education is controlled by district and town councils, the Ministry of Education being responsible for the training and deployment of teachers, curriculum, examinations and the inspectorate. In secondary education 18 schools are community based and controlled by boards of governors. Enrolment in primary schools was 222,549, and in secondary schools 31,019. There is a Polytechnic and an Auto Trades Training School. Throughout the country, Brigades provide lower level vocational training. The Department of Non-Formal Education offers secondary level correspondence courses and is the executing agency for the National Literacy Programme. The University of Botswana had 1,700 full-time students in 1986–87.

In 1987, 63% of those over 15 years could read and write.

Health (1986). There were 13 general hospitals, a mental hospital, 7 health centres, 81 clinics and 246 health posts. There were also 438 stops for mobile health teams. In 1986 there were 156 registered medical practitioners, 14 dentists, and 1,530 nurses. The health facilities are the concern of central and local government, medical missions, mining companies and voluntary organizations.

DIPLOMATIC REPRESENTATIVES

Of Botswana in Great Britain (6 Stratford Pl., London, W1N 9AE)
High Commissioner: G. U. S. Matlhabaphiri (accredited 3 July 1986).

Of Great Britain in Botswana (Private Bag 0023, Gaborone)
High Commissioner: P. A. Raftery, CVO, MBE.

Of Botswana in the USA (4301 Connecticut Ave., NW, Washington, D.C., 20008)
Ambassador: Serara T. Ketlogetswe.

Of the USA in Botswana (PO Box 90, Gaborone)
Ambassador: Natale H. Bellocchi.

Of Botswana to the United Nations
Ambassador: Legwaila Joseph Legwaila.

Books of Reference

General Information: The Director of Information and Broadcasting, PO Box 0060, Gaborone, Botswana publishes *Botswana Handbook*, the monthly *Kutlwano, The Botswana Daily News, Botswana in Brief* and *Botswana Up To Date*.
Botswana '86: An Official Handbook. Department of Information and Broadcasting, Gaborone, 1986
Statistical Bulletins. Quarterly. Central Statistical Office, Gaborone
Report on the Population Census, 1981. Government Printer, Gaborone, 1982
Campbell, A. C., *The Guide to Botswana.* Gaborone, 1980
Colclough, C. and McCarthy, S., *The Political Economy of Botswana.* OUP, 1980
Harvey, C., (ed.), *Papers on the Economy of Botswana.* London and Nairobi, 1981
Parson, J., *Botswana: Liberal Democracy and Labour Reserve in Southern Africa.* Aldershot, 1984

BRAZIL

Capital: Brasília, DF
Population: 141·3m. (1987)
GNP per capita: US$1,740 (1986)

República Federativa do Brasil

HISTORY. Brazil was discovered on 22 April 1500 by the Portuguese Admiral Pedro Alvares Cabral, and thus became a Portuguese settlement; in 1815 the colony was declared 'a kingdom', and it was proclaimed an independent Empire in 1822. The monarchy was overthrown in 1889 and a republic declared. Following a *coup* in 1964 the armed forces retained overall control until civilian government was restored on 15 March 1985.

AREA AND POPULATION. Brazil is bounded east by the Atlantic and on its northern, western and southern borders by all the South American countries except Chile and Ecuador. The area is 8,511,965 sq. km (3,286,487 sq. miles) including 55,457 sq. km of inland water. Population as at 1 Sept. 1980 (census) and 1 July 1986 (estimate):

State and Capital	Area (sq. km)	Census 1980	Estimate 1986
North	3,581,180 [1]	5,880,268	7,586,000
Rondônia (Pôrto Velho)	243,044	491,069	776,000
Acre (Rio Branco)	152,589	301,303	365,000
Amazonas (Manaus)	1,564,445	1,430,089	1,781,000
Roraima (Boa Vista)	230,104	79,159	107,000
Pará (Belém)	1,248,042	3,403,391	4,337,000
Amapá (Macapá)	140,276	175,257	220,000
North-east	1,548,672 [2]	34,812,356	39,884,000
Maranhão (São Luís)	328,663	3,996,404	4,751,000
Piauí (Teresina)	250,934	2,139,021	2,480,000
Ceará (Fortaleza)	148,016	5,288,253	5,996,000
Rio Grande do Norte (Natal)	53,015	1,898,172	2,163,000
Paraíba (João Pessoa)	56,372	2,770,176	3,059,000
Pernambuco (Recife)	98,281	6,141,993	6,882,000
Alagoas (Maceió)	27,731	1,982,591	2,290,000
Fernando de Noronha [3]	26	1,279	1,300
Sergipe (Aracajú)	21,994	1,140,121	1,313,000
Bahia (Salvador)	561,026	9,454,346	10,949,000
South-east:	924,935	51,734,125	60,613,000
Minas Gerais (Belo Horizonte)	587,172	13,378,553	14,808,000
Espírito Santo [4] (Vitória)	45,597	2,023,340	2,334,000
Rio de Janeiro (Rio de Janeiro) [5]	44,268	11,291,520	13,021,000
São Paulo (São Paulo)	247,898	25,040,712	30,450,000
South	577,723	19,031,162	20,932,000
Parana (Curitiba)	199,554	7,629,392	8,150,000
Santa Catarina (Florianópolis)	95,985	3,627,933	4,174,000
Rio Grande do Sul (Pôrto Alegre)	282,184	7,773,837	8,608,000
Central West	1,879,455	7,544,795	9,338,000
Mato Grosso (Cuiabá) [6]	881,001	1,138,691	1,539,000
Mato Grosso do Sul (Campo Grande) [6]	350,548	1,369,567	1,645,000
Goiás (Goiânia)	642,092	3,859,602	4,455,000
Distrito Federal (Brasília)	5,814	1,176,935	1,649,000
Total	8,511,965	119,002,706	138,403,000

For notes *see* p. 228.

Population (estimate, 1987) 141·3m.; density, 16·6 per sq. km.
The 1980 census showed 59,123,361 males and 59,879,345 females. The urban
population comprised 72·7% in 1985.
The language is Portuguese.
Population of principal cities (1980 census):

São Paulo	7,033,529	Brasília	411,305	São José dos	
Rio de Janeiro	5,090,700	Santos	411,023	Campos	268,073
Salvador	1,506,602	Guarulhos	395,117	Olinda	266,392
Belo Horizonte	1,442,483	Niterói	386,185	Londrina	258,054
Recife	1,184,215	São Bernardo do		Sorocaba	254,718
Pôrto Alegre	1,108,883	Campo	381,261	Uberlândia	230,400
Curitiba	843,733	Natal	376,552	Diadema	228,594
Belém	758,117	Maceió	376,479	Feira de Santana	225,003
Goiânia	703,263	Teresina	339,264	Campina Grande	222,229
Fortaleza	648,815	Duque de Caxias	306,057	São Gonçalo	221,278
Manaus	613,068	Ribeirao Prêto	300,704	Joinville	217,074
Campinas	566,517	Juiz de Fora	299,728	Canoas	214,115
Santo André	549,278	João Pessoa	290,424	São João de Meriti	210,548
Nova Iguaçu	491,802	Aracajú	288,106	Jundiaí	210,015
Osasco	473,856	Campo Grande	282,844	Mauá	205,817

The principal metropolitan areas (estimate, 1985) were São Paulo (15,280,375),
Rio de Janeiro (10,217,269), Belo Horizonte (3,059,727) and Salvador (2,125,792).

CLIMATE. Because of its latitude, the climate is predominantly tropical, but factors such as altitude, prevailing winds and distance from the sea cause certain variations, though temperatures are not notably extreme. In tropical parts, winters are
dry and summers wet, while in Amazonia conditions are constantly warm and
humid. The N.E. sertao is hot and arid, with frequent droughts. In the south and
east, spring and autumn are sunny and warm, summers are hot, but winters can be
cold when polar air-masses impinge. Brasilia. Jan. 72°F (22·2°C), July 64°F
(17·8°C). Annual rainfall 64″ (1,600 mm). Bahia. Jan. 80°F (26·7°C), July 74°F
(23·3°C). Annual rainfall 76″ (1,900 mm). Belem. Jan. 79°F (26°C), July 79°F
(26°C). Annual rainfall 97″ (2,438 mm). Manaus. Jan. 81°F (27·2°C), July 82°F
(27·8°C). Annual rainfall 72″ (1,811 mm). Recife. Jan. 81°F (27·2°C), July 75°F
(24°C). Annual rainfall 64″ (1,610 mm). Rio de Janeiro. Jan. 78°F (25·6°C), July
69°F (20·6°C). Annual rainfall 43″ (1,082 mm).

CONSTITUTION AND GOVERNMENT. The present Constitution was
adopted on 24 Jan. 1967 and came into force on 15 March. However, in Feb. 1987,
the Congress became a Constituent Assembly, to draft a new Constitution. The
present Constitution grants powers to the President to issue decree-laws on matters
connected with the economy and national security; it gives the President authority
to intervene in any of the 23 states without consultation with Congress and the
right to declare a state of siege and to rule by decree. President and Vice-President
are elected for a 6-year term and are not immediately re-eligible.
Congress consists of a 69-member Senate (3 Senators per state) and a
487-member Chamber of Deputies. The Senate is two-thirds directly elected (50%
of these elected for 8 years in rotation) and one-third indirectly elected. Following
partial elections held on 15 Nov. 1986, the *Partido do Movimento Democrático
Brasiliero* (PMDB) held 44 seats, its ally the *Partido da Frente Liberal* (PLL) 16
seats, and others 12 seats in the Senate. The Chamber of Deputies is elected by

[1] Including litigious area between states of Amazonas and Pará (2,680 sq. km).
[2] Including litigious area between states of Piauí and Ceará (2,614 sq. km).
[3] The archipelago comprises the main isle (of the same name), Rocas atoll and the islets of
São Pedro and São Paulo.
[4] Including the islands of Trindade and Martin Vaz.
[5] The former States of Rio de Janeiro and Guanabara were consolidated, from 15 March
1975, into a single State of Rio de Janeiro.
[6] The former state of Mato Grosso was divided into 2 new states from 1979.

universal franchise for 4 years. At the General Election held on 15 Nov. 1986, the PMDB won 259 seats in the Chamber, the PFL 115 seats, and others 113 seats.

Voting is compulsory for men and women between the ages of 18 and 65 and optional for persons over 65. Enlisted men (who numbered 339,849 at the 1980 census) may not vote. The Constitutional Amendment number 25 of 15 May 1985 granted illiterate persons (until then disenfranchised) the right to vote and also provided for the direct election of the President.

Former Presidents since 1956 have been as follows:

Juscelino Kubitschek de Oliveira, 31 Jan. 1956–31 Jan. 1961.

Jânio da Silva Quadros, 31 Jan. 1961–25 Aug. 1961 (resigned).

João Belchior Marques Goulart, 7 Sept. 1961–31 March 1964 (deposed).

Marshal Humberto de Alencar Castelo Branco, 15 April 1964–15 March 1967.

Marshal Artur da Costa e Silva, 15 March 1967–31 Aug. 1969 (resigned).

Gen. Emilio Garrastazu Medici, 30 Oct. 1969–15 March 1974.

Gen. Ernesto Geisel, 15 March 1974–15 March 1979.

Gen. João Baptista de Oliveira Figueiredo, 15 March 1979–15 March 1985.

President of the Republic: José Sarney, assumed office 15 March 1985 and became President on 22 April 1985 when President-elect Tancredo de Almeida Neves died.

The cabinet was composed as follows in Jan 1988:

Head of President's Civil Household: Marco Antonio de Oliveira Maciel. *Head of President's Military Household:* Gen. Rubens Bayma Denys. *Head of National Information Service:* Gen. Ivan de Souza Mendes. *Head of General Armed Forces* (EMFA): Col. Paulo Campos Paiva. *Air Force:* Brig. Octávio Júlio Moreira Lima. *Agriculture:* Iris Rezende Machado. *Science and Technology:* Renato Bayma Archer da Silva. *Communications:* Antonio Carlos Peixoto de Magalhães. *Culture:* Celso Monteiro Furtado. *Urban Development and Environment:* Deni Lineu Schwartz. *Education:* José Konder Bornhausen. *Army:* Gen. Leônidas Pires Gonçalves. *Finance:* Mailson da Nobrega. *Industry and Commerce:* José Hugo Castelo Branco. *Interior:* Ronaldo Costa Couto. *Justice:* Paulo Brossard de Souza Pinto. *Navy:* Adm. Henrique Saboia. *Mines and Energy:* Dr Antônio Aureliano Chaves de Mendonça. *Social Welfare:* Raphael de Almeida Magalhães. *Foreign Affairs:* Roberto Abreu Sodré. *Health:* Roberto Figueira Santos. *Labour:* Almir Pazzianotto Pinto. *Transport:* José Reinaldo Carneiro Tavares. *Administration:* Aluizio Alves. *Land Reform and Development:* Jader Barbalho. *Extraordinary Minister of Debureaucratization:* Paulo de Tarso Lustosa da Costa. *Head of the Secretariat for Planning:* João Sayad. *Irrigation:* Vicente Cavalcante Fialho.

National flag: Green, with yellow lozenge on which is placed a blue sphere, containing 24 white stars and crossed with a band bearing the motto *Ordem e Progresso.*

National anthem: Ouviram do Ipiranga . . . (words by J. O. Duque Estrada; tune by F. M. da Silva).

Local Government. Brazil consists of 23 states, 3 federal territories (Roraima, Amapá, Fernando de Noronha) and 1 federal district. Each state has its distinct administrative, legislative and judicial authorities, its own constitution and laws, which must, however, agree with the constitutional principles of the Union. Taxes on interstate commerce, levied by individual states, are prohibited. The governors and members of the legislatures are elected for 4-year terms, but magistrates are appointed and are not removable from office save by judicial sentence. The states and territories are sub-divided into 3,963 *municipos*, each under an elected mayor *(prefeito)* and municipal council, and then further sub-divided into *distritos.* The Federal District is the national capital, inaugurated in 1960; it is divided into 8 administrative Regions the first Region being Brasília.

DEFENCE.

Army. The Army is organized in 8 divisions, each with 4 armoured, 4 mechanized cavalry brigades and 12 motorized infantry brigades; in addition there are 7 light 'jungle' infantry battalions, 27 artillery groups and 1 independent parachute brigades; total strength (1988) 197,000. An Aviation Corps is being formed.

Navy. The principal ship of the Brazilian Navy:

Completed	Name	Standard displacement Tons	Aircraft	Guns	Shaft horsepower	Speed Knots
			Aircraft Carrier			
1945	Minas Gerais [1]	15,890	{ 16 fixed-wing / 4 helicopters }	10 40mm AA	40,000	24·0

[1] Ex-*Vengeance*, purchased from Great Britain in 1956.

There are also 8 diesel-powered submarines (1 new built in FR Germany, 3 modern built in Britain and 4 old *ex*-US), 6 modern frigates (the *Constituição, Defensora, Liberal* and *Niteroi*, built in Britain, and the *Independencia* and *Uniao*, built in Brazil), 10 old *ex*-US destroyers, 9 fleet tug type corvettes, 6 coastal minesweepers, 1 river monitor, 5 river patrol ships, 6 coastal gunboats, 1 submarine rescue ship, 2 tank landing ships, 4 transports, 19 local transports, 4 oilers, 1 repair ship, 6 training ships, 9 survey ships (2 carrying a helicopter), 6 survey launches, 35 minor landing craft, 6 coastal training craft, 12 tenders, 14 auxiliaries, 17 tugs and 3 floating docks.

Two small diesel-powered patrol submarines and 4 corvettes are being built and 3 more submarines, 8 corvettes and 6 minehunters are planned.

Naval bases are at Rio de Janeiro, Aratu (Bahia), Belém, Natal, Recife, Salvador, with river bases at Ladário and Rio Negro.

The Fleet Air Arm was formed on 26 Jan. 1965. Aircraft for service on the carrier include 4 Sea King SH-3 helicopters and 12 S-2A/E Tracker anti-submarine aircraft from USA. Three Westland Wasp HAS-1 light helicopters are operated on utility and search and rescue duties with 16 Bell 206B Jet Ranger, 3 more Sea King and 20 Esquilo (AS 350) helicopters. Eight Westland Lynx WG13 helicopters and a Sea Lynx HAS-23 were provided for the destroyer leader/frigates of the 'Niteroi' class. Six Super Puma AS-332 helicopters were on order in 1987.

The active personnel in 1988 totalled 50,300 (6,300 officers and 44,000 men), including 14,500 marines and auxiliary corps.

Air Force. The Air Force, formed in 1918, has been independent of the Army and Navy since 1941. It is organized in 6 zones, centred on Belém, Recife, Rio de Janeiro, São Paulo, Porto Alegre and Brasília. The 1a ALADA (air defence wing) has 12 Mirage IIIE fighters and 2 Mirage IIID trainers, integrated with Roland mobile short-range surface-to-air missile systems deployed by the Army, and a radar/communications/computer network. Two fighter groups have 3 squadrons of F-5E Tiger II supersonic fighter-bombers and two-seat F-5Bs; 4 others operate AT-26 (Aermacchi MB 326G) Xavante light jet attack/trainers, licence-built by Embraer in Brazil. Counter-insurgency squadrons are also equipped with Neiva Regente lightplanes, Universal armed piston-engined trainers, Puma transports and UH-1D/H Iroquois and armed Ecureuil helicopters for liaison and observation. There is an ASW group of S-2A/E Trackers for shore-based and carrier-based operations; a maritime patrol group (2 squadrons) with 12 EMB-111 (P-95) twin-turboprop aircraft developed from the Embraer Bandeirante transport; and 2 air-sea rescue units with Bandeirantes. Equipment of transport units includes 1 squadron of C-130E/H Hercules transports; 1 squadron of Boeing 707 and KC-130H Hercules tanker/transports; 1 group made up of a squadron of HS 748 and a second squadron of Bandeirante turboprop transports; 2 troop-carrier groups with DHC-5 Buffaloes; 1 group with Bandeirantes; and 7 independent squadrons with Bandeirantes and Buffaloes. Light aircraft for liaison duties include 30 Embraer U-7s (licence-built Piper Senecas). The VIP transport group has 2 Boeing 737s, 11 HS 125 twin-jet light transports, some Brasilias, 6 Embraer Xingu (VU-9) twin-turboprop pressurized transports and Ecureuil and JetRanger helicopters. Training is performed primarily on locally-built T-25 Universal and turboprop

T-27 Tucano (EMB-312) basic trainers, and AT-26 Xavante armed jet basic trainers. Future equipment will include 79 AM-X jet attack aircraft, produced jointly by Embraer and Aeritalia/Aermacchi of Italy, Super Puma helicopters plus small quantities of F-5 and Mirage III fighters.

Personnel strength (1988) about 50,700, with more than 600 aircraft of all types.

INTERNATIONAL RELATIONS

Membership. Brazil is a member of UN, OAS and LAIA (formerly LAFTA).

ECONOMY

Planning. A 3-year 'Targets' Plan was introduced in July 1986, providing for a new National Development Fund with a budget of US$20,000m. for investment.

Budget. In 1985 the budget balanced at 88,872,115m. Cruzeiros (1986, 656,126,100m. Cruzeiros).

Chief items of revenue were in 1983 as follows (in Cr$1m.): Taxes, 8,836,691; government property, 90,480. Principal items of expenditure: Transport, 969,785; education and culture, 766,629; army, 453,703; aviation and navy, 807,688; welfare and security, 271,332; finance, 149,369.

The foreign debt (including states and municipalities) of Brazil on 31 Dec. 1985 amounted to US$95,857m. Internal federal debt, June 1986 was Cz$685,350m. Internal states and municipalities (main securities outstanding), June 1986, Cz$56,660m.

Currency. The *cruzado* (Cz$) is the monetary unit which was introduced in March 1986. 1 *cruzado* = 1,000 *cruzeiros*. The exchange rate was in March 1988 US$1 = Cz$99·20; £1 = Cz$173·96.

Banking. The Bank of Brazil (founded in 1853 and reorganized in 1906, with an authorized capital of NCr$60m. from 1967) is not a central bank of issue but a state-owned commercial bank; it had 2,489 branches in 1985 throughout the republic. On 31 Dec. 1985 deposits were Cr$47,064m.

On 31 Dec. 1964 the Banco Central do Brasil was founded as the national bank of issue; assets (1985) Cr$639,424m.

The country's currency held by the public on 31 Dec. 1985 was Cr$23,494m. Since Sept. 1939 gold and dollar supply has risen from US$40m. to US$420m., of which the government's gold was US$288m. in May 1961. All banks had on 31 Dec. 1985 deposits of Cr$211,033m.

Weights and Measures. The metric system has been compulsory since 1872.

ENERGY AND NATURAL RESOURCES

Electricity. Brazil's hydraulic potential capacity for electric power production was estimated at 106,500 mw. in Dec. 1984, one of the largest in the world, of which 34% belongs to the Amazon hydrographic basin. Installed capacity (1984) 40,869 mw, excluding the Itaipú complex (12,600 mw) which began production in Oct. 1984. A new dam on the Xingu river is planned with 17,000 mw capacity. Production (1985) 167,000m. kwh (94% hydro-electric). Supply 110, 127 and 220 volts; 60 Hz.

Oil. There are 13 oil refineries, of which 11 are state owned. Crude oil output (excluding NGL) was 31,709,403 cu.metres in 1985, of which 72% was from the continental shelf. Promising results have been obtained with the exploration of that area which in 1974 represented only 9% of all the national oil production.

The country imported substantial amounts of oil in 1985: 26,798,497 tonnes (value f.o.b. US$5,418m.) representing 41% of total value of all Brazilian imports. Imports come mainly from Iraq and Nigeria.

In Dec. 1984 a major oil field was reported on the fringes of the existing Campos Basin oil field; reserves are estimated at 4,000m. bbls. Total proven reserves (1986) 2,194m. bbls.

Gas. Production (1985) 2,118m. cu. metres; proven reserves (1986) 93,000m. cu. metres.

Minerals. Brazil is the only source of high-grade quartz crystal in commercial quantities; output, 1984, 109,964 tonnes raw, 8,271 tonnes processed. It is the largest western producer of chrome ore (reserves of 8·4m. tonnes; output, 1984, 708,634 tonnes); other minerals are mica (406 tonnes in 1984); zirconium, 7,287; beryllium 10; graphite 290,007; titanium ore 2,870,335 tonnes, and magnesite 724,280 tonnes. Along the coasts of the states of Rio de Janeiro, Espírito Santo and Bahia are found monazite sands containing thorium; output, 1984, 4,165 tonnes; reserves are estimated at 14,000 tonnes. Manganese ores of high content are important (reserves in 1984 were estimated at 70m. tonnes); output, 1984, 3,494,237 tonnes. Output of bauxite, 1984, 10,355,126 tonnes; salt (1983), 3,529,291; tungsten ore, 432,990, unrough, 1,892; lead, 366,129; asbestos, 1,869,326; coal (1983), 21,367,472. Deposits of coal exist in Rio Grande do Sul, Santa Catarina, Paraná and Minas Gerais. Total reserves were estimated at 4,159·5m. tonnes in 1984.

Iron is found chiefly in Minas Gerais, notably the Cauê Peak at Itabira. The Government is now opening up what is believed to be one of the richest iron-ore deposits in the world, situated in Carajás, in the northern state of Pará, with estimated reserves of 35,000m. tonnes, representing the largest concentration of high-grade (66%) iron ore in the world. Total output of iron ore, 1984, mainly from the Cia. Vale do Rio Doce mine at Itabira, was 143,841,535 tonnes.

Production of tin ore (cassiterite, processed) was 33,920 tonnes in 1984. Output of barytes, 101,301 tonnes. Output of phosphate rock, 22·7m. tonnes.

Gold is chiefly from Pará (17·5 tonnes in 1984), Mato Grosso (8·7 tonnes) and Minas Gerais (4·7 tonnes); total production (1984), 37·2 tonnes processed. Silver output (processed in 1984) 25·8 tonnes. Diamond output in 1984 was 122,827 carats (52,949 carats from Minas Gerais, 55,204 carats from Mato Grosso).

Agriculture. In 1984, 29·8% of the labour force was employed in agriculture, with 8·9% of the land area under cultivation. In 1980, there were 5·16m. farms (61% family operated). Production (in tonnes):

	1984 [1]	1985 [1]		1984 [1]	1985 [1]
Bananas			Grapes	603,172	718,157
(1,000 bunches)	470,815	500,330	Cocoa	329,903	419,268
Kidney beans	2,625,676	2,547,197	Coffee	2,840,563	3,753,379
Cassava	21,466,222	23,072,526	Cotton, raw	1,889,359	2,648,133
Castor beans	222,678	415,879	Jute	19,091	20,081
Oranges	64,722,620	70,995,596	Maize	21,164,138	22,817,154
Potatoes	2,933,736	1,989,261	Soya	15,540,792	18,278,422
Rice	9,027,363	8,019,156	Sugar-cane	222,317,847	245,904,175
Sisal	224,759	290,901	Wheat	1,983,157	4,247,197
Groundnuts	...	339,335	Tobacco	413,598	410,902
Tomatoes	...	1,931,810			

[1] Preliminary.

Harvested coffee area, 1986, 2,259,000 hectares, principally in the 4 states of São Paulo, Paraná, Espírito Santo and Minas Gerais. Harvested cocoa area, 1986, 658,000 hectares. Bahia furnished 87% of the output in 1985. Two crops a year are grown. Harvested castor-bean area, 1986, 458,000 hectares. Tobacco output was 386,000 tonnes in 1986 grown chiefly in Rio Grande do Sul and Santa Catarina.

Rubber is produced chiefly in the states of Acre, Amazonas and Pará. Output, 1986, 44,000 tonnes (natural). Brazilian consumption of rubber in 1984, was 336,726 tonnes. Jute output, 1986, 63,000 tonnes. Plantations of tung trees established in 1930 are beginning to yield tung oils in commercial quantities; output, 1984, 5,426 tonnes.

Livestock (in 1,000): 1986, 128,918 cattle, 33,000 swine, 18,473 sheep, 9,800 goats, 5,500 horses, 1,250 asses and 2,000 mules. In 1985, 10,234,000 cattle, 12·7m. swine, 1·8m. sheep and lambs, 2m. goats and (1982) 798m. poultry were slaughtered for meat.

Forestry. Production (1984) 222m. cu. metres.

Fisheries. The fishing industry had a 1984 catch of 958,908 tonnes.

INDUSTRY AND TRADE

Industry. The total number of persons engaged in industry (1980) was 5,004,522 and the value of production Cr$9,738,340m.

The National Iron and Steel Co. at Volta Redonda, State of Rio de Janeiro, furnishes a substantial part of Brazil's steel. Brazil's total output, 1985: Pig-iron, 18,960,635 tonnes; crude steel, 20,456,000 tonnes.

Cement output, 1985, was 20,612,000 tonnes. Brazil's output of paper, 1985, was 4,021,400 tonnes. Production (1984) of rubber tyres for motor vehicles, 23m. units; rubber tubes for motor vehicles, 14m. units.

Labour. The work force in 1984 numbered 50,208,765, of whom 29·8% were in agriculture, 26·8% in service industries, 15·9% in mining and manufacturing, 10·7% in commerce, 5·8% in construction, 4·3% in defence and public administration and 3·6% in transport and communications.

Commerce. Imports and exports for calendar years in Cr$1m.:

	1981	1982	1983	1984	1985
Imports	1,968,271	3,338,626	8,288,170	5,966,160	77,947,888
Exports	2,054,525	3,368,796	11,652,923	49,422,908	148,571,718

Principal imports in 1985 were (in US$1m.): Mineral products, 6,455; chemical products, 1,479; machinery and mechanical appliances, electrical equipment, 1,972; vegetable products, 958.

Principal exports in 1984 were (in US$1m.): Coffee (green), 2,582; iron ore, 1,512; soybean bran, 1,464; orange juice, 1,425; footwear, hats etc., 1,082; machinery, 1,051.

Of exports (in US$1m.) in 1985, USA took 6,956; Netherlands, 1,558; Japan, 1,398; Germany (Fed. Rep.), 1,309; Italy, 1,150; Nigeria, 915; China, 818; France, 800; UK, 632; Iraq, 630; Belgium, 577. Of 1985 imports, USA furnished 2,616; Iraq, 1,800; Nigeria, 1,348; Saudi Arabia, 945; Germany (Fed. Rep.), 864; Japan, 550; Argentina, 469; China, 419; Canada, 398; Mexico, 380; France, 302.

Total trade between Brazil and UK (according to British Department of Trade returns, in £1,000 sterling):

	1983	1984	1985	1986	1987
Imports to UK	560,277	637,702	610,624	552,259	636,675
Exports and re-exports from UK	157,758	238,717	211,512	295,152	347,916

Tourism. In 1984, 1,595,726 tourists visited Brazil (1986, 1,934,000). 446,055 were Argentinian, 166,753 Uruguayan, 205,034 US citizens, 119,880 Paraguayan, 58,305 German, 51,963 Bolivian, 46,908 Chilean, 67,575 Italian, 41,055 French, 29,721 Spanish, 21,633 Canadian, 24,460 Peruvian, 26,279 Portuguese, 26,858 UK citizens, 26,029 Swiss, 19,877 Japanese.

COMMUNICATIONS

Roads. There were (1985) 1,583,172 km of highways. In 1984 Brazil had 12,600,572 motor vehicles, including 9,162,384 passenger cars, 1,798,192 commercial vehicles, 129,131 buses and minibuses. 839,816 motor vehicles of all types were produced in 1984.

Railways. Public railways are operated by two administrations, the Federal Railways (RFFSA) formed in 1957 and São Paulo Railways (FEPASA) formed in 1971, which is confined to the state of São Paulo. RFFSA had a route-length of 22,837 km (776 km electrified) in 1985 and FEPASA 5,072 km (1,099 km electrified). Principal gauges are metre (24,373 km) and 1,600 mm (3,449 km). Traffic moved by RFFSA in 1985 amounted to 82·4m. tonnes of freight and 547·6m. passengers. FEPASA carried 21m. tonnes and 77·8m. passengers.

There are several important independent freight railways, including the Vitoria à Minas (729 km with (1985) 103·1m. tonnes of freight), the Carajas (890 km, opened in 1985) and the Amapa (194 km). There are rapid-transit railways (metros) operating in São Paulo (from 1975), Rio de Janeiro city (1979), Belo Horizonte, Pôrto Alegre (all in 1985), and small systems in Fortaleza and Salvador.

Aviation. There were 34 companies (30 foreign) operating in 1985. The 4 Brazilian companies cover the whole territory and in 1985 they carried 13,182,409 passengers (11,290,384 in domestic traffic) and 2,045m. tonne-km of freight. Their commercial fleet consisted of 248 aircraft on 31 Dec. 1984. There were 243 taxiplane companies on 31 Dec. 1985. The 4 airlines are Viação Aérea Rio Grande do Sul (VARIG), Cruzeiro do Sul, Trans Brasil and VASP. In 1986 there were 126 airports with scheduled flights.

Shipping. Inland waterways, mostly rivers, are open to navigation over some 43,000 km; number of vessels in 1984, 1,348. Rio de Janeiro and Santos are the 2 leading ports; there are 19 other large ports. During 1984, 46,325 vessels entered and cleared the Brazilian ports.

The Lloyd Brasileiro is owned and operated by the Government; its fleet comprised (1984), 39 vessels of 604,733 DWT. Brazilian shipping, 1984 (registered with Lloyds) amounted to 1,636 vessels of 10,001,356 DWT. Petrobrás, the government oil monopoly, took over the government tanker fleet of 26 vessels in 1958; total tanker fleet in 1984 was 70 vessels of 5,090,494 DWT (private and government-owned).

Post and Broadcasting. Of the telegraph system of the country, about half, including all interstate lines, is under control of the Government. There were 7,246 post and telegraph offices in 1984. There were 7,363,586 telephones in 1984 (São Paulo, 2,755,534; Rio de Janeiro, 1,204,701; Brasilia, 210,197). In 1986 there were 2,073 radio and 177 television stations, with an estimated 67m. radio and 26m. television receivers.

Cinemas (1983). Cinemas numbered 1,971.

Newspapers (1983). There were 312 daily newspapers with a total yearly circulation of 1,454m. Foreigners and corporations (except political parties) are not allowed to own or control newspapers or wireless stations.

JUSTICE, RELIGION, EDUCATION AND WELFARE

Justice. There is a Supreme Federal Court of Justice at Brasília composed of 11 judges, and a Federal Court of Appeal of 13 judges; all are appointed by the President with the approval of the Senate. There are also federal courts in each state and territory and the federal district military courts to arraign members of the armed forces, as well as 'electoral courts' to protect the elections, and labour tribunals. Each state organizes its own judicial system in accordance with state law, but in Brasília federal justice is administered. Judges are appointed for life.

Religion. At the 1980 census Roman Catholics numbered 105,861,113 (89% of the total), Protestants, 7,885,846 (6·6%) and Spiritualists, 1,538,230.

Education. Elementary education is compulsory. In 1985 there were 66,255,000 persons aged 15 years or over who could read and write; this was 79·3% of that age group (80·4% among men; 78·3% among women).

In 1984 there were 37,348 pre-primary schools with 2,493,381 pupils and 107,338 teachers; 190,983 primary schools, with 24,825,545 pupils and 1,022,096 teachers; 9,104 secondary schools, with 2,946,657 pupils and 214,969 teachers; and 847 higher education institutions, with 1,399,539 pupils and 113,844 teachers: This tertiary level comprises 67 universities (including 20 private) and 780 other institutions (589 private)

Of the 35 Federal universities, the principal are at Rio de Janeiro (30,000 students), Niterói (20,713), Belo Horizonte (20,044), João Pessoa (19,849), Salvador (18,431), Pôrto Alegre (17,626), Recife (18,500), Manaus (17,000), Curitiba (14,882), Fortaleza (14,700) and Natal (14,000). Largest of the 10 State universities is that of São Paulo (44,159 students, founded 1934), and there are 2 Municipal universities.

The 20 private universities include 11 Catholic universities in Rio de Janeiro, São Paulo, Pôrto Alegre, Campinas, Recife, Belo Horizonte, Goiânia, Curitiba, Pelotas, Salvador and Petrópolis.

Health. In 1984 there were 27,552 hospitals and clinics of which 6,861 were for inpatients; total number of beds, 538,721 (411,184 in private institutions). In 1980 there were 97,100 doctors, 56,015 dentists, 5,129 pharmacists, 2,526 midwives and 306,411 nursing personnel.

Social Welfare. In 1983, receipts for programmes of social security totalled Cr$8,605,500m. and expenditure Cr$8,290,000m.

DIPLOMATIC REPRESENTATIVES

Of Brazil in Great Britain (32 Green St., London, W1Y 4AT)
Ambassador: Celso de Souza e Silva (accredited 9 Dec. 1986).

Of Great Britain in Brazil (Setor de Embaixadas Sul, Quadra 801, Conjunto K, Brasília, D.F.)
Ambassador: M. J. Newington.

Of Brazil in the USA (3006 Massachusetts Ave., NW, Washington, D.C., 20008)
Ambassador: Marcílio Marques Moreira.

Of the USA in Brazil (Ave das Noções, Lote 3, Brasília, D.F.)
Ambassador: Harry W. Shlaudeman.

Of Brazil to the United Nations
Ambassador: George Alvares Maciel.

Books of Reference

Anuário do Transporte Aéreo. Ministério da Aeronáutica, DAC. Rio de Janeiro, 1985
Anuário Estatístico do Brasil. Vol. 46. Fundação Instituto Brasileiro de Geografia e Estatística, Rio de Janeiro, 1985
Anuário Mineral Brasileiro. Departamento Nacional da Produção Mineral. Brasília, 1985
Boletim do Banco Central do Brasil. Banco Central do Brasil. Brasília. Monthly
A Profile of Brazil. Banco do Brazil, 1984
Anuario Sunamam, Superintendência Nacional da Marinha Mercante, 1984
Bruneau, T. C., *The Church in Brazil: The Politics of Religion.* Univ. of Texas Press, 1982
Burns, E. B., *A History of Brazil.* 2nd ed. Columbia Univ. Press, 1980
Dickenson, J. P., *Brazil.* Harlow, 1982
Hanbury-Tenison, R., *A Question of Survival for the Indians of Brazil.* London, 1973
McDonough, P., *Power and Ideology in Brazil.* Princeton Univ. Press, 1981
Mainwaring, S., *The Catholic Church and Politics in Brazil, 1916–86.* Stanford Univ. Press, 1986
Micallef, J., (ed.), *Brazil: Country with a Future.* London, 1982
Moraes, R. Borba de., *Bibliographia Brasiliana (1504–1900).* 2 vols. 1958
Selcher, W. E. (ed.), *Brazil in the International System: The Rise of a Middle Power.* Boulder, 1981
Trebat, T. J., *Brazil's State-Owned Enterprises.* CUP, 1983
Tyler, W. G., *The Brazilian Industrial Economy.* Aldershot, 1981
Young, J. M., *Brazil: Emerging World Power.* Malabar, 1982

National Library: Biblioteca Nacional Avenida Rio Branco 219–39, Rio de Janeiro, RJ.

BRITISH ANTARCTIC TERRITORY

HISTORY. The British Antarctic Territory was established on 3 March 1962, as a consequence of the entry into force of the Antarctic Treaty, to separate those areas of the then Falkland Islands Dependencies which lay within the Treaty area from those which did not.

AREA AND POPULATION. The territory encompasses the lands and islands within the area south of 60°S latitude lying between 20°W and 80°W longitude (approximately due south of the Falkland Islands and the Dependencies). It covers an area of some 700,000 square miles, and its principal components are the South Orkney and South Shetland Islands, the Antarctic Peninsula (Palmer Land and Graham Land) and Coats Land.

British Antarctic Territory has no indigenous or permanently resident population. There is however an itinerant population of scientists and logistics staff of about 300, manning a number of research stations.

The territory is administered by a High Commissioner. Designated personnel of the scientific stations of the British Antarctic Survey are also appointed to exercise certain legal and administrative functions.

High Commissioner: Gordon W. Jewkes, CMG (resides in Port Stanley).

Fox, R., *Antarctica and the South Atlantic.* London, 1985

BRITISH INDIAN OCEAN TERRITORY

HISTORY. This territory was established by an Order in Council on 8 Nov. 1965, consisting then of the Chagos Archipelago (formerly administered from Mauritius) and the islands of Aldabra, Desroches and Farquhar (all formerly administered from Seychelles). The latter islands having become part of Seychelles when that country achieved independence on 29 June 1976, the territory now comprises the Chagos Archipelago, lying 1,180 miles (1,899 km) north-east of Mauritius.

AREA AND POPULATION. The group, with a total land area of 23 sq. miles (60 sq. km) comprises 5 coral atolls (Diego Garcia, Peros Banhos, Salomon, Eagle and Egmont) of which the largest and southern-most, Diego Garcia, covers 17 sq. miles (44 sq. km). The British Indian Ocean Territory was established to meet UK and US defence requirements in the Indian Ocean. In accordance with the terms of Exchanges of Notes between the UK and US governments in 1966 and 1976, a US Navy support facility has been established on Diego Garcia. There is no permanent population in the British Indian Ocean Territory.

Commissioner: W. Marsden (non-resident).
Administrator: T. C. S. Stitt (non-resident).

BRUNEI

Capital: Bandar Seri Begawan
Population: 221,900 (1985)
GNP per capita: US$15,989 (1985)

Negara Brunei Darussalam

HISTORY. The Sultanate of Brunei was a powerful state in the early 16th century, with authority over the whole of the island of Borneo and some parts of the Sulu Islands and the Philippines. At the end of the 16th century its power had begun to decline and various cessions were made to Great Britain, the Rajah of Sarawak and the British North Borneo Company in the 19th century to combat piracy and anarchy. By the middle of the 19th century the State had been reduced to its present limits.

In 1847 the Sultan of Brunei entered into a treaty with Great Britain for the furtherance of commercial relations and the suppression of piracy, and in 1888, by a further treaty, the State was placed under the protection of Great Britain. As a result of negotiations in June 1978, the Sultan and the British Government signed a new treaty on 7 Jan. 1979 under which Brunei became a fully sovereign and independent State on 31 Dec. 1983.

AREA AND POPULATION. Brunei, on the northwest coast of Borneo, is bounded on all sides by Sarawak territory, which splits the State into two separate parts, with the smaller portion forming Temburong district. Area, about 2,226 sq. miles (5,765 sq. km), with a coastline of about 100 miles. Population (1981 census) was 191,770; estimate (1985) 221,900. The 4 districts are Brunei/Muara (114,310), Belait (49,590), Tutong (21,640), Temburong (6,230). The capital is Bandar Seri Begawan (census, 1981) 63,868, 9 miles from the mouth of Brunei River; other large towns are Seria (23,511) and Kuala Belait (19,281). 50% of the population speak Malay and 26% Chinese.

CLIMATE. The climate is tropical marine, hot and moist, but nights are cool. Humidity is high and rainfall heavy, varying from 100″ (2,500 mm) on the coast to 200″ (5,000 mm) inland. There is no dry season. Bandar Seri Begawan. Jan. 80°F (26·7°C), July 82°F (27·8°C). Annual rainfall 131″ (3,275 mm).

RULER. The Sultan and Yang di-Pertuan is HM Sir Muda Hassanal Bolkiah Mu'izzadin Waddaulah. He succeeded on 5 Oct. 1967 at his father's abdication and was crowned on 1 Aug. 1968.

CONSTITUTION AND GOVERNMENT. On 29 Sept. 1959 the Sultan promulgated a Constitution, but parts of it have been in abeyance since Dec. 1962. At independence, the Privy Council, Council of Ministers, and the posts of Chief Minister and State Secretary were abolished. There is no legislature (the 33-member Legislative Council was dissolved in Feb. 1984) and supreme political powers are vested in the Sultan.

The Council of Ministers was composed as follows in Oct. 1987:
Prime Minister, Minister of Defence: HM The Sultan and Yang di-Pertuan.
Foreign Affairs: Pengiran Muda Mohamad Bolkiah. *Finance:* Pengiran Muda Jefri Bolkiah. *Home Affairs:* Isa Ibrahim. *Communications:* Abdul Aziz Umar. *Attorney-General and Law:* Pengiran Bahrin Abas. *Education:* Abdul Rahman Taib. *Religious Affairs:* Mohd Zain Serudin. *Development:* Dr Ismail Damit. *Culture, Youth and Sports:* Hussein Yusof. *Health:* Dr Johar Noordin.

The official language is Malay, but English may be used for other purposes. The Chinese community mainly use the Hokkien dialect.

Flag: Yellow, with 2 diagonal strips of white over black with the national arms in red placed over all in the centre.

DEFENCE

Army. The armed forces are known as the Royal Brunei Malay Regiment and contain the naval and air elements. Strength (1988) 3,380. Military units include 2 infantry battalions, 1 armoured reconnaissance squadron, 1 engineer squadron and 1 signals squadron. Equipment includes 16 Scorpion light tanks and 24 Sankey AT-104 armoured personnel carriers.

Navy. The Flotilla of the Royal Brunei Armed Forces comprises 3 fast missile-armed attack craft of 200 tons (completed by Vosper, Singapore in 1978–79), 3 coastal patrol boats (built by Vosper-Thornycroft (Singapore)), 2 landing craft, 2 utility craft and 3 small patrol boats. River Division operates 24 fast assault boats. Personnel in 1988 numbered 500 (45 officers and 455 ratings) in the First Flotilla (for offshore work) and in the Special Combat Division and River Division.

Two coastal patrol craft supplied in 1979 for the Marine Police operate with 7 smaller patrol boats.

Air Wing. The Air Wing of the Royal Brunei Malay Regiment was formed in 1965. Current equipment includes up to 6 MBB BO 105, 2 Bell 206B JetRanger, 1 Bell 214, 1 Sikorsky S-70 and 11 Bell 212 helicopters, and 2 SF.260M piston-engined trainers. Personnel (1988) 200.

Police. Establishment provides over 1,750 officers and men (1980). In addition, there is a small auxiliary force mostly employed on static guard duties.

INTERNATIONAL RELATIONS

Membership. Brunei is a member of the UN, the Commonwealth and ASEAN.

ECONOMY

Planning. A fifth Five-Year National Development Plan (1986–90) aims to further improve the economic, social and cultural life of the people.

Budget. The budget for 1985 envisaged expenditure of B$3,200m. and revenue of B$7,000m.

Currency. The currency is the *Brunei dollar* with a par value of 0·290 299 gramme of gold. In March 1988, £1 = B$3·56; US$1 = B$2·01.

Banking. In 1986 there were 9 banks (2 incorporated in Brunei) with a total of 41 branches.

ENERGY AND NATURAL RESOURCES

Electricity. Electric power production (1986) was 470m. kwh. Supply 240 volts; 50 Hz.

Oil. The Seria oilfield, discovered in 1929, has passed its peak production. The high level of crude oil production is maintained through the increase of offshore oilfields production, which exceeds onshore oilfields production. There were 182 offshore structures in 1986. Production was 7·75m. tonnes in 1987. The crude oil is exported directly, and only a small amount is refined at Seria for domestic uses.

Gas. Natural gas is produced (5·1m. tonnes in 1985) at one of the biggest liquefied natural gas plants in the world and is exported to Japan.

Agriculture. The chief agricultural products in 1986 were fruit (6,000 tonnes), rice (3,000 tonnes), roots and tubers (1,000 tonnes), bananas (1,000 tonnes) and cassava (1,000 tonnes).

Livestock in 1986: Cattle, 4,000; buffaloes, 12,000; pigs, 14,000; chickens, 2m.

Forestry. Most of the interior is under forest, containing large potential supplies of serviceable timber. Annual production averages 300,000 cu. metres.

INDUSTRY AND TRADE

Industry. Brunei depends primarily on its oil industry, which employs more than 7% of the entire working population. Other minor products are rubber, pepper, sawn timber, gravel and animal hides. Local industries include boat-building, cloth weaving and the manufacture of brass-and silverware.

Commerce. Crude oil accounts for 56% of the total value of the exports and re-exports. The second main export is liquefied natural gas, which contributes 40% and petroleum products 3%. In 1985 imports totalled B$1,155m.; exports, B$6,140m. Singapore supplied 24% of imports, the USA 15·2% and Japan 20%. Japan took 68% of all exports.

Total trade between Brunei and UK (British Department of Trade returns, in £1,000 sterling):

	1983	1984	1985	1986	1987
Imports to UK	27,154	21,966	23,346	71,624	34,144
Exports and re-exports from UK	106,477	122,651	71,496	154,146	204,129

Tourism. There were 47,043 visitors in 1984.

COMMUNICATIONS

Roads. There were (1983) 1,233 km of road, of which 451 miles are bituminous surfaced. The main road connects Bandar Seri Begawan with Kuala Belait and Seria. In 1983 there were 63,177 passenger cars and 9,603 commercial vehicles.

Aviation. Royal Brunei Airlines (RBA) and Singapore Airlines provide daily services linking Brunei and Singapore. RBA also operates services to Bangkok, Manila, Kuala Lumpur, Kuching, Kota Kinabalu and Hong Kong. Cathay Pacific Airways also operates to Brunei and on to Western Australia from Hong Kong. British Airways provides a weekly service between Brunei and UK. Malaysian Airlines System has air connections from neighbouring regions. In 1985 Brunei International Airport handled 380,000 passengers and 8,500 tons of freight.

Shipping. Regular shipping services operate from Singapore, Hong Kong, and from ports in Sarawak and Sabah to Bandar Seri Begawan. Private companies operate a passenger ferry service between Bandar Seri Begawan and Labuan daily.

Post and Broadcasting. There were 14 post offices (1983) and a telephone network (21,928 telephones in 1982) linking the main centres. Radio Brunei is operated by the Department of Radio and Television and operates on medium- and short-waves in Malay, Iban, Dusun, English and Chinese. Number of receivers (1984): radio 52,000 and television 31,000.

JUSTICE, RELIGION, EDUCATION AND WELFARE

Justice. The Supreme Court comprises a High Court and a Court of Appeal and the Magistrates' Courts. The High Court receives appeals from subordinate courts in the districts and is itself a court of first instance for criminal and civil cases. Appeal from the High Court is to a Court of Appeal. The Judicial Committee of the Privy Council in London is the final court of appeal. Syariah Courts deal with Islamic law.

Religion. The official religion is Islam. In 1982, 63% of the population were Moslem (mostly Malays), 14% Buddhists and 10% Christian.

Education (1986). There is free primary education for 6 years, followed by 3 years secondary education for those who show ability. Scholarships can lead to tertiary education overseas, either in the academic or vocational fields, although vocational training is given locally. In 1986 there were 243 schools of all types (primary and secondary) with 64,090 pupils and 4,087 teachers.

Students have been sent to Al-Azhar University in Cairo since 1960. The University of Brunei Darussalam opened in 1985 with an enrolment of 176 students.

Health. In 1981 there were 5 hospitals with 630 beds; there were also 97 doctors, 12 dentists, 3 pharmacists, 115 midwives and 280 nursing personnel.

DIPLOMATIC REPRESENTATIVES

Of Brunei in Great Britain (49 Cromwell Rd, London, SW7 2ED)
High Commissioner: Pengiran Setia Raja Pengiran Haji Jaya (accredited 14 March 1984).

Of Great Britain in Brunei (Hong Kong Chambers, Jalan Pemancha, Bandar Seri Begawan)
High Commissioner: Roger Westbrook.

Of Brunei in the USA (2600 Virginia Ave., NW, Washington, D.C., 20037)
Ambassador: Pengiran Haji Idriss.

Of the USA in Brunei (Bandar Seri Begawan)
Ambassador: Thomas C. Ferguson.

Of Brunei to the United Nations
Ambassador: Awang Haji Jaya Bin Abdul Latif.

BULGARIA

Narodna Republika Bulgaria

Capital: Sofia
Population: 8·95m. (1987)
GNP per capita: US$6,460 (1985)

HISTORY. The Bulgarian state was founded in 681, but fell under Turkish rule in 1396. By the Treaty of Berlin (1878), the Principality of Bulgaria and the Autonomous Province of Eastern Rumelia, both under Turkish suzerainty, were constituted. In 1885 Rumelia was reunited with Bulgaria. On 5 Oct. 1908 Bulgaria declared her independence of Turkey.

In 1941 Bulgaria signed the Three Power Pact and the Anti-Comintern Pact. After a referendum which abolished the monarchy (for details *see* THE STATESMAN'S YEAR-BOOK, 1986–87) the Fatherland Front government asked for an armistice, which was signed on 28 Oct. 1944 by the USSR, the UK and the USA. A People's Republic was proclaimed on 15 Sept. 1946. The peace treaty was signed in Paris on 10 Feb. 1947. It restored the frontiers as on 1 Jan. 1941.

AREA AND POPULATION. The area of Bulgaria is 110,911·5 sq. km (42,823 sq. miles) and is bounded in the north by Romania, east by the Black Sea, south by Turkey and Greece and west by Yugoslavia.

The country was divided into 28 provinces (*okrŭg,* plur. *okrŭzi).* Area and population in 1985:

Province	Area (sq. km)	Pop. 1,000	Province	Area (sq. km)	Pop. 1,000	Province	Area (sq. km)	Pop. 1,000
Blagoevgrad	6,490	346	Pleven	4,332	367	Sofia (City)	1,194	1,193
Burgas	7,697	446	Plovdiv	5,638	758	Stara Zagora	5,066	415
Gabrovo	2,035	178	Razgrad	2,669	197	Tolbukhin	4,704	256
Khaskovo	4,007	300	Ruse	2,570	303	Tŭrgovishte	2,732	172
Kŭrdzhali	4,036	298	Shumen	3,390	256	Varna	3,825	466
Kyustendil	3,041	193	Silistra	2,842	174	Veliko Tŭrnovo	4,680	338
Lovech	4,136	204	Sliven	3,614	239	Vidin	3,006	165
Mikhailovgrad	3,609	226	Smolyan	3,523	171	Vratsa	3,955	288
Pazardzhik	4,455	326	Sofia	7,166	304	Yambol	4,111	204
Pernik	2,391	176						

In Aug. 1987 these provinces were grouped into 9 regions *(oblast)* which replaced them as administrative units: Mikhailovgrad (Mikhailovgrad, Vidin, Vratsa); Lovech (Lovech, Pleven, Gabrovo, Veliko Tŭrnovo); Razgrad (Razgrad, Ruse, Silistra, Tŭrgovishte); Varna (Varna, Sliven, Yambol); Sofia Region (Sofia Province, Pernik, Kyustendil, Blagoevgrad); Sofia City; Plovdiv (Plovdiv, Pazardzhik, Smolyan); Khaskovo (Khaskovo, Stara Zagora, Kŭrdzhali); Burgas (Burgas, Sliven, Yambol).

The population at the census of Dec. 1985 was 8,942,976 (females, 4,515,936). Population on 1 Jan. 1987 was 8,949,600 (4·5m. males; 5·8m. urban). Population density 80·7 per sq. km.

Ethnic minorities are not identified. Some Turks have been repatriated, but 10–15% of the population may be Turkish. There were attempts forcibly to Bulgarianise these in preparation for the 1985 census. The remainder include Gipsies, Jews, Romanians and Armenians.

Population of principal towns (1985): Sofia, 1,114,962; Plovdiv, 342,201; Varna, 302,208; Ruse, 183,746; Burgas, 182,570; Stara Zagora, 150,906; Pleven, 129,782; Shumen, 100,122; Tolbukhin, 109,069; Sliven, 102,455; Pernik, 94,845; Yambol, 90,215; Khaskovo, 87,788; Gabrovo, 81,531; Pazardzhik, 77,378.

Vital statistics, 1985: Live births, 118,955; deaths, 107,485; marriages, 66,682; divorces, 14,361; birth rate, 13·6 per 1,000 population; death rate, 12; infant mortality, 15·4 per 1,000; growth rate, 1·3. Abortions, 1985: 130,805.

Expectation of life in 1984 was 68·4 years.

CLIMATE. The southern parts have a Mediterranean climate, with winters mild and moist and summers hot and dry, but further north the conditions become more continental, with a larger range of temperature and greater amounts of rainfall in summer and early autumn. Sofia. Jan. 28°F(-2·2°C), July 69°F (20·6°C). Annual rainfall 25·4″ (635 mm).

CONSTITUTION AND GOVERNMENT. The 'Tŭrnovo' Constitution of 1879 was replaced by the 'Dimitrov' Constitution in 1947. This was in turn replaced by a new constitution on 18 May 1971. This provides for a single-chamber National Assembly *(Narodno Sŭbranie).* The highest permanently operating organ of the state is the Council of State elected by the National Assembly from its members. Supreme power is vested in the National Assembly, which consists of 400 deputies elected from areas of equal population by direct, secret and universal suffrage (everybody at age of 18 being eligible to vote and hold office) for a term of 5 years; it is to meet at least three times every year.

A general election was held on 27 Oct. 1946. The Fatherland Front, composed of the Workers (Communist), Agrarian, Socialist and Zveno Parties, and non-party independents, obtained 364 seats (277 of which went to the Communists) and the opposition 101. In Aug. 1947 the oppositional Agrarian Union was dissolved. The Socialist Party was merged with the Workers' Party in Aug. 1948, and the Zveno Party dissolved itself.

The Fatherland Front became, in 1948, a unified mass organization with individual memberships. Inside the Fatherland Front, there remain two political parties, the Bulgarian Communist Party and the Bulgarian People's Agrarian Union. Petŭr Tanchev *(1st Vice-Chairman, Council of State)* is Secretary of the Agrarian Union and Pencho Kubadinski Chairman of the Fatherland Front's National Council.

In 1984 the membership of the Communist Party was 892,000; Young Communist League, (1976) 1·3m.; Agrarian Union (1986), 120,000; Fatherland Front, 3,770,080.

Elections to the National Assembly were held on 8 June 1986. 6,639,562 votes were stated to have been cast (from an electorate of 6,650,739) for the 400 candidates of the Fatherland Front (84 women; 276 Communists; 99 Agrarian Union; 25 independents).

Constitutionally there is no office of Head of State, but Todor Zhivkov *(Chairman of the Council of State, Secretary-General of the Communist Party)*, performs some of its functions. Ministries were radically reorganized in 1987.

Real political power lies with the Bulgarian Communist Party, whose highest policy-making and executive body is its Politburo, elected by and from the Central Committee.

In March 1988 it consisted of: FULL MEMBERS: Todor Zhivkov, Georgi Atanasov *(Prime Minister)*, Stanko Todorov *(Chairman, National Assembly)*, Pencho Kubadinski, Milko Balev, Chudomir Aleksandrov, Gen. Dobri Dzhurov *(Defence Minister)*, Petŭr Mladenov *(Foreign Minister)*, Ognian Doinov, Grisha Filipov, Yordan Yotov. CANDIDATE MEMBERS: Petŭr Dyulgerov, Andrei Lukanov *(Minister of Foreign Economic Relations)*, Georgi Yordanov *(Minister of Culture, Science and Education)*, Grigor Stoichkov *(Deputy Prime Minister)*, Stoian Markov, Dimitŭr Stoianov *(Minister of Internal Affairs)*.

Ministers not in the Politburo include: Stoian Ovcharov, *(Economy and Planning)*, Svetla Daskalova *(Justice)*, Radoi Popivanov *(Health and Social Welfare)*, Georgi Pankov (without portfolio).

In May 1967 a second 20-year treaty of friendship, co-operation and mutual assistance with the Soviet Union was signed.

National flag: Three horizontal stripes of white, green, red, with the national emblem in the canton.

National anthem: An arrangement of Mila Rodino (Dear Fatherland), a popular patriotic song, was declared the national anthem in 1964.

Local Government. People's Councils for the 9 regions, 29 urban areas and 299 other districts are elected for 30 months. In addition to their civic functions they also supervise the management of publicly owned enterprises. The Council's executive organs are Permanent Committees. Elections were held on 28 Feb. 1988, for the first time with multiple candidacies.

DEFENCE. There is a compulsory service of 2 years in the Army and Air Force (3 years in the Navy).

Army. In 1988 the Army had a strength of 110,000, including 70,000 conscripts, and is organized in 8 motor rifle divisions and 5 tank brigades. Bulgaria is divided into 3 Military Districts, based on Sofia, Plovdiv and Sliven. Equipment includes 400 T-34, 1,500 T-54/-55 and 200 T-72 tanks. Paramilitary forces, including border guards, security police and People's Territorial Militia, number some 172,500.

Navy. The Navy consists of 4 *ex*-Soviet 'R' class diesel-powered patrol submarines, 3 *ex*-Soviet 'Riga' class old small frigates, 3 *ex*-Soviet 'Poti' class corvettes, 7 *ex*-Soviet 'Osa' class missile boats, 6 *ex*-Soviet patrol vessels, 6 *ex*-Soviet torpedo boats, 2 fleet minesweepers, 9 coastal minesweepers, 4 inshore minesweepers, 18 minesweeping boats, 24 landing craft, 4 oilers, 3 survey ships, 2 salvage craft, 9 tugs, 3 training ships, 2 degaussing vessels, 2 diving tenders and 20 auxiliaries and service craft. Personnel in 1988 totalled 8,800 officers and ratings of whom 2,100 were afloat, 2,200 on coastal defence, 1,800 in training, 2,500 for shore support and 200 for naval aviation comprising 20 helicopters.

Air Force. The large tactical Air Force had (1987) about 250 Soviet-built combat aircraft and (1988) 34,000 personnel. There are 4 regiments of MiG-21 and MiG-23 interceptors; 2 regiments of fighter/ground attack MiG-23s and MiG-17s; 2 reconnaissance squadrons of MiG-17s and MiG-21s; some Mi-24 helicopter gunships; a total of about 40 Tu-134, Il-14, An-2 and An-24/26 transport aircraft; a total of about 70 Mi-4, Mi-2, Ka-26, and Mi-8 helicopters; and L-29 Delfin, MiG-15UTI, Zlin 42 and MiG-21UTI trainers. Soviet-built 'Guideline', 'Goa' and 'Ganef' surface-to-air missiles have also been supplied to Bulgaria.

INTERNATIONAL RELATIONS

Membership. Bulgaria is a member of UN, Comecon and the Warsaw Pact.

External Debt. Agreements of 1955 and 1963 settled outstanding financial claims by the UK and USA respectively.

ECONOMY

Planning. State economic planning started in 1947. There were planning reforms in 1964, 1969, 1982, 1986 and 1987. An economic code of 1 Jan. 1988 provides for the self-management and self-accounting of all economic enterprises.

For the first eight 5-year plans *see* THE STATESMAN'S YEAR-BOOK for 1987–88. The ninth 5-year plan is running from 1986 to 1990. The emphasis is on technological development.

Budget. The revenue and expenditure of Bulgaria for calendar years were as follows (in 1m. leva):

	1977	1980	1981	1982	1983	1984	1985	1986	1987
Revenue	9,498	13,187	15,385	15,824	16,812	17,754	18,097	...	20,672
Expenditure	9,477	13,167	15,370	15,809	16,663	17,392	18,087	...	20,662

Of the 1984 revenue 92% came from the national economy. 1983 expenditure was: National economy, 8,630m. leva; education, 2,945m.; social security, 2,846m.

Currency. The unit of currency is the *lev* (pl. *leva*) divided into 100 *stotinki* (sing. *stotinka*). It has been linked to the Soviet rouble since May 1952. A new *lev*, equalling 10 old leva, was introduced on 1 Jan. 1962. The parity (clearing value) is 1 rouble = 1·30 *leva*. Official rate of exchange (Feb. 1988) was £1 = 1·52 *leva*; US$1 = 0·82 *leva*. Rate of exchange for non-commercial transactions (1987): £1 = 2·40 leva; US$1 = 1·65 *leva*. Notes are issued for 1, 2, 5, 10 and 20 *leva* and coins for 1, 2, 5, 10, 20, 50 *stotinki* and 1, 2 and 5 *leva*.

Banking. Under a banking reform of 1987 the National Bank remains the central bank and is responsible for issuing currency. The Foreign Trade Bank (founded 1964) and the State Savings Bank also remain, the latter now serving local enterprises as well as the public. In 1985, 10·21m. depositors had savings totalling 13,418m. leva. Five new commercial banks serving various specific industrial sectors, and three more broadly-based (the Economic Bank, the Agricultural Bank and the Bank for Economic Initiative) have been set up. A Bavarian-Bulgarian Bank began operating in May 1987.

Weights and Measures. The metric system is in general use. On 1 April 1916 the Gregorian calendar came into force in Bulgaria.

ENERGY AND NATURAL RESOURCES

Energy. Bulgaria has little oil, gas or high-grade coal and energy policy is based on the exploitation of its low-grade coal and hydro-electric resources, which produce 20% of the electricity supply. Supply 220 volts; 50 Hz.

Electricity. In 1984 there were 135 power stations with a potential of 9·8m. kw. (thermal, (46) 6m. kw.; hydroelectric, (88) 2m. kw.; nuclear, (1) 1·76m. kw.). Output, 1986, 41,836m. kwh. Domestic consumption was rationed in 1987–88.

Oil and Natural Gas. Oil is extracted in the Balchik district on the Black Sea, in an area 100 km north of Varna and at Dolni Dubnik near Pleven. There are refineries at Burgas (annual capacity 5m. tonnes) and Dolni Dubnik (7m. tonnes). 190m. cu. metres of natural gas were produced in 1980.

Minerals. Ore production 1985: Manganese, 11,300 tonnes; iron, 607,000 tonnes. 32·5m. tonnes of coal including 381,000 tonnes of hard coal and 25·3m. tonnes of lignite were mined in 1985. 89 tonnes of salt were extracted in 1985.

Agriculture. In 1986 the National Agro-Industrial Union was replaced by a new Ministry of Agriculture. In 1985 agricultural land covered 6,169,300 hectares, of which 4,652,900 hectares were cultivable.

Size of private plots (maximum, 1 hectare) is based on the number of members of a household. Total area of private plots in 1985 was 609,400 hectares. Collective and state farms have been incorporated into 'agricultural-industrial complexes'. There were 298 of these in 1985. 139,218 tractors (in 15-h.p. units) were in use and 15,141 combine harvesters.

In 1982, 26 irrigation systems and 161 dams irrigated 1,169,900 hectares.

Production in 1986 (in 1,000 tonnes): Wheat, 4,000; rye, 35; maize, 2,750; barley, 1,050; oats, 25; rice, 69; sunflower seed, 475; seed cotton, 17; tobacco, 119; tomatoes, 830; potatoes, 400; grapes, 1,025. Bulgaria produces 80% of the world supply of attar of roses; annual production, 1,200 kg.

Other products (in 1,000 tonnes) in 1985: Meat, 1,254; wool, 34; 2,781m. eggs were produced and 2,462m. litres of milk.

Livestock (1986): 119,558 horses, 1,705,685 cattle, including 669,674 milch cows, 9,723,731 sheep, 3,911,599 pigs, 39,226,550 poultry and 572,069 beehives.

Forestry. The forest area, 1985, was 3,867,000 hectares (34% coniferous, 26% oak). Oak forests are in a poor condition due to indiscriminate felling in the past. 39,798 hectares were afforested in 1985. 7·7m. cu. metres of timber were cut in 1985.

Fisheries. Catch, 1982: 115,600 tonnes (15,600 tonnes freshwater).

INDUSTRY AND TRADE

Industry. All industry was nationalized in 1947 and is divided into 11 associations of up to 150 linked enterprises. A Labour Code of 1986 provides for the self-management of enterprises and the election of management by the workforce.

Industrial production	1980	1981	1982	1983	1984	1985
Crude steel (1,000 tonnes)	2,565	2,484	2,584	2,831	2,878	2,944
Pig-iron (1,000 tonnes)	1,583	1,512	1,558	1,623	1,578	1,702
Cement (1,000 tonnes)	5,359	5,433	5,614	5,644	5,717	5,296
Sulphuric acid (1,000 tonnes)	852	920	916	861	908	810

In 1985 there were also produced (in 1,000 tonnes): Coke, 1,087; rolled steel, 3,326; artificial fertilizers, 3,132; calcinated soda, 1,037; sugar, 457; cotton fabrics, 351m. metres; woollens, 35·11m. metres.

Labour. There is 42½-hour 5-day working week. The average wage (excluding peasantry) was 2,564 leva per annum in 1985. Population of working age (males 16–60; females 16–55), 1985, 5·02m. (2·7m. males). The labour force (excluding peasantry) in 1985 was 4,111,919 (1,979,354 female), of whom 2,870,750 (1,238,935) were manual labourers. 1,412,088 worked in industry, 353,432 in building and 907,737 in agriculture and forestry. There were some 4m. trade union members in 1988.

Commerce. Foreign trade is controlled by the Ministry of Foreign Trade. Bulgarian trade has developed as follows (in 1m. leva):

	1980	1981	1982	1983	1984	1985
Imports	8,283	9,860	10,976	11,966	12,842	14,067
Exports	8,902	9,958	10,880	11,818	12,987	13,739

Structure of imports and exports in 1985: Producers' goods, 88%, 78%; consumer goods, 12%, 22%.

Main exports are food products, tobacco, non-ferrous metals, cast iron, leather articles, textiles and (to Communist countries) machinery; main imports are machinery, oil, natural gas, steel, cellulose and timber.

77% of Bulgaria's trade is with the Communist countries (56% with USSR). Agreements with USSR envisage the co-ordination of the Soviet and Bulgarian 5-year plans in the spirit of 'socialist internationalism'. In 1979 a 10-year plan of economic specialization and co-operation was signed with the USSR. Libya is Bulgaria's biggest non-Communist export market, Federal Republic of Germany her major non-Communist supplier.

Total trade between Bulgaria and UK (British Department of Trade returns, in £1,000 sterling):

	1983	1984	1985	1986	1987
Imports to UK	12,355	17,345	22,291	32,459	24,249
Exports and re-exports from UK	44,577	55,917	109,970	80,504	88,761

Joint Western-Bulgarian industrial ventures are permitted under a law of March 1980 by which Western share participation may exceed 50%. There were 6 in operation in 1985. In Oct. 1987 the Bulgarian government offered to repurchase Bulgarian bonds.

COMMUNICATIONS

Roads. In 1985 there were 36,459 km of roads, including 221 km of motorways and 2,915 km of main roads. 912m. tonnes of freight and 886m. passengers were carried.

Railways. In 1985 Bulgaria had 4,297 km of standard gauge railway, including 2,227 km electrified. 105m. passengers and 83m. tonnes of freight were carried in 1985.

Aviation. BALKAN (Bulgarian Airlines) operates internal flights from Sofia (airport: Vrazhdebna) to Burgas, Khaskovo, Pleven, Plovdiv, Ruse, Silistra, Stara Zagora, Tŭrgovishte, Veliko Tŭrnovo, Varna, Vidin and Yambol and international flights to Algiers, Amsterdam, Athens, Baghdad, Bratislava, Belgrade, Benghazi, Berlin, Brussels, Bucharest, Budapest, Cairo, Casablanca, Copenhagen, Damascus, Dresden, Frankfurt, Istanbul, London, Madrid, Moscow, Nicosia, Paris, Prague, Rome, Stockholm, Syktyvkar, Tunis, Vienna, Warsaw and Zurich. There are also flights from Burgas to Leningrad and Kiev, and from Varna to Leningrad, Kuwait, Athens and Stockholm. In 1985 BALKAN carried 2·6m. passengers and 26,428 tonnes of freight.

Shipping. Ports, shipping and shipbuilding are controlled by the Bulgarian United Shipping and Shipbuilding Corporation. In 1982 it had 194 ocean-going vessels with a loading capacity of 1·6m. DWT. Burgas is a fishing and oil-port open to tankers of 20,000 tons. Varna is the other important port. There is a rail ferry between Varna and Ilitchovsk (USSR). In 1987 Bulgaria set up an exclusive economic zone extending 200 miles into the Black Sea. In 1985, 687,000 passengers and 23m. tonnes of cargo were carried.

Post and Broadcasting. In 1985 there were 4,048 post and telecommunications offices, 1,946,324 telephones, 76 broadcasting stations and 34 television stations. Radio Sofia, the government broadcasting station, transmits 2 programmes on medium- and short-waves. There is also a special tourist service, broadcast *via* the Varna II transmitter on 1,124 kHz. Advertisements are broadcast for half an hour a day. Bulgaria participates in the East European TV link 'Intervision'. Colour programmes by SECAM system. Radio receiving sets licensed in 1985, 2,017,462; television, 1,696,461.

Cinemas and Theatres (1985). There were 37 theatres, 19 puppet theatres, 8 opera houses, 1 operetta house and 3,314 cinemas. 501 films were made (40 full-length).

Newspapers and Books. In 1985 there were 17 dailies with a circulation of 2·6m. The Party newspaper is *Rabotnicheskoto Delo* ('The Workers' Cause') with a circulation of 820,000 in 1984. 4,322 book titles were published in 1985.

JUSTICE, RELIGION, EDUCATION AND WELFARE

Justice. A law of Nov. 1982 provides for the election (and recall) of all judges by the National Assembly. There are a Supreme Court, 28 provincial courts (including Sofia), 105 regional courts and 'Comrades' Courts' for minor offences. Jurors are elected at the local government elections.

The maximum term of imprisonment is now 20 years except for 'exceptionally dangerous crimes' which carry the death penalty. In 1985 harsh penalties were imposed for terrorist acts and drug smuggling following incidences of both.

The Prosecutor General who is elected by the National Assembly for 5 years and subordinate to it alone, exercises supreme control over the observance of the law by all government bodies, officials and citizens. He appoints and discharges all Prosecutors of every grade. The powers of this office were extended and redefined by a law of 1980 to put a greater emphasis on crime prevention and the rights of citizens.

Religion. 'The traditional church of the Bulgarian people' (as it is officially described), is that of the Eastern Orthodox Church. It was disestablished under the 1947 Constitution. In 1953 the Bulgarian Patriarchate was revived. The present Patriarch is Metropolitan Maksim of Lovech (enthroned 1971). The seat of the Patriarch is at Sofia. There are 11 dioceses, each under a Metropolitan, 10 bishops, 2,600 parishes, 1,700 priests, 400 monks and nuns, 3,700 churches and chapels, one seminary and one theological college.

The Constitution provides for freedom of conscience and belief but forbids propaganda against the Government. The State provides 17% of Church funds.

Churches may not maintain schools or colleges, except theological seminaries, or organize youth movements.

In 1987 there were some 60,000 Roman Catholics (including 10,000 Uniates) in 2 bishoprics with (in 1983) 42 priests (20 Uniates) in 50 parishes. In 1984 there were 5 Protestant groups: Pentecostals (10,000 members, 120 churches, 30 pastors); Baptists (1,000 members, 20 churches); Methodists; Congregationalists; Adventists. There were estimated to be about 700,000 practising Moslems in 1984 under a Chief Mufti elected by 7 regional muftis. There were about 1,000 mosques in 1987.

Education. Education is free, and compulsory for children between the ages of 7 and 16. The gradual introduction of unified secondary polytechnical schools offering compulsory education for all children from the ages of 7 to 17 was begun in 1973–74. Complete literacy is claimed. Schools are classified according to which years of schooling they offer: Elementary (1–3), primary (1–8), preparatory (4–8), secondary (9–11), complete secondary (1–11).

Educational statistics for 1985–86: 5,054 kindergartens (360,395 children, 28,864 teachers); 738 elementary schools; 2,187 primary schools; 48 preparatory schools; 70 secondary schools; 465 complete secondary schools. Numbers of teachers and pupils: School years 1 to 3, 24,952 and 429,912; 4 to 8, 36,201 and 651,067; 9 to 11, 9,392 and 163,417. There were also 3 vocational-technical schools (50 teachers, 1,461 students), 267 secondary vocational-technical schools (7,457 teachers, 114,036 students), 232 technical colleges (9,838 teachers, 95,651 students), 21 post-secondary institutions (843 teachers, 9,536 students) and 30 institutes of higher education (14,009 teachers, 101,507 students). University entrance is by competitive examination. Failure rate was 65% in 1985. There are 3 universities: the Kliment Ohrid University in Sofia (founded 1888) had 1,016 teachers and 9,612 students (in 1983–84); the Kirill i Metodii University in Veliko Tŭrnovo (founded 1971) had 243 teachers and 3,138 students and the Paisi Hilendarski University in Plovdiv (founded 1961) had 274 teachers and 3,500 students.

The Academy of Sciences was founded in 1869.

Social Welfare. Retirement and disablement pensions and temporary sick pay are calculated as a percentage of previous wages (respectively 55–80%, 35–100%, 69–90%) and according to the nature of the employment.

Monthly family allowances for children under 16: 18 leva for 1 child, 30 leva for 2 children and 55 leva for 3 children.

In 1985, 2·21m. persons received pensions totalling 2,398m. leva.

All medical services are free. In 1985 there were 187 hospitals (including 16 mental hospitals and addiction treatment centres) with 81,651 beds. There were 25,665 doctors and 5,745 dentists.

DIPLOMATIC REPRESENTATIVES

Of Bulgaria in Great Britain (186 Queen's Gate, London, SW7 5HL)
Ambassador: Dimitar Aleksandrov Zhulev (accredited 25 Feb. 1987).

Of Great Britain in Bulgaria (Blvd. Marshal Tolbukhin 65–67, Sofia)
Ambassador: John Fawcett, CMG.

Of Bulgaria in the USA (1621 22nd St., NW, Washington, D.C., 20008)
Ambassador: Stoyan I. Zhulev.

Of the USA in Bulgaria (1 Stamboliski Blvd., Sofia)
Ambassador: Sol Polansky.

Of Bulgaria to the United Nations
Ambassador: Boris Tsvetkov.

Books of Reference

Kratka Bŭlgarska Entsiklopediia (Short Bulgarian Encyclopaedia), 5 vols. Sofia, 1963–69
Statisticheski Godishnik (Statistical Yearbook). Sofia from 1956
Constitution of the People's Republic of Bulgaria. Sofia, 1971
Information Bulgaria. Oxford, 1985
Modern Bulgaria: History, Politics, Economy, Culture. Sofia, 1981
Normative Acts of the Foreign Economic Relations of the People's Republic of Bulgaria. Sofia, 1982
Atanasova, T., *et al., Bulgarian-English Dictionary.* Sofia, 1975
Bell, J. D., *The Bulgarian Communist Party from Blagoev to Zhivkov.* Stanford, 1985
Crampton, R. J., *A Short History of Modern Bulgaria.* CUP, 1987
Feiwel, G. R., *Growth and Reforms in Centrally Planned Economies: the Lessons of the Bulgarian Experience.* New York, 1977
Lampe, J. R., *The Bulgarian Economy in the Twentieth Century.* London, 1986
Oren, N., *Communism Administered: Agrarianism and Communism in Bulgaria.* Baltimore, 1973
Pundeff, M. V., *Bulgaria: A Bibliographic Guide.* Library of Congress, 1965
Zhivkov, T., *Modern Bulgaria: Problems and Tasks in Building an Advanced Socialist Society.* New York, 1974.—*Marxist Concepts and Practices.* Oxford, 1984

BURKINA FASO

Capital: Ouagadougou
Population: 8·33m. (1987)
GNP per capita: US$160 (1984)

HISTORY. A separate colony of Upper Volta was in 1919 carved out of the colony of Upper Senegal and Niger, which had been established in 1904. In 1932 it was abolished and most of its territory transferred to Ivory Coast, with small parts added to French Sudan and Niger, but it was re-constituted with its former borders on 4 Sept. 1947. Upper Volta became an autonomous republic within the French Community on 11 Dec. 1958 and reached full independence on 5 Aug. 1960.

On 3 Jan. 1966 the government of Maurice Yameogo was overthrown by a military *coup* led by Lieut-Col. Sangoulé Lamizana, who assumed the Presidency. In a further *coup* on 25 Nov. 1980, President Lamizana was overthrown and a military regime assumed power. Further *coups* took place on 7 Nov. 1982, 4 Aug. 1983 and 15 Oct. 1987. The name of the country was changed to Burkina Faso in 1984.

AREA AND POPULATION. Burkina Faso is bounded north and west by Mali, east by Niger, south by Benin, Togo, Ghana and the Côte d'Ivoire. The republic covers an area of 274,122 sq. km; population (census, 1985) 7,967,019 (3,846,518 males). Estimate (1987) 8,334,000. The largest cities (1985 census) are Ouagadougou, the capital (442,223), Bobo-Dioulasso (231,162), Koudougou (51,670), Ouahigouya (38,604), Banfora (35,204), Kaya (25,799), Fada N'Gourma and Tenkodogo.

The areas and populations of the 30 provinces were:

Province	Sq. km	Census 1985	Province	Sq. km	Census 1985
Bam	4,017	164,263	Nahouri	3,843	105,273
Bazéga	5,313	306,976	Namentenga	7,755	198,798
Bougouriba	7,087	221,522	Oubritenga	4,693	303,229
Boulgou	9,033	403,358	Oudalan	10,046	105,715
Boulkiemde	4,138	363,594	Passoré	4,078	225,115
Comoé	18,393	250,510	Poni	10,361	234,501
Ganzourgou	4,087	196,006	Sanguie	5,165	218,289
Gnagna	8,600	229,249	Sanmatenga	9,213	368,365
Gourma	26,613	294,123	Sèno	13,473	230,043
Houet	16,472	585,031	Sissili	13,736	246,844
Kadiogo	1,169	459,138	Soum	13,350	190,464
Kénédougou	8,307	139,722	Sourou	9,487	267,770
Kossi	13,177	330,413	Tapoa	14,780	159,121
Kouritenga	1,627	197,027	Yatenga	12,292	537,205
Mouhoun	10,442	289,213	Zoundwéogo	3,453	155,142

The principal ethnic groups are the Mossi (48%), Fulani (10%), Lobi-Dagari (7%), Mandé (7%), Bobo (7%), Sénoufo (6%), Gourounsi (5%), Bissa (5%), Gourmantché (5%). French is the official language.

CLIMATE. A tropical climate with a wet season from May to Nov. and a dry season from Dec. to April. Rainfall decreases from south to north. Ouagadougou. Jan. 76°F (24·4°C), July 83°F (28·3°C). Annual rainfall 36″ (894 mm).

CONSTITUTION AND GOVERNMENT. Following the *coup* of 15 Oct. 1987, when President Sankara was killed, the ruling National Recovery Council was dissolved and the government re-shuffled. A new Military Council was formed on 31 Oct. 1987

President of CNR, Head of State and Government: Capt. Blaise Compaoré.
The National Recovery Council prior to the *coup* was composed as follows:
Popular Defence: Maj. Boukary Jean-Baptiste Lingani. *Minister of State to the*

248

Presidency, Justice: Capt. Blaise Compaoré. *Foreign Affairs and Co-operation:* Bazomboué Léandre Bassolet. *Interior and Security:* Nongman Ernest Ouedraogo. *Information:* Basile Laetare Guissou. *Culture:* Bernadette Sanou. *Economic Development:* Capt. Henri Zongo. *Financial Resources:* Talata Eugène Dondasse. *Budget:* Adèle Ouedraogo. *Planning and People's Development:* Youssouf Ouedraogo. *Commerce and People's Supply:* Mohamadou Touré. *Agriculture and Animal Husbandry:* Jean-Marc Somda. *Water:* Michel Kouda. *Equipment:* Moussa Michel Tapsoba. *Transport and Communications:* Alain Koeffe. *Labour, Social Security and Civil Service:* Fidèle Toe. *Environment and Tourism:* Noellie Marie Béatrice Damiba. *Family Welfare and National Solidarity:* Joséphine Ouedraogo. *Public Health:* Azara Bamba. *Sports:* Maj. Abdou Salam Kaboré. *National Education:* Sansan Jean-Baptiste Da. *Higher Education and Scientific Research:* Valère Dieudonné Somé. *Rural Affairs:* Jean-Léonard Compaoré. *Secretary-General to the Cabinet:* Nayabtigungu Congo-Kaboré. *Secretary of State for Justice:* Sambo Antoine Komi.

National flag: Horizontally red over green with a yellow star over all in the centre.

Local government: The country is divided into 30 provinces and 250 districts.

DEFENCE

Army. The Army consists of 5 infantry regiments, 1 airborne regiment and support units. Equipment includes about 83 armoured cars. Strength (1988), 7,000 with a further 1,750 men in paramilitary forces.

Air Force. Creation of a small air arm to support the land forces began, with French assistance, in 1964. Equipment now comprises 2 HS.748 twin-turboprop freighters, 2 C-47s, 2 twin-turboprop Nord 262s, an Aero Commander 500, 2 Broussard and 1 Reims/Cessna Super Skymaster for transport and liaison duties, 1 Cessna 172 trainer, and 3 Dauphin and Alouette III helicopters. Eight MiG-21 fighters and 2 MiG-21U trainers and 6 SF.260W Warrior light strike aircraft have been delivered. Personnel total (1988) 200.

INTERNATIONAL RELATIONS

Membership. Burkina Faso is a member of UN, OAU and is an ACP state of the EEC.

ECONOMY

Planning. A 5-year Development Plan (1986–90) aimed at economic sufficiency and envisages expenditure of 630,000m. francs CFA.

Budget. Government revenue in 1987 was 88,000m. francs CFA and expenditure 100,000m. francs CFA.

Currency. The unit of currency is the *franc* CFA with a parity rate of 50 *francs* CFA to 1 French *franc*. In March 1988, £1 = 507·00 *francs*; US$1 = 285·66 *francs*.

Banking. The *Banque Centrale des Etats de l'Afrique de l'Ouest* is the bank of issue. The main commercial bank is the *Banque Internationale du Burkina.* In Dec. 1982 it had deposits of 32,046m. *francs* CFA.

ENERGY AND NATURAL RESOURCES

Electricity. Production of electricity (1986) was 159m. kwh.

Minerals. There are deposits of manganese near Tambao in the north, but exploitation is limited by existing transport facilities. Magnetite, bauxite, zinc, lead, nickel and phosphates have been found in the same area. Gold was discovered in 1987 at Assakan, near the Malian border.

Agriculture. Production (1986, in 1,000 tonnes): Sorghum, 1,012; millet, 687; sugar-cane, 345; maize, 158; groundnuts, 152; rice, 28; seed cotton, 142; sesame, 16. Rice and groundnuts are of increasing importance.

Livestock (1986): 3,106,000 cattle, 2,215,000 sheep, 3,335,000 goats, 70,000 horses, 200,000 donkeys.

Forestry. In 1983, 25% of the land was forested, chiefly in the deep river valleys of the Mouhoun (Black Volta), Nakambe, (Red Volta) and Nazinon (White Volta). Production, 7·15m. cu. metres.

Fisheries. River fishing produced 7,000 tonnes in 1983.

INDUSTRY AND TRADE

Industry. In 1982 gross manufacturing (including energy) was 68,146,600 francs CFA, of which textiles (3,666,600 francs CFA) and metal products (2,795,100 francs CFA).

Labour. In 1982 the labour force was 3,503,610 of whom 2,873,000 (82%) were engaged in agriculture, forestry and fishing. There were (1981) 4 trade unions.

Commerce. In 1983 imports totalled 109,572m. francs CFA and exports 21,712m. francs CFA. The major exports were cotton (55%), karite nuts (12%) and livestock (6%). In 1983 France provided 28%, the Côte d'Ivoire 24% and USA 9% of imports, while the Côte d'Ivoire took 9%, France 12%, Taiwan (27%), China (11%) and UK 8% of exports.

Total trade between Burkina Faso and UK (British Department of Trade returns, in £1,000 sterling):

	1984	1985	1986	1987
Imports to UK	3,695	557	1,369	462
Exports and re-exports from UK	2,065	2,729	3,104	4,168

Tourism. There were 60,000 tourists in 1986.

COMMUNICATIONS

Roads. The road system comprises 13,134 km, of which 4,396 km are national, 1,744 km departmental, 2,364 km regional and 1,940 km unclassified roads. In 1982 there were 33,769 vehicles, comprising 16,463 private cars, 419 buses, 14,852 commercial vehicles, 411 special vehicles and 1,123 tractors.

Railway. Ouagadougou is the terminus of the Abidjan-Niger railway, of which 517 km lie in Burkina Faso. A 355-km extension to the manganese deposits at Tambao is planned with the first 107-km section to Kaya under construction.

Aviation. Ouagadougou and Bobo-Dioulasso are regularly served by UTA and Air Afrique and in 1982 dealt with 120,684 passengers and 6,778 tonnes of freight. Air Burkina operates all internal flights to 47 domestic airports.

Post and Broadcasting. There were, in 1982, some 42 post offices and (1981) 10,625 telephones. There are radio stations at Ouagadougou and Bobo-Dioulasso and (1984) 116,000 receivers. The state television service, Télévision Nationale du Burkina, broadcasts 6 days a week in Ouagadougou; there were (1984) 20,000 receivers.

Cinemas. In 1982 there were 12 cinemas with 14,000 seats.

Newspapers. Four daily newspapers were published in Ouagadougou in 1986.

JUSTICE, RELIGION, EDUCATION AND WELFARE

Justice. There is a Supreme Court in Ouagadougou and Courts of Appeal at Ouagadougou and Bobo-Dioulasso. Revolutionary People's Tribunals have replaced the former lower courts.

Religion. In 1980 45% of the population followed animist religions; 43% were Moslem and 12% Christian (mainly Roman Catholic).

Education. There were (in 1984) 276,732 pupils and 4,796 teachers in 1,037 primary schools, 43,001 pupils and 1,553 teachers in 79 secondary schools, 4,492 students with 484 teachers in 27 technical schools and (1980) 495 students in teacher-training establishments. The Université d'Ouagadougou had 3,870 students and 216 teaching staff in 1984.

Health (1980). There were 5 hospitals, 254 dispensaries, 11 medical centres, 65 regional clinics and 167 mobile clinics with a total of 4,587 beds. There were 119 doctors, 14 surgeons, 52 pharmacists, 163 health assistants, 229 midwives and 1,345 nursing personnel.

A 10-year health programme started in 1979, providing for 7,000 village health centres, 515 district health centres, regional and sub-regional medical centres, 10 departmental hospitals, 2 national hospitals and a university centre of health sciences in Ouagadougou.

DIPLOMATIC REPRESENTATIVES

Of Burkina Faso in Great Britain
Ambassador: Amadé Ouedraogo, resides in Brussels (accredited 11 July 1984).

Of Great Britain in Burkina Faso
Ambassador: V. E. Sutherland (resides in Abidjan).

Of Burkina Faso in the USA (2340 Massachusetts Ave., NW, Washington, D.C., 20008)
Chargé d'Affaires: Jean Kotie Diasso.

Of the USA in Burkina Faso (PO Box 35, Ouagadougou)
Ambassador: Leonardo Neher.

Of Burkina Faso to the United Nations
Ambassador: (Vacant).

Book of Reference

MacFarlane, D. M., *Historical Dictionary of Upper Volta*. Metuchen, 1978

BURMA

Capital: Rangoon
Population: 37·85m. (1987)
GNP per capita: US$180 (1983)

Pyidaungsu Socialist Thammada Myanma Naingngandaw

HISTORY. The Union of Burma came formally into existence on 4 Jan. 1948 and became the Socialist Republic of the Union of Burma in 1974. In 1948 Sir Hubert Rance, the last British Governor, handed over authority to Sao Shwe Thaike, the first President of the Burmese Republic, and Parliament ratified the treaty with Great Britain providing for the independence of Burma as a country not within His Britannic Majesty's dominions and not entitled to His Britannic Majesty's protection. This treaty was signed in London on 17 Oct. 1947 and enacted by the British Parliament on 10 Dec. 1947.

For the history of Burma's connexion with Great Britain *see* THE STATESMAN'S YEAR-BOOK, 1950, p. 836.

AREA AND POPULATION. Burma is bounded east by China, Laos and Thailand, west by the Indian ocean, Bangladesh and India. The total area of the Union is 261,228 sq. miles (676,577 sq. km). The population in 1983 (census) was 35,313,905. Estimate (1987) 37,850,000. Birth rate (1977 estimate), 29·1; death rate, 10·4 per 1,000 population; infant deaths, 56·3 per 1,000 live births. The leading towns are: Rangoon, the capital (1983), 2,458,712; other towns, Mandalay, 532,985; Moulmein, 219,991; Pegu, 150,447; Bassein, 144,092; Sittwe (Akyab), 107,907; Taunggye, 107,607; Monywa, 106,873.

The population of the States and Divisions at the 1983 census (provisional): Kachin State, 903,982; Kayah State, 168,355; Karen State, 1,057,505; Chin State, 368,985; Sagaing Division, 3,855,991; Tenasserim Division, 917,628; Pegu Division, 3,800,240; Magwe Division, 3,241,103; Mandalay Division, 4,580,923; Mon State, 1,682,041; Rakhine State, 2,045,891; Rangoon Division, 3,973,782; Shan State, 3,718,706; Irrawaddy Division, 4,991,057.

The Burmese belong to the Tibeto-Chinese (or Tibeto-Burman) family.

CLIMATE. The climate is equatorial in coastal areas, changing to tropical monsoon over most of the interior, but humid temperate in the extreme north, where there is a more significant range of temperature and a dry season lasting from Nov. to April. In coastal parts, the dry season is shorter. Very heavy rains occur in the monsoon months May to Sept. Rangoon. Jan. 77°F (25°C), July 80°F (26·7°C). Annual rainfall 104" (2,616 mm). Akyab. Jan. 70°F (21·1°C), July 81°F (27·2°C). Annual rainfall 206" (5,154 mm). Mandalay. Jan. 68°F (20°C), July 85°F (29·4°C). Annual rainfall 33" (828 mm).

CONSTITUTION AND GOVERNMENT. A new Constitution came into force on 2 March 1974. Military rule ended and Burma became a one-party socialist republic. For earlier Constitutions *see* THE STATESMAN'S YEAR-BOOK, 1981–82, p. 252.

The sole party is the Burmese Socialist Program Party (BSPP). There is a unicameral People's Assembly of 475 members directly elected for a 4-year term, plus 14 other members appointed by the President. The Assembly elects a 29-member Council of State as the supreme political body, and a Council of Ministers as its executive body.

President of the Republic, Chairman of the Council of State: U San Yu (elected 9 Nov. 1981, re-elected 4 Nov. 1985).

In Jan. 1988 the Council of Ministers consisted of:

Prime Minister: U Maung Maung Kha.
Deputy Prime Minister, Planning and Finance: Thura U Tun Tin. *Deputy Prime Minister, Defence:* Gen. Thura Kyaw Htin. *Agriculture and Forests:* Brig.-Gen. Than Nyunt. *Co-operatives:* U Than Hlaing. *Transport and Communications:* Thura U Saw Pru. *Foreign Affairs:* U Ye Goung. *Industry:* U Tint Swe, U Maung Cho. *Construction:* Maj.-Gen. Myint Lwin. *Mines:* U Than Tin. *Trade:* U Khin Maung Gyi. *Education:* U Kyaw Nyein. *Information and Culture:* U Aung Kyaw Myint. *Home and Religious Affairs:* U Min Gaung. *Labour and Social Welfare:* U Ohn Kyaw. *Health:* U Tun Wai. *Livestock and Fisheries:* Rear Adm. Maung Maung Win. *Energy:* U Sein Tun.

National flag: Red with a blue canton bearing 2 ears of rice within a cog-wheel and a ring of 14 stars, all in white.

Language: The official language is Burmese; the use of English is permitted.

Local government: Burma is divided into 7 states and 7 administrative divisions; these are sub-divided into 314 townships and thence into villages and wards.

DEFENCE

Army. The strength of the Army (1988) was 170,000. The Army is organized into 8 regional commands comprising 7 light infantry divisions, 16 brigades, and 2 armoured, 87 independent infantry and 4 artillery battalions and 1 anti-aircraft battery. Equipment includes 24 Comet tanks, 40 Humber armoured cars and 45 Ferret scout cars. In addition, there are 2 paramilitary units: People's Police Force (38,000) and People's Militia (35,000).

Navy. The fleet includes 2 old escort patrol vessels (*ex*-USA PCE and MSF types), 2 small indigenously built corvettes, 3 new patrol craft, 21 gunboats, 7 river gunboats, 30 small river patrol craft, 1 support ship, 2 survey vessels, 12 fishery protection cutters (3 offshore, 3 coastal, 6 inshore), 10 auxiliaries and 12 landing craft. Personnel in 1988 totalled 7,000 including 800 marines.

Air Force. The Air Force is intended primarily for internal security duties. Its combat force comprises about 5 T-33A jet fighter/trainers supplied under MAP, supplemented by 15 SIAI-Marchetti SF.260W light piston-engined attack/trainers. Other training aircraft include 20 turboprop Pilatus PC-7s and PC-9s, and 10 jet-powered T-37Cs. Transport and second-line units are equipped with 4 FH-227, 7 Turbo-Porter, 1 Citation and 10 Cessna 180 aircraft, 10 Japanese-built Bell 47 (H-13), Bell UH-1, and Alouette III helicopters. Personnel (1988) 9,000.

INTERNATIONAL RELATIONS

Membership. Burma is a member of the UN and Colombo Plan.

ECONOMY

Planning. The Development Plan, 1986–90, envisages a total investment of K.14,000m.

Budget. The budget estimates (in K.1m.) for fiscal year 1 April 1986–31 March 1987 was revenue K.74,372m. and expenditure K.61,686m.

The largest items, in 1986–87, of revenue were commodities and service tax (K.28,496m.) and customs (K.10,600m.); of expenditure, processing and manufacturing (K.24,809m.); trade (K.3,500m.); transport and communication (8,400m.).

Currency. The currency unit is now the *kyat* divided into 100 *pyas*. There are notes of *kyat* 90, 45, 15, 10, 5 and 1, and coins of *kyat* 1; *pyas* 100, 50, 25, 10, 5 and 1.
In March 1988, £1 = K.11·15 and US$1 = K.6·25.

Banking. Banks include the Union of Burma Bank, the Myanma Economic Bank, the Myanma Foreign Trade Bank and the Myanma Agricultural Bank, and the State Insurance Company is the Myanma Insurance Corporation.

ENERGY AND NATURAL RESOURCES

Electricity. In 1983–84 the total installed capacity of the Electric Power Corporation was 635,000 kw., of which 170,000 was hydro-electricity, 74,000 steam-turbine, 300,000 natural gas and 91,000 diesel. Production (1986) 1,750m. kwh. Supply 220 volts; 50 Hz.

Oil. Production (1987) of crude oil was 750,000 tonnes; natural gas 32,596m. cu. feet, petroleum (1986–87) 38,290m. cu. ft.

Minerals. Production in 1986–87 (in tonnes): Copper concentrates, 45,720; refined tin metal, 600; refined lead, 8,128; refined copper metal, 175; tin concentrates, 1,323; tungsten concentrates, 476; tin-tungsten-scheelite concentrates, 2,285; steel billets, 21,000; steel grinding balls, 3,000. Refined silver, 600,000 fine oz.; refined gold, 95 fine oz.

Agriculture. Production (1986–87) in 1,000 tonnes: Paddy, 15,219; sugar-cane, 3,399; maize, 323; jute, 45; cotton, 92; wheat, 245; butter beans, 106; soya beans, 23; rubber, 15.

Livestock (1986–87): Cattle, 9·8m.; buffaloes, 2·2m.; pigs, 3·m.; sheep and goats, 1·5m.; poultry, 38·2m.

In 1986–87 the area irrigated by government-controlled irrigation works was 2,679,000 acres.

Forestry. The area of reserved forests in 1986–87 was 39,037 sq. miles. Teak extracted in 1986–87, 410,000 cu. tons; hardwood, 1,305,000 cu. tons. All the teak and about 50% of the hardwood is from the state sector. Other forest produce included 17,572,000 cu. tons of firewood and 877,000 cu. tons of charcoal.

Fisheries. In 1986–87 sea fishing produced 19,275,000 *viss* and freshwater fisheries 3,494,000 *viss*. [Ed. note 1 *viss* = 3·6 lb.].

INDUSTRY AND TRADE

Industry. Production (1985–86) in 1,000 tonnes: Cement, 477; sheet glass, 4; fertilizers, 354·3; sugar, 65; paper, 21·6; cotton yarn, 14·5. 2,504 motor cars, 611 tractors and 14,000 bicycles were produced in 1985–86.

Labour. Economically active (1985–86) 15·13m.

Commerce. All imports and exports are controlled by the government trading organizations.

Imports and exports (US$1m.) for 1984–85: Imports 694·2 and exports 425·9.

Total trade between Burma and UK (British Department of Trade returns, in £1,000 sterling):

	1983	1984	1985	1986	1987
Imports to UK	4,726	6,420	9,944	5,092	3,826
Exports and re-exports from UK	21,927	16,488	20,221	10,835	24,715

Tourism. There were 46,500 tourists in 1986.

COMMUNICATIONS

Roads. There were 14,477 miles of road in 1986–87, of which 2,452 miles were union highway.

Railways. The Burma Railways were nationalized in 1948 and the present Burma Railways Corporation took over in 1972. In 1985 there were 2,774 miles of route on metre gauge. In 1986–87 the railway carried 2·86m. tons of freight and 61·1m. passengers.

Aviation. Burma Airways Corporation, formerly Union of Burma Airways, started its internal service in Sept. 1948 and its external service in Nov. 1950. International services were in 1963 maintained between Rangoon and Bangkok and Calcutta. The routes were extended to Hong Kong in 1969 and to Dhaka and Káthmándu in 1970 and to Singapore in 1979. There were, in 1987, 37 civil airfields.

Shipping. Burma has 60 miles of navigable canals. The Irrawaddy is navigable up to Myitkyina, 900 miles from the sea, and its tributary, the Chindwin, is navigable for 390 miles. The Irrawaddy delta has nearly 2,000 miles of navigable water. The Salween, the Attaran and the G'yne provide about 250 miles of navigable waters around Moulmein.

Post and Broadcasting. There were 1,127 post offices in 1986–87. Number of telephones was 66,912 in 1986–87. There were (1985) 7 radio stations and one television broadcasting station. In 1985 there were 725,000 radio and 35,000 television receivers.

Cinemas. In 1971 there were about 418 cinemas.

Newspapers. In 1987 there were 6 daily newspapers with a readership of over 800,000.

JUSTICE, RELIGION, EDUCATION AND WELFARE

Justice. The highest judicial authority is the Council of People's Justices, appointed by the People's Assembly from its own members, which serves as the Supreme Court and Central Criminal Court. At lower levels courts are appointed by the local People's Councils from among their own membership.

Religion. The Revolutionary Government, having repealed the amendment of 1961 which made Buddhism the state religion, recognizes 'the right of everyone freely to profess and practise his religion'.

Education. The medium of instruction in all schools is Burmese; English is taught as a compulsory second language from kindergarten level.

Education is free in the primary, junior secondary and vocational schools; fees are charged in senior secondary schools and universities.

In 1986–87 there were 750 state high schools with 238,498 pupils, 1,772 state middle schools with 1,125,632 pupils and 33,499 state primary schools with 5,056,961 pupils; the total teaching staff was 218,206, of which 158,934 were in primary schools.

Beside the Arts and Science University, there are independent degree-giving institutes of engineering, education, medicine, agriculture, economics and commerce, and veterinary sciences. A foreign-languages institute in Rangoon had (1987) 1,127 students learning English, French, German, Russian, Japanese, Chinese and Italian.

There are intermediate colleges at Taunggyi, Magwe, Akyab and Myitkyina, and degree colleges at Moulmein and Bassein, and several technical and agricultural institutes at higher and middle level. 7,040 school teachers were being trained in 16 training colleges in 1986–87. Technical high schools had 5,414 students; agricultural schools, 1,675; other vocational colleges, 4,639, and university colleges 91,748.

Health. In 1986–87 there were 10,579 doctors and 636 hospitals with 26,839 beds.

DIPLOMATIC REPRESENTATIVES

Of Burma in Great Britain (19A Charles St., London, W1X 8ER)
Ambassador: U Tin Tun (accredited 16 July 1985).

Of Great Britain in Burma (80 Strand Rd., Rangoon)
Ambassador: Martin Morland, CMG.

Of Burma in the USA (2300 S. St., NW, Washington, D.C., 20008)
Ambassador: U Myo Aung.

Of the USA in Burma (581 Merchant St., Rangoon)
Ambassador: Burton Levin.

Of Burma to the United Nations
Ambassador: U Maung Maung Gyi.

Books of Reference

Burma: Treaty between the Government of the United Kingdom and the Provisional Government of Burma. (Treaty Series No. 16, 1948.) HMSO, 1948

Cornyn, W. S., and Musgrave, J. K., *Burmese Glossary.* New York, 1958

Lehman, F. K., *The Structure of Chin Society.* Univ. of Illinois Press, 1963

Silverstein, J., *Burma: Military Rule and the Politics of Stagnation.* Cornell Univ. Press, 1978.
 —*Burmese Politics: The Dilemma of National Unity.* Rutgers Univ. Press, 1980

Steinberg, D. I., *Burma.* Boulder, 1982

Stewart, J. A., and Dunn, C. W., *Burmese–English Dictionary.* London, 1940 ff.

Taylor, R. H., *The State of Burma.* London, 1988

BURUNDI

Republika y'Uburundi

Capital: Bujumbura
Population: 4·92m. (1986)
GNP per capita: US$250 (1984)

HISTORY. Tradition recounts the establishment of a Tutsi kingdom under successive Mwamis as early as the 16th century. German military occupation in 1890 incorporated the territory into German East Africa. From 1919 Burundi formed part of Ruanda-Urundi administered by the Belgians, first as a League of Nations mandate and then as a UN trust territory. Internal self-government was granted on 1 Jan. 1962, followed by independence on 1 July 1962.

On 8 July 1966 Prince Charles Ndizeye deposed his father Mwami Mwambutsa IV, suspended the constitution and made Capt. Michel Micombero Prime Minister. On 1 Sept. Prince Charles was enthroned as Mwami Ntare V. On 28 Nov., while the Mwami was attending a Head of States Conference in Kinshasa (Congo), Micombero declared Burundi a republic with himself as president.

On 31 March 1972 Prince Charles returned to Burundi from Uganda and was placed under house arrest. On 29 April 1972 President Micombero dissolved the Council of Ministers and took full power; that night heavy fighting broke out between rebels from both Burundi and neighbouring countries, and the ruling Tutsi, apparently with the intention of destroying the Tutsi hegemony. Prince Charles was killed during the fighting and it was estimated that up to 120,000 were killed. On 14 July 1972 President Micombero reinstated a Government with a Prime Minister. On 1 Nov. 1976 President Micombero was deposed by the Army. as was President Bagaza on 3 Sept. 1987.

AREA AND POPULATION. Burundi is bounded north by Rwanda, east and south by Tanzania and west by Zaïre, and has an area of 27,834 sq. km (10,759 sq. miles).

The population at the census in 1986 was 4,782,000; estimate (1987) 4,927,000. There are three ethnic groups—Hutu (Bantu, forming over 83% of the total): Tutsi (Nilotic, less than 15%); Twa (pygmoids, less than 1%). There are some 3,500 Europeans and 1,500 Asians. In 1980 some 65,000 Tutsi refugees from Rwanda were living in Burundi.

Bujumbura, the capital, had (1986 census) 272,600 inhabitants. Gitega (95,300) was formerly the royal residence.

The local language is Kirundi, a Bantu language. French is also an official language. Kiswahili is spoken in the commercial centres.

CLIMATE. An equatorial climate, modified by altitude. The eastern plateau is generally cool, the easternmost savanna several degrees hotter. The wet seasons are from March to May and Sept. to Dec. Bujumbura. Jan. 73°F (22·8°C), July 73°F (22·8°C). Annual rainfall 33″ (825 mm).

CONSTITUTION AND GOVERNMENT. A new Constitution was promulgated on 21 Nov. 1981 and provides for a one-party state. The 65-member National Assembly elected in Oct. 1982 comprised 52 members elected by universal suffrage from a list of 104 candidates nominated by UPRONA *(Parti de l'Unité et du Progrès National du Burundi)*, together with 13 members appointed by the President. President Bagaza became Party Chairman and Head of the Central Committee for a 5-year term in Jan. 1980 and was re-elected for a second 5-year term in Sept. 1984 but was deposed in Sept. 1987.

President of the Republic, Minister of Defence: Major Pierre Buyoya (assumed office 1 Oct. 1987).

Foreign Affairs and Co-operation: Cyprien Mbonimpa.
Finance: Pierre Binoba.

257

Flag: White diagonal cross dividing triangles of red and green, in the centre a white disc bearing 3 red green-bordered 6-pointed stars.

Local Government: There are 15 provinces, each under a military governor, and sub-divided into 114 districts and then into communes.

DEFENCE. The national armed forces total (1988), 7,200 (there are also about 1,500 in paramilitary units) and include a small naval flotilla and air force flight of 3 SF 260, 3 Cessna 150 and 1 DC3 liaison aircraft, 3 Alouette III and 2 armed Gazelle helicopters. The Army comprises 2 infantry battalions, 1 parachute battalion, 1 commando battalion and 1 armoured-car company.

INTERNATIONAL RELATIONS
Membership. Burundi is a member of UN and OAU and is an ACP state of EEC.

ECONOMY
Planning. The 1983–87 Plan aims at greater diversification of agriculture with an envisaged investment of 107,400m. Burundi francs.

Budget. The 1985 budget envisaged receipts of 17,152m. Burundi francs and expenditure at 18,757m. Burundi francs.

Currency. The currency is the *Burundi franc.* There are coins of 1, 5 and 10 *francs* and bank notes of 10, 20, 50, 100, 500, 1,000 and 5,000 *francs.* The exchange rate was 208·87 *Burundi francs* = £1 and 118·28 *Burundi francs* = US$1 in March 1988.

Banking. The Bank of the Republic of Burundi is the central bank and 4 commercial banks have headquarters in Bujumbura.

Weights and Measures. The metric system operates.

ENERGY AND NATURAL RESOURCES
Electricity. Electricity production was (1986) 44m. kwh. The majority of the electricity is supplied by Zaïre. Supply 220 volts; 50 Hz.

Minerals. Mineral ores such as bastnasite and cassenite were formerly mined but output is now insignificant. Deposits of nickel (280m. tonnes) and vanadium remain to be exploited.

Agriculture. The main economic activity and the main source of employment is subsistence agriculture. Beans, cassava, maize, sweet potatoes, groundnuts, peas, sorghum and bananas are grown according to the climate and the region.

The main cash crop is coffee, of which about 95% is arabica. It accounts for 90% of exports and taxes and levies on coffee constitute a major source of revenue. A coffee board (OCIBU) manages the grading and export of the crop. Production (1985) 36,000 tonnes. The main food crops (production 1986, in 1,000 tonnes) are cassava (520), yams (7), bananas (1,260), dry beans (300), maize (160), sorghum (220), groundnuts (80) and peas (32). Other cash crops are cotton (7) and tea (3).

Cattle play an important traditional role, and there were about 415,000 head in 1986. There were (1986) some 820,000 goats, 370,000 sheep and 80,000 pigs.

Forestry. Production (1983) 3·5m. cu. metres.

Fisheries. There is a small commercial fishing industry on Lake Tanganyika. The catch in 1983 totalled 12,000 tonnes.

INDUSTRY AND TRADE
Industry. Industrial development is rudimentary. In Bujumbura there are plants for the processing of coffee and by-products of cotton, a brewery, cement works, a textile factory, a soap factory, a shoe factory and small metal workshops.

Commerce. The total value of exports in 1984 was 11,828m. Burundi francs, and of imports, 22,383m. Burundi francs. Main exports in 1984 were coffee, 84% and tea,

7%. Main imports, petrol products, food, vehicles and textiles. In 1984, 34% of exports were to the Federal Republic of Germany, while Belgium supplied 15% and France 14% of imports.

Total trade between Burundi and the UK (British Department of Trade returns, in £1,000 sterling):

	1983	1984	1985	1986	1987
Imports to UK	3,485	1,924	3,367	3,074	1,330
Exports and re-exports from UK	3,155	1,710	1,592	2,324	2,867

Tourism. Tourism is developing and there were 66,000 visitors in 1986.

COMMUNICATIONS

Roads. There is a road network of 5,144 km connecting with Rwanda, Zaïre and Tanzania but in 1982 only 310 km were macadamized. In 1984 there were 7,533 cars and 4,364 commercial vehicles.

Aviation. In 1984, 38,141 passengers arrived or departed through Bujumbura International airport, and there are local airports at Gitega, Nyanza-Lac, Kiofi and Nyakagunda.

Shipping. There are lake services from Bujumbura to Kigoma (Tanzania) and Kalémié (Zaïre). The main route for exports and imports is *via* Kigoma, and thence by rail to Dar es Salaam.

Post and Broadcasting. In 1983 there were 38 post offices and 6,033 telephones. In 1985 there were 250 television and 180,000 radio sets.

Cinemas. In 1980 there were 7 cinemas with 2,000 seats.

Newspapers. There was (1984) one daily newspaper *(Le Renouveau)* with a circulation of 20,000.

JUSTICE, RELIGION, EDUCATION AND WELFARE

Justice. There is a Supreme Court, an appeal court and a *tribunal de première instance* at Bujumbura and provincial tribunals in each provincial capital.

Religion. About 60% of the population is Roman Catholic; there is a Roman Catholic archbishop and 3 bishops. About 3% are Pentecostal, 1% Anglican and 1% Moslem, while the balance follow traditional tribal beliefs.

Education. In 1984 the number of children in primary school was 337,329 and 22,061 pupils were receiving secondary education. The university of Bujumbura had (1981) 1,793 students.

Health. In 1979 there were about 130 doctors and 21 hospitals.

DIPLOMATIC REPRESENTATIVES

Of Burundi in Great Britain
Ambassador: Vacant.

Of Great Britain in Burundi
Ambassador: R. L. B. Cormack (resides in Kinshasa).

Of Burundi in the USA (2233 Wisconsin Ave., NW, Washington, D.C., 20007)
Ambassador: Edouard Kadigiri.

Of the USA in Burundi (PO Box 1720, Ave. du Zaïre, Bujumbura)
Ambassador: James Daniel Phillips.

Of Burundi to the United Nations
Ambassador: Jonathas Niyungeko.

Books of Reference
Lemarchand, R., *Rwanda and Burundi.* London, 1970
Weinstein, W., *Historical Dictionary of Burundi.* Metuchen, 1976

CAMBODIA

People's Republic of Kampuchea

Capital: Phnom Penh
Population: 6·23m. (1985)
GNP per capita: No accurate estimate available (1981)

Since April 1975 the situation in Cambodia has been such that it has been impossible to obtain reliable statistical and other information.

HISTORY. The recorded history of Cambodia starts at the beginning of the Christian era with the Kingdom of Fou-Nan, whose territories at one time included parts of Thailand, Malaya, Cochin-China and Laos. The religious, cultural and administrative inspirations of this state came from India. The Kingdom was absorbed at the end of the 6th century by the Khmers, under whose monarchs was built, between the 9th and 13th centuries, the splendid complex of shrines and temples at Angkor. Attacked on either side by the Vietnamese and the Thai from the 15th century on, Cambodia was saved from annihilation by the establishment of a French protectorate in 1863. Thailand eventually recognized the protectorate and renounced all claims to suzerainty in exchange for Cambodia's north-western provinces of Battambang and Siem Reap, which were, however, returned under a Franco-Thai convention of 1907, confirmed in the Franco-Thai treaty of 1937. In 1904 the province of Stung Treng, formerly administered as part of Laos, was attached to Cambodia. For history to 1969 *see* THE STATESMAN'S YEAR-BOOK, 1973–74, p. 1112.

Following a period of increasing economic difficulties and growing indirect involvement in the Vietnamese war Prince Sihanouk was deposed in March 1970 and on 9 Oct. 1970 the Kingdom of Cambodia became the Khmer Republic. From 1970 hostilities extended throughout most of the country involving North and South Vietnamese and US forces as well as Republican and anti-Republican Khmer troops. During 1973 direct American and North Vietnamese participation in the fighting came to an end, leaving a civil war situation which continued during 1974 with large-scale fighting between forces of the Khmer Republic supported by American arms and economic aid and the forces of the United National Cambodian Front including 'Khmer Rouge' communists supported by North Vietnam and China.

After unsuccessful attempts to capture Phnom Penh in 1973 and 1974, the Khmer Rouge ended the 5-year war in April 1975, when the remnants of the republican forces surrendered the city.

From April 1975 the Khmer Rouge instituted a harsh and highly regimented régime. They cut the country off from normal contact with the world and expelled all foreigners. All cities and towns were forcibly evacuated and the population were set to work in the fields.

The régime had difficulties with the Vietnamese from 1975 and this escalated into full-scale fighting in 1977–78. On 7 Jan. 1979, Phnom Penh was captured by the Vietnamese, and the Prime Minister, Pol Pot, fled. In Dec. 1985 the Khmer Rouge still had 30,000 guerrillas fighting the Vietnamese in Kampuchea. Pol Pot formally retired as C.-in-C. of the Khmer Rouge forces on 2 Sept. 1985 but retained an advisory role.

In June 1982 the Khmer Rouge (who claim to have abandoned their Communist ideology and to have disbanded their Communist Party) entered into a coalition with Son Sann's Khmer People's National Liberation Front and Prince Sihanouk's group. This government is recognized by the UN.

President of the Coalition Government: Prince Norodom Sihanouk. *Deputy President:* Khieu Samphan. *Prime Minister:* Son Sann.

AREA AND POPULATION. Cambodia is bounded north by Laos and Thailand, in the west by Thailand, east by Vietnam and south by the Gulf of Thailand. It has an area of about 181,035 sq. km (69,898 sq. miles).

The total population was 5,756,141 (census, 1981) of whom 93% were Khmer, 4% Vietnamese and 3% Chinese. Estimate (1985) 6,232,000.

The capital, Phnom Penh is located at the junction of the Mekong and Tonle Sap rivers. Populations of major towns have fluctuated greatly since 1970 by flows of refugees from rural areas and from one town to another. Phnom Penh formerly had a population of at least 2·5m. but a 1983 estimate puts it at 500,000. Other cities are Kompong Cham and Battambang. Khmer is the official language.

CLIMATE. A tropical climate, with high temperatures all the year. Phnom Penh. Jan. 78°F (25·6°C), July 84°F (28·9°C). Annual rainfall 52″ (1,308 mm).

CONSTITUTION AND GOVERNMENT. Following the ousting of the Khmer Rouge régime, the Vietnamese-backed Kampuchean National United Front for National Salvation (KNUFNS) on 8 Jan. 1979 proclaimed a People's Republic and established a People's Revolutionary Council to administer the country. A 117-member National Assembly was elected on 1 May 1981 for a 5-year term; in June 1981 it ratified a new Constitution under which it appointed a 7-member Council of State and a 16-member Council of Ministers, replacing the Revolutionary Council.

President of the Council of State: Heng Samrin.
Prime Minister: Hun Sen.

National flag: Red with a five-towered silhouette of the temple of Angkor Wat in the centre in yellow.

DEFENCE. Since the end of the war in April 1975 there has been no accurate data on defence and the three sections below should be treated with great reserve. There is conscription into the armed forces.

Army. Strength (1987) 35,000 including 5 infantry divisions and some 50 supporting units. Equipment reported includes 60 T-54/-55 and 10 PT-76 tanks. There are also paramilitary police and militia units.

Navy. The Marine Royale Khmer was established on 1 March 1954 and became Marine Nationale Khmer on 9 Oct. 1970. It recently included 2 fast anti-submarine hydrofoil craft, 1 *ex*-Soviet fast attack craft, 9 coastal patrol craft, 29 river patrol boats, 3 surveying craft, 1 tug, 2 floating docks and 2 landing craft. About a third of this force is operational and the remainder of questionable fighting value. Two patrol vessels and 2 support (landing) gunboats escaped from Khmer Rouge, and 2 torpedo boats were believed to have sunk. Units since stricken include 7 amphibious vessels, 8 coastal patrol craft and 60 river patrol boats and service craft.

Naval personnel provided for in 1988 did not exceed 7,000. In addition there was the Marine Corps numbering some 4,000.

Air Force. Since the Vietnamese invasion in 1978 there has been no established air force.

ECONOMY

Currency. In 1978 money was officially abolished and no wages or salaries were paid, but in 1980 the use of money was restored. The currency is the *riel*, divided into 100 *sen*.

Banking. In 1964 all bank functions were taken over by government banks. In 1972 legislation permitted the re-opening of foreign banks but by the end of Dec. 1973 only a few representational offices had opened. In 1979 there was no longer anything that could be called a normal banking system.

ENERGY AND NATURAL RESOURCES

Electricity. Production (1986) 142m. kwh. Supply 120 and 220 volts; 50 Hz.

Minerals. A phosphate factory, jointly controlled by the State and private interests, was set up in 1966 near a deposit of an estimated 350,000 tons. Another deposit of about the same size is earmarked for exploitation. High-grade iron-ore deposits (possibly as much as 2·5m. tons) exist in Northern Cambodia, but are not exploited commercially because of transportation difficulties. Some small-scale gold panning (6,687 troy oz. in 1963) and gem (mainly zircon) mining is carried out at Pailin where there is potential for considerable expansion.

Agriculture. The overwhelming majority of the population is normally engaged in agriculture, fishing and forestry. Of the country's total area of 44m. acres, about 20m. are cultivable and over 20m. are forest land. In 1980, 1·5m. hectares were cultivated. Before the spread of war the high productivity provided for a low, but well-fed standard of living for the peasant farmers, the majority of whom owned the land they worked. A relatively small proportion of the food production entered the cash economy. The war and unwise pricing policies have led to a disastrous reduction in production to a stage in which the country had become a net importer of rice.

A crop of about 2m. tonnes of paddy was produced in 1986. Rubber production in 1985 amounted to 16,000 tonnes. Production of other crops (1986 in tonnes): Maize, 92,000; dry beans, 37,000; soybeans, 2,000.

Livestock (1986) FAO estimate: Cattle, 1,571,000; buffaloes, 705,000; sheep, 1,000; pigs, 1,299,000; horses, 12,000; poultry, 9m.

Forestry. Much of Cambodia's surface is covered by potentially valuable forests, 3·8m. hectares of which are reserved by the Government to be awarded to concessionaires, and are not at present worked to an appreciable extent. The remainder is available for exploitation by the local residents, and as a result some areas are over-exploited and conservation is not practised. There are substantial reserves of pitch pine. Roundwood production (1982) 5·1m. cu. metres.

Fisheries. Cambodia has the greatest freshwater fish resources in South-East Asia. Production in 1982 84,700 tonnes.

INDUSTRY AND TRADE

Industry. Some development of industry had taken place before the spread of open warfare in 1970. Industry established and in operation in Jan. 1970 included a motor-vehicle assembly plant, 3 cigarette manufacturing concerns, a modern factory, several metal fabricating concerns, a distillery, a saw-mill, textile, fish canning, plywood, paper, cement, sugar sack, tyre, pottery and glassware factories and a cotton-ginnery. In the private sector there are about 3,200 manufacturing enterprises, producing a wide range of goods; most of them are small family concerns. An oil refinery at Kompong Som came into production in 1969 but was put out of action by an attack in early 1971. Since April 1975 a programme for repairing factories has been started and some 70 are back in production.

Commerce. Principal imports by order of value (1972) were petroleum products, metals and machinery (including vehicles), general foodstuffs and chemicals.

The only recorded export in 1972 was 7,328 tonnes of rubber. Much of the country's trade is with Hong Kong and Singapore.

Total trade between Cambodia and UK (British Department of Trade returns, in £1,000 sterling):

	1983	1984	1985	1986	1987
Imports to UK	184	72	77	58	268
Exports and re-exports from UK	826	635	467	217	435

COMMUNICATIONS

Roads. There were, in 1981, 2,670 km of asphalt roads (including the 'Khmer-American Friendship Highway' from outside Phnom Penh to close to Kompong

Som, built under the US aid programme and opened in July 1959), and 10,680 km of unsurfaced roads.

Railways. A line of 385 km (metre gauge) links Phnom Penh to Poipet (Thai frontier). In 1969 traffic amounted to 170m. passenger-km and 76m. ton-km. Work was completed during 1969 on a line Phnom Penh-Kompong Som *via* Takeo and Kampot. Total length, 649 km but by 1973 only a short stretch between Battambang and the Thai border remained in operation, the remainder having been closed by military action. Irregular passenger and freight trains were running over all the network in 1988.

Aviation. The Pochentong airport is 10 km from Phnom Penh. Air Kampuchea has 2 small aircraft.

Shipping. The port of Phnom Penh can be reached by the Mekong (through Vietnam) by ships of between 3,000 and 4,000 tons. In 1970, 97 ocean-going vessels imported 51,300 tons of cargo at Phnom Penh and exported 86,400 tons.

A new ocean port has been built under the French aid programme at Kompong Som (formerly Sihanoukville) on the Gulf of Siam and is being increasingly used by long-distance shipping.

Post. There were 58 post offices functioning in 1968. There are telephone exchanges in all the main towns; number of telephones in 1981, 7,315. There is an International Telex network in Phnom Penh and direct telephone and telegraphic links with Singapore.

RELIGION AND EDUCATION

Religion. In 1980 the majority of the population practised Theravada Buddhism. The Constitution of 1976 ended Buddhism as the State religion. There are small Roman Catholic and Moslem minorities.

Education. The primary education system has now substantially recovered from the disruptions of the 1970's. In 1982 there were 1,430,000 primary school and 40,000 secondary school pupils.

DIPLOMATIC REPRESENTATIVES

UK and USA Embassies have been closed as have Cambodian Embassies in London and Washington.

Of Democratic Kampuchea to the United Nations
Ambassador: Thiounn Prasith.

Books of Reference

Barron, J., and Paul, A., *Murder of a Gentle Land.* New York, 1977.—*Peace with Horror.* London, 1977
Debré, F., *La Révolution de la Forêt.* Paris, 1976
Etcheson, C., *The Rise and Demise of Democratic Kampuchea.* London, 1984
Kiljunen, K., (ed.) *Kampuchea: Decade of the Genocide.* London, 1984
McDonald, M., *Angkor.* London, 1958
Ponchaud, F., *Cambodia, Year Zero.* London, 1978
Vickery, M., *Cambodia: 1975–1982.* London, 1984

CAMEROON

Capital: Yaoundé
Population: 9·88m. (1986)
GNP per capita: US$800 (1983)

République du Cameroun

HISTORY. The former German colony of Kamerun was occupied by French and British troops in 1916. The greater portion of the territory (422,673 sq. km) was in 1919 placed under French administration, excluding the territory ceded to Germany in 1911, which reverted to French Equatorial Africa. The portion under French trusteeship was granted full internal autonomy on 1 Jan. 1959 and complete independence was proclaimed on 1 Jan. 1960.

The portion assigned to British trusteeship consisted of 2 parts where separate plebiscites were held in Feb. 1961. The northern part decided in favour of joining Nigeria, while the southern part decided to join the Cameroon Republic. This was implemented on 1 Oct. 1961 with the formation of a Federal Republic of Cameroon. As a result of a national referendum, Cameroon became a unitary republic on 2 June 1972. In Jan. 1984 the country was renamed the Republic of Cameroon.

AREA AND POPULATION. Cameroon is bounded west by the Gulf of Guinea, north-west by Nigeria and east by Chad, with Lake Chad at its northern tip, and the Central African Republic, and south by Congo, Gabon and Equatorial Guinea. The total area is 465,054 sq. km (179,558 sq. miles). Population (1976 census) 7,663,246 (28·5% urban). Estimate (1986) 9·88m.

The areas, populations and chief towns of the 10 provinces were:

Province	Sq. km	Census 1976	Chief town	Estimate 1981
Adamaoua	63,691	359,227	Ngaoundéré	47,508
Centre	68,926	1,176,206	Yaoundé	435,892
Est	109,011	366,235	Bertoua	18,254
Extrême-Nord	34,246	1,394,958	Maroua	81,861
Littoral	20,239	935,166	Douala	636,980
Nord (Bénoué)	65,576	479,072	Garoua	77,856
Nord-Ouest	17,810	980,531	Bamenda	58,697
Ouest	13,872	1,035,597	Bafoussam	75,832
Sud	47,110	315,739	Ebolowa	22,222
Sud-Ouest	24,471	620,515	Buéa	29,953

Other large towns (1981): Nkongsamba (86,870), Kumba (53,823), Foumban (41,358), Limbe (32,917), Edéa (31,016), Mbalmayo (26,934) and Dschang (21,705).

The population is composed of Sudanic-speaking people in the north (Fulani, Sao and others) and Bantu-speaking groups, mainly Bamileke, Beti, Bulu, Tikar, Bassa, Duala, in the rest of the country. The official languages are French and English.

CLIMATE. An equatorial climate, with high temperatures and plentiful rain, especially from March to June and Sept. to Nov. Further inland, rain occurs at all seasons. Yaoundé. Jan. 76°F (24·4°C), July 73°F (22·8°C). Annual rainfall 62″ (1,555 mm). Douala. Jan. 79°F (26·1°C), July 75°F (23·9°C). Annual rainfall 160″ (4,026 mm).

CONSTITUTION AND GOVERNMENT. The 1972 Constitution, subsequently amended, provides for a President as head of state and government and commander of the armed forces. He is directly elected for a 5-year term, and there is a Council of Ministers whose members must not be members of parliament.

The National Assembly, elected by universal adult suffrage for 5 years, consists of 120 representatives. Elections took place in May 1983. Since 1966 the sole legal party has been the *Union Nationale Camerounaise.* In March 1985 the UNC was renamed the *Rassemblement Démocratique du Peuple Camerounais* (RDPC) and is administered by a 65-member Central Committee and a 12-member Political Bureau.

The Council of Ministers in Dec. 1987 comprised:

President: Paul Biya (assumed office 6 Nov. 1982).

Town Planning and Housing: Ferdinand Léopold Oyono. *Territorial Administration:* Jérôme Emilien Abondo. *National Education:* Georges Ngango. *Higher Education and Scientific Research:* Abdoulaye Babale. *Finance:* Sadou Hayatou. *Information and Culture:* Ibrahim Mbombo Njoya. *Youth and Sports:* Dr Joseph Fofe. *Labour and Social Welfare:* Adolphe Moudiki. *Foreign Affairs:* Philippe Mataga. *Justice, Keeper of the Seals:* Benjamin Itoe. *Plan and Territorial Development:* René Ze Nguele. *Livestock, Fisheries and Animal Husbandry:* Dr Hamadjoda Adjoudji. *Social Affairs:* Rose Zang Nguele. *Posts and Telecommunications:* Léonard-Claude Mpouma. *Transport:* Jean-Bosco Cheuoua. *Equipment:* Herman Maimo. *Agriculture:* Jean-Baptiste Yonke. *Women's Affairs:* Aissatou Yaou. *Trade and Industry:* Tsanga Abanda. *Public Health:* Victor Anomah Ngu. *Mines and Power:* Michael Tabong Kima. *Public Service:* André Bo'oto à Ngon. *Ministers at the Presidency:* Joseph-Charles Doumba, Titus Edzoa. *Ministers-Delegate at the Presidency:* Michel Meva'a M'Eboutou *(Defence),* Francis Nkwain *(Relations with Parliament and ECOSOC),* Paul Kamga Njike *(Contracts and Computer Services),* Mohamadou Labarang *(General State Inspection and Administrative Reforms),* Emmanuel Zoa Oloa *(Stabilization Plan). (Minister-Delegate, Foreign Affairs):* Mahamat Paba Sale.

There were 11 Secretaries of State.

National flag: Three vertical strips of green, red, yellow, with a gold star in the centre.

National anthem: O Cameroun, berceau de nos ancêtres.

Local Government: The 10 provinces are each administered by a governor appointed by the President. They are sub-divided into 49 *départements* (each under a *préfet*) and then into *arrondissements* (each under a *sous-préfet*).

DEFENCE.

Army. The Army consists of 1 armoured car, 1 para-commando, 1 engineer and 4 infantry battalions and 5 artillery batteries. Equipment includes M-8 armoured and Ferret scout cars. Total strength (1987) 6,600, there are an additional 4,000 paramilitary troops.

Navy. The Navy operates 2 fast missile-armed craft, 2 patrol vessels (all 4 French-built), 2 *ex*-Chinese fast gunboats, 12 coastal patrol launches, 12 inshore cutters, 2 landing craft and 32 auxiliaries and service craft. Personnel in 1988 numbered 350.

Air Force. The Air Force has 3 C-130H Hercules turboprop transports, 4 Buffalo and 1 Caribou STOL transports, 3 C-47s for transport and communications duties, 3 Broussard liaison aircraft, 6 Magister armed jet basic trainers, 5 Alpha Jet close support/trainers, and 5 Alouette helicopters. Some of 4 Gazelle light helicopters are armed with anti-tank missiles. A small VIP transport fleet, maintained in civil markings, comprises 1 Boeing 727 jet aircraft, 1 Gulfstream III and 3 Aerospatiale helicopters. Radar-equipped Dornier 128-6 twin-turboprop aircraft were delivered in 1982 for offshore oilfield patrol. Personnel total (1988) 350.

INTERNATIONAL RELATIONS

Membership. Cameroon is a member of UN, OAU, the Non-Aligned Movement and is an ACP state of EEC.

ECONOMY

Planning. The Sixth 5-year Development Plan (from 1 July 1986 to 30 June 1991) gives priority to rural development and food self-sufficiency.

Budget. The budget for 1986–87 balanced at 800,000m. francs CFA.

Currency. The unit of currency is the *franc CFA*, with a parity rate of 50 *francs CFA* to 1 French *franc*. In March 1988, £1 = 507 *francs CFA*; US$1 = 285·66 *francs CFA*.

Banking. The Banque des Etats de l'Afrique Centrale is the sole bank of issue. The main banks are Banque Internationale pour l'Afrique Occidentale, Société Camerounaise de Banque, Société Générale de Banques au Cameroun, Banque International pour le Commerce et l'Industrie du Cameroun, Cameroon Bank, Banque Camerounaise de Développement, Bank of Credit and Commerce Cameroon, Paribas Cameroun, Boston Bank Cameroon, Chase Bank Cameroon and Bank of America Cameroon. Most of the banks operate in all the large cities and towns throughout the Republic.

ENERGY AND NATURAL RESOURCES

Electricity. There are 3 hydro-electric power stations at Edéa on the Sanaga river with a capacity of 180,000 kw. Total production (1986) 4,200m. kwh. Supply 127 and 220 volts; 50 Hz.

Oil. Production (estimate, 1985) mainly from Kole oilfield was 9·2m. tonnes.

Minerals. There are considerable deposits of bauxite and kyanite around Ngaoundéré. Further deposits of bauxite and cassiterite remain to be exploited in the Adamawa plateau.

Agriculture. At the 1976 Census, 80% of the working population were engaged in agriculture. The main food crops (with 1986 production in 1,000 tonnes): Cassava, 690; millet, 400; maize, 350; plantains, 986; yams, 400; groundnuts, 140; bananas, 67. Cash crops include palm oil, 85; palm kernels, 52·3; cocoa, 120; coffee, 122; rubber, 19; cotton, 38; raw sugar, 76.
Livestock (1986): 4,361,000 cattle, 2·5m. sheep, 2·6m. goats, 1·8m. pigs.

Forestry. Over 50% of Cameroon consists of forests, ranging from tropical rain forests in the south (producing hardwoods such as mahogany, ebony and sapele) to semi-deciduous forests in the centre and wooded savannah in the north. Production in 1983 amounted to 9·9m. cu. metres.

Fisheries. In 1984–85 the industrial output of fish was 10,790 tonnes of which shrimp, 686 tonnes.

INDUSTRY AND TRADE

Industry. There is a major aluminium smelting complex at Edéa; aluminium production in 1983 amounted to 77,600 tonnes. Production of cement totalled 227,000 tonnes in 1980. There are also factories producing shoes, beer, soap, oil and food products, cigarettes. Agro-industrial production (1984–85, in tonnes): Rubber, 17,679; palm-oil, 76,954; sugar, 73,717; oil palm, 14,849; tea, 2,279.

Labour. In 1982 the work-force numbered 3,543,000 of whom 73% were occupied in agriculture. The principal trade union federation is the *Organisation des syndicats des travailleurs camerounais* (OSTC) established on 7 Dec. 1985 to replace the former body, the UNTC.

Commerce. Imports and exports in 1m. francs CFA were as follows:

	1982–83	1983–84	1984–85
Imports	429,466	462,891	482,297
Exports	407,203	484,144	495,977

In 1984–85, exports (in 1m. francs CFA) went mainly to the Netherlands (136,057), France (127,966), Italy (58,333), Federal Republic of Germany (35,089), USA (30,098) and Spain (25,517), while imports were mainly from France (193,176), USA (51,687), Japan (36,354), Federal Republic of Germany (31,220) and Italy (26,610); the main exports were crude oils (123,398), coffee and by-products (111,201) and cocoa and by-products (105,858).

Total trade between Cameroon and UK (British Department of Trade returns, in £1,000 sterling):

	1983	1984	1985	1986	1987
Imports to UK	52,481	132,539	73,746	7,634	14,201
Exports and re-exports from UK	26,445	23,254	44,806	34,368	28,057

Tourism. There were an estimated 140,000 foreign visitors in 1986.

COMMUNICATIONS

Roads. In 1986 there were 66,910 km of roads, of which 2,922 km were tarmac. In 1984–85 there were 73,963 passenger cars and 43,165 commercial vehicles.

Railways. Cameroon Railways, *Regifercam* (1,115 km in 1985) link Douala with Nkongsamba and Ngaoundéré, with branches M'Banga–Kumba and Makak–M'Balmayo. In 1984–85 railways carried 2,481,000 passengers and 1,982,000 tonnes of freight.

Aviation. Douala is the main international airport; other airports are at Yaoundé and Garoua. Cameroon Airlines serve 7 domestic airports. In 1981–82, 644,000 passengers and 14,600 tonnes of freight passed through the airports.

Shipping. The merchant-marine consisted (1986) of 48 vessels (over 100 GRT) of 76,433 GRT. The major port of Douala handled (1984) 3m. tonnes of imports and 1m. tonnes of exports and in 1984–85, 671 cargo ships and 2,582 other ships entered the port. Timber is exported mainly through the south-west ports of Kribi and Campo. Other ports are Bota, Tiko, Limbe and Garoua.

Post and Broadcasting. There were (1975) 150 post offices supplemented by a mobile postal service; telephones (1984), 47,200; radio stations, 10 with 785,000 receivers. Television was introduced in 1985.

Cinemas. There were (1979) 52 cinemas with a capacity of 29,000 seats.

Newspapers. There was (1984) 1 daily newspaper with a circulation of 20,000.

JUSTICE, RELIGION, EDUCATION AND WELFARE

Justice. The Supreme Court sits at Yaoundé, as does the High Court of Justice (consisting of 9 titular judges and 6 surrogates all appointed by the National Assembly). There are magistrates' courts situated in the provinces.

Religion. In 1980, 21% of the population was Roman Catholic, 22% Moslem, 18% Protestant, while 39% followed traditional (animist) religions.

Education (1984–85). There were 1,638,569 pupils and 32,082 teachers in primary schools, 238,075 pupils and 8,381 teachers in general secondary schools, 77,551 pupils and 3,239 teachers in technical secondary schools, and 3,880 students in vocational training schools. In 1984–85 there were 13,753 students and 572 teaching staff at higher education institutions of the University of Yaoundé.

Health. In 1981 there were 1,003 hospitals and health centres with 24,541 beds; there were also (1982) 604 doctors and 17 dentists, 96 pharmacists, 399 midwives and 1,086 nursing personnel.

DIPLOMATIC REPRESENTATIVES

Of Cameroon in Great Britain (84 Holland Pk., London, W11 3SB)
Ambassador: Dr Gibering Bol-Alima (accredited 12 May 1987).

Of Great Britain in Cameroon (Ave. Winston Churchill, BP 547, Yaoundé)
Ambassador: Martin Reith.

Of Cameroon in the USA (2349 Massachusetts Ave., NW, Washington, D.C., 20008)
Ambassador: Vincent Paul-Thomas Pondi.

Of the USA in Cameroon (Rue Nachtigal, BP 817, Yaoundé)
Ambassador: Mark L. Edelman.

Of Cameroon to the United Nations
Ambassador: Paul Bamela Engo.

Books of Reference

Statistical Information: The Service de la Statistique Générale, at Douala, set up in 1945, publishes a monthly bulletin (from Nov. 1950)

DeLancey, M. W., and Schraeder, P. J., *Cameroon.* [Bibliography] Oxford and Santa Barbara, 1986
Ndongko, W. A., *Planning for Economic Development in a Federal State: The Case of Cameroon, 1960–71.* New York, 1975
Rubin, N., *Cameroon.* New York, 1972

CANADA

Capital: Ottawa
Population: 25·4m. (1986)
GNP per capita: US$12,940 (1984)

HISTORY. The territories which now constitute Canada came under British power at various times by settlement, conquest or cession. Nova Scotia was occupied in 1628 by settlement at Port Royal, was ceded back to France in 1632 and was finally ceded by France in 1713, by the Treaty of Utrecht; the Hudson's Bay Company's charter, conferring rights over all the territory draining into Hudson Bay, was granted in 1670; Canada, with all its dependencies, including New Brunswick and Prince Edward Island, was formally ceded to Great Britain by France in 1763; Vancouver Island was acknowledged to be British by the Oregon Boundary Treaty of 1846, and British Columbia was established as a separate colony in 1858. As originally constituted, Canada was composed of Upper and Lower Canada (now Ontario and Quebec), Nova Scotia and New Brunswick. They were united under an Act of the Imperial Parliament, 'The British North America Act, 1867', which came into operation on 1 July 1867 by royal proclamation. The Act provided that the constitution of Canada should be 'similar in principle to that of the United Kingdom'; that the executive authority shall be vested in the Sovereign, and carried on in his name by a Governor-General and Privy Council; and that the legislative power shall be exercised by a Parliament of two Houses, called the 'Senate' and the 'House of Commons'.

On 30 June 1931 the British House of Commons approved the enactment of the Statute of Westminster freeing the Provinces as well as the Dominion from the operation of the Colonial Laws Validity Act, and thus removing what legal limitations existed as regards Canada's legislative autonomy. A joint address of the Senate and the House of Commons was sent to the Governor-General for transmission to London on 10 July 1931. The statute received the royal assent on 12 Dec. 1931.

Provision was made in the British North America Act for the admission of British Columbia, Prince Edward Island, Newfoundland, Rupert's Land and Northwest Territory into the Union. In 1869 Rupert's Land, or the Northwest Territories, was purchased from the Hudson's Bay Company. On 15 July 1870, Rupert's Land and the Northwest Territory were annexed to Canada and named the Northwest Territories, Canada having agreed to pay the Hudson's Bay Company in cash and land for its relinquishing of claims to the territory. By the same action the Province of Manitoba was created from a small portion of this territory and they were admitted into the Confederation on 15 July 1870. On 20 July 1871 the province of British Columbia was admitted, and Prince Edward Island on 1 July 1873. The provinces of Alberta and Saskatchewan were formed from the provisional districts of Alberta, Athabaska, Assiniboia and Saskatchewan and originally parts of the Northwest Territories and admitted on 1 Sept. 1905. Newfoundland formally joined Canada as its tenth province on 31 March 1949.

In Feb. 1931 Norway formally recognized the Canadian title to the Sverdrup group of Arctic islands. Canada thus holds sovereignty in the whole Arctic sector north of the Canadian mainland.

In Nov. 1981 the Canadian government agreed on the provisions of an amended constitution, to the end that it should replace the British North America Act and that its future amendment should be the prerogative of Canada. These proposals were adopted by the Parliament of Canada and were enacted by the UK Parliament as the Canada Act of 1982.

The enactment of the Canada Act was the final act of the UK Parliament in Canadian constitutional development. The Act gave to Canada the power to amend the Constitution according to procedures determined by the Constitutional Act 1982, which was proclaimed in force by the Queen on 17 April 1982. The Constitution Act 1982 added to the Canadian Constitution a charter of Rights and Freedoms, and provisions which recognize the nation's multi-cultural heritage, affirm the existing rights of native peoples, confirm the principle of equalization of benefits among the provinces, and strengthen provincial ownership of natural resources.

AREA AND POPULATION. Canada is bounded north-west by the Beaufort Sea, north by the Arctic Ocean, north-east by Baffin Bay, east by the Davis Strait, Labrador Sea and Atlantic Ocean, south by the USA and west by the Pacific Ocean and USA (Alaska). Population of the area now included in Canada:

1851	2,436,297	1901	5,371,315	1951 [1]	14,009,429
1861	3,229,633	1911	7,206,643	1961	18,238,247
1871	3,689,257	1921	8,787,949	1971	21,568,311
1881	4,324,810	1931	10,376,786	1981	24,343,181
1891	4,833,239	1941	11,506,655		

[1] From 1951 figures include Newfoundland.

Population (census), 3 June 1986, was 25,354,054.

Areas of the provinces, etc. (in sq. km) and population at recent censuses:

Province	Land area	Fresh water area	Total land and fresh water area	Population, 1976	Population, 1981	Population, 1986 [1]
Newfoundland	371,634	34,030	405,664	557,725	567,681	568,349
Prince Edward Island	5,660	—	5,660	118,229	122,506	126,646
Nova Scotia	52,840	2,650	55,490	828,571	847,442	873,199
New Brunswick	71,569	1,350	72,919	677,250	696,403	709,442
Quebec	1,357,811	183,890	1,541,701	6,234,445	6,438,403	6,532,461
Ontario	916,733	177,390	1,094,123	8,264,465	8,625,107	9,101,694
Manitoba	547,703	101,590	649,293	1,021,506	1,026,241	1,063,016
Saskatchewan	570,113	81,630	651,743	921,323	968,313	1,009,613
Alberta	638,232	16,800	655,032	1,838,037	2,237,724	2,365,825
British Columbia	892,677	18,070	910,747	2,466,608	2,744,467	2,883,367
Yukon	531,843	4,480	536,323	21,836	22,135	23,504
Northwest Territories	3,246,389	133,300	3,379,689	42,609	45,471	52,238
Total	9,203,204	755,180	9,958,384	22,992,604	24,343,181	25,354,064

[1] Excluding incompletely enumerated Indian reserves and Indian settlements.

Of the total population in 1981, 20,216,340 were Canadian born, 3,867,160 foreign born, 312,015 of the latter being USA born and 2,586,080 European born.

The population (1981) born outside Canada in the provinces was in the following ratio (%): Newfoundland, 1·7; Prince Edward Island, 3·7; Nova Scotia, 4·9; New Brunswick, 3·9; Quebec, 8·2; Ontario, 23·5; Manitoba, 14·2; Saskatchewan, 8·6; Alberta, 16·3; British Columbia, 23; Yukon, 12·5; Northwest Territories, 6·1.

In 1981, figures for the population, according to origin, were [1]:

Single origins	22,244,885	Polish	254,485
Austrian	40,630	Portuguese	188,105
Belgian and Luxembourg	43,000	Romanian	22,485
British	9,674,245	Russian	48,435
Czech and Slovak	67,695	Scandinavian	282,795
Chinese	289,245	Spanish	53,540
Dutch	408,240	Swiss	29,805
Finnish	52,315	Ukrainian	529,615
French	6,439,100	Other single origins:	1,204,685
German	1,142,365		
Greek	154,365	*Multiple origins:*	1,838,615
Magyar (Hungarian)	116,390	British and French	430,255
Italian	747,970	British and Other	859,800
Japanese	40,995	French and Other	124,940
Native Peoples	413,380	Others	423,620

[1] The 1981 Census was the first to accept more than one ethnic origin for an individual. Therefore, this table includes counts of single and multiple origins.

The total status, non-status population numbered 367,810 in 1981 and the Inuit population was 25,390 in 1981.

Populations of Census Metropolitan Areas (CMA) and Cities (proper), 1986 census:

	CMA	City proper		CMA	City proper
Toronto	3,427,168	612,289	Winnipeg	623,304	594,551
Montreal	2,921,357	1,015,420	Quebec	603,267	164,580
Vancouver	1,380,729	431,147	Hamilton	557,029	306,728
Ottawa-Hull	819,263	300,763 [1]	St Catharines-		
Edmonton	785,465	573,982	Niagara	343,258	—
Calgary	671,326	636,104	St Catharines	—	123,455

[1] Ottawa

	CMA	City proper		CMA	City proper
Niagara Falls	—	72,107	Chicoutimi-		
London	342,302	269,140	Jonquière	158,468	—
Kitchener	311,195	150,604	Chicoutimi	—	61,083
Halifax	295,990	113,577	Jonquière	—	58,467
Victoria	255,547	66,303	Sudbury	148,877	88,717
Windsor	253,988	193,111	Sherbrooke	129,960	74,438
Oshawa	203,543	123,651	Trois Rivières	128,888	50,122
Saskatoon	200,665	177,641	Thunder Bay	122,217	112,272
Regina	186,521	175,064	Saint John	121,265	76,381
St John's	161,901	96,216			

The total 'urban' population of Canada in 1981 was 18,435,927, against 17,366,970 in 1976.

While the registration of births, marriages and deaths is under provincial control, the statistics are compiled on a uniform system by Statistics Canada.

The following table gives the results for the year 1986:

Province	Living births Number	Marriages Number	Deaths Number
Newfoundland	8,320	3,280	3,810
Prince Edward Island	1,960	990	1,180
Nova Scotia	12,450	6,960	7,590
New Brunswick	10,190	5,500	5,380
Quebec	86,750	37,870	46,710
Ontario	134,130	75,550	67,940
Manitoba	16,850	8,440	9,090
Saskatchewan	18,100	7,190	8,340
Alberta	44,010	20,430	13,690
British Columbia	43,740	24,020	22,380
Yukon Territory	500	180	110
N.W. Territories	1,260	270	190
	378,260	190,680	186,410

Immigrant arrivals by country of last permanent residence:

Country	1984	1985	1986
UK	5,104	4,454	5,088
France	1,380	1,401	1,610
Germany	1,727	1,578	1,403
Netherlands	545	466	524
Greece	555	551	551
Italy	839	650	715
Portugal	855	910	1,970
Other Europe	9,896	8,849	10,848
Asia	41,920	38,597	41,600
Australia	535	506	338
USA	6,922	6,669	7,275
Caribbean	5,630	6,132	8,874
All other	12,331	13,539	18,423
Total	88,239	84,302	99,219

CLIMATE. The climate ranges from polar conditions in the north to cool temperate in the south, but with considerable differences between east coast, west coast and the interior, affecting temperatures, rainfall amounts and seasonal distribution. Winters are very severe over much of the country, but summers can be very hot inland. *See* individual provinces for climatic details.

CONSTITUTION AND GOVERNMENT. The members of the Senate are appointed until age 75 by summons of the Governor-General under the Great Seal of Canada. Members appointed before 2 June 1965 may remain in office for life. The Senate consists of 104 senators, namely, 24 from Ontario, 24 from Quebec, 10 from Nova Scotia, 10 from New Brunswick, 4 from Prince Edward Island, 6 from Manitoba, 6 from British Columbia, 6 from Alberta, 6 from Saskatchewan, 6 from Newfoundland, 1 from the Yukon Territory and 1 from the Northwest Territories.

Each senator must be at least 30 years of age, a born or naturalized subject of the Queen and must reside in the province for which he is appointed and his total net worth must be at least $4,000. The House of Commons is elected by the people, for 5 years, unless sooner dissolved. Women have the vote and are eligible. From 1867 to the election of 1945 representation was based on Quebec having 65 seats and the other provinces the same proportion of 65 which their population had to the population of Quebec. In the General Election of 1949 readjustments were based on the population of all the provinces taken as a whole. Generally speaking, this format for representation has prevailed in all subsequent elections with readjustments made after each decennial census. Under the Representation Act 1985, effective March 1986, the formula contained in section 51 of the Constitution Act, 1867[1] dealing with the number of seats in the House of Commons and their distribution throughout the country, was changed.

[1] The Constitution Act, 1985 (Representation). Redrawing of Electoral boundaries statutes of Canada 1984–86, Chap. 8.

The thirty-second Parliament, elected in Sept. 1984, comprises 282 members and the provincial and territorial representation are: Ontario, 95; Quebec, 75; Nova Scotia, 11; New Brunswick, 10; Manitoba, 14; British Columbia, 28; Prince Edward Island, 4; Saskatchewan 14; Alberta, 21; Newfoundland, 7; Yukon Territory, 1; Northwest Territories, 2.

State of parties in the Senate (Oct. 1987): Liberals, 65; Progressive Conservatives, 31; Independent, 5; Independent Liberal, 1; Vacant, 2; Social Credit, –; total 102.

State of the parties in the House of Commons (Oct. 1987): Progressive Conservatives, 208; Liberals, 40; New Democratic Party, 32; Independent, 2; Vacancies, –; total, 282. Party standings in the House of Commons 33rd Parliament.

The following is a list of Governors-General of Canada:

Viscount Monck	1867–1868	Viscount Willington	1926–1931
Lord Lisgar	1868–1872	Earl of Bessborough	1931–1935
Earl of Dufferin	1872–1878	Lord Tweedsmuir	1935–1940
Marquess of Lorne	1878–1883	Earl of Athlone	1940–1946
Marquess of Lansdowne	1883–1888	Field-Marshal Viscount	
Lord Stanley of Preston	1888–1893	Alexander of Tunis	1946–1952
Earl of Aberdeen	1893–1898	Vincent Massey	1952–1959
Earl of Minto	1898–1904	Georges Philias Vanier	1959–1967
Earl Grey	1904–1911	Roland Michener	1967–1974
HRH the Duke of Connaught	1911–1916	Jules Léger	1974–1979
Duke of Devonshire	1916–1921	Edward Schreyer	1979–1984
Viscount Byng of Vimy	1921–1926		

Governor-General: Jeanne Sauvé.

National flag: Vertically red, white, red with the white of double width and bearing a stylized red maple leaf.

The office and appointment of the Governor-General are regulated by letters patent, signed by the King on 8 Sept. 1947, which came into force on 1 Oct. 1947. In 1977 the Queen approved the transfer to the Governor-General of functions discharged by the Sovereign. He is assisted in his functions, under the provisions of the Act of 1867, by a Privy Council composed of Cabinet Ministers.

The following is the list of the Conservative Cabinet in Feb. 1988, in order of precedence, which in Canada attaches generally rather to the person than to the office:

Prime Minister: The Rt. Hon. Martin Brian Mulroney.

Minister of Veterans Affairs and Minister of State (Senior Citizens): The Hon. George Harris Hees.

Secretary of State for External Affairs: The Rt. Hon. Charles Joseph Clark.

Minister of Communications: The Hon. Flora Isabel MacDonald.

Minister of Transport: The Hon. John Carnell Crosbie.

Deputy Prime Minister, President of the Privy Council and President of the Treasury Board: The Hon. Donald Frank Mazankowski.

Minister of National Revenue: The Hon. Elmer MacIntosh MacKay.

Minister of National Health and Welfare: The Hon. Jake Epp.
Minister of Agriculture: The Hon. John Wise.
Minister of Justice and Attorney-General of Canada: The Hon. Ramon John Hnatyshyn.
Secretary of State of Canada: The Hon. David Edward Crombie.
Minister of Regional Industrial Expansion and Minister of State for Science and Technology: The Hon. Robert R. de Cotret.
Minister of National Defence: The Hon. Henry Perrin Beatty.
Minister of Finance: The Hon. Michael Holcombe Wilson.
Minister of Consumer and Corporate Affairs: The Hon. Harvie Andre.
Minister of State (Fitness and Amateur Sport): The Hon. Otto John Jelinek.
Minister of Fisheries and Oceans: The Hon. Thomas Edward Siddon.
Minister of State (Grains and Oilseeds): The Hon. Charles James Mayer.
Minister of Indian Affairs and Northern Development: The Hon. William Hunter McKnight.
Minister of the Environment: The Hon. Thomas Michael McMillan.
Minister for International Trade: The Hon. Patricia Carney.
Minister of Employment and Immigration: The Hon. Benoit Bouchard.
Minister of Supply and Services: (Vacant).
Solicitor-General of Canada: The Hon. James Francis Kelleher.
Minister of Energy, Mines and Resources: The Hon. Marcel Masse.
Minister of State (Privatization and Regulatory Affairs): The Hon. Barbara Jean McDougall.
Minister of State (Forestry and Mines): The Hon. Gerald S. Merrithew.
Minister of State (Transport): The Hon. Monique Vezina.
Minister of Public Works: The Hon. Stewart McInnes.
Minister of State (Science and Technology): The Hon. Frank Oberle.
Leader of the Government in the Senate and Minister of State (Federal-Provincial Relations): The Hon. Lowell Murray.
Associate Minister of National Defence: The Hon. Paul Wyatt Dick.
Minister of Labour: The Hon. Pierre H. Cadieux.
Minister of State (Youth): The Hon. Jean J. Charest.
Minister of State (Finance): The Hon. Thomas Hockin.
Minister for External Relations: The Hon. Monique Landry.
Minister of State (Small Businesses and Tourism) and Minister of State (Indian Affairs and Northern Development): The Hon. Bernard Valcourt.
Minister of State (Immigration): The Hon. Gerry Weiner.
Minister of State (Treasury Board): The Hon. Douglas Grinsdale Lewis.
Minister of State (Agriculture): The Hon. Pierre Blais.

The salary of a member of the House of Commons (Jan. 1986) is $56,100 with a tax-free allowance of $18,700. The salary of a senator is $56,100 with a tax-free allowance of $9,000. The salary and allowances of the Prime Minister total $129,755. The salary of the Speaker of the House of Commons is $120,600; the salary of the Speaker of the Senate is $96,200; the salary of the Opposition Leader is $119,600 and that of the National Democratic Party Leader, $100,600; all these also have tax-free allowances of from $18,700–$24,700.

On 10 Jan. 1986 Cabinet decided that, for the calendar year 1986, the salaries of the Prime Minister and Ministers, pursuant to the Salaries Act, would be retained at the actual level paid in 1985. This actual level entailed a 15% and 10% reduction for the Prime Minister and Ministers respectively.

Future increases are to be pegged at 1% less than increases in the consumer price index or industrial composite index, whichever is lower.

An Act to provide retiring allowances, on a contributory basis, to members of the House of Commons was given the Royal Assent on 4 July 1952. Subsequent amendments provide allowances for surviving spouses and for former Prime Ministers or their surviving spouses.

Canadian Parliamentary Handbook. Compiled by John Bejermi, Borealis Press, Ottawa, 1986
Canadian Government Programs and Services. CCH Canadian Limited. Loose-leaf. Don Mills, Ontario, 1973

Index to Federal Programs and Services 1986. Seventh edition. Supply and Services Canada.
  Annual, Ottawa
Organisation of the Government of Canada 1980. 13th edition. Irregular, Ottawa
A consolidation of the *The Constitution Acts 1867 to 1982.* Department of Justice Canada.
  Ottawa, 1986
Bureaucracy in Canadian Government: selected readings. 2nd edition, edited by W. D. K.
  Kernashan, Toronto, 1973
Laskins Canadian Constitutional Law. 5th ed., Vol. 2, Neil Finkelstein. Toronto: Carswell,
  1986
Leading Constitutional decisions: Cases on the British North America Act. Edited and with an
  introduction by Peter H. Russell, 3rd edition. Ottawa, 1982

The Canadian Parliamentary Guide. Annual. Ottawa
Report of the Royal Commission on Dominion–Provincial Relations, Canada 1867–1939.
  3 vols. Ottawa, 1940
Byers, R. B. (ed.), *Canada Challenged: The Viability of the Confederation.* Toronto, 1979
Information Canada, *Organization of the Government of Canada.* Loose-leaf service. Ottawa,
  1970
Kennedy, W. F. M., *Statutes, Treaties and Documents of the Canadian Constitution,
  1713–1929.* Toronto, 1930
Kernaghan, N. (ed.), *Bureaucracy in Canadian Government, Selected Readings.* Toronto, 1969
Morton, W. L., *The Kingdom of Canada; A General History From Earliest Times.* Toronto,
  1969
Olmsted, R. A., *Decisions of the Judicial Committee of the Privy Council Relating to the British
  North America Act, 1867, and the Canadian Constitution, 1867–1954.* Ottawa, Queens'
  Printer, 1954
Russell, P. H. (ed.), *Leading Constitutional Decisions; Cases on the British North America Act.*
  Toronto, 1968

DEFENCE. The Department of National Defence was created by the National Defence Act, 1922, which established one civil Department of Government in place of the previous Departments of Militia and Defence, Naval Service and the Air Board. The Department now operates under authority of RSC 1970, c.N1-4. The Minister of National Defence has the control and management of the Canadian Forces and all matters relating to national defence establishments and works for the defence of Canada. He is the Minister responsible for presenting before the Cabinet, matters of major defence policy for which Cabinet direction is required. He is also responsible for the Canada Emergency Measures Organization which was renamed 'Emergency Planning Canada' in 1976.

In Dec. 1976, the Minister of National Defence was named as minister responsible for all aspects of air Search and Rescue in the areas of Canadian SAR responsibility, and for the overall co-ordination of marine search and rescue including provision of air resources for marine SAR within Canadian territorial waters and in designated oceanic areas off the Pacific and Atlantic Coasts in accordance with agreements made with the United States Coast Guard. A group from Transport Canada, the Department of National Defence and the Department of Fisheries and Oceans was set up at the same time, as a co-ordinating body.

From September 1985 the Minister has shared his responsibilities with a newly appointed Associate Minister of National Defence.

The Canadian Forces (CF) are the military element of the Canadian government and are part of the Department of National Defence (DND). Government policy concerning the CF takes into account national and foreign policy. The roles of the CF are developed within this framework. They are:
- the protection of Canada and Canadian national interests at home and abroad; this includes the provision of aid of the civil power and national development;
- the defence of North America in co-operation with the United States' military forces;
- the fulfillment of such North Atlantic Treaty Organization (NATO) commitments to security as may be agreed upon; the performance of such international peacekeeping roles as Canada may from time to time assume.

Command Structure. The missions and roles of the CF are undertaken by functional and regional commands. Commands and major organizations report directly to

National Defence Headquarters (NDHQ) in Ottawa, Ontario from headquarters situated as follows:
- Mobile Command, St Hubert, Quebec;
- Maritime Command, Halifax;
- Air Command, Winnipeg;
- Canadian Forces Training System, Trenton, Ontario; and
- Canadian Forces Communication Command, Ottawa;
- Canadian Forces Europe, Lahr, Federal Republic of Germany (FRG);
- Northern Region, Yellowknife, NWT.

1. *Mobile Command.* With a 1986 combined Regular Force, Militia and civilian staff of 40,248, Mobile Command (FMC) maintained combat ready land forces to meet Canada's defence commitments. During 1986, FMC units were involved in numerous operations, exercises and other activities.

Defence of North America
  Mobile Command is prepared to undertake defence of North America operations in conjunction with the forces of the United States. Under the Canada-United States Basic Defence Agreement, a number of mutual defence treaties exist. One that directly concerns Mobile Command is Canada-United States Land Operations (CANUS LANDOP). It is designed to provide the co-ordination of the land defence of Canada, Alaska, and the continental United States. Under this plan, Mobile Command is responsible for co-ordinating the land defence of Canada by both Canadian and US forces, if required, and must be prepared to assist US forces in the defence of Alaska and the United States. Both this and the National Security task involves Mobile Command in maintaining a presence in the Canadian North through surveillance and patrols and numerous exercises.

Nato Commitments
  Mobile Command (FMC) provides forces in support of several NATO commitments. FMC NATO commitments are to provide:
(a) A Brigade Group to reinforce ACE (Allied Command Europe) Forces in emergency. That brigade is known as the CAST (Canadian Air/Sea Transportable) Brigade and is committed to operations in North Norway with Norwegian division.
(b) An infantry battle group for operations with the Allied Command Europe Mobile Force (Land (AMF)L). The Canadian contingent is designated to deploy either to North Norway or to the Zeeland Group of Islands in Denmark. The contingent maintains a high degree of operational readiness for this purpose and exercises in its operational areas on a regular basis.
  Although the land force units in Europe are not part of FMC, the command provides trained replacements through individual and sub-unit rotations to sustain peacetime manning requirements. The Command is also tasked to provide personnel augmentation to bring 4 Brigades to full establishment in the event of war, and to provide replacements and reinforcements to sustain the Brigade in combat.

International Peacekeeping or Stability Operations
  Mobile Command is committed to providing forces for international peacekeeping or stability operations. It maintains a ready force of battalion group size on short notice to meet urgent international requirements, and provides the majority of Canadian troops assigned to UN duties. At present, our UN involvement includes a unit in Cyprus and a service support element on the Golan Heights, and a small number of personnel to augment the national commitment to the Multi-National Peacekeeping Force (MFO) in the Sinai.

Budget and Personnel
  In 1986, FMC budgeted approximately $256m. for normal operations and maintenance costs. This excluded salaries for the 18,436 Regular Force members and 5,597 full-time civilian personnel which accounted for about $1,350m. of departmental expenditure. FMC also allocated about $77m. for the 16,221 Militia members. Expenditures in support of British, German and US Army units training on FMC bases were recovered from the nations concerned.

2. *Maritime Command.* The Maritime Command (MARCOM) role is to have a maritime force ready to meet Canada's defence commitments. This role is fulfilled using MARCOM resources and designated Air Command aircraft under MARCOM control.

Maritime Command comprises operational maritime forces, headquarters and supporting units located primarily on the east and west coasts of Canada, but also extending as far north as Frobisher Bay and as far south as Bermuda.

Operational forces include 20 destroyers, 6 coastal patrol and training ships, 3 submarines, 3 operational support ships, 1 diving support ship, as well as Air Command aircraft under the operational control of Maritime Command. In addition there are 5 gate vessels, 2 'R' Class patrol vessels and the FORT STEELE located at Reserve Training Units on both coasts, and 16 minor vessels located at naval reserve units across Canada.

Protection of Canada and National Interests

Maritime Command continues to conduct military surveillance of Canadian territorial waters on both coasts. Surveillance patrols in support of Canadian national interests are conducted in the 370 km Economic zone by surface and air units.

Numerous missions are flown in northern latitudes to establish a Canadian presence and ensure that foreign vessels are operating in accordance with national regulations. CP-121 Tracker reconnaissance aircraft conduct flying operations in aid of the Department of Fisheries and Oceans Canada. Ships of Maritime Command spend time at sea on both the east and west coasts locating, identifying and boarding foreign fishing vessels.

Defence of North America

Combat readiness in the Fleet is maintained through many different training exercises. Early each year units deploy to the Caribbean for intensive training and maintenance period, normally followed by a large-scale NATO exercise. A Combat Training Exercise (COMBATEX) is usually scheduled to take place each May and November. This exercise is designed to provide a realistic at-sea examination for members of the Combat control Officer (CC) Course, culminating a year-long course in maritime warfare.

NATO Exercises

Canada is continuously represented in NATO's Standing Naval Force Atlantic (STANAVFORLANT) by a Halifax based destroyer. This multi-national squadron provides a highly visible demonstration of NATO solidarity in the face of an expanding Soviet naval threat. Ports are visited in Alliance nations throughout Europe, the Mediterranean and the east coast of North America, strengthening ties with NATO's member nations. East coast destroyers participate in the NATO Squadron and are involved in a number of exercises on both sides of the Atlantic. In addition to STANAVFORLANT, Maritime Command ships participate in several NATO exercises each year.

Budget and Personnel

MARCOM's budget for fiscal year 1986–87 was $210.5m.

Personnel

Maritime Command		Maritime Air Group (MAG)	
Regular Force	9,616	Regular Force	4,973
Naval Reserves	3,300	Reserves	13
DND Civilian Employees	6,725	DND Civilian Employees	1,354
Total	19,641	Total	6,340

3. *Air Command.* Air Command is the largest of the Canadian Forces (CF) Commands and is headquartered at Canadian Forces Bases (CFB) Winnipeg, Manitoba. Air Command's six functional groups provide combat-ready air forces to meet Canada's defence commitments. It is also responsible for the Prairie Region.

Personnel and Budget

Air Command consists of 22,209 Regular Force members, 945 Air Reserves, and 8,328 civilians for a total of 31,482 people. The operations and maintenance budget for 1986–87 was $424.1m. The budgets for the Air Reserves, the Prairie Region Cadets and Allied Military Training at CFB Goose Bay were $6.2m., $6.3m. and $15.8m. respectively.

Projects and Plans

During 1986, the projects and plans for Air Command included the following: The developments of Canadian Forces Station Goose Bay; the staffing needs for the North American Air Defence Modernization project; and the acquisition of 97 CF-18 aircraft and 2 CC-130 'Hercules Aircraft'.

Air Command is divided into six functional air groups. The Commander, Air Command, whose headquarters is in Winnipeg, Manitoba, delegates operational control to the commanders of the air groups over their assigned resources. The Commander retains responsibility for flight safety, as well as air doctrine and standards relating to flying operations throughout the Canadian Forces, including units located outside Canada. The air groups are:

(a) Fighter Group (Headquarters at North Bay, Ontario) maintains the sovereignty of Canada's airspace, supports Mobile and Maritime Command training and operations, and fulfills Canada's commitments to NATO and NORAD.

(b) Air Transport Group (Headquarters at Trenton, Ontario) provides airlift resources for the Canadian Forces, and is responsible for Search and Rescue (SAR) forces for Canada and surrounding waters.

(c) Maritime Air Group (Headquarters at Halifax, Nova Scotia) is responsible for the management of all air resources engaged in maritime patrol, maritime surveillance and anti-submarine warfare.

(d) 10 Tactical Air Group (Headquarters at St. Hubert, Quebec) provides combat-ready tactical aviation forces for operational employment in support of Mobile Command operations and training, and of other defence commitments.

(e) 14 Training Group (Headquarters at Winnipeg) trains aircrew and other air personnel to initial classification and trade specifications, and provides other training as directed.

(f) Air Reserve Group (Headquarters at Winnipeg) provides support to Air Command by provision of operational units and individual augmentees.

4. *Canadian Forces Training System.* The Canadian Forces Training System headquarters is located at CFB Trenton, Ontario. Its functions include the planning and conduct of all recruit, trades, specialist and other officer classification training common to more than one command.

5. *Canadian Forces Communication Command (CFCC).* In 1986 the Canadian Forces Communication Command (CFCC) provided strategic communications services, as well as communications research and high frequency radio direction-finding services for the CF. To effect these services CFCC operated and maintained several data networks and voice communications systems.

It is implicit in the provision of strategic communications for the CF and emergency government that the organization be capable of extending services to the various military and civil headquarters during a national emergency. As well, it must supply reliable strategic communications from Canada to CF combat elements anywhere in the world. To these ends, Communication Command personnel exercise their equipment and procedures regularly.

Personnel and Budget

The Canadian Forces Communication Command's (CFCC) 5,475 personnel includes a regular force contingent of 3,304 members, a Communications Reserve of 1,560 and a civilian force of all 611 persons.

The 1986 command budget was $1.8m. Expenses included long distance telephone services and Canada's share of costs to ensure global access to our NORAD NATO and Commonwealth partners.

6. *Canadian Forces Europe (CFE).* Throughout 1986 Canadian Forces Europe (CFE) continued to provide combat-ready land and air forces to Supreme Allied Commander Europe in accordance with Canada's NATO commitment. The two formations stationed permanently in Central Europe, 4 Canadian Mechanized Bri-

gade Group (4 CMBG) and 1 Canadian Air Group (1 CAG), completed challenging and realistic training programmes to maintain their operational readiness at the highest possible state. Support for the two formations was provided by Canadian Forces Bases (CFBs) Lahr and Baden-Soellingen.

Personnel and Budget
During 1986 CFE reached the increase manning establishment authorized in Jan. 1985 of 1,220 personnel, bringing the total number of service members assigned to CFE to 7,160.
During the fiscal year 1986–87, CFE was allocated an operations and maintenance budget of $148.5m.

The Reserve Force consists of officers and men who are enrolled for other than continuing full-time military service. The sub-components of the Reserve Force are the Primary Reserve; the Supplementary Reserve; the Cadet Instructors List; and the Canadian Rangers.
The elements of the Primary Reserve are the Naval Reserve; Militia; Air Reserve; and Communication Reserve. Funded personnel levels for these four elements are 3,082; 19,220; 944; and 1,612 respectively.
The Supplementary Reserve consists of officers and men who, except when on active service, are not required to perform duty or training.
The Cadet Instructors List consists of commissioned officers who may be required to undergo annual training and whose primary duty is the supervision, administration and training of cadets.
The Canadian Rangers consists of officers and men who volunteer to hold themselves in readiness for service but are not required to undergo annual training. Their role is to provide a military force in sparsely settled, northern, coastal and isolated areas of Canada.

Regional organization. In order to most effectively respond to support requirements within Canada, a regional structure has been superimposed over the functional organization. This has been accomplished by dividing Canada into six geographic regions and appointing the senior commander in each region as the Region Commander. Thus the following interrelationship of Functional Command/Region/geographical area has resulted: *Maritime Command* – Atlantic Region (Newfoundland, New Brunswick, Nova Scotia and Prince Edward Island); *Mobile Command* – Eastern Region (Quebec); *Canadian Forces Training System* – Central Region (Ontario); *Air Command* – Prairie Region (Manitoba, Saskatchewan, and Alberta); *Maritime Forces Pacific* – Pacific Region (British Columbia); and *Northern Region Headquarters* – Northern Region (Yukon and Northwest Territories). Functional responsibilities include representation to provincial governments, aid of the Civil Power, emergency and survival operations, and administration of cadets, as well as regional support services for all units in the region.

7. *Northern Region Headquarters.* Situated in Yellowknife, NWT, the Northern Region Headquarters (HRHQ) was formed on 15 May 1970 to assist in maintaining Canadian sovereignty and support ongoing Canadian Forces activities in the North.

Personnel and Budget
NRHQ strength, including detachment personnel, was about 80 Regular Force and civilian personnel located in Yellowknife and Whitehorse.
Seventy-five percent of the region's $2m. annual budget was used to support the Ranger and Cadet programme including National Cadet Camp Whitehorse. The remaining 25% was used for operations and maintenance.

Training
Increasing emphasis on the North during 1986 was felt by NRHQ as more land and air units carried out air defence, tactical airlift and adventure training exercises. These exercises included French army and Royal Air Force units as well as elements of the CF.

The Estimated net Program Expenditures for the Department of National Defence for 1986–1987 is $9,955,000,000.

The strength of the Regular Forces for 1986 was 86,036.

Royal Canadian Mounted Police. The Royal Canadian Mounted Police is a civil force maintained by the federal government. It was established in 1873, as the North-West Mounted Police for service in what was then the North-West Territories and, in recognition of its services, was granted the use of the prefix 'Royal' by King Edward VII in 1904. Its sphere of operations was expanded in 1918 to include all of Canada west of Thunder Bay. In 1920 the force absorbed the Dominion Police, and its headquarters was transferred from Regina to Ottawa, and its title was changed to Royal Canadian Mounted Police. The force is responsible to the Solicitor-General of Canada and is controlled and managed by a Commissioner who holds the rank and status of a Deputy Minister. The Commissioner is empowered under the Royal Canadian Mounted Police Act to appoint members to be peace officers in all provinces and territories of Canada.

The responsibilities of the Royal Canadian Mounted Police are national in scope. The administration of justice within the provinces, including the enforcement of the Criminal Code of Canada, is part of the power and duty delegated to the provincial governments.

All provinces except Ontario and Quebec have entered into contracts with the Royal Canadian Mounted Police to enforce criminal and provincial laws under the direction of the respective Attorneys-General. In addition, in these 8 provinces the Force is under agreement to provide police services to 187 municipalities, thereby assuming the enforcement responsibility of municipal as well as criminal and provincial laws within these communities. The Royal Canadian Mounted Police is also responsible for all police work in the Yukon and Northwest territories enforcing federal law and territorial ordinances. The 16 Operational Divisions, alphabetically designated, make up the strength of the Force across Canada; they comprise 47 sub-divisions which include 718 detachments. Headquarters Division, as well as the Office of the Commissioner, is located in Ottawa. The Force maintains liaison officers in 18 countries and represents Canada in the International Criminal Police Organization which has its headquarters in Paris.

Thorough training is emphasized for members of the Force. Recruits receive 6 months of basic training at the Royal Canadian Mounted Police Academy in Regina. This is followed by a further 6 months of supervised on-the-job training. The RCMP also operates the Canadian Police College at which its members and selected representatives of other Canadian and foreign police forces may study the latest advances in the fields of crime prevention and detection.

Many of these advances have been incorporated into the operation of the Force. A teletype system links the widespread divisional headquarters with the administrative centre at Ottawa and a network of fixed and mobile radio units operates within the provinces. The focal point of the criminal investigation work of the Force is the Directorate of Laboratories and Identification; its services, together with those of divisional and sub-divisional units, and of 8 Crime Detection Laboratories, are available to police forces throughout Canada. The Canadian Police Information Centre at RCMP Headquarters, a duplexed computer system, is staffed and operated by the Force. Law Enforcement agencies throughout Canada have access *via* a series of remote terminals of information on stolen vehicles, licences and wanted persons.

In Oct. 1986, the Force had a total strength of 19,365 including regular members, special constables, civilian members and Public Service employees. It maintained 6,500 motor vehicles, 77 police service dogs and 145 horses.

The Force has 13 divisions actively engaged in law enforcement, 1 Headquarters Division and 2 training divisions. Maritime services are divisional responsibilities and the Force currently has 350 boats at various points across Canada. The Air Directorate has stations throughout the country and maintains a fleet of 20 fixed-wing aircraft and 8 helicopters.

Eayrs, J., *In Defence of Canada: Growing up Allied.* Univ. of Toronto Press, 1980
Feasby, W. R. (ed.), *Official History of the Canadian Medical Services, 1939–45.* 2 vols. Dept. of National Defence. Ottawa, 1953–56

INTERNATIONAL RELATIONS

Membership. Canada is a member of UN, the Commonwealth, OECD, NATO and Colombo Plan.

ECONOMY

Budget. Budgetary revenue and expenditure of the Government of Canada for years ended 31 March (in Canadian $1m.):

	1983–84	1984–85	1985–86	1986–87	1987–88 [1]
Revenue	64,211	70,891	76,823	85,793	93,220
Expenditure	96,610	109,215	111,227	116,395	122,550

[1] Estimate.

Budgetary revenue, main items, 1986–87 (estimates in Canadian $1m.):

Income tax, personal	37,878	Non-resident tax	1,356
Income tax, corporation	9,885	Oil export charge	–
Sales tax	11,973	Natural gas tax	1
Customs import duties	4,187	Non-tax revenue	1,669

Details of budget estimates[1], 1986–87 (in Canadian $1m.):

Economic and regional		External affairs and aid	2,892
development	11,789	Defence	10,006
Social development	54,566	Parliament	206
Public debt charges	26,658	Services to government	3,976

[1] The Department of Finance now manages expenditure under a new system of broad categories (listed above) called 'envelopes'.

On 31 March 1987 the net public debt was $264,101m.

Canadian Tax Foundation. *The National Finances: An Analysis of the Revenues and Expenditures of the Government of Canada.* Toronto. Annual

Currency. The denominations of money in the currency of Canada are dollars and cents. The cent is one-hundredth part of a dollar. Circulating coins are in denominations of 1, 5, 10, 25, 50 and 100 cents. The monetary standard is gold of 900 millesimal fineness (23·22 grains of pure gold equal to 1 gold dollar). The Currency Act provides for gold coins in the denominations of $5, $10 and $20, which are legal tender. The British and US gold coins are also legal tender, at the par rate of exchange. The legal equivalent of the British sovereign is $4.86⅔.

Since 1935 the Bank of Canada has the sole right to issue paper money for circulation in Canada. Restrictions introduced by the 1944 revisions of the Bank Act cancelled the right of chartered banks to issue or re-issue notes after 1 Jan. 1945; and in Jan. 1950 the chartered banks' liability for such of their notes as then remained outstanding was transferred to the Bank of Canada in return for payment of a like sum to the Bank of Canada. On 31 May 1970 the Canadian dollar which was stabilized at 92·50 US cents was allowed to fluctuate. The value of the US$ in Canadian funds was $1·26 and £1 sterling = Canadian $2·24 in March 1988.

The Bank of Canada notes in circulation are in denominations of $1, $2, $5, $10, $20, $50, $100 and $1,000. On 25 March 1986, the Government of Canada announced the introduction of a circulating dollar coin with the eventual withdrawal of one dollar bank note in 1989. The exportation of gold from Canada is prohibited except by licence issued by the Minister of Finance to the Bank of Canada or a chartered bank.

The Ottawa Mint was established in 1908 as a branch of the Royal Mint, in pursuance of the Ottawa Mint Act, 1901. In Dec. 1931 control of the Mint was passed over to the Canadian Government, and since that time it has operated as the Royal Canadian Mint. The Mint issues nickel, bronze and cupronickel coins for circulation in Canada. In 1967, in celebration of Canada's Centennial of Confederation, a $20 gold piece was minted, the first gold coin struck since 1919. In 1935, on the occasion of His Majesty's Silver Jubilee, the Royal Canadian Mint issued the first Canadian silver dollars. Commemorative dollars were also issued in

1939 on the occasion of the visit of King George VI and Queen Elizabeth to Canada; in 1949, when Newfoundland became the tenth Province of Canada; in 1958, the one-hundredth anniversary of the establishment of the Colony of British Columbia; in 1964, the centennial of the Charlottetown and Quebec Conferences which paved the way to confederation. The silver dollar bearing the design of the canoe manned by an Indian and a Voyageur has been issued in the years 1935–38, 1945–48, 1950–57, 1959–63, 1965 and 1966. In 1968, the coin bore the same design but its composition changed from silver to nickel. This composition remained for all the following years. The design was used again in 1969, 1972, 1975–87. For centennial year the Canada goose replaced the usual canoe design on the silver dollar. Because of a world-wide shortage of silver, the Government, in Aug. 1967, authorized the Mint to change the metal content of the 25-cent and 10-cent coins. Commencing in Sept. 1968, 10-cent, 25-cent, 50-cent and $1 coins were minted in pure nickel. Gold refining is one of the principal activities of the Mint. In 1986 the refinery treated over 5·3m. troy oz. of gold-containing materials and returned over 2·4m. troy oz. of fine gold to its clients. Of this total, 2,418,413 troy oz. of rough bullion were received from Canadian gold mines for treatment, containing 2,012,352 troy oz. of fine gold and 328,498 troy oz. of fine silver. Coins issued (1986): Gold, $2,842,100; silver, $5,292,161.

Banking. Commercial banks in Canada are known as chartered banks and are incorporated under the terms of the Bank Act, which imposes strict conditions as to capital, returns to the Federal government, types of lending operations and other matters. In Aug. 1987 there were 69 chartered banks (10 domestic banks and 59 foreign bank subsidiaries) incorporated under the provisions of the Bank Act; the 10 had 7,000 branches serving 1,700 communities in all provinces in Canada and 237 branches in other countries. The foreign bank subsidiaries operate 378 offices in Canada including 59 head offices. The Bank Act is subject to revision by Parliament every 10 years. Bank charters expire every 10 years and are renewed at each decennial revision of the Bank Act. The chartered banks make detailed monthly and yearly returns to the Minister of Finance and are subject to periodic inspection by the Superintendent of Financial Institutions, an official appointed by the Government.

There were 10 domestic banks in Aug. 1987 with assets of gold coin and bullion, $810m.; Bank of Canada deposits and notes, $6,811m.; deposits with banks, $45,589m.; cheques and other items in transit, $672,559m.; loans, $290,810m. (including mortgage loans, $63,241m.); total assets, $424,898m.

The Bank of Canada Act, passed on 3 July 1934, provided for the establishment of a central bank for the Dominion. This bank commenced operations on 11 March 1935 with a paid-up capital of $5m. By reason of certain changes introduced into the composition of stockholders of the bank (for which *see* THE STATESMAN'S YEAR-BOOK, 1944 pp. 322–23), the Minister of Finance on behalf of Canada is the sole registered owner of the capital stock of the bank. The revised Bank Act, which came into force on 1 Dec. 1980, requires chartered banks to maintain a statutory primary reserve of 10% on demand deposits, 3% on foreign-currency deposits and 2% on notice deposits, with an additional 1% on the portion of notice deposits exceeding $500m. This reserve is required to be maintained in the form of notes and deposits with the Bank of Canada. A secondary reserve of 4% in the form of treasury bills, government bonds, etc., is also required. All gold held in Canada by the chartered banks was transferred to the Bank of Canada along with the gold held by the Government as reserve against Dominion notes outstanding at the time of the commencement of operations of the Bank of Canada. The liability of the Dominion notes outstanding at the commencement of business of the Bank of Canada was assumed by the bank.

In the year ending 31 March 1987, the Federal Business Development Bank authorized 5,685 loans for a total of $927·9m.

Weights and Measures. The legal weights and measures are in transition from the Imperial to the International system of units. The Metric Commission, established in June 1971, co-ordinates Canada's conversion to the metric system.

ENERGY AND NATURAL RESOURCES

Electricity. The net generation of electricity in 1986 was 457,187,989 mwh., of which utilities accounted for 419,155,729 mwh. Of the total, 308,572,356 mwh. was from hydro-electricity, 81,382,666 mwh. from conventional steam plants and 67,232,969 mwh. from nuclear plants. The demand in 1986 was 423,210,034 mwh. Supply 115 volts; 60 Hz.

Oil and Natural Gas. With the discovery of large oilfields in Alberta and development of the Alberta oil sands, the production of petroleum became a major Canadian industry. The Interprovincial Pipeline, Canada's largest oil pipeline, moves crude oil from Edmonton, Alberta, to Montreal, Quebec. The pipeline serves Canadian refineries from Edmonton to Montreal and since the middle of 1982, Canadian crude has been delivered from Montreal to the Atlantic provinces and many in the USA. Another pipeline, Trans-Mountain, extends from Edmonton to Vancouver. Nine refineries, 5 in Canada and 4 in Washington State, are served by the pipeline. At the end of 1986 Canada's oil pipeline system had 43,436 km in operation. Net oil deliveries in 1986 were 151,180,658 cu. metres. The Trans-Canada natural gas pipeline is the longest in the world (10,632·1 km). It brings natural gas from the Alberta–Saskatchewan border across the prairies, through northern Ontario to Toronto, then eastward to Montreal. Natural gas pipeline mileage totalled 231,126·8 km in 1986. Total deliveries of marketable natural gas to transportation and delivery systems distribution in 1986, 71,864·8m. cu. metres; total gas sales 48,052·9m. cu. metres.

Minerals. Alberta, British Columbia, Saskatchewan and Quebec are the chief mining provinces. Total value of minerals produced in 1986 (preliminary) was $33,854,397,000. Principal minerals produced in 1986 (preliminary) were as follows:

	Quantity (1,000)	Value ($1,000)
Metallics		
Copper (kg)	768,244	1,567,988
Nickel (kg)	180,599	1,075,467
Zinc (kg)	283,557	350,476
Iron ore (tonnes)	36,096	1,254,758
Gold (grammes)	104,655	1,715,392
Lead (kg)	303,503	204,427
Silver (kg)	1,219	310,102
Molybdenum (kg)	12,914	113,942
Others	...	2,351,607
Total metallics	...	8,944,159
Non-metallics		
Asbestos (tonnes)	640	300,586
Potash (K$_2$O) (tonnes)	6,969	579,022
Salt (tonnes)	11,088	241,611
Sulphur, elemental (tonnes)	6,868	927,063
Gypsum (tonnes)	8,542	80,613
Others	...	539,875
Total non-metallics	...	2,668,790
Fuels		
Crude petroleum (cu. metres)	84,964	9,719,155
Natural gas (1,000 cu. metres)	76,365	6,743,835
Natural gas by-products (cu. metres)	18,906	1,825,439
Coal (tonnes)	57,800	1,716,000
Total fuels	...	20,004,429
Structural materials		
Cement (tonnes)	10,058	790,846
Sand and gravel (tonnes)	242,548	596,603
Stone (tonnes)	91,200	426,306
Clay products (bricks, tiles, etc.)	...	160,353
Lime (tonnes)	2,364	206,400
Total structural materials	...	2,200,508

Value (in Canadian $1,000) of mineral production by provinces:

Provinces	1985	1986	Provinces	1985	1986
Newfoundland	869,727	764,169	Saskatchewan	3,796,550	2,572,809
Pr. Ed. Island	1,917	1,700	Alberta	27,029,638	17,462,731
Nova Scotia	325,379	356,673	British Columbia	3,540,930	3,365,598
New Brunswick	508,897	526,046	Yukon Territory	60,069	183,533
Quebec	2,243,274	2,275,750	N.W. Territories	864,657	789,840
Ontario	4,630,344	4,797,195			
Manitoba	862,158	758,353	Total	44,733,540	33,854,397

Agriculture. Though the manufacturing and service industries now predominate, agriculture is still very important to the Canadian economy. As a percentage of the GDP, agriculture in 1986 equalled 3·4% of the net value of production; it also accounted for about 8·2% of the total value of commodities exported (1985).

According to the census of 1986 the total land area is 2,278·6m. acres of which 167·6m. acres are agricultural land.

Grain growing, dairy farming, fruit farming, ranching and fur farming are all carried on successfully. Total farm cash receipts (1986) $20,485·7m.

The following table shows the value of farm cash receipts for 1986 (revised), for selected agricultural commodities, in Canadian $1,000:

Wheat [1]	2,829,384	Tobacco	452,487
Oats and barley [1]	838,180	Cattle and calves	3,564,389
Rapeseed	560,333	Hogs	2,121,228
Potatoes	285,785	Sheep and lambs	33,035
Vegetables	587,789	Dairy products	2,804,459
Fruit	311,754	Poultry and eggs	1,444,771

[1] Includes Canadian Wheat Board payments.

Number of occupied farms (census of 1986) was 293,089; average farm size, 231 hectares.

Field Crops. The estimated acreage and yield of the principal field crops, by provinces, 1986 were:

	Wheat		Tame hay		Oats	
	1,000	1,000	1,000	1,000	1,000	1,000
Provinces	acres	bu.	acres	bu.	acres	bu.
Prince Edward Island	12	610	127	267	27	1,830
Nova Scotia	6	320	169	425	16	992
New Brunswick	10	430	171	356	32	1,790
Quebec	132	6,100	2,409	6,720	250	14,520
Ontario	718	37,888	2,500	8,404	245	14,900
Manitoba	4,950	164,500	1,450	3,400	450	30,000
Saskatchewan	21,660	675,000	1,860	3,100	800	49,000
Alberta	7,600	265,000	3,950	8,700	1,300	94,000
British Columbia	100	3,100	790	1,900	60	3,700
Total, Canada	35,188	1,152,948	13,426	33,272	3,180	210,732

	Barley		Rye		Corn for Grain	
	1,000	1,000	1,000	1,000	1,000	1,000
Provinces	acres	bu.	acres	bu.	acres	bu.
Prince Edward Island	68	4,000	—	—	—	—
Nova Scotia	13	671	—	—	5	165
New Brunswick	26	1,380	—	—	—	—
Quebec	425	23,650	—	—	579	44,490
Ontario	590	35,400	57	1,980	1,830	185,000
Manitoba	1,550	85,000	77	2,400	34	2,400
Saskatchewan	3,550	181,000	420	11,300	—	—
Alberta	5,550	330,000	215	8,000	7	680
British Columbia	160	8,000	9	300	—	—
Total, Canada	11,932	669,101	778	23,980	2,455	232,735

Provinces	Canola-Rapeseed-Colza		Mixed grains		Soybeans	
	1,000 acres	1,000 bu.	1,000 acres	1,000 bu.	1,000 acres	1,000 bu.
Prince Edward Island	—	—	67	4,500	—	—
Nova Scotia	—	—	3	154	—	—
New Brunswick	—	—	4	215	—	—
Quebec	—	—	75	4,066	—	—
Ontario	93	3,240	535	33,794	940	35,200
Manitoba	1,000	25,500	80	4,000	—	—
Saskatchewan	2,520	66,000	50	2,400	—	—
Alberta	2,800	71,000	125	8,000	—	—
British Columbia	110	2,200	4	220	—	—
Total, Canada	6,523	167,940	943	57,349	940	35,200

Livestock. In parts of Saskatchewan and Alberta stockraising is still carried on as a primary industry, but the livestock industry of the country at large is mainly a subsidiary of mixed farming. The following table shows the numbers of livestock (in 1,000) by provinces in July 1987:

Provinces	Milch cows	Other cattle	Sheep and lambs	Swine
Newfoundland	3·9	4·0	6·6	16·0
Prince Edward Island	20·0	74·0	6·5	124·0
Nova Scotia	34·0	96·0	39·5	140·0
New Brunswick	26·5	78·5	9·3	96·0
Quebec	555·0	937·0	111·0	3,015·0
Ontario	450·0	1,800·0	204·0	3,360·0
Manitoba	65·0	1,025·0	23·0	1,148·0
Saskatchewan	53·0	1,997·0	52·0	685·0
Alberta	125·0	3,675·0	190·0	1,670·0
British Columbia	74·5	597·5	55·0	222·0
Total	1,406·9	10,284·0	696·9	10,476·0

Net production[1] of farm eggs in 1985, 487·9m. doz. ($518·6m.); 1986, 491·5m. doz. ($512m.).

[1] Includes exports.

Wool production (in tonnes), 1982, 1,417; 1983, 1,380; 1984, 1,386; 1985, 1,310·8; 1986, 1,220·8.

Dairying. The dairy products industry has shown a marked tendency towards centralization; the number of establishments decreased between 1961 and 1984[1] from 1,710 to 401 (76·5%), whereas the number of employees has decreased to 20·6%. Production, 1986: Creamery butter, 97,743 tonnes; cheddar cheese, 111,560 tonnes[2]; concentrated whole milk products, 92,921 tonnes; skim milk powder, 106,133 tonnes.

[1] The number of establishments/employees are based on the 1980 Standard Industrial Classification.
[2] Includes cheddar used to make processed cheese.

Fruit Farming. The value of fruit production (excluding apples) in 1985 was (estimated in $1,000): Ontario, 80,037; British Columbia, 89,335 ; Quebec, 25,638; Nova Scotia, 10,189; New Brunswick, 3,498; Prince Edward Island, 1,290. Total apple production in Canada in 1985 was 478,605 tonnes.

Tobacco. Commercial production of tobacco is confined to Ontario and Quebec. Farm cash receipts in 1985 totalled $158m. (1986, $453m.). The large drop in 1985 cash receipts could be attributed to all of the 1985 crop being sold in 1986 due to a delay in the Ontario Auction.

Forestry. As of 1982, the total area of land covered by forests is estimated at about 4,364,000 sq. km, of which 2,641,000 sq. km are classed as productive forest land.
    Lumber production (in cu. metres) in 1984 was 48,988,638.
    Lumber shipments from sawmills and planing mills in 1984 was 46,801,846 cu.

metres valued at $4,735·5m. Pulp production was 20·5m. tonnes in 1984 and 20·2m. tonnes in 1983. In 1984 mill shipments of paper amounted to 14·1m. tonnes valued at $8,194,242,000.

Fur Trade. In 1985–86 (year ended 30 June), 4,143,414 pelts valued at $99,577,798, were taken. In wild-life pelt production beaver led in total value, followed by marten, muskrat and lynx. The most important animal raised on fur farms is mink, with 50% of the total production. The value of mink pelts from fur farms in 1985-86 was $66,122,570. There were, in 1986, 851 fur farms reporting fox and 570 mink.

Fisheries. During 1985, landings in Canadian commercial fisheries reached 1,446,330 tonnes. The landed value was $1,131·3m. and the estimated market value was $2,475·7m. The landed value of principal fish in 1985 was (in $1,000): Salmon, 250,964; cod, 187,043; lobster, 193,238; herring, 87,003; scallops, 62,312; freshwater fish, 65,500; halibut, 26,227. Exports of fisheries' products, 1985, were valued at $1,868·9m.

Canadian Mines Handbook. Annual. Toronto, from 1931
Canadian Fisheries, Highlights 1983. Dept. of Fisheries and Oceans, 1984

INDUSTRY AND TRADE

Industry. Industry groups ranked by value of shipments, survey of 1985 (based on 1980 Standard Industrial Classification):

Industry	Production workers	Wages ($1,000)	Cost of materials ($1,000)	Value of shipments ($1,000)
Food industries	135,226	2,774,064	22,502,053	32,792,936
Beverage industries	17,445	506,206	2,020,693	4,863,698
Tobacco products	4,178	136,801	685,135	1,640,901
Rubber products	18,029	459,548	1,227,071	2,554,187
Plastic products	30,890	571,650	2,042,618	3,860,925
Leather and allied industries	19,954	295,758	663,016	1,308,180
Primary textile	19,589	395,031	1,383,846	2,669,665
Textile industries	25,152	409,979	1,450,182	2,650,075
Clothing industries	98,854	1,321,426	2,703,750	5,543,164
Wood industries	90,988	2,203,516	6,164,466	11,121,616
Furniture and fixtures	42,576	748,740	1,574,847	3,398,624
Paper and allied industries	86,477	2,699,480	8,711,530	18,074,629
Printing, publishing and allied industries	74,386	1,802,150	3,515,739	9,534,831
Primary metal industries	80,989	2,660,807	8,906,869	16,970,955
Metal fabricating industries	112,386	2,578,832	7,195,841	13,971,012
Machinery industries	53,286	1,263,801	3,759,316	7,450,789
Transport equipment	63,192	4,735,027	29,125,931	43,182,266
Electrical and electronic products	88,224	2,002,149	6,651,939	13,270,246
Non-metallic mineral products	38,763	1,001,780	2,303,654	5,879,141
Refined petroleum products	6,436	265,859	21,090,561	24,420,831
Chemical and chemical prods.	46,274	1,269,796	9,649,600	18,268,582
Other manufacturing	51,865	970,395	2,487,540	5,065,381
All industries	1,205,159	31,072,595	145,817,198	248,492,634

Labour. In 1986 (annual average) the industrial distribution of the employed was estimated as follows (in 1,000): Service, 4,150; manufacturing, 2,210; trade, 2,274; transport, communication and other utilities, 965; construction, 761; public administration, 866; finance, insurance and real estate, 687; agriculture, 518; non-agriculture, 12,256; other primary industries, 342; total employed, 11,634; un-employed, 1,236. Union returns filed for 1985 in compliance with the Corporations and Returns Act (1962), show 395 labour organizations reporting on 14,909[1] local union branches in Canada. Union membership in 1985 was 3·49m. 34·4% of paid workers in major industry groups were members of reporting labour organizations, with about 58·9% of the organized workers members of unions affiliated with the Canada Labour Congress. Over 1·38m. of the union members were in international unions, which have branches both in Canada and the USA and in most cases belong to central labour organizations in both countries.

It is generally established by legislation, both federal and provincial, that a trade union to which the majority of employees in a unit suitable for collective bargaining belong, is given certain rights and duties. An employer is required to meet and negotiate with such a trade union to determine wage-rates and other working conditions of his employees. The employer, the trade union and the employees affected are bound by the resulting agreement. If an impasse is reached in negotiation conciliation services provided by the appropriate government board are available. Generally, work stoppages do not take place until an established conciliation or mediation procedure has been carried out and are prohibited while an agreement is in effect. Almost 23% of the workers affected by collective agreements are in the manufacturing industry.

Freedom of association is a civil right in Canada, and under common law workers are at liberty to join unions and participate in their activities. This right has also been guaranteed by statutes which make it an offence to interfere with freedom of association.

Certain specific minimum standards in regard to working conditions are set by law, for the most part by provincial labour legislation. Minimum wages, maximum hours of work or an overtime rate of pay after a specified number of hours, minimum weekly rest periods, annual vacations with pay, statutory holidays, maternity leave and notice of termination of employment are established for the majority of workers.

Dept. of Labour, *Working Conditions in Canadian Industry*. Annual, Ottawa

Commerce. In the past the custom tariff of Canada has been protective, with a preferential tariff in favour of the UK, the Dominions, a number of Crown Colonies, and the Irish and South African Republics. At the Imperial Economic Conference of 1932, held in Ottawa, the UK developed further the policy of preferential tariffs to the Dominions, and on the part of the latter there was a general lowering of the existing tariffs against certain lines of UK manufacturers. Canada is one of the signatories of the General Agreement on Tariffs and Trade (GATT) and of the Kennedy Round agreements.

Imports for home consumption and domestic exports (in Canadian $1,000) for calendar years (merchandise only):

	Imports	Exports		Imports	Exports
1960	5,842,695	5,255,575	1984	95,459,996	109,436,610
1970	13,951,903	16,820,098	1985 [1]	104,355,196	116,145,111
1980	69,273,844	74,445,976	1986 [2]	112,677,998	116,587,685
1983	75,608,386	88,154,564		[1] Revised	[2] Estimate.

Exports (domestic) by countries in 1986 (in Canadian $1,000):

Australia	624,132	Kenya	48,774
Bahamas	26,305	Leeward and Windward Islands	77,300
Bahrain	7,604	Malaŵi	847
Bangladesh	101,320	Malaysia	104,324
Barbados	41,305	Malta	1,064
Belize	3,973	Mauritius and Dependencies	987
Bermuda	29,818	New Zealand	149,446
Britain (UK)	2,551,925	Nigeria	18,943
British Oceania	109	Pakistan	64,841
Cyprus	9,907	Qatar	7,642
Falkland Islands	—	Sierra Leone	156
Fiji	5,908	Singapore	146,304
Gambia	61	South Africa, Republic of	151,397
Ghana	28,672	Sri Lanka	28,896
Gibraltar	108	Tanzania	24,556
Guyana	4,517	Trinidad and Tobago	85,987
Hong Kong	315,167	Uganda	1,311
India	350,984	Zambia	12,691
Ireland	84,681		
Jamaica	70,026	Afghánistán	132

Exports *(continued)*

Albania	49	Kuwait	24,366
Algeria	190,339	Lebanon	17,561
Angola	1,248	Liberia	2,459
Argentina	60,015	Libya	74,123
Austria	49,404	Madagascar	1,398
Belgium and Luxembourg	821,285	Mauritania	268
Benin	2,348	Mexico	397,438
Bolivia	8,926	Morocco	154,590
Brazil	654,077	Mozambique	6,531
Burma	319	Netherlands	970,021
Cameroon Republic	12,452	Netherlands Antilles	6,773
Chile	86,317	Nicaragua	22,683
China	1,104,477	Norway	311,474
Colombia	159,162	Panama	40,624
Costa Rica	26,302	Paraguay	2,386
Côte d'Ivoire	7,293	Peru	110,918
Cuba	361,238	Philippines	49,477
Czechoslovakia	13,265	Poland	19,487
Denmark	107,689	Portugal	153,983
Dominican Republic	52,995	Portuguese Africa	2,340
Ecuador	79,309	Puerto Rico	202,059
Egypt (UAR)	132,952	Romania	119,331
El Salvador	11,261	St Pierre and Miquelon	27,167
Ethiopia	31,549	Saudi Arabia	211,985
Finland	82,674	Senegal	15,118
France	962,841	Somalia	1,817
French Africa	22,371	Spain	132,276
French Guiana	3,303	Spanish Africa	2,184
French Oceania	2,708	Sudan	23,112
French West Indies	1,889	Suriname	1,308
Gabon	12,630	Sweden	221,138
German Democratic Rep.	117,666	Switzerland	338,301
Germany, Fed. Rep. of	1,263,535	Syria	12,307
Greece	63,668	Taiwan	599,358
Greenland	3,402	Thailand	105,325
Guatemala	15,065	Togo	4,798
Guinea	2,736	Tunisia	75,550
Haiti, Republic of	20,769	Turkey	201,848
Honduras	13,971	USSR	1,215,585
Hungary	10,909	United Arab Emirates	24,278
Iceland	4,339	USA	90,297,227
Indonesia	240,898	US Oceania	6,748
Iran	35,683	US Virgin Islands	4,899
Iraq	105,435	Uruguay	12,653
Israel	127,191	Venezuela	323,186
Italy	692,390	Vietnam	2,845
Japan	5,914,802	Yemen (South)	10,295
Jordan	6,090	Yugoslavia	40,872
Korea, North	1,273	Zaïre	16,504
Korea, South	964,180	Zimbabwe	7,370

Imports (for consumption) by countries in 1985 (in Canadian $1,000):

Australia	504,668	Gibraltar	217
Bahamas	29,808	Guyana	26,917
Bahrain	3,594	Hong Kong	1,040,970
Bangladesh	18,492	India	165,405
Barbados	21,278	Ireland	244,817
Belize	1,211	Jamaica	149,903
Bermuda	27,091	Kenya	20,868
Britain (UK)	3,721,155	Leeward and Windward Islands	5,386
British Oceania	45	Malawi	1,560
Cyprus	500	Malaysia	150,204
Falkland Islands	—	Malta	3,389
Fiji	4,809	Mauritius and Dependencies	13,474
Gambia	84	New Zealand	174,808
Ghana	65	Nigeria	368,210

Imports *(continued)*

Pakistan	146,858	Israel	129,955
Qatar	594	Italy	1,671,352
Sierra Leone	8,211	Japan	7,626,298
Singapore	210,030	Jordan	1,633
South Africa, Republic of	373,163	Korea, North	614
Sri Lanka	35,824	Korea, South	1,749,446
Tanzania	3,062	Kuwait	293
Trinidad and Tobago	54,090	Lebanon	1,060
Uganda	2,360	Liberia	1,260
Zambia	84	Libya	22,727
		Madagascar	7,848
Afghánistán	45	Mauritania	24
Albania	39	Mexico	1,179,552
Algeria	11,502	Morocco	19,358
Angola	42,428	Mozambique	110
Argentina	87,269	Netherlands	694,138
Austria	212,961	Netherlands Antilles	16,299
Belgium and Luxembourg	618,228	Nicaragua	34,111
Benin	12	Norway	167,561
Bolivia	9,591	Panama	27,965
Brazil	821,641	Paraguay	7,243
Burma	1,556	Peru	65,724
Cameroon Republic	304	Philippines	109,411
Chile	127,338	Poland	67,931
China	566,591	Portugal	78,294
Colombia	124,050	Portuguese Africa	—
Costa Rica	56,557	Puerto Rico	194,747
Côte d'Ivoire	15,760	Romania	55,868
Cuba	71,123	St Pierre and Miquelon	389
Czechoslovakia	62,438	Saudi Arabia	186,894
Denmark	233,493	Senegal	58
Dominican Republic	36,049	Somalia	134
Ecuador	92,227	Spain	441,421
Egypt (UAR)	5,118	Spanish Africa	380
El Salvador	64,188	Sudan	27
Ethiopia	2,156	Suriname	1,665
Finland	253,959	Sweden	788,209
France	1,585,290	Switzerland	591,284
French Africa	16,616	Syria	48
French Guiana	66	Taiwan	1,744,665
French Oceania	837	Thailand	150,267
French West Indies	1,268	Togo	3,182
Gabon	5,770	Tunisia	9,359
German Democratic Rep.	26,852	Turkey	56,753
Germany, Fed. Rep. of	3,453,227	USSR	25,448
Greece	70,250	United Arab Emirates	2,100
Greenland	3,260	USA	77,336,970
Guatemala	40,362	US Oceania	341
Guinea	15,169	US Virgin Islands	40,799
Haiti, Republic of	12,265	Uruguay	14,862
Honduras	20,678	Venezuela	516,069
Hungary	41,951	Vietnam	6,671
Iceland	11,883	Yemen (South)	755
Indonesia	114,189	Yugoslavia	45,463
Iran	208,682	Zaïre	33,945
Iraq	815	Zimbabwe	6,737

Categories of imports in 1986, estimate (in Canadian $1,000):

Live animals	158,696	Fabricated materials, inedible	19,979,359
Food, feed, beverages		End products, inedible	76,983,995
and tobacco	6,541,222	Special transactions	1,746,936
Crude materials, inedible	7,267,791		

Categories of exports (Canadian produce) in 1986, estimate (in Canadian $1,000):

Live animals	348,574	Fabricated materials, inedible	38,392,321
Food, feed, beverages		End products, inedible	52,690,815
and tobacco	9,510,609	Special transactions	317,139
Crude materials, inedible	15,328,226		

Total trade of Canada with UK (British Department of Trade returns, in £1,000 sterling):

	1983	1984	1985	1986	1987
Imports to UK	1,522,187	1,618,057	1,652,974	1,499,600	1,568,305
Exports and re-exports from UK	968,269	1,183,613	1,693,557	1,698,372	1,938,237

Tourism. The number of visitors to Canada in 1986 was 40,459,341 (1985, 35,925,417). In 1986, 38,199,514 came from USA (1985, 34,117,379).

COMMUNICATIONS

Roads. The total length of federal and provincial territorial roads and highways in Canada at the end of March 1986 was 280,251 km. Expenditures by these two levels of government on roads and highways during the fiscal year 1985–86 amounted to approximately $5,347·7m.

Federal expenditures were directed largely to the maintenance of national park highways, Indian Reserve roads and designated provincial/territorial highway construction in projects. In general highways are controlled and maintained by the province who also have the responsiblity of providing assistance to their municipalities and townships.

The Alaska Highway is part of the Canadian highway system. For the Trans-Canada Highway *see* map in THE STATESMAN'S YEAR-BOOK, 1962.

Registered motor vehicles totalled 14,818,625 in 1985 (revised); they included 11,118,071 passenger cars and taxis, 3,095,243 trucks and buses and 452,526 motor cycles.

Urban Transit. There are metros in Montreal, Toronto and Vancouver, and tram/light rail systems in Calgary, Edmonton and Toronto. In 1985 urban transit systems (urban and suburban passenger transport, electrical railway, trolly coach, bus or subway) carried 1,448,275,000 fare passengers 726,914,174 km for an operating revenue of $1,861,907,499. In 1985, intercity and rural bus operations carried 26,943,000 fare passengers 173,612,914 km, earning revenues of $329,769,413.

Railways. The total length of track operated during 1985 in Canada was 95,670 km. Mainline track, 39,307 km; branch line, 30,928 km; industrial and siding track, 25,435 km.

Canada has 2 great trans-continental systems: the Canadian National Railway system (CN), a government-owned body which operates 51,745 km (1985) of track, and the Canadian Pacific Railway, a joint-stock corporation operating 34,015 km (1985). From 1 April 1978, a government funded organization known as Via Rail took over passenger services formerly operated by CP and CN; 7·8m. passengers were carried in 1986.

Selected statistics of Canadian railways for 1985: Passenger revenue $244·7m.; freight revenue, $6,137·4m.; total railway operating revenues, $7,668·7m.; total operating expenses, $6,845m.

Aviation. Civil aviation in Canada is under the jurisdiction of the federal government. The technical and administrative aspects are supervised by Transport Canada, while the economic functions are assigned to the National Transportation agency.

In 1986 Canadian airports handled 48,825,000 passengers, 157,900 tonnes of mail and 540,074 tonnes of cargo. Operating revenue (1986) was $5,980·6m.; operating expenditure, $5,738·4m.

Shipping. The registered shipping on 31 Dec. 1985, including vessels for inland navigation, totalled 38,129 with a gross tonnage of 5,776,882. A total of 52,993 vessels (international shipping) visited Canadian ports in 1985, loading and unloading 204m. tonnes of cargo.

The major canals in Canada are those of the St Lawrence–Great Lakes waterway with their 7 locks, providing navigation for vessels of 26-ft draught from Montreal to Lake Ontario; the Welland Canal by-passing the Niagara River between Lake Ontario and Lake Erie with its 8 locks; and the Sault Ste Marie Canal and lock between Lake Huron and Lake Superior. These 16 locks overcome a drop of 582 ft from the head of the lakes to Montreal. The St Lawrence Seaway was opened to navigation on 1 April 1959 (*see* map in THE STATESMAN'S YEAR-BOOK, 1957). In 1986, traffic on the Montreal–Lake Ontario Section of the Seaway numbered 3,307 transits carrying 37·6m. cargo tonnes; on the Welland Canal Section, 3,959 transits with 41·6m. cargo tonnes. Value of fixed assets was $598,739,000 and investments, $30,614,000 at 31 March 1987.

Coast Guard. The Canadian Coast Guard is responsible to the Minister of Transport. In 1986 it comprised 1 heavy icebreaker; 7 medium icebreakers; 8 light icebreakers/nav. aid tenders; 16 ice strengthened/nav. aid tenders; 1 hydraulic survey and founding vessel; 76 search and rescue vessels (all types and sizes); 4 hovercraft and 34 helicopters; 1 fixed-wing aircraft (DC-3).

Post. In 1985–86 there were 8,000 postal facilities in operation and 7,938m. pieces of mail were processed in 1986–87. Total revenue (estimate 1986–87) was $2,970m.; total expenditure, $3,099m.

There were 919,143 miles (1,479,216 km) of telegraph wire in Canada in 1979 (including external cable landed in Canada). There were 15·5m. telephones in Sept. 1986.

Broadcasting. There were 920 originating stations operating in Canada at 31 March 1987, of which 124 were Canadian Broadcasting Corporation stations, 54 were CBC affiliates and 489 were privately owned and operated. Included were 422 AM radio stations, 276 FM radio stations and 132 television stations. Radio and television licence fees were abolished in 1953.

Wireless 'beam' stations are operated at Montreal for direct communications with the UK and Australia, and a station at Louisburg, N.S., provides a long-distance service to ships.

Cinemas (1984). There were 860 cinemas with a seating capacity of 568,068 and 248 drive-in theatres with a capacity of 125,993 cars.

Newspapers (1985). There were 115 daily newspapers, of which 99 were in English, 11 in French and 5 others.

JUSTICE, RELIGION, EDUCATION AND WELFARE

Justice. There is a Supreme Court in Ottawa, having general appellate jurisdiction in civil and criminal cases throughout Canada. There is an Exchequer Court, which is also a Court of Admiralty. There is a Superior Court in each province and county courts, with limited jurisdiction, in most of the provinces, all the judges in these courts being appointed by the Governor-General. Police, magistrates and justices of the peace are appointed by the provincial governments.

For the year ended 31 Dec. 1986, 2,277,749 Criminal Code Offences were reported and 392,742 adults were charged.

Canadian Legal and Directory. Toronto. Annual

Religion. Membership of the leading denominations in 1981:

Province	Roman Catholic	United Church of Canada	Anglican Church of Canada	Presbyterian	Lutheran
Newfoundland	204,430	104,835	153,530	2,700	460
Prince Edward Island	56,415	29,645	6,850	12,620	210
Nova Scotia	310,140	169,605	131,130	38,285	12,315
New Brunswick	371,100	87,460	66,260	12,070	1,810
Quebec	5,609,685	126,275	132,115	34,625	17,655
Ontario	2,986,175	1,655,550	1,164,315	517,020	254,175
Manitoba	269,070	240,395	108,220	23,910	58,830
Saskatchewan	279,840	263,375	77,725	16,065	88,785
Alberta	573,495	525,480	202,265	63,890	144,675
British Columbia	526,355	548,360	374,055	89,810	122,395
Yukon	5,470	3,310	4,665	615	915
Northwest Territories	18,215	3,725	15,295	505	665
Total, Canada	11,210,385	3,758,015	2,436,375	812,110	702,905

Other denominations: Baptist, 696,850; Greek Orthodox, 314,870; Jewish, 296,425; Ukrainian (Greek) Catholic, 190,585; Pentecostal, 338,790; Mennonite, 189,370; other, 3,136,815.

Education. Under the Constitution the various provincial legislatures have power over education. These powers are subject to certain qualifications respecting the rights of denominational and minority language schools. Newfoundland and Quebec legislations provide for Roman Catholic and Protestant school boards. School Acts in Ontario, Saskatchewan and Alberta provide tax support for both public and separate schools. School board revenues derive from local taxation on real property and government grants from general provincial revenue.

Except in Quebec the number of private elementary and secondary schools is small; their enrolments in 1986–87 were less than 4·6% of the total elementary-secondary enrolment. Indian and Northern Affairs Canada finances schools for Indian and Inuit children; the enrolment in 1986–87 was 42,080.

In 1986–87, 475,414 full-time regular students (graduates and undergraduates) were enrolled in universities. In 1986 some 35,009 took first degrees in social sciences, commerce, economics, law, political science and geography; 15,594 in education; 10,091 in humanities; 8,271 in engineering and applied sciences; 5,790 in agriculture; 6,612 in health subjects; 7,872 in mathematics and physical sciences and 3,038 in fine and applied arts. Unclassified, 7,691.

The following statistics give information, for 1986–87, about all elementary and secondary schools, public, federal, private and blind and deaf:

Province	Schools	Teachers	Pupils
Newfoundland	596	8,078	139,820
Prince Edward Island	73	1,291	25,005
Nova Scotia	581	10,190	174,400
New Brunswick	471	7,631	141,330
Quebec	2,852	70,450	1,144,530
Ontario	5,471	98,210	1,865,750
Manitoba	837	12,334	219,370
Saskatchewan	1,038	11,405	214,590
Alberta	1,713	25,280	470,910
British Columbia	1,886	26,242	524,170
Yukon	25	290	4,800
Northwest Territories	75	700	13,300
National Defence (overseas)	9	250	3,590
Total	15,627	272,351	4,941,665

Health. Constitutional responsibility for personal health care services rests with the ten provinces of Canada. Accordingly, Canada's national health insurance system consists of an interlocking set of provincial hospital and medical insurance plans conforming to certain national standards rather than a single national programme. These national standards, which are set out in the Canada Health Act, include: Provision of a comprehensive range of hospital and medical benefits; universal population coverage; access to necessary services on uniform terms and conditions; portability of benefits; and public administration of provincial insurance plans

Provinces satisfying these national standards are eligible for federal financial assistance according to the provisions of the Federal-Provincial Fiscal Arrangements and Federal Post-Secondary Education and Health Contributions Act. Under this Act, the provinces are entitled to receive equal-per-capita federal health contributions escalated annually by the three year average increase in nominal Gross National Product. These federal contributions are paid in the form of a combination of tax point and cash transfers, which together account for approximately 50% of provincial expenditures on insured hospital and medical care services. Over and above these health insurance transfers, the federal government also provides unconditional financial support for such provincial extended health care service programmes as nursing home care, certain home care services and adult residential care services. These supplementary equal-per-capita cash payments to the provinces are also escalated annually by provincial population increases and increases to nominal GNP.

The health insurance programmes were introduced in stages. The Hospital Insurance and Diagnostic Services Act was passed in 1958, providing prepaid coverage to all Canadians for in-patient and, at the option of each province, out-patient hospital services. The Medical Care Act was introduced in 1968 to extend universal coverage to all medically-required services provided by medical practitioners. The Canada Health Act, which took effect 1 April 1984, consolidated the original federal health insurance legislation and clarified the national standards provinces are required to meet in order to qualify for full federal health contributions.

The approach taken by Canada is one of state-sponsored health insurance. Accordingly, the advent of insurance programmes produced little change in the ownership of hospitals, almost all of which are owned by non-government non-profit corporations, or in the rights and privileges of private medical practice. Patients are free to choose their own general practitioner without losing their insured benefits (there is a minor exception in Quebec involving the non-emergency services of a few physicians). Except for 0·5% of the population whose care is provided for under other legislation (such as serving members of the Canadian Armed Forces), all residents are eligible, regardless of whether they are in the work force. Benefits are available without upper limit so long as they are medically necessary, provided any registration obligations are met. Benefits are also portable during any temporary absence from Canada anywhere in the world—subject to any limitation a province may impose upon treatment electively sought outside the particular province without prior approval.

In addition to the benefits qualifying for federal contributions, provinces provide additional benefits at their own discretion. All provinces provide benefits covering a variety of services (e.g., optometric care, children's dental care, drug benefits). Most provinces fund their portion of health costs out of general provincial revenues. Three provinces levy health premiums which meet part of the provincial costs, 2 provinces impose a levy on employers, and 2 provinces utilize a tax based on income for this purpose. Only 1 province has nominal co-charges for short-term hospital care. Several provinces have charges for long-term hospital care geared, approximately, to the room and board portion of this OAS–GIS payment mentioned under Social Welfare. In 1987, total health expenditures were about $45,900m., representing 8·6% of GNP. Public sector spending accounts for about 75% of total national health expenditure.

Social Welfare. The social security system provides financial benefits to individuals and their families through a variety of programmes administered by federal, provincial and municipal governments. Federally, the Department of National Health and Welfare is responsible for research into the areas of health and social issues, provision of grants and contributions for various social services, improvement and construction of health facilities and the administration of several of Canada's income security programmes. These programmes are: The Family Allowances programme, introduced in 1945 and amended in 1973; the Old Age Security programme, introduced in 1952 and to which were added the Guaranteed Income Supplement in 1967 and the Spouse's Allowance in 1975; and the Canada Pension Plan and Canada Assistance Plan which came into being in 1966. Several income security programmes are administered by other federal departments – the Child Tax Credit, Unemployment Insurance, and two financial benefit programmes for veterans. Workers' Compensation is run by provincial Boards; the provincial governments administer social assistance and social service programmes which are cost-shared under the Canada Assistance Plan, as well as various taxation and income supplementation programmes.

The 1973 Family Allowances Act provides for the payment of a monthly Family Allowance ($32.38 in 1988) in respect of a dependent child under the age of 18 who is a resident of Canada and is wholly or substantially maintained by a parent or guardian. At least one parent must be a Canadian citizen, or admitted to Canada as a permanent resident under the Immigration Act, or admitted to Canada for a period of not less than 1 year, if during that time his or her income is subject to Canadian income tax. Benefits are also paid under prescribed circumstances to

Canadian citizens living abroad. Eligibility for Family Allowances (FA) is a precondition for receipt of the refundable Child Tax Credit discussed below. A Special Allowance ($48.31 monthly in 1988) is paid on behalf of a child under the age of 18 who is maintained by a welfare agency, a government department or an institution. In some cases, payment is made directly to a foster parent.

The Family Allowances Act specifies that a provincial government may request the federal government to vary the allowance rates payable within the province subject to the fulfillment of stipulated conditions. Only the provinces of Alberta and Quebec have exercised this option. During the month of March 1987, over 3·7m. Canadian families (including 6·6m. eligible children) received Family Allowances; the Special Allowance was paid on behalf of 32,000 of these children. The total bill for FA and Special Allowances for 1986–87 was $2,534m.

The Old Age Security (OAS) pension is payable to persons 65 years of age and over who satisfy the residence requirements stipulated in the Old Age Security Act. The amount payable, whether full or partial, is also governed by stipulated conditions, as is the payment of an OAS pension to a recipient who absents himself from Canada. OAS pensioners with little or no income apart from OAS may, upon application, receive a full or partial supplement known as the Guaranteed Income Supplement (GIS). Entitlement is normally based on the pensioner's income in the preceding year, calculated in accordance with the Income Tax Act. The spouse of an OAS pensioner, aged 60 to 64, meeting the same residence requirements as those stipulated for OAS, may be eligible for a full or partial Spouse's Allowance (SPA). SPA is payable, on application, depending on the annual combined income of the couple (not including the pensioner spouse's basic OAS pension or GIS). In 1979, the SPA programme was expanded to include a spouse, who is eligible for SPA in the month the pensioner spouse dies, until the age of 65 or until remarriage (Extended Spouse's Allowance). Since Sept. 1985, SPA has also been available to low income widow(er)s aged 60–64. For the first quarter of 1988, the basic OAS pension was $310·65 monthly; the maximum Guaranteed Income Supplement was $369·21 monthly for a single pensioner or a married pensioner whose spouse was not receiving a pension or a Spouse's Allowance, and $240·47 monthly for each spouse of a married couple where both were pensioners. The maximum Spouse's Allowance for the same quarter was $551·13 monthly (equal to the basic pension plus the maximum GIS married rate), and $608·46 for widow(er)s. Total OAS/GIS/SPA benefit expenditures for 1986–87 were $13,445m.; in March 1987, almost 2·9m. Canadians received benefits through these programmes.

The Canada Pension Plan (CPP) is designed to provide workers with a basic level of income protection in the event of retirement, disability or death. Benefits may be payable to a contributor, a surviving spouse or an eligible child. As of 1987, reduced retirement benefits may be paid as early as age 60; eligibility prior to age 65 is subject to a test of cessation of employment. Formerly, retirement benefits began no earlier than age 65. Benefits are determined by the contributor's earnings and contributions made to the Plan. Contribution is compulsory for most employed and self-employed Canadians 18 to 65 years of age. The Canada Pension Plan does not operate in Quebec, which has exercised its constitutional prerogative to establish a similar plan, the Quebec Pension Plan (QPP), to operate in lieu of CPP; there is reciprocity between the two to ensure coverage for all adult Canadians in the labour force. In 1987 both CPP and QPP were funded by equal contributions of 1·9% of pensionable earnings from the employer and 1·9% from the employee (self-employed persons contribute the full 3·8%), in addition to the interest on the investment of excess funds. In 1987, the range of yearly pensionable earnings was from $2,500 to $25,900; a person who earned and contributed at less than the maximum level receives monthly benefits at rates lower than the maximum allowable under CPP/QPP. In March 1987, about 2·7m. Canadians received Canada or Quebec Pension Plan benefits. Total expenditures in 1986–87 for both plans were about $7,849m.

OAS and CPP legislation authorizes reciprocal agreements with other countries to achieve portability of pensions. Such agreements have been made with Italy, France, Portugal, the United States, Greece, Jamaica, Barbados, Belgium, Denmark, Norway and Sweden. In general, such agreements also provide for the conclusion of arrangements with the province of Quebec to cover QPP contributors on a similar basis.

Under the Canada Assistance Plan, the federal government pays 50% of the cost to the provinces and territories of: Assistance to persons in need; welfare services provided to persons who are in need or likely to become in need if they do not receive such services (welfare services means services having as their object the lessening, removal or prevention of the causes and effects of poverty, child neglect or dependence on public assistance); and work activity projects which are designed to improve the employability of persons who have unusual difficulty in finding or retaining jobs or in undertaking job training. For the direct financial assistance programmes, 'need' is determined by the 'budget deficit' method, that is, the difference between an applicant's requirements and his income and resources. The rates of assistance payable are also determined by provincial authorities. Through the Plan, the federal government shares in the costs of many personal social service programmes. The funding, administration, and delivery of such services are particular to each province and municipality. In March 1987, close to 1·9m. Canadians (representing 1,048,900 households) were in receipt of direct financial assistance from provincial programmes shareable under the Canada Assistance Plan. Total payments to the provinces under the Plan (including direct financial assistance, welfare services and work activity projects) for the 1986–87 financial year were almost $4,438m. Revenue Canada, Taxation administers the Child Tax Credit (CTC) which was introduced in 1978. The programme provides benefits to low and middle income families, in addition to those provided through Family Allowances (described above). The maximum credit payable in 1988 (in respect of the 1987 taxation year) is $488 for each eligible child (i.e. the parent must be entitled to receive a Family Allowance in respect of that child for Jan. 1988 or at any time during 1987 if the child died during 1987), where the net annual family income for the 1987 taxation year was below a specified level ($23,500 for 1 child); CTC entitlement is reduced by 5% of the amount by which the family's income exceeded this level. As of 1986, a partial payment of the CTC is made in Nov. of the taxation year; the remainder is paid after application is made through the income tax system. It is estimated that approximately $1,460m. was paid out to approximately 2·4m. Canadian families in 1986 for the 1985 taxation year.

The Unemployment Insurance programme, administered by Employment and Immigration Canada, was introduced in 1940 and revised in 1971; it provides income protection to workers suffering temporary employment interruptions such as loss of work, illness and pregnancy. Lump sum retirement benefits are also paid to workers aged 65 whether or not they leave the labour force. Approximately 95% of workers in Canada are covered through the UI programme. To be insurable, workers must be employed by the same employer for at least 15 hours a week, or make $113 a week or more (in 1988). Neither the self-employed (except specified fishermen) nor those over 65 years are eligible. The programme is funded by employer and employee contributions and provides a benefit of 60% of average weekly insurable earnings. In 1988, the maximum weekly benefit was $339. Approximately 1·25m. Canadians collected UI benefits in March 1987; programme expenditures for 1986–87 were approximately $10,540m.

The Department of Veterans Affairs offers two direct financial assistance programmes – the Veterans' and Civilians' Disability Pensions programme and the War Veterans' and Civilian War Allowances programme, which were introduced in 1919 and 1930 respectively and both amended to include civilians in 1962. The first programme provides pensions to military personnel disabled during service as defined in the legislation, a surviving spouse or dependents. Benefits are based on the degree of disability ranging from 5% to 100%. In March 1987, there were approximately 143,775 persons/families receiving pensions for a cost of just under $764m. in 1986–87. War Veterans' and Civilian War Allowances provide financial benefits to persons, or their dependents, who meet service eligibility requirements and who, due to age or incapacity, are unable to work and have insufficient income for maintenance, as determined by an income test. Benefits vary depending upon the family composition of the applicant. In March 1987, about 82,400 persons were receiving benefits under the programme; benefit expenditures in 1986–87 were $425m.

Workers' Compensation, administered by provincial Boards, provides compulsory coverage against wage loss due to work-related injury or disease for workers in specified trades and industries. The programme is employer-funded and precludes legal action by the worker against his employer. Benefits are based upon previous earnings and degree of impairment and may be of a long or short term nature. Maximum compensation is set at 75% of a fixed maximum gross earnings level or 90% of a fixed maximum net earnings level, depending on the province. Benefits are also available to surviving spouses and dependent children and are calculated in the above manner; however, additional sums may be available for funeral and related expenses. Medical support and rehabilitation services are also intrinsic to the programme. Benefit expenditures for Workers' Compensation in 1986 were approximately $3,005m.

Ismael, J. S., (ed.) *Canadian Welfare State: Evolution and Transition.* Univ. of Alberta Press, 1987

DIPLOMATIC REPRESENTATIVES

Of Canada in Great Britain (Macdonald House., Grosvenor Sq., London, W1X 0AB)
High Commissioner: R. Roy McMurtry, QC.

Of Great Britain in Canada (80 Elgin St., Ottawa, K1P 5K7)
High Commissioner: Sir Alan Urwick, KCVO, CMG.

Of Canada in the USA (1746 Massachusetts Ave., NW, Washington, D.C., 20036)
Ambassador: Allan E. Gotlieb.

Of the USA in Canada (100 Wellington St., Ottawa, K1P 5TI)
Ambassador: Thomas M. T. Niles.

Of Canada to the United Nations
Ambassador: Stephen Lewis.

Books of Reference

Statistical Information: Statistics Canada, Ottawa, has been the official central statistical organization for Canada since 1918. The Bureau, which reports to Parliament through the Minister of Supply and Services, serves as the statistical agency for federal government departments; co-ordinates the statistics of the provincial governments along national lines; and channels all Canadian statistical data to internal organizations. *Chief Statistician of Canada:* Dr I. P. Felligi.

Publications of Statistics Canada are classified as periodical (issued more frequently than once a year), annual, biennial and occasional publications. The occasional publications frequently supplement the annual reports and usually contain historical information. A complete list is contained in the 1986 edition of the Current Publications Index, available at a nominal cost. Official publications include:

The Canada Year Book. Annual, from 1905
Canada, Official Handbook. Annual, from 1930
Canadian Statistical Review. Monthly, with weekly supplements, from 1926
Twelfth Decennial Census of Canada, 1981. Ottawa, 1982
Atlas and Gazetteer of Canada. Dept. of Energy, Mines and Resources. Ottawa, 1969
Cambridge History of the British Empire. Vol. VI. Canada and Newfoundland. Cambridge, 1930
Canadian Almanac and Directory. Toronto. Annual
Canadian Annual Review. Annual, from 1960
Canadian Dictionary: French–English. Toronto, 1970
Canadian Encyclopedia. 3 vols. Edmonton, 1985
Canadiana; A List of Publications of Canadian Interest. National Library, Ottawa. Monthly, with annual cumulation. 1951 ff.
Cook, R., *French-Canadian Nationalism; An Anthology.* Toronto, 1970.—*The Maple Leaf Forever; Essays on Nationalism and Politics in Canada.* Toronto, 1971
Creighton, Donald G., *Canada's First Century.* Toronto, 1970.—*Towards the Discovery of Canada.* Toronto, 1974

Dewitt, D. B., and Kirton, J. J., *Canada as a Principal Power: A Study in Foreign Policy.* Toronto, 1983
Dictionnaire Bélisle de la langue française au Canada; dictionnaire oxford. 1970
Dictionnaire canadien; français–anglais–français. Toronto, 1962
Encyclopedia Canadiana. 10 vols. Rev. ed. Ottawa, 1967
Granatstein, J. L., *Twentieth Century Canada.* Toronto, 1983
Hardy, W. G., *From Sea to Sea; Canada, 1850–1920: The Road to Nationhood.* Toronto, 1960
Hockin, T. A., *Government in Canada.* London, 1976
Kerr, D. G. G., *Historical Atlas of Canada.* Toronto, 1960
Leacy, F. H., (ed.) *Historical Statistics of Canada.* Government Printer, Ottawa, 1983
Lower, A. R. M., *Colony to Nation: A History of Canada.* 4th ed. Toronto, 1964
McCann, L. D., (ed.) *Heartland and Hinterland: A Geography of Canada.* Scarborough, Ontario, 1982
Newman, P. C., *Company of Adventurers: The Story of the Hudson's Bay Company.* Vol. 1, London, 1986
Nurgitz, N., and Segal, H., *No Small Measure: The Progressive Conservatives and the Constitution.* Ottawa, 1983
Smith, D. L., (ed.) *History of Canada: An Annotated Bibliography.* Oxford and Santa Barbara, 1983

National Library: The National Library of Canada, Ottawa, Ontario. *Librarian:* J. Guy Sylvestre.

CANADIAN PROVINCES

The 10 provinces have each a separate parliament and administration, with a Lieut.-Governor, appointed by the Governor-General in Council at the head of the executive. They have full powers to regulate their own local affairs and dispose of their revenues, provided only they do not interfere with the action and policy of the central administration. Among the subjects assigned exclusively to the provincial legislatures are: the amendment of the provincial constitution, except as regards the office of the Lieut.-Governor; property and civil rights; direct taxation for revenue purposes; borrowing; management and sale of Crown lands; provincial hospitals, reformatories, etc.; shop, saloon, tavern, auctioneer and other licences for local or provincial purposes; local works and undertakings, except lines of ships, railways, canals, telegraphs, etc., extending beyond the province or connecting with other provinces, and excepting also such works as the Dominion Parliament declares are for the general good; marriages, administration of justice within the province; education.

Local Government. Under the terms of the British North America Act the provinces are given full powers over local government. All local government institutions are, therefore, supervised by the provinces, and are incorporated and function under provincial acts.

The acts under which municipalities operate vary from province to province. A municipal corporation is usually administered by an elected council headed by a mayor or reeve, whose powers to administer affairs and to raise funds by taxation and other methods are set forth in provincial laws, as is the scope of its obligations to, and on behalf of, the citizens. Similarly, the types of municipal corporations, their official designations and the requirements for their incorporation vary between provinces. The following table sets out the classifications as at 1 Jan. 1983.

Type and size of group	Nfld.	PEI	NS	NB	Que.	Ont.	Man.
Type:							
Regional municipalities	—	—	—	—	96	39	—
Metropolitan and regional municipalities [1]	—	—	—	—	3	12	—
Counties and regional districts	—	—	—	—	93	27	—
Unitary municipalities	169	39	66	114	1,518	792	185
Cities [2]	2	1	3	6	65	49	5
Towns	167	8	39	23	192	145	35
Villages	—	30	—	85	243	119	40
Rural municipalities [3]	—	—	24	—	1,018	479	105
Quasi-municipalities [4]	141	—	—	—	—	7	17
Total	310	39	66	114	1,614	838	202

Type and size of group	Nfld.	PEI	NS	NB	Que.	Ont.	Man.
Population size group (1981 census):							
Unitary municipalities—							
Over 100,000	—	—	1	—	4	17	1
50,000 to 99,999	1	—	2	2	16	14	—
10,000 to 49,999	5	1	17	4	76	78	4
Under 10,000	163	38	46	108	1,422	683	180
Total	169	39	66	114	1,518	792	185

Type and size of group	Sask.	Alta.	BC	YT	NWT	Canada
Type:						
Regional municipalities	—	—	28	—	—	163
Metropolitan and regional municipalities [1]	—	—	—	—	—	15
Counties and regional districts	—	—	28	—	—	148
Unitary municipalities	805	332	142	3	7	4,172
Cities [2]	12	11	35	2	1	192
Towns	142	111	10	1	5	878
Villages	352	162	55	—	1	1,087
Rural municipalities [3]	299	48	42	—	—	2,015
Quasi-municipalities [4]	—	19	285	5	26	500
Total	805	351	455	8	33	4,835
Population size group (1981 census):						
Unitary municipalities—						
Over 100,000	2	2	3	—	—	30
50,000 to 99,999	—	2	9	—	—	46
10,000 to 49,999	6	15	30	1	—	237
Under 10,000	797	313	100	2	7	3,859
Total	805	332	142	3	7	4,172

[1] Includes urban communities in Quebec; and Metropolitan Toronto, regional municipalities and the district municipality of Muskoka in Ontario.

[2] Includes the 5 boroughs of Metropolitan Toronto.

[3] Includes municipalities in Nova Scotia; parishes, townships, united townships and municipalities without designation in Quebec; townships in Ontario; rural municipalities in Manitoba and Saskatchewan; municipal districts and counties in Alberta; and districts in British Columbia.

[4] Includes local government communities and the metropolitan area in Newfoundland; improvement districts in Ontario and Alberta; local government districts in Manitoba; local improvement districts in British Columbia the Yukon Territory; and hamlets in the Northwest Territories.

ALBERTA

HISTORY. The southern half of the province of Alberta was part of Rupert's land which was granted by royal charter in 1670 to the Hudson's Bay Company. The intervention by the North West Company in the fur trade after 1783 led to the establishment of trading posts. In 1869 Rupert's land was transferred from the Hudson's Bay Company (which had absorbed its rival in 1821) to the new Dominion, and in the following year this land was combined with the former Crown land of the North Western Territories to form the Northwest Territories.

In 1882 'Alberta' first appeared as a provisional 'district', consisting of the southern half of the present province. In 1905 the Athabasca district to the north was added when provincial status was granted to Alberta.

Four parties have held office: the Liberals 1905–21; the United Farmers 1921–35; Social Credit 1935–71, and Progressive Conservative since Sept. 1971.

AREA AND POPULATION. The area of the province is 661,188 sq. km; 644,392 sq. km being land area and 16,796 sq. km water area. The population (estimate 1 Oct. 1987) was 2,381,500; the urban population (1986), centres of 1,000 or over, was 1,877,758 and the rural 488,067. Population of the cities (30 June 1987): Calgary, 647,285; Edmonton, 576,249; Lethbridge, 60,610; Red Deer,

54,309; Medicine Hat, 41,804; St Albert, 37,008; Fort McMurray, 34,949; Grande
Prairie, 26,471; Leduc, 13,126; Camrose, 12,968; Fort Saskatchewan, 11,963;
Spruce Grove, 11,918; Airdrie, 10,461; Lloydminster (Alberta portion), 10,201;
Wetaskiwin, 10,103; Drumheller, 6,366.

Vital statistics, *see* p. 271.

Religion, *see* p. 290.

CLIMATE. A continental climate: long, cold winters and mild summers. Rainfall amounts are greatest between May and Sept. Edmonton. Jan. 5°F (−15°C), July 61°F (16·1°C). Annual rainfall 18″ (439 mm).

CONSTITUTION AND GOVERNMENT. The constitution of Alberta is contained in the British North America Act of 1867, and amending Acts; also in the Alberta Act of 1905, passed by the Parliament of the Dominion of Canada, which created the province out of the then Northwest Territories. All the provisions of the British North America Act, except those with respect to school lands and the public domain, were made to apply to Alberta as they apply to the older provinces of Canada. On 1 Oct. 1930 the natural resources were transferred from the Dominion to provincial government control. The province is represented by 6 members in the Senate and 21 in the House of Commons of Canada.

The executive is vested nominally in the Lieut.-Governor, who is appointed by the federal government, but actually in the Executive Council or the Cabinet of the legislature. Legislative power is vested in the Assembly in the name of the Queen.

Members of the Legislative Assembly are elected by the universal vote of adults over the age of 18 years.

There are 83 members in the legislature (elected 8 May 1986): 61 Progressive Conservative, 16 New Democratic Party, 4 Liberal, 2 Representative.

Lieut.-Governor: Hon. Helen Hunley (sworn in 22 Jan. 1985).

Flag: Blue with the shield of the province in the centre.

The members of the Ministry were as follows in Sept. 1987:

Premier, President of Executive Council: Hon. D. R. Getty.

Deputy Premier and Minister of Advanced Education: Hon. D. J. Russell. *Municipal Affairs and Deputy Government House Leader:* Hon. D. Anderson. *Attorney-General, Minister of Federal and Intergovernmental Affairs:* Hon. J. D. Horsman. *Economic Development and Trade:* Hon. L. R. Shaben. *Provincial Treasurer:* Hon. D. Johnston. *Energy:* Hon. Dr P. N. Webber. *Technology, Research and Telecommunications:* Hon. L. Young. *Transportation and Utilities:* Hon. J. A. Adair. *Hospitals and Medical Care:* Hon. M. E. Moore. *Tourism:* Hon. D. Sparrow. *Labour:* Hon. Dr I. Reid. *Social Services:* Hon. C. E. Osterman. *Forestry, Lands and Wildlife:* Hon. E. L. Fjordbotten. *Environment and Deputy Government House Leader:* Hon. K. Kowalski. *Public Works, Supply and Services:* Hon. E. D. Isley. *Agriculture:* Hon. P. Elzinga. *Associate Minister of Agriculture and Deputy Government House Leader:* Hon. S. Cripps. *Culture:* Hon. G. Stevens. *Recreation and Parks:* Hon. N. Weiss. *Career Development and Employment:* Hon. R. Orman. *Education:* Hon. N. Betkowski. *Solicitor General and Minister of Housing and Native Affairs:* Hon. K. Rostad. *Consumer and Corporate Affairs and Minister responsible for Women's Issues:* Hon. E. McCoy. *Community and Occupational Health:* Hon. J. Dinning. *Special Projects:* Hon. N. S. Crawford.

Local Government. The local government units are City, Town, New Town, Village, Summer Village, County, Municipal District and Improvement District.

There are 16 cities in Alberta, namely: Airdrie, Calgary, Camrose, Drumheller, Edmonton, Fort McMurray, Fort Saskatchewan, Grande Prairie, Leduc, Lethbridge, Lloydminster, Medicine Hat, Red Deer, St Albert, Spruce Grove and Wetaskiwin. These cities operate under the Municipal Government Act. The governing body consists of a mayor and a council of from 6 to 20 members. A city can be incorporated by order of the Lieut.-Governor-in-Council. A population of 10,000 is required.

There are no limits of area specified in the statutes for any of the different local government units. The population requirement for a Town as specified in the

Municipal Government Act is 1,000 people, and the area at incorporation is that of the original village.

A Village must contain 75 separate and occupied dwellings. The Municipal Government Act requires each dwelling to have been occupied continuously for a period of at least 6 months. A Summer Village must contain 50 separate dwellings.

A rural county area is an area incorporated through an order of the Lieut.-Governor-in-Council under the provisions of the County Act. One board of councillors deal with both municipal and school affairs.

A rural Municipal District is an area which has been incorporated under the Municipal Government Act. In Municipal Districts separate boards control municipal and school affairs.

Areas not incorporated as counties or Municipal Districts are termed Improvement Districts or Special Areas. Sparsely populated, such districts are administered and taxed by the Department of Municipal Affairs of the provincial government. There are no requirements as to the minimum number of residents of a County or Municipal District.

FINANCE. The budgetary revenue and expenditure (in Canadian $) for years ending 31 March were as follows:

	1983–84	1984–85	1985–86	1986–87	1987–88 [1]
Revenue [2]	9,282,373,000	10,122,287,000	9,873,259,000	8,308,000,000	8,627,000,000
Expenditure [2]	9,341,747,000	9,078,938,000	10,331,460,000	10,806,849,000	10,416,113,000

[1] Estimates.
[2] Excludes funds allocated to Alberta Heritage Savings Trust Fund for 1983–84 to 1986–87.

Personal income *per capita* (1986), $17,672.

ENERGY AND NATURAL RESOURCES

Oil. In 1986, 68,970,000 cu. metres of crude oil were produced with gross sales value of $7,970,208,000. Alberta produced 82% of Canada's crude petroleum output in 1986. Production of natural gas by-products was 18,295,000 cu. metres, valued at $1,762,164,000.

The 4 major deposits of oil sands are found in northern and eastern Alberta: The Athabasca, Cold Lake, Peace River and Buffalo Head Hills deposits; total area, 140,800 sq. km. A limited part of the deposits along the Athabasca River can be exploited through open-pit mining. The rest of the Athabasca, and all the deposits in the other areas, are deeper reserves which must be developed through in situ techniques. These reserves reach depths of 760 metres. By 31 Dec. 1986 there were 638 enhanced oil recovery projects operating. Production of bitumen was estimated at 12,000 cu. metres per day in Dec. 1985.

Two oil sands mining plants in the Fort McMurray area produced 10·8m. cu. metres of synthetic crude oil in 1986.

Gas. Natural gas is found in abundance in numerous localities. In 1986, 67,029m. cu. metres valued at $6,106,362,000 were produced.

Minerals. In 1986 the ultimate remaining recoverable coal resources of Alberta were estimated at 26,000m. tonnes. Production (1986) 25·02m. tonnes valued at $438m.

Value of total mineral production decreased from $27,029,638,000 in 1985 to $17,462,731,000 in 1986.

Agriculture. Total area of farms (1986) 51,040,463 acres; improved land, 31,891,516; (under crops, 22,641,092; improved pasture, 3,402,183; summer fallow, 5,255,965; other improved land, 592,276); unimproved land, 19,148,947; (unimproved pasture, 16,057,185; woodland, 713,699; other unimproved land, 2,378,063). Number of farms (1986) 57,777.

For particulars of agricultural production and livestock, *see under* CANADA, pp. 283–84. Farm cash receipts in 1986 totalled $3,758,869,000, of which crops contributed $1,726,859,000; livestock and products, $1,764,319,000, and other sources, $267,691,000.

Forestry. Total forest lands (1986–87) 338,000 sq. km, of which 186,000 sq. km were productive (supporting 2,500m. cu. metres of wood) and 18,300 sq. km had the potential to produce forest products. In 1986–87, 7·3m. cu. metres of lumber and plywood were produced.

Fisheries. The largest catch in commercial fishing is whitefish. Perch, tullibee, walley, pike and lake trout are also caught in smaller quantities. In 1984 a provincial fish marketing policy was implemented and a new commercial fishery licensing system was approved for implementation in 1986. Commercial fish production in 1986–87 was 2·1m. kg, value $2,718,800.

INDUSTRY. The leading manufacturing industries are food and beverages, petroleum refining, metal fabricating, wood industries, primary metal, chemical and chemical products and non-metallic mineral products industries. There were in 1985 approximately 2,536 manufacturing establishments, in which were employed 74,684 persons, who earned in salaries and wages $2,080,991,000.

Manufacturing shipments had a total value of $15,473,134,000 in 1986. Chief among these shipments were: Food and beverages, $3,827,459,000; refined petroleum and coal products, $4,514,175,000; chemicals and chemical products, $2,009,101,000; fabricated metal products, $713,422,000; primary metals, $642,972,000; non-metallic mineral products, $566,694,000; printing, publishing and allied, $647,695,000; wood, $574,565,000; paper and allied products, $455,372,000; machinery, $560,892,000; furniture and fixtures, $103,193,000; other, $143,669,000.

Total retail sales (1986) $14,338,357,000.

Tourism is of increasing importance and in 1986 contributed $2,276,623,000 to the economy.

COMMUNICATIONS

Roads. In 1987 there were 152,395 km of roads and highways, including 106,043 km gravelled and 18,551 km paved.

At 31 March 1987 there were 2,115,036 motor vehicles registered, including 1,306,382 passenger cars, 386,035 commercial vehicles, 320,438 trailers, 6,048 buses and 42,762 motor cycles.

Railways. In 1987 the length of main railway lines was 10,135·8 km. In 1986 there was a rail rapid transit network in Edmonton (10·5 km) and Calgary (22·5 km).

Post and Telecommunications. Alberta's modern telephone system is owned and operated by the provincial government, except in the city of Edmonton (owned and operated by Edmonton) and some rural lines. There were 1,210,052 telephones in service in April 1987.

JUSTICE AND EDUCATION

Justice. The Supreme Judicial authority of the province is the Court of Appeal. Judges of the Court of Appeal and Court of Queen's Bench are appointed by the Dominion Government and hold office until retirement at the age of 75. There are courts of lesser jurisdiction in both civil and criminal matters. The Court of Queen's Bench has full jurisdiction over civil proceedings. A Provincial Court which has jurisdiction in civil matters up to $1,000 is presided over by provincially appointed judges. Juvenile Courts have power to try boys and girls 16 and under for offences against the Juvenile Delinquents Act.

The jurisdiction of all criminal courts in Alberta is enacted in the provisions of the Criminal Code. The system of procedure in civil and criminal cases conforms as nearly as possible to the English system.

Education. Schools of all grades are included under the term of public school (including those in the separate school system which are publicly supported). The same board of trustees controls the schools from kindergarten to university entrance. In 1986–87 there were 426,987 pupils enrolled in elementary, junior high schools and high schools. The University of Alberta (in Edmonton), organized in 1907, had, in 1986–87, 24,302 full-time students. The University of Calgary, formerly part of the University of Alberta and autonomous from April 1966, had in 1986–87, 16,142 full-time students. The University of Lethbridge, organized in 1966, had in 1986–87, 2,763 full-time students. The Athabasca University had in 1986–87, 10,772 part-time students. Banff Centre for Continuing Education had in 1986–87, 1,360 part-time students. The full-time enrolment at Alberta's 11 public colleges totalled 18,166 students in 1986–87.

Books of Reference

Statistical Information: The Alberta Bureau of Statistics (Dept. of Treasury, Edmonton), which was established in 1939, collects, compiles and distributes information relative to Alberta. Among its publications are: *Alberta Statistical Review* (Quarterly).—*Alberta Economic Accounts* (Annual).—*Alberta Facts* (Annual).—*Population Projections, Alberta* (Occasional).—*Alberta Population Growth* (Quarterly).
Dept. of Economic Development, *Alberta Profile*. Edmonton, (Annual)

MacGregor, J. G., *A History of Alberta*. 2nd ed. Edmonton, 1981
Masson, J., *Alberta's Local Governments and their Politics*. Univ. of Alberta Press, 1985
Richards, J., *Prairie Capitalism: Power and Influence in the New West*. Toronto, 1979
Wiebe, Rudy., *Alberta, a Celebration*. Edmonton, 1979

BRITISH COLUMBIA

HISTORY. Vancouver Island was organized as a colony in 1849; the mainland as far as the watershed of the Rocky Mountains was organized as a colony following a gold rush on the Fraser River in 1859. The two were united as the colony of British Columbia in 1866; this became a Canadian Province in 1871.

AREA AND POPULATION. British Columbia has an area of 948,596 sq. km. The capital is Victoria. The province is bordered westerly by the Pacific ocean and Alaska Panhandle, northerly by the Yukon and Northwest Territories, easterly by the Province of Alberta and southerly by the USA along the 49th parallel. A chain of islands, the largest of which are Vancouver Island and the Queen Charlotte Islands, affords protection to the mainland coast.

The June 1986 census population was 2,889,207.

The principal cities and their 1986 census populations are as follows: Greater Vancouver, 1,266,152; Greater Victoria, 264,614; Prince George, 67,621; Kamloops, 61,773; Kelowna, 61,213; Nanaimo, 49,029; Penticton, 23,588; Vernon, 20,241; Port Alberni, 18,241; Prince Rupert, 15,755; Cranbrook, 15,893; Fort St. John, 13,355.

Vital statistics, *see* p. 271.
Religion, *see* p. 290.

CLIMATE. The climate is cool temperate, but mountain influences affect temperatures and rainfall very considerably. Driest months occur in summer. Vancouver. Jan. 36°F (2·2°C), July 64°F (17·8°C). Annual rainfall 58″ (1,458 mm).

CONSTITUTION AND GOVERNMENT. British Columbia (then known as New Caledonia) originally formed part of the Hudson's Bay Company's concession. In 1849 Vancouver Island and in 1858 British Columbia were constituted Crown Colonies; in 1866 the two colonies amalgamated. The British North America Act of 1867 provided for eventual admission into Canadian Confederation, and on 20 July 1871 British Columbia became the sixth province of the Dominion.

British Columbia has a unicameral legislature of 69 elected members. Government policy is determined by the Executive Council responsible to the Legislature. The Lieut.-Governor is appointed by the Governor-General of Canada, usually for a term of 5 years, and is the head of the executive government of the province.

Lieut.-Governor: The Hon. Robert Gordon Rogers.

Flag: A banner of the arms, *i.e.*, blue and white wavy stripes charged with a setting sun in gold, across the top of a Union Flag with a gold coronet in the centre.

The Legislative Assembly is elected for a maximum term of 5 years. Every male or female Canadian citizen 19 years and over, having resided a minimum of 6 months in the province, duly registered, is entitled to vote. Representation of the parties in Sept. 1987: Social Credit Party, 46; New Democratic Party, 22; Independent, 1.

The province is represented in the Federal Parliament by 28 members in the House of Commons, and 6 Senators.

The Executive Council was composed as follows, Dec. 1987:

Premier and President of the Executive Council: William N. Vander Zalm.

Minister of Economic Development: Grace M. McCarthy. *Provincial Secretary, Minister of Government Services:* Elwood N. Veitch. *Attorney General:* Brian R. D. Smith, QC. *Agriculture and Fisheries:* J. Savage. *Education:* Anthony J. Brummet. *Energy, Mines and Petroleum Resources:* John Davis, PC. *Environment and Parks:* W. Bruce Strachan. *Forests and Lands:* Dave Parker. *Health:* P. A. Dueck. *Social Services and Housing:* Claude H. Richmond. *Intergovernmental Relations:* C. Stephen Rogers.. *Labour and Consumer Services:* L. F. Hansen. *Municipal Affairs:* Rita M. Johnston. *Advanced Education and Job Training:* S. Hagen. *Tourism, Recreation and Culture:* William E. Reid. *Transportation and Highways:* S. Rogers. *Finance and Corporation Relations:* M. Couvelier.

Agent-General in London: Garde Gardom (British Columbia House, 1 Regent St., London, SW1Y 4NS).

Local Government. Vancouver City was incorporated by statute and operates under the provisions of the Vancouver Charter of 1953 and amendments. This is the only incorporated area in British Columbia not operating under the provisions of the Municipal Act. Under this Act municipalities are divided into the following classes: *(a)* a village with a population between 500 and 2,500, governed by a council consisting of a mayor and 4 aldermen; *(b)* a town with a population between 2,500 and 5,000, governed by a council consisting of a mayor and 4 aldermen; *(c)* a city where the population exceeds 5,000 governed by a council consisting of a mayor and 6 or 8 aldermen depending on population; *(d)* a district where the area exceeds 810 hectares and the average density is less than 5 persons per hectare, governed by a council consisting of a mayor and 6 or 8 aldermen depending on population.

There are two other forms of local government: The regional district covering a number of areas both incorporated and unincorporated, governed by a board of directors; and the improvement district governed by a board of 3 trustees.

Revenue for municipal services is derived mainly from real-property taxation, although additional revenue is derived from licence fees, business taxes, fines, public utility projects and grants-in-aid from the provincial government.

ECONOMY

Budget. Current provincial revenue and expenditure, including all capital expenditures, in Canadian $1m. for fiscal years ending 31 March:

	1984–85	1985–86	1986–87	1987–88
Revenue	7,789·9	8,179·8	8,578·0	9,370·0
Expenditure	8,783·8	9,146·3	9,749·0	10,220·0

The main sources of current revenue are the income taxes, contributions from the federal government, and privileges, licences and natural resources taxes and royalties.

The main items of expenditure in 1987–88 (preliminary) are as follows: Health and social services, $4,582·6m.; education, $2,118·7m.; transport and communications, $835·3m.

Banking. On 31 Dec. 1986, Canadian chartered banks maintained 823 branches and had total assets of $34,600m. in British Columbia; credit unions at 284 locations had total assets of $6,711m. Several foreign banks have Canadian head offices in Vancouver and several others have branches.

ENERGY AND NATURAL RESOURCES

Electricity. Generation in 1986 totalled 50,759m. kwh. of which a net 4,709m. kwh. were exported. Consumption within the province was 49,395m. kwh.

Minerals. Copper, coal, natural gas, crude oil, gold and silver are the most important minerals produced. The 1986 total of mineral production was estimated at $3,237m. Total value of mineral fuels produced in 1986 was estimated at: Coal, $1,000m.; oil and gas, $738m.

Agriculture. Only 2·4m. hectares or 3% of the total land area is arable or potentially arable. Farm cash receipts, in 1986, were $1,003·1m.

Forestry. About 55% of British Columbia's land is forest land, with 47·8m. hectares bearing commercial forest. Over 94% of the forest area is owned or administered by the provincial government. The total cut from forests in 1986 was 77·5m. cu. metres.

Fisheries. In 1985 the wholesale market value of fish products was $725m.

INDUSTRY AND TRADE

Industry. The selling value of factory shipments from all manufacturing industries reached an estimated $20,639m. in 1986.

Commerce. Exports through British Columbia customs ports during 1986 totalled $17,931m. in value, while imports amounted to $11,020m. About 32% of exports through British Columbia customs ports are products from other provinces, primarily grains, potash and fuels from the Prairie Provinces. USA is the largest market for products exported through British Columbia customs ports ($6,626m. in 1986) followed by Japan ($4,667m.).

Exports were valued at $12,714·8m. in 1986. The leading exports were: Lumber, $3,091m.; pulp, $1,980·5m.; coal, $1,493·7m.; newsprint, $880·9m.

COMMUNICATIONS

Roads. At 31 March 1986 there were 45,570 km of provincial roads and rights of way in the province, of which 21,101 km were paved.

Railways. The province is served by two transcontinental railways, the Canadian Pacific Railway and the Canadian National Railway. Passenger service is provided by VIA Rail, a Crown Corporation. British Columbia is also served by the publicly owned British Columbia Railway, the Railway Freight Service of the B.C. Hydro and Power Authority, the Northern Alberta Railways Company and the Burlington Northern Inc. The combined route-mileage of mainline track operated by the CPR, CNR and BCR totals 7,500 km. The system also includes CPR and CNR railcar barge connections to Vancouver Island, between Prince Rupert and Alaska, and interchanges with American railways at southern border points. A metro line was opened in Vancouver in 1986.

Aviation. International airports are located at Vancouver and Victoria. Daily interprovincial and intraprovincial flights serve all main population centres. Small public and private airstrips are located throughout the province.

Shipping. The major ports are Vancouver, New Westminster, Victoria, Nanaimo and Prince Rupert. The volume of domestic cargo handled during 1985 was 42·3m. tonnes.

The British Columbia Ferries connect Vancouver Island with the mainland and also provide service to other coastal points. Service by other ferry systems is also provided between Vancouver Island and the USA. The Alaska State Ferries connect Prince Rupert with centres in Alaska.

Post and Broadcasting. The British Columbia Telephone Company have approximately 1·5m. telephones in service. In March 1986 there were 67 AM radio, 19 FM radio, 10 television stations and 2 pay-television networks originating in British Columbia. In addition there were 575 re-broadcasting stations in the province.

EDUCATION AND WELFARE

Education. Education, free up to Grade XII levels, is financed jointly from municipal and provincial government revenues. Attendance is compulsory from the age of 6 to 15. There were approximately 486,200 pupils enrolled in public schools from kindergarten to Grade XII in Sept. 1986.

The universities had a full-time enrolment of approximately 35,000 for 1986–87. They include University of British Columbia, Vancouver; University of Victoria, Victoria and Simon Fraser University, Burnaby. The regional colleges are Camosun College, Victoria; Capilano College, North Vancouver; Cariboo College, Kamloops; College of New Caledonia, Prince George; Douglas College, New Westminister; East Kootenay Community College, Cranbrook; Fraser Valley College, Chilliwack/Abbotsford; Kwantlen College, Surrey; Malaspina College, Nanaimo; North Island College, Comox; Northern Lights College, Dawson Creek/Fort St John; Northwest Community College, Terrace/Prince Rupert; Okanagan College, Kelowna with branches at Salmon Arm and Vernon; Selkirk College, Castlegar; Vancouver Community College, Vancouver.

There are also the British Columbia Institute of Technology, Burnaby; Emily Carr College of Art and Design, Vancouver; Justice Institute of British Columbia, Vancouver; Open Learning Institute, Richmond; Pacific Marine Training Institute, North Vancouver; Pacific Vocational Institute, Burnaby/Maple Ridge/Richmond. A televised distance education and special programmes through KNOW, the Knowledge Network of the West is provided.

Health. The Government operates a hospital insurance scheme giving universal coverage after a qualifying period of 3 months' residence in the province. The province has come under a national medicare scheme which is partially subsidized by the provincial government and partially by the federal government.

Books of Reference

Statistical Information: Central Statistics Bureau (Ministry of Economic Development, Hon. Grace McCarthy—Minister, Parliament Buildings, Victoria, B.C., V8V 1X4), collects, compiles and distributes information relative to the Province.
  Publications include *B.C. Industry Review* (annual); *Manufacturers' Directory; External Trade Report* (annual); *British Columbia Facts and Statistics* (annual); *British Columbia Economic Accounts* (annual); *British Columbia Population Forecast* (annual).

Ministry of Finance, *British Columbia Financial and Economic Review.* Victoria, B.C. (annual)
Morley, J. T., *The Reins of Power: Governing British Columbia.* Vancouver, 1983
Ormsby, M., *British Columbia: A History.* Vancouver, 1958

MANITOBA

HISTORY. The Hudson's Bay Company formed a colony on the Red River in 1812, which was part of territory annexed to Canada in 1870. The Metis colonists (part-Indian, mostly French-speaking, Catholic) objected to the arrangements for the purchase of the Company territory by Canada and the province of Manitoba was created to accommodate them. It was extended northwards and westwards in 1881 and to Hudson Bay in 1912.

AREA AND POPULATION. The area of the province is 250,946 sq. miles (649,046 sq. km), of which 211,721 sq. miles are land and 39,225 sq. miles water. From north to south it is 793 km and at the widest point it is 493 km.

The population (census, 1986) was 1,071,232. Estimate (April 1987), 1,082,800. Population of Winnipeg, the capital (June 1986), 625,304; other principal cities (census, 1986): Brandon, 38,708; Thompson, 14,701; Portage la Prairie, 13,198; Selkirk, 10,013; Flin Flon (Manitoba portion), 7,243.

Vital statistics, *see* p. 271.

Religion, *see* p. 290.

CLIMATE. The climate is cold continental, with very severe winters but pleasantly warm summers. Rainfall amounts are greatest in the months May to Sept. Winnipeg. Jan. –3°F (–19·3°C), July 67°F (19·6°C). Annual rainfall 21" (539 mm).

CONSTITUTION AND GOVERNMENT. Manitoba was known as the Red River Settlement before its entry into the Dominion in 1870. The provincial government is administered by a Lieut.-Governor assisted by an Executive Council (Cabinet) which is appointed from and responsible to a legislative assembly of 57 members elected for 5 years. Women were enfranchised in 1916. The Electoral Division Act, 1955, created 57 single-member constituencies and abolished the transferable vote. The Electoral Divisions Act, 1979, created 27 rural electoral divisions, and 30 urban electoral divisions. The province is represented by 6 members in the Senate and 14 in the House of Commons of Canada.

Lieut.-Governor: Dr George Johnson (sworn in 12 Dec. 1986).

Flag: The British Red Ensign with the shield of the province in the fly.

State of parties in the Legislative Assembly: New Democratic Party, 30; Progressive Conservative, 26; Liberal, 1.

The members of the New Democratic Party Ministry (sworn in 30 Nov. 1981) are as follows (Jan. 1988):

Premier, President of the Council, Minister of Federal-Provincial Relations: Howard Russell Pawley.

Employment Services and Economic Security, Minister responsible for and charged with the administration of The Manitoba Data Services Act: Leonard Salisbury Evans. *Municipal Affairs, Minister charged with the Administration of the Manitoba Public Insurance Act:* Billie Uruski. *Co-operative Development:* Jay Marine Cowan. *Health, Sport, Minister charged with the administration of The Boxing and Wrestling Commission Act, The Fitness and Amateur Sport Act:* Wilson D. Parasiuk. *Industry, Trade and Technology, Attorney-General, Keeper of the Great Seal, Minister responsible for The Development Corporation Act:* Victor Schroeder. *Community Services:* Maureen Lucille Hemphill. *Finance, Minister responsible for and having general supervision of The Civil Service Act, The Civil Service Superannuation Act, The Public Servants Insurance Act, Minister responsible for A. E. McKenzie Co. Ltd:* Eugene Michael Kostyra. *Education, Minister responsible for Constitutional Affairs:* Roland Penner. *Deputy Premier, Housing, Labour, Minister responsible for the Status of Women:* Muriel Ann Smith. *Business Development and Tourism, Consumer and Corporate Affairs:* Alvin Henry Mackling. *Energy and Mines, Minister responsible for The Natural Gas Act, The Manitoba Natural Resources Development Act (with respect to Channel Area Loggers Ltd or to Moose Lake Loggers Ltd) and Manitoba Forestry Resources Ltd:* Jerry Thomas Storie. *Natural Resources, Minister responsible for and charged with the administration of The Communities Economic Development Fund Act:* John S. Plohman. *Highways and Transportation:* John Bucklaschuk. *Environment and Workplace Safety and Health:* Gerard Lecuyer. *Government Services, Minister responsible for The Workers Compensation Act (except as it relates to Worker Advisers):* Harry M. Harapiak. *Urban Affairs, Crown Investments, Minister responsible for the administration of The Manitoba Telephone Act, The Crown Corporation Accountability Act and The Liquor Control Act:* Gary A. Doer. *Agriculture:* Leonard E. Harapiak. *Culture, Heritage and Recreation, Minister charged with the administration of The Manitoba Lotteries Foundation Act:* Judith Wasylycia-Leis. *Northern Affairs, Minister responsible for Native Affairs:* Elijah Harper.

Local Government. Rural Manitoba is organized into rural municipalities which vary widely in size. Some have only 4 townships (a township is 36 sq. miles), while the largest has 22 townships. The province has 105 rural municipalities, as well as 35 incorporated towns, 39 incorporated villages and 5 incorporated cities.

On 1 Jan. 1972, the cities and towns comprising the metropolitan area of Winnipeg were amalgamated to form the City of Winnipeg. A mayor and council are elected to a central government, but councillors also sit on 'community committees' which represent the areas or wards they serve. These committees are advised by non-elected residents of the area on provision of municipal services within the community committee jurisdiction. Taxing powers and overall budgeting rest with the central council. The mayor is elected at the same time as the councillors in a city-wide vote. Revisions to the City of Winnipeg Act came into effect with the municipal elections held in Oct. 1977.

Since Jan. 1945, 17 Local Government Districts have been formed in the less densely populated areas of the province. They are administered by a provincially appointed person, who acts on the advice of locally elected councils.

In the extreme north, many communities have locally elected councils, while others are administered directly by the Department of Northern Affairs. This department provides most of the funding in all these northern settlements.

FINANCE. Provincial revenue and expenditure (current account) for fiscal years ending 31 March (in Canadian $):

	1983–84	1984–85	1985–86	1986–87 [1]	1987–88 [2]
Revenue	2,797,155,000	2,924,600,000	3,116,600,000	3,385,800,000	3,772,600,000
Expenditure	3,226,104,000	3,407,200,000	3,644,900,000	3,945,600,000	4,187,900,000

[1] Preliminary unaudited. [2] Budgeted.

ENERGY AND NATURAL RESOURCES

Electricity. The total generating capacity of Manitoba's power stations is 4·1m. kw. The Manitoba Hydro system, owned by the province, provides most of this power, while the city-owned Winnipeg Hydro provides about 190,000 kw. The systems have about 436,000 customers and consumption was 13·6m. kwh. in 1986.

Oil. Crude oil production in 1986 was valued at $195m. for the 825,000 cu. metres produced.

Minerals. Total value of minerals in 1986 was about $758·4m. Principal minerals mined are nickel, zinc, copper, and small quantities of gold and silver. Manitoba has the world's largest deposits of caesium ore.

Agriculture. Rich farmland is the main primary resource, although the area of Manitoba in farms is only about 14% of the total land area. In 1986 the total value of agricultural production in Manitoba was $2,200m., with $1,500m. from crops, $737m. from livestock and from the sale of other products including furs, hides and honey.

Forestry. About 40% of the land area is wooded, of which 149,000 sq. km is productive forest land. Total sales of wood-using industries (1986, estimate) $500m.

Fur Trade. Value of fur production to the trapper was $5m. in 1986.

Fisheries. From 22,000 sq. miles of rivers and lakes fisheries production was about $18m. in 1985–86. Whitefish, sauger, pickerel, pike, trout and perch are the principal varieties of fish caught.

INDUSTRY AND TRADE

Industry. Manufacturing, the largest industry in the province, encompasses almost every major industrial activity in Canada. Estimated shipments in 1986 totalled $5,611m. Manufacturing employed about 57,000 persons. Due to the agricultural base of the province, the food and beverage group of industries is by far the largest, valued at $1,902m. in 1986, accounting for about 33·9% of the total value. The next largest segments are transportation equipment, $409m. (7·3%), clothing and textiles, $399m. (7·1%) and printing and allied products, $344m. (6·1%).

Trade. Products grown and manufactured in Manitoba find ready markets in other parts of Canada, in the USA, particularly the upper midwest region, and in other countries. Export shipments to foreign countries from Manitoba in 1986 were valued at about $2,462m., with $1,331m. (54·1%) going to the US. Of total exports about 28% are raw materials and about 72% are processed and manufactured products.

Tourism. In 1986, non-Manitoban tourists numbered 2·4m. All tourists including Manitobans contributed $657m. to the economy.

COMMUNICATIONS

Roads. Highways and provincial roads totalled 19,721 km in 1987.

Railways. At 30 June 1987 the province had 6,250 km of track, not including industrial track, yards and sidings.

Aviation. A total of 108 licensed commercial air carriers operate from bases in Manitoba, as well as 6 regularly scheduled major national and international airlines.

Post. All of the Manitoba Telephone System's 502,400 (1986) telephones are dial-operated. There are some privately-owned fixtures and extension phones; all service is operated by MTS.

EDUCATION. Education is controlled through locally elected school divisions. There are about 199,000 children enrolled in the province's elementary and secondary schools. Manitoba has 3 universities with an enrolment of about 33,800 during the 1986–87 year; the University of Manitoba, founded in 1877, in Winnipeg, the University of Winnipeg, and Brandon University. Expenditure (estimate) on education in the 1987–88 fiscal year was $747m.

Three community colleges, in Brandon, The Pas and Winnipeg, offer 2-year diploma courses in a number of fields, as well as specialized training in many trades. They also give a large number and variety of shorter courses, both at their campuses and in many communities throughout the province.

Books of Reference

General Information: Inquiries may be addressed to the Information Services Branch, Room 29, Legislative Building, Winnipeg, R3C OV8.

The Department of Agriculture publishes: *Year Book of Manitoba Agriculture*
Information Services Branch publishes: *Manitoba Facts*
Manitoba Statistical Review. Manitoba Bureau of Statistics, Quarterly
Twelfth Census of Canada: Manitoba. Statistics Canada, 1981
Jackson, J. A., *The Centennial History of Manitoba.* Toronto, 1970
Morton, W. L., *Manitoba: A History.* Univ. of Toronto Press, 1967

NEW BRUNSWICK

HISTORY. Touched by Jacques Cartier in 1534, New Brunswick was first explored by Samuel de Champlain in 1604. It was ceded by the French in the Treaty of Utrecht in 1713 and became a permanent British possession in 1763. It was separated from Nova Scotia and became a province in June 1784, as a result of the great influx of United Empire Loyalists. Responsible government came into being in 1848, and consisted of an executive council, a legislative council (later abolished) and a House of Assembly.

AREA AND POPULATION. The area of the province is 28,354 sq. miles

(73,000 sq. km), of which 27,633 sq. miles (71,569 sq. km) are land area. The population (census 1986) was 710,422. Of the individuals identifying a single ethnic origin (at the 1981 census), 53·5% were British and 36·4% French. Other significant ethnic groups were German, Dutch and Scandinavian. Among those who provided a multiple response 3·3% were of British and French descent and 1·6% British and other. In 1981 there were 5,515 Native People or Native People and other. Census 1986 population of urban centres: Saint John, 76,381; Moncton, 55,468; Fredericton (capital), 44,352; Bathurst, 14,683; Edmundston, 11,497; Campbellton, 9,073.

Vital statistics, see p. 271.

Religion, see p. 290.

CLIMATE. A cool temperate climate, with rain at all seasons but temperatures modified by the influence of the Gulf Stream. Saint John. Jan. 14°F (–10°C), July 63°F (17·2°C). Annual rainfall 51″ (1,278 mm).

CONSTITUTION AND GOVERNMENT. The government is vested in a Lieut.-Governor and a Legislative Assembly of 58 members each of whom is individually elected to represent the voters in one constituency or riding. A simultaneous translation system is used in the Assembly. Any Canadian subject of full age and 6 months' residence is entitled to vote. As a result of the provincial election held on 10 Oct. 1982 and subsequent by-elections, the Assembly is composed of 37 Progressive Conservatives, 17 Liberals and 1 New Democratic Party members. The province has 10 members in the Canadian Senate and 10 members in the federal House of Commons.

Lieut.-Governor: Gilbert Finn (appointed Aug. 1987).

Flag: A banner of the Arms, *i.e.*, yellow charged with a black heraldic ship on wavy lines of blue and white; across the top a red band with a gold lion.

The members of the Liberal government are as follows (Oct. 1987):

Premier and Minister responsible for the Advisory Council on the Status of Women, and for Regional Development: Francis J. McKenna.

President of the Executive Council and Intergovernmental Affairs: Aldéa Landry.

Attorney General and Justice: James Lockyer. *Finance and responsibility for the New Brunswick Liquor Corporation:* Allan Maher. *Chairman of Board of Management:* Gerald Clavette. *Supply and Services:* Bruce Smith. *Transportation:* Sheldon Lee. *Natural Resources and Energy:* Morris Green. *Agriculture:* Alan Graham. *Health and Community Services:* Ray Frenette. *Income Assistance:* Laureen Jarrett. *Labour and responsibility for Multiculturalism:* Michael McKee. *Education:* Shirley Dysart. *Advanced Education and Training:* Dr Russ King. *Municipal Affairs and Environment:* Vaughn Blaney. *Commerce and Technology:* A. W. Lacey. *Fisheries:* Douglas Young. *Tourism, Recreation and Heritage:* Roland Beaulieu. *Housing:* Peter Trites. *Chairman of the New Brunswick Electric Power Commission:* Rayburn Doucett. *Solicitor General:* Conrad Landry.

Local Government. Under the reforms introduced in 1967 the province has assumed complete administrative and financial responsibility for education, health, welfare and administration of justice. Local government is now restricted to provision of services of a strictly local nature. Under the new municipal structure, units include existing and new cities, towns and villages. Counties have disappeared as municipal units. Areas with limited populations have become local service districts. The former local improvement districts have become towns, villages or local service districts depending on their size.

FINANCE. The ordinary budget (in Canadian $) is shown as follows (financial years ended 31 March):

	1984	1985	1986	1987
Gross revenue	2,213,420,941	2,373,169,361	2,662,864,912	2,765,646,061
Gross expenditure	2,345,326,419	2,510,960,922	2,714,257,315	2,837,964,380

Funded debt and capital loans outstanding (exclusive of Treasury Bills) as of 31 March 1987 was $3,567m. Sinking funds held by the province at 31 March 1987, $956m. The ordinary budget excludes capital spending.

ENERGY AND NATURAL RESOURCES

Electricity. Hydro-electric, thermal and nuclear generating stations of the New Brunswick Electric Power Commission had an installed capacity of 3,190,000 kw. at 31 March 1986, consisting of 14 generating stations. The Mactaquac hydro-electric development near Fredericton, has a name plate capacity of 653,400 kw. The largest thermal generating station, Coleson Cove, near Saint John, has over 1m. kw. of installed capacity. Atlantic Canada's first nuclear generating station, a 630,000 kw. CANDU plant built on a promontory jutting out in the Bay of Fundy, near Saint John, went into commercial operation in Jan. 1983. New Brunswick is electrically inter-connected with utilities in neighbouring provinces of Quebec, Nova Scotia and Prince Edward Island, as well as the New England States. Electricity export sales accounted for over 40% of revenue in 1985–86; energy purchases, mainly from the large Hydro Quebec system, supplied about 35% of in-province energy requirements.

Minerals. In 1985, a total of 22 different metals, minerals and commodities were produced. These included lead, zinc, copper, cadmium, bismuth, gold, silver, antimony, potash, salt, limestone, dolomite, gypsum, oil, gas, coal, oil shales, sand, gravel, clay, peat and marl. The total value of minerals produced in 1985 declined to (preliminary) $552,132,000 from $619,969,438 in 1984. The largest contributors to mineral production are zinc, silver, lead and potash with zinc accounting for over 53% of total value in 1985. These 4 minerals recorded significant reductions in price during the year, especially zinc which declined nearly 40%. In Canada in 1985, New Brunswick ranked first in bismuth production; second in antimony, tungsten, peat and potash; third in sulphur, lead, silver and zinc, and fifth in copper and clay products. Antimony is mined at Lake George and production resumed at the Durham Resources mine near Fredericton in 1985. Peat, rapidly becoming a major industry, is produced from 15 operations in the north. Three potash mines are in operation in the Sussex area, including the Denison-Potacan mine where production commenced in 1985. Oil and natural gas continue to be produced in the Stoney Creek and Hillsborough areas. Gordex Minerals produced its first gold in 1986 using the heap leach process. Coal is strip-mined at Grand Lake, producing some 555,000 tonnes annually. Not all of the province's minerals have been explored sufficiently and research continues. Provincial government programmes are being supplemented by a 5-year, $22m. Mineral Development Agreement between the Canada Department of Energy, Mines and Resources and the province. Federal and Provincial agencies are co-operating on field, laboratory and other projects.

Agriculture. The total area under crops is estimated at 129,475 hectares. Farms numbered 3,554 and averaged 115 hectares each (census 1986). Potatoes account for 19% of total farm cash income. Mixed farming is common throughout the province. Dairy farming is centred around the larger urban areas, and is located mainly along the Saint John River Valley and in the south-eastern sections of the province. Income from dairy operations provides about 24% of farm cash income. New Brunswick is self-sufficient in fluid milk and supplies a processing industry. For particulars of agricultural production and livestock, *see under* CANADA, pp. 283–84. Farm cash receipts in 1986 were approximately $226m.

Forestry. New Brunswick contains some 62,000 sq. km of productive forest lands. The gross value of forest production is over $1,300m. and it accounts for almost one-quarter of all goods produced in the province. The pulp and paper and allied industry group is the largest component of the industry contributing about 70% of the value of output. Timber-using plants employ about 15,000 people for all aspects of the forest industry, including harvesting, processing and transportation. Practically all forest products are exported from the province's numerous ports and harbours near which many of the mills are located or sent by road or rail to the USA.

Fisheries. Commercial fishing is one of the most important primary industries of the province, employing 6,488. Nearly 50 commercial species of fish and shellfish are landed, including scallop, shrimp, crab, herring and cod. Landings in 1986 (141,125 tonnes) amounted to $97·9m. In 1986 there were 150 fish processing plants employing 14,000 people in peak periods. The total market value of 94,383 tonnes of fish products in 1985 was $315·2m. Estimate (1985) $350m. Exports (1986) $305·2m., mainly to the USA and Japan.

INDUSTRY. In 1987 there were 1,477 manufacturing and processing establishments, employing about 42,300 persons. New Brunswick's location, with deep-water harbours open throughout the year and container facilities at Saint John, makes it ideal for exporting. Industries include food and beverages, paper and allied industries, timber products. About 20% of the industrial labour force work in Saint John.

TOURISM. Tourism is a major industry. During 1986, 4·3m. tourists spent approximately $464m. Over 26,000 people are employed in the industry.

COMMUNICATIONS

Roads. There are about 1,541·9 km of arterial highways and 2,381·7 km of collector roads, all of which are hard-surfaced. 12,279·9 km of local roads provide access to most areas in the province. The main highway system, including 596·4 km of the Trans-Canada Highway, links the province with the principal roads in Quebec and Nova Scotia, and Prince Edward Island, as well as the Interstate Highway System in the eastern seaboard states of the USA. Passenger vehicles, 31 March 1987, numbered 286,037; commercial vehicles, 122,052; motor cycles, 11,393.

Railways. New Brunswick is served by main lines of both Canadian Pacific and Canadian National railways.

Post and Broadcasting. In 1984 the New Brunswick Telephone Co. Ltd had 439,446 telephones in service. The province is served by 21 radio stations. Sixteen are privately owned and 3 owned by the Canadian Broadcasting Corporation and 2 are university stations. Three stations broadcast in the French language, 3 are bilingual and the CBC International Service broadcasts in several languages from its station at Sackville. The province is served by 3 television stations, 1 of which broadcasts in French.

Newspapers. New Brunswick had (1987) 6 daily newspapers, 2 in French, and 23 weekly newspapers, 7 in French or bilingual.

EDUCATION. Public education is free and non-sectarian. There are 4 universities. The University of New Brunswick at Fredericton (founded 13 Dec. 1785 by the Loyalists, elevated to university status in 1823, reorganized as the University of New Brunswick in 1859) had 6,617 full-time students at the Fredericton campus and 1,097 full-time students at the Saint John campus (1986–87); Mount Allison University at Sackville had 1,750 full-time students; the Université de Moncton at Moncton, 3,405 full-time students; St Thomas University at Fredericton, 1,267 full-time students. During the period 1 July 1986 to 30 June 1987, there were 12,197 students enrolled full-time at 9 Community College campuses and at various campus training centres.

There were, in Sept. 1986, 139,023 students and 7,600 full-time (equivalent) teachers in the province's 434 schools. There are 41 school boards.

Books of Reference

Industrial Information: Dept. of Commerce and Technology, Fredericton. *Economic Information:* Dept. of Finance, Economics and Statistics Branch. Fredericton. *General Information:* NB Information Service, Fredericton.
Directory of Products and Manufacturers. Department of Commerce and Development; Annual
Thompson, C., *New Brunswick Inside Out.* Ottawa, 1977
Trueman, S., *The Fascinating World of New Brunswick.* Fredericton, 1973

NEWFOUNDLAND AND LABRADOR

HISTORY. Archaeological finds at L'Anse-au-Meadow in northern New-foundland show that the Vikings had established a colony there at about A.D. 1000. This site is the only known Viking colony in North America. Newfoundland was discovered by John Cabot 24 June 1497, and was soon frequented in the summer months by the Portuguese, Spanish and French for its fisheries. It was formally occupied in Aug. 1583 by Sir Humphrey Gilbert on behalf of the English Crown, but various attempts to colonize the island remained unsuccessful. Although British sovereignty was recognized in 1713 by the Treaty of Utrecht, disputes over fishing rights with the French were not finally settled till 1904. By the Anglo-French Convention of 1904, France renounced her exclusive fishing rights along part of the coast, granted under the Treaty of Utrecht, but retained sovereignty of the offshore islands of St Pierre and Miquelon.

AREA AND POPULATION. Area, 143,501 sq. miles (371,690 sq. km) of which freshwater, 13,139 sq. miles (34,030 sq. km). In March 1927 the Privy Council decided the boundary between Canada and Newfoundland in Labrador. This area, now part of the Province of Newfoundland and Labrador, is 102,699 sq. miles. The coastline is extremely irregular. Bays, fiords and inlets are numerous and there are many good harbours with deep water close to shore. The coast is rugged with bold rocky cliffs from 200 to 400 ft high; in the Bay of Islands some of the islands rise 500 ft, with the adjacent shore 1,000 ft above tide level. The interior is a plateau of moderate elevation and the chief relief features trend north-east and south-west. Long Range, the most notable of these, begins at Cape Ray and extends north-east for 200 miles, the highest peak reaching 2,673 ft. Approximately one-third of the area is covered by water. Grand Lake, the largest body of water, has an area of about 200 sq. miles. The principal rivers flow towards the north-east. On the borders of the lakes and water-courses good land is generally found, particularly in the valleys of the Terra Nova River, the Gander River, the Exploits River and the Humber River, which are also heavily timbered.

Census population, 1986, was 568,349.

The capital of Newfoundland is the City of St John's (161,901, metropolitan area). The only other city is Corner Brook (22,719); important towns are Labrador City (8,664), Gander (10,207), Stephenville (7,994), Grand Falls (9,121), Happy Valley–Goose Bay (7,248), Marystown (6,660), Channel-Port aux Basques (5,901), Windsor (5,545), Carbonear (5,337), Bonavista (4,605), Wabana (4,057), Wabush (2,637).

Vital statistics, see p. 271.

Religion, see p. 290.

CLIMATE. The cool temperate climate is marked by heavy precipitation, distributed evenly over the year, a cool summer and frequent fogs in spring. St. John's. Jan. 23°F (–5°C), July 59°F (15°C). Annual rainfall 54″ (1,367 mm).

CONSTITUTION AND GOVERNMENT. Until 1832 Newfoundland was ruled by the Governor under instructions of the Colonial Office. In that year a Legislature was brought into existence, but the Governor and his Executive Council were not responsible to it. Under the constitution of 1855, which lasted until its suspension in 1934, the government was administered by the Governor appointed by the Crown with an Executive Council responsible to the House of Assembly of 27 elected members and a Legislative Council of 24 members nominated for life by the Governor in Council. Women were enfranchised in 1925. At the Imperial Conference of 1917 Newfoundland was constituted as a Dominion.

In 1933 the financial situation had become so critical that the Government of Newfoundland asked the Government of the UK to appoint a Royal Commission to investigate conditions. On the strength of their recommendations, the parliamentary form of government was suspended and Government by Commission was inaugurated on 16 Feb. 1934.

A National Convention, elected in 1946, made, in 1948, recommendations to H.M. Government in Great Britain as to the possible forms of future government to be submitted to the people at a national referendum. Two referenda were held. In the first referendum (June 1948) the three forms of government submitted to the people were: Commission of government for 5 years, confederation with Canada and responsible government as it existed in 1933. No one form of government received a clear majority of the votes polled, and commission of government, receiving the fewest votes, was eliminated. In the second referendum (July 1948) confederation with Canada received 78,408 and responsible government 71,464 votes.

In the Canadian Senate on 18 Feb. 1949 Royal assent was given to the terms of union of Newfoundland and Labrador with Canada, and on 23 March 1949, in the House of Lords, London, Royal assent was given to an amendment to the British North America Act made necessary by the inclusion of Newfoundland and Labrador as the tenth Province of Canada.

Under the terms of union of Newfoundland and Labrador with Canada, which was signed at Ottawa on 11 Dec. 1948, the constitution of the Legislature of Newfoundland and Labrador as it existed immediately prior to 16 Feb. 1934 shall, subject to the terms of the British North America Acts, 1867 to 1946, continue as the constitution of the Legislature of the Province of Newfoundland and Labrador until altered under the authority of the said Acts.

The franchise was in 1965 extended to all male and female residents who have attained the age of 19 years and are otherwise qualified as electors.

The House of Assembly (Amendment) Act, 1979, established 52 electoral districts and 52 members of the Legislature.

In Jan. 1988 there were 35 Progressive-Conservatives, 15 Liberals and 2 New Democrats.

The province is represented by 6 members in the Senate and by 7 members in the House of Commons of Canada.

Lieut.-Governor: Hon. James W. McGrath (assumed office 5 Sept. 1986).

Flag: White, in the hoist 4 solid blue triangles; in the fly 2 red triangles voided white, and between them a yellow tongue bordered in red.

The Progressive-Conservative Executive Council was, at 6 Jan. 1988, composed as follows:

Premier and Minister of Energy: Brian Peckford.
Deputy Premier and Minister of Health: Dr John Collins. *Finance and Minister responsible for Newfoundland and Labrador Hydro:* Neil Windsor. *President of Treasury Board, President of Executive Council and Government House Leader:* Leonard A. Simms. *Intergovernmental Affairs:* Ronald G. Dawe. *Transportation:* Norman Doyle. *Justice:* Lynn Verge. *Development and Tourism:* Harold M. Barrett. *Education:* Loyola Hearn. *Fisheries:* Thomas G. Rideout. *Career Development and Advanced Studies:* William B. Matthews. *Social Services:* Glenn Tobin. *Forest Resources:* Robert J. Aylward. *Municipal Affairs:* Charles Brett. *Rural and Agricultural Development:* Charles Power. *Mines:* Jerome Dinn. *Public Works and Services:* Dr Hugh M. Twomey. *Labour:* T. A. Blanchard. *Culture, Recreation and Youth:* John C. Butt. *Environment and Lands:* James Russell. *Consumer Affairs and Communications:* D. Haig Young. *Minister responsible for Newfoundland and Labrador Housing:* Milton Peach. *Minister responsible for Northern Development:* Garfield Warren.

Agent-General in London: H. Watson Jamer (60 Trafalgar Sq., WC2).

FINANCE. Budget[1] in Canadian $1,000 for fiscal years ended 31 March:

	1982–83	1983–84	1984–85	1985–86	1986–87[2]	1987–88[3]
Gross revenue	1,652,046	1,768,464	1,867,470	2,072,581	2,233,077	2,316,349
Gross expenditure	1,689,339	1,827,839	1,954,762	2,117,012	2,273,981	2,489,022

[1] Current amount only. [2] Revised estimates. [3] Estimates.

Capital account:

	1984–85	1985–86	1986–87 [2]	1987–88 [3]
Gross revenue	78,205,000	63,952,000	54,711,000	132,475,000
Gross expenditure	243,074,000	273,347,000	264,414,000	336,038,000

[1] Current amount only.   [2] Revised estimates.   [3] Estimates.

Public debenture debt as at 31 March 1987 (preliminary) was $3,687·4m.; sinking fund, $911·2m.

ENERGY AND NATURAL RESOURCES

Electricity. The electrical energy requirements of the province are met mainly by hydro-electric power, with petroleum fuels being utilized to provide the balance. The total amount of energy generated in the province in 1986 (preliminary) was 40,407,174 mwh., of which approximately 97% was derived from hydro-electric facilities. The greater part of the energy produced in 1986 (preliminary) came from Churchill Falls, of which 30,694,787 mwh. was sold to Hydro-Quebec under the terms of a long-term contract. Energy consumed in the province during 1986 (preliminary) totalled 9,712,387 mwh., with approximately 8,434,333 mwh., or 87%, coming from hydro-electric facilities.

At Dec. 1986 total electrical generating capacity in the province was 7,237 mw., with hydro-electric plants accounting for 6,538 mw., or 90%. It is estimated that potential additional hydro-electric generating capacity of up to 4·5m. kw. can be developed at various sites in Labrador.

Oil. In 1981 the province consumed refined petroleum at the rate of 39,000 bbls a day.

Since 1965, 129 wells have been drilled on the Continental Margin of the Province. In 1986 it was estimated that offshore exploration expenditures would be approximately $377·9m.

By 31 Dec. 1985 there had been 20 significant hydrocarbon discoveries off Newfoundland and delineation drilling had been initiated or was ongoing at 6: Terra Nova, Ben Nevis, Whiterose, North Ben Nevis and Mara. In 1986 only the Hibernia discovery had commercial capability and the Canada-Newfoundland Offshore Petroleum Board approved Mobil Oil Canada's development plan for the Hibernia Project, with production starting in the early 1990's.

In 1979, a discovery of oil was made on the Hibernia geological structure located 164 nautical miles east of Cape Spear. The discovery well, Hibernia P-15, tested medium gravity, sweet crude from several intervals with a reported total producing capability in excess of 20,000 bbls of oil per day.

By 31 Dec. 1985 there had been 20 significant hydrocarbon discoveries off Newfoundland but by Nov. 1986 only one (Hibernia) was considered commercially viable.

In June 1986, the Canada–Newfoundland Offshore Petroleum Board approved Mobil Oil Canada's development plan for the Hibernia Project. Production is currently expected to begin in the early 1990's.

Minerals. The mineral resources are vast but only partially documented. Large deposits of iron ore, with an ore reserve of over 5,000m. tons at Labrador City, Wabush City and in the Knob Lake area are supplying approximately half of Canada's production. Other large deposits of iron ore are known to exist in the Julienne Lake area.

There are a variety of other minerals being produced in the province in more limited amounts.

Uranium deposits in the Kaipokak Bay area near Makkovik in Labrador are presently being studied by Brinex. The Central Mineral Belt, which extends from the Smallwood Reservoir to the Atlantic coast near Makkovik, holds uranium, copper, beryllium and molybdenite potential.

In 1986 a gold mine was being developed at Hope Brook on the south coast east of Port aux Basques. Full production from an underground operation using conventional carbon-in-pulp gold processing is planned to start in late 1988.

Production in 1986 (preliminary): Iron ore, 19,465,000 tonnes ($702,483,000);

zinc, 6,686 kg ($8,264,000); asbestos, 45,000 tonnes ($18m.); gypsum, 449,000 tonnes ($5,507,000); pyrophyllite, soapstone and talc ($1,308,000); cement ($9·3m.); clay products ($1·48m.); sand and gravel, 2,700,000 tonnes ($13,345,000); stone, 529,000 tonnes ($2,612,000); quartz ($1·6m.); barite ($24,000); peat, 1,000 tonnes ($238,000); gemstones ($8,000).

Agriculture. The estimated value of agricultural products sold, including livestock, 1986, was $44·9m.

Forestry. The forestry economy in the province is mainly dependent on the operation of 3 newsprint mills. In 1986 the value of newsprint exported from these 3 mills totalled $369m. Lumber mills, saw-log operations produced 38m. f.b.m. in 1983–84.

Fisheries. The principal fish landings are cod, flounder, redfish, Queen crabs, lobster, salmon and herring. In 1986 (preliminary) a yearly average of some 9,500 persons were employed by the fish-processing industry and there were 26,939 licensed full-, part-time and casual fishermen engaged in harvesting operations. Approximately 206 processing operations were licensed in 1986. The production of fresh and frozen fish products was $449·8m. in 1984.

The total catch in 1986 (preliminary) was 493,845 tonnes valued at $197,581,000, which comprised: Cod, 270,172 tonnes ($103,451,000); flounders and soles, 64,675 ($19,525,000); herring, 14,448 tonnes ($2,469,000); redfish, 22,254 ($4,532,000); lobster, 1,917 ($11,625,000); salmon, 1,191 ($4,572,000); capelin, 64,788 ($20,867,000); crab, 9,175 ($10,439,000); other, 45,185 ($20,101,000).

INDUSTRY. The total value of manufacturing shipments in 1986 was $1,645m. This consists largely of first-stage processing of primary resource products with two of the largest components being paper and fish products.

TRADE UNIONS. There were (1984) 428 unions representing 81,182 members of international and national unions and government employee associations.

COMMUNICATIONS

Roads. In 1986 there were 8,618 km, of which 5,574 were paved.

Railways. In 1981 there were 1,457·8 km of main track railway, of which the Canadian National Railways operated 1,130·6 (3 ft 6 in.), the Quebec North Shore and Labrador Railway 324·8 (4 ft 8½ in.) and there were 2·4 km of private line. Car and passenger ferries operate from Port aux Basques and Argentia to North Sydney, Nova Scotia. On the island of Newfoundland, the Terra Transport operates a trans-island bus and rail freight service in addition to a coastal service for both passengers and freight. In the months that the Labrador coast is ice-free, usually from June to Nov., the CN Marine operates a scheduled coastal steamer service every week.

Aviation. The province is linked to the rest of Canada by regular air services provided by Air Canada, Canadian International Airways, Quebecair and a number of smaller air carriers.

Shipping. At 31 Dec. 1986 there were 1,531 ships registered in Newfoundland.

Post. There were 460 post offices open in 1986, and 2 telegraph offices in the Newfoundland and Labrador postal district. Telephone access lines in the province numbered 196,900 in 1985.

EDUCATION. The number of schools in 1986–87 was 594. The enrolment was 139,378; teachers numbered 8,954. The Memorial University, offering courses in arts, science, engineering, education, nursing and medicine, had approximately 15,018 full- and part-time students in 1985–86. Total expenditure for education by the Government in 1985–86 was $547·2m.

Books of Reference

Blackburn, R. H. (ed.), *Encyclopaedia of Canada: Newfoundland Supplement.* Toronto, 1949
Bruet, E., *Le Labrador et le Nouveau-Québec.* Paris, 1949
Horwood, H.,*Newfoundland.* Toronto, 1969
Loture, R. de, *Histoire de la grande pêche de Terre-Neuve.* Paris, 1949
Mercer, G. A., *The Province of Newfoundland and Labrador: Geographical Aspects.* Ottawa, 1970
Perlin, A. B., *The Story of Newfoundland, 1497–1959.* St John's, 1959
Tanner, V., *Outlines of Geography. Life and Customs of Newfoundland–Labrador.* 2 vols. Helsinki, 1944, and Toronto, 1947
Taylor, T. G., *Newfoundland: A Study of Settlement.* Toronto, 1946

NOVA SCOTIA

HISTORY. The first permanent settlement was made by the French early in the 17th century, and the province was called Acadia until finally ceded to the British by the Treaty of Utrecht in 1713.

AREA AND POPULATION. The area of the province is 21,425 sq. miles (55,000 sq. km), of which 20,401 sq. miles are land area, 1,024 sq. miles water area. The population (census 1986) was 873,199.

Population of the principal cities and towns (census 1986): Halifax, 113,577; Dartmouth 65,243; Sydney, 27,754; Glace Bay, 20,467; Truro, 12,124; New Glasgow, 10,022; Amherst, 9,671; New Waterford, 8,326; Sydney Mines, 8,063; Bedford, 8,010; North Sydney, 7,472; Yarmouth, 7,617.

Vital statistics, *see* p. 271.

Religion, *see* p. 290.

CLIMATE. A cool temperate climate, with rainfall occurring evenly over the year. The Gulf Stream moderates the temperatures in winter so that ports remain ice-free. Halifax. Jan. 23°F (–5°C), July 64°F (17·8°C). Annual rainfall 56″ (1,412 mm).

CONSTITUTION AND GOVERNMENT. Under the British North America Act of 1867 the legislature of Nova Scotia may exclusively make laws in relation to local matters, including direct taxation within the province, education and the administration of justice. The legislature of Nova Scotia consists of a Lieut.-Governor, appointed and paid by the federal government, and holding office for 5 years, and a House of Assembly of 52 members, chosen by popular vote not more than every 5 years. The province is represented in the Canadian Senate by 10 members, and in the House of Commons by 11.

The franchise and eligibility to the legislature are granted to every person, male or female, if of age (19 years), a British subject or Canadian citizen, and a resident in the province for 1 year and 2 months before the date of the writ of election in the county or electoral district of which the polling district forms part, and if not by law otherwise disqualified. State of parties in Jan. 1987: 41 Progressive Conservatives, 6 Liberals, 3 New Democrats, 1 Labour, 1 Independent.

Lieut.-Governor: Alan R. Abraham.

Flag: A banner of the Arms, *i.e.*, white with a blue diagonal cross, bearing in the centre the royal shield of Scotland.

The members of the Progressive Conservative Ministry were as follows in Dec. 1987:

Premier, President of the Executive Council, Minister of Intergovernmental Affairs: Rt Hon. John M. Buchanan, PC, QC.

Deputy Premier, Environment, Industry, Trade and Technology, Minister Responsible for the Nova Scotia Research Foundation and the Advisory Council on Applied Science and Technology: Roland J. Thornhill. *Agriculture and Marketing:* Roger S. Bacon. *Lands and Forests:* Jack MacIsaac. *Mines and Energy:* Kenneth Streatch. *Education:* Ronald C. Giffin, QC. *Attorney-General, Labour:* Terence R.

B. Donahue, QC. *Community Services, Minister Responsible for the Human Rights Acts:* Thomas J. McInnis. *Health and Fitness, Registrar General, Minister in Charge of the Drug Dependency Act and Reporting of the Handicapped:* Joel R. Matheson, QC. *Municipal Affairs:* Laird Stirling. *Advanced Education and Job Training:* Edmund L. Morris. *Solicitor General, Provincial Secretary, Minister in Charge of the Regulations Act and the Liquor Control Act:* Ronald S. Russell. *Finance, Minister in Charge of the Lottery Act:* Greg Kerr. *Government Services:* Michael E. Laffin. *Fisheries:* John E. Leefe. *Chairman of the Management Board, Minister Responsible for the Communications and Information Act, Civil Service Act and Nova Scotia Purchasing Agency:* George C. Moody. *Housing, Minister Responsible for the Emergency Measures Organization:* Mel C. Pickings. *Small Business Development, Minister Responsible for the Nova Scotia Business Capital Corporation:* David Nantes. *Consumer Affairs, Minister Responsible for the Residential Tenancies Act and Advisory Council on the Status of Women:* Maxine Cochran. *Transportation and Communications:* Guy LeBlanc. *Tourism and Culture, Minister Responsible for the Heritage Property Act:* Brian A. Young.

Agent-General in London: Donald M. Smith (14 Pall Mall, SW1Y 5LU).

Local Government. The main divisions of the province for governmental purposes are the 3 cities, the 39 towns and the 24 rural municipalities, each governed by a council and a mayor or warden. The cities have independent charters, and the various towns take their powers from and are limited by The Towns Act, and the various municipalities take their powers from and are limited by The Municipal Act as revised in 1967. The majority of municipalities comprise 1 county, but 6 counties are divided into 2 municipalities each. In no case do the boundaries of any municipality overlap county lines. The 18 counties as such have no administrative functions.

Any city (of which there are 3) or incorporated town (of which there are 39) that lies within the boundaries of a municipality is excluded from any jurisdiction by the municipal council and has its own government.

FINANCE. Revenue is derived from provincial sources, payments from the federal government under the Federal-Provincial Fiscal Arrangements and Established Programs Financing Act. Recoveries consist generally of amounts received under various federal cost-shared programmes. Main sources of provincial revenues include income and sales taxes.

Revenue, expenditure and debt (in Canadian $1m.) for fiscal years ending 31 March:

	1984	1985	1986	1987	1988 [1]
Budgetary Transactions					
Current Expenditure	2,558·8	2,789·8	2,983·6	3,093·1	3,289·7
Current Revenues and Recoveries	2,323·9	2,549·6	2,714·6	2,903·9	3,104·4
Operating Deficit (Surplus)	234·9	240·3	269·0	189·2	185·3
Sinking fund Instalments and Serial Retirements	51·3	65·1	77·2	87·3	86·4
Net Capital Expenditures	203·7	231·2	192·0	198·5	241·2
Net Budgetary Transactions	489·9	536·5	538·2	475·0	512·9
Non-Budgetary Transactions					
Capital Expenditures	10·3	6·8	2·7	0·9	3·0
Net Increase (Decrease) in Advances and Investments	(9·3)	(12·1)	(7·4)	28·1	1·9
Net Other Transactions	(7·7)	7·0	6·7	7·2	7·2
Non-Budgetary Transactions	(8·7)	1·6	2·0	36·2	12·1
	498·6	538·1	540·2	511·2	525·0

[1] Estimate.

Banking. All major Canadian banks are represented with numerous branch locations throughout the Province. In March 1987 total deposits with chartered banks in Nova Scotia totalled $3,395m.

NATURAL RESOURCES

Minerals. Principal minerals in 1986 were: Coal, 2·9m. tonnes, valued at $176·5m.; gypsum, 6·2m. tonnes, valued at $50·8m.; sand and gravel, 8·3m. tonnes, valued at $25·2m. Total value of mineral production in 1986 was about $356·7m.

Agriculture. Dairying, poultry and egg production, livestock and fruit growing are the most important branches. Farm cash receipts for 1986 were estimated at $268m., with an additional $5·8m. going to persons on farms as income in kind.

Cash receipts from sale of dairy products were $79·9m., with total milk production of 181,117,000 litres.

The production of poultry meat in 1986 was 20,496 tonnes, of which 18,376 tonnes were chickens and fowls and 2,120 tonnes were turkeys. Egg production was 17·9m. dozen.

The main 1986 fruit crops were apples, 34,292 tonnes; blueberries, 7,489 tonnes; and strawberries, 1,985 tonnes.

Forestry. The estimated forest area of Nova Scotia is 15,555 sq. miles (40,298 sq. km), of which about 25% is owned by the province. The principal trees are spruce, balsam fir, hemlock, pine, larch, birch, oak, maple, poplar and ash. 3,532,840 cu. metres of round forest products were produced in 1986.

Fisheries. The fisheries of the province in 1986 had a landed value of $407·8m. of sea fish including scallop fishery, $62·5m., and lobster fishery, $133·6m. In 1984 there were about 5,793 employees in the fish processing industry; the value of shipment of goods was $388·8m.

INDUSTRY. The number of manufacturing establishments was 820 in 1985; the number of employees was 35,149; wages and salaries, $774·6m.; value of shipments was $4,634·8m. The value of shipments in 1986, was $4,747·4m., and the leading industries were food, paper and allied industries and transportation equipment.

TRADE UNIONS. Total union membership during 1987 was 105,326 belonging to 97 unions comprised of 609 individual locals. The largest percentage of the total union membership was in the service sector followed by public administration and defence sector. An estimated 48,250 members in 381 locals were affiliated with the Canadian Labour Congress.

COMMUNICATIONS

Roads. In April 1986 there were 25,797 km of highways; 2,642 km of paved arterial highways; 4,725 km of collector highways (of which 4,500 km are paved); 18,430 km of local highways (of which 5,137 km are paved).

Railways. The province is covered with a network of 1,100 km of mainline track.

Aviation. There is a direct air service to all Canadian points and international service to Boston, New York, Bermuda, London, Glasgow, Orlando and Tampa.

Shipping. Ferry services connect Nova Scotia with Newfoundland, Prince Edward Island, New Brunswick and Maine. Direct service by container vessels is provided from the Port of Halifax to ports in Europe, Asia and the Caribbean.

JUSTICE AND EDUCATION

Justice. There is a Supreme Court which is a Court of common law and equity possessing original and appellate jurisdiction in civil and in criminal cases. The Supreme Court consists of an appeal division of 8 judges and a trial division of 12 judges. There are also county courts, family courts, probate courts, magistrates' courts, small claims courts, municipal and justices' courts. Bodies, sometimes referred to as courts, are established for the revision of assessment rolls, voters' lists and like purposes.

Young offenders under 16 years are now tried by Youth Courts. The Courts were established in April 1984. In 1985, the Youth Courts have the jurisdiction to adjudicate charges against 16- and 17- year-old offenders.

For the year fiscal ending 31 March 1987 there were 4,150 admissions to provincial custody; of these, 2,564 were sentenced.

Education. Public education in Nova Scotia is free, compulsory and undenominational through elementary and high school. Attendance is compulsory to the age of 16. In addition to 540 public schools there are the Atlantic Provinces Resource Centres for the Hearing Handicapped and for the Visually Impaired; the Shelburne Youth Centre for young offenders and the Nova Scotia Residential Centre for delinquent children; and the Nova Scotia Youth Training Centre for mentally handicapped children. The province has 13 universities and colleges of which the largest is Dalhousie University in Halifax. The Nova Scotia Agricultural College and the Nova Scotia Teachers' College are located at Truro. The Technical University of Nova Scotia at Halifax grants degrees in engineering and architecture.

The Department of Vocational and Technical Training administers 2 institutes of technology and a nautical institute. It also provides in-school training for the Department of Labour Apprenticeship programme.

The Nova Scotia government offers financial support and organizational assistance to local school boards for provision of weekend and evening courses in academic and avocational subjects, and citizenship for new Canadians. It also provides local authorities with specialist support services to assist them in providing community workshops and it operates a correspondence study service for children and adults.

Occupational courses at the high school level are provided by 14 regional vocational schools under the jurisdiction (except in 3 school areas) of the Department of Vocational and Technical Training in the public school system.

Total estimated expenditure on education for the year 1986 was $621·5m., of which 80% was borne by the provincial government. In 1986–87, classrooms operated in 540 schools, with 10,422 teachers and 170,964 pupils.

Books of Reference

Nova Scotia Fact Book. N.S. Department of Development, Halifax, 1986
Nova Scotia Resource Atlas. N.S. Department of Development, Halifax, 1986

Atlantic Provinces Economic Council. *The Atlantic Vision, 1990.* Halifax, 1979
Public Archives of Nova Scotia. *Place Names and Places of Nova Scotia.* Halifax, 1967
Beck, M., *The Evolution of Municipal Government in Nova Scotia, 1749–1973.* 1973
Fergusson, C. B., *Nova Scotia in Encyclopedia Canadiana,* Vol. VII. Toronto, 1968
Hamilton, W. B., *The Nova Scotia Traveller.* Toronto, 1981
McCormick, P., *A Guide to Halifax.* Tantallon, 1984
McCreath, P., and Leefe, J., *History of Early Nova Scotia.* Halifax, 1982
Vaison, R., *Nova Scotia Past and Present: A Bibliography and Guide.* Halifax, 1976

ONTARIO

HISTORY. The French explorer Samuel de Champlain explored the Ottawa River from 1613. The area was governed by the French, first under a joint stock company and then as a royal province, from 1627 and was ceded to Great Britain in 1763. A constitutional act of 1791 created there the province of Upper Canada, largely to accommodate loyalists of English descent who had immigrated after the United States war of independence. Upper Canada entered the Confederation as Ontario in 1867.

AREA AND POPULATION. The total area is about 412,582 sq. miles

(1,068,630 sq. km), of which some 344,100 sq. miles (891,200 sq. km) are land area and some 64,490 sq. miles (189,196 sq. km) are lakes and fresh water rivers.

The province extends 1,050 miles (1,690 km) from east to west and 1,075 miles (1,730 km) from north to south.

Ontario is bounded on the north by the waters of Hudson and James Bay, on the east by Quebec, on the west by Manitoba, and on the south by the states of New York, Pennsylvania, Ohio, Michigan, Wisconsin and Minnesota.

The population of the province (census, 1 June 1981) was 8,625,107. Estimate (1985) 9·1m. Population of the principal cities (1985): Hamilton, 307,690 (city), 421,264 (metropolitan area); Kitchener, 147,439 (city), 287,801 (census metropolitan area); London, 276,000 (city); Ottawa (federal capital), 304,448 (city), 562,782 (census metropolitan area); Sudbury, 90,453 (city), 154,387 (regional municipality); Toronto (provincial capital), 606,247 (city), 2,998,947 (census metropolitan area); Windsor, 195,028 (city).

Vital statistics, see p. 271.

Religion, see p. 290.

CLIMATE. A temperate continental climate, but conditions are quite severe in winter, though proximity to the Great Lakes has a moderating influence on temperatures. Ottawa. Jan. 12°F (–11·1°C), July 69°F (20·6°C). Annual rainfall 35″ (871 mm). Toronto. Jan. 23°F (–5°C), July 69°F (20·6°C). Annual rainfall 33″ (815 mm).

CONSTITUTION AND GOVERNMENT. The provincial government is administered by a Lieut.-Governor, a cabinet and one chamber elected by a general franchise for a period of 5 years. Women were granted the right to vote and be elected to the chamber in 1917. The minimum voting age is 18 years.

In Aug. 1987 the provincial legislature was composed as follows: Progressive Conservatives, 51; Liberals, 51; New Democrats, 23; total 125.

Lieut.-Governor: Right Hon. Lincoln M. Alexander, PC, QC (appointed Sept. 1985).

Flag: The British Red Ensign with the shield of Ontario in the fly.

The members of the Executive Council in June 1985 were as follows (all Liberals):

Premier and President of the Council and Minister of Intergovernmental Affairs: Hon. David Peterson.

Treasurer and Minister of Economics and of Revenue: Hon. Robert F. Nixon. *Agriculture and Food:* Hon. Jack Riddell. *Attorney-General and Minister for Women's Issues and for Native Affairs:* Hon. Ian G. Scott, QC. *Citizenship and Culture:* Hon. Lily Munro. *Colleges and Universities and Skills Development:* Hon. Gregory Sorbara. *Community and Social Services:* Hon. John Sweeney. *Consumer and Commercial Relations:* Hon. Monte Kwinter. *Correctional Services and Solicitor General:* Hon. Ken Keyes. *Education:* Hon. Sean Conway. *Energy and Natural Resources:* Hon. Vincent Kerrio. *Environment:* Hon. James Bradley. *Government Services and Chairman of Management Board of Cabinet:* Hon. Sean Conway (Acting). *Health:* Murray J. Elston. *Housing:* Hon. Alvin Curling. *Industry, Trade and Technology:* Hon. Hugh P. O'Neil. *Labour:* Hon. William Wrye. *Municipal Affairs and Francophone Affairs:* Hon. Bernard Grandmaitre. *Northern Affairs and Mines:* Hon. David Peterson (Acting). *Tourism and Recreation:* Hon. John Eakins. *Transportation and Communications:* Hon. Ed Fulton. *Ministers Without Portfolio:* Hon. Ron Van Horne, Hon. Tony Ruprecht.

Local Government. Local government in Ontario is divided into two branches, one covering municipal institutions and the other education.

The present municipal system dates from The Municipal Corporations Act enacted by The Province of Canada in 1849. It has been considerably modified in recent years with the creation of the Municipality of Metropolitan Toronto in 1954 and the launching of the Government of Ontario's local government restructuring programme in 1968. Generally, there are two levels of municipal government in Ontario. The upper level consists of 27 counties plus 12 restructured regional municipalities. The local level comprises more than 800 cities, towns and townships. Cities in the traditional county system function independently of the county in which they lie, as do 4 towns which have been separated for municipal purposes. There are no separated municipal units in regional governments.

Ontario's local municipalities are governed by councils elected by popular vote.

A city council usually consists of a mayor, aldermen and, sometimes, an executive committee known as a board of control.

Councils of towns, villages and townships usually consist of a mayor, reeve, deputy reeve, councillors and, in the case of the newer regional municipalities, one or more regional councillors who represent the area municipalities on the regional council.

County and regional government councils are federated assemblies.

A county council consists of the reeves and deputy reeves of the towns, villages and townships. The head of the county council is the warden, who is elected by the council from among its own members.

A regional council consists of the heads of council of the local municipalities, as well as a varying number of regional councillors, who are elected on the basis of representation, either directly or indirectly. The head of the regional council is the chairman who is elected by council but who, unlike a county warden, need not have been a council member.

No municipality in Ontario may incur long-term debts without the sanction of the tribunal created by the Provincial Legislature and known as the Ontario Municipal Board. Debenture obligations incurred by municipalities for utility undertakings (water-works and electric light and power systems) are discharged ordinarily out of revenues derived from the sale of utility services and do not fall upon the ratepayers.

Municipal councils have no jurisdiction for education beyond the collection of taxes for school purposes. Responsibility for providing, operating and maintaining school facilities, and for the supply of teachers, rests with local education authorities known as Boards of Education or School Boards. These Boards are now generally organized on a county or regional basis. Apart from some of the larger cities, local municipal school boards no longer exist.

Municipal institutions come under the jurisdiction of the Provincial Ministry of Intergovernmental Affairs. One of the principal functions of the Ministry is to advise and assist municipalities on such matters as accounting, reporting, auditing, budgeting and planning. Educational support and guidance at the provincial level is the responsibility of the Ministry of Education, which deals with the training of teachers and the formulation of curriculum. (At the university and community college level, education support services are provided by the Ministry of Colleges and Universities.)

There are considerable areas in the northernmost parts of Ontario where as yet there is little or no settlement of population. In such areas no municipal organization exists, and control for all purposes over such areas remains in the hands of the Provincial Government.

FINANCE. The gross revenue and expenditure and the net cash requirements (in Canadian $1,000) for years ending 31 March were as follows:

	1982–83	1983–84	1984–85	1985–86	1986–87
Gross revenue	20,395	21,313	23,765	26,228	28,454
Gross expenditure	22,943	24,553	26,430	32,562	31,031
Net cash requirement	2,548	2,289	1,701	2,134	1,544

Gross revenue and expenditure figures include all non-budgetary transactions, *i.e.*, the lending and investment activity of the Government to Crown corporations, agencies and municipalities as well as the repayment of these loans or recovery of investments. Transactions on behalf of Ontario Hydro are excluded.

ENERGY AND NATURAL RESOURCES

Electricity (1986). Ontario Hydro recorded for the calendar year an installed generating capacity of 30,701m. kw. and a net energy output generated and purchased of 126,626m. kwh.

Minerals (1986, preliminary). The total value of shipments from mines was $4,777m. in 1986. Important commodities (in $1m.) were: Nickel, 816; copper, 590; uranium, 476; gold, 766; zinc, 375. The mining industry employed about 23,579 people in 1986.

Agriculture. In 1985, 3·5m. hectares were under field crops with total farm receipts of $5,179m.

Forestry. According to the most recent inventory (1985) the total area of productive forest is 39·9m. hectares, comprising: Softwoods, 26·3m.; hardwoods, 13·6m. The growing stock equals 5,102m. cu. metres. The estimated value of shipments by the forest products industry (including logging) was (1984) $8,483m.

INDUSTRY AND TRADE

Industry (1986). Ontario is Canada's most highly industrialized province. About 73% of value added in commodity-producing industries is accounted for by manufacturing. Construction is next with 10%.

In 1986, the labour force was 4·9m. Total labour income was $103,351·6m. The 1985 Gross Provincial Product (GPP) was $185,724m.

The leading manufacturing industries are motor vehicles and parts, iron and steel, meat and meat preparations, dairy products, paper and paperboard, chemical products, petroleum and coal products, machinery and equipment, metal stamping and pressing and communications equipment.

Trade. In 1985 Ontario exported 49·8% ($59,382m.) of Canada's total foreign trade.

COMMUNICATIONS

Roads. There were, in 1985, 154,043·5 km of roads. Motor licences numbered (1985) approximately 9m., of which 6·3m. were passenger cars, 1·3m. trucks and tractors, 31,358 buses, 916,803 trailers, 241,394 motor cycles and 209,477 snow vehicles.

Railways. The provincially-owned Ontario Northland Railway has about 550 miles of track and the Algoma Central Railway 325 miles. The Canadian National and Canadian Pacific Railways operate a total of about 9,500 miles in Ontario. There is a metro and tramway network in Toronto.

Post (1985). Telephone service is provided by 30 independent systems (178,527 telephones) and Bell Canada (10m. telephones).

EDUCATION. There is a complete provincial system of elementary and secondary schools as well as private schools. In 1986 publicly financed elementary and secondary schools had a total enrolment of 1,781,924 pupils.

In 1965 Ontario established Colleges of Applied Arts and Technology (CAATS). There are now 22 of these publicly owned colleges with full-time enrolment (1985) of 96,269 in academic courses.

The University of Toronto, founded in 1827 (full-time enrolment, 1985, 34,346), and 14 other major universities (total full-time enrolment, 1985, 185,012), all receive provincial grants. The net general expenditure of the provincial ministries of education and colleges of universities for the fiscal year ending 31 March 1986 was $5,552m.

Books of Reference

Statistical Information: Annual publications of the Ontario Ministry of Treasury and Economics include: *Ontario Statistics; Ontario Budget; Public Accounts; Financial Report.*
Guillet, E. C., *Pioneer Days in Upper Canada.* Toronto, 1933
McDonald, D. C. (ed.), *The Government and Politics of Ontario.* 2nd ed. Toronto, 1980
Middleton, J. E., *The Province of Ontario: A History 1615–1927.* Toronto, 1927, 4 vols.
Schull, J., *Ontario since 1867.* Toronto, 1978

PRINCE EDWARD ISLAND

HISTORY. The earliest discovery of the island is not satisfactorily known, but the first recorded visit was by Jacques Cartier in 1534, who named it Isle St-Jean; it was first settled by the French, but was taken from them in 1758. It was annexed to Nova Scotia in 1763, and constituted a separate colony in 1769. Prince Edward Island entered the Confederation on 1 July 1873.

AREA AND POPULATION. The province, which is the smallest in Canada, lies in the Gulf of St Lawrence, and is separated from the mainland of New Brunswick and Nova Scotia by Northumberland Strait. The area of the island is 2,184 sq. miles (5,656 sq. km). Total population (census, 1981), 124,200; (estimate, 1987), 128,300. Population of the principal cities: Charlottetown (capital), 15,776; Summerside, 8,020.

Vital statistics, *see* p. 271.
Religion, *see* p. 290.

CLIMATE. The cool temperate climate is affected in winter by the freezing of the St. Lawrence, which reduces winter temperatures. Charlottetown. Jan. 19°F (−7·2°C), July 67°F (19·4°C). Annual rainfall 43″ (1,077 mm).

CONSTITUTION AND GOVERNMENT. The provincial government is administered by a Lieut.-Governor-in-Council (Cabinet) and a Legislative Assembly of 32 members who are elected for up to 5 years. In Sept. 1987, parties in the Legislative Assembly were: Liberals, 22; Progressive Conservatives, 10.

Lieut.-Governor: Lloyd G. MacPhail (sworn in 1 Aug. 1985).
Flag: A banner of the arms, *i.e.*, a white field bearing 3 small trees and a larger tree on a compartment, all green, and at the top a red band with a golden lion; on 3 sides a border of red and white rectangles.

Premier and President of Executive Council: Hon. Joseph A. Ghiz, QC.
Finance and Community and Cultural Affairs: Hon. Gilbert R. Clements.
Energy and Forestry: Hon. Allison Ellis. *Industry:* Hon. Leonce Bernard. *Fisheries:* Hon. Johnny Ross Young. *Transportation and Public Works:* Hon. Robert Morrissey. *Education:* Hon. Betty Jean Brown. *Agriculture:* Hon. Tim Carroll. *Justice and Attorney-General and Labour:* Hon. Wayne Cheverie. *Tourism and Parks:* Hon. Gordon MacInnis. *Health and Social Services:* Hon. Keith Milligan.

Local Government. The Municipalities Act, 1983, provides for the incorporation of Towns and Communities. The City of Charlottetown and the town of Summerside are incorporated under private Acts of the Legislature.

FINANCE. Revenue and expenditure (in Canadian $) for 6 financial years ending 31 March:

	1982–83	1983–84	1984–85	1985–86	1986–87	1987–88
Revenue	380,883,900	394,641,400	432,222,600	446,850,500	486,328,400	522,352,800
Expenditure	386,878,700	415,444,500	440,300,700	450,806,600	509,642,900	532,090,200

ENERGY AND NATURAL RESOURCES

Electricity. Electric power is supplied to 100% of the population. The province's net generated and purchased consumption of electricity during 1986 was 607·6m. kwh. In 1986, peak demand for electricity was 115·3 mw. In 1977 the province completed the laying of an undersea power cable which links the island with New Brunswick and the Maritime Power Grid. In 1980, 30 miles of additional 138 kv transmission line was added to the PEI system. In 1986, about 98% of power requirements were supplied through this system.

Agriculture. Total area of farms occupied approximately 673,196 acres in 1986 out of the total land area of 1,399,040 acres. Farm cash receipts in 1986 were $190m. with cash receipts from potatoes accounting for 30% of the total. Cash receipts from dairy products, cattle and hogs followed in importance. The land in forest covered 700,000 acres in 1986 and total value of forest products sold in 1986 was about $7m. For particulars of agricultural production and livestock, *see under* CANADA, pp. 283–84.

Fisheries. The fishery in 1986 had a landed value of $67·1m. Lobsters and shellfish accounted for 81% of the total. Value of groundfish landings accounted for 8%; pelagic and estuarial, 7%; Irish moss, 3%.

INDUSTRY AND TRADE

Industry. Value of manufacturing shipments for all industries in 1986 was $312·5m.

Commerce. Average personal income rose from $10,606 in 1985 to $10,938 in 1986. The average weekly wage (industrial aggregate) rose from $339.30 in 1985 to $348.10 in 1986. The labour force averaged 60,000 in 1986, while employment averaged 52,000.

In 1984, provincial GDP for manufacturing was $78·9m.; construction, $56m. In 1986, total value of retail trade was $577·3m.

Tourism. The value of the tourist industry was estimated at $62·4m. in 1986 with 223,883 tourist parties.

COMMUNICATIONS

Roads. The province has a total of 5,280 km of road, including 3,725 km of paved highway.

Railways. Rail service is provided over 235 miles of track within the province and connects with the national railways system *via* the New Brunswick–Prince Edward Island ferry service.

Aviation. In 1987 air service for passengers, mail and cargo provided 15 flights daily in each direction between the province and various points in eastern Canada. A daily bus service operates between various centres in the province as well as to the mainland.

Shipping. A ferry service provides rail and highway communication with New Brunswick by means of 4 large ferries, 2 of which are powerful ice-breakers. Another ferry service employing 2 ferries plus an additional 2 for summertime operates between the province and Nova Scotia throughout the season of open navigation. A third ferry service employing 1 ferry operates between the province and Magdalen Islands, Quebec, during the open navigation season.

Post. In 1987 there were approximately 86,547 telephones.

EDUCATION (1986–87). Under the regional school boards there are 66 public schools, 1,377 teaching positions, 24,773 students. There is one undergraduate university (over 1,837 full-time students), and a college of applied arts and technology (1,951 full-time students), both in Charlottetown. Total expenditure in education in the year ending 31 March 1988 was forecast to be $123,868,800.

Books of Reference

Baldwin, D. O., *Abegweit: Land of the Red Soil*. Charlottetown, 1985
Bolger, F. W. P., *Canada's Smallest Province*. Charlottetown, 1973
Clark, A. H., *Three Centuries and the Island*. Toronto, 1959
Hocking, A., *Prince Edward Island*. Toronto, 1978
MacKinnon, F., *The Government of Prince Edward Island*. Toronto, 1951

QUEBEC—QUÉBEC

HISTORY. Quebec was formerly known as New France or Canada from 1534 to 1763; as the province of Quebec from 1763 to 1790; as Lower Canada from 1791 to 1846; as Canada East from 1846 to 1867, and when, by the union of the four original provinces, the Confederation of the Dominion of Canada was formed, it again became known as the province of Quebec (Québec).

The Quebec Act, passed by the British Parliament in 1774, guaranteed to the people of the newly conquered French territory in North America security in their religion and language, their customs and tenures, under their own civil laws.

In the referendum held 20 May 1980, 59·5% voted against and 40·5% for 'separatism'.

AREA AND POPULATION. The area of Quebec (as amended by the Labrador Boundary Award) is 1,667,926 sq. km (594,860 sq. miles), of which 1,315,134 sq. km is land area and 352,792 sq. km water. Of this extent, 911,106 sq. km represent the Territory of Ungava, annexed in 1912 under the Quebec Boundaries Extension Act. The population (census 1986) was 6,532,461.

Principal cities (1986): Quebec (capital), 164,580; Montreal, 1,015,420; Laval, 284,164; Sherbrooke, 74,438; Verdun, 60,246; Hull, 58,722; Trois-Rivières, 50,122.

Vital statistics, see p. 271.

Religion, see p. 290.

CLIMATE. Cool temperate in the south, but conditions are more extreme towards the north. Winters are severe and snowfall considerable, but summer temperatures are quite warm. Rain occurs at all seasons. Quebec. Jan. 10°F (−12·2°C), July 66°F (18·9°C). Annual rainfall 40″ (1,008 mm). Montreal. Jan. 11°F (−11·7°C), July 67°F (19·4°C). Annual rainfall 30″ (776 mm).

CONSTITUTION AND GOVERNMENT. There is a Legislative Assembly consisting of 122 members, elected in 122 electoral districts for 4 years. At the provincial general elections held 2 Dec. 1985, Liberals won 99 seats and *Parti Québecois*, 23. The Liberal Party was led by Robert Bourassa who failed to win a seat but did so at a subsequent by-election on 20 Jan. 1986.

Lieut.-Governor: The Hon. Gilles Lamontagne.

Flag: The Fleurdelysé flag, blue with a white cross, and in each quarter a white fleur-de-lis.

Senior members of the Executive Council as in Jan. 1988, were as follows:

Prime Minister: Robert Bourassa.

Finance: Gérard D. Lévesque. *Education:* Claude Ryan. *Justice:* Herbert Marx. *External Trade:* Pierre MacDonald. *International Relations:* Gil Rémillard.

General-delegate in London: Patrick Hyndman (59 Pall Mall, London SW1Y 5JH).

General-delegate in New York: Léo Paré (17 West 50th St., Rockefeller Center, New York 10020).

General-delegate in Paris: Jean-Louis Roy (66 Pergolèse, Paris 75116).

ECONOMY

Budget. Ordinary revenue and expenditure (in Canadian $1,000) for fiscal years ending 31 March:

	1981–82	1982–83	1983–84	1984–85	1985–86
Revenue	17,471,594	19,210,266	21,410,969	23,310,027	24,080,778
Expenditure	20,359,807	22,259,296	24,523,514	25,542,499	27,222,178

The total net debt at 31 March 1986 was $21,997,000,000.

ENERGY AND NATURAL RESOURCES

Electricity. Water power is one of the most important natural resources of the province of Quebec. Its turbine installation represents about 40% of the aggregate of Canada. At the end of 1986 the installed generating capacity was 32,599 mw. Production, 1986, was 144,534 gwh.

Minerals (1986). The estimated value of the mineral production (metal mines only) was $2,278,271,000. Chief minerals: Iron ore, (confidential); copper, $136,840,000; gold, $482,944,000; zinc, $51,912,000.

The second major iron-ore development in northern Quebec is, like the one at Knob Lake which gave birth to Schefferville, based on the Quebec–Labrador Trough which extends from Lac Jeannine to the northern tip of Ungava peninsula. The port of Sept-Iles and the railway connecting it with Schefferville allow easy shipment to the furnaces and steel mills of Canada, the USA and Europe.

Non-metallic minerals produced include: Asbestos ($232,986,000; about 78% of Canadian production), titane-dioxide (confidential), industrial lime, dolomite and brucite, quartz and pyrite. Among the building materials produced were: Stone, $153,024,000; cement, $200,700,000; sand and gravel, $54,083,000; lime, (confidential).

Agriculture. In 1986 the total area (estimate) of the principal field crops was 2,185,600 hectares. The yield of the principal crops was (in 1,000 tonnes):

Crops	Yield	Crops	Yield
Tame hay	6,100	Fodder corn	2,300
Oats for grain	260	Maize for grain	1,450
Potatoes	420	Barley	580
Mixed grains	120	Buckwheat	18

The farm cash receipts from farming operations estimated in 1986 amounted to $3,232,219,000. The principal items being: Livestock and products, $2,390,162,000; crops, $502,430,000; dairy supplements payments, $131,231,000, forest and maple products, $79,322,000.

Forestry. Forests cover an area of 764,279 sq. km. About 556,044 sq. km are classified as productive forests, of which 652,956 sq. km are provincial crown land and 108,992 sq. km are privately owned. Quebec leads the Canadian provinces in pulpwood production, having nearly half of the Canadian estimated total.

In 1984 production of lumber was softwood and hardwood, 7,477,939 cu. metres; woodpulp, 6,371,393 tonnes.

Fisheries. The principal fish are cod, herring, red fish, lobster and salmon. Total catch of sea fish, 1986, 87,949 tonnes, valued at $82,207,000.

INDUSTRY AND TRADE

Industry. In 1984 there were 10,649 industrial establishments in the province; employees, 484,883; salaries and wages, $11,178,303,358; cost of materials, $35,829,698,342; value of shipments, $61,537,262,869. Among the leading industries are petroleum refining, pulp and paper mills, smelting and refining, dairy products, slaughtering and meat processing, motor vehicle manufacturing, women's clothing, saw-mills and planing mills, iron and steel mills, commercial printing.

Commerce. In 1986 the value of Canadian exports through Quebec custom ports was $19,877,162,000; value of imports, $18,170,584,000.

COMMUNICATIONS

Roads. In 1986 there were 58,045 km of roads and 3,467,200 registered motor vehicles.

Railways. There were (1985) 4,507 km of railway. There is a metro system in Montreal.

Aviation. In 1986 Quebec had 2 international airports, Dorval (Montreal) with landing runway of 8·4 km and Mirabel (Montreal) with 7·3 km.

Post and Broadcasting. Telephones numbered 3,174,238 in 1985 and there were 35 television and 116 radio stations.

Newspapers (1986). There were 10 French- and 2 English-language daily newspapers.

EDUCATION. The province has 7 universities: 3 English-language universities, McGill (Montreal) founded in 1821, Bishop (Lennoxville) founded in 1845 and the Concordia University (Montreal) granted a charter in 1975; 4 French-language universities: Laval (Quebec) founded in 1852, Montreal University, opened in 1876 as a branch of Laval and became independent in 1920, Sherbrooke University founded in 1954 and University of Quebec founded in 1968.

In 1984–85 there were 108,656 full-time university students and 111,781 part-time students.

In 1985–86, in pre-kindergartens, there were 6,413 pupils; in kindergartens, 94,741; primary schools, 568,613; in secondary schools, 568,613; in colleges (post-secondary, non-university), 158,733; and in classes for children with special needs, 110,453. The school boards had a total of 61,200 teachers.

Expenditure of the Department of Education for 1985–86, $7,031,274,000 net. This included $1,106,875,000 for universities, $4,168,228,000 for public primary and secondary schools, $207,933,000 for private primary and secondary schools and $891,279,000 for colleges.

Books of Reference

Statistical Information: The Quebec Bureau of Statistics was established in 1912. The Bureau, which reports to the Finance Dept. since March 1983, collects, compiles and distributes statistical information relative to Quebec. *Director:* Nicole Gendreau.

A statistical information list is available on request. Among the most important publications are: *Le Québec Statistique, Statistiques* (quarterly), *Comptes économiques du Québec* (annual), *Perspectives démographiques* (annual), *Situation démographique* (annual), *Commerce international du Québec* (annual), *Investissements privés et publics* (annual).

Atlas du Québec: L'Agriculture. Ministère de l'Industrie et du Commerce, Quebec, 1966
Baudoin, L., *Le Droit civil de la province de Québec.* Montreal, 1953
Blanchard, R., *Le Canada-français.* Paris, 1959
Hamelin, J., *Histoire du Québec.* St-Hyacinthe, 1978
Jacobs, J., *The Question of Separatism: Quebec and the Struggle for Sovereignty.* London, 1981
McWhinney, E., *Quebec and the Constitution.* Univ. of Toronto Press, 1979
Ouellet, F., *Histoire de la Chambre de Commerce de Québec, 1809–1959.* Québec, 1959
Raynauld, A., *Croissance et structure économiques de la province de Québec.* Québec, 1961
Trofimenkoff, S. M., *Action Française.* Univ. of Toronto Press, 1975
Wade, F. M., *The French Canadians, 1760–1967.* Toronto, 1968.—*Canadian Dualism: Studies of French–English Relations.* Quebec–Toronto, 1960

SASKATCHEWAN

HISTORY. Saskatchewan derives its name from its major river system, which the Cree Indians called 'Kis-is-ska-tche-wan', meaning 'swift flowing'. It officially became a province when it joined the Confederation on 1 Sept. 1905.

In 1670 King Charles II granted to Prince Rupert and his friends a charter covering exclusive trading rights in 'all the land drained by streams finding their outlet in the Hudson Bay'. This included what is now Saskatchewan. The trading company was first known as The Governor and Company of Adventurers of England; later as the Hudson's Bay Company. In 1869 the Northwest Territories was formed, and this included Saskatchewan. In 1882 the District of Saskatchewan was formed. By 1885 the North-West Mounted Police had been inaugurated, with headquarters in Regina (now the capital), and the Canadian Pacific Railway's transcontinental line had been completed, bringing a stream of immigrants to southern Saskatchewan. The Hudson's Bay Company surrendered its claim to territory in return for cash and land around the existing trading posts. Legislative government was introduced.

AREA AND POPULATION. Saskatchewan is bounded on the west by Alberta, on the east by Manitoba, to the north by the Northwest Territories; to the south it is bordered by the US states of Montana and North Dakota. The area of the province is 251,700 sq. miles (570,113 sq. km), of which 220,182 sq. miles is land area and 31,518 sq. miles is water. The population, 1986 census, was 1,010,198. Population of cities, 1986 census: Regina (capital), 175,064; Saskatoon, 177,641; Moose Jaw, 35,073; Prince Albert, 33,686; Yorkton, 15,574; Swift Current, 15,666; North Battleford, 14,876; Estevan, 10,161; Weyburn, 10,153; Lloydminster, 7,155; Melfort, 6,078; Melville, 5,123.

Vital statistics, see p. 271.

Religion, see p. 290.

CLIMATE. A cold continental climate, with severe winters and warm summers. Rainfall amounts are greatest from May to Aug. Regina. Jan. 0°F (–17·8°C), July 65°F (18·3°C). Annual rainfall 15″ (373 mm).

CONSTITUTION AND GOVERNMENT. The provincial government is vested in a Lieut.-Governor, an Executive Council and a Legislative Assembly, elected for 5 years. Women were given the franchise in 1916 and are also eligible for election to the legislature. State of parties in Sept. 1987: Progressive Conservative, 37; New Democratic Party, 25; Liberal, 1; vacant, 1.

Lieut.-Governor: F. W. Johnson.

Flag: Green over gold, with the shield of the province in the canton, and a green and red prairie lily in the fly.

The Progressive Conservative Ministry in Oct. 1987 was composed as follows:

Premier and Agriculture: Grant Devine.

Deputy Premier, Provincial Secretary, SaskPower: Eric Berntson. *Finance, SaskTel, Saskatchewan Pension Plan:* Gary Lane. *Economic Development and Trade, Justice:* Bob Andrew. *Consumer and Commercial Affairs, Saskatchewan Government Insurance:* Joan Duncan. *Rural Development, Crop Insurance Corporation:* Neal Hardy. *Education, Public Service Commission:* Lorne Hepworth. *Highways and Transportation:* Grant Hodgins. *Urban Affairs, Saskatchewan Housing Corporation:* Jack Klein. *Parks, Recreation and Culture:* Colin Maxwell. *Health, Saskatchewan Forest Products Corporation:* George McLeod. *Science and Technology:* Ray Meiklejohn. *Social Services, Human Resources, Labour and Employment:* Grant Schmidt. *Energy and Mines, Saskoil:* Pat Smith. *Environment and Public Safety, Sask Water:* Herb Swan. *Tourism, Small Business and Co-operatives, SEDCO, Liquor Board, Saskatchewan Property Management Corporation:* Graham Taylor.

Agent-General in London: R. A. Larter, 21 Pall Mall, SW1Y 5LP.

Local Government. The organization of a city requires a minimum population of 5,000 persons; that of a town, 500; that of a village, 100 people. No requirements as to population exist for the rural municipality and the local improvement district.

Cities, towns, villages and rural municipalities are governed by elected councils, which consist of a mayor and 6–20 aldermen in a city; a mayor and 6 councillors in a town; a mayor and 2 other members in a village; a reeve and a councillor for each division in a rural municipality (usually 6). Local improvement districts are administered by the Department of Municipal Affairs.

FINANCE. Budget and net assets (years ending 31 March) in Canadian $1,000:

	1984–85	1985–86	1986–87	1987–88
Budgetary revenue	2,793,213	3,048,650	3,358,742	3,202,508
Budgetary expenditure	3,230,223	3,396,230	3,747,892	3,779,743

ENERGY AND NATURAL RESOURCES. Agriculture used to dominate the history and economics of Saskatchewan, but the 'prairie province' is now a rapidly developing mining and manufacturing area. It is a major supplier of oil; has the world's largest deposits of potash; and net value of non-agricultural production accounts for (1985 estimate) 83·7% of the provincial economy.

Electricity. The Saskatchewan Power Corporation generated 13,912m. kwh. in 1986.

Minerals. The 1986 mineral sales were valued at $3,597,300,000, including (in $1,000): Petroleum 1,175,587; natural gas, 11,721; coal and others, 108,952; gold, 474; silver, 598; copper, 6,983; zinc, 6,270; potash, 549,791; salt and others, 20,319; uranium, 457,173; sodium sulphate, 29,723.

Agriculture. Saskatchewan normally produces about two-thirds of Canada's wheat. Wheat production in 1986 (in 1,000 tonnes), was 18,643 from 21·7m. acres; oats, 941 from 1m. acres; barley, 4,006 from 3·6m. acres; rye, 274·5 from 400,000 acres; rapeseed, 1,497 from 2·6m. acres; flax, 432 from 800,000 acres. Livestock (1 July 1987): Cattle and calves, 2·05m.; swine, 676,000; sheep and lambs, 52,000. Poultry in 1986: Chickens, 4,435,000; turkeys 450,000. Cash income from the sale of farm products in 1986 was $4,130m. At the June 1986 census there were 63,431 farms in the province, each being a holding of 1 acre or more with sales of agricultural products during the previous 12 months of $250 or more.

The South Saskatchewan River irrigation project, whose main feature is the Gardiner Dam, was completed in 1967. It will ultimately provide for an area of 200,000 acres of irrigated cultivation in Central Saskatchewan. In 1987, 206,768 acres were irrigated. Total irrigated land in the province, 295,327 acres.

Forestry. Half of Saskatchewan's area is forested, but only 115,000 sq. km are of commercial value at present. Forest products valued at $163m. were produced in 1986. The province's first pulp-mill, at Prince Albert, went into production in 1968; its daily capacity is 1,000 tons of high-grade kraft pulp.

Fur Production. In 1985–86 wild fur production was estimated at $5,007,639. Ranch-raised fur production amounted to $102,454.

Fisheries. The lakeside value of the 1985–86 commercial fish catch of 3·7m. kg was $3·3m.

INDUSTRY. In 1985 Saskatchewan had 791 manufacturing establishments, employing 19,245 persons. Manufacturing contributed $941m., construction $745m. to the total gross domestic product at factor cost of $17,442m. in 1985.

TOURISM. An estimated 1,063,000 out of province tourists spent $193m. in 1986.

COMMUNICATIONS

Roads. In 1987 there were 23,966 km of provincial highways, 207,500 km of municipal roads (including prairie trails). Motor vehicles registered totalled (1985) 697,160. Bus services are provided by 2 major lines.

Railways. There were (1987) approximately 12,089 km of main railway track in operation.

Aviation. Saskatchewan had 2 major airports, 176 airports and landing strips in 1987.

Post and Broadcasting. There were (1986) 720 post offices (excluding sub-post offices), 87 TV and re-broadcasting stations and 52 AM and FM radio stations. 738,709 telephones were connected to the Saskatchewan Telecommunications system.

EDUCATION. The University of Saskatchewan was established at Saskatoon on 3 April 1907. In 1987–88 it had 13,500 full-time students, 4,000 part-time students and 1,200 full-time teaching staff. The University of Regina was established 1 July 1974; in 1987–88 it had 5,950 full-time and 3,966 part-time students and 379 full-time faculty members.

The Saskatchewan education system in 1986–87 consisted of 112 school divisions and 4 school boards, of which 22 are Roman Catholic separate school divisions, serving 144,435 elementary pupils, 58,369 high-school students and 3,086 students enrolled in special classes. In addition, provincial technical and vocational schools had 7,058 students enrolled in autumn 1986. In addition there are 16 community colleges with an enrolment of approximately 86,000 per year.

Books of Reference

Tourist and industrial publications, descriptive of the Government's programme, are obtainable from the Department of Industry and Commerce; other government publications from Government Information Services (Legislative Building, Regina).
Saskatchewan Economic Review. Executive Council, Regina. Annual
Archer, J. H., *Saskatchewan: A History.* Saskatoon, 1980
Arora, V., *The Saskatchewan Bibliography.* Regina, 1980
Richards, J. S., and Fung, K. I. (eds.), *Atlas of Saskatchewan.* Univ. of Saskatchewan, 1969

THE NORTHWEST TERRITORIES

HISTORY. The Territory was developed by the Hudson's Bay Company and the North West Company (of Montreal) from the 17th century. The Canadian Government bought out the Hudson's Bay Company in 1869 and the Territory was annexed to Canada in 1870. The Arctic Islands lying north of the Canadian mainland were annexed to Canada in 1880 by Queen Victoria.

AREA AND POPULATION. The total area of the Territories is 1,304,903 sq. miles (3,379,700 sq. km), divided into 5 administrative regions: Fort Smith, Inuvik, Kitikmeot, Keewatin and Baffin. The population in June 1986 was 51,384, 29,602 of whom were Inuit (Eskimo) or Dene (Indian) and Metis. When the transfer of governmental responsibility from Ottawa to the Territorial capital at Yellowknife took place in 1967, the population of Yellowknife increased by the influx of civil servants from 3,741 in 1966 to 11,077 in 1985. Main centres (June 1985): Inuvik (3,166), Fort Smith (2,468), Hay River (3,142), Frobisher Bay (2,954), Rankin Inlet (1,315), Cambridge Bay (902).

CLIMATE. Conditions range from cold continental to polar, with long hard winters and short cool summers. Precipitation is low. Yellowknife. Jan. −15°F (−26°C), July 61°F (16·1°C). Annual rainfall 10″ (256 mm).

CONSTITUTION AND GOVERNMENT. The Northwest Territories comprises all that portion of Canada lying north of the 60th parallel of N. lat. except those portions within the Yukon Territory and the Provinces of Quebec and Newfoundland: it also includes the islands in Hudson Bay, James Bay and Ungava Bay except those within the Provinces of Manitoba, Ontario and Quebec.

The Northwest Territories is governed by a Government Leader, with a 7-member cabinet and a Legislative Assembly. The Assembly is composed of 24 members elected for a 4-year term of office. A Commissioner of the Northwest Territories acts as a lieutenant-governor and is the federal government's senior representative in the Territorial government. The seat of government was transferred from Ottawa to Yellowknife when it was named Territorial capital on 18 Jan. 1967.

Government Leader: Nick Sibbeston.
Commissioner: J. H. Parker.
Flag: Vertically, blue, white, blue, with the white of double width and bearing the shield of the Territory.

Legislative powers are exercised by the Executive Council on such matters as taxation within the Territories in order to raise revenue, maintenance of justice, licences, solemnization of marriages, education, public health, property, civil rights and generally all matters of a local nature.

The Territorial Government has assumed most of the responsibility for the administration of the Northwest Territories but political control of Crown lands and non-renewable resources still rests with the Federal Government. In a Territory-wide plebiscite in April 1982, a majority of residents voted in favour of dividing the Northwest Territories into two jurisdictions, east and west. Two forums for each jurisdiction have been created to develop constitutions for the proposed new territories and to negotiate a dividing boundary.

ENERGY AND NATURAL RESOURCES

Oil and Gas. As of Sept. 1987, 71 licences for oil and gas exploration were held for over 7·2m. hectares, of which 44 were for the mainland, 14 were for the arctic islands and 16 for the marine coast.

Crude oil is produced at Norman Wells and piped to Alberta. In 1986, oil production was 117,520 cu. metres.

Minerals. Metallic mineral production for the year 1986, from 7 producing mines, was valued at $630m. The Northwest Territories produces 26·5% of Canada's lead, 23% of zinc, 12·9% of gold and 3% of Canadian silver.

Trapping and Game. The 180,000 pelts, furs and hides sold by Northwest Territories hunters and trappers in the 1984–85 season were valued at $5·5m. The pelts of highest value are those of the marten, muskrat, polar bear and lynx. A herd of some 6,500 buffalo is protected in Wood Buffalo National Park. Barren ground caribou are plentiful.

Forestry. The principal trees are white and black spruce, jack-pine, balsam, poplar and birch. In 1985–86, 70,600 cu. metres of lumber, valued at $2·8m., was produced.

Fisheries. Commercial fishing, principally on Great Slave Lake, in 1983–84 produced fish valued at $1·7m., principally trout, arctic char and whitefish.

CO-OPERATIVES. There are 46 active co-operatives, including 6 housing co-operatives and one central organization to service local co-operatives, in the Northwest Territories. They are active in handicrafts, furs, fisheries, retail stores and print shops. Total revenue in 1985 was about $31m.

COMMUNICATIONS

Roads. The Mackenzie Route connects Grimshaw, Alberta, with Hay River, Pine Point, Fort Smith, Fort Providence, Rae-Edzo and Yellowknife. The Mackenzie Highway extension to Fort Simpson and a road between Pine Point and Fort Resolution have both been opened.

Highway service to Inuvik in the Mackenzie Delta was opened in spring 1980, extending north from Dawson, Yukon as the Dempster Highway. The Liard Highway connecting the communities of the Liard River valley to British Columbia opened in 1984.

Railways. There is one small railway system in the north which runs from Pine Point and Hay River, on the south shore of Great Slave Lake, 435 miles south to Grimshaw, Alberta, where it connects with the CN Rail's main system.

Aviation (1979). Fourteen licensed and 1 unlicensed airports are operated by the federal Ministry of Transport and there are 17 licensed and 18 unlicensed airports operated by the Government of the Northwest Territories. Two licensed and 10 unlicensed airports are operated by private owners. Regular mail, passenger and express services are maintained throughout the Territories. A seaplane base is operated by the Ministry of Transport and there are 17 private seaplane bases. Scheduled services join major points with centres in southern Canada.

Shipping. A direct inland-water transportation route for about 1,700 miles is provided by the Mackenzie River and its tributaries, the Athabasca and Slave rivers. Subsidiary routes on Lake Athabasca, Great Slave Lake and Great Bear River and Lake total more than 800 miles.

Post and Broadcasting (1987). There were 79 post offices. The CBC northern service operated radio stations at Yellowknife, Inuvik, Frobisher Bay and Rankin Inlet. Virtually all communities of 150 or over were receiving television *via* satellite. Telephone service is provided by common carriers to nearly all communities in the Northwest Territories. Those few communities without service have high frequency or very high frequency radios for emergency use.

EDUCATION AND WELFARE

Education. In 1986–87 the Government of the Northwest Territories operated 72 schools with 769 teachers. In addition, 2 public school districts operated at Yellowknife, one Roman Catholic separate school district at Yellowknife, and one school society operated a school at Rae-Edzo. The total enrolment in grades kindergarten to 12 was 13,296 in 1986–87. Three large and 4 small residences accommodate 400 students. Free correspondence courses are available to any pupil in a settlement where appropriate instruction is not available. There is a full range of courses available in the school system: academic, industrial arts, home economics, commercial, technical and occupational training. The continuing and special education programme provides courses and financial assistance to residents who have left the school system or are taking post high school training.

Health. In 1987 there were 7 hospitals in the Territories, 5 operated by the territorial government (Yellowknife, Hay River, Inuvik, Iqaluit and Fort Smith) and 2 operated by the federal government. The territorial government also operated 12 nursing stations, 2 boarding homes (Winnipeg, Montreal), 2 regional health boards (Keewatin and Kitimeot) and 1 transient centre. The federal government operated 30 nursing stations, 5 health stations and 5 health centres.

Welfare. Welfare services are provided by professional social workers. Facilities included (1986) for children: 13 group homes, 2 residential treatment centres, 3 secure custody facilities for young offenders and 1 receiving home, as well as 4 homes for the aged.

Books of Reference

Annual Report of the Government of the Northwest Territories
Government Activities in the North, 1983–84. Indian and Northern Affairs, Canada
NWT Data Book 84/85. Yellowknife, 1985
Boyle, E., and Sprudz, A., *Arctic Cooperatives, Canada 1965–68*
Dawson, C. A., *The New North-West.* Toronto, 1947
MacKay, D., *The Honorable Company.* Toronto, 1949
Rasmussen, K., *The People of the Polar North, A Record.* Philadelphia, 1908

YUKON TERRITORY

HISTORY. Formerly part of the North-West Territory, Yukon was joined to the Dominion as a separate territory in 1898.

AREA AND POPULATION. The Yukon Territory is situated in the extreme north-western section of Canada and comprises 482,515 sq. km. of which 4,481 fresh water. The census population in 1981 was 23,153; 1986 (estimate), 26,166. Principal centres are Whitehorse (capital), 18,385; Watson Lake, 1,595; Dawson City, 1,553; Mayo-Elsa, 869; Faro, 727.

Vital statistics, see p. 271.

Religion, see p. 290.

CLIMATE. A cold climate, with considerable annual range of temperature and moderate rainfall. Whitehorse. Jan. 5°F (–15°C), July 56°F (13·3°C). Annual rainfall 10″ (250 mm). Dawson City. Jan. –22°F (–30°C), July 57°F (13·9°C). Annual rainfall 13″ (320 mm).

CONSTITUTION AND GOVERNMENT. The Yukon Territory was constituted a separate territory in June 1898. It is governed by a 5-member Executive Council (Cabinet) appointed from among the 16-member elected Legislative

Assembly. The members are elected for a 4-year term. The seat of government is at Whitehorse. A federally appointed Commissioner has the final signing authority for all legislation passed by the Assembly.

Commissioner: Ken McKinnon (appointed 27 March 1986)

Flag: Vertically green, white, blue, in the proportions 2 : 3 : 2, charged in the centre with the arms of the Territory.

The legislative authority of the Assembly includes direct taxation, education, property and civil rights, territorial civil service, municipalities and generally all matters of local or private nature. All other major administration including Crown lands, income tax, natural resources and particularly that which requires the spending of large sums of money, is federally controlled.

ECONOMY

Planning. The three main sectors of the Yukon economy are government, tourism and mining. Government expenditures will exceed $400m. in 1986–87. The tourism industry remains strong, benefiting from Vancouver's Expo '86. Curragh Resources reopened the Cyprus Anvil lead-zinc mine in 1986, employing 405 people. In 1985 gold production from Yukon's placer mines was approximately $43m., silver production, mostly from the United Keno Hill mine, was $13m. and exploration expenditures were $30m. One modest gold mine commenced production in 1986. In general, in 1986 the economy had recovered strongly from the recession of 1981–85.

Finance. The territorial revenue and expenditure (in Canadian $1,000) for fiscal years ended 31 March was:

	1981–82	1982–83	1983–84	1984–85
Revenue	145,021	173,559	184,749	199,586
Expenditure	142,047	161,682	173,864	192,636

ENERGY AND NATURAL RESOURCES

Electricity. Power is supplied through hydroelectric plants at Whitehorse Rapids (capacity 40 mw) and Aishihik.

Oil. Dome Petroleum, Gulf, Esso Resources, Petro Canada and Shell were exploring (1986) extensively for oil in the Beaufort Sea.

Minerals. Mining remains the main industry. Lead, zinc, silver and gold are the chief minerals. Production figures for year ending 31 Dec. 1985 (provisional) in tonnes were: Lead, 1,675; silver, 50; gold, 3,098 kg. The value of mining production sales in 1985 was approximately $56·7m.

Agriculture. There are areas where the climate is suitable for the production of forage crops (occupying the largest acreage and used as feed for the estimated 2,500 horses), early maturing varieties of cereals and grains and vegetables. In 1984 cereal crop and forage fertility trials were initiated and the Yukon New Crop Development Project began in 1985. In 1985 there were 25–30 full time and 75 part-time farmers. The total improved acreage was 4,500 acres and the estimated value of agricultural products (farm gate not retail) $1·3m.

Forestry. The forests are part of the great Boreal forest region of Canada which stretches from the east coast of Canada into Alaska and north well above the Arctic Circle. Vast areas are covered by coniferous stands in the southern portion of Yukon with white spruce and lodgepole pine forming pure stands on wet sites and in northern aspects. Deciduous species form pure stands or occur mixed with conifers throughout forest areas.

The value of forest production in 1985 was approximately $2·8m.

Fisheries. Commercial fishing concentrates on chinook salmon, chum salmon, lake trout and whitefish. The value of the raw catch in 1985 was $328,000.

Game and Furs. The country abounds with big game, such as moose, goat, caribou, mountain sheep and bear (grizzly and black). In 1985, 27,017 pelts were taken for a market value of $1,279,705. Lynx was the most valuable fur and made up 50·3% of the total harvest bringing in $643,615 in revenues.

TOURISM. In 1984, 422,094 tourists visited Yukon and spent $84m. In 1985 tourists spent $87m.

COMMUNICATIONS

Roads. The Alaska Highway and its side roads connect Yukon's main communities with Alaska and the provinces and with adjacent mining centres. Interior roads connect the mining communities of Elsa (silver–lead), Faro (lead–zinc–silver). Tungsten (tungsten) and mineral exploration properties (lead–zinc and tungsten) north of Ross River. The 725 km Dempster Highway north of Dawson City connects with Inuvik, on the Arctic coast; this highway, the first public road to be built to the Arctic ocean, was opened in Aug. 1979. The Carcross–Skagway road was opened in May 1979, providing a new access to the Pacific Ocean. There are 4,688 km of roads in the Territory, of which about 250 km are paved. The rest are all-weather gravel of which 1,364 km are accessible during the summer months only.

Railways. The 176-km White Pass and Yukon Railway connected Whitehorse with year-round ocean shipping at Skagway, Alaska, but was closed in 1982.

Aviation. Commercial airlines provide regular services between Whitehorse, Watson Lake, Edmonton and Vancouver. Regularly scheduled air services extend from Whitehorse to interior communities of Faro, Mayo, Dawson City, Old Crow, Ross River, Watson Lake, MacMillan Pass, Juneau with connecting service to Anchorage, Seattle, Fairbanks and other points in Alaska. There are several commercial bush plane operations for charter service.

Shipping. Most goods are shipped into the Territory by truck over the Alaska and Stewart–Cassiar Highways. A recent development has been the shipment of food-stuffs *via* container ship to Skagway, Alaska, and then by truck to Whitehorse. Some goods are transported within the Territory by air. Although navigable, the rivers are no longer used for shipping.

Post and Broadcasting. There are 3 radio stations in Whitehorse and 13 low-power relay radio transmitters operated by CBC. There are also 12 cable-TV channels in Whitehorse, TV channels in Whitehorse and private cable operations in Faro (provided by Canadian Satellite), Dawson City and Watson Lake. Live CBC national television is provided by the Anik satellite to virtually every community in the Territory. All telephone and telecommunications in the Territory are provided by NorthwesTel, a subsidiary of Canadian National Telecommunications. Almost all pole lines have been replaced with microwave transmission.

Newspapers. In 1985 there were 3 newspapers, 2 published 3 days a week and 1 twice a month, in Whitehorse. Elsa and Dawson City both have newsletters.

EDUCATION AND WELFARE

Education. In 1985–86, the Territory had 26 schools with 289 teachers and 4,477 pupils attending classes from kindergarten to grade 12. In 1983–84 approximately 850 students were involved in full-time programmes at Yukon College, while 900 persons were enrolled in part-time courses in Whitehorse and the rural communities. In 1984 French schooling for francophone children was introduced. In addition to the courses given at Yukon College, there are a number of post-secondary courses through the University of Alberta, University of Victoria and Red Deer College. A Yukon Teacher Education Programme started in 1977 to train local residents to obtain Bachelor of Education degrees in Education and a Teaching Certificate. The course is conducted by the University of British Columbia. The Government provides financial assistance to students requiring further education elsewhere.

Health. The health care system provides all residents with the care demanded by illness or accident. The federal government operates 1 general hospital at Whitehorse, 3 cottage hospitals, 2 nursing stations, with a total of 160 beds, 11 health centres and 4 health stations. The territorial government also operates a medical evacuation programme to send patients to Edmonton or Vancouver for specialized treatment not available in the Territory.

Books of Reference

Annual Report of the Commissioner.
Yukon Executive Council, *Statistical Review.*
Berton, P., *Klondike.* Toronto, 1963
Coults, R., *Yukon Places and Names.* Sidney, 1980
McCourt, E., *The Yukon and Northwest Territories.* Toronto, 1969
William, A. A., *The Discovery and Exploration of the Yukon.* Sidney, 1976

CAPE VERDE

República de Cabo Verde

Capital: Praia
Population: 350,000 (1987)
GNP per capita: US$320 (1983)

HISTORY. The Cape Verde Islands were discovered in 1460 by Diogo Gomes, the first settlers arriving in 1462. In 1587 its administration was unified under a Portuguese governor. The colony became an Overseas Province on 11 June 1951.

On 30 Dec. 1974 Portugal transferred power to a transitional government headed by the Portuguese High Commissioner. Full independence was granted on 5 July 1975.

AREA AND POPULATION. Cape Verde is situated in the Atlantic Ocean 620 km WNW of Senegal and consists of 10 islands and 5 islets. Praia is the capital. The islands are divided into 2 groups, named Barlavento (windward) and Sotavento (leeward). The total area is 4,033 sq. km (1,557 sq. miles). The population (census, 1980) was 296,093. Estimate (1987) 350,000. About 600,000 Cape Verdeans live abroad.

The areas and populations (1980, census) of the islands are:

	Sq. km	Population		Sq. km	Population
Santo Antão	779	43,198	Maio	269	4,103
São Vicente [1]	227	41,792	São Tiago	991	145,923
São Nicolau	388	13,575	Fogo	476	31,115
Sal	216	6,006	Brava	67	6,984
Boa Vista	620	3,397			
			Sotavento	1,803	188,125
Barlovento	2,230	107,968			
			Total	4,033	296,093

[1] Includes Santa Luzia which is uninhabited.

The main towns (1980 census) are Praia, the capital (37,676) on São Tiago; and Mindelo (36,746) on Sao Vicente. 70% of the inhabitants are of mixed origins, and another 28% are black. Crioulo serves as the common language of the islands, although the official language is Portuguese.

Vital statistics (1985): Births, 10,949; deaths, 2,804.

CLIMATE. The climate is arid, with a cool dry season from Dec. to June and warm dry conditions for the rest of the year. Rainfall is sparse, rarely exceeding 5" (127 mm) in the northern islands or 12" (304 mm) in the southern ones. There are periodic severe droughts. Praia. Jan. 72°F (22·2°C), July 77°F (25°C). Annual rainfall 10" (250 mm).

CONSTITUTION AND GOVERNMENT. The Constitution adopted on 12 Feb. 1981 removed all reference to possible future union with Guinea-Bissau, and the *Partido Africano da Independencia de Cabo Verde*, founded 20 Jan. 1981, became the sole legal party. The legislature consists of a unicameral People's National Assembly of 83 members elected for 5 years by universal suffrage; it elects the President, who appoints and leads a Council of Ministers. Elections were held on 7 Dec. 1985.

President: Arístides Maria Pereira (assumed office 5 July 1975; re-elected 1981 and 1986).

In Jan. 1988 the Council of Ministers comprised:

Prime Minister, Co-operation and Planning, Finance: Gen. Pedro Verona Rodrigues Pires.

Foreign Affairs: Col. Silvino Manuel da Luz. *Armed Forces and Security:* Col. Júlio de Carvalho. *Transport, Trade and Tourism:* Maj. Osvaldo Lopez da Silva. *Education:* André Corsino Tolentino. *Health, Labour and Social Welfare:* Dr

Ireneu Gomes. *Justice:* Dr José Eduardo Araújo. *Information, Culture and Sport:* Dr David Hopffer Cordeiro Almada. *Agriculture and Fisheries:* Maj. João Pereira Silva. *Local Government and Town Planning:* Tito Livio Santos de Oliveira Ramos. *Industry and Energy:* Adão Silva Rocha. *Public Works:* Adriano de Oliveira Lima. *Deputy Ministers:* Herculano Vieira *(to Prime Minister)*, Dr Arnaldo Vasconcellos Franca *(Finance)*. *Secretaries of State:* Virgilio Burgo Fernandes *(Trade and Tourism)*, Miguel Lima *(Fisheries)*, Aguinaldo Lisboa Ramos *(Foreign Affairs)*, Renato Cardoso *(Public Administration)*, João de Deus Maximiano *(Assistant to Prime Minister)*.

National flag: Horizontally yellow over green, with a vertical red strip in the hoist charged slightly above the centre with a black star surrounded by a wreath of maize, and beneath this a yellow clam shell.

Local government: The 2 *distritos* (Barlovento and Sotavento) are sub-divided into 14 *conçelhos* – Ribeira Grande, Paúl, Porto Novo (these 3 covering Santo Antão island), São Vicente (including Santa Luzia), São Nicolau, Sal, Boa Vista, Maio, Praia, Santa Catarina, Tarrafal, Santa Cruz (these 4 covering São Tiago island), Fogo and Brava.

DEFENCE

Army. The Popular Revolutionary Armed Forces had a strength of 1,000 in 1988. There is also a paramilitary People's Militia.

Navy. There are 3 fast gunboats and 3 fast attack craft (*ex*-torpedo boats), all 6 *ex*-Soviet and 1 hydrographic survey vessel. Personnel (1988) 120.

Air Force. An embryo air force has been formed with three An-26 twin-turboprop transports and about 25 personnel.

INTERNATIONAL RELATIONS

Membership. Cape Verde is a member of UN, OAU and an ACP state of EEC.

ECONOMY

Planning. The second 5-year development plan (1985–89) is concentrated on the fishing industry and small-scale enterprises.

Budget. In 1984, the budget included revenue of 1,630m. escudos Caboverdianos and expenditure, 2,134·5m.

Currency. *Escudo Caboverdiano* of 100 *centavos.* There are coins of 20 and 50 *centavos* and of 1, 2½, 10, 20 and 50 *escudos*, and banknotes of 100,500 and 1,000 *escudos.* In March 1988, 130·21 *Escudo* = £1 and 73·42 *Escudo* = US$1.

Banking. The Banco de Cabo Verde is the bank of issue and commercial bank, with branches at Praia, Mindelo and Espargos airport (Sal).

ENERGY AND NATURAL RESOURCES

Electricity. Production in 1986 amounted to 18m. kwh; capacity (1986), 14,000 kw.

Minerals. Salt is obtained on the islands of Sal, Boa Vista and Maio. Volcanic rock (pozzolana) is mined for export.

Agriculture. Mostly confined to irrigated inland valleys, the chief crops (production, 1986, in 1,000 tonnes) are: Coconuts, 10; sugar-cane, 10; bananas, 4; potatoes, 3; cassava, 4; sweet potatoes, 7; maize, 12; beans, groundnuts and coffee. Bananas and coffee are mainly for export.

Livestock (1986): 66,000 goats, 13,000 cattle, 54,000 pigs and 6,000 asses.

Fisheries. The catch in 1983 was 13,205 tonnes, of which tuna comprised 46%. About 200 tonnes of lobsters are caught annually.

COMMERCE. Imports in 1984 totalled 5,988m. escudos Caboverdianos, of which 24% came from Portugal, 22% from the Netherlands; exports in 1984 totalled 222m. escudos Caboverdianos, of which 30% went to Algeria, 22% to Portugal, 19% to Italy. In 1983, expatriated earnings from Cape Verdeans abroad totalled 2,800m. escudos Caboverdianos. Exports: Fish, salt and bananas.

Total trade of Cape Verde with UK (British Department of Trade returns, in £1,000 sterling):

	1983	1984	1985	1986	1987
Imports to UK	122	211	370	426	301
Exports and re-exports from UK	1,245	1,162	2,282	1,618	1,208

COMMUNICATIONS

Roads. There were 2,250 km of roads (660 km paved) in 1981 and there were 4,000 private cars and 1,343 commercial vehicles.

Aviation. Amilcar Cabral International Airport, at Espargos on Sal, is a major refuelling point on flights to Africa and South America, with 21,200 passengers disembarking and 23,106 embarking in 1982. Transportes Aéros de Cabo Verde provides regular services to smaller airports on most of the other islands.

Shipping. The main ports are Mindelo and Praia. In 1982 the ports handled 371,812 tonnes of imports and 146,822 tonnes of exports. In 1986, the merchant marine comprised 25 vessels of 14,095 GRT.

Broadcasting. There are 2 radio stations, at Praia and Mindelo; both are government-owned. There were (1983) 46,857 radio receivers and (1981) 1,739 telephones.

Cinemas. In 1972 there were 6 cinemas with 2,800 seats.

JUSTICE, RELIGION, EDUCATION AND WELFARE

Justice. There is a network of People's Tribunals, with a Supreme Court in Praia.

Religion. In 1982, over 98% of the population were Roman Catholic.

Education. In 1983 there were 57,262 pupils and 1,959 teachers at 449 primary schools, 7,262 pupils and 500 teachers at 13 preparatory schools, 3,192 pupils and 103 teachers at 3 secondary schools, and 724 students and 103 teachers at a technical school. There were 199 students and 36 teachers in 3 teacher-training colleges and about 500 students were at foreign universities.

In 1981, 49% of the adult population were literate.

Health. In 1980 there were 21 hospitals and dispensaries with 632 beds; there were also 51 doctors, 3 dentists, 7 pharmacists, 9 midwives and 184 nursing personnel.

DIPLOMATIC REPRESENTATIVES

Of Great Britain in Cape Verde
Ambassador: J. E. C. Macrae, CMG (resides in Dakar).

Of Cape Verde in the USA (3415 Massachusetts Ave., NW, Washington, D.C., 20007)
Ambassador: José Luis Fernandes Lopes.

Of the USA in Cape Verde (Rua Hojl Ya Yenna 81, Praia)
Ambassador: Vernon D. Penner, Jr.

Of Cape Verde to the United Nations
Ambassador: Humberto Bettencourt Santos.

Books of Reference

Annuario Estatistico de Cabo Verde. Praia. Annual
Andrade, E., *The Cape Verde Islands: From Slavery to Modern Times.* Dakar, 1973
Carreira, A., *The People of the Cape Verde Islands.* London, 1982
Lobban, R., *The Cape Verde Islands.* New York, 1974

CAYMAN
ISLANDS

Capital: George Town
Population: 22,900 (1987)
GNP per capita: US$9,000 (1987)

HISTORY. The islands were discovered by Columbus on 10 May 1503 and were ceded (with Jamaica) to Britain in 1670. Grand Cayman was settled in 1734 and the other islands in 1833. They became a separate Crown Colony on 4 July 1959, administered by the same governor as Jamaica until the latter's independence on 6 Aug. 1962 when they received their own Administrator (From 1972 a governor).

AREA AND POPULATION. Cayman Islands consist of Grand Cayman, Little Cayman and Cayman Brac. Situated in the Caribbean Sea, about 200 miles NW of Jamaica. Area, 100 sq. miles (260 sq. km). Census population of 1979, 16,677 (11,282 Caymanians by birth); estimate (1987) 22,900. The spoken language is English. The chief town is George Town, estimate (1985) 8,900. Vital statistics (1987): Births, 359; marriages, 272; deaths, 98.

The areas and populations of the islands are:

	Sq. km	Census 1979	Estimate 1987
Grand Cayman	197	15,000	21,485
Cayman Brac	36	1,607	1,345
Little Cayman	26	70	70

CLIMATE. The climate is tropical maritime, with a cool season from Nov. to March and temperatures some 10°F warmer for the remaining months. Rainfall averages 56″ (1,400 mm) a year at George Town. Hurricanes may be experienced between July and Nov.

CONSTITUTION AND GOVERNMENT. A new Constitution came into force in Aug. 1972. The Legislative Assembly consists of the Governor (as President), 3 official members, and 12 elected members.

The Executive Council consists of Govenor (as Chairman), the 3 official members and 4 elected members elected by the elected members of the Legislative Assembly.

Governor: A. J. Scott, CVO, CBE.

Flag: British Blue Ensign with the arms of the Colony on a white disc in the fly.

ECONOMY

Budget. Revenue 1987, CI$75·5m.; expenditure, CI$71·8m. Public debt (31 Dec. 1986), CI$14m.; total reserves, CI$8·3m.

Currency. The Cayman Island dollar (CI$) is divided into 100 cents and is fixed at a rate of CI$1 = US$1.20.

Banking. 510 commercial banks and trust companies held licences in 1987, which permit the holders to offer services to the public, over 30 domestically. Barclays Bank International has offices at George Town and Cayman Brac.

INDUSTRY AND TRADE

Electricity. Production (1987) 161·4m. kwh.

Industry. Finance and tourism are the main industries. 17,400 companies are registered in the islands.

Commerce. Exports, 1986 (f.o.b.), totalled CI$2m. Imports, (c.i.f.), CI$134m.; principally foodstuffs, manufactured items, textiles, building materials, automobiles and petroleum products.

Total trade between Cayman Islands and UK (British Department of Trade returns, in £1,000 sterling):

	1985	1986	1987
Imports to UK	826	2,422	1,318
Exports and re-exports from UK	6,410	11,403	6,442

Tourism. Tourism is the chief industry of the islands, after financial services, and there were (1988) over 2,680 beds in hotels and over 2,350 in apartments, guest-houses and cottages. There were 480,792 visitors in 1987, including 209,044 by air, an increase of 26% over 1986.

COMMUNICATIONS

Roads. There were (1988) about 110 miles of road and (1986) 10,709 motor vehicles.

Aviation. Cayman Airways provides regular services between Grand Cayman and Miami, Houston, Tampa, Atlanta and Jamaica. Eastern and Northwest Airlines provide a daily service between Miami and Grand Cayman. CAL provides a regular inter-island service. Air Jamaica also provides services between Grand Cayman and Jamaica.

Shipping. Motor vessels ply regularly between the Cayman Islands, Jamaica, Costa Rica and Florida. Shipping registered at George Town, 696 vessels (Nov. 1987).

Post and Broadcasting. There were 13,677 telephones in 1986 and there are 2 radio broadcasting stations in the islands, with (1988) 20,000 receivers.

Newspapers. The *Caymanian Compass* is published 5 days a week.

JUSTICE, RELIGION, EDUCATION AND WELFARE

Justice. There is a Grand Court, sitting 6 times a year at George Town under a Chief Justice. 2 Summary Courts sit at other times.

Religion. There are Anglican, Roman Catholic, Presbyterian and other Christian communities represented in the islands.

Education. In 1986 there were 10 government primary schools with 1,209 pupils, 6 private elementary schools with 885 pupils and 4 private secondary schools with 212 pupils. Post-primary education at the government high schools and the government middle school and private schools was attended by 2,278 pupils. There was also a private institution for further education and a government school for special educational needs.

Health. In 1988 there was a fully-equipped general hospital in George Town with 15 doctors, a dental clinic, 4 district clinics and a hospital in Cayman Brac.

Books of Reference

Annual Report, 1986. Cayman Islands Government, 1987
Statistical Abstract of the Cayman Islands, 1986. Cayman Islands Government Statistics Unit, 1987

CENTRAL
AFRICAN
REPUBLIC

Capital: Bangui
Population: 2·78m. (1987)
GNP per capita: US$280 (1984)

République centrafricaine

HISTORY. Central African Republic became independent on 13 Aug. 1960, after having been one of the 4 territories of French Equatorial Africa (under the name of Ubangi Shari) and from 1 Dec. 1958 a member state of the French Community. A new Constitution was adopted by a special congress of the *Mouvement pour l'évolution sociale de l'Afrique noire* on 4 Dec. 1976. It provided for the country to be a parliamentary democracy and to be known as the Central African Empire. President Bokassa became Emperor Bokassa I. The Emperor was overthrown in a *coup* on 20–21 Sept. 1979 and the empire was abolished. On 15 March 1981 David Dacko was re-elected President but Army Chief General André Kolingba took power in a bloodless *coup* on 1 Sept. 1981 at the head of a Military Committee for National Recovery (CMRN), which held supreme power until 21 Sept. 1985 when President Kolingba dissolved it and initiated a return towards constitutional rule.

AREA AND POPULATION. The Central African Republic is bounded north by Chad, east by Sudan, south by Zaïre and Congo, and west by Cameroon. The area covers 622,436 sq. km (240,324 sq. miles); its population in 1975 census, 2,054,610 and estimate in 1987 was 2,775,000. The capital is Bangui (473,817 inhabitants in 1984): other towns, Bambari (44,500), Bouar (42,000), Berbérati (38,000), Bossangoa (36,000) and Bria (31,000).

French is the official language.

CLIMATE. A tropical climate with little variation in temperature. The wet months are May, June, Oct. and Nov. Bangui. Jan. 80°F (26·5°C), July 77°F (25°C). Annual rainfall 61″ (1,525 mm). Ndele. Jan. 83°F (28·3°C), July 77°F (25°C). Annual rainfall 57″ (1,417 mm).

CONSTITUTION AND GOVERNMENT. Under the Constitution adopted by a national referendum on 21 Nov. 1986, the sole legal political party is the *Rassemblement Démocratique Centrafricaine (RDC).* Legislative elections for the 52-member National Assembly were held on 31 July 1987. The President is elected by popular vote for a term of 6 years, and appoints and leads a Council of Ministers.

The Council of Ministers in Aug. 1987 was composed as follows:

Chairman of CMRN, Head of State and Government, Minister of Defence and Veterans' Affairs: Gen. André Kolingba (assumed office 1 Sept. 1981, re-elected 21 Nov. 1986).

Foreign Affairs: Jean-Louis Psimhis. *Economy, Finance and Budget:* Dieudonné Wazoua. *Interior:* Lieut.-Col. Christophe Grelombe. *Justice:* Lieut.-Col. Jean-Louis Gervil Yambala. *Rural Development and Water Power:* Basil Erepe. *Public Works and Territorial Planning:* Jacques Kitte. *Education:* Jean-Paul Ngoupande. *Public Health and Social Affairs:* Bernard Belloun. *Posts and Telecommunications:* Cmdte. Joseph Stanislas Pollagba. *Transport and Civil Aviation:* Pierre Gonifei Gaibounanou. *Trade and Industry:* Justin Njapou. *Planning, Statistics and International Co-operation:* Guy Darlan. *Civil Service, Labour and Social Security:* Daniel Sehoulia. *Tourism, Water Resources, Forestry, Hunting and Fishing:* Raymond Mbitikon. *Scientific and Technical Research:* Jean-Claude Kazgui.

Energy and Mines: Lieut. Michel Salle. *Information, Arts, Culture, Youth, Sport and National Organisations:* Joaquim da Silva Nzengue.

National flag: Four horizontal stripes of blue, white, green, yellow; over all in the centre a vertical red strip, and in the canton a yellow star.

Local Government: Central African Republic is divided into 14 prefectures, 2 'economic prefectures' and the autonomous commune of Bangui (the capital).

DEFENCE. Selective national service for a 2-year period is in force. There are some 10,000 para-military personnel in the 3 services.

Army. The Army consisted (1988) of about 4,000 men, comprising an infantry battalion, with supporting engineer, signals and transport companies. Equipment includes 4 T-55 tanks, 39 armoured personnel carriers and 10 Ferret scout cars.

Navy. The naval force has 9 river patrol craft and (1988) 85 personnel.

Air Force. The Air Force has 2 Rallye Guerrier armed light aircraft, 1 twin-jet Caravelle, 1 DC-4 and 2 C-47 transports, 2 Reims-Cessna 337, 6 Aermacchi AL.60 and 5 Broussard liaison aircraft, 1 Alouette and 1 Ecureuil helicopters. It also maintains and operates the Caravelle and Falcon 20 twin-jet VIP aircraft. Personnel strength (1988) about 300.

INTERNATIONAL RELATIONS

Membership. Central African Republic is a member of UN, OAU and an ACP state of EEC.

ECONOMY

Planning. The new recovery plan (1983–86) provided for expenditure of 31,300m. francs CFA for development of agriculture, transport and infrastructure.

Budget. The budget for 1985 provided for expenditure of 52,510m. francs CFA, and for revenue of 41,420m. francs CFA.

Currency. The unit of currency is the *franc CFA* with a parity of 50 *francs CFA* to 1 French *franc*. There are coins of 1, 2, 5, 10, 25, 50, 100 and 500 *francs* CFA, and banknotes of 100, 500, 1,000, 5,000 and 10,000 *francs* CFA. In March 1988, £1 = 507 *francs* CFA; US$1 = 285·66 *francs* CFA.

Banking. The *Banque des Etats de l'Afrique Centrale* is the bank of issue.

ENERGY AND NATURAL RESOURCES

Electricity. Production in 1986 totalled 61m. kwh. Supply 220 volts; 50 Hz.

Minerals. 295,000 carats of gem diamonds and 134 kg of gold were mined in 1983. There are significant regions of uranium in the Bakouma area.

Agriculture. Over 86% of the working population is occupied in subsistence agriculture. The main crops (production 1986, in 1,000 tonnes) are cassava, 708; groundnuts, 142; bananas, 83; plantains, 65; millet, 40; maize, 53; seed cotton, 63; coffee, 18; rice, 16.

Livestock (1986): Cattle, 2,135,000; goats, 1·1m.; sheep, 112,000; pigs, 360,000.

Forestry. The extensive hardwood forests, particularly in the south-west, provide mahogany, obeche and limba for export. Production (1983) 3·05m. cu. metres.

Fisheries. Catch (1983) 13,000 tonnes.

INDUSTRY AND TRADE

Industry. The small industrial sector includes factories producing cotton fabrics (5m. sq. metres in 1981) footwear, beer and radios.

Commerce. Imports and exports in 1m. francs CFA:

	1980	1981	1982	1983
Imports	17,009	25,646	41,307	52,100
Exports	24,384	21,323	35,454	43,700

In 1983, France took 30% of exports and provided 46% of imports. Of all exports, coffee comprised 29% (by value), diamonds 24%, timber 19% and cotton 13%.

Total trade of Central African Republic with UK (British Department of Trade returns, in £1,000 sterling):

	1984	1985	1986	1987
Imports to UK	357	1,739	1,452	233
Exports and re-exports from UK	722	1,151	787	1,127

Tourism. There were about 4,000 visitors in 1986.

COMMUNICATIONS

Roads. In 1984 there were 22,560 km of roads and 46,982 vehicles in use.

Railways. There are no railways, but a proposal exists (1985) for an 800 km line (1,435 mm gauge) from Bangui through Cameroon and Congo to connect with the Trans-Gabon railway at Belinga.

Aviation. There are international airports at Mpoko, near Bangui and Berbérati. Air Centrafrique operates extensive internal services to several airstrips.

Shipping. Timber and barges are taken to Brazzaville (Congo).

Post and Broadcasting. There were (1982) 1,200 television and 135,000 radio receivers and (1984) 5,000 telephones.

Cinemas. In 1971 there were 8 cinemas.

Newspapers. In 1984 there was one daily newspaper.

JUSTICE, RELIGION, EDUCATION AND WELFARE

Justice. The Criminal Court and Supreme Court are situated in Bangui. There are 16 high courts throughout the country.

Religion. About 57% of the population follow animist beliefs, 20% are Roman Catholic, 15% Protestant and 8% Moslem.

Education. The University of Bangui was founded in 1970 and had 1,489 students in 1980. In 1983 there were 291,444 pupils at primary schools and 52,417 at secondary schools; technical schools held 1,325 students, while 327 were at the 2 teacher-training establishments.

Health. In 1979 there were 85 hospitals and dispensaries with 3,605 beds. In 1980 there were 108 doctors, 3 dentists, 18 pharmacists and 149 midwives.

DIPLOMATIC REPRESENTATIVES

Of Central African Republic in Great Britain
Ambassador: (Vacant).

Of Great Britain in Central African Republic
Ambassador: (Vacant).

Of Central African Republic in the USA (1618 22nd St., NW, Washington, D.C. 20008)
Ambassador: Christian Lingama-Toleque.

Of the USA in Central African Republic (Ave. President Dacko, Bangui)
Ambassador: David C. Fields.

Of Central African Republic to the United Nations
Ambassador: Michel Gbezera-Bria.

Book of Reference

Kalck, H. P., *Historical Dictionary of the Central African Republic.* Metuchen, 1980

CHAD

Capital: N'djaména
Population: 5·24m. (1987)
GNP per capita: US$88 (1984)

République du Tchad

HISTORY. France proclaimed a protectorate over Chad on 5 Sept. 1900, and in July 1908 the territory was incorporated into French Equatorial Africa. It became a separate colony March 1920, and in 1946 one of the four constituent territories of French Equatorial Africa. On 28 Nov. 1958 Chad became an autonomous republic within the French Community and achieved full independence on 11 Aug. 1960, although the northern prefecture of Borkou-Ennedi-Tibesti remained under French military administration until 1965.

Conflicts between the central government and secessionist groups, particularly in the Moslem north and centre of Chad, began in 1965 and flared into a prolonged and confused civil war that continued under different protagonists, with occasional pauses during attempts at reconciliation. On 7 June 1982 the *Forces Armées du Nord* (FAN) led by Hissène Habré gained control of the country. In June 1983 the Libyan-backed forces of former President Goukouni Oueddei re-occupied Bourkou-Ennedi-Tibesti, but by April 1987 most of the rebels rallied to the government side, which then forced the Libyans back into the Aozou Strip, a 114,000 sq. km region in the extreme north of Chad occupied by Libyan forces since 1973.

AREA AND POPULATION. Chad is bounded west by Cameroon, Nigeria and Niger, north by Libya, east by Sudan and south by the Central African Republic. Area, 1,284,000 sq. km; its population in 1987 was estimated at 5,241,000 (census 1975, 4,029,917). The capital is N'djaména, formerly Fort Lamy with 511,700 inhabitants in 1985, other large towns (1985) being Sarh (124,000), Moundou (87,000), Abéché (71,000), Bongor (69,000) and Doba (64,000).

The areas, populations and chief towns of the 14 prefectures were:

Préfecture	sq. km	Population Estimate 1984	Capital
Borkou-Ennedi-Tibesti	600,350	103,000	Faya (Largeau)
Biltine	46,850	200,000	Biltine
Ouaddaï	76,240	411,000	Abéché
Batha	88,800	410,000	Ati
Kanem	114,520	234,000	Mao
Lac	22,320	158,000	Bol
Chari-Baguirmi	82,910	719,000	N'djaména
Guéra	58,950	234,000	Mongo
Salamat	63,000	121,000	Am Timan
Moyen-Chari	45,180	582,000	Sarh
Logone Oriental	28,035	350,000	Doba
Logone Occidental	8,695	324,000	Moundou
Tandjilé	18,045	341,000	Laï
Mayo-Kabbi	30,105	757,000	Bongor

The official language is French but more than 100 different languages and dialects are spoken. The largest ethnic group is the Sara of southern Chad. Arabic serves as a common language throughout the semi-tropical (Sahelian) centre and the Saharan north.

CLIMATE. A tropical climate, with adequate rainfall in the south, though Nov. to April are virtually rainless months. Further north, desert conditions prevail. N'djaména. Jan. 75°F (23·9°C), July 82°F (27·8°C). Annual rainfall 30″ (744 mm).

CONSTITUTION AND GOVERNMENT. From June 1982 a State Council administered the country until 21 Oct. 1982, when Hissène Habré was sworn in as President and appointed a Council of Ministers to administer the country. A provisional constitution had been promulgated on 29 Sept. 1982, under which a new official political party was established on 22 June 1984, the *Union nationale pour l'independence et la révolution* (UNIR), administered by a 15-member Executive Bureau. A National Consultative Assembly was also formed on 21 Oct. 1982, comprising 2 representatives from each of the 14 prefectures and 2 from the capital, N'djaména.

President, Minister of Defence, Veterans and War Victims: Hissène Habré.

Foreign Affairs and Co-operation: Capt. Gouara Lassou.

National flag: Three vertical strips of blue, yellow, red.

Local Government: The 14 *préfectures* are divided into 53 *sous-préfectures.*

DEFENCE

Army. A new national army, the Forces Armées Nationales Tchadiennes (FANT) was formed in Dec. 1982. In 1988 the strength was over 17,000 and there was a paramilitary force of 5,700.

Air Force. The Air Force has 3 C-130 Hercules, 1 VIP Caravelle, 1 C-54, 2 Aviocar and 6 C-47 transports, 4 Reims-Cessna F337 light aircraft, 2 Turbo-Porters, 2 Broussard communications aircraft and about 10 Gazelle, Puma and Alouette III helicopters. 2 armed PC-7 and 2 armed Rallye Guerrier aircraft have recently been supplied by France. Personnel (1988) about 200.

INTERNATIONAL RELATIONS

Membership. Chad is a member of UN, OAU and is an ACP state of EEC.

ECONOMY

Budget. The budget for 1984 envisaged expenditure of 37,635m. francs CFA of which defence amounted to 17,496m. and revenue, 11,200m. francs CFA.

Currency. The unit of currency is the *franc CFA* with a parity value of 50 *francs CFA* to 1 French *franc*. In March 1988, £1 = 507 *francs*; US$1 = 285·66 *francs.*

Banking. The *Banque des Etats de l'Afrique Centrale* is the bank of issue, and the principal commercial banks are the *Banque de Développement du Tchad* and the *Banque Tchadienne de Crédit et de Dépôts.*

ENERGY AND NATURAL RESOURCES

Electricity. Production (1986) amounted to 66m. kwh. Supply 220 volts; 50 Hz.

Oil. The oilfield in Kanem préfecture has been linked by pipeline to a new refinery at Laï (in Tandjilé) but production has remained minimal due to war disruption.

Minerals. Salt (about 4,000 tonnes per annum) is mined around Lake Chad, and deposits of uranium, gold and bauxite are to be exploited.

Agriculture. Cotton growing (in the south) and animal husbandry (in the central zone) are the most important industries. Production (1986, in 1,000 tonnes) was: Millet, 600; sugar-cane, 290; yams, 219; seed cotton, 70; groundnuts, 90; cassava, 306; rice, 25; dry beans, 42; sweet potatoes, 41; mangoes, 32; dates, 33; maize, 53; cotton seed, 40.

Livestock (1986): Cattle, 5,017,000; sheep, 2·62m.; goats, 2·62m.; chickens, 4m.

Fisheries. Fish production from Lake Chad and the Chari and Logone rivers, was estimated at 110,000 tonnes in 1983.

INDUSTRY AND TRADE

Industry. Cotton ginning is the principal activity, undertaken in some 22 mills. Sugar refineries produced 23,000 tonnes in 1984. A textile factory produced 13·1m. metres of woven fabric in 1980, a brewery 130,000 hectolitres of beer and a cigarette factory 259m. cigarettes. There are also rice and flour mills and other factories involved in food processing or light industry.

Commerce. Trade (in 1 m. francs CFA):

	1981	1982	1983
Imports	29,349	35,701	13,540
Exports	22,665	18,968	4,120

The main trading partners are France and Nigeria. Cotton formed 91% of exports in 1983 as civil war has decimated other exporting industries.

Total trade with UK (British Department of Trade returns, in £1,000 sterling):

	1983	1984	1985	1986	1987
Imports to UK	8	626	1,099	2,806	1,101
Exports and re-exports from UK	2,244	3,521	1,847	1,250	1,006

COMMUNICATIONS

Roads. In 1976 there were 30,725 km of roads, of which only 240 km are surfaced. In 1977 there were 7,636 private cars and 9,668 commercial vehicles.

Aviation. There is an international airport at N'djaména, from which UTA and Air Afrique run 4 flights per week to Paris; there are also flights to Douala, Bangui and Kinshasa. Air Tchad operates internal services to 12 secondary airports.

Post and Broadcasting. In 1978 there were 3,850 telephones and (1983), 75,000 radios in use.

Cinemas. In 1977 there were 13 cinemas with 12,400 seats.

JUSTICE, RELIGION, EDUCATION AND WELFARE

Justice. There are criminal courts and magistrates courts in N'djaména, Moundou, Sarh and Abéché, with a Court of Appeal situated in N'djaména.

Religion. The northern and central parts of the country are predominantly Moslem (44% of the total population) and the southern part is mainly animist (38%) or Christian (17%).

Education. In 1977 there were 229,191 pupils in primary schools, 18,382 in secondary schools, 649 in technical schools and 549 students in teacher-training establishments. The University of Chad (founded 1971) at N'djaména had (1980) 800 students and 62 teaching staff.

Health. There were 33 hospitals with 3,353 beds in 1977 and in 1978 90 doctors, 4 dentists, 9 pharmacists, 98 midwives and 993 nursing personnel.

DIPLOMATIC REPRESENTATIVES

Of Chad in Great Britain
Ambassador: Abdoulaye Lamana (resides in Brussels).

Of Great Britain in Chad
Ambassador: M. G. Fort (resides in London).

Of Chad in the USA (2002 R. St., NW, Washington, D.C., 20009)
Ambassador: Mahamat Ali Adoum.

Of the USA in Chad (Ave., Felix Eboue, N'djaména)
Ambassador: John Blane.

Of Chad to the United Nations
Ambassador: Mahamat Ali Adoum.

Books of Reference

Kelley, M. P., *Conditions of the State's Survival.* Oxford, 1986
Thompson, V., and Adloff, R., *Conflict in Chad.* London and Berkeley, 1981
Westebbe, R., *Chad: Development Potential and Constraints.* Washington, D.C., 1974

CHILE

República de Chile

Capital: Santiago
Population: 12·07m. (1986)
GNP per capita: US$1,590 (1984)

HISTORY. The Republic of Chile threw off allegiance to the crown of Spain, constituting a national government on 18 Sept. 1810, finally freeing itself from Spanish rule in 1818.

AREA AND POPULATION. Chile is bounded north by Peru, east by Bolivia and Argentina, and south and west by the Pacific ocean.

Chile has an area of 736,905 sq. km (284,520 sq. miles) excluding the claimed Antarctic territory. Many islands to the west and south belong to Chile: the Islas Juan Fernández (179 sq. km with 516 inhabitants in 1982) lie about 600 km west of Valparaíso, and the volcanic Isla de Pascua (Easter Island or Rapa Nui, 118 sq. km with 1,867 inhabitants in 1982), discovered in 1722, lies about 3,000 km WNW of Valparaíso. Small uninhabited dependencies include Sala y Goméz (400 km east of Easter Is.), San Ambrosio and San Félix (1,000 km northwest of Valparaíso, and 20 km apart) and Islas Diego Ramírez (100 km SW of Cape Horn).

In 1940 Chile declared, and in each subsequent year has reaffirmed, its ownership of the sector of the Antarctic lying between 53° and 90° W. long.; and asserted that the British claim to the sector between the meridians 20° and 80° W. long. overlapped the Chilean by 27°. Seven Chilean bases exist in Antarctica. A law promulgated 21 July 1955 put the Intendente (*now* Gobernador) of the Province (*now* Region) of Magallanes in charge of the 'Chilean Antarctic Territory' which has an area of 1,269,723 sq. km. and a population (1982) 1,368.

The total population at the census in 1982 was 11,275,440. Estimate (31 March 1986) 12,070,000.

The areas of the 13 regions and their populations (census, 1982) were as follows:

Region	Sq. km	Census 1982	Capital	Estimate 1985
Tarapacá	58,073	273,427	Iquique	120,732
Antofagasta	125,306	341,203	Antofagasta	175,486
Atacama	78,268	183,071	Copiapó	70,241 [1]
Coquimbo	39,647	419,178	La Serena	87,456 [1]
Aconcagua	16,109	1,204,693	Valparaíso	267,025
Metropolitan	13,808	4,294,938	Santiago	4,318,305
Liberador	18,193	584,989	Rancagua	152,132
Maule	30,518	723,224	Talca	144,656
Bíobío	36,823	1,516,552	Concepción	217,756
Araucanía	31,760	692,924	Temuco	171,831
Los Lagos	67,090	843,430	Puerto Montt	81,353 [1]
Aisén	108,998	65,478	Coihaique	31,167 [1]
Magallanes	132,033	132,333	Punta Arenas	105,265

[1] Census, 1982

Vital statistics (1984): Birth rate 21·2 per 1,000 population; death rate, 6·3; marriage rate, 7 (1982); infantile mortality rate, 20·1 per 1,000 live births. Life expectancy (1981): men, 65·4 years, women, 70·1.

Over 92% of the population is mixed or *mestizo*; only about 2% are European immigrants and their descendants, while the remainder are indigenous amerindians of the Araucanian, Fuegian and Chango groups. Language and culture remain of European origin, with the 675,000 Araucanian-speaking (mainly Mapuche) Indians the only sizeable minority.

Other large towns (estimate, 1985) are: Viña del Mar (315,947), Talcahuano (220,910), Chillán (128,920), Arica (127,925), Valdivia (119,977) and Osorno (100,982).

CLIMATE. With its enormous range of latitude and the influence of the Andean Cordillera, the climate of Chile is very complex, ranging from extreme aridity in the north, through a Mediterranean climate in Central Chile, where winters are wet and summers dry, to a cool temperate zone in the south, with rain at all seasons. In the extreme south, conditions are very wet and stormy. Santiago. Jan. 67°F (19·5°C), July 46°F (8°C). Annual rainfall 15″ (375 mm). Antofagasta. Jan. 69°F (20·6°C), July 57°F (14°C). Annual rainfall 0·5″ (12·7 mm). Valparaíso. Jan. 64°F (17·8°C), July 53°F (11·7°C). Annual rainfall 20″ (505 mm).

CONSTITUTION AND GOVERNMENT. The Marxist coalition government of President Salvador Allende Gossens was ousted on 11 Sept. 1973 by the 3 Armed Services and the *Carabineros* (para-military police). These forces formed a government headed by a Junta of the 4 Commanders-in-Chief. Gen. Augusto Pinochet Ugarte, Commander-in-Chief of the Army, took over the presidency. President Allende died on the day of the *coup*.

Marxist parties were outlawed and all political activities banned. The new Government assumed wide-ranging powers but the 'state of siege' ended in March 1978. A new Constitution was approved by 67·5% of the voters on 11 Sept. 1980 and came into force on 11 March 1981. It provided for a return to democracy after a minimum period of 8 years. Gen. Pinochet would remain in office during this period after which the Junta would nominate a single candidate for President.

The capital is Santiago, founded on 12 Feb. 1541.

National flag: Two horizontal bands, white, red, with a white star on blue square in top sixth next to staff.

National anthem: Dulce patria, recibe los votos (words by E. Lillo, 1847; tune by Ramón Carnicer, 1828).

The following is a list of the presidents since 1946:

Gabriel González Videla, 3 Nov. 1946–3 Nov. 1952.

Carlos Ibáñez del Campo, 3 Nov. 1952–3 Nov. 1958.

Jorge Alessandri Rodriguez, 3 Nov. 1958–3 Nov. 1964.

Eduardo Frei Montalva, 3 Nov. 1964–3 Nov. 1970.

Salvador Allende Gossens, 3 Nov. 1970–11 Sept. 1973 (deposed).

President of the Republic: Gen. Augusto Pinochet Ugarte (assumed office 17 Dec. 1974).

The *Junta Militar de Gobierno* consisted in Jan. 1986 of Lieut.-Gen. Humberto Gordon (Army), Adm. José Toribio Merino Castro (Navy C.-in-C.), Gen. Rodolfo Strange (Carabiñeros Dir.-Gen.) and Gen. Fernando Matthei Aubel (Air Force C.-in-C.).

The Cabinet in March 1988 was composed as follows:

Interior: Sergio Fernandez. *Foreign Affairs:* Ricardo Garcia Rodriguez. *Defence:* Vice-Adm. Patricio Carvajal. *Economy, Development and Building:* Brig.-Gen. Manuel Concha. *Exchequer:* Hernan Buchi: *Education.* Juan Antonio Guzman. *Justice:* Hugo Rosende. *Public Works:* Maj.-Gen. Bruno Siebert. *Agriculture:* Jorge Prado. *Treasury:* Jorge Veloso. *Employment and Social Welfare:* Alfonso Marzquez de la Plata. *Health:* Juan Giaconi. *Mining:* Samuel Lira. *Housing and Urbanism:* Miguel Angel Produje. *Transport and Telecommunications:* Gen. Jorge Maza. *General Secretary of State:* Orlando Poblete. *General Secretary to the Presidency:* Brig.-Gen. Sergio Valenzuela. *Planning Office:* Sergio Melnick. *Development Corporation:* Col. Guillermo Letelier. *Energy:* Lieut.-Gen. Herman Brady.

Local Government. For the purposes of local government the Military Junta in pursuance of its policy of administrative decentralization, has divided the republic into 13 regions (12 and Greater Santiago). Each Region is presided over by an *Intendente,* while the provinces (40) included in it are in charge of a *Gobernador* who represents the central government. The provinces are divided into munici-palities under an *alcalde* (mayor). All these officials are appointed by the President.

DEFENCE. Military service is for a period of 2 years at the age of 19.

Army. The Army is organized in 1 armoured, 10 cavalry and 23 infantry regiments; 7 artillery and 7 engineer battalions; and 1 helicopter-borne ranger unit. Equip-ment includes 150 M-4A3 and 21 AMX-30 tanks, 110 light tanks and 300 armoured cars. The service operates over 50 aircraft including 6 Aviocar trans-ports, 12 Puma, 2 Super Puma, 2 Iroquois, 2 Jet Ranger and 12 Lama helicopters, 4 Navajo communications aircraft and 18 Cessna Hawk XP trainers. Strength (1987) 57,000 (30,000 conscripts) and 100,000 reserves.

Navy. The principal ships[1] of the Chilean Navy are the 4 ex-British guided missile armed destroyers *Norfolk*, 5,440 tons standard, completed in 1970, purchased in 1982 and re-named *Prat* on transfer; *Antrim* of the same age, purchased in 1984 and re-named *Cochrane*; *Glamorgan*, completed in 1966, purchased in 1986 and re-named *Almirante Latorre* and *Fife*, completed in 1966, handed over in 1987 and re-named *Blanco Encalada*.

There are 2 modern Federal German-built small diesel-electric patrol sub-marines, 2 diesel powered patrol submarines (British 'Oberon' class), 4 other dest-royers (2 old British built and 2 ancient *ex*-US), 2 frigates (modern British 'Leander' class, *Condell* and *Lynch*), 2 fast missile craft, 4 torpedo boats, 5 patrol vessels, 26 coastal patrol craft, 1 submarine support vessel, 3 landing ships, 2 land-ing craft, 1 survey ship, 4 transports, 2 training ships, 1 antarctic patrol ship, 2 harbour patrol boats, 4 oilers, 4 floating docks and 2 tugs.

The Naval Air Service has 4 squadrons: 1 with Bandeirante and Aviocar trans-ports; 1 with Alouette and JetRanger ASW helicopters; 1 with EMB-111 maritime patrol aircraft; and 1 with Pilatus PC-7 trainers.

Naval personnel in 1988 totalled 29,000 all ranks including 5,200 marines and 500 in the maritime air service.

[1] The over 50-years-old cruiser *O'Higgins* (ex-USS *Brooklyn*), 10,000 tons standard, is still listed, but her equally ancient sister-ship *Prat* (ex-USS *Nashville*) was scrapped in 1986. The over 40-year-old cruiser *Latorre* (ex-Swedish *Göta Lejon*), 8,200 tons was unlisted in 1987.

Air Force. Approximate strength (1988) is 15,000 personnel, with (1987) 105 first-line and 150 second-line aircraft, divided among 12 groups, each comprising 1 squadron, within 4 combat and support wings. Groups 1 and 12 have twin-jet A-37Bs, from a total of 34 acquired for light strike/reconnaissance duties. Group 2 is equipped for photo-reconnaissance with 2 Canberras. Group 4 has 14 Mirage 50 fighters. Group 5 has 14 Twin Otters for light transport and survey duties. Group 7 received 15 F-5E Tiger II fighter-bombers and 3 F-5F trainers. Groups 8 and 9 are also fighter-bomber units, with a total of 30 Hunter F.71s, *ex*-RAF FGA.9s, and T.72s. Group 10 is a transport wing, with 2 C-130H Hercules, 2 Boeing 707s, 1 Boeing 727, 9 Beech 99As and various helicopters. An aerial survey unit has 3 Learjets and 3 Beech twin-engined aircraft. Training aircraft include piston-engined Piper Dakota and T-35 Pillan basic trainers and T-37 jets have been superseded by Spanish-built CASA C-101BB Aviojets. The A-37Bs are being replaced by CASA C-101CC Aviojets.

INTERNATIONAL RELATIONS

Membership. Chile is a member of the UN, OAS and LAIA (formerly LAFTA).

ECONOMY

Budget. In 1985 revenue was US$6,633·7m. and expenditure, US$7,518·3m.

Currency. In Jan. 1960 a system came into force based on the *escudo* (equivalent of 1,000 *pesos*), the *centésimo* (10 *pesos*) and the *milésimo* (1 *peso*). On 29 Sept. 1975 the currency reverted to *pesos* with a value of 1,000 escudos to the new peso.

In March 1988 there were 432·73 *pesos* = £1 and 244·51 *pesos* = US$1.

Banking. There is a Central Bank and State Bank and in 1986 18 domestic and 19 foreign banks were operating.

Commercial banks' total assets/liabilities in June 1985 were 1,422,700m. pesos.

Notes in circulation and deposits in currency were 1,187,882m. pesos at 31 Dec. 1985; total deposits in the commercial banks stood at 959,297m. pesos (1985).

Weights and Measures. The metric system has been legally established in Chile since 1865, but the old Spanish weights and measures are still in use to some extent.

ENERGY AND NATURAL RESOURCES

Electricity. In 1985 production of electricity was 14,209m. kwh, of which 70% hydro-electric. Supply 220 volts; 50 Hz.

Oil. Petroleum was discovered in 1945 in the southern area of Magallanes. Production (1987) 1·4m. tonnes.

Gas. Production (1985) 4,638 m. cu. metres.

Minerals. The wealth of the country consists chiefly in its minerals, especially in the northern provinces of Atacama and Tarapacá.

Copper is the most important source of foreign exchange (about 45% of exports) and government revenues (over 30%). The copper industry's output in 1985 was 1,256,400 tonnes. Exports during 1985 were valued at US$1,770·1m.

Nitrate of soda is found in the Atacama deserts. Exports were US$84·9m. in 1985. Production was 870,000 tonnes in 1985. Iodine is a by-product: 1984 production totalled 2,661 tonnes. The use of solar evaporation as a means of reducing costs has developed the production of potassium salts as an additional by-product.

Iron ore, of which high-grade deposits estimated at over 1,000m. tons exist in the provinces of Atacama and Coquimbo, has overtaken nitrate as Chile's second mineral. Production in 1985 was 6,493,833 tonnes, of which some 3,400,000 were in pellet form.

Coal reserves exceed 2,000m. tons, partially low in thermal unit. Net 1985 production was 1,240,978 tonnes.

In 1985 other minerals included molybdenum (11,389 tonnes, pure), zinc (22,040 tonnes), manganese (35,658 tonnes), lead (2,349 tonnes).

Agriculture. Agriculture and forestry contribute one-tenth of the national product, although one-third of the population take part in it. Total area of land available for agricultural use in 1986 was 29m. hectares, of which 12% was sown crops, 38% grassland and 15% forested.

Some principal crops were as follows:

Crop	Area harvested, 1,000 hectares 1986	Production, 1,000 tonnes 1986	Crop	Area harvested, 1,000 hectares 1986	Production, 1,000 tonnes 1986
Wheat	569	1,626	Potatoes	53	792
Oats	64	124	Dry beans	90	89
Barley	23	68	Lentils	37	29
Maize	105	721	Green peas	4	20
Rice	32	127	Sugar-beet	51	2,638

In 1985 fruit plantations had expanded to 86,620 hectares with 9 types of fruit, mainly apples and table grapes. Production, 1986 (in 1,000 tonnes): Apples, 480; grapes, 1,100; pears, 70; peaches and nectarines, 165; plums, 51; oranges, 80; lemons and limes, 66. Exports in the season ended May 1986 totalled 64m. cases valued at US$450m.

Production of animal products in 1985 was (in 1,000 tonnes): Cattle, 174·8; sheep, 13·5; pork, 66; poultry, 73. Eggs, 1,577m.; milk, 1,000m. litres.

Livestock (1986): Cattle, 3·5m.; horses, 500,000; asses, 28,000; sheep, 5·98m.; goats, 600,000; pigs, 1·13m.; poultry, 19m.

Forestry. According to the Forestry Institute, by late 1985, there were 1,050,000 hectares of artificial forests from Maule to Magallanes, the most important species being the pine (*pinus radiata*) which covers 850,000 hectares. Eucalyptus and poplar cover some 72,000 hectares. Native species of importance amounted to 9·4m. hectares in 1983.

Production during 1985 amounted to about 245m. in. of sawn timber. Exports of forestry products in 1985 were valued at US$320m.

Fisheries. Chile has 4,200 km of coastline and exclusive fishing rights to 1·6 m. sq. km. There are 220 species of edible fish. Catch of fish and shellfish in 1985 was 5m. tonnes; shellfish, 144,000 tonnes. Exports of seafood in 1985 were US$275m., of which fishmeal accounted for US$244m. The industry employs 70,000 (1·5% of the working population).

INDUSTRY AND TRADE

Industry. A nationally-owned steel plant operates from Huachipato, near Concepción. Output, 1985, 654,500 tonnes of steel ingots. Cellulose and wood-pulp are two industries which are rapidly developing; in 1985, 657,500 tonnes of cellulose were produced. Cement (1·4m. tonnes) and fishmeal (723,100 tonnes) are also important.

Labour. In March 1986 the total workforce numbered 4·36m., of which 607,100 were employed in agriculture, fishing, construction and manufacturing industries, 925,100 in service industries and 97,100 in transport and communications.

Trade unions began in the middle 1880s.

Commerce. Imports and exports in US$1m.:

	1982	1983	1984	1985	1986	1987
Imports	3,580	2,969	3,357	2,955	...	3,967
Exports	3,798	3,835	3,650	3,743	...	5,046

In 1985 imports (in US$1m.) from USA, were valued at 655; Venezuela, 268; Brazil, 249; Japan, 188; Federal Republic of Germany, 209; Argentina, 106; Spain, 106; France, 79; UK, 84; Italy, 50.

In 1985 the principal imports were (in US$1m.): Fuels, 522; chemicals, 461; industrial equipment, 432; transport equipment, 129; spares, 194, and live animals and foodstuffs, 38. The principal exports in 1985 were (in US$1m.): Copper, 1,770; paper and pulp, 200; iron ore, 90; timber, 112; nitrate, 85.

Total trade between Chile and UK for 5 years (British Department of Trade returns, in £1,000 sterling):

	1983	1984	1985	1986	1987
Imports to UK	107,644	108,420	134,750	128,007	112,843
Exports and re-exports from UK	43,520	74,997	73,914	67,459	105,838

Tourism. There were 547,000 tourists in 1986.

COMMUNICATIONS

Roads. In 1986 there were in Chile 78,025 km of highways. There were in 1982 (estimate), 850,000 automobiles, 185,000 goods vehicles and 22,500 buses.

Railways. The total length of state railway lines was (1986) 7,205 km, including 1,884 km electrified, of broad- and metre-gauge. In 1986 the State Railways carried 13·1m. tonnes and 6·2m. passengers. Further electrification is in progress between Concepción and Puerto Montt (600 km). An underground railway in Santiago was opened in Sept. 1975. The Antofagasta (Chili) and Bolivia Railway (702 km, metre-gauge) links the port of Antofagasta with Bolivia and Argentina.

Aviation. There are 7 international airports, 16 domestic airports and about 300 landing grounds. Chile is served by 19 commercial air companies (2 Chilean). In 1980, 325,800 passengers were carried into and out of Chile on international services; 265,400 passengers were carried on internal routes.

Shipping. The mercantile marine had, in 1982, 60 ships of over 100 tons (825,076 DWT) but most of the fleet operates under flags of convenience. Valparaíso is the chief port. The free ports of Magallanes, Chiloé and Aysén serve the southern provinces.

Post and Broadcasting. There are 1,486 post offices and agencies. In 1983 there were 608,200 (Santiago, 360,053) telephones in use.

At the end of 1982 there were 267 commercial broadcasting stations. Three television stations are operated by the Universities and there is a national television station using NTSC 525 line colour standards. On 9 Aug. 1968 the satellite station at Longovilo, 50 miles south-west of Santiago, was inaugurated to cover transmissions (including colour) from the USA and Europe. In 1977 there were 2m. radio receivers and (1976) 710,000 television receivers.

Cinemas (1986). Cinemas numbered 170; 60 of them are in Santiago.

Newspapers (1986). There were 65 daily newspapers and 100 magazines.

JUSTICE, RELIGION, EDUCATION AND WELFARE

Justice. There are a High Court of Justice in the capital, 12 courts of appeal distributed over the republic, tribunals of first instance in the departmental capitals and second-class judges in the sub-delegations. The police force had (1975) about 27,000 officers and men; it is organized and regulated by the Ministry of Defence.

Religion. 89·5% of the population are Catholics. There are 1 cardinal-archbishop, 5 archbishops, 22 bishops and 2 vicars apostolic. Latest estimates show 6·7m. Roman Catholics, 880,500 Protestants and 25,000 Jews.

Education. Education is in 3 stages: Basic (6–14 years), Middle (15–18) and University (19–23). Enrolment (1981): 2,139,319 pupils in the basic schools, 392,940 pupils in the middle schools and 161,809 pupils in technical schools; teachers in 1980 numbered 66,354 in basic, 24,387 in middle and 4,176 in technical schools.

University education is provided in the state university, University of Chile (founded in 1842), the Catholic University at Santiago (1888), the University of Concepción (1919), the Catholic University at Valparaíso (1928), the Universidad Técnica Federico Santa María at Valparaíso (1930), the Universidad Técnica del Estado (1952), Universidad Austral, Valdivia (1954) and Universidad del Norte, Antofagasta (1957) with a total student population of 118,978 in 1981.

Health. In 1982 there were 5,416 doctors, 1,644 dentists, 201 pharmacists, 1,930 midwives and 25,889 nursing personnel. 205 hospitals, 296 health centres and 888 emergency posts.

DIPLOMATIC REPRESENTATIVES

Of Chile in Great Britain (12 Devonshire St., London, W1N 2FS)
Ambassador: Juan Carlos Délano (accredited 26 Nov. 1987).

Of Great Britain in Chile (La Concepción 177, Casilla 72-D, Santiago)
Ambassador: Alan White, CMG, OBE.

Of Chile in the USA (1732 Massachusetts Ave., NW, Washington, D.C., 20036)
Ambassador: Hernán Felipe Errázuriz.

Of the USA in Chile (Agustinas 1343, Santiago)
Ambassador: Harry G. Barnes Jr.

Of Chile to the United Nations
Ambassador: Pedro Daza.

Books of Reference

Statistical Information: The Instituto Nacional de Estadística (Santiago), was founded 17 Sept. 1847. *Director General:* Alvaro Vial Donoso. Principal publications: *Anuario Estadística* and the bi-monthly *Estadística Chilena*.
    Other sources are: *Geografía Económica,* by the Corporación de Fomento de la Production, and *Boletín Mensual,* by the Banco Central de Chile.

Davis, N., *The Last Two Years of Salvador Allende*. London, 1985
Horne, A., *Small Earthquake in Chile. A Visit to Allende's South America*. London, 1972
Lasaga, M., *The Copper Industry in the Chilean Economy. An Econometric Analysis.* Aldershot, 1981
Porteous, J. D., *The Modernization of Easter Island.* Victoria, B.C., 1981
Smith, B. H., *Church and Politics in Chile: Challenges to Modern Catholicism.* Princeton Univ. Press, 1983

PEOPLE'S REPUBLIC OF CHINA

Capital: Beijing (Peking)
Population: 1,072·2m. (1988)
GNP per capita: US$250 (1986)

Zhonghua Renmin
Gonghe Guo

HISTORY. In the course of 1949 the Communists obtained full control of the mainland of China, and in 1950 also over most islands off the coast, including Hainan.

On 1 Oct. 1949 Mao Zedong (Tse-tung) proclaimed the establishment of the People's Republic of China.

AREA AND POPULATION. China is bounded north by the USSR and Mongolia, east by Korea, the Yellow Sea and the East China Sea, with Hong Kong and Macao as enclaves on the south-east coast; south by Vietnam, Laos, Burma, India, Bhután and Nepál; west by India, Pakistan, Afghánistán and the USSR.

The capital is Beijing (Peking).

See map in THE STATESMAN'S YEAR-BOOK, 1968–69.

The total area (including Taiwan) is estimated at 9,572,900 sq. km (3,696,100 sq. miles).

At the 1982 census population was 1,008,175,288. Han Chinese numbered 936·7m. There are 55 ethnic minorities; those numbering more than 3m. were with percentage of total population: Zhuang (1·3%), Hui (0·7%), Uighur (0·6%), Yi (0·54%), Miao (0·5%), Manchu (0·43%), Tibetan (0·39%) and Mongolian (0·34%).

Since 1979 married couples in urban areas have been permitted to have only one child (usually two in rural areas), a policy enforced by compulsory abortions and economic sanctions. It was admitted in 1987, however, that this demographic curb was failing, and that the population target of not more than 1,200m. by 2000 was in jeopardy.

Population, 1988: 1,072·2m. (1986: males, 530·11m.; urban, 382·44m.). Vital statistics, 1985: birth rate, 1·8%; death rate, 0·7%; growth rate, 1·12%. Population density, 109 per sq. km. in 1986. There were 8,290,588 marriages and 457,938 divorces in 1985. Expectation of life was 67 in 1985.

Estimates of persons of Chinese race outside China, Taiwan and Hong Kong in 1980 varied from 15m. to 20m. Since 1982 China has permitted the emigration of a quota of 75 persons per day to Hong Kong.

A number of widely divergent varieties of Chinese are spoken. The official 'Modern Standard Chinese' is based on the dialect of North China. The ideographic writing system of 'characters' is uniform throughout the country, and has undergone systematic simplification. In 1958 a phonetic alphabet (*Pinyin*) was devised to transcribe the characters, and in 1979 this was officially adopted for use in all texts in the Roman alphabet. The previous transcription scheme (Wade) is still used in Taiwan.

China is administratively divided into 21 provinces, 5 autonomous regions (originally entirely or largely inhabited by ethnic minorities, though in some regions now outnumbered by Han immigrants) and 3 government-controlled municipalities. These are in turn divided into 165 prefectures, 321 cities, 2,046 counties and 620 urban districts. (For earlier administrative divisions *see* THE STATESMAN'S YEAR-BOOK, 1986–87.)

Government-controlled municipalities	Area (in 1,000 sq. km)	Population in 1985 (in 1,000s)	Density per sq. km	Capital
Beijing	17·8	9,470	564	—
Tianjin	4·0	7,990	707	—
Shanghai	5·8	12,050	1,944	—
Provinces				
Hebei	202·7	54,870	293	Shijiazhuang
Shanxi	157·1	26,000	167	Taiyuan
Liaoning	151·0	36,550	251	Shenyang
Jilin	187·0	22,840	122	Changchun
Heilongjiang	463·6	32,950	70	Harbin
Jiangsu	102·2	61,710	602	Nanjing
Zhejiang	101·8	39,930	392	Hangzhou
Anhui	139·9	51,030	366	Hefei
Fujian	123·1	26,770	221	Fuzhou
Jiangxi	164·8	34,210	205	Nanchang
Shandong	153·3	76,370	499	Jinan
Henan	167·0	76,460	458	Zhengzhou
Hubei	187·5	48,760	260	Wuhan
Hunan	210·5	55,610	264	Changsha
Guangdong	231·4	61,660	291	Guangzhou
Sichuan	569·0	101,120	179	Chengdu
Guizhou	174·0	29,320	167	Guiyang
Yunnan	436·2	33,620	85	Kunming
Shaanxi	195·8	29,660	145	Xian
Gansu	530·0	20,160	45	Lanzhou
Qinghai	721·0	4,020	6	Xining
Autonomous regions				
Inner Mongolia	450·0	19,850	17	Hohhot
Guangxi	220·4	38,060	165	Nanning
Tibet [1]	1,221·6	1,970	2	Lhasa
Ningxia	170·0	4,060	61	Yinchuan
Xinjiang	1,646·8	13,440	8	Urumqi

[1] See also paragraph on Tibet below.

Population of largest cities in 1986: Shanghai, 6·98m.; Beijing (Peking), 5·86m.; Tianjin, 5·38m.; Shenyang, 4·2m.; Wuhan, 3·4m.; Guangzhou (Canton), 3·29m.; Chongqing, 2·78m.; Harbin, 2·63m.; Chengdu, 2·58m.; Xian, 2·33m.; Zibo, 2·3m.; Nanjing, 2·25m.; Changchun, 1·88m.; Changchun, 1·86m.; Dalian, 1·63m.; Zhengzhou, 1·59m.; Kunming, 1·49m.; Jinan, 1·43m.; Tangshan, 1·39m.; Guiyang, 1·38m.; Lanzhou, 1·35m.; Anshan, 1·28m.; Qiqihar, 1·26m.; Hangzhou, 1·25m.; Qingdao, 1·25m.; Fushun, 1·24m.; Fuzhou, 1·19m.; Changsha, 1·16m.; Shijazhuang, 1·16m.; Jilin, 1·14m.; Nanchang, 1·12m.; Baotau, 1·1m.; Huainan, 1·07m.; Luoyang, 1·05m.; Ningbo, 1·02m.; Datong, 1m.; Urumqi, 1m.

Tibet. For events before the revolt of 1959 *see* THE STATESMAN'S YEAR-BOOK, 1964–65, under TIBET. After the revolt was suppressed the Preparatory Committee for the Autonomous Region of Tibet (set up 1955) took over the functions of local government, led by its Vice-Chairman, the Banqen Lama, in the absence of its Chairman, the Dalai Lama, who had fled to India in 1959. In Dec. 1964 both the Dalai and Banqen Lamas were removed from their posts and on 9 Sept. 1965 Tibet became an Autonomous Region. 301 delegates were elected to the first People's Congress, of whom 226 were Tibetans. The Banqen Lama was re-elected to the Standing Committee of the Chinese People's Political Consultative Conference in March 1978—he became one of its Vice-Chairmen in July 1979—and has made several appeals to the Dalai Lama to return to China. In 1985 the Tibetan population of Tibet was 1·9m., Han 400,000. Population of the capital, Lhasa, in 1986 was 310,000. Expectation of life was 45 years in 1985. 4·25m. Tibetans live outside Tibet, in China, and in India and Nepál. Chinese efforts to modernize Tibet include irrigation, road-building and the establishment of light industry: in 1985 296 small and medium-sized factories and mines were producing electric power, coal, building materials, lumber, textiles, chemicals and animal products.

In 1979, 1·6m. were engaged in agriculture, including 0·5m. nomadic herdsmen. By 1984, a large measure of autonomy for the peasantry had been re-introduced: compulsory deliveries and some taxes were abolished and private ownership of livestock and 30-year disposition of land were granted. There were 23m. cattle in 1984. In 1975 Tibet became self-sufficient in grain for the first time. There are now 21,000 km of highways, and air routes link Lhasa with Chengdu, Xian and Kathmandu. Six more were opened in 1987. 30,000 tourists visited Tibet in 1986.

The borders were opened for trade with neighbouring countries in 1980. In July 1988 Tibetan was reinstated as a 'major official language', competence in which is required of all administrative officials.

Efforts are being made to revive Tibetan culture as part of China's new liberal policy towards minorities. Since 1980 178 monasteries and 743 shrines have been renovated and reopened. There were some 15,000 monks and nuns in 1987. In 1984 a Buddhist seminary in Lhasa opened with 200 students. Circulation of the Tibetan-language *Xizang Daily* now totals 38,000. In 1986 there were 2,315 primary schools, 56 secondary schools, 14 technical schools and 3 higher education institutes. The total number of students was 146,000. A university was established in 1985. In 1985 there were almost 7,000 medical personnel (of whom 59% were Tibetan) and 927 medical institutions, with a total of 4,738 beds.

In Oct. 1987 there were anti-Chinese demonstrations in which several people were killed.

The Dalai Lama, *My Land and My People* (ed. D. Howarth). London, 1962
Grunfeld, A. T., *The Making of Modern Tibet*. London, 1987
Harrer, H., *Return to Tibet*. London, 1984
Jäschke, H. A., *A Tibetan–English Dictionary*. London, 1934
Shakabpa, T. W. D., *Tibet: A Political History*. New York, 1984
Sharabati, D., *Tibet and its History*. London, 1986

CLIMATE. Most of China has a temperate climate but, with such a large country, extending far inland and embracing a wide range of latitude as well as containing large areas at high altitude, many parts experience extremes of climate, especially in winter. Most rain falls during the summer, from May to Sept., though amounts decrease inland. Peking (Beijing). Jan. 24°F (–4·4°C), July 79°F (26°C). Annual rainfall 24·9″ (623 mm). Chongqing. Jan. 45°F (7·2°C), July 84°F (28·9°C). Annual rainfall 43·7″ (1,092 mm). Shanghai. Jan. 39°F (3·9°C), July 82°F (27·8°C). Annual rainfall 45·4″ (1,135 mm). Tianjin. Jan. 24°F (–4·4°C), July 81°F (27·2°C). Annual rainfall 21·5″ (533·4 mm).

CONSTITUTION AND GOVERNMENT. On 21 Sept. 1949 the 'Chinese People's Political Consultative Conference' met in Peking, convened by the Chinese Communist Party. The Conference adopted a 'Common Programme' of 60 articles and the 'Organic Law of the Central People's Government' (31 articles). Both became the basis of the Constitution adopted on 20 Sept. 1954 by the 1st National People's Congress, the supreme legislative body. The Consultative Conference continued to exist after 1954 as an advisory body. In 1986 it had 2,021 members.

New constitutions were adopted in 1975 and 1978 (for details *see* THE STATESMAN'S YEAR-BOOK, 1986–87).

A further Constitution was adopted in 1982. It defines 'socialist modernisation' as China's basic task. Its most striking change is the restoration of the post of State President (*i.e.* Head of State).

The National People's Congress had 2,700 members in 1987. It can amend the Constitution, elects and has power to remove from office the highest State dignitaries, decides on the national economic plan, etc. The Congress elects a *Standing Committee* (which supervises the State Council) and the State President, currently Li Xiannian.

Congress is elected for a 5-year term and meets once a year. It is composed of deputies elected on a constituency basis by direct secret ballot. Any voter, and certain organizations, may nominate candidates. Nominations may exceed seats by 50–100%. 2,978 deputies were elected to the 6th Congress in June 1983.

Government structure was streamlined in 1983 and the number of Ministries reduced. In 1987 there were 32 Ministries and 10 Commissions under the State Council. The Premier is Li Peng. *Vice-Premiers:* Tian Jiyun, Yao Yilin, Wan Li, Qiao Shi, Wu Xuegqian. Other ministers include: Vacant *(Foreign Affairs)*, Zheng Tuobin *(Foreign Trade)*, Zhang Aiping *(Defence)*, Wang Bingqian *(Finance)* Wang Fang *(Public Security)* and Li Tieying *(Commission for Economic Restructure)*.

Since 1970 China's diplomatic relations have expanded considerably. On 25 Oct. 1971 the UN voted for the People's Republic to take over the China seat from the Nationalists by 76 votes to 35 with 17 abstentions. On 1 Jan. 1979 the US recognized the Beijing government as the sole legal government of China and diplomatic relations were established. In 1978 China and Japan signed a 10-year treaty of peace and friendship. China did not renew its treaty of friendship with the USSR which expired in 1980, but since 1985 there have been signs that both countries were endeavouring to normalize their relations and in Jan. 1987 talks on border demarcation were resumed after breaking down in 1978.

State emblem: 5 stars above Peking's Gate of Heavenly Peace, surrounded by a border of ears of grain entwined with drapings, which form a knot in the centre of a cogwheel at the base; the colours are red and gold.

National flag: Red with a large star and 4 smaller stars all in yellow in the canton.

National anthem: 'March of the Volunteers' composed 1935 by Tien Han. (Replacing the 1978 version).

De facto power is in the hands of the Communist Party of China, which had 44m. members in 1987. There are 8 other parties, all members of the Chinese People's Political Consultative Conference. In mid-1966 the Party Chairman, Mao Tse-tung, launched the 'Great Proletarian Cultural Revolution' to eradicate 'revisionism' and numerous Party and State officials were dismissed. The Cultural Revolution can be taken to have terminated by April 1969 when the long-delayed 9th Party Congress was convened. The 9th Congress adopted a new Party Constitution which proclaimed the leading rôle of the Party in the State and designated Lin Biao as Chairman Mao's successor. A factional dispute developed, however, centred on Lin Biao (killed in an air crash in Mongolia in Sept. 1971) and in Aug. 1973 the 10th Party Congress adopted amendments to the Party Constitution, removing references to Lin Biao and the succession to Chairman Mao, and electing a new Central Committee which appointed a new Politburo and Standing Committee. In Jan. 1975 the Central Committee appointed as a vice-chairman of the Politburo Deng Xiaoping, former Party Secretary-General dismissed during the Cultural Revolution. In April 1976 a 'radical' faction in the Politburo engineered a second dismissal of Deng from all his posts, and Hua Guofeng was appointed First Party Vice-Chairman as well as Premier. On the death of Mao Tse-tung on 9 Sept. 1976 Hua became Party Chairman. In Oct. 1976 the 'radical' faction (now identified and branded as the 'Gang of Four': Mao's widow, Jiang Qing, Zhang Chunqiao, Wang Hongwen and Yao Wenyuan) were placed under arrest. At the 11th Party Congress in Aug. 1977 a new Party Constitution was adopted, and a new Central Committee was elected. Changes in the leadership saw the elimination of the 'radical' faction and a second reinstatement of Deng to his Party and government posts. In Feb. 1980 4 Politburo members of Maoist persuasion were dismissed. Hua Guofeng was replaced as Premier by Zhao Ziyang in Sept. 1980. The 'Gang of Four', along with Chen Boda (a former secretary of Mao), were brought to trial only on 20 Nov. 1980. At the same time the trial opened of five generals accused of complicity with Lin Biao in an attempt to seize power. All 10 accused were found guilty on 25 Jan. 1981. Suspended death sentences were passed on Jiang Qing and Zhang Chunqiao. Hua Guofeng was removed from the Party Chairmanship in June 1981 and replaced by Hu Yaobang. In 1985 a nationwide drive to promote younger and better-qualified personnel and favour supporters of Deng

Xiaoping resulted in massive reshuffles at ministerial and Politburo level. In the wake of student demonstrations Hu Yaobang was accused of 'bourgeois liberalism' and forced to resign as Party General Secretary in Jan. 1987. Deng Xiaoping and several colleagues retired from the Politburo in Nov. 1987. The members of the Politburo in March 1988 (the first 5 constituting its Standing Committee) were Zhao Ziyang *(General Secretary)*, Li Peng, Qiao Shi, Hu Qili, Yao Yilin; Hu Yaobang, Wan Li, Tian Jiyun, Jiang Zimin, Li Tieying, Li Ruihuan, Li Ximing, Yang Rudai, Yang Shangkun, Wu Xueqian, Song Ping, Qin Jiwei; candidate member, Ding Guangen.

Local Government. There are 4 administrative levels: (1) Provinces, Autonomous Regions and the municipalities directly administered by the Government; (2) prefectures and autonomous prefectures (*zhou*); (3) counties, autonomous counties and municipalities; (4) towns. Local government organs ('congresses') exist at provincial, county and township levels and in national minority autonomous prefectures, but not in ordinary prefectures which are just agencies of the provincial government. Up to county level congresses are elected directly. By a law of 2 Dec. 1986 multiple candidacies will be permitted at the next local elections due in late 1987.

DEFENCE. Although retired from his political offices in 1987, Deng Xiaoping remains chairman of the Communist Party's Military Commission. China is divided into 7 military regions. The military commander also commands the air, naval and civilian militia forces assigned to each region.

Conscription is compulsory but for organizational reasons selective: only some 10% of potential recruits are called up. Service is 3 years with the Army and 4 years with the Air Force and 5 years with the Navy.

It was announced in 1985 that the armed forces would be reduced by one million by 1988, and most of the regional commanders were replaced by younger officers. A Defence University to train senior officers in modern warfare was established in 1985.

Army. The Army (PLA: 'People's Liberation Army') is divided into main and local forces. Main forces, administered by the military regions in which they are stationed but commanded by the Ministry of Defence, are available for operation anywhere and are better equipped. Local forces concentrate on the defence of their own regions. The Army consists of 191 divisions including 31 artillery, 13 armoured, 118 infantry, 3 airborne and 73 local divisions. Land-based missile forces consisted of (1985 estimate): 4 intercontinental, 60 intermediate range and 50 medium range ballistic missiles. Total strength in 1987 was $2 \cdot 11$m.

The security forces, including the armed police, number some 300,000.

The People's Militia consists of the Armed Militia of up to 6m. strength, the Ordinary Militia of several million, unarmed but with some basic military training, which includes the Urban Militia.

Navy. The steady new construction programme of all classes of warships in modernized yards, many with advanced nuclear and/or missile capability, has been maintained. Chinese naval strength is an important factor in the present and future balance of power in the eastern hemisphere.

Strength comprises 4 nuclear powered and ballistic missile armed submarines, 1 diesel-powered submarine with ballistic missile tubes, 3 nuclear propelled fleet submarines, 3 diesel driven cruise missile submarines, 106 patrol submarines, 20 destroyers, 35 frigates, 14 patrol escorts, 237 missile boats, 21 large patrol boats, 70 fast patrol craft, 395 fast gunboats, 255 fast torpedo boats, 28 ocean minesweepers, 100 coastal minesweepers, 80 mine warfare craft, 100 river patrol craft, 35 coastal patrol craft, 50 survey and research ships, 35 supply ships, 16 support ships, 40 oilers, 12 boom defence vessels, 3 repair ships, 58 landing ships, 530 landing craft, 20 salvage ships, 3 icebreakers, 43 tugs, 375 coast and river defence craft and 525 vessels of the Maritime Militia.

Active personnel in 1988 exceeded 298,000 officers and men, including 30,000 in the naval air force and over 28,000 marines.

Main naval bases: Qingdao (North Sea Fleet); Shanghai (East Sea Fleet); Tsamkong (Zhanjiang) (South Sea Fleet).

The largely land-based naval air force of over 700 aircraft, primarily for defensive and anti-submarine service, includes MiG-17, MiG-19, MiG-21 and Q-5 fighters, some 130 Il-28 torpedo bombers, Be-6 flying boats, Mi-4, Mi-8 and Super Frelon helicopters, and communications, research, training and transport aircraft.

Air Force. In 1984 the Air Force was estimated at 4,500 front-line aircraft, organized in over 100 regiments of jet-fighters and about 12 regiments of tactical bombers, plus reconnaissance, transport and helicopter units. Each regiment is made up of 3 or 4 squadrons (each 12 aircraft), and 3 regiments form a division.

Equipment is predominantly Russian in design and includes about 500 J-7 (MiG-21), 2,000 J-6 (MiG-19) and 500 J-5 (MiG-17) interceptors and fighter-bombers, with about 400 H-5 (Il-28) jet-bombers, about 120 H-6 Chinese-built copies of the Soviet Tu-16 twin-jet strategic bomber, plus 500 Q-5 twin-jet fighter-bombers (known in the west as 'Fantan'), evolved from the MiG-19. Under development is a new fighter designated J-8 (known in the west as 'Finback'). Transport aircraft include about 300 Y-5 (An-2), Y-8 (An-12), An-24/26, 100 Li-2, 30 Il-14 and a few three-turbofan Trident fixed-wing types, plus 300 Z-5 (Mi-4) and Z-6 (Mi-8) helicopters. The MiG fighters and Antonov transports have been manufactured in China, initially under licence, and other types have been assembled there, including several hundred JJ-5 (2-seat MiG-17) trainers. Small quantities of Western aircraft have been procured in the past few years, including 24 Black Hawk and 6 Super Puma transport helicopters and 3 Challenger VIP transports. The US Government is providing technical assistance in developing the J-8 fighter.

Total strength (1988) about 470,000, including 220,000 in air defence organization.

At least 27 nuclear tests have been made since 1964 and a nuclear force capable of reaching large parts of the USSR and Asia is operational. It was announced in 1986 that atmospheric nuclear testing had been abandoned. Land-based missile forces thought to be deployed consist of 4 intercontinental, 60 intermediate-range (approximately 3–5,000 km) and 50 medium-range (1,100 km) ballistic missiles. Missile forces are controlled by the Second Artillery, the missile arm of the PLA.

INTERNATIONAL RELATIONS

Membership. The People's Republic of China is a member of UN, the IMF, the Asian Development Bank, and is an observer at GATT.

ECONOMY

Planning. For planning history 1953–73 *see* THE STATESMAN'S YEAR-BOOK, 1973–74, p. 817.

The long-term aim of the present leadership is to transform China by the year 2000 into a modern developed economic power by the implementation of 'the 4 modernizations', *i.e.,* of agriculture, industry, defence and science and technology. In 1978, as a first step to the realization of the '4 modernizations', a 10-year plan (1976–85) was introduced. However this proved in practice to be over-ambitious; many of the planned targets were too high and the scale of capital construction was too great. The pursuit of the plan caused serious imbalances in the economy. In 1979 a policy of 'readjusting, restructuring, consolidating and improving' the economy was adopted.

Agriculture and light industry now receive higher priority in development targets. The average annual increase in the value of industrial and agricultural output was 9·6% during the 1981–85 plan. A programme for fundamental reform of the urban economy was introduced in 1985, to be fully implemented by 1990. The state plan is being reduced in scope and enterprises are to have a degree of freedom in deciding their production and marketing a portion of it. Wages will vary according to work performed, and prices will gradually be adjusted to reflect market conditions. The seventh 5-year plan is running from 1986 to 1990. It aims to curb investment in order to deal with the symptoms of inflation which had appeared in 1985 and reached 6% in 1986, and to restrict the pace of development to within the limits imposed by infrastructural resources. Production in agriculture is scheduled to rise at an annual average of 6%, and in industry, 7%.

Prices rose 6·3% in the first half of 1987 and a price freeze was imposed.

Budget. 1986 revenue was 220,030m. yuan; expenditure, 229,110m. yuan.

Sources of revenue, 1985 (in million yuan): state enterprise income tax, 51,380; industrial and commercial tax, 110,100; agricultural tax, 4,210. Expenditure, 1986: capital construction, 65,570; culture, 38,000; defence, 20,126; price subsidies, 24,200.

China's foreign exchange reserves in March 1986 were US$10,348m. Gold reserves in 1986 were 12·7m. troy oz. of gold.

Currency. The currency is called Renminbi (RMB, *i.e.*, People's Currency). The unit of currency is the *yuan* which is divided into 10 *jiao*, the *jiao*, into 10 *fen*. In July 1986 the *yuan* was devalued by 15·8%. The official rate of exchange in March 1988 was £1 = 6·58 *yuan*; US$1 = 3·72 *yuan*.

Notes are issued for 1, 2 and 5 *jiao* and 1, 2, 5 and 10 *yuan* and coins for 1, 2 and 5 *fen*.

Banking. A re-organization of the banking system in 1983 resulted in the People's Bank of China assuming the role of a Central Bank. Its former commercial role has been taken over by the Industrial and Commercial Bank. Other specialized banks include the Agricultural Bank of China, the China Investment Bank and the Chinese People's Construction Bank. The Bank of China will continue to be responsible for foreign banking operations. It has branches in London, New York, Singapore, Luxembourg, Macao and Hong Kong, and agencies in Tōkyō and Paris.

Savings bank deposits were 1,622,600m. yuan in 1985.

Weights and Measures. The metric system is in general use alongside traditional units of measurement, for which *see* THE STATESMAN'S YEAR-BOOK, 1975–76, p. 826 and 1954, pp. 877–88.

ENERGY AND NATURAL RESOURCES

Electricity. Sources of energy in 1985: coal 72·8%; oil, 20·9%; hydroelectric power, 4·3%; gas, 2%. Hydroelectric potential is 676m. kw. Generating is not centralized; local units range between 30 and 60 mw of output. Output in 1986: 430,300m. kwh. Supply 220 volts; 50 Hz. There are nuclear energy plants under construction at Shanghai and Liaoning, and a joint venture at Daya Bay in Guangdong. Plans to build further nuclear power plants were postponed in 1986 on economy grounds.

Oil. Exploration in the South China and Yellow Seas had not produced any commercially viable discoveries by 1986. There are on-shore fields at Daqing, Shengli, Dagang and Karamai, and 10 provinces south of the Yangtze River have been opened for exploration in co-operation with foreign companies. Crude oil production was 133m. tonnes in 1987.

Gas. Natural gas is available from fields near Canton and Shanghai and in Sichuan province. Production was 12,930m. cu. metres in 1985, but is only used locally.

Minerals. *Coal.* Most provinces contain coal, and there are 70 major production centres, of which the largest are in Hebei, Shanxi, Shandong, Jilin and Anhui. Coal reserves are estimated at 769,180m. tonnes. Coal production was 870m. tonnes in 1986.

Iron. Iron ore deposits are estimated at 496,410m. tonnes and are abundant in the anthracite field of Shanxi, in Hebei and in Shandong and are found in conjunction with coal and worked in the north-east. Estimated output of iron ore in 1984, 122m. tonnes. The biggest steel bases are at Anshan with a capacity of 6m. tons, Wuhan (capacity 3·5m. tonnes), Baotou and Maanshan (both 2·5m. tonnes) and Baoshan near Shanghai.

Tin. Tin ore is plentiful in Yunnan, where the tin-mining industry has long existed. Tin production was 15,000 tonnes in 1981.

Tungsten. China is the world's principal producer of wolfram (tungsten ore), producing 14,000 tonnes in 1981. Mining of wolfram is carried on in Hunan, Guangdong and Yunnan.

Production of other minerals in 1978 (in tonnes): Phosphate rock, 4·5m.; aluminium, 225,000; copper, 200,000; lead, 120,000; zinc, 125,000; antimony, 9,000; manganese, 2m.; (1973) sulphur, 130,000; (1967) bauxite, 350,000; (1973) salt, 18,000; (1969) asbestos, 160,000. Other minerals produced: barite, bismuth, gold, graphite, gypsum, mercury, molybdenum, silver.

Agriculture. China remains essentially an agricultural country. 144m. hectares are sown to crops. Intensive agriculture and horticulture have been practised for millennia. Present-day policy aims to avert the traditional threats from floods and droughts by soil conservancy, afforestation, irrigation and drainage projects, and to increase the 'high stable yields' areas by introducing fertilizers, pesticides and improved crops. 44·04m. hectares were irrigated in 1985, and 17·8m. tonnes of chemical fertilizer were applied.

Agricultural communes have shed the administrative functions which they had in the Maoist period to become purely economic units. There were 2,048 state farms in 1984.

Since 1978 more flexible methods of management have been adopted comprising 'responsibility systems', whereby individual households or other small units are contracted to supply to the commune or government purchasing agency a quantity of crops to be produced from an allotted area of commune land. Any surplus is at the disposal of the household, to be consumed or marketed. In 1984 peasants were granted contracts to commune land with inheritance rights, and were permitted to hire up to 7 labourers. Initially production was improved considerably, but a fall in the 1985 total grain harvest to 380m. tonnes from the 1984 record of 407m. tonnes led to a more cautious policy of encouraging grain production in 1986. Reasons for the shortfall included the greater profitability in devoting land to cash crops and stock-breeding and the migration of 60m. peasants to industry. Net *per capita* annual peasant income, 1985: 397·60 yuan.

In 1985 there were 852,354 large and medium-sized tractors and 34,573 combine harvesters.

Agricultural production (in 1m. tonnes), 1986: Rice, 177; wheat, 89; maize, 65·56; soybeans, 11·01; roots and tubers, 138·84; tea, 0·49; cotton, 3·5; oilseed crops, 8·29; sugar-cane, 57·1. The gross value of agricultural output in 1985 was 387,300m. yuan.

Livestock, 1986: Horses, 11; cattle, 86·8m.; sheep, 94·2m.; goats, 61·7m.; pigs, 331·4m. Pork, beef and mutton production in 1985 was 17·61m. tonnes.

Forestry. Forest area in 1985 was 115m. hectares, including 2·6m. hectares of timber forest. Timber reserves were 102,600m. cu. metres in 1985. The chief forested areas are in Heilongjiang, Sichuan and Yunnan. Timber output in 1985 was 63·1m. cu. metres.

Fisheries. Total catch, 1985: 7·05m. tonnes. There were 172,582 motor fishing vessels in 1985.

INDUSTRY AND TRADE

Industry. 'Cottage' industry is very old in the economy and persists into the 20th century. Modern industrial development began with the manufacture of cotton textiles, and the establishment of silk filatures, steel plants, flour-mills and match factories. In 1985 there were 463,200 industrial enterprises, of which 367,800 were collectives and 93,700 state-owned. 7,900 were classified as 'large and medium-sized'. In 1985 rural industries expanded by 53% and accounted for 20% of total industrial production. Labour is drawn from the rural surplus. Expanding sectors of manufacture are: steel, chemicals, cement, agricultural implements, plastics and lorries.

1985 production (in tonnes): Chemical fertilizer, 13·3m.; pig-iron, 40m.; cement, 142m.; cotton cloth, 14,360m. metres; motor vehicles, 439,000; tractors, 44,600; bicycles, 32·3m.; chemical fibres, 734,900; steel, 46·6m.; rolled steel, 36·8m.; coke, 33m.; paper, 8·26m.; sugar, 4·6m.; drugs, 58,500; cotton yarn, 3·2m. and 10m. TV sets.

The gross value of industrial output in 1985 was 875,960m. yuan.

Labour. Workforce (excluding peasantry), 1986: 499m. (36·4% female), including 371m. rural workers, 83m. industrial workers, 24m. workers in service trades and commerce, 20·7m. in building and 12·2m. in transport and telecommunications. There were 3·6m. unemployed in 1986. Average annual non-agricultural wage in 1985: 1,184 yuan. There is a 6-day 48-hour working week.

Commerce. Foreign trade is being decentralized and has expanded rapidly since 1978. A trade deficit developed in 1984, and measures to curb this were taken in 1985. Four Special Economic Zones have been set up in the provinces of Guangdong and Fujian, in which concessions are made to foreign businessmen to encourage their investment. In 1984 14 coastal cities and Hainan Island were opened for technological imports. Since 1979 joint ventures with foreign firms have been permitted. By 1986 2,645 equity joint ventures, 4,075 contractual joint ventures and 130 wholly-owned foreign subsidiaries had been launched. About 80% of the investment was from Hong Kong. There is no maximum limit on the foreign share of the holdings; the minimum limit is 25%. A Stock Exchange was opened in Shanghai in 1986. Foreign indebtedness was US$2,500m. in 1987. In 1985 the IMF lent China US$3,000m. repayable over 5 years.

Trade in 1986: Imports, US$42,900m.; exports, US$30,900m.

Main exports are textiles, oil and oil products; others are chemicals, light industrial goods and arms. Major imports are machinery and transport equipment, iron and steel, and chemicals.

Major exports in 1985 (in 1,000 tonnes): crude oil, 30,030; petroleum products, 6,210; tea, 137; cereals, 93,300; tungsten ore, 16; cotton cloth, 16,733m. metres; imports: wheat, 53,800; rolled steel, 20,030; motor vehicles, 353,979 units; chemical fertilizers, 76,100.

In 1984 only 7·2% of China's trade was with Communist countries (2·5% with the USSR), but trade with the USSR rose by 61% in 1985: Imports, US$940m.; exports, US$960m. A trade agreement covering 1986–90 was signed in July 1985. Japan is China's biggest trading partner. Other major trading partners are Hong Kong, USA, Federal Republic of Germany and Canada. Customs duties with Taiwan were abolished in 1980.

Total trade between China and UK (British Department of Trade returns, in £1,000 sterling):

	1983	1984	1985	1986	1987
Imports to UK	231,417	278,474	307,963	327,032	391,766
Exports and re-exports from UK	159,722	317,256	396,156	535,943	416,012

In June 1987 China agreed to settle British claims for assets totalling £23·4m. confiscated by the present Chinese Government when it took power in 1949.

In April 1978 a most-favoured-nation agreement was signed with EEC, and in 1980 the EEC extended preferential tariffs to China.

In July 1979 the USA and China signed a 3-year trade agreement which accorded China most-favoured-nation status from 1980. In 1985 both the UK and the USA signed nuclear power agreements with China, and the UK and China signed a second agreement on economic co-operation valid till 1990.

Tourism. 1·37m. foreigners and 1·63m. overseas Chinese visited China in 1985. Restrictions on Chinese wishing to travel abroad were eased in Feb. 1986.

COMMUNICATIONS

Roads. The total road length was 942,400 km in 1985. Highways are well graded but mostly unmetalled. In 1985 there were 2·2m. lorries and 790,000 passenger vehicles.

In 1985, 762m. tonnes of freight and 4,272m. passengers were transported by road.

Railways. In 1985 there were 52,100 km of railway including 4,200 km electrified. The principal railways are:

(1) The great north–south trunk lines: (*a*) Peking–Canton Railway (over 2,300 km), *via* Zhengzhou–Wuhan–Zhuzhou–Hengyang. (*b*) Tianjin–Shanghai Railway (1,500 km), *via* Pukow and Nanjing (double-tracked in July 1976). (*c*) Baoji–Chongqing Railway, *via* Chengdu (1,174 km). Chongqing with the east–west route from Hengyang to the Vietnam border, and to Kunming, connecting there with the Yunnan Railway to the Vietnam border. Two further lines connect Baoji.

(2) Great east–west trunk lines: (*a*) Longhai Railway; Lianyungkang–Xuzhou–Zhengzhou (on the Peking–Canton line) –Xian–Baoji–Tianshui–Lanzhou (1,500 km). The Baoji–Lanzhou section was upgraded in 1978. (*b*) Lanzhou–Xinjiang Railway: Lanzhou–Yumen–Hami–Turfan–Urumqi (1,800 km); (*c*) Shanghai–Youyiguan (Vietnam border) *via* Hangzhou, Nanchang, Hengyang (on the Peking–Canton line), Guilin, Liuzhou and Nanning. (*d*) Peking–Lanzhou *via* Xining (from which a branch connects with the lines through Mongolia to the Trans–Siberian Railway), Dadong (from which a branch serves the province of Shanxi), Baotou and Yinchuan (Ningxia). (*e*) Zhuzhou–Guiyang (632 km). A new east–west line was opened in 1978 between Xiangfan and Chongqing.

Branches link coastal areas (*e.g.,* Fujian province) and the smaller inland centres with the main parts of the system. Surveys have been made for a new 500-km railway, linking the trunk line with the oilfield of Karamai in Xinjiang.

(3) The Manchurian system: (*a*) Chinese Eastern (Changchun) Railway (2,370 km), from Manzhouli on the Soviet border through northern Inner Mongolia and Manchuria *via* Qiqihar, Harbin and Mudanjiang to the Soviet border near Vladivostok. (*b*) South Manchuria Railway (705 km, 1,120 km with branches), Changchun–Shenyang–Luda. (*c*) Peking–Shenyang Railway, with branches in Manchuria (854 km, 1,350 km with branches).

Branches give connexions with outlying parts of Manchuria and Inner Mongolia as well as international links with Korean railways. Chinese railways are all constructed to the standard gauge except for some 600 mm gauge in Yunnan. Trunk routes are being converted from single to double track. The route between Baoji and Chengdu (676 km) was electrified in 1975 and that between Yangpingguan (on the Baoji–Chengdu route) and Ankang in 1977.

Capacity was expanded under the 1976–85 development plan, with several new lines built to serve primary industries, and much track doubling carried out. In 1986, 14 major construction projects were in progress, totalling over 3,000 km, and 9,000 km of electrification is planned.

In 1986 the railways carried 1,347m. tons of freight and 1,248m. passengers.

Aviation. Since 1985 the Civil Aviation Administration of China has become the administrative body for 5 new airlines: Air China (based on Beijing); Eastern Airways (Shanghai); Southern Airways (Canton); South-Western Airways (Chengdu) and the Capital Helicopter Company. There are services to Pyongyang, Hanoi, Rangoon, Singapore, Bangkok, Karachi, Tōkyō, Moscow, Ulan Bator, Teheran, Addis Ababa, Bucharest, Belgrade, Zürich, Paris, Frankfurt, Manila, New York, San Francisco, London, Sydney and Hong Kong. Route lengths in 1985: international, 106,000 km; domestic, 171,220 km. British Airways have a direct flight London-Beijing. Japan Airlines have a route from Tōkyō to Beijing (*via* Osaka and Shanghai), Air France Paris to Beijing (*via* Athens and Karachi), Pakistan Airlines Karachi to Beijing, Aeroflot Moscow to Beijing, Ethiopian Airlines Addis Ababa to Shanghai, Tarom Bucharest to Beijing, Swissair Geneva to Beijing and Shanghai, Iran Air Paris to Beijing and PANAM Beijing *via* Tōkyō. Singapore Airlines Singapore to Beijing and Thai Airways Bangkok to Beijing.

In 1985 CAAC carried 7·47m. passengers and 195,000 tonnes of freight.

Shipping. In 1980 the ocean-going merchant fleet consisted of 431 vessels with a total DWT of 7·92m.

Cargo handled by the major ports in 1985 (in tonnes): Shanghai, 113m.; Dalian, 44m.; Qinhuangdao, 44m.; Qingdao, 26m.; Huangpu, 18m.; Tianjin, 18m.; Zhanjiang, 12m. In 1985 65·6m. tonnes of freight were carried.

Inland waterways totalled 109,075 km in 1985. 434m. tonnes of freight and 270m. passengers were carried.

Pipeline. A pipeline links the Daqing oilfield to the port of Luda and to refineries in Peking. There is a pipeline from Lanzhou to Lhasa. There were 11,800 km of pipeline in 1985 which carried a load of 136·5m. tonnes.

Post and Broadcasting. There were 53,100 post offices in 1985, and 6,259,829 telephones. The use of *Pinyin* transcription of place names has been requested for mail to addresses in China (*e.g.,* 'Beijing' *not* 'Peking').

In 1984 there were 167 radio and 93 television stations and in 1981 9·02m. TV receivers. Most are communally owned.

Cinemas and Theatres. There were 8,723 cinemas, 182,948 film projection units and 6,651 theatres in 1985. 127 feature films were made in 1985.

Newspapers and books. In 1985 there were 698 newspapers with a circulation of 19,980m. and 5,705 periodicals. The Party newspaper is *Renmin Ribao* (People's Daily). In 1979 it had a daily circulation of 7m. 45,603 book titles were produced in 66,700m. copies in 1985.

JUSTICE, RELIGION, EDUCATION AND WELFARE

Justice. Six new codes of law (including criminal and electoral) came into force in 1980, to regularize the legal unorthodoxy of previous years. There is no provision for *habeas corpus*. An anti-crime campaign was launched in Aug. 1983 which, it was claimed in 1985, had cut the crime rate sharply; by 1986 624,000 sentences of death or long-term imprisonment had been imposed. The death penalty has been extended from treason and murder to include rape, embezzlement, smuggling, drug-dealing, bribery and robbery with violence. Courts will no longer be subject to the intervention of other state bodies, and their decisions will be reversible only by higher courts. 'People's courts' are divided into some 30 higher, 200 intermediate and 2,000 basic-level courts, and headed by the Supreme People's Court. The latter tries cases, hears appeals and supervises the people's courts.

People's courts are composed of a president, vice-presidents, judges and 'people's assessors' who are the equivalent of jurors. 'People's conciliation committees' are charged with settling minor disputes.

There are also special military courts.

Procuratorial powers and functions are exercised by the Supreme People's Procuracy and local procuracies.

Religion. Confucianism, Buddhism and Taoism have long been practised. Confucianism has no ecclesiastical organization and appears rather as a philosophy of ethics and government. Taoism—of Chinese origin—copied Buddhist ceremonial soon after the arrival of Buddhism two millennia ago. Buddhism in return adopted many Taoist beliefs and practices. It is no longer possible to estimate the number of adherents to these faiths. A more tolerant attitude towards religion had emerged by 1979, and the Government's Bureau of Religious Affairs was reactivated.

Ceremonies of reverence to ancestors have been observed by the whole population regardless of philosophical or religious beliefs.

Moslems are found in every province of China, being most numerous in the Ningxia–Hui Autonomous Region, Yunnan, Shaanxi, Gansu, Hebei, Honan, Shandong, Sichuan, Xinjiang and Shanxi. They totalled 14m. in 1986.

Roman Catholicism has had a footing in China for more than 3 centuries. In 1985 there were about 3m. Catholics who are members of the Patriotic Catholic Association, which declared its independence of Rome in 1958. In 1979 there were about 1,000 priests. In 1977 there were 78 bishops and 4 apostolic administrators, not all of whom were permitted to undertake religious activity. This figure included 46 'democratically elected' bishops not recognized by the Vatican. A bishop of

Peking was consecrated in 1979 without the consent of the Vatican and 2 auxiliary bishops of Shanghai in 1984. Archbishop Gong Pinmei, arrested in 1955, was freed in 1988. Protestants are members of the All-China Conference of Protestant Churches.

Education. At the 1982 census 23·5% of the population were illiterate. In 1986 90% of school-age children attended school. In 1985 there were 172,262 kindergartens with 14·8m. children and 798,000 teachers. An educational reform of 1985 is phasing in compulsory 9-year education consisting of six years of primary schooling and three years of secondary schooling, to replace an existing 5-year system. In 1985 there were 832,309 primary schools with 6·02m. teachers and 133·7m. pupils, and 104,848 secondary schools, with 4·18m. teachers and 50·93m. pupils. There were 1,016 institutes of higher education, with 0·87m. teachers and 1·7m. students.

University entry is dependent upon entrance examinations. Since 1985 instead of receiving grants based on parents' income students have been funded by competitive scholarships. Following student demonstrations in Jan. 1987 political education courses and periods of labour service have been restored to university curricula, and political criteria of selection re-applied.

The Academy of Sciences had in 1964 some 20 provincial branches and an Academy of Social Sciences was established in 1977.

Among the universities are the following: People's University of China, Peking (founded 1912 by Dr Sun Yat-sen; reorganized 1950; about 3,000 students); Peking University, Peking (1898, enlarged 1945; about 10,000 students); Xiamen University, Fujian (1921 and 1937); Fudan University, Shanghai (1905); Inner Mongolia University, Hohhot; Lanzhou University, Lanzhou (Gansu Prov.); Nankai University, Tianjin (1919); Nanjing University, Nanjing (1888 and 1928); Jilin University, Changchun (Jilin Prov.); North-West University, Xian (Shanxi Prov.); Shandong University, Qingdao (1926); Sun Yat-sen University, Canton (founded 1924 by Dr Sun Yat-sen); Sichuan University, Chengdu (1931); Qinghua University, Peking, Wuhan University, Wuhan (Hubei Prov.; 1905 and 1928); Yunnan University, Kunming. Between 1978 and 1985 40,000 students went abroad to study.

Chen, T. H., *Chinese Education since 1949.* Oxford, 1981
Heyhoe, R., (ed.), *Contemporary Chinese Education.* London, 1984

Health. Medical treatment is free only for certain groups of employees, but where costs are incurred they are partly borne by the patient's employing organization. In 1985 there were 1,413,000 doctors, of whom 336,000 practise Chinese medicine.

In 1985 there were 59,619 hospitals (including 348 mental hospitals) with 2·23m. beds.

DIPLOMATIC REPRESENTATIVES

Of China in Great Britain (49 Portland Pl., London, W1N 3AH)
Ambassador: Ji Chaozhu (accredited Sept. 1987).

Of Great Britain in China (Guang Hua Lu 11, Jian Guo Men Wai, Beijing)
Ambassador: Sir Richard Evans, KCMG, KCVO.

Of China in the USA (2300 Connecticut Ave., NW, Washington, D.C., 20008)
Ambassador: Han Xu.

Of the USA in China (Xiu Shui Bei Jie 3, Beijing)
Ambassador: Winston Lord.

Of China to the United Nations
Ambassador: Li Luye.

Books of Reference

Beijing Review. Beijing, weekly
China: A Statistics Survey in 1985. Beijing, 1986

China Daily [European ed.]. London, from 1986

China Directory [in Pinyin and Chinese]. Tōkyō, annual

The China Quarterly. London, from 1960

China Reconstructs. Peking, monthly

China's Foreign Trade. Bimonthly. Peking, from 1966

People's Republic of China Yearbook. Beijing, from 1983

Statistical Yearbook of China. Beijing and Oxford, from 1981

Barnett, A. D., *The Making of Foreign Policy in China.* London, 1985

Barnett, A. D., and Clough, R., (eds.), *Modernizing China: Post-Mao Reform and Development.* Boulder, 1986

Bartke, W. (ed.), *Who's Who in the People's Republic of China.* 2nd ed. New York, 1986

Bartke, W., and Schier, P., *China's New Party Leadership: Biographies and Analysis.* London, 1985

Blecher, M., *China: Politics, Economics and Sociology.* London, 1986

Bonavia, D., *The Chinese.* New York, 1980.—*The Chinese: A Portrait.* London, 1981

Boorman, H. L., and Howard, R. C., (eds.) *Biographical Dictionary of Republican China.* 5 vols. Columbia Univ. Press, 1967–79.

Brady, J. P., *Justice and Politics in People's China: Legal Order or Continuing Revolution?* London, 1982

Brown, D. G., *Partnership with China: Sino-foreign Joint Ventures in Historical Perspective.* Boulder, 1985

Bullard, M., *China's Political-Military Evolution.* Boulder, 1985

The Cambridge History of China. 14 vols. CUP, 1978 ff.

Cheng, P., *China.* [Bibliography] Oxford and Santa Barbara, 1983

Chow, G. C., *The Chinese Economy.* New York, 1985

Chu, G. C. and Hsu, F. L., (eds.) *China's New Social Fabric.* London, 1983

Croll, E., *The Family Rice Bowl: Food and the Domestic Economy in China.* London, 1983

Deng Xiaoping, *Speeches and Writings.* 2nd ed. Oxford, 1987

Dietrich, C., *People's China: A Brief History.* OUP, 1986

Domes, J., *The Government and Politics of the PRC.* Boulder, 1985

Fairbank, J. K., *The Great Chinese Revolution 1800–1985.* London, 1987

Ginsburg, N., and Lalor, B. A., (eds.), *China: The 80s Era.* Boulder, 1984

Guide to China's Foreign Economic Relations and Trade. Hong Kong, 1984

Harding, H. (ed.), *China's Foreign Relations in the 1980's.* Yale UP, 1984.—*China's Second Revolution.* Washington, 1987

Hinton, H. C. (ed.), *The People's Republic of China 1949–1979.* 5 vols. Wilmington, 1980

Hook, B. (ed.), *The Cambridge Encyclopaedia of China.* CUP, 1982

Hsieh, C. M., *Atlas of China.* New York, 1973

Jingrong, W. (ed.), *The Pinyin-Chinese Dictionary.* Beijing and San Francisco, 1979

Jones, P., and Kevill S., *China and the Soviet Union, 1949–84.* Harlow, 1984

Kaplan, F. M. (ed.), *Encyclopedia of China Today.* 3rd ed. London, 1982

Kapur, H., *China and the European Economic Community.* Dordrecht, 1986

Kim, S. S. (ed.), *China and the World: Chinese Foreign Policy in the Post-Mao Era.* Boulder, 1984

Klein, D. W., and Clark, A. B., *Biographic Dictionary of Chinese Communism, 1921–1965.* Harvard U.P., 1971

Lamb, M., *Directory of Officials and Organizations in China, 1968–1983.* Armonk, 1984

Lardy, N. R., *Agriculture in China's Modern Economic Development.* CUP, 1983

Leeming, F., *Rural China Today.* London, 1985

Lippit, V. D., *The Economic Development of China.* Armonk, 1987

Mabbett, I., *Modern China: The Mirage of Modernity.* New York, 1985

Mancall, M., *China at the Center: 300 Years of Foreign Policy.* New York, 1984

Marshall, M., *Organizations and Growth in Rural China.* London, 1985

Mathews, R. H., *Chinese-English Dictionary.* Cambridge, Mass., 1943–47

Maxwell, N., and McFarlane, B. (eds.), *China's Changed Road to Development.* Oxford, 1984

Moise, E. E., *Modern China: A History.* London, 1986

Moody, P. R., *Chinese Politics after Mao.* NY, 1983

Moser, L. J., *The Chinese Mosaic: the Peoples and Provinces of China.* Boulder, 1985

Moser, M. J. (ed.), *Foreign Trade Investment and the Law in the People's Republic of China.* OUP, 1984

Nathan, A. J., *Chinese Democracy.* London, 1986

Pan, L., *The New Chinese Revolution.* London, 1987

Pannell, C. W., and Laurence, J. C., *China: the Geography of Development and Modernization.* London, 1983

Riskin, C., *China's Political Economy: The Quest for Development since 1949.* OUP, 1987

Rodzinski, W., *A History of China.* Oxford, 1981–84

Schram, S. R. (ed.), *The Scope of State Power in China.* London, 1985

Segal, G., *Defending China.* OUP, 1985

Segal, G., and Tow, W. T. (eds.), *Chinese Defence Policy*. London, 1984
Song, J., *et al, Population Control in China*. New York, 1985
Teiwes, F. C., *Leadership, Legitimacy and Conflict in China*. London, 1984
Thornton, R. C., *China: A Political History, 1917–1980*. Boulder, 1982
The Times Atlas of China. London, 1974
Walker, K. R., *Food Grain Procurement and Consumption in China*. CUP, 1984
Wong, K., and Chu, D. (eds.), *Modernization in China: The Case of the Shenzhen Special Economic Zone*. OUP, 1986
Yahuda, M. B., *Towards the End of Isolationism: China's Foreign Policy after Mao*. London, 1983
Yin, J., *Government of Socialist China*. Lanham, 1984
Young, G. (ed.), *China: Dilemmas of Modernisation*. London, 1985

TAIWAN [1]

'Republic of China'

Capital: Taipei
Population: 19·5m. (1986)
GNP per capita: US$3,748 (1986)

HISTORY. The island of Taiwan (Formosa) was ceded to Japan by China by the Treaty of Shimonoseki on 8 May 1895. After the Second World War the island was surrendered to Gen. Chiang Kai-shek in Sept. 1945 and was placed under Chinese administration on 25 Oct. 1945. USA broke off diplomatic relations with Taiwan on 1 Jan. 1979 on establishing diplomatic relations with the Peking Government. Relations between the USA and Taiwan are maintained through the American Institute on Taiwan and the Co-ordination Council for North American Affairs in the USA, set up in 1979 and accorded diplomatic status in Oct. 1980.

AREA AND POPULATION. Taiwan lies between the East and South China Seas about 100 miles from the coast of Fujian province. The total area of Taiwan Island and the Penghu Archipelago is 13,969 sq. miles (36,179 sq. km). Population (1986), 19·5m., of whom some 2m. are mainland Chinese who came with the Nationalist Government. There are also some 306,000 aboriginals. Population density: 535 per sq. km.

In 1986, birth rate was 1·6%; death rate, 0·49%; rate of growth, 1·1% per annum (1989 target: 0·94% per annum). Life expectancy, 1986: males, 70·97 years; females, 75·88 years.

Taiwan is divided into two special municipalities (Taipei, the capital, population 2·56m. in 1986 and Kaohsiung, population 1·3m. in 1986), 5 municipalities (Taichung, the seat of the Provincial Government, Keelung, Tainan, Chiayi and Hsinchu) and 16 counties (*hsien*): Changhua, Chiayi, Hsinchu, Hualien, Ilan, Kaohsiung, Miaoli, Nantou, Penghu, Pingtung, Taichung, Tainan, Taipei, Taitung, Taoyuan, Yunlin.

CLIMATE. A tropical climate with hot, humid conditions and heavy rainfall in the summer months but cooler from Nov. to March when rainfall amounts are not so great. Typhoons may be experienced. Taipei. Jan. 59°F (15·3°C), July 83°F (29·2°C). Annual rainfall 100″ (2,500 mm).

CONSTITUTION AND GOVERNMENT. Taiwan is controlled by the remnants of the Nationalist Government. On 1 March 1950, Chiang Kai-shek resumed the presidency of the 'Republic of China'. He died 5 April 1975. His son Chiang Ching-kuo was president from March 1978 to his death in Jan. 1988. He was succeeded by Lee Teng-hui. Until 1986 there were 3 political parties: the ruling Kuomintang (KMT) (2,356,042 members in 1986), which has a youth movement (China Youth Corps) of over 1m. members; the Young China Party, and the China Democratic Socialist Party. Opposition parties were banned.

The National Assembly was elected in 1947. In Dec. 1987 it had 964 delegates.

[1] See note on transcription of names p. 352.

Government is conducted through 5 councils (Executive, Legislative, Judicial, Examination, and Control *Yuan*). The highest administrative organ is the Executive Yuan, headed by the premier, which includes a number of ministers. The highest legislative body is the Legislative Yuan, elected in 1948, which in Dec. 1987 numbered 329 members. The National Assembly, Legislative Yuan and Control Yuan are elected bodies. Their terms of office have been extended indefinitely. As the number of original delegates dwindled, regulations introduced in 1966 and 1972 provided for the election of additional members to the National Assembly and Legislative Yuan, and elections were held in 1969, 1972, 1975, 1980, 1984 and 6 Dec. 1986. Martial law, in force since 1949, was lifted in July 1987, and the ban on opposition parties removed. A new Democratic Progress Party (DPP) was formed in Oct. 1986 and a Democratic Liberal Party in Sept. 1987. In the 1986 elections the DPP contested 44 of the 157 seats to be filled in the National Assembly and Legislative Yuan, gaining 11 in the former and 12 in the latter. The KMT gained 127 seats. Turnout 7·7m. from electorate of 11·8m. There is also a Provincial Assembly of which the current Eighth Assembly with 77 members was elected on 16 Nov. 1985. Electoral turn-out was 72·8%. 60 seats went to the KMT. Further local government elections were held 1 Feb. 1986; the KMT won 1,002 out of 1,146 seats.

State emblem: A 12-pointed white sun in a blue sky.

National flag: Red with a blue first quarter bearing the state emblem in white.

National anthem: 'San Min Chu I', words by Dr Sun Yat-sen; tune by Cheng Mao-yun.

Prime Minister: Yu Kuo-hwa.

Vice-Premier: Lien Chan. *Foreign Minister:* Ding Mou-shih. *Minister of National Defence:* Cheng Wei-yuan. *Minister of the Interior:* Wu Po-hsiung. *Minister of Finance:* Robert Chun Chien. *Minister of Education:* Mao Kao-kuan. *Minister of Justice:* Shih Chi-yang. *Minister of Economic Affairs:* Lee Ta-hai. *Minister of Communications:* Kuo Nan-hung. *Governor of Taiwan Province:* Chiu Chuang-huan.

DEFENCE

Army. The Army, which embodies the remnants of the forces which escaped to Taiwan with Chiang Kai-shek at the end of the civil war in 1949, numbered about 270,000 in 1988. It was reorganized, re-equipped and trained by the USA and in 1985 consisted of 12 heavy and 6 light infantry divisions, 6 armoured infantry and 2 airborne brigades, 4 tank groups, 20 field artillery and 5 SAM battalions. The aviation element has 127 helicopters, O-1 Bird Dog observation aircraft and Bell 47G trainer helicopters. There is a conscription system for 2 years and reserve liability. US supplies of military equipment were resumed in 1980 after a moratorium in 1979. US forces were withdrawn by 1 May 1979.

Navy. There are 2 new Netherlands-built diesel powered patrol submarines, but most of the major vessels in naval service are former US Navy ships now over 40 years old and well overdue for replacement. There are 2 other diesel powered patrol submarines, 24 destroyers, 10 frigates, 3 corvettes (*ex*-fleet minesweepers), 62 fast missile craft, 13 coastal minesweepers, 1 coastal minelayer, 9 minesweeping boats, 28 coastal patrol craft, 2 dock landing ships, 1 amphibious flagship, 26 landing ships, 22 utility landing craft, 260 LCM landing craft, 150 minor landing craft, 2 repair ships, 5 surveying ships, 12 support ships, 3 transports, 7 oilers, 1 supply ship, 17 tugs, 5 floating docks and 25 service craft. Customs have 18 coastguard cutters.

Active personnel in 1988 totalled 38,000 officers and ratings in the Navy and 39,000 officers and men in the Marine Corps. There are 45,000 naval reservists and 35,000 marine reservists.

The Navy has 12 anti-submarine helicopters, 10 search helicopters and operational control of 2 squadrons of Air Force anti-submarine warfare Tracker aircraft; and the Marine Corps operates a number of observation aircraft and helicopters.

Air Force. The Nationalist Air Force is equipped mainly with aircraft of US design, including F-5E fighters built in Taiwan. It has 11 front-line squadrons of F-5E/F Tiger IIs, 3 of F-104G Starfighters and 1 tactical reconnaissance squadron of RF-104G Starfighters. There are 6 reserve fighter squadrons, 4 with F-5A/Bs and 2 with F-100 Super Sabres. The 6 transport squadrons are equipped with a VIP Boeing 720, 4 Boeing 727s, 5 C-54s, 20 C-47s, about 40 C-119Gs, 12 C-130H Hercules and 10 C-123 Providers. There is a naval co-operation squadron with S-2A/E Trackers. Search and rescue units operate Albatross amphibians and S-70 and Iroquois helicopters, and there are other helicopter and large training elements, some equipped with AT-3 twin-jet trainers designed and built in Taiwan and others with US-supplied T-34Cs. Total strength in 1988: 77,000 personnel and (1986) 485 combat aircraft.

INTERNATIONAL RELATIONS. By a treaty of 1 Dec. 1954 the USA was pledged to protect Taiwan, but this treaty lapsed 1 year after the USA established diplomatic relations with the People's Republic of China on 1 Jan. 1979. In April 1979 the US Congress approved a law to maintain commercial, cultural and other relations between USA and Taiwan.

The People's Republic took over the China seat in the UN from the Nationalists on 25 Oct. 1971.

ECONOMY

Planning. There have been a series of development plans. The eighth (1986–89), aims at an annual growth rate of 6·5% (industry 6·1%, agriculture 1·3%).

Budget. There are 2 budgets, the national together with a special defence budget (partly secret) and the provincial (*i.e.,* for Taiwan proper). For the fiscal year July 1988–June 1989 the budget is scheduled for NT$479,673m. Expenditure planned: 37% on defence; 19% on economic development; 18% on welfare; 13% on culture.

Currency. The unit of currency is the New Taiwan dollar, divided into 100 cents. There are coins of NT$ 1, 5 and 10 and notes of NT$ 10, 50, 100, 500 and 1,000. There are no cent coins or notes. Exchange rates (March 1988): £1 = NT$50·78; US$1 = NT$28·63.

Banking. The Central Bank of China (reactivated in 1961) regulates the money market, manages foreign exchange and issues currency.

The Bank of Taiwan is the largest commercial bank and the fiscal agent of the Government. In addition, there are 16 domestic commercial banks and 33 local branches of foreign banks.

ENERGY AND NATURAL RESOURCES

Electricity. Output of electricity in 1986 was 54,000m. kwh.; total generating capacity was 16·2m. kw. There are 3 nuclear power-stations (capacities 1m., 1m. and 0·6m. kw.) and a fourth is envisaged. Supply 110 volts; 60 Hz.

Minerals. There are reserves of coal (182m. tonnes), gold (1·5m. tonnes), copper (4·8m. tonnes), sulphur (2·4m. tonnes), oil (1·2m. kl.) and natural gas (19,240 cu. metres). In 1986, coal production was 1·9m. tonnes; refined oil, 1·7m. kl.; natural gas (1986), 1,023m. cu. metres.

Agriculture. The cultivated area was 883,106 hectares in 1985, of which 493,641 hectares were paddy fields. Production in 1,000 tonnes, in 1985: Rice, 2,174; tea, 23; bananas, 199; pineapples, 150; sugar-cane, 6,823; sweet potatoes, 369; wheat, 2·1; soybeans, 12; peanuts, 89.

Livestock (1986): Cattle, 153,322; pigs, 7,057,099; goats, 237,252.

Forestry. Forest area, 1986: 1,864,420 hectares; forest reserves, 326,189,164 cu. metres; timber production, 562,414 cu. metres.

Fisheries. The fleet comprised 4,951 vessels over 20 GRT in 1986; the catch was 1,094,587 tonnes in 1986.

INDUSTRY AND TRADE

Industry. Output (in tonnes) in 1986 (and 1985): Steel bars, 2·1m. (1·9m.); pig-iron, 197,536 (225,730); shipbuilding, 552,294 (516,173); sugar, 534,980 (645,632); cement, 14·4m. (14·4m.); fertilizers, 1·1m. (1·4m.); paper, 635,075 (530,224); cotton fabrics, 756m. metres (618m.).

Labour. In 1986 the labour force was 7·95m., of whom 1·3m. worked in agriculture, forestry and fisheries, 3·21m. in industry (including 2·61m. in manufacturing and 0·53m. in building), 1·38m. in commerce, 0·41m. in transport and communications, and 1·42m. in other services. 210,000 were registered unemployed.

Commerce. Foreign trade affairs are handled by the China External Trade Development Council (founded 1970), which operates branches in 22 countries under the name of Far East Trade Service. Principal exports: textiles, electronic products, agricultural products, metal goods, plastic products. Principal imports: oil, chemicals, machinery, electronic products. Total trade, in US$1m.:

	1982	1983	1984	1985	1986
Imports	18,888	20,287	21,959	20,102	24,165
Exports	22,204	25,123	30,456	30,723	39,789

The USA, Japan and Hong Kong are Taiwan's major trade partners followed by Kuwait, the Federal Republic of Germany and Saudi Arabia.

Total trade between Taiwan and UK (British Department of Trade returns, in £1,000 sterling):

	1983	1984	1985	1986	1987
Imports to UK	458,307	585,246	582,904	705,775	1,006,880
Exports and re-exports from UK	128,467	150,648	164,776	192,492	292,275

Tourism. In 1986 1,610,385 tourists visited Taiwan, and 812,928 Taiwanese made visits abroad. The ban on Taiwanese travel to Communist China was lifted in 1987.

COMMUNICATIONS

Roads. In 1986 there were 19,885 km of roads (16,602 km surfaced). 8,696,045 motor vehicles were registered in 1986 including 1,046,660 passenger cars, 21,698 buses, 418,212 trucks and 7,194,202 motor cycles. 2,080m. passengers and 200m. tonnes of freight were transported (excluding urban buses).

Railways. Total route length in 1986 was 2,681 km (1,067 mm to 762 mm gauge), of which a large proportion is owned by the Taiwan Sugar Corporation and other concerns. The state network consisted (1986) of 1,087 km. Freight traffic in 1986 amounted to 17·3m. tonnes and passenger traffic to 131·6m.

Aviation. There are 2 international airports: Chiang Kai-shek at Taoyuan near Taipei, and Kaohsiung which operates daily flights to Hong Kong. There are 6 domestic airlines, including China Airlines (CAL), which also operates international services to Bangkok, Hong Kong, Jakarta, Kuala Lumpur, Manila, Seoul, Singapore, Amsterdam, Saudi Arabia, Japan and USA. In 1986 10·13m. passengers and 327,976 tonnes of freight were flown.

Shipping. The merchant marine in 1986 comprised 1 passenger ship, 62 container ships, 47 bulk carriers, 15 tankers and 103 mixed service ships, with a total DWT of 7·1m.

The 4 international ports, Kaohsiung, Keelung, Hualien and T'aichung, are being extensively redeveloped. The first two are container centres. Suao port is an auxiliary port to Keelung.

Post and Broadcasting. In 1986 there were 12,522 postal establishments. Number of telephones in 1986, 6,247,360. In 1986 there were more than 5m. TV receivers. There are 3 TV networks.

Cinemas (1986). Cinemas numbered 567.

Newspapers and Books. There were 31 daily papers with a circulation of 3·7m. and 3,023 periodicals in 1986. 9,730 book titles were published. A 36-year ban on the publication of new dailies was lifted on 1 Jan. 1988.

RELIGION, EDUCATION AND WELFARE

Religion. There were 1·98m. Taoists in 1986 with 7,224 temples and 22,332 priests, 3·11m. Buddhists with 3,265 temples and 5,328 priests, 291,592 Catholics and 477,650 Protestants.

Education. Since 1968 there has been free compulsory education for 9 years (6–15). In that year the curriculum was modernized to give more emphasis to science while retaining the traditional basis of Confucian ethics. Since 1983 school-leavers aged 15-18 receive part-time vocational education. There were, in 1986–87, 2,486 primary schools with 74,838 teachers and 2,364,438 pupils; 1,055 secondary schools with 77,849 teachers and 1,691,516 students; 105 schools of higher learning, including 28 universities and colleges, with 21,769 full-time teachers and 442,648 students.

Health. In 1986 there were 69,053 practising registered medical personnel, including 15,908 doctors, 3,750 dentists and 2,057 doctors of Chinese medicine. There were 85 public hospitals with 29,792 beds and 750 private hospitals with 41,381 beds.

Books of Reference

Statistical Yearbook of the Republic of China. Taipei, annual
Republic of China: A Reference Book. Taipei, from 1983, irreg.
Taiwan Statistical Data Book. Taipei, annual
Annual Review of Government Administration, Republic of China. Taipei, annual
Gold, T. B., *State and Society in the Taiwan Miracle.* Armonk, 1986
Hsieh, C. C., *Strategy for Survival: The Foreign Policy and External Relations of the Republic of China on Taiwan 1949–1979.* London, 1985
Kuo, S. W., *The Taiwan Economy in Transition.* Boulder, 1983
Lasater, M., *The Taiwan Issue in Sino-American Strategic Relations.* Boulder, 1984
Simon, D. F. S., *Taiwan, Technology Transfer, and Transnationalism.* Boulder, 1983

National Library: National Central Library, Taipei (established 1986). *Director:* Wang Chen-ku.

COLOMBIA

Capital: Bogotá
Population: 29·5m. (1985)
GNP per capita: US$1,129 (1986)

República de Colombia

HISTORY. The Vice-royalty of New Granada gained its independence of Spain in 1819, and was officially constituted 17 Dec. 1819, together with the present territories of Panama, Venezuela and Ecuador, as the state of 'Greater Colombia', which continued for about 12 years. It then split up into Venezuela, Ecuador and the republic of New Granada in 1830. The constitution of 22 May 1858 changed New Granada into a confederation of 8 states, under the name of Confederación Granadina. Under the constitution of 8 May 1863 the country was renamed 'Estados Unidos de Colombia', which were 9 in number. The revolution of 1885 led the National Council of Bogotá, composed of 2 delegates from each state, to promulgate the constitution of 5 Aug. 1886, forming the Republic of Colombia, which abolished the sovereignty of the states, converting them into departments, with governors appointed by the President of the Republic, though they retained some of their old rights, such as the management of their own finances.

AREA AND POPULATION. Colombia is bounded north by the Caribbean sea, north-west by Panama, west by the Pacific ocean, south-west by Ecuador and Peru, north-east by Venezuela and south-east by Brazil. The estimated area is 1,141,748 sq. km (440,829 sq. miles). It has a coastline of about 2,900 km, of which 1,600 km are on the Caribbean sea and 1,300 km on the Pacific ocean. Population census, (1985) 29,481,852. Bogotá, the capital, (census, 1985) 4,185,174.

Départmentos	Area (sq. km)	Population census 1985	Capital	Population census 1985
Antioquia	63,612	4,055,064	Medellín	1,506,050
Atlántico	3,388	1,461,925	Barranquilla	920,695
Bolívar	25,978	1,289,891	Cartagena	559,581
Boyacá	23,189	1,149,028	Tunja (M.E.)	95,503
Caldas	7,888	882,193	Manizales	309,821
Caquetá	88,965	254,777	Florencia	87,794
Cauca	29,308	848,603	Popayán	166,178
César (El)	22,905	646,088	Valledupar	208,741
Chocó	46,530	296,914	Quibdó	85,085
Córdoba	25,020	997,597	Montería	238,081
Cundinamarca [1]	22,478	1,481,895	Bogotá	4,185,174
Guajira (La)	20,848	303,110	Riohacha	83,956
Huila	19,890	671,112	Neiva	197,445
Magdalena	23,188	860,841	Santa Marta	225,936
Meta	85,635	436,506	Villavicencio	182,298
Nariño	33,268	1,048,480	Pasto	252,115
Norte de Santander	21,658	943,225	Cúcuta	407,236
Quindío	1,845	400,117	Armenia	199,459
Risaralda	4,140	659,292	Pereira	301,715
Santander	30,537	1,535,021	Bucaramanga	363,909
Sucre	10,917	560,886	Sincelejo	139,519
Tolima	23,562	1,114,990	Ibagué	306,078
Valle del Cauca	22,140	1,955,483	Cali	1,397,433

[1] Excluding Bogotá.

Intendencias	Area (sq. km)	Population census 1985	Capital	Population census 1985
Arauca	23,818	70,085	Arauca	21,279
Casanare	44,640	110,253	El Yopal	23,169
Putumayo	24,885	119,815	Mocoa	20,325
San Andrés y Providencia	44	35,936	San Andrés	32,282

Comisarías	Area (sq. km)	Population census 1985	Capital	Population census 1985
Amazonas	109,665	30,327	Leticia	19,245
Guainía	72,238	9,214	Obando (Puerto Inírida)	9,214
Guaviare	53,460	35,305	San José del Guaviare	31,082
Vaupés	54,135	18,935	Mitú	13,192
Vichada	100,242	13,770	Puerto Carreño	8,081

The bulk of the population lives at altitudes of from 4,000 to 9,000 ft above sea-level. It is divided broadly into: 68% mestizo, 20% white, 7% Indio and 5% Negro. The official language is Spanish.

CLIMATE. The climate includes equatorial and tropical conditions, according to situation and altitude. In tropical areas, the wettest months are March to May and Oct. to Nov. Bogotá. Jan. 58°F (14·4°C), July 57°F (13·9°C). Annual rainfall 42″ (1,052 mm). Baranquilla. Jan. 80°F (26·7°C), July 82°F (27·8°C). Annual rainfall 32″ (799 mm). Cali. Jan. 75°F (23·9°C), July 75°F (23·9°C). Annual rainfall 37″ (915 mm). Medellin. Jan. 71°F (21·7°C), July 72°F (22·2°C). Annual rainfall 64″ (1,606 mm).

CONSTITUTION AND GOVERNMENT. The legislative power rests with a Congress of 2 houses, the Senate, of 112 members, and the House of Representatives, of 199 members, both elected for 4 years. Congress meets annually at Bogotá on 20 July. Women were given the vote, which is now open to citizens of either sex, over 18 years of age, on 25 Aug. 1954.

The President is elected by direct vote of the people for a term of 4 years, and is not eligible for re-election until 4 years afterwards. Congress elects, for a term of 2 years, one substitute to occupy the presidency in the event of a vacancy during a presidential term. There are 13 Ministries. The Governors of Departments and the Mayor of Bogotá are nominated by the national government.

A National Economic Council, functioning since May 1935, went through several transformations, becoming in 1954 a Directorate of Planning.

National Flag: Three horizontal stripes of yellow, blue, red with the yellow of double width.

National anthem: Oh! Gloria inmarcesible (words by R. Núñez; tune by O. Síndici).

The following is a list of presidents since 1953:

Gen. Gustavo Rojas Pinilla, 13 June 1953– 10 May 1957.
Military Junta, Maj.-Gen. Gabriel París and 4 others, 10 May 1957–7 Aug. 1958.
Dr Alberto Lleras Camargo (Lib.), 7 Aug. 1958–7 Aug. 1962.
Dr Guillermo León Valencia (Cons.), 7 Aug. 1962–7 Aug. 1966.
Dr Carlos Lleras Restrepo (Lib.), 7 Aug. 1966–7 Aug. 1970.

Dr Misael Pastrana Borrero (Cons.), 7 Aug 1970–7 Aug. 1974.
Dr Alfonso López Michelsen (Cons./Lib.), 7 Aug. 1974–7 Aug. 1978.
Dr Julio Cesar Turbay Ayala (Lib.), 7 Aug. 1978–7 Aug. 1982.
Dr Belisario Betancur Cuartas (Cons.), 7 Aug. 1982–7 Aug. 1986.

President: Dr Virgilio Barco Vargas (Lib.). He was elected on 25 May 1986 and took office on 7 Aug. 1986.

The Cabinet was composed as follows in Nov. 1987:
Government: Cesar Gaviria Trujillo. *Foreign Affairs:* Col. Julio Londoño Paredes. *Justice:* Enrique Low Murtha. *Finance and Public Credit:* Luis Fernando Alarcón Mantilla. *Defence:* Gen. Rafael Samudio Molina. *Agriculture:* Luis Guillermo Parra Dussan. *Labour and Social Security:* Diego Younes Moreno. *Health:* José Granada Rodriguez. *Economic Development:* Fuad Char Abdala. *Mines and Energy:* Guillermo Perry Rubio. *Education:* Antonio Yepes Parra. *Communications:* Fernando Cepeda Ulloa. *Public Works and Transport:* Luis Fernando Jaramillo.

Local government: The country is divided into 23 *départmentos*, 4 *intendencias*,

5 *comisarías* and a Special District. The governor of each is appointed by the President, but each has also a directly-elected legislature. The *départmentos* are subdivided into municipalities, each with a mayor appointed by the departmental governor.

DEFENCE. Men become liable for 1 year's military service at age 18, although the system is applied selectively. *Ex*-conscripts remain in the reserve, divided into 3 classes, until age 45.

Army. The Army consists of 11 infantry and 1 training brigades, artillery, cavalry, engineer and motorized troops and the usual services. Personnel (1988) 57,000 men (conscripts, 25,800); reserves 116,900. Number of national police, about 55,000.

Navy. Colombia has 2 Federal German-built 1,200-ton diesel-electric powered patrol submarines completed in 1975, 2 Italian-built midget submarines; 4 new German-built missile-armed frigates; 4 old patrol vessels (*ex*-US fleet tugs); 2 fast patrol gunboats; 3 river gunboats; 4 surveying vessels; 4 coastguard patrol vessels; 10 patrol motor launches; 5 small transports, 1 training ship, 5 service craft, and 10 tugs. Personnel in 1988 totalled 700 officers and 6,500 men. The Navy has also a brigade of marines with 2,500 officers and men. An air arm was formed in 1984 and has 4 BO 105 helicopters for ship-based ASW and SAR duties.

Air Force. Formed in 1922, the Air Force has been independent of the Army and Navy since 1943, when its reorganization began with US assistance. In 1986 it had about 300 aircraft, including a squadron of Mirage 5-COA fighter-bombers, 5-COR reconnaissance aircraft and 5-COD two-seat operational trainers; 2 squadrons of A-37B jets for counter-insurgency duties, a transport group equipped with 3 C-130, 12 C-47s, 6 C-54s and a small number of Arava, Beaver and Turbo-Porter light transports; a presidential F-28 Fellowship jet transport; 1 Boeing 707, UH-1B/H utility helicopters; and a reconnaissance unit with Iroquois, Lama, Hughes OH-6A, 300C and TH-55 helicopters. Eight more C-47s, 2 C-54s, 1 F-28 and 2 HS.748 transports are flown by the Air Force operated airline SATENA. Thirty Cessna T-41D primary trainer/light transports were delivered in 1968 and were followed by 10 T-37C jet advanced trainers to supplement piston-engined T-34s and T-33A armed jet trainers. Total strength (1988) 4,200 personnel.

INTERNATIONAL RELATIONS

Membership. Colombia is a member of the UN, OAS, the Andean Group and LAIA (formerly LAFTA).

ECONOMY

Planning. The 1982–86 Development Plan gives priority to agriculture.

Budget. Revenue and expenditure of central government in 1985: Revenue, 659,093,000 pesos; expenditure, 631·89m. pesos. External public debt, 31 Dec. 1986, US$11,512,000.

Currency. Coins include 1, 2, 5, 10, 20 and 50 *pesos*. There are also notes representing 20, 50, 100, 200, 500, 1,000, 2,000 and 5,000 *gold pesos*. Exchange rate March 1988, 483·52 *pesos* = £1 sterling; 273·60 *pesos* = US$1.

Banking. On 23 July 1923 the Banco de la República was inaugurated as a semi-official central bank, with the exclusive privilege of issuing bank-notes in Colombia; its charter, in 1951, was extended to 1973. Its note issues must be covered by a reserve in gold of foreign exchange of 25% of their value.

There are 25 commercial banks, of which 12 are privately owned, 8 jointly owned by Colombian and foreign interest and 5 official in nature, with total assets of 1,387,057 pesos as of May 1986. External public debt was US$6,958m. in 1983.

Weights and Measures. The metric system was introduced in 1857, but in ordinary commerce Spanish weights and measures are generally used; according to new definitions by the Ministry of Development, *e.g., botella* (750 grammes), *galón* (5 *botellas*), *vara* (70 cm), *arroba* (25 lb., of 500 grammes; 4 *arrobas* = 1 quintal).

ENERGY AND NATURAL RESOURCES

Electricity. Capacity of electric power (1985) was 7·16m. kw. Electric power produced in 1986, 29,580m. kwh. Supply 110, 120 and 150 volts; 60 Hz.

Oil. Production in 1987 was 19m. tonnes.

Minerals. Colombia is rich in minerals; gold is found chiefly in Antioquia and moderately in Cauca, Caldas, Tolima, Nariño and Chocó; output in 1986, 1,279,242 troy oz.

Other minerals are silver (149,422 troy oz. in 1986), copper, lead, mercury, manganese, emeralds and platinum; production of platinum, 1986, 14,638 troy oz. The chief emerald mines are those of Muzo and Chivor.

The Government holds the monopoly, which is leased to the Banco de la República, for extracting salts from the outstanding Zipaquirá mines (several hundred feet in depth and several hundred square miles in area) and for evaporating many sea salt pans; salt production in 1986 was 227,601 tonnes of land salt from the Zipaquirá mines and 500,938 tonnes of sea salt from Manaure and Galerazamba on the Caribe coast. Coal reserves were estimated at 16,500m. tonnes in 1983; production (1986) 89m. tonnes.

Agriculture. Very little of the country is under cultivation, but much of the soil is fertile and is coming into use as roads improve. The range of climate and crops is extraordinary; the agricultural colleges have different courses for 'cold-climate farming' and 'warm-climate farming'. In 1987 there were 2,025,428 hectares under temporary cultivation and 1,165,978 under permanent.

Coffee area harvested (1986) 945,000 hectares; production, 708,000 tonnes. Crops are grown by smallholders, and are picked all the year round. Production (1986, in 1,000 tonnes): Potatoes, 2,091; rice, 1,631·8; maize, 788·1; sorghum, 599·8.

The rubber tree grows wild. Fibres are being exploited, notably the 'fique' fibre, which furnishes all the country's requirements for sacks and cordage; output (1986) 23,920 tonnes. Tolú balsam is cultivated, and copaiba trees are tapped but are not cultivated. Tanning is an important industry.

Livestock (1986): 23·59m. cattle, 2·44m. pigs, 2·75m. sheep, 35m. poultry.

Fisheries. Total catch (1984) 34,528 tonnes.

INDUSTRY AND TRADE

Industry. Production (1986): Iron, 508,082 tonnes; cement, 5,915,502 tonnes; motor cars, 35,600; industrial vehicles, 8,056.

Commerce. Imports (c.i.f. values) and exports (f.o.b. values) (excluding export tax) for calendar years (in US$1m.):

	1983	1984	1985	1986
Imports	4,968	4,492	4,131	3,852
Exports	3,081	3,483	3,552	5,108

Important articles of export in 1986 (in US$1m.) were coffee (2,988), bananas (200), flowers (149), sugar (36), clothing and textiles (68). The chief imports are machinery, vehicles, tractors, metals and manufactures, rubber, chemical products, wheat, fertilizers and wool. It was reported (1987) that cocaine exports earn Colombia more than its main export, coffee.

Imports in 1986 (in US$1,000) from USA were valued at 1,343,340; Venezuela, 118,559; Japan, 349,592; Federal Republic of Germany, 255,993; Brazil, 139,183. Exports (in US$1,000) went to USA, 1,449,558; Federal Republic of Germany, 1,051,149; Netherlands, 265,814; Venezuela, 150,198; Italy, 73,812.

Total trade between Colombia and UK (British Department of Trade returns, in £1,000 sterling).

	1983	1984	1985	1986	1987
Imports to UK	56,458	80,387	112,486	94,112	65,331
Exports and re-exports from UK	51,023	43,485	82,639	58,084	61,385

Tourism. Foreign visitors totalled 732,000 in 1986.

COMMUNICATIONS

Roads. Owing to the mountainous character of the country, the construction of arterial roads and railways is costly and difficult. Total length of highways, about 75,000 km in 1983. Of the 2,300-mile Simón Bolívar highway, which runs from Caracas in Venezuela to Guayaquil in Ecuador, the Colombian portion is complete. Buenaventura and Cali are linked by a highway (Carreterra al Mar). Motor vehicles in 1985 numbered 1,091,751, of which 509,478 were passenger cars and 104,639 lorries.

Railways. There are 5 divisions of the State Railway with a total length of 2,622 km in 1985 and a gauge of 914 mm. The Pacific Railway connects Bogotá with the port of Buenaventura. The Atlantic line from Bogotá to Sta. Marta was opened in July 1961. Three connecting links are planned to improve the operating efficiency of the network. Total railway traffic, 1986, was 1·42m. passengers and 1,186,000 tonnes of freight.

Aviation. In civil aviation Colombia ranks perhaps second, after Brazil, among South American countries. There are 670 landing grounds of all kinds. In 1986 the national airports moved 5,448,000 passengers and 84,000 tonnes of cargo.

Shipping. Vessels entering Colombian ports in 1986 unloaded 5,631,000 tonnes of imports and loaded 11·19m. tonnes of exports.

The Magdalena River is subject to drought, and navigation is always impeded during the dry season, but it is an important artery of passenger and goods traffic. The river is navigable for 900 miles; steamers ascend to La Dorada, 592 miles from Barranquilla.

Post and Broadcasting. The length of telephone lines in service is 705,852 km (Bogotá only); instruments in use, 1 Jan. 1984, 2,547,222. The cable company is government owned. Television was established in 1954 and in 1978 there were 1·75m. sets in use. In 1983 there were 485 radio stations, of which 50 were in Bogotá.

Cinemas (1983). There were 623 cinemas, of which 87 were in Bogotá.

Newspapers (1984). There were 31 daily newspapers, with daily circulation totalling 1·5m.

JUSTICE, RELIGION, EDUCATION AND WELFARE

Justice. The Supreme Court, at Bogotá, of 20 members, is divided into 3 chambers—civil cassation (6), criminal cassation (8), labour cassation (6). Each of the 61 judicial districts has a superior court with various sub-dependent tribunals of lower juridical grade. Communism was outlawed by government decree on 5 March 1956.

Religion. The religion is Roman Catholic, with the Cardinal Archbishop of Bogotá as Primate of Colombia and 7 other archbishops in Cartagena, Manizales, Medellín, Pamplona, Popayán, Cali and Tunja, 26 bishops, 1,546 parishes and 4,020 priests. Other forms of religion are permitted so long as their exercise is 'not contrary to Christian morals or to the law'.

Education. Primary education is free but not compulsory, and facilities are limited. Schools are both state and privately controlled. In 1984 there were 4,358 pre-primary schools with 219,016 pupils, 31,229 primary schools with 3,614,074 pupils. In 5,210 secondary schools there were 1,945,134 pupils and in 216 higher education establishments there were 378,999 students.

The National University in Bogotá was founded in 1886 and there are 97 other universities with 171,002 students and 17,963 lecturers.

Health. In 1984 there were 753 hospitals and clinics. There were also 861 health centres.

DIPLOMATIC REPRESENTATIVES

Of Colombia in Great Britain (3 Hans Cres., London, SW1X 0LR)
Ambassador: (Vacant).

Of Great Britain in Colombia (Calle 98, No. 9–03 Piso 4, Bogotá)
Ambassador: Richard Neilson, CMG, LVO.

Of Colombia in the USA (2118 Leroy Pl., NW, Washington, D.C., 20008)
Ambassador: Victor Mosquera Chaux.

Of the USA in Colombia (Calle 38, 8-61, Bogotá)
Ambassador: Charles A. Gillespie Jr.

Of Colombia to the United Nations
Ambassador: Dr Enrique Peñalosa.

Books of Reference

Anuario General de Estadística de Colombia. Bogotá. Annual
Anuario de Comercio Exterior de Colombia. Annual
Anuario Estadístico Bogotá D. E. Annual
Boletín Mensual de Estadística. Monthly
Economía y Estadística. Occasional
Informe Financiero del Contralor General. Annual
Informe del Gerente de la Caja de Crédito Agrario, Industrial y Minero. Annual
Memorias (13) de los Ministros al Congreso Nacional. Annual
Braun, H., *The Assassination of Gaitán: Public Life and Urban Violence in Colombia.* Univ. of
    Wisconsin Press, 1985
Morairetz, D., *Why the Emperor's New Clothes are not made in Colombia.* OUP, 1982

COMOROS

Capital: Moroni
Population: 422,500 (1987)
GNP per capita: US$290 (1985)

République fédérale islamique des Comores

HISTORY. The 3 islands forming the present state became French protectorates at the end of the 19th century, and were proclaimed colonies on 25 July 1912. With neighbouring Mayotte they were administratively attached to Madagascar from 1914 until 1947, when the 4 islands became a French Overseas Territory, achieving internal self-government in Dec. 1961.

In referenda held on each island on 22 Dec. 1974, the 3 western islands voted overwhelmingly for independence, while Mayotte voted to remain French. The Comoran Chamber of Deputies unilaterally declared the islands' independence on 6 July 1975, but Mayotte remained a French dependency.

The first government of Ahmed Abdallah was overthrown on 3 Aug. 1975 by a *coup* led by Ali Soilih (who assumed the Presidency on 2 Jan. 1976), but Ahmed Abdallah regained the Presidency after a second *coup* ousted Ali Soilih in May 1978.

AREA AND POPULATION. The Comoros consists of 3 islands in the Indian ocean between the African mainland and Madagascar. Population (estimate, 1987) 422,500.

	Area sq. km	*Population census 1980*	*Chief town*	*Population census 1980*
Njazídja (Grande Comore)	1,148	192,177	Moroni	20,112
Mwali (Mohéli)	290	17,194	Fomboni	5,663
Nzwani (Anjouan)	424	137,621	Mutsamudu	12,518
	1,862	346,992		

The indigenous population are a mixture of Malagasy, African, Malay and Arab peoples; the vast majority speak Comoran, an Arabised dialect of Swahili, but a small proportion speak Makua (a bantu language), French or Arabic.

CLIMATE. There is a tropical climate, affected by Indian monsoon winds from the north, which gives a wet season from Nov. to April. Moroni. Jan. 81°F (27·2°C), July 75°F (23·9°C). Annual rainfall, 113″ (2,825 mm).

CONSTITUTION AND GOVERNMENT. Under the new Constitution approved by referendum on 1 Oct. 1978 (amended 1983), the Comoros are a Federal Islamic Republic. Mayotte has the right to join when it so chooses.

The President is Head of State, directly elected for a 6-year term (renewable once). He appoints up to 9 other Ministers to form the Council of Government, on which each island's Governor has a non-voting seat. There is a 38-member unicameral Federal Assembly, directly elected for 5 years. Each of the 3 islands is administered by a Governor (nominated by the President), up to 4 Commissioners whom he appoints to assist him, and a Legislative Council directly elected for 5 years.

President: Ahmed Abdallah Abderemane (elected Oct. 1978 and re-elected Sept. 1984).

The Council of Government was composed as follows in Dec. 1986:

Economy, Finance, Domestic Commerce and State Enterprises: Said Ahmed Said Ali. *Foreign Affairs, Co-operation and Foreign Commerce:* Said Madi Kafe. *Health and Population:* Ali Hassanaly. *Interior, Information and Press:* Omar

Tamou. *Justice, Employment and Professional Training and Manpower:* Ben Ali Bacar. *National Education, Culture, Youth and Sports:* Salim Idarousse. *Plan, Equipment, Environment and Urbanism and Housing:* Abdou'Rahim Mikidache. *Production, Rural Development, Industry and Crafts:* Mohamed Ali. *Director General, Central Bank:* Mohamed Halifa.

There were 3 Secretaries of State.

National flag: Green with a crescent and 4 stars all in white in the centre, tilted towards the lower fly.

DEFENCE

Army. The army had a strength of about 700 in 1988.

Navy. An *ex*-British landing craft built in 1945 was transferred from France in 1976 and another vessel, with ramps, was purchased in 1981. Two small patrol boats were supplied by Japan in 1982.

Air Arm. In 1987 only 1 Cessna 402B communications aircraft was in operation. Two survivors of three SIAI-Marchetti SF.260W Warrior armed trainers were returned to the manufacturer.

INTERNATIONAL RELATIONS

Membership. Comoros is a member of UN and an ACP state of EEC.

ECONOMY

Budget. In 1984, current revenue amounted to 6,066m. Comorian francs and current expenditure to 7,008m. Comorian francs; the separate capital budget totalled 593m. Comorian francs revenue against 1,000m. Comorian francs expenditure.

Currency. The unit of currency is the *Comorian franc*. There are banknotes of 500, 1,000, and 5,000 *Comorian francs*. In March 1988, £1 = CF507; US$1 = CF285·66.

Banking. The Institut d'émission des Comores was established as the new bank of issue in 1975. The chief commercial banks are the Banque des Comores, established in 1974 by the separation of the former Comoran section of the Banque de Madagascar et des Comores and the Banque de Développement des Comores.

Weights and Measures. The metric system is in force.

ENERGY AND NATURAL RESOURCES

Electricity. Production (1986) 5m. kwh.

Agriculture. The chief product was formerly sugar-cane, but now vanilla, copra, maize and other food crops, cloves and essential oils (citronella, ylang, lemongrass) are the most important products. Production (1986 in tonnes): Cassava, 93,000; coconuts, 47,000; bananas, 36,000; sweet potatoes, 18,000; rice, 16,000; maize, 6,000 and copra, 3,000.

Livestock (1986): Cattle, 86,000; sheep, 95,000; goats (1985), 94,000; asses, 4,000.

Forestry. Njazídja has a fine forest and produces timber for building.

Fisheries. In 1983 the catch was (estimate) 4,000 tonnes.

COMMERCE. Imports in 1985 amounted to 15,675m. Comorian francs, exports to 6,714m. Comorian francs. In 1981 France provided 57% of imports and in 1984 took 43% of exports. The main exports (1985) were vanilla (66% of value), cloves (20%), ylang-ylang (12%), essences, copra and coffee.

Trade between Comoros and UK (British Department of Trade returns, in £1,000 sterling):

	1983	1984	1985	1986	1987
Imports to UK	278	236	234	...	91
Exports and re-exports from UK	597	316	603	307	527

Tourism. In 1986 there were about 5,000 visitors.

COMMUNICATIONS

Roads. In 1983 there were 750 km of classified roads, of which 262 km were tarmac. There were 3,600 passenger cars and about 2,000 commercial vehicles.

Aviation. There is an international airport at Hahaya (on Njazídja). Air Comores have twice-weekly flights to Antananarivo, Dar es Salaam and Mombasa. Air France and Air Madagascar also have twice-weekly flights to Antananarivo. Air Comores has daily internal flights between Moroni and Nzwani, and 5 per week between Moroni and Mwali.

Shipping. In 1982, vessels entering Comoran ports (excluding internal traffic) discharged 39,000 tonnes and loaded 15,000 tonnes.

Post and Broadcasting. There were 496 telephones in 1983. *Comores-Inter* broadcasts in French and Comorian on short-wave and FM for approximately 8 hours a day. Number of radios (1988) 40,000.

Cinemas. In 1973 there were 2 cinemas with a seating capacity of 800.

JUSTICE, RELIGION, EDUCATION AND WELFARE

Justice. French and Moslem law is in a new consolidated code. The Supreme Court comprises 7 members, 2 each appointed by the President and the Federal Assembly, and 1 by each island's Legislative Council.

Religion. Islam is the official religion, and over 99% of the population are Sunni Moslems; there are about 1,000 Christians.

Education. In 1981 there were 59,709 pupils and 1,292 teachers in 236 primary schools; 32 secondary schools had 13,528 pupils and 432 teachers, 2 technical schools held 151 students with 9 teachers, and a teacher-training college had 119 students and 8 teachers.

Health. In 1978 there were 20 doctors, 1 dentist, 2 pharmacists, 35 midwives and 124 nursing personnel. In 1980 there were 17 hospitals and clinics with 763 beds.

DIPLOMATIC REPRESENTATIVES

Of Great Britain in Comoros
Ambassador: R. B. Crowson, CMG (resides in Port Louis).

Of the Comoros in the USA
Ambassador: Amini Al Moumin.

Of the USA in the Comoros
Ambassador: Patricia Gates Lynch (resides in Antananarivo).

Of the Comoros to the United Nations
Ambassador: Amini Al Moumin.

Book of Reference

Newitt, N., *The Comoro Islands*. London, 1985

CONGO

Capital: Brazzaville
Population: 2·18m. (1987)
GNP per capita: US$1,140 (1984)

République Populaire du Congo

HISTORY. First occupied by France in 1882, the Congo became (as 'Middle Congo') a territory of French Equatorial Africa from 1910–58, when it became a member state of the French Community. It became an independent Republic on 15 Aug. 1960.

The first President, Fulbert Youlou, was deposed on 15 Aug. 1963 by a *coup* led by Alphonse Massemba-Débat, who became President on 19 Dec. Following a second *coup* in Aug. 1968, the Army took power under the leadership of Major Marien Ngouabi, whose colleague, Major Alfred Raoul, was appointed President from 3 Sept. until 1 Jan. 1969, when Ngouabi himself became President.

The country's present name was established on 3 Jan. 1970, when a Marxist-Leninist state was introduced. Ngouabi was assassinated on 18 March 1977, and succeeded by Col. Joachim Yhombi-Opango, who in turn was replaced on 5 Feb. 1979 by Col. Denis Sassou-Nguesso.

AREA AND POPULATION. The Congo is bounded by Cameroon and the Central African Republic in the north, Zaïre to the east and south, the Cabinda province of Angola and the Atlantic to the south-west and Gabon to the west, and covers 342,000 sq. km; census population (1984), 1,912,429. Estimate (1987) 2·18m. The main towns (census, 1984) are Brazzaville, the capital (595,102), Pointe-Noire, the main port and oil centre (297,392), N'kayi (formerly Jacob) (49,458) and Loubomo (formerly Dolisie) (35,628).

The areas, populations and capitals of the Regions in 1983 were:

Region	Sq. km	1984	Capital	Region	Sq. km	1984	Capital
Kouilou	13,694	373,608	Pointe-Noire	Fed. District	65	595,102	Brazzaville
Niari	25,942	159,084	Loubomo	Plateaux	38,400	108,802	Djambala
Lékoumou	20,950	68,301	Sibiti	Cuvette	74,850	133,144	Owando
Bouenza	12,265	194,977	N'kayi	Sangha	55,800	46,367	Ouesso
Pool	33,990	180,051	Kinkala	Likouala	66,044	48,993	Impfondo

In 1984, 45% spoke Kongo dialects, chiefly in the south and south-west; 20% were Teke (in the south-east); 15% Sanka and 16% Ubangi chiefly inhabit the north. There are also about 12,000 pygmies and 12,000 Europeans (mainly French). French is the official language, but 2 local *patois*, Monokutuba (west of Brazzaville) and Lingala (north of Brazzaville), serve as lingua francas.

CLIMATE. An equatorial climate, with moderate rainfall and a small range of temperature. There is a long dry season from May to Oct. in the S.W. plateaux, but the Congo Basin in the N.E. is more humid, with rainfall approaching 100″ (2,500 mm). Brazzaville. Jan. 78°F (25·6°C), July 73°F (22·8°C). Annual rainfall 59″ (1,473 mm).

CONSTITUTION AND GOVERNMENT. In July 1979 a new Constitution was approved by referendum. Executive power was vested in the President, elected for a 5-year term by the National Congress of the *Parti congolais du travail* (the sole legal party since 1969). The President is assisted by a Council of Ministers, appointed and led by him. The PCT Congress elects a Central Committee of 75 members and a Political Bureau of 10 to administer it; it nominates all candidates for the 153-member People's National Assembly and for the regional, district and local councils, all of which were last elected on 11 Aug. 1984. In 1984 a constitu-

379

tional amendment made the President Head of Government and reduced the role of the Prime Minister to that of a co-ordinator.

President, Defence and Security: Col. Denis Sassou-Nguesso (re-elected July 1984).

Prime Minister: Ange-Edouard Poungui.

Foreign Affairs and Co-operation: Antoine Ndinga Oba.

National flag: Red, in the canton the national emblem of a crossed hoe and mattock, a green wreath and a gold star.

Local Government: The republic is divided into the capital district of Brazzaville and 9 regions (each under an appointed Commissioner and an elected Council), which are sub-divided into 46 districts.

DEFENCE

Army. The Army consists of 8 battalions, 2 armoured, 1 artillery, 2 infantry and 1 forming, 1 engineering, and 1 paracommando. Equipment includes 35 T-54/-55 and 15 T-59 tanks. Total personnel (1988) 8,000.

Navy. The flotilla includes 3 new Spanish-built fast attack craft, 1 *ex*-Soviet patrol (*ex*-torpedo) boat, 3 *ex*-Chinese gunboats, 4 *ex*-Chinese river patrol craft, 2 *ex*-Soviet guard vessels, 4 small patrol cutters, 2 French-built modern tugs and 12 small river patrol boats. Personnel in 1988 totalled 250 officers and men.

Air Force. The Air Force had (1988) about 500 personnel, 15 MiG-17 jet fighters, 1 twin-turbofan F28 Fellowship for VIP transport, 5 Antonov An-24/26 turboprop transports, 2 C-47, and 2 Noratlas piston-engined transports, 3 Broussard communications aircraft, 4 L-39 jet trainers and 2 Alouette II and 1 Alouette III light helicopters.

INTERNATIONAL RELATIONS

Membership. Congo is a member of UN, OAU and is an ACP state of EEC.

ECONOMY

Planning. The National 5-year Development Plan 1982–86 envisaged an investment of 1,105,000m. francs CFA.

Budget. The ordinary budget in 1985 balanced at 311,000m. francs CFA. Oil revenues provided 58% of the budget.

Currency. The unit of currency is the *franc CFA* with a parity value of 50 *francs CFA* to 1 French franc. There are coins of 1, 2, 5, 10, 25, 50, 100 and 500 *francs* CFA, and banknotes of 100, 500, 1,000, 5,000 and 10,000 *francs* CFA. In March 1988, £1 = 507 *francs*; US$1 = 285·66 *francs*.

Banking. The *Banque des États de l'Afrique Centrale* is the bank of issue. There are 4 commercial banks situated in Brazzaville, including the *Banque Commerciale Congolaise* and the *Union Congolaise de Banques.*

ENERGY AND NATURAL RESOURCES

Electricity. Production in 1985 was 306m. kwh from a hydro-electric plant at Djoué near Brazzaville and from about 6 thermal plants. Supply 220 volts; 50 Hz.

Oil. Oil reserves are estimated at 500–1,000m. tonnes. Output in 1987 was 5·3m. tonnes from the 26 offshore oil platforms operated by Elf Congo and Agip Congo. A refinery at Pointe-Noire came on stream in Dec. 1982.

Minerals. Lead, copper, zinc and gold (3 kg in 1983) are the main minerals. There are reserves of phosphates, bauxite and iron.

Agriculture. Production (1986, in 1,000 tonnes): Cassava, 620; sugar-cane, 510; pineapples, 110; bananas, 34; plantains, 64; yams, 14; maize, 8; groundnuts, 16; palm-oil, 15·6; coffee, 2; cocoa, 2; rice, 3; sweet potatoes, 14.

Livestock (1986): Cattle, 71,000; pigs, 44,000; sheep, 63,000; goats, 184,000; poultry, 1m.

Forestry. Equatorial forests cover 20m. hectares (60% of the total land area) from which (in 1983) 2,238,000 cu. metres of timber were produced, mainly okoumé from the south and sapele from the north. Hardwoods (mainly mahogany) are also exported.

Fisheries. In 1983 the catch amounted to 31,926 tonnes.

INDUSTRY AND TRADE

Industry. There is a growing manufacturing sector, located mainly in the 4 major towns, producing processed foods, textiles, cement (39,242 tonnes in 1982), metal industries and chemicals; in 1981 it employed 26% of the labour force.

Trade Unions. In 1964 the existing unions merged into one national body, the *Confédération Syndicale Congolaise*.

Commerce. Imports in 1982 totalled 265,250m. francs CFA (mainly machinery) and exports 321,030m. (of which petroleum 90%). In 1982 64% of imports were from France; 51% of exports were to USA, 21% to Italy, 10% to Spain and 10% to France.

Total trade between the Congo and UK (British Department of Trade returns, in £1,000 sterling):

	1983	1984	1985	1986	1987
Imports to UK	4,335	1,958	2,819	2,444	1,930
Exports and re-exports from UK	9,560	6,207	12,112	9,165	19,219

Tourism. There were 39,000 tourists in 1986.

COMMUNICATIONS

Roads. There were (1982) 8,246 km of all-weather roads, of which 849 km were paved. In 1982 there were 30,500 cars and 18,600 commercial vehicles.

Railways. A railway (517 km, 1,067 mm gauge) and a telegraph line connect Brazzaville with Pointe-Noire and a 200 km branch railway links Mont-Belo with Mbinda on the Gabon border. In 1983 railways carried 2·4m. passengers and 2·9m. tonnes of freight.

Aviation. The principal airports are at Maya Maya (near Brazzaville) and Pointe-Noire. In addition there are 22 airfields served by the local airline, Lina-Congo.

Shipping. Pointe-Noire handled (1979) 2·4m. tonnes of goods including manganese from Gabon. There were (1985) 21 vessels of 8,458 GWT registered. There are hydrofoil connexions from Brazzaville to Kinshasa (30 km across the river).

Post and Broadcasting. Telephones (1982) numbered 8,899. In 1985 there were 99,000 radios and 5,000 TV sets in use.

Cinemas. In 1973 there were 7 cinemas with a seating capacity of 5,100.

Newspapers. In 1986 there were 3 daily newspapers with a combined circulation of 24,000.

JUSTICE, RELIGION, EDUCATION AND WELFARE

Justice. The Supreme Court, Court of Appeal and a criminal court are situated in Brazzaville, with a network of *tribunaux de grande instance* and *tribunaux d'instance* in the regions.

Religion. In 1980, 54% of the population were Roman Catholic, 24% Protestant, 19% followed animist beliefs and 3% were Moslem.

Education. In 1982 there were 406,835 pupils and 6,997 teachers in 1,377 primary schools, 171,862 pupils and 3,638 teachers in 122 secondary schools, 18,150 students with 1,261 teachers in 36 technical schools and teacher-training establishments. The Université Marien-Ngouabi (founded 1972) in Brazzaville had 7,255 students and 292 teaching staff in 1980. Adult literacy (1980) 56%.

Health. There were (1978) 274 doctors, 2 dentists, 28 pharmacists, 413 midwives, 1,915 nursing personnel and 473 hospitals and dispensaries with 6,876 beds.

DIPLOMATIC REPRESENTATIVES

Of the Congo in Great Britain
Ambassador: Jean-Marie Ewengue (accredited 12 June 1986, resides in Paris).

Of Great Britain in the Congo (Ave. du General de Gaulle, Plateau, Brazzaville)
Ambassador: T. C. Almond.

Of the Congo in the USA (4891 Colorado Ave., NW, Washington D.C., 20011)
Ambassador: Stanislas Batchi.

Of the USA in the Congo (PO Box 1015, Brazzaville)
Ambassador: Leonard G. Shurtleff.

Of the Congo to the United Nations
Ambassador: Dr Martin Adouki.

Book of Reference

Thompson, V. and Adloff, R., *Historical Dictionary of the People's Republic of the Congo.* 2nd ed. Metuchen, 1984

COSTA RICA

República de Costa Rica

Capital: San José
Population: 2·66m. (1985)
GNP per capita: US$1,280 (1984)

HISTORY. Part of the Spanish Viceroyalty of New Spain from 1540, Costa Rica (the 'Rich Coast') formed part of Central America when the latter acquired independence on 15 Sept. 1821. Central America seceded to Mexico on 5 Jan. 1822 until 1 July 1823, when it became an independent confederation as the United Provinces of Central America. The province of Guanacaste was acquired from Nicaragua in 1825. Costa Rica left the confederation and achieved full independence in 1838. The first Constitution was promulgated on 7 Dec. 1871.

AREA AND POPULATION. Costa Rica is bounded north by Nicaragua, east by the Caribbean, southeast by Panama, and south and west by the Pacific. The area is estimated at 51,100 sq. km (19,730 sq. miles). The population at the census of 1 June 1985 was 2,655,000.

The area and census of population for 1 June 1984 (2,416,809) was as follows:

Province	Area (sq. km)	Population	Capital	Population
San José	4,959·63	890,434	San José	241,464
Alajuela	9,753·23	427,962	Alajuela	34,556
Cartago	3,124·67	271,671	Cartago	23,928
Heredia	2,656·27	197,575	Heredia	21,440
Guanacaste	10,140·71	195,208	Liberia	22,525 [1]
Puntarenas	11,276·97	265,883	Puntarenas	29,224 [1]
Limón	9,188·52	168,076	Limón	52,602 [1]

[1] District

In 1982, 47% lived in urban areas, and 36% were aged under 15; population density (1986) 51 per sq. km.

Vital statistics for calendar years:

	Marriages	Births	Deaths
1984	20,558 [1]	78,197 [1]	9,931 [1]
1985	19,747 [1]	84,252 [1]	10,968 [1]

[1] Preliminary.

The population of European descent, many of them of pure Spanish blood, dwell mostly around the capital of the republic, San José, and in the principal towns of the provinces. Limón, on the Caribbean coast, and Puntarenas, on the Pacific coast, are the chief commercial ports. The United Fruit Co., who in 1941 abandoned their banana plantations on the Atlantic coast in favour of large new plantations on the Pacific coast, have constructed ports at Quepos and Golfito. The Standard Fruit Co. and others have cleared land since 1958 in the Atlantic coast area and now have 2,325 acres producing some 4·2m. stems a year. There are some 15,000 West Indians, mostly in Limón province. The indigenous Indian population is dwindling and is now estimated at 1,200.

Spanish is the language of the country.

CLIMATE. The climate is tropical, with a small range of temperature and abundant rains. The dry season is from Dec. to April. San José. Jan. 66°F (18·9°C), July 69°F (20·6°C). Annual rainfall 72″ (1,793 mm).

CONSTITUTION AND GOVERNMENT. The Constitution was promulgated in Nov. 1949. It forbids the establishment or maintenance of an army. The legislative power is normally vested in a single chamber called the Legislative Assembly, which since 1962 consists of 57 deputies, 1 for every 40,000 inhabitants, elected for 4 years. The President and 2 Vice-Presidents are elected for 4 years; the candidate receiving the largest vote, provided it is over 40% of the total, is declared elected, but a second ballot is required if no candidate gets 40% of the total. Suffrage is universal, there being no exemption for reasons of economic status, race or sex. The vote is direct by secret ballot for all nationals of 18 years or over. Elections are normally held on the first Sunday in February. Voting for President, Deputies and Municipal Councillors is secret and compulsory for all men under 70 years of age. Independent non-party candidates are barred from the ballot.

The Cabinet in Dec. 1988 was composed as follows:

President: Oscar Arias Sánchez, elected 2 Feb. 1986.

Minister at the Presidency: Rodrigo Arias Sánchez. *Foreign Affairs:* Rodrigo Madrigal Nieto. *Interior and Police:* Guido Fernández Saborio. *Finance:* Fernando Naranjo Villalobos. *Health:* Dr Edgar Mohs Villalta. *Public Works and Transport:* Guillermo Constenla Umaña. *Public Security:* Hernán Garrón Salazar. *Agriculture:* Alberto Esquivel Volio. *Education:* Francisco Antonio Pacheco. *Economy and Commerce:* Luis Diego Escalante Vargas. *Industry, Energy and Mines:* Calixto Chávez Zamora. *Culture, Youth and Sports:* Carlos Francisco Echeverría Salgado. *Labour and Social Security:* Edwin León. *Housing and Urban Development:* Fernando Zumbado Jiménez. *Science and Technology:* Rodrigo Zeledón Araya. *Foreign Trade:* Muni Figueres de Jiménez. *Justice:* Luis Paulino Mora. *Planning:* Otón Solís Fallas. *Co-ordinator of Presidential Advisers:* Danilo Jiménez Veiga. *Central Bank President:* Eduardo Lizano Fait. *Vice-President:* Jorge Manuel Dengo. *Vice-President:* Victoria Garrón de Doryan.

The powers of the President are limited by the constitution, which leaves him the power to appoint and remove at will members of his cabinet. All other public appointments are made jointly in the names of the President and of the minister in charge of the department concerned.

National flag: Five unequal stripes of blue, white, red, white, blue, with the national arms on a white disc near the hoist.

National anthem: Noble patria, tu hermosa bandera (words by J. M. Zeledón, 1903; tune by M. M. Gutiérrez, 1851).

DEFENCE

Army. The Army was abolished in 1948, and replaced by a Civil Guard reputed to be 6,000 strong. There has never been compulsory military service or training.

Navy. The flotilla includes 1 fast patrol craft and 1 armed tug on the Atlantic coast and 5 small coastguard cutters on the Pacific coast. Personnel (1988) 100 officers and men.

Air Wing. The Civil Guard operates a small air wing equipped with about 15 lightplanes and helicopters.

INTERNATIONAL RELATIONS

Membership. Costa Rica is a member of UN and OAS.

ECONOMY

Budget. The budget for 1981 balanced at 12,400m. colones. The income-tax law of 10 March 1972 raised the maximum rate to 50% for personal incomes of 350,000 colones and over, and to 40% for corporate incomes of 1m. colones and over.

External government debt on 31 Dec. 1982 was US$3,500m.

Currency. The unit of currency is the *colone* (₡). The official rate in March 1988 was ₡73·45 = US$1; 130·26 = £1. The official rate is used for all imports on an essential list and by the Government and autonomous institutions and a free rate is used for all other transactions.

The currency is chiefly notes. The Banco Central issue notes for 5, 10, 20, 50, 100, 500 and 1,000 colones. Silver coins of 1 colone, 50 centimos and 25 centimos were in 1935 replaced by coins (2 and 1 colones and 50 and 25 centimos) made up of 3 parts copper and 1 part nickel, and given the same value as the subsidiary silver currency. There are copper coins (and chromium stainless steel coins) of 10 and 5 centimos.

Banking. By a law passed on 28 Jan. 1950 a Central Bank was established for the organization and direction of the national monetary system and of dealings in foreign exchange, the promotion of facilities for credit and the supervision of all banking operations in the country. The bank has a board of 7 directors appointed by the Government, including *ex officio* the Minister of Finance and the Planning Office Director.

The National Insurance Institute *(Instituto Nacional de Seguros)* is a Government organization, created in 1924, which has a monopoly of new insurance business.

Weights and Measures. The metric system is legally established; but in the country districts the following old Spanish weights and measures are found: *libra* = 1·014 lb. avoirdupois; *arroba* = 25·35 lb. avoirdupois; *quintal* = 101·40 lb. avoirdupois, and *fanega* = 11 Imperial bushels.

ENERGY AND NATURAL RESOURCES

Electricity. Electricity, derived from water power in the highlands, is increasingly used as motive power. Output, 1986, was 2,770m. kwh. Supply 120 volts; 60 Hz.

Minerals. Gold output is about 3,000 troy oz. per year. Salt production from sea water is about 10,000 tonnes annually. Haematite ore was discovered on the Nicoya Peninsula late in 1960 and sulphur near San Carlos in 1966. The United Nations have offered US$1m. towards a 3-year mining survey.

Agriculture. Agriculture is the principal industry. The cultivated area is about 1m. acres; grass lands cover 1·8m. acres; forests and woodlands, 9,855,000 acres. There are thousands of square miles of public lands that have never been cleared on which can be found quantities of rosewood, cedar, mahogany and other cabinet woods. The principal agricultural products are coffee, bananas, sugar and cattle. Coffee normally accounts for about half the country's foreign-exchange earnings.

Coffee production in 1986 was 128,000 tonnes; sugar-cane, 2·65m.; bananas, 1m.; cocoa, 5,000; maize, 104,000; tobacco, 2,000; rice, 186,000; potatoes, 40,000.

Dairy-farming and cattle-raising are substantial pursuits. In 1986 cattle numbered 2,415,000 and pigs 222,000.

Costa Rica is the seat of the Inter-American Institute of Agricultural Sciences, with headquarters at Turrialba.

INDUSTRY AND TRADE

Industry. The main manufactured goods are foodstuffs, textiles, fertilizers, pharmaceuticals, furniture, cement, tyres, canning, clothing, plastic goods, plywood and electrical equipment.

Industrial production was valued at 25·1m. colones in 1980, compared with 1·499m. in 1972.

Labour. As Costa Rica is still essentially an agricultural country, the organization of labour has made progress only in the larger centres of population, and even there it is not a strong movement. There are two main trade unions, *Rerum Novarum* (anti-Communist) and *Confederación General de Trabajadores Costarricenses* (Communist).

Commerce. The value of imports into and exports from Costa Rica in 5 years was as follows in US$:

	1981	1982	1983	1984	1985
Imports	1,208,529,000	867,000,000	987,826,445	1,093,739,311	1,098,178,489
Exports	1,030,203,040	870,800,000	559,951,375	1,006,389,617	...

The values (in US$1m.) of the principal imports in 1984 were: Machinery, including transport equipment, 219·6; manufactures, 317·5; chemicals, 250·1; fuel and mineral oils, 166·7; foodstuffs, 9.

Chief exports (in US$1m.) in 1984 were: Manufactured goods and other products, 450·6; coffee, 267·8 (mostly to Federal Republic of Germany, USA, UK and Italy); bananas, 251 (to USA); sugar, 35·5; cocoa, 1·5.

Total trade between Costa Rica and UK (British Department of Trade returns in £1,000 sterling):

	1983	1984	1985	1986	1987
Imports to UK	22,299	21,248	22,646	30,318	16,752
Exports and re-exports from UK	11,041	9,138	14,413	12,007	14,407

Tourism. There was a total of 261,000 tourists in 1986.

COMMUNICATIONS

Roads. In 1984 there were about 28,994 km of all-weather motor roads open. On the Costa Rica section of the Inter-American Highway it is possible to motor to Panama during the dry season. The Pan-American Highway into Nicaragua is metalled for most of the way and there is now a good highway open almost to Puntarenas. Motor vehicles, 1984, numbered 217,324.

Railways. The nationalized railway system *(Incofer)*, totalling 828·5 km (128 km electrified) of 1,067 mm gauge, connects San José with Limón, the Atlantic port, and San José with Puntarenas, the Pacific port. Total railway traffic in 1985 was 1m. tonnes of freight and 2m. passengers.

Aviation. There were 92 airports (59 private) in service in 1984. Passenger movement in and out of Costa Rica is almost entirely by air *via* the local company, Lacsa, PANAM and Taca. Passengers carried, 1984, 1,014,559. Lacsa links San José by daily services with all the more important towns.

Shipping. In 1981, 1,221 ships entered and cleared the ports of the republic (Puerto Limón, Puntarenas and Golfito).

Post and Broadcasting. There were 281,042 telephones in 1983.

The commercial wireless telegraph stations are operated by *Cia Radiográfica Internacional de Costa Rica.* The stations are located at Cartago, Limón, Puntarenas, Quepos and Golfito. The Government has 19 wireless telegraph stations in its local network. The principal or central station at San José also maintains international radio-telegraph circuits to Nicaragua, Honduras, San Salvador and Mexico. The Government has 202 telegraph offices and 88 official telephone stations. The official list of broadcasting stations shows 28 long-wave stations and 7 short-wave stations. Television was inaugurated in May 1960; there were 6 stations and (estimate) 277,694 receivers in 1980.

Cinemas (1979). Cinemas numbered 106, with seating capacity of 105,000.

Newspapers (1984). There were 4 daily newspapers all published in San José.

JUSTICE, RELIGION, EDUCATION AND WELFARE

Justice. Justice is administered by the Supreme Court, 5 appeal courts divided into 5 chambers; the Court of Cassation, the Higher and Lower Criminal Courts, and the Higher and Lower Civil Courts. There are also subordinate courts in the separate provinces and local justices throughout the republic. Capital punishment may not be inflicted.

Religion. Roman Catholicism is the religion of the State, which contributes to its maintenance but controls the Church Patronage and insists on lay instruction in history, economics and similar subjects; there is entire religious liberty under the constitution, but religious appeals are forbidden in current political discussions. The Archbishop of Costa Rica has 4 bishops at Alajuela, Limón, San Isidro el General and Tilarán.

Protestants number about 40,000.

Education. Costa Rica has a very low illiteracy rate. Elementary instruction is compulsory and free; secondary education (since 1949) is also free. Elementary schools are provided and maintained by local school councils, while the national government pays the teachers, besides making subventions in aid of local funds. In 1984 there were 3,068 public primary schools with 12,223 teachers and administrative staff and 353,958 enrolled pupils; there were 241 public and private secondary schools with 148,032 pupils. The University of Costa Rica, founded in San José in 1843, had (1980) 2,337 professors in 13 faculties and 38,629 students.

Social Welfare. The labour code of 1943 provides considerable protection for the workers, while a system of social insurance against sickness covering 756,347 workers in 1968, old age and death covering 68,949 is gradually being extended throughout the country.

DIPLOMATIC REPRESENTATIVES

Of Costa Rica in Great Britain (93 Star St., London, W2)
Ambassador: Dr Marcelo Martén (accredited 14 Oct. 1986)

Of Great Britain in Costa Rica (Edificio Centro Colon, Apartado 815, San José)
Ambassador and Consul-General: Michael Daly.

Of Costa Rica in the USA (1825 Connecticut Ave., NW Washington D.C., 20009)
Ambassador: Guido Fernandez.

Of the USA in Costa Rica (Avenida 3 and Calle 1, San José)
Chargé d'Affaires: James L. Tull.

Of Costa Rica to the United Nations
Ambassador: Dr Carlos José Gutierrez.

Books of Reference

Statistical Information: Official statistics are issued by the Director General de Estadística (Ministerio de Industria y Comercio, San José) as they become available. The compilation of statistics was started in 1861.

Ameringer, C. D., *Democracy in Costa Rica.* New York, 1982
Biesanz, R., *(et al), The Costa Ricans.* Hemel Hempstead, 1982
Bird, L., *Costa Rica: Unarmed Democracy.* London, 1984
Fernandez Guardia, L., *Historia de Costa Rica.* 2nd ed., 2 vols. San José, 1941
Seligson, M. A., *Peasants of Costa Rica and the Development of Agrarian Capitalism.* Univ. of Wisconsin Press, 1980

CÔTE D'IVOIRE

Capital: Abidjan
Population: 10·60m. (1986)
GNP per capita: US$720 (1983)

République de la Côte d'Ivoire

HISTORY. France obtained rights on the coast in 1842, but did not actively and continuously occupy the territory till 1882. On 10 Jan. 1889 Ivory Coast was declared a French protectorate, and it became a colony on 10 March 1893; in 1904 it became a territory of French West Africa. On 1 Jan. 1933 most of the territory of Upper Volta was added to the Ivory Coast, but on 1 Jan. 1948 this area was returned to the re-constituted Upper Volta, now Burkina Faso. The Ivory Coast became an autonomous republic within the French Community on 4 Dec. 1958 and achieved full independence on 7 Aug. 1960. From 1 Jan. 1986 the French version of the name of the country became the only correct title.

AREA AND POPULATION. Côte d'Ivoire is bounded west by Liberia and Guinea, north by Mali and Burkina Faso, east by Ghana, and south by the Gulf of Guinea. It has an area of 322,463 sq. km and a population at the 1975 census of 6,702,866 (of whom 31·8% were urban). Estimate (1986) 10,595,000.

The areas and populations of the 34 departments were:

Department	Sq. km	Census 1975	Department	Sq. km	Census 1975
Abengourou	6,900	177,692	Ferkéssédougou	17,728	90,423
Abidjan	14,200	1,389,141	Gagnoa	4,500	174,018
Aboisso	6,250	148,823	Guiglo	14,150	137,672
Adzopé	5,230	162,837	Issia	3,590	104,081
Agboville	3,850	141,970	Katiola	9,420	77,875
Biankouma	4,950	75,711	Korhogo	12,500	276,816
Bondoukou	16,530	296,551	Lakota	2,730	76,105
Bongouanou	5,570	216,907	Man	7,050	278,659
Bouaflé	5,670	164,817	Mankono	10,660	82,358
Bouaké	23,800	808,048	Odienné	20,600	124,010
Bouna	21,470	84,290	Oumé	2,400	85,486
Boundiali	7,895	96,449	Sassandra	17,530	116,644
Dabakala	9,670	56,230	Séguéla	11,240	75,181
Daloa	11,610	265,529	Soubré	8,270	75,350
Danané	4,600	170,249	Tingréla	2,200	35,829
Dimbokro	8,530	258,116	Touba	8,720	77,786
Divo	7,920	202,511	Zuénoula	2,830	98,792

The principal cities (populations, census 1975) are the capital, Abidjan (951,216; estimate 1982, 1·85m.), Bouaké (175,264), Daloa (60,837), Man (50,288), Korhogo (45,250) and Gagnoa (42,362). The new capital will be at Yamoussoukro (70,000 in 1983).

The principal ethnic groups are the Akan-speaking peoples of the south-east (Baule, 12% and Anyi, 11%) and the Bete (20%) and Kru of the south-west; in the north-east are Voltaic groups including Senufo (14%), while Malinké (7%) and other Mandé peoples inhabit the north-west.

French is the official language and there were (1985) about 50,000 French residents.

CLIMATE. A tropical climate, affected by distance from the sea. In coastal areas, there are wet seasons from May to July and in Oct. and Nov., but in central areas the periods are March to May and July to Nov. In the north, there is one wet season from June to Oct. Abidjan. Jan. 81°F (27·2°C), July 75°F (23·9°C). Annual rainfall 84″ (2,100 mm). Bouaké. Jan. 81°F (27·2°C), July 77°F (25°C). Annual rainfall 48″ (1,200 mm).

388

CONSTITUTION AND GOVERNMENT. The 1960 Constitution was amended in 1971, 1975, 1980, 1985 and 1986. The sole legal Party is the *Parti Démocratique de la Côte d'Ivoire*. There is a 175-member National Assembly elected by universal suffrage (Elections were held in Nov. 1985) for a 5-year term. The President is also directly elected for a 5-year term (renewable). He appoints and leads a Council of Ministers who assist him.

The Government was in Jan. 1988 composed as follows:

President: Félix Houphouët-Boigny. (Re-elected for a sixth 5-year term in 1985).

Ministers of State: Auguste Denise, Mathieu Ekra, Camille Alliali, Maurice Seri Gnoleba, Emile Kéi Boguinard, Lamine Diabate, Lanzeni N. P. Coulibaly, Paul Gui Dibo, Amadou Thiam. *Public Health and Population:* Alphonse Djedje Mady. *Information and Culture:* Laurent Dona Fologo. *Commerce:* Nicolas Kouandi Angba. *Labour and 'Ivorization' of Personnel:* Albert Vanié Bi Tra. *Civil Service:* Jean-Jacques Bechio. *Tourism:* Duon Sadia. *Social Affairs:* Yaya Ouattara. *Mining:* Yed Esai Angoran. *Internal Security:* Gen. Oumar N'daw. *Justice, Keeper of the Seals:* Noel Neme. *Defence:* Jean Konan Banny. *Interior:* Siméon Konan. *Foreign Affairs:* Siméon Ake. *Economy and Finance:* Abdoulaye Koné. *Agriculture, Water and Forest Resources:* Denis Bra Kanon. *National Education, responsible for Secondary and Higher Education:* Dr Bala Keita and 14 other ministers.

National flag: Three vertical strips of orange, white, green.

Local government: There are 34 departments, each under an appointed Prefect and an elected Conseil-Général, sub-divided into 163 sub-prefectures.

DEFENCE

Army. The Army consisted in 1988 of 1 armoured battalion, 3 infantry battalions and support units. Equipment includes 5 AMX-13 light tanks and 7 ERC-90 armoured cars. Total strength (1988), 5,500. Paramilitary forces, 7,800.

Navy. Offshore, riverine and coastal patrol squadrons include 2 fast missile craft, 2 patrol vessels, 1 river defence craft, 1 light transport, 4 fast assault boats and 2 minor landing craft. Personnel in 1988 totalled 70 officers and 630 ratings.

Air Force. The Air Force, formed in 1962, has 6 Alpha Jet advanced trainers, with combat potential, 1 turbofan F-28 Fellowship, 1 Super-King Air, 1 Cessna 421, 1 Gulfstream III transport, 2 Reims-Cessna 150s, 6 Beech F-33Cs and 2 Reims-Cessna 337s for liaison and training, and 4 SA330 Puma, 4 Dauphin 2 and 3 Alouette II/III helicopters. Personnel (1988) 930.

INTERNATIONAL RELATIONS

Membership. Côte d'Ivoire is a member of UN, OAU and is an ACP state of EEC.

ECONOMY

Planning. The 1981–85 Five Year Development Plan concentrated on the primary sector, mainly increasing food production.

Budget. The budget for 1987 totalled 480,980m. francs CFA. Capital expenditure 145,879 francs CFA.

Currency. The currency is the *franc CFA* with a parity rate of 50 *francs CFA* to 1 French *franc.* In March 1988, £1 sterling = 507 francs CFA; US$1 = 285·66 francs CFA.

Banking. The *Banque Centrale des Etats de l'Afrique de l'Ouest* is the bank of issue. Numerous foreign and domestic banks have offices in Abidjan, and *Société Générale de Banque, Société Ivoirienne de Banque, Banque Internationale pour le Commerce et l'Industrie de la Côte d'Ivoire* and *Banque Internationale pour l'Afrique Occidentale* maintain wide branch networks throughout the country.

ENERGY AND NATURAL RESOURCES

Electricity. Production in 1985 amounted to 2,162m. kwh mostly from new hydro-electric projects at Kassou and Taabo on the Bandama river, Buyo on the Sassandra river, and from 2 older dams on the Bia river. Supply 220 volts; 50 Hz.

Oil. Petroleum has been produced (offshore) since Oct. 1977. Production (1987) 1m. tonnes.

Minerals. Diamond extraction was 37,000 carats in 1982. Exploitation of iron ore deposits at Bangolo in the west await completion of hydro-electric projects.

Agriculture. The main export crops (production 1986 in 1,000 tonnes) are coffee (280), cocoa (520), bananas (170), pineapples (300), palm oil (180), palm kernels (43), seed cotton (206) and rubber (48); food crops include yams (2,996), cassava (1,500), plantains (1,400), rice (460), maize (550), millet (35) and groundnuts (86). Sugar-cane (1·5m. tonnes in 1986) is grown on new plantations in the north at Ferkéssédougou and elsewhere.

Livestock, 1986: 881,000 cattle, 1·45m. sheep, 1,502,000 goats, 450,000 pigs, 1,000 horses and 1,000 donkeys.

Forestry. Equatorial rain forests, especially in the south, cover 3m. hectares and produce over 30 commercially valuable species including teak, mahogany and ebony. Production in 1983 was 11·8m. cu. metres.

Fisheries. The catch in 1983 amounted to 93,960 tonnes (16% from inland waters).

INDUSTRY AND TRADE

Industry. Industrialization has developed rapidly since independence, particularly food processing, textiles and sawmills. Several factories produce palm-oil, fruit preserves and fruit juice.

Labour. The main trade union is the *Union Générale des Travailleurs de Côte d'Ivoire*, with over 100,000 members.

Commerce. Trade for calendar years in 1m. francs CFA:

	1981	1982	1983	1984	1985
Imports	681,464	718,593	714,828	658,569	772,987
Exports	689,298	747,452	796,774	1,184,347	1,318,059

In 1983 exports of coffee furnished 20% of exports, cocoa 20·4%, timber 13·5% and petroleum products, 8·6%. Of the total 19% went to France, 11·6% to the Netherlands, 12·4% to the USA and 8·8% to Italy. Of the imports, France supplied 35%, the Federal Republic of Germany, 5% and Nigeria, 5%.

Total trade between the Côte d'Ivoire and UK (British Department of Trade returns, in £1,000 sterling):

	1983	1984	1985	1986	1987
Imports to UK	79,255	93,875	116,699	117,058	90,246
Exports and re-exports from UK	25,591	25,347	29,514	34,266	26,834

Tourism. In 1986 there were 187,000 foreign tourists.

COMMUNICATIONS

Roads. In 1984 roads totalled 53,736 km (including 128 km of motorway) and there were 182,956 private cars and 43,001 commercial vehicles.

Railways. From Abidjan a metre-gauge railway runs to Léraba on the border with Burkina Faso (655 km), and thence through Burkina Faso to Ouagadougou. In 1985 the railways carried 2·4m. passengers and 667,659 tonnes of freight.

Aviation. The international airport is at Abidjan-Port-Buet. In 1981 it handled 870,000 passengers and 33,000 tonnes of freight and mail. Air Ivoire provides regular domestic services to 10 regional airports and 15 landing strips.

Shipping. The main ports are Abidjan and San Pedro. In 1981 Abidjan port handled 5·8m. tonnes and San Pedro 1·5m. tonnes. In 1986 the merchant marine comprised 61 vessels of 141,674 tons gross.

Post and Broadcasting. There were 87,700 telephones in 1984 and (1981), 1,181 telex machines. In 1983 there were 562,000 television and 800,000 radio receivers.

Cinemas. There were 60 cinemas in 1977 with a seating capacity of 41,000.

Newspapers. In 1982 there were 3 daily newspapers, the principal being *Fraternité-Matin,* circulation 80,000.

JUSTICE, RELIGION, EDUCATION AND WELFARE

Justice. There are 28 courts of first instance and 3 assize courts in Abidjan, Bouaké and Daloa, 2 courts of appeal in Abidjan and Bouaké, and a supreme court in Abidjan.

Religion. In 1980, 24% were Moslems (mainly in the north), 32% Christians (chiefly Roman Catholics in the south), and 44% animists.

Education. There were, in 1984, 1,179,456 pupils in primary schools, 245,342 pupils in secondary schools and (1979) 22,437 in technical schools. The *Université Nationale de Côte d'Ivoire,* at Abidjan (founded 1964), had 12,755 students in 1984.

Health. In 1978 there were 9,962 hospital beds, 429 doctors, 36 dentists, 615 midwives, 3,052 nurses and 76 pharmacists.

DIPLOMATIC REPRESENTATIVES

Of the Côte d'Ivoire in Great Britain (2 Upper Belgrave St., London, SW1X 8BJ)
Ambassador: Théodore De Mel (accredited 10 Feb. 1987).

Of Great Britain in the Côte d'Ivoire (Immeuble 'Les Harmonies', Blvd. Carde, Abidjan)
Ambassador: V. E. Sutherland.

Of the Côte d'Ivoire in the USA (2424 Massachusetts Ave., NW, Washington, D.C., 20008)
Ambassador: Charles Gomis.

Of the USA in the Côte d'Ivoire (5 Rue Jesse Owens, Abidjan)
Ambassador: Dennis Kux.

Of the Côte d'Ivoire to the United Nations
Ambassador: Amara Essy.

Books of Reference

Statistical Information: Service de la Statistique, Abidjan. It publishes *Bulletin Statistique Mensuel* and *Inventoire Économique de la Côte d'Ivoire.*

Zartman, I. W., and Delgado, C., *The Political Economy of Ivory Coast.* New York, 1984
Zolberg, A. R., *One-Party Government in the Ivory Coast.* Rev. ed. Princeton Univ. Press, 1974

CUBA

Capital: Havana
Population: 10·19m. (1987)
GNP per capita: US$2,696 (1981)

República de Cuba

HISTORY. Cuba, except for the brief British occupancy in 1762–63, remained a Spanish possession from its discovery by Columbus in 1492 until 10 Dec. 1898, when the sovereignty was relinquished under the terms of the Treaty of Paris, which ended the struggle of the Cubans against Spanish rule. Cuba thus became an independent republic, but the United States stipulated under the 'Platt Amendment' (abrogated by Roosevelt in 1934) that Cuba must enter into no treaty relations with a foreign power, which might endanger its independence.

The revolutionary movement against the Batista dictatorship, led by Dr Fidel Castro, started on 26 July 1953 (now a national holiday). It achieved power on 1 Jan. 1959 when Batista fled the country.

An invasion force of émigrés and adventurers landed in Cuba on 17 April 1961; the main body was defeated at the Bay of Pigs (Matanzas province) and mopped up by 20 April.

The US Navy blockaded Cuba from 22 Oct. to 22 Nov. 1962.

AREA AND POPULATION. The island of Cuba forms the largest and most westerly of the Greater Antilles group and lies 135 miles south of the tip of Florida, USA. It has an area of 44,206 sq. miles (114,524 sq. km); the Isle of Youth (formerly Isle of Pines) has 1,180 sq. miles, and other islands about 1,350 sq. miles. Census (1981) 9,723,605; estimate in 1985 was 10·15m.

The area, population and density of population of the 14 provinces and the special Municipality of the Isle of Youth were as follows (1987 estimate):

	Area sq. km	Population		Area sq. km	Population
Pinar del Río	10,860	669,500	Camagüey	14,134	711,200
La Habana	5,671	618,100	Las Tunas	6,373	467,600
Ciudad de La Habana	727	2,025,700	Holguín	9,105	957,800
Matanzas	11,669	586,600	Granma	8,452	765,700
Cienfuegos	4,149	346,600	Santiago de Cuba	6,343	954,000
Villa Clara	8,069	789,200	Guantánamo	6,366	478,000
Sancti Spíritus	6,737	415,600			
Ciego de Ávila	6,485	345,200	Isla de la Juventud	2,199	68,700

The chief cities (1986, estimate) were Habana, the capital (2,014,800), Santiago de Cuba (358,800), Camagüey (260,800), Holguín (194,700), Santa Clara (178,300), Guantánamo (174,400), Cienfuegos (109,300), Matanzas (105,400), Bayamo (105,300), Pinar del Río (100,900), Las Tunas (91,400), Ciego de Ávila (80,500) and Sancti Spíritus (75,600).

Infant mortality (1986) 13·6 per 1,000 live births.

CLIMATE. Situated in the sub-tropical zone, Cuba has a generally rainy climate, affected by the Gulf Stream and the N.E. Trades, though winters are comparatively dry after the heaviest rains in Sept. and Oct. Hurricanes are liable to occur between June and Nov. Havana. Jan. 72°F (22·2°C), July 82°F (27·8°C). Annual rainfall 48″ (1,224 mm).

CONSTITUTION AND GOVERNMENT. The previous Constitution was suspended in Jan. 1959. The first socialist Constitution came into force on 24 Feb. 1976.

Since 1940 the following have been Presidents of the Republic:

	Took office		Took office
Gen. Fulgencio Batista y Zaldívar	10 Oct. 1940	Gen. Fulgencio Batista y Zaldívar	10 March 1952
Dr Ramón Grau San Martín	10 Oct. 1944	Dr Manuel Urratia Lleo	2 Jan. 1959
Dr Carlos Prío Socarrás	10 Oct. 1948	Osvaldo Dórticos Torrado	17 July 1959

Legislative power is vested in the National Assembly of People's Power, consisting of 499 deputies elected for a 5-year term by the Municipal Assemblies; elections were held in 1976, 1981 and 1986. The National Assembly elects a 31-member Council of State as its permanent organ. The Council of State's President, who is head of state and of government, nominates and leads a Council of Ministers approved by the National Assembly.

President: Dr Fidel Castro Ruz became President of the Council of State on 3 Dec. 1976. He is also President of the Council of Ministers, First Secretary of the Cuban Communist Party and C.-in-C. of the Revolutionary Armed Forces.

First Vice-President of the Council of State and of the Council of Ministers, Minister of the Revolutionary Armed Forces: Raúl Castro Ruz. *Foreign Affairs:* Isidoro Octavio Malmierca Peoli. *Interior:* José Abrantes Fernandez. *Justice:* Juan Escalona Reguera. *Foreign Trade:* Ricardo Cabrisas Ruiz.

The Council of Ministers also includes 10 other Vice-Presidents, the Presidents of 9 State Planning Committees and 15 other Ministers.

Dr Castro on 2 Dec. 1961 proclaimed 'a Marxist–Leninist programme adapted to the precise objective conditions existing in our country'. The provisional *Organizaciones Revolucionarias Integradas* (ORI) were established as an intermediate stage towards a single (communist) party, and gave way to the *Partido Unido de la Revolución Socialista* (PURS). This brought together the *Partido Socialista Popular, Movimiento de 26 Julio* and (Students') *Directorio Revolucionario.* The PURS in turn became (3 Oct. 1965) the *Partido Comunista de Cuba.*

The Congress of the PCC elects a Central Committee of 146 full and 79 alternate (non-voting) members, which in turn appoints a Political Bureau comprising 14 full and 10 alternate members.

National flag: 3 blue, 2 white stripes (horizontal); a white 5-pointed star in a red triangle at the hoist.

National anthem: Al combate corred bayameses (words and tune by P. Figueredo, 1868).

Local Government. The country is divided into 14 provinces, the special Municipality (the Isle of Youth) and 169 municipalities. Local Government is the responsibility of the organizations of Peoples' Power. Elections were held in 1976, 1979, 1981 and 1984 for delegates to the Municipal Assemblies by universal suffrage for 2½ year terms; the Municipal Assemblies then elected the Provincial Assemblies for similar terms.

DEFENCE. On 13 Nov. 1963 conscription was introduced for all men between the ages of 16 and 45, later raised to 50 (3 years); women of the 17–35 age groups may volunteer (for 2 years).

Army. The strength was 145,000 officers and men (60,000 conscripts) in 1988. Reserves are estimated at 130,000.

The Army is organized in 4 corps, 1 armoured division, 3 mechanical divisions and 26 artillery regiments for air defence. Equipment includes 150 T-34, 650 T-54/-55, 300 T-62 tanks and 60 PT-64 light-tanks. Para-military forces total 15,000 and the new Territorial Militia, 1·2m. including reservists, all armed.

Navy. The expanding Navy consists of 4 *ex*-Soviet diesel-powered submarines (of which 1 is in static reserve), 2 *ex*-Soviet guided missile-armed frigates, 23 missile boats, 9 hydrofoil attack craft, 4 patrol vessels, 24 fast gunboats, 4 minehunters, 10 inshore minesweepers, 12 motor launches, 14 coastguard vessels, 15 survey vessels, 2 landing ships, 6 landing craft and 15 service craft. The large majority of over 140 craft are former units of the Soviet Navy.

Personnel in 1988 exceeded 12,000 including marines and coastguard. The USA is still in possession of the Guantanámo naval base, but the Cuban Government refuses to accept the nominal rent of US$5,000 per annum.

Air Force. The Air Force has been extensively re-equipped with aircraft supplied by USSR and in 1988 had a strength of some 18,500 officers and men and 300 combat aircraft. About 16 interceptor and 4 ground-attack squadrons fly MiG-23, MiG-21 and MiG-17 jet fighters. There is a squadron of An-26 twin-turboprop transports, some An-24 twin-turboprop transports, piston-engined Il-14s, and about 100 Mi-24 gunship, Mi-8 (some armed), Mi-17 and Mi-4 helicopters, Zlin 326 piston-engined trainers and L-39, MiG-15UTI, MiG-21U and MiG-23U jet trainers. An-2M biplanes are operated by the Air Force, mainly on agricultural and liaison duties. Soviet-built surface-to-air ('Guideline', 'Goa' and 'Gainful') and coastal defence ('Samlet') missiles are in service.

INTERNATIONAL RELATIONS

Membership. Cuba is a member of the UN, Sela, the Non-Aligned Movement and Comecon.

ECONOMY

Planning. The Cuban economy is now centrally planned. Since July 1972 Cuba has been a member of the Council for Mutual Economic Assistance (Comecon) and, since Jan. 1974, of the two Comecon international banks.

Budget. Revenue in 1987 was 11,574·6m. pesos and expenditure, 11,689·6m. pesos.

Currency. The *peso* is not a freely exchangeable currency but an official exchange rate is announced daily reflecting any changes in the strength of the US$. In March 1988, the sterling-peso rate was £1 = 1·342 *pesos*. US currency is accepted in tourist/hotel shops, but is not normally legal tender.

Copper-nickel coins of 1 *peso* and 20, 5, 2 and 1 *cent* are issued. Notes are for 100, 50, 20, 10, 5, 3 and 1 *peso*.

Banking. On 23 Dec. 1948 the president signed the law creating a central bank (with capital of US$10m.) and which began operating 27 April 1950.

On 14 Oct. 1960 all banks were nationalized, except the Royal Bank of Canada and the Bank of Nova Scotia, which were bought out later. All banking is now carried out by the National Bank of Cuba through its 250 agencies, or via the Banco Financiero.

All insurance business was nationalized in Jan. 1964. A National Savings Bank was established in 1983.

Weights and Measures. The metric system of weights and measures is legally compulsory, but the American and old Spanish systems are much used. The sugar industry uses the Spanish long ton (1·03 tonnes) and short ton (0·92 tonne). Cuba sugar sack = 329·59 lb. or 149·49 kg. Land is measured in *caballerías* (of 13·4 hectares or 33 acres).

ENERGY AND NATURAL RESOURCES

Electricity. Production in 1986 was 13,167m. kwh. Supply 115 and 120 volts; 60 Hz.

Oil. Crude oil production (1987) 1m. tonnes.

Minerals. Iron ore abounds, with deposits estimated at 3,500m. tons, of which 90% were held as reserves by American steel interests but are now controlled by the Cuban Ministry of Basic Industry; output (tonnes), wrought iron (1980), 1,180; steel (1985), 412,900. Output of copper concentrate (1986) was 3,257 tonnes; refractory chrome (1982), 27,300 tonnes. Other minerals are nickel and cobalt (1985, 33,400 tonnes), silica and barytes. Gold and silver are also worked. Salt output from the solar evaporation of sea water was 122,300 tonnes in 1986.

Agriculture. In May 1959 all land over 30 *caballerías* was nationalized and has since been turned into state farms. In Oct. 1963 private holdings were reduced to a maximum of 5 *caballerías* (approximately 67 hectares).

In Sept. 1984 there were 1,472 co-operatives comprising 70,000 *caballerías* of land. The total cultivated land (1982) included state-owned, 3,398,200 hectares, and in the private sector, 475,400 hectares.

The most important product is sugar, of which Cuba is the world's second largest producer; with its by-products it furnishes nearly 50% by value of the national exports. The 1986 crop was estimated at 6·7m. tonnes. There are 164 mills, including 40 of the largest, which were taken over from US interests, and which represent 39% of total capacity. Tobacco, coffee, cotton, maize, rice, potatoes and citrus fruit are grown.

Production of other important crops in 1986 was (in tonnes): Tobacco, 42,900; rice, 524,000; maize (1984), 29,963; coffee (1984), 23,417.

Tobacco is grown mainly in the Vuelta–Abajo district, near Pinar del Río. Coffee is grown chiefly in the province of Oriente.

A fast-growing fibre, *kenaf*, originally from India, soft in texture, is replacing jute for sacking (production, 1984, 19,800 tonnes); the tobacco industry uses *majagua*, another local fibre, while a third fibre, *yarey*, from palms is also used. 316,473 tonnes of potatoes were produced in 1986. A nitrate plant has been built at Nuevitas and a large British-built urea plant at Cienfuegos. The principal fruits exported are pineapples, citrus fruit, tomatoes and pimentos. A rice cultivation plan began in 1967 in the south of Havana province. Cultivation is highly mechanized and the area so far sown produces two crops a year.

In 1986 citrus fruit production was 786,330 tonnes. Seed cotton production, 1986, was 3,000.

In 1986 the livestock included 2·4m. pigs; 718,000 horses; 380,000 sheep; 108,000 goats; 6·4m. head of cattle.

Forestry. Cuba has extensive forest lands. These forests contain valuable cabinet woods, such as mahogany and cedar, besides dye-woods, fibres, gums, resins and oils. Cedar is used locally for cigar-boxes, and mahogany is exported. Cedars, mahogany, *majagua*, teca, etc., are also raised. In 1984 saplings planted included: Eucalyptus, 12·4m.; pine, 40·1m.; majagua, 3·5m.; mahogany, 6·6m.; cedar, 1·3m.; casuarina, 17m.

Fisheries. Fishing is the third most important export industry, after sugar and nickel. Catch (1986) 244,589 tonnes.

INDUSTRY AND TRADE

Industry. Production in 1986 was: Textiles, 217m. sq. metres; cement, 3·3m. tonnes; wheat flour, 437,000 tonnes; fuel oil, 3,314,000 tonnes; diesel oil, 991,000 tonnes; 436,000 tyres; 332,200 inner tubes (1984); leather shoes (1985), 12·4m. pairs; paint, 84,800 hectolitres; soft drinks (1985), 2,106,500 hectolitres; 366·3m. cigars (1985); 1,684,000m. cigarettes; fertilizers, 1,045,200 tonnes; 2,351 buses; 236,000 radios; 102,000 TVs.

Trade Unions. All workers have a right to join a trade union. The Workers' Central Union of Cuba, to which 23 unions are affiliated, had 2m. members in 1978.

Commerce. Imports and exports (including bullion and specie) for calendar years (in 1m. pesos):

	1983	1984	1985	1986
Imports	6,224	7,207	7,983	7,569
Exports	5,537	5,462	7,209	6,702

Cuba's principal exports are sugar, minerals, tobacco and fish. The main imports from non-Communist countries are chemicals and engineering and electrical machinery and transport equipment.

In 1985 the USSR provided 67% of imports (by value) and took 75% of exports; in 1984 sugar formed 75% of all exports.

Total trade between Cuba and UK (British Department of Trade returns, in £1,000 sterling):

	1983	1984	1985	1986	1987
Imports to UK	14,010	13,020	7,273	8,555	12,776
Exports and re-exports from UK	45,737	64,377	59,332	58,760	41,510

Tourism. In 1986 there were 194,531 visitors (280,000 in 1957).

COMMUNICATIONS

Roads. In 1986 there were 16,740 km of paved highways open to traffic, traversing the island for 760 miles from Pinar del Río to Santiago. In 1983 there were 49,841 hire cars (including coaches and buses).

Railways. There were (1986) 4,881 km of public railway (mainly 1,435 mm gauge) of which 152 km is electrified. In 1984 it carried 67·4m. passengers and 16·5m. tonnes of freight. In addition, the large sugar estates have 7,773 km of lines on 1,435, 914 and 760 mm gauges.

Aviation. The state airline CUBANA operates all internal services, and from Havana to Mexico City, Madrid, Moscow and East Berlin, Montreal, Prague, Paris and Brussels, and also to Lima, Panama, Kingston, Bridgetown, Port of Spain, Georgetown and Managua. The other regular foreign services are Mexican, Spanish, Soviet, Czech, East German and Canadian.

Shipping. The coastline is over 3,500 miles long and has many fine harbours. The merchant marine, in 1984, consisted of 107 sea-going vessels of 1,071,500 DWT.

Post and Broadcasting. There are 3,545 miles of public and 8,902 miles of private telegraph wires. Cuba has 103 radio broadcasting stations and 2 television stations. Radio receiving sets, 1985, numbered 2·14m.; television sets, 1·53m. The national telephone system (1985) had 493,000 instruments.

Cinemas. In 1986 there were 515 (35mm) and 927 (16mm) cinemas.

Newspapers. In 1983 there were 29 newspapers of which 16 were daily newspapers.

JUSTICE, RELIGION, EDUCATION AND WELFARE

Justice. There is a Supreme Court in Havana and 7 regional courts of appeal. The provinces are divided into judicial districts, with courts for civil and criminal actions, with municipal courts for minor offences. The civil code guarantees aliens the same property and personal rights as are enjoyed by nationals.

The 1959 Agrarian Reform Law and the Urban Reform Law passed on 14 Oct. 1960 have placed certain restrictions on both. Revolutionary Summary Tribunals have wide powers.

Religion. There is no state Church, though Roman Catholics predominate. There is a bishop of the American Episcopal Church in Havana; there are congregations of Methodists in Havana and in the provinces as well as Baptists and other denominations.

Education. Education is compulsory (between the ages of 6 and 14) and free, and now available everywhere. In 1964 illiteracy was officially declared to have been completely eliminated.

In 1984–85 the universities had 212,200 students and (1982–83) 12,222 teaching staff. In 1982–83 there were 1,363,078 pupils and 71,251 teachers at primary schools; 118,072 at pre-primary, 774,400 pupils at intermediate schools; 173,403 students at higher schools; 392,945 students at adult primary and intermediate schools; and 56,721 students at other schools.

Health. There were (1985) 22,910 doctors, (1983) 4,380 dentists and (1986) 254 hospitals with 53,038 beds. The 1984 health and education budget was 2,405m. pesos.

Free medical services are provided by the state polyclinics, though a few doctors still have private practices. All serious tropical diseases are effectively kept under control, and virtually all children under the age of 15 have been vaccinated against poliomyelitis.

DIPLOMATIC REPRESENTATIVES

Of Cuba in Great Britain (167 High Holborn, London, WC1)
Ambassador: Dr Oscar Fernández-Mell.

Of Great Britain in Cuba (Edificio Bolivar, Carcel 101–103, Havana)
Ambassador: A. E. Palmer, CMG, CVO.

Of Cuba to the United Nations
Ambassador: Oscar Oramas-Oliva.

The USA broke off diplomatic relations with Cuba on 3 Jan. 1961 but in 1977 Interest Sections were opened, officially attached to the Swiss Embassy in Havana and to the Czech Embassy in Washington respectively.

Books of Reference

Anuario Estadístico de a República de Cuba. Havana
Boletín Oficial, Ministerio de Comercio. Monthly
Estadística General: Commercio Exterior. Quarterly and Annual.—*Movimiento de Población.* Monthly and Annual. Havana
Anuario azucarero de Cuba. Havana, from 1937
Brundenius, C., *Revolutionary Cuba: The Challenge of Economic Growth with Equity.* Oxford, 1984
Domínguez, J. I., *Cuba: Order and Revolution.* Harvard Univ. Press, 1978
Gravette, A. G., *Cuba: Official Guide.* London, 1987
Guerra y Sánchez, R., and others, *Historia de la Nación Cubana.* 10 vols. Havana, 1952
MacEwan, A., *Revolution and Economic Development in Cuba.* London, 1981
Mesa-Lago, C., *The Economy of Socialist Cuba: A Two-Decade Appraisal.* Univ. of New Mexico Press, 1981
O'Connor, J., *The Origins of Socialism in Cuba.* London, Cornell Univ. Press, 1970
Ritter, A. R. M., *The Economic Development of Revolutionary Cuba: Strategy and Performance.* New York, 1974
Thomas, H., *The Cuban Revolution: 25 Years Later.* Epping, 1984

CYPRUS

Capital: Nicosia
Population: 673,100 (1986)
GNP per capita: US$5,703 (1986)

Kypriaki Dimokratia—
Kıbrıs Cumhuriyeti

HISTORY. About the middle of the 2nd millennium B.C. Greek colonies were established in Cyprus and later it formed part of the Persian, Roman and Byzantine empires. In 1193 it became a Frankish kingdom, in 1489 a Venetian dependency and in 1571 was conquered by the Turks. They retained possession of it until its cession to England for administrative purposes under a convention concluded with the Sultan at Constantinople, 4 June 1878. On 5 Nov. 1914 the island was annexed by Great Britain and on 1 May 1925 given the status of a Crown Colony.

For the history of Cyprus from 1931 to 1974 *see* THE STATESMAN'S YEAR-BOOK, 1958, pp. 237–38, 1959, p. 236, and 1983–84, p. 385.

On 15 July 1974 a *coup* was staged in Cyprus by the men of the Greek ruling junta, for the overthrow of President Makarios. The President left the island and the *coup* was short-lived. On 23 July power was handed over to the President of the House of Representatives, Glafcos Clerides, in accordance with the Constitution. He acted as President until the return of President Makarios on Dec. 7.

Turkey invaded the island on 20 July, eventually landing 40,000 troops supported with heavy armament and tanks. In two military operations 20–30 July and 14–16 Aug. the Turkish troops managed to occupy 40% of the northern part of Cyprus. As a result 200,000 Greek Cypriots fled to live as refugees in the south. The Cyprus crisis was raised in the UN and the General Assembly unanimously adopted resolutions calling for the withdrawal of all foreign troops from Cyprus and the return of refugees to their homes, but without result.

On 13 Feb. 1975 at a special meeting of the executive council and legislative assembly of the Autonomous Turkish Cypriot Administration a Turkish Cypriot Federated State was proclaimed. Rauf Denktash was appointed President and he declared that the state would not seek international recognition. The proclamation was denounced by President Makarios and the Greek Prime Minister but welcomed by the Turkish Prime Minister. In 1984 the UN Secretary-General initiated talks on a possible federal state but these failed in Jan. 1985.

AREA AND POPULATION. The island lies in the eastern Mediterranean, about 50 miles off the south coast of Turkey and (at the nearest points) 65 miles off the coast of Syria. Area 3,572 sq. miles (9,251 sq. km); greatest length from east to west about 150 miles, and greatest breadth from north to south about 60 miles. The Turkish occupied area is 3,400 sq. km (about 37% of the total area). Population by ethnic group:

Ethnic group	1946	1960	1980	1985	1986
Greek Orthodox	361,199	441,656	507,500	532,600	538,900
Turkish Moslem	80,548	104,942	118,000	124,100	125,500
Others	8,367	26,968	3,500	8,500	8,700
Total	450,114	573,566	629,000	665,200	673,100

Population estimate (June 1986) 673,100, of which 81% are Greek Cypriot (Armenian, Maronite and Latin minorities included) and 19% Turkish Cypriot. Principal towns with populations (Dec. 1986 estimate): Nicosia (the capital), 163,700 (Greek Cypriots); Limassol, 113,600; Larnaca, 53,400; Paphos, 23,100.

As a result of the Turkish invasion and the occupation of part of Cyprus, 200,000 Greek Cypriots were displaced and forced to find refuge in the south of the island. The urban centres of Famagusta, Kyrenia and Morphou were completely evacuated. See p. 404 for details of the 'Turkish Republic of Northern Cyprus'.

Vital statistics. The birth rate per 1,000 population in 1986 was 19·5; death rate, 8·4; infantile mortality per 1,000 live births, 12.

CLIMATE. The climate is Mediterranean, with very hot, dry summers and variable winters. Maximum temperatures may reach 112°F (44·5°C) in July and Aug., but minimum figures may fall to 22°F (–5·5°C) in the mountains in winter when snow is experienced. Rainfall is generally between 10 and 27″ (250 and 675 mm) and occurs mainly in the winter months, but it may reach 48″ (1,200 mm) in the Troodos mountains. Nicosia. Jan. 50°F (10·0°C), July 83°F (28·3°C). Annual rainfall 15″ (371 mm).

CONSTITUTION AND GOVERNMENT. The legislative power is exercised by the House of Representatives of 80 members, of whom 56 were elected by the Greek community and 24 by the Turkish community. As from Dec. 1963 the Turkish members have ceased to attend.

On 13 Dec. 1959 Archbishop Makarios was elected President of the Republic. Dr Fazil Kuchuk was elected Vice-President unopposed; he resigned on 4 Jan. 1964. On 13 Feb. 1975, Rauf Denktash the Turkish-Cypriot leader announced the formation of a Turkish-Cypriot state within a federal republic and on 15 Nov. 1983 a unilateral declaration of independence, as the Turkish Republic of Northern Cyprus, was announced.

When President Makarios died in Aug. 1977 Spyros Kyprianou became acting President and was proclaimed President on 31 Aug. 1977 and was elected for a 5-year term in 1978 and re-elected in 1983. In 1988 George Vassilou was installed as President following elections held on 14 Feb.

Flag: White with a copper-coloured outline of the island with 2 green olive-branches beneath.

The elections held on 8 Dec. 1985 returned 16 Democratic Party, 15 Akel Party (Communists), 6 EDEK (Socialist Party), 19 Democratic Rally. The Turks have not participated in the proceedings of the House since Dec. 1963.

The Council of Ministers in Feb. 1988 was as follows:

Foreign Affairs: George Iacovou. *Interior:* Christodoulos Veniamin. *Defence:* Andreas Aloneftis. *Agriculture and Natural Resources:* Andreas Gavrielides. *Commerce and Industry:* Takis Nemitsas. *Health:* Panikos Papageorgiou. *Communications and Works:* Nakos Protopapas. *Finance:* George Syrimis. *Education:* Andreas Philippou. *Labour and Social Insurance:* Takis Christofides. *Justice:* Christodoulos Chrysanthou.

DEFENCE

Army. Total strength (1988) 13,000 organized in 3 reconnaissance/mechanized infantry and 20 infantry battalions, with artillery and support units. The National Guard has a twin-engined Maritime Islander light transport and 2 AB.47 helicopters. There is also a para-military force of 3,666 armed police.

The Turkish-Cypriot Security Force: 25,000 Turkish mainland troops, 5,000 Turkish Cypriots, and some T-34 tanks.

INTERNATIONAL RELATIONS

Membership. Cyprus is a member of UN, the Commonwealth, the Council of Europe and the Non-Aligned Movement.

ECONOMY

Planning. A fourth emergency economic action plan (1982–86) envisaged expenditure of £C398m. for development projects.

Budget. Revenue and expenditure for calendar years (in £C1m.):

	1983	1984	1985	1986	1987
Expenditure	366	418	448	505	540
Revenue	288	343	388	359	404

Main sources of ordinary revenue in 1986 (in £C1m.) were: Import duties, 77·9 (including 17 temporary refugee levy on imports); excise duties, 51·6; income tax, 77·7; rents, royalties and interest, 18·5; sales of goods and services, 20·9; other duties and taxes, 42·2; social security contributions, 71·9.

Main divisions of ordinary expenditure in 1986 (in £C1m.): Wages and salaries, 156·5; pensions and gratuities, 12·6; commodity subsidies, 20·1; expenditures on goods and services, 39; public debt charges, 90·2; social insurance benefits, 56·7.

Development expenditure for 1986 (in £C1m.) included 35·6 for water development, 4·1 for agriculture, forests and fisheries, 2·7 for rural development, 95 for roads, 1·2 for airports and 0·5 for tourism. (An independent Ports Authority with its own funds was set up in 1977.)

The outstanding public debt as at 31 Dec. 1984 was £C383·7m., excluding sinking fund reserves, and accumulated sinking funds totalled £C23·3m. Outstanding loans as at 31 Dec. 1984 totalled £C52·3m.; including £C2·9m. to the Cyprus Telecommunications Authority. Foreign debt (1986) public and private, £C636m.

Currency. From Oct. 1983 the *Cyprus £* has been divided into 100 *cents*. Notes of the following denominations are in circulation: £10, £5, £1, 50 *cents*. Coins in circulation: Cupro-zinc-nickel: 20, 10, 5, 2, 1 *cent* and ½ *cent* in aluminium. Rate of exchange, March 1988: £1 = £C0·804; US$1 = £C2·219.

Banking. There is a Central and Issuing Bank exercising monetary functions, and the Cyprus Development Bank Ltd established by the Government as a major source of loan funds for industrial development. Commercial banks operating in Cyprus are: Bank of Cyprus Ltd, Turkish Bank Ltd, Cyprus Popular Bank Ltd, Barclays Bank International, National Bank of Greece, Hellenic Bank Ltd, Arab Bank Ltd and Turkiye Is Bankasi. There are 2 central co-operative banks (Co-operative Central Bank Ltd and the Cyprus Turkish Co-operative Central Bank Ltd) and 3 specialized financial institutions (Mortgage Bank of Cyprus Ltd, Lombard Banking (Cyprus) Ltd and Housing Finance Corporation). Twelve off-shore banking units were in operation in 1987.

Turkish Bank Ltd, Turkiye Is Bankasi and the Cyprus Turkish Co-operative Central Bank Ltd are operating in the Turkish occupied area of the republic and consequently no control or supervision is exercised by the Central Bank of Cyprus.

The Central Bank of Cyprus, established in 1963, is responsible for the issue of currency, the regulation of money supply and credit, administration of the exchange control law and the foreign-exchange reserves of the republic. The Bank also acts as a banker of the banks operating in Cyprus and of the Government and acts as supervisor of the banking system.

At the end of Dec. 1985 total deposits in banks were £C1,113·3m. The country's foreign exchange reserves at the end of Dec. 1985 were £C389·5m.

Weights and Measures. Weights and measures had been based on the standard weights and measures of the UK. From 1 Jan. 1986 a programme of gradual adoption of the Metric (SI) System is being implemented with the end of 1988 as the target date for completion of the change.

ENERGY AND NATURAL RESOURCES

Electricity. Production (1986) 1,423m. kwh. Supply 240 volts; 50 Hz.

Water Resources. In 1985 £C23·9m. was spent on water dams, water supplies, hydrological research and geophysical surveys. Existing dams had (1984) a capacity of 150m. cu. metres as against 6m. cu. metres before independence.

Minerals. The principal minerals exported during 1986 were (in tonnes): Asbestos, 11,781; flotation pyrites, 65,938; copper precipitates, 1,148. Mining products provided about 1·9% of domestic exports in 1986. Total value of minerals exported in 1986 was £C3·3m.

Agriculture. Chief agricultural products in 1986 (1,000 tonnes): Grapes, 151; potatoes, 172; milk, 112·5; cereals (wheat and barley), 67·5; citrus fruit, 131·5; meat, 50·8; carobs, 2·5; fresh fruit, 23·9; olives, 12; other vegetables, 106; eggs, 8·5m. dozen.

Of the island's 2·3m. acres, approximately 1m. are cultivated. 14·1% (1986) of the economically active population are engaged in agriculture.

Livestock in 1986 (in 1,000): Cattle, 44; sheep, 325; goats, 230; pigs, 225; poultry, 2,400.

Forestry. By Dec. 1982, the reforesting of burnt areas in the Paphos Forest was completed and an area of 7,492 ha (56,000 donums) was reforested. Reforestation work in other bare areas of state forests was carried out in an area of 5,729 ha (42,828 donums). Total forest area, 1,753 sq. km.

In 1986 the chief forest products were timber, valued at £C721,000; firewood, £C133,000; figures relate to the area of Cyprus not occupied by Turkey.

Fisheries. Catch (1986) 2,548 tonnes valued at £C5·9m.

INDUSTRY AND TRADE

Industry. Cyprus has no heavy industry, but a wide variety of light manufacturing industries. Manufacturing industry in 1986 contributed about £C245·1m. to the GDP and gave employment to 43,250 of the economically active population.

The highest increases in output in 1986 were production of food products, wearing apparel, metal products and machinery and equipment. Industrial exports declined to £C126·2m. in 1986 and accounted for 70% of total domestic exports.

Trade Unions and Associations. About 80% of the workforce is organized and the majority of workers belong either to the Pancyprian Federation of Labour or the Cyprus Workers Confederation.

Commerce. The commerce and the shipping, exclusive of coasting trade, for calendar years were (in £C1,000):

	1982	1983	1984	1985	1986
Imports [1]	577,551	641,962	796,520	762,312	659,100
Exports [2]	263,809	260,525	336,826	290,610	260,200

[1] Excluding Naafi imports.
[2] Including re-exports and ships' stores.

Chief civil imports, 1986 (in £C1,000):

Petroleum and petroleum products	78,820	Feeding stuff for animals	10,389
Textile yarn and fabrics made up	55,239	Tobacco and manufactures	15,675
Iron and steel	39,174	Meat and meat preparations	6,732
Cereals and cereal preparations	24,883	Animal and vegetable	
Machinery and Transport		oils, fats and waxes	10,511
equipment	160,252	Non-metallic mineral manufactures	17,503
Paper, paperboard and pulp and		Medicinal and pharmaceutical	
articles thereof	19,807	products	14,196
Artificial resins and		Manufactures of metal, n.e.s.	19,125
plastics	15,234	Dairy products and eggs	5,173

Chief domestic exports, 1986 (in £C1,000):

Grapes	3,758	Cigarettes	2,345
Grapefruit	6,164	Paper products	3,202
Lemons	4,285	Cement	3,539
Oranges	3,400	Clothing	41,038
Potatoes	20,228	Footwear	14,368
Wine	4,282		

In 1986 the EEC countries supplied 60·7% of the imports; Arab countries, 7·2%; others, 32·1%. Of the exports (1986), 37·8% went to Arab countries; 38·3% to EEC countries; 5·4% to Eastern Europe and 18·5% to other countries.

Total trade between Cyprus and UK (British Department of Trade returns, in £1,000 sterling):

	1983	1984	1985	1986	1987
Imports to UK	87,436	94,381	93,689	124,198	118,250
Exports and re-exports from UK	127,837	146,773	150,921	140,387	141,129

Tourism. Foreign tourists (1986), 900,700.

COMMUNICATIONS

Roads. In 1986 the total length of roads was 11,975 km, of which 5,813 km were paved and 6,162 km were earth or gravel roads. The main roads which are maintained by the Ministry of Communications and Works (Public Works Department) totalled 3,012 km, of which 1,279 km were paved. The total of urban streets was 1,785 km, of which 1,270 were paved. Village roads and streets totalled 4,417 km, of which 1,599 km were paved, the rest being of earth or gravel surface. There were also 2,761 km of unpaved forest roads. On 31 Dec. 1986, there were 281,889 motor vehicles including 1,850 buses and 54,928 goods vehicles.

The area controlled by the Government of the Republic and that occupied by Turkey are now served by separate transport systems, and there are no services linking the two areas.

Aviation. Nicosia airport has been closed since Aug. 1974. In 1987, 27 international airlines operated scheduled services between Cyprus and Europe, Africa and the Middle East, and another 16 airlines operated non-scheduled services. A new airport opened in Turkish Cypriot northern Cyprus in 1986. During 1986, 1,903,882 persons travelled and 24,744 tonnes of commercial air-freight was handled through Larnaca and Paphos airports. Paphos International airport started operations in 1983.

Shipping. In 1986, 4,455 ships of 12,429,280 net tons entered Cyprus ports. Ships under Cyprus registry numbered 1,473 of 9·8m. tons. Famagusta has been closed to international traffic since Oct. 1974.

Post and Broadcasting. In 1983 there were 53 post offices and 583 postal agencies. There are 17 post offices and 368 postal agencies in the Turkish occupied area. Telephones (1983) 158,000. Wireless licences issued (1981) were 247,000, including television licences.

Cyprus Broadcasting Corporation broadcasts mainly in Greek, but also in Turkish, English, and Armenian on medium-waves. The corporation also broadcasts on one TV channel. There are also 2 foreign broadcasting stations.

Cinemas (1982). In the Greek part of Cyprus there were 56 cinemas.

Newspapers (1983). There were 9 Greek, 4 Turkish and 1 English daily newspapers and 10 Greek, 6 Turkish and 1 English weeklies.

JUSTICE, RELIGION, EDUCATION AND WELFARE

Justice. The administration of justice is exercised by separate and independent judiciary. Under the 1960 Constitution and other legislation in force there are the Supreme Court of the Republic, Assize Courts, District Courts, Ecclesiastical Courts and Turkish Family Courts.

The Supreme Court is composed of 5-7 judges one of whom is the President of the Court. There is an Assize Court and a District Court for each district. The Assize Courts have unlimited criminal jurisdiction and may order the payment of compensation up to £C800. The District Courts exercise original civil and criminal jurisdiction, the extent of which varies with the composition of the Bench.

There is a Supreme Council of Judicature, consisting of the Attorney-General of the Republic, the President and Judges of the Supreme Court, entrusted with the appointment, promotion, transfers, termination of appointment and disciplinary control over all judicial officers, other than the Judges of the Supreme Court.

Religion. *See* Area and Population, p. 398.

Education. Until 31 March 1965 each community managed its own schooling through its respective Communal Chamber. Intercommunal education had been placed under the Minister of the Interior, assisted by a Board of Education for Intercommunal Schools, of which the Minister was the Chairman. In 1965 the Greek Communal Chamber was dissolved and a Ministry of Education was established to take its place. Intercommunal education has been placed under this Ministry.

Greek-Cypriot Education. Elementary education is compulsory and is provided free in 6 grades to children between 5½ and 12 years of age. In some towns and large villages there are separate junior schools consisting of the first three grades. Apart from schools for the deaf and blind, there are also 9 schools for handicapped children. In 1986–87 the Ministry ran 186 kindergartens for children in the age group 2½–5½; there were 244 privately run pre-primary schools. There were 373 primary schools with 54,254 pupils and 2,369 teachers in 1986–87.

Secondary education is also free and attendance for the first cycle is compulsory. The secondary school is 6 years, 3 years at the gymnasium followed by 3 years at the lykeion. In 1978–79 the lyceums of optional subjects were introduced, in which students can choose one of the 5 main fields of specialization: Classical, science, economics, commercial/secretarial and foreign languages. There are 6-year technical schools. In 1986–87 there were 103 secondary schools with 3,058 teachers and 44,308 pupils.

Post-secondary education is provided at the Pedagogical Academy, which organizes 3-year courses for the training of pre-primary and primary school teachers, and at the Higher Technical Institute, which provides 3-year courses for technicians in civil, electrical, mechanical and marine engineering. There is also a 2-year Forestry College (administered by the Ministry of Agriculture), a Hotel and Catering Institute, the Mediterranean Institute of Management (Ministry of Labour and Social Insurance) and a 3-year Nurses' School (Ministry of Health). Adult education is conducted through youth centres in rural areas, foreign language institutes in the towns and private institutions offering courses in business administration and secretarial work.

In 1985–86, 10,312 students were studying in universities abroad, mainly in Greece, the UK, USA, Federal Republic of Germany and Italy.

Turkish-Cypriot Education. The Office of Education of the Turkish Community of Cyprus caters for some 18% of the island's population and (1976) administered 10 kindergartens, 167 elementary schools (16,014 pupils), 18 secondary schools (7,190 pupils), 6 technical schools (735 pupils) and 1 teacher-training college (13 students). There were 43 evening institutes for adult education.

Greek is the language of 82% of the population and Turkish of 18%. English is widely spoken. English and French are compulsory subjects in secondary schools. Illiteracy is largely confined to older people.

Social Security. The administration of the social-security services in Cyprus is in the hands of the Ministry of Labour and Social Insurance, with the Ministry of Health providing medical services through public clinics and hospitals on a means test, except medical treatment for employment accidents, which is given free to all insured employees and financed by the Social Insurance Scheme.

DIPLOMATIC REPRESENTATIVES

Of Cyprus in Great Britain (93 Park St., London, W1Y 4ET)
High Commissioner: Tasos Panayides.

Of Great Britain in Cyprus (Alexander Pallis St., Nicosia)
High Commissioner: W. J. A. Wilberforce, CMG.

Of Cyprus in the USA (2211 R. St., NW, Washington, D.C., 20008)
Ambassador: Andrew J. Jacovides.

Of the USA in Cyprus (Therissos St., Nicosia)
Ambassador: Richard W. Boehm.

Of Cyprus to the United Nations
Ambassador: Constantine Moushoutas.

'TURKISH REPUBLIC OF NORTHERN CYPRUS'

HISTORY. See p. 398.

AREA AND POPULATION. The Turkish Republic of Northern Cyprus occupies 3,355 sq. km (about 37% of the island of Cyprus) and its population was estimated in 1986 to be 162,676. Population of principal towns (1985): Nicosia, 37,400; Famagusta, 19,428; Kyrenia, 6,902; Morphou, 10,179; Lefka, 3,785. Ethnic groups: Turks, 158,225; Greeks, 733; Maronites, 368; Others, 961.

CONSTITUTION AND GOVERNMENT. The Turkish Republic of Northern Cyprus was proclaimed on 15 Nov. 1983. The President is Rauf R. Denktash, and there is a council of Ministers comprised in Nov. 1987 of:

Prime Minister: Derviş Eroğlu.
Foreign Affairs and Defence: Kenan Atakol. *Education and Culture:* Salih Coşar. *Economy, Industry and Trade:* Erdal Onurhan. *Health and Social Assistance:* Mustafa Erbilen. *Agriculture and Forestry:* Aytaç Beşeşler. *Housing:* Onay Demirciler. *Finance and Customs:* Mehmet Bayram. *Public Works, Communications and Tourism:* Nazif Borman. *Youth, Sports and Labour:* Günay Caymaz. *Interior, Rural Affairs and Natural Resources:* Taşkent Atasayan.

A 50-seat Legislative Assembly was elected in June 1985; 24 seats were won by the *Ulusal Birlik Partisi* (National Unity Party), 12 by the Cumhuriyetçi Türk Partisi (Turkish Republican Party), 9 by the Toplumcu Kurtuluş Partisi (Communal Liberation Party) and 4 by the Yeni Doğuş Partisi (Revival Party).

Budget. The 1987 Budget balanced at 103,079m. Turkish lire.

Currency. The Turkish lire is used throughout Northern Cyprus.

Trade. Imports in 1986 amounted to 102,461m. and exports to 35,018m. Turkish lire.

Tourism. There were 131,492 tourists in 1986.

Books of Reference

Statistical Information: Statistics and Research Department, Nicosia.
North Cyprus Almanack, London, 1987
Attalides, M., *Cyprus Nationalism and International Politics.* Edinburgh, 1979
Bitsios, D. S., *Cyprus: The Vulnerable Republic.* Thessaloniki, 1975
Crawshaw, N., *The Cyprus Revolt: An Account of the Struggle for Union with Greece.* London, 1978
Denktash, R., *The Cyprus Triangle.* London, 1982
Georghallides, G. S., *A Political and Administrative History of Cyprus 1918–1926.* Nicosia, 1979
Halil, K., *The Rape of Cyprus.* London, 1982
Hill, Sir George F., *A History of Cyprus.* 4 vols. Cambridge, 1940–52
Hitchins, C., *Cyprus.* London, 1984
Hunt, D., *Footprints in Cyprus.* London, 1982
Kitromilides, P. M., and Evriviades, M. L., *Cyprus,* [Bibliography]. Oxford and Santa Barbara, 1982
Kyle, K., *Cyprus.* London, 1984
Loizos, P., *The Heart Grows Bitter: A Chronicle of Cypriot War Refugees.* CUP, 1982
Mayes, S., *Makarios.* London, 1981
Oberling, P., *The Road to Bellapais: The Turkish Cypriot Exodus to Northern Cyprus.* Boulder, 1982
Polyviou, P. G., *Cyprus: The Tragedy and the Challenge.* London, 1975.—*Cyprus in Search of a Constitution.* Nicosia, 1976.—*Cyprus: Conflict and Negotiation, 1960–1980.* London, 1980
St John-Jones, L. W., *The Population of Cyprus.* London, 1983

CZECHOSLOVAKIA

Capital: Prague
Population: 15·5m. (1986)
GNP per capita: US$8,700 (1985)

Československá Socialistická Republika

HISTORY. The Czechoslovak State came into existence on 28 Oct. 1918, when the Czech *Národní Výbor* (National Committee) took over the government of the Czech lands upon the dissolution of Austria–Hungary. Two days later the Slovak National Council manifested its desire to unite politically with the Czechs. On 14 Nov. 1918 the first Czechoslovak National Assembly declared the Czechoslovak State to be a republic with T. G. Masaryk as President (1918–35).

The Treaty of St Germain-en-Laye (1919) recognized the Czechoslovak Republic, consisting of the Czech lands (Bohemia, Moravia, part of Silesia) and Slovakia. To these lands were added as a trust the autonomous province of Subcarpathian Ruthenia.

This territory was broken up for the benefit of Germany, Poland and Hungary by the Munich agreement (29 Sept. 1938) between UK, France, Germany and Italy.

In March 1939 the German-sponsored Slovak government proclaimed Slovakia independent, and Germany incorporated the Czech lands into the Reich as the 'Protectorate of Bohemia and Moravia'. A government-in-exile, headed by Dr Beneš, was set up in London in July 1940.

Liberation by the Soviet Army and US Forces was completed by May 1945.

Territories taken by Germans, Poles and Hungarians were restored to Czechoslovak sovereignty. Subcarpathian Ruthenia was transferred to the USSR.

Elections were held in May 1946, at which the Communist Party obtained about 38% of the votes.

A coalition government under a Communist Prime Minister, Klement Gottwald, remained in power until 20 Feb. 1948, when 12 of the non-Communist ministers resigned in protest against infiltration of Communists into the police.

In Feb. a predominantly Communist government was formed by Gottwald. In May elections resulted in an 89% majority for the government and President Beneš resigned.

In the first months of 1968 mounting pressure for liberalization culminated in the overthrow of the Stalinist President and Party Secretary, Antonín Novotný, and his associates. Under a new leadership the Communist Party introduced in April 1968 an 'Action Programme' of far-reaching political and economic reforms.

Soviet pressure to abandon this programme was exerted between May and Aug. 1968, and finally, Warsaw Pact forces occupied Czechoslovakia on 21 Aug. The enforced Moscow agreement of 26 Aug. bound the Czechoslovak government to a policy of 'normalization' (*i.e.*, abandonment of most reforms) and to the stationing of Soviet forces on Czechoslovak soil. This situation was confirmed by the Czechoslovak–Soviet 'Status of Forces Agreement' of 16 Oct. In 1969–1970 Soviet pressure led to extensive changes in the Party and Government. In Oct. 1969 Czechoslovakia repudiated its condemnation of the Warsaw Pact invasion.

A Czechoslovak–Soviet 20-year Treaty of Friendship, Co-operation and Mutual Assistance was signed in May 1970. Since 1977 a dissident civil rights movement 'Charter 77' has been active despite official efforts to suppress it.

On 11 Dec. 1973 the German Federal Republic and Czechoslovakia signed a treaty normalizing relations and annulling the Munich agreement of 1938. This was ratified by both countries' parliaments in July 1974.

AREA AND POPULATION. Czechoslovakia is bounded north-west by the German Democratic Republic, north by Poland, east by the USSR, south by

Hungary and Austria and south-west by the Federal Republic of Germany. At the census of 11 Nov. 1980 the population was 15,283,095 (4,991,168 in Slovakia; 7·9m. females). Population in 1986, 15,520,839 (Slovakia, 5,177,441; females 7,960,979). There are 12 administrative regions *(Kraj)*, one of which is the capital, Prague (Praha) and one the capital of Slovakia, Bratislava.

Region	Chief city	Area in sq. km	Population 1986
Czech			
Prague	—	495	1,190,576
Středočeský	Prague (Praha)	11,003	1,139,116
Jihočeský	České Budějovice	11,345	694,928
Západočeský	Plzeň (Pilsen)	10,876	874,152
Severočeský	Ústí nad Labem	7,810	1,181,818
Východočeský	Hradec Králové	11,240	1,245,474
Jihomoravský	Brno	15,028	2,075,180
Severomoravský	Ostrava	11,067	1,956,753
Slovak			
Bratislava	—	367	413,002
Západoslovenský	Bratislava	14,491	1,713,750
Středoslovenský	Banská Bystrica	17,986	1,575,887
Východoslovenský	Košice	16,195	1,457,452

The area of Czechoslovakia is 127,903 sq. km (Slovakia, 49,039 sq. km). Population density in 1986: 121 per sq. km. Growth rate in 1985, 2·7 per 1,000. Expectation of life in 1985 was 67 (males); 74 (females).

Ethnic minorities have equal political and cultural rights. In 1985 there were (in 1,000): Czechs, 9,805; Slovaks, 4,809; Hungarians, 588; Poles, 71; Germans, 58; Ukrainians, 47; Russians, 8. There were 303,000 gipsies in 1983.

Official languages are Czech and Slovak.

The population of the principal towns in 1986 was as follows (in 1,000):

Prague (Praha)	1,194	Hradec Králové	100	Prešov	83
Bratislava	417	Pardubice	94	Banská Bystrica	78
Brno	385	České Budějovice	94	Karviná	75
Ostrava	328	Havířov	92	Kladno	73
Košice	222	Žilina	92	Trnava	70
Plzeň	175	Ústí nad Labem	91	Most	65
Olomouc	106	Gottwaldov	86	Frýdek-Místek	63
Liberec	101	Nitra	85	Martin	62

Vital statistics for calendar years:

	Live births	Marriages	Divorces	Deaths
1983	228,701	120,458	36,254	185,688
1984	226,595	121,376	37,422	182,351
1985	225,193	119,176	38,289	182,581

Infant mortality in 1985 (per 1,000 live births), 14·5. Abortion rate per 1,000 live births, in 1985: Czech Lands, 728; Slovakia, 504. Abortion law was liberalized in 1986.

CLIMATE. A humid continental climate, with warm summers and cold winters. Precipitation is generally greater in summer, with thunderstorms. Autumn, with dry, clear weather and spring, which is damp, are each of short duration. Prague. Jan. 29·5°F (−1·5°C), July 67°F (19·4°C). Annual rainfall 19·3″ (483mm). Brno. Jan. 31°F (−0·6°C), July 67°F (19·4°C). Annual rainfall 21″ (525mm).

CONSTITUTION AND GOVERNMENT. The 1960 constitution remains in force as amended by Constitutional Acts 143 and 144 of 1968. For details of previous constitutions, *see* THE STATESMAN'S YEAR-BOOK, 1968–69, pp. 927–28.

Since 1 Jan. 1969 Czechoslovakia has been a federal socialist republic consisting of two nations of equal rights: the Czech Socialist Republic (the Czech lands, previously Bohemia, Moravia and part of Silesia), and the Slovak Socialist Republic (Slovakia). Each Republic is governed by a National Council (the Czech with 200 deputies, the Slovak with 150), which delegates to an overall Federal Assembly responsibility for constitutional and foreign affairs, defence and important economic decisions. The Federal Assembly consists of the Chamber of Nations, which has 75 Czech and 75 Slovak delegates, and the Chamber of the People, which has 200 deputies. Both Chambers are elected by direct universal suffrage. Since 1971 deputies are elected for a 5-year term so as to coincide with Communist Party congresses. Minimum age of voters is 18, of deputies, 21 years. At the elections of May 1986 a single list of National Front candidates was presented. Turnout was 10,884,947 from an electorate of 10,950,675 (99·39%).

President of the Republic: Gustáv Husák (born 1913), *President of the Federal Assembly:* Alois Indra.

The *de facto* primary source of power is the Communist Party of Czechoslovakia, of which the Communist Party of Slovakia (*First Secretary:* Jozef Lenárt) is a constituent part. Communists head the National Front, which incorporates the remaining political parties (Czechoslovak Socialist Party, Czechoslovak People's Party, Slovak Reconstruction Party, Slovak Freedom Party) and the trade unions and youth organizations. The Communist Party had 1,675,000 members in 1986. In March 1988 the Presidium consisted of Miloš Jakeš (*General Secretary*); Ladislav Adamec (*Deputy Prime Minister*); Vasil Bil'ak; Peter Colotka (*Deputy Prime Minister*); Gustáv Husák; Karel Hoffmann; Alois Indra; Antonín Kapek; Josef Kempný; Jozef Lenárt; Lubomír Štrougal (*Prime Minister*). Candidate members: Jan Fojtík, Josef Hamán, Vladimír Herman, Miloslav Hruškovič, Ignác Janák, František Pitra.

In March 1988 members of the government not in the Party Presidium included: Rudolf Rohlíček (*First Deputy Prime Minister*); 7 Deputy Prime Ministers Ladislav Gerle; Pavol Hrivák; Karol Laco; Matej Lúčan; Jaromír Obzina (*Chairman, State Commission for Scientific and Technological Development*); Svatopluk Potáč (*Chairman, State Planning Commission*); Miroslav Toman (*Agriculture*); (*other ministers*) Jan Sterba (*Foreign Trade*); Milán Václavík (*Defence*); František Ondřich (*Chairman, People's Control Commission*); Bohuslav Chňoupek (*Foreign*); Jaromír Žák (*Finance*); Vratislav Vajnar (*Interior*).

The Czech Prime Minister is Ladislav Adamec; the Slovak, Peter Colotka.

Local government is carried on by National Committees consisting of deputies elected for 5-year terms. There are 10 regional Committees, 2 City Committees with the same status for Prague and Bratislava, 108 district Committees and 7,979 town and community Committees. Elections were held in 1986. 197,404 candidates were elected.

National flag: White and red (horizontal), with a blue triangle of full depth at the hoist, point to the fly.

National anthem: Kde domov můj (words by J. K. Tyl; tune by F. J. Škroup, 1834); combined with, Nad Tatru sa blyska (words by J. Matuška, 1844).

DEFENCE. Defence is the responsibility of the Defence Council set up in Feb. 1969 and headed by the First Secretary of the Party.

The Warsaw Pact invasion of Aug. 1968 brought an estimated 500,000 occupation troops into the country. By early 1970 this number had been reduced to 80,000 Soviet troops, the presence of which is legalized by the Czech–Soviet 'Status of Forces' Agreement of Oct. 1968.

In Feb. 1969 the government announced an increase in defence capacity, and Czechoslovakia resumed participation in Warsaw Pact meetings.

Military service is for 2 years in the Army and in the Air Force.

Army. The Army had a strength (1988) of 145,000 (100,000 conscripts). It consists of 5 armoured, 5 motor rifle and 1 artillery divisions, 1 airborne brigade, 6 engineer battalions and 5 regiments of Civil Defence Troops. Equipment includes 3,500 T-54/-55/-72 tanks. There are also 2 paramilitary forces: Border Troops (11,000) and People's Militia (120,000).

Air Force. The Air Force is organized as a tactical force, under overall army command, and had a strength of some 56,000 personnel and 468 combat aircraft in 1988. Three interceptor regiments (each 3 squadrons of 14 aircraft) are equipped with MiG-23 and MiG-21 jets, and there are 4 regiments of Su-7, Su-20, Su-25, MiG-23 and MiG-21 ground attack aircraft, as well as Mi-24 gunship helicopters. MiG-21s and modified L-39 Albatros jet trainers are used for tactical reconnaissance. Transport units have a total of 60 Let L-410, An-24/26, Il-14 and Tu-134 aircraft and about 100 Mil Mi-2 (some armed), Mi-4, Mi-8 and Mi-17 helicopters. Training units are equipped with 2-seat MiG-23s and MiG-21s and Czech-built aircraft, including L-29 and L-39 Albatros jet advanced trainers and Zlin primary trainers. Surface-to-air ('Guideline', 'Goa', 'Ganef', 'Gainful' and 'Gaskin') missile units are operational.

INTERNATIONAL RELATIONS

Membership. Czechoslovakia is a member of UN, COMECON and the Warsaw Pact.

ECONOMY

Planning. For the first six 5-year plans *see* THE STATESMAN'S YEAR-BOOK, 1985–86. In 1980 some rationalizations in the planning system, which have become known as the 'Set of measures', were applied. The 7th 5-year plan ran from 1981 to 1985. National income rose by 11%, industrial production by 13%, agricultural by 9% (Targets were 14%, 18% and 10%). The eighth 5-year plan covers 1986–90. Targets include a growth in national income of 18% and in agricultural production of 6%. Emphasis is laid on intensive rather than extensive development and a more efficient use of resources. Cautious proposals for restructuring the economy after 1990 were outlined in the 'Principles of Reconstruction' announced in Jan. 1987.

Budget. Budgets for calendar years (in Kčs. 1m.):

	1979	1980	1981	1982	1983	1984	1985
Revenue	294,638	306,262	311,568	314,203	324,127	343,805	359,692
Expenditure	292,403	304,182	310,928	314,046	323,890	342,192	358,028

Main items of the 1988 budget were (in Kčs. 1,000m.): Revenue: from the economy, 258; direct taxes, 47. Expenditure: national economy, 90; health and social services, 96; defence, 27; administration, 4.

Currency. The monetary unit in the Czechoslovak Republic is the *koruna* (Kčs.) or crown of 100 *haler*. Notes in circulation: Kčs. 10, 20, 50, 100, 500. Coin: 5, 10, 20, 50 *halers*, and Kčs. 1, 2, 5. The *koruna* is based on a gold content of 0·123426 gramme of pure gold and pegged on the rouble at Kčs. 1·80 = R.1. The IMF did not approve this change of the par value, and Czechoslovak membership was terminated in 1954. Foreign currency reserves were US$4,832m. in 1987; gold reserves were US$1,832m. Official rates of exchange (Feb. 1988): £1 = Kčs. 16·10; US$1 = Kčs. 5·15. Commercial: £1 = Kčs. 9·25. Tourist: £1 = Kčs. 15·49.

The return of 18·4 tonnes of gold seized by Nazi Germany and held in London and New York since the nationalization of Western assets in 1948 was agreed in Jan. 1982 by the Czech, British and US governments in exchange for compensation of the asset-holders.

Banking. For previous banking history *see* THE STATESMAN'S YEAR-BOOK, 1971–72, pp. 858–59. The central bank and bank of issue is the State Bank (Statní Banka), which controls foreign exchange reserves, and is a savings bank and a commercial credit bank to enterprises, except foreign trade enterprises. These are financed by the Commercial Bank (Obchodní Banka) which carries out all foreign trade transactions. The Trade Bank (Živnostenská Banka) provides banking services for private foreign clients, and maintains branches abroad. There is also an Investment Bank (Investiční Banka), one of whose functions is to manage foreign securities. 'Foreign exchange points' (*e.g.*, hotels) have partial foreign exchange authorization. There were 18·8m. savings accounts totalling 5,069m. Kčs in 1985.

Weights and Measures. The metric system is in force.

ENERGY AND NATURAL RESOURCES

Electricity. Production of electricity in 1985: 80,627m. kwh. In 1986 there were 2 nuclear power stations, producing 14·5% of all electricity. Supply 120, 127 and 220 volts; 50 Hz.

Oil. There is an oil pipeline from the USSR with branches to Bratislava and Zaluzi.

Gas. A natural gas pipeline which supplies the German Federal and Democratic Republics, Austria and Italy as well as Czechoslovakia. A second is under construction.

Minerals. Czechoslovakia is not rich in minerals. There are hard and soft coal reserves (chief coalfields: Most, Chomutov, Kladno, Ostrava and Sokolov). There is also uranium, glass sand and salt, and small quantities of iron ore, graphite, copper and lead. Gold deposits were found near Prague in 1985. Production in 1985 (in tonnes): Coal, 25,738,000; lignite and brown coal, 104,315,000.

Agriculture. In 1985 there were 6·8m. hectares of agricultural land (4·8m. hectares arable, 0·8m. meadow, 0·8m. pasture), of which 4·3m. were held by collective farms, 2·1m. by state farms and 87,000 as private plots (maximum size 1 hectare).

In 1985 there were 1,677 collective farms with 997,798 members and 226 state farms with 166,432 employees. Crop production in 1986 (in 1,000 tonnes): Sugarbeet, 7,135; wheat, 5,305; potatoes, 3,512; barley, 3,530; maize, 992; rye, 547.

Livestock. In 1986: Cattle, 5,073,000 (including 1,815,000 milch cows); horses, 46,000; pigs, 6,833,000; sheep, 1,104,000; poultry, 49m. In 1985 production of meat was 1,748,680 tonnes (live weight); milk, 6,676m. litres; 5,499m. eggs. In 1985 there were 137,054 tractors. 45,509 hectares were irrigated in 1985.

Forestry. Czechoslovakia is a richly wooded country, and the timber industry is important. Forest area in 1986 was 4,585,814 hectares (50% spruce, 16% beech and pine, 7% oak). The area reafforested in 1985 was 75,751 hectares. The timber yield was 19·65m. cu. metres in 1984.

Fisheries. Total catch was 20m. tonnes in 1985.

INDUSTRY AND TRADE

Industry. Industrialization is well developed and antedates the Communist régime. All industry is nationalized.

Output in 1985 (in 1,000 tonnes): Pig-iron, 9,562; crude steel, 15,036; coke, 10,237; rolled-steel products, 11,040; cement, 10,265; paper, 964; sulphuric acid, 1,298; nitrogenous fertilizers, 582; phosphate fertilizers, 353; plastics, 1,100; synthetic fibres, 193; sugar, 969; beer, 23m. hectolitres; cars, 183,701 (no.).

Textile production (in 1m. metres) in 1985: Cotton, 606; linen, 95; woollen, 63; shoes, 131·4m. pairs (57·9m. leather).

Labour. There were 8,733,829 persons of employable age in 1985 (*i.e.*, males, 15–59; females 15–54), of whom 7·65m. (3·5m. women) were employed: 5·8m. in production (industry, 2·9m.; agriculture, 0·9m.; building, 0·6m.; commerce, 0·7m.); and 1·9m. in services.

A 5-day 42-hour week with 4 weeks annual holiday is standard. A new wage system of norms and differentials linked to productivity was introduced in 1985. Average monthly wage in 1984: Kčs. 2,837. In 1988 the trade union movement had 7·7m. members; chairman, Miroslav Zavadil.

Commerce. Total trade (in Kčs. 1m.) for calendar years:

	1980	1981	1982	1983	1984	1985
Imports	81,540	86,276	94,177	103,012	113,737	120,323
Exports	80,163	87,689	95,314	103,838	114,230	119,818

In 1985, trade with Communist countries amounted to 189,311m. Kčs. (107,650m. Kčs. with the USSR, 22,461m. Kčs. with the German Democratic Republic, 18,778m. Kčs. with Poland). The UK is Czechoslovakia's third biggest non-Communist trade partner after the Federal German Republic and Austria.

Major exports in 1985 (percentage of total): Machinery, 53; industrial consumer goods, 16·7; other finished products, 11·3. Imports: Machinery, 31·1; fuel, 31.

There are 11 foreign trade agencies (independent legal entities with their own capital run by state-appointed managers). Joint economic ventures with Western firms holding up to 49% of the equity have been permitted since 1985. Foreign hard-currency indebtedness was US$4,089m. in 1986.

In 1972 an Anglo-Czech Agreement on Co-operation was signed. Under this an Anglo-Czech Joint Commission was established to further the development of trade and industrial and scientific co-operation.

UK-Czechoslovak trade has been conducted since 1 Jan. 1975 on the basis of autonomous EEC measures.

Total trade between Czechoslovakia and UK for calendar years (British Department of Trade returns, in £1,000 sterling):

	1983	1984	1985	1986	1987
Imports to UK	101,302	117,188	120,017	125,399	141,472
Exports and re-exports from UK	69,456	78,075	100,452	108,841	114,101

Tourism. In 1985, 10,499,385 tourists visited Czechoslovakia (1,302,951 from the West) and 7,492,049 Czechoslovak tourists made visits abroad (194,141 to the West).

COMMUNICATIONS

Roads. In 1985 there were 73,809 km of motorways and first-class roads and in 1984 2,639,564 passenger cars. In 1985 state road transport carried 2,274m. passengers and 339m. tonnes of freight.

Railways. In 1986 the length of railway track was 13,116 km. Of this, 3,530 km were electrified. In 1986, 19,935m. passenger-km and 69,315m. tonne-km of freight were carried.

Aviation. Air transport is run by ČSA (Czechoslovak Airlines). The main airports are: Prague (Ruzyně), Brno (Cernovice), Bratislava (Vajnory), Olomouc (Holice), Košice (Barca). In 1985, 1·2m. passengers and 25,190 tonnes of freight were flown. There are 6 internal and 53 international flights from Prague. British Airways operates air traffic London–Prague, Air France Paris–Prague–Bucharest.

Shipping. In 1986 Czechoslovak Maritime Shipping had 14 freighters totalling 264,230 DWT, based on Szczecin. In 1985, 1,879m. tonnes of cargo were carried.

There are 475 km of inland waterways. Freight transport totalled 13·33m. tonnes in 1985.

Czechoslovak Danube Shipping operate 5 ships totalling 244,000 DWT in the Mediterranean from Bratislava, and Czechoslovak Elbe-Oder Shipping had a fleet of 284,500 DWT in 1985.

Post and Broadcasting. There were 5,101 post offices in 1985. Number of telephones in service in 1985 was 3,591,045. *Československý Rozhlas*, the governmental broadcasting station, broadcasts on 2 networks; 1 from Prague with 3 programmes in Czech and Slovak and 1 from Bratislava with 2 programmes in Slovak and additional broadcasts in Hungarian and Ukrainian. *Československá Televise* broadcast 2 television programmes nation-wide, including colour broadcasts. In 1984, 4·2m. people held wireless and 4·35m. TV licences.

Cinemas and Theatres (1985). There were 2,818 cinemas and 79 theatres. 44 full-length films were made.

Newspapers and Books (1985). There were 30 daily newspapers, including 12 in Slovak, and 1,047 other periodicals. The party daily *Rudé Právo* ('Red Justice') has a circulation of about 1m. 6,956 book titles were published in 102m. copies.

JUSTICE, RELIGION, EDUCATION AND WELFARE

Justice. The criminal and criminal procedure codes date from 1 Jan. 1962, as amended in April 1973.

There is a Federal Supreme Court and federal military courts, with judges elected by the Federal Assembly. Both republics have Supreme Courts and a network of regional and district courts whose professional judges are elected by the republican

National Councils. Lay judges are elected by regional or district local authorities. Local authorities and social organizations may participate in the decision-making of the courts.

Religion. Official surveys suggest that 20% of the population are religious believers. Churches are controlled by the Federal Secretariat for Church Affairs and the Ministries of Culture. In 1987 there were 18 different faiths with 5,500 clergy and 7,500 churches. The largest single church is the Roman Catholic (3·7m. members, 4,336 parishes 5,085 churches and 3,175 priests, 1985): its main support is in Slovakia. Cardinal František Tomášek was installed as archbishop of Prague in 1978. The archbishopric of Trnava is held by a bishop and that of Olomouc by an administrator. In 1988, 8 of the remaining 10 dioceses were directed by Government-appointed capitulary vicars. There were 2 seminaries authorized to train priests in 1986.

In 1986 there were 1·3m. non-Catholic church members, including 475,000 Hussites, 81,000 Czech Brethren with 670 congregations, 370,000 Slovak Lutherans in 2 districts with 15 associations of parishes, 36,000 Silesian Lutherans and 120,000 Reformed Christians with 7 associations of parishes. In 1981 there were 15,000 Jews (mainly in Prague, where there is a synagogue and, since 1984, a rabbi). In 1986 there were 150,000 Orthodox with 100 congregations in 4 dioceses. The Uniate Church was suppressed in 1950 but maintains a clandestine existence.

Education. In 1985–86 there were 11,477 kindergartens for children from 3 to 6 years of age, with 51,104 teachers and 681,515 pupils. Education is free and compulsory for 10 years. Children of 6 to 14 yrs attend primary school (grades 1 to 9). Selection then takes place for secondary schools (4 years), vocational secondary schools (4 years) or apprentice centres (2–4 years). University entrance is from secondary schools. The respective proportions of entrants are approximately 20%:20%:60%. In 1985–86 there were 6,332 primary schools with 2,074,403 pupils and 96,414 teachers, 343 secondary schools with 9,465 teachers and 134,392 pupils and 562 secondary vocational schools with 261,422 students and 16,740 teachers. In higher education in 1985–86, there were 136,944 (60,224 women) full-time students, and 19,131 teachers. There are 36 institutions of higher education, with 110 faculties. These include 5 universities—the Charles University in Prague (founded 1348); the Purkyně (formerly Masaryk) University in Brno (1919); the Comenius University in Bratislava (1919); the Palacký University in Olomouc (1573); the Šafárik University in Košice (1959); and 12 technical universities or institutes.

Welfare. Medical care is free. In 1985 Kčs. 30,993m. were spent on health insurance benefits. There were, in 1985, 229 hospitals with a total of 123,194 beds, and 55,871 doctors and dentists. Family allowances (Kčs. per month): 1 child, 200; 2 children, 650; 3, 1,210. Old age pensions averaging 67% of salary are paid at the age of 60 (men), 53–57 (women).

DIPLOMATIC REPRESENTATIVES

Of Czechoslovakia in Great Britain (25 Kensington Palace Gdns., London, W8 4QY)
Ambassador: Jan Fidler (accredited 30 May 1986).

Of Great Britain in Czechoslovakia (Thunovská 14, 11800 Prague 1)
Ambassador: Stephen Barrett, CMG.

Of Czechoslovakia in the USA (3900 Linnean Ave., NW, Washington, D.C., 20008)
Ambassador: Dr Miroslav Houštecký.

Of the USA in Czechoslovakia (Tržiste 15–12548 Praha, Prague)
Ambassador: Julian M. Niemczyk.

Of Czechoslovakia to the United Nations
Ambassador: Evžen Zápotocký.

Books of Reference

The Constitution of the Czechoslovak Socialist Republic. Prague, 1960
Statistická ročenka ČSSR [Statistical Yearbook]. Prague, annual since 1958
Historická statistická ročenka ČSSR. Prague, 1985
Czechoslovak Foreign Trade. Prague, monthly
August, F., and Rees, D., *Red Star over Prague.* London, 1984
Bradley, J. F. N. *Politics in Czechoslovakia, 1945–1971.* Lanham, 1981
Czechoslovak Chamber of Commerce and Industry. *Facts on Czechoslovak Foreign Trade.* Prague, annual since 1965.—*Your Trade Partners in Czechoslovakia.* Prague, 1986
Demek, J., and others, *Geography of Czechoslovakia.* Prague, 1971
Eidlin, F. H. *The Logic of 'Normalization': The Soviet Intervention in Czechoslovakia of 21 August 1968 and the Czechoslovak Response.* Columbia Univ. Press, 1980
Hermann, A. H., *A History of the Czechs.* London, 1975
Hejzlar, Z., and Kusin, V. V., *Czechoslovakia, 1968–1969.* New York, 1975
Husák, G., *Speeches and Writings.* Oxford, 1986
Jičinský, J., and Skála, J. *The Czechoslovak Federation,* Prague, 1969
Kalvoda, J., *The Genesis of Czechoslovakia.* New York, 1986
Kolafová, V., and Slaba, D. *Czech-English and English-Czech dictionary.* Prague, 1979
Korbel, J., *Twentieth-Century Czechoslovakia: The Meanings of its History.* Columbia Univ. Press, 1977
Krystufek, Z., *The Soviet Régime in Czechoslovakia.* Columbia Univ. Press, 1981
Kusin, V. V., *From Dubček to Charter 77.* Edinburgh, 1978
Littell, R. (ed.), *The Czech Black Book; prepared by the Institute of History of the Czechoslovak Academy of Sciences.* London, 1969
Mamatey, V. S., and Luža, R. (eds.), *A History of the Czechoslovak Republic 1918–1948.* Princeton Univ. Press, 1973
Mlynař, Z., *Night Frost in Prague: the End of Humane Socialism.* New York, 1980
Procházka, J., *English–Czech and Czech–English Dictionary.* 16th ed. London, 1959
Sejna, J. *We Will Bury You.* London, 1982
Short, D., *Czechoslovakia.* [Bibliography] Oxford and Santa Barbara, 1986
Sperling. W., *Tschechoslowakei: Beiträge zur Landeskunde Ostmitteleurapas.* Stuttgart, 1981
Stevens, J. N., *Czechoslovakia at the Crossroads: The Economic Dilemmas of Communism in Postwar Czechoslovakia.* Boulder, 1986
Suda, Z. L., *Zealots and Rebels: A History of the Communist Party in Czechoslovakia.* Stanford, 1980
Teplý, J., *Economie Nationale de la Tchécoslovaquie Contemporaine.* Paris, 1977
Wallace, W. V., *Czechoslovakia.* London, 1977

DENMARK

Kongeriget Danmark

Capital: Copenhagen
Population: 5·12m. (1987)
GNP per capita: US$7,533 (1985)

HISTORY. First organized as a unified state in the 10th century, Denmark acquired approximately its present boundaries in 1815, having ceded Norway to Sweden and its north German territory to Prussia. Denmark became a constitutional monarchy in 1849.

AREA AND POPULATION. According to the census held on 9 Nov. 1970 the area of Denmark proper was 43,075 sq. km (16,631 sq. miles) and the population 4,937,579. Population, Jan. 1987: 5,124,794.

Administrative divisions		Area (sq. km) 1987	Population 1970	Population 1987	Population 1987 per sq. km
København (Copenhagen)	(city)	88	622,773	469,706	5,328
Frederiksberg	(borough)	9	101,874	86,558	9,870
Københavns	(county)	526	615,343	606,870	1,154
Frederiksborg	,,	1,347	259,442	339,627	252
Roskilde	,,	891	153,199	213,476	240
Vestsjællands	,,	2,984	259,057	282,397	95
Storstrøms	,,	3,398	252,363	257,880	76
Bornholms	,,	588	47,239	46,839	80
Fyns	,,	3,486	432,699	456,483	131
Sønderjyllands	,,	3,938	238,062	249,805	63
Ribe	,,	3,131	197,843	216,967	69
Vejle	,,	2,997	306,263	328,849	110
Ringkøbing	,,	4,853	241,327	266,088	55
Aarhus	,,	4,561	533,190	589,108	129
Viborg	,,	4,122	220,734	230,760	56
Nordjyllands	,,	6,173	456,171	483,381	78
Total		43,092	4,937,579	5,124,794	119

The population is almost entirely Scandinavian; in Jan. 1987, of the inhabitants of Denmark proper, 95·4% were born in Denmark, including Faroe Islands and Greenland.

On 1 Jan. 1987 the population of the capital, Copenhagen (comprising Copenhagen, Frederiksberg and Gentofte municipalities), was 622,275 (including suburbs, 1,346,666); Aarhus, 255,932; Odense, 173,331; Aalborg, 154,853; Esbjerg, 80,825; Randers, 61,094; Kolding, 57,148; Helsingør, 56,618; Herning, 56,195; Horsens, 54,676.

Vital statistics for calendar years:

	Living births	Still births	Marriages	Divorces	Deaths	Emigration	Immigration
1982	52,658	269	24,330	14,621	55,368	28,328	28,223
1983	50,822	265	27,096	14,763	57,156	25,999	27,718
1984	51,800	230	28,624	14,490	57,109	25,053	29,035
1985	53,749	240	29,322	14,385	58,378	26,715	36,214
1986	55,312	242	30,773	14,490	58,100	27,928	38,932

Illegitimate births: 1983, 40·6%; 1984, 41·9%; 1985, 43%; 1986, 43·9%.

CLIMATE. The climate is much modified by marine influences, and the effect of the Gulf Stream, to give winters that are cold and cloudy but warm and sunny summers. In general, the east is drier than the west, though few places have more than 27″ (675 mm) of rain a year. Long periods of calm weather are exceptional and windy conditions are common. Copenhagen. Jan. 33°F (0·5°C), July 63°F

(17°C). Annual rainfall 22·8″ (571 mm). Esbjerg. Jan. 33°F (0·5°C), July 59°F (15°C). Annual rainfall 32″ (800 mm).

REIGNING QUEEN. Margrethe II, born 16 April 1940; married 10 June 1967 to Prince Henrik, born Count de Monpezat; *offspring:* Crown Prince Frederik, born 26 May 1968; Prince Joachim, born 7 June 1969. She succeeded to the throne on the death of her father, King Frederik IX, on 14 Jan. 1972.

Mother of the Queen: Queen Ingrid, born Princess of Sweden, 28 March 1910.
Sisters of the Queen: Princess Benedikte, born 29 April 1944 (married 3 Feb. 1968 to Prince Richard of Sayn-Wittgenstein-Berleburg); Princess Anne-Marie, born 30 Aug. 1946 (married 18 Sept. 1964 to King Constantine of Greece).

The crown of Denmark was elective from the earliest times. In 1448 after the death of the last male descendant of Swein Estridsen the Danish Diet elected to the throne Christian I, Count of Oldenburg, in whose family the royal dignity remained for more than 4 centuries, although the crown was not rendered hereditary by right till 1660. The direct male line of the house of Oldenburg became extinct with King Frederik VII on 15 Nov. 1863. In view of the death of the king, without direct heirs, the Great Powers signed a treaty at London on 8 May 1852, by the terms of which the succession to the crown of Denmark was made over to Prince Christian of Schleswig-Holstein-Sonderburg-Glücksburg, and to the direct male descendants of his union with the Princess Louise of Hesse-Cassel, niece of King Christian VIII of Denmark. In accordance with this treaty, a law concerning the succession to the Danish crown was adopted by the Diet, and obtained the royal sanction 31 July 1853. Linked to the constitution of 5 June 1953, a new law of succession, dated 27 March 1953, has come into force, which restricts the right of succession to the descendants of King Christian X and Queen Alexandrine, and admits the sovereign's daughters to the line of succession, ranking after the sovereign's sons.

Subjoined is a list of the kings of Denmark, with the dates of their accession, from the time of election of Christian I of Oldenburg:

House of Oldenburg

Christian I	1448	Christian IV	1588	Frederik V	1746
Hans	1481	Frederik III	1648	Christian VII	1766
Christian II	1513	Christian V	1670	Frederik VI	1808
Frederik I	1523	Frederik IV	1699	Christian VIII	1839
Christian III	1534	Christian VI	1730	Frederik VII	1848
Frederik II	1559				

House of Schleswig-Holstein-Sonderburg-Glücksburg

Christian IX	1863	Christian X	1912	Margrethe II	1972
Frederik VIII	1906	Frederik IX	1947		

CONSTITUTION AND GOVERNMENT. The present constitution of Denmark is founded upon the 'Grundlov' (charter) of 5 June 1953.

The legislative power lies with the Queen and the *Folketing* (Diet) jointly. The executive power is vested in the Queen, who exercises her authority through the ministers. The judicial power is with the courts. The Queen must be a member of the Evangelical-Lutheran Church, the official Church of the State. The Queen cannot assume major international obligations without the consent of the *Folketing*. The *Folketing* consists of one chamber. All men and women of Danish nationality of more than 18 years of age and permanently resident in Denmark possess the franchise and are eligible for election to the *Folketing*, which is at present composed of 179 members; 135 members are elected by the method of proportional representation in 17 constituencies. In order to attain an equal representation of the different parties, 40 *tillægsmandater* (additional seats) are divided among such parties which have not obtained sufficient returns at the constituency elections. Two members are elected for the Faroe Islands and 2 for Greenland. The term of the legislature is 4 years, but a general election may be called at any time.

The *Folketing* must meet every year on the first Tuesday in October. Besides its legislative functions, it appoints every 6 years judges who, together with the ordinary members of the Supreme Court *(Højesteret),* form the *Rigsret,* a tribunal which can alone try parliamentary impeachments. The ministers have free access to the House, but can vote only if they are members.

Folketing, elected 8 Sept. 1987: 54 Social Democrats, 11 Radical Liberals, 38 Conservatives, 27 Socialist People's Party, 9 Centre Democrats, 5 Common Cause, 4 Christian People's Party, 19 Liberals, 5 Left Socialists, 9 Progress Party, 2 Faroe Islands and 2 Greenland representatives.

The executive (called the State Council *(Statsraadet)* when acting with the Queen presiding) is a minority non-Socialist coalition government, consisting of the Conservatives, the Liberals, the Centre Democrats and the Christian People's Party; it was in Jan. 1987 as follows:

Prime Minister: Poul Schlüter.

Foreign Affairs: Uffe Ellemann-Jensen. *Finance:* Palle Simonsen. *Economy:* Knud Enggaard. *Justice:* Erik Ninn-Hansen. *Interior:* Thor Pedersen. *Environment:* Christian Christensen. *Education:* Bertel Haarder. *Social Affairs:* Mimi Stilling Jakobsen. *Agriculture:* Laurits Tørnae. *Inland Revenue:* Anders Fogh Rasmussen. *Defence:* Bernt Johan Collet. *Ecclesiastical Affairs:* Mette Madsen. *Energy:* Svend Erik Hovmand. *Fisheries and Nordic Affairs:* Lars P. Gammelgaard. *Labour:* Henning Dyremose. *Housing:* Flemming Kofod-Svendsen. *Culture and Communication:* H. P. Clausen. *Industry:* Niels Wilhjelm. *Public Works:* Frode Nør Christensen. *Health:* Agnette Laustsen.

The ministers are individually and collectively responsible for their acts, and if impeached and found guilty, cannot be pardoned without the consent of the *Folketing.*

In 1948 a separate legislature *(Lagting)* and executive *(Landsstyre)* were established for the Faroe Islands, to deal with specified local matters and in 1979 a separate legislature *(Landsting)* and executive *(Landsstyre)* were established for Greenland, also to deal with specified local matters.

National flag: Red with white Scandinavian cross (Dannebrog).

National anthems: Kong Kristian stod ved højen Mast (words by J. Ewald, 1778; tune by J. E. Hartmann, 1780) and Der er et yndigt land.

Local Government. For administrative purposes Denmark is divided into 275 municipalities *(kommuner)*; each of them has a district council of between 5 and 25 members, headed by an elected mayor. The city of Copenhagen forms a district by itself and is governed by a city council of 55 members, elected every 4 years, and an executive *(magistraten)*, consisting of the chief burgomaster *(overborgmesteren)* and 6 burgomasters, appointed by the city council for 4 years. There are 14 counties *(amtskommuner)*, each of which is administered by a county council *(amstråd)* of between 13 and 31 members, headed by an elected mayor. All councils are elected directly by universal suffrage and proportional representation for 4-year terms. A third council, the Metropolitan Council, with a constitution similar to the counties was established 1 April 1974. The Metropolitan Council is responsible for overall development within Metropolitan Copenhagen.

The counties and Copenhagen are superintended by the Ministry of Interior Affairs. The municipalities are superintended by 14 local supervision committees, headed by a state county prefect *(statsamtmand)* who is a civil servant appointed by the Queen.

DEFENCE. The Danish military defence is organized in accordance with the Defence Act of May 1982 and the overall organization of the Danish Armed Forces comprises the Defence Command, the Army, the Navy, the Air Force and interservice authorities and institutions. To this should be added the Home Guard, which is an indispensable part of Danish military defence. The Home Guard is based on the Home Guard Act of May 1982.

In accordance with the Defence Act the Chief of Defence has full command of the three services: the Army, the Navy and the Air Force. The Chief of Defence, and the Defence Staff constitute the Defence Command. The Inspector Generals of the Army, the Navy and the Air Force are members of the Defence Staff.

The Minister of Defence is assisted by a Defence Council consisting of the Chief of Defence, the Chief of Defence Staff, the Chief of Danish Operational Forces, the Inspector Generals of the Army, the Navy and the Air Force and the Chief of the Home Guard.

The Constitution of 1849 declared it the duty of every fit man to contribute to the national defence, and this provision is still in force. According to the Personnel Act of May 1982, the military personnel comprises officers, n.c.o.s and privates. Private personnel are provided by enlistment and by recruiting of volunteers. Selection of conscripts takes place at the age of 18–19 years, and the conscripts are normally called up for 9 months service ½–1½ years later. Afterwards conscripts may be recalled for refresher training or musters. The initial training period for conscripts in combat and engineer units is 12 months.

Army. The Army comprises field army formations and the local defence forces. The field army formations are organized in a covering force and in reserve units (comprising 6 regimental combat teams and some independent battalions). The covering force numbers about 13,600 men and comprises a standing force (regulars and conscripts with more than six months' service), and a supplementary force consisting of men newly released from service. The standing force are organized in standing brigade units, headquarters units and support units. The brigade units are organized in 5 mechanized infantry brigades. The field army is equipped with 200 medium battle tanks, 50 light tanks and about 650 armoured personnel carriers as well as artillery including 72 self-propelled howitzers. The Army has 14 Hughes 500 helicopters and 8 Supporter aircraft for observation and liaison. The local defence units consist of about 18,000 men organized in 9 infantry battalions and some artillery battalions. The men of the latest annual service groups form the troops of the line, while those of the previous years form the local defence, the reserve and the reserve for the Home Guard. The mobilization units of the field army and the local defence force will total about 58,000 men.

Navy. The Navy comprises the fleet and coast-defence which includes several permanent fortifications. The fleet includes 5 submarines, 2 frigates, 3 small frigates, 5 ocean escorts (for fishery protection and surveying duties), 10 fast missile craft, 6 fast torpedo boats, 4 ocean minelayers, 2 coastal minelayers, 6 coastal minesweepers, 3 torpedo recovery vessels, 22 patrol vessels, 7 coastal patrol launches, 2 oilers, 20 auxiliary vessels and the royal yacht. The Naval Air Arm comprises 8 Lynx helicopters (one is carried in each of the ocean escorts).

Total strength of the Navy is 7,900 officers and men (1,200 officers, 3,200 regular ratings, 990 national service, 2,500 civilians). Reserves total 10,000 (the mobilization force is 4,600 men).

The Naval Home Guard has 35 vessels and 4,800 officers and men.

Air Force. The operational units of the Air Force comprise 8 surface-to-air missile squadrons and 6 flying squadrons.

The air defence force consists of the 8 Hawk surface-to-air missile squadrons and 4 all-weather air-defence squadrons with a total of 52 F-16s. All squadrons have an air-defence and a fighter-bomber rôle.

The fighter bomber force comprises 2 squadrons with a total of 32 F 35 Drakens, one unit having a secondary reconnaissance role.

In addition the Air Force has a number of supplementary units, including 1 transport squadron (C-130 Hercules and Gulfstream III), 1 helicopter rescue squadron (S-61As), and a control and warning system.

Total strength of the Air Force is about 9,200, and the mobilization force about 10,000 men.

Home Guard. The overall Home Guard organization comprises the Home Guard Command, the Army Home Guard, the Naval Home Guard and the Air Force Home Guard.

The personnel of the Home Guard is recruited on a voluntary basis. The personnel establishment of the Home Guard is at present about 74,500 persons (58,000 in the Army Home Guard, 4,800 in the Navy Home Guard and 11,700 in the Air Force Home Guard).

INTERNATIONAL RELATIONS

Membership. Denmark is a member of UN, NATO, OECD and the European Communities.

ECONOMY

Budget. The budget *(Finanslovforslag)* must be laid before the Parliament *(Folketing)* not later than 4 months before the beginning of a new fiscal year.

The following shows the actual revenue and expenditure as shown in central government accounts for the calendar years 1984, 1985 and 1986, the approved budget figures for 1987 and the budget for 1988 (in 1,000 kroner):

	1984	1985	1986	1987	1988
Revenue	142,377,099	160,156,688	193,545,000	199,051,000	206,678,000
Expenditure	186,019,866	186,495,042	185,703,000	199,915,000	208,248,000

Receipts and expenditures of special government funds and expenditures on public works are included.

The 1988 budget envisages revenue of 106,540m. kroner from income and property taxes and 117,180m. from consumer taxes.

The central government debt on 31 Dec. 1986 amounted to 421,049m. kroner.

Currency. The monetary unit is the *krone* of 100 *øre*. In 1931 Denmark went off the gold standard, as established in 1873.

Small change: 10-kroner and 5-kroner pieces of copper-nickel, 1-krone pieces of copper-nickel; 25-øre and 10-øre pieces of copper-nickel, and 5-øre pieces of copper–steel–copper clad. In March 1988, £1 = 11·44 *kroner*; US$1 = 6·45 *kroner*.

Banking. On 31 Dec. 1986 the accounts of the National Bank balanced at 124,437m. kroner. The assets included official net foreign reserves of 35,864m. kroner. The liabilities included notes and coin of 21,339m. kroner. On 31 Dec. 1986 there were 78 commercial banks, with deposits of 293,293m. kroner, and 144 savings banks, with deposits of 114,063m. kroner. Their advances amounted to 245,921m. kroner and 105,067m. kroner respectively. On 31 Dec. 1986 the money supply was 347,779m. kroner.

On 31 Dec. 1984 there were 71 other banks for commercial, agricultural and industrial purposes; their deposits amounted to 219,503m. kroner; advances were 147,818m. kroner.

Weights and Measures. The use of the metric system of weights and measures has been obligatory in Denmark since 1 April 1912.

ENERGY AND NATURAL RESOURCES

Electricity. Production (1986) 26,994m. kwh. Supply 220 volts; Hz 50.

Oil. Production (1987) 4·5m. tonnes.

Agriculture. Land ownership is widely distributed. In June 1986 (census) there were 89,659 holdings with at least 5 hectares of agricultural area (or at least a production equivalent to that from 5 hectares of barley). About 10,000 holdings were below the sample threshold. There were 17,364 small holdings (with less than 10 hectares), 57,767 medium sized holdings (10–50 hectares) and 14,528 holdings with more than 50 hectares.

The number of agricultural workers declined from 120,442 in July 1961 to 25,743 in June 1985.

In June 1986 the cultivated area was utilized as follows (in 1,000 hectares): Grain, 1,578; peas and beans, 145; root crops, 221; other crops, 306; green fodder and grass, 566; fallow, 3; total cultivated area, 2,819.

		Area (1,000 hectares)			*Production (in 1,000 tonnes)*	
Chief crops	*1984*	*1985*	*1986*	*1984*	*1985*	*1986*
Wheat	333	339	353	2,446	1,972	2,177
Rye	122	126	120	608	565	546
Barley	1,180	1,094	1,078	6,072	5,251	5,134
Oats [1]	34	42	27	158	168	111
Potatoes	31	30	31	1,121	1,100	1,129
Other root crops	206	198	190	12,304	11,379	10,563

[1] Including mixed grain.

Livestock, 1986: Horses, 30,000; cattle, 2,495,000; pigs, 9,321,000; poultry, 14,008,000.

Production (in 1,000 tonnes) in 1986: Milk, 5,111; butter, 112; cheese, 254; beef, 264; pork and bacon, 1,195; eggs, 81.

In June 1986 farm tractors numbered 168,574 and harvester-threshers, 34,054.

Fisheries. The total value of the fish caught was (in 1m. kroner): 1950, 156; 1955, 252; 1960, 376; 1965, 650; 1970, 854; 1975, 1,442; 1980, 2,888; 1984, 3,645; 1985, 3,542; 1986, 3,554.

INDUSTRY AND TRADE

Industry. The following table sets forth the gross factor income (in 1m. kroner) by industrial origin in 3 calendar years:

	1984		1985		1986	
	Current Prices	1980 Prices	Current Prices	1980 Prices	Current Prices	1980 Prices
Agriculture, fur-farming, forestry, etc.	28,549	21,376	27,970	21,215	27,733	21,451
Fishing	2,481	2,211	2,451	2,100	2,684	1,911
Total	31,030	23,588	30,421	23,316	30,417	23,363
Mining and quarrying	4,253	2,973	6,719	4,836	4,745	6,486
Manufacturing	94,736	69,907	102,933	72,031	113,766	73,971
Electricity, gas and water	5,686	5,450	6,323	5,478	8,195	6,017
Construction	27,073	18,288	30,214	19,143	35,759	21,565
Total	131,748	96,616	146,189	101,489	162,465	108,040
Wholesale and retail trade	64,971	45,807	73,697	48,278	79,010	50,951
Restaurants and hotels	6,032	4,484	6,825	4,633	8,173	4,872
Transport and storage	30,395	20,706	33,537	20,976	35,341	21,801
Communication	8,659	5,204	9,684	5,689	9,766	5,771
Financing and insurance	15,278	11,178	17,365	11,979	22,041	13,383
Dwellings	44,118	30,404	47,407	30,714	50,485	31,154
Business services	24,590	17,376	28,648	19,355	30,955	19,803
Market services of education, health	5,929	4,247	6,265	4,343	6,692	4,472
Recreational and cultural services	4,397	3,099	4,725	3,063	4,819	3,182
Household services, incl. auto repair	13,278	9,082	14,386	9,379	15,553	9,767
Total	217,647	151,586	242,539	158,408	262,835	165,157
Other producers, excl. government	3,076	2,207	3,410	2,345	3,770	2,459
Producers of government services	108,646	79,391	114,950	81,037	118,719	81,473
Total	111,722	81,598	118,360	83,382	122,488	83,932

	1984		1985		1986	
	Current Prices	1980 Prices	Current Prices	1980 Prices	Current Prices	1980 Prices
Imputed bank service charges	−15,220	−11,109	−16,894	−11,545	−21,416	−13,994
Gross domestic product at factor cost	476,926	342,280	520,656	355,048	556,789	366,496
Plus indirect taxes	102,353 }	62,507	113,123 }	66,772	130,163 }	69,630
Less subsidies	18,539 }		18,554 }		19,766 }	
Gross domestic product at market prices	560,740	404,787	615,225	421,820	667,186	436,127

According to the registration of business units for VAT settlement there were in 1983 a total of 33,000 manufacturing enterprises. In the following table 'number of wage-earners' refers to 6,600 establishments with 6 employees or more (1985), while 'gross-output' and 'value-added' cover 3,240 kind-of-activity units of enterprises with 20 employees or more (1985).

Branch of industry	Number of wage-earners (1,000)[1]	Gross output in factor values (1m. kroner)	Value added in factor values (1m. kroner)
Mining and quarrying	0·8	657	487
Food products	45·2	85,431	25,448
Beverages	7·2	6,934	4,041
Tobacco	1·7	2,031	1,009
Textiles	11·6	7,930	3,429
Wearing apparel	9·1	3,830	1,853
Leather and products	0·7	451	186
Footwear	1·7	1,015	399
Wood products	7·5	4,803	2,057
Furniture and fixtures	11·9	6,385	3,228
Paper and products	7·0	6,759	2,781
Printing, publishing	14·0	11,178	7,151
Industrial chemicals	12·5	23,748	11,450
Other chemical products, petroleum refineries, petroleum coal products and rubber	2·6	12,311	1,765
Plastic products	6·3	4,645	2,408
Pottery, china, glass and products	3·8	1,531	1,030
Non-metal products	9·3	8,077	4,591
Iron, steel and non-ferrous metals	4·6	4,486	1,696
Metal products	26·3	17,980	8,460
Machinery	40·4	27,702	14,698
Electrical machinery	16·7	12,681	6,589
Transport equipment	21·2	13,932	6,061
Controlling equipment	6·1	5,047	3,105
Other industries	4·4	3,560	1,957
Total manufacturing	272·6	273,104	115,879

[1] Preliminary, excluding dairies.

Labour. In 1986, 6% of the working population lived on agriculture, forestry and fishery, 21% on industries and handicrafts, 7% on construction, 14% on commerce, etc., 7% on transport and communication, and 45% on administration, professional services, etc.

Commerce. The following table shows the value, in 1,000 kroner, of special trade imports and exports (including trade with the Faroe Islands and Greenland) for calendar years:

	1982	1983	1984	1985	1986[1]
Imports	138,864,990	148,896,460	171,825,816	191,562,564	184,639,543
Exports	128,172,776	146,800,268	179,338,909	179,577,142	171,613,867

[1] Preliminary.

Imports and exports (in 1m. kroner) for calendar years:

| | 1985 | | 1986 [1] | |
Leading commodities	Imports	Exports	Imports	Exports
Live animals, meat, etc.	575	20,774	768	19,524
Dairy products, eggs	648	7,388	617	6,878
Fish and fish preparations	3,812	8,973	4,729	102,187
Cereals and cereal preparations	1,392	4,495	1,358	4,279
Sugar and sugar preparations	634	1,237	719	1,283
Coffee, tea, cocoa, etc.	2,669	564	2,915	609
Feeding stuff for animals	3,921	1,502	3,786	1,383
Wood, lumber and cork	2,676	568	2,861	495
Textiles, fibres, yarns, fabrics, etc.	7,112	4,124	6,972	4,025
Fuels, lubricants, etc.	33,152	9,719	16,409	5,282
Pharmaceutical products	2,343	5,260	2,615	5,429
Fertilizers, etc.	2,642	1,309	2,084	966
Metals, manufactures of metals	13,325	6,738	13,346	7,086
Machinery, electrical, equipment, etc.	35,493	35,101	38,956	35,298
Transport equipment	15,241	8,438	19,336	6,010

[1] Preliminary.

Distribution of Danish foreign trade (in 1,000 kroner) according to countries of origin and destination, for calendar years:

| | Imports | | | Exports | | |
Countries	1984	1985	1986 [1]	1984	1985	1986 [1]
Belgium	5,051,661	6,363,654	6,738,785	2,803,521	3,253,814	3,307,503
Finland	6,013,288	6,337,703	5,631,728	3,230,781	3,711,536	3,837,687
France	7,655,780	8,527,353	9,318,732	7,313,209	7,924,526	8,911,679
Germany (Fed. Rep.)	35,002,130	40,383,642	43,563,835	26,644,433	28,460,093	28,870,780
Norway	7,066,888	7,747,222	6,744,475	10,515,953	12,071,284	13,068,324
Sweden	23,944,744	24,991,263	22,777,949	18,874,379	21,692,076	19,474,585
Switzerland	3,176,132	3,589,022	3,956,351	3,067,615	3,412,264	3,565,046
UK	15,458,651	18,009,597	14,005,205	21,228,401	21,908,237	20,076,696
USA	8,930,259	11,339,399	9,744,057	15,914,502	18,148,661	14,542,162
Allied forces in Fed. Rep. Germany	—	—	—	210,042	223,572	192,930

[1] Preliminary.

Total trade between Denmark (without the Faroe Islands) and UK (British Department of Trade returns, in £1,000 sterling):

	1983	1984	1985	1986	1987
Imports to UK	1,512,620	1,660,447	1,715,233	1,752,174	1,873,495
Exports and re-exports from UK	1,159,184	1,197,381	1,371,556	1,211,637	1,231,097

Tourism. In 1986, foreigners visiting Denmark spent some 14,232m. kroner. In 1986 foreigners spent 4.34m. nights in hotels and 3.78m. nights at camping sites.

Industrial Statistics. Danmarks Statistik. Copenhagen (annually)
Quarterly Statistics for the Industry: Commodity Statistics. Danmarks Statistik, Copenhagen
Statistics on Agriculture, Horticulture and Forestry. Danmarks Statistik. Copenhagen (annually)
Agricultural Statistics 1900–1965. Vol. I: *Agricultural Area and Harvest and Utilization of Fertilizers.*—Vol. II: *Livestock and Livestock Products, and Consumption of Feeding Stuffs.* Danmarks Statistik. Copenhagen, 1968–69
External Trade of Denmark. Danmarks Statistik, Copenhagen
Danish Industry in Facts and Figures. Federation of Danish Industries. Copenhagen (annually)
Energy Supply of Denmark, 1900–58 and 1948–65. Danmarks Statistik. Copenhagen, 1959, 1967. Annual Supplements 1966–75 have been published in Statistical News
Report on Fisheries. Ministry of Fisheries, Copenhagen (annually)
Nash, E. F., and Attwood, E. A., *The Agricultural Policies of Britain and Denmark.* London, 1961

COMMUNICATIONS

Roads. Denmark proper had (1 Jan. 1986), 593 km of motorways, 3,996 km of other state roads, 7,049 km of provincial roads and 58,509 km of commercial roads. Motor vehicles registered at 31 Dec. 1986 comprised 1,545,704 passenger cars, 274,991 lorries, 12,176 taxicabs (including 5,528 for private hire), 8,105 buses and 41,868 cycles.

Railways. In 1986 there were 2,471 km of State railways (199 km electrified), which carried 4,536m. passenger-km and 1,791m. tonne-km. There were also 494 km of private railways in 1985.

Aviation. On 1 Oct. 1950 the 3 Scandinavian airlines, Det Danske Luftfartsselskab, ABA and DNL, combined in Scandinavian Airlines System. In 1985–86 SAS flew 136m. km and carried 11,708,000 passengers.

SAS inaugurated its transpolar routes Copenhagen–Los Angeles on 15 Nov. 1954 and Copenhagen–Tôkyô on 25 Feb. 1957, and its trans-Asian express route Copenhagen–Bangkok–Singapore *via* Tashkent on 4 Nov. 1967.

Shipping. On 31 Dec. 1986 the Danish merchant fleet consisted of 2,795 vessels (above 20 GRT) of 5,040,433 GRT.

In 1986, 36,751 vessels of 64m. GRT entered the Danish ports, unloading 45m. tonnes and loading 21m. tonnes of cargo; traffic by passenger ships and ferries is not included.

Post and Broadcasting. There were, in 1985, 1,293 post offices. On 31 Dec. 1985 the length of telephone circuits of private companies was 13,247,560 km. On 31 Dec. 1985 there were 4,005,495 telephone instruments. Postal revenues, 1985, 10,070m. kroner; expenditure, 8,166m. kroner.

Danmarks Radio is the government broadcasting station and is financed by licence fees. Television is broadcast by *Danmarks Radio* with colour programmes by PAL system. Number of receivers (1986): Combined radio and television, 1·98m., including 1·63m. colour sets; radio only, 0·15m.

Cinemas. In 1985 there were 429 cinema rooms with a seating capacity of 75,919.

Newspapers. In 1986 there were 47 daily newspapers with a combined circulation of 1·88m. on weekdays.

JUSTICE, RELIGION, EDUCATION AND WELFARE

Justice. The lowest courts of justice are organized in 84 tribunals *(byretter)*, where cases are dealt with by a single judge. The tribunals at Copenhagen have 34 judges, Aarhus 13, Odense 10, Aalborg 9, and the other tribunals have 1 to 4. Cases of greater consequence are dealt with by the superior courts *(Landsretterne)*; these courts are also courts of appeal for the above-named cases. Of superior courts there are two: *Østre Landsret* in Copenhagen with 46 judges, *Vestre Landret* in Viborg with 23 judges. From these an appeal lies to the Supreme Court *(Højesteret)* in Copenhagen, composed of 15 judges. Judges under 65 years of age can be removed only by judicial sentence.

In 1985, 13,674 men and 1,484 women were convicted of violations of the criminal code, fines not included. In 1986, the daily average population in penal institutions, local prisons, etc., was 3,274 men and 134 women, of whom 743 men and 47 women were on remand.

Religion. At the Reformation in 1536 the Danish Church ceased to exist as a legally independent unit, a part of the Roman Catholic Church, and became instead a Lutheran Church under the direction of the State. Since that time the State has, in one form or another, continued to exercise supreme authority in the affairs of the Church, and has regulated these by the passing of laws, by royal decree, or other appropriate means. The great majority of Danish citizens (about 90%) belongs to the National Church. Administratively, Denmark is divided into 10 dioceses each with a Bishop who, within the framework of the law, is the supreme diocesan authority in ecclesiastical affairs. The Bishop together with the Chief Administrative Officer of the county make up the diocesan governing body, responsible for all matters of ecclesiastical local finance and general administration. Bishops are appointed by the Crown after an election at which the clergy and parish council members of the diocese have had the opportunity of voting for the candidates nominated. Each diocese is divided into a number of deaneries (107 in the whole country) each with its Dean and Deanery Committee, who have certain financial powers. Local government at parish level (there are about 2,100 parishes in all) is in the hands of Parish Councils, who are elected for a 4-year period of office.

Since the Constitution of 1849 complete religious toleration is extended to every sect, and no civil disabilities attach to Dissenters.

Kjær, J. C., *History of the Church of Denmark.* Blair, Nebr., 1945
Roesen, August, *Religion in Denmark.* Copenhagen, 1963

Education. Education has been compulsory since 1814. The *folkeskole* (public primary and lower secondary school) comprises a pre-school class *(børnehave-klasse)*, a 9-year basic school corresponding to the period of compulsory education and a 1-year voluntary tenth form. Compulsory education may be fulfilled either through attending the *folkeskole* or private schools or through home-instruction, on the condition that the instruction given is comparable to that given in the *folkeskole.* The *folkeskole* is mainly a municipal school and no fees are paid. In the year 1986–87, 2,557 primary and lower secondary schools had 707,135 pupils and employed 65,154 teachers. Approximately 16% of the total number of schools were private schools and they were attended by over 9% of the total number of pupils. The 9-year basic school is in practice not streamed. However, a certain differentiation may take place in the eighth and ninth forms.

On completion of the eighth and ninth forms the pupils may sit for the leaving examination of the *folkeskole (folkeskolens afgangsprøve).* On completion of the tenth form the pupils may sit for either the leaving examination of the *folkeskole (folkeskolens afgangsprøve)* or the advanced leaving examination of the *folkeskole (folkeskolens udvidede afgangsprøve).*

For 14–18 year olds there is an alternative of completing compulsory education at continuation schools, with the same leaving examinations as in the *folkeskole.* In the year 1985–86 there were 188 continuation schools with 14,140 pupils.

Under certain conditions the pupils may continue school either in the 3-year gymnasium (upper secondary school) or 2-year *studenterkursus* (adult upper secondary school) ending with *studentereksamen* (upper secondary school leaving examination) or in the 2-year higher preparatory examination course ending with the *højere forberedelseseksamen.* There were (1985–86) 164 of these upper secondary schools with 73,581 pupils and 7,578 teachers.

Vocational education and training consists of apprenticeship training, *lærlingeuddannelse*; vocational education, *EFG-uddannelse,* consisting of a 1-year basic course, *EFG-basisår,* followed by a second part, *EFG-2.del,* and courses preparing for a vocation, leading to a diploma.

Vocational education and training cover courses in commerce and trade, iron and metal industry, chemical industry, construction industry, graphic industry, service trades, food industry, agriculture, horticulture, forestry and fishery, transport and communication, and health related auxiliary programmes.

In 1985–86 68,818 students were enrolled within trade and commerce, of whom 6,690 were in apprenticeship training and 46,167 in vocational education. 81,945 students were enrolled within technical education, of whom 34,071 were in apprenticeship training and 34,653 in vocational education. 15,961 students were admitted to the diploma courses within the field of trade and commerce, and 13,221 students were admitted to the technical diploma courses.

Tertiary education comprises all education after the 12th year of education, no matter whether the 3 years after the 9th form of the *folkeskole* have been spent on a course preparing for continued studies *(studentereksamen* or *højere forberedel-seseksamen),* or a course preparing for a vocation *(lærlingeuddannelse, EFG-uddannelse,* etc.). Tertiary education can be divided into 2 main groups, short courses of further education and long courses of higher education. There was a total of 27,417 students at short courses of further education.

There were 28 teacher-training colleges with 6,042 students and 20 colleges for training of teachers for kindergartens and leisure-time activities with 5,385 students.

Degree-courses in engineering: The Technical University of Denmark had 5,022 students. The Engineering Academy had 2,065 students and 8 engineering colleges had 5,100 students.

Universities: The University of Copenhagen (founded 1479) 24,150 students. The University of Aarhus (founded in 1928) 12,129 students. The University of Odense (founded in 1964) 4,996 students. Roskilde University Centre (founded in 1972) 2,161 students. Aalborg University Centre (founded in 1974) 4,473 students.

Other types of post-secondary education: The Royal Veterinary and Agricultural University had 2,441 students. The two dental colleges had 894 students. The Danish School of Pharmacy had 839 students. The 11 colleges of economics, business administration and modern languages had 18,387 students. The 2 schools of architecture had 1,830 students. Five academies of music had 813 students. Two schools of librarianship had 667 students. The Royal Danish School of Educational Studies had 2,038 students. The 5 schools of social work had 873 students. The Danish School of Journalism had 712 students. Nine colleges of physical therapy had 1,369 students. Two schools of Midwifery Education had 109 students. Two colleges of home economics had 403 students. The School of Visual Arts had 157 students. Two schools of nursing had 412 students. Three military academies had 348 students and 4 colleges for ship's officers 112 students.

Among adult education the most well-known are *Folkeskolehøjskoler*, folk high schools. Adult education in general programmes, single subjects (since 1978) and courses for semi-skilled workers and for skilled workers is organized by counties.

Andresén, A., *The Danish Folk High School To-day.* Copenhagen, 1981
Struve, K., *Schools and Education in Denmark.* Copenhagen, 1981
Thorsen, L., *Public Libraries in Denmark.* English and French eds., Copenhagen, 1972

Social Security. The main body of Danish social welfare legislation is consolidated in 7 acts concerning (1) public health security, (2) sick-day benefits, (3) social pensions (for early retirement and old age), (4) employment injuries insurance, (5) employment services and unemployment insurance, (6) social assistance including assistance to handicapped, rehabilitation, child and juvenile guidance, day-care institutions, care of the aged and sick, and (7) family allowances.

Public health security, covering the entire population, provides free medical care, substantial subsidies for certain essential medicines together with some dental care and a funeral allowance. Hospitals are primarily municipal and the hospital treatment is normally free. All employed workers are granted daily sickness allowances, others can have limited daily sickness allowances. Daily cash benefits are granted in the case of temporary incapacity for work because of illness, injury or child-birth to all persons who earn an income derived from personal work. The benefit is paid at the rate of 90% of the average weekly earnings. There was a maximum rate of 2,126 kroner a week (July 1987).

Social pensions cover the entire population. Entitlement to old-age pensions at the full rates is subject to the condition that the beneficiary has been ordinarily resident in Denmark for a number of years (40). For a shorter period of residence, the benefits are reduced proportionally. The basic amount of the old-age pension in Oct. 1986 was 70,896 kroner a year to married couples and 38,592 to single persons. Various supplementary allowances, depending on age and income, may be payable with the basic amount. Persons aged 55–66 may, depending on health and income, apply for an early-retirement pension. Persons over 67 years of age are entitled to the basic amount. The pensions to a married couple are calculated and paid to the husband and the wife separately. Early retirement pension to a disabled person is payable, having regard to the degree of disability, at a rate of up to 89,076 kroner to a single person. Early-retirement pensions may be subject to income regulation. The same applies to the basic amount of the old age pension to persons aged 67–69. *Employment injuries insurance* provides for disablement or survivors' pensions and compensations. The scheme covers practically all employees.

Employment services are provided by regional public employment agencies. The insurance against unemployment provides daily allowances. The unemployment insurance funds had in March 1987 a membership of 1,930,374.

The *Social Assistance Act* applies to the field of social legislation which rules the individually granted benefits in contrast to the other fields of social legislation which apply to fixed benefits.

Total social expenditure, including hospital and health services, statutory pensions, etc, amounted in the financial year 1986 to 168,929m. kroner.

Bibliography of Foreign Language Literature on Industrial Relations and Social Services in Denmark. Ministries of Labour and Social Affairs, Copenhagen, 1975
Social Conditions in Denmark. Vols. 1–8. Ministries of Labour and Social Affairs, Copenhagen
Marcussen, E., *Social Welfare in Denmark.* 4th ed. Copenhagen, 1980

THE FAROE ISLANDS
Færøerne/Føroyar

HISTORY. A Norwegian province 1380–1709, the islands secured the restoration of their Parliament in 1852 and since 1948 they have been a self-governing region of the Kingdom of Denmark. From 1 Jan. 1972 the Faroe Islands were no longer members of EFTA.

AREA AND POPULATION. The archipelago is situated due north of Scotland and lies equidistant between Norway and Iceland, with a total land area of 1,399 sq. km (540 sq. miles). There are 17 inhabited islands (the main ones being Strømø, Østerø, Vagø, Suderø, Sandø and Bordø) and numerous islets, all mountainous and volcanic. The census population in 1977 was 41,969; estimate (31 Dec. 1986) 46,312. The capital is Tórshavn (15,287 inhabitants on 31 Dec. 1986) on Strømø. The inhabitants speak Færøese, a Scandinavian language which has official status along with Danish.

CONSTITUTION AND GOVERNMENT. The parliament *(Lagting)*, comprises 32 members elected by proportional representation by universal suffrage at age 18. The *Lagting* elected on 8 Nov. 1984 consists of 7 Samband Party, 8 Social Democrats, 7 Folkeflok, 2 Progressive Party, 2 Home Rule Party and 6 Republicans. Parliament elects from among its members a government of from 4 to 6 members *(Landsstyre)* which administers Færøese affairs. Denmark is represented by an appointed commissioner *(Rigsombudsmand)* who administers other matters. The Færøes are represented by 2 members in the Danish parliament.

Chief Minister (Lagmand): Atli P. Dam.

Flag: White with a red blue-edged Scandinavian cross.

ECONOMY

Budget. The 1983–84 Budget balanced at 1,143 Færøese kroner.

Currency. Since 1940 the currency has been the *Færøese krone* (of 100 øre) which remains freely interchangeable with the Danish krone.

ENERGY AND NATURAL RESOURCES

Electricity. There is a hydro-electric station at Vestmanhavn on Strømø. Total production (1986) 225m. kwh.

Agriculture. Only 2% of the surface is cultivated, the main crop being potatoes (1,282 tonnes in 1984). The chief use is for grazing, the traditional mainstay of the economy. Livestock (1982): Sheep, 47,314; cattle, 1,494.

Fisheries. Deep sea fishing now forms the most important sector of the economy, primarily in the 200-mile exclusive zone but also off Greenland and Newfoundland. Total catch (1986) 354,000 tonnes, primarily cod, blue whiting, coalfish, mackerel and herring.

COMMERCE. The main industries are fisheries and crafts. Exports, mainly fresh, frozen, filleted and salted fish, amounted to 1,999m. kroner in 1986; imports to 2,670m. kroner. In 1986 Denmark supplied 46% of imports, Norway 13% and Federal Republic of Germany 9%; exports were mainly to Denmark (18%), the USA (14%), Federal Republic of Germany (13%) and UK (13%).

Total trade with UK (British Department of Trade returns, in £1,000 sterling):

	1983	1984	1985	1986	1987
Imports to UK	15,932	17,649	21,383	21,380	19,239
Exports and re-exports from UK	2,332	5,140	5,605	5,709	7,165

COMMUNICATIONS

Roads. In 1984 there were 200 km of roads. In 1983 there were 10,942 passenger cars and 2,360 commercial vehicles.

Aviation. The airport is on Vagø, from which there are regular services to Copenhagen, Bergen, Reykjavík and Kirkwall (Orkney).

Shipping. The chief port is Tórshavn, with smaller ports at Klaksvig, Vestmanhavn, Ejde, Fuglafjørdur and Skalafjørdur.

Post and Broadcasting. In 1986 there were 28,872 telephones. *Utvarp Føroya* broadcasts from Tórshavn about 40 hours a week on 4 transmitters. In 1984 there were 16,800 radio and 9,000 television receivers.

RELIGION, EDUCATION AND WELFARE

Religion. About 75% are Evangelical Lutherans and 20% are Plymouth Brethren. There are small Baptist and Roman Catholic communities.

Education. In 1986–87 there were 5,606 primary and 2,904 secondary school pupils with 534 teachers.

Health. In 1985 there were 75 doctors, 34 dentists, 8 pharmacists, 13 midwives and 235 nursing personnel. In 1985 there were 3 hospitals with 370 beds.

Books of Reference

Årbog for Færøerne. 1985
Faroes in Figures. Thorshavn, annual, from 1956
Rutherford, G. K., (ed.) *The Physical Environment of the Færoe Islands.* The Hague, 1982
West, J. F., *Faroe.* London, 1973

GREENLAND
Grønland/Kalaallit Nunaat

HISTORY. A Danish possession since 1380, Greenland became on 5 June 1953 an integral part of the Danish kingdom. Following a referendum in Jan. 1979, home rule was introduced from 1 May 1979, and full internal self-government was attained in Jan. 1981 after a transitional period.

AREA AND POPULATION. Area 2,175,600 sq. km (840,000 sq. miles), made up of 1,833,900 sq. km of ice cap and 341,700 sq. km of ice-free land. The population, 1 Jan. 1987, numbered 53,733; West Greenland, 48,424; East Greenland, 3,366; North Greenland (Thule), 794, and 1,149 not belonging to any specific municipality. Of the total in 1986, 9,303 were born outside Greenland. Capital, Godthaab (Nuuk) (1986), 11,209.

CONSTITUTION. Greenland has the same rights as other counties in Denmark with a democratically elected council *(landsråd).* Denmark is represented by an appointed commissioner. At the elections held on 26 May 1987 for the

Parliament, *Landsting*, the *Siumut* gained 11 seats, the *Atassut*, 11 seats, the *Inuit Ataqatigiit*, 4 seats and the *Isittup Partii-a* the remaining 1 seat. The Premier, Jonathan Motzfeldt, formed a 6-member administration, *Landsstyre*.

ECONOMY

Budget. The Budget for 1984 balanced at 1,156·7m. kroner.

Currency. The Danish kroner remains the legal currency.

ENERGY AND NATURAL RESOURCES

Electricity. Production (1984) 181·7m. kwh.

Fisheries. In 1983 the catch totalled 107,360 tonnes; there were also 92,794 seals and 2,308 whales killed.

INDUSTRY. Until the beginning of this century, the hunting of land and sea mammals, especially seals, was the main occupation of the population; now fishing is most important. Fish-processing industries, construction and trade are also important occupations.

Coal production ceased in 1972. A deposit of the valuable mineral cryolite has been mined at Ivigtut. The mine is now worked out, but exports from stock will continue for some years. In 1973 the Danish company Greenex A/S began producing lead and zinc concentrate near Umanak. Annual production of lead and zinc concentrates was in 1984 about 27,000 tonnes and 129,000 tonnes respectively.

Public authorities are investigating uranium and coal deposits in Greenland as well as possibilities of hydro-electric power and there are other private prospectors for various minerals.

COMMERCE. Imports (c.i.f. Greenland) (in 1m. kroner): 1979, 1,448; 1980, 1,848; 1981, 2,096; 1982, 2,319; 1983, 2,421; 1984, 2,836; 1985, 3,140; 1986 (provisional), 2,912. Exports (f.o.b. Greenland) (in 1m. kroner): 1979, 867; 1980, 1,199; 1981, 1,325; 1982, 1,432; 1983, 1,653; 1984, 1,751; 1985, 1,842; 1986 (provisional), 2,078. Trade is mainly with Denmark.

Total trade with UK (British Department of Trade returns, in £1,000 sterling):

	1983	1984	1985	1986	1987
Imports to UK	3,114	3,983	3,168	4,789	838
Exports and re-exports from UK	140	99	348	452	735

COMMUNICATIONS

Roads. There were (1970) 150 km of roads, of which 60 km were paved.

Aviation. There is an international airport at Søndre Srømfjord, and about 12 local airports with scheduled services.

Broadcasting. *Grønlands Radio* broadcasts in Greenlandic and Danish. The short wave transmitters are located at Godthaab. Several towns have local television stations. In 1984 there were 11,554 telephones, 10,000 television sets and 13,500 radio sets.

JUSTICE, RELIGION, EDUCATION AND WELFARE

Justice. The High Court *(Landsret)* in Godthaab comprises one professional judge and 2 lay magistrates, while there are 18 district courts under lay assessors.

Religion. About 98% of the population are Evangelical Lutherans.

Education. There were (1986–87) 9,148 pupils in primary comprehensive schools, of whom 7,141 were in the course of compulsory education (9 years). On 1 July 1986, 1,469 students were enrolled in vocational training.

Health. The medical service is free to all inhabitants. There is a central hospital in Godthaab and 16 smaller district hospitals. In 1985 there were 63 doctors and 601 hospital beds.

Books of Reference

Greenland. R. Danish Ministry of Greenland. Copenhagen. Annual from 1968

Indkomst- og erhvervsforholdene i Grønland ved Hjemmestyrets indførelse (Income and Business Conditions in Greenland at the Introduction of Home Rule), Statistiske Undersøgelser nr. 40, Danmarks Statistik 1984

Meddelelser om Grønland. Ed. Kommissionen for videnskabelige undersøgelser i Grønland. Copenhagen, 1899 ff. Since 1979 issued in 3 separate series: 'Bioscience', 'Geoscience' and 'Man and Society'

Statistiske Efterretninger (Statistical News), from 1983 special series: *Færøerne og Grønland* (Faroe Islands and Greenland)

Gad, F., *A History of Greenland.* Vol. 1. London, 1970.—Vol. 2. London, 1973

Hertling, K. (ed.), *Greenland Past and Present.* Copenhagen, 1970

DIPLOMATIC REPRESENTATIVES

Of Denmark in Great Britain (55 Sloane St., London, SW1X 9SR)
Ambassador: Peter Dyvig (accredited 20 May 1986).

Of Great Britain in Denmark (36–40 Kastelsvej, DK-2100, Copenhagen)
Ambassador: Peter William Unwin, CMG.

Of Denmark in the USA (3200 Whitehaven St., NW, Washington, D.C., 20008)
Ambassador: Eigil Jørgensen.

Of the USA in Denmark (Dag Hammarskjolds Alle 24, Copenhagen)
Ambassador: Terence A. Todman.

Of Denmark to the United Nations
Ambassador: Ole Bierring.

Books of Reference

Statistical Information: Danmarks Statistik (Sejrøgade 11, 2100 Copenhagen Ø.) was founded in 1849 and reorganized in 1966 as an independent institution; it is administratively placed under the Minister of Economic Affairs. *Chief:* N. V. Skak-Nielsen. Its main publications are: *Statistisk Årbog* (Statistical Yearbook). From 1896; *Statistiske Efterretninger* (Statistical News). *Statistiske Månedsoversigt* Monthly Review of Statistics), *Statistisk hårsoversigt* (Statistical Ten-Year Review).

Ministry of Foreign Affairs, *Danish Foreign Office Journal. Commercial and General Review.—Denmark.* 1961.—*Economic Survey of Denmark* (annual).—*Facts About Denmark.* 1959.—Hæstrup, J., *From Occupied to Ally: the Danish Resistance Movement.* 1963

Atlas over Danmark. R. Danish Geog. Society. Copenhagen, 1963

Bibliografi over Danmarks Offentlige Publikationer. Institut for International Udveksling, Copenhagen. Annual

Dania polyglotta. Annual Bibliography of Books ... in Foreign Languages Printed in Denmark. State Library, Copenhagen. Annual

Kongelig Dansk Hof og Statskalender. Copenhagen. Annual

Brynildsen, F., *A Dictionary of the English and Dano-Norwegian Languages.* 2 vols. Copenhagen, 1902–07

Danstrup, J., *History of Denmark.* 2nd ed. Copenhagen, 1949

Johansen, H. C., *The Danish Economy in the Twentieth Century.* London, 1987

Krabbe, L., *Histoire de Danemark.* Copenhagen and Paris, 1950

Miller, K. E., *Denmark.* [Bibliography] Oxford and Santa Barbara, 1987

Nielsen, B. K., *Engelsk–Dansk Ordbog.* Copenhagen, 1964

Trap, J. P., *Kongeriget Danmark.* 5th ed. 11 vols. Copenhagen, 1953 ff.

Vinterberg, H., and Bodelsen, C. A., *Dansk-Engelsk Ordbog.* Copenhagen, 1966

National Library: Det Kongelige Bibliotek, Copenhagen. *Librarian:* P. Birkelund.

DJIBOUTI

Capital: Djibouti
Population: 470,000 (1987)
GNP per capita: US$760 (1984)

Jumhouriyya Djibouti

HISTORY. At a referendum held on 19 March 1967, 60% of the electorate voted for continued association with France rather than independence and the new statute for the territory came into being on 5 July 1967. In Jan. 1976, following discussions between Ali Aref and President Giscard d'Estaing, it was announced that the French Government affirmed that the Territory of the Afars and the Issas was destined for independence but no date was fixed. Legislative elections were held on 8 May and independence as the Republic of Djibouti was achieved on 27 June 1977.

AREA AND POPULATION. Djibouti is bounded north-east by the Gulf of Aden, south-east by Somalia and all other sides by Ethiopia.

Djibouti has an area of 23,200 sq. km (8,960 sq. miles). The population was estimated in 1987 at 470,000, of whom 47% were Somali (Issa), 37% Afar, 8% European (mainly French) and 6% Arab. There were (1985) about 32,000 refugees from Ethiopia. Djibouti, the seat of government, had (1987) 250,000 inhabitants; other towns are Tadjoura, Obock, Dikhil and Ali-Sabieh. There are 5 administrative districts.

CLIMATE. Conditions are hot throughout the year, with very little rain. Djibouti. Jan. 78°F (25·6°C), July 96°F (35·6°C). Annual rainfall 5″ (130 mm).

CONSTITUTION AND GOVERNMENT. Under an organic law approved by the Constituent Assembly on 10 Feb. 1981, the President is directly elected for a 6-year term (renewable once) and the Constituent Assembly became a 65-member Chamber of Deputies, with a 5-year term. In Oct. 1981, the Assembly declared Djibouti a one-Party state, the ruling Party being the *Rassemblement Populaire pour le Progrès.* Elections for the Chamber of Deputies were held 21 May 1982, when 26 Somali, 23 Afar and 16 Arab members were elected.

President: Hassan Gouled Aptidon (elected 1977 and re-elected 1981).

The Council of Ministers in Sept. 1987 was composed as follows:

Prime Minister, Port Affairs: Barkat Gourad Hamadou.

Justice: Omar Kamil Warsama. *Interior, Posts and Telecommunications:* Youssouf Ali Chirdon. *Foreign Affairs and Co-operation:* Moumin Bahdon Farah. *Defence:* Habib Mumammed Loita. *Finance and Economy:* Mohamed Djama Elabeh. *Commerce, Transport and Tourism:* Moussa Bouraleh Robleh. *Industry:* Salem Abdou Yaya. *Education, Youth and Sport:* Souleiman Farah Lodon. *Public Health and Social Affairs:* Mohamed Adabo Kako. *Labour and Social Security:* Mohamed Del Wais. *Public Works, Town Planning and Housing:* Bourhan Ali Warki. *Civil Service and Administrative Reform:* Helem Houmed. *Agriculture and Rural Development:* Ahmed Hassan Liban Gouhad.

National flag: Horizontally blue over green, with a white triangle based on the hoist charged with a red star.

DEFENCE

Army. The Army comprises 1 infantry regiment, 1 armoured squadron, 1 support battalion, 1 border commando battalion and 1 parachute company. Equipment includes 30 armoured cars. The strength of the Army (of which the Navy and Air

Force form part) was (1988) 3,000 men. There is also a paramilitary force of some 1,200 men.

Navy. The nucleus of a naval force was acquired in 1977 with the commissioning of a coastal patrol craft transferred by France with 3 minor landing craft and 2 new patrol launches were given by France in 1985. Personnel (1988) 60.

Air Force. There is a small air force, all equipment *via* French aid. There are 2 Noratlas transports, 1 Falcon 20 VIP aircraft, 1 Cessna 206 for liaison, 1 Rallye trainer, and 5 helicopters (Alouette II and Ecureuil). Personnel (1988) 100.

INTERNATIONAL RELATIONS

Membership. Djibouti is a member of UN, OAU, the Arab League and an ACP State of the EEC.

ECONOMY

Budget. The ordinary budget for 1984 envisaged an expenditure of 21,855m. Djibouti francs.

Currency. The currency is the *Djibouti franc*. In March 1988, £1 = 313 *Djibouti francs*; US$1 = 177 *Djibouti francs*.

Banking. The Banque Nationale de Djibouti is the bank of issue. There are 6 commercial banks.

ENERGY AND NATURAL RESOURCES

Electricity. Production (1986) 140m. kwh. Installed capacity 80,100 kw.

Minerals. Minerals supposed to exist are gypsum, mica, amethyst and sulphur.

Agriculture. Mainly market gardening at the oasis of Ambouli and near urban areas. Tomato production (1982) 278 tonnes. Livestock (1986): 47,000 cattle, 500,000 sheep, 410,000 pigs, 8,000 donkeys, 57,000 camels.

Fisheries. The catch in 1980 was 2,000 tonnes.

INDUSTRY AND TRADE

Industry. In 1982 there were 2,309 persons employed in construction and 726 in manufacturing.

Commerce. The main economic activity is the operation of the port. The chief imports are cotton goods, sugar, cement, flour, fuel oil and vehicles; the chief exports are hides, cattle and coffee (transit from Ethiopia). Trade in 1m. Djibouti francs:

	1979	1980	1981	1982
Imports	28,436	33,782	36,654	40,197
Exports	14,147	19,171	20,348	...

In 1980 France provided 50% of imports and took 66% of exports.

Total trade between Djibouti and UK (British Department of Trade returns, in £1,000 sterling):

	1983	1984	1985	1986	1987
Imports to UK	184	59	293	53	175
Exports and re-exports from UK	7,712	8,896	21,546	12,537	12,501

Tourism. There were 19,000 visitors in 1986.

COMMUNICATIONS

Roads. There were (1983) 2,906 km of roads, of which 300 km were hard-surfaced. In 1982 there were 9,000 passenger cars and 1,500 commercial vehicles.

Railway. For the line Djibouti–Addis Ababa, of which 106 km lies within Djibouti *see* p. 462. In 1983 the railway carried 249,000 tonnes of freight and 1·4m. passengers.

Aviation. Air Djibouti provides services to Addis Ababa, Nairobi, Jidda and the

Gulf. Other airlines serving Djibouti international airport (Ambouli) are Ethiopian Airlines, Air France, Air Tanzania and Yemen Airways Corporation. In 1984, 63,662 passengers and 6,542 tonnes of freight arrived at Ambouli, and 58,479 passengers and 1,575 tonnes of freight departed.

Shipping. In 1981 there entered at Djibouti 1,753 vessels, unloading 307,800 tonnes and loading 151,900 tonnes of merchandise. In 1981 the merchant marine comprised 8 vessels of 3,185 GRT. Djibouti became a free port in 1981.

Post and Broadcasting. Number of telephones (1984), 6,400. *Radiodiffusion-Télévision de Djibouti* broadcasts on medium- and short-waves in French, Somali, Afar and Arabic. There is a television transmitter in Djibouti, broadcasting for 19 hours a week. Number of receivers (1984): radio, 17,500; TV, 11,200.

Cinemas. In 1975 there were 4 cinemas with a seating capacity of 5,800.

JUSTICE, RELIGION, EDUCATION AND WELFARE

Justice. There is a Court of First Instance and a Court of Appeal in the capital. The judicial system is based on Islamic law.

Religion. The vast majority of the population is Moslem, with about 24,000 Roman Catholics.

Education. In 1984 there were 21,847 pupils and 503 teachers at primary schools, 6,331 pupils and 280 teachers at secondary and technical schools.

Health. In 1984 there were 29 hospitals and dispensaries with 1,182 beds, 46 physicians, 3 dentists and 4 pharmacists.

DIPLOMATIC REPRESENTATIVES

Of Djibouti in Great Britain
Ambassador: Ahmed Ibrahim Abdi (resides in Paris).

Of Great Britain in Djibouti
Ambassador: M. A. Marshall (resides in San'a).

Of the USA in Djibouti (Plateau du Serpent Blvd., Djibouti)
Ambassador: John P. Ferriter.

Of Djibouti to the United Nations and in the USA
Ambassador: Saleh Haji Farah Dirir.

Books of Reference

Poinsot, J.-P., *Djibouti et la Côte française des Somalis.* Paris, 1965
Thompson, V., and Adloff, R., *Djibouti and the Horn of Africa.* Stanford Univ. Press, 1967

COMMONWEALTH
OF DOMINICA

Capital: Roseau
Population: 94,191 (1987)
GNP per capita: US$970 (1983)

HISTORY. Dominica was discovered by Columbus. It was a British possession from 1805, a member of the Federation of the West Indies 1958–62, an Associated State of the UK, 1967–78 and became an independent republic as the Commonwealth of Dominica on 3 Nov. 1978.

AREA AND POPULATION. Dominica is an island in the Windward group of the West Indies situated between Martinique and Guadeloupe. It has an area of 751 sq. km (290 sq. miles) and a population at the 1981 Census of 74,851; estimate (1987) 94,191. The chief town, Roseau, had about 20,000 inhabitants in 1981.

The population is mainly of Negro and mixed origins, with small white and Asian minorities. There is a Carib settlement of about 500, almost entirely of mixed blood.

CLIMATE. A tropical climate, with pleasant conditions between Dec. and March, but there is a rainy season from June to Oct., when hurricanes may occur. Rainfall is heavy, with coastal areas having 70″ (1,750 mm) but the mountains may have up to 250″ (6,250 mm). Roseau. Jan. 76°F (24·2°C), July 81°F (27·2°C). Annual rainfall 78″ (1,956 mm).

CONSTITUTION AND GOVERNMENT. The House of Assembly has 21 elected and 9 nominated members. The Speaker is elected from among the members of the House or from outside. The Cabinet is presided over by the Prime Minister and consists of 6 other Ministers including the Attorney-General (official member). Elections were held in July 1985. The Dominica Freedom Party won 15 seats, the Dominica Labour Party 5 seats and the United Dominica Labour Party 1 seat.

President: C. A. Seignoret.
The Cabinet in March 1987 was composed as follows:
Prime Minister and Minister for Finance, Economic Development and External Affairs: Mary Eugenia Charles.
Attorney-General and Minister for Legal Affairs and Labour: Brian G. K. Alleyne. *Agriculture, Trade, Industry and Tourism:* Charles A. Maynard. *Health, Water, Sewerage and Fire:* Ronan David. *Community Development, Housing and Social Affairs:* Heskeith Alexander. *Education and Sports:* Henry George. *Communications and Works, Electricity, Telecommunications and Feeder Roads:* Alleyne Carbon.

National flag: Green with a cross over all of yellow, black, and white pieces, and in the centre a red disc charged with a Sisserou parrot in natural colours within a ring of 10 green yellow-bordered stars.

INTERNATIONAL RELATIONS
Membership. The Commonwealth of Dominica is a member of UN, OAS, CARICOM, the Commonwealth and is an ACP state of EEC.

ECONOMY
Budget. In 1986 there was a deficit of EC$12·4m.

Currency. The French *franc,* the £ sterling and the East Caribbean *dollar* are legal tender. In March 1988, EC$2·70 = US$1 and EC$4·79 = £1.

Banking. Savings bank (Dec. 1982), 2,862 depositors, with $593,659 deposits. There are branches of Barclays Bank International and Royal Bank of Canada in Roseau, and branches of Barclays and National Commercial and Development Bank at Portsmouth. The National Commercial and Development Bank was opened in 1977 and Banque Française Commerciale opened in 1979.

ENERGY AND NATURAL RESOURCES

Electricity. Production (1987) 16m. kwh.

Agriculture. Hurricanes in 1979 and 1980 devastated large agricultural areas and damaged infrastructure. Production (1986): Bananas, 39,000 tonnes; coconuts, 13,000; beef (1982), 457,428 lb; pork (1982), 588,993 lb. Livestock (1986): Cattle, 4,000; pigs, 9,000; sheep, 4,000; goats, 6,000; poultry, (1982) 115,000.

INDUSTRY AND TRADE

Industry. The main industries are agriculture and tourism.

Commerce (1984). Imports, EC$156,103,731; exports, EC$67,307,045. Chief products: Bananas, soap, fruit juices, essential oils, coconuts, vegetables, fruit and fruit preparations, and alcoholic drinks.

Total trade between Dominica and UK (British Department of Trade returns, in £1,000 sterling):

	1984	1985	1986	1987
Imports to UK	14,961	18,110	26,612	37,083
Exports and re-exports from UK	8,359	10,257	8,780	10,431

Tourism. Tourists (1986) totalled 36,310.

COMMUNICATIONS

Roads. In 1976 there were 467 miles of road and 282 miles of track. Vehicles totalled (Sept. 1983) 5,717.

Post and Broadcasting. Telephone lines, 136 route miles; number of telephones, 6,685 (Dec. 1987). Radio receivers (1982) 13,405.

Cinemas. In 1987 there was 1 cinema with a seating capacity of 1,000.

JUSTICE, RELIGION, EDUCATION AND WELFARE

Justice. There are 4 magistrates' courts. There is also a supreme court which dealt with 38 criminal and 319 civil cases in 1981. The police force consists of 10 officers and 431 other ranks.

Religion. 80% of the population is Roman Catholic.

Education. In 1987–88 there were 65 primary schools with 15,060 pupils and in 1986–87 there were 10 secondary schools with 3,287 pupils, and 2 colleges of higher education.

Health. In Sept. 1983 there were 3 hospitals with 237 beds, 26 doctors, 7 dentists, 10 pharmacists and 153 nursing personnel.

DIPLOMATIC REPRESENTATIVES

Of Great Britain in Dominica
High Commissioner: K. F. X. Burns, CMG (resides in Bridgetown).

Of Dominica in the USA and to the United Nations
Ambassador: Franklin Andrew Baron.

Book of Reference

Myres, R. A., *Dominica.* [Bibliography] Oxford and Santa Barbara, 1987
Library: Public Library, Roseau. *Librarian:* Mrs. C. Williams.

DOMINICAN REPUBLIC

Capital: Santo Domingo
Population: 6·6m. (1985)
GNP per capita: US$1,090 (1984)

República Dominicana

HISTORY. On 5 Dec. 1492 Columbus discovered the island of Santo Domingo, which he called La Española; for a time it was called Hispaniola. The city of Santo Domingo, founded by his brother, Bartholomew, in 1496, is the oldest city in the Americas. The western third of the island—now the Republic of Haiti—was later occupied and colonized by the French, to whom the Spanish colony of Santo Domingo was also ceded in 1795. In 1808 the Dominican population, under the command of Gen. Juan Sánchez Ramirez, routed an important French military force commanded by Gen. Ferrand, at the famous battle of Palo Hincado. This battle was the beginning of the end for French rule in Santo Domingo and culminated in the successful siege of the capital. Eventually, with the aid of a British naval squadron, the French were forced to capitulate and the colony returned again to Spanish rule, from which it declared its independence in 1821. It was invaded and held by the Haitians from 1822 to 1844, when they were expelled, and the Dominican Republic was founded and a constitution adopted. Independence day 27 Feb. 1844. Great Britain, in 1850, was the first country to recognize the Dominican Republic. The country was occupied by American Marines from 1916 until 1924. In 1936 the name of the capital city was changed from Santo Domingo to Ciudad Trujillo; and back again in 1961.

AREA AND POPULATION. The Dominican Republic occupies the eastern portion (about two-thirds) of the island of Hispaniola, Quisqueya or Santo Domingo, the western division forming the Republic of Haiti. It consists of the National District (containing the capital, Santo Domingo; population, census 1,550,739), and 26 provinces.

Area is 48,442 sq. km (18,700 sq. miles) with 870 miles of coastline, 193 miles of frontier line with Haiti (marked out in 1936).

The populations of the 26 provinces at the 1981 census were:

La Altagracia	100,112	Puerto Plata	206,757
Azua	142,770	La Romana	109,769
Bahoruco	78,636	Salcedo	99,191
Barahona	137,160	Samaná	65,699
Dajabón	57,709	Sánchez Ramírez	126,567
Duarte	235,544	San Cristóbal	446,132
Espaillat	164,017	San Juan	239,957
La Estrelleta	65,384	San Pedro de Macorís	152,890
Independencia	38,768	Santiago	550,372
María Trinidad Sánchez	112,629	Santiago Rodríguez	55,411
Montecristi	83,407	El Seibo	157,866
Pedernales	17,006	Valverde	100,319
Peravia	168,123	La Vega	385,043

Census (1981) 5,647,977. Estimate (1985) 6,588,000.

Population of the principal municipalities (Census 1981): Santo Domingo, 1,313,172; Santiago de los Caballeros, 278,638; La Romana, 91,571; San Pedro de Macoris, 78,562; San Francisco de Macoris, 64,906; La Vega, 52,432; San Juan de la Managuana, 49,764; Barahona, 49,334; Puerto Plata, 45,348.

The population is partly of Spanish descent, but is mainly composed of a mixed race of European and African blood.

CLIMATE. A tropical maritime climate with most rain falling in the summer months. The rainy season extends from May to Nov. and amounts are greatest in the north and east. Hurricanes may occur from June to Nov. Santo Domingo. Jan. 75°F (23·9°C), July 81°F (27·2°C). Annual rainfall 56″ (1,400 mm).

CONSTITUTION AND GOVERNMENT. A new Constitution was promulgated on 28 Nov. 1966.

The President is elected for 4 years, by direct vote. In case of death, resignation or disability, he is succeeded by the Vice-president. There are 12 secretaries of state, a judicial adviser with secretary-of-state rank and 2 ministers without portfolio in charge of departments. Citizens are entitled to vote at the age of 18, or less when married.

President: Dr Joaquín Balaguer (elected 16 May 1986; took office 16 Aug.).
Foreign Affairs: Dr Donald J. Reid Cabral.

There is a bicameral legislature, comprising a 27-member Senate and a 120-member Chamber of Deputies, both elected for 4-year terms at the same date as the President.

National flag: Blue, red; quartered by a white cross.
National anthem: Quisqueyanos valientes, alzemos (words by E. Prud'homme; tune by J. Reyes, 1883).

Local Government: The republic consists of a National District (containing the capital, Santo Domingo, and surrounding areas) and 26 provinces, divided into 97 municipalities.

DEFENCE

Army. The Army has a strength (1988) of about 13,000. It is organized in 4 infantry brigades and 1 artillery regiment. There were (1988) some light tanks and armoured cars.

Navy. The Navy, largely comprising former US vessels, consists of 1 very old frigate (built 1944) acting as the staff flagship (former training ship, *ex*-presidential yacht), 2 very old escort (*ex*-fleet) minesweepers, 3 very old patrol vessels (*ex*-netlayers), 1 medium landing ship, 2 landing craft, 8 coastguard vessels, 8 patrol cutters, 4 small training craft, 2 oilers, 1 survey craft and 10 tugs. Personnel in 1988 totalled 4,000 officers and men.

Air Force. The Air Force, with HQ at San Isidoro, has 1 squadron with a total of about 25 Bell 205A-1, UH-1, UH-12E, OH-6A and Alouette II/III helicopters; 1 transport squadron with 5 C-47s and some smaller communications aircraft; a Presidential Dauphin 2 helicopter; and an assortment of trainers, including 10 T-34B Mentors, 10 Cessna T-41s and 3 T-6 Texans. Personnel strength was (1988) 3,765.

INTERNATIONAL RELATIONS

Membership. The Dominican Republic is a member of UN and OAS.

ECONOMY

Planning. The 1983–85 development plan envisaged investment of RD$1,666m.

Budget. The 1983 budget balanced at RD$1,172·6m. In 1985 external debt was RD$3,551m.

Currency. In Oct. 1947 the *peso oro*, then equal to the US$, was formally made the unit of currency. In March 1988, £1 = RD$8·81; US$1 = RD$4·97.

There are silver coins for 50, 25 and 10 centavos, a copper-nickel 5-centavo piece and a copper 1-centavo piece.

Banking. There are 4 foreign banks—the Royal Bank of Canada with 12 branches, the Bank of Nova Scotia with 11 branches, the Citibank with 6 branches, the Chase

Manhattan Bank with 7 branches and the Bank of America with 4 branches. An agricultural and mortgage bank, with paid-up capital of RD$500,000, was established in 1945; in 1950 its capital was increased to RD$5m. In 1947 the Central Bank of the Dominican Republic was established. A Banco Popular Dominicano, with an authorized capital of RD$5m., opened in Jan. 1964.

Weights and Measures. The metric system was nominally adopted on 1 Aug. 1913, but English and Spanish units have remained in common use in ordinary commercial transactions; on 17 Sept. 1954 a more drastic law requiring the decimal metric system was passed.

ENERGY AND NATURAL RESOURCES

Electricity. In 1986, 3,800m. kwh. of electricity was generated. Supply 110 and 220 volts; 60 Hz.

Minerals. Bauxite output in 1982 was 152,250 tonnes. Silver and platinum have been found, and near Neiba there are several hills of rock salt. Ferronickel production (1983) 52,278 tonnes. The Rosario Dominicana goldmines were nationalized in Oct. 1979. Production of gold (1983) 354,023 troy oz.; silver, 1,329,138.

Agriculture. Agriculture and its processing industries are the chief source of wealth, sugar cultivation being the principal industry. Of the total area, 27,411 hectares are cultivable.

Livestock in 1986: 2,055,000 cattle, 2·5m. pigs, 80,000 sheep.

The largest sugar estates are in the south-eastern part of the republic. Sugar-cane production, 1986, was 7·3m. tonnes.

Coffee is exported mainly to USA. Output, 1986, 55,000 tonnes. Production of rice for home consumption and export is fostered; output, 1986, 298,000 tonnes. Cocoa is the second principal crop and covers 2m. *tareas* (340,000 acres); output in 1986, 37,000 tonnes. There are useful crops of yucca and beans for local consumption. Scientific growing of bananas (1986: 422,000 tonnes) and of leaf tobacco (1986: 12,000 tonnes) is progressing.

Fisheries. The total catch (1981) was 14,500 tonnes.

INDUSTRY AND TRADE

Industry. In 1975, 1,286 industrial establishments employed 130,000 men and women, who earned RD$157·57m. Important products are sugar (1,105,263 tonnes of crude and 104,194 of refined sugar in 1983), cement (960,000 tonnes in 1981). Value of textile manufactures (1983), RD$30·4m.; tobacco products, RD$63·5m.

Commerce. Total imports and exports in RD$1m. (equal to US$1m.):

	1980	1981	1982	1983	1984	1985
Imports	1,498·4	1,450·2	1,255·8	1,297·0	1,257·1	1,285·9
Exports	961·9	1,188·0	767·7	785·9	868·1	739·3

The principal exports in 1983 were (in RD$1m.): Sugar, 263·5; coffee, 76·3; ferronickel, 83·5; Doré, 164·5.

Total trade between the Dominican Republic and UK (British Department of Trade returns, in £1,000 sterling):

	1983	1984	1985	1986	1987
Imports to UK	6,662	5,620	7,900	7,599	8,637
Exports and re-exports from UK	11,594	12,535	14,595	15,178	23,887

Tourism. About 800,000 tourists visited the Dominican Republic in 1986.

COMMUNICATIONS

Roads. Three main trunk highways, with branches, extend from Santo Domingo eastward to Higuey (106 miles), northward to Santiago and Montecristi and Dajabón (204 miles) and westward to San Juan (128 miles) and Elías Piña on the

Haitian border (161 miles). At Elías Piña the road joins the Haitian road to Port-au-Prince. Total highway system in 1977 was 5,224 km first-, 1,538 km second- and 2,505 km third-class roads; there were 647 bridges. Road transport is the chief means of travel. There were 82,001 cars, 40,626 commercial vehicles and 34,967 motor cycles in 1977.

Railways. Some 142 km of the Dominican Government Railway remains in use between La Vega and the port of Sánchez. Twelve lines, including the Central Romana Railway, exist to serve the sugar industry, totalling 1,600 km.

Aviation. The country is reached from the American continent and the Caribbean islands by 8 international airlines. Two local aviation companies provide interior services and connect Santo Domingo with San Juan in Puerto Rico, Curaçao, Aruba and Miami.

Shipping. Santo Domingo is the leading port; Puerto Plata ranks next. In 1971, vessels of 9,833,000 tons entered the ports to discharge 3,009,000 tonnes of cargo, and vessels of 5,276,000 tons cleared the ports having loaded 1,986,000 tonnes.

Post and Broadcasting. Number of telephone instruments (1983), 175,054, of which 138,169 in Santo Domingo. The telegraph has a total length of about 500 km, privately owned; they have been leased to All-America Cables, Inc., which also controls submarine cables connecting, in the north, Puerto Plata with Puerto Rico and New York, and in the south, Santo Domingo with Puerto Rico, Cuba and Curaçao.

There were (1980) 105 broadcasting stations in Santo Domingo and other towns; this includes the 2 government stations. There are 4 television stations.

Cinemas (1978). Cinemas numbered 72, with seating capacity of about 40,000.

Newspapers (1984). There were 7 daily newspapers with a circulation of 155,000.

JUSTICE, RELIGION, EDUCATION AND WELFARE

Justice. The judicial power resides in the Supreme Court of Justice, the courts of appeal, the courts of first instance, the communal courts and other tribunals created by special laws, such as the land courts. The Supreme Court consists of a president and 8 judges chosen by the Senate, and the procurator-general, appointed by the executive; it supervises the lower courts. Each province forms a judicial district, as does the *Distrito Nacional*, and each has its own procurator fiscal and court of first instance; these districts are subdivided, in all, into 72 municipalities and 18 municipal districts, each with one or more local justices. The death penalty was abolished in 1924.

Religion. The religion of the state is Roman Catholic; other forms of religion are permitted.

Education. Primary instruction (5,956 schools) is free and obligatory for children between 7 and 14 years of age; there are also secondary, normal, vocational and special schools, all of which are either wholly maintained by the State or state-aided; in 1981, primary schools had 22,672 teachers and 1·1m. pupils; 1,963 intermediate and secondary schools had 11,716 teachers and 331,471 pupils.

The University of Santo Domingo (founded 1538) had (1975) 27,675 students; 5 other universities had 14,573 students.

Health. In 1978, 18 towns had complete waterworks. There were, in 1975, 1,310 doctors, 121 hospitals, health centres and polyclinics with 8,389 beds.

DIPLOMATIC REPRESENTATIVES

Of Dominican Republic in Great Britain
Ambassador: (Vacant).

Of Great Britain in the Dominican Republic
Ambassador: Giles Fitzherbert (resides in Caracas).

Of the Dominican Republic in the USA (1715 22nd St., NW, Washington, D.C., 20008)
Ambassador: Eduardo Leon.

Of the USA in the Dominican Republic (Calle Cesar Nicolas Penson, Santo Domingo)
Ambassador: Lowell C. Kilday.

Of the Dominican Republic to the United Nations
Ambassador: Dr Juan Arístides Taveras-Guzman.

Books of Reference

Anuario estadístico de la República Dominicana, 1944–45. Ciudad Trujillo. 1949. This has been succeeded by separate annual reports covering foreign trade, vital statistics, banking, insurance, housing and communications.

Official Guide to the Dominican Republic, 79–80. Tourist Information Center, Santo Domingo, 1980

Atkins, G. P., *Arms and Politics in the Dominican Republic.* London, 1981

Bell, I., *The Dominican Republic.* London, 1980

Black, J. K., *The Dominican Republic: Politics and Development in an Unsovereign State.* London, 1986

Diederich, B., *Trujillo: The Death of the Goat.* London, 1978

Wiarda, H. J., and Kryzanek, M. J., *The Dominican Republic: A Caribbean Crucible.* Boulder, 1982

ECUADOR

República del Ecuador

Capital: Quito
Population: 9·64m. (1986)
GNP per capita: US$1,160 (1985)

HISTORY. The Spaniards under Francisco Pizarro founded a colony after their victory at Cajamarca (16 Nov. 1532). Their rule was first challenged by the rising of 10 Aug. 1809. Marshal Sucre defeated the Spaniards at Pichincha in 1822, and in 1822 Bolívar persuaded the new republic to join the federation of Gran Colombia. The Presidency of Quito became the Republic of Ecuador by amicable secession 13 May 1830.

AREA AND POPULATION. Ecuador is bounded on the north by Colombia, on the east and south by Peru, on the west by the Pacific ocean. The frontier with Peru has long been a source of dispute between the two countries. The latest delimitation of it was in the treaty of Rio, 29 Jan. 1942, when, after being invaded by Peru, Ecuador lost over half her Amazonian territories. Ecuador unilaterally denounced this treaty in Sept. 1961. *See* map in THE STATESMAN'S YEAR-BOOK, 1942. Fighting between Peru and Ecuador began again in Jan. 1981 over this border issue but a ceasefire was agreed in early Feb.

No definite figure of the area of the country can yet be given, as a portion of the frontier has not been delimited. One estimate of the area of Ecuador is 270,670 sq. km, excluding the litigation zone between Peru and Ecuador, which is 190,807 sq. km, but including the Galápagos Islands (7,844 sq. km).

Mainland Ecuador has 3 distinct zones: the *Sierra* or uplands of the Andes, consisting of high mountain ridges with valleys, with 3·76m. of the population and high-priced farming land; the *Costa*, the coastal plain between the Andes and the Pacific, with 4·03m., whose permanent plantations furnish bananas, cacao, coffee, sugar-cane and many other crops; the *Oriente*, the upper Amazon basin on the east and the site of the main oilfields, consisting of tropical jungles threaded by large rivers (0·26m.).

The population is predominantly of Mestizos and Amerindians, with some proportion of people of European or African descent.

The official language is Spanish. The Amerindians of the highlands also speak the Quechua language; in the Oriental Region various tribes have languages of their own.

Census population in 1982, 8,072,702. Estimate (1986) 9·64m.

The population 28 Nov. 1982 was distributed by provinces as follows:

Province	Sq. km	Census 1982	Capital	Census 1982
Azuay	8,092	443,044	Cuenca	272,397
Bolívar	4,142	141,566	Guaranda	14,155 [1]
Cañar	3,481	174,674	Azogues	13,840 [1]
Carchi	3,744	125,452	Tulcán	33,635 [1]
Chimborazo	6,056	320,268	Riobamba	149,757
Cotopaxi	5,198	279,765	Latacunga	55,979
El Oro	5,908	337,818	Machala	117,243
Esmeraldas	15,162	247,311	Esmeraldas	141,030
Guayas	21,382	2,047,001	Guayaquil	1,300,868
Imbabura	4,976	245,745	Ibarra	60,719 [1]
Loja	11,472 [2]	358,952	Loja	86,196
Los Ríos	6,370	457,065	Babahoyo	42,583 [1]
Manabi	18,105	858,780	Portoviejo	167,070
Pichincha	16,587	1,376,831	Quito	1,110,248
Tungurahua	3,110	324,286	Ambato	221,392
Napo [3]	52,318 [2]	115,110	Tena	4,735 [1]
Pastaza [3]	30,269 [2]	31,779	Puyo	...
Morona-Santiago [3]	26,418 [2]	70,217	Macas	...
Zamora-Chinchipa [3]	18,394 [2]	46,691	Zamora	6,365
Colon (Galápagos)	7,994	6,119	Baquerizo Moreno	...

[1] 1983 estimate.   [2] Excluding Peru-Ecuador litigation zone.
[3] Comprising 'Región Oriental'.

Vital statistics for calendar years: Births, (1985) 209,974; deaths, (1985) 51,134.

CLIMATE. The climate varies from equatorial, through warm temperate to mountain conditions, according to altitude which affects temperatures and rainfall. In coastal areas, the dry season is from May to Dec., but only from June to Sept. in mountainous parts, where temperatures may be 20°F colder than on the coast. Quito Jan. 59°F (15°C), July 58°F (14.4°C). Annual rainfall 44″ (1,115 mm). Guayaquil. Jan. 79°F (26.1°C), July 75°F (23.9°C). Annual rainfall 39″ (986 mm).

CONSTITUTION AND GOVERNMENT. On 22 June 1970 President José Maria Velasco Ibarra assumed dictatorial powers, following months of strife between student and security forces. For details of governments 1963–70, *see* THE STATESMAN'S YEAR-BOOK, 1974–75, pp. 875–76. On 15 Feb. 1972 President Velasco Ibarra was deposed. A National Military Government under Gen. Guillermo Rodriguez Lara was formed and the 1945 Constitution reintroduced. President Rodriguez Lara resigned in Jan. 1976 and a military Junta assumed power until the 1979 elections. A new Constitution came into force on 10 Aug. 1979. Elections in May 1984 were won by León Febres Cordero.

National flag: Three horizontal stripes of yellow, blue, red, with the yellow of double width, and in the centre over all the national arms.

National anthem: Indignados tus hijos del yugo (words by J. L. Mera; music by A. Neumann, 1866).

The following is a list of the presidents and provisional executives since 1948:

Galo Plaza Lasso, 1 Sept. 1948–31 Aug. 1952.

Dr José María Velasco Ibarra, 1 Sept. 1952–31 Aug. 1956.

Dr Camilo Ponce Enríquez, 1 Sept. 1956–31 Aug. 1960.

Dr José María Velasco Ibarra, 1 Sept. 1960–8 Nov. 1961 (withdrew).

Dr Carlos Julio Arosemena Monroy, 8 Nov. 1961–11 July 1963 (deposed).

Military Junta, 11 July 1963–31 March 1966.

Clemente Yerovi Indaburu, 31 March–16 Nov. 1966 (interim).

Dr Otto Arosemena Gómez, 17 Nov. 1966–1 Sept. 1968.

Dr José María Velasco Ibarra, 1 Sept. 1968–15 Feb. 1972 (deposed).

Gen. Guillermo Rodriguez Lara, 16 Feb. 1972–11 Jan. 1976 (resigned).

Adm. Alfredo Poveda Burbano, 11 Jan. 1976–10 Aug. 1979.

Jaime Roldós Aguilera, 10 Aug. 1979–24 May 1981.

Osvaldo Hurtado Larrea, 24 May 1981–10 Aug. 1984.

President: León Febres Cordero (sworn in on 10 Aug. 1984).

The Cabinet in Dec. 1987 was as follows:

Vice-President: Blasco Peñaherrera. *Agriculture and Livestock:* Marcos Espinel. *Education and Culture:* Ivan Gallegos. *Finance and Credit:* Rodrigo Espinosa. *Foreign Relations:* Rafael Garcia Velasco. *Government and Justice:* Luis Robles. *Industry, Commerce, Integration and Fishing:* Ricardo Noboa. *Labour:* Guillermo Chang. *Defence:* Gen. Medardo Salazar. *Energy and Mines:* Fernando Santos. *Public Health:* Dr José Thoume. *Public Works and Communications:* Cesar Rodriguez. *Social Welfare:* Aquiles Rigail. *Secretary of Administration:* Patricio Quevedo. *General Manager of the Central Bank:* Fernando Sevilla. *President of the Monetary Board:* Federico Arteta.

Local Government. The country is divided politically into 20 provinces; 4 of them comprise the 'Región Oriental' and one the Archipelago of Galápagos, situated in the Pacific ocean about 600 miles to the west of Ecuador and comprising 15 islands. The provinces are administered by governors, appointed by the Government; their sub-divisions, or cantons, by political chiefs and elected cantonal councillors; and the parishes by political lieutenants. The Galápagos Archipelago is administered by the Ministry of National Defence. The 20 provinces are made up of 115 cantons, 212 urban parishes and 715 rural parishes.

DEFENCE. Military service is selective, with a 1-year period of conscription.

The country is divided into 4 military zones, with headquarters at Quito, Guayaquil, Cuenca and Pastaza.

Army. The Army consists of 7 infantry, 2 armoured and 2 'jungle' brigades. Strength (1988) 29,000, with about 50,000 reservists. Equipment includes 40 American M-3 and 92 French AMX-13 light tanks. The aviation element has 3 Arava, 5 Turbo-Porter and 2 King Air transports, 5 survey aircraft, 2 Cessna light aircraft and over 30 helicopters including 8 Super Pumas and 5 Pumas.

Navy. The Navy consists of 2 Federal Republic of Germany-built diesel-electric powered patrol submarines; 1 old *ex*-US destroyer (completed in 1946), 1 old *ex*-US frigate (built in 1943), 6 Italian-built new corvettes, 6 fast missile boats, 7 coastal patrol craft, 1 landing ship, 1 medium landing ship, 1 supply ship, 2 survey vessels and 6 tugs. The Maritime Air Force has 15 aircraft, including 8 Cessna light aircraft, 2 Alouette III helicopters and 3 Beech trainers. Naval personnel in 1988 totalled 3,800 officers and men. There are 17 Coast Guard cutters.

Air Force. The Air Force, formed with Italian assistance in 1920, was reorganized and re-equipped with US aircraft after Ecuador signed the Rio Pact of Mutual Defence in 1947 but latest equipment acquired from Europe and Brazil. 1988 strength of about 4,000 personnel and 70 combat aircraft includes a strike squadron equipped with 9 single-seat and 2 two-seat Jaguars; an interceptor squadron of 15 single-seat and 1 two-seat Mirage F.1; an interceptor squadron with 12 Kfirs; 3 counter-insurgency units equipped with 11 Cessna A-37B, 25 T-33 and 10 Strikemaster light jet attack and training aircraft, 1 squadron with 4 piston-engined C-47 and 2 C-130, 2 Buffalo and 4 HS 748 turboprop transports; Alouette III, AS 332 Super Puma, SA 330 Puma, Bell 47, Bell 212, UH-1 Iroquois and SA 315B Lama helicopters; and Cessna 150, T-33, T-34C-1 and T-41A/D trainers. Other transports are operated by the military airline TAME.

INTERNATIONAL RELATIONS

Membership. Ecuador is a member of UN, OAS, Grupo Andino and LAIA (formerly LAFTA).

ECONOMY

Planning. The 1985–89 medium term objectives aim at private investment in agriculture, fishing, mining, petroleum and gas. Improvement in infrastructure is envisaged.

Budget. Estimated revenue in 1986 was 186,824m. sucres and expenditure, 216,466m. sucres.

Net international reserves, 31 Dec. 1987, were US$55m.

Currency. The monetary unit is the *sucre,* divided into 100 *centavos.* In circulation are a pure nickel 1-sucre and copper-nickel and copper-zinc 50-, 20-, 10- and 5-centavo pieces. The currency consists mainly of the notes of the Central Bank in denominations of 5, 10, 20, 50, 100, 500 and 1,000 sucres. In March 1988, US$1 = 386; £1 = 638·27.

Banking. The Central Bank of Ecuador, at Quito, with a capital and reserves of 3,462m. sucres at Dec. 1986, is modelled after the Federal Reserve Banks of US: through branches opened in 16 towns it now deals in mortgage bonds. All commercial banks must be affiliated to the Central Bank. American and European banks include the Bank of London and Canada with branches in Quito and Guayaquil.

Weights and Measures. By a law of 6 Dec. 1856 the metric system was made the legal standard but the Spanish measures are in general use. The quintal is equivalent to 101·4 lb.

The meridian of Quito has been adopted as the official time.

ENERGY AND NATURAL RESOURCES

Electricity. In 1985, total capacity of hydraulic and thermal plants was 1,795,100 kw. Estimated output was 4,805m. kwh. Supply 110,120 and 220 volts; 60 Hz.

Oil. Production of crude oil in 1987 was 8·5m. tonnes. Ecuador has to import some refined oil.

Gas. In 1985, natural gas production was 608,453·5m. cu. metres.

Minerals. Production (1983): Silver, 3,137·6 troy oz; gold, 607·6 troy oz; copper, 7,900 kg; zinc, 14,820 kg.
The country also has some iron, uranium, lead and coal.

Agriculture. Ecuador is divided into two agricultural zones: the coast and lower river valleys, where tropical farming is carried on in an average temperature of from 18° to 25° C.; and the Andean highlands with a temperate climate, adapted to grazing, dairying and the production of cereals, potatoes, pyrethrum and other flowers, and vegetables suitable to temperate climes. Some wheat has to be imported.
124,000 acres of rich virgin land in the Santo Domingo de los Colorados area has been set aside for settlement of smallholders.
Excepting the two agricultural zones and a few arid spots on the Pacific coast, Ecuador is a vast forest. Roughly estimated, 10,000 sq. miles on the Pacific slope extending from the sea to an altitude of 5,000 ft on the Andes, and the Amazon Basin below the same level containing 80,000 sq. miles, nearly all virgin forest, are rich in valuable timber, but much of it is still not commercially accessible.
The staple export products are bananas, cacao and coffee. Main crops, in 1,000 tonnes, in 1986: Rice, 510; potatoes, 505; maize, 328; coffee, 118; barley, 40; cocoa, 112; bananas, 2,100.
Livestock (1986): Cattle, 3,727,000; sheep, 1,959,000; pigs, 4,986,000; horses, 340,000; poultry, 45m.

Forestry. In 1981, 4·5m. cu. metres of timber were cut. Exports approximately US$10m. per annum.

Fisheries. Fisheries and fish product exports were valued at US$387·6m. in 1986 (268,000 tonnes).

INDUSTRY AND TRADE

Industry. Production in 1978: Sugar, 178,000 tonnes; beer, 1,560,000 hectolitres; cement 1·06m. tonnes.

Commerce. Imports and exports for calendar years, in US$1m.:

	1982	1983	1984	1985	1986
Imports (f.o.b.)	2,187	1,421	1,567	1,611	1,631
Exports (f.o.b.)	2,327	2,348	2,622	2,905	2,186

Of the total exports (1985): petroleum, US$1,926m.; bananas, US$220m.; cocoa, US$138·4m.; coffee, US$190·8m.
USA furnished 30% of imports in 1985 and took 61% of the exports.
Total trade between Ecuador and UK (British Department of Trade returns, in £1,000 sterling):

	1983	1984	1985	1986	1987
Imports to UK	11,022	12,951	19,015	11,339	14,002
Exports and re-exports from UK	35,008	34,323	58,628	46,673	37,934

Tourism. There were 252,443 visitors in 1986, spending US$170m.

COMMUNICATIONS

Roads. In 1983, there were 35,900 km of roads of all types in this mountainous country. A trunk highway through the coastal plain is under construction which will link Machala in the extreme south-west with Esmeraldas in the north-west and with Quito and the northern section of the Pan-American Highway. In 1984, there were 314,360 cars and 32,379 commercial vehicles.

Railways. A 1,067 mm gauge line runs from San Lorenzo through Quito to Guayaquil and Cuenca, total 971 km.

Aviation. There are 2 international airports. The following international lines operate: Air France, Avianca, Eastern, Ecuatoriana de Aviación, KLM, Lufthansa, Pan-Am, Iberia, LAN Chile, Aerovías Peruanas, Aereolinas Argentinas, Air Panama and Varig. They connect Quito with North and Central America, other countries in South America and Europe. All the leading towns are connected by an almost daily service.

Shipping. Ecuador has 3 major seaports, of which Guayaquil is the chief and 6 minor ones. The merchant navy comprises 39,964 tons of seagoing and 21,232 tons of river craft. In 1980 ships totalling 26·58m. GRT entered Ecuadorean ports, unloading 2·28m. tons, and loading 8·59m. tons.

There is river communication, improved by dredging, throughout the principal agricultural districts on the low ground to the west of the Cordillera by the rivers Guayas, Daule and Vinces (navigable for 200 miles by river steamers in the rainy season).

Post and Broadcasting. Quito is connected by telegraph with Colombia and Peru, and by cable with the rest of the world. The main towns in the country are connected by radio-telephone. There are over 470 radio stations.

In 1984 there were 295,650 telephones in use, 104,000 in Quito and 104,000 in Guayaquil; most were operated by the Government; 99% were automatic. Television was inaugurated in 1960 in Guayaquil, in 1961 in Quito and in 1967 in Cuenca. In 1980 there were 1·8m. radio receivers and 1·3m. television receivers.

Cinemas. (1974). Cinemas numbered about 185 with total seating capacity of 114,600.

Newspapers (1984). There were 22 daily newspapers with an aggregate daily circulation of 526,000; 7 papers in Quito and Guayaquil have the bulk of the circulation.

JUSTICE, RELIGION, EDUCATION AND WELFARE

Justice. The Supreme Court in Quito, consisting of a President and 15 Justices, comprises 5 chambers each of 3 Justices. There is a Superior Court in each province, comprising chambers (as appointed by the Supreme Court) of 3 magistrates each. There are numerous lower and special courts. Capital punishment and all forms of torture are prohibited by the constitution, as are imprisonment for debt and contracts involving personal servitude or slavery.

Religion. The state recognizes no religion and grants freedom of worship to all. Civil registration of births, deaths and marriages is obligatory. Divorce is permitted. Illegitimate children have the same rights as legitimate ones with respect to education and inheritance.

Education. Primary education is free and obligatory. Private schools, both primary and secondary, are under some state supervision. In 1982, 13,291 primary schools had 1,676,681 pupils; 1,633 secondary schools with 687,085 pupils and 17 universities and other higher education establishments with 274,353 students.

Health. In 1979 there were 261 hospitals with 14,316 beds. In 1977 there were 4,660 doctors, 1,370 dentists and 1,225 nursing staff.

DIPLOMATIC REPRESENTATIVES

Of Ecuador in Great Britain (3 Hans Cres., London, SW1X 0LS)
Ambassador: Rafael Pérez y Reyna (accredited 17 Dec. 1987).

Of Great Britain in Ecuador (Calle Gonzalez Suarez 111, Quito)
Ambassador: M. W. Atkinson, CMG, MBE.

Of Ecuador in the USA (2535 15th St., NW, Washington, D.C., 20009)
Ambassador: Mario Ribadeneira.

Of the USA in Ecuador (Avenida 12 de Octubre y Avenida Patria, Quito)
Ambassador: Fernando E. Rondon.

Of Ecuador to the United Nations
Ambassador: Carlos Tobar-Zaldumbide.

Books of Reference

Anuario de Legislación Ecuatoriana. Quito. Annual
Boletín del Banco Central. Quito
Boletín General de Estadística. Tri-monthly
Boletín Mensual del Ministerio de Obras Públicas. Monthly
Informes Ministeriales. Quito. Annual
Bibliografía Nacional, 1756–1941. Quito, 1942
Invest in Ecuador. Banco Central del Ecuador, Quito, 1980
Buitrón, A., and Collier, Jr, J., *The Awakening Valley: Study of the Otavalo Indians.* New York, 1950
Cueva, A., *The Process of Political Domination in Ecuador.* London, 1982
Hickman, J., *The Enchanted Islands: The Galapagos Discovered.* Oswestry, 1985
Martz, J. D., *Ecuador: Conflicting Political Culture and the Quest for Progress.* Boston, 1972.—*Politics and Petroleum in Ecuador.* New Brunswick, 1987
Middleton, A., *Class, Power and the Distribution of Credit in Ecuador.* Glasgow, 1981

EGYPT

Jumhuriyat
Misr al-Arabiya

Capital: Cairo
Population: 49·28m. (1987)
GNP per capita: US$466 (1984)

HISTORY. Part of the Ottoman Empire from 1517 until Dec. 1914 when it became a British protectorate, Egypt became an independent monarchy on 28 Feb. 1922. Following a revolution on 23 July 1952, a Republic was proclaimed on 18 June 1953. Egypt merged with Syria on 22 Feb. 1958 to form the United Arab Republic, retaining that name when Syria broke away from the union on 28 Sept. 1961, finally re-adopting the name of Egypt on 2 Sept. 1971.

AREA AND POPULATION. Egypt is bounded east by Israel, the Gulf of Aqaba and the Red Sea, south by Sudan, west by Libya and north by the Mediterranean. The total area is 1,002,000 sq. km (386,900 sq. miles), but the cultivated and settled area, that is, the Nile valley, delta and oases, covers only about 35,580 sq. km.

The area, population (1976 Census and 1985 estimate) and capitals of the governorates are:

Governorate	Sq. km	1976 census	1985 estimate	Capital
Sinai al-Janûbîya	33,140 ⎫	10,104	⎧ 24,000	At-Tur
Sinai ash-Shamâlîya	25,574 ⎭		⎩ 152,000	Al-Arish
Suez	17,840	194,001	254,000	Suez
Ismailia	1,442	351,889	465,000	Ismâilya
Port Said	72	262,620	374,000	Port Said
Sharqîya	4,180	2,621,208	3,318,000	Zaqâziq
Daqahlîya	3,471	2,732,756	3,469,000	Mansûra
Damietta	589	557,115	728,000	Damietta
Kafr el Sheikh	3,437	1,403,468	1,795,000	Kafr el-Sheikh
Alexandria	2,679	2,318,655	2,821,000	Alexandria
Behera	10,130	2,517,292	3,199,000	Damanhur
Gharbîya	1,942	2,294,303	2,847,000	Tanta
Menûfîya	1,532	1,710,982	2,157,000	Shibin el-Kom
Qalyûbîya	1,001	1,674,006	2,186,000	Benha
Cairo	214	5,084,463	6,205,000	Cairo
Gîza	85,105	2,419,247	3,159,000	Gîza
Faiyûm	1,827	1,140,245	1,495,000	Faiyûm
Beni Suef	1,322	1,108,615	1,424,000	Beni-Suef
Minya	2,262	2,055,739	2,692,000	Minyâ
Asyût	1,530	1,695,378	2,179,000	Asyût
Sohag	1,547	1,924,960	2,455,000	Sohag
Qena	1,851	1,705,594	2,159,000	Qinâ
Aswân	679	619,932	781,000	Àswân
al-Bahr al-Ahmar	203,685	56,191	70,000	Al-Ghurdaqah
al-Wadi al-Jadid	376,505	84,645	113,000	Al-Kharijah
Mersa Matruh	212,112	112,772	173,000	Matruh
Total		36,656,180	46,694,000	

The principal towns, with their census 1985 populations, were:

Cairo	6,205,000	Asyût	274,400	Aswân	182,700
Alexandria	2,821,000	Zaqâziq	266,800	Sani Suwayf	151,200
Gaza	1,608,000	Suez	254,000	Uqsur (Luxor)	137,300
Shubrâ al-Khayma	515,500	Damanhûr	221,500	Qinâ	137,100
Port Said	374,000	Fayyûm	218,500	Sawhâj	131,300
Tantâ	364,700	Kafr ad-Dawwar	210,000	Shibin al-Kawm	129,600
Mahalla al-Kubrâ	362,700	Minyâ	191,800	Dumyât	118,100
Hulwan	345,600	Ismâiliya	191,700	Banhâ	115,500
Mansûra	328,700				

444

Population (1987) 49·28m. and of Greater Cairo 13·3m.
The official language is Arabic, although French and English are widely spoken.

CLIMATE. The climate is mainly dry, but there are winter rains along the Mediterranean coast. Elsewhere, rainfall is very low and erratic in its distribution. Winter temperatures are everywhere comfortable, but summer temperatures are very high, especially in the south. Cairo. Jan. 56°F (13·3°C), July 83°F (28·3°C). Annual rainfall 1·2″ (28 mm). Alexandria. Jan. 58°F (14·4°C), July 79°F (26·1°C). Annual rainfall 7″ (178 mm). Aswân. Jan. 62°F (16·7°C), July 92°F (33·3°C). Annual rainfall trace. Giza. Jan. 55°F (12·8°C), July 78°F (25·6°C). Annual rainfall 16″ (389 mm). Ismailia. Jan. 56°F (13·3°C), July 84°F (28·9°C). Annual rainfall 1·5″ (37 mm). Luxor. Jan. 59°F (15°C), July 86°F (30°C). Annual rainfall trace. Port Said. Jan. 58°F (14·4°C), July 78°F (27·2°C). Annual rainfall 3″ (76 mm).

CONSTITUTION AND GOVERNMENT. The Constitution was approved by referendum on 11 Sept. 1971. It defines Egypt as 'an Arab Republic with a democratic, socialist system' and the Egyptian people as 'part of the Arab nation' with Islam as the state religion and Arabic as the official language.

The President of the Republic is nominated by the People's Assembly and confirmed by plebiscite for a 6-year term. He is the supreme commander of the armed forces and presides over the defence council.

Presidents since the establishment of the Republic have been:

Gen. Mohamed Neguib, 18 June 1953–14 Nov. 1954 (deposed).

Col. Gamal Abdel Nasser, 14 Nov. 1954–28 Sept. 1970 (died).

Col. Muhammad Anwar Sadat, 28 Sept. 1970–6 Oct. 1981 (assassinated).

Lieut.-Gen. Muhammad Hosni Mubarak, 7 Oct. 1981–.

The People's Assembly is a unicameral legislature consisting of 448 members directly elected for a 5-year term; the President of the Republic may appoint up to 10 additional members. At the general elections held in April 1987, the National Democratic Party gained 346 seats, the New *Wafd* Party 35, SLP-led alliance 60, Independent 7.

The President may appoint one or more Vice-Presidents, and appoints a Prime Minister and a Council of Ministers, whom he may remove as he wishes.

A 210-member consultative body, the Shura Council, was established in 1980. Two-thirds of its members are elected and one-third appointed by the President.

President of the Republic: Hosni Mubarak, sworn in for second 6-year term Oct. 1987.

The Council of Ministers in Jan. 1988 was composed as follows:

Prime Minister: Dr Atef Mohamed Naguib Sidki.

Deputy Prime Minister and Minister of Defence and Military Production: Field Marshal Mohamed Abdul Halim Abu Ghazala. *Deputy Prime Minister and Minister of Foreign Affairs:* Dr Ahmed Esmat Abdul Meguid. *Deputy Prime Minister and Minister of Planning:* Dr Kamal Ahmed el-Ganzuri. *Deputy Prime Minister and Minister of Agriculture and Food Sufficiency:* Dr Youssef Amin Wali. *Insurance and Social Affairs:* Dr Amal Abdul Rehim Osman. *Housing, Utilities and New Communities:* Hassaballah Mohamed el Kafrawi. *Minister of State for Foreign Affairs:* Dr Boutros Boutros-Ghali. *Transport, Communications and Marine Transport:* Soliman Metwalli Soliman. *Electricity and Energy:* Mohamed Maher Abaza. *Minister of State for Military Production:* Dr Gamal el Sayed Ibrahim. *Information:* Mohamed Safwat el Sherif. *Public Works and Water Resources:* Esam Abdul Hamid Radi. *Industry:* Mohamed Mahmoud Abdul Wahhab. *Petroleum and Mineral Wealth:* Abdul Hadi Mohamed Kandil. *Cabinet Affairs and Minister of State for Administrative Development:* Dr Atef Mohamed Ebeid. *Tourism and Civil Aviation:* Fuad Abdul Latif Sultan. *Interior:* Zaki Mostafa Badr. *Supply and Home Trade:* Dr Mohamed Galal Abul Dahab. *Minister of State for Scientific Research:* Dr Adel Abdul Hamid Ez. *Health:* Dr Mohamed Ragheb Dwidar. *Economy and Foreign Trade:* Dr Yusri Ali Mustafa.

People's Assembly and Shura Council Affairs: Dr Ahmed Salama Mohamed. *Education:* Dr Ahmed Fathi Serour. *Finance:* Dr Mohamed Ahmed el Razzaz. *Wakfs:* Dr Mohamed Ali Mahgoub. *Manpower and Training:* Assem Abdul Haq Saleh. *Justice:* Farouk Seiful Nasr. *Minister of State for International Co-operation:* Dr Mouris Makramallah. *Minister of State for Emigration and Expatriates' Affairs:* Dr Fuad Iskandar. *Culture:* Farouk Hosni.

National flag: Three horizontal stripes of red, white, black, with the national emblem in the centre in gold.

Local Government. There are 26 governorates: 16 provinces, 5 cities and 5 frontier districts.

DEFENCE. Conscription is for 3 years, between the ages of 20 and 35. Graduates serve for 1 year.

Army. The Army comprises 4 armoured, 6 mechanized infantry, and 2 infantry divisions; 1 Republican Guard, 1 independent armoured, 3 independent infantry, 2 airmobile, 1 parachute, 3 artillery, 2 heavy mortar, and 6 anti-tank guided weapon brigades; 7 commando groups; and 2 surface-to-surface missile regiments. Strength (1988) 320,000 (180,000 conscripts) and about 500,000 reservists. Equipment includes 900 T-54/-55, 600 T-62 and 753 M-60A3 tanks.

Navy. There are 12 elderly diesel-driven *ex*-Soviet and *ex*-Chinese submarines (most nearing the end of their hull lives and of which only 8 can be operational – 2 having been used for spares and 2 being overhauled), 1 old destroyer, 2 new Chimere-built frigates, 2 new Spanish-built frigates, 27 missile boats, 3 torpedo boats, 7 fast attack craft, 8 new patrol gunboats, 1 submarine parent ship (*ex*-frigate), 4 fleet minesweepers, 2 inshore minesweepers, 3 medium landing ships, 14 landing craft, 10 minor landing craft, 2 survey vessels, 10 service craft, 2 tenders, 3 minelaying hovercraft, 1 large training ship (*ex*-Royal Yacht), 7 auxiliaries and 4 tugs. There are 108 coast guard cutters.

Naval bases are at Alexandria, Port Said, Mersa Matruh, Port Tewfik, Hurghada and Safaqa. The Naval Academy is at Abu Qir.

Naval personnel in 1988 totalled 20,000 officers and men, including the Coastguard, but not reserves of about 15,000.

Air Force. Until 1979, the Air Force was equipped largely with aircraft of USSR design, but subsequent re-equipment involves aircraft bought in the West, as well as some supplied by China. Strength (1988) is about 25,000 personnel and 500 combat aircraft, of which the interceptors are operated by an independent Air Defence Command, in conjunction with many 'Guideline', 'Goa', 'Gainful', Hawk and Crotale missile batteries. There are about 12 Tu-16 twin-jet strategic bombers, some equipped to carry 'Kelt' air-to-surface missiles. Other interceptor/ground attack fighter divisions are equipped with 75 F-16 Fighting Falcons, 60 Mirage 5s, 33 F-4E Phantoms, 80 F-6s (Chinese-built MiG-19s), 15 Alpha Jets, 50 Su-7s, more than 120 MiG-21s, and 60 F-7s (Chinese-built MiG-21s). Airborne early warning capability is provided by 5 E-2C Hawkeyes. Transport units have 19 C-130H Hercules turboprop heavy freighters, 12 An-12s, 9 twin-turboprop Buffaloes and up to 175 Gazelle, Mi-4, Mi-6, Mi-8, Sea King/Commando and Agusta-built CH-47C helicopters; some Commando helicopters and 2 EC-130H Hercules are equipped for electronic warfare duties. Training units are equipped with Gomhouria piston-engined trainers, Embraer Tucanos, Czech-built L-29 Delfin and Alpha Jet jet trainers, two-seat versions of the MiG-15, MiG-17s, two-seat FT-6s, Mirage IIIs, MiG-21Us and Su-7Us, and UH-12E helicopters. Main aircrew training centre is the EAF Academy at Bilbeis.

INTERNATIONAL RELATIONS

Membership. Egypt is a member of UN, OAU, the Arab League and OAPEC.

ECONOMY

Planning. A 5-year development plan runs 1987/88–1991–92 and envisages investments totalling £E46,500m.

Budget. Ordinary revenue and expenditure for fiscal years ending 30 June, in £E1m.:

	1985–86	1986–87	1987–88
Revenue	15,010	14,451	17,910
Expenditure	19,910	20,246	23,060

Currency. By decree of 18 Oct. 1916 (20 Zi-El-Higga 1934), the monetary unit of Egypt is the gold Egyptian pound of 100 *piastres* of 1,000 *millièmes*. Coins in circulation are 20, 10, 5, 2 piastres (silver); 2, 1 piastre, 5 millièmes, 1 millième (bronze). Gold coins are no longer in circulation. Silver coin is legal tender only up to £E1, and bronze coins up to 10 piastres. The Treasury issues 5- and 10-piastre currency notes. Bank-notes are issued by the National Bank in denominations of 5, 10, 25 and 50 piastres, £E1, 5, 10, 20, and 100.

In March 1988, £1 sterling = £E3·96; US$ = £E0·70.

Banking. On 18 Aug. 1960 a Central Bank of Egypt was established by decree. It manages the note issue, the Government's banking operations and the control of commercial banks. At the same date the National Bank founded in 1898 ceased to be the central bank and became a purely commercial bank. In 1986 there were 27 commercial banks, 33 business and investment banks (joint ventures and 22 foreign currency branches) and 4 specialized banks. There were also 29 representative offices of foreign banks.

Weights and Measures. In 1951 the metric system was made official with the exception of the feddân and its subdivisions.

Capacity. Kadah = 1/96th ardeb = 3·36 pints. *Rob* = 4 kadahs = 1·815 gallons. *Keila* = 8 kadahs = 3·63 gallons. *Ardeb* = 96 kadahs = 43·555 gallons, or 5·44439 bu., or 198 cu. decimetres.

Weights. Rotl = 144 dirhems = 0·9905 lb. *Oke* = 400 dirhems = 2·75137 lb. *Qantâr* or 100 rotls or 36 okes = 99·0493 lb. 1 *Qantâr* of unginned cotton = 315 lb. 1 *Qantâr* of ginned cotton = 99·05 lb. The approximate weight of the ardeb is as follows: Wheat, 150 kg; beans, 155 kg; barley, 120 kg; maize, 140 kg; cotton seed, 121 kg.

Surface. Feddân, the unit of measure for land = 4,200·8 sq. metres = 7,468·148 sq. pics = 1·03805 acres. 1 sq. pic = 6·0547 sq. ft = 0·5625 sq. metre.

ENERGY AND NATURAL RESOURCES

Electricity. Electricity generated in 1986 was 40,600m. kwh. Supply 110 and 220 volts; 50 Hz.

Oil. The first commercial discovery of oil in the Middle East outside Iran was made in Egypt in 1909, but production long remained low and often insufficient to meet Egypt's domestic requirements. Policy is controlled by the Egyptian General Petroleum Corporation (EGPC) a wholly state-owned corporation answerable to the Minister of Petroleum. EGPC is whole or part-owner of the various production and refining companies and controls supplies to the domestic marketing companies. With the agreement of EGPC several foreign oil companies were exploring for oil in 1986.

Production 1987, was 45m. tonnes of crude oil. Net oil earnings (1983–84) US$2,340m.

Gas. The first gas field, at Abu Madi in the Nile delta, became operational in 1974 and produced 4,306,000 tonnes in 1986. The 2 other fields are at Abu Gharadeq in the Western Desert and Abu Qir near Alexandria.

Water. The Aswân High Dam, completed in 1970, allows for a perennial irrigation system.

Minerals. Production (1981 in tonnes): Phosphate rock, 1m. (1985); iron ore, 2,130,000; marine salt, 869,000. Other minerals discovered include manganese, chrome, tantalum, molybdenum and uranium.

Agriculture. The cultivated area of Egypt proper was estimated in 1982 at 11·17m. feddâns (1 feddân = 1·038 acres) and of this, 4,945,000 feddâns were under winter crops, 5,017,000 under summer crops, 818,000 under Nile crops and 390,000 under orchards.

Irrigation occupies a predominant place in the economic development of the country. An intricate irrigation system now reaches most cultivated areas but only about 6·5% of the total land area is arable. The 'vertical' development policy calls for improved methods, better drainage and the introduction of stiff penalties for encroachment of farmland. Under the first phase of the 'horizontal' expansion programme, which aims to add 2·8m. feddâns to the arable area over 20 years, 24,000 feddâns are being added near Alexandria. Export earnings from agriculture have fallen and Egypt is no longer self sufficient in food production partly due to the increase in population. No priority has been given in government planning and because of inadequate investment earnings have fallen for its three most important export crops, cotton, oranges and rice.

In 1985–86 the area sown with cotton rose 7% to 440,705 hectares; output increased 8% to 1,985,000 bales.

The major summer crops are cotton, rice, maize and sorghum. Berseem (Egyptian clover), wheat and beans are the main winter crops.

Production (1986, in 1,000 tonnes): Sugar cane, 9,450; maize, 3,801; tomatoes, 2,840; rice, 2,450; wheat, 1,929; potatoes, 1,275; oranges, 1,170; lint cotton, 434.

Livestock (1986): 2·75m. cattle, 2·6m. buffaloes, 2·55m. sheep, 2·7m. goats, 170,000 camels and 56,000 pigs.

Forestry. In 1982 total removal of roundwood was 1·89m. cu. metres of which 1·8m. was fuel wood.

Fisheries. The catch of the Egyptian sea, Nile and lake fisheries in 1982 amounted to 155,000 tonnes.

INDUSTRY AND TRADE

Industry. (1987) Almost all large-scale enterprises are in the public sector and these account for about two-thirds of total output. The private sector, dominated by food processing and textiles, consists of about 150,000 small and medium businesses, most employing less than 50 workers. A car industry is being established.

Production in 1985–86 (in 1,000 tonnes) included: Phosphates, 766; fertilizer phosphates, 100·1; fertilizer nitrates, 4,482; cement, 7,735; cotton yarn, 225; cotton fabrics, 608,000 metres.

Trade Unions. Trade unions were first recognized in 1942.

Commerce. Imports and exports for 5 years (in £E1,000):

	1981	1982	1983	1984	1985
Imports	6,187,486	6,354,517	7,192,657	7,536,100	6,276,300
Exports	2,262,982	2,184,122	2,250,295	2,197,900	2,600,000

In 1985 major exports (in £E1m.) included: Crude petroleum, 1,402·1; refined petroleum, 362·5; cotton, 299. Major imports (1984–85) included: Machinery and transport equipment, 1,915·2; foodstuffs, 1,848·5.

Exports, 1985 (in US$1m.), were mainly to Italy (656·6), Israel (462), Romania (434·2), France (430), USSR (177·8), Netherlands (152·1), Greece (119·2), Japan (113·8), Spain (100·2) and Republic of Korea (99·7); imports were mainly from USA (1,295·7), Federal Republic of Germany (953·8), Italy (757·3), France (700·9), Japan (514·7), UK (425·3), Spain (390·1), Romania (369·7), Netherlands (356·5) and Australia (335·7).

Total trade between Egypt and UK (British Department of Trade returns, in £1,000 sterling):

	1983	1984	1985	1986	1987
Imports to UK	79,826	164,946	162,162	328,053	127,261
Exports and re-exports from UK	370,489	427,688	471,091	371,007	342,195

Tourism. In 1986 there were 1·36m. tourists (43% from Arab countries) spending £E251·3m.

COMMUNICATIONS

Roads. In 1980, the total length of roads was 21,637 km, of which 16,182 km were paved. Motor vehicles, in 1981, 580,000 private cars, 165,000 commercial vehicles (including buses).

Railways. In 1986 there were 4,321 km of state railways (1,435 mm gauge) which carried 28,340m. passenger-km and 8.6m. tonnes of freight. An underground rail system was opened in Cairo in 1987.

Aviation. There is an international airport at Cairo. There are 95 airfields (77 unusable). The national airline Egyptair operates scheduled flights connecting Cairo with Athens, Rome, Frankfurt, Zürich, London, Khartoum, Tōkyō, Bombay, Aden, Jeddah, Doha, Dharan, Kuwait, Beirut, Baghdad, Tripoli, Benghazi, Algiers, Entebbe, Nairobi, Dar-es-Salaam, Kano, Lagos, Accra, Abidjan, Damascus, Amman, Manilla, Paris, Munich, Copenhagen, Nicosia, Karachi, Aleppo, Bahrain, Abu Dhabi, Dubai, Sharjah, Sanaa and Vienna. In addition, Egyptair operates scheduled flights on a widespread domestic network connecting Cairo with Port Said, Mersa Matruh, Asyût, Luxor, Aswân. In 1982, 62,000 tonnes of cargo were carried.

Shipping. The Egyptian merchant navy in 1980 consisted of 75 steamers of 387,460 tons.

In 1977, 3,050 ships of 11,432,000 tons entered the port of Alexandria and 876 ships of 4,583,000 tons entered Port Said.

Suez Canal. The Suez Canal was opened for navigation on 17 Nov. 1869. By the convention of Constantinople of 29 Oct. 1888 the canal is open to vessels of all nations and is free from blockade, except in time of war, but the UAR Government did not allow Israeli ships to use the canal until May 1979, when the embargo was lifted. It is 173 km long (excluding 11 km of approach channels to the harbours), connecting the Mediterranean with the Red Sea. Its minimum width is 197 ft at a depth of 33 ft, and its depth permits the passage of vessels up to 38 ft draught.

In 1976 a 2-stage development project was started. The first stage which was completed in 1980 allowing vessels, of up to 150,000 tons, fully loaded, and up to 370,000 tons in ballast to pass through the canal and give a draught of 53 ft.

During the war with Israel in June 1967 the Canal was blocked. The canal was cleared and re-opened to shipping on 5 June 1975. This is part of a programme to develop and rebuild the whole area of Suez to make it one of the largest tax-free industrial zones. Canal toll fees reached US$980m. in 1984, and in 1983 22,224 vessels (378.2m. tons) went through the canal. The first tunnel below the canal, located 10 miles north of Suez City, was completed on 30 April 1980 and the first phase of a £E4,000m. development plan, to widen and deepen the canal, was completed in 1980.

Post and Broadcasting. There were, in 1980–81, 1,821 postal agencies, 1,812 mobile offices (1978), 1,747 government and 2,956 private post offices. Number of telephones in 1984, 600,000. Number of wireless licences in 1984, 12m. and 4m. TV licences.

The internal telecommunications system is owned and operated by the Telecommunications Organization. Government landlines connect with those of the Gaza sector and the Sudan.

Cinemas (1971). There were 152 cinemas with a seating capacity of 140,900.

Newspapers. In 1984 there were 11 dailies published in Cairo and 6 in Alexandria.

JUSTICE, RELIGION, EDUCATION AND WELFARE

Justice. The National Courts in 1981 were as follows: Court of Cassation with a bench of 5 judges which constitutes the highest court of appeal in both criminal and civil cases; Courts of Appeal with 3 judges situated in Cairo and 4 other cities; Assize Courts with 3 judges which deal with all cases of serious crime; Central Tribunals with 3 judges which deal with ordinary civil and commercial cases; Summary Tribunals presided over by a single judge which hear civil disputes in matters up to the value of £E3,250, and criminal offences punishable by a fine or imprisonment of up to 3 years.

Religion. In 1986 about 90% of the population were Moslems, mostly of the Sunni sect, and about 7% Coptic Christians, the remainder being Roman Catholics, Protestants or Greek Orthodox, with a small number of Jews.

There are in Egypt large numbers of native Christians connected with the various Oriental Churches; of these, the largest and most influential are the Copts, who adopted Christianity in the 1st century. Their head is the Coptic Patriarch. There are 25 metropolitans and bishops in Egypt; 4 metropolitans for Ethiopia, Jerusalem, Khartoum and Omdurman, and 12 bishops in Ethiopia. Priests must be married before ordination, but celibacy is imposed on monks and high dignitaries. The Copts use the Diocletian (or Martyrs') calendar, which begins in A.D. 284.

Education. Primary education (6 years) was made free in 1944, secondary and technical education in 1950. Compulsory education is provided in primary schools (6 years).

In 1982–83 there were 503 nurseries and kindergartens with 84,539 pupils. In 1982–83 there were in basic education (6–15 years) 5,036,608 primary stage pupils in 12,013 schools and 1,769,768 preparatory stage pupils in 3,151 schools. In secondary education there were 517,998 general secondary pupils in 823 schools; 441,636 commercial secondary pupils in 639 schools; 208,468 industrial secondary pupils in 170 schools and 84,527 agricultural secondary pupils in 65 schools. Ninety-two teacher training schools had 63,429 pupils and 144 rehabilitation schools had 8,215 pupils.

El Azhar institutes educate students who join the faculties of El Azhar University after graduation. In 1982–83, 1,287 institutes had 308,370 students.

Government experimental language schools, which teach in foreign languages, had 5,000 nursery and kindergarten pupils in 1982–83, and 2,700 primary stage pupils in 1983–84.

Higher education: In 1982, there were 64,870 students in 17 higher commercial institutes and 22,341 students in 16 industrial institutions.

There were 11 universities in Egypt (apart from El Azhar University), with 558,527 students and 74,945 graduates in 1980–81. El Azhar University had 65,451 students and 5,346 graduates in 1980–81.

Health. In 1983–84 there were about 73,300 doctors and 85,350 hospital beds.

DIPLOMATIC REPRESENTATIVES

Of Egypt in Great Britain (26 South St., London, W1Y 8EL)
Ambassador: Yousef Sharara (accredited 29 Nov. 1984).

Of Great Britain in Egypt (Ahmed Ragheb St., Garden City, Cairo)
Ambassador: W. J. Adams, CMG.

Of Egypt in the USA (2310 Decatur Pl., NW, Washington, D.C., 20008)
Ambassador: Abdel Raouf El-Ridy.

Of the USA in Egypt (5 Sharia Latin America, Cairo)
Ambassador: Frank G. Wisner.

Of Egypt to the United Nations
Ambassador: Abdel Halim Badawi.

Books of Reference

Egypt: Facts and Figures 1985. Ministry of Information, 1985
The Egyptian Almanac. Annual
Le Mondain Egyptien (Who's Who). Cairo. Annual
Aliboni, R., (et al) *Egypt's Economic Potential.* London, 1984
Hart, V., *Modern Egypt.* Cairo, 1984
Heikal, M., *Autumn of Fury: Assassination of Sadat.* London, 1983
Hopwood, D., *Egypt: Politics and Society 1945–1981.* London, 1982
Kepel, G., *Muslim Extremism in Egypt.* Univ. of California Press, 1986
Makar, R. N., *Egypt.* [Bibliography] Oxford and Santa Barbara, 1988
Springberg, R., *Family, Power and Politics in Egypt.* Univ. of Pennsylvania Press, 1982
Waterbury, J., *The Egypt of Nasser and Sadat.* Princeton Univ. Press, 1983

EL SALVADOR

República de El Salvador

Capital: San Salvador
Population: 5·48m. (1985)
GNP per capita: US$880 (1985)

HISTORY. In 1839 the Central American Federation, which had comprised the states of Guatemala, El Salvador, Honduras, Nicaragua and Costa Rica, was dissolved, and El Salvador declared itself formally an independent republic in 1841.

AREA AND POPULATION. El Salvador is the smallest and most densely populated (256 inhabitants per sq. km) of the Central American states. Its area (including 247 sq. km of inland lakes) is estimated at 21,393 sq. km (8,236 sq. miles) with population estimate (1985) 5·48m.

The republic is divided into 14 departments, each under an appointed governor. Their areas and populations in 1981 were:

Department	Sq. km	1981	Chief town	1984
Ahuachapán	1,281	241,323	Ahuachapán	20,153
Sonsonate	1,133	321,989	Sonsonate	47,489
Santa Ana	1,829	445,462	Santa Ana	135,186
La Libertad	1,650	388,538	Nueva San Salvador	52,226
San Salvador	892	979,683	San Salvador	452,614
Chalatenango	2,507	235,757	Chalatenango	28,675 [1]
Cuscatlán	766	203,978	Cojutepeque	31,108
La Paz	1,155	249,635	Zacatecoluca	25,650
San Vicente	1,175	206,959 [1]	San Vicente	26,461
Cabañas	1,075	179,909	Sensuntepeque	50,448 [1]
Usulután	1,780	399,912	Usulután	31,349
San Miguel	2,532	434,047	San Miguel	86,722
Morazán	1,364	215,163	San Francisco	13,015 [1]
La Unión	1,738	309,879	La Unión	27,186

[1] 1980.

CLIMATE. Despite its proximity to the equator, the climate is warm rather than hot and nights are cool inland. Light rains occur in the dry season from Nov. to April while the rest of the year has heavy rains, especially on the coastal plain. San Salvador. Jan. 71°F (21·7°C), July 75°F (23·9°C). Annual rainfall 71″ (1,775 mm). San Miguel. Jan. 77°F (25°C), July 83°F (28·3°C). Annual rainfall 68″ (1,700 mm).

CONSTITUTION AND GOVERNMENT. A new Constitution was enacted in Dec. 1983. The Executive Power is vested in a President elected for a non-renewable term of 5 years, with Ministers and Under-Secretaries appointed by him. The Legislative power is an Assembly of 60 members elected by universal suffrage and proportional representation for a term of 3 years. The judicial power is vested in a Supreme Court, of a President and 9 magistrates elected by the Legislative Assembly for renewable terms of 3 years; and subordinate courts. For governments, 1961–79 see STATESMAN'S YEAR-BOOK 1982–83, p. 436.

Elections were held in March 1984.

President: José Napoleon Duarte (elected May 1984).

In Jan. 1988 the Cabinet was composed as follows:

Vice-President: Rodolfo Castillo Claramont. *Foreign Affairs:* Dr Ricardo Acevedo Peralta. *Planning and Co-ordination of Economic and Social Development:* Dr Fidel Chávez Mena. *Interior:* Dr Edgar Ernesto Belloso. *Justice:* Dr Julio Alfredo Samayoa. *Finance:* Ricardo J. López. *Foreign Trade:* Dr Ricardo González Camacho. *Economics:* Dr Ricardo Perdomo. *Education:* Professor Alberto Buendía Flores. *Defence and Public Safety:* Carlos Eugenio Vides Casanova.

Labour and Social Security: Dr Miguel Alejandro Gallegos. *Public Health and Social Welfare:* Dr Benjamín Valdez H. *Agriculture and Livestock:* Carlos Aquilino Duarte Funes. *Works:* Luis Lopez Cerón.

National flag: Blue, white, blue (horizontal): the white stripe charged with the arms of the republic.
National anthem: Saludemos la patria orgullosos (words by J. J. Cañas; tune by J. Aberle).

DEFENCE. There is selective national service for 2 years.

Army. The Army comprises 6 infantry brigades, 1 mechanized cavalry regiment, 1 artillery brigade, 1 engineer, 1 anti-aircraft, 1 parachute, 14 light infantry and 6 counter-insurgency battalions. Equipment includes 12 AMX-13 light tanks and 10 AML-90 armoured cars. Strength was (1988) 43,000. There are also National Guard, National Police and Treasury Police, paramilitary units, numbering (1988) about 12,000 and a territorial civil defence force of up to 12,000.

Navy. The Navy includes 4 patrol boats, 1 modern French-built tug, 6 cutters and 25 service launches. Personnel in 1988 totalled 300 officers and men.

Air Force. The Air Force underwent a major re-equipment programme in 1974–75, with most aircraft coming from Israel and US aid for transport units, but lost 18 aircraft in a guerrilla attack in Jan. 1982. Counter-insurgency equipment includes 8 A-37B and 6 Magister attack aircraft, 3 armed C-47 transports and 4 Hughes 500MD helicopters. Other aircraft are 12 C-47, 3 Arava, 1 DC-6 and 2 C-123 transports, 10 Cessna O-2 patrol aircraft, plus 3 Lamas, 3 Alouette III and 50 UH-1H helicopters. Training types include about 15 piston-engined T-41Cs, T-6s and T-34s. Strength totalled about 2,500 personnel in 1988.

INTERNATIONAL RELATIONS

Membership. El Salvador is a member of UN and OAS.

ECONOMY

Planning. The development plan 1985–89 envisages investment of ₡6,294m.

Budget. Revenue and expenditure for fiscal years ending 31 Dec., in 1,000 cólones:

	1980	1981	1982	1983	1984	1985
Revenue	1,376,337	1,740,424	1,730,899	1,723,333	2,817,730	2,391,010
Expenditure	1,606,335	1,757,600	1,864,699	1,847,065	2,685,009	2,276,052

External debt amounted to US$1,650m. in 1983.

Currency. The monetary unit is the *colón* (₡) of 100 *centavos*. The *colón* (₡) is issued in denominations of 1, 2, 5, 10, 25 and 100 *cólones*; 25 and 50 *centavos* and 1 *colón* (silver); 1, 2, 5 and 10 *centavos* (copper–nickel and copper–zinc); 1 centavo (nickel). In March 1988, £1 = ₡8·85; US$1 = ₡5·00.

Banking. There are 10 native commercial banks, including the Banco Salvadoreño (paid-up capital, 6m. cólones). The Citibank Bank of America and the Bank of Santander and Panama S. A. are the only foreign institutions. The Central Reserve Bank of El Salvador, constructed in 1934 out of the Banco Agricola Comercial, was nationalized on 20 April 1961.

Weights and Measures. On 1 Jan. 1886 the metric system was made obligatory. But other units are still commonly in use, of which the principal are as follows: *Libra* = 1·014 lb. av.; *quintal* = 101·4 lb. av.; *arroba* = 25·35 lb. av.; *fanega* = 1·5745 bushels.

ENERGY AND NATURAL RESOURCES

Electricity. A 200 ft high dam completed in 1954 was constructed across the (unnavigable) Lempa River, 35 miles north-east of San Salvador, with an annual capacity of 344m. kwh. The San Lorenzo dam, completed in 1983, has an annual capacity of 722m. kwh. Production in 1986, 1,710m. kwh.; consumption (1984), 1,415m. kwh. Supply 120 and 240 volts; 60 Hz.

Oil. Production of petroleum derivatives during 1984 totalled ₡608,473,000.

Minerals. The mineral output of the republic is now negligible, but the Ministry of Public Works has recently started to investigate 2 new silver mines in the department of Morazán.

Agriculture. El Salvador is predominantly agricultural; 32·5% of its total area is used for crops and 30·2% for pasture. Area devoted to coffee (1982–83) was about 516,615 acres, entirely owned by nationals. In 1981, 35·5% of the working population was engaged in farming.

Production (1986, in 1,000 tonnes): Coffee, 141; seed cotton, 55; maize, 391; dry beans, 50; rice, 53; sorghum, 135; sugar-cane, 3,175. A little rubber is exported.

Livestock (1986): 1·01m. cattle, 400,000 pigs, 4,000 sheep, 14,000 goats.

Forestry. In the national forests are found dye woods and such woods as mahogany, cedar and walnut. Balsam trees also abound: El Salvador is the world's principal source of this medicinal gum. Production, 1981, ₡36,148,000.

Fisheries. In 1983, fish products were valued at ₡82·2m. Total catch 1983, 7,600 tonnes.

INDUSTRY AND TRADE

Industry. Total production was valued at ₡4,579,322m. in 1984, which included (in 1,000 colones): Food, ₡1,827,983; textiles, ₡273,573; chemicals, ₡310,922; footwear and clothing, ₡218,287; beverages, ₡352,224.

Commerce. The imports (including parcels post) and exports have been as follows in calendar years in 1,000 colónes:

	1979	1980	1981	1982	1983	1984
Imports	2,529,900	2,404,269	2,461,458	2,141,852	2,228,700	2,443,575
Exports	2,579,300	2,683,953	1,991,940	1,748,616	1,840,800	1,793,432

Of total exports (1984), coffee furnished about 34·6% by weight and 61·7% by value. The coffee is of the 'mild' variety; it is sold in bags of 60 kg, but trade statistics use a bag of 69 kg.

In 1984 US took 669,933,000 colónes of exports and furnished 811,347,000 colónes of the imports. The chief imports in 1984 were manufactured goods (26·9%), chemical and pharmaceutical products (23%), non-edible crude materials, mainly crude oil (17·2%), electric machinery, tools and appliances and transport equipment (15·4%). The other Central American Republics, the Federal Republic of Germany, Japan, Canada, Mexico, Spain, France and the Netherlands are also important trading partners.

Total trade between El Salvador and UK (British Department of Trade returns, in £1,000 sterling):

	1983	1984	1985	1986	1987
Imports to UK	425	2,551	1,662	1,323	1,890
Exports and re-exports from UK	7,653	7,589	8,507	6,917	9,595

Tourism. There were 134,000 visitors in 1986.

COMMUNICATIONS

Roads. In 1982 there were 12,297 km of national roads in the republic, including 1,695 km of main paved roads; 3,295 km main asphalted roads; other roads, 7,308·1 km. Motor vehicles registered, 1983, 150,079.

Railways. All railways (602 km) came under the control of National Railways of El Salvador *(Fenadesal)* in 1975. Lines run from Acajutla to San Salvador; Cutuco to San Salvador; between San Salvador and Santa Ana, San Miguel and Sonsonate;

there is also a link to the Guatemalan system. Total railway traffic in 1984 was 315,000 tonnes of freight and 290,100 passengers.

Aviation. The airport at Ilopango, 8 km from San Salvador, now a military airport, and the new international airport at Cuscatlán, 40 km from San Salvador, opened in 1979. In 1984, 144,576 passengers arrived and 164,654 departed.

Shipping. The principal ports are La Unión, La Libertad and Acajutla, all on the Pacific. Passengers (and some freight) use the Guatemalan port of Puerto Barrios on the Atlantic, reaching El Salvador by rail or road.

Post and Broadcasting. The telephone and telegraph systems are government-owned; the radio-telephone systems are partly private, partly government-owned. Telephone instruments, 1983, 82,158. There were (1986) over 50 radio stations. Radio El Salvador is state-owned. There were (1986) 4 commercial television channels and 2 educational channels sponsored by the Ministry of Education.

Cinemas (1976). Cinemas numbered 65.

Newspapers (1987). There are 4 daily newspapers in San Salvador and 1 in Santa Ana.

JUSTICE, RELIGION, EDUCATION AND WELFARE

Justice. Justice is administered by the Supreme Court of Justice, courts of first and second instance, besides minor tribunals. Magistrates of the Supreme Court and courts of second instance are elected by the Legislative Assembly for a renewable 3-year term.

An anti-Communist law, effective 29 Sept. 1962, has made the propagation of totalitarian or Communist doctrines an offence punishable by imprisonment; supplementary offences, contrary to democratic principles, are punished by prison terms of from 3 to 7 years.

Religion. The dominant religion is Roman Catholicism. Under the 1962 Constitution churches are exempted from the property tax; the Catholic Church is recognized as a legal person, and other churches are entitled to secure similar recognition. There is an archbishop in San Salvador and bishops at Santa Ana, San Miguel, San Vicente, Santiago de María, Usulafter, Sonsonate and Zacatecoluca.

Education. Education is free and obligatory. In 1929 the State took over control of all schools, public and private, but the provision that the teaching in government schools must be wholly secular was removed in 1945.

In 1984 there were 60,902 pupils in nursery schools, 969,120 in secondary schools, 74,113 students at universities and polytechnics and (1983) 42,700 students receiving adult education.

Social Welfare. The Social Security Institute now administers the sickness, old age and death insurance, covering industrial workers and employees earning up to ₡700 a month. Employees in other private institutions with salaries over this amount are included but are excluded from the medical and hospital benefits.

DIPLOMATIC REPRESENTATIVES

Of El Salvador in Great Britain (62 Welbeck St., London, W1)
Ambassador: Dr Mauricio Rosales-Rivera (accredited 26 Feb. 1986).

Of Great Britain in El Salvador
Ambassador: D. Joy, CBE.

Of El Salvador in the USA (2308 California St., NW, Washington, DC., 20008)
Ambassador: Dr Ernesto Rivas-Gallont.

Of the USA in El Salvador (25 Ave. Norte, Colonia Dueñas, San Salvador)
Ambassador: Edwin G. Corr.

Of El Salvador to the United Nations
Ambassador: Dr Roberto Meza.

Books of Reference

Statistical Information: The Dirección General de Estadística y Censos (Villa Fermina, Calle Arce, San Salvador) dates from 1937. *Director General:* Lieut.-Col. José Castro Meléndez. Its publications include *Anuario Estadístico.* Annual from 1911.—*Boletín Estadístico.* Quarterly.—*El Salvador en Gráficas.* Annual.—*Atlas Censal de El Salvador.* 1955 only.— Revista Mensual, Banco Central de Reserva de El Salvador.

Angel Gallardo, M., *Cuatro Constituciones Federales de Centro América y Las Constituciones Políticas de El Salvador.* San Salvador, 1945

Armstrong, R., and Shenk, J., *El Salvador: The Face of Revolution.* London, 1982

Baloyra, E. A., *El Salvador in Transition.* Univ. of North Carolina Press, 1982

Bevan, J., *El Salvador. Education and Repression.* London, 1981

Browning, D., *El Salvador: Landscape and Society.* OUP, 1971

Devire, F. J., *El Salvador: Embassy under Attack.* New York, 1981

Didion, J., *Salvador.* London, 1983

Erdozain, P., *Archbishop Romero: Martyr of El Salvador.* Guildford, 1981

Montgomery, T.S., *Revolution in El Salvador: Origins and Evolution.* Boulder, 1982

North, L., *Bitter Grounds: Roots of Revolt in El Salvador.* London, 1981

Schmidt, S. W., *El Salvador: America's Next Vietnam.* Salisbury (N.C.), 1983

EQUATORIAL GUINEA

Capital: Malabo
Population: 384,000 (1987)
GNP per capita: US$420 (1983)

República de Guinea Ecuatorial

HISTORY. Equatorial Guinea was a Spanish colony (Territorios Españoles del Golfo de Guinea) until 1 April 1960, the territory was then divided into two Spanish provinces with a status comparable to the metropolitan provinces until 20 Dec. 1963, when they were re-joined as an autonomous Equatorial Region. It became an independent Republic on 12 Oct. 1968 as a federation of the two provinces, and a unitary state was established on 4 Aug. 1973. The first President, Francisco Macías Nguema, was declared President-for-Life on 14 July 1972, but was overthrown by a military *coup* on 3 Aug. 1979. A Supreme Military Council then created was the sole political body until constitutional rule was resumed on 12 Oct. 1982.

AREA AND POPULATION. The mainland part of Equatorial Guinea is bounded north by Cameroon, east and south by Gabon, and west by the Gulf of Guinea in which lie the islands of Bioko (formerly Macías Nguema, formerly Fernando Póo) and Annobón (called Pagalu from 1973 to 1979). The total area is 28,051 sq. km (10,831 sq. miles) and the population at the 1983 census was 300,000. Estimate (1987) 384,000. Another 110,000 are estimated to remain in exile abroad.

The 7 provinces are grouped into 3 regions with areas and populations as follows:

	Sq. km	Census 1983	Chief town
Annobón	17	2,006	Palé
Bioko Norte ⎱		46,221	Malabo
Bioko Sur ⎰	2,017	10,969	Luba
Centro Sur ⎫		52,393	Kogo
Kié-Ntem ⎪		70,202	Mikomeseng
Litoral ⎬	26,017 [1]	66,370	Bata
Wele-Nzas ⎭		51,839	Mongomo

[1] Including the adjacent islets of Corisco, Elobey Grande and Elobey Chico (17 sq. km).

In 1986 the largest towns were Bata (17,000) and the capital Malabo (10,000).

The main ethnic group on the mainland (Río Muni) is the Fang; there are several minority groups along the coast and adjacent islets. On Bioko the indigenous inhabitants (Bubis) constitute 60% of the population there, the balance being mainly Fang and coast people from Río Muni; the formerly numerous immigrant workers from Nigeria and Cameroon have mostly been repatriated. On Annobón the indigenous inhabitants are the descendents of Portuguese slaves and still speak a Portuguese patois. The official language is Spanish.

CLIMATE. The climate is equatorial, with alternate wet and dry seasons. In Río Muni, the wet season lasts from Dec. to Feb.

CONSTITUTION AND GOVERNMENT. A new Constitution was approved in Aug. 1982 by 95% of the votes cast in a plebiscite, which also confirmed the President in office for a further 7-year term. A 41-member National Assembly was elected on 28 Aug. 1983 for a 5-year term.

President and Minister of Defence Security and Political Affairs: Col. Teodoro Obiang Nguema Mbasogo (from 3 Aug. 1979).
Prime Minister, Health: Capt. Cristino Seriche Bioko Malabo.
Deputy Prime Minister, Territorial Administration (Interior) and National

Security: Isidoro Eyi Monsui Andeme. *Foreign Affairs:* Marcelino Nguema Ongueme.

National flag: Three horizontal stripes of green, white, red; a blue triangle based on the hoist; in the centre the national arms.

DEFENCE. Under President Macías the *Guardia Nacional* consisted mainly of Fang soldiers with Cuban and Chinese military advisers. Total active strength (1988) of 1,400 with some 2,000 para-military personnel. Since the 1979 *coup,* Moroccan troops and Spanish military and police personnel have replaced Soviet bloc advisers.

INTERNATIONAL RELATIONS

Membership. Equatorial Guinea is a member of UN, OAU and is an ACP state of EEC.

ECONOMY

Budget. The 1982 budget envisaged income at 2,980m. Bikuele and expenditure at 4,038m. Bikuele.

Currency. In July 1973 the Guinean *peseta* was redesignated the *Ekuele* (plural, *Bikuele*). On 2 Jan. 1985 the country joined the franc zone and the *Ekuele* was replaced by the *franc CFA.*

Banking. The *Banque des Etats de l'Afrique Centrale* became the bank of issue in Jan. 1985. There are 2 commercial banks.

ENERGY AND NATURAL RESOURCES

Electricity. Production (1986) 17m. kwh.

Agriculture. The chief products are cocoa (75,000 hectares in 1986), coffee (18,000 hectares) and wood; in 1984 production was about 10,000 tonnes of cocoa, most of it high-grade exported to Spain and the US. Coffee, of mediocre quality, is chiefly a Fang product. Production (1986) of coffee 7,000 tonnes; palm oil, 7,000; palm kernels, 2,900; bananas, 19,000. Food crops include cassava, 55,000; sweet potatoes, 35,000. Plantations in the hinterland have been abandoned by their Spanish owners and except for cocoa, commercial agriculture is under serious difficulties.

Livestock (1986): Cattle, 4,000; sheep, 35,000; goats, 8,000.

Forestry. Wood was almost entirely exported from Río Muni to Spain and the Federal Republic of Germany. Production: 1981, 465,000 cu. metres. Since 1979 the lumber industry has resumed activity but there was (1981) a shortage of labour.

Fisheries. Catch (1983) 2,500 tonnes.

INDUSTRY AND TRADE

Industry. Bioko has very few industries. Rio Muni has no industry except lumbering. Post-independence political conditions have not been conducive to private investment.

Commerce. In 1981 imports amounted to 7,982m. Bikuele (of which 80% came from Spain) and exports to 2,502m. Bikuele (of which Spain took 87%). Cocoa amounted to 71% of all exports and timber to 24%.

Total trade between Equatorial Guinea and UK (British Department of Trade returns, in £1,000 sterling):

	1984	1985	1986	1987
Imports to UK	559	...	1	...
Exports and re-exports from UK	553	191	633	1,572

COMMUNICATIONS

Roads. Length (1982) 2,760 km of which 330 km surfaced.

Aviation. There are international airports at Malabo and Bata. The line Madrid–Malabo–Bata is subsidized by Spain. Links with Douala (from Malabo) and Libreville (Gabon) exist.

Shipping. Malabo is the main port. The other ports are Luba, formerly San Carlos (bananas, cocoa) in Bioko and Bata, Kogo and Mbini (wood) in Río Muni. A new harbour in Bata has been completed. In 1981 47,731 tonnes were unloaded and 50,843 loaded.

Post and Broadcasting. Estimated number of telephones (1969), 1,451. In 1984 there were 90,000 radio and 2,100 TV receivers.

JUSTICE, RELIGION, EDUCATION AND WELFARE

Justice. The Constitution guarantees an independent judiciary. The Supreme Tribunal is the highest court of appeal and is located at Malabo. There are Courts of First Instance and Courts of Appeal at Malabo and Bata.

Religion. The population of Equatorial Guinea is nominally Roman Catholic with influential Protestant groups in Malabo and Río Muni. By order of the President most churches were closed in 1975 and in June 1978 the Roman Catholic Church was banned. Since 1979, religious services have been restored.

Education. There were in 1981 about 40,110 pupils and 647 teachers in 511 primary schools and 3,013 pupils and 288 teachers in 14 secondary schools.

Health. In 1975 there were 5 doctors, 2 midwives and 248 nursing personnel.

DIPLOMATIC REPRESENTATIVES

Of Equatorial Guinea in Great Britain
Ambassador: (Vacant).

Of Great Britain in Equatorial Guinea
Ambassador: M. Reith (resides at Yaoundé).

Of the USA in Equatorial Guinea (Calle de Los Ministros, Malabo)
Ambassador: Francis S. Ruddy.

Of Equatorial Guinea to the USA and the United Nations
Ambassador: Florencio Maye Ela.

Books of Reference

Atlas Historico y Geográfico de Africa Española. Madrid, 1955
Plan de Desarrollo Económico de la Guinea Ecuatorial. Presidencia del Gobierno. Madrid, 1963
Berman, S., *Spanish Guinea: An Annotated Bibliography.* Microfilm Service, Catholic University. Washington, D.C. 1961
Liniger-Goumaz, M., *La Guinée équatoriale un pays méconnu.* Paris, 1980.—*Connaître la Guinée Equatoriale.* Paris, 1986
Pélissier, R., *Les Territoires espagnols d'Afrique.* Paris, 1963.—*Los territorios españoles de Africa.* Madrid, 1964.—*Etudes Hispano-Guinéennes.* Orgeval, 1969

ETHIOPIA

Hebretesebawit
Ityopia

Capital: Addis Ababa
Population: 46m. (1986)
GNP per capita: US$110 (1984)

HISTORY. The ancient empire of Ethiopia has its legendary origin in the meeting of King Solomon and the Queen of Sheba. Historically, the empire developed in the centuries before and after the birth of Christ, at Aksum in the north, as a result of Semitic immigration from South Arabia. The immigrants imposed their language and culture on a basic Hamitic stock. Ethiopia's subsequent history is one of sporadic expansion southwards and eastwards, checked from the 16th to early 19th centuries by devastating wars with Moslems and Gallas. Modern Ethiopia dates from the reign of the Emperor Theodore (1855–68).

Menelik II (1889–1913) defeated the Italians in 1896 and thereby safeguarded the empire's independence in the scramble for Africa. By successful campaigns in neighbouring kingdoms within Ethiopia (Jimma, Kaffa, Harar, etc.) he united the country under his rule and created the empire as it is today.

In 1936 Ethiopia was conquered by the Italians, who were in turn defeated by the Allied forces in 1941 when the Emperor returned.

The former Italian colony of Eritrea, from 1941 under British military administration, was in accordance with a resolution of the General Assembly of the UN, dated 2 Dec. 1950, handed over to Ethiopia on 15 Sept. 1952. Eritrea thereby became an autonomous unit within the federation of Ethiopia and Eritrea.

This federation became a unitary state on 14 Nov. 1962 when Eritrea was fully integrated with Ethiopia although a secessionist movement has also been active.

A provisional military government assumed power on 12 Sept. 1974 and deposed the Emperor. On 24 Nov. 1974 the Provisional Military Government announced that on 23 Nov. it had executed 60 former military and civilian leaders including Gen. Aman Andom who was Chairman of the Provisional Military Administrative Council.

On 3 Feb. 1977, Brig.-Gen. Teferi Bante, the Chairman of PMAC and 6 other members of the ruling military council were killed and Lieut.-Col. Mengistu Haile Mariam became Chairman.

In mid-1977 Somalia invaded Ethiopia and took control of the Ogaden region. After an offensive mounted with strong USSR and Cuban support the area was recaptured and in March Somalia withdrew all troops from the area. Control was re-established by Ethiopia later in 1978 and nationalist guerrillas were pushed back. Sporadic fighting continued in the Ogaden and along the border. Talks about the normalization between Ethiopia and Somalia commenced in 1986.

AREA AND POPULATION. Ethiopia is bounded north-east by the Red Sea, east by Djibouti and Somalia, south by Kenya and west by Sudan. It has a total area of 1,221,900 sq. km (471,800 sq. miles). The first census was carried out in 1984: Population (preliminary) 42,019,418. Estimate (1986) 46m. There were 204,000 refugees in Ethiopia in Aug. 1987.

The dominant race of Ethiopia, the Amhara, inhabit the central Ethiopian highlands. To the north of them are the Tigréans, akin to the Amhara and belonging to the same Christian church, but speaking a different, though related, language. Both these races are of mixed Hamitic and Semitic origin, and further mixed by intermarriage with Oromo (Galla) and other races. The Oromos, some of whom are Christian, some Moslem and some pagan, comprise about 40% of the entire population, and are a pastoral and agricultural people of Hamitic origin. Somalis, another Hamitic race, inhabit the south-east of Ethiopia, in particular the Ogaden desert region. These like the closely related Afar people, are Moslem. The Afar stretch northwards from Wollo region into Eritrea.

Region	Area (sq. km)	Population May. 1984	Chief town	Population May 1984
Addis Ababa	218	1,412,575	—	—
Arussi	23,500	1,662,233	Assela	36,720
Bale	124,600	1,006,491	Goba	22,963
Eritrea	117,600	2,614,700	Asmara	275,385
Gemu Gofa	39,500	1,248,034	Arba Minch	23,030
Gojjam	61,600	3,244,882	Debre Markos	39,808
Gondar (Begemdir)	74,200	2,905,362	Gondar	68,958
Hararge	259,700	4,151,706	Harar	62,160
Illubabor	47,400	963,327	Mattu	12,491
Kefa	54,600	2,450,369	Jimma	60,992
Shoa	85,200	8,090,565	—	—
Sidamo	117,300	3,790,579	Awassa	36,169
Tigre	65,900	2,409,700	Mekele	61,583
Wollega	71,200	2,369,677	Lekemti	28,824
Wollo	79,400	3,609,918	Dessie	68,848

Other large towns (population, May 1984): Dire Dawa, in Hararge, 98,104; Nazret, in Shoa, 76,284; Bahr Dar, 54,800; Debre Zeit, 51,143.

Local Government. From Sept. 1987 the country is divided into 24 administrative and 5 autonomous regions. Each region governed by a regional *shengo*.

CLIMATE. The wide range of latitude produces many climatic variations between the high, temperate plateaus and the hot, humid lowlands. The main rainy season lasts from June to Aug., with light rains from Feb. to April, but the country is very vulnerable to drought. Addis Ababa. Jan. 59°F (15°C), July 59°F (15°C). Annual rainfall 50″ (1,237 mm). Harar. Jan. 65°F (18·3°C), July 64°F (17·8°C). Annual rainfall 35″ (897 mm). Massawa. Jan. 78°F (25·6°C), July 94°F (34·4°C). Annual rainfall 8″ (193 mm).

CONSTITUTION AND GOVERNMENT. The People's Democratic Republic of Ethiopia was inaugurated on 10 Sept. 1987 at the first meeting of the newly elected *Shengo* (National Assembly). A new Constitution, on a Marxist model, was approved on 1 Feb. 1987 in a referendum. On 14 June 1987 Ethiopia held its first parliamentary election when 813 members belonging to the single political party the Workers' Party of Ethiopia were elected to the new civilian legislature.

President: Mengistu Haile Mariam.
Vice President: Fisseha Desta.
Prime Minister: Fikre-Selassie Wogderess.

National flag: Three horizontal stripes of green, yellow and red.
National anthem: Ityopya, Ityopia Kidemi (tune by Daniel Yohannes, 1975).

DEFENCE. Ethiopia's revolutionary rulers have moved away from US military assistance since they came to power and from 1977 have relied on USSR for most of their military aid.

Selective conscription was introduced in 1983 for a period of 30 months.

Army. The Army, comprises 22 infantry divisions with some 32 tank battalions, 8 para-commando brigades, 37 artillery battalions and 12 air defence battalions. Equipment includes 600 T-54/-55, 40 T-34 and 65 M-47 tanks. Strength (1988) 313,000 including a People's Militia.

Navy. The Navy consists of 2 *ex*-Soviet light frigates, 4 *ex*-Soviet fast missile boats, 2 *ex*-Soviet fast torpedo boats, 1 hydrofoil fast attack craft, 1 training ship (1,768 tons; *ex*-US seaplane tender), 1 *ex*-Netherlands coastal minesweeper, 1 patrol craft (*ex*-US coastguard motor gunboat), 3 patrol boats, 3 *ex*-Soviet coastal cutters, 4 harbour defence craft, 2 medium landing ships, 2 landing craft and 4 minor landing craft. The Naval Base and College are at Massawa.

Personnel in 1988 totalled 1,500 officers and men. Soviet advisers remained embarked in the 6 attack craft acquired until Ethiopian naval officers and ratings had sufficient experience to operate independently the missiles and torpedoes.

Air Force. The Air Force, trained originally by Swedish and American personnel, but now operating aircraft of Soviet origin, has its headquarters at Debre Zeit, near Addis Ababa. It includes a training school and a central workshop. Fighter equipment is understood to comprise 140 MiG-17s, MiG-21s and MiG-23s. There is a squadron of Mi-24 helicopter gunships, and a transport squadron equipped with An-12s, and An-26s. Training aircraft include two-seat MiG-21s and L-39 jet basic trainers. More than 40 Mi-8 helicopters are in service. Most equipment surviving from the 1960s and '70s (such as F-5 fighters, Canberra bombers and US-built transports) is in storage. However since 1984 India has delivered 10 Chetak (Alouette III) helicopters and Italy 21 SF-260TP turboprop trainers. Personnel, (1988) 4,000 officers and men.

INTERNATIONAL RELATIONS

Membership. Ethiopia is a member of UN, OAU and is an ACP state of EEC.

ECONOMY

Planning. A 10-year development plan (1984–94) places emphasis on socialist development and a growth rate of 6%.

Budget. Revenue for 1983–84 (ending 7 July) was EB2,897·6m. and expenditure EB3,459·8m.

Of the estimated revenue in 1983–84, EB1,706m. is expected to come from taxes.

Currency. The Ethiopian *birr*, divided into 100 cents, is the unit of currency; it is based on 5·52 grains of fine gold. It consists of notes of EB1, 2, 10, 50 and 100 denominations, and bronze 1-, 5-, 10-, 25- and 50-cent coins. *Birr* 3·64 = £1 sterling; *Birr* 2·07 = US$1 (in March 1988).

Banking. The State Bank was renamed the National Bank of Ethiopia in Oct. 1963, when its commercial activities were transferred to the newly established Commercial Bank of Ethiopia. At the same time another new bank, the Investment Bank of Ethiopia, was set up with a capital of EB10m., of which the Government held the majority of shares. In Sept. 1965 it became the Ethiopian Investment Corporation, which is a substantial shareholder in a number of industrial and other ventures. There is also the Agricultural and Industrial Development Bank, SC.

On 1 Jan. 1975 the Government nationalized all banks, mortgage and insurance companies.

Weights and Measures. The metric system of weights and measures is officially in use. Traditional weights and measures vary considerably in the various provinces: the principal ones are: *Frasilla* = approximately 37½ lb.; *gasha*, the principal unit of land measure, which is normally about 100 acres but can vary between 80 and 300 acres, depending on the quality of the land.

ENERGY AND NATURAL RESOURCES

Electricity. Production in 1986 totalled 722m. kwh. Supply 220 volts; 50 Hz.

Oil. A Russian built state-owned oil refinery at Assab came on stream in 1967 with a capacity of 600,000 tonnes of crude per annum.

Gas. A natural gas-strike was made offshore near Massawa in Dec. 1969, but it was not exploited. Traces of gas and oil have been found in south-east Ethiopia.

Minerals. Ethiopia has little proved mineral wealth. Salt is produced mainly in Eritrea, while a placer goldmine is worked by the Government of Adola in the south. Gold production, in 1980, was 373 kg. Small quantities of other minerals are produced including platinum.

Agriculture. Coffee is by far the most important source of rural income accounting for 70% of foreign earnings in 1982. Harari coffee (long berry Mocha) is cultivated in the east.

Teff (*Eragrastis abyssinica*) is the principal food grain, followed by barley, wheat, maize and durra. Pulses and oilseeds are imported for local consumption and export. Cane sugar is an important crop.

Production (1986 in 1,000 tonnes): Maize, 1,500; sorghum, 1,100; barley, 1,000; pulses, 945.

Livestock (1986): 26·3m. cattle, 23·55m. sheep, 17·28m. goats; smaller numbers of donkeys, horses, mules and camels. Hides and skins and butter (ghee) are important for home consumption and export. Sheep, cattle and chickens are the main providers of meat. In 1983 85% of the population were engaged in agriculture, producing 40% of GDP. The continuing drought has had a devastating effect on production.

Fisheries. Catch (1983) 3,900 tonnes.

INDUSTRY AND TRADE

Industry. The most important products of the small but growing industries are cotton yarn (9,000 tonnes in 1982) and fabrics, cement (159,000 tonnes in 1982), sugar, salt, cigarettes, canned foodstuffs, beer, building materials, footwear, pharmaceuticals, tyres and paint. Most industry is centred around Addis Ababa and Asmara. Industry around Asmara has been severely hit by actions of Eritrean guerrillas.

Commerce. Imports and exports (in EB1m.) for 3 years.

	1979	1980	1982	1983
Imports	1,175	1,495	1,529	1,810
Exports	864	879	835	...

Total trade between Ethiopia and UK (British Department of Trade returns, in £1,000 sterling):

	1983	1984	1985	1986	1987
Imports to UK	12,071	13,733	13,805	22,343	12,875
Exports and re-exports from UK	34,092	63,434	66,089	50,049	46,146

Tourism. There were 59,000 tourists in 1986.

COMMUNICATIONS

Roads. There were (1984) 30,000 km of roads. Addis Ababa is linked with Nairobi by a highway.

Motor vehicles (1984): Cars, 41,300; lorries and trucks, 8,800; buses, 3,041.

Railways. The former Franco-Ethiopian Railway Co. (782 km, metre-gauge) became the Ethiopian-Djibouti Railway Corp. in 1982, when the remaining France-owned shares were bought out. In 1983 the railway carried 249,000 tonnes of freight and 1·4m. passengers.

Aviation. Ethiopian Air Lines, formed in 1946, carried 242,924 passengers in 1980 and 8,613 tonnes of freight.

Shipping. A state shipping line was established in 1964. The ports unloaded 1·75m. tonnes in 1982 and loaded 547,000.

Post and Broadcasting. The postal system serves 301 offices, mainly by air-mail. All the main centres are connected with Addis Ababa by telephone or radio telegraph. International telephone services are available at certain hours to most countries in Europe, North America and India. Number of telephones (1983), 100,783.

The Ethiopian Broadcasting Service makes sound broadcasts on the medium and short waves in English, Amharic and in the vernacular languages spoken within the country. There were about 45,000 television sets and 2m. radio receivers in 1986.

Cinemas (1974). There were 31 cinemas, with seating capacity of about 25,600.

Newspapers. There were (1984) 3 government-controlled daily newspapers with a combined circulation of about 47,000.

JUSTICE, RELIGION, EDUCATION AND WELFARE

Justice. The legal system is said to be based on the Justinian Code. A new penal code came into force in 1958 and Special Penal Law in 1974. Codes of criminal procedure, civil, commercial and maritime codes have since been promulgated.

The extra-territorial rights formerly enjoyed by foreigners have been abolished, but any person accused in an Ethiopian court has the right to have his case transferred to the High Court, provided he asks for this before any evidence has been taken in the court of first instance.

Provincial and district courts have been established, and High Court judges visit the provincial courts on circuit. The Supreme Court at Addis Ababa is presided over by the Chief Justice.

Religion. About 45% of the population are Moslem and 40% Christian, mainly belonging to the Ethiopian Orthodox Church.

Education. In the academic year 1980–81 there were more than 2·13m. pupils in primary schools. In secondary schools there were 400,000 students. Higher education is co-ordinated under the National University, chartered in 1961; in 1979–80, there were 14,562 students. The University College, the Engineering, Building and Theological Colleges are in Addis Ababa, the Agricultural College in Harar and the Public Health College in Gondar.

The government claims to have reduced illiteracy from 95% to 54% since 1974.

Health. In 1977 there was one doctor for every 75,000 people.

DIPLOMATIC REPRESENTATIVES

Of Ethiopia in Great Britain (17 Prince's Gate, London, SW7 1PZ)
Ambassador: Ato Teferra Haile-Selassie (accredited 10 July 1985).

Of Great Britain in Ethiopia (Fikre Mariam Abatechan St., Addis Ababa)
Ambassador: Harold Walker, CMG.

Of Ethiopia in the USA (2134 Kalorama Rd., NW, Washington D.C., 20008)
Chargé d'Affaires: Girma Amara.

Of the USA in Ethiopia (Entoto St., Addis Ababa)
Chargé d'Affaires: James R. Cheek.

Of Ethiopia to the United Nations
Ambassador: Tesfaye Tadesse.

Books of Reference

Halliday, F. and Molyneaux, M., *The Ethiopian Revolution.* London, 1981
Hancock, G., *Ethiopia: The Challenge of Hunger.* London, 1985
Pool, D., *Eritrea: Africa's Longest War.* London, 1982
Schwab, P., *Ethiopia: Politics, Economics and Society.* Boulder, 1985.

FALKLAND ISLANDS

Capital: Stanley
Population: 1,916 (1986)

HISTORY. France established a settlement in 1764 and Britain a second settlement in 1765. In 1770 Spain bought out the French and drove off the British. In 1806 Spanish rule was overthrown in Argentina, and the Argentine claimed to succeed Spain in the French and British settlements in 1820. The British objected and reclaimed their settlement in 1832 as a Crown Colony.

On 2 April 1982 Argentine forces invaded the Falkland Islands and the Governor was expelled. At a meeting of the UN Security Council, held on 3 April, the voting was 10 to 1 in favour of the resolution calling for Argentina to withdraw. Britain regained possession on 14–15 June after the Argentine surrendered.

AREA AND POPULATION. The Crown Colony is situated in the South Atlantic Ocean about 480 miles north-east of Cape Horn. The numerous islands cover 4,700 sq. miles. The main East Falkland Island, 2,610 sq. miles; the West Falkland, 2,090 sq. miles, including the adjacent small islands.

The population of the Falkland Islands at census 1986 was 1,916. The only town is Stanley, in East Falkland, with a population of just over 1,200. The population of the Falkland Islands is nearly all of British descent, with about 67% born in the islands. A large garrison of British servicemen was stationed near Stanley in 1987.

CLIMATE. A cool temperate climate, much affected by strong winds, particularly in spring. Stanley. Jan. 49°F (9·4°C), July 35°F (1·7°C). Annual rainfall 27″ (681 mm).

CONSTITUTION AND GOVERNMENT. A new Constitution came into force on 3 Oct. 1985. This incorporated a chapter protecting fundamental human rights and in the preamble recalled the provisions on the right of self-determination contained in international covenants.

Executive power is vested in the Governor who must consult the Executive Council except on urgent or trivial matters. He must consult the Commander British Forces on matters relating to defence and internal security (except police).

There is a Legislative Council consisting of 8 elected members and 2 *ex officio* members, the Chief Executive and Financial Secretary. Only elected members have a vote. The Commander British Forces has a right to attend and take part in its proceedings but has no vote. The Attorney General also has a similar right to take part in proceedings with the consent of the person presiding. The Governor presides over sittings. He also presides over sittings of the Executive Council which consists of 3 elected members (elected by and from the elected members of Legislative Council) and the Chief Executive and Financial Secretary (*ex officio*) who do not vote. The Commander British Forces and Attorney General have a right to attend but may not vote.

Offices in the Public Service are constituted by the Governor and he makes appointments and is responsible for discipline. The Constitution allows for the establishment of a public service commission.

Governor: G. W. Jewkes, CMG.
Chief Executive: B. R. Cummings.
Financial Secretary: H. T. Rowlands, OBE.
Attorney General: D. G. Lang.
Government Secretary: C. Redston.

Flag: British Blue Ensign with arms of Colony on a white disc in the fly.

DEFENCE. Since 1982 the Islands have been defended by a large garrison of British servicemen. The Commander British Forces is responsible for all military matters in the Islands. He liaises with the Governor on civilian and political matters, and advises him on matters of defence and internal security, except police.

ECONOMY

Budget. Revenue and expenditure (in £ sterling) for fiscal years ending 30 June:

	1982–83	1983–84	1984–85	1985–86	1986–87	1987–88 [1]
Revenue	3,655,000	5,314,000	5,163,000	6,003,315	19,646,310	22,774,680
Expenditure	3,119,000	3,867,000	4,358,000	5,344,048	12,212,805	21,968,150

[1] Estimate

Currency. The Falkland £ is at parity with the £ sterling.

Banking. On 1 Dec. 1983 the government savings bank was dissolved, and all savings bank deposits were transferred to the Standard Chartered Bank, which has a branch in Stanley, and provides a full range of banking facilities.

SHEEP FARMING. Most of the Colony is divided into large sheep runs. Subdivision into smaller family units is gradually being effected. Wool is the principal product, but hides are exported. In 1986 there were 699,000 sheep, 7,000 cattle and 2,000 horses in the islands.

DEVELOPMENT. The economy was formerly based solely on agriculture, principally sheep farming with a little dairy farming for domestic requirements and crops for winter fodder. Since the establishment of a 150-mile interim conservation and management zone around the Islands and the consequent introduction, on 1 Feb. 1987, of a licensing regime for vessels fishing within the zone the economy has diversified and income from the associated fishing activities is now the largest source of revenue. The Falkland Islands Development Corporation was established by statute in June 1984 with the aim of encouraging economic development. The first projects assisted by the Corporation include inshore and offshore fisheries surveys to establish potential catch size and value, agricultural improvement schemes to encourage investment in the land, a wool spinning and knitting factory to process a portion of the islands' main product, a new dairy and a hydroponic market garden.

TRADE. Total imports, 1981, amounted to £3,193,437 and exports to £2,304,446.

Total trade between the Falkland Islands and UK (British Department of Trade returns, in $1,000 sterling):

	1985	1986	1987
Imports to UK	7,434	14,286	8,148
Exports and re-exports from UK	9,502	11,135	7,353

COMMUNICATIONS

Roads. There are 27 km of made-up roads in and around Stanley and another 54 km of all-weather road between Stanley and Mount Pleasant Airport. Other settlements outside Stanley are linked by tracks, which are passable, with high axle clearing four-wheel drive vehicles in all but the worst weather. Work has recently recommenced on the construction of an all-weather track linking the Estancia Farm with the Stanley to Mount Pleasant Road which will help towards opening up the north of East Falkland. The Government is also providing assistance to farms which wish to improve tracks and bridges to their immediate area.

Aviation. Air communication is currently *via* Ascension Island. A new airport, completed in 1986, is sited at Mount Pleasant on East Falkland. RAF Tristar aircraft operate a twice-weekly service between the Falklands and the UK. Internal air links are provided by the government operated air service, which carries passengers, mail, freight and medical patients between the settlements and Stanley on non-scheduled flights in Islander aircraft.

Shipping. A charter vessel calls 4 or 5 times a year to/from the UK. There is occasional direct communication with South Georgia, the South Sandwich Islands and the British Antarctic Territory by the Royal research ships *John Biscoe* and *Bransfield* and by the ice-patrol vessel HMS *Endurance*. Vessels of the Royal Fleet Auxiliary run regularly to South Georgia.

Post and Broadcasting. Number of telephones (1987) 560. International direct dialling is available, as are international telex and facsimile links. Plans to update the telecommunications network were being considered in 1987. There is a government-operated broadcasting station at Stanley.

JUSTICE, EDUCATION AND WELFARE

Justice. There is a Supreme Court, and a Court of Appeal sits in the United Kingdom; appeals may go from that court to the judicial committee of the Privy Council. Judges have security of tenure and may only be removed for inability or misbehaviour on the advice of the judicial committee of the Privy Council. The senior resident judicial officer is the Senior Magistrate. There is an Attorney General and a Crown Solicitor but no lawyers in private practice.

Education. Education is compulsory between the ages of 5 and 15 years. In Feb. 1987 there were 351 children receiving education in the Colony. Almost 75% attended schools in Stanley, the others were taught in settlement schools or by itinerant teachers. 5 children were being educated abroad.

Health. The Government Medical Department is responsible for all medical services to civilians. The Chief Medical Officer advises the Government on policy, and is chairman of the Board of Health responsible for public health. Medical services for the Islands are run from a temporary hospital; a new hospital and some sheltered accommodation was completed in March 1987. Services include all primary care for Stanley and the flying doctor service for outlying farm settlements.

WILD LIFE. The Falkland Islands are noted for their outstanding wild life, including penguin and seal. Four Nature Reserves have been declared and 18 Wild Animal and Bird Sanctuaries gazetted. The brown trout introduced between 1947 and 1952 can now be found in nearly all the rivers and there are good runs of sea-trout during spring and autumn.

Books of Reference

Falkland Islands: The Facts. HMSO, London, 1982
Falkland Islands Journal. Stanley, from 1967
Falkland Islands Review [Franks Report] Cmnd. 8787. HMSO, London, 1983
Falklands/Malvinas, Whose Crisis? Latin American Bureau, London, 1982
Calvert, P., *The Falklands Crisis: The Rights and the Wrongs.* London, 1982
Hanrahan, B., and Fox, R., *'I counted them all out and I counted them all back'.* London, 1982
Hastings, M., and Jenkins, S., *The Battle for the Falklands.* London, 1983
Hoffmann, F. L., and Hoffmann, O. M., *Sovereignty in Dispute.* London, 1984
Phipps, C., *What Future for the Falklands?* London, 1977
Shackleton, E., *Falkland Islands Economic Study 1982.* HMSO, London, 1982
Strange, I. J., *The Falkland Islands.* 3rd ed. Newton Abbot, 1983.—*The Falkland Islands and their Natural History.* Newton Abbot, 1987

FIJI

Capital: Suva
Population: 714,000 (1986)
GNP per capita: US$1,700 (1985)

HISTORY. The Fiji Islands were discovered by Tasman in 1643 and visited by Capt. Cook in 1774, but first recorded in detail by Capt. Bligh after the mutiny of the *Bounty* (1789). In the 19th century the search for sandalwood, in which enormous profits were made, brought many ships. Deserters and shipwrecked men stayed on; firearms salvaged from wrecks were used in native wars, new diseases swept the islands, and rum and muskets became regular articles of trade. Tribal wars became bloody and general until Fiji was ceded to Britain on 10 Oct. 1874, after a previous offer of cession had been refused. British administrators produced order out of chaos, and since then there has been steady political, social and economic progress. Fiji gained independent status on 10 Oct. 1970.

AREA AND POPULATION. Fiji comprises about 332 islands and islets (about 110 inhabited) lying between 15° and 22° S. lat. and 174° E. and 177° W. long. The largest is Viti Levu, area 10,429 sq. km (4,027 sq. miles), next is Vanua Levu, area 5,556 sq. km (2,145 sq. miles). The island of Rotuma (47 sq. km, 18 sq. miles), about 12° 30′ S. lat., 178° E. long., was added to the colony in 1881. Total area, 7,078 sq. miles (18,333 sq. km).

A population census is taken every 10 years. Total population (census, Aug. 1986), 714,000; average annual increase about 1.9%. The 1986 total population consisted of the following: 330,000 (46.2%) Fijians; 347,000 (48.6%) Indians; 37,000 (5.2%) were of other races.

Suva, the capital, is on the south coast of Viti Levu; population (1982), 71,255. Suva was proclaimed a city on 2 Oct. 1953. Lautoka had 26,000 in 1982.

Vital statistics, 1984: Crude birth rate per 1,000 population, Fijian, 29.2, Indian, 27.5; crude death rate per 1,000 population, Fijian, 4.2, Indian, 4.9.

CLIMATE. A tropical climate, but oceanic influences prevent undue extremes of heat or humidity. The S.E. Trades blow from May to Nov., during which time nights are cool and rainfall amounts least. Suva. Jan. 80°F (26.7°C), July 73°F (22.8°C). Annual rainfall 117″ (2,974 mm).

CONSTITUTION AND GOVERNMENT. Following a military *coup* in May 1987 the government was removed from office by the Governor-General who took temporary control of the administration. A second *coup* led by Col. Rabuka took place in Sept. and Fiji was declared a Republic and membership of the Commonwealth lapsed.

President: Ratu Sir Penaia Ganilau, GCMG, KCVO, KBE, DSO.
Prime Minister and Minister for Foreign Affairs: Ratu Sir Kamisese Mara, GCMG, KBE.

Home Affairs, National Youth Service and Auxiliary Army Services: Brig. Sitiveni Rabuka. *Fijian Affairs:* Col. Vatiliai Navunisaravi. *Finance and Economic Planning:* Josefata Kamikamica. *Education:* Filipe Bole. *Primary Industries:* Viliame Gonelevu. *Trade and Commerce:* Berenado Vunibobo. *Health:* Dr Apenisa Kurisaqila. *Communications, Works and Transport:* Apisai Tora. *Attorney-General and Justice:* Sailosi Kepa. *Tourism, Civil Aviation and Energy:* David Pickering. *Youth and Sport:* Col. Ilaisa Kacisolomone. *Rural Development and Rural Housing:* Col. Apolosi Biuvakaloloma. *Indian Affairs:* Irene Jai Narayan. *Forests:* Ratu Sir Josaia Tavaiqia. *Employment and Industrial Relations:* Taniela Veitata. *Co-operatives and National Marketing Authority:* Ishwari Bajpai. *Women's Affairs and Social Welfare:* Finau Tabakaucord. *Housing and Urban Development:* Tomasi Vakatora. *Lands and Mineral Resources:* Ratu William Toganivalu. *Information:* Charles Walker.

Flag: Light blue with the Union Flag in the canton and the shield of Fiji in the fly.

Local Government. Fiji is divided into 14 provinces, each with its own council under which 188 Tikina Councils have been established. The number of Tikina Councils within a province varies from 4 to 22. Tikina Councils have wide powers to make by-laws and levy rates to raise revenue. 50% of the rates collected is credited to the Provincial Council treasury for the running of the Council and 50% is used for the financing of the Tikina and village projects.

DEFENCE. The Fiji Military Forces are for the defence of Fiji, maintenance of law and order and provision of forces to international peace-keeping agencies overseas. The forces have two overseas battalions and regular and territorial units at home. Total active strength (1988) 2,600 (reserves, 5,000).

Navy. A naval division was authorized in 1974 to perform fishery protection, surveillance, hydrographic surveying and coastguard duties. Present strength is 3 coastal minesweepers (*ex*-US MSC), 1 utility vessel and 2 survey craft. Naval personnel in 1988 numbered 150 officers and ratings. Training is carried out in Australia, New Zealand, USA and Hong Kong. The naval base is HMFS *Viti* in Suva.

INTERNATIONAL RELATIONS

Membership. Fiji is a member of the UN, the Colombo Plan, the South Pacific Forum and is an ACP state of the EEC.

ECONOMY

Budget. The financial year corresponds with the calendar year. All figures are in $1m. Fijian.

	1981	1982	1983	1984	1985
Revenue	259·4	258·3	296·4	337·7	349·9
Expenditure	239·6	273·2	304·1	344·4	349·3

Currency. Fiji changed to decimal currency on 13 Jan. 1969, with the major unit being $F1. In March 1988, £1 = $F2·57; US$ = $F1·46.

Banking. The National Bank of Fiji had, in 1985, deposits amounting to $F62·3m. due to 241,375 accounts. The headquarters are at Suva, and there are 11 branches, 35 postal agencies and 9 private agencies throughout Fiji. The Westpac Banking Corporation has 9 branches, 2 sub-branches and 18 agencies; the Bank of New Zealand has 8 branches, and 18 agencies; the Australia and New Zealand Bank has 9 branches and 7 agencies and the Bank of Baroda has 8 branches and 3 agencies in Fiji.

ENERGY AND NATURAL RESOURCES

Electricity. Production (1986) 220m. kwh. Supply 240 volts; 50 Hz.

Agriculture. Some 600,000 acres of land are in agricultural use. Sugar-cane is the principal cash crop (production, 1986, 4·3m. tonnes), accounting for more than two-thirds of Fiji's export earnings; one quarter of the population depend on it directly or their livelihood. Copra, Fiji's second major cash crop (output, 1986, 22,000 tonnes), provides coconut oil and other products for export. Ginger is the third major export crop replacing bananas which has declined through disease and hurricane. Production, 1986 (in 1,000 tonnes): Rice, 28; maize, 2; fruit, 18; vegetables, 16. Tobacco and cocoa are also cultivated. There is a small, but fast developing, livestock industry.

Livestock (1986): Cattle, 159,000; horses, 42,000; goats, 56,000; pigs, 31,000; poultry, 1m.

Forestry. Fiji supplies the bulk of its own timber requirements. A comprehensive pine scheme has been implemented with the aim of planting 186,000 acres by 1988.

Fisheries. Catch (1985) 15,900 tonnes. Exports (1986) F$20m.

INDUSTRY AND TRADE

Industry. Major industries include 4 large sugar-mills, the goldmines (1,865 kg in 1985) and 2 mills which process copra into coconut oil and coconut meal. There is a great variety of light industries.

Trade Unions. In 1985 there were 46 trade unions operating with about 45,000 members.

Commerce. Exports in 1985, $F263,887,000 (including re-exports). Imports, $F508,191,000. Chief exports: Sugar, gold, molasses and canned fish.

Total trade between Fiji and UK (British Department of Trade returns, in £1,000 sterling):

	1982	1983	1984	1985	1986	1987
Imports to UK	39,826	46,943	70,209	36,328	66,500	53,062
Exports and re-exports from UK	9,088	12,184	11,281	9,843	8,775	7,381

Tourism. In 1986, there were 260,000 visitors. Earnings (1986) $F185m.

COMMUNICATIONS

Roads. Total road mileage is 2,996, of which 376 are sealed (paved), 2,534 are gravelled and 86 are unimproved. In 1985, there were 66,287 vehicles including 27,699 private cars, 21,539 goods vehicles, 1,260 buses, 4,366 tractors, 4,754 taxis and 6,669 rental and hire cars and others.

Railway. Fiji Sugar Cane Corporation runs 600 mm gauge railways at four of its mills on Viti Levu and Vanua Levu, totalling 595 km.

Aviation. Fiji provides an essential staging point for long-haul trunk-route aircraft operating between North America, Australia and New Zealand. Under the South Pacific Air Transport Council, which comprises the UK, Australia, New Zealand and Fiji, the international airport at Nadi has been developed and administered. Eighteen other airports are in use for domestic services.

Shipping. The 3 ports of entry are Suva, Lautoka and Leuuka. In 1985, 1,313 vessels called at Suva, 780 at Lautoka and 1,004 at Leuuka. Local shipping provides services to scattered outer islands of the group.

Post. There are 43 post offices and 176 postal agencies. Overseas telephone and telegram services are available through the Commonwealth cable to most countries except those in the South Pacific, which are served by direct radio circuits. The automatic telex network operates through New Zealand into the international telex system. There are ship-to-shore radio facilities. There were 53,228 telephones in 1985.

Cinemas. In 1979 there were 48 cinemas with a seating capacity of 28,100.

JUSTICE, RELIGION AND EDUCATION

Justice. An independent Judiciary is guaranteed under the Constitution of Fiji. The Constitution allows for a Supreme Court of Fiji which has unlimited original jurisdiction to hear and determine any civil or criminal proceedings under any law.

The Supreme Court also has jurisdiction to hear and determine constitutional and electoral questions including the membership of members of the House of Representatives and the Senate.

The Chief Justice of Fiji is appointed by the Governor-General acting after consultation with the Prime Minister and the Leader of the Opposition.

The Fiji Court of Appeal of which the Chief Justice is *ex officio* President is formed by four specially appointed Justices of Appeal. The Justices of Appeal are appointed by the Governor-General acting after consultation with the Judicial and Legal Services Commission. Generally any person convicted of any offence has a right of appeal from the Supreme Court to the Fiji Court of Appeal. The final appellant court is the Privy Council. Most matters coming before the Superior Courts originate in Magistrates' Courts.

Police. The Royal Fiji Police Force had (1986) a total strength of 1,510.

Religion. The 1976 census showed: Christians, 299,960; Hindus, 234,520; Moslems, 45,247; Confucians, 731.

Education (1984). School attendance is not compulsory in Fiji. There were 1,069 schools scattered over 56 islands, staffed by 7,615 teachers, of whom about 93% were trained. There were also 219 pre-schools. The 665 primary and 139 secondary schools had 166,617 pupils. The technical and vocational schools had 3,708 students and the teachers' colleges 181. There were 3 teacher-training colleges, 1 medical and 2 agricultural schools.

The University of the South Pacific (USP) opened in Feb. 1968 at Laucala Bay in Suva. In 1985 there were about 2,000 students enrolled in courses on campus and about 6,000 enrollments in extension services. The University has an operating budget of $F12·13m. a year provided by the 11 countries it serves.

Total government expenditure on education in 1984 (including USP) was $F80,863,000.

Health. In 1984 there were 27 hospitals with 1,736 beds, 339 doctors, 50 dentists and 1,406 nurses.

DIPLOMATIC REPRESENTATIVES

Of Fiji in Great Britain (34 Hyde Park Gate, London, SW7 5DN)
Ambassador: Brig. Ratu Epeli Nailatikau.

Of Great Britain in Fiji (47 Gladstone Rd., Suva)
Ambassador: R. A. R. Barltrop, CMG, CVO.

Of Fiji in the USA (2233 Wisconsin Ave., NW, Washington, D.C., 20007)
Chargé d'Affaires: Abdul Yusuf.

Of the USA in Fiji (31 Loftus St., Suva)
Ambassador: Edric Sherman.

Of Fiji to the United Nations
Ambassador: Winston Thompson.

Books of Reference

Statistical Information: A Bureau of Statistics was set up in 1950 (Government Buildings, Suva).
Trade Report. Annual (from 1887 [covering 1883–86]). Bureau of Statistics, Suva.
Journal of the Fiji Legislative Council. Annual (from 1914 [under different title from 1885]). Suva
Fiji Today. Suva, Annual
Fiji Facts and Figures. Suva, 1986
Report of Commission of Inquiry Into Natural Resources and Population Trends in Fiji. Suva, Government Press, 1960
Ali, A., *Plantations to Politics, studies on Fiji Indians.* Suva, 1980
Capell, A., *New Fijian Dictionary.* 2nd ed. Glasgow, 1957
Ravuvu, A., *Vaka i Taukei: The Fijian Way of Life.* Suva, 1983
Scarr, D., *Fiji, A Short History.* Sydney, 1984
Wright, R., *On Fiji Islands.* London, 1987

FINLAND

Capital: Helsinki
Population: 4·93m. (1986)
GNP per capita: US$14,302 (1986)

Suomen Tasavalta— Republiken Finland

HISTORY. Since the Middle Ages Finland was a part of the realm of Sweden. In the 18th century parts of south-eastern Finland were conquered by Russia, and the rest of the country was ceded to Russia by the peace treaty of Hamina in 1809. Finland became an autonomous grand-duchy which retained its previous laws and institutions under its Grand Duke, the Emperor of Russia. After the Russian revolution Finland declared itself independent on 6 Dec. 1917. The Civil War began in Jan. 1918 between the 'whites' and 'reds', the latter being supported by Russian bolshevik troops. The defeat of the red guards in May 1918 consequently meant freeing the country from Russian troops. A peace treaty with Soviet Russia was signed in 1920.

On 30 Nov. 1939 Soviet troops invaded Finland, after Finland had rejected territorial concessions demanded by the USSR. These, however, had to be made in the peace treaty of 12 March 1940, amounting to 32,806 sq. km and including the Carelian Isthmus, Viipuri and the shores of Lake Ladoga.

When the German attack on the USSR was launched in June 1941 Finland again became involved in the war against the USSR. On 19 Sept. 1944 an armistice was signed in Moscow. Finland agreed to cede to Russia the Petsamo area in addition to cessions made in 1940 (total 42,934 sq. km) and to lease to Russia for 50 years the Porkkala headland to be used as a military base. Further, Finland undertook to pay 300m. gold dollars in reparations within 6 years (later extended to 8 years). The peace treaty was signed in Paris on 10 Feb. 1947. The payment of reparations was completed on 19 Sept. 1952. The military base of Porkkala was returned to Finland on 26 Jan. 1956.

AREA AND POPULATION. Finland is bounded north-west and north by Norway, east by the USSR, south by the Baltic Sea and west by the Gulf of Bothnia and Sweden. The area and the population of Finland on 31 Dec. 1986 (Swedish names in brackets):

Province	Area (sq. km) [1]	Population [2]	Population per sq. km [2]
Uusimaa (Nyland)	9,898	1,200,485	121·3
Turku-Pori (Åbo-Björneborg)	22,170	713,896	32·2
Ahvenanmaa (Åland)	1,527	23,640	15·5
Häme (Tavastehus)	17,010	680,091	40·0
Kymi (Kymmene)	10,783	338,983	31·4
Mikkeli (St Michel)	16,342	208,726	12·8
Pohjois-Karjala (Norra Karelen)	17,782	177,288	10·0
Kuopio	16,511	256,213	15·5
Keski-Suomi (Mellersta Finland)	16,230	247,995	15·3
Vaasa (Vasa)	26,447	444,777	16·8
Oulu (Uleåborg)	56,866	432,979	7·6
Lappi (Lappland)	93,057	200,571	2·2
Total	304,623	4,925,644	16·2

[1] Excluding inland water area which totals 33,522 sq. km.   [2] Resident population.

The growth of the population, which was 421,500 in 1750, has been:

End of year	Urban	Rural	Total	Percentage urban
1800	46,600	786,100	832,700	5·6
1900	333,300	2,322,600	2,655,900	12·5
1950	1,302,400	2,727,400	4,029,800	32·3
1960	1,707,000	2,739,200	4,446,200	38·4
1970	2,340,300	2,258,000	4,598,300	50·9
1980	2,865,100	1,922,700	4,787,800	59·8
1986	2,948,000	1,977,600	4,925,600	59·9

The population on 31 Dec. 1986 by language primarily spoken: Finnish, 4,611,856; Swedish, 298,295; other languages, 13,767; Lappish, 1,726.

The principal towns with resident census population, 31 Dec. 1986, are (Swedish names in brackets):

Helsinki (Helsingfors)—capital	487,581	Kajaani	36,127
(metropolitan area)	965,233	Imatra	34,802
Tampere (Tammerfors)	169,994	Kokkola (Gamlakarleby)	34,615
(metropolitan area)	256,080	Rovaniemi	32,769
Turku (Åbo)	161,188	Kouvola	31,917
(metropolitan area)	260,532	Mikkeli (St Michel)	31,763
Espoo (Esbo)	160,406	Rauma (Raumo)	30,909
Vantaa (Vanda)	146,425	Savonlinna (Nyslott)	28,608
Oulu (Uleåborg)	97,869	Järvenpää	27,976
Lahti	94,205	Seinäjoki	26,578
Kuopio	78,529	Kerava	26,510
Pori (Björneborg)	77,805	Kemi	26,218
Jyväskylä	65,442	Varkaus	25,039
Kotka	58,367	Riihimäki	24,599
Vaasa (Vasa)	54,253	Nokia	24,549
Lappeenranta (Villmanstrand)	53,917	Iisalmi	23,617
Joensuu	47,017	Tornio	22,465
Hämeenlinna (Tavastehus)	42,326	Valkeakoski	22,442
Hyvinkää (Hyvinge)	38,843	Kuusankoski	21,976

Vital statistics in calendar years:

	Living births	Of which illegitimate	Still-born	Marriages	Deaths (exclusive of still-born)	Emigration
1980	63,064	8,247	266	29,388	44,398	14,824
1981	63,469	8,431	260	30,100	44,404	10,042
1982	66,106	9,007	263	30,459	43,408	7,403
1983	66,076	9,386	268	29,474	45,388	6,822
1984	65,076	9,825	260	28,550	45,098	7,467
1985	62,796	10,292	241	25,751	48,198	7,739
1986	60,799	...	191	25,866	47,117	8,517

In 1986 the rate per 1,000 was: Births, 12·4; marriages, 5·6; deaths, 9·6, and infantile deaths (1985, per 1,000 live births), 6·2.

Population and Housing Census 1980. 19 vols. Helsinki, 1981–83
Population. Annual. Helsinki

CLIMATE. The climate is severe in winter, which lasts about 6 months, but mean temperatures in south and south-west are less harsh, 21°F (–6°C). In the north, mean temperatures may fall to 8·5°F (–13°C). Snow covers the ground for three months in the south and for over six months in the far north. Summers are short but quite warm, with occasional very hot days. Precipitation is light throughout the country, with one third falling as snow, the remainder mainly as convectional rain in summer and autumn. Helsinki (Helsingfors). Jan. 21°F (–6°C), July 62°F (16·5°C). Annual rainfall 24·7″ (618 mm).

CONSTITUTION AND GOVERNMENT. Finland is a republic according to the Constitution of 17 July 1919.

Parliament consists of one chamber of 200 members chosen by direct and proportional election in which all Finnish citizens (men or women) who are 18 years have the vote (since 1972). The country is divided into 15 electoral districts with a representation proportional to their population. Every citizen over the age of 18 is eligible for Parliament, which is elected for 4 years, but can be dissolved sooner by the President.

The President is elected for 6 years by a college of 301 electors, elected by the votes of the citizens in the same way as the members of Parliament.

President of Finland: Dr Mauno Koivisto (elected 1982, re-elected 1988).

State of Parties for Parliament elected on 15–16 March 1987: Conservative 53; Swedish Party, 13 (including 1 for Coalition of Åland); Centre, 40; Rural, 9; Social Democratic Party, 56; People's Democratic League, 16; Christian League, 5; the Greens, 4; Democratic Alternative, 4.

The Council of State (Cabinet), composed as follows in Jan. 1988:
Prime Minister: Harri Holkeri.
Deputy Prime Minister and Foreign Affairs: Kalevi Sorsa. *Minister of State, Prime Minister's Office:* Ilkka Kanerva. *Finance:* Erkki Liikanen. *Finance (Deputy):* Ulla Puolanne. *Education:* Christoffer Taxell. *Education (Deputy):* Anna-Liisa Piipari. *Social Affairs and Health:* Helena Pesola. *Social Affairs and Health (Deputy):* Tarja Halonen. *Justice:* Matti Louekoski. *Agriculture and Forestry:* Toivo T. Pohjala. *Transport and Communication:* Pekka Vennamo. *Labour:* Matti Puhakka. *Trade and Industry:* Ilkka Suominen. *Defence:* Ole Norrback. *Environment:* Kaj Bärlund. *Interior:* Jarmo Rantanen. *Foreign Trade:* Pertti Salolainen.

National flag: White with a blue Scandinavian cross.

National anthem: Maamme; Swedish: Vårt land (words by J. L. Runeberg, 1843; tune by F. Pacius, 1848).

Finnish and Swedish are the official languages of Finland.

Local Government. For administrative purposes Finland is divided into 12 provinces (*lääni*, Sw.: *län*). The administration of each province is entrusted to a governor (*maaherra*, Sw.: *landshövding*) appointed by the President. He directs the activities of the provincial office (*lääninhallitus*, Sw.: *länsstyrelse*) and of local sheriffs (*nimismies*, Sw.: *länsman*). In 1986 the number of sheriff districts was 225.

The unit of local government is the commune. Main fields of communal activities are local planning, roads and harbours, sanitary services, education, health services and social aid. The communes raise taxes independent from state taxation. Two different kinds of communes are distinguished: Urban communes (*kaupunki*, Sw.: *stad*) and rural communes. In 1987 there were altogether 461 communes of which 94 were urban and 367 rural. In all communes communal councils are elected for terms of 4 years; all inhabitants (men and women) of the commune who have reached their 18th year are entitled to vote and eligible. The executive power is in each commune vested in a board which consists of members elected by the council and one or a few chief officials of the commune. Several communes often form an association for the administration of some common institution, *e.g.*, a hospital or a vocational school.

The autonomous county *(landskap)* of Åland has a county council *(landsting)* of one chamber, elected according to rule corresponding to those for parliamentary elections. In addition to its provincial governor it has a county board with executive power in matters within the field of the autonomy of the county.

Constitution Act and Parliament Act of Finland. Helsinki, 1978

DEFENCE. The period of military training is 240 to 330 days and refresher training obligation 40 to 100 days between conscript service and age 50 (officers and NCOs age 60). Total strength of trained and equipped reserves is about 700,000.

Army. The country is divided into 7 military areas. The Army consists of 1 armoured brigade, 7 infantry brigades, 7 independent infantry battalions, 2 field-artillery regiments, 2 independent field-artillery battalions, 2 coastal artillery regiments, 3 independent coastal artillery battalions, 1 anti-aircraft regiment, 4 independent anti-aircraft battalions, 2 engineering battalions, 1 signals regiment and 1 signals battalion, making a total strength in 1988, of about 32,200.

Navy. The Fleet comprises 1 *ex*-Soviet modified minelayer/training frigate, 2 corvettes, 1 coastal minelayer, 8 missile craft, 1 missile experimental craft, 6 fast patrol boats, 6 inshore minesweepers, 5 patrol boats capable of minelaying, 10 coastal patrol craft, 6 support ships, 1 headquarters ship, 10 transport craft, 14 landing craft, 2 tugs, 1 supply ship, 9 icebreakers and 1 cable ship. There is a naval academy. Personnel in 1988 totalled 2,500 (200 officers and 2,300 ratings).

Air Force. The Air Force has 3 fighter squadrons, 1 transport squadron, a military school of aviation, a technical school, a signal school and a depot. The fighter squadrons have MiG-21bis and Saab J35 Draken aircraft. Other equipment includes 30 Valmet Vinka piston-engined primary trainers of Finnish design, 48 Hawk trainers, MiG-21U and Saab J35C jet advanced trainers, Fokker F.27 transport aircraft, Piper Arrow liaison aircraft, Learjet 35A target tugs, Piper Chieftain utility transports, and Mi-8 and Hughes 500 helicopters. Personnel (1988) 2,500 officers and men.

Frontier Guard. Comprises 5 large patrol craft, 10 coastal craft and 36 coastal patrol boats. Personnel (1988) 3,500.

INTERNATIONAL RELATIONS

Membership. Finland is a member of UN, the Nordic Council, OECD and EFTA.

Treaties. A Treaty of friendship, co-operation and mutual assistance between Finland and the USSR was concluded in Moscow on 6 April 1948 for 10 years, extended on 19 Sept. 1955 to cover a period of 20 years, extended on 19 July 1970 for a further period of 20 years and extended again on 6 June 1983 for a further period of 20 years.

Treaty of Peace with Finland (10 Feb. 1947). Cmd. 7484

ECONOMY

Budget. Actual revenue and expenditure for the calendar years 1981–86, the ordinary budget for 1987 and the proposed budget for 1988 in 1m. marks:

	1981	1982	1983	1984	1985	1986	1987	1988
Revenue	58,795	63,043	76,354	86,611	96,408	96,769	102,660	113,817
Expenditure	57,797	68,008	77,190	85,748	95,803	95,172	102,628	113,816

Of the total revenue, 1986, 26% derived from sales tax, 26% from income and property tax, 12% from excise duties, 11% from other taxes and similar revenue, 13% from loans and 12% from miscellaneous sources. Of the total expenditure, 1985, 16% went to education and culture, 17% to social security, 8% to transport, 9% to agriculture and forestry, 9% to general administration, public order and safety, 8% to health, 4% to communities and housing policy, 5% to defence, 3% to promotion of industry and 21% to other expenditures.

At the end of Dec. 1986 the foreign loans totalled 26,981m. marks. The internal loans amounted to 25,013m. marks, of which, 20,872m. were long-term loans. The cash surplus was 145m. marks. The total public debt was 46,981m. marks.

Currency. The unit of currency, starting 1 Jan. 1963, is the new *mark* of 100 *pennis*, equalling 100 old *marks*. The gold standard was suspended on 12 Oct. 1931. Aluminium bronze coins are 5 *marks* 50, 20 and 10 *pennis*; copper coins, 5 *pennis*; aluminium coins, 10 and 5 *pennis*; silver, 1 *mark* pieces. Exchange rate in March 1988: 7·22 marks = £1; 4·08 marks = US$1.

Banking. The Bank of Finland (founded in 1811) is owned by the State and under the guarantee and supervision of Parliament. It is the only bank of issue, and the limit of its right to issue notes is fixed equal to the value of its assets of gold and foreign holdings plus 500m. marks. Notes of 1,000, 500, 100, 50 and 10 marks are in circulation, and their total value at the end of 1985 was 7,303m. marks.

At the end of 1985 the deposits in banking institutions totalled 148,222m. marks and the loans granted by them 150,717m. marks. The most important groups of banking institutions were:

	Number of institutions	Number of offices	Deposits (1m. marks)	Loans (1m. marks)
Commercial banks	7	1,535	54,534	62,871
Savings banks	254	1,332	41,562	36,982
Postipankki	1	48 [1]	17,380	15,271
Co-operative banks	370	1,465	34,746	35,593

[1] In addition: 2,997 post offices.

Bank of Finland Monthly Bulletin. Helsinki, from 1926
Unitas. Quarterly Review, issued by Union Bank of Finland. Helsinki, from 1929
Economic Review (issued quarterly by Kansallis–Osake–Pankki). Helsinki, from 1948

Weights and Measures. The metric system of weights and measures was introduced in 1887 and is officially and universally employed.

Economic Survey of Finland. Annual

ENERGY AND NATURAL RESOURCES

Electricity. Electricity production was (in 1m. kwh.) 8,605 in 1960; 22,562 in 1970; 38,710 in 1980; 39,354 in 1982; 40,120 in 1983; 43,311 in 1984; 47,316 in 1985, of which 26% was hydro-electric; 45,590 in 1986. Supply 220 volts; 50 Hz.

Minerals. The most important mines are Outokumpu (copper, discovered in 1910) and Otanmäki (iron, discovered in 1953). In 1986 the metal content (in tonnes) of the output of copper concentrates was 24,100, of zinc concentrates 60,300, of nickel concentrates 11,300, of iron concentrates and pellets 643,000 and of lead concentrates 1,980.

Agriculture. The cultivated area covers only 9% of the land and of the economically active population 10·3% were employed in agriculture and forestry in 1985. The arable area was divided in 1983 into 208,229 farms, and the distribution of this area by the size of the farms was: Less than 5 hectares cultivated, 61,764 farms; 5–20 hectares, 115,157 farms; 20–50 hectares, 28,091 farms; 50–100 hectares, 2,835 farms; over 100 hectares, 382 farms.

The principal crops (area (1987) in 1,000 hectares, yield in tonnes) were in 1986:

Crop	Area	Yield	Crop	Area	Yield
Rye	27	70,600	Oats	407	1,174,500
Barley	598	1,713,800	Potatoes	40	773,200
Wheat	166	529,100	Hay	387	1,564,100

The total area under cultivation in 1986 was 2,157,700 hectares. Production of dairy butter in 1986 was 65,605 tonnes, and of cheese, 83,370 tonnes.

Livestock (1987): Horses, 18,400; cattle, 1,497,900; pigs, 1,341,900; poultry, 6,790,700; reindeer, 366,000.

Forestry. The total forest land amounts to 30–31m. hectares. The productive forest land covers 19·73m. hectares. The growing stock was valued at 1,520m. cu. metres in 1971–76 and the annual growth at 57·4m. cu. metres.

In 1984 there were exported: Round timber, 1,056,334 cu. metres; sawn wood, 4,820,969 cu. metres; plywood and veneers, 685,530 cu. metres.

Monthly Review of Agriculture. Board of Agriculture
Agriculture 1982: Annual Statistics of Agriculture. Helsinki

INDUSTRY AND TRADE

Industry. The following data cover establishments with a total personnel of 5 or more in 1986 [1]:

Industry	Establishments [2]	Personnel [3]	Gross (1m. marks)	Value added (1m. marks)
Mining and quarrying	118	5,647	2,010	1,272
Metal ore mining	11	2,590	798	568
Other mining	107	3,059	1,215	706
Manufacturing	7,208	478,746	220,152	84,032
Manufacture of food, beverages and tobacco	1,029	57,110	42,687	11,491
Textile, wearing apparel and leather industries	877	52,144	11,360	5,201
Manufacture of textiles	278	14,536	3,908	1,785
Manufacture of wearing apparel, except footwear	426	28,342	5,235	2,526
Manufacture of wood and wood products, incl. furniture	1,045	45,562	15,257	5,350
Manufacture of paper and paper prod., printing, publishing	966	79,454	51,728	19,103
Manufacture of paper and paper products	199	41,381	38,491	11,372
Printing, publishing, etc.	767	38,317	13,488	7,904
Manufacture of chemicals and chemical, petroleum, coal, rubber and plastic products	476	38,333	25,984	9,005
Manufacture of industrial chemicals	163	14,123	10,230	4,093
Manufacture of other chemical products	104	10,189	4,313	2,325
Petroleum refineries	2	2,580	7,573	616
Manufacture of non-metallic mineral products	443	20,616	6,584	3,634
Basic metal industries	85	18,400	14,536	3,744
Iron and steel basic industries	57	13,498	9,936	2,936
Non-ferrous metal basic industries	28	4,904	4,605	808

[1] Preliminary.   [2] 1985.   [3] Working proprietors, salaried employees and wage earners.

Industry	Establish-ments [1]	Person-nel [2]	Value of production Gross (1m. marks)	Value added (1m. marks)
Manufacture of fabricated metal products, machinery, etc.	2,184	162,148	51,379	25,762
Manufacture of fabricated metal products, excl. machinery	791	32,259	9,568	4,972
Manufacture of machinery, except electrical	757	55,680	17,982	9,683
Manufacture of electrical machinery, apparatus, etc.	240	31,953	10,548	5,647
Manufacture of transport equipment	306	36,831	11,690	4,534
Other manufacturing industries	103	4,778	1,160	677
Electricity, gas and water	536	28,325	27,870	10,171
All industry	7,862	512,793	249,753	95,426

[1] 1985. [2] Working proprietors, salaried employees and wage earners.

GDP (at market prices) *per capita* (1986) 72,526 marks.

Industrial Statistics of Finland. Annual

Commerce. Imports and exports for calendar years, in 1m. marks:

	1982	1983	1984	1985	1986
Imports	64,751	71,528	74,682	81,520	77,602
Exports	63,026	69,692	80,904	84,028	82,579

The trade with some principal import and export countries was (in 1,000 marks):

Country	Imports 1985	Imports 1986	Exports 1985	Exports 1986
Australia	241,037	249,647	943,954	818,998
Austria	461,400	1,015,166	596,620	780,888
Belgium–Luxembourg	1,632,396	1,898,600	1,267,176	1,409,646
Brazil	601,474	519,441	145,691	199,120
Canada	572,790	409,536	998,244	909,917
China	216,009	276,537	633,938	558,831
Colombia	473,702	627,620	118,702	89,360
Czechoslovakia	368,615	387,442	275,936	296,835
Denmark	2,036,248	2,180,946	3,402,643	3,321,407
France	2,763,937	3,458,835	3,298,297	3,690,723
German Dem. Rep.	406,498	438,378	388,681	271,343
Germany (Fed. Rep.)	12,179,977	13,159,293	7,778,974	8,016,002
Greece	141,113	157,584	419,525	409,177
Hungary	283,096	269,456	291,341	253,182
Iran	984,592	192,140	220,995	129,322
Iraq	142	323	264,792	197,534
Ireland	374,586	309,516	418,429	455,568
Israel	193,106	174,024	256,409	270,110
Italy	2,754,045	3,526,004	1,687,567	1,741,234
Japan	4,308,854	5,021,830	1,223,447	1,265,633
Netherlands	2,400,413	2,369,031	2,773,066	2,854,576
Norway	1,955,231	1,713,455	3,518,820	3,714,877
Poland	1,211,386	954,877	333,179	237,709
Portugal	576,859	677,560	258,343	215,028
Saudi Arabia	1,332,715	731,005	535,196	380,919
Spain	811,634	872,452	687,501	876,116
Sweden	9,620,478	10,558,463	11,084,644	12,228,313
Switzerland	1,364,127	1,579,115	1,210,567	1,331,434
USSR	17,152,616	11,933,002	18,099,425	16,773,798
UK	5,848,002	5,055,640	9,075,999	8,667,112
USA	4,400,990	3,721,745	5,308,200	4,479,560

Principal imports 1985 (in 1m. marks): Machinery, apparatus and appliances, 24,246; mineral fuels, lubricants, etc., 19,887; chemicals, 7,919; food and live animals, 4,027; road vehicles, 5,494; crude materials, inedible, except fuels, 5,018; textile yarn, fabrics, etc., 3,048; iron and steel, 2,852.

Principal exports in 1985 (in 1m. marks): Paper and paper-board, 21,067;

machinery and transport equipment, 21,128; wood shaped or simply worked, 4,000; wood pulp, 3,428; ships, 5,506; clothing, 3,233; veneers, plywood, etc., and other wood manufactures, 1,513; food and live animals, 2,490; road vehicles, 1,474.

Total trade between Finland and UK (British Department of Trade returns, in £1,000 sterling):

	1983	1984	1985	1986	1987
Imports to UK	995,017	1,248,561	1,324,792	1,346,058	1,539,011
Exports and re-exports from UK	539,721	684,477	705,365	664,451	797,236

Foreign Trade. Annual

Tourism. In 1986 tourism contributed 3,026m. marks to the economy.

COMMUNICATIONS

Roads. In Jan. 1987 there were 76,223 km of public roads, of which 42,989 km were paved. At the end of 1986 there were 1,619,848 registered cars, 51,747 lorries, 135,718 vans and pick-ups, 9,166 buses and coaches and 12,470 special automobiles.

Railways. On 31 Dec. 1986 the total length of the line operated was 5,905 km (1,445 km electrified), of which all except 6 km was owned by the State. The gauge was 1,524 mm. In 1986 the number of passengers carried was 35m. and the amount of goods carried was 97·7m. tonnes. The total revenue in 1986 was 2,797m. marks and the total expenditure 3,904m. marks.

Aviation. The scheduled traffic of Finnish airlines covered 38m. km in 1986. The number of passengers was 2,987,844 and the number of passenger-km 2,935,896 The air transport of freight and mail amounted to 93m. tonne-km.

Shipping. The total registered mercantile marine on 31 Dec. 1986 was 427 vessels of 1·65m. gross tons. In 1986 the total number of vessels arriving in Finland from abroad was 15,350 and the goods discharged amounted to 29·9m. tonnes. The goods loaded for export from Finland ports amounted to 20·9m. tonnes.

The lakes, rivers and canals are navigable for about 6,100 km. Timber floating is important, and there are about 9,200 km of floatable inland waterways. In 1986 bundle floating was about 4·8m. tonnes and free floating 1·3m. tonnes.

On 27 Aug. 1963 the USSR leased to Finland the Russian part of the canal connecting Lake Saimaa with the Gulf of Finland. After extensive rebuilding the canal was opened for traffic in 1968. The Saimaa Canal and deepwater channels on Lake Saimaa (755 km) can be used by vessels with dimensions not larger than as follows: length 82 metres, width 11·8 metres, draught 4·2 metres and height of mast 24·5 metres.

Post and Broadcasting. In 1986 there were 3,583 post offices and 576 telegraph offices. The total length of telegraph wires was 582,973 km and that of domestic trunk and net group telephone wires 6·8m. km. The number of telephones was (1985), 3,028,000. All post and telegraph systems are administered by the State jointly with a large part of the telephone services. The total revenues from postal services were 3,020m. marks and from (wire and radio) telegraph services 3,072m. marks.

On 31 Dec. 1985 the number of television licences was 1,822,372, of which licences for colour television, 1,534,899. *Oy Yleisradio AB* broadcasts 2 programmes in Finnish and 1 in Swedish on long-, medium- and short-waves, and on FM. Three TV programmes (1 commercial) are broadcast.

Cinemas. In Dec. 1986 there were 344 cinemas with a seating capacity of 73,000.

Newspapers. In 1985 the number of newspapers published more often than 3 times a week was 77, of which 66 were in Finnish and 11 in Swedish.

JUSTICE, RELIGION, EDUCATION AND WELFARE

Justice. The lowest courts of justice are the municipal courts in towns and district courts in the country. Municipal courts are held by the burgomaster and at least 2 members of court, district court by judge and 5 jurors, the judge alone deciding, unless the jurors unanimously differ from him, when their decision prevails. From these courts an appeal lies to the courts of appeal *(Hovioikeus)* in Turku, Vaasa, Kuopio, Helsinki, Kouvola and Rovaniemi. The Supreme Court *(Korkein oikeus)* sits in Helsinki. Appeals from the decisions of administrative authorities are in the final instance decided by the Supreme Administrative Court *(Korkein hallinto-oikeus)*, also in Helsinki. Judges can be removed only by judicial sentence.

Two functionaries, the *Oikeuskansleri* or Chancellor of Justice, and the *Oikeusasiamies* (ombudsman), or Solicitor-General, exercise control over the administration of justice. The former acts also as counsel and public prosecutor for the Government; while the latter, who is appointed by the Parliament, exerts a general control over all courts of law and public administration.

At the end of 1986 the prison population numbered 4,128 men and 124 women; the number of convictions in 1985 was 325,057, of which 298,925 were for minor offences with maximum penalty of fines and 25,885 with penalty of imprisonment. 11,319 of the prison sentences were unconditional.

Religion. Liberty of conscience is guaranteed to members of all religions. National churches are the Lutheran National Church and the Greek Orthodox Church of Finland. The Lutheran Church is divided into 8 bishoprics (Turku being the archiepiscopal see), 78 provostships and 595 parishes. The Greek Orthodox Church is divided into 3 bishoprics (Kuopio being the archiepiscopal see) and 25 parishes, in addition to which there are a monastery and a convent.

Percentage of the total population at the end of 1985: Lutherans, 89·2; Greek Orthodox, 1·1; others, 0·8; not members of any religion, 8·9.

Education (1985–86). *Primary and Secondary Education:*

	Number of institutions	Teachers	Students
First-level Education	4,233	...	380,509
(Lower sections of the comprehensive schools, grades I–VI)			
Second-level Education	1,673	...	414,871
General education	1,093	...	300,748
(Upper sections of the comprehensive schools, grades VII–IX, and senior secondary schools)			
Vocational education	580	15,993	114,123

Higher Education. Education at the third level (including universities and third level education at vocational colleges) was provided for 127,976 students. Education at universities was provided at 20 institutions with 7,169 teachers and 92,230 students.

University Education. Universities and similar types of institutions and the number of teachers and students are:

	Founded	Teachers	Students Total	Students Women
Universities				
Helsinki	1640	1,749	25,167	14,467
Turku (Swedish)	1919	301	4,375	2,558
Turku (Finnish)	1922	740	9,114	5,371
Jyväskylä	1958	515	6,457	4,103
Oulu	1958	806	7,669	3,556
Tampere	1966	553	9,183	5,653
Joensuu	1969	321	3,803	2,392
Kuopio	1972	250	2,116	1,274
Lapland	1979	93	1,000	488
Vaasa	1968	97	1,614	816
Universities of Technology				
Lappeenranta	1969	131	1,519	228
Helsinki	1849	571	8,667	1,416
Tampere	1972	222	3,166	373
College of Veterinary Medicine, Helsinki	1946	51	291	220
Schools of Economics and Business Administration				
Helsinki (Finnish)	1911	170	3,099	1,330
Helsinki (Swedish)	1927	92	1,644	699
Turku (Finnish)	1950	67	1,463	682
Swedish school of social work and local administration [1]				

[1] Previously Swedish Civic College since 1943. Was united to Helsinki University 1984.

	Founded	Teachers	Students Total	Women
Universities of Art				
Sibelius Academy	1939	263	980	536
University of Industrial Arts	1949	130	757	473
Theatre Academy	1979	47	146	69

General adult education (at civic institutes, folk high schools and study centres) had 894,000 students.

General Education. Central Statistical Office, Helsinki (annual), *Higher Education.* Central Statistical Office, Helsinki (annual), *Vocational Education.* Helsinki (annual)

Health. In 1985 there were 11,072 physicians, 4,595 dentists and 73,888 hospital beds.

Social Security. The Social Insurance Institution administers general systems of old age pensions (to all persons over 65 years of age and disabled younger persons) and of health insurance. An additional system of compulsory old age pensions paid for by the employers is in force and works through the Central Pension Security Institute. Systems for child welfare, care of vagrants, alcoholics and drug addicts and other public aid are administered by the communes and supervised by the National Social Board and the Ministry of Social Affairs and Health.

The total cost of social security amounted to 87,253m. marks in 1985. Out of this 25,216m. (28·9%) was spent for health, 1,546m. (1·8%) for industrial accidents, 5,589m. (6·4%) for unemployment, 33,624m. (38·5%) old age and disability, 14,324m. (16·4%) for family allowances and child welfare, 818m. (0·9%) for general welfare purposes, 2,237m. (2·6%) for war-disabled, etc., 1,156m. (1·3%) as tax reductions for children. Out of the total expenditure 30% was financed by the State, 16% by local authorities, 42% by employers, 8% by the beneficiaries and 4% by users.

Labour Protection in Finland. Helsinki, 1980
Social Welfare in Finland. Helsinki, 1980
Social Security in the Nordic Countries 1981. Statistical Reports of the Nordic Countries, vol. 44. Helsinki, 1984

DIPLOMATIC REPRESENTATIVES

Of Finland in Great Britain (38 Chesham Pl., London, SW1X 8HW)
Ambassador: Ilkka Olavi Pastinen, KCMG (accredited 24 Feb. 1983).

Of Great Britain in Finland (16–20 Uudenmaankatu, Helsinki 00120)
Ambassador: H. A. J. Staples, CMG.

Of Finland in the USA (3216 New Mexico Ave., NW, Washington, D.C., 20016)
Ambassador: Paavo Rantanen.

Of the USA in Finland (Itäinen Puistotie 14A, Helsinki 00140)
Ambassador: Rockwell A. Schnabel.

Of Finland to the United Nations
Ambassador: Dr Keijo Korhonen.

Books of Reference

Statistical Information: The Central Statistical Office (Tilastokeskus, Swedish: Statistikcentralen; address: PO Box 504, SF-00101 Helsinki 10) was founded in 1865 to replace earlier official statistical services dating from 1749 (in united Sweden–Finland). Statistics on foreign trade, agriculture, forestry, navigation, health and social welfare are produced by other state authorities. Its publications include: *Statistical Yearbook of Finland* (from 1879) and *Bulletin of Statistics* (monthly, from 1924). A bibliography of all official statistics of Finland was published in Finnish, Swedish and English in *Statistical publications 1856–1979.* Helsinki, 1980.
Constitution Act and Parliament Act of Finland. Helsinki, 1978
Suomen valtiokalenteri–Finlands statskalender (State Calendar of Finland). Helsinki. Annual
Facts About Finland. Helsinki. Annual (Union Bank of Finland)
Facts about Finland. Helsinki, 1987
Finland in Figures. Helsinki, Annual

Finland in Maps. Helsinki, 1979
Finnish Press Laws. Helsinki, 1984
Making and Applying Law in Finland. Ministry of Justice, 1983
Statistical Yearbook of Finland. Helsinki, Annual
Yearbook of Finnish Foreign Policy. Helsinki, Annual
The Finnish Banking System. Helsinki, 1983
Finnish Industry. Helsinki, 1986
Finnish Local Government. Helsinki, 1982
Health Care in Finland. Helsinki, 1986
Hurme-Malin-Syväoja, *Finnish-English General Dictionary.* Helsinki, 1984
Hurme-Pesonen, *English–Finnish General Dictionary.* Helsinki, 1982
Jutikkala, E., and Pirinen, K., *A History of Finland.* 3rd ed. New York, 1979
Kekkonen, U., *President's View.* London, 1982
Kirby, D. G., *Finland in the Twentieth Century.* 2nd ed. London, 1984
Klinge, M., *A Brief History of Finland.* Helsinki, 1987
Nousiainen, J., *The Finnish Political System.* Harvard Univ. Press, 1971
Paasivirta, J., *Finland and Europe. The Period of Autonomy and the International Crises 1808–1914.* London, 1981
Polvinow, T., *Between East and West – Finland in International Politics 1944–1947.* Minnesota Univ. Press, 1986
Puntila, L. A., *The Political History of Finland, 1809–1966.* Helsinki, 1974
University of Turku, *Political Parties in Finland.* Turku, 1984

FRANCE

Capital: Paris
Population: 55·62m. (1987)
GNP per capita: US$9,280 (1985)

République Française

HISTORY. The republic proclaimed on the fall of the Bourbon monarchy in 1792 lasted until the First Empire, under Napoleon I, was established in 1804. The Bourbon monarchy was restored in 1814 and (with an interval during 1815) lasted until the abdication of Louis Philippe in 1848. The Second Republic was established on 12 March 1848, the Second Empire (under Louis Napoleon) on 2 Dec. 1852. The Third Republic was established on 4 Sept. 1870 following the capture and imprisonment of Louis Napoleon in the Franco-Prussian war, and lasted until the German occupation of 1940. The Fourth Republic was established on 24 Dec. 1946 and lasted until 4 Oct. 1958.

AREA AND POPULATION. France is bounded north by the English Channel *(La Manche)*, north-east by Belgium and Luxembourg, east by Federal Republic of Germany, Switzerland and Italy, south by the Mediterranean (with Monaco as a coastal enclave), south-west by Spain and Andorra, and west by the Atlantic Ocean The total area is 543,965 sq. km (210,033 sq. miles).

The population (present in actual boundaries) at successive censuses has been:

1801	27,349,003	1881	37,672,048	Mar. 1946	40,506,639
1821	30,461,875	1891	38,342,948	May 1954	42,777,174
1841	34,230,178	1901	38,961,945	Mar. 1962	46,519,997
1861	37,386,313	1911	39,604,992	Mar. 1968	49,778,540
1866	38,067,064	1921	39,209,518	Feb. 1975	52,655,802
1872	36,102,921	1931	41,834,923	Mar. 1982	54,334,871

The 1982 total included 3,680,100 foreigners, of whom 795,920 were Algerian, 764,860 Portuguese, 431,120 Moroccan, 333,740 Italian and 321,440 Spanish.

The latest population estimate (at 1 July 1987) is 55,622,000.

Vital statistics for calendar years:

	Marriages	Divorces	Live births	Stillborn	Deaths
1981	315,117	87,600	805,483	6,644	554,823
1982	312,405	93,900	797,223	6,334	543,104
1983	300,513	98,700	748,525	5,723	559,655
1984	281,402	104,000	759,939	5,835	542,490

Live birth rate in 1985 was 13·9 per 1,000 inhabitants; death rate, 10; marriage rate, 4·9; divorce rate, 2; infant mortality, 8 per 1,000 live births. Life expectation at birth (1984); men, 71·2; women, 79·3. Population growth rate (1985), 3·9 per 1,000. Average density (1987) 102 persons per sq. km.

The areas, populations and chief towns of the 22 Metropolitan regions were as follows:

Regions	Area (sq. km)	Census March 1982	Estimate Jan. 1986	Chief town
Alsace	8,280	1,566,048	1,599,800	Strasbourg
Aquitaine	41,308	2,656,544	2,718,200	Bordeaux
Auvergne	26,013	1,332,678	1,334,400	Clermont-Ferrand
Basse-Normandie	17,589	1,350,979	1,373,400	Caen
Bourgogne (Burgundy)	31,582	1,596,054	1,607,200	Dijon
Bretagne (Brittany)	27,208	2,707,886	2,764,200	Rennes
Centre	39,151	2,264,164	2,324,400	Orléans
Champagne-Ardenne	25,606	1,345,935	1,352,500	Reims
Corse (Corsica)	8,680	240,178	248,700	Ajaccio
Franche-Comté	16,202	1,084,049	1,085,900	Besançon
Haute-Normandie	12,317	1,655,362	1,692,800	Rouen

Regions	Area (sq. km)	Census March 1982	Estimate Jan. 1986	Chief town
Île-de-France	12,012	10,073,059	10,250,900	Paris
Languedoc-Roussillon	27,376	1,926,514	2,011,900	Montpellier
Limousin	16,942	737,153	735,800	Limoges
Lorraine	23,547	2,319,905	2,313,200	Nancy
Midi-Pyrénées	45,348	2,325,319	2,355,100	Toulouse
Nord-Pas-de-Calais	12,414	3,932,939	3,923,200	Lille
Pays de la Loire	32,082	2,930,398	3,017,700	Nantes
Picardie	19,399	1,740,321	1,774,000	Amiens
Poitou-Charentes	25,810	1,568,230	1,583,600	Poitiers
Provence-Côte d'Azur	31,400	3,965,209	4,058,800	Marseille
Rhône-Alpes	43,698	5,015,947	5,153,600	Lyon

Populations of the principal conurbations and towns at Census 1982:

	Conurbation	Town		Conurbation	Town
Paris	8,706,963 [1]	2,188,918	Limoges	171,689	144,082
Lyon	1,220,844 [2]	418,476	Mantes-la-Jolie	170,265	43,585
Marseille	1,110,511	878,689	Amiens	154,498	136,358
Lille	936,295 [3]	174,039	Thionville	138,034	41,448
Bordeaux	640,012	211,197	Perpignan	137,915	113,646
Toulouse	541,271	354,289	Nîmes	132,343	129,924
Nantes	464,857	247,227	Pau	131,265	85,766
Nice	449,496	338,486	Saint-Nazaire	130,271	68,947
Toulon	410,393	181,985	Montbéliard	128,194	33,362
Grenoble	392,021	159,503	Bayonne	127,477	42,970
Rouen	379,879	105,083	Aix-en-Provence	126,552	124,550
Strasbourg	373,470	252,264	Troyes	125,240	64,769
Valenciennes	349,505	40,881	Besançon	120,772	119,687
Lens	327,383	38,307	Hagondange-Briey	119,669	9,091
Saint-Étienne	317,228	206,688	Annecy	112,632	51,593
Nancy	306,982	99,307	Valence	106,041	68,157
Cannes	295,525	72,787	Maubeuge	105,714	36,156
Tours	262,786	136,483	Lorient	104,025	64,675
Béthune	258,383	26,105	Angoulême	103,552	50,151
Clermont-Ferrand	256,189	151,092	Poitiers	103,204	82,884
Le Havre	254,595	200,411	La Rochelle	102,143	78,231
Rennes	234,418	200,390	Calais	100,823	76,935
Montpellier	221,307	201,067	Forbach	99,606	27,321
Mulhouse	220,613	113,794	Boulogne-sur-Mer	98,566	48,349
Orléans	220,478	105,589	Chambéry	96,163	54,896
Dijon	215,865	145,569	Bourges	92,202	79,408
Douai	202,366	44,515	Cherbourg	85,485	30,112
Brest	201,145	160,355	Saint-Brieuc	83,900	51,399
Reims	199,388	181,985	Creil	82,505	36,128
Angers	195,859	141,143	Melun	82,479	36,218
Dunkerque	195,705	73,618	Colmar	82,468	63,764
Le Mans	191,080	150,331	Saint-Chamond	82,059	40,571
Metz	186,437	118,502	Roanne	81,786	49,638
Caen	183,526	117,119	Béziers	81,347	78,477
Avignon	174,264	91,474	Arras	80,477	45,364

[1] Including towns of Boulogne-Billancourt (102,595), Argenteuil (96,045), Versailles (95,240), Montreuil (93,394), Saint-Denis (91,275), Nanterre (90,371) and Vitry-sur-Seine (85,820).
[2] Including towns of Villeurbanne (118,330) and Vénissieux (64,982).
[3] Including towns of Roubaix (101,836) and Tourcoing (97,121).

Recensement de la population de 1982. Paris, Institut National de la Statistique et des Etudes Economiques, 1983
Scargill, I., *Urban France.* London, 1983

CLIMATE. The north-west has a moderate maritime climate, with small temperature range and abundant rainfall, but inland, rainfall becomes more seasonal, with a summer maximum, and the annual range of temperature increases. Southern France has a Mediterranean climate, with mild moist winters and hot dry summers. Eastern France has a continental climate and a rainfall maximum in summer, with thunderstorms prevalent.

Paris. Jan. 37°F (3°C), July 64°F (18°C). Annual rainfall 22·9″ (573 mm).
Bordeaux. Jan. 41°F (5°C), July 68°F (20°C). Annual rainfall 31·4″ (786 mm).
Lyon. Jan. 37°F (3°C), July 68°F (20°C). Annual rainfall 31·8″ (794 mm).

CONSTITUTION AND GOVERNMENT. The Constitution of the Fifth
Republic, superseding that of 1946, came into force on 4 Oct. 1958. It consists of a
preamble, dealing with the Rights of Man, and 92 articles.

France is a Republic, indivisible, secular, democratic and social; all citizens are
equal before the law (Art. 2). National sovereignty resides with the people, who
exercise it through their representatives and by referenda (Art. 3). Political parties
carry out their activities freely, but must respect the principles of national
sovereignty and democracy (Art. 4).

The President of the Republic sees that the Constitution is respected; he ensures
the regular functioning of the public authorities, as well as the continuity of the
state. He is the protector of national independence and territorial integrity (Art. 5).
He is elected for 7 years by direct universal suffrage (Art. 6). He appoints a Prime
Minister and, on the latter's advice, appoints and dismisses the other members of
the Government (Art. 8). He presides over the Council of Ministers (Art. 9). He can
dissolve the National Assembly, after consultation with the Prime Minister and the
Presidents of the two Houses (Art. 12). He appoints to the civil and military offices
of the state (Art. 13). In times of crisis, he may take such emergency powers as
the circumstances demand; the National Assembly cannot be dissolved during
such a period (Art. 16).

Previous Presidents of the Fifth Republic:
General Charles André Joseph de Gaulle, 8 Jan. 1959–28 April 1969 (resigned);
Alain Poher (interim), 28 April 1969–20 June 1969; Georges Jean Raymond
Pompidou, 20 June 1969–2 April 1974 (died); Alain Poher (interim), 2 April
1974–27 May 1974; Valéry Giscard d'Estaing, 27 May 1974–21 May 1981.

President of the Republic: François Mitterrand (elected 10 May 1981; took office
21 May 1981).

The government determines and conducts the policy of the nation (Art. 20). The
Prime Minister directs the operation of the Government, is responsible for national
defence and ensures the execution of laws (Art. 21). Members of the Government
must not be members of Parliament (Art. 23).

The Council of Ministers was composed as follows in Jan. 1988:

Prime Minister: Jacques Chirac (RPR).
Minister of State for Economics, Finance and Privatization: Edouard Balladur
(RPR).
Justice, Keeper of the Seals: Albin Chalandon (RPR).
Defence: André Giraud (UDF-PR).
Culture and Communication: François Léotard (UDF-PR).
Foreign Affairs: Jean-Bernard Raimond.
Interior: Charles Pasqua (RPR).
Housing, Transport and Urban Affairs: Pierre Méhaignerie (UDF-CDS).
Overseas Departments and Territories: Bernard Pons (RPR).
Education: René Monory (UDF-CDS).
Employment and Social Affairs: Philippe Séguin (RPR).
Industry, Posts and Telecommunications, Tourism: Alain Madelin (UDF-PR).
Agriculture: François Guillaume.
Co-operation: Michel Aurillac (RPR).
Relations with Parliament: André Rossinot (UDF-Rad.).
Ministers-Delegate: Bernard Bosson *(European Affairs)*, Gérard Longuet *(Posts
and Telecommunications)*, Hervé de Charette *(Planning and Public Offices)*, Alain
Juppé *(Budget)*, Michel Noir *(Foreign Trade)*, Camille Cabana *(Privatization and
Repatriates)*, Georges Chavanes *(Commerce and Small Businesses)*, Robert
Pandraud *(Security)*, Dr Michèle Barzach *(Health)*, Hélène Gisserot *(Women's
Affairs)*, Jacques Douffiagues *(Transport)*, Alain Carignon *(Environment)*, Yves
Galland *(Local Government)*, Jacques Valade *(Research and Higher Education)*,
André Santini *(Communication)*.

The Government also includes 15 Secretaries of State.
Secretary-General to the Government: Renaud Denoix de Saint Marc.

Parliament consists of the National Assembly and the Senate; the National Assembly is elected by direct suffrage and the Senate by indirect suffrage (Art. 24). It convenes as of right in two ordinary sessions per year, the first on 2 Oct. for 80 days and the second on 2 April for not more than 90 days (Art. 28).

The National Assembly comprises 577 Deputies, elected for a 5-year term from multi-member constituencies by proportional representation – 555 in Metropolitan France and 22 in the various overseas departments and dependencies. The latest General Election, held in March 1986, resulted in a composition (by group, including 'affiliates') of 155 *Rassemblement Pour la République* (Gaullists), 131 *Union de la Démocracie Française* (Giscardians and Centrists) and 5 others supporting the Government, and an opposition consisting of 212 *Parti Socialiste* (including 2 *Mouvement des Radicaux de Gauche* and 14 other 'affiliates'), 35 *Parti Communiste Française*, 4 other 'unaffiliated left' and 35 *Front National*.

The Senate comprises 319 Senators elected for 9-year terms (one-third every 3 years) by an electoral college in each Department or overseas dependency, made up of all members of the Departmental Council or its equivalent in overseas dependencies, together with all members of Municipal Councils within that area; there are 296 Senators for Metropolitan France, 13 for the Overseas Departments and dependencies, and 10 for French citizens residing outside France and its dependencies. Following the partial elections held in Sept. 1986, the Senate was composed of (by group, including 'affiliates') 154 UDF, 77 RPR, 73 *Groupe Socialiste* (including 9 MRG) and 15 *Groupe Communiste*.

The Constitutional Council is composed of 9 members whose term of office is 9 years (non-renewable), one-third every 3 years; 3 are appointed by the President of the Republic, 3 by the President of the National Assembly, and 3 by the President of the Senate; in addition, former Presidents of the Republic are, by right, life members of the Constitutional Council (Art. 56). It oversees the fairness of the elections of the President (Art. 58) and Parliament (Art. 59) and of referenda (Art. 60), and acts as a guardian of the Constitution (Art. 61).

The Economic and Social Council advises on Government and Private Members' Bills (Art. 69). It comprises representatives of employers', workers' and farmers' organizations in each Department and Overseas Territory.

National flag: The Tricolour of three vertical stripes of blue, white, red.

National anthem: La Marseillaise (words and music by C. Rouget de Lisle, 1792).

Local Government: France is divided into 22 regions for national development work, for planning and for budgetary policy. Under far-reaching legislation on decentralisation promulgated in March 1982, state-appointed Regional Prefects were abolished and their executive powers transferred to the Presidents of the Regional Councils, which are to be directly elected.

There are 96 *départements* within the 22 regions each governed by a directly-elected *Conseil Général.* From 1982 their Presidents' powers are greatly extended to take over local administration and expenditure from the former Departmental prefects, now called 'Commissioners of the Republic' with responsibility for public order. The *arrondissement* (325 in 1982) and the *canton* (3,714 in 1982), have little administrative significance.

The unit of local government is the *commune*, the size and population of which vary very much. There were, in 1982, in the 96 metropolitan departments, 36,433 communes. Most of them (31,122) had less than 1,500 inhabitants, and 16,144 had less than 300, while 227 communes had more than 30,000 inhabitants. The local affairs of the commune are under a Municipal Council, composed of from 9 to 36 members, elected by universal suffrage for 6 years by French citizens of 21 years or over after 6 months' residence. Each Municipal Council elects a mayor, who is both the representative of the commune and the agent of the central government.

In Paris the *Conseil de Paris* is composed of 109 members elected from the 20 *arrondissements.* It combines the functions of departmental *Conseil Général* and Municipal Council.

DEFENCE. The President of the Republic exercises command over the Armed Forces. He is assisted by the High Council of Defence *(Conseil Supérieur de Défense)*, which studies defence problems, and by two Committees *(Comité de Défense* and *Comité de Défense restreint)* which formulate directives. The Prime Minister is responsible for national defence; he exercises his military responsibilities and co-ordinates inter-ministry defence activities through the General Secretariat of National Defence (SGDN). Under the Prime Minister's authority, the Minister of Defence is responsible for the execution of military policy, in particular the organization and administration of the Armed Forces.

On 5 July 1969 the Ministry of State for National Defence assumed responsibility from the former individual service Ministries for the Army, Air Force and Navy. The Ministry prepares general directives for negotiations relating to defence. The preparation and control of the Armed Forces is exercised by the Chief of Staff of the Armed Forces, the Chiefs of Staff of the 3 services—Army, Navy and Air—and the head of the *Gendarmerie.*

French forces are not formally under the NATO command structure. About 48,000 French service personnel are stationed in the Federal Republic of Germany, with a further 28,000 stationed in other overseas locations.

Army. The Army consists of regular officers and n.c.o.s, long-term n.c.o.s and soldiers, and conscripts serving 12 months.

The peace-time units comprise 6 armoured divisions, 2 light armoured divisions and 2 motorized rifle divisions, plus artillery, engineering, signals, parachute, transport, supply, and naval infantry and artillery units. In addition, there are the Foreign Legion, the Rapid Action Force (comprising a parachute division, an airportable marine division, a light armoured division, an alpine division and an airmobile division), and other specialized units. 5 artillery units can deliver the 'Pluton' nuclear missile.

In 1988 the effective strength of the Army was 279,900 all ranks (excluding *Gendarmerie).* Equipment included 1,340 AMX-30 and 300 AMX-13 main battle tanks.

Higher military instruction is provided in 3 stages: the staff school *(École d'État-major)* for officers of formation staffs; the *École Supérieure de Guerre* for officers earmarked for the higher command; the *Institut des Hautes Études de Défense Nationale* where high-ranking officers and civilians study together the problems of national defence.

Formed in 1952, the *Aviation Légère de l'Armée de Terre* (ALAT) is a well-equipped force, with 12 light aeroplanes and more than 483 helicopters for observation, reconnaissance, combat area transport, liaison and supply duties. Effective strength, 1988, about 7,000.

Gendarmerie. The *Gendarmerie* is an integral part of the Armed Forces but also co-operates with the civil administration in maintaining public order. Effective strength, 1988, 89,816.

Navy. The Navy is under the supreme direction of the Minister of Defence, being administered by the Chief of Naval Staff and his deputies.

All naval aircraft and coastal defences are under the control of the Navy, and are organized in 3 maritime regions (with headquarters in Cherbourg, Brest and Toulon).

The French Navy is manned partly by conscription but mainly by voluntary enlistment. In 1988 the active personnel was 67,000 officers and men.

The following is a summary of the strength of the fleet at the end of the years shown:

	1979	1980	1981	1982	1983	1984	1985	1986	1987
Aircraft carriers	3[1]	3[1]	3[1]	3[1]	3[1]	3[1]	3[1]	3[1]	3[1]
Capital submarines[2]	5	5	5	5	6	6	6	6	6
Other submarines	24	23	22	23	18	20	16	17	18
Cruisers	1	1	1	1	1	1	1	1	1
Destroyers	20	19	20	20	18	18	16	17	17
Frigates	24	22	22	25	26	26	25	25	25

[1] Including 1 helicopter-carrier.   [2] Nuclear-powered ballistic missile type.

The principal ships of the French Navy are as follows:

Com-pleted	Name	Standard displace-ment Tons	Aircraft	Principal armament	Shaft horse-power	Speed Knots

Aircraft Carriers

| 1963 | Foch } | 27,307 | 40 fixed wing, | 2 Crotale | 126,000 | 32·0 |
| 1961 | Clemenceau } | | 4 helicopters } | | | |

[1] 8 single 3·9in guns replaced by 2 *Crotale* missile launchers during 1986–88.

Helicopter Carrier

| 1964 | Jeanne d'Arc[1] | 10,000 | 8 helicopters [2] | 6 'Exocet' (singles) 4 single 3·9 in. | 40,000 | 26·5 |

[1] Cruiser type forward, flat-topped midships to aft.   [2] Four in peacetime.

Cruiser

| 1959 | Colbert | 8,500 | — | 4 'Exocet' (singles) 1 twin 'Masurca' 2 single 3·9 in. | 86,000 | 31·5 |

Capital (Strategic) Submarines

Class	No.	Displacement (submerged) tons	Missile Tubes (vertical)	Nuclear Reactors	Shaft horse-power	Speed Knots
'611'	5	8,940	16 M 20	1	16,000	25 dived 20 surface
'615'	1	8,920	16 M 4	1	16,000	25

The '611' class comprises *Le Redoubtable* (completed 1971), *Le Terrible* (1973), *Le Foudroyant* (1974), *L'Indomptable* (1976) and *Le Tonnant* (1980). *L'Inflexible* (1985) of the '615' class is of intermediate type between her predecessors and an ordered class of 14,200 tonnes to be laid down in 1988.

All the named vessels above are also armed with four 21-inch torpedo tubes.

There are also 4 nuclear-powered fleet submarines (*Rubis*, 1983, *Saphir*, 1984, *Casabianca*, 1986, and *Emeraude*, 1987) of 2,670 tons (submerged), 14 diesel-powered submarines, 17 destroyers, 25 frigates, 3 fast missile craft, 10 fast attack craft, 5 patrol vessels, 10 large mine counter hunters (*ex*-ocean minesweepers), 12 coastal minehunters, 12 coastal minesweepers (3 used as patrol vessels and 4 as diving ships), 8 inshore minesweepers (used as diving and utility tenders), 7 survey-ing vessels, 2 dock landing ships, 6 tank landing ships, 8 landing craft, 27 minor landing craft, 6 maintenance, repair and depot ships, 6 oilers, 13 boom defence vessels, 8 support ships, 13 transports, 17 training vessels, 40 auxiliary ships and 110 tugs.

A 34,000 ton nuclear-powered aircraft carrier (*Charles de Gaulle*, for comple-tion in 1995), a seventh nuclear-powered ballistic missile submarine, 4 more nuclear-powered fleet (torpedo-armed) submarines and 3 guided missile destroyers are under construction. A second nuclear-powered aircraft carrier, 2 guided missile destroyers, 3 frigates, 4 surveying ships and 5 mine-hunters are projected.

The naval air arm, known usually as *Aéronavale*, includes 3 squadrons of Super Etendard transonic fighter-bombers, 1 squadron of Etendard reconnaissance fighters, 1 squadron of US-built Crusader all-weather fighters, 2 squadrons of Alizé turboprop anti-submarine aircraft, 4 squadrons of Atlantic maritime reconnais-sance aircraft and 5 anti-submarine and assault helicopter squadrons with Super Frelon and Lynx helicopters. Strength is 400 aircraft comprising 300 fixed-wing and 100 helicopters.

Air Force. Formed as the *Service Aéronautique* in April 1910, the *Armeé de l'Air* is organized in 7 major commands. The *Commandement des Forces Aériennes Stratégiques* (CFAS) commands the airborne nuclear deterrent force. The *Com-*

mandement de la Force Aérienne Tactique (FATAC) directs the tactical air forces and is responsible for support of the ground forces. Under FATAC the 1st *Commandement Aérien Tactique* (1° CATAC) controls tactical air units based in eastern France; the 2nd *Commandement Aérien Tactique* (2° CATAC) controls the reserve forces and the air component of the *Force d'Intervention.* The *Commandement du Transport Aérien Militaire* (COTAM) is responsible for air transport operations and participates also in the training and transport of airborne forces. The *Commandement de la Défense Aérienne* (DA) controls French airspace. The *Commandement des Écoles de l'Armée de l'Air* (CEAA) is responsible for training the personnel for all branches of the Air Force. The *Commandement des Transmissions* has responsibility for communications and electronic warfare. Finally, the *Commandement du Génie de l'Air,* made up mainly of Army personnel, undertakes airbase construction and maintenance under Air Force control.

The home-based French Air Force is divided territorially among 4 metropolitan air regions (Metz, Villacoublay, Bordeaux, Aix-en-Provence); overseas, small air units are integrated into the local joint-service commands. There are about 40 combat squadrons plus about 30 transport, helicopter and support squadrons, and the Air Force uses a total of 60 bases.

The strategic, tactical and air defence forces are equipped entirely with jet aircraft. The CFAS has 26 Mirage IV supersonic nuclear bombers, deployed in 2 wings (total 3 squadrons) supported by 11 C-135F in-flight refuelling tanker transports. The FATAC deploys 6 wings (18 squadrons), with about 105 Mirage III-E and 5F ground-attack fighters, and 120 Jaguar strike aircraft, 3 reconnaissance squadrons with Mirage F1-CRs, and operational conversion units equipped with Mirage III-Bs and Jaguars. The air defence forces have 4 wings, comprising 9 squadrons with 120 Mirage F1-C and 3 squadrons with 30 Mirage 2000C interceptors. The COTAM is organized into 3 wings, equipped with 74 Transall C.160 turboprop transports, 5 DC-8s, 3 C-130s and 105 helicopters. Training aircraft include CAP-10/20/230 piston-engined primary trainers, Epsilon piston-engined and Fouga-Magister jet basic trainers, Mirage F1Bs, Mirage III-Bs, Mirage 2000Bs and two-seat Jaguars in wings for operational transformation; 25 Embraer 121-Xingus bought from Brazil are dual-purpose training/liaison aircraft. Delivery of the Mirage 2000N strike aircraft began in 1987. Total officers and other ranks (1987) 95,978; 450 combat aircraft.

INTERNATIONAL RELATIONS

Membership. France is a member of UN, the Council of Europe, NATO and the European Communities.

ECONOMY

Planning. For the history of planning in France from 1947 to 1980, *see* THE STATESMAN'S YEAR-BOOK, 1982–83, p. 474. The Eighth Plan, covering the 1981–85 period, was set aside after the change of government in May 1981 and replaced by an interim plan for 1982–83, followed by a new Ninth Plan for 1984–88.

Budget. Receipts and expenditure (in 1 m. francs) for calendar years:

Receipts	1984	%	1985	%
Direct taxation				
Income tax	203,397	20·0	204,155	18·9
Corporation tax	89,290	8·8	93,720	8·7
Indirect taxation				
Value-added tax	415,800	41·0	444,624	41·1
Petrol tax	67,396	6·6	85,291	7·9
Payroll and other taxes	174,154	18·3	181,314	16·7
Non-fiscal receipts	54,002	5·3	60,475	5·6
Gross total	1,004,039		1,069,579	
Net budget receipts (gross total taxes minus various deductions)	833,130		867,374	

Expenditure	1985	%	1986	%
Public authorities and general administration	116,113	11·4	128,700	12·2
Education and culture	238,565	23·4	246,500	23·4
Social affairs, health, employment	200,859	19·7	199,000	18·9
Agriculture and countryside	25,179	2·5	25,700	2·4
Housing and town planning	46,938	4·6	48,000	4·6
Transport and communications	42,920	4·2	43,100	4·1
Industry and services	50,852	5·0	51,300	4·9
External affairs	26,150	2·6	26,200	2·5
Defence	159,531	15·7	167,800	15·9
Miscellaneous expenditure	111,059	10·9	117,400	11·1
Total expenditure	1,018,170		1,053,800	

The accounts of revenue and expenditure are examined by a special administrative tribunal (*Cour des Comptes*), instituted in 1807.

Currency. The unit of currency is the *franc*. Coins are issued for 5, 10, 20 and 50 centimes, 1, 2, 5 and 10 francs; and bank-notes for 10, 20, 50, 100, 200 and 500 francs. In March 1988, £1 sterling = 10·14 *francs*; US$1 = 5·71 *francs*.

Banking. The *Banque de France*, founded in 1800, and nationalized on 2 Dec. 1945, has the monopoly (since 1848) of issuing bank-notes throughout France. Note circulation at 31 Dec. 1981 was 151,900m. francs. As a Central Bank, it puts monetary policy into effect and supervises its application.

The National Credit Council, formed in 1945 to regulate banking activity and consulted in all political decisions on monetary policy, comprises 45 members nominated by the Government; its president is the Minister for the Economy, its vice-president is the Governor of the *Banque de France*. Four principal deposit banks were nationalized in 1945 and the remainder in 1982, the chief ones being the Crédit Lyonnais (founded 1863), Banque Nationale de Paris (founded by amalgamation 1966), Société Générale (founded 1864), Crédit Industriel et Commercial, Crédit Commercial de France, the Banque de Paris et des Pays-Bas and the Crédit du Nord. Total deposits and short- and medium-term held bills by the banks at 31 Dec. 1981 was 1,302,800m. francs. The rest of the banking system comprises the popular banks, the Crédit agricole, the Crédit mutuel, the Banque française du commerce exterieur and the various financial establishments.

The state savings organization (*Caisse nationale d'epargne*) is administered by the post office on a giro system. On 31 Dec. 1981 the private savings banks (*Caisses d'epargne et de prévoyance*), numbering about 500 had 434,000m. francs in deposits; the state savings banks had 206,300m. francs in deposits. Deposited funds are centralized by a non-banking body, the *Caisse de Dépôts et Consignations*, which finances a large number of local authorities and state aided housing projects, and carries an important portfolio of transferable securities.

Weights and Measures. The metric system is in general use.

ENERGY AND NATURAL RESOURCES

Electricity. Production (in 1m. kwh.): 1985, 332,016, of which 24% was hydroelectric and 49% nuclear. Supply 127 and 220 volts; 50 Hz.

Oil. In 1987 3·3m. tonnes of crude oil were produced. The greater part came from the Parentis oilfield in the Landes. Reserves (1985) total 221m. bbls. France has an important oil-refining industry, chiefly utilizing imported crude oil. The principal plants are situated in Seine-Maritime and in Bouches-du-Rhône. In 1985, 72·49m. tonnes of petroleum products were refined. There are 7,802 km of pipelines.

There has been considerable development of the production of natural gas and sulphur in the region of Lacq in the foothills of the Pyrenees. Production of natural gas was 10,574m. cu. metres in 1984; reserves (1985) 41,000m. cu. metres.

Minerals. Principal minerals and metals produced in 1983, in 1,000 tonnes: Coal, 33,396; crude steel, 17,616; iron ore, 15,972; pig iron, 13,752; bauxite, 1,660; potash salts, 1,651.

Agriculture. Of the total area of France (54·9m. hectares) 17·9m. were under cultivation, 12·3m. were pasture, 1·3m. were under vines, 14·6m. were forests and 8·8m. were uncultivated land in 1985.

The following table shows the area under the leading crops and the production for 3 years:

	Area (1,000 hectares)			Produce (1,000 tonnes)		
	1983	1984	1985	1983	1984	1985
Wheat	4,825	4,828	4,828	24,748	32,977	29,012
Rye	101	100	88	293	347	297
Barley	2,143	2,107	2,255	8,773	11,509	11,426
Oats	436	440	431	1,419	1,874	1,744
Potatoes	204	205	211	5,317	6,125	6,961
Sugar-beet	490	526	490	26,320	28,752	28,684
Maize	1,646	1,702	1,810	10,390	10,359	11,714

Other crops for 1984 (1983 in brackets) include (in 1,000 tonnes): Rice, 42 (38); tobacco, 37 (36); flax, 78 (62).

France is the world's second largest producer of wine (after Italy); production in 1985 amounted to 15·92m. hectolitres.

The production of fruits (other than for cider making) for 4 years was (in 1,000 tonnes) as follows:

	1982	1983	1984	1985		1982	1983	1984	1985
Apples	2,102	1,648	2,119	1,815	Cherries	142	109	140	112
Pears	459	446	480	442	Nuts	72	58	49	47
Plums	190	193	240	222	Grapes	229	199	205	197
Peaches	421	469	488	485	Strawberries	89	84	90	92
Apricots	75	107	85	102	Oranges	38	31	27	31

In 1986 the numbers of farm animals (in 1,000) were (figures for 1985 in brackets): Horses, 310 (310); cattle, 22,896 (23,099); sheep, 10,790 (10,824); goats, 969 (962); pigs, 10,956 (10,975); poultry, 217,000 (215,000).

Forestry. The total area of forested land (1984) was 138,383 sq. km. Timber sold (1982), 28,342m. cu. metres valued at 7,581m. francs.

Fisheries. (1986). There were 18,165 fishermen, and 9,227 sailing-boats, steamers and motor-boats. Catch (in tonnes): Fish, total, 473,211; crustaceans, 25,991; shell fish, 185,923.

INDUSTRY AND TRADE

Industry. Industrial production (in 1,000 tonnes) for 3 years was as follows:

	1983	1984	1985
Sulphuric acid	4,325	4,531	4,322
Caustic acid	1,393	1,497	1,467
Sulphur	1,833	1,775	1,570
Polystyrene	480	485	497
Polyvinyl	817	797	809
Polyethylene	971	1,005	1,019
Wool	44	45	50
Cotton	154	151	142
Linen	2·1	2·2	1·2
Silk	52	57	61
Man-made fibres, yarns	38	29	...
Jute	2·7	3·2	5
Cheese	1,153	1,191	1,219
Chocolate	124	122	120
Biscuits	397	400	402
Sugar	3,562	3,956	3,978
Fish preparations	99	102	101
Jams and jellies	122	128	130
Cement	24,503	22,724	22,224

Engineering production (in 1,000 units) for 3 years:

	1983	1984	1985
Motor vehicles	3,336	3,062	3,016
Television sets	2,033	2,001	1,913
Radio sets	2,489	2,128	2,632
Tyres	45,606	47,817	47,742

Employment (1985). Out of an economically active population of 21,257,200 persons, there were 1·56m. engaged in agriculture; 1,518,000 in building and public works; 4,181,900 in other manufacturing industries; 889,200 in transport; 609,900 in business, banking and insurance; 3,270,900 in services; 2,950,400 in commerce. In 1984, there were 23,594,000 employed (42·5% female), of whom 1·9m. were foreign workers; in April 1987, there were 2,592,700 unemployed.

Trade Unions. The main confederations recognized as nationally representative are: the CGT (Confédération Générale du Travail), founded in 1895; the CGT-FO (Confédération Générale du Travail–Force Ouvrière) which broke away from the CGT in 1948 as a protest against Communist influence therein; the CFTC (Confédération Française des Travailleurs Chrétiens), which was founded in 1919 and divided in 1964, with a breakaway group retaining the old name and the main body continuing under the new name of CFDT (Confédération Française Démocratique du Travail); and the CGC (Confédération Générale des Cadres) formed in 1944 which only represents managerial and supervisory staff.

Membership is estimated because unions are not required to publish figures; but at elections held on 8 Dec. 1982 for labour tribunals, the CGT was supported by 2·8m. members, the CGT-FO by 1·4m., the CFDT by 1·8m., the CFTC by 650,000 and the CGC by 740,000. Except for the CGC unions operate within the framework of industries and not of trades.

Commerce. Imports (c.i.f.) and exports (f.o.b.) in 1m. francs for 5 calendar years were (including gold):

	1982	1983	1984	1985	1986
Imports	757,595	799,754	903,775	962,746	863,172
Exports	606,094	694,651	813,003	870,812	863,652

The chief imports for home use and exports of home goods are to and from the following countries, in 1m. francs (including gold):

	Imports (c.i.f)		Exports (f.o.b.)	
Countries	1985	1986	1985	1986
Belgium-Luxembourg	82,288	83,944	73,931	74,906
Germany, Fed. Rep. of	159,057	172,362	130,513	133,085
Italy	96,796	103,388	95,322	97,249
Japan	26,887	32,227	10,736	11,160
Spain	36,535	36,961	29,340	33,780
Switzerland	20,275	22,174	36,499	37,733
UK	78,992	58,078	71,553	72,708
USA	73,246	67,008	75,349	61,027

Total trade between France and UK (British Department of Trade returns, in £1,000 sterling):

	1983	1984	1985	1986	1987
Imports to UK	5,043,118	5,885,715	6,632,410	7,348,574	8,381,984
Exports and re-exports from UK	5,651,521	7,082,389	7,751,751	6,210,216	7,781,546

Tourism. In 1986 there were 36·08m. tourists.

COMMUNICATIONS

Roads. In 1984 the French road system consisted of 6,290 km of motorway, out of a total road network of 1,521,351 km. In 1985, there were 20·8m. passenger cars and 3·31m. commercial vehicles in use.

Railways. As from 1 Jan. 1938 all the independent railway companies were merged with the existing state railway system in a Société Nationale des Chemins de Fer Français, which became a public industrial and commercial establishment in 1983.

In 1986, the State railway totalled 34,665 km (11,549 km electrified) of 1,435 mm gauge, and carried 146m. tonnes of freight and 774m. passengers. A new railway for high-speed trains was completed in 1983 between Paris and Lyon and another is under construction to serve Western France.

The Paris transport network consisted in 1985 of 472 km of underground railway (métro) and regional express railways and 2,134 km of bus routes. In 1985 it carried 1,477m. passengers on the métro and 747m. by bus.

Aviation. Air France, UTA and Air Inter, the national airlines, had (31 Dec. 1985) a fleet of 137 aircraft, servicing Europe, North America, Central and South America, West and East Africa, Madagascar, the Near, Middle and Far East. There are local networks in the West Indies and Central America. In 1985 Air France, UTA and Air Inter flew 2,900m. tonne-km (excluding mail) and 39,655m. passenger-km. There were (1984) 60 airports with scheduled services.

Shipping. Merchant ships, on 1 Jan. 1985, numbered 1,174 vessels of 8,945,046 GRT. During 1985, 74,485 vessels entered French ports to discharge 199,081,100 tonnes and load 75,175,800 tonnes, principal ports being Marseille, Le Havre, Dunkerque, Rouen and Nantes/St Nazaire; Calais (8·2m. passengers in 1985) and Boulogne-sur-Mer (3·03m.) are the main passenger ports.

In 1986 there were 8,500 km of navigable rivers, waterways and canals (of which 1,647 km accessible to vessels over 3,000 tons), with a total traffic in 1985 of 64·12m. tonnes.

Post and Broadcasting. On 31 Dec. 1983 the telephone system (government-owned) had 29,373,663 subscribers; the Paris region (including the Paris and Seine-et-Marne, Yvelines, Essonne, Hauts-de-Seine, Seine-Saint-Denis, Val-de-Marne and Val-d'Oise departments) accounted for 5,396,726. In 1984 there were 17,035 post offices.

Radio and television broadcasting was reorganized under the Act of 7 Aug. 1974 which replaced the Office de Radiodiffusion Télévision Française with 4 broadcasting companies, a production company and an audio-visual institute. Organization, development, operation and the maintenance of networks and installations became the responsibility of the Public Broadcasting Establishment. Radio programmes are broadcast from 363 transmitters by 3 stations: *France Inter, France Musique* and *France Culture*. Television programmes are broadcast from 325 transmitters and 4,661 relay stations on 3 channels. There were about 20m. radio and 19m. TV sets in use in 1983 (of which 8·9m. in colour).

Cinemas (1984). There were 5,098 cinemas with a seating capacity of 1,306,500; attendances totalled 187·8m.

Newspapers (1987). There were 72 daily papers published in the provinces with a circulation of 6·7m. copies, and 14 published in Paris with a national circulation of 2·5m. Among Paris dailies *France-Soir* sells 539,000; *Le Monde* 445,000; *Le Parisien Libéré* 421,000; *Le Figaro* 465,000, *Le Matin* 224,000 and *L'Aurore* 220,000. Among provincial dailies *Ouest-France* (Rennes) sells 783,000; *Le Progrés* (Lyon) 447,000; *La Voix du Nord* (Lille) 372,000; *Sud-Ouest* (Bordeaux) 430,000; *La Dauphine Libérée* (Grenoble) 401,000 and *Le Provençal* (Marseilles) 345,000.

JUSTICE, RELIGION, EDUCATION AND WELFARE

Justice. Since 1958, 471 *tribunaux d'instance* (11 in overseas departments), under a single judge each and with increased material and territorial jurisdiction, have replaced the former *juges de paix* (1 in each canton); and 181 *tribunaux de grande instance* (6 in overseas departments) have taken the place of the 357 *tribunaux de première instance* (1 in each *arrondissement*).

The *tribunaux de grande instance* usually have a collegiate composition, however a law dated 10 July 1970 has allowed them to administer justice under a single judge in some civil cases.

All petty offences (*contraventions*) are disposed of in the Police Courts (*Tribun-*

aux de Police) presided over by a Judge on duty in the *tribunal d'instance*. The Correctional Courts pronounce upon all graver offences (*délits*), including cases involving imprisonment up to 5 years. They have no jury, and consist of 3 judges who administer both criminal and civil justice. An Act of 29 Dec. 1972 established that there is only 1 judge; in some cases, the correctional courts may consist of a single judge each. In all cases of a *délit* or a *crime* the preliminary inquiry is made in secrecy by an examining magistrate (*juge d'instruction*), who either dismisses the case or sends it for trial before a court where a public prosecutor (*Procureur*) endeavours to prove the charge.

The 282 Conciliation Boards (*Conseils des Prud'hommes*) are composed of an equal number of employers and employees deal with labour disputes. Commercial litigation goes to one of the 227 Commercial Courts (*Tribunaux de Commerce*) composed of tradesmen and manufacturers elected for 2 years. The judges hold office for 2 years and they can be re-elected; 3 years for the President.

When the decisions of any of these Tribunals are susceptible of appeal, the case goes to one of the 35 Courts of Appeal (*Cours d'Appel*), (including 3 in overseas departments and 2 in overseas territories), composed each of a president and a variable number of members.

The Courts of Assizes (*Cours d'Assises*), composed each of a president, assisted by 2 other magistrates who are members of the Courts of Appeal, and by a jury of 9 people, sit in every *département*, when called upon to try very important criminal cases. The decisions of the Courts of Appeal and the Courts of Assizes are final; however, the Court of Cassation (*Cour de Cassation*) has discretion to verify if the law has been correctly interpreted and if the rules of procedure have been followed exactly. The Court of Cassation may annul any judgment, and the cases have to be tried again by a Court of Appeal or a Court of Assizes.

The State Security Court, established in 1963, was abolished by law on 4 Aug. 1981. Capital punishment was abolished in the same month.

On 24 Jan. 1973 the first Ombudsman (*médiateur*) was appointed for a 6-year period.

The French penal institutions consist of: (1) *maisons d'arrêt* and *de correction*, where persons awaiting trial as well as those condemned to short periods of imprisonment are kept; (2) central prisons (*maisons centrales*) for those sentenced to long imprisonment; (3) special establishments, namely (*a*) schools for young adults, (*b*) hostels for old and disabled offenders, (*c*) hospitals for the sick and psychopaths, (*d*) institutions for recidivists. Special attention is being paid to classified treatment and the rehabilitation and vocational re-education of prisoners including work in open-air and semi-free establishments. There are 2 penal institutions for women.

Juvenile delinquents go before special judges and courts; they are sent to public or private institutions of supervision and re-education.

The population at 31 Dec. 1984 of all penal establishments was 43,001 men and 1,497 women.

Religion. No religion is officially recognized by the State. Under the law promulgated on 9 Dec. 1905, which separated Church and State, the adherents of all creeds are authorized to form associations for public worship (*associations culturelles*). The law of 2 Jan. 1907 provided that, failing *associations culturelles*, the buildings for public worship, together with their furniture, would continue at the disposition of the ministers of religion and the worshippers for the exercise of their religion; but in each case there was required an administrative act drawn up by the *préfet* as regards buildings belonging to the State or the departments and by the *maire* as regards buildings belonging to the communes.

There were (1985) 125 archbishops and bishops of the Roman Catholic Church, with (1974) 43,557 clergy of various grades and (1986) 42.35m. members. The Protestants of the Augsburg confession are, in their religious affairs, governed by a General Consistory, while the Reformed Church is under a Council of Administration, the seat of which is in Paris. In 1986 there were about 800,000 Protestants and 2.5m. Moslems.

Education. The primary, secondary and higher state schools constitute the 'Université de France'. The Supreme Council of 84 members has deliberative, administrative and judiciary functions, and as a consultative committee advises respecting the working of the school system, the inspectors-general are in direct communication with the Minister. For local education administration France is divided into 25 academic areas, each of which has an Academic Council whose members include a certain number elected by the professors or teachers. The Academic Council deals with all grades of education. Each is under a Rector, and each is provided with academy inspectors, 1 for each department.

Compulsory education is now provided for children of 6–16. The educational stages are as follows:

1. Non-compulsory pre-school instruction for children aged 2–5, to be given in infant schools or infant classes attached to primary schools.

2. Compulsory elementary instruction for children aged 6–11, to be given in primary schools and certain classes of the *lycées*. It consists of 3 courses: preparatory (1 year), elementary (2 years), intermediary (2 years). Physically or mentally handicapped children are cared for in special institutions or special classes of primary schools.

3. Lower secondary education (*Enseignement du premier cycle du Second Degré*) for pupils aged 11–15, consists of 4 years of study in the *lycées* (grammar schools), *Collèges d'Enseignement Secondaire* or *Collèges d'Enseignement Général*.

4. Upper secondary education (*Enseignement du second cycle du Second Degré*) for pupils aged 15–18:

> *Long, général* or *professionel* provided by the *lycées* and leading to the *baccalauréat* or to the *baccalauréat de technicien* after 3 years.

> *Court*, professional courses of 3, 2 and 1 year are taught in the *lycées d'enseignement professionel*, or the specialized sections of the *lycées*, CES or CEG.

The following table shows the various types of schools in 1984–85 and the numbers of enrolled pupils:

Description	State	Private	Total
Pre-primary	2,196,645	328,979	2,525,624
Primary	3,504,227	622,208	4,126,435
Secondary	4,180,730	1,129,565	5,310,295
Higher	1,084,261	79,642	1,163,903
Specialized	199,536	93,752	293,288
Total	11,165,399	2,254,146	13,419,545

The state schools in 1984–85 had 73,872 nursery, 166,623 primary, 33,003 special school and 321,128 secondary school teachers.

Higher Instruction is supplied by the State in the universities and in special schools, and by private individuals in the free faculties and schools. The law of 12 July 1875 provided for higher education free of charge. This law was modified by that of 18 March 1880, which granted the state faculties the exclusive right to confer degrees. A decree of 28 Dec. 1885 created a general council of the faculties, and the creation of universities, each consisting of several faculties, was accomplished in 1897, in virtue of the law of 10 July 1896.

The law of 12 Nov. 1968 laying down future guidelines for higher education redefined the activities and working of universities. Bringing several disciplines together, 780 units for teaching and research (UER–Unités d'Enseignement et de Récherche) were formed which decided their own teaching activities, research programmes and procedures for checking the level of knowledge gained. They and the other parts of each university must respect the rules designed to maintain the national standard of qualifications.

The UERs form the basic units of 69 Universities and 3 National Polytechnic Institutes (with university status), grouped into 25 *académies* with 944,434 students (of which 59,824 in the Institutes) in 1984–85.

There are also Catholic university facilities in Paris, Angers, Lille, Lyon and

Toulouse with (1981–82) 34,118 students and private universities with (1984–85) 17,646 students.

Outside the university system, higher education (academic, professional and technical) is provided by over 400 schools and institutes, including the various Grand Écoles. In 1984–85 there were 139,827 students in state establishments and 61,996 in private establishments. In 1984–85 there were also 46,258 students in preparatory classes leading to the Grande Écoles, 105,101 in the Sections de Techniciens Supérieurs and 31,513 in the Écoles d'ingénieurs; there were also 18,951 students in Écoles normales d'instituteurs (teacher-training).

Health. On 1 Jan. 1983 there were 114,534 physicians, 43,662 pharmacists, 33,048 dentists, 271,253 nursing personnel and 8,660 midwives practising. On 1 Jan. 1984 there were 3,364 hospitals with 622,552 beds.

Social Welfare. An order of 4 Oct. 1945 laid down the framework of a comprehensive plan of Social Security and created a single organization which superseded the various laws relating to social insurance, workmen's compensation, health insurance, family allowances, etc. All previous matters relating to Social Security are dealt with in the Social Security Code, 1956; this has been revised several times, and finally by orders laid down on 21 Aug. 1967, which were ratified on 31 July 1968. The Social Security general scheme covers all wage-earning workers in industry and commerce that are not covered by a special scheme of their own.

Contributions. All wage-earning workers or those of equivalent status are insured regardless of the amount or the nature of the salary or earnings. The funds for the general scheme are raised mainly from professional contributions, these being fixed within the limits of a ceiling (assessed at 68,760 francs per annum on 1 Jan. 1981) and calculated as a percentage of the salaries. The calculation of contributions payable for family allowances, old age and industrial injuries relates only to this amount; on the other hand, the amount payable for sickness, maternity expenses, disability and death is calculated partly within the limit of the 'ceiling' and partly on the whole salary. These contributions are the responsibility of both employer and employee, except in the case of family allowances or industrial injuries, where they are the sole responsibility of the employer.

Contributions and benefits paid in 1984 (in 1m. francs) were:

	Contributions	Benefits
Health service	259,258	219,476
Industrial injuries	34,049	25,551
Old age pensions	135,243	123,414
Family benefits	93,948	91,561

Self-employed Workers. From 17 Jan. 1948 allowances and old-age pensions were paid to self-employed workers by independent insurance funds set up within their own profession, trade or business. Schemes of compulsory insurance for sickness were instituted in 1961 for farmers and in 1966, with modifications in 1970, for other non-wage-earning workers.

Social Insurance. The orders laid down in Aug. 1967 ensure that the whole population can benefit from the Social Security Scheme; at present all elderly persons who have been engaged in the professions, as well as the surviving spouse, are entitled to claim an old-age benefit; 98% of the population, both working and retired, are covered by a compulsory scheme of insurance for sickness, the remaining 2% who are not covered by a compulsory insurance scheme have been able to participate in a voluntary scheme since 1967; the whole population benefit from the legislation regarding family allowances.

Sickness Insurance refunds the costs of treatment required by the insured and the needs of dependants. A decree of 12 Oct. 1976 laid down conditions on which students of 20 or over at public or private educational institutions, who do not benefit from a social security scheme in their own right, are guaranteed insurance benefits for sickness or maternity, holding their parents entitlement until the end of the academic year in which they attain their 21st birthday, provided they have proof that their studies have been interrupted by illness. The general principles relating to medical care consist of: A free choice by the patient of his doctor, his pharmaceutical chemist, his place of treatment, etc.; the medical practitioner is granted freedom of prescription. Reimbursement is not as a rule made in full; the insured person usually pays between 10% and 30% of the legal rate except in cases of exemption. The insured who is recognized as medically unfit for work receives daily allowances equal to half of the wage which has been used to calculate the contributions, or to two-thirds of this if the person has 3 or more children. These allowances may be paid for 3 years, plus 1 additional year if the insured undergoes readaptation treatment or takes up fresh vocational training.

Maternity Insurance covers the costs of medical treatment relating to the pregnancy, confinement and lying-in period; the beneficiaries being the insured person or the spouse. The daily allowances are equal to 90% of the salary on which contributions were calculated.

Insurance for Invalids is divided into 3 categories: (1) those who are capable of working; (2) those who cannot work; (3) those who, in addition, are in need of the help of another person. According to the category, the pension rate varies from 30 to 50% of the average salary for the last 10 years, with additional allowance for home help for the third category.

Old-age Pensions for workers were introduced in 1910 and are now fixed by the Social Security Code of 28 Jan. 1972. Since 1983 people who have paid insurance for at least 37½ years (150 quarters) receive at 60 a pension equal to 60% of basic salary. People who have paid insurance for less than 37½ years but no less than 15 years can expect a pension equal to as many 1/150ths of the full pension as their quarterly payments justify. In the event of death of the insured person, the husband or wife of the deceased person receives half the pension received by the latter. Compulsory supplementary schemes ensure benefits equal to 70% of previous earnings.

Family Allowances. The system comprises: (a) Family allowances proper, equivalent to 25·5% of the basic monthly salary (1,246 francs) for 2 dependent children, 46% for the third child, 41% for the fourth child, and 39% for the fifth and each subsequent child; a supplement equivalent to 9% of the basic monthly salary for the second and each subsequent dependent child more than 10 years old and 16% for each dependent child over 15 years. (b) Family supplement (519 francs) for persons with at least 3 children or one child aged less than 3 years. (c) Antenatal grants. (d) Maternity grant equal to 260% of basic salary; increase for multiple births or adoptions, 198%; increase for birth or adoption of third or subsequent child, 457%. (e) Allowance for specialized education of handicapped children. (f) Allowance for orphans. (g) Single parent allowance. (h) Allowance for opening of school term. (i) Allowance for accommodation, under certain circumstances. (j) Minimum family income for those with at least 3 children. Allowances (b), (g), (h) and (j) only apply to those whose annual income falls below a specified level.

Workmen's Compensation. The law passed by the National Assembly on 30 Oct. 1946 forms part of the Social Security Code and is administered by the Social Security Organization. Employers are invited to take preventive measures. The application of these measures is supervised by consulting engineers (assessors) of the local funds dealing with sickness insurance, who may compel employers who do not respect these measures to make additional contributions; they may, in like manner, grant rebates to employers who have in operation suitable preventive measures. The injured person receives free treatment, the insurance fund reimburses the practitioners, hospitals and suppliers chosen freely by the injured. In cases of temporary disablement the daily payments are equal to half the total daily wage received by the injured. In case of permanent disablement the injured person receives a pension, the amount of which varies according to the degree of disablement and the salary received during the past 12 months.

A law promulgated on 11 Oct. 1946 has created a medical labour service of doctors who hold a diploma of 'industrial health specialists'. These doctors are entrusted with the control of hygiene and health matters in all industrial undertakings or groups of undertakings. In addition, it is the duty of this medical service to examine wage-earners when they are engaged, to carry out periodical medical examinations and to ensure the application of the existing rules relating to safety in work.

Unemployment Benefits vary according to circumstances (full or partial unemployment) which are means-tested. Since 1926 unemployment benefits have been paid from public funds. Full unemployment benefit amounts to 13·50 francs per day for the head of the family and 5·40 francs for the spouse or a dependent person. After 3 months the payment is reduced to 12·40 francs.

A collective agreement signed on 31 Dec. 1958 between the national council of employers and certain trade unions has established a system of special allowances for totally unemployed workers in industry and trade. The costs are shared by employers (2·76% of wages) and employees (0·84%) and the benefits vary according to circumstances. The system is now governed by the law of 16 Jan. 1979. A similar agreement of 21 Feb. 1968 extends the system to partial unemployment.

DIPLOMATIC REPRESENTATIVES

Of France in Great Britain (58 Knightsbridge, London, SW1X 7JT)
Ambassador: Vicomte Luc de la Barre de Nanteuil (accredited 28 Feb. 1986).

Of Great Britain in France (35 rue du Faubourg St Honoré, 75383 Paris)
Ambassador: Sir Ewen Fergusson, KCMG.

Of France in the USA (4101 Reservoir Rd., NW, Washington, D.C., 20007)
Ambassador: Emmanuel de Margerie.

Of the USA in France (2 Ave. Gabriel, Paris)
Ambassador: Joe M. Rodgers.

Of France to the United Nations
Ambassador: Pierre-Louis Blanc.

Books of Reference

Statistical Information: The Institut national de la Statistique et des Études économiques (18, Boulevard Adolphe Pinard, 75014 Paris) is the central office of statistics. It was established by a law of 27 April 1946, which amalgamated the Service National des Statistiques (created in 1941 by merging the Direction de la Statistique générale de la France and the Service de la Démographie) with the Institut de Conjoncture (set up in 1938) and some statistical services of the Ministry of National Economy. The Institut comprises the following departments: Metropolitan statistics, Overseas statistics, Market research and economic studies, Documentation, Research statistics and economics, Informatics, Foreign Economic Studies.
The main publications of the Institut include:

Annuaire statistique de la France (from 1878)
Annuaire statistique des Territoires d'Outre-Mer (from 1959)
Bulletin mensuel de statistique (monthly)
Documentation économique (bi-monthly)
Données statistiques africaines et Malgaches (quarterly)
Economie et Statistique (monthly)
Tableaux de l'Economie Française (biennially, from 1956)
Tendances de la Conjoncture (monthly)

Caron, F., *An Economic History of Modern France.* London, 1979
Chambers, F. J., *France.* [Bibliography] London and Santa Barbara, 1984
Crozier, M., *A Strategy for Change: The Future of French Society.* MIT Press, 1982
Dyer, C., *Population and Society in Twentieth Century France.* London, 1978
Peyrefitte, A., *The Trouble with France.* New York, 1981
Tuppen, J. N., *France.* Folkestone, 1981

OVERSEAS DEPARTMENTS

On 19 March 1946 the French colonies of Guadeloupe, French Guiana, Martinique and Réunion each became an Overseas Department of France, with the same status as the departments comprising Metropolitan France. The former territory of Saint Pierre and Miquelon held a similar status from July 1976 until June 1985, when it became a *collectivité territorial.*

GUADELOUPE

HISTORY. Discovered by Columbus in Nov. 1493, the two main islands were then known as *Karukera* (Isle of Beautiful Waters) to the Carib inhabitants, who resisted Spanish attempts to colonize. A French colony was established on 28 June 1635, and apart from short periods of occupancy by British forces, Guadeloupe has since remained a French possession. On 19 March 1946 Guadeloupe became an Overseas Department; in 1974 it additionally became an administrative region.

AREA AND POPULATION. Guadeloupe consists of a group of islands in the Lesser Antilles. The two main islands, Basse-Terre to the west and Grande-Terre to the east, are separated by a narrow channel, called Rivière Salée. Adjacent to these are the islands of Marie Galante *(Ceyre* to the Caribs) to the south-east, La Désirade to the east, and the Îles des Saintes to the south. The islands of St Martin and St Barthélemy lie 250 km to the north-west.

	Area in sq. km	Census 1974	Census 1982	Chief town
St Martin[1]	54 [2]	6,191	8,072	Marigot
St Barthélemy	21	2,491	3,059	Gustavia
Basse-Terre	848	135,746	135,341	Basse-Terre
Grande-Terre	590	159,424	163,668	Pointe-à-Pitre
Îles des Saintes	13	3,084	2,901	Terre-de-Bas
La Désirade	20	1,682	1,602	Grande Anse
Marie-Galante	158	15,912	13,757	Grand-Bourg
	1,705	324,530	328,400	

[1]Northern part only; the southern third is Dutch.   [2]Includes uninhabited Tintamarre.

Population (estimate, 1987) 335,300. 77% are mulatto, 10% black and 10% mestizo, but the populations of St Barthélemy and Les Saintes are still mainly descended from 17th-century Breton and Norman settlers. French is the official language, but a Creole dialect is spoken by the vast majority except on St Martin.

The seat of government is Basse-Terre (13,656 inhabitants in 1982) at the south-west end of that island but the largest towns are Pointe-à-Pitre (25,310 inhabitants), the economic centre and main port, and its suburb, Les Abymes.

Vital statistics (1985): Live births, 6,760; deaths, 2,313; marriages, 1,611.

CONSTITUTION AND GOVERNMENT. Guadeloupe is administered by a *Conseil Général* of 42 members (assisted by an Economic and Social Committee of 40 members) and a Regional Council of 39 members, both directly elected for terms of 6 years. It is represented in the National Assembly by 4 deputies, in the Senate by 2 senators and on the Economic and Social Council by 2 councillors. There are 3 *arrondissements*, sub-divided into 34 communes, each administered by an elected municipal council. The French government is represented by an appointed Commissioner.

Commissioner: Yves Bonnet.
President of the Conseil Général: Dominique Larifla.
President of the Regional Council: Félix Proto.

ECONOMY

Budget. The budget for 1983 balanced at 1,633m. francs.

Banking. The main commercial banks are the Banque des Antilles Françaises (with 6 branches), the Banque Populaire de la Guadeloupe (with 6 branches), the Banque Nationale de Paris (14 branches), the Crédit Agricole (26), the Banque Française Commerciale (8), the Société Generale de Banque aux Antilles (5) and the Chase Manhattan Bank (1). The Caisse Centrale de Coopération économique is the official bank of the department and issues its bank-notes.

ENERGY AND NATURAL RESOURCES

Electricity. Production in 1986 totalled 315m. kwh.

Agriculture. Chief products (1986) are bananas (157,000 tonnes), sugar-cane (773,000 tonnes), rum (64,883 hectolitres of pure alcohol in 1984). Other fruits and vegetables are grown for domestic consumption. 11·8m. flowers were grown in 1984.

Livestock (1986): Cattle, 82,000; goats, 36,000; sheep, 4,000; pigs, 44,000.

Forestry. In 1985, there were 395 sq. km of forests. In 1984, 51,848 cu. metres of wood were produced.

Fisheries. The catch in 1984 was 8,500 tonnes; crustacea (120 tonnes), shell fish (300 tonnes).

COMMERCE. Trade for 1985 (in 1m. francs) was imports 5,745 and exports 669, 60% of imports were from France, while 63% of exports went to France and 18% to Martinique. In 1985 bananas formed 43% of the exports, sugar 10% and rum 7%. St Martin and St Barthélemy are free ports.

Tourism. In 1986 there were 212,000 tourists.

COMMUNICATIONS

Roads. In 1984 there were 3,500 km of roads. There were 87,785 passenger cars and 33,350 commercial vehicles in 1981.

Aviation. Air France and 7 other airlines call at Guadeloupe. In 1984 there were 31,451 arrivals and departures of aircraft and 1,325,500 passengers at Raizet (Pointe-à-Pitre) airport and, 6,682 aircraft movements and 116,000 passengers at Marie-Galante airport.

Shipping. Guadeloupe is in direct communication with France by means of 12 steam navigation companies. In 1983, 1,239 vessels arrived to disembark 74,921 passengers and 1,035,800 tonnes of freight and to embark 74,999 passengers and 470,600 tonnes of freight.

Post and Broadcasting. In 1984 there were 47 post offices and 64,916 telephones. RFO broadcasts for 17 hours a day in French and television broadcasts for 6 hours a day. There were (1983) 25,000 radio and (1981) 32,886 TV receivers.

Newspapers. There was (1984) 1 daily newspaper *(France-Antilles)* with a circulation of 25,000.

JUSTICE, RELIGION, EDUCATION AND WELFARE

Justice. There are 4 *tribunaux d'instance* and 2 *tribunaux de grande instance* at Basse-Terre and Pointe-à-Pitre; there is also a court of appeal and a court of assizes at Basse-Terre.

Religion. The majority of the population are Roman Catholic.

Education. In 1984 there were 62,303 pupils at 284 primary schools and 45,843 at secondary schools. The *University Antilles-Guyane* had 4,809 students in 1984–85, of which Guadeloupe itself had 1,870.

Health. The medical services in 1985 included 11 public hospitals (2,891 beds) and 18 private clinics (1,256 beds). There were 416 physicians, 127 dentists, 127 pharmacists, 70 midwives and 1,131 nursing personnel.

Books of Reference

Information: Office du Tourisme du départemente, Point-à-Pitre. *Director:* Eric W. Rotin.
Lasserre, G., *La Guadeloupe, étude géographique.* 2 vols. Bordeaux, 1961

GUIANA
Guyane Française

HISTORY. A French settlement on the island of Cayenne was established in 1604 and the territory between the Maroni and Oyapock rivers finally became a French possession in 1817. Convicts settlements were established from 1852, that on off-shore Devil's Island being most notorious; all were closed by 1945. On 19 March 1946 the status of Guiana was changed to that of an Overseas Department and in 1974 also became an administrative region.

AREA AND POPULATION. French Guiana is situated on the north-east coast of South America, and has an area of about 83,533 sq. km (32,252 sq. miles) and a population at the 1982 Census of 73,012, of whom 3,000 were tribal Indians; estimate (1987) 89,000. The chief towns (1982 populations) are Cayenne, the capital (38,091), Kourou (7,061) and Saint-Laurent-du-Maroni (5,042). These figures exclude the floating population of miners, officials and troops.

In 1982, 43% of the inhabitants were of Creole origin, 14% Chinese, 11% from Metropolitan France and 8% Haitian. 90% of the population speak Creole.

Vital statistics (1985): Live births, 2,473; deaths, 492; marriages, 317.

CONSTITUTION AND GOVERNMENT. French Guiana is administered by a *Conseil Général* of 19 members and a Regional Council of 31 members, both directly elected for terms of 6 years. It is represented in the National Assembly by 2 deputies and in the Senate by 1 senator. The French government is represented by an appointed Commissioner. There are 2 *arrondissements* (Cayenne and Saint-Laurent-du-Maroni) sub-divided into 20 communes.

Commissioner: Jacques Dewatre.
President of the Conseil Général: Elie Castor.
President of the Regional Council: Georges Othily.

ECONOMY

Budget. The budget for 1984 balanced at 675m. francs, excluding duplicated items and national expenditure.

Banking. The Banque de la Guyane has a capital of 10m. francs and reserve fund of 2·39m. francs. Loans totalled 206m. francs in 1981. Other banks include Banque National de Paris-Guyane and Banque Française Commerciale.

ENERGY AND NATURAL RESOURCES

Electricity. Production in 1986 totalled 156m. kwh. Supply 220 volts; 50 Hz.

Agriculture. Only 10,436 hectares are under cultivation. The crops (1986, in tonnes) consist of rice (9,000), roots and tubers (13,000), manioc (8,000), plantains (1,000), limes (1984, 650) and sugar-cane (8,000) as well as a large variety of other fruits, vegetables and spices.

Livestock (1986): 15,000 cattle, 10,000 swine and (1982) 100,000 poultry.

Forestry. The country has immense forests (about 80,511 sq. km in 1987) rich in many kinds of timber. Roundwood production (1984) 69,200 cu. metres.

Fisheries. The fishing fleet for shrimps comprises 59 US, 22 Japanese and 11 French boats. The catch in 1982 totalled 4,503 tonnes (of which shrimps comprised 3,227 tonnes), exports 2,750 tonnes. Production of *Macrobrachium Rosenbergii* (an edible river shrimp) is now established.

COMMERCE. Trade in 1m. francs:

	1982	1983	1984	1985
Imports	1,643	2,137	2,158	2,287
Exports	212	294	327	331

In 1985, 14% of imports came from Trinidad and Tobago, 60% from France and 5% from the USA, while 38% of exports went to the USA, 17% to Japan and 19% to France. In 1985, shrimps formed 53% of exports and timber, 9%.

Total trade between Guiana and UK (British Department of Trade returns, in £1,000 sterling):

	1983	1984	1985	1986	1987
Imports to UK	853	795	124	55	380
Exports and re-exports from UK	897	3,106	1,146	1,052	1,134

TOURISM. There were 21,600 tourists in 1982.

COMMUNICATIONS

Roads. Three chief and some secondary roads connect the capital with most of the coastal area by motor-car services. There are (1981) 321 km of national and 269 km of departmental roads. In 1981 there were 16,789 passenger cars and 2,013 commercial vehicles. Connexions with the interior are made by waterways which, despite rapids, are navigable by local craft.

Aviation. In 1985, 75,056 passengers and 2,608 tonnes of freight arrived and 76,934 passengers and 1,237 tonnes of freight departed by air at Rochambeau International Airport (Cayenne). There are regular internal flights to 4 other airports.

Shipping. The chief ports are: Cayenne, St-Laurent-du-Maroni and Kourou. Dégrad des Cannes (the port of Cayenne) is visited regularly by ships of the Compagnie Général Maritime, the Compagnie Maritime des Chargeurs Réunis and Marseille Fret. In 1985, 215 vessels arrived (180 at Dégrad-des-Cannes) to discharge 276,500 tonnes and load 50,800 tonnes of freight. Inland waterways total 3,760 km.

Post and Broadcasting. Number of telephones (1984), 22,143. There are wireless stations at Cayenne, Oyapoc, Régina, St-Laurent-du-Maroni and numerous other locations.

RFO-Guyane (Guiana Radio) broadcasts for 116 hours each week on medium- and short-waves and FM in French. Television is broadcast for 43 hours each week on 7 transmitters. In 1983 there were 40,000 radio and 9,500 TV receivers.

Newspapers. There was (1984) 1 daily newspaper *(Presse de la Guyane)* with a circulation of 16,000, a bi-weekly paper *(France-Guyane)* with a circulation of 3,500 and a weekly *(Debout Guyane)*.

JUSTICE, RELIGION, EDUCATION AND WELFARE

Justice. At Cayenne there is a *tribunal d'instance* and a *tribunal de grande instance*, from which appeal is to the regional *cour d'appel* in Martinique.

Religion. In 1980, 87% of the population was Roman Catholic and 4% Protestant.

Education. Primary education has been free since 1889 in lay schools for the two sexes in the communes and many villages. In 1981 public primary schools had 580 teachers and 11,953 pupils, the *lycées* and *collèges d'enseignement secondaire*, 510 teachers and 7,277 pupils. Private schools had 119 teachers and 2,528 pupils. The *Institut Henri Visioz* forms part of the *Université des Antilles-Guyane,* with 236 students.

Health. There were (1981) 80 physicians, 14 dentists, 18 pharmacists, 16 midwives and 309 nursing personnel. In 1980 there were 5 hospitals with 907 beds and 3 private clinics.

MARTINIQUE

HISTORY. Discovered by Columbus in 1493, the island was known to its inhabitants as *Madinina*, from which its present name was corrupted. A French colony was established in 1635 and, apart from brief periods of British occupation, has since remained under French control. On 19 March 1946 its status was altered to that of an Overseas Department, and in 1974 it also became an administrative region.

AREA AND POPULATION. The island, situated in the Lesser Antilles between Dominica and St Lucia, occupies an area of 1,079 sq. km (417 sq. miles). The total population, 1982 Census, was 326,717 (estimate, 1987, 328,500), of whom 99,844 lived in Fort-de-France, the capital and chief commercial town, which has a landlocked harbour nearly 40 sq. km in extent.

French is the official language, but the majority of the population use a Creole dialect.

Vital statistics (1985): Live births 5,722; deaths 2,257; marriages 1,331.

CONSTITUTION AND GOVERNMENT. The island is administered by a *Conseil Général* of 44 members and a Regional Council of 41 members, both directly elected for terms of 6 years. The French government is represented by an appointed Commissioner. There are 3 *arrondissements*, sub-divided into 34 communes, each administered by an elected municipal council. Martinique is represented in the National Assembly by 4 deputies, in the Senate by 2 senators and on the Economic and Social Council by 2 councillors.

Commissioner: Edouard Lacroix.
President of the Conseil Général: Émile Maurice.
President of the Conseil Régional: Aimé Cesaire.

ECONOMY

Budget. The budget, 1985, balanced at 1,738m. francs.

Banking. The Institut d'Émission des Départements d'Outre-mer is the official bank of the department. The Caisse Centrale de Coopération économique is used by the Government in assisting the economic development of the department.

The Banque des Antilles Françaises (with a capital of 32·5m. francs), the Crédit Martiniquais (30·4m. francs), the Société Générale de Banque aux Antilles (15m. francs), the Banque Française Commerciale (49m. francs), the Banque Nationale de Paris, Crédit Agricole and the Chase Manhattan Bank are operating at Fort-de-France.

ENERGY AND NATURAL RESOURCES

Electricity. Production in 1986 totalled 330m. kwh.

Agriculture. Bananas, sugar and rum are the chief products, followed by pineapples, food and vegetables. In 1984 there were 4,100 hectares under sugar-cane, 7,300 hectares under bananas and 800 hectares under pineapples. Production (1985): Sugar, 8,610 tonnes; industrial rum, 3,260 hectolitres; agricultural rum, 74,514 hectolitres; cane for sugar, 90,200 tonnes; cane for rum, 108,253 tonnes; bananas (1984) 185,000 tonnes; pineapples (1984) 23,000 tonnes.

Livestock (1985): 52,000 cattle, 73,000 sheep, 42,000 pigs, 27,000 goats and 1,000 horses.

Forestry. Production (1983) 11,000 cu. m. Forests comprise 26% of the land area.

Fisheries. The catch in 1983 was 5,174 tonnes.

COMMERCE. Trade in 1m. francs:

	1982	1983	1984	1985
Imports	4,835	5,672	5,983	6,050
Exports	1,016	1,314	1,351	1,300

In 1985 the main items of import were crude petroleum and foodstuffs; main items of export were petroleum products (15%), bananas (47%) and rum (9%); 58% of imports came from France and 65% of exports went to France and 23% to Guadeloupe.

Total trade between Martinique and UK (British Department of Trade returns, in £1,000 sterling):

	1983	1984	1985	1986	1987
Imports to UK	35	229	126	14	712
Exports and re-exports from UK	3,029	2,980	2,776	21,230	10,705

Tourism. In 1986 there were 183,000 tourists.

COMMUNICATIONS

Roads. In 1986 there were 7 km of motorway, 260 km of national roads, 618 km of district roads and 755 km of local roads. In 1985 there were 8,179 passenger cars and 1,828 commercial vehicles registered.

Aviation. In 1985, 815,261 passengers arrived and departed by air at Fort-de-France airport.

Shipping. The island is visited regularly by French and American vessels. In 1985, 903 commercial vessels called at Martinique and discharged 141,000 passengers and 1,254,100 tonnes of freight and embarked 140,000 passengers and 631,000 tonnes of freight.

Post and Broadcasting. There were, in 1985, 46 post offices and, 81,985 telephones. Radio-telephone service to Europe is available. In 1984 there were 46,000 radio and 42,500 TV receivers.

Newspapers. In 1987 there was 1 daily newspaper with a circulation of 30,000.

JUSTICE, RELIGION, EDUCATION AND WELFARE

Justice. Justice is administered by 2 *tribunaux d'instance*, a *tribunal de grande instance*, a regional court of appeal, a commercial court, a court of assizes and an administrative court.

Religion. In 1982, 94% of the population was Roman Catholic.

Education. Education is compulsory between the ages of 6 and 16 years. In 1984–85, there were 54,132 pupils in primary schools, 44,426 pupils in secondary schools, 2,144 pupils in technical schools and 3,460 students at the teacher-training college. The *Institut Henri Visioz*, which forms part of the *Centre Universitaire Antilles-Guyane*, had (1983) 1,299 students.

Health. There were (1982) 16 hospitals with 3,671 beds and in 1985 there were 544 physicians, 155 pharmacists and 127 dentists.

Books of Reference

Annuaire statistique I.N.S.E.E. 1977–80. Martinique, 1982
La Martinique en quelques chiffres. Martinique, 1982
Guide Economique des D.O.M.-T.O.M., Paris, 1982

RÉUNION

HISTORY. Réunion (formerly Île Bourbon) became a French possession in 1638 and remained so until 19 March 1946, when its status was altered to that of an Overseas Department; in 1974 it also became an administrative region.

AREA AND POPULATION. The island of Réunion lies in the Indian Ocean, about 640 km east of Madagascar and 180 km south west of Mauritius. It has an area of 2,512 sq. km (968·5 sq. miles) and population of 515,798 (March 1982 census); estimate (1987) 564,600. The capital is Saint-Denis (1982 census) 109,072; Saint-Pierre, 58,412. Most inhabitants speak a creole language, but French is official and Gujurati is also spoken.

Vital statistics (1985): Live births, 13,111; deaths, 3,050.

The small islands of Juan de Nova, Europa, Bassas da India, Îles Glorieuses and Tromelin, with a combined area of 32 sq. km, are all uninhabited and lie at various points in the Indian Ocean adjacent to Madagascar. They remained French after Madagascar's independence in 1960, and are now administered by Réunion. Both Mauritius and the Seychelles claim Tromelin (transferred by the UK from the Seychelles to France in 1954), and Madagascar claims all 5 islands.

CLIMATE. A sub-tropical maritime climate, free from extremes of weather, though the island lies in the cyclone belt of the Indian Ocean. Conditions are generally humid and there is no well-defined dry season. Saint-Denis. Jan. 80°F (26·7°C), July 70°F (21·1°C). Annual rainfall 56″ (1,400 mm).

CONSTITUTION AND GOVERNMENT. The island is administered by a *Conseil Général* of 36 members and a Regional Council of 45 members, both directly elected for terms of 6 years. Réunion is represented in the National Assembly by 5 deputies, in the Senate by 2 senators, and in the Economic and Social Council by 1 councillor. There are 4 *arrondissements*, sub-divided into 24 communes each administered by an elected municipal council. The French government is represented by an appointed Commissioner.

Commissioner: Jean Anciaux.
President of the Conseil Général: Auguste Legros.
President of the Conseil Régional: Pierre Lagourgue.

ECONOMY

Budget. The budget for 1984 balanced at 2,265m. French francs.

Banking. The Institut d'émission des Départements d'Outre-mer has the right to issue bank-notes. Banks operating in Réunion are the Banque de la Réunion (Crédit Lyonnais), the Banque Nationale de Paris Internationale, the Caisse Régionale de Crédit Agricole Mutuel de la Réunion, the Banque Française Commerciale (BFC) CCP, Trésorerie Générale, and the Banque de la Réunion pour l'Economie et la Développement.

ENERGY AND NATURAL RESOURCES

Electricity. Production (1986) 394m. kwh.

Agriculture (1986). The chief produce is sugar (241,000 tonnes), molasses (1984, 69,353 tonnes), bananas (5,000 tonnes), rum (1984, 98,037 hectolitres), maize (14,000 tonnes), potatoes (4,000 tonnes), onions (1984, 1,831 tonnes), bananas (5,000 tonnes), pineapples (4,000 tonnes), tomatoes (3,000 tonnes), vanilla (1984, 168 tonnes), essences and tobacco.

Livestock (1986): 20,000 cattle, 72,000 pigs, 3,000 sheep, 44,000 goats and 4m. poultry.

Forestry. There were (1985) 103,330 hectares of forest. Roundwood production (1983) 33,000 cu. metres.

Fisheries. In 1985 the catch was 2,180 tonnes.

INDUSTRY AND TRADE

Industry (1985). Total number of workers (in 418 firms employing 10 or more) 16,000. The sugar industry employed 2,900.

Commerce. Trade in 1m. French francs:

	1980	1981	1982	1983	1984	1985
Imports	3,749	4,311	5,304	6,410	6,895	7,457
Exports	554	571	688	662	695	802

The chief export is sugar, forming (1985) 72% by value. In 1985 (by value) 65% of imports were from, and 53% of exports to, France.

Total trade between Réunion and UK (British Department of Trade returns, in £1,000 sterling):

	1983	1984	1985	1986	1987
Imports to UK	73	407	1,391	12,259	1,056
Exports and re-exports from UK	3,684	3,327	4,081	4,225	8,624

Tourism. There were 78,952 tourists in 1985.

COMMUNICATIONS

Roads. There were, in 1984, 1,711 km of roads. There were 92,900 registered vehicles in 1984.

Railways. In 1984 there were 614 km of railways serving only the sugar plantations.

Aviation. Air France maintains an air service 6 times a week. In 1985, 210,121 passengers and 6,625 tonnes of freight arrived and 210,764 passengers and 3,666 tonnes of freight departed at Saint-Denis-Gillot airport.

Shipping. Four shipping lines serve the island. In 1985, 362 vessels visited the island to discharge 1,122,800 tonnes of freight and 1,900 passengers, and load 340,000 tonnes of freight and 1,900 passengers at Pointe-des-Galets.

Post and Broadcasting. There are telephone and telegraph connexions with Mauritius, Madagascar and metropolitan France. There are 38 post offices and a central telephone office; number of telephones (1984), 85,861.

France Régions 3 broadcast in French on medium- and short-waves for more than 18 hours a day. There are 2 television channels broadcasting for 70 hours a week. In 1984 there were 114,500 radio and 107,500 TV receivers.

Cinemas. In 1986 there were 25 cinemas with a seating capacity of 10,200.

Newspapers. There were (1985) 3 daily newspapers with a combined circulation of 70,000.

JUSTICE, RELIGION, EDUCATION AND WELFARE

Justice. There are 3 *tribunaux d'instance*, 2 *tribunaux de grande instance*, 1 *Cour d'Appel*, 1 *tribunal administratif* and 2 *conseils de prud'homme*.

Religion. In 1980, 96% of the population was Roman Catholic and 2% Moslem.

Education. Secondary education is provided in (1983–84) 6 *lycées*, 50 *collèges*, and 9 *lycées d'enseignement technique* with 66,653 pupils altogether and in 13 private secondary schools with 3,407 pupils. Primary education is given in 336 public schools with 4,018 teachers and 106,437 pupils; and in 28 private schools, with 306 teachers, and 8,827 pupils. The *Université Française de l'Océan Indien* (founded 1971) had 2,674 students and 82 teaching staff in 1984.

Health. In 1984 there were 21 hospitals with 3,879 beds; in 1984 there were 762 physicians, 183 dentists, 180 pharmacists, 102 midwives and 1,791 nursing personnel.

Books of Reference

Bulletin de l'Académie de la Réunion. Biennial
Bulletin de la Chambre d'Agriculture de la Réunion
Panorama de l'Economie de la Reunion. 1983
Statistiques et Indicateurs Economiques. 1983

TERRITORIAL COLLECTIVITIES

MAYOTTE

HISTORY. Mayotte was a French colony from 1843 until 1914, when it was attached, with the other Comoro islands, to the government-general of Madagascar. The Comoro group was granted administrative autonomy within the French Republic and became an Overseas Territory.

When the other 3 islands voted to become independent (as the Comoro state) in 1974, Mayotte voted against this and remained a French dependency. In Dec. 1976, it became (following a further referendum) a Territorial Collectivity.

AREA AND POPULATION. Mayotte, east of the Comoro Islands, consists of a main island (362 sq. km) with 57,363 inhabitants at the 1985 Census, containing the chief town, Mamoundzou (12,119); and the smaller island of Pamanzi (11 sq. km) lying 2 km to the east, with 9,775 inhabitants in 1985, containing the old capital of Dzaoudzi (5,675). The whole territory covers 373 sq. km (144 sq. miles) and had a 1985 Census population of 67,138; estimate (1987) 73,900. The spoken language is Mahorian (akin to Comoran, an Arabized dialect of Swahili), but French remains the official and commercial language.

CONSTITUTION AND GOVERNMENT. The island is administered by a *Conseil Général* of 17 members, directly elected for a 6-year term. The French government is represented by an appointed Commissioner. Mayotte is represented by 1 deputy in the National Assembly and by 1 member in the Senate. There are 17 communes, including 2 on Pamanzi.

Commissioner: Akli Khider.
President of the Conseil Général: Younoussa Bamana.

ECONOMY

Budget. In 1984, revenue was 137·1m. francs (44% being subsidies from France) and expenditure 148·4m. francs. The 1985 Budget balanced at 313m. francs.

Currency. Since Feb. 1976 the currency has been the (metropolitan) *French franc.*

Banking. The *Institut d'Emission d'Outre-mer* and the *Banque Française Commerciale* both have branches in Dzaoudzi.

ENERGY AND NATURAL RESOURCES

Electricity. Production (1982) 5m. kwh.

Agriculture. The main food crops (1983 production in tonnes) are mangoes (1,500), bananas (1,300), breadfruit (700), cassava (500) and pineapples (200). The chief cash crops are ylang-ylang, vanilla, coffee, copra, cinnamon and cloves.

Livestock (1982): Cattle, 3,000; goats, 10,000; pigs, 2,000.

Fisheries. A lobster and shrimp industry has recently been created. Annual catch is about 2,000 tonnes.

COMMERCE. In 1984, exports totalled 34m. francs (57% to France in 1983) and imports 182·8m. francs (53% from France). Ylang-ylang formed 48% of exports, vanilla 33% and coffee 12%. Total trade between Mayotte and UK (1984): Imports to UK, £67,000 and exports and re-exports from UK, £343,000.

Total trade between Mayotte and UK (British Department of Trade returns, in £1,000 sterling):

	1985	1986	1987
Imports to UK	22	9	185
Exports and re-exports from UK	2,000	506	2,352

COMMUNICATIONS

Roads. In 1984 there were 93 km of main roads and 137 km of local roads, with 1,528 motor vehicles.

Aviation. In 1985, 17,426 passengers and 172 tonnes of freight arrived and departed by air.

Post and Broadcasting. In 1984 there were 6,000 radio receivers. Telephones (1981) 400.

Newspapers. There is 1 daily newspaper, *le Journal de Mayotte.*

JUSTICE, RELIGION, EDUCATION AND WELFARE

Justice. There is a *tribunal d'instance* and a *tribunal supérieur d'appel.*

Religion. The population is 97% Sunni Moslem, with a small Christian (mainly Roman Catholic) minority.

Education. In 1984 there were 14,992 pupils and 407 teachers in 72 primary schools; 1,374 pupils in 1 secondary school; and 475 students in 2 technical and teacher-training establishments.

Health. In 1980 there were 9 doctors, 1 dentist, 1 pharmacist, 2 midwives and 51 nursing personnel. In 1981 there were 2 hospitals with 86 beds.

ST PIERRE AND MIQUELON
Îles Saint-Pierre et Miquelon

HISTORY. The tiny remaining fragment of the once extensive French possessions in North America, the archipelago was settled from France in the 17th century and finally became a French territory from 1816 until July 1976, when its status was altered to that of an Overseas Department. In June 1985 it became a Territorial Collectivity.

AREA AND POPULATION. The archipelago consists of 8 small islands off the south coast of Newfoundland, with a total area of 242 sq. km, comprising the Saint-Pierre group (26 sq. km) and the Miquelon-Langlade group (216 sq. km). The population (census, 1982) was 6,041 of whom 5,415 were on Saint-Pierre and 626 on Miquelon; estimate (1987) 6,300. The chief town is St Pierre.

Vital statistics (1986): Births, 89; marriages, 16; deaths, 48.

CONSTITUTION AND GOVERNMENT. The dependency is administered by a *Conseil Général* of 14 members, directly elected for a 6-year term. It is represented in the National Assembly by 1 deputy, in the Senate by 1 senator and in the Economic and Social Council by 1 councillor. The French government is represented by an appointed Commissioner.

Commissioner: Jean-René Garnier.
President of the Conseil Général: Marc Plantegenest.

ECONOMY

Budget. The ordinary budget for 1986 balanced at 50m. francs.

Banking. Banks include the Banque des Îles Saint-Pierre et Miquelon and the Crédit Saint-Pierrais.

ENERGY AND NATURAL RESOURCES

Electricity. Production (1986) 36m. kwh.

Agriculture. The islands, being mostly barren rock, are unsuited for agriculture, but some vegetables are grown and livestock kept for local consumption.

Fisheries. The catch (the islands' main industry) amounted in 1986 to 12,000 tonnes, chiefly cod.

COMMERCE. Trade in 1m. francs:

	1980	1981	1982	1983
Imports	177·2	220·9	275·4	348·3
Exports	24·2	38·7	41·0	113·3

In 1986, 76% of imports came from Canada, while 35% of exports were to USA, 37% to France and 11% to UK.

The main exports are fish (88%), shellfish (6%) and fishmeal (5%).

Total trade between St Pierre and Miquelon and UK (British Department of Trade returns in £1,000 sterling):

	1983	1984	1985	1986	1987
Imports to UK	578	743	497	474	77
Exports and re-exports from UK	250	523	370	367	604

Tourism. There were (1986) 15,546 visitors.

COMMUNICATIONS

Roads. In 1985 there were 120 km of roads, of which 60 km were paved. In 1986 there were 1,932 passenger cars and 637 commercial vehicles.

Aviation. Air Saint-Pierre connects St Pierre with Montreal, with Halifax and Sydney (Nova Scotia), and there are occasional flights to and from St John's (Newfoundland), Gander and New York.

Shipping. St Pierre has regular services to Fortune (Newfoundland) and Halifax. In 1986, 73,043 tonnes of freight were unloaded and 7,586 tonnes loaded, while 892 ships (of 810,474 gross tonnage) entered the harbour.

Post and Broadcasting. There were 3,860 telephones in 1986. RFO broadcasts in French on medium-waves. St Pierre is connected by radio-telecommunication with most countries of the world. Radio licences totalled 4,400 and TV 3,800 in 1985.

Cinemas. There were (1983) 2 cinemas with a seating capacity of 760.

JUSTICE, RELIGION, EDUCATION AND WELFARE

Justice. There is a *tribunal de premier instance* and a *tribunal supérieur d'appel* at St Pierre.

Religion. The population is chiefly Roman Catholic.

Education. Primary instruction is free. There were, in 1987, 8 nursery and primary schools with 916 pupils and 4 secondary schools (including 2 technical schools) with 773 pupils.

Health. There was (1986) 1 hospital on St Pierre with 100 beds; 13 doctors and 3 dentists.

Books of Reference

De Curton, E., *Saint-Pierre et Miquelon.* Paris, 1944
De La Rüe, E. A., *Saint-Pierre et Miquelon.* Paris, 1963
Ribault, J. Y., *Histoire de Saint-Pierre et Miquelon: Des Origines à 1814.* St Pierre, 1962

OVERSEAS TERRITORIES

Among the 7 French Overseas Territories remaining since Algerian independence in 1962, the Comoro Islands declared their independence on 6 July 1975 (recognized by France on 31 Dec.), but the island of Mayotte remained French and in Dec. 1976 was classed as a 'territorial collectivity'. The territory of Saint Pierre and Miquelon became a fifth Overseas Department in July 1976, but in June 1985 it acquired the same status as Mayotte. The former French Somaliland (subsequently Territory of the Afars and Issas) became independent on 27 June 1977 as the Republic of Djibouti. The remaining French Overseas Territories are New Caledonia (with its dependancies), French Polynesia, Wallis and Futuna, and the French Southern and Antarctic Territories.

SOUTHERN AND ANTARCTIC TERRITORIES

Terres Australes et Antarctiques Françaises

The Territory of the TAAF was created on 6 Aug. 1955. It comprises the Kerguelen and Crozet archipelagoes, the islands of Saint Paul and Amsterdam (formerly Nouvelle Amsterdam), all in the southern Indian ocean, and Terre Adélie.

The Administrator is assisted by a 7-member consultative council which meets twice yearly in Paris; its members are nominated by the Government for 5 years. The 12 members of the Scientific Council are appointed by the Senior Administrator after approval by the Minister in charge of scientific research. A 15-member Consultative Committee on the Environment, created in Nov. 1982, meets at least once a year to discuss all problems relating to the preservation of the environment. The administration has its seat in Paris.

Administrateur supérieur: Vice-Adm. Claude Piéri.

The staff of the permanent scientific stations of the TAAF (210 in 1985) is renewed annually and forms the only population.

Kerguelen islands, situated 48–50° S. lat., 68–70° E. long., consists of 1 large and 85 smaller islands and over 200 islets and rocks with a total area of 7,215 sq. km (2,786 sq. miles), of which Grande Terre occupies 6,675 sq. km (2,577 sq. miles). It was discovered in 1772 by Yves de Kerguelen, but was effectively occupied by France only in 1949. Port-aux-Français has several scientific research stations (100 members). Reindeer, trout and sheep have been acclimatized.

Crozet islands, situated 46° S. lat., 50–52° E. long., consists of 5 larger and 15 tiny islands, with a total area of 505 sq. km (195 sq. miles); the western group includes Apostles, Pigs and Penguins islands; the eastern group, Possession and Eastern islands. The archipelago was discovered in 1772 by Marion Dufresne, whose mate, Crozet, annexed it for Louis XV. A meteorological and scientific station (40 members) at Base Alfred-Faure on Possession Island was built in 1964.

Amsterdam Island and **Saint-Paul Island,** situated 38–39° S. lat., 77° E. long. Amsterdam, with an area of 54 sq. km (21 sq. miles) was discovered in 1522 by Magellan's companions; Saint-Paul, lying about 100 km to the south, with an area of 7 sq. km (2·7 sq. miles), was probably discovered in 1559 by Portuguese sailors. Both were first visited in 1633 by the Dutch explorer, Van Diemen, and were annexed by France in 1843. They are both extinct volcanoes. The only inhabitants are at Base Martin de Vivies, established in 1949 on Amsterdam Island, with several scientific research stations, hospital, communication and other facilities (40 members). Crayfish are caught commercially on Amsterdam.

Terre Adélie comprises that section of the Antarctic continent between 136° and 142° E. long., south of 60° S. lat. The ice-covered plateau has an area of about 432,000 sq. km (166,800 sq. miles), and was discovered in 1840 by Dumont d'Urville. A research station (30 members) is situated at Base Dumont d'Urville, which is maintained by the French Polar Expeditions.

Book of Reference

T.A.A.F. Revue trimestrielle. Paris, 1957 ff.

NEW CALEDONIA

Nouvelle Calédonie et Dépendances

HISTORY. New Caledonia was annexed by France in 1853 and, together with most of its former dependencies, became an Overseas Territory in 1958.

AREA AND POPULATION. The territory comprises the island of New Caledonia and various outlying islands, all situated in the south-west Pacific with a total land area of 18,576 sq. km (7,172 sq. miles). In 1983 the population (census) was 145,368, including 53,974 Europeans (majority French), 61,870 Melanesians (Kanaks), 7,700 Vietnamese and Indonesians, 5,570 Polynesians, 12,174 Wallisians, 4,080 others; 1987 (estimate) 153,500. The capital, Nouméa had (1983) 60,112 inhabitants. Vital statistics (1986): Live births, 3,779; deaths, 851.

The main islands are:

1. The island of New Caledonia with an area of 16,372 sq. km, has a total length of about 400 km, and an average breadth of 50 km, and a population (census, 1983) of 127,885. The east coast is predominantly Melanesian, the Nouméa region predominantly French, and the rest of the west coast of mixed population.

2. The Loyalty Islands, 100 km (60 miles) east of New Caledonia, consisting of 3 large islands, Maré, Lifou and Uvéa, and many small islands with a total area of 1,981 sq. km and a population (census, 1983) of 15,510, nearly all Melanesians except on Uvéa, which is partly Polynesian. The chief culture in the islands is that of coconuts: the chief export, copra.

3. The Isle of Pines, 50 km (30 miles) to the south-east of Nouméa, with an area of 152 sq. km and a population of 1,287 (census 1983), is a tourist and fishing centre.

4. The Bélep Archipelago, about 50 km north-west of New Caledonia, with an area of 70 sq. km and a population of 686 (census 1983).

The remaining islands are all very small and none have permanent inhabitants. The largest are the Chesterfield Islands, a group of 11 well-wooded coral islets with a combined area of 10 sq. km, about 550 km west of the Bélep Archipelago. The Huon Islands, a group of 4 barren coral islets with a combined area of just 65 hectares, are 225 km north of the Bélep Archipelago. Walpole, a limestone coral island of 1 sq. km, lies 150 km east of the Isle of Pines; Matthew Island (20 hectares) and Hunter Island (2 sq. km), respectively 250 km and 330 km east of Walpole, are spasmodically active volcanic islands also claimed by Vanuatu.

CONSTITUTION AND GOVERNMENT. Following constitutional changes introduced by the French government in Sept. 1985, the Territory is administered by a 5-member Executive Council consisting of the President of the Territorial Congress (as President) and the Presidents of the 4 Regional Councils which were elected on 29 Sept. 1985. The French government is represented by an appointed High Commissioner. In Sept. 1987 the electorate voted in favour of remaining a French possession.

There is a 46-member Territorial Congress consisting of the complete membership of the 4 Regional Councils, which has replaced the former 42-member Territorial Assembly. The *Rassemblement Pour la Calédonie dans la République* (Gaullists) gained 25 seats, the *Front de Libération Nationale Kanake Socialiste* (nationalists) 16 seats and others 5 seats.

New Caledonia is represented in the National Assembly by 2 deputies, in the Senate by 1 senator and in the Economic and Social Council by 1 councillor.

The Territory is divided into 4 regions (Nord, Centre-Sud-Est, Nouméa and Îles Loyauté), each under a directly-elected Regional Council. They are sub-divided into 32 communes administered by locally-elected councils and mayors.

High Commissioner: Jean Montpezat.
President of the Executive Council: Dick Ukeiwé.

ECONOMY

Budget. The budget for 1986 balanced at 38,690m. francs CFP.

Currency. The unit of currency is the *franc* CFP, with a parity of CFP *francs* 18·18 to the French *franc*.

Banking. There are branches of the Banque de Indosuez, the Banque Nationale de Paris, the Banque de Paris et des Pays-Bas, and the Société Générale, and the Banque de la Nouvelle-Calédonie (Crédit Lyonnais).

ENERGY AND NATURAL RESOURCES

Electricity. In 1986, production totalled 1,015m. kwh.

Minerals. The mineral resources are very great; nickel, chrome and iron abound; silver, gold, cobalt, lead, manganese, iron and copper have been mined at different times. The nickel deposits are of special value, being without arsenic. Production of nickel ore in 1986, 3,125,000 tonnes and chrome ore 163,325 tonnes. About 3,270 sq. km of mining land are owned, and 300 sq. km have been granted for exploitation. In 1986 the furnaces produced 9,160 tonnes of matte nickel and 33,001 tonnes of ferro-nickel.

Agriculture. 271,864 hectares are pasture land; about 10,035 hectares are commercially cultivated. The chief agricultural products are beef, pork, poultry, coffee, copra, maize, fruit and vegetables.
Livestock (1986): Cattle, 123,000; pigs, 41,000; goats, 18,000.

Forestry. There are about 250,000 hectares of forest. Roundwood production (1983) 12,000 cu. metres.

Fisheries. The catch in 1985 totalled 5,763 tonnes.

INDUSTRY AND TRADE

Industry. Local industries include chlorine and oxygen plants, cement, soft drinks, barbed wire, nails, pleasure and fishing boats, clothing, pasta, household cleaners and confectionery.

Labour. The working population (1983 census) was 58,000 of whom 19,700 worked in agriculture.

Commerce. Imports and exports in 1m. francs CFP for 5 years:

	1982	1983	1984	1985	1986
Imports	43,735	42,201	49,605	55,931	62,939
Exports	27,707	22,035	33,452	43,938	26,249

In 1986, 50·3% of the imports came from France and 7·4% from Australia, while 56·5% of the exports went to France and most of the rest to Japan. Refined minerals (mainly ferro-nickel and nickel) formed 68·8% of exports by value, nickel ore 9·5% and chrome ore 3·8%.

Tourism. In 1986 there were 59,000 tourists.

COMMUNICATIONS

Roads. There were, in 1984, 6,273 km of roads, of which 1,867 were paved. There were (1986) 44,551 vehicles.

Aviation. New Caledonia is connected by air routes with France (by UTA), Australia (UTA and Qantas), New Zealand (UTA and Air New Zealand), Fiji and Wallis and Futuna (by Air Cal International), Vanuatu and Tahiti (by UTA), and Nauru (by Air Nauru). In 1986, 101,584 passengers arrived and 101,736 departed *via* La Tontouta airport, near Nouméa. Internal services connect Nouméa with 17 domestic air fields.

Shipping. In 1986, 363 vessels entered Nouméa unloading 813,000 tonnes of goods and loading 1,334,900 tonnes. A new harbour for deep-water alongside discharge was completed in 1974.

Post and Broadcasting. There were (1985) 52 post offices and telex, telephone, radio and television services. There were (1983) 30,578 telephones. RFO broadcasts in French on medium- and short-wave radio (there are also 3 private stations) and on 1 television channel 58 hours a week. Number of receivers (1983): radio, 78,000; TV, 30,000.

Cinemas. In 1985 there were 9 cinemas.

Newspapers. In 1984 there was 1 daily newspaper with a circulation of 16,000 and 16 other periodicals.

JUSTICE, RELIGION, EDUCATION AND WELFARE

Justice. There is a *Tribunal de Grande Instance* and a *Cour d'Appel* in Nouméa.

Religion. In 1980 over 72% of the population was Roman Catholic, 16% Protestant and 4% Moslem.

Education. In 1986, there were 31,875 pupils and 1,560 teachers in primary schools, 13,193 pupils in 45 secondary schools, 5,721 students in 29 technical and vocational schools, and 859 students and 66 teaching staff in 5 higher education establishments.

Health. In 1985 there were 194 physicians, 33 dentists, 42 pharmacists, 27 midwives and 823 paramedical personnel. In 1985, 5 hospitals and 25 dispensaries had a total of 991 beds.

Books of Reference

Journal Officiel de la Nouvelle Calédonie et Dépendances
Annuaire Statistique de la Nouvelle Calédonie et Dépendances
Tableaux de l'Economie Caledonienne, 1983–1985

FRENCH POLYNESIA

Territoire de la Polynésie Française

HISTORY. French protectorates since 1843, these islands were annexed to France 1880–82 to form 'French Settlements in Oceania', which opted in Nov. 1958 for the status of an Overseas Territory within the French Community.

AREA AND POPULATION. The total land area of these 5 archipelagoes, scattered over a wide area in the Eastern Pacific is 3,521 sq. km (1,359 sq. miles). The population, Census, 1983, was 166,753; estimate (1987) 184,600. The islands are administratively divided into 5 *circonscriptions:*

1. The **Windward Islands** (Îles du Vent) (123,069 inhabitants in 1983) comprise Tahiti with an area of 1,042 sq. km and 115,820 inhabitants; Moorea with an area of 132 sq. km and 7,000 inhabitants; Maio (Tubuai Manu) with an area of 9 sq. km and 200 inhabitants, and the smaller Mehetia and Tetiaoro. The capital is Papeete (78,814 inhabitants including suburbs).

2. The **Leeward Islands** (Îles sous le Vent), comprise the volcanic islands of Raiatéa, Tahaa, Huahine, Bora-Bora and Maupiti, together with 4 small atolls, the group having a total land area of 404 sq. km and 19,060 inhabitants in 1983. The chief town is Uturoa on Raiatéa.

The Windward and Leeward Islands together are called the Society Archipelago (Archipel de la Société). Tahitian, a Polynesian language, is spoken throughout the archipelago and used as a *lingua franca* in the rest of the territory.

3. The **Tuamotu Archipelago**, consisting of two parallel ranges of 78 atolls lying north and east of the Society Archipelago, have a total area of 690 sq. km; the most populous atolls are Rangiroa, Hao and Turéia. Mururoa and Fangataufa atolls in the south-east of the group have been used by France for nuclear tests since 1966, having been ceded to France in 1964 by the Territorial Assembly.

The *circonscription* (total 11,793 inhabitants) also includes the **Gambier Islands** further east (of which Mangareva is the principal), with an area of 36 sq. km and a population of 556 (1977); the chief centre is Rikitea on Mangareva.

4. The **Austral or Tubuai Islands**, lying south of the Society Archipelago, comprise a 1,300 km chain of volcanic islands and reefs. They include Rimatara, Rurutu, Tubuai, Raivaevae and, 500 km to the south, Rapa-Iti, with a combined area of 148 sq. km and 6,283 inhabitants; the chief centre is Mataura on Tubuai.

5. The **Marquesas Islands**, lying north of the Tuamotu Archipelago, with a total

area of 1,049 sq. km and 6,548 inhabitants, comprise Nukuhiva, Uapu, Uahuka, Hivaoa, Tahuata, Fatuhiva and 4 smaller (uninhabited) islands; the chief centre is Taiohae on Nukuhiva.

Vital statistics (1984): Births, 5,016; marriages, 1,099; deaths, 818.

CLIMATE. Papeete. Jan. 81°F (27·1°C), July 75°F (24°C). Annual rainfall 83″ (2,106 mm).

CONSTITUTION AND GOVERNMENT. Under the 1984 Constitution, the Territory is administered by a Council of Ministers, whose President is elected by the Territorial Assembly from among its own members; he appoints a Vice-President and 9 other ministers. There is an advisory Economic and Social Committee. French Polynesia is represented in the National Assembly by 2 deputies, in the Senate by 1 senator, and in the Economic and Social Council by 1 councillor. The French government is represented by a High Commissioner. The Territorial Assembly comprises 41 members elected every 5 years by universal suffrage.

At the elections held in March 1986, the *Tahoeraa Huiraatiraa* (Gaullists) won 22 seats, the *Amuitahiraa No Porinesia* 5 seats, Nationalists 5 seats and others 9 seats.

High Commissioner: Pierre Angéli.
President of the Council of Ministers: Jacques Teheiura

Flag: Three horizontal stripes of red, white, red, with the white of double width containing the emblem of French Polynesia in yellow.

ECONOMY

Budget. The ordinary budget for 1986 balanced at 51,600m. francs CFP.

Currency. The unit of currency is the *franc* CFP, with a parity of CFP *francs* 18·18 to the French *franc*.

Banking. There are 5 commercial banks, the Bank Indosuez, the Bank of Tahiti, the Banque de Polynésie, Paribas Pacifique and Société de Crédit et de Développement de l'Océanie.

ENERGY AND NATURAL RESOURCES

Electricity. Production in 1985 (Tahiti only) amounted to 203m. kwh (16% hydro-electric).

Agriculture. An important product is copra (coconut trees covering the coastal plains of the mountainous islands and the greater part of the low-lying islands), production (1986) 14,000 tonnes. Tropical fruits, such as bananas, pineapples, oranges, etc., are grown only for local consumption.

Livestock (1986): Cattle, 7,000; horses, 2,000; pigs, 48,000; sheep, 2,000; goats, 3,000; poultry, 1m.

Fisheries. The catch in 1985 amounted to 1,868 tonnes of fish.

COMMERCE. Trade in 1m. francs CFP:

	1981	1982	1983	1984	1985
Imports	54,843	62,307	74,241	85,622	88,939
Exports	2,861	3,349	4,823	5,084	6,564

Total trade between the French possessions in the Pacific and UK (British Department of Trade returns, in £1,000 sterling):

	1984	1985	1986	1987
Imports to UK	2	23	95	18
Exports and re-exports from UK	3,276	3,961	4,890	5,275

Chief exports are coconut oil and cultured pearls. In 1985, France provided 46% of imports and USA 16%, while 44% of exports went to France and 21% to USA.

Tourism. Tourism is very important, earning almost half as much as the visible exports. There were 161,000 tourists in 1986 (50% from the USA).

COMMUNICATIONS

Roads. In 1984 there were 798 km of roads and (1985) 5,374 registered vehicles.

Aviation. Seven international airlines connect Tahiti with Paris, Los Angeles and many Pacific locations. There is also a regular air service between Faaa airport (on Tahiti), Moorea and the Leeward Isles with occasional connexions to the other groups. In 1985, 154,504 international passengers arrived and 152,567 departed *via* the airports at Faaa and on Mooréa and Bora-Bora. Thirty other airfields have regular domestic services.

Shipping. Several shipping companies connect France, San Francisco, New Zealand, Japan, Australia, South East Asia and most Pacific locations with Papeete.

Post and Broadcasting. Number of telephones (1985), 28,192. *Radio Tele Tahiti* belongs to *Société de Radiodiffusion et de Télévision pour l'Outre-mer* (RFO) and broadcasts in French, Tahitian and English on medium- and short-waves and also broadcasts 1 television programme *via* 5 transmitters. There are also 9 private radio stations. Number of receivers (1983): radio, 77,000; TV, 25,500.

Cinemas. In 1986 there were 8 cinemas in Papeete.

Newspapers. In 1987 there were 3 daily newspapers with a combined circulation of 23,000.

JUSTICE, RELIGION, EDUCATION AND WELFARE

Justice. There is a *tribunal de grande instance* and a *cour d'appel* at Papeete.

Religion. In 1980 it was estimated that 46·5% of the inhabitants were Protestants, 39·4% Roman Catholic and 5·1% Mormon.

Education. Education was reorganized in 1975. There were, in 1985-86, 41,107 pupils in 254 primary schools, 13,372 pupils in secondary schools, and 3,944 pupils in technical schools and teacher-training colleges.

Health. There were (1980) 143 physicians, 47 dentists, 20 pharmacists, 15 midwives and 257 nursing personnel. There was (1983) a main hospital at Mamao (on Tahiti), 7 secondary hospitals, and 12 medical centres with 903 hospital beds.

DEPENDENCY. The uninhabited Clipperton Island, 1,000 km off the west coast of Mexico, is administered by the High Commissioner for French Polynesia but does not form part of the Territory; it is an atoll with an area of 5 sq. km.

Books of Reference

Journal Officiel des Etablissements Françaises de l'Océanie, and *Supplement Containing Statistics of Commerce and Navigation.* Papeete
Andrews, E., *Comparative Dictionary of the Tahitian Language.* Chicago, 1944
Bounds, J. H., *Tahiti.* Bend, Oregon, 1978
Luke, Sir Harry, *The Islands of the South Pacific.* London, 1961
O'Reilly, P., and Reitman, E., *Bibliographie de Tahiti et de la Polynésie française.* Paris, 1967
O'Reilly, P., and Teissier, R., *Tahitiens. Répertoire bio-bibliographique de la Polynésie française.* Paris, 1963

WALLIS AND FUTUNA

HISTORY. French dependencies since 1842, the inhabitants of these islands voted on 22 Dec. 1959 by an overwhelming majority in favour of exchanging their status to that of an Overseas Territory, which took effect from 29 July 1961.

AREA AND POPULATION. The Territory comprises two groups of islands (total area 274 sq. km) in the central Pacific, The Îles de Hoorn lie 240 km north-east of Fiji and consist of 2 main islands–Futuna (64 sq. km) and uninhabited Alofi (51 sq. km). The Wallis Archipelago lies another 160 km further north-east, and comprises one main island – Uvea (159 sq. km), with a surrounding coral reef. The capital is Mata-Utu (815 inhabitants, 1983) on Uvea.

The resident population (census March 1982) was 11,943 (estimate, 1987, 14,800), comprising 7,843 on Uvea and 4,100 on Futuna. About 12,000 Wallisians and Futunians live abroad, mainly in New Caledonia. Wallisian and Futunian are distinct Polynesian languages.

CONSTITUTION AND GOVERNMENT. The Senior Administrator carries out the duties of Head of the Territory, assisted by a 20-member Territorial Assembly directly elected for a 5-year term. The territory is represented by 1 deputy in the National Assembly, by 1 senator in the Senate, and by 1 member on the Economic and Social Council. There are 3 districts: Singave and Alo (both on Futuna) and Wallis.

Administrateur supérieur: Jacques Le Ilénaff.
President of the Territorial Assembly: Falakiko Gata.

ECONOMY

Budget. The 1982 budget provided for expenditure of 303·8m. francs CFP.

Currency. The unit of currency is the *franc* CFP, with a parity of CFP *francs* 18·18 to the French *franc*.

AGRICULTURE. The chief products are copra, cassava, yams, taro roots and bananas.

Livestock: Pigs, 27,000 (1986); goats, 7,000 (1986).

COMMERCE. Imports (1981) amounted to 667m. francs CFP. There are few exports.

COMMUNICATIONS

Roads. In 1977 there were 100 km of roads on Uvea.

Aviation. In 1980 there were 581 aircraft arrivals and departures at Hihifo airport, on Uvea. There is a weekly flight *via* Vila (Vanuatu) to Nouméa (New Caledonia) and three flights each week to Futuna (Point Vele air strip).

Shipping. A regular service links wharves at Mata-Utu and at Singave (Futuna) with Nouméa (New Caledonia), Suva (Fiji) and Vila and Santo (Vanuatu).

Post and Broadcasting. In 1979 a radio station was established on Uvea. In 1983 there were 225 telephones.

RELIGION, EDUCATION AND WELFARE

Religion. The majority of the population is Roman Catholic.

Education. In 1983, there were 3,962 pupils in 13 primary and lower secondary schools.

Health. In 1981 there were 4 physicians, 1 pharmacist, 1 dentist and 1 midwife. There were (1981) 3 hospitals with 108 beds.

GABON

Capital: Libreville
Population: 1·22m. (1987)
GNP per capita: US$4,250 (1983)

République Gabonaise

HISTORY. First colonized by France in the mid-19th century, Gabon was annexed to French Congo in 1888 and became a separate colony in 1910 as one of the 4 territories of French Equatorial Africa. It became an autonomous republic within the French Community on 28 Nov. 1958 and achieved independence on 17 Aug. 1960. The first President, Leon M'ba, died on 30 Nov. 1967 and was succeeded on 2 Dec. by his Vice-President, Albert-Bernard (now Omar) Bongo.

AREA AND POPULATION. Gabon is bounded west by the Atlantic ocean, north by Equatorial Guinea and Cameroon and east and south by Congo. The area covers 267,667 sq. km; its population at the 1970 census was 950,007; estimate (1987) is 1,224,000. The capital is Libreville (350,000 inhabitants, 1983), other large towns being Port-Gentil (123,300), Masuku (formerly Franceville, 38,030), Lambaréné (26,257 in 1978) and Mouanda (22,909 in 1978).

Vital statistics (1975): Birth rate, 3·22%; death rate, 2·22%.

Provincial areas, populations (estimate 1978, in 1,000) and capitals are as follows:

Province	Sq. km	1978	Capital	Province	Sq. km	1978	Capital
Estuaire	20,740	359	Libreville	Nyanga	21,285	98	Tchibanga
Woleu-Ntem	38,465	166	Oyem	Ngounié	37,750	118	Mouila
Ogooué-Ivindo	46,075	53	Makokou	Ogooué-Lolo	25,380	49	Koulamoutou
Moyen-Ogooué	18,535	49	Lambaréné	Haut-Ogooué	36,547	213	Masuku
Ogooué-Maritime	22,890	194	Port-Gentil				

The largest ethnic groups are the Fang (30%) in the north, Eshira (25%) in the south-west, and the Adouma (17%) in the south-east. French is the official language.

CLIMATE. The climate is equatorial, with high temperatures and considerable rainfall. Mid-May to mid-Sept. is the long dry season, followed by a short rainy season, then a dry season again from mid-Dec. to mid-Feb., and finally a long rainy season once more. Libreville. Jan. 80°F (26·7°C), July 75°F (23·9°C). Annual rainfall 99″ (2,510 mm).

CONSTITUTION AND GOVERNMENT. The 1967 Constitution (as subsequently revised) provides for an Executive President directly elected for a 7-year term, who appoints a Council of Ministers to assist him. The unicameral National Assembly consists of 111 members, directly elected for a 5-year term (latest elections, Feb. 1985) and a further 9 members nominated by the President.

The sole legal political party is the *Parti democratique gabonais* founded in 1968. It is governed by a Central Committee of 297 members and a 44-member Political Bureau, both elected.

President: Omar Bongo (re-elected in 1973, 1979 and 1986).
Prime Minister: Léon Mébiame.
Deputy Prime Ministers: Georges Rawiri, Etienne-Guy Mouvagha Tchioba, Emile Kassa-Mapsi, Simon Essimengane.
Foreign Minister: Martin Bongo.
Flag: Three horizontal stripes of green, yellow, blue.
Local government: The 9 provinces, each administered by a governor appointed by the President, are divided into 37 *départements*, each under a prefect.

DEFENCE

Army. The Army consists of 1 all-arms Presidential Guard battalion group with support units, totalling (1988), 1,900 men.

Navy. The small naval flotilla in 1988 comprised 2 new French-built vedettes, 4 fast attack craft, 1 patrol craft, 1 frigate-size amphibious ship, and 10 landing craft with a base at Port-Gentil. Personnel in 1988 totalled 350 officers and men. The Coastguard has 11 small patrol craft and 1 service tender.

Air Force. The Air Force has 6 single-seat and 3 two-seat Mirage 5 ground-attack aircraft, and 1 EMB-111 maritime patrol aircraft. Transport duties are performed primarily by 4 Hercules and 1 EMB-110 Bandeirante turboprop aircraft, supported by 3 C-47s and 3 Nord 262s. Single Mystère 20, F-28 and DC-8 aircraft are used for VIP duties. Three T-34C-1 armed turboprop aircraft, 5 armed Magister trainers and an EMB-110 Bandeirante are operated for *La Présidentiale Garde.* Also in service are 4 Puma, 5 Gazelle, 2 Ecureuil and 4 Alouette III helicopters. Personnel (1988) 600.

INTERNATIONAL RELATIONS

Membership. Gabon is a member of UN, OAU and OPEC; it is an ACP state of the EEC.

ECONOMY.

Planning. The Fifth 5-year Plan (1984–88) envisages public expenditure of 1,228,478m. francs CFA, of which 595,662m. were to develop the infrastructure.

Budget. The 1986 budget provided for expenditure of 720,000m. francs CFA and revenue of 600,000m.

Currency. The unit of currency is the franc CFA, with a parity value of 50 francs CFA to 1 French franc. There are coins of 1, 2, 5, 10, 25, 50, 100 and 500 *francs* CFA, and banknotes of 100, 500, 1,000, 5,000 and 10,000 *francs* CFA. In March 1988 £1 = 507 *francs* CFA; US$1 = 285·66 *francs* CFA.

Banking. The *Banque des États de l'Afrique Centrale* is the bank of issue. There are 9 commercial banks situated in Gabon. The *Banque Gabonaise de Développement* and the *Union Gabonaise de Banque* are Gabonese controlled.

ENERGY AND NATURAL RESOURCES

Electricity. The semi-public *Société d'energie et d'eau du Gabon* produced 736m. kwh. in 1985, mainly from thermal plants but increasingly from hydro-electric schemes at Kinguélé (near Libreville), Tchimbélé and Poubara (near Masuku). Supply 220 volts; 50 Hz.

Oil. Extraction from offshore fields totalled 7·9m. tonnes in 1987. Gabon operates 2 refineries, at Port-Gentil and at nearby Pointe Clairette. Proven reserves (1984) 490m. bbls.

Gas. Natural gas production (1983) was 82m. cu. metres.

Minerals. Production (1985) of manganese ore (from deposits around Moanda in the south-east) amounted to 2·3m. tonnes. Uranium is mined nearby at Mounana (918 tonnes in 1985). An estimated 850m. tonnes of iron ore deposits, discovered 1971 at Mékambo (near Bélinga in the north-east) await completion of the branch railway line to be exploited. Gold (18 kg in 1982), zinc and phosphates also occur.

Agriculture. The major crops (production, 1986, in 1,000 tonnes) are: Sugar-cane, 130; cassava, 255; plantains, 170; maize, 11; groundnuts, 8; bananas, 8; palm oil, 3·6; cocoa, 2; coffee, 1 and rice, 1.

Livestock (1986): 8,000 cattle, 82,000 sheep, 62,000 goats, 152,000 pigs.

Forestry. Gabon's equatorial forests covering 78% of the land area produced 1·38m. cu. metres of *okoumé* and other softwoods in 1985. Hardwoods (mahogany, ebony and walnut) are also exported.

Fisheries. The total catch (1982) amounted to 52,638 tonnes.

INDUSTRY AND TRADE

Industry. A sugar refinery at Masuku produced (1984) 15,000 tonnes raw sugar. Most manufacturing is based on the processing of food, timber and mineral resources.

Labour. The workforce in 1984 numbered 533,000 of whom 74% were agricultural.

Commerce. In 1983 imports totalled 324,900m. francs CFA and exports 746,600m. francs CFA. France and USA are Gabon's principal trading partners. In 1983 petroleum made up 83·5% of exports; metals, 7·5% and timber, 7%.

Total trade between Gabon and the UK (British Department of Trade returns, in £1,000 sterling):

	1983	1984	1985	1986	1987
Imports to UK	66,135	70,775	48,292	36,642	5,357
Exports and re-exports from UK	18,798	20,548	30,588	16,627	11,962

COMMUNICATIONS

Roads. There were (1983) 7,513 km of roads and in 1982 there were 16,043 passenger cars and 10,695 commercial vehicles.

Railways. A 1,435-mm gauge (Transgabonais) railway runs from Owendo *via* N'Djole to Booué and Lastourville, Mouanda and Masuku, opened throughout in 1986, which is connected to the Congo railways. A branch from Booué to Belinga is also under construction. Total 523 km of 1,437 mm gauge. In 1985, 137,111 passengers and 724,928 tonnes of freight were transported.

Aviation. There are 3 international airports at Port-Gentil, Masuku, and Libreville; internal services link these to 65 domestic airfields.

Shipping. Owendo (near Libreville), Mayumba and Port-Gentil are the main ports. In 1982, 6·8m. tonnes were loaded and 733,000 tonnes unloaded at the ports.

Post and Broadcasting. In 1985 there were 11,700 telephones, 21,000 television and 100,000 radio licences.

Cinemas. In 1974 there were 6 cinemas with a seating capacity of 4,100.

Newspapers. There were (1984) 2 newspapers published in Libreville; *Gabon-Matin* (daily) has a circulation of 18,000 and *L'Union* (weekly) 15,000.

JUSTICE, RELIGION, EDUCATION AND WELFARE

Justice. There are *tribunaux de grande instance* at Libreville, Port-Gentil, Lambaréné, Mouila, Oyem, Masuku and Koulamoutou, from which cases move progressively to a central Criminal Court, Court of Appeal and Supreme Court, all 3 located in Libreville. Civil police number about 900.

Religion. 84% of the population is Christian (65% Roman Catholic), the majority of the balance following animist beliefs. There are about 10,000 Moslems.

Education. Education is compulsory between 6–16 years. In 1982–83 there were 165,559 pupils with 3,781 teachers in primary schools; 22,350 pupils with 1,161 teachers in 47 secondary schools; 10,545 students with 582 teachers in 29 technical and teacher-training establishments.

The Université Omar Bongo, founded in 1970 in Libreville, had (1982–83) 2,651 students and 297 teaching staff.

Health In 1980 there were 265 doctors, and 1977, 20 dentists, 28 pharmacists, 99 midwives and 823 nursing personnel. In 1981 there were 16 hospitals and 87 medical centres, with a total of 4,815 beds, as well as 258 local dispensaries.

DIPLOMATIC REPRESENTATIVES

Of Gabon in Great Britain (48 Kensington Ct., London, W8 5DB)
Ambassador: Charles Mamadou Diop (accredited 20 Nov. 1986).

Of Great Britain in Gabon (Immeuble CK2, Blvd de l'Indépendence, Libreville)
Ambassador: M. A. Goodfellow.

Of Gabon in the USA (2034 20th St., NW, Washington, D.C., 20009)
Ambassador: Jean Robert Odzaga.

Of the USA in Gabon (Blvd de la Mer, Libreville)
Ambassador: Warren Clark, Jr.

Of Gabon to the United Nations
Ambassador: Laurent-Marie Biffot.

Books of Reference

Bory, P., *The New Gabon*. Monaco, 1978
Remy, M., *Gabon Today*. Paris, 1977

THE GAMBIA

Capital: Banjul
Population: 698,817 (1986)
GNP per capita: US$170 (1984)

HISTORY. The Gambia was discovered by the early Portuguese navigators, but they made no settlement. During the 17th century various companies of merchants obtained trading charters and established a settlement on the river, which, from 1807, was controlled from Sierra Leone; in 1843 it was made an independent Crown Colony; in 1866 it formed part of the West African Settlements, but in Dec. 1888 it again became a separate Crown Colony. The boundaries were delimited only after 1890. The Gambia achieved full internal self-government on 4 Oct. 1963 and became an independent member of the Commonwealth on 18 Feb. 1965. The Gambia became a republic within the Commonwealth on 24 April 1970. The Gambia, with Senegal formed the Confederation of Senegambia on 1 Feb. 1982.

AREA AND POPULATION. The Gambia is bounded west by the Atlantic ocean and on all other sides by Senegal. Area of Banjul (formerly Bathurst) and environs, 87·8 sq. km. In the provinces (area, 10,601·5 sq. km) the settled population (1971) was 275,469, not including temporary immigrants. Total population (census, April 1983), 687,817; (estimate, 1986) 698,817. The largest tribe is the Mandingo (251,997), followed by the Fulas (117,092), Woloffs (91,004), Jolas (64,494) and Sarahulis (51,137). The capital is Banjul, 1983 census (44,188), and the surrounding urban area, Kombo St Mary (101,504). Other principal towns are Serekunda (68,433), Bakau (19,309), Birkama (19,584), Sukuta (7,227), Gunjur (7,115) and Farafenni (10,168).

Birth rate (1983) 49 per 1,000; death rate, 21.

CLIMATE. The climate is characterized by two very different seasons. The dry season lasts from Nov. to May, when precipitation is very light and humidity moderate. Days are warm but nights quite cool. The SW monsoon is likely to set in with spectacular storms and produces considerable rainfall from July to Oct., with increased humidity. Banjul. Jan. 73°F (22·8°C), July 80°F (26·7°C). Annual rainfall 52″ (1,295 mm).

CONSTITUTION AND GOVERNMENT. Parliament consists of the House of Representatives which consists of a Speaker, Deputy Speaker and 35 elected members; in addition, 4 Chiefs are elected by the Chiefs in Assembly; 5 nominated members are without votes and the Attorney-General is appointed and has no vote. *See* Senegal for details about Senegambia.

A general election was held on 4–5 May 1982. State of parties (Jan. 1984): The People's Progressive Party 29, the National Convention Party 3, and Independents 3 seats.

The Government was in Nov. 1987 composed as follows:

President: Sir Dawda Kairaba Jawara.
Vice-President, Education, Youth, Sports and Culture: Bakary B. Darbo. *External Affairs:* Alhaji Omar Sey. *Finance and Trade:* Sherif Sisay. *Agriculture:* Saikou Sabally. *Health, Labour, Social Welfare and Environment:* Louise Njie. *Works and Communications:* Alhaji Momodou Cadi Cham. *Economic Planning and Industrial Development:* Mbemba Jatta. *Justice and Attorney-General:* Hassan Jallow. *Water Resources:* Omar A. Jallow. *Information and Tourism:* Dr Lamin Saho. *Interior:* (Vacant). *Local Government and Lands:* Landing Jallow Sonko.

National flag: Three horizontal stripes of red, blue, green, with the blue edged in white.

Local Administration. The Gambia is divided into 36 districts, each traditionally under a Chief, assisted by Village Heads and advisers. These districts are grouped into 6 Area Councils containing a majority of elected members, with the Chiefs of the district as *ex-officio* members. The city of Banjul is administered by a City Council.

INTERNATIONAL RELATIONS

Membership. The Gambia is a member of UN, OAU, the Commonwealth, the Non-Aligned Conference and is an ACP state of EEC.

ECONOMY

Budget. Revenue and expenditure for years ending 30 June are (in dalasi):

	1983–84	1984–85	1985–86	1986–87
Revenue	150,500,000	172,300,050	218,080,000	266,730,000
Expenditure	164,908,621	189,279,550	207,524,639	262,531,520

Currency. The currency is the *dalasi* and is divided into 100 *butut*. 12·90 *dalasi* = £1 sterling; 7·27 *dalasi* = US$1 (March 1988).

Banking. There are 5 banks in the Gambia, the Standard Bank of Gambia Ltd, Central Bank of the Gambia, Commercial and Development Bank, la Banque Internationale pour le Commerce et l'Industrie (BICI) and Agricultural Development Bank. On 30 Nov. 1978 the government savings bank had about 36,000 depositors holding approximately 992,496 dalasi.

ENERGY AND NATURAL RESOURCES

Electricity. Production (1986) 63m. kwh. Supply 230 volts; 50 Hz.

Minerals. Heavy minerals, including ilmenite, zircon and rutile, have been discovered (1m. tons up to 31 Dec. 1980) in Sanyang, Batakunku and Kartong areas.

Agriculture. Almost all commercial activity centres upon the marketing of groundnuts, which is the only export crop of financial significance; in 1986, 100,000 tonnes were produced. Cotton is also exported on a limited scale. Rice is of increasing importance for local consumption; production (1986) 45,000 tonnes.

Livestock (1986): 290,000 cattle, 200,000 goats, 191,000 sheep, 12,000 pigs and (1982) 300,000 poultry.

Fisheries. Total catch (1981) 9,700 tonnes, of which 1,100 tonnes were from inland waters.

LABOUR. There are 4 large and 10 small trade unions.

TRADE. Chief items of imports are textiles and clothing, vehicles and machinery, metal goods and petroleum products.

Imports and exports, in 1,000 dalasi:

	1982–83	1983–84	1984–85	1985–86
Imports	262,107	346,706	358,569	567,631
Exports	114,712	163,261	163,890	204,195

Chief items of export (1985–86, in 1,000 dalasi): Groundnuts shelled, 33,570; groundnut oil, 15,132; groundnut cake, 4,142; cotton lint, 3,862; fish and fish preparations, 2,507; hides and skins, 1,652. Main imports: Food and live animals, 175,280; basic manufactured goods, 113,916; machinery and transport equipment, 97,850; mineral fuels and lubricants, 56,630.

Total trade between the Gambia and UK (British Department of Trade returns, in £1,000 sterling):

	1983	1984	1985	1986	1987
Imports to UK	3,781	3,407	2,823	2,273	3,038
Exports and re-exports from UK	13,251	10,233	11,918	16,707	19,765

TOURISM. In 1985–86, 78,268 tourists visited the Gambia.

COMMUNICATIONS

Roads. There are 2,990 km of motorable roads, of which 1,718 km rank as all-weather roads including 306 km of bituminous surface and 531 km of laterite gravel. Number of licensed motor vehicles (1983): 3,420 private cars, 775 buses and coaches, 1,219 motorcycles, scooters and mopeds.

Aviation. The Gambia is served by Air Guinea, Air Mali, British Caledonian Airways, Ghana Airways and Nigeria Airways. The number of aircraft landing at Yundum Airport in 1984–85 was 1,576.

Shipping. The chief port is Banjul. In 1985–86, 125,959 tonnes of goods were loaded and 300,212 tonnes unloaded. Internal communication is maintained by steamers and launches. The Gambia River Development Organization was founded in 1978 as a joint project with Senegal to develop the river and its basin. Guinea and Guinea-Bissau were also members in 1984.

Post and Broadcasting. There are several post offices and agencies; postal facilities are also afforded to all river towns by means of a travelling post office on the government river mail-steamers. Banjul is connected with St Vincent (Cape Verde islands) and with Sierra Leone by cable. Banjul is in wireless communication with London and the main centres up river. A trans-Gambia telephone system provides direct communications with Dakar and Ziguinchor. Telephones numbered 3,476 in Jan. 1980.

Radio Gambia, a government station, broadcasts for about 15 hours a day; Radio Syd, a commercial station, broadcasts for 20 hours. Number of radio receivers (1983, estimate), 66,000.

Cinemas. In 1984 there were 14 cinemas.

Newspapers. There is an official newspaper and several news-sheets.

JUSTICE, RELIGION, EDUCATION AND WELFARE

Justice. Justice is administered by a Supreme Court consisting of a chief justice and puisne judges. It has unlimited jurisdiction but there is a Court of Appeal. Two magistrates' courts and divisional courts are supplemented by a system of travelling magistrates. There are also Moslem courts, group tribunals dealing with cases concerned with customs and traditions, and one juvenile court.

Religion. About 70% of the population is Moslem. Banjul is the seat of an Anglican and a Roman Catholic bishop. There are some Methodist missions. Some sections of the population retain their original animist beliefs.

Education (1983–84). There were 180 primary schools (2,445 teachers, 60,630 pupils), 16 secondary technical schools (475 teachers, 8,923 pupils), 8 secondary high schools (231 teachers, 4,037 pupils). In 1982–83 there were 8 post-secondary schools (148 teachers, 1,058 pupils). Gambia College, which replaced Yundum College as a teacher-training and vocational centre, opened for agricultural and health students in 1979.

Health. In 1980 there were 43 government doctors, 23 private doctors and about 635 hospital beds.

DIPLOMATIC REPRESENTATIVES

Of the Gambia in Great Britain (57 Kensington Ct., London, W8 5DG)
High Commissioner: Horace R. Monday, Jr.

Of Great Britain in the Gambia (48 Atlantic Rd., Fajara, Banjul)
High Commissioner: Alec Ibbott.

Of the USA in the Gambia (Fajara (East), Kairaba Ave., Banjul)
Ambassador: Herbert E. Horowitz.

Books of Reference

The Gambia since Independence 1965–1980. Banjul, 1980
Tomkinson, M., *The Gambia: A Holiday Guide.* London, 1983

GERMANY

POST-WAR HISTORY. Since the unconditional surrender of the German armed forces on 8 May 1945 there has been no central authority whose writ runs in the whole of Germany. Consequently no peace treaty has been signed with a government representing the whole of Germany, and the country is virtually partitioned between the Federal Republic of Germany and the German Democratic Republic.

By the Berlin Declaration of 5 June 1945 the governments of the USA, the UK, the USSR and France assumed supreme authority over Germany. Each of the 4 signatories was given a zone of occupation, in which the supreme power was to be exercised by the C.-in-C. in that zone (*see* map in THE STATESMAN'S YEAR-BOOK, 1947). Jointly these 4 Cs.-in-C. constituted the Allied Control Council in Berlin, which was to be competent in all 'matters affecting Germany as a whole'. The territory of Greater Berlin, divided into 4 sectors, was to be governed as an entity by the 4 occupying powers.

At the Potsdam Conference (17 July–2 Aug. 1945) the northern part of the Province of East Prussia, including its capital Königsberg (renamed Kaliningrad), was transferred to the Soviet Union, pending final ratification by a peace treaty; and it was agreed that, pending the final peace settlement, Poland should administer those parts of Germany lying east of a line running from the Baltic Sea immediately west of Swinemünde along the river Oder to its confluence with the Western Neisse and thence along the Western Neisse to the Czechoslovak frontier.

The agreements between the war-time allies concerning the occupation zones (12 Sept. 1944) and control of Germany (1 May 1945) were repudiated by the USSR on 27 Nov. 1958.

A Treaty was signed in East Berlin between the German Democratic Republic and the Federal Republic of Germany on 21 Dec. 1972 agreeing the basis of relations between the two countries.

GERMAN DEMOCRATIC REPUBLIC

Capital: Berlin (East)
Population: 16·6m. (1986)
GNP per capita: US$10,400 (1985)

Deutsche Demokratische Republik

HISTORY. For the immediate post-war history *see* p. 522. An agreement proclaiming the Oder–Neisse line the permanent frontier between Germany and Poland was concluded between the German Democratic Republic (GDR) and Poland on 6 July 1950. A protocol on the delimitation of the frontier was signed on 27 Jan. 1951.

AREA AND POPULATION. The GDR is bounded north by the Baltic Sea, east by Poland, south-east by Czechoslovakia and west by Federal Germany. Its area is 108,333 sq. km. Population at the census of 31 Dec. 1981 was 16,705,635. Population in 1986, 16,639,877 (7·88m. male; 12·74m. urban). Population density: 153 per sq. km. There were some 110,000 Sorbs, a Slav minority, in 1985. Administratively, the country is divided into 15 counties (*Bezirk*), subdivided in 1986 into 38 urban districts, 191 rural districts and 7,567 communities, Berlin (East) has county status. Area and population, 1986:

Counties	Area in sq. km	Population (1,000s) Total	Female	Per sq. km
Berlin (East)	403	1,223·3	647·4	3,035
Cottbus	8,262	883·3	458·1	107
Dresden	6,738	1,771·6	941·6	263
Erfurt	7,349	1,235·0	647·9	168
Frankfurt	7,186	707·6	366·5	98
Gera	4,004	740·5	390·0	185
Halle	8,771	1,785·8	940·5	204
Karl-Marx-Stadt	6,009	1,870·0	998·8	311
Leipzig	4,966	1,373·8	732·9	277
Magdeburg	11,526	1,250·0	656·7	108
Neubrandenburg	10,948	619·2	318·6	57
Potsdam	12,568	1,120·3	583·7	89
Rostock	7,075	903·0	466·0	128
Schwerin	8,672	592·1	307·7	68
Suhl	3,856	549·2	287·2	142

The capital is Berlin (East).

Resident population of the principal towns in 1986:

Berlin (East)	1,223,309	Rostock	245,606	Schwerin	127,823
Leipzig	552,133	Halle	234,768	Cottbus	125,784
Dresden	519,737	Erfurt	216,646	Zwickau	120,573
Karl-Marx-Stadt	314,437	Potsdam	140,198	Jena	107,369
Magdeburg	288,798	Gera	132,303	Dessau	103,508

Vital statistics:

	Live births	Marriages	Divorces	Deaths
1983	233,756	125,429	49,624	222,702
1984	228,135	133,898	50,320	221,204
1985	227,648	131,514	51,240	225,362
1986	222,269	137,208	52,439	223,521

Rates per 1,000, 1986: Birth, 13·4; marriage, 8·3; divorce, 3·2; death, 13·4; infant mortality, 4·7 stillborn, 9·2 under 1 year.

CLIMATE. The continental-type climate makes winters crisp and clear, but with cold easterly winds bringing very low temperatures and appreciable snowfall. Summers are hot, but with much convectional rainfall. Berlin. Jan. 31°F (–0·5°C), July 66°F (19°C). Annual rainfall 22·5″ (563 mm). Dresden. Jan. 30°F (–1°C), July 65°F (18·5°C). Annual rainfall 27·2″ (680 mm). Leipzig. Jan. 31°F (–0·6°C), July 65°F (18·5°C). Annual rainfall 24″ (605 mm).

CONSTITUTION AND GOVERNMENT. Upon the establishment of the Federal Republic of Germany, the People's Council of the Soviet-occupied zone, appointed in 1948, was converted into a provisional People's Chamber.

On 7 Oct. 1949 the provisional People's Chamber enacted a constitution of the 'German Democratic Republic'.

A new 'socialist constitution' was approved by a referendum on 6 April 1968 (revised in 1974), when 94·54% of the electorate voted for the constitution; it came into force on 8 April 1968. The People's Chamber, is 'the supreme organ of state power'; it elects the Council of State, the Council of Ministers, the National Defence Council and the judges of the Supreme Court.

Council of State. The Council is authorized to issue decisions and to interpret existing laws. The Chairman of the Council of State represents the GDR in international law. In March 1988 it consisted of: *Chairman:* Erich Honecker; *Deputy Chairmen:* Manfred Gerlach, Gerald Götting, Heinrich Homann, Egon Krenz, Günter Maleuda, Günter Mittag, Horst Sindermann, Willi Stoph; 16 other members and a secretary.

In March 1988 the Council of Ministers consisted of a Presidium, composed as follows:

Chairman (i.e. Premier): Willi Stoph.

First Deputy Chairmen: Alfred Neumann, Werner Krolikowski.

Deputy Chairmen: Günther Kleiber, Wolfgang Rauchfuss *(Minister of Materials)*, Gerhard Schürer *(Chairman, State Planning Commission)*, Dr Herbert Weiz *(Minister of Science)*, Manfred Flegel, Hans-Joachim Heusinger *(Minister of Justice)*, Dr Hans Reichelt *(Minister for the Environment)*, Rudolph Schulze *(Minister for Posts and Telecommunications)*, Horst Sölle; Walter Halbritter *(Director, Office of Prices)*, Ernst Höfner *(Minister of Finance)*; and 31 other ministers, including: Gen. Heinz Kessler *(Defence)*, Oskar Fischer *(Foreign Affairs)*, Gerhard Beil *(Foreign Trade)*, and Friedrich Dickel *(Interior)*.

Supreme political power is in the hands of the Socialist Unity (*i.e.* Communist) Party of Germany (SED), which had 2·2m. members in 1985, and which is united in the National Front with 4 puppet parties (1985 membership in brackets): Christian Democratic Union (120,000), Democratic Farmers (100,000), Liberal Democratic Party (90,000) and the National Democratic Party (90,000). At the June 1986 elections to the People's Chamber 703 National Front candidates stood for the 500 seats. Unsuccessful candidates were placed on a reserve list. 99·74% of the 12,434,444 electorate voted; 99·94% of votes were for National Front candidates. 161 women were elected.

The Politburo of the SED in March 1988 consisted of: Erich Honecker *(General Secretary)*; Hermann Axen; Hans-Joachim Böhme; Horst Dohlus; Werner Eberlein; Werner Felfe; Kurt Hager; Joachim Herrmann; Werner Jarowinsky; Heinz Kessler; Günther Kleiber; Egon Krenz; Werner Krolikowski; Siegfried Lorenz; Erich Mielke; Günter Mittag; Erich Mueckenberger; Alfred Neumann; Günther Schabowski; Horst Sindermann; Willi Stoph; Harry Tisch; candidate members: Ingeburg Lange; Gerhard Müller; Margarete Müller; Gerhard Schürer; Werner Walde.

National flag: Black, red, golden (horizontal); in the centre, on both sides, the coat of arms showing a hammer and compass with a wreath of grain entwined with a black, red and golden ribbon.

National hymn: Auferstanden aus Ruinen (tune by Hanns Eisler).

Local government is conducted by assemblies at each administrative level. 3,235 representatives were elected to the County Assemblies in June 1986.

DEFENCE. On 18 Jan. 1956 the People's Chamber established a 'national people's army' and a defence ministry. A 12-member defence council, under the chairmanship of E. Honecker, General Secretary of the SED, was set up on 10 Feb. 1960.

The 'law for the defence of the GDR', of 20 Sept. 1960, makes military service (in case of emergency) and civil defence compulsory for all citizens.

Conscription for men between 18 and 25 years was introduced on 24 Jan. 1962 (18 months' service in the army, 2 years in the navy and air force).

Some 422,000 Soviet troops with about 1,000 heavy tanks and 6,000 armoured vehicles are stationed in the German Democratic Republic, chiefly along the Polish border.

Army. The Army, set up on 1 March 1956, is organized in 2 army corps, including 2 armoured divisions and 4 motorized infantry divisions. Operationally these divisions are subordinate to the Soviet formations of the Warsaw Pact forces. They are armed with about 3,000 tanks (mostly Soviet T-54, T-55, T-62 and T-72), 280 self-propelled guns and ground-to-air 'Guideline' missiles. The Border Police was taken out of the Army in 1974. Total army strength was (1988) 120,000 (71,500 conscripts) with a reserve of 330,000 men.

Police. The Police force *(Volkspolizei)* numbered 25,000 security and 46,500 border troops. There are also 450,000 militiamen organized in combat groups. The militia receive military instruction from the People's Police.

Navy. The 'People's Navy' *(Volksmarine)* includes 3 frigates, 21 corvettes, 11 missile boats, 27 torpedo boats, 46 coastal minesweepers, 3 intelligence ships, 12 tank landing ships, 10 oilers, 2 training ships, 4 supply ships, 5 survey vessels, 9 small survey craft, 13 buoy tenders, 3 diving vessels, 1 cable layer, 2 torpedo recovery craft, 2 icebreakers, 30 auxiliary ships and service craft and 13 tugs. The Navy operates one squadron of 8 Mi-14 helicopters. Personnel in 1988 totalled 16,000 officers and men, including the GBK Coastal Frontier Guards *(Grenz Brigade Küste)* which operates 40 vessels, many of them *ex*-Navy.

Air Force. The *ex*-'air-police', set up in Nov. 1950, had in 1988 a strength of about 40,000 officers and men and 375 combat aircraft. Two air defence divisions consist respectively of 2 and 4 regiments (each with 3 squadrons of 12 aircraft), plus a fighter training division, equipped with MiG-21, MiG-23, and Su-20 supersonic fighters. There is 1 squadron of MiG-21 reconnaissance fighters. Mi-24 gunship helicopters have been delivered to the German Democratic Republic. Other units include a regiment of Mi-2, Mi-4 and Mi-8 helicopters, a regiment of An-2, Let L-410, Il-14, An-26 and Tu-134 transports and a Flight Training Division with Yak-18, Trener, L-29 Delfin, L-39 Albatross, MiG-15UTI and MiG-21U training aircraft. 'Guideline' and 'Goa' surface-to-air missile units are operational.

INTERNATIONAL RELATIONS

Membership. The German Democratic Republic is a member of UN and Comecon.

ECONOMY

Planning. The economy is one of the most successful of the centrally-planned type. Although there have been small concessions to 'market forces', improvement is sought rather in 'comprehensive intensification': rationalization, cutting production costs and combining production units. Extrasystemic features favouring economic performance include the beneficial special relationship with Federal Germany and special support from the USSR. The current 5-year plan is running from 1986 to 1990. Annual increase targets: National income, 4·4%; industrial production, 8·3%.

Budget. The budget of the GDR was as follows (in M 1m.) for calendar years:

	1981	1982	1983	1984	1985	1986
Revenue	167,466	182,836	192,410	213,535	235,535	247,013
Expenditure	167,159	182,071	191,689	211,778	234,392	246,368

Of the 1986 expenditures, M 13,014m. were earmarked for health and social services, M 12,895m. for education and M 34,186 for social benefits and pensions.

Currency. The circulating Reichsmark notes were in June 1948 exchanged for 'Deutsche Mark' (East), renamed 'Mark of the German Bank of Issue' (MDN) from 1 Aug. 1964 and further renamed 'the Mark of the GDR' (M) from 1967. Money in circulation, 1985: M 13,651m. In March 1988, £1 = 2·99 M; US$1 = 1·69 M.

Banking. The most important banking institutions are the State Bank, which is the bank of issue, the Foreign Trade Bank and the Industrial and Trade Bank. Savings in 1986, totalled M 132,315m.

Weights and Measures. The metric system is in force.

ENERGY AND NATURAL RESOURCES

Electricity. Sources of energy in 1986 included lignite, 83·3%, nuclear power, 9·5% and hydroelectric power, 1·5%. Electricity generation (1986): 115,291 kwh. Supply 220 volts; 50 Hz.

Minerals. The GDR is a major producer of lignite. Production in 1986, 311m. tonnes. Uranium, cobalt, bismuth, arsenic and antimony are exploited in the western Erzgebirge and eastern Thuringia.

Agriculture. In 1986 the agricultural area was 6·2m. hectares including 4·7m. hectares arable and 1·25m. hectares grassland. In 1986 there were 3,890 collective farms with 5·27m. hectares of arable land, and 465 state farms with 446,154 hectares of land.

The yield of the main crops in 1986 was as follows (in 1,000 tonnes): Potatoes, 9,997; sugar-beet, 7,747; barley, 4,293; wheat, 4,195; rye, 2,406; oats, 666.

Livestock (in 1,000) in 1986: Cattle, 5,804 (including 2,045 milch cows); pigs, 12,840; sheep, 2,647; poultry, 50,216.

In 1986 there were 161,515 tractors and 17,461 combine harvesters.

Forestry. In 1985 there were 2,977,600 hectares of forest. Timber production was 10,115,000 cu. metres in 1986. The industry employed 50,454 people in 1985.

Fisheries. Total catch (1986) 272,500 tonnes. Inland catch was 24,821 tonnes.

INDUSTRY AND TRADE

Industry. Industry produced about 80% of the national income in 1985. There were 3,449 state and co-operative industrial enterprises in 1986. The percentage of privately owned enterprises was 32·8 in 1950 and 2·9 in 1982.

Production of iron and steel (in 1,000 tonnes):

	1980	1981	1982	1983	1984	1985	1986
Crude steel	7,308	7,467	7,168	7,219	7,573	7,853	7,967
Rolled steel	5,128	5,061	4,959	5,084	5,386	5,637	9,361

Other products in 1986 (in 1,000 tonnes): Sulphuric acid, 883; potash fertilizers, 3,485; nitrogen fertilizers, 1,252; petrol, 4,329; diesel fuel, 6,324; caustic soda, 638; cement, 11,988; passenger cars (no.), 218,000; television receivers (no.), 712,000; shoes, 85·5m. pairs; plastics and synthetic resins, 1,045.

Labour. In 1986 the workforce was 8·55m., of whom 37·7% worked in industry, 21·1% in the service sector, 10·8% in agriculture and 10·3% in commerce. Membership of the trade union organization was 9·45m. (4·98m. women) in 1986.

Commerce. Total trade was as follows (in 1m. Valuta-Mark):

	Total			Total	
	Imports	Exports		Imports	Exports
1981	67,000	65,927	1984	83,501	90,402
1982	69,878	75,231	1985	86,701	93,490
1983	76,197	84,227	1986	90,465	91,505

In 1986 machinery made up 47% of exports and fuels and metal ores 40% of imports; 67% of trade is with Communist countries. Largest trading partners: USSR (39%), Czechoslovakia, Poland, Federal Republic of Germany.

Total trade between the German Democratic Republic and UK (British Department of Trade returns, in £1,000 sterling):

	1983	1984	1985	1986	1987
Imports to UK	157,625	190,130	204,293	195,513	180,299
Exports and re-exports from UK	60,997	92,270	63,797	81,276	81,489

COMMUNICATIONS

Roads. There were, in 1986, 47,210 km of classified roads including 1,855 km of motorways. 3,486m. passengers and 143·2m. tonnes of goods were carried by public transport. There were 3,462,184 cars, 219,415 lorries, 1,321,832 motorcycles and 57,600 buses. There were 45,203 road accidents in 1986, with 1,484 fatalities.

Railways. There were, in 1986, 13,730 km of standard gauge line, of which 2,754 km were electrified. 609m. passengers and 346m. tonnes of freight were carried.

Aviation. Interflug operates services between Berlin and Prague, Warsaw, Budapest, Bucharest, Moscow, Sofia, Belgrade, Tirana, Cairo, Baghdad, Beirut and other capitals. Passengers carried (1985), 1,446,000; freight, 39,678 tonnes.

Shipping. In 1986 the merchant fleet had 174 vessels of 1,344,795 GRT. 11·4m. tonnes of freight were carried in 1985. Navigable inland waterways had a total length of 2,319 km. 6m. passengers and 18·5m. tonnes of freight were carried. In 1986 a rail ferry was opened from the Island of Rügen to the ice-free Soviet port of Klaipeda, by-passing Poland.

Pipeline. 1,307 km in 1986. Materials transported in 1984: 37·3m. tonnes.

Post and Broadcasting. In 1983 there were 11,971 post offices and agencies and 3,441,484 telephone subscribers. *Staatliches Komitee für Rundfunk*, the governmental broadcasting system, broadcasts 4 programmes on long-, medium-and short-waves, and on FM. The foreign service is broadcast in 11 languages on medium-and short-waves, using the name Radio Berlin International. The transmitters are located at Königswusterhausen, Leipzig and Nauen. Radio Volga transmits on long-waves from Burg and broadcasts in Russian for the Soviet Armed Forces in Germany. More than 80% of the programmes are relays from Radio Moscow. Radio Moscow is using relay transmitters on medium-waves at Leipzig for programmes in German. *Deutsche Freiheitssender 904* and *Deutsche Soldatensender* are clandestine stations claiming to be operating from the Federal Republic although they are located not far from Burg. *Fernsehen der DDR* broadcasts 2 TV programmes in colour, using SECAM-system. Number of wireless licences (1986), 6·7m.; TV licences, 6·14m.

Cinemas and Theatres (1986). There were 823 cinemas with a seating capacity of 243,982, and 200 theatres with a capacity of 56,243.

Newspapers. There were 541 newspapers and periodicals in 1986. 6,543 book titles were published in 148·6m. copies.

JUSTICE, RELIGION, EDUCATION AND WELFARE

Justice. The death penalty was abolished in July 1987.

Religion. According to the census of 1950, 80·5% of the population were Protestants and 11% were Roman Catholics. The Synod of Lutheran Churches was founded in 1969 and embraces 8 regional churches. There were some 1·5m. Lutherans in 1986 with 4,300 priests. In 1988 there were 1·05m. Catholics with 1,200 priests.

Education. In 1986 779,700 children were in 13,265 pre-school educational institutions. General education schools numbered 5,895 in 1986 with 170,277 teachers and 2,041,013 pupils. Of these schools 5,198 with 1,942,525 pupils offered 10 years schooling and the remainder 12.

In addition there were 959 vocational schools *(Berufsschulen)* with 16,244 teachers and 369,100 trainees, and 239 technical schools with 160,379 students. There were also 54 universities and other higher education institutes with 131,560 full-time students, including 66,228 women.

Health. In 1986 there were 169,179 hospital beds. There were 598 health centres. There were 39,157 doctors and 12,182 dentists.

DIPLOMATIC REPRESENTATIVES

Of the German Democratic Republic in Great Britain (34 Belgrave Sq., London, SW1X 8QB)
Ambassador: Dr Gerhard Lindner (accredited 27 July 1984).

Of Great Britain in the German Democratic Republic (108 Berlin, Unter den Linden 32/34)
Ambassador: Nigel Broomfield.

Of the German Democratic Republic in the USA (1717 Massachusetts Ave., NW, Washington, D.C., 20036)
Ambassador: Dr Gerhard Herder.

Of the USA in the German Democratic Republic (1080 Berlin, Neustädtische Kirchstrasse 4-5)
Ambassador: Francis J. Meehan.

Of the German Democratic Republic to the United Nations
Ambassador: Harry Ott.

Books of Reference

Statistical Information: The central statistical agency is the Staatliche Zentralverwaltung für Statistik (Hans-Beimler-Str. 70–72, 102, Berlin).
Statistisches Jahrbuch der Deutschen Demokratischen Republik, annual (from 1956).—
Statistisches Taschenbuch der DDR (annual, from 1959; also Arabic, English, French, Russian, Spanish editions).—*Statistische Praxis* (from 1946).
The Constitution of the German Democratic Republic. 3rd ed. Berlin, 1974
DDR-Handbuch. 3rd ed. Cologne, 1985
Handbook of the Economy of the German Democratic Republic. Farnborough, 1979

Åslund, A., *Private Enterprise in Eastern Europe: The Non-Agricultural Private Sector in Poland and the GDR.* London, 1985
Beyme, K, von, and Zimmerman, H., (eds.) *Policy-making in the German Democratic Republic.* Aldershot, 1984
Childs, D., *The GDR: Moscow's German Ally.* London, 1983.— (ed.), *Honecker's Germany.* London, 1985
Dennis, M., *German Democratic Republic.* London, 1987
Edwards, G. E., *GDR Society and Social Institutions.* London, 1985
Honecker, E., *Reden und Aufsätze.* Berlin, 1975.—*The German Democratic Republic, Pillar of Peace and Socialism.* New York, 1979.—*Aus meinem Leben.* Berlin, 1980
Krisch, H., *The German Democratic Republic.* Boulder, 1985
McAdams, A. J., *East Germany and Detente.* CUP, 1985
McCauley, M., *The German Democratic Republic since 1945.* London, 1983
Scharf, C. B., *Politics and Change in East Germany.* London, 1984
Schulz, E., (ed.) *GDR Foreign Policy.* New York, 1982
Staritz, D., *Geschichte der DDR, 1949–1985.* Frankfurt-am-Main, 1985
Weber, H., *Geschichte der DDR.* Munich, 1985

National Library: Deutsche Bücherei, Leipzig C.1. *Director:* Helmut Rötzsch.—Deutsche Staatsbibliothek, Berlin. *Director:* Professor H. Kunze.

FEDERAL REPUBLIC OF GERMANY

Capital: Bonn
Population: 61m. (1985)
GNP per capita: US$10,300 (1985)

Bundesrepublik Deutschland

HISTORY. The Federal Republic of Germany became a sovereign independent country on 5 May 1955.

In June 1948 USA, UK and France agreed on a central government for the 3 western zones. An Occupation Statute, which came into force on 30 Sept. 1949, reduced the responsibilities of the occupation authorities. Formally, the Federal Republic of Germany came into existence on 21 Sept. 1949. The Petersberg Agreement of 22 Nov. 1949 freed the Federal Republic of numerous restrictions of the Occupation Statute. In 1951 USA, UK and France as well as other states terminated the state of war with Germany; the Soviet Union followed on 25 Jan. 1955. On 5 May 1955 the High Commissioners of USA, UK and France signed a proclamation revoking the Occupation Statute. On the same day, the Paris and London treaties, signed in Oct. 1954, came into force and established the sovereignty of the Federal Republic of Germany.

AREA AND POPULATION. Federal Germany is bounded north by Denmark and the North and Baltic Seas, east by the German Democratic Republic, and Czechoslovakia, south-east and south by Austria, south by Switzerland and west by France, Luxembourg, Belgium and the Netherlands. West Berlin is an enclave within the German Democratic Republic. Area: 248,706 sq. km. Population, at 31 Dec. 1986, 61,140,000; at 30 June 1986, 61,066,000 (29,232,000 males). Density 246 per sq. km.

The capital is Bonn.

The Federation comprises 11 Länder (states).

Area and population of the Länder as at 30 June 1986:

Länder	Area in sq. km	Population (in 1,000's) (Males in brackets)		Per sq. km
Schleswig-Holstein	15,727	2,612·7	(1,264·9)	166
Hamburg	755	1,575·7	(732·2)	2,088
Lower Saxony	47,438	7,149·3	(3,455·5)	152
Bremen	404	675·5	(308·5)	1,627
North Rhine-Westphalia	34,068	16,665·3	(7,956·0)	489
Hessen	21,115	5,531·3	(2,659·1)	262
Rhineland-Palatinate	19,848	3,610·4	(1,730·5)	182
Baden-Württemberg	35,751	9,295·1	(4,480·3)	260
Bavaria	70,553	10,993·4	(5,270·6)	156
Saarland	2,569	1,043·4	(496·2)	406
Berlin (West)	480	1,867·7	(865·4)	3,892

Vital statistics for calendar years:

	Marriages	Live births	Of these illegitimate	Deaths	Divorces
1983	369,963	594,177	52,442	718,337	121,475
1984	364,140	584,157	52,998	696,118	130,894
1985	364,661	586,155	55,070	704,296	128,268
1986	372,008	625,963	59,808	701,890	...

Crude birth rate in 1986 was 10·3 per 1,000 population; marriage rate, 6·1; death rate, 11·5; infantile mortality 8·6; growth rate, -1·2.

In 1986 there were 4,512,700 resident foreigners, including 1,434,300 Turks,

529

591,200 Yugoslavs, 537,100 Italians and 278,500 Greeks; 34,913 persons were naturalized in 1985, including 12,153 from Romania and 5,925 from Poland.

In 1985 there were 428,700 emigrants and 512,100 immigrants. In 1986 99,650 persons sought asylum. There were 28,435 immigrants from, and 2,039 emigrants to, the German Democratic Republic in 1985.

Populations of towns of over 100,000 inhabitants on 30 June 1986 (in '000):

Town	Land	Population	Town	Land	Population
Berlin (West)	Berlin (West)	1,868·7	Kassel	Hessen	184·2
Hamburg	Hamburg	1,575·7	Herne	N. Rhine-Westph.	171·5
Munich	Bavaria	1,269·4	Mülheim a.d.		
Cologne	N. Rhine-Westph.	914·0	Ruhr	N. Rhine-Westph.	171·0
Essen	N. Rhine-Westph.	617·7	Hamm	N. Rhine-Westph.	166·2
Frankfurt am			Solingen	N. Rhine-Westph.	158·0
Main	Hessen	593·4	Leverkusen	N. Rhine-Westph.	154·7
Dortmund	N. Rhine-Westph.	569·8	Osnabrück	Lower Saxony	153·2
Stuttgart	Baden-Württ.	564·5	Ludwigshafen		
Düsseldorf	N. Rhine-Westph.	561·2	am Rhein	Rhinel.-Pal.	153·0
Bremen	Bremen	524·7	Neuss	N. Rhine-Westph.	143·5
Duisburg	N. Rhine-Westph.	516·6	Oldenburg	Lower Saxony	138·9
Hanover	Lower Saxony	506·4	Heidelberg	Baden-Württ.	135·8
Nuremburg	Bavaria	466·5	Göttingen	Lower Saxony	133·7
Bochum	N. Rhine-Westph.	381·0	Darmstadt	Hessen	133·6
Wuppertal	N. Rhine-Westph.	375·3	Bremerhaven	Bremen	132·8
Bielefeld	N. Rhine-Westph.	299·2	Würzburg	Bavaria	127·5
Mannheim	Baden-Württ.	295·5	Regensburg	Bavaria	124·1
Bonn	N. Rhine-Westph.	290·8	Wolfsburg	Lower Saxony	122·0
Gelsenkirchen	N. Rhine-Westph.	284·4	Remscheid	N. Rhine-Westph.	121·0
Münster	N. Rhine-Westph.	268·9	Recklinghausen	N. Rhine-Westph.	117·6
Karlsruhe	Baden-Württ.	267·6	Bottrop	N. Rhine-Westph.	112·1
Wiesbaden	Hessen	266·7	Heilbronn	Baden-Württ.	111·4
Mönchenglad-			Koblenz	Rhinel.-Pal.	110·6
bach	N. Rhine-Westph.	254·7	Paderborn	N. Rhine-Westph.	109·8
Braunschweig	Lower Saxony	247·3	Siegen	N. Rhine-Westph.	107·4
Augsburg	Bavaria	245·6	Offenbach am		
Kiel	Schleswig-Holstein	244·7	Main	Hessen	107·2
Aachen	N. Rhine-Westph.	238·6	Salzgitter	Lower Saxony	105·5
Oberhausen	N. Rhine-Westph.	222·1	Pforzheim	Baden-Württ.	104·5
Krefeld	N. Rhine-Westph.	216·7	Witten	N. Rhine-Westph.	102·2
Lübeck	Schleswig-Holstein	209·8	Bergisch		101·4
Hagen	N. Rhine-Westph.	206·1	Gladbach	N. Rhine-Westph.	
Mainz	Rhinel.-Pal.	188·5	Hildesheim	Lower Saxony	100·7
Saarbrücken	Saarland	185·1	Ulm	Baden-Württ.	100·4
Freiburg im					
Breisgau	Baden-Württ.	184·8			

CLIMATE. Oceanic influences are only found in the north-west where winters are quite mild but stormy. Elsewhere a continental climate is general. To the east and south, winter temperatures are lower, with bright frosty weather and considerable snowfall. Summer temperatures are fairly uniform throughout. Frankfurt. Jan. 33°F (0·6°C), July 66°F (18·9°C). Annual rainfall 24″ (601 mm). Hamburg. Jan. 31°F (–0·6°C), July 63°F (17·2°C). Annual rainfall 29″ (726 mm). Hanover. Jan. 33°F (0·6°C), July 64°F (17·8°C). Annual rainfall 24″ (604 mm). Köln. Jan. 36°F (2·2°C), July 66°F (18·9°C). Annual rainfall 27″ (676 mm). Munich. Jan. 28°F (–2·2°C), July 63°F (17·2°C). Annual rainfall 34″ (855 mm). Stuttgart. Jan. 33°F (0·6°C), July 66°F (18·9°C). Annual rainfall 27″ (677 mm).

CONSTITUTION. The Constituent Assembly (known as the 'Parliamentary Council') met in Bonn on 1 Sept. 1948, and worked out a Basic Law which was approved by a two-thirds majority of the parliaments of the participating Länder and came into force on 23 May 1949.

The Basic Law *(Grundgesetz)* consists of a preamble and 146 articles. The first section deals with the basic rights which are legally binding for legislation, administration and jurisdiction.

The Federal Republic is a democratic and social constitutional state on a parliamentary basis. The federation is constituted by the 11 Länder (states): Baden-Württemberg, Bavaria, Bremen, Berlin (West), Hamburg, Hessen, Lower Saxony, North Rhine-Westphalia, Rhineland-Palatinate, Saarland and Schleswig-Holstein. In Berlin (West) the Basic Law applies with certain restrictions. The Basic Law decrees that the general rules of international law form part of the federal law. The constitutions of the Länder must conform to the principles of a republican, democratic and social state based on the rule of law. Executive power is vested in the Länder, unless the Basic Law prescribes or permits otherwise. Federal law takes precedence over state law.

Legislative power is vested in the Federal Assembly *(Bundestag)* and the Federal Council *(Bundesrat)*.

The Federal Assembly, elected in universal, direct, free, equal and secret elections, for a term of 4 years.

The Federal Council consists of 45 members appointed by the governments of the Länder in proportions determined by the number of inhabitants. Each Land has at least 3 votes.

The Head of State is the Federal President *(Bundespräsident)* who is elected for a 5-year term by a Federal Convention specially convened for this purpose. This Convention consists of all the members of the Federal Assembly and an equal number of members elected by the Länder parliaments according to proportional representation. Presidents may be re-elected for one further term only.

Executive power is vested in the Federal Government, which consists of the Federal Chancellor, elected by the Federal Assembly on the proposal of the Federal President, and the Federal Ministers, who are appointed and dismissed by the Federal President upon the proposal of the Federal Chancellor.

The Federal Republic has exclusive legislation on: (1) foreign affairs (2) federal citizenship; (3) freedom of movement, passports, immigration and emigration, and extradition; (4) currency, money and coinage, weights and measures, and regulation of time and calendar; (5) customs, commercial and navigation agreements, traffic in goods and payments with foreign countries, including customs and frontier protection; (6) federal railways and air traffic; (7) post and telecommunications; (8) the legal status of persons in the employment of the Federation and of public law corporations under direct supervision of the Federal Government; (9) trade marks, copyright and publishing rights; (10) co-operation of the Federal Republic and the Länder in the criminal police and in matters concerning the protection of the constitution, the establishment of a Federal Office of Criminal Police, as well as the combating of international crime; (11) federal statistics.

For concurrent legislation in which the Länder have legislative rights if and as far as the Federal Republic does not exercise its legislative powers, *see* THE STATESMAN's YEAR-BOOK, 1956, p. 1038.

Federal laws are passed by the Federal Assembly and after their adoption submitted to the Federal Council, which has a limited veto. The Basic Law may be amended only upon the approval of two-thirds of the members of the Federal Assembly and two-thirds of the votes of the Federal Council.

The foreign service, federal finance, railways, postal services, waterways and shipping are under direct federal administration.

In the field of finance the Federal Republic has exclusive legislation on customs and financial monopolies and concurrent legislation on: (1) excise taxes and taxes on transactions, in particular, taxes on real-estate acquisition, incremented value and on fire protection; (2) taxes on income, property, inheritance and donations; (3) real estate, industrial and trade taxes, with the exception of the determining of the tax rates.

The Federal Republic can, by federal law, claim part of the income and corporation taxes to cover its expenditures not covered by other revenues. Financial jurisdiction is uniformly regulated by federal legislation.

National flag: Three horizontal stripes of black, red, gold.

National anthem: Einigkeit und Recht und Freiheit (words by H. Hoffmann, 1841; tune by J. Haydn, 1797).

Local Government. Below *Land* level local government is carried on by elected councils to counties *(Landkreise)*, county boroughs *(Kreisfreie Städte)* and local communities *(Gemeinden)*.

GOVERNMENT. The 11th Federal Assembly, elected 25 Jan. 1987, is composed of 520 members. These include 22 members for Berlin with limited voting rights. Electoral turnout was 84·4%. The government is formed by a coalition of the Christian Democrat/Christian Socialist (CDU/CSU) alliance with the Free Democrats (FDP). (The CSU is a Bavarian party where the CDU does not stand). Percentage votes, and seats gained (1983 electoral results in brackets): CDU/CSU 44·3%, 223 (48·8%, 244); Social Democratic Party (SPD), 37%, 186 (38·2%, 193); FDP, 9·1%, 46 (7%, 34); Greens, 8·3%, 42 (5·6%, 27).

Federal President: Dr Richard von Weizsäcker (sworn in 1 July 1984).

The Cabinet, in March 1988, was as follows:

Chancellor: Dr Helmut Kohl (CDU).
Without Portfolio: Wolfgang Schäuble (CDU).
Deputy Chancellor, Minister of Foreign Affairs: Hans-Dietrich Genscher (FDP).
Interior: Dr Friedrich Zimmermann (CSU).
Justice: Hans A. Engelhard (FDP).
Finance: Dr Gerhard Stoltenberg (CDU).
Economics: Martin Bangemann (FDP).
Food, Agriculture and Forestry: Ignaz Kiechle (CSU).
Intra-German Relations: Dorothée Wilms (CDU).
Labour and Social Affairs: Dr Norbert Blüm (CDU).
Defence: Dr Manfred Wörner (CDU).
Youth, Family Affairs and Health: Rita Süssmuth (CDU).
Transport: Jürgen Warnke (CSU).
Posts and Telecommunications: Dr Christian Schwarz-Schilling (CDU).
Regional Planning, Building and Urban Development: Dr Oscar Schneider (CSU).
Research and Technology: Dr Heinz Riesenhuber (CDU).
Education and Science: Jürgen Möllemann (CDU).
Economic Co-operation: Hans Klein (CSU).
Environment: Walter Wallman.

DEFENCE. The Paris Treaties, which entered into force in May 1955, stipulated a contribution of the Federal Republic to western defence within the framework of NATO and the Western European Union. The Federal Armed Forces *(Bundeswehr)* had a total strength (1988) of 488,400 all ranks (223,450 conscripts) and a further 750,000 reserves.

Army. The Army is divided into the Field Army, containing the units assigned to NATO in event of war, and the Territorial Army. The Field Army is organized in 3 corps, comprising 17 armoured, 15 armoured infantry, 1 mountain and 3 airborne brigades. Equipment includes 650 M-48, 2,437 Leopard I and 1,800 Leopard II tanks. An air component operates 210 BO 105P anti-armour helicopters, 105 CH-53G and 187 UH-1D Iroquois transport helicopters, plus 148 Alouette II and 95 BO 105M liaison/observation helicopters. The Territorial Army is organized into 5 Military Districts, under 3 Territorial Commands. Its main task is to defend rear areas and remains under national control even in wartime. Total strength was (1988) 332,100 (conscripts 175,900; Territorial Army 41,700).

Navy. The Federal Navy comprises 24 diesel-powered coastal submarines, 7 destroyers, 9 frigates, 5 corvettes, 40 fast missile boats (Exocet armed), a light cruiser type training ship, 10 frigate-type support ships, 6 coastal minesweepers, 12 minehunters, 21 fast minesweepers, 18 inshore minesweepers, 22 utility landing craft, 28 smaller landing craft, 12 supply and support ships, 2 fleet replenishment ships, 8 oilers, 8 coast patrol boats, 10 torpedo recovery vessels, 13 coastguard cutters, 2 repair ships, 28 tugs and 50 auxiliaries and service craft.

The projected construction programme includes 12 submarines, 2 frigates, 10 fast mine warfare craft and 20 minehunters.

The Naval Air Arm operates 116 fixed-wing aircraft, including 47 Tornados, 17 Starfighters, 15 Atlantics and 6 DO28s; and 36 helicopters (22 Sea Kings and 14 Lynx). About 20 more Tornados and 5 Lynx were on order for delivery, 1988.

Navy personnel in 1988 totalled 5,640 officers and 32,860 men, including 6,700 in the Naval Air Arm.

Air Force. Since Oct. 1970, the *Luftwaffe* has comprised the following commands: German Air Force Tactical Command, German Air Force Support Command (including two German Air Force Regional Support Commands—North and South) and General Air Force Office. Its strength in 1988 was approximately 108,700 officers and other ranks and about 500 first-line combat aircraft. Combat units, including 12 heavy fighter-bomber squadrons, 7 light ground attack/ reconnaissance squadrons, 4 reconnaissance squadrons, 8 surface-to-surface missile squadrons, and an air defence force of 4 interceptor squadrons, 24 batteries of *Nike-Hercules* and 36 batteries of *Improved Hawk* surface-to-air missiles, are assigned to NATO. There are 4 F-4F Phantom interceptor squadrons, 8 Tornado attack squadrons, 4 attack squadrons of F-4Fs, 4 RF-4E Phantom reconnaissance squadrons, and 7 light attack/reconnaissance squadrons of Alpha Jets. Four transport squadrons (each 15 aircraft) with turboprop Transall C-160 aircraft and 1 wing of 5 helicopter squadrons with UH-1D Iroquois add to the air mobility of the *Bundeswehr*. There are also VIP, support and light transport aircraft, and Piaggio P.149D initial training aircraft. Guided weapons in service include 8 squadrons of *Pershing* surface-to-surface missiles and 6 battalions of *Nike-Hercules* and 9 battalions of *Improved Hawk* surface-to-air missiles.

Pilots undergo basic and advanced training in USA.

INTERNATIONAL RELATIONS

Membership. The Federal Republic of Germany is a member of UN, OECD, European Communities, WEU, NATO and the Council of Europe.

ECONOMY

Budget. Since 1 Jan. 1979 tax revenues have been distributed as follows: Federal Government. Income tax, 42·5%; capital yield and corporation tax, 50%; turnover tax, 67·5%; trade tax, 15%; capital gains, insurance and accounts taxes, 100%; excise duties (other than on beer), 100%. Länder. Income tax, 42·5%; capital yield and corporation tax, 50%; turnover tax, 32·5%; trade tax, 15%; other taxes, 100%. Local authorities. Income tax, 15%; trade tax, 70%; local taxes, 100%.

Budgets for 1987 and 1986 (in DM1m.):

Revenue	All public authorities		Federal portion	
	1987	1986	1987	1986
	Current			
Taxes	456,352	435,261	222,270	213,541
Economic activities	34,898	41,521	12,716	18,037
Interest	3,223	3,191	1,267	1,269
Current allocations and subsidies	102,593	96,248	1,093	1,264
Other receipts	30,984	29,743	4,447	4,428
minus equalising payments	95,658	89,597	...	...
	532,390	516,367	241,792	238,539
	Capital			
Sale of assets	7,838	5,471	3,521	637
Allocations for investment	25,968	25,139	15	17
Repayment of loans	7,056	6,669	2,318	2,037
Public sector borrowing	2,433	2,555	...	...
minus equalising payments	24,615	24,008	...	...
	18,679	15,826	5,853	2,691
Totals	551,276	532,010	247,645	241,230

| | All public authorities | | Federal portion | |
Expenditure	1987	1986	1987	1986
		Current		
Staff	185,653	178,120	39,192	37,913
Materials	94,822	92,238	40,942	39,944
Interest	60,169	59,489	30,878	30,382
Allocations and subsidies	257,167	244,403	124,810	120,983
minus equalising payments	95,658	89,597	...	...
	502,152	484,653	235,821	229,222
		Capital		
Construction	45,094	42,837	6,194	6,060
Acquisition of property	10,977	10,456	1,699	1,511
Allocations and subsidies	47,981	47,342	18,101	17,963
Loans	19,158	19,935	8,442	9,209
Acquisition of shares	3,028	3,277	1,471	1,514
Repayments in the public sector	1,517	1,373	...	...
minus equalising payments	24,615	24,008	...	...
	103,142	101,212	35,909	36,256
Totals	602,583	584,866	270,312	265,220

Major areas of expenditure in 1987 (and 1986) in DM1,000m.: Social, 87·2 (85·7); defence, 53·5 (52·5); transport and communications, 13·1 (12·9); economy, 10·2 (10).

Currency. 100 *pfennig* (pf.)=1 *deutsche Mark* (DM). There are 1, 2, 5, 10, 50 pf., 1, 2, 5 and 10 DM coins and 5, 10, 20, 50, 100, 500 and 1,000 DM notes. Money in circulation in 1984, DM 104,700m. In March 1988, £1 = 2·99 DM; US$1 = 1·69

Banking. On 14 Feb. 1948 the Bank deutscher Länder was established in Frankfurt as the central bank.

The Länder and Berlin central banks were merged from 1 Aug. 1957 to form the Deutsche Bundesbank. Its assets were DM 220,851m. in 1986.

Weights and Measures. The metric system is in force.

ENERGY AND NATURAL RESOURCES

Electricity. In 1986, 414,000m. kwh. were produced. Supply 220 volts; 50 Hz.

Oil. The chief oilfields are in Emsland (Lower Saxony). In 1986, 27·68m. tonnes of petroleum and benzine, and 11·68m. tonnes of diesel oil were produced.

Minerals. The main production areas are: North Rhine-Westphalia (for coal, iron and metal smelting-works), Central Germany (for brown coal), and Lower Saxony (Salzgitter for iron ore; the Harz for metal ore).

Production (in 1,000 tonnes):

Minerals	1981	1982	1983	1984	1985	1986
Coal	88,460	89,014	82,202	79,426	82,398	80,801
Lignite	130,619	127,307	124,281	126,739	120,667	114,310
Iron ore	1,572	1,304	976	977	1,034	717
Potash	28,192	22,536	27,200	29,543	29,248	24,775
Crude oil	4,459	4,256	4,116	4,055	4,105	4,017

Production of iron and steel (in 1,000 tonnes):

	1981	1982	1983	1984	1985	1986
Pig-iron	31,876	27,621	26,598	30,203	31,919	29,443
Steel	41,610	35,880	35,729	39,389	40,908	37,533
Rolled products finished	...	25,702	26,063	27,962	28,919	27,409

Agriculture. Area cultivated, 1986: 11·91m. hectares (arable, 7·25m.; pasture, 4·5m.).

In 1986 the number of agricultural holdings classified by area farmed was:

	Total	1–5 hectares	5–20 hectares	20–100 hectares	Over 100 hectares
Schleswig-Holstein	30,210	6,292	5,573	17,028	1,317
Hamburg	1,295	788	283	211	13
Lower Saxony	110,949	30,023	31,054	47,888	1,984
Bremen	466	153	114	196	3
North Rhine-Westphalia	90,022	27,568	31,661	30,198	595
Hessen	54,996	20,500	21,115	13,075	266
Rhineland-Palatinate	54,050	22,262	19,777	11,839	172
Baden-Württemberg	120,466	47,840	48,590	23,669	367
Bavaria	241,225	62,242	121,925	56,421	637
Saarland	3,836	1,583	1,135	1,067	51
Berlin (West)	143	84	35	24	—
Federal Republic	*707,658*	*219,335*	*281,302*	*201,616*	*5,405*

Area (in 1,000 hectares) and yield (in 1,000 tonnes) of the main crops:

	Area				Yield			
	1983	1984	1985	1986	1983	1984	1985	1986
Wheat	1,655	1,634	1,618	1,648	8,990	10,223	9,866	10,406
Rye	445	439	424	414	1,599	1,931	1,821	1,768
Barley	2,035	2,006	1,944	1,947	8,944	8,284	9,690	9,377
Oats	601	555	582	506	2,068	2,507	2,807	2,276
Potatoes	224	219	218	210	5,669	7,272	7,905	7,390
Sugar-beet	393	406	403	391	...	...	20,813	20,260

Wine must production (in 1m. hectolitres): 8 in 1984; 5·4 in 1985; 10 in 1986.

Livestock, 1986: Cattle, 15,806,300 (including 5,419,000 milch cows); horses, 259,900; sheep, 1,779,000; pigs, 23,905,500; poultry, 72,123,700.

Forestry. Forestry is of great importance, conducted under the guidance of the State on scientific lines. In recent years enormous depredation has occurred through pollution with acid rain. Forest area in 1986 was 5·29m. hectares, of which 2·22m. were owned by the State. In 1985 31m. cu. metres of timber were cut.

Fisheries. In 1986 the yield of sea fishing was 161,280 tonnes live weight.

In 1986 the fishing fleet consisted of 15 trawlers (25,884 gross tons), 1 lugger and 648 cutters.

INDUSTRY AND TRADE

Industry. In 1985 there were 51,757 manufacturing firms (with 20 and more employees) employing 8·17m. persons, made up of 0·28m. in energy and water services, 0·22m. in mining, 1·4m. in raw materials processing, 3·6m. in the manufacture of producers' goods, 1·3m. in the manufacture of consumer goods, 0·47m. in food and tobacco and 0·95m. in building.

Production of major industrial products:

Products (1,000 tonnes)	1982	1983	1984	1985	1986
Aluminium	723	743	777	745	765
Artificial fertilizers	1,505	1,618	1,691	1,651	1,425
Sulphuric acid, SO_3	3,601	3,543	3,518	3,428	3,351
Soda, Na_2CO_3	1,105	1,218	1,364	1,412	1,442
Cement	30,079	30,466	28,909	25,758	26,580
Plastics	6,335	7,100	7,505	7,666	7,943
Cotton yarn	168	181	194	131	128
Woollen yarn	47	46	49	42	41
Passenger cars (1,000)	3,771	3,875	3,505	3,867	3,952
Bicycles (1,000)	3,089	3,334	3,024	2,891	3,209

Labour. 26·61m. persons were employed in 1985, including 10·17m. women and 2·1m. foreign workers. Major categories: manufacturing industries, 10·46m.; services, 9m.; commerce and transport, 4·67m.; self-employed, 2·43m.; agriculture, forestry and fishing, 1·37m. Unemployed (1986): 2·05m.; unfilled vacancies, 165,257.

Trade Unions. The majority of trade unions belong to the *Deutscher Gewerkschaftsbund* (DGB, German Trade Union Federation), which had (women in brackets) 7·76m. (1·76m.) members in 1986, including 5·19m. (0·86m.) manual workers, 1·76m. (0·74m.) white-collar workers and 0·82m. (0·16m.) civil servants. Of these 2·6m. (0·39m.) worked in the metal industries, 1·2m. (0·37m.) in public services, 0·49m. in building and 0·36m. in mining and energy. DGB unions are organized in industrial branches such that only one union operates within each enterprise. Outside the DGB lie several smaller unions: The *Deutscher Beamtenbund* (DBB) or civil servants union with 0·8m. (0·2m.) members, the *Deutsche Angestellten-Gewerkschaft* (DAG) or union of salaried staff with 0·5m. (0·2m.) members and the *Christlicher Gewerkschaftsbund Deutschlands* (CGD, Christian Trade Union Federation of Germany) with 0·3m. (0·08m.) members.

Commerce. Imports and exports in DM 1m.:

	Imports				Exports		
1983	1984	1985	1986	1983	1984	1985	1986
390,192	434,257	463,811	413,744	432,281	488,223	537,164	526,363

Distribution of imports and exports by categories of countries in 1986 (in DM 1m.): EEC, 216,020, 267,454; developing countries, 52,796, 55,913; Communist countries, 21,157, 25,892. Most important trading partners in 1986 (trade figures in DM 1m.): *imports* Netherlands, 57,798; France, 47,083; Italy, 38,091; UK, 29,758; Belgium with Luxembourg, 29,250; USA, 26,864; Japan, 24,030; Switzerland, 18,494; Austria, 16,383; Sweden, 9,984; USSR, 9,299: *exports* France, 61,336; USA, 55,206; Netherlands, 45,458; UK, 44,600; Italy, 42,879; Belgium with Luxembourg, 37,172; Switzerland, 31,033; Austria, 28,199; Sweden, 14,747; Denmark, 12,215; Spain, 12,135; USSR, 9,374.

Distribution by commodities in 1986 (in DM 1m.): *imports and exports* live animals, 554, 996; foodstuffs, 44,256, 21,280; luxury foods and tobacco, 9,941, 5,044; raw materials, 30,873, 7,279; semi-finished products, 60,180, 30,635; manufactures, 259,805, 457,617.

Total trade between the Federal Republic of Germany and UK (British Department of Trade returns, in £1,000 sterling):

	1983	1984	1985	1986	1987
Imports to UK	9,667,444	11,090,227	12,601,387	14,139,097	15,783,904
Exports and re-exports from UK	6,063,989	7,458,042	8,947,055	8,542,196	9,404,257

Tourism. In 1985–86, 12·07m. arrivals and 27·3m. overnight stays by foreign visitors were registered.

COMMUNICATIONS

Roads. On 1 Jan. 1986 the total length of classified roads was 173,240 km, including 8,350 km of motorway *(Autobahn)*, 31,372 km of federal highways, 63,296 km first-class and 70,222 km second-class country roads. Motor vehicles licensed on 1 July 1986: 31,748,300 (including 26,917,400 passenger cars, 1,411,700 trucks, 69,300 buses and 1,721,200 tractors.

Road casualties in 1986 totalled 443,217 injured and 8,948 killed.

Railways. Length of Federal Railway in 1986 was 27,484 km (1,435 mm gauge) of which 11,433 km was electrified. In 1986 it carried 1,125m. passengers and 315·4m. tonnes of freight. There were also 2,919 km of privately-owned and other minor railways.

Aviation. Deutsche Lufthansa was set up in 1953 with a capital of DM 900m. The Federal Republic owns 74·3%, Land North Rhine-Westphalia 2·2%, the Federal Railways, 0·9%, Federal Post 1·8%, Kreditanstalt für Wiederaufbau 3% and private industry 17·8%. In 1985 it had 88 Boeings and 16 Airbuses.

Lufthansa operate internal, European, African, North and South Atlantic, Near and Far East routes. In 1986 it carried 43m. passengers and 0·8m. tonnes of freight.

Shipping. On 31 Dec. 1985 the mercantile marine comprised 1,950 ocean-going vessels of 5,627,000 BRT.

The inland-waterways fleet on 31 Dec. 1985 included 2,186 motor freight vessels totalling 2m. tonnes and 430 tankers of 545,844 tonnes. The length of the navigable rivers and canals in use was 4,429 km.

Sea-going ships in 1986 carried 134·9m. tonnes of cargo. Inland waterways carried 229·5m. tonnes in 1986.

Pipeline. In 1986 there were 1,715 km of pipeline. 59·1m. tonnes of oil were transported.

Post and Broadcasting. In 1986 there were 17,719 post offices and 39·1m. telephones.

The post office savings banks had, in 1986, 21,090,000 depositors with DM 36,217m. to their credit.

In 1986 postal revenues amounted to DM 52,549m. and expenditure to DM 49,280m.

There are 9 regional broadcasting stations. The *Arbeitsgemeinschaft der öffentlich-rechtlichen Rundfunkanstalten der Bundesrepublik Deutschland* (ARD) organizes co-operation between them and also broadcasts a federal-wide TV programme of its own. Number of wireless licences, (1986) 25·92m.; of television licences, 23·01m.

Cinemas and Theatres. In 1985 there were 3,418 cinemas and 282 theatres with seating capacities of 723,199 and 155,147 respectively. 64 feature films were made in 1985.

Newspapers and Books. In 1985, 357 newspapers and 6,893 periodicals were published with respective circulations of 25·44m. and 268·33m. 57,623 book titles were published.

JUSTICE, RELIGION, EDUCATION AND WELFARE

Justice. Justice is administered by the federal courts and by the courts of the Länder. In criminal procedures, civil cases and procedures of non-contentious jurisdiction the courts on the Land level are the local courts *(Amtsgerichte)*, the regional courts *(Landgerichte)* and the courts of appeal *(Oberlandesgerichte)*. Constitutional federal disputes are dealt with by the Federal Constitutional Court *(Bundesverfassungsgericht)* elected by the Federal Assembly and Federal Council. The Länder also have constitutional courts. In labour law disputes the courts of the first and second instance are the labour courts and the Land labour courts and in the third instance, the Federal Labour Court *(Bundesarbeitsgericht)*. Disputes about public law in matters of social security, unemployment insurance, maintenance of war victims and similar cases are dealt with in the first and second instances by the social courts and the Land social courts and in the third instance by the Federal Social Court *(Bundessozialgericht)*. In most tax matters the finance courts of the Länder are competent and in the second instance, the Federal Finance Court *(Bundesfinanzhof)*. Other controversies of public law in non-constitutional matters are decided in the first and second instance by the administrative and the higher administrative courts *(Observerwaltungsgerichte)* of the Länder, and in the third instance by the Federal Administrative Court *(Bundesverwaltungsgericht)*.

For the inquiry into maritime accidents the admiralty courts *(Seeämter)* are competent on the Land level and in the second instance the Federal Admiralty Court *(Bundesoberseeamt)* in Hamburg.

The death sentence has been abolished.

Religion. Census (1970) 49% of the population were Protestants, 44·6% Roman Catholics and 0·1% Jews.

The Evangelical (Protestant) Church consists of 18 member-churches in the Federal Republic and West Berlin (7 Lutheran Churches, 8 United-Lutheran-Reformed, 2 Reformed Churches and 1 Confederation of United member Churches: 'Church of the Union'). Its organs are the Synod, the Church Conference and the Council under the chairmanship of Bishop Dr Eduard Lohse (Hanover). There are also some 12 Evangelical Free Churches. In 1983 there were 10,648 parishes, 16,302 priests and 25·5m. members.

There are 5 Catholic archbishops and 17 bishoprics. Chairman of the German

Bishops' Conference is Cardinal Höffner, Archbishop of Cologne. A concordat between Germany and the Holy See was signed on 20 July and ratified on 10 Sept. 1933.

The 'Old Catholics', who are in full communion with the Anglican Churches, numbered about 30,000 in 1977; they have a bishop at Bonn.

Evangelische Kirche in Deutschland. Hanover, 1979
Taschenbuch der evangelischen Kirche in Deutschland. Frankfurt, 1980
Kirchliches Handbuch. Amtliches statistisches Jahrbuch der Katholischen Kirche Deutschlands
Pastoral der Kirche fremden—Eroffnungsreferat der Deutschen Bischofskonferenz 1979 in Fulda—von Kardinal Joseph Höffner. Bonn, 1979
Alt-Katholisches Jahrbuch. Bonn, 1978
Katholiken und ihre Kirche, Protestanten und ihre Kirche. Munich, 1977

Education. Schools providing general education are primary and post-primary schools *(Grund- und Hauptschulen)*, special schools *(Sonderschulen)*, secondary modern schools *(Realschulen)*, grammar schools *(Gymnasien)* and comprehensive schools *(Gesauntschulen)*. Primary schools: Attendance is compulsory for all children having completed their 6th year of age. Compulsory education extends 9 years. After the first 4 (or 6) years at primary school children may attend post-primary schools, secondary modern schools, grammar schools and other schools of general secondary education. The secondary modern school comprises 6, the grammar school 9 years. The final Grammar School Certificate (Abitur-Higher School Certificate) entitles the holder to enter any institution of higher education. There are also special schools for retarded, physically or mentally handicapped and socially maladjusted children.

In 1985 there were 19,280 primary and post-primary schools with 3,827,875 pupils and 234,385 teachers; 2,826 special schools with 271,424 pupils and 41,622 teachers, 2,617 secondary modern schools with 1,049,010 pupils and 60,596 teachers; 2,486 grammar schools with 1,750,377, pupils and 126,010 teachers; 314 comprehensive schools with 217,461 pupils and 28,695 teachers.

Vocational education is provided in part-time, full-time and advanced vocational schools *(Berufs-, Berufsaufbau-, Berufsfach-* and *Fachschulen,* including *Fachschulen für Technik* and *Schulen des Gesundheitswesens).* Running parallel to the occupation, part-time vocational schools offer 6 to 12 hours per week of additional compulsory schooling. All young people who are apprentices, in some other employment or even unemployed have to attend them in general up to the age of 18 years or until the completion of the practical vocational training. Full-time vocational schools comprise courses of at least one year. They prepare for commercial and domestic occupations as well as specialized occupations in the field of handicrafts. Advanced full-time vocational schools are attended by pupils having completed their 18th year of age; courses vary from 6 months to 3 or more years.

In 1985 there were 5,328 full- and part-time vocational schools with 81,825 teachers and 2,562,619 pupils (1,153,722 female); 2,896 advanced vocational schools with 9,390 teachers and 213,816 pupils (140,909 female).

Higher Education. There are universities at Augsburg, Bamberg, Bayreuth, Berlin (West), Bielefeld, Bochum, Bonn, Bremen, Cologne, Dortmund, Düsseldorf, Eichstatt, Erlangen-Nuremberg, Frankfurt-am-Main, Freiburg im Breisgau, Giessen, Göttingen, Hamburg, Hanover, Heidelburg, Hildesheim, Hohenheim, Kaiserslautern, Karlsruhe, Kiel, Konstanz, Lüneburg, Mainz, Mannheim, Marburg, Munich, Münster, Oldenburg, Osnabrück, Passau, Regensburg, Saarbrücken, Stuttgart, Trier, Tübingen, Ulm and Würzburg, and in 1985 there were 17 other institutions of equivalent status.

Teachers in 1985: universities, 103,842; technical universities, 22,639; polytechnics, 7,670; art colleges, 4,861.

Students in 1986–87 (women in brackets): universities and equivalent institutions, 931,348 (381,237); polytechnics, 88,151 (27,770); teachers' training colleges, 10,244 (7,179); theological colleges, 3,469 (1,159); art schools, 22,019 (10,903); technical universities, 279,387 (76,284); business colleges, 33,081 (13,900).

Health. In 1985 there were 153,895 doctors (including 73,010 in hospitals) and 34,415 dentists. There were 3,098 hospitals (including 945 private) with 674,742 beds.

Social Welfare. *Social Health Insurance* (introduced in 1883). Wage-earners and apprentices, salaried employees with an income below a certain limit and social-insurance pensioners are compulsorily insured. Voluntary insurance is also possible.

Benefits: Medical treatment, medicines, hospital and nursing care, maternity benefits, death benefits for the insured and their families, sickness payments and out-patients' allowances.

36m. persons were insured in 1985 (21·1m. compulsorily) and 10·6m. persons (including 6·6m. women) were drawing pensions. Number of cases of incapacity for work totalled 23m., and 378m. working days were lost. Total disbursements DM 114,108m.

Accident Insurance (introduced in 1884). Insured are all persons in employment or service, apprentices and the greater part of the self-employed and the unpaid family workers.

Benefits in the case of industrial injuries and occupational diseases: Medical treatment and nursing care, sickness payments, pensions and other payments in cash and in kind, surviving dependants' pensions.

Number of insured in 1985, 29·9m.; number of current pensions, 0·97m.; total disbursements, DM 13,101m.

Workers' and Employees' Old-Age Insurance Scheme (introduced in 1889). All wage-earners and salaried employees, the members of certain liberal professions and—subject to certain conditions—self-employed craftsmen are compulsorily insured. The insured may voluntarily continue to insure when no longer liable to do so or increase the insurance.

Benefits: Measures designed to maintain, improve and restore the earning capacity; pensions paid to persons incapable for work, old age and surviving dependants' pensions.

Number of insured in 1985, 31·7m. (15·3m. women); number of current pensions, 1985: 13·3m.; pensions to widows and widowers, 3·8m.; pensions to orphans, 0·5m. Total disbursements in 1985, DM 187,978m.

There are also special retirement and unemployment pension schemes for miners and farmers, assistance for war victims and compensation payments to members of German minorities in East European countries expelled after the Second World War and persons who suffered damage because of the war or in connexion with the currency reform.

Family Allowances. The monthly allowance for the first child is DM 50, for the second, DM 70-100 (varying according to income) for the third DM 140-220 and the fourth DM 140-240. DM 10,849 were dispersed to 6·3m. recipients in 1986.

Unemployment Allowances. In 1986 0·8m. persons (0·37m. women) were receiving unemployment benefit and 0·6m. (0·16m. women) earnings-related benefit. Total expenditure on these and similar benefits (e.g. short-working supplement, job creation schemes) was DM 31,862m. in 1986.

Accommodation Allowances averaging DM 119 a month were paid in 1985 to 1·5m. persons whose monthly income averaged DM 1,329.

Public Welfare. Benefits were instituted in 1962. In 1985 DM 20·82m. were distributed to 2·81m. recipients.

Public Youth Welfare. For supervision of foster children, official guardianship, assistance with adoptions and affiliations, social assistance in juvenile courts, educational assistance and correctional education under a court order. Total expenditure in 1985, DM 6,367m.

Übersicht über die soziale Sicherung. Bundesministerium für Arbeit und Sozialordnung. 9th ed. Bonn, 1977

Tietz, G., *Zahlenwerk zur Sozialversicherung in der Bundesrepublik Deutschland* (and supplements). Berlin, 1963
Arbeits- und Sozialstatistik. Bundesminister für Arbeit und Sozialordnung, Bonn (from 1950)
Fachserie 13 Sozialleistungen. Statistisches Bundesamt (from 1951)
Fachserie 12 Gesundheitswesen. Statistisches Bundesamt (from 1946)

DIPLOMATIC REPRESENTATIVES

Of the Federal Republic of Germany in Great Britain (21–23 Belgrave Sq., London, SW1X 8PZ)
Ambassador: Baron Rüdiger von Wechmar, GCVO (accredited 7 Feb. 1984).

Of Great Britain in the Federal Republic of Germany (Friedrich-Ebert-Allee 77, 5300 Bonn 1)
Ambassador: Sir Christopher Mallaby, KCMG.

Of the Federal Republic of Germany in the USA (4645 Reservoir Rd, NW, Washington, D.C., 20007)
Ambassador: Guenther van Well.

Of the USA in the Federal Republic of Germany (Deichmanns Ave., 5300, Bonn)
Ambassador: Richard R. Burt.

Of the Federal Republic of Germany to the United Nations
Ambassador: Dr Hans Werner Lautenschlager.

Books of Reference

Statistical Information: The central statistical agency is the Statistisches Bundesamt, 62 Wiesbaden, Gustav Stresemann Ring 11. *President:* Egon Hölder. Its publications include:

Statistisches Jahrbuch für die Bundesrepublik Deutschland; Wirtschaft und Statistik (monthly, from 1949); *Das Arbeitsgebiet der Bundesstatistik* (latest issue 1981; also in English: *Survey of German Federal Statistics*).

Berghahn, V. R., *Modern Germany: Society, Economy and Politics in the Twentieth Century.* CUP, 1982
Beyme, K. von, *The Political System of the Federal Republic of Germany.* New York, 1983
Burdick, C., *et al.* (eds.), *Contemporary Germany: Politics and Culture,* Boulder, 1984
Carr, J., *Helmut Schmidt, Helmsman of Germany.* London, 1985
Childs, D., *Germany since 1918.* 2nd ed. New York, 1980
Conradt, D. P., *The German Polity.* 2nd ed. New York, 1982
Craig, G. A., *Germany, 1866–1945.* OUP, 1981—*The Germans.* Harmondsworth, 1984
Detwiler, D. S., and Detwiler, I. E., *West Germany.* [Bibliography] Oxford and Santa Barbara, 1988
Edinger, L. J., *West German Politics.* New York, 1986
Eley, G., *From Unification to Nazism: Reinterpreting the German Past.* London, 1986
Hardach, K., *The Political Economy of Germany in the Twentieth Century.* California Univ. Press, 1980
Hubatsch, W., *Studies in Medieval and Modern German History.* Basingstoke, 1985
Johnson, N., *State and Government in the Federal Republic of Germany: the Executive at Work.* 2nd ed. Oxford, 1983
Jonas, M., *The United States and Germany: A Diplomatic History.* Cornell Univ. Press, 1984
Koch, H. W., *A Constitutional History of Germany in the Nineteenth and Twentieth Centuries.* London, 1984
Kohl, W. L., and Basevi, G., *West Germany: A European and Global Power.* London, 1982
Kolinsky, E., *Parties, Opposition and Society in West Germany.* London, 1984
König, K., *et al.* (eds.) *Public Administration in the Federal Republic of Germany.* Boston, 1983
Laqueur, W., *Germany Today: a Personal Report.* London, 1985
Markovits, A. S. (ed.), *The Political Economy of West Germany: Modell Deutschland.* New York, 1982
Pachter, H., *Modern Germany: A Social, Cultural and Political History.* Boulder, 1978
Pasley, M., (ed.). *Germany: a Companion to German Studies.* 2nd ed. London, 1982
Schweitzer, D.-C., (ed.) *Politics and Government in the Federal Republic of Germany: Basic Documents.* Leamington Spa, 1984
Smith, E. O., *The West German Economy.* London, 1983
Smith, G., *Democracy in Western Germany.* 3rd ed. Aldershot, 1986

Wallach, P. and Romoser, G. K. (eds.) *West German Politics in the Mid-Eighties: Crisis and Continuity.* New York, 1985
Who's Who in Germany, 1982–1983. Munich, 1983
Wild, T., (ed). *Urban and Rural Change in West Germany.* London, 1983

National Library: Deutsche Bibliothek, Zeppelinallee 4–8; Frankfurt (Main). *Director:* Professor Dr Kurt Köster.

THE LÄNDER

BADEN–WÜRTTEMBERG

AREA AND POPULATION. Baden-Württemberg comprises 35,751 sq. km, with a population (at 31 March 1987) of 9,335,893 (4,504,450 males, 4,831,442 females).

The Land is administratively divided into 4 areas, 9 urban and 35 rural districts, and numbers 1,111 communes. The capital is Stuttgart.

Vital statistics for calendar years:

	Live births	Marriages	Divorces	Deaths
1984	94,000	54,349	16,252	90,870
1985	94,442	54,901	15,984	93,295
1986	101,616	55,705	15,294	93,003

CONSTITUTION. The Land Baden-Württemberg is a merger of the 3 Länder, Baden, Württemberg-Baden and Württemberg-Hohenzollern, which were formed in 1945. The merger was approved by a plebiscite held on 9 Dec. 1951, when 70% of the population voted in its favour.

The Diet, elected on 25 March 1984, consists of 68 Christian Democrats, 41 Social Democrats, 8 Free Democrats, 9 Ecologists.

The Government is formed by Christian Democrats, with Lothar Späth (CDU) as Prime Minister.

AGRICULTURE. Area and yield of the most important crops:

	Area (in 1,000 hectares)			Yield (in 1,000 tonnes)		
	1984	1985	1986	1984	1985	1986
Rye	16.0	16.4	17.0	72.6	80.7	75.6
Wheat	222.4	218.5	216.3	1,279.6	1,330.6	1,166.0
Barley	197.8	200.8	197.4	955.0	995.9	810.7
Oats	86.3	85.3	77.7	373.1	437.6	329.4
Potatoes	17.4	15.5	14.9	559.6	838.8	807.1
Sugar-beet	23.7	23.4	23.3	1,260.8	1,228.6	1,293.5

Livestock (3 Dec. 1986): Cattle, 1,770,918 (including 656,969 milch cows); horses, 51,516; pigs, 2,386,342; sheep, 231,529; poultry, 6,005,209.

INDUSTRY. In 1986 9,338 establishments (with 20 and more employees) employed 1,424,233 persons; of these, 255,468 were employed in machine construction (excluding office machines, data processing equipment and facilities); 74,577 in textile industry; 244,696 in electrical engineering; 223,908 in car building.

LABOUR. The economically active persons totalled 4,298,000 at the 1%-EC-sample survey of June 1985. Of the total 530,500 were self-employed (including family workers), 3,768,100 employees; 218,200 were engaged in agriculture and forestry; 2,038,300 in power supply, mining, manufacturing and building, 669,700 in commerce and transport, 1,372,400 in other industries and services.

ROADS. On 1 Jan. 1987 there were 28,323 km of 'classified' roads, including 1,345 km of autobahn, 4,972 km of federal roads, 10,173 km of first-class and 11,833 km of second-class highways. Motor vehicles, at 1 July 1987, numbered 5,217,788, including, 4,443,426 passenger cars, 8,520 buses, 197,960 lorries, 310,763 tractors and 199,732 motor cycles.

JUSTICE. There are a constitutional court *(Staatsgerichtshof)*, 2 courts of appeal, 17 regional courts, 108 local courts, a Land labour court, 9 labour courts, a Land social court, 8 social courts, a finance court, a higher administrative court *(Verwaltungsgerichtshof)*, 4 administrative courts.

RELIGION. On 1 Jan. 1987, 43·8% of the population were Protestants and 47·2% Roman Catholics.

EDUCATION. In 1986–87 there were 3,621 primary schools *(Grund* and *Hauptschule)* with 31,690 teachers and 543,247 pupils; 570 special schools with 7,988 teachers and 43,731 pupils; 442 intermediate schools with 11,745 teachers and 190,031 pupils; 415 high schools with 19,102 teachers and 252,427 pupils; 27 *Freie Waldorf* schools with 1,096 teachers and 14,657 pupils. Other schools together had 965 teachers and 12,910 pupils; there were also 40 *Fachhochschulen* (colleges of engineering and others) with 45,528 students.

In the winter term 1986–87 there were 9 universities (Freiburg, 22,576 students; Heidelberg, 26,687; Konstanz, 6,412; Tübingen, 22,963; Karlsruhe, 18,055; Stuttgart, 18,244; Hohenheim, 5,330; Mannheim, 10,798; Ulm, 4,766); 8 teacher-training colleges with 8,227 students; 5 colleges of music with 2,762 students and 2 colleges of fine arts with 1,016 students.

Statistical Information: Statistisches Landesamt Baden-Württemberg (P.O.B. 898, D7000 Stuttgart 1) *(President:* Prof. Max Wingen), publishes: *'Baden-Württemberg in Wort und Zahl'* (monthly); *Jahrbücher für Statistik und Landeskunde von Baden-Württemberg; Statistik von Baden-Württemberg* (series); *Statistisch-prognostischer Bericht* (latest issue 1986–87); *Statistisches Taschenbuch* (latest issue 1986–87).

State Library: Württembergische Landesbibliothek, Konrad-Adenauer-Str. 8, 7000 Stuttgart 1. *Director:* Dr Hans-Peter Geh. Badische Landesbibliothek Karlsruhe, Lamm-Str. 16, 7500 Karlsruhe 1. *Director:* Dr Römer.

BAVARIA
Bayern

AREA AND POPULATION. Bavaria has an area of 70,553 sq. km. The capital is Munich. There are 7 areas, 96 urban and rural districts and 2,051 communes. The population (31 Dec. 1986) numbered 11,026,490 (5,290,422 males, 5,736,068 females).

Vital statistics for calendar years:

	Live births	Marriages	Divorces	Deaths
1984	111,183	66,005	18,877	122,057
1985	111,365	66,012	19,252	121,941
1986	118,439	67,061	18,352	120,489

CONSTITUTION. The Constituent Assembly, elected on 30 June 1946, passed a constitution on the lines of the democratic constitution of 1919, but with greater emphasis on state rights; this was agreed upon by the Christian Social Union and the Social Democrats.

The elections for the Diet, held on 12 Oct. 1986, had the following results: 128 Christian Social Union, 61 Social Democrats, 15 Green Party. The cabinet of the Christian Social Union is headed by Minister President Dr Franz Josef Strauss (CSU).

AGRICULTURE. Area and yield of the most important products:

	Area (1,000 hectares)			Yield (1,000 tonnes)		
	1985	1986	1987[1]	1985	1986	1987[1]
Wheat	487·6	493·1	501·0	2,984·2	2,829·1	2,685·6
Rye	60·1	56·4	52·5	260·5	219·1	189·4
Barley	530·8	521·5	496·3	2,642·2	2,193·4	2,012·5
Oats	129·8	121·2	115·3	639·8	558·5	473·9
Potatoes	80·9	72·4	68·4	2,732·9	2,426·1	1,730·4
Sugar-beet	83·8	79·1	76·9	4,845·7	4,544·4	...

[1] Preliminary figures.

Livestock (3 Dec. 1986): 5,130,500 cattle (including 1,999,500 milch cows); 62,600 horses; 334,400 sheep; 4,220,300 pigs; 11,888,400 poultry.

INDUSTRY. In 1986, 9,423 establishments (with 20 or more employees) employed 1,344,953 persons; of these, 248,567 were employed in electrical engineering; 183,232 in mechanical engineering; 122,985 in clothing and textile industries.

LABOUR. The economically active persons totalled 5,333,700 at the 1% sample survey of the microcensus of April 1986. Of the total, 530,300 were self-employed, 283,000 unpaid family workers, 4,520,400 employees; 2,284,700 in power supply, mining, manufacturing and building; 856,400 in commerce and transport; 1,768,200 in other industries and services.

ROADS. There were, on 1 Jan. 1987, 40,821 km of 'classified' roads, including 1,925 km of autobahn, 7,113 km of federal roads, 13,781 km of first-class and 18,002 km of second-class highways. Number of motor vehicles, at 1 July 1987, was 6,315,305, including 5,113,450 passenger cars, 235,170 lorries, 13,018 buses, 577,367 tractors, 309,098 motor cycles.

JUSTICE. There are a constitutional court *(Verfassungsgerichtshof)*, a supreme Land court *(Oberstes Landesgericht)*, 3 courts of appeal, 21 regional courts, 72 local courts, 2 Land labour courts, 11 labour courts, a Land social court, 7 social courts, 2 finance courts, a higher administrative court *(Verwaltungsgerichtshof)*, 6 administrative courts.

RELIGION. At the census of 27 May 1970 there were 69·9% Roman Catholics and 25·7% Protestants.

EDUCATION. In 1986–87 there were 2,810 primary schools with 42,752 teachers and 718,317 pupils; 384 special schools with 5,139 teachers and 38,324 pupils; 335 intermediate schools with 8,684 teachers and 135,729 pupils; 396 high schools with 19,887 teachers and 278,614 pupils; 264 part-time vocational schools with 7,901 teachers and 366,206 pupils, including 54 special part-time vocational schools with 531 teachers and 7,913 pupils; 563 full-time vocational schools with 3,755 teachers and 54,722 pupils including 225 schools for public health occupations with 888 teachers and 13,869 pupils; 283 advanced full-time vocational schools with 2,095 teachers and 25,640 pupils; 82 vocational high schools *(Berufsoberschulen, Fachoberschulen)* with 1,745 teachers and 25,640 pupils.

In the winter term 1986–87 there were 11 universities with 162,708 students (Augsburg, 8,104; Bamberg, 4,911; Bayreuth, 5,309; Eichstätt, 2,115; Erlangen-Nürnberg, 24,619; München, 60,185; Passau, 4,566; Regensburg, 11,554; Würzburg, 16,708; the Technical University of München, 22,049; München University of the Federal Armed Forces (Universität der Bundeswehr), 2,588); 1 *Gesamthochschule* with 309 students, the college of philosophy, München, 345 and a philosophical-theological college in Benediktbeuern with 119 students. There were also 2 colleges of music, 2 colleges of fine arts and 1 college of television and film, with together 2,450 students; 13 vocational colleges *(Fachhochschulen)* with 51,847 students including one for the civil service *(Bayerische Beamtenfachhochschule)* with 3,867 students.

Statistical Information: Bayerisches Landesamt für Statistik und Datenverarbeitung, 51 Neuhauser Str. 8000 Munich, was founded in 1833. *President:* Dr Hans Helmut Schiedermaier. It publishes: *Statistisches Jahrbuch für Bayern.* 1894 ff.—*Bayern in Zahlen.* Monthly (from Jan. 1947).—*Zeitschrift des Bayerischen Statistischen Landesamts.* July 1869–1943; 1948 ff.—*Beiträge zur Statistik Bayerns.* 1850 ff.—*Statistische Berichte.* 1951 ff.—*Schaubilderhefte.* 1951 ff.—*Kreisdaten.* 1972 ff.—*Gemeindedaten.* 1973 ff.

Nawiasky, H., and Luesser, C., *Die Verfassung des Freistaates Bayern vom 2. Dez. 1946.* Munich, 1948; supplement, by H. Nawiasky and H. Lechner, Munich, 1953

State Library: Bayerische Staatsbibliothek, Munich 22. *Director:* Dr Franz G. Kaltwasser.

BERLIN

GOVERNMENT. Greater Berlin was under quadripartite Allied government (Kommandatura) until 1 July 1948, when the Soviet element withdrew. On 30 Nov. 1948, a separate Municipal Government was set up in the Soviet Sector (*see* p. 522).

AREA. The total area of Berlin is 883 sq. km, of which Western Berlin covers 480 sq. km and the Soviet Sector 403 sq. km. The *British Sector* includes the administrative districts of Tiergarten, Charlottenburg, Wilmersdorf and Spandau; the *American Sector* those of Kreuzberg, Neukölln, Tempelhof, Schöneberg, Zehlendorf and Steglitz; the *French Sector* covers the administrative districts of Wedding and Reinickendorf, and the *Soviet Sector*, those of Mitte, Friedrichshain, Prenzlauer Berg, Pankow, Weissensee, Lichtenberg, Treptow and Köpenick. The British, American and French sectors form an administrative unit, called Berlin (West).

In 1961 the East German Government tried to stop the outflow by erecting a heavily fortified barrier, the 'Berlin Wall', along the border. A minefield which accompanied it was removed in 1985.

BERLIN (WEST)

POPULATION. Population, 31 Dec. 1986, 1,879,225 (872,057 males, 1,007,168 females). According to the census of 27 May 1970, 70·2% were Protestants and 12·5% Roman Catholics.

Vital statistics for calendar years:

	Live births	Marriages	Divorces	Deaths
1984	17,799	12,239	6,471	32,411
1985	17,921	12,277	6,597	32,614
1986	18,688	11,941	6,060	31,727

CONSTITUTION AND GOVERNMENT. According to the constitution of 1 Sept. 1950, Berlin is simultaneously a Land of the Federal Republic (though not yet formally incorporated) and a city. It is governed by a House of Representatives (at least 200 members); the executive power is vested in a Senate, consisting of the Governing Mayor, the Mayor and not more than 16 senators.

In the municipal elections, held on 10 March 1985, the Christian Democrats obtained 69 seats; the Social Democrats, 48; the Alternative List, 15; the Free Democrats, 12.

Governing Mayor: Eberhard Diepgen (Christian Democrat).

ECONOMY

Currency. The legal tender of Berlin (West) is the German Mark (DM).

Banking. On 20 March 1949 when the DM (West) became the only legal tender of the Western Sectors, the Zentralbank of Berlin was established. Its functions were similar to those of the Zentralbanks of the Länder of the Federal Republic. The Berlin Central Bank was merged with the Bank deutscher Länder as from 1 Aug. 1957, when the latter became the Deutsche Bundesbank. The legal tender for the Western Sectors of Berlin is being issued by the Deutsche Bundesbank (formerly Bank deutscher Länder).

AGRICULTURE. Agricultural area (April 1987), 1,320 hectares, including 860 hectares arable land and 96 hectares gardens, orchards, nurseries.

Livestock (Dec. 1986): Cattle, 641; pigs, 3,122; horses, 3,517; sheep, 1,126.

INDUSTRY. In 1986 (monthly averages), 983 establishments (with 20 or more employees) employed 164,367 persons; of these, 58,519 were employed in electrical engineering, 15,949 in machine construction, 12,296 in the manufacture of chemicals, 3,831 in steel construction and 3,495 in textiles.

LABOUR. The economically active persons totalled 849,300 at the 1%-sample survey of the microcensus of June 1985. Of the total, 69,800 were self-employed including unpaid family workers, 779,500 employees; 7,800 were engaged in agriculture and forestry; 259,400 in power supply, manufacturing and building; 159,700 in commerce and transport; 422,400 in other industries and services.

ROADS. There were, on 1 Jan. 1986, 140 km of 'classified' roads, including 42 km of autobahn and 98 km of federal roads. On 1 July 1985, 753,994 motor vehicles were registered, including 596,291 passenger cars, 40,204 lorries (1986), 37,846 motor cycles, and (1986) 2,285 buses.

JUSTICE. There are a court of appeal *(Kammergericht)*, a regional court, 7 local courts, a Land Labour court, a labour court, a Land social court, a social court, a higher administrative court, an administrative court and a finance court.

EDUCATION. In 1986–87 (preliminary figures) there were 446 schools providing general education (excluding special schools) with 181,256 pupils; 58 special schools with 7,087 pupils. There were a further 176 vocational schools with 61,197 pupils.

In the winter term 1986–87 there was 1 university (54,213 students); 1 technical university (27,217); 1 theological (evangelical) college (570); 1 college of fine arts with 4,441 students; 1 vocational college (for economics) (1,532); 2 colleges for social work (1,222); 1 technical college (4,788), 1 college of the Federal postal administration (548) and 2 colleges for public administration (2,560).

Statistical Information: The Statistisches Landesamt Berlin was founded in 1862 (Fehrbelliner Platz 1, 1000 Berlin 31). *Director:* Günther Appel. It publishes: *Statistisches Jahrbuch* (from 1867): *Berliner Statistik* (monthly, from 1947).—*100 Jahre Berliner Statistik* (1962).

Childs, D. and Johnson, J., *West Berlin: Politics and Society.* London, 1981
Hillenbrand, M. J., *The Future of Berlin.* Monclair, 1981

State Library: Amerika-Gedenkbibliothek-Berliner Zentralbibliothek-, Blücherplatz 1, D1000 Berlin 61. *Director:* Dr Peter K. Liebenow.

BREMEN
Freie Hansestadt Bremen

AREA AND POPULATION. The area of the Land, consisting of the towns and ports of Bremen and Bremerhaven, is 404 sq. km. Population, 31 Dec. 1986, 654,170 (306,831 males, 347,339 females).

Vital statistics for calendar years:

	Live births	Marriages	Divorces	Deaths
1984	5,240	3,632	2,006	8,493
1985	5,294	3,804	1,999	8,545
1986	5,745	3,904	1,680	8,707

CONSTITUTION. Political power is vested in the House of Burgesses *(Bürgerschaft)* which appoints the executive, called the Senate.

The elections of 13 Sept. 1987 had the following result: 54 Social Democratic Party, 25 Christian Democrats, 10 Free Democratic Party, 10 Die Grünen, 1 Deutsche Volksunion. The Senate is only formed by Social Democrats; its president is Klaus Wedemeier (Social Democrat).

AGRICULTURE. Agricultural area comprised (1983), 10,510 hectares: yield of grain crops (1986), 8,378 tonnes; potatoes, 295 tonnes.

Livestock (3 Dec. 1986): 16,816 cattle (including 5,120 milch cows); 4,351 pigs; 459 sheep; 1,031 horses; 22,456 poultry.

INDUSTRY. In 1986, 345 establishments (20 and more employees) employed 75,965 persons; of these, 8,937 were employed in shipbuilding (except naval engineering); 7,109 in machine construction; 9,891 in electrical engineering; 1,843 in coffee and tea processing.

LABOUR. The economically active persons totalled 255,400 at the 1%-sample survey of the microcensus of June 1985. Of the total, 19,000 were self-employed, 235,300 employees; 85,100 in power supply, mining, manufacturing and building, 64,700 in commerce and transport, 104,100 in other industries and services.

ROADS. On 1 Jan. 1987 there were 127 km of 'classified' roads, including 45·4 km of autobahn, 81·6 km of federal roads, 7 km of first-class and 5 km of second-class highways. Registered motor vehicles on 1 July 1986 numbered 289,757, including 259,346 passenger cars, 13,792 trucks, 2,402 tractors, 628 buses and 10,051 motor cycles.

SHIPPING. Vessels entered in 1986, 9,882 of 43,455,176 net tons; cleared, 9,859 of 43,608,757 net tons. Sea traffic, 1986, incoming 17,670,589 tonnes; outgoing, 11,822,101 tonnes.

JUSTICE. There are a constitutional court *(Staatsgerichtshof)*, a court of appeal, a regional court, 3 local courts, a Land labour court, 2 labour courts, a Land social court, a social court, a finance court, a higher administrative court, an administrative court.

RELIGION. On 27 May 1970 (census) there were 82·4% Protestants and 10·2% Roman Catholics.

EDUCATION. In 1986 there were 313 new system schools with 5,454 teachers and 67,150 pupils; 27 special schools with 588 teachers and 3,237 pupils; 21 part-time vocational schools with 30,804 pupils; 34 full-time vocational schools with 6,945 pupils; 7 advanced vocational schools (including institutions for the training of technicians) with 812 pupils; 11 schools for public health occupations with 1,010 pupils.

In the winter term 1986–87 about 9,321 students were enrolled at the university. In addition to the university there were 4 other colleges in 1986–87 with about 6,073 students.

Statistical Information: Statistisches Landesamt Bremen (An der Weide 14–16 (P.B. 101309), D2800 Bremen 1), founded in 1850. *Director:* Ltd Reg. Dir. Volker Hannemann. Its current publications include: *Statistische Mitteilungen Freie Hansestadt Bremen* (from 1948).—*Monatliche Zwischenberichte* (1949–53); *Statistische Monatsberichte* (from 1954).—*Statistische Berichte* (from 1956).—*Statistisches Handbuch für das Land Freie Hansestadt Bremen (1950–60,* 1961; *1960–64,* 1967; *1965–69,* 1971; *1970–74,* 1975; *1975–80,* 1982).—*Bremen im statistischen Zeitvergleich 1950–1976.* 1977.—*Bremen in Zahlen.* 1981–85, 1987.

State and University Library: Bibliotheks Str., D2800 Bremen 33. *Director:* Prof. Dr Hans-Albrecht Koch.

HAMBURG

Freie und Hansestadt Hamburg

AREA AND POPULATION. In 1938 the territory of the town was re-organized by the amalgamation of the city and its 18 rural districts with 3 urban and 27 rural districts ceded by Prussia. Total area, 754·7 sq. km (1986), including the islands Neuwerk and Scharhörn (7 sq. km). Population (31 Dec. 1986), 1,571,267 (735,790 males, 835,477 females).

Vital statistics for calendar years:

	Live births	Marriages	Divorces	Deaths
1984	12,407	8,885	5,213	22,021
1985	12,711	8,768	4,916	22,266
1986	13,404	9,180	4,556	21,973

CONSTITUTION. The constitution of 6 June 1952 vests the supreme power in the House of Burgesses *(Bürgerschaft)* of 120 members. The executive is in the hands of the Senate, whose members are elected by the Bürgerschaft.

The elections of 17 May. 1987 had the following results: Social Democrats, 55; Christian Democrats, 49; Green Alternatives, 8; Free Democrats, 8. The First Burgomaster is Dr Klaus von Dohnanyi (Social Democrat).

The territory has been divided into 7 administrative districts.

AGRICULTURE. The agricultural area comprised 15,500 hectares in 1986. Yield, in tonnes, of cereals, 24,500; potatoes, 700.

Livestock (3 Dec. 1986): Cattle, 12,263 (including 2,874 milch cows); pigs, 6,767; horses, 2,654; sheep, 2,552; poultry, 24,736.

FISHERIES. In 1986 the yield of sea and coastal fishing was 1,190 tonnes valued at DM 3m.

INDUSTRY. In June 1986, 775 establishments (with 20 and more employees) employed 135,654 persons; of these, 20,951 were employed in electrical engineering; 16,907 in machine construction; 8,393 in shipbuilding (except naval engineering); 13,392 in chemical industry.

LABOUR. The economically active persons totalled 721,600 at the 0·4%-sample survey of the microcensus of June 1983. Of the total, 57,200 were self-employed, 4,000 unpaid family workers, 660,400 employees; 4,800 were engaged in agriculture and forestry, 202,600 in power supply, mining, manufacturing and building, 196,600 in commerce and transport, 318,200 in other industries and services.

ROADS. On 31 Dec. 1985 there were 3,872 km of roads, including 78 km of autobahn, 153 km of federal roads. Number of motor vehicles (1 July 1986), 677,246, including 604,709 passenger cars, 34,197 lorries, 1,742 buses, 4,828 tractors, 22,699 motor cycles and 9,071 other motor vehicles.

SHIPPING. Hamburg is the largest port in the Federal Republic.

Vessels		1938	1958	1978	1985	1986
Entered:	Number	18,149	19,033	16,636	14,315	13,740
	Tonnage	20,567,311	27,454,640	61,785,643	58,926,086	53,033,000
Cleared:	Number	19,316	20,363	17,414	14,415	13,950
	Tonnage	20,547,148	27,579,914	62,028,141	58,978,175	53,080,000

JUSTICE. There is a constitutional court *(Verfassungsgericht)*, a court of appeal *(Oberlandesgericht)*, a regional court *(Landgericht)*, 6 local courts *(Amtsgerichte)*, a Land labour court, a labour court, a Land social court, a social court, a finance court, a higher administrative court, an administrative court.

RELIGION. On 27 May 1970 (census) Evangelical Church and Free Churches 73·6%, Roman Catholic Church 8·1%.

EDUCATION. In 1986 there were 369 schools of general education (not including *Internationale Schule*) with 7,484 teachers and 151,744 pupils; 61 special schools with 872 teachers and 6,867 pupils; 46 part-time vocational schools with 50,474 pupils; 22 schools with 1,813 pupils in their vocational preparatory year; 23 schools with 2,062 pupils in manual instruction classes; 59 full-time vocational schools with 11,734 pupils; 10 economic secondary schools with 2,592 pupils; 24 advanced vocational schools with 3,266 pupils; 38 schools for public health occupations with 2,416 pupils; 6 vocational introducing schools with 194 pupils and 21 technical superior schools with 2,411 pupils; all these vocational and technical schools have a total number of 2,951 teachers.

In the summer term 1986 there was 1 university with 41,102 students; 1 technical university with 335 students; 1 college of music and 1 college of fine arts with together 1,966 students; 1 university of the *Bundeswehr* with 1,645 students; 1 professional high school *(Fachhochschule)* with 12,699 students; 1 high school for economics and politics with 1,821 students; 1 high school of public administration with 1,044 students, as well as 1 private professional high school with 172 students.

Statistical Information: The Statistisches Landesamt der Freien und Hansestadt Hamburg (Steckelhörn 12, D2000 Hamburg 11) publishes: *Hamburg in Zahlen, Statistische Berichte, Statistisches Taschenbuch, Statistik des Hamburgischen Staates.*

Klessmann, E., *Geschichte der Stadt Hamburg.* Hamburg, 1981
Meyer-Marwitz, B., *Das Hamburg Buch.* Hamburg, 1981
Ohlig, J., *Porträt einer Weltstadt.* Hamburg, 1974
Plagemann, V., *Industriekultur in Hamburg.* Hamburg, 1984
Studt, B., and Olsen, H., *Hamburg—eine kurzgefaßte Geschichte der Stadt.* Hamburg, 1964

State Library: Staats- und Universitätsbibliothek, Carl von Ossietzky, Von-Melle-Park 3, D2000 Hamburg 13. *Director:* Prof. Dr Horst Gronemeyer.

HESSEN

AREA AND POPULATION. The state of Hessen comprehends the areas of the former Prussian provinces Kurhessen and Nassau (excluding the exclaves belonging to Hessen and the rural counties of Westerwaldkreis and Rhine-Lahn) and of the former Volkssstaat Hessen, the provinces Starkenburg (including the parts of Rheinhessen east of the river Rhine) and Oberhessen. Hessen has an area of 21,114 sq. km. Its capital is Wiesbaden. Since 1 Jan. 1981 there have been 3 areas with 5 urban and 21 rural districts and 421 communes. Population, 31 March 1987, was 5,547,912 (2,669,372 males, 2,878,540 females).

Vital statistics for calendar years:

	Live births	Marriages	Divorces	Deaths
1984	49,844	31,424	12,097	62,012
1985	49,682	31,823	11,877	63,360
1986	52,587	32,520	11,380	63,385

CONSTITUTION. The constitution was put into force by popular referendum on 1 Dec. 1946. The Diet, elected on 5 April 1987, consists of 44 Social Democrats, 47 Christian Democrats, 9 Free Democrats, 10 *Die Grünen.*

The Christian Democrat cabinet is headed by Minister President Walter Wallmann (CDU).

AGRICULTURE. Area and yield of the most important crops:

	Area (in 1,000 hectares)			Yield (in 1,000 tonnes)		
	1984	1985	1986	1984	1985	1986
Wheat	136.4	141.7	144.1	837.1	850.1	913.5
Rye	34.7	31.5	29.5	159.1	138.5	132.9
Barley	142.1	141.6	146.6	750.1	707.8	727.9
Oats	63.8	63.2	55.9	261.4	294.3	243.0
Potatoes	10.5	9.7	8.7	298.5	304.7	303.7
Sugar-beet	22.7	21.7	21.8	1,049.9	1,061.4	1,061.0

Livestock, Dec. 1986: Cattle, 828,600 (including 272,200 milch cows); horses 31,600; Dec. 1984, pigs, 1·24m.; sheep, 133,900; poultry, 3·39m.

INDUSTRY. In June 1987, 3,628 establishments (with 20 and more employees) employed 626,861 persons; of these, 95,947 were employed in chemical industry; 86,495 in electrical engineering; 91,712 in car building; 78,826 in machine construction; 30,020 in food industry.

LABOUR. The economically active persons totalled 2·48m. at the 1% sample survey of the microcensus of April 1986. Of the total, 206,000 were self-employed, 44,600 unpaid family workers, 2,233,000 employees; 68,300 were engaged in agriculture and forestry, 997,000 in power supply, mining, manufacturing and building, 499,300 in commerce and transport, 919,000 in other services.

ROADS. On 1 Jan. 1987 there were 16,644 km of 'classified' roads, including 929 km of autobahn, 3,569 km of federal highways, 7,120 km of first-class highways and 5,026 km of second-class highways. Motor vehicles licensed on 1 July 1987 totalled 3,105,165, including 2,703,144 passenger cars, 5,778 buses, 119,335 trucks, 140,815 tractors and 105,246 motor cycles.

JUSTICE. There are a constitutional court *(Staatsgerichtshof)*, a court of appeal, 9 regional courts, 58 local courts, a Land labour court, 12 labour courts, a Land social court, 7 social courts, a finance court, a higher administrative court *(Verwaltungsgerichtshof)*, 5 administrative courts.

RELIGION. In 1980 there were 51·7% Protestants and 35·3% Roman Catholics.

EDUCATION. In 1986 there were 1,248 primary schools with 14,336 teachers and 262,948 pupils (including *Förderstufen*); 234 special schools with 2,728 teachers and 18,972 pupils; 154 intermediate schools with 2,601 teachers and 45,913 pupils; 153 high schools with 8,845 teachers and 116,922 pupils; 191 *Gesamtschulen* (comprehensive schools) with 11,114 teachers and 156,652 pupils; 118 part-time vocational schools with 4,718 teachers and 176,499 pupils; 248 full-time vocational schools with 2,402 teachers and 35,492 pupils; 100 advanced vocational schools with 526 teachers and 8,302 pupils; 177 schools for public health occupations with 10,119 pupils.

In the winter term 1986–87 there were 3 universities (Frankfurt/Main, 29,373 students; Giessen, 16,592; Marburg, 14,378); 1 technical university in Darmstadt (14,257); 1 *Gesamthochschule* (9,782); 15 *Fachhochschulen* (34,865); 2 Roman Catholic theological colleges and 1 Protestant theological college with together 535 students; 1 college of music and 2 colleges of fine arts with together 1,322 students.

Statistical Information: The Hessisches Statistisches Landesamt (Rheinstr. 35–37, D6200 Wiesbaden). *President:* Götz Steppuhn. Main publications: *Statistisches Taschenbuch für das Land Hessen* (zweijährlich; 1980–81 ff.).—*Staat und Wirtschaft in Hessen* (monthly).— *Beiträge zur Statistik Hessens.—Statistische Berichte. —Hessische Gemeindestatistik 1960–61* (5 vols., 1963 ff.).—*Hessische Gemeindestatistik 1970* (5 vols., 1972 ff.).—*Hessische Gemeindestatistik* (annual, 1980 ff.).

State Library: Hessische Landesbibliothek, Rheinstr. 55–57, D6200 Wiesbaden. *Director:* Dr Helmut Schwitzgebel.

LOWER SAXONY
Niedersachsen

AREA AND POPULATION. Lower Saxony (excluding the town of Bremerhaven, and the districts on the right bank of the Elbe in the Soviet Zone) comprises 47,439 sq. km, and is divided into 4 administrative districts, 38 rural districts, 9 towns and 1,019 communes; capital, Hanover.

Estimated population, on 31 Dec. 1986, was 7,196,127 (3,458,468 males, 3,737,659 females).

Vital statistics for calendar years:

	Live births	Marriages	Divorces	Deaths
1984	66,803	40,415	14,100	83,684
1985	67,223	40,778	13,885	84,432
1986	71,226	42,740	13,198	84,071

GOVERNMENT. The Land Niedersachsen was formed on 1 Nov. 1946 by merging the former Prussian province of Hanover and the *Länder* Brunswick, Oldenburg and Schaumburg-Lippe. The Diet, elected on 15 June 1986, consists of 69 Christian Democrats, 66 Social Democrats; Free Democrats, 9 and *Die Grünen*, 11.

The cabinet of the Christian Democratic Union is headed by Minister President Dr Ernst Albrecht (CDU).

AGRICULTURE. Area and yield of the most important crops:

	Area (in 1,000 hectares)			Yield (in 1,000 tonnes)		
	1984	1985	1986	1984	1985	1986
Wheat	283	280	280	1,699	1,619	2,119
Rye	183	178	176	773	742	747
Barley	483	455	454	2,326	2,204	2,290
Oats	133	136	110	579	678	519
Potatoes	71	78	79	2,563	3,103	3,011
Sugar-beet	153	152	146	6,735	7,238	6,850

Livestock, 3 Dec. 1986: Cattle, 3,314,709 (including 1,089,765 milch cows); horses, 76,853; pigs, 7,774,344; sheep, 191,013; poultry, 35,239,391.

FISHERIES. In 1986 the yield of sea and coastal fishing was 83,314 tonnes valued at DM 61m.

INDUSTRY. In Sept. 1986, 4,215 establishments (with 20 and more employees) employed 647,216 persons; of these 59,129 were employed in machine construction; 146,926 in car building; 65,992 in electrical engineering.

LABOUR. The economically active persons totalled 2,986,500 in 1985. Of the total 268,300 were self-employed, 105,400 unpaid family workers, 2,574,600 employees; 212,700 were engaged in agriculture and forestry, 1,125,400 in power supply, mining, manufacturing and building, 551,100 in commerce and transport, 1,097,300 in other industries and services.

ROADS. At 1 Jan. 1986 there were 27,939 km of 'classified' roads, including 1,125 km of autobahn, 4,956 km of federal roads, 8,718 km of first-class and 13,140 km of second-class highways.

Number of motor vehicles, 1 Jan. 1987, was 3,722,545 including 3,141,105 passenger cars, 146,537 lorries, 8,417 buses, 245,664 tractors, 141,818 motor cycles.

JUSTICE. There are a constitutional court *(Staatsgerichtshof)*, 3 courts of appeal, 11 regional courts, 79 local courts, a Land labour court, 15 labour courts, a Land social court, 8 social courts, a finance court, a higher administrative court (together with Schleswig-Holstein), 4 administrative courts.

RELIGION. On 27 May 1970 (census) there were 74·6% Protestants and 19·6% Roman Catholics.

EDUCATION. In 1986 there were 2,245 primary schools with 23,531 teachers and 373,019 pupils; 299 special schools with 4,583 teachers and 28,617 pupils; 327 stages of orientation with 8,837 teachers and 125,966 pupils; 270 intermediate schools with 8,115 teachers and 118,688 pupils; 243 grammar schools with 13,083 teachers and 156,633 pupils; 9 evening high schools with 196 teachers and 1,661 pupils; 24 integrated comprehensive schools with 2,011 teachers and 20,902 pupils; 17 co-operative comprehensive schools with 1,614 teachers and 19,790 pupils; 139 part-time vocational schools with 225,189 pupils; 118 year of basic vocational training with 23,973 pupils; 538 full-time vocational schools with 38,008 pupils; 92 *Fachgymnasien* with 11,403 pupils; 142 *Fachoberschulen* with 8,151 pupils (full-time vocational schools leading up to vocational colleges); 36 vocational extension schools with 509 pupils; 196 advanced full-time vocational schools (including schools for technicians) with 9,439 pupils; 241 public health schools with 14,290 pupils.

In the winter term 1986–87 there were 4 universities (Göttingen, 29,138 students; Hanover, 25,177; Oldenburg, 9,467; Osnabrück, 7,957); 2 technical universities (Braunschweig, 14,970; Clausthal, 3,784); the medical college of Hanover (3,657), the veterinary college in Hanover (1,899) and the colleges of Hildesheim (1,944) and Lüneburg (1,883).

Statistical Information: The Niedersächsisches Landesverwaltungsamt—Statistik' (Geibelstr. 65, D3000 Hanover 1) fulfils the function of the 'Statistisches Landesamt für Niedersachsen'. *Head of Division:* Abteilungsdirektor Dr Günter Koop. Main publications are: *Statistisches Jahrbuch Niedersachsen* (from 1950).—*Statistische Monatshefte Niedersachsen* (from 1947).—*Statistik Niedersachsen.*

State Library: Niedersächsische Staats- und Universitätsbibliothek, Prinzenstr. 1, 3400, Göttingen. *Director:* Helmut Vogt; Niedersächsische Landesbibliothek, Waterloostr. 8, D3000 Hannover 1. *Director:* Dr Wilhelm Totok.

NORTH RHINE-WESTPHALIA
Nordrhein-Westfalen

AREA AND POPULATION. The Land comprises 34,069 sq. km. It is divided into 5 areas, 23 urban and 31 rural districts. Capital Düsseldorf. Population, 31 Dec. 1986, 16,676,501 (7,963,134 males, 8,713,367 females).

Vital statistics for calendar years:

	Live births	Marriages	Divorces	Deaths
1984	158,309	102,035	39,560	188,515
1985	159,713	101,321	38,203	191,161
1986	171,891	103,402	36,933	191,430

GOVERNMENT. The Land Nordrhein-Westfalen is governed by Social Democrats; Minister President, Johannes Rau (SPD). The Diet, elected on 12 May 1985, consists of 125 Social Democrats, 88 Christian Democrats and 14 Free Democrats.

AGRICULTURE. Area and yield of the most important crops:

	Area (in 1,000 hectares)			Yield (in 1,000 tonnes)		
	1984	1985	1986	1984	1985	1986
Wheat	223·6	235·4	236·4	1,447·1	1,464·6	1,636·3
Rye	54·6	53·4	50·9	254·1	232·6	235·1
Barley	358·9	327·4	338·7	1,995·0	1,714·0	1,871·0
Oats	81·4	85·7	71·1	363·8	395·9	333·2
Potatoes	16·9	18·3	17·6	615·6	706·6	643·3
Sugar-beet	81·2	81·6	80·5	3,791·8	4,099·3	4,019·4

Livestock, 3 Dec. 1986: Cattle, 2,015,770 (including 609,669 milch cows); pigs, 6,465,980; sheep, 176,881; horses, 80,901; poultry, 12,196,102.

INDUSTRY. In June 1986, 10,797 establishments (with 20 and more employees) employed 1,959,031 persons; of these, 159,272 were employed in mining; 280,085 in machine construction; 149,882 in iron and steel production; 194,389 in chemical industry; 181,956 in electrical engineering; 58,136 in textile industry.

Output and/or production in 1,000 tonnes, 1986: Hard coal, 69,834; lignite, 108,651; pig-iron, 18,600; raw steel ingots, 22,094; rolled steel, 14,784; castings (iron and steel castings), 1,244; cement, 9,562; fireproof products, 1,146; sulphuric acid (including production of cokeries), 1,764; staple fibres and rayon, 315; metalworking machines, 105; equipment for smelting works and rolling mills, 114; machines for mining industry, 228; cranes and hoisting machinery, 73; installation implements, 1,218,369,000 (pieces); cables and electric lines, 237; springs of all kinds, 205; chains of all kinds, 92; locks and fittings, 362; spun yarns, 209; electric power, 165,484m. kwh. Of the total population, 11·8% were engaged in industry.

LABOUR. The economically active persons totalled 6,774,800 at the 1%-sample survey of the microcensus of June 1985. Of the total, 567,500 were self-employed, 96,700 unpaid family workers, 6,110,600 employees; 170,200 were engaged in agriculture and forestry, 3,017,100 in power supply, mining, manufacturing and building, 1·21m. in commerce and transport, 2,381,700 in other industries and services.

ROADS. There were (1 Jan. 1987) 29,834 km of 'classified' roads, including 1,979 km of autobahn, 5,542 km of federal roads, 12,386 km of first-class and 9,927 km of second-class highways. Number of motor vehicles, 1 July 1987, 8,388,438, including 6,760,826 passenger cars, 680,493 lorries, 327,226 motor lorries/trucks, 16,760 buses, 210,300 tractors and 315,080 motor cycles.

JUSTICE. There are a constitutional court *(Verfassungsgerichtshof)*, 3 courts of appeal, 19 regional courts, 130 local courts, 3 Land labour courts, 30 labour courts, a Land social court, 8 social courts, 3 finance courts, a higher administrative court, 7 administrative courts.

RELIGION. On 27 May 1970 (census) there were 41·9% Protestants and 52·5% Roman Catholics.

EDUCATION. In 1986 there were 4,630 primary schools with 66,070 teachers and 1,033,133 pupils; 734 special schools with 12,464 teachers and 84,051 pupils; 552 intermediate schools with 16,261 teachers and 265,778 pupils; 107 *Gesamtschulen* (comprehensive schools) with 7,810 teachers and 76,738 pupils; 639 high schools with 38,504 teachers and 512,075 pupils; in 1986 there were 288 part-time vocational schools with 486,674 pupils; vocational preparatory year 225 with 17,199 pupils; 319 full-time vocational schools with 98,218 pupils; 25 schools offering upgrading courses to raise the general level of education and quality for vocational colleges with 439 pupils; 218 full-time vocational schools leading up to vocational colleges with 22,976 pupils; 151 advanced full-time vocational schools with 18,432 pupils; 570 schools for public health occupations with 10,268 teachers and 32,732 pupils; 24 schools within the scope of a pilot system of courses with 58,862 pupils and 2,225 teachers.

In the winter term 1986–87 there were 8 universities (Bielefeld, 12,948 students; Bochum, 30,709; Bonn, 38,591; Dortmund, 17,405; Düsseldorf, 14,772; Cologne, 46,581; Münster, 43,185; Witten, 225); the Technical University of Aachen (34,481); 4 Roman Catholic and 2 Protestant theological colleges with together 1,191 students. There were also 3 colleges of music, 1 college of fine arts and the college for physical education in Cologne with together 10,566 students; 20 *Fachhochschulen* (vocational colleges) with 91,663 students, and 6 *Gesamthochschulen* with together 78,412 students.

Statistical Information: The Landesamt für Datenverarbeitung und Statistik Nordrhein-Westfalen (Mauerstr. 51, D4000 Düsseldorf 30) was founded in 1946, by amalgamating the provincial statistical offices of Rhineland and Westphalia. *President:* A. Benker. The Landesamt publishes: *Statistisches Jahrbuch Nordrhein-Westfalen.* From 1949. More than 550 other publications yearly.

Först, Walter, *Kleine Geschichte Nordrhein-Westfalens.* Münster, 1986.

Land Library: Universitätsbibliothek, Universitätsstr. 1, D4000 Düsseldorf. *Director:* Dr G. Gattermann.

RHINELAND-PALATINATE
Rheinland-Pfalz

AREA AND POPULATION. Rhineland-Pfalz comprises 19,848 sq. km. Capital Mainz. Population (at 31 Dec. 1986), 3,611,437 (1,732,019 males, 1,879,418 females).

Vital statistics for calendar years:

	Live births	Marriages	Divorces	Deaths
1984	35,504	23,016	7,266	42,890
1985	34,899	22,971	7,215	42,587
1986	37,181	22,814	7,354	43,214

CONSTITUTION. The constitution of the Land Rheinland-Pfalz was approved by the Consultative Assembly on 25 April 1947 and by referendum on 18 May 1947, when 579,002 voted for and 514,338 against its acceptance.

The elections of 17 May 1987 returned 48 Christian Democrats, 40 Social Democrats, 7 Free Democrats, 5 Greens.

The cabinet is headed by Bernhard Vogel (Christian Democrat).

AGRICULTURE. Area and yield of the most important products:

	Area (1,000 hectares)			Yield (1,000 tonnes)		
	1984	1985	1986	1984	1985	1986
Wheat	114·2	106·9	105·7	683·0	592·4	557·8
Rye	29·2	29·1	28·1	141·5	130·8	115·3
Barley	133·8	138·4	137·3	633·2	636·4	617·8
Oats	42·9	44·9	38·4	170·6	183·4	151·2
Potatoes	11·8	12·5	12·4	351·8	379·9	381·5
Sugar-beet	22·2	23·1	22·7	1,179·4	1,176·8	1,213·0
Wine (1,000 hectolitres)	60·0	60·7	61·0	5,668·7	4,144·2	6,729·1

Livestock (3 Dec. 1986): Cattle, 604,300 (including 216,100 milch cows); horses, 19,900; sheep, 113,100; pigs, 639,300; poultry, 2,904,800.

INDUSTRY. In Sept. 1986, 2,606 establishments (with 20 and more employees) employed 371,426 persons; of these 73,772 were employed in chemical industry; 18,314 in production of leather goods and footwear; 49,718 in machine construction; 14,301 in processing stones and earthenware.

LABOUR. The economically active persons totalled 1,558,900 at the census of April 1986. Of the total, 145,500 were self-employed, 47,400 unpaid family workers, 1,366,000 employees; 89,000 were engaged in agriculture and forestry, 658,000 in power supply, mining, manufacturing and building, 250,600 in commerce and transport, 561,300 in other industries and services.

ROADS. There were (1 Jan. 1987) 18,640 km of 'classified' roads, including 766 km of autobahn, 3,218 km of federal roads, 6,978 km of first-class and 7,678 km of second-class highways. Number of motor vehicles, 1 July 1987, was 2,078,662, including 1,738,639 passenger cars, 78,676 lorries, 5,034 buses, 146,712 tractors and 90,662 motor cycles.

JUSTICE. There are a constitutional court *(Verfassungsgerichtshof)*, 2 courts of appeal, 8 regional courts, 47 local courts, a Land labour court, 5 labour courts, a Land social court, 4 social courts, a finance court, a higher administrative court, 4 administrative courts.

RELIGION. On 27 May 1970 (census) there were 40·7% Protestants and 55·7% Roman Catholics.

EDUCATION. In 1986 there were 1,187 primary schools with 14,532 teachers and 223,504 pupils; 156 special schools with 2,725 teachers and 12,606 pupils; 108 intermediate schools with 3,180 teachers and 51,132 pupils; 137 high schools with 7,021 teachers and 98,917 pupils; 97 vocational schools with 118,533 pupils; 138 advanced vocational schools and institutions for the training of technicians (full-and part-time) with 6,943 pupils; 107 schools for public health occupations with 320 teachers and 6,799 pupils.

In the winter term 1986–87 there were the University of Mainz (25,068 students), the University of Kaiserslautern (6,880 students), the University of Trier

(7,100 students), the *Hochschule für Verwaltungswissenschaften* in Speyer (409 students), the Koblenz School of Corporate Management *(Wissenschaftliche Hochschule für Unternchmensführnng in Koblenz)* with 122 students, the Roman Catholic Theological College in Trier (277 students) and the Roman Catholic College in Vallendar (70 students). There were also the Teacher-Training College of the Land Rheinland-Pfalz *(Erziehungswissenschaftliche Hochschule)* with 2,620 students, the *Fachhochschule des Landes Rheinland-Pfalz* (college of engineering) with 15,476 students and 4 *Verwaltungsfachhochschulen* with 2,100 students; also 2 private colleges for social-pedagogy (865 students).

Statistical Information: The Statistisches Landesamt Rheinland-Pfalz (Mainzer Str., 14–16, D5427 Bad Ems) was established in 1948. *President:* Dr Weis. Its publications include: *Statistisches Jahrbuch für Rheinland-Pfalz* (from 1948); *Statistische Monatshefte Rheinland-Pfalz* (from 1958); *Statistik von Rheinland-Pfalz* (from 1949) 324 vols. to date; *Rheinland-Pfalz im Spiegel der Statistik* (1968); *Die kreisfreien Städte und Landkreise in Rheinland-Pfalz* (1977); *Rheinland-Pfalz heute* (from 1973); *Benutzerhandbuch des Landesinformationssystems* (1976); *Rheinland-Pfalz heute und morgen* (Mainz, 1985); *Raumordnungsbericht 1985 der Landesregierung Rheinland-Pfalz* (Mainz, 1985). *Landesentwicklungsprogramm 1980* (Mainz, 1980).

Klöpper, R., and Korber, J., *Rheinland-Pfalz in seiner Gliederung nach zentralörtlichen Bereichen.* Remagen, 1957
Süsterhenn, A., and Schäfer, H., *Verfassung von Rheinland-Pfalz: Kommentar.* Koblenz, 1950

SAARLAND

HISTORY. In 1919 the Saar territory was placed under the control of the League of Nations. Following a plebiscite, the territory reverted to Germany in 1935. In 1945 the territory became part of the French Zone of occupation, and was in 1947 accorded an international status inside an economic union with France. In pursuance of the German–French agreement signed in Luxembourg on 27 Oct. 1956 the territory returned to Germany on 1 Jan. 1957. Its re-integration with Germany was completed by 5 July 1959.

AREA AND POPULATION. Saarland has an area of 2,568 sq. km. Estimated population, 31 Dec. 1986, 1,042,135 (495,918 males, 546,217 females). The capital is Saarbrücken.

Vital statistics for calendar years:

	Live births	Marriages	Divorces	Deaths
1984	9,696	7,095	2,644	12,387
1985	9,800	6,964	2,418	12,765
1986	10,493	7,214	2,370	12,912

CONSTITUTION. Saarland now ranks as a *Land* of the Federal German Republic and is represented in the Federal Diet by 8 members. The constitution passed on 15 Dec. 1947 is being revised.

The Saar Diet, elected on 10 March 1985, is composed as follows: 26 Social Democrats, 20 Christian Democrats, 5 Free Democrats.

Saarland is governed by Social Democrats in Parliament. Minister President: Oskar Lafontaine (Social Democrat).

AGRICULTURE AND FORESTRY. The cultivated area occupies 120,500 hectares or slightly more than half the total area; the forest area comprises nearly 33% of the total (256,804 hectares).

Area and yield of the most important crops:

	Area (1,000 hectares)			Yield (1,000 tonnes)		
	1984	1985	1986	1984	1985	1986
Wheat	7.0	6.1	6.6	36.9	32.2	30.5
Rye	5.7	6.2	6.1	25.0	25.9	23.5
Barley	10.5	10.7	10.5	47.0	47.0	42.7
Oats	6.0	6.3	5.6	24.0	27.0	20.2
Potatoes	0.5	0.5	0.4	11.2	13.7	13.3
Sugar-beet	...	...	...	0.3	0.2	...

Livestock, Dec. 1986: Cattle, 70,137 (including 23,974 milch cows); pigs, 44,964; sheep, 13,264; horses, 3,746; poultry, 302,765.

INDUSTRY. In June 1987, 583 establishments (with 20 and more employees) employed 134,430 persons; of these 23,505 were engaged in coalmining, 17,168 in iron and steel production, 12,204 in machine construction, 7,950 in steel construction. In 1986 the coalmines produced 10·4m. tonnes of coal. Four iron foundries had 5 blast furnaces working and produced 3·7m. tonnes of pig-iron and 4·1m. tonnes of crude steel.

LABOUR. The economically active persons totalled 406,300 at the 1%-sample survey of the microcensus of June 1985. Of the total, 34,300 were self-employed, 6,500 unpaid family workers, 365,500 employees; 8,100 were engaged in agriculture and forestry, 180,500 in power supply, mining, manufacturing and building, 76,400 in commerce and transport, 141,300 in other industries and services.

ROADS. At 1 Jan. 1986 there were 2,188 km of 'classified' roads, including 222 km of autobahn, 421 km of federal roads, 762 km of first-class and 783 km of second-class highways. Number of motor vehicles, 31 Dec. 1986, 542,835, including 479,661 passenger cars, 21,258 lorries, 1,408 buses, 12,946 tractors and 22,861 motor cycles.

JUSTICE. There are a constitutional court *(Verfassungsgerichtshof)*, a court of appeal, a regional court, 11 local courts, a Land labour court, 3 labour courts, a Land social court, a social court, a finance court, a higher administrative court, an administrative court.

RELIGION. On 27 May 1970 (census) 73·8% of the population were Roman Catholics and 24·1% were Protestants.

EDUCATION. In 1986–87 there were 330 primary schools with 3,870 teachers and 59,393 pupils; 51 special schools with 552 teachers and 3,348 pupils; 37 intermediate schools with 1,055 teachers and 13,516 pupils; 37 high schools with 2,004 teachers and 24,596 pupils; 8 *Gesamtschulen* (comprehensive high schools) with 225 teachers and 2,607 pupils; 2 *Freie Waldorfschulen* with 51 teachers and 651 pupils; 1 *Abendhauptschule* with 12 pupils; 4 *Abendrealschulen* with 229 pupils; 2 *Abendgymnasien* and 1 *Saarland-Kolleg* with 20 teachers and 372 pupils; 42 part-time vocational schools with 31,967 pupils; year of commercial basic training: 90 institutions with 3,673 pupils; 22 advanced full-time vocational schools and schools for technicians with 3,018 pupils; 52 full-time vocational schools with 5,716 students; 13 vocational extension schools with 630 pupils; 26 *Fachoberschulen* (full-time vocational schools leading up to vocational colleges) with 2,819 pupils; 43 schools for public health occupations with 2,373 pupils. The number of pupils visiting the vocational schools amounts to 50,196. They are instructed by 1,818 teachers.

In the winter term 1986–87 there was the University of the Saarland with 17,488 students; 1 music-conservatory with 306 students; 1 vocational college (economics, engineering and design) with 2,837 students; 1 vocational college for social affairs with 215 students; 1 vocational college for public administration with 228 students.

Statistical Information: The Statistisches Amt des Saarlandes (Hardenbergstrasse 3, D6600 Saarbrücken 1) was established on 1 April 1938. As from 1 June 1935, it was an independent agency; its predecessor, 1920–35, was the Statistical Office of the Government Commission of the Saar. *Chief:* Direktor Josef Mailänder. The most important publications are: *Statistisches Handbuch für das Saarland,* from 1950.—*Statistisches Taschenbuch für das Saarland,* from 1959.—*Saarländische Bevölkerungs-und Wirtschaftszahlen.* Quarterly, from 1949. —*Saarland in Zahlen* (special issues).—*Einzelschriften zur Statistik des Saarlandes,* from 1950—*Statistische Nachrichten,* from 1981.

Fischer, P., *Die Saar zwischen Deutschland und Frankreich.* Frankfurt, 1959
Osang, R.M., *Saarland ABC.* Saarbrücken, 1975
Schmidt, R. H., *Saarpolitik 1945–57.* 3 vols. Berlin, 1959–62

SCHLESWIG-HOLSTEIN

AREA AND POPULATION. The area of Schleswig-Holstein is 15,728 sq. km; it is divided into 4 urban and 11 rural districts and 1,131 communes. The capital is Kiel. The population (estimate, 31 Dec. 1986) numbered 2,612,672 (1,265,399 males, 1,347,273 females).

Vital statistics for calendar years:

	Live births	Marriages	Divorces	Deaths
1984	22,958	15,045	6,231	30,778
1985	23,099	15,042	5,803	31,330
1986	24,693	15,631	5,290	30,979

GOVERNMENT. The elections of 13 Sept. 1987 gave the Christian Democrats 33, the Social Democratic Party 36, the Free Democratic Party 4 and the South Schleswig Association 1 seat.

AGRICULTURE. Area and yield of the most important crops:

	Area (1,000 hectares)			Yield (1,000 tonnes)		
	1984	1985	1986	1984	1985	1986
Wheat	152·1	145·8	154·6	1,112·1	1,081·8	1,230·0
Rye	52·2	50·0	48·0	226·4	213·8	221·8
Barley	143·2	142·8	139·6	865·1	726·9	149·3
Oats	22·9	32·0	24·4	113·6	164·0	132·6
Potatoes	5·1	4·5	4·1	187·2	177·6	151·8
Sugar-beet	18·8	17·3	17·2	831·1	775·6	768·9

Livestock, 3 Dec. 1986: 33,134 horses, 1,539,913 cattle (including 514,397 milch cows), 1,718,253 pigs, 183,844 sheep, 3,213,920 poultry.

FISHERIES. In 1986 the yield of small-scale deep-sea and inshore fisheries was 54,706 tonnes valued at DM63·4m.

INDUSTRY. In 1986 (average), 1,539 establishments (with 20 and more employees) employed 166,833 persons; of these, 11,454 were employed in shipbuilding (except naval engineering); 32,040 in machine construction; 22,281 in food and kindred industry; 17,193 in electrical engineering.

LABOUR. The economically active persons totalled 1,146,400 in 1985. Of the total, 102,300 were self-employed, 24,200 unpaid family workers, 1,019,900 employees; 59,800 were engaged in agriculture and forestry, 350,600 in power supply, mining, manufacturing and building, 243,900 in commerce and transport, 492,100 in other industries and services.

ROADS. There were (1 Jan. 1987) 9,787·1 km of 'classified' roads, including 384·8 km of autobahn, 1,931·6 km of federal roads, 3,536·5 km of first-class and 3,934·2 km of second-class highways. Number of motor vehicles, 1 Jan. 1987, was 1,297,674, including 1,114,645 passenger cars, 52,972 lorries, 2,801 buses, 73,435 tractors, 38,943 motor cycles.

SHIPPING. The Kiel Canal, 98·7 km (51 miles) long, is on Schleswig-Holstein territory. In 1938, 53,530 vessels of 22·6m. net tons passed through it; in 1981, 52,641 vessels of 53·3m. net tons; in 1982, 49,100 vessels of 52·7m. net tons; in 1983, 49,320 vessels of 50·9m. net tons; in 1984, 50,920 vessels of 53m. net tons; in 1985, 48,387 vessels of 53·5m. net tons; in 1986, 46,543 vessels of 47·5m. net tons.

JUSTICE. There are a court of appeal, 4 regional courts, 30 local courts, a Land labour court, 6 labour courts, a Land social court, 4 social courts, a finance court, an administrative court.

RELIGION. On 27 May 1970 (census) there were 86·5% Protestants and 6% Roman Catholics.

EDUCATION. In 1986–87 there were 691 primary schools with 5,434 teachers and 140,688 pupils; 167 special schools with 1,454 teachers and 13,634 pupils; 175 intermediate schools with 2,801 teachers and 58,563 pupils; 99 high schools with 4,153 teachers and 71,134 pupils; 6 *Integrierte Gesamtschulen* (comprehensive schools) with 260 teachers and 4,412 pupils; 42 part-time vocational schools with 1,563 teachers and 92,870 pupils; 142 full-time vocational schools with 469 teachers and 11,603 pupils; 56 advanced vocational schools with 278 teachers and 5,242 pupils; 59 schools for public health occupations with 4,219 pupils; 50 vocational grammar schools with 354 teachers and 6,081 pupils; 6 *Fachhochschulen* (vocational colleges) with 10,860 pupils in the summer term 1987.

In the summer term 1987 the University of Kiel had 16,422 students, 2 teacher-training colleges had 1,827 students, 1 music college had 320 students, 1 *Medizinische* University in Lübeck had 1,047 students and 1 *Nordische* University in Fiensburg had 31 students.

Statistical Information: Statistisches Landesamt Schleswig-Holstein (Fröbel Str. 15–17, D2300 Kiel 1). *Director:* Dr Mohr. Publications: *Statistisches Taschenbuch Schleswig-Holstein,* since 1954.—*Statistisches Jahrbuch Schleswig-Holstein,* since 1951.—*Statistische Monatshefte Schleswig-Holstein,* since 1949.—*Statistische Berichte,* since 1947.—*Beitrage zur historischen Statistik Schleswig-Holstein,* since 1967.—*Lange Reihen,* since 1977.

Baxter, R. R., *The Law of International Waterways.* Harvard Univ. Press, 1964
Brandt, O., *Grundriss der Geschichte Schleswig-Holsteins.* 5th ed. Kiel, 1957
Handbuch für Schleswig-Holstein. 22nd ed. Kiel, 1984

State Library: Schleswig-Holsteinische Landesbibliothek, Kiel, Schloss. *Director:* Prof. Dr Dieter Lohmeier.

GHANA

Capital: Accra
Population: 12·21m. (1984)
GNP per capita: US$390 (1986)

HISTORY. The State of Ghana came into existence on 6 March 1957 when the former Colony of the Gold Coast and the Trusteeship Territory of Togoland attained Dominion status. The name of the country recalls a powerful monarchy which from the 4th to the 13th century A.D. ruled the region of the middle Niger.

The Ghana Independence Act received the royal assent on 7 Feb. 1957. The General Assembly of the United Nations in Dec. 1956 approved the termination of British administration in Togoland and the union of Togoland with the Gold Coast on the latter's attainment of independence.

The country was declared a Republic within the Commonwealth on 1 July 1960 with Dr Kwame Nkrumah as the first President. On 24 Feb. 1966 the Nkrumah regime was overthrown in a military *coup* and ruled by the National Liberation Council until 1 Oct. 1969 when the military regime handed over power to a civilian regime under a new constitution. Dr K. A. Busia was the Prime Minister of the Second Republic. On 13 Jan. 1972 the armed forces and police took over power again from the civilian regime in a *coup*.

In Oct. 1975 the National Redemption Council was subordinated to a Supreme Military Council (SMC). In 1979 the SMC was toppled in a *coup* led by Flight-Lieut. J. J. Rawlings. The new government permitted elections already scheduled and these resulted in a victory for Dr Hilla Limann and his People's National Party. However on 31 Dec. 1981 another *coup* led by Flight-Lieut. Rawlings dismissed the government and Parliament, suspended the Constitution and established a Provisional National Defence Council to exercise all government powers.

AREA AND POPULATION. Ghana is bounded west by the Côte d'Ivoire, north by Burkina Faso, east by Togo and south by the Gulf of Guinea. The area of Ghana is 92,010 sq. miles (238,305 sq. km); census population 1984, 12,205,574.

Ghana is divided into 10 regions:

Regions	Area (sq. km)	Population census 1984	Capital	Population census 1970
Eastern	19,977	1,679,483	Koforidua	69,804
Western	23,921	1,116,930	Sekondi-Takoradi	254,543
Central	9,826	1,145,520	Cape Coast	71,594
Ashanti	24,390	2,089,683	Kumasi	348,880 [1]
Brong-Ahafo	39,557	1,179,409	Sunyani	61,772
Northern	70,383	1,162,645	Tamale	136,828 [1]
Volta	20,572	1,201,095	Ho	46,348
Upper East	8,842	771,584	Bolgatanga	18,896
Upper West	18,477	439,161	Wa	...
Greater Accra	2,593	1,420,066	Accra	964,879 [1]

[1] Census 1984.

The capital is Accra, other chief towns (population, census, 1970); Asamankese, 101,144; Tema, 99,608 (1984); Nsawam, 57,350; Tarkwa, 50,570; Oda, 40,740; Obuasi, 40,001; Winneba, 36,104; Keta, 27,461; Agona Swedru, 23,843.

Estimated birth rate, between 47 and 52 per 1,000; death rate, about 23 per 1,000.

In the south and centre of Ghana, the people are of the Kwa ethno-linguistic group, mainly Akan (Ashanti, Fante, etc.), Ewe (in the Volta region) and Ga, while the 20% living in the north belong to Gur peoples (Dagbane, Gurma and Grusi).

CLIMATE. The climate ranges from the equatorial type on the coast to savannah in the north and is typified by the existence of well-marked dry and wet seasons.

Temperatures are relatively high throughout the year. The amount, duration and seasonal distribution of rain is very marked, from the south, with over 80″ (2,000 mm) to the north, with under 50″ (1,250 mm). In the extreme north, the wet season is from March to Aug., but further south it lasts until Oct. Near Kumasi, two wet seasons occur, in May and June and again in Oct. and this is repeated, with greater amounts, along the coast of Ghana. Accra. Jan. 80°F (26·7°C), July 77°F (25°C). Annual rainfall 29″ (724 mm). Kumasi. Jan. 77°F (25°C), July 76°F (24·4°C). Annual rainfall 58″ (1,402 mm). Sekondi-Takoradi. Jan. 79°F (25°C), July 76°F (24·4°C). Annual rainfall 47″ (1,181 mm). Tamale. Jan. 82°F (27·8°C), July 78°F (25·6°C). Annual rainfall 41″ (1,026 mm).

CONSTITUTION AND GOVERNMENT. Since the *coup* of 31 Dec. 1982, supreme power is vested in the Provisional National Defence Council, which in Dec. 1987 consisted of: Flight-Lieut. Jerry John Rawlings (Chairman), Aanaa Enin, Ebo Tawiah, D. F. Annan, Mahama Iddrisu, Capt. Kojo Tsikata, P. V. Obeng, Maj.-Gen. Mensah-Wood and Lieut.-Gen. A. Quianoo. Ministerial responsibilities are exercised by Secretaries appointed by the PNDC, comprising in Dec. 1987:

Chairman of Committee of Secretaries: P. V. Obeng.
Finance and Economic Planning: Dr Kwesi Botchwey. *Foreign Affairs:* Dr Obed Asamoah. *Fuel and Power:* Ato Ahwoi. *Mobilization and Productivity:* George Adamu. *Justice and Attorney-General:* G. E. K. Aikins. *Lands and Natural Resources:* Kwame Peprah. *Local Government and Rural Development:* W. H. Yeboah. *Youth and Sports:* Ato Austin. *Roads and Highways:* Mensah Gbedemah. *Education and Culture:* Dr Mohammed Ben Abdallah. *Acting Interior:* Nii Okaijah Adamafio. *Works and Housing:* E. Appiah-Korang. *Health:* F. W. K. Klutse. *Information:* Kofi Totobi Quakyi. *Transport and Communications:* Yaw Donkor. *Trade and Tourism:* Kofi Djin. *Industries, Science and Technology:* Dr Francis Acquah. *Agriculture:* Cmdre Steve Obimpeh. *Chief of Staff, PNDC:* Lieut.-Col. E. K. T. Donkoh. *Political Counsellor for the Economic Development of CDRs:* Lieut.-Col. J. Y. Assassie. There are 7 Secretaries of various Committees.

National flag: Red, gold, green (horizontal); a black star in the centre.
National anthem: Hail the name of Ghana.

Local government: The 10 Regions, each under a Regional Secretary appointed by the PNDC, are divided into 105 districts.

DEFENCE.

Army. The Ghana Army consists of 6 infantry battalions, 1 reconnaissance battalion, 1 field engineer battalion, 3 border battalions, 1 parachute battalion, 1 signal battalion, 1 mortar battalion, 5 with armoured cars and ancillary units. Total strength, (1988) 9,000. There is also a people's militia and Committees for the Defence of the Revolution.

Navy. The Ghana Navy was formed in 1959. It comprises 2 British-built 500-ton corvettes, 4 fast attack craft, 2 patrol craft, 2 coastal patrol boats and 2 service craft. Naval personnel in 1988 numbered 1,200 officers and ratings.

Air Force. The Ghana Air Force was formed in 1959, when an Air Force Training School was established at Accra. Its first combat unit has 4 Italian-built Aermacchi M.B.326K light ground attack jets ordered in 1976. It has, for training, transport, search and rescue, and air survey operations, 5 Fokker Friendship twin-turboprop transports, and a twin-turbofan Fokker Fellowship for Presidential use, all built in the Netherlands, 8 Islander piston-engined light transports, 6 Shorts Skyvan twin-turboprop STOL transports, and 10 Bulldog primary trainers, all built in the UK; 2 Bell 212 helicopters built in the US; 4 French-built Alouette III helicopters, and 5 Aermacchi M.B.326F and 2 M.B.339 jet trainers. There are air bases at Takoradi and Tamale. Personnel strength (1988) about 800.

INTERNATIONAL RELATIONS

Membership. Ghana is a member of UN, the Commonwealth, OAU, ECOWAS and is an ACP state of EEC.

ECONOMY

Planning. The Development Plan, 1983–86, aimed at the reform of prices and the restoration of production incentives, arresting a runaway inflation, reducing budget deficits, rehabilitating the rundown productive infrastructure and exchange resources.

Budget. In 1987 budget provided for revenue estimated at ₵ 109,711m. and expenditure estimated at ₵ 109,407m.

Currency. The monetary unit is the *cedi* (₵), divided into 100 *pesewas* (P). Notes are issued of 1, 2, 5, 10, 50, 200 and 500 ₵; cupro-nickel coins of 2½, 5, 10 and 20 P and 1₵. In March 1988, £1 = ₵ 324·64; US$1 = ₵ 183.

Banking. The Bank of Ghana was established in Feb. 1957 as the central bank of the country. The Ghana Commercial Bank, also established in Feb. 1957, is a purely commercial institution with agricultural financing as one of its priorities. It had 150 full branches in Sept. 1987, 1 in London and 1 subsidiary in Lomé (Togo). Barclays Bank of Ghana Ltd has 39 branches and agencies and the Standard Bank (Ghana) Ltd has 38 branches.

The National Investment Bank, established in 1963, is an autonomous joint state-private development finance institution. The former post office savings bank has been transformed into the National Savings and Credit Bank. The Bank for Housing and Construction opened in 1973; The Merchant Bank (Ghana) Ltd in 1972; The Ghana Co-operative Bank was established and re-organized in 1974; The Agricultural Development Bank in 1967; The Consolidated Discount House Ltd in Nov. 1987.

ENERGY AND NATURAL RESOURCES

Electricity. Production (1986) 4,372m. kwh, mainly from the Volta Dam at Akosombo, which has a capacity of 1,072 mw. Supply 240 volts; 50 Hz.

Oil. The Government announced in Jan. 1978 that oil had been found in commercial quantities with known reserves (1980) 7m. bbls and in Oct. 1983 formed the Ghanaian National Petroleum Corporation with exploration rights in all areas not covered by existing agreements.

Minerals. In 1986 gold production was 8,950 kg; diamonds, 559,200 carats; manganese, 259,300 tonnes; bauxite, 204,000 tons.

Agriculture. In southern and central Ghana main food crops are maize, rice, cassava, plantain, groundnuts, yam and cocoyam, and in northern Ghana groundnuts, rice, maize, sorghum, millet and yams.

Production of main food crops (1986 in 1,000 tonnes) was: Maize, 471; rice, 95; millet, 130; sorghum, 210; cassava, 3,692; cocoyam (1985), 581; yam, 937; plantain, 677.

Cocoa is by far Ghana's main cash crop. Production (1985–86) 216,000 tonnes. Output has fallen considerably since the 1970s, and Ghana has lost its long-held position as the world's leading producer to the Côte d'Ivoire. While there is smuggling to that country, Ghana's low cocoa production was due to ageing trees and declining interest in cocoa growing because of poor prices. Since 1982 the PNDC has carried out a rehabilitation programme for cocoa as well as increased producer prices for farmers, which has halted the decline and raised production considerably.

Among other cash crops, tobacco and coffee are important, and improved types of palm oil and coconuts are being planted on an increased scale; progress has been made with clonal rubber in the south-west; pepper, ginger, pineapple, avocado, citrus and other crops are being grown for export, and efforts are being made to increase local supplies of cotton, kenaf, tobacco, palm oil, mango, pineapple and sugar-cane for local industries.

Livestock, 1986: Cattle, 1,188,000; sheep, 2,175,000; goats, 2·4m.; horses, 4,000; pigs, 586,000; poultry, 10m.

Forestry. Forests form 12% of the total land area. Production (1985): Logs, 580,000 cu. metres; lumber, 200,000 cu. metres.

Fisheries. Catch (1986) 269,154 tonnes (43,000 from inland waters).

INDUSTRY AND TRADE

Industry. The aluminium smelter at Tema is the centre of industrial development, mainly concentrated on Accra/Tema, Kumasi and Takoradi/Sekondi. In 1984 the Volta Aluminium Company (VALCO), which operates the smelter, reached an agreement with the government on the use of Volta dam electricity. Production (1986) 120,000 tonnes.

Commerce. In 1984 exports were US$566m.; imports, US$533m. In 1983, USA took 16% of exports; UK, 11%; Japan, 10% and Federal Republic of Germany, 9%. Imports came from Nigeria, 21%; UK, 18%; USA, 17% and Federal Republic of Germany 7%. Principal exports: cocoa, timber and gold; imports were raw materials, capital equipment, petroleum and food.

Total trade between Ghana and UK (British Department of Trade returns, in £1,000 sterling):

	1983	1984	1985	1986	1987
Imports to UK	58,192	61,561	99,410	103,480	113,859
Exports and re-exports from UK	82,234	82,897	116,883	113,218	138,081

Tourism. In 1986 there were 92,550 tourists.

COMMUNICATIONS

Roads. The total mileage of roads maintained by the Public Works Department in 1986 was 14,000 and there were also about 18,000 km of feeder roads. The number of vehicles in use (1986) was 54,196, of which private cars, 26,590.

Railways. Total length of railways open in 1985 was 953 km of 1,067 mm gauge. In 1985 railways carried 510,000 tonnes and 2·1m. passengers.

Aviation. There is an international airport at Kotoka (Accra), domestic airports at Takoradi, Kumasi, Tamale and Sunyani and airstrips at Wa, Navrongo and Ho. Services are operated by Ghana Airways, Nigeria Airways, Swissair, KLM, British Caledonian, Swiss Air, Egypt Air, Air India, Aeroflot, Air Afrique and Bulgarian Airlines. Total aircraft freight in 1986 was 8,661,971 tonnes.

Shipping. The chief ports are Takoradi and Tema. In 1983, 1,299,146 tonnes of cargo were imported and 1,682,519 tonnes were exported by 663 ships.

Post and Broadcasting. There were 444 telephone exchanges and 766 call offices with (1986) 72,000 telephones in use. There are internal wireless stations at Accra, Kumasi, Bawku, Lawra, Kete-Krachi, Tamale, Yendi, Kpandu, Tumu and Sekondi-Takoradi. In 1985 there were over 2m. radio and 140,000 television receivers.

Cinemas. In 1987 there were 83 cinemas with an average seating capacity of 1,200.

Newspapers. There were (1987) 3 daily and 48 weekly and monthly newspapers.

JUSTICE, RELIGION, EDUCATION AND WELFARE

Justice. In June 1983 the legal system was being re-organized. The Courts were constituted as follows:

Supreme Court. The Supreme Court consists of the Chief Justice who is also the President and not less than 4 other Justices of the Supreme Court. The Supreme Court is the final court of appeal in Ghana. The final interpretation of the provisions of the constitution has been entrusted to the Supreme Court.

Court of Appeal. The Court of Appeal consists of the Chief Justice together with not less than 5 other Justices of the Appeal court and such other Justices of Superior Courts as the Chief Justice may nominate. The Court of Appeal is duly constituted by 3 Justices. The Court of Appeal is bound by its own previous decisions and all courts inferior to the Court of Appeal are bound to follow the decisions of the Court of Appeal on questions of law. Divisions of the Appeal Court may be created, subject to the discretion of the Chief Justice.

High Court of Justice. The Court has jurisdiction in civil and criminal matters as well as those relating to industrial and labour disputes including administrative complaints. The High Court of Justice has supervisory jurisdiction over all inferior Courts and any adjudicating authority and in exercise of its supervisory jurisdiction has power to issue such directions, orders or writs including writs or orders in the nature of habeas corpus, certiorari, mandamus, prohibition and quo qarrantto. The High Court of Justice has no jurisdiction in cases of treason. The High Court consists of the Chief Justice and not less than twelve other judges and such other Justices of the Superior Court as the Chief Justice may appoint.

The PNDC has established Public Tribunals in addition to the traditional courts of justice.

There is a Public Tribunal Board consisting of not less than 5 members and not more than 15 members of the public appointed by the PNDC, at least one of whom shall be a lawyer of not less than 5 years' standing as a lawyer. The Board is responsible for the administration of all tribunals.

A tribunal consists of at least three persons and not more than five persons, selected by the Board from among persons appointed by the Council as members of public tribunals.

Religion. Christians represent 52% of the population (Protestant, 37%; Roman Catholic, 15%), Moslem, 13%, others, 30%.

Education. In 1985–86 there were 2,399 kindergartens for the age-groups 4–6 years with 171,182 pupils. Primary schools are free and attendance is compulsory. In 1985–86 there were 9,004 primary schools with 1,491,162 pupils. In 1986 there were 5,310 middle schools with 617,613 pupils; 110 junior secondary schools with 18,372 pupils and 233 secondary schools with 133,435 students. In 1986 there were 45 training colleges with 15,210 students and 26 vocational-technical schools with 19,547 students at the beginning of the academic year. In 1985–86 there were 3,265 students at the 3 universities (University of Ghana, the University of Science and Technology at Kumasi, and the University of the Cape Coast). University education is free.

Health. Medical facilities include 46 government hospitals, 252 health centres and posts, 3 university hospitals, 3 mental hospitals, 5 leprosaria, 8 military hospitals, 1 police hospital, 35 mission hospitals, 34 mission clinics and 40 private hospitals. In addition, there are 26 nurses and midwives training schools. There were 600 doctors, 5,190 nurses and 2,830 midwives in 1986.

DIPLOMATIC REPRESENTATIVES

Of Ghana in Great Britain (13 Belgrave Sq., London, SW1X 8PR)
High Commissioner: Dr J. L. S. Abbey (accredited 15 Oct. 1986).

Of Great Britain in Ghana (Osu Link, off Gamel Abdul Nasser Ave., Accra)
High Commissioner: A. H. Wyatt, CMG.

Of Ghana in the USA (2460 16th St., NW, Washington, D.C., 20009)
Ambassador: Eric K. Otoo.

Of the USA in Ghana (Ring Rd. East, Accra)
Ambassador: Stephen Lyne.

Of Ghana to the United Nations
Ambassador: James Victor Gbeho.

Books of Reference

Digest of Statistics. Accra. Quarterly (from May 1953)
Ghana. Official Handbook. Annual
Davidson, B., *Black Star.* London, 1973
James, C. L. R., *Nkrumah and the Ghana Revolution.* London, 1977
Jones, T., *Ghana's First Republic 1960–1966.* London, 1975
Killick, T., *Development Economics in Action: A Study of Economic Policies in Ghana.* London, 1978
Ray, D. I., *Ghana: Politics, Economics and Society.* London, 1986

GIBRALTAR

Population: 29,166 (1986)
GNP per capita: US$5,420 (1983)

HISTORY. The Rock of Gibraltar was settled by Moors in 711; they named it after their chief Jebel Tariq, 'the Mountain of Tarik'. In 1462 it was taken by the Spaniards, from Granada. It was captured by Admiral Sir George Rooke on 24 July 1704, and ceded to Great Britain by the Treaty of Utrecht, 1713. The cession was confirmed by the treaties of Paris (1763) and Versailles (1783).

On 10 Sept. 1967, in pursuance of a United Nations resolution on the decolonization of Gibraltar, a referendum was held in Gibraltar in order to ascertain whether the people of Gibraltar believed that their interests lay in retaining their link with Britain or in passing under Spanish sovereignty. Out of a total electorate of 12,762, 12,138 voted to retain the British connexion, while 44 voted for Spain.

On 15 Dec. 1982 the border between Gibraltar and Spain was re-opened for Spaniards and Gibraltarian pedestrians who are residents of Gibraltar. The border had been closed by Spain in June 1969. Following an agreement signed in Brussels in Nov. 1984 the border was fully opened on 5 Feb. 1985.

AREA AND POPULATION. Area, 2½ sq. miles (6·5 sq. km). Total population, including port and harbour (census, 1981), 28,719. Estimate (31 Dec. 1986) 29,166 (of which 20,071 were British Gibraltarian, 5,502 Other British and 3,593 Non-British). The population is mostly of Genoese, Portuguese and Maltese as well as Spanish descent.

Vital statistics (1986): Births, 507; marriages, 637; deaths, 290.

CLIMATE. The climate is warm temperate, with westerly winds in winter bringing rain. Summers are pleasantly warm and rainfall is low. Frost or snow is very rare. Jan. 55°F (12·8°C), July 75°F (23·9°C). Annual rainfall 29″ (772 mm).

CONSTITUTION AND GOVERNMENT. Following a Constitutional Conference held in July 1968, a new Constitution was introduced in 1969. The Legislative and City Councils were merged to produce an enlarged legislature known as the Gibraltar House of Assembly. Executive authority is exercised by the Governor, who is also Commander-in-Chief. The Governor, while retaining certain reserved powers, is normally required to act in accordance with the advice of the Gibraltar Council, which consists of 4 *ex-officio* members (the Deputy Governor, the Deputy Fortress Commander, the Attorney-General and the Financial and Development Secretary) together with 5 elected members of the House of Assembly appointed by the Governor after consultation with the Chief Minister. Matters of primarily domestic concern are devolved to elected Ministers, with Britain responsible for other matters, including external affairs, defence and internal security. There is a Council of Ministers presided over by the Chief Minister.

The House of Assembly consists of a Speaker appointed by the Governor, 15 elected and 2 *ex-officio* members (the Attorney-General and the Financial and Development Secretary).

A Mayor of Gibraltar is elected by the elected members of the Assembly.

Governor and C.-in-C.: Air Chief Marshal Sir Peter Terry, GCB, AFC.

Chief Minister: Adolfo Canepa.

Flag: White with a red strip along the bottom, a red triple-towered castle with a gold key depending from the gateway.

DEFENCE. The Gibraltar Regiment is a part-time unit consisting of 1 infantry company, 1 battery of 105 mm light guns and an air defence troop equipped with blowpipe missiles with a small regular cadre. There is also a resident battalion from the British Army, an RAF Base and a Naval Base.

ECONOMY

Budget. Revenue and expenditure (in £ sterling):

	1984–85	1985–86	1986–87	1987–88
Revenue	60,184,807	62,930,849	75,387,665	78,343,477
Expenditure	62,854,244	70,082,715	72,868,043	82,063,600

Currency. The legal currency consists of Gibraltar government notes in denominations of £50, £20, £10, £5 and £1 and UK silver and copper-cupro-nickel coins. The amount of local currency notes in circulation at 31 March 1986 was £9,065,910.

Banking. Domestic and offshore banking services are provided by 11 banks: Barclays Bank PLC (with 3 branches), Lloyds Bank PLC, Hambros Bank Ltd, Bank of Credit and Commerce Gibraltar Ltd, United Bank of Gibraltar Ltd, Algemene Bank Gibraltar Ltd, Banque Indosuez, Lombard North Central PLC, A L Galliano Bankers Ltd, Banco de Bilbao (Gibraltar) Ltd and Banco Central SA. In addition there are 7 offshore banks: Gibraltar and Iberian Bank Ltd, Hong Kong Bank and Trust Co. Ltd, Hambros Bank Ltd, Laredo Investment Bank (Gibraltar) Ltd, Republic National Bank of New York (Gibraltar) Ltd, Gibraltar Trust Bank Ltd and Banco Hispano Americano SA. Total assets of commercial banks were £224·2m. in Sept. 1985.

INDUSTRY AND TRADE

Industry. There are a number of relatively small industrial concerns engaged in the bottling of beer and mineral waters, etc., mainly for local consumption. There is a small but important commercial ship-repair yard with 3 dry docks for vessels of up to 75,000 DWT, and a yacht repair yard.

Employment. The total insured labour force at 31 Dec. 1986, was 13,633. There were (1986) 12 registered trade unions and 9 employers associations. Approximately 50% of the local labour force is employed by the UK departments of the Gibraltar Government. In the private sector the main sources of employment are the construction industry, ship repairing, hotel and catering services, shipping services, trading agencies and retail distribution.

Commerce. Imports and exports (in £ sterling):

	1983	1984	1985	1986
Imports	61,600,000	66,098,000	113,200,000	111,700,000
Exports	24,500,000	25,072,000	48,300,000	44,300,000

Britain and the Commonwealth provide the bulk of imports, but fresh vegetables and fruit come mainly from Morocco and Spain. Foodstuffs accounted for 16% of total imports (about £18m.) in 1986. About 40% of non-fuel imports originate from the UK. Other sources include Japan, Spain and USA. Value of non-fuel imports, 1986, £82m. Exports are mainly re-exports of petroleum and petroleum products supplied to shipping. Gibraltar depends largely on tourism, offshore banking and other financial sector activity, the entrepôt trade and the provision of supplies to visiting ships. Exports of local produce are negligible.

Total trade between Gibraltar and UK (British Department of Trade returns, in £1,000 sterling):

	1985	1986	1987
Imports to UK	3,582	6,021	3,367
Exports and re-exports from UK	47,052	46,200	49,986

Tourism. The number of tourists in 1986 was 2,807,900 of which 89,842 arrived by air, 83,808 by sea and 2,634,250 by land.

COMMUNICATIONS

Roads. There are 31 miles of roads including 4·25 miles of pedestrian way.

Aviation. There are regular flights between London and Gibraltar operated by GB Airways and British Airways. GB Airways operate daily flights between Gibraltar and Tangier. Air Europe operate regular flights between London and Gibraltar and Manchester and Gibraltar.

Shipping. Gibraltar is a naval and air base of strategic importance. There is a deep Admiralty harbour of 440 acres. A total of 2,493 merchant ships, 32,662,935 GRT, entered the port during 1986, including 1,692 deep-sea ships of 32,454,137 GRT. In 1986, 5,407 calls were made by yachts, 113,088 GRT and 78 cruise liners called during 1986.

Post and Broadcasting. An automatic telephone system exists in the town; number of telephones (1986), 11,751. There is also world-wide communication *via* the cable and/or wireless circuits of Cable & Wireless Ltd and international direct dialling facilities. Air-mails arrive by British Airways daily. A direct air-mail service between Gibraltar and Tangier is run by Gibraltar Airways Ltd. Surface mails arrive direct and through France, Spain and Tangier. Radio Gibraltar broadcasts for 17 hours daily, in English and Spanish, and GBC Television operates for 5 hours daily in English. Number of receivers (31 Dec. 1986), TV (including radio), 6,706.

Cinemas. In 1986 there was 1 cinema with a seating capacity of 1,680.

Newspapers. There were (1986) 1 daily and 5 weeklies.

JUSTICE, RELIGION, EDUCATION AND WELFARE

Justice. The judicial system is based on the English system. There is a Court of Appeal, a Supreme Court, presided over by the Chief Justice, a court of first instance and a magistrates' court.

Religion. Religion of civil population mostly Roman Catholic; 1 Anglican and 1 Roman Catholic cathedral and 2 Anglican and 6 Roman Catholic churches; 1 Presbyterian and 1 Methodist church and 4 synagogues; annual subsidy to each communion, £500.

Education. Free compulsory education is provided for children between ages 5 and 15 years. Scholarships are made available for universities, teacher-training and other higher education in Britain. The comprehensive system was introduced in Sept. 1972. There were (1986) 12 primary and 2 comprehensive schools. Primary schools are mixed and divided into first schools for children aged 4-8 years and middle schools for children aged 8-12 years. The comprehensives are single-sex. In addition, there are 2 Services primary schools and 1 private primary school. A new purpose-built Special School for severely handicapped children aged 2-16 years was opened in 1977, and there are 2 Special Units for children with special educational needs (1 attached to a first school, the other to a middle school), 2 nurseries for children aged 3-4 years and an occupational therapy centre for handicapped adults. Technical education is available at the Gibraltar College of Further Education managed by the Gibraltar Government. In Sept. 1986, there were 1,339 pupils at government first schools, 1,406 at government middle schools, 165 at private and 802 at services schools; 19 at the special school; 838 at the boy's comprehensive school and 840 at the girls' comprehensive. In addition there were 50 full-time and 101 part-time students in the Gibraltar College of Further Education. Total full-time pupils in all educational institutions, 5,560. In 1985–86, government expenditure on education was £4,195,900.

Health. In 1986 there were 3 hospitals with 262 beds and 25 doctors. Total expenditure on medical and health services during year ended 31 March 1986 was £6,426,535.

Books of Reference

Gibraltar Year Book. Gibraltar, (Annual)
Ellicott, D., *Our Gibraltar.* Gibraltar, 1975
Green, M. M., *A Gibraltar Bibliography.* London, 1980.—*Supplement.* London, 1982
Hills, G., *Rock of Contention: A History of Gibraltar.* London, 1974
Jackson, W. G. F., *The Rock of the Gibraltarians.* Farleigh Dickinson Univ. Press, 1987
Magauran, H. C., *Rock Siege: The Difficulties with Spain 1964–85.* Gibraltar, 1986
Shield, G. I., *Gibraltar.* [Bibliography] Oxford and Santa Barbara, 1988

GREECE

Elliniki Dimokratia

Capital: Athens
Population: 9·97m. (1985)
GNP per capita: US$3,300 (1985)

HISTORY. Greece gained her independence from Turkey in 1821–29, and by the Protocol of London, of 3 Feb. 1830, was declared a kingdom, under the guarantee of Great Britain, France and Russia. For details of the subsequent history to 1947 *see* THE STATESMAN'S YEAR-BOOK, 1957, pp. 1069–70 and for details of the monarchy *see* THE STATESMAN'S YEAR-BOOK, 1973–74, p. 1000.

AREA AND POPULATION. Greece is bounded north by Albania, Yugoslavia and Bulgaria, east by Turkey and the Aegean Sea, south by the Mediterranean and west by the Ionian Sea. The total area is 131,957 sq. km (50,949 sq. miles), of which the islands account for 25,042 sq. km (9,669 sq. miles).

The population was 9,740,417 according to the census of 5 April 1981. Estimate (1985) 9·97m.

Athens is the capital; population of Greater Athens, in 1981, 3,027,331.

The following table shows the prefectures *(Nomoi)* and their population:

Nomoi	Area in sq. km	Population 1981	Capital	Population 1981
Greater Athens [1]	433	3,027,331	Athens	885,737
			(Piraeus)	196,389
Central Greece and Euboea [2]	24,475	1,099,841		
Aetolia and Acarnania	5,447	219,764	Missolonghi	10,164
Attica [2]	2,496	342,093	Athens	885,737
Boeotia	3,211	117,175	Levadeia	16,864
Euboea	3,908	188,410	Chalcis	44,867
Evrytania	2,045	26,182	Karpenissi	5,100
Phthiotis	4,368	161,995	Lamia	41,667
Phokis	2,121	44,222	Amphissa	7,156
Peloponnessos	21,439	1,012,528		
Argolis	2,214	93,020	Nauplion	10,609
Arcadia	4,419	107,932	Tripolis	21,311
Akhaïa	3,209	275,193	Patras	141,529
Elia	2,681	160,305	Pyrgos	21,958
Korinthia	2,289	123,042	Korinthos	22,658
Lakonia	3,636	93,218	Sparte	11,911
Messenia	2,991	159,818	Calamata	41,911
Ionian Islands	2,307	182,651		
Zakynthos	406	30,014	Zante	9,764
Kerkyra	641	99,477	Kerkyra	33,561
Kefallenia	935	31,297	Argostolion	6,788
Levkas	325	21,863	Levkas	6,415
Epirus	9,203	324,541		
Arta	1,612	80,044	Arta	18,283
Thesprotia	1,515	41,278	Hegoumenitsa	5,879
Yannina	4,990	147,304	Yannina	44,829
Preveza	1,086	55,915	Preveza	12,662
Thessaly	13,904	695,654		
Karditsa	2,576	124,930	Karditsa	27,291
Larissa	5,354	254,295	Larissa	102,048
Magnessia	2,636	182,222	Volos	71,378
Trikkala	3,338	134,207	Trikkala	40,857

[1] Comprising parts of Attica (2,551,027) and Piraeus (476,304) prefectures.
[2] Excluding figures for the parts of Attica and Piraeus prefectures within Greater Athens.

Nomoi	Area in sq. km	Population 1981	Capital	Population 1981
Macedonia	34,203	2,121,953		
Grevena	2,338	36,421	Grevena	7,433
Drama	3,468	94,772	Drama	36,109
Imathia	1,699	133,750	Verria	37,087
Thessaloniki	3,560	871,580	Thessaloniki	406,413
Kavalla	2,109	135,218	Kavalla	56,375
Kastoria	1,685	53,169	Kastoria	17,133
Kilkis	2,597	81,562	Kilkis	11,148
Kozani	3,562	147,051	Kozani	30,994
Pella	2,506	132,386	Edessa	16,054
Pieria	1,548	106,859	Katerini	38,016
Serres	3,987	196,247	Serres	45,213
Florina	1,863	52,430	Florina	12,562
Khalkidiki	2,945	79,036	Polyghyros	4,075
Aghion Oros (Mount Athos)	336	1,472	Karyai (locality)	235
Thrace	8,578	345,220		
Evros	4,242	148,486	Alexandroupolis	34,535
Xanthi	1,793	88,777	Xanthi	31,541
Rodopi	2,543	107,957	Komotini	34,051
Aegean Islands	9,071	428,533		
Cyclades	2,572	88,458	Hermoupolis	13,876
Lesvos	2,154	104,620	Mitylini	24,115
Samos	778	40,519	Samos	5,575
Khios	904	49,865	Khios	24,070
Dodecanese	2,663	145,071	Rhodes	40,392
Crete	8,331	502,165		
Heraklion	2,641	243,622	Heraklion	101,634
Lassithi	1,818	70,053	Aghios Nikolaos	8,130
Rethymnon	1,496	62,634	Rethymnon	17,736
Canea	2,376	125,856	Canea	47,338

In 1981 cities (i.e., communes of more than 10,000 inhabitants, including Greater Athens) had 5,659,528 inhabitants (58·1%), towns (i.e., communes with between 2,000 and 9,999 inhabitants), 1,125,547 (11·6%), villages and rural communities (under 2,000 inhabitants), 2,955,342 (30·3%).

Mount Athos, the easternmost of the three prongs of the peninsula of Chalcidice, is a self-governing community composed of 20 monasteries. (*See* THE STATESMAN'S YEAR-BOOK, 1945, p. 983.) For centuries the peninsula has been administered by a Council of 4 members and an Assembly of 20 members, 1 deputy from each monastery. The Greek Government on 10 Sept. 1926 recognized this autonomous form of government; Articles 109–112 of the Constitution of 1927 gave legal sanction to the Charter of Mount Athos, drawn up by representatives of the 20 monasteries on 20 May 1924. Article 103 of the 1952 Constitution and Article 105 of the 1975 Constitution confirmed the special status of Mount Athos.

Vital statistics (1983): 132,608 live births; 1,174 still births; 2,050 illegitimate live births; 71,143 marriages; 90,580 deaths.

The Greek language consists of 2 branches, *katharevousa*, a conscious revival of classical Greek and *demotiki*. Demotiki is the official language both spoken and written.

CLIMATE. Coastal regions and the islands have typical Mediterranean conditions, with mild, rainy winters and hot, dry, sunny summers. Rainfall comes almost entirely in the winter months, though amounts vary widely according to position and relief. Continental conditions affect the northern mountainous areas, with severe winters, deep snow cover and heavy precipitation, but summers are hot. Athens. Jan. 48°F (8·6°C), July 82·5°F (28·2°C). Annual rainfall 16·6″ (414·3 mm).

CONSTITUTION AND GOVERNMENT. A *coup d'état* took place on 21 April 1967, 'to avert the danger of a communist threat against the nation'. A Military Government was formed, which suspended the 1952 Constitution. Following the unsuccessful counter-*coup* in 1967, King Constantine went abroad.

Voting took place on 29 July 1973 in the referendum to change Greece from a Monarchy to a Republic and to elect a President. 77·2% of the valid votes were cast for a republican régime.

On 25 Nov. 1973, in a bloodless *coup*, President Papadopoulos was overthrown and Lieut.-Gen. Phaedon Ghizikis was sworn in. The military dictatorship collapsed on 23 July 1974 and the 1952 Constitution was reintroduced in a modified form. A new Constitution was introduced in June 1975. Parliamentary elections took place on 12 Nov. 1974.

A further referendum on the Monarchy took place on 8 Dec. 1974 and 69·2% of the valid votes were cast for an 'uncrowned democracy'.

Elections were held on 2 June 1985. The results were New Democracy, 126; Pan-Hellenic Socialist Movement, 161; Communists, 13; Euro-Communists, 1.

President: Christos Sartzetakis (elected President in March 1985).

The Cabinet in Feb. 1988:

Prime Minister: Andreas G. Papandreou.
Vice-Premier and National Defence: Yiannis Charalambopoulos. *Vice-Premier and Justice:* Agamemnon Koutsogiorgas. *Minister to the Prime Minister:* Apostolos Kaklamanis. *Foreign Affairs:* Karolos Papoulias. *Interior:* Akis Tsochatzopoulos. *National Economy:* Panagiotis Roumeliotis. *Finance:* Dimitris Tsovolas. *Health, Welfare and Social Services:* Giannis Floros. *Education and Religion:* Antonis Tritsis. *Culture:* Melina Mercouri. *Public Order:* Antonis Drossoyiannis. *Northern Greece:* Stelios Papathemelis. *The Aegean:* Petros Valvis. *Agriculture:* Yiannis Pottakis. *Environment, Town Planning and Public Works:* Evangelos Kouloumbis. *Industry, Energy and Technology:* Athanassios Peponis. *Labour:* George Gennimatas. *Commerce:* Nikos Akritidis. *Transport and Communications:* Kostas Badouvas. *Merchant Marine:* Evangelos Yannopoulos. *Without Portfolio:* Athanassios Filippopoulos.

National flag: Nine horizontal stripes of blue and white, with a canton of blue with a white cross.

National anthem: Hymn to Freedom, Imnos eis tin Eleftherian (words by Dionysios Solomos, 1824; tune by N. Mantzaros, 1828).

DEFENCE. In Aug. 1950 the Ministries of War, Marine and Military Aviation were fused into a single Ministry of National Defence. The General Staff of National Defence is directly responsible to the Minister on general defence questions, besides the special staffs for Army, Navy and Air Force. Military service in the Armed Forces is compulsory and universal. Liability begins in the 21st year and lasts up to the 50th. The normal terms of service are Army 21 months, Navy 25 months, Air Force 23 months, followed by 19 years in the First Reserve and 10 years in the Second Reserve.

Army. The Army is organized into 3 Military Regions, comprising 1 armoured, 1 mechanized, 1 para-commando and 11 infantry divisions; 5 armoured brigades; 12 field artillery, 8 anti-aircraft, 2 surface-to-surface missile, 2 surface-to-air missile, and 3 army aviation battalions; and 1 independent aviation company. Equipment includes 359 M-47, 1,125 M-48, 250 AMX-30 and 193 Leopard I main battle tanks. Hellenic Army Aviation has over 100 helicopters, including 43 AB-205 and 50 UH-1H Iroquois, 5 Chinooks, 20 Nardi-Hughes 300s, and 25 Cessna U-17A observation aircraft, 2 Aero Commander and 1 Super King Air transports. Strength (1988) 165,500 (108,500 conscripts), with a further 350,000 reserves. There is also a paramiltary gendarmerie of 25,000 men.

Navy. The Hellenic Navy includes 2 modern Netherlands-built leader-size guided missile frigates, 10 submarines (8 modern German (Fed. Rep.)-built small and 2 old *ex*-US large), 14 very old *ex*-US destroyers, 1 *ex*-German support frigate, 1 new armed training ship carrying a helicopter, 4 very old *ex*-US frigates (small DE type), 2 coastal minelayers, 14 fast missile vessels, 6 fast torpedo boats, 2 fast attack craft, 14 coastal minesweepers, 9 coastal patrol boats, 1 dock landing ship, 8 tank landing ships, 5 medium landing ships, 10 landing craft, 88 minor landing craft, 1 ammunition ship, 5 oilers, 2 transports, 1 depot ship, 4 surveying craft, 2 light-house tenders, 5 water carriers, 1 netlayer and 14 fleet tugs.

The Navy operates 10 HU-16 Albatross patrol amphibians (manned by Air Force crews) and 11 AB-212ASW anti-submarine helicopters and 4 Alouettes for SAR and liaison.

Personnel in 1988 totalled 2,500 officers and 17,000 ratings (200 women).

Air Force. The Hellenic Air Force had a strength (1988) of about 24,000 officers and men and 275 combat aircraft, consisting of 3 squadrons of F-4E Phantom air-superiority fighters, 2 squadrons of F-104G Starfighters, 2 squadrons of Mirage F.1 fighters, 3 squadrons of A-7H Corsair II attack aircraft, 2 squadrons of F-5 fighters, 1 squadron of RF-4E and RF-84F reconnaissance fighters and 1 squadron of HU-16B Albatross ASW amphibians (under Navy control). There are also transport squadrons equipped with C-130H Hercules (12), Noratlas, NAMC YS-11, DO28 and C-47 aircraft, 12 Canadair CL-215 twin-engined amphibians, 36 T-2E Buckeye training/attack aircraft, other training and helicopter equipment, and anti-aircraft units equipped with Nike-Hercules and Hawk surface-to-air missiles. Forty F-16 Fighting Falcon and 40 Mirage 2000 fighters are on order.

The HAF is organized into Tactical, Training and Air Materiel Commands.

INTERNATIONAL RELATIONS

Membership. Greece is a member of UN, EEC, the Council of Europe and the military and political wings of NATO.

ECONOMY

Budget. The estimated revenue and expenditure for calendar years were as follows (in 1m. drachmai):

	1982	1983	1984	1985
Revenue	590,000	736,000	933,000	1,114,412
Expenditure	787,000	1,055,000	1,470,058	1,776,937

Currency. On 11 Nov. 1944 the Greek currency was stabilized at 1 new *drachma* equalling 50,000m. old *drachmai*. Further readjustments took place in 1946, 1949 and 1953. A 'new issue' of notes and coins was put into circulation on 1 May 1954, 1 new drachma equalling 1,000 old drachmai (72 drachmai = £1; 30 drachmai = US$1). The 'new issue' comprises notes of 50, 100, 500 and 1,000 drachmai and metal coins of 1, 2, 5, 10 and 20 drachmai and 10, 20 and 50 *lepta*. Rate of exchange, March 1988, £1 = 239·75 drachmai; US$1 = 135·30.

Banking. The Bank of Greece *(Trapeza Tis Ellados)* is the bank of issue.

The National Investment Bank for industrial development was set up in Dec. 1963; of its capital of 180m. drachmai, the National Bank provided 60%.

Other important banks are the Ionian and Popular Bank of Greece, the Commercial Bank of Greece, the National Mortgage Bank, the Hellenic Industrial Development Bank, the Investment Bank, the Commercial Credit Bank, the Agricultural Bank, the Bank of Central Greece and the General Bank of Greece.

Weights and Measures. The metric system was made obligatory in 1959; the use of other systems is prohibited. The Gregorian calendar was adopted in Feb. 1923.

ENERGY AND NATURAL RESOURCES

Electricity. Total installed capacity of the Public Power Corporation was 6,093m. mw as at 31 Dec. 1980. Total net production in 1986 was 29,580m. kwh. Supply 220 volts; 50 Hz.

Minerals. Greece produces a variety of ores and minerals, including iron-pyrites (115,976 tonnes in 1982), bauxite (2·84m. tonnes, 1982), nickel (523,405 tonnes, 1982), magnesite (967,106 tonnes, 1982), dead burnt magnesite (285,572 tonnes, 1982), mixed sulphur ores (752,000 tonnes, 1976), barytes, chromite, marble (white and coloured) and various other earths, chiefly from the Laurium district, Thessaly, Euboea and the Aegean islands. There is little coal, and lignite of indifferent quality (27·19m. tonnes, 1982). Salt production (1982) 115,675 tonnes.

Agriculture. Of the total area (131,957 sq. km) 39,452 sq. km is arable and fallow. Another 52,550 sq. km is grazing land, 29,511 sq. km is forest.

Agriculture accounted for some 19% of GDP in 1986, and in 1984 provided 23% of export earnings. Production (1986, in 1,000 tonnes):

Wheat	2,200	Grapes	1,712
Tobacco	153	Wine	507
Seed cotton	535	Citrus fruit	1,069
Sugar-beet	2,700	Other fruit	2,979
Raisins	141	Milk	1,642
Olive oil	267	Meat	507

Olive production (1986) about 1·2m. tonnes.

Rice is cultivated in Macedonia, the Peloponnese, Epirus and Central Greece. Successful experiments have been made in growing rice on alkaline land previously regarded as unfit for cultivation. The main kinds of cheese produced are white cheese in brine (commercially known as Fetta) and hard cheese, such as Kefalotyri.

Livestock (1986): 740,000 cattle, 1,000 buffaloes, 1,095,000 pigs, 10,122,000 sheep, 5·6m. goats, 81,000 horses, 90,000 mules, 200,000 asses, 31m. poultry.

Fisheries. In 1985, over 10,000 fishermen were active and landed 105,478 tonnes of fish. 37,182 kg of sponges were produced in 1981.

INDUSTRY AND TRADE

Industry. Manufacturing contributed 411,185m. drachmai to GDP in 1982. The main products are canned vegetables and fruit, fruit juice, beer, wine, alcoholic beverages, cigarettes, textiles, yarn, leather, shoes, synthetic timber, paper, plastics, rubber products, chemical acids, pigments, pharmaceutical products, cosmetics, soap, disinfectants, fertilizers, glassware, porcelain sanitary items, wire and power coils and household instruments.

Production, 1982 (1,000 tonnes): Textile yarns, 199; cement, 12,860; fertilizers, 1,785; ammonia, 272; iron (concrete-reinforcing bars), 826; alumina, 404; aluminium, 173; electrical domestic goods (1,000 pieces), 680; processed fruit and juices, 160; beer, 293; bottled wine, 100; paper, 223; chemical acids, 1,707; iron wire, 127; glass products, 76; packing materials, 79.

Labour. Of the economically active population in 1981, 972,090 were engaged in agriculture. 664,322 in manufacturing and 1,907,385 in other employment.

Pepelasis, A. A., and Yotopoulos, P. A., *Surplus Labor in Greek Agriculture, 1953–60.* Athens, 1962

Trade Unions. The status of trade unions in Greece is regulated by the Associations Act 1914. Trade-union liberties are guaranteed under the Constitution, and a law of June 1982 altered the unions' right to strike.

The national body of trade unions in Greece is the Greek General Confederation of Labour.

Commerce. Foreign trade (in US$1m.) for 4 calendar years was:

	1982	1983	1984	1985
Imports	8,910	8,400	8,624	10,561
Exports	4,141	4,106	4,394	4,293

In 1984 exports (in US$1m.) included: Manufactures, 2,003; petroleum products, 893; food and beverages, 872; minerals and ores, 217; tobacco, 155; raw materials and semi-finished products, 135. Imports included: Fuels and lubricants, 3,080; manufactured consumer goods, 2,215; capital goods, 1,743; raw materials, 1,445; food, 1,208.

Of the exports (1984) 15·4% went to the Federal Republic of Germany, 11·4% to the USA, 9·1% to Italy, 6·2% to France, 5·4% to the UK, 4% to Saudi Arabia and 2·1% to the USSR. Of the imports (1984) 15·8% came from the Federal Republic of Germany, 13·9% from the USA, 8·2% from Italy, 6·7% from France, 6·5% from Saudi Arabia, 5·9% from the USSR and 5·7% from the Netherlands.

Total trade between Greece and UK (British Department of Trade returns, in £1,000 sterling):

	1983	1984	1985	1986	1987
Imports to UK	164,917	279,367	320,131	308,644	355,320
Exports and re-exports from UK	280,204	354,332	335,352	356,020	444,500

Tourism. Tourists visiting Greece in 1986 numbered 7,025,000. In 1984 they spent the equivalent of US$1,310m.

COMMUNICATIONS

Roads. There were, in 1982, 37,365 km of roads, of which 8,689 were national and 28,676 provincial roads.

Number of motor vehicles in Dec. 1984: 1,740,293, of which (1983) 1,073,411 were passenger cars, 519,194 goods vehicles, 19,121 buses.

Railways. In 1986 the State network, Hellenic Railways (OSE), totalled 2,479 km comprising 1,565 km of 1,435 mm gauge, 892 km of 1,000 mm gauge, and 22 km of 750 mm gauge, and carried 4·2m. tonnes of freight and 11·7m. passengers.

Aviation. Olympic Airways connects Athens with all important cities of the country, Europe, the Middle East and USA. Thirty-four foreign companies connect Athens with the principal cities of the world.

The principal airport is at Athens. In 1983, 95,923 aircraft arrived, carrying 8·4m. passengers.

Shipping. In Dec. 1985 the merchant navy comprised 2,456 vessels of 28,646,000 GRT. Greek-owned ships under foreign flags totalled 5,856,000 GRT in 1985.

There is a canal (opened 9 Nov. 1893) across the Isthmus of Corinth (about 4 miles).

Post and Broadcasting. In 1983 there were 2,691 telephone exchanges, handling 4,700m. calls. There were (1983) 3,331,143 telephones.

Elliniki Radiophonia Tileorasis (ERT), the Hellenic National Radio and Television Institute, is the government broadcasting station. ERT broadcasts 2 TV programmes. Number of receivers: radio, 5m.; television, 1·4m.

Cinemas (1981). There were 1,150 cinemas.

Newspapers (1984). There were 35 daily newspapers published in Athens, 6 in Piraeus and 102 elsewhere.

JUSTICE, RELIGION, EDUCATION AND WELFARE

Justice. Under the 1975 Constitution judges are appointed for life by the President of the Republic, after consultation with the judicial council. Judges enjoy personal and functional independence. There are three divisions of the courts: administrative, civil and criminal and they must not give decisions which are contrary to the Constitution. Final jurisdiction lies with a Special Supreme Tribunal.

Some laws, passed before the 1975 Constitution came into force, and which are not contrary to it, remain in force.

Religion. The Christian Eastern Orthodox faith is the established religion to which 98% of the population belong.

The Greek Orthodox Church is under an archbishop and 67 metropolitans, 1 archbishop and 7 metropolitans in Crete, and 4 metropolitans in the Dodecanese. The Roman Catholics have 3 archbishops (in Naxos and Corfu and, not recognized by the State, in Athens) and 1 bishop (for Syra and Santorin). The Exarchs of the Greek Catholics and the Armenians are not recognized by the State.

Complete religious freedom is recognized by the Constitution of 1968, but prose-lytizing from, and interference with, the Greek Orthodox Church is forbidden.

Education. Public education is provided in nursery, primary and secondary schools, starting at 6 years of age and since 1963 free at all levels.

In 1983–84 there were 5,003 nursery schools with 6,913 staff and 158,816 pupils; 9,077 public day primary schools with 36,825 staff and 888,440 pupils; 861 secondary schools with 15,098 staff and 252,594 pupils. In 1981–82 there were 611 public and 155 private secondary, technical and vocational schools (with 108,212 pupils and 7,410 staff); 73 public and 34 private higher technical schools (29,965 and 3,613); 21 higher education schools (7,253 and 208).

In 1981–82 there were 13 universities with 87,476 students and 7,489 lecturers.

Illiteracy in the age groups of 10 years and over was 8·6% in 1981 (3·6% among men).

Health (1983). There were 626 hospitals and sanatoria with a total of 57,496 beds. There were 27,607 doctors and 8,286 dentists.

DIPLOMATIC REPRESENTATIVES

Of Greece in Great Britain (1A Holland Park, London, W11 3TP)
Ambassador: Stephanos G. Stathatos (accredited 12 Feb. 1986).

Of Great Britain in Greece (1 Ploutarchou St., 106 75 Athens)
Ambassador: Sir Jeremy Thomas, KCMG.

Of Greece in the USA (2221 Massachusetts Ave., NW, Washington, D.C., 20008)
Ambassador: George D. Papoulias.

Of the USA in Greece (91 Eleftheriou Venizelou St., Athens)
Ambassador: Robert V. Keeley.

Of Greece to the United Nations
Ambassador: Coustantine Zepos.

Books of Reference

Clogg, R., *Greece in the 1980s.* London, 1983
Clogg, R. and M. J., *Greece.* [Bibliography] Oxford and Santa Barbara, 1980
Freris, A. F., *The Greek Economy in the Twentieth Century.* London, 1986
Holden, D., *Greece Without Columns: The Making of the Modern Greeks.* London, 1972
Kousoulas, D. G., *Revolution and Defeat: The Story of the Greek Communist Party.* OUP, 1965
Kykkotis, I., *English–Modern Greek and Modern Greek–English Dictionary.* 3rd ed. London, 1957
Mouzelis, N. P., *Modern Greece.* London, 1978
Pring, J. T., *The Oxford Dictionary of Modern Greek, Greek-English, English-Greek.* OUP, 1965–82
Tsoukalis, L., *Greece and the European Community.* Farnborough, 1979
Woodhouse, C. M., *The Struggle for Greece, 1941–1949.* London, 1976.—*Karamanlis: The Restorer of Greek Democracy.* OUP, 1982
Xydis, S. G., *Greece and the Great Powers, 1944–47.* Thessaloniki, 1963

GRENADA

Capital: St George's
Population: 88,000 (1985)
GNP per capita: US$940 (1984)

HISTORY. Grenada became an independent nation within the Commonwealth on 7 Feb. 1974. Grenada was formerly an Associated State under the West Indies Act, 1967. The 1973 Constitution was suspended in 1979 following a revolution.

On 19 Oct. 1983 the army took control after a power struggle led to the killing of Maurice Bishop the Prime Minister. At the request of a group of Caribbean countries, Grenada was invaded by US-led forces on 24–28 Oct. On 1 Nov. a State of Emergency was imposed which ended on 15 Nov. when an interim government was installed.

AREA AND POPULATION. Grenada is the most southerly island of the Windward Islands with an area of 120 sq. miles (311 sq. km); the state also includes the Southern Grenadine Islands to the north, chiefly Carriacou and Petite Martinique, with an area of 13 sq. miles (34 sq. km). The total population (Census, 1981) was 89,099 including 4,671 on the Southern Grenadines; estimate (1987) 92,000. The Borough of St. George's, the capital, had 29,369 inhabitants in 1981, but its urban area had a population of only 4,788. In 1983, 84% of the people were black and a further 12% of mixed origins.

Vital statistics (1983): Births, 2,880; deaths, 794.

CLIMATE. The tropical climate is very agreeable in the dry season, from Jan. to May, when days are warm and nights quite cool, but in the wet season there is very little difference between day and night temperatures. On the coast, annual rainfall is about 60″ (1,500 mm) but it is as high as 150–200″ (3,750–5,000 mm) in the mountains.

CONSTITUTION AND GOVERNMENT. The British sovereign is represented by an appointed Governor-General. There is a bicameral legislature, consisting of a 13-member Senate, appointed by the Governor-General, and a 15-member House of Representatives, elected by universal suffrage. Elections were held for the 15-seat House of Representatives on 3 Dec. 1984. The New National Party won 14 seats and the Grenada United Labour Party, 1.

Governor-General: Sir Paul Scoon, GCMG, GCVO, OBE.

Prime Minister, Finance, Security and Home Affairs: Rt. Hon. Herbert Blaize PC.

National flag: Divided into 4 triangles of yellow, top and bottom, and green, hoist and fly; in the centre a red disc bearing a gold star; along the top and bottom edged red stripes each bearing 3 gold stars; on the green triangle near the hoist a pod of nutmeg.

Local government: Elected local councils were re-introduced in 1986; there are 7 district councils (including 1 for Carriacou/Petite Martinique) and the Borough Council of St. George's.

DEFENCE

Army. A People's Revolutionary Army was created in 1979. Personnel about 6,500 organized into 3 infantry battalions and an artillery battery.

INTERNATIONAL RELATIONS

Membership. Grenada is a member of the UN, OAS, Caricom, the Commonwealth and is an ACP state of EEC.

ECONOMY

Budget. The 1986 estimates balanced at EC$236·4m. Value added tax is to replace income tax.

Currency. The currency is the *Eastern Caribbean dollar*. In March 1988, £1 = EC$4·79; US$ = EC$2·70.

Banking. In 1981 there were 5 commercial banks in Grenada: The National Commercial Bank, Barclays Bank International, Royal Bank of Canada, Bank of Nova Scotia and the Grenada Co-operative Bank. The Grenada Agricultural Bank was established in 1965 to encourage agricultural development. In 1981, bank deposits were EC$164·7m.

ENERGY AND NATURAL RESOURCES

Electricity. Production (1986) 24m. kwh.

Agriculture (1981). The principal crops (production in lb.) are: Cocoa (1986, 3,000 tonnes), nutmegs (6,767,199), bananas (1986, 8,000 tonnes), and mace (506,950); coconuts, corn and pigeon peas, citrus, sugar-cane, root-crops and vegetables are also grown, in addition to small scattered cultivations of cotton, cloves, cinnamon, pimento, coffee and fruit trees The fish catch was about 3m. lb.

Livestock (1986): Cattle, 4,000; sheep, 17,000; goats, 14,000; pigs, 11,000; poultry (1982), 260,000.

Fisheries. The catch (1983) was 1,801 tonnes.

COMMERCE (1986). Total value of imports, EC$225m. The main exports are cocoa (EC$10·6m.), nutmegs (EC$26·1m.) and fruit (EC$15·3m.).

Of exports in 1981, UK took 35·6%; Netherlands, 15·8%; Trinidad, 15·6%; Federal Republic of Germany, 9%; Canada, 2·8%; USA, 2·5%. Of 1981 imports, Trinidad furnished 19·2%; USA, 18·6%; UK, 16·6%; Canada, 5·5%; Netherlands, 1·6%; Federal Republic of Germany, 1·3%.

Total trade between Grenada and UK (British Department of Trade returns, in £1,000 sterling):

	1983	1984	1985	1986	1987
Imports to UK	5,387	5,703	6,735	7,011	6,302
Exports and re-exports to UK	7,293	8,319	8,820	8,628	8,772

TOURISM. In 1986, there were 171,000 visitors; including 114,000 cruise ship passengers.

COMMUNICATIONS

Roads. The scheduled road mileage is 577, of which 377 have an oiled surface and 210 are graded as third- and fourth-class roads. Vehicles registered (1979) 6,676.

Aviation. A new international airport was inaugurated in Oct. 1984 at Point Salines. Pearls Airport has daily connexions to London, New York and South America *via* nearby islands. There is a small airstrip on Carriacou.

Shipping. Total shipping for 1978 was 927 motor and steamships and 166 sailing and auxiliary vessels, with a total net tonnage of 2,210,532 and 7,479 respectively.

Post and Broadcasting. The telephone system is owned and operated by the Grenada Telephone Co. Ltd. The Government of Grenada is a shareholder. The system is completely automatic, and in 1983 served 5,544 subscribers. Cable & Wireless (W.I.) Ltd operates a VHF radio system (telephone and telegraph) to Trinidad and Barbados, from where connexion is made to all other parts of the world. There were (1978) 63,500 radios.

JUSTICE, RELIGION, EDUCATION AND WELFARE

Justice. The Grenada Supreme Court, situated in St George's, comprises a High Court of Justice, a Court of Magisterial Appeal (which hears appeals from the lower Magistrates' Courts exercising summary jurisdiction) and an Itinerant Court of Appeal (to hear appeals from the High Court).

Religion. The majority of the population are Roman Catholic; the Anglican and Methodist churches are also well represented.

Education. There are 20 primary schools, 4 junior schools and 16 secondary schools, as well as 46 schools taking the full age range. There is a Technical Centre in each district and a Technical Institute in St George's, where there is also a Teacher Training College and a branch of the University of the West Indies. There were 22,093 primary and 6,249 secondary school pupils in 1981.

Health. In 1980 there were 6 hospitals and clinics with 325 beds. In 1979 there were 34 doctors, 5 dentists, 1 pharmacist (1978), 107 midwives (1978) and 259 nursing personnel.

DIPLOMATIC REPRESENTATIVES

Of Grenada in Great Britain (1 Collingham Gdns., London, SW5)
High Commissioner: O. M. Gibbs, CMG (accredited 15 March 1984).

Of Great Britain in Grenada
High Commissioner: K. F. X. Burns, CMG (resides at Bridgetown).

Of Grenada in the USA (1701 New Hampshire Ave., NW, Washington, D.C., 20009)
Ambassador: Albert O. Xavier.

Of the USA in Grenada (P.O. Box 54, St George's)
Chargé d'Affaires: John C. Leary.

Of Grenada to the United Nations
Ambassador: Dr Lamuel A. Stanislaus.

Books of Reference

Gilmore, W. G., *The Grenada Intervention: Analysis and Documentation.* London, 1984
Hodge, M. and Searle, C. (eds), *Is Freedom We Making.* Govt. Information Service, 1981
O'Shaughnessy, H., *Grenada: Revolution, Invasion and Aftermath.* London, 1984
Page, A., Sutton, P., and Thorndike, T., *Grenada and Invasion.* London, 1984
Searle, C., *Grenada: The Struggle against Destabilization.* London, 1983
Searle, C. and Rojas, D. (eds), *To Construct from Morning.* Grenada, 1982
Sinclair, N., *Grenada: Isle of Spice.* London, 1987
Thorndike, T., *Grenada: Politics, Economics and Society.* London, 1985
Wheaton, P. and Sunshine, C. (eds), *Grenada: The Peaceful Revolution.* Washington, 1982

GUATEMALA

Capital: Guatemala City
Population: 8·99m. (1987)
GNP per capita: US$1,150 (1985)

República de Guatemala

HISTORY. From 1524 to 1821 Guatemala was a Spanish captaincy-general, comprising the whole of Central America. It became independent in 1821 and formed part of the Confederation of Central America from 1823 to 1839, when Rafael Carrera dissolved the Confederation.

AREA AND POPULATION. Guatemala is bounded on the north and west by Mexico, south by the Pacific ocean and east by El Salvador, Honduras and Belize, and the area is 108,889 sq. km (42,042 sq. miles). In March 1936 Guatemala, El Salvador and Honduras agreed to accept the peak of Mount Montecristo as the common boundary point.

The census population was 6,054,227 in 1981. Estimate (1987) 8·99m. In 1983, 53% were pure Indians, of 21 different groups descended from the Maya; most of the remainder are mixed Indian and Spanish and these supply the ruling classes. Density of population, 1985, 77 per sq. km.

Vital statistics, 1984: Births, 302,921; deaths, 75,462; marriages, 31,351.

Guatemala is administratively divided into 22 departments, each with a governor appointed by the President. Population, 1985:

Departments	Area (sq. km)	Population	Departments	Area (sq. km)	Population
Alta Verapaz	8,686	393,446	Petén	35,854	118,116
Baja Verapaz	3,124	160,567	Quezaltenango	1,951	478,030
Chimaltenango	1,979	283,887	Quiché	8,378	460,956
Chiquimula	2,376	220,067	Retalhuleu	1,858	228,563
El Progreso	1,922	106,115	Sacatepéquez	465	148,574
Escuintla	4,384	565,215	San Marcos	3,791	590,152
Guatemala	2,126	2,050,673	Santa Rosa	2,955	263,060
Huehuetenango	7,403	571,292	Sololá	1,061	181,816
Izabal	9,038	330,546	Suchitepéquez	2,510	327,763
Jalapa	2,063	171,542	Totonicapán	1,061	249,067
Jutiapa	3,219	348,032	Zacapa	2,690	155,496

The capital is Guatemala City with about 1·3m. inhabitants (1983). Other towns are Quezaltenango (65,733), Puerto Barrios (38,956), Mazatenango (38,319), Antigua (26,631), Zacapa (35,769) and Cobán (43,538).

CLIMATE. A tropical climate, with little variation in temperature and a well marked wet season from May to Oct. Guatemala City. Jan. 63°F (17·2°C), July 69°F (20·6°C). Annual rainfall 53″ (1,316 mm).

CONSTITUTION AND GOVERNMENT. A new Constitution, drawn up by the Constituuent Assembly elected on 1 July 1984, was promulgated in June 1985 and came into force on 14 Jan. 1986. The President and Vice-President are elected for a term of 5 years by direct election (with a second round of voting if no candidate secures 50% of the first-round votes). The Legislative Assembly comprises 100 members. Presidential, congressional and municipal elections were held on 3 Nov. 1985, with a second round of voting on 8 Dec. 1985.

President: Marco Vinicio Cerezo Arévalo (assumed office 14 Jan. 1986).

Vice-President: Roberto Carpio Nicolle.

Foreign Relations: Alfonso Cabrera Hidalgo. *Finance:* Rodolfo Paiz Andrade. *Defence:* Gen. Héctor Gramaso Morales.

National flag: Three vertical strips of blue, white, blue, with the national arms in the centre.

National anthem: ¡Guatemala! feliz (words by J. J. Palma; tune by R. Alvarez).

DEFENCE. There is selective conscription into the armed forces for 30 months.

Army. The Army numbered (1988) 38,000, organized in 39 infantry, 1 armoured and 1 engineer battalions, 4 field artillery groups, 1 anti-aircraft artillery group, 1 Special Forces brigade, 1 Presidential Guard brigade and 7 reconnaissance squadrons. Equipment includes light tanks and armoured cars. Reserves, 1988, 35,000. Territorial militia, 725,000.

Navy. A Naval force was formed in 1959. It comprises 8 small patrol craft, 1 landing craft, 2 small troop carriers, 6 motor launches, 30 river patrol craft, 1 survey craft and 1 tug. Since 1973 the base at Santo Tomas has had a 230-ton marine elevator (synchrolift), greatly improving naval repair facilities. Personnel in 1988 numbered 1,000 comprising 125 officers and 875 men (including marines).

Air Force. There is a small Air Force with 10 A-37B and 2 T-33 light attack aircraft, 1 DC-6, 10 C-47, 3 F.27 and 7 Israeli-built Arava transports, 10 Pilatus PC-7 turboprop trainers, and a number of Cessna light aircraft and Bell helicopters, including a few armed UH-1 Iroquois. Strength was (1988) about 700 personnel and 90 aircraft.

INTERNATIONAL RELATIONS

Membership. Guatemala is a member of UN, OAS and Cacom.

External Debt. In 1984 the external debt was Q.539.9m.

ECONOMY

Planning. The 1979–82 National Economic Development Plan involved government investment of Q.1,937.5m.

Budget. In 1985 expenditure was 1,076m. quetzales; revenue, 865m. quetzales

Currency. The gold *quetzal* was established 7 May 1925 equal to 60 old Guatemala paper pesos, with a gold content equal to that of the US$. Coins of 25, 10, 5 and 1 *centavos* were issued by the Banco de Guatemala on 16 Sept. 1965; they are of a lower content value than the previous ones. There are also paper notes of 100, 50, 20, 10, 5, 1 and ½ *quetzales* (50 *centavos*). In March 1988, £1 = Q.1·77; US$1 = Q.1.

Banking. On 4 Feb. 1946 the Central Bank of Guatemala (founded in 1926 as a mixed central and commercial bank) was superseded by a new institution, the Banco de Guatemala, to operate solely as a central bank. Savings and term deposits at commercial banks were Q.1,652·1m. at the end of 1984. Total currency circulation (backed by a gold reserve fixed by law at a minimum of 40%) on 31 Dec. 1984 was Q.1,162·6m.; total net international reserves amounted to Q.–26·4m. on 31 Dec. 1984.

There are 19 banks, including the Banco de Guatemala, Banco Nacional de Desarollo, set up in 1971 to promote agricultural development, its counterpart for small industries (Banco de los Trabajadores) set up in Jan. 1966 with initial capital of US$1·3m., a branch of Lloyds Bank International Ltd and a branch of the Bank of America.

Weights and Measures. The metric system has been officially adopted, but is little used in local commerce.

Libra of 16 oz.	= 1·014 lb.	*League*	= 3 miles
Arroba of 25 libras	= 25·35 lb.	*Vara*	= 32 in.
Quintal of 4 arrobas	= 101·40 lb.	*Manzana*	= 100 varas sq.
Tonelada of 20 quintals	= 18·10 cwt	*Caballeria* of 64 man-	
Fanega	= 1½ Imp. bushels	zanas	= 110 acres

ENERGY AND NATURAL RESOURCES

Electricity. 2,250m. kwh. of electricity were generated in 1986. A large hydro-electric plant was inaugurated in Dec. 1985. Supply 115 and 230 volts; 60 Hz.

Oil. Guatemala began exporting crude oil in 1980; exports, 1984, were valued at Q.34m. Production is from wells in Alta Verapaz department from where the oil is piped to Santo Tomas de Castilla. Further exploration is proceeding in the Petén.

Minerals. Mineral production includes zinc and lead concentrates, some antimony and tungsten, a small amount of cadmium and silver; some copper is also being mined. Exports (1983) Q.2m.

Agriculture. The Cordilleras divide Guatemala into two unequal drainage areas, of which the Atlantic is much the greater. The Pacific slope, though comparatively narrow, is exceptionally well watered and fertile between the altitudes of 1,000 and 5,000 ft, and is the most densely settled part of the republic. The Atlantic slope is sparsely populated, and has little of commercial importance beyond the chicle and timber-cutting of the Petén, coffee cultivation of Cobán region and banana-raising of the Motagua Valley and Lake Izabal district. Soil erosion is serious and a single week of heavy rains suffices to cause flooding of fields and much crop destruction.

The principal crop is coffee; there are about 12,000 coffee plantations with 138m. coffee trees on about 338,000 acres, but 80% of the crop comes from 1,500 large coffee farms employing 426,000 workers. Production (1986) 156,000 tonnes. Coffee exports in 1984 were valued at Q.360.7m. mainly to USA and Federal Republic of Germany.

Bananas are still an important export crop, but exports have at times been seriously reduced, partly by labour troubles and by hurricanes. Production (1986) 690,000 tonnes. Exports 1984 were worth Q.59m.

Cotton exports in 1984 were valued at Q.70.4m. Cotton lint production (1986) 41,000 tonnes. Other important exports (1984) were sugar, Q.74.5m.; beef, Q.11.6m. Guatemala is, after Mexico, the largest producer of chicle gum (used for chewing-gum manufacture in USA). Rubber development schemes are under way, assisted by US funds. Guatemala is one of the largest sources of essential oils (citronella and lemon grass); exports in 1984 were valued at Q.1.7m. Cardamom, exported mainly to the Arab countries, was valued at Q.9.4m. in 1984.

Livestock (1986): Cattle, 2,284,000; pigs, 862,000; sheep, 680,000; horses, 100,000; poultry, 15m.

Forestry. The forest area has an extent of 17,784,000 acres. The department of Petén is rich in mahogany and other woods. Production (1980) 11.23m. cu. metres.

Fisheries. Exports were about Q.11.8m. in 1984.

INDUSTRY AND TRADE

Industry. The principal industries are food and beverages, tobacco, chemicals, hides and skins, textiles, garments and non-metallic minerals. New industries include electrical goods, plastic sheet and metal furniture.

Trade Unions. Trade unions are small. In 1954 the trade unions were ordered to reorganize and there are now two main federations.

Commerce. Values in Q.1,000 (1 quetzal = US$1) were:

	1980	1981	1982	1983	1984
Imports (c.i.f.)	1,615,000	1,773,600	1,387,000	1,135,000	1,278,496
Exports (f.o.b.)	1,522,000	1,281,200	1,120,000	1,150,000	1,122,286

Total trade between Guatemala and UK (British Department of Trade returns, in £1,000 sterling):

	1983	1984	1985	1986	1987
Imports to UK	9,764	9,565	5,176	8,098	7,536
Exports and re-exports from UK	7,440	10,660	13,397	9,288	13,926

Tourism. There were 287,000 foreign visitors in 1986.

COMMUNICATIONS

Roads. In 1985 there were 18,000 km of roads, of which 2,850 are paved. There is a trunk highway from coast to coast *via* Guatemala City. There are 2 trunk highways from the Mexican to the Salvadorean frontier: the Pacific Highway serving the fertile coastal plain and the Pan-American Highway running through the highlands and Guatemala City. Motor vehicles number about 200,000.

Railways. The principal railway system is the government-owned (since 1968) *Ferrocarriles de Guatemala.* All railways are of 914 mm gauge. Total length of all lines was (1988) 953 km. Passengers carried, 1986, numbered 379,789, and freight carried 650,000 tonnes.

Aviation. The government-owned airline, Aviateca, furnishes both domestic and international services; 6 other airlines handle international traffic.

Shipping. The chief ports on the Atlantic coast are Puerto Barrios and Santo Tomás de Castilla: on the Pacific coast, San José and Champerico. Total tonnage handled was, 1983, 6·17m. tons.

Post and Broadcasting. The Government own and operate the telegraph and telephone services; there were (1982) 97,670 telephone instruments. There are some 70 broadcasting stations. Radio receiving sets in use, 1976, numbered about 1m. There are 4 commercial TV stations, 1 government station and about 192,000 TV receivers.

Cinemas (1984). Cinemas numbered approximately 100.

Newspapers (1984). There are 4 daily newspapers.

JUSTICE, RELIGION, EDUCATION AND WELFARE

Justice. Justice is administered in a Supreme Court, 6 appeal courts and 28 courts of first instance. Supreme Court and appeal court judges are elected by Congress. Judges of first instance are appointed by the Supreme Court.

All holders of public office have to show on entering office, and again on leaving, a full account of their private property and income.

Religion. Roman Catholicism is the prevailing faith; but all other creeds have complete liberty of worship. Guatemala has an archbishopric.

Education. In 1984 there were 11,587 schools with 45,611 teachers and an attendance of 1,331,294 pupils; these figures include private schools. There are 1,237 secondary and other schools having 13,891 teachers and an attendance of 194,484 pupils; the autonomous University of San Carlos de Borromeo, founded in 1678, was reopened in 1910 with 7 faculties and schools and there are 4 new universities. Students at state university (1984) approximately 45,552. All education is in theory free, but owing to a grave shortage of state schools private schools flourish. The 1964 census showed that 63% of those 10 years of age and older were illiterate.

Social Welfare. A comprehensive system of social security was outlined in a law of 30 Oct. 1946. Medical personnel include about 1,250 doctors and 275 dentists for the whole republic. There are about 60 public hospitals and about 100 dispensaries.

DIPLOMATIC REPRESENTATIVES

Of Great Britain in Guatemala (7a Avenida 5-10, Zona 4, Guatemala City)
Ambassador: Bernard Everett.

Of Guatemala in Great Britain (13 Fawcett St., London, SW10 9HN)
Ambassador: Dr Erwin Blandon.

Of Guatemala in the USA (2220 R. St., NW, Washington, D.C., 20008)
Ambassador: Dr Oscar Ernesto Padilla Vidaurre.

Of the USA in Guatemala (7–01 Avenida de la Reforma, Zone 10, Guatemala City)
Ambassador: (Vacant).

Of Guatemala to the United Nations
Ambassador: Fernando Andrade-Díaz-Durán.

Books of Reference

The official gazette is called *Diario de Centro America.*

Banco de Guatemala, *Memoria annual, Estudio económico* and *Boletín Estadístico*
Bloomfield, L. M., *The British Honduras–Guatemala Dispute.* Toronto, 1953
Franklin, W. B., *Guatemala.* [Bibliography] Oxford and Santa Barbara, 1981
Glassman, P., *Guatemala Guide.* Dallas, 1977
Humphreys, R. A., *The Diplomatic History of British Honduras 1638–1901.* London, 1961
Immerman, R. H., *The CIA in Guatemala: The Foreign Policy of Intervention.* Univ. of Texas Press, 1982
Mendoza, J. L., *Britain and Her Treaties on Belize.* Guatemala, 1946
Morton, F., *Xeláhuh.* London, 1959
Plant, R., *Guatemala: Unnatural Disaster.* London, 1978
Schlesinger, S., and Kinzer, S., *Bitter Front: The Untold Story of the American Coup in Guatemala.* London and New York, 1982

National Library: Biblioteca Nacional, 5a Avenida y 8a Calle, Zona 1, Guatemala City.

GUINEA

Capital: Conakry
Population: 6·34m. (1987)
GNP per capita: US$300 (1984)

République de Guinée

HISTORY. Guinea was proclaimed a French protectorate in 1888 and a colony in 1893. It became a constituent territory of French West Africa in 1904. The independent republic of Guinea was proclaimed on 2 Oct. 1958, after the territory of French Guinea had decided at the referendum of 28 Sept. to leave the French Community. Following the death of the first President, Ahmed Sekou Touré on 27 March 1984, the armed forces staged a *coup* and dissolved the National Assembly.

AREA AND POPULATION. Guinea, a coastal state of West Africa, is bounded north-west by Guinea-Bissau and Senegal, north-east by Mali, south-east by the Côte d'Ivoire, south by Liberia and Sierra Leone, and west by the Atlantic Ocean.

The area is 245,857 sq. km (94,926 sq. miles), and the population, census, 1983, was 5,781,014; estimate, 1987, 6,339,000. The capital is Conakry. In 1985, 25% were urban.

The areas, populations and chief towns of the major divisions are:

	Sq. km	Census 1983	Chief town	Census 1983
Conakry (city)	308	705,280	Conakry	705,280
Guinée-Maritime	43,980	1,147,301	Kindia	55,904
Moyenne-Guinée	51,710	1,595,007	Labé	65,439
Haute-Guinée	92,535	1,086,679	Kankan	88,760
Guinée-Forestière	57,324	1,246,747	Nzérékoré	23,000 [1]

[1] 1972.

The ethnic composition is Fulani (40·3%, predominant in Moyenne-Guinée), Malinké (or Mandingo, 25·8%, prominent in Haute-Guinée), Susu (11%, prominent in Guinée-Maritime), Kissi (6·5%) and Kpelle (4·8%) in Guinée-Forestière, and Dialonka, Loma and others (11·6%).

CLIMATE. A tropical climate, with high rainfall near the coast and constant heat, but conditions are a little cooler on the plateau. The wet season on the coast lasts from May to Nov., but only to Oct. inland. Conakry. Jan. 80°F (26·7°C), July 77°F (25°C). Annual rainfall 172″ (4,293 mm).

CONSTITUTION AND GOVERNMENT. Following the *coup* of 3 April 1984, supreme power rests with a *Comité Militaire de Redressement National*, ruling through a Council of Ministers appointed by the President composed as follows in Dec. 1986:

President, Head of CMRN, National Defence, Security, Planning and Co-operation: Brig.-Gen. Lansana Conté.

Ministers-Delegate to Presidency: Lieut.-Col. Sory Doumbouya *(National Defence)*, Maj. Alfa Oumar Diallo *(Interior and Decentralization)*, Edouard Benjamin *(Planning and International Co-operation)*, Zaïnoul Sanoussi Abidiné *(Information and Culture)*.

Resident (Regional) Ministers: Maj. Jean Kolipé Lama *(Guinée-Maritime)*, Maj. Sekou Mantong Camara *(Moyenne-Guinée)*, Capt. Mamadou Baldet *(Haute-Guinée)*, Capt. Faciné Touré *(Guinée-Forestière)*.

There are also 10 Ministers and 11 Secretaries of State.

Local Government: The administrative division comprises the capital Conakry and 32 provinces divided into 175 districts, grouped into 4 'supra-regions' which correspond to the 4 major geographical and ethnic areas: Guinée-Maritime; Moyenne-Guinée; Haute-Guinée and Guinée-Forestière.

National flag: Three vertical strips of red, gold, green.

Besides French, there are 8 official languages taught in schools: Fulani, Malinké, Susu, Kissi, Kpelle, Loma, Basari and Koniagi.

DEFENCE

Army. The Army of 8,500 men (1988), comprises 1 armoured, 5 infantry, 1 commando and 1 engineer, 1 artillery and 1 special force battalions. Equipment includes 45 T-34 and 20 PT-76 tanks. There are also 3 paramilitary forces: People's Militia (7,000), Gendarmerie (1,000) and Republican Guard (1,600).

Navy. The Navy comprises 1 patrol ship (*ex*-Soviet ocean minesweeper), 6 fast gunboats, 4 fast attack craft, 13 coastal patrol craft, and 4 small landing craft. There are bases at Conakry and Kakanda. Personnel in 1988 exceeded 600 officers and men.

Air Force. The Air Force, formed with Soviet assistance, is reported to be equipped with 6 MiG-17 jet-fighters and 2 MiG-15UTI trainers, 2 Il-18 turboprop transports, 4 An-14 and 4 Il-14 piston-engined transports and a Yak-40 jet aircraft for VIP duties, all Russian built, plus a few helicopters, piston-engined Yak-18 and L-29 jet trainers. Personnel about 800.

INTERNATIONAL RELATIONS

Membership. Guinea is a member of UN, OAU and is an ACP state of EEC.

ECONOMY

Planning. The Fourth Development Plan, 1981–85 envisaged expenditure of 38,000m. sylis.

Budget. The budget for 1983 balanced at US$444m.

Currency. The monetary unit is the *Guinea franc*, which replaced the *Syli* in Jan. 1986. In March 1988, £1 = 532 *francs*; US$1 = 440 *francs*.

Banking. In 1986 the Central Bank was restructured and commercial banking returned to the private sector.

ENERGY AND NATURAL RESOURCES

Electricity. Production of electrical energy was 236m. kwh. in 1986. The development of 2 new dams (1981) on the Konkouré river will expand capacity, primarily for the aluminium industry.

Minerals. Bauxite is mined at Fria, Boké and Kindia; output (1983) 12·38m. tonnes, alumina 578,000 tonnes. Production of iron ore from the Nimba and Simandou mountains commenced in 1981, following exhaustion of the Kaloum peninsula deposits. Diamond mining was suspended in 1978 but resumed in 1982; output (1983) 23,000 carats.

Agriculture. There are experimental fruit gardens at Camayenne near Conakry, Kindia and Dalaba, 2 stations for rice selection (Kankan, Koba) and an experimental quinine station at Seredou. Coffee is grown in forest districts. Fouta Djallon contains cattle in abundance.

The chief crops (production, 1986, in 1,000 tonnes) are: Cassava, 500; rice, 480; plantains, 350; sugar-cane, 200; bananas, 105; groundnuts, 75; sweet potatoes, 70; yams, 61; maize, 50; palm-oil, 40; palm kernels, 46; pineapples, 20; pulses, 50; coffee, 15; coconuts, 15.

Livestock (1986): Cattle, 1,838,000; sheep, 465,000; goats, 470,000; pigs, 49,000.

Forestry: There were 5,756 sq. km of classified forests in 1977. Round-wood production amounted to 3·64m. cu. metres in 1983.

Fisheries: Catch (1983) 18,453 tonnes, 90% in coastal waters.

COMMERCE. In 1984 imports totalled US$403m.; exports, US$537m. Alumina forms about 30% and bauxite 58% of the exports.

Total trade between Guinea and the UK (British Department of Trade returns, in £1,000 sterling):

	1983	1984	1985	1986	1987
Imports to UK	668	1,171	9,064	23,892	19,538
Exports and re-exports from UK	7,190	6,469	10,301	10,679	10,675

COMMUNICATIONS

Roads. There are 28,400 km of roads and tracks, of which 520 km are bitumenized. In 1978 there were 9,948 cars and 9,992 commercial vehicles.

Railways. A railway connects Conakry with Kankan (662 km) and is to be extended to Bougouni in Mali. A line 134 km long linking bauxite deposits at Sangaredi with Port Kamsar was opened in 1973 and a third line links Conakry and Fria (144 km).

Aviation. There are airports at Conakry and Kankan; in 1978, 71,000 passengers disembarked and embarked.

Shipping. There are ports at Conakry and for bauxite exports at Kamsar (opened 1973). There were (1983) 18 vessels of 6,944 GRT registered in Guinea.

Post and Broadcasting. The territory is connected by cable with France and Pernambuco; also with Freetown, Monrovia and other places. There is a wireless station at Conakry affording communication with all territories of West Africa. Telephones, 1981, numbered about 10,000. There were 125,000 radio receivers and 7,600 television receivers in 1984.

Newspapers. In 1979 there was 1 daily newspaper (circulation 20,000).

JUSTICE, RELIGION, EDUCATION AND WELFARE

Justice. There are *tribunaux du premier degré* at Conakry and Kankan, and a *juge de paix* at Nzérékoré. The High Court, Court of Appeal and Superior Tribunal of Cassation are at Conakry.

Religion. In 1980, about 69% of the population was Moslem, 1% Christian (mainly Roman Catholic) and 30% followed tribal religions.

Education. In 1980–81, 257,547 pupils and 7,165 teachers in primary schools, 89,900 pupils and 3,520 teachers in secondary schools, 2,776 students in technical schools and 8,437 in teacher-training colleges and 18,270 in higher education.

Health. In 1976 there were 314 hospitals and dispensaries with 7,650 beds; there were also 277 doctors, 21 dentists, 159 pharmacists, 394 midwives and 1,533 nursing personnel.

DIPLOMATIC REPRESENTATIVES

Of Guinea in Great Britain (resides in Paris)
Ambassador: Sekou Decazi Camara (accredited on 13 June 1985).

Of Great Britain in Guinea
Ambassador: J. E. C. Macrae, CMG (resides in Dakar).

Of Guinea in the USA (2112 Leroy Pl., NW, Washington, D.C., 20008)
Ambassador: Tolo Beavogui.

Of the USA in Guinea (2nd Blvd. and 9th Ave., Conakry)
Ambassador: Samuel E. Lupo.

Of Guinea to the United Nations
Ambassador: Mohamed Traore.

Books of Reference

Bulletin Statistique et Economique de la Guinée. Monthly. Conakry
Adamolekun, L., *Sékou Touré's Guinea.* London, 1976
Camara, S. S., *La Guinée sans la France.* Paris, 1976
Rivière, C., *Guinea: The Mobilization of a People.* Cornell Univ. Press, 1977
Taylor, F. W., *A Fulani-English Dictionary.* Oxford, 1932

GUINEA-BISSAU

Capital: Bissau
Population: 935,000 (1987)
GNP per capita: US$180 (1983)

Republica da Guiné-Bissau

HISTORY. Guinea-Bissau, formerly Portuguese Guinea, on the coast of Guinea, was discovered in 1446 by Nuno Tristão. It became a separate colony in 1879. It is bounded by the limits fixed by the convention of 12 May 1886 with France. In 1951 Guinea-Bissau became an overseas province of Portugal. The struggle against colonial rule began in 1963. Independence was declared on 24 Sept. 1973. In 1974 Portugal formally recognized the independence of Guinea-Bissau.

AREA AND POPULATION. Guinea-Bissau is bounded by Senegal in the north, the Atlantic ocean in the west and by Guinea in the east and south. It includes the adjacent archipelago of Bijagós. Area, 36,125 sq. km (13,948 sq. miles); population (census, 1979), 767,739, of whom 109,214 resided in the capital, Bissau; (estimate, 1987) 935,000.

The areas and populations (census 1979) of the regions were as follows:

Region	Sq. km	Census 1979	Region	Sq. km	Census 1979
Bissau City	78	109,214	Gabú	9,150	104,315
Bafatá	5,981	116,032	Oio	5,403	135,114
Biombo	838	56,463	Quinara	3,138	35,532
Bolama-Bijagós	2,624	25,473	Tombali	3,736	55,099
Cacheu	5,175	130,227			

In 1979, 14% of the population were urban, 48·2% were male and 44·3% were under the age of 15.

The main ethnic groups were (1979) the Balanta (27%), Fula (23%), Malinga (12%), Manjaco (11%) and Papel (10%). Portuguese remains the official language, but Crioulo is spoken throughout the country.

CLIMATE. The tropical climate has a wet season from June to Nov., when rains are abundant, but the hot, dry Harmattan wind blows from Dec. to May. Bissau. Jan. 76°F (24·4°C), July 80°F (26·7°C). Annual rainfall 78″ (1,950 mm).

CONSTITUTION AND GOVERNMENT. A new Constitution was promulgated on 16 May 1984. The Revolutionary Council, established following the 1980 *coup,* was replaced by a 15-member Council of State, while in April 1984 a new National People's Assembly was elected comprising 150 Representatives elected by and from the directly-elected regional councils. The sole political movement is the *Partido Africano da Independencia da Guiné e Cabo Verde* (PAIGC). The President is Head of State and Government, leading a Council of Ministers which in Dec. 1987 was composed as follows:

President: Gen. João Bernardo Vieira.

Ministers of State: Col. Iafai Camara *(Armed Forces),* Dr Vasco Cabral *(Justice),* Carlos Correia *(Rural Development and Fisheries),* Tiago Alelua Lopes *(Presidency).*

Foreign Affairs: Júlio Semedo. *Education, Culture and Sports:* Dr Fidelis Cabral d'Almada. *Commerce and Tourism:* Maj. Manuel dos Santos. *Public Works:* Avito da Silva. *National Security and Public Order:* Maj. José Pereira. *Natural Resources and Industry:* Filinto de Barros. *Finance:* Dr Vítor Freire Monteiro. *Public Health:* Adelino Nunes Correia. *Planning:* Bartolomeu Simões Pereira. *Civil Service and Labour:* Henriqueta Godinho Gomes. *Information and Telecommunications:* Mussa Djassi. *Minister-Governor of Central Bank:* Dr Pedro A. Godinho Gomes.

There are 11 Secretaries of State.

National flag: Horizontally yellow over green with red vertical strip in the hoist bearing a black star.

Local government: The administrative division is into 3 provinces, 8 regions (each under an elected regional council), in turn subdivided into 37 sectors; and the city of Bissau, treated as a separate region.

DEFENCE

Army. The Army consisted in 1988 of 5 infantry battalions, 1 engineer unit and 1 tank squadron. Equipment includes 10 T-34 tanks. Personnel, 6,800 men.

Navy. The naval flotilla includes 8 fast attack craft, 11 coastal patrol craft, 4 utility landing craft, 2 river craft and 4 minor landing craft. Based at Bissau. Personnel in 1987 totalled 250 officers and men.

Air Force. Formation of a small Air Force began in 1978 with the delivery of a French-built Cessna FTB-337 twin-engined counter-insurgency and general-purpose light transport. It has been followed by an Mi-8 and 2 Alouette III helicopters and 2 Dornier Do 27 utility aircraft. Personnel (1988) 75.

INTERNATIONAL RELATIONS

Membership. Guinea-Bissau is a member of UN, OAU and is an ACP state of EEC.

ECONOMY

Planning. The Development Plan ending 1990 aims at self-sufficiency in food.

Budget. The revenue in 1981 was 1,137m. pesos; the expenditure, 1,944m. pesos.

Currency. The monetary unit is the *peso* of 100 *centavos.* In March 1988, £1 = 1,152·78 *pesos*; US$1 = 650 *pesos.*

Banking. The Banco Nacional da Guiné-Bissau, founded 1976, is the bank of issue and also the commercial bank. There are also state-owned savings institutions.

ENERGY AND NATURAL RESOURCES

Electricity. Production (1986) 28m. kwh.

Minerals. Mining is very little developed although bauxite (200m. tonnes) has been located in the Boé area. Exploration for oil is taking place but no finds have been reported.

Agriculture. Chief crops (production, 1986, in 1,000 tonnes) are: Groundnuts, 29; sugar-cane, 5; plantains, 25; coconuts, 25; rice, 125; rubber, 23 (1981); palm kernels, 14; millet, 18; palm-oil, 2·8; sorghum, 33; maize, 29; cashew nuts, 10; timber, hides, seeds and wax.

Livestock (1986): Cattle, 333,000; sheep, 200,000; goats, 205,000; pigs, 286,000; poultry (1982), 420,000.

Forestry. Production (1983) 528,000 cu. metres.

Fisheries. Total catch (1984) 2,617 tonnes. Fishing is an important export industry.

COMMERCE. Imports in 1983, 1,586m. pesos of which 33% from Portugal; exports, 358m. of which 66% went to Portugal, 11% to Senegal and 10% to Guinea. In 1980, fish formed 33% of exports, groundnuts, 24% and coconuts, 17%.

Total trade between Guinea-Bissau and UK (British Department of Trade returns, in £1,000 sterling):

	1984	1985	1986	1987
Imports to UK	–	2	214	17
Exports and re-exports from UK	499	1,209	1,319	1,152

COMMUNICATIONS

Roads. There were (1982) 5,058 km of roads and (1981) 3,807 vehicles.

Aviation. There is an international airport at Bissalanca (for Bissau).

Shipping. The main port is Bissau; minor ports are Boloma, Cacheu and Catió. In 1974, 169 vessels entered the ports unloading 134,000 tonnes.

Post. In 1984 there were 3,000 telephones and 26,000 radio receivers.

Cinemas. There were 7 cinemas (1972) with a seating capacity of 3,000.

Newspapers (1984). There was one weekly newspaper, with a circulation of 3,000.

RELIGION, EDUCATION AND WELFARE

Religion. In 1985 about 30% of the population were Moslem and about 5% Christian (mainly Roman Catholic).

Education. There were, in 1982, 83,155 pupils in 732 primary schools with 3,256 teachers; 10,740 pupils in 8 secondary schools with 432 teachers and 827 students in 4 technical schools and teacher-training establishments with 96 teachers.

Health. In 1981 there were 17 hospitals and clinics with 1,570 beds and in 1980 there were 108 doctors, 2 dentists, 3 pharmacists, 2 midwives and 56 nursing personnel.

DIPLOMATIC REPRESENTATIVES

Of Guinea-Bissau in Great Britain (resides in Brussels)
Ambassador: Bubacar Turé (accredited 26 Nov. 1986).

Of Great Britain in Guinea-Bissau
Ambassador: J. E. C. Macrae, CMG (resides in Dakar).

Of Guinea-Bissau in the USA
Ambassador: Alfredo Lopes Cabral.

Of the USA in Guinea-Bissau (Ave. Domingos Ramos, Bissau)
Ambassador: John Dale Blacken.

Of Guinea-Bissau to the United Nations
Ambassador: Alfredo Lopes Cabral.

Books of Reference

Relatório e Mapas do Movimento Comercial e Maritimo da Guiné. Bolama, Annual
Cabral, A., *Revolution in Guinea.* London, 1969.—*Return to the Source.* New York, 1973
Davidson, B., *Growing from the Grass Roots.* London, 1974
Gjerstad, O., and Sarrazin, C., *Sowing the First Harvest: National Reconstruction in Guinea-Bissau.* Oakland, 1978
Rudebeck, L., *Guinea-Bissau: A Study of Political Mobilization.* Uppsala, 1974

GUYANA

Capital: Georgetown
Population: 812,000 (1987)
GNP per capita: US$510 (1984)

HISTORY. The territory, including the counties of Demerara, Essequibo and Berbice, named from the 3 rivers, was first partially settled by the Dutch West Indian Company about 1620. The Dutch retained their hold until 1796, when it was captured by the English. It was finally ceded to Great Britain in 1814 and named British Guiana. On 26 May 1966 British Guiana became an independent member of the Commonwealth under the name of Guyana and the world's first Co-operative Republic on 23 Feb. 1970.

AREA AND POPULATION. Guyana is situated on the north-east coast of South America on the Atlantic ocean, with Suriname on the east, Venezuela on the west and Brazil on the south and west. Area, 83,000 sq. miles (214,969 sq. km). Estimated population (1987), 812,000. The official language is English, and in 1980 the population comprised 51% (East) Indians, 30% Africans, 10% mixed race, 5% Amerindian and 4% others. The capital is Georgetown, whose metropolitan area had 188,000 inhabitants in 1983; other towns are New Amsterdam, Linden, Rose Hall and Corriverton.

Vital statistics (1983): Birth rate 2·90%; death rate 0·70%.

Venezuela demanded the return of the Essequibo region in 1963. It was finally agreed in March 1983 that the UN Secretary-General should mediate. There was also an unresolved claim (1984) by Suriname for the return of an area between the New river and the Courantyne river.

CLIMATE. A tropical climate, with rainy seasons from April to July and Nov. to Jan. Humidity is high all the year but temperatures are moderated by sea-breezes. Rainfall increases from 90″ (2,280 mm) on the coast to 140″ (3,560 mm) in the forest zone. Georgetown. Jan. 79°F (26·1°C), July 81°F (27·2°C). Annual rainfall 87″ (2,175 mm).

CONSTITUTION AND GOVERNMENT. A new Constitution was promulgated in Oct. 1980. The National Assembly consists of 65 elected members. Elections are held under the single-list system of proportional representation, with the whole of the country forming one electoral area and each voter casting his vote for a party list of candidates. The legislature is elected for 5 years unless earlier dissolved.

The elections held on 9 Dec. 1985 gave the People's National Congress 42 seats, the People's Progressive Party 8 seats, the United Force 2 seats and the Working People's Alliance 1 seat.

The Cabinet was in Dec. 1987 composed as follows:

President: H. Desmond Hoyte.
Prime Minister: Hamilton Green.
Vice-Presidents: Mohamed Shahabuddeen *(Attorney-General)*; Ranji Chandisingh *(National Development)*; Viola Burnham *(Education and Social Development)*.
Deputy Prime Ministers: William Haslyn Parris *(Planning and Development)*; Robert H. O. Corbin *(Agriculture)*. *Foreign Affairs:* Rashleigh Jackson. *Finance:* Carl Greenidge. *Labour:* Seeram Prashad. *Trade and Tourism:* Winston S. Murray. *Information:* Yvonne Harewood-Benn.

587

National flag: Green with a yellow triangle based on the hoist, edged in white, charged with a red triangle edged in black.

Local government: There are 10 administrative regions: Barima/Waini, Pomeroon /Supernaam, Essequibo Islands/West Demerara, Demerara/Mahaica, Mahaica/ Berbice, East Berbice/Corentyne, Cuyuni/Mazaruni, Potaro/Siparuni, Upper Takutu/Upper Essequibo, Upper Demerara/Berbice.

DEFENCE

Army. The Guyana Army had (1988) a strength of 5,200 (which includes airforce), including a women's army corps. It comprises 2 infantry battalions and 1 artillery battery.

Navy. In 1988 the naval force had 150 personnel and comprised 6 fast patrol craft, 9 coastal patrol boats, 2 service vessels and a landing craft.

Air Force. The Air Command is equipped with light aircraft and helicopters, including 1 Super King Air 200 twin-turboprop transport, 6 Islander twin-engined STOL transports, a Cessna U206F utility lightplane, and 5 Bell 206/212/412 and 2 Mi-8 helicopters. Personnel (1988) 200.

INTERNATIONAL RELATIONS

Membership. Guyana is a member of UN, the Commonwealth, Caricom, the Non-Aligned Movement and is an ACP state of the EEC.

ECONOMY

Budget. Revenue and expenditure for calendar years (in G$1,000):

	1981	1982	1983	1984	1985	1986
Revenue	1,009,936	818,136	887,539	1,537,928	1,200,208	1,618,125
Expenditure	1,176,678	1,621,814	1,236,878	1,585,840	1,562,858	2,858,467

Currency. The Bank of Guyana, established in 1965, issued Guyana dollar notes of $1, 5, 10 and 20 and coins of 1-, 5-, 10-, 25- and 50-cent pieces. In March 1988: £1 = 15·94 G$; US$1 = 10 G$.

Banking. Of the 6 commercial banks operating in Guyana 3 are foreign-owned (Barclays Bank International with branches, Bank of Baroda and Bank of Nova Scotia) and 3 locally controlled (Guyana National Co-operative Bank, the National Bank of Industry and Commerce and the Republic Bank). The Guyana Agricultural and Industrial Development Bank (Gaibank) for farmers and agri-based industries and the Guyana Co-operative Mortgage Finance Bank for housing.

ENERGY AND NATURAL RESOURCES

Electricity. Production (1986) 500m. kwh. Supply 110 volts; 60 Hz and 240 volts; 50 Hz.

Minerals. Placer gold mining commenced in 1884, and was followed by diamond mining in 1887. Output of gold was 14,040 oz. in 1986. Production of diamonds was 10,200 in 1980. Total production of the 4 grades of bauxite (calcined, chemical, metallurgical and abrasive) was 1·5m. tonnes in 1986. Full-scale production of manganese began in 1960 and other minerals include uranium, oil, copper and molybdenum.

Agriculture. Production, 1985: Sugar-cane, 3·52m. tonnes; rice, 183,000 tonnes. Important products are coconuts, 40,000 tonnes, 1985 and oranges 11,000 tonnes. Other tropical fruits and vegetables are grown mostly in scattered plantings; they include mangoes, papaws, avocado pears, melons, bananas and gooseberries. Other important crops are tomatoes, cabbages, black-eye peas, peanuts, carrots, onions, turmeric, ginger, pineapples, red kidney beans, soybeans, eschallot and tobacco. Large areas of unimproved land in the coastal region, which vary in width up to about 30 miles from the sea, are still available for agricultural and cattle-grazing projects.

Livestock estimate (1986): Cattle, 200,000; pigs, 180,000; sheep, 120,000; goats, 77,000; poultry, 15m.

Forestry. Guyana can be divided roughly into 3 regions: (1) A low coastal region varying in width up to about 30 miles and constituting the agricultural area; (2) an intermediate area about 100 miles wide, of slightly higher undulating land containing the chief mineral and forest resources of the country; and (3) a hinterland of several mountain ranges and extensive savannahs. 19,844,170 hectares of the land area is forested out of 21,497,000 hectares. Production (1986) 4·7m. cu. ft.

Fisheries. Production (1986) of fish, 39,000 tons and shrimp, 3,500 tons.

COMMERCE. Imports and exports (in G$) for calendar years:

	1982	1983	1984	1985	1986
Imports	840,442,362	745,000,000	821,300,000	959,500,000	1,618,000,000
Exports	775,544,161	580,000,000	831,300,000	914,400,000	1,092,000,000

Chief imports (1983): Fuel and lubricants, 19,367,367 kg, $272,513,835; milk, 1,386,887 kg, $8,674,714.

Chief domestic exports (1983): Sugar, 210,734 tonnes, $195,814,993; rice, 41,721 tonnes, $64,939,971; bauxite, dried, 779,768 tonnes, $66,629,072; bauxite, calcined, 340,709 tonnes, $136,201,592; alumina, 29,301 tonnes, $7,019,133; rum, 20,442,180 litres, $6,987,107; timber, 49,720 cu. metres, $10,837,689; molasses, 53,938,864 litres, $2,019,371; shrimps, 7,318,145 kg, $14,067,860.

Imports (exclusive of transhipments), 1981, from CARICOM Territories, 35%; from USA, 25%; from UK, 16%; from Canada, 4%; exports (exclusive of transhipments) to UK, 26%; to CARICOM Territories, 17%; to Canada, 5%.

Total trade between Guyana and UK (British Department of Trade returns, in £1,000 sterling):

	1983	1984	1985	1986	1987
Imports to UK	42,810	57,884	52,377	55,535	58,502
Exports and re-exports from UK	13,585	14,845	18,406	13,737	15,371

COMMUNICATIONS

Roads. Roads and vehicular trails in the national, provincial and urban systems amount to 8,870 km. Motor vehicles, as of 31 Dec. 1987, totalled 53,446, including 8,401 passenger cars, 3,682 lorries and vans, 8,958 tractors and trailers, and 15,893 motor cycles. The main road on the Atlantic Coast, some 290 km (180 miles) long extends from Charity on the Pomeroon River to Crabwood Creek on the Corentyne, there are two unbridged gaps made by the Berbice and Essequibo Rivers, and the banks of the Demerara River are linked by a 1,853 metre (6,074 ft) floating bridge.

Railways. There is a government-owned railway in the North West District, while the Guyana Mining Enterprise operates a standard gauge railway of 133 km from Linden on the Demerara River to Ituni and Coomacka.

Aviation. Guyana Airways Corporation operates 11 flights weekly on its international service and 21 flights locally. In 1985 Guyana Airways Corporation carried 108,936 passengers on its international service and 59,113 passengers locally. Other services in operation: British Airways 4 times weekly to the Caribbean, Europe and North America: PANAM 3 times weekly to North, Central and South America: Air France, to and from Guadeloupe, Paramaribo and Cayenne 4 times a week; British West Indian Airways, Ltd, to and from Trinidad twice a week, providing direct connexion with New York and London; Cubana Airlines once a fortnight; Suriname Airways and Tropical Airways once weekly. The International Airport at Timehri serves Arrow Air Airlines, BWIA, Cubana Airways, and Suriname Airways.

Shipping. There are 217 nautical miles of river navigation. There are ferry services across the mouths of the Demerara, Berbice and Essequibo rivers, the last providing a link between the islands of Leguan and Wakenaam and the mainland at Adventure, and a number of coastal and river-boat services carrying both passengers and cargo. A number of launch services are operated in the more remote areas by private concerns.

Georgetown harbour, about ½ mile wide and 2½ miles long, has a minimum depth of 24 ft. New Amsterdam harbour is situated at the mouth of the Berbice River; there are wharves for coastal vessels only. Bauxite is loaded on ocean-going freighters at Mackenzie, 67 miles up the Demerara River, and at Everton on the Berbice River, about 10 miles from the mouth of the waterway. The Essequibo River has several timber-loading berths ranging from 20 to 40 ft. Springlands on the Corentyne River is the point of entry and departure of passengers travelling by launch services to and from Suriname. In 1984 the merchant marine comprised 84 vessels of 20,248 GRT.

Post and Broadcasting. The inland public telegraph and radio communication services are operated and maintained by the Telecommunication Corporation, established on 1 March 1967. On 31 Aug. 1987 there were 57 post offices and 28 agencies.

The telephone exchanges had at 31 Aug. 1987 a total of 28,450 direct exchange lines with (1987), 20,000 telephone instruments. The number of route miles in the coastal and inland areas was 2,982 km. 39 land-line stations were maintained at post offices in the coastal area, and 8 telegraph stations in the interior provide communication with the coastal area through a central telegraph office in Georgetown.

The Guyana Broadcasting Corporation, which came into operation on 1 July 1980, has 2 channels. In 1985 there were 350,000 radio receivers.

Cinemas (1987). There are 52 cinemas.

Newspapers (1987). There is 1 daily newspaper with a circulation of 60,000 and 5 weekly papers with a combined circulation of about 120,000.

JUSTICE, RELIGION, EDUCATION AND WELFARE

Justice. The law, both civil and criminal, is based on the common and statute law of England, save that the principles of the Roman–Dutch law have been retained in respect of the registration, conveyance and mortgaging of land.

The Supreme Court of Judicature consists of a Court of Appeal and a High Court.

Religion. In 1980, 34% of the population were Hindu, 34% Protestant, 18% Roman Catholic and 9% Muslim.

Education. In Sept. 1976 the Government assumed total responsibility for education from nursery school to university. Private education was abolished. In Sept. 1984, the total number of schools was 876: Nursery, 368; primary, 418; community high, 34; general secondary, 56.

There are now 5 technical and vocational schools and 2 schools for the teaching of home economics and domestic crafts. Training in co-operatives is provided by the Kuru-Kuru Co-operative College and agriculture by the Guyana School of Agriculture and the Burnham Agricultural Institute. Art training is provided by the Burrowes School of Art. The training of primary and secondary school teachers is undertaken by 3 institutions. Higher education is also provided by the University of Guyana which was established in 1963 with faculties of medicine, natural science, social science, art, technology and education as well as first year students in law. There were 2,004 students in July 1983. The total number of pupils in all schools was 233,723 in 1983.

Health. In 1987 there were 213 health facilities including hospitals. There were (1987) 142 doctors, 19 dentists and (1982) 32 pharmacists, 546 midwives and 881 nursing personnel.

DIPLOMATIC REPRESENTATIVES

Of Guyana in Great Britain (3 Palace Ct., London, W2 4LP)
High Commissioner: Cecil S. Pilgrim (accredited 5 Dec. 1986).

Of Great Britain in Guyana (44 Main St., Georgetown)
High Commissioner: D. P. Small, MBE.

Of Guyana in the USA (2490 Tracy Place, NW, Washington, D.C., 20008)
Ambassador: Dr Cedric Hilburn Grant.

Of the USA in Guyana (31 Main St., Georgetown)
Ambassador: Theresa A. Tull.

Of Guyana to the United Nations
Ambassador: Samuel R. Insanally.

Books of Reference

Baber, C., and Jeffrey, H. B., *Guyana: Politics, Economics and Society.* London, 1986
Braveboy-Wagner, J. A., *The Venezuela-Guyana Border Dispute: Britain's Colonial Legacy in Latin America.* London, 1984
Daly, P. H., *From Revolution to Republic.* Georgetown, 1970
Daly, Vere T., *A Short History of the Guyanese People.* Rev. ed. London, 1975
Hope, K. R., *Development Policy in Guyana: Planning, Finance and Administration.* London, 1979
Latin American Bureau, *Guyana: Fraudulent Revolution.* London, 1984
Spinner, T. J., *A Political and Social History of Guyana, 1945–83.* Epping, 1985

HAITI

Capital: Port-au-Prince
Population: 5·3m. (1985)
GNP per capita: US$320 (1983)

République d'Haiti

HISTORY. Haiti occupies the western third of the large island of Hispaniola which was discovered by Christopher Columbus in 1492. The Spanish colony was ceded to France in 1697 and became her most prosperous colony. After the extirpation of the Indians by the Spaniards (by 1533) large numbers of African slaves were imported whose descendants now populate the country. The slaves obtained their liberation following the French Revolution, but subsequently Napoleon sent his brother-in-law, Gen. Leclerc, to restore French authority and re-impose slavery. Toussaint Louverture, the leader of the slaves who had been appointed a French general and governor, was kidnapped and sent to France, where he died in gaol. However, the reckless courage of the Negro troops and the ravages of yellow fever forced the French to evacuate the island and surrender to the blockading British squadron.

The country declared its independence on 1 Jan. 1804, and its successful leader, Gen. Jean-Jacques Dessalines, proclaimed himself Emperor of the newly-named Haiti. After the assassination of Dessalines (1806) a separate régime was set up in the north under Henri Christophe, a Negro general who in 1811 had himself proclaimed King Henry. In the south and west a republic was constituted, with the mulatto Alexander Pétion as its first President. Pétion died in 1818 and was succeeded by Jean-Pierre Boyer, under whom the country became re-united after Henry had committed suicide in 1820. From 1822 to 1844 Haiti and the eastern part of the island (later the Dominican Republic) were united. After one more monarchical interlude, under the Emperor Faustin (1847–59), Haiti has been a republic. From 1915 to 1934 Haiti was under United States occupation.

Following a military *coup* in 1950, and subsequent uprisings, Dr François Duvalier was elected President on 22 Oct. 1957 and subsequently became President for Life in 1964. He died on 21 April 1971 and was succeeded as president for life by his son, Jean-Claude Duvalier who fled the country on 7 Feb. 1986.

AREA AND POPULATION. The area is 27,750 sq. km (10,700 sq. miles), of which about three-quarters is mountainous. The population at the census in 1982 was 5,053,792 of which 21% urban and 48·5% male. Estimate (1985) 5,272,000.

The areas and populations of the 9 *départements* are as follows:

Département	Sq. km	1982	Chief town	1982
Nord-Ouest	2,094	293,531	Port-de-Paix	21,733 [1]
Nord	2,175	564,002	Cap Haïtien	64,406
Nord-Est	1,698	189,573	Fort-Liberté	…
L'Artibonite	4,895	732,932	Gonaïves	34,209
Centre	3,597	361,470	Hinche	…
Ouest	4,595	1,551,792	Port-au-Prince	449,831 [2]
Sud-Est	2,077	367,911	Jacmel	…
Sud	2,602	502,624	Les Cayes	34,090
Grande Anse	3,100	489,957	Jérémie	17,117 [3]

[1] 1975.   [2] Metropolitan area, 763,188.   [3] 1971.

The Île de la Gonave, some 40 miles long, lies in the gulf of the same name. Among other islands is La Tortue, off the north peninsula. 95% of the population is black, with an important minority of mulattoes and only about 5,000 white residents, almost all foreign.

Haiti is the only French-speaking republic in the Americas. The standard French of government, parliament and the press is spoken by the small literate minority (about 10%), but the great majority of the people habitually speak the dialect known as Créole.

CLIMATE. A tropical climate, but the central mountains can cause semi-arid conditions in their lee. There are rainy seasons from April to June and Aug. to Nov. Hurricanes and severe thunderstorms can occur. The annual temperature range is small. Port-au-Prince. Jan. 77°F (25°C), July 84°F (28·9°C). Annual rainfall 53″ (1,321 mm).

CONSTITUTION AND GOVERNMENT. The 1983 Constitution, provided for an Executive President who was elected for life and could nominate his successor. He nominated a Cabinet to assist him and, in cases of national emergency, could dismiss both the Cabinet and the National Assembly and govern by decree. A new draft Constitution was approved in March 1987. The unicameral National Assembly comprises 59 deputies elected for 6-year terms (renewable) by universal suffrage at age 18.

Following the departure of President Jean-Claude Duvalier the 5-man Council of Government formed in Feb. 1986 was composed of Gen. Henry Namphy; Col. Max Valles, Commander of the Presidential Guard; Col. William Regala, Inspector-General; Alix Cinéas and Gérard Gourgue. Presidential elections were planned for 29 Nov. 1987 but were postponed because of violence. They took place on 17 Jan. 1988 and on 24 Jan. Leslie Manigat was declared elected President with 534,080 votes, 50·29% of the total cast. President Manigat was sworn in on 5 Feb. and the country nominally returned to civilian rule.

The Cabinet in April 1987 was composed as follows:

President: Gen. Henri Namphy.

Interior and Defence: Brig.-Gen. Williams Regala. *Finance and Economy:* Leslie Delatour. *Trade and Industry:* Mario Célestin. *Agriculture:* Gustave Menager. *Foreign Affairs:* Col. Hérard Abraham. *Justice:* François St. Fleur. *Public Health and Population:* Lieut-Col. Jean Verly. *Public Works, Transport and Communications:* Col. Jacques Joachim. *Education, Youth and Sport:* Patrick Delencourt. *Social Affairs:* Gérard Noel. *Planning:* Jacques Villegrain. *Information:* Jacques Lorthe. *Without Portfolio:* Luc Hector.

National flag: Horizontally blue over red with the national arms on a white panel in the centre.

National anthem: 'La Dessalinienne': Pour le pays, pour les ancêtres (words by J. Lhérisson; tune by N. Geffrard, 1903).

DEFENCE. The Haitian Defence Force (*Forces Armées d'Haiti*) totalling about 7,600 men, was divided into Army, Navy, and Air Force. The President is Commander-in-Chief and appoints the officers.

Army. Total strength, about 7,000 (1988), organized into 9 Military Departments and the 'Leopards'. Three of the Departments are in Port-au-Prince and consist of the Presidential Guard, 1 infantry battalion, 1 special forces battalion, 2 artillery battalions and 6 garrison departments.

Navy. The Navy/coastguard of 45 officers and 280 men has 1 *ex*-US armed tug, and 14 coastal patrol boats. The base is at Port-au-Prince.

Air Force. Personnel strength was (1988) about 275, with (1987) about 30 aircraft of some 12 varieties. They include 7 Summit/Cessna O2-337 Sentry twin piston-engined counter-insurgency aircraft, 1 DC-3, 6 light transports, 15 training and liaison aircraft, including 4 S.211 jet trainers, 4 turboprop-powered SF.260 TPs, and 3 helicopters.

INTERNATIONAL RELATIONS

Membership. Haiti is a member of UN and OAS.

ECONOMY

Budget. Revenue (fiscal year ending 30 Sept.) in US$1m. (5 gourdes = US$1), 1981–82, 204m.; expenditure, 270m.

Currency. The unit of currency is the *gourde* and its value fixed at 5 *gourdes* = US$1. In March 1988, £1 = 8·87 *gourdes*. There are copper–nickel coins for 50, 20, 10 and 5 *centimes* and copper–zinc–nickel coins of 10 and 5 centimes.

Banking. Banque Nationale de Credit, owned by the State, was established 21 Oct. 1910 with a capital of US$5m., and has a monopoly of the note issue. US dollars may be included in the minimum required reserves. The Royal Bank of Canada, the Citibank, the Bank of Nova Scotia, the Bank of Boston, the Banque de l'Union Haitienne (mainly local capital with participation from American, Canadian and Dominican Republic Banks), Banque Nationale de Paris and Banque Nationale de République d'Haiti (the central bank) all have branches in Port-au-Prince.

Weights and Measures. The metric system is officially accepted.

ENERGY AND NATURAL RESOURCES

Electricity. Production (1986) 332m. kwh. Supply 110 and 220 volts; 60 Hz.

Minerals. Copper exists but is at present uneconomic to exploit. Haiti may possess undeveloped mineral resources of oil, gold, silver, antimony, sulphur, coal and lignite, nickel, gypsum and porphyry.

Agriculture. Only one-third of the country is arable and most people own the tiny plots they farm; the resulting pressure of population is the main cause of rural poverty. Number of farms is estimated at over 500,000.

The occupations of Haiti are nine-tenths agricultural, carried on in 7 large plains, from 200,000 to 25,000 acres, and in 15 smaller plains down to 2,000 acres. Irrigation is used in some areas. Haiti's most important product is coffee of good quality, classified as 'mild', and grown by peasants. Production in 1986 totalled about 38,000 tonnes. Second most important crop is sugar. Sisal is grown extensively. Much of the fibre is exported as or for cordage. New types of cotton are being tried with success. New varieties of rice should significantly boost future production, especially in the Artibonite Valley. Output of main crops in 1986 (in 1,000 tonnes) was: Sugar-cane, 3,150; mangoes, 350; plantains; 275; sweet potatoes, 360; cassava, 270; bananas, 235; maize, 160; sorghum, 110; rice, 180; sisal, 10; cotton, 6; cocoa, 5.

Rum and other spirits are distilled. Essential oils from vetiver, neroli and amyris are important. Cattle and horse breeding are encouraged.

Livestock (1986); Cattle, 1·4m.; sheep, 92,000; goats, 1·1m.; horses, 425,000; poultry, 8m.

Fisheries. Production (1984) 5,000 tonnes.

INDUSTRY AND TRADE

Industry. Light manufacturing industries assembling or finishing goods for re-export constitute the fastest growing sector. Soap factories produce laundry soap, toilet soap and detergent. A cement factory located near the capital produced 243,000 tonnes in 1980. A steel plant making rods, beams and angles was opened in 1974. There are also a pharmaceutical plant, a tannery, a plastics plant, 2 paint works, 5 shoe factories, a large factory producing enamel cookingware, 2 pasta-making factories, a tomato cannery and a flour-mill, all located in or near Port-au-Prince.

Labour. Trade unions were recognized in Feb. 1946. Strong government influence is exercised over the insignificant portion of the labour force that is unionized and organized labour has virtually no strength in Haiti.

Commerce. In 1984 exports were US$250m. and imports, US$365m.

The leading imports are foodstuffs, textiles, machinery, mineral oils, raw materials for transformation industries and vehicles.

Total trade between Haiti and UK (British Department of Trade returns, in £1,000 sterling):

	1983	1984	1985	1986	1987
Imports to UK	1,646	1,402	1,512	899	621
Exports and re-exports from UK	4,171	3,736	5,048	5,147	5,327

Tourism. In 1986, 112,000 tourists visited Haiti.

COMMUNICATIONS

Roads. Total length of roads is some 4,000 km, little of which is practicable in ordinary motors in the rainy season. There were (1984) about 50,000 vehicles in Haiti.

Railways. The only railway is owned by the Haitian American Sugar Company.

Aviation. An airport capable of handling jets was opened at Port-au-Prince in 1965. US and French carriers provide daily direct services to New York, Miami, Jamaica, Puerto Rico and the French Antilles. There are also services to the Dominican Republic and the Netherlands Antilles. A Haitian company provides a cargo service to the US and Puerto Rico. Air services connecting Port-au-Prince with other Haitian towns are operated by Haiti Air Inter.

Shipping. US, French, Federal Republic of Germany, Dutch, British, Canadian and Japanese lines connect Haiti with the US, Latin America (except Cuba), Canada, Jamaica, Europe and the Far East.

Post and Broadcasting. Most principal towns are connected by the government telegraph system, telephones and wireless.

The telephone company, of which the Haitian Government is now the majority stockholder, is in process of being modernized. Telephone subscribers totalled 34,000 in 1984.

In 1982 there were 105,000 radio and 65,000 television receivers.

Cinemas (1984). There were 10 cinemas in Port-au-Prince.

Newspapers (1984). There were 6 daily newspapers in Port-au-Prince, also a monthly in English and 1 weekly newspaper in Cap Haïtien.

JUSTICE, RELIGION, EDUCATION AND WELFARE

Justice. Judges, both of the lower courts and the court of appeal, are appointed by the President. The legal system is basically French. The divorce law has recently been amended to permit parties to obtain 'quick and painless' divorces at a moderate cost, in the hope of attracting the US trade, now that the Mexican 'divorce mills' have closed down. This has developed a useful flow of dollar revenue.

Police. The Police number about 1,200 in Port-au-Prince and are part of the armed forces.

Religion. Since the Concordat of 1860, the official religion is Roman Catholicism, under an archbishop with 5 suffragan bishops. There are still quite a number of foreigners, French and French Canadians mainly, among the clergy but the first Haitian archbishop took office in 1966. The Episcopal Church now has its first Haitian bishop who was consecrated in 1971. Other Christian churches number perhaps 10% of the population. The folk religion is Voodoo.

Education. Education is divided into primary (first 6 years), secondary (the next 7 years) and finally superior or university. The school system is modelled on that of France. The law calls for free and compulsory elementary education in the French language.

In 1983 there were 3,321 primary schools with 14,927 teachers and 658,102 pupils. Secondary schools had 98,562 pupils in 1980.

Higher education is offered at the University of Haiti with 4,100 students in 1980.

Health. There were, in 1972, 332 doctors and 104 dentists in practice, 44 hospitals, and 196 health centres and rural clinics. The hospitals had 3,329 beds, of which 776 were in private and charitable establishments.

DIPLOMATIC REPRESENTATIVES

Of Haiti in Great Britain. The Embassy closed on 30 March 1987.

Of Great Britain in Haiti
Ambassador: Alan J. Payne, CMG (resides in Kingston).

Of Haiti in the USA (2311 Massachusetts Ave., NW, Washington, D.C., 20008)
Ambassador: Pierre Sam.

Of the USA in Haiti (Harry Truman Blvd., Port-au-Prince)
Ambassador: Brunson McKinley.

Of Haiti to the United Nations
Ambassador: Yves L. Auguste.

Books of Reference

The official gazette is *Le Moniteur.*

Revue Agricole d'Haïti. From 1946. Quarterly
Bellegarde, D., *Histoire du Peuple Haïtien.* Port-au-Prince, 1953
Chambers, F. J., *Haiti.* [Bibliography] Oxford and Santa Barbara, 1983
Ferguson, J., *Papa Doc, Baby Doc: Haiti and the Duvaliers.* Oxford, 1987
Laguerre, M. S., *The Complete Haitiana.* [Bibliography] London and New York, 1982
Lundahl, M., *The Haitian Economy: Man, Land and Markets.* London, 1983
Nicholls, D., *From Dessalines to Duvalier: Race, Colour and National Independence in Haiti.*
    CUP, 1979.—*Haiti in Caribbean Context: Ethnicity, Economy and Revolt.* London, 1985

National Library: Bibliothèque Nationale, Rue du Centre, Port-au-Prince.

HONDURAS

Capital: Tegucigalpa
Population: 4·3m. (1986)
GNP per capita: US$750 (1984)

República de Honduras

HISTORY. On 5 Nov. 1838 Honduras declared itself an independent sovereign state, free from the Federation of Central America, of which it had formed a part.

AREA AND POPULATION. Honduras is bounded north by the Caribbean, east and south-east by Nicaragua, west by Guatemala, south-west by El Salvador and south by the Pacific ocean. Area is 112,088 sq. km (43,277 sq. miles), with a population, census (1974) of 2,656,948. Estimate (1986) 4·3m.

The chief cities (populations, 1985) were Tegucigalpa, the capital (571,400), San Pedro Sula (372,800), El Progreso (55,500), Choluteca (57,200), Danli (18,200) and the Atlantic coast ports of La Ceiba (61,900), Puerto Cortés (39,900) and Tela (26,700); other towns include Olanchito (12,400), Juticalpa (13,800), Comayagua (28,800), Signatepeque (24,100) and Santa Rosa de Copan (19,400).

The areas and populations of the 18 departments and federal district were as follows:

Department	Sq. km	1983	Department	Sq. km	1983
Atlántida	4,251	242,235	Intibucá	3,072	111,412
Choluteca	4,211	289,637	Islas de la Bahía	261	18,744
Colón	8,875	128,370	La Paz	2,331	86,627
Comayagua	5,196	211,465	Lempira	4,290	174,916
Copán	3,203	217,258	Ocotepeque	1,680	64,151
Cortés	3,954	624,090	Olancho	24,350	228,122
El Paraíso	7,218	206,601	Santa Bárbara	5,115	286,854
Federal District	1,648	532,519	Valle	1,565	125,640
Francisco Morazán	6,298	203,753	Yoro	7,939	304,310
Gracias a Dios	16,630	35,471			

Aboriginal tribes number over 35,000, principally Miskito, Payas and Xicaques Indians and Sambos (the latter a mixture of Miskito and Negro), each speaking a different dialect. The Spanish-speaking inhabitants are chiefly *mestizos*, Indians with an admixture of Spanish blood. Gracias a Dios is still largely unexplored and is inhabited by pure native races who speak little or no Spanish.

In 1985 the population growth rate was 3·1%; infant mortality rate 70 per 1,000 live births; life expectancy 62.

CLIMATE. The climate is tropical, with a small annual range of temperature but with high rainfall. Upland areas have two wet seasons, from May to July and in Sept. and Oct. The Caribbean Coast has most rain in Dec. and Jan. and temperatures are generally higher than inland. Tegucigalpa. Jan. 66°F (19°C), July 74°F (23·3°C). Annual rainfall 64″ (1,621 mm).

CONSTITUTION AND GOVERNMENT. Presidential and Congressional elections were held on 24 Nov. 1985. A new Constitution was promulgated on 20 Jan. 1982. The President is directly elected for a 4-year term.

At the 1985 Presidential elections the National Party's leading candidate obtained 41% of the vote, but the leading Liberal, José Azcona Hoyo, was declared President-elect since the combined Liberal vote was 51% against 45% for the National Party candidates.

President: José Azcona Hoyo (sworn in 27 Jan. 1986).

The legislature is a 134-member Congress of Deputies, composed following the

597

elections of 24 Nov. 1985 of 46 deputies of the official *Partido Liberal,* 63 of the *Partido Nacional* and the remaining 25 seats were won by a rival Liberal Party faction and 2 smaller political parties.

National flag: Three horizontal stripes of blue, white, blue, with 5 blue stars in the centre.

National anthem: Tu bandera (words by A. C. Coello; tune by C. Hartling).

Local government: Honduras comprises a Federal District (containing the cities of Tegucigalpa and Comayaguela) and 18 departments (each administered by an appointed Governor), sub-divided into 282 municipalities.

DEFENCE. Conscription is for approximately 24 months.

Army. The Army consists of 3 infantry brigades, 1 armed cavalry regiment, 1 artillery and 1 engineer battalion. Equipment includes 12 Scorpion light tanks. Strength (1987) 17,000 (12,000 conscripts). There is also a paramilitary Public Security Force of 5,000 men.

Air Force. Equipment includes 6 J52-engined Super Mystère and a few F-86 fighters, both of which are to be replaced by 12 F-5E/F Tiger IIs now being delivered, 12 A-37B jet light attack aircraft, 4 Spanish-built CASA C-101BB armed jet trainers, 4 four-engined Douglas and Lockheed transports, 6 C-47, 4 Israeli-built Arava and 2 Westwind transports, some helicopters and Tucano and T-41A trainers. Total strength was (1988) about 1,500 personnel, of whom many are civilian maintenance staff.

INTERNATIONAL RELATIONS

Membership. Honduras is a member of UN, OAS and ODECA.

ECONOMY

Budget. In 1988 revenue (in 1m. lempiras) was 2,165 (1987, 1,932); expenditure, (1987) 2,059.

Total external debt (1986) was (in 1m. lempiras), 4,882 and net reserves of foreign currency, 280.

Currency. The unit of the monetary system is the *lempira* also known as a *peso*, comprising 100 *centavos*. Notes are issued by the Banco Central de Honduras which has the sole right to issue, in denominations of 100, 50, 20, 10, 5, 2 and 1 *lempiras*. Coins in circulation are 50 and 20 *centavos* in silver, 10 and 5 *centavos* in cupro-nickel and 2 and 1 *centavos* in copper.

Rate of exchange, March 1988: £1 = 3·54 *lempiras;* US$1 = 2 *lempiras.*

Banking. The central bank of issue is the Banco Central de Honduras. The Banco Atlántida has branches in Tegucigalpa, San Pedro Sula, Comayaguela, Puerto Cortés, La Ceiba, Tela, El Progreso, Choluteca and other towns. The Banco de Honduras which operates in many parts of the country is controlled by the Citibank. The Bank of London and Montreal has branches in Tegucigalpa, San Pedro Sula, Comayaguela and La Ceiba. The Central American Bank for Economic Integration has its head office in Tegucigalpa.

Weights and Measures. The metric system has been legal since 1 April 1897, but English pounds and yards and the old Spanish system are still in use: 1 *vara* = 32 in.; 1 *manzana* (10,000 sq. *varas*) = 700 sq. metres; 1 *arroba* = 25 lb.; 1 *quintal* = 100 lb.; 1 *tonelada* = 2,000 lb.

ENERGY AND NATURAL RESOURCES

Electricity. Production (1986) 1,400m. kwh. Supply 110 and 220 volts; 60 Hz.

Minerals. Mineral resources include gold, silver, lead, copper, zinc and iron ore, which are exported. There are probably reserves of other minerals which have not yet been exploited. The Rosario Resources Company, closed down the only important mine but a West German consortium were considering re-opening it in 1987. The Compañia Minera Los Angeles SA has a mine currently extracting lead, zinc and silver at Valle de Angeles (Department of Francisco Morazán).

Agriculture. Although Honduras is essentially an agricultural country, less than a quarter of the total land area is cultivated and by far the larger portion of this is on the Caribbean and Pacific coastal plains. Agriculture employs 58·9% of the working population and provides 80% of the exports. The main agricultural crops are: Bananas, coffee, sugar and tobacco. Meat and lobster were important exports in 1987.

Livestock (1986): Cattle, 2,848,000; sheep, 7,000; pigs, 563,000; goats, 28,000; horses, 170,000; poultry, 5m.

Forestry. Forests cover nearly 45% of the total land area. Honduras has an abundance of hard- and soft-woods. Large stands of mahogany and other hardwoods—granadino, guayacán, walnut and rosewood—grow in the north-eastern part of the country, in the interior valleys, and near the southern coast. Stands of pine occur almost everywhere in the interior, but are severely damaged by bark beetle and fires. In 1985, total wood exports amounted to 200,000 cu. metres valued at 65·1m. lempiras.

Fisheries. Commercial fishing in territorial waters is restricted to Honduran nationals and Honduran companies in which the controlling share of the capital is owned by a Honduran national. Shrimps and lobsters are important catches; exports (1985) 102·4m. lempiras.

INDUSTRY AND TRADE

Industry. Small-scale local industries include beer and mineral waters, cement, flour, vegetable lard, coconut oil, sweets, cigarettes, cigars, textiles and clothing, panama hats, plastics, nails, matches, plywood, furniture, paper bags, soap, candles, fruit juices and household chemicals. Electricity from an important hydro-electric scheme, EL CAJON, built at Rio Lindo to serve the Central and North Coast regions, came on stream in 1985 (290 mw). The manufacturing industry employed 12% of the working population in 1985.

Labour. The organization of trade unions was begun in 1954 with the assistance of ORIT (Inter-American Regional Organization) sponsored by the USA trade unions. In 1972 there were 166 trade unions, of which only 119 were active, with about 67,956 members. A 'Charter of Labour' was granted in Feb. 1955 and an advanced Labour Code and Social Security Bill passed into law in May 1959. A Ministry of 'Labour, Social Assistance and the Middle Class' was created in 1955; the last four words of its title were expunged in 1957.

Commerce. Imports in 1986 were valued at 1,940m. lempiras and exports at 1,800m. lempiras.

Imports (1985) in 1m. lempiras: Fuel and lubricants, 327; consumer goods, 426; raw materials, 576; capital goods, 432.

Exports (1986) in 1m. lempiras: Bananas, 530; coffee, 612; timber, 74; refrigerated meats, 40; shrimp and lobster, 88.

Trade with main countries in 1m. lempiras (1985) was: USA, 718; Japan, 104·6; Federal Republic of Germany, 125·6; Italy, 135·2; Netherlands, 54·7; Belgium, 112·7; Spain, 49·9; UK, 43·5.

Total trade between Honduras and UK (British Department of Trade returns, in £1,000 sterling):

	1983	1984	1985	1986	1987
Imports to UK	7,082	12,360	11,139	5,280	4,703
Exports and re-exports from UK	9,539	7,382	9,026	9,213	10,449

Tourism. There were 204,000 visitors in 1986.

COMMUNICATIONS

Roads. Honduras is connected with Guatemala, El Salvador and Nicaragua by the

Pan-American Highway. Out of a total of 17,022 km of road (1985), 2,102 were asphalted and 8,366 were unpaved but of all-weather construction. There are good asphalted highways between Puerto Cortés in the north and Choluteca in the south passing through San Pedro Sula and Tegucigalpa with branches to Guatemala and El Salvador. In 1986 there were 114,675 motor vehicles.

Railways. Only 4 railways exist; they are confined to the north coastal region and are used mainly for transportation of bananas. Tegucigalpa, the capital, is not served by any railway, and there are no international railway connexions. The total railways operating in 1986 were 955 km of 1,067 mm and 914 mm gauge, which carried 1 m. passengers and 1·2 m. tonnes of freight.

Aviation. Over a large part of the country the aeroplane is the normal means of transport for both passengers and freight. There are international airports at Tegucigalpa, San Pedro Sula, La Ceiba and over 30 smaller airstrips in various parts of the country.

Shipping. Sailings to the Atlantic coast port of Puerto Cortés from Europe are frequent, mainly operated by the Harrison Line, Cia Generale Transatlantique, the Royal Netherlands Steamships Co., Hapag Lloyd and vessels owned or chartered by the Tela Railroad Co., a subsidiary of United Brands, and the Standard Fruit Co.

Post and Broadcasting. The Government in April 1972 operated 18,845 km of telephone lines and 12,526 km of telegraph lines. Number of telephones in use, 1984, 37,278; telephone exchanges, 56; number of telegraph offices, 262; combined telephone and telegraph offices, 184; radio stations, 187; commercial television channels, 4. There were (1979) about 27,000 receivers in use. Transmission in colour commenced mid-1973.

Cinemas (1982). Cinemas numbered about 60 with seating capacity of some 60,000.

Newspapers (1984). The 4 most important daily papers are *El Heraldo* and *La Tribuna* in Tegucigalpa, *La Prensa* and *El Tiempo* in San Pedro Sula. Several others exist but their circulation is low and their influence is very limited.

JUSTICE, RELIGION, EDUCATION AND WELFARE

Justice. The judicial power resides in the Supreme Court, with 7 judges elected by the National Congress for 6 years; it appoints the judges of the courts of appeal, labour tribunals and the district attorneys who, in turn, name the justices of the peace.

Religion. Roman Catholicism is the prevailing religion, but the constitution guarantees freedom to all creeds, and the State does not contribute to the support of any.

Education. Instruction is free, compulsory (from 7 to 15 years of age) and secular. In 1983 the 6,422 primary schools had 704,612 children (19,300 teachers); the 354 secondary, normal and technical schools had 129,606 pupils (5,916 teachers); the teachers' training college had 3,220 students in 1985. In 1985, the three universities had a total of 30,616 students.

The illiteracy rate was 40% of those 10 years of age and older in 1983.

Health. In 1981 there were about 1,370 doctors. In 1987 there were 46 public hospitals and 25 private, with 5,601 beds, and 617 health centres.

DIPLOMATIC REPRESENTATIVES

Of Honduras in Great Britain (47 Manchester St., London, W1M 5PB)
Ambassador: Max Velásquez-Diaz (accredited 7 June 1984).

Of Great Britain in Honduras (Edificio Palmira, 3er Piso, Colonia Palmira, Tegucigalpa)
Ambassador: D. Joy, CBE.

Of Honduras in the USA (4301 Connecticut Ave., NW, Washington, D.C., 20008)
Ambassador: Roberto Martinez Ordoñez.

Of the USA in Honduras (Ave. La Paz, Tegucigalpa)
Ambassador: Everett Ellis Briggs.

Of Honduras to the United Nations
Ambassador: Dr Jorge Ramón Hernández Alcerro.

Books of Reference

The *Anuario Estadístico* (latest issue, *Comercio Exterior de Honduras,* 1983) is published by the Dirección de Estadísticas y Censos, Tegucigalpa. *Director:* Elizabeth Zavala de Turcios.

Monthly Bulletin.—Honduras en Cifras. Banco Central de Honduras, 1980
Checchi, V. (and others), *Honduras, a Problem in Economic Development.* New York, 1959
Morris, J. A., *Honduras: Caudillo Politics and Military Rulers.* Boulder, 1984
Rubio Melhado, A., *Geografía General de la Republica de Honduras.* Tegucigalpa, 1953
Stokes, W. S., *Honduras: An Area Study in Government.* Madison, Wisc., 1950

HONG KONG

Population: 5·59m. (1986)
GDP per capita: US$6,841 (1986)

HISTORY. Hong Kong Island and the southern tip of the Kowloon peninsula were ceded by China to Britain after the first and second Anglo-Chinese Wars respectively by the Treaty of Nanking 1842 and the Convention of Peking 1860. Northern Kowloon was leased to Britain for 99 years by China in 1898. Since then, Hong Kong has been under British administration, except from Dec. 1941 to Aug. 1945 during the Japanese occupation. Talks began in Sept. 1982 between Britain and China over the future of Hong Kong after the lease expiry in 1997. On 19 Dec. 1984, the two countries signed a joint declaration whereby China would recover sovereignty over Hong Kong (including Hong Kong Island, Kowloon and the New Territories) from 1 July 1997 and establish it as a Special Administrative Region where the existing social and economic systems, and the present life-style, would remain unchanged for another 50 years.

AREA AND POPULATION. Hong Kong island is 32 km east of the mouth of the Pearl River and 130 km south-east of Canton. The area of the island is 79·45 sq. km. It is separated from the mainland by a fine natural harbour. On the opposite side is the peninsula of Kowloon (11·44 sq. km), which was added to the Territory by the Convention of Peking, 1860. By a further convention, signed at Peking on 9 June 1898, about 979·23 sq. km, consisting of all the immediately adjacent mainland and numerous islands in the vicinity, were leased to Great Britain by China for 99 years. This area is known as the New Territories. Total area of the territory is 1,070·12 sq. km (including recent reclamations), a large part of it being steep and unproductive hillside. Some 38% of the territory is conserved as country parks. Shortage of land suitable for development for housing and industry is a serious problem. Since 1945, the Government has reclaimed about 2,305 hectares from the sea, principally from the seafronts of Hong Kong and Kowloon, facing the harbour. In the New Territories, the new town of Tsuen Wan, incorporating Tsuen Wan, Kwai Chung and Tsing Yi, already houses 700,000 of its planned ultimate population of 890,000. The construction of 7 further new towns at Sha Tin, Tuen Mun, Tai Po, Fanling, Yuen Long, Junk Bay and Tin Shui Wai is now well underway, with planned ultimate population of about 710,000, 570,000, 305,000, 220,000, 190,000, 220,000 and 125,000 respectively.

The population was 5,431,200 at 1986 census. Estimate (31 Dec. 1986) 5,588,000. During the war years the population of Hong Kong fluctuated sharply. In Sept. 1945, at the end of the Japanese occupation, it was about 600,000. In mid-1950 it was estimated at 2·24m. Since 1976 the average annual growth rate has been 2·1%. Of the present population about 23% are under 15 years of age. About 59% of the population was born in Hong Kong.

CLIMATE. The climate is warm sub-tropical being much affected by monsoons, the winter being cool and dry and the summer hot and humid, May to Sept. being the wettest months. Jan. 60°F (15·6°C), July 83°F (28·3°C). Annual rainfall 85″ (2,162 mm).

CONSTITUTION AND GOVERNMENT. The administration is in the hands of a Governor, aided by an Executive Council, composed of the Chief Secretary, the Commander British Forces, the Financial Secretary, the Attorney-General (who are members *ex officio*) and such other members, as may be appointed by the Queen upon the Governor's nomination. In Nov. 1987 there were, in addition to the 4 *ex-officio* members, 1 nominated official and 9 appointed members. There is also a Legislative Council, presided over by the Governor. From Oct. 1985 it consisted of 3 *ex-officio* members, namely the Chief Secretary, the Financial Secretary, the Attorney-General, 7 official members, 22 appointed members and 24 elected members. Chinese and English are the official languages. District boards with elected members were set up in 1982 in the 19 administrative districts of Hong Kong. They have mainly an advisory role to perform and have a substantial influence over district affairs.

Governor and C.-in-C.: Sir David Wilson, KCMG.
Commander British Forces: Maj.-Gen. Garry Johnson, OBE, MC.
Chief Secretary: David Ford, LVO, OBE, JP.
Flag: British Blue Ensign with the arms of the Territory on a white disc in the fly.

DEFENCE. The Hong Kong garrison, under the Commander British Forces, comprises units of all three services. Its principal rôle is to assist the Hong Kong Government in maintaining security and stability.

Army. The Army constitutes the bulk of the garrison. It comprises a UK battalion, based at Stanley Fort, and 3 Gurkha infantry battalions, all based in the New Territories; supporting units include the Queen's Gurkha Engineers, the Queen's Gurkha Signals, the Gurkha Transport Regiment, and 660 Squadron Army Air Corps.

Navy. The Naval Base is at HMS *Tamar*. The Hong Kong Squadron comprises five Peacock class patrol craft which are specially designed for patrol duties during typhoons and perform Search and Rescue operation in both Hong Kong waters and international waters in the South China Sea. The vessels, HMS *Peacock*, HMS *Plover*, HMS *Starling*, HMS *Swallow*, HMS *Swift*, were built by Hall Russell, Aberdeen, Scotland in 1984–85.

Air Force. The Royal Air Force is based at Shek Kong. No. 28 (Army Co-operation) Squadron operates Wessex helicopters. In addition to its operational rôle in support of the army and navy, the RAF carries out search and rescue and medical evacuation tasks. It is also responsible for air traffic control services at Shek Kong, and provides a territory-wide air traffic advisory service.

Auxiliary Forces. The local auxiliary defence units, consisting of the Royal Hong Kong Regiment and the Royal Hong Kong Auxiliary Air Force, are administered by the Hong Kong Government, but, if called out, would come under the command of the Commander British Forces. The Royal Hong Kong Regiment (The Volunteers) has a strength of about 950. It is fully mobile and its rôle is to operate in support of regular army battalions stationed in Hong Kong. The Royal Hong Kong Auxiliary Air Force is intended mainly for internal security and air-sea rescue duties. It has a strength of about 131, operating a fleet of nine aircraft – a twin-engined Britten-Norman Islander, a twin-engined Beech King Air 200, two Scottish Aviation Bulldog and two Slingsby T-67 trainers, and three Aérospatiale Dauphin 365C1 helicopters.

ECONOMY

Budget. The public revenue and expenditure for financial years ending 31 March were as follows (in HK$):

	1984–85	1985–86	1986–87	1987–88 [1]
Revenue	36,342,500,000	41,241,000,000	43,870,000,000	46,176,000,000
Expenditure	36,901,700,000	39,798,200,000	39,928,000,000	44,409,000,000

[1] Estimate.

The revenue is derived chiefly from rates, licences, tax on earnings and profits, land sales, duties on tobacco, hydrocarbon oils, methyl alcohol, intoxicating liquor, non-intoxicating liquor, non-alcoholic beverages and cosmetics and various duties.

Currency. The unit of currency is the Hong Kong *dollar*. Banknotes (of denominations of $10 upwards) are issued by the Hongkong and Shanghai Banking Corporation, and the Standard Chartered Bank. Their combined note issue was, at 31 Dec. 1986, HK$20,626m. Subsidiary currency consisting of HK$5, HK$2, HK$1,

50-cent, 20-cent, 10-cent, 5-cent copper-nickel-alloy coins and 1-cent notes is issued by the Hong Kong Government and at 31 Dec. 1986 totalled HK$1,786m.

Since Oct. 1983 the HK$ has been linked to the US$1 at a fixed exchange rate of US$1 = HK$7·80. In March 1988, £1 = HK$13·80.

The Hong Kong Government has issued a set of 14 Hong Kong commemorative HK$1,000 gold coins over the years. The set comprises 2 coins commemorating the Queen's visit to Hong Kong in 1975 and in 1986 and 12 coins depicting the animals of the Chinese lunar calendar. The last coin in the lunar series was issued in 1987 to commemorate the Year of the Rabbit.

Banking. At 31 Dec. 1986: There were 151 banks licensed under the Banking Ordinance with a total of 1,386 banking offices, and 134 representative offices of foreign banks; bank deposits were HK$491,353m. and loans and advances HK$390,747m.; there were 254 deposit taking companies registered, and 38 licensed, under the Deposit-taking Companies Ordinance with total deposits of HK$71,176.

Weights and Measures. Metric, British Imperial, Chinese and US units are all in current use in Hong Kong. However Government departments have now effectively adopted metric units; all new legislation uses metric terminology and existing legislation is being progressively metricated. Metrication is also proceeding in the private sector.

The statutory equivalent for the *chek* is 14 5/8 inches. The variation of the size of the *chek* with usage still persists in Hong Kong but the *chek* and derived units are now used much less than in the past.

ENERGY AND NATURAL RESOURCES

Electricity. Production (1986) 18,868m. kwh. Supply 220 volts; 50 Hz.

Water. The provision of sufficient reservoir capacity to store the summer rainfall in order to meet supply requirements has always been a serious problem. Over the years no less than 17 impounding reservoirs have been constructed with a total capacity of 586m. cu. metres. The major among these are the Plover Cove Reservoir (230m. cu. metres) finally completed in 1973 and the High Island Reservoir (280m. cu. metres) completed in 1978, both involving the conversion of sea water inlets into fresh water lakes.

There are no sites remaining in Hong Kong suitable for development as storage reservoirs. Consequently the purchase of water from China has been of increasing importance and the future needs of Hong Kong will be met to a large extent from this source. In 1986 water purchased from China was in the order of 360m. cu. metres which represents about 50% of Hong Kong's demand. The agreement with China allows for annual increases up to a total figure of 620m. cu. metres per annum by 1994–95 which will represent around 60% of Hong Kong's demand.

These resources can be further supplemented when necessary by up to 181,000 cu. metres of fresh water a day from a desalting plant completed in 1976 and now considered as a reserve resource.

Agriculture. Only 8·8% of the total land area is suitable for crop farming and most vegetables are produced through intensive market gardening cultivation, with 34% self-sufficiency. In 1986, 158,400 tonnes of vegetables and 2,040 tonnes of fruit were produced. Poultry production was 47,320 tonnes, with 40% self-sufficiency. Livestock (1986): Cattle, 970; pigs, 563,840.

Fisheries. The fishing fleet of 4,714 vessels supplies 83% of fresh marine fish consumed locally. In 1986 the total catch was 205,480 tonnes, valued at HK$1,895m. Inland freshwater farming and coastal marine farming provided 5,740 tonnes of freshwater fish valued at HK$70m. and 2,100 tonnes of marine products valued at HK$136m.

INDUSTRY AND TRADE

Industry. An economic policy based on free enterprise and free trade; an industrious work force; an efficient and aggressive commercial infrastructure; modern and efficient sea-port (including container shipping terminals) and airport facilities; its geographical position relative to markets in North America and its traditional trading links with Britain have all contributed to Hong Kong's success as a modern industrial territory.

In Sept. 1986, there were 48,623 factories employing 869,753 people out of a total population of over 5·5m. The type of factory involved ranges from the small sub-contractor type to large highly complex modern establishments. Given the scarcity of land it is most common for light industry to operate in multi-storey buildings specially designed for this purpose. The main industry is textiles and clothing, which employed 43% of the total industrial workforce and accounted for 41% of total domestic exports in 1986. Other major light manufacturing industries include electronic products, clocks and watches, toys, plastic products, electrical products, metalware, footwear, cameras and travel goods. Heavy industry includes ship-building, ship-repairing, aircraft engineering and the manufacture of machinery.

Commerce. Hong Kong's industries are mainly export oriented. The total value of domestic exports in 1986 was HK$153,983m. The major markets were USA (41·7%), China (11·7%), Federal Republic of Germany (7·1%), UK (6·4%), Japan (4%) and Canada (3·2%). There is also a sizeable and flourishing entrepôt trade which accounted for another HK$122,546m. in 1986.

The total value of imports in 1986 was HK$275,955m., mainly from China (29·6%), Japan (20·4%), Taiwan (8·7%), USA (8·4%), Republic of Korea (4%) and Singapore (3·9%).

The chief import items were manufactured goods (29·1%), machinery and transport equipment (24%), foodstuffs (8·1%), chemicals (7·7%), mineral fuel, lubricants and related materials (3·2%).

Duties are levied only on tobacco, hydrocarbon oils, methyl alcohol, alcoholic liquors, non-alcoholic beverages and cosmetics, whether imported into or manufactured in Hong Kong for local consumption.

All imports (apart from foodstuffs, which are subject to a flat declaration charge irrespective of the value of the consignment) and exports are subject to an *ad valorem* declaration charge at the rate of HK50 cents for every $1,000 value (or part thereof) of the goods shipped.

Visible trade normally carries an adverse balance which is offset by a favourable balance from exchange, shipping and insurance transactions, an inflow of capital, ship-repairing, a flourishing tourist industry, etc.

Hong Kong has a free exchange market. Foreign merchants may remit profits or repatriate capital. Import and export controls are kept to the minimum, consistent with strategic requirements.

Total trade between Hong Kong and UK (British Department of Trade returns, in £1,000 sterling) is given as follows:

	1983	1984	1985	1986	1987
Imports to UK	1,178,343	1,266,965	1,175,984	1,530,786	1,531,681
Exports and re-exports from UK	726,711	897,419	949,180	960,956	1,013,038

Tourism. 3·7m. tourists spent HK$17,860m. in Hong Kong during 1986.

COMMUNICATIONS

Roads. In June 1987 there were 1,350 km of roads, distributed as follows: Hong Kong Island, 380; Kowloon and New Kowloon, 359, and New Territories, 611. A cross-harbour tunnel, 1·8 km in length, opened to traffic in Aug. 1972, now links Hong Kong Island with the Kowloon peninsula. The 1·4 km twin-tube Lion Rock Tunnel, which links Kowloon with Sha Tin New Town and other areas of the north-eastern New Territories, became fully operational in Oct. 1978. The 1·8 km twin-tube Aberdeen Tunnel, which connects Aberdeen and Wanchai, became operational in March 1983. A 34 km Light Railway Transit System was scheduled for 1988 and will connect Tuen Mun and Yuen Long in the New Territories.

Railways. There is an electric tramway with a total track length of 30·4 km, and a cable tramway connecting the Peak district with the lower levels in Victoria. The electrified Kowloon-Canton Railway runs for 34 km from the terminus at Hung Hom in Kowloon to the border point at Lo Wu. It carried 114·2m. passengers and 4·2m. tonnes of freight in 1986. A light rail system operated by KCR opens in the Tuen Mun area in 1988.

An underground Mass Transit Railway system, comprising 38 km with 37 stations, is now in operation. The system consists of three lines, one linking the Central District of Hong Kong Island with Tsuen Wan in the west of Kowloon, the second linking Kwun Tong in East Kowloon with Yau Ma Tei in Nathan Road and the third Island line links Sheung Wan and Chai Wan. A second cross-harbour line is under construction linking Kwun Tong and Quarry Bay. It carried 532m. passengers in 1986.

Aviation. Hong Kong International Airport is situated on the north shore of Kowloon Bay. It is regularly used by some 32 airlines and many charter airlines which provide frequent services throughout the Far East to Europe, North America, Africa, the Middle East, Australia and New Zealand. British Airways operates 7 flights per week via India or the Gulf to the UK. Cathay Pacific Airways, one of the two Hong Kong-based airlines, operates more than 400 passenger and cargo services to Europe, the Far and Middle East, Australia and North America weekly. Hong Kong Dragon Airlines Ltd, which was set up in July 1985, operates B-737 non-scheduled services between Hong Kong and a number of cities in Asia, the People's Republic of China and Micronesia. British Caledonian Airways operates scheduled services on the Hong Kong to London route. About 1,000 scheduled flights are operated weekly to and from Hong Kong by various airlines. In 1986, 64,770 aircraft arrived and departed on international flights, carrying 10·6m. passengers and 500,000 tonnes of freight.

Shipping. The port of Hong Kong, which ranks among the top three container ports in the world, handled 2·77m. twenty-foot equivalent units in 1986. The Kwai Chung Container Port has six berths with more than 2,300 metres of quay backed by about 103 hectares of cargo handling area. In 1986, some 14,100 ocean-going vessels called at Hong Kong and loaded and discharged some 62m. tonnes of cargo. This included 34m. tonnes of general goods, 44% of which was containerized cargo.

Telecommunications, Post and Broadcasting. There were 103 post offices in 1986; postal revenue totalled HK$1,038·2m.; expenditure, HK$655m.; 618m. letters and parcels were handled. Telephone service is provided by the Hong Kong Telephone Co. Ltd., a member of the Cable and Wireless Worldwide Communications Group. It provides local, and in association with Cable and Wireless (HK) Ltd., international voice, data and facsimile transmission services for Hong Kong. At 31 Dec. 1986 there were over 2·5m. telephones served by 1·8m. lines. Cable and Wireless (Hong Kong) Ltd, which is owned jointly by Cable and Wireless PLC and the Hong Kong Government, provides the international telecommunication services as well as local telegram and telex services. These include public telegram, telex, telephone, television programmes transmission and reception, leased circuits, facsimile, switched data, ship-shore and air-ground communications. International facilities are provided through submarine cables, microwave and satellite radio systems.

There is a government broadcasting station, Radio Television Hong Kong, with daily transmissions in English and Chinese. A commercial station, the Commercial Broadcasting Co. Ltd, transmits daily in English and Cantonese. Two radio stations operate 8 channels with 4 providing 24-hour service.

Television Broadcasts Ltd and Asia Television Ltd transmit commercial television in English and Chinese on 4 channels, in colour.

Cinemas. In June 1987 there were 103 cinemas with a seating capacity in excess of 110,000.

Newspapers. In June 1987 there were 69 daily or weekly newspapers, registered and in circulation, including 8 English-language papers, one bilingual paper, 51 Chinese-language dailies and a number of news agency bulletins.

JUSTICE, EDUCATION AND WELFARE

Justice. There is a Supreme Court which comprises the Court of Appeal and the High Court. While the Court of Appeal hears appeals on all matters, civil and criminal from the lower courts, the High Court has unlimited jurisdiction in both civil and criminal matters including bankruptcy, company winding-up, adoptions, probate and lunacy matters. The District Court has civil jurisdiction to hear monetary claims up to HK$60,000 or, where the claims are for recovery of land, the annual rent or rateable value does not exceed HK$45,000. In its criminal jurisdiction, it may try more serious offences except murder, manslaughter and rape; the maximum term of imprisonment it can impose is seven years. The Magistrates' Court exercises criminal jurisdiction over a wide range of indictable and summary offences. Its powers of punishment are generally restricted to a maximum of two years' imprisonment, or a fine of HK$10,000, though cumulative sentences of imprisonment up to three years may be imposed. The Coroner's Court inquires into the identity of a deceased person and the cause of death. The Juvenile Court has jurisdiction to hear charges against young people aged under 16 for any offence other than homicide. Children under the age of seven are not deemed to have reached the age of criminal responsibility. The Lands Tribunal determines on statutory claims for compensation over land and certain landlord and tenant matters. The Labour Tribunal provides inexpensive and speedy settlements to individual monetary claims arising from disputes between employers and employees. The Small Claims Tribunal deals with monetary claims involving amounts not exceeding HK$8,000.

Police. At the end of 1986, the establishment of the Royal Hong Kong Police Force was 31,673. In addition, there were over 5,600 auxiliary officers. During the year, 81,411 crimes were reported. The overall detection rate was 47·9% and a total of 37,863 people were arrested and prosecuted.

The Marine Police is responsible for patrolling some 1,850 sq. km of territorial waters and involved in the control of some 33,000 local craft with a maritime population of between 50,000 and 60,000. At the end of 1986, it consisted of a disciplined staff of more than 2,900 and a fleet of over 120 vessels.

Education. The majority of schools have to be registered with the Education Department under the Education Ordinance. They are required to comply with regulations as to staff, building, fire and health requirements. From Sept. 1971, free and compulsory primary education was introduced in government and the majority of government-aided schools. Free junior secondary education of 3 years' duration was introduced in 1978 and it was made compulsory in Sept. 1979.

In March 1987 there were 231,610 pupils in kindergartens (all private), another 531,993 in primary schools and 446,193 in secondary schools.

There are 7 technical institutes with a total full-time enrolment of 49,000, 1 technical teachers' college and 3 colleges of education with a total enrolment of 5,511.

The University of Hong Kong had 6,530 undergraduates in 1986 and the Chinese University of Hong Kong, inaugurated in Oct. 1963, had 5,791 undergraduates. The Hong Kong Polytechnic, 1986, had a total of 25,596 students. In Oct. 1984, the City Polytechnic was opened and had a total of 4,183 students in 1986.

Health. In Feb. 1987 there were 5,080 doctors and about 24,550 hospital beds.

Social Security. The Government co-ordinates and implements expanding programmes in social welfare, which include social security, family services, child care, services for the elderly, youth and community work, probation and corrections and rehabilitation. 149 voluntary welfare agencies are subsidised by public funds.

The Government gives non-contributory cash assistance to needy families, unemployed able-bodied adults, the severely disabled and the elderly. Caseload in July 1987 totalled 360,878. Victims of natural disasters, crimes of violence and traffic accidents are financially assisted.

Books of Reference

Statistical Information: The Census and Statistics Department is responsible for the preparation and collation of Government statistics. These statistics are published mainly in the *Hong Kong Monthly Digest of Statistics* which is also available in a collected annual edition. The Department also publishes monthly trade statistics, economic indicators, annual review of overseas trade, etc. Statistical information is also published in the annual reports of Government departments. *Hong Kong 1987*, and other government publications are available from the Hong Kong Government Publications Centre, GPO Building, Connaught Place, Hong Kong, and the Hong Kong Government Office in London, 6 Grafton Street, London, W1X 3LB.

The Hong Kong Trade Development Council, Connaught Centre, Connaught Place, Hong Kong, issues a monthly *Hong Kong Enterprise* and other publications.

Hong Kong 1987. Hong Kong Government Press, 1987

Beazer, W. F., *The Commercial Future of Hong Kong.* New York, 1978

Benton, G., *The Hong Kong Crisis.* London, 1983

Bonavia, D., *Hong Kong 1997.* London, 1984

Cheng, J. Y. S. (ed.), *Hong Kong: In Search of a Future.* OUP, 1984

Chill, H., *et al* (eds.) *The Future of Hong Kong: Toward 1997 and Beyond.* Westport, 1987

Endacott, G. B., *A History of Hong Kong.* 2nd ed. OUP, 1973.–*Government and People in Hong Kong, 1841–1962. A Constitutional History.* OUP, 1965

Hopkins, K., *Hong Kong: The Industrial Colony.* OUP, 1971

Rabushka, A., *The Changing Face of Hong Kong: New Departures in Public Policy.* Washington, 1973

Tregear, E. R., *Land Use in Hong Kong.* Hong Kong Univ. Press, 1958.—*Hong Kong Gazetteer.* Hong Kong Univ. Press, 1958.—*The Development of Hong Kong as Told in Maps.* Hong Kong Univ. Press, 1959

Youngson, A. J., *Hong Kong: Economic Growth and Policy.* OUP, 1982

HUNGARY

Magyar Népköztársaság

Capital: Budapest
Population: 10·62m. (1987)
GNP per capita: US$2,150 (1983)

HISTORY. Hungary first became an independent kingdom in 1001. For events in Hungary since 1918 *see* THE STATESMAN'S YEAR-BOOK, 1945, pp. 1006–7, and 1957, p. 1096.

On 23 Oct. 1956 an anti-Stalinist revolution broke out, and the newly formed coalition government of Imre Nagy on 1 Nov. withdrew from the Warsaw Pact and asked the UN for protection. János Kádár, formed a counter-government on 3 Nov. and asked the USSR for support.

Russian troops suppressed the revolution and abducted Nagy and his Ministers, who were later secretly executed.

On 7 Sept. 1967 the Soviet-Hungarian treaty of friendship was renewed for 20 years.

In 1978 the crown of St Stephen, the symbol of Hungarian nationhood, which had been in US hands since 1945, was returned to Hungary.

AREA AND POPULATION. Hungary is bounded north by Czechoslovakia, north-east by the USSR, east by Romania, south by Yugoslavia and west by Austria. The peace treaty of 10 Feb. 1947 restored the frontiers as of 1 Jan. 1938. The area of Hungary is 93,032 sq. km (35,911 sq. miles).

The official language is Hungarian (Magyar), which is a member of the Finno-Ugrian group.

At the census of 1 Jan. 1980 the population was 10,709,550 (5,195,300 males). Population in 1987: 10,622,000 (males, 5,126,000). Ethnic composition, 1984: Hungarians, 96·6%; Germans, 1·6%; Slovaks, 1·1%; Romanians, 0·2%; others, 0·5%. There were 0·32m. Gypsies in 1985. A Gypsy Council was set up in 1985.

57% of the population is urban (20% in Budapest). Population density, 114·2 per sq. km. Birth rate, 1986, 12·1 per 1,000; death rate, 13·8 per 1,000. The population is decreasing, by 2 per 1,000 in 1984; expectation of life (1985): males, 66; females, 74. There is a world-wide Hungarian diaspora, and Hungarian minorities in Romania, Yugoslavia and Czechoslovakia.

Vital statistics, 1986: Births, 128,453; marriages, 72,516 (of which 22,600 remarriages); divorces, 29,301; deaths, 146,384; abortions, 84,000 (approx.); infant mortality, 18·9 per 1,000 live births.

Area (in sq. km) and population (in 1,000) of counties and county towns:

Counties (1985)	Area	Population	Chief town (1985)	Population
Baranya	4,487	432	Pécs	179
Bács-Kiskun	8,362	556	Kecskemét	104
Békés	5,632	419	Békéscsaba	71
Borsod-Abaúj-Zemplén	7,247	784	Miskolc	211
Csongrád	4,263	457	Szeged	186
Fejér	4,373	426	Székesfehérvár	113
Győr-Sopron	4,012	427	Győr	130
Hajdú-Bihar	6,211	550	Debrecen	212
Heves	3,637	339	Eger	66
Komárom	2,251	320	Tatabánya	76
Nógrád	2,544	231	Salgótarján	49
Pest	6,394	985	Budapest	2,089
Somogy	6,036	351	Kaposvár	74
Szabolcs-Szatmár	5,938	583	Nyíregyháza	117
Szolnok	5,607	432	Szolnok	81
Tolna	3,704	265	Szekszárd	39
Vas	3,337	278	Szombathely	87
Veszprém	4,689	387	Veszprém	65
Zala	3,784	311	Zalaegerszeg	62
Budapest	525	2,089	(has county status)	

CLIMATE. A humid continental climate, with warm summers and cold winters. Precipitation is generally greater in summer, with thunderstorms. Dry, clear weather is likely in autumn, but spring is damp and both seasons are of short duration. Budapest. Jan. 32°F (0°C), July 71°F (21·5°C). Annual rainfall 25" (625 mm). Pécs. Jan. 30°F (–0·7°C), July 71°F (21·5°C). Annual rainfall 26·4" (661 mm).

CONSTITUTION AND GOVERNMENT. On 1 Feb. 1946 the National Assembly proclaimed a republic.

The present People's Republic was established by a constitution adopted on 18 Aug. 1949. Supreme power is vested in Parliament. Parliament elects a Presidential Council, which exercises the functions of Parliament between sessions. It can dissolve government bodies and annul legislation. The 1949 Constitution was amended in 1972. The distinction between 'working people' and 'citizens' disappears. Citizens are stated to have both indirect (through elected representatives) and direct (through local and enterprise councils) democratic rights. State and co-operative property are recognized as co-existing with equal status. Personal property is 'recognized and protected' up to the limit set by law (this includes for private artisans and, since 1 Jan. 1982, for various classes of small companies and 'economic working groups', places of business and machinery).

Ethnic minorities have equal rights and education in their own tongue.

National flag: Three horizontal stripes of red, white, green.

National anthem: God bless the Hungarians–Isten áldd meg a magyart (words by Ferenc Kölcsey, tune by Ferenc Erkel).

Chairman of the Presidential Council (Head of State): Károly Németh, appointed June 1987. *Deputy Chairmen:* Sándor Gáspár and Rezső Trautmann.

In 1949 the Hungarian Working People's Party (Communists), the Smallholders' Party, the National Peasant Party, the Trade Union Federation, the Association of Working Peasants, the Democratic Women's Association and the Federation of Working Youth were merged in the Hungarian People's Independence Front. In 1954 a new comprehensive organization was formed, the People's Patriotic Front. The Communist Youth Association (Kɪsz) had 912,000 members in 1986.

The Communist Party was reorganized after the 1956 revolution and changed its name to 'Hungarian Socialist Workers' Party'. It had 852,000 members in 1983 (32% women; 46% manual workers and peasants in 1980). Supreme *de facto* power is in the hands of the Party's Politburo, composed in March 1988 of: János Kádár, *(General Secretary)*; György Lázár *(Deputy General Secretary)*; György Aczél; János Berecz; Judit Cséhak; Sándor Gáspár; Károly Grosz; Csaba Hámori; Ferenc Havasi; László Maróthy; Károly Németh; Miklos Óvári; István Szabó.

Prominent members of the Government in March 1988 were:

Prime Minister: Károly Grosz.

Deputy Prime Ministers: Judit Cséhak, Péter Medgyessy, József Marjai *(Minister of Trade). Finance:* Miklós Villányi. *Foreign Affairs:* Péter Várkonyi. *Speaker, National Assembly:* István Sárlos. *Interior:* Dr István Horváth. *Chairman, National Planning Office:* Lászlo Hoos. *Defence:* Col.-Gen. Ferenc Kárpáti. *Justice:* Imre Markója.

Parliament consists of 352 deputies, elected for a 5-year term by all citizens over 18 years.

The right to select candidates is vested solely in pre-election nomination meetings open to all voters. In order to stand candidates must receive one-third of the votes of those present. Since 1983 more than one candidate must stand in each constituency. All candidates must support the policies of the Patriotic People's Front (PPF). To be elected candidates must gain at least 50% of the votes cast. Candidates who receive more than 25% of the votes become alternate deputies. In addition a 'national slate' of 35 prominent personalities is voted on by all citizens.

At the elections of 8 June 1985 93·9% of the 7,728,280 electors voted (97% in 1980) for the 762 candidates, including 71 not sponsored by the PPF, of whom 25 were elected. 5·4% of the votes were invalid, and 1·2% negative. 77% of those elected were Communist Party members. In 42 constituencies no candidate gained an absolute majority, and a second vote was taken on 22 June after new nomination meetings. Turnout here was 83%.

Local Government. Hungary is divided into 19 counties *(megyék)* and the capital city, Budapest, which has county status. Counties are sub-divided into towns and boroughs. These are administered by a hierarchy of local councils which in turn elect Executive Committees to carry on day-to-day administration. There are 42,734 local council constituencies. Elections are held at the same time as general elections. Members of county councils are elected by the lower councils. At the June 1985 elections 41,885 councillors and 30,885 alternate councillors were elected. County districts were abolished in 1983.

DEFENCE. The 1947 Treaty authorized Hungary to have an army up to a strength of 65,000 personnel, and an air force of 90 aircraft, of which not more than 70 may be combat types with a personnel strength of 5,000.

By a law of 1976 the Presidential Council may establish a National Defence Council which in times of war would exercise supreme control over defence.

Men between the ages of 18 and 23 are liable for 18 months' conscription in the Army, 24 months in the Air Force. Compulsory military service age-limits are 18 to 55 (18 to 45 women).

The security police (BKH) is controlled by the Ministry of the Interior.

The Workers' Militia is a para-military organization armed with automatic weapons. Strength (1988), 60,000.

Four Soviet divisions are stationed in Hungary.

Army. Hungary is divided into 4 army districts: Budapest, Debrecen, Kiskunfélegyháza, Pécs. The strength of the Army was (1988) 84,000 (including 50,000 conscripts). It is organized in 1 tank division, 5 motor rifle divisions, 1 artillery and 1 surface-to-surface missile brigade, 1 anti-aircraft regiment, 4 surface-to-air missile regiments and 1 airborne battalion. Equipment includes 1,200 T-54/-55, 100 T-72 and 100 PT-76 tanks.

Navy. The maritime wing of the Army, still very active along the Danube, in 1988 deployed 500 officers and men operating 51 vessels, comprising 10 patrol craft, 26 mine warfare craft, 15 river patrol craft, and over 30 other craft including 5 utility landing craft, several troop transports of up to 1,000 tons, river monitors, ice-breakers and tugs, constituting the River Guard, and Army amphibious logistic and bridging vessels.

Air Force. The Air Force is an integral part of the Army, with a strength (1988) of about 22,000 officers and men and 200 combat aircraft. The combat aircraft strength comprises 2 regiments of MiG-23 fighters, 2 of MiG-21 interceptors, 1 of Su-25 ground attack aircraft, and a regiment of Mi-8 and Mi-24 armed helicopters. Transport units are equipped with An-2, An-24, An-26 and Il-14 aircraft. Other types in service include Ka-26, Mi-2 and Mi-8 helicopters and L-29 Delfin and MiG-15UTI trainers. 'Guideline' and 'Goa' surface-to-air missiles are also operational.

INTERNATIONAL RELATIONS

Membership. Hungary is a member of UN, the Warsaw Pact and Comecon and, since 1982, IMF and IBRD.

External Debt. Hungary settled its debt to the UK in 1967. By an agreement of 6 March 1973 Hungary is to meet US claims of US$189m. arising from war damage and nationalization in 20 yearly instalments. Hungarian indebtedness to the West was US$8,300m. in 1983. A US$400m. loan was made by IBRD in 1983.

ECONOMY

Planning. The 'New Economic Mechanism' introduced in 1968, allows decentralisation in planning and responsiveness to market forces. For details of this and previous economic plans *see* THE STATESMAN'S YEAR-BOOK, 1985–86. New forms of enterprise management were introduced in 1985, under which some 25% of enterprises will elect their own management and a further 50% will be run by enterprise councils. Remaining enterprises will continue to be state-administered. The seventh 5-year plan covers 1986 to 1990. There were large price increases in 1983, 1985 and 1987. Income tax and VAT were introduced in Jan. 1988. Inflation was 15% in 1988.

Budget. The budget for calendar years was as follows (in 1,000 forints):

	1981	1982	1983	1984	1985	1986	1987
Revenue	472,600	485,792	543,735	572,920	638,130	615,000	650,700
Expenditure	482,400	498,007	549,822	576,580	651,310	643,700	694,500

1985 revenue included: Direct taxes, 51·9%; wages tax, 24·8%; profits tax, 20·2%; indirect taxes, 31·1%. Expenditure included: Price subsidies 26·7%; social security, 20·2%; wealth and education, 16·5%; defence, 5·7%.

Currency. A decree of 26 July 1946 instituted a new monetary unit, the *forint* sub-divided into 100 *fillér*. The rate of exchange (March 1988) 84·54 forints to the £1 sterling, 47·05 forints = US$1. A uniform exchange rate was established in Oct. 1981 as a final step before the introduction of external, central-bank convertibility for foreign trade. Since 1983 the forint has been devalued several times by a total of 28%.

Banking. In 1987 a two-tier system was established. The National Bank remained the central state financial institution, responsible for the circulation of money and foreign currency exchange, but also became a central clearing bank, with general (but not operational) control over 5 new second-tier commercial banks and 10 specialized development banks. 9 other commercial banks were set up in 1985 to finance development. In 1987 the State Development Institute was established to issue Government bonds to cover the budgetary deficit.

The Hungarian International Trade Bank opened in London in 1973. In 1980 the Central European International Bank was set up in Budapest with 7 Western banks holding 66% of the shares. The National Savings Bank handles local government as well as personal accounts. Deposits in 1986: 274,300m. forints.

Weights and Measures. The metric system is in use.

ENERGY AND NATURAL RESOURCES

Electricity. Sources of energy in 1986: Oil, 33%, gas, 27·8%; coal, 25·5%; others, 13·7%. Imported, 51·3%. Capacity of all power stations in 1986 was 6,806 mw. There is an 880-mw nuclear power station at Paks. A 750 kv power line links Albertirsa with the Soviet grid at Vinnitsa. 28,042m. kwh were produced in 1986 (7,424 kwh by nuclear power), and 11,862m. kwh imported. Supply 220 volts; 50 Hz.

Oil. Oil and natural gas have been found in the Szeged basin and in Zala county. Production in 1986: oil, 2m. tonnes; gas, 7,098m. cu. m. There are pipelines for crude oil ('Friendship' I and II from USSR, section of the Adria oil pipeline from Rijeka to Czechoslovakia) and natural gas totalling 5,340 km in 1986.

Minerals. Production in 1986 (in 1,000 tonnes): coal, 2,324; lignite, 6,983; brown coal, 13,821; bauxite, 3,022; iron ore, nil.

Agriculture. Agricultural land was collectivised in 1950. A law of 1968 permits collectives to own land, and guarantees individuals' rights to private plots. Collectives meet in a National Council of Agricultural Co-operatives.

In 1986 the agricultural area was (in 1,000 hectares) 6,524, of which 4,705 were arable, 1,234 meadows and pastures, and 247 orchards and vineyards.

In 1987 there were 1,267 collective farms with 5·5m. hectares of land (including 293,500 hectares of household plots) and 129 state farms with 914,200 hectares of land. The irrigated area was 163,000 hectares; 55,000 tractors were in use.

In 1985 state farms were transformed from state-administered into self-governing bodies under the Ministry of Agriculture.

Production statistics (in 1,000 tonnes):

Crops	1984	1985	1986	Crops	1984	1985	1986
Wheat	7,367	6,555	5,744	Maize	6,514	6,619	7,024
Rye	192	164	169	Potatoes	1,048	975	812
Barley	1,208	1,039	845	Sugar-beet	4,360	4,072	3,764
Oats	151	130	121	Sunflower seed	596	673	855

Livestock in 1987 was (in 1,000 head) as follows: Cattle, 1,725; pigs, 8,687; poultry, 37,174; sheep, 2,337; horses, 95,000.

Livestock products (1986): Eggs, 4,049m.; milk, 2,652m. litres; wool, 10,759 tonnes; animals for slaughter, 2,236,000 tonnes.

The north shore of Lake Balaton and the Tokaj area are important wine-producing districts. Wine production in 1986 was 414m. litres.

Forestry. The area under forest in 1986 was 1·66m. hectares. 29,000 hectares were afforested and 8·5m. cu. metres of timber were cut.

Fisheries. There are fisheries in the rivers Danube and Tisza and Lake Balaton, and in 1984 there were 26,000 hectares of commercial fishponds. Catch in 1984: 38,976 tonnes.

INDUSTRY AND TRADE

Industry. Production (in 1,000 tonnes):

	1982	1983	1984	1985	1986
Pig-iron	2,183	2,047	2,097	2,095	2,054
Crude steel	3,703	3,617	3,750	3,646	3,715
Rolled steel	2,856	2,820	2,953	2,863	2,903
Aluminium	74	74	74	74	74
Alumina	745	836	839	798	856
Cement	4,369	4,243	4,145	3,678	3,846
Artificial fertilizers	726	761	742	733	747
Synthetic materials (PVC, etc.)	326	344	385	389	423
Sulphuric acid	569	606	549	520	543
Sugar	459	476	407	483	421
Cotton cloth (1 m. sq. metres)	310	307	303	310	314
Woollen (1 m. sq. metres)	41	37	39	36	34
Silk and rayon (1 m. sq. metres)	57	55	57	59	58
Leather footwear (1 m. pairs)	44	44	45	45	42

By a law of 1986 creditors may proceed against insolvent companies which may be liquidated. Workers laid off receive 12 months' 'relocation support'.

Labour. In 1986 there were 4,892,500 wage-earners (2,252,600 female) in the following categories: working-class, 55·3%; white-collar, 29·6%; co-operative peasantry, 11·8%; self-employed tradesmen, 3·3%. 4,643,700 worked in the socialist sector. Percentage distributions of the workforce: industry, 31·4; agriculture, 20·2; social and cultural services, 11·9; trade, 10·4; transport and communications, 8·2; building, 7·1. A 40-hour 5-day week was introduced in 1984. Average monthly wages in 1987: 7,700 forints. Minimum wage in 1984: 2,000 forints. There were some 30,000 unemployed in 1988. Retirement age: Men, 60; women, 55. Leave entitlement, 15-24 days in 1985.

Trade Unions. Trade union membership was 4·9m. in 1984, 3·9m. in 1988.

Commerce. The economy is heavily dependent on foreign trade. Trade for calendar years (in 1m. forints):

	1980	1981	1982	1983	1984	1985	1986
Imports	299,900	314,300	324,800	365,000	390,500	410,100	439,700
Exports	281,000	299,400	324,500	374,150	414,000	424,600	420,300

In 1986 Hungary's trade with communist countries (in 1,000m. forints): imports, 451·1; exports, 252·7. In 1985 USSR was Hungary's major trading partner (31% of imports, 40% of exports), ahead of the Federal Republic of Germany (12·4%, 8·4%) and the German Democratic Republic (6·7%, 6·4%).

Commodity structure of foreign trade (%), 1985:

	Imports		Exports	
	Communist countries	Other countries	Communist countries	Other countries
Fuels and electricity	32·4	7·2	0·6	6·4
Raw materials	13·6	12·1	2·2	9·8
Semi-finished products	11·9	31·4	10·0	25·4
Spare parts	7·8	12·1	10·4	3·1
Machinery and capital goods	20·3	13·4	46·0	13·6
Industrial consumer goods	11·2	12·1	16·7	15·6
Agricultural produce	0·5	4·8	4·2	10·5
Food industry products	2·4	6·9	10·0	15·6

All exports and imports require licensing by the Ministry of Foreign Trade, and may be handled by 29 specialized foreign-trade agencies. Enterprises may handle their own foreign trade relations, set up companies abroad and participate in foreign companies. Hard currency is available through the National Bank. Tax-free zones for foreign companies exporting their own products were established in 1983. The Marketexpo branch of the Hungarian National Market Research Institute will conduct research for foreign firms. The agency Interag acts for Western firms in Hungary.

Joint ventures with Western firms holding more than 50% of the capital are permitted, and may be declared duty-free zones. Foreign companies may set up offices in Hungary. In 1985 there were 3 Hungarian-British companies. In Nov. 1978 the US and Hungary signed a most-favoured-nation trade agreement. Foreign indebtedness was some £5,000m. in 1987.

Total trade between Hungary and UK (British Department of Trade returns, in £1,000 sterling):

	1983	1984	1985	1986	1987
Imports to UK	53,834	75,905	84,114	77,229	83,267
Exports and re-exports from UK	91,845	100,502	107,226	101,557	101,300

Tourism. In 1986, 16·65m. foreigners visited Hungary (4·08m. from the West), of whom 10·61m. were tourists (2·04m. from the West); and 6·28m. Hungarians travelled abroad (0·89m. to the West) of whom 5·63m. (0·71m.) were tourists. Restrictions on travel to the West were eased in Jan. 1988.

COMMUNICATIONS

Roads. In 1986 there were 29,796 km of roads, including motorways, 227 km; highways, 97 km and other first class main roads, 1,952 km. In 1986 passenger cars numbered 1,538,900 (1,500,800 private), lorries 163,151 and coaches and buses 25,920. 244m. tonnes of freight and 650m. passengers were transported by road in 1986 (excluding intra-urban passengers). In 1986 there were 19,332 road accidents with 1,632 fatalities.

Railways. Route length of public lines in 1986, 7,767 km, of which 1,918 km were electrified. 119m. tonnes of freight and 233m. passengers were carried.

Aviation. Hungarian Air Lines (Malév) operate from Ferihegy airport, 16 km from Budapest. Passengers carried, 1986, 1·2m. Malév has 24 aircraft and flies 41 routes (including one to UK). British Airways, PANAM, Air France, SABENA, Swissair, OS, Lufthansa and KLM as well as Aeroflot and East European lines have services to Budapest.

Shipping. Permanently navigable waterways have a length of 1,688 km. The Hungarian Shipping Company (MAHART) has agencies at Amsterdam, Alexandria, Algiers, Beirut, Rijeka and Trieste. It has 17 sea-going ships. 4·3m. tonnes of cargo were carried in 1986 and 4·1m. passengers.

Post and Broadcasting. Number of post offices (1986), 2,573; number of telephones, 770,200 (524,600 private). Radio licences were abolished in 1980; television licences, (1986) 2,930,000. *Magyar Rádió és Televízió* broadcasts 3 programmes on medium-waves and FM and also regional programmes, including transmissions in German, Romanian and Serbo-Croat. Two TV programmes are broadcast, averaging 95 hours a week in 1985. Colour broadcasts are only transmitted in Budapest, using the SECAM system.

Cinemas and Theatres (1986). There were 3,600 cinemas; attendance 68m. 23 full-length feature films were made. There were 41 theatres; attendance 5·96m.

Newspapers and Books. In 1986 there were 29 dailies and 1,678 other periodicals. The Party daily is *Népszabadság* ('People's Freedom') (average daily circulation, 727,000). 8,206 book titles were published in 1986 in 95·6m. copies.

JUSTICE, RELIGION, EDUCATION AND WELFARE

Justice. The administration of justice is the responsibility of the Procurator-General, who is elected by Parliament for a term of 6 years. Civil and criminal cases fall under the jurisdiction of the district courts, county courts and the Supreme

Court in Budapest. Criminal proceedings are dealt with by district courts through 3-member councils and by county court and the Supreme Court in 5-member councils. A new Civil Code was adopted in 1978 and a new Criminal Code in 1979.

District Courts act only as courts of first instance; county courts as either courts of first instance or of appeal. The Supreme Court acts normally as an appeal court, but may act as a court of first instance in cases submitted to it by the Public Prosecutor. All courts, when acting as courts of first instance, consist of 1 professional judge and 2 lay assessors, and, as courts of appeal, of 3 professional judges. Local government Executive Committees may try petty offences.

District or county judges and assessors are elected by the district or county councils, all members of the Supreme Court by Parliament.

There are also military courts of the first instance. Military cases of the second instance go before the Supreme Court.

Judges are elected by the Presidential Council. 63,384 sentences were imposed on adults in 1986, including 30,745 of imprisonment. Juvenile convictions: 6,513.

Religion. There are 20 authorized religious denominations which share proportionally an annual state subsidy of 70m. forints. 8·5m. of the population professed a religious faith in 1976; the number of active church members was put between 1m. and 1·5m.

Senior church appointments require the consent of the Presidential Council. Lower ones are ratified by the State Office for Church Affairs. Certain appointments become valid if the Office makes no comment within 15 days, and for the most minor church appointments neither state consent nor prior notification is required. Ecclesiastics are required to take an oath of allegiance to the state.

In 1976 there were 5·25m. Roman Catholics with 4,400 churches, and 500,000 Uniates. In 1979 there were 3 seminaries and 1 Uniate seminary, a theological academy, and 8 secondary schools. There were 2,400 Roman Catholic priests in 1986. There are also lay co-operators of both sexes who perform some priestly duties. The Primate of Hungary is Archbishop László Pacskai, appointed Aug. 1986. There are 11 dioceses, all with bishops or archbishops. There is one Uniate bishopric.

In 1976 there were 2m. Calvinists with 4 dioceses, 1,300 ministers and 1,567 churches. There were 2 theological colleges (20% of students female) with 16 teachers, and 1 secondary school. There were 500,000 Lutherans with 16 dioceses, 374 ministers and 673 churches. There is a theological college with 6 teachers. The 10 denominations in the Association of Free Churches had 37,000 members, 230 ministers and 675 churches. There are 4 Orthodox denominations with 40,000 members in 1979. The Unitarian Church has 10,000 members, 11 ministers and 6 churches. In 1988 there were 80,000 Jews (825,000 in 1939) with 136 synagogues, 26 rabbis and a rabbinical college which enrols 10 students a year.

Education. Education is free and compulsory from 6 to 14. Primary schooling ends at 14; thereafter education may be continued at secondary, secondary technical or secondary vocational schools, which offer diplomas entitling students to apply for higher education, or at vocational training schools which offer tradesmen's diplomas. Students at the latter may also take the secondary school diploma examinations after 2 years of evening or correspondence study.

In 1986–87 there were 4,804 kindergartens with 33,716 teachers and 405,995 pupils; 3,540 primary schools with 89,611 teachers and 1,299,500 pupils; 587 secondary schools with 18,527 teachers and 236,900 pupils; and 278 vocational training schools with 175,200 students and 11,591 teachers. There are 4 universities proper (Budapest, Pécs, Szeged, Debrecen), and 14 specialized universities (6 technical, 4 medical, 3 arts, 1 economics). At these and at 36 other institutions of higher education there were 64,900 students and 15,111 teachers.

Libraries and Museums. In 1986 there were 4,644 public and 5,003 trade union libraries. Major national libraries (1985): National Széchenyi, 6·3m. volumes; Budapest University, 3·4m.; Academy of Sciences, 1·7m.; National Technical Library and Documentation Centre, 1·4m. In 1986 there were 661 museums with 19·6m. visitors.

Health. In 1986 there were 34,930 doctors and dentists and 103,777 hospital beds.

Social Security. Medical treatment is free. Patients bear 15% of the cost of medicines. Sickness benefit is 75% of wages, old age pensions (at 60 for men, 55 for women) 60–70%. In 1986, 147,700m. forints were paid out in social insurance benefits including 21,467m. in family allowances, 12,700m. in sick pay and 99,176m. in pensions. There were 2·31m. pensioners in 1986. In 1986 family allowances were paid to 1,336,000 families. Family support measures were improved in 1985. Allowances range from 410 forints per month.

DIPLOMATIC REPRESENTATIVES

Of Hungary in Great Britain (35 Eaton Pl., London, SW1X 8BY)
Ambassador: Dr Mátyás Domokos (accredited 22 Nov. 1984).

Of Great Britain in Hungary (Harmincad Utca 6, Budapest V)
Ambassador: L. V. Appleyard, CMG.

Of Hungary in the USA (3910 Shoemaker St., NW, Washington, D.C., 20008)
Ambassador: Dr Vencel Hazi.

Of the USA in Hungary (Szabadság Tér 12, Budapest V)
Ambassador: Mark Palmer.

Of Hungary to the United Nations
Ambassador: Ferenc Esztergalyos.

Books of Reference

Statisztikai Évkönyv. Budapest, annual; since 1871, abridged English version, *Statistical Year-Book*
Statistical Pocket Book of Hungary (in English). Budapest, annual from 1959
State Budget. Budapest, annual from 1983
Hungarian Digest. Budapest, 6 a year from 1980
The Hungarian Economy: a Quarterly Economic and Business Review. Budapest, since 1972
Hungary 66 (67 etc.). Budapest, annual from 1966
Managers in Hungary: A Biographical Directory. Budapest, 1986
Marketing in Hungary. Budapest, quarterly
Quarterly Review of the National Bank of Hungary. From 1983
Information Hungary. Budapest, 1980
The Constitution of the Hungarian People's Republic. Budapest, 1972
The 13th Congress of the Hungarian Workers' Party, March 25–28, 1985. Budapest, 1986

Bako, E., *Guide to Hungarian Studies.* 2 vols. Stanford Univ. Press, 1973
Berend, I. T., and Ranki, G., *Hungary: A Century of Economic Development.* New York and Newton Abbot, 1974.—*Underdevelopment and Economic Growth: Studies in Hungarian Social and Economic History.* Budapest, 1979.—*The Hungarian Economy in the Twentieth Century.* London, 1985
Bernat, T., (ed.) *An Economic Geography of Hungary.* Budapest, 1985
Cave, M., *Alternative Approaches to Economic Planning.* London, 1981
Fekete, J., *Back to the Realities: Reflections of a Hungarian Banker.* Budapest, 1982
Gati, C., *Hungary and the Soviet Bloc.* Duke Univ. Press, 1986
Hare, P. G., and others (eds.), *Hungary: a Decade of Economic Reform.* London, 1981
Hegedüs, A., *The Structure of Socialist Society.* London, 1977
Heinrich, H.-G., *Hungary: Politics, Economics and Society.* London, 1986
Kabdebó, T., *Hungary.* [Bibliography] Oxford and Santa Barbara, 1980
Kádár, J., *For a Socialist Hungary.* Budapest, 1974.—*Socialism and Democracy in Hungary.* Budapest, 1984
Kovrig, B., *Communism in Hungary.* Stanford, 1979
Kozma, F., *Economic Integration and Economic Strategy.* The Hague, 1982
Kulcsár K., *Contemporary Hungarian Society.* Budapest, 1984
Macartney, C. A., *Hungary: A Short History.* London, 1962
Németh, G. (ed.), *Hungary: A Comprehensive Guide.* Budapest, 1980
Országh, L., *Hungarian-English Dictionary.* Budapest, 1977.—*English-Hungarian Diction-ary.* Budapest, 1970
Pamlényi, E. (ed.), *A History of Hungary.* Budapest, 1975
Pécsi, M. and Sárfalvi, B., *Physical and Economic Geography of Hungary.* 2nd ed. Budapest, 1979
Rába, A. and Schenk, K.-E., (eds.) *Investment System and Foreign Trade Implications in Hungary.* New York, 1987
Szoboszlai, G. (ed.), *Politics and Public Administration in Hungary.* Budapest, 1985
Vardy, S. B., and Vardy, A. H., (eds.) *Society in Change.* Boulder, 1983

ICELAND

Lýðveldið Ísland

Capital: Reykjavík
Population: 244,009 (1986)
GNP per capita: US$11,410 (1985)

HISTORY. The first settlers came to Iceland in 874. Between 930 and 1264 Iceland was an independent republic, but by the 'Old Treaty' of 1263 the country recognized the rule of the King of Norway. In 1381 Iceland, together with Norway, came under the rule of the Danish kings, but when Norway was separated from Denmark in 1814, Iceland remained under the rule of Denmark. Since 1 Dec. 1918 it has been acknowledged as a sovereign state. It was united with Denmark only through the common sovereign until it was proclaimed an independent republic on 17 June 1944.

AREA AND POPULATION. Iceland is a large island in the North Atlantic, close to the Arctic Circle, and comprises an area of about 103,000 sq. km (39,758 sq. miles), with its extreme northern point (the Rifstangi) lying in 66° 32′ N. lat., and its most southerly point (Kötlutangi) in 63° 23′ N. lat., not including the islands north and south of the land; if these are included, the country extends from 67° 10′ N. (the Kolbeinsey) to 63° 17′ N. (Surtsey, one of the Westman Islands). It stretches from 13° 30′ (the Gerpir) to 24° 32′ W. long. (Látrabjarg). The skerry *Hvalbakur* (The Whaleback) lies 13° 16′ W. long.

There are 8 regions:

Region	Inhabited land (sq. km)	Mountain pasture (sq. km)	Waste-land (sq. km)	Total area (sq. km)	Population (1 Dec. 1986)
Capital area	1,266	716	—	1,982	134,773
Southwest Peninsula					14,334
West	5,011	3,415	275	8,711	14,941
Western Peninsula	4,130	3,698	1,652	9,470	10,230
Northland West	4,867	5,278	2,948	13,093	10,690
Northland East	9,890	6,727	5,751	22,368	25,786
East	16,921	17,929	12,555	21,991	13,157
South				25,214	20,098
Iceland	42,085	37,553	23,181	102,819	244,009

The census population (1980) was 229,187. In 1986, 25,151 were domiciled in rural districts and 218,858 in towns and villages (of over 200 inhabitants.) The population is almost entirely Icelandic.

In 1986 foreigners numbered 3,553; of these 949 were Danish, 675 US, 349 British, 263 Norwegian and 255 German nationals.

The capital, Reykjavík, had on 1 Dec. 1986, a population of 91,394; other towns were Akranes, 5,373; Akureyri, 13,750; Bolungarvík, 1,265; Dalvík, 1,339; Eskifjörður, 1,056; Garðabær, 6,231; Grindavík, 1,997; Hafnarfjörður, 13,431; Húsavík, 2,454; Ísafjörður, 3,398; Keflavík, 6,993; Kópavogur, 14,609; Neskaupstaður, 1,748; Njarðvík, 2,254; Ólafsfjörður, 1,145; Sauðárkrókur, 2,401; Selfoss, 3,718; Seltjarnarnes, 3,773; Seyðisfjörður, 964; Siglufjörður, 1,917; Vestmannaeyjar, 4,785.

Vital statistics for calendar years:

	Living births	Still-born	Marriages	Divorces	Deaths	Infant deaths
1984	4,113	17	1,413	449	1,584	25
1985	3,856	9	1,252	543	1,656	22
1986	3,908	18	1,229	498	1,597	21

The official language is Icelandic *(íslenska).*

CLIMATE. The climate is cool temperate oceanic and rather changeable, but mild for its latitude because of the Gulf Stream and prevailing S.W. winds. Precipitation is high in upland areas, mainly in the form of snow. Reykjavik. Jan. 34°F (1°C), July 52°F (11°C). Annual rainfall 34″ (860 mm).

617

CONSTITUTION AND GOVERNMENT. On 24 May 1944 the people of Iceland decided in a referendum to sever all ties with the Danish Crown. The voters were asked whether they were in favour of the abrogation of the Union Act, and whether they approved of the bill for a republican constitution: 70,725 voters were for severance of all political ties with Denmark and only 370 against it; 69,048 were in favour of the republican constitution, 1,042 against it and 2,505 votes were invalid. On 17 June 1944 the republic was formally proclaimed, and as the republic's first president the Alþingi elected Sveinn Björnsson for a 1-year term (re-elected 1945 and 1949; died 25 Jan. 1952). The President is now elected for a 4-year term.

President of the Republic of Iceland: Vigdís Finnbogadóttir (elected 29 June 1980, with 43,611 out of 129,049 valid votes, inaugurated 1 Aug. 1980); re-elected unopposed in 1984.

National flag: Blue with a red white-bordered Scandinavian cross.

National anthem: Ó Guð vors lands (words by M. Jochumsson, 1874; tune by S. Sveinbjörnsson).

The *Alþingi* (Parliament) is divided into two Houses, the Upper House and the Lower House. The former is composed of one-third of the members elected by the whole Alþingi in common sitting. The remaining two-thirds of the members form the Lower House. The members of the Alþingi receive payment for their services.

The budget bills must be laid before the two Houses in joint session, but all other bills can be introduced in either of the Houses. If the Houses do not agree, they assemble in a common sitting and the final decision is given by a majority of two-thirds of the voters, with the exception of budget bills, where a simple majority is sufficient. The ministers have free access to both Houses, but can vote only in the House of which they are members.

The electoral law enacted in 1984 provides for an Alþingi of 63 members. Of these, 54 seats are distributed among the 8 constituencies as follows: 14 seats are allotted to Reykjavík, 8 to Reykjanes (i.e. the Southwest excluding Reykjavík) and 5 or 6 to each of the remaining 6. From the 9 seats then left, 8 are divided beforehand among the constituencies according to the number of registered voters in the preceding elections. Finally, one seat is given to a constituency after the elections, to compensate the party with the fewest seats as compared to its number of votes.

At the elections held on 25 April 1987 the following parties were returned: Independence Party, 18; Progressives, 13; Social Democrats, 10; People's Alliance, 8; Citizen's Party, 7; Women's Alliance, 6; Association for Equality and Social Justice, 1.

The executive power is exercised under the President by the Cabinet. The coalition Cabinet, as constituted in July 1987, was as follows:

Prime Minister: Þorsteinn Pálsson (Ind.).

Foreign Affairs: Steingrímur Hermannsson (Progress). *Finance:* Jón Baldvin Hannibalsson (Soc. Dem.). *Social Affairs:* Jóhanna Sigurðardóttir (Soc. Dem.). *Fisheries:* Halldór Ásgrímsson (Progress). *Agriculture:* Jón Helgason (Progress). *Health and Social Security:* Guðmundur Bjarnason (Progress). *Commerce, Justice and Church:* Jón Sigurðsson (Soc. Dem.). *Communications:* Matthías Á. Mathiesen (Ind.). *Education:* Birgir Ísleifur Gunnarsson (Ind.). *Energy and Industry:* Friðrik Sophusson (Ind.).

Local Administration. Iceland is divided into 221 communes, of which 23 have the status of towns, while the 198 remaining communes make up 23 counties (*sýslur*). The commune and county councils are elected by universal suffrage (men and women 18 years of age and over), in town and other urban communes by proportional representation, but in rural communes by simple majority. The county councils consist of one representative for each of the constituent communes, their purpose being the superintendence of local government within the county. Town councils and county councils come under the supervision of the Ministry of Social Affairs. For national government there are 27 divisions, consisting of towns and counties, single or combined, with the exception of Keflavik Airport. In the capital the different branches of national government are independent (courts, police, customs), while in other national government divisions they are the charge of one official, who, in the case of counties, presides over the county council as well.

DEFENCE. Iceland possesses neither an army nor a navy. Under the North Atlantic Treaty, US forces are stationed in Iceland as the Iceland Defence Force. Three armed fishery protection vessels are maintained by the Coastguard, with 1 patrol aircraft and 2 helicopters. Coastguard Service personnel in 1986 totalled about 125 officers and men.

INTERNATIONAL RELATIONS

Membership. Iceland is a member of UN, EFTA, OECD, the Council of Europe, NATO and the Nordic Council.

ECONOMY

Budget. Total revenue and expenditure for calendar years (in 1m. kr.):

	1980	1981	1982	1983	1984	1985
Revenue	3,929	6,304	10,328	16,282	22,088	28,746
Expenditure	3,790	6,129	9,479	17,717	20,474	30,716

Main items of the Treasury accounts for 1985 (in 1m. kr.):

Revenue		Expenditure	
Direct taxes	3,698	Administration, justice and police	2,752
Indirect taxes	23,646	Foreign service	282
Other	1,403	Education, culture and	
		State Church	5,064
		Health and social security	13,168
		Subsidies	987
		Agriculture	1,457
		Fisheries	943
		Manufacturing and energy	1,219
		Communications	2,529
		Other	2,216

The public debt of Iceland was on 31 Dec. 1985, 26,700m. kr.

Currency. The Icelandic monetary units are the *króna*, pl. *krónur* and the *eyrir*, pl. *aurar*. There are 100 *aurar* to the *króna*. In March 1988, US$1 = kr. 39·46; £1 = kr. 65·47. Note and coin circulation, 31 Dec. 1986, was 1,692m. kr.

Banking. By Act of 29 March 1961 the Central Bank of Iceland was established, which took over the central bank function up to that date exercised by the *Landsbanki Íslands* (The National Bank of Iceland, owned entirely by the State). Other banks are: *Búnaðarbanki Íslands* (the Agricultural Bank of Iceland), a state bank, founded in 1930; *Útvegsbanki Íslands* (the Fisheries Bank of Iceland), founded in 1930 as a joint-stock bank, which in 1957 became a state bank; *Iðnaðarbanki Íslands* (Industrial Bank of Iceland Ltd), a joint-stock bank, established 1953, part of the shares being owned by the Government; *Verzlunarbanki Íslands* (Iceland Bank of Commerce Ltd), established in 1961; *Samvinnubanki Íslands* (The Icelandic Co-operative Bank), established in 1963; *Alþýðubankinn* (The People's Bank Ltd) established 1971. On 31 Dec. 1986 the accounts of the Central Bank balanced at 25,949m. kr.

At the end of 1986 there were 38 savings banks with deposits amounting to 7,714m. kr. and total deposits of the commercial banks amounted to 42,750m. kr.

Weights and Measures. The metric system of weights and measures is obligatory.

ENERGY AND NATURAL RESOURCES

Electricity. The installed capacity of public electrical power plants at the end of 1986 totalled 922,350 kw., of which 752,000 kw. comprised hydro-electric plants. Total electricity production in public-owned plants in 1986 amounted to 4,058m. kwh.; in privately-owned plants, 10m. kwh. Supply 220 volts; 50 Hz.

Agriculture. Of the total area of Iceland, about six-sevenths is unproductive, but only about 1·3% is under cultivation, which is largely confined to hay, potatoes and turnips. In 1986 the total hay crop was 3,499,000 cu. metres; the crop of potatoes, 16,600 tonnes, and of turnips 1,000 tonnes. At the end of 1986 the livestock was as follows: Horses, 56,400; cattle, 71,400 (including 33,900 milch cows); sheep, 675,500; pigs, 2,700; poultry, 310,000.

Fisheries. Fishing vessels at the end of 1986 numbered 822 with a gross tonnage of 112,391. Total catch in 1985, 1,680,000 tonnes; 1986, 1,656,000 tonnes.

The Icelandic Government announced that the fishery limits off Iceland were extended from 12 to 50 nautical miles from Sept. 1972. An interim agreement for 2 years signed by the UK and Iceland in Nov. 1973 expired in Nov. 1975.

On 15 July 1975 the Icelandic Government issued a decree that from 15 Oct. 1975 the fishery limits of Iceland were extended from 50 to 200 nautical miles. The Icelandic Government maintain that this extension is necessary to protect the fish stocks in Icelandic waters because the fishing industry is of vital importance to the national economy.

COMMERCE. Total value of imports (c.i.f.) and exports (f.o.b.) in 1,000 kr.:

	1982	1983	1984	1985	1986
Imports	11,644,752	20,605,978	26,780,309	37,600,289	45,905,230
Exports	8,478,796	18,632,993	23,556,960	33,749,626	44,967,770

Leading exports (in 1,000 kg and 1,000 kr.):

	1985		1986	
	Quantity	Value	Quantity	Value
Marine products	694,243	25,226,194	714,954	34,627,277
Aluminium	70,600	3,339,704	77,490	4,124,712
Ferro-silicon	56,845	1,219,588	64,990	1,334,417

Leading imports (in 1,000 tonnes and 1,000 kr.):

	1985		1986	
	Quantity	Value	Quantity	Value
Ships (number)	2	446,198	9	1,301,492
Fuel oil	99,985·7	791,396	89,339	457,500
Gas oils	255,399·6	2,570,087	253,244	1,729,800
Jet fuel	65,764·0	709,363	63,547	464,700
Cereals	12,944·0	218,003	14,102	245,500
Animal feed	59,796·6	500,813	52,549	450,900
Gasoline	91,711·9	993,762	116,804	877,700
Motor vehicles (number)	7,202·0	1,368,976	16,055	3,512,700
Fishing nets and other gear	1,400·7	342,182	841	336,900

Value of trade with principal countries for 3 years (in 1,000 kr.):

	1984		1985		1986	
	Imports (c.i.f.)	Exports (f.o.b.)	Imports (c.i.f.)	Exports (f.o.b.)	Imports (c.i.f.)	Exports (f.o.b.)
Austria	160,417	10,259	204,353	32,970	322,485	38,691
Belgium	593,617	446,097	897,870	422,846	1,058,839	430,997
Brazil	164,283	34,725	185,555	50,073	296,787	43,897
Canada	147,507	60,059	135,572	102,292	183,245	135,477
Czechoslovakia	103,609	118,270	97,819	74,240	153,404	57,619
Denmark	2,451,579	685,112	3,410,894	950,284	4,745,348	1,713,553
Faroe Islands	3,932	136,395	18,151	281,830	34,673	248,476
Finland	629,311	456,543	951,339	680,324	1,212,184	834,180
France	680,880	869,278	1,080,935	1,346,481	1,374,778	2,152,271
German Dem. Rep.	93,387	2,921	92,822	25,984	114,871	37,354
Germany, Fed. Rep. of	3,377,204	2,558,308	4,984,664	2,810,308	6,964,772	4,079,811
Greece	7,610	220,653	19,157	291,544	25,188	391,881
Hungary	25,809	12,296	14,685	23,223	15,007	9,008
India	30,417	—	40,371	—	30,845	—
Ireland	82,311	10,484	94,784	28,442	124,155	55,962
Israel	29,483	20,466	34,801	12,498	23,963	15,206
Italy	726,689	538,088	978,963	611,296	1,334,697	1,329,494
Japan	1,220,598	883,921	1,631,711	1,672,187	2,993,567	2,147,361

| | 1984 | | 1985 | | 1986 | |
	Imports (c.i.f.)	Exports (f.o.b.)	Imports (c.i.f.)	Exports (f.o.b.)	Imports (c.i.f.)	Exports (f.o.b.)
Netherlands	2,342,590	530,999	3,354,926	485,754	3,923,719	508,010
Nigeria	607	41,630	1,054	27,853	269	774,918
Norway	1,653,973	301,260	2,854,835	715,865	3,322,749	1,153,656
Poland	273,689	225,780	66,295	247,996	82,972	446,297
Portugal	716,032	1,000,070	866,629	1,909,337	439,552	2,915,100
Spain	300,746	1,081,039	371,097	1,308,908	532,291	1,592,764
Sweden	2,260,863	340,120	2,994,644	384,590	4,099,720	1,097,525
Switzerland	259,574	887,628	417,820	1,082,207	503,762	1,425,111
USSR	2,477,365	1,844,049	3,016,431	2,271,996	2,607,005	1,924,609
UK	2,208,763	3,152,981	3,591,482	6,214,810	3,754,209	9,177,626
USA	1,826,678	6,685,915	2,557,771	9,118,359	3,208,469	9,770,811

Total trade between Iceland and UK (British Department of Trade returns, in £1,000 sterling):

	1983	1984	1985	1986	1987
Imports to UK	66,505	86,104	128,281	173,140	178,314
Exports and re-exports from UK	65,176	64,242	76,194	73,640	84,866

TOURISM. There were 113,528 visitors to Iceland in 1986.

COMMUNICATIONS

Roads. On 31 Dec. 1986 the length of the public roads (including roads in towns) was 12,435 km. Of these 8,230 km were national main roads and 3,137 km were provincial roads. Total length of surfaced roads was 2,192 km. Motor vehicles registered at the end of 1986 numbered 126,995, of which 112,760 were passenger cars and 12,144 trucks; there were also 869 motor cycles.

Aviation. One large and some small companies maintain regular services between Reykjavík and various places in Iceland (the large one 1985: 244,027 passengers; 1,027 tonnes of mail; 2,232 tonnes of freight). The large company maintains regular services between Iceland and the UK, the Scandinavian countries, some other European countries and USA. In 1985 the company carried in scheduled foreign flights 485,696 passengers, 1,565 tonnes of mail and 4,577 tonnes of freight.

Shipping. Total registered vessels, 951 (179,005 GRT) on 31 Dec. 1986, of these 822 were sea-going fishing vessels.

Post and Broadcasting. At the end of 1985 the number of post offices was 139 and telephone and telegraph offices 109; number of telephone subscribers, 102,700. The government station, *Rikisútvarpid*, broadcasts 1 radio programme on long and medium-waves and on FM and a second programme on FM, as well as 2 local programmes for the capital region and the central north coast. *Rikisútvarpid* uses 200 transmitters and broadcasts 1 TV programme. Number of licensed receivers (1986): radio, about 79,000; television, about 71,000.

Cinemas (1986). In Reykjavík there were 8 cinemas (18 cinema halls) with a seating capacity of about 5,000.

Newspapers (1986). There are 6 daily newspapers, 5 in Reykjavík and one in Akureyri, with a combined circulation of about 100,000.

JUSTICE, RELIGION, EDUCATION AND WELFARE

Justice. The lower courts of justice are those of the provincial magistrates (*sýslumenn*) and town judges (*bæjarfógetar*). From these there is an appeal to the Supreme Court (*hæstiréttur*) in Reykjavík, which has 8 judges.

Religion. The national church, and the only one endowed by the State, is Evangelical Lutheran. But there is complete religious liberty, and no civil disabilities are attached to those not of the national religion. The affairs of the national church are under the superintendence of a bishop. In 1986, 4,905 persons (2%) were Dissenters and 3,060 persons (1·3%) did not belong to any religious community.

Education. Compulsory education for children began in 1907, and a university was founded in Reykjavík in 1911. There is in Reykjavík a teachers' training college and a technical high school; various specialized institutions of learning and a number of second-level schools are scattered throughout the country. There are many part-time schools of cultural activities, including music.

Compulsory education comprises 9 classes, 7-15 years of age. After completion of a facultative 9th class, attended by 93%-95% of the relevant age group, there is access to further schooling free of charge. Some 53-74% of the age groups 16-19 years old attend schools. Around 15%-20% of each age group go into handicraft apprenticeship. About 30% pass matriculation examination, generally at the age of 20. Approximately one third-level student out of every four goes abroad for studies, two-thirds of them to Scandinavia, the rest mainly to English- and German-speaking countries.

Immatriculation in Iceland in autumn 1985: Preceding the first level, 4,528. First-level (1st-6th class) 24,603. Second-level first stage (7th-9th class) 12,248. Second-level second stage (4-year courses) 15,311. Third-level studies, 4,949.

Social Welfare. The main body of the Icelandic social welfare legislation is consolidated in six main acts:

(i) The social security legislation (a) health insurance, including sickness benefits; *(b)* social security pensions, mainly consisting of old age pension, disablement pension and widows' pension, and also children's pension; *(c)* employment injuries insurance.

(ii) The unemployment insurance legislation, where daily allowances are paid to those who have met certain conditions.

(iii) The subsistence legislation. This is controlled by municipal government, and social assistance is granted under special circumstances, when payments from other sources are not sufficient.

(iv) The tax legislation. In 1975 family allowances were abolished and children's support included in the tax legislation, according to which a certain amount for each child in a family is subtracted from income taxes or paid out to the family.

(v) The rehabilitation legislation.

(vi) Child and juvenile guidance.

Health insurance covers the entire population. Citizenship is not demanded and there is no waiting period. Most hospitals are both municipally and state run, a few solely state run and all offer free medical help. Medical treatment out of hospitals is partly paid by the patient, the same applies to medicines, except medicines of lifelong necessary use, which are paid in full by the health insurance. Dental care is free for the age groups 6-15, but is paid 75% for those five years or younger and the age group 16 but 50% for old age and disabled pensioners. Sickness benefits are paid to those who lose income because of periodical illness. The daily amount is fixed and paid from the 11th day of illness.

The pension system is composed of the public social security system and some 90 private pension funds. The social security system pays basic old age and disablement pensions of a fixed amount regardless of past or present income, as well as supplementary pensions to individuals with low present income. The pensions are index-linked, i.e. are changed in line with changes in wage and salary rates in the labour market. The private pension funds pay pensions that depend on past payments of premiums that are a fixed proportion of earnings. The payment of pension fund premiums is compulsory for all wage and salary earners. The pensions paid by the funds differ considerably between the individual funds, but are generally index-linked. In the public social security system, entitlement to old age and disablement pensions at the full rates is subject to the condition that the beneficiary has been resident in Iceland for 40 years at the age period of 16-67. For shorter period of residence, the benefits are reduced proportionally. Entitled to old age pension are all those who are 67 years old, and have been residents in Iceland for 3 years of the age period of 16-67. Entitled to disablement pension are those who have lost 75% of their working capacity and have been residents in Iceland for 3 years before application or have had full working capacity at the time when they became residents. Old age and disablement pension are of equally high amount, in the year 1986 the total sum was 74,028 kr. for an individual. Married pensioners are paid 90% of two individuals' pensions. In addition to the basic amount, supplementary allowances are paid according to social circumstances and income possibilities. Widows' pensions are the same amount as old age and disablement pension, provided the applicant is over 60 when she becomes widowed. Women at the age 50–60 get reduced pension. Women under 50 are not entitled to widows' pensions.

The employment injuries insurance covers medical care, daily allowances, disablement pension and survivors' pension and is applicable to practically all employees.

All benefits within the above-mentioned laws shall go up in step with general wages within 6 months from their increase.

Social assistance is primarily municipal and granted in cases outside the social security legislation. Domestic assistance to old people and disabled is granted within this legislation, besides other services.

Child and juvenile guidance is performed by chosen committees according to special laws, such as home guidance and family assistance. In cases of parents' disablement the committees take over the guidance of the children involved.

DIPLOMATIC REPRESENTATIVES

Of Iceland in Great Britain (1 Eaton Terrace, London, SW1W 8EY)
Ambassador: Ólafur Egilsson (accredited 28 Nov. 1986).

Of Great Britain in Iceland (Laufásvegur 49, 101 Reykjavík)
Ambassador and Consul-General: Mark F. Chapman, CVO.

Of Iceland in the USA (2022 Connecticut Ave., NW, Washington, D.C., 20008)
Ambassador: Ingvi S. Ingvarson.

Of the USA in Iceland (Laufásvegur 21, 101 Reykjavík)
Ambassador: L. Nicholas Ruwe.

Of Iceland to the United Nations
Ambassador: Hans G. Andersen.

Books of Reference

Statistical Information: The Statistical Bureau of Iceland, Hagstofa Íslands (Reykjavík) was founded in 1914. *Director:* Hallgrimur Snorrason. Its main publications are:

Statistical Abstract. (latest issue 1984)
Hagskýrslur Íslands. Statistics of Iceland (from 1912)
Hagtíðindi (Statistical Bulletin) (from 1916)
Economic Statistics. Central Bank of Iceland (quarterly from 1980)
Icelandic Currency Reform January 1st 1981. Central Bank of Iceland, 1980
Heilbrigðisskýrslur. Public Health in Iceland (latest issue for 1983; published 1986)
Cleasby, R., *An Icelandic-English Dictionary.* 2nd ed. Oxford, 1957
Foss, H. (ed.), *Directory of Iceland.* Annual. Reykjavík, 1907–40, 1948 ff.
Hermannsson, Halldór, *Islandica.* An annual relating to Iceland and the Fiske Icelandic Collection in Cornell University Library. Ithaca (from 1908)
Hood, J. C. F., *Icelandic Church Saga.* London, 1946
Horton, J. J., *Iceland.* [Bibliography] Oxford and Santa Barbara, 1983
Leaf, H., *Iceland Yesterday and Today.* London, 1949
Magnússon, S. A., *Northern Sphinx: Iceland and the Icelanders from the Settlement to the Present.* London, 1977
Nordal, J., and Kristinsson, V. (eds), *Iceland 1986.* Central Bank of Iceland, Reykjavík, 1987
Þórðarson, Matthias, *The Althing, Iceland's Thousand-Year-Old Parliament, 930–1930.* Reykjavík, 1930
Þorsteinsson, Þorsteinn, *Iceland, 1946: A Handbook Published on the 60th Anniversary of the National Bank of Iceland.* 4th ed. Reykjavík, 1946
Zoëga, G. T., *Íslensk-ensk (and Ensk-íslensk) orðabók.* 3rd ed. 2 vols. Reykjavík, 1932–51

National Library: Landsbókasafnið, Reykjavík, *Librarian:* Dr Finnbogi Guðmundsson.

INDIA

Capital: New Delhi
Population: 748m. (1984)
GDP per capita: US$260 (1983)

Bharat

HISTORY. The Indus civilization was fully developed by *c.* 2500 B.C., and collapsed *c.* 1750 B.C. An Aryan civilization spread from the west as far as the Ganges valley by 500 B.C.; separate kingdoms were established and many of these were united under the Mauryan dynasty established by Chandragupta in *c.* 320 B.C. The Mauryan Empire was succeeded by numerous small kingdoms. The Gupta dynasty (A.D. 320–600) was followed by the first Arabic invasions of the north-west. Moslem, Hindu and Buddhist states developed together with frequent conflict until the establishment of the Mogul dynasty in 1526. The first settlements by the East India Company were made after 1600 and the company established a formal system of government for Bengal in 1700. During the decline of the Moguls frequent wars between the Company, the French and the native princes led to the Company's being brought under British Government control in 1784; the first Governor-General of India was appointed in 1786. The powers of the Company were abolished by the India Act, 1858, and its functions and forces transferred to the British Crown. Representative government was introduced in 1909, and the first parliament in 1919. The separate dominions of India and Pakistan became independent within the Commonwealth in 1947 and India became a republic in 1950.

AREA AND POPULATION. India is bounded north-west by Pakistan, north by China, Tibet, Nepál and Bhután, east by Burma, south-east, south and south west by the Indian ocean. The far eastern states and territories are almost separated from the rest by Bangladesh as it extends northwards from the Bay of Bengal. The area of the Indian Union (excluding the Pakistan and China-occupied parts of Jammu and Kashmir) is 3,166,829 sq. km. Its population according to the 1981 census (preliminary figures) is 683,810,051 (excluding the occupied area of Jammu and Kashmir); this represents an increase of 24·8% since 1971. Sex ratio was 940 females per 1,000 males (929 in 1971); density of population, 221 per sq. km. About 23·7% of the population was urban in 1981 (in Maharashtra, 35%; in Himachal Pradesh, 7·7%).

Many births and deaths go unregistered. Data from certain areas of better registration and field studies suggest that the average annual birth rate for the decade 1971–80 was about 36 per 1,000 population, the death rate 14·8 per 1,000. In 1980 (estimate) the age-group 0–14 years represented 39·7% of the population and only 5·5% were over 60. In 1981 expectation of life for men was 52 years, for women 50.

Marriages and divorces are not registered. The minimum age for a civil marriage is 18 for women and 21 for men; for a sacramental marriage, 14 for girls and 18 for youths.

The main details of the census of 1 March 1971 and of 1 March 1981 are:

Name of State	Land area in sq. km (1981)	Population 1971	1981
States			
Andhra Pradesh	276,814	43,502,708	53,403,619
Assam	78,438	14,625,152	19,902,826
Bihar	173,876	56,353,369	69,823,154
Gujarat	195,984	26,697,475	33,960,905
Haryana	44,222	10,036,808	12,850,902
Himachal Pradesh	55,673	3,460,434	4,237,569
Jammu and Kashmir[1]	101,283	4,617,000	5,981,600
Karnataka	191,773	29,299,014	37,043,451

[1] Excludes the Pakistan-occupied area.

624

Name of State	Land area in sq. km (1981)	Population 1971	Population 1981
Kerala	38,864	21,347,375	25,403,217
Madhya Pradesh	442,841	41,654,119	52,131,717
Maharashtra	307,762	50,412,235	62,693,898
Manipur	22,356	1,072,753	1,433,691
Meghalaya	22,489	1,011,699	1,327,824
Nagaland	16,527	516,449	773,281
Orissa	155,782	21,944,615	26,272,054
Punjab	50,362	13,551,060	16,669,755
Rajasthan	342,214	25,765,806	34,102,912
Sikkim	7,299	...	315,682
Tamil Nadu	130,069	41,199,168	48,297,456
Tripura	10,477	1,556,342	2,060,189
Uttar Pradesh	294,413	88,341,144	110,858,019
West Bengal	87,853	44,312,011	54,485,560
Union Territories			
Andaman and Nicobar Islands	8,293	115,133	188,254
Arunachal Pradesh [1]	83,578	467,511	628,050
Chandigarh	114	257,251	450,061
Dadra and Nagar Haveli	491	74,170	103,677
Daman and Diu	110	62,648	78,981
Delhi	1,485	4,065,698	6,196,414
Goa [2]	3,701	795,123	1,003,136
Lakshadweep	32	31,810	40,237
Mizoram [1]	21,087	332,390	487,774
Pondicherry	480	471,707	604,136
Grand total	3,166,829	547,949,809	683,810,051

[1] Achieved statehood 1986.   [2] Achieved statehood 1987.

Greatest density occurs in Delhi (4,178 per sq. km), Chandigarh (3,948), Lakshadweep (1,257) and Pondicherry (1,228). The lowest occurs in Arunachal Pradesh (7).

There were (1981) 353,347,249 males and 330,462,802 females.

In 1981, 502m. were rural (*c.* 76%) and 156m. were urban.

Cities and Urban Agglomerations (with states in brackets) having more than 250,000 population at the 1981 census were (1,000):

City	Pop.	City	Pop.	City	Pop.
Agra (U.P.)	770	Erode (T.N.)	275	Nasik (Mah.)	429
Ahmedabad (Guj.)	2,515	Faridabad		Patna (Bih.)	916
Ajmer (Raj.)	374	agglomeration	327	Pondicherry	251
Aligarh (U.P.)	320	Ghaziabad (U.P.)	292	Pune (Mah.)	1,685
Allahabad (U.P.)	642	Gorakhpur (U.P.)	306	Raipur (M.P.)	339
Amravati (Mah.)	261	Guntur (A.P.)	367	Rajahmundry (A.P.)	268
Amritsar (Pun.)	589	Gwalior (M.P.)	560	Rajkot (Guj.)	444
Asansol (W.B.)	365	Hubli-Dharwar (Kar.)	526	Ranchi (Bih.)	501
Aurangabad (Mah.)	316	Hyderabad (A.P.)	2,528	Rourkela (Ori.)	321
Bangalore (Kar.)	2,914	Indore (M.P.)	827	Saharanpur (U.P.)	294
Bareilly (U.P.)	438	Jabalpur (M.P.)	758	Salem (T.N.)	515
Belgaum (Kar.)	300	Jaipur (Raj.)	1,005	Sangli (Mah.)	269
Bhavnagar (Guj.)	308	Jalandhar (Pun.)	406	Sholapur (Mah.)	514
Bhopal (M.P.)	672	Jamnagar (Guj.)	317	Srinagar (J. & K.)	520[1]
Bikaner (Raj.)	280	Jamshedpur (Bih.)	670	Surat (Guj.)	913
Bokaro Steel City		Jhansi (U.P.)	281	Thana (Mah.)	389
(Bih.)	261	Jodhpur (Raj.)	494	Tiruchirapalli	
Bombay (Mah.)	8,227	Kanpur (U.P.)	1,688	(T.N.)	608
Calcutta (W.B.)	9,166	Kolhapur (Mah.)	351	Tirunelveli (T.N.)	324
Calicut (Ker.)	546	Kotah (Raj.)	347	Trivandrum (Ker.)	520
Chandigarh (Ch.)	421	Lucknow (U.P.)	1,007	Tuticorin (T.N.)	251
Cochin (Ker.)	686	Ludhiana (Pun.)	606	Ujjain (M.P.)	282
Coimbatore (T.N.)	917	Madras (T.N.)	4,277	Ulhasnagar (Mah.)	648
Cuttack (Ori.)	326	Madurai (T.N.)	904	Vadodara (Guj.)	744
Dehra Dun (U.P.)	294	Mangalore (Kar.)	306	Varanasi (U.P.)	794
Delhi	5,714	Meerut (U.P.)	538	Vijayawada (A.P.)	545
Dhanbad (Bih.)	677	Moradabad (U.P.)	348	Visakhapatnam	
Durgapur (W.B.)	306	Mysore (Kar.)	476	(A.P.)	594
Durg-Bhilainagar (M.P.)	490	Nagpur (Mah.)	1,298	Warangal (A.P.)	336

[1] Estimate.

Report of the Officials of the Government of India and the People's Republic of China on the Boundary Question. New Delhi, Ministry of External Affairs, 1961

Census of India: Reports and Papers, Decennial Series. (Government of India.)

Annual Report on the Working of Indian Migration. Government of India, from 1956

Report of the Commissioner for Scheduled Castes and Scheduled Tribes. Government of India. Annual

Public Health. Report of the Public Health Commission with the Government of India. Annual

Agarwala, S. N., *India's Population Problems.* New York, 1973

CLIMATE. India has a variety of climatic sub-divisions. In general, there are four seasons. The cool one lasts from Dec. to March, the hot season is in April and May, the rainy season is June to Sept., followed by a further dry season till Nov. Rainfall, however, varies considerably, from 4″ (100 mm) in the N.W. desert to over 400″ (10,000 mm) in parts of Assam.

Range of temperature and rainfall: New Delhi. Jan. 57°F (13·9°C), July 88°F (31·1°C). Annual rainfall 26″ (640 mm). Bombay. Jan. 75°F (23·9°C), July 81°F (27·2°C). Annual rainfall 72″ (1,809 mm). Calcutta. Jan. 67°F (19·4°C), July 84°F (28·9°C). Annual rainfall 64″ (1,600 mm). Cherrapunji. Jan. 53°F (11·7°C), July 68°F (20°C). Annual rainfall 432″ (10,798 mm). Cochin. Jan. 80°F (26·7°C), July 79°F (26·1°C). Annual rainfall 117″ (2,929 mm). Darjeeling. Jan. 41°F (5°C), July 62°F (16·7°C). Annual rainfall 121″ (3,035 mm). Hyderabad. Jan. 72°F (22·2°C), July 80°F (26·7°C). Annual rainfall 30″ (752 mm). Madras. Jan. 76°F (24·4°C), July 87°F (30·6°C). Annual rainfall 51″ (1,270 mm). Patna. Jan. 63°F (17·2°C), July 90°F (32·2°C). Annual rainfall 46″ (1,150 mm).

CONSTITUTION AND GOVERNMENT. On 26 Jan. 1950 India became a sovereign democratic republic. India's relations with the British Commonwealth of Nations were defined at the London conference of Prime Ministers on 27 April 1949.

Unanimous agreement was reached to the effect that the Republic of India remains a full member of the Commonwealth and accepts the Queen as 'the symbol of the free association of its independent member nations and, as such, the head of the Commonwealth'. This agreement was ratified by the Constituent Assembly of India on 17 May 1949.

The constitution was passed by the Constituent Assembly on 26 Nov. 1949 and came into force on 26 Jan. 1950. It has since been amended 57 times.

India is a Union of States and comprises 25 States and 7 Union territories. Each State is administered by a Governor appointed by the President for a term of 5 years while each Union territory is administered by the President through an administrator appointed by him.

The capital is New Delhi.

Presidency. The head of the Union is the President in whom all executive power is vested, to be exercised on the advice of ministers responsible to Parliament. He is elected by an electoral college consisting of all the elected members of Parliament and of the various state legislative assemblies. He holds office for 5 years and is eligible for re-election. He must be an Indian citizen at least 35 years old and eligible for election to the Lower House. He can be removed from office by impeachment for violation of the constitution.

There is also a Vice-President who is *ex-officio* chairman of the Upper House of Parliament.

Central Legislature. The Parliament for the Union consists of the President, the Council of States *(Rajya Sabha)* and the House of the People *(Lok Sabha)*. The Council of States, or the Upper House, consists of not more than 250 members; in 1988 there were 232 elected members and 12 members nominated by the President. The election to this house is indirect; the representatives of each State are elected by the elected members of the Legislative Assembly of that State. The Council of States is a permanent body not liable to dissolution, but one-third of the members retire every second year. The House of the People, or the Lower House, consists of 546 members, 532 directly elected on the basis of adult suffrage from territorial constituencies in the States, and 13 members to represent the Union territories, chosen in such manner as the Parliament may by law provide; in Dec. 1987 there were 544 elected members and 2 members nominated by the President. The House of the People unless sooner dissolved continues for a period of 5 years from the date appointed for its first meeting; in emergency, Parliament can extend the term by 1 year.

State Legislatures. For every State there is a legislature which consists of the Governor, and *(a)* 2 Houses, a Legislative Assembly and a Legislative Council, in the States of Bihar, Jammu and Kashmir, Karnataka, Madhya Pradesh (where it is provided for but not in operation), Maharashtra and Uttar Pradesh, and *(b)* 1 House, a Legislative Assembly, in the other States. Every Legislative Assembly, unless sooner dissolved, continues for 5 years from the date appointed for its first meeting. In emergency the term can be extended by 1 year. Every State Legislative Council is a permanent body and is not subject to dissolution, but one-third of the members retire every year. Parliament can, however, abolish an existing Legislative Council or create a new one, if the proposal is supported by a resolution of the Legislative Assembly concerned.

Legislative Councils have one-third of the total membership of the Assemblies but not less than 40 members, of whom one-third are elected by local authorities, one-third by members of the Assembly, one-twelfth by state university graduates and one-twelfth by teachers of secondary school upwards; the rest are named by the Governor. Legislative Assemblies have between 60 and 500 directly elected members.

Legislation. The various subjects of legislation are enumerated in three lists in the seventh schedule to the constitution. List I, the Union List, consists of 97 subjects (including defence, foreign affairs, communications, currency and coinage, banking and customs) with respect to which the Union Parliament has exclusive power to make laws. The State legislature has exclusive power to make laws with respect to the 66 subjects in list II, the State List; these include police and public order, agriculture and irrigation, education, public health and local government. The powers to make laws with respect to the 47 subjects (including economic and social planning, legal questions and labour and price control) in list III, the Concurrent List, are held by both Union and State governments, though the former prevails. But Parliament may legislate with respect to any subject in the State List in circumstances when the subject assumes national importance or during emergencies.

Other provisions deal with the administrative relations between the Union and the States, interstate trade and commerce, distribution of revenues between the States and the Union, official language, etc.

Fundamental Rights. Two chapters of the constitution deal with fundamental rights and 'Directive Principles of State Policy'. 'Untouchability' is abolished, and its practice in any form is punishable. The fundamental rights can be enforced through the ordinary courts of law and through the Supreme Court of the Union. The directive principles cannot be enforced through the courts of law; they are nevertheless fundamental in the governance of the country.

Citizenship. Under the Constitution, every person who was on the 26 Jan. 1950, domiciled in India and *(a)* was born in India or *(b)* either of whose parents was born in India or *(c)* who has been ordinarily resident in the territory of India for not less than 5 years immediately preceding that date became a citizen of India. Special provision is made for migrants from Pakistan and for Indians resident abroad. Under the Citizenship Act, 1955, which supplemented the provisions of the Constitution, Indian citizenship is acquired by birth, by descent, by registration and by naturalization. The Act also provides for loss of citizenship by renunciation, termination and deprivation. The right to vote is granted to every person who is a citizen of India and who is not less than 21 years of age on a fixed date and is not otherwise disqualified.

Parliament. Parliament and the state legislatures are organized according to the following schedule (figures show distribution of seats in Dec. 1987):

| | Parliament | | State Legislatures | |
	House of the People (Lok Sabha)	Council of States (Rajya Sabha)	Legislative Assemblies (Vidhan Sabhas)	Legislative Councils (Vidhan Parishads)
States:				
Andhra Pradesh	42	18	294	–
Arunachal Pradesh	2	1³	30	–
Assam	14	7	126	–
Bihar	54	22	324	96
Goa	3	–	31	–
Gujarat	26	11	182	–
Haryana	10	5	90	–
Himachal Pradesh	4	3	68	–
Karnataka	28	12	224	75
Kerala	20	9	140	–
Madhya Pradesh	40	16	320	–
Maharashtra	48	19	288	63
Manipur	2	1	60	–
Meghalaya	2	1	60	–
Mizoram	1	1	30	–
Nagaland	1	1	60	–
Orissa	21	10	147	–
Punjab	13	7	117	–
Rajasthan	25	10	200	–
Sikkim	1	1	32	–
Tamil Nadu	39	18	234	–
Tripura	2	1	60	–
Uttar Pradesh	85	34	425	108
West Bengal	42	16	294	–
Jammu and Kashmir	6	4	76²	36⁴
Union Territories:				
Andaman and Nicobar Islands	1	–	–	–
Chandigarh	1	–	–	–
Dadra and Nagar Haveli	1	–	–	–
Delhi	7	3	61	–
Daman and Diu	1	–	–	–
Lakshadweep	1	–	–	–
Pondicherry	1	1	30	–
Nominated by the President under Article 80 (1) (a) of the Constitution	–	12	–	–
Total	546¹	244	4,003	378

¹ Includes 2 nominated members to represent Anglo-Indians.
² Excludes 25 seats for Pakistan-occupied areas of the State which are in abeyance.
³ Nominated by the President.   ⁴ Excludes seats for the Pakistan-occupied areas.

The number of seats allotted to scheduled castes and scheduled tribes in the House of the People is 79 and 40 respectively. Out of the 3,997 seats allotted to the Legislative Assemblies, 557 are reserved for scheduled castes and 315 for scheduled tribes.

In Dec. 1987 the composition of the House of the People was: Indira Congress 408; Telugu Desam, 30; Communist Party (Marxist) 22; All India Anna DMK, 11; Janata, 13; Bharatiya Janata, 2; Communist Party, 6; others, 44; nominated, 2; vacant, 8.

The Council of States was composed as follows: Indira Congress 151; CPI (Marxist) 14; All-India Anna DMK 11; Janata, 10; Bharatiya Janata, 9; Lok Dal, 9; others, 32; Nominated 6; Vacant 2.

National flag: Three horizontal stripes of saffron (orange), white and green, with the wheel of Asoka in the centre in blue.

National anthem: Jana-gana-mana (words by Rabindranath Tagore).

Indian Independence Act, 1947. (Ch. 30.) London, 1947
The Constitution of India (Modified up to 15 April 1967). Delhi, 1967
Appadorai, A., *Indian Political Thinking in the Twentieth Century: From Naoroji to Nehru.*
   OUP, 1971.—*Documents on Political Thought in Modern India.* OUP, 1974
Austin, G., *The Indian Constitution.* OUP, 1972
Mansergh, N., ed. *The Transfer of Power 1942–47.* 5 vols. HMSO, 1970–75
Pylee, M. V., *Constitutional Government in India.* 2nd ed. Bombay, 1965
Rao, K. V., *Parliamentary Democracy of India.* 2nd ed. Calcutta, 1965
Seervali, H. M., *Constitutional Law of India.* Bombay, 1967

Language. The Constitution provides that the official language of the Union shall be Hindi in the Devanagari script. It was originally provided that English should continue to be used for all official purposes until 1965. But the Official Languages Act 1963 provides that, after the expiry of this period of 15 years from the coming into force of the Constitution, English might continue to be used, in addition to Hindi, for all official purposes of the Union for which it was being used immediately before that day, and for the transaction of business in Parliament. According to the Official Languages (Use for official purposes of the Union) Rules 1976, an employee may record in Hindi or in English without being required to furnish a translation thereof in the other language and no employee possessing a working knowledge of Hindi may ask for an English translation of any document in Hindi except in the case of legal or technical documents.

The 56th amendment to the Constitution (26 Nov. 1987) authorised the preparation of a Constitution text in Hindi.

The following 15 languages are included in the Eighth Schedule to the Constitution: Assamese, Bengali, Gujarati, Hindi, Kannada, Kashmiri, Malayalam, Marathi, Oriya, Punjabi, Sanskrit, Sindhi, Tamil, Telugu, Urdu.

There are numerous mother tongues grouped under each language. Hindi, Bengali, Telugu, Tamil and Marathi languages (including mother tongues grouped under each) are spoken by 264·2m., 51·5m., 54·2m., 44·7m. and 49·6m. of the popu-lation respectively.

Ferozsons English–Urdu, Urdu–English Dictionary. 2 vols. 4th ed. Lahore, 1961
Fallon, S. W., *A New English–Hindustani Dictionary.* Lahore, 1941
Grierson, Sir G. A., *Linguistic Survey of India.* 11 vols. (in 19 parts). Delhi, 1903-28
Mitra, S. C., *Student's Bengali–English Dictionary.* 2nd ed. Calcutta, 1923
Scholberg, H. C., *Concise Grammar of the Hindi Language.* 3rd ed. London, 1955
University of Madras, *Tamil Lexicon.* 7 vols. Madras, 1924-39
Vyas, V. G., and Patel, S. G., *Standard English–Gujarati Dictionary.* 2 vols. Bombay, 1923

Government. *President of the Republic:* R. Venkataraman (sworn in 25 July 1987). Vice-President: S. Dayal Sharma (elected 4 Sept. 1987).

There is a Council of Ministers to aid and advise the President of the Republic in the exercise of his functions; this comprises Ministers who are members of the Cabinet and Ministers of State who are not. A Minister who for any period of 6 consecutive months is not a member of either House of Parliament ceases to be a Minister at the expiration of that period. The Prime Minister is appointed by the President; other Ministers are appointed by the President on the Prime Minister's advice.

The salary of each Minister is Rs 27,000 per annum, and that of each Deputy Minister is Rs 21,000 per annum. Each Minister is entitled to the free use of a furnished residence and a chauffeur-driven car throughout his term of office. A Cabinet Minister has a sumptuary allowance of Rs 1,000 per month, Ministers of State, Rs 500 and Deputy Ministers, Rs 300. At the administrative head of each Ministry is a Secretary of the Government.

Following was the composition of the Cabinet in Jan. 1988:

Prime Minister: Rajiv Gandhi.
Portfolios held by the Prime Minister assisted by Ministers of State:
Science and Technology, External Affairs, Atomic Energy and Space.
Ministers:
Industry: J. Vengal Rao.
Commerce and Finance: N. Dutt Tiwari.

Urban Development and Tourism: Mohsinha Kidwai.
Water Resources: Dinesh Singh.
Agriculture: Bhajan Lal.
Parliamentary Affairs, Information and Broadcasting: H. K. L. Bhagat.
Steel and Mines: M. Lal Fotedar.
Human Resources Development: P. V. Narasimha Rao.
Home: Buta Singh.
Energy and Communications: Vasant Sathe.
Defence: K. Chandra Pant.
Planning, Programme Implementation: P. Shivshankar.
Law and Justice: Bindeshwari Dubey.
Textiles: R. N. Mirdha.
Health, Family Welfare, Civil Aviation: Motilal Vora.

There were also 7 Ministers of State with independent charge, 30 other Ministers of State and 7 Deputy Ministers.

Local Government. There were in 1981, 42 municipal corporations, 2,165 municipalities, 420 notified area committees and 59 cantonment boards (all figures exclude Assam). The municipal bodies have the care of the roads, water supply, drainage, sanitation, medical relief, vaccination and education. Their main sources of revenue are taxes on the annual rental value of land and buildings, octroi and terminal, vehicle and other taxes. The municipal councils enact their own bye-laws and frame their budgets, which in the case of municipal bodies other than corporations generally require the sanction of the State government. All municipal councils are elected on the principle of adult franchise.

For rural areas there is a 3-tier system of *panchayati raj* at village, block and district level, although the 3-tier structure may undergo some changes in State legislation to suit local conditions. All *panchayati raj* bodies are organically linked, and representation is given to special interests. Elected directly by and from among villagers, the *panchayats* are responsible for agricultural production, rural industries, medical relief, maternity and child welfare, common grazing grounds, village roads, tanks and wells, and maintenance of sanitation. In some places they also look after primary education, maintenance of village records and collection of land revenue. They have their own powers of taxation. There are some judicial *panchayats* or village courts.

Panchayati raj now cover all the States with the exception of Mizoram, Nagaland and Meghalaya, although Nagaland has area, range and tribal councils. They exist in all the Union Territories except Lakshadweep.

The powers and responsibilities of *panchayati raj* institutions are derived from State Legislatures, and from the executive orders of State governments.

NAGARLOK (Municipal Affairs Quarterly). Quarterly. Institute of Public Administration. Delhi
Proceedings of the 13th Meeting of the Central Council of Local Self Government. Delhi, 1970
Report of the Committee on Budgetary Reforms in Municipal Administration. Delhi, 1974
State Machinery for Municipal Supervision. Institute of Public Administration. Delhi, 1970
Statistical Abstract of India. Annual. Delhi.

DEFENCE. The Supreme Command of the Armed Forces vests in the President of the Indian Republic. Policy is decided at different levels by a number of committees, including the Political Affairs Committee presided over by the Prime Minister and the Defence Minister's Committee. Administrative and operational control rests in the respective Service Headquarters, under the control of the Ministry of Defence.

The Ministry of Defence is the central agency for formulating defence policy and for co-ordinating the work of the three services. Among the organizations directly administered by the Ministry are the Research and Development Organization, the Production Organization, the National Defence College, the National Cadet Corps and the Directorate-General of Armed Forces Medical Services.

The Research and Development Organization (headed by the Scientific Adviser to the Minister) has under it about 30 research establishments. The Production Organization controls 8 public-sector undertakings and 28 ordnance and 2 departmental factories.

The National Defence College, New Delhi, was established in 1960 on the pattern of the Imperial Defence College (UK): the 1-year course is for officers of the rank of brigadier or equivalent and for senior civil servants. The Defence Services Staff College, Wellington, trains officers of the three Services for higher command for staff appointments. There is an Armed Forces Medical College at Pune.

The National Defence Academy, Khadakvasla, gives a 3-year basic training course to officer cadets of the three Services prior to advanced training at the respective Service establishments.

Army. The Army Headquarters functioning directly under the Chief of the Army Staff is divided into the following main branches: General Staff Branch; Adjutant General's Branch; Quartermaster-General's Branch; Master-General of Ordnance Branch; Engineer-in-Chief's Branch; Military Secretary's Branch.

The Army is organized into 5 commands each divided into areas, which in turn are subdivided into sub-areas.

Recruitment of permanent commissioned officers is through the Indian Military Academy, Dehra Dun. It conducts courses for ex-National Defence Academy, National Cadet Corps and direct-entry cadets, and for serving personnel and technical graduates.

The Territorial Army came into being in Sept. 1949, its role being to: (1) relieve the regular Army of static duties and, if required, support civil power; (2) provide anti-aircraft units, and (3) if and when called upon, provide units for the regular Army. The Territorial Army is composed of practically all arms of the Services.

The authorized strength of the Army is 1·1m., that of the Territorial Army, 50,000. There are 2 armoured, 1 mechanized, 20 infantry and 9 mountain divisions, 7 independent armoured brigades, 10 independent infantry, 10 independent artillery brigades, 1 parachute brigade, 1 mountain brigade and 3 independent engineer brigades. An Aviation Corps was formed in 1986.

Navy. Since 26 Jan. 1950 the former Royal Indian Navy, which traced its history in an unbroken line from the foundation in 1613 of the East India Company's Marine, has been known as 'Indian Navy', and the ships referred to as 'INS' instead of 'HMIS'. There are 3 commands: Eastern, Western and Southern; and 2 fleets: Eastern and Western.

Principal ships of the Indian Navy:

Completed	Name	Standard displacement Tons	Aircraft	Principal armament	Shaft horse-power	Speed Knots
		Aircraft Carriers [1]				
1959	Viraat (ex-Hermes)	23,900	5 Sea Harriers; 9 Sea King helicopters	2 quadruple Seacat missile launchers	78,000	28·0
1961	Vikrant (ex-Hercules)	16,000	22 capacity	4 40 mm. AA	40,000	24·5

[1] The cruiser *Delhi* (ex-*Achilles*) completed in 1933, was scrapped in 1979; and the cruiser *Mysore* (ex-*Nigeria*), completed in 1940, was deleted from the List in 1986.

The fleet also includes 2 new German (FR)-built submarines, 10 ex-Soviet submarines, 4 new Soviet-built guided missile armed destroyers, 3 new 'stretched', or improved 'Leander' type missile frigates and 6 broad-beamed 'Leander' class general purpose frigates (all nine built in India), 2 anti-submarine frigates and 2 anti-aircraft frigates (all four built in Great Britain), 1 very old ex-British frigate,

5 corvettes, 13 fast missile boats, 14 fast attack craft, 8 *ex*-Soviet ocean mine-sweepers, 10 inshore minesweepers, 11 landing ships, 5 landing craft, 13 survey ships, 1 repair ship, 1 submarine parent ship, 1 submarine rescue ship, 6 oilers, 22 service craft and 6 tugs.

New construction includes 2 Federal German-built patrol submarines, 2 indigenously built similar submarines, 4 Soviet built larger submarines, 3 more Soviet destroyers, 3 more frigates and 7 corvettes. India plans to build an aircraft carrier and/or an aviation support/HQ ship.

The major training establishments of the Navy include INS *Venduruthy* at Cochin (Basic and Divisional, Gunnery, Torpedo and Anti-Submarine, Navigation and Direction, Communication), INS *Vaisura* at Jamnagar (Electrical), INS *Shivaji* at Lonavla (Engineering), INS *Hansa* at Goa (Aviation), INS *Hamla* at Bombay (Supply and Secretariat) and INS *Satyavahana* (Submarine) and INS *Circars* (Boys') at Vishakhapatnam.

The Fleet Requirement Unit of the Naval Aviation Station, INAS *Garuda*, is at Cochin. The 115 aircraft include Sea Harriers and Sea King anti-submarine helicopters for the aircraft carriers, Chetak utility/SAR, and Alize anti-submarine aircraft.

Naval personnel in 1988 exceeded 47,000 officers and ratings, including the Naval Air Arm.

The Coast Guard was constituted as an independent para-military service by 1978 Act of Parliament. It comprised the frigates *Kirpan* and *Kuthar* and five patrol craft all transferred from the Indian Navy and 2 larger patrol vessels custom-built. It has since been augmented by new specifically built ships and aircraft, including six 1,040-ton offshore patrol vessels with aircraft and hangar, 5 inshore protection craft, 4 fast patrol craft, 8 South Korean-built launches and 11 Japanese-designed vedettes (10 built indigenously). There are 19 aircraft. The Coast Guard is administered by a Director-General (Vice-Admiral) and a Deputy Director-General (Commodore). It functions under the Defence Ministry but is funded by the Revenue Department.

Personnel in 1988 comprised 80 officers and 400 ratings.

Air Force. The Indian Air Force Act was passed in 1932, and the first flight was formed in 1933.

The Air Headquarters, under the Chief of Air Staff, consists of 4 main branches, viz., Air Staff, Administration, Policy and Plans, and Maintenance. Units of the IAF are organized into 5 operational commands–Western at Delhi, Central at Allahabad, Eastern at Shillong, Southern at Trivandrum and South-Western at Jodhpur. Training Command HQ is at Bangalore, Maintenance Command at Nagpur. Nominal strength in 1986 was 13,000 personnel and 1,400 aircraft of all types, in 45 squadrons of fixed-wing aircraft, 14 helicopter squadrons and about 30 squadrons of 'Guideline' and 'Goa' surface-to-air missiles, and close-range missiles such as 'Gainful' and Tigercat.

Air defence units include 2 squadrons of MiG-23 variable-geometry interceptors, 2 squadrons of MiG-29s, 18 squadrons of MiG-21s and 3 of Mirage 2000s. Initial delivery of MiG-21s from the Soviet Union was followed by large-scale licence production in India. There are 2 squadrons of MiG-27s, 3 of Ajeet (Gust Mk 2) fighters, 2 of Canberras, 4 of Jaguars, 1 of Hunter F56s, 3 of MiG-23 super-sonic fighter-bombers and one of MiG-25 reconnaissance aircraft plus a MiG-25U two seat trainer. Canberra and Hunter squadrons are being re-equipped with 124 Jaguars, assembled in India, to create a force of 5 Jaguar squadrons. Some of those flying MiG-21s will re-equip with MiG-27s.

The large transport force includes An-12s, An-32s, Il-76s, HS 748s, 2 Boeing 737s, and smaller aircraft and helicopters for VIP and other duties. Otters are being replaced with Dornier 228s. Helicopter units have Mi-8s and Mi-17s (10 squadrons), Mi-26s, Chetaks (Aerospatiale Alouette IIIs) and licence-built Cheetahs (Aerospatiale Lamas), plus Mi-24 gunships; main training types are the Hindustan HPT-32 and Kiran, Polish-built TS-11 Iskra, Hunter T.66, MiG-21UT1 and MiG-23U.

Primary flying training is provided at the Elementary Flying School, Bidar, and advanced flying training at the Air Force Academy, Dundigal, Hyderabad. There is a Navigation and Signals School at Begumpet. The IAF Technical College, Jalahalli, imparts technical training, while the IAF Administrative College, Coimbatore, trains officers of the ground duty branch. There are also land-air warfare, flying instructors' and medical schools.

INTERNATIONAL RELATIONS

Membership. India is a member of the UN, the Commonwealth and the Colombo Plan.

External Debt. At the end of Nov. 1987 India's external public debt was estimated at Rs 319,100m.

Treaties. India pursues a general policy of non-alignment; the exception is a Treaty of Peace, Friendship and Cooperation with the USSR, 1971; the parties agreed to mutual support short of force in the event of either being attacked by a third party.

ECONOMY

Planning. The sixth plan (1980–85) envisaged total investment of Rs 1,587,100m., of which Rs 975,000m. was for the public sector. The seventh plan (1985–89) aims at an annual 5·2% growth. The priority sections are power generation, irrigation and hydro carbons. Total planned outlay, Rs 3,200,000m., 56% from the public sector. Annual plan outlay (1986–87) Rs 390,520m.

Ministry of Agriculture. *Serving the Small Farmer: Policy Choices in Indian Agricultural Development.* 1975

Dutt, A. K. (ed.), *India: Resources, Potentialities and Planning.* Rev. ed. Dubuque, India, 1973

Singh, T., *India's Development Experience.* London, 1975

Budget. Revenue and expenditure (on revenue account) of the central government[1] for years ending 31 March, in crores of rupees:

	1984–85 [2]	1985–86 [2]	1986–87 [3]
Revenue	24,930	28,430	30,956
Expenditure	28,300	33,617	36,850

[1] Excluding states' share of excise duties and other taxes.
[2] Revised.   [3] Budget estimates.

Important items of revenue and expenditure on the revenue account of the central government for 1985–86 (estimates), in Rs 1m.:

Revenue		Expenditure	
Net tax revenue	209,400	General Services	183,108
Non-tax revenue	62,312	Defence	71,970
		Grants in aid to States, etc.	72,330

Total capital account receipts (1986–87 budget), Rs 196,700m.; capital account disbursements, Rs 160,120m. Total (revenue and capital) receipts, Rs 492,120m.; disbursements, Rs 528,620m.

Under the Constitution (Part XII and 7th Schedule), the power to raise funds has been divided between the central government and the states. Generally, the sources of revenue are mutually exclusive. Certain taxes are levied by the Union for the sake of uniformity and distributed to the states. The Finance Commission (Art. 280 of the Constitution) advises the President on the distribution of the taxes which are distributable between the centre and the states, and on the principles on which grants should be made out of Union revenues to the states. The main sources of central revenue are: customs duties; those excise duties levied by the central government; corporation, income and wealth taxes; estate and succession duties on non-agricultural assets and property, and revenues from the railways and posts and telegraphs. The main heads of revenue in the states are: taxes and duties levied by the state governments (including land revenues and agricultural income tax); civil administration and civil works; state undertakings; taxes shared with the centre; and grants received from the centre.

Currency. A decimal system of coinage was introduced in 1957. The Indian *rupee* is divided into 100 *paise* (until 1964 officially described as *naye paise*), the decimal coins being 1, 2, 3, 5, 10, 20, 25 and 50 *paise*.

The rupee is valued in relation to a package of main currencies. The £ is the currency of intervention. In March 1988 Rs 22.90 = £1; Rs 13.05 = US$1.

The paper currency consists of: (1) Reserve Bank notes in denominations of Rs 2, 5, 10, 20, 50 and 100; and (2) Government of India currency notes of denominations of Re 1 deemed to be included in the expression 'rupee coin' for the purposes of the Reserve Bank of India Act, 1934.

According to the Reserve Bank of India, the total money supply with the public on the last Friday of Oct. 1986 was Rs 26,204 crores. Foreign exchange reserves, Feb. 1987, Rs 69,644·8m.

100,000 rupees are called 1 lakh; 100 lakhs are called 1 crore.

Banking. The Reserve Bank, the central bank for India, was established in 1934 and started functioning on 1 April 1935 as a shareholder's bank; it became a nationalized institution on 1 Jan. 1949. It has the sole right of issuing currency-notes. The Bank acts as adviser to the Government on financial problems and is the banker for central and state governments, commercial banks and some other financial institutions. The Bank manages the rupee public debt of central and state governments. It is the custodian of the country's exchange reserve and supervises repatriation of export proceeds and payments for imports. The Bank gives short-term loans to state governments and scheduled banks and short and medium-term loans to state co-operative banks and industrial finance institutions. The Bank has extensive powers of regulation of the banking system, directly under the Banking Regulation Act, 1949, and indirectly by the use of variations in Bank rate, variation in reserve ratios, selective credit controls and open market operations. Bank rate was raised to 10% in July 1981.

Except refinance for food credit and export credit, the Reserve Bank's refinance facility to commercial banks has been placed on a discretionary basis. The net profit of the Reserve Bank of India for the year ended June 1986, after making the usual or necessary provisions, amounted to Rs 210 crores.

The commercial banking system consisted of 275 scheduled banks (*i.e.*, banks which are included in the 2nd schedule to the Reserve Bank Act) and 4 non-scheduled banks on 30 June 1986; scheduled banks included 194 Regional Rural Banks. Total deposits in commercial banks, Nov. 1986, stood at Rs 95,164 crores. The business of non-scheduled banks forms less than 0·1% of commercial bank business. Of the 275 scheduled banks, 21 are foreign banks which specialize in financing foreign trade but also compete for domestic business. The largest scheduled bank is the State Bank of India, constituted by nationalizing the Imperial Bank of India in 1955. The State Bank acts as the agent of the Reserve Bank and the subsidiaries of the State Bank act as the agents of the State Bank for transacting government business as well as undertaking commercial functions. Fourteen banks with aggregate deposits of not less than Rs 50 crores were nationalized on 19 July 1969. Six banks were nationalized in April 1980. The 28 public sector banks (which comprise the State Bank of India and its seven associate banks and 20 nationalised banks) account for over 90% of deposits and bank credit of all scheduled commercial banks.

Reserve Bank of India: Report on Currency and Finance.—Report on the Trend and Progress of Banking in India.—Report of the Central Board of Directors. Annual. Bombay

Weights and Measures. Uniform standards of weights and measures, based on the metric system, were established for the first time by the Standards of Weights and Measures Act, 1956, which provided for a transition period of 10 years. So far the system has been fully adopted in trade transactions but there are a few fields such as engineering, survey and land records and the building and construction industry where it has not; efforts are being made to complete the change as early as possible.

In order to align this legislation with the latest international trends an expert committee (Weights and Measures (Law Revision) Committee) was set up by the central government to suggest a revised Bill which was passed by Parliament in April 1976. The new Standards of Weights and Measures Act, 1976, has recognized the International System of Units and other units recommended by the General Conference on Weights and Measures and is in line with the recommendations of the International Organisation of Legal Metrology (OIML). The new Act also covers the system of numeration, the approval of models of weights and measures, regulation and control of inter-state trade in relation to weights and measures. The Act also protects consumers through proper indication of weight, quantity, identity, source, date and price on packaged goods. A draft Standards of Weights and Measures (Enforcement) Bill has also been prepared by the committee for adoption either by Parliament or State legislatures, as enforcement is now in the 'concurrent' list of legislation.

The provisions of the 1976 Act came into force in Sept. 1977, as did the accompanying Standards of Weights and Measures (Packaged Commodities) Rules, 1977.

While the Standards of Weights and Measures are laid down in the Central Act, enforcement of weights and measures laws is entrusted to the state governments; the central Directorate of Weights and Measures is responsible for co-ordinating activities so as to ensure national uniformity.

An Indian Institute of Legal Metrology trains officials of the Weights and Measures departments of India and different developing countries. The Institute is being modernized with technical assistance from the Federal Republic of Germany.

There are 2 Regional Reference Standards laboratories at Ahmedabad and Bhubaneswar which (besides calibrating secondary standards of physical measurements) also provide testing facilities in metrological and industrial measurements. These laboratories are equipped with Standards next in line to the National Standards of physical measurements which are maintained at the National Physical Laboratory in New Delhi.

For weights previously in legal use under the Standards of Weight Act, 1956, *see* THE STATESMAN'S YEAR-BOOK, 1961, p. 171.

Calendar. The dates of the Saka era (named after the north Indian dynasty of the first century A.D.) are being used alongside Gregorian dates in issues of the *Gazette of India*, news broadcasts by All-India Radio and government-issued calendars, from 22 March 1957, a date which corresponds with the first day of the year 1879 in the Saka era.

ENERGY AND NATURAL RESOURCES

Electricity. In March 1986 about 68% of all villages had electricity. Total installed capacity (1985–86) was 46·6m. kw. Production of electricity in 1985–86 was 170,037m. kwh., of which 119,104m. kwh. came from thermal and nuclear stations and 50,933m. kwh from hydro-electric stations. Supply 230 and 250 volts; 50 Hz.

Oil and Gas. The Oil and Natural Gas Commission, Oil India Ltd and the Assam Oil Co. are the only producers of crude oil. Estimated production, 1986–87, about 31m. tonnes, about 60% of consumption. The main fields are in Assam and offshore in the Gulf of Cambay (the Bombay High field). Natural gas production, 1984–85, 6,600m. cu. metres.

Water. The net area of 57m. hectares (1982) under irrigation exceeds that of any other country except China, and equals about 38% of the total area under cultivation. Irrigation projects have formed an important part of all three Five-Year Plans. The possibilities of diverting rivers into canals being nearly exhausted, the emphasis is now on damming the monsoon surplus flow and diverting that. Ultimate potential of irrigation is assessed at 107m. hectares, total cultivated land being 142m. hectares. In 1985 India and Bangladesh reached an agreement to monitor the water of the Ganges at the Farakka barrage.

1987 was a year of severe drought, affecting both agriculture and water-supplies to cities.

Minerals. Bihar, West Bengal and Madhya Pradesh produce 42%, 25% and 19% of all coal, respectively. The coal industry was nationalized in 1973. Production, 1984–85, 147m. tonnes; reserves (including lignite) are estimated at 155,902m.

tonnes. Production of other minerals, 1986 estimates (in 1,000 tonnes): Iron ore, 48,441; bauxite, 2,273; chromite 642; copper ore, 4,420; manganese ore, 1,275; gold, 1,929 kg. Other important minerals are lead, zinc, limestone, apatite and phosphorite, dolomite, magnesite and silver. Value of mineral production, 1982 (provisional), Rs 53,912m. of which mineral fuels produced Rs 48,140m., metallic minerals Rs 2,671m. and non-metallic Rs 3,102m.

Agriculture. The chief industry of India has always been agriculture. About 70% of the people are dependent on the land for their living. In 1983-84 it provided 39·8% of GDP.

In 1984–85 agricultural commodities accounted for about 20% by value of Indian exports, while agricultural commodities, machinery and fertilizers accounted for about 20% of imports. Tea accounted for about 30% of agricultural exports.

An increase in food production of at least 2% per annum is necessary to keep pace with the rising population. Foodgrain production, 78·4m. tons in 1962–63, was 150·5m. tonnes in 1985–86.

The Indian Council of Agricultural Research works through 41 institutes, 7 national research centres, 4 project directorates, and 68 national research projects. There are 4 national research bureaux and 23 agricultural universities.

The farming year runs from July to June through three crop seasons: kharif (monsoon); rabi (winter) and summer.

Agricultural production, 1986-87 (in 1,000 tons): rice, 60,420; wheat, 45,580; total foodgrains, 144,070; sugar-cane 182,480; oilseeds, 11,450; cotton, 7·01m. bales (of 170 kg); jute is grown in West Bengal (half total yield), Bihar and Assam, total yield, 7·4m. bales (of 180 kg); potatoes, 12,730; tobacco, 460; chillies, 780. The coffee industry is growing: the main cash varieties are Arabica and Robusta (main growing areas Karnataka, Kerala and Tamil Nadu).

The tea industry is important, with production concentrated in Assam, West Bengal, Tamil Nadu and Kerala. Total crop in 1986–87, about 621,000 tonnes from 370,000 hectares.

Livestock (1986). Cattle, 200m.; sheep, 54·46m.; pigs, 8·7m.; horses, 910,000; asses, 1,001,000; goats, 102·87m.; buffaloes, 75·01m.

Fertilizer consumption in 1985–86 was 8·7m. tonnes.

Land Tenure. There are three main traditional systems of land tenure: *ryotwari* tenure, where the individual holders, usually peasant proprietors, are responsible for the payment of land revenues; *zamindari* tenure, where one or more persons own large estates and are responsible for payment (in this system there may be a number of intermediary holders); and *mahalwari* tenure, where village communities jointly hold an estate and are jointly and severally responsible for payment.

Agrarian reform, initiated in the first Five-Year Plan, being undertaken by the state governments includes: (1) The abolition of intermediaries under *zamindari* tenure. (2) Tenancy legislation designed to scale down rents to ¼ – ⅕ of the value of the produce, to give permanent rights to tenants (subject to the landlord's right to resume a minimum holding for his personal cultivation), and to enable tenants to acquire ownership of their holdings (subject to the landlord's right of resumption for personal cultivation) on payment of compensation over a number of years. (3) Fixing of ceilings on existing holdings and on future acquisition; the holding of a family is between 4·05 and 7·28 hectares if it has assured irrigation to produce two crops a year; 10·93 hectares for land with irrigation facilities for only one crop a year; and 21·85 hectares for all other categories of land. Tea, coffee, cocoa and cardamom plantations have been exempted. (4) The consolidation of holdings in community project areas and the prevention of fragmentation of holdings by reform of inheritance laws. (5) Promotion of farming by co-operative village management (*see* p. 638).

The average size of holding for the whole of India is 2·63 hectares. Andhra Pradesh, 2·87; Assam, 1·46; Bihar, 1·53; Gujarat, 4·49; Jammu and Kashmir, 1·43; Karnataka, 4·11; Kerala, 0·75; Madhya Pradesh, 3·99; Maharashtra, 4·65; Orissa, 1·98; Punjab, 3·85; Rajasthan, 5·5; Tamil Nadu, 1·49; Uttar Pradesh, 1·78; West Bengal, 1·56.

Of the total 71m. rural households possessing operational holdings, 34% hold on the average less than 0·20 hectare of land each.

Opium. By international agreement the poppy is cultivated under licence, and all raw opium is sold to the central government. Opium, other than for wholly medical use, is available only to registered addicts.

Fisheries. Total catch (1986–87) was 2·92m. tons, of which Kerala, Tamil Nadu, and Maharashtra produced about half. Of the total catch, 1,720,000 tons were marine fish. There were 96 deep-sea (20 metres and above) fishing boats at end Dec. 1986, and 63 under construction. There were 22,000 mechanised boats (1985–86). There were 7,452 fishermen's co-operatives with 783,000 members in 1984–85; total sales, Rs 205·4m.

Forestry. The lands under the control of the state forest departments are classified as 'reserved forests' (forests intended to be permanently maintained for the supply of timber, etc., or for the protection of water supply, etc.), 'protected forests' and 'unclassed' forest land.

In 1984–85 the total forest area was 75m. hectares. Main types are teak and sal. About 16% of the area is inaccessible, of which about 45% is potentially productive. In 1985–86 3m. saplings were planted. Some states have encouraged planting small areas around villages.

INDUSTRY AND TRADE

Industries. Railways, air transport, armaments and atomic energy are government monopolies. In a number of industries (including the manufacture of iron and steel and mineral oils, shipbuilding and the mining of coal, iron and manganese ores, gypsum, gold and diamonds) new units are set up only by the state. In a further group of industries (road transport, manufacture of chemicals such as drugs, dyestuffs, plastics and fertilizers) the state established new undertakings, but private enterprise may develop either on its own or with state backing, which may take the form of loans or purchase of equity capital. Nationalized industries employed 4m. in 1981. Under the Industries (Development and Regulation) Act, 1951, as amended, industrial undertakings are required to be licensed; 162 industries are within the scope of the Act. The Government are authorized to examine the working of any undertaking, to issue directions to it and to take over its control if this be deemed necessary. A Central Advisory Council has been set up consisting of representatives of industry, labour, consumers and primary producers. There are Development Councils for individual industries and (1981) 4 national development banks.

Foreign investment is encouraged by a tax holiday on income up to 6% of capital employed for 5 years. There are special depreciation allowances, and customs and excise concessions for export industries.

Oil refinery installed capacity, Dec. 1985, was 45·55m. tonnes; production of refined oils (1984–85), 33·2m. tonnes. The Indian Oil Corporation was established in 1964 and had (1984) most of the market.

Industry, particularly steel, has suffered from a shortage of power and coal. There is expansion in petrochemicals, based on the oil and associated gas of the Bombay High field, and gas from Bassein field. Small industries (initial outlay on capital equipment of less than Rs 3·5m.) are important; they employ about 9m. and produced (1984–85) goods worth Rs 505,200m. The industrial growth rate, 1985–86 was 6·3%.

Industrial production, 1986 (in 1,000 tonnes): Pig-iron and ferro-alloys, 10,724; steel ingots, 11,332; finished steel, 7,753; aluminium, 235; motor cycles and scooters, 887,814; buses and trucks, 94,905; cars and jeeps, 130,090; petroleum products, 41,943; sulphuric acid, 2,709; cement, 33,651; board and paper, 1,573; nitrogen fertilizer, 5,077; phosphate fertilizer, 1,593; jute goods, 1,381; cotton yarn, 1,262; cotton cloth, 9,272m. metres; man-made fibre, 299·8; diesel engines, 190,200 engines; electric motors (1985), 5·1m. h.p.; sugar, 7,027.

Lal, V. B., (et al) *The Aluminium Industry in India: Promise, Prospects, Constraints and Impact.* New Delhi, 1985

Labour. At the 1981 census there were 222·5m. workers, of whom 92·5m. were cultivators, 55·5m. agricultural labourers; in 1984 there were 7·4m. in manufacturing, 11·3m. in social, community and personal services, 1·5m. in construction and 3·53m. in transport, communications and storage. There were 36,606 registered trade unions. The bond labour system was abolished in 1975. Man-days lost by industrial disputes, 1986, 22·12m., of which 2·05m. were in the public sector. An ordnance of July 1981 gave the government power to ban strikes in essential services; the ordnance was to remain in force for six months and would then be renewable.

Dasgupta, A. K., *A Theory of Wage Policy.* OUP, 1976

Companies. The total number of companies limited by shares at work in India, 31 March 1986, was 122,159; aggregate paid-up capital was Rs 31,943·3 crores. There were 16,122 public limited companies with an aggregate paid-up capital of Rs 7,159·9 crores, and 106,037 private limited companies (Rs 24,783·4 crores). There were also 298 companies with unlimited liability.

During 1985–86, 15,056 new limited companies were registered in the Indian Union under the Companies Act 1956 with a total authorized capital of Rs 4,409·9 crores; 1,589 were public limited companies (Rs 3,198·5 crores) and 13,467 were private limited companies (Rs 1,211·4 crores). There were 3 private companies with unlimited liability also registered in 1985–86. Of the new non-government limited companies, 419 had an authorized capital of Rs 1 crore and above, and 331 of between Rs 50 lakhs and Rs 1 crore. During 1985–86, 133 companies with an aggregate paid-up capital of Rs 12·17 crores went into liquidation and 129 companies (Rs 0·81 crores) were struck off the register.

On 31 March 1986 there were 1,020 government companies at work with a total paid-up capital of Rs 25,284·3 crores; 440 were public limited companies and 580 were private limited companies.

On 31 March 1986, 335 companies incorporated elsewhere were reported to have a place of business in India; 122 were of UK and 69 of USA origin.

Department of Company Affairs, Govt. of India. *Annual Report on the Working and Administration of the Companies Act, 1956.* New Delhi, 1983

Co-operative Movement. On 30 June 1986 there were about 315,000 co-operative societies with a total membership of about 145m. These included Primary Co-operative Marketing Societies, State Co-operative Marketing Federations and the National Agricultural Co-operative Marketing Federation of India. There were also 15 State Co-operative Commodity Marketing Federations, and 10 State Tribal Co-operative Development Corporations/Federations.

There were, on 30 June 1985, 28 State Co-operative Banks, 350 Central Co-operative Banks, 92,408 Primary Agricultural Societies, 19 State Land Development Banks, and 881 primary or district Land Development Banks/branches which provide long-term investment credit.

Total agricultural credit disbursed by Co-operatives in 1985–86 was Rs 3,206 crores including Rs 2,409 crores in short-term credit, Rs 258 crores in medium-term credit and Rs 539 crores in long-term credit. Total credit disbursed in 1983–84, Rs 2,905 crores.

Value of agricultural produce marketed by Co-operatives in 1985–86 was about Rs 4,193 crores.

In June 1985–86 there were 2,429 processing units; in 1985–86, 195 sugar factories produced 4·16m. tons; 92 spinning mills (capacity 2·44m. spindles) produced 122m. kg. (1984–85) of yarn; there were 294 oil mills and similar units; total storage capacity was 8·49m. tons.

In 1985–86 there were 64,000 retail depots distributing 3·8m. tons of fertilizers.

Indian Labour Guide. Monthly. Delhi
Co-operative Movement in India, Statistical Statements Relating to. Annual. Reserve Bank of India, Bombay

Commerce. The external trade of India (excluding land-borne trade with Tibet and Bhután) was as follows (in 100,000 rupees):

	Imports	Exports and Re-exports
1981–82	1,360,735	780,591
1982–83	1,429,274	880,337
1983–84	1,563,146	977,071
1984–85	1,717,325	1,185,515
1985–86	1,837,128	1,042,037
1986–87 [1]	2,006,257	1,255,006

[1] Provisional.

The distribution of commerce by countries and areas was as follows in the year ended 31 March 1986 (in 100,000 rupees):

Countries	Exports to	Imports from	Countries	Exports to	Imports from
Afghánistán	1,573	1,450	Malaysia	12,805	40,556
Algeria	1,854	250	Morocco	845	15,284
Argentina	64	4,094	Nepál	14,164	5,027
Australia	12,453	42,180	Netherlands	17,142	29,216
Austria	1,967	6,476	New Zealand	1,582	2,951
Bahrain	3,975	15,014	Nigeria	2,203	43
Bangladesh	14,403	972	Norway	1,635	5,749
Belgium	22,865	92,661	Pakistan	1,703	2,506
Brazil	368	37,047	Poland	6,622	8,954
Bulgaria	4,281	5,407	Qatar	1,955	7,734
Burma	90	3,679	Romania	10,467	14,534
Canada	12,968	47,602	Saudi Arabia	21,302	81,114
Czechoslovakia	6,865	7,269	Singapore	14,304	36,323
Denmark	4,346	7,010	Spain	3,040	16,576
Egypt	9,973	11,579	Sri Lanka	8,333	1,128
Federal Rep.			Sudan	2,027	165
of Germany	50,698	154,216	Sweden	4,344	14,004
Finland	885	8,680	Switzerland	11,829	14,359
France	19,999	61,512	Tanzania	1,167	1,952
German Dem.			Thailand	2,734	8,870
Republic	9,109	7,834	Turkey	1,043	3,605
Ghana	1,431	272	United Arab		
Hong Kong	23,134	7,509	Emirates	28,837	62,845
Hungary	2,615	4,551	USSR	193,744	167,282
Indonesia	1,505	5,532	UK	53,823	124,876
Iran	9,486	89,989	USA	199,448	208,586
Iraq	3,549	54,660	Yemen, Arab Rep.	2,665	—
Italy	21,684	31,974	Yemen, People's		
Japan	119,097	179,784	Dem. Rep.	2,412	—
Kenya	3,069	873	Yugoslavia	2,329	7,597
Korea,			Zaïre	51	4,815
Republic of	9,289	27,161	Zambia	684	10,988
Kuwait	12,216	33,478			

The value (in 100,000 rupees) of the leading articles of merchandise was as follows in the year ended 31 March 1986 (provisional):

Exports	Value
Meat and meat preparations	7,219
Fish, crustaceans, molluscs and preparations thereof	38,860
Rice	19,294
Vegetables and fruits	39,049
Coffee and coffee substitutes	23,564
Tea and mate	61,191
Spices	25,500
Oilcake	12,354
Tobacco unmanufactured and tobacco refuse	12,040
Raw cotton	6,582
Iron ore	55,459
Crude vegetable materials	11,436
Cotton fabrics	37,157
Cotton madeup articles	10,253

Exports	Value
Readymade garments	100,750
Jute manufactures including twist and yarn	26,960
Leather and leather manufactures (except footwear)	48,766
Pearls, precious and semi-precious stones	142,991
Works of art	12,334
Handmade carpets	22,861
Metal manufactures except iron and steel	15,635
Machinery including transport equipments	60,394
Mineral fuel, lubricants and related products	51,792
Chemicals and allied products	28,589
Iron and steel	4,812
Jewellery	6,829
Sugar and sugar preparations	1,099

Imports	
Wheat	4,921
Milk and cream	2,890
Crude rubber including synthetic and reclaimed	8,185
Synthetic and regenerated fibre	5,572
Fertilizers, crude	12,444
Sulphur and unroasted iron pyrites	14,984
Metalliferous ores and metal scrap	28,620
Petroleum, Petroleum products and related materials	499,014
Edible oil	61,427
Organic chemicals	43,730
Inorganic chemicals	44,208
Medical and pharmaceutical products	16,357
Fertilizers, manufactured	82,253
Artificial resins, plastic materials etc	29,148
Chemical materials and products	11,657
Paper, paper board and manufactures thereof	19,524
Textile yarn, fabrics and madeup articles	13,304
Pearls, precious and semi-precious stones	110,626
Non-metallic mineral manufactures exclg. pearls	8,148
Iron and steel	123,085
Non-ferrous metal	46,851
Manufactures of metal	18,580
Machinery other than electric	247,857
Electrical machinery	56,714
Transport equipment	45,222
Professional, scientific, controlling instruments, photographic, optical goods, watches and clocks	34,799

Total trade between India and UK (British Department of Trade returns, in £1,000 sterling):

	1983	1984	1985	1986	1987
Imports to UK	366,928	571,470	431,785	440,681	536,704
Exports and re-exports from UK	804,779	780,997	894,708	941,169	1,090,146

Annual Statement of the Foreign Trade of India. 2 vols. Calcutta
Monthly Statistics of the Foreign Trade of India. Calcutta
Review of the Trade of India. Annual. Delhi
India–Handbook of Commercial Information. 3 vols. Calcutta
Guide to Official Statistics of Trade, Shipping, Customs and Excise Revenue of India. Rev. ed. Calcutta

Tourism. There were 1·08m. visitors (excluding nationals of Pakistan and Bangladesh) in 1986 bringing about Rs 16,000m. in foreign exchange; 160,685 from UK, 125,364 from USA, 75,631 from Sri Lanka.

COMMUNICATIONS

Roads. In 1984–85 there were 1,770,000 km of roads, of which 832,000 km were surfaced. Roads are divided into 5 main administrative classes, namely, national highways, state highways, major district roads, other district roads and village roads. The national highways (31,803 km in 1986) connect capitals of states, major ports and foreign highways. The national highway system is linked with the ESCAP (Economic and Social Commission for Asia and the Pacific) international highway system. The state highways are the main trunk roads of the states, while the major district roads connect subsidiary areas of production and markets with distribution centres, and form the main link between headquarters and neighbouring districts.

There were (31 March 1985) 8,796,000 motor vehicles in India, comprising 1,380,000 private cars and jeeps, 4·9m. motor cycles and scooters, 160,000 taxis, 210,000 buses and 850,000 goods vehicles.

Railways. The Indian railway system is government-owned and (under the control of the Railway Board) is divided into 9 zones; route-km at 31 March 1986:

Zone	Headquarters	Route-km
Central	Bombay	6,486 km (943·34 km electrified)
Eastern	Calcutta	4,281 km (1,229·06 km)
Northern	Delhi	10,977 km (884·29 km)
North Eastern	Gorakhpur	5,163 km
North East Frontier	Gauhati	3,763 km
Southern	Madras	6,729 km (431·95 km)
South Central	Secunderabad	7,138 km (393·04 km)
South Eastern	Calcutta	7,075 km (1,972·63 km)
Western	Bombay	10,224 km (496·13 km)

Principal gauges are 1,676 mm. and metre, with networks also of 762 and 610 mm. gauge.

Passengers carried in 1985–86 were approximately 3,433m.; freight, 286·4m. tonnes. Revenue (1985–86) from passengers, Rs 1,720 crores; from goods, Rs 4,232 crores.

Indian Railways pay to the central government a fixed dividend of 4·5% on capital-at-charge. Railway finance in Rs 1m.:

Financial years	Gross traffic receipts	Working expenses	Net revenues (traffic and miscellaneous)	Net surplus or deficit (after dividend)
1986–87[1]	75,030	53,920	5,810	+110
1987–88[2]	81,790	75,500	7,210	+690

[1] Revised estimate.   [2] Budget.

Aviation. The air transport industry in India was nationalized in 1953 with the formation of two Air Corporations: Air India for operating long-distance international air services, and Indian Airlines for operating air services within India and to adjacent countries. A third airline, Vayudoot, was formed in 1981 as an internal feeder airline.

Air India runs Boeing 747s and 707s, Airbus A-300 and A-310s; it operates from Bombay, Delhi, Madras, Trivandrum, Hyderabad, Goa and Calcutta to Africa (Nairobi, Lagos, Seychelles, Mauritius, Dar es Salaam, Lusaka and Harare); to Europe (London, Paris, Amsterdam, Frankfurt, Geneva, Zurich, Brussels, Moscow and Rome); to western Asia (Doha, Abu Dhabi, Dharan, Dubai, Bahrain, Kuwait, Muscat, Jeddah, Ras al Khaymah, Sharjah and Baghdad); to east Asia (Bangkok, Hong Kong, Tōkyō, Osaka, Kuala Lumpur, Singapore and Sydney); to North America (New York).

Indian Airlines has a fleet of 53 aircraft consisting of Airbus A-300BS, Boeing 737, F-27 and HS-748 aircraft (Sept. 1986). During 1985–86 they carried 9·2m. passengers; net profit Rs 58·75 crores. Flights cover over 83,000 unduplicated route km. Vayudoot serves remote areas of India; it has a network of 62 stations.

The National Airports Authority maintains and operates 84 civil aerodromes and 25 terminals at military aerodromes. The management of the 4 international airports at Bombay (Santa Cruz), Calcutta (Dum Dum), Delhi (Palam) and Madras is vested in the International Airports Authority of India.

Shipping. In Dec. 1985, 428 ships totalling 6,388,772 GRT were on the Indian Register; of these, 111 ships of 355,108 GRT were engaged in coastal trade, and

317 ships of 6,033,664 GRT in overseas trade. Traffic of major ports, 1985–86, was as follows:

Port	Ships cleared	Imports (1m. tonnes)	Exports (1m. tonnes)
Calcutta	813	3·04	0·87
Bombay	2,064	11·8	13·1
Madras	1,323	10·4	7·8
Cochin	652	4·5	0·6
Mormugao	457	1·4	14·5
Vishakhapatnam	689	6·4	7·0
Kandla	770	15·2	1·3
Paradip	173	0·9	2·4
New Mangalore	303	1·0	2·7
Tuticorin	452	4·0	0·2
Haldia	567	5·36	2·61

The shipyard at Vishakhapatnam is capable of building vessels of a maximum of 21,500 DWT. Present capacity is about 64,500 DWT per year. The Cochin Shipyard can build Panamax type bulk carriers of 85,000 DWT each. On full development the capacity of the shipyard will be 2 such ships a year. Garden Reach Shipbuilders and Engineers are building bulk carriers of 26,000 DWT, ferry ships (6,000 DWT), hydrographic research ships, tugs and fast patrol craft. There are about 5,200 km of major rivers navigable by motorised craft, of which 1,700 km are used. Canals, 4,300 km, of which 485 km are navigable by motorised craft (331 km are used).

Post and Broadcasting. On 30 Sept. 1986 there were 144,257 post offices and 36,161 telegraph offices. Of the post offices, 128,470 were rural and 15,787 urban.

The telephone system is in the hands of the Indian Posts and Telegraphs Department. In Sept. 1986 there were 3,259,000 telephones. There were 213 telex exchanges and 31,755 subscribers.

There were 88 radio stations on 31 March 1986, and programmes were sent out from 167 transmitters. There were 44 high-power and 135 low-power television transmission centres. In 1985 television covered 36% of the national area and 58% of the population. Entertainment films occupy 29·3% of broadcasting time, news and current affairs, 21·3%. A communications satellite ('APPLE') went into operation in July 1981.

Cinemas. In 1976 there were 9,017 cinemas, including about 2,660 touring cinemas: about 500 feature films were produced.

Newspapers. In 1982 the total number of newspapers and periodicals was 19,937; about 30% were published in Delhi, Bombay, Calcutta and Madras. There were 1,334 daily and 5,898 weekly papers. Circulation of dailies (1981), 13·2m., of weeklies, 12·9m. Hindi papers have the highest number and circulation, followed by English, then Bengali, Urdu and Marathi.

Annual Report of the Register of Newspapers for India. New Delhi

JUSTICE, RELIGION, EDUCATION AND WELFARE

Justice. All courts form a single hierarchy, with the Supreme Court at the head, which constitutes the highest court of appeal. Immediately below it are the high courts and subordinate courts in each state. Every court in this chain, subject to the usual pecuniary and local limits, administers the whole law of the country, whether made by Parliament or by the state legislatures.

The states of Andhra Pradesh, Assam (in common with Nagaland, Meghalaya, Manipur, Mizoram, Tripura and Arunachal Pradesh), Bihar, Gujarat, Himachal Pradesh, Jammu and Kashmir, Karnataka, Kerala, Madhya Pradesh, Maharashtra, Orissa, Punjab (in common with the state of Haryana and the Union Territory of Chandigarh), Rajasthan, Tamil Nadu, Uttar Pradesh, West Bengal and Sikkim have each a High Court. The jurisdiction of Bombay High Court extends to the Territory of Goa. There is a separate High Court for Delhi. For the Andaman and Nicobar Islands the Calcutta High Court, for Pondicherry the High Court of Madras, and for Lakshadweep the High Court of Kerala are the highest judicial authorities; in Dadra and Nagar Haveli the High Court of Bombay is the relevant high court. The Allahabad High Court has a Bench at Lucknow, the Bombay High Court has Benches at Nagpur and Aurangabad, the Madhya Pradesh High Court has Benches at Gwalior and Indore, the Patna High Court has a Bench at Ranchi and the Rajasthan High Court has a Bench at Jaipur. Judges and Division Courts of the Gauhati High Court also sit in Meghalaya, Manipur, Nagaland and Tripura. Below the High Court each state is divided into a number of districts under the jurisdiction of district judges who preside over civil courts and courts of sessions. There are a number of judicial authorities subordinate to the district civil courts. On the criminal side magistrates of various classes act under the overall supervision of the High Court.

The Code of Criminal Procedure, 1898, has been replaced by the Code of Criminal Procedure, 1973 (2 of 1974), which came into force with effect from 1 April 1974. The new Code provides for complete separation of the Judiciary from the Executive throughout India.

Police. The states control their own police force through the state Home Ministers. The Home Minister of the central government co-ordinates the work of the states and controls the Central Detective Training School, the Central Forensic Laboratory, the Central Fingerprint Laboratory as well as the National Police Academy at Mount Abu (Rajasthan) where the Indian Police Service is trained. This service is recruited by competitive examination of university graduates and provides all senior officers for the state police forces. The Central Bureau of Investigation functions under the control of the Cabinet Secretariat.

The cities of Pune, Ahmedabad, Nagpur, Bangalore, Calcutta, Madras, Bombay and Hyderabad have separate police commissionerates.

Sarkar, P. C., *Civil Laws of India and Pakistan*. 2 vols. Calcutta, 1953.—*Criminal Laws of India and Pakistan*. 2nd ed. 2 vols. Calcutta, 1956
Setalvad, M. C., *The Common Law of India*. London, 1960
Sharma, S. R., *Supreme Court in the Indian Constitution*. Delhi, 1959

Religion. The principal religions in 1971 (census) were: Hindus, 453·2m. (82·7%); Moslems, 61·4m. (11·21%); Christians, 14·2m. (2·6%); Sikhs, 10·3m. (1·89%); Buddhists, 3·8m. (0·7%); Jains, 2·6m. (0·47%).

In 1971 the Christian population consisted of 8·2m. Roman Catholics, 2·69m. Anglicans of the Church of South India, 1·37m. Anglicans of the Church of North India and about 2m. nonconformists.

Sundkler, B., *Church of South India*. London, 1954

Education. Literacy. According to the 1981 census the literacy percentage in the country (excluding age-group, 0-4) was 36·23 (34·45 in 1971): 46·74% among males, 24·88% among females. Of the states and territories, Chandigarh and Kerala have the highest rates.

Educational Organization. Education is the concurrent responsibility of state and Union governments. In the union territories it is the responsibility of the central government. The Union Government is also directly responsible for the central universities and all institutions declared by parliament to be of national importance; the promotion of Hindi as the federal language; coordinating and maintaining standards in higher education, research, science and technology. Professional education rests with the Ministry or Department concerned, e.g., medical education, the Ministry or Department of Health. The Department of Education is a part of the Union Ministry of Human Resource Development, headed by a cabinet minister. There are several autonomous organizations attached to the Department of Education. These include the University Grants Commission, the National Institute of Educational Planning and Administration and the National Council of Educational Research and Training. There is a Central Advisory Board of Education to advise the Union and the State Governments on any educational question which may be referred to it.

School Education. The school system in India can be divided into four stages: primary, middle, secondary and senior secondary.

Primary education is imparted either at independent primary (or junior basic) schools or primary classes attached to middle or secondary schools. The period of instruction in this stage varies from 4 to 5 years and the medium of instruction is in most cases the mother tongue of the child or the regional language. Free primary education is available for all children. Legislation for compulsory education has been passed by some state governments and Union Territories but it is not practicable to enforce compulsion when the reasons for non-attendance are socioeconomic. Residential schools are planned for country children.

The period for the middle stage varies from 2 to 3 years.

Higher Education. Higher education is given in arts, science or professional colleges, universities and all-India educational or research institutions. In 1985–86 there were 132 universities, 10 institutions of national importance and 17 institutions deemed as universities. Of the universities, 9 are central: Aligarh Muslim University; Banaras Hindu University; University of Delhi; University of Hyderabad; Jawaharlal Nehru University; North Eastern Hill University; Visva Bharati; Pondicherry; Indira Gandhi National Open. The rest are state universities. Total enrolment at universities, 1985–86, 3·57m., of which 3·14m. were undergraduates. Women students, 1·05m.

Grants are paid through the University Grants Commission to the central universities and institutions deemed to be universities for their maintenance and development and to state universities for their development projects only; their maintenance is the concern of state governments. During 1985–86 the University Grants Commission sanctioned grants of Rs 192·37 crores.

Technical Education. The number of institutions awarding degrees in engineering and technology in 1986 was 184 (in 1947: 38), and those awarding diplomas in engineering and technology numbered 422 (in 1947: 53); the former admitted about 34,800, the latter about 66,400 students. There were also 47 Girls' Polytechnics with about 5,900 students. There were 108 Community Polytechnics. For training high-level engineers and technologists 5 Institutes of Technology, the Indian Institute of Science, Bangalore, and 104 other institutions conduct postgraduate and research courses. There are (1986) 4 national Management Institutions and 42 other management units, admitting about 3,000 annually.

Adult Education. In spite of the improvement in the literacy rate, the number of adult illiterates over 14 was over 424·26m. in 1981. Adult education is, therefore, being accorded a high priority; it formed part of the Minimum Needs Programme under the seventh Five-Year Plan (1985–90). The National Literacy Mission aims to cover all illiterate persons in the age-group 15–35 by 1990. The Directorate of Adult Education, established in 1971, is the national resource centre; with state resource centres it is responsible for producing teaching/learning materials, training and orientation, monitoring and evaluating the programme.

Educational statistics for the year 1985–86:

Type of recognized institution	No. of institutions	No. of students on rolls	No. of teachers
Primary/junior basic schools	528,079	86,465,189	1,509,910
Middle/senior basic schools	134,074	28,124,756	967,988
High/higher secondary schools	61,314	15,105,934	1,158,745
Training schools and colleges	1,416	182,777[1]	–
Arts, Science and Commerce colleges	4,078	3,014,186[2]	–

[1] Enrolment by stages of teachers' training courses at school and college level.
[2] Enrolment by stages of all post-graduate and graduate courses.

School pupils represent 93·4% of the age-group 6–11 and 52% of 11s-14s.

Expenditure. Total public expenditure on education 1985–86 is estimated at Rs 8,143 crores. Total public expenditure on education, sport, arts and youth welfare during the Seventh Plan, Rs 6,382·65 crores; Seventh Plan spending on adult education, Rs 130 crores in the central and Rs 230 crores in the state sectors.

Health. Health programmes are primarily the responsibility of the state governments. The Union Government has sponsored and supported major schemes for disease prevention and control which are implemented nationally. These include the prevention and control of malaria, filaria, tuberculosis, leprosy, venereal diseases, smallpox, trachoma and cancer. There are also Union Government schemes in connexion with water supply and sanitation, and with nutrition. The Nutrition Advisory Committee of the Indian Council of Medical Research sponsors schemes for research and advises the Government. The National Nutrition Advisory Committee is to formulate a national nutrition policy and recommend measures for improving national standards.

Medical relief and service is primarily the responsibility of the states. Medical education is also a state responsibility, but there is a co-ordinating Central Health Educational Bureau. Family planning is centrally sponsored and locally implemented. The goal is to reduce the birth-rate by means of education in family planning methods.

The central government budget for 1984–85 provided Rs 469·7 crores for family welfare (including family planning) and Rs 343 crores for health; Rs 124·4 crores was for prevention and control of disease.

DIPLOMATIC REPRESENTATIVES

Of India in Great Britain (India House, Aldwych, London, WC2B 4NA)
High Commissioner: (Vacant).

Of Great Britain in India (Chanakyapuri, New Delhi 1100-21)
High Commissioner: Sir David Goodall, KCMG.

Of India in the USA (2107 Massachusetts Ave., NW, Washington, D.C., 20008)
Ambassador: P. K. Kaul.

Of the USA in India (Shanti Path, Chanakyapuri, New Delhi 21)
Ambassador: John G. Dean.

Of India to the United Nations
Ambassador: Chinmaya Rajaninath Gharekhan.

Books of Reference

Special works relating to States are shown under their separate headings.

India: A Reference Annual. Delhi Govt. Printer. Annual
Cambridge History of India. 6 vols. CUP, 1922-47. Supp., 1953
The Times of India Directory and Yearbook. Bombay and London. Annual
Akbar, M. J., *India: The Siege Within.* Harmondsworth, 1985
Balasubramanyam, V. N., *The Economy of India.* London, 1985
Bardham, P., *The Political Economy of Development in India.* Oxford, 1984
Brown, J., *Modern India: The Origins of an Asian Democracy.* OUP, 1985
Chatterjee, S. P., *Indian Climatology.* Calcutta, 1956. (ed.), *National Atlas of India (Preliminary* (Hindi) *edition).* Calcutta, 1957
Fishlock, T., *India File: Inside the Subcontinent.* London, 1983
von Fürer-Haimendorf, C., *Tribes of India: the Struggle for Survival.* Univ. of California Press, 1983
Kesavan, B. S., and Kulkarni, V. Y. (eds), *The National Bibliography of Indian Literature, 1901–53,* New Delhi, 1963 ff.
Gupta, G. K. and Kharbas, D. S., *India.* [Bibliography] Oxford and Santa Barbara, 1984
Hall, A., *The Emergence of Modern India.* Columbia Univ. Press, 1981
Hart, D., *Nuclear Power in India: a Comparative Analysis.* London, 1983
Majumdar, R. C., Raychandhuri, H. C., and Datta, K., *An Advanced History of India.* 2nd ed. London, 1950
Mitra, H. N., *The Indian Annual Register.* Calcutta, from 1953
Moore, R. J., *Making the New Commonwealth.* Oxford, 1987
Nanda, B. R. (ed.), *Socialism in India.* Delhi, Bombay, Bangalore, Kanpur, London, 1972
Pachauri, R. K., *Energy and Economic Development in India.* New York, 1977
Philips, C. H. (ed.), *The Evolution of India and Pakistan: Select Documents.* OUP, 1962 ff.— *Politics and Society in India.* London, 1963
Poplai, S. L. (ed.), *India, 1947–50* (select documents). 2 vols. Bombay and London, 1959
Ray, R. K., *Industrialisation of India.* OUP, 1983
Roach, J. R., (ed.) *India 2000: The Next Fifteen Years.* Riverdale, My, 1986
Smith, V. E., *Oxford History of India.* 3rd ed. OUP, 1958

Spear, P., *India: A Modern History.* 2nd ed. Univ. of Michigan Press, 1972
Sutton, S. C., *Guide to the India Office Library (founded in 1801).* HMSO, 1952
Thomas, R., *India's Emergence as an Industrial Power.* Royal Institute of International Affairs, London, 1982
Yasdani, C. (ed.), *Early History of the Deccan.* 2 vols. London, 1960

STATES AND TERRITORIES

The Republic of India is composed of the following 25 States and 7 centrally administered Union Territories:

States	Capital	States	Capital
Andhra Pradesh	Hyderabad	Manipur	Imphal
Arunachal Pradesh	Itanagar	Meghalaya	Shillong
Assam	Dispur	Mizoram	Aizawl
Bihar	Patna	Nagaland	Kohima
Goa	Panaji	Orissa	Bhubaneswar
Gujarat	Ahmedabad	Punjab	Chandigarh
Haryana	Chandigarh	Rajasthan	Jaipur
Himachal Pradesh	Shimla	Sikkim	Gangtok
Jammu and Kashmir	Srinagar	Tamil Nadu	Madras
Karnataka	Bangalore	Tripura	Agartala
Kerala	Trivandrum	Uttar Pradesh	Lucknow
Madhya Pradesh	Bhopal	West Bengal	Calcutta
Maharashtra	Bombay		

Union Territories

Andaman and Nicobar Islands; Chandigarh; Dadra and Nagar Haveli; Delhi; Daman and Diu; Lakshadweep; Pondicherry.

States Reorganization. The Constitution, which came into force on 26 Jan. 1950, provided for 9 Part A States (Assam, Bihar, Bombay, Madhya Pradesh, Madras, Orissa, Punjab, Uttar Pradesh and West Bengal) which corresponded to the previous governors' provinces; 8 Part B States (Hyderabad, Jammu and Kashmir, Madhya Bharat, Mysore, Patalia-East Punjab (PEPSU), Rajasthan, Saurashtra and Travancore-Cochin) which corresponded to Indian states or unions of states; 10 Part C States (Ajmer, Bhopal, Bilaspur, Coorg, Delhi, Himachal Pradesh, Kutch, Manipur, Tripura and Vindhya Pradesh) which corresponded to the chief commissioners' provinces; and Part D Territories and other areas (*e.g.*, Andaman and Nicobar Islands). Part A States (under governors) and Part B States (under rajpramukhs) had provincial autonomy with a ministry and elected assembly. Part C States (under chief commissioners) were the direct responsibility of the Union Government, although Kutch, Manipur and Tripura had legislatures with limited powers. Andhra was formed as a Part A State on its separation from Madras in 1953. Bilaspur was merged with Himachal Pradesh in 1954.

The States Reorganization Act, 1956, abolished the distinction between Parts A, B and C States and established two categories for the units of the Indian Union to be called States and Territories. The following were the main territorial changes: the Telugu districts of Hyderabad were merged with Andhra; Mysore absorbed the whole Kannada-speaking area (including Coorg, the greater part of 4 districts of Bombay, 3 districts of Hyderabad and 1 district of Madras); Bhopal, Vindhya Pradesh and Madhya Bharat were merged with Madhya Pradesh, which ceded 8 Marathi-speaking districts to Bombay; the new state of Kerala, comprising the majority of Malayalam-speaking peoples, was formed from Travancore-Cochin with a small area from Madras; Patalia-East Punjab was included in Punjab; Kutch and Saurashtra in Bombay; and Ajmer in Rajasthan; Hyderabad ceased to exist.

On 1 May 1960 Bombay State was divided into two parts: 17 districts (including Saurashtra and Kutch) in the north and west became the new state of Gujarat; the remainder was renamed the state of Maharashtra.

In Aug. 1961 the former Portuguese territories of Dadra and Nagar Haveli became a Union territory. The Portuguese territory of Goa and the smaller territories of Daman and Diu, occupied by India in Dec. 1961, were constituted a Union territory in March 1962. In Aug. 1962 the former French territories of Pondicherry, Karikal, Mahé and Yanaon were formally transferred to India and became a Union territory. In Sept. 1962 the Naga Hills Tuensang Area was constituted a separate state under the name of Nagaland. On 1 Nov. 1966, under the Punjab Reorganization Act 1966, a new state of Haryana and a new Union Territory of Chandigarh were created from parts of Punjab (India); for details, see pp. 655 and 687. On 26 Jan. 1971 Himachal Pradesh became a state. In 1972 the North East Frontier Agency and Mizo hill district were made Union territories (as Arunachal Pradesh and Mizoram) and Manipur, Meghalaya and Tripura full states. Sikkim became a state in 1975. Statehood for Mizoram was passed by parliament in July 1986; for Arunachal Pradesh in Dec. 1986; for Goa in May 1987.

Report of the States Reorganization Commission. Government of India. Delhi, 1956

ANDHRA PRADESH

HISTORY. Andhra was constituted a separate state on 1 Oct. 1953, on its partition from Madras, and consisted of the undisputed Telugu-speaking area of that state. To this region was added, on 1 Nov. 1956, the Telangana area of the former Hyderabad State, comprising the districts of Hyderabad, Medak, Nizamabad, Karimnaga, Warangal, Khammam, Nalgonda and Mahbubnaga, parts of the Adilabad district and some taluks of the Raichur, Gulbarga and Bidar districts, and some revenue circles of the Nanded district. On 1 April 1960, 221·4 sq. miles in the Chingleput and Salem districts of Madras were transferred to Andhra Pradesh in exchange for 410 sq. miles from Chittoor district. The district of Prakasam was formed on 2 Feb. 1970. Hyderabad was split into 2 districts on 15 Aug. 1978. A new district, Vizianagaram, was formed in 1979.

AREA AND POPULATION. Andhra Pradesh is in south India and is bounded south by Tamil Nadu, west by Karnataka, north and northwest by Maharashtra, northeast by Madhya Pradesh and Orissa, east by the Bay of Bengal. The state has an area of 275,100 sq. km and a population (1981 census) of 53·5m. Density, 195 per sq. km. Growth rate 1971–81, 23·19%. The principal language is Telugu. Cities with over 250,000 population (1981 census), see p. 625. Other large cities (1981): Nellore (236,879); Kakinada (226,600); Kurnool (206,700); Nizamabad (183,135); Eluru (168,100); Machilipatnam (138,500); Anantapur (119,536); Tenali (119,200); Tirupati (115,200); Vizianagaram (115,200); Adoni (108,900); Proddatur (107,100); Cuddapah (103,100); Bheemavaram (101,940).

CONSTITUTION AND GOVERNMENT. Andhra Pradesh has a unicameral legislature; the Legislative Council was abolished in June 1985. There are 295 seats in the Legislative Assembly. At the election of March 1985, the Telegu Dasam party continued in office.

For administrative purposes there are 23 districts in the state. The capital is Hyderabad.

Governor: M. S. Kumud Ben Joshi.
Chief Minister: N. T. Rama Rao.

BUDGET. The budget (estimate) for 1986–87 showed total receipts on revenue account of Rs 3,226·88 crores, and expenditure of Rs 3,242·62 crores.

ENERGY AND NATURAL RESOURCES

Electricity. There are 6 hydro-electric plants including Machkund, Upper Sileru and Nizam Sagar and 5 thermal stations including Nellore and Kothagudam. Installed capacity, 1986–87, 3,366 mw., power generated 12,225m. kwh. In 1985–86 there were 23,680 electrified villages and 733,000 electric pump sets.

Gas. Natural gas was found at Reyzole in 1983.

Water. The irrigation potential of the state in 1983–84 was 10,300,000 hectares; actual area under irrigation, 3,880,000 hectares. The Telugu Ganga joint project with Tamil Nadu, now in execution, will irrigate about 233,000 hectares, besides supplying drinking water to Madras city (Tamil Nadu).

Minerals The state is an important producer of asbestos and barytes. Other important minerals are copper ore, coal, iron and limestone, steatite, mica and manganese.

Agriculture. There were (1983–84) about 13·04m. hectares of cropped land, of which 35·9% is irrigated. 9·2m. hectares were under food-grains. Yield per hectare, in kg: Sugar-cane, 7,332; rice, 2,161; ground-nuts, 1,029; tobacco, 881; jowar, 569; cotton, 360; castor, 208.

Livestock (1983 provisional): Cattle, 13·12m.; buffaloes, 8·7m.; goats, 5·5m.; sheep, 7·5m.

Forests. In 1982 it was estimated that forests occupy 23·2% of the total area of the state or 63,771 sq. km; main forest products are teak, eucalyuptus, cashew, casuarina, softwoods and bamboo.

Fisheries. Production 1985–86, 150,000 tonnes of marine fish and 150,000 tonnes of inland water fish. The state has a coastline of 974 km.

INDUSTRY. The main industries are textile manufacture, sugar-milling machine tools, pharmaceuticals, cement, chemicals, glass, fertilizers, electronic equipment, heavy electrical machinery, aircraft parts and paper-making. There is an oil refinery at Vishakhapatnam, where India's only major shipbuilding yards are situated. In 1983 a steel plant was under construction at Vishakhapatnam and a railway repair shop at Tirupathi.

Cottage industry includes the manufacture of carpets, wooden and lacquer toys, brocades, bidriware, filigree and lace-work. The wooden toys of Nirmal and Kondapalli are particularly well known. Sericulture is developing rapidly. District Industries Centres have been set up to promote small-scale industry.

Tourism is growing; the main centres are Hyderabad, Nagarjunasagar, Warangal, Araku Valley, Horsley Hills and Tirupathi.

COMMUNICATIONS

Roads. On 31 March 1986 there were 2,357 km of national highways, 8,387 km of state highways, 25,419 km of major district roads, 85,156 km of other roads. Number of vehicles: 408,341 motor cycles and scooters, 64,173 cars and jeeps, 61,252 goods vehicles and 13,237 buses.

Railways. In 1985–86 there were approximately 5,090 route-km of railway, of which 3,079 km were broad gauge.

Aviation. There are airports at Hyderabad, Tirupathi, Vijayawada and Vishakapatnam, with regular scheduled services to Bombay, Delhi, Calcutta, Bangalore and Madras. A feeder airline serves Rajahmundry and Cuddapah.

Shipping. The chief port is Vishakhapatnam. There are minor ports at Kakinada, Machilipatnam, Bheemunipatnam, Narsapur, Krishnapatnam, Vadarevu and Kalingapatnam.

JUSTICE, RELIGION AND EDUCATION

Justice. The high court of Judicature at Hyderabad has a Chief Justice and 22 puisne judges.

Religion. At the 1981 census Hindus numbered 47,525,681; Moslems, 4,533,700; Christians, 1,433,327; Jains 18,642; Sikhs, 16,222; Buddhists, 12,930.

Education. In 1981, 29·94% of the population were literate (39·13% of men and 20·52% of women). There were, in 1984–85 41,702 primary schools (4,835,050 students); 5,445 upper primary (1,693,586); 4,679 secondary (2,248,201). Education is free for children up to 14.

There were in 1985–86 353 degree colleges, 635 junior colleges, 53 oriental colleges and 13 universities: Osmania University, Hyderabad; Andhra University,

Waltair; Sri Venkateswara University, Tirupathi; Kakatiya University, Warangal; Nagarjuna University, Guntur; Sri Jawaharlal Nehru Technological University, Hyderabad; Central University, Hyderabad; A.P. Agricultural University, Hyderabad; Sri Krishnadevaraya University, Anantapur; Smt. Padmarathi Mahila Vishwaridyalayam (University for Women), Tirupathi; A. P. Open University, Hyderabad; Telugu University, Hyderabad and A. P. Medical University, Vijayawada.

ARUNACHAL PRADESH

HISTORY. In Jan. 1972 the former North East Frontier Agency of Assam was created a Union Territory. In Dec. 1986, by the Constitution (55th Amendment) and State of Arunachal Pradesh Acts, the Territory became the 24th state of India.

AREA AND POPULATION. The state is in north-east India and is bounded by Assam, Bhután, China and Burma; it comprises the former frontier divisions of Kameng, Tirap, Subansiri, Siang and Lohit; it has an area of 81,426 sq. km and a population (1981 census) of 628,050; growth, 1971–81, 34·34%; density, 7 per sq. km.

The state is mainly tribal; there are over 80 tribes using about 50 tribal dialects.

CONSTITUTION AND GOVERNMENT. There is a Legislative Assembly of 30 members. Elections were to be held during 1987. The capital is Itanagar.

Lieut.-Governor: B. Narayan Singh.
Chief Minister: Gegong Apang.

NATURAL RESOURCES. About 60% of the land area is forest, and most is mountainous. There is some farming on terraced land; crops include rice, rubber, coffee, fruits and spices. Agriculture employs about 46% of the population.

ASSAM

HISTORY. Assam first became a British Protectorate at the close of the first Burmese War in 1826. In 1832 Cachar was annexed; in 1835 the Jaintia Hills were included in the East India Company's dominions, and in 1839 Assam was annexed to Bengal. In 1874 Assam was detached from Bengal and made a separate chief commissionership. On the partition of Bengal in 1905, it was united to the Eastern Districts of Bengal under a Lieut.-Governor. From 1912 the chief commissionership of Assam was revived, and in 1921 a governorship was created. On the partition of India almost the whole of the predominantly Moslem district of Sylhet was merged with East Bengal (Pakistan). Dewangiri in North Kamrup was ceded to Bhután in 1951. The Naga Hill district, administered by the Union Government since 1957, became part of Nagaland in 1962. The autonomous state of Meghalaya within Assam, comprising the districts of Garo Hills and Khasi and Jaintia Hills, came into existence on 2 April 1970, and achieved full independent statehood in Jan. 1972, when it was also decided to form a Union Territory, Mizoram (now a state), from the Mizo Hills district.

EVENTS. In Aug. 1985 there was an agreement between central government and anti-immigration parties, led by the Assam Peoples' Front. Settlers coming in illegally between 1966 and 1971 are disenfranchised for 10 years; those coming illegally since 1971 are to be expelled.

AREA AND POPULATION. Assam is in eastern India, almost separated from central India by Bangladesh. It is bounded west by West Bengal, north by Bhután and Arunachal Pradesh, east by Nagaland, Manipur and Burma, south by Meghalaya, Bangladesh, Mizoram and Tripura. The area of the state is now approximately 78,438 sq km. Its population (1981 census) 19·9m. Density, 254 per sq. km. Growth rate since 1971, 36·09%. Principal towns with population (1971) are; Guwahati, 122,981; Dibrugarh, 80,344; Tinsukia, 55,392; Nowgong, 52,892; Silchar, 52,612. The principal language is Assamese.

The central government is surveying the line of a proposed boundary fence to prevent illegal entry from Bangladesh.

CONSTITUTION AND GOVERNMENT. Assam has a unicameral legislature of 126 members. In Dec. 1985 elections were held and an Asom Gana Parishad government was returned. The temporary capital is Dispur.

Governor: B. N. Singh.
Chief Minister: P. Kumar Mahanta.

BUDGET. The revised budget estimates for 1985–86 showed revenue account receipts of Rs 938·84 crores and expenditure of Rs 992·12 crores.

ENERGY AND NATURAL RESOURCES

Electricity. In 1985–86 there was an installed capacity of 428 mw and 13,648 villages (out of 21,995) with electricity. New power stations are under construction at Lakwa, and Karbi-Langpi hydro-electricity project.

Oil. Assam contains important oilfields and produces about 50% of India's crude oil. There is also natural gas.

Water. In 1986–87, 448,000 hectares were irrigated; 2 major and 18 medium projects were in hand.

Minerals. Coal production (1985), 834,000 tonnes. The state also has limestone, refractory clay, dolomite, and corundum.

Agriculture. There are 802 tea plantations, and growing tea is the principal industry. Production in 1985, 352m. kg, over 50% of Indian tea. Over 72% of the cultivated area is under food crops, of which the most important is rice. Total foodgrains, 1985–86, 30·3m. tonnes. Main cash crops: jute, tea, cotton, oilseeds, sugar-cane, fruit and potatoes. Wheat has been introduced recently and yielded 100,500 tonnes in 1985–86. Cattle are important.

Forestry. There are 17,400 sq. km of reserved forests under the administration of the Forest Department and 10,063·81 sq. km of unclassed forests, altogether about 30% of the total area of the state. Revenue from forests, 1985–86, Rs 216m.

INDUSTRY. Sericulture and hand-loom weaving, both silk and cotton, are important home industries together with the manufacture of brass, cane and bamboo articles. Hand-loom weaving of silk is stimulated by state and central development schemes. There are two silk-spinning mills and 26 cotton-mills. The main heavy industry is petro-chemicals; there are 3 oil refineries. Other industries include manufacturing paper, fertilizers, sugar, jute and plywood products, rice and oil milling.

COMMUNICATIONS

Roads. In 1984–85 there were 26,352 km of road maintained by the Public Works Department in Assam, including national highway. There were 135,322 motor vehicles in the state in 1985.

Railways. The route km of railways in 1985–86 was 2,338 km, of which 105·22 km are broad gauge.

Aviation. Daily scheduled flights connect the principal towns with the rest of India. There are airports at Guwahati, Tezpur, Jorhat, North Lakhimpur, Silchar and Dibrugarh.

Shipping. Water transport is important in Lower Assam; the main waterway is the Brahmaputra River. Cargo carried in 1986 was 65,000 tonnes.

JUSTICE, RELIGION AND EDUCATION

Justice. The seat of the High Court is Guwahati. It has a Chief Justice and 6 puisne judges.

Religion. At the 1971 census Hindus numbered 10,604,618; Moslems, 3,592,124; Christians, 381,010; Buddhists, 22,565; Jains, 12,914; Sikhs, 11,920.

Education. In 1984–85 there were 25,770 primary/junior basic schools; 4,757 middle/senior basic; 2,580 high/higher secondary. There were 156 colleges for general education, 3 medical colleges, 3 engineering and 1 agricultural, 8 teacher-training colleges and 3 universities.

Goswami, P. C., *Economic Development of Assam*. London, 1963
Reid, Sir Robert, *History of the Frontier Areas Bordering on Assam*. Shillong, 1942

BIHAR

The state contains the ethnic areas of North Bihar, Santhalpargana and Chota Nagpur. In 1956 certain areas of Purnea and Manbhum districts were transferred to West Bengal.

AREA AND POPULATION. Bihar is in north India and is bounded north by Nepál, east by West Bengal, south by Orissa, south-west by Madhya Pradesh and west by Uttar Pradesh. The area of Bihar is 173,877 sq. km and its population (1981 census, revised), 69,914,734, a density of 402 per sq. km. Growth rate since 1971, 23.9%. Population of principal towns, *see* p. 625. Other large towns (1981): Muzaffarpur, 189,765; Darbhanga, 175,879; Biharsharif, 151,305; Munghyr, 129,187; Arrah, 124,614; Katihar, 121,693; Dhanbad, 119,807; Chapra, 111,407; Purnea, 109,649; Bermo, 101,502.

The official language is Hindi (55·8m. speakers at the 1981 census), the second, Urdu (6·9m.), the third, Bengali (2m.).

CONSTITUTION AND GOVERNMENT. Bihar has a bicameral legislature. The Legislative Assembly consists of 324 elected members and the Council, 96. After the elections in March 1985 a Congress government was returned. For the purposes of administration the state is divided into 10 divisions covering 39 districts. The capital is Patna.

Governor: Govind Narayan Singh.
Chief Minister: Bhagwat Jha Azad.

BUDGET. The budget estimates for 1981–82 show total receipts of Rs 15,221·3m and expenditure of Rs 14,443·5m. Per capita income (1983) Rs 870.

ENERGY AND NATURAL RESOURCES

Electricity. Installed capacity (1985–86) 1,379·68 mw. Power generated (1985–86), 3,348m. kw.; there were 34,992 villages with electricity. Hydro-electric projects in hand will add about 149·2mw. capacity.

Minerals. Bihar is very rich in minerals, with about 40% of national production. There are huge deposits of copper, capatite and kyanite and sizeable deposits of coal, mica and china clay. Bihar is a principal producer of iron ore. Other important minerals: manganese, limestone, graphite, chromite, asbestos, barytes, dolomite, feldspar, columbite, pyrites, saltpetre, glass sands, slate, lead, silver, building stones and radio-active minerals.

Agriculture. About 26% of the cultivable area is irrigated. Cultivable land, 11·6m. hectares, of a total area of 17·4m. hectares. Total cropped area, 1984, 8·4m. hectares. Production (1985–86): Rice, 6·1m. tonnes; wheat, 3·2m.; total foodgrains, 11·5m. Other food crops are maize, rabi and pulses. Main cash crops are jute, sugar-cane, oilseeds, tobacco and potato.

Forests in 1984 covered 30,896 hectares. There are 12 protected forests.

INDUSTRY. Main plants are the Tata Iron and Steel Co., the Tata Engineering and Locomotive Co., the steel plant at Bokaro, oil refinery at Barauni, Heavy Engineering Corporation and Foundry Forge project at Ranchi, and aluminium plant at Muri. Other important industries are machine tools, fertilizers, electrical engineering, sugar-milling, paper-milling, silk-spinning, manufacturing explosives and cement. There is a copper smelter at Ghatsila and a zinc plant at Tundo.

TOURISM. The main tourist centres are Bodh Gaya, Patna, Nalanda, Jamshedpur, Sasaram, Betla, Hazaribagh and Vaishali.

COMMUNICATIONS

Roads. In 1983–84 the state had 84,185 km of highway . Passenger transport has been nationalized in 7 districts. There were 286,734 motor vehicles in March 1984.

Railways. The North Eastern and Eastern railways traverse the state; route-km, 1985–86, 5,362.

Aviation. There are airports at Patna and Ranchi with regular scheduled services to Calcutta and Delhi.

Shipping. The length of waterways open for navigation is 900 miles.

JUSTICE, RELIGION, EDUCATION AND WELFARE

Justice. There is a High Court (constituted in 1916) at Patna, and a bench at Ranchi, with a Chief Justice, 32 puisne judges and 4 additional judges.

Police. The police force is under a Director General of Police; in 1983 there were 957 police stations (and 56 for railway police).

Religion. At the 1981 census Hindus numbered 58,011,070; Moslems, 9,874,993; Christians, 740,186; Sikhs, 77,704; Jains, 27,613; Buddhists, 3,003.

Education. At the census of 1981 the number of literates was 18.16m. (26%: males 37.78%; females, 13.58%). There were, 1985–86, 3,666 high and higher secondary schools with (1984–85) 1.4m. pupils, 11,841 middle schools with 2.1m. pupils, 50,798 primary schools with 8,203,000 pupils. Primary and middle schools had 211,719 teachers, higher secondary, high schools and junior colleges, 43,593. Education is free for children aged 6-11.

There were 9 universities in academic year 1985–86; Patna University (founded 1917) with 18,895 students (1984–85); Bihar University, Muzaffarpur (1952) with 57 constituent colleges, 10 affiliated colleges and 75,886 students (1981–82); Bhagalpur University (1960) with 40,182 students (1983–84); Ranchi University (1960) with 66,296 students (1982–83); Darbhanga Sanskrit University (1961); Magadha University, Gaya (1962) and Lalit Narayan Mithila University (1972), Darbhanga.

Health. In 1983 there were 259 hospitals with 19,583 beds, and 861 dispensaries with 4,166 beds.

Das, A. N., *Agrarian Movements in India: Studies in 20th Century Bihar.* London, 1982

GOA

HISTORY. The coastal area was captured by the Portuguese in 1510 and the inland area was added in the 18th century. In Dec. 1961 Portuguese rule was ended and Goa incorporated into the Indian Union as a Territory together with Daman and Diu. Goa was granted statehood as a seperate unit on 30 May 1987. Daman and Diu remained Territories (see p. 688).

AREA AND POPULATION. Goa, bounded on the north by Maharashtra and on the east and South by Karnataka, has a coastline of 105 km. The area is 3,702 sq. km. (Population, 1981 census, 1,007,749). Density, 272 per sq. km.

Panaji is the largest town; population (urban agglomeration, 1981) 76,839. The languages spoken are Konkani (official language) Marathi, Hindi, English.

GOVERNMENT. The Indian Parliament passed legislation in March 1962 by which Goa became a Union Territory with retrospective effect from 20 Dec. 1961. On 30 May 1987 Goa attained statehood, it is represented by 3 elected and one nominated representatives in Parliament. There is a Legislative Assembly of 31 members of which 3 are nominated. The Capital is Panaji. There are 196 village Panchayats.

Governor: Dr Gopal Singh.
Chief Minister: Pratapsing Rane.

BUDGET. The total budget for 1987–88 was Rs 238·07 crores. Annual plan 1988–89, Rs 92 crores.

ENERGY AND NATURAL RESOURCES

Electricity. Seventeen towns and 396 villages were supplied with electric power by March 1987; Goa receives its power supply from the neighbouring states of Maharashtra and Karnataka.

Minerals. Resources include manganese ore and iron ore, both of which are exported. There are also reserves of bauxite, lime stone and clay.

Agriculture. Agriculture is the main occupation, important crops are rice, pulses, ragi, mango, cashew and coconuts. Area irrigated under paddy (1986–87) 37,050 hectares of high yielding grains (production 106,607 tonnes). Area under pulses 4,323, sugar-cane 1,751, groundnut 570.

Government poultry and dairy farming schemes produced 77·5m. eggs and 7·74m. litres of milk in 1986–87.

Fisheries. Fish is the territory's staple food. In 1986–87 the catch of seafish was 60,116 tonnes (value Rs 109,975 lakhs). There is a coastline of about 105 km and about 4,074 active fishing vessels.

INDUSTRY. In 1986–87 there were 31 large and medium industrial projects and 3,527 small units registered. There were 11 Government industrial estates. Small units were mainly occupied in making nylon fishing-nets, ready made clothing, pesticides, pharmaceuticals and footwear.

In 1986 there were 46 small-scale industry units employing 23,730 persons.

ROADS. In 1986 there were 4,164 km of motorable roads (National Highway, 224 km).

JUSTICE. There is a bench of the Bombay High Court at Panaji.

GUJARAT

HISTORY. On 1 May 1960, as a result of the Bombay Reorganization Act, 1960, the state of Gujarat was formed from the north and west (predominantly Gujarati-speaking) portion of Bombay State, the remainder being renamed the state of Maharashtra. Gujarat consists of the following districts of the former state of Bombay: Banas Kantha, Mehsana, Sabar Kantha, Ahmedabad, Kaira, Panch Mahals, Vadodara, Bharuch, Surat, Dangs, Amreli, Surendranagar, Rajkot, Jamnagar, Junagadh, Bhavnagar, Kutch, Gandhinagar and Bulsar.

AREA AND POPULATION. Gujarat is in western India and is bounded north by Pakistan and Rajasthan, east by Madhya Pradesh, south-east by Maharashtra, south and west by the Indian ocean and Arabian sea. The area of the state is 195,984 sq. km and the population at the 1981 census (revised) was

34,086,000; a density of 174 per sq. km. Growth rate 1971–81, 27·2%. The chief cities, *see* p. 625. Gujarati and Hindi in the Devanagari script are the official languages.

CONSTITUTION AND GOVERNMENT. Gujarat has a unicameral legislature, the Legislative Assembly, which has 182 elected members. After the elections in March 1985 a Congress government was returned.

The capital is Gandhinagar. There are 19 districts.

Governor: Ram Krishna Trivedi.
Chief Minister: Amarsinh Chaudhury.

BUDGET. The budget estimates for 1986–87 showed an overall deficit of Rs 41·21 crores.

ENERGY AND NATURAL RESOURCES

Electricity. In 1985 the total generating capacity was 3,383 mw of electricity, serving 34,500 towns and villages and 322,681 wells and tube-wells.

Water. The Karjan Dam, under construction, will provide a reservoir of 630m. cu. metres capacity; it is designed to irrigate 56,000 hectares through 2 main canals.

Oil and Gas. There were crude oil and gas reserves in 23 fields in 1982–83. Production: Crude oil, 3·2m. tonnes; gas, 658·5m. cu. metres.

Minerals. Chief minerals produced in 1983 (in tonnes) included lime stone (3·6m.), agate stone (541), calcite (612), quartz and silica (204,459), bauxite (520,000), crude china clay (10,557), refined china clays (10,335), dolomite (279,232), crude fluorite (105,886), graded fluorite (348), calcareous and sea sand (630,000) and lignite (646,000). Enormous reserves of coal were found under the Kalol and Mehsana oil and gas fields in May 1980. The deposit, mixed with crude petroleum, is estimated at 100,000m. tonnes, extending over 500 km.

Agriculture. In 1985–86 drought was exceptionally severe. Cropped area, 1981–82, was 10·9m. hectares. Area and production of principal crops, 1984–85 (in 1,000 hectares and 1,000 tonnes): Rice, 566 and 835; groundnuts, 2,061 and 1,572; cotton, 1,383 and 2,069,000 bales of 170 kg. Total cropped area 3·9m. hectares producing 4·7m. tonnes.

Livestock (1982): Buffaloes, 4·43m.; other cattle, 6·93m.; sheep, 2·33m.; goats, 3·26m.; horses and ponies, 24,000.

Fisheries. There were (1984) about 225,000 people engaged in fisheries. There were 11,774 fishing vessels (4,245 motor vessels). The catch for 1982–83 (estimate) was 212,419 tonnes.

INDUSTRY. Gujarat is one of the 4 most industrialized states. In 1985 there were more than 70,000 small-scale units and 13,000 factories including 1,328 textile factories. There were 167 industrial estates. Principal industries are textiles, general and electrical engineering, petrochemicals, machine tools, heavy chemicals, pharmaceuticals, dyes, sugar, soda ash and cement. Large fertilizer plants have been set up and there is an oil refinery at Koyali near Vadodara, with a developing petro-chemical complex.

State production of soda-ash is 90·4% of national output, and of salt, about 60%. Salt production (1984) 8·4m. tonnes; cement production, 142,100 tonnes.

COMMUNICATIONS

Roads. In 1985 there were 57,845 km of roads. Gujarat State Transport Corporation operated 13,284 routes.

Railways. In 1983 the state had 5,633 km of railway line.

Aviation. Ahmedabad is the main airport. There are 5 services daily between Ahmedabad and Bombay, Jaipur and Delhi. There are 8 other airports: Baroda, Bhavnagar, Bhuj, Jamnagar, Kandla, Keshod, Porbandar and Rajkot.

Shipping. The largest port is Kandla. There are 39 other ports, 11 intermediate, 28 minor.

Post. There were (March 1984–85) 9,000 post offices, 2,000 telegraph offices. Ahmedabad has direct dialling telephone connexion (or night S.T.D.) with 273 cities and 16 foreign countries. There were 227,000 telephone connexions in the state.

JUSTICE, RELIGION, EDUCATION AND WELFARE

Justice. The High Court of Judicature at Ahmedabad has a Chief Justice and 18 puisne judges.

Religion. At the 1971 census Hindus numbered 23,835,471; Moslems, 2,249,055; Jains, 451,578; Christians, 109,341; Sikhs, 18,233; Buddhists, 5,469.

Education. In 1981 the number of literates was 14·85m. (43·7%). Primary and secondary education up to Standard XI are free. Education above Standard XII is free for girls. In 1984–85 there were 27,087 primary schools; nearly all villages with more than 200 people have one within 1·5 km. There were 4,125 secondary schools including 1,416 higher secondary schools.

There are 7 universities in the state. Gujarat University, Ahmedabad, founded in 1949, is teaching and affiliating; it has 149 affiliated colleges. The Maharaja Sayajirao University of Vadodara (1949) is residential and teaching. The Sardar Patel University, Vallabh-Vidyanagar, (1955) has 16 constituent and affiliated colleges. The 2 newer universities (1967) are Saurashtra University at Rajkot with 54 affiliated colleges, and South Gujarat at Surat with 37. Bhavnagar University (1978) is residential and teaching with 7 affiliated colleges. North Gujarat University was established at Patan in 1986. Gujarat Vidyapith at Ahmedabad is deemed a university under the University Grants Commission Act. There were also 1 agricultural and 1 Ayurvedic university.

There are 9 engineering colleges, 24 polytechnics, 5 medical colleges, 6 agricultural, 3 pharmaceutical and 2 veterinary. In 1984–85 the total number of higher education institutes was 400, with 213,000 students.

Health. In 1985 there were 260 primary health centres and 4,869 sub-centres.

Rushbrook Williams, L. F., *The Black Hills: Kutch in History and Legend.* London, 1958
Desai, I. F., *Untouchability in Rural Gujarat.* Bombay, 1977

HARYANA

HISTORY. The state of Haryana, created on 1 Nov. 1966 under the Punjab Reorganization Act, 1966, was formed from the Hindi-speaking parts of the state of Punjab (India). It comprises the districts of Hissar, Mohindergarh, Gurgaon, Rohtak and Karnal; parts of Sangrur and Ambala districts; and part of Kharar tehsil.

AREA AND POPULATION. Haryana is in north India and is bounded north by Himachal Pradesh, east by Uttar Pradesh, south and west by Rajasthan and north-west by Punjab. Delhi forms an enclave on its eastern boundary. The state has an area of 44,222 sq. km and a population (1981) of 12,850,902; density, 291 per sq. km. Growth rate, 1971–81, 28·04%. The principal language is Hindi.

CONSTITUTION AND GOVERNMENT. The state has a unicameral legislature with 90 members. After the elections of June 1987 when 87 seats were contested, Lok Dal held 58 seats; Bharatiya Janata, 15; Congress (I), 5; independents, 6 and others, 3. The state shares with Punjab (India) a High Court, a university and certain public services. The capital (shared with Punjab) is Chandigarh (*see* p. 687). Its transfer to Punjab, intended for 1986, has been postponed. There are 12 districts.

Governor: H. R. Barari.
Chief Minister: Devi Lal.

BUDGET. Budget estimates for 1981–82 show income of Rs 872 crores and expenditure of Rs 921 crores. Annual plan 1988–89, Rs 600 crores.

ENERGY AND NATURAL RESOURCES

Electricity. Approximately 1,000 mw are supplied to Haryana, mainly from the Bhakra Nangar system. In 1982–83 installed capacity was 1,385 mw and all the 3,302 villages had electric power.

Minerals. Minerals include placer gold, barytes and rare earths. Value of production, 1984–85, Rs 39m.

Agriculture. Haryana has sandy soil and erratic rainfall, but the state shares the benefit of the Sutlej-Beas scheme. Agriculture employs over 82% of the working population; in 1981 there were about 900,000 holdings (average 3·7 hectares), and the gross irrigated area was 1·97m. hectares. Area under high-yielding varieties of foodgrains, 2·2m. hectares. During 1983–84 foodgrain production was 6·9m. tonnes; sugar (gur), oilseeds, and wheat, are important.

Forests cover 3·3% of the state.

INDUSTRY. Haryana has a large market for consumer goods in neighbouring Delhi. In 1984–85 there were 348 large and medium scale industries employing 120,000 and producing goods worth over Rs 10,000m. There were 58,250 small units. The main industries are cotton textiles (27 mills in 1984–85), agricultural machinery, woollen textiles, scientific instruments, glass, cement, paper and sugar milling, cars, tyres and tubes, motor cycles, bicycles, steel tubes, engineering goods, electrical and electronic goods.

COMMUNICATIONS

Roads. There were (1984) about 19,415 km of metalled roads, linking all villages. Road transport is nationalized. There were 139,890 motor vehicles in 1982–83.

Railways. The state is crossed by lines from Delhi to Agra, Ajmer, Ferozepur and Chandigarh. Route km, 1983–84, 1,501. The main stations are at Ambala and Kurukshetra.

Aviation. There is no airport within the state but Delhi is on its eastern boundary.

JUSTICE AND EDUCATION

Justice. Haryana shares the High Court of Punjab and Haryana at Chandigarh.

Education. In 1981 the number of literates was 4·6m. In 1984-85 there were 7,962 schools and colleges with 2,433,000 attending. This includes 4,928 primary schools, 1,801 high and higher secondary schools, 1,105 middle schools and 128 colleges.

HIMACHAL PRADESH

HISTORY. The territory came into being on 15 April 1948 and comprised 30 former Hill States. The state of Bilaspur was merged with Himachal Pradesh in 1954. The 6 original districts were: Mahasu, Sirmur, Mandi, Chamba, Bilaspur and Kinnaur. On 1 Nov. 1966, under the Punjab Reorganization Act, 1966, certain parts of the state of Punjab (India) were transferred to Himachal Pradesh. These comprise the districts of Shimla, Kulu, Kangra, and Lahaul and Spiti; and parts of Hoshiarpur and Ambala districts.

AREA AND POPULATION. Himachal Pradesh is in north India and is bounded north by Kashmir, east by Tibet, south-east by Uttar Pradesh, south by Haryana, south-west and west by Punjab. The area of the state is 55,673 sq. km and it had a population at the 1981 census of 4,280,818. Density, 77 per sq. km. Growth rate, 1971–81, 23·71%. Principal language is Pahari.

CONSTITUTION AND GOVERNMENT. Full statehood was attained, as the 18th state of the Union, on 25 Jan. 1971.

On 1 Sept. 1972 districts were reorganized and 2 new districts created, Hamirpur and Una, making a total of 12. The capital is Shimla.

There is a unicameral legislature. After the elections in March 1985 a Congress government was returned.

Governor: Vice Adm. (Retd.) R. K. S. Ghandhi.
Chief Minister: Vir Bhadra Singh.

BUDGET. Budget estimates for 1987–88 showed revenue receipts of Rs 549·19 (1986–87, Rs 529·75 crores) crores (including central assistance and centrally-sponsored schemes) and expenditure on revenue account of Rs 567·37 crores (Rs 494·79 crores). The capital account showed expenditure of Rs 244·56 crores (Rs 226·19 crores). Annual plan, 1988–89, Rs 260 crores.

ENERGY AND NATURAL RESOURCES

Electricity. In March 1987, 16,141 villages had electricity. Power generation is the first priority of the 7th five-year plan.

Water. An artificial confluence of the Sutlej and Beas rivers has been made, directing their united flow into Govind Sagar Lake.

Minerals. The state has rock salt, slate, gypsum, limestone, barytes, dolomite and pyrites.

Agriculture. Farming employs 76% of the people. Irrigated area is 26% of the area sown. Main crops are seed potatoes, wheat, maize, rice and fruits such as apples, peaches, apricots, nuts, pomegranates.

Production of foodgrains (1986) 1·32m. tonnes.

Livestock (1977 census): Buffaloes, 384,497; other cattle, 2,106,220; goats, 1,035,337.

Forestry. Himachal Pradesh forests cover 38·3% of the state and supply the largest quantities of coniferous timber in northern India. They are the main source of revenue of Pradesh. The forests also ensure the safety of the catchment areas of the Jumna, Sutlej, Beas, Ravi and Chenab rivers.

INDUSTRY. The main sources of employment are the forests and their related industries; there are factories making turpentine and rosin. The state also makes fertilizers, cement and TV sets. There is a foundry and a brewery. Other industries include salt production and handicrafts, including weaving.

COMMUNICATIONS

Roads. The national highway from Chandigarh runs through Shimla; other main highways from Shimla serve Kulu, Manali, Kangra, Chemba and Pathankot. The rest are minor roads. Pathankot is also on national highways from Punjab to Kashmir.

Railways. There is a line from Chandigarh to Shimla, and the Jammu-Delhi line runs through Pathankot. A Nangal-Talwara rail link has been approved by the central government (1985).

Aviation. The state has airports at Bhuntar near Kulu and at Jubbarhathi near Shimla.

JUSTICE. The state has its own High Court at Shimla.

EDUCATION. In 1987, 43·91% of the population was literate.

JAMMU AND KASHMIR

HISTORY. The state of Jammu and Kashmir, which had earlier been under Hindu rulers and Moslem sultans, became part of the Mogul Empire under Akbar from 1586. After a period of Afghan rule from 1756, it was annexed to the Sikh kingdom of the Punjab in 1819. In 1820 Ranjit Singh made over the territory of Jammu to Gulab Singh. After the decisive battle of Sobraon in 1846 Kashmir also was made over to Gulab Singh under the Treaty of Amritsar. British supremacy was recognized until the Indian Independence Act, 1947, when all states decided on accession to India or Pakistan. Kashmir asked for standstill agreements with both. Pakistan agreed, but India desired further discussion with the Government of Jammu and Kashmir State. In the meantime the state became subject to armed attack from the territory of Pakistan and the Maharajah acceded to India on 26 Oct. 1947, by signing the Instrument of Accession. India approached the UN in Jan. 1948; India-Pakistan conflict ended by ceasefire in Jan. 1949. Further conflict in 1965 was followed by the Tashkent Declaration on Jan. 1966. Following further hostilities between India and Pakistan a ceasefire came into effect on 17 Dec. 1971, followed by the Simla Agreement in July 1972, whereby a new line of control was delineated bilaterally through negotiations between India and Pakistan and came into force on 17 Dec. 1972.

AREA AND POPULATION. The state is in the extreme north and is bounded north by China, east by Tibet, south by Himachal Pradesh and Punjab and west by Pakistan. The area is 222,236 sq. km, of which about 78,932 sq. km is occupied by Pakistan and 42,735 sq. km by China; the population of the territory on the Indian side of the line, 1981 census, was 5,981,600. Growth rate, 1971–81, 29·57%. The official language is Urdu; other commonly spoken languages are Kashmiri (3·1m. speakers at 1981 census), Hindi (1m.), Dogri, Balti, Ladakhi and Punjabi.

CONSTITUTION AND GOVERNMENT. The Maharajah's son, Yuvraj Karan Singh, took over as Regent in 1950 and, on the ending of hereditary rule (17 Oct. 1952), was sworn in as Sadar-i-Riyasat. On his father's death (26 April 1961) Yuvraj Karan Singh was recognized as Maharajah by the Indian Government; he decided not to use the title while he was elected head of state.

The permanent Constitution of the state came into force in part on 17 Nov. 1956 and fully on 26 Jan. 1957. There is a bicameral legislature; the Legislative Council has 36 members and the Legislative Assembly has 76. Since the 1967 elections the 6 representatives of Jammu and Kashmir in the central House of the People are directly elected; there are 4 representatives in the Council of States. After a period of President's rule, a National Conference–Indira Congress coalition government was formed in March 1987.

Kashmir Province has 8 districts and Jammu Province has 6 districts. Srinagar (population, 1981, 586,038) is the summer and Jammu (206,135) the winter capital.

Governor: Jag Mohan.
Chief Minister: Farooq Abdullah.

BUDGET. Total planning expenditure for 1987–88 is Rs 375 crores.

ENERGY AND NATURAL RESOURCES

Electricity. Installed capacity (1986–87) 208·93 mw.; 5,468 villages had electricity.

Minerals. Minerals include coal, bauxite and gypsum.

Agriculture. About 80% of the population are supported by agriculture. Rice, wheat and maize are the major cereals. The total area under food crops (1983-84) was estimated at 860,900 hectares. Total foodgrains produced, 1985–86, 1·3m. tonnes. Fruit is important; production, 1985–86, 800,000 tonnes; exports, Rs 2,000m.

The Agrarian Reforms Act came into force in July 1978; the Debtors Relief Act and the Restriction of Mortgage Properties Act also alleviate rural distress. The redistribution of land to cultivators is continuing.

Livestock (1982): Cattle, 2,325,200; buffaloes, 5,631,000; goats, 1,003,900; sheep, 1,908,700; horses, 973,000, and poultry, 2,406,760.

Forestry. Forests cover about 20,891·89 sq. km., forming an important source of revenue, besides providing employment to a large section of the population. About 20,174 sq. km of forests yield valuable timber; state income in 1985–86 was Rs 477m.

INDUSTRY. There are 2 central public sector industries and 30 medium-scale (latter employing 6,468 in 1984). The largest industrial complex is the Bari Brahmara estate in Jammu which covers 320 acres and accommodates diverse manufacturing, as does the Khanmuh estate. The Sopore industrial area in Kashmir Division is intended for industries based on horticulture. There are 19,000 small units (1985–86) employing 86,713. The main traditional handicraft industries are silk spinning, wood-carving, papier-maché and carpet-weaving. Value of total industrial production, 1983–84, Rs 1,573m.

COMMUNICATIONS

Roads. Kashmir is linked with the rest of India by the motorable Jammu-Pathankot road. The Jawahar Tunnel, through the Banihal mountain, connects Srinagar and Jammu, and maintains road communication with the Kashmir Valley during the winter months. In 1983 there were 11,863 km of roads.

There were 52,930 motor vehicles in 1983–84.

Railways. Kashmir is linked with the Indian railway system by the line between Jammu and Pathankot; route km of railways in the state, 1985–86, 77 km.

Aviation. Major airports, with daily service from Delhi, are at Srinagar and Jammu. There is a third airport at Leh. Srinagar airport is being developed as an international airport.

Post. There were 1,290 post offices in 1980, 82 telephone exchanges and approximately 12,120 private telephones.

JUSTICE, RELIGION, EDUCATION AND WELFARE

Justice. The High Court, at Srinagar and Jammu, has a Chief Justice and 4 puisne judges.

Religion. The majority of the population, except in Jammu, are Moslems. At the 1981 census Moslems numbered 3,843,451; Hindus, 1,930,448; Sikhs, 133,675; Buddhists, 69,706; Christians, 8,481; Jains, 1,576.

Education. The proportion of literates was 27% in 1981. Education is free. There were (1984–85) 909 secondary schools, 2,113 middle and 7,646 primary schools; total, 739,000 pupils. Jammu University (1969) has 3 constituent and 11 affiliated colleges, with 8,118 students (1984–85); Kashmir University (1948) has 6 constituent, 12 affiliated and 6 oriental institutions (11,900 students); the third university is Sher-E-Kashmir University of Agricultural Sciences and Technology. There are 2 medical colleges, an engineering college, 1 agricultural college, 2 polytechnics, 12 professional colleges, 8 oriental colleges and an Ayurvedic college.

Health. In 1983–84 there were 45 hospitals, 93 primary health centres and 425 units, 679 clinics and dispensaries, and 483 other units. There were 2,036 doctors. There is a National Institute of Medical Sciences.

Bamzai, P. N. K., *A History of Kashmir.* Delhi, 1962
Gupta, S., Kashmir: *A Study in IndiaPakistan Relations.* London, 1967

KARNATAKA

HISTORY. The state of Karnataka, constituted as Mysore under the States Reorganization Act, 1956, brought together the Kannada-speaking people distributed in 5 states, and consisted of the territories of the old states of Mysore and Coorg, the Bijapur, Kanara and Dharwar districts and the Belgaum district (except one taluk) in former Bombay, the major portions of the Gulbarga, Raichur and Bidar districts in former Hyderabad, and South Kanara district (apart from the Kasaragod taluk) and the Kollegal taluk of the Coimbatore district in Madras. The state was renamed Karnataka in 1973.

AREA AND POPULATION. The state is in south India and is bounded north by Maharashtra, east by Andhra Pradesh, south by Tamil Nadu and Kerala, west by the Indian ocean and north-east by Goa. The area of the state is 191,791 sq. km, and its population (1981 census), 37,135,714, an increase of 26·43% since 1971. Density, 194 per sq. km. Kannada is the language of administration and is spoken by about 66% of the people. Other languages include Telugu (8·17%), Urdu (9%), Marathi (4·5%), Tamil (3·6%), Tulu and Konkani. Principal cities, *see* p. 625.

CONSTITUTION AND GOVERNMENT. Karnataka has a bicameral legislature. The Legislative Council has 63 members. The Legislative Assembly consists of 225 elected members. After elections in March 1985 the Janata party formed a government.

The state has 20 districts (of which Bangalore Rural is one) in 4 divisions: Bangalore, Mysore, Belgaum and Gulbarga. The capital is Bangalore.

Governor: P. Venkatasubiah.
Chief Minister: Ramakrishna Hegde.

BUDGET. Budget estimates for 1986–87 showed a deficit of Rs 38·89 crores; for 1987–88, Rs 60·96 crores. Annual plan, 1988–89, Rs 900 crores.

ENERGY AND NATURAL RESOURCES

Electricity. In 1983 the state's installed capacity was 2,009·8 mw. Electricity generated, 1986–87, 8,125m. kwh.

Water. About 1·69m. hectares were irrigated in 1985.

Minerals. Karnataka is an important source of gold and silver. The estimated reserves of high grade iron ore are 5,000m. tonnes. These reserves are found mainly in the Chitradurga belt. The National Mineral Development Corporation of India has indicated total reserves of nearly 1,000m. tonnes of magnesite and iron ore (with an iron content ranging from 25 to 40) which have been found in Kudremukh Ganga-Mula region in Chickmagalur District. The estimated reserves of manganese are over 275m. tonnes.

Limestone is found in many regions; deposits (1986) are about 4,248m. tonnes.

Karnataka is the largest producer of chromite. It is one of the only two states of India producing magnesite. The other minerals of industrial importance are corundum and garnet.

Agriculture. Agriculture forms the main occupation of more than three-quarters of the population. Physically, Karnataka divides itself into four regions–the coastal region, the southern and northern 'maidan' or plain country, comprising roughly the districts of Bangalore, Tumkur, Chitaldrug, Kolar, Bellary, Mandya and Mysore, and the 'malnad' or hill country, comprising the districts of Chickmagalur, Hassan and Shimoga. Rainfall is heavy in the 'malnad' tracts, and in this area there is dense forest. The greater part of the 'maidan' country is cultivated. Coorg district is essentially agricultural.

The main food crops are rice and jowar, and ragi which is also about 30% of the national crop. Total foodgrains production (1985–86), 5·74m. tonnes of which rice, 1·87m. tonnes. Sugar, groundnut, castor-seed, safflower, mulberry silk and cotton are important cash crops. The state grows about 70% of the national coffee crop.

Production, 1985–86 (1,000 tonnes): Sugar-cane, 12,574; tobacco (1983–84), 158·2; chillies, 131·3; ground nuts, 615; castor seed, 134; cotton, 503 bales (170 kg).

Livestock (1986): Buffaloes, 3,647,967; other cattle, 11,300,223; sheep, 4,791,650; goats, 4,546,928.

Forestry. Total forest in the state (1984–85) is 3,047,102 acres, producing sandal wood, bamboo and other timbers, and ivory.

INDUSTRY. The Vishweswaraya Iron and Steel Works is situated at Bhadravati, while at Bangalore are national undertakings for the manufacture of aircraft, machine tools, light engineering and electronics goods. Other industries include textiles, vehicle manufacture, cement, chemicals, sugar, paper, porcelain and soap. In addition, much of the world's sandalwood is processed, the oil being one of the most valuable productions of the state. Sericulture is a more important cottage industry giving employment, directly or indirectly, to about 2·7m. persons; production of raw silk, 1985–86, 4,300 tonnes, over two-thirds of national production.

COMMUNICATIONS

Roads. In 1985–86 the state had 112,610 km of roads. There were (31 March 1984) 578,352 motor vehicles.

Railways. In 1985–86 there were 3,024 km of railway (including 154 km of narrow gauge) in the state.

Aviation. There are airports at Bangalore, Mangalore, Bellary and Belgaum, with regular scheduled services to Bombay, Calcutta, Delhi and Madras.

Shipping. Mangalore is a deep-water port for the export of mineral ores. Karwar is being developed as an intermediate port.

JUSTICE, RELIGION AND EDUCATION

Justice. The seat of the High Court is at Bangalore. It has a Chief Justice and 11 puisne judges.

Religion. At the 1981 census there were 31,906,793 Hindus; 4,104,616 Moslems; 764,449 Christians; 297,974 Jains; 42,147 Buddhists; 6,401 Sikhs.

Education. The number of literates, according to the 1981 census, was 38·5m. In 1985–86 the state had 37,271 primary schools, 4,777 high schools, 636 schools for professional and technical education and 128 polytechnic and engineering schools. Education is free up to pre-university level.

Universities: Mysore (1916); Karnatak (1950) at Dharwar; University of Agricultural Sciences (1964) at Hebbal, Bangalore; Gulbarga, and Mangalore. Mysore has 6 university and 117 affiliated colleges (1983–84); Karnatak, 5 and 115; Bangalore, 126 affiliated; Hebbal, 8 constituent colleges.

The Indian Institute of Science, Bangalore, is unaffiliated; it conducts diploma courses in engineering, metallurgy and technology. There are 417 other colleges, including medical, law and commercial.

Learmouth, A. T. A., and Bhat, L. T., *Mysore State.* 2 vols. London, 1961–62

KERALA

HISTORY. The state of Kerala, created under the States Reorganization Act, 1956, consists of the previous state of Travancore-Cochin, except for 4 taluks of the Trivandrum district and a part of the Shencottah taluk of Quilon district. It took over the Malabar district (apart from the Laccadive and Minicoy Islands) and the Kasaragod taluk of South Kanara (apart from the Amindivi Islands) from Madras State.

AREA AND POPULATION. Kerala is in south India and is bounded north by Karnataka, east and south-east by Tamil Nadu, south-west and west by the Indian ocean. The state has an area of 38,863 sq. km. The 1981 census showed a population of 25,453,680; density of population was 655 per sq. km (highest of any state). Growth rate, 1971–81, 19%. Population of principal cities, see p. 625.

Languages spoken in the state are Malayalam, Tamil and Kannada.

The physical features of the land fall into three well-marked divisions: (1) the hilly tracts undulating from the Western Ghats in the east and marked by long spurs, extensive ravines and dense forests; (2) the cultivated plains intersected by numerous rivers and streams; and (3) the coastal belt with dense coconut plantations and rice fields.

CONSTITUTION AND GOVERNMENT. The state has a unicameral legislature of 140 members including the Speaker. After the elections of March 1987 the Indian National (I) Congress Party and allies held 60 seats, the Left Front (CPI, CPI (M) and allies), 76.

The state has 14 districts. The capital is Trivandrum.

Governor: R. Dulari Sinha.
Chief Minister: K. Karunakaran.

BUDGET. Revised budget estimates for 1985–86 showed total revenue receipts of Rs 1,156·30 crores, expenditure Rs 1,235·42 crores. Annual Plan expenditure, Rs 369 crores.

ENERGY AND NATURAL RESOURCES

Electricity. Installed capacity (1983), 1,011·5 mw.; energy generated in 1982–83 was 4,487·7m. kw. Stage I of the Idukki hydro-electric plant has a capacity of 390 mw, the Sabarigiri scheme 300mw.

Minerals. Next to Bihar, Kerala possesses the widest variety of economic mineral resources among the Indian States. The beach sands of Kerala contain monazite, ilmenite, rutile, zircon, sillimanite, etc. There are extensive whiteclay deposits; other minerals of commercial importance include mica, graphite, limestone, quartz sand and lignite. Iron ore has been found at Kozhikode (Calicut). Value of mineral production, 1983–84, Rs 2·45m.

Agriculture. The chief agricultural products are rice, tapioca, coconut, arecanut, cashewnut, oilseeds, pepper, sugar-cane, rubber, tea, coffee and cardamom. About 98% of Indian black pepper and about 95% of Indian rubber is produced in Kerala. Area and production of principal crops, 1983–84 (in 1,000 hectares and 1,000 tonnes): Rice, 740, 1,208; black pepper, 106, 25; arecanut, 60, 8,318 (million nuts); bananas and other plantains, 49·3, 293·8; cashewnuts, 142, 77; coconuts, 682·5, 2,602 (million nuts); tea, 36·1, 48·7; coffee, 57·9, 21·7; rubber, 271, 162; tapioca, 233, 3,924; cardamom, 54·5, 1·9.

Livestock (1982, provisional); Buffaloes, 7·4m.; other cattle, 3m.; goats, 2m. In 1982–83 milk production was 1m. tonnes. Egg production, 1,018m.

Forestry. About 24% of the area is comprised of forests, including teak, sandal wood, ebony and blackwood and varieties of softwood. Net forest revenue, 1983–84, Rs 40·53 crores, from timber, bamboos, reeds and ivory.

Fisheries. Fishing is a flourishing industry; the catch in 1983 was about 412,000 tonnes. Fish exports, 1983–84, 32,840 tonnes valued at Rs 140·8 crores. A shrimp-culture project was approved in 1986, investment Rs 134·7 crores.

INDUSTRIES. Most of the major industrial concerns are either owned or sponsored by the Government. Among the privately owned factories are the numerous cashew and coir factories. Other important factory industries are rubber, tea, tiles, oil, textiles, ceramics, fertilizers and chemicals, zinc-smelting, sugar, cement, rayon, glass, matches, pencils, monazite, ilmenite, titanium oxide, rare earths, aluminium, electrical goods, paper, shark-liver oil, etc.

The number of factories registered under the Factories Act 1948 on 31 Dec. 1984 was 10,000, with daily average employment of 286,000.

Among the cottage industries, coir-spinning and handloom-weaving are the most important, forming the means of livelihood of a large section of the people. Other industries are the village oil industry, ivory carving, furniture-making, bell metal, brass and copper ware, leather goods, screw-pines, mat-making, rattan work, bee-keeping, pottery, etc. These have been organized on a co-operative basis.

COMMUNICATIONS

Roads. In 1983–84 there were 101,200 km of roads in the state; national highways, 839 km. There were 277,000 motor vehicles in 1983–84.

Railways. There is a coastal line from Mangalore (Karnataka) which serves Cannanore, Mahe, Kozhikode (Calicut), Ernakulam (for Cochin), Quilon and Trivandrum, and connects them with main towns in Tamil Nadu. In 1982–83 there were 806 km broad gauge and 113 km metre gauge lines.

Aviation. There are airports at Cochin and Trivandrum with regular scheduled services to Bombay and Madras; international flights leave Trivandrum for Sri Lanka.

Shipping. Port Cochin, administered by the central government, is one of India's major ports; in 1983 it became the out-port for the Inland Container Depot at Coimbatore (Tamil Nadu). There are 13 other ports and harbours.

JUSTICE, RELIGION AND EDUCATION

Justice. The High Court at Ernakulam has a Chief Justice and 14 puisne judges and 3 additional judges.

Religion. The majority are Hindus; other important faiths are Christianity and Islam. There are also some Jains.

Education. Kerala is the most literate Indian State with 17m. literates at the 1981 census (70%). Education is free up to the age of 14.

In 1983–84 there was a total school enrolment of 5·66m. students. There were 6,842 lower primary schools 2,822 upper primary schools and 2,331 high schools.

Kerala University (established 1937) at Trivandrum, is affiliating and teaching; in 1982–83 it had 99 affiliated arts and science colleges. The University of Cochin is federal, and for post-graduate studies only. The University of Calicut (established 1968) is teaching and affiliating and has 69 affiliated colleges. Kerala Agricultural University (established 1971) has 3 constituent colleges. Gandhiji University at Kottayam was established in 1983.

MADHYA PRADESH

HISTORY. Under the provisions of the States Reorganization Act, 1956, the State of Madhya Pradesh was formed on 1 Nov. 1956. It consists of the 17 Hindi districts of the previous state of that name, the former state of Madhya Bharat (except the Sunel enclave of Mandsaur district), the former state of Bhopal and Vindhya Pradesh and the Sironj subdivision of Kotah district, which was an enclave of Rajasthan in Madhya Pradesh.

For information on the former states, *see* THE STATESMAN'S YEAR-BOOK, 1958, pp. 180–84.

AREA AND POPULATION. The state is in central India and is bounded north by Rajasthan and Uttar Pradesh, east by Bihar and Orissa, south by Andhra Pradesh and Maharashtra, west by Gujarat. Madhya Pradesh is the largest Indian state in size, with an area of 443,446 sq. km. In respect of population it ranks sixth. Population (1981 census), 52,138,467, an increase of 25·15% since 1971. Density, 118 per sq. km.

Cities with over 250,000 population, *see* p. 625. Other large cities (1981): Sagar, 207,401; Bilaspur, 186,885; Ratlam, 156,490; Burhanpur, 141,142; Mudwari-Katni, 125,096; Khandwa, 114,463; Rewa, 100,519.

The number of persons speaking each of the more prevalent languages (1981 census) were: Hindi, 43,870,242; Urdu, 1,131,288; Marathi, 1,184,128; Gujarati, 581,084.

CONSTITUTION AND GOVERNMENT. Madhya Pradesh is one of the 9 states for which the Constitution provides a bicameral legislature, but the Vidhan

Parishad or Upper House (to consist of 90 members) has yet to be formed. The Vidhan Sabha or Lower House has 320 elected members. Following the election of March 1985, a Congress government was returned, with 250 out of 350 seats.

For administrative purposes the state has been split into 11 divisions with a Commissioner at the head of each; the headquarters of these are located at Bhopal, Bilaspur, Gwalior (2), Hoshangabad, Indore, Jabalpur, Raipur, Rewa, Sagar and Ujjain. There are 45 districts.

The seat of government is at Bhopal.

Governor: Prof. K. M. Chandy.
Chief Minister: Arjun Singh.

BUDGET. Budget estimates for 1985–86 showed total revenue of Rs 23,627m. and expenditure of Rs 22,800m.

ENERGY AND NATURAL RESOURCES

Electricity. Madhya Pradesh is rich in low-grade coal suitable for power generation, and also has immense potential hydro-electric energy. Power generated, 9,871m. kwh. in 1984–85. The thermal power stations are at Korba in Bilaspur district, Amarkantak in Shahdol district and Satpura in Betul district; new stations are being built. The only hydro-electric power station is at Gandhi Sagar lake in Mandsaur district; this, with a maximum water surface of 165 sq. miles, is the biggest man-made lake in Asia.

Water. Major irrigation projects include the Chambal Valley scheme (started in 1952 with Rajasthan), the Tawa project in Hoshangabad district, the Barna and Hasdeo schemes, the Mahanadi canal system and schemes in the Narmada valley at Bargi and Narmadasagar. Total irrigation potential in 1983, 10m. hectares, of which 3m. had been achieved.

Minerals. The state has extensive mineral deposits including coal (35% of national deposits), iron ore (30%) and manganese (50%), bauxite (44%), ochre, sillimanite, limestone, dolomite, rock phosphate, copper, lead, tin, fluorite, barytes, china clay and fireclay, corundum, gold, diamonds, pyrophyllite and diaspore, lepidolite, asbestos, vermiculite, mica, glass sand, quartz, felspars, bentonite and building stone. New and very large reserves of copper were found in the Malanjkhand area in 1986.

In 1985 the output of major minerals was (in tonnes): Coal, 41·3m.; limestone, 11·7m.; dolomite, 695,000; diamonds, 16,324 carats; bauxite, 641,000; iron ore, 8·7m.; manganese ore, 262,000. Value of production, 1985, Rs 8,907m.

Agriculture. Agriculture is the mainstay of the state's economy and 80% of the people are rural. Over 42% of the land area is cultivable, of which 14% is irrigated. The Malwa region abounds in rich black cotton soil, the low-lying areas of Gwalior, Bundelkhand and Baghelkhand and the Chhatisgarh plains have a lighter sandy soil, while the Narmada valley is formed of deep rich alluvial deposits. Production of principal crops, 1985–86 (in tonnes): Foodgrains, 15·5m. of which rice, 5·76m.; sugar-cane 1,519,000; oilseeds, 1,310,600, and cotton, 141,300.

Livestock (1985–86): Buffaloes, 6,861,000; other cattle, 26,503,000; sheep, 1,120,000; goats, 7,636,000; horses and ponies, 112,000.

Forestry. In 1982 155,411 sq. km, or about 35% of the state's area was covered by forests. The forests are chiefly of sal, saja, bija, bamboo and teak. They are the chief source in India of best-quality teak; they also provide firewood for about 60% of domestic fuel needs, and form valuable watershed protection. Forest revenue, 1984–85, Rs 2,730m.

INDUSTRY. The major industries are the steel plant at Bhilai, Bharat Heavy Electricals at Bhopal, the aluminium plant at Korba, the security paper mills at Hoshangabad, the Bank Note Press at Dewas, the newsprint mill at Nepanagar and alkaloid factory at Neemuch, cement factories, vehicle factory, ordnance factory, and gun carriage factory. There are also 23 textile mills, 7 of them nationalized.

The Bhilai steel plant near Durg is one of the 6 major steel mills. A power station at Korba (Bilaspur) with a capacity of 420 mw serves Bhilai, the aluminium plant and the Korba coalfield.

The heavy electricals factory was set up by the Government of India at Bhopal during the second-plan period. This is India's first heavy electrical equipment factory and also one of the largest of its type in Asia. It makes a variety of highly complicated equipment required for generation, transmission, distribution and utilization of electric power.

Other industries include cement, sugar, straw board, paper, vegetable oil, refractories, potteries, textile machinery, steel casting and rerolling, industrial gases, synthetic fibres, drugs, biscuit manufacturing, engineering, tools, rayon and art silk. The number of heavy and medium industries in the state is 193, with 181 ancillary industries; the number of small-scale industries in production is 77,360. Thirty-nine out of 45 districts in the state are categorized as industrially backward districts.

The main industrial development agencies are Madhya Pradesh Financial Corporation, Madhya Pradesh Audyogik Vikas Nigam Ltd, Madhya Pradesh State Industries Corporation, Madhya Pradesh Laghu Udyog Nigam, Madhya Pradesh State Textile Corporation, Madhya Pradesh Handicrafts Board, Khadi and Village Industries Board and Madhya Pradesh State Mining Corporation.

The state is known for its traditional village and home crafts such as handloom weaving, best developed at Chanderi and Maheshwar, toys, pottery, lacework, woodwork, zari work, leather work and metal utensils. The ancillary industries of dyeing, calico printing and bleaching are centred in areas of textile production.

COMMUNICATIONS

Roads. Total length of roads in 1982–83 was 113,176 km, of which 58,230 km were surfaced. In 1983–84 there were 395,727 motor vehicles.

Railways. Bhopal, Bilaspur, Katni, Khandwar and Ratlam are important junctions for the central and northern networks. Route km of railways (1985–86), 5,779 km.

Aviation. There are airports at Bhopal, Indore, Jabalpur, Khajuraho and Raipur with regular scheduled services to Bombay, Calcutta and Delhi.

JUSTICE, RELIGION AND EDUCATION

Justice. The High Court of Judicature at Jabalpur has a Chief Justice and 21 puisne judges.

Religion. At the 1981 census Hindus numbered 48,504,575; Moslems, 2,501,919; Christians, 351,972; Buddhists, 75,312; Sikhs, 143,020, Jains, 444,960.

Education. The 1981 census showed 14·5m. people to be literate. Education is free for children aged up to 14.

In 1984–85 there were 377 higher educational institutions. Primary schools had 6·1m. pupils and higher secondary schools, 1,035,005 pupils.

There are 11 universities in Madhya Pradesh: Dr. Hari Singh Gour University (established 1946), at Sagar, had 73 affiliated colleges and 40,000 students in 1984–85; Rani Durgavati University (1957) had 28 affiliated colleges and 8,539 students; Vikram University (1957), at Ujjain, had 35 affiliated and 29 constituent colleges and 34,053 students; Indira Kala Sangeet Vishwavidyalaya (1956), at Khairagarh, had 33 affiliated colleges and 6,720 students on roll (this university teaches music and fine arts); Devi Ahilya University (1964) had 25 affiliated colleges and 23,884 students; Jiwagi University (1963), at Gwalior, had 47 affiliated colleges and 41,358 students; Jawaharlal Nehru Krishi University (1964), at Jabalpur, had 10 constituent colleges and 2,871 students in 1983–84; Ravishankar University (1964), at Raipur, had 61 affiliated colleges. In 1984–85 there were 338 degree-granting colleges, 20 teacher-training colleges, and 39 professional colleges, 12 polytechnics and 51 technical-industrial arts and craft schools.

MAHARASHTRA

HISTORY. Under the States Reorganization Act, 1956, Bombay State was formed by merging the states of Kutch and Saurashtra and the Marathi-speaking areas of Hyderabad (commonly known as Marathwada) and Madhya Pradesh (also called Vidarbha) in the old state of Bombay, after the transfer from that state of the Kannada-speaking areas of the Belgaum, Bijapur, Kanara and Dharwar districts which were added to the state of Mysore, and the Abu Road taluka of Banaskantha district, which went to the state of Rajasthan.

By the Bombay Reorganization Act, 1960, which came into force 1 May 1960, 17 districts (predominantly Gujarati-speaking) in the north and west of Bombay State became the new state of Gujarat, and the remainder was renamed Maharashtra.

The state of Maharashtra consists of the following districts of the former Bombay State: Ahmednagar, Akola, Amravati, Aurangabad, Bhandara, Bhir, Buldana, Chanda, Dhulia (West Khandesh), Greater Bombay, Jalgaon (East Khandesh), Kolaba, Kolhapur, Nagpur, Nanded, Nasik, Osmanabad, Parbhani, Pune, Ratnagiri, Sangli, Satara, Sholapur, Thana, Wardha, Yeotmal; certain portions of Thana and Dhulia districts have become part of Gujarat.

AREA AND POPULATION. Maharashtra is in central India and is bounded north and east by Madhya Pradesh, south by Andhra Pradesh, Karnataka and Goa, west by the Indian ocean and north-west by Daman and Gujarat. The state has an area of 307,762 sq. km. The population at the 1981 census (revised) was 62,784,174 (an increase of 24.36% since 1971), of whom about 30m. were Marathi-speaking. Density, 204 per sq. km. The area of Greater Bombay was 603 sq. km. and its population 8,227,000. For other principal cities, *see* p. 625.

CONSTITUTION AND GOVERNMENT. Maharashtra has a bicameral legislature. The Legislative Council has 78 members. The Legislative Assembly has 288 elected members and 1 member nominated by the Governor to represent the Anglo-Indian community. Following the election of March 1985 Congress (I) held 159 seats; Congress (U), 54; Janata, 21; B.J.P., 16; P.W.P., 13; others, 25.

The Council of Ministers consists of the Chief Minister, 7 other Ministers, and 12 Ministers of State.

The capital is Bombay.

Governor: K. Brahmananda Reddy
Chief Minister: S. B. Chavan.

BUDGET. Budget estimates, 1986–87, show a deficit of Rs 341·63 crores.

ENERGY AND NATURAL RESOURCES

Electricity. Installed capacity, 31 March 1986, 6,940 mw. (5,477 mw. thermal, 1,303 mw. hydro-electricity and 160 mw. nuclear).

Minerals. Value of main mineral production, 1985, Rs 215 crores. The state has coal, silica, sand, dolomite, kyanite, sillimanite, limestone, iron ore, manganese, bauxite.

Agriculture. About 12·5% of the cropped area is irrigated. In 1984–86 there was severe drought in 18 of the state's 30 districts. The monsoon-season harvest failed, and the winter-season harvest was poor.

In normal seasons the main food crops are rice, wheat, jowar, bajri and pulses. Main cash crops: cotton, sugar-cane, groundnuts.

Livestock (1978 census): Buffaloes, 3,898,716; other cattle, 6,916,355; sheep, 2,636,001; goats, 7,562,925; horses and ponies, 48,817; poultry, 18,750,817.

Forestry. Forests occupy 20·8% of the state.

INDUSTRY. Industry is concentrated mainly in Bombay, Pune and Thana. The main groups are chemicals and products, textiles, electrical and non-electrical machinery, petroleum and products, and food products. The state industrial development corporation had invested Rs 5,000 crores in 4,400 industrial units by 1986.

COMMUNICATIONS

Roads. On 31 March 1985 there were 151,724 km of roads, of which 88,117 km were surfaced. There were 1,391,641 motor vehicles on 31 March 1985, of which 441,084 were in Greater Bombay. Passenger and freight transport has been nationalized.

Railways. The total length of railway on 31 March 1984 was 5,297 km; 60% was broad gauge, 19% metre gauge and 21% narrow gauge. The main junctions and termini are Bombay, Manmad, Akola, Nagpur, Pune and Sholapur.

Aviation. The main airport is Bombay, which has national and international flights. Nagpur airport is on the route from Bombay to Calcutta and there are also airports at Pune and Aurangabad.

Shipping. Maharashtra has a coastline of 720 km. Bombay is the major port, and there are 48 minor ports.

JUSTICE, RELIGION AND EDUCATION

Justice. The High Court has a Chief Justice and 37 judges. The seat of the High Court is Bombay, but it has benches at Nagpur, Aurangabad and Panaji (Goa).

Religion. At the 1981 census Hindus numbered 51,109,457; Moslems, 5,805,785; Buddhists, 3,946,149; Christians, 795,464; Jains, 939,392; Sikhs, 107,255. Other religions, 155,692; religion not stated, 1,394.

Education. The number of literates, according to the 1981 census, was 29·6m.
    The total number of recognized institutions in 1984–85 was 62,452, with 14,288,000 students. Higher and secondary schools numbered 7,683 with 4,263,000 pupils; primary schools, 53,420, with 9,235,000 pupils; pre-primary schools, 701 with 78,000.
    Bombay University, founded in 1857, is mainly an affiliating university. It has 145 colleges with a total (1984–85) of 215,692 students. Colleges in Goa can affiliate to Bombay University. Nagpur University (1923) is both teaching and affiliating. It has 94 colleges with 81,872 students. Pune University, founded in 1948, is teaching and affiliating; it has 165 colleges and 169,859 students. The SNDT Women's University had 10 colleges with a total of 10,083 students. Marathwada University, Aurangabad, was founded in 1958 as a teaching and affiliating body to control colleges in the Marathwada or Marathi-speaking area, previously under Osmania University; it has 115 colleges and 81,691 students. Shiwaji University, Kolhapur, was established in 1963 to control affiliated colleges previously under Pune University. It has 127 colleges and 100,055 students. Amravarti University has 81 colleges and 57,633 students.

Statistical Information: The Director of Publicity, Sachivalaya, Bombay.
Tindall, G., *City of Gold*, London, 1982

MANIPUR

HISTORY. Formerly a state under the political control of the Government of India, Manipur, on 15 Aug. 1947, entered into interim arrangements with the Indian Union and the political agency was abolished. The administration was taken over by the Government of India on 15 Oct. 1949 under a merger agreement, and it is centrally administered by the Government of India through a Chief Commissioner. In 1950–51 an Advisory form of Government was introduced. In 1957 this was replaced by a Territorial Council of 30 elected and 2 nominated members. Later in 1963 a Legislative Assembly of 30 elected and 3 nominated members was established under the Government of Union Territories Act 1963. Because of the unstable party position in the Assembly, it had to be dissolved on 16 Oct. 1969 and President's Rule introduced. The status of the administrator was raised from Chief Commissioner to Lieut.-Governor with effect from 19 Dec. 1969. On the 21 Jan. 1972 Manipur became a state and the status of the administrator was changed from Lieut.-Governor to Governor.

AREA AND POPULATION. The state is in north-east India and is bounded north by Nagaland, east by Burma, south by Burma and Mizoram, and west by Assam. Manipur has an area of 22,356 sq. km and a population (1981) of 1,433,691. Density, 64 per sq. km. Growth rate, 1971–81, 33·65%. The valley, which is about 1,813 sq. km, is 2,600 ft above sea-level. The hills rise in places to nearly 10,000 ft, but are mostly about 5,000–6,000 ft. The average annual rainfall is 65 in. The hill areas are inhabited by various hill tribes who constitute about one-third of the total population of the state. There are about 40 tribes and sub-tribes falling into two main groups of Nagas and Kukis. Manipuri and English are the official languages. A large number of dialects are spoken, while Hindi is gradually becoming prevalent.

CONSTITUTION AND GOVERNMENT. With the attainment of state-hood, Manipur has a Legislative Assembly of 60 members, of which 19 are from reserved tribal constituencies. There are 6 districts. Capital, Imphal (population, 1981, 155,639). Presidential rule was imposed in Feb. 1981.

Governor: Gen. K. V. Krishna Rao.

BUDGET. Revised estimates for 1977–78 show revenue of Rs 4,247·82 lakhs and expenditure on revenue account of Rs 4,774·24 lakhs.

ENERGY AND NATURAL RESOURCES

Electricity. Installed capacity (1983) is 22 mw. from diesel generators. This has been augmented since 1981 by the North Eastern Regional Grid. In 1983 there were 488 villages with electricity.

Water. The main power, irrigation and flood-control schemes are the Loktak Lift Irrigation scheme (irrigation potential, 40,000 hectares of which (1983) 19,000 have been achieved); the Singda scheme (potential 4,000 hectares, and improved water supply for Imphal); the Thoubal scheme (potential 34,000 hectares, 7·5 mw. of electricity and 10 MGD of water supply), and four other large projects.

Agriculture. Rice is the principal crop; with wheat, maize and pulses. Total food-grains, 1982–83, 358,000 tonnes.

Agricultural work force, about 348,000. Only 210,000 hectares are cultivable, of which 186,000 are under paddy. Fruit and vegetables are important in the valley, including pineapple, oranges, bananas, mangoes, pears, peaches and plums. Soil erosion, produced by shifting cultivation, is being halted by terracing.

Forests. Forests occupy about 15,154 sq km. The main products are teak, jurjan, pine; there are also large areas of bamboo and cane, especially in the Jiri and Barak river drainage areas, yielding about 300,000 tonnes annually. Total revenue from forests, 1981–82, Rs 3·9m.

Fisheries. Landings in 1981–82, 3,450 tonnes.

INDUSTRY. Handloom weaving is a popular industry. Larger-scale industries include sugar, cement, starch and glucose. Sericulture produces about 45 tonnes of raw silk annually. Estimated non-agricultural work force, 240,000.

COMMUNICATIONS. A national highway from Kazirangar (Assam) runs through Imphal to the Burmese frontier. There are no railways, but the highway runs through Dimapur which has a rail-head, 215 km. from Imphal. There is an airport at Imphal with regular scheduled services to Guwahati and Calcutta.

EDUCATION AND HEALTH

Education. The 1981 census gave the number of literates as 600,000. In 1982–83 there were 2,821 primary schools, 459 middle schools, 301 high and higher schools and 23 colleges, as well as Manipur University.

Health. In 1977–78 there were 33 hospitals (including primary health centres) and 125 dispensaries (including primary health centres).

MEGHALAYA

HISTORY. The state was created under the Assam Reorganization (Meghalaya) Act 1969 and inaugurated on 2 April 1970. Its status was that of a state within the State of Assam until 21 Jan. 1972 when it became a fully independent state of the Union. It consists of the former Garo Hills district and United Khasi and Jaintia Hills district of Assam.

AREA AND POPULATION. Meghalaya is bounded north and east by Assam, south and west by Bangladesh. In 1981 (census figure) the area was 22,429 sq. km and the population 1,335,819. Density 59 per sq. km. Growth rate, 1971–81, 31·25%. The people are mainly of the Khasi, Jaintia and Garo tribes.

CONSTITUTION AND GOVERNMENT. Meghalaya has a unicameral legislature. The Legislative Assembly has 60 seats. Party position in summer 1984: Meghalaya Democratic Front, 37 (including 31 Congress I); opposition, 13.

There are 2 districts. The capital is Shillong (population, 1981, 109,244).

Governor: B. N. Singh.
Chief Minister: Purno A. Sangma.

BUDGET. Budget estimates for 1981–82 showed a deficit of Rs 6·6m. Annual Plan expenditure, 1988–89, Rs 130 crores.

ENERGY AND NATURAL RESOURCES

Electricity. Total installed capacity (1982–83) was 125·2 mw. 997 villages had electricity.

Minerals. The United Khasi and Jaintia Hills district produces coal, sillimanite (95% of India's total output), limestone, white clay and corundum. The state also has deposits of coal (estimated reserves 1,200m. tonnes), limestone (2,100m.), fire clay (100,000) and sandstone which are virtually untapped because of transport difficulties. Value of production, 1976, Rs 3·26m.

Agriculture. About 80% of the people depend on agriculture, and 27% of the cultivable area is irrigated. Principal crops are potatoes, fresh fruit and cotton. Production 1983–84 (in 1,000 tonnes): Foodgrains, 163; potatoes, 141; tapioca, 5; jute, 43,900 bales (of 180 kg). Annual production (in 1,000 tonnes, estimated) of pineapples, 70; oranges, 80; bananas, 35.

Forest products are the state's chief resources.

INDUSTRY. Apart from agriculture the main source of employment is the extraction and processing of minerals; there are also important timber processing mills. Meghalaya Industrial Development Corporation has set up industrial units. There is a new industrial area in Byrnihat, and two industrial estates in Shillong and Mendipathar.

COMMUNICATIONS. A national highway from Guwahati (Assam) runs through Dispur and Shillong. The state has no railways. Umroi airport (20 km from Shillong) connects the state with main air services.

JUSTICE. There is a High Court at Shillong which is common to Assam, Meghalaya, Nagaland, Manipur, Mizoram, Tripura and state of Arunachal Pradesh.

MIZORAM

HISTORY. On 21 Jan. 1972 the former Mizo Hills District of Assam was created a Union Territory. A long dispute between the Mizo National Front (originally Seperatist) and the central government was resolved in 1985. Mizoram became a state by the Constitution (53rd Amendment) and the State of Mizoram Acts, July 1986.

AREA AND POPULATION. Mizoram is one of the eastern-most Indian states, lying between Bangladesh and Burma, and having on its northern boundaries Tripura. Assam and Manipur. The area is about 21,090 sq. km and the population (1981 census) 487,774. Density, 23 per sq. km; growth rate 1971–81, 46·75%.

CONSTITUTION AND GOVERNMENT. Mizoram has a unicameral Legislative Assembly with 30 seats. Elections in February 1987 returned a Mizo National Front government.

The capital is Aizawl.

Governor: H. Saikia.
Chief Minister: Laldenga.

EMPLOYMENT. About 46% of the people are employed in agriculture, either on terraced holdings or in shifting cultivation. Industry is based on the extensive forests.

COMMUNICATIONS. Aizawl is connected by road and air with Silchar in Assam.

RELIGION. The mainly tribal population is 90% Christian.

NAGALAND

HISTORY. The territory was constituted by the Union Government in Sept. 1962. It comprises the former Naga Hills district of Assam and the former Tuensang Frontier division of the North-East Frontier Agency; these had been made a Centrally Administered Area in 1957, administered by the President through the Governor of Assam. In Jan. 1961 the area was renamed and given the status of a state of the Indian Union, which was officially inaugurated on 1 Dec. 1963.

For some years a section of the Naga leaders sought independence. Military operations from 1960 and the prospect of self-government within the Indian Union led to a general reconciliation, but rebel activity continued. A 2-month amnesty in mid 1963 had little effect. A 'ceasefire' in Sept. 1964 was followed by talks between a Government of India delegation and rebel leaders. The peace period was extended and the 'Revolutionary Government of Nagaland' (a breakaway group from the Naga Federal Government) was dissolved in 1973. Further talks with the Naga underground movement resulted in the Shillong Peace Agreement of Nov. 1975.

AREA AND POPULATION. The state is in the extreme north-east and is bounded west and north by Assam, east by Burma and south by Manipur. Nagaland has an area of 16,527 sq. km and a population (1981) census of 773,281.

Density 47 per sq. km. Growth rate, 1971–81, 49·73%. Towns include Kohima, Mokokchung, Tuensang and Dimapur. The chief tribes in numerical order are: Angami, Ao, Sema, Konyak, Chakhesang, Lotha, Phom, Khiamngan, Chang, Yimchunger, Zeliang-Kuki, Rengma and Sangtam.

CONSTITUTION AND GOVERNMENT. An Interim Body (Legislative Assembly) of 42 members elected by the Naga people and an Executive Council (Council of Ministers) of 5 members were formed in 1961, and continued until the State Assembly was elected in Jan. 1964. The initial strength of this Assembly was 46, with 8 cabinet ministers. Since 1974 there have been 60 members. The Governor has extraordinary powers, which include special responsibility for law and order. In Nov. 1987 a Congress (I) government was re-elected.

There are 10 cabinet ministers and 10 ministers of state.

The state has 7 districts (Kohima, Mon, Zunheboto, Wokha, Phek, Mokokchung and Tuensang). The capital is Kohima.

Governor: Gen. K. V. Krishna Rao.
Chief Minister: Hokishe Sema.

BUDGET. The budget (estimate) for 1984–85 is Rs 187·18 crores. Annual plan, 1988–89, Rs 110 crores.

ENERGY AND NATURAL RESOURCES

Electricity. Installed capacity (1984) 5·12 mw; 580 towns and villages (out of 814) had electricity in 1984.

Agriculture. More than 80% of the people derive their livelihood from agriculture. The Angamis, in Kohima district, practise a fixed agriculture in the shape of terraced slopes, and wet paddy cultivation in the lowlands. In the other two districts a traditional form of shifting cultivation (*jhumming*) still predominates, but some farmers have begun tea and coffee plantations and horticulture. About 66,120 hectares were under terrace cultivation and 44,810 under *jhumming* in 1982. Production of rice (1981) was 135,000 tonnes.

Forests covered 288,252 hectares in 1981.

INDUSTRY. There is a forest products factory at Tijit; a paper-mill (100 tonnes daily capacity) at Tuli, a distillery unit and a sugar-mill (1,200 tonnes daily capacity) at Dimapur. There are also over 1,000 small units.

COMMUNICATIONS. There is a national highway from Kaziranga (Assam) to Kohima and on to Manipur. There are state highways connecting Kohima with the district headquarters. There were 16,972 motor vehicles in 1983. Dimapur has a rail-head and a daily air service to Calcutta.

RELIGION AND EDUCATION

Religion. Christianity is the main religion; there are also Hindus, Moslems, and followers of indigenous faiths.

Education. The 1981 census records 300,000 literates, or 41·9%: 49·16% of men and 33·72% of women. In 1984 there were 3 government and 10 private colleges, 59 government and 50 private high schools, 173 government and 147 private middle schools and 1,224 primary schools, 1 polytechnic, 1 agricultural college, 2 law colleges. The North Eastern Hill University opened in 1978.

Aram, M., *Peace in Nagaland,* New Delhi, 1974

ORISSA

HISTORY. Orissa, ceded to the Mahrattas by Alivardi Khan in 1751, was conquered by the British in 1803. In 1803 a board of 2 commissioners was appointed to administer the province, but in 1805 it was designated the district of Cuttack and was placed in charge of a collector, judge and magistrate. In 1829 it was split up into 3 regulation districts of Cuttack, Balasore and Puri, and the non-regulation tributary states which were administered by their own chiefs under the ægis of the British Government. Angul, one of these tributary states, was annexed in 1847, and with the Khondmals, ceded in 1835 by the tributary chief of the Boudh state, constituted a separate non-regulation district. Sambalpur was transferred from the Central Provinces to Orissa in 1905. These districts formed an outlying tract of the Bengal Presidency till 1912, when they were transferred to Bihar, constituting one of its divisions under a commissioner. Orissa was constituted a separate province on 1 April 1936, some portions of the Central Provinces and Madras being transferred to the old Orissa division.

The rulers of 25 Orissa states surrendered all jurisdiction and authority to the Government of India on 1 Jan. 1948, on which date the Provincial Government took over the administration. The administration of 2 states, viz., Saraikella and Kharswan, was transferred to the Government of Bihar in May 1948. By an agreement with the Dominion Government, Mayurbhanj State was finally merged with the province on 1 Jan. 1949. By the States Merger (Governors' Provinces) Order, 1949, the states were completely merged with the state of Orissa on 19 Aug. 1949.

EVENTS. Serious flooding in Aug. 1982 caused the deaths of about 1,000 people.

AREA AND POPULATION. Orissa is in eastern India and is bounded north by Bihar, north-east by West Bengal, east by the Bay of Bengal, south by Andhra Pradesh and west by Madhya Pradesh. The area of the state is 155,707 sq. km, and its population (1981 census), 26,370,271, density 169 per sq. km. Growth rate, 1971–81, 20·17%. The largest cities are Cuttack (327,412 in 1981), Rourkela (322,610) and Bhubaneswar (219,211). The principal and official language is Oriya.

CONSTITUTION AND GOVERNMENT. The Legislative Assembly has 147 members. After the election in March 1985 a Congress government was returned.

The state consists of 13 districts.

The capital is Bhubaneswar (18 miles south of Cuttack).

Governor: B. N. Pandey.
Chief Minister: J. B. Patnaik.

BUDGET. Budget estimates, 1980–81 showed total revenue of Rs 1,257·3 crores and expenditure of Rs 1,235·6 crores (capital and revenue accounts).

ENERGY AND NATURAL RESOURCES

Electricity. The Hirakud Dam Project on the river Mahanadi (started 1949) irrigates 628,000 acres and has a scheduled capacity of 270,000 kw. The dam (the largest earth dam in the world) was completed in 1957. Hydro-electric power is now serving a large part of the state. Hydro-electric installed capacity (1985) 664 mw. (Balimela Hydel project, 360 mw.), Talcher thermal plant, 470 mw. Under construction, 1985, were Rengali Hydel project (100 mw.) and thermal plants at the Rourkela Steel Plant and NALCO plant. Total installed capacity, 1985, 1,134 mw.; there were 23,762 electrified villages in 1984–85.

Minerals. Orissa is India's leading producer of chromite (95% of national output), dolomite (50%), manganese ore (25%), graphite (80%), iron ore (16%), fire-clay (34%), limestone (20%), and quartz-quartzite (18%). Production in 1984 (1,000 tonnes): iron ore, 6,603; manganese ore, 435; chromite, 400; coal, 5,101; limestone, 2,877; dolomite, 909; fire-clay, 91; china clay, 28; graphite, 29; quartz and quartzite, 64; lead ore, 66. About 60,000 workers are employed in the mines. Value of mineral production (1984), Rs 1,840m.

Agriculture. The cultivation of rice is the principal occupation of nearly 80% of the population. Production amounted to 5·05m. tonnes in 1983–84; only a very small amount of other cereals is grown. Production of foodgrains (1983–84) totalled 6·84m. tonnes from 6·8m. hectares. Jute (340,000 bales of 180 kg.), wheat (121,000 tonnes), oilseeds (603,000 tonnes) and sugar-cane (2·86m. tonnes) are also grown. Turmeric is cultivated in the uplands of the districts of Ganjam, Phulbani and Koraput, and is exported.

Livestock (1977 census): Buffaloes, 1,358,451; other cattle, 12·1m.; sheep, 1·5m.; goats, 3·4m.; horses and ponies, 3,675.

Forests. Forests occupy about 43% of the area of the state, the most important species being sal, teak, kendu, sandal, sisu, bija, kuruma, kongada and bamboo.

Fisheries. There were, in 1981, 484 fishery co-operative societies.

INDUSTRY. Over 100 large and medium industries have been set up (1984), mostly based on minerals, including the steel plant of Hindustan Steel Ltd at Rourkela, a pig-iron plant near Barbil, 3 ferrochrome plants, 2 ferromanganese plants at Joda and Rayagada, 1 ferrosilicon plant at Theruvelli and an aluminium smelter plant at Hirakud, 4 refractory plants and 2 cement plants. There are 3 large paper mills at Rayagada, Chowdwar and Brajrajnagar, three fertilizer plants, a caustic soda plant, a salt manufacturing unit and an industrial explosives plant. There are aluminium-alumina plants at Damanjodi and Angul.

Other industries of importance are sugar, glass, aluminium, heavy machine tools, a re-rolling mill and textile mills.

There are cottage and small-scale industries in the state, e.g., handloom weaving and the manufacture of baskets, wooden articles, hats and nets; silver filigree work and hand-woven fabrics are specially well known.

TOURISM. Tourist traffic is concentrated mainly on the 'Golden Triangle', Konark, Puri and Bhubaneswar, and its temples. Tourists also visit Gopalpur, the Similipal Forest and Chilka Lake.

COMMUNICATIONS

Roads. On 31 March 1982 length of roads was: State highway, 2,834 km; national highway, 1,631 km; other Public Works Department roads, 13,522 km; village council roads, 938 km. There were 74,304 motor vehicles in 1982. A 144-km expressway, part national highway, connects the Daitari mining area with Paradip Port.

Railways. The total length of railway in 1983–84 was 1,982 km, of which 1,310 km was single line.

Aviation. There is an airport at Bhubaneswar with regular scheduled services to New Delhi, Calcutta, Visakhapatnam and Hyderabad.

Shipping. Paradip was declared a 'major' port in 1966 and has been developed to handle 4m. tons of traffic. Other minor ports at Chandbali and Gopalpur.

JUSTICE, RELIGION AND EDUCATION

Justice. The High Court of Judicature at Cuttack has a Chief Justice and 6 puisne judges.

Religion. There were in 1981: Hindus (including scheduled castes and scheduled tribes), 25,161,725; Christians, 480,426; Moslems, 422,266; Sikhs, 14,270; Buddhists, 8,028; Jains, 6,642.

Education. The percentage of literates in the population is 34·12% (males, 46·9%, females, 21·11%).

In 1981–82 there were 32,797 primary, 7,413 middle English and 2,466 high schools.

Utkal University was established in 1943 at Cuttack and moved to Bhubaneswar in 1962; it is both teaching and affiliating. It has 2 university colleges (law) and 113 affiliated colleges. Berhampur University has 20 affiliated colleges and Orissa University of Agriculture and Technology 4 constituent colleges. Sambalpur University has 42 affiliated colleges. Sri Jagannath Sanskrit Viswavidyalaya University was established in 1981 for oriental studies.

PUNJAB (INDIA)

HISTORY. The Punjab was constituted an autonomous province of India in 1937. In 1947, the province was partitioned between India and Pakistan into East and West Punjab respectively, under the Indian Independence Act, 1947, the boundaries being determined under the Radcliffe Award. The name of East Punjab was changed to Punjab (India) under the Constitution of India. On 1 Nov. 1956 the erstwhile states of Punjab and Patiala and East Punjab States Union (PEPSU) were integrated to form the state of Punjab. On 1 Nov. 1966, under the Punjab Reorganization Act, 1966, the state was reconstituted as a Punjabi-speaking state comprising the districts of Gurdaspur (excluding Dalhousie), Amritsar, Kapur-thala, Jullundur, Ferozepore, Bhatinda, Patiala and Ludhiana; parts of Sangrur, Hoshiarpur and Ambala districts; and part of Kharar tehsil. The remaining area comprising an area of 18,000 sq. miles and an estimated (1967) population of 8·5m. was shared between the new state of Haryana and the Union Territory of Himachal Pradesh. The existing capital of Chandigarh was made joint capital of Punjab and Haryana; its transfer to Punjab alone (due in 1986) has been delayed while the two states seek agreement as to which Hindi-speaking districts shall be transfered to Haryana in exchange.

AREA AND POPULATION. The Punjab is in north India and is bounded at its northernmost point by Kashmir, north-east by Himachal Pradesh, south-east by Haryana, south by Rajasthan, west and north-west by Pakistan. The area of the state is 50,362 sq. km, with census (1981) population of 16,788,915. Density 333 per sq. km. Growth rate, 1971–81, 23·01%. The largest cities, *see* p. 625. The official language is Punjabi.

CONSTITUTION AND GOVERNMENT. Punjab (India) has a uni-cameral legislature, the Legislative Assembly, of 117 members. Presidential rule was imposed in May 1987 after outbreaks of communal violence.

There are 12 districts. The capital is Chandigarh (*see* p. 687). There are 106 municipalities, 118 community development blocks and 9,331 elected village *panchayats*.

Governor: S. Shankar Ray.

BUDGET. Budget estimates, 1985–86, showed a surplus of Rs 36·89 crores on revenue account and a deficit of Rs 344·96 crores on capital account.

ENERGY AND NATURAL RESOURCES

Electricity. Installed capacity, 1986–87, was 2,460 mw; all villages had electricity.

Agriculture. About 70% of the population depends on agriculture. Agricultural prosperity is mainly due to irrigation. The irrigated area rose from 2·21m. hectares in 1950–51 to 6·5m. hectares in 1985–86: total production of foodgrains was 1,719·9m. tonnes in 1985–86. Wheat production was 10·9m. tonnes, rice, 5·4m. Sugar-cane yield is 6,468 kg. per hectare. Punjab produced 1·4m. bales of cotton.

Livestock (1977 census): Buffaloes, 4,110,000; other cattle, 3·31m.; sheep and goats, 1,219,600; horses and ponies, 75,900; poultry, 5·5m.

Forestry. In 1986–87 there were 260,235 hectares of forest land, of which 136,734 hectares belonged to the Forest Department.

INDUSTRY. In March 1987 the number of registered industrial units in the

Punjab (India) was 122,766, employing about 800,000 people. The chief manufactures are textiles (especially hosiery), sewing machines, sports goods, sugar, bicycles, electronic goods, machine tools, hand tools, vehicle parts, surgical goods and vegetable oils.

COMMUNICATIONS

Roads. The total length of metalled roads on 31 March 1987 was 35,501 km. State transport services cover 822,000 route km daily with a fleet of 3,405 buses carrying a daily average of over 1m passengers. Coverage by private operators is estimated as 40%.

Railways. The Punjab possesses an extensive system of railway communications, served by the Northern Railway. Total length, (1986) 3,630·04 km.

Aviation. There is an airport at Amritsar, and Chandigarh airport is on the north-eastern boundary; both have regular scheduled services to Delhi. There are also Vayudoot services to Ludhiana, Amritsar and Bathinda.

JUSTICE, RELIGION, EDUCATION AND WELFARE

Justice. The Punjab and Haryana High Court exercises jurisdiction over the states of Punjab and Haryana and the territory of Chandigarh. It is located in Chandigarh. It consists (1987) of a Chief Justice and 18 puisne judges.

Religion. At the 1971 census Hindus numbered 5,037,235; Sikhs, 8,159,172; Moslems, 114,447; Christians, 162,202; Jains, 21,383; Buddhists, 1,374.

Education. Compulsory education was introduced in April 1961; at the same time free education was introduced up to 8th class for boys and 9th class for girls as well as fee concessions. The aim is education for all children of 6-11.

At 31 March 1987 there were 12,339 primary schools, 1,388 middle schools, 25 old-pattern higher secondary schools, 272 higher secondary and 2,428 high schools.

Punjab University was established in 1947 at Chandigarh as an examining, teaching and affiliating body. In 1962 Punjabi University was established at Patiala and an agricultural university at Ludhiana. Guru Nanak University has been established at Amritsar to mark the 500th anniversary celebrations for Guru Nanak Dev, first Guru of the Sikhs. Altogether there are 205 affiliated colleges, 163 for arts and science, 18 for teacher training, 9 medical, 3 engineering and 11 for other studies.

Health. Punjab claims the longest life expectancy (60·6 years for women, 60·7 for men) and lowest death rate (9 per 1,000). There were (1986) 266 hospitals, 467 Ayurvedic and Unani hospitals and dispensaries, 130 primary health centres, 2,703 sub-centres and 1,791 dispensaries.

Singh, Khushwant, *A History of the Sikhs.* 2 vols. Princeton and OUP, 1964–67

RAJASTHAN

HISTORY. As a result of the implementation of the States Reorganization Act, 1956, the erstwhile state of Ajmer, Abu Taluka of Bombay State and the Sunel Tappa enclave of the former state of Madhya Bharat were transferred to the state of Rajasthan on 1 Nov. 1956, whereas the Sironj subdivision of Rajasthan was transferred to the state of Madhya Pradesh.

EVENTS. An instance of *suttee* on 4 Sept. 1987 brought about state legislation (Rajasthan Sati (Prevention) Ordinance) promulgated on 1 Oct., and the central government's Sati Prevention Act (strengthening existing penalties) in Dec. 1987.

AREA AND POPULATION. Rajasthan is in north-west India and is bounded north by Punjab, north-east by Haryana and Uttar Pradesh, east by Madhya

Pradesh, south by Gujarat and west by Pakistan. The area of the state is 342,239 sq. km and its population (census 1981, revised), 34,261,862, density 100 per sq. km. Growth rate, 1971–81, 32.36%. The chief cities, *see* p. 625.

CONSTITUTION AND GOVERNMENT. There is a unicameral legislature, the Legislative Assembly, having 200 members. After the election in March 1985 a Congress government was returned.

The capital is Jaipur. There are 27 districts.

Governor: Sukhdev Prasad.
Chief Minister: Shiv Charan Mathur.

BUDGET. Revised estimates for 1986–87 show total revenue receipts of Rs 1,637 crores, and expenditure of Rs 1,707 crores. Receipts included: share in Central taxes, Rs 356.9 crores; state excise, Rs 96 crores, sales tax, Rs 386.9 crores; vehicles taxes, Rs 76 crores; non-tax revenue, Rs 333.3 crores. Expenditure included: Education, art and culture, Rs 389.4 crores; medical and family welfare, Rs 124.2 crores; water supply and public health, Rs 164.5 crores; agriculture, Rs 249.2 crores; irrigation, Rs 329.1 crores. Annual plan 1988–89, Rs 710 crores.

ENERGY AND NATURAL RESOURCES

Electricity. Installed capacity in Feb. 1988, 1,803 mw.; 21,409 villages and 289,574 wells had electric power.

Water. In 1984 the Bhakra Canal irrigated 300,000 hectares, the Chambal Canal, 200,000 and the Rajasthan Canal, 450,000. The Rajasthan (now the Indira Gandhi canal) is the main canal system, of which (1984) 189 km. of main canal and 2,950 km of distributors had been built. Cost, at 1 March 1984, Rs 419 crores. There were 2,909 villages with drinking water in 1984–85.

Minerals. The state is rich in minerals. In 1985–86, 305,670m. tonnes of gypsum and 172,989 tonnes of rock phosphate were produced. Other minerals include silver (9,852 kg., 1984 estimate), asbestos, felspar, copper, limestone and salt. Total sale value of mineral production in 1984 (estimate) was about Rs 233 crores. Lead-zinc reserves have been found near Rampura-Agucha, estimated at 61m. tonnes.

Agriculture. The state has suffered drought and encroaching desert for several years. The cultivable area is (1985–86) about 26.6m. hectares, of which 4m. is irrigated. Production of principal crops (in 1,000 tonnes), 1984–85: pulses, 1,300; sugar-cane (gur), 1,300; total oilseeds, 1,000; cotton, 300,000 bales (of 180 kg). Total foodgrains (1985–86) 6,337.

Livestock (1983): Buffaloes, 6,034,743; other cattle, 13,466,474; sheep, 15,389,100; goats, 15,397,993; horses and ponies, 45,381; camels, 7,528,287.

INDUSTRY. In March 1986 there were 8,233 registered factories and 122,304 small industrial units. There were 171 industrial estates. Total capital investment Rs 4,750.7m. Chief manufactures are textiles, cement, glass, sugar, sodium, oxygen and acetylene units, pesticides, insecticides, dyes, caustic soda, calcium, carbide, nylon tyre cords and refined copper.

COMMUNICATIONS

Roads. In 1986 there were 49,311 km of roads including 37,617 km of good and surfaced roads in Rajasthan; there were 15,134 km of national highway. Motor vehicles numbered 554,388 in Dec. 1985.

Railways. Jodhpur, Marwar, Udaipur, Ajmer, Jaipur, Khota, Bikaner and Sawai Madhopur are important junctions of the north-western network.

Aviation. There are airports at Jaipur, Jodhpur, Khota and Udaipur with regular scheduled services by Indian Airlines.

JUSTICE, RELIGION, EDUCATION AND WELFARE

Justice. The seat of the High Court is at Jodhpur. There is a Chief Justice and 11 puisne judges. There is also a bench of High Court judges at Jaipur.

Religion. At the 1971 census Hindus numbered 23,093,895; Moslems, 1,778,275; Jains, 513,548; Sikhs, 341,182; Christians, 30,202.

Education. The proportion of literates to the total population was 24·39% at the 1981 census.

In 1985–86 there were 35,508 primary and upper primary schools, 2,052 secondary and 892 higher secondary schools. Elementary education is free but not compulsory.

In 1985–86 there were 266 colleges. Enrolment at these was 171,000 in 1985. Rajasthan University, established at Jaipur in 1947, is teaching and affiliating (6 affiliated colleges); Jodhpur University and Udaipur University were founded in 1962. There are 2 others, at Vanasthali and Pilani. There are also 11 medical and nursing colleges, 5 engineering colleges, 21,436 adult and other education centres, 32 sanskrit institutions, 34 teacher-training colleges and 13 polytechnics.

Health. In 1984 there were 995 hospitals and dispensaries, 348 primary health centres, 72 Unani, 80 homoepathic and 3 naturopathy hospitals. There were 111 maternity centres, and 3,046 Ayurvedic hospitals and dispensaries.

SIKKIM

HISTORY. Sikkim became the twenty-second state of the Indian Union in May 1975. It is inhabited chiefly by the Lepchas, who are a tribe indigenous to Sikkim with their own dress and language, the Bhutias, who originally came from Tibet, and the Nepális, who entered from Nepál in large numbers in the late 19th and early 20th century. The main languages spoken are Bhutia, Lepcha and Nepáli. Being a small country Sikkim had frequently been involved in struggles over her territory, and as a result her boundaries have been very much reduced over the centuries. In particular the Darjeeling district was acquired from Sikkim by the British East India Company in 1839. The Namgyal dynasty had been ruling Sikkim since the 14th century; the first consecrated ruler was Phuntsog Namgya I who was consecrated in 1642 and given the title of 'Chogyal', meaning 'King ruling in accordance with religious laws', derived from Cho–religion and Gyalpo–king. The last Chogyal was deposed in 1975 and died in America in 1982.

Sikkim is a land of wide variation in altitude, climate and vegetation, and is known for the great number and variety of birds, butterflies, wild flowers and orchids to be found in the different regions. It is a fertile land and to the Sikkimese is known as Denjong, The Valley of Rice.

AREA AND POPULATION. Sikkim is in the Eastern Himalayas and is bounded north by Tibet, east by Tibet and Bhután, south by West Bengal and west by Nepál. Area, 7,298 sq. km. Census population (1981), 314,999, of whom 36,768 lived in the capital, Gangtok. Density 43 per sq km. Growth rate, 1971–81, 50·01%.

CONSTITUTION AND GOVERNMENT. Sikkim was joined to the British Empire by a treaty in 1886 until 1947, but that relationship ceased when Britain withdrew from India in 1947. Thereafter there was a standstill agreement between India and Sikkim until a treaty was signed on 5 Dec. 1950 between India and Sikkim by which Sikkim became a protectorate of India and India undertook to be responsible for Sikkim's defence, external relations and strategic communications. The Chogyal had governed Sikkim with the help of the Sikkim Council, consisting of 18 elected members and 6 members nominated by the Chogyal. Sikkim parties represented were: National Party, Sikkim National Congress and, later, Sikkim Janta Congress.

Political reforms were demanded by the National Congress and the Janta Congress in March-April 1973 and Indian police took over control of law and order at the request of the Chogyal. On 13 April it was announced that the Chogyal had agreed to meet most of the political demands. Elections were held in April 1974 to a popularly-elected assembly. By the Government of Sikkim Act, June 1974, the Chogyal became a constitutional monarch with power of assent to the Assembly's legislation. By the Constitution (Thirty-Sixth Amendment) Act 1974 Sikkim became a state associated with the Indian Union. The office of Chogyal was abolished in April 1975. By the Constitution (Thirty-Eighth Amendment) Act 1975 Sikkim became the twenty-second state of the Indian Union. The Assembly has 32 members with a cabinet of 10 ministers including the Chief Minister. After the election of March 1985 a Sangram Parishad government was returned.

Governor: T. V. Rajeshwar.
Chief Minister: N. Bahadur Bhandari.

The official language of the Government is English. Lepcha, Bhutia, Nepáli and Limboo have also been declared official languages.

Sikkim is divided into 4 districts for administration purposes, Gangtok, Mangan, Namchi and Gyalshing being the headquarters for the Eastern, Northern, Southern and Western districts respectively. Each district is administered by a District Collector. Within this framework are the Panchayats or Village Councils.

ECONOMY

Planning. The seventh Five-Year Plan covered 1985–90.

Budget. The annual budget for 1987–88 is Rs 57 crores.

ENERGY AND NATURAL RESOURCES

Electricity. There are 4 operational hydro-electric power stations; the Lagyap project is also being implemented by the Government of India as aid to meet the growing demand for electrical power for new industries. The first of its two 6 mv generators was commissioned 1 Sept. 1979.

Agriculture. The economy is mainly agricultural; main food crops are rice, maize, millet, wheat and barley; cash crops are cardamom (a spice), mandarin oranges, apples, potatoes, and buckwheat. Foodgrain production, 1983, 84,000 tonnes. A tea plantation has recently been started. Forests occupy about 1,000 sq. km. of the land area (excluding hill pastures) and the potential for a timber and wood-pulp industry is being explored. Some medicinal herbs are exported.

INDUSTRY AND TRADE

Industry. There is a state Industrial Development Investment Corporation and an Industrial Training Institute offering 7 trades. There are two cigarette factories (at Gangtok and Rangpo), two distilleries and a tannery at Rangpo and a fruit preserving factory at Singtam. Copper, zinc and lead are mined by the Sikkim Mining Corporation. A recent survey by the Geological Survey of India and the Indian Bureau of Mines has confirmed further deposits of copper, zinc, silver and gold in Dikchu, North Sikkim. There is a jewel-bearing factory for the production of industrial jewels. A watch factory has been set up in collaboration with Hindustan Machine Tools (India). A number of small manufacturing units for leather, wire nails, storage cells batteries, candles, safety matches and carpets, are already producing in the private sector. Local crafts include carpet weaving, making handmade paper, wood carving and silverwork. To encourage trading in indigenous products, particularly agricultural produce, the State Trading Corporation of Sikkim has been established.

Tourism. There is great potential for the tourist industry; a 78-bed lodge at Gangtok and a 50-bed tourist lodge in West Sikkim have been opened. Tourism has been stimulated by the opening of new roads from Pemayangtse to Yuksam in West Sikkim and from Yuksam to the Dzongri Glacier.

COMMUNICATIONS

Roads. There are 1,201 km. of metalled roads, all on mountainous terrain, and 18 major bridges under the Public Works Department. Public transport and road haulage is nationalized.

Railways. The nearest railhead is at Siliguri (115 km from Gangtok).

Aviation. The nearest airport is at Bagdogra (128 km from Gangtok), linked to Gangtok by helicopter service.

Post and Broadcasting. There are 1,445 telephones (1987) and 37 wireless stations. A radio broadcasting station, Akashvani Gangtok, was built in 1982, and a permanent station in 1983. Gangtok also has a low-power TV transmitter.

RELIGION, EDUCATION AND WELFARE

Religion. The state religion is Mahayana Buddhism, but a large proportion of the population is Hindu. There are some Christians, Moslems and members of other religions.

Education. At the 1981 census there were 100,000 literates. Sikkim has (1987) 528 pre-primary schools, 246 primary schools, 123 junior high schools, 55 secondary and 13 senior secondary schools. Education is free up to class XII; text books are free up to class V. There are 500 adult education centres. There is also a training institute for primary teachers, a law college and a degree college.

Health. There are (1983) 4 district hospitals at Singtam, Gyalshing, Namchi and Mangan, and one central referral hospital at Gangtok, besides 20 primary health centres, 109 sub-centres and 8 dispensaries, a maternity ward, chest clinic and 2 blocks for tuberculosis patients. There is a blood bank at Gangtok. There are 110 doctors. Medical and hospital treatment is free; there is a health centre for every 20,000 of the population. Small-pox and Kala-azar have been completely eliminated and many schemes for the provision of safe drinking water to villages and bazaars have been implemented. A leprosy hospital (20 beds) was being built near Gangtok in 1987.

Coelho, V. H., *Sikkim and Bhutan.* New Delhi, 1970
Mele, F., *Sikkim.* Paris, 1974

TAMIL NADU

HISTORY. The first trading establishment made by the British in the Madras State was at Peddapali (now Nizampatnam) in 1611 and then at Masulipatnam. In 1639 the English were permitted to make a settlement at the place which is now Madras, and Fort St George was founded. By 1801 the whole of the country from the Northern Circars to Cape Comorin (with the exception of certain French and Danish settlements) had been brought under British rule.

Under the provisions of the States Reorganization Act, 1956, the Malabar district (excluding the islands of Laccadive and Minicoy) and the Kasaragod district taluk of South Kanara were transferred to the new state of Kerala; the South Kanara district (excluding Kasaragod taluk and the Amindivi Islands) and the Kollegal taluk of the Coimbatore district were transferred to the new state of Mysore; and the Laccadive, Amindivi and Minicoy Islands were constituted a separate Territory. Four taluks of the Trivandrum district and the Shencottah taluk of Quilon district were transferred from Travancore-Cochin to the new Madras State. On 1 April 1960, 405 sq. miles from the Chittoor district of Andhra Pradesh were transferred to Madras in exchange for 326 sq. miles from the Chingleput and Salem districts. In Aug. 1968 the state was renamed Tamil Nadu.

AREA AND POPULATION. Tamil Nadu is in south India and is bounded north by Karnataka and Andhra Pradesh, east and south by the Indian ocean and west by Kerala. Area, 130,357 sq. km. Population (1981 census), 48,297,456, density of 371 per sq. km. Growth rate, 1971–81, 17·23%. Tamil is the principal language and has been adopted as the state language with effect from 14 Jan. 1958. The principal towns, see p. 625.

CONSTITUTION AND GOVERNMENT. The Governor is aided by a Council of 16 ministers. There is a unicameral legislature; the Legislative Assembly has 234 members. The Assembly was dissolved and Presidents' Rule imposed on 30 Jan. 1988.

There are 18 districts. The capital is Madras.

Governor: P. C. Alexander.

BUDGET. Budget estimates for 1984-85, revenue receipts, Rs 2,065·4 crores, revenue account expenditure, Rs 1,946·4 crores. Capital outlay, Rs 883·5 crores; capital account receipts, Rs 577·9. Annual plan 1988–89, Rs 1,457 crores.

ENERGY AND NATURAL RESOURCES

Electricity. Installed capacity 1983 amounted to 3,344 mw of which 1,344 mw was hydro-electricity and 1,170 mw thermal. 99·8% of villages were supplied with electricity. The Kalpakkam nuclear power plant became operational in 1983; initial capacity, 230 mw.

Water. A joint project with Andhra Pradesh was agreed in 1983, to supply Madras with water from the Krishna river, also providing irrigation, *en route,* for Andhra Pradesh. In 1981–82 3·4m. hectares were irrigated.

Minerals. Value of mineral exports, 1983, Rs 1·5 crores. The state has magnesite, salt, coal, chromite, bauxite, limestone, manganese, mica, quartz, gypsum and feldspar.

Agriculture. In 1981 there were 5·5m. cultivators and 5·9m. agricultural labourers. The land is a fertile plain watered by rivers flowing east from the Western Ghats, particularly the Cauvery and the Tambaraparani. Temperature ranges between 18°C. and 43°C., rainfall between 25 in. and 75 in. Of the total land area (13·01m. hectares), 6,909,357 hectares were cropped and 335,462 hectares of waste were cultivable. The staple food crops grown are paddy, maize, jawar, bajra, pulses and millets. Important commercial crops are sugar-cane, oilseeds, cashewnuts, cotton, tobacco, coffee, tea, rubber and pepper. Production 1983–84, in 1,000 tons, (and area, 1,000 hectares): rice 5,000 (2,282); millet 1,900 (1,652); sugar-cane 2,500 (132); pulses 115 (333); cotton 3m. bales (169); oilseeds 752 (825).

Livestock (1982 census): Buffaloes, 3,212,242; other cattle, 10,365,500; sheep, 5,536,514; goats, 5,246,192; swine, 693,735; horses, ponies, mules, camels and donkeys, 90,632; poultry, 18,283,720.

Forestry. Forest area, 1983, 2,201,000 hectares, of which 1,812,000 were reserved forest. Forests cover about 17% of land area. Main products are teak, soft wood, wattle, sandalwood, pulp wood, cashew and cinchona bark.

Fisheries. There were 93,825 active marine fishermen working the 1,000 km coastline in 1984.

INDUSTRY AND TRADE

Industry. The number of working factories was 10,800 in 1982, employing about 771,000 workers. The consumption of power in the industrial sector was 43% of total state consumption in 1982–83. The biggest central sector project is Salem steel plant.

Cotton textiles is one of the major industries. There are nearly 180 cotton textile mills and many spinning mills supplying yarn to the decentralized handloom industry. Other important industries are cement, sugar, manufacture of textile machinery, power-driven pumps, bicycles, electrical machinery, tractors, rubber tyres and tubes, bricks and tiles and silk.

Public sector undertakings include the Neyveli lignite complex, integral coach factory, high-pressure boiler plant, photographic film factory, surgical instruments factory, teleprinter factory, oil refinery, continuous casting plant and defence vehicles manufacture. Main exports: cotton goods, tea, coffee, spices, engineering goods, motor-car ancillaries.

In 1982 there were 3,932 registered trade unions. Man-days lost by strikes, 1,396,452; by lockouts, 409,526.

Tourism. In 1982, 229,000 foreign tourists visited the state.

COMMUNICATIONS

Roads. On 1 April 1982 the state had approximately 35,746 km of national and state highways, major and other district roads. In 1983 there were 100,037 registered motor vehicles and 326,977 others not covered by permits.

Railways. In 1983 there were 6,563 km of railway track (3,853 route km). Madras and Madurai are the main centres.

Aviation. There are airports at Madras, Tiruchirapalli and Madurai, with regular scheduled services to Bombay, Calcutta and Delhi. Madras is the main centre of airline routes in South India.

Shipping. Madras and Tuticorin are the chief ports. Important minor ports are Cuddalore and Nagapattinam. Madras handled 13·3m. tonnes of cargo in 1983–84, Tuticorin, 3·5m. The Inland Container Depot at Coimbatore has a capacity of 50,000 tonnes of export traffic; it is linked to Cochin (Kerala).

JUSTICE, RELIGION AND EDUCATION

Justice. There is a High Court at Madras with a Chief Justice and 18 judges. *Police.* Strength of armed police battalions, 1973, 4,420; strength of the armed reserve (1972) in the state and in Madras, 356,461.

Religion. At the 1971 census Hindus numbered 36,674,150 (89·2%), Christians, 5·75%; Moslems, 5·11%.

Education. At the 1981 census 22·6m. people were literate (14·3m. males).

Education is free up to pre-university level. In 1983-84 there were 37,989 schools for general education, 10·2m. students and 281,149 teachers. There were 188 general colleges (189,060 students and 13,934 teachers); 80 professional colleges (38,313 and 5,519); 19 special education colleges (2,348 and 246).

There are 3 universities. Madras University (founded in 1857) is affiliating and teaching. Annamalai University, Annamalainagar (founded 1928) is residential; Madurai University (founded 1966) is an affiliating and teaching university.

Statistical Information: The Department of Statistics (Fort St George, Madras) was established in 1948 and reorganized in 1953. *Director:* D. S. Rajabushanam, MA. Main publications: *Annual Statistical Abstract; Decennial Statistical Atlas; Season and Crop Report; Quinquennial Wages Census; Quarterly Abstract of Statistics.*

TRIPURA

HISTORY. A Hindu state of great antiquity having been ruled by the Maharajahs for 1,300 years before its accession to the Indian Union on 15 Oct. 1949. With the reorganization of states on 1 Sept. 1956 Tripura became a Union Territory, and was so declared on 1 Nov. 1957. The Territory was made a State on 21 Jan. 1972.

AREA AND POPULATION. Tripura is bounded by Bangladesh, except in the north-east where it joins Assam and Mizoram. The major portion of the state is hilly and mainly jungle. It has an area of 10,477 sq. km and a population of 2,060,189 (1981 census); Density, 196 per sq. km. Growth rate, 1971-81, 32·37%.

The official languages are Bengali and Kokbarak. Manipuri is also spoken.

CONSTITUTION AND GOVERNMENT. There is a Legislative Assembly of 60 members. The election of Jan. 1983 was won by the Communist Party of India (Marxist). The territory has 3 districts, divided into 10 administrative subdivisions, namely, Sadar, Khowai, Kailasahar, Dharmanagar, Sonamura, Udaipur, Belonia, Kamalpur, Sabroom and Amarpur.

The capital is Agartala (population, 1981, 132,186).

Governor: Gen. K. V. Krishna Rao.
Chief Minister: Sudhir Ranjan Majumdar.

BUDGET. Budget estimates 1985-86 balance at Rs 289 crores.

ENERGY AND NATURAL RESOURCES

Electricity. Installed capacity (1984), 15 mw (demand 23 mw); there were (1985) 1,710 electrified villages.

Agriculture. About 24% of the land area is cultivable. The tribes practise shifting cultivation, but this is being replaced by modern methods. The main crops are rice, wheat, jute, mesta, potatoes, oilseeds and sugar-cane. Foodgrain production (1983-84), about 370,000 tonnes. There are 49 registered tea gardens producing 4,500,000 kg. per year, and employing about 10,000.

Forestry. Forests cover about 55% of the land area. They have been much depleted by clearance for shifting cultivation and, recently, for refugee settlements of Bangladeshis. About 8% of the forest area still consists of dense natural forest; losses elsewhere are being replaced by plantation. Commercial rubber plantation has also been encouraged. In 1984, 4,167 hectares were under new rubber plantations.

INDUSTRY. Tea is the main industry. There is also a jute mill producing about 15 tonnes per day and employing about 2,000. The main small industries: aluminium utensils, saw-milling, soap, piping, fruit canning, handloom weaving and sericulture. Handloom weaving products (1983–84) were valued at Rs 9·75 crores.

COMMUNICATIONS

Roads. Total length of motorable roads (1974) 3,692 km, of which 1,123 km were surfaced. Vehicles registered, 31 March 1984, 9,924, of which 3,191 were lorries.

Railways. There is a railway between Dharmanagar and Kalkalighat (Assam).

Aviation. There is 1 airport and 2 airstrips. The airport (Agartala) has regular scheduled services to Calcutta.

EDUCATION AND WELFARE

Education. In autumn 1985 there were 1,974 primary schools (325,504 pupils); 308 middle schools (70,010); 240 high schools (40,964). There were 9 colleges of general education, 17 colleges of professional and technical education and 1,203 social education centres.

Health. There were (1980) 12 hospitals, with 1,357 beds, 128 dispensaries, 297 doctors and 459 nurses. There were 26 primary health centres and about 35 other medical units.

UTTAR PRADESH

HISTORY. In 1833 the then Bengal Presidency was divided into two parts, one of which became the Presidency of Agra. In 1836 the Agra area was styled the North-West Province and placed under a Lieut.-Governor. The two provinces of Agra and

Oudh were placed, in 1877, under one administrator, styled Lieut.-Governor of the North-West Province and Chief Commissioner of Oudh. In 1902 the name was changed to 'United Provinces of Agra and Oudh', under a Lieut.-Governor, and the Lieut.-Governorship was altered to a Governorship in 1921. In 1935 the name was shortened to 'United Provinces'. On Independence, the states of Rampur, Banaras and Tehri-Garhwal were merged with United Provinces. In 1950 the name of the United Provinces was changed to Uttar Pradesh.

AREA AND POPULATION. Uttar Pradesh is in north India and is bounded north by Himachal Pradesh, Tibet and Nepál, east by Bihar, south by Madhya Pradesh and west by Rajasthan, Haryana and Delhi. The area of the state is 294,413 sq. km. Population (1981 census), 110,862,013, a density of 377 per sq. km. Growth rate, 1971–81, 25·52%. Cities with more than 250,000 population, *see* p. 625. The official language is Hindi.

CONSTITUTION AND GOVERNMENT. Uttar Pradesh has had an autonomous system of government since 1937. There is a bicameral legislature. The Legislative Council has 108 members; the Legislative Assembly has 426, of which 423 are elected. After the elections in March 1985 a Congress government was returned.

There are 12 administrative divisions, each under a Commissioner, and 57 districts.

The capital is Lucknow.

Governor: M. Usman Arif.
Chief Minister: V. B. Singh.

BUDGET. Budget estimates 1984–85 show revenue and capital receipts of Rs 4,356·28 crores; revenue and capital account expenditure, Rs 4,629 crores.

ENERGY AND NATURAL RESOURCES

Electricity. The State Electricity Board had, 31 March 1985, an installed capacity of 4,084 mw. There were 68,301 villages with electricity in Sept. 1986.

Minerals. The state has magnesite, fire-clay, coal, copper, dolomite, limestone, soapstone, gypsum, bauxite, diaspore, ochre, phosphorite, pyrophyllite, silica sand and steatite among others.

Agriculture. Agriculture occupies 78% of the work force. About 9m. hectares are irrigated. The state is India's largest producer of foodgrains; production (1982–83), 26·5m. tonnes; sugar-cane 81·4m.; oilseeds, 1·22m. The state is one of India's main producers of sugar. There were (1982) 1,199 veterinary centres for cattle.

Forests cover (1982) about 5·3m. sq. km.

The state government in 1985 began a management programme for the ravines of the Chambal river catchment area. The programme includes stabilizing ravines, soil conservation, afforestation, pasture development and ravine reclamation. Estimated cost of a six-year programme, Rs 453·96m.

INDUSTRY. Sugar production is important; other industries include edible oils, textiles, distilleries, brewing, leather working, agricultural engineering, paper and chemicals. There is an aluminium smelter at Renukoot. An oil refinery at Mathura has capacity of 6m. tonnes per annum. Large public-sector enterprises have been set up in electrical engineering, pharmaceuticals, locomotive building, general engineering, electronics and aeronautics. Village and small-scale industries are important; there were 90,237 small units in 1983. About one-third of cloth output is from hand-looms. Total working population (1981) 30·8m., of whom 6·8m. were non-agricultural.

COMMUNICATIONS

Roads. There were, 31 March 1983, 273,011 km of motorable roads, of which

66,034 km were metalled. (This excludes forest roads.) In 1983 there were 674,049 motor vehicles of which 391,307 were motorcycles.

Railways. Lucknow is the main junction of the northern network; other important junctions are Agra, Kanpur, Allahabad and Varanasi.

Aviation. There are airports at Lucknow, Kanpur, Varanasi, Allahabad, Agra, Jhansi, Lalitpur and Gorakhpur.

JUSTICE, RELIGION AND EDUCATION

Justice. The High Court of Judicature at Allahabad (with a bench at Lucknow) has a Chief Justice and 49 puisne judges including additional judges. There are 56 sessions divisions in the state.

Religion. At the 1981 census Hindus numbered 92,365,968; Moslems, 17,657,735; Sikhs, 458,647; Christians, 162,199; Jains, 141,549; Buddhists, 54,542.

Education. At the 1981 census 30·1m. people were literate. In 1985–86 there were 73,424 junior basic schools, 14,240 senior basic schools and 5,709 higher secondary schools.

Uttar Pradesh has 19 universities: Allahabad University (founded 1887); Agra University (1927); the Banaras Hindu University, Varanasi (1916); Lucknow University (1921); Aligarh Muslim University (1920); Roorkee University (1948), formerly Thomason College of Civil Engineering (established in 1847); Gorakhpur University (1957); Varanasaya Sanskrit Vishwavidyalaya, Varanasi (1958); Kashi Vidyapith, Varanasi (1963). Kanpur University and Meerut University were founded in 1966. Govind Ballabh Pant University, Pantnagar (1969); Garhwal University, Srinagar, (1973). Two universities of agriculture were founded in 1974–75 and Avadh, Kumaon, Rohilkhand and Jhansi Universities in 1975.

There are also two institutions with university status: Gurukul Kangri and Dayal Bagh Educational Institute. There are 9 medical colleges.

HEALTH. In 1984–85 there were 3,405 allopathic and 1,669 ayurvedic and unani hospitals. There were 5,187 allopathic doctors and 3,556 allopathic nurses in state service. There were TB hospitals and clinics with 3,437 beds.

WEST BENGAL

HISTORY. For the history of Bengal under British rule, from 1633 to 1947, *see* THE STATESMAN'S YEAR-BOOK, 1952, p. 183.

Under the terms of the Indian Independence Act, 1947, the Province of Bengal ceased to exist. The Moslem majority districts of East Bengal, consisting of the Chittagong and Dacca Divisions and portions of the Presidency and Rajshahi Divisions, became what was then East Pakistan (now Bangladesh).

AREA AND POPULATION. West Bengal is in north-east India and is bounded north by Sikkim and Bhután, east by Assam and Bangladesh, south by the Bay of Bengal and Orissa, west by Bihar and north-west by Nepál. The total area of West Bengal is 87,853 sq. km. At the 1981 census its population was 54,580,647, an increase of 23·17% since 1971, the density of population 621 per sq. km. Population of chief cities, *see* p. 625. The principal language is Bengali.

CONSTITUTION AND GOVERNMENT. The state of West Bengal came into existence as a result of the Indian Independence Act, 1947. The territory of Cooch-Behar State was merged with West Bengal on 1 Jan. 1950, and the former French possession of Chandernagore became part of the state on 2 Oct. 1954. Under the States Reorganization Act, 1956, certain portions of Bihar State (an area of 3,157 sq. miles with a population of 1,446,385) were transferred to West Bengal.

The Legislative Assembly has 295 seats. Distribution March 1987: Communist Party of India (Marxist), 187; Forward Bloc, 26; Revolutionary Socialist Party, 18; Communist Party of India, 11; Revolutionary Communist Party of India, 1; Forward Bloc (Marxist), 2; Democratic Socialist Party, 2; Socialist Party, 4. Total 'Left Front', 251. Opposition: Indian National Congress, 40; others, 3; nominated, 1.

The capital is Calcutta.

For administrative purposes there are 3 divisions (Jalpaiguri, Burdwan and Presidency), under which there are 16 districts, including Calcutta. The Calcutta Metropolitan Development Authority has been set up to co-ordinate development in the metropolitan area (1,350 sq. km). For the purposes of local self-government there are 16 *zilla parishads* (district boards), 339 *panchayat samities* (regional boards), and 3,305 *gram* (village) *panchayats*. There are 99 municipalities, 3 Corporations and 9 Notified Areas. The Calcutta Corporation has a mayor and deputy mayor, a commissioner, aldermen and standing committees.

Governor: S. Nurul Hasan.
Chief Minister: J. Basu.

BUDGET. Budget estimates for 1987–88 showed a deficit of Rs 597m.

ENERGY AND NATURAL RESOURCES

Electricity. Installed capacity, 1985–86, 3,278 mw; 20,531 villages had electricity at 31 March 1986.

Water. The major irrigation and power scheme at present under construction is (1987) the Teesta barrage. Major irrigation schemes are the Mayurakshi Reservoir, Kansabati Reservoir, Mahananda Barrage and Aqueduct and Damodar Valley. During 1984–85 government canals irrigated 989,689 hectares. At March 1986 there were 5,674 tubewells and 3,155 riverlift irrigation schemes.

Minerals. Value of production, 1985, Rs 4,952·6m. The state has coal (the Raniganj field is one of the 3 biggest in India) including coking coal. Coal production (1985) 19·36m. tonnes.

Agriculture. About 5m. hectares are rice-paddy, one-third of it irrigated. Total foodgrain production, 1985–86, 9·13m. tonnes; oilseeds (provisional), 233,700 tonnes; jute, 7·4m. bales (180 kg); wheat, 738,700 tonnes. The state produces 57·3% of the national output of jute.

Livestock (1976 census): 11,968,000 cattle, 758,000 buffaloes; 1981 census, 758,000 sheep and goats, and 15,052,000 poultry.

Forests cover 13·4% of the state.

Fisheries. Landings, 1985–86, about 424,000 tonnes. During 1985–86 Rs 74·4m. was invested in fishery schemes.

INDUSTRY. The total number of registered factories, 1984, was 7,628; average daily employment in public sector industries, 1·6m. The coalmining industry had 116 units with average daily employment of 128,000.

There is a large automobile factory at Uttarpara, and there are aluminium rolling-mills at Belur and Asansol. Durgapur has a large steel plant and other industries under the state sector—a thermal power plant, coke oven plant, fertilizer factory, alloy steel plant and ophthalmic glass plant. There are a locomotive factory and cable factory at Chittaranjan and Rupnarayanpur. A refinery and fertilizer factory are operating at Haldia.

Small industries are important; 225,760 units were registered at 31 March 1986, (estimated employment, 1·6m.).

COMMUNICATIONS

Roads. In 1981–82 the length of national highway was 1,631 km, of state highway. On 31 March 1984 the state had 453,113 motor vehicles.

Railways. The length of railways within the state (1985–86) is 3,771 km. The main centres are Howrah, Sealdah, Kharagpur, Asansol and New Jalpaiguri. The Calcutta Metro was 75% complete by July 1987.

Aviation. The main airport is Calcutta which has national and international flights. The second airport is at Bagdogra in the extreme north, which has regular scheduled services to Calcutta. Vayudoot domestic airline flies between Calcutta and district headquarters.

Shipping. Calcutta is the chief port: a barrage has been built at Farakka to control the flow of the Ganges and to provide a rail and road link between North and South Bengal. A second port is being developed at Haldia, halfway between the present port and the sea, which is intended mainly for bulk cargoes. West Bengal possesses 779 km of navigable canals.

JUSTICE, RELIGION AND EDUCATION

Justice. The High Court of Judicature at Calcutta has a Chief Justice and 36 puisne judges. The Andaman and Nicobar Islands *(see below)* come under its jurisdiction.

Police. At 1 June 1987 the police force numbered 54,959, under a director-general and an inspector-general. Calcutta has a separate force under a commissioner directly responsible to the Government; its strength was 21,140 at 1 June 1987.

Religion. At the 1981 census Hindus numbered 42,007,159; Moslems, 11,743,259; Christians, 319,670; Buddhists, 156,296; Sikhs, 49,054; Jains, 38,663.

Education. At the 1981 census 22·2m. people were literate. In 1985–86 there were 50,811 primary schools, 3,890 junior high and 6,580 high and higher secondary schools. Education is free up to higher secondary stage.

The University of Calcutta (founded 1857) is affiliating and teaching; in 1983–84 it had 140,671 students. Visva Bharati, Santiniketan, was originally established in 1951 and is residential and teaching; it had 3,189 students in 1983–84. The University of Jadavpur, Calcutta (1955), had about 5,000 students in 1983–84. Burdwan University was established 15 June 1960 with 30 affiliated colleges previously under the supervision of the University of Calcutta; in 1983–84 there were 49,139 students. Kalyani University was established in 1960 (1,672 students in 1981–82). The University of North Bengal (1962) had 16,000 students in 1981–82. Rabindra Bharati University with 3 affiliated colleges had 2,995 students in 1981–82. Bidhan Chandra Krishi Viswavidyalaya (1974) had 1,239 students in 1981–82.

UNION TERRITORIES

ANDAMAN AND NICOBAR ISLANDS. The Andaman and Nicobar Islands are administered by the President of the Republic of India acting through a Lieut.-Governor. There is a Pradesh Council, 5 members of which are selected by the Administrator as advisory counsellors. The seat of administration is at Port Blair, which is connected with Calcutta (1,255 km away) and Madras (1,190 km) by steamer service which calls about every 10 days; there are air services from Calcutta and Madras. Roads in the islands, 722 km black-topped and 20 km others. There are 2 districts.

The population (1981 census) was 188,741; density 23 per sq. km.; growth rate 1971–81, 63·5%. Port Blair (1981), 49,634.

The climate is tropical, with little variation in temperature. Heavy rain (125″ annually) is mainly brought by the south-west monsoon. Humidity is high.

Budget figures for 1985–86 show total revenue receipts of Rs 1,59,892 lakhs, and total expenditure on revenue account of Rs 5,78,162 lakhs.

On 31 March 1987 there were 296 educational institutions, including a B. Ed. college, another teachers' training college, and a polytechnic. Literacy (1981 census), 51·56%.

Lieut.-Governor: Lieut.-Gen. (Ret'd.) T. S. Oberoi.

The **Andaman Islands** lie in the Bay of Bengal, 193 km from Cape Negrais in Burma, 1,255 from Calcutta and 1,190 from Madras. Five large islands grouped together are called the Great Andamans, and to the south is the island of Little Andaman. There are some 204 islets, the two principal groups being the Ritchie Archipelago and the Labyrinth Islands. The total area is about 6,340 sq. km. The Great Andaman group is about 467 km long and, at the widest, 51 km broad.

The original inhabitants live in the forests by hunting and fishing; they are of a small Negrito type and their civilization is about that of the Stone Age. Their exact numbers are not known, as they avoid all contact with civilization. The total population of the Andaman Islands (including about 430 aboriginals) was 158,287 in 1981. Main aboriginal tribes, Andamanese, Onges, Jarawas and Sentinelese. Under a central government scheme started in 1953, some 4,000 displaced families, mostly from East Pakistan, had been settled in the islands by May 1967.

Japanese forces occupied the Andaman Islands on 23 March 1942. Civil administration of the islands was resumed on 8 Oct. 1945.

From 1857 to March 1942 the islands were used by the Government of India as a penal settlement for life and long-term convicts, but the penal settlement was abolished on re-occupation in Oct. 1945.

The Great Andaman group, densely wooded, contains many valuable trees, both hardwood and softwood. The best known of the hardwoods is the *padauk* or Andaman redwood; *gurjan* is in great demand for the manufacture of plywood. Large quantities of softwood are supplied to match factories. Annually the Forest Department export about 25,000 tons of timber to the mainland. Coconut, coffee and rubber are cultivated. The islands are slowly being made self-sufficient in paddy and rice, and now grow approximately half their annual requirements. Livestock (1982): 27,400 cattle, 9,720 buffaloes, 17,600 goats and 21,220 pigs. Fishing is important. There is a sawmill at Port Blair and a coconut-oil mill. Little Andaman has a palm-oil mill.

The islands possess a number of harbours and safe anchorages, notably Port Blair in the south, Port Cornwallis in the north and Elphinstone and Mayabandar in the middle.

The **Nicobar Islands** are situated to the south of the Andamans, 121 km from Little Andaman. The British were in possession 1869–1947. There are 19 islands, 7 uninhabited; total area, 1,953 sq. km. The islands are usually divided into 3 subgroups (southern, central and northern), the chief islands in each being respectively, Great Nicobar, Camotra with Nancowrie and Car Nicobar. There is a fine land-locked harbour between the islands of Camotra and Nancowrie, known as Nancowrie Harbour.

The population numbered, in 1981, 30,454, including about 22,200 of Nicobarese and Shompen tribes. The coconut and arecanut are the main items of trade, and coconuts are a major item in the people's diet.

The Nicobar Islands were occupied by the Japanese in July 1942; and Car Nicobar was developed as a big supply base. The Allies reoccupied the islands on 8 Oct. 1945.

CHANDIGARH. On 1 Nov. 1966 the city of Chandigarh and the area surrounding it was constituted a Union Territory. Population (1981), 450,061; density, 3,948 per sq. km.; growth rate, 1971–81, 74·9%. Area, 114 sq. km. It serves as the joint capital of both Punjab (India) and the state of Haryana, and is the seat of a High Court and of a university serving both states. The city will ultimately be the capital of just the Punjab; joint status is to last while a new capital is built for Haryana.

There is some cultivated land and some forest (27·5% of the territory).

Evenson, N., *Chandigarh*. Berkeley, Cal., 1966

DADRA AND NAGAR HAVELI. Formerly Portuguese, the territories of Dadra and Nagar Haveli were occupied in July 1954 by nationalists, and a pro-India administration was formed; this body made a request for incorporation into the Union, 1 June 1961. By the 10th amendment to the constitution the territories became a centrally administered Union Territory with effect from 11 Aug. 1961, forming an enclave at the southernmost point of the border between Gujarat and Maharashtra. Area 491 sq. km.; population (1981), 103,676 (males 52,515, females 51,161); density 211 per sq. km; growth rate, 1971–81, 39·78%. There is an Administrator appointed by the Government of India. The day-to-day business is done by various departments, co-ordinated by the Administrator's secretary and headed by a Collector. Headquarters are at Silvassa. The territory and 78·82% of the population is tribal and organized in 72 villages. Languages used are Bhilli, Gujarat, Bhilodi (83%), Marathi and Hindi.

Administrator: Dr Gopal Singh.
Collector: S. M. S. Chaudhary.

Electricity. Electricity is supplied by Gujarat, and all villages have been electrified.

Water. As the result of a joint project with the governments of Gujarat, Goa, Daman and Diu there is a reservoir at Damanganga with irrigation potential of 8,280 hectares.

Agriculture. Farming is the chief occupation, and about 24,000 hectares were under crops in 1986–87. Much of the land is terraced and there is a 100% subsidy for soil conservation. The major food crops are rice and ragi; wheat, small millets and pulses are also grown. There is little irrigation (1,000 hectares). There are 9 veterinary centres, a veterinary hospital, an agricultural research centre and breeding centres to improve strains of cattle and poultry. During 1986–87 the Administration distributed 268 tonnes of high yielding paddy seed, and high yielding wheat seed, and 366 tonnes of fertilizer.

Forests. About 20,311 hectares or 41·2% of the total area is forest, mainly of teak, sadad and khair. Timber production provides the largest simple contribution to the territory's revenue. There was (1985) a moratorium on commercial felling, to preserve the environmental function of the forests and ensure local supplies of firewood, timber and fodder.

Industry. There is no heavy industry, and the Territory is a "No Industry District". Industrial estates for small and medium units have been set up at Piparia, Masat and Khadoli. There are 286 small units, and 16 medium scale, employing about 5,700. Concessions (25% subsidy, 15 years' sales tax holiday) are available for small industries.

Communications. There are (1986) 292 km of motorable road. The railway line from Bombay to Ahmedabad runs through Vapi near Silvassa. The nearest airport is Bombay.

Tourism. The territory is a rural area between the industrial centres of Bombay and Surat-.Vapi. The Tourism Department is developing areas of natural beauty to promote acceptable tourism.

Justice. The territory is under the jurisdiction of the Bombay (Maharashtra) High Court. There is a District and Sessions Court and one Junior Division Civil Court at Silvassa.

Education. Literacy was 26·67% of the population at the 1981 census. In 1986–87 there were 86 adult education centres (4,500 students); there were 144 government primary schools, 16 government-aided mission schools and one unaided; there were 2 higher secondary schools and 5 high schools. Total primary enrolment was 17,198; high-school and higher secondary, 2,616.

Health. The territory has 1 cottage hospital, 3 primary health centres and 7 dispensaries; there is also a mobile dispensary.

DAMAN AND DIU. Daman (Damão) on the Gujarat coast, 100 miles (160 km) north of Bombay, was seized by the Portuguese in 1531 and ceded to them (1539) by the Shar of Gujarat. The island of Diu, captured in 1534, lies off the south-east coast of Kathiawar (Gujarat); there is a small coastal area. Former Portuguese forts on either side of the entrance to the Gulf of Cambay, in Dec. 1961 the territories were occupied by India and incorporated into the Indian Union; they were administered as one unit together with Goa, to which they were attached until 30 May 1987, when Goa was seperated from them and became a state.

Area and Population. Daman, 72 sq. km, population (1981) 48,560; Diu, 38 sq. km, population 30,421. The main language spoken is Gujarati.

The chief towns are Daman (population, 1981, 21,003) and Diu (8,020).

Daman and Diu have been governed as parts of a Union Territory since Dec. 1961, becoming the whole of that Territory on 30 May 1987.

The main activities are tourism, fishing and tapping the toddy palm. In Daman there is rice-growing, some wheat and dairying. Diu has fine tourist beaches, grows coconuts and pearl millet, and processes salt.

DELHI. Delhi became a Union Territory on 1 Nov. 1956.

Area and Population. The territory forms an enclave inside the eastern frontier of Haryana in north India. Delhi has an area of 1,483 sq. km. At the 1981 census its population was 6,220,406 (density per sq. km, 4,194). Estimate, 1 July 1987, 8·04m. Growth rate, 1971–81, 53%. In the rural area of Delhi there are 214 inhabited and 17 deserted villages and 27 census towns. They are distributed in 5 community development blocks.

Government. The Lieut-Governor is the Administrator, assisted by 4 Executive Councillors (1 Chief Executive Councillor and 3 Executive Councillors) appointed by the President of India on the recommendation of the Union Home Ministry. There is a Metropolitan Council of 61 members including 5 nominated by the President of India. The Territory is covered by 3 local bodies: Delhi Municipal Corporation, New Delhi Municipal Committee and Delhi Cantonment Board.

Lieut.-Governor: Air Vice Marshall (Rtd.) H. Lal Kapoor.
Chief Executive Councillor: J. Pravesh Chandra.

Budget. Revised estimates 1986–87 show total revenue of Rs 5,728m. and expenditure including plan expenditure: Rs 11,100m. of which plan, Rs 4,950m.; power, Rs 1,820m.; transport, Rs 624m.; water and sewerage, Rs 533m.; rural and urban development, Rs 535m.; medical services and public health, Rs 379m.

Sanctioned budget 1987–88, Rs 11,021m. Annual plan, 1988–89, Rs 510 crores.

Agriculture. The contribution to the economy is not significant. About 81,377 hectares are cropped (of which 46,747 are irrigated). Animal husbandry is increasing and mixed farms are common. Chief crops are wheat, jowar, bajra, grain, sugarcane and vegetables.

Industry. The modern city is the largest commercial centre in northern India and an important industrial centre. Since 1947 a large number of industrial concerns have been established; these include factories for the manufacture of razor blades, sports goods, radios and television and parts, bicycles and parts, plastic and PVC goods including footwear, textiles, chemicals, fertilizers, medicines, hosiery, leather goods, soft drinks, hand tools. There is also metal forging, casting, galvanising and electro-plating, and printing. The number of industrial units functioning was about 65,000 in 1985–86; average number of workers employed was 595,000. Production was worth Rs 34,500m. and investment was about Rs 12,600m.

Some traditional handicrafts, for which Delhi was formerly famous, still flourish; among them are ivory carving, miniature painting, gold and silver jewellery and papier mâché work. The handwoven textiles of Delhi are particularly fine; this craft is being successfully revived.

Delhi publishes major daily newspapers, including the *Times of India, Hindustan Times, The Hindu, Indian Express* and *Statesman* (all in English); *Nav Bharat Times, Jansatta* and *Hindustan* (in Hindi), and 3 Urdu dailies

Roads. Five national highways pass through the city. There were (1986) 1,075,486

registered motor vehicles in Delhi. The Transport Corporation had 4,077 buses in daily service in 1986.

Railways. Delhi is an important rail junction with three main stations: Delhi, New Delhi, Hazart Nizamuddin. There is an electric ring railway for commuters.

Aviation. Indira Gandhi International Airport operates international flights; Palam airport operates internal flights.

Religion. At the 1981 census Hindus numbered 5,200,432; Sikhs, 393,921; Moslems, 481,802; Jains, 73,917; Christians, 61,609; Buddhists, 7,117; others, 1,608.

Education. The proportion of literates to the total population was 61·54% at the 1981 census (68·4% of males and 53·07% of females).

The total number of educational institutions in 1985–86 was 4,868, with an enrolment of 1·79m.

The University of Delhi was founded in 1922; it had 66 constituent colleges and institutions in 1985–86, with a total of 101,412 students. There are also Jawaharlal Nehru university, Indira Gandhi National Open University and the Jamia Millia Islamia; the Indian Institute of Technology at Haus Khaz; the Indian Agricultural Research Institute at Pusa; the All India Institute of Medical Science at Ansari Nagar and the Indian Institute of Public Administration are deemed universities.

LAKSHADWEEP. The territory consists of an archipelago of 36 islands (10 inhabited), about 300 km off the west coat of Kerala. It was constituted a Union Territory in 1956 as the Laccadive, Minicoy and Amindivi Islands, and renamed in Nov. 1973. The total area of the islands is 32 sq. km. The northern portion is called the Amindivis. The remaining islands are called the Laccadives (except Minicoy Island). The inhabited islands are: Androth (the largest), Amini, Agatti, Bitra, Chetlat, Kadmat, Kalpeni, Kavaratti, Kiltan and Minicoy. Androth is 4·8 sq. km, and is nearest to Kerala. An Advisory Committee associated with the Union Home Minister and an Advisory Council to the Administrator assist in the administration of the islands; these are constituted annually. Population (1981 census), 40,249, nearly all Moslems. Density, 1,258 per sq. km.; growth rate, 1971–81, 26·53%. The language is Malayalam, but the language in Minicoy is Mahl. There were, in autumn 1986, 9 high schools and 9 nursery schools, 19 junior basic schools, 4 senior basic schools and 2 junior colleges. There are 2 hospitals and 7 primary health centres. The staple products are copra and fish. There is a tourist resort at Bangarem, an uninhabited island with an extensive lagoon. Headquarters of administration, Kavaratti Island.

Administrator: Wajahat Habibullah.

PONDICHERRY. Formerly the chief French settlement in India, Pondicherry was founded by the French in 1674, taken by the Dutch in 1693 and restored to the French in 1699. The English took it in 1761, restored it in 1765, re-took it in 1778, restored it a second time in 1785, retook it a third time in 1793 and finally restored it to the French in 1814. Administration was transferred to India on 1 Nov. 1954. A Treaty of Cession (together with Karikal, Mahé and Yanam) was signed on 28 May 1956; instruments of ratification were signed on 16 Aug. 1962 from which date (by the 14th amendment to the Indian Constitution) Pondicherry, comprising the 4 territories, became a Union Territory.

Area and Population. The territory is composed of enclaves on the Coromandel Coast of Tamil Nadu and Andhra Pradesh, with Mahé forming an enclave on the coast of Kerala. The total area of Pondicherry is 492 sq. km, divided into 4 Districts. On Tamil Nadu coast: Pondicherry (293 sq. km; population, 1981 census, 444,417), Karikal (160; 120,010). On Kerala coast: Mahé (9; 28,413). On Andhra Pradesh coast: Yanam (30; 11,631). Total population (1981 census), 604,471; density, 1,228 per sq. km.; growth rate, 1971–81, 28·14%. Pondicherry Municipality had (1981) 162,639 inhabitants. The principal languages spoken are Tamil, Telegu, Malayalam, French and English.

Government. By the Government of Union Territories Act 1963 Pondicherry is governed by a Lieut.-Governor, appointed by the President, and a Council of Ministers responsible to a Legislative Assembly. The election in March 1985 returned a Congress (I) government.

Lieut.-Governor: Thiru T. P. Tewary.

Planning. Approved outlay for 1987–88 was Rs 470m. Of this, Rs 14m. was for agriculture, Rs 12·2m. for rural development, Rs 16m. for co-operatives, Rs 110m. for education, Rs 8·5m. for public works, Rs 34·5m. for electricity, Rs 10·4m. for fisheries.

Budget. Budget estimates for 1987–88 show revenue receipts of Rs 49·6 crores.

Electricity. Power is bought from neighbouring states. All 292 villages have electricity. Consumption, 1986–87, 386 units per head. Peak demand, 62 mw.; total consumption, 233·23m. units.

Agriculture. Nearly 45% of the population is engaged in agriculture and allied pursuits; 90% of the cultivated area is irrigated. The main food crop is rice. Foodgrain production, 101,000 tonnes from 38,582 hectares in 1986–87, of which 89,713 tonnes was paddy; cash crops include oilseeds, cotton (7,700 bales of 180 kg) and sugar-cane (330,000 tonnes). Crops suffered from drought, as rains failed in the Mettur Dam catchment area.

Industry. There are (1987) 12 large and 24 medium-scale industries manufacturing consumer goods such as textiles, sugar, cotton yarn, paper, spirits and beer, potassium chlorate, rice bran oil, vehicle parts and soap, and employing 18,000 people. There were 17,500 people employed in 2,619 small industrial units engaged in varied manufacturing.

Railways. Pondicherry is on a branch from the main Madurai–Madras line.

Aviation. The nearest airport is Madras.

Education. There were, in Sept. 1987, 112 pre-primary schools (6,087 pupils and 195 teachers), 353 primary schools (50,884 and 1,680), 102 middle schools (47,959 and 1,592), 65 high schools (39,365 and 1,470) and 22 higher secondary schools (23,450 and 680). There were 9 general education colleges (5,409 and 656); a medical college, a law college, a technical higher secondary school and a polytechnic had a total of 1,713 students.

Health. On 31 March 1986 there were 8 hospitals, 40 health centres and dispensaries and 73 sub-centres. Family schemes have reduced the birth rate to 22·2, the infant mortality rate to 38 per 1,000 live births.

INDONESIA

Capital: Jakarta
Population: 172m. (1987)
GNP per capita: US$510 (1986)

Republik Indonesia

HISTORY. In the 16th century Portuguese traders in quest of spices settled in some of the islands, but were ejected by the British, who in turn were ousted by the Dutch (1595). From 1602 the Netherlands East India Company conquered the Netherlands East Indies, and ruled them until the dissolution of the company in 1798. Thereafter the Netherlands Government ruled the colony from 1816 to 1941, when it was occupied by the Japanese until 1945. An independent republic was proclaimed by Dr Sukarno and Dr Hatta on 17 Aug. 1945.

Complete and unconditional sovereignty was transferred to the Republic of the United States of Indonesia on 27 Dec. 1949, except for the western part of New Guinea, the status of which was to be determined through negotiations between Indonesia and the Netherlands within one year after the transfer of sovereignty. A union was created to regulate the relationship between the two countries. A settlement of the New Guinea (Irian Jaya) question was, however, delayed until 15 Aug. 1962, when, through the good offices of the United Nations, an agreement was concluded for the transfer of the territory to Indonesia on 1 May 1963. In Feb. 1956 Indonesia abrogated the union and in Aug. 1956 repudiated Indonesia's debt to the Netherlands.

During 1950 the federal system which had sprung up in 1946–48 (*see* THE STATESMAN'S YEAR-BOOK, 1950, p. 1233) was abolished, and Indonesia was again made a unitary state. The provisional constitution was passed by the Provisional House of Representatives on 14 and came into force on 17 Aug. 1950. On 5 July 1959 by Presidential decree, the Constitution of 1945 was reinstated and the Constituent Assembly dissolved. For history 1960–66 *see* THE STATESMAN'S YEAR-BOOK, 1982–83, p. 678.

On 11–12 March 1966 the military commanders under the leadership of Lieut.-Gen. Suharto took over the executive power while leaving President Sukarno as the head of State. The Communist Party was at once outlawed and the National Front was dissolved in Oct. 1966. On 22 Feb. 1967 Sukarno handed over all his powers to Gen. Suharto.

AREA AND POPULATION. Indonesia, covering a total land area of 741,098 sq. miles (1,919,443 sq. km), consists of some 13,700 islands (6,000 of which are inhabited) extending about 3,200 miles east to west through three time-zones (East, Central and West Indonesian Standard time) and 1,250 miles north to south. The largest islands are Sumatra, Java, Kalimantan (Indonesian Borneo), Sulawesi (Celebes) and Irian Jaya (the western part of New Guinea). Most of the smaller islands except Madura and Bali are grouped together. The two largest groups of islands are Maluku (the Moluccas) and Nusa Tenggara (the Lesser Sundas).

The total population in 1980 (census) was 147,490,298, distributed as follows:

Province	Sq. km	Census 1980	Chief town	Census 1980
Aceh (D.I.)	55,392	2,611,271	Banda Aceh	72,090
Sumatera Utara	70,787	8,360,894	Medan	1,378,955
Sumatera Barat	49,778	3,406,816	Padang	480,922
Riau	94,562	2,168,535	Pakanbaru	186,262
Jambi	44,924	1,445,994	Telanaipura	230,373
Sumatera Selatan	103,688	4,629,801	Palembang	787,187
Bengkulu	21,168	768,064	Bengkulu	64,783
Lampung	33,307	4,624,785	Tanjungkarang	284,275
Sumatera	473,606	28,016,160		

Province	Sq. km	Census 1980	Chief town	Census 1980
Jakarta Raya (D.C.I.)	590	6,503,449	Jakarta	6,503,449
Jawa Barat	46,300	27,453,525	Bandung	1,462,637
Jawa Tengah	34,206	25,372,889	Semarang	1,026,671
Yogyakarta (D.I.)	3,169	2,750,813	Yogyakarta	398,727
Jawa Timur	47,922	29,188,852	Surabaya	2,027,913
Jawa and Madura	132,187	91,269,528		
Kalimantan Barat	146,760	2,486,068	Pontianak	304,778
Kalimantan Tengah	152,600	954,353	Palangkaraya	60,447
Kalimantan Selatan	37,660	2,064,649	Banjarmasin	381,286
Kalimantan Timur	202,440	1,218,016	Samarinda	264,718
Kalimantan	539,460	6,723,086		
Sulawesi Utara	19,023	2,115,384	Menado	217,159
Sulawesi Tengah	69,726	1,289,635	Palu	298,584
Sulawesi Selatan	72,781	6,062,212	Ujung Padang	709,038
Sulawesi Tenggara	27,686	942,302	Kendari	41,021
Sulawesi	189,216	10,409,533		
Bali	5,561	2,469,930	Denpasar	261,263
Nusu Tenggara Barat	20,177	2,724,664	Mataram	68,964
Nusu Tenggara Timur	47,876	2,737,166	Kupang	403,110
Timor Timur [1]	14,874	555,350	Dili	60,150
Maluku	74,505	1,411,006	Amboina	208,898
Irian Jaya	421,981	1,173,875	Jayapura	149,618
Palau–Palau Lain	584,974	11,071,991		

[1] Formerly Portuguese East Timor.

Other major cities (census 1980): Malang, 511,780; Surakarta, 469,888; Bogor, 247,409; Cirebon, 223,776; Kediri, 221,830; Madiun, 150,562; Pematangsiantar, 150,376; Pekalongan, 132,558; Tegal, 131,728; Magelang, 123,484; Jember, 122,712; Sukabumi, 109,994 and Probolinggo, 100,296 (all on Java); Balikpapan (on Kalimantan), 280,875. Estimate (1987) 172·25m.

The principal ethnic groups are the Aceh, Bataks and Minangkabaus in Sumatra, the Javanese and Sundanese in Java, the Madurese in Madura, the Balinese in Bali, the Sasaks in Lombok, the Menadonese, Minahas, Torajas and Buginese in Sulawesi, the Dayaks in Kalimantan, Irianese in Irian Jaya, the Ambonese in the Moluccas and Timorese in Timor Timur.

Bahasa Indonesian, a Malay dialect, is the official language of the Republic although Dutch is spoken as an unofficial language.

CLIMATE. Conditions vary greatly over this spread of islands, but generally the climate is tropical monsoon, with a dry season from June to Sept. and a wet one from Oct. to April. Temperatures are high all the year and rainfall varies according to situation on lee or windward shores. Jakarta. Jan. 78°F (25·6°C), July 78°F (25·6°C). Annual rainfall 71″ (1,775 mm). Padang. Jan. 79°F (26·7°C), July 79°F (26·7°C). Annual rainfall 177″ (4,427 mm). Surabaya. Jan. 79°F (27·2°C), July 78°F (25·6°C). Annual rainfall 51″ (1,285 mm).

CONSTITUTION AND GOVERNMENT. Indonesia is a sovereign, independent republic.

The People's Consultative Assembly is the supreme power. It has 1,000 members and it sits at least once every 5 years. The House of People's Representatives has 500 members, 400 of them elected and 100 nominated by the President upon recommendation and sits for a 5-year term.

General elections to the 360 elected seats in the House of Representatives were held on 23 April 1987 and 299 seats were won by the Golkar Party.

President, Prime Minister and Minister of Defence: Gen. Raden Suharto, elected by the People's Consultative Assembly in 1968 and re-elected in 1973, 1978, 1983 and 1988.

Vice-President: Gen. Umar Wirahadikusumah. *Minister Coordinator for Political Affairs and Security:* Gen. Reksodimedjo Surono. *Minister Coordinator for the Economy, Finance, Industry and Development Supervision:* Dr Ali Wardhana. *Minister Coordinator for Public Welfare:* H. Alamsjah Ratu Perwiranegara. *State Minister and Secretary of State:* Sudharmono. *State Minister for National Development Planning and Chairman of the National Development Planning Agency:* Dr J. B. Sumarlin. *State Minister for Research and Technology and Chairman of the Agency for Research and Applied Technology:* Prof. B. J. Habibie. *State Minister for Population Affairs and the Environment:* Dr Emil Salim. *State Minister for Housing:* Dr Cosmas Batubara. *State Minister for Youth Affairs and Sports:* Dr Abdul Gafur. *State Minister for Administrative Reform and Vice Chairman of the National Development Planning Agency:* Dr Saleh Afiff. *State Minister for Women's Affairs:* L. Soetanto. *Minister of Home Affairs:* Soepardjo Roestam. *Foreign Affairs:* Dr Mochtar Kusumaatmadja. *Defence and Security:* Gen. S. Poniman. *Justice:* Ismail Saleh. *Information:* H. Harmoko. *Finance:* Dr Radius Prawiro. *Trade:* Dr Rachmat Saleh. *Cooperatives:* Bustanil Arifin. *Agriculture:* Achmad Affandi. *Forestry:* Soedjarwo. *Industries:* Hartarto. *Mines and Energy:* Dr Subroto. *Public Works:* Suyono Sosrodarsono. *Communications:* Roesmin Nurjadin. *Tourism, Post and Telecommunications:* Achmad Tahir. *Manpower:* Sudomo. *Transmigration:* Martono. *Education and Culture:* Dr Nugroho Notosusanto. *Health:* Dr Suwardjono Surjaningrat. *Religious Affairs:* H. Munawir Sjadzali. *Social Affairs:* Nani Soedarsono. *Commander-in-Chief of the Armed Forces:* Gen. L. B. Murdani.

There are 5 junior ministers.

National flag: Horizontally red over white.
National anthem: Indonesia Raya (tune by Wage Rudolf Supratman, 1928).

Local government: There are 24 provinces and 2 special districts (Aceh and Yogyakarta), each administered by a Governor appointed by the President; they are divided into 301 *kabupatens*, each under a *bupati*, and thence into over 3,000 *kecamatans*, each headed by a *camat*. The capital, Jakarta, forms a separate metropolitan district.

DEFENCE. The Indonesian Armed Forces were formally set up on 5 Oct. 1945. On 11 Oct. 1967 the Army, Navy, Air Force and Police were integrated under the Department of Defence and Security. Their commanders no longer hold cabinet rank. There is selective military service.

Army. There are 2 infantry divisions: 1 armoured cavalry brigade, 3 infantry brigades, 2 airborne infantry brigades, 3 artillery regiments, 1 engineer regiment and 3 special warfare groups. There are 67 independent infantry battalions, 15 independent artillery battalions and 7 independent cavalry battalions. Equipment includes 100 AMX-13 and 41 PT-76 light tanks. The Army has over 70 aircraft, including 4 Aviocars, 2 C-47s and 16 other fixed-wing types, and 16 Iroquois, 12 BO 105, 9 Hughes 300 and 6 Alouette III helicopters. Delivery of 28 locally-built Bell 412 helicopters was under way in 1988. Total strength in 1988 was 216,000.

Navy. The fleet comprises 2 diesel powered patrol submarines, 12 frigates, 4 fast missile boats, 2 fast attack craft, 1 fast gunboat, 12 patrol vessels, 2 fleet minesweepers, 8 small patrol craft, 15 landing ships, 2 landing craft, 3 training ships, 6 surveying vessels, 2 command and submarine support ships, 1 destroyer depot ship, 1 repair ship, 1 cable ship, 6 oilers, 10 auxiliaries, 60 minor landing craft, 20 service craft and 6 tugs. Of the 104 ships acquired from the USSR very few now remain.

The Naval Air Arm has 60 aircraft, including 31 helicopters. There are 78 customs patrol cutters, 10 maritime security agency boats, 35 Army vessels, 6 Air Force boats and 60 armed marine police craft.

Naval personnel in 1988 numbered 35,800 officers and men, including 5,000 of the Marine Commando Corps and 1,000 in the Naval Air Arm.

Air Force. Operational combat units comprise two squadrons of A-4E Skyhawk attack aircraft, and single squadrons of F-5E Tiger II fighters and OV-10F Bronco twin-turboprop counter-insurgency aircraft. There are 3 transport squadrons, equipped with turboprop C-130 Hercules, Nurtanio/CASA NC-212 Aviocar and F27 Friendship aircraft, and piston-engined C-47s, plus 3 specially-equipped Boeing 737 dual-purpose maritime surveillance/transports; and an assortment of other aircraft in transport, helicopter and training units including 16 Hawk attack/trainers, 25 T-34C-1 armed turboprop trainers, and 40 Swiss-built AS 202 Bravo piston-engined primary trainers. On order are 32 CN-235 twin-turboprop transports, 12 F-16 Fighting Falcon interceptors, and Super Puma and Bell 412 helicopters, all from Nurtanio of Indonesia. Personnel (1988) approximately 26,000.

INTERNATIONAL RELATIONS

Membership. Indonesia is a member of UN, OPEC and ASEAN.

ECONOMY

Planning. The fourth Five-Year Development Plan (1984–89) gives priority to increasing production and services in agriculture, manufacturing, mining, communications and transportation, and tourist industries.

Budget. The ordinary budget (in Rp.1m.) in 1987–88, balanced at 22,783,100m.

Currency. The monetary unit is the *rupiah* (abbreviated Rp.), divided into 100 *sen*. There are banknotes of 1, 2·5, 5, 10, 25, 50, 100, 500, 1,000, 5,000 and 10,000 rupiahs and aluminium coins of 1, 5, 10, 25 and cupro-nickel coins of 50 sen.
In March 1988 there were 2,951 rupiahs = £1 sterling; 1,660 rupiahs = US$1.

Banking. The Bank Indonesia, successor to De Javasche Bank established by the Dutch in 1828, was made the central bank of Indonesia on 1 July 1953. It had an original capital of Rp. 25m.; a reserve fund of Rp. 18m. and a special reserve of Rp. 84m.
There are 117 commercial banks, 28 development banks and other financial institutions, 8 development finance companies and 9 joint venture merchant banks. Commercial banking is dominated by 5 state-owned banks: Bank Rakyat Indonesia provides services to smallholder agriculture and rural development; Bank Bumi Daya, estate agriculture and forestry; Bank Negara Indonesia 1946, industry; Bank Dagang Negara, mining; and Bank Expor-Impor Indonesia, export commodity sector. All state banks are authorized to deal in foreign exchange.
There are 101 private commercial banks owned and operated by Indonesians. The 11 foreign banks, which specialize in foreign exchange transactions and direct lending operations to foreign joint ventures, include the Chartered Bank, the Hong-kong and Shanghai Banking Corporation, the Bank of America, the City Bank, the Bank of Tōkyō, Chase Manhattan and the American Express International Banking Corporation. The government owns one Savings Bank, Bank Tabungan Negara, and 1,000 Post Office Savings Banks. There are also over 3,500 rural and village savings bank and credit cooperatives.

Weights and Measures. The metric system of weights and measures was officially introduced in Feb. 1923, and came into full operation on 1 Jan. 1938.
The following are the old weights and measures: *Pikol* = 136·16 lb. avoirdupois; *Katti* = 1·36 lb. avoirdupois; *Bau* = 1·7536 acres; *Square Pal* = 227 hectares = 561·16 acres; *Jengkal* = 4 yd; *Pal* (Java) = 1,506 metres; *Pal* (Sumatra) = 1,852 metres.

ENERGY AND NATURAL RESOURCES

Electricity. Three large-scale hydro-electric plants are operating on the Jatiluhur and Brantas rivers in Java and on the Asahan River in Sumatra. Electricity produced (1986) 30,000m. kwh. Supply 127 and 220 volts; 50 Hz.

Oil. Indonesia is the principal producer of petroleum in the Far East, production coming from Sumatra, Kalimantan (Indonesian Borneo) and Java. Proven reserves (1986) 8,500m. bbls. The 1987 output of crude oil was 64·1m. tonnes.

Gas. Pertamina, the state oil company, started to pump natural gas to Jakarta in 1979. Production (1985) 1,749,000m. cu. ft.

Minerals. The high cost of extraction means that little of the large mineral resources outside Java is exploited; however, there is copper mining in Irian Jaya, nickel mining and processing on Sulawesi, aluminium smelting in northern Sumatra. Coal production (1986) 3m. tonnes; bauxite (1985), 800,000 tonnes. Output (in 1,000 tonnes, 1982) of iron sand was 136·52; copper, 223·70; silver, 3,051·74 kg; gold, 222·37 kg; nickel 1,640·92. In 1986 tin production was 26,500 tonnes.

Agriculture. Production (1986, in 1,000 tonnes): Rice, 26,706; cassava, 12,667; corn, 5,361; sweet potatoes, 2,125; cane sugar, 1,986; coconuts and copra, 1,864; palm oil, 1,419; soyabeans, 1,177; rubber, 1,034; coffee, 346.

Livestock (1986): Cattle, 6,465,000; buffaloes, 2,936,000; horses, 702,000; sheep, 5,193,000; goats, 12,289,000; pigs, 5,643,000.

Forestry. The forest area is 113m. hectares. Production (1985): Plywood, 4·2m. cu. metres and exports (1986) US$840m.

Fisheries. In 1984 the catch of sea fish was 1·67m. tonnes; inland fish was 550,000 tonnes.

INDUSTRY AND TRADE

Industry. There are shipyards at Jakarta Raya, Surabaya, Semarang and Amboina. There were (1985) more than 2,000 textile factories (total production in 1982–83, 1,708·9m. metres), large paper factories (342,300 tons, 1984–85), match factories, automobile and bicycle assembly works, large construction works, tyre factories, glass factories, a caustic soda and other chemical factories. Production (1984–85): Cement, 8,813,300 tons; fertilizers, 2,910,000 tons; 6·1m. tyres; automobiles, 153,000.

Trade Unions. All unions must be affiliated to the All Indonesia Labour Federation (FBSI). About 40% of the labour force belong to unions. Strikes are forbidden by law. The total labour force (1985, estimate) was 64m.

Commerce. Imports and exports (including oil) in US$1m. for year April–March:

	1983	1984	1985	1986
Imports	16,351·8	13,882·1	14,450·0	12,540·0
Exports	21,151·7	...	19,910·0	18,100·0

The main export items (in US$1m.) in 1986 were: Gas and oil, 7,971·5; timber, 1,417·2; handicrafts, 952·7; coffee, 823·6; rubber, 719·8; shrimps, 288·6; tin, 180·6; copper, 157·9; pepper, 139·3; palm oil, 102·4. Exports went mainly to Japan (44·8%), USA (19·6%), Singapore (8·4%), Netherlands (3·1%), Republic of Korea (2·4%), Federal Republic of Germany (2·3%) and Hong Kong (2·3%).

The main import items are non-crude oil, rice, consumer goods, fertilizer, chemicals, weaving yarn, iron and steel, industrial and business machinery. In 1986 imports came mainly from Japan (29·2%), USA (13·8%), Singapore (9%), Federal Republic of Germany (6·7%), Australia (3·9%), UK (3·2%) and China (3·1%).

Total trade between Indonesia and UK (British Department of Trade returns, in £1,000 sterling):

	1983	1984	1985	1986	1987
Imports to UK	169,454	181,490	155,934	141,242	144,819
Exports and re-exports from UK	193,642	186,736	172,818	196,629	236,027

Tourism. In 1986 about 825,000 tourists visited Indonesia mainly from USA, Australia, Japan, Netherlands, Germany, France, UK and Singapore.

COMMUNICATIONS

Roads. Most cities on Java, Sumatra, Sulawesi and Bali are connected by highways or secondary roads. The Trans-Sumatra trunk road connecting Aceh (north) and Lampung (south) and the Trans-Sulawesi highway were nearing completion in 1984. The feeder-road between West Sumatra and Riau provinces was completed with the building of the bridge over the Kampar River at Pekanbaru in 1974. Motor vehicles, at 31 Dec. 1979, totalled 577,345 passenger cars, 383,648 vans and trucks, 69,545 buses and about 2,266,183 motor cycles.

Railways. In 1985 the State Railways totalled 6,877 km, comprising 4,922 km of 1,067 mm gauge on Java, and 1,458 km of 1,067 mm gauge and 497 km of 750 mm gauge on Sumatra. In 1985–86, railways carried 4,877m. passenger-km and 7,047m. tonne-km.

Aviation. Indonesia has 14 major airports: 4 on Java, 3 on Sumatra, 2 on Sulawesi and one each on Bali, Kalimantan, Timor, Maluku and Irian Jaya. A new international airport, 18 miles west of Jakarta at Cengkareng, was opened in 1985. This will replace Jakarta's present international airport. The Government and KLM in 1949 set up 'Garuda Indonesian Airways' as a mixed enterprise on a 50–50 capital basis under KLM management.

Shipping. There are 16 ports for oceangoing ships, the largest of which is Tanjung Priok, which serves the Jakarta area and has a container terminal. The national shipping company Pelajaran Nasional Indonesia (PELNI) maintains interinsular communications. The Jakarta Lloyd maintains regular services between Jakarta, Amsterdam, Hamburg and London.

Post and Broadcasting. In 1979 the postal and telegraph services of Indonesia included 2,796 post offices. There were 660 telegraph offices which handled 3·9m. domestic and 488,000 international cables. Post offices handled 176m. letters and Rp. 250,000m. in money orders, Giro and postal cheques. Deposits with post office savings accounts, Rp. 31,210m. Number of telephones (1983), 669,301.

Radio Republik Indonesia, under the Department of Information, operates 26 stations. In 1982 there were 1·8m. television and 20m. radio receivers.

Newspapers (1980). There were about 120 daily newspaper publishers with estimated daily circulation of 1·7m. There were 270 publishers of weekly papers and magazines with a circulation of 3·5m.

JUSTICE, RELIGION, EDUCATION AND WELFARE

Justice. There are courts of first instance, high courts of appeal in every provincial capital and a Supreme Court of Justice for the whole of Indonesia in Jakarta. Administrative matters on judicial organization are under the direction of the Department of Justice.

In civil law the population is divided into three main groups: Indonesians, Europeans and foreign Orientals, to whom different law systems are applicable. When, however, people from different groups are involved, a system of so-called 'inter-gentile' law is applied.

The present criminal law, which has been in force since 1918, is codified and is based on European penal law. This law is equally applicable to all groups of the population. For private and commercial law, however, there are various systems applicable for the various groups of the population. For the Indonesians, a system of private and agrarian law is applicable; this is called Adat Law, and is mainly uncodified. For the other groups the prevailing private and commercial law system is codified in the Private Law Act (1847) and the Commercial Law Act (1847). These Acts have their origins in the French *Code Civile* and *Code du Commerce* through the similar Dutch codifications. These Acts are entirely applicable to Indonesian citizens and to Europeans, whereas to foreign Orientals they are applicable with some exceptions, mainly in the fields of family law and inheritance. Penal law was in the process of being codified in 1981.

Religion. Religious liberty is granted to all denominations. About 78% of the Indonesians were Moslems in 1985 and 11% Christians. There are also about 1m. Buddhists, probably for the greater part Chinese. Hinduism has 6m. members, of whom 2·5m. are on Bali.

Education. Pupils and teachers in 1984 (1,000):

	Schools	Pupils	Teachers
Primary	129	25,804	926
Secondary	19	6,447	384
Technological	1	316	29

English is the first foreign language taught in schools. Literacy rate was 72% in 1984.

Total number of students in higher education (1981) 597,000 attending the 41 state, or 450 private universities and technical institutes.

Health. In 1983 there were 10,262 doctors, 1,292 dentists and 1,244 hospitals with 103,500 beds; in 1982 there were 16,928 midwives and 62,615 nursing personnel.

DIPLOMATIC REPRESENTATIVES

Of Indonesia in Great Britain (157 Edgware Rd., London W2 2HR)
Ambassador: S. Suhartoyo.

Of Great Britain in Indonesia (Jalan M.H. Thamrin 75, Jakarta 10310)
Ambassador: M. K. K. White.

Of Indonesia in the USA (2020 Massachusetts Ave., NW, Washington, D.C., 20036)
Ambassador: Soesilo Soedarman.

Of the USA in Indonesia (Medan Merdeka Selatan 5, Jakarta)
Ambassador: Paul D. Wolfowitz.

Of Indonesia to the United Nations
Ambassador: Ali Alatas.

Books of Reference

Economic Update 1984. National Development Information Office, Jakarta, 1984
Indonesia 1984. Department of Information, Jakarta, 1984
Bee, O. J., *The Petroleum Resources of Indonesia.* OUP, 1982
Bemmelen, R. W. van, *Geology of Indonesia.* 2 vols. The Hague, 1949
Echols, J. M., and Shadily, H., *An Indonesian–English Dictionary.* 3rd ed. Cornell Univ. Press, 1975
International Commission of Jurists, *Indonesia and the Rule of Law.* London, 1987
Leifer, M., *Indonesia's Foreign Policy.* London, 1983
McDonald, H., *Suharto's Indonesia.* Univ. Press of Hawaii, 1981
Palmier, L., *Understanding Indonesia.* London, 1986
Papenek, G., *The Indonesian Economy.* Eastbourne, 1980
Polomka, P., *Indonesia Since Sukarno.* London, 1971
Robison, R., *Indonesia: The Rise of Capital.* Sydney, 1986

IRAN

Jomhori-e-Islami-e-Irân

Capital: Tehrán
Population: 49·86m. (1986)
GNP per capita: US$1,690 (1986)

HISTORY. Persia was ruled by the Shahs as an absolute monarchy until 30 Dec. 1906 when the first Constitution was granted. Reza Khan took control after a *coup d'état* on 31 Oct. 1925 deposed the last Shah of the Qajar Dynasty, and became Reza Shah Pahlavi on 12 Dec. 1925. The country's name was changed to Iran on 21 March 1935. Reza Shah abdicated on 16 Sept. 1941 (and died 25 July 1944) in favour of his son, Mohammad Reza Pahlavi (born 26 Oct. 1919).

Following widespread civil unrest, the Shah left Iran with his family on 17 Jan. 1979 (and died in Egypt 27 July 1980). The Ayatollah Ruhollah Khomeini, spiritual leader of the Shi'a Moslem community, returned from 15 years' exile on 1 Feb. 1979 and appointed a provisional government on 5 Feb. The Shah's government resigned and Parliament dissolved itself on 11 Feb. Following a referendum in March, an Islamic Republic was proclaimed on 1 Apr. 1979.

In Sept. 1980 war began with Iraq with destruction of some Iranian towns and damage to the oil installations at Abadán. The war was still in progress in early 1988.

AREA AND POPULATION. Iran is bounded north by the USSR and the Caspian Sea, east by Afghánistán and Pakistan, south by the Gulf of Oman and the Persian Gulf, and west by Iraq and Turkey. It has an area of 1,648,000 sq. km (634,724 sq. miles), but a vast portion is desert, and the average density is only (1987) 31 inhabitants to the sq. km.

The population at recent censuses was as follows: (1956) 18,944,821; (1966) 25,781,090; (1976) 33,708,744; (1986) 49,857,384.

The areas, populations and capitals of the 24 provinces *(ostán)* were:

Province	Area (sq. km)	Census 1976	Census 1986	Capital
Azárbáiján, East	67,102	3,197,685	4,180,376	Tabriz
Azárbáiján, West	38,850	1,407,604	1,989,935	Orúmiyeh [2]
Bakhtárán [1]	23,667	1,030,714	1,471,224	Bakhtarán [3]
Boyer ahmadi and Kohkiluyeh	14,261	244,370	413,096	Yásúj
Búshehr	27,653	347,863	578,556	Búshehr
Chahár Mahál and Bakhtiári	14,870	394,357	637,167	Shahr Kord
Esfáhán	104,650	2,176,694	3,317,081	Esfáhán
Fárs	133,298	2,035,582	3,229,226	Shiráz
Gilán	14,704	1,581,872	2,086,659	Rasht
Hamadán	19,784	1,088,024	1,533,885	Hamadan
Hormozgán	66,870	462,440	760,014	Bandár-e-Abbas
Ilám and Poshtkuh	19,044	246,024	384,417	Ilám
Kermán	179,916	1,091,148	1,639,031	Kermán
Khorásán	313,337	3,264,398	5,312,991	Mashhad
Khuzestán	67,282	2,187,118	2,702,533	Ahváz
Kordestán	24,998	782,440	1,091,064	Sánándáj
Lorestán	28,803	933,939	1,369,897	Khorramabád
Markazi	39,895	1,090,374	1,092,214	Arák
Mázándárán	47,375	2,387,171	3,449,359	Sári
Semnán	90,039	289,463	418,152	Semnán
Sistán and Balúchestan	181,578	664,292	1,205,980	Záhedán
Tehrán (formed from Markazi)	19,118	5,331,166	8,719,480	Tehrán
Yazd	70,011	356,849	582,300	Yazd
Zanján	36,398	1,117,157	1,600,237	Zanján

[1] Formerly Kermánsháhán.   [2] Formerly Rezáyeh.   [3] Formerly Kermánsháh.

The principal cities were:

	Census 1976	Census 1986		Census 1976	Census 1986
Tehrán	4,530,223	6,022,078	Ardabil	147,865	283,710
Esfáhán	661,510	1,001,248	Khorramshahr	140,490	...
Mashhad	667,770	1,466,018	Kermán	140,761	254,786
Tabriz	597,976	994,377	Karaj	137,926	276,592
Shiráz	425,813	848,011	Qazvin	139,258	248,874
Ahváz	334,399	589,529	Yazd	135,925	234,003
Abadán	294,068	...	Arák	116,832	268,405
Bakhtárán	290,600	565,544	Desful	121,251	142,116
Qom	247,219	550,630	Khorramábád	104,912	208,212
Rasht	188,957	293,881	Borujerd	101,345	184,763
Orúmiyeh	164,419	304,823	Zanján	100,351	215,458
Hamadán	165,785	274,274			

The national language is Farsi or Persian, spoken by 45% of the population. 23% spoke related languages, including Kurdish and Luri in the west and Baluchi in the south-east, while 26% spoke Turkic languages, primarily the Azerbáijáni-speaking peoples of the north-west and the Turkomen of Khorásan in the north-east.

CLIMATE. Mainly a desert climate, but with more temperate conditions on the shores of the Caspian Sea. Seasonal range of temperature is considerable. Abadán. Jan. 54°F (12·2°C), July 97°F (36·1°C). Annual rainfall 8″ (204 mm). Tehrán. Jan. 36°F (2·2°C), July 85°F (29·4°C). Annual rainfall 10″ (246 mm).

CONSTITUTION AND GOVERNMENT. The Constitution of the Islamic Republic was approved by a national referendum in Dec. 1979. It gives supreme authority to a religious leader (*wali faqih*), which position will be held by Ayatollah Khomeini for the rest of his natural life, and thereafter be elected by the Moslem clergy.

The President of the Republic is popularly-elected for a 4-year term and is head of the executive; he appoints a Prime Minister and other Ministers, subject to approval by the *Majlis*.

Presidents since the establishment of the Islamic Republic:

Abolhassan Bani-Sadr, 4 Feb. 1980–22 June 1981 (deposed)

Mohammad Ali Raja'i, 24 July 1981–30 Aug. 1981 (assassinated).

The Cabinet was composed as follows in Dec. 1985.

President: Hojatolislam Sayed Ali Khamenei (from 12 Oct. 1981, sworn in for second term 4 Sept. 1985).

Prime Minister: Mir Hosein Musavi-Khamenei.

Agriculture and Rural Development: Abas Ali Zali. *Commerce:* Hasan Abedi-Jafari. *Construction Jihad:* Bizhan Namdar-Zangeneh. *Culture and Higher Education:* Mohammad Farhadi. *Defence:* Mohammed Hosein Jalali. *Economic Affairs and Finance:* Mohammad Javad Iravani. *Education and Training:* Kazem Akrami. *Energy:* Mohammad Taqi Banki. *Foreign Affairs:* Ali Akbar Velayati. *Health and Medical Education:* Ali Reza Marandi. *Heavy Industries:* Behzad Nabavi. *Housing and Urban Development:* Seraj-ed-Din Kazeruni. *Industries:* Qolam Reza Shafei. *Information and Security:* Mohammad Mohammadai-Reyshahri. *Interior:* Ali Akbar Mohtashemi-Pur. *Islamic Guidance:* Mohammad Khatami. *Justice:* Hasan Habibi. *Labour and Social Affairs:* Abol Qasem Sarhadi-zadeh. *Mines and Metals:* Mohammad Reza Ayatollahi. *Petroleum:* Qolam Reza Aqazadeh. *Plan and Budget:* Masud Roqani-Zanjani. *Post, Telegraph and Telephone:* Mohammad Qarazi. *Revolutionary Guard:* Mohsen Rafiq-Dust. *Roads and Transport:* Mohammad Sayyed-Kia.

Legislative power is held by a 270-member Islamic Consultative Assembly *(Majlis),* directly elected for a 4-year term on 17 May 1984; but all legislation is subject to approval by a 12-member Council of Guardians who ensure it is in accordance with the Islamic code and with the Constitution. Six members of this constitutional Council are appointed by the *wali faqih* and six by the judiciary.

National flag: Three horizontal stripes of green, white and red; on the borders of the green and red stripes the legend *Allah Akbar* in white Kufi script repeated 22 times in all; in the centre of the white stripe the national emblem in red.

Local Government. The country is divided into 24 provinces *(ostán)* and 2 governor-generalships, these are sub-divided into 172 *shahrestán* (counties), each under a *farmándár* (governor) and thence into 499 *bakhsh* (districts), each under a *bakhshdár*. The districts are sub-divided into *dehistán* (groups of villages) each under a *dehdár,* each village having its elected *kadkhodá* (headman).

DEFENCE. Two years' military service is compulsory.

Army. The Army consisted (1988) of 305,000 men (about 250,000 conscripts), with some 350,000 reservists. It is organized in 3 armoured, 7 infantry and 1 airborne divisions, and auxiliary units. Equipment includes T-54/-55/-62, T-72, 300 Chieftain, M-47/-48 and M-60A1 main battle tanks. There is also a 300,000-strong Revolutionary Guard Corps. The Army does operate aircraft, but strength is not known.

Navy. The fleet, declining since the revolution, before the war comprised 3 very old destroyers, 4 frigates, 2 old corvettes, 8 fast attack craft (some missile-armed), 3 old coastal minesweepers, 2 inshore minesweepers, 7 patrol boats, 14 hovercraft, 4 logistic landing ships, 2 tank landing ships, 4 landing craft, 2 supply ships, 1 repair ship, 1 replenishment ship, 4 survey vessels, 3 water carriers and 5 tugs. There were also 150 coastguard cutters and 40 customs craft. The Navy air service had a fleet of 20 helicopters and 14 fixed-wing aircraft.

The construction of 12 fast missile craft in France was to have been completed by mid-1979, but later boats did not receive their missiles and the last 3 boats were embargoed in France. They eventually sailed on 2 Aug. 1981 but one was seized by a Royalist group off Cadiz and after she surrendered to the French all three were sent to Iran in a merchant ship to obviate further trouble. Four were reported sunk during the war with Iraq. Two corvettes were also sunk.

Naval personnel nominally totalled 20,000 officers and ratings including marines, but (1987) fewer than 12,000 were reportedly active.

With war following revolution and withdrawal of UK and US maintenance teams the fleet lacks spares and the navy has run down, several ships being laid up. The situation was worsened by cessation of foreign help in training semi-illiterate conscripts and with poor morale following general instability and casualties the above ships do not represent an efficient maritime force.

Claims of sinkings during the Iran-Iraq war have not been officially confirmed. Figures for ship and personnel strengths should be interpreted with caution.

Air Force. In Aug. 1955 the Air Force became a separate and independent arm, and had a strength of about 23 first-line squadrons (each 15 aircraft, plus reserves), with 100,000 personnel before the 1979 revolution. Strength (1988) was estimated at 35,000 personnel and 100 serviceable combat aircraft. The latter include some MiG-19/Chinese-built F-6 fighter-bombers, supplied via North Korea, and surviving US fighters that include F-14 Tomcat, F-5E Tiger II and F-4D/E Phantom II fighter-bombers, plus a few RF-4E reconnaissance-fighters. Transport aircraft include F27s, C-130 Hercules, PC-6 Turbo-Porters, Boeing 707s and 747s, some equipped as flight refuelling tankers. The status of the large fleet of CH-47C Chinook, Bell Model 214 and other helicopters is not known; but two P-3F Orion maritime patrol aircraft remain operational. Training aircraft include Bonanza basic trainers and 35 turboprop PC-7 Turbo-Trainers.

INTERNATIONAL RELATIONS

Membership. Iran is a member of UN, OPEC and the Colombo Plan.

ECONOMY

Planning. The development plan, 1983–88 envisages an investment of 14,191,300m. rials (60% state).

Budget. Budget estimate for year commencing March 1985: Revenue 3,780,400m. *rials*; expenditure 4,134,800m. *rials*.

Currency. The Iranian unit of currency is the *rial* sub-divided into 100 *dinars*.

Notes in circulation are of denominations of 100, 200, 500, 1,000, 2,000, 5,000 and 10,000 *rials*. Coins in circulation are bronze–aluminium and copper, 50 *dinar*; silver alloy, 1, 2, 5, 10, 20 and 50 *rials*. In March 1988, US$1 = 67·81 *rials*; £1 = 120·20 *rials*.

Banking. The *Bank Markazi Iran* was established in 1960 as the note-issuing authority and government bank of Iran. All other banks and insurance companies were nationalized in June 1979, and re-organized into 8 new state banking corporations. The 'Law for Usury-Free Banking' was given final approval in Aug.-Sept. 1983. From 21 March 1985 interest on accounts was abolished.

Weights and Measures. By a law passed on 8 Jan. 1933, the official weights and measures are those of the metric system.

The Iranian year is a solar year running from 21 March to 20 March; the Hejira year 1362 corresponds to the Christian year 21 March 1984–20 March 1985.

ENERGY AND NATURAL RESOURCES

Electricity. Capacity of generators installed at institutions affiliated to Ministry of Energy, 1985, was 12,369,000 kw., and 36,720m. kwh. was generated. Supply 220 volts; 50 Hz.

Oil. For a history of Iran's oil industry 1951–79, *see* STATESMAN'S YEAR-BOOK, 1982–83.

The petroleum industry was seriously disrupted by the 1979 revolution, and many facilities, including the vast refinery at Abadan, the new refinery at Bandar Khomeini and the tanker terminal at Kharg Island, have been destroyed or put out of action during the Gulf war with Iraq. All operating companies were nationalized in 1979 and operations are now run by the National Petrochemical Company.

Crude oil production, 112·5m. tonnes, 1987.

Gas. Natural gas production (1983) was 315,000m. cu. ft.

Minerals. Iran has substantial mineral deposits relatively underdeveloped. Production figures for 1985 (in 1,000 tonnes): Iron ore, 2,099; coal, 614; zinc and lead, 56; manganese, 46; chromite, 56; salt, 618.

Agriculture. In 1982, cultivatable land totalled 14,867,000 hectares, of which 4,069,000 were irrigated and 4,929,000 hectares fallow land. Forests totalled 12·7m. hectares and pastures 90m.

Crop production for 1986 (in 1,000 tonnes): Wheat, 7,128; barley, 2,500; rice, 1,569; sugar-beet, 4,700; sugar-cane, 1,100; tobacco, 22.

Wool comes principally from Khorásán, Bakhtarán, Mázandarán and Azerbáiján. Production, 1972, 20,000 tonnes.

Rice is grown largely on the Caspian shores.

Cigarette tobacco is grown mainly in Hormozgán, Bushehr and West Azerbáiján *ostáns*. It is purchased by the Tobacco Monopoly and manufactured in the government factory at Tehrán.

Opium, until 1955, was an important export commodity in Iran. On 7 Oct. 1955 an Act was approved by Parliament to prohibit the cultivation and usage of opium.

Livestock (1986): 34·5m. sheep, 13·6m. goats, 8·35m. cattle, 316,000 horses, 27,000 camels, (1984) 20,000 pigs, 230,000 buffaloes, and 1·8m. donkeys.

Fisheries. The Caspian Fisheries Co. (Shilát) is a government monopoly. Exports of caviar (1975) were valued at US$72m. In 1984–85 the catch (in tonnes) in the north was: Non-caviar fish, 4,385; caviar, 247; clupeonella deliculata, 1,660. In the south (1984): Canned fish, 6,196; non-canned fish, 16,452; shrimp, 973.

INDUSTRY AND TRADE

Industry. Production of industrial goods, 1984: Vegetable oil, 426,580 tonnes;

sugar, 639,514 tonnes; finished cloth, 668,305,947 metres; footwear, 66,292,000 pairs; bricks, 10,824,612; cement, 12,064,027 tonnes; tractors, 14,513; combines, 612; tillers and threshers, 18,637; agricultural discs, 25,136; small vans, 68,644; trucks and small trucks, 14,932; private cars, 57,790; buses, 2,532; mini-buses, 8,170; ambulances, 559; motor cycles, 199,782. In 1984 there were 7,512 large-scale manufacturing establishments and the labour force was 619,332.

Commerce. Imports totalled 1,332,673m. rials in 1984–85. Exports totalled 33,041m. rials in 1984–85, excluding oil and hydrocarbon solvents obtained from oil.

Total trade between Iran and UK (British Department of Trade returns, in £1,000 sterling):

	1983	1984	1985	1986	1987
Imports to UK	100,545	368,572	63,317	100,303	187,572
Exports and re-exports from UK	629,980	703,097	525,589	399,373	307,853

COMMUNICATIONS

Roads. In 1985 the total length of roads was 139,368 km, of which 504 km were freeways, 16,346 km main roads, 35,930 km by-roads, 33,618 km rural roads and 52,366 km other roads.

In 1984 private motor vehicles numbered 2,246,143; rented vehicles, 377,745; government vehicles, 144,248.

Railways. The State Railways totalled 4,567 km of main lines in 1985, of which 146 km electrified. In 1986 the railways carried 5,585m. passenger-km and 6,888 tonne-km. Construction began in 1983 of a link from Kermán to Zahedán to connect the network to Pakistan.

Aviation. In 1985, 1,470,000 passengers arrived at Mehrabad Airport (1,157,000 on domestic flights and 313,000 on international flights) and 1,516,000 passengers departed (1,155,000 domestic and 361,000 international). The state airline carried 3,166,000 passengers and 52,303 tons of cargo and mail in 1983.

Shipping. In 1985, 1,345 ships, capacity 11,998,000 tonnes, entered commercial ports, unloading 12,660,000 tonnes and loading 447,000 tonnes of goods (excluding oil products).

Post and Broadcasting. Postal, telegraph and telephone services are administered by the Iranian Ministry of Posts, Telegraphs and Telephones.

In 1985 the number of telephones was 1,305,122, of which some 488,516 were in Tehrán province. Wireless sets numbered 10m. in 1980, and television sets 2·1m.

Cinemas (1983). There were 277 cinemas with 174,366 seats.

Newspapers. There were in 1982, 17 daily papers in Tehrán and other cities. Their circulation is relatively small, *Ettela'át* and *Kayhán* leading with about 220,000 and 350,000 respectively. Two English-language and a French-language daily ceased publication in March 1979.

JUSTICE, RELIGION, EDUCATION AND WELFARE

Justice. A new legal system based on Islamic law was introduced by the new constitution in 1979. The President of the Supreme Court and the public Prosecutor-General are appointed by the *wali faqih* (Ayatollah Khomeini). The Supreme Court has 16 branches and 109 offences carry the death penalty.

Religion. The official religion is the Shi'a branch of Islam, known as the *Ithna-Ashariyya,* which recognizes 12 Imáms or spiritual successors of the Prophet Mohammad. Of the total population, 96% are Shi'a, 3% are Sunni and 1% non-Moslem (including about 300,000 of the Bahai faith).

Education. The great majority of primary and secondary schools are state schools. Elementary education in state schools and university education are free; small fees are charged for state-run secondary schools. Text-books are issued free of charge to pupils in the first 4 grades of elementary schools.

In 1984 there were 634,200 pupils in elementary schools, 2,021,520 in orientation schools and 901,056 in general secondary schools; there were 184,520 students in technical and vocational schools, 37,247 in teacher-training schools, 18,590 gifted children, and 182,239 in adult education courses. Universities and other institutes of higher education had 145,809 students in 1984. The Free Islamic University was established after the revolution and in 1983 the International University of Islamic Studies was being organized.

A literacy movement was established in 1981 and by 1985, 3m. citizens had participated.

Health. In 1984 70,152 hospital beds were available in 589 hospitals. Medical personnel included 15,945 physicians and 2,340 dentists in 1982.

DIPLOMATIC REPRESENTATIVES

Of Iran in Great Britain (27 Prince's Gate, London, SW7 1PX)
Chargé d'Affaires: Mohammad Mehdi Akhoond Zadeh Basti.

Of Great Britain in Iran (Ave. Ferdowsi, Tehrán)
Head of Interests Section: (Vacant) (at Swedish Embassy).

Of Iran in the USA (3005 Massachusetts Ave., NW, Washington, D.C., 20008)
Ambassador: (Vacant).

Of the USA in Iran (260 Takhte Jamshid Ave., Tehrán)
Ambassador: (Vacant).

Of Iran to the United Nations
Ambassador: Dr Said Rajaie-Khorassani.

Books of Reference

Statistical Information. Statistical Centre of Iran, Dr Fakemi Avenue, Tehrán, Iran, 14144.

Afshar, H., *Iran: A Revolution in Turmoil.* London, 1985
Arberry, A. J. (ed.), *The Cambridge History of Iran.* 8 vols. CUP, 1968ff.
Bakhash, S., *The Reign of the Ayatollahs.* London, 1984
Benard, C., and Zalmay, K., *'The Government of God' Iran's Islamic Republic.* Columbia Univ. Press, 1984
Haim, S., *Shorter Persian–English Dictionary.* Tehrán, 1958
Heikal, M., *Iran: The Untold Story.* New York, 1982
Hiro, D., *Iran under the Ayatollahs.* London, 1985
Hussain, A., *Islamic Iran: Revolution and Counter-Revolution.* London, 1985
Katouzian, H., *The Political Economy of Iran.* London, 1981
Keddie, N., *Roots of Revolution.* Yale Univ. Press, 1981
Lambton, A. K. S., *Landlord and Peasant in Persia.* OUP, 1953.—*Persian Vocabulary.* CUP, 1954
Looney, R. E., *The Economic Development of Iran: A Recent Survey with Projections to 1981.* New York, 1973
Nashat, G., *Women and Revolution in Iran.* Boulder, 1983
Navabpour, A. R., *Iran.* [Bibliography] Oxford and Santa Barbara, 1987
Sick, G., *All Fall Down.* London, 1985
Steinglass, F. J., *A Comprehensive Persian–English Dictionary.* 2nd ed. London, 1930
Stempel, J. D., *Inside the Iranian Revolution.* Indiana Univ. Press, 1981
Sullivan, W. H., *Mission to Iran.* New York, 1981
Zabih, S., *Iran's Revolutionary Upheaval: An Interpretive Essay.* San Francisco, 1979.—*The Mosadegh Era: Roots of the Iranian Revolution.* Chicago, 1982.—*Iran since the Revolution.* London, 1982.—*The Left in Contemporary Iran.* London and Stamford, 1986

IRAQ

Capital: Baghdad
Population: 17·09m. (1987)
GNP per capita: US$2,140 (1986)

al Jumhouriya al 'Iraqia

HISTORY. Part of the Ottoman Empire from the 16th century, Iraq was captured by British forces in 1916 and became in 1921 a Kingdom under a League of Nations mandate, administered by Britain. It became independent on 3 Oct. 1932 under the Hashemite Dynasty, which was overthrown on 14 July 1958 by a military *coup* which established a Republic, controlled by a military-led Council of Sovereignty under Gen. Qassim. The republican régime terminated the adherence of Iraq to the Arab Federation (*see* THE STATESMAN'S YEAR-BOOK, 1958, p. 806). In 1963 Qassim was overthrown and Gen. Abdul Salam Aref became President, to be succeeded in 1966 by his brother Abdul Rahman Aref. In 1968 a successful *coup* was mounted by the Ba'th Party, which brought Gen. Ahmed Al Bakr to the Presidency. His Vice-President, from 1969, Saddam Hussein, became President in a peaceful transfer of power in 1979.

An attempt at succession by the Kurdish minority in the north-east of Iraq flared up in 1962, and fighting continued until the acceptance of a peace plan in June 1966. The Revolutionary Command Council formed after the 17 July 1968 *coup* announced in March 1970 a complete and constitutional settlement of the Kurdish issue. This was not, however, fully accepted by the Kurdish opposition leader.

In Sept. 1980 Iraq invaded Iran in a dispute over territorial rights in the Shatt-al-Arab waterway. Fighting was continuing in early 1988.

AREA AND POPULATION. Iraq is bounded north by Turkey, east by Iran, south-east by the Gulf, south by Kuwait and Saudi Arabia, and west by Jordan and Syria. The country has an area of 434,924 sq. km (167,925 sq. miles) and its population census (1977) was 12,000,497 and (estimate) 1987, 17,093,000.

The areas, populations (1977) and capitals of the governorates were:

Governorate	sq. km	Census 1977	Capital	1970
Al-Anbar	83,740	466,059	Ar-Ramadi	79,488
Babil (Babylon)	5,270	592,016	Al-Hillah	128,811
Baghdad	5,150	3,189,700	Baghdad	2,183,760
al-Basrah	19,070	1,008,626	Al-Basrah	333,684
Dahuk [1]	8,824	250,575	Dahuk	19,736
Dhi Qar	13,626	622,979	an-Nasiriyah	62,368
Diyala	19,301	587,754	Ba'qubah	39,186
Irbil [1]	14,471	541,456	Irbil	107,355
Karbala	57,880	269,822	Karbala	107,496
Maysan	14,103	372,575	Al-Amarah	80,078
Al-Muthanna	49,111	215,637	As-Samawah	33,473 [2]
an-Najaf	27,494	389,680	An-Najaf	179,160
Ninawa (Nineveh)	35,726	1,105,671	Mosul	293,079
al-Qadisiyah	8,507	423,006	Ad-Diwaniyah	60,553 [2]
Salah ad-Din	29,004	363,819	Samarra	62,008
As-Sulaymaniyah [1]	15,756	690,557	As-Sulaymaniyah	98,063
Ta'mim	9,659	495,425	Kirkuk	207,852
Wasit	17,308	415,140	Al-Kut	58,647

[1] Forming Kurdish Autonomous Region   [2] Census 1965

The national language is Arabic, spoken by 81% of the population. There is a major minority group of Kurdish-speakers in the north-east (15·5%) and smaller groups speaking Turkic, Aramaic and Iranian languages.

CLIMATE. The climate is mainly arid, with small and unreliable rainfall and a large annual range of temperature. Summers are very hot and winters cold. Al-Basrah. Jan. 55°F (12·8°C), July 92°F (33·3°C). Annual rainfall 7″ (175 mm).

Baghdad. Jan. 50°F (10°C), July 95°F (35°C). Annual rainfall 6″ (140 mm). Mosul. Jan. 44°F (6·7°C), July 90°F (32·2°C). Annual rainfall 15″ (384 mm).

CONSTITUTION AND GOVERNMENT. The Provisional Constitution was published on 22 Sept. 1968 and promulgated on 16 July 1970. The highest state authority remains the 9-member Revolutionary Command Council (RCC) but some legislative power has now been given to the 250-member National Assembly, elected 20 June 1980 for a 4-year term.

The only legal political grouping is the National Progressive Front (founded July 1973) comprising the Arab Socialist Renaissance (Ba'th) Party and various Kurdish parties; the Iraqi Communist Party left the Front in March 1979.

The President and Vice-President are elected by the RCC; the President appoints and leads a Council of Ministers responsible for administration.

President: Saddam Hussein at-Takriti (assumed office 17 July 1979).
Vice-President: Taha Moheddin Marouf.

The RCC was composed as follows in Dec. 1987:

Saddam Hussein at-Takriti *(Chairman)*, Taha Moheddin Marouf, Izzat Ibrahim *(Vice-Chairman)*, Na'im Hamid Haddad *(Secretary-General of the National Progressive Front)*, Taha Yasin Ramadan *(First Deputy Prime Minister)*, Gen. Adnan Khairallah *(Deputy Prime Minister, Defence)*, Tariq Aziz Isa *(Deputy Prime Minister, Foreign Affairs)*, Sa'doun Shakir Mahmud *(Interior)*, Hasan Ali Nasar al-Amiri *(Trade)*.

Besides those named above, the Council of Ministers comprises 7 Ministers of State, 19 other Ministers and 7 Presidential advisors with ministerial status.

National flag: Three horizontal stripes of red, white, black, with 3 green stars on the white stripe.

Local Government. Iraq is divided into 18 governorates *(liwa),* each administered by an appointed Governor; three of the governorates form a (Kurdish) Autonomous Region, with an elected 57-member Kurdish Legislative Council. Each governorate is divided into *qadhas* (under Qaimaqams) and *nahiyahs* (under Mudirs).

DEFENCE. Military training is compulsory for all men when they reach the age of 18. This consists of 21-24 months' service (extended for war) with the colours.

Army. The Army is organized into 5 armoured, 3 mechanized and 30 infantry divisions including People's Army and Reserve brigades; 1 Presidential Guard division, 6 special forces divisions. Equipment includes 4,500 Soviet T-54/-55/-62/-72 and 1,500 Chinese Type-69 main battle tanks. Strength (1988 estimate) 955,000, including 480,000 active reserves.

Navy. The Navy comprises 4 new Italian-built frigates, 1 modern frigate/training ship, 6 new Italian-built missile corvettes, 12 *ex*-Soviet missile boats, 6 *ex*-Soviet torpedo boats, 3 Danish-built tank landing ships, 3 *ex*-Soviet but Polish-built medium landing ships, 3 *ex*-Soviet anti submarine craft, 2 fleet minesweepers, 5 inshore minesweepers, 1 training ship, 16 gunboats, 8 coastal patrol craft, 10 harbour patrol boats, 1 oiler, 1 presidential yacht, 1 harbour authority craft (former presidential yacht), 5 diving craft and 10 service tenders.

In 1988 naval personnel totalled over 3,000 officers and ratings.

Air Force. Except for a few Hunter jet fighter-bombers bought from Britain and 100 Mirage F.1E/B fighters, about 40 Alouette III, 10 Super Frelon, 40 Puma and 59 Gazelle helicopters acquired from France, the combat and transport squadrons are equipped primarily with aircraft of Soviet design, including 6 Tu-22 supersonic medium bombers, 30 Su-7 and 50 Su-20 fighter-bombers, some MiG-29 and 90 MiG-23 interceptors and fighter-bombers, and 100 Chinese-built F-7 and MiG-21 interceptors, 60 Chinese-built F-6 (MiG-19) fighters, 40 Mi-24 gunship helicopters, 100 Mi-8 helicopters, and four-turbofan Il-76, turboprop An-12 and An-24/26 transports. USSR was also reported (1987) to have supplied Su-25 ground attack aircraft. A few Il-14s and smaller types are used in a transport/ communications role. Hunter, L-29 Delfin and L-39 Albatross aircraft are employed for training, with Swiss-built Bravo piston-engined primary trainers, and Tucano and Pilatus PC-7 turboprop basic trainers, Soviet MiG-15UTI trainers and other types in the Air Force College and operational conversion units. Total strength (1988) 40,000 personnel and 500 combat aircraft. Soviet 'Guideline', 'Goa', 'Gainful', 'Gaskin' and Roland surface-to-air missiles are operational.

INTERNATIONAL RELATIONS

Membership. Iraq is a member of UN, Arab League and the Non-Aligned Movement.

ECONOMY

Planning. The plan for 1981–85 was introduced but has been affected, to some extent, by the hostilities with Iran.

Budget. Revenue and expenditure (in 1,000 Iraqi dinars) for 1981 balanced at I.D. 19,250m.

Oil revenues account for nearly 50%, customs and excise for about 26% of the total revenue.

Currency. The monetary unit is the *Iraqi dinar* (I.D.) = 1,000 *fils* = 10 *riyals* = 20 *dirhams.* Silver alloy coins for 100 and 50 fils (*dirham*) and 25 fils are in circulation, and other coins for 10, 5 and 1 fils. Notes are for ¼, ½ and 1 dinar, and for 5 and 10 dinars. In March 1988, £1 = 0·53 *dinar*; US$1 = 0·311 *dinar*.

Banking. All banks were nationalized on 14 July 1964. The Central Bank of Iraq is the sole bank of issue. In 1941 the Rafidain Bank, financed by the Iraqi Government, was instituted to carry out normal banking transactions with head office in Baghdad and branches in the chief towns and abroad, including London. In addition, there are 4 government banks which are authorized to issue loans to companies and individuals: the Industrial Bank, the Agricultural Bank, the Estate Bank, and the Mortgage Bank.

Weights and Measures. The metric system is in general use.

ENERGY AND NATURAL RESOURCES

Electricity. Production in 1986 amounted to 22,560m. kwh. Supply 220 volts; 50 Hz.

Oil. Following the nationalization of the Iraqi oil industry in June 1972, the Iraqi National Oil Company (INOC) is responsible for the exploration, production, transport and marketing of Iraqi crude oil and oil products.

The total crude petroleum production was (1987) 101·2m. tonnes and of natural gas (1980) 1,760m. cu. ft. Oil exports are essential for the economy but oil terminals in the Gulf were destroyed in 1980 and the trans-Syria pipeline closed in 1982. Iraq is now wholly reliant on the 625 mile pipeline from Kirkuk to the Mediterranean *via* Turkey.

Agriculture. The chief winter crops (1986) are wheat, 1·1m. tonnes and barley, 1·3m. tonnes. The chief summer crop is rice, 145,000 tonnes. The date crop is important (100,000 tonnes), the country furnishing about 80% of the world's trade in dates; the chief producing area is the totally irrigated riverain belt of the Shatt-el-Arab. Wool and cotton are also important exports.

Livestock (1986): Cattle, 1·55m.; buffaloes, 150,000; sheep, 8·8m.; goats, 2·4m.; horses, 53,000; camels, 60,000; chickens, 75m.

INDUSTRY AND TRADE

Industry. Iraq is still relatively under-developed industrially but work has begun on new industrial plants which are being established with Soviet equipment and technical assistance.

Commerce. Imports and exports for 4 calendar years were (in US$1m.):

	1981	1982	1983	1984
Imports	10,530	10,250	9,785	11,260
Exports	20,922	21,728	12,275	11,720

In 1983, crude oil formed 98·6% of all exports, of which 23% to Brazil and 12·5% to Italy. 13·8% of imports came from Federal Republic of Germany and 11% from Kuwait.

Total trade between Iraq and UK for 5 years (British Department of Trade returns, in £1,000 sterling):

	1983	1984	1985	1986	1987
Imports to UK	30,334	69,047	44,125	66,129	33,871
Exports and re-exports from UK	400,259	343,120	444,749	443,890	271,655

Tourism. About 1,004,000 tourists visited Iraq in 1986.

COMMUNICATIONS

Roads. There were 25,500 km of main roads in 1985. Vehicles registered in 1982 totalled 230,000 passenger cars and 145,000 commercial vehicles.

Railways. The Iraqi Republic Railways were originally largely metre gauge but now comprise a 1,435 mm gauge main line from Um Qasr through Basra to Baghdad, Mosul and Tel-Kotchek on the Syrian frontier, and the remaining metre gauge route from Baghdad to Khanaqin, Kirkuk and Erbil. A 1,435 mm gauge line was opened in 1983 from Baghdad to Husaiba (404 km) on the Syrian frontier, which will form part of a through route to the Mediterranean port of Latakia, together with a branch of 155 km to serve phosphates deposits at Akashat. Total length 2,029 km. In 1986 the railways carried 2,360 tonne-km and 1,005m. passenger-km.

Aviation. Baghdad airport is served by British Airways, Lufthansa, Alitalia, SAS, Swissair, KLM, Middle East Air Lines, PIA, Iraqi Airways, Air Liban, United Arab Airlines and Aeroflot. In 1982 passenger-km were 1,476m. and cargo, 37·5m. tonne-km.

Shipping. The merchant fleet in 1980 comprised 142 vessels (over 100 gross tons) with a total tonnage of 1,465,949. The ports of Basra and Um Qasr have been closed since Sept. 1980.

Post and Broadcasting. Wireless telegraph services exist with UK, USA, UAR, Lebanon and Saudi Arabia, and wireless telephone services with UK, USA, Italy, UAR and USSR. Telephones, 1983, 624,685 (Baghdad, 302,219). In 1986 there were 2·5m. radio and 750,000 television receivers.

Cinemas (1979). There were 87 cinemas.

Newspapers (1983). In Baghdad there are 4 main daily newspapers (one of which is in English with a circulation of 200,000).

JUSTICE, RELIGION, EDUCATION AND WELFARE

Justice. The courts are established throughout the country as follows: For civil matters: the court of cassation in Baghdad; 6 courts of appeal at Baghdad (2), Basra, Babylon, Mosul and Kirkuk; 18 courts of first instance with unlimited powers and 150 courts of first instance with limited powers, all being courts of single judges. In addition, 6 peace courts have peace court jurisdiction only. Tribal law was abolished in Aug. 1958.

For *Shara'* (religious) matters: the Shara' courts at all places where there are civil courts, constituted in some places of specially appointed Qadhis (religious judges) and in other places of the judges of the civil courts. For criminal matters: the court of cassation; 6 sessions courts (2 being presided over by the judge of the local court of first instance and 4 being identical with the courts of appeal). Magistrates' courts at all places where there are civil courts, constituted of civil judges exercising magisterial powers of the first and second class. There are also a number of third-class magistrates' courts, powers for this purpose being granted to municipal councils and a number of administrative officials. Some administrative officials are granted the powers of a peace judge to deal with cases of debts due from cultivators.

Religion. In 1965 there were 7,711,712 Moslems, 232,406 Christians (1979), 2,500 Jews, 69,653 Yazidis and 14,262 Sabians.

Education. Primary and secondary education is free and primary education became compulsory in Sept. 1976. Primary school age is 6–12. Secondary education is for 6 years, of which the first 3 are termed intermediate. The medium of instruction is Arabic; Kurdish is used in primary schools in northern districts.

There were, in 1981, 10,816 primary schools with 2,637,023 pupils, and 1,579 secondary schools with 1,028,348 pupils. 155 vocational schools had 82,307 students and 62 teacher-training colleges had 102,430 students.

There are 6 universities with (1977) 71,536 students and 15 other higher educational establishments with 9,962 students.

Health. In 1981 there were 7,634 doctors, and 25,443 hospital beds.

DIPLOMATIC REPRESENTATIVES

Of Iraq in Great Britain (21 Queen's Gate, London, SW7 5JG)
Ambassador: Dr Mohammed Sadiq Al-Mashat.

Of Great Britain in Iraq (Zukaq 12, Mahala 218, Hai Al Khelood, Baghdad)
Ambassador: T. J. Clark, CMG, CVO.

Of Iraq in the USA (1801 P St., NW, Washington, D.C., 20036)
Ambassador: Nizar Hamdoon.

Of the USA in Iraq (PO Box 2447, Alwiyah, Baghdad)
Chargé d'Affaires: David G. Newton.

Of Iraq to the United Nations
Ambassador: Ismat Taha Kittani.

Books of Reference

Statistical Information: The Central Statistical Organization, Ministry of Planning, Baghdad *(President:* Dr Salah Al-Shaikhly) publishes an annual *Statistical Abstract* (latest issue 1973). Foreign Trade statistics are published annually by the Ministry of Planning.

Abdulrahman, A. J., *Iraq* [Bibliography]. Oxford and Santa Barbara, 1984
Axelgrad, F. W., *Iraq in Transition: A Political, Economic and Strategic Perspective.* London, 1986
Ghareeb, E., *The Kurdish Question in Iraq.* Syracuse Univ. Press, 1981
Postgate, E., *Iraq: International Relations and National Development.* London, 1983

IRELAND

Éire

Capital: Dublin
Population: 3·54m. (1986)
GNP per capita: US$4,040 (1985)

HISTORY. In April 1916 an insurrection against British rule took place and a republic was proclaimed. The armed struggle was renewed in 1919 and continued until 1921. The independence of Ireland was reaffirmed in Jan. 1919 by the National Parliament (*Dáil Éireann*), elected in Dec. 1918.

In 1920 an Act was passed by the British Parliament, under which separate Parliaments were set up for 'Southern Ireland' (26 counties) and 'Northern Ireland' (6 counties). The Unionists of the 6 counties accepted this scheme, and a Northern Parliament was duly elected on 24 May 1921. The rest of Ireland, however, ignored the Act.

On 6 Dec. 1921 a treaty was signed between Great Britain and Ireland by which Ireland accepted dominion status subject to the right of Northern Ireland to opt out. This right was exercised, and the border between *Saorstát Éireann* (26 counties) and Northern Ireland (6 counties) was fixed in Dec. 1925 as the outcome of an agreement between Great Britain, the Irish Free State and Northern Ireland. The agreement was ratified by the three parliaments.

Subsequently the constitutional links between *Saorstát Éireann* and the UK were gradually removed by the *Dáil*. The remaining formal association with the British Commonwealth by virtue of the External Relations Act, 1936, was severed when the Republic of Ireland Act, 1948, came into operation on 18 April 1949.

AREA AND POPULATION. The Republic of Ireland lies in the Atlantic ocean, separated from Great Britain by the Irish Sea to the east, and bounded north-east by Northern Ireland.

Counties and county boroughs	Area in hectares [1]	Males	Population, 1986 Females	Total
Province of Leinster				
Carlow	89,635	20,813	20,145	40,948
Dublin County Borough	11,499	237,770	264,567	502,337
Dublin-Belgard	78,937	99,075	100,403	199,478
Dublin-Fingal	...	68,652	69,822	138,474
Dun Laoghaire-Rathdown	1,720	86,320	94,187	180,507
Kildare	169,425	59,445	56,570	116,015
Kilkenny	206,167	37,280	35,814	73,094
Laoighis	171,954	27,519	25,751	53,270
Longford	104,387	16,165	15,326	31,491
Louth	82,334	45,419	46,279	91,698
Meath	233,587	52,878	50,884	103,762
Offaly	199,774	30,814	28,992	59,806
Westmeath	176,290	31,986	31,320	63,306
Wexford	235,143	51,708	50,748	102,456
Wicklow	202,483	46,973	47,509	94,482
Total of Leinster	1,963,335	912,817	938,317	1,851,134
Province of Munster				
Clare	318,784	46,901	44,442	91,343
Cork County Borough	3,731	64,438	68,758	133,196
Cork	742,257	141,922	137,505	279,427
Kerry	470,142	63,162	60,760	123,922
Limerick County Borough	1,904	27,498	28,743	56,241
Limerick	266,676	54,957	53,006	107,963
Tipperary, N. R.	199,622	30,285	29,168	59,453
Tipperary, S. R.	225,836	39,350	37,701	77,051

[1] Exclusive of certain rivers, lakes and tideways.

710

Counties and county boroughs	Area in hectares [1]	Population, 1986		
		Males	Females	Total
Province of Munster—contd.				
Waterford County Borough	3,809	19,356	20,160	39,516
Waterford	179,977	26,287	25,295	51,582
Total of Munster	2,412,738	514,156	505,538	1,019,694
Province of Connacht				
Galway County Borough	...	22,524	24,484	47,008
Galway	593,966	67,834	63,338	131,172
Leitrim	152,476	14,197	12,803	27,000
Mayo	539,846	58,620	56,396	115,016
Roscommon	246,276	28,335	26,216	54,551
Sligo	179,608	28,114	27,865	55,979
Total of Connacht	1,712,172	219,624	211,102	430,726
Province of Ulster (part of)				
Cavan	189,060	28,170	25,711	53,881
Donegal	483,058	65,723	63,705	129,428
Monaghan	129,093	27,009	25,323	52,332
Total of Ulster (part of)	801,211	120,902	114,739	235,641
Total	6,889,456	1,767,499	1,769,696	3,537,195

[1] Exclusive of certain rivers, lakes and tideways.

Principal towns (1981 census): Greater Dublin including Dún Laoghaire, 915,115; Cork, 149,792; Limerick, 75,520; Galway, 41,861; Waterford, 39,636.
Vital statistics for 6 calendar years:

	Births	Marriages	Deaths		Births	Marriages	Deaths
1981	72,158	20,612	32,929	1984	64,237	18,355	32,154
1982	70,224	20,224	32,457	1985	62,250	18,552	33,222
1983	67,117	19,467	32,976	1986	61,425	18,322	33,627

CLIMATE. Influenced by the Gulf Stream, there is an equable climate with mild south-west winds, making temperatures almost uniform over the whole country. The coldest months are Jan. and Feb. (39–45°F, 4–7°C) and the warmest July and Aug. (57–61°F, 14–16°C). May and June are the sunniest months, averaging 5·5 to 6·5 hours each day, but over 7 hours in the extreme S.E. Rainfall is lowest along the eastern coastal strip. The central parts vary between 30–44″ (750–1,125 mm), and up to 60″ (1,500 mm) may be experienced in low-lying areas in the west. Dublin. Jan. 41°F (5°C), July 59°F (15°C). Annual rainfall 30″ (750 mm). Cork. Jan. 43°F (6·1°C), July 60°F (15·6°C). Annual rainfall 41″ (1,025 mm).

CONSTITUTION AND GOVERNMENT. Ireland is a sovereign independent, democratic republic. Its parliament exercises jurisdiction in 26 of the 32 counties of Ireland.

The first Constitution of the Irish Free State came into operation on 6 Dec. 1922. Certain provisions which were regarded as contrary to the national sentiments were gradually removed by successive amendments, with the result that at the end of 1936 the text differed considerably from the original document. On 14 June 1937 a new Constitution was approved by Parliament (*Dáil Éireann*) and enacted by a plebiscite on 1 July 1937. This Constitution came into operation on 29 Dec. 1937. Under it the name Ireland (Éire) was restored.

The Constitution provides that, pending the reintegration of the national territory, the laws enacted by the Parliament established by the constitution shall have the same area and extent of application as those of the Irish Free State.

The *Oireachtas* or National Parliament consists of the President and two Houses, viz., a House of Representatives, called *Dáil Éireann*, and a Senate, called *Seanad Éireann*, consisting of 60 members. The *Dáil*, consisting of 166 members, is elected by adult suffrage. Of the 60 members of the Senate, 11 are nominated by the *Taoiseach* (Prime Minister), 6 are elected by the universities and the remaining 43 are elected from 5 panels of candidates established on a vocational basis, representing the following public services and interests: (1) national language and culture, literature, art, education and such professional interests as may be defined by law for the purpose of this panel; (2) agricultural and allied interests, and fisheries; (3) labour, whether organized or unorganized; (4) industry and commerce, including banking, finance, accountancy, engineering and architecture; (5) public administration and social services, including voluntary social activities. The electing body is a college of about 1,109 members, comprising members of the *Dáil*, Senate, county boroughs and county councils.

A maximum period of 90 days is afforded to the Senate for the consideration or amendment of Bills sent to that House by the *Dáil*, but the Senate has no power to veto legislative proposals.

No amendment of the Constitution can be effected except with the approval of the people given at a referendum.

Irish is the first official language; English is recognized as a second official language. For further details of the Constitution *see* THE STATESMAN'S YEAR-BOOK, 1952, pp. 1123–34.

President: Pádraig Óhlrighile (Patrick Hillery), installed on 3 Dec. 1976 and re-elected for a second 7-year term in 1983.

Former Presidents: Dr Douglas Hyde (1938–45); Seán T. O. Ceallaigh (1945–59; 2 terms); Éamon de Valéra (1959–73; 2 terms); Erskine Childers (1973–74; died in office); Cearbhall Ó Dálaigh (1974–76; resigned).

A general election was held Feb. 1987: Fianna Fáil, 81 (Nov. 1982 election, 75); Fine Gael, 51 (70); Labour Party, 12 (16); Progressive Democrats, 14; Workers' Party, 4 (2); Democratic Socialists, 1; Independents, 3 (3).

There are no formal party divisions in the Senate.

The Government consisted of the following members in March 1987:

Taoiseach (Prime Minister) and Minister for the Gaeltacht: Charles Haughey.

Tanaiste (Deputy Prime Minister) and Minister for Foreign Affairs: Brian Lenihan. *Finance:* Ray McSharry. *Justice:* Gerry Collins. *Agriculture and Food:* Michael O'Kennedy. *Social Welfare:* Dr Michael Woods. *Industry and Commerce:* Albert Reynolds. *Energy and Communications:* Ray Burke. *Marine:* Brendan Daly. *Environment:* Padraig Flynn. *Labour:* Bertie Ahern. *Health:* Dr Rory O'Hanlon. *Defence:* Michael J. Noonan. *Education:* Mary O'Rourke. *Tourism and Transport:* John Wilson.

There were 15 Ministers of State.

National flag: Three vertical strips of green, white, orange.

National anthem: The Soldier's Song (words by P. Kearney; music by P. Heaney).

Local Government. The elected local authorities comprise 27 county councils, 5 county borough corporations, 6 borough corporations, 49 urban district councils and 25 Boards of Town Commissions. All the members of these authorities are elected under a system of proportional representation, normally every 5 years. All residents of an area who have reached the age of 18 are entitled to vote in the local election for their area. Women are eligible for election as members of local authorities in the same manner and on the same conditions as men. Elected members are not paid, but provision is made for the payment of travelling expenses and subsistence allowances.

The range of services for which local authorities are responsible is broken down into 8 main programme groups as follows: Housing and Building; Road Transportation and Safety; Water Supply and Sewerage; Development Incentives and Controls; Environmental Protection; Recreation and Amenity; Agriculture, Education, Health and Welfare and Miscellaneous Services. Because of the small size of their administrative areas the functions carried out by town commissioners and some of the smaller urban district councils have tended to become increasingly limited, and the more important tasks of local government have tended to become the responsibility of the county councils.

The local authorities have a system of government which combines an elected council and a whole-time manager. The elected members have specific functions reserved to them which include the striking of rates (local tax), the borrowing of money, the adoption of development plans, the making, amending or revoking of bye-laws and the nomination of persons to other bodies. The managers, who are paid officers of their authorities, are responsible for the performance of all functions which are not reserved to the elected members, including the employment of staff, making of contracts, management of local authority property, collection of rates and rents and the day-to-day administration of local authority affairs. The manager for a county council is manager also for every borough corporation, urban district council and board of town commissioners whose functional area is wholly within the county.

DEFENCE. Under the direction of the President, and subject to the provisions of the Defence Act, 1954, the military command of the Defence Forces is exercisable by the Government through the Minister for Defence. To aid and counsel the Minister for Defence on all matters in relation to the business of the Department of Defence on which he may consult it, there is a Council of Defence consisting of the Minister for State at the Department of Defence, the Secretary of the Department of Defence, the Chief of Staff, the Adjutant-General and the Quartermaster-General. Establishments provide at present for a Permanent Defence Force of approximately 13,600 all ranks including the Air Corps and the Naval Service. The Reserve Defence Force has 15,800 all ranks. Recruitment is on a voluntary basis. Minimum term of enlistment is 3 years in the Permanent Defence Force and 6 years in the Reserve.

Since May 1978 an Irish contingent has formed part of the United Nations force in Lebanon. The contingent now comprises 746 men (all ranks). 21 Irish officers are at present serving with the UN Truce Supervision Organization and the UN Disengagement Observer Force in the Middle East. There is a small detachment with the UN force in Cyprus.

Army. The Army has 4 brigades and an infantry force. Three of the brigades have two infantry battalions and one brigade has three infantry battalions. Each brigade has a field artillery regiment and a squadron/company size unit for each of the support corps. The infantry force has two infantry battalions. The establishment strength of the Army was (1988) 11,900 all ranks.

Navy. The Naval Service comprises 4 offshore patrol vessels and 1 helicopter offshore patrol vessel. All 5 ships were built in Cork. Two of the 5 AC Dauphin helicopters are for Naval use on board the helicopter patrol vessel. The Naval Base is at Haulbowline Island in Cork Harbour. The establishment strength of the Naval Service is 1,277 officers and men but in 1988 personnel were about 800.

Air Force. The Air Corps has an establishment of 1,227 all ranks, and 41 aircraft. There are 6 Magister armed jet trainers, 9 SF 260W armed piston-engined trainers, 7 Alouette III, 5 Dauphin and 2 Gazelle helicopters, 3 twin-turbo prop Super Beech King 200 for coastal fishery patrol, 8 Cessna 172, and a BAe 125/700 twin turbofan transport.

INTERNATIONAL RELATIONS

Membership. Ireland is a member of UN, OECD, the Council of Europe and the European Communities.

ECONOMY

Budget. Current revenue and expenditure (in IR£1m.):

	1985	1986
Current revenue		
Customs duties	96·8	104·0
Excise duties	1,316·1	1,377·7
Capital taxes	32·6	35·0
Stamp duties	119·5	167·0
Income tax	2,103·1	2,356·4
Income levy	74·0	34·0
Corporation tax	217·2	249·9
Value-added tax	1,402·3	1,562·4
Agricultural levies (EEC)	14·5	13·0
Motor vehicle duties	122·1	130·7
Youth employment levy	82·9	87·0
Non-Tax Revenue	749·8	675·0
Total	6,330·9	6,792·1
Current expenditure		
Debt service	1,967	2,020
Industry and Labour	243	274
Agriculture	412	428
Fisheries, Forestry, Tourism	72	71
Health	1,094	1,130
Education	950	1,003
Social Welfare	2,315	2,524
Less: Receipts, e.g. social security	(–)1,342	(–)1,431
Total (including other items)	7,615	8,042

Capital expenditure amounted to £1,875m. in 1984, and £1,761m. in 1985.

On 31 Dec. 1984 the liabilities totalled £18,492m. The assets included: Electricity scheme, £37m.: local loans fund, £2,307·9m.; national transport organization, £44·5m.; industrial credit company, £41·2m.; turf development, £33·6m.; reconstruction finance, £61·2m.; shares in companies established under State auspices, £967m.; other assets, £1,098·4m.; total, £4,599·8m.

Currency. The unit of currency is the Irish *pound* or *an punt Éireannach*. From 10 Sept. 1928 when the first Irish legal-tender notes were issued, the Irish currency was linked to Sterling on a one-for-one basis. This relationship was discontinued on 30 March 1979 when, following Ireland's adherence to the European Monetary System, it became inconsistent with Ireland's obligations under that system.

The Central Bank has the sole right of issuing legal tender notes; token coinage is issued by the Minister for Finance through the Bank. In March 1988, £1 = IR£1·12; US$ = IR£1·58.

The volume of legal-tender notes outstanding in Dec. 1986 was £1,067m. Total notes and coins outstanding amounted to £1,127m.

Banking. The Central Bank, which was established as from 1 Feb. 1943, in accordance with the Central Bank Act, 1942, replaced the Currency Commission, which was set up under the Currency Act, 1927, and had been responsible *inter alia* for the regulation of the note issue. In addition to the powers and functions of the Currency Commission the Central Bank has the power of receiving deposits from banks and public authorities, of rediscounting Exchequer bills and bills of exchange, of making advances to banks against such bills or against Government securities, of fixing and publishing rates of interest for rediscounting bills, or buying and selling certain Government securities and securities of any international bank or financial institution formed wholly or mainly by governments. The Bank also collects and publishes information relating to monetary and credit matters. The Central Bank Act, 1971, gives further powers to the Central Bank in the regulation of banking including licensing of banks, the supervision of their operations and control of liquidity and reserve ratios. The capital of the Bank is £40,000, of which £24,000 has been paid up and is held by the Minister for Finance.

The Board of Directors of the Central Bank consists of a Governor, appointed by the President on the advice of the Government, and 8 directors, all appointed by the Minister for Finance, 6 direct and 2 from among directors of the Associated Banks (the term applied to the 4 shareholding banks associated with the former Currency Commission).

The principal independent commercial banks are known (following the Central Bank Act, 1942) as the Associated Banks. They are Allied Irish Banks Ltd., Bank of Ireland and two smaller banks, Ulster Bank and Northern Bank (Ireland). They operate the branch banking system; on 15 July 1987 their total deposit and current accounts within Ireland amounted to £6,742m. and their total gross assets in Ireland, £11,385m.

There are also 33 Non-Associated Banks of which 23 are merchant and commercial banks and 10 are industrial banks whose main activity is installment credit. Four of the merchant or commercial banks are subsidiaries of the Associated Banks; 10 are from other EEC countries and 6 from outside the EEC (mainly US) and the remainder are Irish. On 15 July 1987 their current and deposit accounts and interbank borrowings amounted to £8,072m. (46·5% of total bank resources) and their lending to £5,355m. (44·4% of lending to residents); total gross assets in Ireland, £9,090m.

There are two state-owned credit corporations, one industrial and one agricultural, and several building societies. There are 4 Trustee Savings Banks and the Post Office Savings Bank which together had deposits of £1,065m. in March 1987.

Weights and Measures. Conversion to the metric system is in progress; the imperial system is still legal (1987).

ENERGY AND NATURAL RESOURCES

Electricity. The total generating capacity was (1986) 3,852 mw. In the 9 months ending 31 Dec. 1986 the total sales of electricity amounted to 7,295m. units supplied to 1,207,051 consumers. Electricity generated by fuel source (last 9 months of 1986): Oil, 48%; natural gas, 16%; peat, 12%; hydro, 7%; coal, 17%. Supply 220 volts; 50 Hz.

Oil. About 551,000 sq. km of the continental shelf has been made an exploration area; at the furthest point the limit of jurisdiction is 520 nautical miles from the coast. Since 1970, 93 exploratory offshore oil wells have been drilled. A number of encouraging oil and gas flows have been recorded. In 1987, 88 blocks were held under exclusive offshore licences and offshore petroleum leases. A total of 4,696 sq. km were held under onshore petroleum prospecting licences.

Gas. There has been one commercial discovery of natural gas, off the south-west coast at Kinsale Head. Of the total reserves of 1·35m. cu. ft. it was estimated that at 31 Dec. 1987 approximately 60% would remain to be produced. At 1987 estimated take-off this should last until 1999. Gas Transmission is controlled by the Irish Gas Board (BGE), who sell the gas into electricity generation, fertilizer production, and distribution systems for domestic, commercial and industrial use.

Peat. The country has very little indigenous coal, but possesses large reserves of peat, the development of which is handled by Bord na Mona (Peat Board). To date, the Board has acquired over 200,000 acres of bog and has established 21 locations around the country. In the year ending 31 March, 1987, production totalled 4m. tonnes. From this 2·5m. tonnes of peat went to generate electricity and 1·6m. tonnes for the domestic market. In addition moss peat production for the year was 1·4m. cu. metres.

Minerals. Lead and zinc concentrates are important. Metal content of production, 1986: zinc, 181,700 tonnes; lead, 36,400 tonnes. Barytes, gypsum, limestone and aggregates are also important, and there is some coal, silver, quartz, dolomite, silica sand, green and black marbles. Exploration activity is centred on base metals, precious metals, industrial minerals and coal and about 30 companies are prospecting.

Agriculture. General distribution of surface (in hectares) in 1986: Crops and pasture, 4,688,164; other land, including grazed mountain, 2,201,086; total, 6,889,250.

Estimated area (hectares) under certain crops calculated from sample returns:

		Area		
Crops	1983	1984	1985	1986
Wheat	59,000	77,200	78,100	76,100
Oats	22,600	24,900	23,300	20,900
Barley	313,400	304,300	298,400	282,800
Potatoes	33,500	35,700	33,000	30,500
Sugar-beet	36,400	34,900	33,900	37,000

Gross agricultural output (excluding value of changes in stocks) for the year 1986 was valued at £2,795·1m.

Livestock (1986): Cattle, 6,717,800; sheep, 4,233,700; pigs, 1,002,900; horses, 55,800; poultry, 8,794,600.

Forestry. The total area of state forests at 31 Dec. 1985 was 403,950 hectares, of which 325,656 was planted; 78,294 were reserve land for planting, the rest roads, water etc.

Fisheries. The number of vessels engaged in fishing in 1984 were 3,135, of which 1,611 accounted for the greater part of the fishing effort; men 7,806. The quantities and values of fish landed during 1985 were: Demersal fish, 42,000 tonnes, value IR£23,685,000; pelagic fish, 123,000 tonnes, value IR£13,786,000; shellfish, 23,000 tonnes, value IR£14,294,000. Total quantity: 188,000 tonnes; total value, IR£51,765,000.

INDUSTRY AND TRADE

Industry. The census of industrial production for 1984 gives the following details of the values (in IR£1m.) of gross and net output for the principal manufacturing industries. The figures for net output are those of gross output minus cost of materials, including fuel, light and power, repairs to plant and machinery and amounts paid to others in connexion with products made.

	Gross output	Net output
Slaughtering, preparing and preserving meat	1,344·0	203·2
Manufacture of dairy products	1,466·6	194·4
Bread, biscuit and flour confectionery	222·6	99·5
Cocoa, chocolate and sugar confectionery	223·7	69·8
Animal and poultry foods	403·0	67·5
Brewing and malting	244·7	146·7
Spirit distilling and compounding	120·7	63·2
Paper and paper products	181·3	71·1
Printing and publishing	284·9	185·8
Manufacture of metal articles	443·8	195·6
Manufacture of non-metallic mineral products	711·2	333·3
Chemicals, including manmade fibres	1,618·4	906·5
Mechanical engineering	300·9	155·3
Office machinery and data-processing machinery	1,521·2	568·7
Electrical engineering	939·6	499·0
Manufacture and assembly of motor vehicles, parts and accessories	148·7	53·6
Manufacture of other means of transport	157·8	69·6
Instrument engineering	387·5	235·2
Textiles	457·4	160·2
Manufacture of footwear and clothing	291·8	137·8
Timber and wooden furniture	227·6	92·3
Processing rubber and plastics	331·9	147·2
Mineral oil refining	274·5	14·6
Gas, water and electricity	1,031·3	631·1
All other industries	1,668·8	890·5
Total (all industries)	15,003·9	6,191·7

Labour. The total labour force at mid-April 1986 was about 1,302,000, of which about 227,000 persons were out of work. Of the estimated 1,075,000 persons at work, 168,000 were in the agricultural sector, 301,000 in industry and 606,000 in services.

The number of trade unions in Dec. 1986 was 77; total membership, 518,000. About 250,000 were organized in 4 general unions catering both for white collar and manual workers. There were 16 employers' associations holding negotiation licences, with membership of 11,400.

Commerce. Value of imports and exports of merchandise for calendar years (in £):

	1981	1982	1983	1984	1985
Imports	6,578,406,480	6,816,154,975	7,366,775,383	8,912,170,063	9,430,492,317
Exports	4,777,570,799	5,691,441,609	6,943,836,265	8,897,524,535	9,743,028,594

The values of the chief imports and total exports are shown in the following table (in IR£):

	Imports		Exports	
	1984	1985	1984	1985
Live animals and food	932,969,575	994,439,722	2,064,173,762	2,204,971,595
Raw materials	295,802,229	297,350,224	505,116,665	450,070,889
Mineral fuels and lubricants	1,106,717,585	1,122,026,740	106,838,590	123,667,458
Chemicals	1,031,930,198	1,103,239,819	1,236,288,522	1,406,424,449
Manufactured goods	1,369,689,876	1,415,039,112	845,105,966	904,081,576
Machinery and transport equipment	2,778,477,214	2,945,833,546	2,550,254,190	2,889,334,829
Manufactured articles [1]	1,031,807,006	1,090,507,160	991,166,311	1,080,401,748

[1] Not elsewhere specified.

Exports, in IR£1m., for 1986 (and 1985): UK, 3,201·3 (3,211·1); Federal Republic of Germany, 1,022·1 (985·3); France, 887·3 (821·7); USA, 819·2 (953·9); Netherlands, 555·6 (663·7); Belgium and Luxembourg, 450·2 (396·4); Italy, 334·3 (363·9); Sweden, 173·5 (170·9); Japan, 170·6 (154·3); Switzerland, 155 (127·6); Spain, 137·3 (111·2); Canada, 118·5 (171·7). Imports: UK, 3,586·8 (4,026·1); USA, 1,364·8 (1,602·2); Federal Republic of Germany, 771·4 (729·3); France, 438·6 (456·2); Netherlands, 331·9 (356·9); Japan, 328·4 (334·4); Italy, 227·7 (214); Belgium and Luxembourg, 188·4 (205·8); Sweden, 139·8 (149·1); Spain, 119·6 (101).

An Anglo-Irish free-trade agreement to remove progressively all duties between July 1966 and July 1975 was signed in London on 14 Dec. 1965.

Total trade between Ireland and UK (British Department of Trade returns, in £1,000 sterling):

	1983	1984	1985	1986	1987
Imports to UK	2,290,067	2,635,039	2,816,007	3,053,807	3,488,406
Exports and re-exports from UK	3,055,275	3,393,499	3,642,844	3,558,372	3,831,737

Tourism. Total number of visits by foreigners (including cross-border traffic) in 1986 was 1,991,000; they spent £649m.

COMMUNICATIONS

Roads. At 31 Dec. 1985 there were 92,302 km of public roads, consisting of 8 km of motorway, 5,365 km of national roads, 10,616 km of main (trunk and link) roads other than national roads, 73,975 km of county roads and 2,338 km of county borough and urban roads; of the total length 87,687 km (95%) was paved.

Number of licensed motor vehicles at 30 Sept. 1985: Private cars, 709,546; public-service vehicles, 7,653; goods vehicles, 93,369; agricultural tractors, 66,040; motor cycles, 26,025; other vehicles, 12,125.

The total number of km run by road motor passenger vehicles of the omnibus type during 1985 was 92,662,000. Passengers carried numbered 224,459,000 and the gross receipts from passengers were £119,862,000.

Railways. The total length of railway open for traffic at 31 Dec. 1985 was 1,944 km (38 km electrified), all 1,600 mm gauge. Córas Iompair Éireann, the national transport undertaking, operates all rail services in the State.

Railway statistics for years ending 31 Dec.	1985	1986
Passengers (no.)	20,090,000	21,735,000
Km run by coaching trains	9,336,000	9,665,000
Merchandise and mineral traffic conveyed (tonnes)	601,014,000	574,355,000
Km run by freight trains	4,305,000	4,239,000
Receipts (£)	131,865,000	135,936,000
Expenditure (£)	132,059,000	124,207,000

Aviation. Aer Lingus PLC is a state owned company. Incorporated in 1936, it operates air services within Ireland and between Ireland and Britain and Europe. Air services between Ireland and the USA are operated by Aerlinte Eireann PLC, a state owned company incorporated in 1947. During the year ended 31 March 1987 Aer Lingus carried 2,098,165 passengers, 33,439 short tons of cargo and 1,241 short tons of mail on its European services and 339,463 passengers, 14,886 short tons of cargo and 630 short tons of mail on its trans-Atlantic services.

In addition to Aer Lingus, there were in 1987 9 independent air transport operators, the largest of which, Ryanair, which operates scheduled services between Dublin, Cork, Connaught, Waterford and Luton and between Connaught and Manchester/Birmingham.

Shipping. The Irish merchant fleet, of vessels of 100 gross tonnes or over, consisted of 69 vessels totalling 123,306 GRT at 31 Aug. 1986. Total cargo traffic passing through the country's ports amounted to 20m. tonnes in 1985.

Inland Waterways. The principal inland waterways open to navigation are the Shannon Navigation (130 miles) and the Grand Canal and Barrow Navigation (156 miles). Merchandise traffic is not now transported on them and navigation is confined to pleasure craft operated either privately or commercially.

Post and Broadcasting. Telecommunication services are provided by Bord Telecom Eireann as a statutory body set up under the Postal and Telecommunications Services Act, 1983. Number of telephones (April 1986), 694,000; public telephones, 5,000; telephone exchanges, 1,000; telex lines, 7,300; data lines, 4,200.

Postal services are provided by An Post, a statutory body set up under the Postal and Telecommunications Services Act, 1983. Number of Post Offices as of Dec. 1985, 2,168.

Radio and television broadcasting is operated by Radio Telefis Éireann, a statutory body appointed by the Minister for Communications under the Broadcasting Authority Acts. On 31 Dec. 1985 there were 717,023 holders of current television licences.

Cinemas. There were (1986) 124 cinemas and 169 (estimate) screens.

Newspapers (1986). There are 7 daily newspapers (all in English) with a combined circulation of 647,912; 5 of them are published in Dublin (circulation, 555,282).

JUSTICE, RELIGION, EDUCATION AND WELFARE

Justice. The Constitution provides that justice shall be administered in public in Courts established by law by Judges appointed by the President on the advice of the Government. The jurisdiction and organization of the Courts are dealt with in the Courts (Establishment and Constitution) Act, 1961, the Courts (Supplemental Provisions) Acts, 1961–86. These Courts consist of Courts of First Instance and a Court of Final Appeal, called the Supreme Court. The Courts of First Instance are the High Court with full original jurisdiction and the Circuit and the District Courts with local and limited jurisdiction. A judge may not be removed from office except for stated misbehaviour or incapacity and then only on resolutions passed by both Houses of the *Oireachtas.* Judges of the Supreme, High and Circuit Courts are appointed from among practising barristers. Judges of the District Court (called District Justices) may be appointed from among practising barristers or practising solicitors.

The Supreme Court, which consists of the Chief Justice (who is *ex officio* an additional judge of the High Court) and 5 ordinary judges, has appellate jurisdiction from all decisions of the High Court. The President may, after consultation with the Council of State, refer a Bill, which has been passed by both Houses of the *Oireachtas* (other than a money bill and certain other bills), to the Supreme Court for a decision on the question as to whether such Bill or any provision thereof is repugnant to the Constitution.

The High Court, which consists of a President (who is *ex officio* an additional Judge of the Supreme Court) and 14 ordinary judges, has full original jurisdiction in and power to determine all matters and questions, whether of law or fact, civil or criminal. In all cases in which questions arise concerning the validity of any law having regard to the provisions of the Constitution, the High Court alone exercises original jurisdiction. The High Court on Circuit acts as an appeal court from the Circuit Court.

The Court of Criminal Appeal consists of the Chief Justice or an ordinary Judge of the Supreme Court, together with either 2 ordinary judges of the High Court or the President and one ordinary judge of the High Court. It deals with appeals by persons convicted on indictment where the appellant obtains a certificate from the trial judge that the case is a fit one for appeal, or, in case such certificate is refused, where the court itself, on appeal from such refusal, grants leave to appeal. The decision of the Court of Criminal Appeal is final, unless that court or the Director of Public Prosecutions certifies that the decision involves a point of law of exceptional public importance, in which case an appeal is taken to the Supreme Court.

The Offences against the State Act, 1939 provides in Part V for the establishment of Special Criminal Courts. A Special Criminal Court sits without a jury. The rules of evidence that apply in proceedings before a Special Criminal Court are the same as those applicable in trials in the Central Criminal Court. A Special Criminal Court is authorised by the 1939 Act to make rules governing its own practice and procedure. An appeal against conviction or sentence by a Special Criminal Court may be taken to the Court of Criminal Appeal. On 30 May 1972 Orders were made establishing a Special Criminal Court and declaring that offences of a particular class or kind (as set out) were to be scheduled offences for the purposes of Part V of the Act, the effect of which was to give the Special Criminal Court jurisdiction to try persons charged with those offences.

The High Court exercising criminal jurisdiction is known as the Central Criminal Court. It consists of a judge or judges of the High Court, nominated by the President of the High Court. The Court sits in Dublin and tries criminal cases which are outside the jurisdiction of the Circuit Court.

The country is divided into a number of circuits for the purposes of the Circuit Court. The President of the Circuit Court is *ex officio* an additional judge of the High Court. The jurisdiction of the court in civil proceedings is limited to £15,000 in contract and tort, £15,000 in actions founded on hire-purchase and credit-sale agreements, £5,000 in equity and £5,000 in probate and administration, save by consent of the parties, in which event the jurisdiction is unlimited. In criminal matters it has jurisdiction in all cases except murder, treason, piracy and allied offences. The Circuit Court acts as an appeal court from the District Court.

The District Court has summary jurisdiction in a large number of criminal cases where the offence is not of a serious nature. In civil matters the Court has jurisdiction in contract and tort (except slander, libel, seduction, slander of title and false imprisonment) where the claim does not exceed £2,500; in proceedings founded on hire-purchase and credit-sale agreements, the jurisdiction is £2,500.

All criminal cases, except those of a minor nature, are tried by a judge and a jury of 12. Juries are also used in many civil cases in the High Court. In a criminal case a majority vote of the jury (10 must agree) is necessary to determine a verdict, but in a civil case the agreement of 9 members is sufficient.

Religion. According to the census of population taken in 1981 the principal religious professions were as follows:

	Leinster	Munster	Connacht	Ulster (part of)	Total
Roman Catholics	1,645,489	949,938	406,811	202,238	3,204,476
Church of Ireland	58,356	18,076	5,973	12,961	95,366
Presbyterians	4,337	542	345	9,031	14,255
Methodists	3,339	1,285	324	842	5,790
Other religious denominations	9,148	2,586	753	483	12,970
Not stated or no religion	69,852	25,888	10,204	4,604	110,548

Education. *Elementary.* Elementary education is free and was given in about 3,387 national schools (including 118 special schools) in 1986. The total number of pupils on rolls in 1985–86 was 567,086, including pupils in special schools and classes; the number of teachers of all classes about 21,144, including remedial teachers and teachers of special classes. The estimated state expenditure on elementary education for 1987 is £444,015,000, excluding the cost of administration.

Special provision is made for handicapped and deprived children in special schools which are recognized on the same basis as primary schools, in special classes attached to ordinary schools and in certain voluntary centres where educational services appropriate to the needs of the children are provided. Categories of children include visually handicapped, hearing impaired, physically handicapped, mentally handicapped, emotionally disturbed, travelling children and other socially disadvantaged children. Provision is also made, on an increasing scale, for children with dual or multiple handicaps. Each class in such schools is very much smaller than ordinary classes in a primary school and, because of the size of the catchment areas involved, an extensive system of school transport has been developed. Many handicapped children who have spent some years in a special school or class are integrated into normal schools for part of their school career, if necessary with special additional facilities such as nursing services, special equipment, etc. For others who cannot progress within the ordinary school system the special schools or classes provide both the primary and post-primary level of education. There are also part-time teaching facilities in hospitals, child guidance clinics, rehabilitation workshops, special 'Saturday-morning' centres and home teaching schemes.

Special schools (1985–86) numbered 118 with 8,650 pupils. There were 248 special classes attached to ordinary schools with 2,711 pupils. 797 remedial teachers were employed for backward pupils in ordinary primary schools. 30 peripatetic teachers were employed for children with hearing or visual impairments, and for travelling children.

Secondary. Voluntary secondary schools are under private control and are conducted in most cases by religious orders; all schools receive grants from the State and are open to inspection by the Department of Education. The number of recognized secondary schools during the school year 1986–87 was 503, and the number of pupils in attendance was 215,833.

Vocational Education Committee schools provide courses of general and technical education. The number of vocational schools during the school year 1986–87 was 252, full-time students, 83,278. These schools are controlled by the local Vocational Education Committees; they are financed mainly by state grants and also by local rating authorities and VECs.

Comprehensive Schools which are financed by the State combine academic and technical subjects in one broad curriculum so that each pupil may be offered educational options suited to his needs, abilities and interests. Pupils are prepared for the State examinations and for entrance to universities and institutes of further education. The number of comprehensive schools during the school year 1986–87 was 15 with 8,937 students.

Community Schools continue to be established through the amalgamation of existing voluntary secondary and Vocational Education Committee schools where this is found feasible and desirable and in new areas where a single larger school is considered preferable to 2 smaller schools under separate managements. These schools provide second-level education and also provide adult education facilities for their own areas. They also make facilities available to voluntary organizations and to the adult community generally. The number of community schools during the school year 1986–87 was 44 with 30,455 students.

The estimated State expenditure for post-primary education for 1987 was £498,558,000.

Regional Technical Colleges and Colleges of Technology. Apprentice, technician and professional courses (and some degree courses) are provided in the Dublin Institute of Technology under the auspices of the City of Dublin Vocational Education Committee; the Limerick College of Art, Commerce and Technology; the Cork School of Art and School of Music and 9 regional technical colleges at Athlone, Carlow, Cork, Dundalk, Galway, Letterkenny, Sligo, Tralee and Waterford. Students (full-time) 1985–86, 18,952.

University Education is provided by the National University of Ireland, founded in Dublin in 1908, and by the University of Dublin (Trinity College), founded in 1592. The National University comprises 3 constituent colleges–University College, Dublin, University College, Cork, and University College, Galway.

St Patrick's College, Maynooth, Co. Kildare, is a national seminary for Catholic priests and a pontifical university with the power to confer degrees up to doctoral level in philosophy, theology and canon law. It also admits lay students (men and women) to the courses in arts, Celtic studies, science and education which it provides as a recognized college of the National University.

Besides the University medical schools, the Royal College of Surgeons in Ireland provides medical qualifications which are internationally recognized. Courses to degree level are available at the National College of Art and Design, Dublin.

There are six Colleges of Education for training primary school teachers. For degree awarding purposes, three of these colleges are associated with Trinity College, two with University College, Dublin, and one with University College, Cork. The Thomond College of Education, Limerick, trains post-primary teachers in physical education, rural and general science, metalwork and engineering science, woodwork and building science and commercial and secretarial subjects.

Third-level courses with a technological bias, leading to degree, diploma and certificate qualifications are also provided by the National Institutes for Higher Education, Limerick and Dublin. There are also 2 Home Economics Colleges, one associated with Trinity College and the other with University College, Galway.

Agricultural. An Chomhairle Óiliuna Talmhaíochta (ACOT) is the agency responsible for providing agricultural advisory and training services. Full-time instruction in agriculture is provided for all sections of the farming community. There are 4 agricultural colleges for young people, administered by ACOT, and 8 private ACOT- aided agricultural colleges, at each of which a 1-year course in agriculture is given. A second-year course in farm machinery is provided at one college. Scholarships tenable at these colleges, all of which are residential, are awarded by ACOT which also provides a comprehensive agricultural advisory service and conducts winter classes in agriculture and horticulture at local centres.

Horticultural. Two of the agricultural colleges mentioned above also provide a commercial horticultural course. A third college aided by ACOT also provides this course. A 3-year course in amenity horticulture is provided at the National Botanic Gardens in Dublin.

A comprehensive 3-year training programme for young entrants to farming leading to a 'Certificate in Farming' involving both formal instruction and a period of supervised on-farm work experience, was introduced by ACOT in 1982. Students taking the Certificate in Farming can follow a course in general agriculture, pigs, poultry or horticulture. In the case of horticulture, the major part of this course is taken at one of the three horticultural colleges.

Health Services. There are 3 categories of entitlement, based on a person's income:
(i) Persons on a low income and their dependants, who qualify for the full range of health services, free of charge, i.e. family doctor, drugs and medicines, hospital and specialist services as well as dental, aural and optical services. Maternity care and infant welfare services are also provided. There is no fixed limit, but guidelines laid down by health boards, determine eligibility – each application is considered on its merit. There is provision for hardship cases.
(ii) Persons whose income for the year ended 5 April 1987 was under £15,000. They and their dependants are entitled to free hospital services, both as an in-patient and an out-patient, a full maternity and infant welfare service and assis-

tance towards the cost of prescriptions. The latter limits the nett outlay on medicines used in a calendar month to £28.

(iii) Persons whose income for the year ended 5 April 1987 was £15,000 or more. They are entitled to in-patient and out-patient hospital services but they are liable for the fees of consultants. They are also entitled to assistance towards the cost of prescriptions. Drugs and medicines are made available free of charge to all persons suffering from specified long-term ailments such as diabetes, multiple sclerosis, epilepsy, etc. Hospital in-patient and out-patient services are free of charge to all children under 16 years of age, suffering from specified long-term conditions such as cystic fibrosis, spina bifida, cerebral palsy, etc. Immunization and diagnostic services as well as hospital services are free of charge to everyone suffering from an infectious disease. A maintenance allowance is also payable in necessitous cases.

From 18 May 1987 persons in categories *(ii)* and *(iii)* are liable for in-patient and out-patient charge. A charge of £10 is made for each day or part of a day during which in-patient services are availed of subject to a maximum payment of £100 in any period of 12 consecutive months. A charge of £10 for out-patient services is made for the first and subsequent instances relating to the same matter. Persons in category *(i)*, women receiving service in respect of motherhood, children suffering from certain diseases etc. are not liable for these charges.

Services for Children: Health Boards are involved, with the co-operation of a wide network of voluntary organizations, in the provision of a range of child care services including adoption, fostering, residential care, day care and social work services for families in need of support.

Welfare Services: There are various services provided for the elderly, the chronic sick, the disabled and families in stress, such as social support service, day care services for children, home helps, home nursing, meals-on-wheels, day centres, cheap fuel, etc. Health Boards also provide disabled persons, without charge, with training for employment and place them in jobs.

Grants and Allowances: Disabled Persons' Maintenance Allowance is payable to the chronically disabled over the age of 16 who are not in long term care. Recipients are entitled to free travel and subject to certain conditions to electricity allowance, free TV licence, telephone rental and fuel vouchers. Mobility allowance is payable to severely disabled persons between 16 and 66 years who are unable to walk. Allowance for the Domiciliary Care of Severely Handicapped Children is payable to the mother of a severely handicapped child, maintained at home, but needing constant care and supervision. Blind welfare allowance: This allowance is in addition to the benefits for the blind operated by the Department of Social Welfare. Grants up to £1,500 are paid, subject to a means test, to disabled persons towards the purchase of a car, in order that they might obtain or retain employment.

Health contributions: A health contribution of 1·25% of income up to a ceiling of £15,000 is payable by all.

Social Security. Social-welfare services concerned primarily with income maintenance are under the general control of the Minister for Social Welfare. The services administered by the Department of Social Welfare are divided into Insurance and Assistance schemes.

Insurance Services. All employees irrespective of their level of earnings are compulsorily insured from age 16 to 66 years and are liable for pay-related social insurance contributions. The majority of employees pay a contribution of 7·75% of their earnings prescribed up to a ceiling of £15,000 while a contribution of 6·5% of their earnings continues to be deducted up to a ceiling of £15,500. Their employers pay a further 12·33% up to a prescribed ceiling of £15,500. (The insured population is approximately 1·2m.) Subject to appropriate statutory conditions (but without regard to the recipients' means) the following flat-rate insurance benefits are available: Disability benefit, invalidity pension, unemployment benefit, maternity benefit, widow's pension, deserted wife's benefit, orphan's allowance, treatment benefit, retirement pension payable at 65, old-age pension payable at 66 and a death grant. Pay-related benefit is payable with disability benefit, unemployment benefit, maternity allowance and injury benefit to persons whose employment is insurable at certain class rates of pay-related social insurance contribution. The cost of the flat-rate and pay-related benefits is met by pay-related social insurance contributions from employers and employees and by a state grant.

The insurance services also provide for payment of benefits in respect of injury, disablement or death, as well as medical care resulting from an occupational accident or disease. These benefits are available to employees, irrespective of age, and are paid from an Occupational Injuries Fund which is financed by employers' contributions and income from investments.

Assistance Services. Child Benefit is payable without a means test in respect of each child under 16 years of age and children between 16 and 18 who are at school or incapacitated for a prolonged period. The following Assistance services are subject to a means test: Non-contributory widows' and orphans' pensions to the survivors of persons whose lack of insurance (or inadequate insurance record) precludes payment of contributory pensions; deserted wife's allowance to women who have been deserted by their husbands and for whom the deserted wife's benefit is similarly precluded; allowances for unmarried mothers, prisoners' wives and single women between the ages of 58 and 66 years; old age pensions payable at age 66 to persons not entitled to insurance pensions; blind pensions (under the same general conditions as apply to old age pensions) payable at age 18; unemployment assistance payable during unemployment to persons not entitled to receive unemployment benefit; supplementary welfare allowance, payable when a person has no other resources or when such resources are insufficient to meet his needs.

DIPLOMATIC REPRESENTATIVES

Of Ireland in Great Britain (17 Grosvenor Pl., London, SW1X 7HR)
Ambassador: Andrew O'Rourke.

Of Great Britain in Ireland (33 Merrion Rd., Dublin, 4)
Ambassador: Nicholas Fenn, CMG.

Of Ireland in the USA (2234 Massachusetts Ave., NW, Washington, D.C., 20008)
Ambassador: Padraic N. MacKernan.

Of the USA in Ireland (42 Elgin Rd., Ballsbridge, Dublin)
Ambassador: Margaret M. Heckler.

Of Ireland to the United Nations
Ambassador: Robert McDonagh.

Books of Reference

Statistical Information: The Central Statistics Office (Earlsfort Terrace, Dublin, 2) was established in June 1949, and is attached to the Department of the Taoiseach. *Director:* T. P. Linehan, B.E., B.Sc.

Principal publications of the Central Statistics Office are *National Income and Expenditure* (annually), *Statistical Abstract* (annually), *Census of Population Reports, Census of Industrial Production Reports, Trade and Shipping Statistics* (annually and monthly), *Trend of Employment and Unemployment* (annually), *Reports on Vital Statistics* (annually), *Irish Statistical Bulletin* (quarterly).

Aspects of Ireland. (Series). Dublin Department of Foreign Affairs.
Atlas of Ireland. Royal Irish Academy, Dublin, 1979
Facts About Ireland. Dublin Department of Foreign Affairs, 6th ed. 1985
The Gill History of Ireland. 11 vols. Dublin
Bartholomew, P. C., *The Irish Judiciary.* Dublin, Institute of Public Administration, 1974
Brown, T., *Ireland: A Social and Cultural History, 1922–1979.* London, 1981
Chubb, B., *The Constitution and Constitutional Change in Ireland.* Dublin, 1978
Eager, A. R., *A Guide to Irish Bibliographical Material.* 2nd ed. London, 1980
Encyclopaedia of Ireland. Dublin, 1968
Hickey, D. J. and Doherty, J. E., *A Dictionary of Irish History since 1800.* Dublin, 1980
Johnston, T. J., and others, *A History of the Church of Ireland.* Dublin, 1953
Lehane, B., *The Companion Guide to Ireland.* London, 1973
McDunphy, Michael, *The President of Ireland: His Powers, Functions and Duties.* Dublin, 1945
Nevill, W. E., *Geology and Ireland.* Dublin, 1963
Shannon, M. O., *Irish Republic.* [Bibliography] Oxford and Santa Barbara, 1986
Thom's Directory of Ireland. 2 vols. (Dublin, Street Directory, Commercial). Dublin, 1979–80
Tobin, F., *Ireland in the 1960s.* Dublin, 1984

ISRAEL

Capital: Jerusalem
Population: 4·33m. (1986)
GNP per capita: US$6,350 (1986)

Medinat Israel—State of Israel

HISTORY. The State of Israel was established on 14 May 1948. In 1967, following some years of uneasy peace, local clashes on the Israeli-Syrian border were followed by Egyptian mass concentration of forces on the borders of Israel. The UN emergency force was expelled and a blockade of shipping to and from Israel was imposed by Egypt in the Red Sea. Israel struck out at Egypt on land and in the air on 5–9 June 1967. Jordan joined in the conflict which spread to the Syrian borders. By 11 June the Israelis had occupied the Gaza Strip and the Sinai peninsula as far as the Suez Canal in Egypt, West Jordan as far as the Jordan valley and the heights east of the Sea of Galilee, including Quneitra in Syria.

A further war broke out on 6 Oct. 1973 when an Egyptian offensive was launched across the Suez Canal and Syrian forces struck on the Golan Heights. Following UN Security Council resolutions a ceasefire finally came into being on 24 Oct. In Dec. agreement was reached by Egypt and Israel on disengagement and a disengagement agreement was signed with Syria on 31 May 1974. A further disengagement agreement was signed between Israel and Egypt in Sept. 1975.

Developments in 1977 included President Sadat of Egypt's visit to Israel and peace inititative and in March 1978 Israeli troops entered southern Lebanon but later withdrew after the arrival of a UN peace-keeping force.

In Sept. 1978 President Carter convened the Camp David conference at which Egypt and Israel agreed on frameworks for peace in the Middle East with treaties to be negotiated between Egypt and her neighbours. Negotiations began in USA between Egypt and Israel in Oct. 1978 and a peace treaty was signed in Washington 26 March 1979.

Under the Israel-Egypt peace treaty signed in Washington on 26 March 1979, Israel withdrew from the Sinai Desert in two phases, part was achieved on 26 Jan. 1980 and the final withdrawal by 26 April 1982.

AREA AND POPULATION. The area of Israel, within the boundaries defined by the 1949 armistice agreements with Egypt, Jordan, the Lebanon and Syria, is 20,770 sq. km (8,017 sq. miles), with a population (June 1983 census) of 4,037,600 (estimated, 1986, 4,331,300). Population of areas under Israeli administration as a result of the 6-day war was, at 31 Dec. 1986: Judaea and Samaria (West Bank), 836,000, Gaza Strip, 545,000.

Crude birth rate per 1,000 population of Jewish population (1986), 21·2; non-Jewish: Moslems, 33·8; Christians, 22; Druzes and others, 30·8. Crude death rate, Jewish, 7·5; non-Jewish: Moslems, 3·4; Christians (1985), 5·2; Druzes and others (1985), 3·4. Infant mortality rate per 1,000 live births, Jewish, 9·5; non-Jewish: Moslems, 18; Christians (1985), 13·8; Druzes and others (1985), 12·9. Life expectancy (1985): Males, 73·5 years; females, 77.

Israel is administratively divided into 6 districts:

District	Area (sq. km)	Population [1]	Chief town
Northern	4,501	718,900	Nazareth
Haifa	854	596,100	Haifa
Central	1,242	907,700	Ramla
Tel Aviv	170	1,018,800	Tel Aviv
Jerusalem [2]	627	518,200	Jerusalem
Southern	14,107	518,100	Beersheba

[1] 1986.   [2] Includes East Jerusalem.

On 23 Jan. 1950 the Knesset proclaimed Jerusalem the capital of the State and on 14 Dec. 1981 extended Israeli law into the Golan Heights. Population of the main towns (1986): Tel-Aviv/Jaffa, 320,300; Jerusalem, 468,900; Haifa, 223,400; Ramat Gan, 115,500; Bat-Yam, 132,000; Holon, 140,700; Petach-Tikva, 130,700; Beersheba, 115,000.

The official languages are Hebrew and Arabic.

Immigration. The following table shows the numbers of Jewish immigrants entering Palestine (Israel), including persons entering as travellers who subsequently registered as immigrants. For a year-by-year breakdown, *see* THE STATESMAN'S YEAR-BOOK, 1951, p. 1167.

1919–48	482,857	1958–68	384,870	1980–86	103,784
1948–57	905,740	1969–79	384,066		

During the period 1948–68, 45.5% of the immigrants came from Europe and America and 54.5% from Asia and Africa; in 1985, 27.5% came from Europe and America and 72.5% from Asia and Africa.

The Jewish Agency, which, in accordance with Article IV of the Palestine Mandate, played a leading role in laying the political, economic and social foundations on which the State of Israel was established, continues to be instrumental in organizing immigration.

CLIMATE. From April to Oct., the summers are long and hot, and almost rainless. From Nov. to March, the weather is generally mild, though colder in hilly areas, and this is the wet season. Jerusalem. Jan. 48°F (9°C), July 73°F (23°C). Annual rainfall 21″ (528 mm). Tel Aviv. Jan. 57°F (14°C), July 81°F (27°C). Annual rainfall 22″ (550 mm).

CONSTITUTION AND GOVERNMENT. Israel is an independent sovereign republic, established by proclamation on 14 May 1948. For the history of the British Mandate, *see* THE STATESMAN'S YEAR-BOOK, 1920–49, under PALESTINE.

In 1950 the Knesset (*Parliament*), which in 1949 had passed the Transition Law dealing in general terms with the powers of the Knesset, President and Cabinet, resolved to enact from time to time fundamental laws, which eventually, taken together, would form the Constitution. Fundamental laws that have been passed are: The Knesset (1958), Israel Lands (1960), the President (1964), the Government (1968), the State Economy (1975), the Army (1976), Jerusalem, capital of Israel (1980), and the Judicature (1984).

National flag: White with 2 horizontal blue stripes, the blue Shield of David in the centre.

National anthem: Hatikvah (The Hope). Words by N. N. Imber (1878); adopted as the Jewish National Anthem by the first Zionist Congress (1897).

The Knesset, a one-chamber Parliament, consists of 120 members. It is elected for a 4-year term by secret ballot and universal direct suffrage. The system of election is by proportional representation. After the July 1984 elections the Knesset was composed as follows: Alignment, 44; Likud, 41; National Religious Party, 5; Tehiya, 5; Hadash, 4; Shas, 4; Shinui, 3; Civil Rights, 3; Yahad, 3; PLP, 2; Agudat Israel, 2; Morasha, 2; Tami, 1; Kach, 1; Ometz, 1. It was agreed that for the first 25 months of the parliamentary term Shimon Peres should be Prime Minister and Yitzhak Shamir, Deputy Prime Minister and after that the roles would be reversed. The President is elected by the Knesset by secret ballot by a simple majority; his term of office is 5 years. He may be re-elected once.

Former Presidents of the State: Chaim Weizmann (1949–52); Izhak Ben-Zvi (1952–63); Zalman Shazar (1963–68); Ephraim Katzir (1968–78); Yitzhak Navon (1978–83).

President: Chaim Herzog, elected 22 March 1983 by 61 votes to 56 against with 3 abstentions.

The Cabinet in Dec. 1987 was composed as follows:

Prime Minister: Yitzhak Shamir.

Vice Prime Minister and Foreign Minister: Shimon Peres. *Deputy Prime Minister and Minister of Housing and Construction:* David Levy. *Deputy Prime Minister and Minister of Education and Culture:* Yitzhak Navon. *Health:* Shoshana Arbeli Almoslino. *Police:* Haim Bar-Lev. *Minister:* Yigael Hurvitz. *Religious Affairs:* Zevulun Hammer. *Minister:* Ezer Weizman. *Economy, Planning and Communications:* Gad Ya'acobi. *Minister:* Yitzhak Moda'i. *Agriculture:* Aryeh Nehamkin. *Finance:* Moshe Nissim. *Science and Development:* Gideon Patt. *Immigrants' Absorption:* Ya'acov Tzur. *Transport:* Haim Corfu. *Labour and Social Affairs:* Moshe Katzav. *Defence:* Yitzhak Rabin. *Energy and Infrastructure:* Moshe Shahal. *Minister:* Yosef Shapira. *Industry and Trade:* Ariel Sharon. *Justice and Tourism:* Avraham Sharir.

Local Government. Local authorities are of three kinds, namely, municipal corporations, local councils and regional councils. Their status, powers and duties are prescribed by statute. Regional councils are local authorities set up in agricultural areas and include all the agricultural settlements in the area under their jurisdiction. All local authorities exercise their authority mainly by means of bye-laws approved by the Minister of the Interior. Their revenue is derived from rates and a surcharge on income tax. Local authorities are elected for a 4-year term of office concurrently with general elections.

There were (1988) 40 municipalities (3 Arab), 137 local councils (61 Arab and Druze) and 54 regional councils (1 Druze).

DEFENCE. The Defence Service Law, provides a compulsory 36-month conscription for men (Jews and Druze only). Unmarried women (Jews only) serve 24 months.

The Israel Defence Force is a unified force, in which army, navy and air force are subordinate to a single chief-of-staff. The Minister of Defence is *de facto* commander-in-chief but from Oct. 1973 the cabinet formed a defence committee with authority to make decisions on military operations.

Army. The Army is organized in 11 armoured divisions, 33 armoured brigades, 9 mechanized infantry brigades, 12 territorial/border infantry brigades, 5 parachute brigades and 15 artillery brigades. Equipment includes some 3,900 main battle tanks and 5,000 other armoured fighting vehicles. Strength (1988) 104,000 (conscripts 88,000), rising to 598,000 on mobilization.

Navy. The Navy includes 3 diesel-electric patrol submarines (built in Britain), 25 missile vessels (4 of 500 tons with helicopter and hangar, 8 of 415 tons, 12 of 220 tons and 1 of 47 tons, the smallest missile craft yet built), 3 missile-armed hydrofoils of 105 tons, 40 coastal patrol craft, 2 transports, 3 medium landing ships, 6 landing craft, 1 'firefish', 1 support ship, 1 training ship, 4 coastguard cutters, and 12 minor landing craft. The Navy controls 3 Westwind patrol aircraft and 12 Dauphin helicopters were ordered in 1986.

New construction planned includes 4 missile armed corvettes of 850 tons to be built in Israel.

The former Nautical School in Haifa has been reorganized as a Naval Officers' School in Acre. The repair base at Eilat has a syncrolift. Naval personnel in 1988 totalled 800 officers and 5,800 men, of whom 3,500 are conscripts, including a Naval Commando. There are also 1,000 naval reservists available on mobilization.

Air Force. The Air Force has a personnel strength (1988) of 28,000, with about 629 first-line aircraft, all jets, of Israeli and US manufacture. There are 3 squadrons with about 50 F-15s, 2 squadrons with about 100 Israeli-built Kfirs, and 3 squadrons with the first 120 of a planned 144 F-16s in an interceptor role; 4 squadrons with 110 F-4E Phantoms, 3 squadrons with 65 Kfirs, and 3 squadrons with A-4E/H/N Skyhawks in the fighter-bomber/attack role; and 15 RF-4E reconnaissance fighters; supported by 4 E-2C Hawkeye airborne early warning and control aircraft and a few OV-1 Mohawk, RC-12 and RU-21 aircraft. There are transport squadrons of turboprop C-130/KC-130 Hercules, C-47, Arava, Islander, and

Boeing 707 (some equipped for tanker or ECM duties) aircraft, helicopter squadrons of CH-53, Super Frelon, AH-1 HueyCobra, Hughes 500MD/TOW Defender, JetRanger, Dauphin, Agusta-Bell 205, 206 and 212 aircraft, and training units with locally-built Magister jet trainers, which can be used also in a light ground attack role. Missiles in service include surface-to-air Hawks and surface-to-surface Lances.

INTERNATIONAL RELATIONS

Membership. Israel is a member of UN.

ECONOMY

Budget. The budget year runs from 1 April to 31 March and in 1987 balanced at 39,294m. new shekels.

Currency. The unit of currency is the *new shekel* introduced in Jan. 1986 its value is 1,000 old *shekels*. Currency in circulation on 31 Dec. 1984 was I£161,651m. (bank-notes and coins). In March 1988, £1 = 2·79 *shekel*; US$ = 1·58 *shekel*.

Banking. The Bank of Israel was established by law in 1954 as Israel's central bank. Its Governor is appointed by the President on the recommendation of the Cabinet for a 5-year term. He acts as economic adviser to the Government and has ministerial status. There are 26 commercial banks headed by Bank Leumi Le Israel, Bank Hapoalim and Israel Discount Bank, 2 merchant banks, 1 foreign bank, 15 mortgage banks and 9 lending institutions specifically set up to aid industry and agriculture.

Weights and Measures. The metric system is in general use. The (metrical) *dunam* = 1,000 sq. metres (about 0·25 acre).

Jewish Year. The Jewish year 5747 corresponds to 4 Oct. 1986–23 Sept. 1987; 5748 to 24 Sept. 1987–11 Sept. 1988; 5749 to 12 Sept. 1988 to 29 Sept. 1989.

ENERGY AND NATURAL RESOURCES

Electricity. Electric-power production amounted during 1986 to 15,503m. kwh. Supply 230 volts; 50 Hz.

Oil and Gas. The only significant indigenous hydrocarbon known to be found is oil shale. In 1988 recoverable potential was estimated to be 250m. tons of oil.

Minerals. The most valuable natural resources of the country are the potash, bromine and other salt deposits of the Dead Sea, which are exploited by the Dead Sea Works, Ltd. Geological research and exploration of the natural resources in the Negev are undertaken by the Israel Mining Corporation. Potash production in 1986 was 2,035,000 tons.

Agriculture. In the coastal plain (Sharon, Emek Hefer and the Shephelah) mixed farming, poultry raising, citriculture and vineyards are the main agricultural activities. The Emek (the Valley of Jezreel) is the main agricultural centre of Israel. Mixed farming is to be found throughout the valleys; the sub-tropical Beisan and Jordan plainlands are also centres of banana plantations and fish breeding. In Galilee mixed farming, olive and tobacco plantations prevail. The Hills of Ephraim are a vineyard centre; many parts of the hill country are under afforestation. In the northern Negev farming has been aided by the Yarkon–Negev water pipeline. This has become part of the overall project of the 'National Water Carrier', which is to take water from the Sea of Galilee (Lake Kinnereth) to the south. The plan includes a number of regional projects such as the Lake Kinnereth –Negev pipeline which came into operation in 1964; it has an annual capacity of 320m. cu. metres.

The area under cultivation (in 1,000 dunams) in 1985–86 was 4,358, of which 2,335 were under irrigation. Of the total cultivated area 2,367 dunams were under field crops, 405 under vegetables, potatoes, pumpkins and melons, 900 under citrus and orchards, 28 under fish ponds and the rest under miscellaneous crops, including auxiliary farms, nurseries, flowers, etc.

Industrial crops, such as cotton, have successfully been introduced. In 1985–86 the area under cotton totalled 465,000 dunams.

Livestock (1986) included 321,000 cattle, 232,000 sheep, 127,000 goats, 130,000 pigs, 4,000 horses, 27m. poultry.

Characteristic types of rural settlement are, among others, the following: (1) The *Kibbutz* and *Kvutza* (communal collective settlement), where all property and earnings are collectively owned and work is collectively organized. (126,700 people lived in 269 settlements in 1986). (2) The *Moshav* (workers' co-operative smallholders' settlement) which is founded on the principles of mutual aid and equality of opportunity between the members, all farms being equal in size. (146,400 in 411) (3) The *Moshav Shitufi* (co-operative settlement), which is based on collective ownership and economy as in the *Kibbutz*, but with each family having its own house and being responsible for its own domestic services. (10,900 in 47). (4) Other rural settlements in which land and property are privately owned and every resident is responsible for his own well-being. In 1986 there were 229 villages with a population of 114,800.

INDUSTRY AND TRADE

Industry. A wide range of products is manufactured, processed or finished in the country, including chemicals, metal products, textiles, tyres, diamonds, paper, plastics, leather goods, glass and ceramics, building materials, precision instruments, tobacco, foodstuffs, electrical and electronic equipment.

Labour. The General Federation of Labour (Histadrut) founded in 1920, had, in 1987, 1·6m. members (including 170,000 Arab and Druze members); including workers' families, this membership represents 71·5% of the population covering 87% of all wage-earners. Several trades unions also exist representing other political and religious groups.

Commerce. External trade, in US$1m., for calendar years:

	1980	1982	1983	1984	1985	1986
Imports	8,070	8,173	8,667	8,257	8,202	9,550
Exports	5,874	5,639	5,603	6,242	6,682	7,712

The main exportable commodities are citrus fruit and by-products, fruit-juices, wines and liquor, sweets, polished diamonds, chemicals, tyres, textiles, metal products, machinery, electronic and transportation equipment, flowers. The main exports were, in 1986 (US$1m.): Diamonds, 1,879; chemical and oil products, 790; agricultural products including citrus fruit, 560; manufactured goods, machinery and transport equipment, 4,328. In 1986 62·7% of imports came from Europe, 18·6% from Canada and USA, 8·1% from Africa and Asia. Of exports, 36·4% went to Europe, 34% to Canada and USA, 12% to Africa and Asia.

Total trade between Israel and UK (British Department of Trade returns, in £1,000 sterling):

	1983	1984	1985	1986	1987
Imports to UK	314,148	392,757	403,952	385,164	437,014
Exports and re-exports from UK	354,860	393,025	434,470	452,407	523,591

Tourism. In 1986 there were about 1·2m. tourists.

COMMUNICATIONS

Roads. There were 12,823 km of paved roads in 1986. Registered motor vehicles in 1986 totalled 819,102, including 8,191 buses, 120,842 trucks and 648,847 private cars.

Railways. Internal communications (1986–87) are provided by 528 km of standard gauge line. Construction is in progress of 215 km of new line linking Eilat on the Gulf of Aqaba with Sedom and the existing rail network. In 1986–87, 2·5m. passengers and 6·4m. tonnes of freight were carried.

Aviation. Air communications are centred in the airport of Ben Gurion, near Tel-Aviv. In 1986, 10,091 planes landed at Israeli airports on international flights;

1,542,000 passengers arrived, 1,556,000 departed. In 1986, 83,732 tons of freight were loaded and 78,603 tons unloaded. The Israeli airline El Al maintains regular flights to London, Paris, Rome, Amsterdam, Brussels, Cairo, Madrid, Lisbon, Bucharest, Athens, Vienna, New York, Montreal, Zurich, Munich, Istanbul, Johannesburg, Nairobi, Frankfurt and Copenhagen. In 1986–87 El Al carried 1·5m. passengers.

Shipping. Israel has 3 commercial ports, Haifa, Ashdod and Eilat. In 1986, 3,054 ships departed from Israeli ports; 17m. tons. of freight were handled. The merchant fleet consisted in 1986 of 73 vessels, totalling 1,571,000 GRT.

Post and Broadcasting. The Ministry of Communications controls the postal service, and a public company responsible to the Ministry administers the tele-communications service. In 1986 there were 594 post offices and postal agencies, 50 mobile post offices and (1986) 1·94m. telephones.

Israeli television and the state radio station, *Kol Israel* are controlled by the Israel Broadcasting Authority, established in 1965. Radio licences in 1985 numbered approximately 1·12m. and television licences (1986) 936,000.

Cinemas In 1987 there were 162 cinemas.

Newspapers (1987). There were 21 daily newspapers.

JUSTICE, RELIGION, EDUCATION AND WELFARE

Justice. *Law.* Under the Law and Administration Ordinance, 5708/1948, the first law passed by the Provisional Council of State, the law of Israel is the law which was obtaining in Palestine on 14 May 1948 in so far as it is not in conflict with that Ordinance or any other law passed by the Israel legislature and with such modifications as result from the establishment of the State and its authorities.

Capital punishment was abolished in 1954, except for support given to the Nazis and for high treason.

The law of Palestine was derived from three main sources, namely, Ottoman law, English law (Common Law and Equity) and the law enacted by the Palestine legislature, which to a great extent was modelled on English law. The Ottoman law in its turn was derived from three main sources, namely, Moslem law which had survived in the Ottoman Empire, French law adapted by the Ottomans and the personal law of the non-Moslem communities.

Civil Courts. Municipal courts, established in certain municipal areas, have criminal jurisdiction over offences against municipal regulations and bye-laws and certain specified offences committed within a municipal area.

Magistrates courts, established in each district and sub-district, have limited jurisdiction in both civil and criminal matters.

District courts, sitting at Jerusalem, Tel-Aviv and Haifa, have jurisdiction, as courts of first instance, in all civil matters not within the jurisdiction of magistrates courts, and in all criminal matters, and as appellate courts from magistrates courts and municipal courts.

The Supreme Court has jurisdiction as a court of first instance (sitting as a High Court of Justice dealing mainly with administrative matters) and as an appellate court from the district courts (sitting as a Court of Civil or of Criminal Appeal).

In addition, there are various tribunals for special classes of cases, such as the Rents Tribunals and the Tribunals for the Prevention of Profiteering and Speculation. Settlement Officers deal with disputes with regard to the ownership or possession of land in settlement areas constituted under the Land (Settlement of Title) Ordinance.

Religious Courts. The rabbinical courts of the Jewish community have exclusive jurisdiction in matters of marriage and divorce, alimony and confirmation of wills of members of their community other than foreigners, concurrent jurisdiction with the civil courts in such matters of members of their community who are foreigners if they consent to the jurisdiction, and concurrent jurisdiction with the civil courts in all other matters of personal status of all members of their community, whether foreigners or not, with the consent of all parties to the action, save that such courts may not grant a decree of dissolution of marriage to a foreign subject.

The courts of the several recognized Christian communities have a similar jurisdiction over members of their respective communities.

The Moslem religious courts have exclusive jurisdiction in all matters of personal status over Moslems who are not foreigners, and over Moslems who are foreigners, if under the law of their nationality they are subject in such matters to the jurisdiction of Moslem religious courts.

Where any action of personal status involves persons of different religious communities, the President of the Supreme Court will decide which court shall have jurisdiction, and whenever a question arises as to whether or not a case is one of personal status within the exclusive jurisdiction of a religious court, the matter must be referred to a special tribunal composed of 2 judges of the Supreme Court and the president of the highest court of the religious community concerned in Israel.

Religion. Religious affairs are under the supervision of a special Ministry, with departments for the Christian and Moslem communities. The religious affairs of each community remain under the full control of the ecclesiastical authorities concerned: in the case of the Jews, the Sephardi and Ashkenazi Chief Rabbis, in the case of the Christians, the heads of the various communities, and in the case of the Moslems, the Qadis. The Druze were officially recognized in 1957 as an autonomous religious community.

In 1986 there were: Jews, 3,561,400; Moslems, 586,300; Christians, 100,200; Druze and others, 73,000.

The Jewish Sabbath and Holy Days are observed as days of rest in the public services. Full provision is, however, made for the free exercise of other faiths, and for the observance by their adherents of their respective days of rest and Holy Days.

Education. Laws passed by the Knesset in 1949 and 1978 provide for free and compulsory education from 5 to 16 years of age. There is free education until 18 years of age.

The State Education Law of 12 Aug. 1953 established a unified state-controlled elementary school system with a provision for special religious schools. The standard curriculum for all elementary schools is issued by the Ministry with a possibility of adding supplementary subjects comprising not more than 25% of the total syllabus. Most schools in towns are maintained by municipalities, a number are private and some are administered by teachers' co-operatives or trustees.

Statistics relating to schools under government supervision, 1986–87:

Type of School [1]	Schools	Teachers	Pupils
Hebrew Education			
Primary schools	1,310	37,799	480,616
Schools for handicapped children	198	3,055	12,071
Schools of intermediate division	291	12,952	109,365
Secondary schools	516		191,519
Vocational schools	308	22,864	91,720
Agricultural schools	26		4,683
Arab Education			
Primary schools	308	6,610	140,777
Schools for handicapped children	16	176	1,262
Schools of intermediate division	55	1,578	23,393
Secondary schools	83		35,805
Vocational schools	37	2,208	5,696
Agricultural schools	2		640

[1] Schools providing more than one type of education are included more than once.

There are also a number of private schools maintained by religious foundations—Jewish, Christian and Moslem—and also by private societies.

The Hebrew University of Jerusalem, founded in 1925, comprises faculties of the humanities, social sciences, law, science, medicine and agriculture. In

1986–87 it had 16,870 students. The Technion in Haifa had 9,090 students. The Weizmann Institute of Science in Rehovoth, founded in 1949, had 570 students.

Tel Aviv University had 19,400 students. The religious Bar-Ilan University at Ramat Gan, opened in 1965 had 9,480 students. The Haifa University had 6,550 students. The Ben Gurion University had 5,200 students.

Social Welfare. In 1986 Israel had 150 hospitals with 27,399 beds and 9,500 doctors.

The National Insurance Law, which took effect in April 1954, provides for old-age pensions, survivors' insurance, work-injury insurance, maternity insurance, family allowances and unemployment benefits.

DIPLOMATIC REPRESENTATIVES

Of Israel in Great Britain (2 Palace Green, London, W8 4QB)
Ambassador: Yehuda Avner (accredited 3 Aug. 1983).

Of Great Britain in Israel (192 Hayarkon St., Tel Aviv 63405)
Ambassador: C. W. Squire, CMG, LVO.

Of Israel in the USA (3514 International Dr., NW, Washington, D.C., 20008)
Ambassador: Ovadia Sofer.

Of the USA in Israel (71 Hayarkon St., Tel Aviv)
Ambassador: Thomas R. Pickering.

Of Israel to the United Nations
Ambassador: Benjamin Netanyahu.

Books of Reference

Statistical Information: There is a Central Bureau of Statistics at the Prime Minister's Office, Jerusalem. It publishes monthly bulletins of statistics (economic and social), foreign trade statistics and price statistics.
Atlas of Israel. 3rd ed. 1985
Government Yearbook. Government Printer, Jerusalem. 1951 ff. (latest issue, 1971/72)
Facts about Israel. Ministry of Foreign Affairs, Jerusalem, 1985
Statistical Abstract of Israel. Government Printer, Jerusalem (from 1949/50)
Israel Yearbook. Tel-Aviv, 1948–49 ff.
Statistical Bulletin of Israel. 1949 ff.
Reshumoth (Official Gazette)
Middle East Record, ed. Y. Oron. London, 1960 ff.
Laws of the State of Israel. Authorized translation. Government Printer, Jerusalem, 1958 ff.
Alkalay, R., *The Complete English–Hebrew Dictionary.* 4 vols. Tel-Aviv, 1959–61
Ben-Gurion, D., *Ben-Gurion Looks Back.* London, 1965.—*The Jews in Their Land.* London, 1966.—*Israel: A Personal History.* New York, 1971
Gilbert, M., *The Arab-Israeli Conflict: Its History in Maps.* 3rd ed. London, 1981
Harris, W., *Taking Root: Israeli Settlement in the West Bank, The Golan and Gaza Sinai 1967–1980.* Chichester, 1981
Kieval, G. R., *Party Politics in Israel and the Occupied Territories.* Westport, 1983
Likhovski, E. S., *Israel's Parliament: The Law of the Knesset.* Oxford, 1971
O'Brien, C. C., *The Siege.* London, 1986
Peri, Y., *Between Battles and Ballots: Israeli Military in Politics.* CUP, 1983
Reich, B., *Israel: Land of Tradition and Conflict.* London, 1986
Sachar, H. M., *A History of Israel.* 2 vols. OUP, 1976 and 1987
Sager, S., *The Parliamentary System of Israel.* Syracuse Univ. Press, 1986
Segev, T., *1949: The First Israelis.* New York, 1986
Sharkansky, I., *The Political Economy of Israel.* Oxford and Santa Barbara, 1986
Shimshoni, D., *Israeli Democracy: The Middle of the Journey.* New York, 1982
Snyder, E. M., and Kreiner, E., *Israel.* [Bibliography] Oxford and Santa Barbara, 1985
Wolffsohn, M., *Politik in Israel.* Opladen, 1983

National Library: The Jewish National and University Library, Jerusalem.

ITALY

Capital: Rome
Population: 57·3m. (1986)
GNP per capita: US$6,096 (1984)

Repubblica Italiana

HISTORY. On 10 June 1946 Italy became a republic on the announcement by the Court of Cassation that a majority of the voters at the referendum held on 2 June had voted for a republic. The final figures, announced on 18 June, showed: For a republic, 12,718,641 (54·3% of the valid votes cast, which numbered 23,437,143); for the retention of the monarchy, 10,718,502 (45·7%); invalid and contested, 1,509,735. Total 24,946,878, or 89·1% of the registered electors, who numbered 28,005,449. For the results of the polling in the 13 leading cities, *see* THE STATESMAN'S YEAR-BOOK, 1951, p. 1175. Voting was compulsory, open to both men and women 21 years of age or older, including members of the Civil Service and the Armed Forces; former active Fascists and a few other categories were excluded.

On 18 June the then Provisional Government without specifically proclaiming the republic, issued an 'Order of the Day' decreeing that all court verdicts should in future be handed down 'in the name of the Italian people', that the *Gazzetta Ufficiale del Regno d'Italia* should be re-named *Gazzetta Ufficiale della Repubblica Italiana,* that all references to the monarchy should be deleted from legal and government statements and that the shield of the House of Savoy should be removed from the Italian flag.

Thus ended the reign of the House of Savoy, whose kings had ruled over Piedmont for 9 centuries and as Kings of Italy since 18 Feb. 1861. (For fuller account of the House of Savoy, *see* THE STATESMAN'S YEAR-BOOK, 1946, p. 1021.) The Crown Prince Umberto, son of King Victor Emmanuel III, became Lieut.-Gen. (*i.e.*, Regent) of the kingdom on 5 June 1944. Following the abdication and retirement to Egypt of his father on 9 May 1946, Umberto was declared King Umberto II; his reign lasted to 13 June, when he left the country. King Victor Emmanuel III died in Alexandria on 28 Dec. 1947.

AREA AND POPULATION. Italy is bounded north by Switzerland and Austria, east by Yugoslavia and the Adriatic Sea, south-east by the Ionian Sea, south by the Mediterranean Sea, south-west by the Tyrrhenian Sea and Ligurian Sea and west by France. The population (present in actual boundaries) at successive censuses were as follows:

31 Dec. 1881	29,277,927	21 April 1936	42,302,680
10 Feb. 1901	33,370,138	4 Nov. 1951	47,158,738
10 June 1911	35,694,582	15 Oct. 1961	49,903,878
1 Dec. 1921	37,403,956	24 Oct. 1971	53,744,737
21 April 1931	40,582,043	25 Oct. 1981	56,243,935

The following table gives area and population of the Regions (census 1981 and estimate, 1986):

Regions	Area in sq. km (1981)	Resident pop. census, 1981	Resident pop. estimate, 1985	Density per sq. km (1981)
Piemonte	25,399	4,479,031	4,389,430	175
Valle d'Aosta	3,262	112,353	113,855	35
Lombardia	23,856	8,891,652	8,876,787	373
Trentino-Alto Adige	13,613	873,413	880,237	64
Bolzano-Bozen	7,400	430,568	435,377	58
Trento	6,213	442,845	444,860	71
Veneto	18,364	4,345,047	4,372,869	235
Friuli-Venezia Giulia	7,846	1,233,984	1,214,557	157
Liguria	5,416	1,807,893	1,758,961	332
Emilia Romagna	22,123	3,957,513	3,931,014	178
Toscana	22,992	3,581,051	3,571,538	155
Umbria	8,456	807,552	817,852	95
Marche	9,694	1,412,404	1,426,965	145
Lazio	17,203	5,001,684	5,116,125	289

Regions	Area in sq. km (1981)	Resident pop. census, 1981	Resident pop. estimate, 1985	Density per sq. km (1981)
Abruzzi	10,794	1,217,791	1,254,129	113
Molise	4,438	328,371	334,195	73
Campania	13,595	5,463,134	5,690,431	398
Puglia	19,347	3,871,617	4,026,151	199
Basilicata	9,992	610,186	620,260	60
Calabria	15,080	2,061,182	2,139,301	135
Sicilia	25,708	4,906,878	5,112,073	189
Sardegna	24,090	1,594,175	1,643,789	66
Total	301,268	56,556,911	57,290,519	187

Vital statistics for calendar years:

		Living births				Deaths excl. of
	Marriages	Legitimate	Illegiti-mate	Total	Still-born	still-born
1980	322,968	612,945	27,456	640,401	5,453	554,510
1981	316,953	595,514	27,589	623,103	4,728	545,291
1982	310,938 [1]	590,042	29,055	619,097	4,757	534,935
1983	300,855 [1]	572,641	29,287	601,928	4,396	564,330
1984 [1]	298,028	556,810	29,162	585,972	4,160	531,899
1985 [1]	295,990	545,027	30,468	575,495	3,833	544,811
1986 [1]	296,539	523,801	31,044	554,845	3,658	542,127

[1] Provisional.

Emigrants to non-European countries, by sea and air: 1978, 23,589; 1979, 21,302; 1980, 20,360; 1981, 20,628; 1982, 22,324; 1983, 20,443; 1984, 16,776; 1985, 16,151. Since 1960 nearly nine-tenths of these emigrants have gone to Canada, USA and Australia.

Communes of more than 100,000 inhabitants, with population resident at the census of 25 Oct. 1981 and on 31 Dec. 1986:

	1981	1986		1981	1986
Roma (Rome)	2,840,259	2,815,457	Perugia	142,348	146,713
Milano (Milan)	1,604,773	1,495,260	Ravenna	138,034	136,016
Napoli (Naples)	1,212,387	1,204,211	Pescara	131,330	131,027
Torino (Turin)	1,117,154	1,035,565	Reggio nell'E.	130,376	130,086
Genova (Genoa)	762,895	727,427	Rimini	127,813	130,698
Palermo	701,782	723,732	Monza	123,145	122,064
Bologna	459,080	432,406	Bergamo	122,142	118,959
Firenze (Florence)	448,331	425,835	Sassari	119,596	120,152
Catania	380,328	372,486	Siracusa (Syracuse)	117,615	122,857
Bari	371,022	362,524	La Spezia	115,392	108,937
Venezia (Venice)	346,146	331,454	Vicenza	114,598	110,449
Verona	265,932	259,151	Terni	111,564	111,157
Messina	260,233	268,896	Forlì	110,806	110,482
Trieste	252,369	239,031	Piacenza	109,039	105,626
Taranto	244,101	244,997	Cosenza	106,801	106,026
Padova (Padua)	234,678	225,769	Ancona	106,498	104,409
Cagliari	233,848	222,574	Bolzano	105,180	101,515
Brescia	206,661	199,286	Pisa	104,509	104,384
Modena	180,312	176,880	Torre del Greco	103,605	105,066
Parma	179,019	175,842	Novara	102,086	102,742
Livorno (Leghorn)	175,741	174,065	Udine	102,021	100,211
Reggio di C.	173,486	178,821	Catanzaro	100,832	102,558
Prato	160,220	164,595	Alessandria	100,523	–
Salerno	157,385	154,848	Trento	99,179	100,202
Foggia	156,467	159,051	Lecce	91,289	100,981
Ferrara	149,453	143,950			

CLIMATE. The climate varies considerably with latitude. In the south, it is warm temperate, with little rain in the summer months, but the north is cool temperate with rainfall more evenly distributed over the year.

Florence, Jan. 42°F (5.6°C), July 76°F (25°C). Annual rainfall 36″ (901 mm). Milan, Jan. 35°F (2°C), July 75°F (24°C). Annual rainfall 32″ (802 mm). Naples, Jan. 48°F (8.9°C), July 77°F (25.6°C). Annual rainfall 34″ (850 mm). Palermo, Jan. 52°F (11.1°C), July 79°F (26.1°C). Annual rainfall 28″ (702 mm). Rome, Jan. 44.5°F (7°C), July 77°F (25°C). Annual rainfall 26″ (657 mm). Venice, Jan. 38°F (3.3°C), July 75°F (23.9°C). Annual rainfall 29″ (725 mm).

CONSTITUTION AND GOVERNMENT. The new Constitution was passed by the constituent assembly by 453 votes to 62 on 22 Dec. 1947; it came into force on 1 Jan. 1948. The Constitution consists of 139 articles and 18 transitional clauses. Its main dispositions are as follows:

Italy is described as 'a democratic republic founded on work'. Parliament consists of the Chamber of Deputies and the Senate. The Chamber is elected for 5 years by universal and direct suffrage and it consists of 630 deputies. The Senate is elected for 5 years on a regional basis; each Region having at least 7 senators, consisting of 315 elected senators; the Valle d'Aosta is represented by 1 senator only. The President of the Republic can nominate 5 senators for life from eminent men in the social, scientific, artistic and literary spheres. On the expiry of his term of office, the President of the Republic becomes a senator by right and for life, unless he declines.

The President of the Republic is elected in a joint session of Chamber and Senate, to which are added 3 delegates from each Regional Council (1 from the Valle d'Aosta). A two-thirds majority is required for the election, but after a third indecisive scrutiny the absolute majority of votes is sufficient. The President must be 50 years or over; his term lasts for 7 years. The President of the Senate acts as his deputy.

The President can dissolve the chambers of parliament, except during the last 6 months of his term of office.

The Cabinet can be forced to resign only on a motivated motion of censure; the defeat of a government bill does not involve the resignation of the Government.

A Constitutional Court, consisting of 15 judges who are appointed, 5 each, by the President of the Republic, Parliament (in joint session) and the highest law and administrative courts, has rights similar to those of the Supreme Court of the USA. It can decide on the constitutionality of laws and decrees, define the powers of the State and Regions, judge conflicts between the State and Regions and between the Regions, and try the President of the Republic and the Ministers. The court was set up in Dec. 1955.

The reorganization of the Fascist Party is forbidden. Direct male descendants of King Victor Emmanuel are excluded from all public offices, have no right to vote or to be elected, and are banned from Italian territory; their estates are forfeit to the State. Titles of nobility are no longer recognized, but those existing before 28 Oct. 1922 are retained as part of the name.

National flag: Three vertical strips of green, white, red.

National anthem: Fratelli d'Italia (words by G. Mameli; tune by M. Novaro, 1847).

Head of State: On 3 July 1985 Chamber and Senate in joint session elected by an absolute majority (752 votes out of 977 votes cast) Francesco Cossiga (Christian Democrat; born 1928), President of the Republic.

Former Presidents of the Republic: Luigi Einaudi (1948–55); Giovanni Gronchi (1955–62); Antonio Segni (1962–64); Giuseppe Saragat (1964–71); Giovanni Leone (1971–78); Alessandro Pertini (1978–85).

General elections for the Senate and Chamber of Deputies took place on 14 June 1987.

Senate. Christian Democrats, 125; Communists, 101; Socialists, 36; Italian Social Movement, 16; Social Democrats, 5; Republicans, 8; Liberals, 3; other groups, 21. Total: 315.

Chamber. Christian Democrats, 234; Communists, 177; Socialists, 94; Italian Social Movement, 35; Republicans, 21; Social Democrats, 17; Liberals, 11; Radical Party, 13; Green Party, 13; other groups, 15. Total: 630.

The coalition government was composed as follows in Jan. 1988.

Prime Minister and Southern Affairs (ad interim): Giovanni Goria (DC).
Vice Prime Minister and Treasury: Giuliano Amato (PSI).
Foreign Affairs: Giulio Andreotti (DC).
Interior: Amintore Fanfani (DC).
Justice: Giuliano Vassalli (PSI).

Budget: Emilio Colombo (DC).
Finance: Antonio Gava (DC).
Defence: Valerio Zanone (PLI).
Education: Giovanni Galloni (DC).
Public Works: Emilio De Rose (PSDI).
Agriculture: Filippo Pandolfi (DC).
Transport: Calogero Mannino (DC).
Post: Oscar Mammi (PRI).
Industry: Adolfo Battaglia (PRI).
Labour: Rino Formica (PSDI).
Foreign Trade: Renato Ruggera (PSI).
Merchant Navy: Giovanni Prandini (DC).
State Industry: Luigi Granelli (DC).
Health: Carlo Donat Cattin (DC).
Tourism: Franco Carraro (PSI).
Culture: Carlo Vizzini (PSDI).
EEC Affairs: Antonio La Pergola (PSDI/PSI).
Public Administration: Giorgio Santuz (DC).
Scientific Research: Antonio Ruberti (PSI).
Regional Affairs: Aristide Gunnella (PRI).
Relations with Parliament: Sergio Mattarella (DC).
Civil Protection: Remo Gaspari (DC).
Ecology: Giorgio Ruffolo (PSI).
Urban Problems: Carlo Tognoli (PSI).
Special Affairs: Rosa Russo Jervolino (DC).

Regional Administration. Italy is administratively divided into regions (*regioni*), provinces (*province*) and municipalities (*comuni*).

Art. 116 of the 1948 constitution provided for the establishment of 5 autonomous regions with special statute (*regioni autonome con statuto speciale*) and 15 autonomous regions with ordinary statute (*regioni autonome con statuto normale*). The regions have their own parliaments (*consiglio regionale*) and governments (*giunta regionale e presidente*) with certain legislative and administrative functions adapted to the circumstances of each region.

A government commissioner co-ordinates regional and national activities. The results of the last regional elections were as follows:

Regions	Election date	Christian Democrats	Communists	Socialists	Social Movement	Social Democrats	Republicans	Liberals	Others	Total
Piemonte	12 May 1985	19	18	8	3	3	3	3	3	60
Valle d'Aosta [1]	26 June 1983	7	6	3	1	1	1	1	15	35
Lombardia	12 May 1985	31	22	12	4	2	4	1	4	80
Trentino-Alto Adige [1]	20 Nov. 1983	19	6	4	3	1	3	1	33	70
Veneto	12 May 1985	30	12	8	2	1	2	1	4	60
Friuli-Venezia Giulia [1]	26 June 1983	23	14	7	3	3	3	1	8	62
Liguria	12 May 1985	13	15	4	2	1	2	1	2	40
Emilia-Romagna	12 May 1985	13	26	4	2	1	2	1	1	50
Toscana	12 May 1985	14	25	5	2	1	1	–	2	50
Umbria	12 May 1985	9	14	4	2	–	1	–	–	30
Marche	12 May 1985	15	15	4	2	1	1	1	1	40
Lazio	12 May 1985	21	18	7	6	2	2	1	3	60
Abruzzi	12 May 1985	19	11	5	2	1	1	1	–	40
Molise	12 May 1985	18	5	3	1	1	1	1	–	30
Campania	12 May 1985	24	14	9	5	3	2	1	2	60
Puglia	12 May 1985	20	13	8	5	2	1	1	–	50
Basilicata	12 May 1985	14	7	5	1	2	1	–	–	30
Calabria	12 May 1985	16	10	8	2	2	1	–	1	40
Sicilia [1]	22 June 1986	36	14	13	8	4	5	3	7	90
Sardegna [1]	24 June 1984	27	24	8	3	4	3	–	12	81

[1] Autonomous regions with special statute.

DEFENCE. Most of the restrictions imposed upon Italy in Part IV of the peace treaty signed on 10 Feb. 1947 were repudiated by the signatories on 21 Dec. 1951, only the USSR objecting.

Head of the armed forces is the Defence Chief of Staff. In 1947 the ministries of war, navy and air were merged into the ministry of defence. The technical and scientific council for defence directs all research activities.

National service lasts 12 months in the Army and Air Force, and 18 months in the Navy.

Army. The Army consists of 3 corps, one of which is alpine and others include mechanized, armoured and support brigades. In peninsular defence there are 2 independent motorized brigades. In addition there is a rapid intervention force, 2 amphibious battalions and a support brigade with missiles. Equipment includes 500 M-47, 300 M-60A1 and 920 Leopard I main battle tanks. The Army air corps operates 100 light aircraft and 330 helicopters. Strength (1988) 265,000 (215,000 conscripts), with 520,000 reserves. There is also the paramilitary Carabinieri of 90,000 men.

Navy. Particulars of the principal surface ships in the Italian Navy:

Completed	Name	Standard displacement Tons	Aircraft	Principal armament	Torpedo tubes	Shaft horsepower	Speed Knots
			Light Aircraft Carrier				
1985	Giuseppe Garibaldi (fitted with 6·5° VSTOL launching ramp)	10,100	16 Sea King helicopters	4 Teseo 2 launchers for Otomat; 2 Albatross systems with octuple Aspide missiles (48)	6 A/S	80,000	30
			Cruisers				
1969	Vittorio Veneto (fitted as aircraft carrier aft)	7,500	9 helicopters	8 3-in.; 4 Teseo launchers; twin 'Terrier' missile launcher	6	73,000	32
1964 1964	Andrea Doria [1] Caio Duilio [1]	6,000	4 helicopters	8 3-in.; twin 'Terrier' missile launcher	6	60,000	31

[1] Rated as guided-missile escort cruisers.

There are also 10 diesel-powered submarines, 4 guided-missile destroyers, 16 frigates, 8 corvettes, 4 ocean minesweepers, 15 minehunters, 10 coastal minesweepers, 7 hydrofoil missile boats, 1 dock landing ship, 2 tank landing ships, 3 surveying vessels, 2 salvage ships, 1 transport, 1 support ship, 5 training ships, 2 replenishment oilers, 14 water carriers, 1 netlayer, 6 repair craft, 20 auxiliaries, 5 coastal transports (landing craft), 5 motor transports (minor landing craft), 6 harbour oilers and 60 tugs. The Naval Air Arm has 100 anti-submarine and training helicopters.

One submarine, 1 dock landing ship and 4 corvettes are under construction. Two destroyers, 8 corvettes and 8 minehunters are projected.

The coastline of the peninsula is divided into zones, with headquarters at Spezia, Naples, Taranto and Ancona; all are under the jurisdiction of flag officers with the status of C.-in-C. The admirals commanding on the coasts of Sardinia and Sicily do not rank as C.-in-C.

Other localities of strategic importance under naval administration are Brindisi, where there is an admiral commanding, and Genoa, Leghorn, Augusta and Venice, each of which is under a senior naval officer.

The personnel of the Navy in 1988 numbered 44,500 officers and ratings, including the naval air arm and the marine battalion.

Air Force. Control is exercised through 2 regional HQ near Taranto and Milan. Units assigned to NATO comprise the 1st air brigade of Nike-Hercules surface-to-air missiles, 4 fighter-bomber, 3 light attack, 9 interceptor and 2 tactical reconnaissance squadrons, with supporting transport, search and rescue, and training units. Two of the fighter-bomber squadrons have Tornados, others have Aeritalia G91Ys. The light attack squadrons operate G91Rs and MB.339s. F-104S Starfighters have been standardized throughout the interceptor squadrons. The reconnaissance force operates RF-104G Starfighters. A total of 187 AM-X jet aircraft, built jointly by Aeritalia, Aermacchi and Embraer of Brazil, will replace G91R, G91Y and F-104G/S aircraft in eight squadrons in 1988–90.

One transport squadron has turboprop C-130H Hercules aircraft; 2 others have turboprop Aeritalia G222s. There is a VIP and personnel transport squadron, equipped with AS-61, DC-9, Gulfstream III and Falcon 50 aircraft. Electronic warfare duties are performed by specially equipped G222s, PD-808s and MB 339s. Two land-based anti-submarine squadrons operate Breguet Atlantics. Search and rescue are performed by 20 Agusta-Sikorsky HH-3F helicopters, Canadair CL-215 amphibians and smaller types. There are also strong support and training elements; some MB 339 jet trainers have armament provisions for secondary close air support and anti-helicopter roles.

Air Force strength in mid-1987 was about 73,000 officers and men, about 300 combat aircraft, 300 fixed-wing second-line aircraft and over 100 helicopters.

INTERNATIONAL RELATIONS

Membership. Italy is a member of UN, NATO and the European Communities.

ECONOMY

Budget. Total revenue and expenditure for fiscal years, in 1 m. lire:

	Revenue	Expenditure		Revenue	Expenditure
1981	105,343,000	149,246,000	1984	199,986,000	292,348,000
1982	150,842,000	206,444,000	1985	218,973,000	319,099,000
1983	177,142,000	250,203,000	1986	266,301,009	384,344,429

In the revenue for 1986 turnover and other business taxes accounted for 60,017,295m. lire, customs duties and indirect taxes for 21,615,563m. lire.

The public debt at 31 Dec. 1985 totalled 585,899,796m. lire, including consolidated debt of 42,090m. lire and the floating debt 261,548,138m. lire.

Currency. The standard coin is the *lira*. From 30 March 1960 the gold standard was formally established as equal to 0·00142187 gramme of gold per lira.

State metal coins are of 5, 10, 20, 50, 100, 200, and 500 lire. There are in circulation bank-notes of 1,000, 2,000, 5,000, 10,000, 20,000, 50,000 and 100,000 lire; they are neither convertible into gold as foreign moneys nor exportable abroad, nor importable from abroad into Italy (except for certain specified small amounts).

Circulation of money at 31 Dec. 1986: State coins and notes, 1,074,600m. lire; bank-notes, 50,499,800m. lire.

In March 1988 the rate of exchange was 1,244 lire per US$1 and 2,207 lire per £1 sterling.

Banking. According to the law of 6 May 1926 there is only one bank of issue, the Banca d'Italia. Its gold reserve amounted to 35,203,000m. lire in Dec. 1986; the foreign credit reserves of the Exchange Bureau (*Ufficio Italiano Cambi*) amounted to 18,495,000m. lire at the same date.

Since 1936, all credit institutions have been under the control of a State organ, named 'Inspectorate of Credit'; the Bank of Italy has been converted into a 'public institution', whose capital is held exclusively by corporate bodies of a public nature. Other credit institutions, totalling 1,102, are classified as: (1) 6 chartered banks (Banco di Napoli, Banco di Sicilia, Banca Nazionale del Lavoro, Monte dei Paschi di Siena, Istituto di S. Paolo di Torino, Banca di Sardegna); (2) 3 banks of national interest (Banca Commerciale Italiana in Milan, Credito Italiano in Genoa and Banco di Roma); (3) banks and credit concerns in general, including 153 joint-stock banks and 135 co-operative banks; (4) 87 savings banks and Monti di pegno (institutions granting loans against personal chattels as security); (5) 713 *Casse rurali e agrarie* (agricultural banks, established as co-operative institutions with unlimited liability of associates); (6) 5 Istituti di Categoria.

At 31 Dec. 1986 there were 285 credit institutes handling 95% of all deposits and current accounts, with capital and reserves of 51,585,000m. lire.

On 31 Dec. 1986 the post office savings banks had deposits and current accounts of 86,851,000m. lire; credit institutions, 499,948,000m. lire.

Insurance. By a decree of 29 April 1923 life-assurance business is carried on only by the National Insurance Institute and by other institutions, national and foreign, authorized by the Government. At 31 Dec. 1985 the insurances vested in the *Istituto Nazionale delle Assicurazioni* amounted to 14,189,386m. lire, including the decuple of life annuities.

Weights and Measures. The metric system is in general use.

ENERGY AND NATURAL RESOURCES

Electricity. Italy has greatly developed her water-power resources. In 1986 the total power generated was 189,570m. kwh., of which 44,531m. kwh. were generated by hydro-electric plants. Supply 220 volts; 50 Hz and 120, 125, 160 and 260 volts; 60 Hz.

Oil. Production in 1986 amounted to 2,510,564 tonnes, of which 837,827 came from Sicily. Natural gas production (1986) 558,000m. cu. ft.

Minerals. The Italian mining industry is most developed in Sicily (Caltanissetta), in Tuscany (Arezzo, Florence and Grosseto), in Sardinia (Cagliari, Sassari and Iglesias), in Lombardy (particularly near Bergamo and Brescia) and in Piedmont.

Italy's fuel and mineral resources are wholly inadequate. Only sulphur and mercury outputs yield a substantial surplus for exports. In 1986 outputs, in tonnes, of raw steel were 22,881,951; rolled iron, 20,096,897; cast-iron ingots, 11,837,020.

Production of metals and minerals (in tonnes) was as follows:

	1981	1982	1983	1984	1985	1986
Iron pyrites	680,988	666,964	646,209	442,674	690,395	760,860
Iron ore	345,604	195,034	67,700	273,700	–	–
Manganese	8,756	8,727	7,205	9,528	8,621	6,336
Zinc	82,094	74,142	83,462	81,291	87,380	50,515
Crude sulphur	96,172	88,848	40,858	20,639	4,911	–
Bauxite	19,000	23,810	3,118	–	–	2,250
Mercury	20,017	17,163	–	–	–	–
Lead	35,556	36,360	37,429	37,558	37,051	27,219
Aluminium	273,845	232,861	195,694	230,207	226,300	262,562

Agriculture. The area of Italy in 1986 comprised 301,277 sq. km, of which 262,975 sq. km was agricultural and forest land and 38,302 sq. km was unproductive; the former was mainly distributed as follows (in 1,000 hectares): Forage and pasture, 8,205; woods, 6,727; cereals, 4,832; vines, 1,099; olive trees, 1,177; garden produce, 519; leguminous plants, 270.

At the third general census of agriculture (24 Oct. 1982) agricultural holdings numbered 3,270,560 and covered 23,559,924 hectares. 3,063,010 owners (93·6%) farmed directly 16,597,798 hectares (70·4%); 152,250 owners (4·7%) worked with hired labour on 6,209,702 hectares (26·4%); 130,648 share-croppers (3·6%) tilled 1,271,485 hectares (5·1%); the remaining 55,300 holdings (1·7%) of 752,424 hectares (3·2%) were operated in other ways.

According to the labour force survey in July 1978 persons engaged in agriculture numbered 3·17m. (2·02m. males and 1·15m. females).

In 1985, 1,227,134 farm tractors were being used.

The production of the principal crops (in 1,000 metric quintals) in 1986: Sugar beet, 149,578; wheat, 90,698; maize, 62,471; tomatoes, 45,156; potatoes, 25,511; oranges, 22,175; rice, 10,851; barley, 15,482; lemons, 8,132; oats, 3,973; olive oil, 3,563; tangerines, 5,318; other citrus fruit, 510; rye, 221.

Production of wine, 1986, 76,987,000 hectolitres; of tobacco, 156,100 tonnes.

In 1985 consumption of chemical fertilizers in Italy was as follows (in 1,000 tons): Perphosphate, 722; nitrate of ammonia, 838·1; sulphate of ammonium, 352·6; potash salts, 131·3; nitrate of calcium¹⁵⁄₁₆, 87·6; deposed slags, 38·3.

Livestock estimated in 1986: Cattle, 8,921,000; pigs, 9,278,000; sheep, 11,451,000; goats, 1,201,000; horses, 253,000; donkeys, 91,000; mules, 52,000.

Fisheries. The Italian fishing fleet comprised in 1982, 23,385 motor boats (323,512 gross tons) and 11,694 sailing vessels (14,612 gross tons). The catch in 1984 was 428,691 tonnes.

INDUSTRY AND TRADE

Industry. The main branches of industry are: (% of industrial value added at factor cost in 1982) Textiles, clothing, leather and footwear (17·7%), food, beverages and tobacco (10·4%), energy products (7·9%), agricultural and industrial machines (7·7%), metal products except machines and means of transport (7%), mineral and non-metallic mineral products (7%), timber and wooden furniture (6·6%), electric plants and equipment (6·3%), chemicals and pharmaceuticals (6·2%), means of transport (6·1%).

Production, 1986: Steel, 22,695,400; motor vehicles, 1,831,827; cement, 35,938,446 tonnes; artificial and synthetic fibres (including staple fibre and waste), 699,255 tonnes; polyethylene resins, 683,840 tonnes.

Labour. As at April 1982, 20·1m. persons were employed, 1·9m. unemployed (figures from a new series of statistics on the labour force, 1977, which is not comparable with previous series).

Trade Unions. There are 4 main groups: Confederazione Generale Italiana del Lavoro (Communist-dominated); Confederazione Italiana Sindacati Lavoratori (Catholic); Unione Italiana del Lavoro and Confederazione Italiana Sindacati Nazionali Lavoratori.

Commerce. The territory covered by foreign trade statistics includes Italy, the Republic of San Marino, but excludes the municipalities of Livigno and Campione.

The following table shows the value of Italy's foreign trade (in 1m. lire):

	1981	1982	1983	1984	1985	1986
Imports	103,674,405	116,215,679	121,978,334	148,162,029	172,809,202	149,044,966
Exports	86,039,719	99,230,877	110,530,106	129,026,980	149,723,608	145,322,982

The following table shows trade by countries in 1m. lire:

Countries	Imports into Italy from			Exports from Italy to		
	1984	1985	1986	1984	1985	1986
Argentina	775,711	951,177	530,848	419,735	428,378	454,044
Australia	990,700	1,079,687	905,868	1,124,992	1,473,117	1,049,510
Austria	2,698,224	3,084,146	3,187,843	2,912,338	3,293,871	3,447,341
Belgium-Luxembourg	5,464,553	6,412,172	6,919,195	3,732,440	4,442,557	4,842,643
France	18,436,260	21,546,182	21,705,037	18,078,148	21,003,252	22,703,882
Germany, Fed. Rep. of	23,665,941	28,742,482	30,467,639	20,781,721	24,172,063	26,354,658
Japan	2,371,574	2,827,485	3,119,697	1,481,441	1,765,431	1,965,898
Netherlands	7,246,042	8,795,999	8,771,113	3,708,591	4,630,021	4,755,345
Switzerland	6,099,618	6,666,741	6,484,644	5,245,889	6,070,302	6,608,396
USSR	7,096,887	5,692,204	3,464,130	2,786,132	2,913,927	2,412,583
UK	6,384,263	8,540,121	7,606,296	8,715,611	10,423,757	10,298,190
USA	9,110,937	10,294,233	8,473,707	14,045,308	18,356,745	15,604,124
Yugoslavia	1,934,286	2,194,954	2,006,592	1,702,205	2,262,840	2,013,352

In 1986 the main imports were maize, wood, greasy wool, metal scrap, pit-coal, petroleum, raw oils, meat, paper, rolled iron and steel, copper and alloys, mechanical and electric equipment, motor vehicles. The main exports were fruit and vegetables, fabrics, footwear and other clothing articles, rolled iron and steel, machinery, motor vehicles, plastic materials and petroleum by-products.

Italy's balance of trade (in 1,000m. lire) has been estimated as follows:

	Export	*Goods and services* Import	Balance	*Income from investments and work, balance*	*Net balance*
1980	83,815	94,316	−10,501	+669	−9,832
1981	107,251	116,240	−8,989	−2,323	−11,312
1982	123,757	129,859	−6,102	−3,622	−9,724
1983	138,894	134,247	+4,647	−4,196	+451
1984	163,867	165,930	−2,063	−4,736	−6,799
1985	183,406	186,955	−3,549	−5,360	−8,909
1986	179,242	164,986	+14,256	−5,002	+9,254

Remittances from Italians abroad (in US$1m. until 1969 and then 1,000m. lire): 1950, 72; 1960, 214; 1970, 289; 1980, 1,059; 1981, 1,325; 1982, 1,607; 1983, 1,727; 1984, 1,963; 1985, 2,226; 1986, 1,792.

Total trade between Italy and UK (British Department of Trade returns, in £1,000 sterling):

	1983	1984	1985	1986	1987
Imports to UK	3,188,219	3,814,163	4,293,941	4,658,036	5,216,751
Exports and re-exports from UK	2,292,788	2,902,666	3,466,495	3,472,364	4,145,659

Tourism. In 1986, 53·3m. foreigners visited Italy; they included 9·6m. German, 11·3m. Swiss, 8·6m. French, 5·4m. Austrian, 3·9m. Yugoslav, 2m. British, 1·7m. Dutch and 1·6m. US citizens. They spent about 14,691,006m. lire.

COMMUNICATIONS

Roads. Italy's roads totalled (31 Dec. 1986) 300,292 km, of which 45,779 km were state roads, 106,850 km provincial roads, 141,666 km communal roads. Motor vehicles, Dec. 1984: Cars, 20·9m.; buses, 71,981; lorries, 1,720,445; motor cycles, light vans, etc., 5,552,717.

Railways. Railway history in Italy begins in 1839, with a line between Naples and Portici (8 km). Length of railways (31 Dec. 1986), 19,726 km, including 16,166 km of state railways, of which 7,231 had not yet been electrified. The first section of a new high-speed direct railway linking Rome and Florence opened in Feb. 1977. In 1986 the state railways carried 397·1m. passengers and 52·6m. tonnes of goods. The Rome Underground opened in Feb. 1980.

Aviation. The Italian airline Alitalia (with a capital of 421,900m. lire, of which 99·1% is owned by the State) operates flights to every part of the world. Airports include 25 international, 36 national and 75 club airports. Domestic and international traffic in 1986 registered 16,838,339 passengers arrived and 16,858,787 departed, while freight and mail (excluding luggage) amounted to 190,133 tonnes unloaded and 242,799 tonnes loaded.

Shipping. The mercantile marine at 31 Dec. 1985 consisted of 2,045 vessels of 8,003,394 gross tons, not including pleasure boats (yachts, etc.), sailing and motor vessels. There were 1,344 motor vessels of 100 gross tons and over.

In 1985, 249,021,570 tonnes of cargo were unloaded, and 88,246,680 tonnes of cargo were loaded in Italian ports.

Post and Broadcasting. On 31 Dec. 1985 there were 14,276 post offices and 13,759 telegraph offices. The maritime radio-telegraph service had 20 coast stations. On 1 Jan. 1986 the telephone service had 25,614,597 apparatus. *Radiotelevisione Italiana* broadcasts 3 programmes and additional regional programmes, including transmissions in English, French, German and Slovenian on medium- and short-waves and on FM. It also broadcasts 2 TV programmes. Radio licences numbered 381,521; television and radio licences, 14,212,781.

Cinemas. There were 4,885 cinemas in 1985.

Newspapers. There were (1985) 72 daily newspapers with a combined circulation of 6·71m. copies; of the papers 14 are published in Rome and 7 in Milan. One daily each is published in German, Slovene and English.

JUSTICE, RELIGION, EDUCATION AND WELFARE

Justice. Italy has 1 court of cassation, in Rome, and is divided for the administration of justice into 23 appeal court districts (and 3 detached sections), subdivided into 159 tribunal *circondari* (districts), and these again into *mandamenti* each with its own magistracy (*Pretura*), 899 in all. There are also 90 first degree assize courts and 26 assize courts of appeal. For civil business, besides the magistracy above mentioned, *Conciliatori* have jurisdiction in petty plaints (those to a maximum amount of 1m. lire).

On 31 Dec. 1983 there were 25,016 male and 1,448 female prisoners in establishments for preventive custody, 10,819 males and 409 females in penal establishments and 1,255 males and 98 females in establishments for the execution of safety measures.

Religion. The treaty between the Holy See and Italy, of 11 Feb. 1929, confirmed by article 7 of the Constitution of the republic, lays down that the Catholic Apostolic Roman Religion is the only religion of the State. Other creeds are permitted, provided they do not profess principles, or follow rites, contrary to public order or moral behaviour.

The appointment of archbishops and of bishops is made by the Holy See; but the Holy See submits to the Italian Government the name of the person to be appointed in order to obtain an assurance that the latter will not raise objections of a political nature.

Catholic religious teaching is given in elementary and intermediate schools. Marriages celebrated before a Catholic priest are automatically transferred to the civil register. Marriages celebrated by clergy of other denominations must be made valid before a registrar. In 1972 there were 279 dioceses with 28,154 parishes and 43,714 priests. There were 187,153 members (154,796 women) of about 20,000 religious houses.

In 1962 there were about 100,000 Protestants and about 50,000 Jews.

Education. Education is compulsory from 6 to 14 years of age. An optional pre-school education is given to the children between 3 and 5 years in the preparatory schools (kindergarten schools). Illiteracy of males over 6 years was 2·2% in 1981, of females 3·8%.

Compulsory education can be classified as primary education (5-year course) and junior secondary education (3-year course).

Senior secondary education is subdivided in classical (*ginnasio* and classical *liceo*), scientific (scientific *liceo*), language lyceum, professional institutes and technical education: agricultural, industrial, commercial, technical, nautical institutes, institutes for surveyors, institutes for girls (5-year course) and teacher-training institutes (4-year course).

University education is given in Universities and in University Higher Institutes (4, 5, 6 years, according to degree course).

Statistics for the academic year 1986–87:

Elementary schools	No.	Pupils
Kindergarten	28,507	1,621,471
Public elementary schools	24,828	3,255,161
Private elementary schools		
Private elementary recognized schools (*parificate*)	2,360	275,664

Government secondary schools		Total students
Junior secondary schools	10,031	2,714,038
Classical lyceum	742	212,359
Lyceum for science	992	384,612
Language lyceum	360	50,196
Teachers' schools	199	25,446
Teachers' institutes	679	164,987
Professional institutes	1,680	515,239
Technical institutes, of which:		
Industrial institutes	609	323,038
Commercial institutes	1,208	614,569
Surveyors' institutes	494	149,265
Agricultural institutes	94	30,017
Nautical institutes	48	11,969
Technical institutes for tourism	37	20,196
Managerial institutes	149	50,077
Girls technical schools	72	27,041
Artistic studies	261	79,577

Universities and higher institutes	Date of foundation	Students 1985–86	Teachers 1985–86	Universities and higher institutes	Date of foundation	Students 1985–86	Teachers 1985–86
Ancona	1965	6,768	304	Napoli	1224	113,965	4,346
Arezzo	1971	1,087	75	Padova	1222	44,673	2,373
Bari	1924	56,453	1,833	Palermo	1805	42,153	2,081
Bergamo	1970	3,459	140	Parma	1502	14,865	987
Bologna	1200	60,660	3,110	Pavia	1390	18,355	1,250
Brescia	1970	6,244	200	Perugia	1276	18,975	1,154
Cagliari	1626	18,864	1,114	Pescara	1965	9,212	213
Camerino				Piacenza	1924	643	91
(Macerata)	1727	3,226	233	Pisa	1338	30,235	2,031
Cassino				Potenza	1983	1,341	81
(Frosinone)	1968	2,841	51	Reggio di C.	1968	4,737	103
Catania	1434	33,727	1,422	Roma	1303	166,950	6,992
Catanzaro	1983	5,129	–	Salerno	1944	22,056	481
Chieti	1965	4,339	135	Sassari	1677	8,419	488
Cosenza	1972	6,257	457	Siena	1300	10,135	724
Feltre (Belluno)	1969	551	30	Teramo	1965	5,018	118
Ferrara	1391	5,129	491	Torino	1404	62,528	2,751
Firenze	1924	45,022	2,351	Trento	1965	3,860	253
Genova	1243	31,515	1,904	Trieste	1924	13,807	966
L'Aquila	1956	6,456	609	Udine	1969	3,997	349
Lecce	1959	7,103	321	Urbino	1564	11,723	468
Macerata	1290	4,783	177	Venezia	1868	22,866	758
Messina	1549	29,246	1,798	Verona	1969	8,585	489
Milano	1924	128,701	3,991	Viterbo	1980	1,145	61
Modena	1678	7,939	642				

Health. In 1985 there were 237,579 doctors and 470,579 hospital beds.

Social Security. Social expenditure is made up of transfers which the central public departments, local departments and social security departments, make to families. Payment is principally for pensions, family allowances and health services. Expenditure on subsidies, public assistance to various classes of people and people injured by political events or national disasters are also included.

DIPLOMATIC REPRESENTATIVES

Of Italy in Great Britain (14 Three Kings Yard, London, W1Y 2EH)
Ambassador: Boris Biancheri (accredited 11 Nov. 1987).

Of Great Britain in Italy (Via XX Settembre 80A, 00187, Rome)
Ambassador: Sir Derek Thomas, KCMG.

Of Italy in the USA (1601 Fuller St., NW, Washington, D.C., 20009)
Ambassador: Rinaldo Petrignani.

Of the USA in Italy (Via Veneto 119/A, Rome)
Ambassador: Maxwell M. Rabb.

Of Italy to the United Nations
Ambassador: Maurizio Bucci.

Books of Reference

Statistical Information: The Istituto Centrale di Statistica (16 Via Cesare Balbo 00100 Rome) was set up by law of 9 July 1926 as the central institute in charge of census and all statistical information. *President:* Prof. Guido Mario Rey. *Director-General:* Dr Luigi Pinto. Its publications include:

Annuario statistico italiano. 1987, *Compendio statistico italiano.* 1987, *Bollettino mensile di statistica.* Monthly, from 1950, *Annuario di statistiche industriali.* 1986, *Annuario di statistiche demografiche.* 1984, *Annuario di statistica agraria.* 1984, *Annuario statistico della navigazione marittima.* 1987, *Annuario statistico del commercio interno e del turismo.* 1986, *Statistica annuale del commercio con l'estero.* 1987, *Statistica mensile del commercio con l'estero.* Monthly, *Annuario di statistiche del lavoro.* 1986, *Censimento generale dell'agricoltura.* 1982, *Censimento generale della popolazione, 1981.* Vol. I, II and III, *Censimento generale dell'industria e del commercio.* 1981 *Sommario di Statistiche Storiche, 1926–1985.*

Italy. Documents and Notes. Servizi delle Informazioni, Rome. 1952 ff.
Italian Books and Periodicals. Bimonthly from 1958
Banco di Roma, *Review of the Economic Condition in Italy* (in English). Bimonthly, 1947 ff.
Credito Italiano, *The Italian Economic Situation.* Bimonthly. Milan, from June 1961 (in Italian), from June 1962 (in English)
Compendio Economico Italiano. Rome, Unione Italiana delle Camere di Commercio. Annually from 1954
Carone, G., *Il Turismo nell'economia internazionale.* Milan, 1959
Clark, M., *Modern Italy 1871–1982.* London, 1984
Di Vittorio, G. (ed.), *I sindacati in Italia.* Bari, 1955
Finer, S. E., and Mastropaolo, A. (eds.), *The Italian Party System, 1945–80.* London, 1985
Grindrod, M., *The Rebuilding of Italy, 1945–55.* R. Inst. of Int. Affairs, 1955
Nichols, P., *Italia, Italia.* London, 1974
Spotts, F., and Wieser, T., *Italy: A Difficult Democracy.* CUP, 1986
Woolfe, S. J. (ed.), *The Rebirth of Italy, 1943–50.* New York, 1972

National Library: Biblioteca Nazionale Centrale Vittorio Emanuele II Viale Castro Pretorio, Rome. *Director:* Dr L. M. Crisari.

JAMAICA

Capital: Kingston
Population: 2·3m. (1987)
GNP per capita: US$909 (1986)

HISTORY. Jamaica was discovered by Columbus in 1494, and was occupied by the Spaniards between 1509 and 1655, when the island was captured by the English; their possession was confirmed by the Treaty of Madrid, 1670. Self-government was introduced in 1944 and gradually extended until Jamaica achieved complete independence within the Commonwealth on 6 Aug. 1962.

AREA AND POPULATION. The island of Jamaica lies in the Caribbean Sea about 150 km south of Cuba. The area is 4,411 sq. miles (11,425 sq. km). The population at the census of 8 June 1982 was 2,095,878, distributed on the basis of the 14 parishes of the island as follows: Kingston and St Andrew, 565,487; St Thomas, 76,347; Portland, 70,787; St Mary, 101,442; St Ann, 132,475; Trelawny, 65,038; St James, 127,994; Hanover, 60,420; Westmoreland, 116,163; St Elizabeth, 132,353; Manchester, 136,517; St Catherine, 315,970; Clarendon, 194,885.

Chief towns (census, 1982): Kingston and St Andrew, 524,638, metropolitan area; Spanish Town, 89,097; Montego Bay, 70,265; May Pen, 40,962; Mandeville, 34,502.

Estimated population, in 1987, was 2·3m. The population is 76% of African ethnic origin, 3% European and 21% mixed and other groups.

Vital statistics (1986): Births, 54,067 (23 per 1,000 population); deaths, 13,341 (5·7); migration loss, 20,079.

CLIMATE. A tropical climate but with considerable variation. High temperatures on the coast are usually mitigated by sea breezes, while upland areas enjoy cooler and less humid conditions. Rainfall is plentiful over most of Jamaica, being heaviest in May and from Aug. to Nov. The island lies in the hurricane zone. Kingston. Jan. 76°F (24·4°C), July 81°F (27·2°C). Annual rainfall 32″ (800 mm).

CONSTITUTION AND GOVERNMENT. A new Constitution was enacted with independence in Aug. 1962. The Crown is represented by a Governor-General appointed by the Crown on the advice of the Prime Minister. The Governor-General is assisted by a Privy Council.

The Legislature comprises two chambers, an elected House and a nominated Senate. The executive is chosen from both chambers.

The Executive comprises the Prime Minister, who is the leader of the majority party, and Ministers appointed by the Prime Minister. Together they form the Cabinet, which is the highest executive power. An Attorney-General is a member of the House and is legal adviser to the Cabinet.

The Senate consists of 21 senators appointed by the Governor-General, 13 on the advice of the Prime Minister, 8 on the advice of the Leader of the Opposition. The House of Representatives (60 members, Dec. 1976) is elected by universal adult suffrage for a period not exceeding 5 years. Electors and elected must be Jamaican or Commonwealth citizens resident in Jamaica for at least 12 months before registration. The powers and procedure of Parliament correspond to those of the British Parliament.

The Privy Council consists of 6 members appointed by the Governor-General in consultation with the Prime Minister.

Governor-General: Sir Florizel Glasspole, GCMG, GCVO.

National flag: A yellow diagonal cross dividing triangles of green, top and bottom, and black, hoist and fly.

The elections to the House of Representatives, held on 15 Dec. 1983, returned 60 members of the Jamaica Labour Party. The People's National Party did not contest the election.

The Cabinet in Dec. 1986 was comprised as follows:

Prime Minister and Minister of Finance, Planning and Information: Right Hon. Edward Seaga, PC.

Deputy Prime Minister and Minister of Foreign Affairs and Foreign Trade and Commerce: Hugh Shearer. *Construction with responsibility for Electoral Matters:* Bruce Golding. *Agriculture:* Dr Percival Broderick. *Public Service:* Clifton Stone. *Social Security and Consumer Affairs:* Dr Mavis Gilmour. *Labour and Leader of Government Business in the House of Representatives:* J. A. G. Smith. *Education:* Neville Gallimore. *Health:* Dr Kenneth Baugh. *Local Government:* Neville Lewis. *Youth and Community Development:* Edmund Bartlett. *Mining, Energy and Tourism:* Hugh Hart. *Justice:* Oswald G. Harding. *Public Utilities and Transport:* Pernel Charles.

DEFENCE

Army. The Jamaica Defence Force consists of a Regular and a Reserve Force. The Regular Force is comprised of the 1st battalion, Jamaica Regiment and Support Services which include the Air Wing and Coast Guard. The Reserve Force consists of the 3rd battalion, Jamaica Regiment. Total strength (all services, 1988), 2,520. Reserves, 745.

Air Force. The Air Wing of the Jamaica Defence Force was formed in July 1963 and has since been expanded and trained successively by the British Army Air Corps and Canadian air force personnel. Equipment for army liaison, search and rescue, police co-operation, survey and transport duties includes 2 Defender armed STOL transports; 1 Beech King Air and 1 Cessna 337 light transports; 4 JetRanger and 3 Bell 212 light helicopters. Personnel (1988) 170.

INTERNATIONAL RELATIONS

Membership. Jamaica is a member of UN, the Commonwealth, OAS, CARICOM and is an ACP state of EEC.

ECONOMY

Budget. Revenue and expenditure for fiscal years ending 31 March (in J$1m.):

	1983–84	1984–85	1985–86	1986–87
Revenue	1,751	2,623	3,207	4,467
Expenditure	2,420	2,849	4,529	5,631

The chief heads of recurrent revenue are income tax; consumption, customs and stamp duties. The other major share of current resources is generated by the Bauxite levy. The chief items of recurrent expenditure are public debt, education and health.

Net external debt at 31 Dec. 1986, US$2,106·1m.

Currency. The currency is the *dollar*, divided into 100 cents. Currency circulation at 31 May 1987 was J$806·6m. In March 1988, £1 = J$9·56; US$1 = J$5·50.

Banking. On 1 May 1961 the Bank of Jamaica opened as Jamaica's Central Bank. It has the sole right to issue notes and coins in Jamaica, acts as Banker to the Government and to the commercial banks, and administers the island's external reserves and exchange control.

There are 9 commercial banks with about 171 branches and agencies in operation, with main offices in Kingston. Six of these banks are subsidiaries of major British and North American banks, of which 4 are incorporated locally. The Workers' Savings and Loan Bank is owned by the Government, Trade Unions and the private sector. The National Commercial Bank (Jamaica) Ltd, formerly Barclays Bank Jamaica Ltd, is 49% government-owned. The other 6 banks which operate are: The Bank of Nova Scotia (Jamaica) Ltd, City Bank of North America, Mutual Security Bank (formerly Royal Bank Jamaica Ltd), Bank of Commerce,

Jamaica Citizens Bank Ltd, First National Bank of Chicago (Jamaica) Ltd and Century National Bank Ltd.

Total deposits in commercial banks, 31 Dec. 1986, J$6,203·5m., of which J$1,993·9m. were time deposits and J$2,867·4m. were savings.

ENERGY AND NATURAL RESOURCES

Electricity. The Jamaica Public Service Co. is the public supplier of electricity. The bauxite companies, sugar estates and the Caribbean Cement Co. and Goodyear generate their own electricity. Total installed capacity, 1986, 1,119,000. kw. Production (1986) 1,520m. kwh. Supply 110 and 220 volts; 50 Hz.

Minerals. Bauxite, ceramic clays, marble, silica sand and gypsum are commercially viable. Jamaica has become the world's third largest producer of bauxite and alumina. The bauxite deposits are worked by a Canadian, an American and a Jamaican company. In 1986, 6·9m. tonnes of bauxite ore was mined; gypsum, 117,000 tonnes; marble, 200 tonnes; sand and gravel, 320,000m. cu. metres; industrial lime, 1,960 cu. metres.

Agriculture (1986). Production: Sugar-cane, 2,185,000 tons; sugar (commercial), 203,000 tons; rum, 4,638,000 proof gallons; molasses, 80,200 tons; bananas, 20,700 tons; citrus fruit, 929,000 boxes; cocoa, 2,400,000 tons; spices, 2,429,824 tons; copra, 2,322,000 tons; domestic food crops, 514,646 tons.

Livestock (1986): Cattle, 361,000; goats, 326,000; pigs, 152,000; poultry, 5m.

INDUSTRY AND TRADE

Industry. Three bauxite-mining companies also process bauxite into alumina; production, 1986, 1·5m. tonnes. From processing only a few agricultural products—sugar, rum, condensed milk, oils and fats, cigars and cigarettes—the island is now producing clothing, footwear, textiles, paints, building materials (including cement), agricultural machinery and toilet articles. There is an oil refinery in Kingston. In 1986 manufacturing contributed J$2,949m. to the total GDP at current prices.

Labour. Average total labour force (1986), 1,059,000, of whom 820,600 were employed. Government and services employed 384,400; agriculture, forestry, fishing and mining, 278,450; manufacture 109,950; construction and installation, 32,600.

Commerce. Value of imports and domestic exports for calendar years (in US$1m.):

	1983	1984	1985	1986
Imports	1,284	1,183	1,144	969
Domestic exports	673	731	535	566

Principal imports in 1986 (in US$1m.): Minerals, fuels, lubricants and related materials, 199·1 (20·5%), with imports of 56·9 from USA and 72·4 from Venezuela; food, 166·2 (17·1%), with 101 from USA; machinery and transport equipment, 174·8 (18%); manufactured goods, 166·9 (17·2%).

Principal domestic exports in 1986 (in US$1m.): Crude materials, 300·9 (50·5%), of which alumina, 205·4 (34·5%) and bauxite, 90·1 (15·1%), with crude materials exports of 90·2 to USA, 84·2 to Canada and 29·4 to UK; food, 135 (22·7%), of which sugar, 62·3 (10·5%), with food exports of 84·4 to UK and 25·3 to USA; miscellaneous manufactures, 65·6 (11%).

Total trade between Jamaica and UK (British Department of Trade returns, in £1,000 sterling):

	1983	1984	1985	1986	1987
Imports to UK	95,036	77,895	89,684	87,416	85,655
Exports and re-exports from UK	116,188	48,088	44,290	43,378	54,644

Tourism. In 1986, 954,621 tourists arrived in Jamaica, spending about US$512m.

COMMUNICATIONS

Roads (1984). The island has 7,826 miles of main roads, and over 2,874 miles of parochial and subsidiary roads. Main roads are constructed and maintained by the Ministry of Construction (Works), while other roads are constructed and maintained by parish councils. In 1986 there were 74,982 licensed vehicles.

Railways. There are 294 km of railway open of 1,435 mm gauge, operated by the Jamaica Railway Corporation, which also operates 31 km (Alcoa Mineral Railway) on behalf of one of the bauxite companies. In 1984 the railway carried 3m. tonnes and 958,893 passengers.

Aviation. Scheduled commercial international airlines operate through the Norman Manley and Sangster international airports at Palisadoes and Montego Bay. In 1986 Norman Manley airport had 27,764 aircraft movements, handled 827,944 passengers and 18,522 tonnes of freight. Sangster had 27,912 movements, with 1,675,603 passengers and 4,314 tonnes of freight. Trans-Jamaica Airlines Ltd operates internal flights; in 1984 it carried 37,800 passengers. Air Jamaica, originally set up in conjunction with BOAC and BWIA in 1966, became a new company, Air Jamaica (1968) Ltd, and is affiliated to Air Canada. In 1969 it began operations as Jamaica's national airline. In 1984 Air Jamaica carried 985,000 passengers and operated at a net loss of J$10·9m.

Shipping. In 1986 there were 2,096 visits to all ports; 9·24m. tons of cargo were handled. Kingston had 1,298 visits and handled 2·46m. tons. The outports had 798 visits and handled 6·78m. tons, of which 7·2m. was loaded and 1·6m. landed.

Post and Broadcasting. In 1986 there were 318 post offices and 504 postal agencies and sub-agencies.

In Dec. 1986 there were 152,295 telephones.

There was (1986) 1 commercial and 1 publicly owned broadcasting stations; the latter also operates a television service.

Cinemas. In 1986 there were 34 cinemas and 3 drive-in cinemas.

JUSTICE, RELIGION, EDUCATION AND WELFARE

Justice. The Judicature comprises a Supreme Court, a court of appeal, a revenue court, resident magistrates' courts, petty sessional courts, coroners' courts, a traffic court and a family court which was instituted in 1975. The Chief Justice is head of the judiciary. All prosecutions are initiated by the Director of Public Prosecutions.

Police. The Constabulary Force in 1986 stood at approximately 5,601 officers, sub-officers and constables (men and women).

Religion. Freedom of worship is guaranteed under the Constitution. The main Christian denominations are Anglican, Baptist, Roman Catholic, Methodist, Church of God, United Church of Jamaica, and Grand Cayman (Presbyterian–Congregational) Moravian, Seventh-Day Adventists, Pentecostal, Salvation Army, Quaker, and Disciples of Christ. Pocomania is a mixture of Christianity and African survivals. Non-Christians include Hindus, Jews, Moslems and Bahai followers. There is also a growing number of Rastafarians who believe in the deity of the late Emperor Hailé Selassié of Ethiopia.

Education. In Sept. 1973 education became free for all government grant-aided schools (the majority of all schools) and for all Jamaicans entering the University of the West Indies, the College of Arts, Science and Technology and the Jamaica School of Agriculture. In 1985–86 there were 1,581 pre-primary schools and departments (125,046 pupils); 290 primary schools (171,452 pupils); 498 all-age schools (229,538 pupils).

There were 141 secondary and vocational schools (165,308). Teacher-training colleges had 2,724 students; community colleges had 6,721; the College of Arts, Science and Technology had 3,475; the College of Agriculture, 199 and the University of the West Indies, 4,792.

Health. In 1986 the public health service had 4,049 staff in medicine, nursing and pharmacology; 328 in dentistry; 344 public health inspectors; 67 in nutrition. In 1984 there were 382 primary health centres, 5,639 public hospital beds and 250 private beds.

DIPLOMATIC REPRESENTATIVES

Of Jamaica in Great Britain (63 St James's St., London, SW1A 1LS)
High Commissioner: H. S. Walker.

Of Great Britain in Jamaica (Trafalgar Rd., Kingston 10)
High Commissioner: Alan J. Payne, CMG.

Of Jamaica in the USA (1850 K. St., NW, Washington, D.C., 20006)
Ambassador: Keith Johnson.

Of the USA in Jamaica (2 Oxford Rd., Kingston 5)
Ambassador: Michael G. Sotirhos.

Of Jamaica to the United Nations
Ambassador: Lloyd M. H. Barnett.

Books of Reference

Statistical Information: The Department of Statistics, now Statistical Institute of Jamaica (2c Constant Spring Rd., Kingston 10), was set up in 1945—the nucleus being the Census Office, which undertook the operations of the 1943 Census of Jamaica and its Dependencies. *Director:* Mrs C. P. McFarlane. Publications of the Bureau include the *Bulletin of Statistics on External Trade* and the *Annual Abstract of Statistics.*

Economic and Social Survey, Jamaica. Planning Institute of Jamaica, Kingston (Annual)
Social and Economic Studies. Institute of Social and Economic Research, Univ. of the West Indies. Quarterly
A Review of the Performance of the Jamaican Economy 1981–1983. Jamaica Information Service, 1985
Quarterly Economic Report. Planning Institute of Jamaica, Kingston
Beckford, G. and Witter, M., *Small Garden ... Bitter Weed. The Political Struggle and Change in Jamaica.* 2nd ed. London, 1982
Cassidy, F. G., and Le Page, R. B., *Dictionary of Jamaican English.* CUP, 1966
Floyd, B., *Jamaica: An Island Microcosm.* London, 1979
Ingram, K. E., *Jamaica.* [Bibliography] Oxford and Santa Barbara, 1984
Kuper, A., *Changing Jamaica.* London and Boston, 1976
Lacey, T., *Violence and Politics in Jamaica, 1960–70.* Manchester Univ. Press, 1977
Manley, M., *A Voice at the Work Place.* London, 1975.—*Jamaica: Struggle in the Periphery.* London, 1983
Post, K., *Strike the Iron, A Colony at War: Jamaica 1939–1945.* 2 vols. Atlantic Highlands, N.J., 1981
Sherlock, P., *Keeping Company with Jamaica.* London, 1984
Stephens, E. H., and Stephens, J. D., *Democratic Socialism in Jamaica.* London, 1986
Stone, C., *Class, Race and Political Behaviour in Urban Jamaica.* Kingston, 1973.
—*Democracy and Clientalism in Jamaica.* London and New Brunswick, N.J., 1981
Bibliography of Jamaica, 1900–1963. Jamaica Library Service, 1963

Libraries: National Library of Jamaica, Kingston. Jamaica Library Service, Kingston.

JAPAN

Nippon (*or* Nihon)

Capital: Tōkyō
Population: 121·67m. (1986)
GNP per capita: US$13,447 (1985)

HISTORY. The house of Yamato, from about 500 B.C. the rulers of one of several kingdoms, in about A.D. 200 united the nation; the present imperial family are their direct descendants. From 1186 until 1867 successive families of Shoguns exercised the temporal power. In 1867 the Emperor Meiji recovered the imperial power after the abdication on 14 Oct. 1867 of the fifteenth and last Tokugawa Shogun Keiki (in different pronunciation: Yoshinobu). In 1871 the feudal system (Hōken Seido) was abolished; this was the beginning of the rapid westernization.

At San Francisco on 8 Sept. 1951 a Treaty of Peace was signed by Japan and representatives of 48 countries. For details *see* THE STATESMAN'S YEAR-BOOK, 1953, p. 1169. On 26 Oct. 1951 the Japanese Diet ratified the Treaty by 307 votes to 47 votes with 112 abstentions. On the same day the Diet ratified a Security Treaty with the US by 289 votes to 71 votes with 106 abstentions. The treaty provided for the stationing of American troops in Japan until she was able to undertake her own defence. The peace treaty came into force on 28 April 1952, when Japan regained her sovereignty. In 1960 Japan signed the Japan–US Mutual Security Treaty, valid for 10 years, which was renewed in 1970. Of the islands under US administration since 1945, the Bonin (Ogasawara), Volcano, and Daito groups and Marcus Island were returned to Japan in 1968, and the southern Ryukyu Islands (Okinawa) in 1972.

AREA AND POPULATION. Japan consists of 4 major islands, Honshu, Hokkaido, Kyushu and Shikoku, and many small islands, with an area of 377,815 sq. km. Census population (1 Oct. 1985) 121,047,196 (males 59,495,663, females 61,551,553). Estimate (1986) 121,672,000 (males 59,805,000, females 61,867,000). Foreigners registered 31 Dec. 1986 were 867,237, of whom 677,959 were Koreans, 84,397 Chinese, 30,695 Americans, 18,897 Filipinos, 7,426 British, 4,388 Vietnamese, 3,193 West Germans, 2,981 Thais, 2,685 Canadians, 2,601 Indians, 2,494 French, 1,493 stateless persons.

Japanese overseas, Oct. 1985, 480,739; of these 146,104 lived in USA, 120,276 in Brazil, 19,889 in UK, 16,995 in Canada, 16,073 in the Federal Republic of Germany, 15,660 in Argentina, 12,156 in France, 8,974 in Hong Kong, 8,415 in China, 8,077 in Singapore.

The areas, populations and capitals of the principal islands (and regions) are:

Island/Region	Sq. km	Census 1985	Chief cities
Hokkaido	83,519	5,679,500	Sapporo
Honshu/Tohoku	66,971	9,730,000	Sendai
/Kanto	32,377	36,786,200	Tokyo
/Chubu	66,774	20,595,000	Nagoya
/Kinki	33,070	21,828,000	Osaka
/Chugoku	31,881	7,748,500	Hiroshima
Shikoku	18,806	4,227,400	Matsuyama
Kyushu	42,150	13,276,000	Fukuoka
Ryukyu	2,254	1,179,000	Naha

The leading cities, with population, 31 March 1985 (in 1,000), are:

Akashi	263	Fukuyama	360	Ibaraki	250
Akita	296	Funabashi	507	Ichinomiya	257
Amagasaki	509	Gifu	412	Ichikawa	398
Aomori	294	Hachiōji	427	Iwaki	351
Asahikawa	364	Hakodate	319	Kagoshima	530
Chiba	789	Hamamatsu	514	Kanazawa	430
Fujisawa	328	Higashiosaka	523	Kashiwa	273
Fukui	250	Himeji	453	Kasugai	257
Fukuoka	1,160	Hirakata	382	Kawagoe	285
Fukushima	271	Hiroshima	1,044	Kawaguchi	403

Kawasaki	1,089	Naha	304	Suita	349
Kitakyushu	1,056	Nara	328	Takamatsu	327
Kobe	1,411	Neyagawa	258	Takatsuki	349
Kōchi	312	Niigata	476	Tokorozawa	275
Kōriyama	302	Nishinomiya	421	Tokushima	258
Koshigaya	254	Oita	390	Tōkyō	8,354
Kumamoto	556	Okayama	572	Toyama	314
Kurashiki	414	Okazaki	285	Toyohashi	322
Kyoto	1,479	Omiya	373	Toyonaka	413
Machida	321	Osaka	2,636	Toyota	308
Maebashi	277	Sagamihara	483	Urawa	377
Matsudo	427	Sakai	818	Utsunomiya	405
Matsuyama	427	Sapporo	1,543	Wakayama	401
Miyazaki	279	Sasebo	251	Yao	276
Nagano	337	Sendai	700	Yokkaichi	263
Nagasaki	449	Shimonoseki	269	Yokohama	2,993
Nagoya	2,116	Shizuoka	468	Yokosuka	427

Vital statistics (in 1,000) for calendar years:

	1979	1980	1981	1982	1983	1984	1985
Births	1,643	1,577	1,529	1,515	1,509	1,490	1,432
Deaths	690	723	720	712	740	740	752

Crude birth rate of Japanese nationals in present area, 1985, was 11·9 per 1,000 population (1947: 34·3); crude death rate, 6·3; crude marriage rate, 6·1; infant mortality rate per 1,000 live births, 5·5.

CLIMATE. The islands of Japan lie in the temperate zone, north-east of the main monsoon region of S.E. Asia. The climate is temperate with warm, humid summers and relatively mild winters except in the island of Hokkaido and northern parts of Honshu facing the Japan Sea. There is a month's rainy season in June-July, but the best seasons are spring and autumn, though Sept. may bring typhoons. There is a summer rainfall maximum. Tōkyō. Jan. 40·5°F (4·7°C), July 77·4°F (25·2°C). Annual rainfall 63″ (1,460 mm). Hiroshima. Jan. 39·7°F (4·3°C), July 78°F (25·6°C). Annual rainfall 61″ (1,603 mm). Nagasaki. Jan. 43·5°F (6·4°C), July 79·7°F (26·5°C). Annual rainfall 77″ (2,002 mm). Osaka. Jan. 42·1°F (5·6°C), July 80·6°F (27°C). Annual rainfall 53″ (1,400 mm). Sapporo. Jan. 23·2°F (−4·9°C), July 68·4°F (20·2°C). Annual rainfall 47″ (1,158 mm).

EMPEROR. The Emperor bears the title of Nihon-koku Tennō ('Emperor of Japan'). **Hirohito,** born in Tōkyō, 29 April 1901; succeeded his father, Yoshihito, 25 Dec. 1926; married 26 Jan. 1924, to Princess Nagako, born 6 March 1903. Living sons: (1) Prince Akihito (Tsugunomiya), born 23 Dec. 1933; formally installed as Crown Prince on 10 Nov. 1952; married to Michiko Shoda (born 20 Oct. 1934), 10 April 1959. *Offspring:* Prince Naruhito (Hironomiya), born 23 Feb. 1960; Prince Fumihito (Ayanomiya), born 30 Nov. 1965; Princess Sayako (Norinomiya), born 18 April 1969. (2) Prince Masahito (Hitachinomiya), born 28 Nov. 1935; married to Hanako Tsugaru, 30 Sept. 1964.

By the Imperial House Law of 11 Feb. 1889, revised on 16 Jan. 1947, the succession to the throne was fixed upon the male descendants.

CONSTITUTION AND GOVERNMENT. Japan's Government is based upon the Constitution of 1947 which superseded the Meiji Constitution of 1889. In it the Japanese people pledge themselves to uphold the ideas of democracy and peace. The Emperor is the symbol of the States and of the unity of the people. Sovereign power rests with the people. The Emperor has no powers related to government. Japan renounces war as a sovereign right and the threat or the use of force as a means of settling disputes with other nations. Fundamental human rights are guaranteed.

National flag: White, with a red disc.

National anthem: Kimi ga yo wa (words 9th century, tune by Hiromori Hayashi, 1881).

Legislative power rests with the Diet, which consists of the House of Representatives (of 512 members), elected by men and women over 20 years of age for a 4-year term, and the House of Councillors of 252 members (100 elected by party list system with proportional representation according to the d'Hondt method and 152 from prefectural districts), one-half of its members being elected every 3 years. The Lower House controls the budget and approves treaties with foreign powers.

The former House of Peers is replaced by the House of Councillors, whose members, like those of the House of Representatives, are elected as representatives of all the people. The House of Representatives has pre-eminence over the House of Councillors.

On 5 Nov. 1987 the House of Representatives consisted of 302 Liberal-Democrats, 87 Socialists, 57 Komeito, 29 Democratic Socialists, 27 Japan Communist Party, and 5 Independents.

The Cabinet, as constituted in Nov. 1987, was as follows:

Prime Minister: Noboru Takeshita.
Justice: Yukio Hayashida.
Foreign Affairs: Sosuke Uno.
Finance: Kiichi Miyazawa.
Education: Gentaro Nakajima.
Health and Welfare: Takao Fujimoto.
Agriculture, Forestry and Fishery: Takashi Sato.
Trade and Industry: Hajime Tamura.
Transport: Shintaro Ishihara.
Postal Service: Masaaki Nakayama.
Labour: Taro Nakamura.
Construction: Ihei Ochi.
Home Affairs: Seiroku Kajiyama.

Local Government. The country is divided into 47 prefectures (*Todōfuken*), including Tōkyō-to (the capital), Ōsaka-fu and Kyōto-fu, Hokkai-dō, and 43 *Ken.* Each *Todōfuken* has its governor (*Chiji*) elected by the voters in the area. The prefectural government of Tōkyō-to is also responsible for the urban part (formerly Tōkyō-shi) of the prefecture. Each prefecture, city, town and village has a representative assembly elected by the same franchise as in parliamentary elections.

New legislation, which came into effect on 1 July 1954, has given the central government complete control of the police throughout the country.

DEFENCE

Army. The 'Ground Self-Defence Force' had in 1988 an authorized strength of 156,000 uniformed personnel, plus a reserve of 44,000 men. The Army is organized in 12 infantry divisions, 1 armoured division, 1 airborne brigade, 2 air defence brigades, 1 artillery, 5 engineer, 1 signal, 2 composite and 1 helicopter brigades in addition to 4 anti-aircraft artillery groups. Equipment includes 1,150 tanks, over 400 transport, observation and training helicopters including anti-tank helicopters, plus about 19 fixed-wing aircraft.

The Northern Army, stationed in Hokkaido, consists of 4 divisions (1 of which is armoured), an artillery brigade, an anti-aircraft artillery brigade, a tank group and an engineering brigade. The Western Army, stationed in Kyushu, consists of 2 divisions and 1 composite brigade. The North-Eastern Army (2 divisions), the Eastern Army (2 divisions) and 1 airborne brigade, the Middle Army (3 divisions and 1 composite brigade). The infantry division establishment is approximately 9,000 with 4 infantry regiments or 7,000 (lower establishment) with 3 infantry regiments. Each infantry division has an artillery unit, an anti-tank unit, a tank battalion and an engineering battalion in addition to administrative units.

Navy. The 'Maritime Self-Defence Force' comprises 52 destroyers including 2 training and 8 converted, 18 frigates, 14 submarines, 39 mine warfare vessels, 15 patrol vessels, 8 landing ships, 40 landing craft, 4 survey vessels, 25 oilers, 33 auxiliary ships, 2 submarine rescue vessels, 1 ice breaker, 3 training vessels, and 39 support ships.

The Fleet Air Arm, numbering 6 air wings, includes 86 patrol aircraft and flying boats for anti-submarine patrol, 80 trainers and 71 helicopters plus transports, rescue planes and others.

Personnel in 1987 numbered 45,600 officers and ratings including the Naval Air Arm. There are also 4,150 in civil maritime defence.

Air Force. An 'Air Self-Defence Force' was inaugurated on 1 July 1954. In 1987 its equipment included 5 interceptor squadrons of F-15J/DJ Eagles (total of 142 aircraft to be acquired by 1990) and 5 of F-4EJ Phantoms; 3 squadrons of Mitsubishi F-1 close-support fighters; 1 squadron of RF-4E reconnaissance fighters; 8 E-2C Hawkeye AWACS aircraft; ECM flight with 2 YS-11Es; 3 squadrons of turbofan Kawasaki C-1 and turboprop C-130H Hercules and NAMC YS-11 transports. About 35 helicopters, mostly KV-107s (to be replaced with CH-47 Chinooks), and MU-2 twin-turboprop aircraft perform search, rescue and general duties. Training units use piston-engined Fuji T-3 basic trainers, Fuji T-1 jet intermediate trainers, T-33 jet trainers and supersonic Mitsubishi T-2 jet advanced trainers. The T-1s and T-33s will be replaced with Kawasaki T-4s in the late '80s. Six surface-to-air missile groups (19 squadrons) are in service. Total strength (1987) about 311 combat aircraft and 45,000 officers and men.

INTERNATIONAL RELATIONS

Membership. Japan is a member of UN, the Colombo Plan and OECD.

ECONOMY

Planning. The 1980s Plan envisages an onward real growth rate of 4% and a nominal between 5% and 6%. The real growth rate for 1988 is envisaged at 3·8% and the nominal 4·8%.

Budget. Ordinary revenue and expenditure for fiscal year ending 31 March 1988 balanced at 54,101,000m. yen.

Of the proposed revenue in 1987, 41,194,000m. was to come from taxes and stamps, 10,501,000m. from public bonds. Main items of expenditure: Social security, 10,089,600m.; public works, 6,082,400m.; local government, 10,184,100m.; education, 4,849,700m.; defence, 3,517,400m.

The outstanding national debt incurred by public bonds was estimated in March 1986 to be 136,611,000m. yen, including 800m. yen of Japan's foreign currency bonds.

The estimated 1987 budgets of the prefectures and other local authorities forecast a total revenue of 54,380,000m. yen, to be made up partly by local taxes and partly by government grants and local loans.

Currency. Coins of 1, 5, 10, 50, 100 and 500 *yen* are in circulation as well as notes of the Bank of Japan, of 1,000, 5,000 and 10,000 *yen*. Bank-notes for 500 *yen* are still in circulation but are gradually being replaced by coins. In March 1988, £1 = 228 *yen*; US$1 = 128·50 *yen*.

In Dec. 1986 the currency in circulation consisted of 26,884,900m. yen Bank of Japan notes and 2,664,200m. yen subsidiary coins.

Banking. The modern banking system dates from 1872. The Nippon Ginko (Bank of Japan) was founded in 1882. The Bank of Japan has undertaken to finance the Government and the banks; its function is similar to that of a Central Bank in other countries. The Bank undertakes the actual management of Treasury funds and foreign exchange control.

Gold bullion and cash holdings of the Bank of Japan at 31 Dec. 1986 stood at 361,000m. yen.

There were on 31 Dec. 1986, 13 city banks, 64 regional banks, 7 trust banks, 3 long-term credit banks, 68 Sogo banks (mutual savings and loan banks), 455 Shinkin banks (credit associations), 446 credit co-operatives, and 79 foreign banks. There are also various governmental financial institutions, including postal savings which amounted to 112,768,400m. yen in June 1987. Total savings by individuals, including insurance and securities, stood at 540,019,800m. yen on 30 June 1987, and more than 60% of these savings were deposited in banks and the post-office.

Many foreign banks operate branches in Japan including: Bank of Indo-China, Hongkong & Shanghai Banking Corporation, Chartered Bank of India, Australia and China, Bank of India, Mercantile Bank of India, Bank of Korea, Bank of China, Algemene Bank Nederland NV, National Handelsbank NV, Bank of America, National City Bank of New York, Chase Manhattan Bank, Bangkok Bank and American Express Co.

Weights and Measures. The metric system was made obligatory by a law passed in March 1921, and the period of grace for its compulsory use ended on 1 April 1966.

ENERGY AND NATURAL RESOURCES

Electricity. In 1985 generating facilities were capable of an output of 169,399,000 kw.; electricity produced was 671,952m. kwh. Supply 100 and 200 volts; 50 or 60 Hz.

Oil and Gas. Output of crude petroleum, 1985, was 625,000 kl, almost entirely from oilfields on the island of Honshu, but 198,330,000 kl crude oil had to be imported. Output of natural gas, 1985, 2,225m. cu. metres.

Minerals. Ore production in tonnes, 1985, of chromite, 11,920; coal, 16,383,000; iron, 338,343; zinc, 253,021; molybdenum (1982), 97; manganese, 21,140; copper, 43,208; lead, 49,951; tungsten, 1,922; silver, 339,485 kg.; gold, 5,309 kg.

Agriculture. Agricultural workers in 1986 were 6,274,000, including 567,000 subsidiary and seasonal workers; 8·4% (1985) of the labour force as opposed to 24·7% in 1962. The arable land area in 1986 was 5,358,000 hectares (5,796,000 in 1970). Division of ordinary fields to non-agricultural use accounted largely for this decrease. Rice cultivation accounted for 2,303,000 hectares in 1986. The area planted with industrial crops such as rapeseed, tobacco, tea, rush, etc., was 256,900 hectares in 1985.

In 1986 there were 4,388,000 power cultivators and tractors in use together with 2,151,000 (1985) power sprayers and power dusters and 2,098,000 rice power planters.

Output of rice was 10·26m. tonnes in 1981, 10·27m. in 1982, 10,366,000 in 1983, 11,878,000 in 1984 and 11,662,000 in 1985.

Production in 1986 (in 1,000 tonnes) of barley was 344; wheat, 876; soybeans, 228. Sweet potatoes, which in the past mitigated the effects of rice famines, have, in view of rice over-production, decreased from 4,955,000 tons in 1965 to 1,507,000 tons in 1986. Domestic sugar-beet and sugar-cane production accounted for only 31·5% of requirement in 1985. In 1985, 1,924,000 tonnes were imported, 28·3% of this being imported from Australia, 23·5% from Cuba, 19·8% from South Africa, 15·9% from Thailand, 6% from Philippines.

Fruit production, 1985 (in 1,000 tonnes): Mandarins, 2,491; apples, 910; pears, 471; grapes, 311; peaches, 205; and persimmons, 290.

Livestock (1986): 4,742,000 cattle (including about 2·1m. milch cows), 23,000 horses, 11,061,000 pigs, 26,000 sheep, 48,000 goats, 337m. chickens. Milk (1985), 7·38m. tonnes.

Forestry. Forests and grasslands cover about 25m. hectares (nearly 70% of the whole land area), with an estimated timber stand of 2,716m. cu. metres in 1984. In 1984, 41,248,000 cu. metres were felled.

Fisheries. Before the War, Japanese catch represented one-half to two-thirds of the world's total fishing, in 1984 it was 14·5%. The catch in 1985 was 12·17m. tonnes, excluding whaling.

INDUSTRY AND TRADE

Industry. Japan's industrial equipment, 1984, numbered 739,581 plants of all sizes, employing 11,382,000 production workers.

Since 1920 there has been a shift from light to heavy industries. The production of electrical appliances and electronic machinery has made great strides: television sets (1986: 13,885,000), radio sets (1985: 12,996,000), cameras (1986: 17,598,000), computing machines and automation equipment are produced in increasing quantities. The chemical industry ranks third in production value after machinery and metals (1984). Production, 1985, included (in tonnes): Sulphuric acid, 6,580,000; caustic soda, 2,982,000; ammonium sulphate, 1,837,000; calcium superphosphate, 529,000.

Output (1985), in 1,000 tonnes, of pig iron was 80,569; crude steel, 105,279; ordinary rolled steel, 82,731.

In 1985 paper production was 11,790,000 tonnes; paperboard, 8,679,000 tonnes.

Japan's textile industry before the War had 13m. cotton-yarn spindles. After the War she resumed with 2·78m. spindles; in 1964, 8·42m. spindles were operating. Output of cotton yarn, 1985, 437,000 tonnes, and of cotton cloth, 2,061m. sq. metres.

In wool, Japan aims at wool exports sufficient to pay for the imports of raw wool. Output, 1985, 123,400 tonnes of woollen yarns and 326m. sq. metres of woollen fabrics.

Output, 1985, of rayon woven fabrics, 656m. sq. metres; synthetic woven fabrics, 3,068m. sq. metres; silk fabrics, 115m. sq. metres.

Shipbuilding has been decreasing and in 1985, 8,897,000 gross tons were launched, of which 1,528,000 GRT were tankers.

Labour. Total labour force, 1986, was 58·53m., of which 4·5m. were in agriculture and forestry, 450,000 in fishing, 80,000 in mining, 5·34m. in construction, 14·44m. in manufacturing, 15·64m. in commerce and finance, 3·85m. in transport and other public utilities, 12·05m. in services (including the professions) and 1·97m. in government work.

In 1986 there were 12,343,000 workers organized in 74,183 unions. The largest federation is the 'General Council of Japanese Trade Unions' (Sōhyō) with 4,268,000 members. The 'Japanese Confederation of Labour' (Dōmei Kaigi) had 2,126,000 members. The 'Federation of Independent Unions' (Chūritsu Rōren) founded in 1956 had 1,601,000 members.

In 1986, 1·67m. (2·8%) were unemployed. In 1986, 253,000 working days were lost in industrial stoppages.

Commerce. Trade (in US$1m.)

	1980	1981	1982	1983	1984	1985	1986
Imports	140,528	152,030	138,831	126,393	136,503	129,539	126,408
Exports	129,807	143,289	131,931	146,927	170,114	175,638	209,151

Distribution of trade by countries (customs clearance basis) (US$1m.):

	Exports		Imports	
	1985	1986	1985	1986
Africa	3,539	3,533	2,896	3,585
Australia	5,379	5,227	7,452	6,980
Canada	4,520	5,526	4,773	4,895
China	12,477	9,856	6,483	5,652
Fed. Rep. of Germany	6,938	10,477	2,928	4,298
Hong Kong	6,509	7,161	767	1,073
Latin America	8,486	9,494	6,242	6,194
South-east Asia	33,248	41,778	30,264	29,489
Korea, Republic of	7,097	10,475	4,092	5,292
Taiwan	5,025	7,852	3,386	4,691
USSR	2,751	3,150	1,429	1,972
UK	4,723	6,647	1,817	3,573
USA	65,278	80,456	25,793	29,054

Principal items in 1986, with value in 1m. yen were:

Imports, c.i.f.		Exports, f.o.b.	
Mineral fuels	6,437,000	Machinery and transport equipment	26,146,000
Foodstuffs	3,233,000	Metals and metal products	3,073,000
Metal ores and scrap	985,000	Textile products	1,161,000
Machinery and transport equipment	2,477,000	Chemicals	1,603,000

Total trade between Japan and UK (British Department of Trade returns, in £1,000 sterling):

	1983	1984	1985	1986	1987
Imports to UK	3,355,450	3,768,019	4,117,024	4,932,497	5,463,116
Exports and re-exports from UK	797,848	925,311	1,012,436	1,193,933	1,495,111

Tourism. In 1986, 2,021,450 foreigners visited Japan, 482,670 of whom came from USA, 142,697 from UK. Japanese travelling abroad totalled 5,516,193 in 1986.

COMMUNICATIONS

Roads. The total length of roads (including urban and other local roads) was 1,127,504 km at 1 April 1985; the 'national' roads extended 46,435 km, of which 44,880 km were paved. Motor vehicles, at 31 Dec. 1986, numbered 46,995,000, including 28,654,000 passenger cars and 18,109,000 commercial vehicles.

Railways. The first railway was completed in 1872, between Tōkyō and Yokohama (29 km). From 1 April 1987 the National Railways organization was disbanded and replaced by six regional operating authorities, plus separate companies for the Shinkansen (high-speed) and freight networks prior to privatization. Total length of railways, in March 1985, was 26,899 km, of which the national railways had 21,091 km (9,038 km electrified) and private railways, 5,808 km (4,986 km electrified). In 1985 the national railways carried 6,941m. passengers (private, 12,048m.) and 69m. tons of freight (private, 31m.).

Aviation. The principal airlines are Japan Airlines and All Nippon Airways. Japan Airlines, founded in 1953, operate international services from Tōkyō to the USA, Europe, the Middle East and Southeast Asia, including flights to London over the North Pole and to Moscow by way of Siberia. In 1985 Japanese companies carried 44,717,000 passengers in domestic services and 6,234,000 passengers in international services.

Shipping. On 30 June 1986 the merchant fleet consisted of 8,024 vessels of 100 gross tons and over; total tonnage 36m. gross tons; there were 708 ships for passenger transport (1,176,000 gross tons), 2,459 cargo ships (1,799,000 gross tons) and 1,333 oil tankers (11,611,000 gross tons).

Coastguard. The 'Maritime Safety Agency' (Coastguard) consists of 11 regional MS headquarters, 65 MS offices, 52 MS stations, 14 air stations, 1 special rescue station, 8 district communications centres, 2 traffic advisory service centres, 4 hydrographic observatories and 124 navigation aids offices (with 4,992 navigation aids facilities) and controls 44 large patrol vessels, 47 medium patrol vessels, 19 small patrol vessels, 231 patrol craft, 22 hydrographic service vessels, 5 firefighting vessels, 10 firefighting boats, 67 guard and rescue boats and 79 navigation aids service supply vessels. Personnel in 1986 numbered 12,047 officers and men.

The Coastguard aviation service includes 22 fixed-wing aircraft and 38 helicopters.

Post and Broadcasting. The telephone services, operated by a public corporation, at 31 March 1985 had 66,636,000 instruments.

On 31 March 1986, 98·9% of all households owned colour television sets.

Cinemas (1986). Cinemas numbered 2,109 with an annual attendance of 161m. (1960: 1,014m.).

Newspapers (1985). Daily newspapers numbered 125 with aggregate circulation of 68,296,000, including 4 major English-language newspapers.

JUSTICE, RELIGION, EDUCATION AND WELFARE

Justice. The Supreme Court is composed of the Chief Justice and 14 other judges. The Chief Justice is appointed by the Emperor, the other judges by the Cabinet. Every 10 years a justice must submit himself to the electorate. All justices and judges of the lower courts serve until they are 70 years of age.

Below the Supreme Court are 8 regional higher courts, district courts (*Chihōsai-bansho*) in each prefecture (4 in Hokkaidō) and the local courts.

The Supreme Court is authorized to declare unconstitutional any act of the Legislature or the Executive which violates the Constitution.

Religion. There has normally been religious freedom, but Shintō (literally, The Way of the Gods) was given the status of *quasi*-state-religion in the 1930s; in 1945 the Allied Supreme Command ordered the Government to discontinue state support of Shintō. State subsidies have ceased for all religions, and all religious teachings are forbidden in public schools.

In Dec. 1985 Shintoism claimed 115,602,000 adherents, Buddhism 92,065,000; these figures obviously overlap. Christians numbered 1,688,000.

Education. Education is compulsory and free between the ages of 6 and 15. Almost all national and municipal institutions are co-educational. On 1 May 1986 there were 15,092 kindergartens with 97,758 teachers and 2,018,523 pupils; 24,036 elementary schools with 454,760 teachers and 10,665,404 pupils; 11,028 junior high schools with 289,885 teachers and 6,105,749 pupils; 5,295 senior high schools with 270,630 teachers and 5,259,307 pupils; 548 junior colleges with 18,205 teachers and 396,455 pupils.

There were also 822 special schools for handicapped children (40,074 teachers, 95,857 pupils).

Japan has 7 main state universities, formerly known as the Imperial Universities: Tōkyō University (1877); Kyōto University (1897); Tohoku University, Sendai (1907); Kyushu University, Fukuoka (1910); Hokkaido University, Sapporo (1918); Osaka University (1931), and Nagoya University (1939). In addition, there are various other state and municipal as well as private universities of high standing, such as Keio (founded in 1859), Waseda, Rikkyo, Meiji universities, and several women's universities, among which Tōkyō and Ochanomizu are most notable. There are 465 colleges and universities with (1 May 1986) 1,879,532 students and 113,877 teachers.

Social Welfare. Hospitals at the end of 1985 numbered 9,608 with 1,495,328 beds. Physicians at the end of 1984 numbered 181,101; dentists, 63,145.

There are in force various types of social security schemes, such as health insurance, unemployment insurance and old-age pensions. The total population come under one or more of these schemes.

In 1985 17,173,407 persons and 9,366,083 households received some form of regular public assistance, the total of which came to 1,537,642m. yen.

DIPLOMATIC REPRESENTATIVES

Of Japan in Great Britain (43-46 Grosvenor St., London, W1X 0BA)
Ambassador: Kazuo Chiba.

Of Great Britain in Japan (1 Ichiban-cho, Chiyoda-ku, Tōkyō 102)
Ambassador: Sir John Whitehead, KCMG, CVO.

Of Japan in the USA (2520 Massachusetts Ave., NW, Washington, D.C., 20008)
Ambassador: Nobuo Matsunaga.

Of the USA in Japan (10–1, Akasaka 1-chome, Minato-Ku, Tōkyō)
Ambassador: Michael J. Mansfield.

Of Japan to the United Nations
Ambassador: Kiyoaki Kikuchi.

Books of Reference

Statistics Bureau of the Prime Minister's Office: *Statistical Year-Book* (from 1949).— *Statistical Abstract* (from 1950).—*Statistical Handbook of Japan 1977.—Monthly Bulletin* (from April 1950)

Economic Planning Agency: *Economic Survey* (annual), *Economic Statistics* (monthly), *Economic Indicators* (monthly)

Ministry of International Trade: *Foreign Trade of Japan* (annual)

Kodansha Encyclopedia of Japan. 9 vols. Tōkyō, 1983

Japan Times Year Book. (I. Year Book of Japan. II. Who's Who in Japan. III. Business Directory of Japan.) Tōkyō, first issue 1933

Labor in Tokyo. Tōkyō Metropolitan Government, 1986
Treaty of Peace with Japan. (Cmd. 8392). HMSO, 1951; (Cmd. 8601). HMSO, 1952
Allen, G. C., *The Japanese Economy.* London, 1981
Baerwald, H. H., *Japan's Parliament.* CUP, 1974.—*Party Politics in Japan.* Boston, 1986
Burks, A. W., *Japan: Profile of an Industrial Power.* Boulder, 1981
Kenkyusha's *New Japanese–English [and English–Japanese] Dictionary.* 2 vols. New ed. Cambridge, Mass., and Berkeley, Cal., 1960
Miyazaki, S., *The Japanese Dictionary Explained in English.* Tōkyō, 1950
Morishima, U. *Why has Japan 'Succeeded'?* CUP, 1984
Murata, K., *An Industrial Geography of Japan.* London, 1980
Nippon: A Chartered Survey of Japan. Tsuneta Yano Memorial Society. Tōkyō, annual
Okita, S., *The Developing Economics of Japan: Lessons in Growth.* Univ. of Tōkyō Press, 1983
Prindl, A., *Japanese Finance: Guide to Banking in Japan.* Chichester, 1981
Sansom, G. B., *A History of Japan.* 3 vols. London, 1958–64
Tsoukalis, L., (ed.), *Japan and Western Europe.* London, 1982
Vogel, E. F., *Japan as Number One.* Harvard Univ. Press, 1979
Ward, P., *Japanese Capitals.* Cambridge, 1985

THE HASHEMITE KINGDOM OF JORDAN

Capital: Amman
Population: 2·85m. (1987) E. Bank
834,000 (1987) W. Bank
GNP per capita: US$1,900 (1984)

Al Mamlaka al Urduniya al Hashemiyah

HISTORY. By a Treaty, signed in London on 22 March 1946, Britain recognized Transjordan as a sovereign independent state. On 25 May 1946 the Amir Abdullah assumed the title of King, and when the treaty was ratified on 17 June 1946 the name of the territory was changed to that of 'The Hashemite Kingdom of Jordan' in 1949. A new Anglo-Transjordan treaty was signed in Amman on 15 March 1948. The treaty was to remain in force for 20 years, but by mutual consent was terminated on 13 March 1957.

The Arab Federation between the Kingdoms of Iraq and Jordan, which was concluded on 14 Feb. 1958, lapsed after the revolution in Iraq of 14 July 1958, and was officially terminated by royal decree on 1 Aug. 1958.

Since the occupation of the West Bank in June 1967 by Israeli forces, that part of Palestine has not been administratively controlled by the Jordanian government. All statistics in this section, unless otherwise stated, are thus relative to the East Bank only.

AREA AND POPULATION. The part of Palestine remaining to the Arabs under the armistice with Israel on 3 April 1949, with the exception of the Gaza strip, was in Dec. 1949 placed under Jordanian rule and formally incorporated in Jordan on 24 April 1950. For the frontier lines *see* map in THE STATESMAN'S YEAR-BOOK, 1951. In June 1967 this territory, known as the West Bank, was occupied by Israeli forces and has since been under Israel administration.

The area presently administered by the Jordanian government, known as the East Bank, comprises 89,206 sq. km (34,443 sq. miles) following an exchange of territory with Saudi Arabia on 10 Aug. 1965. Its population at the 1979 Census was 2,132,997; latest estimate (1987) 2·85m. The area and population of the 5 districts were:

Muhafaza	Sq. km	1986
Asimah	17,882	1,160,000
Balqa	1,069	193,800
Irbid	22,654	680,200
Karak	4,601	120,100
Ma'an	43,000	97,500

The largest towns, with estimated population, 1984: Amman, the capital, 777,500; Zarqa, 265,700; Irbid, 136,200.

West Bank: The former part of Palestine, incorporated into Jordan in 1950 but occupied by Israel since June 1967, has an area of 5,879 sq. km (2,270 sq. miles) and was divided into 3 further districts *(muhafaza)*; population (estimate, 1985) 1·25m.

In 1984 registered births numbered 102,521; deaths, 8,303; marriages, 18,189; divorces, 2,652.

CLIMATE. Predominantly a Mediterranean climate, with hot dry summers and cool wet winters, but in hilly parts summers are cooler and winters colder. Those areas below sea-level are very hot in summer and warm in winter. Eastern parts have a desert climate. Amman. Jan. 46°F (7·5°C), July 77°F (24·9°C). Annual rainfall 12" (290 mm). Aqaba. Jan. 61°F (16°C), July 89°F (31·5°C). Annual rainfall 1·5" (35 mm).

KING. The Kingdom is a constitutional monarchy headed by HM King **Hussein**, GCVO, eldest son of King Talal, who, being incapacitated by mental illness, was deposed by Parliament on 11 Aug. 1952 and died 8 July 1972. The King was born 14 Nov. 1935, and married Princess Dina Abdul Hamid on 19 April 1955 (divorced 1957), Toni Avril Gardiner (Muna al Hussein) on 25 May 1961 (divorced 1972), Alia Toukan on 26 Dec. 1972 (died in air crash 1977) and Elizabeth Halaby on 15 June 1978. *Offspring:* Princess Alia, born 13 Feb. 1956; Prince Abdulla, born 30 Jan. 1962; Prince Faisal, born 11 Oct. 1963; Princesses Zein and Aisha, born 23 April 1968; Princess Haya, born 3 May 1974; Prince Ali, born 23 Dec. 1975; Prince Hamzah, born 1 April 1980; Prince Hashem, born 10 June 1981; Princess Iman, born 4 April 1983; Princess Raya, born 9 Feb. 1986. *Crown Prince* (appointed 1 April 1965): Prince Hassan, younger brother of the King.

CONSTITUTION AND GOVERNMENT. The Constitution passed on 7 Nov. 1951 provides that the Cabinet is responsible to Parliament.

The legislature consists of a lower house of 60 members elected by universal suffrage (30 from East Jordan and 30 from West Jordan), and a senate of 30 members nominated by the King.

On 5 Feb. 1976 both Houses of Parliament approved amendments to the Constitution by which the King was empowered to postpone calling elections until further notice. The lower house was dissolved. This step was taken because no elections could be held in the West Bank which has been under Israeli occupation since June 1967.

Parliament was reconvened on 9 Jan. 1984. By-elections were held in March 1984 and 6 members were nominated for the West Bank bringing Parliament to 60 members. Women voted for the first time in 1984.

The Cabinet, in Oct. 1987, was composed as follows:

Prime Minister and Defence: Zaid Rifai.

Deputy Prime Minister and Education: Abdul Wahab Al Majali. *Minister of State for Prime Ministry Affairs:* Thogan Al-Hindawi. *Minister of State for Parliamentary Affairs:* Dr Sami Judeh. *Interior:* Rafai Al-Dajanée. *Labour and Social Development:* Khalid Al Haj Hassan. *Communications:* Mohyeddin Al Husseini. *Foreign Affairs:* Taher Al Masri. *Municipal and Rural Affairs and the Environment:* Yousef Jaber. *Awqaf and Islamic Affairs:* Dr Abdul Aziz Al Khayyat. *Public Works:* Mahmoud Al Hawamdeh. *Supply, Industry and Trade:* Dr Rajai Muasher. *Finance:* Dr Hanna Odeh. *Transport:* Ahmad Dakhqan. *Energy and Mineral Resources:* Dr Hisham Al Khatib. *Planning:* Dr Taher Kana'an. *Higher Education:* Dr Nasseruddeen Al Assad. *Agriculture:* Marwan Al Hmoud. *Information, Culture, Tourism and Antiquities:* Mohammad Al Katib. *Justice:* Riyadh Al Shaka's. *Health:* Dr Zaid Hamzeh. *Occupied Territories Affairs:* Dr Marwan Dodean. *Youth:* Eid Al Dahheait.

National flag: Three horizontal stripes of black, white, green, with a red triangle based on the hoist, bearing a white 7-pointed star.

The official language of the country is Arabic.

DEFENCE

Army. The Army is organized in 3 armoured, 1 special forces and 6 mechanized brigades, 4 anti-aircraft brigades, 1 independent Royal Guards brigade and 16 artillery battalions. Total strength (1988) 70,000 men.

Navy. The Coastal Guard or Jordan Sea Force has 14 patrol launches and 1 support craft based at Aqaba. Personnel (1988) totalled 300 officers and ratings.

Air Force. The Air Force has 2 interceptor and 3 ground attack squadrons equipped respectively with Mirage F1 and F-5E Tiger II fighters, and 2-seat F-5Fs, plus an OCU equipped with F-5A fighters and 2-seat F-5Bs. Two anti-armour squadrons have Bell AH-1S Huey Cobra helicopters. There are 6 C-130B/H Hercules and 2 CASA Aviocar turboprop transports, S-70 Blackhawk, S-76, Gazelle, Alouette III and Hughes 500D helicopters, piston-engined Bulldog basic trainers and CASA Aviojet and T-37B jet trainers. Hawk surface-to-air missiles equip 14 batteries. Strength (1988) about 10,000 officers and men.

INTERNATIONAL RELATIONS

Membership. Jordan is a member of the UN and the Arab League.

ECONOMY

Planning. A 5-year plan (1986–90) aims at improving agriculture and the development of water resources.

Budget. The budget estimates for the year 1985 provide for revenue of JD.794,500,000 and expenditure of JD.811,200,000 which included 206m. for defence.

Currency. The Jordan *dinar,* divided into 1,000 *fils.* The following bank-notes and coins are in circulation: 10, 5 dinars, 1 dinar, 500 fils (notes), 250, 100, 50, 25, 20 fils (cupronickel), 10, 5, 1 fils (bronze). In March 1988, £1 = JD.0·599; US$ = JD.0·344.

Banking. The Central Bank of Jordan was established in 1964. In 1986 there were 9 local commercial banks including Arab Bank (the largest, with a capital of JD.22m.), 8 foreign commercial banks including Grindlays Bank and 6 foreign banks with representative offices. In 1985 there were 2 investment banks, 5 finance companies, 3 Islamic institutions and 3 real estated-linked savings and loan associations.

Assets and liabilities of the Jordanian banking system (including the Central Bank, commercial banks and the Housing Bank) totalled JD.2,404·34m. in 1984.

Weights and Measures. The metric system is in force.

ENERGY AND NATURAL RESOURCES

Electricity. Production (1986) 2,955m. kwh. Supply 220 volts; 50 Hz.

Oil. Oil was discovered in 1982 at Azraq, 70 km east of Amman and 7 new wells were under development in 1985. Deposits of oil shale, estimated at 10,000m. tonnes, have been discovered at Lajjun.

Minerals. Phosphates production in 1986 was 6·25m. tonnes. Potash is found in the Dead Sea. Reserves, over 800m. tonnes. A potash plant built on the southeast shore to extract compounds by solar evaporation produced 486,868 tonnes in 1984. Cement production (1984), 1,994,082 tonnes.

Agriculture. The country east of the Hejaz Railway line is largely desert; northwestern Jordan is potentially of agricultural value and an integrated Jordan Valley project began in 1973. The agricultural cropping pattern for irrigated vegetable cultivation was introduced in 1984 to regulate production and diversify the crops being cultivated. In 1987 Jordan was self-sufficient in the production of potatoes and onions. In 1986 the government began to lease state-owned land in the semi-arid southern regions for agricultural development by private investors, mostly for wheat and barley. Jordan is self-sufficient in poultry meat. The main crops are tomatoes and other vegetables, citrus fruit, wheat and olives.

Production in 1985 included (in tonnes): Tomatoes, 220,000; olives, 40,000; citrus fruit, 63,000; wheat, 100,000.

Livestock (1986): 1·1m. sheep; 500,000 goats; 35,000 cattle; 14,000 camels.

INDUSTRY AND TRADE

Industry. Production (1984): Phosphates, 6,213,000 tons; petroleum products, 2,511,000 tons; cement, 2,026,000 tons; iron, 165,000 tons; fertilizer, 30,000 tonnes and phosphoric acid as a by-product, 105,000 tonnes.

Other industries include cigarettes, cosmetics, textiles, shoes, batteries, plastic products, leather tanning, pharmaceutical products, iron pipes, detergents, aluminium and ceramics. Some 50% of industry is based in Amman.

Commerce. Imports in 1985 were valued at JD.1,072·51m. and exports and re-exports at JD.310·89m. Total remittances from Jordanians working abroad reached US$1,187·5m. in 1984.

Major exports in 1984 (in JD.1m.) included phosphates, 69·6; chemicals, 67·6; food and live animals, 41·7; manufactured goods, 33·7. Major imports included machinery and transport equipment, 215·8; crude oil, 203·9.

Exports in 1984 (in JD.1m.) were mainly to Iraq, 67·7; Saudi Arabia, 38·6 and India, 34·1. Imports were mainly from Saudi Arabia, 208·7 and the USA, 119.

Total trade between Jordan and UK (British Department of Trade returns, in £1,000 sterling):

	1983	1984	1985	1986	1987
Imports to UK	28,680	18,114	86,077	49,766	29,285
Exports and re-exports from UK	262,503	192,508	154,270	130,385	188,998

Tourism. In 1986, 2,835,217 tourists visited Jordan spending JD186m.

COMMUNICATIONS

Roads. Total length of public highways, 4,095 km. Motor vehicles in 1980 included 73,078 private passenger cars, 11,207 taxis, 1,415 buses, 29,517 goods vehicles, 4,888 motor cycles.

Railways. The 1,050 mm gauge Hejaz Jordan and Aqaba Railway runs from the Syrian border at Nassib to Ma'an and Naqb Ishtar and Aqaba Port (total, 618 km). In 1986 the railways carried 31,304 passengers and 2,789,524 tons of freight.

Aviation. The Queen Alia International airport, at Zizya, 30 km south of Amman was inaugurated in 1983. There are other international airports at Amman and Aqaba. Jordan is served by over 20 international airlines.

Shipping (1980). The port of Aqaba handled 6,598,591 tons of cargo. JD.65m. was spent between 1980–85 on developing facilities and US$1,000m. is to be provided under the 1986–90 plan on further developments including a special oil terminal and 4 new wharves.

Post and Broadcasting. In 1982 there were 791 post offices and 82,000 telephones in 1986. There were 280,000 TV receivers and 550,000 radios in 1985.

Cinemas (1975). Cinemas numbered 40 with a total attendance of 4,341,900.

Newspapers (1987). There were 4 daily (including 1 in English) and 5 weekly papers, with a total circulation of 188,000.

RELIGION, EDUCATION AND WELFARE

Religion. About 80% of the population are Sunni Moslems.

Education (1985–86). There were 358 pre-primary schools with 1,336 teachers and 27,495 pupils; 1,239 elementary schools with 16,979 teachers and 530,906 pupils; 1,099 preparatory schools with 9,943 teachers and 208,646 pupils; 485 secondary schools with 7,131 teachers and 96,400 pupils and 24 vocational educational schools with 2,127 teachers and 30,789 pupils. The University of Jordan, in-augurated on 15 Dec. 1962 had in 1985-86, 11,629 students. The Yarmouk University (Irbid) was inaugurated in 1976 with (1985-86) 14,370 students. The Mu'tah University was inaugurated in 1981 with (1985–86) 712 students.

Health (1980). There were 1,715 physicians, 351 dentists and 35 hospitals with 2,743 beds.

DIPLOMATIC REPRESENTATIVES

Of Jordan in Great Britain (6 Upper Phillimore Gdns., London, W8 7HB)
Ambassador: Dr Albert Butros.

Of Great Britain in Jordan (Third Circle, Jebel Amman)
Ambassador: Anthony Reeve.

Of Jordan in the USA (3504 International Dr., NW, Washington, D.C., 20008)
Ambassador: Mohammad Kamal.

Of the USA in Jordan (Jebel Amman, Amman)
Ambassador: Roscoe S. Suddarth.

Of Jordan to the United Nations
Ambassador: Abdullah Salah.

Books of Reference

The Department of Statistics, Ministry of National Economy, publishes a *Statistical Yearbook* (in Arabic and English), latest issue 1968, and a *Statistical Guide,* latest issue 1965.—*External Trade Statistics*, 1968.—*National Accounts and Input-Output Analysis, 1959–65,* 1967

The Constitution of the Hashemite Kingdom of Jordan. Amman, 1952

Gubser, P., *Jordan.* Boulder, 1982

Haas, J., *Husseins Königreich: Jordaniens Stellung in Nahen Osten.* Munich, 1975

Seton, C. R. W., *Legislation of Transjordan, 1918-30.* London, 1931. [Continued by the Government of Jordan as an annual publication: *Jordan Legislation.* Amman, 1932 ff.]

Toni, Y. T., and Mousa, S., *Jordan: Land and People.* Amman, 1973

KENYA

Jamhuri ya Kenya

Capital: Nairobi
Population: 20·03m. (1987)
GNP per capita: US$280 (1985)

HISTORY. Until Kenya became independent on 12 Dec. 1963, it consisted of the colony and the protectorate. The protectorate comprised the mainland dominions of the Sultan of Zanzibar, viz., a coastal strip of territory 10 miles wide, to the northern branch of the Tana River; also Mau, Kipini and the Island of Lamu, and all adjacent islands between the rivers Umba and Tana. The Sultan on 8 Oct. 1963 ceded the coastal strip to Kenya with effect from 12 Dec. 1963.

The colony and protectorate, formerly known as the East African Protectorate were, on 1 April 1905, transferred from the Foreign Office to the Colonial Office and in Nov. 1906 the protectorate was placed under the control of a governor and C.-in-C. and (except the Sultan of Zanzibar's dominions) was annexed to the Crown as from 23 July 1920 under the name of the Colony of Kenya, thus becoming a Crown Colony.

The territories on the coast became the Kenya Protectorate.

A Treaty was signed (15 July 1924) with Italy under which Great Britain ceded to Italy the Juba River and a strip from 50 to 100 miles wide on the British side of the river. Cession took place on 29 June 1925. The northern boundary is defined by an agreement with Ethiopia in 1947. A Constitution conferring internal self-government was brought into force on 1 June 1963, and full independence was achieved on 12 Dec. 1963. On 12 Dec. 1964 Kenya became a republic.

AREA AND POPULATION. Kenya is bounded by Sudan and Ethiopia in the north, Uganda in the west, Tanzania in the south and the Somali Republic and the Indian ocean in the east. The total area is 224,960 sq. miles (582,600 sq. km), of which 219,790 sq. miles is land area. In the 1979 census, the population was 15,327,061, of which 15,100,000 were Africans, 78,600 Asians, 39,900 Europeans, 39,140 Arabs. Estimate (1987) 20·03m.

Population of the provinces (1979): Rift Valley, 3·24m.; Eastern, 2,719,000; Nyanza, 2,643,000; Central, 2,345,000; Coast, 1,342,000; Western, 1,832,000; Nairobi district, 835,000; North-Eastern, 373,000.

Nairobi is the capital, and the 1979 census showed a population of 827,775. Estimate (1985) 827,800.

Population of the largest towns: Mombasa, 341,000; Kisumu, 152,600; Nakuru, 92,900; Machakos, 84,000; Meru, 70,000; Eldoret, 51,000; Thika, 41,000. A new town is being developed (in 1981) at Bura, which will be the centre of a production area using irrigated water from the Tana river.

Kiswahili is the official language, but 21% speak Kikuyu as their mother tongue, 14% Luhya, 12% Luo, 11% Kamba, 11% Kalenjin, 6% Gusii, 6% Meru and 5% Mijikenda. English is spoken in commercial centres.

CLIMATE. The climate is tropical, with wet and dry seasons, but considerable differences in altitude make for varied conditions between the hot, coastal lowlands and the plateau, where temperatures are very much cooler. Heaviest rains occur in April and May, but in some parts there is a second wet season in Nov. and Dec. Nairobi. Jan. 65°F (18·3°C), July 60°F (15·6°C). Annual rainfall 39″ (958 mm). Mombasa. Jan. 81°F (27·2°C), July 76°F (24·4°C). Annual rainfall 47″ (1,201 mm).

CONSTITUTION AND GOVERNMENT. There is a unicameral National Assembly of 172 members, comprising 158 elected by universal suffrage for a 5-year term, 12 members appointed by the President, and the Speaker and Attorney-General ex-officio. The President is also directly elected for 5 years; he

763

appoints a Vice-President and other Ministers to a Cabinet over which he presides. The sole legal political party is the Kenya African National Union (KANU).

Elections are due on 21 March 1988.

President of the Republic: Daniel T. arap Moi (elected 1978, re-elected 1983).

Vice-President and Home Affairs: Mwai Kibaki. *Foreign Affairs:* Zachary Onyonka. *Planning and National Development:* Dr John Onko.

National flag: Three horizontal stripes of black, red, green, with the red edged in white; bearing in the centre an African shield in black and white with 2 crossed spears behind.

Administration. The country is divided into the Nairobi Area and 7 provinces and there are 40 districts.

DEFENCE

Army. The Army consists of 2 armoured, 1 armoured reconnaissance, 6 infantry, 2 artillery, 1 parachute, 1 independent air cavalry and 2 engineer battalions. Equipment includes 76 Vickers Mk 3 main battle tanks. 40 Hughes Defender helicopters, of which 15 are armed with TOW missiles and 8 new Hughes 530 helicopters. Total strength (1988) 13,000.

Navy. The Navy in 1988 consists of 2 new British built missile armed fast attack craft, 4 British built smaller missile armed attack craft, 3 British built patrol craft, 2 patrol boats and 1 tug. Personnel totalled 350 officers and ratings. The base is at Mombasa which has a dry dock with a capacity of 18,000 tons. There are also 2 British-built small marine police cutters, and up to 15 larger customs/police craft are planned.

Air Force. An air force, formed 1 June 1964, was built up with RAF assistance and is under Army command. Equipment includes 11 F-5E/F-5F supersonic combat aircraft/trainers, 12 Hawk and 5 BAC 167 Strikemaster light jet attack/trainers, 8 twin-turboprop Buffaloes for transport, air ambulance, anti-locust spraying and security duties, 8 Skyservant light twins, 12 Bulldog piston-engined primary trainers and Puma, Gazelle and Alouette helicopters.

INTERNATIONAL RELATIONS

Membership. Kenya is a member of UN, the Commonwealth, OAU and is an ACP state of EEC.

ECONOMY

Planning. The 1984–88 development plan aimed at an average annual growth rate of 6·3%. In 1984 GDP grew by 0·9% (agriculture declining by 3·7%; manufacture increasing by 4·3% and distribution by 4%).

Budget. Ordinary revenue and expenditure for 1986–87: Revenue, KSh.28,456m.; expenditure, KSh.38,962m.

Currency. The monetary unit is the Kenya *Shilling* divided into 100 *cents*; 20 shillings = K£1. Notes of the Central Bank of Kenya are circulated in denominations of KSh.5, 10, 20, 50 and 100 and coins in denominations of 5, 10 and 50 cents and KSh.1 and 5. Currency in circulation at March 1986: Notes, K£296,121,000; coins, K£9·4m. In March 1988, £1 = 30 *Shilling*; US$1 = 15·87 *Shilling*.

Banking. Banks operating in Kenya: The National & Grindlays Bank International, Ltd; the Standard Bank, Ltd; Barclays Bank of Kenya Ltd; Algemene Bank Nederland NV; Bank of India, Ltd; Bank of Baroda, Ltd; Habib Bank (Overseas), Ltd; Commercial Bank of Africa, Ltd; Citibank; The Co-operative Bank of Kenya, Ltd; National Bank of Kenya, Ltd; Agricultural Finance Corporation; The Kenya Commercial Bank; The Central Bank of Kenya. In Jan. 1985 there were 43 non-bank finance institutions.

The Kenya Post Office Savings Bank, a state savings bank established in 1978, had 1,250,000 ordinary savings accounts with total deposits of KSh.750m. at 31 Dec. 1984.

ENERGY AND NATURAL RESOURCES

Electricity. Installed generating capacity was 544 mw in 1986; two-thirds was provided by hydropower from power stations on the Tana river, 30% by oil-fired power stations and the rest by geothermal power. Production (1986) 1,950m. kwh. Supply 220 volts; 50 Hz.

Minerals. Production, 1985 (in K£1,000): Soda ash, 13,002; fluorspar ore, 3,550; salt, 1,029; gold, 61·1. Other minerals included raw soda, lime and limestone, diatomite, garnets and vermiculite.

Agriculture. As agriculture is possible from sea-level to altitudes of over 9,000 ft, tropical, sub-tropical and temperate crops can be grown and mixed farming can be advocated. Four-fifths of the country is range-land which produces mainly live-stock products and wild game which constitutes the major attraction of the country's tourist industry.

The main areas of crop production are the Central, Rift Valley, Western and Nyanza Provinces and parts of Eastern and Coastal Provinces. Coffee, tea, sisal, pyrethrum, maize and wheat are crops of major importance in the Highlands, while coconuts, cashew nuts, cotton, sugar, sisal and maize are the principal crops grown at the lower altitudes. All production in 1984 was affected by drought but good seasonal rains returned for the 1985 crop year and output grew by 3·5%. Production, 1985 (in 1,000 tonnes), of principal food crops: Maize, 2,650; wheat, 250; rice, 35; barley, 50; millet, 50; sorghum, 100; potatoes, 650; sweet potatoes, 280; cassava, 400; sugar-cane, 3,960. Main cash crops (1985–86): Tobacco, 9,000; coffee, 115; tea, 147; vegetables, 439; fruit, 670; flowers.

Livestock (1986): Cattle, 9m.; sheep, 7·1m.; goats, 8·5m.; pigs, 98,000; poultry, 21m.

Forestry. The total area of gazetted forest reserves in Kenya amounts to 16,800 sq. km, of which the greater part is situated between 6,000 and 11,000 ft above sea-level, mostly on Mount Kenya, the Aberdares, Mount Elgon, Tinderet, Londiani, Mau watershed, Elgeyo and Charangani ranges. These forests may be divided into coniferous, broad-leaved or hardwood and bamboo forests. The upper parts of these forests are mainly bamboo, which occurs mostly between altitudes of 8,000 and 10,000 ft and occupies some 10% of the high-altitude forests. Production (1985): Softwood, 407,000 cu. metres; hardwood, 542,000.

Fisheries. Landings in 1985 were 99,764 tonnes of fresh water fish, 5,777 tonnes of marine fish, 274 tonnes of crustaceans and 158 tonnes of other marine products; total value K£15,588,500.

INDUSTRY AND TRADE

Industry. In 1986 industry accounted for some 13% of GDP and employed about one-fifth of the wage-earning labour force. The main activities were textiles, chemicals, vehicle assembly and transport equipment, leather and footwear, printing and publishing, food and tobacco processing. An important sub-sector was the refining of crude petroleum at Mombasa.

Commerce. Total domestic exports (1984, provisional) K£745m.; imports K£1,116m.

Chief imports in 1984 were petroleum and petroleum products (31·1%of total), industrial supplies (26·4%), machinery and other capital equipment (16·9%), food and drink (10·7%) and transport equipment (10·4%). Chief exports were coffee (27%), tea (25·1%) and petroleum products (18·3%). By 1986 fresh vegetables, fruits and flowers became the fourth largest foreign exchange earner.

Imports in 1985 were mainly from the UK (14·7%), Saudi Arabia (12·3%), Japan (10%), Federal Republic of Germany (8%) and USA (6·8%). Exports were mainly to the UK (17·8%), Federal Republic of Germany (11·4%), Uganda (9·1%), USA (7·1%) and Pakistan (5·8%).

Total trade between Kenya and UK (British Department of Trade returns, in £1,000 sterling):

	1983	1984	1985	1986	1987
Imports to UK	128,464	203,243	185,622	163,745	129,236
Exports and re-exports from UK	111,249	176,061	160,651	170,671	199,059

Tourism. In 1986, about 604,000 tourists visited Kenya and spent KSh.4,960m.

COMMUNICATIONS

Roads. In 1981 there were 6,540 km of bitumen surfaced roads and 47,037 km of gravel-surfaced roads.

Railways. On 11 Feb. 1977 the independent Kenya Railways Corporation was formed following break-up of the East African Railways administration. The network totals 2,654 km of metre-gauge. In 1985, the railways carried 1·9m. passengers and 3·2m. tonnes of freight.

Aviation. Total number of passengers handled at the 3 main airports (1984) was 2,058,000. Jomo Kenyatta Airport, Nairobi, handles nearly 30 international airlines as well as Kenya Airways.

Shipping. A national shipping service is planned (1984) to be based in Mombasa, the Kenyan main port at Kilindini on the Indian Ocean. The port handles cargo freight both for Kenya as well as for the neighbouring East African states. The Port Authority also runs a modern harbour college.

Post and Broadcasting. The Voice of Kenya operates 2 national services (Swahili–English) from Nairobi and regional services in Kisumu, Nairobi and Mombasa. The television service provides programmes mainly in English and Swahili. A new television station opened in Mombasa in 1970. Telephones (1983) 216,674.

Cinemas (1971). Cinemas numbered 32, with seating capacity of 18,800.

JUSTICE, RELIGION, EDUCATION AND WELFARE

Justice. The courts of justice comprise the High Court, established in 1921, with full jurisdiction both civil and criminal over all persons and all matters in Kenya, including Admiralty jurisdiction arising on the high seas and elsewhere, and Subordinate Courts. The High Court has its headquarters at Nairobi and consists of the Chief Justice and 24 puisne judges; it sits continuously at Nairobi, Mombasa, Nakuru and Kisumu; civil and criminal sessions are held regularly at Eldoret, Nyeri, Meru, Kitale, Kisii and Kericho.

The Subordinate Courts are presided over by Senior Resident, Resident or District Magistrates and are established in the main centres of all districts. They sit throughout the year. There are also Moslem Subordinate Courts established in areas where the local population is predominantly Moslem; they are presided over by Kadhis and exercise limited jurisdiction in matters governed by Moslem law.

Religion. In 1987, the Roman Catholic Church had nearly 6m. adherents (27% of the population), Protestants 4m. (19%) and other Christian churches over 6m. (27%), while Islam had 1·3m. (6%), traditional tribal religions 4m. (19%) and others 400,000 (2%).

Education. *Primary* (1983). 11,966 primary schools with 4·3m. pupils and 82,983 teachers.

Secondary (1983). There were 2,230 secondary schools with a total enrolment of 494,000 and 8,797 teachers.

Technical (1983). 18 technical colleges with 9,258 pupils and 368 teachers.

Teacher training (1982). 14,000 students were training as teachers in 20 colleges with 900 lecturers.

Higher Education. The University of Nairobi was inaugurated on 10 Dec. 1970 and provides courses in arts, science, education, agriculture, medicine, art, architecture, engineering, veterinary, law and domestic science. In 1983 there were 8,761 students and 928 lecturers. Moi University opened in 1985 with 90 students.

Health. In 1981 beds in hospitals (including mission hospitals) totalled 28,108. 1,328 health centres, including sub-centres and dispensaries, were in operation. Free medical service for all children and adult out-patients was launched in 1965.

DIPLOMATIC REPRESENTATIVES

Of Kenya in Great Britain (24-25 New Bond St., London, W1Y 9HD)
High Commissioner: Dr Sally J. Kosgei.

Of Great Britain in Kenya (Bruce Hse., Standard St., Nairobi)
High Commissioner: J. R. Johnson, CMG.

Of Kenya in the USA (2249 R. St., NW, Washington, D.C., 20008)
Ambassador: Sospeter O. Mageto.

Of the USA in Kenya (Moi/Haile Selassie Ave., Nairobi)
Ambassador: Elinor G. Constable.

Of Kenya to the United Nations
Ambassador: Raphael Muli Kiilu.

Books of Reference

Kenya Development Plan, 1984–88. Nairobi, 1984
Kenya Economic Survey, 1983. Nairobi, 1984
Statistical Abstract. Government Printer, Nairobi, 1982
Standard English–Swahili Dictionary. Ed. Inter-territorial Language Committee of East Africa. 2 vols. London, 1939
Who's Who in Kenya 1982–1983. London, 1983
Arnold, G., *Kenyatta and the Politics of Kenya.* London, 1974.—*Modern Kenya.* London, 1982
Bienen, H., *Kenya: The Politics of Participation and Control.* Princeton Univ. Press, 1974
Bigsten, A., *Education and Income Distribution in Kenya.* Brookfield, Vermont, 1984
Bolton, K., *Haramble Country: A Guide to Kenya.* London, 1970
Collison, R. L., *Kenya.* [Bibliography] London and Santa Barbara, 1982
Harbeson, J. W., *Nation-Building in Kenya: The Role of Land Reform.* Northwestern Univ. Press, 1973
Hazlewood, A., *The Economy of Kenya: The Kenyatta Era.* OUP, 1980
Langdon, S. W., *Multinational Corporations in the Political Economy of Kenya.* London, 1981
Miller, N. N., *Kenya, the Quest for Prosperity.* Boulder and London, 1984
Tomkinson, M., *Kenya: A Holiday Guide.* 5th ed. London and Hammamet, 1981

KIRIBATI

Capital: Tarawa
Population: 66,250 (1987)
GNP per capita: US$390 (1985)

HISTORY. The Gilbert and Ellice Islands were proclaimed a protectorate in 1892 and annexed (at the request of the native governments) as the Gilbert and Ellice Islands Colony on 10 Nov. 1915 (effective on 12 Jan. 1916). On 1 Oct. 1975 the former Ellice Islands severed its constitutional links with the Gilbert Islands and took a new name Tuvalu.

Internal self-government was obtained on 1 Nov. 1976 and independence achieved on 12 July 1979 as the Republic of Kiribati.

AREA AND POPULATION. Kiribati (pronounced Kiribass) consists of 3 groups of coral atolls and one isolated volcanic island, spread over a large expanse of the Central Pacific with a total land area of 717·1 sq. km (276·9 sq. miles). It comprises Banaba or Ocean Island (5 sq. km), the 16 Gilbert Islands (295 sq. km), the 8 Phœnix Islands (55 sq. km), and 8 of the 11 Line Islands (329 sq.km), the other 3 Line Islands (Jarvis, Palmyra and Kingman Reef) being uninhabited dependencies of the US. Population, 1985 census, 63,848; estimate (1987) 66,250. Banaba, all 16 Gilbert Islands, and 3 atolls in the Line Islands (Teraina, Tabuaeran and Kiritimati—formerly Washington, Fanning and Christmas Islands respectively) are inhabited; their populations in 1985 (census) were as follows:

Banaba (Ocean Is.)	189	Abemama	2,966	Onotoa	1,927
Makin	1,777	Kuria	1,052	Tamana	1,348
Butaritari	3,622	Aranuki	984	Arorae	1,470
Marakei	2,693	Nonouti	2,930	Phœnix Island	24
Abaiang	4,386	Tabiteuea	4,493	Teraina	416
Tarawa	24,598	Beru	2,702	Tabuaeran	445
Maiana	2,141	Nikunau	2,061	Kiritimati	1,737

The remaining 13 atolls have no permanent population; the 8 Phœnix Islands comprise Birnie, Rawaki (formerly Phœnix), Enderbury, Kanton (or Abariringa), Manra (formerly Sydney), Orona (formerly Hull), McKean and Nikumaroro (formerly Gardner), while the others are Malden and Starbuck in the Central Line Islands and Caroline, Flint and Vostok in the Southern Line Islands. The population is almost entirely Micronesian.

CLIMATE. The Line Islands, Phœnix Islands and Banaba have a maritime equatorial climate, but the islands further north and south are tropical. Annual and daily ranges of temperature are small and mean annual rainfall ranges from 50″ (1,250 mm) near the equator to 120″ (3,000 mm) in the north. Tarawa. Jan. 83°F (28·3°C), July 82°F (27·8°C). Annual rainfall 79″ (1,977 mm).

CONSTITUTION AND GOVERNMENT. Under the independence Constitution the republic has a unicameral legislature, comprising 36 members elected from 20 constituencies for a 4-year term. The *Beretitenti* (President) is both Head of State and of Government.

In Sept. 1985 the government was composed as follows:

President and Foreign Affairs: Ieremia Tabai, GCMG.

Vice-President, Home Affairs and Decentralization: Teatao Teannaki. *Trade, Industry and Labour:* Teewe Arobati. *Finance:* Boanareke Boanareke. *Health and Family Planning:* Binata Tetaeka. *Natural Resource Development:* Babera Kirata, OBE. *Education:* Baitika Toum. *Communications:* Taomati Iuta, OBE. *Minister for the Line and Phœnix Group of Islands:* Uera Rabaua. *Works and Energy:* Tiwau Awira. *Attorney-General:* Michael Takabwebwe.

National flag: Red, with blue and white wavy lines in base, and in the centre a gold rising sun and a flying frigate bird.

768

National anthem: Teirake Kain Kiribati.

INTERNATIONAL RELATIONS

Membership. Kiribati is a member of the Commonwealth, South Pacific Forum and is an ACP state of the EEC.

ECONOMY

Budget. Budget estimates for 1985 show revenue, $A16,243,000; principal items: fishing licences, $A2,178,000; customs duties, $A3,400,000; direct taxation, $A920,000. Expenditure amounted to $A16,243,000.

Currency. The currency in use is the Australian *dollar.*

ENERGY AND NATURAL RESOURCES

Electricity. Electric power production (1986) was 8m. kwh.

Minerals. Phosphate production was discontinued in 1979.

Agriculture. Land under agriculture and permanant cultivation, 50·7%; forest, 2·8%; other, 46·5%. The land is basically coral reefs upon which coral sand has built up, and then been enriched by humus from rotting vegetation and flotsam which has drifted ashore. The principal tree is the coconut, which grows prolifically on all the islands except some of the Phœnix Islands. Other food-bearing trees are the pandanus palm and the breadfruit. As the amount of soil is negligible, the only vegetable which grows in any quantity is a coarse calladium (alocasia) with the local name 'babai', which is cultivated most laboriously in deep pits. Pigs and fowls are kept throughout Kiribati.

Copra production is mainly in the hands of the individual landowner, who collects the coconut products from the trees on his own land. Production (1986) 12,000 tonnes; coconuts, 90,000 tonnes.

Livestock (1986): Pigs, 10,000; poultry (1982), 163,000.

Fisheries. Tuna fishing is an important industry and licenses have been granted to USSR fleets.

TRADE. The principal imports (1984, in A$1m.) are: Machinery and transport equipment, 8·5; food, 5·5; manufactured goods, 3·1; fuels, 2·25. The value of exports for 1981 amounted to $A3·6m. Exports are almost exclusively copra.

Total trade between Kiribati and UK (British Department of Trade returns, in £1,000 sterling):

	1985	1986	1987
Imports to UK	209	4	8
Exports and re-exports from UK	775	179	301

COMMUNICATIONS

Roads. There are 640 km of roads, of which 483 km suitable for vehicles.

Shipping. The main port is at Betio (Tarawa). Other ports of entry are Christmas Island and Banaba. In 1980, 71 vessels were handled at Betio.

Aviation. Air Tungaru is the national carrier. It operates services from Tarawa to the other 15 outer Islands in the Gilbertese Group, services varying between one and four flights each week. There is a charter service weekly to Christmas Island, in the Line Islands, which continues to Honolulu. A fortnightly service operates to Funafuti and weekly to Majuro and Nandi. Air Nauru has a weekly flight between Nauru and Tarawa.

Post and Broadcasting. There were 1,400 telephones in 1984. Radio Tarawa transmits daily in English and I-Kiribati. A telephone line to Australia was installed in 1981. There were (1983 estimate) 10,000 radio receivers.

Cinemas. In 1974 there were 5 cinemas with a seating capacity of 2,000.

Newspapers. There was (1984) 1 bi-lingual weekly newspaper.

JUSTICE, RELIGION, EDUCATION AND WELFARE

Justice. In 1985 Kiribati had a police force of 236 under the command of a Commissioner of Police. The Commissioner of Police is also responsible for prisons, immigration, fire service (both domestic and airport) and firearms licensing.

Religion. The majority of the population belong to the Roman Catholic or Protestant (Congregational) church; there are small numbers of Seventh-day Adventist, Mormons, Baha'i and Church of God.

Education. In 1985 the government maintained boarding school had an enrolment of 467 pupils and there were 108 primary schools, with a total of 13,308 pupils, 5 secondary schools with 970 pupils, and 2 community high schools with 587 pupils. The Government also maintains a teachers' training college with 90 students in 1985 and a marine training school which offers training for about 70 merchant seamen each year. The Tarawa Technical Institute at Betio offers a variety of part-time and evening technical and commercial courses and had 461 students in 1985.

In 1978, 120 islanders were in overseas countries for secondary and further education or training.

Welfare. Government maintains free medical and other services. There are few towns, and the people are almost without exception landed proprietors, thus eliminating child vagrancy and housing problems to a large extent, except in the Tarawa urban area. Destitution is almost unknown. There were 16 doctors in 1986. There is a general hospital on Tarawa and dispensaries on other islands, with 283 beds.

DIPLOMATIC REPRESENTATIVES

Of Kiribati in Great Britain
High Commissioner: (Vacant).

Of Great Britain in Kiribati (Tarawa)
High Commissioner: Charles Thompson.

Of Kiribati in the USA
Ambassador: Atenroi Ba'teke, OBE (resides in Tarawa).

Books of Reference

Kiribati, Aspects of History. Univ. of South Pacific, 1979
Bailey, E., *The Christmas Island Story.* London, 1977
Cowell, R., *Structure of Gilbertese.* Suva, 1950
Grimble, Sir Arthur, *A Pattern of Islands.* London, 1953.—*Return to the Islands.* London, 1957
Maude, H. E., *Of Islands and Men.* London, 1968.—*Evolution of the Gilbertese Boti.* Suva, 1977
Sabatier, E., *Astride the Equator.* Melbourne, 1978
Whincup, T., *Nareau's Nation.* London, 1979

KOREA

Capital: Seoul
Population: 41·8m. (1987)
GNP per capita: US$2,850 (1987)

Han Kook

HISTORY. Korea was united in a single kingdom under the Silla dynasty from 668. China, which claimed a vague suzerainty over Korea, recognized Korea's independence in 1895. Korea concluded trade agreements with the USA (1882), Great Britain, Germany (1883). After the Russo-Japanese war of 1904–5 Korea was virtually a Japanese protectorate until it was formally annexed by Japan on 29 Aug. 1910 thus ending the rule of the Yi dynasty which had begun in 1392.

Following the collapse of Japan in 1945, American and Russian forces entered Korea to enforce the surrender of the Japanese troops there, dividing the country for mutual military convenience into two portions separated by the 38th parallel of latitude. Negotiations between the Americans and Russians regarding the future of Korea broke down in May 1946.

On 25 June 1950 the North Korean forces crossed the 38th parallel and invaded South Korea. The same day, the Security Council of the United Nations asked all member states to render assistance to the Republic of Korea. When the UN forces had reached the Manchurian border Chinese troops entered the war on the side of the North Koreans on 26 Nov. 1950 and penetrated deep into the south. By the beginning of April 1951, however, the UN forces had regained the 38th parallel. On 23 June 1951 Y. A. Malik, President of the Security Council, suggested a cease-fire, and on 10 July representatives of Gen. Ridgway met representatives of the North Koreans and of the Chinese Volunteer Army. An agreement was signed on 27 July 1953.

For the contributions of member-nations of the United Nations to the war, *see* THE STATESMAN'S YEAR-BOOK, 1954, p. 1195, and 1956, p. 1180.

On 16 Aug. 1953 the USA and Korea signed a mutual defence pact and on 28 Nov. 1956 a treaty of friendship, commerce and navigation.

On 4 July 1972 it was announced in Seoul and Pyongyang (North Korea) that talks had taken place aimed at 'the peaceful unification of the fatherland as early as possible'. In Nov. 1984 agreement was reached to form a joint economic committee.

A North Korean–UN agreement of 6 Sept. 1976 established a joint security area 850 metres in diameter, divided into 2 equal parts to ensure the separation of the two sides.

AREA AND POPULATION. South Korea is bounded north by the demilitarized zone (separating it from North Korea), east by the Sea of Japan, south by the Korea Strait (separating it from Japan) and west by the Yellow Sea. The area was (1985) 99,022 sq. km (38,232 sq. miles). The population (census, 1 Nov. 1985) was 40,466,577 (male, 20,280,857). Estimate (1987) 41,826,706.

The areas (in sq. km) and 1985 census populations of the Regions were as follows:

Region	sq. km	1985	Region	sq. km	1985
Seoul (city)	627	9,645,824	South Chungchong	8,807	3,001,538
Pusan (city)	433	3,516,768	North Cholla	8,052	2,202,218
Taegu (city)	455	2,030,649	South Cholla	12,189	3,748,442
Inchon (city)	201	1,387,475	North Kyongsang	19,427	3,013,276
Kyonggi	10,875	4,794,240	South Kyongsang	11,850	3,519,121
Kangwon	16,894	1,726,029	Cheju	1,825	489,458
North Chungchong	7,430	1,391,084			

The chief cities (populations, census 1985) are:

Seoul	9,645,824	Kwangchu	905,896	Masan	449,236
Pusan	3,516,768	Taejon	866,303	Seongnam	447,832
Taegu	2,030,649	Ulsan	551,219	Suweon	430,827
Inchon	1,387,475	Puch'on	456,311	Chonchu	426,490

CLIMATE. The extreme south has a humid warm temperate climate while the rest of the country experiences continental temperate conditions. Rainfall is concentrated in the period April to Sept. and ranges from 40″ (1,020 mm) to 60″ (1,520 mm). Pusan. Jan. 36°F (2·2°C), July 76°F (24·4°C). Annual rainfall 56″ (1,407 mm). Seoul. Jan. 23°F (–5°C), July 77°F (25°C). Annual rainfall 50″ (1,250 mm).

CONSTITUTION AND GOVERNMENT. A new constitution was approved by national referendum in Oct. 1987 and came into force on 25 Feb. 1988. It provides for a President, to be directly elected for a single 7-year term (by an electoral college of 5,271 directly-elected members), a State Council of ministers whom he appoints and leads, and a National Assembly (276 members) directly elected for 4 years (184 from 2-member constituencies and 92 by proportional representation).

The National Assembly elected on 25 March 1981 comprised 151 members of the Democratic Justice Party, 81 Democratic Korea Party, 25 Korean National Party, 8 from other parties and 11 independents.

President of the Republic: Roh Tae-woo (took office 25 Feb. 1988).

The Cabinet at Feb. 1988 was composed as follows:

Prime Minister: Lee Hyun-jae.

Deputy Prime Minister and Economic Planning: Rha Woong-bae. *Foreign Affairs:* Choi Kwang-soo. *Home Affairs:* Lee Sang-hee. *Finance:* SaKong-Il. *Justice:* Chung Hae-chang. *National Defence:* Oh Ja-bok. *Education:* Kim Young-sik. *Sports:* Cho Sang-ho. *Agriculture, Forestry-Fisheries:* Yun Kun-hwan. *Trade and Industry:* Ahn Byong-wha. *Energy and Resources:* Lee Bong-suh. *Construction:* Choe Dong-sup. *Health and Social Affairs:* Kwon E-hyock. *Labour Affairs:* Choi Myung-hun. *Transportation:* Rhee Bomb-june. *Communications:* Oh Myung. *Culture and Information:* Chung Han-mo. *Government Administration:* Kim Yong-kap. *Science and Technology:* Lee Kwan. *National Unification:* Lee Hong-koo. *Second State Minister for Political Affairs:* Cho Kyung-hee. *Office of Legislation:* Hyun Hong-choo. *Patriots and Veterans Affairs Agency:* Juhn Suk-hong.

National flag: White charged in the centre with the *yang-um* in red and blue and with 4 black *pal-kwar* trigrams.

Local government: South Korea is divided into 9 provinces *(Do)* and 4 cities with provincial status (Seoul, Pusan, Taegu and Inchon); the provinces are sub-divided into 139 districts *(Gun)* and 57 cities *(Si)*.

DEFENCE. Military service is compulsory for 30-36 months in all services.

Army. The Army is organized in 19 infantry divisions, 2 mechanized infantry divisions, 7 independent special forces brigades, 2 anti-aircraft artillery brigades, 2 surface-to-air missile brigades, 1 army aviation brigade and 2 surface-to-surface battalions. Equipment includes 350 M-47 and 950 M-48A5 main battle tanks. Army aviation equipment includes about 200 Hughes 500 and 8 AH-1G Huey Cobra helicopters for anti-armour operations, observation and liaison, plus 60 UH-1 Iroquois transport helicopters. Strength (1988) 542,000, with a Regular Army Reserve of 1·4m. and a Homeland Reserve Defence Force of 3·3m. Para-military Civilian Defence Corps, 3·5m.

Navy. The Fleet comprises 2 new very small submarines (built in South Korea), 2 indigenously built modern frigates, 11 aged (1943–46) *ex*-US destroyers, 4 equally old *ex*-US frigates (former fast transports, *ex*-destroyer escorts), 4 new missile corvettes, 12 gun corvettes, 11 fast missile patrol craft, 65 fast attack craft, 10 fast gunboats, 3 coastal patrol boats, 8 coastal minesweepers, 8 landing ships, 7 medium landing craft, 20 utility landing craft, 1 repair ship, 7 surveying vessels, 2 salvage ships, 4 supply ships, 6 oilers, 13 auxiliary ships, 35 service craft, and 2 tugs. Nearly all South Korea's naval vessels are *ex*-US ships. The Navy has a small aviation element with 20 S-2A/F Tracker anti-submarine aircraft. Ten 500MD helicopters and 12 Alouette helicopters are operated by the Marine Corps.

It was reported that the first submarine built in South Korea entered service in 1983. Probably the first of a class of four or five, she displaces only 175 tons.

The South Korean Coastguard operates 25 small ships and over 200 light vessels including rescue craft and tugs.

Personnel in 1988 totalled 29,000 in the Navy; plus 25,000 in the Marine Corps.

Air Force. With a 1988 strength of about 33,000 men, the Air Force is undergoing rapid expansion with US assistance. Its combat aircraft include 36 F-16C/D Fighting Falcons being delivered in 1986–87, about 75 F-4D/E Phantoms, 78 F-5A/B tactical fighters, more than 200 F-5E/F tactical fighters (being delivered from local production), 20 OV-10 Bronco light strike aircraft, 6 RF-5A reconnaissance fighters, 10 O-2A forward air control aircraft and 10 Hughes 500-D Defender helicopters. There are also 10 C-54 and 10 C-123 piston-engined transports, 2 HS.748s, 1 Boeing 737 and 1 DC-6 for VIP transport; UH-1, Bell 212 and Bell 412 transport helicopters, and T-41, T-28, T-33 and T-37C trainers.

ECONOMY

Planning. The fifth 5-year social and economic plan (1982–86) was revised in 1983 to aim at an annual growth rate of 7·5% from 1984–86.

Budget. The 1986 budget balanced at 13,800,000m. won of which 31% defence and 20% education.

Currency. Notes are issued by the Bank of Korea in denominations of 10,000, 5,000, 1,000 and 500 *won* and coin in denominations of 500, 100, 50, 10, 5 and 1 *won*. The exchange rate is determined daily by the Bank of Korea. In March 1988, 761 *won*=US$1; 1,347·38 *won*=£1 sterling.

Banking. State-run banks include the Bank of Korea, the Korean Development Bank, the Medium & Small Industry Bank, the Citizen's National Bank, the Korea Exchange Bank, the National Agricultural Co-operatives Federation, the Federation of Fisheries Co-operatives serving as banking and credit institutions for farmers and fishermen, the Korea Housing Bank, the Export and Import Bank of Korea.

There are 5 commercial banks: the Bank of Seoul & Trust Co. Ltd, the Cho Heung Bank Ltd, the Commercial Bank of Korea, the Korea First Bank, the Hanil Bank, Ltd, the Taegu Bank Ltd. The Bank of Korea is the central bank and the only note-issuing bank, the authorized purchaser of domestically produced gold.

In addition, there are non-bank financial institutions consisting of 19 insurance companies, the Land Bank of Korea, the Credit Guarantee Fund, 10 short-term financial companies, 211 mutual credit companies, and the Merchant Banking Corporation.

ENERGY AND NATURAL RESOURCES

Electricity. Electricity generated (1986) was 65,000m. kwh. Supply 100 and 220 volts; 60 Hz.

Oil. The KODECO Energy Co. and the Indonesian state-run oil company Pertamin are developing an oil field off the coast of Indonesia's Madura Island. KODECO began drilling operations in 1982 and began producing oil in Sept. 1985 from the Madura field, which contains 22·1m. bbls of proven oil deposits. The state-run Korean Petroleum Development Corp. (PEDCO) and the US company Hadson Petroleum International are exploring for oil in the southern part of the

Fifth Continental Shelf oil mining block off the coast of the Korean Peninsula. Oil worth US$6,490m. was imported in 1985.

Minerals. Mineral deposits are mostly small, with the exception of tungsten; the Sangdong mine is one of the world's largest deposits of tungsten. Output, 1985, included (in tonnes): Anthracite coal, 22·4m.; iron ore, 670,000; tungsten ore, 4,643; kaolin, 634,202; copper ore, 1,228; lead ore, 18,947; gold, 2,345; silver, 126,133; zinc ore, 92,509.

Agriculture. The arable land in South Korea comprised 2,144,000 hectares in 1985, of which 1,325,000 hectares were rice paddies and 819,000 hectares dry fields.

Production (1985, in 1,000 tonnes) of rice was 5,262; of total crops from dry fields, 1,364, including barley, 584; of cash crops: Vegetables, 7,083; fruits, 1,463.

Output of tobacco manufactures, a government monopoly, was 94,524 tonnes in 1983. In 1986 cattle numbered 2,864,000; pigs, 2,853,000; poultry, 52m.

Fisheries. Fishery exports (1985) US$960m. In 1985, 603 Korean deep-sea fishing vessels were operating overseas. In 1982, there was a total of 86,515 boats (808,570 gross tons). The fish catch (inland and marine) was 2,990,000 tonnes in 1985.

INDUSTRY AND TRADE

Industry. Manufacturing industry, which (1985) employed 3,654,000 persons, was concentrated primarily in 1985 on oil, petrochemical, chemical fibre, construction, iron and steel, cement, machinery, shipbuilding, automobile and electronics.

Commerce. In 1986 the total exports were US$33,913m., while imports were US$29,707m. In 1985 USA provided 20·8% and Japan 24·3% of imports; USA received 35·5% of exports, Japan 15%.

Major exports, 1985, included (in US$1m.): Heavy and chemical products, 16,466; light industrial products, 11,173. Major imports included: Crude oil and raw materials, 17,400; capital goods, 11,079; grain and other goods, 1,637.

Total trade between Korea and UK (British Department of Trade returns, in £1,000 sterling):

	1984	1985	1986	1987
Imports to UK	443,819	480,448	661,975	936,038
Exports and re-exports from UK	219,406	247,887	288,421	427,229

Tourism. In 1986 there were 1,659,000 foreign tourists. They spent about US$784m. in 1985.

COMMUNICATIONS

Roads. In 1983 there were 53,936 km of roads. In 1985 motor vehicles totalled 1,113,430 including 412,739 trucks, 128,309 buses, 556,659 passenger cars.

Railways. In Dec. 1985, 6,285 km of railways existed, including 3,113·4 km of commercial railways, 441 km of which were electrified. In 1985 railways carried 519m. passengers and 58m. tonnes of freight.

Aviation. In Dec. 1985, 35 countries maintained aviation agreement with Korea and had 34 air routes with 24 cities in 16 countries. The Ministry of Transportation opened Seoul-Kuala Lumpur-Bangkok cargo route and Seoul-Singapore-Bangkok and Cheju-Pusan-Tōkyō passenger routes in 1985.

In Dec. 1985 Korea had 108 commercial aircraft (46 Korean Air Lines passenger-cargo planes, 18 light planes and 35 helicopters). In 1985, 3·47m. passengers and 66,000 tons of cargo were carried on domestic routes and 4·41m. passengers on international routes.

Shipping. In Dec. 1985, there were 24 first-grade ports and 22 second-grade ports, and 7,516,000 gross tons in various vessels. Of the total tonnage, national-flag ocean-going vessels accounted for 6,118,000 tons, chartered vessels for 966,000 tons and coastal passenger-cargo vessels for 432,000 tons. Passenger ships accounted for 43,000 tons, cargo vessels 5,954,000 tons and oil tankers 1,519,000.

Post and Telecommunications. Post offices total 2,556 (1985); telephones (all government-owned) were 6,517,395 in 1985. The fourth satellite earth station was opened in Jan. 1985, bringing the number of communications circuits *via* satellite to 2,290. There were 4·73m. television receivers in 1985.

Cinemas. In 1983 there were 452 with a seating capacity of 400,000.

Newspapers (1985). There were 25 daily papers, including 6 national dailies and 2 in English appearing in Seoul.

RELIGION, EDUCATION AND WELFARE

Religion. Basically the religions of Korea have been Animism, Buddhism (introduced A.D. 372) and Confucianism, which was the official faith from 1392 to 1910. Catholic converts from China introduced Christianity in the 18th century, but the ban on Roman Catholics was not lifted until 1882. Christian population in 1983 was 6,927,833.

Education. In 1985 Korea had 4,856,752 pupils enrolled in 6,519 elementary schools, 2,782,173 pupils in 2,371 middle schools and 2,152,802 pupils in 1,602 high schools (including 635 vocational schools).

For higher education, 1,018,236 students attended 312 universities, colleges and junior colleges in 1985. There are 86 graduate schools granting master's degrees in 2 years and doctor's degrees in 4 years, where 14,274 students attended in 1985. An Open University was inaugurated in March 1982.

The Korean language belongs to the Ural–Altaic group, is polysyllabic, agglutinative and highly developed syntactically. The modern Korean alphabet of 10 vowels and 14 consonants forms a script known as Hangul.

Health. In 1985 there were 29,596 physicians, 3,789 oriental medical doctors, 5,436 dentists, 6,247 midwives, 59,104 nurses, and 29,866 pharmacists. There were 16,679 hospitals and clinics in 1985 with 74,365 beds.

DIPLOMATIC REPRESENTATIVES

Of Korea in Great Britain (4 Palace Gate, London, W8 5NF)
Ambassador: Jay Hee Oh (accredited 16 Dec. 1987).

Of Great Britain in Korea (4 Chung-Dong, Chung-Ku, Seoul)
Ambassador and Consul-General: Lawrence J. Middleton, CMG.

Of Korea in the USA (2370 Massachusetts Ave., NW, Washington, D.C., 20008)
Ambassador: Kim Kyong-Won.

Of the USA in Korea (Sejong-Ro, Seoul)
Ambassador: James R. Lilley.

Books of Reference

A Handbook of Korea. 4th ed. Seoul, 1982
Guide to Investment in Korea. Economic Planning Board. Seoul, 1980
Korea Annual 1983. 20th ed. Seoul, 1983
Korea Statistical Year Book. Seoul, 1981
Major Economic Indicators, 1979–80. Seoul, 1980
Monthly Statistics of Korea. Seoul
Hastings, M., *The Korean War.* London, 1987
Lew, H. J., *New Life Korean–English, English–Korean Dictionary.* 2 vols. Seoul, 1947–50
Martin, S. F. (ed.), *A Korean–English Dictionary.* Yale Univ. Press, 1968
Srivastava, M.P., *The Korean Conflict: Search for Unification.* New Delhi, 1982

NORTH KOREA

Capital: Pyongyang
Population: 20·55m. (1986)
GNP per capita: US$1,180 (1985)

Chosun Minchu-chui
Inmin Konghwa-guk

HISTORY. In northern Korea the Russians, arriving on 8 Aug. 1945, one month ahead of the Americans, established a Communist-led 'Provisional Government'. The newly created Korean Communist Party merged in 1946 with the New National Party into the Korean Workers' Party. In July 1946 the KWP, with the remaining pro-Communist groups and non-party people, formed the United Democratic Patriotic Front. On 25 Aug. 1948 the Communists organized elections for a Supreme People's Assembly, both in Soviet-occupied North Korea (212 deputies) and in US-occupied South Korea (360 deputies, of whom a certain number went to the North and took their seats). A People's Democratic Republic was proclaimed on 9 Sept. 1948. Proposals for talks between North and South Korea on reunification began in 1980, but have repeatedly broken down. A series of North-South economic talks began in 1985, and an exchange of visits between divided families was held. Relations with the USSR have intensified since 1985.

AREA AND POPULATION. North Korea is bounded north by China, east by the sea of Japan, west by the Yellow Sea and south by South Korea, from which it is separated by a demilitarized zone of 1,262 sq km. Its area is 120,538 sq. km. Population estimate in 1986, 20·55m. Rate of population increase, 2·2% per annum. Death rate, 1979: 4·4 per mille. Marriage is discouraged before the age of 32 for men and 29 for women. Expectation of life in 1986 was 74 years. The capital is Pyongyang, with 1·28m. inhabitants in 1981. Other large towns (with 1981 population): Hamhung (775,000); Chongjin (490,000); Kimchaek (formerly Songjin) (490,000); Wonsan (398,000); Sinuiju (305,000); Kaesong (259,000); Nampo (241,000); Haeju (213,000 in 1983).

CLIMATE. There is a warm temperate climate, though winters can be very cold in the north. Rainfall is concentrated in the summer months. Pyongyang. Jan. 18°F (–7·8°C), July 75°F (23·9°C). Annual rainfall 37" (916 mm).

CONSTITUTION AND GOVERNMENT. The political structure is based upon the Constitution of 27 Dec. 1972. The Constitution provides for a Supreme People's Assembly elected every 4 years by universal suffrage. Citizens of 17 years and over can vote and be elected. Elections were held in 1948, 1957, 1962, 1972, 1977, 1982 and 2 Nov. 1986. At the latter it was claimed that 100% of the electorate voted for the list of single candidates presented. There are 655 deputies. The government consists of the Administration Council directed by the Central People's Committee (*Secretary,* Chi Chang Ik). In Nov. 1985 several Commissions were set up superordinate to ministries within the Council.

In practice the country is ruled by the Korean Workers' (*i.e.,* Communist) Party which elects a Central Committee which in turn appoints a Politburo. In March 1988 this was composed of: Marshal Kim Il Sung, *(General Secretary of the Party, President of the Republic, Chairman of the Central People's Committee, Supreme Commander of the Armed Forces)*; Kim Jong Il (Kim Il Sung's son and designated successor) *(Vice-President of the Republic)*; O Jin U *(Defence Minister)* (The latter 3 constituting the Politburo's Presidium); Kang Song San; Li Jong Ok *(Vice-President of the Republic)*; Pak Sung Chul *(Vice-President of the Republic)*; Rim Chun Chu *(Vice-President of the Republic)*; So Chol; Kim Yong Nam *(Deputy Prime Minister, Foreign Minister)*; Kim Hwan; Yon Hyong Muk; O Guk Ryol; So Yun Sok; Li Gun Mo *(Prime Minister)*; Ho Dam *(Deputy Prime Minister)*; Hong

Song Nam *(First Deputy Prime Minister)*. There were also 10 candidate members.

Ministers not full members of the Politburo include Kim Yun Hyok *(Deputy Prime Minister)*; Yun Gi Jong *(Finance)*; Chong Song Nam *(Foreign Economic Affairs)*; Pak Nam Gi *(Chairman, State Planning Commission)*; Kim Bok Sin; Chong Jun Gi, Kim Yun Hyok, Kim Chang Ju *(Deputy Prime Ministers)*; Choe Jong Gun *(Foreign Trade)*; Paek Hak Rim *(Public Security)*.

In 1981 the Party had some 2m. members.

There are also the puppet religious Chongu and Korean Social Democratic Parties and various organizations combined in a Fatherland Front.

National flag: Blue, red and blue horizontal stripes separated by narrow white bands. The red stripe bears a white circle within which is a red 5-pointed star.

National anthem: 'A chi mun bin na ra i gang san' (Shine bright, o dawn, on this land so fair'). Words by Pak Se Yong; music by Kim Won Gyun.

The country is divided into 13 administrative units: 4 cities (Pyongyang, Chongjin, Hamhung and Kaesong) and 9 provinces (capitals in brackets): South Pyongan (Nampo), North Pyongan (Sinuiju), Jagang (Kanggye), South Hwanghai (Haeju), North Hwanghai (Sariwon), North Kangwon (Wonsan), South Hamgyong (Hamheung), North Hamgyong (Chongjin), Yanggang (Hyesan). These are subdivided into 152 counties.

Local government is administered by 26,539 deputies in People's Assemblies at city/province, county and commune level. The latest elections were on 15 Nov. 1987.

DEFENCE. Military service is compulsory at the age of 16 for periods of 5-8 years in the Army and Navy and 3–4 years in the Air Force. In 1987 defence spending was 22% of GNP. North Korea adhered to the 1968 Non-Proliferation Treaty on nuclear weapons in 1985.

Army. The Army is organized in 2 armoured, 5 motorized infantry, 25 infantry and 2 anti-aircraft divisions; 8 armoured, 21 infantry and 25 special forces brigades; 250 artillery, 82 multiple-rocket-launcher and 6 surface-to-surface missile battalions. Equipment includes 2,900 T-34/-55/-62 and 175 Type-59 main battle tanks. Strength (1988) 750,000, with 500,000 reserves. There is also a paramilitary militia of some 3m. men and a ranger commando force of 100,000. The militia (men of 18–40 not in the armed forces or reserves, single women of 18–30) is estimated at 3m. It was announced in Jan. 1988 that 100,000 troops had been demobilized.

Navy. The Navy comprises 19 diesel-powered patrol submarines (15 *ex*-Chinese and indigenously-built and 4 *ex*-Soviet), 2 small frigates, 28 fast missile boats, 156 fast torpedo boats, 139 fast gunboats, 32 patrol vessels, 30 coastal patrol craft, 30 light gunboats, 8 medium landing ships, 25 utility landing craft, 20 mechanised landing craft, 100 small assault landing craft, 30 trawlers and auxiliaries, 2 *ex*-Soviet ocean tugs and 100 service craft. Up to 20 small submarines are reported as built locally with a dozen X-craft in commission. Personnel in 1988 totalled 33,000 officers and men with 40,000 reserves.

Air Force. The Air Force had a total of about 854 combat aircraft and 55,000 personnel in 1987. Since 1985 the USSR has supplied 50 supersonic MiG-23 interceptors and 30 SA3 surface-to-air missiles. Other equipment is believed to include about 160 supersonic MiG-21 interceptors, more than 100 F-6s (Chinese-built MiG-19s), 250 MiG-17s for ground attack and reconnaissance, 30 Su-7 fighter-bombers, 60 Il-28 twin-jet light bombers, 250 AN-2 light transport aircraft, 40 Mi-4 and Mi-8 transport helicopters and 80 US Hughes 300 and 500 helicopters.

INTERNATIONAL RELATIONS

North Korea is a member of WHO and an observer at UN.

ECONOMY

Planning. For previous plans *see* THE STATESMAN'S YEAR-BOOK, 1987–88. After a hiatus it was announced in Oct. 1986 that a third 7-year plan would run from 1987 to 1993. Steel production targets have been reduced (to 10m. tonnes) and more emphasis placed on export items, non-ferrous metals and fishery products.

Budget (in 1m. won) for calendar years:

	1982	1983	1984	1985	1986	1987
Revenue	22,680	24,384	26,305	27,439	28,539	30,308
Expenditure	22,204	24,018	26,158	27,329	28,396	30,308

Defence spending was 13·8% of the budget in 1987 (14% in 1986). Local government revenue in 1987: 4,185m. *won*; expenditure, 3,427m. *won*.

Currency. The monetary unit is the *won*, divided into 100 *jun*. In March 1988, US$1 = 0·94 *won*; £1 = 1·65 *won*. Tourist rate: US$1 = 2·26 *won*.

Weights and Measures. While the metric system is in force traditional measures are in frequent use. The *jungbo* = 1 hectare; the *ri* = 3,927 metres.

ENERGY AND NATURAL RESOURCES

Electricity. There are 3 thermal power stations and 4 hydro-electric plants. A nuclear power plant is being built with Soviet help. Output in 1986, was 40,000m. kwh. Installed capacity was 6·11m. kw in 1987. Hydro-electric potential exceeds 8m. kw. A hydro-electric plant and dam under construction on the Pukhan near Mount Kumgang has been denounced as a flood threat by the South Koreans, who are constructing a defensive 'Peace Dam' in retaliation.

Oil. Oilwells went into production in 1957. An oil pipeline from China came on stream in 1976. Crude oil refining capacity was 70,000 barrels a year in 1986.

Minerals. North Korea is rich in minerals. Estimated reserves in tonnes: Iron ore, 3,300m.; copper, 2·15m.; lead, 6m.; zinc, 12m.; coal, 11,990m.; uranium, 26m.; manganese, 6,500m. 37·5m. tonnes of coal were mined in 1986. 16m. tonnes of iron ore were extracted in 1984.

Agriculture. In 1982 there were 2·1m. hectares of arable land, including 635,000 hectares of paddy fields. In 1982, 38% of the population made a living from agriculture.

Collectivization took place between 1954 and 1958. 90% of the cultivated land is farmed by co-operatives. Land belongs either to the State or to co-operatives, and it is intended gradually to transform the latter into the former, but small individually-tended plots producing for 'farmers' markets' are tolerated as a 'transition measure'. Livestock farming is mainly carried on by large state farms.

There is a large-scale tideland reclamation project. There were 37,600 km of irrigation canals in 1976, making possible 2 rice harvests a year. In 1982 there were 133,000 tractors (15 h.p. units). The technical revolution in agriculture (nearly 95% of ploughing, etc., is mechanized) has considerably increased the yield of grain (sown on 2·3m. *jungbo* of land); rice production, 1986, was 2m. tonnes, other grains, 4·83m. tonnes. 1,895,000 tonnes of potatoes were produced in 1986.

Livestock, 1986: 1,122,000 cattle, 2·92m. pigs, 19m. poultry.

Forestry. Between 1961 and 1970, 800,000 hectares were afforested.

Fisheries. Catch in 1983: 1·6m. tonnes. There is a fishing fleet of 28,000 vessels including 19,000 motor vessels.

INDUSTRY AND TRADE

Industry. Industries were intensively developed by the Japanese, notably cotton spinning, hydro-electric power, cotton, silk and rayon weaving, and chemical fertilizers. Production (in tonnes) in 1982: Pig-iron, 4m.; crude steel, 4m.; rolled steel, 3·2m.; lead, 30,000; zinc, 140,000; copper, 48,000; ship-building, 400,000; chemical fertilizers, 620,000; chemicals, 20,000; synthetic resins, 90,000; cement (1986), 9,040; textiles (1986), 600m. metres; woven goods, 600m. metres; shoes, 40m. pairs; motor-cars (1986), 20,000; TV sets (1986), 240,000; refrigerators, 10,000. Annual steel production capacity was 4·3m. tonnes in 1987.

Labour. The economically-active population was 9m. in 1985. Industrial workers make up some 60% of the work force. Average monthly wage, 1984: 90 *won.*

Commerce. North Korea's largest trade partners have been USSR, China and Japan. Estimated exports, 1985: US$1,234·6m. (US$785·3m. to Communist countries); imports US$1,991·5m. (US$1,198·6m. from Communist countries). In Aug. 1987 140 Western banks declared North Korea in default on US$770m. in outstanding loans. In 1984 foreign debt was estimated at US$4,000m. (US$2,230m. to non-Communist countries). The chief exports are metal ores and products, the chief imports machinery and petroleum products.

Joint ventures with foreign firms have been permitted since 1984.

Trade with the USSR is based on 5-year agreements, the last of which was signed in 1986.

Exports to the USSR in 1986 (and 1985) were worth 450·7m. (404·4m.) roubles; imports from the USSR, 757·2m. (654·8m.) roubles.

Total trade between North Korea and UK (British Department of Trade returns, in £1,000 sterling):

	1983	1984	1985	1986	1987
Imports to UK	362	456	1,983	1,374	641
Exports and re-exports from UK	2,527	2,935	2,608	3,331	2,198

Tourism. A 40-year ban on non-Communist tourists was lifted in 1986.

COMMUNICATIONS

Roads. There were 22,000 km of road in 1984, including 240 km of motorways. There were 180,000 motor cars in 1982.

Railways. The two trunk-lines Pyongyang–Sinuiju and Pyongyang–Myongchon are both electrified, and the Pyongyang–Sariwon trunk is in course of electrification. The 'Wonra' line runs from Wonsan to Rajin and is electrified from Myongchon to Rajin and beyond to Tumangang. The Namdokchon–Toknam line was opened in 1983. Lines are under construction from Pukchong to Toksong, from Palwon to Kujang and Kanggye *via* Hyesan to Musan. The Hyesan–Samsok section of the latter opened to traffic in 1971. In 1988 there were 4,549 km of track, (2,706 km were electrified in 1984). In 1986, 89% of trains were hauled by electricity. In 1987 86% of all freight was transported by rail. A weekly service from Pyongyang to Beijing opened in 1983, and a twice-weekly service to Moscow in 1987.

Aviation. There are services to Moscow, Khabarovsk, Beijing and Hong Kong. An agreement envisaging a service from Pyongyang to Tōkyō was signed in 1986. There are domestic flights from Pyongyang to Hamhung and Chongjin.

Shipping. The leading ports are Chongjin, Wonsan and Hungnam. Nampo, the port of Pyongyang, has been dredged and expanded. Pyongyang is connected to Nampo by railway and river. In 1987 the ocean-going merchant fleet numbered 71 vessels totalling 407,253 GRT.

The biggest navigable river is the Yalu, 698 km up to the Hyesan district.

Post and Broadcasting. There is a central TV station at Pyongyang and stations at Kaesong and Mansudae. In 1982 there were some 200,000 television receivers. The central broadcasting station is Radio Pyongyang. There are several local stations and a station for overseas broadcasts. There were some 10,000 telephones in 1983.

Newspapers. There were 11 newspapers in 1984. The party newspaper is *Nodong* (or *Rodong*) *Sinmun* (Workers' Daily News). Circulation about 600,000.

JUSTICE, RELIGION, EDUCATION AND WELFARE

Justice. The judiciary consists of the Supreme Court, whose judges are elected by the Assembly for 3 years; provincial courts; and city or county people's courts. The procurator-general, appointed by the Assembly, has supervisory powers over the judiciary and the administration; the Supreme Court controls the judicial administration.

Religion. According to the 1972 Constitution 'The people shall enjoy the freedom of religion as well as the freedom of anti-religious propaganda'. There are 3 religious organizations: The Buddhist League, the Chondoist Society and the Christians' League.

Education. Free compulsory universal technical education lasts 11 years: 1 preschool year, 4 years primary education starting at the age of 6, followed by 6 years secondary.

In 1988 there were 47,600 kindergartens. In 1980 there were some 10,000 11-year schools. In 1982–83 there were 5·2m. pupils and 110,000 teachers, and nearly 1m. students in higher education. In 1985 there were 216 institutes of higher education, including 3 universities—Kim Il Sung University (founded 1946), Kim Chaek Technical University, Pyongyang Medical School—and an Academy of Sciences (founded 1952).

In 1977–78 Kim Il Sung University had some 17,000 students.

Health. Medical treatment is free. In 1982 there were 1,531 general hospitals, 979 specialised hospitals and 5,414 clinics. There were 24 doctors and 130 hospital beds per 10,000 population in 1983.

DIPLOMATIC REPRESENTATIVE

Of North Korea to the United Nations
Ambassador: Pak Gil Yon.

Books of Reference

An, T. S., *North Korea in Transition.* Westport, 1983;–*North Korea: a Political Handbook.* Washington, 1983

Baik Bong, *Kim Il Sung: Biography.* 3 vols. New York, 1969–70

Chung, C.-S., (ed.), *North Korean Communism: A Comparative Analysis.* Seoul, 1980

Kihl, Y. W., *Politics and Policies in Divided Korea.* Boulder, 1984

Kim Han Gil, *Modern History of Korea.* Pyongyang, 1979

Kim Il Sung, *Works.* Pyongyang, 1980–83

Kim, Y. S., (ed.), *The Economy of the Korean Democratic People's Republic, 1945–1977.* Kiel, 1979

Koh, B. C., *The Foreign Policy Systems of North and South Korea.* Berkeley, 1984

Park, J. K., and Kim, J.-G., *The Politics of North Korea.* Boulder, 1979

Scalapino, R. A., and Lee, C.-S., *Communism in Korea. Part I: The Movement. Part II: The Society.* Univ. of Calif. Press, 1972—and Kim, J-Y. (eds.), *North Korea Today: Strategic and Domestic Issues.* Univ. of California Press, 1983

Suh, D.-S., *Korean Communism, 1945–1980: A Reference Guide to the Political System.* Honolulu, 1981

Yang, S. C., *Korea and Two Regimes: Kim Il Sung and Park Chung Hee.* Cambridge, Mass., 1981

KUWAIT

Capital: Kuwait
Population: 1·77m. (1986)
GNP per capita: US$11,510 (1985)

Dowlat al Kuwait

HISTORY. The ruling dynasty was founded by Shaikh Sabah al-Owel, who ruled from 1756 to 1772. In 1899 the then ruler Shaikh Mubarak concluded a treaty with Great Britain wherein, in return for the assurance of British protection, he undertook not to alienate any of his territory without the agreement of Her Majesty's Government. In 1914 the British Government recognized Kuwait as an independent government under British protection. On 19 June 1961 an agreement reaffirmed the independence and sovereignty of Kuwait and recognized the Government of Kuwait's responsibility for the conduct of internal and external affairs; the agreement of 1899 was terminated and Her Majesty's Government expressed their readiness to assist the Government of Kuwait should they request such assistance.

AREA AND POPULATION. Kuwait is bounded east by the Gulf, north and west by Iraq and south by Saudi Arabia, with an area of about 6,880 sq. miles (17,819 sq. km); the total population at the census of 1985 was 1,695,128, of which about 60% were non-Kuwaitis. Estimate (1986) 1·77m. Over 78% speak Arabic, the official language, while 10% speak Kurdish and 4% Iranian (Farsi). English is also used as a second language.

The country is divided into 4 governorates: The capital (comprising Kuwait City, Kuwait's 9 islands and territorial and shared territorial waters), with an area of 983 sq. km (population 167,750 at 1985 census); Hawalli, 620 sq. km (943,250); Ahmadi, 4,665 sq. km (304,662) and Jahra, 11,550 sq. km (279,466).

The chief cities were (1980) Kuwait, the capital (60,525), and its suburbs Hawalli (152,402) and as-Salimiya (145,991).

The Neutral Zone (3,560 sq. miles, 5,700 sq. km), jointly owned and administered by Kuwait and Saudi Arabia from 1922 to 1966, was partitioned between the two countries in May 1966, but the exploitation of the oil and other natural resources will continue to be shared.

CLIMATE. Kuwait has a dry, desert climate which is cool in winter but very hot and humid in summer. Rainfall is extremely light. Kuwait. Jan. 56°F (13·5°C), July 99°F (36·6°C). Annual rainfall 5″ (125 mm).

RULER. HH Shaikh Jabir al-Ahmad al-Jabir al-Sabah the 13th Amir of Kuwait, succeeded on 31 Dec. 1977.

CONSTITUTION AND GOVERNMENT. In 1976 the Amir dissolved the Assembly and at the same time parts of the Constitution were suspended. Elections were held in Feb. 1985 for the 50-member National Assembly.

The Cabinet in Jan. 1988 was composed as follows:

Prime Minister: HRH Crown Prince Shaikh Saad al-Abdullah as Salim as Sabah.
Deputy Prime Minister, Foreign Affairs: Shaikh Sabah al Ahmad al Jabir as Sabah. *Finance and Economy:* Jassim Mohammed al Kharafi. *Education:* Anwar Abdullah al Nuri. *Waqfs and Islamic Affairs:* Khaled Ahmed Saad al Jasir. *Defence:* Shaikh Nawaf al Ahmad al Jabir as Sabah. *Justice, Legal and Administrative Affairs:* Dari Abdullah al Uthman. *Public Works:* Abdel Rahman Ibrahim al Houti. *Public Health:* Dr Abdurrahman Abdullah al Awadi. *Planning:* Mohammed Soleiman Said Ali. *Oil:* Shaikh Ali al Khalifa al Adhibi as Sabah. *Communications:* Khalid Jumayan Salim al Jumayan. *Electricity and Water:* Mohammed as Saad Abdel Moshin al Rifai. *Information:* Shaikh Nasser Mohammed al Ahmad al Jabir as Sabah. *Social Affairs and Labour:* Jabir Mubarak

al Hamad. *Interior:* Shaikh Salim as Sabah as Salim as Sabah. *Trade and Industry:* Faisal Abdel Razzaq al Khaled.

There are 5 Ministers of State.

Flag: Three horizontal stripes of green, white, red, with a black trapezium based on the hoist.

DEFENCE. Military service is compulsory for 24 months (university students, 12 months).

Army. Kuwait maintains a small, well-equipped and mobile army of 2 armoured and 2 mechanized infantry brigades and 1 surface-to-surface missile battalion. Equipment includes 90 Vickers Mk I, 10 Centurion and 160 Chieftain main battle tanks. Strength (1988) about 13,000 men.

Navy. The flotillas comprise 6 fast missile craft, 2 larger fast missile gunboats (all eight West German-built); 40 coastal patrol craft built by Vosper/Thornycroft; 13 light patrol boats; 27 US-built very fast cutters; 6 general purpose launches; 6 Vosper Singapore-built landing craft, 4 other amphibious ships and 4 tugs.

Six hovercraft are reportedly to be ordered, and probably fast attack craft, patrol vessels and mine countermeasures vessels.

A Japanese firm was awarded the contract for the construction of a base to accommodate the planned expansion of the coastguard force.

In 1988 personnel totalled 1,100 officers and men.

Air Force. From a small initial combat force the Air Force has grown rapidly. It has 2 squadrons with 25 Mirage F1-C fighters and 4 Mirage F1-B 2-seat trainers; and 2 squadrons with 30 A-4KU/TA-4KU Skyhawk attack aircraft. Other equipment includes 2 DC-9 jet transports, 4 L-100-30 Hercules turboprop transports and 12 Hawk jet trainers, 10 Puma, 6 Exocet missile-armed Super Puma and 25 missile-armed Gazelle helicopters. Hawk surface-to-air missiles are in service. Personnel strength (1988) about 2,000.

INTERNATIONAL RELATIONS

Membership. Kuwait is a member of UN, the Arab League, OPEC and OAPEC.

ECONOMY

Budget. The financial year runs 1 April–31 March. In 1985–86 revenue, KD 3,116m.; expenditure, KD 4,175m.

Currency. The Kuwait *dinar* of 1,000 *fils* replaced the Indian external rupee on 1 April 1961. Coins in circulation are, 1, 5, 10, 20, 50 and 100 fils and notes of KD, 10, 5, 1, ½ and ¼. In March 1988, £1 sterling = KD 0·488; US$1 = KD 0·278.

Banking. In addition to the Central Bank, 7 commercial banks (Bank of Kuwait and the Middle East, National Bank of Kuwait, Commercial Bank, Gulf Bank, Al-Ahli Bank, Burgan Bank and Bank of Bahrain and Kuwait) and 3 specialized banks (Credit and Savings Bank, Kuwait Real Estate Bank and Industrial Bank of Kuwait) operate in Kuwait. There is also the Kuwait Finance House, which is not subject to the control of the Central Bank.

Weights and Measures. The metric system was adopted in 1962.

ENERGY AND NATURAL RESOURCES

Electricity. 16,360m. kwh. were produced in 1986. Supply 240 volts; 50 Hz.

Oil. The Kuwait Petroleum Corporation (KPC) was set up in 1980 to reorganize, integrate and develop the oil sector. The functions of the operating oil companies have been reallocated: Kuwait Oil Company (KOC) specializes in exploration, drilling and production in all areas; Kuwait National Petroleum Company (KNPC) is responsible for refining, local marketing and gas liquefaction operations; Kuwait Oil Tankers Company (KOTC) is in charge of transporting crude oil, liquefied gas and oil products to various world markets; Petrochemical Industries

Company is in charge of use of hydrocarbon resources to set up diverse petro-chemical industries, and the International Marketing Department of KPC markets and sells oil and gas worldwide.

Oil revenues in 1983–84 were KD2,787·6m. Crude oil production in 1987, 61m. tonnes. As well as selling crude oil, Kuwait is refining, marketing refined products, and prospecting and producing abroad. Production of petroleum products in 1984, 24,266,000 tonnes.

Gas. Production (1983) 170,200m. cu. ft.

Agriculture. Cultivable land area is 8·6%. A five-year development plan was initiated in 1981–82 to increase vegetable growing areas with the aim of meeting 40% of projected domestic demand. Major crops (production, 1986, in tonnes) were melons (2,000), tomatoes (15,000), onions (2,000), dates (2,000), radishes, clover.

Livestock (1986): Cattle, 21,000; sheep, 265,000; goats, 344,000; poultry, 8m.

Fisheries. Shrimp fishing is becoming one of the important non-oil industries.

INDUSTRY AND TRADE

Industry. Industries, apart from oil, include boat building, fishing, food produc-tion, petrochemicals, gases and construction. The manufacture or import of alcoholic drinks is prohibited.

Labour. In 1980 the labour force totalled 813,000, with 492,000 employed.

Commerce. The port of Kuwait formerly served mainly as an entrepôt for goods for the interior, for the export of skins and wool, and for pearl fishing. Entrepôt trade continues but, with the development of the oil industry, is declining in importance. Pearl fishing is now on a small scale. Dhows and launches of traditional construc-tion are still built.

In 1984 total imports were valued at KD2,778m.; exports, KD3,517m. Oil accounted for 83·5% of exports at KD2,938m.

Total trade between Kuwait and UK (British Department of Trade returns, in £1,000 sterling):

	1983	1984	1985	1986	1987
Imports to UK [1]	67,281	141,606	156,912	58,517	81,530
Exports and re-exports from UK	333,273	301,520	347,915	300,586	225,168

[1] Including oil.

Tourism. There were 116,000 visitors in 1985.

COMMUNICATIONS

Roads. In 1985 there were 3,590 km and the number of vehicles was 535,730.

Aviation. There were 29,000 scheduled and unscheduled flights to and from Kuwait International Airport in 1983, carrying about 3m. passengers and 72,000 tonnes of freight. Kuwait Airways flew over 5,000 flights in 1983, carrying about 1·5m. passengers. Forty airlines operate at the airport.

Shipping. The Kuwaiti merchant fleet in 1982 comprised 217 vessels (of over 100 tonnes) with a total gross tonnage of 2,014,379. The oil terminal is at Mina al-Ahmadi (receiving 3,400 oil tankers a year), while the main ports for other traf-fic are at Shuwaikh, Doha and Shuaiba.

Post and Broadcasting. There were (1984), 419,200 telephones and there is a broadcasting and a television station. In 1985 there were 580,000 TV receivers and 750,000 radios.

Cinemas. In 1984 there were 14 cinemas, including 2 drive-ins.

Newspapers. In 1987 there were 5 daily newspapers in Arabic and 2 in English, with a combined circulation of about 418,000.

JUSTICE, RELIGION, EDUCATION AND WELFARE

Justice. In 1960 Kuwait adopted a unified judicial system covering all levels of courts. These are: Courts of Summary Justice, Courts of the First Instance, Supreme Court of Appeal, Court of Cassation, Constitutional Court and State Security Court. Islamic Sharia is a major source of legislation.

Religion. In 1980 about 78% of the population were Sunni Moslems, 14% Shia Moslems, 6% Christians and 2% others.

Education. In 1983–84 there were 346,350 pupils in 485 government schools: 21,502 in kindergartens, 130,073 in primary schools, 120,325 in intermediate schools and 74,450 in secondary schools. There were also (1983–84) 87,000 pupils in 72 Arab and foreign private schools. In 1983–84 there were 2,378 students in the Teachers' Training Institute, 1,186 in the Institute of Applied Technology, 1,500 in the Religious Institute, 2,603 in the Commercial Institute and 340 in the Clinical Institute. The University of Kuwait had 14,000 students in 1984.

Health. Medical services are free to all residents. There were (1983) 15 hospitals with 6,952 beds in the State and 54 clinics and health centres. The Ministry of Health employed 2,872 doctors and 8,926 nursing staff in 1983.

DIPLOMATIC REPRESENTATIVES

Of Kuwait in Great Britain (45 Queen's Gate, London, SW7)
Ambassador: Ghazi Mohammed Amin Al-Rayes (accredited 12 Feb. 1981).

Of Great Britain in Kuwait (Arabian Gulf St., Kuwait)
Ambassador: P. R. M. Hinchcliffe, CMG, CVO.

Of Kuwait in the USA (2940 Tilden St., NW, Washington, D.C., 20008)
Ambassador: Shaikh Saud Nasir Al-Sabah.

Of the USA in Kuwait (PO Box 77, Safat, Kuwait)
Ambassador: W. Nathaniel Howell.

Of Kuwait to the United Nations
Ambassador: Mohammad A. Abulhasan.

Books of Reference

Arabian Year Book. Kuwait, 1978
Annual Statistical Abstract of Kuwait. Kuwait
The Oil of Kuwait: Facts and Figures. 3rd ed. Kuwait Government Press, 1970
Sabah, Y. S. F., *The Oil Economy of Kuwait.* London, 1980

LAOS

Capital: Vientiane
Population: 3·67m. (1986)
GNP per capita: US$220 (1984)

HISTORY. The Lao People's Democratic Republic was founded on 2 Dec. 1975. Until that date Laos was a Kingdom, once called Lanxang (the land of a million elephants).

In 1893 Laos became a French protectorate and in 1907 acquired its present frontiers. In 1941 French authority was suppressed by the Japanese. When the Japanese withdrew in 1945 an independence movement known as Lao Issara (Free Laos) set up a government under Prince Phetsarath, the Viceroy of Luang Prabang. This government collapsed with the return of the French in 1946 and the leaders of the movement fled to Thailand.

Under a new Constitution of 1947 Laos became a constitutional monarchy under the Luang Prabang dynasty, and in 1949 became an independent sovereign state within the French Union. Most of the Lao Issara leaders returned to Laos but a few remained in dissidence under Prince Souphanouvong, who allied himself with the Vietminh and subsequently formed the 'Pathet Lao' (Lao State) rebel movement.

The war in Laos from 1953 to 1973 between the Royal Lao Government (supported by American bombing and Thai mercenaries) and the Patriotic Front *Pathet Lao* (supported by large numbers of North Vietnamese troops) ended in 1973 when an agreement and a protocol were signed. A provisional coalition government was formed by the two sides in 1974. However, after the communist victories in neighbouring Vietnam and Cambodia in April 1975, the *Pathet Lao* took over the running of the whole country, although maintaining the façade of a coalition. On 29 Nov. 1975 HM King Savang Vatthana signed a letter of abdication and the People's Congress proclaimed a People's Democratic Republic of Laos on 2 Dec. For the history of *Pathet Lao* and the military intervention of the Vietminh, *see* THE STATESMAN'S YEAR-BOOK, 1971–72, pp. 1126–28 and 1975–76 ed., pp. 1115–16.

AREA AND POPULATION. Laos is a landlocked country of about 91,400 sq. miles (236,800 sq. km) bordered on the north by China, the east by Vietnam, the south by Cambodia and the west by Thailand and Burma. Apart from the Mekong River plains along the border of Thailand, the country is mountainous, particularly in the north, and in places densely forested.

The population (census, 1985) was 3,584,803 (1,757,115 male); estimate (1986) 3·67m. The most heavily populated areas are the Mekong River plains by the Thailand border. Otherwise, the population is sparse and scattered, particularly in the northern provinces, and the eastern part of the country has been depopulated by war. The majority of the population is officially divided into 4 groups: about 56% Lao-Lum (Valley-Lao), 34% Lao-Theung (Lao of the mountain sides); and 9% Lao-Soung (Lao of the mountain tops), who comprise the Meo and Yaoe. Other minorities include Vietnamese, Chinese, Europeans, Indians and Pakistanis.

The Lao-Lum and Lao-Tai belong to the Lao branch of the Tai peoples, who migrated into South-East Asia at the time of the Mongol invasion of South China. The valley Lao are Buddhists, following the Hinayana (Theravada) form. The majority of the Lao-Theungma diverse group consisting of many tribes but mostly belonging to the Mon-Khmer group—are animists.

The Meo and Yaoe live in northern Laos. Far greater numbers live in both North Vietnam and China, having migrated over the last century. Their religions have strong Confucian and animistic features but some are Christians.

There are 16 provinces. Compared with other parts of Asia, Laos has few towns. The administrative capital and largest town is Vientiane, with a population of census (1985) 377,409. Other important towns (1973) are Luang Prabang, 44,244; Pakse, 44,860, in the extreme south, and Savannakhet, 50,690.

Language: Lao is the official language of the country. The liturgical language of Theravada Buddhism is Pali.

CLIMATE. A tropical monsoon climate, with high temperatures throughout the year and very heavy rains from May to Oct. Vientiane. Jan. 70°F (21·1°C), July 81°F (27·2°C). Annual rainfall 69″ (1,715 mm).

CONSTITUTION AND GOVERNMENT. On 2 Dec. 1975 a national congress of 264 people's representatives met and declared Laos a People's Democratic Republic. A People's Supreme Council was appointed to draw up a new Constitution.

Acting President: Phoumi Vongvichit.
Prime Minister, Secretary General of the Central Committee of the Lao People's Revolutionary Party: Kaysone Phomvihane.
First Deputy Prime Minister, Deputy Secretary General of the Central Committee of the Lao People's Revolutionary Party: Nouhak Phounsavanh.
The Politbureau of the LPRP comprises the above 3 plus: Phoumi Vongvichit [1], Gen. Phoune Sipraseuth [1] *(Minister of Foreign Affairs),* Gen. Khamtai Siphandon [1] *(Minister of National Defence, Supreme Commander of the Lao People's Army)* and Sisomphon Lovansay *(Vice-President of the Supreme People's Assembly).* Ministers not in the Politbureau include Saly Vongkhamsao [1] *(Chairman of State Planning Committee).*

[1] Vice-Chairman of the Council of Ministers.

There are 4 deputy prime ministers.

National flag: Three horizontal stripes of red, blue, red, with blue of double width with in the centre a large white disc.
National anthem: Peng Sat Lao (Hymn of the Lao People).

Provincial Administration: All provincial administration is in the hands of the Lao People's Revolutionary Party. Orders come from the Central Committee through a series of 'People's Revolutionary Committees' at the province, town and village level.

DEFENCE. Military service is compulsory for 18 months.

Army. The Army is organized in 5 engineering and 1 artillery divisions; 7 independent infantry regiments and 65 independent infantry companies; and 5 artillery and 9 anti-aircraft battalions. Equipment includes 30 T-34, T-55 main battle tanks. Strength (1988) about 52,500.

Navy. There were nominally 4 squadrons comprising 42 small river patrol craft of 6 different types, of which 14 were in commission and 28 in reserve; but the situation is very uncertain. Some 70 river patrol boats were reportedly transferred from Vietnam and 46 river patrol craft from the USSR in 1986 for operations on the Mekong. Naval personnel in 1988 totalled about 1,700 officers and ratings.

Air Force. Since 1975, the Air Force has received aircraft from the USSR, including 40 MiG-21 fighters, 6 An-24 and 3 An-26 turboprop transports and 10 Mi-8 helicopters. They may be supplemented by a few of the C-47 and C-123 transports, and UH-1 Iroquois, supplied by the USA to the former régime. Personnel strength, about 2,000 in 1988.

INTERNATIONAL RELATIONS

Membership. Laos is a member of UN.

Aid. Foreign aid in 1983 (estimate), was US$50m.

ECONOMY

Planning. Following the completion of the original 3-year Development Plan 1978–80, a 5-year plan (1981–85), which was basically a list of investment projects, was drawn up by the government with Soviet assistance.

Budget. Total revenue 1983, K.3,496m.; total expenditure, K.6,695m.

Currency. The currency is the new *kip*. 1 *kip* = 100 *att*. Coinage, 1, 2 and 5 *att*; banknotes, 1, 5, 10, 20 and 50 *kip*. The official rate of exchange was (March 1988) K.350 = US$1; £1 = K620·73.

ENERGY AND NATURAL RESOURCES

Electricity. Only a few towns in Laos have an electricity service. The Nam Ngum Dam situated about 45 miles north of Vientiane was inaugurated in Dec. 1971 with an initial installed capacity of 30,000 kw. and a planned ultimate capacity of 150,000 kw. The generators of Phase II of the scheme were brought into operation in 1978, giving an installed capacity of 110,000 kw. The installation of a fifth generator (Phase III) was due for completion in 1984. Transmission lines to Vientiane and to Thailand have been constructed. Production (1986) 900m. kwh. Supply 127 and 220 volts; 50 Hz.

Minerals. Various minerals are found, but only tin is mined to any significant extent at present, and only at 2 mines. Production of tin concentrates (1983) 352 tonnes. There are extremely rich deposits of high-quality iron in Xieng Khouang province and potash near Vientiane.

Agriculture. The chief products are rice (production in 1986, 1·49m. tonnes), maize (production 37,000 tonnes), tobacco (3,000 tonnes), seed-cotton (18,000 tonnes), citrus fruits, sticklack, benjohn tea and in the Boloven plateau coffee (6,000 tonnes), potatoes, cardamom and cinchara. Opium is produced but its manufacture is controlled by the state.

Livestock (1986): Cattle, 593,000; buffaloes, 1,017,000; horses, 42,000; pigs, 1,516,000; goats, 71,000; poultry, 8m.

Forestry. The forests, which cover over 50% of the country, produce valuable woods such as teak.

INDUSTRY AND TRADE

Industry. Industry is limited to beer, cigarettes, matches, soft drinks, plastic bags, saw-mills, rice-mills, weaving, pottery, distilleries, ice, plywood, bricks, etc. but most factories have been working at limited capacity in recent years. Plans for increased production are limited by lack of funds and skilled machine operators.

Commerce. In 1981 imports (estimate) amounted to US$121m. and exports to US$48m. The main imports were food and beverages, petroleum products and agricultural and other machinery. The chief supplying countries were Thailand and Japan. The main exports were timber, coffee and electricity.

Total trade between Laos and UK (British Department of Trade returns, in £1,000 sterling):

	1983	1984	1985	1986	1987
Imports to UK	56	238	6	150	621
Exports and re-exports from UK	626	721	523	1,460	1,742

COMMUNICATIONS

Roads. In 1981 the national road network, consisted of 1,300 km paved, 5,300 km gravel and 3,600 km earth roads.

Railways. There is no railway in Laos, but the Thai railway system extends to Nongkhai, on the Thai bank of the Mekong, which is connected by ferry with Thadeua about 12 miles east of Vientiane.

Aviation. Lao Aviation provides scheduled domestic air services linking major towns in Laos and international services to Bangkok, Phnom Penh and Hanoi. Thai Airways, Aeroflot and Air Vietnam provide flights from Bangkok, Hanoi, Rangoon, Ho Chi Min City and Moscow.

Shipping. The river Mekong and its tributaries are an important means of transport, but rapids, waterfalls and narrow channels often impede navigation and make trans-shipments necessary.

Telecommunications. There is a radio network in Laos as well as a limited TV service with the main station at Vientiane. There were (1984) about 225,000 radio and 30,000 television receivers. A ground station constructed near Vientiane under the Soviet aid programme enables USSR television programmes to be received in the capital. It also provides a telephone service to Hanoi and Eastern Europe.

In 1974 there were 5,506 telephones in Laos.

RELIGION, EDUCATION AND WELFARE

Religion. The majority of the population is Buddhist (Hinayana) but 34% follow tribal religions.

Education. In 1982–83 school year there were 6,525 elementary schools (481,000 pupils); 420 secondary schools (65,000 pupils); 60 senior high schools (17,000 pupils); and 55 vocational schools (13,000 students).

Literacy has improved from 40% in 1975, 65% in 1978 to 85% in 1981 according to official reports.

There is 1 teachers' training college, 1 college of education, 1 school of medicine, 1 agricultural college and an advanced school of Pali.

Sisavangvong University in Vientiane (founded 1958) had 1,600 students in 1984, and there are regional technical colleges in Luang Prabang, Savannakhét and Champasak.

Health. In 1982 there were about 40 qualified doctors and 8,729 hospital beds.

DIPLOMATIC REPRESENTATIVES

The Embassy in London closed on 22 July 1985.

Of Great Britain in Laos
Ambassador: Derek Tonkin, CMG (resides in Bangkok).

Of Laos in USA (2222 S St., NW, Washington, D.C., 20008)
Chargé d'Affaires: Done Somvorachit.

Of USA in Laos (Rue Bartholonie, Vientiane)
Chargé d'Affaires: D. Steven May.

Of Laos to the United Nations
Ambassador: Dr Kithong Vongsay.

Books of Reference

Deuve, J., *Le royaume du Laos 1949–1965.* Paris, 1984
Stuart-Cox, M., *Contemporary Laos.* Univ. of Queensland Press, 1983.—*Laos: Politics, Economics and Society.* London, 1986
Zasloff, J. J., *The Pathet Lao: Leadership and Organization.* Lexington, Toronto and London, 1973

LEBANON

al-Jumhouriya al-Lubnaniya

Capital: Beirut
Population: 3·5m. (1984)
GNP per capita: No reliable figures available.

HISTORY. After 20 years' French mandatory regime, Lebanon was proclaimed independent at Beirut on 26 Nov. 1941. On 27 Dec. 1943 an agreement was signed between representatives of the French National Committee of Liberation and of Lebanon, by which most of the powers and capacities exercised hitherto by France were transferred as from 1 Jan. 1944 to the Lebanese Government. The evacuation of foreign troops was completed in Dec. 1946.

In early May 1958 the opposition to President Chamoun, consisting principally (though not entirely) of Moslem pro-Nasserist elements, rose in insurrection; and for 5 months the Moslem quarters of Beirut, Tripoli, Sidon and the northern Bekaa were in insurgent hands. On 15 July the US Government acceded to President Chamoun's request and landed a considerable force of army and marines who re-established the authority of the Government.

Israeli attacks on Lebanon resulted from the presence and activities of armed Palestinian resistance units. Internal problems, which had long been latent in Lebanese society, were exacerbated by the politically active Palestinian population and by the deeply divisive question of the Palestine problem itself. An attempt to regulate the activities of Palestinian fighters through the secret Cairo agreement of 1969 was frustrated both by the inability of the Government to enforce its provisions and by an influx of battle-hardened fighters expelled from Jordan in Sept. 1970. A further attempt to control the guerrillas in 1973 also failed. From March 1975, Lebanon was beset by civil disorder causing considerable loss of life and economic life was brought to a virtual standstill.

By Nov. 1976 however, large scale fighting had been brought to an end by the intervention of the Syrian-dominated Arab Deterrent Force which ensured sufficient security to permit Lebanon to establish quasi-normal conditions under President Sarkis. Large areas of the country, however, remained outside Governmental control, including West Beirut which was the scene of frequent conflict between opposing militia groups. The South, where the Arab Deterrent Force could not deploy, remained unsettled and subject to frequent Israeli attacks. In March 1978 there was an Israeli invasion following a Palestinian attack inside Israel. Israeli troops eventually withdrew in June, but instead of handing over all their positions to UN Peacekeeping Forces they installed Israeli-controlled Lebanese militia forces in border areas. Severe disruption continued in the South. In June 1982, following on the attempted assassination of the Israeli ambassador in London, Israeli forces once again invaded, this time in massive strength, and swept through the country, eventually laying siege to and devastatingly bombing Beirut. In Sept. Palestinian forces, together with the PLO leadership, evacuated Beirut. On 23 Aug. 1982 Bachir Gemayel was elected President of Lebanon. On 14 Sept. he was assassinated. His brother, Amin Gemayel, was elected in his place on 21 Sept. Since then there has been a state of 'no peace, no war' with intermittent clashes between the various *de facto* forces on the ground. Israeli forces started a complete withdrawal on 16 Feb. 1985. A peace agreement was signed by the leaders of the Druse, Amal and (Christian) Lebanese Forces to end the civil war on 28 Dec. 1985 but its terms were not implemented. Syrian forces were acting as a peace keeping force between rival militias in early 1987.

AREA AND POPULATION. Lebanon is a mountainous country about 135 miles long and varying between 20 and 35 miles wide, bounded on the north and east by Syria, on the west by the Mediterranean and on the south by Israel. Between the two parallel mountain ranges of Lebanon and Anti-Lebanon lies the fertile Bekaa Valley. About one-half of the country lies at an altitude of over 3,000 ft.

The area of Lebanon is estimated at 10,452 sq. km (4,036 sq. miles) and the population at 3·5m. (1984, estimate) but there are no reliable estimates. The principal towns, with estimated population (1980), are: Beirut (the capital), 702,000; Tripoli 175,000; Zahlé, 46,800; Saida (Sidon), 24,740; Tyre, 14,000.

The official language is Arabic. French and, increasingly, English are widely spoken in official and commercial circles.

CLIMATE. A Mediterranean climate with short, warm winters and long, hot and rainless summers, with high humidity in coastal areas. Rainfall is largely confined to the winter months and can be torrential, with snow on high ground. Beirut. Jan. 55°F (13°C), July 81°F (27°C). Annual rainfall 35·7″ (893 mm).

CONSTITUTION AND GOVERNMENT. Lebanon is an independent republic. The first Constitution was established under the French Mandate on 23 May 1926. It has since been amended in 1927, 1929, 1943 (twice) and 1947. It is a written constitution based on the classical separation of powers, with a President, a single chamber elected by universal adult suffrage, and an independent judiciary. The Executive consists of the President and a Prime Minister and Cabinet appointed by him. The system is, however, adapted to the peculiar communal balance on which Lebanese political life depends. This is done by the electoral law which allocates deputies according to the confessional distribution of the population, and by a series of constitutional conventions whereby, *e.g.*, the President is always a Maronite Christian, the Prime Minister a Sunni Moslem and the Speaker of the Assembly a Shia Moslem. There is no highly developed party system other than on religious confessional lines.

Former Presidents of the Republic:

Bishara al-Khuri, 1 Jan. 1944–23 Sept. 1952

Camille Chamoun, 23 Sept. 1952–23 Sept. 1958

Gen. Fouad Chehab, 23 Sept. 1958–23 Sept. 1964

Charles Hélou, 23 Sept. 1964–17 June 1970

Suleiman Frangié, 17 June 1970–13 Sept. 1976

Elias Sarkis, 13 Sept. 1976–23 Sept. 1982

Bachir Gemayel, 23 Aug. 1982–14 Sept. 1982 (assassinated)

President of the Republic: Amin Gemayel (elected on 21 Sept. 1982 and took office on 23 Sept.).

On 1 May 1984, a new government was formed and aims to achieve constitutional and power-sharing reforms on the basis of a wide measure of consensus.

The Cabinet was composed as follows in Dec. 1987:

Acting Prime Minister, Foreign Affairs, Labour and Education: Dr Selim Hoss.
Public Works, Transport and Tourism: Walid Jumblatt. *Posts and Communications, Health and Social Affairs:* Joseph Hashem. *Finance, Housing and Co-operatives:* Camille Chamoun. *Justice, Hydroelectricity, Minister of State for Reconstruction and for Southern Lebanon:* Nabih Berri. *Defence, Agriculture:* Adel Osseirane. *Information:* Joseph Skaff. *Interior:* Abdullah al-Rassi. *Economy, Trade and Industry:* Victor Kassir.

National flag: Three horizontal stripes of red, white, red, with the white of double width and bearing in the centre a green cedar of Lebanon.

National anthem: Kulluna lil watan lil 'ula lil' alam (words by Rashid Nachleh, tune by Mitri El-Murr).

Local government: The 6 governorates (including the city of Beirut) are sub-divided into 26 districts.

DEFENCE.

Army. The strength of the Army was about 15,000 in 1988 but it is in a state of flux and most of its units are well below strength. Its equipment includes M-48 and AMX-13 tanks and Saladin armoured cars. In addition, there are numerous private militias under arms in Lebanon, divided between the Maronite-Christian factions, notably the Phalange of some 10,000 men, and the Moslem-Leftist groups, such as the Druze Free Lebanese Militia led by Walid Jumblatt.

Navy. The small flotilla includes 4 old French-built patrol boats (replacement craft to be acquired), 2 new French-built landing craft and 8 coastal patrol craft (2 British-built). Personnel in 1988 totalled 250 officers and men.

Air Force. The Air Force had (1987) about 1,100 men and 50 aircraft. In addition to 6 Hunter jet fighter-bombers, it has (in storage) 9 Mirage III supersonic fighters and 1 Mirage 2-seat trainer. Other aircraft include 1 Dove light transport, 12 Alouette II and III, 4 Gazelle, 11 Puma and 9 Agusta-Bell 212 helicopters, and 5 Fouga Magister jet and 5 piston-engined Bulldog trainers. Serviceability of most aircraft is low because of the troubled national political situation.

INTERNATIONAL RELATIONS

Membership. Lebanon is a member of UN and the Arab League.

ECONOMY

Planning. Since the civil war a Development and Reconstruction Council has been responsible for co-ordinating all efforts.

Budget. The budget for 1985 provides for a total expenditure of £Leb.10,000m.

Currency. The Lebanese *pound*, divided into 100 *piastres*, is issued by the Banque du Liban, which commenced operations on 1 April 1964. There is a fluctuating official rate of exchange, fixed monthly (March 1988: £Leb.712·04 = £1 sterling; £Leb.370 = US$1), this in practice is used only for the calculation of *ad-valorem* customs duties on Lebanese imports and for import statistics. For other purposes the free market is used.

Banking. Beirut was an important international financial centre, and there were about 80 banks registered with the central bank in 1979. As a result of the civil war, Beirut has lost much of its status as an international and regional banking centre; in general only local offices for banks remain.

Weights and Measures. The use of the metric system is legal and obligatory throughout the whole of the country. In outlying districts the former weights and measures may still be in use. They are: 1 *okiya* = 0·47 lb.; 6 *okiyas* = 1 *oke* = 2·82 lb.; 2 *okes* = 1 *rottol* = 5·64 lb.; 200 *okes* = 1 *kantar*.

ENERGY AND NATURAL RESOURCES

Electricity. Electric power production (1986) was 2,270m. kwh. Supply 110 and 120 volts; 50 Hz.

Oil. There are 2 oil refineries in Lebanon, one at Tripoli, which refines oil brought by ship from Iraq, and the other at Sidon, which refines oil brought from Saudi Arabia by a pipeline owned by the Trans-Arabian Pipeline Co. These refineries were not fully active in 1987 and the country depends on imports.

Minerals. Iron ore exists but is difficult to work. Other minerals known to exist are iron pyrites, copper, bituminous shales, asphalt, phosphates, ceramic clays and glass sand; but the available information is of doubtful value.

Agriculture. Lebanon is essentially an agricultural country, although owing to its physical character only about 38% of the total area of the country is at present cultivated.

The estimated production (in 1,000 tonnes) of the main crops in 1986 was as follows: Citrus fruits, 366; apples, 133; grapes, 158; potatoes, 230; sugar-beet, 80; wheat, 13; bananas, 19; olives, 9.

Livestock (estimated, 1986): Goats, 460,000; sheep, 137,000; cattle, 50,000; pigs, 21,000; horses, 2,000; donkeys, 10,000; mules, 4,000.

Forestry. The forests of the past have been denuded by exploitation.

INDUSTRY AND TRADE

Industry. Industry suffered badly during the civil war. The manufacturing industry was small but had doubled in size in the 10 years before the war. As a result of the war some industrial concerns have closed but others are working at reduced capacity.

Commerce. Foreign as well as local wholesale and retail trade is the principal source of income in Lebanon. Because of the protectionist policies followed in some neighbouring countries, this sector has been declining, the sectors to gain being those of banking, real estate, government and services.

Reliable trade figures have not been published in recent years.

Total trade between Lebanon and UK (British Department of Trade returns, in £1,000 sterling):

	1983	1984	1985	1986	1987
Imports to UK	11,521	6,859	7,888	9,845	9,528
Exports and re-exports from UK	81,435	76,223	52,751	55,867	40,707

Tourism. Receipts from tourism were £Leb.573m. in 1973; since 1975 they have been negligible, this sector having suffered badly as a result of the war.

COMMUNICATIONS

Roads. The main roads in Lebanon are not good by international standards. The surface is normally of asphalt and they are well maintained in normal times. Roads between Beirut and the provinces were (1984) controlled by various militia.

In 1985 there were about 300,000 cars and taxis.

Railways. There are 3 railway lines in Lebanon, all operated by the *Office des Chemins de Fer de l'Etat Libanais* (CFL): (1) Nakoura–Beirut–Tripoli (standard gauge); the Nakoura–Sidon section has been idle since the establishment of Israel: (2) a narrow-gauge line running from Beirut to Riyak in the Bekaa Valley (now closed) and thence to Damascus, Syria; (3) a standard-gauge line from Tripoli to Homs and Aleppo in Syria, providing access to Ankara and Istanbul. From Homs a branch of the CFL line extends south and re-enters Lebanon, terminating at Riyak. Total length 417 km. Apart from a short section near Beirut these lines were idle in 1984–85 because of insecurity and large sections needed repairs.

Aviation. Beirut International Airport is used by a few international airlines. There are 2 national airlines, Middle East Airlines/Air Liban and Trans-Mediterranean Airways. Over the past few years, Beirut airport was closed several times.

Shipping. Beirut is the largest port, followed by Tripoli, Jounieh and Sidon. Illegal ports have mushroomed on the coast, very much reducing the legal ports' activity. No reliable figures about tonnage were available in 1987.

Post and Broadcasting. There is an automatic telephone system in Beirut which is being extended to other parts of the country. There are no telegraph, postal or telephone communications with Israel. Number of telephones (1986), 150,000.

The state radio transmits in Arabic, French, English and Armenian. Teté-Liban, which is 50% government-owned was the only television station in operation in 1984. There were 450,000 TV sets in 1986 and 1·5m. radios.

Cinemas (1973). There were 161 cinemas with a seating capacity of about 77,400.

Newspapers (1985). There were about 30 daily newspapers in Arabic, 2 in French, 1 in English and 4 in Armenian.

RELIGION, EDUCATION AND WELFARE

Religion. Probably less than half the population are Christians. The Christian faith has been indigenous since the earliest times. The Christians include the Maronites,

Greek Orthodox, Armenians, Greek and Roman Catholics, Armenian Catholics and the Protestants. Moslems include the Sunnis, the Shiites and the Druzes. No reliable figures on the numbers of these communities are available. Most Jews left the country after the 1975 disturbances.

Education. Government schools in 1984 comprise primary and secondary schools. There were also private primary and secondary schools. There are also 5 universities, namely the Lebanese (State) University, the American University of Beirut, the French University of St Joseph (founded in 1875), the Arab University, a branch of Alexandria University and Beirut University College. The French Government runs the École Supérieure de Lettres and the Centre d'Études Mathématiques. The Maronite monks run the University of the Holy Spirit at Kaslik.

The Lebanese Academy of Fine Arts includes schools of architecture, art, music, political and social science.

Health. There are several government-run hospitals, and many private ones.

DIPLOMATIC REPRESENTATIVES

Of Lebanon in Great Britain (21 Kensington Palace Gdns., London, W8 4QM)
Ambassador: Gen. Ahmad al-Hajj (accredited 25 May 1983).

Of Great Britain in Lebanon (Shamma Bldg., Raouché, Ras Beirut)
Ambassador: J. W. D. Gray, CMG.

Of Lebanon in the USA (2560 28th St., NW, Washington, D.C., 20008)
Ambassador: Dr Abdallah Bouhabib.

Of the USA in Lebanon
Ambassador: John Kelly.

Of Lebanon to the United Nations
Ambassador: Rachid Fakhoury.

Books of Reference

Statistical Information: Import and export figures are produced by the Conseil Supérieur des Douanes. The Service de Statistique Généralé (M. A. G. Ayad, *Chef du Service*) publishes a quarterly bulletin (in French and Arabic) covering a wide range of subjects, including foreign trade, production statistics and estimates of the national income.

Cobban, H., *The Making of Modern Lebanon.* London, 1985
Deeb, M., *The Lebanese Civil War.* New York, 1980
Gilmour, D., *Lebanon: The Fractured Country.* Oxford and New York, 1983
Gordon, D. C., *The Republic of Lebanon: Nation in Jeopardy.* London, 1983
Khairallah, S., *Lebanon.* [Bibliography] Oxford and Santa Barbara, 1979
Laffin, J., *The War of Desperation: Lebanon 1982–85.* London, 1985
Rabanovich, I., *The War for Lebanon, 1970–1983.* Cornell Univ. Press, 1984
Randal, J., *The Tragedy of Lebanon.* London, 1982
Weinberger, N. J., *Syrian Intervention in Lebanon.* New York, 1986

National Library: Dar el Kutub, Parliament Sq., Beirut.

LESOTHO

Capital: Maseru
Population: 1·63m. (1987)
GNP per capita: US$470 (1983)

HISTORY. Basutoland first received the protection of Britain in 1868 at the request of Moshoeshoe I, the first paramount chief. In 1871 the territory was annexed to the Cape Colony, but in 1884 it was restored to the direct control of the British Government through the High Commissioner for South Africa.

On 4 Oct. 1966 Basutoland became an independent and sovereign member of the Commonwealth under the name of the Kingdom of Lesotho.

AREA AND POPULATION. Lesotho, an enclave within the Republic of South Africa is bounded on the west by the Orange Free State, on the north by the Orange Free State and Natal, on the east by Natal, and on the south by Transkei. The altitude varies from 1,500 to 3,482 metres. The area is 11,720 sq. miles (30,355 sq. km). Lesotho is a purely African territory, and the few European residents are government officials, traders, missionaries and artisans.

The census taken on 12 April 1976 showed a total population of 1,216,815 persons. Estimate (1987) 1,626,500. The capital is Maseru (population, 1986, 109,382).

The official languages are Sesotho and English.

CLIMATE. A healthy and pleasant climate, with variable rainfall, but averaging 29″ (725 mm) a year over most of the country. The rain falls mainly in the summer months of Oct. to April, while the winters are dry and may produce heavy frosts in lowland areas and frequent snow in the highlands. Temperatures in the lowlands range from a maximum of 90°F (32·2°C) in summer to a minimum of 20°F (–6·7°C) in winter.

CONSTITUTION AND GOVERNMENT. Lesotho is a constitutional monarchy with HM the King as ceremonial Head of State.

Parliament consists of the National Assembly (60 members elected by adult suffrage) and a Senate (22 principal chiefs and 11 members nominated by the King). The elections of 27 Jan. 1970 were declared invalid on 31 Jan. Parliamentary rule, with a National Assembly of nominated members, was reintroduced in April 1973. Chief Jonathan was deposed in a bloodless military *coup* on 20 Jan. 1986.

Ruler: Constantine Bereng Seeiso Motlotlehi Moshoeshoe II, Paramount Chief of the Sotho people since 1940, became King at independence on 4 Oct. 1966.

Chairman of the Military Council: Maj.-Gen. Justin Lekhanya.

The College of Chiefs settles the recognition and succession of Chiefs and adjudicates cases of inefficiency, criminality and absenteeism among them.

National flag: Diagonally white over blue over green with the white of double width charged with a brown Basotho shield in the upper hoist.

Local Government. The country is divided into 10 districts as follows: Maseru, Qacha's Nek, Mokhotlong, Leribe, Butha–Buthe, Teyateyaneng, Mafeteng, Mohale's Hoek, Quthing, Thaba–Tseka. Each district is subdivided into 22 wards, most of which are presided over by hereditary chiefs allied to the Moshoeshoe family.

DEFENCE

Police Mobile Unit. Formed in 1978, to facilitate deployment of men and equipment to less accessible regions, this small air wing has 2 Skyvan and 1 King Air twin-turboprop transports, and a total of 6 Bell 412, BO 105, and Bell 47 helicopters. The Skyvans are available also as ambulance aircraft.

INTERNATIONAL RELATIONS

Membership. Lesotho is a member of UN, OAU, the Commonwealth and is an ACP state of the EEC.

ECONOMY

Planning. A third 5-year plan (1980–85), aimed to exploit natural resources and promote investment in industry. Envisaged investment US$915m.

Budget. Expenditure (1986–87) M463m.; revenue, M385m.

Currency. The currency is the *Loti* (plural *Maloti*) divided into 100 *Lisente* which is at par with the South African *Rand*. In March 1988, £1 = 3·69 *Maloti*; US$1 = 2·11 *Maloti*.

Banking. The Standard Bank of South Africa and Barclays Bank International have branches at Maseru, Mohale's Hoek and Leribe. The Lesotho Bank has branches throughout the country.

ENERGY AND NATURAL RESOURCES

Electricity. A feasibility study was announced (1982) to be undertaken by the Republic of South Africa and Lesotho to divert river waters from Lesotho to South Africa and to provide hydro-electricity for Lesotho. Production (1985) 1m. kwh. Supply 230 volts; 50 Hz.

Agriculture. The chief crops were (1986 production in 1,000 tonnes): wheat, 11; maize, 86; sorghum, 33; barley, oats, beans, peas and other vegetables are also grown. Soil conservation and the improvement of crops and pasture are matters of vital importance. A total area of 1,006,817 acres has been protected against soil erosion by means of terracing, training banks, tree planting and grass strips. Efforts are being made to secure the general introduction of rotational grazing in the mountain area.

Livestock (1986): Cattle, 520,000; horses, 108,000; donkeys, 108,000; pigs, 65,000; sheep, 1·42m.; goats, 1·01m.; mules, 1,000; poultry, 1m.

INDUSTRY AND TRADE

Industry. Industrial development is progressing under the National Development Corporation. Diamond mining ceased in 1982.

Commerce. Lesotho, Botswana and Swaziland are members of the South African customs union, by agreement dated 29 June 1910.

Total values of imports and exports into and from Lesotho (in Mm.):

	1979	1980	1981	1982
Imports	312	372	453	541
Exports	38	45	43	38

Principal imports were food, livestock, drink and tobacco, machinery and transport equipment, mineral fuels and lubricants; principal exports were wool and mohair and diamonds.

The majority of international trade is with the Republic of South Africa.

Total trade between Lesotho and UK (British Department of Trade returns, in £1,000 sterling):

	1983	1984	1985	1986	1987
Imports to UK	216	78	290	277	486
Exports and re-exports from UK	2,080	633	3,023	2,128	1,112

Tourism. In 1986 there were 213,000 visitors.

COMMUNICATIONS

Roads. There were (1983) 311 km of tarred roads and 1,500 km of gravel-surfaced roads. In addition to the main roads there were (1983) 931 km of food aid tracks leading to trading stations and missions. Communications into the mountainous interior are by means of bridlepaths suitable only for riding and pack animals, but a mountain road of 80 miles has been constructed, and some parts are accessible by air transport, which is being used increasingly. In 1982 there were 11,962 commercial vehicles and 5,129 passenger cars.

Railways. A railway built by the South African Railways, 1 mile long, connects Maseru with the Bloemfontein–Natal line at Marseilles.

Aviation. There is a scheduled passenger service between Maseru and Jan Smuts Airport, Johannesburg, operated jointly by Lesotho National Airways and SAA. There are also 30 airstrips for light aircraft.

Post and Broadcasting. There were 5,409 telephones in 1983. Radio Lesotho transmits daily in English and Sesotho. Radio receivers (1986), 600,000.

Cinemas. In 1971 there were 2 cinemas with a seating capacity of 800.

Newspapers. In 1985, 3 daily newspapers had a combined circulation of 44,000.

JUSTICE, RELIGION, EDUCATION AND WELFARE

Justice. An appeal court for Lesotho was established at Maseru on 4 Oct. 1966.

The police force on 31 Dec. 1982 had an establishment of 348 officers and subordinate officers and 1,530 other ranks.

Religion. About 93% of the population are Christians, 44% being Roman Catholics.

Education. Education is largely in the hands of the 3 main missions (Paris Evangelical, Roman Catholic and English Church), under the direction of the Ministry of Education. In 1984–85 the total enrolment in 1,141 primary schools was 314,003; in 143 secondary schools, 35,423; in the National Teacher-Training College and 8 technical schools enrolment 2,221. University education is provided at the National University of Lesotho established in 1975 at Roma; enrolment in 1985, 1,119 and 146 teaching staff.

Health. The government medical staff of the territory consists of 1 Permanent Secretary for Health, 1 Director of Health Services, 1 medical superintendent, 8 district medical officers and a total of 102 doctors including 20 specialists.

There are 11 government hospitals staffed by 308 matrons, sisters and nurses. There is accommodation for 2,175 patients in government hospitals.

DIPLOMATIC REPRESENTATIVES

Of Lesotho in Great Britain (10 Collingham Rd., London, SW5 ONR)
High Commissioner: Dr John T. Kolane (accredited 2 June 1986).

Of Great Britain in Lesotho (PO Box Ms 521, Maseru 100)
High Commissioner: P. E. Rosling, CMG, LVO.

Of Lesotho in the USA (1430 K. St., NW, Washington, D.C., 20005)
Ambassador: W. T. Van Tonder.

Of the USA in Lesotho (PO Box 333, Maseru, 100)
Ambassador: Robert M. Smalley.

Of Lesotho to the United Nations
Ambassador: (Vacant).

Books of Reference

Statistical Information: Bureau of Statistics, PO Box 455, Maseru, Lesotho.
Ashton, H., *The Basuto.* 2nd ed. OUP, 1967
Murray, C., *Families Divided: The Impact of Migrant Labour in Lesotho.* OUP, 1981
Spence, J. E., *Lesotho.* OUP, 1968
Stevens, C., *Food, Aid and the Developing World.* London, 1979

LIBERIA

Capital: Monrovia
Population: 2·5m. (1987)
GNP per capita: US$490 (1984)

HISTORY. The Republic of Liberia had its origin in the efforts of several American philanthropic societies to establish freed American slaves in a colony on the West African coast. In 1822 a settlement was formed near the spot where Monrovia now stands. On 26 July 1847 the State was constituted as the Free and Independent Republic of Liberia. The new State was first recognized by Great Britain and France, and ultimately by other powers.

On 12 April 1980, President Tolbert was assassinated; his government was overthrown and the Constitution suspended. President Tolbert's party, the True Whig Party, was formed in 1860 and had been in power since 1870. Recent economic decline and pressure for change had undermined the Government. In March 1980, the newly formed People's Progressive Party was banned and its leaders arrested. The *coup* was led by Master-Sergeant Doe who was later installed as Head of State and Commander-in-Chief of the army.

AREA AND POPULATION. Liberia has about 350 miles of coastline, extending from Sierra Leone, on the west, to the Côte d'Ivoire, on the east. It stretches inland to a distance, in some places, of about 250 miles and is bounded in the north by Guinea.

The total area is about 42,989 sq. miles (111,370 sq. km). At the census (1984) population 2,232,000. Estimate (1987) 2·5m. The indigenous natives belong in the main to 3 linguistic groups: Mande, West Atlantic, and the Kwa. These are in turn subdivided into 16 ethnic groups: Bassa, Bella, Gbandi, Mende, Gio, Dey, Mano, Gola, Kpelle, Kissi, Krahn, Kru, Lorma, Mandingo, Vai and Grebo.

Monrovia, the capital, had (1984) a population of 425,000. It is one of the 4 ports of entry, the others being Buchanan (Grand Bassa), River Cess, Greenville (Sinoe), Harper (Maryland). Other towns are Kolba City, Voinjama, Tubmanburg, Bensonville, Zorzor, Kakata, Suakoko, Gbarnga, Ganta, Sanniquellie, Saclape, Tappita, Robertsport, Bendja, Yekepa and Zwedru.

The country is divided into 13 counties and the district of Careysburg.

CLIMATE. An equatorial climate, with constant high temperatures and plentiful rainfall, though Jan. to May is drier than the rest of the year. Monrovia. Jan. 79°F (26·1°C), July 76°F (24·4°C). Annual rainfall 206″ (5,138 mm).

CONSTITUTION AND GOVERNMENT. A new Constitution was approved by referendum in July 1984 and came into force on 6 Jan. 1986. The National Assembly consists of a 26-member Senate and a 64-member House of Representatives.

General elections were held on 15 Oct. 1985. The National Democratic Party of Liberia gained 21 seats in the Senate; the Liberal Action Party, 3 seats and the Liberian Unification Party and the Unity Party one each.

President and Commander-in-Chief: Samuel Kanyon Doe.
Vice President: Harry F. Moniba.
The official language is English.

National flag: Six red and 5 white horizontal stripes alternating. In the upper corner, nearest the staff, is a square of blue covering a depth of 5 stripes. In the centre of this blue field is a 5-pointed white star.

National anthem: All hail, Liberia, hail! (words by President Warner; tune by O. Lucas, 1860).

DEFENCE

Army. The establishment organized on a militia basis numbers 5,300 (1988), divided into 6 infantry battalions with support units.

Navy. The small naval service or coastguard comprises 3 cutters, 3 small patrol boats, and 1 aircraft. Personnel in 1988 totalled 440 officers and men.

Air Force. The nucleus of an Air Force has been formed, as the Air Reconnaissance Unit, to support the Liberian Army. Equipment includes 2 C-47 transports, 3 Israeli-built Arava twin-turboprop light transports and a small number of Cessna 172, 185 and 337G light aircraft. Personnel about 250.

INTERNATIONAL RELATIONS

Membership. Liberia is a member of UN, OAU, ECOWAS and is an ACP state of EEC.

ECONOMY

Planning. The 1981–85 Development Plan envisaged expenditure of US$615m. of which US$203m. was devoted to the development of agriculture.

Budget. Revenue and expenditure was as follows (in US$1,000):

	1984–85	1985–86	1986–87
Revenue	315,000	237,600	366,400
Expenditure	371,000	366,700	366,400

Currency. The legal currency of Liberia is the *dollar* which is equivalent to US$1 which itself has been in circulation since 3 Nov. 1942, but there is a Liberian coinage in silver and copper. Official accounts are kept in dollars and cents. The Liberian coins are as follows: Silver,$5, $1, 50-, 25-, 10- and 5-cent pieces; alloy, 2-cent and copper 1-cent pieces. The Government has not yet issued paper money. In March 1988, £1 = 1·77 Liberian $; US$1 = 1 Liberian $.

Banking. The First National City Bank (Liberia) was founded in 1935. An Italian bank, Tradevco, started business in 1955. The International Trust Co. of Liberia opened a commercial banking department at the end of 1960. The Liberian Bank of Development and Investment (LBDI) was founded in 1964 and began operations in 1965. The National Bank of Liberia opened on 22 July 1974, to act as a central bank. The National Housing and Savings Bank opened on 20 Jan. 1972. The Liberian Finance & Trust Corporation was incorporated Oct. 1976 and began operations in May 1977. The Liberian Agricultural and Co-operative Development Bank started operations in 1978. The Bank of Credit & Commerce International opened in Sept. 1978 and Meridien Bank of Liberia in July 1985.

Weights and Measures. Weights and measures are the same as in UK and USA.

ENERGY AND NATURAL RESOURCES

Electricity. Production (1986) was 655m. kwh. Supply 120 volts; 60 Hz.

Minerals. Iron ore production was valued at US$241·1m. tonnes in 1982. Total employment in iron ore mining was 8,815 in 1981. Gold production (1986) 21,125 oz valued at US$7·3m. and diamond production (1982) 337,732 carats valued at US$20·8m.

Agriculture. Over 65% of the labour force is engaged in agriculture. The soil is productive, but due to excessive rainfall (from 160 to 180 in. per year), there are large swamp areas. Rice, cassava, coffee, citrus and sugar-cane are cultivated. The Government is negotiating the financing of large-scale investment in rice production aimed at making the country self-sufficient in rice production. Coffee, cocoa and palm-kernels are produced mainly by the traditional agricultural sector.

The Liberia Produce Marketing Corporation (LPMC) operates an oil-mill in Monrovia, processing most of the palm-kernels. There were 2 large commercial oil-palm plantations in the country. The Liberia Industrial Co-operative (LBINC) has 6,000 acres of oil-palm (of which 5,000 acres are in production) in Grand Bassa County, and West Africa Agricultural Co. (WAAC) has 4,020 acres in production in Grand Cape Mount County.

Production (1986, in 1,000 tonnes): Rice, 295; cassava, 326; coffee, 9; citrus, 7; sugar-cane, 159; cocoa, 5; palm-kernels, 8.

Livestock (1986): Cattle, 43,000; pigs, 131,000; sheep, 246,000; poultry, 4m.

Forestry. The Firestone Plantation Co. have large rubber plantations, employing over 40,000 men. Their concession comprises about 1m. acres and expires in the year 2025. About 100,000 acres have been planted. Independent producers have a further 65,000 acres planted. In 1976 the total area under rubber cultivation was 294,400 acres, of which 195,800 acres were under actual production.

The foreign concessions produced 131·6m. lb. in 1981 while independent Liberian farmers produced 148·7m. lb. in 1981.

The production of logs in 1981 was 451m. cu. metres; 1980, 745m.

Fisheries. Catch (1982) 13,600 tonnes.

INDUSTRY AND TRADE

Industry. There are a number of small factories (brick and tile, soap, nails, mattresses, shoes, plastics, paint, oxygen, acetylene, tyre retreading, a brewery, soft drinks, cement, matches, candy and biscuits).

Commerce. Foreign trade for 6 calendar years was as follows (in US$1m.):

	1978	1979	1980	1981	1982	1983
Imports	486	537	533·8	477·4	353·9	424
Exports	481	505	600·4	529·2	...	429

In 1987, iron ore accounted for about 70% of total export earnings, rubber 15% and sawn timber over 5%. Other exports were coffee, cocoa, palm-kernel oil, diamonds and gold.

Total trade between Liberia and UK (British Department of Trade returns, in £1,000 sterling):

	1983	1984	1985	1986	1987
Imports to UK	7,181	6,975	7,967	7,574	7,284
Exports and re-exports from UK	13,877	30,980	15,957	22,056	13,538

The figures for exports from the UK include the value of shipping transferred to the Liberian flag; the genuine exports are considerably lower.

COMMUNICATIONS

Roads. In 1981, there were 4,794 miles of public roads (1,165 primary, 366 paved, 799 all-weather, 3,629 secondary and feeder) and 1,474 miles of private roads (93 paved, 1,381 laterite and earth). The principal highway connects Monrovia with the road system of Guinea, with branches leading into the Eastern and Western areas of Liberia. The latter branch reaches the Sierra Leone border and joins the Sierra Leone road system. A bridge over the St Paul River carries road traffic to the iron-ore mines at Bomi Hills.

Railway. A railway (for freight only) was built in 1951, connecting Monrovia with the Bomi Hills iron-ore mines about 69 km distant; this has been extended to the National Iron Ore Co. area by 79 km. A line from Nimba to Lower Buchanan was completed in 1963 and another line from Bong to Monrovia (78 km) was completed in 1965.

Aviation. The airport for Liberia is Roberts International Airport (30 miles from Monrovia). The James Spriggs Payne Airfield, 5 miles from Monrovia, can be used by light aircraft and mini jumbo jets. Air services are maintained by Ghana Airways, Swissair, British Caledonian, Air Guinea, SABENA, Iberia Airlines, Romanian Airlines and Air Liberia.

Shipping. Over 2,000 vessels enter Monrovia each year. The Liberian merchant navy, in 1976, consisted of 2,666 ships of 76,412,842 GRT. The Liberian Government requires only a modest registration fee and an almost nominal annual charge and maintains no control over the operation of ships flying the Liberian flag.

Post and Broadcasting. There is cable communication with Europe and America *via* Dakar, and a wireless station is maintained by the Government at Monrovia. There is a telephone service (8,510 telephones, 1983), in Monrovia, which is gradually being extended over the whole country.

There are wireless stations at Monrovia, Bassa, Harper, Kolahun, Cape Mount and Sinoe. There were (1986) 320,000 radio and 21,000 television receivers.

JUSTICE, RELIGION, EDUCATION AND WELFARE

Justice. Justice is administered by a Supreme Court of 5 judges, 14 circuit courts and lower courts. A new Liberian code of laws has been published (5 vols. to 1956).

Religion. The main denominations represented in Liberia are Methodist, Baptist, Episcopalian, African Methodist, Pentecostal, Seventh-day Adventist, Lutheran and Roman Catholic, working through missionaries and mission schools. There were (1985) about 670,000 Moslems.

Education. Schools are classified as: (1) Public schools, maintained and run by the Government; (2) Mission schools, supported by foreign Missions and subsidized by the Government, and operated by qualified Missionaries and Liberian teachers; (3) Private schools, maintained by endowments and sometimes subsidized by the Government.

In 1986 there were estimated to be 1,830 schools with 8,744 teachers and 443,786 pupils.

Health. There were 236 doctors in 1981 and about 3,000 hospital beds.

DIPLOMATIC REPRESENTATIVES

Of Liberia in Great Britain (2 Pembridge Pl., London, W2)
Ambassador: W. A. Givens.

Of Great Britain in Liberia (Mamba Point, Monrovia)
Ambassador and Consul-General: M. E. J. Gore.

Of Liberia in the USA (5201 16th St., NW, Washington, D.C., 20011)
Ambassador: Eugenia Wordsworth-Stevenson.

Of the USA in Liberia (United Nations Drive, Monrovia)
Ambassador: James K. Bishop.

Of Liberia to the United Nations
Ambassador: Sylvester O. Jarrett.

Books of Reference

Economic Survey of Liberia, 1981. Ministry of Planning and Economic Affairs
Dunn, D. E., *The Foreign Policy of Liberia during the Tubman Era, 1944–71.* London, 1979
Fraenkel, M., *Tribe and Class in Monrovia.* OUP, 1964
Wilson, C. M., *Liberia: Black Africa in Microcosm.* New York, 1971

LIBYA

Capital: Tripoli
Population: 3·96m. (1986)
GNP per capita: US$7,180 (1985)

Al-Jamahiriya Al-Arabiya
Al-Libiya Al-Shabiya
Al-Ishtirakiya Al-Uzma

HISTORY. Tripoli fell under Turkish domination in the 16th century, and though in 1711 the Arab population secured some measure of independence, the country was in 1835 proclaimed a Turkish vilayet. In Sept. 1911 Italy occupied Tripoli and on 19 Oct. 1912, by the Treaty of Ouchy, Turkey recognized the sovereignty of Italy in Tripoli.

After the expulsion of the Germans and Italians in 1942 and 1943, Tripolitania and Cyrenaica were placed under British, and the Fezzan under French, military administration. Britain recognized the Amir Mohammed Idris Al-Senussi as Amir of Cyrenaica in June 1949.

Libya became an independent, sovereign, federal kingdom under the Amir of Cyrenaica, Mohammed Idris Al-Senussi, as King of the United Kingdom of Libya, on 24 Dec. 1951, when the British Residents in Tripolitania and Cyrenaica and the French Resident in the Fezzan transferred their remaining powers to the federal government of Libya, in pursuance of decisions passed by the United Nations in 1949 and 1950.

On 1 Sept. 1969 King Idris was deposed by a group of army officers. Twelve of the group of officers formed the Revolutionary Command Council chaired by Col. Muammar Qadhafi and proclaimed a republic.

AREA AND POPULATION. Libya is bounded north by the Mediterranean Sea, east by Egypt and Sudan, south by Chad and Niger and west by Algeria and Tunisia. The area is estimated at 1,759,540 sq. km (679,358 sq. miles). The population, at the census on 31 July 1984, was 3,637,488; estimate (1986) 3,955,000.

In 1985, 65% of the population was urban. The chief cities (1981) were: Tripoli, the capital (858,000), Benghazi (368,000) and Misurata (117,000).

The populations (1984) of the municipalities were as follows:

Ajdabiya	100,547	Jabal al-Akhdar	120,662	Shati	46,749
Awbari	48,701	Khums	149,642	Surt	110,996
Aziziyah	85,068	Kufrah	25,139	Tarhunah	84,640
Benghazi	485,386	Marzuq	42,294	Tobruk	94,006
Derna	105,031	Misurata	178,295	Tripoli	990,697
Fatah	102,763	Nigat al-Khums	181,584	Yafran	73,420
Ghadames	52,247	Sabha	76,171	Zavia	220,075
Gharyan	117,073	Sawfajjin	45,195	Zlitan	101,107

CLIMATE. The coastal region has a warm temperate climate, with mild wet winters and hot dry summers, though most of the country suffers from aridity. Tripoli. Jan. 52°F (11·1°C), July 81°F (27·2°C). Annual rainfall 16″ (400 mm). Benghazi. Jan. 56°F (13·3°C), July 77°F (25°C). Annual rainfall 11″ (267 mm).

CONSTITUTION AND GOVERNMENT. In March 1977 a new form of direct democracy, the 'Jamahiriya' (state of the masses) was promulgated and the official name of the country was changed to Socialist Peoples Libyan Arab Jamahiriya. Under this system, every adult is supposed to be able to share in policy making through the Basic People's Congresses of which there are some 2,000 throughout Libya. These Congresses appoint Popular Committees to execute policy. Provincial and urban affairs are handled by Popular Committees responsible to Municipality People's Congresses, of which there are 13. Officials of these

Congresses and Committees form at national level the General People's Congress which now normally meets for about a week each December or January. This is the highest policy-making body in the country. The General People's Congress appoints its own General Secretariat and the General People's Committee, whose members (the equivalents of ministers under other forms of government) head the 10 government departments which execute policy at national level.

Until 1977 Libya was ruled by a Revolutionary Command Council headed by Col. Muammar Qadhafi. Upon its abolition in that year the 5 surviving members of the RCC became the General Secretariat of the General People's Congress, still under Qadhafi's direction. In 1979 they stood down to be replaced by elected officials. Since then, Col. Qadhafi has retained his position as Leader of the Revolution. But neither he nor his former RCC colleagues have any formal posts in the present administration, although they continue to wield authority.

Arabic is the official language. Tripoli is the capital.

Secretary-General of the General Secretariat of the General People's Congress: Omar al-Muntasir.

Foreign Affairs: Jadallah Azzuz al-Talhi.

National flag: Plain green.

DEFENCE. There is selective conscription with terms varying from 3-4 years. Enrolment in the reserves, numbering about 40,000, continues until age 49.

Army. The Army is organized into 30 tank battalions, 50 mechanized infantry, 1 National Guard, 10 artillery, 2 anti-aircraft, 2 surface-to-surface missile battalions and 14 parachute commando battalions. Equipment includes 2,100 T-54/-55/-62 and 180 T-72 main battle tanks. The Army has an aviation component; equipment includes over 70 helicopters, notably 40 armed Gazelles, and about 10 O-1 Bird Dog observation aircraft. Strength (1987) 55,000. The paramilitary Pan-African Legion numbers 7,000.

Navy. The fleet comprises 6 *ex*-Soviet diesel-driven submarines, 6 *ex*-Yugoslav 2-man midget submarines, 3 missile-armed frigates, 7 missile-armed corvettes, 1 gun corvette, 8 ocean minesweepers, 25 fast missile craft, 14 fast gunboats, 8 patrol boats, 1 medium (dock type) logistic support ship, 2 landing ships, 3 medium landing ships, 16 landing craft, 1 maintenance repair craft, 1 diving ship, 1 salvage ship, 1 transport and 10 tugs. Under construction are 4 missile-armed fast attack craft.

One missile-armed fast corvette was sunk on 24 March 1986 and one severely damaged next day by US naval forces.

Libya has procured naval equipment and weapons from both the East (particularly the USSR) and the West; and the modern fleet constitutes a force of some importance in the Mediterranean, although training, maintenance and logistic support are questionable.

Personnel in 1988 exceeded 4,000 officers and ratings, including coastguard. A large proportion of personnel have trained in the Soviet Union since 1975.

Air Force. The creation of an Air Force began in 1959. In 1974, delivery was completed of a total of 110 Mirage 5 combat aircraft and trainers, of which about 50 remain. They have been followed by 10 Tu-22 supersonic reconnaissance bombers, 70 MiG-25 interceptors and reconnaissance aircraft, 100 Su-22 ground attack fighters, 94 MiG-21s, and about 140 MiG-23 variable-geometry fighters and fighter-bombers from the USSR. Other equipment includes 40 Mirage F1 fighters from France, 6 Mirage F1-B two-seat trainers, 20 Mi-24 gunship helicopters, Mi-14 anti-submarine helicopters, 9 C-130H Hercules and 20 Aeritalia G222T transports, 8 Super Frelon and 20 Agusta-built CH-47C Chinook heavy-lift helicopters, and a total of 16 Bell 212, Bell 47, Alouette III and Mi-8 helicopters. Training is performed on piston-engined SF.260Ms (some of which are armed for light attack duties) from Italy; L-39 Albatross, Galeb and Magister jet aircraft; and twin-engined L-410s built in Czechoslovakia. Personnel total (1988) about 10,000, with many of the combat aircraft operated by foreign aircrew.

INTERNATIONAL RELATIONS

Membership. Libya is a member of UN, OAU, OIC, OPEC and the Arab League.

ECONOMY

Planning. Declining oil revenues (50% down on 1980 levels) has meant postponing of most projects envisaged in the 5-year development plan (1981–85) and no new development plan had been announced by Dec. 1987.

Budget. A development budget of LD1,450m. was announced for 1987 but is likely to be under-spent.

Currency. The currency is the Libyan *dinar* which is divided into 1,000 *millemes*. Rate of exchange, March 1988: LD 0·50 = £1; LD 0·28 = US$1.

Banking. A National Bank of Libya was established in 1955; it was renamed the Central Bank of Libya in 1972. All foreign banks were nationalized by Dec. 1970. In 1972 the government set up the Libyan Arab Foreign Bank whose function is overseas investment and to participate in multinational banking corporations. The National Agricultural Bank, which has been set up to give loans and subsidies to farmers to develop their land and to assist them in marketing their crops, has offices in Tripoli, Benghazi, Sebha and other agricultural centres. The National Industrial and Real Estate Bank has been divided to form a Real Estate Bank to provide loans for house-buyers and the Development Bank to finance industrial projects.

Weights and Measures. Although the metric system has been officially adopted and is obligatory for all contracts, the following weights and measures are still used: *oke* = 1·282 kg; *kantar* = 51·28 kg; *draa* = 46 cm; *handaza* = 68 cm.

ENERGY AND NATURAL RESOURCES

Electricity. Electricity capacity (1985) 5,615 mw. Production (1986) 2,126m. kwh. Supply 110, 115 and 220 volts; 50 Hz.

Oil. Production (1987) 46·5m. tonnes. Reserves (1985) 21,000m. bbls. The Libyan National Oil Corporation (NOC) was established in March 1970 to be the state's organization for the exploitation of Libya's oil resources. NOC does not participate in the production of oil but has a majority share in all the operating companies with the exception of two small producers Aquitaine-Libya and Wintershall Libya.

The largest producers are Waha (formerly Oasis, until the withdrawal of US oil companies at the end of June 1986) and AGOCO who together produce more than 50% of total production. The other significant producers are Zuweitina (formerly Occidental Libya), AGIP, Sirte Oil Company, and Veba (also known as Mobil Oil Libya, although Mobil Inc. withdrew in July 1982 after EXXON's withdrawal from the Sirte Oil Company in Oct. 1981).

Gas. Reserves (1985) 600,000m. cu. metres. Production (1982) 29,000m. cu. metres. In 1983 a gas pipeline was under construction which will take gas from Brega, along the coast to Misurata. In 1987 agreement was reached with Algeria and Tunisia to construct a gas pipeline to supply western Libya with Algerian gas.

Water. Since 1984 a major project has been under way to bring water from wells in southern Libya to the coast. This scheme, called the 'Great Man-made River', is planned, on completion, to irrigate some 185,000 acres of land with water brought along some 4,000 km of pipes. Factories for the construction of the 4 metre diametre pipes which will be used were opened in Aug. 1986.

Minerals. There were (1984) 5 cement factories with a capacity of 4·75m. tonnes per annum. Two new plants were under construction in 1984 with a capacity of 2·5m. tonnes. Gypsum output (1982) 172,400 tonnes. Iron ore deposits have been found in the south and uranium has reportedly been found in the region of Ghat in the south-west.

Agriculture. Tripolitania has 3 zones from the coast inland—the Mediterranean, the sub-desert and the desert. The first, which covers an area of about 17,231 sq.

miles, is the only one properly suited for agriculture, and may be further sub-divided into: (1) the oases along the coast, the richest in North Africa, in which thrive the date palm, the olive, the orange, the peanut and the potato; (2) the steppe district, suitable for cereals (barley and wheat) and pasture; it has olive, almond, vine, orange and mulberry trees and ricinus plants; (3) the dunes, which are being gradually afforested with acacia, robinia, poplar and pine; (4) the Jebel (the mountain district, Tarhuna, Garian, Nalut-Yefren), in which thrive the olive, the fig, the vine and other fruit trees, and which on the east slopes down to the sea with the fertile hills of Msellata. Of some 25m. acres of productive land in Tripolitania, nearly 20m. are used for grazing and about 1m. for static farming. The sub-desert zone produces the alfa plant. The desert zone and the Fezzan contain some fertile oases, such as those of Ghadames, Ghat, Socna, Sebha, Brak.

Cyrenaica has about 10m. acres of potentially productive land, most of which, however, is suitable only for grazing. Certain areas, chief of which is the plateau known as the Barce Plain (about 1,000 ft above sea-level), are suitable for dry farming; in addition, grapes, olives and dates are grown. With improved irrigation, production, particularly of vegetables, could be increased, but stock raising and dry farming will remain of primary importance. About 143,000 acres are used for settled farming; about 272,000 acres are covered by natural forests. The Agricultural Development Authority plans to reclaim 6,000 hectares each year for agriculture. In the Fezzan there are about 6,700 acres of irrigated gardens and about 297,000 acres are planted with date palms.

Production (1985, in tonnes): Wheat, 149,000; barley, 80,000; milk, 98,000; meat, 153,000. Olive trees number about 3·4m. and productive date-palm trees about 3m.

Livestock (1985): 5·5m. sheep, 900,000 goats, 200,000 cattle, 25m. poultry.

Fisheries. The catch in 1982 was 7,425 tonnes.

INDUSTRY AND TRADE

Industry. Among the traditional industries of Tripolitania and Cyrenaica are sponge fishing, tunny fishing, tobacco growing and processing, dyeing and weaving of local wool and imported cotton yarn, and olive oil. Tripolitania also produces bricks, salt, leather and esparto grass for paper-making. Home industries of both territories include the making of matting, carpets, leather articles and fabrics embroidered with gold and silver. The Government has embarked on an ambitious programme of industrial development aimed at the local manufacture of building materials (steel and aluminium pipes and fittings, electric cables, cement, bricks, glass, etc.), foodstuffs (dairy products, flour, tinned fruits and vegetables, dates, fish processing and canning, etc.), textiles and footwear (ready-made clothing, woollen and cotton cloth, blankets, leather footwear, etc.) and development of mineral deposits (iron ore, phosphates, mineral salts). Small scale private sector industrialization is encouraged by government loans and subsidies. From 21 Sept. 1969 all businesses, except oil and banks, were Libyan-owned.

Commerce. Total imports in 1986 were valued at US$4,553 (f.o.b.) and exports at US$6,412 (f.o.b.), virtually all crude oil. In 1986, 23% of imports came from Italy, while 28% of exports were to Italy, 14% to the Federal Republic of Germany and 13% to Spain.

Total trade between Libya and UK (British Department of Trade returns, in £1,000 sterling):

	1983	1984	1985	1986	1987
Imports to UK	224,050	155,276	311,764	136,390	133,649
Exports and re-exports from UK	274,169	246,467	237,639	260,529	220,626

Tourism. There were 100,000 visitors in 1984.

COMMUNICATIONS

Roads. In 1986 there were 25,675 km of roads. In 1982 there were 415,509 passenger cars and 334,405 commercial vehicles.

Railways. In 1988 there were no operating railways.

Aviation. A national airline, the Libyan Arab Airlines (LAA), was inaugurated on 30 Sept. 1965. Benghazi and Tripoli are linked by LAA and other international airlines to Athens, Rome, Madrid, Moscow, Frankfurt, Paris, Amsterdam, Vienna and Zurich.

Post and Broadcasting. Tripoli is connected by telegraph cable with Malta and by microwave link with Bengardane (Tunis). There are overseas wireless-telegraph stations at Benghazi and Tripoli, and radio-telephone services connect Libya with most countries of western Europe. In 1982 some 102,000 telephones were in use and in 1983 there were 165,000 radio sets and 170,000 television receivers.

Newspapers. There was (1984) one daily in Tripoli with a circulation of about 40,000.

JUSTICE, RELIGION, EDUCATION AND WELFARE

Justice. The Civil, Commercial and Criminal codes are based mainly on the Egyptian model. Matters of personal status of family or succession matters affecting Moslems are dealt with in special courts according to the Moslem law. All other matters, civil, commercial and criminal, are tried in the ordinary courts, which have jurisdiction over everyone.

There are civil and penal courts in Tripoli and Benghazi, with subsidiary courts at Misurata and Derna; courts of assize in Tripoli and Benghazi, and courts of appeal in Tripoli and Benghazi.

Religion. Islam is declared the State religion, but the right of others to practise their religions is provided for. In 1982, 97% were Sunni Moslems.

Education. There were (1981–82) 718,124 pupils in primary schools, 286,414 in preparatory and secondary schools, 44,789 pupils in technical schools and 25,700 students in higher education. There are 2 universities of Al Fatah (in Tripoli) and Garyounes (in Benghazi).

Health. In 1981 there were 74 hospitals with 15,375 beds, 4,690 physicians, 314 dentists, 420 pharmacists, 1,080 midwives and 5,346 nursing personnel.

DIPLOMATIC REPRESENTATIVES

UK broke off diplomatic relations with Libya on 22 April 1984. Saudi Arabia looks after Libyan interests in UK and Italy looks after UK's interests in Libya.

USA suspended all embassy activities in Tripoli on 2 May 1980.

Of Libya to the United Nations
Ambassador: Dr Ali Treiki.

Books of Reference

Allen, J. A., *Libya: The Experience of Oil.* London and Boulder, 1981.—*Libya since Independence.* London, 1982
Bearman, J., *Qadhafi's Libya.* London, 1986
Blundy, D. and Lycett, A., *Qadhafi and the Libyan Revolution.* London, 1987
Cooley, J. K., *Libyan Sandstorm: The Complete Account of Qaddafi's Revolution.* London and New York, 1983
Fergiani, M. B., *The Libyan Jamahiriya.* London, 1984
Harris, L. C., *Libya: Qadhafi's Revolution and the Modern State.* Boulder and London, 1986
Lawless, R. I., *Libya.* [Bibliography] Oxford and Santa Barbara, 1987
Waddhams, F. C., *The Libyan Oil Industry.* London, 1980
Wright, J., *Libya: A Modern History.* London, 1982

LIECHTENSTEIN

Capital: Vaduz
Population: 27,400 (1986)
GNP per capita: US$15,000 (1984)

HISTORY. The Principality of Liechtenstein, situated between the Austrian province of Vorarlberg and the Swiss cantons of St Gallen and Graubünden, is a sovereign state whose history dates back to 3 May 1342, when Count Hartmann III became ruler of the county of Vaduz. Additions were later made to the count's domains, and by 1434 the territory reached its present boundaries. It consists of the two former counties of Schellenberg and Vaduz (until 1806 immediate fiefs of the Roman Empire). The former in 1699 and the latter in 1712 came into the possession of the house of Liechtenstein and, by diploma of 23 Jan. 1719, granted by the Emperor Charles VI, the two counties were constituted as the Principality of Liechtenstein.

AREA AND POPULATION. Liechtenstein is bounded on the east by Austria and the west by Switzerland. Area, 160 sq. km (61·8 sq. miles); population, of Alemannic race (census 1980), 25,215; estimate, 1986, 27,400. In 1986 there were 351 births and 188 deaths. Population of Vaduz (census 1980), 4,606; estimate, 1986, 4,920. The language is German.

REIGNING PRINCE. Francis Joseph II, born 16 Aug. 1906; succeeded his great uncle, 26 July 1938; married on 7 March 1943 to Countess Gina von Wilczek; there are 4 sons, Prince Hans Adam (Has exercised the prerogatives to which the Sovereign is entitled from 26 Aug. 1984, born 14 Feb. 1945; married on 30 July 1967 to Countess Marie Aglaë Kinsky), Prince Philipp Erasmus (married on 11 Sept. 1971 to Isabelle de l'Arbre de Malander), Prince Nikolaus Ferdinand (married on 20 March 1982 to Princess Margaretha of Luxembourg) and Prince Franz Josef Wenzel, and one daughter, Princess Nora Elisabeth. The monarchy is hereditary in the male line.

CONSTITUTION AND GOVERNMENT. Liechtenstein is a constitutional monarchy ruled by the princes of the House of Liechtenstein. The present constitution of 5 Oct. 1921 provides for a unicameral parliament (Diet) of 15 members elected for 4 years. Election is on the basis of proportional representation. The prince can call and dismiss the parliament. On parliamentary recommendation, he appoints the prime minister and the 4 councillors for a 4-year term. Any group of 900 persons or any 3 communes may propose legislation (initiative). Bills passed by the parliament may be submitted to popular referendum. A law is valid when it receives a majority approval by the parliament and the prince's signed concurrence. The capital and seat of government is Vaduz and there are 10 more communes all connected by modern roads. The 11 communes are fully independent administrative bodies within the laws of the principality. They levy additional taxes to the state taxes. Since Feb. 1921 Liechtenstein has had the Swiss currency, and since 29 March 1923 has been united with Switzerland in a customs union.

At the elections for the Diet, on 2 Feb. 1986, the Fatherland Union obtained 8 seats, the opposition Progressive Citizens' Party, 7 seats.

Head of Government: Hans Brunhart.

National flag: Horizontally blue over red, with a gold coronet in the first quarter.
National anthem: Oben am jungen Rhein (words by H. H. Jauch, 1850; tune, 'God save the Queen').

INTERNATIONAL RELATIONS

Membership. Liechtenstein is a member of EFTA, the Council of Europe and the International Court of Justice.

ECONOMY

Budget. Budget estimates for 1987: Revenue, 347,378,000 Swiss francs; expenditure, 331,914,000 Swiss francs. There is no public debt.

Currency. The Swiss *franc*.

Banking. There were (1988) 3 banks: Liechtensteinische Landesbank, Bank in Liechtenstein Ltd, Verwaltungs-und Privatbank Ltd.

Weights and Measures. The metric system is in force.

ENERGY AND NATURAL RESOURCES

Electricity. Electricity produced in 1986 was 43,371,000 kwh.

Agriculture. The rearing of cattle, for which the fine alpine pastures are well suited, is highly developed. In March 1987 there were 6,487 cattle (including 2,999 milk cows), 189 horses, 2,337 sheep, 80 goats, 2,606 pigs. Total production of dairy produce, 1986, 13,338,845 kg.

INDUSTRY AND TRADE

Industry. The country has a great variety of light industries (textiles, ceramics, steel screws, precision instruments, canned food, pharmaceutical products, heating appliances, etc.).

Since 1945 Liechtenstein has changed from a predominantly agricultural country to a highly industrialized country. The farming population has gone down from 70% in 1930 to only 3% in 1986. The rapid change-over has led to the immigration of foreign workers (Austrians, Germans, Italians, Spaniards). Industrial undertakings affiliated to the Liechtenstein Chamber of Industry and Commerce in 1986 employed 6,657 workers earning 315,336,000 Swiss francs.

Commerce. Exports of home produce, for firms in membership of the Chamber of Commerce, in 1986 amounted to 1,291m. Swiss francs. 25·8% went to EFTA countries, of which Switzerland took 248·1m. (19·2%) and 40% went to EEC countries.

Total trade with UK is included with Switzerland from 1968.

Tourism. In 1986, 76,440 visitors arrived in Liechtenstein.

COMMUNICATIONS

Roads. There are 250 km of roads. Postal buses are the chief means of public transportation within the country and to Austria and Switzerland.

Railways. The 18·5 km of main railway passing through the country is operated by Austrian Federal Railways.

Post and Broadcasting. In 1986 there were 13,156 telephones, 468 telex, 9,218 wireless sets and 8,674 television sets. The post and telegraphs are administered by Switzerland.

Cinemas. There were 2 cinemas in 1988.

Newspapers. In 1987 there were 2 daily newspapers with a total circulation of 15,000.

JUSTICE, RELIGION, EDUCATION AND WELFARE

Justice. The principality has its own civil and penal codes. The lowest court is the county court, *Landgericht*, presided over by one judge, which decides minor civil cases and summary criminal offences. The criminal court, *Kriminalgericht*, with a bench of 5 judges is for major crimes. Another court of mixed jurisdiction is the court of assizes (with 3 judges) for misdemeanours. Juvenile cases are treated in the Juvenile Court (with a bench of 3 judges). The superior court, *Obergericht*, and

Supreme Court, *Oberster Gerichtshof*, are courts of appeal for civil and criminal cases (both with benches of 5 judges). An administrative court of appeal from government actions and the State Court determines the constitutionality of laws.

The death penalty was abolished in 1987.

Police. The principality has no army. Police force, 42; auxiliary police, 29 (1987).

Religion. In 1986, 87·1% of the population was Roman Catholic and 8·6% was Protestant.

Education (1987–88). In 14 primary, 3 upper, 5 secondary, 1 grammar and 3 (for backward children) schools there were 3,486 pupils and 204 teachers. There is also an evening technical school, a music school and a children's pedagogic-welfare day school.

Health. In 1984 there was 1 hospital, but Liechtenstein has an agreement with the Swiss cantons of St Gallen and Graubünden and the Austrian Federal State of Vorarlberg that her citizens may use certain hospitals.

DIPLOMATIC REPRESENTATIVES

In 1919, Switzerland agreed to represent the interests of Liechtenstein in countries where she has diplomatic missions and where Liechtenstein is not represented in her own right. In so doing Switzerland always acts only on the basis of mandates of a general or specific nature, which she may either accept or refuse, while Liechtenstein is free to enter into direct relations with foreign states or to set up her own additional diplomatic missions.

British Consul-General: G. A. Duggan (resident in Zürich).
USA Consul-General: L. Segesvary (resident in Zürich).

Books of Reference

Statistical Information: Amt für Volkswirtschaft, Vaduz.

Rechenschaftsbericht der Fürstlichen Regierung. Vaduz. Annual, from 1922
Jahrbuch des Historischen Vereins. Vaduz. Annual since 1901
Kranz, W., *The Principality of Liechtenstein.* Press and Information Office. 5th ed. Vaduz, 1981
The Economy of the Principality of Liechtenstein. Press and Information Office, Vaduz, 1984
Batliner, E. H., *Das Geld- und Kreditwesen des Fürstentums Liechtenstein in Vergangenheit und Gegenwart.* 1959
Green, B., *Valley of Peace.* Vaduz, 1967
Larke, T. A. T., *Index and Thesaurus of Liechtenstein.* 2nd ed. Berkeley, 1984
Malin, G., *Kunstführer Fürstentum Liechtenstein.* Berne, 1977
Raton, P., *Liechtenstein: History and Institutions of the Principality.* Vaduz, 1970
Seger, O., *A Survey of Liechtenstein History.* 4th English ed. Vaduz, 1984
Steger, G., *Fürst und Landtag nach Liechtensteinischem Recht.* Vaduz, 1950

LUXEMBOURG

Capital: Luxembourg
Population: 369,500 (1987)
GNP per capita: US$12,990 (1985)

Grand-Duché de Luxembourg

HISTORY. The country formed part of the Holy Roman Empire until it was conquered by the French in 1795. In 1815 the Grand Duchy of Luxembourg was formed under the house of Orange-Nassau, also sovereigns of the Netherlands. In 1839 the Walloon-speaking area was joined to Belgium. In 1890 the personal union with the Netherlands ended with the accession of a member of another branch of the house of Nassau, Grand Duke Adolphe of Nassau-Weilburg.

AREA AND POPULATION. Luxembourg has an area of 2,586 sq. km (998 sq. miles) and is bounded on the west by Belgium, south by France, east by the Federal Republic of Germany. The population (1987) was 369,500. The capital, Luxembourg, had 76,640 inhabitants; Esch-Alzette, the centre of the mining district, 23,720; Differdange, 16,000; Dudelange, 14,060, and Petange, 11,590. In 1984 the foreign population was about 96,700.

Vital statistics (1986): 4,309 births, 3,970 deaths, 1,892 marriages.

CLIMATE. Cold, raw winters with snow covering the ground for up to a month are features of the upland areas. The remainder resembles Belgium in its climate, with rain evenly distributed throughout the year. Jan. 31°F (0·5°C), July 63°F (17·5°C). Annual rainfall 29·6″ (740 mm).

REIGNING GRAND DUKE. Jean, born 5 Jan. 1921, son of the late Grand Duchess Charlotte and the late Prince Felix of Bourbon-Parma; succeeded 12 Nov. 1964 on the abdication of his mother; married to Princess Joséphine-Charlotte of Belgium, 9 April 1953. *Offspring:* Princess Marie-Astrid, born 17 Feb. 1954, married Christian of Habsbourg-Lorraine 6 Feb. 1982 (*Offspring:* Marie Christine, born 31 July 1983; Imre, born 8 Dec. 1985); Prince Henri, *heir apparent,* born 16 April 1955, married Maria Teresa Mestre 14 Feb. 1981; (*Offspring:* Prince Guillaume, born 11 Nov. 1981, Prince Felix, born 3 June 1984, Prince Louis, born 3 Aug. 1986). Prince Jean, born 15 May 1957, married Hélène Vestur; Princess Margaretha, born 15 May 1957, married Prince Nikolaus of Liechtenstein 20 March 1982; Prince Guillaume, born 1 May 1963.

The civil list is fixed at 300,000 gold francs per annum, to be reconsidered at the beginning of each reign.

On 28 Sept. 1919 a referendum was taken in Luxembourg to decide on the political and economic future of the country. The voting resulted as follows: For the reigning Grand Duchess, 66,811; for the continuance of the Nassau-Braganza dynasty under another Grand Duchess, 1,286; for another dynasty, 889; for a republic, 16,885; for an economic union with France, 60,133; for an economic union with Belgium, 22,242. But France refused in favour of Belgium, and on 22 Dec. 1921 the Chamber of the Grand Duchy passed a Bill for the economic union between Belgium and Luxembourg. The agreement, which is for 60 years, provides for the disappearance of the customs barrier between the two countries and the use of Belgian, in addition to Luxembourg, currency as legal tender in the Grand Duchy. It came into force on 1 May 1922.

The Grand Duchy was under German occupation from 10 May 1940 to 10 Sept. 1944. The Grand Duchess Charlotte and the Government carried on an independent administration in London. Civil government was restored in Oct. 1944.

National flag: Three horizontal stripes of red, white and light blue.

National anthem: Ons Hemecht (words by M. Lentz, 1859; tune by J. A. Zinnen).

CONSTITUTION AND GOVERNMENT. The Grand Duchy of Luxembourg is a constitutional monarchy, the hereditary sovereignty being in the Nassau family. The constitution of 17 Oct. 1868 was revised in 1919, 1948, 1956 and 1972. The revision of 1948 has abolished the 'perpetually neutral' status of the country and introduced the concepts of right to work, social security, health services, freedom of trade and industry, and recognition of trade unions. The revision of 1956 provides for the devolution of executive, legislative and judicial powers to international institutions.

The national language is Luxemburgish; French, German and English are widely used.

The country forms 4 electoral districts. An elector must be a citizen (male or female) of Luxembourg and have completed 18 years of age; to be eligible for election the citizen must have completed 21 years of age.

The Chamber of Deputies consists of 25 Christian Social, 21 Socialists, 14 Democrats, and 2 Communists, and 1 Green alternative (Ecologist) and 1 non-attached deputy (elections of 17 June 1984). Members are elected for 5 years; they receive a salary and a travelling allowance.

The head of the state takes part in the legislative power, exercises the executive power and has a certain part in the judicial power. The constitution leaves to the sovereign the right to organize the Government, which consists of a Minister of State, who is President of the Government, and of at least 3 Ministers.

The Cabinet was, in Jan. 1986, composed as follows:

President of the Government, Minister of State, Minister for Finance: Jacques Santer.
Vice-President of the Government, Foreign Affairs, Foreign Trade and Co-operation, Economy and Middle Classes, Exchequer: Jacques F. Poos. *Health and Social Security:* Benny Berg. *Justice, Cultural Affairs, Environment:* Robert Krieps. *National Education and Youth, Tourism:* Fernand Boden. *Interior, Family Affairs, Social Solidarity:* Jean Spautz. *Labour, Finance and Budget:* Jean-Claude Juncker. *Transport, Public Works, Energy:* Marcel Schlechter. *Agriculture and Viticulture, Armed Forces, Civil Service, Physical Education and Sports:* Marc Fischbach. *Secretary of State for Economy:* Johny Lahure. *Secretary of State for Agriculture and Viticulture:* René Steichen. *Secretary of State for Foreign Affairs, Foreign Trade and Co-operation, Middle Classes:* Robert Goebbels.

Besides the Cabinet there is a Council of State. It deliberates on proposed laws and Bills, and on amendments; it also gives administrative decisions and expresses its opinion regarding any other question referred to it by the Grand Duke or the Government. The Council of State is composed of 21 members chosen for life by the sovereign, who also chooses a president from among them each year.

DEFENCE. A law passed by Parliament on 29 June 1967 abolished compulsory service and instituted a battalion-size army of volunteers enlisted for 3 years. Strength (1988) 630. The defence estimates for 1987 amounted to 2,018m. francs. Luxembourg is an original member of NATO and the battalion is committed to NATO ACE mobile force.

INTERNATIONAL RELATIONS

Membership. Luxembourg is a member of the UN, Benelux, the European Communities, OECD, the Council of Europe, NATO and WEU.

ECONOMY

Budget. Revenue and expenditure (including extraordinary) for years ending 30 April (in 1m. francs):

	1983	1984	1985	1986	1987	1988[1]
Revenue	71,828·6	75,047·9	81,363·8	78,625·9	80,063·9	84,738·7
Expenditure	74,075·3	73,599·3	79,536·8	78,280·4	80,217·8	84,141·6

[1] Provisional.

Consolidated debt at 31 Dec. 1986 amounted to 17,084m. francs (long-term) and 3,432·1m. francs (short-term).

Currency. On 14 Oct. 1944 the Luxembourg *franc* was fixed at par value with the Belgian franc. Notes of the Belgian National Bank are legal tender in Luxembourg.

Banking. On 31 Dec. 1986 depositors in the State Savings Bank with a total of 45,466m. francs to their credit. There were (1987) 122 banks and 21 non-bank credit institutions established in Luxembourg which has become an international financial centre.

Weights and Measures. The metric system is in force.

ENERGY AND NATURAL RESOURCES

Electricity. Power production was 976m. kwh. in 1986.

Minerals. In 1986 production (in tonnes) of pig-iron, 2,649,700; of steel, 3,705,300.

Agriculture. Agriculture is carried on by about 7,000 of the population; 126,960 hectares were under cultivation in 1986. The principal crops are potatoes, barley, beet, oats, wheat and maize. In 1986, 159,700 hectolitres of wine were produced from 1,163 hectares.

Livestock (1986): 1,699 horses, 222,864 cattle, 75,609 pigs, 5,900 sheep.

INDUSTRY AND TRADE

Commerce. By treaty of 5 Sept. 1944, signed in London, and the treaty of 14 March 1947, signed in The Hague, the Grand Duchy, together with Belgium and the Netherlands, became a party to the Benelux Customs Union, which came into force on 1 Jan. 1948. For further particulars *see* p. 198.

Total trade between Luxembourg and UK included with Belgium from 1974.

Tourism. In 1986 there were 462,000 tourists.

COMMUNICATIONS

Roads. In 1987 the network had a total of 5,220 km. Motor vehicles registered in Luxembourg on 1 Jan. 1987 included 162,481 passenger cars, 9,627 trucks, 701 buses, 18,871 tractors and special vehicles.

Railways. In 1986 there were 270 km of railway (standard gauge) of which 162 km electrified. It carried 604m. tonne-km and 278m. passenger-km.

Aviation. Findel is the airport for Luxembourg and 877,000 passengers and 78,372 tonnes of freight were handled in 1986.

Post and Broadcasting. In 1982 the telephone system had more than 5,200 km of telegraph and telephone line, 157,100 telephones (1986), 106 post offices and 387 telegraph offices (1985). *Compagnie Luxembourgeoise de Télédiffusion* broadcasts 1 programme in Luxembourgian on FM. Powerful transmitters on long-, medium- and short-waves are used for commercial and religious programmes in French, Dutch, German, English and Italian. Ten TV programmes are broadcast. Colour transmission by SECAM system.

Cinemas (1987). There were 11 cinemas.

Newspapers (1986). There were 6 daily newspapers with a circulation of 130,000.

RELIGION, EDUCATION AND WELFARE

Religion. The population is 95% Roman Catholic. The remaining 5% is mainly Protestant or Jewish, or does not belong to any religion. The Protestant Church is organized on an interdenominational basis.

Education (1986–87). Education is compulsory for all children between the ages of 6 and 15. The nursery schools had 8,315 pupils; primary schools had 22,059 pupils; technical secondary schools, 13,135 pupils; secondary schools, 7,197 pupils; the Superior Institute of Technology, 262 pupils; pedagogic education, 145 pupils; university studies (1984–85), 587 pupils.

Health. In 1986 there were 686 doctors and 4,616 hospital beds.

DIPLOMATIC REPRESENTATIVES

Of Luxembourg in Great Britain (27 Wilton Crescent, London, SWIX 8SD)
Ambassador: Jean Wagner (accredited 4 March 1986).

Of Great Britain in Luxembourg (14 Blvd Roosevelt, Luxembourg)
Ambassador and Consul-General: Juliet Campbell.

Of Luxembourg in the USA (2200 Massachusetts Ave., NW, Washington, D.C., 20008)
Ambassador: André Philippe.

Of the USA in Luxembourg (22 Blvd. Emmanuel Servais, Luxembourg)
Ambassador: Jean Broward-Shevlin Gerard.

Of Luxembourg to the United Nations
Ambassador: Jean Feyder.

Books of Reference

Statistical Information: The Service Central de la Statistique et des Études Économiques was founded in 1900 and reorganized in 1962 (19–21 boulevard Royal, C.P. 304 Luxembourg-City). *Director:* Georges Als. Main publications: *Bulletin du Statec.—Annuaire statistique.— Cahiers économiques.*

Bulletin de Documentation. Government Information Service. From 1945 (monthly)
The Institutions of the Grand Duchy of Luxembourg. Press and Information Service, Luxembourg, 1982
Als, G., *Le Luxembourg, situation politique, économique et sociale.* Luxembourg, 1982
Calmes, C., *Au Fil de l'Histoire.* Luxembourg, 1977
Heiderscheid, A., *Aspects de Sociologie Religieuse du Diocèse de Luxembourg.* 2 vols. Luxembourg, 1961
Hury, C. and Christophory, J., *Luxembourg.* [Bibliography] Oxford and Santa Barbara, 1981
Majerus, P., *Le Luxembourg independant.* Luxembourg, 1948.—*L'État Luxembourgeois.* Luxembourg, 1983
Newcomer, J., *The Grand Duchy of Luxembourg: The Evolution of Nationhood, 963 A.D. to 1983.* Washington, 1983
Trausch, G., *Le Luxembourg à l'Époque Contemporaine.* Luxembourg, 1975

Archives of the State: Luxembourg-City. *Director:* Paul Spang.
National Library: Luxembourg-City, 37 Boulevard Roosevelt. *Director:* Jules Christophory.

MADAGASCAR

Capital: Antananarivo
Population: 10·57m. (1987)
GNP per capita: US$250 (1984)

Repoblika Demokratika n'i Madagaskar

HISTORY. Madagascar was discovered by the Portuguese, Diego Diaz, in 1500. The island was unified under the Imérina monarchy between 1797 and 1861, but French claims to a protectorate led to hostilities culminating in the establishment of a protectorate on 30 Sept. 1895. The monarchy was abolished and Madagascar became a French Colony on 6 Aug. 1896.

Madagascar became an Overseas Territory in 1946, and on 14 Oct. 1958, following a referendum, was proclaimed the autonomous Malagasy Republic within the French Community, achieving full independence on 26 June 1960.

The government of Philibert Tsiranana, President from independence, resigned on 18 May 1972 and executive powers were given to Maj.-Gen. Gabriel Ramanantsoa, who replaced Tsiranana as President on 11 Oct. 1972. On 5 Feb. 1975, Col. Richard Ratsimandrava became Head of State, but was assassinated 6 days later. A National Military Directorate under Brig.-Gen. Gilles Andriamahazo was established on 12 Feb. On 15 June it handed over power to a Supreme Revolutionary Council (SRC) under Didier Ratsiraka.

AREA AND POPULATION. Madagascar is situated off the south-east coast of Africa, from which it is separated by the Mozambique channel, the least distance between island and continent being 250 miles (400 km); its length is 980 miles (1,600 km); greatest breadth, 360 miles (570 km).

The area is 587,041 sq. km (226,658 sq. miles). In 1975 (census) the population was 7,603,790. Estimate (1987) 10,568,000.

Province	Area in sq. km	Population 1978	Chief town	Population 1982
Antseranana	43,046	620,228	Antseranana	49,000
Mahajanga	150,023	857,610	Mahajanga	80,881
Toamasina	71,911	1,254,639	Toamasina	82,907
Antananarivo	58,283	2,322,019	Antananarivo	662,585 [1]
Fianarantsoa	102,373	1,908,465	Fianarantsoa	72,901
Toliary	161,405	1,084,083	Toliary	48,929

[1] 1985.

Vital statistics, 1984: Births, 456,000; deaths, 146,000.

The indigenous population are of Malayo-Polynesian stock, divided into 18 ethnic groups of which the principal are Merina (26%) of the central plateau, the Betsimisaraka (15%) of the east coast, and the Betsileo (12%) of the southern plateau. Foreign communities include Europeans, mainly French (30,000), Indians (15,000), Chinese (9,000), Comorians and Arabs.

CLIMATE. A tropical climate, but the mountains cause big variations in rainfall, which is very heavy in the east and very light in the west. Antananarivo. Jan. 70°F (21·1°C), July 59°F (15°C). Annual rainfall 54″ (1,350 mm). Toamasina. Jan. 80°F (26·7°C), July 70°F (21·1°C). Annual rainfall 128″ (3,256 mm).

CONSTITUTION AND GOVERNMENT. The new Constitution of the Democratic Republic of Madagascar was approved by referendum on 21 Dec. 1975 and came into force on 30 Dec. It provides for a National People's Assembly of 137 members elected by universal suffrage for a 5-year term from the single list of the *Front National pour la Défense de la Révolution Socialiste Malgache;* following the general elections held on 28 Aug. 1983, this comprised 117 members of the

Avant-garde de la Révolution Malgache, 9 of the *Parti du Congrès de l'Indépendence* and 11 others. Executive power is vested in the President, directly elected for 7 years, who appoints a Council of Ministers to assist him, with the guidance of the 20-member Supreme Revolutionary Council.

President: Adm. Didier Ratsiraka (re-elected 7 Nov. 1982).
The Council of Ministers in Feb. 1988 was composed as follows:

Prime Minister: Lieut.-Col. Victor Ramahatra.
Foreign Affairs: Jean Bemananjara. *Defence:* Gen. Christophe Bienaimé Raveloson-Mahasampo. *Interior:* Ampy Portos. *Civil Service and Labour:* Georges Ruphin. *Finance and Economy:* Pascal Rakotomavo. *Health:* Dr Jean-Jacques Séraphin. *Commerce:* Georges Solofoson. *Industry, Energy and Mines:* José Rakotomavo. *Animal Production, Water Resources and Forestry:* Joseph Randrianasolo. *Agricultural Production and Agrarian Reform:* José-Michel Andrianoélison. *Posts and Telecommunications:* Rakotovoa Andriantiana. *Secondary and Basic Education:* Charles Zeny. *Higher Education:* Ignace Rakoto. *Scientific Research:* Antoine Zafera. *Information and Ideological Guidance:* Simon Pierre. *Revolutionary Art and Culture:* Gisêle Rabesahala. *Transport and Tourism:* Jean Emile Tsaranazy. *Public Works:* (Vacant). *Population, Social Welfare, Youth and Sport:* Jean-André Ndremanjary. *Justice:* Joseph Bedo. *Special Economic Advisor:* Nirina Andriamanerasoa.

National flag: Horizontally red over green, in the hoist a vertical white strip.
National anthem: Ry tanindrazanay malala ô!

Malagasy, which is a language of Malayo-Polynesian origin, is the official language. French and English are understood and taught in Malagasy schools.

Local Government: The six provinces are sub-divided into 110 *Fivondronana,* which in turn are divided into 1,252 *Firaisana* and finally into 11,393 *Fokontany* (the traditional communal divisions). Each level is governed by an elected council.

DEFENCE

Army. The Army is organized in 2 battalion groups, and 1 engineer, 1 signals, 1 service and 7 construction regiments. Equipment includes PT-76 light tanks and M-8 armoured cars. Strength (1988) 20,000 and gendarmerie 7,500.

Navy. The small maritime guard in 1988 had a strength of 600 (including 120 marines), equipped with 1 large patrol craft, 5 patrol boats, 1 medium landing ship, 1 landing craft, 4 minor landing craft and a large trawler training ship.

Air Force. Created in 1961, the Malagasy Air Force received its first combat equipment in 1978, with the arrival of 8 MiG-21 and 4 MiG-17 fighters, plus flying and ground staff instructors, from North Korea. Other equipment includes 1 An-12 and 4 An-26 turboprop transports, 1 Britten-Norman Defender armed transport, 5 C-47s, 1 HS. 748 and 1 Yak-40 for VIP use, 1 Aztec, 3 Cessna Skymasters, 4 Cessna 172Ms and 6 Mi-8 helicopters. Personnel (1988) 500.

INTERNATIONAL RELATIONS

Membership. Madagascar is a member of UN, OAU and is an ACP state of EEC.

ECONOMY

Planning. The 1984–87 agricultural plan aimed at food self-sufficiency and envisaged investment of US$219m.

Budget. The budget 1985, envisaged revenue of 241,000m. FMG and expenditure of 436,200m. FMG.

Currency. The Malagasy *franc* is the unit of currency. There are coins of 1, 2, 5, 10, 50 and 100 francs and banknotes of 50, 100, 500, 1,000 and 5,000 francs. In March 1988, £1 = 1,967 FMG; US$1 = 1,277·60 FMG.

Banking. A Central Bank was formed in July 1973, replacing the former *Institut* *d'Emission Malgache* as the central bank of issue. All commercial banking and insurance was nationalised in June 1975. Industrial development is financed through the *Bankin'ny Indostria,* and other commercial banking undertaken by the *Bankin'ny Tantsaha Mpamokatra* and the *Banky Fampandrosoana ny Varotra.*

Weights and Measures. The metric system is in use.

ENERGY AND NATURAL RESOURCES

Electricity. Production (1986) 479m. kwh. Supply 127 and 220 volts; 50 Hz.

Oil. The oil refinery at Toamasina has a capacity of 12,000 bbls a day.

Minerals. Mining production in 1986 included: Graphite, 161,788 tonnes; chromite, 82,910 tonnes; zircon (1985), 650 kg; beryl (1985), (industrial), 129,507 kg; mica, 1,775 kg; gold (1985), 181·6 grammes; industrial garnet (1985), 52·2 kg.

Agriculture. The principal agricultural products in 1985 were (in 1,000 tonnes): Rice, 2,178; cassava, 2,142; mangoes, 172; bananas, 225; potatoes, 264; sugar-cane, 1,744; maize, 140; sweet potatoes, 450; coffee, 82; oranges, 82; pineapples, 51; cotton, 37; groundnuts, 32; sisal, 20; tobacco, 5.

Cattle breeding and agriculture are the chief occupations. There were, in 1986, 10,485,000 cattle, 1·35m. pigs, 604,000 sheep, 1,225,000 goats and 25m. poultry.

Forestry. The forests contain many valuable woods, while gum, resins and plants for tanning, dyeing and medicinal purposes abound. Production (1984) 6·26m. cu. metres.

Fisheries. The fish catch in 1983 was 54,500 tonnes.

INDUSTRY AND TRADE

Industry. Industry, hitherto confined mainly to the processing of agricultural products, is now extending to cover other fields.

Commerce. Trade in 1m. FMG:

	1983	1984	1985	1986
Imports (c.i.f)	166,750	213,531	265,916	238,458
Exports (f.o.b)	127,257	192,267	181,530	205,875

The chief exports in 1984 were coffee (41%), cloves (13%) and vanilla (16%). France took 42% of exports, the USA, 15% and Japan, 9%, while France took 36% of imports, the USA, 7%, Federal Republic of Germany 4% and Japan 4%.

Total trade between Madagascar and UK (British Department of Trade returns, in £1,000 sterling):

	1984	1985	1986	1987
Imports to UK	4,529	6,236	6,432	6,925
Exports and re-exports from UK	6,936	9,484	6,872	6,382

Tourism. There were 27,000 tourists in 1986.

COMMUNICATIONS

Roads. In 1982 there were 49,637 km of roads of which 4,774 km bitumenized. In 1983 there were 33,000 private cars and lorries.

Railways. In 1985 there were 883 km of railways, all metre gauge. In 1986, 3,161,000 passengers and 735,000m. tonnes of cargo were transported.

Aviation. Air France and Air Madagascar connect Antananarivo (International airport, Ivato) with Paris, Alitalia connects with Rome. Several weekly services operated by Air Madagascar connect the capital with the ports and the chief inland towns. In 1985, 138,362 passengers and 5,144 tonnes of cargo arrived and departed.

Shipping. In 1986, 705,824 tonnes were loaded and 1,153,133 tonnes unloaded at

Toamasina, Mahajanga and other ports. In 1980, registered merchant marine was 56 vessels (of more than 100 GRT) with a total of 91,211 GRT.

Post and Broadcasting. There were in 1978, 547 post offices and agencies. There were (1983) 37,100 telephone subscribers, 910,000 radio receivers and 71,000 television receivers.

Newspapers. In 1985 there were 7 daily newspapers with a total circulation of 68,000.

Cinemas. There were, in 1974, 31 cinemas with a seating capacity of 12,500.

JUSTICE, RELIGION, EDUCATION AND WELFARE

Justice. The Supreme Court and the Court of Appeal are in Antananarivo. In most towns there are Courts of First Instance for civil and commercial cases. For criminal cases there are ordinary criminal courts in most towns.

Religion. 47% of the population follow animist religions; 28% are Roman Catholic, 22% Protestant (mainly belonging to the Fiangonan'i Jesosy Kristy eto Madagaskar) and 3% Moslem.

Education. Education is compulsory from 6 to 14 years of age in the primary schools. In 1978 there were 1,311,000 pupils and 23,937 teachers in public primary schools, while in 1976 there were 114,468 pupils in secondary schools and about 7,000 in technical schools. The University of Madagascar has a main campus at Antananarivo and 5 university centres in the other provincial capitals, with 32,599 students in 1984. There are also 4 agricultural schools at Nanisana, Ambatondrazaka, Marovoay and Ivoloina.

Health. In 1978 there were 749 hospitals and dispensaries with 20,625 beds; there were (1981) 901 doctors, 52 dentists, 87 pharmacists, 839 midwives and 770 nursing personnel.

DIPLOMATIC REPRESENTATIVES

Of Madagascar in Great Britain
Ambassador: François de Paul Rabotoson (resides in Paris)

Of Great Britain in Madagascar (Immeuble Ny Havana, Cite de 67 Ha, Antananarivo)
Ambassador: A. V. Hayday.

Of Madagascar in the USA (2374 Massachusetts Ave., NW, Washington, D.C., 20008)
Ambassador: Leon M. Rajaobelina.

Of the USA in Madagascar (14 rue Rainitovo, Antsahavola, Antananarivo)
Ambassador: Patricia Gates Lynch.

Of Madagascar to the United Nations
Ambassador: Blaise Rabetafika.

Books of Reference

Statistical Information: The Service de Statistique Générale in Antananarivo published the *Bulletin mensuel de Madagascar* (from 1971); continuation of the trimestrial *Bulletin de statistique générale* (1949–71), the *Revue de Madagascar,* the *Madagascar à travers ses provinces* (latest issue, 1953) and the *Statistiques du Commerce Extérieur de Madagascar.*
Bulletin de l'Académie Malgache (from 1902)
Brown, M., *Madagascar Rediscovered.* London, 1978
Deschamps, H., *Histoire de Madagascar.* Paris, 4th ed. 1972

MALAŴI

Capital: Lilongwe
Population: 7·1m. (1985)
GNP per capita: US$210 (1983)

HISTORY. Malaŵi was formerly the Nyasaland (until 1907 British Central Africa) Protectorate, constituted on 15 May 1891.

Nyasaland became a self-governing country on 1 Feb. 1963, and on 6 July 1964 an independent member of the Commonwealth under the name of Malaŵi. It became a republic on 6 July 1966.

AREA AND POPULATION. Malaŵi lies along the southern and western shores of Lake Malaŵi (the third largest lake in Africa), and is otherwise bounded north by Tanzania, south by Mozambique and west by Zambia. Land area (excluding inland water of Lakes Palombe, Chilwa and Chiuta) 36,325 sq. miles, divided into 3 regions and 24 districts, each administered by a District Commissioner.

Lake Malaŵi waters belonging to Malaŵi are 9,250 sq. miles and the whole Lake Malaŵi (including the waters under Mozambique by an agreement made between the two countries in 1950) is 11,650 sq. miles.

Population at census 1977, 5,547,460 (males, 2,673,589). Estimate (1985), 7,058,800. Over 90% of the population live in rural areas.

Population of main towns (estimate 1985) was as follows: Blantyre, 355,200; Lilongwe, 186,800; Mzuzu, 82,700; Zomba, 53,000.

Population of the regions, 1986 (and census 1977): Northern, 815,000 (648,853); Central, 2,938,300 (2,143,716); Southern, 3,525,600 (2,754,891).

The official languages are Chichewa, spoken by over 50% of the population, and English.

CLIMATE. The tropical climate is marked by a dry season from May to Oct. and a wet season for the remaining months. Rainfall amounts are variable, within the range of 29–100″ (725–2,500 mm), and maximum temperatures average 75–89°F (24–32°C), and minimum temperatures 58–67°F (14·4–19·4°C). Lilongwe. Jan. 73°F (22·8°C), July 60°F (15·6°C). Annual rainfall 36″ (900 mm). Blantyre. Jan. 75°F (23·9°C), July 63°F (17·2°C). Annual rainfall 45″ (1,125 mm). Zomba. Jan. 73°F (22·8°C), July 63°F (17·2°C). Annual rainfall 54″ (1,344 mm).

CONSTITUTION AND GOVERNMENT. The President of the republic is also head of Government and of the Malaŵi Congress Party. Malaŵi is a one-party state. Parliament is composed of 102 elected members elected for up to 5 years, and 5 nominated by the President.

Life President, External Affairs, Agriculture, Justice, Works and Supplies: Ngwazi Dr H. Kamuzu Banda. (Took office 6 July 1966 and became Life President on 6 July 1971).

The Cabinet in Jan. 1988 was composed as follows:

Finance: Dalton S. Katopola. *Trade, Industry and Tourism:* Wadson B. Deleza. *Education and Culture:* Solomon J. Tseka Phiri. *Local Government:* Richard Mussa Banda. *Health:* Louis J. Chimango. *Labour:* Stanford Demba. *Transport and Communications:* Edward Chitsulo Isaac Bwanali. *Community Services:* Elia C. Katola Phiri. *Forestry and Natural Resources:* B. L. Kapichira Banda. *At Large:* Sydney B. Somanje. *Without Portfolio, Administrative Secretary of Malaŵi Congress Party:* Maxwell Pashane.

National flag: Three equal horizontal stripes of black, red, green, with a red rising sun on the centre of the black stripe.

DEFENCE. All services form part of the Army and have a strength (1988) 5,250.

Army. The army is organized into 3 infantry battalions and 1 support battalion. Equipment includes scout cars.

Navy. There are 3 small lake patrol boats and 2 gunboats. Uniformed personnel in 1988 totalled 36.

Air Wing. To support the infantry battalion, the Air Wing has 3 Do 28D Skyservant and 3 Do 228 light transports, and 2 Puma, 1 Ecureuil, 1 Dauphin, and 1 Alouette III helicopters. An HS 125 jet is used for VIP transport. Personnel (1988) 150.

INTERNATIONAL RELATIONS

Membership. Malaŵi is a member of UN, the Commonwealth, OAU, SADCC and is an ACP state of EEC.

ECONOMY

Planning. The Government of Malaŵi operates a 3-year 'rolling' public-sector investment programme, revised annually to take into account changing needs and the expected level of resources available. The greatest part of the development programme is annually financed from external aid, and priority in the use of resources has always been given to providing the counterpart contributions to funds received from external sources. The balance of these local resources is used for financing projects commanding high national priority for which no external funds can be secured.

Budget. Revenue Account receipts and expenditure (in K.1,000) for years ending 31 March:

	1983–84	1984–85	1985–86	1986–87
Revenue	458,140	353,200	450,200	512,300
Expenditure	449,747	416,800	523,600	547,000

Currency. The currency is the *kwacha* (dawn), which is subdivided into 100 *tambala* (cockerels). From 9 June 1975 the kwacha has been pegged to Special Drawing Rights. In March 1988: £1 sterling = K.4·42, US$1 = K.2·53.

Banking. In July 1964 the Reserve Bank of Malaŵi was set up with a capital of K.1m. to be responsible for the issue of currency and the holding of external reserves and to issue treasury bills and local registered stock on behalf of the Government. Since then, the Reserve Bank has fully assumed the responsibilities of a Central Bank.

The National Bank of Malaŵi has a total of 14 branches in major urban areas and 25 static and 41 mobile agencies in rural areas. The Commercial Bank of Malaŵi Ltd opened in 1970 and has branches at Limbe, Lilongwe, Mzuzu and Zomba and an agency in Dedza and headquarters at Blantyre. It has 4 permanent and 65 mobile agencies.

In 1972 The Investment Development Bank of Malaŵi was established in Blantyre. Its resources are derived from domestic and foreign official sources and its objective is to provide medium and long-term credits to private entities considered of importance to the economy.

The post office savings bank had (1985) 257 offices conducting savings business throughout the country, and the New Building Society has agencies in Limbe, Mzuzu, Zomba, Muloza and Blantyre with its head office in Lilongwe.

Weights and Measures. The metric system became fully operational in 1982.

ENERGY AND NATURAL RESOURCES

Electricity. The Electricity Supply Commission of Malaŵi is the sole supplier of electrical power and energy and the demand and supply of electricity and power on the inter-connected system was met from the hydro-electric generator sets installed at Tedzani Falls and Nkula Falls stations which together have a total capacity of 124 mw as at 1984. The inter-connected system extends from the Shire River hydro stations and covers most areas of the Southern and Central Regions, and part of the Northern Region. Production (1986) 466m. kwh. Supply 230 volts; 50 Hz.

Thermal plant of 23·8 mw capacity is available on the inter-connected system and there are stations at Blantyre, Lilongwe, Mtunthama, Kasungu, and Mzuzu.

The capacity of the isolated station at Karonga was increased to 480 kw with the installation of 120 kw diesel generator set.

Minerals. The main product in 1976 was marble (149,254 tonnes) for the manufacture of cement. Coal mining began in 1985.

Agriculture. Malaŵi is predominantly an agricultural country. In 1983 agriculture contributed about 43% to the GDP, and agricultural produce accounted for 90% of total exports. Maize is the main subsistence crop and is grown by over 95% of all smallholders; production (1986) 1,374,000 tonnes. Tea cultivation is of growing importance; in 1986, 42,000 tonnes were produced. Almost all the surplus crops produced by smallholders are sold to the Agricultural Development and Marketing Corporation. Production (1986): Tobacco, 71,000 tonnes; sugar-cane, 1·6m. tonnes.

Livestock in 1986: Cattle, 930,000; sheep, 180,000; goats, 690,000; pigs, 240,000.

Forestry. In 1983–84, 11,108 cu. metres of sawn timber were removed.

Fisheries. Landings in 1984 were 65,073 tonnes.

INDUSTRY AND TRADE

Industry. Index of manufacturing output in 1985 (1970 = 100): manufacturing for domestic consumption 419·7 (229·5 in 1980); of this consumer goods were at 183·4 (252·5) and intermediate goods mainly for building and construction were at 111·1 (150·4). Manufacturing for export, 236·3 (201·6).

Commerce. Exports 1985 (in K.1m.): Tobacco, 229·9; tea, 113·3; sugar, 28·9; pulses, 6·4; groundnuts, 1·1; rice, 3; other crops including manufactures, 53·4.

Trade statistics for calendar years are (in K.1m.):

	1983	1984	1985
Imports	363·7	381·5	492·5
Exports	270·6	446·2	419·6

Total trade between Malaŵi and UK (British Department of Trade returns, in £1,000 sterling):

	1984	1985	1986	1987
Imports to UK	65,327	87,218	56,983	44,223
Exports and re-exports from UK	22,995	20,525	28,557	18,069

Tourism. There were 41,145 visitors to Malaŵi in 1985.

COMMUNICATIONS

Roads. In 1985 there were 2,671 km of main road, of which 1,776 km were bitumen surfaced and 410 km gravel; 2,781·5 km of secondary roads, of which 285 km were surfaced, 204·8 km of gravel and 2,291·7 km of earth roads. In 1984 there were 15,584 cars, 12,605 commercial vehicles and 1,115 buses and hire vehicles.

Railways. Malaŵi Railways (789 km–1,067 mm gauge) operates a main line from Salima to the Mozambique border near Nsanje, from which running powers over the Trans-Zambesia Railway allow access to the port of Beira; a branch opened in 1970 runs eastwards from a point 16 km south of Balaka to the Mozambique border to give a direct route to the deep-water port of Nacala. The 26-km section from Nsanje to the border is operated by the Central Africa Railway Co. Ltd. An extension of 111 km from Salima to the new state capital of Lilongwe was opened in Feb. 1979, and a further extension to Mchinji on the Zambian border (120 km) was completed in 1981. In 1985–86, 461,000 tonnes hauled, 121·5m. passenger-km run.

Aviation. In 1983 the Kamuzu International Airport at Lilongwe was inaugurated. It handled (1984) 56,580 passengers and 893 tonnes. In 1982 Chileka Airport handled 184,700 passengers and 5,598 tonnes of freight.

Shipping. In 1982 lake ships carried 1·48m. passengers.

Post and Broadcasting. Number of telephones (1982) 16,445. The Malaŵi Broadcasting Corporation broadcasts in English and Chichewa. There were 1m. radio sets in 1983.

Newspapers (1984). *The Daily Times* (English, Monday to Friday); 14,000 copies daily. *Malaŵi News* (English and Chichewa, Saturdays); 21,000 copies weekly. *The Odini* (English and Chichewa, 7,000 fortnightly).

JUSTICE, RELIGION, EDUCATION AND WELFARE

Justice. Justice is administered in the High Court, the magistrates' courts and traditional courts. There are 23 magistrates' courts, 176 traditional courts and 23 local appeal courts.

Appeals from traditional courts are dealt with in the traditional appeal courts and in the national traditional appeal court. Appeals from magistrates' courts lie to the High Court, and appeals from the High Court to Malaŵi's Supreme Court of Appeal.

Religion. In 1983 the Roman Catholic Church claimed 1·2m. members; Church of Central Africa Presbyterian, 366,377; Diocese of Southern Malaŵi and Lake Malaŵi (part of the Province of Central Africa (the Anglican Communion), 70,606; Seventh Day Adventist Church (1984), 59,319. Zambezi Evangelical Church (formerly Nyasa mission), 26,000; Assembly of God, 10,000; Seventh Day Baptist (Central Africa Conference), 5,198; Church of Christ, 50,000+; African Evangelical Church, 6,000. Moslems are estimated to number about 500,000.

Education In 1983–84 the number of pupils in primary schools was 847,157; in secondary schools, 22,245. There were 14,499 teachers in primary schools and 1,079 in secondary schools. The primary school course is of 8 years' duration, followed by a 4-year secondary course. English is taught from the 1st year and becomes the general medium of instruction from the 4th year. There were 1,890 students in teacher training schools and 522 in government technical schools.

The University of Malaŵi was inaugurated in 1965. In 1983–84 there were 1,961 students taking degree and diploma courses.

Health. In 1984 there were two central hospitals, one general hospital, one mental hospital, 43 hospitals of which 21 are government district hospitals. There are 6,596 hospital beds of which 1,448 are for maternity.

DIPLOMATIC REPRESENTATIVES

Of Malaŵi in Great Britain (33 Grosvenor St., London, W1X 0DE)
High Commissioner: Bernard Brenn Mtawali.

Of Great Britain in Malaŵi (Lingadzi Hse., Lilongwe, 3)
High Commissioner: Dr D. G. Osborne.

Of Malaŵi in the USA (1400 20th St., NW, Washington, D.C., 20036)
Ambassador: T. S. Mangwazu.

Of the USA in Malaŵi (PO Box 30016, Lilongwe)
Chargé d'Affaires: Dennis C. Jett.

Of Malaŵi to the United Nations
Ambassador: T. S. Mangwazu.

Books of Reference

General Information: The Chief Information Officer, PO Box 494, Blantyre.
Boeder, R. B. *Malawi.* [Bibliography] Oxford and Santa Barbara, 1981
McMaster, C., *Malawi: Foreign Policy and Development.* London, 1974

MALAYSIA

Capital: Kuala Lumpur
Population: 16·5m. (1987)
GNP per capita: US$1,870 (1985)

HISTORY. On 16 Sept. 1963 Malaysia came into being, consisting of the Federation of Malaya, the State of Singapore and the colonies of North Borneo (renamed Sabah) and Sarawak. The agreement between the UK and the 4 territories was signed on 9 July (Cmnd. 2094); by it, the UK relinquished sovereignty over Singapore, North Borneo and Sarawak from independence day and extended the 1957 defence agreement with Malaya to apply to Malaysia. Malaysia became automatically a member of the Commonwealth of Nations. *See* map in THE STATESMAN'S YEAR-BOOK, 1964–65.

On 9 Aug. 1965, by a mutual agreement dated 7 Aug. 1965 between Malaysia and Singapore, Singapore seceded from Malaysia to become an independent Sovereign nation.

AREA AND POPULATION. Malaysia comprises 11 states and a federal territory in the Malay Peninsula (bounded north by Thailand), together with a further 2 states and a second federal territory lying on the island of Borneo (bounded south by Indonesia). Singapore and Brunei form enclaves along the coasts of these two parts.

The area of Malaysia is 329,759 sq. km (127,317 sq. miles) and the population (1987 estimate) is 16,527,000. The growth of Census population has been:

Year	Peninsular Malaysia	Sarawak	Sabah/Labuan	Total Malaysia
1970	8,809,557	975,918	655,295	10,440,770
1980	11,426,613	1,307,582	1,011,046	13,745,241

The areas, populations and chief towns of the states and federal territories are:

State	Sq. km	Census 1980 [1]	Capital	Census 1980
Johor	18,985	1,638,229	Johor Baharu	249,880
Kedah	9,425	1,116,140	Alor Setar	71,682
Kelantan	14,931	893,753	Kota Baharu	170,559
Kuala Lumpur [2]	243	977,102	Kuala Lumpur	937,875
Melaka	1,658	464,754	Melaka	88,073
Negeri Sembilan	6,646	573,578	Seremban	136,252
Pahang	35,960	798,782	Kuantan	136,625
Perak	21,005	1,805,198	Ipoh	300,727
Perlis	795	148,276	Kangar	12,956
Pinang	1,033	954,638	Pinang (Georgetown)	250,578
Selangor	7,956	1,515,536	Shah Alam	24,138
Terengganu	12,955	540,627	Kuala Terengganu	186,608
Peninsular Malaysia	131,592	11,426,613		
Labuan [2]	98	12,219	Victoria	...
Sabah	73,613	998,827	Kota Kinabalu	55,997
Sarawak	124,449	1,307,582	Kuching	74,229
East Malaysia	198,160	2,318,628		

[1] Revised figures   [2] Federal Territories.

Other large cities (1980 Census): Petaling Jaya (207,805), Kelang (192,080), Taiping (146,002), Sibu (85,231), Sandakan (70,420) and Miri (52,125).

Of the total population in 1980, 47% were Malay, 32% Chinese, 8% Indian and 13% others. Over 58% speak Malay, the official language, 9% Chinese, 4% Tamil and 3% Iban.

CLIMATE. Malaysia is affected by the monsoon climate. The N.E. monsoon prevails from Oct. to Feb., bringing rain to the east coast of the peninsula. The S.W. monsoon lasts from mid-May to Sept. and affects the opposite coastline the most. Temperatures are uniform throughout the year. Kuala Lumpur. Jan. 81°F (27.2°C), July 81°F (27.2°C). Annual rainfall 97.6" (2,441 mm). Penang. Jan. 82°F (27.8°C), July 82°F (27.8°C). Annual rainfall 109.4" (2,736 mm).

CONSTITUTION AND GOVERNMENT. The Constitution of Malaysia is based on the Constitution of the former Federation of Malaya, but includes safeguards for the special interests of Sabah and Sarawak. It was amended in 1983.

The federal capital is Kuala Lumpur, established on 1 Feb. 1974 with an area of approximately 94 sq. miles. The official language is Bahasa Malaysia.

The Constitution provides for one of the 9 Rulers of the Malay States to be elected from among themselves to be the *Yang di-Pertuan Agong* (Supreme Head of the Federation). He holds office for a period of 5 years. The Rulers also elect from among themselves a Deputy Supreme Head of State, also for a period of 5 years.

Supreme Head of State (Yang di-Pertuan Agong): HM Sultan Mahmood Iskandar ibni Al-Marhum Sultan Ismail DK, SPMJ, SPDK, DK (Brunei) SSIJ, PIS, BSI, elected as 8th *Yang di-Pertuan Agong* from 26 April 1984, proclaimed 15 Nov. 1984.

Raja of Perlis: HRH Tuanku Syed Putra ibni Al-Marhum Syed Hassan Jamalullail, DK, DKM, DMN, SMN, SPMP, SPDK, acceded 12 March 1949.

Sultan of Kedah: HRH Tuanku Haji Abdul Halim Mu'adzam Shah ibni Al-Marhum Sultan Badlishah, DK, DKH, DKM, DMN, DUK, SPMK, SSDK, acceded 20 Feb. 1959.

Regent of Johor: HRH Tengku Ibrahim Ismail ibni Sultan Mahmood Iskandar Al-Haj, DK, SPMJ, appointed from 15 Nov. 1984.

Sultan of Selangor: HRH Sultan Salahuddin Abdul Aziz Shah ibni Al-Marhum Sultan Hisamuddin 'Alam Shah Al-Haj, DK, DMN, SPMS, SPDK, acceded 3 Sept. 1960.

Raja of Perak: HRH Raja Tun Azlan Shah, DK, DMN, PMN, SPCM, SPMP, acceded 3 Feb. 1984.

Yang di-Pertuan Besar of Negeri Sembilan: HRH Tuanku Ja'afar ibni Al-Marhum Tuanku Abdul Rahman, DMN, DK, acceded 8 April 1968.

Sultan of Kelantan: HRH Sultan Ismail Petra ibni Al-Marhum Sultan Yahya Petra, DK, SPMK, SJMK, SPSM, appointed 29 March 1979.

Sultan of Trengganu: HRH Sultan Mahmud Al Marhum ibni Al-Marhum Tuanku Al-Sultan Ismail Nasiruddin Shah, DK, SPMT, SPCM, appointed 2 Sept. 1979.

Sultan of Pahang: Sultan Haji Ahmad Shah Al-Musta'in Billah ibni Al-Marhum Sultan Abu Bakar Ri'Ayatuddin Al-Mu'Adzam Shah, DKM, DKP, DK, SSAP, SPCM, SPMJ.

Yang di-Pertua Negeri Pulau Pinang: HE Tun Dr Awang bin Hassan, DUPN, SPMJ, appointed 1 May 1981.

Governor of Malacca: HE Tuan Yang Terutama Tan Sri Datuk Sri Utama Syed Ahmad Al-Haj bin Syed Mahmud Shahabudin, PSM, SPMK, DUNM, SSDK, PNBS, PGDK, JMN, JP, appointed 4 Dec. 1984.

Yang di-Pertua Negeri Sarawak: HE Datuk Patinggi Haji Ahmad Zaidi Adruce bin Muhammed Noor, DPSS, DP, PNBS, appointed 2 April 1985.

Yang di-Pertua Negeri Sabah: HE Datuk Mohamad Adnan Robert, SMN, SPDK, SPMP, DUPN, DP, appointed 26 June 1978.

Parliament consists of the *Yang di-Pertuan Agong* and two *Majlis* (Houses of Parliament) known as the *Dewan Negara* (Senate) of 68 members and *Dewan Rakyat* (House of Representatives) of 177 members. There are 169 members from the states in Malaysia and 8 from the Federal Territory. Appointment to the Senate is for 3 years. The maximum life of the House of Representatives is 5 years, subject to its dissolution at any time by the *Yang di-Pertuan Agong* on the advice of his Ministers.

National flag: Fourteen horizontal stripes of red and white, with a blue quarter bearing a crescent and a star of 14 points, all in gold.

The elections to the House of Representatives held on 2–3 Aug. 1986, returned the following members: National Front, 148; Democratic Action Party, 24; PAS, 1; Independent, 4.

The Cabinet was in Jan. 1988 composed as follows:

Prime Minister and Minister of Home Affairs: Datuk Seri Dr Mahathir Mohamad, SSDK, SSAP, SPMS, SPMJ, DP(Sk), DUPN, SPNS, SPDK, SPCM, SSMT, DUMN.

Deputy Prime Minister, Minister of National and Rural Development: Abdul Ghafar Baba. *Ministers in the Prime Minister's Department:* Dr Yusof Mohd Nor; Kasitah Gadam. *Works:* S. Samy Vellu. *Primary Industries:* Dr Lim Keng Yaik. *Information:* Dato Mohamed Rahmat. *Trade and Industry:* Datin Paduka Rafidah Aziz. *Energy, Telecommunications and Posts:* Leo Moggie. *Public Enterprises:* Dato Napsiah Omar. *Land and Regional Development:* Dr Sulaiman Daud. *Agriculture:* Sanusi Junid. *Defence:* Tenglen Ahmad Rithandeen. *Foreign Affairs:* Abu Hassan Omar. *Science, Technology and Environment:* Amar Stephen Yong. *Welfare:* Mustaffa Mohammad. *Education:* Anwar Ibrahim. *Finance:* Daim Zainuddin. *Transport:* Dr Ling Liong Sik. *Health:* Chan Siang Sun. *Labour:* Lee Kim Sai. *Youth and Sports:* Najib Tun Razak. *Housing and Local Government:* Ng Cheng Kiat. *Justice:* Vacant. *Culture and Tourism:* Sabbaruddin Chik.

DEFENCE. The Malaysian Constitution provides for the *Yang di-Pertuan Agong* (Supreme Head of State) to be the Supreme Commander of the Armed Forces who exercises his powers and authority in accordance with the advice of the Cabinet. Under the general authority of the Yang di-Pertuan Agong and the Cabinet, there is the Armed Forces Council which is responsible for the command, discipline and administration of all other matters relating to the Armed Forces, other than those relating to their operational use.

The Armed Forces Council is chaired by the Minister of Defence and its membership consists of the chief of the Defence Forces, the 3 Service Chiefs and 2 other senior military officers, the Secretary-General of the Ministry of Defence, a representative of State Rulers and an appointed member.

The chief of the Armed Forces Staff is the professional head of the Armed Forces and the senior military member in the Armed Forces Council. He is the principal adviser to the Minister of Defence on the military aspects of all defence matters. The chief of the Armed Forces Staff's committee, established under the authority of the Armed Forces Council, is the highest level at which joint planning and co-ordination with the Armed Forces are carried out. The Committee is chaired by the chief of the Armed Forces Staff and its membership consists of the chief of the Army, Navy and Air Force, the chief of Personnel Staff, the chief of logistic Staff and the chief of Staff of the Ministry of Defence.

Army. The Army is organized into 4 divisions, comprising 9 infantry brigades made up of 36 infantry battalions; 4 cavalry, 5 field artillery, 5 engineer and 5 signals regiments and 2 anti-aircraft battalions. There is also a special service regiment. Equipment includes 26 Scorpion light tanks. Strength (1988) about 90,000, with as reserves the Malaysian Territorial Army (45,000) and the regular reservists who have completed their full-time service.

Navy. The Royal Malaysian Navy is commanded by the Chief of the Navy from the integrated Ministry of Defence in Kuala Lumpur. The main naval bases are KD Malaya at Lumut Perak, KD Sri Labuan on Labuan Island and KD Pelandok in Lumut, Perak. These establishments are responsible for the operation and administration of the ships, and KD Pelandok for the training of personnel.

The ships include 2 new German-built (Kiel) frigates, 2 British (Yarrow)-built frigates (including the former HMS *Mermaid*), 2 new corvettes, 4 new Italian-built minehunters, 2 logistic support ships, 8 fast missile craft, 6 fast gunboats, 21 patrol craft, 2 landing ships, 1 diving tender, 2 survey vessels, 200 very small amphibious craft and 6 tugs. The peace-time tasks include fishery protection and anti-piracy patrols. There are also 50 armed patrol launches, 48 operated by the Royal Malaysian Police and 2 by the Government of Sabah (North Borneo) which also operates 4 other patrol boats, 1 landing craft and a yacht.

Naval personnel in 1988 totalled over 11,000 officers and ratings.

Air Force. Formed on 1 June 1958, the Royal Malaysian Air Force is equipped primarily to provide air defence and air support for the Army, Navy and Police. Its secondary rôle is to render assistance to Government departments and civilian organizations, especially during periods of national disasters. There were in late 1987 12 squadrons, of which 9 operated transport aircraft and helicopters. 39 *ex*-US Navy A-4L/C Skyhawks equip 2 squadrons as the primary attack force. Other equipment includes 14 F-5E Tiger II jet fighter-bombers, 2 RF-5E reconnaissance-fighters, and 3 F-5F trainers, 2 F.28 Fellowship and 2 Challenger VIP transports, 9 C-130 Hercules four-engined transport and patrol aircraft, 15 Caribou twin-engined STOL transports, 2 HU-16 amphibians, 35 Sikorsky S-61A-4 Nuri heavy troop and cargo transport helicopters, 20 Alouette III, and 9 Bell 47 helicopters, 11 Cessna 402Bs for twin-engine training and liaison, 44 PC-7 Turbo-Trainers, 11 MB.339 jet trainers and 2 H.S. 125 Merpati twin-jet executive transports. Personnel (1988) totalled about 12,000.

Volunteer Forces. The Army Volunteer Force (Territorial Army) consists of first-line infantry, signals, engineer and logistics units able to take the field with the active army, and a second-line organization to provide local defence. There is also a small Naval Volunteer Reserve with Headquarters in Penang and Kuala Lumpur. The Royal Malaysian Air Force Volunteer Reserve has both air and ground elements.

INTERNATIONAL RELATIONS

Membership. Malaysia is a member of UN, the Commonwealth, Non-Aligned countries, the Colombo Plan, Organization of Islamic Conference and ASEAN.

ECONOMY

Planning. The fifth 5-year plan, 1986–90 envisages an expenditure of M$74,000m. and aims at stimulating economic growth through development of manufacturing industries, revitalization of agriculture and improvement of productivity in all sectors.

Budget. Revenue and expenditure for calendar years, in M$1m.:

	1982	1983	1984	1985	1986	1987[1]
Revenue	16,434	18,608	20,805	21,114	19,518	17,278
Operating expenditure	16,185	16,124	17,506	20,066	20,075	20,793
Development expenditure	10,434	9,416	8,074	6,756	6,949	6,192

[1] Estimate.

Currency. Bank Negara Malaysia (Central Bank of Malaysia) assumed sole currency issuing authority in Malaysia on 12 June 1967. The unit of currency issued by Bank Negara Malaysia is the Malaysian *ringgit* ($) which is divided into 100 *sen.* Currency notes are of denominations of $1, 5, 10, 20, 50, 100, 500 and $1,000. Coins are of denominations of 1 *sen*, 5, 10, 20, 50 *sen* and $1, $5 and $100. On 31 Dec. 1984, currency issued by Bank Negara Malaysia amounted to M$6,561·4m., of which M$6,147·6m. (93%) was notes and M$413·8m. (6·3%) coins.

Rate of exchange, March 1988: 2·58 *ringgit* = US$1; 4·57 *ringgit* = £1.

Banking. Thirty-nine banks were operating in Aug. 1985; of these 23 were domestic banks with over 650 banking offices. Five were banks incorporated in Singapore with 63 banking offices and the remaining 12 banks were foreign incorporated with 85 banking offices. Total deposits amounted to M$56,453·1m. on 30 June 1987 and loans and advances amounted to M$51,235·4m.

The National Savings Bank (formerly known as the post office savings bank) held M$973·8m. due to 3,600,948 depositors at 31 Dec. 1978.

Weights and Measures. The standard measures are the imperial yard, pound and gallon. The Weights and Measures Act of 1972 provides for a 10-year transition to the metric system, and was completed by 31 Dec. 1981.

ENERGY AND NATURAL RESOURCES

Oil. Production (1987) 23·5m. tonnes.

Gas. Natural gas reserves, 1987, 1,400,000m. cu. metres. Production of LNG in 1986 was approximately 5·3m. tonnes, most of which was exported to Japan.

Minerals. Production (1986, in 1,000 tonnes): Bauxite, 566; iron ore, 208; copper, 115; tin, 29.

Agriculture. Production, 1986: Pineapples, 188,000 tonnes; tobacco leaves, 12,000 tonnes from 15,000 hectares; pepper (1984), 15,000 tonnes from 10,550 hectares; cocoa, 130,000 tonnes from 245,000 hectares.

Livestock (1986): Cattle, 620,000, buffaloes, 250,000; sheep, 69,000; pigs, 2·15m.; goats, 347,000.

INDUSTRY AND TRADE.

Industry. The total labour force was 6,259,000 in 1987, of whom 5,687,800 were employed: 2,005,500 in agriculture, 820,500 in manufacturing, 843,900 in government.

Production, 1987 (1,000 tonnes): Rubber, 1,600; tin, 32; crude palm oil, 4,400; sawlogs, 30,700,000 cu. metres.

Commerce. In 1987 exports totalled M$41,036m. and imports M$31,087m.

Chief imports (1987, provisional): Machinery and transport equipment, M$13,585m.; manufactured goods, M$4,787m.; food, beverages and tobacco M$3,233m.; crude petroleum and related products, M$2,054m.

Chief exports (1986): Manufactured goods (M$18,147m.); rubber (M$3,784m.); crude petroleum (M$6,223m.); palm oil (M$3,038m.); saw logs (M$3,218m.); tin, M$857.

In 1986 imports came chiefly from Japan (20·5%); USA (18·8%); and Singapore (15%). Exports in 1986 went chiefly to Japan (22·7%), Singapore (17·1%) and USA (16·6%).

Total trade of Malaysia with UK (British Department of Trade returns, in £1,000 sterling):

	1984	1985	1986	1987
Imports to UK	320,325	383,860	350,058	397,122
Exports and re-exports from UK	283,269	281,671	226,912	257,970

COMMUNICATIONS

Post and Broadcasting. The Postal Services in Malaysia are under the Ministry of Energy, Telecommunications and Post and are headed by the Director-General of Post, Malaysia. There were 849,129 telephone subscribers in 1984; telephone connections between Peninsular Malaysia, Sabah and Sarawak are by satellite and submarine cable. As at 31 Dec. 1979, 445 post offices, 1,381 postal agencies, 177 mobile post offices and 1 riverine postal office were operating in Malaysia, and the cash turnover for the year amounted to M$4,688,113,241.

In 1984, 279,370 radio licences and 1,414,960 television licences were issued.

Cinemas. In 1974 there were 500 cinemas with a seating capacity of 345,400.

Newspapers. Papers are published in Malay (1,226,000 daily sales in 1984), English (830,000), Chinese (387,000) and Tamil (19,000).

JUSTICE. By virtue of Art. 121(1) of the Federal Constitution judicial power in the Federation is vested on 2 High Courts of co-ordinate jurisdiction and status namely the High Court of Malaya and the High Court of Borneo, and the inferior courts. The Federal Court with its principal registry in Kuala Lumpur is the Supreme Court in the country.

The Lord President as the supreme head of the Judiciary, the 2 Chief Justices of the High Courts and 6 other Judges form the constitution of the Federal Court. Apart from having exclusive jurisdiction to determine appeals from the High Court the Federal Court is also conferred with such original and consultative jurisdiction as is laid out in Articles 128 and 130 of the Constitution.

A panel of 3 Judges or such greater uneven number as may be determined by the Lord President preside in every proceeding in the Federal Court.

The right of appeal to the Yang di-Pertuan Agong (who in turn refers the appeal to the Judicial Committee of the British Privy Council) from a decision of the Federal Court in respect of criminal and constitutional matters was abolished on 1 July 1978.

DIPLOMATIC REPRESENTATIVES

Of Malaysia in Great Britain (45 Belgrave Sq., London, SW1X 8QT)
High Commissioner: Datuk Jamaluddin Abu Bakar.

Of Great Britain in Malaysia (Wisma Damansara, Jalan Semantan, Kuala Lumpur)
High Commissioner: J. Nicholas T. Spreckley, CMG.

Of Malaysia in the USA (2401 Massachusetts Ave., NW, Washington, D.C., 20008)
Ambassador: Albert S. Talalla.

Of the USA in Malaysia (376 Jalan Tun Razak, Kuala Lumpur)
Ambassador: John C. Monjo.

Of Malaysia to the United Nations
Ambassador: Yusof M. Hitam.

Books of Reference

Statistical Information: The Department of Statistics, Malaysia, Kuala Lumpur, was set up in 1963, taking over from the Department of Statistics, States of Malaya. *Chief Statistician:* Khoo Teik Huat. Main publications: *Peninsular Malaysia Monthly* and *Annual Statistics of External Trade; Malaysia External Trade* (quarterly); *Peninsular Malaysia Statistical Bulletin* (monthly); *Rubber Statistics* (monthly); *Rubber Statistics Handbook* (annual); *Oil Palm Statistics* (monthly); *Oil Palm, Coconut and Tea Statistics* (annual). *Malaysia 1985,* The Department of Information, Kuala Lumpur, 1986

Anand, S., *Inequality and Poverty in Malaysia.* OUP, 1983
Brown, I., and Ampalavanar, R., *Malaysia.* [Bibliography] Oxford and Santa Barbara, 1986
Gullick, J., *Malaysia: Economic Expansion and National Unity.* Boulder and London, 1982
Meerman, J., *Public Expenditure in Malaysia.* OUP, 1980
Snodgrass, D. R., *Inequality and Economic Development in Malaysia.* OUP, 1982

PENINSULAR MALAYSIA

AREA AND POPULATION. The total area of Peninsular Malaysia is about 50,810 sq. miles (131,598 sq. km). Population (1986 estimate) 13,324,000. The federal capital is Kuala Lumpur (244 sq. km).

CONSTITUTION AND GOVERNMENT. The States of the Federation of Malaya, now known as Peninsular Malaysia, comprises the 11 States of Johore, Pahang, Negeri Sembilan, Selangor, Perak, Kedah, Perlis, Kelantan, Trengganu, Penang and Malacca.

For earlier history of the States and Settlements *see* THE STATESMAN'S YEAR-BOOK, 1957, p. 241.

The Constitution is based on the agreements reached at the London conference of Jan.-Feb. 1956, between HM Government in the UK, the Rulers of the Malay states and the Alliance Party (which at the first federal elections on 27 July 1955 obtained 51 of the 52 elected members), and subsequently worked out by the Constitutional Commission appointed after that conference.

ECONOMY

Budget. See p. 824.

ENERGY AND NATURAL RESOURCES

Electricity. In 1986, 10,700m. kwh. were generated. Supply 240 volts; 50 Hz.

Oil. Production (1985) 20·2m. tonnes of crude oil.

Minerals. Production (in tonnes): Tin-in-concentrates: 1983, 41,400; 1982, 52,300. Iron ore: 1983, 113,700; 1982, 340,300. Bauxite: 1983, 501,800; 1982, 589,000. Copper: 1983, 123,400; 1982, 128,800. Gold: 1980, 4,621 troy oz.; 1979, 5,273.

Agriculture. Production in 1985 (in tonnes): Rice, 1,895,000 from 675,000 hectares; rubber, 1·54m.; palm oil, 4·13m.; palm kernels, 1·21m.; cocoa, 100,000; coconuts, 1,721,000; copra, 216,000; vegetables, 481,000; fruit, 898,000; sugarcane, 1·2m.; tea, 4,000; cassava, 370,000; sweet potatoes, 50,000; roots and tubers, 505,000; maize, 24,000.

Forestry (1984). Reserved forests, 4·7m. hectares. Production of logs (1984), 10·7m. cu. metres; sawn timber, 5·8m. cu. metres; plywood, 630,000 cu. metres.

Fisheries. Landings in 1983 493,117 tonnes. Fishermen (1985) 87,000; 70% offshore.

INDUSTRY AND TRADE

Trade Unions. There were, in Aug. 1985, 287 registered trade unions with over 500,000 members in Peninsular Malaysia.

Tourism. In 1986 there were 3,027,000 tourists.

COMMUNICATIONS

Roads. In 1985 the Public Works Department maintained 25,540 km of roads of which 79% were paved. In 1985 the 8-mile road bridge between the mainland and Penang island opened.

In 1983, 3,229,371 motor vehicles were registered, including 974,170 private cars, 16,069 buses, 195,752 lorries and vans, 1,948,342 motor cycles.

Railways. The Malayan Railway main line runs from Singapore to Butterworth opposite Penang Island. From Bukit Mertajam 8 miles south of Butterworth a branch line connects Peninsular Malaysia with the State Railways of Thailand at the frontier station of Padang Besar. Other branch lines connect the main line with Port of Klang, Teluk Anson, Port Dickson and Ampang. The east-coast line, branching off the main line at Gemas, runs for over 300 miles to Tumpat, Kelantan's northernmost coastal town; a 13-mile branch line linking Pasir Mas with Sungei Golok makes a second connexion with Thailand.

In 1986 there were 1,639 km (metre gauge) which carried 6·7m. passengers and 2·8m. tonnes of freight.

Aviation (1985). International air services are operated into Kuala Lumpur Johor and Penang airports. The national carrier, Malaysian Airlines System (MAS), began operation on 1 Oct. 1972 to provide both domestic and international services.

Civil aviation statistics for airports in Peninsular Malaysia (1984): Aircraft movements, 97,890; terminal passengers, 6,078,273; freight, 80,232 tonnes; mail, 7,163 tonnes.

Shipping. The major ports of Peninsular Malaysia are Port Kelang, Penang, Johor and Kuantan. In 1984 Port Kelang handled 12,357,262 tonnes of cargo valued at M\$16,318·4m., of which imports totalled 7,744,789 tonnes (M\$9,532·9m.) and exports 4,612,473 tonnes (M\$6,785·5m.). A total of 4,630 ships, GRT 35m. tonnes, called in 1984. In 1984 the Port of Penang handled 7,960,506 tonnes of cargo, of which 5,220,550 tonnes were imports and 2,739,956 tonnes exports. The total cargo handled in all ports during 1984 was 31,986,000 tonnes.

JUSTICE, RELIGION, EDUCATION AND WELFARE

Justice. Unlike the Federal Court and the High Court which were established under the Constitution, the subordinate courts in Peninsular Malaysia comprising the sessions court, the Magistrate's court and the Penghulu's court were established under a Federal Law (the subordinate Courts Act, 1948 (Revised 1972)).

All offences other than those punishable with death are tried before a Sessions Court President who is empowered to pass any sentence allowed by law other than the sentence of death. In civil matters, the sessions court has jurisdiction to hear all actions and suits where the amount in dispute does not exceed M\$25,000.

A First Class Magistrate's criminal jurisdiction is limited to offences for which the maximum term provided by law does not exceed 10 years' imprisonment and to certain specified offences where the term of imprisonment provided for may be extended to 14 years' imprisonment or which are punishable with fine only.

Juvenile courts established under the Juvenile Courts Act, 1947 for juvenile offenders below the age of 18 are presided over by a First Class Magistrate assisted by 2 advisers. There are 30 penal institutions, including Borstal establishments and an open prison camp.

Religion. More than half the population are Moslems, and Islam is the official religion. In 1970 there were 4,673,670 Moslems, 765,250 Hindus, 220,897 Christians and 2,495,739 Buddhists.

Education. In 1984 there were 4,459 state assisted primary schools with 1,756,825 pupils and 67,244 teachers and in 1980, 208 private primary schools with 5,130 pupils and 224 teachers.

In 1984 there were 929 secondary schools with 1,079,424 pupils and 48,098 teachers.

There were (1980): 10 special schools with 1,312 pupils and 104 teachers; 401 classes for further education with 10,281 students and 997 teachers; 25 teacher training colleges with over 12,000 students.

In the academic year 1981–82 there were 10 institutions of higher learning:

	1981–82	
	Staff	Students
Ungku Omar Polytechnic, Ipoh	112	2,449
Kuantan Polytechnic, Kuantan	49	575
MARA Institute of Technology, Shah Alam	665	11,108
Tunku Ab. Rahman College, Kuala Lumpur	156	6,285
University of Malaya, Kuala Lumpur	1,085	9,310
University of Kebangsaan, Bangi	864	7,514
University of Science, Penang	417	4,387
University of Agriculture, Serdang	502	4,136
University of Technology, Kuala Lumpur	431	4,862

The International Islamic University opened in 1983.

Health. In 1983 Government maintained 60 general, district hospitals with 21,164 beds and 4 special medical institutions with 8,497 beds, and there were 99 private hospitals, nursing and maternity homes with 3,024 beds. In 1983 there were 4,082 doctors, 774 dentists, 13,874 midwives and 17,916 nurses.

Books of Reference

Morris, M. W., *Local Government in Peninsular Malaysia.* London, 1980
Wilkinson, R. J., *Malay-English Dictionary.* 2 vols. New ed. London, 1956
Winstedt, Sir R., *Malaya and Its History.* 3rd ed. London, 1953.—*An English–Malay Dictionary.* 3rd ed. Singapore, 1949.—*The Malays: A Cultural History.* London, 1959

SABAH

HISTORY. The territory now named Sabah, but until Sept. 1963 known as North Borneo, was in 1877-78 ceded by the Sultans of Brunei and Sulu and various other rulers to a British syndicate, which in 1881 was chartered as the British North Borneo (Chartered) Company. The Company's sovereign rights and assets were transferred to the Crown with effect from 15 July 1946. On that date, the island of Labuan (ceded to Britain in 1846 by the Sultan of Brunei) became part of the new Colony of North Borneo. On 16 Sept. 1963 North Borneo joined the new Federation of Malaysia and became the State of Sabah.

AREA AND POPULATION. Area, about 28,460 sq. miles (73,710 sq. km), with a coastline of 973 miles (1,577 km). The interior is mountainous, Mount Kinabalu being 13,455 ft (4,175 metres) high. Population, 1980 census 1,011,046, (1987 estimate, 1,322,000), of whom, 838,141 were Pribumis, 163,996 Chinese, 5,613 Indians, 3,296 others. The native population comprises Kadazans (largest and mainly agricultural), Bajaus and Bruneis (agriculture and fishing), Muruts (hill tribes), Suluks (mainly seafaring) and several smaller tribes.

The island of Labuan became Federal territory on 16 April 1984, 35 sq. miles (75 sq. km) in area, lying 6 miles (9·66 km) off the north-west coast of Borneo is a free port. It has a fine port, Victoria Harbour.

The principal towns are situated on or near the coast. They include Kota Kinabalu, the capital (formerly Jesselton), 1980 census population (preliminary), 108,725, Tawau (113,708), Sandakan (113,496), Keningau in the hinterland (41,204), and Kudat (38,397).

CLIMATE. The climate is tropical monsoon, but on the whole is equable, with temperatures around 80°F (26·5°C) throughout the year. Annual rainfall varies, according to locality, from 10″ (250 mm) to 148″ (3,700 mm). The north-east monsoon lasts from Dec. to April and chiefly affects the east coast, while the south-west monsoon from May to Aug. gives the west coast its wet season.

CONSTITUTION AND GOVERNMENT. The Constitution of the State of Sabah provides for a Head of State, called the *Yang Dipertua Negeri Sabah.* Executive authority is vested in the State Cabinet headed by the Chief Minister.

Head of State: Tan Seri Mohamad Said Keruak.
Chief Minister: Datuk Joseph Pairin Kittingan.

Flag: Horizontally blue over white with a red triangle based on the hoist.

The Legislative Assembly consists of the Speaker, 48 elected members and not more than 6 nominated members.

The official language was English for a period of 10 years from Sept. 1963 but in Aug. 1973 Bahasa Malaysia was introduced and in 1974 was declared the official language. English is widely used especially for business.

ECONOMY

Budget. Budgets for calendar years, in M$1,000:

Ordinary Budget	1980	1981	1982	1983	1984
Revenue	1,538,251	1,206,110	1,481,738	1,315,650	1,336,171
Expenditure	1,383,482	1,738,218	1,340,536	1,645,666	1,437,179
Development Budget					
Revenue	331,754	898,051	546,902	492,806	195,099
Expenditure	396,635	798,727	555,460	328,983	299,889

Banking. There are branches of The Chartered Bank at Kota Kinabalu, Sandakan, Tawau, Labuan, Kudat, Tenom and Lahad Datu. The Hongkong and Shanghai

Bank has branches at Kota Kinabalu, Sandakan, Labuan, Beaufort, Papar and Tawau. The Hock Hua Bank (S) has branches at Kota Kinabalu, Sandakan and Tawau. The Chung Khiaw Bank has branches at Kota Kinabalu, Tuaran and Sandakan. Malayan Banking Ltd has branches at Kota Kinabalu, Tawau, Semporna and Sandakan. United Overseas Bank and the Overseas Chinese Banking Corporation have each a branch at Kota Kinabalu. Bank Bumiputra Malaysia has branches at Kota Kinabalu. Lahad Datu, Sandakan and Keningau. Overseas Union Bank and the Development and Commercial Bank have each a branch at Sandakan. The Sabah Bank Berhad and Sabah Development Bank were established in Kota Kinabalu in 1979.

The National Savings Bank has taken over the functions of the post office savings bank as from 1 Dec. 1974 and had (1984) M$28·3m. due to 148,180 depositors. It also provides additional services to depositors including the granting of loans for housing.

COMMERCE. The main imports are machinery, tobacco, provisions, petroleum products, metals, rice, textiles and apparel, vehicles, sugar, building material. Statistics for calendar years, in M$:

	1980	1981	1982	1983	1984
Imports	3,060,819,153	3,644,281,463	3,217,971,724	3,802,333,624	3,647,743,664
Exports	4,455,982,812	4,357,069,182	5,726,240,301	5,432,972,223	5,522,111,454

Tourism. In 1984 some 60,923 tourists visited Sabah.

COMMUNICATIONS

Roads (1984). There were 6,652 km of roads, of which 1,997 km were bitumen surfaced, 4,484 km gravel surfaced and 171 km of earth road. Work is in progress on a network of roads, notably the Kota Kinabalu-Sandakan and Sandakan-Lahad Datu road links.

Railways. A metre-gauge railway, 134 km, runs from Kota Kinabalu on Gaya Bay to Tenom in the interior. It carried 445,937 passengers and 168,936 tonnes in 1986.

Aviation. External communications are provided from the international airport at Kota Kinabalu by Cathay Pacific Airways Ltd to Hong Kong; Malaysian Airways to Hong Kong, Manila, Brunei, Kuching, Singapore and Kuala Lumpur; Brunei Airways to Brunei and Kuching and Philippine Airlines to Manila.

The total air traffic handled at Sabah airports during 1984 was 2,386,304 passengers, 18,154,314 kg freight and 3,162,385 kg mail.

Shipping (1985). Merchant shipping totalling 13,339,002 NRT used the ports, handling 15,813,000 tonnes of cargo.

Post. As at 31 Dec. 1984 there were 39 post offices, 18 mobile post offices and 128 postal agencies. There were 75,514 telephones on 31 Dec. 1984. As at 31 Dec. 1984, there were 55,203 wireless and 85,376 television licences issued.

JUSTICE, EDUCATION AND WELFARE

Justice. Pursuant to the Subordinate Courts Ordinance (Cap. 20) (1951) Courts of a Magistrate of the First Class, Second Class and Third Class were established to adjudicate upon the administration of civil and criminal law. The civil jurisdiction of a First Class Magistrate is limited to cases where the amount in dispute does not exceed M$1,000. but provision is made for the Chief Justice to enlarge that jurisdiction to M$3,000. This has been established so as to confer this jurisdiction on all stipendiary magistrates. A Second Class Magistrate can only try suits where the amount involved does not exceed M$500 and a Third Class Magistrate where it does not exceed M$100.

The criminal jurisdiction of these Magistrates' Courts is limited to offences of a less serious nature although stipendiary magistrates have enhanced jurisdiction. There are no Juvenile Courts.

There are also Native Courts with jurisdiction to try cases arising from breach of native law and custom (including Moslem Law and custom) where all parties are natives or one of the party is a native (if the matter is a religious, matrimonial or sexual one). Appeals from Native Courts lie to a District Judge or a Native Court of Appeal presided over by a Judge.

In 1984, 4,228 convictions were obtained in 1,212 cases taken to court.

Education. In 1985, there were 194,808 primary and (1984) 80,377 secondary pupils. There are 837 primary schools (659 government, 167 grant-aided and 11 private), and 113 general secondary schools (62 government, 37 grant-aided and 14 private) throughout the State. There were 3 teacher-training colleges, with (1984) 1,290 students.

The Government also runs 5 vocational schools in Kota Kinabalu and Sandakan offering carpentry, motor mechanics, electrical installation, fitting/turning, radio and television and heavy plant fitting.

The Department of Education also runs further education classes in most towns and districts. The main medium of instruction in primary schools is Bahasa Malaysia although there are some Chinese medium primary schools. Secondary education is principally English but this is being replaced by Bahasa Malaysia.

Health. The principal diseases are malaria, pulmonary tuberculosis and intestinal infestations. Specific control programmes for malaria and tuberculosis have drastically reduced the incidence of these two diseases.

As at 31 Dec. 1984 there were 16 hospitals (2,596 beds). Sixty-four fixed dispensaries in outlying districts providing in-patient and out-patient care are staffed by hospital assistants under the supervision of district medical officers. There is one mental hospital at Kota Kinabalu. There are 18 district health centres and 45 travelling clinics throughout the State providing maternal and child health care.

Book of Reference

Statistical Information: Director, Federal Department of Information, Kota Kinabalu.
Tregonning, K. G., *North Borneo.* HMSO, 1960

SARAWAK

HISTORY. The Government of part of the present territory was obtained on 24 Sept. 1841 by Sir James Brooke from the Sultan of Brunei. Various accessions were made between 1861 and 1905. In 1888 Sarawak was placed under British protection. On 16 Dec. 1941 Sarawak was occupied by the Japanese. After the liberation the Rajah took over his administration from the British military authorities on 15 April 1946. The Council Negeri, on 17 May 1946, authorized the Act of Cession to the British Crown by 19 to 16 votes, and the Rajah ceded Sarawak to the British Crown on 1 July 1946.

On 16 Sept. 1963 Sarawak joined the Federation of Malaysia.

AREA AND POPULATION. The area is about 48,250 sq. miles (124,449 sq. km), with a coastline of 450 miles and many navigable rivers.

The population at 1980 census was 1,294,753 (1985 estimate, 1,477,000, including 439,000 Ibans; 300,000 Malays; 434,000 Chinese; 123,000 Bidayuhs; 85,000 Melanaus; 78,000 other indigenous; 18,000 others).

The chief towns are the capital, Kuching, about 21 miles inland, on the Sarawak River (1983 population: 300,000), Sibu, 80 miles up the Rejang River, which is navigable by large steamers (1984 population: 170,000), and Miri, the headquarters of the Sarawak Shell Ltd (1983 population: 120,000).

CONSTITUTION AND GOVERNMENT. On 24 Sept. 1941 the Rajah began to rule through a constitution. Since 1855 two bodies, known as Majlis Mesyuarat Kerajaan Negeri (Supreme Council) and the Dewan Undangan Negeri (State Legislature), had been in existence. By the constitution of 1941 they were given, by the Rajah, powers roughly corresponding to those of a colonial executive council and legislative council respectively. Sarawak has retained a considerable measure of local autonomy in state affairs. The State or Legislature consists of 48 elected members and sits for 5 years unless sooner dissolved. In 1985 the Assembly approved a bill to increase its seats to 56 but this has not been implemented.

A ministerial system of government was introduced in 1963. The Chief Minister presides over the Supreme Council, which contains no more than 8 other Council Negeri members, all of whom are Ministers.

Elections to the State Legislature on 15 and 16 April 1987 returned 28 members of the Sarawak Barisan Nasional comprising the Party Pesaka Bumiputera Bersatu (PBB), the Sarawak United Peoples' Party and the Sarawak National Party.

Sarawak has 24 seats in the Malaysia House of Representatives (154 members) and 5 seats in the Senate (58 members).

Sarawak has 9 divisions each under a Resident.

Head of State: Tun Datuk Patinggi Haji Ahmad Zaidi Adruce bin Muhammed Noor, SSM, DP, PNBS, Bintang Mahaputera Adipradana (Indonesia).

Chief Minister: Datuk Patinggi Haji Abdul Taib Mahmud, DP, SPMJ, PGDK, Kt. WE (Thailand) KOU (Korea), KEPN (Indonesia).

Deputy Chief Ministers: Tan Sri Datuk Amar Sim Kheng Hong, DA, PSM, PGDK, JMN. Datuk Alfred Jabu anak Numpang, PNBS, KMN. *Environment and Tourism:* Datuk Amar James Wong Kim Min, DA, PNBS. *Infrastructure Development:* Datuk Dr Wong Soon Kai, PNBS, PBS. *Housing:* Datuk Celestine Ujang anak Jilan, PNBS. *Industrial Development:* Abang Abdul Rahman Zohari bin Tun Datuk Abang Haji Openg, JBS. *Land Development:* Encik Adenan bin Haji Satem, JBS. *Special Functions:* Dr George Chan Hong Nam, KMN, PBS.

State Secretary: Datuk Amar Haji Bujang Mohd. Nor, DA, PNBS, JSM, AMN. *State Attorney-General:* Datuk Haji Mohammad Jemuri bin Serjan, PNBS, JMN, PPC. *State Financial Secretary:* Datuk Liang Kim Bang, PNBS, JBS, PPC, KMN.

The official language is Bahasa Malaysia. The use of English as official language in Sarawak was abolished in 1985.

Flag: Horizontally red over white with a blue triangle on the hoist.

ECONOMY

Budget. In 1987 State revenue was M$772·1m.; expenditure, M$802·4m. The revenue is mainly derived from royalties on oil, timber and gas.

The fifth Malaysia 5-year development plan (1986-90) provides for Sarawak an expenditure of M$4,731m.; of this sum about 90% was to be spent on infrastructure, public utilities, agriculture and land development, education and medical services.

Currency. The Malaysian *ringgit* is on a par of £0·334 or US$0·426.

Banking. The National savings bank had 150,000 depositors in Aug. 1987; the amount to their credit was M$64m. There are branches of Bank Negara Malaysia in Kuching, and branches of the Chartered Bank, the Hongkong & Shanghai Bank, Bank Bumiputera Malaysia, the Overseas Chinese Banking Corporation, the Malayan Bank.

Nine local banks have branches in major towns. Sibu is the centre for local commercial banking with Hock Hua Bank (established in 1951, 13 branches and assets of M$872·4m. in 1983) and Kwong Ming Bank (established in 1964, 8 branches and assets of M$170m. in 1983). Both are locally owned and have branches in Kuala Lumpur and other towns.

INDUSTRY AND TRADE

Industry. Industry includes petroleum and petroleum products, natural gas, timber and timber products and rubber. Emphasis is being given to the development of petro-chemical, timber-based and agro-based industries.

Commerce. Exports in 1986 totalled M$6,685m. Crude petroleum, the chief export, accounted for 26% of the total, with 6,348,000 tonnes, value M$1,755m., exported to Japan (28%), Korea (24%), Peninsular Malaysia (15%), Philippines (12%), Singapore (8%), Taiwan (5%) and Thailand (3%) in 1986. Liquified natural gas accounted for 28% of the total at M$1,848m., exported solely to Japan, in 1986. The other main exports in 1986 were sawn logs (19% of the total; 10·3m. cu. metres, value M$1,291m.) and petroleum products (5% of the total). The major agricultural exports, which together accounted for 4% of the total in 1986, were pepper, cocoa beans, crude palm oil and rubber.

Total import value, 1986, M$3,312m.

Sarawak's major trading partners in 1986 were Japan (export, 48%; import, 13%), Peninsular Malaysia (export, 7%, import, 37%); Singapore (export, 11·3%, import, 11%); Korea (export, 10%, import, 4%); Sabah (export, 7%, import, 0·8%).

Tourism. In 1986 there were 189,452 foreign tourists.

COMMUNICATIONS

Roads. In 1985 there were 4,620 km of roads, consisting of 1,490 km of bitumen surfaced, 2,980 km of gravel or stone surfaced and 150 km of earth roads. There are no railways.

Aviation. There are daily Malaysian Airline System (MAS) B737 and Airbus flights between Kuching and Kuala Lumpur *via* Singapore, and also scheduled flights between Kuching, Brunei and Hong Kong. Major towns in Sarawak are linked up by internal air routes.

Shipping. In 1986 Sarawak ports handled a total of 27m. tonnes of cargo. Kuching wharf, operational since 1974, can accommodate vessels up to 15,000 tonnes. The Bintulu Port, the largest in the State, handled more than 4m. tonnes in 1984.

Post and Broadcasting. There are 54 post offices, 18 mobile offices and 203 postal agencies. The Telecommunications department was privatized in 1986 and renamed Syarikat Telekoms Malaysia (STM). A telephone system with 65 automatic exchanges (84,048 telephones) covers the country. There are International Subscribers Dialling (ISD) links with 75 countries and Atur system was introduced in 1985. The government radio and television service had, in 1986, 245 electric radio, 28,693 battery radio and 92,739 TV registered receivers.

Newspapers (1987). There are 1 Malay bi-weekly, 3 English and 7 Chinese dailies. One Malay and 1 Iban monthly newspapers are published by Government.

JUSTICE, RELIGION, EDUCATION AND WELFARE

Justice (1987). In Sarawak there are the High Court and the Subordinate Court. High Court cases go on appeal to the Supreme Court which sits in Sarawak and Sabah twice a year. The Subordinate Courts (Amendment) Act 1987 was extended to Sarawak on 1 Sept. 1987 in which the jurisdiction of the Sessions Court judges and magistrates of the First Class and Second Class was enhanced.

In 1986 a Moslem Court was established.

Police. There is a Royal Malaysia Police, Sarawak Component, with a total establishment of about 9,000 regular officers and men.

Religion. There are Church of England, Roman Catholic, American Methodist, Seventh-day Adventist and Borneo Evangelical missions. There is a large Moslem population and many Buddhists. Islam is the national religion.

Education (1987). There were 1,266 government and government-aided primary schools with 219,405 pupils and 10,735 teachers, and 121 secondary schools with 120,321 pupils and 5,106 teachers. There were 3 teacher-training centres and an agricultural university campus conducting pre-university courses. The MARA Institute of Technology campus, established in 1973, had 960 students in 1987 and offers 3-year courses leading to diploma in accountancy, stenography and business studies and a 6-month pre-commerce course.

Health. In 1987 there were 17 government hospitals, 154 static and 118 travelling dispensaries, 145 public dental and school dental clinics and 130 maternal and child health centres. There were 302 doctors and 55 registered dentists.

Books of Reference

Population and Housing Census of Malaysia, 1980. Dept. of Statistics, Kuala Lumpur
Sarawak Annual of Statistics. Dept. of Statistics, Kuching, 1981
Sarawak Annual External Trade Statistics. Dept. of Statistics, Kuching, 1982
1983 Sarawak Budget. Information Dept., Sarawak
Milne, R. S., and Ratnam, K. J., *Malaysia, New States in a New Nation: Political Development of Sarawak and Sabah in Malaysia.* London, 1974
Runciman, S., *The White Rajahs.* CUP, 1960
Scott, N. C., *Sea Dyak Dictionary.* Govt. Printing Office, Kuching, 1956

National Library: The Sarawak Central Library, Kuching.

MALDIVES

Divehi Jumhuriya

Capital: Malé
Population: 189,000 (1986)
GNP per capita: US$470 (1985)

HISTORY. The islands were under British protection from 1887 until complete independence was achieved on 26 July 1965. Maldives became a republic on 11 Nov. 1968.

AREA AND POPULATION. The Republic of Maldives, some 400 miles to the south-west of Sri Lanka, consists of 1,200 low-lying coral islands (only 202 inhabited), grouped into 12 clearly defined clusters of atolls. Area 115 sq. miles (298 sq. km). Population (census 1985), 181,453, of which 45% under 15 years. Estimate (1986) 189,000. Capital, Malé (46,334).

CLIMATE. The islands are hot and humid, and affected by monsoons. Malé. Average temperature 81°F (27°C). Annual rainfall 59″ (1,500 mm).

CONSTITUTION AND GOVERNMENT. The President is elected every 5 years by universal adult suffrage. He is assisted by the Ministers' *Majlis*, a cabinet of ministers of his own choice whom he may dismiss at will. There is also a Citizens' *Majlis* (Parliament) which consists of 48 members, 8 of whom are nominated by the President and 40 directly elected (2 each from Malé and the 19 administrative districts) for a term of 5 years. There are no political parties.

President, Minister of Defence and National Security: Maumoon Abdul Gayoom.

Attorney-General: Ahmed Zaki. *Atolls Administration:* Abdullah Hameed. *Education:* Mohamed Zahir Hussain. *Fisheries:* Abdul Sattar Moosa Didi. *Foreign Affairs:* Fathulla Jameel. *Health:* Abdulla Jameel. *Home Affairs and Social Services:* Umar Zahir. *Trade and Industry:* Ilyas Ibrahim. *Transport and Shipping:* Ahmed Mujuthaba.

The official and spoken language is Divehi, which is akin to Elu or old Sinhalese.

National flag: Red with a green panel bearing a white crescent.

Local government: Maldives is divided into the capital and 19 other administrative districts, each under an appointed governor *(verin)* assisted by local chiefs *(katheebun)*, who are also appointed.

INTERNATIONAL RELATIONS.

Membership. The Maldives is a member of UN and the Commonwealth.

ECONOMY

Budget. In 1985 revenue totalled 177m. rufiyaa and expenditure 165·5m. rufiyaa.

Currency. The *rufiyaa* is divided into 100 *laari*; there are notes of 1, 2, 5, 10, 20, 50 and 100 *rufiyaa*. In March 1988, £1 = 17·91 *rufiyaa*; US$1 = 10·10 *rufiyaa*.

ENERGY AND NATURAL RESOURCES

Electricity. Production, 1986, 9m. kwh.

Agriculture. The islands are covered with coconut palms and yield millet, cassava, yams, melons and other tropical fruit as well as coconut produce.
Production in 1985 included (in 1,000 tonnes): Coconuts, 10; copra, 2.

Fisheries. Catch, mainly tuna (1985) 61,900 tonnes.

INDUSTRY AND TRADE

Industry. The main industries are fishing, tourism, shipping, reedware, lacquerwork, coconut processing and garment manufacturing.

Commerce. Bonito ('Maldive fish') is the main export commodity. It is exported principally to Thailand, Singapore, Sri Lanka, Japan and some European markets.

Total trade between the Republic of Maldives and UK (British Department of Trade returns, in £1,000 sterling):

	1983	1984	1985	1986	1987
Imports to UK	44	529	73	276	440
Exports and re-exports from UK	840	747	1,243	1,321	2,772

Tourism. Tourism, introduced in 1972, is expanding and there were 114,544 visitors in 1985.

COMMUNICATIONS

Roads. In 1985 there were 336 cars, 941 motorbikes, 432 handcarts and 13,162 other vehicles.

Aviation. There are direct flights to Europe, Dubai, Karachi, Singapore and neighbouring countries. Service to Australia is available *via* Singapore. In 1985, 3,027 aircraft, 259,497 passengers and 2,731,045 kg of freight were handled at Malé International Airport. There are 2 domestic airports. Air Maldives operates domestic flights only.

Shipping. The Maldives Shipping Line operated (1984) 32 vessels.

Post and Broadcasting. There were (1985) 2,429 telephones. There is one AM and one FM radio station broadcasting to (1985) 19,146 receivers. In 1987 there were 3,828 television sets and 2 television transmitters.

Newspapers. There were (1985) 2 daily newspapers, 1 weekly and 1 monthly magazine.

JUSTICE, RELIGION EDUCATION AND WELFARE

Justice. Justice is based on the Islamic Shari'ah.

Religion. The State religion is Islam.

Education. In 1983–84 there were 65 primary schools with 42,598 pupils and 590 teachers and 4 secondary schools with 841 students and 93 teachers.

Health. There is an 84-bed hospital in Malé and 3 regional hospitals. In 1987 there were 7 doctors, 1 dentist and 19 nurses.

DIPLOMATIC REPRESENTATIVES

Of Great Britain in the Republic of Maldives
High Commissioner: D. A. S. Gladstone (resides in Colombo).

Of the Republic of Maldives to the United Nations
Ambassador: (Vacant).

Books of Reference

Bell, H. C. P., *History, Archaeology and Epigraphy of the Maldive Islands.* Ceylon Govt. Press, Colombo, 1940
Bernini, F. and Corbin, G., *Maldives.* Turin, 1973

MALI

Capital: Bamako
Population: 8·73m. (1987)
GNP per capita: US$150 (1983)

République du Mali

HISTORY. Annexed by France between 1881 and 1895, the region became the territory of French Sudan as a part of French West Africa. It became an autonomous state within the French Community on 24 Nov. 1958, and on 4 April 1959 joined with Sénégal to form the Federation of Mali. The Federation achieved independence on 20 June 1960, but Sénégal seceded on 22 Aug. and Mali proclaimed itself an independent republic on 22 Sept. The National Assembly was dissolved on 17 Jan. 1968 by President Modibo Keita, whose government was then overthrown by an Army *coup* on 19 Nov. 1968; power was assumed by a Military Committee for National Liberation led by Lieut. (now General) Moussa Traoré, who became President on 19 Sept. 1969.

AREA AND POPULATION. Mali is a landlocked state, consisting of the Middle and Upper Niger basin in the south, the Upper Sénégal basin in the southwest, and the Sahara in the north. It is bounded west by Sénégal, north-west by Mauritania, north-east by Algeria, east by Niger and south by Burkina Faso, Côte d'Ivoire and Guinea. The republic covers an area of 1,240,142 sq. km (478,832 sq. miles) and had a population of 6,398,914 at the 1976 Census; the latest estimate (1987) is 8·73m. In 1985, 21% lived in urban areas.

The areas, populations and chief towns of the regions are:

Region	Sq. km	Estimate 1986	Chief town	Census 1976
Kayes	197,760	1,093,100	Kayes	44,736
Koulikoro	89,833	1,169,600	Koulikoro	16,876
Capital District	267	862,600	Bamako	404,022
Sikasso	76,480	1,383,300	Sikasso	47,030
Ségou	56,127	1,316,000	Ségou	64,890
Mopti	88,752	1,416,000	Mopti	53,885
Tombouctou	408,977	601,400	Tombouctou	20,483
Gao	321,996	461,000	Gao	30,714

The various indigenous languages belong chiefly to the Mande group; of these the principal are Bambara (spoken by 60% of the population), Soninké, Malinké and Dogon; non-Mande languages include Fulani, Songhai, Senufo and Tuareg. The official language is French.

CLIMATE. A tropical climate, with adequate rain in the south and west, but conditions become increasingly arid towards the north and east. Bamako. Jan. 76°F (24·4°C), July 80°F (26·7°C). Annual rainfall 45" (1,120 mm). Kayes. Jan. 76°F (24·4°C), July 93°F (33·9°C). Annual rainfall 29" (725 mm). Tombouctou. Jan. 71°F (21·7°C), July 90°F (32·2°C). Annual rainfall 9" (231 mm).

CONSTITUTION AND GOVERNMENT. A new constitution was announced on 26 April 1974 and approved by a national referendum on 2 June; it was amended by the National Assembly on 2 Sept. 1981. The sole legal party is the *Union démocratique du peuple malien* (UDPM), formally constituted on 30 March 1979 and governed by a 19-member Central Executive Bureau responsible to a 137-member National Council who nominate all candidates for election.

The President is directly elected for a term of 6 years. The 82-member National Assembly is also directly elected, for a term of 3 years. Elections for both were held on 9 June 1985.

The Council of Ministers in Aug. 1987 comprised:

President, Head of Government, Secretary-General of UDPM: Gen. Moussa

837

Traoré (assumed office Sept. 1969, re-elected 1985).

Prime Minister: Dr Mamadou Dembélé.

Foreign Affairs and International Co-operation: Modibo Keita. *Defence:* Gen. Sékou Ly. *Planning:* Ousmane Mohamed Diallo. *State Companies and Enterprises:* Anthioumane N'Diaye. *Industrial Development and Tourism:* Drissa Keita. *Finance and Trade:* Zoumane Sacko. *Justice:* Diango Sissoko. *National Education:* Oumar Isslaka Bah. *Agriculture:* Lieut.-Col. Issa Ongoiba. *Natural Resources and Animal Husbandry:* Oumar Tall. *Labour and Civil Service:* Hama Ag Mahmoud. *Public Works and Transport:* Oumar Doumbia. *Public Health and Social Affairs:* Sidibé Aissata Cissé. *Interior (Territorial Administration and Basic Development):* Lieut.-Col. Abdourahmane Maiga. *Information and Telecommunications:* Fatou Gakou Niang. *Sports, Arts and Culture:* Bakari Traoré.

National flag: Three vertical stripes of green, yellow, red.

Local Government: Mali is divided into the Capital District of Bamako and 7 regions, sub-divided into 46 *cercles* and then into 279 *arrondissements*.

DEFENCE. There is a selective system of 2 years' military service.

Army. The Army consists of 4 infantry battalions, 2 tank, 1 engineer, 1 parachute, 1 special force, 2 artillery battalions and support units. Equipment includes 21 T-34 tanks. Strength (1988) 6,900. There is also a paramilitary force of 7,800 men.

Air Force. The Air Force has 5 MiG-17 jet fighters, 1 MiG-15UTI jet trainer, some Yak-18 piston-engined trainers, 2 An-24, 2 An-26 and 3 An-2 transports, and 3 Mi-8 and Mi-4 helicopters from USSR. A twin-turbofan Corvette is used for VIP transport. Personnel (1988) total about 400.

INTERNATIONAL RELATIONS

Membership. Mali is a member of UN, OAU and is an ACP state of EEC.

ECONOMY

Planning. The 1981–85 Four Year Plan provided for expenditure of MF 795,200m.

Budget. The budget for 1986 provided for revenue of 69,180m. francs CFA and expenditure of 69,080m. francs CFA, of which 19% was on defence and 13% on education.

Currency. Mali introduced its own currency, the *Mali franc,* in July 1962 but reverted to the *franc CFA* on 1 June 1984 at a rate of 2 *Mali francs* to 1 *franc CFA.* There are coins of 1, 2, 5, 10, 25, 50 and 100 *francs CFA*, and notes of 50, 100, 500, 1,000, 5,000 and 10,000 *francs CFA.*

Banking. The *Banque Centrale du Mali* (founded in 1968) is the bank of issue. There are 4 domestic and 2 French-owned banks.

ENERGY AND NATURAL RESOURCES

Electricity. Production (1986) totalled 161m. kwh. Supply 220 volts; 50 Hz.

Minerals. Mineral resources are limited, but marble (at Bafoulabé) and limestone (at Diamou) are being extracted in the Upper Sénégal valley; iron ore deposits in this area await development. Salt is mined at Taoudenni in the far north (3,000 tonnes a year) and phosphates at Bouren (10,000 tonnes).

Agriculture. Production in 1986 included (in 1,000 tonnes): Millet, 1,284; sugarcane, 210; groundnuts, 120; rice, 249; maize, 200; seed cotton, 195; cotton lint, 70; cassava, 76; sweet potatoes, 50.

Livestock, 1986: Cattle, 4,676,000; horses, 62,000; asses, 550,000; sheep, 5·5m.; goats, 5·5m.; camels, 241,000; chickens, 15m.

Fisheries. About 100,000 tonnes of fish per annum are caught in the rivers.

TRADE. Exports in 1985 totalled 77,200m. francs CFA. Chief imports are foodstuffs, automobiles, petrol, building material, sugar, salt and beer. France and Côte d'Ivoire are the main sources of imports. Cotton formed 41% of exports and livestock in 1983; 25% went to Belgium and 16% to France.

Total trade between Mali and UK (British Department of Trade returns, in £1,000 sterling):

	1983	1984	1985	1986	1987
Imports to UK	3,833	5,646	4,804	8,282	6,937
Exports and re-exports from UK	15,856	5,471	7,294	4,121	5,573

Tourism. There were 54,000 foreign tourists in 1986.

COMMUNICATIONS

Roads. There were (1981) 15,700 km of roads. There were 25,000 road vehicles in 1982.

Railways. Mali has a railway from Kayes to Koulikoro by way of Bamako, a continuation of the Dakar–Kayes line in Sénégal. Total length 642 km (metre-gauge) and in 1985 carried 695,563 passengers and 574,972 tonnes of freight.

Aviation. Air services connect the republic with Paris, Dakar and Abidjan. There are international airports at Bamako and Mopti, and Air Mali operates domestic services to 10 other airports.

Shipping. For about 7 months in the year small steamboats perform the service from Koulikoro to Tombouctou and Gao, and from Bamako to Kouroussa.

Post and Broadcasting. There were, in 1984, 9,537 telephones and 110,000 radio receivers.

JUSTICE, RELIGION, EDUCATION AND WELFARE

Justice. The Supreme Court was established at Bamako in 1969 with both judicial and administrative powers. The Court of Appeal is also at Bamako, at the apex of a system of regional tribunals and local *juges de paix.*

Religion. In 1980, 90% of the population were Sunni Moslems, 9% animists and 1% Christians.

Education. In 1982–83 there were 364,382 pupils and 10,912 teachers in 1,558 primary and intermediate schools, 13,227 pupils and 890 teachers in 20 senior schools, 12,612 students in 11 technical schools. There were 5,792 students and 491 teaching staff in 7 higher educational establishments in 1979.

Health. In 1980 there were 12 hospitals, 327 health centres and 445 dispensaries, with a total of 3,200 beds; there were 319 doctors, 18 surgeons, 14 dentists (1978), 24 pharmacists (1978), 250 midwives and 1,312 nursing personnel.

DIPLOMATIC REPRESENTATIVES

Of Mali in Great Britain
Ambassador: Lamine Keita (accredited 18 Feb. 1988).

Of Great Britain in Mali
Ambassador: John Macrae, CMG (resides in Dakar).

Of Mali in the USA (2130 R. St., NW, Washington, D.C., 20008)
Ambassador: Nouhoum Samassekou.

Of the USA in Mali (Rue Testard and Rue Mohamed V, Bamako)
Ambassador: Robert J. Ryan, Jr.

Of Mali to the United Nations
Ambassador: Seydou Niare.

MALTA

Capital: Valletta
Population: 343,334 (1986)
GNP per capita: US$3,103 (1984)

Repubblika Ta' Malta

HISTORY. Malta was held in turn by Phoenicians, Carthaginians and Romans, and was conquered by Arabs in 870. From 1090 it was joined to Sicily until 1530, when it was handed over to the Knights of St John, who ruled until dispersed by Napoleon in 1798. The Maltese rose in rebellion against the French and the island was subsequently blockaded by the British aided by the Maltese from 1798 to 1800. The Maltese people freely requested the protection of the British Crown in 1802 on condition that their rights and privileges be preserved. The islands were finally annexed to the British Crown by the Treaty of Paris in 1814.

On 15 April 1942, in recognition of the steadfastness and fortitude of the people of Malta during the Second World War, King George VI awarded the George Cross to the island.

Malta became independent on 21 Sept. 1964 and became a republic within the Commonwealth on 13 Dec. 1974. For earlier constitutional and government history *see* THE STATESMAN'S YEAR-BOOK, 1980–81, p. 837.

In 1971 Malta began to follow a policy of strict non-alignment and closed the NATO base. In March 1972 agreement was reached on the phasing out of the British Military base which was closed down completely on 31 March 1979.

AREA AND POPULATION. The area of Malta is 246 sq. km (94·9 sq. miles); Gozo, 67 sq. km (25·9 sq. miles); Comino, 3 sq. km (1·1 sq. miles); total area, 316 sq. km (121·9 sq. miles). Population, census 16 Nov. 1985, 345,418; estimate (1986) 343,334. Malta, 318,222; Gozo and Comino, 25,112. Chief town and port, Valletta, population 9,263 but the urban harbour area, 213,600.

Vital statistics, 1986, estimate: Births, 5,245; deaths, 2,824; marriages, 2,619; emigrants, 737; returned emigrants, 622 (estimate).

CLIMATE. The climate is Mediterranean, with hot, dry and sunny conditions in summer and very little rain from May to Aug. Rainfall is not excessive and falls mainly between Oct. and March. Average daily sunshine in winter is 6 hours and in summer over 10 hours. Valletta. Jan. 55°F (12·8°C), July 78°F (25·6°C). Annual rainfall 23" (578 mm).

CONSTITUTION AND GOVERNMENT. Malta is a democratic republic and the Constitution, provides for a Parliament consisting of a President of the Republic, a House of Representatives of elected members and a Cabinet consisting of the Prime Minister and such number of Ministers as may be appointed. The Constitution which is founded on work, makes provision for the protection of fundamental rights and freedom of the individual, and ensures that all persons in Malta shall have full freedom of conscience and religious worship. In Jan. 1987 the 2 Political Parties agreed to amend the Constitution to provide that any political party winning more than 50% of all valid votes (but less than 50% of elected members) shall have the number of its members increased in order to have a majority in the House of Representatives. Elections were held in May 1987 in which the Nationalist Party obtained 50·91% of the votes but less seats than the Malta Labour Party. As a result of the above Amendment the Nationalist Party now commands a majority with 35 seats to the MLP 34 seats.

Maltese and English are the official languages.

Elections were held on 9 May 1987. State of parties on 31 Dec. 1987: Malta Labour Party, 34; Nationalist Party, 35.

Acting President: Paul Xuereb.

The Cabinet (Nationalist Party) was as at Dec. 1987:

Prime Minister: Dr Eddie Fenech Adami. *Deputy Prime Minister and Minister for Internal Affairs and Justice:* Dr Guido De Marco. *Foreign Affairs:* Dr Censu Tabone. *Education:* Dr Ugo Mifsud Bonnici. *Social Policy:* Dr Louis Galea. *Finance:* Dr George Bonello Dupuis. *Development of Infrastructure:* Michael Falzon. *Productive Development:* Lawrence Gatt. *Development of Tertiary Sector:* Dr Emmanuel Bonnici. *Gozo:* Anton Tabone.

There are 8 Parliamentary Secretaries.

National flag: Vertically white and red, with a representation of the George Cross medal in the canton.

DEFENCE. The Maltese armed forces include 910 personnel, organized into 1 infantry battalion, and support companies including a Helicopter Flight equipped with 3 Agusta-Bell 47G light helicopters and 2 AB.204s. Duties of the Flight include patrol, search and rescue. There is also a para-military force of 900.

A coastal patrol force of small craft was formed in 1973. It is manned by the Maltese Regiment and primarily employed as a coastguard. In 1988 it comprised 11 patrol and 4 support craft.

INTERNATIONAL RELATIONS

Membership. Malta is a member of UN, the Commonwealth and the Council of Europe.

ECONOMY

Planning. National economic strategy aims especially at the attraction of new investment and the creation of new employment in the directly productive and market services (tertiary) sectors as a means of stimulating export-oriented growth. The objective is to promote the location in Malta of new manufacturing industry with higher skill production and to develop the island as an offshore financial centre. Other important economic activities include ship repair and shipbuilding, food production and tourism. Plans are also under way to encourage foreigners to take up permanent residence in Malta and to convert Marsaxlokk port into a free-port zone for transhipment and related activities. Malta's economic orientation is largely geared towards private sector initiative. The Government's declared long-term economic strategic aim is that of seeking full membership by Malta of the European Communities with suitable terms of accession.

Budget. Revenue and expenditure (in Lm):

	1982	1983	1984	1985	1986
Revenue	210,724,438	224,522,930	218,557,730	220,548,389	225,853,367
Expenditure	216,494,068	220,908,608	223,982,512	227,644,950	240,463,632

The most important sources of revenue are customs duties, income tax, National Insurance contributions and receipts from the Central Bank of Malta.

Currency. The Maltese currency is (Lm) *Lira Maltija* (Maltese Lira). Central Bank of Malta notes of Lm2, Lm5, Lm10 and Lm20 denominations are in circulation. Malta coins are issued in the following denominations: Lm1, 50, 25, 10, 5, 2 and 1 cents; 5, 3 and 2 *mils*. Total notes and coins in circulation on 31 Aug. 1987, Lm294·8m. In March 1988, £1 sterling = Lm 0·576; US$1 = Lm 0·305.

Banking. The Central Bank of Malta was founded in 1968. Commercial banking facilities are provided by Bank of Valletta Ltd, Lombard Bank (Malta) Ltd and Mid-Med Bank Ltd. The other domestic banking institutions are the Investment Finance Bank (long-term industrial loans), the Apostleship of Prayer Savings Bank Ltd, Lohombus Corporation Ltd (house mortgage) and Melita Bank International Ltd (offshore bank).

ENERGY AND NATURAL RESOURCES

Electricity. Up to Sept. 1986 the islands obtained their electricity power supplies from 2 interconnected power stations located at Marsa, having a total installed generating capacity of 192 mw. The larger station with a capacity of 164 mw is also equipped with multi-stage sea water distillation plants for the production of fresh water for public consumption. Supply 240 volts; 50 Hz.

The gross electricity generated in 1985–86 was 822·93m. kwh.

Agriculture. In 1985 agriculture contributed Lm18·8m. to the Gross Domestic Product as against Lm18·7m. in 1984. (The 1985 figure represents a share of 4·4% in the GDP.) In 1983 there was a slight decrease in the cultivable area, which totalled 11,491 hectares as against 11,639 hectares in 1982. In 1983 agriculture employed 4,373 full-time farmers, 341 full-time wage earners and 10,903 part-time farmers against, 4,332, 346 and 11,026 respectively in 1982.

In 1986 the value of Malta's main agricultural exports reached Lm1,124,500. The 1986 exports consisted mainly of: Potatoes, Lm417,859; seeds, cut-flowers and plants, Lm578,802; wine, Lm14,947; hides and skins, Lm93,832; capers, Lm19,783.

Livestock (1986): Cattle, 14,000; pigs, 95,000; sheep, 5,000; goats 5,000; poultry, 1m.

Fisheries. In 1986 the fishing industry occupied 1,270 power propelled and 86 other fishing boats, engaging 269 full-time and 676 part-time fishermen. The catch in 1986 was 1,067 tonnes valued at Lm858,998.

INDUSTRY AND TRADE

Industry. Foreign investors in industry in Malta are offered the following advantages: political stability, excellent industrial relations, a strategic geographic location, a special association agreement with the EEC, a fully developed and highly functional infrastructure, free repatriation of profits and capital, easily trainable and highly adaptable labour force, financing facilities at favourable rates of interest, ready-built factories at subsidized rents, tax holidays, training grants, soft loans. Over 300 state-aided manufacturing enterprises are in operation in various industrial sectors, of which the majority are foreign-owned or have foreign interests. The Malta Development Corporation is the Government agency responsible for promoting and implementing new industrial projects.

Labour. The total work force in Dec. 1986 was 124,137; males, 93,851; females, 30,286, distributed as follows: Agriculture and fisheries, 3,291; manufacturing, 30,452; building, construction and quarrying, 6,646; services, 37,610; electricity, gas and drydocks, 5,831; government, 27,475; armed forces, 869; Dejma and auxiliary workers, 2,935. The number of registered unemployed under Part I of the Employment Register was 8,499, and under Part II, 529.

There were 21 trade unions registered as at 30 June 1987, with a total membership of 60,625 and 21 employers' associations with a total membership of 5,534.

Commerce. Imports and exports including bullion and specie (in Lm1,000):

	1980	1981	1982	1983	1984	1985	1986
Imports	323,737	332,269	325,073	316,633	330,489	354,139	347,909
Exports	166,722	173,725	169,036	156,748	181,364	187,099	194,668

In 1986 the principal items of imports were: Semi-manufactures, Lm101·6m.; machinery and transport, Lm96·5m.; food, Lm38·8m.; fuels, Lm21m.; manufactures, Lm38·5m.; chemicals, Lm27·9m.; others, Lm23·7m. Of domestic exports: Manufactures, Lm101·9m.; machinery and transport, Lm45m.; semi-manufactures, Lm20·2m.; beverages and tobacco, Lm4·9m.; food, Lm4·6m.; others, Lm3·8m.

In 1986, Lm81·1m. of the imports came from Italy, Lm61·6m. from UK, Lm65·8m. from Federal Republic of Germany, Lm18·2m. from USA, Lm22·5m. from Asia, Lm14·7m. from the EFTA, Lm9·3m. from Africa, Lm1·7m. from

Oceania, Lm66·7m. from other European countries; of domestic exports, Lm59·3m. to Federal Republic of Germany, Lm25·6m. to UK, Lm20m. to Italy, Lm9·6m. to Africa, Lm12·5m. to Asia, Lm14·3m. to USA, Lm5·2m. to EFTA and Lm32m. to other European countries.

Total trade between Malta and UK (British Department of Trade returns, in £1,000 sterling):

	1983	1984	1985	1986	1987
Imports to UK	40,852	45,076	51,794	49,197	52,105
Exports and re-exports from UK	71,895	89,468	101,247	101,877	107,941

Tourism. In 1986, 574,189 tourists visited Malta, 329,390 from UK, 36,475 from Italy, 23,177 from Scandinavia, 59,711 from Federal Republic of Germany, 23,141 from Libya, 25,482 from France and 5,199 from USA. In 1986, gross tourist expenditure was Lm79m. (estimate).

COMMUNICATIONS

Roads. Every town and village is served by motor omnibuses. There are ferry services running between Malta and Gozo; cars can be transported on the ferries. In 1984 there were 1,324 km of roads. Motor vehicles registered at 31 Dec. 1986 totalled 114,197, of which 82,580 were private cars, 3,022 hire cars, 18,544 commercial vehicles, 646 buses and 9,405 motor cycles.

Aviation. In 1987 the main scheduled airlines, Air Malta, Alitalia, British Airways, Corse Air, Interflug, JAT, KLM, Lufthansa, Libyan Arab Airlines, Balkan Bulgarian Airlines, Czechoslovakian Airlines, Austrian Airlines, Swissair, Aeroflot and Tunisavia, operated scheduled services between Malta and UK, German Democratic Republic, Federal Republic of Germany, France, Italy, Libya, Netherlands, Switzerland, Yugoslavia, Bulgaria, Czechoslovakia, Austria, USSR, Tunisia, Greece and Hungary. In 1986 there were 13,631 civil aircraft movements at Luqa Airport. 1,243,357 passengers, 5,975 tonnes of freight and 641 tonnes of mail were handled.

Shipping. The number of yachts and ships registered in Malta on 31 Dec. 1986 was 660; 1,740,150 GRT. Ships entering harbour, excluding yachts and fishing vessels, during 1986, 1,894.

Post and Telecommunications. Telegraph and telephone services are administered by Telemalta Corporation with exchanges at Malta and Gozo. On 31 Dec. 1987 there were 154,000 telephones. In 1985 there were 90,500 television and 151,000 radio sets.

Cinemas (1985). There were 22 cinemas with a seating capacity of 15,939.

Newspapers. There were (1987) 1 English, 2 Maltese daily newspapers and 5 weekly papers.

JUSTICE, RELIGION, EDUCATION AND WELFARE

Justice. The number of persons convicted of crimes in 1986 was 1,024; those convicted for contraventions against various laws and regulations numbered 8,823. Fifty-three were committed to prison and 6,461 were awarded fines.

Police. On 31 Dec. 1986 police numbered 50 officers and 1,333 other ranks, including 65 women police.

Religion. The majority of the population belong to the Roman Catholic Church.

Education. Education in Malta is compulsory between the ages of 6 and 16 and free in government schools. Kindergarten education is provided for 4-year old children. The primary level enrols children between 5 and 11 years in a 6-year course. In 1986, there were 25,227 children (13,205 boys and 12,072 girls) in 80 government schools. Another 1,188 pupils were enrolled in preparatory (secondary) classes and classes for weaker pupils. Six Junior Lyceums (4 in Malta and 2 in Gozo) had a total of 5,234 students (2,112 boys, 3,122 girls). There were 31 other government secondary schools with a total of 7,833 (3,098 boys, 4,735 girls). Secondary schools run

5-year courses leading to GCE 'O' level. Two-year courses leading to GCE 'A' level on a worker/pupil system which alternates work with study periods are provided for in the New Lyceum, *i.e.*, upper secondary schools (1,375 students). A higher Secondary School catering for students at GCE O and A level enrolled 777 students. Enrolment in craft and technician courses in 3 technical institutes amounted to 1,050, while 4,149 (2,776 boys and 701 girls) were enrolled in the 12 trade schools for boys and 6 trade schools for girls. Junior Craft Schools for students of lower ability enrolled 1,190 boys and 701 girls. Other students are enrolled in specialized vocational schools. Trade schools offer 2- to 4-year courses in specialized trades and are open to students who finish their third year of secondary education. The number of children in special education amounted to 773.

There were 80 private schools with a population of 4,426 at the nursery level, 10,005 at the primary level and 6,835 at the secondary level.

About 5,000 students attended evening courses in academic, commercial, technical and practical subjects established in 82 centres. Other schools run on a mainly part-time basis by the Education Department for adult students are the School of Art, the School of Music and the School of Art and Design.

The University of Malta consists of 6 faculties: Law, Medicine and Surgery, Engineering and Architecture, Dental Surgery, Education and Management Studies (1,386 students in 1984–85).

Social Security. The National Insurance Act, 1956, provides cash benefits for marriage, maternity, sickness, unemployment, widowhood, orphanhood, invalidity, old age, children's allowances and industrial injury.

The total number of persons in receipt of benefits on 31 Dec. 1986 was 86,615, viz., 647 in receipt of sickness benefit, 505 unemployment benefit, 206 special unemployment benefit, 59 injury benefit, 279 disablement benefit, 91 death benefit, 21,675 retirement pensions, 9,120 widows' pensions, 9 widows' special allowance, 13 guardian's allowance, 5,398 invalidity pensions, 48,223 children's allowances and 390 maternity benefit.

The National Assistance Act, 1956, provides for the payment of social assistance and medical assistance, while the Old Age Pensions Act of 1948 provides for the payment of non-contributory pensions to persons over 60 years of age, to blind persons over the age of 14 years and to handicapped persons over the age of 16 years.

The number of households in receipt of social assistance and of medical assistance on 31 Dec. 1986 was 7,205 and 6,836 respectively, and the number of pensioners in receipt of a non-contributory pension under the Old Age Pensions Act, 1948, was 6,712.

Health. In 1982 there were 413 doctors, 57 dentists, 369 pharmacists, 225 midwives, 2,962 nursing personnel and (1983) 7 hospitals with 3,431 beds.

DIPLOMATIC REPRESENTATIVES

Of Malta in Great Britain (16 Kensington Sq., London, W8 5HH)
High Commissioner: John A. Manduca.

Of Great Britain in Malta (7 St Anne St., Floriana)
High Commissioner: Brian Hitch.

Of Malta in the USA (2017 Connecticut Ave., NW, Washington, D.C., 20008)
Ambassador: Alfred Falzon.

Of the USA in Malta (Development Hse., St Anne St., Floriana)
Ambassador: Peter R. Sommer.

Of Malta to the United Nations
Ambassador: Dr Alexander Borg Olivier.

Books of Reference

Statistical Information: The Central Office of Statistics (Auberge d'Italie, Valletta) was set up in 1947. It publishes *Statistical Abstracts of the Maltese Islands*, a quarterly digest of statistics, quarterly and annual trade returns, annual vital statistics and annual publications on shipping and aviation, education, agriculture and industry and National Accounts and Balance of Payments.

Government publications: Department of Information (Auberge de Castille, Malta), set up in 1955, publishes *The Malta Government Gazette* (twice weekly), *Il-Gzejjer* (monthly), *Malta Review* (bi-monthly), *Malta Handbook, Economic Survey, Malta: Guidelines for Progress, Development Plan for Malta 1981–85* and *Supplement Paper Currency in Malta, Heritage of an Island, Reports on the Working of Government Departments.* Malta, 1982.

Annual Reports. Central Bank of Malta

Trade Directory. Chamber of Commerce (annual)

The Year Book. Sliema (annual)

Malta Independence Constitution (Cmnd 2406). HMSO, 1964

Constitution of the Republic of Malta. Information Division, 1975

Malta Manufacturers and Exporters. Department of Industry, 1981

Economic Survey 1985. Malta, 1985

Bannerman, D. A., and Vella-Gaffiero, J. A., *Birds of the Maltese Archipelago.* Valletta, 1976

Blouet, Brian, *The Story of Malta.* London, Rev. ed. 1981

Cremona, J. J., *The Malta Constitution of 1835 and its Historical Background.* Malta, 1959.— *The Constitutional Developments of Malta under British Rule.* Malta Univ. Press, 1963.—*Human Rights Documentation in Malta.* Malta Univ. Press, 1966

Gerada, E. and Zuber, C., *Malta: An Island Republic.* Paris, 1979

Haslam, S. M., Sell, P. D., and Wolseley, P. A., *A Flora of the Maltese Islands.* Malta Univ. Press, 1977

Luke, Sir Harry, *Malta.* 2nd ed. London, 1962

Price, G. A., *Malta and the Maltese: A Study in 19th-century Migration.* Melbourne, 1954

Thackrah, J. R., *Malta.* [Bibliography] Oxford and Santa Barbara, 1985

MAURITANIA

Capital: Nouakchott
Population: 2·01m. (1987)
GNP per capita: US$450 (1985)

République Islamique de Mauritanie

HISTORY. Mauritania became a French protectorate in 1903 and a colony in 1920. It became an autonomous republic within the French Community on 28 Nov. 1958 and achieved full independence on 28 Nov. 1960. Under its first President, Moktar Ould Daddah, Mauritania became a one-party state in 1964, but following his deposition by a military *coup* on 10 July 1978, the ruling *Parti du peuple mauritanien* was dissolved.

Following the Spanish withdrawal from Western Sahara on 28 Feb. 1976, Mauritania occupied the southern part (88,667 sq. km) of this territory and incorporated it under the name of Tiris el Gharbia. In Aug. 1979 Mauritania renounced sovereignty and withdrew from Tiris el Gharbia.

Following the *coup* of 10 July 1978, power was placed in the hands of a Military Committee for National Recovery (CMRN); the constitution was suspended and the 70-member National Assembly dissolved. On 6 April 1979 the CMRN was renamed the Military Committee for National Salvation (CMSN).

AREA AND POPULATION. Mauritania is bounded west by the Atlantic ocean, north by Western Sahara, north-east by Algeria, east and south-east by Mali, and south by Sénégal. The total area is 1,030,700 sq. km (398,000 sq. miles) of which 47% is desert, and the population at the Census of 1976 was 1,419,939 including 12,897 in Tiris el Gharbia; latest estimate (1987) 2,015,000. The capital Nouakchott had a population of over 500,000 in 1985; other towns (1976) were Nouâdhibou (21,961), Kaédi (20,848), Zouérate (17,474), Rosso (16,466) and Atâr (16,326).

The areas and populations of the Capital District and 12 Regions are:

Region	Sq. km	Estimate 1982	Region	Sq. km	Estimate 1982
Nouakchott District	120	150,000	Adrar	215,300	60,000
Hodh ech-Chargui	182,700	235,000	Dakhlet Nouâdhibou	22,300	30,000
Hodh el-Gharbi	53,400	154,000	Tagant	95,200	84,000
Açâba	36,600	152,000	Guidimaka	10,300	102,000
Gorgol	13,600	169,000	Tiris Zemmour	252,900	28,000
Brakna	33,000	171,000	Inchiri	46,800	23,000
Trarza	67,800	242,000			

In 1983, 34% of the population were urban and 25% were nomadic. In 1980 81% of the inhabitants were Moorish, speaking the Hassaniyah dialect of Arabic, while the other 19% consist of Negro peoples, mainly Fulfulde-speaking Tukulor (8%) and Fulani (5%) who together with the Soninike (Sarakole) and Wolof groups all inhabit the Sénégal valley in the extreme south.

The official languages are Arabic and French.

CLIMATE. A tropical climate, but conditions are generally arid, even near the coast, where the only appreciable rains come in July to Sept. Nouakchott. Jan. 71°F (21·7°C), July 82°F (27·8°C). Annual rainfall 6″ (158 mm).

CONSTITUTION AND GOVERNMENT. The 24-member CMSN wields all executive and legislative powers, working through an appointed Council of Ministers composed as follows in Nov. 1987:

President, Prime Minister, Minister of Defence and Secretary-General of CMSN: Col. Moaouia Ould Sidi Mohamed Taya (assumed office 12 Dec. 1984).

Foreign Affairs and Co-operation: Capt. Mohamed Lemine Ould N'Diayane. *Interior:* Lieut.- Col. Djibril Ould Abdallahi. *Justice and Islamic Affairs:* Hamdi Samba Diop. *Finance and Economy:* Cdr Mohamed Salem Ould Lekhal. *Fisheries and Maritime Economy:* Sidi Ould Cheikh Abdallahi. *Mines and Industry:* Mahfoud Ould Lemrabott. *Energy and Water:* Soumare Oumar. *Rural Development:* Messmoud Ould Belkhair. *Equipment:* Lieut.-Col. Brahim Ould Alioune Ndiaye. *Transport and Trade:* Capt. Dia al-Hadj Abderahmane. *National Education:* Hassiny Ould Didi. *Civil Service, Cadre Training, Labour, Youth and Sports:* Lieut.-Col. Mohamed Mahmoud Ould Deh. *Public Health and Social Affairs:* Maj. N'Daye Kane. *Information, Posts and Telecommunications:* Mohamed Mahmoud Ould Weddadi. *Secretary-General to the Government:* Barou Abdallah. *Deputy Interior Minister:* N'Gam Lirwane.

National flag: Green, with a crescent beneath a star in yellow in the centre.

Local Government: Mauritania is divided into a capital district and 12 regions and sub-divided into 49 *départements.*

DEFENCE

Army. The Army consists of 2 infantry and 1 artillery battalion, 1 Camel Corps, 3 armoured car squadrons and support units; total strength, 14,400 in 1988.

Navy. The Navy consists of 4 patrol vessels, 4 small patrol craft and 2 light aircraft. Personnel (1988) 320.

Air Force. The Air Force has 6 Britten-Norman Defender armed light transports, 2 Maritime Surveillance Cheyennes for coastal patrol, 2 Buffalo and 2 Skyvan transports, 4 Reims-Cessna 337 Milirole twin-engined counter-insurgency, forward air control and training aircraft and 4 Hughes 500 helicopters for communications. Personnel (1988) 150.

INTERNATIONAL RELATIONS

Membership. Mauritania is a member of UN, OAU, the Arab League and is an ACP state of EEC.

ECONOMY

Planning. The 1981–85 development plan stressed the development of agriculture and light industry.

Budget. The ordinary budget for 1986 balanced at 18,600m. ouguiyas.

Currency. The monetary unit is the *ouguiya* which is divided into 5 *khoums.* Banknotes of 1,000, 500, 200 and 100 *ouguiya* and coins of 20, 10, 5 and 1 *ouguiya* and 1 *khoum* are in circulation. In March 1988, £1 = 128·42 *ouguiya*; US$1 = 72·41 *ouguiya.*

Banking. *The Banque Centrale de Mauritanie* (created 1973) is the bank of issue, and there are 5 commercial banks situated in Nouakchott.

ENERGY AND NATURAL RESOURCES

Electricity. Production (1986) 74m. kwh.

Minerals. Iron ore production (1984) 9·5m. tonnes. Copper mining at Akjoujt (by the state-owned SOMIMA), suspended in 1978, resumed in 1983.

Agriculture. Agriculture is mainly confined to the south, in the Sénégal river valley. Production in tonnes (1986) of millet, 94,000; dates, 12,000; potatoes, 1,000; maize, 1,000; sweet potatoes, 2,000; rice, 16,000; groundnuts, 2,000.

In 1986 there were 787,000 camels, 1m. cattle, 149,000 asses, 16,000 horses, 3m. sheep, 3·25m. goats.

Forestry. There are 151,340 sq. km of forests, chiefly in the southern regions, where wild acacias yield the main product, gum arabic.

Fisheries. About 350,000 tonnes of fish are caught in Mauritanian coastal waters each year, but only 50,000 tonnes (1985) are landed in the country (mainly at Nouâdhibou) with another 10,000 tonnes caught in inland waters.

TRADE. In 1985 imports totalled 15,758m. ouguiya, and exports, 28,887 ouguiya of which iron ore comprised 40% of exports and salted and dried fish 60%; 24% of all exports went to Italy, 22% to Japan, 18% to Belgium and 15% to France, while France provided 22% of imports and Spain 20%.

Total trade between Mauritania and UK (British Department of Trade returns, in £1,000 sterling):

	1983	1984	1985	1986	1987
Imports to UK	6,044	10,343	6,311	2,184	8,724
Exports and re-exports from UK	1,719	2,656	2,069	2,495	3,862

Tourism. In 1975 there were 20,700 tourists.

COMMUNICATIONS

Roads. There were 8,900 km of roads in 1983. In 1981 there were 11,262 passenger cars and 8,437 commercial vehicles.

Railways. A 652-km railway links Zouérate with the port of Point-Central, 10 km south of Nouâdhibou, and is used primarily for iron ore exports. In 1984 it carried 9·1m. tonnes and 19,353 passengers.

Aviation. There are international airports at Nouakchott, Nouâdhibou and Néma.

Shipping. The major ports are at Point-Central (for mineral exports), Nouakchott and Nouâdhibou.

Post and Broadcasting. There were, in 1985, 3,161 telephones and (1983) 95,000 radio receivers and about 750 television receivers.

Cinemas. In 1977 there were 12 cinemas with a seating capacity of 8,800.

JUSTICE, RELIGION, EDUCATION AND WELFARE

Justice. There are *tribunaux de première instance* at Nouakchott, Atar, Kaédi, Aïoun el Atrouss and Kiffa. The Appeal Court and Supreme Court are situated in Nouakchott. Islamic jurisprudence was adopted in Feb. 1980.

Religion. Over 99% of Mauritanians are Sunni Moslem, mainly of the Qadiriyah sect.

Education. In 1982 there were 107,390 pupils in primary schools, 25,700 in secondary schools, 1,004 (1981) in technical schools, 1,027 in teacher-training establishments and 400 (1984) students in higher education. The University of Nouakchott (founded 1983) had 974 students in 1984.

Health. In 1979 there were 12 hospitals and clinics with 561 beds. In 1977 there were 99 doctors, 4 dentists, 6 pharmacists, 19 midwives and 192 nursing personnel.

DIPLOMATIC REPRESENTATIVES

Of Mauritania in Great Britain
Ambassador: (Vacant).

Of Great Britain in Mauritania
Ambassador: John Macrae, CMG (resides in Dakar).

Of Mauritania in the USA (2129 Leroy Pl., NW, Washington, D.C., 20008)
Ambassador: Abdellah Ould Daddah.

Of the USA in Mauritania (PO Box 222, Nouakchott)
Ambassador: Robert L. Pugh.

Of Mauritania to the United Nations
Ambassador: Mohamed Mahjoub Ould Boye.

Books of Reference

Stewart, C. C., and Stewart, E. K., *Islam and Social Order in Mauritania.* New York, 1970
Westebbe, R. M., *The Economy of Mauritania.* New York, 1971

MAURITIUS

Capital: Port Louis
Population: 1,041,000 (1987)
GNP per capita: US$1,150 (1983)

HISTORY. Mauritius was known to Arab navigators probably not later than the 10th century. It was probably visited by Malays in the 15th century, and was discovered by the Portuguese between 1507 and 1512, but the Dutch were the first settlers (1598). In 1710 they abandoned the island, which was occupied by the French under the name of Ile de France (1715). The British occupied the island in 1810, and it was formally ceded to Great Britain by the Treaty of Paris, 1814. Mauritius attained independence on 12 March 1968. In 1965 the Chagos Archipelago was transferred to the British Indian Ocean Territory.

AREA AND POPULATION. Mauritius, the main island, lies 500 miles (800 km) east of Madagascar. Rodrigues (formerly a dependency and now a part of Mauritius) is about 350 miles (560 km) east of Mauritius. The outer islands consist of Agalega and the St Brandon Group. Population estimate (1987) 1,041,000.

Island	Area in sq. km	Census 1972	Census 1983
Mauritius	1,865	826,199	966,863
Rodrigues	104	24,769	33,082
Dependencies			
Agalega	70	366	487
St Brandon	1	–	–
Total	2,040	851,334	1,000,432

Port Louis is the capital (138,482, 1986). Other towns, Beau Bassin-Rose Hill, 92,896; Curepipe, 64,417; Quatre Bornes, 64,732; Vascoas-Phoenix, 55,023.

Vital statistics, 1986: Births, 18,225 (18·3 per 1,000); marriages, 10,337; deaths, 6,622 (6·7 per 1,000).

The official language is English.

CLIMATE. The sub-tropical climate produces quite a difference between summer and winter, though conditions are generally humid. Most rain falls in the summer so that the pleasantest months are Sept. to Nov. Rainfall amounts vary between 40″ (1,000 mm) on the coast to 200″ (5,000 mm) on the central plateau, though the west coast only has 35″ (875 mm). Mauritius lies in the cyclone belt, whose season runs from Nov. to April, but is seldom affected by intense storms. Port Louis. Jan. 73°F (22·8°C), July 81°F (27·2°C). Annual rainfall 40″ (1,000 mm).

CONSTITUTION AND GOVERNMENT. Mauritius became an independent state and a monarchial member of the British Commonwealth on 12 March 1968 after 7 months of internal self-government. The Governor-General is the local representative of HM the Queen, who remains the Head of the State.

The Cabinet is presided over by the Prime Minister. Each of the other 18 members of the Cabinet is responsible for the administration of specified departments or subjects and is bound by the rule of collective responsibility. 10 Parliamentary Secretaries may also be appointed by the Governor-General on the advice of the Prime Minister.

The Legislative Assembly consists of a Speaker, elected from its own members, and 62 elected members (3 each for the 20 constituencies of Mauritius and 2 for Rodrigues) and 8 additional seats in order to ensure a fair and adequate representation of each community within the Assembly. General Elections are held every 5 years on the basis of universal adult suffrage.

At the General Election held on 30 Aug. 1987, 41 of the 62 seats were won by the ruling *Alliance* (Mouvement Socialiste Mauricien, 26; Mauritius Labour Party, 9; Parti Mauricien Social-Démocrate, 4; Organisation du Peuple Rodriguais, 2) and 21 by the opposition *Union for the Future* (the Mouvement Militant Mauricien and its allies); of the 8 additional seats awarded to the highest losers in each community, 5 went to the *Alliance* and 3 to the *Union.*

Governor-General: Sir Veerasamy Ringadoo, GCMG, QC.
The Cabinet was composed as follows in Jan. 1988:

Prime Minister, Defence and Internal Security, Information, External Communication and the Outer Islands: Rt Hon. Anerood Jugnauth, PC, QC.
Deputy Prime Minister, Employment and Tourism: Sir Gaetan Duval, QC. *Attorney-General, Justice, External Affairs and Emigration:* Sir Satcam Boolell, QC. *Finance:* Seetanah Lutchmeenaraidoo. *Economic Planning and Development:* Beergoonath Ghurburrun. *Education, Arts and Culture:* Armoogum Parsuraman. *Trade and Shipping:* Dwarkanath Gungah. *Energy and Internal Communications:* Mahyendrah Utchanah. *Industry:* Joseph Herve Duval. *Labour and Industrial Relations, Women's Rights and Family Welfare:* Sheilabai Bappoo. *Youth and Sports:* Michael James Kevin Glover. *Health:* Jagdishwar Goburdhun. *Agriculture, Fisheries and Natural Resources:* Murlidas Dulloo. *Social Security, National Solidarity and Reform Institutions:* Dineshwur Ramjuttun. *Works:* Ramduthsing Jaddoo. *Rodrigues:* Louis Serge Clair. *Housing, Lands and the Environment:* Ramesh Jeewoolall. *Local Government:* Joseph Clarel Desire Malherbe. *Co-operatives:* Vishwanath Sajadah.

National flag: Horizontally 4 stripes of red, blue, yellow and green.

DEFENCE. The Mauritius Police, which is responsible for defence, is equipped with arms; its strength was (1987) 5,367 officers and men.

INTERNATIONAL RELATIONS

Membership. Mauritius is a member of UN, the Commonwealth, OAU and is an ACP state of EEC.

ECONOMY

Budget. Revenue and expenditure (in Rs1m.) for years ending 30 June:

	1983–84	1984–85	1985–86	1986–87
Revenue	3,256	3,559	4,131	5,009
Expenditure	4,073	4,261	4,488	4,635

Principal sources of revenue, 1986–87 (estimate): Direct taxes, Rs 761·3m.; indirect taxes, Rs 3,563·2m.; receipts from public utilities, Rs 212·4m.; receipts from public services Rs 127·9m.; interest and reimbursement, Rs 334·8m. Capital expenditure was Rs 1,764·9m. Capital revenue, Rs 1,448m. On 30 June 1987 the public debt of Mauritius was Rs 8,293·1m.

Currency. The unit of currency is the Mauritius *Rupee*, divided into 100 *cents.*
The currency consists of: (i) Bank of Mauritius notes of Rs 200, 100, 50, 25, 10 and 5; (ii) Cupro-nickel coins of 1 rupee, ½ rupee, ¼ rupee and 10 cents; (iii) Bronze coins of 5 cents, 2 cents and 1 cent. In March 1988, £1 = 22·50 *rupees*; US$1 = 12·85.

Banking. The Bank of Mauritius was established in 1966, with an authorized capital of Rs 10m., to exercise the function of a central bank. There are 13 commercial banks, the Mauritius Commercial Bank Ltd (established 1838), Barclays Bank PLC, the Bank of Baroda Ltd, The Hong Kong and Shanghai Banking Corporation, the Mauritius Co-operative Central Bank Ltd, Banque Nationale de Paris (Intercontinentale), the Habib Bank Ltd, the State Commercial Bank, the Bank of Credit and Commerce International SA, Indian Ocean International Bank Ltd, Mauritius Commercial Bank Finance Corporation Ltd, Union International Bank Ltd and Habib Bank (Zurich).

On 31 Dec. 1987 the Post Office Savings Bank held deposits amounting to Rs 205·4m., belonging to 252,686 depositors.

ENERGY AND NATURAL RESOURCES

Electricity. Electric power production (1986) was 373m. kwh. Supply 230 volts; 50 Hz.

Agriculture. In 1986 84,900 hectares were planted with sugar-cane. There were 19 factories and sugar production (1986 in tonnes) was: Raw sugar, 668,710; white sugar, 38,129; molasses, 173,402.

The main secondary crops in 1986 were tea (4,000 hectares from which 8,000 tonnes were produced), tobacco (1,000 tonnes), potatoes (25,000 tonnes) and maize (5,000 tonnes).

In 1984 poultry production totalled 6,500 tonnes, beef 980 tonnes, pork 620 tonnes and goat meat 110 tonnes.

Livestock (1986): Cattle, 61,000; goats, 71,000; poultry, 2m.

Forestry. The total forest area was estimated (1987) at 21,161 hectares including some 11,730 hectares of plantations. In 1983 sales of forest produce from Crown land totalled 29,876 cu. metres, round wood.

Fisheries. Total catch (1984) 4,176 tonnes.

INDUSTRY AND TRADE

Industry. Manufactures include: Knitwear, clothing, footwear, diamond cutting, jewellery, furniture, watchstraps, sunglasses, plastic ware and chemical products. Total employment in manufacturing 91,800 out of a total labour force of 238,300.

Labour. In 1986 the labour force was 360,000, 13% of whom were employed in sugar production. There were 291 registered trade unions.

Commerce. Total trade (in Rs1m.) for calendar years:

	1984	1985	1986
Imports c.i.f.	6,494	8,010	9,090
Exports f.o.b.	5,180	6,644	9,063

In 1986, Rs 1,242m. of the imports came from France, Rs 910m. from the Republic of South Africa, Rs 686m. from UK, Rs 249m. from Australia. Rs 2,415m. of the exports went to UK, Rs 2,108m. to France, Rs 1,455m. to USA and Rs 661m. to Federal Republic of Germany.

Sugar exports in 1985 were 624,950 tonnes, Rs 3,553m. Other major exports (1984) included clothing, Rs 1,592m.; tea, Rs 249m. and toys, Rs 100m. Major imports, 1984, included textiles and fabrics, Rs 1,296m.; petroleum products, Rs 1,038m. and machinery and transport equipment, Rs 752m.

Total trade between Mauritius and UK (British Department of Trade returns, in £1,000 sterling):

	1983	1984	1985	1986	1987
Imports to UK	128,437	160,042	122,829	153,271	163,271
Exports and re-exports from UK	22,499	24,358	28,512	32,087	44,395

Tourism. In 1987, 180,000 tourists visited Mauritius.

COMMUNICATIONS

Roads. In 1987 there were 27 km of motorway, 840 km of main roads, 934 km of rural roads. At 31 Dec. 1986 there were 23,560 cars, 1,360 buses, 9,005 motor cycles, 20,211 auto cycles and 7,463 lorries and vans.

Aviation. Mauritius is linked by air with Europe, Africa, Asia and Australia by the following airlines: Air France, Air India, Air Malawi, Air Mauritius, British Airways, Lufthansa, South African Airways and Zambia Airways. In addition to passenger services a weekly cargo flight is operated by Air France on the Mauritius–Paris route. In 1984, 192,920 passengers arrived at Plaisance airport and 2,789 tonnes of freight were unloaded.

Shipping. In 1986 1,286 vessels entered Port Louis; total tonnage of cargo, about 2,084,000 tonnes.

Post and Broadcasting. In Dec. 1983 there were 31 telephone exchanges and 48,462 individual telephone installations in Mauritius and Rodrigues. Communication with other parts of the world is established *via* satellite.

At 31 Dec. 1986 there were 115,000 television sets and (1984) 719,112 radio sets.

Cinemas (1987). There were 36 cinemas, with a seating capacity of about 40,000.

Newspapers. There were (1987) 5 French daily papers (with occasional articles in English) and 2 Chinese daily papers with a combined circulation of about 80,000.

RELIGION, EDUCATION AND WELFARE

Religion. At the 1983 Census (excluding Rodrigues), Hindus formed 53% of the population, Roman Catholics 26%, Moslems 13% and Protestants 4%.

Education. Education is free but not compulsory. In 1986 there were 138,765 pupils at 273 primary schools and 68,604 pupils at 127 secondary schools.

In 1987 over 618 students were enrolled at the University of Mauritius.

Health. In 1986 there were 761 doctors, including 144 specialists, and 2,841 hospital beds.

DIPLOMATIC REPRESENTATIVES

Of Mauritius in Great Britain (32–33 Elvaston Pl., London, SW7)
High Commissioner: Soo Soobiah (accredited 18 Feb. 1988).

Of Great Britain in Mauritius (King George V Ave., Port Louis)
High Commissioner: R. B. Crowson, CMG.

Of Mauritius in the USA (4301 Connecticut Ave., NW, Washington, D.C., 20008)
Ambassador: Chitmansing Jesseramsing.

Of the USA in Mauritius (Rogers Bldg., John Kennedy St., Port Louis)
Ambassador: Ronald D. Palmer.

Of Mauritius to the United Nations
Ambassador: Dr S. Peerthum.

Books of Reference

Statistical Information: The Central Statistical Information Office (Rose Hill, Mauritius) was founded in July 1945. Its main publication is the *Bi-annual Digest of Statistics.*

Buckory, S., *Our Constitution.* Port Louis, 1971.—*An Outline of Local Government.* Port Louis, 1970

Ministry of Information and Broadcasting, *Fruits of Political and Social Democracy.— Mauritius Facts and Figures 1980*

Simmons, A. S., *Modern Mauritius: The Politics of Decolonization.* Indiana Univ. Press, 1982

Société de l'Histoire de l'Ile Maurice. *Dictionnaire de biographie mauricienne.* Port Louis, 1967

Toussaint A., *History of Mauritius.* London, 1978

Library: The Mauritius Institute Public Library, Port Louis.

MEXICO

Estados Unidos Mexicanos

Capital: Mexico City
Population: 76m. (1987)
GNP per capita: US$2,200 (1984)

HISTORY. Mexico's history falls into four epochs: the era of the Indian empires (before 1521), the Spanish colonial phase (1521–1810), the period of national formation (1810–1910), which includes the war of independence (1810–21) and the long presidency of Porfirio Díaz (1876–80, 1884–1911), and the present period which began with the social revolution of 1910–21 and is regarded by Mexicans as the period of social and national consolidation.

AREA AND POPULATION. Mexico is at the southern extremity of North America and is bounded in the north by USA, west and south by the Pacific, south-east by Guatemala, Belize and the Caribbean, and north-east by the Gulf of Mexico. It comprises 1,958,201 sq. km (756,198 sq. miles), including uninhabited islands (5,073 sq. km) offshore.

The population at recent censuses has been as follows:

| 1900 | 13,607,272 | 1950 | 25,791,017 | 1970 | 48,225,238 |
| 1930 | 16,552,722 | 1960 | 34,923,129 | 1980 | 66,846,833 |

The areas (in sq. km), populations and capitals of the states are:

States	Sq. km	Census 1980	Estimate 1983	Capital
Aguascalientes	5,471	519,439	593,623	Aguascalientes
Baja California	69,921	1,177,886	1,289,023	Mexicali
Baja California Sur	73,475	215,139	256,463	La Paz
Campeche	50,812	420,553	494,497	Campeche
Chiapas	74,211	2,084,717	2,306,271	Tuxtla Gutiérrez
Chihuahua	244,938	2,005,477	2,152,094	Chihuahua
Coahuila	149,982	1,557,265	1,735,586	Saltillo
Colima	5,191	346,293	383,621	Colima
Distrito Federal	1,479	8,831,079	9,663,360	México City
Durango	123,181	1,182,320	1,289,775	Victoria de Durango
Guanajuato	30,491	3,006,110	3,287,919	Guanajuato
Guerrero	64,281	2,109,513	2,332,230	Chilpancingo
Hidalgo	20,813	1,547,493	1,692,791	Pachuca de Soto
Jalisco	80,836	4,371,998	4,811,551	Guadalajara
México	21,355	7,564,335	9,223,725	Toluca de Lerdo
Michoacán de Ocampo	59,928	2,868,824	3,134,536	Morelia
Morelos	4,950	947,089	1,091,280	Cuernavaca
Nayarit	26,979	726,120	790,932	Tepic
Nuevo León	64,924	2,513,044	2,834,325	Monterrey
Oaxaca	93,952	2,369,076	2,542,094	Oaxaca de Juárez
Puebla	33,902	3,347,685	3,704,627	Puebla de Zaragoza
Querétaro	11,449	739,605	837,003	Querétaro
Quintana Roo	50,212	225,985	290,242	Chetumal
San Luis Potosí	63,068	1,673,893	1,846,726	San Luis Potosí
Sinaloa	58,328	1,849,879	2,089,168	Culiacán Rosales
Sonora	182,052	1,513,731	1,661,898	Hermosillo
Tabasco	25,267	1,062,961	1,180,689	Villahermosa
Tamaulipas	79,384	1,924,484	2,111,730	Ciudad Victoria
Tlaxcala	4,016	556,597	611,650	Tlaxcala
Veracruz	71,699	5,387,680	6,001,856	Jalapa Enríquez
Yucatán	38,402	1,063,733	1,182,180	Mérida
Zacatecas	73,252	1,136,830	1,209,951	Zacatecas

At the 1980 census 33,039,307 were males, 33,807,526 females. Estimate (1987) 76m. Urban population was 66·3% and rural population was 33·7%. Estimate (1986) 81,315,000. The official language is Spanish, the mother tongue of over 92%

of the population, but there are 5 indigenous language groups (Náhuatl, Maya, Zapotec, Otomi and Mixtec) from which are derived a total of 59 dialects spoken by 5,181,038 inhabitants (1980 census). In 1980, about 16% of the population were of European ethnic origin, 55% mestizo and 29% Amerindian.

The populations (1980 Census) of the largest cities were:

México [1]	12,932,116	Saltillo	321,758	Ensenada	175,425
Guadalajara [2]	2,244,715	Victoria de Durango	321,148	Poza Rica de Hidalgo	166,799
Monterrey [3]	1,916,472	Veracruz Llave	305,456	Tuxtla Gutiérrez	166,476
Puebla de Zaragoza	835,759	Querétaro	293,586	Ciudad Obregón	165,572
Léon de los Aldamas	655,809	Tampico	267,957	Salamanca	160,040
Ciudad Juárez	567,365	Villa Hermosa	250,903	Oaxaca de Juárez	157,284
Culiacán Rosales	560,011	Mazatlán	249,988	Ciudad Victoria	153,206
Mexicali	510,554	Irapuato	246,308	Campeche	151,805
Tijuana	461,257	Matamoros	238,840	Uruapan	146,998
Mérida	424,529	Cuernavaca	232,355	Minatitlán	145,268
Acapulco de Juárez	409,335	Celaya	219,010	Pachuca de Soto	135,248
Chihuahua	406,830	Jalapa Enríquez	212,769	Ciudad Madero	132,444
San Luis Potosí	406,630	Reynosa	211,412	Cordoba	126,179
Torreón	363,886	Nuevo Laredo	203,286	Los Mochis	122,531
Aguascalientes	359,454	Atizapán de Zaragoza	188,497	Monclova	119,609
Toluca de Lerdo	357,071	Coatzacoalcos	186,129	Gómez Palacio	116,967
Morelia	353,055	Tepic	177,007	Orizaba	114,848
Hermosillo	340,779				

[1] Metropolitan Area, including Netzahualcóyotl (1,341,230).
[2] Metropolitan Area, including Zapopan (345,390) and Tlaquepaque (135,500).
[3] Metropolitan Area, including Guadalupe (370,524) and San Nicolás de los Garzas (280,696).

Vital statistics for calendar years:

	Births	Deaths	Marriages	Divorces
1982	2,392,849	412,345	528,963	25,901
1983	2,609,088	413,403	507,550	29,427

Crude birth rate in 1983 was 35 per 1,000 population; crude death rate, 5·5; marriage rate 6·8. In 1980 there were 73,260 permanent immigrants.

There were 500,000 (estimate) refugees from Central America.

CLIMATE. Latitude and relief produce a variety of climates. Arid and semi-arid conditions are found in the north, with extreme temperatures, whereas in the south there is a humid tropical climate, with temperatures varying with altitude. Conditions on the shores of the Gulf of Mexico are very warm and humid. In general, the rainy season lasts from May to Nov. Mexico City. Jan. 55°F (12·6°C), July 61°F (16·1°C). Annual rainfall 30" (747 mm). Guadalajara. Jan. 59°F (15·2°C), July 69°F (20·5°C). Annual rainfall 36" (902 mm). La Paz. Jan. 64°F (17·8°C), July 85°F (29·4°C). Annual rainfall 6" (145 mm). Mazatlan Jan. 66°F (18·9°C), July 82°F (27·8°C). Annual rainfall 33" (828 mm). Merida. Jan. 72°F (22·2°C), July 83°F (28·3°C). Annual rainfall 38" (957 mm). Monterrey. Jan. 58°F (14·4°C), July 81°F (27·2°C). Annual rainfall 23" (588 mm). Puebla de Zaragoza. Jan. 54°F (12·2°C), July 63°F (17·2°C). Annual rainfall 34" (850 mm).

CONSTITUTION AND GOVERNMENT. A new Constitution was promulgated on 5 Feb. 1917 and has been amended from time to time. Mexico is a representative, democratic and federal republic, comprising 31 states and a federal district, each state being free and sovereign in all internal affairs, but united in a federation established according to the principals of the Fundamental Law. Citizenship, including the right of suffrage, is vested in all nationals of 18 years of age and older who have 'an honourable means of livelihood'.

There is complete separation of legislative, executive and judicial powers (Art. 49). Legislative power is vested in a General Congress of 2 chambers, a Chamber of Deputies and a Senate (Art.50). The Chamber of Deputies consists of 400 members directly elected for 3 years, 300 of them from single-member constituencies and 100 chosen under a system of proportional representation (Arts.51–55). In Nov. 1986 a programme of electoral reform was introduced which would have the effect of increasing opposition representation in the Chamber of Deputies. At the general elections held on 7 July 1985, 289 of the single-member seats were won by the *Partido Revolucionario Institucional* (PRI), 9 by the *Partido de Acción Nacional* (PAN) and 2 by the *Partido Auténtico de la Revolución* (PARM); of the extra 100 seats, 32 were won by PAN, 12 by the *Partido Socialista Unificado de México*, 11 by the *Partido Popular Socialista*, 12 by the *Partido Socialista de los Trabajadores*, 12 by the *Partido Demócrata Mexicano*, 7 by the PARM, 6 by the *Partido Revolucionario de los Trabajadores*, 6 by the *Partido Mexicano de los Trabajadores* and 2 others. The Senate comprises 64 members, 2 from each state and 2 from the federal district, directly elected for 6 years (Arts.56–58). At the elections of 4 July 1982, the PRI won all 64 seats. Members of both chambers are not immediately re-eligible for election (Art.59). Congress sits from 1 Sept. to 31 Dec. each year; during the recess there is a permanent committee of 15 deputies and 14 senators appointed by the respective chambers. The PRI won all the elections for State Governors held in 1986.

The President is the supreme executive authority. He appoints the members of the Council of Ministers and the senior military and civilian officers of the state. He is directly elected for a single 6-year term.

The names of the presidents from 1958 are as follows:

Adolfo López Mateos, 1 Dec. 1958–30 Nov. 1964.

Gustavo Díaz Ordaz, 1 Dec. 1964–30 Nov. 1970.

Luis Echeverría Alvarez, 1 Dec. 1970–30 Nov. 1976.

José López Portillo y Pacheco, 1 Dec. 1976–30 Nov. 1982.

President: Miguel de la Madrid Hurtado (born in 1934), formerly Minister of Planning, elected 4 July 1982. He assumed office on 1 Dec. 1982.

In Jan. 1987 the Council of Ministers was composed as follows:

Agrarian Reform: Rafael Rodríguez Barrera. *Agriculture and Water Resources:* Eduárdo Pesqueira Olea. *Commerce and Industrial Development:* Héctor Hernández Cervantes. *Communication and Transport:* Daniel Díaz Díaz. *Finance and Public Credit:* Gustavo Petricioli Iturbide. *Foreign Relations:* Bernardo Sepúlveda Amor. *Interior:* Manuel Bartlett Díaz. *Health and Assistance:* Dr Guillermo Soberón Acevedo. *Urban Development and Environment:* Victor Manuel Camacho Solis. *Labour and Social Welfare:* Arsenio Farell Cubillas. *National Defence:* Gen. Juan José Arévalo Gardoqui. *Navy:* Adm. Miguel Angel Gómez Ortega. *Energy, Mines and State Industries:* Alfredo del Mazo González. *Planning and Budget:* Carlos Salinas de Gortari. *Public Education:* José Miguel González Avelar. *Tourism:* Antonio Enríquez Savignac. *Fisheries:* Pedro Ojeda Paullada. *Comptroller-General:* Ignacio Pichardo Pagaza. *Attorney-General:* Dr Sergio García Ramírez. *Governor of the Federal District:* Ramón Aguirre Velázquez. *Attorney-General of the Federal District:* Renato Sales Gasque. *Head of Petróleos Mexicanos (PEMEX):* Francisco Rojas González. *Governor of the Bank of Mexico:* Miguel Mancera Aguayo.

National flag: Three vertical strips of green, white, red, with the national arms in the centre.

National anthem: Mexicanos, al grito de guerra (words by F. González Bocanegra; tune by Jaime Nunó, 1854).

Local Government. Mexico is divided into 31 states and a Federal District. The latter is co-extensive with Mexico City and is administered by a Governor appointed by the President. Each state has its own constitution, with the right to legislate and to levy taxes (but not inter-state customs duties); its Governor is directly elected for 6 years and its unicameral legislature for 3 years; judicial officers are appointed by the state governments. Mexico City is sub-divided into 16 municipalities and the 31 states into 2,378 municipalities.

DEFENCE.

Army. Enlistment into the regular army is voluntary, but there is conscription into a part-time militia, which numbers some 250,000. The regular army consists of 3 infantry brigades (one of which is mechanized), 3 armoured regiments, a garrison for each of the country's 36 military zones, and support units. Equipment includes 45 M-3/-8 tanks and some 140 armoured cars. Strength of the regular army (1988) 105,000; reserve, 60,000.

Navy. The fleet comprises 3 very old *ex*-US destroyers, 5 very old *ex*-US frigates (including 4 former destroyer escort transports), 8 modern light frigate or corvette-type with small helicopter and hangar and 1 frigate-size listed as patrol ships, 1 ancient frigate-size armed transport used as patrol ship, 18 old *ex*-US fleet mine-sweepers, 12 old *ex*-US escort minesweepers, 21 fishery protection cutters of 130 tons built in Britain in 1974–76 and 15 similar-design patrol craft built in Mexico in 1978–88, 7 patrol boats, 25 river patrol craft, 7 survey ships, 1 transport, 3 armed landing ships (2 used for rescue and 1 (with helicopter landing deck) for light forces repair), 2 oilers, 1 training ship, 21 auxiliary vessels and 8 tugs. There are 6 naval zones on the Gulf and 11 on the Pacific coast and 6 naval air bases holding 54 aircraft, including 10 Aviocars and 12 HU-16 Albatross for maritime patrol, and about 20 transports and 20 helicopters and other aircraft for SAR and communications. Naval personnel in 1988 totalled nearly 24,000 officers and men including naval air force and over 3,800 marines.

Air Force. The Air Force had (1988) a strength of about 6,500 officers and men, and has nine operational groups, each with one or two squadrons. No. 1 Group comprises No. 208 Squadron with 10 IAI Aravas for transport, search and rescue and counter-insurgency duties; and No. 209 Squadron with Bell 205A, 206B Jet-Ranger, Alouette III and Puma helicopters. No. 2 Group has two Squadrons (Nos. 206 and 207) of Swiss-built Pilatus PC-7 Turbo-Trainers for light attack duty. No. 3 Group (203 and 204 Squadrons) also operates PC-7s; No. 4 Group (201 and 205 Squadrons) is equipped with PC-7s. No. 5 Group consists of No. 101 communications Squadron and a photo-reconnaissance unit, both equipped with Aero Commander 500S piston-engined light twins. Nos. 301 and 302 Squadrons, in No. 6 Group, operate a total of 5 C-54, 2 C-118A and 1 DC-7 piston-engined transports. The main combat Group, No. 7, comprises No. 401 Squadron with 11 F-5E Tiger II and F-5F 2-seat fighters; and No. 202 Squadron with AT-33A jet trainer/fighter-bombers. No. 8 Group has 7 C-47s in a VIP transport squadron. No. 9 Group operates the Air Force's remaining 12 or more C-47s in Nos. 311 and 312 transport Squadrons. There is a Presidential Squadron with 7 Boeing 727s, 2 737s, 1 HS.125, 1 Electra, 1 JetStar, 1 Islander and 1 Bell 212. The Military Academy continues to fly 14 veteran Stearman PT-17 biplanes. Other training aircraft include 20 Mudry CAP-10Bs, 20 Beech Musketeers, 40 Bonanzas, over 30 T-28 Trojans and PC-7 Turbo-Trainers.

INTERNATIONAL RELATIONS

Membership. Mexico is a member of UN, OAS and ALADI (formerly LAFTA).

ECONOMY

Budget. The 1984 budget provides for expenditure of 12,023,282m. pesos.

Currency. The monetary unit is the *peso*. There are coins of 1, 5, 10, 20, 50, 100 and 200 *pesos*; and banknotes of 500, 1,000, 2,000, 5,000 10,000, 20,000, and 50,000 *pesos*. Total currency in circulation (1984) was 1,192,000m. *pesos*.
Rate of exchange, March 1988: 2,300 pesos = US$1; 4,095 pesos = £1.

Banking. The Bank of Mexico, established 1 Sept. 1925, is the central bank of issue; it is modelled on the Federal Reserve system, with large powers to 'manage' the currency. On 1 Sept. 1982 the private banking sector was nationalized. The total external debt (June 1986) was US$97,000m.

Weights and Measures. The metric system was introduced in 1896, and its sole use is enjoined by law of 14 Dec. 1928.

ENERGY AND NATURAL RESOURCES

Electricity. In 1985 the 498 generating plants had installed capacity of 21,492,000 kw. (34% hydro-electric). Production (1986) 90,490m. kwh. Supply 120 volts; 50 Hz and some 120 volts; 60 Hz.

Oil. The chief Mexican oilfields had proven reserves of oil and gas, in 1983, of 72,500m. bbls. Since the nationalization of the industry in 1938, Petróleos Mexicanos, a government-owned enterprise, has exclusive rights to the exploitation, refining and sale of oil and its by-products. Initially centred on the northeast coasts of the Gulf of Mexico, the industry developed with the discovery of rich fields in the south and southeast, particularly in Veracruz, Tabasco and Chiapas. Offshore wells and those from the southeast now provide the main yields. Exploration has been primarily in recent years in deep waters on the continental shelf in the Gulf coast area, as well as in the northern and southern zones inland. Crude petroleum output was 165m. tonnes in 1985.

Gas. Natural gas production came to 37,160m. cu. metres in 1985.

Minerals. Uranium deposits were discovered in the states of Chihuahua, Durango, Sonora and Queretaro in 1959, rich deposits have been located in Nuevo León. Total reserves (proven 1982) 15,000 tonnes of uranium 308; potential reserves, 150,000 tonnes. Silver output (tonnes) was 2,153 in 1985; gold 7,524 kg.

Mexico has large coal resources, calculated at 5,448m. tonnes, including 1,675m. tonnes (65% cokeable) including high-grade coking coal in Coahuila.

Output, 1985 (in 1,000 tonnes): Lead, 207; copper, 179; zinc, 275; fluorite, 708; pig iron, 5,244; sulphur, 2,052; manganese, 153; gypsum, 2,300 (1984); phosphorus, 518 (1984); barite, 475.

Agriculture. About 80% of Mexico's territory is unsuitable for agriculture. In 1981 Mexico had 21·9m. hectares of arable land, 74·4m. hectares of meadows and pastures, 48·1m. hectares of forests, 1·6m. hectares of permanent crops and 40·6m. hectares of other land. Grains occupy most of the cultivated land, with about 43% given to maize, 10% to sorghum and 5% to wheat. In 1982 there were 146,083 tractors. It is estimated that Mexico should be self-supporting with at least 17m. hectares of land under irrigation and 20·3m. hectares under cultivation.

Livestock (1985): Cattle, 37·45m.; sheep, 6·5m.; pigs, 19m.; horses, 6,135,000; goats, 10·5m.; mules, 3·13m.; donkeys, 3,183,000; poultry, 216m.

Mexico's basic food crop is maize, and a rapid expansion of this crop is one of the chief aims of Mexican agricultural policy, balanced by the demand for 'cash crops' for export, such as cotton, sugar, garbanzos (chick peas), bananas, winter vegetables and coffee.

Production of crops for 1984 was as follows (in 1,000 tonnes):

Crop	1984	Crop	1984	Crop	1984
Maize	12,932	Sugar-cane	34,910	Oranges	1,720
Sorghum	4,974	Tomatoes	1,687	Bananas	2,093
Wheat	4,506	Potatoes	1,017	Lemons	847
Barley	619	Dry beans	974	Pineapples	453
Rice	484	Soybeans	685	Apples	459
Chickpeas	173	Coconuts	1,008	Grapes	539
Cotton	828	Coffee	240	Mangoes	850

Forestry. Forests extended over 48m. hectares in 1981, containing pine, spruce, cedar, mahogany, logwood and rosewood. There are 14 forest reserves (nearly 800,000 hectares) and 47 national park forests of 750,000 hectares. In 1984 total roundwood production amounted to 9·45m. cu. metres.

Fisheries. Catch (1984, in tonnes): sardines, 284,204; anchoveta, 125,884; shrimp and prawns, 76,114; oysters, 42,807; tunny, 57,420; shark, 20,488; sea perch (*mojarras*), 75,273; sea bass, 20,750. Total catch in 1984 was 1,134,592 tonnes.

INDUSTRY AND TRADE

Industry. In 1983, the primary sector (agriculture etc.) provided 7·9% of GDP, the mining, oil and petrochemical industry 11·2%, manufacturing and construction 27·4% and the service sector (commerce, transport and communications, power supply and other services) 54·6%.

Labour. In 1987 unemployment was estimated to be over 50%. Real wages had fallen by about 45% since 1982. In 1980, the economically active population was 22,066,084, of whom 5·7m. were engaged in the primary sector and 2·6m. in manufacturing. Approximately 5m. people belong to trade unions, of whom 85% are affiliated to the *Congreso del Trabajo*.

Commerce. Trade for calendar years in US$1m.:

	1982	1983	1984	1985
Imports	15,057	9,006	11,788	13,994
Exports	21,230	22,312	24,054	21,820

Of total imports in 1985, 63·7% came from USA, 3·8% from Federal Republic of Germany and 5·2% from Japan. Leading imports were mechanical and transport equipment, machine tools, parts and spares.

Of total exports in 1985, 61·1% went to USA, 7·8% to Spain, 7·8% to Japan, 3·7% to France and 3·1% to UK. The main exports (1984) were crude petroleum (62%) vehicles (6%) and petroleum products (5%).

The 1,200 in-bond assembly plants situated along the US-Mexican border generate the second largest flow of foreign exchange after oil, earning US$1,300m. in 1986 and employing 300,000 people.

Total trade between Mexico and UK (British Department of Trade returns, in £1,000 sterling):

	1983	1984	1985	1986	1987
Imports to UK	160,978	175,487	236,811	116,078	244,719
Exports and re-exports from UK	95,674	150,126	203,404	162,328	198,992

Tourism. In 1986, there were 4,625,000 tourists; gross revenue (1983), including border visitors, amounted to US$1,625m.

COMMUNICATIONS

Roads. Total length, (1982) 214,073 km, of which 1,178 km were motorways. Motor vehicles registered in 1982 comprised 5,221,159 passenger cars, and 1,978,327 commercial vehicles.

Railways. The principal group is the *Ferrocarriles Nacionales de México*, with 25,474 km of track. In 1984, FNM carried 60m. tonnes of freight and 20·8m. passengers. Several lines were privately owned including a new line *Ferrocarril Norte de México* completed in 1984 from Los Mochís to Chihuahua. In Mexico City an urban railway system opened in 1969 had 120 km of route and 7 lines in 1985. In 1985 it carried 1,324m. passengers.

Aviation. There are 32 international and 40 national airports. Each of the larger states has a local airline which links them with main airports, which, in turn, furnish services to US, Central and South America and Europe. Thirty-four companies maintained international services, of which *Aeromexico* and *Mexicana de Aviacion* are Mexican. Domestic flights are handled by 77 companies. In 1983 commercial aircraft carried 20m. national and international passengers and some 127,000 tonnes of mail and freight.

Shipping. Mexico has 49 ocean ports, of which, on the Gulf coast, the most important include Coatzacoalcos, Carmen (Campeche), Tampico, Veracruz and Tuxpan. On the Pacific are Salina Cruz, Isla de Cedros, Guaymas, Santa Rosalia, Manzanillo, Lázaro Cárdenas and Mazatlán.

Merchant shipping loaded 72·4m. tonnes and unloaded 11m. tonnes of international traffic in 1984. Passengers (1982), embarked and disembarked 2·8m. In 1982, the merchant marine comprised 545 vessels (of over 100 GRT) with a total tonnage of 1,251,630 GRT.

Post and Broadcasting. In 1980 the telegraph and telephone system had 7,140 offices and 184,641 km of telegraph lines and 30·56m. km of telephone line. *Teléfonos de México*, a state-controlled company, controls about 98% of all the telephone service. Telephones in use, Jan. 1983, 6,395,000.

In 1983 there were 1,014 commercial radio stations and 47 cultural government radio stations while (1982) 10,338,024 homes had receiving sets. In 1982 commercial television stations numbered 191 and cultural stations 8; there were 4,589,170 homes with receiving sets.

Cinemas (1983). Cinemas numbered 1,751 with annual attendance of 271·8m.

Newspapers (1982). There were 362 dailies and 36 weeklies, with an aggregate circulation of 9·5m. In Mexico City the main dailies are, *Excelsior, El Sol de México, Uno más Uno, La Prensa, El Heraldo de México, Novedades, El Universal* and *Esto,* with a combined circulation (1984) 1·8m.

JUSTICE, RELIGION, EDUCATION AND WELFARE

Justice. Magistrates of the Supreme Court are appointed for 6 years by the President and confirmed by the Senate; they can be removed only on impeachment. The courts include the Supreme Court with 21 magistrates, 12 collegiate circuit courts with 3 judges each and 9 unitary circuit courts with 1 judge each, and 68 district courts with 1 judge each.

The penal code of 1 Jan. 1930 abolished the death penalty, except for the armed forces, and set up a commission of alienists and other specialists, in place of courts, to deal with criminal cases (for federal offences); each state also appoints its own local magistrates.

The Mexican Constitution provides a guarantee of individual rights by means of a judicial procedure known as *amparo,* which gives any injured person whose constitutional rights have, in his opinion, been infringed, right to immediate access to the courts and full remedy, combining the swiftness of the Anglo-Saxon writ of *habeas corpus* and the breadth of remedy available through the injunction.

Religion. The prevailing religion is the Roman Catholic (92·6% of the population in 1980); with (1983) 3 cardinals, 12 archbishops and 87 bishops, but by the constitution of 1857, the Church was separated from the State, and the constitution of 1917 provided strict regulation of this and all other religions. No ecclesiastical body may acquire landed property, and since 1917 the property of the Church has been held to belong to the State. In the 1920s the Government suppressed the political influence of the priesthood and temporarily (1929–31) closed the churches. An understanding between State and Church was, however, reached, and all churches eschewing public affairs flourish freely. At the 1980 census there were also 3·3% Protestants, and 4·1% members of other religions.

Education. Primary and secondary education is free and compulsory, and secular. Clergy are forbidden to establish primary schools. All private schools must conform to government standards. In the Federal District education is controlled by the national government; elsewhere by the state authorities.

In 1984–85 there were:

	Establishments	Teachers	Students
Nursery	31,022	72,325	2,147,495
Primary	76,183	437,408	15,219,245
Secondary	17,620	230,656	4,396,087
Preparatory/Vocational	4,300	112,775	1,734,737
Teacher-training	515	13,930	106,886
Higher education	1,305 [1]	92,338 [1]	1,121,252 [1]

[1] 1983–84.

The most important university is the Universidad Nacional Autónoma de México (UNAM) in México City which, with its associated institutions, had, in 1982, 136,534 students (excluding post-graduates). UNAM was founded in 1551, re-organized in 1910, and granted full autonomy in 1920. Other universities of particular importance in México City are the Instituto Politécnico Nacional, specializing in technology and applied science, with 52,694 students, and the Universidad Autónoma Metropolitana with 27,452 students, opened in 1973.

Outside México City the principal universities are the Universidad de Guadalajara (in Guadalajara) with 65,799 students; the Universidad Veracruzana (in Jalapa) with 57,755 students; the Universidad Autónoma de Nueva León (in Monterrey) with 48,124 students; the Universidad Autónoma de Puebla (in Puebla) with 39,505 students; the Universidad Autónoma de Sinaloa (in Culiacán) with 33,366 students; and the Universidad Michoacana (in Morelia) with 23,935 students.

Health. In 1980 Mexico had 66,373 physicians; there were 6,315 state and private hospitals and clinics with 82,717 beds.

Social Welfare. The social welfare system administered mainly by the Mexican Social Security Institute covered 27m. on 31 Dec. 1983.

DIPLOMATIC REPRESENTATIVES

Of Mexico in Great Britain (8 Halkin St., London, SW1X 7DW)
Ambassador: Jorge Eduardo Navarrete.

Of Great Britain in Mexico (Lerma 71, Col. Cuauhtémoc, México City 06500, D.F.)
Ambassador: John A. Morgan, CMG.

Of Mexico in the USA (2829 16th St., NW, Washington, D.C., 20009)
Ambassador: Jorge Espinosa de los Reyes.

Of the USA in Mexico (Paseo de la Reforma 305, México City 5, D.F.)
Ambassador: Charles J. Pilliod, Jr.

Of Mexico to the United Nations
Ambassador: Mario Moya-Palencia.

Books of Reference

Anuario Estadístico de los Estados Unidos Mexicanos. Annual
Revista de Estadística (Monthly); *Revista de Economia* (Monthly)
Alba, V., *A Concise History of Mexico.* London, 1973
Banco de México S.A., Annual report
Banco Nacional de Comercio Exterior. *Comercio Exterior,* monthly.—*Mexico.* Annual (in Spanish or English)
Bazant, J., *A Concise History of Mexico.* CUP, 1977
Carrada-Bravo, F., *Oil, Money, and the Mexican Economy.* Boulder, 1982
Dominguez, J. I., (ed.) *Mexico's Political Economy: Challenges at Home and Abroad.* London, 1982
Hamilton, N., and Harding, T. F., (eds.) *Mexico: State, Economy and Social Conflict.* London, 1986
Kaufman, S., (ed.) *The Politics of Mexican Oil.* Univ. of Pittsburgh Press, 1981
Newell, R. G., and Rubio, L. F., *Mexico's Dilemma: The Political Origins of Economic Crisis.* Epping, 1984
Philip, G., (ed.) *Politics in Mexico.* London, 1985
Riding, A., *Distant Neighbours.* London, 1985.—*Mexico: Inside the Volcano.* London, 1987
Robbins, N., *Mexico.* [Bibliography] Oxford and Santa Barbara, 1984
Velasco, S. J-A., *Impacts of Mexican Oil Policy on Economic and Political Developments.* Aldershot, 1983
Wyman, D. L., (ed) *Mexico's Economic Crisis: Challenges and Opportunities.* San Diego, 1983

MONACO

Capital: Monaco
Population: 27,063 (1982)

HISTORY. Monaco is a small Principality on the Mediterranean, surrounded by the French Department of Alpes Maritimes except on the side towards the sea. From 1297 it belonged to the house of Grimaldi. In 1731 it passed into the female line, Louise Hippolyte, daughter of Antoine I, heiress of Monaco, marrying Jacques de Goyon Matignon, Count of Torigni, who took the name and arms of Grimaldi. The Principality was placed under the protection of the Kingdom of Sardinia by the Treaty of Vienna, 1815, and under that of France in 1861. Prince Albert I (reigned 1889–1922) acquired fame as an oceanographer; and his son Louis II (1922–49) was instrumental in establishing the International Hydrographic Bureau.

AREA AND POPULATION. The area is 195 hectares or 481 acres. The Principality is divided into 4 districts: Monaco-Ville, la Condamine, Monte-Carlo and Fontvieille. Population (1982), 27,063. The official language is French.

CLIMATE. A Mediterranean climate, with mild moist winters and hot dry summers. Monaco. Jan. 50°F (10°C), July 74°F (23·3°C). Annual rainfall 30″ (758 mm).

REIGNING PRINCE. Rainier III, born 31 May 1923, son of Princess Charlotte, Duchess of Valentinois, daughter of Prince Louis II, 1898–1977 (married 19 March 1920 to Prince Pierre, Comte de Polignac, who had taken the name Grimaldi, from whom she was divorced 18 Feb. 1933). Prince Rainier succeeded his grandfather Louis II, who died on 9 May 1949. He married on 19 April 1956 Miss Grace Kelly, a citizen of the USA (died 14 Sept. 1982). *Issue:* Princess Caroline Louise Marguerite, born 23 Jan. 1957; married Philippe Junot on 28 June 1978, divorced, 9 Oct. 1980, married Stefano Casiraghi on 29 Dec. 1983, offspring; Andrea, born 8 June 1984, Charlotte, born 3 Aug. 1986, Pierre, born 7 Sept. 1987. Prince Albert Alexandre Louis Pierre, born 14 March 1958 *(heir apparent).* Princess Stephanie Marie Elisabeth, born 1 Feb. 1965.

CONSTITUTION AND GOVERNMENT. Prince Rainier III on 28 Jan. 1959 suspended the Constitution of 5 Jan. 1911, thereby dissolving the National Council and the Communal Council. On 28 March 1962 the National Council (18 members elected every 5 years, last elections 1983) and the Communal Council (15 members elected every 4 years, last elections 1987) were re-established as elected bodies.

On 17 Dec. 1962 a new constitution was promulgated. It maintains the hereditary monarchy, though Prince Rainier renounces the principle of divine right. The supreme tribunal becomes the custodian of fundamental liberties, and guarantees are given for the right of association, trade union freedom and the right to strike. It provides for votes for women and the abolition of the death penalty.

The constitution can be modified only with the approval of the elected National Council. Women were given the vote in 1945.

Monegasque relations with France were based on a convention of neighbourhood and administrative assistance of 1951. This was terminated by France on 11 Oct. 1962, but has been replaced by several new conventions signed on 18 May 1963.

National flag: Horizontally red over white.

ECONOMY

Planning. A 55-acre site has been reclaimed from the sea at Fontvieille. This land has been earmarked for office and residential development. The present industrial zone is to be reorganized and developed with a view to attracting new light industry to the Principality.

Budget. The budget (in 1,000 francs) was as follows:

	1983	1984	1985	1986	1987
Revenue	1,811,896	1,842,237	1,964,790	2,139,305	2,232,032
Expenditure	1,266,623	1,460,102	1,550,748	1,999,764	2,229,806

Currency. The monetary unit is the French *franc* divided into 100 *centimes.*

Weights and Measures. The metric system is in use.

INDUSTRY AND TRADE

Trade Unions. Membership of trade unions is estimated at 2,000 out of a work force of 25,000 (1986).

Commerce. International trade is included with France.

Tourism. There were 210,558 tourists in 1986.

COMMUNICATIONS

Roads. There were 47·8 km of roads in 1984.

Railways. The 1·6m. km of main line passing through the country is operated by the French National Railways (SNCF).

Aviation. The nearest airport is at Nice, France and a heliport at Fontvieille.

Shipping. The harbour has an area of 40 acres, depth at the entrance 98 ft, and alongside the quay 23 ft at least.

Post and Broadcasting. Telephone subscribers numbered about 20,830 in 1986 and telex subscribers (1984), 597. Monaco issues its own postage stamps.

Radio Monte Carlo broadcasts FM commercial programmes in French (long- and medium-waves). Radio Monte Carlo owns 55% of Radio Monte Carlo Relay Station on Cyprus. The foreign service is dedicated exclusively to religious broadcasts and is maintained by free-will contributions. It operates in 36 languages under the name 'Trans World Radio' and has relay facilities on Bonaire, West Indies, and is planning to build relay facilities in the southern parts of Africa. *Télé Monte-Carlo* broadcasts TV programmes in French, Italian and English.

Cinemas. In 1986 there were 4 cinemas (one open air) with seating capacity of 1,000.

JUSTICE, RELIGION, EDUCATION AND WELFARE

Justice. There are the following courts, *Juge de Paix*, Tribunal of the First Instance, a Court of Appeal, Criminal Tribunal, *Cour de Révision Judiciaire* and a Supreme Tribunal.

Police: There is an independent police force *(Sûreté Publique)* which comprised (1986) 390 policemen and inspectors.

Religion. There has been since 1887 a Roman Catholic bishop elevated since 1982 to an archbishop, directly dependent on the Holy See.

Education. In 1987 there were 5,160 pupils with over 420 teachers.

Health. In 1986 there were 432 hospital beds and 53 physicians.

DIPLOMATIC REPRESENTATIVES

British Consul-General (resident in Marseille): T. E. J. Mound, OBE.
British Honorary Consul (resident in Nice): Lieut.-Col. R. W. Challoner, OBE.
Consul-General for Monaco in London: I. S. Ivanovic.

Books of Reference

Journal de Monaco. Bulletin Officiel. 1858 ff.
Handley-Taylor, G., *Bibliography of Monaco.* London, 1968

MONGOLIAN PEOPLE'S REPUBLIC

Capital: Ulan Bator
Population: 1·97m. (1987)
GNP per capita: US$940 (1978)

Bügd Nayramdakh Mongol Ard Uls

HISTORY. Outer Mongolia was a Chinese province from 1691 to 1911, an autonomous state under Russian protection from 1912 to 1919 and again a Chinese province from 1919 to 1921. On 13 March 1921 a Provisional People's Government was established which declared the independence of Mongolia and on 5 Nov. 1921 signed a treaty with Soviet Russia annulling all previous unequal treaties and establishing friendly relations. On 26 Nov. 1924 the Government proclaimed the country the Mongolian People's Republic.

On 5 Jan. 1946 China recognized the independence of Outer Mongolia after a plebiscite in Mongolia (20 Oct. 1945) had resulted in an overwhelming vote for independence. A Sino-Soviet treaty of 14 Feb. 1950 guaranteed this independence. In Aug. 1986 a consular agreement, and in June 1987 a boundary agreement, were signed with China.

AREA AND POPULATION. Mongolia is bounded north by the USSR, east and south and west by China. Area, 1,567,000 sq. km (605,022 sq. miles); population (1987) 1,965,300 (52·5% urban; 51% male). Density (1987), 1·22 per sq. km. Birth rate (1983), 36·2 per 1,000; death rate, 9·8 per 1,000; marriage rate, 5·7 per 1,000; divorce rate, 0·3 per 1,000. Rate of increase (1987), 27·5 per 1,000. The population is predominantly made up of Mongolian peoples (77·5% Khalkha). There is a Turkic Kazakh minority (5·3% of the population) and 8 Mongol minorities. The official language is Mongolian. Expectation of life in 1987 was 65 years. 45% of the population is under 16.

The republic is administratively divided into 3 cities (Ulan Bator, the capital, population 479,500 (1984), Darkhan, 63,600 (1984) and Erdenet 40,000 (1984)), and 18 provinces *(aimag)*. Local government is administered by People's Deputies' Khurals. The provinces are sub-divided into 258 districts *(somon)*.

CLIMATE. A very extreme climate, with six months of mean temperatures below freezing, but much higher temperatures occur for a month or two in summer. Rainfall is very low and limited to the months mid-May to mid-Sept. Ulan Bator. Jan. −14°F (−25·6°C), July 61°F (16·1°C). Annual rainfall 8″ (208 mm).

CONSTITUTION AND GOVERNMENT. According to the fourth Constitution (1960) legislative power is vested in the *Great People's Khural* of deputies elected for 5 years by universal suffrage of voters over 18 years of age on a basis of 1 deputy per 2,500 inhabitants. It elects from its number 9 members of the Presidium, which carries on current state affairs.

At the election of 22 June 1986 it was stated that turn-out was 99·99%, and 99·99% of votes were cast for the 370 deputies (92 women).

De facto power is in the hands of the only political party, the Mongolian People's Revolutionary (*i.e.*, Communist) Party, which had 89,588 members and candidates in 1987 (workers, 33·2%; white collar, 50%; peasants, 16·8%; women, 30·9%; 15·6% under 30). The youth organization had over 180,000 members in 1982. The *Chairman of the Presidium of the Khural* (head of state) and *General Secretary of*

863

the Party is Dr Jambyn Batmunkh. The other members of the Politburo of the Party are: Dumaagiyn Sodnom, *Prime Minister*; B.-O. Altangerel, *First Deputy Prime Minister*; D. Molomjamts, Ts. Namsra, B. Dejid. *Candidate members:* N. Jagvaral, B. Lamjav, S. Luvsangombo. Ministers not in the Politburo include: *Chairman, State Planning Commission:* P. Jasrai. *Minister of Defence:* Col.-Gen. J. Yondon; *Minister of Public Security:* A. Jamsranjav; *Foreign Minister:* Mangalyn Dugersuren; *Minister of Foreign Trade:* J. Dulmaa. *Minister of Agriculture:* S. Sodnomdorj.

National flag: Red–sky-blue–red (vertical), with a golden 5-pointed star and under it the golden *soyombo* emblem on the red stripe nearest to the flagpole.

The last local elections to the 380 *khurals* took place in June 1984. Turn-out was announced to be 99·99% of the electorate. There are some 15,000 councillors. White-collar, 50%; collective farmers, 30%; industrial workers, 20%; Communist Party members, 60%; women, 33%; under-30, 20%, first term of office, 50%.

DEFENCE. Military service is 3 years.

Army. The Army comprises 4 infantry divisions. Equipment includes T-54/-55/-62 main battle tanks. Strength (1988) 30,000, with reserves of 200,000. There is a paramilitary Ministry of Public Security force of about 15,000 men. A civil defence force was set up in 1970. There were some 75,000 Soviet service personnel in Mongolia, but in Aug. 1987 the USSR announced it had withdrawn one division of about 10,000 troops.

Air Force. The Air Force has about 100 pilots and more than 70 aircraft, including 12 MiG-21 and 10 MiG-17 fighters; a total of about 30 An-2, An-24 and An-26 transports used mainly on civil air services; 3 Wilga utility aircraft; 10 Mi-4 and 3 Mi-8 helicopters; and Yakovlev trainers.

INTERNATIONAL RELATIONS

Membership. Mongolia is a member of UN and Comecon.

Aid. Mongolia receives economic aid from the USSR and other communist countries. There is also a UN development aid programme running at US$2m. per annum.

Treaties. Relations with the USSR are based on a 15-year treaty of economic and technical co-operation (1985).

Sino-Mongolian relations deteriorated after the estrangement between China and USSR, but have improved slightly recently.

ECONOMY

Planning. Mongolia has had for centuries a traditional nomadic pastoral economy, which the Government aims to transform into an 'agricultural–industrial economy'. The eighth 5-year plan is running from 1986 to 1990. For earlier plans *see* THE STATESMAN'S YEAR-BOOK, 1987–88.

Budget (in 1 m. tugriks):

	1978	1980	1982	1983	1984	1985
Revenue	3,660	4,070	4,830	5,255	...	5,743
Expenditure	3,650	4,058	3,131	3,356	...	5,693

Sources of revenue, 1983: turnover tax, 64%; profits tax, 28%; social insurance, 3·5%. Expenditure: economy, 40%; social and cultural, 40%.

Currency. 100 *möngö* = 1 *tugrik*. Notes are issued for 1, 3, 5, 10, 20, 50 and 100 *tugriks*; and coins for 1, 3, 5, 10, 15, 20, 50 *möngö* and 1 *tugrik*. Official exchange rates: £1 = 5·9 *tugriks*; 1 rouble = 4·76 *tugriks*; US$1 = 3·36 *tugriks*.

Banking. The Mongolian State Bank (established 1924) is the sole bank, being at once a bank of issue and a commercial, savings and development bank. It has 21 main branches.

Weights and Measures. The metric system is in use.

ENERGY AND NATURAL RESOURCES

Electricity. There are 6 thermal electric power stations. Production of electricity, 1986, 2,800m. kwh.

Minerals. There are large deposits of copper, nickel, zinc, molybdenum, phosphorites, tin, wolfram and fluorspar; production of the latter in 1984, 747,000 tonnes, entirely exported to the USSR. The copper/molybdenum ore-dressing plant at Erdenet was completed in 1981. Coal reserves are 17,000m. tonnes. Coal accounted for 74·6% of energy production in 1980. There are major coalmines near Ulan Bator and Darkhan. Coal (mainly lignite) production in 1984 was 5·4m. tonnes.

Agriculture. 68% of agricultural production derives from cattle-raising. In 1985 there were 1,971,000 horses, 2,408,000 cattle, 13,248,800 sheep, 559,000 camels and 4,298,600 goats.

Ownership of livestock (in 1m.) in 1983:

	Collective farms	State farms	Private
Cattle	1·14	0·02	0·98
Camels	0·48	0·01	0·08
Horses	1·11	0·08	0·73
Sheep	10·92	1·04	1·93
Goats	3·55	0·07	0·91

In 1983 there were 45,100 pigs and 240,200 poultry. 230,300 tonnes of meat and 6·5m. litres of fermented mare's milk were produced in 1984. Milk production was 44·7m. litres in 1986. In 1983 there were 255 collective farms, 39 inter-farm associations, 14 fodder supply farms and 51 state farms.

All cultivated land belongs to collective or state farms. The total agricultural area in 1983 was 124·98m. hectares, of which 1·3m. were arable (1·2m. sown) and 12·37m. meadows and pastures. 78·5% of the sown area belongs to state farms, 21·2% to collectives. In 1985 81% was sown to cereals, 17% to fodder and 2% to vegetables. The 1986 crop was 664,000 tonnes of wheat; 1,700 tonnes of rye (1980); 50,000 tonnes of oats; 146,000 tonnes of barley. In 1986, 133,000 tonnes of potatoes were harvested. In 1981 there were 7,500 tractors (15 h.p. units) and 2,000 combine harvesters.

Forestry. Forests, chiefly larch, cedar, fir and birch, occupy 156,700 sq. km. Production, 1983: 683,100 cu. metres of timber.

INDUSTRY AND TRADE

Industry. Industry though still small in scale and local in character, is being vigorously developed and now accounts for a greater share of GNP than agriculture. The food industry accounts for 20% of industrial production. The main industrial centre is Ulan Bator; others are at Erdenet and Baga-Nuur, and a northern territorial industrial complex is being developed based on Darkhan and Erdenet to produce copper and molybdenium concentrates, lime, cement, machinery and wood- and metal-worked products. Production figures (1983): wool, 12,100 tonnes; cement, 165,300 tonnes; leather footwear, 2·2m. pairs; meat, 64,400 tonnes; soap, 10,800 tonnes.

Employment. The labour force was 365,000 in 1983, including 82,200 in industry, 41,200 in agriculture, 26,700 in building, 39,700 in transport and communications and 38,900 in trade. In 1983 48·4% of the labour force was female. Average wage was 500 tugriks per month in 1981. Trade union membership was 530,000 in 1988.

There is a labour shortage necessitating the employment of military personnel, and workers from the USSR and Eastern Europe.

Commerce. Foreign trade is a state monopoly. Trade figures for 1983 (in 1m. tugriks): exports, 1,816; imports, 2,764. The main exports are live cattle and horses, wool and hair, meat, grain, hides, furs, ores, and butter. 97% of foreign trade is with communist countries. Just over 25% of imports are consumer goods and the remainder are machinery and industrial raw materials. Imports from the USSR totalled 1,014·6m. roubles in 1984, exports to the USSR, 387·4m. roubles.

Total trade between Mongolia and UK (British Department of Trade returns, in £1,000 sterling):

	1984	1985	1986	1987
Imports to UK	4,561	3,264	4,750	3,847
Exports and re-exports from UK	100	142	1,031	941

COMMUNICATIONS

Roads. There are fewer than 1,000 km of surfaced roads running around Ulan Bator, from Ulan Bator to Darkhan, at points on the frontier with USSR and towards the south. Truck services run where there are no surfaced roads. 30·8m. tonnes of freight were carried in 1983, and 144·9m. passengers.

Railways. The Trans-Mongolian Railway (1,423 km in 1983) connects Ulan Bator with the Soviet Union and China. The Moscow–Ulan Bator–Beijing express runs each way once a week. There are spur lines to Erdenet and to the coalmines at Nalaykha and Sharin Gol. A separate line connects Choybalsan in the east with Borzya on the Trans-Siberian railway. 1·9m. passengers and 12m. tonnes of freight were carried in 1983.

Aviation. Mongolian Airlines (MIAT) operates internal services, a flight to Irkutsk which links with the Soviet airlines (Aeroflot) stopping service to Moscow and a thrice-weekly non-stop service to Moscow from Ulan Bator. 10,000 tons of freight were carried in 1983 and 500,000 passengers. Some charter flights were operated to Beijing in 1986. Ulan Bator airport (Buyant Uhaa) was modernized and expanded in 1985.

Shipping. There is a steamer service on the Selenge River and a tug and barge service on Hobsgol Lake. 3,000 tonnes of freight were carried in 1976.

Post and Broadcasting. There were, in 1983, 414 post offices and 264 telephone exchanges. Number of telephones (1983), 44,600.

There are wireless stations at Ulan Bator, Gobi Altai and Olgiy. In 1983 there were 186,600 radio and 70,700 television receivers. Television services began in 1967. A Mongolian television station opened in 1970. Mongolia is a member of the international TV organization Intervision.

Cinemas. In 1983 there were 26 cinemas, 493 mobile cinemas and 20 theatres.

Newspapers and books. In 1983, 37 newspapers and 39 journals were published. The Party daily paper *Ünen* ('Truth') had a circulation of 112,000 in 1978. 400 book titles were published in 1982 in 70m. copies

JUSTICE, RELIGION, EDUCATION AND WELFARE

Justice. The Procurator-General is appointed, and the Supreme Court elected, by the *Khural* for 5 years. There are also courts at province, town and district level. Lay assessors sit with professional judges.

Religion. Tibetan Buddhist Lamaism was the prevalent form of religion. It was suppressed in the 1930s, and only one functioning monastery exists today, at Ulan Bator, with about 100 lamas.

Education. In 1985 there were 680 nurseries with 62,500 children. Schooling begins at the age of 7. In 1984-85 there were 911 general education schools with 444,000 pupils and 15,900 teachers, 28 specialized secondary schools with 23,000 students and 1,200 teachers and 40 vocational technical schools with 25,000 pupils. There is a state university (founded 1942) at Ulan Bator (40 professors, 240 lecturers and 10,000 students in 1982), and 7 other institutes of higher learning (teacher training, medicine, agriculture, economics, etc.) with 26,000 students in 1983 and 1,400 teachers under the supervision of an Academy of Sciences (founded 1961) which has 15 institutes and 190 research workers. Some 6,000 students a year are sent to study abroad, principally in the USSR.

In 1946 the Mongolian alphabet was replaced by a modern Cyrillic alphabet.

Health and Welfare. In 1983 68·3m. tugriks were spent on maternity benefits.

Annual average per capita consumption (in kilogrammes) of foodstuffs over 1981–83: Meat, 91·4; milk and products, 147·7; sugar, 21·3; flour, 97·7; potatoes, 17·9; fresh vegetables, 14·5. In 1987 there were 24 doctors and 111 hospital beds per 10,000 population.

DIPLOMATIC REPRESENTATIVES

Of Mongolia in Great Britain (7 Kensington Ct., London, W8 5DL)
Ambassador: Ishetsogyin Ochirbal.

Of Great Britain in Mongolia (30 Enkh Taivny Gudamzh, Ulan Bator)
Ambassador: G. W. P. Hart, OBE.

Of Mongolia to the United Nations
Ambassador: Gendengiin Nyamdoo.

In Jan. 1987 the USA announced it would be establishing diplomatic relations with Mongolia at ambassadorial level.

Books of Reference

The Central Statistical Office: *National Economy of the MPR, 1924–1984: Anniversary Statistical Collection.* Ulan Bator, 1984

Bawden, C. R., *The Modern History of Mongolia.* London, 1968
Boberg, F., *Mongolian–English, English–Mongolian Dictionary.* 3 vols. Stockholm, 1954–55
Haltod, M. (ed.), *Mongolian–English Dictionary.* Berkeley, Cal., 1961
Jagchid, S., and Hyer, P. *Mongolia's Culture and Society.* Folkestone, 1979
Lattimore, O., *Nationalism and Revolution in Mongolia.* Leiden, 1955.—*Nomads and Commissars.* OUP, 1963
Lörinc, L., *Histoire de la Mongolie des Origines à nos Jours.* Budapest, 1984
Mongol'skaia Narodnaia Respublika: Spravochnik. Moscow, 1986
News from Mongolia. Ulan Bator, fortnightly, Jan. 1980
Rupen, R. A., *How Mongolia is Really Ruled: A Political History of the Mongolian People's Republic, 1900–1978.* Stanford, 1979
Sanders, A. J. K., *The People's Republic of Mongolia: A General Reference Guide.* OUP, 1968.—*Mongolia: Politics, Economics and Society.* London, 1987
Shirendev, B., and Sanjdorj, M. (eds.), *History of the Mongolian People's Republic.* Vol. 3 (vols. 1 and 2 not translated). Harvard Univ. Press, 1976
Socialist Mongolia. Ulan Bator, 1981

MONTSERRAT

Capital: Plymouth
Population: 11,852 (1985)
GNP per capita: US$3,127 (1985)

HISTORY. Montserrat was discovered by Columbus in 1493 and colonized by Britain in 1632 who brought Irish settlers to the island. Montserrat formed part of the federal colony of the Leeward Islands from 1871 until 1956, when it became a separate colony following the dissolution of the Federation. The island's Constitution came into force in 1960 and the title Administrator was changed to that of Governor in 1971.

AREA AND POPULATION. Montserrat is situated in the Caribbean Sea 25 miles south-west of Antigua. The area is 39·5 sq. miles (106 sq. km). Population, 1985, 11,852. Chief town, Plymouth, 3,500 inhabitants.

CLIMATE. A tropical climate but with no well-defined rainy season, though July to Dec. shows slightly more rainfall, with the average for the year being about 60″ (1,500 mm). Dec. to March is the cooler season while June to Nov. is the hotter season, when hurricanes may occur. Plymouth. Jan. 76°F (24·4°C), July 81°F (27·2°C). Annual rainfall 65″ (1,628 mm).

CONSTITUTION AND GOVERNMENT. Montserrat is a crown colony. The Executive Council is composed of 4 elected Ministers (the Chief Minister and 3 other Ministers) and 2 civil service officials (Attorney-General and Financial Secretary). The Legislative Council consists of 7 elected and 2 civil service officials (the Attorney-General and Financial Secretary) and 2 nominated members. The Executive Council is presided over by the Governor and the Legislative Council by the Speaker.

In elections to the Legislative Council in 1987, 4 seats were won by the People's Liberation Movement, 2 by the National Development Party and 1 by the Progressive Democratic Party.

Governor: C. J. Turner, OBE.
Chief Minister: Hon. J. A. Osborne.
Flag: The British Blue Ensign with the shield of Montserrat in the fly.

ECONOMY.

Budget. In 1986 the budget expenditure was at EC$25m. of which EC$7m. was capital expenditure. In 1981 the territorial budget ceased to be grant-aided by the British Government.

Currency. 100 cents = 1 Eastern Caribbean dollar (EC$). Coins: 1, 2, 5, 25, 50 cents. Notes: 1, 5, 10, 20 and 100 dollars.

Banking. There are 5 recognized banks on Montserrat. These are the Barclays Bank, the Royal Bank of Canada, The First American Bank, the Government Savings Bank and the Montserrat Building Society.

ENERGY AND NATURAL RESOURCES

Electricity. Production (1986) 11·6m. kwh.

Agriculture. Agriculture has been in decline for several years, but is likely to recover with the progress of the Integrated Sea Island Cotton Project and revised land tenure and settlement arrangements associated with the government's acquisition of a number of estates. Attempts are being made to bring about self-sufficiency in selected foodstuffs with any surplus for export.

Livestock (1986); Cattle, 3,500; pigs, 1,000; sheep, 5,000; goats, 6,500.

Fisheries. Catch (1983) 150 tonnes.

INDUSTRY AND TRADE

Industry. Considerable light industry was attracted to the territory from abroad during 1979–81 and there is 83,000 sq. ft of modern factory space available.

Commerce. Imports in 1986 totalled EC$55m.; domestic exports, EC$5m. Chief imports were manufactured goods, food and beverages, machinery and transport equipment and fuel. Chief exports in 1986 were electronic parts and lighting fittings.

Total trade between Montserrat and UK (British Department of Trade returns, in £1,000 sterling):

	1984	1985	1986	1987
Imports to UK	115	414	358	139
Exports and re-exports from UK	1,999	2,330	3,926	2,432

Tourism. In 1986, 26,076 tourists arrived in Montserrat.

COMMUNICATIONS

Roads. In 1986 there were 290 km of roads, 212 km paved, 1,217 passenger cars and 215 commercial vehicles.

Aviation. At Blackburne airport 4,422 aircraft landed in 1985, disembarking 25,380 passengers and 132·4 tonnes of cargo.

Shipping. In 1986, 299 cargo vessels arrived, landing 22,207 and loading 66 tonnes of cargo.

Post and Broadcasting. Number of telephones (1986), 3,738; telex, 33. In 1984 there were 4,000 radio and 1,100 TV receivers.

JUSTICE, RELIGION, EDUCATION AND WELFARE

Justice. There are 2 magistrates' courts, at Plymouth and Cudjoe Head. Strength of the police force (1986), 3 gazetted officers, 3 inspectorate and 89 other ranks.

Religion. In 1980 (census) there were 1,368 Roman Catholics, 3,676 Anglicans, 2,742 Methodists, 1,041 Seventh Day Adventists, 1,503 Pentecostals and 285 members of the Church of God. There is also a Christian Council of Churches.

Education. There are 9 government and 4 private nursery schools for children up to age 5; 9 government, 2 grant-aided and 3 private primary schools for children between 5-12 years; 1 comprehensive secondary school with 3 campuses and 2 private secondary schools for students 12 years and above. In 1986, 1,351 children were enrolled in the primary schools, with 67 teachers; 1,016 in the secondary schools, with 74 teachers. There is 1 government owned technical college with 53 students and 11 teachers.

Health. In 1985 there were 8 doctors and 67 hospital beds.

Books of Reference

Population Census 1980. Montserrat
Overseas Trade 1983. Montserrat Government
Preliminary National Account Statistics, 1975–1982. 1982
Vital Statistics Report. Montserrat Government, 1983
Statistical Digest 1984. Montserrat Government
Fergus, H.A., *Montserrat: Emerald Isle of the Caribbean.* London, 1983

Library: Public Library, Plymouth. *Librarian:* Miss Ruth Allen.

MOROCCO

Capital: Rabat
Population: 23m. (1987)
GNP per capita: US$500 (1984)

al-Mamlaka al-Maghrebia

HISTORY. From 1912 to 1956 Morocco was divided into a French protectorate (established by the treaty of Fez concluded between France and the Sultan on 30 March 1912), a Spanish protectorate (established by the Franco-Spanish convention of 27 Nov. 1912) and the international zone of Tangier (set up by France, Spain and Great Britain on 18 Dec. 1923).

On 2 March 1956 France and the Sultan terminated the treaty of Fez; on 7 April 1956 Spain relinquished her protectorate, and on 29 Oct. 1956 France, Spain, Great Britain, Italy, USA, Belgium, the Netherlands, Sweden and Portugal abolished the international status of the Tangier Zone. The northern strip of Spanish Sahara was ceded by Spain on 10 April 1958, and on 30 June 1969 the former Spanish province of Ifni was returned to Morocco.

A tripartite agreement was announced on 14 Nov. 1975 providing for the transfer of power from Spanish Sahara (Western Sahara) to the Moroccan and Mauritanean governments on 28 Feb. 1976. Spanish troops left El Aaiún on 20 Dec. 1975. On 14 April 1976 a Convention was signed by Mauritania and Morocco in which the 2 countries agreed to partition the former Spanish territory, but on 14 Aug. 1979 Mauritania renounced its claim to its share of the territory (Tiris El-Gharbiya) which was added by Morocco to its area.

AREA AND POPULATION. Morocco is bounded by Algeria to the east and south-east, Western Sahara to the south-west, the Atlantic ocean to the north-west and the Mediterranean to the north. Excluding the Western Saharan territory claimed and occupied since 1976 by Morocco, the total area is 458,730 sq. km and its total population at the Sept. 1982 census was 20,255,687; the latest estimate (1987) is 23m.

The areas (in sq. km) and populations (census 1982) of the provinces are:

Province	Sq. km	1982	Province	Sq. km	1982
Agadir	5,910	579,741	Nador	6,130	593,255
Taroudant	16,460	558,501	Ouarzazate	41,550	533,892
Al-Hoceima	3,550	311,298	Oujda	20,700	780,762
Azilal	10,050	387,115	Rabat-Salé [1]	1,275	1,020,001
Beni Mellal	7,075	668,703	Safi	7,285	706,618
Ben Slimane	2,760	174,464	Settat	9,750	692,359
Boulemane	14,395	131,470	Tangier	1,195	436,227
Casablanca-Anfa [1]		923,630	Tan-Tan	17,295	47,040
Aïn Chok-Hay Hassani [1]		298,376	Taounate	5,585	535,972
Ben Msik-Sidi Othmane [1]	1,615	639,558	Tata	25,925	99,950
Hay Mohamed-Aïn Sebâa [1]		421,272	Taza	15,020	613,485
Mohamedia-Znata [1]		153,828	Tétouan	6,025	704,205
Chechaouèn	4,350	309,024	Tiznit	6,960	313,140
El Jadida	6,000	763,351			
El Kelâa-Srarhna	10,070	577,595	Morocco	458,730	20,255,687
Er Rachidia	59,585	421,207			
Es Saouira	6,335	393,683			
Fez	5,400	805,464	Boujdour		
Figuig	55,990	101,359	(Bojador)	100,120	8,481
Guelmim	28,750	128,676	Es Semara		
Kénitra	4,745	715,967	(Smara)	61,760	20,480
Sidi Kacem	4,060	514,127	Laâyoune		
Khémisset	8,305	405,836	(Ál Aaiún)	39,360	113,411
Khénifra	12,320	363,716	Oued Ed		
Khouribga	4,250	437,002	Dahab	50,880	21,496
Marrakesh	14,755	1,266,695			
Meknès	3,995	626,868	Sahara	252,120	163,868
Ifrane	3,310	100,255			

[1] Urban prefectures

Population of cities (estimates, 1981): Casablanca, 2,408,600; Rabat-Salé, 841,800; Fez, 562,900; Marrakesh, 548,700; Meknès, 486,600; Oujda, 470,500; Kénitra, 449,700; Tétouan, 371,700; Tangier, 304,000; Safi, 255,700; Agadir, 245,800; Khouribga, 229,600; Beni Mellal, 204,800, Settat, 167,000; Al-Jadida, 164,000; Taza, 146,500; Nador, 115,300; Khémisset, 100,100.

The official language is Arabic, spoken by 75% of the population; the remainder speak Berber. French and Spanish are considered subsidiary languages.

CLIMATE. The climate ranges from semi-arid in the south to warm temperate Mediterranean conditions in the north, but cooler temperatures occur in the mountains. Rabat. Jan. 55°F (12·9°C), July 72°F (22·2°C). Annual rainfall 23" (564 mm). Agadir. Jan. 57°F (13·9°C), July 72°F (22·2°C). Annual rainfall 9" (224 mm). Casablanca. Jan. 54°F (12·2°C), July 72°F (22·2°C). Annual rainfall 16" (404 mm). Marrakesh. Jan. 52°F (11·1°C), July 84°F (28·9°C). Annual rainfall 10" (239 mm). Tangier. Jan. 53°F (11·7°C), July 72°F (22·2°C). Annual rainfall 36" (897 mm).

REIGNING KING. Hassan II, born on 9 July 1929, succeeded on 3 March 1961, on the death of his father Mohammed V, who reigned 1927–61. The royal style was changed from 'His Sherifian Majesty the Sultan' to 'His Majesty the King' on 18 Aug. 1957. *Heir apparent:* Crown Prince Sidi Mohammed, born 21 Aug. 1963.

The King holds supreme civil and religious authority; the latter in his capacity of Emir-el-Muminin or Commander of the Faithful. He resides usually at Rabat, but occasionally in one of the other traditional capitals, Fez (founded in 808), Marrakesh (founded in 1062), or at Skhirat.

CONSTITUTION AND GOVERNMENT. A new Constitution was approved by referendum in March 1972 and amendments were approved by referendum in May 1980. The Kingdom of Morocco is a constitutional monarchy with a legislature of a single chamber composed of 306 deputies. Deputies for 102 seats are elected by indirect vote through an electoral college representing the town councils, the regional assemblies, the chambers of commerce, industry and agriculture, and the trade unions. Deputies for the remaining 204 seats are by general election. The King, as sovereign head of State, appoints the Prime Minister and other Ministers, has the right to dissolve Parliament and approves legislation.

In the General Elections held on 14 Sept. 1984, the new *Union constitutionelle* (founded Jan. 1983) won 83 seats, the *Rassemblement nationale des indépendants* 61 seats, the *Union socialiste des forces populaires* 36 seats, the *Mouvement populaire* 47 seats, *Istiqlal* (Independence) 41 seats; others 38 seats.

National flag: Red, with a green pentacle star in the centre.

Cabinet in Dec. 1987:

Prime Minister: N. Azzeddine Laraki.

Justice: Moulay Mustapha Belarbi Alaoui. *Interior:* Driss Basri. *Foreign Affairs, Co-operation and Information:* Abdellatif Filali. *Planning:* Rachid Ghazouani. *National Education:* Mohamed Hilali. *Economic Affairs:* Moulay Zine Zahidi. *Finance:* Abdellatif Jouahri. *Trade, Industry and Tourism:* Abdallah al-Azmani. *Handicrafts and Social Affairs:* Mohamed Labied. *Transport:* Mohamed Bouamoud. *Energy and Mining:* Mohamed Fettah. *Health:* Tayeb Bencheikh. *Maritime Fishing and Merchant Navy:* Bensalem Smili. *Secretary-General of the Government:* Abbas Kaissi. *Cultural Affairs:* Mohamed Benaissa. *Housing and Land Management:* Abderrahmane Boufettas. *Equipment, Executive and Professional Training:* Mohamed Kabbaj. *Posts and Telecommunications:* Mohand Laensar. *Agriculture and Land Reform:* Otman Demnati. *Relations with Parliament:* Tahar Afifi. *Youth and Sports:* Abdellatif Semlali. *Labour:* Hassan Abbadi. *Islamic Affairs:* Abdelkbar Alaoui Medaghri. *Administrative Affairs:* Abderrahim Ben Abdeljalil. *Saharan Province:* Khali H. Ould Rachid. *Relations with the European Community:* Azzedine Guessous. There was 1 Minister of State.

Local Government: The country is administratively divided into 39 provinces and 8 urban prefectures.

DEFENCE. Military service is compulsory for 18 months.

Army. The Army comprises 2 mechanized infantry, 1 light security, 1 parachute brigade and 1 anti-aircraft group; 4 mechanized infantry regiments; 9 artillery groups; 7 armoured, 1 Royal Guard, 3 camel corps, 2 desert cavalry, 1 mountain, 4 commando and 10 engineer battalions; and 7 armoured car squadrons. Equipment includes 110 M-48A5 main battle tanks, 110 light tanks and 1,400 armoured cars. Strength (1988) 170,000 men. There are also 35,000 paramilitary troops.

Navy. Navy includes 1 modern missile-armed light frigate, 4 new missile armed large patrol vessels or small corvettes, 2 modern fast attack (corvette size) gunboats, 1 *ex*-coastal minesweeper used for patrol duties, 1 patrol vessel, 1 gunboat, 1 seaward patrol craft, 9 coastal patrol boats, 4 landing craft acquired from France and 2 logistic support vessels. Six corvettes of new design have been ordered. There were also 13 small customs cutters and 24 more building. Personnel in 1988 was considerably increased to 6,000 officers and ratings including 600 marines.

Air Force. The Air Force was formed in Nov. 1956. Equipment in current use is mainly of US and West European origin. It includes 40 Mirage F1s, a total of 25 F-5A/B/E/F fighter-bombers and RF-5A reconnaissance-fighters, 4 OV-10 Bronco counter-insurgency aircraft, 2 Falcon 20s for electronic warfare, and 24 Gazelle armed helicopters, 24 Alpha Jet advanced trainers, 22 Magister armed jet basic trainers, 12 T-34C-1 turboprop basic trainers, 10 Swiss-built Bravo primary trainers, 2 Mudry CAP 10B aerobatic trainers, 4 Broussard liaison aircraft, 85 Agusta-Bell 205 and 212, Puma and JetRanger helicopters, 10 Do 28D Skyservants for coastal patrol, 11 CH-47C heavy-lift helicopters, 20 C-130H turboprop transport aircraft, 3 KC-130H tanker/transports, a Falcon 50 and a Gulfstream III VIP transport, 2 Boeing 707s and 5 turboprop King Air light transports. Personnel strength (1988) about 15,000.

INTERNATIONAL RELATIONS

Membership. Morocco is a member of UN, the Non-Aligned Movement, the Islamic Conference and the Arab League.

ECONOMY

Planning. The Development Plan, 1981–85, envisaged an investment of DH110,900m. and gave priority to housing, health services, industry and agriculture.

Budget. The budget for 1986 envisaged revenue of 51,100m. DH and expenditure of 59,700m. DH.

Debt. In April 1985 foreign debt was estimated at US$12,500m. (£9,800m.).

Currency. In Oct. 1959, a national currency was introduced. Its unit is the *dirham* (abbreviated DH), equalling 100 *centimes*. Notes: 10, 50, 100 DH; coins: 0·10, 0·20, 0·50, 1 DH. The exchange rate in March 1988 was £1 sterling = 14·10 DH; US$1 = 8·06 DH.

Banking. The central bank is the Banque al Maghrib. Authorized banks are: La Banque Marocaine du Commerce Extérieur, La Banque Marocaine pour le Commerce et l'Industrie, La Banque Commerciale du Maroc, Compagnie Marocaine du Crédit et de Banque, Société Générale Marocaine de Banque, Crédit du Maroc, Union Marocaine de Banque, Société de dépôt et de crédits, Arab Bank Ltd, Bank of America, Banco Espagnol en Maruecos, Banque de Paris et des Pays-Bas, First National City Bank, Société Hollandaise de Banque et de Gestion, The British Bank of the Middle East, Société de Dépôt et de Crédits, Wafabank, Citibank, Algemene Bank Nederland and Banque Américano-Suisse pour le Maroc. The Banque Centrale Populaire and regional Banques populaires also provide banking services for small and medium businesses. There are 3 development banks: Banque Nationale du Development Economique, whose major area of investment has been industry; Credit Industrial et Hotelier, which finances housing on easy terms; Caisse Nationale du Credit Agricole, which specializes in agriculture. La Banque National pour le Développement économique grants loans to the industrial sector. Le Crédit Immobilier et Hôtelier grants loans for construction. La Caisse de Dépôt et de Gestion is responsible for the centralization of savings and their management.

Weights and Measures. The metric system of weights and measures is the sole legal system.

ENERGY AND NATURAL RESOURCES

Electricity. Electric power-plants produced 6,920m. kwh. in 1986. Supply 110, 127 and 220 volts; 50 Hz.

Oil. Crude oil production, 17,500 tonnes 1981. Refined oil production (including imported crude), 4·5m. tonnes in 1983.

Minerals. The principal mineral exploited is phosphate, the output of which was 21·4m. tonnes in 1986. Other important minerals (in tonnes, 1985) are: Anthracite (774,500), iron ore (190,258), lead (153,636), copper (59,245), zinc (27,153), manganese (43,690), baryt (463,380), fluorine (74,350), salt (118,173).

Agriculture. Land suitable for cultivation, 1984, 7·7m. hectares, of which (in 1,000 hectares): Cereals, 4,500; leguminous vegetables, 400; market gardening, 150; oil-producing and industrial cultivation, 130; fodder, 110; dense fruit plantations, 400; fallows, 2,000.

Production in 1986 (in 1,000 tonnes): Wheat, 3,809; barley, 3,563; maize, 307; fruit, 1,725 (of which citrus fruits, 1,224); pulses, 393; sunflower seeds, 21; groundnuts, 36; sugar beets, 2,500; sugar-cane, 790; olives, 330; potatoes, 56; tomatoes, 400; onions, 260.

Dairy production in 1986 included: Milk, 910,000 tonnes; butter, 13,723 tonnes; cheese, 6,396 tonnes. Meat production (1986) 327,000 tonnes.

Livestock (in 1,000 heads), 1984–85: Cattle, 2,870; sheep, 14,640; goats, 6,320.

Forestry. Forests cover 5m. hectares (8% of land area) and employed (1984) 50,000. They produce mainly firewood, building and industrial timber, some cork and charcoal.

Fisheries. The industry employed 83,000 workers in 1987. Total catch in 1986 was 591,000 tonnes, value 2,442,404,000 DH. The value of fish exports in 1986 was 2,860,552,000 DH.

INDUSTRY AND TRADE

Industry. In 1984 industry represented 14% of the GNP. Manufacturing industries are concentrated in Casablanca (metallurgy, car assembly, sugar-producing and pharmaceutical products), Fez, Rabat, Muhammadia (textile), Safi (chemicals, manure, fish treatment) and Agadir (fish treatment, canning factories). There are 8 cement factories, with an output of 3,848,200 tonnes in 1983, when self-sufficiency was achieved.

The agricultural and food industries produce 40% of the whole industrial output. The sugar industry meets 76% of the country's needs and produced 426,800 tonnes of crude sugar in 1983.

Trade Unions. In 1984 there were 8 trade unions.

Commerce. Imports and exports were (in US$1m.):

	1983	1984	1985	1986
Imports	3,530	3,880	3,750	3,800
Exports	2,030	2,150	2,160	2,500

Exports (1986) of phosphates 13·7m. tonnes, value DH3,840m.
Exports in 1985 went mainly to France (24%), Spain (7%), Federal Republic of

Germany (7%), Italy (6%) and UK (3%). Imports were mainly from France (25%), Spain (14%), Federal Republic of Germany (8%), Italy (6%) and UK (3%).

Total trade between Morocco and UK (British Department of Trade returns, in £1,000 sterling):

	1983	1984	1985	1986	1987
Imports to UK	75,602	79,738	74,820	65,419	61,108
Exports and re-exports from UK	99,727	79,850	92,658	84,510	94,487

Tourism. In 1986, 1·47m. visitors came to Morocco, spending (1985) DH6,200m.

COMMUNICATIONS

Roads. In 1983 there were 57,592 km of classified roads, of which 19,099 km were surfaced. A motorway links Rabat to Casablanca. At the end of 1981 there were in use 207,370 lorries, 445,000 private cars and 18,424 motor cycles.

Railways. In 1984 there were 1,779 km of railways, of which 794 km were electrified. The principal standard-gauge lines are from Casablanca eastward to the Algerian border, forming part of the continuous rail line to Tunis; Casablanca to Marrakesh with 2 important branches, one eastward to Oued Zem tapping the Khouribga phosphate mines, the other westward to the port of Safi. Another branch serves the manganese mines at Bou Arfa. Two new double-track electrified lines are to serve a new deep-water port at Jorf Lasfar.

In 1986 the railways carried 958m. passenger-km and 4,502 tonne-km.

Aviation. There are 15 international airports as well as national airports. The most important, Mohamed V airport in Casablanca, handled 18,154 flights with 1,367,548 passengers and 24,968·8 tonnes of freight including mail in 1983. Total flights, 1983, 44,606 with 3,176,648 passengers and 29,882·7 tonnes of freight including mail.

Shipping. In 1983, 17,555 vessels entered and cleared the ports of Morocco and 19,393,000 tonnes of merchandise, including 13,891,500 tonnes of phosphate, were loaded and 11,260,000 tonnes unloaded.

Post and Broadcasting. In 1983 there were 359 post offices. Telephone subscribers totalled 265,672 in 1983.

There are broadcasts in Arabic, Berber, French, Spanish and English from Rabat and Tangier; television in Arabic and French began in 1962. In 1984 there were 2·5m. radio receivers and in 1983 1,044,895 television receivers.

Cinemas. There were about 235 cinemas in 1971.

Newspapers. In 1984 there were 12 daily newspapers (7 Arabic, 5 French) and 18 main weeklies and monthlies (10 Arabic, 8 French).

JUSTICE, RELIGION, EDUCATION AND WELFARE

Justice. A uniform legal system is being organized, based mainly on French and Islamic law codes and French legal procedure. The judiciary consists of a Supreme Court, courts of appeal, regional tribunals and magistrates' courts.

Religion. Islam is the established state religion. 98% are Sunni Moslems of the Malekite school and 2% are Christians, mainly Roman Catholic.

Education. In 1959 a standardization of the various school systems (French, Spanish, Israeli, Moslem, etc.) was begun. Education is compulsory from the age of 7 to 13.

In 1984 there were 2,550,000 pupils and 75,094 teachers in 3,144 state primary schools; 1,050,000 pupils and 51,711 teachers in secondary schools; 10,020 (1981) students in technical schools and 16,148 (1981) students in teacher-training establishments.

The language of instruction in primary and secondary schools is Arabic. Some scientific courses were (1985) still taught in French.

Professional and vocational colleges had 6,942 students in 1983. There were 30,000 students abroad.

There are six universities, Mohamed V at Rabat, Hassan II at Casablanca, Mohamed Ben Abdallah at Fez, Quaraouyine at Fez, Mohamed I at Oujda and Cadi Ayyad at Marrakesh with a total enrolment of 99,637 students and 3,146 teaching staff in 1984.

Health. In the public sector, 1984, there were 1,048 medical centres and dispensaries, 5,258 doctors, 63 chemists and 4,424 (1983) registered nurses. In the private sector, 1984, there were 1,971 doctors, 6,713 (1983) chemists and 709 registered nurses. There were 14,847 qualified nurses in 1983.

DIPLOMATIC REPRESENTATIVES

Of Morocco in Great Britain (49 Queen's Gate Gdns., London, SW7 5NE)
Ambassador: Abdeslam Zenined, GCVO.

Of Great Britain in Morocco (17 Blvd de la Tour Hassan, Rabat)
Ambassador: J. W. R. Shakespeare, CMG, LVO.

Of Morocco in the USA (1601 21st St., NW, Washington, D.C., 20009)
Ambassador: M'hamed Bargach.

Of the USA in Morocco (2 Ave. de Marrakech, Rabat)
Ambassador: Thomas A. Nassif.

Of Morocco to the United Nations
Ambassador: Driss Slaoui.

Books of Reference

Statistical Information: The Service Central des Statistiques (BP 178, Rabat) was established in 1942. Its publications include: *Annuaire de Statistique Générale.—La Conjoncture Économique Marocaine* (monthly; with annual synthesis).—*Bulletin économique et social du Maroc* (trimestral)

Bulletin Official (in Arabic and French). Rabat. Weekly
Findlay, A. M. and A. M., and Lawless, R. I., *Morocco.* [Bibliography] Oxford and Santa Barbara, 1984
Kinross, Lord, and Hales-Gary, D., *Morocco.* London, 1971

National Library: Bibliothèque Générale et Archives, Rabat.

MOZAMBIQUE

República Popular de Moçambique

Capital: Maputo
Population: 14·54m. (1987)
GNP per capita: US$90 (1986)

HISTORY. Trading settlements were established by Arab merchants at Sofala (Beira), Quelimane, Angoche and Mozambique Island in the fifteenth century. Mozambique Island was visited by Vasco da Gamba's fleet on 2 March 1498, and Sofala was occupied by Portuguese in 1506. At first ruled as part of Portuguese India, a separate administration was created in 1752, and on 11 June 1951 Mozambique became an Overseas Province of Portugal. Following a decade of guerrilla activity, Portugal and the nationalists jointly established a transitional government on 20 Sept. 1974. Independence was achieved on 25 June 1975. In March 1984 the Republic of South Africa and Mozambique signed a non-agression pact.

AREA AND POPULATION. Mozambique is bounded east by the Indian ocean, south by South Africa, south-west by Swaziland, west by South Africa and Zimbabwe and north by Zambia, Malaŵi and Tanzania. It has an area of 799,380 sq. km (308,642 sq. miles) and a population, according to the census of 1980, of 11,673,725. Estimate (1987) 14,543,000 of whom (1986) 882,800 lived in the capital, Maputo. Other chief cities are Beira (1986 population, 269,700) and Nampula (182,600). The areas, populations and capitals of the provinces are:

Province	Sq. km	Census 1980	Estimate 1986	Capital
Cabo Delgado	82,625	940,000	1,098,700	Pemba
Niassa	129,056	514,100	600,900	Lichinga
Nampula	81,606	2,402,700	2,808,300	Nampula
Zambézia	105,008	2,500,200	2,922,300	Quelimane
Tete	100,724	831,000	971,300	Tete
Manica	61,661	641,200	749,500	Chimoio
Sofala	68,018	1,065,200	1,245,000	Beira
Inhambane	68,615	997,600	1,166,000	Inhambane
Gaza	75,709	990,900	1,158,200	Xaixai
Province of Maputo	25,756	491,800	574,800	Maputo
City of Maputo	602	755,300	882,800	

The main ethnolinguistic groups are the Makua/Lomwe (52% of the population), mainly in the 4 provinces in the north, the Malaŵi (12%), Shona (6%) and Yao (3%) in Tete, Manica and Sofala, and the Thonga (24%) in the 3 provinces in the south. Portuguese remains the official language, but Swahili serves as a lingua franca north of the Zambézi.

CLIMATE. A humid tropical climate, with a dry season from June to Sept. In general, temperatures and rainfall decrease from north to south. Maputo. Jan. 78°F (25·6°C), July 65°F (18·3°C). Annual rainfall 30″ (760 mm). Beira. Jan. 82°F (27·8°C), July 69°F (20·6°C). Annual rainfall 60″ (1,522 mm).

CONSTITUTION AND GOVERNMENT. Under the Constitution adopted at independence on 25 June 1975, the directing power of the state is vested in the *Frente de Libertação de Moçambique* (FRELIMO), the liberation movement, which in Feb. 1977 was reconstituted as sole political Party. A new Constitution was under discussion in 1987. The legislative organ is the People's Assembly of 250 members, elected in Dec. 1986.

The Council of Ministers in Dec. 1987 consisted of:

President, and Commander-in-Chief of the Armed Forces: Joaquim Alberto Chissano.
Prime Minister and Planning: Mário da Graça Machungo.

Foreign Affairs: Pascoal Mocumbi. *Defence:* Alberto Joaquim Chipande. *Deputy Minister of Defence, Chief of Staff of the Armed Forces:* Antonio Hama Thai. *Co-operation:* Jacinto Veloso. *Minister in the Presidency:* Feliciano Gundana. *Minister in the Presidency for State Administration:* José Oscar Monteiro. *Security:* Mariano de Araújo Matsinhe. *Health:* Fernando Everard do Rosario Vaz. *Education:* Graça Machel. *Interior:* Manuel António. *Finance:* Abdul Magid Osman. *Construction and Water:* João Salomão. *Trade:* Manuel Aranda da Silva. *Agriculture:* João Ferreira. *Transport and Communications:* Armando Emílio Guebuza. *Industry and Energy:* António José Lima Rodrigues Branco. *Justice:* Ali Ossumane Dauto. *Information:* Teodato Hunguana. *Mineral Resources:* John Kachamila. *Labour:* Aguiar Real Mazula. *Culture:* Luis Bernardo Honwana.

There are 14 Deputy Ministers and 11 Secretaries of State.

National flag: Horizontally green, black, yellow with the black fimbriated in white; a red triangle based on the hoist, charged with a yellow star surmounted by an open white book and a crossed rifle and hoe in black.

Local Government. The capital of Maputo and 10 provinces, each under a Governor who is automatically a member of the Council of Ministers, are sub-divided into 112 districts.

DEFENCE. Selective conscription for 2 years is in force.

Army. The Army consists of 1 tank brigade and 7 infantry brigades, 2 independent mechanized and 7 anti-aircraft artillery battalions. Equipment includes T-34/-54/-55 main battle tanks. Strength (1988) 30,000. There are also 9,500 Border Guards and various militias.

Navy. The small flotilla comprises 4 Indian-built (Goa) patrol craft, 2 *ex*-Soviet anti-submarine vessels, 6 former Portuguese coastal patrol boats, 6 *ex*-Soviet gunboats, 4 *ex*-Netherlands patrol craft, 10 Goa-built inshore patrol boats and 2 *ex*-Portuguese minor landing craft. Naval personnel in 1988 totalled 800 officers and men.

Air Force. The Air Force is reported to have about 20 MiG-17 and 30 MiG-21 fighters, probably flown by Cuban pilots, An-26 turboprop transports, and a few C-47 piston-engined transports. About 10 Mi-24 armed helicopters and 8 Mi-8 transport helicopters, a small number of L-39 jet trainers, Zlin 326 primary trainers and a few *ex*-Portuguese Air Force Alouette liaison helicopters. Personnel (1988) 1,000.

INTERNATIONAL RELATIONS

Membership. Mozambique is a member of UN, OAU, SADCC and is an ACP state of EEC.

ECONOMY

Planning. The Economic Recovery Programme (1987–90) aims to stimulate production and to restore the real value of wages and earnings as an incentive to productivity in industry and agriculture.

Budget. In 1987 the revenue was US$2·77·87m.; expenditure, US$427·91m. Foreign debt (1986) US$3,200m.

Currency. In June 1980 the currency became the *metical* (pl. *meticais*) divided into 100 *centavos*. The *metical* was established at par with the former *escudo*. In March 1988, £1 = 806 *meticais*; US$1 = 454 *meticais*.

Banking. Most banks had been nationalized by 1979. The *Banco de Moçambique* (bank of issue) and the *Banco Popular de Desenvolvimento* (state investment bank) each have a capital of 1,000m. meticais.

Weights and Measures. The metric system is in force.

ENERGY AND NATURAL RESOURCES

Electricity. Production (1986) 1,640m. kwh. Capacity (1986) 2,225,000 kw. Supply 220 volts; 50 Hz. The hydro-electric dam at Cabora Bassa on the Zambezi is the largest producer in Africa.

Minerals. Coal is the main mineral being exploited. Output was 380,000 tonnes in 1983. Coal reserves (estimate) 400m. tonnes. Small quantities of bauxite, gold, titanium, fluorite and colombo-tantalite are produced. Iron ore deposits and natural gas are known to exist.

Agriculture. Production in tonnes (1986): Cereals, 610,000; tea, 15,000; maize, 350,000; bananas, 75,000; sisal, 3,000; rice, 60,000; groundnuts, 65,000; copra, 67,000; vegetables, 191,000; citrus, 42,000; potatoes, 65,000; cashews, 30,000; sunflower seed, 20,000; cotton (lint), 17,000; sugar, 26,000.

Livestock 1986: 1·34m. cattle, 365,000 goats, 116,000 sheep, 150,000 pigs, 20,000 asses.

Forestry. Forests represent 20% of land area. Production (1985) 35,000 cu. metres of cut timber.

Fisheries. In 1984 the prawn catch was 5,800 tonnes; other fish 11,700 tonnes.

INDUSTRY AND TRADE

Industry. Although the country is overwhelmingly rural, there is some substantial industry in and around Maputo (steel, engineering, textiles, processing, docks and railways).

Commerce. Imports in 1986 totalled US$546·8m. and exports US$79m. In 1985 20% of imports came from the USSR, 12% from the Republic of South Africa and 12% from the USA. 23% of exports were to Spain, 19% to the USA, 16% to Japan and 12% to the Federal Republic of Germany. Shrimps made up 44% of exports; cashews, 15%; cotton fibre, 7%; sugar, 9%; copra, 7% and petroleum products, 5%.

Total trade between Mozambique and UK (British Department of Trade returns, in £1,000 sterling):

	1983	1984	1985	1986	1987
Imports to UK	9,176	8,549	6,908	1,335	6,580
Exports and re-exports from UK	28,618	15,671	11,343	13,175	21,168

COMMUNICATIONS

Roads. There were, in 1982, 26,000 km of roads, of which 4,600 km were tarred. Motor vehicles, in 1980, included 99,400 passenger cars and 24,700 lorries and buses. The Government is devoting effort to constructing a new North/South road link, and to improving provincial rural feeder road systems.

Railways. The Mozambique State Railways consist of 5 independent networks known as the Maputo, Mozambique, Sofala (Beira), Inhambane and Gaza, and Quelimane systems. The Maputo system has a link at Komatipoort with the Republic of South Africa, Swaziland and Zimbabwe railways; the Sofala system links with Zimbabwe at Machipanda (near Umtali); and the Mozambique system links with Malawi at Entre Lagos. Total route-km (1986), 2,988 km (1,067 mm gauge), and 143 km (762 mm gauge). In 1986, 6·8m. passengers and 301m. tonne-km of goods were carried.

Aviation. There are international airports at Maputo, Beira and Nampula with regular services to European and Southern African destination by several foreign airlines and by *Linhas Aéreas de Moçambique*, who also serve 13 domestic airports.

Shipping. The total tonnage handled by Mozambique ports (1981) was 9·12m. The principal ports are Maputo, Beira, Nacala and Quelimane.

Post and Broadcasting. Maputo is connected by telegraph with the Transvaal system. Quelimane has telegraphic communication with Chiromo. Number of telephones (1982), 56,305.

Radio Moçambique broadcasts 5 programmes in Portuguese, English, Afrikaans, Ronga and Shangane as well as 4 regional programmes in 8 languages. Number of receivers (1985): radio, 450,000; TV, 6,500.

Cinemas. There were, in 1971, 31 cinemas with a seating capacity of 20,195.

Newspapers. There were (1984) 2 daily newspapers in Mozambique: *Noticias,* published in Maputo (circulation, 45,000), and *Diario de Mozambique* in Beira (15,000).

JUSTICE, RELIGION, EDUCATION AND WELFARE

Justice. A system of People's Courts exists at all levels.

Religion. About 60% of the population follow traditional animist religions, while some 18% are Christian (mainly Roman Catholic) and 16% Moslem.

Education. In 1983 there were 1,402,541 pupils in 8,528 primary schools and 106,975 in 136 secondary schools. The *Universidade Eduardo Mondlane* had 2,500 students in 1985. About 500,000 attend adult literacy classes.

Health. There were (1985) 258 hospitals and medical centres with 12,472 beds; there were 317 doctors, 871 midwives and 2,590 nursing personnel. In 1980 there were 96 dentists and 8 pharmacists.

DIPLOMATIC REPRESENTATIVES

Of Great Britain in Mozambique (Ave. Vladimir 1 Lenine 310, Maputo)
Ambassador: J. N. Allan, CBE.

Of Mozambique in the USA (1990 M. St., NW, Washington, D.C., 20036)
Ambassador: Valeriano Ferrao.

Of the USA in Mozambique (35 Rua Da Mesquita, Maputo)
Chargé d'Affaires: Michael E. Ranneberger.

Of Mozambique to the United Nations
Ambassador: Manuel dos Santos.

Books of Reference

Darch, C., *Mozambique.* [Bibliography] Oxford and Santa Barbara, 1987
Hanlon, J., *Mozambique: The Revolution under Fire.* London, 1984
Henriksen, T. H., *Mozambique: A History.* London and Cape Town, 1978
Houser, G., and Shore, H., *Mozambique: Dream the Size of Freedom.* New York, 1975
Isaacman, A., *A Luta Continua: Building a New Society in Mozambique.* New York, 1978.
    —*Mozambique: From Colonization to Revolution, 1900–1982.* Aldershot and Boulder, 1984
Mondlane, E., *The Struggle for Mozambique.* London, 1983
Munslow, B., *Mozambique: The Revolution and its Origins.* London and New York, 1983

NAURU

Population: 8,042 (1983)
GNP per capita: US$9,091 (1985)

HISTORY. The island was discovered by Capt. Fearn in 1798, annexed by Germany in Oct. 1888, and surrendered to the Australian forces in 1914. It was administered under a mandate, effective from 17 Dec. 1920, conferred on the British Empire and approved by the League of Nations until 1 Nov. 1947, when the United Nations General Assembly approved a trusteeship agreement with the governments of Australia, New Zealand and UK as joint administering authority. Independence was gained in 1968.

AREA AND POPULATION. The island is situated 0° 32′ S. lat. and 166° 56′ E. long. Area, 5,263 acres (2,130 hectares). It is an oval-shaped upheaval coral island of approximately 12 miles in circumference, surrounded by a reef which is exposed at low tide. There is no deep water harbour but offshore moorings, reputedly the deepest in the world, are capable of holding medium-sized vessels, including 30,000 tonne capacity bulk carriers. On the seaward side the reef dips abruptly into the deep waters of the Pacific at an angle of 45°. On the landward side of the reef there is a sandy beach interspersed with coral pinnacles. From the sandy beach the ground rises gradually, forming a fertile section ranging in width from 150 to 300 yd and completely encircling the island. There is an extensive plateau bearing phosphate of a high grade, the mining rights of which were vested in the British Phosphate Commissioners until 1 July 1970, subject to the rights of the Nauruan landowners. In July 1970 the Nauru Phosphate Corporation assumed control and management of the enterprise. It is chiefly on the fertile section of land between the sandy beach and the plateau that the Nauruans have established themselves. With the exception of a small fringe round a shallow lagoon, about 1 mile inland, the plateau, which contains the phosphate deposits, has few foodbearing trees and is not settled by the Nauruans.

At the census held on 13 May 1983 the population totalled 8,042, of whom 4,964 were Nauruans.

Vital statistics, 1982: Births, 286 (224 Nauruan); deaths, 77 (42 Nauruan).

CLIMATE. A tropical climate, tempered by sea breezes, but with a high and irregular rainfall, averaging 82″ (2,060 mm). Jan. 81°F (27·2°C), July 82°F (27·8°C). Annual rainfall 75″ (1,862 mm).

CONSTITUTION AND GOVERNMENT. A Legislative Council was established by the Nauru Act, passed by the Australian Parliament in Dec. 1965 and was inaugurated on 31 Jan. 1966. The trusteeship agreement terminated on 31 Jan. 1968, on which day Nauru became an independent republic but having special relationship with the Commonwealth. An 18-member Parliament is elected on a 3-yearly basis.

President and Minister for Foreign Affairs: Hammer DeRoburt, GCMG, OBE.

National flag: Blue with a narrow horizontal gold stripe across the centre, beneath this near the hoist a white star of 12 points.

FINANCE. Revenue and expenditure (in $A) for financial year ending 30 June 1983 (estimate): revenue, 97,279,300; expenditure, 111,284,800 (health, 1,602,200; education, 2,004,200).

The interests in the phosphate deposits were purchased in 1919 from the Pacific Phosphate Company by the governments of the UK, the Commonwealth of Australia and New Zealand at a cost of £Stg3·5m., and a Board of Commissioners representing the 3 governments was appointed to manage and control the working of the deposits. In May 1967, in Canberra, the British Phosphate Corporation agreed to hand over the phosphate industry to Nauru and on 15 June 1967 agreement was reached that the Nauruans could buy the assets of the B.P.C. for approximately $A20m. over 3 years. It is estimated that the deposits will be exhausted by 1993. Phosphate sales (1984–85) $A100m.

COMMERCE. The export trade consists almost entirely of phosphate shipped to Australia, New Zealand and Japan. The imports consist almost entirely of food supplies, building construction materials and machinery for the phosphate industry.

Total trade between Nauru and UK (British Department of Trade returns, in £1,000 sterling):

	1983	1984	1985	1986	1987
Imports to UK	1,421	916	479	148	674
Exports from UK	1,715	1,332	1,199	1,239	394

COMMUNICATIONS

Aviation. There is an airfield on the island capable of accepting medium size jet aircraft. Air Nauru, a wholly owned government subsidiary, operates services with Boeing 727 and 737 aircraft to Melbourne, Sydney, Apia, Honiara, Guam, Tarawa, Majuro, Kagoshima, Okinawa, Noumea, Port Vila, Suva, Nadi, Ponape, Manila, Taipei, Truk, Saipan, Korer (Pelan), Honolulu, Singapore, Auckland, Pago Pago and Niue.

Shipping. The Nauru Local Government Council, through its agency the Nauru Pacific Shipping Line, owns 6 ships and 2 fishing boats. These ships ply between Australia, Pacific Islands, west coast of USA, New Zealand, Japan, Singapore etc. Other shipping coming to the island consists of those under charter to the phosphate industry.

Telecommunications. Number of telephones (1978) 1,500 and (1984) 5,500 radio receivers. Direct daily high frequency service is maintained with Tarawa and both long- and short-wave transmissions with merchant shipping. A separate tele-radio service exists between Nauru and Ocean Island.

Cinemas. In 1978 there were 7 cinemas with seating capacity of 1,500.

JUSTICE, RELIGION AND EDUCATION

Justice. The highest Court is the Supreme Court of Nauru. It is the Superior Court of record and has the jurisdiction to deal with constitutional matters in addition to its other jurisdiction. There is also a District Court which is presided over by the Resident Magistrate who is also the Chairman of the Family Court and the Registrar of Supreme Court. The laws applicable in Nauru are its own Acts of Parliament and a large number of British statutes and the common law have been adopted for Nauru.

Religion. The population is mainly Roman Catholic or Protestant.

Education. Attendance at school is compulsory for all children between the ages of 6 and 16. In June 1983 there were 8 infant and primary schools and 2 secondary schools. There were 44 teachers and 2,164 pupils in infant, primary and secondary schools. In addition, there is a trade school with 4 instructors and an enrolment of 74 trainees. Scholarships are available for Nauruan children to receive secondary and higher education and vocational training in Australia and New Zealand. In 1984, 88 Nauruans were receiving secondary and tertiary education abroad.

DIPLOMATIC REPRESENTATIVES

Of Great Britain in Nauru
High Commissioner: R. A. R. Barltrop, CVO (resides in Suva).

Of Nauru in the USA
Ambassador: T. W. Star (resides in Melbourne).

Books of Reference

Packett, C. N., *Guide to the Republic of Nauru.* Bradford, 1970
Pittman, G. A., *Nauru, the Phosphate Island.* London, 1959
Viviani, N., *Phosphate and Political Progress.* Canberra, 1970

NEPÁL

Nepal Adhirajya

Capital: Káthmándu
Population: 16·63m. (1985)
GNP per capita: US$170 (1983)

HISTORY. From 1846 to 1951 Nepál was virtually ruled by the Ráná family, a member of which always held the office of prime minister, the succession being determined by special rules. The last Ráná prime minister (and, until 18 Feb. 1951, Supreme C.-in-C.) was HH Máhárája Mohan Shumsher Jung Bahádur Ráná, who resigned in Nov. 1951.

AREA AND POPULATION. Nepál, is bounded on the north by Tibet, on the east by Sikkim and West Bengal, on the south and west by Bihar and Uttar Pradesh. There are 3 geographical regions: The fertile Tarai plain in the south; a central belt containing the Mahabharat Lekh and Churia Hills and the basins of the Inner Tarai; and the Himalayas in the north. Area 56,827 sq. miles (147,181 sq. km); population (estimate, 1985), 16,625,439; (census, 1981) 15,022,839 of whom 52·4% were Nepali-speaking and 18·5% Bihari-speaking.

Capital, Káthmándu, 75 miles from the Indian frontier; population (census 1981) 235,160. Other towns include Pátan (also called Lalitpur), 79,875; Moráng (Biratnagar), 93,544; Bhádgáon (Bhaktapur), 48,472.

The aboriginal stock is Mongolian with a considerable admixture of Hindu blood from India. They were originally divided into numerous hill clans and petty principalities, one of which, Gorkha or Gurkha, became predominant in 1559 and has since given its name to men from all parts of Nepál. The 15 feudal chieftain-ships were integrated into the kingdom on 10 April 1961.

CLIMATE. The rainfall is high, with maximum amounts from May to Sept., but conditions are very dry from Nov. to Jan. The range of temperature is moderate. Káthmándu. Jan. 50°F (10°C), July 76°F (24·4°C). Annual rainfall 57″ (1,428 mm).

RULING KING. The sovereign is HM Mahárájádhirája **Birendra Bir Bikram Sháh Dev**, who succeeded his father Mahendra Bir Bikram Sháh Dev on 31 Jan. 1972.

CONSTITUTION AND GOVERNMENT. On 18 Feb. 1951 the King pro-claimed a constitutional monarchy, and on 16 Dec. 1962 a new Constitution of the 'Constitutional Monarchical Hindu State'. The village and town *panchayat*, re-cognized as the basic units of democracy, elect the district *panchayat*, these elect the zonal *panchayat*, and these finally the 112 members of the national *panchayat*. The Constitution was amended in 1975 and 1980. In addition, 28 representatives of professional organizations and royal nominees not exceeding 15% of the elected members, will be included in the national *panchayat*. The executive power is vested in the King, who appoints a council of ministers from the national *panchayat*. A state council will advise the King and proclaim the successor or, if the heir is a minor, a regency council. Art. 81 empowers the King to declare a state of emergency and to suspend the Constitution.

The Cabinet in Jan. 1987 was as follows (for reshuffle March 1988 *see* Addenda):

Prime Minister, Defence, General Administration and Royal Palace Affairs: Marich Man Singh Shrestha.

Finance: Bharat Bahadur Pradhan. *Foreign Affairs and Land Reform:* Shilendra Kumar Upadhayay. *Transport, Public Works and Communications:* Hari Bahadur. *Panchayat and Local Development:* Pashupati Shumshere Rana. *Agri-culture, Law and Justice:* Hari Narayan Rajauriya. *Forests and Soil Conservation:* Hem Bahadur Malla. *Commerce:* Bijaya Prakash Thebey. *Water Resources:* Yadav

Prasas Pant. *Local Supply:* Parshu Narayan Chaudhury. *Public Health:* Gunjeswori Prasad Singh.

There were also 4 Ministers of State.

National flag: Two triangular parts of red, with a blue border all round, bearing symbols of the moon and the sun in white.

National anthem: 'May glory crown our illustrious sovereign' (1952).

Local Government: The country is administratively divided into 14 zones (Bágmati, Bheri, Dhaulagiri, Gandaki, Janakpur, Karnali, Kosi, Lumbini, Mahakali, Mechi, Náráyani, Rápti, Sagarmatha and Seti) and thence into 75 districts and over 3,500 villages.

DEFENCE

Army. The Army consists of 6 infantry brigades, and single artillery, engineer, signals, parachute and transport battalions, and 1 air squadron. Equipment includes AMX-13 light tanks. Strength of all services (1988) about 30,000, and there is also a 25,000-strong paramilitary police force.

Air Force. Independent of the army since 1979, the Air Force has 3 Skyvan transport aircraft, 1 Puma helicopter and 3 Chetak helicopters. An H.S. 748 turboprop transport and 1 Super Puma and 1 Puma helicopter are operated by the Royal Flight.

INTERNATIONAL RELATIONS

Membership. Nepál is a member of UN and the Colombo Plan.

ECONOMY

Planning. The seventh (1985–90) plan envisages expenditure of NRs 50,500m. Priority will be given to education, transport, communications, power, agriculture and irrigation.

Budget. The general budget for the fiscal year 1987–88 envisaged current expenditure of NRs 4,307m. Domestic revenue were estimated at NRs 5,875m.

Currency. The Nepalese *rupee* is 171 grains in weight, as compared with the Indian rupee, which weighs 180 grains. The rate of exchange is 135 Nepalese rupees for 100 Indian rupees. 100 Nepalese *pice* = 1 Nepalese rupee. Coins of all denominations are minted. The Rástra Bank also issues notes of 1, 5, 10, 100 and 1,000 rupees. In March 1988, US$1 = 21·00 *rupees*; £1 = 37·24 *rupees*.

ENERGY AND NATURAL RESOURCES

Electricity. Production (1986) 395m. kwh. A hydro-electric power scheme on the Karnali river costing US$4,500m. was being planned in 1986.

Agriculture. Nepál has valuable forests in the southern part of the country. In the northern part, on the slopes of the Himálayas, there grow large quantities of medicinal herbs which find a world-wide market. Of the total area, nearly one-third (11·2m. acres) is under forest; 5·4m. acres is covered by perpetual snow; 9·6m. acres is under paddy, 2·9m. maize and millet, 800,000 wheat. Production (1986 in 1,000 tonnes): Rice, 2,350; maize, 880; wheat, 598; sugar-cane, 558; potatoes, 357; millet, 138.

Livestock (1985): Cattle, 7·05m., including about 438,000 cows; 4·5m. buffaloes; sheep, 2·55m.; goats, 2·65m.; pigs, 400,000; poultry, 25m.

Fisheries. Catch (1983) 2,100 tonnes.

INDUSTRY AND TRADE

Industry. Industries, such as jute- and sugar-mills, match, leather, cigarette, and shoe factories, and chemical works have been established, including two industrial estates at Pátan and Balaju. Production (1982 in 1,000 tonnes): Jute goods, 15·7; sugar, 21·1; cement, 30; iron goods, 7·4.

Commerce. The principal articles of export are food grains, jute, timber, oilseeds, ghee (clarified butter), potatoes, medicinal herbs, hides and skins, cattle. The chief imports are textiles, cigarettes, salt, petrol and kerosene, sugar, machinery, medicines, boots and shoes, paper, cement, iron and steel, tea.

Imports and exports in NRs 1,000:

	1982	1983	1984	1985
Imports	4,930,200	6,172,500	6,514,300	7,742,000
Exports	1,491,400	1,132,000	1,703,900	2,741,000

Total trade between Nepál and UK (British Department of Trade returns, in £1,000 sterling):

	1983	1984	1985	1986	1987
Imports to UK	6,115	5,564	9,347	5,966	8,331
Exports and re-exports from UK	5,011	6,453	7,835	4,672	8,707

Tourism. There were 223,000 tourists in 1986.

COMMUNICATIONS

Roads. With the co-operation of India and the USA 900 miles of motorable roads are being constructed, including the East-West Highway through southern Nepál. A road from the Tibetan border to Káthmándu was recently completed with Chinese aid. There are about 1,300 miles motorable roads. A ropeway for the carriage of goods covers the 14 miles from Dhursing above Bhimphedi into the Káthmándu valley. A road connects Káthmándu with Birgung.

Railways. Railways (762 mm gauge) connect Jayanagar on the North Eastern Indian Railway with Janakpur and thence with Bizalpura (54 km).

Aviation. The Royal Nepál Airline Corporation has linked Káthmándu, the capital, with 11 districts of Nepál; and in 1984, 30 airfields were in regular use. The airline carried 424,000 passengers and 2,900 tonnes of freight in 1983–84. The Royal Nepalese Airline Corporation has services between Káthmándu and Calcutta, Patna, New Delhi, Bangkok, Rangoon and Dacca, employing Boeing 727 jet aircraft.

Post and Broadcasting. Káthmándu is connected by telephone with Birganj and Raxaul (North Eastern Indian Railway) on the southern frontier with Bihar; and with the eastern part of the Terai foothills; an extension to the western districts is being completed. Number of telephones (1978) 9,425, of which 5,431 were in Káthmándu. Under an agreement with India and the USA, a network of 91 wireless stations exists in Nepál, with further stations in Calcutta and New Delhi. Radio Nepál at Káthmándu broadcasts in Nepáli and English. In 1983 there were 300,000 radio receivers and in 1985 the first television station opened.

Newspapers. In 1983 there were 7 daily newspapers with a circulation of 75,000.

JUSTICE, RELIGION, EDUCATION AND WELFARE

Justice. The Supreme Court Act, established a uniform judicial system, culminating in a supreme court of a Chief Justice and no more than 6 judges. Special courts to deal with minor offences may be established at the discretion of the Government.

Religion. Hinduism is the religion of 90% of the people. Buddhists comprise 5% and Moslems 3%. Christian missions are permitted, but conversion is forbidden.

Education. In 1984 there were 1,748,000 primary school pupils, 454,000 secondary school pupils and the Tribhuvan University (founded 1960).

In 1981, 23% of the population were literate.

Health. There were about 420 doctors and 2,586 hospital beds in 1979.

DIPLOMATIC REPRESENTATIVES

Of Nepál in Great Britain (12a Kensington Palace Gdns., London, W8 4QU)
Ambassador: Ishwari Raj Pandey, GCVO (accredited 4 Aug. 1983).

Of Great Britain in Nepál (Láincháur, Káthmándu)
Ambassador: R. E. Burges Watson, CMG.

Of Nepál in the USA (2131 Leroy Pl., NW, Washington, D.C., 20008)
Ambassador: (Vacant).

Of the USA in Nepál (Pani Pokhari, Káthmándu)
Ambassador: Leon J. Weil.

Of Nepál to the United Nations
Ambassador: Jai Pratap Rana.

Books of Reference

Statistical Information: A Department of Statistics was set up in Káthmándu in 1950.

Baral, L. S., *Political Development in Nepal.* London, 1980
Bezruchka, S., *A Guide to Trekking in Nepal.* Leicester, 1981
Turner, R. L., *Nepali Dictionary.* 1980.
Wadhwa, D. N., *Nepal.* [Bibliography] Oxford and Santa Barbara, 1986

THE NETHERLANDS

Capital: Amsterdam
Seat of Government: The Hague
Population: 14·62m. (1987)
GNP per capita: US$8,500 (1984)

Koninkrijk der Nederlanden

HISTORY. William of Orange (1533–84), as the German count of Nassau, inherited vast possessions in the Netherlands and the Princedom of Orange in France. He was the initiator of the struggle for independence from Spain (1568–1648); in the Republic of the United Netherlands he and his successors became the 'first servants of the Republic' with the title of 'Stadhouder' (governor). In 1689 William III acceded to the throne of England, becoming joint sovereign with Mary II, his wife. William III died in 1702 without issue, and after a stadhouderless period a member of the Frisian branch of Orange–Nassau was nominated hereditary stadhouder in 1747; but his successor, Willem V, had to take refuge in England, in 1795, at the invasion of the French Army. In Nov. 1813 the United Provinces were freed from French domination.

The Congress of Vienna joined the Belgian provinces, the 'Austrian Netherlands' before the French Revolution, to the Northern Netherlands. The son of the former stadhouder Willem V was proclaimed King of the Netherlands at The Hague on 16 March 1815 as Willem I. The union was dissolved by the Belgian revolution of 1830, and the treaty of London, 19 April 1839, constituted Belgium an independent kingdom.

Netherlands Sovereigns

Willem I	1815–1840 (died 1843)	Wilhelmina	1890–1948 (died 1962)
Willem II	1840–1849	Juliana	1948–1980
Willem III	1849–1890	Beatrix	1980–

AREA AND POPULATION. The Netherlands is bounded north and west by the North Sea, south by Belgium and east by the Federal Republic of Germany. Growth of census population:

1829	2,613,298	1909	5,858,175	1960	11,461,964
1849	3,056,879	1920	6,865,314	1971	13,060,115
1869	3,579,529	1930	7,935,565		
1889	4,511,415	1947	9,625,499		

Area, density and estimated population on 1 Jan. 1977 and 1987:

Province	Land area (in sq. km) 1987	Population 1977	Population 1987	Density per sq. km 1987
Groningen	2,345·52	544,264	558,378	238
Friesland	3,353·06	566,042	599,061	179
Drenthe	2,653·91	409,874	434,038	164
Overijssel	3,339·20	948,009	1,003,915	301
Flevoland [1]	1,442·01	85,619	185,365	131
Gelderland	5,011·35	1,653,516	1,771,972	354
Utrecht	1,331·43	873,753	953,957	716
Noord-Holland	2,665·03	2,299,410	2,334,209	876
Zuid-Holland	2,907·99	3,049,570	3,186,249	1,096
Zeeland	1,791·97	335,624	335,434	198
Noord-Brabant	4,946·01	1,991,176	2,139,626	433
Limburg	2,169·87	1,055,619	1,091,553	503

[1] The new province Flevoland, former Ijsselmeerpolders, established on 1 Jan. 1906. The Noordoostpolder (drained in 1942) and the Zuidelijke Ijsselmeerpolders (drained in 1957) are parts of the former Zuiderzee, now called Ijsselmeer.

Province	Land area (in sq. km) 1987	Population 1977	1987	Density per sq. km 1987
Central Population Register [2]	—	2,019	1,368	—
Total	33,937·33	13,814,495	14,615,125	431

[2] The Central Population Register includes persons who are residents of the Netherlands but who have no fixed residence in any particular municipality (living in caravans and houseboats, population on inland vessels, etc.).

Of the total population on 1 Jan. 1987, 7,224,323 were males, 7,390,802 females.

The total area of the Netherlands is 41,863 sq. km (16,163 sq. miles), of which 33,937 sq. km (13,103 sq. miles) is land area.

On 14 June 1918 a law was passed concerning the reclamation of the Zuiderzee. The work was begun in 1920; the following sections have been completed: 1. The Noordholland–Wieringen Barrage (2·5 km), 1924; 2. The Wieringermeer Polder (210 sq. km), 1930 (inundated by the Germans in 1945, but drained again in the same year); 3. The Wieringen–Friesland Barrage (30 km), 1932; 4. The Noordoost Polder (501 sq. km), 1942; 5. Oost Flevoland (604 sq. km), 1957; 6. Zuidelijk Flevoland (499 sq. km), 1967.

The reclamation of the Markerwaard is still a subject of political discussion. A portion of what used to be the Zuiderzee behind the barrage will remain a fresh-water lake: Ijsselmeer (1,400 sq. km). The 'Delta-project', completed in 1986, comprises (semi) enclosure dams in the estuaries between the islands in the south-western part of the country, excluding the sea-entrances to the ports of Rotterdam and Antwerp. See map in THE STATESMAN'S YEAR-BOOK, 1959.

Vital statistics for calendar years:

	Live births Total	Illegitimate	Still births	Marriages	Divorces	Deaths	Net migration
1983	170,246	11,857	1,002	78,451	32,589	117,761	+ 5,978
1984	174,436	13,445	1,036	81,655	34,068	119,812	+ 8,053
1985	178,136	14,766	1,054	82,747	34,044	122,704	+ 24,147

Population of principal municipalities on 1 Jan. 1987:

Aalsmeer	21,456	Deurne	29,054	Hardenberg	31,923
Achtkarspelen	27,216	Deventer	65,423	Harderwijk	33,866
Alkmaar	87,034	Doetinchem	40,682	Heemskerk	32,494
Almelo	62,222	Dongen	20,816	Heemstede	26,380
Almere	50,881	Dongeradeel	24,726	Heerenveen	37,528
Alphen a/d Rijn	57,184	Dordrecht	106,987	Heerhugowaard	35,264
Amersfoort	91,587	Dronten	22,617	Heerlen	93,888
Amstelveen	68,581	Edam-Volendam	24,251	Heiloo	20,622
Amsterdam	682,702	Ede	90,186	Den Helder	62,943
Apeldoorn	145,696	Eindhoven	190,962	Hellendoorn	33,967
Arnhem	127,671	Elburg	20,266	Hellevoetsluis	31,974
Assen	48,131	Emmen	91,968	Helmond	63,909
Baarn	24,764	Enschede	144,227	Hengelo (O.)	76,714
Barneveld	40,283	Epe	33,845	's-Hertogenbosch	89,732
Bergen op Zoom	46,353	Ermelo	25,165	Hilversum	85,449
Best	20,601	Etten-Leur	31,906	Hoogeveen	45,282
Beuningen	20,263	Franekeradeel	21,074	Hoogezand-	
Beverwijk	34,809	Geldermalsen	21,541	Sappemeer	34,745
De Bilt	31,688	Geldrop	25,837	Hoorn	53,788
Borne	20,444	Geleen	34,078	Houten	20,104
Boxtel	24,667	Gendringen	20,052	Huizen	40,285
Breda	119,427	Gilze en Rijen	21,817	Kampen	32,527
Brummen	20,540	Goes	31,497	Katwijk	39,034
Brunssum	29,804	Gorinchem	28,016	Kerkrade	52,827
Bussum	32,540	Gouda	61,458	Krimpen a/d Ijssel	27,809
Capelle a/d Ijssel	55,919	's-Gravenhage	445,127	Landgraaf	40,049
Castricum	22,658	Groningen	168,019	Leeuwarden	85,191
Culemborg	20,607	Haaksbergen	22,407	Leiden	106,808
Delft	87,736	Haarlem	149,099	Leiderdorp	21,340
Delfzijl	24,042	Haarlemmermeer	89,447	Leidschendam	31,762

Lelystad	58,663	Ridderkerk	46,247	Veenendaal	45,501
Leusden	26,587	Rijssen	23,370	Veghel	25,492
Lisse	20,449	Rijswijk	48,551	Veldhoven	37,149
Loon op Zand	20,640	Roermond	38,291	Velsen	56,802
Losser	22,408	Roosendaal en		Venlo	63,598
Maarssen	35,671	Nispen	57,930	Venray	33,964
Maassluis	32,890	Rosmalen	25,636	Vlaardingen	75,430
Maastricht	115,272	Rotterdam	572,642	Vlissingen	44,863
Meerssen	20,283	Rucphen	20,622	Voorburg	41,196
Meppel	23,106	Schiedam	69,349	Voorschoten	22,161
Middelburg	39,044	Schijndel	21,023	Voorst	23,598
Naaldwijk	26,933	Sittard	44,251	Vught	23,477
Nieuwegein	56,719	Skarsterlân	23,182	Waalwijk	28,557
Nijkerk	24,984	Sliedrecht	22,734	Waddinxveen	23,865
Nijmegen	146,639	Smallingerland	50,757	Wageningen	32,418
Noordoostpolder	37,820	Sneek	29,578	Wassenaar	26,188
Noordwijk	24,776	Soest	40,931	Weert	39,793
Nuenen c.a.	20,619	Spijkenisse	62,394	Weststellingwerf	24,533
Nunspeet	23,766	Stadskanaal	33,506	Wierden	21,940
Oldebroek	20,751	Steenwijk	20,861	Wijchen	31,855
Oldenzaal	29,188	Stein	26,445	Winschoten	20,030
Oosterhout	47,401	Terneuzen	35,411	Winterswijk	27,937
Ooststellingwerf	24,895	Tiel	30,568	Woerden	27,226
Opsterland	26,410	Tietjerksteradeel	29,975	Zaanstad	128,388
Oss	50,636	Tilburg	153,625	Zeist	59,873
Papendrecht	26,589	Uden	34,434	Zevenaar	26,329
Purmerend	52,257	Uithoorn	21,372	Zoetermeer	85,349
Putten	20,469	Utrecht	229,326	Zutphen	31,127
Raalte	26,251	Valkenswaard	29,396	Zwijndrecht	40,772
Renkum	33,911	Veendam	28,359	Zwolle	89,348
Rheden	46,762				

Urban agglomerations as at 1 Jan. 1987: Rotterdam, 1,030,696; Amsterdam, 1,015,916; The Hague, 678,173; Utrecht, 516,064; Eindhoven, 378,247; Arnhem, 295,380; Heerlen-Kerkrade, 266,642; Enschede-Hengelo, 248,832; Nijmegen, 239,535; Tilburg, 224,050; Haarlem, 214,418; Groningen, 206,910; Dordrecht-Zwijndrecht, 201,121; 's-Hertogenbosch, 190,842; Leiden, 181,095; Geleen-Sittard, 177,432; Maastricht, 159,632; Breda, 155,033; Zaanstad, 140,538; Velsen-Beverwijk, 124,105; Hilversum, 102,775.

CLIMATE. A cool temperate maritime climate, marked by mild winters and cool summers, but with occasional continental influences. Coastal temperatures vary from 37°F (3°C) in winter to 61°F (16°C) in summer, but inland the winters are slightly colder and the summers slightly warmer. Rainfall is least in the months Feb. to May, but inland there is a well-defined summer maximum in July and Aug.

The Hague. Jan. 37°F (2·7°C), July 61°F (16·3°C). Annual rainfall 32·8″ (820 mm). Amsterdam. Jan. 36°F (2·3°C), July 62°F (16·5°C). Annual rainfall 34″ (850 mm). Rotterdam. Jan. 36·5°F (2·6°C), July 62°F (16·6°C). Annual rainfall 32″ (800 mm).

REIGNING QUEEN. Beatrix Wilhelmina Armgard, born 31 Jan. 1938 daughter of Queen Juliana and Prince Bernhard; married to Claus von Amsberg on 10 March 1966; succeeded to the crown on 1 May 1980, on the abdication of her mother. *Offspring:* Prince Willem-Alexander, born 27 April 1967; Prince Johan Friso, born 25 Sept. 1968; Prince Constantijn, born 11 Oct. 1969.

Mother of the Queen: Queen Juliana Louise Emma Marie Wilhelmina, born 30 April 1909, daughter of Queen Wilhelmina (born 31 Aug. 1880, died 28 Nov. 1962) and Prince Henry of Mecklenburg-Schwerin (born 19 April 1876, died 3 July 1934); married to Prince Bernhard Leopold Frederick Everhard Julius Coert Karel Godfried Pieter of Lippe-Biesterfeld (born 29 June 1911) on 7 Jan. 1937. Abdicated in favour of her daughter, the Reigning Queen, on 30 April 1980.

Sisters of the Queen: Princess Irene Emma Elisabeth, born 5 Aug. 1939, married to Prince Charles Hugues de Bourbon-Parma on 29 April 1964, divorced 1981 (*sons:*

Prince Carlos Javier Bernardo, born 27 Jan. 1970; Prince Jaime Bernardo, born 13 Oct. 1972; *daughters:* Princess Margarita Maria Beatriz, born 13 Oct. 1972; Princess Maria Carolina Christina, born 23 June 1974); Princess Margriet Francisca, born in Ottawa, 19 Jan. 1943, married to Pieter van Vollenhoven on 10 Jan. 1967 (*sons:* Prince Maurits, born 17 April 1968; Prince Bernhard, born 25 Dec. 1969; Prince Pieter-Christiaan, born 22 March 1972; Prince Floris, born 10 April 1975); Princess Maria Christina, born 18 Feb. 1947, married to Jorge Guillermo on 28 June 1975 (*sons:* Bernardo, born 17 June 1977; Nicolas Daniel Mauricio, born 6 July 1979; *daughter:* Juliana, born 8 Oct. 1981).

CONSTITUTION AND GOVERNMENT. According to the Constitution of the Kingdom of the Netherlands, the Kingdom consists of the Netherlands, Aruba and the Netherlands Antilles. Their relations are regulated by the 'Statute' for the Kingdom, which came into force on 29 Dec. 1954. Each part enjoys full autonomy; they are united, on a footing of equality, for mutual assistance and the protection of their common interests.

The first Constitution of the Netherlands after its restoration as a Sovereign State was promulgated in 1814. It was revised in 1815 (after the addition of the Belgian provinces, and the assumption by the Sovereign of the title of King), 1840 (after the secession of the Belgian provinces), 1848, 1884, 1887, 1917, 1922, 1938, 1946, 1948, 1953, 1956, 1963, 1972 and 1983.

The Netherlands is a constitutional and hereditary monarchy. The royal succession is in the direct male or female line in the order of primogeniture. The Sovereign comes of age on reaching his/her 18th year. During his/her minority the royal power is vested in a Regent—designated by law—and in some cases in the Council of State.

The central executive power of the State rests with the Crown, while the central legislative power is vested in the Crown and Parliament (the *Staten-Generaal*), consisting of 2 Chambers. After the 1956 revision of the Constitution the Upper or First Chamber is composed of 75 members, elected by the members of the Provincial States, and the Second Chamber consists of 150 deputies, who are elected directly from all Netherlands nationals who are aged 18 or over on polling day. Members of the States-General must be Netherlanders or recognized as Netherlands subjects and 21 years of age or over; they may be men or women. They receive an allowance.

First Chamber (as constituted in 1987): Labour Party, 26; Christian Democratic Appeal, 26; People's Party for Freedom and Democracy, 12; Democrats '66, 5; Party of Political Radicals, 1; Communist Party, 1; Pacifist Socialist Party, 1; Calvinist Party, 1; Reformed Political Federation, 1; Calvinist Political Union, 1.

Second Chamber (elected on 21 May 1986): Christian Democratic Appeal, 54; Labour Party, 52; People's Party for Freedom and Democracy, 27; Democrats '66, 9; Party of Political Radicals, 2; Pacifist Socialist Party, 1; Calvinist Party, 3; Reformed Political Federation, 1; Calvinist Political Union, 1.

The revised Constitution of 1917 has introduced an electoral system based on universal suffrage and proportional representation. Under its provisions, members of the Second Chamber are directly elected by citizens of both sexes who are Netherlands subjects not under 18 years (since 1972).

The members of the First Chamber and of the Second Chamber are elected for 4 years, and retire in a body. The Sovereign has the power to dissolve both Chambers of Parliament, or one of them, subject to the condition that new elections take place within 40 days, and the new House or Houses be convoked within 3 months.

Both the Government and the Second Chamber may propose Bills; the First Chamber can only approve or reject them without inserting amendments. The meetings of both Chambers are public, though each of them may by a majority vote decide on a secret session. It is a fixed custom, that Ministers and Secretaries of State, on their own initiative or upon invitation of the Parliament, attend the sessions to defend their policy, their budget, their proposals of Bills, etc., when these are in discussion. A Minister or Secretary of State, however, cannot be a member of Parliament at the same time.

The Constitution can be revised only by a Bill declaring that there is reason for introducing such revision and containing the proposed alterations. The passing of this Bill is followed by a dissolution of both Chambers and a second confirmation by the new States-General by two-thirds of the votes. Unless it is expressly stated, all laws concern only the realm in Europe, and not the oversea part of the kingdom, the Netherlands Antilles.

Every act of the Sovereign has to be covered by a responsible Minister.

The Ministry, a coalition of Christian Democrats and Liberals, was composed as follows in July 1986:

Prime Minister: Ruud Lubbers (CDA).

Deputy Prime Minister and Economic Affairs: Rudolf de Korte (VVD). *Foreign Affairs:* Hans van den Broek (CDA). *Finance:* Onno Ruding (CDA). *Defence:* Willem van Eekelen (VVD). *Development Aid Co-operation:* Piet Bukman (CDA). *Social Affairs and Employment:* Jan de Koning (CDA). *Home Affairs:* Kees van Dijk (CDA). *Justice:* Frits Korthals Altes (VVD). *Agriculture and Fisheries:* Gerrit Braks (CDA). *Welfare, Public Health and Culture:* Eelco Brinkman (CDA). *Education and Science:* Wim Deetman (CDA). *Transport and Public Works:* Neelie Smit-Kroes (VVD). *Housing, Physical Planning and Environment:* Ed Nijpels (VVD).

There are also 11 state secretaries.

The Council of State *(Raad van State)*, appointed by the Crown, is composed of a vice-president and not more than 28 members. The Queen is president, but the day-to-day running of the council is in the hands of the vice-president. The Council can be consulted on all legislative matters. Decisions of the Crown in administrative disputes are prepared by a special section of the Council.

The Hague is the seat of the Court, Government and Parliament; Amsterdam is the capital.

National flag: Three horizontal stripes of red, white, blue.

National anthem: Wilhelmus van Nassoue (words by Philip Marnix van St Aldegonde, c. 1570).

Local Government. The kingdom is divided in 12 provinces and 714 municipalities. Each province has its own representative body, the Provincial States. The members must be 21 years of age or over; they are elected for 4 years, directly from the Netherlands inhabitants of the province who are 18 years of age or over. The electoral register is the same as for the Second Chamber. The members retire in a body and are subject to re-election. The number of members varies according to the population of the province, from 83 for Zuid-Holland to 39 for Flevoland (a new province in the Zuiderzee area). The Provincial States are entitled to issue ordinances concerning the welfare of the province, and to raise taxes pursuant to legal provisions. The provincial budgets and the provincial ordinances and resolutions relating to provincial property, loans, taxes, etc., must be approved by the Crown. The members of the Provincial States elect the First Chamber of the States-General. They meet twice a year, as a rule in public. A permanent commission composed of 6 of their members, called the 'Deputy States', is charged with the executive power and, if required, with the enforcement of the law in the province. Deputy as well as Provincial States are presided over by a Commissioner of the Queen, appointed by the Crown, who in the former assembly has a deciding vote, but attends the latter in only a deliberative capacity. He is the chief magistrate in the province. The Commissioner and the members of the Deputy States receive an allowance.

Each municipality forms a Corporation with its own interests and rights, subject to the general law, and is governed by a Municipal Council, directly elected from the Netherlands inhabitants, and, under certain circumstances, non-Netherlands inhabitants of the municipality who are 18 years of age or over, for 4 years. All Netherlands inhabitants and non-Netherlands inhabitants who meet certain requirements aged 21 or over are eligible, the number of members varying from 7 to 45, according to the population. The Municipal Council has the right to issue bye-laws concerning the communal welfare. The Council may levy taxes pursuant to legal provisions; these ordinances must be approved by the Crown. All bye-laws may be vetoed by the Crown. The Municipal Budget and resolutions to alienate municipal property require the approbation of the Deputy States of the province. The Council meets in public as often as may be necessary, and is presided over by a Burgomaster, appointed by the Crown. The day-to-day administration is carried out by the Burgomaster and 2–7 Aldermen *(wethouders)*, elected by and from the Council; this body is also charged with the enforcement of the law. The Burgomaster may suspend the execution of a resolution of the council for 30 days, but is bound to notify the Deputy States of the province. In maintaining public order, the Burgomaster acts as the chief of police. The Burgomaster and Aldermen receive allowances.

DEFENCE. The Netherlands are bordered on the south by Belgium, on the east by the Federal Republic of Germany. On both sides the country is quite level and has no natural defences, except the barriers of some large rivers, running east to west and south to north. The country has an excellent roadnet and a vast railway system, enabling rapid movement. The western part of the country is densely populated.

Army. Service is partly voluntary and partly compulsory; the voluntary enlistments are of small proportion to the compulsory. The total peacetime strength amounts to 68,000, including Military Police. The number of regulars is 25,000. The Army also employs 13,000 civilians. The legal period of active service for national servicemen is 22–24 months; the actual service period is 16 months for reserve-officers and n.c.o.s and 14 months for other ranks. The balance is spent as 'short leave'. After their period of actual service or short leave, conscript personnel are granted long leave. However, they will be liable to being called up for refresher training or in case of mobilization until they have reached the age of 35 (n.c.o.s 40, reserve officers 45).

The 1st Netherlands Army Corps is assigned to NATO. It consists of 10 brigades and Corps troops. The active part of the Corps comprises 2 armoured brigades and 4 armoured infantry brigades, grouped in two divisions and 40% of the Corps troops. Part of this force is stationed in the Federal Republic of Germany. The peacetime strength of the active brigades is 80% of the war-authorized strength.

The mobilizable part of the Corps comprises 1 armoured brigade, 2 armoured infantry brigades, 1 infantry brigade and the remaining Corps troops.

The mechanized brigades comprise tank battalions (Leopard I improved and Leopard 2), armoured infantry battalions (YP-408 and YPR-765), medium artillery battalions (155 mm self-propelled), armoured engineer units and armoured anti armour units. The Corps troops comprise headquarters units, combat-support units, including Engineer and Corps artillery (203 mm, 155 mm and Lance) and service-support units. Helicopter squadrons are also available.

The National Territorial Command forces consist of territorial brigades, security forces, some logistical units and staffs. The major part of these units is mobilizable. Some units in the Netherlands are earmarked for assignment to the United Nations as peace-keeping forces. The army is responsible for the training of these units. In time of war, the civil defence operations will be closely co-ordinated with the local civilian authorities.

Navy. The Royal Netherlands Navy has its main base in the Netherlands at Den Helder and minor bases at Flushing and Curaçao (Netherlands Antilles). The Ministry of Defence is located in The Hague.

The fleet comprises 6 diesel-electric patrol submarines, 18 frigates, 2 large (fast) combat support ships (aircraft carrying capacity 5 helicopters), 1 mine countermeasures support ship (*ex*-ocean minesweeper), 15 coastal minehunters, 11 coastal minesweepers, 2 diving vessels, 1 torpedo tender, 3 minelayer survey ships, 11 minor landing craft, 3 training ships, 12 tugs and 30 small auxiliary ships.

Four diesel-electric patrol submarines, 4 frigates, 2 coastal minehunters and 9 minor landing craft are under construction. The future construction programme includes 2 more diesel-electric patrol submarines.

In 1988 personnel totalled 16,880 officers and other ranks, including 1,700 in the Naval Air Service, 560 female, and 2,800 in the Royal Netherlands Marine Corps.

The naval air service maintains 13 Orion P3C, 16 Westland Lynx SH14B/C embarked and 5 Lynx UH 14A for SAR, utility and transport.

Air Force. The Royal Netherlands Air Force (RNLAF) was established 1 July 1913. Its strength (1987) was 18,300 personnel and it has a first-line combat force of 9 squadrons of aircraft and 3 groups of surface-to-air missiles in the Federal Republic of Germany. All squadrons are operated by Tactical Air Command. Aircraft operated are F-16A/B (5 squadrons for air defence and ground attack, 1 for tactical reconnaissance), and NF-5A/B fighter-bombers (3 squadrons, to be re-equipped with F-16s in 1988 through 1994). Also under control of Tactical Air Command is 1 squadron of the USAF, flying F-15C/D Eagles in the air defence role. 3 squadrons of Alouette III and Bölkow Bö 105C helicopters are under control of the Royal Netherlands Army, but flown and maintained by the RNLAF for use in the communications and observation roles. Also operated is 1 squadron of F.27 Friendship/Troopship transport aircraft, and another (based in Curaçao) with F.27 maritime patrol aircraft.

Training of RNLAF pilots is undertaken in the USA, Belgium and the Netherlands. The surface-to-air missile force consists of 1 group of Nike Hercules (to be disbanded in 1988), 1 group of Hawk and Patriot missile systems and 1 group of Hawk (to be partly re-equipped with Patriot as of 1989). Hawk missiles are also used for air defence in the Netherlands.

INTERNATIONAL RELATIONS

Membership. The Netherlands is a member of UN, the European Communities, OECD, the Council of Europe and NATO.

ECONOMY

Budget. The revenue and expenditure of the central government (ordinary and extraordinary) were, in 1m. guilders, for calendar years:

	1980[2]	1981[2]	1982[2]	1983[2]	1984[3]	1985[4]	1986[6]
Revenue[1]	107,162	110,913	113,967	115,002	127,918	138,605	159,633
Expenditure[5]	121,090	130,589	142,586	146,622	157,709	162,085	167,366

[1] Without the revenue of loans.   [2] Accounts.   [3] Preliminary accounts.
[4] Revised budget figures.   [5] Without redemption of loans.   [6] Budget figures.

The revenue and expenditure of the Agriculture Equalization Fund, the Fund for Central Government roads, the Property Acquisition Fund and of the Investment Account Fund (established in 1978) have been incorporated in the general budget.

The national debt, in 1m. guilders, was on 31 Dec.:

	1982	1983	1984	1985	1986
Internal funded debt	122,777	153,262	183,312	208,484	219,466
,, floating ,,	21,878	21,535	19,806	19,799	19,969
Total	144,655	174,797	203,118	228,283	239,435

Currency. The monetary unit is the *gulden* (guilder, florin) of 100 *cents*. In March 1988 the rate of exchange was US$1 = 1·89 guilders; £1 = 3·36 guilders.

Legal tender are bank-notes, silver 10-guilder pieces, nickel 2½- and 1-guilder pieces, 25-cent, 10-cent pieces and bronze 5-cent pieces.

Banking. The Netherlands Bank, founded as a private institution, was nationalized on 1 Aug. 1948, the shareholders receiving, for a share of 1,000 guilders, a security of 2,000 guilders on the 2½% National Debt. Since 1863 the bank has the sole right of issuing bank-notes. The capital amounts to 75m. guilders.

Weights and Measures. The metric system of weights and measures was adopted in the Netherlands in 1820.

ENERGY AND NATURAL RESOURCES

Electricity. The total production of electrical energy (in 1m. kwh.) amounted in 1938 to 3,688; 1958, 13,854; 1970, 40,859; 1980, 64,806; 1984, 62,778; 1985, 62,936; 1986, 67,148. Supply 220 volts; 50 Hz.

Gas. Production of manufactured gas (milliard k joule): 1978, 181,033; 1979, 233,553; 1980, 210,011; 1981, 197,586; 1982, 244,438; 1983, 258,515; 1984, 267,643. Production of natural gas in 1950, 8m. cu. metres; 1955, 139; 1960, 384; 1970, 31,688; 1980, 91,153; 1981, 84,617; 1982, 72,035; 1983, 76,536; 1984, 77,251; 1985, 80,721; 1986, 74,037.

Minerals. On 1 Jan. 1975 all coalmines were closed.

The production of crude petroleum (in 1,000 tonnes) amounted in 1943 (first year) to 0·2; 1953, 820; 1970, 1,919; 1978, 1,402; 1979, 1,316; 1980, 1,280; 1981, 1,348; 1982, 1,637; 1983, 2,589; 1984, 3,102; 1985, 3,729.

There are saltmines at Hengelo and Delfzijl; production (in 1,000 tonnes), 1950, 412·6; 1960, 1,096; 1970, 2,871; 1978, 2,939; 1979, 3,951; 1980, 3,464; 1981, 3,578; 1982, 3,191; 1983, 3,124; 1984, 3,674; 1985, 4,154; 1986, 3,763.

Agriculture. The net area of all holdings was divided as follows (in hectares):

	1982	1983	1984	1985	1986
Field crops	726,591	728,663	738,808	749,722	763,075
Grass	1,178,098	1,181,297	1,178,534	1,164,290	1,141,978
Market gardening	69,906	66,828	68,110	72,288	72,352
Land for flower bulbs	14,189	14,165	14,558	15,055	15,564
Flower cultivation	5,472	5,615	5,824	5,965	6,216
Nurseries	6,386	6,431	6,498	6,738	7,037
Fallow land	4,577	5,713	3,763	4,965	6,367
Total	2,005,219	2,008,712	2,016,095	2,019,023	2,012,589

The net areas under special crops were as follows (in hectares):

Products	1985	1986	Products	1985	1986
Autumn wheat	121,385	110,636	Colza	10,120	5,849
Spring wheat	6,734	5,677	Flax	4,368	3,136
Rye	4,571	4,140	Agricultural seeds	15,959	19,559
Autumn barley	6,765	9,198	Potatoes, edible [1]	108,745	107,075
Spring barley	32,072	32,786	Potatoes, industrial [2]	60,241	59,961
Oats	11,278	6,475	Sugar-beet	130,507	137,691
Peas	19,879	22,411	Fodder-beet	2,242	1,986

[1] Including early and seed pototoes.   [2] Including seed potatoes.

The yield of the more important products, in tonnes, was as follows:

Crop	Average 1940–49	Average 1950–58	1984	1985	1986 [1]
Wheat	322,003	348,464	1,131,329	851,034	872,832
Rye	439,055	454,992	24,650	19,265	19,442
Barley	145,892	258,049	191,747	197,387	256,390
Oats	315,642	464,041	57,906	58,133	36,561
Field beans	15,799	5,693	9,377	10,448	...
Peas	65,460	93,664	56,406	71,290	114,521
Colza	24,763	18,358	37,771	30,580	19,880
Flax, unrippled	82,906	138,165	32,260	35,714	25,633
Potatoes, edible [2]	2,861,793	2,745,505	4,344,458	4,688,386	4,561,099
Potatoes, industrial	1,242,326	1,003,994	2,328,579	2,461,220	...
Sugar-beet	1,667,711	2,935,881	6,955,462	6,334,835	...
Fodder-beet	...	...	170,804	189,113	...

[1] 1986 figures provisional.   [2] Including early potatoes.

Livestock, May 1986: 5,122,950 cattle, 13,481,358 pigs; 63,060 horses and ponies; 868,112 sheep, 92·3m. poultry.

In 1985 the production of butter, under state control, declined to 230,169 tonnes; that of cheese, under state control, increased to 541,407 tonnes. Export value (processed and unprocessed) of arable crops amounted to 18,883m. guilders; animal produce, 19,834m. guilders and horticultural produce, 10,769m. guilders.

Fisheries. The total produce of fish landed from the sea and inshore fisheries in 1981 was valued at 595m. guilders; the total weight amounted to 399,438 tonnes. In 1981 the herring fishery had a value of 26m. guilders and a weight of 16,710 tonnes. The quantity of oysters produced in 1981 amounted to 573 tonnes (10m. guilders).

INDUSTRY AND TRADE

Industry. Numbers employed (in 1,000) and turnover (in 1m. guilders) in manufacturing enterprises with 10 employees and more, excluding building:

Class in industry	Numbers employed		Turnover	
	1984	1985	1984	1985
Mining and quarrying	8.3	8.0	38.8	34.9
Manufacturing industry	788.4	798.3	256.8	264.2
Foodstuffs and tobacco products	133.9	132.8	75.2	74.1
Textile industry	23.3	23.5	4.7	5.0
Clothing	10.5	10.4	1.3	1.4
Leather and footwear	6.0	6.0	0.9	1.0
Wood and furniture industry	23.8	23.9	3.8	3.9
Paper industry	22.8	23.4	6.5	6.9
Graphic industry, publishers	60.7	61.6	10.6	11.4
Petroleum industry	9.7	9.7	30.2	29.6
Chemical industry, artificial yarns and fibre industry	83.6	84.4	41.6	43.6
Rubber and synthetic materials processing industry	25.2	25.9	5.6	6.0
Building industry, earthenware and glass	28.7	29.2	5.8	6.0
Basic metal industry	30.0	30.3	9.8	10.3
Metal products (excl. machinery and means of transport)	68.9	69.7	11.5	12.7
Machinery	75.8	79.1	14.6	14.5
Electrical industry	112.7	116.8	21.5	23.7
Means of transport	61.3	60.0	11.9	12.6
Instrument making and optical industry	7.0	7.3	0.9	0.9
Other industries	4.4	4.2	0.6	0.7
Public utilities	25.6	...	22.9	25.9

Commerce. On 5 Sept. 1944 and 14 March 1947 the Netherlands signed agreements with Belgium and Luxembourg for the establishment of a customs union. On 1 Jan. 1948 this union came into force and the existing customs tariffs of the Belgium–Luxembourg Economic Union and of the Netherlands were superseded by the joint Benelux Customs Union Tariff. It applies to imports into the 3 countries from outside sources, and exempts from customs duties all imports into each of the 3 countries from the other two. The Benelux tariff has 991 items and 2,400 separate specifications.

Returns of special imports and special exports for calendar years (in 1,000 guilders):

	Imports	Exports		Imports	Exports
1949	5,331,569	3,851,126	1983	173,544,395	184,352,354
1959	14,968,454	13,702,927	1984	198,813,498	210,663,054
1969	39,955,406	36,205,110	1985	216,031,008	226,017,400
1979	134,885,386	127,689,416	1986	184,791,270	196,976,543

Value of the trade with leading countries (in 1,000 guilders):

Country	Imports			Exports		
	1984	1985	1986	1984	1985	1986
Belgium–Luxembourg	22,359,926	26,640,785	26,254,666	29,392,295	31,901,604	28,059,944
France	12,957,439	14,459,136	13,295,354	21,842,951	23,411,539	21,252,072
Germany (Fed. Rep.)	43,708,174	48,326,397	48,831,569	62,516,199	67,683,921	55,660,199
Indonesia	782,072	792,064	636,218	875,737	534,332	485,836
Italy	5,791,941	6,531,097	7,032,609	11,628,047	13,006,527	12,479,537
Kuwait	2,794,530	3,124,506	1,533,321	374,133	350,155	298,297
Sweden	3,719,399	4,087,953	4,076,202	3,741,810	3,745,261	3,538,064
UK	17,299,342	21,541,672	15,128,266	19,887,707	21,408,907	20,086,964
USA	17,718,030	17,834,450	14,554,444	10,574,458	11,842,083	9,325,971
Venezuela	304,107	301,908	83,875	366,256	303,207	268,014

Total trade between the Netherlands and UK (British Department of Trade returns, in £1,000 sterling):

	1983	1984	1985	1986	1987
Imports to UK	5,097,673	6,147,298	6,550,735	6,615,851	7,148,036
Exports and re-exports from UK	5,440,701	6,127,991	7,344,681	5,442,503	5,856,164

Tourism. There were 3,142,000 foreign visitors in 1986 (hotels only). 636,000 came from the Federal Republic of Germany, 578,000 from UK and 390,000 from USA. Total income from tourism (1986) US$2,228m.

COMMUNICATIONS

Roads. In 1986 the length of the Netherlands network of surfaced inter-urban roads was 54,525 km, of which 2,040 km were motor highways. Number of private cars (1986), 4·9m.

Railways. All railways are run by the mixed company 'N.V. Nederlandse Spoorwegen'. Length of line in 1986 was 2,817 km, of which 1,841 km were electrified. Passengers carried (1986), 210m.; goods transported, 18·3m. tonnes.

Aviation. The Royal Dutch Airlines (KLM) was founded on 7 Oct. 1919. Revenue traffic, 1986–87: Passengers, 5·7m.; freight, 342m. kg; mail, 18m. kg.

Sea-going Shipping. Survey of the Netherlands mercantile marine as at 1 Jan. (capacity in 1,000 GRT):

	1986		1987	
Ships under Netherlands flag	Number	Capacity	Number	Capacity
Passenger ships [1]	4	20	4	49
Freighters (100 GRT and over)	489	2,736	476	2,506
Tankers	65	631	69	721
	558	3,387	549	3,276

[1] With accommodation for 13 or more cabin passengers.

In 1986, 44,847 sea-going ships of 361m. gross tons entered Netherlands ports.

Total goods traffic by sea-going ships in 1986 (with 1985 figures in brackets), in 1m. tonnes, amounted to 258 (250) unloaded, of which 122 (114) tankshipping, and 79 (79) loaded, of which 28 (26) tankshipping. The total seaborne freight traffic at Rotterdam was 258m. (251m.) and at Amsterdam 29m. (28m.) tonnes.

The number of containers (excluding flats) at Rotterdam in 1986 (with 1985 figures in brackets) was: unloaded from ships, 979,834 (920,548), of which 287,632 (258,208) from North America, and 997,295 (946,160) loaded into ships, of which 156,300 (158,228) to North America.

Inland Shipping. The total length of navigable rivers and canals is 4,832 km, of which about 2,387 km is for ships with a capacity of 1,000 and more tonnes. On 1 Jan. 1986 the Netherlands inland fleet actually used for transport (with carrying capacity in 1,000 tonnes) was composed as follows:

	Number	Capacity
Self-propelled barges	5,323	3,057
Dumb barges	429	437
Pushed barges	541	1,184
	6,293	5,479

In 1986, 271m. (1985: 254m.) tonnes of goods were transported on rivers and canals, of which 188m. (179m.) was international traffic. Goods transport on the Rhine across the Dutch–German frontier near Lobith amounted to 137m. (133m.) tonnes.

Post and Broadcasting. On 1 Jan. 1987 there were 6m. telephone connexions (41 per 100 inhabitants). Number of telex lines, 40,000. *Nederlandse Omroep Stichting* (NOS) provides 5 programmes on medium-waves and FM in co-operation with broadcasting organizations. Regional programmes are also broadcast.

Advertisements are transmitted. NOS broadcasts 2 TV programmes. Advertisements, in the last quarter of 1980, were restricted to 4% of the transmission time in the evening. Television sets (1 Jan. 1985) totalled 4·5m.; holders of television licences may, in addition, have wireless receiving sets.

Cinemas (end 1986). There were 451 cinemas with a seating capacity of 119,000.

Newspapers (Sept. 1986). There were 85 daily newspapers with a total circulation of nearly 4·6m.

JUSTICE, RELIGION, EDUCATION AND WELFARE

Justice. Justice is administered by the High Court of the Netherlands (Court of Cassation), by 5 courts of justice (Courts of Appeal), by 19 district courts and by 62 cantonal courts; trial by jury is unknown. The Cantonal Court, which deals with minor offences, is formed by a single judge; the more serious cases are tried by the district courts, formed as a rule by 3 judges (in some cases one judge is sufficient); the courts of appeal are constituted of 3 and the High Court of 5 judges. All judges are appointed for life by the Sovereign (the judges of the High Court from a list prepared by the Second Chamber of the States-General). They can be removed only by a decision of the High Court.

At the district court the juvenile judge is specially appointed to try children's civil cases and at the same time charged with administration of justice for criminal actions committed by young persons between 12 and 18 years old, unless imprisonment of more than 6 months ought to be inflicted; such cases are tried by 3 judges.

Number of sentences, and cases in which prosecution was evaded by paying a fine to the public prosecutor (excluding violation of economic and tax laws):

	Major offences		Minor offences
1983	90,010	1983	1,059,902
1984	91,145	1984	1,029,334
1985	93,855	1985	972,863

In addition, prosecution was evaded by paying a fine to the police in 1,550,130 cases in 1985.

Police. There are both State and Municipal Police. The State Police, about 8,900 men strong, serves 593, and the Municipal Police, about 20,700 men strong, serves 148 municipalities. The State Police includes ordinary as well as water, mounted and motor police. The State Police Corps is under the jurisdiction of the Police Department of the Ministry of Justice, which also includes the Central Criminal Investigation Office, which deals with serious crimes throughout the country, and the International Criminal Investigation Office, which informs foreign countries of international crimes.

Religion. Entire liberty of conscience is granted to the members of all denominations. The royal family belong to the Dutch Reformed Church.

The number of adherents of the Churches according to survey estimates of 1983 was: Roman Catholics, 5,180,000; Dutch Reformed Church, 2,770,000; Reformed Churches, 1,134,000; other creeds, 631,000; no religion, 4,635,000.

The government of the Reformed Church is Presbyterian. On 1 July 1972 the Dutch Reformed Church had 1 synod, 11 provincial districts, 54 classes, 147 districts and 1,905 parishes.

Their clergy numbered 2,000. The Roman Catholic Church had, Jan. 1973, 1 archbishop (of Utrecht), 6 bishops and 1,815 parishes and rectorships. The Old Catholics had (1 July 1972) 1 archbishop (Utrecht), 2 bishops and 29 parishes. The Jews had, in 1970, 46 communities.

Education. Statistics for the scholastic year 1985–86:

	Full-time			Part-time [1]		
	Pupils/Students			Pupils/Students		
	Schools	Total	Female	Schools	Total	Female
Basic schools	8,401	1,468,720	724,010	—	—	—
Special schools	987	99,545	31,249	—	—	—
Secondary general schools	1,382	803,782	425,118	79	103,580	74,923
Secondary vocational schools:						
Junior—						
Technical, nautical	385	186,080	16,152	183	5,776	37
Agricultural	132	35,367	10,096	82	1,530	497
Domestic science	510	93,466	88,432	1	122	120
Other	246	44,339	26,687	—	—	—
Senior—						
Technical, nautical	130	81,029	7,687	51	7,070	287
Agricultural	61	19,188	3,622	39	5,251	672
Service trade and health						
care training	291	72,617	66,485	62	10,827	7,367
Teachers' training (nursery						
schools)	47	2,138	2,097	47	2,669	2,646
Other	200	101,269	46,563	503	163,276	59,054
Third level non-university						
training:						
Technical, nautical	70	37,457	4,083	23	4,303	438
Agricultural	18	6,599	1,403	8	362	58
Arts	48	15,401	8,451	27	4,813	2,410
Teachers' training	159	26,067	15,575	115	44,954	20,524
Other	137	63,339	36,579	53	18,167	9,249

[1] Including apprenticeship schemes, young workers' educational institutes.

	Academic Year 1985–86				
		Full-time		Part-time	
		Students		Students	
	Schools	Total	Female	Total	Female
University education:					
Humanities		29,835	16,449	825	443
Social sciences		67,009	26,562	9,105	3,350
Natural sciences	21	14,545	3,400	161	37
Technical sciences		22,476	1,896		
Medical sciences		18,398	7,670	93	56
Agricultural sciences		6,412	2,188		

Health. On 1 Jan. 1987 there were 33,330 doctors and about 67,545 licensed hospital beds.

DIPLOMATIC REPRESENTATIVES

Of the Netherlands in Great Britain (38 Hyde Park Gate, London, SW7 5DP)
Ambassador: Hans Jonkman, GCVO (accredited 20 Feb. 1987).

Of Great Britain in the Netherlands (Lange Voorhout, 10, The Hague)
Ambassador: M. R. H. Jenkins.

Of the Netherlands in the USA (4200 Linnean Ave., NW, Washington, D.C., 20008)
Ambassador: Richard H. Fein.

Of the USA in the Netherlands (Lange Voorhout, 102, The Hague)
Ambassador: John S. Shad.

Of the Netherlands to the United Nations
Ambassador: Adriaan Jacobovits de Szeged.

Books of Reference

Statistical Information: The 'Centraal Bureau voor de Statistiek' at Voorburg and Heerlen, is the official Netherlands statistical service. *Director-General of Statistics:* Prof. Dr W. Begeer.
  The Bureau was founded in 1899. Prior to that year, statistical publications were compiled by the 'Centrale commissie voor de statistiek', the 'Vereniging voor staathuishoudkunde en

statistiek' and various government departments. These activities have gradually been taken over and co-ordinated by the Central Bureau, which now compiles practically all government statistics.

Its current publications include:

Statistical Yearbook of the Netherlands. From 1923/24 (preceded by *Jaarcijfers voor het Koninkrijk der Nederlanden, 1898–1922);* latest issue, 1987 (in English)
Statistisch zakboek (Pocket Year Book). From 1899/1924 (1 vol.); latest issue, 1987
CBS Select (Statistical Essays). From 1980; latest issue, 1987
Statistisch Bulletin (From 1945; weekly statistical bulletin)
Maandschrift (From 1944; monthly bulletin)
85 Jaren Statistiek In Tijdreeksen (historical series of the Netherlands 1899–1984)
Nationale Rekeningen (National Accounts). From 1948–50; latest issue, 1987
Statistisch Magazine. From 1981
Statistische onderzoekingen. From 1977
Statistical Studies. From 1953
Regionaal Statistisch Zakboek (Regional Pocket Yearbook). From 1972, latest issue 1986
Environmental Statistics of the Netherlands, 1987 (in English)

Other Official Publications

Central Economic Plan. Centraal Plan bureau, The Hague (Dutch text), annually, from 1946
Netherlands. Organization for Economic Co-operation and Development. Paris, annual from 1964
Staatsalmanak voor het Koninkrijk der Nederlanden. Annual. The Hague, from 1814
Staatsblad van het Koninkrijk der Nederlanden. The Hague, from 1814
Staatscourant (State Gazette). The Hague, from 1813
Atlas van Nederland. Government Printing Office, The Hague, 1970 and supplements up to and including 1973
Memoranda on the Condition of the Netherlands State Finances. Ministry of Finance, The Hague, from 1906
Basic Guide to the Establishing of Industrial Operations in the Netherlands 1976. Ministry of Economic Affairs, The Hague, 1976
The Kingdom of the Netherlands. Ministry of Foreign Affairs, The Hague, Occasional
Huggett, F. E., *The Dutch Today.* Ministry of Foreign Affairs, The Hague, 1973.—*The Dutch Connection.* Ministry of Foreign Affairs, The Hague, 1982
Aspects of Dutch Agriculture. Ministry of Agriculture and Fisheries, The Hague, 1976

Non-Official Publications

Jansonius, H., *Nieuw Groot Nederlands—Engels Woordenboek Voor Studie en Praktijk.* 3 vols. Leiden, 1973 (Vols. 1–3)
King, P. K., and Wintle, M., *The Netherlands.* [Bibliography] Oxford and Santa Barbara, 1988
Newton, G., *The Netherlands: An Historical and Cultural Survey, 1795–1977.* Boulder, 1978
Pinder, D., *The Netherlands.* Folkestone, 1976
Pyttersen's Nederlandse Almanak. Zaltbommel, annual, from 1899
Commerce and Industry in the Netherlands. Amsterdam–Rotterdam Bank. Amsterdam, 1977
Foreign Investment in the Netherlands. The Hague, 1975
A Compact Geography of the Netherlands. Utrecht, 1980
National Library: De Koninklijke Bibliotheek, Prinz Willem Alexanderhof 5, The Hague.
   Director: Dr C. Reedijk.

ARUBA

HISTORY. Discovered by Alonzo de Ojeda in 1499, the island of Aruba was claimed for Spain but not settled. It was acquired by the Dutch in 1634, but apart from garrisons was left to the indigenous Caiquetios (Arawak) Indians until the 19th century. From 1828 it formed part of the Dutch West Indies and, from 1845, part of the Netherlands Antilles, with which on 29 Dec. 1954 it achieved internal self-government.

Following a referendum in March 1977, the Dutch government announced on 28 Oct. 1981 that Aruba would proceed to independence separately from the other islands. Aruba was constitutionally separated from the Netherlands Antilles from 1 Jan. 1986, and full independence has been promised by the Netherlands after a 10-year period.

AREA AND POPULATION. The island, which lies in the southern Caribbean 24 km north of the Venezuelan coast and 68 km west of Curaçao, has an area of 193 sq. km (75 sq. miles) and a population at the 1981 census of 60,312; estimate (1985) 61,000. The chief towns are Oranjestad, the capital (17,000) and Sint Nicolaas, site of the former oil refinery (17,000). Dutch is the official language, but the language usually spoken is Papiamento, a creole language. Unlike other Caribbean islands, over half the population is of Indian stock, with the balance chiefly of Dutch, Spanish and mestizo origin.

CLIMATE. Aruba has a tropical marine climate, with a brief rainy season from Oct. to Dec. Oranjestad. Jan. 79°F (26·0°C), July 84°F (29·0°C). Annual rainfall 17″ (432 mm).

CONSTITUTION AND GOVERNMENT. Under the separate constitution inaugurated on 1 Jan. 1986, Aruba is an autonomous part of the Kingdom of the Netherlands with its own legislature, government, judiciary, civil service and police force. The Netherlands is represented by a Governor appointed by the monarch. The unicameral legislature *(Staten)* consists of 21 members; at the general elections held on 27 Nov. 1985, 8 seats were won by the *(Movimento Electoral di Pueblo*, 7 by the *Arubaanse Volks Partij*, and 2 each by 3 smaller parties with whom the AVP formed a coalition government.

Governor: Felipe B. Tromp.
Prime Minister, Minister of General Affairs: J. Henny Eman.
Deputy Prime Minister, Transport and Communications: Benny Nisbet.
Economic Affairs and Labour: Leonard Berlinski. *Justice:* Watty Vos. *Education and Welfare:* Mito Croes. *Utilities and Public Works:* Charo Kelly. *Finance:* Armand W. Englebrecht.

Flag: Blue, with 2 narrow horizontal yellow stripes, and in the canton a red 4-pointed star fimbriated in white.

ECONOMY

Budget. The 1984 budget totalled 207m. guilders revenue and 278m. guilders expenditure.

Currency. From 1 Jan. 1986 the currency has been the Aruban florin, at par with the Netherlands Antilles guilder. In March 1988, £1 = 3·17 *Aruban florins*; US$1 = 1·79 *Aruban florins*.

Banking. As well as the Aruba Bank, there are local branches of the Algemene Bank Nederland, Barclays Bank International, Caribbean Mercantile Bank and Citibank.

ENERGY AND NATURAL RESOURCES

Electricity. Generating capacity totals 310,000 kw. Production (1986) 945m. kwh.

Oil. The Exxon refinery dominated the economy from 1929–85, when it was closed, resulting in unemployment reaching 40% by the end of 1985.

Minerals. Gold, first discovered in 1825, is still found but in uneconomic quantities.

INDUSTRY AND TRADE

Trade. Total trade between Aruba and UK (British Department of Trade returns, in £1,000 sterling):

	1986	1987
Imports to UK	572	296
Exports and re-exports from UK	6,972	5,652

Tourism. Tourism is now the main economic sector. In 1986 there were 181,000 tourists.

COMMUNICATIONS

Roads. In 1984 there were 380 km of surfaced highways. In 1984 there were 23,409 passenger cars and 582 commercial vehicles.

Aviation. There is an international airport (Prinses Beatrix) served by numerous airlines.

Post and Broadcasting. In 1983 there were 5 radio stations and 1 television station. In 1983 there were 17,000 telephones.

JUSTICE, RELIGION, EDUCATION AND WELFARE

Justice. The Aruban judiciary is now separated from that of the Netherlands Antilles. There is a Court of First Instance and a Court of Appeal situated in Oranjestad.

Religion. In 1981, 89% of the population were Roman Catholic and 7% Protestant.

Education. In 1983 there were 33 elementary schools with 6,763 pupils, 10 junior high schools with 3,082 pupils and 4 senior schools and colleges with 881 students.

Health. In 1985 there were 59 doctors, 16 dentists, 9 pharmacists, 189 nursing personnel and one hospital with 279 beds.

THE NETHERLANDS ANTILLES
De Nederlandse Antillen

HISTORY. Bonaire and Curaçao islands, originally populated by Caiquetios Indians, were discovered in 1499 by Amerigo Vespucci and Alonso de Ojeda respectively, and claimed for Spain. They were settled in 1527, and the indigenous population exterminated and replaced by a slave-worked plantation economy. The 3 Windward Islands, inhabited by Caribs, were discovered by Columbus in 1493. They were taken by the Dutch in 1632 (Saba and Sint Eustatius), 1634 (Curaçao and Bonaire) and 1648 (the southern part of Sint Maarten, with France acquiring the northern part). With Aruba, the islands formed part of the Dutch West Indies from 1828, and the Netherlands Antilles from 1845, with internal self-government being granted on 29 Dec. 1954. Aruba was separated from 1 Jan. 1986.

AREA AND POPULATION. The Netherlands Antilles comprise two groups of islands, the Leeward group (Curaçao and Bonaire) being situated 100 km north of the Venezuelan coast and the Windward Islands situated 800 km away to the north-east, at the northern end of the Lesser Antilles. The total area is 800 sq. km (308 sq. miles) and the Census population in 1981 was 171,620. Estimate (1985) 183,000. Willemstad is the capital.

The areas, populations and chief towns of the islands are:

Island	Sq. km	1981 Census	Chief town	Population
Bonaire	288	8,753	Kralendijk	1,200
Curaçao	444	147,388	Willemstad	50,000
Saba	13	965	Leverock	–
Sint Eustatius	21	1,358	Oranjestad	–
Sint Maarten [1]	34	13,156	Philipsburg	6,000

[1] The southern part belongs to the Netherlands Antilles, the northern to France.

Dutch is the official language, but the languages usually spoken are Papiamento (a creole language) on Curaçao and Bonaire, and English in the Windward Islands.

Vital statistics (1980, including Aruba): Live births, 4,018; marriages, 1,340; deaths, 1,132.

CLIMATE. All the islands have a tropical marine climate, with very little difference in temperatures over the year. There is a short rainy season from Oct. to Jan. Willemstad. Jan. 79°F (26·1°C), July 82°F (27·8°C). Annual rainfall 23″ (582 mm).

CONSTITUTION AND GOVERNMENT. On 29 Dec. 1954, the Netherlands Antilles became an integral part of the Kingdom of the Netherlands but are fully autonomous in internal affairs, and constitutionally equal with the Netherlands and Aruba. The Sovereign of the Kingdom of the Netherlands is Head of State and Government, and is represented by a Governor.

The executive power in internal affairs rests with the Governor and the Council of Ministers, who together form the Government. The Ministers are responsible to a unicameral legislature *(Staten)* consisting of 22 members (since 1985, 14 from Curaçao, 3 from Bonaire, 3 from Sint Maarten, and 1 each from Saba and Sint Eustatius) elected by universal suffrage. In general elections held on 22 Nov. 1985, 9 seats were won by the *Democratische Partij*, 6 by the *Nationale Volks Partij*, 4 by the *Movimento Antijas Nobo*, and 1 each by three smaller parties.

The executive power in external affairs is vested in the Council of Ministers of the Kingdom, in which the Antilles is represented by a Minister Plenipotentiary with full voting powers. On each of the insular communities, local autonomous power is divided between an Island Council (elected by universal suffrage), the Executive Council and the Lieut.-Governor, responsible for law and order.

Governor: Dr Rene A. Römer.
Prime Minister: Domenico Felip Martina.
Economic Affairs: Marco de Castro. *Labour and Social Affairs:* Winston Laurens. *Finance:* Leslie Navarro. *Health:* Frank Rosendal. *Justice, Transport and Communications:* Leo Chance. *Co-operation and Development:* Jopie Abraham.

Flag: White, with a red vertical strip crossed by a blue horizontal strip bearing 5 white stars.

ECONOMY.

Budget. The central budget for 1984 envisaged 342·3m. NA guilders revenue and 394·5m. guilders expenditure.

Currency. The currency is the *Netherlands Antilles guilder* of 100 cents. There are notes of 250, 100, 50, 25, 10, 5, 2½ and 1 *guilder*, and coins of 2½ and 1 *guilder* and 25, 10, 5, 2½ and 1 *cent*. The official rate of exchange was £1 = 3·17 *NA guilder*; US$1 = 1·79 *NA guilder* in March 1988.

ENERGY AND NATURAL RESOURCES

Electricity. Production (1986) totalled 365m. kwh.

Oil. The economy was formerly based largely on oil refining at the Shell refinery on Curaçao, but following an announcement by Shell that closure was imminent, this was sold to the Netherlands Antilles government in Sept. 1985, and leased to Petróleos de Venezuela to operate on a reduced scale thus retaining some (1,500) employment.

Minerals. About 100,000 tons of calcium phosphate are mined annually.

Agriculture. Livestock (1986): Cattle, 9,000; goats, 23,000. Figures include Aruba.

Fisheries. Catch (1982) 11,000 tonnes.

INDUSTRY AND TRADE

Industry. Curaçao has one of the largest ship-repair dry docks in the western hemisphere. Curaçao has a paint factory, 2 cigarette factories, a textile factory, a brewery and some smaller industries. The Texas Instruments Co. and Electronic Fabriek have established electronic factories. Bonaire has a textile factory and a modern-equipped salt plant. Sint Maarten has a rum factory and fishing is important. Sint Eustatius and Saba are of less economic importance.

Trade (1980). Total imports amounted to US$5,944m., total exports to US$6,054m.

Total trade between the Netherlands Antilles and UK (British Department of Trade returns, in £1,000 sterling):

	1983	1984	1985	1986 [1]	1987 [1]
Imports to UK	25,871	221,012	163,236	78,509	5,133
Exports and re-exports from UK	78,879	20,235	19,844	17,260	19,635

[1] Excluding Aruba.

Tourism. In 1986, 594,000 tourists visited the islands (Sint Maarten, 439,000; Curaçao, 128,000; Bonaire, 27,000) excluding 441,000 cruise passengers (Curaçao, 126,000; Sint Maarten, 314,000).

COMMUNICATIONS

Roads. In 1984, the Netherlands Antilles had 820 km of surfaced highway distributed as follows: Curaçao, 550; Bonaire, 210; Sint Maarten, 3. Number of motor vehicles (31 Dec. 1975): 41,955 in Curaçao.

Aviation. There are international airports on Curaçao (Dr Albert Plesman Airport), Bonaire (Flamingo Field) and Sint Maarten (Juliana Airport).

Shipping (1977). There entered the port of Curaçao, 11,432 vessels of 95m. gross tons. Curaçao has a dry dock of 120,000 tons.

Post and Broadcasting. Number of telephones, 1 Jan. 1983, 48,000. Eight radio stations are operating on medium-waves from Curaçao, Aruba, Bonaire, and Sint Maarten. These stations broadcast in *Papiamento*, Dutch, English and Spanish and are mainly financed by income from advertisements. In addition, Radio Nederland and Trans World Radio have powerful relay stations operating on medium- and short-waves from Bonaire. There were (1984, including Aruba) 160,000 radio and 57,000 TV receivers.

Cinemas (1973). Curaçao and Aruba had 13 cinemas with a seating capacity of 11,000. There is a drive-in for 500 cars in Curaçao, and for 200 cars in Sint Maarten.

Newspapers. In 1985 there were 4 daily newspapers with a total circulation of 44,500.

JUSTICE, RELIGION, EDUCATION AND WELFARE

Justice. There is a Court of First Instance, which sits in each island, and a Court of Appeal in Willemstad.

Religion. In 1981, 84% of the population were Roman Catholics, 10% were Protestants (Sint Maarten and Sint Eustatius being chiefly Protestant).

Education. In 1983 there were 24,578 pupils and 1,248 teachers in 91 primary schools, 8,623 pupils and 633 teachers in 22 secondary schools, 732 students and 79 teachers in 3 technical and teacher-training colleges, and 677 students with 53 teaching staff in higher education.

Health. In 1985 there were 184 doctors and 1,500 hospital beds.

DIPLOMATIC REPRESENTATIVE

USA Consul-General: Martin McLean.

Books of Reference

Statistical Information: Statistical publications (on population, trade, cost of living, etc., are obtainable on request from the Statistical Office, Willemstad, Curaçao. *Statistical Jaarboek 1970* (text in Dutch, English and Spanish).

De West Indische Gids. The Hague. Monthly from 1919

NEW ZEALAND

Capital: Wellington
Population: 3·3m. (1987)
GNP per capita: US$5,276 (1985)

HISTORY. The first European to discover New Zealand was Tasman in 1642. The coast was explored by Capt. Cook in 1769. From about 1800 onwards, New Zealand became a resort for whalers and traders, chiefly from Australia. By the Treaty of Waitangi, in 1840, between Governor William Hobson and the representatives of the Maori race, the Maori chiefs ceded the sovereignty to the British Crown and the islands became a British colony. Then followed a steady stream of British settlers.

The Maoris are a branch of the Polynesian race, having emigrated from the eastern Pacific before and during the 14th century. Between 1845 and 1848, and between 1860 and 1870, misunderstandings over land led to war, but peace was permanently established in 1871, and the development of New Zealand has been marked by racial harmony and integration.

AREA AND POPULATION. New Zealand lies south-east of Australia in the south Pacific, Wellington being 1,983 km from Sydney by sea. There are two principal islands, the North and South Islands, besides Stewart Island, Chatham Islands and small outlying islands, as well as the territories overseas (*see* pp. 918–20).

New Zealand (*i.e.*, North, South and Stewart Islands) extends over 1,750 km from north to south. Area, excluding territories overseas, 268,046 sq. km comprising North Island, 114,685 sq. km; South Island, 149,813 sq. km; Stewart Island, 1,746 sq. km; Chatham Islands, 963 sq. km; minor islands, 829 sq. km. Growth in census population, exclusive of territories overseas:

	Total population	Average annual increase %		Total population	Average annual increase %
1858	115,462	—	1926	1,408,139	2·06
1874	344,984	—	1936	1,573,810	1·13
1878	458,007	7·33	1945[1]	1,702,298	0·83
1881	534,030	5·10	1951[1]	1,939,472	2·37
1886	620,451	3·05	1956[1]	2,174,062	2·31
1891	668,632	1·50	1961[1]	2,414,984	2·12
1896	743,207	2·13	1966[1]	2,676,919	2·10
1901[1]	815,853	1·89	1971[1]	2,862,631	1·34
1906	936,304	2·75	1976[1]	3,129,383	1·71
1911	1,058,308	2·52	1981[1]	3,175,737	0·20
1916[1]	1,149,225	1·50	1986[1]	3,307,084	0·82
1921	1,271,644	2·27			

The census of New Zealand is quinquennial, but the census falling in 1931 was abandoned as an act of national economy, and owing to war conditions the census due in 1941 was not taken until 25 Sept. 1945.

[1] Excluding members of the Armed Forces overseas.

The areas and populations of local government regions (with principal centres) at 4 March 1986 were as follows [1]:

Local Government Region (and principal centre)	Area [2] (sq. km)	Total Population 1981 census	Total Population 1986 census	Intercensal change (%)
Northland (Whangarei)	12,604	113,994	126,999	11·4
Auckland (Auckland) [1]	5,201	827,408	887,448	7·3
Thames Valley (Thames–Coromandel)	4,666	54,343	58,665	8·0
Bay of Plenty (Tauranga)	9,126	172,480	187,462	8·7
Waikato (Hamilton)	13,241	221,850	228,303	2·9
Tongariro (Taupo)	12,085	40,089	40,793	1·8
East Cape (Gisborne)	11,461	53,295	53,968	1·3
Hawke's Bay (Napier, Hastings)	12,396	137,840	140,709	2·1
Taranaki (New Plymouth)	7,876	103,798	107,600	3·7
Wanganui (Wanganui)	9,171	68,702	69,439	1·1
Manawatu (Palmerston North)	6,669	113,238	115,500	2·0
Horowhenua (Levin)	1,614	49,296	53,592	8·7
Wellington (Wellington)	1,379	323,162	328,163	1·5
Wairarapa (Masterton)	6,894	39,689	39,608	−0·2
Total, North Island [2]	*114,383*	*2,319,184*	*2,438,249*	*5·1*

Local Government Region (and principal centre)	Area [2] (sq. km)	Total Population 1981 census	Total Population 1986 census	Intercensal change (%)
Nelson Bays (Nelson)	10,197	65,934	69,648	5·6
Marlborough (Blenheim)	12,882	37,557	38,225	1·8
West Coast (Greymouth)	22,893	34,178	34,942	2·2
Canterbury (Christchurch)	17,465	336,846	348,712	3·5
Aorangi (Timaru)	19,910	84,772	81,294	−4·1
Clutha–Central Otago	28,982	45,402	48,771	7·4
Coastal–North Otago (Dunedin)	10,590	138,164	137,393	−0·6
Southland (Invercargill)	27,716	107,905	104,618	−3·0
Total, South Island [2]	150,635	850,758	863,603	1·3
Total, New Zealand [2]	265,018	3,169,942	3,301,852	4·2

[1] Excludes Great Barrier Island and Chatham Island Counties.
[2] Excludes Extra County Islands.

New Zealand-born residents made up 84·5% of the population at the 1986 census. Foreign-born (provisional): UK, 196,872; Australia, 46,839; Netherlands, 24,159; Samoa, 33,864; Cook Islands, 15,540; others (including USA and Ireland), 187,644.

Maori population: 1896, 42,113; 1936, 82,326; 1945, 98,744; 1951, 115,676; 1961, 171,553; 1971, 227,414; 1976, 270,035; 1981, 279,255; 1986, 294,201.

Populations of statistical divisions and main urban areas as at 31 March 1987 were as follows:

Auckland	889,200	Invercargill	52,400
Christchurch	333,200	Nelson	44,900
Dunedin	113,300	New Plymouth	47,400
Hamilton	169,000	Rotorua	52,200
Napier–Hastings	115,700	Tauranga	60,500
Palmerston North	93,700	Timaru	28,500
Wellington	351,400	Wanganui	40,900
Urban areas:		Whangarei	43,600
Gisborne	32,000		

Vital statistics for calendar years:

	Total live births	Ex-nuptial births	Deaths	Marriages	Divorces (decrees absolute)
1984	51,636	12,556	25,378	25,272	9,166
1985	51,798	12,921	27,480	24,657	8,607
1986	52,824	14,237	27,045	24,037	...

Birth rate, 1986, 16·11 per 1,000; death rate, 8·25 per 1,000; marriage rate, 7·33 per 1,000; infant mortality, 11·21 per 1,000 live births.

External migration (exclusive of crews and through passengers) for years ended 31 March:

	Arrivals	Departures		Arrivals	Departures
1982	946,287	951,030	1985	1,017,212	1,016,995
1983	915,463	900,021	1986	1,111,926	1,130,444
1984	922,868	912,311	1987	1,321,729	1,317,372

Population and Migration: Part B—External Migration. Dept. of Statistics, Wellington, Annually

CLIMATE. Lying in the cool temperate zone, New Zealand enjoys very mild winters for its latitude owing to its oceanic situation, and only the extreme south has cold winters. The situation of the mountain chain produces much sharper climatic contrasts between east and west than in a north-south direction. Observations for 1983: Auckland. Jan. 65·5°F (18·6°C), July 50°F (10·2°C). Annual rainfall 41·5″ (1,053 mm). Christchurch. Jan. 61·3°F (16·3°C), July 42·4°F (5·8°C). Annual rainfall 29″ (737 mm). Dunedin. Jan. 57·4°F (14·1°C), July 43·2°F (6·2°C). Annual rainfall 38·1″ (968 mm). Hokitika. Jan. 56·1°F (13·4°C), July 43·5°F (6·4°C). Annual rainfall 132·2″ (3,357 mm). Rotorua. Jan. 61·2°F (16·2°C), July 43·7°F (6·5°C). Annual rainfall 49·9″ (1,268 mm). Wellington. Jan. 59·9°F (15·5°C), July 46·4°F (8·0°C). Annual rainfall 51·2″ (1,300 mm).

CONSTITUTION AND GOVERNMENT. Definition was given the status of New Zealand by the (Imperial) Statute of Westminster of Dec. 1931, which had received the antecedent approval of the New Zealand Parliament in July 1931. The Governor-General's assent was given to the Statute of Westminster Adoption Bill on 25 Nov. 1947.

The powers, duties and responsibilities of the Governor-General and the Executive Council under the present system of responsible government are set out in Royal Letters Patent and Instructions thereunder of 11 May 1917, published in the *New Zealand Gazette* of 24 April 1919. In the execution of the powers vested in him the Governor-General must be guided by the advice of the Executive Council.

The following is a list of Governors-General, the title prior to June 1917 being Governor:

Earl of Liverpool	1917–20	Viscount Cobham	1957–62
Viscount Jellicoe	1920–24	Sir Bernard Fergusson	1962–67
Sir Charles Fergusson, Bt	1924–30	Sir Arthur Porrit, Bt	1967–72
Lord Bledisloe	1930–35	Sir Denis Blundell	1972–77
Viscount Galway	1935–41	Sir Keith Holyoake	1977–80
Sir Cyril Newall	1941–46	Sir David Beattie	1980–85
Lord Freyberg, VC	1946–52	Sir Paul Reeves	1985–
Lord Norrie	1952–57		

National flag: The British Blue Ensign with 4 stars of the Southern Cross in red, edged in white, in the fly.

National anthems: God Save the Queen; God Defend New Zealand (words by Thomas Bracken, music by John J. Woods).

Since Nov. 1977 both 'God Save the Queen' and 'God Defend New Zealand' have equal status as national anthems.

Parliament consists of the House of Representatives, the former Legislative Council having been abolished since 1 Jan. 1951.

The statute law on elections and the life of Parliament is contained in the Electoral Act, 1956. In 1974 the voting age was reduced from 20 to 18 years.

The House of Representatives from Aug. 1987 consists of 97 members, including 4 members representing Maori electorates, elected by the people for 3 years. The 4 Maori electoral districts cover the whole country and adult Maoris of half or more Maori descent are the electors. From 1976 a descendant of a Maori is entitled to register either for a general or a Maori electoral district. Women's suffrage was instituted in 1893: women became eligible as members of the House of Representatives in 1919. The House in 1987 included 12 women members.

During Parliamentary sittings the proceedings of the House are broadcast regularly on sound radio.

House of Representatives as composed following the General Election in Aug. 1987: Labour, 58; National Party, 39.

The Executive Council was composed as follows in Aug. 1987:

Governor-General and C.-in-C.: The Most Rev. Sir Paul Reeves (from Nov. 1985).

Prime Minister, Education, Security Intelligence Service: David R. Lange.

Deputy Prime Minister, Attorney-General, Justice, Environment: Geoffrey W. R. Palmer.

Overseas Trade and Marketing: Michael K. Moore.

Finance: Roger O. Douglas.

State Owned Enterprises, Postmaster-General, Works and Development, Pacific Island Affairs, Broadcasting, Public Trust Office, Railways: Richard W. Prebble.

Maori Affairs: Koro T. Wetere.

Health, Trade and Industry: David F. Caygill.

Foreign Affairs, Disarmament and Arms Control: Cedric R. Marshall.

Internal Affairs, Local Government, Civil Defence, Arts and Culture: Michael E. R. Bassett.

Minister of State, Leader of the House: Jonathon L. Hunt.

Defence, Science and Technology: Robert J. Tizard.

Agriculture, Fisheries: Colin J. Moyle.

Labour, Immigration, State Services: Stanley J. Rodger.
Employment, Youth Affairs, Tourism: Philip B. Goff.
Women's Affairs, Consumer Affairs, Statistics: Margaret K. Shields.
Police, Forestry, Lands, Recreation and Sport, Survey and Land Information, Valuation Department: Peter Tapsell.
Housing, Conservation: Helen Clark.
Social Welfare, War Pensions: Michael J. Cullen.
Transport, Civil Aviation, Meteorological Services: William P. Jeffries.
Energy, Regional Development: David J. Butcher.

Ministers not in Cabinet but on Executive Council: Trevor A. de Cleene, Fran Wilde, Philip T. E. Woollaston, Peter Neilson.

The Prime Minister (provided with residence) had in 1987 a salary of NZ$129,250 plus a tax-free expense allowance of $23,400 per annum; Ministers with portfolio, $90,200 plus a tax-free expense allowance of $9,600 (Minister of Foreign Affairs $15,600) per annum; Minister without portfolio, $73,150 plus a tax-free expense allowance of $7,500 per annum; Parliamentary Under-Secretaries, $70,400 plus an expense allowance of $7,500 per annum. In addition, Ministers and Parliamentary Under-Secretaries not provided with residence at the seat of Government receive $1,000 per annum house allowance. An allowance of $200 per day while travelling within New Zealand on public service is payable to Ministers.

The Speaker of the House of Representatives receives $83,600 plus an expense allowance of $12,600 per annum in addition to his electorate allowance, and residential quarters in Parliament House, and the Leader of the Opposition $90,200 plus expense allowance of $9,600 per annum, and allowances for travelling and housing.

Members were paid $49,500 per annum, plus an expense allowance varying from $7,000 to $17,000 according to the area of electorate represented.

There is a compulsory contributory superannuation scheme for members; retiring allowances are payable to a member after 9 years' service and the attainment of 45 years of age.

Dollimore, H. N., *The Parliament of New Zealand and Parliament House.* 3rd ed. Wellington, 1973

Scott, K. J., *The New Zealand Constitution.* OUP, 1962

Local Government. New Zealand is divided into 22 regions, excluding the Chatham Islands and various uninhabited minor islands. Of these, two (Auckland and Wellington Regions) are under directly-elected Regional Councils with direct rating powers, while the other twenty are under United Councils, appointed by constituent second-tier authorities upon which they precept. The regions are subdivided into (at 31 March 1987) 85 counties, 18 districts, 118 boroughs (and cities) and 3 town districts; further districts are being formed by the amalgamation of counties, boroughs and town districts, which they will eventually replace fully. Great Barrier Island and the Chatham Islands form the 86th and 87th counties outside the regional structure. There are also numerous other local authorities created for specific functions.

DEFENCE. The control and co-ordination of defence activities is obtained through the Ministry of Defence. This is a unitary department combining not only all joint-Service functions but also the former Departments of Army, Navy and Air.

Army. The Chief of the General Staff commands the Army, assisted by the General Staff and the staffs of Defence Headquarters. A regular force battalion is stationed in Singapore.

There are 2 infantry battalions, 1 artillery battery, 1 light armoured squadron.

Regular personnel, in 1987, totalled 5,848 all ranks; reserves, 1,338, territorial personnel totalled 5,759; the cadet corps totalled (1987) 1,190 Army School cadets.

Navy. The Royal New Zealand Navy is administered by the Chief of Naval Staff and the Deputy Chief of Naval Staff at Defence Headquarters.

The RNZN ships include 4 frigates (including *Wellington* (ex-*Bacchante*) and

Southland (ex-*Dido*) transferred from the Royal Navy in 1982 and 1983 respectively), 1 large fleet supply ship with helicopter deck, 1 surveying vessel, 4 patrol craft, 4 new inshore defence boats, 1 old harbour defence motor launch, 2 survey boats, 2 oceanographic research ships, 1 diving tender, 1 training ship and 1 tug.

Personnel, in 1987, totalled 2,626 officers and ratings and 447 in the naval reserve.

Air Force. The Chief of Air Staff and Air Officer Commanding the RNZAF exercises command and administration of the RNZAF. Operational units of the RNZAF comprise a utility helicopter support unit (UH-1H Iroquois) based in Singapore as part of the NZ force, South-east Asia. Maritime (P-3B Orion), long and medium-range transport (Boeing 727, C-130H Hercules, Andover, F.27 Friendship) and helicopter (Sioux, Iroquois, Wasp) squadrons are based at RNZAF Base Auckland; and Hobsonville; and offensive support (A-4 Skyhawk) at RNZAF Base Ohakea. Flying training units (Airtrainer, Strikemaster, TA-4 Skyhawks, Sioux) are located at RNZAF Bases Wigram and Ohakea; ground training is carried out at RNZAF Bases Auckland, Woodbourne and Wigram.

The strength as at 31 March 1987 was 4,195 regular personnel, 1,016 reserves.

INTERNATIONAL RELATIONS

Membership. New Zealand is a member of UN, the Commonwealth, OECD, South Pacific Forum and the Colombo Plan.

ECONOMY

Budget. The following tables of revenue and expenditure relate to the Consolidated Account, which covers the ordinary revenue and expenditure of the general government—*i.e.*, apart from capital items, commercial and special undertakings, advances, etc. Revenue in the Account (in NZ$1m.) was as follows:

Year ended 31 March	Customs and excise	Sales tax	Income tax	Other taxes	Trading profits and departmental receipts	Interest	Total
1984	805·6	1,312·3	7,453·3	617·8	759·9	796·2	11,744·9
1985	1,003·6	1,561·0	8,348·5	666·4	884·7	984·7	13,448·9
1986	966·9	1,553·6	10,567·2	724·5	1,287·3	1,446·7	16,546·2
1987	1,577·0	1,016·7	12,431·8	1,963·6	1,470·0	1,616·5	20,075·6

Expenditure from Consolidated Account, year ended 31 March, was as follows (in NZ$1m.):

	Debt services	Social services [1]	Industrial development	Defence	Total (including other)
1984	2,229·2	7,618·5	2,134·8	673·0	14,221·5
1985	2,781·4	8,254·1	1,984·8	756·4	16,162·4
1986	3,622·4	10,041·1	1,697·3	870·5	18,317·6
1987	4,411·9	12,334·9	11,531·5	1,096·0	32,039·5

[1] Includes education, health and social welfare.

Taxation receipts in 1986–87 for all purposes amounted to $17,408m., giving an average of $5,301 per head of mean population. Included in the total taxation is $419m. National Roads Fund taxation. The estimate for 1987–88 is $21,250m., the total being inclusive of an estimated $465m. of National Roads Fund taxation.

The gross public debt at 31 March 1987 was $42,479m., of which $20,744m. was held in New Zealand, $5,872m. in Europe, $8,969m. in USA and $6,894m. in Canada, Australia and other sources. The gross annual interest charge on the public debt at 31 March 1987 was $4,069,438,000.

New Zealand System of National Accounts. This replaces the National Income and Expenditure Accounts which have been produced since 1948. National Accounts aggregates for 4 years are given in the following table (in NZ$1m.):

Year ended 31 March	Gross domestic product	Gross national product	National income
1983	31,160	30,300	28,084
1984	34,329	33,031	30,416
1985	38,667	36,763	33,678
1986	44,868	42,824	39,068

Currency. The monetary unit is the New Zealand *dollar*, divided into 100 *cents*. In March 1988, £1 = 2·66NZ$; US$1 = 1·51NZ$.

Banking. The Reserve Bank is the sole note-issuing authority. Seven denominations of Reserve Bank notes are issued: NZ$1, 2, 5, 10, 20, 50, 100.

The New Zealand banking system comprises a central bank, the Reserve Bank of New Zealand, and 4 commercial or trading banks. There are also 12 trustee savings banks and the Post Office Savings Bank, while each trading bank has a private savings bank subsidiary. In addition, a number of trading companies, investment societies, etc., perform quasi-banking functions, accepting deposits and granting credits to clients.

The primary functions of the Reserve Bank are to act as the central bank, to advise the Government on matters relating to monetary policy, banking and overseas exchange, and to give effect to the monetary policy of the Government.

At the end of March 1987 the amount on deposit at trading banks was NZ$17,362·5m., while advances amounted to NZ$14,051·4m. The weekly average of bank debits for 1986 was NZ$11,189·6m. excluding government.

The number of accounts with the post office savings bank at 31 March 1987 was 3·72m.; amount deposited during year ended March 1987, $9,647m.; withdrawn, $9,518m., total amount to credit of depositors at end of year, $3,052m. At 31 March 1987, $4,418m. was on deposit in Trustee Savings Banks to the credit of 3·31m. depositors. The amount to the credit of depositors with savings accounts in the trading banks was $435·9m. at 31 March 1987.

Weights and Measures. The metric system of weights and measures operates.

ENERGY AND NATURAL RESOURCES

Electricity. The general policy of the Government in regard to electric power is to supply power in bulk, leaving the reticulation and retail supply in the hands of local authorities; some of these are cities and boroughs but most are electric power boards. During the year ending 31 March 1986 hydro energy provided 73% of the national electricity supply, the balance coming from coal, oil, natural gas and geothermal energy. The last is obtained from Wairakei in the thermal region; natural steam is used to drive the turbines.

The transmission systems of the North and South Islands are linked by a high-voltage direct-current transmission and 40 km of submarine cable in Cook Strait. Supply 230 volts; 50 Hz.

Principal statistics for 4 years ended 31 March are:

	1983	1984	1985	1986
Number of establishments	82	89	94	95
Generators (capacity) AC (1,000 kw.)	5,820	6,382	6,988	7,435
Units generated (1m. kwh.)	24,301	25,855	26,765	27,017
Revenue ($1,000)	1,720,058	1,852,830	2,014,438	2,524,772
Expenditure:				
Operating ($1,000)	947,179	978,261	1,070,187	1,394,049
Management, etc. ($1,000)	163,403	168,655	185,057	220,022
Capital charges ($1,000)	359,989	383,720	461,946	568,540
Capital outlay:				
During year ($1,000)	491,286	488,700	411,100	456,300
To date ($1,000)	4,116,100	4,493,200	4,770,900	5,067,700

Natural Gas. In 1987 there were 4 gasfields in production: Kapuri (on stream 1970), Maui (1979), McKee (1984) and Kaimaro (1984). Natural gas represents 29% of primary energy consumption.

Minerals. New Zealand's production of minerals in 1986 included 1,265 kg of gold, 3,140 tonnes of bentonite, 104,532 tonnes of clay for bricks, tiles, etc., 28,464 tonnes of potters' clays, 2,689,000 tonnes of iron sand, 723,000 tonnes of limestone for agriculture and 257,600 tonnes of limestone for industry, 1,012,000 tonnes of limestone, marl, etc., for cement, 43,800 tonnes of pumice, 22,400 tonnes of serpentine, 114,200 tonnes of silica sand. Mineral fuel production amounted to 2,517,000 tonnes of coal.

Agriculture. Two-thirds of the surface of New Zealand is suitable for agriculture and grazing. The total area under cultivation at 30 June 1986 was 21,331,194 hectares (including residential area and domestic orchards). There were 13,831,833 hectares of grassland, lucerne and tussock, 90,071 hectares of land for horticulture, 417,740 hectares of grain or fodder crops and 1,150,331 hectares of plantations. The area of Crown lands (other than reserves) leased under various tenures at 31 March 1987 was 4,714,766 hectares.

The largest freehold estates are held in the South Island. The extent of occupied holdings as at 30 June 1986 (exclusive of holdings within borough boundaries) was as follows:

Size of holdings (hectares)	Number of farms	Aggregate area (hectares)	Size of holdings (hectares)	Number of farms	Aggregate area (hectares)
Under 5	10,167	30,278	400–799	4,409	2,403,793
5–19	15,216	150,402	800–1,199	1,242	1,200,428
20–39	8,036	227,153	1,200–1,999	934	1,425,968
40–59	7,360	356,255	2,000–3,999	571	1,554,245
60–99	10,100	779,949	4,000 and over	595	8,855,987
100–199	11,476	1,645,056			
200–399	9,718	2,701,680	Total	79,824	21,331,194

The area and yield for each of the principal crops are given as follows (area and yield for threshing only, not including that grown for chaff, hay, silage, etc.):

	Wheat		Maize		Barley	
Crop years	Area (1,000 hectares)	Yield (1,000 tonnes)	Area (1,000 hectares)	Yield (1,000 tonnes)	Area (1,000 hectares)	Yield (1,000 tonnes)
1985	71·8	309·6	17·8	174·6	152·3	644·4
1986	91·4	379·7	19·5	187·7	138·6	556·2

Private air companies are carrying out such aerial work as top-dressing, spraying and crop-dusting, seed-sowing, rabbit poisoning, aerial photography and surveying, and dropping supplies to deer cullers and dropping fencing materials in remote areas. In 1986 a total area of 4,719,731 hectares was top-dressed with fertilizer and lime.

Livestock 1986: 8,279,000 cattle, 67·5m. sheep and 435,000 pigs. Total meat produced in the year ended 30 Sept. 1986 was estimated at 1·13m. tonnes (including 451,600 tonnes of beef and 465,000 tonnes of lamb). Total liquid milk produced in the year ended 31 May 1986 was 7,963m. litres.

Production of wool for 1985–86, 358,000 tonnes (greasy basis).

Agricultural Statistics. Dept. of Statistics, Wellington. Annual.

Forestry. Of the 6·2m. hectares of indigenous forest, most is protected in National Parks or State Forests. Declining quantities of indigenous timber are being produced from restricted areas of State Forest and from privately owned forest. There are just over 1m. hectares of productive exotic forest, and this produces far more timber than the indigenous forests. Introduced pines form the bulk of the large exotic forest estate and among these radiata pine is the best multi-purpose tree, reaching log size in 25–30 years. Other species planted are Douglas fir and Eucalyptus species. The table below shows production of rough sawn timber in cu. metres for years ending 31 March:

	Indigenous			Exotic			All Species
	Rimu and Miro	Beech	Total	Exotic Pines	Douglas Fir	Total	Total
1983–84	99,541	15,651	136,286	1,748,467	170,950	1,959,284	2,095,570
1984–85	101,792	17,076	140,766	1,636,000	174,780	2,164,880	2,305,646
1985–86	96,153	12,620	132,740	2,043,759	182,911	2,264,873	2,397,613

Forest industries consist of 449 saw-mills, 9 plywood and veneer plants, 3 particle board mills, 8 pulp and paper mills and 2 fibreboard mills.

The basic products of the pulp and paper mills are mechanical and chemical pulp which are converted into newsprint, kraft and other papers, paperboard and fibreboard. Production of woodpulp, 31 March 1986, amounted to 1·11m. tonnes and of paper (including newsprint paper and paperboard) to 671,000 tonnes.

Fisheries. The total value of New Zealand Fisheries exports during the year ended 30 June 1985 was $513·7m., an increase of $144·4m. (39·1%) over the previous year.

| | Exports, 1986 | | Exports, 1987 | |
	Quantity kg (1,000)	Value $ (1,000)	Quantity kg (1,000)	Value $ (1,000)
Finfish or wetfish	91,593	319,808	110,949	457,107
Rock lobster	2,894	89,262	2,871	109,023
Shellfish (squid, mussels, oysters, etc)	36,883	97,704	42,961	145,339
Total	131,370	506,774	156,782	711,469

INDUSTRY AND TRADE

Industry. Major industrial developments in recent years have included the establishment of an oil refinery, an iron and steel industry using New Zealand iron sands, a petro-chemical industry and an aluminium smelter using hydro-electric power.

Statistics of manufacturing industries:

Production year	Persons engaged	Salaries and wages paid (NZ$1,000)	Cost of materials (NZ$1,000)	Sales and other income (NZ$1,000)	Value added (NZ$1,000)
1985–86	304,640	5,479,271	17,502,521	31,799,989	9,342,728

The following is a statement of the provisional value of the products (including repairs) of the principal industries for the year 1985–86 (in NZ$1,000):

Industry group	Purchases & operating expenses	Sales and other income	Value added	Additions to fixed tangible assets
		(NZ$1,000)		
Food, beverage and tobacco manufacturing	8,651,628	9,174,803	2,395,813	469,275
Textile, wearing apparel, leather industries	2,740,161	2,914,926	911,462	151,353
Wood and wood products (including furniture)	1,948,056	2,086,568	707,513	167,887
Paper and paper products, printing and publishing	3,126,013	3,385,798	1,207,900	247,746
Chemicals and chemical, petroleum, coal, rubber and plastic products	3,883,330	3,847,384	986,496	1,374,006
Non-metallic mineral products (excludes products of petroleum and coal)	1,011,316	1,153,771	358,202	58,513
Basic metal industries	1,128,821	1,222,812	345,503	531,083
Fabricated metal products, machinery and equipment	7,352,124	7,728,508	2,333,535	344,495
Other manufacturing industries	259,679	285,419	96,304	14,438
Total	30,101,128	31,799,989	9,342,728	3,358,796

Enterprise Survey. Dept. of Statistics, Wellington. Annual

Labour. In Dec. 1986 there were 215 industrial unions of workers with a total of 489,763 members.

The industrial distribution of the labour force as estimated in Feb. 1984 was: Primary industries, 148,400; manufacturing, 302,300; construction, 87,700; commerce, 220,900; transport and communication, 103,100; services, 315,200; armed forces, 13,000; unemployed, 77,500; total labour force, 1,371,100.

By the Accident Compensation Act 1972 immediate compensation without proof of fault is provided for every injured person and wherever the accident occurred. Compensation is paid both for permanent physical disability and also—in the case of earners—for income losses on an income related basis. Regular adjustment in the level of payment is provided for in accordance with variations in the value of money. Non-earners such as tourists, housewives, children, students, retired people do not normally qualify for earnings related compensation but are eligible for all other benefits. These are not taxable. Housewives—including visiting women from overseas—who are non-earners are eligible for the benefits available to non-earners and home help can be paid for or the husband compensated for loss of earnings while he is looking after the home until the injured wife can resume her duties.

After the first week's incapacity and for the ensuing 4 weeks the earner can be paid 80% of his average earnings for the 28 days preceding the accident; after that the 80% is related to average earnings over the 12 preceding months. In addition—for earners—lump sums are payable for impairment, pain and disfigurement and for funeral expenses and weekly sums and lump payments to their widows and dependent children. All employees are covered by the Accident Compensation Act 1972.

Commerce. Trade (excluding specie and bullion) in NZ$1m. for 12 months ended 30 June:

	Total merchandise imported (v.f.d.) [1]	Exports of domestic produce	Re-exports	Total merchandise exported (f.o.b.)
1983–84	8,197·9	8,366·1	257·7	8,623·8
1984–85	11,344·2	11,011·9	303·9	11,315·8
1985–86	10,468·3	10,139·0	432·7	10,571·7
1986–87	10,803·4	11,723·9	383·3	12,107·2

[1] Value for duty.

The principal imports for the 12 months ended 30 June 1987:

Commodity (c.i.f.)	Value (NZ$1,000)
Cereals and cereal preparations	39,334
Fruit and vegetables	190,040
Sugar and sugar preparations	71,369
Coffee, tea, cocoa, spices, etc.	102,128
Beverages	96,556
Tobacco and manufactures	28,249
Crude rubber	37,984
Textile fibres	32,146
Crude fertilizers and minerals other than coal	88,253
Petroleum and petroleum products	759,469
Organic chemicals	199,333
Inorganic chemicals	147,382
Dyeing, tanning, etc. materials	93,676
Medicinal and pharmaceutical products	288,169
Fertilizers, manufactured	59,781
Plastic materials, etc.	438,661
Miscellaneous chemical materials and products	151,742
Rubber manufactures [1]	108,652
Paper and paperboard manufactures	288,219
Textile yarn and fabrics, etc.	742,465
Non-metallic mineral manufactures [1]	199,782
Iron and steel	453,128
Non-ferrous metals	174,600
Manufactures of metals	297,051
General industrial machinery	526,229
Electrical machinery	595,658
Road vehicles	1,320,644
Professional scientific instruments	238,999
Miscellaneous manufactured articles [1]	593,744
Total merchandise imported [2]	11,800,187

[1] Not elsewhere specified.   [2] Including commodities not listed.

The principal exports of New Zealand produce for the 12 months ended 30 June 1987 were:

Commodity	Value (NZ$1m.)	Commodity	Value (NZ$1m.)
Meat, fresh, chilled or frozen		Forest products	
Beef and veal	1,024·5	Sawn timber	92·8
Lamb	952·9	Radiata pine logs	40·6
Mutton	141·5	Wood pulp	252·9
Dairy products		Fruit and vegetables	800·3
Skimmed milk powder	221·2	Inedible tallow	60·7
Butter	510·1	Casein and caseinates	281·1
Cheese	276·7	Iron ore and concentrates	30·3
Hides, skins and fur skins	537·8	Aluminium and aluminium alloys	503·9
Wool	1,566·9	Carpets and carpeting	81·0
Sausage casings	94·0	Domestic electrical equipment	
Fish, fresh, chilled or frozen	457·1	(incl. parts)	66·7
Rock lobster (crayfish)	108·3		
		Total produce exported	12,107·2

The following table shows the trade with different countries for the year ended 30 June (in NZ$1,000):

Countries	Imports v.f.d. from 1986	1987	Exports and re-exports f.o.b. to 1986	1987
Australia	1,725,495	1,942,097	1,821,754	1,794,912
Bahrain	104,930	8,627	10,624	8,891
Belgium	82,130	96,857	121,994	161,457
Canada	226,566	236,447	172,717	198,854
China	83,778	84,667	229,578	425,488
Fiji	20,748	24,837	119,523	123,106
France	175,556	191,383	147,772	226,003
Germany, Fed. Rep. of	622,635	641,557	269,868	310,773
Greece	1,994	1,590	71,748	72,975
Hong Kong	129,669	182,648	161,075	186,232
India	38,112	41,980	52,761	71,483
Iran	487	982	300,967	195,084
Italy	168,131	240,279	227,144	301,890
Japan	2,194,371	2,235,401	1,531,459	1,823,080
Korea, Republic of	83,927	178,340	153,027	244,970
Kuwait	64	9,401	20,247	19,902
Malaysia	50,327	48,418	117,726	133,376
Netherlands	131,176	156,564	158,106	165,451
Philippines	20,958	24,552	58,110	94,428
Saudi Arabia	210,986	203,903	85,041	99,006
Singapore	396,297	184,955	171,462	170,167
Sweden	103,515	118,345	16,109	18,755
UK	985,521	1,060,655	933,870	1,125,092
USSR	5,353	7,828	241,257	205,081
USA	1,823,091	1,729,477	1,612,219	1,944,831

Total trade between New Zealand and UK was as follows (British Department of Trade returns, in £1,000 sterling):

	1983	1984	1985	1986	1987
Imports to UK	486,305	483,749	533,047	455,694	487,332
Exports and re-exports from UK	266,054	367,512	396,595	343,145	378,368

Tourism. The country has a growing tourist industry. In the year ended 31 March 1987, 763,209 travellers visited New Zealand (including 598,700 tourists), compared with 689,073 (including 544,517 tourists) in 1986.

COMMUNICATIONS

Roads. Total length of formed roads and streets in New Zealand at 31 March 1986 was 92,971 km. There were 14,949 bridges of over 3 metres in length with a total length of 335,000 metres at 31 March 1986. The network of state highways comprised, at 31 March 1986, 11,555 km, including the principal arterial traffic routes.

Total expenditure on roads, streets and bridges by the central government and local authorities combined for the financial year 1985–86 amounted to $339·9m.

At 31 March 1986 motor vehicles licensed numbered 2,437,329, of which 1,531,425 were cars and 5,038 omnibuses and service vehicles. Included in the remaining numbers were 134,214 motor cycles, 895 power cycles, 305,984 trucks, 385,916 trailers and caravans and 62,827 farm tractors and other farm equipment.

Railways. On 31 March 1987 there were 4,273 km of 1,067 mm gauge railway open for traffic (519 km electrified). In 1985–86, railways carried 9m. tonnes and 15·1m. passengers. Operating earnings from government railways, 1986–87, $468,865,000. Three rail/road ferries maintain a regular service between the North and South Islands.

The total revenue (including road motor and other subsidiary services) amounted to $666·1m., and total expenditure $690·1m. in 1986–87.

Aviation. International services are operated to and from New Zealand by a state-owned company, Air New Zealand Ltd, and by a number of overseas companies. Air New Zealand Ltd also operates most domestic scheduled passenger services. Non-scheduled services are run by the main companies and also by a number of small operators and aero clubs.

Domestic scheduled services during the 12 months ended Dec. 1985: Passengers carried, 3,255,000. International services: Passengers carried, 2,061,000; mail, 3,936 tonnes; freight, 92,227 tonnes.

Shipping. Container ships operate from Auckland, Wellington, Lyttelton and Port Chalmers to the UK, Europe, North America and Japan. The government-owned New Zealand Shipping Corporation has begun to increase its activity into New Zealand—UK and Pacific trades.

Entrances and clearances of vessels from overseas:

	Entrances		Clearances	
	No.	Tons	No.	Tons
1984	3,193	14,001,000	3,174	13,934,000
1985	2,932	14,607,000	2,935	14,613,000
1986	2,519	13,388,000	2,527	13,365,000

Post and Broadcasting. Receipts of the Post Office for year ended 31 March 1987 were $2,271·6m.; total expenditure was $1,912·6m. The average staff for 1986–87 was 40,891.

The telegraph and telephone systems are operated by the Post Office. At 31 March 1987 there were 2,315,000 telephones. The telecommunications receipts for the year 1986–87 were $1,529m.

An earth satellite station has been built north of Auckland to link with the Pacific satellite Intelsat III to augment the Compac and Seacon telecommunications systems which link New Zealand with overseas countries.

There are 2 TV channels both operated by the state-owned New Zealand Broadcasting Corporation, which also operates most of the broadcasting stations. Over 85% of New Zealand households have TV sets. There are 64 medium-wave broadcasting stations and 2 short-wave transmitters. Some commercial material is broadcast by both sound and TV services. Number of TV receiving licences at 31 March 1987 was 914,689.

Cinemas. There were in 1981, 154 cinemas with a seating capacity of 89,364.

Newspapers. There were (1987), 34 daily newspapers (10 morning and 24 evening) with a combined circulation of 1,134,835. Seven of these newspapers (2 each in Auckland, Wellington and Christchurch and 1 in Dunedin) had a circulation of 711,538.

JUSTICE, RELIGION, EDUCATION AND WELFARE

Justice. The judiciary consists of the Court of Appeal, the High Court and District Courts. All exercise both civil and criminal jurisdiction. Other special courts include the Maori Land Court, Family Courts and Young Persons' Courts. At the end of Dec. 1986 the gaols and Borstal institutions contained 2,690 prisoners, 2,578 males and 112 females. The death penalty for murder was replaced by life imprisonment in 1961.

The Criminal Injuries Act, 1963, which came into force on 1 Jan. 1964, provided for compensation of persons injured by certain criminal acts and the dependants of persons killed by such acts. However, this has now been phased out in favour of the Accident Compensation Act, 1972, except in the residual area of property damage caused by escapers. Since 1970 legal aid in civil proceedings (except divorce) has been available for persons of small or moderate means. For the year ended 31 Dec. 1986 expenditure amounted to $8,505,761 and 31,295 applications for aid were granted.

Police. The police in New Zealand are a national body maintained wholly by the central government. The total strength at 31 March 1987 was 5,291, the proportion of police to population being 1 to 627. The total cost of police services for the year 1986–87 was NZ$321m., equivalent to $97 per head of population. In New Zealand the police do not control traffic.

Ombudsmen. The office of Ombudsman was created in 1962. From 1975 additional Ombudsmen have been authorized. There are currently two. Ombudsmen's functions are to investigate complaints from members of the public relating to administrative decisions of government departments, local authorities and statutory organizations.

During the year ended 31 March 1987, 1,747 complaints were received, 93 of which were sustained.

Religion. No direct state aid is given to any form of religion. For the Church of England the country is divided into 7 dioceses, with a separate bishopric (Aotearoa) for the Maoris. The Presbyterian Church is divided into 23 presbyteries and the Maori Synod. The Moderator is elected annually. The Methodist Church is divided into 10 districts; the President is elected annually. The Roman Catholic Church is divided into 4 dioceses, with the Archbishop of Wellington as Metropolitan Archbishop.

Religious denomination	Number of clergy (April 1977)	Number of adherents 1981 census	1986 census [1]
Church of England	780	814,740	784,059
Presbyterian	686	523,221	586,530
Roman Catholic (including 'Catholic' undefined)	931	456,858	495,300
Methodist	349	148,512	152,955
Baptist	254	50,043	67,716
Brethren	187	24,324	
Ratana	142	35,781	
Protestant (undefined)	—	16,986	
Salvation Army	241	20,490	
Latter-day Saints (Mormon)	162	37,686	
Congregationalist	10	3,825	
Seventh-day Adventist	55	11,523	871,689
Ringatu	88	6,114	
Christian (undefined)	—	101,901	
Jehovah's Witnesses	125	13,737	
Hebrew	7	3,360	
All other religious professions	—	279,768	
Agnostic	—	24,201	
Atheist	—	21,528	
Not specified	—	108,015	59,385
Object to state	—	473,115	244,152
Total	4,712	3,175,737	3,261,786

[1] Provisional.

Education. New Zealand has 6 universities, the University of Auckland, University of Waikato (at Hamilton), Victoria University of Wellington, Massey University (at Palmerston North), the University of Canterbury (at Christchurch) and the University of Otago (at Dunedin). There is, in addition, Lincoln College near Christchurch, a university college of agriculture, which is a constituent college of the University of Canterbury. The number of students in 1986 was 61,979. There were 6 teachers' training colleges with 3,553 students in 1986.

At 1 July 1986 there were 315 state secondary schools with 14,344 full-time teachers and 214,300 pupils. There were also 36 district high schools with 3,191 scholars in the secondary division. At 1 July 1986, 84,617 part-time pupils attended technical classes, and 33,598 received part-time instruction from the technical correspondence institute. At 1 July 1986, 1,109 pupils received tuition from the secondary department of the correspondence school. There were 21 registered private secondary schools with 433 teachers and 11,816 pupils.

At 1 July 1986, there were 2,418 state primary schools (including intermediate schools and departments), with 414,731 pupils; the number of teachers was 18,830. A correspondence school for children in remote areas and those otherwise unable to attend school had 1,606 primary pupils. There were 69 registered private primary schools with 336 teachers and 11,417 pupils.

Education is compulsory between the ages of 6 and 15. Children aged 3 and 4 years may enrol at the 552 free kindergartens maintained by Free Kindergarten Associations, which receive government assistance. There are also 657 play centres which also receive government subsidy. In July 1986 there were 41,822 and 14,509 children on the rolls respectively.

Total expenditure out of government funds in 1986–87 upon education was NZ$2,598m.

The universities and the affiliated agricultural colleges are autonomous bodies. Most secondary schools are controlled by their own boards. Virtually all state primary schools are controlled by the district education boards: there are 10 education districts. The Department of Education exercises certain defined functions in connexion with the general supervision of the education provided in state primary and secondary schools and disburses the government grants payable to controlling authorities for the running of those schools. Education in state schools is free for children under 19 years of age. Private schools are regularly visited by state school inspectors.

Report of the Minister of Education ('E.1. Report'). Annually. Wellington, Government Printer

NZ Committee on Secondary Education. *Towards Partnership.* Dept. of Education, 1976

Health. At 30 June 1987 there were 8,312 doctors on the medical register. At 31 March 1986 there were 23,759 public hospital beds, of which 2,070 were for maternity cases.

Social Welfare. New Zealand's record for progressive legislation reaches back to 1898, when it was second only to Denmark in introducing non-contributory old-age pensions.

The present system came into operation from 1 April 1972. It provides for retirement, unemployment, widowhood, invalidity and sickness, as well as hospital and other medical care. Since 1 April 1969 the scheme has been financed from general taxation. Previously there was a special social security tax on virtually all income of individuals and companies in excess of $4 a week which met approximately three-quarters of the cost of the scheme, the balance being met from general taxation.

At 31 March 1987 the current weekly rates of widows', invalids', sickness, domestic purposes, unemployment and miners' benefits were $218·60 for a married couple, $131·16 for an unmarried person aged 18 years or over, and $106·13 for those under 18 years.

There are additional payments for dependent children.

All benefits except superannuation and family allowances are subject to an income test.

Family Benefit. A family benefit of $6 a week is payable for each dependent child.

Unemployment Benefit. The payment is subject to the condition that the applicant is capable and willing to undertake suitable employment.

Sickness Benefit. Payment is subject to medical evidence of incapacity of a person who has suffered a loss of weekly earnings as a result.

Other benefits include emergency benefits and additional benefits for those in need but who either do not qualify for one of the standard benefits or who have special needs or commitments for which a benefit at the standard rate is insufficient.

Medical, Hospital and Related Benefits. Medical, hospital and other related benefits are also provided under the Social Welfare scheme. These consist mainly of the payment of certain fees for medical attention by private practitioners, free treatment in public and mental hospitals, certain fees for treatment in private hospitals, maternity benefits (including ante-natal and post-natal treatment and services of doctors and nurses at confinements), pharmaceutical benefits (medicines, drugs, etc., prescribed by medical practitioners), etc. There are also benefits in connexion with dental services up to the age of 16, X-ray diagnosis, massage, home-nursing, artificial aids, etc.

Pensions. Provision is made for the payment of pensions and allowances to members or dependants of disabled, deceased or missing members, of the New Zealand Forces who served in the South African War, the two World Wars, the Korean War and the Vietnam War, to members of the New Zealand Mercantile Marine during the Second World War, or in connexion with any emergency whether arising out of the obligations undertaken by New Zealand in the Charter of the United Nations or otherwise. Principal rates are payable to widows at a rate of $68·28 a week, together with a mother's allowance of $36 a week, increased by $16 a week for each additional child, in addition to the normal child allowances of $6 per week for each child. These rates may be increased by an amount not exceeding $46·82 per week if the pensioner is suffering from total blindness, two or more serious disabilities or one extremely severe disability.

An 'economic pension' is defined as a supplementary pension granted on economic grounds and is additional to any pension payable as of right in respect of death or disablement. The maximum weekly rates are $218·60 to a married person (if unmarried, $131·16); to the widow or dependent widowed mother of a member, $178·60.

War veterans' allowances are $131·16 weekly for a single person and $218·60 for a married person, plus an equal amount to a wife, increased by $1.50 a week each at age 65, subject to income qualifications.

Domestic Purposes Benefit. A domestic purposes benefit is payable to unsupported male and female solo parents including divorced, separated and unmarried persons, prisoners' spouses and also to those who are required to give full-time care to a person (other than their spouse) who would otherwise have to be admitted to hospital.

Death Benefit. A death benefit of $1,260 is payable to a widow or widower if totally dependent on the deceased plus $630 for each dependent child but not exceeding $1,600.

Social Welfare Benefits and War Pensions:

Benefits	Number in force at 31 March 1987	Total payments 1986–87 (NZ$1,000)
SOCIAL WELFARE:		
Monetary—		
Superannuation	473,401	3,650,165
Widows	13,019	94,732
Family care	246,495	68,969
Family	450,072	273,248
Invalids	23,087	159,823
Miners and orphans	506	1,774
Unemployment	63,922	459,685
Sickness	11,116	124,292
Domestic purposes	69,146	709,568
Total	1,350,764	5,542,256

Benefits	Total payments 1986–87 (NZ$1,000)
SOCIAL WELFARE (contd.):	
Health, etc.—	
Medical	93,943
Hospital	65,318
Maternity	30,445
Pharmaceutical	444,295
Supplementary	58,002
Total	692,003

WAR PENSIONS as at 31 March 1987:

Type of Person	Number in Force	Dependent Wives Included	Annual Value (NZ$ 1,000)
War disablement	21,481	–	34,775
Dependants of disabled	50	–	283
Widows	4,211	–	14,989
Other dependants of deceased	30		
Economic	1,307	48	8,976
War service	1,825	1,079	17,456
War veteran's allowance	745	328	7,127
Police	32	–	59
Total	29,681	1,455	83,665

Reciprocity with Other Countries. There are reciprocal arrangements between New Zealand and Australia in respect of age, invalids', widows', family, unemployment and sickness benefits, and between New Zealand and the UK in respect of family, age, superannuation, widows', orphans', invalids', sickness and unemployment benefits.

Superannuation. Following the change of Government in Dec. 1975 the earnings-related superannuation scheme described in THE STATESMAN'S YEAR-BOOK, 1977–78, was abolished. Under the new system (operative from Feb. 1977) superannuation is payable to all New Zealanders on reaching the age of 60. It is taxable but not subject to an income test. The rates are based on the national average wage, of which married couples now receive 80% and single persons 60% of the married rate.

MINOR ISLANDS

The minor islands (total area, 320 sq. miles, 829 sq. km) included within the geographical boundaries of New Zealand (but not within any local government area) are the following: Kermadec Islands (34 sq. km), Three Kings Islands (8 sq. km), Auckland Islands (606 sq. km), Campbell Island (114 sq. km), Antipodes Islands (606 sq. km), Bounty Islands (1 sq. km), Snares Islands (3 sq. km), Solander Island (1 sq. km). With the exception of meteorological station staff on Raoul Island in the Kermadec Group (5 in 1986) and Campbell Island (10 in 1986) there are no inhabitants.

The **Kermadec Islands** were annexed to New Zealand in 1887, have no separate administration and all New Zealand laws apply to them. Situation, 29° 10' to 31° 30' S. lat., 177° 45' to 179° W. long., 1,000 miles NNE of New Zealand. The largest of the group is Raoul or Sunday Island, 29 sq. km, smaller islands being Macauley and Curtis, while Macaulay Island is 3 miles in circuit.

TERRITORIES OVERSEAS

Territories Overseas coming within the jurisdiction of New Zealand consist of Tokelau and the Ross Dependency.

Tokelau. Situated some 480 km to the north of Western Samoa between 8° and 10° S. lat., and between 171° and 173° W. long., are the 3 atoll islands of Atafu, Nukunonu and Fakaofo of the Tokelau (Union) group. Formerly part of the Gilbert and Ellice Islands Colony, the group was transferred to the jurisdiction of New Zealand on 11 Feb. 1926. By legislation enacted in 1948, the Tokelau Islands were declared part of New Zealand as from 1 Jan. 1949. The area of the group is 1,011 hectares; the population at 10 Oct. 1986 was 1,690.

By the Tokelau Islands Act 1948 the Tokelau Group was included within the territorial boundaries of New Zealand; legislative powers are now invested in the Governor-General in Council. The inhabitants are British subjects and New Zealand citizens. In Dec. 1976 the territory was officially renamed 'Tokelau', the name by which it has customarily been known to its inhabitants.

From 8 Nov. 1974 the office of Administrator was invested in the Secretary of Foreign Affairs. Certain powers are delegated to the district officer in Apia, Western Samoa.

Because of the very restricted economic and social future in the atolls, the islanders agreed to a proposal put to them by the Minister of Island Territories in 1965 that over a period of years most of the population be resettled in New Zealand. Up to March 1975, 528 migrants entered New Zealand as permanent residents under Government sponsorship. At the request of the people the scheme has now been suspended.

New Zealand Government aid to Tokelau totalled $3·3m. for the year ended 31 March 1987.

Ross Dependency. By Imperial Order in Council, dated 30 July 1923, the territories between 160° E. long. and 150° W. long. and south of 60° S. lat. were brought within the jurisdiction of the New Zealand Government. The region was named the Ross Dependency. From time to time laws for the Dependency have been made by regulations promulgated by the Governor-General of New Zealand.

The mainland area is estimated at 400,000–450,000 sq. km and is mostly ice-covered. In Jan. 1957 a New Zealand expedition under Sir Edmund Hillary established a base in the Dependency. In Jan. 1958 Sir Edmund Hillary and 4 other New Zealanders reached the South Pole.

The main base—Scott Base—at Pram Point, Ross Island—is manned throughout the year, about 12 people being present during winter. Vanda Station in the dry ice-free Wright Valley is manned every summer.

Quartermain, L. B., *New Zealand and the Antarctic.* Wellington, 1971

SELF-GOVERNING TERRITORIES OVERSEAS

THE COOK ISLANDS

HISTORY. The Cook Islands, which lie between 8° and 23° S. lat., and 156° and 167° W. long., were proclaimed a British protectorate in 1888, and on 11 June 1901 were annexed and proclaimed part of New Zealand. In 1965 the Cook Islands became a self-governing territory in 'free association' with New Zealand.

AREA AND POPULATION. The islands within the territory fall roughly into two groups—the scattered islands towards the north (Northern group) and the islands towards the south known as the Lower group. The names of the islands with their populations as at the census of 1 Dec. 1981 were as follows:

Lower Group—	Area sq. km	Population	Northern Group—	Area sq. km	Population
Rarotonga	67·2	9,530	Nassau	1·2	134
Mangaia	51·8	1,364	Palmerston (Avarau)	2·0	51
Atiu	26·9	1,225	Penrhyn (Tongareva)	9·8	608
Aitutaki	18·0	2,335	Manihiki (Humphrey)	5·4	405
Mauke (Parry Is.)	18·4	681	Rakahanga (Reirson)	4·1	272
Mitiaro	22·3	256	Pukapuka (Danger)	5·1	796
Manuae and Te au-o-tu	6·2	12	Suwarrow (Anchorage)	0·4	—
Takutea	1·3	—			
			Total	293	17,754

Vital statistics (1985): Births, 418; marriages, 105; deaths, 117.

CONSTITUTION AND GOVERNMENT. The Cook Islands Constitution Act 1964, which provides for the establishment of internal self-government in the Cook Islands, came into force on 4 Aug. 1965.

The Act establishes the Cook Islands as fully self-governing but linked to New Zealand by a common Head of State, the Queen, and a common citizenship, that of New Zealand. It provides for a ministerial system of government with a Cabinet consisting of a Premier and 6 other Ministers. The New Zealand Government is represented by a New Zealand Representative and the position of a Queen's Representative has recently been created by changes in the Constitution. New Zealand continues to be responsible for the external affairs and defence of the Cook Islands, subject to consultation between the New Zealand Prime Minister and the Prime Minister. The changed status of the Islands does not affect the consideration of subsidies or the right of free entry into New Zealand for exports from the group. The capital is Rarotonga, which was devastated by a hurricane in Jan. 1987.

The unicameral Parliament comprises 24 members elected for a term of 5 years; at general elections held in Nov. 1983, the Democratic Party won 13 seats and the Cook Islands Party 11 seats. There is also an advisory council composed of hereditary chiefs, the 15-member House of Ariki, without legislative powers.

Prime Minister: Dr Pupuke Robati.

ECONOMY AND TRADE

Budget. Budget 1987–88, NZ$40,104,700. Revenue is derived chiefly from customs duties which follow the New Zealand customs tariff, income tax and stamp sales.

Grants from New Zealand, mainly for medical, educational and general administrative purposes totalled NZ$7m. in 1982–83.

Currency. The Cook Island *dollar* is at par with the New Zealand *dollar*.

Agriculture. Livestock (1986): Pigs, 17,000; goats, 3,000.

Fisheries. Catch (1984) 800 tonnes.

Commerce. Exports, mainly to New Zealand, were valued at $6·5m. in 1984. Main items of export were fresh fruit and vegetables, fruit juice, copra and clothing. Imports totalled $30m. in 1984. The main items were foodstuffs, manufactured goods (including transport equipment), petrol and petroleum products.

COMMUNICATIONS

Roads. In 1984 there were 280 km of roads and 1,417 vehicles.

Aviation. New Zealand has financed the construction of an international airport at Rarotonga which became operational for jet services in Sept. 1973.

Shipping. A fortnightly cargo shipping service is provided between New Zealand, Niue and Rarotonga.

Telecommunications. Wireless stations are maintained at all the permanently inhabited islands. In 1983 there were 2,052 telephones. There are 2 radio stations on Rarotonga with (1983) 10,000 receivers.

Newspapers. The *Cook Islands News* (circulation 2,000) is the sole daily newspaper.

JUSTICE, RELIGION, EDUCATION AND HEALTH

Justice. There is a High Court and a Court of Appeal, from which further appeal is to the Privy Council in the UK.

Religion. Some 60% of the population belong to the Cook Islands Congregational Church, about 20% are Roman Catholics, and the rest chiefly Mormons and Seventh-Day Adventists.

Education. In 1986 there were 30 primary schools with 165 teachers and 3,183 pupils, and 8 secondary schools with 146 teachers and 2,156 pupils on Rarotonga, Aitutaki, Mangaia, Atiu, Mauke and Pukapuka.

Health. All Cook Islanders receive free medical and surgical treatment in their villages, the hospital and the tuberculosis sanatorium. Cook Islands Maori patients in the hospital and the sanatorium and all schoolchildren receive free dental treatment.

NIUE

History. Niue achieved internal self-government in Oct. 1974.

Area and Population. Distance from Auckland, New Zealand, 1,343 miles; from Rarotonga, 580 miles. Area, 258 sq. km; height above sea-level, 220 ft. Population at 31 Dec. 1987 was 2,442. During 1987 births registered numbered 50, deaths 15. Migration to New Zealand is the main factor in population change. The capital is Alofi (986 inhabitants in 1981).

Constitution and Government. There is a Legislative Assembly of 20 members, and legislative measures apply as in the case of the Cook Islands.

Premier: Robert R. Rex, CMG, OBE.

Budget. Financial aid from New Zealand, 1987–88, totalled $8,500,000.

Agriculture. The most important products of the island are coconuts, honey, limes and root crops.

Trade. Exports, 1985, $175,924 (main export, coconut cream); imports, $3,753,384.

Communications. There is a wireless station at Alofi, the port of the island. A weekly commercial air service links Niue with New Zealand. Telephones (1986) 460.

Justice. There is a High Court under a Chief Justice, with a right of appeal to the New Zealand Supreme Court.

Religion. 75% of the population belong to the Congregational (Ekalesia Niue); 10% are Mormons and 5% Roman Catholics.

Education. There were 7 government schools with 702 pupils in 1987.

Health. In 1986 there were 3 doctors, 3 dentists, 7 midwives and 27 nursing personnel. There is a 25-bed hospital at Alofi.

DIPLOMATIC REPRESENTATIVES

Of New Zealand in Great Britain (New Zealand Hse, Haymarket, London, SW1Y 4TQ)
High Commissioner: Bryce Harland.

Of Great Britain in New Zealand (Reserve Bank of New Zealand Bldg., 2 The Terrace, Wellington, 1)
High Commissioner: R. A. C. Byatt, CMG.

Of New Zealand in the USA (37 Observatory Cir., NW, Washington, D.C., 20008)
Ambassador: H. H. (Tim) Francis.

Of the USA in New Zealand (29 Fitzherbert Terrace, Wellington)
Ambassador: Paul Cleveland.

Of New Zealand to the United Nations
Ambassador: David K. McDowell.

Books of Reference

Statistical Information: The central statistical office for New Zealand is the Department of Statistics (Wellington, 1).

The beginning of a statistical service may be seen in the early 'Blue books' prepared annually from 1840 onwards under the direction of the Colonial Secretary, and designed primarily for the information of the Colonial Office in England. A permanent statistical authority was created in 1858. The Department of Statistics functions under the Statistics Act 1975 and reports to Parliament through the Minister of Statistics. A comprehensive statistical service has been developed to meet national requirements, and close contact is maintained with the United Nations Statistical Office and other international statistical organizations; through the Conference of Asian Statisticians assistance is being given with the development of statistics in the region. The oldest publications consist of *(a)* census results from 1858 onwards and *(b)* annual volumes of statistics (first published 1858 but covering years back to 1853). Main current publications:

New Zealand Official Yearbook. Annual, from 1893
Catalogue of New Zealand Statistics. 1972
Statistical Reports of New Zealand. Annual
Monthly Abstract of Statistics. From 1914
Pocket Digest of Statistics. Annual, 1927–31, 1938 ff.

Parliamentary Reports of Government Departments. Annual
Pacific Islands Yearbook. Sydney, 1977
Dictionary of New Zealand Biography. 2 vols. Wellington, 1940
Encyclopaedia of New Zealand. 3 vols. Wellington, 1966
National Bibliography. Wellington, 1968
Alley, R., *New Zealand and the Pacific.* Boulder, 1984
Bedggood, D., *Rich and Poor in New Zealand.* Sydney, 1980
Bush, G., *Local Government and Politics in New Zealand.* Sydney, 1980
Easton, B., *Social Policy and the Welfare State in New Zealand.* Auckland, 1980
Grover, R. R., *New Zealand.* [Bibliography] Oxford and Santa Barbara, 1981
Hawke, G. R., *The Making of New Zealand: An Economic History.* CUP, 1985
Holcroft, M. H., *The Shaping of New Zealand.* Auckland, 1975
Morrell, W. P., and Hall, D. O. W., *A History of New Zealand Life.* Christchurch and London, 1957
Oliver, W. H. (ed.), *The Oxford History of New Zealand.* OUP, 1981
Robson, J. L. (ed.), *New Zealand: The Development of its Laws and Constitution.* 2nd ed. London, 1967
Sinclair, K., *A History of New Zealand.* Rev. ed. London, 1980
Thakur, R., *In Defence of New Zealand.* Wellington, 1984
Wards, I., *A Descriptive Atlas of New Zealand.* Wellington, Government Printer, 1976

NICARAGUA

Capital: Managua
Population: 3·5m. (1987)
GNP per capita: US$960 (1985)

República de Nicaragua

HISTORY. Active colonization of the Pacific coast was undertaken by Spaniards from Panama, beginning in 1523. After links with other Central American territories, and Mexico, Nicaragua became completely independent in 1838, but subject to a prolonged feud between the 'Liberals' of León and the 'Conservatives' of Granada. Mosquitia remained an autonomous kingdom on the Atlantic coast, under British protection until 1860.

On 5 Aug. 1914 the Bryan–Chamorro treaty between Nicaragua and the US was signed, under which the US in return for US$3m. acquired a permanent option for a canal route through Nicaragua and a 99-year option for a naval base in the Bay of Fonseca on the Pacific coast and Corn Islands on the Atlantic coast. It was ratified by Nicaragua on 7 April 1916 and by the US on 22 June 1916. US Marines finally left in 1933. The Bryan–Chamorro treaty was abrogated on 14 July 1970 and the Corn Islands handed back in 1971.

The 46-year political domination of Nicaragua by the Somoza family ended on 17 July 1979, after the 17 years long struggle by the Sandinista National Liberation Front flared into civil war. A Government Junta of National Reconstruction was established by the revolutionary government on 20 July 1979 and a 51-member Council of State later created; both were dissolved on 10 Jan. 1985 following new Presidential and legislative elections.

On 9 Jan. 1987 the President signed the new Constitution, but immediately reimposed a state of emergency, suspending many of the liberties granted under the Constitution.

AREA AND POPULATION. Nicaragua is bounded north by Honduras, east by the Caribbean, south by Costa Rica and west by the Pacific. Area 127,849 sq. km (49,363 sq. miles) or 118,558 sq. km (45,775 sq. miles) if the lakes are excluded. The coastline runs 540 km on the Atlantic and 350 km on the Pacific. Population at the census of April 1971 was 1,877,972. Estimate (1987) 3·5m.

Nicaragua is the largest in area and most thinly populated of the Central American republics, 30 inhabitants per sq. km in 1987. In 1984, births, 139,800; marriages, 13,600; deaths, 30,700.

The people of the western half of the republic are principally of mixed Spanish and Indian extraction, some of pure Spanish descent and many Indians. The population of the eastern half is composed mainly of Mosquito and other Indians and Zambos, and Negroes from Jamaica and other islands of the Caribbean. The main ethnic groups in 1980 were: Mestizo, 69%; white, 14%; black, 8%; amerindian, 4%.

The areas, estimated populations (1985) and capitals of the 6 regions and 3 special zones are as follows:

Region	Capital	Sq. km	1985	Special Zone	Capital	Sq. km	1985
1	Estelí	7,598	334,717	Zelaya Norte	Rosita	59,094	325,454
2	León	9,896	545,321	Zelaya Sur	Bluefields	¹	¹
3	Managua	3,597	903,998	Rio San Juan	San Carlos	7,448	34,330
4	Jinotepe	4,726	514,113				
5	Juigalpa	9,929	209,218	¹ Included in Zelaya Norte.			
6	Matagalpa	16,370	406,913				

The capital is Managua, situated on the lake of the same name, 180 ft above sea level, with (1985) 682,111 inhabitants. Other cities: León, 100,982; Granada, 88,636; Masaya, 74,946; Chinandega, 67,792; Matagalpa, 36,983; Esteli, 30,635; Tipitapa, 30,078; Chichigalpa, 28,889; Juigalpa, 25,625; Corinto, 24,250; Jinotepe, 23,538.

CLIMATE. The climate is tropical, with a wet season from May to Jan. Temperatures vary with altitude. Managua. Jan. 79°F (26°C), July 86°F (30°C). Annual rainfall 45″ (1,140 mm).

CONSTITUTION AND GOVERNMENT. The National Assembly drafted and approved on 19 Nov. 1986 the new Constitution which was promulgated on 9 Jan. 1987. It provided for a unicameral National Assembly comprising 90 members directly elected by proportional representation, together with unsuccessful presidential election candidates obtaining a minimum level of votes. The President and Vice-President are directly elected for a 6-year term commencing on the 10 Jan. following their date of election.

Under Article 185 of the Constitution, the President is empowered to declare a state of emergency and suspend certain of the civil rights provisions enshrined therein; this was done by the President immediately upon the promulgation of the Constitution.

President: Daniel Ortega Saavedra (elected 4 Nov. 1984, took office 10 Jan. 1985).

Vice-President: Sergio Ramírez Mercado.

The Council of Ministers in Aug. 1987 was composed as follows:

Foreign Affairs: Miguel d'Escoto Brockman. *Defence:* Gen. Humberto Ortega Saavedra. *Interior:* Cdr Tomas Borge Martinez. *Presidency:* René Núñez Téllez, Cdr Luis Carrión Cruz *(First Vice-Minister)*. *International Co-operation:* Cdr Henry Ruiz Hernández. *Agriculture:* Cdr Jaime Wheelock Román. *Industry:* Emilio Baltodano. *Foreign Trade:* Dr Alejandro Martínez Cuenca. *Domestic Trade:* Cdr Ramón Cabrales. *Transport:* Cdr William Ramírez Solórazano. *Finance:* William Hupper Argello. *Environment:* Miguel Ernesto Vigil Icaza. *Housing and Construction:* Cdr Mauricio Valenzuala. *Labour:* Benedicto Meneses Fonseca. *Health:* Dora Maria Téllez Argello. *Education:* Fernando Cardenal Martínez. *Justice:* Dr Rodrigo Reyes Portocarrero. *Culture:* Ernesto Cardenal Martínez.

National flag: Three horizontal stripes of blue, white, blue, with the national arms in the centre.

National anthem: Salve a ti Nicaragua (words by S. Ibarra Mayorga, 1937).

Local government. Since 26 July 1982 the country has been divided into 6 administrative regions and 3 special zones. Article 181 of the new Constitution provides for autonomous governments for Zelaya Norte and Zelaya Sur to offer self-government for the ethnic minorities who chiefly inhabit the Atlantic coast – Miskitos, Sumos, Ramos, creoles, garifunas (mixed black and amerindian) and mestizos.

DEFENCE. Conscription for 2 years was introduced in 1983 for men between 17 and 22 years.

Army. The Army is organized into 1 motorized infantry brigade, 5 armoured, 10 infantry, and 4 engineer battalions; 4 field artillery brigades and 1 anti-aircraft artillery group. Equipment includes 150 T-54/-55 main battle tanks. Strength (1988) 74,000 including reservists and Militia.

Navy. To picket the east and west coasts the Marina de Guerre Sandinista operates 8 *ex*-Soviet fast gunboats, 2 *ex*-North Korean fast torpedo boats, 2 *ex*-Soviet inshore minehunters, 4 *ex*-Soviet minesweeping boats, 4 coastguard cutters, 18 coastal patrol craft and 3 minor landing craft. Personnel in 1988 totalled 600 officers and men.

Air Force. Formed in June 1938 as the Nicaraguan Army Air Force, the Air Force has been semi-independent since 1947. Its combat units are reported to have 10 L-39 Albatross light jet attack/trainers, 4 T-33 armed jet trainers, and 3 T-28 armed piston-engined trainers but confirmation is not available. Other equipment includes 4 C-47s, 2 Spanish-built Aviocar and 2 Israeli-built Arava STOL transports and smaller communications aircraft and helicopters, including 10 Mi-8s, 2 Mi-2s and 5 Mi-24 gunships and 6 SF.260s for counter-insurgency duties.

INTERNATIONAL RELATIONS

Membership. Nicaragua is a member of the UN, OAS and the Central American Common Market.

ECONOMY

Budget. Revenue in 1984 was 11,460m. córdobas and expenditure 14,311m. córdobas.

Currency. The monetary unit is the new *córdoba* (C$), divided into 100 *centavos*. Bills form the greater part of the currency, in denominations from 1,000 córdobas to 1 córdoba. Coins are 5 and 1 *cordobas* and 50, 25, 10 and 5 *centavos*. March 1988, US$1 = 10 new *córdobas*; £1 = 17·05 new *córdobas*.

Banking. The Central Bank of Nicaragua came into operation on 1 Jan. 1961 as an autonomous bank of issue, absorbing the issue department of the National Bank. In July 1979 private financial banking was nationalized and branches of foreign banks were prohibited from receiving deposits.

Weights and Measures. Since 1893 the metric system of weights and measures has been recommended.

ENERGY AND NATURAL RESOURCES

Electricity. Installed capacity for electric energy was 398,000 kw. in 1986 and 1,200 kwh. was produced. Supply 120 volts; 60 Hz.

Minerals. Production of gold in 1980 was 67,000 troy oz.; of silver, 167,000 troy oz.; of copper, 3,000 tonnes. Large deposits of tungsten in Nueva Segovia were reported in 1961.

Agriculture. Agriculture is the principal source of national wealth, finding work for 65% of the labour force.

Of the total land area (about 36·5m. acres), about 17·5m. acres are under timber 900,000 acres are used for grazing and 2·1m. acres are arable. The unit of area used locally is the *manzana* (= 1·73 acres). Of the arable only 1·2m. acres are actively cultivated, 780,000 in annual crops such as cotton and rice and the remainder in perennial crops such as coffee and sugar-cane, or in two harvests a year in the cases of maize, sorghum and beans.

The products of the western half are varied, the most important being cotton, coffee, now under the aegis of the new *Instituto del Café*, sugar-cane, cocoa, maize, sesame and beans. Production (1986): Coffee, 44,000 tonnes; sugar-cane, 2,810,000 tonnes; cotton, 46,000 tonnes.

There were about 2·1m. head of cattle in 1986 and 750,000 pigs.

Forestry. Timber production has been declining, though the forests, which cover 10m. acres, contain mahogany and cedar, which were formerly largely exported, three varieties of rosewoods, guayacán (*lignum vitae*) and dye-woods. Production of sawn wood in 1983, 222,000 tonnes.

Fisheries. On the Atlantic coast fisheries are an important subsistence activity. Catch (1984) 4,300 tonnes.

INDUSTRY AND TRADE

Industry. Chief local industries are cane sugar, cooking oil, cigarettes, beer, leather products, plastics, textiles, chemical products, metal products, cement (100,000 tonnes in 1982), strong and soft drinks, soluble coffee, dairy products, meat, plywood. Production of oil products (1983) 489,000 tonnes.

Labour. In 1980 there were some 813,000 persons gainfully employed.

Commerce. The foreign trade of Nicaragua, in US$1m. (1984): Exports, 390m. consisting of cotton, coffee, chemical products, meat, sugar; imports, 750m.

Total trade between Nicaragua and UK (British Department of Trade returns, in £1,000 sterling):

	1983	1984	1985	1986	1987
Imports to UK	1,810	2,176	1,324	1,307	717
Exports and re-exports from UK	2,367	4,755	6,368	7,349	7,883

COMMUNICATIONS

Roads. In 1984, 4,000 km were paved, out of a total of 25,000 km. The whole 368·5 km of the Nicaraguan section of the Pan-American Highway is now paved. The all-weather Roosevelt Highway linking Managua with the river port Rama was completed in 1968, to provide the first overland link with the Atlantic coast. There are paved roads to San Juan del Sur, Puerto Sandino and Corinto. In 1981 there were 66,000 vehicles in use including 23,000 cars.

Railways. The Pacific Railroad of Nicaragua, owned and operated by the Government, has a total length of 334 km, all single-track, and connects Corinto, Chinandega, León, Managua, Masaya and Granada. Passengers carried (1986) 3·5m. and 2·5m. tonnes of freight.

Aviation. LANICA, the Nicaraguan airline has daily flights to Miami and 6 flights a week to Guatemala and to the inner cities of Bluefields, Puerto Cabezas and the mining towns of Siuna and Bonanza. PANAM and TACA (Transportes Aéreos Centroamericanos), COPA (Compañía Panameña de Aviacíon), have daily services to Panama, Mexico, the other Central American countries and USA. SAM (Servicio Aéreo de Medellín) has 3 flights a week to Nicaragua and Colombia.

Shipping. The Pacific ports are Corinto (the largest), San Juan del Sur and Puerto Sandino through which pass most of the external trade. The chief eastern ports are El Bluff (for Bluefields) and Puerto Cabezas. The merchant marine consists solely of the Mamenic Line with 8 vessels. In 1980, 471,000 tonnes of goods were loaded and 1·14m. tonnes unloaded at Nicaraguan ports.

Post and Broadcasting. In 1984 there were 51,237 telephones.

The Tropical Radio Telegraph Company maintains a powerful station at Managua, and branch stations at Bluefields and Puerto Cabezas. The Government operates the National Radio with 47 broadcasting stations: there are 31 commercial stations and some 70 others. Number of wireless sets in 1984 was 200,000 and television sets 127,000. There are 2 television stations at Managua.

Cinemas. Cinemas numbered over 100 in 1977 and seated over 60,000.

Newspapers. In 1984 there were 3 daily newspapers (2 in Managua and 1 in León), with a total circulation of about 105,000.

JUSTICE, RELIGION, EDUCATION AND WELFARE

Justice. The judicial power is vested in a Supreme Court of Justice at Managua, 5 chambers of second instance (León, Masaya, Granada, Matagalpa and Bluefields) and 153 judges of inferior tribunals.

Religion. The prevailing form of religion is Roman Catholic, but religious liberty is guaranteed by the Constitution. The republic constitutes 1 archbishopric (seat of Managua) and 7 bishoprics (León, Granada, Estelí, Matagalpa, Juigalpa, Masaya and Puerto Cabezas). Protestants, established principally on the Atlantic coast, numbered 54,100 in 1966.

Education. There were, in 1983, 4,976 primary schools, with a total of 534,996 pupils and 14,105 teachers; and 323 secondary schools, with 151,012 pupils. It was claimed that the illiteracy rate was 12% in 1983. In 1977 there were 6 universities and technical colleges with 1,204 professors and 23,171 students.

Health. In 1984 there were 2,172 doctors, 222 dentists, 5,649 nursing personnel and 49 hospitals with 5,045 beds.

DIPLOMATIC REPRESENTATIVES

Of Nicaragua in Great Britain (8 Gloucester Rd., London, SW7 4PP)
Ambassador: Francisco d'Escoto.

Of Great Britain in Nicaragua
Ambassador and Consul-General: M. F. Daly (resides in San José).

Of Nicaragua in the USA (1627 New Hampshire Ave., NW, Washington, D.C., 20009)
Ambassador: Dr Carlos Tunnermann.

Of the USA in Nicaragua (Km. 4½ Carretera Sur., Managua)
Ambassador: (Vacant).

Of Nicaragua to the United Nations
Ambassador: Nora Astorga-Gadea.

Books of Reference

Dirección General Estadística y Censos, *Boletín de Estadística* (irregular intervals); and *Indicadores Economicos*.

Black, G., *Triumph of the People: The Sandinista Revolution in Nicaragua.* London, 1981

Boletín de la Superintendencia de Bancos. Banco Central, Managua

Booth, J. A., *The End of the Beginning: The Nicaraguan Revolution.* Boulder, 1982

Christian, S., *Nicaragua: Revolution in the Family.* New York, 1985

McGinnis, J., *Solidarity with the People of Nicaragua.* New York, 1985

Rosset, P., and Vandermeer, J., (eds.) *The Nicaragua Reader: Documents of a Revolution under Fire.* New York, 1984

Walker, T. W., *Nicaragua: The Land of Sandino.* Boulder, 1982.—*Nicaragua: The First Five Years.* New York, 1985

Weber, H., *Nicaragua: The Sandinista Revolution.* London and New York, 1981

Woodward, R. L., *Nicaragua.* [Bibliography] Oxford and Santa Barbara, 1983

National Library: Biblioteca Nacional, Managua, D.N.

NIGER

République du Niger

Capital: Niamey
Population: 6·6m. (1987)
GNP per capita: US$240 (1985)

HISTORY. Niger was occupied by France between 1883 and 1899, and constituted a military territory in 1901, which became a part of French West Africa in 1904. It became an autonomous republic within the French Community on 18 Dec. 1958 and achieved full independence on 3 Aug. 1960.

On 15 April 1974 the first President, Hamani Diori, was overthrown in a military *coup* led by Lieut.-Col. Seyni Kountché, who suspended the constitution, dissolved the National Assembly and banned political groups.

AREA AND POPULATION. Niger is bounded north by Algeria and Libya, east by Chad, south by Nigeria, south-west by Benin and Burkina Faso, and west by Mali. Area, 1,186,408 sq. km (458,075 sq. miles), with a population at the 1977 census of 5,098,657. Estimate (1987) 6,608,000. The major towns (populations 1983) are: Niamey, the capital (399,100 inhabitants), Zinder (82,800), Maradi (65,100), Tahoua (41,900), Agadèz (27,000). Arlit (28,000), Akouta (26,000). In 1985, 16% of the population was urban, and 47% were under 15 years. The population is composed chiefly of Hausa (54%), Songhai and Djerma (23%), Fulani (10%), Beriberi-Manga (9%) and Tuareg (3%).

The official language is French but Hausa is understood by 85% of the population.

CLIMATE. Precipitation determines the geographical division into a southern zone of agriculture, a central zone of pasturage and a desert-like northern zone. The country lacks water, with the exception of the south-western districts, which are watered by the Niger and its tributaries, and the southern zone, where there are a number of wells. Niamey, 95°F (35°C). Annual rainfall varies from 22" (560 mm) in the south to 7" (180 mm) in the Sahara zone.

CONSTITUTION AND GOVERNMENT. The country is administered by a Supreme Military Council of 12 officers led by the President, who appoints a Council of Ministers to assist him. A system of elected Development Councils at all levels has been created, culminating in a 150-member National Development Council with limited legislative powers charged with drafting a new constitution.

The Council of Ministers, in Oct. 1987, comprised:

Head of State, President of SMC, Defence and Interior: Col. Ali Seybou.
Prime Minister: Hamid Algabid.
Foreign Affairs and Co-operation: Mahamane Sani Bako. *Finance:* Boukari Adji. *Planning:* Almoustapha Somaila. *Commerce, Industry and Transport:* Madou Mahamadou. *Culture and Communication:* Daouda Diallo. *Civil Service and Labour:* Lieut-Col. Mamadou Beidari. *Mines and Energy:* Amadou Noudou. *Agriculture and Environment:* Allele Habibou. *Animal and Water Resources:* Salha Haladou. *National Education and Professional Training:* Amadou Madougou. *Higher Education, Research and Technology:* Illa Maikassoua. *Public Works and Housing:* Abdou Aboubacar. *Youth and Sport:* Maj. Toumba Boubacar. *Public Health and Social Affairs:* Maj. Mainassara Bare. *Justice:* Capt. Malam Oubandawaki. *Ministers-Delegate:* Amadou Fity Maiga *(Interior)*, Maina Moussa Boukar *(Public Establishments, State Enterprises and Companies).* *Secretaries of State:* Amadou Mamadou *(Agriculture and Environment)*, Brigi Rafini *(Interior).*

National flag: Three horizontal strips of orange, white and green, with an orange disc in the middle of the white strip.

Local government: Niger is divided into 7 *départements* (Agadez, Diffa, Dosso, Maradi, Niamey, Tahoua and Zinder), each under a prefect, sub-divided into 38 *arrondissements*, each under a sub-prefect, and some 150 communes.

DEFENCE. Selective military service for 2 years operates.

Army. The Army consists of 2 armoured reconnaissance squadrons, 6 infantry, 1 engineer, 1 parachute and 1 support company. Equipment includes 10 M-8, 18 AML-90 and 18 AML-60-7 armoured cars. Strength (1988) 3,150. There are additional paramilitary forces of some 2,550 men.

Air Force. The Air Force had (1988) 140 officers and men, 2 C-130H and 3 Noratlas transports, 1 Boeing 737 VIP transport, 2 Cessna Skymasters and 3 Do 28D Skyservants and 1 Do 228 for communications duties.

INTERNATIONAL RELATIONS

Membership. Niger is a member of UN, OAU and is an ACP state of the EEC.

ECONOMY

Planning. The 10-year plan (1981–90) provided for an investment of 520,000m. francs CFA in the first phase (1981–85) with a prime aim of obtaining self-sufficiency in food and developing the mining sector.

Budget. The ordinary budget for 1986–87 balanced at 105,575m. francs CFA.

Currency. The unit of currency is the *franc CFA*, with a parity rate of 50 francs CFA to 1 French franc.

Banking. The *Banque Centrale des États de l'Afrique de l'Ouest* is the bank of issue, and there are 9 commercial banks in Niamey.

ENERGY AND NATURAL RESOURCES

Electricity. Production (1986) amounted to 265m. kwh. Supply 220 volts; 50 Hz.

Oil. Deposits in the Lake Chad area, located in 1978, are to be exploited.

Minerals. Large uranium deposits are mined at Arlit and Akouta, in the Aïr mountains of northern Niger, with French and Japanese assistance. Concentrate production (1983) 3,416 tonnes. Phosphates are mined in the Niger valley, and coal reserves are being exploited by open-cast mining. Salt and natron are produced at Manga and Agadez, tin ore in Aïr, iron ore at Say.

Agriculture. The chief foodcrops in 1986 (in 1,000 tonnes) were: Millet, 1,383; pulses, 313; sorghum, 360; cassava, 200; sugar-cane, 110; onions, 120; rice, 75. The main cash crops are ground-nuts (42), cotton and gum arabic.

Livestock (1986): Cattle, 3·3m.; horses, 292,000; asses, 507,000; sheep, 3·5m.; goats, 7·5m.; camels, 415,000; chickens, 14m.

Forestry. Production (1984) 3·81m. cu. metres.

Fisheries. Catch (1983) 6,840 tonnes.

INDUSTRY AND TRADE

Industry. Some small manufacturing industries, mainly in Niamey, produce textiles, food products, furniture and chemicals.

Trade Unions. The sole national body is the *Union Nationale des Travailleurs du Niger,* which has 15,000 members in 31 unions.

Commerce. Imports in 1983 were valued at 123,288m. francs CFA and exports at 113,896m. francs CFA. In 1981, France provided 36% of imports and took 36% of the exports. Main exports were uranium (79%) and livestock, 12%.

Total trade between Niger and UK (British Department of Trade returns, in £1,000 sterling):

	1983	1984	1985	1986	1987
Imports to UK	6,854	391	399	848	10,556
Exports and re-exports from UK	9,650	10,682	12,076	10,367	7,026

COMMUNICATIONS

Roads. In 1981 there were 8,547 km of roads. Niamey and Zinder are the termini of two trans-Sahara motor routes; the Hoggar–Aïr–Zinder road extends to Kano and the Tanezrouft-Gao-Niamey road to Benin. A 648-km 'uranium road' runs from Arlit to Tahoua. There were (1984), 23,100 private cars and 5,074 goods vehicles.

Aviation. There are international airports at Niamey, Zinder and Maradi. Air Niger operates domestic services to over 20 other public airports.

Shipping. Sea-going vessels can reach Niamey (300 km. inside the country) between Sept. and March.

Post and Broadcasting. There were (1981) 9,320 telephones. In 1984 there were 160,000 radio and 11,000 television receivers.

Cinemas. In 1970 there were 4 cinemas with a seating capacity of 3,800.

Newspapers. In 1984 there was 1 daily newspaper, *Le Sahel*, with a circulation of 5,000.

JUSTICE, RELIGION, EDUCATION AND WELFARE

Justice. There are Magistrates' and Assize Courts at Niamey, Zinder and Maradi, and justices of the peace in smaller centres. The Court of Appeal is at Niamey.

Religion. In 1980, 97% of the population was Moslem and the remainder mainly followed animist beliefs. There were about 30,000 Christians.

Education. There were, in 1980–81, 228,855 pupils and 5,518 teachers in 1,664 primary schools, 45,846 (1981) and 1,371 teachers in secondary schools, and 2,351 students and 120 teachers in the technical and teacher-training colleges. In 1982 there were 1,825 students and 273 teaching staff at the University of Niamey.

Health. In 1982 there were 2 hospitals, 36 medical centres and 116 dispensaries. In 1980 there were 136 doctors, and (in 1978) 10 dentists, 12 pharmacists, 88 midwives and 1,080 nursing personnel.

DIPLOMATIC REPRESENTATIVES

Of Niger in Great Britain
Ambassador: Abdou Garba (resides in Paris).

Of Great Britain in Niger
Ambassador and Consul-General: V. E. Sutherland (resides in Abidjan).

Of Niger in the USA (2204 R. St., NW, Washington, D.C., 20008)
Ambassador: Joseph Diatta.

Of the USA in Niger (PO Box 11201, Niamey)
Ambassador: Richard W. Bogosian.

Of Niger to the United Nations
Ambassador: Joseph Diatta.

Books of Reference

Bonardi, P., *La République du Niger*. Paris, 1960
Fugelstad, F., *A History of Niger, 1850–1960*. OUP, 1984
Séré de Rivières, E., *Histoire du Niger*. Paris, 1965

NIGERIA

Capital: Lagos
Population: 105m. (1988)
GNP per capita: US$730 (1986)

Federal Republic of Nigeria

HISTORY. The Federal Republic comprises a number of areas formerly under separate administrations. Lagos, ceded in Aug. 1861 by King Dosunmu, was placed under the Governor of Sierra Leone in 1866. In 1874 it was detached, together with Gold Coast Colony, and formed part of the latter until Jan. 1886, when a separate 'colony and protectorate of Lagos' was constituted. Meanwhile the United African Company had established British interests in the Niger valley, and in July 1886 the company obtained a charter under the name of the Royal Niger Company. This company surrendered its charter to the Crown on 31 Dec. 1899, and on 1 Jan. 1900 the greater part of its territories was formed into the protectorate of Northern Nigeria. Along the coast the Oil Rivers protectorate had been declared in June 1885. This was enlarged and renamed the Niger Coast protectorate in 1893; and on 1 Jan. 1900, on its absorbing the remainder of the territories of the Royal Niger Company, it became the protectorate of Southern Nigeria. In Feb. 1906 Lagos and Southern Nigeria were united into the 'colony and protectorate of Southern Nigeria', and on 1 Jan. 1914 the latter was amalgamated with the protectorate of Northern Nigeria to form the 'colony and protectorate of Nigeria', under a Governor. On 1 Oct. 1954 Nigeria became a federation under a Governor-General. In 1967, 12 states were created and in 1976 this was increased to 19.

On 1 Oct. 1960 Nigeria became sovereign and independent and a member of the Commonwealth and on 1 Oct. 1963 Nigeria became a republic.

For the history of Nigeria from 1961 to 1978, see THE STATESMAN'S YEAR-BOOK, 1979–80, pp. 923-924.

AREA AND POPULATION. Nigeria is bounded north by Niger, east by Chad and Cameroon, south by the Gulf of Guinea and west by Benin. It has an area of 356,669 sq. miles (923,773 sq. km). Census population, Nov. 1963, 55,670,052. The results of the 1973 census have been officially repudiated. There is considerable uncertainty over the total population, but one estimate based on electoral registration in 1978 is 95m. Estimate (1988) 105m.

There are 19 states and a Federal Capital Territory (Abuja):

States	Area (in sq. km)	Population 1984	States	Area (in sq. km)	Population 1984
Anambra	17,675	6,029,500	Kwara	66,869	2,884,400
Bauchi	64,605	4,075,800	Lagos	3,345	2,825,200
Bendel	35,500	4,125,500	Niger	65,037	1,961,800
Benue	45,174	4,068,600	Ogun	16,762	2,596,000
Borno	116,400	5,025,000	Ondo	20,959	4,617,200
Cross River	27,237	5,830,800	Oyo	37,705	8,732,300
Gongola	91,390	4,367,600	Plateau	58,030	3,397,500
Imo	11,850	6,157,000	Rivers	21,850	2,883,300
Kaduna	70,245	6,868,800	Sokoto	102,535	7,608,900
Kano	43,285	9,681,000			

The populations (1983) of the largest towns were as follows:

Lagos	1,097,000	Ilesha	273,400	Aba	216,000
Ibadan	1,060,000	Onitsha	268,700	Ife	214,500
Ogbomosho	527,400	Ado-Ekiti	265,800	Ila	189,700
Kano	487,100	Iwo	261,600	Oyo	185,300
Oshogbo	344,500	Kaduna	247,100	Ikerre-Ekiti	176,800
Ilorin	343,900	Mushin	240,700	Benin City	165,900
Abeokuta	308,800	Maiduguri	230,900	Iseyin	157,000
Port Harcourt	296,200	Enugu	228,400	Katsina	149,300
Zaria	274,000	Ede	221,900	Jos	149,000

Sokoto	148,000	Ondo	122,600	Shomolu	106,800
Ilobu	143,800	Akure	117,300	Oka-Akoko	103,500
Offa	142,300	Gusau	114,100	Ikare	101,700
Owo	132,600	Ijebu-Ode	113,100	Sapele	100,600
Calabar	126,000	Effon-Alaiye	110,600	Minna	98,900
Shaki	125,800	Kumo	107,000	Warri	91,100

It was announced in Feb. 1976 that the federal capital would be moved from Lagos to the Abuja area and, in Sept. 1982, Abuja was established as the future capital.

CLIMATE. Lying wholly within the tropics, temperatures everywhere are high. Rainfall varies very much, but decreases from the coast to the interior. The main rains occur from April to Oct. Lagos. Jan. 81°F (27·2°C), July 78°F (25·6°C). Annual rainfall 72″ (1,836 mm). Ibadan. Jan. 80°F (26·7°C), July 76°F (24·4°C). Annual rainfall 45″ (1,120 mm). Kano. Jan. 70°F (21·1°C), July 79°F (26·1°C). Annual rainfall 35″ (869 mm). Port Harcourt. Jan. 79°F (26·1°C), July 77°F (25°C). Annual rainfall 100″ (2,497 mm).

CONSTITUTION AND GOVERNMENT. Under the Constitution drafted and ratified in 1977–78, Nigeria is a sovereign, federal republic comprising 19 states and a federal capital district. Elections were held in Aug. 1983 and President Shagari was returned with 48% of the vote but in Dec. 1983 the military again took over control in a *coup* and in Jan. 1984 a Supreme Military Council under Maj.-Gen. Mohammed Buhari took office. In Aug. 1985 there was a *coup* following which a 29-member Armed Forces Ruling Council was sworn in on 30 Aug. 1985. Return to civilian rule is envisaged for 1992.

Head of State, Chairman of AFRC and C.-in-C. of the Armed Forces: Maj.-Gen. Ibrahim Babangida.

On 12 Sept. 1985 the AFRC appointed a National Council of Ministers comprising the following in Dec. 1987:

Agriculture, Water Resources and Rural Development: Maj.-Gen. Gado Nasko . *Communications:* Col. David Mark. *Defence:* Maj.-Gen. Domkat Yah Bali. *Education:* Jibril Aminu. *External Affairs:* Maj.-Gen. Ike Nwachukwa. *Federal Capital Territory:* Air Cmdre. Hamza Abdullah. *Finance:* Chu Okongwu. *Health:* Koye Ransome-Kuti. *Industry:* Lieut.-Gen. A. I. Akinrinade. *Information:* Prince Tony Momoh. *Internal Affairs:* Lieut.-Col. J. N. Shagaya. *Justice:* Prince Bola Ajibola. *Mines, Power and Steel:* Buna Sherrif Musa. *National Planning:* Dr Kalu I. Kalu. *Petroleum Resources:* Rilwanu Lukman. *Science and Technology:* Emmanuel Emovon. *Social Development, Youth and Culture:* Air Cmdre. Bayo Lawal. *Special Duties:* Air Vice-Marshal Aboyi I. Shekari. *Trade:* Samaila Mamman. *Transport:* Dr Kalu I. Kalu. *Works and Housing:* Abubakar Umar. *Aviation:* Air Vice-Marshal Tony Okper.

National flag: Three vertical strips of green, white, green.

Local Government: Each of the 19 states is administered by a military governor, who appoints and presides over a State Executive Council.

DEFENCE

Army. The Army consists of 1 armoured division, 2 mechanized divisions and 1 airborne and amphibious forces division, each with supporting artillery and engineer and reconnaissance units. Equipment includes 60 T-55 and 72 Vickers Mk 3 main battle tanks. Strength (1988) 80,000 men.

Navy. The Nigerian Navy was established in 1958. It comprises the frigates *Aradu* (completed in the Federal Republic of Germany in 1982) and *Obuma* (*ex*-Nigeria) acting as training ship (completed in the Netherlands in 1965), 4 corvettes built in Britain in 1970–72 (*Dorina* and *Otobo*), and 1975–80 (*Erinmi* and *Enyimiri*), 6 fast missile-armed attack vedettes (3 built in France and 3 in FR Germany), 2 mine-hunters, 9 patrol craft, 16 coastal patrol boats, 2 tank landing ships, 2 utility landing craft, 1 survey ship, 1 training ship, 57 launches and 8 tugs.

The new construction programme provided for the delivery of 30 fast light craft ordered from Great Britain (6), United States (6), France (6) and Netherlands (12), this urgent expansion of armed light forces being necessitated by the continuing maritime lawlessness apparently endemic off the Nigerian coast. There are also over 80 small patrol launches operated by the Nigerian Police.

The Navy has a small aviation component, formed recently, equipped with 3 Lynx anti-submarine helicopters.

Naval personnel in 1988 totalled 550 officers and 4,500 ratings.

Air Force. The Nigerian Air Force was established in Jan. 1964. Pilots were trained initially in Canada, India and Ethiopia. The Air Force was built up subsequently with the aid of a Federal Republic of Germany mission; much first-line equipment has since been received from the Soviet Union. It has 18 MiG-21 supersonic jet-fighters, 16 Jaguar attack aircraft and MiG-21U fighter-trainers, and 22 Alpha Jet light attack/trainers. About 20 BO 105 twin-turbine helicopters have been acquired from the Federal Republic of Germany for search and rescue, while 2 F.27MPAs were recently delivered for maritime patrol. Transport units operate 9 C-130H-30 and C-130H Hercules 4-turboprop heavy transports, 5 twin-turboprop Aeritalia G222s, 3 DO 228s, a Boeing 727 and a Gulfstream II for VIP use, 16 Dornier 128-6 twin-turboprop and 20 DO 28D twin-piston utility aircraft, 2 Navajos and a Navajo Chieftain. Training types include 25 Bulldog primary trainers and about 12 MB 339 jets for instrument training, transport and ambulance duties. Fourteen medium-lift Aérospatiale Puma helicopters are also in service. Personnel (1988) total about 9,500.

INTERNATIONAL RELATIONS

Membership. Nigeria is a member of UN, the Commonwealth, ECOWAS, OAU, OPEC and is an ACP state of EEC.

ECONOMY

Planning. The fourth plan (1981–85) was launched in 1981 but was rescheduled because of lower oil prices.

Budget. The 1987–88 budget provided for expenditure (capital and recurrent) of ₦24,300m. and revenue of ₦15,700m.

Currency. Since 1 Jan. 1973 a decimal currency has been issued by the Central Bank of Nigeria, consisting of *Naira* (₦) and divided into 100 *kobo* (k). Notes in circulation ₦20, ₦10, ₦5, ₦1, 50k. Coins, 25k, 10k, 5k, 1k, ½k.

In March 1988, £1 = ₦7·77; US$1 = ₦4·23. The currency is unconvertible and subject to stringent exchange controls.

Banking. There are 16 commercial banks: First Bank of Nigeria, Union Bank, United Bank for Africa, International Bank for West Africa, Nigeria Arab Bank, Allied Bank of Nigeria, Savannah Bank of Nigeria, National Bank of Nigeria, African Continental Bank, Bank of the North New Nigeria Bank, Habib Bank Nigeria, Societe Generale Bank, Progress Bank Nigeria, Commercial Credit and Commercial International (Nigeria Limited).

Weights and Measures. The metric system is in force.

ENERGY AND NATURAL RESOURCES

Electricity. The National Electric Power Authority generated 10,730m. kwh. in 1986. Supply 230 volts; 50 Hz.

Oil. There are refineries at Port Harcourt, Warri and at Kaduna. Oil represents 95% of exports. Production, 1987, 64m. tonnes.

Gas. Natural gas is being used at electric power stations at Afam and Ughelli. Reserves: 4,000,000m. cu.metres.

Minerals. Production: Tin, 1980, 2,527 tonnes; columbite, 1977 (the world's largest producer), 800 tonnes; coal (1981) 114,875 tonnes. There are large deposits of iron ore, coal (reserves estimate 245m. tonnes), lead and zinc. There are small quantities of gold and uranium.

Agriculture. Main food crops are millet and sorghum in the north, plantains and oil palms in the south, and maize, yams, cassava and rice in much of the country, the north being, however, the main food producing area. 1985 production figures (in 1,000 tonnes) are: Millet, 3,600; sorghum, 3,500; plantains, 1,350; maize, 3; yams, 18,300; cassava, 13,000; rice, 1,430.

In the 1970s food imports rose rapidly, especially of rice, but import curbs have cut this since 1982 and rice production has risen rapidly. In 1985–86 imports of rice, maize and vegetable oil were banned to encourage higher local production.

Production of crops for export or local industry has greatly declined since the early 1970s. Groundnut production in 1985 was 600,000 tonnes, but very little was sold to the government marketing board which until 1986 bought supplies for export and industry. Cotton lint production (1985) 17,000 tonnes. Cocoa production has declined in recent years, to 112,000 tonnes in 1985; palm kernel was 370,000 tonnes and palm oil, 770,000 tonnes.

In 1986 the marketing boards were abolished. State governments and private and co-operative buyers are all now able to buy any crops, all monopolies being ended.

Livestock (1986). There were 12,169,000 cattle, 13·16m. sheep, 26,328,000 goats, 1,351,000 pigs and 169m. poultry.

Forestry. There are plywood factories at Epe, Sapele and Calabar, and numerous saw-mills. The most important timber species include mahogany, iroko, obeche, abwa, ebony and camwood.

Fisheries. The total catch (1984) was 373,800 tonnes.

INDUSTRY AND TRADE

Industry. There were more than 2,000 industrial establishments in 1982. Timber and hides and skins are major export commodities. Industrial products include soap, cigarettes, beer, margarine, groundnut oil, meat and cake, concentrated fruit juices, soft drinks, canned food, metal containers, ply-wood, textiles, ceramic products and cement (3m. tonnes, 1985). Of growing importance is the local assembly of motor vehicles, bicycles, radio equipment, electrical goods and sewing machines. In 1982, the Delta Steel Plant opened at Ovwian—Aladja.

Under a decree on indigenization Nigerians must have a minimum of 40% shareholding in all foreign enterprises.

Trade Unions. All trade unions were dissolved in 1976 and 42 new unions, each organized around a particular occupation, have since been created.

Commerce. There is a great deal of internal commerce in local foodstuffs and imported goods moving by rail, lorry and pack animals overland, and by launches, rafts and canoes along an extensive and complex network of inland waterways.

Total trade in ₦m. for 4 years:

	1983	1984	1985	1986
Imports (c.i.f.)	6,588	7,200	8,300	6,700
Exports and re-exports (f.o.b.)	7,723	8,700	12,600	6,800

Total trade between Nigeria and UK (according to British Department of Trade returns, in £1,000 sterling):

	1983	1984	1985	1986	1987
Imports to UK	387,975	375,796	660,410	329,036	159,386
Exports and re-exports from UK	798,276	768,449	960,703	566,176	481,568

Tourism. There were 340,000 foreign visitors in 1985.

COMMUNICATIONS

Roads (1980). There were 108,000 km of maintained roads and 633,268 vehicles were registered.

Railways. There are 3,505 route-km of line 1,067 mm gauge, which in 1984 ran 1,246m. tonne-km and carried 15·3m. passengers.

Aviation. There is an extensive system of internal and international air routes, serving Europe, USA, Middle East and South and West Africa. Regular services are operated by Nigerian Airways (WAAC), British Caledonian, UTA, KLM, SABENA, Swissair, PANAM and other lines. In 1981, 2·3m. passengers were carried on domestic and international routes.

Shipping. The principal ports are Lagos, Port Harcourt, Warri and Calabar.

Post and Broadcasting. Postal facilities are provided at 1,667 offices and agencies; telegraph, money order and savings bank services are provided at 280 of these. Most internal letter mail is carried by air at normal postage rates. External telegraph services are owned and operated by Nigerian External Telecommunications, Ltd, at Lagos, from which telegraphic communication is maintained with all parts of the world. There were 708,390 telephones in use in 1982, of which 249,150 were in Lagos and 33,138 in Ibadan. There is also a telex service.

Federal and some state governments have established commercial corporations for sound and television broadcasting, which are widely used in schools. In 1985 there were 15·7m. radio and 500,000 television receivers.

Cinemas (1974). There were 120 cinemas, with a seating capacity of 60,000. Mobile cinemas are used by the Federal and States Information Services.

Newspapers. In 1984 there were 18 daily and 30 weekly newspapers. The aggregate circulation is about 1m., of which the *Daily Times* (Lagos) has about 400,000. (Another 2 dailies were published in Lagos, 4 in Ikeja, 3 in Enugu, and 4 in Ibadan.)

JUSTICE, RELIGION, EDUCATION AND WELFARE

Justice. The highest court is the Federal Supreme Court, which consists of the Chief Justice of the Republic, and up to 15 Justices appointed by AFRC. It has original jurisdiction in any dispute between the Federal Republic and any State or between States; and to hear and determine appeals from the Federal Court of Appeal, which acts as an intermediate appellate Court to consider appeals from the High Court.

High Courts, presided over by a Chief Justice, are established in each state. All judges are appointed by the AFRC. Magistrates' courts are established throughout the Republic, and customary law courts in southern Nigeria. In each of the northern States of Nigeria there are the Sharia Court of Appeal and the Court of Resolution. Moslem Law has been codified in a Penal Code and is applied through Alkali courts.

Religion. Moslems, 48%; Christians, 34% (17% Protestants and 17% Roman Catholic); others, 18%. Northern Nigeria is mainly Moslem; Southern Nigeria is predominantly Christian and Western Nigeria is evenly divided between Christians, Moslems and animists.

Education. In 1976 primary education became free throughout the country. Literacy rate (1973) 25%.

In 1982–83 there were 15,021,100 primary school pupils, and 2,421,625 secondary grammar/commercial school pupils.

Teacher-training institutions totalled 157 in 1973, and in 1982–83 there were 309,442 students enrolled in Grade II teacher-training colleges and 36,772 in advanced teachers' colleges/colleges of education. There were also in 1982–83 86,290 students in secondary technical/vocational schools and 46,244 in polytechnics/colleges of technology.

There are 24 universities with 121,430 full-time students in 1984 in Nigeria, providing 3–5-year courses leading to the award of a first degree in various disciplines; these include 7 Federal Universities of Technology. There are also opportunities for taking higher degrees. Free tuition was provided from 1977.

Health. Most tropical diseases are endemic to Nigeria. Blindness, yaws, leprosy, sleeping sickness, worm infections, malaria are major health problems which, however, are yielding to remedial and preventative measures. In co-operation with the World Health Organization river blindness and malaria are being tackled on a large scale, while annual campaigns are undertaken against the danger of smallpox epidemics. Dispensaries and travelling dispensaries are found in most parts of the country.

In 1980 there were 8,000 doctors and 75,000 hospital beds.

DIPLOMATIC REPRESENTATIVES

Of Nigeria in Great Britain (9 Northumberland Ave., London, WC2 5BX)
High Commissioner: George Dove-Edwin (accredited 29 May 1986).

Of Great Britain in Nigeria (11 Eleke Cres., Victoria Island, Lagos)
High Commissioner: Sir Martin Ewans, KCMG.

Of Nigeria in the USA (2201 M. St., NW, Washington, D.C., 20037)
Ambassador: Hamzat Ahmadu.

Of the USA in Nigeria (2 Eleke Cres., Lagos)
Ambassador: Princeton N. Lyman.

Of Nigeria to the United Nations
Ambassador: Maj.-Gen. Joseph N. Garba.

Books of Reference

Nigeria Digest of Statistics. Lagos, 1951 ff. (quarterly)
Annual Abstract of Statistics. Federal Office of Statistics. Lagos, 1960 ff.
Nigeria Trade Journal. Federal Ministry of Commerce and Industries (quarterly)
Achebe, C., *The Trouble with Nigeria.* London, 1984
Adamolekun, L., *Politics and Administration in Nigeria.* Ibadan, 1986
Barbour, K. M. (ed.), *Nigeria in Maps.* London, 1982
Burns, A., *History of Nigeria.* 8th ed. London, 1978
Crowder, M., and Abdullahi, G., *Nigeria, an Introduction to its History.* London, 1979
Ikoku, S. G., *Nigeria's Fourth Coup: Options for Modern Statehood.* Enugu, 1984
Kirk-Greene, A., and Rimmer, D., *Nigeria since 1970.* London, 1981
Nwabueze, B. O., *The Presidential Constitution of Nigeria.* Lagos and London, 1982
Oyediran, O., *Nigerian Government and Politics under Military Rule, 1966–1979.* New York, 1980
Oyovbaine, S.E., *Federalism in Nigeria: A Study in the Development of the Nigerian State.* London, 1985
Shaw, T. M., and Aluko, O., *Nigerian Foreign Policy: Alternative Perceptions and Projections.* London, 1984
Simmons, M., and Obe, O. A., *Nigerian Handbook 1982–83.* London, 1982
Tijjani, A. and Williams, D., (eds.) *Shehu Shagari: My Vision of Nigeria.* London, 1981
Van Apeldoorn, G. J., *Perspectives on Drought and Famine in Nigeria.* London, 1981
Williams, D., *President and Power in Nigeria.* London, 1982
Zartman, I. W., *The Political Economy of Nigeria.* New York, 1983

NORWAY

Capital: Oslo
Population: 4·2m. (1986)
GNP per capita: US$16,400 (1986)

Kongeriket Norge

HISTORY. By the Treaty of 14 Jan. 1814 Norway was ceded to the King of Sweden by the King of Denmark, but the Norwegian people declared themselves independent and elected Prince Christian Frederik of Denmark as their king. The foreign Powers refused to recognize this election, and on 14 Aug. a convention proclaimed the independence of Norway in a personal union with Sweden. This was followed on 4 Nov. by the election of Karl XIII (II) as King of Norway. Norway declared this union dissolved, 7 June 1905, and Sweden agreed to the repeal of the union on 26 Oct. 1905. The throne was offered to a prince of the reigning house of Sweden, who declined. After a plebiscite, Prince Carl of Denmark was formally elected King on 18 Nov. 1905, and took the name of Haakon VII.

Norwegian Sovereigns

Inge Baardssøn	1204	Erik of Pomerania	1389
Haakon Haakonssøn	1217	Kristofer af Bavaria	1442
Magnus Lagabøter	1263	Karl Knutssøn	1449
Eirik Magnussøn	1280	Same Sovereigns as in Denmark	1450–1814
Haakon V Magnussøn	1299	Christian Frederik	1814
Magnus Erikssøn	1319	Same Sovereigns as in Sweden	1814–1905
Haakon VI Magnussøn	1343	Haakon VII	1905
Olav Haakonssøn	1381	Olav V	1957
Margrete	1388		

AREA AND POPULATION. Norway is bounded north by the Arctic ocean, east by the USSR, Finland and Sweden, south by the Skagerrak Straits and west by the North Sea.

Fylker (counties)	Area (sq. km)	Census population 1 Nov. 1980	Population 1 Jan. 1987	Pop. per sq. km (total area) 1987
Oslo (City)	454·0	452,023	451,099	993·6
Akershus	4,916·5	369,193	399,443	81·3
Østfold	4,183·4	233,301	235,655	56·3
Hedmark	27,388·3	187,223	186,065	6·8
Oppland	25,259·7	180,765	181,436	7·2
Buskerud	14,927·3	214,571	221,182	14·8
Vestfold	2,215·9	186,691	192,823	87·0
Telemark	15,315·1	162,050	162,448	10·6
Aust-Agder	9,211·7	90,629	95,377	10·4
Vest-Agder	7,280·5	136,718	141,165	19·4
Rogaland	9,140·7	305,490	326,489	35·7
Hordaland	15,633·8	391,463	402,086	25·7
Sogn og Fjordane	18,633·5	105,924	105,862	5·7
Møre og Romsdal	15,104·2	236,062	237,279	15·7
Sør-Trøndelag	18,831·4	244,760	247,154	13·1
Nord-Trøndelag	22,463·4	125,835	126,549	5·6
Nordland	38,327·1	244,493	240,763	6·3
Troms	25,953·8	146,818	146,476	5·6
Finnmark	48,637·3	78,331	74,654	1·5
Mainland total	323,877·7 [1]	4,092,340	4,174,005	12·9

Svalbard and Jan Mayen have an area of 63,080 sq. km. Persons staying on Svalbard and Jan Mayen are registered as residents of their home Norwegian municipality.

[1] 125,049 sq. miles.

On 1 Nov. 1980, 2,874,990 persons lived in densely populated areas and 1,197,939 in sparsely populated areas.

Population of the principal towns at 1 Jan. 1987:

Oslo	451,099	Sandnes	41,938	Gjøvik	25,929
Bergen	208,809	Sandefjord	35,441	Halden	25,802
Trondheim	134,496	Ålesund	35,314	Moss	24,660
Stavanger	95,437	Bodø	34,962	Lillehammer	22,186
Kristiansand	63,293	Porsgrunn	31,289	Harstad	22,093
Drammen	51,324	Haugesund	26,878	Molde	21,625
Tromsø	48,829	Ringerike	26,776	Kongsberg	21,199
Skien	47,237	Fredrikstad	26,650	Steinkjer	20,393

Vital statistics for calendar years:

	Marriages	Divorces	Births	Still-born	Illegitimate [1]	Deaths
1983	20,803	7,668	49,937	303	9,616	42,224
1984	20,537	7,974	50,274	261	10,687	42,581
1985	20,221	8,090	51,134	279	13,203	44,372
1986 [2]	...	...	52,514	268	14,673	...

[1] Excluding still-born.   [2] Provisional.

CLIMATE. There is considerable variation in the climate because of the extent of latitude, the topography and the varying effectiveness of prevailing westerly winds and the Gulf Stream. Winters along the whole west coast are exceptionally mild but precipitation is considerable. Oslo. Jan. 25°F (–3·9°C), July 63°F (17°C). Annual rainfall 27" (683 mm). Bergen. Jan. 35°F (1·5°C), July 61°F (16·1°C). Annual rainfall 78·3" (1,958 mm). Trondheim. Jan. 26°F (–3·5°C), July 57°F (14°C). Annual rainfall 32·1" (870 mm).

REIGNING KING. Olav V, born 2 July 1903, married on 21 March 1929 to Princess Märtha of Sweden (born 28 March 1901, died 5 April 1954), daughter of the late Prince Carl (son of King Oscar II). He succeeded on the death of his father, King Haakon VII, on 21 Sept. 1957. *Offspring:* Princess Ragnhild Alexandra, born 9 June 1930 (married, 1953, Erling Lorentzen); Princess Astrid Maud Ingeborg, born 12 Feb. 1932 (married, 12 Jan. 1961, Hr. Johan Martin Ferner); Crown Prince Harald, born 21 Feb. 1937, married, 29 Aug. 1968, Sonja Haraldsen. *Offspring:* Princess Märtha Louise, born 22 Sept. 1971; Prince Haakon Magnus, born 20 July 1973.

CONSTITUTION AND GOVERNMENT. Norway is a constitutional and hereditary monarchy. The royal succession is in direct male line in the order of primogeniture. In default of male heirs the King may propose a successor to the Storting, but this assembly has the right to nominate another, if it does not agree with the proposal.

The Constitution, voted by the constituent assembly at Eidsvoll on 17 May 1814 and modified at various times, vests the legislative power of the realm in the Storting (Parliament). The royal veto may be exercised; but if the same Bill passes two Stortings formed by separate and subsequent elections it becomes the law of the land without the assent of the sovereign. The King has the command of the land, sea and air forces, and makes all appointments.

Since June 1938 all branches of the Government service, including the state church, are open to women.

National flag: Red with a blue white-bordered Scandinavian cross.

National anthem: Ja, vi elsker dette landet (words by B. Bjørnson, 1865; tune by R. Nordraak, 1865).

The Storting assembles every year. The meetings take place *suo jure,* and not by any writ from the King or the executive. They begin on the first weekday in Oct. each year, until June the following year. Every Norwegian subject of 18 years of age is entitled to vote, unless he is disqualified for a special cause. Women are, since 1913, entitled to vote under the same conditions as men. The mode of election is direct and the method of election is proportional. The country is divided into 19 districts, each electing from 4 to 15 representatives.

At the elections for the Storting held in 1985 the following parties were elected: Labour, 71; Conservative, 50; Centre Party, 12; Christian Democratic Party, 16; Socialist Left Party, 6; Party of Progress, 2.

The Storting, when assembled, divides itself by election into the *Lagting* and the *Odelsting*. The former is composed of one-fourth of the members of the Storting, and the other of the remaining three-fourths. Each Ting (the Storting, the Odelsting and the Lagting) nominates its own president. Most questions are decided by the Storting, but questions relating to legislation must be considered and decided by the Odelsting and the Lagting separately. Only when the Odelsting and the Lagting disagree, the Bill has to be considered by the Storting in plenary sitting, and a new law can then only be decided by a majority of two-thirds of the voters. The same majority is required for alterations of the Constitution, which can only be decided by the Storting in plenary sitting. The Storting elects 5 delegates, whose duty it is to revise the public accounts. The Lagting and the ordinary members of the Supreme Court of Justice (the *Høyesterett*) form a High Court of the Realm (the *Riksrett*) for the trial of ministers, members of the *Høyesterett* and members of the Storting. The impeachment before the *Riksrett* can only be decided by the Odelsting.

The executive is represented by the King, who exercises his authority through the Cabinet or Council of State *(Statsråd)*, composed of a Prime Minister *(Statsminster)* and (at present) 17 ministers *(Statsråder)*. The ministers are entitled to be present in the Storting and to take part in the discussions, but without a vote.

A Labour Government was formed and took office on 9 May 1986. The members of the Government were in Oct. 1987:

Prime Minister: Gro Harlem Brundtland.
Foreign Affairs: Thorvald Stoltenberg. *Cultural and Scientific Affairs:* Hallvard Bakke. *Environment:* Sissel Rønbeck. *Industry:* Finn Kristensen. *Petroleum and Energy:* Arne Øien. *Local Government and Labour:* William Engeseth. *Development:* Vesla Vetlesen. *Trade and Shipping:* Kurt M. Mosbakk. *Fisheries:* Bjarne Mørk Eidem. *Defence:* Johan Jørgen Holst. *Communications:* Kjell Borgen. *Justice:* Helene Bøsterud. *Finance:* Gunnar Berge. *Church and Education:* Kirsti Kolle Grøndahl. *Health and Social Affairs:* Tove Strand Gerhardsen. *Agriculture:* Gunhild Øyangen. *Customer Affairs and Government Administration:* Anne-Lise Bakken.

The official languages are Bokmål (or Riksmål) and Nynorsk (or Landsmål).

Local Government. For the purposes of administration the country is divided into 19 counties *(fylker)*, in each of which the central government is represented by a county governor *(fylkesmannen)*. In addition, there are 47 urban districts *(bykommuner)* and 407 rural districts *(herredskommuner)*, each of which usually corresponds in size to a parish *(prestegjeld)*. The districts are administered by district councils *(kommunestyrer)*, whose membership may vary between 13 and 85 councillors, and by a committee *(formannskap)* which is elected by and from the members of the council. The council is four times the size of the committee. The council elects a chairman and a vice-chairman from among the committee members.

Each of the 18 counties forms a county district *(fylkeskommune)*, while the remaining one, Oslo, comprises an urban district. The supreme authority in a county district is the county council *(fylkesting)*. The members of the county council are elected directly by the electors of the county and the number of representatives varies between 25 and 85. In a county district the county committee *(fylkesutvalg)* occupies a position corresponding to that of the committee *(formannskap)* in the primary districts. The county committee is elected by and from among the members of the county council. The number of county committee members is one-fourth of the membership of the county council, but must be not more than 15. The county council elects from among the members of the county committee a county sheriff *(fylkesordfører)* and a deputy sheriff.

DEFENCE. Service is universal and compulsory, liability in peace-time commencing at the age of 19 and continuing till the age of 44. The training period in the Army is 12 months, in the Navy and Air Force, 15 months. The Norwegian Defence forces are organized into 2 integrated regional commands.

Army. In Northern Command the largest standing element is Brigade North. There are also 2 infantry battalions and 1 tank platoon, 1 SP field artillery battery and 1 AD battery in the North. Southern Command comprises 1 infantry battalion, 1 tank company and 1 self-propelled field artillery battery. Equipment includes 80 Leopard I and 39 M-48A5 main battle tanks. Strength (1988) 19,000 (including 13,200 conscripts). Reserves number 146,000.

Navy. The Royal Norwegian Navy comprises the Navy, the Coast Guard and the Coastal Artillery. The main combatants include 11 coastal submarines, 5 frigates, 2 corvettes, 38 missile-armed fast attack craft, 8 fast torpedo boats, 7 coastal minesweepers, 1 minehunter, 2 minelayers, 1 submarine and missile torpedo boat tender, 7 landing craft and 27 auxiliaries. In addition all 6 Coast Guard Vessels are prepared for the escort role. The Coastal Artillery includes 55 coastal batteries and other static defence systems. Personnel strength (1988) totalled 9,000 officers and ratings.

Coastguard. The Coastguard main tasks are Fishery Protection and Economic Zone Patrol. The Coastguard assists other government agencies in rescue service, environment, surveillance and police duties. It comprises 3 frigate-size monitors each equipped with a Lynx helicopter, 3 corvette type cutters, 12 survey ships and 7 inspection vessels.

Air Force. The Royal Norwegian Air Force consists of 4 squadrons of F-16 Fighting Falcons, 1 squadron of F-5 fighter-bombers, 1 maritime patrol squadron of P-3B Orions, 1 squadron of C-130H Hercules transports and Jet Falcons equipped for EW duties, 1 squadron with Twin Otter light transports and 2 squadrons of UH-1B helicopters, being replaced by Bell 412SPs, in 1988–89. Ground based air defence forces deploy 4 Nike surface-to- air missile batteries and several light anti-aircraft artillery units. Hawk missiles provide area and airfield defence. Nine Westland Sea King helicopters are used for search and rescue duties; 6 Lynx helicopters are operated for the Coast Guard.

Total strength (1988) is about 9,100 personnel, including 5,300 conscripts.

Home Guard. The Home Guard is organized in small units equipped and trained for special tasks. Service after basic training is 1 week a year. The total strength is approximately 85,000.

INTERNATIONAL RELATIONS

Membership. Norway is a member of UN, NATO, EFTA, OECD, the Council of Europe and the Nordic Council.

ECONOMY

Budget. Current revenue and expenditure for years ending 31 Dec. (in 1,000 kroner):

	1982	1983 [1]	1984 [1]	1985 [1]	1986 [1]	1987 [1] [2]
Revenue	110,539,000	165,421,000	192,896,000	222,994,000	246,466,000	247,612,000
Expenditure	100,898,000	157,432,000	171,369,000	198,332,000	225,144,000	247,534,000

[1] Including National Insurance.   [2] Voted budget.

National debt [1] for years ending 31 Dec. (in 1,000 kroner):

1978	86,556,000	1981	107,662,000	1984	115,805,000
1979	103,605,000	1982	103,799,400	1985	142,392,600
1980	106,908,000	1983	92,406,100	1986	194,287,500

[1] At the rate of par on foreign loans: including treasury bills (in 1m. kroner) which amounted to 6,000 in 1978; 9,600 in 1979; 14,600 in 1980, 17,200 in 1981, 13,880 in 1982, 13,413 in 1983, 24,558 in 1984, 35,111 in 1985 and 48,975 in 1986.

Currency. The Norwegian *krone*, of 100 øre, is of the value of about 11 *kroner* to £1 sterling. National bank-notes of 50, 100, 500 and 1,000 *kroner* are legal means of payment. March 1988, US$1 = 6·38 *kroner*; £1 = 11·27 *kroner*.

On 31 Aug. 1987 the nominal value of the coin in circulation was 1,779m. kroner; notes in circulation, 25,169m. kroner.

Banking. The Bank of Norway is governed by laws enacted by the State, and its directors are elected by the Storting, except the president and vice-president of the head office, who are nominated by the King. It is the only bank of issue.

At the end of 1986 there were 29 private joint-stock banks. Their total amount of capital and funds was 13,222m. kroner (capital 6,456m., funds 6,766m.). Deposits amounted to 188,129m. kroner, of which 46,848m. kroner were at call and notice, and 141,271m. kroner on time.

The number of savings banks at the end of 1986 was 192. The total amount of funds of the savings banks amounted to 8,975m. kroner, and total deposits 149,766m. kroner, of which 37,330m. kroner were at call and notice and 112,436m. kroner on time.

Weights and Measures. The metric system of weights and measures has been obligatory since 1875.

ENERGY AND NATURAL RESOURCES

Electricity. Norway is a large producer of hydro-electric energy. The potential total hydro-electric power at regulated mean water flow is estimated at 162,000m. kwh. annually.

By the end of 1985 the capacity of the installations for production of thermo-electric energy was 255 mw. and the capacity for production of hydro-electric energy was 23,513 mw. In 1986 the total production of electricity amounted to 97,156m. kwh. of which 99·6% was produced by hydro-electric plants.

Most of the electricity is used for industrial purposes, especially by the chemical and basic metal industries for production of nitrate of calcium and other nitrogen products, carbide, ferrosilicon and other ferro-alloys, aluminium and zinc. The paper and pulp industries are also big consumers of electricity. Supply 130, 150, 220 and 230 volts; 50 Hz.

Oil. In 1963 sovereignty was proclaimed over the Norwegian continental shelf and in 1966 the first exploration well was drilled. By 1986 production was 6 times the domestic consumption of petroleum and is valued at about 11% of the GNP. Production (1987) 50m. tonnes.

Gas. Production (1986) 953,370m. cu. ft.

Minerals. Production and value of the chief concentrates, metals and alloys were:

	1984		1985	
Concentrates and minerals	Tonnes	1,000 kroner	Tonnes	1,000 kroner
Copper concentrates	96,286	231,285	97,035	261,621
Pyrites	428,438	74,637	395,162	70,973
Titanium ore	651,834	...	735,842	...
Zinc and lead concentrates	60,218	141,546	59,084	110,413
Metals and alloys				
Copper	36,821	...	37,828	...
Nickel	35,548	...	37,513	...
Aluminium	765,083	8,529,557	742,686	7,841,702
Ferro-alloys	1,003,286	3,573,347	921,903	3,318,867
Pig-iron	545,972	...	596,031	...
Zinc	94,248	...	97,762	...
Lead and tin	62	...	61	...

Agriculture. Norway, including Svalbard and Jan Mayen, is a barren and mountainous country. The arable soil is found in comparatively narrow strips, gathered in deep and narrow valleys and around fiords and lakes. Large, continuous tracts fit for cultivation do not exist. Of the total area, 79·3% is unproductive, 18% productive forest and 2·7% under cultivation.

Principal crops	Area [1] (hectares)			Produce [1] (tonnes)		
	1984	1985	1986	1984	1985	1986
Wheat	33,450	39,090	39,570	170,400	169,900	158,400
Rye	1,670	1,060	1,000	6,700	3,500	3,100
Barley	171,220	170,550	174,230	657,600	600,000	544,700
Oats	123,640	129,260	127,230	581,200	494,200	400,400
Potatoes	19,170	18,610	17,130	488,700	440,100	398,300
Hay	428,870	424,460	424,860	3,147,300	2,978,300	2,880,300

Livestock, 1986 [1]: 16,300 horses, 967,500 cattle (363,200 milch cows), 2,339,900 sheep, 94,600 goats, 737,900 pigs, 4,082,800 hens.

Fur production in 1985–86 was as follows (1984–85 in brackets): Silver fox, 97,800 (67,000); silver-blue fox, 74,000 (90,900); blue fox, 303,000 (240,700); mink, 553,000 (516,000).

[1] Holdings with at least 5 decares agricultural area in use.

Forestry. About 83% of the total forest area consists of conifers and 17% of broadleaves. The annual increment (estimate, 1987) is about 19m. cu. metres with bark. The area of productive forests is 66,600 sq. km. Forests in public ownership cover 8,470 sq. km of this area. Between 1976–77 and 1985–86 an annual average of 8·4m. cu. metres was cut for sale: 8·1m. for industrial use, 300,000m. for fuel. Of industrial use, 4·5m. cu. metres in the lumber industry, 3m. as pulp, 200,000 as particle board. About 800,000 cu. metres are consumed annually on farms.

Fisheries. The total number of registered fishermen in 1986 was 29,981, of whom 7,362 had another chief occupation. In 1985, the number of fishing vessels (all with motor) was 23,202, and of these, 15,256 were open boats.

The value of sea fisheries in 1m. kroner in 1986 was: Cod, 1,613; capelin, 188; mackerel, 205; coal-fish (saithe), 478; deep-water prawn, 823; haddock, 287; herring, 366; dogfish, 11. The catch totalled in 1986, 2·1m. tons, valued at 5,035m. kroner.

Fish farming is a growth industry, exports (1986) 1,664m. kroner.

INDUSTRY AND TRADE

Industry. Industry is chiefly based on raw materials produced within the country (wood, fish, etc.) and on water power, of which the country possesses a large amount. Crude petroleum and natural gas production, the manufacture of paper and paper products, industrial chemicals and basic metals are the most important export manufactures. In the following table are given figures for industrial establishments in 1985, excluding one-man units. Electrical plants, construction and building industry are not included. The values are given in 1m. kroner.

Industries	Establish-ments	Number of Employees	Gross value of production	Value added
Coalmining	1	770	238	105
Crude petroleum and natural gas	8	12,818	105,210	91,010
Metal-mining	14	3,213	1,675	404
Other-mining	413	3,170	1,830	815
Food manufacturing	2,257	49,660	47,154	5,681
Beverages	63	4,344	3,973	2,556
Tobacco	4	928	2,305	1,888
Textiles	414	8,454	3,165	1,150
Clothing, etc.	304	4,678	1,417	548
Footwear	33	684	211	84
Leather	55	804	270	85
Wood	1,485	19,933	10,975	3,380
Furniture and fixtures	528	8,877	4,228	1,519
Pulp and paper	131	13,709	13,295	3,451
Printing and publishing	1,771	34,608	15,124	6,698
Chemical, industrial	63	8,991	12,742	3,640
Chemical, other	172	6,158	4,899	1,620

Industries	Establish-ments	Number of Employees	Gross value of production	Value added
Petroleum, refined	3	898	15,784	208
Petroleum and coal	74	1,714	2,059	547
Rubber	73	1,733	817	363
Plastics	322	6,620	3,719	1,312
Ceramics	32	1,084	275	156
Glass	66	1,982	1,012	443
Other mineral products	487	7,695	5,558	1,917
Iron, steel and ferro-alloys	51	9,950	9,074	2,377
Non-ferrous metals	64	12,791	15,854	4,737
Metal products, except machinery	1,587	25,426	10,748	4,369
Machinery and equipment	1,280	41,600	36,984	9,707
Electrical apparatus and supplies	445	20,782	10,502	4,384
Transport equipment	902	30,698	14,764	4,937
Professional and scientific instruments, photographic and optical goods	56	1,379	754	349
Other manufacturing industries	303	2,938	1,069	442
Total (all included)	13,461	349,039	357,684	160,884

The following table sets forth the estimated value of net production, at factor cost by industries, in 1m. kroner:

	1981	1982	1983	1984	1985[1]	1986[1]
Agriculture	8,852	10,090	9,366	10,608	10,500	10,794
Forestry	2,260	2,164	2,054	2,458	2,503	2,718
Fishing	2,048	1,655	2,335	2,536	2,780	3,299
Mining and quarrying	1,179	1,147	1,370	1,531	1,392	1,518
Manufacturing	44,845	46,869	51,748	59,522	63,298	71,911
Crude petroleum and gas production	37,395	39,879	47,968	59,720	65,076	26,968
Electricity, gas and water	5,852	7,168	9,072	10,543	11,952	12,875
Construction [2]	17,274	19,949	21,011	21,626	23,765	25,281
Wholesale and retail trade	27,405	31,073	32,413	35,240	38,565	41,371
Restaurants and hotels	3,674	4,277	5,029	5,675	6,521	7,335
Water transport	6,263	3,469	2,473	5,228	6,339	7,331
Other transport [3]	12,912	14,866	16,486	16,996	17,867	22,907
Financial institutions	12,726	15,320	16,874	16,266	17,253	24,351
Real estate	9,710	11,244	12,643	13,993	15,052	16,538
Business services	7,600	9,372	10,502	13,086	16,648	21,277
Government services, social and personal services	57,074	64,954	71,906	77,924	85,600	95,820
Imputed bank service charge	−11,349	−14,318	−15,960	−15,443	−15,857	−22,008
Net production at factor cost	245,720	269,178	297,289	337,509	369,254	370,286
+ Indirect taxes	55,696	61,747	69,733	78,200	91,992	101,084
− Subsidies	21,795	23,662	24,439	25,709	26,936	29,686
Net domestic product (market price)	279,621	307,263	342,583	390,000	434,310	441,684

[1] Provisional figures.
[2] Including drilling of crude oil and natural gas wells.
[3] Including pipeline transport of oil and gas.

Labour. Distribution of employed persons by occupation in 1986 showed 444,000 (21%) in technical, physical science, humanistic and artistic work; 134,000 (6%) administration; 228,000 (11%) clerical; 211,000 (10%) sales; 141,000 (7%) agriculture, forestry, fishing etc.; 11,000 (0·5%) mining and quarrying; 147,000 (7%) transport and communication; 468,000 (23%) manufacturing; 271,000 (13%) service, and 16,000 (1%) military and occupations not specified.

Source: Labour Force Sample Surveys.

Commerce. Total imports and exports in calendar years (in 1,000 kroner):

	1981	1982	1983	1984	1985	1986
Imports	89,687,802	99,747,271	98,407,773	113,102,212	132,563,356	150,052,325
Exports	104,265,370	113,236,296	131,396,960	154,034,540	170,732,779	133,847,404

Trading according to countries was as follows (in 1,000 kroner):

Countries	1985 Imports	1985 Exports	1986 Imports	1986 Exports
Argentina	326,011	80,108	318,704	32,553
Australia and New Zealand	695,539	471,756	622,742	399,595
Belgium and Luxembourg	3,698,414	1,646,708	4,397,737	1,585,464
Brazil	1,182,491	416,100	1,046,830	651,742
Canada	2,512,297	625,132	2,000,803	705,812
Czechoslovakia	303,439	193,074	328,908	138,475
Denmark	8,961,950	6,165,410	10,704,384	5,969,916
Fed. Republic of Germany	21,297,332	26,548,826	25,418,960	25,313,058
Finland	5,382,342	2,686,649	5,995,158	2,343,720
France	5,536,511	8,951,789	6,109,453	4,639,154
India	143,303	448,775	168,589	313,182
Italy	4,435,407	2,232,488	5,657,178	2,456,464
Netherlands	4,686,170	10,360,395	5,726,149	8,118,643
Poland	423,841	268,244	805,715	198,272
Portugal	1,053,081	595,337	1,247,301	462,650
Spain	1,291,799	591,546	1,509,911	759,112
Sweden	23,699,533	15,016,633	26,950,235	13,377,274
Switzerland	2,058,802	1,186,504	2,548,454	1,118,668
UK	13,222,638	61,039,782	13,194,894	3,678,950
USA	9,554,428	8,722,732	10,288,375	7,304,233
USSR	1,450,358	629,210	805,715	671,899

Principal items of import in 1986 (in 1,000 kroner): Machinery, transport equipment, etc., 60,796,759; fuel oil, etc., 8,859,517; base metals and manufactures thereof, 13,898,325; chemicals and related products, 10,123,453; textiles, 3,744,734.

Principal items of export in 1986 (in 1,000 kroner): Machinery and transport equipment, 23,718,106; base metals and manufactures thereof, 17,417,106; crude oil and natural gas, 53,076,842; edible animal products, 8,684,375; pulp and paper, 6,624,607.

Total trade between Norway and UK (British Department of Trade returns, in £1,000 sterling):

	1983	1984	1985	1986	1987
Imports to UK	2,820,760	3,852,657	4,367,154	3,265,157	3,290,339
Exports and re-exports from UK	828,612	968,404	1,140,376	1,147,790	1,220,844

COMMUNICATIONS

Roads. On 31 Dec. 1986 the length of the public roads (including roads in towns) was 86,143 km. Of these, 52,708 km were main roads; 55,453 km had some kind of paving, mostly bituminous and oil-gravel treatment, the rest being gravel-surfaced.

Number of registered motor vehicles (31 Dec. 1986) was 2,780,311, including 1,592,195 passenger cars (including taxis), 264,517 lorries and vans, 18,278 buses, 170,838 motor cycles and mopeds. The scheduled bus and lorry services in 1986 drove 3,877m. passenger-km and 699m. net ton-km.

Railways. The length of state railways on 31 Dec. 1986 was 4,219 km; of private companies, 16 km. On 2,451 km of state and 16 km of private railways electric traction is installed. Total receipts of the state railways and road traffic in 1986 were 2,798m. kroner; total expenses (excluding depreciation and interest on capital), 4,024m. kroner. The state railways carried 25·7m. tonnes of freight (of which 14m. was iron ore on the Ofoten railway) and 35m. passengers.

Aviation. Det Norske Luftfartselskap (DNL) started its post-war activities on 1 April 1946. On 1 Aug. 1946 DNL, together with DDL (Danish Airlines) and ABA/SILA (Swedish Airlines), formed the 'Scandinavian Airlines System'—SAS. The 3 companies remained independent units, but all services were co-ordinated. In 1951 a new agreement was signed (retroactive from 1 Oct. 1950) according to which the 3 national companies became holding partners in a new organization which took over the entire operational system. Denmark and Norway hold each two-sevenths and Sweden three-sevenths of the capital, but they have joint responsibility towards third parties.

In the autumn of 1986 SAS had a fleet of 104 jet planes. Length of route network, about 252,000 km. Scheduled air services are run by SAS, Braathens South-American and Far East Air transport service (SAFE) and Widerøes Flyveselskap service. The Norwegian share of the scheduled air service run by SAS is two-sevenths of the SAS service on international routes and the total SAS service in Norway.

	1,000 km flown	Passengers carried	1,000 passenger-km	Post, luggage, freight and passengers (1,000 ton-km) Total	Of which post
1983	59,638	5,610,866	4,345,000	514,000	19,000
1984	59,359	6,114,038	4,533,000	534,000	18,000
1985	63,666	6,799,735	4,791,000	557,000	19,000
1986	73,774	7,490,448	5,030,000	578,000	20,000

Shipping. The total registered mercantile marine on 1 Jan. 1987 was 1,335 vessels, 7m. gross tons (steam and motor vessels above 100 gross tons). These figures do not include fishing and catching boats, tugs, salvage vessels, icebreakers and similar special types of vessels, totalling 767 vessels of 340,000 gross tons.

Vessels entering Norway from foreign countries 1983	Total No.	Net tons
Norwegian	6,970	17,470
Foreign	10,013	31,264
Total entered	16,983	48,734

Goods (in 1,000 tonnes) in 1985 discharged, 19,012; loaded, 53,309, of which 14,564 was Swedish iron ore shipped from Narvik.

Post and Broadcasting. Number of telephone connexions on 31 Dec. 1986 was 1,861,412 (44·6 per 100 of population). Receipts, 11,909·9m. kroner; expenses, 11,003·2m. kroner (interest on capital included) for State Telecommunications. *Norsk Rikskringkasting* is a non-commercial enterprise operated by an independent state organization and broadcasts 1 programme (P1) on long-, medium-, and short-waves and on FM and 1 programme (P2) on FM. Local programmes are also broadcast. It broadcasts 1 TV programme from 1,980 transmitters. Colour programmes are broadcast by PAL system. Number of television licences, 1,443,020.

Cinemas. There were 448 cinemas with a seating capacity of 123,090 in 1985.

Newspapers. There were 63 daily newspapers with a combined circulation of 2,008,000 in 1986.

JUSTICE, RELIGION, EDUCATION AND WELFARE

Justice. The judicature is common to civil and criminal cases. The same professional judges, who are legally educated, preside over both kinds of cases. These judges are as such state officials. The participation of lay judges and jurors, both summoned for the individual case, varies according to the kind of court and kind of case.

The ordinary Court of First Instance *(Herredsrett* and *Byrett)* is in criminal cases composed of one professional judge and 2 lay judges, chosen by ballot from a panel elected by the district council. In civil cases 2 lay judges may participate. The ordinary Court of First Instance is in general competent in all kinds of cases with the exception of criminal cases where the maximum penalty prescribed in the Criminal Code for the offence in question exceeds five years imprisonment. Altogether there are about 100 ordinary courts of first instance.

In every community there is a Conciliation Council *(Forliksråd)* composed of 3 lay persons elected by the district council. A civil lawsuit usually begins with mediation in the council which also has judicial authority in minor civil cases.

The ordinary Courts of Second Instance *(Lagmannsrett),* of which there are 5, are composed of 3 professional judges. Additionally, in civil cases 2 or 4 lay judges may be summoned. In criminal cases a jury of 10 lay persons is summoned to determine whether the defendant is guilty according to the charge. Four lay persons take part in the assessment of the punishment. In civil cases, the Court of Second

Instance is an ordinary court of appeal. In criminal cases in which the lower court does not have judicial authority, it is itself the court of first instance. In other criminal cases it is an appeal court as far as the appeal is based on an attack against the lower court's assessment of the facts when determining the guilt of the defendant. An appeal based on any other alleged mistakes is brought directly before the Supreme Court.

The Supreme Court *(Høyesterett)* is the court of last resort. There are 18 Supreme Court judges. Each individual case is heard by 5 judges. Some major cases are determined in plenary session. The Supreme Court may in general examine every aspect of the case and the handling of it by the lower courts. However, in criminal cases the Court may not overrule the lower court's assessment of the facts as far as the guilt of the defendant is concerned.

The Court of Impeachment *(Riksretten)* is composed of 5 judges of the Supreme Court and 10 members of Parliament.

All serious offences are prosecuted by the State. The Public Prosecution Authority *(Påtalemyndigheten)* consists of the Attorney General *(Riksadvokaten)*, the district attorneys *(statsadvokater)* and legally qualified officers of the ordinary police force. Counsel for the defence is in general provided for by the State.

Religion. There is complete freedom of religion, the Evangelical Lutheran Church, however, being the national church, endowed by the State. Its clergy are nominated by the King. Ecclesiastically Norway is divided into 11 *Bispedømmer* (bishoprics), 91 *Prostier* (provostships or archdeaconries) and 620 *Prestegjeld* (clerical districts). There were 140,202 members of registered religious communities outside the Evangelical Lutheran Church, subsidized by central government and local authorities in 1984. The Roman Catholics are under a Bishop at Oslo, a Vicar Apostolic at Trondheim and a Vicar Apostolic at Tromsø.

Education. In Norway the children normally start their school attendance the year they are 7 years of age and finish compulsory school the year they complete 16 years of age.

On 1 Oct. 1986 the number of primary schools and pupils were as follows: 3,509 primary schools, 519,867 pupils; 87 special schools for the handicapped, 2,911 pupils.

On 1 Oct. 1985 the number of pupils in upper secondary schools, *i.e.*, folk high schools, secondary general schools and vocational schools, was 209,629.

There are in Norway 4 universities and 9 institutions equivalent to universities. In autumn 1986 the total number of students was 43,341. The University of Oslo, founded in 1811, had 19,202 students. The University of Bergen, founded in 1948, had 8,368 students. The University of Trondheim consists of the Norwegian Institute of Technology, founded in 1910, and the College of Arts and Science, founded in 1925. At each of them the number of students was in autumn 1986, 5,463 and 3,292 respectively. The University of Tromsø was established in 1968; 2,240 students were registered in autumn 1986. The other university institutions had 4,647 students.

On 1 Oct. 1985 there were at other schools of higher education, 45,901 students. These included 12,391 at colleges for teachers, 7,755 at colleges for engineers and 6,806 at district colleges.

In 1985–86 there were 6,673 Norwegian students and pupils attending foreign universities and schools.

Health. In 1985 there were 10,324 doctors and 66,539 hospital beds.

Social Security. In 1986, about 82,000m. kroner were paid under different social insurance schemes, amounting to approximately 19% of the net national income.

The National Insurance Act of 17 June 1966, which came into force on 1 Jan. 1967, replaced the schemes relating to old age pensions, disability benefits, widows' and mothers' pensions, benefits to unmarried women, 'survivors' benefit for children and rehabilitation aid. Schemes relating to health insurance, unemployment insurance and occupational injury insurance were revised and incorporated in National Insurance Scheme on 1 Jan. 1971. As from 1 Jan. 1981, benefits to divorced and separated supporters also are covered by the National Insurance Scheme.

The following conspectus gives a survey of schemes established by law. Many municipalities grant additional benefits to old-age, disablement and survivor's pensions.

Type of scheme	Introduced[1]	Scope	Principal benefits as from 1 May 1987
National insurance	1967 (1987)		
Medical care and sickness cash benefits[2]	1911	All residents	Medical benefits: all hospital expenses; cost share of expense of medical consultation, important medicines, travel expenses, etc. (such costs exceeding 880kr. a calendar year are paid in full by the National Insurance).
		Nearly all wage-earners	Daily sickness allowances: kr. 58 to 690 per day cash (5 days a week). The new sickness allowance scheme (1 July 1978) entitles employees to a daily allowance equal to 100% of their gross earned income (within certain limits) from and including the first day of absence; self-employed persons, ordinarily 65% of gross earned income as from the 15th day. Supplementary insurance available
		All female residents giving birth	Maternity allowances: same as sickness allowances for 100 days (time sharing with the father is possible) or a lump sum of kr. 4,360 per child
Unemployment benefits[2]	1939	Nearly all wage-earners	Daily allowance during unemployment kr. 46 to 359 per day, excluding supplement for supported child(ren) (six days a week). Contributions to training and retraining, removal expenses, wage subsidies
Rehabilitation benefits[3]	1961	Persons unfit for work because of disablement and persons who have a substantially limited general functional capacity	Training; treatment; rehabilitation allowance grants and loans Full rehabilitation allowance equals old age pension (however, no special supplement is granted, see below.)
Disability benefits[3]	1961	All residents	A basic grant and an assistance grant to persons with special needs. Basic grant: kr. 4,104 to kr. 13,656 per annum (However, for many diabetes cases kr. 2,004 per annum.) Assistance grant: kr. 6,828, may be increased for children below 18 years of age to a maximum of kr. 38,232 per annum
		All residents between 16 and 67 years of age	Disability pension to persons between 16 and 67 years of age, occupationally disabled by at least 50%, unfit for rehabilitation Full disability pension equals old age pension

For notes see p. 948.

Type of scheme	Introduced [1]	Scope	Principal benefits as from 1 May 1987
Occupational injury benefits [2] (industrial workers 1895; fishermen 1909; seamen 1913; military personnel 1953, combined in the act of occupational injury insurance 1960)	1960	All employed persons, school children and students; self-employed on a voluntary basis	The ordinary benefits of the National Insurance, alternative calculation of pensions etc. which in many cases are more favourable for the insured person—or his survivors than the ordinary rules *An occupational injury compensation,* alone or in addition to a disability pension
Old age pensions [3]	1937	All persons above 67 years of age	Basic pensions: Single, kr. 29,900; couples, kr. 44,850 per annum; supplementary pensions based on previous pensionable income; supplement for supported spouse kr. 14,950 per annum; supplement for supported child(ren) kr. 7,475 or kr. 3,738 per child per annum; *see below* under 'Special supplement' and 'Compensation supplement'
Death grants	1967	All residents	A certain amount fixed by the Storting, for the time being kr. 4,000
Survivors' benefits [3]	1965	All residents	Full pension = kr. 29,900 per annum + 55% of the supplementary pension due to the deceased, *transitional benefits,* child care allowance and educational allowances (*see below* under 'Special supplement' and 'Compensation supplement')
Children's pension [3]	1958	Under 18 (20) years of age, after loss of one or both parents	40% of basic amount (kr. 11,960) for first child, 25% (kr. 7,475) for each additional child. If both parents are dead, full survivors' pension for first, 40% of basic amount for second, 25% third, etc., child
Benefits to unmarried supporters [3]	1965	Unmarried mothers or fathers	An additional maternity benefit of kr. 8,282, transitional benefit, full amount kr. 29,900 per annum, child care allowance and educational allowances (*see below* under 'Special supplement' and 'Family allowances')
Benefits to divorced and separated supporters [4]	1972	Divorced and separated supporters	Same kind of benefits as unmarried supporters above
Benefits to unmarried persons forced to live at home [3]	1965	Unmarried persons under 67 years of age having stayed at home for at least 5 years to give necessary care and attention to parents or other near relatives	Transitional benefit or a pension kr. 29,900 per annum, educational allowances (*see below* under 'Special supplement' and 'Compensation supplement')
Special supplement to National Insurance pensions or transitional benefits	1969 (1984)	Pensioners and persons with transitional allowance on basic rates	Full special supplement, 54·5% of basic amount, *i.e.* kr. 16,296. For a married pensioner full supplement is lower when spouse has her/his own pension (49·75%)

For notes *see* p. 948.

Type of scheme	Introduced [1]	Scope	Principal benefits as from 1 May 1987
Compensation supplement to National Insurance pensions or transitional benefits	1970 (1984)	Pensioners, persons with transitional benefits (except unmarried, divorced and separated supporters) or rehabilitation allowances	Full compensation supplement kr. 500 for single persons and kr. 750 for married couples
Family allowances	1946 (1986)	All families with children under 16 years of age	Kr. 6,180 per annum for the first child, kr. 6,672 for the second, kr. 8,088 for the third, kr. 8,712 for the fourth and kr. 9,096 for the fifth and each additional child. Single supporters receive benefits for one child more than the actual number
War pensions	1946 (1986)	War victims, 1939–45	Pensions up to kr. 118,344 per annum for single pensioners/ couples (excluding supplement for supported child(ren); widows' and children's pensions
Special pension schemes:		Persons with at least: [5]	Maximum old-age pension:
Forestry workers	1952 (1987)	750 premium weeks (1,500 „ „)	Kr. 29,900 per annum (for supported spouse an additional 33⅓%, 10% supplement per child, maximum 5 children)
Fishermen	1958 (1987)	750 premium weeks (1,500 „ „)	Kr. 29,900 per annum (for supported spouse an additional 50%, 30% supplement per child)
Seamen	1948 (1987)	150 months service (360 „ „)	Kr. 97,978 [6] per annum (officers) Kr. 69,984 [6] „ „ (others) (no spouse supplement, an additional 10% per child)

[1] Date of latest revision of law in brackets.
[2] Transferred to national insurance scheme and revised in 1971.
[3] Transferred to national insurance scheme and revised in 1967.
[4] Transferred to national insurance scheme and revised in 1981.
[5] Requirements for maximum pensions in brackets.
[6] Supplements for service during war not included.

Provisions have been laid down for the integration of more than one benefit, pension, etc., so as to limit the total amount.

As a main rule all running benefits are taxable, while lump sums are not taxed. Certain tax modifications apply to all pensioners and pensioners with no other income than minimum benefits are not charged for tax.

SVALBARD

An archipelago situated between 10° and 35° E. long. and between 74° and 81° N. lat. Total area, 62,000 sq. km (24,000 sq. miles).

The main islands of the archipelago are Spitsbergen (formerly called Vestspitsbergen), Nordaustlandet, Edgeøya, Barentsøya, Prins Karls Forland, Bjørnøya, Hopen, Kong Karls Land, Kvitøya, and many small islands. The arctic climate is tempered by mild winds from the Atlantic.

The archipelago was probably discovered by Norsemen in 1194 and rediscovered by the Dutch navigator Barents in 1596. In the 17th century the very lucrative whale-hunting caused rival Dutch, British and Danish–Norwegian claims to sovereignty and quarrels about the hunting-places. But when in the 18th century the whale-hunting ended, the question of the sovereignty of Svalbard lost its significance; it was again raised in the 20th century, owing to the discovery and exploitation of coalfields. By a treaty, signed on 9 Feb. 1920 in Paris, Norway's sovereignty over the archipelago was recognized. On 14 Aug. 1925 the archipelago was officially incorporated in Norway.

Coal is the principal product. Of the 3 Norwegian and 3 Soviet mining camps,

2 Norwegian and 2 Soviet camps are operating. Total population on 31 Dec. 1986 was 3,942, of which 1,387 were Norwegians, 2,535 Soviet citizens, and 10 Poles. In 1986, 349,204 tonnes of coal were exported from the Norwegian and 510,086 tonnes from the Soviet mines.

Norwegian and foreign companies have been prospecting for oil. So far 5 deep drillings have been made, but oil and gas finds have not been reported.

There are Norwegian meteorological and/or radio stations at the following places: Bjørnøya (since 1920), Hopen (1945), Isfjord Radio (1933), Longyearbyen (1930), Svalbard Lufthavn (1975) and Ny-Ålesund (1961). A research station, administered by Norsk Polarinstitutt, was erected at Ny-Ålesund in 1968 for various observations and investigations. An airport near Longyearbyen (Svalbard Lufthavn) opened in 1975.

Norsk Polarinstitutt, Skrifter, Oslo, from 1948 (under different titles from 1922)
Greve, T., Svalbard: Norway in the Arctic. Oslo, 1975
Hisdal, V., Geography of Svalbard. Norsk Polarinstitutt, Oslo, rev. ed., 1984
Orvin, A. K., 'Twenty-five Years of Norwegian Sovereignty in Svalbard 1925–1950' (in The Polar Record, 1951)

JAN MAYEN

This bleak, desolate and mountainous island of volcanic origin and partly covered by glaciers, is situated 71° N. lat. and 8° 30′ W. long., 300 miles NNE of Iceland. The total area is 380 sq. km (147 sq. miles). Beerenberg, its highest peak, reaches a height of 2,277 metres. Volcanic activity, which had been dormant, was reactivated in Sept. 1970.

The island was possibly discovered by Henry Hudson in 1608, and it was first named Hudson's Tutches (Touches). It was again and again rediscovered and re-named. Its present name derives from the Dutch whaling captain Jan Jacobsz May, who indisputably discovered the island in 1614. It was uninhabited, but occasionally visited by seal hunters and trappers, until 1921 when Norway established a radio and meteorological station. On 8 May 1929 Jan Mayen was officially proclaimed as incorporated in the Kingdom of Norway. Its relation to Norway was finally settled by law of 27 Feb. 1930. A LORAN station (1959) and a CONSOL station (1968) have been established.

BOUVET ISLAND
Bouvetøya

This uninhabited volcanic island, mostly covered by glaciers and situated 54° 25′ S. lat. and 3° 21′ E. long., was discovered in 1739 by a French naval officer, Jean Baptiste Loziert Bouvet, but no flag was hoisted till, in 1825, Capt. Norris raised the Union Jack. In 1928 Great Britain waived its claim to the island in favour of Norway, which in Dec. 1927 had occupied it. A law of 27 Feb. 1930 declared Bouvetøya a Norwegian dependency. The area is 50 sq. km (19 sq. miles). From 1977 Norway has had an automatic meteorological station on the island, and 5 men operated a meteorological station there during the 1978–79 season.

PETER I ISLAND
Peter I Øy

This uninhabited island, situated 68° 48′ S. lat. and 90° 35′ W. long., was sighted in 1821 by the Russian explorer, Admiral von Bellingshausen. The first landing was made in 1929 by a Norwegian expedition which hoisted the Norwegian flag. On 1 May 1931 Peter I Island was placed under Norwegian sovereignty, and on 24 March 1933 it was incorporated in Norway as a dependency. The area is 180 sq. km (69 sq. miles).

QUEEN MAUD LAND
Dronning Maud Land

On 14 Jan. 1939 the Norwegian Cabinet placed that part of the Antarctic Continent from the border of Falkland Islands dependencies in the west to the border of the Australian Antarctic Dependency in the east (between 20° W. and 45° E.) under Norwegian sovereignty. The territory had been explored only by Norwegians and hitherto been ownerless. Since 1949 expeditions from various countries have explored the area. In 1957 Dronning Maud Land was given the status of a Norwegian dependency.

DIPLOMATIC REPRESENTATIVES

Of Norway in Great Britain (25 Belgrave Sq., London, SW1X 8QD)
Ambassador: Rolf T. Busch.

Of Great Britain in Norway (Thomas Heftyesgate 8, 0264 Oslo, 2)
Ambassador: J. A. Robson, CMG.

Of Norway in the USA (2720 34th St., NW, Washington, D.C., 20008)
Ambassador: Kjell Eliassen.

Of the USA in Norway (Drammensveien 18, 0255 Oslo, 2)
Ambassador: Robert D. Stuart Jr.

Of Norway to the United Nations
Ambassador: Tom Eric Vraalsen.

Books of Reference

Statistical Information: The Central Bureau of Statistics, Statistisk Sentralbyrå (Skippergaten 15, P.B.8131 Dep.0033, Oslo 1), was founded in 1876 as an independent state institution. *Director general:* Arne Øien. The earliest census of population was taken in 1769. The Sentralbyrå publishes the series *Norges Offisielle Statistikk,* Norway's official statistics (from 1828), and *Social Economic Studies* (from 1954). The main publications are:

    Statistisk Årbok for Norge (annual, from 1880; from 1952 bilingual Norwegian–English)
    Økonomisk Utsyn (annual, from 1935; with English summary from 1952)
    Historisk Statistikk 1978 (historical statistics; bilingual Norwegian–English)
    Statistisk Månedshefte (monthly, from 1880; with English index)
    Sosialt Utsyn 1983 (social survey). Irregular
    Miljóstatistikk 1983 (environmental statistics). Irregular
Norges Statskalender. From 1816; annual from 1877
Facts about Norway. Ed. by Aftenposten. 20th ed. Oslo, 1986–87
Arntzen, J. G., and Knudsen, B. B., *Political Life and Institutions in Norway.* Oslo, 1981
Derry, T. K., *A History of Modern Norway, 1814–1972.* OUP, 1973.—*A History of Scandinavia.* London, 1979
Glässer, E., *Norwegen* [Bibliography] Darmstadt, 1978
Gleditsch, Th., *Engelsk–norsk ordbok,* 2nd ed. Oslo, 1948
Greve, T., *Haakon VI of Norway, Founder of a New Monarchy.* London, 1983
Grønland, E., *Norway in English, Books on Norway . . . 1742–1959.* Oslo, 1961
Haugen, E., *Norwegian–English Dictionary,* Oslo, 1965
Helvig, M., *Norway: Land, People, Industries, a Brief Geography.* 3rd ed. Oslo, 1970
Holtedahl, O. (ed.), *Geology of Norway.* Oslo, 1960
Hornby, A. S., and Svenkerud, H., *Oxford engelsk-norsk ordbok.* Oslo, 1983
Hove, O., *The System of Education.* Oslo, 1968
Imber, W., *Norway.* Oslo, 1980
Knudsen, O., *Norway at Work.* Oslo, 1972
Larsen, K., *A History of Norway.* New York, 1948
Midgaard, J., *A Brief History of Norway.* Oslo, 1969
Nielsen, K., and Nesheim, A., *Lapp Dictionary: Lapp–English–Norwegian.* 5 vols., Oslo 1963
Orvik, N. (ed.), *Fears and Expectations: Norwegian Attitudes Toward European Integration.* Oslo, 1972
Paine, R., *Coast Lapp Society.* 2 vols. Tromsø, 1957–65
Popperwell, R. G., *Norway.* London, 1972
Sather, L. B., *Norway.* [Bibliography] Oxford and Santa Barbara, 1986
Udgaard, N. M., *Great Power Politics and Norwegian Foreign Policy.* Oslo, 1973
Vorren, Ø. (ed.), *Norway North of 65.* Oslo, 1960

National Library: The University Library, Drammensvein 42b, 0255 Oslo. *Director:* Ben Rugaas.

OMAN

Capital: Muscat
Population: 1·2m. (1987)
GNP per capita: US$7,080 (1985)

Sultanate of Oman

HISTORY. Oman was dominated by Portugal from 1507–1649. The Al-Busaid family assumed power in 1744 and have ruled to the present day. The Sultanate of Oman, known as the Sultanate of Muscat and Oman until 1970, is an independent sovereign state, situated in south-east Arabia.

AREA AND POPULATION. Its coastline is over 1,000 miles long and extends from the Ras al Khaimah Shaikdom near Bukha on the west side of the Musandum Peninsula to Fujairah Shaikdom on the east side, then again from the southern boundary of Fujairah to Ras Dharbat Ali, which marks the boundary between Oman and the territory of the People's Democratic Republic of Yemen. The Sultanate extends inland to the borders of the Rub' al Khali ('Empty Quarter') across three geographical divisions—a coastal plain, a range of hills and a plateau. The coastal plain varies in width from 10 miles near Suwaiq to practically nothing in the vicinity of Mutrah and Muscat towns, where the hills descend abruptly into the sea. These hills are for the most part barren except at the highest part of the mountainous region of the Jebel Akhdar (summit 9,998 ft) where there is some cultivation. The plateau has an average height of 1,000 ft. With the exception of oases there is little or no cultivation. North-west of Muscat the coastal plain, known as the Batinah, is fertile and prosperous. The date gardens extend for over 150 miles. Whereas the coastline between the capital, Muscat, and the southern province of Dhofar is barren, Dhofar itself is highly fertile. Its principal town is Salalah on the coast which is served by the port of Raysut.

The area has been estimated at about 105,000 sq. miles (300,000 sq. km) and the population at 1·2m., chiefly Arabs; of these, some 40,000 live in Dhofar. The town of Muscat is the capital which, while formerly of some commercial importance, has now lost most of its trade to the adjacent port of Mutrah, the starting point for the trade routes into the interior. The population of both towns consists of pure Arabs, Indians, Pakistanis and Negroes; numerous merchants are Khojas (from Sind and Kutch) and Hindus (mostly from Gujarat and Bombay). Estimated population of the Capital area (comprising Muscat, Mutrah, Ruwi and Seeb), 1985, 250,000. Other principal towns are Nizwa, 10,000 and Salalah, 10,000. Other ports are Sohar, Khaburah and Sur on the Gulf of Oman and Raysut in the south; only Raysut affords shelter from bad weather.

The port of Gwadur and a small tract of country on the Balúchistán coast of the Gulf of Oman were handed over to Pakistan on 8 Sept. 1958.

The **Kuria Muria** islands were ceded to the UK in 1854 by the Sultan of Muscat and Oman. On 30 Nov. 1967 the islands were retroceded to the Sultan of Muscat and Oman, in accordance with the wishes of the population.

CLIMATE. Oman has a desert climate, with exceptionally hot and humid months from April to Oct., when temperatures may reach 117°F (47°C). From Dec. to the end of March, the climate is more pleasant. Light monsoon rains fall in the south from June to Sept., with highest amounts in the western highland region. Muscat. Jan. 72°F (22·2°C), July 91°F (33·3°C). Annual rainfall 4·0″ (99·1 mm). Salalah. Jan. 72°F (22·2°C), July 78°F (25·6°C). Annual rainfall 3·3″ (81·3 mm).

RULER. The present Sultan is Qaboos bin Said (born Nov. 1940). He took over from his father Said bin Taimur, on 23 July 1970 in a Palace *coup*.

In Oct. 1981 the Sultan issued three decrees establishing a 45-member State consultative council. The number of Council members was increased to 55 in 1983.

CONSTITUTION AND GOVERNMENT. Oman is an absolute monarchy and there is no formal constitution. The Sultan legislates by decree and appoints a Cabinet to assist him; he holds the posts of Prime Minister and Minister of Foreign Affairs, Defence and Finance. Besides 17 departmental Ministers, the Cabinet also includes:

Deputy Prime Minister for Security and Defence: Sayyid Fahar Bin-Taimur al-Said. *Deputy Prime Minister for Finance and Economy:* Qais bin Abdal Munim al-Zawawi. *Deputy Prime Minister for Legal Affairs:* Sayyid Fahad Bin-Mahmoud al-Said. *Special Adviser to Sultan, Governor of Muscat:* Sayyid Thuwaini Bin-Shihab al-Said. *Special Adviser to Sultan on Religious and Historical Affairs:* Mohammad Bin-Ahmad Al Bu Saidi. *Minister of State for Foreign Affairs:* Yusuf Bin Alawi Bin Abdullah. *Minister of State, Governor of Dhofar:* Musallim Bin Ali Bu Saidi.

National flag: Red, with a white panel in the upper fly and a green one in the lower fly, and in the canton the national emblem in white.

Local government: Oman is divided into 10 provinces *(liwas)* and sub-divided into 41 governates *(wilayats)* each under a governor *(wali).*

DEFENCE

Army. The Army consists of 2 headquarter brigades; 1 armoured, 1 reconnaissance and 3 artillery regiments; 8 infantry battalions; 1 special force, 1 signals regiment, 1 engineer regiment and 1 parachute regiment. Equipment includes 6 M-60A1 and 33 Chieftain main battle tanks. Strength (1988) about 16,500.

Navy. The Navy comprises 4 new very fast missile-armed corvettes, 4 fast gun-boats, 4 inshore patrol craft, 1 training ship/offshore patrol vessel, 2 logistic support ships, 5 landing craft, 1 troop transport,, 1 survey craft, 1 supply ship and 1 training ship. All the warships are British-built. Naval personnel in 1988 totalled 2,400 officers and ratings. The marine police operate 12 coastal patrol boats, 2 logistics support craft, 3 inshore patrol boats and 8 launches.

Air Force. The Air Force, formed in 1959, had in 1987 two strike/interceptor squadrons of Jaguars, a ground attack/interceptor squadron of Hunters, a squadron of Strikemaster light jet training/attack aircraft, 1 DC-8, 3 BAC One-Eleven and 1 Falcon VIP transports, 3 C-130H Hercules, 6 Defender and 15 Skyvan light transports, 35 Agusta-Bell 205, 212, 214B and JetRanger, and Bell 214 ST helicopters for security duties, 2 Super Puma VIP helicopters and 2 Bravo piston-engined trainers. Air defence force has batteries of Rapier low-level surface-to-air missiles. Personnel (1988) about 3,000.

INTERNATIONAL RELATIONS

Membership. Oman is a member of UN, the Arab League, the Islamic Conference Organisation and the Gulf Co-operation Council.

Treaties. The Treaty of Friendship, Commerce and Navigation between Britain and the Sultan signed on 20 Dec. 1951, reaffirmed the close ties which have existed between the British Government and the Sultanate of Oman for over a century and a half. A Memorandum of Understanding signed in June 1982 provided for regular consultations on international and bilateral issues.

ECONOMY

Planning. The third 5-year plan (1986–90) envisages expenditure of R.O. 9,250m.

Budget. Revenue (1987) R.O. 1,335m. (1,081m. from oil); expenditure, 1,610m.

Currency. The *Rial Omani* was introduced in Nov. 1972 replacing the *Rial Saidi.* It is divided into 1,000 *baiza.* There are notes of 100, 200 and 500 *baiza* and 1, 5, 10, 20 and 50 *Rial Omani* and coins of 2, 5, 10, 25, 50, 100, 250 and 500 *baiza.* The exchange rate in March 1988 was £1 = 683 *baiza*; US$1 = 385 *baiza.*

Banking. In Dec. 1986 there were 22 commercial banks operating in Oman, of which 13 were foreign institutions. There are 3 specialized banks: The Oman Development Bank, the Oman Housing Bank and the Oman Bank for Agriculture and Fisheries. The Central Bank of Oman commenced operations in 1975.

Weights and Measures. The metric system of measurement is in operation. Transactions in the former measurements are now illegal.

ENERGY AND NATURAL RESOURCES

Electricity. Production (1986) 2,920m. kwh. Supply 240 volts; 50 Hz.

Oil. The economy of Oman is dominated by the oil industry, which provides nearly all Government revenue. In 1937 Petroleum Concessions (Oman) Ltd, a subsidiary of the Iraq Petroleum Co., was granted a 75-year oil concession extending over the whole of Oman, although it relinquished Dhofar in 1950. In 1951 the company's name was changed to Petroleum Development (Oman) Ltd. The company (PDO) regained the Dhofar concession area in 1969. When some of the IPC partners withdrew from Oman in 1960, Shell took over the management of PDO with an 85% interest (minority interests were held by Compagnie Française des Pétroles, 10% and Gulbenkian, 5%). At the beginning of 1974 the Oman Government bought a 25% share in PDO, increasing this retroactively to 60% in July. A Joint Management Committee was established. Other companies active in exploration activities in Oman, with mixed success, include Amoco, Elf-Acquitaine and a consortium of Deminex, Agip and Hispanoil with BP as operator.

Oil in commercial quantities was discovered in 1964 and production began at a rate of 200,000 bbls per day in 1967. Production has fluctuated from year to year, peaking in 1976 at 366,000 bbls per day. Production in 1987 was 28·25m. tonnes. Total proven reserves were estimated in 1986 to be 4,200m. bbls, or sufficient for 22 years at the current rate of production. Since the first oil refinery became operational in 1982, Oman has been self-sufficient in most oil-derived products.

Oman is not a member of OPEC or OAPEC but tends to follow OPEC pricing policy.

Gas. Production (1982) 290m. cu. ft per day. In 1987 reserves were estimated at 7·7m. cu. ft.

Water Resources. Oman relies on a combination of water and desalination plants for its water. Two desalination plants at Ghubriah, built in 1972 and 1982, provide most of the water needs of the capital area.

Minerals. Production of refined copper at the smelter at Sohar was about 14,000 tonnes in 1984.

Agriculture. About 41,000 hectares are under cultivation. In the valleys of the interior, as well as on the Batinah, date cultivation has reached a high level, and there are possibilities of agricultural development subject to present water resources and soil surveys. The crop of dates was 77,000 tonnes in 1986, most of which is exported to India. Other main crops are limes, bananas, coconuts, mangoes and alfalfa. Camels (79,000 in 1986) are bred in large numbers by the inland tribes.

Fisheries. Catch (1985) 114,000 tonnes.

INDUSTRY AND TRADE

Industry. Manufacturing accounts for 3% of GDP and apart from oil production, copper mining and smelting and cement production there are no industries of any importance. Fishing, water resources, soil and agricultural surveys are being undertaken. The government gives priority to import substitute industries.

Commerce. The total imports for 1985 were valued at R.O. 1,162m., including machinery and transport equipment (455m.), manufactured goods (240·9m.), food and live animals (124·1m.), petroleum products (19·7m.) and chemicals (31·7m.).

In 1985, 18·9% of imports came from Japan, 15·4% from UK, 5·3% from USA and 7·3% from the Federal Republic of Germany; 66·3% of oil exports went to Japan, 14·1% to South Korea, 6·7% to Thailand, 2·9% to Singapore and 2·7% to Taiwan.

Total trade between Oman and UK (British Department of Trade returns, in £1,000 sterling):

	1983	1984	1985	1986	1987
Imports to UK	91,216	82,655	69,015	87,235	49,487
Exports and re-exports from UK	448,900	390,275	489,926	399,647	249,916

COMMUNICATIONS

Roads. A network of adequate graded roads links all the main sectors of population, and only a few mountain villages are not accessible by Land-Rover. In Dec. 1983 there were 3,222 km of paved roads and 18,667 km of graded roads. In 1985 there were 200,000 vehicles.

Aviation. Gulf Air run regional services in and out of Seeb international airport (20 miles from Muscat) to Bahrain, Doha, Abu Dhabi, Dubai, Karachi, Bombay and operate daily flights to and from London. Other airlines serving Muscat are British Airways, KLM, Thai International, British Caledonian, Air Tanzania, MEA, Kuwait Airlines, PIA, Air India, Iran Air, TMA (cargo) and Trade Winds (cargo). Domestic flights are provided by Oman Aviation Services.

Shipping. In Mutrah a deep-water port (named Mina Qaboos) was completed in 1974 at a cost of R.O. 18·2m. It provides 12 berths, 9 of which are deep-water berths, warehousing facilities and a harbour for dhows and coastal vessels. The annual handling capacity has been raised to 1·5m. tons. Mina Raysut, the port of Salalah, has a capacity of 1m. tons per year.

Post and Broadcasting. There are Sultanate post offices in Muscat and Mutrah, relying solely upon a Post Office Box system for delivery. Omantel maintain a telegraph office at Muscat and an automatic telephone exchange (23,000 lines, 1984) which includes Mutrah, Bait-al-Falaj and Mina al-Fahal, the oil company terminal. A high-frequency radio link with Bahrain was opened in Aug. 1972 providing communications with other parts of the world. Internally, there are radio telephone, telex and telegraph services direct between Salalah and Muscat, and a VHF radio link between Seeb international airport and Muscat. The airport is also served by a SITA telex system. Radio Oman broadcasts daily for 17 hours in Arabic and 2 hours in English.

A colour television service covering Muscat and the surrounding area started transmission in Nov. 1974. A television service for Dhofar opened in 1975. Total number of televisions, 23,500 and radios, 800,000 in 1985.

Newspapers. There were (1987) 2 Arabic and 1 English daily newspapers and 2 English weekly newspapers.

EDUCATION AND WELFARE

Education. In 1985–86, there were 531 schools with 195,847 pupils and (1984–85) 9,236 teachers. Plans have been implemented for the development of technical and agricultural training and craft training at intermediate and secondary level. Oman's first university, the Sultan Qaboos University, opened in Sept. 1986. There are also programmes to combat adult illiteracy.

Health. Health services in 1984 were widely spread with 15 hospitals in use with 2,142 beds, and 1 more hospital planned, 21 health centres, 74 dispensaries, 572 doctors and 1,753 nurses. There are also Save the Children Fund Welfare Clinics at Sohar and Sur.

DIPLOMATIC REPRESENTATIVES

Of Oman in Great Britain (44A Montpelier Sq., London, SW7 1JJ)
Ambassador: Hussain Bin Mohammad Bin Ali.

Of Great Britain in Oman (PO Box 300, Muscat)
Ambassador: Robert John Alston, CMG.

Of Oman in the USA (2342 Massachusetts Ave., NW, Washington, D.C., 20008)
Ambassador: Ali Salim Bader Al-Hinai.

Of the USA in Oman (PO Box 966, Muscat)
Ambassador: G. C. Montgomery.

Of Oman to the United Nations
Ambassador: Salim Bin Mohammed Al-Khussaiby.

Books of Reference

Oman in 10 years. Ministry of Information. Oman, 1980
Oman: A MEED Practical Guide. London, 1981
Carter, J. R. L., *Tribes of Oman.* London, 1981
Clements, F. A., *Oman: The Reborn Land.* London and New York, 1980.—*Oman.* [Bibliography] Oxford and Santa Barbara, 1981
Graz, L., *The Omani's: Sentinels of the Gulf.* London, 1982
Hawley, D., *Oman and its Rennaissance.* London, 1977
Peterson, J. E., *Oman in the Twentieth Century.* London and New York, 1978
Peyton, W. D., *Oman before 1970: The End of an Era.* London, 1985
Pridham, B. R., (ed.) *Oman: Economic, Social and Strategic Developments.* London, 1987
Shannon, M. O., *Oman and South-eastern Arabia: A Bibliographic Survey.* Boston, 1978
Skeet, I., *Muscat and Oman: The End of an Era.* London, 1974
Thesiger, W., *Arabian Sands.* London, 1959
Townsend, J., *Oman.* London, 1977
Ward, P., *Travels in Oman.* Cambridge, 1987
Wikan, U., *Behind the Veil in Arabia: Women in Oman.* Johns Hopkins Univ. Press, 1982

PAKISTAN

Capital: Islamabad
Population: 102·2m. (1987)
GNP per capita: US$390 (1983)

Islamic Republic of Pakistan

HISTORY. Pakistan was constituted as a Dominion on 14 Aug. 1947, under the provisions of the Indian Independence Act, 1947, which received the royal assent on 18 July 1947. The Dominion consisted of the following former territories of British India: Balúchistán, East Bengal (including almost the whole of Sylhet, a former district of Assam), North-West Frontier, West Punjab and Sind; and those States which had acceded to Pakistan.

On 23 March 1956 an Islamic republic was proclaimed after the Constituent Assembly had adopted the draft constitution on 29 Feb.

On 7 Oct. 1958 President Mirza declared martial law in Pakistan, dismissed the central and provincial Governments, abolished all political parties and abrogated the constitution of 23 March 1956. Field Marshal Mohammad Ayub Khan, the Army Commander-in-Chief, was appointed as chief martial law administrator and assumed office on 28 Oct. 1958, after Maj.-Gen. Iskander Mirza had handed all powers to him. His authority was confirmed by a ballot in Feb. 1960. He proclaimed a new constitution on 1 March 1962.

On 25 March 1969 President Ayub Khan resigned and handed over power to the army under the leadership of Maj.-Gen. Agha Muhammad Yahya Khan who immediately proclaimed martial law throughout the country, appointing himself chief martial law administrator on the same day. On 29 March 1970 the Legal Framework Order was published, defining a new constitution: Pakistan to be a federal republic with a Moslem Head of State; the National Assembly and Provincial Assemblies to be elected in free and periodical elections, the first of which was held on 7 Dec. 1970.

At the general election the Awami League based in East Pakistan and led by Sheikh Mujibur Rahman gained 167 seats and the Peoples' Party 90. Martial law continued pending the settlement of differences between East and West, which developed into civil war in March 1971. The war ended in Dec. 1971 and the Eastern province declared itself an independent state, Bangladesh. On 20 Dec. 1971 President Yahya Khan resigned and Mr Z. A. Bhutto became President and chief martial law administrator. On 30 Jan. 1972, Pakistan withdrew from the Commonwealth.

A new Constitution was adopted by the National Assembly on 10 April 1973 and enforced on 14 Aug. 1973. It provided for a federal parliamentary system with the President as constitutional head and the Prime Minister as chief executive. President Bhutto stepped down to become Prime Minister and Fazal Elahi Chaudhry was elected President.

The Chief of the Army Staff, Gen. M. Zia-ul-Haq, proclaimed martial law on 5 July 1977 and the armed forces took control of the administration; scheduled elections were postponed. Mr Bhutto was hanged (for conspiracy to murder) on 4 April 1979. Gen. M. Zia-ul-Haq succeeded Fazal Elahi Chaudhry as President in Sept. 1978.

Governors-General of Pakistan: Quaid-I-Azam Mohammed Ali Jinnah (14 Aug. 1947–11 Sept. 1948); Khawaja Nazimuddin (14 Sept. 1948–18 Oct. 1951; took over the premiership after the assassination of Liaquat Ali Khan); Ghulam Mohammad (19 Oct. 1951–6 Aug. 1955); Maj.-Gen. Iskander Mirza (assumed office of President on 6 Oct. 1955, elected President on 5 March 1956).

Presidents of Pakistan: Maj.-Gen. Iskander Mirza (23 March 1956–28 Oct. 1958); Field Marshal Mohammad Ayub Khan (28 Oct. 1958–25 March 1969); Maj.-Gen. Agha Muhammad Yahya Khan (31 March 1969–20 Dec. 1971);

Zulfiqar Ali Bhutto (20 Dec.1971–14 Aug. 1973); Fazal Elahi Chaudhri (14 Aug. 1973–16 Sept. 1978); Gen. Mohammad Zia ul-Haq (16 Sept. 1978–).

AREA AND POPULATION. Pakistan is bounded north-west by Afghánistán, north by the USSR and China, east by India and south by the Arabian Sea. The total area of Pakistan is 307,293 sq. miles (796,095 sq. km); population (1981 census), 84·25m.; males, 44,232,000; females, 40,021,000. Density, 105·8 per sq. km. Estimate (1987) 102·2m. Urban population, 28·3%.

The population of the principal cities is:

Census of 1981

Islamabad	201,000	Multan	730,000	Jhang	195,000
Karachi	5,103,000	Gujranwala	597,000	Sukkur	191,000
Lahore	2,922,000	Peshawar	555,000	Bahawalpur	178,000
Faisalabad	1,092,000	Sialkot	296,000	Kasur	155,000
Rawalpindi	928,000	Sargodha	294,000	Gujrat	154,000
Hyderabad	795,000	Quetta	285,000	Okara	154,000

Population of the provinces (census of 1981) was (1,000):

	Area (sq. km)	1981 census population				1981 density per sq. km (number)	Estimated total 1985
		Total	Male	Female	Urban		
North-west Frontier Province	74,521	11,061	5,761	5,300	1,665	148	12,287
Federally admin. Tribal Areas	27,219	2,199	1,143	1,056	–	81	2,467
Fed. Cap. Territory Islamabad	907	340	185	155	204	376	379
Punjab	205,344	47,292	24,860	22,432	13,051	230	53,840
Sind	140,914	19,029	9,999	9,030	8,243	135	21,682
Balúchistán	347,190	4,332	2,284	2,048	677	12	4,908

By Jan. 1987 there were 3m. Afghan refugees in Pakistan, of whom most were in the North-west Frontier Province, and small numbers in Baluchistan and the Punjab.

Language. The commonest languages are Urdu and Punjabi. Urdu is the national language while English is used in business and in central government. Provincial languages are Punjabi, Sindhi, Pushtu (North-West Frontier Province), Baluchi and Brahvi.

CLIMATE. A weak form of tropical monsoon climate occurs over much of the country, with arid conditions in the north and west, where the wet season is only from Dec. to March. Elsewhere, rain comes mainly in the summer. Summer temperatures are high everywhere, but winters can be cold in the mountainous north.
Islamabad. Jan. 50°F (10°C), July 90°F (32·2°C). Annual rainfall 36″ (900 mm).
Karachi. Jan. 61°F (16·1°C), July 86°F (30°C). Annual rainfall 8″ (196 mm).
Lahore. Jan. 53°F (11·7°C), July 89°F (31·7°C). Annual rainfall 18″ (452 mm).
Multan. Jan. 51°F (10·6°C), July 93°F (33·9°C). Annual rainfall 7″ (170 mm).
Quetta. Jan. 38°F (3·3°C), July 80°F (26·7°C). Annual rainfall 10″ (239 mm).

CONSTITUTION AND GOVERNMENT. Under the Constitution of 1973 Parliament is bi-cameral, comprising the National Assembly and the Senate. The strength of the National Assembly is 210 including 10 women. The Senate consists of 63 members, 14 from each province, 5 from Federally Administered Tribal Areas and 2 from the federal capital area, elected by the members of the Provincial Assemblies. A constitutional amendment of 29 March 1976 provided 6 National Assembly seats reserved for non-Moslem minority representatives.

With the proclamation of martial law the Constitution was kept in abeyance, but not abrogated.

The Constitution obliges the Government to use such ways and means as may enable the people to order their lives collectively and individually in accordance with the principles of Islam. The Constitution (Ninth Amendment) Bill, 1986, consolidated Islam as the basis of law.

An Ombudsman was appointed in Jan. 1983.

National elections were held in Feb. 1985 on the basis of the 1973 Constitution, amended to provide wider presidential powers. On 19 Dec. 1984 a referendum had been held to determine whether the President should continue in office for a 5-year term, following the elections; results were announced as 98% in favour.

The Pakistan People's Party won 47 seats in the new Assembly, the Muslim League 17 and the Jamaat Islami Party, 9. In March 1985 the President set up a new National Security Council, led by himself; he assumed power to appoint and dismiss ministers and retained the final decision on legislation.

In April 1985 the Council was replaced by a Federal Cabinet. On 30 Dec. 1985 martial law ended.

President, Establishment: Gen. M. Zia-ul-Haq.

Federal Cabinet in March 1988:

Prime Minister: Mohammad Khan Junejo. *Acting Foreign Affairs:* Zain Noorani. *Finance and Economic Affairs, Petroleum and Natural Resources:* Mian M. Y. K. Wattoo. *Communications and Railways:* M. A. Khan Khattak. *Education, Health, Special Education, Social Welfare:* Nasim A. Aheer. *Food and Agriculture:* M. I. Baluch. *Industries and Production:* C. S. Husain. *Information and Broadcasting, Water and Power:* Q. A. M. Abid. *States and Frontier Areas:* S. Q. Shah. *Justice, Parliamentary Affairs, Interior:* W. Sajjad. *Housing:* H. H. Tayyeb. *Local Government, Rural Development:* A. A. Chaudhary. *Federal Minister:* I. A. Khan. *Commerce, Planning and Development:* M. Haq. *Labour, Manpower and Overseas Pakistanis:* S. M. Pasha Khuro. *Religious and Minority Affairs:* H. M. Saifullah Khan.

There are 4 Ministers of State.

On 18 Jan. 1986 the Prime Minister was elected leader of the Muslim League Party.

National flag: Green, charged at the centre, with a white crescent and white 5-pointed star, a white vertical stripe at the mast to one-quarter of the flag.

Local Government. Pakistan comprises the Federal Capital Territory (Islamabad), the provinces of the Punjab, the North-West Frontier, Sind and Balúchistán, and the tribal areas of the north-west. The provincial capitals are Peshawar (NW Frontier Province), Lahore (Punjab), Karachi (Sind) and Quetta (Balúchistán). Provincial governors are appointed by the President and are assisted by elected provincial councils.

Within the provinces there are divisions administered by Commissioners appointed by the President; the divisions are divided into districts and agencies administered by Deputy Commissioners or Political Agents who are responsible to the Provincial Governments.

The tribal areas (Khyber, Kurram, Malakand, Mohmand, North Waziristan, South Waziristan) are administered by political agents responsible to the federal government.

Kashmir. Pakistan controls the northern and western portions of Kashmir, an area of about 84,160 sq. km with a population of about 2·8m. in 1985. Under a United Nations resolution of 1949 its future was to be decided by plebiscite; it is still a disputed territory.

The people of Azad Kashmir (the west) have their own Assembly (42 members including 2 women), their own Council (of 14 members), High Court and Supreme Court. There is a Parliamentary form of Government with a Prime Minister as the executive head and the President as the Constitutional head. Elections to the Legislative's 40 general seats are to be held within 10 days of the general elections in Pakistan, according to a presidential proclamation of 8 Oct. 1977. The seat of government is Muzaffarabad.

The Pakistan Government is directly responsible for Gilgit and Baltistan (the north).

DEFENCE

Army. The Army consists of 2 armoured and 17 infantry divisions; 4 independent armoured, 8 independent infantry, 8 artillery and 3 anti-aircraft brigades; 6 armoured reconnaissance regiments, 7 surface-to-air missile batteries and 1 Special Services Group. Equipment includes 450 M-47/-48, 51 T-54/-55 and 1,100 Type-59 main battle tanks. The Army has an air component with about 70 fixed-wing aircraft for transport, reconnaissance and observation duties and over 100 helicopters for anti-armour operations, transport, liaison and training. Strength (1988) 450,000, with a further 500,000 reservists. There are also 164,000 men in paramilitary units: National Guard, Frontier Corps, Pakistan Rangers, Coast Guard and Frontier Constabulary.

Navy. The fleet comprises 6 diesel-powered patrol submarines (completed in France in 1969–80), 3 midget submarines, 1 'County' class destroyer, *Babur* (*ex*-HMS *London*) transferred from the Royal Navy in 1982, the ex-British very old light cruiser (harbour training ship) *ex*-HMS *Diadem*, re-named *Jahangir*, 7 very old destroyers (6 *ex*-US and 1 *ex*-British), 4 *ex*-Chinese corvette-type patrol vessels, 8 *ex*-Chinese fast missile craft, 12 *ex*-Chinese fast gunboats, 4 *ex*-Chinese fast (hydrofoil) torpedo boats, 1 seaward defence boat, 1 oceanographic survey ship, 3 coastal minesweepers, 1 fleet replenishment ship, 1 degaussing vessel, 1 rescue ship, 2 landing craft, 1 water carrier and 4 tugs. The naval air arm has 3 Atlantics and 1 Fokker for patrol and transport duties, 6 Sea King anti-submarine warfare helicopters and 4 Alouette III liaison helicopters.

The principal naval base and dockyard are at Karachi. Naval personnel in 1988 totalled 1,250 officers and 14,550 ratings.

Air Force. The Pakistan Air Force came into being on 14 Aug. 1947. It has its head-quarters at Peshawar and is organized within 3 air defence sectors, in the northern, central and southern areas of the country. Air defence units include 2 squadrons of F-16 Fighting Falcons and at least 6 squadrons of Chinese-built F-6s (MiG-19). Tactical units include 5 squadrons of Mirage III-EP/5 supersonic fighters and 5 with A-5 fighter-bombers, 1 squadron equipped with Mirage III-RP reconnaissance aircraft, and 1 with C-130 Hercules turboprop transports. Flying training schools are equipped with Masshaq (Saab Supporter) armed piston-engined primary trainers, T-37B/C jet trainers supplied by the USA, Mirage III-DPs and Chinese-built FT-5s (two-seat MiG-17s) and FT-6s (two-seat MiG-19s). A VIP transport squadron operates the Presidential F27 turboprop aircraft, 3 twin-jet Falcon 20s and smaller types. There is a flying college at Risalpur and an aeronautical engineering college at Korangi Creek. Total strength in 1988 was about 381 combat aircraft and 17,600 all ranks.

INTERNATIONAL RELATIONS

External Debt (30 June 1986), US$16,349·8m.

Membership. Pakistan is a member of the UN, the Colombo Plan, and Regional Co-operation for Development.

Treaties. A mutual defence assistance agreement between Pakistan and the USA was signed in Karachi on 19 May 1954.

ECONOMY

Planning. The sixth 5-year plan (1983–88) envisages a total fixed investment of Rs 495,000m. including Rs 77,000m. for industry, of which Rs 62,000m. would be spent in the private sector. Real growth in GDP is planned at 6·5% annually (agriculture 5%; industry 9%). Expenditure will be met mainly (75%) from internal resources. Allocations for energy (Rs 116,000m.), agriculture and irrigation (Rs 88,000m.), special development programmes (Rs 22,000m.) and family planning (Rs 1,800m.) have been made.

Budget. The following table shows the budget for the years 1985–86 and 1986–87 in Rs 1m.:

	1985–86 Revised	1986–87 Budget
Revenue receipts	93,716·4	105,396·9
of which taxes	58,207·9	61,194·6
Capital receipts	57,866·7	52,426·0
of which External	19,962·0	25,944·4
Revenue expenditure	98,783·1	114,654·4
Capital expenditure	45,008·0	39,918·9

Currency. The monetary unit is the Pakistan *rupee.* In March 1988 Rs 30·60 = £1; Rs 17·59 = US$1. Decimal coinage was introduced on 1 Jan. 1961. The rupee, which previously consisted of 64 *pice,* now consists of 100 *paisas.* The notes are of Rs 100, 50, 10 and 5 denominations issued by the State Bank in the name of the Government, and Rs 1 issued by the State Bank incurring no liability; the coinage in the decimal series is 0·5, 0·25, 0·1, 0·05 and 0·01 rupee.

Total monetary assets (including currency in circulation and deposits) on 31 March 1987 amounted to Rs 230,978m. Currency in circulation, Rs 73,596m.

Banking. As from 1 Jan. 1985, banks and other financial institutions will abandon the payment of interest on new transactions. This does not apply to international business, but does apply to the domestic business of foreign banks operating in Pakistan. Investment partnerships, between bank and customer, are to replace straight loans at interest. The aim is to bring all domestic financial transactions into conformity with Islamic teaching. The State Bank of Pakistan has prepared a schedule of acceptable practice.

The State Bank of Pakistan is the central bank; it came into operation as the Central Bank on 1 July 1948 with an authorized capital of Rs 30m. and was nationalized in Jan. 1974. At end June 1987 total assets or liabilities of the issue department amounted to Rs 78,181m. and those of the banking department Rs 79,165m.; total deposits, Rs 48,675m. It is the sole bank of issue for Pakistan, custodian of foreign exchange reserves and banker for the federal and provincial governments and for scheduled banks. It also manages the rupee public debt of federal and provincial governments. It provides short-term loans to the Government and commercial banks and short- and medium-term loans to specialized banks. The Bank's subsidiary Federal Bank for Co-operatives makes loans to provincial co-operative banks.

There were 32 scheduled banks in Pakistan on 30 June 1987. Of these 9 were Pakistani (nationalized since 1974). Total liabilities or assets of all scheduled banks stood at Rs 399,692·6m., of which time liabilities, Rs 105,389·5m., on the last working day of June, 1987. The National Bank of Pakistan acts as an agent of the State Bank for transacting Government business and managing currency chests at places where the State Bank has no offices of its own.

Weights and Measures. The metric system is in general use.

ENERGY AND NATURAL RESOURCES

Electricity. Installed capacity of the state power system (1986–87) by type of generation: Thermal 3,263 mw., hydro-electric, 2,898 mw.; the Karachi Electric Supply Corporation had 17·9%. Total generated electrical energy in 1986–87, 28,236m. kwh; 15,241m. kwh of this was hydro-electricity, the main source being the Tarbela Dam. By June 1986 21,846 villages (of a total 43,244) had access to electric power. Supply 230 volts; 50 Hz.

Oil. Oil comes mainly from the Potowar Plain, from fields at Meyal, Tut, Balkassar, Joya Mair and Dhullian. Production in 1987 was 2·4m. tonnes. Oil reserves were also found at Dhodak in Dec. 1976. Exploitation is mainly through government incentives and concessions to foreign private sector companies. The Pak-Arab refinery pipeline runs 865 km. from Karachi to Multan; capacity, 4·5m. tonnes of oil annually.

Gas. Gas pipelines from Sui to Karachi (345 miles) and Multan (200) supply natural gas to industry and domestic consumers. A pipeline between Quetta and

Shikarpur was constructed in 1982. There are 4 other productive fields. Reserves (1983), 500,000m. cu. metres; production in 1986–87 was 11,045m. cu. metres.

Water. The Indus water treaty of 1960, concluded between India and Pakistan, has created the basis for a large-scale development programme. The Indus Basin Development Fund Agreement has been subscribed by Australia, Canada, Federal Republic of Germany, New Zealand, UK and USA and is administered by the International Bank; the works to be constructed call for expenditure of US$1,000m. The main purpose of the treaty is the division of the water power of the Indus and its 5 tributaries between India and Pakistan. After the construction of some 460 miles of canals, the Indus and the 2 western tributaries will serve Pakistan and the entire flow of the 3 eastern tributaries will be released for use in India.

The largest project is the construction of the Tarbela Dam, an earth-and-rock filled dam on the river Indus, 485 ft high, which has a gross storage capacity of 11·1m. acre feet of water for irrigation.

The Lloyd Barrage and Canal Construction Scheme, consists of a barrage across the river Indus at Sukkur and 7 canals—4 on the left and 3 on the right bank. Another barrage across the Indus, 4½ miles north of Kotri, called the Ghulam Muhammad Barrage, was completed in 1955. The Taunsa barrage on the Indus, 80 miles downstream of Kalabagh, was completed in 1958. The Gudu barrage, 10 miles from Kashmore, was completed in 1962.

The province of the Punjab set up in 1949 the Thal Development Authority to colonize the Thal desert between the Indus and Jhelum rivers.

The Chashma canal will carry water 172 miles across Dera Ismail Khan from the Chashma barrage on the Indus. The Mangla Dam on the Jhelum was inaugurated in Nov. 1967.

Minerals. The main agencies are the Pakistan Mineral Development Corporation, the Resource Development Corporation and the Gemstone Corporation of Pakistan. Coal is mined at Sharigh and Harnai on the Sind–Pishin railway and in the Bolan pass, also in Sor Range and Degari in the Quetta–Pishin district and in the Punjab; total recoverable reserves, about 480m. tonnes, mainly low-grade. A further 55m. tonnes was found at Lakhra in 1980 and reserves of over 500m. tonnes were found in the 300 sq. mile Thatta Sadha field in 1981. Copper ore reserves at Saindak, in Balúchistán, 412m. tons, containing (1984 estimate) 1·69m. tons of copper; 2·24m. oz. of gold; 2·2m. oz. of silver. Chromite is extracted in and near Muslimbagh. Limestone is quarried generally. Gypsum is mined in the Sibi district and elsewhere; reserves (1983), about 370m. tonnes. Iron ore is being worked in Kalabagh and elsewhere; reserves, about 400m. tonnes, low-grade. A further 18m. tonnes, high-grade, has been found in Balúchistán. Uranium has been found in Dera Ghazi Khan.

Production (tonnes, 1986–87): Coal, 2·14m.; chromite, 7,873; limestone, 6·6m.; gypsum, 379,000; rock salt, 546,000; fire clay, 94,820. Other minerals of which useful deposits have been found are magnesite, sulphur, barites, marble, bauxite, antimony ore, bentonite, celestite, dolomite, fireclay, fluorite, fuller's earth, phosphate rock, silica sand and soapstone.

Agriculture. The entire area in the north and west is covered by great mountain ranges. The rest of the country consists of a fertile plain watered by 5 big rivers and their tributaries. Agriculture is dependent almost entirely on the irrigation system based on these rivers. It employs (1986) 54% of labour and provides about 26% of GNP and 45% of foreign exchange earnings. Growth rate, 1986–87, 5·86%. The main crops are wheat, cotton, maize, sugar-cane and rice, while the Quetta and Kalat divisions (Balúchistán) are known for their fruits and dates.

Pakistan is self-sufficient in wheat, rice and sugar.

Production, 1985–86, in 1,000 tonnes: Rice (cleaned), 2,918·9; wheat, 13,923; sugar-cane, 27,856·3; cotton (lint, 1,000 bales), 7,155.

An ordinance of Jan. 1977 reduced the upper limit of land holding to 100 irrigated or 200 non-irrigated acres; it also replaced the former land revenue system with a new agricultural income tax, from which holders of up to 25 irrigated or 50 unirrigated acres are exempt. Of about 4m. farms, 89% are of less than 25 acres. Of the surveyed area of 156m. acres, cultivated land accounts for 63m. acres, of which 11m. acres consist of fallow land, so that the net area sown is 52m. acres.

Livestock (estimate, 1987): Cattle, 16,900,000; buffaloes, 13,700,000; sheep, 26,600,000; goats, 31,900,000; poultry, 121·7m.

Forestry. In 1983–84 the forest departments managed 6·8m. hectares, including range-lands. Productive forests covered 1·29m. hectares, and produced (1986–87) 733,000 cu. metres of timber and firewood. Forest lands are also used as national parks, wildlife and game reserves.

Fisheries. In 1985 landings were 320,000 tonnes of marine and 70,600 of inland water fish.

INDUSTRY AND TRADE

Industry. Industry employs about 10% of the population, contributing (1984–85) about 19% of GDP. The growth rate in manufacturing, 1986–87, was an estimated 7·44%. In 1972 public sector companies were re-organized under a Board of Industrial Management. Government policy since 1977 has been to encourage private industry, particularly small industry. The public sector, however, is still dominant in large industries; in 1981–82 its gross value added was Rs. 4,291·8m., number of employees 81,689, investment Rs. 45,886·98m., of which 60% was for Pakistan Steel. Steel, cement, fertilizer and vegetable ghee are the most valuable public sector industries.

A public sector steel-mill (Pakistan Steel) has been built at Port Qasim near Karachi, capacity 1·1m. tonnes; production of coke and pig-iron began in autumn 1981 and of steel in 1983. A private sector ferrous alloys plant has been approved near Peshawar, capacity 40 tonnes of ferrous silicon and manganese per day. There is an Export Processing Zone at Karachi, covering 500 acres; at 30 June 1981 investment here stood at US$58·8m. The largest project (approved Aug. 1981) is a Pakistan-Saudi aluminium extrusion plant.

Production 1986–87 (tonnes): Refined sugar, 1·3m.; vegetable products, 590,278; jute textiles, 109,748; soda ash, 130,274; sulphuric acid, 77,610; caustic soda, 41,931; chip board and paper board, 66,945; cycle tyres and tubes, 10·6m. units; bicycles, 593,058 units; cotton cloth, 234·7m. sq. metres; cotton yarn, 578·1m. kg.; cement, 5·4m.; steel billets 253,848; hot-rolled steel sheets and coils, 399,613; cold-rolled, 122,887; mild steel products, 746,189; pre-recorded cassettes, 8·2m. units.

Labour. The 1981 census gave the total work force as 22·62m. Estimates (1985–86) give 28·9m., employed workforce 27·86m. of whom 15·05m. (54%) were engaged in agriculture, forestry and fishing, 3·73m. (13%) in manufacturing; the textile industry was the largest single manufacturing employer. Of the home work force, 26·26% were unpaid family helpers, 26·77% were wage employees.

Commerce. Total value of exports during 1985–86 amounted to Rs 49,592·2m., and the total value of imports to Rs 90,946·3m. In 1986–87, exports were Rs 63,267·9m., imports, Rs 92,430·8m. The value of the chief articles imported into and exported from Pakistan (in Rs 1m.):

Imports			Exports		
	1985–86	1986–87		1985–86	1986–87
Minerals, fuels, lubricants	17,629·8	14,806·2	Raw cotton	8,290·5	7,675·8
Machinery and			Cotton cloth	5,082·7	5,931·1
transport equipment	27,247·7	27,543·5	Textile yarns	4,572·5	8,765·6
Edible oils	8,874·0	5,003·4	Rice	5,527·2	5,052·6
Chemicals	11,663·2	15,773·1	Carpets, tapestries	2,668·4	3,419·5

Of exports (1986–87), Rs 17,503·5m. went to the European Community; Rs 9,608·6m. to the middle east, of which Rs 4,509·6m. was to Saudi Arabia; Rs 6,421·8m. went to USA. Of imports, Rs 22,423·4m. came from the European Community; Rs 10,195m. from USA; Rs 16,613·6m. from the middle east, of which Rs 4,920·3m. was from Saudi Arabia.

Total trade between Pakistan and UK (British Department of Trade returns, in £1,000 sterling):

	1983	1984	1985	1986	1987
Imports to UK	80,277	93,136	119,006	131,296	167,315
Exports and re-exports from UK	191,647	282,356	255,419	227,064	252,978

Tourism. In 1986 there were 432,000 tourist arrivals spending US$180·2m.

COMMUNICATIONS

Roads. In 1985–86 Pakistan had 106,580 km of roads, of which 45,686 km were all-weather roads. The Karakoram highway to the Chinese border, through Kohistan and the Hunza valley, was opened in 1978. An all-weather road linking Skardu and the remote NE Indus valley to the highway was built in 1980.

In 1985 there were 1·8m. vehicles registered, including 925,977 motor-cycles and 426,419 cars, jeeps and station wagons.

Railways. Pakistan Railways had (1986) a route of 8,775 km (of which 290 km electrified) mainly on 1,676 mm. gauge, with some metre gauge and narrow gauge line. In 1985–86 there were 82·9m. passengers and 11·8m. tonnes of freight. Gross earnings, 1985–86, Rs 4,367·7m.

Aviation. Karachi is served by British Airways, KLM, PANAM, Lufthansa, Swissair, SAS, Iran National Airlines, Air France, Garuda, Gulf Air and by Philippine, Japanese, Chinese, East African, Syrian, Iraqui, Kuwait, Jordanian, Saudi Arabian, Romanian, Egyptian and Russian airlines.

Pakistan International Airlines (founded 1955; the majority of shares is held by the Government) had 4 DC-10s, 7 Boeing 707Cs, 5 720Bs, 2 747Bs and 8 Fokker F27s in 1977; 2 other Boeing 720Bs were on lease to Air Malta. Services operate to 20 home airports, New York, Paris, Amsterdam, Copenhagen, İstanbul, Athens, Rome, Cairo, Tripoli, Nairobi, Dhahran, Damascus, Amman, Baghdad, Persian Gulf points, Tōkyō, Peking (Beijing), Zahedan, Singapore, Manila, Kuala Lumpur, Bangkok, Colombo, London, Frankfurt, Bombay, Delhi, Dacca, Kábul, Tehrán and Jeddah.

Shipping. There is a seaport at Karachi, dry-cargo-handling capacity 6m. tonnes a year, oil-handling, 10m. The second port, 26 miles east of Karachi, is Port Muhammad Bin Qasim; it has iron and coal berths for Pakistan Steel Mills, multi-purpose berths, bulk-cargo handling, oil and container-traffic terminals; the first seven berths were operational in 1983. Shipping entered and cleared (1985–86): Karachi 1,828 and 1,787 vessels; Port Qasim 239 and 243. Cargo handled: Karachi 15·8m. tonnes, Port Qasim 4·4m. The Pakistan National Shipping Corporation had 35 vessels in 1985, of 596,973 DWT. National flag carriers now operate between Pakistan and UK; USA and Canada; the Far East; the (Persian) Gulf, Arabian Gulf, Red Sea, Black Sea and Mekran Coast; Continental Europe and the Middle East. The Karachi Shipyard and Engineering Works Ltd construct all types of vessels up to 27,000 DWT and repairs all types; dry-dock and under-water repairs can be done on vessels up to 29,000 DWT, above-water repairs on vessels and drilling rigs of all sizes.

Post and Broadcasting. The telegraph and telephone system is government-owned. Telephones, on 31 March 1987, numbered 643,500; a nationwide dialling system is in operation between 46 cities. In 1987 there were 12,116 post offices. Pakistan has international telephone connections by 102 satellite, 7 HF, 4 microwave and 10 carrier circuits. An international direct-dialling exchange with 25,000 connections was opened in July 1980. The Pakistan Broadcasting Corporation had 16 radio stations in Dec. 1984. Television stations operate in Lahore, Karachi, Peshawar, Quetta and Rawalpindi–Islamabad.

Cinemas (1983). There are about 600 cinemas.

Newspapers. Dailies and periodicals numbered 1,156 in 1983: 763 were in Urdu, 272 in English and 70 in Sindhi; 121 were dailies, 315 weeklies, 562 monthlies and 158 quarterlies. Top circulation 300,000 for an Urdu daily paper.

JUSTICE, RELIGION, EDUCATION AND WELFARE

Justice. The Central Judiciary consists of the Supreme Court of Pakistan, which is a court of record and has three-fold jurisdiction, namely, original, appellate and advisory. There are 4 High Courts in Lahore, Peshawar, Quetta and Karachi. Under the Constitution, each has power to issue directions of writs of *Habeas Corpus, Mandamus, Certiorari* and others. Under them are district and sessions courts of first instance in each division; they have also some appellate jurisdiction. Criminal cases not being sessions cases are tried by district magistrates and subordinate magistrates. There are subordinate civil courts also.

The Constitution provides for an independent judiciary, as the greatest safeguard of citizens' rights. The Laws (Continuance in Force) (Eleventh Amendment) Order, 1980, prescribed the date of 14 Aug. 1981 by which the judiciary shall be separated from the executive. There is an Attorney-General, appointed by the President, who has right of audience in all courts.

A Federal Shariat Court at the Supreme Court level has been established to decide whether any law is wholly or partially un-Islamic. Islamic law is to be enforced as the law of the state; penalties for offences involving intoxicating liquor, offences against property and sexual offences have been specified. Imprisonment remains as a penalty in general use, but some offences in all the above categories are liable to whipping and some property offences, to amputation.

Religion. Religious groups (1981 census): Moslems, 96·68%; Christians, 1·55%; Hindus, 1·51%; Parsees, Buddhists, and others. There is a Minorities Wing at the Religious Affairs Ministry to safeguard the constitutional rights of religious minorities.

Education. At the census of 1981, 23·3% of the population were able to read and write. Estimate (1985), 26%. Adult literacy programmes have been established.

The principle of free and compulsory primary education has been accepted as the responsibility of the state; duration has been fixed provisionally at 5 years. About 49% of children aged 5-9 are enrolled at school. Present policy stresses vocational and technical education, disseminating a common culture based on Islamic ideology. Figures for 1985–86 in 1,000:

	Enrolment	Teachers	Institutions
Primary	7,735	199·7	86·1
Middle	1,891	61·8	6·2
High	739	91·6	5·1
Colleges	61·5	22·4	584 [1]
Universities	56·6	3·8	20 [1]

[1] Numbers.

Sixth plan (1983–88) expenditure: Rs. 11,000m. on primary and secondary schools; Rs. 1,300m. on colleges and Rs. 2,100m. on universities.

Health. In 1986 (provisional) there were 670 hospitals and 3,441 dispensaries (57,709 beds) and 46,494 doctors. Sixth plan (1983–88) expenditure: Rs. 15,750m.

Social Security. In 1981–82 expenditure on cash benefits under the employees' social security scheme was Rs15·3m., on medical care, Rs.93·2m.

DIPLOMATIC REPRESENTATIVES

Of Pakistan in Great Britain (35 Lowndes Sq., London, SW1X 9JN)
Ambassador: Shaharyar M. Khan (accredited 26 Feb. 1987).

Of Great Britain in Pakistan (Diplomatic Enclave, Ramna 5, Islamabad)
Ambassador: N. J. Barrington, CMG, CVO.

Of Pakistan in the USA (2315 Massachusetts Ave., NW, Washington, D.C., 20008)
Ambassador: Jamsheed K. A. Marker.

Of the USA in Pakistan (Diplomatic Enclave, Ramna, 5, Islamabad)
Ambassador: Arnold L. Raphel.

Of Pakistan to the United Nations
Ambassador: S. Shah Nawaz.

Books of Reference

Pakistan Economic Survey 1984–85. Ministry of Finance, Islamabad, 1985
Pakistan Year-Book, Annual
Ahmed, A. S., *Religion and Politics in Muslim Society: Order and Conflict in Pakistan.* CUP, 1973
Ali, T., *Can Pakistan Survive? The Death of the State.* Harmondsworth, 1983
Burke, S. M., *Pakistan's Foreign Policy.* OUP, 1973
Burki, S. J., *Pakistan Under Bhutto.* London, 1980
Griffin, K., and Khan, A. R. (ed.), *Growth and Inequality in Pakistan.* London and New York 1972
Hasan, M., (ed.) *Pakistan in a Changing World.* Karachi, 1978
Jennings, Sir Ivor, *Constitutional Problems in Pakistan.* CUP, 1957
Siddiqui, K., *Conflict, Crisis and War in Pakistan.* London, 1972

PANAMA

Capital: Panama City
Population: 2·28m. (1987)
GNP per capita: US$2,060 (1985)

República de Panamá

HISTORY. A revolution, supported by the USA, led to the separation of Panama from the United States of Colombia and the declaration of its independence on 3 Nov. 1903. The *de facto* Government was on 5 Nov. recognized by the USA, and soon afterwards by the other Powers. In 1924 Colombia agreed to recognize the independence of Panama. On 8 May 1924 diplomatic relations between Colombia and Panama were established. On 1 Oct. 1979 Panama assumed sovereignty over what was previously known as the Panama Canal Zone and now called the Canal Area.

For the treaties regulating the relations between Panama and the USA *see* pp. 967–68.

AREA AND POPULATION. Panama is bounded north by the Caribbean, east by Colombia, south by the Pacific and west by Costa Rica. Extreme length is about 480 miles (772 km); breadth between 37 (60) and 110 miles (177 km); coastline, 426 miles (685 km) on the Atlantic and 767 (1,234 km) on the Pacific; total area is 29,768 sq. miles (77,046 sq. km); population according to the census of 11 May 1980 was 1,830,175. Estimate (1987) 2,277,000. Over 75% are of mixed blood and the remainder Indians, negroid, white and Asiatic.

The largest towns (census, 1980) are Panama City, the capital on the Pacific coast (386,393); its suburb San Miguelito (156,361); Colon, the port on the Atlantic coast (59,043); and David (50,621).

The areas and populations of the 9 provinces and the Special Territory were:

Province	Sq. km	Census 1980	Estimate 1985	Capital
Bocas del Toro	5,711	53,579	75,400	Bocas del Toro
Chiriquí	8,758	287,801	347,500	David
Veraguas	11,086	173,195	206,800	Santiago
Herrera	2,427	81,866	99,800	Chitré
Los Santos	3,867	70,200	83,600	Las Tablas
Coclé	5,035	140,320	156,500	Penonomé
Colón	8,167 }	166,439	{ 158,500	Colón
Terr. de San Blas	3,206 }		{ 39,100	El Porvenir
Panama	12,022	830,278	976,800	Panama City
Darién	16,803	26,497	36,900	La Palma

Vital statistics (1980): Births, 52,626; marriages, 8,850; deaths, 7,959.

CLIMATE. A tropical climate, unvaryingly with high temperatures and only a short dry season from Jan. to April. Rainfall amounts are much higher on the north side of the isthmus. Panama City. Jan. 79°F (26·1°C), July 81°F (27·2°C). Annual rainfall 70″ (1,770 mm). Colón. Jan. 80°F (26·7°C), July 80°F (26·7°C). Annual rainfall 127″ (3,175 mm). Balboa Heights. Jan. 80°F (26·7°C), July 81°F (27·2°C). Annual rainfall 70″ (1,759 mm). Cristóbal. Jan. 80°F (26·7°C), July 81°F (27·2°C). Annual rainfall 130″ (3,255 mm).

CONSTITUTION AND GOVERNMENT. The 1972 Constitution, as amended in 1978 and 1983, provides a president and two vice-presidents to be elected by direct popular vote and a 67 seat Legislative Assembly to be elected on a party basis; in 28 of the 40 constituencies the party winning the vote obtaining one seat; in the other 12, the 39 remaining seats being allocated on a system of proportional party representation. There is also a 505-member National Assembly elected, one member for each electoral district. However effective power is held by the commander of the defence forces, Gen. Manuel Antonio Noriega.

Elections, the first to be held in Panama for 16 years, were held in May 1984. Nicholas Barletta was elected president and took office in Nov. 1984, but he resigned in Sept. 1985 and was succeeded by one of his vice-presidents. In the Legislative Assembly the National Democratic Union (UNADE), a coalition party, won 40 seats; the Democratic Opposition Alliance (ADO) 27 seats.

On 26 Feb. 1988 General Manuel Antonio Noriega deposed President Eric Arturo Delvalle and appointed Manuel Solis Palma in his place. *See* Addenda.

The official language is Spanish.

National flag: Quarterly: first a white panel with a blue star, second red, third blue, fourth white with a red star.

National anthem: Alcanzamos por fin la victoria (words by J. de la Ossa; tune by Santos Jorge, 1903).

Local government: The 9 provinces and a Special Territory (another is envisaged) are sub-divided into 65 municipal districts and are further sub-divided into 505 *corregimientos* (electoral districts).

DEFENCE

Army. The Army (National Guard) numbered (1988) 4,500 men organized in 8 light infantry companies, equipped with 16 V-150 and 12 V-300 armoured cars. There is one air-borne group.

Navy. Divided between both coasts, the flotilla comprises 2 patrol craft, 2 coast-guard cutters, 4 coastal launches, 3 medium landing ships, 3 utility landing craft and 3 logistic support vessels. In 1988 personnel totalled some 550 officers and men.

Air Force. The air force has 3 CASA 212, 2 Islander and 3 Twin Otter transports, 4 Cessna and 2 DHC-3 Otter liaison aircraft, a Shorts Skyvan, a Falcon 20 and a Boeing 727 for VIP transport, 21 UH-1B/D/H Iroquois and twin-engined UH-1N helicopters plus a Super Puma for official use. Personnel (1988) 200.

INTERNATIONAL RELATIONS

Membership. Panama is a member of UN and OAS.

ECONOMY

Budget. The 1987 budget provided for expenditure of 1,705m. balboas and revenue of 1,405m. balboas. Public sector debt was US$3,691m. in 1985.

Currency. The monetary unit is the *balboa*. Other coins are the half-balboa (equal to 50 cents US); the quarter and tenth of a balboa piece; a cupro-nickel coin of 5 cents, and a copper coin of 1 cent. US coinage is also legal tender. The only paper currency used is that of the USA. In March 1988, US$1 = 1 *balboa*; £1 = 1·77 *balboas*.

Banking. There is no statutory central bank. The Government accounts are handled through the *Banco Nacional de Panama.* The number of commercial banks was 132 in June 1986; 67 have a general licence, 30 an international licence, 13 a representational licence and 14 a fiduciary licence. Leading banks are the Citibank, Lloyds Bank International (Bahamas) Ltd., and the Chase Manhattan Bank of New York. Other foreign-owned banks include the Bank of America, as well as Canadian. Panama is a relatively small offshore banking centre. The total assets of Panamanian banks increased to US$41,000m. between 1976–83.

Weights and Measures. English weights and measures are in general use; those of the metric system are also used.

ENERGY AND NATURAL RESOURCES

Electricity. Production (1986) 3,120m. kwh. Supply 110 and 120 volts; 60 Hz.

Minerals. There are known to be copper deposits in the provinces of Chiriquí, Colón and Darien. The most important, containing possibly the largest undeveloped reserves in the world, is Cerro Colorado (Chiriquí) on which a feasibility study was undertaken by the Rio Tinto Zinc Corporation Ltd. If it is eventually decided to develop the mine, it is expected that the annual production of copper will reach 260,000 to 280,000 tonnes within a few years. The deposit has estimated reserves of 1,300m. tonnes, with an average grade of 0·76% copper.

Agriculture. Of the whole area (1981) 15·6% is cultivated, 57·6% is natural or artificial pasture land and 8·6% is fallow. Of the remainder only a small part is cultivated, though the land is rich in resources. About 60% of the country's food requirements are imported. Production in 1985 totalled 1·1m. tonnes of bananas and 160,000 tonnes of raw sugar. Oranges (34,000 tonnes) and mangoes (28,000 tonnes) are also produced. Most important food crop, for home consumption, is rice, grown on 80% of the farms; Panama's *per capita* consumption is very high. Production of rice was 199,000 tonnes in 1985. Other products are maize (70,000 tonnes in 1985), cocoa (1,000 tonnes), coffee (16,000 tonnes) and coconuts (22,000 tonnes). Beer, whisky, rum, 'seco', anise and gin are produced. Coffee is mainly grown in the province of Chiriquí, near the Costa Rican frontier. The country has great timber resources, notably mahogany. Livestock (1986): 1,443,000 cattle, 205,000 pigs and 8m. poultry.

Forestry. Production (1984) 2·05m. cu. metres.

Fisheries. The catch in 1982 was 337,000 tonnes.

INDUSTRY AND TRADE

Industry. Local industries include cigarettes, clothing, food processing, shoes, soap, cement factories; foreign firms are being encouraged to establish industries, and a petrol refinery is operating at Colón.

Commerce. The imports and exports (including re-exports) for the Republic of Panama, for 4 calendar years are as follows (in 1,000 balboas; 1 balboa = US$1):

	Imports	Exports		Imports	Exports
1982	1,569,300	308,100	1984	1,423,000	251,500
1983	1,441,900	299,300	1985	3,140,800	789,000

Chief exports (36·7% to the USA) in 1983 were: Food and live animals, petroleum products and manufactured goods.

Chief imports (17·4% from USA), 1983, were valued (in 1m. balboas f.o.b.) were: Mineral fuels 392·3, machines and transport equipment 324·7, basic manufactures 233·5, and chemicals 166·7.

Total trade between Panama (including Colón Free Zone) and UK (British Department of Trade returns, in £1,000 sterling):

	1983	1984	1985	1986	1987
Imports to UK	5,341	9,681	14,612	4,950	4,919
Exports and re-exports from UK [1]	42,276	74,322	55,424	44,975	40,020

[1] Including new ships built for foreign owners and registered in Panama.

Tourism. In 1986, 467,000 people visited Panama.

COMMUNICATIONS

Roads. Panama had in 1985, 9,694 km of roads. The road from Panama City westward to the cities of David and Concepción and to the Costa Rican frontier, with several branches, is part of the Pan-American Highway. A concrete highway connects Panama City and Colón.

On 1 Jan. 1981 registered motor vehicles, private and commercial, numbered 166,498.

Railways. The *Ferrocarril de Panama* (Panama Railroad) (1,524 mm gauge) (through the Canal area), which connects Ancón on the Pacific with Cristóbal on the Atlantic, is the principal railway. It is 190 km long and runs along the banks of the Canal. As most vessels unload their cargo at Cristóbal (Colón), on the Atlantic side, the greater portion of the merchandise destined for Panama City is brought overland by the *Ferrocarril de Panama.* The United Brands Company runs 376 km of railway, and the Chiriqui National Railroad 171 km.

Aviation. Eastern Airlines, Swissair, Varig, JAL, Alitalia, KLM, Iberia Airlines, Aeromexico, VIASA, Air France and other international companies operate at Tocumen Airport, 12 miles from Panama City. Air Panama provides services between Panama City and New York, Los Angeles, Miami, Central America and some countries in South America. The *Compañia Panameña de Aviación* (COPA) and *Aerolineas Las Perlas* provide a local service between Panama City and the provincial towns. COPA also provides an international service to Central America.

Shipping. Ships under Panamanian registry in 1986 numbered 12,000 of 44m. gross tons; most of these ships elect Panamanian registry because fees are low and labour laws lenient. All the international maritime traffic for Colón and Panama runs through the Canal ports of Cristóbal, Balboa and Bahia Las Minas (Colón); Almirante is used for both the provincial and international trade. There is an oil transfer terminal at Puerto Armuelles on the Pacific coast.

Panama Canal. On 18 Nov. 1903 a treaty between the USA and the Republic of Panama was signed making it possible for the US to build and operate a canal connecting the Atlantic and Pacific oceans through the Isthmus of Panama. The treaty granted the US in perpetuity the use, occupation and control of a Canal Zone, approximately 10 miles wide, in which the US would possess full sovereign rights 'to the entire exclusion of the exercise by the Republic of Panama of any such sovereign rights, power or authority'. In return the US guaranteed the independence of the republic and agreed to pay the republic $10m. and an annuity of $250,000. The US purchased the French rights and properties—the French had been labouring from 1879 to 1899 in an effort to build the Canal—for $40m. and in addition, paid private landholders within what would be the Canal Zone a mutually agreeable price for their properites.

Two new treaties between Panama and USA were agreed on 10 Aug. and signed on 7 Sept. 1977. One deals with the operation and defence of the canal until the end of 1999 and the other guarantees permanent neutrality.

The USA maintains operational control over all lands, waters and installations, including military bases, necessary to manage, operate and defend the canal until 31 Dec. 1999. A new agency of the US Government, the Panama Canal Commission, operates the canal, replacing the Panama Canal Co. A policy-making board of 5 US citizens and 4 Panamanians serves on the Commission's board of directors. Until 1990 the canal administrator will be a US citizen and the deputy will be Panamanian. After that date the position will be reversed.

Six months after the exchange of instruments of ratification Panama assumed general territorial jurisdiction over the former Canal Zone and became able to use portions of the area not needed for the operation and defence of the canal. Panamanian penal and civil codes became applicable. At the same time Panama assumed responsibility for commercial ship repairs and supplies, railway and pier operations, passengers, police and courts, all of which were among other areas formerly administered by the Canal Co. and the Canal Zone Government.

66% of the electorate of Panama agreed to the ratification of the treaties when a referendum was held on 23 Oct. 1977 and on 18 April 1978 the treaty was ratified by the US Congress. The treaty went into effect on 1 Oct. 1979.

At the end of 1962 the US completed the construction of a high-level bridge over the Pacific entrance to the Canal, and the flags of Panama and the US were flown jointly over areas of the Canal Zone under civilian authority. Following the devaluation of the dollar in 1972 and 1973, the annuity was adjusted proportionally to US$2·1m. and US$2·33m. respectively.

In 1986 a tripartite commission, formed by Japan, Panama and the USA, began studies on alternatives to the Panama Canal. Options are: To build a sea-level canal, to enlarge the existing canal with more locks, to improve the canal alongside upgraded rail and road facilities, to continue with the existing facilities.

The Panama Canal Commission, a US Government Agency, is concerned primarily with the actual operation of the Canal. On 8 July 1974, 18 Nov. 1976 and 10 Oct. 1979 tolls were increased. These were the first increases of toll rates in the history of the Canal. Tolls were raised again on 12 March 1983. The new rates are US$1.83 a Panama Canal ton for vessels carrying passengers or cargo and US$1·46 per ton for vessels in transit in ballast. A Panama Canal ton is equivalent to 100 cu. ft of actual earning capacity. The new toll rate for warships, hospital ships and supply ships, which pay on a displacement basis, is US$1·02 a ton.

The changes were designed to continue the approximately break-even financial operating results after paying its own expenses and paying interest on the net direct investment of the US in the Canal.

Administrator of the Panama Canal Commission: Dennis P. McAuliffe.
Deputy Administrator: Fernando Manfredo Jr. (Panama).

The total civilian and military population of the Canal area is 29,000 (estimate). The total permanent force employed by the Panama Canal Commission on 30 Sept. 1987 was 7,555, comprising 1,167 US citizens, 6,247 Panamanians and 141 others.

The Canal was opened to commerce on 15 Aug. 1914. It is 85 ft above sea-level. It is 51·2 statute miles in length from deep water in the Caribbean Sea to deep water in the Pacific ocean, and 36 statute miles from shore to shore. The channel ranges in bottom-width from 500 to 1,000 ft; the widening of Gaillard Cut to a minimum width of 500 ft was completed in 1969. Normally, the average time of a vessel in Canal waters is about 24 hours, 8–12 of which are in transit through the Canal proper. A map showing the Panama, Suez and Kiel canals on the same scale will be found in THE STATESMAN'S YEAR-BOOK, 1959 and a further map in the 1978–79 edition.

Particulars of the ocean-going commercial traffic through the canal are given as follows (vessels of 300 tons Panama Canal net and 500 displacement tons and over; cargo in long tons):

Fiscal year ending 30 Sept.	North-bound (Pacific to Atlantic)		South-bound (Atlantic to Pacific)		Total		Tolls levied [1]
	Vessels	Cargo	Vessels	Cargo	Vessels	Cargo	(in US$)
1984	5,455	62,211,519	5,775	78,259,299	11,230	140,470,818	289,155,035
1985	5,612	64,492,298	5,903	74,150,945	11,515	138,643,243	300,807,914
1986	5,712	67,229,841	6,214	72,580,652	11,926	139,810,493	322,734,202
1987	5,766	61,683,921	6,464	87,006,459	12,230	148,690,380	329,858,775

[1] All annual tolls figures have been revised to show total tolls collected instead of oceangoing commercial tolls.

In the fiscal year ending 30 Sept. 1987, 12,230 ships passed through the Canal. Transits by flag included 2,467 Panamanian; 1,225 Liberian; 1,170 Japanese; 665 US; 678 Greek; 635 Russian; 533 Ecuadorian; 396 British; 269 Fed. German; 448 Cyprian; 305 Filippino.

Statistical Information: The Panama Canal Commission Office of Public Affairs.

Annual Reports on the Panama Canal, by the Administrator of the Panama Canal Commission.
Rules and Regulations Governing Navigation of the Panama Canal. The Panama Canal Commission, Miami, Florida *or* Washington, DC
Cameron, I., *The Impossible Dream.* London, 1972
Le Feber, W., *The Panama Canal: The Crisis in Historical Perspective.* OUP, 1978
McCullough, D., *The Path Between the Seas.* New York and London, 1978

Post and Broadcasting. There are telegraph cables from Panama to North America and Central and South American ports, and from Colón to the USA and Europe. There is also inter-continental communication by satellite. There were (1985) 97 licensed commercial broadcasting stations, nearly all operated by private companies, one of which functions in the canal. There are 12 television stations, one of them run by the US Army at Fort Clayton. In 1985 there were 295,000 radio and 400,000 television sets. On 1 Jan. 1983 there were 202,627 telephones.

Cinemas. In 1977 there were 52 cinemas in the district of Panama. All films must have Spanish subtitles.

Newspapers. There were (1986) 1 English language and 7 Spanish language daily morning newspapers and 1 English/Spanish evening newspaper.

JUSTICE, RELIGION, EDUCATION AND WELFARE

Justice. The Supreme Court consists of 9 justices appointed by the executive. There is no death penalty.

Religion. 85% of the population is Roman Catholic, 5% Protestant, 4·5% Moslem. There is freedom of religious worship and separation of Church and State. Clergymen may teach in the schools but may not hold public office.

Education. Elementary education is compulsory for all children from 7 to 15 years of age, with an estimated 552,172 students in schools in 1985. The University of Panama at Panama City, inaugurated on 7 Oct. 1935, had a total enrolment (1985) of 55,000 students. The Catholic university Sta. Maria La Antigua, inaugurated on 27 May 1965, had 1,916 students in Sept. 1978.

Health. In 1983 there were 2,149 doctors, 409 dentists, 1,962 nursing personnel and 50 hospitals with 7,448 beds.

DIPLOMATIC REPRESENTATIVES

Of Panama in Great Britain (119 Crawford St., London, W1)
Ambassador: Guillermo Vega (accredited 29 May 1984).

Of Great Britain in Panama (Via España 120, Panama City 1)
Ambassador: Margaret Bryan, CMG.

Of Panama in the USA (2862 McGill Terr., NW, Washington, D.C., 20008)
Ambassador: Juan B. Sosa.

Of the USA in Panama (Apartado 6959, Panama City 5)
Ambassador: Arthur Davis.

Of Panama to the United Nations
Ambassador: Dr Jorge Ritter.

Books of Reference

Statistical Information: The Comptroller-General of the Republic (Contraloria General de la República, Calle 35 y Avenida 6, Panama City) publishes an annual report and other statistical publications.

Jorden, W. J., *Panama Odyssey.* Univ. of Texas Press, 1984
Langstaff, E. DeS., *Panama.* [Bibliography] Oxford and Santa Barbara 1982
Ropp, S. C., *Panamanian Politics.* New York, 1982

National Library: Biblioteca Nacional, Departamento de Información. Calle 22, Panama.

PAPUA
NEW GUINEA

Capital: Port Moresby
Population: 3·48m. (1987)
GNP per capita: US$751 (1986)

HISTORY. To prevent that portion of the island of New Guinea not claimed by the Netherlands or Germany from passing into the hands of a foreign power, the Government of Queensland annexed Papua in 1883. This step was not sanctioned by the Imperial Government, but on 6 Nov. 1884 a British Protectorate was proclaimed over the southern portion of the eastern half of New Guinea, and in 1887 Queensland, New South Wales and Victoria undertook to defray the cost of administration, and the territory was annexed to the Crown the following year. The federal government took over the control in 1901; the political transfer was completed by the Papua Act of the federal parliament in Nov. 1905, and on 1 Sept. 1906 a proclamation was issued by the Governor-General of Australia declaring that British New Guinea was to be known henceforth as the Territory of Papua. The northern portion of New Guinea was a German colony until the First World War. It became a League of Nations mandated territory in 1921, administered by Australia, and later a UN Trust Territory (of New Guinea).

The Papua New Guinea Act 1949–1972 provides for the administration of the UN Australian Trust Territory of New Guinea in an administrative union with the Territory of Papua, in accordance with Art. 5 of the New Guinea Trusteeship Agreement, under the title of Papua New Guinea.

Australia granted Papua New Guinea self-government on 1 Dec. 1973 and, on 16 Sept. 1975, Papua New Guinea became a fully independent state.

AREA AND POPULATION. Papua New Guinea extends from the equator to Cape Baganowa in the Louisiade Archipelago to 11° 40′ S. lat. and from the border of West Irian to 160° E. long. with a total area of 462,840 sq. km. According to the census the 1980 population was 3,010,727. Estimate (1987) 3·48m. Port Moresby, (1980) 123,624; Lae, 61,617; Rabaul, 14,954; Madang, 21,335; Mount Hagen, 13,441. Area and population of the provinces:

Provinces	Sq.km	Census 1980	Estimate 1987	Capital
Milne Bay	14,000	127,975	153,800	Alotau
Northern	22,800	77,442	92,200	Popondetta
Central	29,500	116,964	135,000	Port Moresby
National Capital District	240	123,624	145,300	—
Gulf	34,500	64,120	72,600	Kerema
Western	99,300	78,575	93,600	Daru
Southern Highlands	23,800	236,052	262,400	Mendi
Enga	12,800	164,534	180,100	Wabag
Western Highlands	8,500	265,656	304,800	Mount Hagen
Chimbu	6,100	178,290	186,800	Kundiawa
Eastern Highlands	11,200	276,726	310,300	Goroka
Morobe	34,500	310,622	364,400	Lae
Madang	29,000	211,069	251,100	Madang
East Sepik	42,800	221,890	260,000	Wewak
West Sepik	36,300	114,192	130,100	Vanimo
Manus	2,100	26,036	30,500	Lorengau
West New Britain	21,000	88,941	110,600	Kimbe
East New Britain	15,500	133,197	157,800	Rabaul
New Ireland	9,600	66,028	78,900	Kavieng
North Solomons	9,300	128,794	159,100	Arawa

Vital statistics (1987, estimate): Crude birth rate, 35 per 1,000; crude death rate, 13.

CLIMATE. There is a monsoon climate, with high temperatures and humidity the year round. Port Moresby is in a rain shadow and is not typical of the rest of

Papua New Guinea. Jan. 82°F (27·8°C), July 78°F (25·6°C). Annual rainfall 40″ (1,011 mm).

CONSTITUTION AND GOVERNMENT. Papua New Guinea has a Westminster type of government. A single legislative house, known as the National Parliament, is made up of 109 members from all parts of the country. The members are elected under universal suffrage and general elections are held every 5 years. All persons over the age of 18 who are Papua New Guinea citizens are eligible to vote and stand for election. Voting is by secret ballot and follows the preferential system.

The first Legislative Council was established in 1951. It was abolished in 1964 and replaced with the House of Assembly. In 1950 the first village council was formed which established the basis of an extensive local government system. A system of provincial government was introduced in 1976 and, since then, the importance of lower-level local government has diminished.

In the national elections of 1982 a Pangu government, supported by the United Party, came to power with 67 members of Parliament. In Nov. 1985 a vote of no confidence resulted in a coalition government led by the People's Democratic Movement.

The administrative centre and capital is located at Port Moresby. National administration is carried out by a public service under the direction of 25 ministries. The country is divided into the National Capital District and 19 provinces: Western, Gulf, Central, Milne Bay, Northern, Southern Highlands, Enga, Western Highlands, Chimbu, Eastern Highlands, Morobe, Madang, East Sepik, West Sepik, Manus, New Ireland, East New Britain, West New Britain, and North Solomons. Each of the provincial governments has a secretariat headed by an Administrative Secretary. In many provinces the system of local governments still operates, although the provinces may make changes to this if they wish.

Governor-General: Sir Kingsford Dibela, GCMG.

A coalition government led by the People's Democratic Movement was elected in 1987.

The Cabinet in Aug. 1987 was as follows:

Prime Minister: Rt. Hon. Paias Wingti, PC.

Deputy Prime Minister, Trade and Industry: Sir Julius Chan. *Administrative Services:* Johnson Maladina. *Agriculture and Livestock:* Gai Duwabane. *Civil Aviation, Tourism and Culture:* Hugo Berghuser. *Communications:* Gabriel Ramoi. *Correctional Services:* Aron Noaio. *Defence:* James Pokasui. *Education and Foreign Affairs:* (Vacant). *Environment and Conservation:* Parry Zeipi. *Finance:* Galeva Kwarara. *Fisheries and Marine Resources:* Allen Marai Ebu. *Forests:* Tom Horik. *Health:* Timothy Ward. *Home Affairs and Youth:* Esorom Burege. *Housing:* Tom Amaiu. *Justice:* Albert Kipalan. *Labour and Employment:* Masket Iangalio. *Lands and Physical Planning:* Kala Swokin. *Minerals and Energy:* John Kaputin. *Police:* Legu Vagi. *Provincial Affairs:* Jacob Lemeki. *Public Services:* Dennis Young. *Transport:* Roy Yaki. *Works:* Aita Ivarato. *Without Portfolio:* Ted Diro.

The seat of the Government is at Port Moresby.

National flag: Diagonally ochre-red over black, on the red a bird of paradise in gold, and on the black 5 stars of the Southern Cross in white.

DEFENCE. The Papua New Guinea Defence Force has a total strength of 3,525 (1988) consisting of land, maritime and air elements. The Army is organized in 2 infantry battalions, 1 engineer and 1 signals battalion with logistic units. The Navy has 4 attack class patrol craft and 2 heavy landing craft. The Defence Force has an Air Transport Squadron with (1988) about 130 personnel. Current equipment comprises 6 C-47 transports, and 4 Australian-built N22B Nomads and 3 Israeli-built Aravas for both transport and border patrol duties.

INTERNATIONAL RELATIONS

Membership. Papua New Guinea is a member of UN, the Commonwealth, the Colombo Plan, the South Pacific Commission and is an ACP state of EEC.

ECONOMY

Budget. Revenue (in K1,000) for calendar years was:

Source	1984	1985	1986
Customs, excise and export tax	171,700	179,200	202,900
Other taxes	195,100	219,800	217,100
Foreign government grants [1]	231,900	215,500	205,000
Loans	45,100	44,800	82,500
Other revenue	101,800	105,200	123,600
Total	745,600	764,500	831,100

[1] Mainly from Australia.

Expenditure (in K1,000) for the same periods:

Source	1984	1985	1986
Consumption	396,830	517,030	513,350
Capital	84,390	62,940	138,830
Other expenditure [1]	264,380	184,530	178,930
Total	745,600	764,500	831,100

[1] Includes transfers to provincial governments.

Currency. The unit of currency is the *kina* divided into 100 *toea* and is the sole legal tender. In March 1988, £1 = K1·58; US$1 = K0·90.

Banking. The Bank of Papua New Guinea assumed the central banking functions formerly undertaken by the Reserve Bank of Australia on 1 Nov. 1973.

A national banking institution which has been named the Papua New Guinea Banking Corporation, has been established. This bank has assumed the Papua New Guinea business of the Commonwealth Trading Bank of Australia except where certain accounts give rise to special financial or contractual problems.

The subsidiaries of 3 Australian commercial banks also operate in Papua New Guinea. These are the Australia and New Zealand Banking Group (PNG) Ltd, the Bank of New South Wales (PNG) Ltd, and the Bank of South Pacific Ltd, all of which offer trading and savings facilities. As from 1 Nov. 1973 these banks operated under Papua New Guinea banking legislation.

In 1983, two additional commercial banks Indosuez Niugini Bank Ltd and Niugini Lloyds International Bank Ltd began operating, each with 51% national ownership, and the remaining 49% held by the affiliate of a major international bank.

In addition to these five commercial banks, the Agriculture Bank of Papua New Guinea (formerly the Development Bank) has provided long-term development finance with a particular attention to the needs of small-scale enterprises since 1967. The country's first merchant bank, Resources and Investment Finance Ltd (RIFL), specializing in large-scale financial services began business in late 1979. Its shares are owned by the Hong Kong and Shanghai Banking Corporation, the Commonwealth Trading Bank of Australia and the Papua New Guinea Banking Corporation.

On 30 June 1987 commercial banks deposits totalled K762·2m.

Weights and Measures. The metric system is in force.

ENERGY AND NATURAL RESOURCES

Electricity. In 1986 installed capacity was 494,300 mw, production 1,602·4m. kwh.

Minerals. Copper is the main mineral product. Oil companies have been searching for oil, but by 1986 no commercial deposits had been found. Gold, copper and silver are the only minerals produced in quantity. Major copper deposits in the Kieta district of Bougainville have proved reserves of about 800m. tonnes and have been worked by Bougainville Copper Ltd since 1972. Copper and gold deposits in the Star Mountains of the Western Province are being developed by Ok Tedi Mining Ltd at the Mt. Fubilan mine. Production of gold commenced in 1984 and of copper concentrates in 1987. In 1986, B.C.L. produced 586,552 tonnes of copper concentrate containing approximately 178,593 tonnes of copper, 16,367 kg of gold and 50,385 kg of silver; Ok Tedi Mining Ltd produced 18,277 kg of gold and 5,677 kg of silver.

Agriculture. At 31 Dec. 1983, the total area of larger holdings was 397,081 hectares, of which 180,000 hectares were for agricultural purposes, the principal crops being coffee, copra, cocoa and palm oil. Minor commercial crops include pyrethrum, tea, peanuts and spices. Locally consumed food crops include sweet potatoes, taro, bananas, rice and sago. Tropical fruits grow abundantly. There is extensive grassland. A newly-established sugar industry has made the country self-sufficient in this commodity while a beef-cattle industry is being developed.

Production (1986, in 1,000 tonnes): Coffee, 54; copra, 145; cocoa beans, 30; palm oil, 125.

Livestock (1986): Cattle, 123,000; pigs, 1,489,000; goats, 16,000; poultry, 4m.

Forestry. Timber production is of growing importance for both local consumption and export. In 1986, 1·7m. cu. metres of logs were harvested; logs exported, 1·3m. cu. metres.

Production of sawn timber, 1986, 84,000 cu. metres, exports, 7,438 cu. metres; exports of woodchips, 81,037 tonnes.

Fisheries. Tuna, both skipjack and yellowfin species, is the major fisheries resource; in 1980 the catch was 33,000 tonnes but has diminished sharply since then due to oversupply conditions on world markets. Exports of various crustacea, 1986, 1,575 tonnes, value K10·47m.

INDUSTRY AND TRADE

Industry. Secondary and service industries are expanding for the local market. Industries include the manufacture of paint, gases, concrete, twist tobacco and cigarettes, matches, soap, brewing, boat-building, furniture and the assembly of electrical appliances. In 1985 there were 707 factories employing 27,195 persons. Value of output K695m.

Labour. In 1980 about 733,000 were gainfully employed.

Trade. Imports (in K1,000) for calendar years:

	1983	1984	1985
Food and live animals	134,813	154,767	153,734
Beverages and tobacco	8,269	11,248	9,604
Crude materials, inedible, except fuels	4,876	6,289	6,928
Mineral fuels, lubricants and related materials	167,380	156,278	153,793
Oils and fats (animal and vegetable)	2,525	3,927	3,399
Chemicals	64,050	68,171	65,455
Manufactured goods, chiefly by material	130,559	140,064	134,336
Machinery and transport equipment	232,770	243,538	262,074
Miscellaneous manufactured articles	60,339	70,064	74,594
Commodities and transactions of merchandise trade, not elsewhere specified	9,285	12,485	10,856
Total imports	814,866	866,831	874,774

Exports (in K1,000) for calendar years:

	1983	1984	1985
Coconut and copra products—			
Copra	23,891	49,372	33,922
Copra (coconut) oil	20,038	40,421	22,706
Copra cake and pellets	1,433	1,389	938
Total	45,452	91,182	57,566
Coffee beans	94,659	113,317	117,110
Cocoa beans	41,376	67,084	62,764
Crude rubber	2,153	2,543	3,736
Tea	10,391	19,057	13,330
Pyrethrum extract	397	442	704

	1983	1984	1985
Forest and timber products			
Logs	43,576	61,698	55,394
Sawn timber	2,495	2,690	1,845
Plywood	1,394	1,285	211
Other	6,517	6,903	4,985
Total	53,982	72,576	62,435
Crocodile skins	936	2,294	2,370
Crayfish and prawns	8,788	6,843	9,782
Gold	8,058	25,175	175,451
Copper concentrate	364,862	302,396	307,038
Other domestic produce	31,878	79,742	78,232
Total domestic produce	662,932	782,651	890,518
Re-exports	19,236	22,896	27,106
Total exports	682,168	805,547	917,624

Of exports in 1985, Japan took 22%, Federal Republic of Germany, 29% and Australia, 11%; of imports, Australia furnished about 40%, Singapore, 10% and Japan, 17%.

Total trade between Papua New Guinea and UK (British Department of Trade returns, in £1,000 sterling):

	1983	1984	1985	1986	1987
Imports to UK	28,142	68,245	59,642	38,474	46,045
Exports and re-exports from UK	18,236	14,643	12,592	12,084	16,693

Tourism. In 1986, there were 30,934 visitors.

COMMUNICATIONS

Roads. In 1981 there were approximately 18,500 km of roads including approximately 1,020 km of urban roads. Motor vehicles numbered (1986) 45,713 including 16,499 cars and station wagons.

Aviation. Frequent air services operate to and from Australia (Sydney, Brisbane and Cairns), and there are regular flights to Djayapura (Indonesia), Manila and Singapore. A service is also maintained to Honiara in the Solomon Islands. In addition to Air Niugini, the national flag carrier, Qantas operates in and out of Papua New Guinea.

Shipping. There are regular shipping services between Australia and Papua New Guinea ports, and also services to New Zealand, Japan, Hong Kong, US west coast, Singapore, Solomon Islands, Vanuatu, Taiwan, Philippines and Europe. Small coastal vessels run between the various ports. In 1985 cargo discharged from overseas was 1·5m. tonnes; cargo loaded for overseas was 2·1m. tonnes.

Post and Broadcasting. Telephones numbered 63,212 on 31 Dec. 1986. The National Broadcasting Commission operates three networks. A national service is relayed throughout the country by a series of transmitters on medium- and short-wave bands. Local services operate in each of the 19 provinces, mainly on shortwave, while the larger urban centres are also covered by a commercial FM network relayed from Port Moresby. Two commercial television stations broadcast to Port Moresby which had plans (1987) to extend their services to other areas.

JUSTICE, EDUCATION AND WELFARE

Justice. In 1983, over 1,500 criminal and civil cases were heard in the National Court and an estimated 120,000 cases in district and local courts.

Police. Total uniformed strength at 31 Dec. 1986, 4,756.

Education. At 30 June 1986 about 374,950 children attended 2,461 primary schools and 60,052 enrolled in 234 secondary, technical and vocational schools.

The University of Papua New Guinea and the Papua New Guinea University of Technology had 3,029 students enrolled in full-time courses in 1986.

Health. In 1986, there were 19 hospitals, 459 health centres, 2,231 aid posts and 283 doctors.

DIPLOMATIC REPRESENTATIVES

Of Papua New Guinea in Great Britain (14 Waterloo Pl., London, SW1R 4AR)
High Commissioner: Ilinome Frank Tarua, OBE (accredited 25 Oct. 1983).

Of Great Britain in Papua New Guinea (Kiroki St., Port Moresby)
High Commissioner: M. E. Howell, OBE.

Of Papua New Guinea in the USA (1330 Connecticut Ave., NW, Washington D.C., 20036)
Ambassador: Renagi Lohia.

Of the USA in Papua New Guinea (Armit St., Port Moresby)
Ambassador: Everett Bierman.

Of Papua New Guinea to the United Nations
Ambassador: Renagi Lohia.

Books of Reference

The Territory of Papua. Annual Report. Commonwealth of Australia. 1906–1940–41 and from 1945–46
The Territory of New Guinea. Annual Report. Commonwealth of Australia. 1914–1940–41 and from 1946–47
Papua New Guinea, Annual Report. From 1970–71
Hasluck, P., *A Time for Building.* Melbourne Univ. Press, 1976
Ross, A. C., and Langmore, J., *Alternative Strategies for Papua New Guinea.* OUP, 1974
Ryan, J., *The Hot Land.* London, 1970
Ryan, P. (ed.), *Encyclopaedia of Papua and New Guinea.* Melbourne Univ. Press, 1972
Skeldon, R. (ed.), *The Demography of Papua New Guinea.* Institute of Applied Social and Economic Research, 1979

PARAGUAY

Capital: Asunción
Population: 3·79m. (1986)
GNP per capita: US$1,175 (1984)

República del Paraguay

HISTORY. The Republic of Paraguay gained its independence from Spain on 14 May 1811. In 1814 Dr José Gaspar Rodríguez de Francia was elected dictator, and in 1816 perpetual dictator by the National Assembly. He died 20 Sept. 1840. In 1844 a new constitution was adopted, under which Carlos Antonio López (first elected in 1842, died 10 Sept. 1862) and his son, Francisco Solano López, ruled until 1870. During the devastating war against Brazil, Argentina and Uruguay (1865–70) Paraguay's population was reduced from about 600,000 to 232,000. Argentina, in Aug. 1942, and Brazil, in May 1943, voided the reparations which Paraguay had never paid. Further severe losses were incurred during the war with Bolivia (1932–35) over territorial claims in the Chaco. A peace treaty by which Paraguay obtained most of the area her troops had conquered was signed in July 1938.

AREA AND POPULATION. Paraguay is bounded north-west by Bolivia, north-east and east by Brazil, south-east, south and south-west by Argentina. The area of the Oriental province is officially estimated at 159,827 sq. km (61,705 sq. miles) and the Occidental province at 246,925 sq. km (95,337 sq. miles), making the total area of the republic 406,752 sq. km (157,042 sq. miles).

The population in 1986 was 3,788,196. In 1984 the capital, Asunción (and metropolitan area), had 729,307 inhabitants; other principal cities: Presidente Stroessner (110,000), Pedro Juan Caballero (80,000), Encarnación (31,445), Pilar (26,352), Concepción (25,607).

The capital district and 19 departments had the following populations in 1982:

Asunción (city) }	729,307	Misiones	79,278
Central		Neembucu	70,689
Caaguazú	299,227	Amambay	68,422
Itapua	263,021	Canendiyú	65,807
Paraguari	202,152	*Oriente*	*2,959,568*
Cordillera	194,826	Presidente Hayes	43,787
San Pedro	189,751	Boquerón	14,685
Alto Paraná	188,351	Alto Paraguay	4,535
Guairá	143,374	Chaco	286
Concepción	135,068	Nueva Asunción	231
Caazapá	109,510	*Occidente*	*63,524*

Number of births, 1985, was 121,716; deaths, 14,094.

The population is overwhelmingly *mestizo* (mixed Spanish and Guaraní Indian) forming a homogeneous stock. There are some 46,700 unassimilated Indians of other tribal origin, in the Chaco and the forests of eastern Paraguay. There are some small traces of Negro descent. 40·1% of the population speak only Guaraní; 48·2% are bilingual (Spanish/Guaraní); and 6·4% speak only Spanish.

Mennonites who arrived in 3 groups (1927, 1930 and 1947) are settled in the Chaco and Oriental Paraguay and were estimated in 1969 to number 13,000, of whom 2,000 came from Canada and 11,000 from Germany. The Japanese colonists in the Oriental section, who first came in 1935, were reckoned to number 7,000 in 1983. Under an agreement signed with Japan in 1959 up to 85,000 Japanese were to be admitted over 30 years. An agreement with Korea was signed in 1966 and there were (1988) about 7,575 Korean families living in Paraguay.

CLIMATE. A tropical climate, with abundant rainfall and only a short dry season from July to Sept., when temperatures are lowest. Asunción. Jan. 81°F (27·2°C), July 64°F (17·8°C). Annual rainfall 53″ (1,316 mm).

978

CONSTITUTION AND GOVERNMENT. A new constitution replacing that of 1940 was drawn up by a Constituent Convention in which all legally recognized political parties were represented and was signed into law on 25 Aug. 1967. It provides for a two-chamber parliament consisting of a 30-seat Senate and a 60-seat Chamber of Deputies, each elected for a 5-year term. Two-thirds of the seats in each Chamber are allocated to the majority party and the remaining one-third shared among the minority parties in proportion to the votes cast. Voting is compulsory for all citizens over 18. The President is directly elected for a 5-year (renewable) term; he appoints the Cabinet and during parliamentary recess can govern by decree through the Council of State, the members of which are representatives of the Government, the armed forces and other bodies.

The state of siege in force since 1947 was lifted on 8 April 1987.

President: Gen. Alfredo Stroessner, Commander-in-Chief, elected 11 July 1954 to complete the presidential period of his predecessor. He was re-elected as 'Colorado' candidate in 1958, 1963, 1968, 1973, 1978, 1983 and 1988.

The following is a list of past presidents since 1940, with the date on which each took office:

Gen. Higinio Morínigo, 7 Sept. 1940 (re-signed).
Dr Juan Manuel Frutos, 3 June 1948.[1]
Dr J. Natalicio González, 15 Aug. 1948 (deposed).
Gen. Raimundo Rolón, 30 Jan. 1949.

Dr Felipe Molas López, 26 Feb. 1949[1] (re-signed).
Dr Federico Chávez, 16 July 1950 (resigned).
Tomás Romero Pereira, 4 May 1954.

[1] Provisional, *i.e.,* following a *coup d'état.*

The President has a cabinet of 10 ministers which in July 1987 was composed as follows:

Interior: Dr Sabino A. Montanaro. *Foreign Affairs:* Dr Carlos A. Saldívar. *Finance:* César Barrientos. *Education and Worship:* Dr Carlos Ortiz Ramirez. *Public Works and Communications:* Juan A. Cáceres. *Agriculture and Livestock:* Hernando Bertoni. *National Defence:* Gen. Germán G. Martínez. *Public Health and Social Welfare:* Dr Adán Godoy Giménez. *Justice and Labour:* Eugenio Jaquet. *Industry and Commerce:* Dr Delfín Ugarte Centuríon.

National flag: Red, white, blue (horizontal); the white stripe charged with the arms of the republic on the obverse, and, on the reverse, with a lion and the inscription *Paz y Justicia*—the only flag in the world with different obverse and reverse.

National anthem: ¡ Paraguayos, república o muerte! (words by F. Acuña de Figueroa; tune by F. Dupey).

The country is divided into 2 provinces: the 'Oriental', east of Paraguay River, and the 'Occidental', west of the same river. The Oriental section is divided into 14 departments and the capital. The more important departments are supervised by a *Delegado* appointed by and directly responsible to the central government. The Occidental province, or Chaco, is divided into 5 departments.

DEFENCE. The army, navy and air forces are separate services under a single command. The President of the Republic is the active Commander-in-Chief. The armed forces totalled (1988) about 17,050 officers and men.

Army. The Army consists of 1 cavalry division, 8 infantry divisions, 2 independent infantry battalions, 1 Presidential Escort Regiment, 2 infantry regiments and supporting artillery, engineer and signals units. Equipment includes 12 M-4A3 main battle and 12 M-3A1 light tanks. Strength (1988) 12,500 (including 8,100 conscripts), and there are 30,500 reserves.

Navy. The flotilla comprises 6 armoured river defence gunboats (1 new Brazilian-built, 2 ancient monitors of 636 tons built in Italy and 3 old *ex*-Argentinian minesweepers of 620 tons), 1 converted landing ship with helicopter deck, 1 river patrol boat, 6 coastal patrol craft, 2 landing craft, 1 survey craft, 1 transport training ship, 12 service craft and 2 tugs. There are 5 naval fixed-wing aircraft and 6 helicopters. Personnel in 1988 totalled 2,500 officers and men including coastguard and 500 marines.

Air Force. The Air Force came into being in the early thirties. After operating only transport and training aircraft for a number of years, it received 9 Xavante light jet strike/training aircraft from Brazil in 1980. Other types in service include about 6 C-47 and 4 Aviocar twin-engined transports, 1 Convair C-131A, a Twin Otter, an Otter, 8 Brazilian-built Uirapuru primary trainers, 12 T-6 Texan and 5 Brazilian-supplied Universal armed basic trainers and a number of light aircraft and helicopters. HQ and flying school are at Campo Grande, Asunción. Personnel (1988) 1,400.

INTERNATIONAL RELATIONS

Membership. Paraguay is a member of UN, OAS and LAIA (formerly Lafta).

ECONOMY

Budget. In 1985 budget balanced at Gs. 463,652,966,167.

Currency. The *guaraní* was established on 5 Oct. 1943 equal to 100 old paper pesos. Total monetary circulation was Gs.81,531m. in Dec. 1983. The official rate of exchange for essential imports was (1985) Gs.240 = US$1.
Rate of exchange, March 1988: 320 *guaraníes* = US$1; 566 *guaraníes* = £1.

Banking. The Banco Central del Paraguay opened 1 July 1952 to take over the central banking functions previously assigned to the National Bank of Paraguay, which had opened in March 1943 and been reorganized as the Banco del Paraguay in Sept. 1944 with a monetary, a banking and a mortgage department. The Banco del Paraguay closed in Nov. 1961 and has been replaced, with the aid of a US loan of US$3m., by the Banco Nacional de Fomento.

The Banco Nacional de Fomento, Bank of London and South America, Ltd, Banco Exterior do Brasil, Citibank, Banco de Asunción, Banco Exterior SA, Banco Unión SA, Banco Paraguayo de Comercio, Banco Real del Paraguay SA, Banco Aleman Transatlantico, Banco Holandés Unido, Banco Nacional del Estado de São Paulo, Yegros y Azara, Interbanco, Banco Paraná and Banco de Inversiones all have agencies in Asunción and branches in some main towns.

Weights and Measures. The metric system was officially adopted on 1 Jan. 1901.

ENERGY AND NATURAL RESOURCES

Electricity. Electricity requirements are supplied by Acaray hydro-electric power plant. Production in 1986 was 1,130m. kwh. Supply 220 volts; 50 Hz.

Itaipú, the largest hydro-electric dam in the world, a joint effort of the governments of Brazil and Paraguay was inaugurated in 1982 and it is estimated that the whole project will be completed in 1990. Eventually it will have 18 turbogenerators, each with a capacity of 700,000 kw. In 1984 the first turbine started generating power.

The Yacyretá project is being carried out by the Binational Commission Yacyretá which was created by a treaty between the governments of Argentina and Paraguay. Work is being carried out on this project and it is hoped that the plant will be in full operation by the end of this decade. Initially 20 turbines each of 135,000 kw generating capacity will be installed giving the plant an initial output of 2·7m. kw.

Oil. The oil refinery at Villa Elisa, which has been in operation since 1966, has a production of about 3,500 bbls a day. Exploration for petroleum in the Chaco yielded negative results but prospecting was continuing in 1983–84.

Minerals. Iron, manganese and other minerals have been reported but have not been shown to be commercially exploitable. There are large deposits of limestone, and also salt, kaolin and apatite. National and international firms have acquired licences to prospect for oil and natural gas in the Chaco.

Agriculture. In 1981 it was estimated that agriculture absorbs some 51·4m. hectares. In 1986, the main agricultural products (in 1,000 tonnes) were: Mandioca (cassava), 2,875; soybeans, 662; maize, 469; seed cotton, 375; wheat, 253; rice, 77; tobacco, 18; sugar-cane, 1,296; coffee, 18.

Wheat, soybeans, cotton, sugar, tobacco, coffee are increasing in importance, as are also essential oils and oilseeds. *Yerba maté*, or strongly flavoured Paraguayan tea, continues to be produced but is declining in importance.

Livestock (1986). Paraguay had about 7,151,000 cattle, 317,000 horses, 1,403,000 pigs, 388,000 sheep.

Forestry. In the Oriental section there are reserves of hardwoods and cedars that have scarcely been exploited. Palms, tung and other trees are exploited for their oils. The Japanese are experimenting with mulberries for silk growing. Pines and firs have been introduced under a United Nations project. In the Chaco the accessible Quebracho forests have nearly been worked out but plans are being made to open up new areas. In 1986, 181,355 tons of timber were exported.

INDUSTRY AND TRADE

Industry. Production, 1983 (tons): Hides, 11,036; frozen meat, 7,506; cotton fibre, 77,157 (1,000 metres); tannin, 12,678; petit grain, 86; tung oil, 17,033; cement, 152,953; sugar, 98,199; cigarettes (1m. packets), 46,598; matches (1,000 boxes), 8,979. There are 3 meat-packing plants and other factories producing vegetable oils. A textile industry in Pilar and Asunción meets a large part of local needs.

Labour. Trade unionists number about 30,000 (*Confederación Paraguaya de Trabajadores* and *Confederación Cristiana de Trabajadores*).

Commerce. Imports and exports (in US$1m.):

	1982	1983	1984	1985	1986
Imports	581·4	478·3	513·0	442·3	509·3
Exports	329·7	251·5	334·5	303·9	232·5

Chief exports in 1986 included (in US$1,000): Cotton, 80,745; soybeans, 43,867; vegetable oil, 9,215; sawn wood, 17,657; expellers, 8,776; tobacco, 5,448; cattle hides, 9,732; tannin extract, 3,762; processed meat, 33,918; essential oils, 3,762.

Chief imports 1986 (in US$1,000): Fuels and lubricants, 96,918; machinery, 163,529; chemical and pharmaceutical products, 29,561; transport and accessories, 30,663; drinks and tobacco, 33,945; foodstuffs, 17,013; iron and manufactures, 28,803; agricultural implements and accessories, 6,361.

Imports and exports (in US$), by country, 1984:

Country	Imports	Exports
Argentina	80,959	40,525
Belgium	1,151	9,753
Brazil	167,890	53,219
Federal Republic of Germany	16,062	39,557
France	25,965	8,065
Italy	3,174	6,013
Japan	60,741	7,900
Netherlands	6,669	41,264
Spain	2,495	12,108
Switzerland	5,096	12,755
UK	21,455	651
Uruguay	4,764	6,800
USA	44,905	17,464

Total trade between Paraguay and UK (British Department of Trade returns, in £1,000 sterling):

	1983	1984	1985	1986	1987
Imports to UK	3,129	2,961	2,086	1,455	1,409
Exports and re-exports from UK	15,263	16,884	15,540	31,010	25,409

Tourism. Visitors numbered 200,000 in 1986.

COMMUNICATIONS

Roads. In 1983 there were 20,000 km of roads, of which 2,000 were paved. The principal paved roads are Route No. 2/7 running from Asunción to the bridge over the Paraná at Puerto Presidente Stroessner, and thence down to the ocean at Paranaguá; and Route No. 1 to Encarnación in the south. The other main arteries are Coronel Oviedo-Pedro Juan Caballero road (unpaved from Coronel Oviedo) in the north and the Trans-Chaco road which starts from the bridge across the river Paraguay north of Asunción and ends at Nueva Asunción on the Bolivian border. Unpaved roads are closed when it rains. In the Argentine, a paved road starts from Pilcomayo, opposite Asunción, and provides good communication with Buenos Aires. Motor cars, 1976, numbered 17,600; commercial vehicles, 15,200, and passenger vehicles, 7,580.

Railways. The President Carlos Antonio López (formerly Paraguay Central) Railway runs from Asunción to Encarnación, on the Río Alto Paraná, with a length of 441 km (1,435 mm gauge). In 1986, traffic amounted to 156,231 tonnes and 348,535 passengers.

Aviation. International services are operated by 8 airlines (1 domestic and 7 foreign) and internal routes by military airlines and some small private lines.

Shipping. In flood the Paraguay River, which divides the country into two distinct parts, is navigable for 12ft-draught vessels as far as Concepción, 180 miles north of Asunción, and for smaller vessels for a further distance of 600 miles northward. Drought conditions often restrict navigation to lighter traffic. The Paraná River is navigable by large boats from Corrientes up to Puerto Aguirre, at the mouth of the Yguazú River. Boats of a few hundred tons capacity navigate the tributary rivers.

Asunción, the chief port, is 950 miles from the sea. The cargo fleet includes 25 vessels of 300–1,000 tons, 3 tankers of 1,100–1,700 tons, 2 passenger river boats and 1 ocean-going freighter of 713 tons.

Post and Broadcasting. The national telegraph (137 offices) connects Asunción with Corrientes and Posadas in the Argentine Republic, and thus with the outside world; new direct links have been opened with the Federal Republic of Germany, USA, Bolivia and Chile. In addition, 34 stations are operated by the President Carlos Antonio López Railway; total, 2,070 miles. Three companies (12 stations) offer radio-telegraph and telex services to several countries. Telephones, 1983, 77,983, of which 59,113 were in Asunción and were automatic. There are 1 state and 9 commercial radio stations in Asunción, 22 in provincial towns, 2 commercial television stations in Asunción and 1 in Encarnación in the south.

Cinemas (1986). Cinemas numbered 6 in Asunción. The larger country towns usually have an outdoor cinema.

Newspapers (1988). There were 5 daily newspapers in Asunción.

JUSTICE, RELIGION AND EDUCATION

Justice. The highest court is the Supreme Court with 5 members. There are special Chambers of Appeal for civil and commercial cases, and criminal cases. Judges of first instance deal with civil, commercial and criminal cases in 6 departments. Minor cases are dealt with by Justices of the Peace.

The Attorney-General represents the State in all jurisdictions, with representatives in each judicial department and in every jurisdiction. In matters of revenue, taxes, etc., the State is represented by the *Abogado del Tesoro*.

Religion. Religious liberty is guaranteed by the 1967 constitution. Article 6 thereof recognizes Roman Catholicism as the official religion of the country. The same article states that relations between Paraguay and the Holy See shall be regulated by concordats or other bilateral agreements, but no such agreements have yet been negotiated.

The Roman Catholic Church is organized into the Archdiocese of Asunción, 3 other dioceses (San Juan Bautista de las Misiones, Concepción and Villarrica); 4 Prelatures (Coronel Oviedo, Encarnación, Alto Paraná and Caacupé); and 2 Vicariates Apostolic (Chaco and Pilcomayo). The bishops meet in a Conference of Paraguayan Bishops. Only civil marriages are legally valid. There are numerous non-catholic communities, the largest of whom are the Mennonites. There is a small Anglican church in Asunción, with missions in the Chaco, which comes under the jurisdiction of an Anglican Bishop resident in Asunción.

Education. Education is free and nominally compulsory. In 1985 there were 3,993 government primary schools with 570,775 pupils and 22,764 teachers; (1984) 587 private schools, with 80,807 pupils and (1983) 13,810 teachers. In 1985, 740 secondary schools had 149,140 students and (1982) 2,448 teachers. The National University in Asunción had, in 1985, 19,209 students and 2,694 professors; the Catholic University had 9,945 students and (1984) 900 professors.

DIPLOMATIC REPRESENTATIVES

Of Paraguay in Great Britain (51 Cornwall Gdns, London, SW7 4AQ)
Ambassador: Antonio R. Zuccolillo.

Of Great Britain in Paraguay (Calle Presidente Franco, 706, Asunción)
Ambassador and Consul-General: John G. MacDonald, MBE.

Of Paraguay in the USA (2400 Massachusetts Ave., NW, Washington, D.C., 20008)
Ambassador: Dr Marcos Martínez Mendieta.

Of the USA in Paraguay (1776 Mariscal López Ave., Asunción)
Ambassador: Clyde Taylor.

Of Paraguay to the United Nations
Ambassador: Dr Alfredo Cañete.

Books of Reference

Gaceta Official, published by Imprenta Nacional, Estrella y Estero Bellaco, Asunción
Anuario Daumas. Asunción
Anuario Estadístico de la República del Paraguay. Asunción. Annual
Lewis, P. H., *Paraguay under Stroessner.* Univ. of North Carolina Press, 1980
Maybury-Lewis, D. and Howe, J., *The Indian Peoples of Paraguay: Their Plight and Their Prospects.* Cambridge, Mass., 1980
Nickson, R. A., *Paraguay.* [Bibliography] Oxford and Santa Barbara, 1987

National Library: Biblioteca Nacional, De la Rosidenta, Asunción.

PERU

República del Perú

Capital: Lima
Population: 20·2m. (1986)
GNP per capita: US$970 (1985)

HISTORY. The Republic of Peru, formerly the most important of the Spanish vice-royalties in South America, declared its independence on 28 July 1821; but it was not till after a war, protracted till 1824, that the country gained its actual freedom.

AREA AND POPULATION. Peru is bounded north by Ecuador and Colombia, east by Brazil and Bolivia, south by Chile and west by the Pacific ocean. Area 1,285,216 sq. km (496,093 sq. miles).

The long-standing dispute with Chile over the provinces of Tacna and Arica (*see* THE STATESMAN'S YEAR-Book, 1928, p. 1198) reached an amicable settlement on 3 June 1929 at Lima, Tacna going to Peru and Arica to Chile. In response to demands by Bolivia for permanent access to the Pacific Coast, proposals for a Bolivian corridor to the sea and a new Bolivian port to be built in the disputed area have been put forward by Chile and Peru. To date, little progress has been made. One result has been increased tension along the Chilean–Peruvian border, there is no sign of a settlement of the border dispute, and the armed forces of both countries remain on the alert in the disputed border area. Fighting broke out between Peruvian and Ecuadorean Forces, in early 1981, along part of the disputed border (the Cordillera del Condor) which has to date not been adequately mapped. A number of proposals for settling the issue permanently have been put forward but a final settlement is unlikely to be reached in the near future. For an account of the settlement of other boundary disputes, *see* THE STATESMAN'S YEAR-Book, 1948, p. 1173.

The census taken in 1981 gave the population as 17,005,210. Estimate (1986) 20,207,100 (10,179,000 male). Lima, the capital, had (1983) 5,258,600 population. Birth rate per 1,000 population (1986), 35·4; death rate, 9·7; infant mortality rate per 1,000 live births, 90·5.

The area and population (at Census, 12 July 1981) of the 24 departments and the constitutional province of Callao, together with their capitals, are shown below:

Department	Sq. km	Census 1981	Capital	Census 1981
Amazonas	41,297	254,560	Chachapoyas	11,853
Ancash	36,669	818,289	Huaraz	45,116
Apurimac	20,550	323,346	Abancay	19,807
Arequipa	63,528	706,580	Arequipa	447,431
Ayacucho	44,181	503,392	Ayacucho	69,533
Cajamarca	34,930	1,045,569	Cajamarca	60,280
Callao	148	443,413	Callao	260,581
Cuzco[1]	76,329	832,504	Cuzco	181,604
Huancavelica	21,079	346,797	Huancavelica	20,889
Huánuco	34,094	484,780	Huánuco	52,628
Ica	21,251	433,897	Ica	111,087
Junín	41,296	852,238	Huancayo	165,132
La Libertad	23,241	962,949	Trujillo	354,557
Lambayeque	13,737	674,442	Chiclayo	280,244
Lima	33,821	4,745,877	Lima	375,957[4]
Loreto	379,025	445,368	Iquitos	178,738
Madre de Dios	78,403	33,007	Puerto Maldonado	12,693
Moquegua	15,709	101,610	Moquegua	22,224[3]
Pasco	24,035	213,125	Cerro de Pasco	71,558
Piura	36,403	1,125,865	Piura	186,354
Puno	72,382[2]	890,258	Puno	66,477
San Martín	52,309	319,751	Moyobamba	14,376
Tacna	15,232	143,085	Tacna	97,173
Tumbes	4,732	103,839	Tumbes	47,939
Ucayali	100,831	200,669	Pucallpa	89,604

[1] Constitutional province. [2] Includes Peruvian zone of Lake Titicaca (4,996 sq. km). [3] Estimate 1984. [4] Municipality proper; Lima/Callao metropolitan area 4,605,043. Other major cities (1981 Census) include Chimbote (216,406).

The official languages are Spanish (spoken by 68% of the population) and Quechua (spoken by 27%); 3% speak Aymará.

CLIMATE. There is a very wide variety of climate, ranging from equatorial to desert, (or perpetual snow on the high mountains). In coastal areas, temperatures vary very little, either daily or annually, though humidity and cloudiness show considerable variation, with highest humidity from May to Sept. Little rain is experienced in that period. In the Sierra, temperatures remain fairly constant over the year, but the daily range is considerable. There the dry season is from April to Nov. Desert conditions occur in the extreme south, where the climate is uniformly dry, with a few heavy showers falling between Jan. and March. Lima. Jan. 74°F (23·3°C), July 62°F (16·7°C). Annual rainfall 2″ (48 mm). Cuzco. Jan. 56°F (13·3°C), July 50°F (10°C). Annual rainfall 32″ (804 mm).

CONSTITUTION AND GOVERNMENT. On 3 Oct. 1968 a military junta overthrew the government of President Fernando Belaúnde Terry and installed Gen. Juan Velasco Alvarado as President of a 'Revolutionary Government' with a cabinet composed entirely of officers of the armed services. Gen. Velasco was ousted in bloodless *coup* in Aug. 1975 and was replaced by Gen. Francisco Morales Bermudez. The new democratic government, under President Fernando Belaúnde Terry, took office on 28 July 1980.

The new Constitution, which became effective when a civilian government was installed in July 1980, provides for a Legislature consisting of a Senate (60 members) and a Chamber of Deputies (180 members) and an Executive formed of the President of the Republic and a Council of Ministers appointed by him. Elections were held in April 1985. They are held every 5 years with the President and Congress elected, at the same time, by separate ballots. All Peruvians over the age of 18 are eligible to vote; in May 1980 the number of registered voters was over 6m., including 1m. in Lima province. Voting is compulsory; women were fully enfranchised in 1955.

Presidents since 1956 were:

Dr Manuel Prado y Ugarteche, 28 July 1956–July 1962.

Gen. Ricardo Pérez Godoy, 18 July 1962–3 March 1963.[1]

Gen. Nicolás Lindley López, 3 March–28 July 1963.

Fernando Belaúnde Terry, 28 July 1963–3 Oct. 1968.[1]

Gen. Juan Velasco Alvarado, 3 Oct. 1968–29 Aug. 1975.[1]

Gen. Francisco Morales Bermudez, 29 Aug. 1975–28 July 1980.

Fernando Belaúnde Terry, 28 July 1980–28 July 1985.

[1] Deposed.

President: Alan García Pérez (sworn in 28 July 1985).

The Cabinet was in Dec. 1987 composed as follows:

Prime Minister and Minister of the Presidency: Guillermo Larco Cox. *Foreign Affairs:* Dr Allan Wagner Tizon. *Interior:* José Barsallo Burga. *Finance:* Gustavo Saberbein Chevalier. *Industry:* Alberto Vera La Rosa. *Agriculture:* Remigio Morales Bermudez. *Energy and Mines:* Abel Salinas Izaguirre. *Education:* Mercedes Cabanillas de Llanos de la Mata. *Health:* Hilda Urizar Peroni de Arias. *Transport:* Gen. German Parra Herrera. *Justice:* Carlos Blancas Bustamante. *Labour:* Orestes Rodriguez Campos. *Housing:* Luis Bedoya Velez. *Fisheries:* Javier Labarthe. *Defence:* Jorge Torres Flores.

There are 24 departments divided into 179 provinces (plus the constitutional province of Callao) and 1,764 districts; the province of Callao has some of the functions of a department.

National flag: Three vertical strips of red, white, red, with the national arms in the centre.

National anthem: Somos Libres, seámoslo siempre (words by J. de la Torre Ugarte; tune by J. B. Alcedo, 1821).

DEFENCE.

Army. While military service is compulsory youths are only conscripted to fill the annual quota. The term of service is 2 years and all males of 20–25 years of age are liable. The country is divided into 5 military regions.

The Army comprises (1988) approximately 75,000 men (including 50,000 conscripts). There are 5 military regions with 2 armoured, 1 cavalry, 7 infantry, 1 airborne and 1 jungle divisions. Of independent groups there are 2 artillery, 1 anti-aircraft, 4 infantry battalions, 7 jungle battalions and 4 engineering battalions. There is an air element of 25 Mil Mi-8 and 6 Alouette II helicopters. Equipment consists of approximately 140 tanks (T-54/-55 and AMX-13), over 400 light armoured fighting vehicles and 105-mm./130-mm./155-mm. field artillery.

The section of the national police force with a para-military role is known as the *Guardia Civil* and comprises approximately 36,000 personnel.

Navy. The principal surface ships of the Peruvian Navy are the cruisers:–

Completed	Name	Standard Displacement (tons)	Main Guns	Aircraft	Shaft horsepower	Max. Speed (knots)
1953	Almirante Grau ex-Aguirre (ex-De Zeven Provincien)	9,850	4 6in.	3	85,000	32
1953	Proyecto 01 ex-Almirante Grau [1] (ex-De Ruyter)	9,530	8 6in.	–	85,000	32

[1] When the Dutch cruiser *De Ruyter* was purchased in 1973 she was re-named *Almirante Grau* after Peru's principal naval hero. In consequence the cruiser whose name had been changed from *Newfoundland* to *Almirante Grau* when she was purchased from Britain in 1959 was again re-named *Capitan Quinones*, after an air force hero; but this ship has since been retired (latterly used as harbour training ship); and her sister ship *Colonel Bolognesi* (ex-HMS *Ceylon*) was laid up in 1983. *Aquirre* was bought from the Netherlands in 1976 (in 1986 this ship assumed the name *Almirante Grau* and the former *Almirante Grau* became *Proyecto 01*, a very confusing recent history of renaming).

There are also 12 submarines comprising 6 completed in Federal Republic of Germany in 1974–82, 4 completed in USA in 1954–57 and 2 old ex-USN built in 1944; 2 reconstructed 'Daring' class destroyers delivered from Britain during 1973; 6 old destroyers purchased from the Netherlands in 1980–82, 2 Italian-built frigates completed in 1979 and 2 Peruvian completed to same design in 1985–86, 6 new French-built fast missile-armed corvettes, 2 medium landing ships; 5 river gunboats; 3 river patrol boats; 2 transports; 3 hospital craft; 1 research craft; 5 oilers; 7 survey vessels; 1 repair ship; 1 torpedo recovery vessel; 1 floating workshop, 4 floating docks; 4 water carriers, and 7 tugs.

All naval training takes place in the Callao area at various schools. The main naval base and dockyard are also in Callao. Smaller bases are at Iquitos on the Amazon, and at San Lorenzo.

Naval personnel in 1988 totalled 2,100 officers and 19,000 men including the Naval Air Arm which recently operated 14 ship-borne anti-submarine helicopters and 12 land-based maritime patrol aircraft. There is a Marine Brigade of 3,000 men.

The Coast Guard (originally set up with light forces transferred from the Navy) includes 6 modern patrol vessels built in Peru in 1976–82, 3 fast patrol craft built in Britain in 1964–65, 2 former US gunboats, 4 coastal patrol boats and 5 river patrol craft.

Air Force. The operational force consists of 5 combat groups. No. 13 Group has 2 squadrons of Mirage 5 jet fighters; No. 9 Group has 2 squadrons of Canberra light jet bombers; No. 7 Group has 2 squadrons of A-37B light attack aircraft; No. 12 Group has Soviet-built Su-22 variable-geometry fighter bombers in 2 operational squadrons; No. 11 Group has one squadron of Su-22s and one with A-37Bs. Other aircraft in service include medium transports (1 F.28 Fellowship, 16 An-26, 6 L-100 Hercules), light transports (19 Twin Otter, 15 Buffalo, 1 twin-jet Falcon and 12 Turbo-Porter), helicopters (2 Mi-6 and 6 Mi-8, Bell 212 and 214ST, BO 105, Alouette III and Bell 47G), 70 training aircraft (including Aermacchi MB 339,

T-37 and T-41D) and a small number of miscellaneous types for photographic and communications duties. There are military airfields at Talara, Chiclayo, Piura, Pisco, Lima (2), Iquitos and La Joya, and a seaplane base at Iquitos. All officers and pilots are trained at the Air Academy at Lima (Las Palmas). The approximate strength of the Peruvian Air Force (1988) 15,000 personnel and 100 combat aircraft.

INTERNATIONAL RELATIONS

Membership. Peru is a member of UN, OAS, Andean Group and LAIA (formerly LAFTA).

ECONOMY

Planning. A Public Investment Programme for 1981–85 envisages expenditure of US$11,670m.

Budget. The authorized budget for 1985 envisaged expenditure of S/.23,869,000m.

Currency. The monetary unit is the *inti* introduced 1986. One *inti* = 1,000 *soles*. In March 1988, £1 = 58·43 *inti*; US$1 = 33·00 *inti*.

Coins include 50,000 soles (gold) and 10,000 soles (silver) coins as well as 10- and 5-sole pieces (copper 75%; nickel 25%), the sol and half sol (copper 30%; zinc 70%); the 20, 10 and 5 centavos (copper–zinc) and the 2- and 1-centavo pieces (zinc) have been discontinued. Peru has a paper currency issued by the Banco Central de la Reserva in denominations of 5,000, 1,000, 500, 200, 100 and 50. The 10 and 5 soles notes have been discontinued.

Banking. The government bank of issue is the Banco Central de la Reserva del Perú, which was established in 1922.

The Government's fiscal agent is the Banco de la Nación which, since May 1970, has control of the 'giro' market through which most non-trade foreign currency transactions are channelled.

There were in 1983, 7 commercial banks (of which 3 state-owned), 4 foreign commercial banks, 9 development banks (5 state-owned), 6 regional commercial banks and a savings bank.

Weights and Measures. The metric system of weights and measures was established by law in 1869, and since 1916 has come into general use.

ENERGY AND NATURAL RESOURCES

Electricity. In 1985 the production of electric energy was 12,809m. kwh (9·883m kwh hydro-electric). An electrification programme to construct a series of large hydro-electric power stations, was started in 1980. Supply 220 volts; 60 Hz.

Oil. Proven oil reserves in the jungle region amount to about 900m. bbls. The new 850 km pipeline, linking the new jungle oilfields to coastal terminals, was opened in 1977. Output amounted to 8m. tonnes in 1987 and Peru became an oil exporter in 1985.

Minerals. Peru's mining industry produces 13 metals and 25 non-metallic minerals. Lead, copper, iron, silver, zinc and petroleum are the chief minerals exploited. In 1984 prospecting for uranium was in progress. Mineral exports in 1980: Copper, US$752m.; lead, US$383m.; zinc, US$210m.; silver, US$312m.; iron ore, US$95m.; gold, US$40m. Mineral production (in 1,000 tonnes, 1986) of iron, 3,290; zinc, 598; copper, 397; lead, 194; silver, 1,926,000 kg.

Agriculture. There are 4 natural zones: the coast strip, with an average width of 80 km; the Sierra or Uplands, formed by the coast range of mountains and the Andes proper; the Montaña or high wooded region which lies on the eastern slopes of the Andes, and the jungle in the Amazon Basin, known as the Selva. In 1984 irrigation was increasing the amount of cultivable acreage in the arid coastal sections of the country, using the abundance of water flowing from the Andes mountains.

Production in 1986 (in 1,000 tonnes): Sugar-cane, 6,273; potatoes, 1,687; cotton, 304; coffee, 97; rice, 745; maize, 864.

Livestock (1986): 2,435,000 alpacas, 3·95m. cattle, 13·06m. sheep, 2,174,000 pigs, 48m. poultry.

Forestry. There are 209m. acres of forests containing valuable hardwoods; oak and cedar account for about 40%. In 1983, total roundwood removals totalled 7·8m. cu metres.

Fisheries. Production (1986 in tonnes) 5·53m., including anchoveta, 3,482,000; sardine, 1,721,000.

INDUSTRY AND TRADE

Industry. About 70% of Peru's manufacturing industries are located in or around the Lima/Callao metropolitan area. Products include pig-iron, blooms, billets, largets, round and round-deformed bars, wire rod, black and galvanized sheets and galvanized roofing sheets. Refractories are manufactured at Lima.

The Government has a monopoly of the import and/or local manufacture and sale of guano, salt, alcohol and explosives.

Labour. In 1986 the total labour force was considered to number 6,767,900 persons. The population was distributed as follows: Agriculture, forestry, hunting and fishing, 2,422,900; manufacturing industry, 690,300; commerce, 981,300; construction, 243,700; mining, 162,400; services, 1·78m.; others, 487,300.

Trade Unions. Trade unions have about 2m. members (approximately 1·5m. in peasant organizations and 500,000 in industrial). The major trade union organization is the *Confederación de Trabajadores del Perú*, which was reconstituted in 1959 after being in abeyance for some years. The other labour organizations recognized by the Government are the *Confederación General de Trabajadores del Perú*, the *Confederación Nacional de Trabajadores* and the *Central de Trabajadores de la Revolución Peruana*.

Commerce. The value of trade has been as follows (in US$1m.):

	1981	1982	1983	1984	1985	1986
Imports	3,803	3,678	2,698	2,140	1,806	2,525
Exports	3,255	3,293	3,015	3,147	2,978	2,509

In 1984 the principal imports were: Machinery and appliances, chemicals, foodstuffs; fuel, lubricants and other non-metallic minerals. Of exports, 36% went to USA, 15% to Japan; of imports, 41% came from USA and 8% from Japan. In 1986 the chief export was minerals, US$1,023,000.

Total trade between Peru and UK (British Department of Trade returns, in £1,000 sterling):

	1983	1984	1985	1986	1987
Imports to UK	118,414	119,423	108,943	82,141	91,689
Exports and re-exports from UK	32,947	33,841	40,371	48,275	49,324

Tourism. There were 305,000 visitors in 1986; revenue US$325m.

COMMUNICATIONS

Roads. In 1985 there were 68,363 km, of which 7,325 km were paved and 13,627 km gravel. In 1981 there were 529,000 registered motor vehicles.

Railways. Total length (1984), 1,628 km on 1,435- and 914-mm gauges. In 1983 railways carried 2·6m. short tons and 3·1m. passengers.

Aviation. There are 3 international and 61 other airports.

Shipping. In 1983, 23·5m. tonnes of goods were loaded and unloaded, including 10·4m. coastal traffic.

Post and Broadcasting. An earth satellite ground communication station at Lurin connects Peru through Intelsat. III to the US and Europe. In 1983 there were

519,703 telephones, 371,673 in Lima. Radio-telephone circuits connect Lima with distant towns. There are 153 broadcasting stations, of which 29 are in Lima. Radio receivers (1984) 2·24m. and television receivers 520,000.

Cinemas. In 1972 there were 276 cinemas.

Newspapers. The main Lima newspapers are *La Prensa, El Comercio, Expreso, Correo* and *La Crónica.*

JUSTICE, RELIGION, EDUCATION AND WELFARE

Justice. The Peruvian judicial system is a pyramid at the base of which are the justices of the peace who decide minor criminal cases and civil cases involving small sums of money. The apex is the Supreme Court with a President and 12 members; in between are the judges of first instance, who usually sit in the provincial capitals, and the superior courts.

Religion. Religious liberty exists, but the Roman Catholic religion is protected by the State, and since 1929 only Roman Catholic religious instruction is permitted in schools, state or private. In 1972 there were 1 Roman Catholic cardinal, 7 archbishops, 14 bishops, 3 vicars-general, 8 vicars apostolic, 2,672 priests, 506 cloistered monks and 4,558 members of religious orders.

Education. Elementary education is compulsory and free for both sexes between the ages of 7 and 16; secondary education is also free.

In 1986 there were 3·68m. pupils in primary schools and 1,676,000 pupils in secondary schools.

In 1986 the total number of students at 35 universities was 394,000.

Health. There were in 1986, 353 hospitals and 920 health centres.

DIPLOMATIC REPRESENTATIVES

Of Peru in Great Britain (52 Sloane St., London, SW1X 9SP)
Ambassador: Carlos Raffo.

Of Great Britain in Peru (Edificio El Pacifico Washington, Ave. Arequipa, Lima)
Ambassador: A. J. Beamish.

Of Peru in the USA (1700 Massachusetts Ave., NW, Washington, D.C., 20036)
Ambassador: Cesar G. Atala.

Of the USA in Peru (PO Box 1995, Lima)
Ambassador: Alexander F. Watson.

Of Peru to the United Nations
Ambassador: Carlos Alzamora.

Books of Reference

The official gazette is *El Peruano*, Lima.

Anario Estadistico del Perú. Annual.—*Boletin de Estadistica Peruana.* Quarterly.— *Demarcación Política del Perú.* (Dirección Nacional de Estadística), Lima
Estadística del Comercio Exterior (Superintendencia de Aduanas). Lima
Banco Central de Reserva. Monthly Bulletin.—*Renta Nacional del Perú.* Annual, Lima

Figueroa, A., *Capitalist Development and the Peasant Economy of Peru.* CUP, 1984
Hemming, J., *The Conquest of the Incas.* London, 1970
McClintock, C., and Lowental, A. F., (eds.) *The Peruvian Experiment Reconsidered.* Princeton Univ. Press, 1983
Mejía Baca, J., and Tauro, A., *Diccionário Enciclopédico del Perú.* 3 vols. 1966
Thorpe, R., and Bertram, G., *Peru 1890–1977: Growth and Policy in an Open Economy.* London, 1978

National Library: Avenida Abancay, Lima.

PHILIPPINES

Capital: Manila
Population: 57·36m. (1987)
GNP per capita: US$614 (1986)

Republika ng Pilipinas

HISTORY. Before the Spanish discovery of the Philippines, the native Filipinos came in contact with India, China and Arabia. According to the early records of China, 'some Filipinos from the country of Ma-i arrived in Canton and sold their merchandise' as early as 982. The Philippine islands were discovered by Magellan in 1521 and conquered by Spain in 1565. Following the Spanish–American war, the islands were ceded to the USA on 10 Dec. 1898, after the Filipinos had tried in vain to establish an independent republic in 1896.

The Philippines acquired self-government as a Commonwealth of the USA by Act of Congress signed by President Roosevelt on 24 March 1934 and ratified by plebiscite on 14 May 1935. This provided for independence after a 10-year transitional period, at the end of which the Philippines became completely independent on 4 July 1946.

AREA AND POPULATION. The Philippines is situated between 21° 25′ and 4° 23′ N. lat. and between 116° and 127° E. long. It is composed of 7,100 islands and islets, 2,773 of which are named. Approximate land area, 115,830 sq. miles (300,000 sq. km). The largest islands (in sq. km) are Luzon (104,684), Mindanao (94,627), Samar (13,079), Negros (12,706), Palawan (11,784), Panay (11,515), Mindoro (9,735), Leyte (7,215), Cebu (4,421), Bohol (3,864), Masbate (3,268).

Census population 1980 was 48,098,460; 36% urban. Estimate (1987) 57·36m. (41% in 1987).

The area and population of the 13 regions are as follows (from north to south):

Region	Sq. km	Estimate 1987	Region	Sq. km	Estimate 1987
Ilocos	21,568	3,950,000	Central Visayas	14,951	4,359,000
Cagayan Valley	36,403	2,626,000	Eastern Visayas	21,432	3,199,000
Central Luzon	18,231	5,679,000	Northern Mindanao	28,328	3,392,000
National Capital	636	7,322,000	Southern Mindanao	31,693	4,174,000
Southern Tagalog	46,924	7,465,000	Central Mindanao	23,293	2,579,000
Bicol	17,633	3,961,000	Western Mindanao	18,685	2,948,000
Western Visayas	20,223	5,233,000			

The major cities (with 1980 census populations) are as follows; all on Luzon unless indicated in parenthesis.

Manila	1,630,485 [1]	Batangas	143,570
Quezon City	1,165,865 [1]	Cabanatuan	138,298
Davao (Mindanao)	610,375	San Pablo	131,655
Cebu (Cebu)	490,281	San Juan del Monte	130,088 [1]
Caloocan	467,816 [1]	Cadiz (Negros)	129,632
Makati	372,631 [1]	Navotas	126,146 [1]
Zamboanga (Mindanao)	343,722	Lipa	121,166
Pasay	287,770 [1]	Baguio	119,009
Pasig	268,570 [1]	Silay (Negros)	111,131
Bacolod (Negros)	262,415	Mandaue (Cebu)	110,590
Iloilo (Panay)	244,827	Lucena	107,880
Cagayan de Oro (Mindanao)	227,312	Calbayog (Samar)	106,719
Valenzuela	212,363 [1]	Ormoc (Leyte)	104,978
Marikina	211,613 [1]	Tacloban (Leyte)	102,523
Parañaque	208,552 [1]	San Carlos (Luzon)	101,243
Mandaluyong	205,366 [1]	Legaspi	99,766
Angeles	188,834	Dagupan	98,344
Butuan (Mindanao)	172,489	Malolos	95,699
Iligan (Mindanao)	167,358	San Carlos (Negros)	91,627
Olongapo	156,430	Naga	90,712
General Santos (Mindanao)	149,396		

[1] City within Metropolitan Manila (total population 5,925,884).

In 1980 the national language, Pilipino (based on Tagalog, a Malayan dialect) was spoken by 55% of the population, but as a mother tongue by only 23·8%; among the 76 other indigenous languages spoken, all of the Malayo-Polynesian family, Cebuano was spoken as a mother tongue by 24·4%, Ilocano by 11·1%, Hiligaynon by 8% and Bikol by 5%.

CLIMATE. Some areas have an equatorial climate while others experience tropical monsoon conditions, with a wet season extending from May to Nov. Mean temperatures are high all year, with very little variation. Manila. Jan. 77°F (25°C), July 82°F (27·8°C). Annual rainfall 82″ (2,083 mm).

CONSTITUTION AND GOVERNMENT. Presidential elections were held on 7 Feb. 1986. Ferdinand E. Marcos was opposed by Corazón Aquino. The elections proved to be fraudulent and although Marcos was proclaimed President, by the National Assembly, on 15 Feb., on 25 Feb. he fled the country. President Corazón Aquino was sworn in on 25 Feb.

On 25 March 1986 the President abolished the Parliament and declared a provisional government. A new Constitution was ratified by referendum in 1987 with 78·5% of the voters endorsing it. It aims 'to secure to ourselves and our posterity the blessings of independence and democracy under the rule of law and a regime of truth, justice, freedom, love, equality and peace'.

At congressional elections held on 11 May 1987, 24 senators were elected in the Upper House and 200 congressmen in the House of Representatives.

President: Corazón Aquino.
Vice President: Salvador Laurel.
Foreign Affairs: Raul Manglapus. *Finance:* Vicente Jayme. *Justice:* Sedfrey Ordoñez. *National Defence:* Fidel Ramos. *Agriculture and Food:* Carlos Dominguez. *Environment and Natural Resources:* Fulgencio Factoran Jr. *Agrarian Reform:* Philip Juico. *Education, Culture and Sports:* Lourdes Quisumbing. *Local Government:* Lito Monico Lorenzana. *Labour and Employment:* Franklin Drilon. *Public Works and Highways:* Fiorello Estuar. *Trade and Industry:* José Concepcion Jr. *Transport and Communications:* Reinerio Reyes. *Tourism:* José Antonio Gonzales. *Health:* Alfredo Bengzon. *Science and Technology:* Antonio Arizabal. *Social Welfare and Development:* Mita Pardo de Tavera. *Budget and Management:* Guillermo Carague. *National Economic and Development Authority:* Solita Monsod. *Executive Secretary:* Catalino Macaraeg Jr. *Press Secretary:* Teodoro Benigno Jr. *Presidential Commission on Good Government:* Ramon Díaz. *Central Bank Governor:* Jose Fernández.

National flag: Horizontally blue over red, with a white triangle based on the hoist bearing a gold sun of 8 rays and 3 gold stars.

National hymn: 'Tierra Adorada', 'Land of the Morning', lyric in English by M. A. Sane and C. Osias, in Spanish by José Palma (1899), tune by Julian Felipe (1898); 'Pambansang Awit ng Pilipinas', Tagalog lyric by the Institute of National Language, music by Julian Felipe.

Local Government. The country is administratively divided into 13 regions, 73 provinces, 60 cities, 1,532 municipalities, 21 municipal districts and 40,761 *barangays.* On 14 Nov. 1975 the name of provincial boards and city or municipal boards or councils was changed into *Sangguniang Bayan.*

DEFENCE. On 14 March 1947 the Philippine and US Governments signed a 99-year military-base arrangement since reduced to 25 years and will end in 1991. The USA was granted the use of a series of army, navy and air bases, with the right to use a number of others on mutual agreement. On 21 March a second agreement provided for a US Military Advisory Group as well as military assistance. A treaty of mutual assistance was signed in Washington on 30 Aug. 1951; the instruments of ratification were exchanged in Manila on 27 Aug. 1952. The Philippines is also a signatory of the S.E. Asia Collective Defence Treaty.

The Chief of Staff of the Armed Forces has overall command over the Army, Air Force, Navy and Constabulary.

Army. The Army comprises 5 infantry divisions, 1 ranger regiment, 3 engineer brigades, 1 light armoured regiment and 4 artillery regiments. Equipment includes 28 Scorpion light tanks. Strength (1988) 62,000, with reserves totalling 95,000. There are also paramilitary forces; the Philippine Constabulary (50,000) and the Civil Home Defence Force (65,000).

Navy. The fleet includes 3 very old frigates (former US destroyer escorts built in 1943), 10 corvettes (3 ex-US fleet minesweepers and 7 ex-US escorts), 2 ex-US PC-type patrol vessels, 8 other patrol craft, 5 gunboats, 70 coastal patrol craft, 1 training ship, 24 landing ships, 4 medium landing ships, 6 landing craft (3 LSSL and 3 LCU), 3 repair ships, 2 oilers, 3 water carriers, 1 supply ship, 6 survey ships, 5 tenders, 70 minor landing craft, 2 yachts (command ships), 6 tugs and 20 auxiliaries. There are 30 patrol craft and 60 cutters and tenders in the coast guard.

The Philippine Navy was considerably increased in 1976 by taking over many vessels (nearly all former US warships) from the Vietnamese Navy which escaped from Indo-China when the Saigon government collapsed in 1975. But some 60 of the larger ships are well over 40 years old. The 4 largest are now non-operational, 4 patrol vessels built in 1979 are unserviceable, and all LSTs seriously in need of refit. Of some 250 ships only 100 are servicable and 30 regularly operational.

Naval personnel in 1988 totalled 14,700 officers and men. There are also 9,250 officers and enlisted men in the marine corps (was to be raised to 15,400), and 2,000 officers and men in the coast guard.

Air Force. The Air Force had (1988) a strength of 17,000 officers and men, with 390 aircraft, and was built up with US assistance. Its fighter-bomber wing is equipped with 1 squadron of F-5A and 1 squadron of F-8H Crusaders. A strike wing is equipped with armed trainers, 2 squadrons having T-28s and 1 squadron SF.260WPs. Other units include a maritime patrol squadron with F27 Maritimes and HU-16 Albatross amphibians and 7 transport squadrons (1 with C-130/L-100 Hercules, 1 with F27s, 1 with Nomads, 1 with C-47s, 2 with UH-1 Iroquois helicopters and 1 with S-76 helicopters). Training aircraft include T-41s, T-34s and T-33 jets. Two S-70 helicopters are used as VIP transports.

Police. Public order is maintained partly through the Philippine constabulary and partly through the local police forces. The constabulary now forms part of the Armed Forces and has 27,000 personnel.

INTERNATIONAL RELATIONS

Membership. The Republic of the Philippines is a member of UN and the Colombo Plan.

External Debt. At 31 March 1987 the external debt (monetary and non-monetary) amounted to US$28,581m.

ECONOMY

Planning. A development plan, 1983–87, aimed at an average growth rate of 6·5%.

Budget. The revenues and expenditures of the central government for calendar years were, in 1m. Philippine pesos, as follows:

	1983	1984	1985	1986	1987[1]
Revenue	46,642	57,150	68,961	79,245	109,529
Expenditure	50,271	67,797	80,148	114,505	160,416

[1] Estimate.

Expenditure (1987) included (in 1m. pesos): National defence, 8,222; education, health and social services, 31,251; economic development, 28,660; debt service, 65,895.

At Jan. 1987 the total internal public debt outstanding of the national and local governments and monetary institutions, including those of the government corporations, stood at P.140,978·7m.

Currency. Total money supply, July 1987, was P.41,887·6m., of which

P.27,588·8m. was currency in circulation and P.14,298·8m. were demand deposits. The coins used are: 5 *peso*, 1 *peso*, one-half *peso*, quarter *peso*, media *peseta* (10 *centavos*), all contain 70 grammes copper, 18 grammes zinc and 12 grammes nickel; 5 *centavo* in copper and zinc, and 1 *centavo* in aluminium and magnesium zinc. Central Bank notes are issued in 2, 5, 10, 20, 50, 100, 500 *pesos* denominations.

In March 1988, £1 = 36·20 *pesos*; US$1 = 21·01 *pesos*.

Banking. In 1986 there were 30 head offices and 1,735 branches of commercial banks, with 4 overseas, 1 each in New York, Hong Kong, Taipei and London. Agencies exist in Honolulu, San Francisco and Los Angeles. Total deposits of the commercial banks in June 1987 were P.138,587·8m. Total number of Philippine banking institutions, 1986, 3,615 with total assets P.661,569·1m.

Under the law passed 15 June 1948 the Central Bank of the Philippines was created to have sole control of the credit and monetary supply, independent of the Treasury. It has a capital of P.10m. furnished solely by the Government. Its total assets, at 31 Dec. 1986 were P.313,892m. Central Bank's total assets at July 1987 were P.318,308·5m.

Weights and Measures. The metric system of weights and measures was established by law in 1869, and since 1916 has come into general use but there are local units including the picul (63·25 kg) for sugar and fibres, and the cavan (16·5 gallons) for cereals.

ENERGY AND NATURAL RESOURCES

Electricity. Government and private electric systems furnish the Philippines with electric power, with total installed capacity of 6,462,000 mw (1986); production 22,865m. kwh. Supply 110 and 220 volts; 60 Hz.

Minerals. Mineral production in 1986 (in tonnes): Nickel metal, 12,740; zinc metal, 1,570; copper metal, 217,020; cobalt metal, 90; coal, 1,235,500; salt, 442,110; gold, 35,430 kg; silver, 51,530 kg. Other minerals include chromite, cement, rock asphalt, sand and gravel.

Agriculture. Of the total area of 30m. hectares, 7·04m. hectares are commercial forests; 5·4m. hectares non-commercial forests; 794,000 hectares open grassland; 115,000 hectares mangrove and marshes; 14,794,000 hectares cultivated.

About 98·4% of the total cultivated area is owned by Filipinos; the average size of the farm was 2·63 hectares in 1980. The principal products are unhusked rice (palay), Manila hemp (abaca), copra, sugar-cane, maize and tobacco. During the first quarter of 1987 10,013,000 persons were employed in agriculture (48·48% of the working population).

The products (in 1,000 tonnes) are (1986, provisional): Rough rice, 9,097; copra, 2,314; coconuts, 3,162; sugar (centrifugal muscovado and molasses), 2,135; shelled corn, 3,922; bananas, 3,820; tobacco, 47; abaca fibre, 84.

Minor crops are fruits, nuts, root crops, vegetables, onions, beans, coffee, cacao, peanuts, ramie, rubber, maguey and kapok.

Livestock, estimated in 1986: 2,984,440 carabaos (water buffaloes), 1,814,460 cattle, 7,274,830 pigs, 2,176,930 goats and 58,212,180 poultry.

Forestry. The forests covered some 10,765,279 hectares in 1984. Log production, 1986, 3,567,720 cu. metres.

Fisheries. Fish production from all sources was 2,089,484,000 kg and was valued at P.36,911,321,000 in 1986.

INDUSTRY AND TRADE

Industry. Manufacturing is a major source of economic development contributing 25·19% to GNP in 1986. Leading growth sectors were food manufacturing, textile, footwear and wearing apparel, machinery except electrical, fabricated metal products, wood and cork products, industrial chemicals and other chemical products, furniture and fixtures and publishing and allied industries. In 1985 (annual survey), there were 5,369 large manufacturing establishments, of which 1,331 were engaged in food; 413 wearing apparel; 132 footwear; 312 textile; 354 publishing and allied industries; 328 machinery except electrical; 262 fabricated metal products; 294 industrial chemicals and other chemical products; 284 wood and cork products; 157 plastic products and 161 transport equipment. The non-agricultural labour force during the first quarter of 1987 was 10,639,000 out of a total of 20,652,000 employed.

Commerce. The values of imports and exports (f.o.b.) for calendar years are stated as follows in US$1m.:

	1983	1984	1985	1986
Imports	7,487	6,070	5,111	5,044
Exports	5,005	5,391	4,629	4,842

The principal exports in 1985 were (in US$1m.): Electronics, 1,020; garments, 623; coconut oil (crude), 347; copper concentrates, 84; gold, 100; fresh bananas, 113; petroleum products refined, 39; nickel, 52.

Main imports in 1985 (in US$1m.): Petroleum products and related materials, 1,392; machinery other than electric, 125; textile yarns, fabrics, made-up articles and related products, 140; electric machinery apparatus and appliances, 253; cereals and cereal preparations, 278; iron and steel, 135; industrial machinery, equipment and machine parts, 107; metal manufactures, 74; organic chemicals, 137; artificial resins and plastic materials, 94.

For over a half-century the foreign trade has been chiefly with the USA.

Total trade between the Philippines and UK (British Department of Trade returns, in £1,000 sterling):

	1983	1984	1985	1986	1987
Imports to UK	160,701	199,659	179,979	182,852	202,707
Exports and re-exports from UK	102,949	91,751	94,370	79,809	113,784

Tourism. In 1986, 764,000 tourists visited the Philippines spending US$647m.

COMMUNICATIONS

Roads. In 1985 highways totalled 161,709 km; of this, 9,188 km were concrete; 12,050, asphalt; 9,722, earth; 9,722, macadam. In 1986 there were registered 1,185,832 motor vehicles of all types.

Railways. The National Railways totals 1,027 km of 1,067 mm gauge on Luzon, and Phividec Railways operates 116 km on Panay Island. In 1986, 3,744,000 passengers and 64,000 tonnes of freight were carried by rail.

Aviation. The Philippine Air Lines, Inc., with a working capital of P.3,061m., in 1986 carried 4,865,689 passengers and 54,980,763 kg of cargo.

Shipping. In 1985 there were 302 public and 240 private ports, many serving coastal shipping. In 1984, 63,726 vessels of 24,097,000 net tons entered and 63,175 vessels of 23,449,000 net tons cleared all ports.

Post and Broadcasting. In 1986 there were in operation 2,096 post offices and 2,131 telegraph stations. The Philippine Long Distance Telephone Co. had 856,014 telephones in service (company-owned and subscriber-owned) in 1986. Other major operators had 62,429 connexions in 1983.

Licensed radio stations in 1986 numbered 11,006, including 1,257 ship stations and 160 aircraft stations.

Newspapers (1986). There were 472 registered publications (288 published in Manila), 20 of which were dailies in 1986.

JUSTICE, RELIGION, EDUCATION AND WELFARE

Justice. There is a Supreme Court which is composed of a chief justice and 14 associate justices; it can declare a law or treaty unconstitutional by the concurrent votes of the majority sitting. There is an intermediate appellate court, which consists of a presiding appellate justice and 49 associate appellate justices. There are 13 regional trial courts, one for each judicial region, with a presiding regional trial judge in its 720 branches. There is a metropolitan trial court in each metropolitan area established by law, a municipal trial court in each of the other cities or municipalities and a municipal circuit trial court in each area defined as a municipal circuit comprising one or more cities and/or one or more municipalities.

The Supreme Court may designate certain branches of the regional trial courts to handle exclusively criminal cases, juvenile and domestic relations cases, agrarian cases, urban land reform cases which do not fall under the jurisdiction of quasijudicial bodies and agencies and/or such other special cases as the Supreme Court may determine.

Religion. In 1970 there were 31,169,488 Roman Catholics, 1,434,688 Aglipayans, 1,584,963 Moslems, 1,122,999 Protestants, 475,407 members of the Iglesia ni Kristo, 33,639 Buddhists and 863,302 others.

The Roman Catholics are organized in 12 archbishoprics, 30 bishoprics, 12 prelatures nullius, 4 apostolic vicariates, 4 apostolic prefectures and some 1,633 parishes. The Philippine Independent Church, founded in 1902, and comprising about 3·9% of the population, denies the spiritual authority of the Roman Pontiff. It is divided into two groups, one of which has accepted ordinations by the Episcopalian Church.

Education. Formal education consists of 3 levels: elementary, secondary and further education. Public elementary education is free and public elementary schools are established in almost every *barangay* or *barrio*. The majority of the secondary and post-secondary schools are private, sectarian or non-sectarian. The number of years required to complete the elementary and secondary levels are 6 and 4 years respectively, while the tertiary level requires at least 4 years for an academic degree. Pre-school education is also offered mostly in private schools to children from ages 3–6.

Non-formal education consists of adult literacy classes, agricultural and farming training programmes, occupation skills training, youth clubs, and community programmes of instructions in health, nutrition, family planning and co-operatives.

Public and private schools in 1986–87 enrolled 9,230,378 pupils in primary schools, 3,420,921 in secondary schools and 1,704,618 students in further education. The University of the Philippines (founded in 1908) had 15,316 students in 1984.

Health. In 1982 there were 46,579 registered physicians and (1986) 89,171 hospital beds.

DIPLOMATIC REPRESENTATIVES

Of the Philippines in Great Britain (9A Palace Green, London, W8 4QE)
Ambassador: Juan T. Quimson (accredited 8 July 1986).

Of Great Britain in the Philippines (115 Esteban St., Manila)
Ambassador: Keith MacInnes, CMG.

Of the Philippines in the USA (1617 Massachusetts Ave., NW, Washington, D.C., 20036)
Ambassador: Emmanuel N. Pelaez.

Of the USA in the Philippines (1201 Roxas Blvd., Manila)
Ambassador: Nicholas Platt.

Of the Philippines to the United Nations
Ambassador: Emmanuel Pelaez.

Books of Reference

Philippine Yearbook 1987. National Statistics Office, Manila, 1987
National Power Corporation. Annual Report '83
Foreign Trade Statistics of the Philippines, 1985. National Statistics Office, Manila, 1985
Bresnan, J. (ed.), *Crisis in the Philippines: The Marcos Era and Beyond.* Princeton Univ. Press, 1986
Burley, T. M., *The Philippines. An Economic and Social Geography.* London, 1973
Lightfort, K., *The Philippines.* London, 1973
May, R. J., and Nemenzo, F. (eds.), *The Philippines after Marcos.* London and Sydney, 1985
Poole, F., and Vanzi, M., *Revolution in the Philippines.* New York, 1984

PITCAIRN
ISLAND

Only settlement: Adamstown
Population: 57 (1986)

HISTORY. It was discovered by Carteret in 1767, but remained uninhabited until 1790, when it was occupied by 9 mutineers of HMS *Bounty*, with 12 women and 6 men from Tahiti. Nothing was known of their existence until the island was visited in 1808. In 1856 the population having become too large for the island's resources, the inhabitants (194 in number) were, at their own request, removed to Norfolk Island; but 43 of them returned in 1859–64.

AREA AND POPULATION. Pitcairn Island (1·75 sq. miles; 4·6 sq. km) is situated in the Pacific Ocean, nearly equidistant from New Zealand and Panama (25° 04′S. lat., 130° 06′ W. long.). Adamstown is the only settlement. The population on 31 Dec. 1986 was 57.

The uninhabited islands of Henderson (12 sq. miles), Ducie (1½ sq. miles) and Oeno (2 sq. miles) were annexed in 1902 and are included in the Pitcairn group.

CLIMATE. An equable climate, with average annual rainfall of 80″ (2,000 mm), spread evenly throughout the year. Mean monthly temperatures range from 75°F (24°C) in Jan. to 66°F (19°C) in July.

CONSTITUTION. Pitcairn was brought within the jurisdiction of the High Commissioner for the Western Pacific in 1898 and transferred to the Governor of Fiji in 1952. When Fiji became independent in Oct. 1970, the British High Commissioner in New Zealand was appointed Governor.

The Local Government Ordinance of 1964 constitutes a Council of 10 members, of whom 4 are elected, 5 are nominated (3 by the 4 elected members and 2 by the Governor) and the Island Secretary is an *ex-officio* member. The Island Magistrate, who is elected triennially, presides over the Council; other members hold office for only 1 year. Liaison between Governor and Council is through a Commissioner in the Auckland, New Zealand, office of the British Consulate-General.

Governor: R. A. C. Byatt, CMG (resides in Wellington).
Island Magistrate: Brian Young (elected Dec. 1984).

Flag: British Blue Ensign with the whole arms of Pitcairn in the fly.

TRADE. Fruit, vegetables and curios are sold to passing ships; fuel oil, machinery, building materials, flour, sugar and other foodstuffs are imported.

ROADS. There were (1987) 6 km of roads. In Aug. 1987 motor cycles provided the sole means of personal automotive transport; there were 9 2-wheelers, 16 3-wheelers and 1 4-wheeled motor cycle.

JUSTICE. The Island Court consists of the Island Magistrate and 2 assessors.

EDUCATION. In 1987 there was 1 teacher and 12 pupils.

Books of Reference

A Guide to Pitcairn. Pitcairn Island Administration, Auckland, revised ed. 1982
Ball, I., *Pitcairn: Children of the Bounty.* London, 1973
Ross, A. S. C., and Moverly, A. W., *The Pitcairnese Language.* London, 1964

POLAND

Capital: Warsaw
Population: 37·6m. (1987)
GNP per capita: US$6,420 (1985)

Polska Rzeczpospolita Ludowa

HISTORY. In 1966 Poland celebrated its millennium, but modern Polish history begins with the partitions of the once-powerful kingdom between Russia, Austria and Prussia in 1772, 1793 and 1795. For 19th century events *see* THE STATESMAN'S YEAR-BOOK 1980–81.

On 10 Nov. 1918 independence was proclaimed by Józef Piłsudski, the founder of the Polish Legions during the war. On 28 June 1919 the Treaty of Versailles recognized the independence of Poland.

On 1 Sept. 1939 Germany invaded Poland, on 17 Sept. 1939 Russian troops entered eastern Poland, and on 29 Sept. 1939 the fourth partition of Poland took place. After the German attack on Russia, the Germans occupied the whole of Poland. By March 1945 the country had been liberated by the Russians.

In July 1944 the USSR recognized the Polish Committee of National Liberation *(Polski Komitet Wyzwolenia Narodowego)* established in Lublin as an executive organ of the National Council of the Homeland *(Krajowa Rada Narodowa)*. The Committee was transformed into the Provisional Government in Dec. 1944, and on 28 June 1945, supplemented by members of the Polish Government in London (which had been recognized by the UK and USA), it was re-established—in Moscow—as the Polish Provisional Government of National Unity and on 6 July recognized as such by the UK and USA.

Elections were held on 19 Jan. 1947. Of the 12·7m. votes cast, 11·24m. were recognized as valid and 9m. were given for the Communist-dominated 'Democratic Bloc'. After riots in Poznań in June 1956 nationalist anti-Stalinist elements gained control of the Communist Party, under the leadership of Wladyslaw Gomułka.

In 1970 the Federal Republic of Germany recognized Poland's western boundary as laid down by the Potsdam Conference of 1945 (the 'Oder–Neisse line').

In Dec. 1970 strikes and riots in Gdańsk, Szczecin and Gdynia led to the resignation of a number of leaders including Gomułka. He was replaced by Edward Gierek.

The introduction of price rises in June 1976 was again followed by strikes and riots. The rises were withdrawn and some demonstrators were imprisoned. In the campaign of protest which followed a Committee for the Defence of the Workers (KOR) was formed.

The raising of meat prices on 1 July 1980 resulted in a wave of strikes which broadened into generalized wage demands and eventually by mid-Aug. acquired a political character. Workers in Gdańsk, Gdynia and Sopot elected a joint strike committee, led by Lech Wałęsa.

On 24 Aug. Gierek reshuffled the Party and Government leadership. On 31 Aug. the Government and Wałęsa signed the 'Gdańsk Agreements' permitting the formation of independent Trade Unions.

On 5 Sept. Gierek suffered a heart attack and was replaced as First Secretary by Stanislaw Kania (Gierek was expelled from the Party in July 1981). On 17 Sept. various Trade Unions decided to form a national confederation ('Solidarity') and applied for legal status, which was granted on 24 Oct. after some Government resistance.

On 9 Feb. the Defence Minister, Gen. Wojciech Jaruzelski became Prime Minister. At an extraordinary Communist Party congress in July a new leadership was elected. At Solidarity's first national congress (4–10 Sept. and 2–8 Oct. 1981) Wałęsa was re-elected chairman and a radical programme of action was adopted. On 18 Oct. Kania resigned from the Party leadership and was replaced by Jaruzelski. On 13 Dec. 1981 the Government imposed martial law (*stan wojenny*), banning a wide range of civil liberties, and establishing the rule of a 20-member Military Council of National Salvation (WRON). Solidarity was proscribed and its leaders detained. Martial law was approved by the Sejm on 26 Jan. 1982 with one dissident vote and 5 abstentions. The Party Central Committee approved the measure on 25 Feb. Wałęsa was released in Nov. 1982. On 8 Oct. the Sejm voted (with 12 dissident votes and 9 abstentions) a law dissolving all registered trade unions including Solidarity. These have been replaced by workplace unions which are required to pledge support for the Communist Party and the Constitution. Martial law was suspended in Dec. 1982 and finally lifted in July 1983. An amnesty of 21 July 1984 freed 35,000 common and 652 political prisoners, including 7 Solidarity and 4 KOR leaders. In Nov. 1985 Jaruzelski resigned the Prime Ministership in favour of Zbigniew Messner, and was elected Chairman of the Council of State. In July and Sept. 1986 the Government granted an amnesty to all political prisoners except those accused of terrorism or spying. In Dec. the government established a 56-member Advisory Council of independents from various social spheres.

AREA AND POPULATION. Poland is bounded north by the Baltic and the RSFSR, east by Lithuania, White Russia and the Ukraine, south by Czechoslovakia and west by the German Democratic Republic. Poland comprises an area of 312,683 sq. km (120,628 sq. miles). The country is divided into 49 voivodships (*wojewodztwo*) and these in turn are divided into 813 towns and 2,122 wards (*gmina*). The capital is Warsaw (Warszawa).

Area (in sq. km) and population (in 1,000) in 1986 (1984 % urban in brackets).

Voivodship	Area	Population	Voivodship	Area	Population
Biała Podlaska	5,348	300 (32·5)	Opole	8,535	1,020 (50·9)
Białystok	10,055	672 (57·7)	Ostrołęka	6,498	372 (30·9)
Bielsko–Biała	3,704	879 (48·9)	Piła	8,205	469 (53·9)
Bydgoszcz	10,349	1,090 (62·8)	Piotrków	6,266	637 (45·3)
Chełm	3,866	243 (39·9)	Płock	5,117	511 (45·7)
Ciechanów	6,362	420 (33·0)	Poznań	8,151	1,308 (69·7)
Częstochowa	6,182	770 (51·2)	Przemyśl	4,437	398 (35·7)
Elbląg	6,103	470 (58·6)	Radom	7,294	733 (44·5)
Gdańsk	7,394	1,411 (76·2)	Rzeszów	4,397	698 (37·7)
Gorzów	8,484	487 (60·4)	Siedlce	8,499	640 (28·7)
Jelenia Góra	4,378	512 (65·3)	Sieradz	4,869	403 (33·1)
Kalisz	6,512	700 (44·5)	Skierniewice	3,960	412 (42·2)
Katowice	6,650	3,946 (87·7)	Słupsk	7,453	400 (53·8)
Kielce	9,211	1,113 (44·4)	Suwałki	10,490	454 (49·9)
Konin	5,139	461 (38·6)	Szczecin	9,981	951 (73·9)
Koszalin	8,470	494 (61·0)	Tarnobrzeg	6,283	584 (34·6)
Kraków (Cracow)	3,254	1,214 (69·1)	Tarnów	4,151	647 (34·2)
Krosno	5,702	480 (32·8)	Toruń	5,348	646 (60·8)
Legnica	4,037	497 (66·6)	Wałbrzych	4,168	738 (88·5)
Leszno	4,154	378 (46·1)	Warsaw	3,788	2,422 (73·0)
Łódź	1,523	1,150 (91·4)	Włocławek	4,402	427 (44·9)
Łomża	6,684	341 (35·7)	Wrocław	6,287	1,119 (72·4)
Lublin	6,792	992 (55·5)	Zamość	6,980	489 (24·9)
Nowy Sącz	5,576	674 (35·5)	Zielona Góra	8,868	654 (59·0)
Olsztyn	12,327	733 (56·4)			

Population (in 1,000) of the largest towns (1985):

Warsaw	1,649	Bydgoszcz	361	Gliwice	213
Łódź	849	Lublin	324	Kielce	201
Kraków (Cracow)	716	Sosnowiec	255	Zabrze	198
Wrocław (Breslau)	636	Częstochowa	247	Toruń	186
Poznań	553	Białystok	245	Tychy	182
Gdańsk (Danzig)	467	Gdynia	243	Bielsko-Biala	174
Szczecin (Stettin)	391	Bytom	239	Ruda Śląska	165
Katowice	363	Radom	214	Olsztyn	147

At the census of 6 Dec. 1984 the population was 37,026,000 (18m. males; 60% urban). Population on 1 Jan. 1987, 37,572,000 (19·2m. females; 22·7m. urban),

density, 120 per sq. km. Vital statistics, 1986 (per 1,000): Marriages, 6·9; divorces, 1·4; live births, 17; deaths, 10·1; infant mortality (per 1,000 live births), 17·3.
The rate of natural growth, 1986, 6·9 per 1,000. Expectation of life in 1984 was 66·8 years. In 1984, 55% of the population was under 30.
Ethnic minorities are not identified. There were estimated to be 1·2m. Germans in 1984. In 1982 there were 900 immigrants and 32,100 emigrants. In 1983 19,200 Germans emigrated. There is a large Polish diaspora, some 65% in USA.

CLIMATE. Climate is continental, marked by long and severe winters. Rainfall amounts are moderate, with a marked summer maximum. Warsaw. Jan. 25°F (−3·9°C), July 66°F (18·9°C). Annual rainfall 22·1″ (553 mm). Gdańsk. Jan. 29°F (−1·7°C), July 63°F (17·2°C). Annual rainfall 22″ (559 mm). Kraków. Jan. 27°F (−2·8°C), July 67°F (19·4°C). Annual rainfall 29″ (729 mm). Poznań. Jan. 30°F (−1·1°C), July 67°F (19·4°C). Annual rainfall 21″ (523 mm). Stettin. Jan. 30°F (−1·1°C), July 65°F (18·3°C). Annual rainfall 22″ (550 mm). Wrocław. Jan. 30°F (−1·1°C), July 66°F (18·9°C). Annual rainfall 23″ (574 mm).

CONSTITUTION AND GOVERNMENT. The present Constitution was adopted on 22 July 1952. Amendments were adopted in 1976 and 1983.
The titular head of state is the Chairman of the Council of State, Wojciech Jaruzelski. Deputy Chairmen: Kazimierz Barcikowski, Zenon Komender, Tadeusz Mlynczak, Tadeusz Szelachowski.
Since 1983 the Constitution has defined the position of political parties as follows: 'The alliance and cooperation of the Polish United Workers' (*i.e.* Communist) Party with the United Peasant Party and the Democratic Party in the construction of socialism and their cooperation with those social organizations and associations that are grounded in the principles of the system of the Polish People's Republic form the basis of the Patriotic Movement of National Renaissance.' (PRON). The latter was set up on 15 Oct. 1982.
At the 9th, extraordinary, congress of the Communist Party on 19 July 1981 a new Politburo was elected. In March 1988 the Politburo consisted of: Wojciech Jaruzelski *(First Secretary)*; Kazimierz Barcikowski; Józef Baryla; Józef Czyrek; Jan Główczyk; Gen. Czesław Kiszczak *(Minister of the Interior)*; Zbigniew Messner *(Prime Minister)*; Alfred Miodowicz; Włodzimierz Mokrzyszczak; Zygmunt Murański; Marian Orzechowski *(Foreign Minister)*; Tadeusz Porebski; Gen. Florian Siwicki *(Defence Minister)*; Zofia Stepień; Marian Wozniak. Candidate members: Stanisław Bejger; Mieczysław Rakowski *(Chairman, Socio-Economic Council)*; Janusz Kubasiewicz; Zbigniew Michalek; Gabriela Rembisz. Ministers not in the Politburo include 3 *Deputy Prime Ministers:* Zdzisław Sadowski *(Chairman, Planning Commission)*; Józef Koziol; Zbigniew Szałajda; Gen. Tadeusz Hupałowski *(Chairman, Supreme Chamber of Control)*; Bazyli Samojlik *(Finance)*; Władysław Gwiazda *(Foreign Economic Co-operation)*; Jerzy Jozwiak *(Home Trade)*; Lech Domeracki *(Justice)*; Janusz Pawlowski *(Labour and Social Policy)*; Stanisław Zięba *(Agriculture and Food)*; Janusz Komender *(Health and Welfare)*; Jerzy Bilip *(Industry)*; Jerzy Urban *(Head of Government Press Office)*.
In 1986 the Polish United Workers' Party had 2,129,000 (3,091,900 in 1980) members (39% workers, 89% over 30 in 1984), the United Peasants' Party had 498,200 in 1986, and the Democratic Party, 117,700 members. The Socialist Youth Union had 1·5m. members in 1986 (2m. in 1980).
The authority of the republic is vested in the Sejm, elected for 4 years by all citizens over 18. The Sejm elects a Council of State and a Council of Ministers.
The last elections for the Sejm were held on 13 Oct. 1985, having been postponed from March 1984. 410 seats were contested by 2 candidates each, and 50 seats by one candidate who had to obtain 50% of the vote, these latter being mainly Government leaders and 16 independents. All candidates had to support the policies of PRON. Turn-out was said officially to be 78·86%. Solidarity, which had called for a boycott of the election, claimed a turn-out of 66%. (Turn-out was 98·87% in the 1980 election). The 460 seats are distributed as follows: 245 United Workers' Party, 106 United Peasants' Party, 35 Democratic Party, 74 independents, including 21 Catholics. The Speaker of the Sejm is Roman Malinowski.

At a referendum of 29 Nov. 1987 the 28m. voters were asked *(i)* if they would accept two or three years of sacrifice to save the economy *(ii)* if they wanted deep democratization of political life. Turn-out was 68%. 44% of the electorate voted for *(i)* (26% against), 46% for *(ii)* (24% against), falling short of the 50% approval stipulated to make the conditions legally binding.

Local government is carried out by People's Councils elected every 4 years at voivodship and community level. Alongside these are the offices of state administration. The chairman of the People's Council is the Secretary of the regional organization for the area. Local elections due in 1982 were postponed until 17 June 1984. The Government announced that 74·95% of the 25·9m. electorate had voted (a figure claimed by Solidarity to be inflated by 12-15%). There were some 220,000 candidates, all selected by PRON.

National flag: Horizontally white over red.

National anthem: Jeszcze Polska nie zginęła (words by J. Wybicki, 1797; tune by M. Ogiński, 1796).

DEFENCE. A National Defence Committee was set up in Nov. 1983 with Gen. Jaruzelski at its head. Poland is divided into 3 military districts: Warsaw (the eastern part of Poland); Pomerania (Baltic coast, part of central Poland; headquarters at Bydgoszcz); Silesia (Silesia and southern Poland; headquarters at Wrocław).

Armed forces are on Soviet lines and divided into army and air force (2 years' conscription), navy (3 years), anti-aircraft, rocket and radio-technological units (3 years) and internal security forces (2 years). In 1965 the security forces were taken away from the Ministry of Internal Affairs and placed under the Defence Ministry. The military age extends from the 19th to the 50th year. The strength of the armed forces was (1988) 394,000, plus 87,000 security and frontier forces. Security forces include armoured brigades.

Army. The Army consists of 5 armoured, 8 mechanized, 1 airborne and 1 amphibious assault divisions; 5 artillery brigades; 3 anti-tank regiments; 4 surface-to-surface missile brigades; 1 air defence brigade. Equipment includes 3,400 T-54/-55 and 270 T-72 main battle tanks. Strength (1988) 230,000 (including 168,000 conscripts).

Navy. The fleet comprises 3 *ex*-Soviet diesel electric propelled patrol submarines, 1 new frigate, 2 missile armed modern corvettes, 24 fleet minesweepers, 12 fast missile craft, 15 patrol boats, 40 coastguard patrol boats, 24 minesweepers, 8 inshore minesweepers, 23 medium landing ships, 3 intelligence vessels, 8 training ships, 3 degaussing vessels, 2 salvage ships, 2 torpedo recovery vessels, 18 minor landing craft, 6 surveying vessels, 7 oilers, 20 tugs and 40 auxiliaries and tenders. The Fleet Air Arm has 90 somewhat dated fixed-wing aircraft (including 40 MiG-17s and 40 MiG-21s) and over 60 helicopters. Personnel in 1988 totalled 19,500 comprising 5,200 afloat, 2,500 under training, 4,100 of coastal defence, 2,500 in naval aviation and 5,200 on shore support.

Air Force. The Air Force had a strength (1988) of some 80,000 officers and men and 675 first-line jet aircraft of Soviet design, forming 4 air divisions. There are 11 air defence regiments (33 squadrons) with about 400 MiG-21 and MiG-23 supersonic interceptors, and 6 regiments (18 squadrons) operating variable-geometry MiG-23BM and Su-20, Su-7B and MiG-17 close-support fighters. There are also reconnaissance, ECM, transport, helicopter (including Mi-2s for observation and Mi-24 gunships) and training units. Soviet 'Guideline' 'Goa', 'Ganef', 'Gainful' and 'Gaskin' surface-to-air missiles are operational.

Two Soviet armoured divisions are stationed on Polish territory.

INTERNATIONAL RELATIONS

Membership. Poland is a member of UN, Comecon and the Warsaw Pact and was readmitted to IMF in May 1986.

ECONOMY

Planning. For planning history until 1980 *see* THE STATESMAN'S YEAR-BOOK 1981–82, p.1002. Industrialization without sufficient expenditure on infrastructure; neglect of agriculture and the inefficiency of the planning mechanism, exacerbated by higher prices and declining Western demand for exports, and the social unrest since 1980, brought the economy to a state of paralysis. Some foodstuffs are rationed, and price increases were introduced in 1982 and 1984–88. The economy since 1983 has shown some signs of recovery. Economic reforms involving a closer linking of credits, profits and wages with market forces and efficiency were introduced in 1982 and Oct. 1987. A 5-year National Socio-Economic Plan is running from 1986 to 1990, and into this Central Annual Plans are integrated.

Budget. Budget in 1m. złotys, for calendar years:

	1981	1982	1983	1984	1985	1986
Revenue	1,334,700	2,345,300	2,629,100	3,299,700	3,854,200	4,902,700
Expenditure	1,465,600	2,434,200	2,654,400	3,367,800	3,979,200	4,193,200

Main items of 1986 revenue (in 1m. złotys): State enterprises, 3,129,300; finance and insurance, 664,200; income tax, 81,700.

Main items of 1986 expenditure (in 1m. złotys): The economy, 1,933,500; welfare, 511,400; defence, 381,800; administration, 268,500; education, 483,500.

Currency. The currency unit is the *złoty*, divided into 100 *groszy*. The currency consists of notes of 10, 20, 50, 100, 500, 1,000, 2,000 and 5,000 złotys; and of coins of 10, 20 and 50 groszy and 1, 2, 5, 10, 20 and 50 złotys. In Jan. 1982 the złoty was substantially devalued against Western currencies. In March 1988, £1 sterling = 313·7 złotys, US$1 = 675·93 złotys.

Banking. The National Bank of Poland (established 1945) is the central bank, has exclusive authority to issue currency, is charged with control of money and credit, and has responsibility for financial implementation of the national economic plan. Since its merger with the former Investment Bank on 1 Jan. 1970 it exercises centralized control over investment financing. The Food Economics Bank (Bank Gospodarki Żywnościowej) has exclusive responsibility for direct financing of rural areas through both short-term and investment loans. It operates banks. The General Savings Bank (Powszechna Kasa Oszczędności) exercises central control over savings activities, transfers and checking transactions, including activities of workers' co-operative banks.

In addition to the National Bank of Poland other authorized foreign-exchange banks are, the Polish Welfare Bank (Bank Polska Kasa Opieki SA) and the Commercial Bank of Warsaw (Bank Handlowy w Warszawie SA). An Export Development Bank was established in 1986.

Deposits in savings institutions amounted to 2·09m. złotys in 1986.

Weights and Measures. The metric system is in general use.

ENERGY AND NATURAL RESOURCES

Electricity. Electricity production (1986) 140,000m. kwh. In 1984 97·5% of electricity was produced by coal-powered thermal plants. Supply 127 and 220 volts; 50 Hz. A nuclear power station is being built at Zarnowiec.

Minerals. Poland is a major producer of coal (reserves of some 120,000m. tonnes) and sulphur. Copper reserves are estimated at 56m. tonnes. Production in 1986 (in 1m. tonnes): Coal, 192; brown coal, 67·3; copper ore (1985), 29·4; silver, 829 tonnes. Oil was discovered 80 km off the port of Leba in 1985. Total oil reserves amount to some 100m. tonnes. Crude oil production was 190,000 tonnes in 1987, natural gas 5,825m. cu. metres in 1984.

Agriculture. In 1986 there were 18·8m. hectares of agricultural land, of which 14·4m. hectares were in private hands, 3·5m. in state farms, 0·7m. in co-operatives and 0·07m. in agricultural associations. 14·5m. hectares were arable, 260,000 orchards, 2·5m. meadows, 1·6m. pasture lands.

Collectivization has been largely abandoned. There were 2,317 co-operatives in

1986, 1,271 state farms and 392 agricultural associations. In Dec. 1987 a private, Catholic, Foundation for the Development of Polish Agriculture was set up to aid farmers with Western finance. A compulsory contributory pension scheme was introduced in 1978 for farmers who turn over their farms to their successors or the State. Private holdings may not exceed 100 hectares. There were 2·84m. in 1986, of which 0·86m. were less than 2 hectares.

Crops	Area (1,000 hectares)			Yield (1,000 tonnes)		
	1984	1985	1986	1984	1985	1986
Wheat	1,706	1,885	2,025	6,010	6,461	7,502
Rye	3,545	3,083	2,760	9,540	7,600	7,074
Barley	1,055	1,242	1,335	3,555	4,086	4,412
Oats	934	1,086	924	2,604	2,682	2,486
Potatoes	2,147	2,095	2,009	37,437	36,546	39,037
Sugar-beet	473	436	423	16,048	14,664	14,217

Livestock (1986, in thousands): 10,919 cattle (5,207 cows), 18,949 pigs, 4,991 sheep, 1,272 horses, 65,000 poultry. Milk production in 1986 was 15,284m. litres, meat, 3·14m. tonnes.

Tractors in use in 1986: 990,000 (in 15-h.p. units).

Forestry. In 1986, 8·7m. hectares were forests (predominantly coniferous). 68,000 hectares were afforested in 1986, and 25·3m. cu. metres of timber gained.

Fisheries. In 1985 the fishing fleet had 93 deep-sea vessels totalling 314,000 GRT. In 1985 the catch was 650,600 tonnes.

INDUSTRY AND TRADE

Industry. Production in 1985 (and 1984) (in 1,000 tonnes): Coke, 16,000 (16,600); pig-iron, 9,807 (9,981); crude steel, 16,126 (16,533); rolled steel, 11,845 (12,195); cement, 15,000 (16,600); sulphuric acid (100%), 2,863 (2,769); fertilizers, 2,270 (2,356); aluminium, 47 (46); electrolytic copper, 387 (372); lead, 87 (84); zinc, 180 (176); salt, 4,865 (4,711); sugar, 1,708 (1,767). In 1985, 41 ships over 100 DWT were built (343,000 DWT). 283,000 cars, 54,100 lorries and 8,000 buses were built in 1985.

Output of light industry in 1985 (and 1984): Cotton fabrics, 831m. metres (812); woollen fabrics, 105m. metres (103); synthetic fibres. 75m. metres (75); shoes, 164m. pairs (165); household glass, 88,100 tonnes (81,000); paper, 1,071,000 tonnes (1,042,000); washing machines 739,000 (730,000), refrigerators 578,000 (543,000), and TV sets 610,000 (587,000).

Labour. In 1986 the total number in employment was 17·2m. (8·1m. women in 1984), of whom 4·9m. worked in the private sector, and including in agriculture 4·9m., industry 4·9m., building 1·3m., trade 1·5m. and transport and communications 1·1m. There were 5,000 'seeking jobs'. Founded in Aug. 1980 the 'independent self-governing union' organization Solidarity (Chairman Lech Wałęsa) was dissolved in Oct. 1982 along with all other trade unions. New official unions (OPZZ) established in 1983 took over Solidarity's funds in 1985. OPZZ claimed 7m. members in 1987. There are also some 4,000 small unions not affiliated to OPZZ. Average wage in 1986, 24,095 złotys per month. A law of Oct. 1982 makes voluntary unemployment an offence; offenders are liable for compulsory labour for the state. There is a standard, statutory 42-hour working week which may be compulsorily extended in certain workplaces, with 38 free Saturdays a year.

Commerce. Trade statistics for calendar years (in 1m. złotys):

	1981	1982	1983	1984	1985	1986
Imports	963,447	868,908	970,203	1,209,695	1,594,900	1,964,000
Exports	846,209	951,162	1,060,177	1,336,125	1,691,000	2,115,600

Main imports in 1986 (in tonnes): Petroleum, 14·1m.; iron ore, 16·6m.; fertilizers, 5·3m.; wheat, 1·7m.; coal, 1·2m.; passenger cars, 34,300 units.

Main exports in 1986 (in tonnes): Coal, 34·3m.; coke, 1·5m.; copper, 169,000; sulphur, 3·8m.; pharmaceuticals, 46,336m. zlotys; ships, 381,000 DWT.

Foreign trade deals should be made directly with the appropriate foreign trade enterprise. Information may be obtained from the Polish Chamber of Foreign Trade, Trebacka 4, 00–950 Warsaw. Joint ventures with Western firms are encouraged both at home and abroad. The Western partner may own up to 49% of the shares of ventures on Polish soil, and is guaranteed a share of profits and interest.

57% of Poland's trade is with Comecon countries (30% with the USSR). Soviet exports include plant and equipment and raw materials; Polish exports, machinery, ships, coal, chemicals and consumer goods. In Oct. 1985 Poland signed a trade agreement with the USSR for 1986–90. This gives the USSR a wider role in the Polish economy, particularly in the supply of oil, and reschedules Poland's 5,000m. rouble debt beyond 1990. Federal Germany and UK are Poland's major non-communist trading partners.

In July 1985 Western bankers agreed to reschedule Poland's hard currency debts, spreading total repayment over 1991–97. Polish indebtedness to the West was some US$33,000m. in 1987. In 1985 a 2% levy was imposed on firms' fixed asset to help repay hard currency debts. Poland does not accept liability for the £495,000 debts of pre-war Danzig (Gdańsk).

Total trade between Poland and UK (British Department of Trade returns £1,000 sterling):

	1983	1984	1985	1986	1987
Imports to UK	177,057	266,961	320,276	309,746	303,418
Exports and re-exports from UK	151,721	169,962	184,143	182,841	181,451

An Anglo-Polish 10-year agreement on the development of economic, industrial, scientific and technical co-operation was signed on 20 March 1973, and a 10-year programme implementing this was signed on 4 Sept. 1975. Some Polish imports are subject to quota restrictions.

In Feb. 1987 the US restored Poland's most-favoured-nation status and removed other economic sanctions introduced as a response to the imposition of martial law (1981–83).

Tourism. In 1986, 3,851,000 tourists visited Poland (746,000 from the West) and 4,313,000 Polish citizens made visits abroad (957,000 to the West). More liberal passport regulations were introduced for Polish citizens in 1987.

COMMUNICATIONS

Roads. In 1984 Poland had 153,000 km of hard-surfaced roads. Number of motor vehicles: Passenger cars, 3,671,000 (of which, 3,611,000 private); lorries, 780,000 (297,000 private); motor cycles, 1,547,000.

In 1984 road transport carried 2,438m. passengers and 1,421m. tonnes of freight. There were 4,688 fatal road accidents in 1985.

Railways. The length of the standard gauge railway system was (1986) 24,333 km (9,452 km electrified) and ran 121,775m. tonne-km and 48,932m. passenger-km.

Aviation. In 1985 the state airline 'Lot' had 39 aircraft including 5 Il-62s, operated 9 internal and 34 international routes. 1,853,000 passengers were flown and 9,000 tonnes of freight in 1984. There are British Airways, SABENA, KLM, PANAM, Alitalia, Swissair, Air France, Austrian Airlines and Lufthansa services to Okęcie (Warsaw) airport.

Shipping. The principal ports are Gdynia, Gdańsk (Danzig) and Szczecin (Stettin). The merchant marine is grouped into Polish Ocean Lines (150 vessels totalling 1·1m. DWT in 1985) based on Gdynia and operating regular liner services, and the Polish Shipping Company based on Szczecin and operating cargo services. Poland also has a share in the Gdynia America Line. 35·4m. tonnes of freight and 297,000 passengers were carried in 1984.

In 1986 the merchant marine had 261 vessels totalling 2·8m. GRT (including 9 tankers and 17 vessels over 30,000 tons). There are regular lines to London, Hull, China, Indonesia, Australia, Vietnam and some African and Latin-American countries.

Total shipping entering Polish ports in 1984 was 10,081 vessels of 27·2m. NRT.

There are 3,997 km of inland navigable waterways. 15·4m. tonnes of freight and 6·5m. passengers were carried in 1984.

Pipeline. In 1986 there were 1,986 km of oil pipeline.

Post and Broadcasting. In 1986 there were 8,297 post offices. In 1987 there were 2·63m. telephones of which 1·98m. were private.

Polskie Radio i Telewizja broadcasts 3 programmes in Polish on long-, medium- and short-waves and on FM. There are 2 TV programmes. Colour programmes are transmitted by SECAM system. Wireless licences in 1984 numbered 9·29m.; television licences, 8·77m.

Cinemas and Theatres. In 1987 there were 2,041 cinemas, 98 theatres and 49 concert halls. In 1986 cinema attendance was 94·3m.; theatres, 7·9m. 39 full-length films were made.

Newspapers (1986). There were 97 newspapers with an overall circulation of 10·63m. and 2,889 other periodicals. The Party newspaper is *Trybuna Ludu* (People's Tribune), weekend circulation 1·1m.

JUSTICE, RELIGION, EDUCATION AND WELFARE

Justice. The penal code was adopted in 1969. Espionage and treason carry the severest penalties. For minor crimes there is provision for probation sentences and fines.

There exist the following courts: The Supreme Court; voivodship, district and special courts. Judges and lay assessors are elected. The State Council elects the judges of the Supreme Court for a term of 5 years, and appoints the Prosecutor-General. The office of the Prosecutor-General is separate from the judiciary. An ombudsman's office was established in 1987.

Family courts were established (1977) for cases involving divorce and domestic relations. Crimes reported in 1983 (and 1984) 466,205 (538,930) including 478 (593) homicides and 1,875 (2,184) rapes.

Religion. In 1978, 93% of the population was baptized into the Catholic Church, and 78% of the population attended church regularly. According to a survey published in the Communist Party journal *Nowe drogi* in 1985, 90% of the population held religious beliefs. Church–State relations are regulated by agreements of 1950, 1956 and 1972. A joint government-episcopal commission was reactivated in Sept. 1980, and religious broadcasting began. The Church has a university (Lublin), an Academy of Catholic Theology and in 1983 46 seminaries. Religious education of children is conducted in 'catechism centres' of which there were some 20,000 in 1985.

The archbishop of Warsaw and Gniezno is the primate of Poland (since 1981, Cardinal Józef Glemp). The Vatican considers the archbishoprics of Lwów and Vilnius (incorporated in the USSR in 1940) as still being under Polish jurisdiction. In 1983 there were 5 archbishoprics, 27 dioceses and 7,496 parishes, 84 bishops, 37,132 monks and nuns and 14,498 churches and 4,201 chapels. In 1986 there were 3 cardinals and 22,381 priests. In Oct. 1978 Cardinal Karol Wojtyla, archbishop of Cracow, was elected Pope as John Paul II.

On 28 June 1972 the Vatican adjusted the Church boundaries, to coincide with the State's western frontier ('Oder–Neisse line') and the 4 apostolic administrators in the former German territories became bishops. In Oct. 1984, the radical priest, Jerzy Popiełuszko was murdered by secret policemen who were subsequently sentenced to long terms of imprisonment.

Figures for other churches in 1983: Polish Autocephalous Orthodox, 5 dioceses, 218 parishes, 301 churches, 226 priests, 1 monastery, 1 nunnery, 600,000 adherents. Lutheran, 6 dioceses, 121 parishes, 173 churches, 153 chapels, 100 parsons (100,000 adherents in 1975). Uniate, 3 dioceses, 85 parishes, 98 churches, 90 priests (200,000 adherents in 1975). Old-Catholic Mariavite, 3 dioceses, 42 parishes, 55 churches, 29 priests (30,000 adherents in 1975). Methodist, 5 districts, 60 parishes, 57 chapels, 36 parsons (4,133 adherents in 1975). United Evangelical, 200 congregations, 56 chapels, 180 parsons. Seventh-day Adventist, 123 communities, 123 churches, 61 parsons. Baptist, 128 congregations, 58 chapels, 58 parsons (2,300 adherents in 1975). Jews, 16 congregations, 10 synagogues (12,000 adherents in 1978). Epiphany World Mission, 9 chapels and 426 priests. In 1985 there were 2,500 Moslems with 3 mosques and 5 priests.

Education. Basic education from 7 to 15 is free and compulsory. Free secondary education is then optional in general or vocational schools. Primary schools are organized in complexes based on wards under one director ('gmina collective schools'). In 1986–87 there were: Kindergartens, 25,971 with 1·4m. pupils and 86,000 teachers; primary schools, 17,778 with 5,027,600 pupils and 273,000 teachers; secondary schools, 1,135 with 400,000 pupils and 22,000 teachers; vocational schools, 9,333 with 1,600,000 pupils and 83,000 teachers, and 92 institutions of higher education (including 11 universities, 18 polytechnics, 9 agricultural schools, 6 schools of economics, 11 teachers' training colleges and 10 medical schools) with 335,300 students and 57,305 teaching staff.

In 1984 administration of schools was transferred from central to local government.

Health. In 1986 there were 706 hospitals (including 42 mental hospitals) with 248,000 beds, 6,473 dispensaries and 3,289 health centres. There were 75,400 doctors and 17,400 dentists.

Social Security. In 1984, 257,671m. złotys were paid out in 2·1m. retirement pensions, 76,955 zlotys in family allowances and 77,830 złotys in sick pay. Pensions were increased by 15% in 1986.

DIPLOMATIC REPRESENTATIVES

Of Poland in Great Britain (47 Portland Pl., London, W1N 3AG)
Ambassador: Dr Zbigniew Gertych

Of Great Britain in Poland (Aleje Roz No. 1, Warsaw)
Ambassador: Brian L. Barder.

Of Poland in the USA (2640 16th St., NW, Washington, D.C., 20009)
Ambassador: Jan Kinast.

Of the USA in Poland (Aleje Ujazdowskie 29/31, Warsaw)
Ambassador: John R. Davis, Jr.

Of Poland to the United Nations
Ambassador: Dr Eugeniusz Noworyta.

Books of Reference

Statistical Information: The Central Statistical Office, Warsaw (Wawelska 1–3), publishes *Rocznik statystyczny* (annual, 1930–39; 1947–); *Concise Statistical Yearbook of Poland* (1959–); *Statystyka Polski* (irreg., 1947–); *Biuletyn statystyczny* (monthly, 1957–).

Constitution of the Polish People's Republic. Warsaw, 1964
Ascherson, N., *The Struggles for Poland.* London, 1987
Ash, T. G., *The Polish Revolution: Solidarity 1980–82.* London, 1983
Åslund, A., *Private Enterprise in Eastern Europe: the Non-Agricultural Private Sector in Poland and the GDR, 1945–83.* London, 1985
Beneš, V. L., and Pounds, N. G. J., *Poland.* London, 1970
Bielasiak, J. and Simon, M. D. (eds.), *Polish Politics: Edge of the Abyss.* New York, 1984
Brandys, K., *Warsaw Diary 1978–1981.* New York, 1984
Bromke, A., *Poland: the Protracted Crisis.* Oakville (Ontario), 1983.—*The Meaning and Uses of Polish History.* New York, 1987
Brumberg, A., *Poland: Genesis of a Revolution.* New York, 1983
Bulas, K., and others, *English–Polish and Polish–English Dictionary.* 2 vols. The Hague, 1959
Burda, A., *Parliament of the Polish People's Republic.* Wrocław, 1978
Davies, N., *Poland, Past and Present: A Select Bibliography of Works in English.* Newtonville, 1977.—*God's Playground: A History of Poland.* 2 vols. OUP, 1981.—*Heart of Europe: a Short History of Poland.* OUP, 1984
De Weydenthal, J. B., et al. *The Polish Drama, 1980–1982.* Lexington, 1983
Dziewanowski, M. K., *Poland in the Twentieth Century.* Columbia Univ. Press, 1977
Eringer, R., *Strike for Freedom: The Story of Lech Wałesa and Polish Solidarity.* New York, 1982
Gieysztor, A., and others, *History of Poland. 2nd ed.* Warsaw, 1979
Halecki, O., *A History of Poland. 4th ed.* London, 1983
Jaruzelski, W., *Jaruzelski, Prime Minister of Poland: Selected Speeches.* Oxford, 1985

Karpiński, J., *Countdown: the Polish Upheavals of 1956, 1968, 1970, 1976, 1980*. NY, 1982

Kieniewicz, S. (ed.) *History of Poland*. 2nd ed. Warsaw, 1979

Landau, Z., *The Polish Economy in the Twentieth Century*. London, 1985

Leslie, R. F., (ed.) *The History of Poland since 1863*. CUP, 1980

Lewanski, R. C., *Poland*. [Bibliography] Oxford and Santa Barbara, 1984

Lipski, J. J., *KOR: a History of the Workers' Defense Committee in Poland, 1976–1981*. Univ. of California Press, 1985

Michnik, A., *Letters from Prison and Other Essays*. London, 1985

Misztal, B., (ed.), *Poland after Solidarity*. New Brunswick, 1985

Polonsky, A. and Drukier, B., *The Beginnings of Communist Rule in Poland*. London, 1980

Pomian-Srzednicki, M. *Religious Change in Contemporary Poland: Secularization and Politics*. London, 1982

Potel, J.-I., *The Summer Before the Frost: Solidarity in Poland*. London, 1982

Preibisz, J. M., (ed.) *Polish Dissident Publications: an Annotated Bibliography*. New York, 1982

Raina P., *Independent Social Movements in Poland*. London, 1981.—*Poland 1981: Towards Social Renewal*. London, 1985

Ruane, K., *The Polish Challenge*. London, 1982

Sanford, G., *Polish Communism in Crisis*. London, 1983

Singer, D., *The Road to Gdańsk: Poland and the USSR*. New York and London, 1981

Staniszkis, J., *Poland's Self-Limiting Revolution*. Princeton, 1984

Steven, S., *The Poles*. London, 1982

Szczypiorski, A., *The Polish Ordeal: The View from Within*. London, 1982

Taras, R., *Poland: Socialist State, Rebellious Nation*. Boulder, 1986

Wedel, J., *The Private Poland*. New York, 1986

Weschler, L., *Solidarity: Poland in the Season of its Passion*. NY, 1982

Who's Who in Poland. New York, 1983

Wielka Encyklopedia Powszechna. 13 vols. Warsaw, 1962–70

Woodall, J., (ed.) *Policy and Politics in Contemporary Poland: Reform, Failure and Crisis*. London, 1982

National Library: Biblioteka Narodowa, Rakowiecka 6, Warsaw.

PORTUGAL

República Portuguesa

Capital: Lisbon
Population: 10·29m. (1986)
GNP per capita: US$2,190 (1983)

HISTORY. Portugal has been an independent state since the 12th century, apart from one period of Spanish rule (1580–1640). The monarchy was deposed on 5 Oct. 1910 and a republic established.

A *coup* on 28 May 1926 established a military provisional government from 1 June. A corporatist constitution was adopted on 19 March 1933 under which a civil dictatorship governed until a fresh *coup* on 25 April 1974 established a Junta of National Salvation.

Following an attempted revolt on 11 March 1975, the Junta was dissolved and a Supreme Revolutionary Council formed which ruled until 25 April 1976 when constitutional government was resumed; the SRC was renamed the Council of the Revolution, becoming a consultative body until its abolition in 1982.

AREA AND POPULATION. Mainland Portugal is bounded north and east by Spain and south and west by the Atlantic ocean. The Atlantic archipelagoes of the Azores and of Madeira form autonomous but integral parts of the republic, which has a total area of 91,985 sq. km (35,516 sq. miles) and census populations:

1940	7,755,423	1960	8,889,392	1981	9,833,014
1950	8,510,240	1970	8,648,369		

The areas and populations of the districts and Autonomous Regions are:

Districts:	sq. km	Census 1981	Estimate 31 Dec. 1986	Districts:	sq. km	Census 1981	Estimate 31 Dec. 1986
Aveiro	2,808	622,988	660,500	Porto	2,295	1,562,287	1,657,700
Beja	10,225	188,420	179,900	Santarém	6,747	454,123	460,800
Braga	2,673	708,924	763,900	Setúbal	5,064	658,326	761,000
Bragança	6,608	184,252	185,600	Viana de			
Castelo				Castelo	2,225	256,814	265,500
Branco	6,674	234,230	226,000	Vila Real	4,328	264,381	264,100
Coimbra	3,947	436,324	446,200	Viseu	5,007	423,648	424,800
Evora	7,393	180,277	175,600	Total			
Faro	4,960	323,534	339,200	mainland	88,941	9,336,760	9,707,000
Guarda	5,518	205,631	198,300	*Autonomous*			
Leiria	3,515	420,229	435,200	*Regions:*			
Lisboa	2,761	2,069,467	2,124,100	Azores	2,247	243,410	253,500
Portalegre	6,065	142,905	138,600	Madeira	794	252,844	269,500

At the 1981 census, 29·7% of the population was urban (living in towns of 10,000 and more) and 48·2% were male. The chief cities at 31 Dec. 1984 (and census, 1981) are Lisbon, the capital 807,937 (817,627) and Porto 327,368 (330,199); other towns are Amadora 95,518 (93,663), Setúbal 77,885 (76,812), Coimbra 74,616 (71,782), Braga 63,033 (63,771), Vila Nova de Gaia 62,469 (60,962), Barreiro 50,863 (50,745), Funchal 44,111 (48,638), Almada 42,607 (41,468), Queluz 42,241 (41,112), Odivelas 38,322 (38,546), Evora 34,851 (34,072), Agualva-Cacem 34,341 (34,041) and Oeiras 32,529 (32,046).

The Azores islands lie in the mid-Atlantic ocean, between 1,200 and 1,600 km west of Lisbon. They are divided into 3 widely separated groups with clear channels between, São Miguel (747 sq. km) together with Santa Maria (97 sq. km) being the most easterly; about 100 miles north-west of them lies the central cluster of Terceira (397 sq. km), Graciosa (61 sq. km), São Jorge (238 sq. km), Pico (433 sq. km) and Faial (172 sq. km); still another 150 miles to the north-west are Flores (143 sq. km) and Corvo (17 sq. km), the latter being the most isolated and primitive of the islands. São Miguel contains over half the total population of the archipelago.

Madeira comprises the island of Madeira (740 sq. km), containing the capital, Funchal; the smaller island of Porto Santo (42 sq. km), lying 46 km. to the north-east of Madeira; and two groups of uninhabited islets, Ilhas Desertas being 20 km. south-east of Funchal and Ilhas Selvagens near the Canaries.

Vital statistics for calendar years:

	Live-births	Still-births	Marriages	Divorces	Deaths	Emigrants
1982	151,029	1,894	73,660	6,769	92,551	10,276
1983	144,327	1,791	74,417	7,837	96,150	7,096
1984	142,805	1,664	69,875	7,034	97,227	6,556
1985	130,492	1,510	68,461	8,988	97,339	7,149
1986	126,748	1,390	69,271	8,411	95,828	6,253

In 1986 the births included 65,427 boys and 61,321 girls; deaths, 50,036 males and 45,792 females. In 1986, 924 emigrants went to France, 2,704 to USA and 868 to Australia.

CLIMATE. Because of westerly winds and the effect of the Gulf Stream, the climate ranges from the cool, damp Atlantic type in the north to a warmer and drier Mediterranean type in the south. July and Aug. are virtually rainless every-where. Inland areas in the north have greater temperature variation, with con-tinental winds blowing from the interior. Lisbon. Jan. 52°F (11°C), July 72°F (22°C). Annual rainfall 27·4″ (686 mm). Porto. Jan. 48°F (8·9°C), July 67°F (19·4°C). Annual rainfall 46″ (1,151 mm).

CONSTITUTION AND GOVERNMENT. A new Constitution, replacing that of 1976, was approved by the Assembly of the Republic (by 197 votes to 40) on 12 Aug. 1982 and promulgated in Sept. It abolished the (military) Council of the Revolution and reduced the role of the President of the Republic.

Portugal is a sovereign, unitary republic with all citizens possessing fundamental rights and duties before the law. Executive power is vested in the President of the Republic, directly elected for a 5-year term (for a maximum of 2 consecutive terms). Presidents since 1926:

Marshal António Oscar de Fragoso Carmona, 29 Nov. 1926–18 April 1951 (died).

Dr Antonio de Oliveira Salazar (acting), 18 April 1951–22 July 1951.

Marshal Francisco Higino Craveiro Lopez, 22 July 1951–9 Aug. 1958.

Rear-Adm. Américo de Deus Rodrigues Tomás, 9 Aug. 1958–25 April 1974. (deposed).

Gen. Antonio Sebastião Ribeiro de Spinola, 25 April 1974–30 Sept. 1974 (resigned).

Gen. Francisco da Costa Gomes, 30 Sept. 1974–14 July 1976.

Gen. Antonio Ramalho Eanes, 14 July 1976–9 March 1986.

President of the Republic: Mario Soares, elected 16 Feb. 1986 (took office 9 March 1986).

The President appoints a Prime Minister and, upon the latter's nomination, other members of the Council of Ministers, as well as Secretaries and Under-Secretaries of State, who are outside the Council.

The Social Democrat government was composed in Aug. 1987:

Prime Minister: Anibal Cavaco Silva.

Deputy Prime Minister, Defence: Eurico de Melo. *Minister of State and Justice:* Fernando Nogueira. *Parliamentary Affairs:* Antonio Capucho. *Finance:* Miguel Riberio Cadilhe. *Planning and Territorial Administration:* Luis Valente de Oliveira. *Interior:* José Silveira Godinho. *Foreign Affairs:* João de Deus Pinheiro. *Agriculture, Fisheries:* Alvaro Barreto. *Industry and Energy:* Luis Mira Amaral. *Education:* Roberto Carneiro. *Public Works and Communication:* João Oliveira Martins. *Health:* Leonor Beleza. *Labour and Social Security:* José Silva Peneda. *Trade and Tourism:* Joaquim Ferreira do Amaral. *Youth:* Antonio Couto dos Santos.

There is a unicameral legislature, the Assembly of the Republic, comprising 250 deputies elected for 4 years by universal adult suffrage under a system of propor-tional representation. At the General Election of 19 July 1987, there were 148 seats won by the *Partido Social Democrata* (PSD), 60 by the *Partido Socialista* (PS), 7 by the Democratic Renewal Party, 31 by the Communist Party and 4 by the Christian Democrats.

National flag: Vertical green and red, with the red of double width, and over all on the dividing line the national arms.

National anthem: A Portuguesa (words by Lopes de Mendonça, 1890; tune by Alfredo Keil).

Local government: Since 1976, the archipelagoes of the Azores and of Madeira are Autonomous Regions with their own legislatures and governments. Pending the formation of other regional governments, Continental Portugal is divided into 18 districts. Regions and districts are divided into 305 municipal authorities *(concelhos)* and sub-divided into 4,050 parishes. Each level is governed by an assembly elected by direct universal suffrage under a system of proportional representation, with an executive body responsible to the assembly.

DEFENCE. Military service is compulsory for 12–15 months in the Army and 18–20 months in the Navy and Air Force. Reserves for all services number about 190,000.

Army. The Army consists of 1 brigade, 2 cavalry regiments, 1 armoured regiment, 11 infantry regiments, 1 commando regiment and 3 independent battalions, 1 special forces brigade, 3 field, 1 air-defence and 1 coast artillery regiments, 2 engineer and 1 signals regiments and 1 regiment of military police. Equipment includes 60 M-48A5 main battle tanks and 105 M113 armed personnel carriers. Strength (1988) 44,000 (including 35,000 conscripts). Security forces are National Republic Guard (14,600), Public Security Police, 15,300 and the Border Guard (7,400).

Navy. The fleet comprises 3 small French-built diesel-powered patrol submarines, 17 frigates, 10 patrol vessels, 4 coastal minesweepers, 24 patrol launches, 1 sail training ship, 3 surveying vessels, 1 fleet oiler, 1 logistic support ship, 3 landing craft, 13 minor landing craft, 3 tugs, 2 training yachts and 3 harbour tankers. The building programme includes 3 frigates and 1 surveying vessel. Navy personnel in 1988 totalled 14,000 officers and men including 2,600 marines.

Air Force. Formed in 1912, the Air Force has been independent since 1952, when it was combined with the naval air service and given equal status with the Army and Navy. In 1988, it had a strength of about 13,350 officers and men.

Equipment comprises 2 strike squadrons with 40 A-7P Corsair IIs; 2 squadrons of G.91Rs for ground attack; 1 squadron of 5 C-130H Hercules and 4 squadrons of CASA 212 Aviocars for transport and search and rescue operations; 32 Cessna 337 Skymasters and a force of Puma and Alouette III helicopters. Other aircraft in service include Chipmunk piston-engined trainers, T-37C jet basic trainers, T-33, T-38A Talon and G.91T jet advanced trainers. Six P-3B Orion maritime patrol aircraft and 18 Epsilon trainers are on order.

INTERNATIONAL RELATIONS

Membership. Portugal is a member of UN, the European Communities, OECD, NATO and the Council of Europe.

ECONOMY

Planning. The aim of the 1981–84 plan was to modernize existing industry and pave the way for entry into the European Community.

Budget. Revenue in 1986, 866·5m.; expenditure, 1,216·9m. (in escudos).

Currency. The unit of currency is the *escudo* of 100 *centavos*, which contains 0·06651 gramme of fine gold. It was stabilized on 9 June 1931, and the paper currency re-linked to gold when the notes of the Bank of Portugal became payable in gold or its equivalent in foreign currency. 1,000 *escudos* is called a *conto*.

In 1986 there were bank notes of 5,000, 1,000, 500 and 100 *escudos*; cupro-nickel coins of 50, 25, 20, 5 and 2½ *escudos*; nickel-brass coins of 1 *escudo*; bronze coins of 1 and ½ *escudo*. In March 1988, £1 = 244·50 *escudos*; US$1 = 138·33 *escudos*.

Banking. Since 1931, the central bank for Portugal and the only bank of issue for the country (including the Azores and Madeira) has been the Banco de Portugal, founded 19 Nov. 1846 and nationalized on 13 Sept. 1974. Its capital is fixed at 200m. escudos. All other Portuguese banks and insurance companies were nationalized on 14 March 1975 but from Feb. 1984 new private banks were allowed to operate.

The National Development Bank began operations on 4 Jan. 1960. Its total capital (1985) is 10,500m. escudos.

In 1986 there were 27 banks operating in Portugal: 21 commercial banks, 2 investment banks and 4 savings banks. In Feb. 1987 commercial banks' total credits were 1,791,427m. escudos and deposits 3,199,726m. escudos; investment banks' total credits 250,659m. escudos and deposits 141,124m. escudos; savings banks' total credits 1,125,148m. escudos and deposits 1,663,658m. escudos.

There are also 9 foreign banks, the Bank of Brazil, Lloyds Bank International Ltd., Manufactures Hanover Trust, Chase Manhattan, Citibank, Crédit Franco-Portugais, Barclays Bank International Ltd, Banque Nationale de Paris and General Bank.

Weights and Measures. The metric system is the legal standard. The arroba (of 14·69 kg) is sometimes used locally.

ENERGY AND NATURAL RESOURCES

Electricity. Total production of electrical power in 1985 was 19,103m. kwh.; the installed capacity totalled 6,831,753 kva. of which 3,243,074 was hydro-electric. Supply 110 and 220 volts; 50 Hz.

Minerals. Portugal possesses considerable mineral wealth. Production in tonnes:

	1983	1984	1985		1983	1984	1985
Coal	185,228	194,856	233,414	Gold (refined)	0·199	0·193	0·229
Cupriferous pyrites	279,960	334,371	355,519	Uranium	122	135	139
Tin ores	525	453	379	Wolframite	2,010	2,549	2,977
Kaolin	101,594	104,388	104,055				

Uranium mining commenced in Aug. 1979. Annual production, 115 tonnes; reserves, 7,000 tonnes.

Agriculture. About 30% of the workforce is engaged in agriculture. The following figures show the area (in 1,000 hectares) and production (in 1,000 tonnes) of the chief crops:

	1984		1985		1986	
Crop	Area	Quantity	Area	Quantity	Area	Quantity
Wheat	291·1	465·6	282·0	394·8	315·0	499·7
Maize	251·1	491·1	240·3	530·8	252·7	618·4
Oats	194·1	151·9	190·0	118·9	194·1	152·7
Barley	83·7	91·1	85·9	65·2	87·1	89·6
Rye	130·0	103·4	122·7	96·9	124·4	99·9
Rice	29·9	134·0	30·3	146·5	32·3	149·4
Dried beans	211·2	42·1	194·9	43·8	198·4	44·4
Potatoes	122·6	1,038·0	125·6	1,135·9	118·8	1,067·3

Wine production (in hectolitres), 1986, 7·6m.; olive oil (hectolitres), 411,000 (estimate). In 1986, 68,303 tonnes of port wine were exported.

Livestock (1986). 30,000 horses, 89,500 mules, 175,000 asses, 1·2m. cattle, 750,000 goats, 3m. sheep and 2,400,000 pigs.

Forestry. Forest area covers 3m. hectares, of which 1·38m. are pine, 680,390 cork oak, 534,370 other oak, 243,180 eucalyptus, 30,230 chestnut and 160,890 other species.

Portugal surpasses the rest of the world in the production of cork; 103,543 tonnes in 1985. Most of it is exported crude. Production of resin was 107,586 tonnes in 1985; more than two-thirds are exported.

Fisheries. The fishing industry for the continent and adjacent isles is of importance. At 31 July 1986 there were 40,058 men and boys employed, with 11,120 boats. The sardine catch, 1986, was 103,832 tonnes valued at 3,329,315 contos; The most important centres of the sardine industry are at Matosinhos, Figueira di Foz, Peniche, Setúbal, Portimão and Olhão.

INDUSTRY AND TRADE

Industry. Industrial growth rate, 1983, 0·6%; manufacturing provided 30% of GDP and employed about 25% of the workforce. The main groups are textiles, shoes, leather goods, wood and cork products and ceramics; these are produced mainly by small companies. Nationalized steel, oil and engineering industries employed about 5% of the industrial workforce in 1983.

Trade Unions. 331 unions had in 1976 a membership of 1,436,142.

Commerce. Imports for consumption and exports (exclusive of coin and bullion and re-exports) for calendar years, in 1 m. escudos:

	1981	1982	1983	1984	1985
Imports	609,014	753,981	899,340	1,160,633	1,302,737
Exports	256,913	331,743	508,568	760,580	967,404

The principal exports in 1985 were clothing (18% by value), textile yarns and fabrics (12%), machinery and transport equipment (6%), petroleum products (4%), chemicals (7%), cork and cork products (4%), footwear (5%), pulp and waste paper (5%) and wine (3%).

The distribution of the imports and exports (in 1 m. escudos):

From or to	Imports (c.i.f.)			Exports (f.o.b.)		
	1984	1985	1986	1984	1985	1986
Angola	5,550	13,984	11,196	22,721	26,432	13,785
Belgium	24,151	28,101	41,682	25,138	34,510	37,037
France	91,699	104,589	145,157	94,587	122,715	164,234
Germany, Fed. Rep. of	117,916	148,497	205,420	103,957	133,328	158,627
Italy	54,632	66,908	114,487	32,765	38,439	42,915
Mozambique	1,478	1,018	...	5,919	3,680	3,073
Netherlands	40,169	41,375	57,053	44,869	66,907	72,232
Spain	82,807	95,685	157,059	33,527	39,598	71,681
UK	77,802	97,577	108,281	116,857	141,144	154,010
USA	156,185	126,563	100,592	67,248	89,387	75,557

Total trade between Portugal (excluding the Azores and Madeira) and UK (British Department of Trade returns, in £1,000 sterling):

	1983	1984	1985	1986	1987
Imports to UK	475,902	644,520	695,744	768,470	847,980
Exports and re-exports from UK	396,988	385,799	439,499	472,078	699,915

Tourism. Tourism is of increasing importance for the invisible balance of payments. In 1986 there were 13,056,871 visitors.

COMMUNICATIONS

Roads (1985). There were 18,815 km of road. There were registered in continental Portugal in 1986, 2,365,645 motor vehicles (excluding 106,925 motor cycles, 153,326 tractors and vehicles used by the armed forces).

Railways. In 1986 total railway length was 3,588 km (1,668 mm and metre gauges), of which 458 km of broad-gauge was electrified. In 1986, 5,803m. passenger-km were carried and 1,448m. tonne-km of merchandise transported.

Aviation. There are international airports at Portela (Lisbon), Pedras Rubras (Porto), Faro (Algarve), Santa Maria (Azores) and Funchal (Madeira). Services connect Lisbon with most major centres in North and South America, Western Europe and Africa. Airlines in 1985 carried 2m. passengers and (1986) 44,163 tonnes of freight. The national airline changed its name to Air Portugal in 1979.

Shipping. In 1985, 12,539 vessels of 57·6m. tons entered the ports (continental and islands), of which 3,791 (14·2m. tons) were Portuguese, 305 (1·7m. tons) British and 606 (2·1m. tons) Spanish. In 1984 the merchant marine consisted of 91 transport vessels of 1,396,051 gross tons.

Post and Broadcasting (1985). The number of telegraph offices was 1,564. The State owned 7,693,529 km of telephone line through the *Telefones de Lisboa e Porto* (nationalized in 1977). Number of telephones was 1,835,331 (1985).

Radio Difusão Portuguesa broadcasts 3 programmes on medium-waves and on FM as well as 3 regional services. *Radiotelevisão Portuguesa* broadcasts 2 commercial TV programmes. *Radio Renascença* is a commercial, nationwide network. In addition there are 6 local, commercial stations, operating on medium-waves. Radio Trans Europe is a high-powered short-wave station, retransmitting programmes of different broadcasting organizations, *e.g.*, IBRA, Radio Canada and Deutsche Welle. Radio Free Europe also has relay facilities on short-waves in Portugal. Number of receivers: Radio (1984), 2,155,000; TV (1986), 1,618,391.

Cinemas (1986). There were 373 cinemas with a seating capacity of 178,957.

Newspapers (1986). There were 33 daily newspapers with a combined circulation of 173,327m.; 15 of these, with a combined circulation of 104,273m., appeared in Lisbon.

JUSTICE, RELIGION, EDUCATION AND WELFARE

Justice. Portuguese law distinguishes civil (including commercial) and penal, labour, military, administrative and fiscal branches, having low courts and high courts.

The republic is divided for civil and penal cases into 217 *comarcas*; in every comarca there is at least one court or tribunal. In the comarca of Lisbon there are 39 lower sub divisional courts *(juizoo)* (22 for criminal procedure and 17 for civil or commercial cases); in the comarca of Oporto there are 20 such courts (11 for criminal and 9 for civil or commercial cases); at Braga, Coimbra, Loures, Setúbal, Sintra and Vila Nova de Gaia there are 4 functioning courts; at Almada, Cascais, Funchal, Guimarães, Leiria, Matosinhos, Oeiras, Santarém, Torres Vedras, Viana do Castelo, Vila do Conde, Vila da Feira and Viseu there are 3 courts; 22 comarcas have 2 courts each. There are 4 courts of appeal *(Tribunal de Relação)* at Lisbon, Coimbra, Evora and Oporto, and a Supreme Court in Lisbon *(Supremo Tribunal de Justiça)*.

Capital punishment was abolished completely in the Constitution of 1976.

The prison population as at 31 Dec. 1983 was 6,633.

Religion. In 1981, 94·5% of the population were Roman Catholic, but there is freedom of worship, both in public and private, with the exception of creeds incompatible with morals and the life and physical integrity of the people.

Education. Compulsory education has been in force since 1911. In 1984–85 there were 10,448 public primary schools with 837,760 pupils and 40,773 teachers. In 1984–85 private elementary schools numbered 668 with 61,611 pupils and 2,882 teachers. Basic preparatory schools numbered 1,918 with 375,516 pupils and 31,248 teachers. In 1984–85 there were 499 secondary schools, with 604,727 pupils and 45,559 teachers. There were also 27 schools which taught art activities (cinema, music and theatre) with 14,749 students. There are 13 universities, of which 8 are in Lisbon: the University of Lisbon (founded 1911), the Technical University (1930), the private Catholic University (1968), the New University (1973), the Free University (1977) and the International University (1984); the other six are Coimbra (founded 1290), Porto (1911), Aveiro (1973), Minho, at Braga (1974), Evora (1979), Azores, at Ponta Delgado (1980) and Algarve, at Faro (1983). Including other colleges, there were 102,837 students in higher education in 1984–85 with 10,745 teaching staff.

Health. In 1986 there were 227 hospitals, 363 health centres, 25,696 doctors, 312 dentists, 597 stomatologists, 4,285 pharmacists and 25,199 nursing personnel.

DIPLOMATIC REPRESENTATIVES

Of Portugal in Great Britain (11 Belgrave Sq., London, SW1X 8PP)
Ambassador: João Hall Themido, GCVO.

Of Great Britain in Portugal (35-37 Rua de S. Domingos à Lapa, Lisbon)
Ambassador: M. K. O. Simpson-Orlebar, CMG.

Of Portugal in the USA (2125 Kalorama Rd., NW, Washington, D.C., 20008)
Ambassador: João Eduardo M. Pereira Bastos.

Of the USA in Portugal (Ave. das Forcas Armadas, 1600 Lisbon)
Ambassador: (Vacant).

Of Portugal to the United Nations
Ambassador: João de Matos Proença.

Books of Reference

Statistical Information: The Instituto Nacional de Estatistica (Avenida Dr António José de Almeida, Lisbon) was set up in 1935 in succession to the Direcção-Geral de Estatistica. The Centro de Estudos Económicos and the Centro de Estudos Demográficos were affiliated to the Instituto in 1944. The main publications are:

Anuário Estatístico. Annuaire statistique. Annual, from 1875
Estatísticas do Comércio Externo. 2 vols. Annual from 1967 (replacing *Comércio Externo,* 1936–66, and *Estatística Comercial,* 1865–1935)
Censo da População de Portugal. 1864 ff. Decennial (latest ed. 1972)
Estatística da Organização Corporativa. 1938–49. Estatísticas da Organização Corporativa e Previdência Social. 1950 ff.
Estatísticas das Finanças, Publicas and *Estatísticas Nometárias.* 1969 ff. (replacing *Estatísticas Financeiras.* 1947–68 and *Situação Bancária,* 1919–46)
Estatísticas Agrícolas. Statistique Agricole. 1943–64; replaced by *Estatísticas Agrícolas e Alimentares.* From 1965. Annual
Estatísticas Industrials. 1967 ff. (replacing *Estatística Industrial. Statistique Industrielle.* 1943–66)
Estatísticas Demográficas. From 1967 (replacing *Anuário Demográfico,* 1929–66)
Boletim Mensal do Instituto Nacional de Estatística. Monthly since 1929
Centro de Estudos Económicos. Revista. 1945 ff.
Centro de Estudos Demográficos. Revista. 1945 ff.
Estatísticas das Contribuições e Impostos. Annual from 1967 (replacing *Anuário Estatístico das Contribuições e Impostos,* 1936–66)
Estatistica da Cultura, Reveio e Resporto, 1979 ff.
Estatísticas da Educação. 1940 ff.
Estatísticas da Justica. 1968 ff. (replacing *Estatísticas Judiciária.* 1936–66)
Estatísticas das Sociedades. 1939 ff.
Estatísticas da Saúde, 1969 ff.
Estatísticas do Turismo. 1969 ff.
Estatísticas do Energia. 1969 ff.

Azevedo, Gonzaga de, *Historia de Portugal.* 6 vols. Lisbon, 1935–44
Ferreira, H. G., and Marshall, M. W., *Portugal's Revolution: Ten Years On.* CUP, 1986
Ferreira, J. A., *Dictionario inglês-portugês.* 2 vols. Porto, 1948
Gallagher, T., *Portugal: A Twentieth Century Interpretation.* Manchester Univ. Press, 1983
Graham, L. S., and Wheeler, D. L., (eds.) *In Search of Modern Portugal: The Revolution and its Consequences.* Univ. of Wisconsin Press, 1983
Harvey R., *Portugal: Birth of a Democracy.* London, 1978
Robertson, I., *Blue Guide: Portugal.* London, 1982
Rogers, F. M., *Atlantic Islanders of the Azores and Madeiras.* North Quincy, 1979
Soares, M., *Le Portugal Bâillonné: Une Témoignage.* Paris, 1972
Spinola, A. de, *Portugal e o Futoro.* Lisbon, 1974
Taylor, J. L., *Portuguese-English Dictionary.* London, 1959
Unwin, P. T. H., *Portugal.* [Bibliography] Oxford and Santa Barbara, 1987

National Library: Biblioteca Nacional, Campo Grande, Lisbon. *Director:* A. H. C. Marques.

MACAO

HISTORY. Macao was visited by Portuguese traders from 1513 and became a Portuguese colony in 1557; it remains a Portuguese-administered territory by virtue of a Sino-Portuguese treaty of 1 Dec. 1887. It was an Overseas Province of Portugal, 1961–74. Discussions on the future of Macao were taking place with the People's Republic of China in 1986–87 and in 1999 Macao will be handed to China.

AREA AND POPULATION. The territory, which lies at the mouth of the Canton (Pearl) River, comprises a peninsula (6·05 sq. km) connected by a narrow isthmus to the People's Republic of China, on which is built the city of Nome de Deus de Macao, and the islands of Taipa (3·78 sq. km), linked to Macao by a 2-km bridge, and Colôane (7·09 sq. km) linked to Taipa by a 2-km causeway (total area, 16·92 sq. km (6 sq. miles). The population (Census, 1981) was 261,680, Estimate (1986) 426,400, of which 51·7% are males and (1984) 91·5% live in the city of Macao. The official language is Portuguese, but Cantonese is used by virtually the entire population.

Vital statistics (1986): Births, 7,477; marriages, 2,845; deaths, 1,324.

CONSTITUTION AND GOVERNMENT. By agreement with Beijing in 1974, Macao is a Chinese territory under Portuguese administration. An 'organic statute' was published on 17 Feb. 1976. It defined the territory as a collective entity, *pessoa colectiva,* with internal legislative authority which, while remaining subject to Portuguese constitutional laws, would otherwise enjoy administrative, economic and financial autonomy. The Governor is appointed by the Portuguese President, who also appoints up to 5 Secretaries-Adjunct on the Governor's nomination. The Legislative Assembly of 17 deputies, chosen for a 3-year term, comprises 6 members directly elected by universal suffrage, 6 indirectly elected by economic, cultural and social bodies and 5 appointed by the Governor.

Governor: Carlos Melancia.

ECONOMY

Budget. In 1986, revenue was 1,567,000,000 *patacas* and expenditure 1,435,000,000 *patacas.*

Currency. The unit of currency is the *pataca,* of 100 *avos,* which is tied to the Hong Kong dollar at a rate of 103 *patacas* = HK$100.

Banking. The bank of issue is the Instituto Emissor de Macau. Commercial business is handled (1986) by 23 banks with 95 branches in Macao, 9 of which are local (with 81·5% of total resident deposits and 67·4% of total domestic credit at 31 Dec. 1984) and 14 foreign (including 4 offshore banking units). Total banks' deposits, June 1985, 8,508·5m. patacas.

INDUSTRY AND TRADE

Industry. Textile and garment manufacturing forms the basis of local industry. In 1983, it represented about 65% of industrial production.

Labour. The estimated total labour force in 1984 was 178,000, 44% of whom were employed in manufacturing, 33% in commerce and services and 8% in construction.

Commerce. The trade, mostly transit, is handled by Chinese merchants. Imports, in 1986, were 7,318·2m. patacas and exports, 8,630·2m. patacas.

In 1986, 46% of imports came from Hong Kong and 20% from China. 33% of exports went to USA, 36% to EEC (mainly Federal Republic of Germany, France and UK); clothing and textiles accounted for 69·7% of exports, toys 11·8%.

Total trade between Macao and UK (British Department of Trade returns, in £1,000 sterling):

	1984	1985	1986	1987
Imports to UK	40,508	36,509	45,286	45,896
Exports and re-exports from UK	1,034	1,595	6,522	5,617

Tourism. There were 4,238,269 visitors in 1986. 81·7% were from Hong Kong.

COMMUNICATIONS.

Roads. In 1984 there were 90 km of roads. In 1986 there were 21,710 passenger cars and 2,576 commercial vehicles.

Shipping. Macao is served by Portuguese, British and Dutch steamship lines. In 1983, 27,686 vessels of 9·14m. gross tons entered the port. Regular services connect Macao with Hong Kong, 65 km to the north-east.

Post and Broadcasting. The territory has 1,577 km of telephone line (47,591 instruments in 1986). One government and 1 private commercial radio station are in operation on medium-waves broadcasting in Portuguese and Chinese. Number of receivers (1977), 70,000. Macao receives television broadcasts from Hong Kong and in 1984 a public bilingual TV station began operating. There were (1979) 50,000 receivers.

Newspapers. In 1986, there were 11 newspapers (5 in Portugese and 6 in Chinese) with a circulation of 114,000.

JUSTICE, RELIGION, EDUCATION AND WELFARE

Justice. There is a court of First Instance, from which there is appeal to the Court of Appeal and then the Supreme Court, both in Lisbon.

In 1986 there were 4,414 cases of crimes known to the police, of which 3,224 were against property. There were 25,577 cases in courts pending on 1 Jan. and presented during 1986, of which 3,344 were in district court, 19,089 in criminal court, 250 in juvenile court and 3,109 in administrative court. At 31 Dec. 1986 there were 416 prisoners, and 22 addicts in the centre for rehabilitation of drugs-abusers.

Religion. The majority of the Chinese population are Buddhists. About 6% are Roman Catholic.

Education. In 1985–86 education was provided at 63 kindergartens (14,488 pupils; 413 teachers), 74 primary schools (31,669; 1,080), 31 secondary schools (13,849; 769), 3 special schools (53; 13), 2 teacher-training schools (52; 13), 5 higher schools (5,840; 75) and 83 adult schools (23,430; 534). The University of East Asia, established in 1981 on Taipa, had 1,165 students in 1983.

Health. In 1985 there were 2 hospitals with 1,216 beds; there were 179 doctors and (1982) 26 pharmacists, 10 midwives and 315 nursing personnel.

Books of Reference

Anuário Estatístico de Macau. Macao, Annual
Macau in Figures. Macao, Annual.
Education Survey, 1984–85, Macao, 1986
Brazáo, E., *Macau.* Lisbon, 1957

QATAR

Dawlat Qatar

Capital: Doha
Population: 371,863 (1987)
GNP per capita: US$22,940 (1984)

HISTORY. The State of Qatar declared its independence from Britain on 3 Sept. 1971, ending the Treaty of 3 Nov. 1916 which was replaced by a Treaty of friendship between the 2 countries.

AREA AND POPULATION. The State of Qatar, which includes the whole of the Qatar peninsula, extends on the landward side from Khor al Odeid to the boundaries of the Saudi Arabian province of Hasa. The territory includes a number of islands in the coastal waters of the peninsula, the most important of which is Halul, the storage and export terminal for the offshore oilfields. Area, 11,437 sq. km; population census (1981) 244,534; estimate in 1987 371,863. In 1987 only 25% were Qatari, with a large majority coming from Pakistan and India.

The capital is Doha (population 1982, 190,000), which is the main port. Other towns are Dukhan, the centre of oil production, Umm Said, oil-terminal of Qatar, and Ruwais, Wakra, Al-Khour, Umm Salal Mohammad and Umm-Bab.

The official language is Arabic.

CLIMATE. The climate is hot and humid. Doha. Jan. 62°F (16·7°C), July 98°F (36·7°C). Annual rainfall 2·5″ (62 mm).

RULER. *The Amir:* HH Shaikh Khalifa bin Hamad Al-Thani, assumed power on 22 Feb. 1972. On 31 May 1977, HH Shaikh Hamad bin Khalifa Al-Thani was appointed Heir Apparent of the State of Qatar, and the portfolio of Minister of Defence was added to his existing responsibility of Commander-in-Chief of the Armed Forces.

Minister of State for Foreign Affairs: Shaikh Ahmad bin Saif Al-Thani.

There is no Parliament, but the Council of Ministers is assisted by a 30-member nominated Advisory Council.

Flag: Maroon, with white serrated border on hoist.

DEFENCE

Army. The Army consists of 1 Royal Guard regiment, 1 tank, 5 infantry battalions and 1 artillery battery. Equipment includes 24 AMX-30 tanks. Personnel (1988) 6,000.

Navy. The Navy has 3 modern French-built fast gunboats, 6 British-built patrol craft and 45 coastal patrol craft. Personnel in 1988 totalled 700 officers and men.

Air Force. The Air Force has 1 squadron of Mirage F1 fighters and 1 Islander transport aircraft, 12 Commando, 3 Lynx and 6 Super Puma helicopters, 6 Alpha Jet and 3 Hunter armed trainers and Tigercat surface-to-air missile systems. Personnel (1988) 300.

INTERNATIONAL RELATIONS

Membership. Qatar is a member of UN and the Arab League.

ECONOMY

Budget. Revenue (1987–88) 6,745m. riyals; expenditure 12,217m. riyals.

Currency. On 13 May 1973 the Qatar *Riyal* (of 100 *dirhams*) was introduced. In March 1988, £1 = 6·46 *riyals*, US$1 = 3·64 *riyals*.

Banking. The 15 banks operating in Qatar include 5 national banks: Qatar National Bank, The Commercial Bank of Qatar, Doha Bank, the Islamic Bank of Qatar and Al Ahli Bank. There are 3 Arab banks: Arab Bank Limited, Bank of Oman and Al Mashrek Bank. The other 7 foreign banks are: Banque Paribas, the British Bank of the Middle East, Chartered Bank, Citibank, Bank Saderat Iran, Grindlays Bank and the United Bank. The Qatar National Bank was established in 1965 with capital of 56m. riyals, 50% of which was contributed by the Government and 50% by the private sector. Deposits in commercial banks were 7,879·8m. riyals by Dec. 1983. Government deposits 455·5m. riyals and private sector's savings deposits 7,419·3m. riyals in 1983.

Weights and Measures. The metric system is in general use.

ENERGY AND NATURAL RESOURCES

Electricity. Production (1986) 4,302·9m. kwh (generation of Abu Samra not included). Supply 240 volts; 50 Hz.

Oil. On 9 Feb. 1977 Qatar gained national control over its 2 natural resources, oil and gas, with the signing of an agreement with Shell Qatar over the procedure for the transfer to the State of the company's remaining 40% share. A similar agreement had been reached with the Qatar Petroleum Co. on 16 Sept. 1976.

The Qatar General Petroleum Corporation (QGPC) had been established by decree in July 1974 to assume overall responsibility for the State's domestic and foreign oil interests and operations. On 16 Oct. 1976 the Qatar Petroleum Producing Authority (QPPA) was established to serve as the executive arm of the QGPC—but in 1980 it was merged into the QGPC, which now directly oversees oil production through two operational divisions, Onshore and Offshore. The National Oil Distribution Company (NODCO) had a daily throughput capacity of 62,000 bbls a day in 1984 following the opening of a 50,000 bbls a day refinery at Umm Said to supplement the existing refinery.

Production, 1987, 15m. tonnes. Proven reserves (1986) 3,300m. bbls.

Gas. The North West Dome oilfield is being developed which contains 12% of the known world gas reserves. Production (1986) 229,100m. cu. ft.

Water Resources. Two main desalination stations, at Ras Abu Aboud and Ras Abu Fontas, together produce 47·08m. gallons of potable water a day. A third station is planned at Al Wasil, with a capacity of 40m. gallons a day. Total water production 1986 (well field and distillate) 17,902m. gallons.

Agriculture. 10% of the working population is engaged in agriculture. The Ministry of Agriculture is implementing a long-term policy aimed at ensuring self-sufficiency in agricultural products. The number of farms rose from 120 in 1960 to 841 in 1985. Production (1986) in tonnes: Barley, 1,847; wheat, 130; tomatoes, 5,799; melons and watermelons, 3,531; other vegetables, 9,692; dates, 4,976; fruits, 2,716; bovine meat, 1,579; poultry meat, 1,162; eggs, 1,278; milk and dairy products, 17,574.

Livestock (1986): Cattle, 7,000; camels, 9,000; sheep, 55,000; goats, 21,000; poultry, 2m.

Fisheries. The produce of local fisheries in 1984 met 77·2% of Qatar's requirements. The state-owned Qatar National Fishing Company has 3 trawlers and its refrigeration unit processes 10 tonnes of shrimps a day. Catch (1985) 2,484 tonnes.

INDUSTRY AND TRADE

Industry. The Qatar Fertiliser Co. plant was opened in 1973 (production, 1986, 658,300 tonnes of ammonia and 746,900 tonnes of urea), the Qatar Steel Co. factory in 1978 (output, 1985, 510,000 tonnes) and the Qatar Petrochemical Co. plant in 1981, all in the Umm Said industrial zone. Production (1986, in tonnes): Cement, 323,600; lime, 15,900; flour, 25,100; bran, 6,200.

Commerce. In 1986 exports totalled 6,710m. riyals, and imports, 4,000 riyals. In 1985 Japan provided 15·8% of imports, the UK 15·8% and the Federal Republic of Germany 9·2%, while 60·2% of exports went to Japan and 9·5% to France; crude oil was 91% of exports.

Total trade between Qatar and UK (British Department of Trade returns, in £1,000 sterling):

	1983	1984	1985	1986	1987
Imports to UK	10,063	28,212	32,607	29,587	13,765
Exports and re-exports from UK	216,385	133,803	142,065	112,143	105,087

COMMUNICATIONS

Roads. In 1981 there were about 800 miles of road.

Aviation. Gulf Air (owned equally by Qatar, Bahrain, Oman and the UAE), operates daily services from Bahrain; British Airways, Middle East and about 15 other airlines operate regular international flights from Doha airport. In 1984, 418,116 passengers arrived, 417,683 departed and 399,331 were in transit; 9,843 aircraft arrived and 9,482 departed.

Shipping. Umm Said 35 km south of Doha is the main port of Qatar. In 1985, 517 vessels, 1,444,692 tonnes of cargo and 2,308 containers were handled.

Post and Telecommunications. There were 24 post offices in Doha and other towns in 1986. Qatar Broadcasting Service, using 12 transmission stations, broadcasts for 41 hours a day in Arabic, English, French and Urdu. Telephone and radio-telephone services connect Qatar with Europe and America; there were 111,000 telephones in 1986. In 1987 there were 75,000 radios and 111,000 television receivers.

Cinemas. In 1986 there were 5 cinemas with a seating capacity of 7,000.

Newspapers. In 1986 there were 4 daily and 2 weekly newspapers and 6 magazines.

JUSTICE, RELIGION, EDUCATION AND WELFARE

Justice. The Judiciary System is administered by the Ministry of Justice which comprises three main departments: Legal affairs, courts of justice and land and real estate register. There are 5 Courts of Justice proclaiming sentences in the name of H. H. the Amir: The Court of Appeal, the Labour Court, the Higher Criminal Court, the Civil Court and the Lower Criminal Court.

All issues related to personal affairs of Moslems under Islamic Law embodied in the Holy Quran and Sunna are decided by Sharia Courts.

Religion. The population is almost entirely Moslem.

Education. There were, in 1985–86, 31,844 pupils at primary schools, 12,031 pupils at intermediate schools, 7,475 pupils at secondary schools and 700 male students at specialist schools. There were 48 Arab and foreign private schools with 13,050 pupils in 1984–85. The University of Qatar had 5,057 students in 1985–86. Students abroad (1986–87) numbered 1,352. In 1985–86, 4,299 men and 2,698 women attended evening classes.

Health. There were 3 hospitals (including 1 for women and 1 for gynaecology and obstetrics) with a total of 915 beds in 1986. There were 19 health centres in 1986. In 1985 there were 891 doctors, and in 1985, 52 dentists, 115 pharmacists and 1,161 qualified nurses.

DIPLOMATIC REPRESENTATIVES

Of Qatar in Great Britain (27 Chesham Pl., London, SWIX 8HG)
Ambassador: Sherida Sa'ad Jubran Al Ka'abi, GCVO (accredited 26 March 1981).

Of Great Britain in Qatar (Doha, Qatar)
Ambassador: P. M. Nixon, OBE.

Of Qatar in the USA (600 New Hampshire Ave., NW, Washington, D.C., 20037)
Ambassador: Ahmed Abdulla Zaid Al-Mahmoud.

Of the USA in Qatar (Fariq Bin Omran, Doha)
Ambassador: Joseph Ghougassian.

Of Qatar to the United Nations
Ambassador: Hamad Abdel Aziz Al-Kawari.

Books of Reference

Qatar Year Book 1982–83. Doha, 1984
El Mallakh, R., *Qatar: The Development of an Oil Economy.* New York, 1979
Unwin, P. T. H., *Qatar.* [Bibliography] Oxford and Santa Barbara, 1982

ROMANIA

Capital: Bucharest
Population: 22·7m. (1986)
GNP per capita: US$2,540 (1981)

Republica Socialistă România

HISTORY. 1918 is celebrated as the year of foundation of the 'unitary national Romanian state'. For the history and constitution of Romania from 1859 to 1947, *see* THE STATESMAN'S YEAR-BOOK, 1947, pp. 1187–89. On 30 Dec. 1947 King Michael abdicated under Communist pressure and parliament proclaimed the 'People's Republic'.

AREA AND POPULATION. Romania is bounded north and north-east by the USSR, east by the Black Sea, south by Bulgaria, south-west by Yugoslavia and north-west by Hungary. The area of Romania is 237,500 sq. km (91,699 sq. miles). Pre-war Romania had an area of 113,918 sq. miles. Population at censuses: 1930, 18,057,208 (14,280,729 within present-day Romania); 1948, 15,872,624 (48·3% male); 1966, 19,103,163 (49% male, 38·2% urban); 1977, 21,559,910 (49·3% male, 47·5% urban).

In 1986 the population was 22,724,836 (49·1% male; 50% urban), density per sq. km, 95·7. Vital statistics, 1985 (per 1,000 population): Live births, 15·8; deaths, 10·9; marriages, 7·1; divorces, 1·43; stillborn (per 1,000 live births), 7·8; infant mortality (per 1,000 live births), 25·6. Expectation of life in 1984, 66·9 years. Welfare incentives and tax penalties (on the childless) are designed to combat a decline in the birthrate. Abortion and contraception are illegal, and the marriageable age of girls has been lowered from 18 to 15. Population growth rate per 1,000 was 4·9 in 1985 and 5·2 in 1984.

Administratively, Romania is divided into 40 counties (*judeţ*), 237 towns (*oraş*) (of which 55 are municipalities) and 2,705 local authorities (*comune*). The capital is Bucharest (Bucureşti), a municipality with county status. It was announced in 1986 that Tîrgovişte might be made a 'second capital'.

District	Area in sq. km	Population 1985	Capital	Population 1985
Alba	6,231	425,428	Alba Iulia	64,369
Arad	7,652	491,287	Arad	185,892
Argeş	6,801	667,355	Piteşti	154,112
Bacău	6,606	736,416	Bacău	175,299
Bihor	7,535	657,670	Oradea	208,507
Bistriţa-Năsăud	5,305	321,738	Bistriţa	73,429
Botoşani	4,965	496,993	Botoşani	104,836
Braşov	5,351	630,455	Braşov	346,640
Brăila	4,724	396,518	Brăila	234,600
Buzău	6,072	535,004	Buzău	132,311
Caraş-Severin	8,503	393,182	Reşiţa	104,362
Călăraşi	5,075	349,307	Călăraşi	68,226
Cluj	6,650	732,057	Cluj-Napoca	309,843
Constanţa	7,055	662,733	Constanţa	323,236
Covasna	3,705	227,409	Sf. Gheorghe	65,868
Dîmboviţa	4,035	563,838	Tîrgovişte	88,663
Dolj	7,413	774,074	Craiova	275,098
Galaţi	4,425	625,792	Galaţi	292,805
Giurgiu	3,810	352,613	Giurgiu	65,792
Gorj	5,641	371,983	Tîrgu Jiu	85,058
Harghita	6,610	355,383	Miercurea-Ciuc	45,651
Hunedoara	7,016	542,915	Deva	76,934
Ialomiţa	4,449	312,974	Slobozia	44,797
Iaşi	5,469	792,099	Iaşi	314,156
Maramureş	6,215	548,054	Baia Mare	135,536
Mehedinţi	4,900	332,578	Drobeta-Turnu Severin	97,862
Mureş	6,696	623,710	Tîrgu Mureş	157,411
Neamţ	5,890	593,497	Piatra-Neamţ	107,581

District	Area in sq. km	Population 1985	Capital	Population 1985
Olt	5,507	545,361	Slatina	73,982
Prahova	4,694	860,354	Ploieşti	234,021
Satu Mare	4,405	415,404	Satu Mare	128,115
Sălaj	3,850	277,042	Zalău	54,676
Sibiu	5,422	494,538	Sibiu	176,928
Suceava	8,555	695,187	Suceava	92,690
Teleorman	5,760	527,502	Alexandria	51,267
Timiş	8,692	665,888	Timişoara	318,955
Tulcea	8,430	272,949	Tulcea	84,353
Vaslui	5,297	487,222	Vaslui	62,372
Vîlcea	5,705	436,438	Rîmnicu Vîlcea	93,271
Vrancea	4,863	400,780	Focşani	83,562
Bucharest [1]	1,521	2,133,109	Bucharest [2]	1,975,808

[1] Total conurbation.   [2] Central area.

The last official figures on the size of the ethnic minorities were published in 1977. Estimates for 1988: Hungarians, 2m. (mainly in Transylvania); Germans, 0·25m.; Gypsies, 1m.; Jews, 30,000. Hungarians are not allowed to emigrate. Germans are permitted to emigrate under an agreement with Federal Germany of 1980: some 11,000 leave annually. The official language is Romanian.

CLIMATE. A continental climate with a large annual range of temperature and rainfall showing a slight summer maximum.

Bucharest. Jan. 27°F (–2·7°C), July 74°F (23·5°C). Annual rainfall 23·1″ (579 mm). Constanţa. Jan. 31°F (–0·6°C), July 71°F (21·7°C). Annual rainfall 15″ (371 mm).

CONSTITUTION AND GOVERNMENT. The Constitution dates from 1965 and supersedes those of 1948 and 1952. The leading role of the Communist Party is affirmed. In 1986 the Constitution was amended to allow for national referendums. For the first to be held *see* DEFENCE, p. 1022. The Grand National Assembly of 369 is elected for 5 years (before 1972 for 4 years). It holds short sessions twice a year, and between sessions delegates its legislative rights to the State Council. Its Speaker is Nicolae Giosan.

The Socialist Democracy and Unity Front (SDUF) functions as a consultative body on home and foreign affairs. It has central and local councils in which workers, peasants, professional bodies, ethnic minorities and the Communist Party are represented.

All citizens of 18 and over have the right to vote and electoral law provides for the nomination of 'one or more' candidates in each constituency. To be elected candidates must secure 50% + 1 of the vote, otherwise re-elections are held.

The last election was held on 17 March 1985 (for previous elections *see* THE STATESMAN'S YEAR-BOOK, 1985–86). From an electorate of 15,733,060 turn-out was 15,732,095 (99·99%) and 15,375,522 votes (97·73%) were cast for SDUF. Anti-SDUF votes come mainly from ethnic minority areas, and are increasing: 1969, 0·2%; 1975, 1·2%; 1980, 1·5%; 1985, 2·27%. 594 candidates stood.

Local government is carried out by People's Councils at the administrative levels mentioned on p 1020. 57,584 councillors were elected from among 117,349 candidates on 15 Nov. 1987.

Real political power is in the hands of the Romanian Communist Party. The Party Congress elects the General Secretary, and its Central Committee elects the Executive Political Committee with its Permanent Bureau and the Secretariat (General Secretary and 7 secretaries). The Party had 3,465,069 members (1m. women) in 1985 (of whom 23% were under 30, 10% ethnic minorities, 56% workers).

President of the Republic and Chairman of the State Council: Nicolae Ceauşescu, succeeded Chivu Stoica in Dec. 1967. *Vice-Chairmen:* Manea Mănescu, Gheorghe Rădulescu, Maria Ghiţulică, Arpad Pall.

In April 1988 the Permanent Bureau of the Party consisted of: Nicolae

Ceaușescu (*General Secretary*); Emil Bobu; Elena Ceaușescu[1]; Constantin Dăscălescu; Manea Mănescu; Gheorghe Oprea; Gheorghe Rădulescu.

[1] Ceaușescu's wife.

Council of Ministers (April 1988). *Chairman* (*Prime Minister*): Constantin Dăscălescu. *First Deputy Prime Ministers:* Elena Ceaușescu, Gheorghe Oprea, Ion Dinca; *Deputy Prime Ministers:* Stefan Andrei; Ludovic Fazekaș; Cornel Pacoste; Lina Ciobanu; Ion Constantinescu; Nicolae Ibanescu; Constantin Radu. Other ministers include: Ștefan Bîrlea (*Chairman, State Planning Committee*) Gheorghe David (*Agriculture*); Gheorghe Paraşchiv (*Finance*); Ioan Totu (*Foreign*); Maj.-Gen. Vasile Milea (*Defence*); Tudor Postelnicu (*Interior*); Maxim Berghianu (*Labour*); Ilie Văduva (*Foreign Trade*); Maria Bobu (*Justice*); Petre Fluture (*Electric Power*); Paula Prioteașa (*Food*).

In July 1970 Romania signed a treaty of friendship, co-operation and mutual assistance with the USSR. A previous such treaty had expired in 1968. Since the mid-1960s Romania has been taking a relatively independent stand in foreign affairs generally, and within Comecon and the Warsaw Pact.

National flag: Three vertical strips of blue, yellow, red, with the national arms in the centre.

National anthem: Trei culori (Three colours). Introduced, 1977. Music by Ciprian Porumbescu.

DEFENCE. Defence is the responsibility of the Defence Council, which is controlled by the Council of State and headed by President Ceaușescu. On 23 Nov. 1986 a referendum was held on reducing defence spending by 5%. Turn-out was 99·9%, and 100% were in favour. Military service is compulsory for 16 months in the Army and Air Force and 24 months in the Navy.

Army. The 4 Army Areas consist of 2 tank and 8 motor rifle divisions; 3 mountain, 2 artillery, 2 anti-aircraft and 2 surface-to-surface missile brigades; and 3 artillery, 1 anti-aircraft, 5 anti-tank and 1 airborne regiments. Equipment includes 200 T-34, 1,000 T-54/-55, 30 T-72 and 200 M-77 main battle tanks. Strength (1988) 140,000 (including 95,000 conscripts), and 500,000 reservists. There are a further 35,000 men in paramilitary border guard and internal security forces.

Navy. The fleet comprises 2 Romanian-built new missile-armed large destroyers each with hangar for 2 helicopters 1 *ex*-Soviet diesel-electric powered patrol submarine, 3 new frigates, 3 corvettes, 6 fast missile boats, 42 fast torpedo boats, 27 fast gunboats, 1 new monitor, 3 old patrol vessels, 2 minelayer/mine counter measures support ships, 4 old minesweepers, 37 inshore minesweepers, 2 logistic support ships, 1 oceanographic ship, 2 training ships, 40 river patrol craft, 3 landing craft and 2 tugs. Headquarters of the Navy is at Mangalia, and of the Danube flotilla at the main river port of Brăila. The naval school is in Constanța. Personnel in 1988 totalled 7,500 officers and ratings including 600 in Coastal Defence, 900 under Training and 2,500 shore support.

Air Force. The Air Force numbered some 32,000 men, with 368 combat aircraft in 2 air divisions (4 regiments) in 1988. These are organized into 12 interceptor squadrons with MiG-21 and MiG-23 fighters, 6 ground-attack and close-support squadrons with MiG-17 fighters, and 1 reconnaissance squadron of Il-28s. There are also more than 150 training aircraft, 20 An-24/26/30 transports and more than 150 helicopters (Mi-2, Mi-4, Mi-8, Alouette and Puma). Under delivery are 185 IAR-93 close-support/interceptors to replace the MiG-17s. 'Guideline' and 'Gainful' surface-to-air missiles are operational, and short-range surface-to-surface missiles have been displayed.

INTERNATIONAL RELATIONS

Membership. Romania is a member of UN, IMF, Comecon and the Warsaw Pact.

ECONOMY

Planning. In Oct. 1982 the Supreme Council of Economic and Social Development, presided over by Nicolae Ceauşescu, was raised to the level of an economic legislative chamber. The seventh 5-year plan covers 1986–90. Annual growth targets: agriculture, 6·1%; industry, 7·5%. Increase in output (and target) under the 1981–85 plan: Industry, 21·6% (54·4%); agriculture, 10% (75·5%). There has been only limited decentralization of planning. (For previous plans *see* THE STATESMAN'S YEAR-BOOK, 1976–77.). Romania is committed to intensive industrialization and agriculture has been neglected. A workers' riot in Braşov on 15 Nov. 1987 was followed by promises of increased food supplies.

Budget. Revenue and expenditure (in 1m. lei) for calendar years:

	1980	1981	1982	1983	1984	1985	1986 [1]
Revenue	298,004	262,227	288,511	301,908	308,917	363,180	340,914
Expenditure	296,787	262,227	288,511	301,908	308,917	342,545	340,914

[1] Estimates.

In 1985 sources of revenue (in 1m. lei) included: Profit payments of state enterprises 29,527; turnover tax, 93,666; personal taxes, 4,251; insurance contributions, 40,009; taxes on enterprise wage funds, 47,125. Expenditure: National economy, 172,559; social and cultural, 90,412; defence, 12,113.

Revenue and expenditure of local councils (included above) was 63,054m. lei and 60,560m. lei in 1985.

Romania has settled UK claims arising out of the peace treaty and on defaulted bonds.

Currency. The monetary unit is the *leu*, pl.*lei* (of 100 *bani*). On 1 Feb. 1954 the gold content of the leu was to 0·148112 gramme of fine gold. Exchange rates (March 1988): £1 = 6·25 lei; US$1 = 4·25 lei; 1 rouble = 6·67 lei. Tourist rates: £1 = 15·31 lei; US$1 = 8·42 lei.

Bank-notes of 1, 5, 10, 25, 50 and 100 *lei* are issued by the National Bank, and there are coins of 5, 10, 15 and 25 *bani* and 1, 3 and 5 *lei*.

Banking. The National Bank of Romania (founded 1880, nationalized 1946) is the State Bank under the Minister of Finance. Half its profits are allotted to the State budget. There are also a Bank of Investments, a Foreign Trade Bank, an Agriculture and Food Industry Bank and a Savings Bank. The US Export-Import Bank has granted Romania borrowing rights. In 1974 the American bank Manufactures Hanover Trust Co. opened a branch in Bucharest, the first Western bank to do so in a Communist country.

Weights and measures. The Gregorian calendar was adopted in 1919. The metric system is in use. Tubes and pipes are measured in *tol* (= 1 inch).

ENERGY AND NATURAL RESOURCES

Electricity. Installed electric power 1984: 18,829,000 kw.; output, 1985, 71,819m. kwh (11,896m. kwh hydroelectric). Supply 220 volts; 50 Hz. There are two joint Romanian–Yugoslav hydro-electric power plants on the Danube at the 'Iron Gates' with a combined yearly output of 22,250m. kwh. A nuclear power programme has been subject to cut-backs and delays. In Oct. 1985 a state of emergency was declared in the energy sector and its administration handed over to the military. This was still in force in 1988.

Oil. The oilfields are in the Prahova, Băcau, Gorj, Crişana and Argeş districts. Oil production in 1987 was 10·5m. tonnes. Oil reserves are expected to be exhausted by the mid-1990s. Refining capacity was enlarged from 16m. tonnes per annum in 1970 to 30m. tonnes in 1985. Crude oil has to be imported.

Minerals. The principal minerals are oil and natural gas, salt, brown coal, lignite, iron and copper ores, bauxite, chromium, manganese and uranium. Salt is mined in the lower Carpathians and in Transylvania; production in 1985 was 5m. tonnes.

Output, 1985 (and 1984) (in 1,000 tonnes): Iron ore, 2,287 (1,916); coal, 46,581 (47,799, including lignite 37,140); methane gas (cu. metres), 27,719m. (27,196m.). The share of coal in the overall production of energy rose from 28% in 1975 to 47% in 1985 and is expected to reach 60% by 1990.

Agriculture. There were 15·02m. hectares of agricultural land in 1985, including (in 1,000 hectares): Arable, 9,985; meadows and pasture, 4,398; vineyards and fruit trees, 637.

Production in 1986 (in 1,000 tonnes): Wheat and rye, 7,947; barley, 2,200; maize, 20,000; potatoes, 8,513; sunflower seeds, 1,004; sugar-beet, 7,000.

Livestock (1986): 6,867,000 cattle, 14,319,000 pigs, 18,609,000 sheep and 131m. poultry. The number of horses had fallen to some 200,000 by Feb. 1986, but it was then decided to increase the herd and allow the tractor park to reduce by 30%.

In 1985 there were 4,363 collective farms, with 9·1m. hectares of land (7·2m. arable; 1·4m. private plots). State farms numbered 419, with 2m. hectares of land, of which 1·65m. hectares were arable. A further 2·4m. hectares of land were in the hands of other state agricultural organizations. There were 573 agriculture mechanization stations. Total tractor force, 1985: 184,408. Since 1984 production quotas on private plots must be met on pain of confiscation. The National Union of Agricultural Co-operatives promotes self-management in collective farms, and gives guidance on planning and marketing. A minimum income is guaranteed to peasants. In 1985 there were 2·7m. hectares of irrigated land.

Forestry. Total forest area was 6·34m. hectares in 1985. 52,850 hectares were afforested.

INDUSTRY AND TRADE

Industry. Output of main products in 1985 (and 1984) (in tonnes): Pig-iron, 9,912 (9,557); steel, 13,795 (14,437); steel tubes, 1,513 (1,507); blast furnace coke, 4,743 (4,849); rolled steel, 9,900 (10,329); chemical fertilizers, 3,097 (3,073); washing soda, 836 (912); caustic soda, 814 (805); paper, 741 (795); cement, 12,238 (14,016); sugar, 582 (806); edible oils, 328 (348). Fabrics (in 1m. sq. metres): Cotton, 700 (697); woollens, 131 (123); man-made fibres, 257,205 (281,288). In 1,000 units: Radio sets, 571 (458); TV sets, 522 (406); washing machines, 210 (452); motor cars, 134,169 (125,090).

Labour. The employed population in 1985 was 10·6m., of whom 3m. worked in agriculture and 4·71m. industry and building. In 1985 39·4% of the total workforce, and 42·6% of the industrial workforce, were women. Wage differentials (at a ratio of 5·25:1) are in accordance with the 'social evaluation' of the work and a range of incentives for productivity. The average monthly wage was 2,827 lei in 1985. Wages are cut if a firm's output falls below par. The working week is of 46 hours with alternate Saturdays free. Men retire at 62, women at 57.

Commerce. In 1985 exports totalled 192,295m. lei and imports 148,362m. lei.

Principal exports in 1985 were (in 1,000 tonnes): Petroleum products, 9,691; cement, 2,477; cereals, 842; oilfield equipment, 6,110m. lei; equipment for cement mills, 274m. lei; equipment for chemical factories, 904m. lei; shipbuilding, 966m. lei. Principal imports (in 1,000 tonnes): Iron ore, 15,207; industrial coke, 1,898; rolled ferrous metals, 696; electrical equipment, 4,809m. lei; motor cars, 1,303 units, and industrial and agricultural equipment.

In 1985 Romania's main trading partners (trade in 1m. lei) were: USSR, 74,333; Egypt, 22,304; Federal Republic of Germany, 19,486; Italy, 16,866; Iran, 16,758; German Democratic Republic, 16,737; USA, 15,645.

Total trade between Romania and UK (British Department of Trade returns, in £1,000 sterling):

	1983	1984	1985	1986	1987
Imports to UK	58,865	226,091	102,946	86,730	92,526
Exports and re-exports from UK	82,160	71,641	78,474	82,011	55,688

Both the UK and the USA have joint economic commissions with Romania. The US Congress suspended Romania's most-favoured nation status in 1987. In May 1986 Romania and the USSR signed a co-operation agreement for a 15-year programme of economic, scientific and technical development.

Romania owed some US$5,500m. to Western banks in 1987.

Joint companies with Western firms have been set up; at least 51% of the capital must be in Romanian hands. 4 were in operation in 1985. The 'Romconsult' and 'Publicom' agencies will carry out respectively market research and publicity campaigns on behalf of foreign firms.

Romania has a trade link with EEC under the generalized preference system.

Agreements with the EEC on industrial products and establishing a joint economic commission were reached in March 1980.

On 1 Jan. 1975 a 2-tier tariff system was introduced, graded according to the grant of most-favoured nation status to Romania.

COMMUNICATIONS

Roads. There were in 1985, 14,666 km of national roads of which 12,239 km were modernized. Freight carried, 362m. tonnes; passengers, 837m.

Railways. Length of route (1,435 mm gauge) in 1985 was 10,752 km and (narrow-gauge), 472 km. A total of 3,427 km is electrified. Freight carried, 283m. tons; passengers, 460m.

Aviation. TAROM (*Transporturi Aeriene Române*), the state airline, operates all internal services, and also services to Amsterdam, Athens, Beirut, Belgrade, Berlin, Brussels, Budapest, Cairo, Cologne, Copenhagen, Düsseldorf, Frankfurt, Istanbul, London, Moscow, Paris, Prague, Rome, Sofia, Tel-Aviv, Vienna, Warsaw and Zürich. Bucharest is also served by British Airways, PANAM, SABENA, Aeroflot, Air France, Interflug, ČSA, MALEV, Austrian Air Lines, SAS, Lot, TABSO, El Al, Alitalia, Lufthansa and Swissair. An air agreement with China was signed in 1973.

Bucharest's airports are Băneasa (internal flights) and Otopeni (international flights; 12 miles from Bucharest). Air transport in 1985 carried 2·5m. passengers and 29,000 tonnes of freight.

Shipping. The main ports are Constanţa on the Black Sea and Galaţi and Brăila on the Danube. A new port has been constructed at Agigea on the Black Sea and the 64 km canal between the Danube and the Black Sea was opened in 1984. The largest shipyard is at Galaţi.

In 1985 the mercantile marine (NAVROM) owned some 200 sea-going ships. In 1985 sea-going transport carried 25·72m. tonnes of freight; river transport, 18·4m. tonnes and 1·84m. passengers.

Post and Broadcasting. There were 4,979 post offices in 1985. Number of telephone subscribers, 1·96m. *Radio-televiziunea Româna* broadcasts 3 programmes on medium-waves and FM. There are also 6 regional programmes, including transmission in Hungarian, German and Serbo-Croat. Following the energy crisis of 1984 the two TV channels were merged and broadcasting reduced from 100 to 22 hours a week. Programmes in Hungarian and German have been dropped. Radio receiving sets, in 1985 3·21m.; TV sets, 3·88m.

Cinemas and Theatres. There were, in 1985, 5,558 cinemas and 154 theatres and concert halls. 27 full-length feature films were made.

Newspapers and Books. There were, in 1985, 36 daily and 24 weekly newspapers and 422 periodicals, including 11 dailies, 3 weeklies and 38 other periodicals in minority languages. The Party newspaper is *Scînteia* ('The Spark'). 3,063 book titles were published in 1985 in 66·3m. copies. (376 titles in minority languages).

JUSTICE, RELIGION, EDUCATION AND WELFARE

Justice. Justice is administered by the Supreme Court, the 40 district courts, and lower courts. Lay assessors (elected for 4 years) participate in most court trials, collaborating with the judges. The Procurator-General exercises 'supreme supervisory power to ensure the observance of the law' by all authorities, central and local, and all citizens. The Procurator's Office and its organs are independent of any organs of justice or administration, and only responsible to the Grand National Assembly (which appoints the Procurator-General for 4 years) and between its sessions, to the State Council. The Ministry of the Interior is responsible for ordinary police work. State security is the responsibility of the State Security Council. A new penal code came into force on 1 Jan. 1969. The death penalty is retained for 'specially serious offences' (treason, some classes of murder, theft of property having serious consequences). An amnesty of Jan. 1988 abolished or reduced the sentences of all convicts.

Religion. Churches are organized and function in accordance with art. 30 of the Constitution. Churches administer their own affairs and run seminaries for the training of priests. Expenses and salaries are paid by the State. There are 14 Churches, all under the control of the 'Department of Cults'. The largest is the Romanian Orthodox Church, which claimed some 16m. members in 1985. It is autocephalous, but retains dogmatic unity with the Eastern Orthodox Church. It is administered by the consultative Holy Synod and National Ecclesiastical Assembly and the executive National Ecclesiastical Council and Patriarchal Administration. It is organized into 12 dioceses grouped into 5 metropolitan bishoprics (Hungaro-Wallachia; Moldavia-Suceava; Transylvania; Olt; Banat). and headed by Patriarch Teoctist Arapaşu (since 1986). There are some 11,800 churches, 2 theological colleges and 6 'schools of cantors', as well as seminaries.

The Uniate (Greek Catholic) Church (which severed its connexion with the Vatican in 1698) was suppressed in 1948. It had 1·6m. adherents and 1,818 priests. Estimates for 1973: 700,000 adherents and 600 priests.

Other churches: Serbs have a Serbian Orthodox Vicariate at Timişoara. In 1986 there were 1·2m. Roman Catholics, mainly among the Hungarian and German minorities. There are 8 dioceses. In 1985 6 were vacant. There is a bishop of Alba Iulia and an Apostolic Administrator was appointed to Bucharest in Oct. 1984. There were 734 priests in 1982. The Church has not secured approval for a Statute and has no hierarchical ties with the Vatican.

Calvinists (600,000; mainly Hungarian) have bishoprics at Cluj and Oradea; Lutherans (150,000, mainly Germans) a bishopric at Sibiu and Unitarians (60,000, Hungarians) a bishopric at Cluj. These sects share a seminary at Cluj. In 1987 there were about 200,000 Baptists and 300,000 other neo-Protestants.

In 1988 there were 30,000 Jews under a Chief Rabbi (Moses Rosen). There were 120 synagogues in 1987.

There were 40,000 moslems in 1983 and they have a Muftiate at Constanţa.

Education. Education is free and compulsory from 6 to 16, consisting of 8 years of primary school and 2 years of secondary (gymnasium). Further secondary education is available at *lycées*, professional schools or advanced technical schools.

In 1985–86 there were 12,811 kindergartens with 33,522 teachers and 864,332 children; 14,076 primary and secondary schools with 147,147 teachers and 3,030,666 pupils; 981 *lycées* with 47,693 teachers and 1,226,927 pupils; 753 professional schools with 2,517 teachers and 287,818 pupils; and 296 advanced technical schools with 123 teachers and 22,803 pupils. In 1983–84 there were 3,130 schools for 340,773 pupils of ethnic minorities with 15,922 teachers.

There are universities at Iaşi (founded 1860), Bucharest (1864), Cluj (1919), Timişoara (1962), Craiova (1965) and Braşov (1971). In 1985–86 there were in all 44 institutes of higher education, with 159,798 (71,658 female) students and 12,691 teachers. In 1983–84 there were 11,568 students at institutes of higher education for ethnic minorities with some 1,000 teachers.

The Academy, with seat at Bucharest, has 2 branches at Iaşi and Cluj. The National Council for Scientific Research co-ordinates research.

Health. In 1985 there were 212,953 hospital beds and 47,390 doctors. Some hospitals began to charge fees in 1983.

DIPLOMATIC REPRESENTATIVES

Of Romania in Great Britain (4 Palace Green, London, W8 4QD)
Ambassador: Stan Soare (accredited 6 Nov. 1986).

Of Great Britain in Romania (24 Strada Jules Michelet, Bucharest)
Ambassador: Hugh Arbuthnott, CMG.

Of Romania in the USA (1607 23rd St., NW, Washington, D.C., 20008)
Ambassador: Ion Stoichici.

Of the USA in Romania (7–9 Strada Tudor Arghezi, Bucharest)
Ambassador: Roger Kirk.

Of Romania to the United Nations
Ambassador: Petre Tanasie.

Books of Reference

Anuarul Statistic al R.S.R. Bucharest, annual
Atlas Geografic Republica Socialistă Romania. Bucharest, 1965
Dicţionar Enciclopedic Român. Bucharest, 1962–66
Economic and Commercial Guide to Romania. Bucharest, annual since 1969
Mic Dicţionar Enciclopedic. Bucharest, 1973
Revista de Statistică. Bucharest, monthly
Romania: An Encyclopaedic Survey. Bucharest, 1980
Romania, the Industrialization of an Agrarian Economy under Socialist Planning: Report of a Mission sent to Romania by the World Bank. Washington, 1979
Academia Republicii Socialiste România. *Dicţionar Englez-Român.* Bucharest, 1974
Ceauçescu, N.,. *Romania on the Way of Completing Socialist Construction.* 3 vols. Bucharest, 1968–69.—*Romania on the Way of Completing the Many-sided Developed Socialist Society.* Bucharest, 1970 *ff.*
Deletant, A., and D., *Romania* [Bibliography]. Oxford and Santa Barbara, 1985
Fischer-Galati, S. A., *Rumania: A Bibliographical Guide.* Library of Congress, 1963.—*The New Rumania.* Mass. Inst. of Technology, 1968.—*The Socialist Republic of Rumania.* Baltimore, 1969.—*Twentieth Century Rumania.* New York, 1970
Giurescu, C. C. (ed.), *Chronological History of Romania.* 2nd ed. Bucharest, 1974
Graham, L. S., *Romania, a Developing Socialist State.* Boulder, 1982
Ionescu, A. (ed.), *The Grand National Assembly of the Socialist Republic of Romania: A Brief Outline.* Bucharest, 1974
King, R. R., *History of the Romanian Communist Party.* Stanford, 1980
Leviţchi, L., *Dicţionar Român-Englez.* 2nd ed. Bucharest, 1965
Morariu, T., and others, *The Geography of Rumania.* 2nd ed. Bucharest, 1969
Nelson, D. N. (ed.), *Romania in the 1980's.* Boulder, 1981
Pacepa, I., *Red Horizons.* London, 1988
Shafir, M., *Romania: Politics, Economics and Society.* London, 1985
Stanciu, I. G. and Cernovodeanu, P., *Distant Lands: The Genesis and Evolution of Romanian –American Relations.* Boulder, 1985
Turnock, D., *An Economic Geography of Romania.* London, 1974.—*The Romanian Economy in the Twentieth Century.* London 1986

RWANDA

Republika y'u Rwanda

Capital: Kigali
Population: 6·32m. (1986)
GNP per capita: US$257 (1984)

HISTORY. From the 16th century to 1959 the Tutsi kingdom of Rwanda shared the history of Burundi (*see* p. 257). In 1959 an uprising of the Hutu destroyed the Tutsi feudal hierarchy and led to the departure of the Mwami Kigeri V. Elections and a referendum under the auspices of the United Nations in Sept. 1961 resulted in an overwhelming majority for the republican party, the Parmehutu (*Parti du Mouvement de l'Emancipation du Bahutu*), and the rejection of the institution of the Mwami. The republic proclaimed by the Parmehutu on 28 Jan. 1961 was recognized by the Belgian administration (but not by the United Nations) in Oct. 1961. Internal self-government was granted on 1 Jan. 1962, and by decision of the General Assembly of the UN the Republic of Rwanda became independent on 1 July 1962. The first President, Gregoire Kayibanda, was deposed in a *coup* on 5 July 1973.

AREA AND POPULATION. Rwanda is bounded south by Burundi, west by Zaïre, north by Uganda and east by Tanzania. A mountainous state of 26,338 sq. km (10,169 sq. miles), its western third drains to Lake Kivu on the border with Zaïre and thence to the Congo river, while the rest is drained by the Kagera river into the Nile system.

The population was 4,819,317 at the 1978 Census, of whom over 90% were Hutu, 9% Tutsi and 1% Twa (pygmy); latest estimate (1986) 6,324,000.

The areas and populations (1978 Census) of the 10 prefectures are:

Prefecture	Sq. km	Census 1978	Prefecture	Sq. km	Census 1978
Cyangugu	2,226	331,380	Kigali	3,251	698,063
Kibuye	1,320	337,729	Kibungo	4,134	360,934
Gisenyi	2,395	468,786	Gitarama	2,241	602,752
Ruhengeri	1,762	528,649	Gikongoro	2,192	369,891
Byumba	4,987	519,968	Butare	1,830	601,165

Kigali, the capital, had 156,650 inhabitants in 1981; other towns (1978) being Butare (21,691), Ruhengeri (16,025) and Gisenyi (12,436). Kinyarwanda, the language of the entire population, and French are official languages, and Kiswahili is spoken in the commercial centres, where most of the 1,200 Europeans and 750 Asians reside.

Vital statistics (1975): Live births, 113,154; deaths, 41,385; marriages, 13,899.

CLIMATE. Despite the equatorial situation, there is a highland tropical climate. The wet seasons are from Oct. to Dec. and March to May. Highest rainfall occurs in the west, at around 70″ (1,770 mm), decreasing to 40–55″ (1,020–1,400 mm) in the central uplands and to 30″ (760 mm) in the north and east. Kigali. Jan. 67°F (19·4°C), July 70°F (21·1°C). Annual rainfall 40″ (1,000 mm).

CONSTITUTION AND GOVERNMENT. A new Constitution was approved by referendum on 17 Dec. 1978; under it, the *Mouvement revolutionnaire national pour le développement* (MRND) founded 5 July 1975 becomes the sole political organisation. Executive power is vested in a President, elected by universal suffrage for a (renewable) 5-year term. He presides over a Council of Ministers, whom he appoints and dismisses.

Legislative power rests with a National Development Council of 70 deputies, elected for a 5-year term; elections were held on 26 Dec. 1983.

President: Maj.-Gen. Junéval Habyarimana (took office July 1975; elected Dec. 1978 and re-elected Dec. 1983).

Foreign Affairs and Co-operation: François Ngarukiyintwari.

National flag: Three equal vertical panels of red, yellow and green (left to right), the letter 'R' in black superimposed on the centre panel.

Local government: The 10 prefectures, each under an appointed Prefect, are divided into 144 communes, each with an appointed Burgomaster and an elected Council.

DEFENCE

Army. The Army consists of 1 commando battalion, 1 reconnaissance, 8 infantry and 1 engineer companies. Equipment includes 12 AML-60/-90 armoured cars. Strength (1988) about 5,000.

Air Force. The Air Force currently operates 2 Guerrier armed light aircraft, 1 twin-engined Defender, 2 Noratlas, 1 Islander light transport, 6 Gazelle and 4 Alouette III helicopters. A Caravelle is operated on VIP duties. Personnel (1988) 150.

INTERNATIONAL RELATIONS

Membership. Rwanda is a member of UN, OAU and is an ACP state of EEC. With Burundi and Zaïre it forms part of the Economic Community of Countries of the Great Lakes.

ECONOMY

Planning. The 1982–86 Development Plan of the total investment of 232,300m. Rwanda francs 56% will be devoted to agriculture.

Budget. The budget for 1983 envisaged expenditure of 16,368m. Rwanda francs and revenue of 14,683m.

Currency. The currency is the *Rwanda franc.* The official rate of Rwanda francs 131·75 = £1; 75·46 = US$1 (March 1988).

Banking. The Development Bank of Rwanda *(Banque Rwandaise de Développement—BRD)* had a capital (1983) of 1,000m. Rwanda francs. Other banks are the Central Bank *(Banque Nationale du Rwanda)*; 2 commercial banks which are majority foreign owned—the *Banque Commerciale du Rwanda* and the *Banque de Kigali*; the People's Bank, the Savings Association and the *Caisse Hypothécaire.*

ENERGY AND NATURAL RESOURCES

Electricity. 4 hydro-electric installations and 1 thermal plant produced 110m. kwh in 1986, but over half of the country's needs come from Zaïre. Supply 220 volts; 50 Hz.

Minerals. Cassiterite and wolframite are mined east of Lake Kivu. Production (1983): Cassiterite, 1,526 tonnes; wolfram, 429 tonnes. About 1m. cu. metres of natural gas are obtained from under the lake each year.

Agriculture. Subsistence agriculture accounts for most of the gross national product. Staple food crops (production 1986, in 1,000 tonnes) are sweet potatoes (920), cassava (348), beans (240), sorghum (184), potatoes (270), maize (121), peas and groundnuts. The main cash crops are *aravica* coffee (30), tea (8) and pyrethrum. There is a pilot rice-growing project.

Long-horned Ankole cattle, 639,000 head in 1980, play an important traditional role. Efforts are being made to improve their present negligible economic value. There were (1986) 670,000 cattle, 1,005,000 goats, 343,000 sheep and 104,000 pigs.

INDUSTRY AND TRADE

Industry. There are about 100 small-sized modern manufacturing enterprises in the country. Food manufacturing is the dominant industrial activity (64%) followed by construction (15·3%) and mining (9%). There is a large modern brewery.

Commerce. In 1983 imports amounted to 25,267m. Rwanda francs and exports to

7,427m. of which coffee comprised 70%, tea 12% and tin 11%; Belgium provided 17% of imports, Kenya 21% and Japan 12%.

Total trade between Rwanda and UK (British Department of Trade returns, in £1,000 sterling):

	1983	1984	1985	1986	1987
Imports to UK	2,919	7,842	3,998	7,487	4,291
Exports and re-exports from UK	2,326	2,385	3,565	1,681	2,526

Tourism. In 1984 there were 20,000 visitors to national parks.

COMMUNICATIONS

Roads. There were (1982) 6,760 km of roads. There are road links with Burundi, Uganda, Tanzania and Zaïre. There were in 1982 6,188 cars and 7,168 commercial vehicles.

Aviation. There are international airports at Kanombe, for Kigali, and at Kamembe, with services to Bujumbura, Bukavu, Entebbe, Goma, Lubumbashi, Athens and Brussels.

Post and Broadcasting. Telephones (1983) 6,598. In 1983 there were 2 radio stations and 155,000 receivers.

Cinemas. In 1975 there were 3 cinemas with a seating capacity of 1,000.

JUSTICE, RELIGION, EDUCATION AND WELFARE

Justice. A system of Courts of First Instance and provincial courts refer appeals to Courts of Appeal and a Court of Cassation situated in Kigali.

Religion. The population was (1983) predominantly Roman Catholic (56%); there is an archbishop (Kigali) and 3 bishops. 23% of the population follow traditional religions, 12% are Protestants and 9% Moslems.

Education. In 1981 there were 704,924 pupils attending 1,606 primary schools with 11,912 teachers. There were 118 secondary, technical and teacher-training schools with 10,667 students and 887 teachers. The National University, opened at Butare in 1963, had 1,577 students in 1984.

Health. In 1983 there were 170 hospitals and health centres with (1980) 9,015 beds; there were also 164 doctors, 1 dentist, 10 pharmacists, 464 midwives and 525 nursing personnel.

DIPLOMATIC REPRESENTATIVES

Of Rwanda in Great Britain
Ambassador: Ildephonse Munyeshyaka (resides in Brussels).

Of Great Britain in Rwanda
Ambassador: R. L. B. Cormack (resides in Kinshasa).

Of Rwanda in the USA (1714 New Hampshire Ave, NW, Washington, D.C., 20009)
Ambassador: Simon Insonere.

Of the USA in Rwanda (Blvd. de la Revolution, Kigali)
Ambassador: John E. Upston.

Of Rwanda to the United Nations
Ambassador: Célestin Kabanda.

ST CHRISTOPHER
(ST KITTS)—NEVIS

Capital: Basseterre
Population: 47,000 (1987)
GNP capita: US$820 (1983)

HISTORY. St Christopher (known to its Carib inhabitants as *Liamuiga*) and Nevis were discovered and named by Columbus in 1493. They were settled by Britain in 1623 and 1628 respectively, but ownership was disputed with France until 1713. Forming part of the Leeward Islands Federation from 1871 to 1956, and part of the Federation of the West Indies from 1958 to 1962. In Feb. 1967 the colonial status was replaced by an 'association' with Britain, giving the islands full internal self-government, while Britain remained responsible for defence and foreign affairs. St Christopher–Nevis became fully independent on 19 Sept. 1983.

AREA AND POPULATION. The islands form part of the Lesser Antilles in Eastern Caribbean. Population, estimate (1983) 43,309.

	sq. km	Census 1980	Chief town	Census 1980
St Christopher	174	33,881	Basseterre	14,283
Nevis	93	9,428	Charlestown	1,243
	267	43,309		

In 1980, 94% of the population were black and 36% were urban. Estimate (1987) 47,000. English is the official and spoken language.

CLIMATE. A pleasantly healthy climate, with a cool breeze throughout the year, low humidity and no recognized rainy season. Average annual rainfall is about 55″ (1,375 mm).

CONSTITUTION AND GOVERNMENT. The 1983 Constitution described the country as 'a sovereign democratic federal state'. It allowed for a unicameral Parliament consisting of 11 elected Members (8 from St Kitts and 3 from Nevis) and 3 appointed Senators. Nevis was given its own Island Assembly and the right to secession from St Kitts. At the General Elections held on 21 June 1984, 6 seats from St Kitts were won by the People's Action Movement and 2 by the Labour Party, while the 3 Nevis seats were won by the Nevis Reformation Party.

Governor-General: Sir Clement Athelston Arrindell, GCMG, GCVO.
Prime Minister: Rt. Hon. Dr Kennedy Alphonse Simmonds.
Flag: Diagonally green, black, red, with the black fimbriated in yellow and charged with two white stars.

INTERNATIONAL RELATIONS

Membership. St Christopher–Nevis is a member of the UN, the OAS, the Commonwealth and is an ACP state of EEC.

ECONOMY

Budget. The 1988 budget envisaged expenditure at EC$74·6m. and revenue at EC$74·4m.

Currency. The East Caribbean *dollar* (of 100 *cents*) is in use. In March 1988, £1 = EC$4·79; US$1 = EC$2·70.

Banking. The National Bank operates 4 branches in St. Kitts and Nevis. The main office is located in Basseterre. Other banks include Barclay's Bank International, with a sub-branch in Nevis, Royal Bank of Canada, Bank of Commerce, and the Nevis Co-operative Bank and the Bank of Nevis in Charlestown. Branches of the Bank of Nova Scotia are located in Basseterre and Charlestown. Commercial banks' assets (1987) EC$361·5m.; deposits (1985) EC$246·8m.

ENERGY AND NATURAL RESOURCES

Electricity. Production (1984) 34m. kwh.

Agriculture. The main crops are sugar and cotton. There are 30 sugar estates and 124 acres of cotton. Most of the farms are small-holdings and there are a number of coconut estates amounting to some 1,000 acres under public and private ownership. Sugar production (1987) 28,491 tonnes and 30·5 tonnes of cotton and 260,382 lbs of copra were produced in 1986.

Livestock (1986): Cattle, 6,000; pigs, 10,000; sheep, 14,000; goats, 10,000; donkeys, (1984) 1,365; poultry, (1984) 67,030.

Fisheries. Catch (1983) 1,100 tonnes.

INDUSTRY AND TRADE

Industry. The main employer of labour is the sugar industry. Other industries are: Clothing, footwear and assembly of electronic equipment.

Commerce. Imports, (1984) EC$140·1m. mainly from the USA (EC$55·5m. and UK EC$16·8m.); exports, EC$52·6m. Chief export (1985) was sugar (24,576 tons in 1983), mainly to the USA (EC$24m.) and UK (EC$10·2m.).

Total trade between St Christopher (St Kitts)–Nevis and UK (British Department of Trade returns, in £1,000 sterling):

	1985	1986	1987
Imports to UK	5,634	4,429	4,677
Exports and re-exports from UK	5,256	6,008	7,041

Tourism. In 1986, there were 83,768 tourists, 26,963 arriving by sea.

COMMUNICATIONS

Roads. There were (1983) about 305 km of roads, and (1987) 2,641 passenger cars and 1,494 commercial vehicles.

Railways. There are 36 miles of railway operated by the sugar industry.

Aviation. There is an airport at Golden Rock (St Kitts). 66,590 passengers arrived by air in 1985. There is an airfield on Nevis (Newcastle).

Shipping. A deep water port was opened in 1981 at Bird Rock with accommodation for cargo, tourist, roll-on-roll-off ships and bulk sugar and molasses loading. 1,428 tourists arrived by sea in 1985.

Post and Telecommunications. There is a general post office in Basseterre. Five branches are on the island. Charlestown has a general post office, and there are two branches in Nevis. There were 4,000 telephones at 31 Jan. 1988. In 1985 there were 5,000 television and 21,000 radio receivers.

JUSTICE, RELIGION, EDUCATION AND WELFARE

Justice. Justice is administered by the Supreme Court and by Magistrates' Courts. They have both civil and criminal jurisdiction.

Religion. In 1985, 36·2% were Anglican, 32·3% Methodist, 7·9% other Protestant, and 10·7% Roman Catholic.

Education. Primary education is compulsory for all children between the ages of 5 and 14, but no pupil is required to leave school before the age of 16 years. There is an Extra-Mural Department of the University of the West Indies, a Technical College and a Teachers' Training College.

In 1984 there were 7,655 pupils in primary schools, 4,436 in secondary schools, and 240 students in the Technical and Teacher's Training Colleges.

Health. In 1987 there were 22 doctors, 4 hospitals with 258 beds and 17 health clinics.

DIPLOMATIC REPRESENTATIVES

Of St Christopher and Nevis in Great Britain (10 Kensington Ct., London W8)
High Commissioner: Richard Gunn.

Of Great Britain in St Christopher and Nevis
High Commissioner: Kevin F. X. Burns, CMG (resides in Bridgetown).

Of St Christopher and Nevis to the United Nations
Ambassador: Dr William Herbert.

Books of Reference

National Accounts. Statistics Division, Ministry of Development (annual)
St Kitts and Nevis Quarterly. Statistics Division, Ministry of Development
Gordon, J., *Nevis: Queen of the Caribees.* London, 1985

Library: Public Library, Basseterre. *Librarian:* Miss V. Archibald.

ST HELENA

HISTORY. The island was administered by the East India Company from 1659 and became a British colony in 1834.

AREA AND POPULATION. St Helena, of volcanic origin, is 1,200 miles from the west coast of Africa. Area, 47 sq. miles (121·7 sq. km), with a cultivable area of about 600 acres (243 hectares). Population (1985) 5,895. The port of the island is Jamestown, population (1976) 1,516.

In 1982 there were: Births, 123; deaths, 52; marriages, 26.

CLIMATE. A mild climate, with little variation. Temperatures range from 75–85°F (24–29°C) in summer to 65–75°F (18–24°C) in winter. Rainfall varies between 13″ (325 mm) and 37″ (925 mm) according to altitude and situation.

GOVERNMENT. The Government of St Helena is administered by a Governor, with the aid of a Legislative Council consisting of the Governor, 2 *ex-officio* members (the Government Secretary and the Treasurer) and 12 elected members. Committees of the Legislative Council are responsible for the general oversight of the activities of government departments and have, in addition, statutory and administrative functions.

The Governor is also assisted by an Executive Council consisting of the 2 *ex-officio* members and the chairmen of the five Council committees.

Governor and C.-in-C.: R. F. Stimson.
Government Secretary: E. C. Brooks, OBE.

Flag: The British Blue Ensign with the shield of the colony in the fly.

FINANCE AND TRADE, for years from 1 April–31 March, in £ sterling:

	1977–78	1978–79	1979–80	1980–81	1981–82	1982 [3]
Revenue [1]	2,244,550	2,683,681	4,226,899	4,488,257	5,656,518	4,126,548
Expenditure [1]	2,200,299	2,764,150	4,325,910	4,551,657	5,681,934	3,988,900
Imports [2]	1,758,337	1,164,437	1,835,000	2,117,126	2,485,819	2,381,632

[1] Including imperial grants (1977–78, £1,657,231; 1978–79, £1,771,618; 1979–80, £3,347,631; 1980–81, £3,232,093; 1981–82, £3,296,933; 1982, £2,819,256).
[2] Including government stores.
[3] April–Dec.

The revenue from customs was, in 1982, £305,635.

The colony's liabilities at 31 March 1982 exceeded the assets by £177,060; 31 Dec. 1982, £39,412.

Total trade between Ascension and St Helena and UK (British Department of Trade returns, in £1,000 sterling):

	1983	1984	1985	1986	1987
Imports to UK	457	979	4,515	380	189
Exports and re-exports from UK	10,343	6,294	7,914	8,196	8,065

BANKING. Savings-bank deposits on 31 Dec. 1982, £1,467,079, belonging to 3,800 depositors.

COMMUNICATIONS

Roads. There were (1987) 87 km of all-weather motor roads.

Shipping. The number of merchant vessels that called in 1982 (April–Dec.) was 30; total tonnage entered and cleared was 218,257.

Post and Broadcasting. The Cable & Wireless Ltd cable connects St Helena with Cape Town and Ascension Island. There is a telephone service with 85 miles of wire and (1982), 310 telephones.

St Helena Government Broadcasting Station broadcasts in English on medium-waves. Number of radio receivers (1982), 1,500.

JUSTICE, RELIGION, EDUCATION AND WELFARE

Justice. Police force, 32; cases dealt with by police magistrate, 205 in 1981.

Religion. There are 10 Anglican churches, 4 Baptist chapels, 3 Salvation Army halls, 1 Seventh Day Adventist church and 1 Roman Catholic church.

Education. Three pre-school playgroups, 8 primary, 3 senior and 1 secondary schools controlled by the Government had 980 pupils in Sept. 1982.

Health. There were 3 doctors, 1 dentist and 54 hospital beds in 1982.

Ascension is a small island of volcanic origin, of 34 sq. miles (88 sq. km), 700 miles north-west of St Helena. In Nov. 1922 the administration was transferred from the Admiralty to the Colonial Office and annexed to the colony of St Helena. There are 120 hectares providing fresh meat, vegetables and fruit. Population, 31 March 1985, was 1,708; St Helenians 759, others 866.

The island is the resort of sea turtles, which come to lay their eggs in the sand annually between Jan. and May. Rabbits are more or less numerous on the island, which is, besides, the breeding ground of the sooty tern or 'wideawake', these birds coming in vast numbers to lay their eggs every eighth month. There is also a small herd of feral donkeys.

Cable & Wireless Ltd own and operate a cable station, connecting the island with St Helena, Sierra Leone, St Vincent, Rio de Janeiro and Buenos Aires. There is an airstrip (Miracle Mile) near the settlement of Georgetown which was being extended in 1985.

Administrator: M. T. S. Blick.

Tristan da Cunha, is the largest of a small group of islands in the South Atlantic lying 1,320 miles (2,124 sq. km) south-west of St Helena, of which they became dependencies on 12 Jan. 1938. Tristan da Cunha has an area of 98 sq. km and a population (1982) of 325, all living in the settlement of Edinburgh. Inaccessible Island (10 sq. km) lies 20 miles west and the 3 Nightingale Islands (2 sq. km) lie 20 miles south of Tristan da Cunha; they are uninhabited. Gough Island (90 sq. km) is 220 miles south of Tristan and has a meteorological station.

Tristan consists of a volcano rising to a height of 6,760 ft, with a circumference at its base of 21 miles. The volcano, believed to be extinct, erupted unexpectedly early in Oct. 1961. The whole population was evacuated without loss and settled temporarily in the UK. In 1963 they returned to Tristan where they all dwell in the settlement of Edinburgh. Before the disaster occurred the habitable area was a small plateau on the north west side of about 12 sq. miles, 100 ft above sea-level. Only about 30 acres was under cultivation, three-quarters of it for potatoes. There were apple and peach trees. Potatoes remain the chief crop, cattle, sheep and pigs are now reared, and fish are plentiful.

Population in 1880, 109; in 1983, 296. The original inhabitants were shipwrecked sailors and soldiers who remained behind when the garrison from St Helena was withdrawn in 1817.

At the end of April 1942 Tristan da Cunha was commissioned as HMS *Atlantic Isle*, and became an important meteorological and radio station. In Jan. 1949 a South African company commenced crawfishing operations. An Administrator was appointed at the end of 1948 and a body of basic law brought into operation. The Island Council, which was set up in 1932, in 1982 consisted of a Chief Islander, 3 nominated and 7 elected members under the chairmanship of the Administrator.

Administrator: R. Perry.

Books of Reference

Crawford, A., *Tristan da Cunha and the Roaring Forties.* Edinburgh, 1982
Cross, A., *Saint Helena.* Newton Abbot, 1980
Munch, P. A., *Sociology of Tristan da Cunha.* Oslo, 1945.—*Crisis in Utopia.* New York, 1971

ST LUCIA

Capital: Castries
Population: 143,600 (1987)
GNP per capita: US$1,105 (1984)

HISTORY. St Lucia was discovered about 1500 A.D. Attempts to colonize the island by the English took place in 1605 and 1638. The French settled in 1650 and St Lucia was ceded to Britain in 1814. Self-government was achieved in 1967 and independence on 22 Feb. 1979.

AREA AND POPULATION. St Lucia is a small island of the Lesser Antilles situated in the Eastern Caribbean between Martinique and St Vincent, with an area of 238 sq. miles (617 sq. km); population (census, 1980) 120,300. Estimate (1987) 143,600. The capital is Castries (population, 1980, 45,763). Life expectancy (1985) was 68·6 (men) and 75·5 (women).

CLIMATE. The climate is tropical, with a dry season lasting from Jan. to April, a wet season from May to Aug., followed by an Indian summer for two months, but most rain falls in Nov. and Dec. Amounts vary over the year, according to altitude, from 60″ (1,500 mm) to 138″ (3,450 mm). Temperatures are uniform at about 80°F (26·7°C).

CONSTITUTION AND GOVERNMENT. There is a 17-seat House of Assembly elected for 5 years; an 11-seat Senate appointed by the Governor-General, 6 on the advice of the Prime Minister, 3 on the advice of the Leader of the Opposition, and 2 'after consultation with appropriate religious, economic or social bodies or associations'.

At the elections in April 1987, the United Workers' Party gained 9 seats, and the St Lucia Labour Party, 8.

Governor-General: Sir Vincent Floissac, CMG, QC.
Prime Minister: Rt Hon. John George Melvin Compton.
Flag: Blue with a design of a black triangle edged in white, bearing a smaller yellow triangle, in the centre.

INTERNATIONAL RELATIONS

Membership. St Lucia is a member of UN, OAS, Caricom, the Commonwealth and is an ACP state of the EEC.

ECONOMY

Planning. The aim of the Development Plan, 1977–90, is to develop agriculture to diversify production and to contain rural-urban drift.

Budget. The budget in 1986–87 amounted to EC$232·6m. expenditure.

Banking. There are Barclays Bank International with 4 branches and 2 agencies, the Royal Bank of Canada with 1 branch, the Bank of Nova Scotia with 3 branches, the Canadian Imperial Bank of Commerce and the St Lucia Co-operative bank with 2 branches each, the National Development Bank with 1 branch and the National Commercial Bank with 3 branches.

INDUSTRY AND TRADE

Industry. In 1986, laundry soap, coconut meal, rum, beverages and clothing were the chief products.

Agriculture. Bananas, cocoa, copra and coconut oil are the chief products.
Livestock (1986): Cattle, 12,000; pigs, 12,000; sheep, 15,000; goats, 12,000.

Commerce. Value of imports (1985), EC$337·5m.; of exports, EC$140·5m., including coconut oil, cocoa beans, copra and bananas. Main items of imports were artificial silk and cotton piece-goods, cement, plastic goods, iron and steel products, hardware, motor vehicles, agricultural machinery, fertilizers, wheat flour, codfish and rice, meat and meat preparations.

Total trade between St Lucia and UK (British Department of Trade returns, in £1,000 sterling):

	1985	1986	1987
Imports to UK	44,047	59,855	40,908
Exports and re-exports from UK	11,550	12,441	13,196

Tourism. The total number of visitors during 1986 was 171,000.

COMMUNICATIONS

Roads. The island has 500 miles of main and secondary roads, and 9,133 vehicles in 1984.

Aviation. The island is served on a scheduled basis by Leeward Islands Air Transport, British West Indian Airways, Eastern Airline, British Airways, Pan Am, Caribbean Airways and Air Canada. There are 2 airfields—Hewanorra International Airport, with 9,000 ft runway, and Vigie.

Shipping. There are 2 ports, Castries and Vieux Fort.

Post and Broadcasting. There were (1986) 13,654 telephone instruments coupled to 7,960 exchange lines; 157 telex machines, and telegram service. There were 5,000 TV and 92,000 radio receivers in 1985.

Cinemas. There were 8 cinemas in 1986.

JUSTICE, RELIGION, EDUCATION AND WELFARE

Justice. The island is divided into 2 judicial districts, and there are 9 magistrates' courts. Appeals lie with the Eastern Caribbean Supreme Court of Appeal.

Police establishment in 1986 was 14 officers, 16 inspectors, 11 station sergeants, 39 sergeants, 58 corporals and 333 constables.

Religion. In 1981 over 86% of the population was Roman Catholic.

Education (1985–86). 79 primary schools, with 32,273 pupils on roll. Primary education is free and compulsory by law, but the legislation is not enforced. There are 12 secondary schools (2 Roman Catholic, 1 Seventh-day Adventist, 9 government) with 5,665 pupils. There is 1 technical college with (1985–86) 223 students and 1 teachers' college with (1985–86) 123 students.

Health. Victoria Hospital (in Castries) has 213 beds; there is also a 162-bed mental hospital, 3 other hospitals (150 beds) and 29 health centres. In 1984 there were 58 doctors, 5 dentists and 236 nursing personnel.

DIPLOMATIC REPRESENTATIVES

Of St Lucia in Great Britain (10 Kensington Ct., London, W8)
High Commissioner: Richard Gunn.

Of Great Britain in St Lucia (Colombus Sq., Castries)
High Commissioner: Kevin F. X. Burns, CMG (resides in Bridgetown).

Of St Lucia in the USA and to the United Nations
Ambassador: Dr Joseph Edsel Edmunds.

Book of Reference

Ellis, G., *St Lucia: Helen of the West Indies.* London, 1985
Library: The Central Library, Castries. *Acting Librarian:* Frances Niles.

ST VINCENT AND THE GRENADINES

Capital: Kingstown
Population: 138,000 (1985)
GNP per capita: US$860 (1983)

HISTORY. The date of discovery of St Vincent was 22 January 1498. In 1969 St Vincent became a self-governing Associated State of UK and acquired full independence on 27 Oct. 1979.

AREA AND POPULATION. St Vincent is an island of the Lesser Antilles, situated in the Eastern Caribbean between St Lucia and Grenada, from which latter it is separated by a chain of small islands known as the Grenadines. The total area of 388 sq. km (150 sq. miles) comprise the island of St Vincent itself (345 sq. km) and the Northern Grenadines (43 sq. km) of which the largest are Bequia, Mustique, Canouan, Mayreau and Union.

The population at the 1970 Census was 86,314; latest estimate (1985) was 138,000 of whom 10,000 lived on the Northern Grenadines. The capital, Kingstown, had 33,694 inhabitants in 1982 (including suburbs). The population is mainly of black (66%) and mixed (24%) origin, with small white, Asian and Amerindian minorities.

Vital statistics (1986): Live births, 2,910; still births, 21; deaths, 651; marriages, 349.

CLIMATE. The climate is tropical marine, with north-east Trades predominating and rainfall ranging from 150″ (3,750 mm) a year in the mountains to 60″ (1,500 mm) on the south-east coast. The rainy season is from June to Dec., and temperatures are equable throughout the year.

CONSTITUTION AND GOVERNMENT. The House of Assembly consists of 13 elected members, directly elected for a 5-year term from single-member constituencies, the Attorney-General (elected) and 6 Senators appointed by the Governor-General (4 on the advice of the Prime Minister and 2 on the advice of the Leader of the Opposition). At the General Elections held in July 1984, the New Democratic Party won 9 and the St Vincent Labour Party won 4 of the 13 elective seats in the House of Assembly.

Governor-General: Joseph Lambert Eustace.
Prime Minister: Rt. Hon. James Fitz Allen Mitchell.
Deputy Prime Minister: Edward Griffith.

National Flag: Three vertical stripes of blue, yellow, green, with the yellow of double width and charged with three green diamonds.

INTERNATIONAL RELATIONS

Membership. St Vincent and the Grenadines is a member of UN, OAS, Caricom, the Commonwealth and is an ACP state of the EEC.

ECONOMY

Planning. The Development Plan, 1986–89, aims to encourage exports, reduce imports and to develop agriculture.

Budget. Revenue (estimate), 1986–87, $173,804,000; expenditure, $173,804,000. Public debt at the end of the financial year 1985–86 was $57,905,110.

Currency. The currency is the Eastern Caribbean *dollar*. In March 1988, £1 = EC$4·79; US$1 = EC$2·70.

Banking. There are branches of Barclays Bank International, the Caribbean Banking Corporation, the Canadian Imperial Bank of Commerce, the Bank of Nova Scotia. Locally-owned banks: the National Commercial Bank, St Vincent Co-operative Bank and the St Vincent Agricultural Credit and Loan Bank.

ENERGY AND NATURAL RESOURCES

Electricity. Production (1986) 31m. kwh. Supply 230 volts; 50 Hz.

Agriculture. Agriculture accounted for 18·1% of GDP in 1986. According to the 1985–86 census of agriculture, 29,649 acres of the total acreage of 85,120 were classified as agricultural lands; 5,500 acres were under forest and woodland and all other lands accounted for 1,030 acres. The total arable land was about 8,932 acres, of which 4,016 acres were under temporary crops, 2,256 acres under temporary pasture, 2,289 acres under temporary fallow and other arable land covering 371 acres. 16,062 acres were under permanent crops, of which approximately 5,500 acres were under coconuts and 7,224 acres under bananas; the remainder produce cocoa, citrus, mangoes, avocado pears, guavas and miscellaneous crops. The sugar industry was closed down in 1985 although some sugar-cane will be grown for rum production. Production (1986, in tonnes): Coconuts, 22,000; bananas, 46,000.

Livestock (1986): Cattle, 8,000; pigs, 7,000; sheep, 14,000; goats, 4,000.

INDUSTRY AND TRADE

Industry. Industries include assembly of electronic equipment, manufacture of garments, electrical products, animal feeds and flour, corrugated galvanized sheets, exhaust systems, industrial gases, concrete blocks, plastics, soft drinks, beer and rum, wood products and furniture, and processing of milk, fruit juices and food items.

Commerce (1986). Imports, EC$235,637,439; exports, EC$174,434,598.

Principal exports, 1986 in EC$: Arrowroot starch, 978,163; eddoes and dasheen, 31,636,546; sweet potatoes, 15,430,821; tannias, 14,503,151; bananas, 53,322,040; coconuts, 824,403; mangoes, 951,543; yams, 1,101,959; plantain, 4,673,347.

Total trade between St Vincent and the Grenadines and UK (British Department of Trade returns, in £1,000 sterling):

	1985	1986	1987
Imports to UK	22,339	21,161	20,208
Exports and re-exports from UK	6,600	8,288	8,529

Labour (1987). The Department of Labour is charged with looking after the interest and welfare of all categories of workers, including providing advice and guidance to employers/employees and their organizations and enforcing the labour laws.

Tourism. There were 97,000 visitors in 1986.

COMMUNICATIONS

Roads. There were (1987) 620 km of all-weather roads, 453 km of rough motorable roads and 180 km of tracks.

Aviation. Scheduled services are operated daily by LIAT, Air Martinique and Winlink. Non-scheduled services are operated by Mustique Airways, Tropical Air Services, Aero-Services and St Lucia Airways. Passengers are able to travel daily through the chain of islands stretching as far north as San Juan, Puerto Rico and south to Trinidad. Connexions to the USA, Canada, South America and Europe are possible *via* Barbados, Antigua, Trinidad and St Lucia.

Shipping (1987): 38 auxiliary sailing vessels of 1,510 NRT entered and cleared. 659 motor vessels of 805,261 NRT entered and cleared. 47 tankers of 41,798 NRT bringing 18,925·13 tons of fuel entered.

Post and Broadcasting. There is a General Post Office at Kingstown and 49 district post offices. There is an automatic telephone system with (1987), 6,145 subscribers; 7,950 stations and a digital radio link to Bequia, Mustique and Union Island; VHF links Petit St Vincent and Palm Island. In 1987 there were 12,000 TV and 60,000 radio receivers.

Cinemas. There were 2 cinemas in 1987 with a seating capacity of 1,825.

JUSTICE, RELIGION, EDUCATION AND WELFARE

Justice (1986). There were 3,699 criminal matters disposed of in the 3 magisterial districts which comprise 11 courts. Strength of police force (1982), 525 (including 12 officers).

Religion. At the 1970 Census, 47% of the population was Anglican, 28% Methodist and 13% Roman Catholic.

Education (1986). Sixty-one primary schools; pupils on roll, 24,561. Expenditure on primary education, $13,674,257. There is also a secondary school for girls (684 pupils), a co-educational school (578 pupils), as well as 11 assisted secondary schools (3,246 pupils) and 7 rural secondary schools with 1,729 pupils. Expenditure on secondary education, $3,789,128. There is a private secondary school with 298 pupils.

Health. There were (1987) a General Hospital in Kingstown (204 beds), 5 rural hospitals at Chateaubelair, Georgetown, Mesopotamia, Bequia and Union Island; 1 psychiatric hospital (120 beds); 1 geriatric hospital (120 beds); 35 medical clinics and 1 private hospital (10 beds). In 1987 there were 39 doctors, 2 dentists, 80 technical staff, 236 trained nursing personnel and 85 community health aides.

Library: St Vincent Public Library, Kingstown. *Librarian:* Mrs Lorna Small.

DIPLOMATIC REPRESENTATIVES

Of St Vincent and the Grenadines in Great Britain (10 Kensington Ct, London, W8)
High Commissioner: Richard Gunn.

Of Great Britain in St Vincent and the Grenadines
High Commissioner: K. F. X. Burns, CMG (resides in Bridgetown).

Of St Vincent and the Grenadines to the UN
Ambassador: Jonathan Peters.

SAN MARINO

Capital: San Marino
Population: 22,638 (1986)

Repubblica di San Marino

HISTORY. On 22 March 1862 San Marino concluded a treaty of friendship and co-operation, including a *de facto* customs union with the kingdom of Italy, preserving the independence of the ancient republic, although completely surrounded by Italian territory. The treaty was renewed on 27 March 1872, 28 June 1897 and 31 March 1939, with several amendments 1942–85.

The republic has extradition treaties with Belgium, France, the Netherlands, UK and USA.

AREA AND POPULATION. San Marino is a land-locked state in central Italy, 20 km from the Adriatic. The frontier line is 38·6 km in length, area is 61·19 sq. km (24·1 sq. miles) and the population (31 Dec. 1986), 22,638; some 11,000 citizens live abroad. The capital, San Marino, had 4,363 inhabitants (1986); the largest town is Serravalle (7,109), an industrial centre in the north.

CONSTITUTION AND GOVERNMENT. The legislative power is vested in the Great and General Council of 60 members elected every 5 years by popular vote, 2 of whom are appointed every 6 months to act as regents *(Capitani reggenti).*

The elections held on 29 May 1983 gave 26 seats to the Christian Democrats, 15 to the Communists, 17 to Socialist parties, 2 to others.

The regents (who are Heads of State) exercise executive power together with the Congress of State *(Congresso di Stato),* which comprises the regents, 3 secretaries of state and 7 ministers, and through Commissions on social welfare, public works, etc.

National flag: Horizontally white over light blue, with the national arms over all in the centre.

DEFENCE. Military service is not obligatory, but all citizens between the ages of 16 and 55 can be called upon to defend the State. They may also serve as volunteers in the Military Corps.

ECONOMY. The budget (ordinary and extraordinary) for the financial year ending 31 Dec. 1986 balanced at 259,962,035,017 lire.

Wheat, barley, maize and vines are grown. The chief exports are wood machinery, chemicals, wine, textiles, tiles, varnishes and ceramics.

Italian currency is in general use, but the republic issues its own postage stamps and coins.

In 1985, 3m. tourists visited San Marino.

COMMUNICATIONS

Roads. A bus service connects San Marino with Rimini. There are 237 km of roads and (1986) 16,540 passenger cars and 3,225 commercial vehicles.

Post. In 1986 there were 11,707 telephones.

Cinemas. In 1987 there were 7 cinemas with a seating capacity of 1,000.

JUSTICE, RELIGION, EDUCATION AND WELFARE

Justice. Law is administered by a Commissioner for civil cases and a Commissioner for criminal cases (acting with a penal judge), from whom appeals can be made to a civil appeals judge and a criminal appeals judge respectively. The highest legal authority is, in certain cases, the *Consiglio dei XII*. Civil marriage was instituted in Sept. 1953 and divorce allowed in April 1986.

Religion. 95% of the population are Roman Catholic.

Education. There are 19 infant schools, 16 elementary schools, a secondary school and a grammar school, the diplomas of which are recognized by Italian universities. There is also a foreign languages school, a technical school and a trade and handicraft school.

Health. In 1987 there were 149 hospital beds and 60 doctors.

DIPLOMATIC REPRESENTATIVES

British Consul-General (resides at Florence): Ivor-Jon Rawlinson.
Consul-General in London: Lord Forte.

Books of Reference

Information: Office of Cultural Affairs and Information of the Department of Foreign Affairs.

Garbelotto, A., *Evoluzione storica della costituzione di S. Marino.* Milan, 1956
Matteini, N., *The Republic of San Marino.* San Marino, 1981
Packett, C. N., *Guide to the Republic of San Marino.* Bradford, 1970
Rossi, G., *San Marino.* San Marino, 1954

SÃO TOMÉ E PRINCIPE

Capital: São Tomé
Population: 113,000 (1987)
GNP per capita: US$310 (1983)

HISTORY. The islands of São Tomé and Príncipe, were discovered in 1471 by Pedro Escobar and João Gomes, and from 1522 constituted a Portugese colony. On 11 June 1951 it became an overseas province of Portugal.

On 26 Nov. 1974 the Government of Portugal and the liberation movement of São Tomé e Príncipe signed an agreement granting independence to the archipelago on 12 July 1975.

AREA AND POPULATION. The republic, which lies about 200 km off the west coast of Gabon, in the Gulf of Guinea, comprises the main islands of São Tomé (845 sq. km) and Príncipe and several smaller islets including Pedras Tinhosas and Rolas. It has a total area of 1,001 sq. km (387 sq. miles). Total population (census, 1981) 96,611. Estimate (1987) 113,000.

The areas and populations of the 2 provinces were as follows:

Province	Sq. km	Census 1981	Estimate 1987	Chief town	Estimate 1984
São Tomé	859	91,356	106,900	São Tomé	34,997
Príncipe	142	5,255	6,100	São António	1,000

The official language is Portuguese, but 90% speak Fang, a Bantu language.
Vital statistics (1985): Births, 3,700; deaths, 900.

CLIMATE. The tropical climate is modified by altitude and the effect of the cool Benguela current. The wet season is generally from Oct. to May, but rainfall varies very much, from 40″ (1,000 mm) in the hot and humid north-east to 150–200″ (3,800–5,000 mm) on the plateau. São Tomé. Jan. 79°F (26·1°C), July 75°F (23·9°C). Annual rainfall 38″ (951 mm).

CONSTITUTION AND GOVERNMENT. A new constitution was approved by the Constitutional Assembly (elected 6 July 1975) on 12 Dec. 1975. Under it, the sole legal party is the *Movimento de Libertação de São Tomé e Príncipe*, who nominate candidates for the Presidency and People's Assembly. The President is elected by the People's Assembly for a 4-year term; he is also head of government and appoints a Cabinet of Ministers to assist him. The 40-member People's Assembly is also elected for 4 years.

President, Prime Minister, Economy and Planning: Dr Manuel Pinto da Costa (re-elected 30 Sept. 1985).

Foreign Affairs: Guilherme Posser da Costa.

Flag: Three horizontal stripes of green, yellow, green, with the yellow of double width and bearing 2 black stars; in the hoist a red triangle over all.

Local government: São Tomé province comprises 6 districts, while Príncipe province forms a seventh district.

DEFENCE. About 700 Angolan and 200 Cuban military personnel are stationed on the islands.

INTERNATIONAL RELATIONS

Membership. São Tomé e Príncipe is a member of UN, OAU and is an ACP state of EEC.

ECONOMY

Planning. The 5-year Development Plan (1986–90) gives priority to industry, energy, construction and agriculture.

Budget. In 1984 the budget envisaged revenue of 654·9m. dobra and expenditure of 921m. dobra.

Currency. The currency is the *dobra*, introduced in 1977, divided into 100 *centavos*. In March 1988, £1 = 130·54 *dobra*; US$1 = 73·47 *dobra*.

Banking. *Banco Nacional de São Tomé e Príncipe* (established, 1975) is the central bank.

ENERGY AND NATURAL RESOURCES

Electricity. Production (1986) 3m. kwh.

Agriculture. Most land is state-owned and former plantations run as co-operatives. About 38% of the area is under cultivation. Production (1983 in tonnes): Cacao, 4,451; copra, 3,727; bananas, 3,641; palm oil (1982), 1,100. Food crops include cassava, sweet potatoes and yams. In 1986 there were 4,000 goats, 2,000 sheep, 3,000 pigs and 3,000 cattle.

Fisheries. The fishing industry is being developed, to exploit the rich tuna shoals. Catch (1984) 4,289 tonnes.

COMMERCE. Imports in 1984 amounted to 485·9m. dobras and exports to 539·6m. dobras the main exports being cocoa (80%), copra (15%), coffee, bananas and palm-oil. Portugal provided 30% of imports while the German Democratic Republic took 35% of exports, the Netherlands 18% and Portugal 15%.

Total trade between São Tomé e Príncipe and UK (British Department of Trade returns, in £1,000 sterling):

	1984	1985	1986	1987
Imports to UK	450	197	327	205
Exports and re-exports from UK	962	824	455	329

COMMUNICATIONS

Roads. There were 288 km of roads (198 paved) in 1975.

Aviation. São Tomé airport is linked by regular services to Douala, Lisbon, Luanda, Cabinda, Libreville, Malabo and Brazil, as well as to Príncipe.

Shipping. In 1975, 70 vessels entered the port of São Tomé to unload 26,693 tonnes and load 9,880 tonnes.

Post. There were (1983) 25,000 radio receivers and 6,074 telephones.

Cinemas. In 1972 there was 1 cinema with a seating capacity of 1,000.

Newspapers. In 1986 there were 2 weekly newspapers.

JUSTICE, RELIGION, EDUCATION AND WELFARE.

Justice. Members of the Supreme Court are appointed by the People's Assembly.

Religion. About 80% of the population are Roman Catholic.

Education. In 1984 there were 19,086 pupils and 517 teachers in 63 primary schools, 6,186 pupils and 300 teachers in 11 secondary schools, and 370 students and 35 teachers in 2 technical schools.

Health. In 1981 there were 38 doctors and 118 nursing personnel.

DIPLOMATIC REPRESENTATIVES

Of Great Britain in São Tomé and Príncipe
Ambassador: M. J. C. Glaze (resides in Luanda).

Of São Tomé and Príncipe in the USA and to the United Nations
Ambassador: Joaquim Rafael Branco.

SAUDI ARABIA

Capital: Riyadh
Population: 11·52m. (1986)
GNP per capita: US$8,000 (1985)

al-Mamlaka al-'Arabiya as-Sa'udiya

HISTORY. Saudi Arabia was founded by Abdul Aziz ibn Abdur-Rahman al-Faisal Al Sa'ud, GCB, GCIE (born about 1880; died 9 Nov. 1953), who had been proclaimed King of the Hejaz on 8 Jan. 1926 and had in 1927 changed his title of Sultan of Nejd and its dependencies to that of king, thus becoming 'King of the Hejaz and of Nejd and its Dependencies'. On 20 May 1927 a treaty was signed at Jiddah between Great Britain and Ibn Sa'ud, by which the former recognized the complete independence of the dominions of the latter. The name of the State was changed to 'The Saudi Arabian Kingdom' by decree of 23 Sept. 1932.

AREA AND POPULATION. Saudi Arabia, which occupies over 70% of the Arabian peninsula, is bounded west by the Red Sea, east by the Gulf and the United Arab Emirates, north by Jordan, Iraq and Kuwait, south by the Yemen Arab Republic, the People's Democratic Republic of Yemen and Oman. The total area is estimated to be 849,400 sq. miles (2·2m. sq. km).

The principal cities of the Western Province (formerly *Hejaz*) are Jiddah (561,104 inhabitants at the 1974 Census), Mecca (366,801), Taif (204,857) and Medina (198,196); of the Central Province (formerly *Nejd*) are Riyadh, the national capital (666,840), Buraidah (69,940), Ha'il (40,502), Uneiza and Al-Kharj; of the Northern Province are Tabouk (74,825), Al-Jawf and Sakaka; of the Eastern Province (formerly *Al-Hasa*) are Dammam (127,844), Hofuf (101,271), Haradh (100,000), Al-Mobarraz (54,325), Al-Khobar (48,817) and Qatif; and of the Southern Province (formerly *Asir*) are Khamis-Mushait (49,581), Najran (47,501), Jisan (32,814) and Abha (30,150). New industrial cities are being built at Jubail and Yanbu on the Gulf.

Taif, about 3,800ft above sea-level and some 50 miles from Mecca, is a summer resort.

The total population was (1974 census) 7,012,642, of which 5,128,655 were categorized as settled and 1,883,987 as nomadic. Estimate (1986) 11·52m.

CLIMATE. A desert climate, with very little rain and none at all from June to Dec. The months May to Sept. are very hot and humid, but winter temperatures are quite pleasant. Riyadh. Jan. 58°F (14·4°C), July 92°F (33·3°C). Annual rainfall 4″ (100 mm). Jiddah. Jan. 73°F (22·8°C), July 87°F (30·6°C). Annual rainfall 3″ (81 mm).

KING. Fahd ibn Abdul Aziz; succeeded in May 1982, after King Khalid's death. *Crown Prince:* Prince Abdullah ibn Abdul Aziz, First Deputy Prime Minister, Commander of the National Guard, brother of the King.

National flag: Green, with the text 'There is no God but Allah and Mohammed is his prophet' in white Arabic script, and beneath this a white sabre.

CONSTITUTION AND GOVERNMENT. The Kingdom has been welded together from Hejaz, Nejd, Asir and Al-Hasa. Riyadh is the political capital and Mecca the religious capital. There is no formal Constitution.

The King has the post of Prime Minister.

First Deputy Prime Minister and Commander of the National Guard: Prince Abdullah ibn Abdul Aziz.
Second Deputy Prime Minister and Minister of Defence and Civil Aviation: Prince Sultan ibn Abdul Aziz.

Public Works and Housing: Prince Miteb ibn Abdul Aziz. *Interior:* Prince Naif ibn Abdul Aziz. *Foreign Affairs:* Prince Saud al Faisal. *Labour and Social Affairs:* Muhammad al-Ali al-Fayiz. *Communications:* Hussein Ibrahim al Mansouri. *Finance and National Economy:* Muhammad Ali Aba'l Khail. *Information:* Ali ibn Hasan al-Shaer. *Industry and Electricity:* Dr Abdul Aziz al Zamil. *Commerce:* Dr Sulaiman Abdul Aziz al Sulaim. *Justice:* Sheikh Ibrahim ibn Muhammad ibn Ibrahim al Shaikh. *Education and Acting Higher Education:* Dr Abdul Aziz al Abdullah al Khuwaiter. *Petroleum and Mineral Resources and Planning:* Hisham Nazer. *Haj Affairs, Waqfs:* Abdul Wahhab Ahmad Abdul Wasi. *Municipal and Rural Affairs:* Ibrahim ibn Abdullah al Angari. *Agriculture and Water:* Dr Abdul Rahman ibn Abdul Aziz ibn Hasan al Shaikh. *Health:* Faisal ibn Abdul Aziz al Hejailan. *Posts and Telecommunications:* Dr Alawi Darwish Kayyal. *Without Portfolio:* Fayez Badr. *Pilgrimage and Endowments:* Abdul Wahhab Ahmed Abdul Wasi. There are 7 Ministers of State.

There are provisions for the setting up of certain advisory councils, comprising a consultative Legislative Assembly in Mecca, municipal councils in each of the towns of Mecca, Medina and Jiddah, and village and tribal councils throughout the provinces. The country is divided for administrative purposes into 14 Regions (Emirates).

DEFENCE. The US maintains a Military Mission (with an Air Force element) as do France and Pakistan. Personnel are trained in Saudi Arabia, France, Pakistan, UK and the USA.

Army. The Army comprises 4 armoured brigades, 4 mechanized brigades, 1 airborne brigade, 1 Royal Guard regiment, 23 artillery battalions and 1 infantry brigade. Equipment is mainly US or French (M101, M109 and M198 artillery, M113 APCs, M60 tanks, AMX30 tanks. There are 15 surface-to-air batteries with HAWK and 17 with Shahine. Total strength of Army (1988) approximately 45,000. There are para-military forces with the Ministry of Interior; Frontier Force and Coastguard (approximately 8,500) and Special Security Force (1,800).

National Guard. The National Guard comprises 1 mechanized brigade (trained by the US), 1 Special Security Unit. An additional mechanized brigade is planned. Additionally there are a number of regular and irregular units, the total strength of the National Guard amounting to approximately 25,000. The National Guard's primary role is the protection of the Royal Family and vital points in the Kingdom. It does not come under command of the Ministry of Defence and Aviation. UK provides small advisory teams to the National Guard.

Navy. The Royal Saudi Naval Forces, with recent modernization programme impetus under the aegis of USA and France, comprise 4 new French-built guided missile frigates of 2,600 tons, 4 new US-built missile-armed fast corvettes of 800 tons, 9 fast missile craft of 380 tons (all completed in 1980–82 in USA), 3 *ex*-German torpedo boats, 4 US-built MSC-type coastal minesweepers, 2 new French-built armed replenishment ships of 10,500 tonnes each with 2 helicopters, 1 *ex*-US coastguard cutter, 8 new French-built patrol craft, 40 coastal patrol boats, 18 hovercraft, 2 air-sea rescue launches, 1 training ship, 4 utility landing craft, 12 minor landing craft, 1 salvage vessel, 2 tugs, and 2 royal yachts (with helicopter). New construction planned includes 2 large guided missile frigates, 6 submarines and a submarine parent ship. There are 24 Dauphin helicopters. An intensive training programme continued in USA and Saudi Arabia. $70m. was spent on three naval bases. The main port facilities are at Jubail and Jedda.

Naval personnel in 1988 totalled 7,500 officers and other ranks plus instructors and trainees. RSNF rely on considerable US and Pakistan support.

The Coast Guard operates over 450 craft including 160 coastal patrol craft, 300 inshore patrol cutters, 1 training ship, 3 small oilers, 4 fire-fighting craft, 2 yachts and 12 service craft. Eight large patrol craft are planned.

Air Force. Formed as a small army support unit in 1932, the Air Force has been built up considerably with British and US assistance since 1946. Complete re-equipment began in 1966 and delivery of 45 F-15 Eagles to equip 3 air superiority squadrons was made in 1982–84; they operate in conjunction with 5 E-3A Sentry AWACS aircraft and 8 KC-707 flight refuelling tankers. Current combat units include 3 squadrons of F-5E Tiger II supersonic fighter-bombers and RF-5E Tigereye reconnaissance aircraft, supported by a conversion unit with F-5B/F combat trainers. One squadron has formed with Tornado strike aircraft, of which 48 are on order, plus 24 Tornado interceptors. Two squadrons of Strikemaster light jet attack/trainers are based at the King Faisal Air Academy, Riyadh, together with 12 Reims/Cessna FR172 piston-engined primary trainers, PC-9 basic trainers, Hawk advanced trainers and Jetstream navigation trainers. Other types in current service include 40 C-130E/H KC-130H Hercules transports and tankers, 4 C-130H hospital aircraft, 1 Boeing 747 SP, 1 Boeing 747-200, 1 Boeing 737, 1 Boeing 707, 4 CN-235s and 2 JetStar VIP jet transports, more than 60 Agusta-Bell 205, 212 and JetRanger helicopters, 2 Agusta AS-61A-4 VIP transport helicopters and communications aircraft. Personnel (1988), about 15,000.

Air Defence Command. This separate Command was formerly part of the Army, which retains a point air defence capability. It is heavily reliant on Pakistan assistance, particularly manpower. Equipment comprises approximately 18 Crotale missile systems, 15 batteries of Improved Hawk surface-to-air missiles, 30 mm Oerlikon and 20 mm Vulcan guns.

INTERNATIONAL RELATIONS

Membership. Saudi Arabia is a member of UN, the Arab League, the Gulf Co-operation Council and OPEC.

ECONOMY

Planning. The third development plan ran 1980–85, and emphasized industrial development and the training of an indigenous work force. The fourth development plan 1985–90 was launched on 22 March 1985. Expenditure is envisaged at US$277,000m.

Budget. In 1986 the financial year was changed to the calendar year. The 1988 budget provided for expenditure of 141,200m. rials.
There is no public debt.

Currency. The paper *rial* is divided into 100 *halalas*. In March 1988, £1 = 6·64 *rials*; US$1 = 3·75 *rials*.

Banking. The Saudi Arabian Monetary Agency, established in 1953, is the central bank and the government's fiscal agent. There are 11 commercial banks. Two are wholly owned by Saudi interests (National Commercial Bank and the Riyadh Bank). The other 9 are majority-owned by Saudi shareholders. In 1985 total deposits in commercial banks were US$111,000m. and total assets were 143,000m. rials.

ENERGY AND NATURAL RESOURCES

Electricity. 49,925m. kwh. was generated by the main electricity companies in 1985. Supply 127 and 220 volts; 50 and 60 Hz.

Oil. The first general geologic–geographical survey of Saudi Arabia was completed in 1961 under the joint sponsorship of the Saudi Arabian and US governments but surveying continues. Reserves (1986) 167,000m. bbls.
Oil production began in 1938 by Aramco, which is now 100% state-owned and accounts for about 97% of total crude oil production, with Getty and the Arabian Oil Co. accounting for the remainder.
Crude oil production in 1987 was 209·5m. tonnes. Crude oil exports in 1985 were 1,216m. bbls, of which Aramco provided 97·4%, Arabian Oil 1·94% and Getty Oil 0·6%. 1985 oil exports earned US$30,000m. (95m. for crude) and Aramco earned 98% of this total.
Production comes from 14 major oilfields, mostly in the Eastern Region, the

most important of which are Ghawar (believed to be the world's largest oilfield), Abqaiq, Safaniyah (the largest offshore field) and Berri.

New fields have been discovered onshore at Farhah and Assahba and deeper pools offshore at Marjan, Safaniya and Zuluf, and during 1984 117 new wells were drilled and 4 seismic explorations conducted.

In 1981 a pipeline from the eastern oilfields to the Red Sea oil terminal at Yanbu was completed and a link to the Iraqi oilfields was completed in 1985.

In early 1986 there were 5 domestic refineries: Ras Tanura, refining capacity 450,000 bbls per day (Aramco); Riyadh, 120,000 bbls per day, Jiddah, 96,000 bbls per day and Yanbu, 170,000 bbls per day (Petromin); Rasal-Khafji, 13,000 bbls per day (Arabian Oil Co.); as well as 3 joint venture export refineries: Yanbu, 250,000 bbls per day (Petromin/Mobil Oil); Jubail, 250,000 bbls per day (Petromin/Shell Saudi Arabia); Rabigh, 325,000 bbls per day (Petromin/Petrola International). Aramco has added a 300 tonne a day sulphur plant to Ras Tanura and operates a 400 tonnes a day desulphurization plant at Jubail.

Gas. In 1984 production of liquefied natural gas from oilfield associated and dissolved gas was 355,059 bbls per day.

Water Resources. Intensive efforts are underway to provide adequate supplies of water for urban, industrial, rural and agricultural use. There is an important programme to tap non-renewable (3,450m. cu. metres per annum) and renewable (1,145m. cu. metres) water reserves by wells and small dams, and there are plans to reclaim urban waste water. Most investment however has gone into seawater desalination. By early 1985 22 plants in 21 towns had the capacity to produce 2·1m. metres per day and 5 more, totalling 444,200 cu. metres per day were under construction. Another 10, amounting to 475,682 cu. metres per day, were at various stages of planning.

Minerals. Surveys were launched during the second and third development plans to investigate potential mineral wealth other than oil. Deposits of several minerals including viable quantities of coal, iron and gold have been found. There are also reports of uranium deposits.

Agriculture. Since 1970 the Government has devoted huge resources to raise the Kingdom's agricultural potential, and spent substantially on desert reclamation, irrigation schemes, drainage and control of surface water and control of moving sands. Undeveloped land has been distributed to farmers and there are research and extension programmes. Large scale private investment has concentrated on meat, poultry and dairy production.

Production, 1985 (in 1,000 tonnes) were: Dates, 458; tomatoes, 367; water melons, 509; wheat, 1,700; grapes, 79; milk, 550; poultry meat, 250; red meat, 133; eggs, 130.

Livestock estimates for 1985 include 540,000 cattle, 111,000 asses, 171,000 camels, 3·8m. sheep and 2,454,000 goats.

Fisheries. Saudi Fisheries, established in 1981, has introduced a wide variety of fish to the domestic market and opened up a thriving export business in shrimps. Annual catch between 16,000 and 20,000 tonnes.

INDUSTRY AND TRADE

Industry. The Government actively encourages the establishment of manufacturing industries in the country. The policy includes the provision of industrial estates and loans covering 50% of capital investment. The Government has also established two industrial poles at Jubail and Yanbu, to be the focus of heavy industrial development. Linked by gas and oil pipelines both are to have petrochemical complexes producing, initially, ethylene and methanol, for which agreements have been signed with American and Japanese companies. Nine plants for petrochemicals were on stream in 1988. In addition an integrated steel complex (German partners) and a urea fertilizer factory (Taiwanese), both in Jubail started production in 1983. A new pharmaceutical plant is scheduled for completion in 1990.

Employment. The expatriate labour force grew by an average of 11·7% a year between 1980 and 1985. The proportion of non-Saudis in the total labour force rose from 28·2% in 1975 to 60% by 1985.

Commerce. Exports in 1986 (in 1m. rials) 74,377 of which crude oil, 73%; refined oil, 12%; petro-chemicals, 3·5%. Total imports (1986) 70,780m. rials. Major export destinations in 1984 (value in US$1m.) included: Japan, 13,367; USA, 3,644; Singapore, 2,423. Major import sources in 1984 (value in 1m. rials) included: Japan, 23,569; USA, 20,655; Federal Republic of Germany, 9,861; France, 9,253; Italy, 8,595.

Total trade between Saudi Arabia and UK (British Department of Trade returns, in £1,000 sterling):

	1983	1984	1985	1986	1987
Imports to UK	897,702	545,149	483,634	435,930	383,143
Exports and re-exports from UK	1,478,587	1,387,163	1,256,081	1,507,062	1,978,440

Tourism. In 1984 there were nearly 2m. pilgrims to Mecca from abroad.

COMMUNICATIONS

Roads. All the main regions and population centres of the Kingdom are linked by asphalted roads, of which there were 29,655 km in 1985 and 52,226 km of graded, unpaved agricultural roads. An additional 12,492 km of roads were under construction including the Trans-Peninsula Expressway. There are road links with Yemen, Jordan, Kuwait and Qatar, and a causeway link to Bahrain is being built. In 1985 there were 2m. passenger cars, 2m. commercial vehicles and about 41,000 buses.

Railways. A railway from Riyadh to Dammam on the Gulf (571 km, 1,435 mm gauge) *via* Dhahran and the oilfields Abqaiq, Ithmaniya (near Hofuf) and Haradh was completed in Oct. 1951. A 'dry port' at Riyadh station opened in 1981, and a new 465 km Dammam-Riyadh direct line was opened throughout in 1985. There are plans to extend the line *via* Medina to Jiddah. That section of the Hejaz Railway which is in Saudi Arabian territory is not now in working order, but studies have been initiated to restore the whole line from Damascus to Medina. In 1986 railways carried 76m. passenger-km and 758m. tonne-km.

Aviation. Saudi Arabian Air Lines, a government-owned company operates regular internal air services, and international routes to Africa, the Middle East, Europe and the Far East, as well as special flights for pilgrims. There are 3 major international airports at Jiddah, Dhahran and Riyadh and 19 domestic airports. King Fahd International Airport in Eastern Province is due to be completed in 1990. In 1985, 28·6m. passengers and 300,000 tonnes of cargo were carried.

Shipping. The ports of Dammam and Jubail on the Gulf and Jiddah, Yanbu and Jizan on the Red Sea had 143 deep-water piers by 1985 and discharged 35·9m. freight tonnes. Aramco operates a deepwater oil terminal at Ras Tanura.

Post and Broadcasting. Jiddah, Mecca, Taif, Riyadh and Dammam are linked by telephone, Jiddah and Cairo by radio-telephone. An international radio-telephone station at Riyadh was opened in 1956. Number of telephones (1985), 1,216,000. Number of post offices (1985) 591. In 1984 there were (estimate) 2·8m. radio receivers and 2·5m. television receivers.

Newspapers. In 1985 there were 8 daily newspapers in Arabic and 3 in English and 15 weekly or monthly magazines.

JUSTICE, RELIGION, EDUCATION AND WELFARE

Justice. The religious law of Islam is the common law of the land, and is administered by religious courts, at the head of which is a chief judge, who is responsible for the Department of Sharia (legal) Affairs. Sharia courts are concerned primarily with family inheritance and property matters. The Committee for the Settlement of Commercial Disputes is the commercial court. Other specialized courts or committees include one dealing exclusively with labour and employment matters; the Negotiable Instruments Committee, which deals with cases relating to cheques, bills of exchange and promissory notes, and the Board of Grievances, whose preserve is disputes with the government or its agencies and which also has jurisdiction in trademark-infringement cases and is the authority for enforcing foreign court judgements.

Religion. About 85% are Sunni Moslems and 15% Shiites.

Education. Schooling is in three stages, primary, intermediate and secondary which is to prepare older pupils for university; pre-primary schools are being introduced. Education is free in all these stages; monthly scholarships are paid to students in higher education and certain allowances are paid at general education level. Girls' education is administered separately. In 1985 there were 500 pre-primary schools with 55,000 pupils, 7,612 primary schools with 1,242,000 pupils and 79,000 teachers, and 3,314 intermediate/secondary schools with 530,542 students and 40,326 teachers. There were also adult literacy classes (158,521 students, 46% women), and special schools for 2,564 handicapped children. There were 176 teacher-training schools in 1985.

In 1985 there were 24 vocational centres, where 4,515 primary school graduates were instructed in basic trades. There were also 8 technical and 26 commercial secondary schools, taking 11,159 intermediate school graduates, and 2 technical and 3 commercial higher institutes (627 students), 21 more advanced industrial, commercial and agricultural education institutes.

University courses concentrating on science, engineering, agriculture and medicine, but also covering education, commerce and arts, are available at the King Abdul Aziz University, Jiddah, King Saud University, Riyadh and King Faisal University, Dammam and Hofuf. There are two branches of King Saud University at Abha and Qaseem. King Abdul Aziz University had a branch campus at Taif. Specialized engineering studies are available at the University of Petroleum and Minerals, Dhahran, and Arabic and Sharia law studies at the Islamic University, Medina, Imam Mohammad bin Saud University, Riyadh and the Um-AlQura University, Makkah. There were 93,000 university students (35,000 women) and 4,000 post-graduate students in 1984–85.

Welfare. The Ministry of Health is responsible for medical services, serving both Saudi citizens, foreign residents and pilgrims. In 1985 there were 104 hospitals with 20,463 beds, 1,299 clinics and health centres, 8,243 doctors, 16,443 nurses and midwives, 8,858 technical assistants. There were also 73 private hospitals (10,244 beds) employing 6,096 doctors. The Jiddah Quarantine Centre, designed by WHO and primarily for pilgrims, can take 2,400 patients. In 1984 there were 15 schools for female nurses and 14 institutes for male trainees. There is a strict system of health controls for visiting pilgrims and strict supervision of sanitation and water supply.

DIPLOMATIC REPRESENTATIVES

Of Saudi Arabia in Great Britain (30 Belgrave Sq., London, SW1X 8QB)
Ambassador; Sheikh Nasser H. Almanqour, GCVO.

Of Great Britain in Saudi Arabia (PO Box 94351, Riyadh)
Ambassador: Stephen Egerton, CMG.

Of Saudi Arabia in the USA (601 New Hampshire Ave., NW, Washington, D.C., 20037)
Ambassador: HRH Prince Bandar bin Sultan.

Of the USA in Saudi Arabia (PO Box 9041, Riyadh)
Ambassador: Hume Horan.

Of Saudi Arabia to the United Nations
Ambassador: Samir Shihabi.

Books of Reference

Anderson, N., *The Kingdom of Saudi Arabia*. (Rev. ed.). London, 1982
Clements, F. A., *Saudi Arabia*. [Bibliography] Oxford and Santa Barbara, 1979
Hajrah, H. H., *Land Distribution in Saudi Arabia*. London, 1982
Helms, C. M., *The Cohesion of Saudi Arabia*. Baltimore, 1981
Holden, D. and Johns, R., *The House of Saud*. London and New York, 1981
Looney, R. E., *Saudi Arabia's Development Potential*. Lexington, 1982
McMaster, B., *The Definitive Guide to Living in Saudi Arabia*. London, 1980
Niblock, T., *State, Society and Economy in Saudi Arabia*. New York, 1981
Philipp, H.-J., *Saudi Arabia: Bibliography on Society, Politics, Economics*. Munich, 1984
Presley, J. R., *A Guide to the Saudi Arabian Economy*. London, 1984
Quandt, W. B., *Saudi Arabia in the 1980's: Foreign Policy, Security and Oil*. Washington, 1981
Safran, N., *Saudi Arabia: The Ceaseless Quest for Security*. Harvard Univ. Press, 1985

SENEGAL

République du Sénégal

Capital: Dakar
Population: 6·7m. (1986)
GNP per capita: US$360 (1984)

HISTORY. France established a fort at Saint-Louis in 1659 and later acquired other coastal settlements from the Dutch; the interior was occupied in 1854–65. Senegal became a territory of French West Africa in 1902 and an autonomous state within the French Community on 25 Nov. 1958. On 4 April 1959 Senegal joined with French Sudan to form the Federation of Mali, which achieved independence on 20 June 1960, but on 22 Aug. Senegal withdrew from the Federation and became a separate independent republic. Senegal was a one-Party state from 1966 until 1974, when a pluralist system was re-established. Léopold Sédar Senghor, President since independence, resigned on 31 Dec. 1980 and was succeeded by his Prime Minister, Abdou Diouf. From 1 Feb. 1982 Senegal joined with Gambia to form a Confederation of Senegambia.

AREA AND POPULATION. Senegal is bounded by Mauritania to the north and north-east, Mali to the east, Guinea and Guinea-Bissau to the south and the Atlantic to the west with The Gambia forming an enclave along that shore. The republic has a total area of 196,192 sq. km; the population (census, 1976) 4,907,507 (estimate, 1986) 6,700,000.

The areas (in sq. km), Census populations and capitals of the 10 regions are:

Region	sq. km	1976 Census	Capital	1979 Estimate
Casamance [1]	28,350	736,527	Ziguinchor	79,464
Dakar	550	984,660	Dakar	978,553
Diourbel	4,359	425,113	Diourbel	55,307
Louga	29,188	417,137	Louga	37,665 [2]
Saint-Louis	44,127	528,473	Saint-Louis	96,594
Sine-Saloum [3]	23,945	1,007,736	Kaolack	115,679
Tambacounda	57,602	286,148	Tambacounda	29,054
Thiès	6,601	698,994	Thiès	126,886

[1] Before division into Kolda and Ziguinchor regions in July 1984. [2] 1976.
[3] Before division into Fatick and Kaolack regions in July 1984.

Ethnic groups are the Wolof (36% of the population), Serer (19%), Fulani (13%), Tukulor (9%), Diola (8%), Malinké (6%), Bambara (6%) and Sarakole (2%).

CLIMATE. A tropical climate with wet and dry seasons. The rains fall almost exclusively in the hot season, from June to Oct., with high humidity. Dakar. Jan. 72°F (22·2°C), July 82°F (27·8°C). Annual rainfall 22″ (541 mm).

CONSTITUTION AND GOVERNMENT. Under the Constitution promulgated on 7 Mar. 1963 (as subsequently amended) there are simultaneous elections by universal adult suffrage for 5-year terms for both the Presidency and for the unicameral 120-member National Assembly; for the latter 60 members are elected in single-member constituencies and 60 by a form of proportional representation.

In the general election of Feb. 1983 the *Parti socialiste* gained 111 seats, the *Parti démocratique sénégalais* 8 seats and the *Rassemblement national democratique* 1.

On 14 Nov. 1981, President Diouf of Senegal and President Jawara of The Gambia issued a joint communiqué proposing the establishment of a confederation, to be known as Senegambia. Both parliaments ratified the agreement at the end of the year. The instruments of ratification were exchanged in Banjul on 11 Jan. 1982 and the Confederation formally came into existence on 1 Feb.

The agreement stated that each confederal state shall maintain its independence and sovereignty and calls for the integration of the armed security forces, economic and monetary union, co-operation in the fields of communications and external relations, and the establishment of joint institutions (*i.e.* President, Vice President, Council of Ministers, Confederal Parliament). The President of the Confederation would be President Diouf, and the Vice President President Jawara, The Confederal Parliament would have one third Gambian representation and two thirds Senegalese.

President Jawara said in Nov. 1981 that 'the Confederation would not compromise any of the agreements which link The Gambia direct to Britain and the rest of the Commonwealth'.

President of the Republic: Abdou Diouf (took office in Jan. 1981, re-elected 1983 and 1988).

The Council of Ministers was composed as follows in Nov. 1987:

Foreign Affairs: Ibrahima Fall. *Defence:* Medoune Fall. *Interior:* Jean Collin. *Finance and Economic Affairs:* Mamadou Touré. *Supply:* Robert Sagna. *Culture:* Marhili Gassama. *Education:* Dr Iba der Thiam. *Rural Development:* Famara Ibrahima Sagna. *Industrial Development and Handicrafts:* Serigne Lamine Diop. *Housing and Urban Affairs:* Aliaune Diagne Coumba Aita. *Commerce:* Abdourahmane Touré. *Planning and Co-operation:* Cheikh Amidou Kané. *Communications:* Djibo Ka. *Justice and Keeper of the Seals:* Seydou Madani Sy *Civil Service, Employment and Labour:* André Sonko. *Public Health:* Marie Sarr Mbodj. *Social Affairs:* Mantoulaye Guene. *Water Resources:* Samba Yella Diop. *Youth and Sports:* Landing Sané. *Environment:* Cheikh Cissokho. *Emigration:* Mme. Fambaye Fall Diop. *Tourism:* Momar Talla Cissé. *Relations with Parliament:* Thierno Bâ. *Secretaries of State:* Moussa Ndoye *(Decentralisation)*, Mbaye Diouf *(Animal Resources, Fisheries and Livestock)*.

National flag: Three vertical strips of green, yellow, red, with a green star in the centre.

The official language is French.

Local Government. Senegal is divided into 10 *régions,* each with an appointed governor and an elected regional assembly. They are divided into 28 *départements,* each under an appointed *Préfet,* and thence into 99 *arrondissements.*

DEFENCE. There is selective conscription.

Army. The Army had a strength of 8,500 (1988), organized in 5 infantry battalions, 1 engineer, 1 armoured, 1 airborne, 1 commando and 1 artillery battalions, 1 reconnaissance squadron and minor units. Equipment includes about 70 armoured cars. There is also a paramilitary force of some 6,800 men.

Navy. The flotilla includes 1 new corvette, 1 patrol vessel, 3 patrol craft, 3 fast gunboats, 20 small patrol craft, 1 fishery protection trawler, 4 coastal patrol launches, 3 landing craft, 2 minor amphibious craft, 12 service craft, 1 tug and 1 training tender. Personnel (1988) totalled 450 officers and men.

Air Force. The Senegal Air Force, formed with French assistance, has 4 Rallye Guerrier and 5 Magister armed trainers and 1 Twin Otter for maritime patrol, 1 Boeing 727 and 1 Caravelle VIP transports, 6 F.27 twin-turboprop transports, 2 Broussard and 1 Cessna 337 liaison aircraft, 3 Puma, 1 Gazelle and 2 Alouette II helicopters. Personnel (1988) 500.

INTERNATIONAL RELATIONS

Membership. Senegal is a member of UN, OAU and is an ACP state of EEC.

ECONOMY

Planning. The Seventh 4-year Development Plan (1985–89) provides 645,000m. francs CFA for investment in the productive sector, improved infrastructure and for reducing foreign debt.

Budget. The budget for 1985–86 balanced at 316,869m. francs CFA.

Currency. The currency is the *franc* CFA, with a parity value of 50 *francs* CFA to 1 French *franc.*

Banking. The bank of issue is the *Banque Centrale des États de l'Afrique de l'Ouest*. The principal commercial bank is the *Union Sénégalaise de la Banque pour le Commerce et l'Industrie* (established 1961 with assistance from Crédit Lyonnais) in which the Senegalese government has the majority share-holding; also state controlled is the *Banque Nationale de Développement du Sénégal*. There are 3 private banks.

At 31 Dec. 1981 the savings banks had deposits of 85,120m. francs CFA.

ENERGY AND NATURAL RESOURCES

Electricity. Production (1986) was 737m. kwh. Supply 110 volts; 50 Hz.

Minerals. Extraction of phosphate rock in 1984 amounted to 1·9m. tonnes of calcium phosphate and 251,300 of aluminium phosphate. Titanium ores and zirconium are extracted from coastal (sand) deposits. Iron ore deposits amounting to an estimated 980m. tonnes have been located at La Faleme.

Agriculture. Of the total area (19·7m. hectares), 5·35m. were under cultivation, 5·84m. were pasture, 5·45m. were forested and 3·03m. were uncultivated land in 1981. The chief cash crops (1986 production in 1,000 tonnes) are groundnuts (720) and seed cotton (50); the main food crops are millet (703), sugar-cane (800), rice (128), maize (128), tomatoes (25), mangoes (34), onions (32).

Livestock (1986): 2,202,000 sheep, 1,104,000 goats, 2·2m. cattle, 194,000 pigs, 209,000 asses, 6,000 camels and 208,000 horses.

Forestry. Production (1983) amounted to 3·9m. cu. metres.

Fisheries. The 1982 catch totalled 226,481 tonnes; exports, 91,742 tonnes.

INDUSTRY AND TRADE

Industry. Dakar has numerous industrial works. A major ship-repairing complex has been constructed there for vessels of up to 28,000 tonnes. Cement production (1981) 386,000 tonnes; petroleum products, 726,400; groundnut oil, 125,200.

Trade Unions. There are two major unions, the *Union Nationale des Travailleurs Sénégalais* (government-controlled) and the *Confédération Nationale des Travailleurs Sénégalais* (independent) which broke away from the former in 1969.

Commerce. In 1984 imports totalled 437,100m. francs CFA and exports 233,974m. francs CFA. In 1984 28% of imports came from France and 31% of exports went to France. In 1982 petroleum products provided 26% of exports, fisheries 17%, phosphates 10% and groundnut oil 17%.

Total trade between Senegal and UK (British Department of Trade returns, in £1,000 sterling):

	1983	1984	1985	1986	1987
Imports to UK	22,333	23,789	17,671	13,881	11,307
Exports and re-exports from UK	13,212	15,772	13,514	12,328	11,878

Tourism. In 1986, 235,000 tourists visited Senegal.

COMMUNICATIONS

Roads. The length of roads (1983) was 14,700 km of which 3,650 km was bitumenized. In 1980 there were 79,258 passenger cars and 22,767 commercial vehicles.

Railways. There are 4 railway lines: Dakar-Kidira (continuing in Mali), Thiès-Saint-Louis (193 km), Guinguinéo-Kaolack (22 km), and Diourbel-Touba (46 km). Total length (1986), 905 km (metre gauge). In 1984–85 railways carried 32m. passenger-km and 1·5m. tonnes of freight.

Aviation. In 1979 aircraft disembarked 297,170 and embarked 322,921 passengers and disembarked 7,676 tonnes and embarked 5,605 tonnes of freight at Yoff (Dakar). There are also major airports at Saint-Louis, Tambacounda and Ziguinchor.

Shipping. In 1978, 4,870 vessels entered the port of Dakar. There is a river service on the Senegal from Saint-Louis to Podor (363 km) open throughout the year, and to Kayes (924 km) open from July to Oct. The Senegal River is closed to foreign flags. The Saloum River is navigable as far as Kaolack, the Casamance River as far as Ziguinchor.

Post and Broadcasting. There were, in 1978, 74 post offices. Telephones in 1978 numbered 42,105, of which 33,863 were in Dakar. In 1983 there were 2 radio networks with 320,000 radio receivers and 2 television stations with 50,200 receivers.

Cinemas. In 1975 there were 77 with a seating capacity of 33,500.

Newspapers. The main daily is *Le Soleil,* circulation (1984) 30,000.

JUSTICE, RELIGION, EDUCATION AND WELFARE

Justice. There are *juges de paix* in each *département* and a court of first instance in each region. Assize courts are situated in Dakar, Kaolack, Saint-Louis and Ziguinchor, while the Court of Appeal resides in Dakar.

Religion. The population (1980) was 91% Moslem, 6% Christian (mainly Roman Catholic) and 3% animist.

Education. Secondary education is provided at 11 *lycées,* 66 *collèges d'enseignement secondaire,* 2 *lycées techniques,* 2 *écoles normales* and 3 *cours normaux.* In 1981 there were 452,679 pupils and 10,586 teachers in 1,795 primary schools; and 91,081 pupils and 4,834 teachers in secondary schools. The University in Dakar, established on 24 Feb. 1957, had 11,474 students in 1984. A second university was being built (1985) at St Louis.

Health. In 1978 there were 44 hospitals with 7,092 beds; and in 1981, 449 doctors, 70 dentists, 139 pharmacists, 326 midwives and 1,766 state nursing personnel.

DIPLOMATIC REPRESENTATIVES

Of Senegal in Great Britain (11 Phillimore Gdns., London, W8 7QG)
Ambassador: Gen. Idrissa Fall, MBE (accredited 1 Nov. 1984)

Of Great Britain in Senegal (20 Rue du Docteur Guillet, Dakar)
Ambassador: John Macrae, CMG.

Of Senegal in the USA (2112 Wyoming Ave., NW, Washington, D.C., 20008)
Ambassador: Falilou Kane.

Of the USA in Senegal (Ave. Jean XXIII, Dakar)
Ambassador: Lannon Walker.

Of Senegal to the United Nations
Ambassador: Massamba Sarré

Books of Reference

Crowder, M., *Senegal: A Study in French Assimilation.* OUP, 1962
Gellar, S., *Senegal.* Boulder, 1982.—*Senegal: An African Nation between Islam and the West.* Aldershot, 1983
Samb, M. (ed.), *Spotlight on Senegal.* Dakar, 1972

SEYCHELLES

Capital: Victoria
Population: 67,000 (1987)
GNP per capita: US$2,320 (1984)

HISTORY. The islands were first colonized by the French in 1756, in order to establish plantations of spices to compete with the Dutch monopoly. They were captured by the English in 1794 and incorporated as a dependency of Mauritius in 1814. In Nov. 1903 the Seychelles archipelago became a separate colony. Internal self-government was achieved on 1 Oct. 1975 and independence as a republic within the Commonwealth on 29 June 1976. The first President, James Mancham, was deposed in a *coup* on 5 June 1977 and replaced by his Prime Minister.

AREA AND POPULATION. The Seychelles consists of 115 islands and islets in the Indian ocean, north of Madagascar, with a combined area of 175 sq. miles (453 sq. km) within two distinct groups. The Mahé or Granitic group of 41 islands cover 92 sq. miles (239 sq. km); the principal island is Mahé, with 59 sq. miles (153 sq. km) and 59,500 inhabitants at the 1987 census, the other inhabited islands of the group being Praslin, La Digue, Silhouette, Fregate and North, which together have 7,100 inhabitants.

The Outer or Coralline group comprises 74 islands spread over a wide area of ocean between the Mahé group and Madagascar, with a total land area of 83 sq. miles (214 sq. km) and a population of about 400. The main islands are the Amirante Isles (including Desroches, Poivre, Daros and Alphonse), Coetivy Island and Platte Island, all lying south of the Mahé group; the Farquhar, St Pierre and Providence Islands, north of Madagascar; and Aldabra, Astove, Assumption and the Cosmoledo Islands, about 1,000 km south-west of the Mahé group. Aldabra (whose lagoon covers 55 sq. miles), Farquhar and Desroches were transferred to the new British Indian Ocean Territory in 1965, but were returned by Britain to the Seychelles on the latter's independence in 1976. Population (1987, estimate) 67,000.

Vital statistics (1984): Births, 1,739; deaths, 488.

The official languages are Creole, English and French but 95% of the population speak Creole.

CLIMATE. Though close to the equator, the climate is tropical. The hot, wet season is from Dec. to May, when conditions are humid, but south-east trades bring cooler conditions from June to Nov. Temperatures are high throughout the year, but the islands lie outside the cyclone belt. Victoria. Jan. 80°F (26·7°C), July 78°F (25·6°C). Annual rainfall 95" (2,375 mm).

CONSTITUTION AND GOVERNMENT. A new Constitution came into force on 5 June 1979, under which the Seychelles People's Progressive Front is the sole legal Party and nominates all candidates for election. There is a unicameral People's Assembly comprising 23 members elected for 5 years with 2 further nominated members. There is an Executive President directly elected for a 5-year term, who nominates and leads a Council of Ministers.

President: France Albert René.

Education, Information and Youth: James Michel. *National Development:* Jacques Hodoul. *Health and Social Services:* Joseph Belmont. *Political Organization:* Esme Jumeau. *Internal Affairs:* Rita Sinon. *Tourism and Transport:* Ralph Adam. *Manpower:* Jeremie Bonnelame.

National flag: Divided horizontally red over green by a wavy white stripe, with red of double width.

DEFENCE. The Defence Force comprises all services. Personnel (1988) 1,000 organized in 1 infantry battalion, 2 artillery troops and a marine group and an Air

Wing with 1 Islander, 1 Defender and 1 Merlin IIB for transport and 2 Alouette III helicopters. There is also a People's Militia (900).

INTERNATIONAL RELATIONS

Membership. Seychelles is a member of UN, the Commonwealth, OAU and is an ACP state of EEC.

ECONOMY

Planning. The Development Plan, 1985–89 envisages investment of Rs 2,800m. aimed at reducing unemployment and improving the balance of payments.

Budget, in 1m. rupees, for calendar years:

	1982	1983 [1]	1984 [1]	1985
Recurrent revenue	384·3	386·9	395·9	447·7
Recurrent expenditure	410·0	434·6	484·5	632·9

[1] Provisional.

Currency. The currency is the Seychelles *rupee* divided into 100 cents. In March 1988, £1 = 9·24 *rupees;* US$1 = 5·31 *rupees.*

Banking. Central Bank of Seychelles, Development Bank of Seychelles and Seychelles Savings Bank have head offices and Barclays Bank, Standard Bank, Bank of Credit and Commerce International, Banque Francaise Commerçiale, Habib Bank and Bank of Baroda, have branches in Victoria and Mahé.

ENERGY AND NATURAL RESOURCES

Electricity. Production (1986) 59m. kwh.

Agriculture. Coconuts are the main cash crop (production, 1985, 19,000 tonnes). Other main crops produced for export are cinnamon bark (1985, 781 tonnes) and copra (1985, 1,632 tonnes). Tea production, 1985, 117 tonnes. Crops grown for local consumption include cassava, sweet potatoes, yams, sugar-cane, bananas and vegetables. The staple food crop, rice, is imported.

Livestock (1986): Cattle, 2,000; pigs, 15,000; goats, 4,000.

Fisheries. The fishing industry is being expanded for home consumption and export. Catch (1985) 4,361 tonnes.

INDUSTRY AND TRADE

Industry. Local industry is expanding, the largest development in recent years being the brewery, (output, 1985, 4,140,000 litres). Other main activities include production of soft drinks (3,502,000 litres in 1985), cigarettes (56·2m. in 1985) and paints, dairy, processing of cinnamon and coconuts.

Commerce. Total trade, in rupees, for calendar years:

	1982	1983	1984	1985
Imports (less re-exports)	641,300,000	594,100,000	618,700,000	718,700,000
Domestic exports	20,300,000	25,200,000	21,400,000	19,500,000

Principal imports (1985): Manufactured goods, Rs 169·9m.; food, beverages and tobacco, Rs 118·8m.; petroleum products, Rs 184·5m., machinery and transport equipment, Rs 185·8m. mainly from UK (15%), Italy (10%), France (9%) and the Republic of South Africa (9%). Principal exports (1985): Copra, Rs 7·6m.; fresh and frozen fish, Rs 7·9m.; cinnamon bark, Rs 2·4m. mainly to Pakistan (35%), Japan (31%) and Réunion (12%).

Total trade between Seychelles and UK (British Department of Trade returns, in £1,000 sterling):

	1985	1986	1987
Imports to UK	1,663	938	884
Exports and re-exports from UK	9,561	9,639	10,770

Tourism. Tourism has now established itself as an important sector of the economy. The number of visitors has grown very rapidly since the opening of the international airport in 1978 and in 1979 there were 78,852. Tourist numbers declined to 55,867 in 1983 but were 67,000 in 1986.

COMMUNICATIONS

Roads. There is a good system of tarmac (157 km) and earth roads (102 km) in Mahé; extensive roadmaking is being undertaken.

Aviation. Air Seychelles operates 2 services a week between Europe and Seychelles and regular services from Mahé to Praslin and Fregate Islands. British Airways operates 1 service a week between London, Bahrain and Seychelles. Air France operates 3 services a week. Kenya Airways operates a service twice a week. TPC Air also operate services. In 1985 aircraft movements were 1,472; passenger movements, 335,000 (including domestic flights); freight loaded, 171 tonnes, unloaded, 1,326 tonnes.

Shipping. The main port is Victoria. Shipping (1985), goods unloaded, 236,000 tonnes, goods loaded, 4,500 tonnes. There are regular cargo vessels from Australia and the Far East, South Africa and Europe. The vessel *Cinq Juin* travels to and from Mauritius and visits the outlying islands.

Post and Broadcasting. Services operated by Cable & Wireless Ltd provide telegraphic communications with all parts of the world by satellite, the company's radiotelephone service also extends to all principal countries in the world. In 1978, an automatic dialling telex system was introduced. Telephones in Jan. 1983 numbered 4,512. There are 2 radio stations and (1983) 18,000 receivers. There were 3,500 television sets in 1984 and Radio Television Seychelles run radio and television services in Creole, English and French.

Cinemas. In 1983 there were 3 cinemas with seating capacity of 1,038.

Newspapers. In 1986 there were 2 daily newspapers.

JUSTICE, RELIGION, EDUCATION AND WELFARE

Justice. The police force numbered 492 all ranks and 69 special constabulary.

Religion. 90% of the inhabitants are Roman Catholic and 8% Anglican.

Education. Equality of educational opportunity exists for all children for a minimum of 9 years.

In 1986 there were 14,663 pupils and 681 teachers in primary schools, 2,433 pupils and 112 teachers in secondary schools and 1,541 students and 160 teachers in the Polytechnic. In 1983, a total of 239 students were undergoing training overseas, mainly in the UK; 153 were in university, 39 teacher-training and 6 nursing.

Health. In 1985 there were 43 doctors, 288 nurses and 331 hospital beds.

DIPLOMATIC REPRESENTATIVES

Of Seychelles in Great Britain (50 Conduit St., London, W1A 4PE)
High Commissioner: Robert F. Delpech.

Of Great Britain in Seychelles (Victoria Hse., Victoria, Mahé)
High Commissioner: Peter Smart.

Of Seychelles in the USA and to the United Nations
Ambassador: (Vacant).

Of the USA in Seychelles (Victoria Hse., Victoria, Mahé)
Ambassador: (Vacant).

Books of Reference

Statistical Information: Information Office, 52 Kingsgate House, Victoria, Mahé.
Agricultural Survey 1980. Government Printer
Seychelles in Figures. Statistics Division, Mahé, 1986
Benedict, M., and Benedict, B., *Men, Women and Money in Seychelles.* Univ. of California Press, 1983
Franda, M., *The Seychelles: Unquiet Islands.* Boulder, 1982
Lionnet, G., *The Seychelles.* Newton Abbot, 1972
Mancham, J. R., *Paradise Raped: Life, Love and Power in the Seychelles.* London, 1983

SIERRA LEONE

Capital: Freetown
Population: 3·67m. (1987)
GNP per capita: US$380 (1983)

HISTORY. The Colony of Sierra Leone originated in the sale and cession, in 1787, by native chiefs to English settlers, of a piece of land intended as a home for natives of Africa who were waifs in London, and later it was used as a settlement for Africans rescued from slave-ships. The hinterland was declared a British protectorate on 21 Aug. 1896. Sierra Leone became independent as a member state of the Commonwealth on 27 April 1961, and a republic on 19 April 1971.

AREA AND POPULATION. Sierra Leone is bounded on the north-west, north and north-east by the Republic of Guinea, on the south-east by Liberia and on the south-west by the Atlantic ocean. The coastline extends from the boundary of the Republic of Guinea to the north of the mouth of the Great Scarcies River to the boundary of Liberia at the mouth of the Mano River, a distance of about 212 miles (341 km). The area of Sierra Leone is 27,925 sq. miles (73,326 sq. km). Population (census 1985), 3,517,530, of whom about 2,000 are Europeans, 3,500 Asiatics and 30,000 non-native Africans. Estimate (1987) 3,666,000. The capital is Freetown, with 469,776 inhabitants.

Vital statistics (1986); Live births, 75,862; deaths, 6,272.

Sierra Leone is divided into 3 provinces and the Western Area:

	Sq. km	Estimate 1976	Capital	Census 1985
Western Area	557	400,000	Freetown	554,243
Southern province	19,694	744,000	Bo	740,510
Eastern province	15,553	970,000	Kenema	960,551
Northern province	35,936	1,126,000	Makeni	1,262,226

The principal peoples are the Mendes (34% of the total) in the south, the Temnes (31%) in the north and centre, the Konos, Fulanis, Bulloms, Korankos, Limbas and Kissis.

CLIMATE. A tropical climate, with marked wet and dry seasons and high temperatures throughout the year. The rainy season lasts from about April to Nov., when humidity can be very high. Thunderstorms are common from April to June and in Sept. and Oct. Rainfall is particularly heavy at Freetown because of the effect of neighbouring relief. Freetown. Jan. 80°F (26·7°C), July 78°F (25·6°C). Annual rainfall 135" (3,434 mm).

CONSTITUTION AND GOVERNMENT. For earlier Constitutional history *see* THE STATESMAN'S YEAR-BOOK 1978–79, p. 1046. Following a referendum in June 1978, a new Constitution was instituted under which the ruling All People's Congress (APC) became the sole legal Party. The 124-member Parliament comprises 105 members directly elected for a 5-year term (latest elections, 31 May 1986), together with 12 Paramount Chiefs representing the 12 districts and 7 members appointed by the President. The President is elected for a 7-year term by the National Delegates' Conference of the APC; he appoints and leads a Council of Ministers.

President: Maj.-Gen. Dr Joseph Saidu Momoh.

First Vice-President, Minister of Lands, Housing and Planning: Abu B. Kamara.

Finance: Dr Sheka Kanu. *Foreign Affairs:* Abdul Karim Koroma.

National flag: Three horizontal stripes of green, white, blue.

Local Government. The provinces are administered through the Ministry of Internal Affairs and divided into 148 Chiefdoms, each under the control of a Paramount Chief and Council of Elders known as the Tribal Authorities, who are responsible for the maintenance of law and order and for the administration of justice (except for serious crimes). All of these Chiefdoms have been organized into local government units, empowered to raise and disburse funds for the development of the Chiefdom concerned.

DEFENCE

Army. The Army consists of 2 infantry battalions, 2 artillery batteries and 1 engineer squadron. Strength (1988), 3,000 officers and men.

Navy. There are 1 *ex*-Soviet gunboat, 1 coastal patrol craft and 3 landing craft. Personnel in 1988 totalled 150 officers and men.

Air Force. The Air Wing of the Defence Force appears to be inactive, although the Defence Ministry is listed as the owner of 1 BO 105 and 2 AS.355 Ecureuil helicopters carrying civil registrations. Personnel, about 30.

INTERNATIONAL RELATIONS

Membership. Sierra Leone is a member of UN, OAU, ECOWAS, the Commonwealth, the Mano River Union and is an ACP state of EEC.

ECONOMY

Planning. A development plan (1981–84) was launched to achieve self-sufficiency in food, better infrastructure and to increase mineral production.

Budget. Revenue and expenditure (in 1,000 leone) for years ending 30 June:

	1982–83	1983–84	1984–85	1985–86
Revenue	243,300	327,900	317,100	524,700
Expenditure	480,000	537,900	507,100	771,100

Currency. The Bank of Sierra Leone, which was established on 4 Aug. 1964, is responsible for providing the currency in the country. It introduced on 4 Aug. 1964 a decimal currency, the *leone* and the *cent*. The paper currency consists of 1, 2, 5, 10 and 20 *leone* and 50-*cent* notes; the coinage of 1, 5, 10, 20 and 50 *cents*.

At 30 June 1982 total Sierra Leone notes and coins in circulation was Le. 91·75m. In March 1988, £1 = 54·45 *leone*; US$1 = 30·65 *leone*.

Banking. The Standard Chartered Bank Sierra Leone, the National Commercial Bank, International Bank of Credit and Commerce, International Bank of Trade and Industry and Barclays Bank Sierra Leone have their headquarters at Freetown; the Standard Chartered Bank has 14, Barclays Bank 12 and the National Commercial Bank, 8 branches and agencies.

The Post Office Savings Bank had 94,910 depositors with total credit balance of nearly Le. 3,455,469 in 1983.

ENERGY AND NATURAL RESOURCES

Electricity. Production (1986) 85m. kwh. Supply 230 volts; 50 Hz.

Minerals. The chief minerals mined are diamonds (243,500 carats, 1984–85), bauxite (1m. tonnes), gold (12,253 oz.), and rutile (76,900 tonnes). Molybdenite is being prospected. Rutile production started in 1979; potential production 100,000 tonnes per annum. Iron ore production was resumed in Feb. 1983 at Marampa by a new company, Austro Minerals, who withdrew in March 1985, having produced 151·2 tonnes since July 1984.

Agriculture. In the western area farming is largely confined to the production of cassava and garden crops, such as maize, vegetables and mangoes, for local consumption. In the regions the principal products include rice, which is the staple food of the country, cassava, groundnuts and export crops such as palm-kernels, cocoa beans, coffee, ginger and piassava. Cattle production is important in the northern part of the country, and most of the poultry, eggs and pork are produced in the Western Area. Production (1986, in 1,000 tonnes): Rice, 525; cassava, 113; palm oil, 44; palm kernels, 30; coffee, 11; cocoa, 9.

Livestock (1986): Cattle, 333,000; goats, 175,000; sheep, 332,000; chickens, 5m.

Fisheries. The estimated tonnage of catch of all species of fish during 1983 was 126,098 tonnes. The FAO has carried out a 5-year survey of pelagic fish resources along the coastline and continental shelf.

Total catch of fish is still below the demand of the country. In 1980, 247 tonnes of fish value Le. 483,488 were imported.

INDUSTRY AND TRADE

Industry. Four pioneer oil-mills for the expressing of palm-oil are operated by the Sierra Leone Produce Marketing Board. Government also operates 4 rice-mills, and there are a number of privately owned mills. At Kenema the Government Forest Industries Corporation produces sawn timber, joinery products (including prefabricated buildings) and high-class furniture. In addition, there is a smaller privately owned saw-mill at Panguma, Kenema and Hangha, and several small furniture workshops are used internally. Village industries include fishing, fish curing and smoking, weaving and hand methods of expressing palm-oil and cracking palm kernels.

Labour. A large proportion of the population is engaged in agriculture and about 125,000 workers are in wage-earning employment. The number of workers in establishments employing 6 or more persons was 64,092 in 1982, distributed as follows: Services, 24,142; mining and quarrying, 6,170; transport, storage and communications, 4,814; construction, 9,721; commerce, 6,870; manufacturing, 9,407; agriculture, forestry and fishing, 5,834; electricity and water services, 24,142.

Commerce. Total trade (in 1,000 leone) for calendar years:

	1981	1982	1983	1984
Imports	360,440	368,473	289,828	418,286
Exports	168,576	133,245	178,558	334,420

Of the imports (1980) 22% came from the UK, 9% from Japan and 7% from Federal Republic of Germany. Of the exports (1980), 41% went to the UK, 11% to the USA, 8% to the Netherlands and 7% to Switzerland; diamonds formed 45%, coffee 13% and cocoa 13%.

Total trade between Sierra Leone and UK (British Department of Trade returns, in £1,000 sterling):

	1983	1984	1985	1986	1987
Imports to UK	17,710	25,971	17,435	11,599	12,679
Exports and re-exports from UK	13,735	19,532	23,620	17,403	16,221

Tourism. Tourism is being developed and is a major growth industry. In 1986 there were 194,000 tourists.

COMMUNICATIONS

Roads. There were (1977) about 4,406 miles of main roads, of which 665 miles are surfaced with bitumen.

Motor vehicles licensed in 1984 totalled 36,192; passenger cars, 19,040; buses and trucks, 1,818, and motor cycles, 7,056.

Railways. The government railway closed in 1974, though in 1987 there were plans to resume operations, and an 84-km mineral line of 1,067-mm gauge connecting Marampa with the port of Pepel has been rehabilitated.

Aviation. Freetown Airport (Lungi), situated north of Freetown in the Port Loko District, is the only international airport in Sierra Leone.

The airport is served by Sierra Leone Airlines, Ghana/Nigeria Airways, British Caledonian, Union de Transport Aériens, KLM, Air Afrique and Aeroflot. A once weekly non-stop flight from London (Gatwick) to Freetown and *vice versa* is also provided.

Sierra Leone Airlines provide domestic flights daily (except Sundays) from Hastings (14 miles from Freetown) to Gbangbatoke, Bo, Kenema, Yengema; twice weekly to Bonthe, and occasional charter flights to Marampa and Port Loko. Domestic air taxi services also operate.

Shipping. During 1984 the total imports handled by the port of Freetown amounted to 351,205 freight-tons and exports 371,158 freight-tons. In 1982 a total of 576 vessels called at Freetown; 564 were cargo vessels and 12 were tourist ships with a total of 718 passengers.

Bonthe-Sherbro, 80 miles south of Freetown, is used for the shipment of rutile and bauxite. Pepel lies some 12 miles from Freetown and exports iron ore.

Post and Broadcasting. The Posts and Telecommunications Department maintains a trunk network of radio and overhead telephone and telegraph routes of approximately 3,000 miles linking the Western Area with the other regions. Automatic telephone exchanges have been introduced at the regional centres of Bo, Kenema and Makeni; microwave radio relay link now replaces overhead open wire on main trunk routes. An extension programme to link important mining areas at Koidu, Mokanji and Pepel to the national network by microwave links has been established.

The wired broadcasting relay service was replaced in Jan. 1964 by a transistor radio service. Approximately 20,000 transistor radios purchased under this scheme are now in service.

Number of telephones (1981) 220,000. Telegraphic facilities are provided at 58 offices.

There were (1983) 37 post offices and 76 postal agencies.

The number of private wireless-licence holders (1983, estimate) was 600,000 and 22,000 television sets were in operation in 1984.

JUSTICE, RELIGION, EDUCATION AND WELFARE

Justice. The High Court has jurisdiction in civil and criminal matters. Subordinate courts are held by magistrates in the various districts. Native Courts, headed by court Chairmen, apply native law and custom under a criminal and civil jurisdiction. Appeals from the decisions of magistrates' courts are heard by the High Court. Appeals from the decisions of the High Court are heard by the Sierra Leone Court of Appeal. Appeal lies from the Sierra Leone Court of Appeal to the Supreme Court which is the highest court.

Police. The police force at 31 Dec. 1982 had an authorized strength of 136 superior police officers, 485 junior police officers and 4,934 other ranks including 415 women. In the provinces each Chiefdom keeps an additional force known as Chiefdom Police.

A non-pensionable force, known as the Auxiliary Force and consisting of 3 Junior police officers and 260 other ranks, are helping the regular force in maintaining law and order in the diamond protected area in the Eastern region.

Religion. The Moslem community was estimated to comprise 39% of the population in 1980, while 52% followed traditional tribal religions; Protestants were 6% and Roman Catholics 2% of the total. The Temne people are mainly Moslem and the Mende chiefly animists. Spiritualist churches were growing in 1985.

Education (1984). There were over 1,267 registered primary schools; total enrolment (1982) 276,911. Primary education is partially free but not compulsory though parents and guardians are urged to send their children and wards to school. School attendance varies considerably in different parts of the country. There were (1984) 184 secondary schools with (1982) 66,464 pupils; 71 of these schools are fully assisted by the Government. Technical education was provided in 4 technical institutes, 2 trade centres and in the technical training establishments of the mining companies. There is also a rural institute.

Fourah Bay College (1,400 students) and Njala University College are the 2 constituent colleges of the University of Sierra Leone. The Institute of Education, which is part of the University, is now responsible for teacher education, educational research and curriculum development in the country.

There is a paramedical school at Bo in the Southern region.

Health (1984). In the Western Area there are 13 government hospitals (1,108 beds and 217 cots), including a maternity hospital, a children's hospital and an infectious diseases hospital near Freetown. There are 6 government health centres in the Western Area. Three private hospitals are located in Freetown with 108 beds. A mental hospital at Kissy has accommodation for 224 patients. In the provinces there are 14 government hospitals, 6 hospitals associated with mining companies and 7 mission hospitals. There is a school of nursing in Freetown. There are 156 government dispensaries and health treatment centres and two military hospitals with 124 beds.

DIPLOMATIC REPRESENTATIVES

Of Sierra Leone in Great Britain (33 Portland Pl., London,W1N 3AG)
High Commissioner: Caleb Aubee.

Of Great Britain in Sierra Leone (Standard Bank of Sierra Leone Ltd Bldg., Lightfoot Boston St., Freetown)
High Commissioner: D. W. Partridge, CMG.

Of Sierra Leone in the USA (1701 19th St., NW, Washington, D.C., 20009)
Ambassador: Sahr Matturi.

Of the USA in Sierra Leone (Corner Walpole and Siaka Stevens St., Freetown)
Ambassador: Cynthia Perry.

Of Sierra Leone to the United Nations
Ambassador: Dr Thomas Kargbo.

Books of Reference

Atlas of Sierra Leone. Ed. Survey and Lands Dept. Freetown, 1953
Background to Sierra Leone. Freetown, 1980
Cole, B. P., *Sierra Leone Directory of Commerce, Industry and Tourism.* 1985
Fyfe, C., *A History of Sierra Leone.* OUP, 1962.—Fyfe, C., and Jones, E. (ed.), *Freetown.* Sierra Leone Univ. Press and OUP, 1968
Fyfe, C. N. and Jones, E. D., *A Krio–English Dictionary.* OUP and Sierra Leone Univ. Press, 1980
Kup, A. P., *Sierra Leone.* Newton Abbot, 1975
Porter, A. T., *Creoledom: A Study in the Development of Freetown Society.* OUP, 1963

REPUBLIC OF SINGAPORE

Population: 2·59m. (1986)
GNP per capita: US$6,630 (1986)

HISTORY. For the early history of the settlement (1819) and colony (1867) *see* THE STATESMAN'S YEAR-BOOK, 1959, pp. 246 f.

By an agreement entered into between the Governments of Malaysia and of the State of Singapore on 7 Aug. 1965, effective on 9 Aug. 1965, Singapore ceased to be one of the 14 states of the Federation of Malaysia and became an independent sovereign state. The separation was ratified by the Constitution and Malaysia (Singapore Amendment) Act of the Malaysian Parliament on 9 Aug. The 2 governments agreed to enter into a treaty on external defence and mutual assistance. The Singapore Government retains its executive authority and legislative powers under its State Constitution and took over the powers of the Malaysian Government under the Malaysian Constitution in Singapore. The sovereignty and jurisdiction of the head of the Malaysian State was transferred to the Singapore Government. Civil servants working in Singapore for the Federal Departments became Singapore civil servants. Singapore citizens ceased to be Malaysian citizens.

Singapore accepted responsibility for international agreements entered into by the Malaysian Government on its behalf.

AREA AND POPULATION. The Republic of Singapore consists of Singapore Island itself, and some 57 islets.

Singapore Island is situated off the southern extremity of the Malay peninsula, to which it is joined by a causeway carrying a road, railway and water pipeline. The Straits of Johore between the island and the mainland are about three-quarters of a mile wide. The island is some 26 miles (41·8 km) in length and 14 miles (22·9 km) in breadth, and about 238·7 sq. miles (618·2 sq. km) in area, including some 57 adjacent islets, 20 of which are inhabited.

Census of population (1980): 1,856,237 Chinese, 351,508 Malays, 154,632 Indians and 51,568 others; total 2,413,945. Estimate (mid-1986), 2,586,200.

Report on the Census of Population 1980. Dept. of Statistics, Singapore, 1980

CLIMATE. The climate is equatorial, with uniformly high temperatures and no defined wet or dry season, rain being plentiful throughout the year. Jan. 78·1°F (25·6°C), July 80·8°F (27·1°C). Annual rainfall 93·2″ (2,367 mm).

CONSTITUTION AND GOVERNMENT. By a constitutional amendment the name of the state was changed to 'Republic of Singapore', the head of state was named 'President of Singapore' and the legislative assembly was renamed 'Parliament'.

Parliament consists of 77 members, elected by secret ballot from single-member constituencies, and is presided over by a Speaker, chosen by Parliament from its own members or from outside Parliament. In the latter case, the Speaker has no vote. With the customary exception of those serving criminal sentences, all citizens over 21 are eligible to vote irrespective of sex, race, education or property qualification. There is a common roll without communal electorates. Citizenship is automatic by birth; it can also be acquired by registration or by naturalization.

A Presidential Council was established under Part IVA of the Constitution enacted on 9 Jan. 1970. The general function of the Council is to consider and report on matters affecting persons of any racial or religious community in Singapore as referred to it by Parliament or the Government. The Council will draw attention to any bill or subsidiary legislation which in the opinion of the Council is a differentiating measure.

Parliament is composed of 77 People's Action Party members and 1 Singapore Social Democratic Party member.

President of Singapore: Wee Kim Wee (sworn in 2 Sept. 1985).

The People's Action Party Cabinet at Jan. 1988 was composed as follows:
Prime Minister: Lee Kuan Yew.
Senior Minister (Prime Minister's Office): S. Rajaratnam. *First Deputy Prime Minister and Minister for Defence:* Goh Chok Tong. *Second Deputy Prime Minister:* Ong Teng Cheong. *Law:* E. W. Barker. *National Development and Foreign Affairs:* S. Dhanabalan. *Education:* Dr Tony Tan Keng Yam. *Environment:* Dr Ahmad Mattar. *Communications and Information, Second Minister for Defence:* Dr Yeo Ning Hong. *Home Affairs, Second Minister for Law:* S. Jayakumar. *Finance:* Dr Richard Hu Tsu Tau. *Labour:* Lee Yock Suan. *Community Development and Second Minister for Foreign Affairs:* Wong Kan Seng. *Trade and Industry and Second Minister for Defence:* Lee Hsien Loong. *Acting Minister for Health.* Yeo Cheow Tong.

There are 4 Ministers of State.

National flag: Horizontally red over white, charged in the canton with a crescent and a circle of 5 stars, all in white.

Malay, Chinese, Tamil and English are the official languages; English is the language of administration.

DEFENCE. The Ministry of Defence exercises command and control over all armed forces in the republic. It comprises 5 major divisions, *i.e.*, the general staff, manpower, logistic, security and intelligence and finance divisions. Compulsory military service in peace-time was introduced in 1967. Periods of service are officers/n.c.o.s. 30 months, other ranks 24 months. Reserve liability is to 40 for men, 50 for officers.

The governments of Australia, Britain, Malaysia, New Zealand and Singapore continue to co-operate closely in defence arrangements and a 5-nation defence set-up in SE Asia designed to protect Malaysia and Singapore against outside attack came into force on 1 Nov. 1971.

Army. The Army consists of 3 divisions: The 3rd (Tiger) division, the 6th (Cobra) division and the 9th (Panther) division, the latter 2 being reservist formations. Standard infantry weapons are the SAR-80 assault rifle, AR-15 (M-16) rifle, Ultimax 100 light machine gun, 60 mm and 81 mm mortars, 84 mm Carl Gustav anti-tank guns and the Jeep-mounted 106 mm recoilless guns. Most of these weapons and the ammunition are manufactured locally. Strength (1988) 45,000 (including 30,000 conscripts) and 170,000 reserves. Paramilitary forces number 37,500.

Navy. The flotillas comprise 6 fast missile craft, all of German design but 4 built in Singapore, 6 fast patrol craft built by Vosper Thornycroft (2 at Portsmouth, Britain, and 4 in Singapore), 2 *ex*-US coastal minesweepers, 12 coastal patrol boats, 2 training vessels, 6 landing ships (*ex*-USN LST) and 8 small landing craft (2 *ex*-Australian). Six missile corvettes of 600 tons are under construction or on order, and the acquisition of 1 or more 1,000 ton ships is being considered.

Personnel in 1988 numbered 4,500 officers and men. There are over 60 coastal patrol craft deployed by the marine police and 3 small survey craft operated by the Singapore Port Authority.

Air Defence Command. The formation of an Air Defence Command began in 1968. The Republic of Singapore Air Force now has 2 squadrons of F-5E supersonic fighters supported by 2-seat F-5Fs; 3 fighter-bomber squadrons equipped with A-4S Skyhawks, supported by TA-4S two-seat trainers; 1 squadron of Hunter jet fighters and reconnaissance-fighters, supported by Hunter 2-seat trainers; a squadron of Strikemaster armed trainers; a radar unit and Bloodhound, Rapier and Hawk surface-to-air missile squadrons; a transport squadron of C-130s (including 4 equipped as flight refuelling tankers); a squadron of Skyvans equipped for search and rescue; a squadron of Bell UH-1H Iroquois and Bell 212 helicopters; and train-

ing units equipped with SF.260MS piston-engined basic trainers, SIAI-Marchetti
S.211 jets, AS 350 Ecureuil helicopters and four E-2C Hawkeye AWACS aircraft.
Personnel strength (1988) about 6,000.

INTERNATIONAL RELATIONS

Membership. Singapore is a member of UN, the Commonwealth, the Colombo
Plan and ASEAN.

ECONOMY

Planning. The GNP in 1986, at current cost was $39,185·2m., a decrease of 1·8%
over 1985.

Budget. Public revenue and expenditure for financial years (in S$1m.):

	1982	1983	1984	1985	1986[1]
Revenue	9,128	10,632	10,059	13,058	12,396
Expenditure[2]	14,032	16,947	17,243	21,533	25,591

[1] Estimate.

[2] Includes the transfer from the Consolidated Revenue Account to the Development Fund.

Currency. The *Singapore dollar* (S$) is divided in 100 *cents*. Gross circulation in
Dec. 1986 was S$5,484·2m. In March 1988, £1 = 3·56 *dollars*; US$1 = 2·01
dollars.

Banking. The functions of the Commissioner of Banking have been assumed from
1 Jan. 1971 by the Monetary Authority of Singapore, which performs all the functions normally associated with a central bank, except the issuing of currency which
is the responsibility of the Board of Commissioner of Currency.

The Development Bank of Singapore was established as a fully licensed bank in
1968, and is the largest local bank in terms of assets. Primarily it provides long-
term financing of manufacturing and other industries. At 31 Dec. 1986 it had a
paid up capital of S$293·3m. and shareholders' funds amounting to S$1,832·3m.

There were 134 commercial banks with 395 banking offices operating in Singapore in March 1986. The total assets/liabilities amounted to S$76,833·3m. as at
Dec. 1986. Total deposits of non-bank customers amounted to S$30,612·6m.
while loans and advances including bills financing, totalled S$35,792·8m. at 31
Dec. 1986.

There were 58 merchant banks operating in Singapore at 31 Dec. 1986. Of these,
57 had an Asian Currency Unit each and were engaged actively in Asian dollars
transactions. Their main functions included underwritings, portfolio fund management, financial advisory services and loan syndication.

In Dec. 1986, the Singapore Post Office Savings Bank had 3,063,496 savings
accounts and a total deposit balance of all accounts of S$10,166m.

Weights and Measures. The metric system or the International System of Units (SI)
was introduced in 1971 in Singapore.

ENERGY AND NATURAL RESOURCES

Electricity. The Public Utilities Board is responsible for the provision of electricity,
gas and water. Electrical power is generated by 3 oil-fired power stations, with a
total generating capacity of 2,741 mw at the end of 1986. Production (1986)
10,576·5m. kwh. Supply 230 volts; 50 Hz.

Oil. Singapore is the largest oil refining centre in Asia.

Agriculture. Agriculture contributed less than 1% of GDP and employed only 1%
of the labour force in 1987. Most food is imported but Singapore is self-sufficient in
eggs and pork, and vegetables are produced for domestic consumption. Orchids are
a valuable export.

Fisheries. As the prospect of increasing fish production from inshore waters is
poor, in 1967 various projects were introduced with the aim of making Singapore
self-sufficient in fish as well as a major fishing base in the region.

The Jurong fishing port and fish market began operating 26 Feb. 1969. A Fishery Training Institute was established at Changi with the assistance of the United Nations Development Programme (Special Fund) to train youths and fishermen in modern fishing techniques. At Changi, too, a Marine Fisheries Research Department was set up under the sponsorship of the South-East Asian Fisheries Development Centre. Research on fish culture and ornamental fish was carried out at the Freshwater Fisheries Laboratory at Sembawang. The ornamental fish industry is a valuable foreign exchange earner. Export of aquarium fish in 1986, S$47·3m. The total supply of fresh fish in 1986 was 109,529 tonnes.

INDUSTRY AND TRADE

Industry. The largest industrial area is the Jurong Industrial Estate with 1,722 factories employing 97,982 workers in March 1986.

Production, 1986 (in S$1m.), totalled 36,611, including machinery and appliances, 14,260; petroleum, 6,212; food and beverages, 2,544; chemical products, 2,649; transport equipment, 1,984; fabricated metal products, 1,950; paper products and printing, 1,438; wearing apparel, 1,159; rubber processing, 162.

Labour. In June 1986, 1,149,022 persons were employed, of whom 969,343 were employees, 58,890 were employers, 99,278 were self-employed and 21,510 were unpaid family workers. The majority were working in manufacturing, 290,114; trade, 265,645; transport and communications, 114,145.

The Employment Act and the Industrial Relations Act provide principal terms and conditions of employment such as hours of work, sick leave and other fringe benefits. A new labour legislation was introduced allowing youths of 14-16 years to work in industrial establishments, and also children from 12-14 years to be employed in approved apprenticeship schemes. A trade dispute may be referred to the Industrial Arbitration Court which was established in 1960.

The Ministry of Labour operates an employment service to assist job seekers to obtain employment and employers to recruit workers. In addition it provides the handicapped with specialized on-the-job training. The Central Provident Fund was established in 1955 to make provision for employees in their old age. On 31 Dec. 1986 there were 1·9m. members with S$29,337·4m. standing to their credit in the fund. The total number of active employers registered with the board in 1986 was 69,309.

Trade Unions. There were 89 registered trade unions comprising 83 employee unions, 5 employer unions and 1 federation of trade unions at 31 Dec. 1986. The total membership of employee unions numbered 200,613, of whom 194,595 belonged to 68 employee unions affiliated to the National Trades Union Congress. Members of employer unions numbered 1,146.

Commerce.

Imports and exports (in S$1m.), by country, 1986:

	Imports (c.i.f.)	Exports (f.o.b.)
Australia	968·4	1,515·2
China	3,109·6	1,243·8
France	971·6	713·6
Germany, Federal Republic of	1,829·0	1,538·8
Hong Kong	1,310·1	3,182·9
Japan	11,052·2	4,204·4
Kuwait	2,098·1	84·9
Malaysia	7,402·6	7,244·6
Saudi Arabia	1,369·0	483·5
Taiwan	2,244·1	1,097·2
Thailand	1,606·8	1,787·7
United Arab Emirates	687·5	391·0
UK	1886·4	1,283·9
USA	8,317·3	11,447·4

The major trading countries for 1986 were US (18·9%), Japan (14·6%), Malaysia

(14%) and the EEC (11·4%). In 1986, imports (S$55,545·4m.) decreased by 4%. Exports fell from S$50,178m. in 1985 to S$48,985m. in 1986.

Exports (1986, in S$1m.): Machinery and transport equipment, 18,900·5 (of which electric machinery, 10,157·8; transport equipment, 1,322·5); mineral fuels, 10,147·1; crude materials, 2,458·8 (of which rubber, 1,340·8); chemicals, 2,839·9; food, beverages and tobacco, 2,957·6; clothing, 1,469·7; animal and vegetable oils, 880·4; textiles, 929·4; scientific and optical instruments, 755·1; metal goods, 561·1; iron and steel, 433·1.

Imports (1986, in S$1m.): Machinery and transport equipment, 20,780·7; mineral fuels, 10,994·5; food, beverages and tobacco, 4,407·2; chemicals, 3,245·6; crude materials, 1,905 (of which rubber, 903·3); textiles, 2,241·6; iron and steel, 1,463·5; animal and vegetable oils, 720·3; metal goods, 1,133·4; scientific and optical instruments, 1,259·3; non-metal mineral goods, 894; paper and paperboard and related articles, 684·9.

In the following table (British Department of Trade returns, in £1,000 sterling) the imports include produce from Sabah, Sarawak and other eastern places, transhipped at Singapore, which is thus entered as the place of export:

	1983	1984	1985	1986	1987
Imports to UK	404,122	488,421	441,345	462,878	473,814
Exports and re-exports from UK	469,565	556,443	612,920	547,419	602,627

Tourism. There were 3,191,058 visitors in 1986, spending S$4,000m.

COMMUNICATIONS

Roads. There are 2,686 km of public roads, of which 2,572 km are asphalt-paved. In Dec. 1986 motor vehicles numbered 473,659, of which 220,566 were private cars, 8,638 buses, 120,387 motor cycles and scooters, 13,991 public cars including taxis, school taxis and private hire cars.

Railways. A 16-mile (25·8-km) main line runs through Singapore, connecting with the States of Malaysia and as far as Bangkok. Branch lines serve the port of Singapore and the industrial estate at Jurong. A metro opened in 1987.

Aviation. The new international airport at Changi was completed and operational from 1 July 1981. Forty-four international airlines operated 558 scheduled services a week, totalling 68,282 aircraft movements at Singapore International Airport in Changi in 1986. Freight handled (1986) 352,125 tonnes and there were 10m. passengers.

Shipping. A total of 60,863 vessels of 206m. NRT entered Singapore during 1986.

Post and Telecommunications. In March 1986, 87 post offices and 44 postal agencies were in operation. Telephones numbered 1,115,722 in Dec. 1986.

Cinemas (1986). There were 42 cinemas with a total seating capacity of 49,000.

Newspapers (1986). There were 7 daily newspapers, in 4 languages, with a total daily circulation of 684,298.

JUSTICE, RELIGION, EDUCATION AND WELFARE

Justice. There is a Supreme Court in Singapore which consists of the High Court, the Court of Appeal and the Court of Criminal Appeal. The Supreme Court is composed of a Chief Justice and 7 Judges. An appeal from the High Court lies to the Court of Appeal in civil matters and to the Court of Criminal Appeal in criminal matters. Further appeal can in certain cases be made to the Judicial Committee of the Privy Council. The High Court has original civil and criminal jurisdiction as well as appellate civil and criminal jurisdiction in respect of appeals from the Subordinate Courts. There are 12 district courts, 14 magistrates' courts, 1 juvenile and 1 coroner's court and a small claims tribunal.

Religion. The major religions are Buddhism, Taoism, Islam, Christianity and

Hinduism. At the 1980 census 56% of the population aged 10 years and above were Buddhists and Taoists, 16% Moslems, 10% Christians and 4% Hindus.

Education. Statistics of schools in 1986:

	Schools	Pupils	Teachers
Primary			
Government schools	172	205,281	8,100
Government-aided schools	63	63,387	2,407
Private schools	1	152	8
Secondary			
Government schools	109	149,296 [1]	6,461
Government-aided schools	44	51,840 [1]	2,159
Private schools	4	1,952 [1]	75

[1] Includes pre-university classes.

The National University of Singapore was established on 8 Aug. 1980 following the merger of the University of Singapore and the Nanyang University. The National University of Singapore has 8 faculties: Arts and social sciences, law, science, medicine, dentistry, engineering, architecture and building, accountancy and business administration. Post-graduate studies are offered in all the faculties and there are 3 post-graduate schools for medical, dental and management studies. Total enrolment for 1986–87 was 15,599 students.

The Nanyang Technological Institute, situated in the former Nanyang University, was established on 8 Aug. 1981. The institute had an enrolment of 2,202 students in 1986. It will be developed into a University of Technology by 1992. The Singapore Polytechnic had 12,905 students and the Ngee Ann Polytechnic 9,936 students in 1986–87. The Institute of Education, established on 1 April 1973, is now the only institution responsible for teacher education in Singapore and for promoting research in education. There were 1,365 students in 1986–87.

The Adult Education Board and the Industrial Training Board were merged to form the Vocational and Industrial Training Board, on 1 April 1979. The VITB has taken over all the functions and responsibilities in vocational training and continuing education. The VITB runs 16 training institutes and centres offering full-time and part-time courses. The total student enrolment for 1986 was 23,687.

Health. There were 10 government hospitals with a total of 7,898 beds in 1986. There were 2,781 doctors registered.

DIPLOMATIC REPRESENTATIVES

Of Singapore in Great Britain (2 Wilton Cres., London, SW1X 8RW)
High Commissioner: (Vacant).

Of Great Britain in Singapore (Tanglin Rd, Singapore, 1024)
High Commissioner: Michael E. Pike, CMG.

Of Singapore in the USA (1824 R. St., NW, Washington, D.C., 20009)
Ambassador: Tommy Koh Thong Bee.

Of the USA in Singapore (30 Hill St., Singapore, 0617)
Ambassador: Daryl Arnold.

Of Singapore to the United Nations
Ambassador: Kishore Mahbubani.

Books of Reference

Statistical Information: The Department of Statistics (PO Box 3010, Maxwell Road, Singapore 9050) was established 1 Jan. 1922. Its publications include: *Singapore Trade Statistics* (monthly), *Monthly Digest of Statistics, Yearbook of Statistics, Singapore Demographic Bulletin* (monthly), *Census of Population 1980. Singapore Yearbook of Labour Statistics. Chief Statistician:* Khoo Chian Kim.

National Library. *Books About Singapore.* Singapore. Biennial

Singapore. Constitution. The Constitution of Singapore. Singapore, 1966

The Budget for the Financial Year 1986–87. Singapore, 1986

Singapore. Economic Committee, The Singapore Economy: new direction: report of the Economic Committee, Ministry of Trade and Industry, Singapore, 1986

Singapore. Singapore, Information Division, Ministry of Communications and Information

Singapore. Government Gazette (published weekly with supplement)

Economic Survey of Singapore. Ministry of Trade and Industry, Singapore (Annual)

Singapore. Facts and Pictures. Singapore, Information Division, Ministry of Communications and Information

Singapore Government Directory. Singapore, Information Division, Ministry of Communications and Information

Singapore: An Illustrated history, 1941–48. Ministry of Culture, Singapore, 1984

The Statutes of the Republic of Singapore. Rev. 12 vols., 1985 (with annual supplements). Singapore, Law Revision Commission, 1986—.

Chew, P. S. J. (ed.), *Singapore Development: Policies and Trends.* OUP, 1983

Clammer, J. R., *Singapore: Ideology, Society, Culture.* Singapore, 1985

Drysdale, J., *Singapore: Struggle for Success.* Singapore, 1984

Josey, A., *Lee Kuan Yew, The Struggle for Singapore.* London, 1980.—*Singapore: Its Past, Present and Future.* Singapore, 1979

Lim, L., *Trade, Employment and Industrialisation in Singapore.* Geneva, 1986

Quah, J. S., *Government and Politics of Singapore.* OUP, 1985

Saw, S.-H., *Population Control for Zero Growth in Singapore.* Singapore, 1980

Tan, C. H., *Financial Institutions in Singapore.* 4th ed. Singapore, 1985

Turnbull, C. M., *A History of Singapore, 1819–1975.* OUP, 1977

Yeo, K. W., *Political Development in Singapore, 1945–1955.* Singapore Univ. Press, 1973

You, P. S., and Lim, C. Y. (eds.), *Singapore: Twenty-five years of Development.* Singapore, 1984

National Library: National Library, Stamford Rd, Singapore. *Director:* Mrs Hedwig Anuar.

SOLOMON ISLANDS

Capital: Honiara
Population: 270,000 (1985)
GNP per capita: US$640 (1983)

HISTORY. The Solomon Islands were discovered in 1568 by Alvaro de Mendana, on a voyage of discovery from Peru; 200 years passed before European contact was again made with the Solomons. The southern Solomon Islands were placed under British protection in 1893; the eastern and southern outliers were added in 1898 and 1899. Santa Isabel and the other islands to the north were ceded by Germany in 1900. Full internal self-government was achieved on 2 Jan. 1976 and independence on 7 July 1978.

AREA AND POPULATION. The Solomon Islands lie within the area 5° to 12° 30′ S. lat. and 155° 30′ to 169° 45′ E. long. The group includes the main islands of Guadalcanal, Malaita, New Georgia, San Cristobal (now Makira), Santa Isabel and Choiseul; the smaller Florida and Russell groups; the Shortland, Mono (or Treasury), Vella La Vella, Kolombangara, Ranongga, Gizo and Rendova Islands; to the east, Santa Cruz, Tikopia, the Reef and Duff groups; Rennell and Bellona in the south; Ontong Java or Lord Howe to the north; and innumerable smaller islands. The land area of the Solomons is estimated at 10,640 sq. miles (27,556 sq. km). The larger islands are mountainous and forest clad, with flood-prone rivers of considerable energy potential. Guadalcanal has the largest land area and the greatest amount of flat coastal plain.

Population of the Solomon Islands was (1985, estimate) 270,000. Census (1976) 196,823.

The islands are administratively divided into 7 provinces. These provinces are (with 1987 estimated population): Western Province (62,300), Guadalcanal, including Honiara (71,300), Central (20,600), Malaita (80,700), Makira and Ulawa (20,800), Temotu (15,300), Isabel (15,500).

The capital, Honiara, on Guadalcanal, is the largest urban area, with estimated population in 1985 of 26,000.

English is the official language but there are at least 87 vernacular languages.

CLIMATE. An equatorial climate with only small seasonal variations. South-east winds cause cooler conditions from April to Nov., but north-west winds for the rest of the year bring higher temperatures and greater rainfall, with annual totals ranging between 80″ (2,000 mm) and 120″ (3,000 mm).

CONSTITUTION AND GOVERNMENT. The Solomon Islands is a constitutional monarchy with the British Sovereign (represented locally by a Governor-General, who must be a Solomon Island citizen) as Head of State, while legislative power is vested in the unicameral National Parliament composed of 38 members, elected by universal adult suffrage for four years (subject to dissolution), and executive authority is effectively held by the Cabinet, led by the Prime Minister.

The Governor-General is appointed for up to five years, on the advice of Parliament, and acts in almost all matters on the advice of the Cabinet. The Prime Minister is elected by and from members of Parliament. Other Ministers are appointed by the Governor-General on the Prime Minister's recommendation, from members of Parliament. The Cabinet is responsible to Parliament. Emphasis is laid on the devolution of power to provincial governments, and traditional chiefs and leaders have a special role within the arrangement.

At the General election held on 24 Oct. 1984, 13 seats were gained by the Solomon Islands United Party (SIUP), 12 seats by the People's Alliance Party, 4 seats by Solomons Ano Sagufenua (SAS) and 8 seats by others and independents, with one seat vacant.

Governor General: Sir Baddeley Devisi, GCMG, GCVO.
Prime Minister: Ezekiel Alebua.
National flag: Divided blue over green by a diagonal yellow band, and in the canton 5 white stars.

INTERNATIONAL RELATIONS

Membership. The Solomon Islands is a member of UN, the Commonwealth and is an ACP state of EEC.

ECONOMY

Planning. The 1985–89 Development Plan envisages improvement in natural resources, health and education.

Budget. The budget for 1988 envisaged expenditure of SI$170·76m. of which SI$76·47m. was for development.

Currency. The *Solomon Island dollar* (SI$) was introduced in 1977. In March 1988, US$1 = 2·03 *dollars*; £1 = 3·59 *dollars.*

Banking. In 1985 there were 4 commercial banks: Australia and New Zealand, Hong Kong and Shanghai, National Bank of Solomon Islands and Westpac.

Weights and Measures. The metric system is in force.

ENERGY AND NATURAL RESOURCES

Electricity. Production (1986) 23,379,000 kwh. Supply 240 volts; 50 Hz.

Minerals. There are reserves of bauxite and phosphate, and there is a small industry extracting gold (65,807 grams refined, in 1986) and silver (70,158) by panning.

Agriculture. Land is held either as customary land (88% of holdings) or registered land. Customary land rights depend on clan membership or kinship. Only Solomon Islanders own customary land; only Islanders or government members may hold perpetual estates of registered land. Coconuts, cocoa, rice and other minor crops are grown. Main food crops coconut, cassava, sweet potato, yam, taro and banana: Solomon Islands Plantations Ltd has a plantation of about 40,000 hectares of oil-palm, near Honiara. Production of copra (1987), 27,447 tonnes; palm oil, 11,998; cocoa, 2,964; palm kernels, 2,432.

Rice-cropping in 1983 yielded 4,608 tonnes of milled rice. Rice has been imported since the 1986 cyclone.

Livestock (1986): Cattle, 23,000; pigs, 50,000.

Forestry. Forests cover about 2·4m. hectares, with (1987) an estimated 10·4m. cu. metres of commercial timber. Production (1986) of logs, 471,300 cu. metres and sawn timber, 11,000 cu. metres; total exports, 439,700 cu. metres.

Fisheries. Catch of tuna (1986) 44,208 tonnes.

INDUSTRY AND TRADE

Industry. Industries include palm oil milling, rice milling, fish canning, fish freezing, saw milling, food, tobacco and soft drinks. Other products include wood and rattan furniture, fibreglass articles, boats, clothing and spices.

Commerce. The main imports (1986, in SI$1m.) were machinery and transport equipment, 30·8; mineral fuels and lubricants, 19·7; manufactured goods, 16·4; food, 17·5. Total imports SI$104·3m. Main exports included fish products, 52·9; wood products, 35·7; cocoa beans, 6·5; copra, 6; palm oil products, 6. In 1986 imports (in SI$1m.) were mainly from Australia (41·8) and Japan (17·6); exports were mainly to Japan (42·5).

Total trade between Solomon Islands and UK (British Department of Trade returns, in £1,000 sterling):

	1985	1986	1987
Imports to UK	7,714	4,074	4,461
Exports and re-exports from UK	1,862	1,618	1,566

Tourism. In 1984, there were 10,670 visitors.

COMMUNICATIONS

Roads. In 1987 there were 1,300 km of motorable roads of which 100 km of bitumen-topped roads; the rest were coral or gravel. In 1982 there were 1,122 passenger cars and 1,323 commercial vehicles.

Aviation. (1988) An international airport 13 km from Honiara is served by Air Nauru, Air Niugini, Air Pacific and Solomon Islands Airline. There are 27 air-fields. Solomon Islands Airline also provides inter-island transport and scheduled flights to Kieta in Papua New Guinea.

Shipping. International seaports are Honiara, and Yandina in the Russell group. Shipping services are maintained with Australia, New Zealand, UK and the Far East. Honiara port handles about 250 overseas vessels annually. In 1987 the merchant marine comprised 26 vessels of 5,811 GRT.

Post and Broadcasting. In addition to the general post office, there are 9 post offices, 4 sub post offices and 95 Postal Agencies. In addition there are 143 licensed stamp dealers. Number of telephones (Jan. 1985), 3,827. A VHF radio telephone service operates internally as well as overseas. Solomon Islands Broadcasting Corp. transmits 118 hours a week from Honiara, Gizo and Lata. In 1987 there were about 35,000 radio receivers.

Newspapers. In 1987 there were 4 weekly newspapers and 1 monthly.

JUSTICE, RELIGION, EDUCATION AND WELFARE

Justice. Civil and criminal jurisdiction is exercised by the High Court of Solomon Islands, constituted 1975. A Solomon Islands Court of Appeal was established in 1982. Jurisdiction is based on the principles of English law (as applying on 1 Jan. 1981). Magistrates' courts can try civil cases on claims not exceeding $2,000, and criminal cases with penalties not exceeding 14 years' imprisonment. Certain crimes, such as burglary and arson, where the maximum sentence is for life, may also be tried by magistrates. There are also local courts, which decide matters concerning customary titles to land; decisions may be put to the Customary Land Appeal Court. There is no capital punishment.

Religion. At the 1976 census, 34% of the population were Anglican, 19% Roman Catholic, 17% South Sea Evangelical and 25% other Protestant.

Education. In 1987 there were 42,374 pupils and 2,124 teachers in 462 primary schools, and 5,604 pupils and 300 teachers in 12 provincial and 8 national secondary schools.

Training of teachers and trade and vocational training is carried out at the college of Higher Education. There were 413 students on overseas scholarships in 1987.

Health. In 1986 there were 8 hospitals, 128 clinics and 20 doctors.

DIPLOMATIC REPRESENTATIVES

Of the Solomon Islands in Great Britain
High Commissioner: Wilson Ifunaoa (accredited 12 Feb. 1987).

Of Great Britain in the Solomon Islands (Soltel House, Mendana Ave., Honiara)
High Commissioner: John Noss.

Of the Solomon Islands in the USA and to the United Nations
Ambassador: Francis J. Saemala.

Books of Reference

Solomon Islands Hand Book 1983. Government Information Service, Honiara, 1983
Amherst, Lord, and Thompson, B., *The Discovery of the Solomon Islands in 1568.* London, 1967
Kent, J., *The Solomon Islands.* Newton Abbot, 1972

SOMALIA

Capital: Mogadishu
Population: 6·11m. (1987)
GNP per capita: US$250 (1983)

Jamhuriyadda Dimugradiga Somaliya

HISTORY. The Somali Republic came into being on 1 July 1960 as a result of the merger of the British Somaliland Protectorate, which became independent on 26 June 1960, and the Italian Trusteeship Territory of Somalia.

On 21 Oct. 1969 Maj.-Gen. Mohammed Siyad Barre took power in a *coup,* suspended the Constitution and formed a Supreme Revolutionary Council to administer the country, which was renamed the Somali Democratic Republic. Constitutional government was re-established on 23 Sept. 1979.

AREA AND POPULATION. Somalia is bounded north by the Gulf of Aden, east and south by the Indian ocean, and west by Kenya, Ethiopia and Djibouti. Total area 637,657 sq. km (246,201 sq. miles). Census population (1975) 3,253,024 of whom 15% urban. Estimate (1987) 6·11m. In Aug. 1987 there were 700,000 refugees from Ethiopia.

The capital is Mogadishu (1m. including a floating population of about 250,000), other large towns being Hargeisa (400,000), Baidoa (300,000), Burao (300,000), Kismaayo (200,000), Merca (100,000), Kisimayu (70,000) and Berbera (65,000).

CLIMATE. Much of the country is arid, though rainfall is more adequate towards the south. Temperatures are very high on the northern coasts. Mogadishu. Jan. 79°F (26·1°C), July 78°F (25·6°C). Annual rainfall 17" (429 mm). Berbera. Jan. 76°F (24·4°C), July 97°F (36·1°C). Annual rainfall 2" (51 mm).

CONSTITUTION AND GOVERNMENT. A new Constitution was approved by referendum on 25 Aug. 1979 and came into force on 23 Sept. The sole legal Party (since 1 July 1976) is the Somali Revolutionary Socialist Party, administered by a 51-member Central Committee. There is an Executive President nominated by the Central Committee and elected for a 7-year term by direct popular vote; legislative power resides with a People's Assembly consisting of 171 members directly elected for a 5-year term from a single list of 171 SRSP candidates, together with a further 6 members appointed by the President. The President appoints and leads a Council of Ministers.

President: Maj.-Gen. Mohammed Siyad Barre (re-elected for a further 7-year term, Dec. 1986).

First Vice-President, Prime Minister: Lieut.-Gen. Mohammed Ali Samater. *Second Vice-President, Deputy Prime Minister:* Maj.-Gen. Hussein Kulmia Afrah. *Foreign Affairs:* Mohammad Ali Hamoud.

National flag: Light blue with a white star in the centre.

The national language is Somali. Arabic is also an official language and English and Italian are extensively spoken.

Local Government. There are 18 regions, sub-divided into 84 districts.

DEFENCE

Army. The Army consists of 4 tank, 45 mechanized and infantry, 1 commando and 1 surface-to-air missile, 3 field artillery brigades. Equipment includes 140 T-34/-54/-55, 123 M-47 and 30 Centurion main battle tanks. Strength (1988) 61,300. There are additional paramilitary forces: Police (8,000), Border Guards (1,500) and People's Militia (20,000).

Navy. The flotilla includes 4 fast attack/torpedo/patrol craft, 2 fast missile craft, 4 fast torpedo boats, 5 patrol craft, 1 medium landing ship and 4 minor landing craft. All are former Soviet naval units which are deteriorating with the withdrawal of Soviet spares. Personnel totalled 700 officers and men in 1988.

Air Force. Formed with a nucleus of aircraft taken over from the former Italian Air Corps of Somalia, in 1960, the Air Corps was built up with Soviet aid. Current equipment includes 6 MiG-21 and 20 F-6 (Chinese-built MiG-19) supersonic fighters, about 10 MiG-17 jet-fighters and 2 MiG-15UTI two-seat advanced trainers, and small transport, helicopter and training units. Latest equipment includes 2 Aeritalia G222, 6 Aviocar and 2 An-26 twin-turboprop transports, 6 SIAI-Marchetti SF.260W armed trainers and 4 Agusta-Bell 212 helicopters from Italy, plus 4 Islander and 2 P-166 light transports. Serviceability of most aircraft is reported to be low, a squadron of Hunter fighters being stored. Personnel (1988) 2,500.

INTERNATIONAL RELATIONS

Membership. Somalia is a member of UN, OAU, the Arab League, the Islamic League and is an ACP state of EEC.

ECONOMY

Planning. The 1982–86 Development Plan envisaged expenditure of Som.Sh. 16,299m. and a growth rate of 4·8%.

Budget. The budget for 1987 balanced at Som.Sh.17,919m..

Currency. The currency is the *Somali shilling,* divided into 100 cents. The money is issued in notes of 5, 10, 20 and 100 shillings and coins of 1, 5, 10, 50 cents and 1 shilling. In March 1988 £1 = 177·35 Som.Sh.; US$1 = 100·00 Som.Sh.

Banking. The bank of issue is the Central Bank of Somalia (founded in 1960 as the Somali National Bank). All foreign banks were nationalized in May 1970, and the Commercial and Savings Bank of Somalia and the Somali Development Bank, both state-owned, are the only other banks.

Weights and Measures. The metric system is in use.

ENERGY AND NATURAL RESOURCES

Electricity. Electricity production (1986) was 137m. kwh. Supply 220 volts; 50 Hz.

Minerals. Deposits of iron ore in the south and gypsum in the north are known to exist. Beryl and columbite are also found in the north. None are commercially exploited. Several firms hold exploration and drilling licences for oil. Uranium is found in the Juba area.

Agriculture. Somalia is essentially a pastoral country, and about 80% of the inhabitants depend on livestock-rearing (cattle, sheep, goats and camels). In Southern Somalia, especially along the Shebeli and Juba rivers, there are banana and sugarcane plantations with a cultivated area of some 90,000 hectares. Estimated production, 1986 (in 1,000 tonnes): Sugar-cane, 550; bananas, 70; maize, 382; sorghum, 251; grapefruit, 9; seed cotton, 3. Fresh fruit and oil seeds are grown in increasing quantities.

Livestock (1986): 16·2m. goats; 10·1m. sheep; 5·8m. camels; 3·8m. cattle; 1,000 horses, 25,000 asses and 23,000 mules.

Forestry. Production (1984) 5·2m. cu. metres.

Fisheries. 21 co-operatives, including 4,000 full-time and 10,000 part-time fishermen, caught some 15,300 tonnes in 1984.

INDUSTRY AND TRADE

Industry. A few small industries existed in 1986 including sugar refining, food processing, textile and petroleum refining. Production (1981): Textiles, 10·1m. yards; sugar, 26,800 tonnes; flour and pasta, 5,900 tonnes.

Commerce. In 1983 imports were Som.Sh.2,844m. and exports Som.Sh.1,423m. The chief exports are fresh fruit, livestock, hides and skins.

In 1984, 20% of imports came from Italy, 20% from USA and 13% from Saudi Arabia, while 59% of exports went to Saudi Arabia.

Total trade between the Somali Republic and UK (British Department of Trade returns, in £1,000 sterling):

	1983	1984	1985	1986	1987
Imports to UK	581	1,582	1,448	740	825
Exports and re-exports from UK	18,987	14,165	8,646	9,139	11,417

COMMUNICATIONS

Roads. Somalia has no developed transport system. Internal freight and passenger transport is almost entirely by means of road haulage. In 1985 there were 17,215 km of roads (2,500 km were paved), 17,754 passenger cars and 9,533 commercial vehicles.

Aviation. There is a commercial national airline, Somali Airlines. Mogadishu airport is used by Alitalia, Alyemda, Air Tanzania, PIA, Saudi Airways and Kenya Airways.

Shipping. There are 4 deep-water harbours at Kisimayu, Berbera, Marka and Mogadishu. The merchant fleet (1985) amounted to 26 vessels of 28,053 gross tons.

Post and Broadcasting. Number of telephones (1985), about 6,000. The state radio stations transmit in Somali, Arabic, English and Italian from Mogadishu, and Hargeisa. Receivers (1983) 134,000. A television service was started in 1983.

Cinemas. In 1970 there were 26 cinemas with a seating capacity of 23,000.

JUSTICE, RELIGION, EDUCATION AND WELFARE

Justice. There are 84 district courts, each with a civil and a criminal section. There are 8 regional courts and 2 Courts of Appeal (at Mogadishu and Hargeisa), each with a general section and an assize section. The Supreme Court is in Mogadishu.

Religion. The population is almost entirely Sunni Moslems.

Education. The nomadic life of a large percentage of the population inhibits education progress. In 1982 there were 220,680 pupils and 9,460 teachers in primary schools, there were 53,391 pupils and 2,201 teachers in secondary schools, and 1,836 students with 133 teachers at teacher-training establishments. The National University of Somalia in Mogadishu (founded 1959) had 2,332 students in 1980.

Health. In 1986 there were 450 doctors, 180 pharmacists, 2 dentists, 556 midwives and 1,834 nursing personnel.

DIPLOMATIC REPRESENTATIVES

Of Somalia in Great Britain (60 Portland Pl., London, W1N 3DG)
Ambassador: Salah Mohamed Ali (accredited 15 Feb. 1985).

Of Great Britain in Somalia (Waddada Xasan Geedd Abtoow 7/8, Mogadishu)
Ambassador: Jeremy Varcoe.

Of Somalia in the USA (600 New Hampshire Ave., NW, Washington, D.C., 20037)
Ambassador: Abdullah Addou.

Of USA in Somalia (Corso Primo Luglio, Mogadishu)
Ambassador: T. Frank Crigler.

Of Somalia to the United Nations
Ambassador: Abdillahi Said Osman.

Books of Reference

Background to the Liberation Struggle of the Western Somalis. Ministry of Foreign Affairs, Mogadishu, 1978
Darch, C., *Somalia.* [Bibliography] Oxford and Santa Barbara, 1986
Legum, C. and Lee, B., *Conflict in the Horn of Africa.* London, 1977

REPUBLIC OF
SOUTH AFRICA

Capital: Pretoria
Population: 23·39m. (1985)
GNP per capita: US$2,500 (1984)

Republiek van Suid-Afrika

HISTORY. The Union of South Africa was formed in 1910 and comprised the former self-governing British colonies of the Cape of Good Hope, Natal, the Transvaal and the Orange Free State.

The Union remained a member of the British Commonwealth until it became a republic on 31 May 1961.

AREA AND POPULATION. South Africa is bounded north by South West Africa, Botswana and Zimbabwe, north-east by Mozambique and Swaziland, east by the Indian ocean, south and west by the South Atlantic. Lesotho forms an enclave between the Orange Free State and Natal. The total area of the republic was (1983) 433,678[1] sq. miles (1,123,226 sq. km), divided between the provinces as follows: Cape Province, 249,331 (645,767); Natal, 33,578 (86,967); Transvaal, 101,351 (262,499); Orange Free State, 49,418 (127,993).

On 25 Dec. 1947 the Union formally took possession of Prince Edward Island and, on 30 Dec., of Marion Island, about 1,200 miles south-east of Cape Town.

[1] Excludes Walvis Bay (434 sq. miles), which is an integral part of the Cape Province but is administered under Act No. 24 of 1922, and also excludes South West Africa, Transkei, Ciskei, Bophuthatswana and Venda.

The census taken in 1904 in each of the 4 colonies was the first simultaneous census taken in South Africa. In 1911 the first Union census was taken.

| | | All races | | Whites | | Non-whites | |
	Total	Whites	Non-Whites	Males	Females	Males	Females
1904	5,174,827	1,117,234	4,057,593	635,317	481,917	2,046,370	2,011,223
1911	5,972,757	1,276,319	4,696,438	685,206	591,113	2,383,879	2,312,559
1921	6,927,403	1,521,343	5,406,060	783,006	738,337	2,753,188	2,652,872
1936	9,587,863	2,003,334	7,584,529	1,017,557	985,777	3,818,211	3,766,318
1946	11,415,925	2,372,044	9,043,881	1,194,201	1,177,843	4,610,862	4,433,019
1951	12,671,452	2,641,689	10,029,763	1,322,754	1,318,935	5,109,331	4,920,432
1960	15,994,181	3,080,159	12,914,022	1,534,923	1,545,236	6,504,317	6,409,705
1970	21,402,470	3,726,540	17,675,930	1,856,180	1,870,360	8,689,920	8,986,010
1980 [1]	24,885,960	4,528,100	20,357,860	2,265,400	2,262,700	10,393,780	9,964,080
1985 [2]	23,391,245	4,574,339	18,816,906	2,254,801	2,319,538	9,293,081	9,523,825

[1] Excludes Transkei, Bophuthatswana and Venda, but includes Ciskei (677,820).
[2] Also excludes Ciskei.

Of the non-White population in 1985, 15·2m. were Black, 2·8m. Coloured and 821,361 Asiatic. The numerically leading Black nations (1980) are the Zulu (5,682,520), Xhosa (2,987,340), Sepedi (North Sotho) (2,347,600), Seshoeshoe (South Sotho) (1,742,060), Tswana (1,357,360). Population, (1985) of the Black national areas: Kwa Zulu, 3,738,334; Gazankulu, 496,200; Lebowa, 1,833,144; Qwaqwa, 180,924; Ka Ngwane, 391,205; Kwa Ndebele, 235,511. These places are included in the land area figures for the provinces where they lie, but their inhabitants are not included in the provincial population figures. Growth rate 1980–85, 2·7% (Black, 3·1%; Coloured, 3%; Asian, 2%; White, 1·7%).

Vital statistics for calendar years:

| | Whites | | | Immi-grants | Emigrants | Asians and Coloureds | | |
	Births	Deaths	Marriages			Births	Deaths	Marriages
1984	81,550	38,175	44,840	28,793	8,550	111,946	30,895	29,282
1985	79,863	37,348	41,313	17,284	11,401	104,088	27,594	28,006
1986	72,938	38,241	41,575	6,994	13,711	101,331	28,714	28,276

Of the 6,994 immigrants in 1986, 3,818 were from Europe (of whom 2,012, UK); 2,433 from Africa (of whom 1,859, Zimbabwe); 359 from the Americas and 232 from Asia: of the 13,711 emigrants 6,741 went to Europe (of whom 5,407 to UK); 3,978 to Australia; 747 to Africa.

The registration of Black essential data was introduced on a compulsory basis many years ago. However, despite serious efforts on the part of the registering authorities, the Blacks are still largely reluctant to have their essential data registered. Consequently no complete vital statistics are available for this population group.

Principal cities (excluding suburbs) according to the latest statistics (1980) are:

Town	Whites	Africans	Coloureds	Asians	Total
Alberton (Trans.)	45,902	177,123	7,410	232	230,667
Benoni (Trans.)	56,508	135,752	997	13,553	206,810
Bloemfontein (O.F.S.)	90,625	124,768	15,295	...	230,688
Boksburg (Trans.)	61,337	73,385	15,408	157	150,287
Brakpan (Trans.)	31,902	46,135	1,674	21	79,732
Cape Town (C. Prov.)	124,876	5,608	80,748	2,598	213,830
Durban (Natal)	232,616	73,701	44,020	155,626	505,963
East London (C. Prov.)	62,735	77,372	18,150	2,325	160,582
Germiston (Trans.)	117,492	33,740	1,616	2,587	155,435
Johannesburg (Trans.)	435,586	947,290	101,769	51,812	1,536,457
Kempton Park (Trans.)	71,505	217,998	295	17	289,815
Kimberley (C. Prov.)	33,440	66,162	44,125	1,196	144,923
Krugersdorp (Trans.)	46,280	53,752	277	2,631	102,940
Pietermaritzburg (Natal)	53,780	62,330	11,424	51,438	178,972
Port Elizabeth (C. Prov.)	128,605	241,844	115,383	6,308	492,140
Pretoria (Trans.)	351,590	146,766	14,746	15,305	528,407
Roodepoort Maraisburg (Trans.)	83,217	77,511	3,620	967	165,315
Springs (Trans.)	49,752	101,691	1,254	1,277	153,974
Vereeniging (Trans.)	65,500	72,432	7,930	3,548	149,410
Welkom (O.F.S.)	38,027	133,679	4,902	...	176,608

In 1980 (census) Afrikaans was the home language of 2,581,080 Whites, English of 1,763,220 Whites. Of the 15,970,019 Black, Nguni languages (mainly Zulu, Xhosa, Swazi and Ndebele) are spoken by about 10m.; Sotho languages (Northern, Western and Southern) by 5·5m.; Tsonga languages by 900,000 and Venda by 169,700. Bushman and Khoe languages are spoken among nomads. Indian languages in use include Tamil, Hindi, Gujarati, Urdu and Telugu.

CLIMATE. The climate is healthy and invigorating, with abundant sunshine and relatively low rainfall. The factors controlling this include the latitudinal position, the oceanic location of much of the country, and the existence of high plateaus. The south-west has a Mediterranean climate, with rain mainly in winter, but most of the country has a summer maximum, though quantities show a clear decrease from east to west. Temperatures are remarkably uniform over the whole country. Pretoria. Jan. 70°F (21·1°C), July 52°F (11·1°C). Annual rainfall 31″ (785 mm). Bloemfontein. Jan. 73°F (22·8°C), July 47°F (8·3°C). Annual rainfall 23″ (564 mm). Cape Town. Jan. 69°F (20·6°C), July 54°F (12·2°C). Annual rainfall 20″ (508 mm). Durban. Jan. 75°F (23·9°C), July 62°F (16·7°C). Annual rainfall 40″ (1,008 mm). Johannesburg. Jan. 68°F (20°C), July 51°F (10·6°C). Annual rainfall 28″ (709 mm).

CONSTITUTION AND GOVERNMENT. On 2 Nov. 1983 a referendum among white voters approved the South Africa Constitution Bill which had previously been passed in the House of Assembly by 119 votes to 35. Turnout for the referendum was 2,062,469 (76·02%), of whom 1,360,223 voted in favour.

The new constitution became effective on 4 Sept. 1984. It provides for a tri-cameral parliament: the House of Assembly with 178 members of whom 166 are directly elected and 8 indirectly elected by White voters; the House of Representatives with 85 members of whom 80 are directly elected by Coloured voters; the House of Delegates with 45 members of whom 40 are directly elected by Indian voters. The term for all members is 5 years.

These houses choose (from their majority parties) respectively 50 White, 25 Coloured and 13 Indian members of an electoral college which elects an executive President. The President initiates legislation and resolves disputes between houses. He is helped by a 60-member President's Council: 20 members are elected by the House of Assembly, 10 by the House of Representatives and 5 by the House of Delegates; 15 are MPs nominated by himself and 10 are MPs nominated by Opposition parties.

The President appoints a Ministers' Council for each house, choosing 5 members from the majority party; a member chosen from outside the house must become a member of it within one year, and enjoy majority-party support. The Councils handle the affairs of their own population group and administer the departments established for that group. The President also appoints a Cabinet; any member appointed from outside Parliament must become a member of one of the three houses within one year. Any Ministers' Council member may be appointed a Cabinet member for a specific purpose or for an indefinite period. Any Ministers' Council may co-opt a Cabinet member in the same way, providing that member qualifies as a member of the Council in question.

Each house legislates on its own community affairs; the three houses have co-responsibility for national affairs. The State President, on the Cabinet's advice, decides whether a certain matter is a community or a national affair.

To hold an office of profit under the State (with certain exceptions) is a disqualification for membership of either House, as are also insolvency, crime and insanity. Pretoria is the seat of government, and Cape Town is the seat of legislature.

The state of the parties on 4 Sept. 1984: in the House of Assembly, National Party, 114; Progressive Federal Party, 26; Conservative Party, 17; New Republic Party, 8; South African Party, 3. In the House of Representatives, Labour Party, 76; others, 4. In the House of Delegates, National People's Party 18; Solidarity, 17; others, 5.

Indians voting in the elections to the new House of Delegates in Aug. 1984, 20·3% of registered voters; Coloured voters to the new House of Representatives, 30·9%.

President and Prime Minister: P. W. Botha (sworn in, 14 Sept. 1984).

The Cabinet in Jan. 1988 was composed as follows:

Transport Services: H. Schoeman. *Constitutional Development and Planning:* J. C. Heunis. *Foreign Affairs:* R. F. Botha. *Home Affairs and National Education:* F. W. de Klerk. *Law and Order:* A. Vlok. *Communications and Public Works:* Dr L. A. P. A. Munnik. *Health and Welfare and Chairman of the Ministers' Council for White Own Affairs:* Dr C. V. van der Merwe. *Co-operation and Development and (Black) Education:* Dr G. Viljoen. *Defence:* Gen. M. Malan. *Manpower:* P. T. du Plessis. *Industries and Commerce:* Dr D. J. de Villiers: *Justice:* H. J. Coetsee. *Agricultural Economics and Water Affairs:* J. J. G. Wentzel. *Mineral and Energy Affairs:* D. W. Steyn. *Finance:* B. J. du Plessis. *Environment and Tourism:* J. Wiley. *Chairman of the Ministers' Council for Coloured Own Affairs:* A. Hendrickse. *Chairman of the Ministers' Council for Indian Own Affairs:* A. Rajbansi.

The Prime Minister receives an annual salary of R43,000 and a reimbursive allowance of R20,000; a member of the Cabinet an annual salary of R23,500 and a reimbursive allowance of R6,500; and a Deputy Minister an annual salary of R19,000 and a reimbursive allowance of R6,500.

The English and Afrikaans languages are both official, subject to amendments carried by a two-thirds majority in joint session of both Houses of Parliament.

National flag: Three horizontal stripes of orange, white, blue, with the flags of the Orange Free State and the Transvaal, and the Union Jack side by side in the centre.

National anthem: The Call of South Africa/Die Stem van Suid-Afrika (words by C. J. Langenhoven, 1918; tune by M. L. de Villiers, 1921).

Provincial Administration. In each of the 4 provinces there is an Administrator appointed by the State President-in-Council for 5 years. Until 1986 there were provincial councils, each council electing an executive committee of 4 (either members or not of the council), the Administrator acting as chairman. Provincial councils were abolished in 1986; local governments remain, comprising municipal councils, management boards and other local committees, all of which have authority to deal with local matters, of which provincial finance, education (primary and secondary, other than higher education and technical education), hospitals, roads and bridges, townships, horse and other racing, and game and fish preservation are the most important. All ordinances passed by the local councils are subject to the veto of the State President-in-Council.

Black Administration. In 1959 the main ethnic groups received legislative recognition by the passing of the Promotion of Bantu Self-Government Act, which provided *inter alia* for the various ethnic groups to develop into self-governing national units.

As the Act envisages eventual political autonomy for each of the various national units and as representation in the highest White governing bodies is regarded as a retarding factor, the representation of Blacks by Whites in Parliament and the Cape Provincial Administration was abolished with effect from 30 June 1960.

Territorial Authorities were established between 1968 and 1970, and were converted to Legislative Assemblies in 1971.

Each national unit also has an Executive Council. These Councils, each headed by a Chief Councillor, consist of 6 members, except in the case of the South Sotho, where there are only 4. Each of these Councillors is responsible for the administration of a Department. A civil service has been established in each instance, staffed by citizens of the respective homelands. White officials will serve the homeland governments on secondment, until trained Black citizens are able to take over all duties.

There are (1987) 10 homelands of which 4 are recognised by the South African government as Independent:

The Transkei, territory of the Xhosa nation, became independent on 25 Oct. 1976 (*see* p. 1101), Bophuthatswana on 6 Dec. 1977 (*see* p. 1098), Venda on 13 Sept. 1979 (*see* p. 1102) and Ciskei on 4 Dec. 1981 (*see* p. 1104).

There are (1987) 6 territories with a degree of self-government but still forming part of the Republic: Kwa Zulu, Gazankulu (Machangana-Tsonga people), Lebowa (North Sotho), Qwaqwa (South Sotho), Ka Ngwane (Swazi) and Kwa Ndebele (Southern Ndebele).

DEFENCE. The South African Defence Force comprises a Permanent Force, a Citizen Force and a Commando organization. The Permanent Force consists of professional soldiers, airmen and seamen who are responsible for the administration and training of the whole Defence Force in peace-time, but who are gradually absorbed into the Citizen Force in time of war. The Permanent Force and the Citizen Force consist of Army, Air Force and Naval components; the Commando organization is an army and air organization.

Every white male citizen between 18 and 65 is liable to undergo training and to render personal service in time of war. Those between the ages of 16 and 25 are liable to undergo a compulsory course of peace training. Peace-time training in Commando organizations extends over a period of 16 years' intermittent training. Training in the Citizen Force takes the form of 2 years of continuous training, followed by 9 years during which training takes place at regular intervals.

Aliens have become liable for military service after 5 years' residence by Act of Parliament, 1967.

The S.A. Defence Force is administered by the Chief of the Defence Force, his advisers being the Chief of the Army, Chief of the Air Force and Chief of the Navy, Chief of Staff Operations, Chief of Staff Personnel, the Chief of Staff Management Services and the Surgeon-General.

Army. South Africa is divided into 11 territorial Commands. Within the various Commands are training units, of which members of the Permanent Force form the permanent staff. Courses of various types are held also at the S.A. Military College. The Army includes 1 armoured, 1 mechanized, 3 motorized and 1 parachute brigade; 1 special reconnaissance regiment and supporting artillery, engineer and signals units. Equipment includes some 250 Centurion/Olifant main battle tanks. Strength (1988) 76,400 (including 55,000 conscripts) with an Active Reserve of 146,000. Paramilitary forces are Commandos (130,000), South African Police (55,000) and Police Reserves (37,000).

Navy. The South African Navy has its headquarters at Pretoria.

The Navy includes 3 French-built diesel-powered patrol submarines, 2 old British-built anti-submarine frigates (if and when modernised), 9 fast missile armed patrol vessels (6 built in Durban and 3 in Israel), 10 coastal minesweepers (2 converted to minehunters and 2 employed for patrol), 1 British-built survey ship, 1 fleet replenishment ship, 1 small training vessel, 1 torpedo recovery vessel, 3 rescue launches, 30 very small harbour patrol boats and 3 tugs.

A custom-built submarine complex incorporating an operations centre alongside a synchrolift marine elevator capable of docking all South African warships except the large tanker, was opened at Simonstown in July 1972. A new maritime headquarters was opened at Silvermine in March 1973.

Naval personnel in 1988 totalled 7,480 officers and ratings, plus 1,500 national service men.

Air Force. There is 1 bomber squadron with 5 Canberra B.12 and 2 Canberra T.4; 1 bomber squadron with 6 Buccaneer Mk.50; 1 coastal patrol squadron with 18 Piaggio P.166S; 1 coastal patrol squadron with C-47s; 1 fighter-bomber squadron with 30 Mirage F1-AZ ground attack aircraft; 1 general-purpose fighter squadron with Mirage IIICZ interceptors and Mirage IIIRZ reconnaissance fighters; and 1 squadron with Mirage F1-CZ interceptors. Transport squadrons have 9 Transall C-160s, 7 C-130B Hercules, more than 40 C-47s, 7 C-54s, 4 Boeing 707s, 1 Viscount, 4 twin-jet HS.125s and 4 twin-turboprop Merlin IVA light transports. Four helicopter squadrons and No. 22 Flight have more than 80 Alouette IIIs, 60 Pumas, 8 Wasps, and 14 Super Frelons. T-6Gs are used for primary training, followed by advanced training on Impalas and Mirage IIIEZ/DZ, weapons training on Impalas, and multi-engine/crew training on C-47s. Built under licence in the Republic of South Africa, about 150 two-seat Impala Mk. 1s have been followed by 75 single-seat Impala Mk. 2s, based on the Aermacchi MB.326M and 326K respectively. Three squadrons operate C4M Kudu and AM.3C Bosbok liaison aircraft. South African industry is currently modernizing the Mirage combat aircraft (under the name 'Cheetah') and developing an armed helicopter derived from the Puma.

The Citizen Force has 3 squadrons of Impalas for counter-insurgency duties and C4M Kudu and AM.3C Bosbok liaison aircraft. CF personnel have additional functions in regular SAAF squadrons, notably those equipped with C-47 transports and P.166 light transport/coastal patrol aircraft. Total strength (1988) was about 13,000 regular officers and men.

INTERNATIONAL RELATIONS

Membership. The Republic of South Africa is a member of UN.

ECONOMY

Budget. Total revenue and expenditure of the central government's State Revenue Account in R1m.:

	1983–84	1984–85	1985–86
Revenue	20,477·8	24,223·4	29,851·2
Expenditure	22,953·8	27,984·6	33,026·4

The main sources of State Revenue 1985–86 were income tax, R16,158·4m.; general sales tax, R8,085·1m.; excise duties, R1,839·8m.; departmental receipts, R1,144·1m.

Public debt on 31 March 1987, R47,619m., of which R3,220m. was foreign debt; internal debt, R44,399m.

Currency. Decimal coinage was introduced in 1959, the units being the *rand* (abbreviated as R) and the *cent* (abbreviated as c). The rand/cent coinage system came into operation on 14 Feb. 1961. The decimal coins are: *Gold coins*. 2 rand; 1 rand. *Silver coins*. 50 cents; 20 cents; 10 cents; 5 cents. *Bronze coins*. 2 cents; 1 cent. In March 1988, £1 = R3·69; US$1 = R2·86.

Banking. In Dec. 1920, under the South African Currency and Banking Act, 1920, a Central Reserve Bank was established at Pretoria. It commenced operations in June 1921, and began to issue notes in April 1922. The bank has branches in Pretoria (Head Office), Johannesburg, Cape Town, Durban, Port Elizabeth, East London, Bloemfontein, Pietermaritzburg and Windhoek. Total deposits, 31 March 1987, R3,957m.; assets, R12,158m.

In March 1987 there were 14 commercial banks and 22 general banks (formerly hire-purchase and savings banks), with total liabilities, 31 March 1987, commercial banks, R53,369m., general, R15,412m.; 10 merchant banks (R5,352m.) and 3 discount houses (R1,612m.) The Land and Agricultural Bank had R8,342m. total liabilities; Post Office Savings Bank deposits, R3,356m.

Weights and Measures. The Measuring Units and National Measuring Standards Act, 1973, confirmed the adoption of the international metric system.

ENERGY AND NATURAL RESOURCES

Electricity. The total capacity of the power plants controlled by the Electricity Supply Commission was 26,150,000 kw at the end of 1985. There were 20 coal-fired stations, 3 hydro-electric stations (1,540 mw) and 2 gas-turbine stations (342 mw). Production (1986) 145,394m. kwh of which ESCOM generated 133,644m. kwh. Net production (sent out from plants for consumption), 133,293, of which ESCOM, 123,643. Supply 220 and 240 volts; 50 Hz.

Oil. Small amounts of oil and gas were found off-shore (south west of Mossel Bay) in Oct. 1982.

Water. Government activities are governed by the Water Act, 1956 (as amended), which is administered by the Directorate of Water Affairs. A Water Research Commission was established in 1971 to co-ordinate and promote research; it is responsible for hydrological research, major water resource development, water pollution control. The combined average flow of South Africa's rivers is about 52,000m. cu. metres annually, most of it lost by evaporation and spillage. Water demand (now mainly urban-industrial) grows at 7% annually.

The Orange River Project was launched in 1966. It is to embrace 3 major dams on the Orange River, 9 smaller dams or weirs, a 51½-mile tunnel, 20 hydro-electric power stations and a system of canals.

In Oct. 1986 South Africa signed a treaty with Lesotho to allow damming the Orange River head waters within Lesotho and diverting the collected water through tunnels into the Vaal River system of the OFS. Lesotho is to receive royalties and hydro-electric power in exchange.

Minerals. Value of the main mineral production sales (in R1,000):

	1983	1984	1985	1986
Asbestos	113,279	101,207	102,453	99,064
Chrome ore	71,453	121,627	231,669	212,794
Coal	2,539,731	3,348,058	4,962,285	5,245,943
Copper	351,137	365,761	535,853	550,178
Diamonds	525,217	463,019	702,648	647,996
Fluorspar	30,744	49,209	56,510	62,104
Gold	10,180,209	11,556,315	15,296,931	17,287,356
Iron ore	309,919	372,728	472,353	473,510
Lime and limestone	162,493	182,831	203,975	237,311
Manganese	110,219	202,566	298,761	271,024
Phosphate	74,271	97,962	118,855	150,287
Silver	79,342	64,332	78,248	72,087

Total value of all minerals sold (1986), R29,240·1m.

Mineral production (tonnes) 1986: Coal, 170m.; iron ore, 24·5m.; phosphates, 2·9m.; manganese ore, 3·7m.; chromite, 3m.; asbestos, 138,000; copper, 196,000; lime and limestone, 14·3m.; fluorspar, 334,000; gold, 635,233 kg; silver, 216,599 kg; diamonds, 10·1m. carats.

At 31 Dec. 1986 the number of persons engaged in mining was 752,264. Of these, 553,668 were engaged in goldmining.

Minerals. A Quarterly Report of Production and Sales. Department of Mineral and Energy Affairs. Pretoria, from 1936
Mining Statistics. Department of Mineral and Energy Affairs, Pretoria, from 1966

Agriculture. Much of the land suitable for mechanical farming has unreliable rainfall. Of the total area natural pasture occupies 58% (71·3m. hectares); about 14m. hectares are suitable for dry-land farming, of which 10·6m. are actually cultivated.

In 1986, agriculture, forestry and fisheries contributed approximately 6% to GDP.

Production (1986–7, in 1,000 tonnes): Maize, 7,371; sorghum, 467; wheat, 2,592; groundnuts, 85; sunflower seed, 397; sugar-cane, 20,000; oranges, 522; potatoes, 1,072; vegetables, 2,851.

Livestock, in 1,000 (1986): 11,750 cattle, 29,481 sheep, 5,800 goats, 1,445 pigs. The 1983 production of red meat was 957,000 tonnes, poultry meat 457,000 tonnes, wool, 119,000 tonnes. Eggs produced, 272m. dozen; milk, 2,067m. litres.

Cotton-growing is now undertaken by many farmers, the plant being found a better drought resistant than either tobacco or maize. Viticulture and fruit-growing are important. Gross value of production (1986–87), R127·7m.

In 1986–87 the gross value of agricultural production was R12,677m. (field crops, R4,787m.; livestock products, R5,825m.; horticultural products, R2,365m.).

Forestry. The commercial forests occupy about 1·62m. hectares, of which 148,000 hectares are indigenous trees and the rest exotic trees (pine, gum, wattle). The total value of saw logs delivered from plantation was about 45m. cu. metres in 1986.

The Republic is self sufficient in newsprint and exports pulp and paper.

Fisheries. About 90% of the catch is taken from the cold waters off the west coast. In 1983 sea fisheries caught 376,467 tonnes of pelagic shoal fish, mainly anchovy, and trawl fisheries (hake and sole) landed 123,000 tonnes. The fishing fleet consists (1983) of about 5,700 vessels, including 139 purse-seiners and 128 trawlers.

INDUSTRY AND TRADE

Industry. Net value of sales of the principal groups of industries (in R1m.) in 1986: Processed food, 13,667; beverages and tobacco, 3,426; vehicles, 5,318; basic metals, 9,463·3; chemicals and products, 17,756; non-electrical machinery, 4,331; electrical machinery, 3,876; fabricated metal products except machinery, 5,555; printing and publishing, 1,795; wood and cork products except furniture, 1,357; clothing, 1,947; paper and products, 3,785; textiles, 3,497; total net value including other groups, 86,055. Manufacturing industry contributed R28,321m. to gross domestic product of R128,524m. in 1986.

Industrial employment (except mining) at 28 Feb. 1987: Manufacturing employed 1,322,100 workers; construction, 295,600; trade and accommodation services, 742,917 (31 Dec. 1986).

Average monthly earnings of white employee, 1984, R1,402; of black, R364.

In 1985 in private manufacturing 170,900 workers were employed in the food industry (earning R1,264,967,000); textiles employed 102,000 (R657,072,000); clothing, 111,800 (R524,126,000); transport equipment, 99,900 (R1,233,585,000); non-metallic mineral products, 79,100 (R645,653,000); metal products, 123,200 (R1,302,704,000); chemical, petroleum and coal products, 95,200 (R1,351,143,000).

Trade Unions. At 1 Jan. 1984 there were 194 trade unions with an estimated total membership of 1,288,748. There were 56 White unions, 35 Coloured and 23

Black. Thirty-six unions were mixed and 42 had members from all population groups.

The Industrial Conciliation Amendment Act (1979) provides for freedom of association to all workers irrespective of race; it is now possible for a Black trade union (as opposed to a union with some Black members) to register. Unions are barred from political activity.

Commerce. South Africa, Botswana, Lesotho, Swaziland and Transkei are members of a customs union and the foreign trade statistics shown below represent the combined imports and exports of these countries. The total value of the imports and exports was as follows (in R1m.):

	Imports		Exports
1984	21,804·4	1984	25,584·5
1985	22,989·1	1985	36,474·2
1986	26,893·7	1986	41,796·7

The principal commodity groups of imports and exports (in R1m.) in 1986 were:

Imports		Exports	
Machinery	7,317·8	Minerals and products	4,967·2
Vehicles and aircraft	2,963·2	Base metals	4,756·8
Chemical products	3,050·5	Precious stones, metals	
Base metals	1,267·6	and coins	3,036·7
Scientific and special		Textiles	934·4
equipment	1,167·2	Chemical products	1,174·0
Resins and plastics	1,140·0	Food, beverages and tobacco	947·8
Textiles	913·9	Vegetable products	1,059·6

The geographical origin of South Africa's imports and the direction of its export trade were mainly as follows in 1985:

	Imports %	Exports %
Africa	2	4
Europe	42	23
USA	13	9
Japan	10	8

Total trade between South Africa and UK (British Department of Trade returns, in £1,000 sterling):

	1983	1984	1985	1986	1987
Imports to UK	764,909	725,631	989,757	829,305	658,162
Exports and re-exports from UK	1,109,039	1,205,143	1,009,629	849,557	948,584

Tourism. In 1986, 644,502 tourists visited the Republic of South Africa.

COMMUNICATIONS

Roads. The railway administration operates the long-distance road motor services, together with private operators.

There were at 31 March 1982, 184,802 km of roads, of which some 1,967 km of national roads and 46,888 km of provincial roads were surfaced.

South African Transport Services carried 13·2m. passengers and 4·4m. tonnes of goods by road in the year ended 31 March 1986; private operators carried 911,112 passengers and 242·2m. tonnes of goods. Buses have been desegregated in Cape Town and Durban.

Motor vehicles in operation on 30 June 1985 included 2,973,000 passenger cars, 1,055,000 commercial vehicles. New motor vehicles licensed, year ending 30 June 1986, 285,000.

Railways. Railway history in South Africa begins in 1860 with the line Durban–Point. With the formation of the Union in 1910, the state-owned lines in the 4 provinces (12,194 km) were amalgamated into one state undertaking, which also took over the control of the harbours–the South African Railways and Harbours Administration now known as South African Transport Services.

Government-owned lines operated by the administration (1986) totalled 23,821 km (mostly 1,065 mm gauge), of which 7,913 km were electrified. Passenger journeys, 1986, 658·7m.; revenue-earning goods and livestock traffic, 167m. tonnes.

The railways earned R5,410m. in 1986, to which goods contributed R2,646·6m.

Aviation. Civil aviation in South Africa is controlled by the Department of Transport, which administers the following state-owned airports: Jan Smuts Airport, Johannesburg; D. F. Malan Airport, Cape Town; Louis Botha Airport, Durban; J. B. M. Hertzog Airport, Bloemfontein; Ben Schoeman Airport, East London; H. F. Verwoerd Airport, Port Elizabeth; B. J. Vorster Airport, Kimberley; P. W. Botha Airport, George; Pierre van Ryneveld Airport, Upington. At other airports the Department provides air navigation services.

South African Airways, as the national air carrier, operate scheduled international air services within Africa and to Europe, South America, the USA, the Far East and Australia. Twenty independent operators provide internal flights which link up with SAA's internal network.

During 1985 South African Airways carried 4,031,728 passengers (3,494,918 on internal flights) and 78,508 tonnes of freight and mail (44,948).

Shipping. The main ports are Durban, Cape Town, Saldanha, Richards Bay, Port Elizabeth and East London. Smaller ports are Mossel Bay, Port Nolloth, Walvis Bay and Lüderitz. During 1985 main ports handled 93m. tons of cargo, of which Richards Bay handled 47·7m. tons and Durban handled 23·2m. tons.

Post and Broadcasting. On 31 March 1982 there were in South Africa 1,641 money-order post offices and 555 postal agencies.

On 30 Sept. 1982 the international telex switchboard served 26,323 telex subscribers in South Africa. Line capacity of automatic telephone exchanges, 2·1m.; there were (1984) 3,471,519 telephones.

The South African Broadcasting Corporation had, in Sept. 1980, 2·3m. listeners' licences and there were 1·45m. television licences.

Cinemas (1980). There were 620 including 140 drive-ins.

Newspapers (1981). There are 8 Afrikaans and 14 English daily newspapers.

JUSTICE, RELIGION, EDUCATION AND WELFARE

Justice. The common law of the republic is the Roman–Dutch law–that is, the uncodified law of Holland as it was at the date of the cession of the Cape in 1806. The law of England as such is not recognized as authoritative, though by statute the principles of English law relating to evidence and to mercantile matters, *e.g.*, companies, patents, trademarks, insolvency and the like, have been introduced. In shipping and insurance, English law is followed in the Cape Province, and it has also largely influenced civil and criminal procedure throughout the republic. In all other matters, family relations, property, succession, contract, etc., Roman–Dutch law rules, English decisions being valued only so far as they agree therewith–

The Supreme Court of South Africa is constituted as follows: (i) The Appellate Division, consisting of the Chief Justice and as many Judges of Appeal as the State President may stipulate, is the highest court and its decisions are binding on all courts. It has no original jurisdiction, but is purely a Court of Appeal. (ii) The Provincial Divisions: In each province there is a provincial division of the Supreme Court, while in the Cape there are three such divisions possessing both original and appellate jurisdiction. (iii) The Local Divisions: There is a local division each in the Transvaal and Natal exercising the same original jurisdiction within limited areas as the provincial divisions. The judges hold office till they attain the age of 70 years. No judge can be removed from office except by the State President upon an address from both Houses of Parliament on the ground of misbehaviour or incapacity. The circuit system is fully developed.

The Black appeal courts and 3 Black divorce courts have jurisdiction to some extent concurrent with and in certain respects exclusive of that of the Supreme Court in cases in which the parties are Black.

Each province is further divided into districts with a magistrate's court having a prescribed civil and criminal jurisdiction. From this court there is an appeal to the provincial divisions of the Supreme Court, and thence to the appellate division.

Magistrates' convictions carrying sentences above a prescribed limit are subject to automatic review by a judge. In addition, several regional divisions consisting of a number of districts have been constituted. Convictions of such courts are not subject to automatic review by a judge.

Courts of Black affairs commissioners have been constituted in defined areas to hear all civil cases and matters between Black and Black only. An appeal lies to the Black appeal court, whose decision is final, unless the court consents to an appeal to the appellate division of the Supreme Court on a point stated by the court itself. Black affairs commissioners have concurrent criminal jurisdiction with magistrates' courts in respect of certain offences committed by Black, while a limited civil and criminal jurisdiction is conferred upon the Black chief or headman over his own tribe.

Police. In 1980 the staff of the Police department numbered 34,271 (18,370 White). There were 46 police stations manned exclusively by Blacks, 16 by Coloureds and 1 by Indians.

In 1983 there were 242 prisons with (Sept. 1983) a monthly average of 106,000 prisoners.

Religion. A sample tabulation of the 1980 census results as regards religious denominations shows the following: *Whites:* Nederduits Gereformeerde Kerk, 1,693,640; Anglicans, 456,020; Methodists, 414,080; Roman Catholics, 393,640; Nederduits Hervormde Kerk, 246,340; Presbyterians, 128,920; Gereformeerde Kerk, 128,360; Apostolics, 125,920; other Christians, 566,640; Jews, 119,220; others, 255,320. *Blacks:* Methodists, 11,554,280; Black independent churches, 4,954,000; Nederduits Gereformeerde Kerk, 1,103,560; Roman Catholics, 1,676,680; Anglican, 797,040; Lutheran, 698,400; other Christian churches, 1,760,860; non-Christian churches, 101,700; others, 4,277,240. *Coloureds and Asians:* Nederduits Gereformeerde Kerk, 678,380; Hindus, 512,360; Anglican, 360,380; Roman Catholic, 285,980; Islam 318,080; others, 1,279,020.

Membership of the white branch of the Nederduits Gereformeerde Kerk was opened to all races in 1986.

Education. Primary and secondary public education, other than that specifically provided elsewhere, falls under the Provincial Administration. In terms of the National Education Policy Act, 1967, the Minister of Education, Arts and Science may, after consultation with the Provincial Administrators and the National Advisory Education Council, determine general educational policy within the framework of the Act. Black education is the responsibility of the Department of Black Education and Training, while education for Coloureds and Indians is controlled by the Department of Internal Affairs.

Public primary and secondary schools in 1986: For Whites there were 2,452 schools with 955,000 pupils and 67,848 teachers. For Coloureds, 2,044 schools with 807,000 pupils and 30,415 teachers. For Indians there were 450 schools with 232,000 pupils and 10,878 teachers. For Blacks there were 12,484 schools with 4,319,000 pupils and 104,542 teachers. A non-racial school (100 pupils) opened near Durban in 1987.

Private Schools. To a certain extent the activities of private schools are controlled by government regulations. Their pupils generally sit for the state schools' examinations. These schools make provision for kindergarten, elementary and preparatory, general primary, secondary and commercial education.

In 1984, 135 private schools for Whites had 3,130 teachers and 43,111 students; 12 schools for Coloureds had 115 teachers and 2,242 students; 84 for Blacks had 784 teachers and 25,434 students.

Higher Education. In March 1986 tertiary-level students included 233,633 whites (5% of white population), 26,397 coloureds (0·8%), 22,005 Indians (3%) and 79,440 blacks (0·56%).

Of these, 162,627 whites, 20,407 coloureds, 19,345 Indians and 69,301 blacks were at university and Colleges of Education. There are 17 universities in the republic: (1) The University of Cape Town. (2) The University of Natal in Durban and Pietermaritzburg. (3) The University of the Orange Free State at Bloemfontein (teaching in Afrikaans). (4) Potchefstroom University for Christian Higher Education, Potchefstroom (Afrikaans). (5) The University of Pretoria (Afrikaans). (6) Rhodes University, Grahamstown, C.P. (7) The University of Stellenbosch (Afrikaans). (8) The University of the Witwatersrand, Johannesburg. (9) The University of South Africa, with its seat in Pretoria, which conducts a Division of External Studies by means of correspondence and vacation courses (English and Afrikaans); it is also an examining body. (10) The University of Port Elizabeth (English and Afrikaans). (11) Rand Afrikaans University, Johannesburg (All may enrol, white, black, coloured or Asian students).

The University of Fort Hare (12), the University of the North (13) near Pietersburg and the University of Zululand (14) near Empangeni, Natal, are operated by the Department of Education and Training and provide education at university level for Blacks, the University of the Western Cape (15), Bellville (Cape), offers university facilities to the Coloured population and is administered by the Department of Internal Affairs as is the University for Indians (16), the University of Durban-Westville, at Durban. The Medical University of South Africa (17) is for Black students.

Technical and Vocational Education. Technical, vocational and special education for persons other than those for whom specific provision is made: The Department of National Education is responsible for the maintenance, management and control of or the payment of subsidies to colleges for advanced technical education, technical colleges, technical institutes, special schools, schools of industries and reform schools. Colleges for advanced technical education provide education on an advanced level for a variety of technical, commercial and general courses of study as well as secondary education on a part-time basis. Technical colleges and technical institutes are mainly responsible for the training of apprentices and the education, on a part-time basis, of persons not subject to compulsory school attendance. Special schools for handicapped children cater for the educational needs of those who are blind, partially sighted, deaf, hard of hearing, epileptic, cerebral palsied and physically handicapped. Children found to be in need of care by a children's court, are admitted to schools of industries and reform schools.

The Department of Internal Affairs has taken over all schools of this nature for Coloureds.

In 1986, technical and training colleges (except Colleges of Education) had 71,006 white students; 5,990 coloured; 5,047 Indian; 10,139 black.

Health. In 1986 (preliminary) there were 22,525 medical practitioners and specialists, 3,704 dental specialists and dentists, 88,795 nurses; in 1984 there were 629 hospitals. In 1983 there were 14,333 beds in psychiatric hospitals; 652,054 mentally ill were treated as out-patients, and others treated in psychiatric wards in general hospitals.

All public health services rendered by government bodies are free, or charged according to the patient's means. The Department of Health and Welfare works according to the Health Act, 1977. The Department works with the Departments of Internal Affairs and of Co-operation and Development; it also co-operates with the health departments of Black national states.

In preventive medicine there are important programmes for controlling infectious diseases, genetic disorders and malnutrition. Notifiable diseases reported in recent years have been mainly tuberculosis, measles, typhoid, malaria, viral hepatitis, cholera and meningococcal infection.

Social Welfare. Under the Social Pensions Act, 1973, pensions and allowances are made to aged, blind, disabled and war veterans, subject to a means test. Family allowances are paid to families with 3 or more children and inadequate income, and to mothers alone with one or more children and inadequate income.

Welfare Services. South Africa is not a welfare state, yet provides many services for the community. Welfare work on behalf of the Government is done by the Departments of Health and Welfare, Co-operation and Development, and Internal Affairs.

Voluntary organizations are numerous. The work of all these bodies is co-ordinated by the South African Welfare Council and regional welfare boards set up under the National Welfare Act, 1978.

The Children's Act, 1960, provides for the protection of children from neglect, ill-treatment and exploitation; the child is cared for within the family whenever possible, but there are also State subsidies to children's homes, crèches and foster families.

Welfare services for the aged are mainly provided by voluntary bodies with government subsidies; the same principle applies to the care of the handicapped, but there are State settlements for the permanently handicapped, and State sheltered-employment programmes for handicapped adults.

The National Advisory Board on Rehabilitation Matters advises and brings together the voluntary and government agencies working on drug abuse and alcoholism.

In all fields of welfare, State subsidies enable voluntary bodies to employ professional social workers.

DIPLOMATIC REPRESENTATIVES

Of South Africa in Great Britain (South Africa Hse., Trafalgar Sq., London, WC2N 5DP)
Ambassador: P. R. Killen.

Of Great Britain in South Africa (6 Hill St., Arcadia, Pretoria, 0002)
Ambassador: R. W. Renwick, CMG.

Of South Africa in the USA (3051 Massachusetts Ave., NW, Washington, D.C., 20008)
Ambassador: Piet G. Koornhof.

Of the USA in South Africa (225 Pretorius St., Pretoria)
Ambassador: Edward Perkins.

Of South Africa to The United Nations
Ambassador: Albert Leslie Manley.

Books of Reference

Statistical Information: The Bureau (formerly Office) of Census and Statistics (Schoeman St., Pretoria)
    The Customs and Excise Office, Pretoria, publishes *Monthly Abstract of Trade Statistics* (from 1946) and *Trade and Shipping of the Union of South Africa* (annually, 1910–55); *Foreign Trade Statistics* (annually, from 1956)

Benson, M. *Nelson Mandela: The Man and the Movement.* New York, 1986
Bissell, R. E., and Crocker, C. A., *South Africa in the 1980s.* Boulder, 1979
Böhning, W. R., *Black Migration to South Africa.* Geneva, 1981
Branford, J., *A Dictionary of South African English.* Rev. ed. OUP, 1980
Davenport, T. R. H., *South Africa: A Modern History.* 3rd ed. CUP, 1986
de Villiers, L., *South Africa: A Skunk Among Nations.* London, 1975
Gann, L. H. and Duignan, P., *Why South Africa will Survive.* London, 1981
Goldenhuys, D., *The Diplomacy of Isolation: South African Foreign Policy Making.* Johannesburg, 1984
Hill, C. R., *Change in South Africa: Blind Alleys and New Directions.* London, 1983
Musiker, R., *South Africa,* [Bibliography] Oxford and Santa Barbara, 1980
Parker, F. J., *South Africa: Lost Opportunities.* Lexington, 1983
Price, R., and Rossberg, C., *The Apartheid Regime: Political Power and Racial Domination.* Univ. of California Press, 1980
Thompson, L., *The Political Mythology of Apartheid.* Yale Univ. Press, 1985
Oxford History of South Africa. OUP, Vol. 1, 1969; Vol. 2 1971

PROVINCE OF THE CAPE OF GOOD HOPE

Kaapprovinsie

HISTORY. The colony of the Cape of Good Hope was founded by the Dutch in the year 1652. Britain took possession of it from 1795 to 1803 and again in 1806, and it was formally ceded to Great Britain by the Convention of London, 13 Aug. 1814. Letters patent issued in 1850 declared that in the colony there should be a Parliament which should consist of the Governor, a Legislative Council and a House of Assembly. On 31 May 1910 the colony was merged in the Union of South Africa, thereafter forming an original province of the Union.

AREA AND POPULATION. The following table gives the population of the Cape of Good Hope[1] (area (1980) 646,332 sq. km) at the last census:

		All races			Whites		Non-Whites	
	Total	Males	Females	Males	Females	Males	Females
1936	3,527,865	1,663,169	1,864,796	396,058	394,993	1,267,011	1,469,803
1946	4,051,424	1,924,334	2,127,090	433,849	436,300	1,490,485	1,690,790
1951	4,426,726	2,110,674	2,316,052	463,917	471,168	1,646,757	1,844,884
1960	5,360,234	2,553,245	2,806,989	493,370	507,398	2,059,875	2,299,591
1970[2]	4,293,726	2,151,629	2,142,097	546,761	567,448	1,604,868	1,579,649
1980[3]	5,091,360	2,575,460	2,515,900	624,680	639,360	1,950,780	1,876,540
1986[1]	4,901,261	2,371,906	2,529,355	...	...	...	...

[1] Including Walvis Bay (699 sq. km).   [2] Excluding Transkei.
[3] Excluding Transkei, Ciskei and Bophuthatswana.

Present area, 641,379 sq. km (247,637 sq. miles), including the enclave of Walvis Bay 699 sq. km (270 sq. miles) on the coast of South West Africa (Namibia) which forms an administrative part of the Cape Province.

Of the non-White population in 1980, 32,120 were Asians, 1,569,040 were Blacks and 2,226,160 Coloureds.

Vital statistics for calendar years:

	Births	Deaths	Marriages
1979	80,900	32,185	34,243
1980	80,546	34,162	29,334
1983	73,654	39,164	39,162
1984	74,122	41,345	40,165

ADMINISTRATION. In June 1986 the provincial councils were abolished. Cape Town is the seat of the provincial administration.

Administrator: Eugene Louw.

The province is divided into 111 magisterial districts and 35 divisions. Each division has a council of at least 6 members (15 in the Cape Division) elected quinquennially by the owners or occupiers of immovable property. The duties devolving upon divisional councils include the construction and maintenance of roads and bridges, local rating, vehicle taxation (except motor vehicle taxation) and preservation of public health. There are 216 municipalities, each governed by a mayor and councillors. Municipal elections are held biennially.

FINANCE. In 1984–85 revenue amounted to R1,996,920,000 and expenditure to R1,987,920,000.

MINING. For mineral production, *see* p. 1082.

AGRICULTURE. Viticulture in the republic is almost exclusively confined to the Cape Province, but practically all other forms of agricultural and pastoral activity are pursued.

INDUSTRY. The province has brick, tile and pottery works, saw-mills, engineering works, foundries, grain-mills, distilleries and wineries, clothing factories, furniture, boot and shoe factories, etc.

RELIGION. Sample tabulation, 1980 census. Nederduits Gereformeerde Kerk, 1,110,516; Gereformeerde Kerk, 12,714; Nederduits Hervormde Kerk, 115,012; Anglican, 430,102; Presbyterian, 35,126; Methodist, 112,961; Roman Catholic, 251,000; Apostolic, 73,140; Lutheran, 89,134; Islam, 183,000; Hindu, 7,000; Independent Churches, 94,103; other Christian Churches, 440,000; Jews, 31,621; Agnostics, 55,000.

EDUCATION. On 1 April 1986 the Education Department came within the jurisdiction of the Central Government. Education is compulsory for all White children. Primary and secondary education is free to the end of the calendar year in which the age of 19 years is attained.

Whites (1985). There were 828 government and aided schools with 14,205 teachers and 238,853 pupils; 8 teacher-training colleges with 291 lecturers and 1,841 students; 53 private schools with 13,859 pupils.

Coloureds (1985). There were 1,776 government and aided schools with 26,583 teachers and 657,391 pupils; 13 teacher-training colleges with 6,709 students; 18 private schools with 2,652 pupils.

Black (1985). There were 1,137 government schools with 7,105 teachers and 318,541 pupils and 17 private schools with 118 teachers and 6,120 pupils.

Asians (1985). There were 8 government schools with 201 teachers and 5,400 pupils.

PROVINCE OF NATAL

HISTORY. Natal was annexed to Cape Colony in 1844, placed under separate government in 1845, and on 15 July 1856 established as a separate colony. By this charter partially representative institutions were established, and in 1893 the colony attained responsible government. The province of Zululand was annexed to Natal on 30 Dec. 1897. The districts of Vryheid, Utrecht and part of Wakkerstroom, formerly belonging to the Transvaal, were annexed in Jan. 1903. On 31 May 1910 the colony was merged in the Union of South Africa as an original province of the Union.

AREA AND POPULATION. The province (including Kwa Zulu, 36,073 sq. km) has an area of 91,785 sq. km, with a seaboard of about 576 km. The climate is sub-tropical on the coast and somewhat colder inland. The province is divided into 45 magisterial districts.

The census returns of population (excluding Kwa Zulu) for 1985 were:

	All races			Whites		Non-Whites	
	Total	Males	Females	Males	Females	Males	Females
1960	2,979,034	1,443,561	1,535,473	166,404	222,750	1,227,157	1,362,468
1970	4,236,770	2,009,410	2,227,360	171,005	214,960	1,794,430	2,004,610
1980	2,676,340	1,360,600	1,315,740	276,240	285,620	1,084,360	1,030,120
1985	2,145,018	1,072,426	1,072,592	274,987	285,234	797,629	787,358

Of the non-White population in 1980, 665,340 were Asians, 91,020 Coloureds and 1,358,120 Blacks. Population of Kwa Zulu, *see* p. 1077.

ADMINISTRATION. State of parties Oct. 1985: New Republic Party, 14; National Party, 5; Progressive Federal Party, 1.

The seat of provincial government in Natal is Pietermaritzburg. In April 1978 the area of East Griqualand was transferred to Natal from Cape Province.

Administrator: The Hon. Radclyffe Macbeth Cadman.

FINANCE. In 1986–87 revenue amounted to R836,333,000 and expenditure to R831,003,000.

MINING. The province is rich in mineral wealth, particularly coal. For figures of mineral production, see p. 1082.

AGRICULTURE. Sugar and citrus growing are of major importance. On the coast and in Zululand there are vast plantations of sugar-cane (about 375,000 hectares), producing, in 1985, 20,756,000 tons. Cereals of all kinds (especially maize), fruits, vegetables, the *Acacia molissima* (the bark of which is much used for tanning purposes) and other crops are produced. Large areas are devoted to timber plantations and forestry.

INDUSTRY. Natal is highly industrialized. There are metallurgical, chemical, paper, rayon and food-processing plants, iron and steel foundries, petrol refineries, pulp-mills, explosives and fertilizer plants, milk- and meat-canning factories.

EDUCATION. The Department of Education and Culture controls primary and secondary education for Whites. Control was transferred from the province to central government on 1 April 1986, and the classification of government-aided schools changed to private although they continue to receive a subsidy.

Whites (1987). There were 266 government schools with 102,582 pupils; 3 residential teacher-training colleges with 1,116 students; 54 private schools with 11,171 pupils; 11 special schools and training centres with 1,316 pupils and 9 technical colleges with 4,823 pupils.

Coloureds (1987). There were 64 state and state-aided schools with 2,879 teachers and 30,182 pupils; 17 state subsidized pre-primary schools with 43 teachers and 1,093 pupils; 1 teacher-training college with 401 students and 36 lecturers; 1 technical college with 974 full-time students and 319 part-time students.

Blacks (1987). There were 1,074 schools with 5,556 teachers and 192,504 pupils. These schools are situated in the white area of Natal and the south-eastern Transvaal.

Asians (1987). There were 441 state and state-aided schools with 11,652 teachers and 237,163 pupils; 30 pre-primary schools with 2,182 children; 2 schools of industries with 226 pupils; 16 special schools and training centres with 1,482 pupils; 2 technical colleges with 3,040 full-time students; 2 Colleges of Education with 625 students and 1 college for further training for teachers with 137 full-time students.

PROVINCE OF THE TRANSVAAL

HISTORY. The Transvaal was one of the territories colonized by the Boers who left the Cape Colony during the Great Trek in 1831 and following years. In 1852, by the Sand River Treaty, Great Britain recognized the independence of the Transvaal, which, in 1853, took the name of the South African Republic. In 1877 the republic was annexed by Great Britain, but the Boers took up arms towards the end of 1880. In 1881 peace was made and self-government, subject to British suzerainty and certain stipulated restrictions, was restored to the Boers. The London Convention of 1884 removed the suzerainty and a number of these restrictions but reserved to Great Britain the right of approval of the Transvaal's foreign relations, excepting with regard to the Orange Free State. In 1886 gold was discovered on the Witwatersrand, and this discovery, together with the great influx of foreigners which it occasioned, gave rise to many grave problems. Eventually, in 1899, war broke out between Great Britain and the Transvaal. Peace was concluded on 31 May 1902, the Transvaal and the Orange Free State both losing their independence. The Transvaal was governed as a crown colony until 12 Jan. 1907, when responsible government came into force. On 31 May 1910 the Transvaal became one of the four provinces of the Union.

AREA AND POPULATION. The area of the province is 262,499 sq. km or 101,351 sq. miles, including Gazankulu, Lebowa, Ka Ngwane and Kwa Ndebele. The province is divided into 53 districts. The following table shows the population, excluding Gazankulu, Lebowa, Ka Ngwane and Kwa Ndebele in 1985, at each of the last censuses:

| | All races | | | Whites | | Non-Whites | |
	Total	Males	Females	Males	Females	Males	Females
1936	3,341,470	1,846,576	1,494,894	424,470	396,286	1,422,108	1,098,608
1946	4,283,038	2,374,323	1,908,715	541,053	522,068	1,833,270	1,386,647
1951	4,812,838	2,619,314	2,193,524	737,194	731,111	2,575,119	2,230,053
1960	6,270,711	3,310,948	2,959,763	735,845	729,730	2,575,103	2,230,034
1970	6,478,904	3,507,753	2,971,151	957,291	946,802	2,550,462	2,024,349
1980	8,376,042	4,581,054	3,794,988	1,192,484	1,176,055	3,388,570	2,618,933
1985	7,532,179	4,008,070	3,524,109	1,224,064	1,237,300	2,784,006	2,286,809

Of the non-White population in 1985, 4,674,290 were Black, 126,201 Asians and 270,324 Coloureds. Population of Gazankulu, Lebowa, Ka Ngwane and Kwa Ndebele, *see* p. 1077.

Important towns of the province are listed on p. 1078.

ADMINISTRATION. The seat of provincial government is at Pretoria, which is also the administrative capital of the Republic of South Africa.

Administrator: Willem A. Cruywagen.

FINANCE. In 1985–86 revenue amounted to R2,822,726,531 and expenditure to R2,742,739,546.

MINING. For mineral production, *see* p. 1082. Gold output in 1983 was 15,807,760 oz. worth R7,483,932,210.

AGRICULTURE. The province is in the main a stock-raising country, though there are considerable areas well adapted for agriculture, including the growing of tropical crops.

INDUSTRY. The province has iron and brass foundries and engineering works, grain-mills, breweries, brick, tile and pottery works, tobacco, soap, and candle factories, coach and wagon works, clothing factories, etc.

RELIGION. 1980 population census. *Whites:* Christians, 1,927,646; Jews, 76,913; other non-Christians, 4,265.

Non-Whites: Christians, 4,692,362; Moslems, 74,504; Hindus, 37,249; other non-Christians, 15,668.

EDUCATION. All education for Whites except that of universities is under the provincial authority. The province has been divided for the purposes of local control and management into 21 school districts. Instruction in government schools, both primary and secondary, is free. The medium of instruction is the home language of the pupil. The teaching of the other language begins at the earliest stage at which it is appropriate on educational grounds. Both languages are taught as examination subjects to every pupil.

Whites (1982). There were 1,153 public schools with 27,797 teachers and 547,452 pupils; 5 teacher-training colleges with 5,904 students; 84 private schools with 2,009 teachers and 31,597 pupils.

Coloureds (1982). There were 92 state and state-aided schools with 1,898 teachers and 59,547 pupils; 1 teacher-training college with 272 students.

Asians (1982). There were 71 public schools with 1,259 teachers and 28,958 pupils; 1 teacher-training college with 30 teachers and 377 students.

Blacks (1977). There were 2,170 public and private school sections with 15,450 teachers and 735,325 pupils (Homelands excluded).

PROVINCE OF THE ORANGE FREE STATE
Oranje-Vrystaat

HISTORY. The Orange River was first crossed by Europeans in the middle of the 18th century. Between 1810 and 1820, settlements were made in the southern parts of the Orange Free State, and the Great Trek greatly increased the number of settlers during and after 1836. In 1848, Sir Harry Smith proclaimed the whole territory between the Orange and Vaal rivers as a British possession called the 'Orange River Sovereignty'. However, in 1854, by the Convention of Bloemfontein, British sovereignty was withdrawn and the independence of the country was recognized.

During the first 5 years of its existence the Orange Free State was much harassed by incessant raids by the Basutos. These were at length conquered, but, owing to the intervention of the British Government, the treaty of Aliwal North incorporated only part of the territory of the Basutos in the Orange Free State.

On account of the treaty with the South African Republic, the Orange Free State took a prominent part in the South African War (1899–1902) and was annexed on 28 May 1900 as the Orange River Colony. Crown colony government continued until 1907, when responsible government was introduced. On 31 May 1910 the Orange River Colony was merged in the Union of South Africa as the province of the Orange Free State, and on 31 May 1961 became a province of the Republic of South Africa.

AREA AND POPULATION. The area of the province is 127,993 sq. km or 49,418 sq. miles, including Qwaqwa. The province is divided into 43 administrative and 49 magisterial districts. The population has varied as follows:

		All races			Whites		Non-Whites
	Total	Males	Females	Males	Females	Males	Females
1936	772,060	381,903	390,157	101,872	99,106	280,031	291,051
1946	879,071	432,896	446,175	101,874	100,203	331,022	345,972
1951	1,016,570	519,166	497,404	115,637	112,015	403,529	385,389
1960	1,386,202	731,486	654,716	139,304	137,103	601,182	553,613
1970	1,716,350	899,140	817,210	148,110	148,030	751,030	669,180
1980	1,931,860	1,039,220	892,640	166,380	159,840	872,840	732,800
1985	1,776,903	940,000	836,903	164,135	168,192	775,865	668,711
1987	1,863,327	986,220	877,107	166,871	170,995	819,349	706,112

Of the non-White population in 1987, 1,459,851 were Black, 65,555 Coloureds and 55 Indians.

ADMINISTRATION. Provincial councils were abolished on 30 June 1986.

For the Whites there are 69 municipal councils, 2 local management boards and 6 village management boards. For the Non-Whites there are 4 municipal councils, 8 village management boards, 67 village committees and 2 local authority committees.

Administrator: L. J. Botha.

FINANCE. In 1986–87 revenue was R551·5m. and expenditure R574·1m.

MINING. For mineral statistics, *see* p. 1082. The output of gold in 1987 was 165,504 kg valued at R4,800m.

AGRICULTURE. The province consists of undulating plains, affording excellent grazing and wide tracts for agricultural purposes. The rainfall is moderate. The Orange Free State is the largest grain-producing province in the Republic and is also an important sheep- and cattle-farming region.

INDUSTRY. The more important manufacturing industries in the province are the oil-from-coal factory at Sasolburg (as well as industries based on its by-products); grain mills and brick, tile and pottery works. Fertilizers, agricultural implements, blankets, woollen products, clothing, hosiery, cement and pharmaceutical products are also manufactured.

EDUCATION. Primary, secondary and vocational education and the training of teachers are controlled and financed by the Department of Education and Culture. Administration: House of Assembly for Whites and Administration; House of Representatives for Coloureds; Department of Education and Training for Blacks.

Education is free in all public schools up to the university matriculation standard. Attendance is compulsory for White and Coloured between the ages of 7 and 16, but exemption may be granted in special cases. Attendance is not compulsory for Black children, except in areas/communities/towns where a request for compulsory education had been made. In these cases education is compulsory up to Standard 5 or the age of 16. The home language of the pupil is the medium of instruction up to Standard 2; thereafter he has an option of Afrikaans, English or his home language in Black schools.

Further education and training are given at 2 universities, 2 teachers' training colleges, 1 technikon, 1 agricultural college, 2 nursing colleges, 5 technical colleges and 2 training centres.

Whites (1987). There were 209 government and aided schools with 4,519 teachers and 76,416 pupils.

Coloureds (1987). There were 45 government and aided schools with 675 teachers and 16,534 pupils.

Blacks (1987). There were 2,348 government schools with 9,343 teachers and 377,978 pupils.

SOUTH WEST AFRICA
Suidwes-Afrika—Namibia

HISTORY. Britain annexed Walvis Bay in 1878, and incorporated it in the Cape of Good Hope in 1884. In 1884 South West Africa was declared a German protectorate. In 1915 the Union of South Africa occupied German South West Africa at the request of the Allied powers. On 17 Dec. 1920 the League of Nations entrusted South West Africa as a Mandate to the Union of South Africa, to be administered under the laws of the mandatory power. In 1921 the Governor-General of South Africa delegated certain of his functions to the Administrator of the territory. After World War II South Africa refused to place the territory under the UN Trusteeship system, and formally applied for its annexation to the Union. On 18 July 1966 the International Court of Justice decided that Ethiopia and Liberia had no legal right in applying for a decision on the international status of South West Africa, but in Oct. 1966 the General Assembly of the UN terminated South Africa's mandate, and established a UN Council for South West Africa in May 1967. However, South Africa continued to administer the territory, in defiance of various UN resolutions. It speeded up the implementation of the Odendaal Plan (1964), which required massive development aid and the formation of enlarged homelands for the various ethnic groups. In June 1968 the UN changed the name of the territory to Namibia.

In 1971 the International Court of Justice ruled in an advisory opinion that South Africa's presence in Namibia was illegal. In Dec. 1973 the UN appointed a UN Commissioner for Namibia.

After negotiations between South Africa and the UN, a multi-racial Advisory Council was appointed in 1973. Representatives of all the population groups assembled in the Turnhalle in Windhoek for the Constitutional Conference, which on 17 Aug. 1976 decided that a multi-racial interim government was to be formed by early 1977, and that the country should become independent by 31 Dec. 1978. This interim government was rejected by the Western Five, (USA, Britain, Federal Republic of Germany, France and Canada), after which South Africa agreed to universal suffrage elections. An Administrator-General was appointed in Sept. 1977 to govern the territory until independence, and he quickly moved to abolish all laws based on racial discrimination – a precondition for elections. In April 1978 South Africa accepted a plan for UN-supervised elections leading to independence, which was endorsed in UN Security Council Resolution 435 of 27 July 1978. After the final plans for the UN-supervised elections were published, South Africa announced on 20 Sept. 1978 that it was going ahead with internally sponsored elections for a Constitutent Assembly. In the elections held on 4-8 Dec. 1978 the Democratic Turnhalle Alliance (DTA) gained 41 of the 50 seats in a percentage poll of 82%, in spite of the fact that the South West Africa People's Organisation (SWAPO) instructed its members not to take part in the elections.

A 12-member Ministers' Council was instituted, and in Sept. 1981 it was enlarged to 15 members and given executive authority on all matters except constitutional issues, security and foreign affairs. On 11-13 Nov. 1980 elections were held for the second-tier Representative Authorities, which each controls certain administrative functions for a specific ethnic group, but no specific geographical area. In Jan. 1983 the Ministers' Council and the National Assembly were dissolved and executive and legislative powers reverted to the Administrator-General.

On 13 Sept. 1983 the Multi-Party Conference (MPC) was formed. In May 1984 talks were held in Lusaka between the MPC and SWAPO, which were followed in July 1984 by talks between the Administrator-General and SWAPO. SWAPO, which had been waging a terrorist war in the north for almost two decades, was again invited to take part in constitutional talks with the MPC, but again refused. The MPC then petitioned the Republic of South Africa for a form of self-government for Namibia, and on 17 June 1985 the Transitional Government of National Unity was installed, consisting of the six political groups in the MPC.

AREA AND POPULATION. The total area of the Territory, including the Caprivi-Zipfel, is 318,261 sq. miles (824,269 sq. km); this figure includes that of the enclave of Walvis Bay, administered by the Republic of South Africa, 434 sq. miles (1,124 sq. km).

The country is bounded on the north by Angola and Zambia, on the west by the Atlantic ocean, on the south and southern portion of the eastern boundary by the Republic of South Africa, and on the remainder of the eastern boundary by Botswana and Zambia. There are 3 main regions: the Namib, an extremely arid and desolate region stretching along the entire coastline to a width of between 80 to 130 km. The major portion of the Namib receives an annual rainfall of less than 50 mm. The Central Plateau is the region lying to the east of the Namib. It varies in altitude between 1,000 and 2,000 metres and offers a diversified landscape of rugged mountains, rocky outcrops, sand-filled valleys and plains. It covers approximately 50% of the total area; the Kalahari covers the eastern, north-eastern and northern areas of South West Africa.

The rainfall increases steadily from less than 50 mm. in the west and south-west up to 600 mm. in the Caprivi Strip.

The Kunene River and the Okavango, which form portions of the northern border of the country, the Zambesi, which forms the eastern boundary of the Caprivi-Zipfel, the Kwando or Mashi, which flows through the Caprivi-Zipfel from the north between the Okavango and the Zambesi, and the Orange River in the south, are the only permanently running streams. But there is a system of great, sandy, dry river-beds throughout the country, in which water can generally be obtained by sinking shallow wells. In the Grootfontein area there are large supplies of underground water, but except for a few springs, mostly hot, there is no surface water in the country.

The population at the censuses in 1970 and 1981 and estimates 1986, were:

	1970	1981	1986
Ovambos	342,455	506,114	587,000
Whites	90,658	76,430	78,000
Damaras	64,973	76,179	89,000
Hereros	55,670	76,296	89,000
Namas	32,853	48,541	57,000
Kavangos	49,577	95,055	110,000
Caprivians	25,009	38,594	44,000
Coloureds	28,275	42,254	48,000
Basters	16,474	25,181	29,000
Bushmen	21,909	29,443	34,000
Tswanas	4,407	6,706	7,000
Other	...	12,403	12,000
	732,260	1,033,196	1,184,000

Capital, Windhoek (population 110,644, census 1981).

ADMINISTRATION AND GOVERNMENT. For history of the administration from 1949–1985 *see* THE STATESMAN'S YEAR-BOOK 1986–87 p. 1087. Legislative authority is the National Assembly in Windhoek consisting of 62 members nominated by the six political groups represented in the Transitional Government of National Unity; 22 members for the Democratic Turnhalle Alliance, which consists of 11 parties, and 8 members for each of the other parties; the Labour Party (LP), the National Party (NP), the Rehoboth Free Democratic Party (RFDP), the South West Africa National Union (SWANU), and the SWAPO-Democrats (SWAPO-D).

Included in the National Assembly is a Cabinet of eight Ministers and eight Deputy Ministers (three Ministers from the DTA and one each from the other parties), which have full executive authority except for matters regarding foreign affairs and defence (retained by the Republic of South Africa) and constitutional development (which is handled by the Constitutional Council). Chairmanship of the Cabinet rotates three-monthly on an alphabetical basis. The Administrator-General remains in the country as representative of the South African government, with mainly a ceremonial role.

The Constitutional Council consists of a non-voting Chairman and 16 members nominated by the parties in the TGNU (six for the DTA and two each for the other parties). The aim of the Council, which started work in Jan. 1986, is to draft a constitution.

Certain administrative functions for nine of the ethnic groups are controlled by second-tier Representative Authorities first elected in 1980. These are the administrations for Ovambos, Namas, Damaras, Kavangos, Hereros, Whites, Basters, Coloureds and Tswanas. In the case of the Bushmen and Caprivians, these functions are handled by a commissioner and advisory council.

The country is administered by a Government Service founded on 1 July 1980, which consists of 15 departments, as well as the administrations of the nine second-tier Representative Authorities. By mid-1985 98.6% of the civil servants were Namibian citizens.

The third tier of government comprises municipalities which control the civic affairs of larger towns.

The Cabinet in July 1987 consisted of:

Minister of Transport: David Bezuidenhout. *Local Government and Civic Affairs:* Hans Diergaardt. *Manpower, National Health and Welfare:* Moses Katjiuongua. *Information, Justice, Posts and Telecommunications:* Jariretundu Kozonguizi. *National Education, Central Personnel Institution:* Andrew Matjila. *Finance and Governmental Affairs:* Dirk Mudge. *Nature Conservation, Mining,*

Commerce and Tourism: Andreas Shipanga. *Agriculture, Water Affairs and Sea Fisheries:* Jan de Wet.

Administrator-General: Louis Pienaar.

ECONOMY

Budget. The revenue and expenditure (in R1,000) were:

	1982–83	1983–84	1984–85	1985–86	1986–87
Revenue	673,000	801,000	1,000,000	1,199,400	1,569,600
Expenditure	840,111	1,035,884	1,176,687	1,392,449	1,896,660

Banking. Barclays Bank, Standard Bank, Bank Windhoek, Netherlands Bank, Trust Bank, South African Reserve Bank and Boland Bank have branches in the Territory. The only indigenous bank, The Bank of South West Africa, was established in 1973.

A post office savings bank was established in 1916. The number of accounts opened in 1985–86 was 3,398. The balance due to holders as at 31 March 1986 amounted to R2,983,790.

ENERGY AND NATURAL RESOURCES

Electricity. Production (1986) 692m. kwh.

Minerals. Mineral export/sales amounted to R883·1m. in 1986 (excluding uranium). Diamonds, copper ore and lead represent a major share of exports. An open pit gold mine was scheduled to begin operations in March 1988.

Agriculture. Namibia is essentially a stock-raising country, the scarcity of water and poor rainfall rendering agriculture, except in the northern and north-eastern portions, almost impossible. Generally speaking, the southern half is suited for the raising of small stock, while the central and northern portions are better fitted for cattle.

Livestock (1987): 2,003,387 cattle, 2,936,713 sheep, 1,603,915 goats. In 1986, 304,000 head of cattle, 113,745 beef carcasses and 685,246 head of small stock were exported, and 556,483 karakul pelts worth R18·4m. were produced.

In 1986, 8·9m. litres of milk, 120 tonnes of butter and 240 tonnes of cheese were produced. Other products are maize (1986 in tonnes), 22,905; millet, 40-50,000; wheat, 5,600; cotton, 1,250; vegetables, 5,000; sunflower seed, 1,156; sorghum, 500.

Fisheries. The total catch in 1987 was 479,360 tonnes.

COMMERCE. Total imports, R182m. and exports R169m. in 1985.

The bulk of the direct imports into the country is landed at Walvis Bay which handles 750,000 tons of cargo a year.

Total trade between South West Africa and UK (British Department of Trade returns, in £1,000 sterling):

	1983	1984	1985	1986	1987
Imports to UK	62,437	64,015	21,920	6,826	7,681
Exports and re-exports from UK	3,425	5,200	4,084	2,915	3,909

COMMUNICATIONS

Roads. In 1986 there were 4,138 km of trunk roads, 9,049 km of main roads, 28,711 km of district roads and 13,190 km of dirt roads. In 1986 there were 103,715 registered motor vehicles.

Railways. The Namibia system connects with the main system of the South African Railways at De Aar. The total length of the line inside Namibia is 2,349 km of 1,065 mm gauge.

Aviation. In 1985–86 the Territory's 2 major airports handled 275,612 passengers and 2·2m. kg of freight.

Shipping. In 1985 Walvis Bay harbour handled 764 vessels and Luderitz, 152 vessels.

Post and Broadcasting. In 1986 there were 71 post offices and 11 postal agencies, and 1,482 private bag services distributed by rail or road transport.

There were (1987) 69,273 telephones. There were 1,012 telex users.

In 1986, 52,255 radio licences and 24,582 television licences were issued.

EDUCATION AND WELFARE

Education (1986). In 1985–86, R65·84m. was spent on education. There were 1,114 schools for all races, 350,080 pupils and 11,121 teachers. This included 1,071 primary and senior secondary schools, 3 centres for handicapped children, 1 technical school and 2 agricultural schools, 2 technical institutes and 3 agricultural colleges.

Health (1986). There were 61 hospitals and 156 clinics. The ratio of beds per population was 5·71 per 1,000. There were 250 general practitioners, 26 specialists and 41 dentists. Nursing staff numbered 3,916.

Books of Reference

Namibia Information Services, *Namibia: The Economy*. Windhoek, 1987
Namibia Information Service, *Statistical/Economic Review, 1985*. Windhoek, 1985
Human Rights and Namibia. London, 1986
Jaster, R., *South Africa in Namibia: The Botha Strategy*. Univ. Press of America, 1985
Levinson, O., *The Story of Namibia*. Cape Town, 1978
Rotberg, R. I., *Namibia: Political and Economic Prospects*. Lexington, 1983
Schoeman, E. R., and H. S., *Namibia*. [Bibliography] Oxford and Santa Barbara, 1984
Soggot, D., *Namibia: The Violent Heritage*. New York, 1986
Thomas, W. H., *Economic Development in Namibia*. Munich, 1978
van der Merwe, J. H., *National Atlas of South West Africa*. Windhoek, 1983
Vigne, R., *A Dwelling Place of Our Own: The Story of the Namibian Nation*. London, 1973

BOPHUTHATSWANA

HISTORY. Bophuthatswana was first to obtain self-government under the Bantu Homeland Constitution Act of 1971 and was the second black homeland to ask the Republic of South Africa for full independence, which was granted on 6 Dec. 1977.

AREA AND POPULATION. The total area is 44,000 sq. km.

In 1985 there was a *de jure* population of 3·2m., of which 47% lived in the White areas. The remaining 53% (1,740,600) lived in the homeland. Estimate (1985) 1·66m. The capital is Mmabatho.

CONSTITUTION AND GOVERNMENT. The Bophuthatswana Government ment is a compromise between the traditional chief-in-council system and a democratic electoral system. There are 72 elected and 24 nominated members in the Legislative Assembly. Self-government was granted in 1972. Each regional authority (coinciding with the 12 districts of the country) nominates 2 members, and each district elects 6 members to the National Assembly and 12 designated by the President on account of their special knowledge, qualifications or experience.

Executive power vests in the President, who is directly elected by general suffrage of persons who are registered as voters, and he elects his Cabinet.

The first general election was held in Oct. 1972, 2 political parties taking part. Kgosi Lucas Mangope's Bophuthatswana National Party (BNP) won 20 of the 24 contested seats, but in 1974 he formed the Bophuthatswana Democratic Party which in the 1987 elections won 66 seats; the People's Progressive Party, 6 seats.

Members of regional authorities are elected from among the tribal and community authorities in their areas.

The Cabinet in Jan. 1988 consisted of:

President, Minister of Law and Order, Audit and Public Service: Dr Kgosi Lucas Manyane Mangope (took office 6 Dec. 1977; re-elected for another 7 years as from 11 Nov. 1984).

Population Development: T. M. Molatlhwa. *Internal Affairs:* Kgosi B. L. M. I. Motsatsi. *Defence:* Brig. H. F. P. Riekert. *Finance:* L. G. Young. *Posts and Telecommunications and Broadcasting:* K. C. V. A. Sehume. *Manpower and Coordination:* S. M. Seodi. *State Affairs and Civil Aviation:* R. Cronje. *Foreign Affairs:* S. L. L. Rathebe. *Health and Social Welfare:* L. G. Holele. *Water Affairs:* T. M. Tlhabane. *Economic Planning, Energy Affairs and Mines:* E. B. Keikelame. *Agriculture and Natural Resources:* P. H. Mooketsi. *Parliamentary Affairs, Local Government and Housing:* H. F. Tlou. *Education:* G. S. Nkau. *Justice and Transport:* S. G. Mothibe. *Public Works:* S. C. Kgobokoe.

There were 8 Deputy Ministers.

Flag: Blue, crossed by a diagonal orange stripe, and in the canton a white disc charged with a leopard's face in black and white.

DEFENCE. The Air Wing of the Defence Force has 2 Partenavia P-68 patrol aircraft, 2 Aviocar transports, and 2 Alouette III, 1 BK-117 and 1 Ecureuil helicopter. There is an Army Force of 3,100 with 2 infantry battalions.

INTERNATIONAL RELATIONS

Aid. The Republic of South Africa granted aid of R72m. in 1986–87.

ECONOMY

Budget. The 1987–88 budget balanced at R1,517m.

Currency. South African Rand.

Banking. The financial system is controlled by legislation inherited from South Africa on independence, and commercial banks have strong direct links with South African banks which in certain instances are controlled by overseas banking companies.

In 1988 there were 3 commercial banks with branches in all major commercial and agricultural centres offering a full range of banking services. The Agricultural Bank of Bophuthatswana provides finance to farmers. The government-funded Agricultural Development Fund provides loan finance and subsidy support to agricultural co-operative societies. The Bophuthatswana Building Society grants loans for house building.

NATURAL RESOURCES

Water. The Department of Agriculture inherited the following improvements from South Africa: 2,833 reservoirs; 6,845 boreholes, of which more than 4,000 have been equipped; 648 earth dams.

Minerals. The territory is particularly rich in minerals. In 1987 there were 20 mines employing 45,000 people. Minerals include platinum, asbestos, gold, calcite, granite, chrome, vanadium, limestone and diamonds.

Exploration for more platinum, chrome and coal is currently being carried out both by the private sector and by the Mining and Geological Survey Division of the Department of Economic Planning. The platinum mines around Rustenburg produce about 66% of the free world's total production. The major chrome mines are near Rustenburg and Marico, while vanadium is mined in the Odi district near Brits. The Rustenburg, Western and Impala Platinum mines which are shared with the Republic of South Africa produce about 1·9m. oz. a year.

AGRICULTURE. Bophuthatswana is a semi-arid area of bushveld and grass veld suitable for stock farming. The annual rainfall is 300 mm in the west and 700 mm in the east and there are 4 river catchment areas—those of the Molopo, Ngotwane, Sehujwane (Limpopo) and Madikwe (Vaal) rivers.

Although the land tenure system militates against establishing large farms, some land which is suitable for farming is leased by the Government to successful farmers.

Livestock (1986): Cattle, 463,008; sheep, 250,970; goats, 466,088; pigs, 7,601; poultry, 181,151.

Only 6·6% of the territory is suited to dryland farming, but crop yields have shown a steady improvement in recent years. In Ditsobotla district, 3,500 hectares of fertile land has been developed by 3 primary co-operatives comprising 190 Batswana farmers. Silkworm farming was being tried in 1983. By 1981 the country was self sufficient in maize and exported the surplus. Three rice projects are successfully expanding and vegetable production was flourishing in 1987. The budget for 1987–88 is R62m.

INDUSTRY. The first industries were started on an agency basis at Babelegi; the fastest growing industrial area in the homeland, in 1977 it covered 183 hectares and by March 1985 more than R234m. had been invested in the project. Other industries are situated at Garankuwa, Selosesha, Montshiwa and Mogwase. South African border industries are also promoted by the government, notably at Rosslyn where 128 industries had been established by Dec. 1975.

COMMUNICATIONS

Roads. Total length (1985) 6,300 km, of which 810 km are tarred. In 1976–77, 132 km were covered by bus, and 116m. passengers transported.

Aviation. Mmabatho International Airport was opened in 1984.

Post and Broadcasting. There were 18,640 telephones at 30 April 1987, and 107 post offices.

EDUCATION AND WELFARE

Education. In 1986 there were 1,307 educational institutions which included special schools and technical schools. Primary school attendance in 1986 was 349,952; middle schools, 149,815; high schools, 50,499; teacher training colleges, 2,807; special and vocational schools, 1,634; technical schools, 3,648; university (1987), 2,700. There were (1986) 14,250 teachers excluding lecturers.

Education is free apart from nominal contributions to school funds, and hostel fees at post-primary schools.

Instruction from Grade I to Standard 2 is in Setswana, while Standard 3 to senior standards are taught in English. The education is controlled by the Department of Education with a budget of R219m. in 1987–88.

Health. In 1987 there were 11 hospitals, 152 static clinics, 6,303 hospital and clinic beds, 106 doctors and 2,672 nurses. The health budget in 1987–88 was R103m.

Book of Reference

Five Years of Independence: Republic of Bophuthatswana. Mafikeng, 1983

TRANSKEI

HISTORY. Transkei is the homeland of the Xhosa nation and was granted self-government by the Republic of South Africa in 1963. Over 1·5m. Transkeians live permanently in the Republic of South Africa but were deprived of their South African citizenship on independence.

AREA AND POPULATION. The total area is 16,910 sq. miles (43,798 sq. km). Population (1985 estimate) 3m. The capital is Umtata (population (1976)

24,805; 20,196 Blacks, 1,067 Coloured and 3,542 Whites). Other towns include Gcuwa, Kwabhaca, Umzimvubu and Lusikisiki.

CONSTITUTION AND GOVERNMENT. The Status of Transkei Bill of 1976 gave Transkei a unicameral National Assembly instead of the then existing Legislative Assembly. Independence was achieved 26 Oct. 1976.

General elections were held on 29 Sept. 1976 and the Transkei National Independence Party gained 69 of the 75 elective seats in the National Assembly. Members were elected for a 5-year period. In addition there are 75 traditional (co-opted) members (70 chiefs and 5 paramount chiefs).

President: Paramount Chief T. N. Ndamase.

In Sept. 1987 Chief George Mantanzima the Prime Minister, was deposed in a *coup* by Stella Sigcau who in turn was ousted in a bloodless military coup, led by Gen. Bantu Holomisa in Jan. 1988.

Flag: Three horizontal stripes of ochre, white, green.

FINANCE. In 1985 government income was R872m. and expenditure R984m.

AGRICULTURE. Notable examples of successful commercial enterprises in agriculture are the Magwa and Majola tea estates, with approximately 1,700 hectares planted, and various fibre plantations. 70,000 hectares of land are under indigenous forests and 61,000 hectares have been put under exotic plantations. There are 28 sawmills in the country.

Livestock (1976): Cattle, 1·3m.; sheep, 2·5m.; goats, 1·25m.

COMMUNICATIONS

Roads. There are above 8,800 km of roads.

Railways. There is a 209 km railway line linking Umtata with the port of East London in the Republic of South Africa.

Aviation. An international airport exists at Umtata.

Shipping. A start was made in 1978 on a 'free port' at Mnganzana. It will be completed in 5–6 years at a cost of R125m. by a French consortium.

Post. There were 11,498 telephones in 1978.

EDUCATION AND WELFARE

Education. In 1985 there were 690,000 pupils in primary schools and 193,000 pupils in secondary schools. The national university was inaugurated in Umtata in 1977.

Health. There are 31 hospitals with a total of 7,561 beds.

DIPLOMATIC REPRESENTATIVES

No country, other than the Republic of South Africa, has recognized Transkei as an independent state.

VENDA

HISTORY. Traditionally the territory of the Vhavenda, the country was granted self-government in 1973, and became the third Black homeland to be granted independence by the Republic of South Africa on 13 Sept. 1979.

AREA AND POPULATION. The total area is 6,500 sq. km. Of the 381,000 Vhavenda living in the Republic of South Africa in 1970, nearly 70% lived in Venda. In 1980 the *de jure* population of Venda was estimated at 513,890, the *de facto* population at 343,480. The capital is Thohoyandou.

Vital statistics, 1981: Births, 13,568; deaths, 1,069; marriages, 228.

CONSTITUTION AND GOVERNMENT. Executive power is vested in the President, who is elected for the duration of each Parliament, which consists of the President and the National Assembly; legislative power is vested in Parliament. In addition to the National Assembly there is an Executive Council, or Cabinet, and a judiciary independent of the Executive. The National Assembly comprises the 28 chiefs, 15 members designated by 4 regional councils, 42 members elected by popular vote and 3 members nominated by the President. A new Assembly must be elected after every 5 years, but it may be dissolved at any time by the President. All existing tribal, community and regional councils were retained with their status and powers unchanged, like those of the tribal leaders.

The first general election was held in Aug. 1973; the sole political party, the Venda Independence People's Party (VIPP) won 10 of the 18 contested seats. Shortly after, the Chief Minister, Chief Mphephu, formed the Venda National Party (VNP); in the second general election of July 1978 the VIPP won 31 of the 42 contested seats, VNP the remaining 11. Chief Mphephu was re-elected Chief Minister.

President: Paramount Chief P. R. Mphephu.

Foreign Affairs: Chief A. M. Madzivhandila. *Economic Affairs:* Headman F. N. Ravele. *Education:* Headman E. R. B. Nesengani. *Urban Affairs and Land Tenure:* Chief C. A. Nelwamondo. *Justice:* Chief J. R. Rambuda. *Health and Welfare:* Chief C. N. Makuya. *Agriculture and Forestry:* G. M. Ramabulana. *Internal Affairs:* Chief M. M. Mphaphuli. *Transport, Works and Communications:* A. A. Tshivhase. *Deputy for Posts and Telecommunications:* Headman B. R. Nemulodi. *Deputy for Information and Broadcasting and of Public Service Commission:* W. R. Rabuma.

Flag: Three horizontal stripes of green, yellow, and brown, with a brown V on the yellow stripe, and a blue vertical strip in the hoist.

DEFENCE. The Venda Defence Force was formed in 1983. It includes a small aviation component operating 1 Alouette III and 2 BK-117 helicopters.

INTERNATIONAL RELATIONS

Aid. The Republic of South Africa granted aid of R45m. in 1981–82.

ECONOMY

Budget. The 1983–84 budget envisaged expenditure of R152,074,050.

Currency. South African Rand.

NATURAL RESOURCES

Water. In Oct. 1982 there were 118 hectares of canals, 250 dams and 520 boreholes.

Minerals. Venda is relatively poor in mineral resources, although there are large supplies of stone for construction. Coal is the most important mineral; there are large deposits in the west near Makhado and in the north-east, bordering on the Kruger National Park, which it is hoped will soon be exploited. In addition there are deposits of graphite, copper sulphides, phosphates and magnesite; in 1978 the 2 graphite and 2 magnesite mines provided employment for 233 people, and the value of their output was R963,900.

Agriculture. About 85% of Venda is suitable only for the raising of livestock because of insufficient rainfall and poor soils, while some 10% is suited to dry-land crop production. Over 10,965 hectares have been given over to forest, mainly pine and eucalyptus. Eighteen irrigation schemes are being developed and there is extensive reclamation and conservation of eroded or overgrazed land; nearly R2m. were spent on these projects in 1980–81. Only maize is grown on a comparatively large scale, but tea, sisal, groundnuts, coffee and sub-tropical fruits are increasing in importance. A fish-breeding project produced 3 tonnes in 1980–81.

Over 80% of the working population are engaged in agriculture. The Venda Agricultural Corporation (Agriven) was established on 1 April 1982 to promote agricultural development.

INDUSTRY. Industrial development is still in its early stages, and since Venda's location is unfavourable, the Government is concentrating on the promotion of agro-industries utilizing local produce, and small-scale industries. A chutney factory has recently been established, in addition to a tea processing plant, a furniture factory and several saw-mills. A copper-chrome arsenate preservation plant has been established at Phiphidi. At Shayandima a 20-hectare industrial area has been prepared. The construction industry is particularly important owing to the substantial increase in the demand for buildings caused by the recent expansion of government, educational and health services.

In Dec. 1982 total investment in industry was estimated at R18·9m. The Venda Development Corporation was established in 1975 to promote and finance economic developments.

COMMUNICATIONS

Roads. There were (1982) 1,226 km of roads, of which 50 km had a permanent surface.

Aviation. An airline, inaugurated in 1981, operates between Nwangundu in Thohoyandu and Johannesburg *via* Pietersburg and Pretoria.

Post and Broadcasting. In 1983 there were 30 post offices and postal agencies. Telephones (1982) numbered, 1,547. In 1984 the government-owned Radio Thohoyandu broadcast 17 hours daily.

EDUCATION AND WELFARE

Education. The Department of Education assumed responsibility for education on independence. Education is free up to Standard 2, and pupils are taught in the native tongue, Luvenda, for the first 4 years (up to Standard 2), after which English is gradually introduced. Secondary education comprises Standards 6 to 10.

The number of primary schools increased from 233 (1970) to 502 (1984), the number of pupils from 65,500 (1970) to 157,014 (1982) and the number of teachers from 956 (1970) to 4,586 (1982).

In 1970 there were 12 secondary schools, which had increased to 112 by 1982. Pupils numbered 2,465 in 1970, 33,432 in 1982, while the number of teachers increased from 100 (1970) to 1,062 (1982).

In addition there is a technical school at Sibasa with about 320 pupils, an agricultural school at Dimani with 476 pupils, and a school for the handicapped at Shayandima. There are 2 teacher-training colleges; enrolment was 704 in 1982. The University of Venda was established in 1981; 1,358 students (1984).

Health. In 1984 there were 5 hospitals/homes with 1,556 beds and 47 clinics. White doctors numbered 10 and coloured, 3; there were 712 nurses.

Welfare. In 1981–82 the Government spent R7·3m. on grants and pensions to 22,249 recipients. There is one welfare home.

Book of Reference

Venda 1983. Dept. of Information and Broadcasting. Sibasa, 1984

CISKEI

HISTORY. On 4 Dec. 1981 the Republic of South Africa gave independence to Ciskei the fourth of the tribal homelands.

AREA AND POPULATION. Ciskei lies between latitudes 32° and 33°35′

and longitudes 26°20′ and 27°48′, and has a coastal boundary between East London and Port Alfred. The total area is about 8,300 sq. km. The population was (1981) 2·1m. but only 660,000 live in Ciskei. The remainder work in the Republic of South Africa and as a result can be deported as aliens.

Populations of towns (1984): Mdantsane, 300,000; Zwelitsha, 47,000; Sada, 30,000; Dimbaza, 17,800 and Litha, 5,326. The capital, Bisho, is under construction.

CONSTITUTION AND GOVERNMENT. In 1981 Ciskei became an independent democratic republic with an Executive Council consisting of the President, Vice-President and 11 ministers appointed by the President. The legislature is a National Assembly consisting of (1984) 41 Hereditary Chiefs, 22 elected and 5 nominated Members and the Paramount Chief's representatives of 37 are traditional leaders, the others being elected on the basis of adult suffrage every five years.

President: Dr Lennox Sebe.

Flag: Blue, a broad diagonal band from lower hoist to upper fly, charged with a black crane.

National Anthem: Nkosi Sikelel' i Afrika, composed by Enoch Sontonga.

DEFENCE. There is a small Ciskei Defence Force. Its aviation element is equipped with 2 Skyvan and 3 Islander transports, and 3 BK-117 and 1 BO 105 helicopter.

ECONOMY

Budget. In 1984–85, revenue was R366,013,000 and expenditure R438,197,000.

Currency. South African Rand.

ENERGY AND NATURAL RESOURCES

Electricity. Ciskei is totally dependent on power supply lines maintained by the Republic of South Africa.

Minerals. Mineral resources are mainly undeveloped and in 1984 only one mine existed in Ciskei.

Agriculture. In 1977–78, total agricultural production was valued at R8·26m.

In 1983–84, the dryland products included (in tons): Maize, 1,075; wheat, 1,015; dry beans, 304; pumpkins, 14,500; potatoes, 21,750. The main crops produced under irrigation were (1979–80, in tons): Potatoes, 385; lucerne, 364; maize, 333; beans, 77; wheat, 64.

Livestock (1985): 81,177 cattle, 235,550 sheep, 283,877 goats, 15,567 pigs.

Forestry. In 1983–84, 5,500 hectares were planted mainly with conifers. The indigenous forest covered some 18,000 hectares. In 1984–85 (estimate), production of timber was valued at R600,000.

INDUSTRY AND TRADE

Industry. In 1983 total investment was R275·2m. The chief manufactures include textiles, timber products, electronic components, steel products and leather goods.

Commerce. International trade is mainly with the Republic of South Africa and no separate figures are available. The main exports are pineapples, timber and manufactured goods.

Tourism. Tourism is an important and developing industry.

COMMUNICATIONS

Roads. In 1986 there were 324 km of tarred roads and 3,222 km of gravel roads.

Railways. There are two main railway lines serving the southern part of Ciskei only.

Aviation. Ciskei uses East London's airport and there is a new international airport at Bulembu, near Bisho.

Shipping. Ciskei has no harbour of its own but has full access to the facilities of East London in the Republic of South Africa.

Post and Broadcasting. All major centres have post offices and manual and automatic telephone exchanges; telex facilities are available. There were (1986) 13,981 telephones. Radio Ciskei broadcasts from Bisho and Radio Xhosa broadcasts daily.

Newspapers (1986). There were two Ciskeian newspapers, one of which, *Imvo,* was first published in 1884.

JUSTICE, RELIGION, EDUCATION AND WELFARE

Justice. The Supreme Court acts as Court of Appeal for the eight Magistrates' Courts, which in turn act as Courts of Appeal for the chiefs' courts. Appeals from the Supreme Court are heard by the Appellate Division of Ciskei in Bisho.

Religion. In 1980 (estimate) the population was 24% Methodists, 21% Independent, 8% Presbyterian Congregationalists, 7% Anglicans, 6% Roman Catholics, 2% Dutch Reformed Church, 2% other Christians, 28% ancestor worship and 2% other religions.

Education. In 1981 there were 499 primary schools with 184,736 pupils and 4,240 teachers; 126 secondary and teacher-training schools with 48,838 pupils and 1,576 teachers; and 2 vocational schools with 304 pupils and 32 teachers. The University of Fort Hare had a total of 2,304 students in 1981.

Health. In 1983–84, there were 25 hospitals with 2,458 beds, and a total of 2,763 nursing staff.

Social Welfare. Pensions paid in 1984–85:

	Beneficiaries	Amount (R1,000)
Old age	42,573	20,435
Blind	564	270
Disability	5,421	2,602
War veterans	72	38
Leprosy	11	5

Books of Reference

Charlton, N., *Ciskei: Economics and Politics of Dependence in a South African Homeland.* London, 1980
Pauw, B. A., *Christianity and the Xhosa Tradition.* OUP, 1975
Van der Kooy, R, (ed.) *The Republic of Ciskei: A Nation in Transition.* Pretoria, 1981

SOUTH GEORGIA
AND
SOUTH SANDWICH ISLANDS

HISTORY. South Georgia was probably first sighted by a London merchant, Antonio de la Roche, and then in 1756 by a Spanish Captain, Gregorie Jerez. The first landing and exploration was undertaken by Captain James Cook, who formally took possession in the name of George III on 17 Jan. 1775. British sealers arrived in 1788 and American sealers in 1791. Sealing reached its peak in 1800. A German team was the first to carry out scientific studies there in 1882–83. Whaling began in 1904 when the Compania Argentina de Pesca formed by C. A. Larsen, a Norwegian, established a station at Grytviken. Six other stations were established up to 1912. Whaling ceased in 1966 and the civil administration was withdrawn. Argentine forces invaded South Georgia on 3 April 1982. A British naval task force recovered the Island on 25 April 1982.

AREA AND POPULATION. South Georgia lies 800 miles south-east of the Falkland Islands and has an area of 1,450 sq. miles. The South Sandwich Islands are 470 miles south-east of South Georgia and have an area of 130 sq. miles. There has been no permanent population in South Georgia since the whaling station at Leith was abandoned in 1966. There is a small military garrison. The British Antarctic Survey have a biological station on Bird Island. The South Sandwich Islands are uninhabited.

CLIMATE. The climate is wet and cold with strong winds and little seasonal variation. 15°C is occasionally reached on a windless day. Temperatures below –15°C at sea level are unusual.

CONSTITUTION AND GOVERNMENT. Under the new Constitution which came into force on 3 Oct. 1985 the Territories ceased to be dependencies of the Falkland Islands. Executive power is vested in a Commissioner who is the officer for the time being administering the Government of the Falkland Islands. The Commissioner is obliged to consult the officer for the time being commanding Her Majesty's British Forces in the South Atlantic on matters relating to defence and internal security (except police). The Commissioner whenever practicable consults the Executive Council of the Falkland Islands on the exercise of functions that in his opinion might affect the Falkland Islands. There is no Legislative Council. Laws are made by the Commissioner.

Commissioner: G. W. Jewkes, CMG.

Economy. The total revenue of the Territories (estimate, 1987–88) £157,560, mainly from philatelic sales and investment income. Expenditure estimate £243,790.

Communications. There is occasional direct sea communication between the Falkland Islands and South Georgia and the South Sandwich Islands by means of the Royal Research Ships *John Biscoe* and *Bransfield* and the ice patrol vessel *HMS Endurance*. Royal Fleet Auxiliary ships, which serve the garrison, run regularly to South Georgia. Mail is dropped from military aircraft.

Justice. There is a Supreme Court for the Territories and a Court of Appeal in the United Kingdom. Appeals may go from that court to the Judicial Committee of the Privy Council. There is no magistrate permanently in residence. The Officer Commanding the garrison is usually appointed a magistrate.

Book of Reference

Headland, R. K., *The Island of South Georgia*. CUP, 1985

SPAIN

España

Capital: Madrid
Population: 38·9m. (1986)
GNP per capita: US$5,198 (1986)

HISTORY. Although Spain has traditionally been a monarchy there have been two Republics, the first in 1873, which lasted for 11 months, and the second 1931–39; both were democratically and peacefully proclaimed. Part of the army rebelled against the republican government on 18 July 1936, thus beginning the Spanish Civil War, *see* THE STATESMAN'S YEAR-BOOK, 1939, pp. 1325–26. The new regime was led by Gen. Franco, who had been proclaimed Head of State and Government in 1936, and its institutions were based on single party rule, with the *Falange* as the only legal political organization.

In July 1969, Prince Don Juan Carlos de Borbón y Borbón, grandson of Alfonso XIII, was sworn in as successor to the Head of State and he had the title of HRH Prince of Spain until he became King.

Gen. Francisco Franco y Bahamonde died on 20 Nov. 1975 and on 22 Nov. Prince Juan Carlos de Borbón y Borbón took the oath as Juan Carlos I, King of Spain.

On 23 Feb. 1981 there was an attempted military *coup.* For 18 hours the deputies of the lower house of Parliament and the Cabinet were held hostage. The King, the only high authority who kept his liberty, obtained the surrender of the rebels without bloodshed.

AREA AND POPULATION. Spain is bounded north by the Bay of Biscay and the Pyrenees (which form the frontier with France and Andorra), east and south by the Mediterranean and the Straits of Gibraltar, south-west by the Atlantic and west by Portugal and the Atlantic. Continental Spain has an area of 492,592 sq. km, and including the Balearic and Canary Islands and the towns of Ceuta and Melilla 504,750 sq. km (194,884 sq. miles). Population (mid-decennial census, 1986), 38,891,313.

The growth of the population has been as follows:

Census year	Population	Rate of annual increase	Census year	Population	Rate of annual increase
1860	15,655,467	0·34	1950	27,976,755	0·81
1910	19,927,150	0·72	1960	30,903,137	0·88
1920	21,303,162	0·69	1970	33,823,918	0·94
1930	23,563,867	1·06	1981	37,746,260	1·15
1940	25,877,971	0·98			

Area and population of the autonomous communities and provinces, census of 1 March 1981:

Autonomous community Province	Area (sq. km)	Population	Per sq. km	Autonomous community Province	Area (sq. km)	Population	Per sq. km
Andalusia	*87,268*	*6,441,755*	*73*	Zaragoza	17,194	842,386	48
Almería	8,774	405,513	47	*Asturias*	*10,565*	*1,127,007*	*106*
Cádiz	7,385	1,001,716	135	*Baleares*	*5,014*	*685,088*	*136*
Córdoba	13,718	717,213	52	*Basque*			
Granada	12,531	761,734	60	*Country, The*	*7,261*	*2,134,967*	*296*
Huelva	10,085	414,492	41	Álava	3,047	260,580	85
Jaén	13,498	627,598	46	Guipúzcoa	1,997	692,986	347
Málaga	7,276	1,036,261	142	Vizcaya	2,217	1,181,401	532
Sevilla	14,001	1,477,428	105	*Canary Islands*	*7,273*	*1,444,626*	*200*
Aragón	*47,669*	*1,213,099*	*25*	Palmas, Las	4,065	756,353	185
Huesca	15,671	219,813	14	Santa Cruz			
Teruel	14,804	150,900	10	de Tenerife	3,208	688,273	217

Autonomous community Province	Area (sq. km)	Population	Per sq. km	Autonomous community Province	Area (sq. km)	Population	Per sq. km
Cantabria	5,289	510,816	96	Tarragona	6,283	516,078	82
Castilla-La				Extremadura	41,602	1,050,119	25
Mancha	79,226	1,628,005	20	Badajoz	21,657	635,375	29
Albacete	14,858	334,468	22	Cáceres	19,945	414,744	20
Ciudad Real	19,749	468,327	23	Galicia	29,434	2,753,836	93
Cuenca	17,061	210,280	12	Coruña, La	7,876	1,083,415	137
Guadalajara	12,190	143,124	11	Lugo	9,803	399,185	40
Toledo	15,368	471,806	30	Orense	7,278	411,339	56
Castilla-León	94,147	2,577,105	27	Pontevedra	4,477	859,897	192
Ávila	8,048	178,997	22	Madrid	7,995	4,726,986	591
Burgos	14,269	363,474	25	Murcia	11,317	957,903	84
León	15,468	517,973	33	Navarra	10,421	507,367	48
Palencia	8,029	186,512	23	Rioja, La	5,034	253,295	50
Salamanca	12,336	368,055	29	Valencian			
Segovia	6,949	149,286	21	Community	23,305	3,646,765	156
Soria	10,287	98,803	9	Alicante	5,863	1,148,597	195
Valladolid	8,202	489,636	59	Castellón	6,679	431,755	64
Zamora	10,559	224,369	21	Valencia	10,763	2,066,413	192
Catalonia	31,930	5,958,208	186	Ceuta [1]	18	70,864	...
Barcelona	7,773	4,618,734	598	Melilla [1]	14	58,449	...
Gerona	5,886	467,945	80				
Lérida	12,028	355,451	29	Total	504,750	37,746,260	74

[1] Ceuta and Melilla are municipalities located in the northern coast of Morocco.

Population of the autonomous communities, 1 April 1986: Andalusia 6,875,628, Aragón 1,214,729, Asturias 1,114,115, Balearic Islands 754,777, Basque Country, The 2,133,002, Canary Islands 1,614,882, Cantabria 524,670, Castilla-La Mancha 1,665,029, Castilla-León 2,600,330, Catalonia 5,977,008, Extremadura 1,088,543, Galicia 2,785,394, Madrid 4,854,616, Murcia 1,014,285, Navarra 512,676, Rioja, La 262,611, Valencian Community 3,772,002, total (including Ceuta and Melilla), 38,891,313.

The capitals of the autonomous communities are as follows: Andalusia, cap. Sevilla (Seville); Aragón, cap. Zaragoza (Saragossa); Asturias, cap. Oviedo; Baleares (Balearic Islands), cap. Palma de Mallorca; The Basque Country, cap. Vitoria; Canary Islands, dual and alternative capital, Las Palmas and Santa Cruz de Tenerife; Cantabria, cap. Santander; Castilla-León, cap. Valladolid; Catalonia, cap. Barcelona; Extremadura, cap. Mérida; Galicia, cap. Santiago de Compostela; Madrid, cap. Madrid; Murcia, cap. Murcia (but regional parliament in Cartagena); Navarra, cap. Pamplona; La Rioja, cap. Logroño; Valencian Community, cap. Valencia. Castilla-La Mancha had not chosen (1987) a capital town; the actual seat of its legislature and executive is at Toledo.

The capitals of the provinces are in the towns from which they take the name, except in Álava (capital Vitoria), Asturias (Oviedo), Baleares (Palma de Mallorca), Cantabria (Santander), Guipúzcoa (San Sebastián), La Rioja (Logroño), Navarra (Pamplona) and Vizcaya (Bilbao).

In 1981 (census) there were 19,216,496 females and 18,529,764 males. 1985 estimate: 20,000,776 females and 19,309,872 males.

By decree of 21 Sept. 1927 the islands which form the Canary Archipelago were divided into 2 provinces, under the name of their respective capitals: Santa Cruz de Tenerife and Las Palmas de Gran Canaria. The province of Santa Cruz de Tenerife is constituted by the islands of Tenerife, La Palma, Gomera and Hierro, and that of Las Palmas by Gran Canaria, Lanzarote and Fuerteventura, with the small barren islands of Alegranza, Roque del Este, Roque del Oeste, Graciosa, Montaña Clara and Lobos. The area of the islands is 7,273 sq. km; population (mid-decennial census 1986), 1,614,882. Places under Spanish sovereignty in Morocco are: Alhucemas, Ceuta, Chafarinas, Melilla and Peñón de Vélez.

The following were the registered populations of principal towns at census 1981:

Town	Population	Town	Population	Town	Population
Albacete	117,126	Getafe	127,060	Reus	80,710
Alcalá de Henares	142,862	Gijón	255,969	Sabadell	184,943
Alcorcón	140,657	Granada	262,182	Salamanca	167,131
Algeciras	86,042	Hospitalet	294,033	San Baudilio del	
Alicante	251,387	Huelva	127,806	Llobregat	74,550
Almería	140,946	Jerez de la Frontera	176,238	San Fernando	71,846
Avila	86,584	Jaén	96,424	San Sebastián	175,576
Badajoz	114,361	Laguna, La	112,635	Santa Coloma de	
Badalona	227,744	Leganés	163,426	Gramanet	140,588
Baracaldo	117,422	León	131,134	Santa Cruz de	
Barcelona	1,754,900	Lérida	109,573	Tenerife	190,784
Bilbao	433,030	Logroño	110,980	Santander	180,328
Burgos	156,449	Lugo	73,986	Santiago de	
Cáceres	71,852	Madrid	3,188,297	Compostela	93,695
Cádiz	157,766	Málaga	503,251	Sevilla	653,833
Cartagena	172,751	Mataró	96,467	Tarragona	111,689
Castellón	126,464	Móstoles	149,649	Tarrasa	155,360
Córdoba	284,737	Murcia	288,631	Torrejón de Ardoz	75,398
Cornellá	90,956	Orense	96,085	Valencia	751,734
Coruña, La	232,356	Oviedo	190,123	Valladolid	330,242
Elche	162,873	Palencia	74,080	Vigo	258,724
Ferrol, El	91,764	Palma de Mallorca	304,422	Vitoria	192,773
Fuenlabrada	77,626	Palmas, Las	366,454	Zaragoza	590,750
Gerona	87,648	Pamplona	183,126		

Vital statistics for calendar years:

	Marriages	Births	Deaths
1980	213,363	565,401	287,621
1981	199,057	532,255	286,400
1982	188,597	509,685	282,266
1983	183,068	477,291	296,188
1984	192,406	465,709	295,425

Languages. The Constitution states that 'Castilian is the Spanish official language of the State', but also that 'All other Spanish languages will also be official in the corresponding Autonomous Communities'.

Catalan is spoken by a majority of people in Catalonia and Baleares, and by a large minority in Valencian Community (where it is frequently called Valencian); in Aragón, a narrow strip close to Catalonia and Valencian Community boundaries, speaks Catalan.

Galician, a language very close to Portuguese, is spoken by a majority of people in Galicia. Basque, by a significant minority in the Basque Country (33·3%, 1981 census); 54·3% in Guipúzcoa province, 25·7% in Vizcaya province and 11·7% in Álava province. Basque is also spoken by a small minority in north-west Navarra.

In bilingual communities, both Spanish and the regional language are taught in the schools and universities.

CLIMATE. Most of Spain has a form of Mediterranean climate with mild, moist winters and hot, dry summers, but the northern coastal region has a moist, equable climate, with rainfall well-distributed throughout the year, mild winters and warm summers, though having less sunshine than the rest of Spain.

Madrid. Jan. 41°F (5°C), July 77°F (25°C). Annual rainfall 16·8″ (419 mm). Barcelona. Jan. 46°F (8°C), July 74°F (23·5°C). Annual rainfall 21″ (525 mm). Cartagena. Jan. 51°F (10·5°C), July 75°F (24°C). Annual rainfall 14·9″ (373 mm). La Coruña. Jan. 51°F (10·5°C), July 66°F (19°C). Annual rainfall 32″ (800 mm). Sevilla. Jan. 51°F (10·5°C), July 85°F (29·5°C). Annual rainfall 19·5″ (486 mm). Palma de Mallorca (Balearic Islands). Jan. 51°F (11°C), July 77°F (25°C). Annual rainfall 13·6″ (347 mm). Santa Cruz de Tenerife (Canary Islands). Jan. 64°F (17·9°C), July 76°F (24·4°C). Annual rainfall 7·72″ (196 mm).

KING. Juan Carlos I, born 5 Jan. 1938. The eldest son of Don Juan, Conde de Barcelona. Juan Carlos was given precedence over his father as pretender to the Spanish throne in an agreement in 1954 between Don Juan and Gen. Franco. Don

Juan resigned his claims to the throne in May 1977. King (then Prince) Juan Carlos married, in 1962, Princess Sophia of Greece, daughter of the late King Paul of the Hellenes and Queen Frederika. *Offspring:* Elena, born 20 Dec. 1963; Cristina, 13 June 1965; Felipe, Prince of Asturias, Heir to the throne, 30 Jan. 1968.

CONSTITUTION AND GOVERNMENT. The *Cortes* (Parliament) was freely elected on 15 June 1977. The text of the new Constitution was approved by referendum on 6 Dec. 1978, and came into force 29 Dec. 1978. It established a parliamentary monarchy, with King Juan Carlos I as head of state. Legislative power is vested in the *Cortes,* a bicameral parliament composed of the Congress of Deputies (lower house) and the Senate (upper house). The Congress of Deputies has not less than 300 nor more than 400 members (350 in the general elections of 1977, 1979, 1982 and 1986), all elected in a proportional system regarding the population of every province. The members of the Senate are elected in a majority system: the 47 peninsular provinces elect 4 senators each, regardless of population; the insular provinces electing 5 (Baleares, Las Palmas) or 6 (Santa Cruz de Tenerife); and Ceuta and Melilla, 2 senators each. There are 208 senators, to whom are added some other members of the upper house elected by the parliaments of the autonomous communities. Deputies and senators are elected in universal (but not compulsory), direct, free, equal and secret suffrage, for a term of 4 years, liable to dissolution. Executive power is vested in the President of the Government (prime minister), with his Cabinet; he is elected by the Congress of Deputies.

A general election took place on 22 June 1986.

Congress of Deputies (350 members): Spanish Workers Socialist Party (PSOE), 184; Popular Alliance (AP, conservative), 84 (including its ally Liberal Party); Popular Democratic Party (PDP, Christian democrat), 21; Social and Democratic Centre (CDS, centrist), 19; Convergence and Union (CiU, Catalan nationalists), 18; Basque Nationalist Party (PNV), 6; United Left (communist dominated coalition, IU), 7; Herri Batasuna (HB, Basque independentists), 5; Euskadido Eskerra (non-radical Basque independentists), 2; four conservative regional parties from Galicia, the Canaries, Aragón and Valencia, 1 each. *Presidente* (speaker) of the Congress of Deputies, Félix Pons Irazazábal (PSOE).

Senate: 208 members, excluding those elected by regional parliaments (250 including them): PSOE, 124 (145); AP and PDP, 63 (73); CiU, 8 (10); PNV, 7 (9); HB, 1 (1); Independents from the Canaries, 2 (2); CDS, 3 (3). *Presidente* (speaker) of the Senate, José F. de Carvajal (PSOE).

The Council of Ministers appointed 26 July 1986 was composed as follows in Oct. 1987:

President of the Government (Prime Minister): Felipe González Márquez (Secretary-General of PSOE).

Vice-President of the Government (Deputy Premier): Alfonso Guerra González. *Foreign Affairs:* Francisco Fernández Ordóñez. *Economy, Finance and Commerce:* Carlos Solchaga Catalán. *Industry and Energy:* Luis Carlos Croissier. *Interior:* José Barrionuevo. *Defence:* Narcis Serra i Serra. *Public Administration:* Joaquín Almunia Amann. *Education and Science:* José María Maravall. *Public Works:* Javier Sáez de Cosculluela. *Justice:* Fernando Ledesma Bartret. *Culture:* Javier Solana Madariaga. *Agriculture, Fisheries and Food:* Carlos Romero Herrero. *Health and Consumers Affairs:* Julián García Vargas. *Labour and Social Security:* Manuel Chaves. *Transport, Tourism and Communications:* Abel Caballero Álvarez. *Relations with the Cortes and Secretary of the Cabinet:* Virgilio Zapatero.

All ministers are members of PSOE.

National flag: Three horizontal stripes of red, yellow, red, with the yellow of double width, and charged near the hoist with the national arms.

National anthem: Marcha real.

Regional and local government. The Constitution of 1978 establishes a semi-federal system of regional administration, with the autonomous community *(Comunidad Autónoma)* as its basic element. There are 17 autonomous communities, each of them having a Parliament, elected by universal vote, and a regional government; all possess exclusive legislative and executive power in many matters, as listed in the national Constitution and in their own fundamental law *(estatuto de autonomía)*. The Basque Country and Catalonia elected their first parliaments in March 1980, Galicia in Oct. 1981 and Andalusia in May 1982. All others in May 1983 (renewed in June 1987). Basque, Catalan, Galician and Andalusian parliaments were renewed in their regional elections of Feb. 1984, April 1984, Nov. 1985 and June 1986 respectively. Basque parliament, again in Nov. 1986.

There are 7 autonomous communities composed of one only province, i.e., Asturias (*ex*-Oviedo province), Cantabria (*ex*-Santander province), La Rioja (*ex*-Logroño province), Navarra, Baleares, Murcia and Madrid. The other 10 are formed by 2 or more provinces. In all, there are in Spain 50 provinces, since the administrative division established in 1833; Ceuta and Melilla, municipalities in the northern coast of Morocco, are not part of any province. The provincial council *(Diputación Provincial)* is the administrative organ of the province, except in the 7 autonomous communities composed of one province, where there are only the regional legislative and executive powers. The provincial council is indirectly elected. Each of the 7 main islands of the Canaries (provinces of Las Palmas and Santa Cruz de Tenerife) has a directly elected corporation, the *Cabildo Insular*, to rule its special interests; in the main islands of the Balearics there are also elected *Consell Insular*.

The provinces are constituted by the association of municipalities (8,022 in 1981 census). Municipalities are autonomous in their own sphere. At their head stands the municipal council *(Ayuntamiento)*, members of which are elected in a universal ballot every 4 years, and they, in turn, elect one of them as Mayor *(Alcalde)*.

DEFENCE. On 26 Sept. 1953 the US and Spain signed three agreements covering the construction and use of military facilities in Spain by the US, economic assistance, and military end-item assistance. These agreements were renewed several times, the last in July 1982. The American naval and air base at Rota (near Cádiz) is connected by pipelines with the American bomber bases at Morón de la Frontera (near Seville), Torrejón (near Madrid) and Zaragoza. The US will withdraw from Torréjon in 1991.

Length of service is 12 months and 16 months for volunteers.

In March 1986 a referendum was conducted to establish whether Spain should remain in NATO. 52·5% of the voters were for the resolution.

Army. The Army is divided into 2 principal parts: the Immediate Intervention Forces and Territorial Defence Forces. The former consist of 1 armoured, 1 mechanized and 1 motorized divisions; 1 armoured cavalry, 1 parachute and 1 airportable brigades; and supporting artillery, engineer and signals units. The Territorial Defence Forces (to be disbanded 1985–88) are divided between 8 Military Regions, and include 2 mountain divisions and 8 infantry brigades. There are also other reserve and independent units, and the Army Aviation forces. Equipment includes 299 AMX-30, 380 M-47E and 164 M-48 tanks. The aviation element of the Army consists of about 180 helicopters, including 70 BO 105s, 69 UH-1 Iroquois, 12 OH-58 Kiowas, 18 Chinooks and 8 AB.212s. Strength (1988) 230,000 (including 165,000 conscripts). Of these 5,800 are stationed on the Balearic Islands, 10,000 on the Canary Islands and 21,000 in Ceuta/Melilla. The paramilitary Civil Guard number 63,500 men.

Navy. Particulars of the principal ships:

Completed	Name	Standard displacement Tons	Guns	Aircraft	Shaft horse-power	Speed Knots
			Aircraft Carriers			
1988	Principe de Asturias	12,000	4 Meroka 20 mm (12 barrels) CIWS	7 VSTOL aircraft and 13 helicopters	46,400 (gas)	26
1943	Dédalo[1]	13,000	22 40-mm. A.A.	7 VSTOL aircraft and 20 helicopters	100,000 (steam)	32 (original) now 24

[1] The former US fixed-wing aircraft carrier *Cabot*, converted in 1966 and transferred to Spain on loan in 1967 and purchased in 1973. Classed as a helicopter carrier until Harrier 'jump-jet' fixed wing aircraft were embarked.

There are also 8 diesel-powered patrol submarines (4 new French-design, 4 modern French-design), 9 destroyers, 12 frigates, 4 old corvettes, 12 new fast attack craft, 4 patrol ships, 10 new patrol vessels, 4 ocean minesweepers, 8 coastal minesweepers, 38 coastal patrol craft, 33 inshore patrol launches, 1 dock landing ship, 6 survey ships, 3 landing ships, 5 landing craft, 140 minor landing craft, 1 replenishment ship, 12 oilers, 2 attack transports, 2 tenders, 2 training ships, 1 boom defence vessel, 1 fishery protection trawler, 30 tugs, 1 royal yacht, 10 water carriers, 40 auxiliary craft and 36 service barges.

The Spanish Navy is being renewed and modernized. Ships under construction include 4 missile-armed frigates. Ships projected include 3 submarines, 4 destroyers, 1 more missile armed frigate and 6 corvettes, while a modified new construction programme is being considered including 3 submarines, 5 frigates, 8 minesweepers and 4 minehunters.

Shipbuilding is mainly carried on at the dockyards at El Ferrol and Cartagena, Cádiz having a smaller share in it. Barcelona, Bilbao, Seville and Cádiz are the chief naval yards.

There are naval radio telegraphic stations at Cádiz, Barcelona, Mahón, Pontevedra, Cartagena and El Ferrol.

In 1988 naval personnel totalled 64,700, comprising 5,200 naval officers, 37,900 ratings, 9,400 civil branch and 700 marine officers and 11,500 marine other ranks.

The Naval Air Service operates 25 fixed-wing aircraft and 55 helicopters.

Air Force. The Air Force is organized as an independent service, dating from 1939. It is administered through 4 operational commands. These comprise Air Combat Command which controls interceptor squadrons (including USAF elements) and the control and warning radar network, Tactical and Transport Commands, and Air Command of the Canaries. Strength (1988) 32,500 and 215 combat aircraft.

The Tactical Air Command has 2 fighter-bomber squadrons of Spanish-built Northrop SF-5s, 1 aero-naval co-operation squadron with 6 P-3A Orion antisubmarine aircraft, and a liaison flight at Tablada with CASA 127s. Air Combat Command has 2 squadrons of Mirage III-Es, 2 squadrons of F-4C/RF-4C Phantom IIs and 2 squadrons of Mirage F1-Cs, plus a flight of CASA/Dornier Do27 127 liaison aircraft. Five KC-130H tankers support the F-4C squadrons. Three wings of Air Transport Command operate C-130 Hercules, Caribou and Spanish-built CASA Aviocars. Air Command of the Canaries has 3 squadrons, equipped with Aviocar transports; Mirage F1 fighter-bombers; F27 Maritime aircraft and Super Puma helicopters for search and rescue. Other equipment includes 2 DC-8s, 5 Falcons and helicopters for VIP transport; and aircraft for photographic, firefighting, target towing and research duties. Air-sea rescue units have Aviocars and Super Puma helicopters. Delivery of 72 F-18 Hornets began in 1986.

American-built F33 Bonanza and T-34A piston-engined aircraft are used for basic training, after which pupil pilots progress to CASA C-101 jet aircraft. Two-seat versions of operational types are used as advanced trainers. Other training types include Beechcraft King Air C90s for instrument flying and liaison duties. The T-34As are being replaced by Chilean-built Pillan basic trainers.

INTERNATIONAL RELATIONS

Membership. Spain is a member of UN, the Council of Europe, NATO, the European Communities and OECD.

ECONOMY

Budget. Revenue and expenditure in 1m. pesetas:

	1983	1984	1985	1986	1987
Revenue	4,513,305	5,399,997	6,113,086	7,164,232	8,113,442
Expenditure	4,513,305	5,399,997	6,113,086	7,164,232	8,113,442

The budget is made up as follows (in 1m. pesetas):

Revenue (1987)		Revenue (1987) continued	
Direct taxes	2,487,000	Real estate income	94,836
Indirect taxes	2,993,300	Miscellaneous income	199,974
Levies and various revenues	278,465	Deficit (financed with public	
Current transactions	365,813	debt, treasury loans, etc)	1,754,054

Expenditure (1987)		Expenditure (1987) continued	
H.M. House	550	Ministry of Public Works and	
Cortes (Parliament)	9,787	Housing	272,368
Court of Accounts	2,304	,, Education and Science	603,537
Constitutional Court	781	,, Labour and Social	
Council of State	461	Security	1,724,261
Public Debt	1,038,588	,, Industry and Energy	198,009
Civil Service Pensions	423,756	,, Agriculture and Food	222,611
General Council of the Judicial		,, Transport, Tourism and	
Power	1,713	Communications	425,772
Relations with the Cortes and		,, Culture	35,978
Secretariat of the Cabinet	18,431	,, Public Administration	24,570
Ministry of Foreign Affairs	43,746	,, Health and Consumer	
,, Justice	111,640	Affairs	29,420
,, Defence	704,077	Regional governments	1,232,550
,, Finance	142,720	Regional Compensation Fund	124,452
,, Interior	296,124	Expenses in several ministries	425,236

Currency. The *peseta* is divided into 100 *céntimos*; but *céntimos* are no longer in legal use since 1 July 1984.

Bank-notes of 10,000, 5,000, 2,000, 1,000, 500, 200 and 100 *pesetas* and coins of 1 *peseta* (copper and aluminium), 2, 5, 10, 25, 50, 100, 200 *pesetas* (nickel and copper) are in circulation. In Dec. 1985 the circulation of bank-notes was 2,260,600m. *pesetas* and of coins, 131,300m. *pesetas.*

In March 1988, £1 = 202 *pesetas*; US$1 = 113·49.

Banking. On 1 Jan. 1922 the Bank of Spain came under the Bank Ordinance Law, according to which the Government participate in its net profits.

The 10 largest banks are: Banco Central; Banco Español de Crédito; Banco Hispano Americano; Banco de Bilbao; Banco de Vizcaya; Banco de Santander; Banco Popular Español; Banco Exterior de España; Banco Pastor; Banco de Sabadell. All are privately owned except the Banco Exterior de España.

Private banks deposits and savings bank deposits (Popular Savings Banks) in Spain, 30 Sept.1986, amounted to 26,746,800m. pesetas. The Post Office Savings Bank opened on 12 March 1916. Deposits, 30 June 1986, amounted to 499,747m. pesetas.

Weights and Measures. On 1 Jan. 1859 the metric system of weights and measures was introduced.

ENERGY AND NATURAL RESOURCES

Electricity. Electric power-stations in 1986 had a total installed capacity of 41·5m. kw. The total output 1986, amounted to 128,560m. kwh of which 27,260m. hydroelectric and 37,460m. nuclear. Supply 110 and 220 volts; 50 Hz.

Oil. Crude oil production (1987) 1·6m. tonnes.

Gas. Production of natural gas in 1986 was 225,000 tonnes.

Minerals. Spain is relatively rich in minerals. The production of the more important minerals in 1986 was as follows (in 1,000 tonnes; net metal content):

Anthracite	5,477	Iron	2,704	Tin	318
Coal	10,714	Lead	81	Zinc	236
Lignite	22,886	Copper	51	Wolfram	576
Uranium	428	Pyrites	1,211		

Agriculture. Spain is mainly an agricultural country. In 1986 the total value of agricultural produce was 1,681·1m. pesetas; of livestock, 1,076·2m.; of forestry, 82·6m. Land under cultivation in 1985 (in 1,000 hectares) included: Cereals, 7,591·3; vegetables, 480; potatoes, 331. In 1985, 605,468 tractors and (1982) 47,174 harvesters were in use.

Principal		Area (in 1,000 hectares)				Yield (in 1,000 tonnes)		
crops	1983	1984	1985	1986	1983	1984	1985	1986
Wheat	2,603	2,306	2,025	2,096	4,268	6,044	5,326	4,292
Barley	3,735	4,025	4,155	4,334	6,662	10,695	10,680	7,331
Oats	454	479	465	384	464	790	719	422
Rye	217	231	222	223	253	325	295	220
Rice	41	73	74	79	224	437	459	494
Maize	354	440	516	519	1,803	2,495	3,331	3,451
Potatoes	340	348	327	289	5,163	5,949	5,770	4,857
Sugar-beet	249	221	178	195	9,619	8,814	7,349	7,776
Sunflower	...	1,007	1,125	936	682	968	915	844

In 1986, 1,574,000 hectares were under vines; production of wine was (1986) 36·7m. hectolitres. The area of onions was (1986) 34,000 hectares, yielding (1986) 1,149,000 tonnes. Production of oranges and mandarines was 3,119,000 tonnes, lemons, 596,000. Other products are esparto, flax, hemp and pulse. Spain has important industries connected with the preparation of wine and fruits.

Industrial crops (1986 in 1,000 tonnes): Cotton, 254; olives, 246; olive oil, 489; tobacco, 42 (1985).

Livestock products (1986 in 1,000 tonnes): Pigmeat, 1,165; poultry meat, 763; cattle meat, 438; cows' milk, 6,140.

Livestock (1986): Horses, 253,000; asses, 155,000; mules, 139,000; cattle, 5·8m.; sheep, 17·09m.; goats, 2·53m.; pigs, 15·78m.; poultry, 53m.

Forestry. Total forests (1985) 11·7m. hectares; production, 1985, 10,368,000 cu. metres of wood.

Fisheries. The most important catches are those of sardines, whiting, anchovy and hake. The total catch amounted in 1986 to 1·05m. tons. The Spanish fishing fleet in 1985 consisted of 17,665 vessels of 671,804 tonnes, with a total crew of 99,975.

INDUSTRY AND TRADE

Industry. The manufacture of cotton and woollen goods is important, principally in Catalonia. In 1983, the principal textile productions were (in 1,000 tonnes): Wool yarn, 33; cotton yarn, 106; fabrics yarn, 128; wool cloth, 9; cotton cloth, 88; fabrics cloth, 69. In 1983, 2·4m. tonnes of writing, printing, packing and other paper were produced. The production of cement reached 21,880,000 tonnes in 1986. Steel production (1986) 14·19m. tonnes; the three great blast-furnaces concentrations are in Bilbao area, Avilés (Asturias) and Sagunto (Valencia). The chemical industry is located in the areas of Madrid, Barcelona and Bilbao; sulphuric acid production (1982), 2m. tonnes; nitrogenous fertilizers, 822,000 tonnes; plastics (1986), 1,488,000 tonnes. The 9 oil refineries refined (1984) 39,854,000 tonnes of crude oil. In 1982 900,000 TV sets (550,000 colour sets) were manufactured. 816,000 refrigerators, 1,030,000 washing machines and 910,000 bicycles were manufactured in 1986. Spain has important toys and shoe industries, toys especially in Alicante and Barcelona provinces and shoe in Alicante province and the Balearic islands.

Spanish shipyards launched 253,105 BRT in 1986. In 1986, 1,439,000 vehicles were built, including 1,280,000 passenger cars.

Labour. The monthly minimum wage for workers was 44,040 pesetas (Jan. 1988).

The economically active population numbered 13,894,000 in Dec. 1986. Of these, 10,922,000 were employed: 1,741,000 in agriculture and fishing, 2,637,000 in manufactures, 830,000 in construction industry and 5,714,000 in trade and other public and personal services. 21·4% of the active population was unemployed at the end of 1986 (2,972,000 persons).

Trade Unions. The Constitution guarantees the establishment and activities of trade unions provided they have a democratic structure. The two most important trade unions are *Unión General de Trabajadores* (UGT), founded in 1888 by Pablo Iglesias (who had founded in 1879 the Spanish Workers Socialist Party,

PSOE), and *Comisiones Obreras*, which was gradually established 1958–63, then as a clandestine labour organization.

Commerce. Foreign trade of Spain (Peninsula, Baleares, Canaries, Ceuta, Melilla) (in 1 m. pesetas):

	1982	1983	1984	1985	1986
Imports	3,473,208	4,176,470	4,628,991	5,073,239	4,890,768
Exports	2,260,198	2,838,601	3,778,071	4,104,143	3,800,225

In 1986 the most important items of import were (in 1m. pesetas): Crude petroleum, 692,481 (14·16% of total); vehicle parts, 161,368 (3·3%); vehicles 126,433 (2·59%); computers, 117,851 (2·41%), and related machinery, 68,780 (1·41%); petroleum products, 107,336 (2·19%); inner combustion motors, 84,330 (1·72%); coffee, 79,770 (1·63%); oleaginous seeds, 72,851 (1·49%); measuring and precision tools, 66,378 (1·36%).

The most important exports in 1986 (in 1m. pesetas) were: Vehicles, 399,970 (10·52% of total); petroleum products, 220,120 (5·79%); fresh fruit and nuts, 199,897 (5·26%); vehicle parts, 135,013 (3·56%); footwear, 131,867 (3·47%); iron and steel bars, 112,918 (2·97%); iron and steel sheets, 83,774 (2·2%); vegetables, 75,938 (2%); alcoholic beverages, 65,644 (1·73%); computers, 61,749 (1·63%).

Distribution of Spanish foreign trade (in 1m. pesetas) according to origin and destination, for calendar years:

	Imports		Exports	
	1985	1986	1985	1986
Europe	2,232,067	2,829,773	2,512,695	2,589,125
EEC	1,828,360	2,458,106	2,055,225	2,292,173
France	471,091	571,427	636,417	682,748
Germany, Federal Republic	537,432	736,091	393,137	444,686
UK	329,620	377,653	351,254	335,283
Italy	232,726	356,867	289,488	302,261
EFTA	266,077	253,600	256,258	179,837
Comecon	120,174	86,992	120,977	68,601
USA	552,982	482,718	408,562	349,330
LAIA (ex LAFTA)	582,776	347,776	245,159	214,578
Mexico	292,647	127,774	41,552	28,713
Netherlands	...	145,272	...	216,067
Saudi Arabia	59,728	70,498	77,999	50,270
Belgium	...	130,220	...	107,264
Japan	172,778	217,105	53,821	39,211
Libya	186,248	132,654	29,128	17,487
Oceania	34,079	43,065	23,092	14,758

Total trade between Spain and UK (British Department of Trade returns, in £1,000 sterling):

	1984	1985	1986	1987
Imports to UK	1,604,405	1,770,862	1,777,341	2,099,139
Exports and re-exports from UK	1,234,584	1,553,424	1,905,479	2,164,221

Total trade of the Spanish territories and UK (British Department of Trade returns, in £1,000 sterling):

	Imports to UK			Exports from UK		
	1985	1986	1987	1985	1986	1987
Canary Islands	64,625	63,529	77,191	48,946	66,949	86,185
North Africa	...	44	...	2,893	2,762	3,831

Tourism. In 1986, 47,388,000 tourists visited Spain (from France, 11·28m.; Portugal, 9·52m.; Federal Republic of Germany, 5·93m.; UK, 6,043,000). Receipts of foreign currency (1986) US$12·06m. Hotel and similar beds, 1,561,300 (1986).

COMMUNICATIONS

Roads. In 1985 the total length of highways and roads in Spain was 149,471 km, of which about 124,000 km were macadamized or had other good surface. Motorways, 2,074 km. Number of cars (1986) was 9,761,968, lorries, 1,642,371, buses,

42,378 and motorcycles (1985) 739,056. There were 12,284,080 vehicles in Dec. 1986 and 12,345,589 driving licences (3,370,450 for women).

Railways. The total length of the state railways in 1986 was 12,691 km, mostly 1,676-mm gauge (6,226 km electrified). On 1 Feb. 1941 the Spanish railways, of broad gauge only, passed into state ownership; they are under a board known as the *Red Nacional de Ferrocarriles Españoles* (RENFE). The gauge of the principal Spanish railways has, for strategic reasons, been kept different from that of France; passengers therefore must change trains at the French frontier stations except by certain trains having variable gauge axles. In 1986 freight carried was 31·6m. tonnes and 193m. passengers. There are several regional railways including Basque, Catalan and FEVE (narrow gauge) railways.

Aviation. The most important Spanish airline is 'Iberia': it maintains a regular service with Europe, America, Africa and the Middle and Far East. Its fleet included 6 B-747s (for 430 passengers each), 8 DC-10s (for 266), 6 Airbus-300Bs (for 253), 35 B-727s (for 161) and 30 DC-9s (for 110) in 1985. 'Aviaco' operates mainly internal flights. 'Spantax', based on Palma de Mallorca, operates charter flights only. There are 43 airports open to civil traffic; those of Madrid, Palma de Mallorca and Barcelona are the most active. A small airport in Seo de Urgel, in the Pyrenees, used especially for the air service of Andorra was opened in 1982.

Aircraft movements in 1985, 248,245 internal and 282,817 international, carrying 20,967,132 passengers on internal and 22,083,855 on international flights, and 363,100 tonnes of merchandise.

Shipping. The merchant navy in 1984 contained 1,105 vessels of a gross tonnage of 6,377,000.

In 1984, 83,981 ships entered Spanish ports, carrying 12m. passengers and discharging 215m. tonnes of cargo (1985).

Post and Broadcasting. The receipts of the post office in 1984 were 75,075m. pesetas; expenses, 84,345m. pesetas. There were in 1984, 13,299 post offices and 13,825,000 telephones, these all privately operated.

Radio Nacional de España broadcasts 4 programmes on medium-waves and FM, as well as many regional programmes; it does not broadcast advertising. There is another state broadcasting network, *Radio-Cadena Española,* this self-financing with advertising. The greatest radio audience is that of a private network, *Sociedad Española de Radiodifusión* (SER); *Cadena de Ondas Populares Españolas* (COPE) belongs to the Roman Catholic church. Two private broadcasting networks were established in 1982 covering the whole of Spain, *Antena 3* and *Radio 80*. *Televisión Española* broadcasts 2 programmes. Since 1983 *TV3* broadcasts entirely in Catalan and *Eusko Telebista* about 90% in Basque. Colour transmissions are carried by PAL system. Number of receivers (1979): radio, 9·6m.; television, 9·4m. (about 50% colour sets). In 1985 broadcasting on TV in Galician commenced.

Cinemas (1981). There were 3,970 cinemas with an estimated seating capacity of 4m.

Newspapers (1985). There were about 100 daily newspapers with a total daily circulation of about 5m. copies. In 1985 the following dailies had a daily circulation of more than 100,000 copies: *El País* (Madrid, 347,512), *La Vanguardia* (Barcelona, 194,189), *ABC* (Madrid, 157,205), *As* (Madrid, [sports], 143,341), *El Periódico* (Barcelona, 127,777), *Diario 16* (Madrid, 127,514), *Marca* (Madrid, [sports], 113,155) and *El Correo Español-El Pueblo Vasco* (Bilbao, 108,834).

JUSTICE, RELIGION, EDUCATION AND WELFARE

Justice. Justice is administered by *Tribunales* and *Juzgados* (Tribunals and Courts), which conjointly form the *Poder Judicial* (Judicial Power). Judges and magistrates cannot be removed, suspended or transferred except as set forth by law. The Constitution of 1978 has established a new organ, the *Consejo General del Poder Judicial* (CGPJ, General Council of the Judicial Power), formed by 1 President and 20 magistrates, judges, attorneys and lawyers, governing the Judicial Power in full independence from the other two powers of the State, the Legislative (Cortes) and the Executive (President of the Government and his Cabinet); all members of the CGPJ, magistrates, etc., have been appointed by the Cortes since 1985. Its President is that of the *Tribunal Supremo*. The territorial organization of justice is being gradually changed, adapting it to the new map of the country in Autonomous Communities and when completed, in each of these it will be a *Tribunal Superior de Justicia* as the highest judicial organ, responsible only to the national *Tribunal Supremo*.

The Judicature is composed of the *Tribunal Supremo* (Supreme High Court); 16 *Audiencias Territoriales* (Division High Courts); 50 *Audiencias Provinciales* (Provincial High Courts); 518 *Juzgados de Primera Instancia* (Courts of First Instance), 755 *Juzgados de Distrito* (District Courts) and 7,532 *Juzgados Municipales y de paz* (Municipal and Peace Courts, court of lowest jurisdiction held by Justices of the Peace).

The *Tribunal Supremo* consists of a President (appointed by the King, on proposal from the *Consejo General del Poder Judicial*) and various judges distributed among 6 chambers: 1 for trying civil matters, 3 for administrative purposes, 1 for criminal trials and 1 for social matters. The *Tribunal Supremo* has disciplinary faculties; is court of cassation in all criminal trials; for administrative purposes decides in first and second instance disputes arising between private individuals and the State, and in social matters resolves in the last instance all cases involving over 100,000 pesetas.

The *Audiencias Territoriales* have power to try in second instance sentences passed by judges in civil matters.

The *Audiencias Provinciales* try and pass sentence in first instance on all cases filed for delinquency. The jury system, re-established by the art. 125 of the Constitution, had not been applied by Jan. 1987, pending its parliamentary regulation.

The *Juzgados Municipales* try small civil cases and petty offences. The *Juzgados Comarcales* deal with the same charges, but their jurisdiction embraces larger districts.

Military cases are tried by the *Consejo Supremo de Justicia Militar* but its sentences can now pass to the (civil) *Tribunal Supremo*, as final cassation instance.

The *Tribunal Constitucional* (Constitutional Court) has power to solve conflicts between the State and the Autonomous Communities, to determine if legislation passed by the Cortes is contrary to the Constitution and to protect constitutional rights of the individuals violated by any authority. Its 12 members are appointed by the King in the following way: 4, on proposal of the Congress of Deputies; 4, on proposal of the Senate; 2 on proposal of the *Consejo General del Poder Judicial;* and 2 on proposal of the Cabinet. It has a 9 year term, a third of the membership renewed every 3 years.

The death penalty was abolished in 1978 by the Constitution (art. 15). Divorce is again legal since July 1981 and abortion since Aug. 1985.

The prison population was, on 11 Nov. 1986, 26,046.

Religion. Roman Catholicism is the religion of the majority. There are 11 metropolitan sees and 52 suffragan sees, the chief being Toledo, where the Primate resides.

The archdioceses of Madrid-Alcalá and Barcelona depend directly from the Vatican.

The Constitution guarantees full religious freedom and states that no religion has an established legal condition (art. 16); so, since 29 Dec. 1978 there has been no official religion in Spain. A report issued in 1982 by the Episcopal Conference of the Roman Catholic Church claims that $82 \cdot 76\%$ of all children born in 1981 were baptized in that church.

There are about 250,000 other Christians, including several Protestant denominations, Jehovah Witnesses (about 60,000) and Mormons. The British and Foreign Bible Society was, on 10 March 1963, allowed to resume its activities.

The first synagogue since the expulsion of the Jews in 1492 was opened in Madrid on 2 Oct. 1959. The number of Jews is estimated at about 13,000.

Education. Primary education is compulsory and free between 6 and 14 years of age.

In 1985–86 pre-primary education (under 6 years) was conducted by 39,668 schools, with 39,573 teachers and 1,127,348 pupils. Primary or basic education (6 to 14 years): 186,389 schools, 193,445 teachers and 5,594,285 pupils. Secondary education (14-17 years) is conducted on two branches: Middle schools *(Institutos),* and vocational and technical centres *(Formación Profesional),* with 2,635 and 2,248 school units, 75,546 and 49,408 teachers and 1,238,874 and 738,340 pupils. For adult education there were (in 1985–86) 3,048 school units, with 3,341 teachers and 145,062 students. For the physically or mentally disabled there were 5,854 school units, with 5,862 teachers and 98,371 pupils.

In 1986 there were in all 33 universities: 22 State Universities, in Madrid, Barcelona, Valencia, Granada, Sevilla, Santiago de Compostela, Zaragoza, Bilbao (University of the Basque Country), Oviedo, Valladolid, Salamanca (founded in 1215), La Laguna (Canaries), Murcia, Málaga, Córdoba, Badajoz-Cáceres (University of Extremadura), Cádiz, León, Santander, Alicante, Palma de Mallorca and Alcalá de Henares; 4 Polytechnic Universities, in Madrid, Barcelona, Valencia and Las Palmas (Canaries); 2 Autonomous Universities, in Madrid and Barcelona; 4 private (catholic) universities, in Deusto (Bilbao), Pamplona, Salamanca and Madrid (University of Comillas); and the *Universidad Nacional de Educación a Distancia* (National University for Education at Home), which teaches by mail, radio and TV, with its central seat at Madrid (48,491 students, 1985–86). The new (state) University of Castilla-La Mancha started in 1985–86, with 6,625 students and campuses in Albacete, Ciudad Real and other places. There were 826,306 university students (1985–86) including 24,095 students at private universities.

Social Security. The social services budget was 4,367,807 pesetas in 1987, and covered retirement pensions (60·8% of that budget), health and hospital services (25·6%) and other allowances and aids. There is a minimum pension for every retired citizen with yearly earnings under 500,000 pesetas.

In 1987 the system of contributions to the social security and employment scheme was: For pensions, sickness, invalidity, maternity and children, a contribution of 28·8% of the basic wage (24% paid by the employer, 4·8% by the employee); for unemployment benefit, a contribution of 6·3% (5·2% paid by the employer, 1·1% by the employee). There are also minor contributions for a Fund of Guaranteed Salaries, working accidents and professional sicknesses, and vocational training.

DIPLOMATIC REPRESENTATIVES

Of Spain in Great Britain (24 Belgrave Sq., London SW1X 8QA)
Ambassador: José Joaquín Puig de la Bellacasa, GCVO.

Of Great Britain in Spain (Calle de Fernando el Santo, 16, Madrid, 4)
Ambassador: Lord Nicholas Gordon Lennox, KCMG, LVO.

Of Spain in the USA (2700 15th St., NW, Washington, D.C., 20009)
Ambassador: Julián Santamaría.

Of the USA in Spain (Serrano 75, Madrid)
Ambassador: Reginald Bartholomew.

Of Spain to the United Nations
Ambassador: Francisco Villar.

Books of Reference

Statistical Information: The Instituto Nacional de Estadistica (Paseo de la Castellana, 183, Madrid) combines the administrative work of a government department attached to the Presidency of the Government with a centre of statistical studies.

Altamira y Crevea, R., *A History of Spain.* New York and London, 1950
Bell, D., (ed.), *Democratic Politics in Spain: Spanish Politics after Franco.* London, 1983
Carr, R., *Modern Spain, 1875–1980.* OUP, 1980
Collins, R., *The Basques.* Oxford, 1986

Enciclopedia Universal Ilustrada. 70 vols., 10 appendices, 10 supplements. Madrid
Graham, R., *Spain: Change of a Nation.* London, 1984
Gunther, R., (et al) *Spain after Franco: The Making of a Competitive Party System.* Univ. of
   California Press, 1986
Harrison, J., *The Spanish Economy in the Twentieth Century.* London, 1985
Hooper, J., *The Spaniards: A Portrait of The New Spain.* London, 1986
Lieberman, S., *The Contemporary Spanish Economy: A Historical Perspective.* London, 1982
McNair, J. M., *Education for a Changing Spain.* Manchester, 1984
Maravall, J., *The Transition to Democracy in Spain.* London, 1982
Morris, J., *Spain.* London, 1979
Preston, P., *The Triumph of Democracy in Spain.* London and New York, 1986
Preston, P., and Smyth, D., *Spain, the EEC and NATO.* London, 1984
Reay-Smith, J., *Living in Spain in the '80's.* London, 1985
Shields, G. J., *Spain.* [Bibliography] Oxford and Santa Barbara, 1985

National Library: Biblioteca Nacional, Madrid.

FORMER PROVINCE IN AFRICA (WESTERN SAHARA)

The colony of Spanish Sahara became a Spanish province in July 1958. On 14 Nov. 1975 Spain, Morocco and Mauritania had reached agreement on the transfer of power over Western Sahara to Morocco and Mauritania on 28 Feb. 1976. Morocco occupied al-Aaiún in late Nov. and on 12 Jan. 1976 the Spanish army withdrew from Western Sahara which had ceased to be a Spanish province on 31 Dec. 1975. The country was partitioned by Morocco and Mauritania on 28 Feb. 1976; Morocco reorganized its sector into 3 provinces. In Aug. 1979 Mauritania withdrew from the territory it took over in 1976. The area was taken over by Morocco and reorganized into a fourth province.

A liberation movement, *Frente Polisario,* launched an armed struggle against Spanish rule on 20 May 1973 and, in spite of occupation of all western centres by Moroccan troops, Saharawi guerrillas based in Algeria continue to attempt to liberate their country. They have renamed it the Saharawi Arab Democratic Republic and hold most of the desert beyond a defensive line built by Moroccan troops encompassing Smara, Bu Craa and Laâyoune.

In 1982 the Saharawi Arab Democratic Republic became a member of the Organization of African Unity (OAU).

President: Mohammed Abdelaziz.

Area 266,769 sq. km (102,680 sq. miles). The population at the census held by Morocco in Sept. 1982 was 163,868; estimate (1986) 180,000. Another estimated 165,000 Saharawis live in refugee camps around Tindouf in south-west Algeria. The main towns (1982 census) are Laâyoune (al-Aaiún), the capital (96,784), Dakhla (17,822) and as-Smara (17,753). The population is Arabic-speaking, and virtually entirely Sunni Moslem.

Rich phosphate deposits were discovered in 1963 at Bu Craa. Morocco holds 65% of the shares of the former Spanish state-controlled company. While production reached 5·6m. tonnes in 1975, exploitation has been severely reduced by guerrilla activity but in 1984 produced 1m. tonnes. After a nearly complete collapse, production and transportation of phosphate resumed in 1978, ceased again, and then resumed in 1982.

There are about 6,100 km of motorable tracks, but only about 500 km of paved roads. There are airports at Laâyoune and Dakhla. As most of the land is desert, less than 19% is in agricultural use, with about 2,000 tonnes of grain produced annually. There are (1983) about 22,000 sheep, as well as goats and camels raised. Electricity produced (1983) 78m. kwh.

Books of Reference

Damis, J., *Conflict in Northwest Africa: The Western Sahara Dispute.* Stanford, 1983
Hodges, T., *Historical Dictionary of Western Sahara.* London, 1982.—*Western Sahara: The Roots of a Desert War.* London and Westport, 1984
Sipe, L. F., *Western Sahara: A Comprehensive Bibliography.* New York, 1984
Thompson, V. and Adloff, R., *The Western Saharans: Background to Conflict.* London, 1980

SRI LANKA

Capital: Colombo
Population: 15·8m. (1985)
GNP per capita: US$361 (1984)

Ceylon

HISTORY. According to the Mahawansa chronicle, an Indian prince from the valley of the Ganges, named Vijaya, arrived in the 6th century B.C. and became the first king of the Sinhalese. The monarchical form of government continued until the beginning of the 19th century when the British subjugated the Kandyan Kingdom in the central highlands.

In 1505 the Portuguese formed settlements on the west and south, which were taken from them about the middle of the next century by the Dutch. In 1796 the British Government annexed the foreign settlements to the presidency of Madras. In 1802 Ceylon was constituted a separate colony.

Ceylon became an independent Commonwealth state when the Ceylon Independence Act, 1947, came into force on 4 Feb. 1948. Sri Lanka became a republic in 1972. War between northern Tamil separatists and government forces began in 1983.

EVENTS. In July 1987 the governments of Sri Lanka and India signed an agreement on the future of the Tamil community and the resolution of Tamil–Sinhalese differences. Provisions included alterations to the status of the Tamil language, and of the Northern Province. Tamil rebels laid down their arms on 5 Aug., but violence broke out again during operations by an Indian peace-keeping force. By 31 Dec. 1987 there was still no agreed basis for cease-fire between Tamil rebels and Indian forces, and the inter-government agreement remained without effect.

AREA AND POPULATION. Sri Lanka is an island in the Indian Ocean, south of the Indian peninsula from which it is separated by the Palk Strait. On 28 June 1974 the frontier between India and Sri Lanka in the Palk Strait was redefined, giving to Sri Lanka the island of Kachchativu. Area (in sq. km.) and census population on 17 March 1981.

Provinces	Area	Population	Provinces	Area	Population
Western	3,708·61	3,919,807	North-Central	10,723·59	849,492
Central	5,583·50	2,009,248	Uva	8,487·91	914,522
Southern	5,559·15	1,882,661	Sabaragamuwa	4,901·55	1,482,031
Northern	8,882·11	1,109,404			
Eastern	9,951·26	975,251	Total	65,609·86	14,846,750
North-Western	7,812·18	1,704,334			

Population (1981 census), 14,846,750, an increase of 17% since 1971. Population (in 1,000) according to race and nationality at the 1981 census: 10,980 Sinhalese, 1,887 Ceylon Tamils, 1,047 Ceylon Moors, 39 Burghers, 47 Malays, 819 Indian Tamils, 28 others. Non- nationals of Sri Lanka totalled 635,150. By agreement with the Government of India in 1964 and 1974, Indian nationals who have not been granted Sri Lanka citizenship were to be repatriated. The 1964 agreement covered 525,000 people; the 1974 agreement, 75,000.

Vital statistics, 1986 (provisional): birth-rate (per 1,000 population), 22·3; death-rate, 6·0; infant death-rate (per 1,000 live births), 22·6.

The urban population was 21·5% of the total in 1981. The principal towns and their population according to the census of 1981 are: Colombo (the capital), 587,647; Dehiwela-Mt. Lavinia, 173,529; Moratuwa, 134,826; Jaffna, 118,224; Kotte, 101,039; Kandy, 97,872; Galle, 76,863; Negombo, 60,762; Trincomalee, 44,313; Batticaloa, 42,963; Matara, 38,843; Ratnapura, 37,497; Anuradhapura, 35,981; Badulla, 33,068; Kalutara, 31,503. Population of the Greater Colombo area, 1980, about 1m.

The national languages are Sinhala, English and Tamil; Sinhala is the official language and Tamil is used in the northern and eastern provinces.

CLIMATE. Sri Lanka has an equatorial climate with low annual temperature variations, but it is affected by the north-east Monsoon (Dec. to Feb.) and the south-west Monsoon (May to Sept.). Rainfall is generally heavy but never lasts long; it is heaviest in the south-west and central highlands while the north and east are relatively dry. Thirty-year averages, 1951–80: Colombo. Jan. 79·7°F (26·5°C), July 81·1°F (27·3°C). Annual rainfall 99·5″ (2,527 mm). Trincomalee. Jan. 78·6°F (25·9°C), July 86·2°F (30·1°C). Annual rainfall 63·60″ (1,615 mm). Kandy. Jan. 73·9°F (23·3°C), July 75·9°F (24·4°C). Annual rainfall 76·6″ (1,947 mm). Nuwara Eliya. Jan. 58·5°F (14·7°C), July 60·3°F (15·7°C). Annual rainfall 80·04″ (2,044 mm).

CONSTITUTION AND GOVERNMENT. A new constitution for the Democratic Socialist Republic of Sri Lanka was promulgated in Sept. 1978.

The Executive President is directly elected by the people and has to receive more than one-half of the valid votes cast. His term of office is six years and he shall not hold the office for more than two consecutive terms. He is the Head of the State, the Head of the Executive and of the Government and the Commander-in-chief of the Armed Forces. He does not have any veto power over legislation; even in a time of public emergency, he must act with Parliamentary control and approval.

Parliament consists of one chamber, composed of 168 members elected by universal suffrage. The Senate was abolished by constitutional amendment in Oct. 1971.

The term of Parliament is six years. In Nov. 1982 Parliament voted to extend its present term (expiring Aug. 1983) for a further six years. The vote was subject to national referendum on 20 Dec. 1982; 71% of the electorate voted and 55% approved the extension.

The Prime Minister and other Ministers, who must be members of Parliament, are appointed by the President. The President is head of the Cabinet.

The electorate consists of all who are 18 years of age and over.

National flag: A yellow field bearing 2 panels: in the hoist 2 vertical strips of green and orange; in the fly, dark red with a gold lion holding a sword and in each corner a gold 'bo' leaf.

The Cabinet was as follows in March 1988:

President, Defence, Higher Education, Janata Estates Development, State Plantations, and Plan Implementation, Manpower Mobilization and Civil Security: J. R. Jayawardene.

Prime Minister, Leader of the House, Local Government, Highways, Housing and Construction, Emergency Civil Administration: Ranasinghe Premadasa.

Land, Land Development and Mahaweli Development: Gamini Dissanayake. *Foreign Affairs:* A. C. S. Hameed. *Home Affairs:* K. W. Devanayagam. *National Security:* Lalith W. Athulathmudali. *Rural Development:* Wimala Kannangara. *Justice:* N. P. Wijeyeratne. *Finance and Planning:* N. Marikkar. *Labour:* P. C. Imbulana. *Industries and Scientific Affairs:* R. Denzil Fernando. *Cultural Affairs:* E. L. B. Hurulle. *Fisheries:* M. F. W. Perera. *Health:* R. Atapattu. *Post and Telecommunications:* S. Abeysundera. *Parliamentary Affairs and Sports, Chief Government Whip:* M. Vincent Perera. *Transport, Transport Boards, Private Omnibus Transport:* M. H. Mohamed. *Agricultural Development and Research and Food:* D. B. Wijetunge. *Co-operatives:* W. Dahanayake. *Public Administration and Plantation Industries:* M. Jayawickreme. *Textile Industry:* W. Mendis. *Social Services:* Asoka Karunaratne. *Rural Industrial Development:* S. Thondaman. *Youth Affairs, Education and Employment:* R. Wickremasinghe. *State:* A. de Alwis. *Regional Development:* C. Rajadurai. *Women's Affairs and Teaching Hospitals:* S. Ranasinghe. *Trade and Shipping:* M. S. Amarasiri. *Power and Energy:* P. Dayaratne. *Without Portfolio:* M. A. Bakeer Markar.

For purposes of general administration, the island is divided into 25 districts, administered by government agents. There are 12 Municipal Councils and 24 District Councils.

DEFENCE

Army. The Army was constituted on 10 Oct. 1949. It consists of 5 infantry brigades, 2 reconnaissance, 2 field artillery and 1 engineer regiment, and 1 signals battalion. Equipment includes 18 Saladin armoured cars and 15 Ferret scout cars. Strength (1988) 40,000 including active reservists. There are also paramilitary forces: Police Force (28,000), Volunteer Force (eventually 10,000, when fully mobilized) and Home Guard.

Navy. The Navy was constituted on 9 Dec. 1950. It comprises 6 Surveillance Command Ship (*ex*-mercantile), 2 new Colombo-built patrol vessels, 6 (*ex*-Chinese) fast gunboats, 28 small patrol boats, 2 landing craft and 1 service craft. Emphasis is now on indigenous building. *Gemunu* and *Rangalla* are commissioned as shore establishments. The naval base is at Trincomalee. Personnel in 1988 numbered 330 officers and 4,480 ratings. Naval personnel are sent to the UK for training. There is also a Volunteer Naval Reserve of 20 officers and 520 ratings, and a Naval Reserve of 7 officers and 43 men.

Air Force. The Air Force was formed on 10 Oct. 1950. Its flying bases are at Katunayake and China Bay, Trincomalee. Equipment of 4 squadrons comprises 6 SF.260 and 4 Cessna 150/152 trainers, 3 Herons, 2 HS748, 6 Chinese-built Y-12s, 2 DC-3s, 2 Super King Airs, 3 Cessna Skymasters, 1 Cessna 421 and a Cessna Cardinal for general transport and utility purposes; 3 Doves for navigation training; and 2 Dauphin, 12 Bell 212, 4 Bell 412 and up to 20 JetRanger helicopters for internal security operations. Total strength (1988) about 3,700 officers and airmen. There is also an Air Force Reserve.

INTERNATIONAL RELATIONS

Membership. Sri Lanka is a member of UN, the Commonwealth, the Non-Aligned Movement, the South Asian Association for Regional Co-operation and the Colombo Plan.

External debt. External debt in Dec. 1986 was Rs 86,208·2m. (provisional).

ECONOMY

Planning. The 1987–91 plan aims at 4·6% annual growth rate. Investment allocated is mainly for power and water, including the Mahaweli energy and irrigation scheme, road repairs and telecommunication. Total public investment, about Rs154,156m.

Budget. Revenue and expenditure of central government in Rs 1m. for financial years ending 31 Dec.:

		Expenditure		
Year	Revenue	Recurrent	Capital	Total
1985	39,010	33,842	30,529	64,371
1986	41,644	34,772	35,112	69,884
1987 [1]	44,115	37,050	33,000	70,050

[1] Estimate.

The principal sources of revenue in 1986 were (in Rs 1m.): Income tax, 4,787; import duties, 4,476; export duties, 1,574; other indirect taxes, 21,035.

The principal items of recurrent expenditure in 1986 (in Rs 1m.): Administration including defence, 9,279; food subsidies and food stamps, 1,799; education, social services and health, 5,512; interest on public debt, 9,413. Capital expenditure on agriculture, 1,465; communications, 2,476.

Currency. The Monetary Law Act provides that the standard monetary unit is the Sri Lankan *rupee*.

The Central Bank is the sole authority for the issue of currency and all currency notes and coins issued by the Central Bank are legal tender for the payment of any amount, except notes of Rs 50 and Rs 100 dated before 25 Oct. 1970. Currency notes are issued in the denominations of Rs 2, 5, 10, 20, 50, 100, 500 and 1,000. Coins are issued in the denominations of 1, 2, 5, 10, 25 and 50 cents; Rs 1, 2 and 5. The total circulation was Rs 12,246·9m. on 30 June 1986. In May 1988, £1 = Rs 54·10; US$1 = Rs 30·85.

Banking. The narrow money supply (M1) at 30 June 1986 stood at Rs 19,948·8m.

The main commercial banks in Sri Lanka are: The Bank of Ceylon and the People's Bank (state-managed), the State Bank of India, Grindlays Bank, the Hongkong and Shanghai Banking Corporation, the Standard Chartered Bank, the Commercial Bank of Ceylon, the Hatton National Bank, the Habib Bank (Overseas) Ltd., Indo-Suez Bank, Bank of Credit and Commerce International, American Express and the Indian Overseas Bank Ltd. Total assets of 25 commercial banks at 30 June 1986, Rs 63,632·3m.

The state-owned Ceylon Insurance Corporation and the National Insurance Corporation have a monopoly of all insurance business.

Sri Lanka National Savings Bank at 30 June 1986 had a balance to depositors' credit of Rs 13,615·2m. Sri Lanka State Mortgage and Investment Bank, National Development Bank, Development Finance Corporation, the National Housing Authority and the Housing Development Finance Corporation of Sri Lanka Ltd. are the main long-term credit institutions.

Weights and Measures. The metric system has been established by the Weights and Measures (Amendment) Law No. 24 of 1974, and subsequent legislation.

ENERGY AND NATURAL RESOURCES

Electricity. Installed capacity of electric energy (1986), 1,065,250 kw. Energy produced, 2,653m. kwh; the main source is hydro-electricity (producing 2,645m. kwh). The Mahaweli power scheme had 2 large hydro-power plants commissioned in 1985: Victoria and Kothmale. The Randenigala hydro-power plant was commissioned in 1986 (two 61 mw units). Supply 230 volts; 50 Hz.

Water. The Mahaweli Ganga irrigation scheme is (1987) irrigating 41,000 hectares of new land and 77,000 hectares of land already cultivated. There is a Water Resources Board (set up in 1966) and a National Water Supply and Drainage Board (1974). Water supply to the city and area of Colombo comes from the Labugama and Kalatuwawa reservoirs. Consumption within Colombo city limits is estimated at 10,000m. gallons a year.

All domestic consumers receive a free water allowance; commercial consumers do not.

Minerals. Gems are among the chief minerals mined and exported. Precious and semi-precious stones are found among the layers of older alluvium and river gravels of quaternary age in the valleys of the Ratnapura district in the southwest. The most important are sapphire, ruby, crysoberyl, beryl, topaz, spinel, garnet, ziran and tourmaline. Value of gemstones exported in 1986, Rs 755m.

Graphite is also important. The State Graphite Corporation was set up in 1971. There were 3 large mines (Bogala, Kahatagaha and Kalangaha), and several smaller mines. Graphite produced (tonnes), 1985, 7,413; 1986, 7,708.

The Ceylon Mineral Sands Corporation was established in 1957, mainly to extract ilmenite. Production of ilmenite, 1986, 129,907 tonnes. Some rutile is also produced (8,443 tonnes in 1986).

Salt extraction is the oldest industry in Sri Lanka and is now controlled by the National Salt Corporation. The method is solar evaporation of sea-water. Production, 1986, 104,279 tonnes.

Agriculture. The area of the island is 6,561,000 hectares, of which about 2m. hectares are under cultivation. Agriculture engages about 45% of the labour force. The main crops in 1986 were as follows: Paddy (2·6m. tonnes from 836,000 hectares), rubber (137,000 tonnes), tea (211,000 tonnes) and coconuts (3,039m. nuts).

Livestock in 1986 (estimate): 1·78m. cattle, 964,200 buffaloes, 85,800 swine, 562,700 goats and sheep, 7·6m. poultry.

Fisheries. Production for 1986 was 183,056m. tons including 144,266m. tons of coastal water fish, 35,390m. tons of fresh water fish and 3,400m. tons from deepsea fisheries. In 1986 (provisional) there were 27,792 fishing craft, of which 14,387 were not motorized.

INDUSTRY AND TRADE

Industry. The private sector has been encouraged since 1977, with Investment Promotion Zones and freedom for imports; the public sector still accounts for about 60% of total production.

The main industries are food, beverages and tobacco; textiles, clothing and leather goods; chemicals, petroleum, rubber and plastics.

The Greater Colombo Economic Commission has charge of the two Investment Promotion Zones: Katunayake and Biyagama.

Trade Unions. The registration and control of trade unions are regulated by the Trade Unions Ordinance (Ch. 138 of the Legislative Enactments). In 1985 there were 957 registered trade unions with a membership of 1,565,394.

Commerce. The values of total imports and exports (imports excluding bullion, specie and postal articles; exports, including re-exports and ship's stores) for calendar years (in Rs 1,000):

	1982	1983	1984	1985	1986
Imports	36,875,519	42,020,529	46,913,266	49,068,542	51,281,508
Exports	20,728,491	24,843,439	36,540,767	35,034,947	34,092,261

Principal exports (domestic) in 1986 (in Rs 1m.): Tea, 9,253; rubber, 2,622 copra, coconut oil and desiccated coconut, 1,609; other crops, 780; textiles and garments, 9,629; precious and semi-precious stones, 1,182.

Principal imports (Rs 1m.) in 1986 were petroleum, 6,203m.; machinery and equipment, 5,828m.; vehicles and transport equipment, 1,457; food and beverages, 6,746.

In 1986 the principal sources of imports were (in Rs 1m.): Saudi Arabia, 325; Japan, 8,934; UK, 2,882; USA, 3,291; India, 2,222; Iran, 1,069; Singapore, 2,011; FRG. 2,405; South Korea, 1,963.

Principal export destinations 1986 were (in Rs 1m.): UK, 1,893; USA, 8,480; Japan, 1,813; Pakistan, 949; FRG, 2,305; Saudi Arabia, 907.

Total trade between Sri Lanka and UK (British Department of Trade returns, in £1,000 sterling):

	1983	1984	1985	1986	1987
Imports to UK	39,784	77,163	73,956	51,860	53,817
Exports and re-exports from UK	70,136	61,179	79,234	83,315	84,680

Tourism. About 230,000 tourists visited the country in 1986.

COMMUNICATIONS

Roads. There are about 25,650 km. of motorable roads, of which 82% are blacktopped. Number of motor vehicles, 31 Dec. 1985, 523,723, including 148,587 private cars and cabs, 98,859 lorries, 75,474 tractors, 161,373 motor cycles, 38,309 buses.

Railways. In 1986 there were about 1,453 km of railway open, of which 1,394 km were broad gauge and 59 narrow gauge. In 1986 railways ran 1,972m. passenger-km and 204m. tonne-km.

Aviation. Air Lanka operates international services. Foreign airlines which operate scheduled services to Sri Lanka are British Airways, India Airlines Corporation, Aeroflot, KLM, Singapore Airlines, Thai Airways International, Pakistan International Airlines, Gulf Air, Royal Nepal Airlines, Kuwait Airways, Saudi Air, Emirates and UTA French Airlines; various others operate charter services.

Internal services are operated by Upali, Air Taxis and Consolidated Engineering.

Shipping. In 1986, merchant vessels totalling 25·7m. GRT entered the ports of Sri Lanka. The Sri Lanka Shipping Corporation began functioning as ship-owners, charterers, brokers and shipping agents in 1971. The Sri Lanka Port Authority was established in 1979.

Post and Broadcasting. In 1986 there were 487 post offices and 3,221 sub-post offices. In 1982 there were 1,900 telegraph offices and 109,900 telephones. Throughout the Greater Colombo Area inter-dialling facilities are now available between 52 stations.

The Overseas Telecommunication Service operates telegraph and telephone services to most parts of the world. Broadcasting is provided by the Sri Lanka Broadcasting Corporation, which assumed the functions of Radio Ceylon on 5 Jan. 1967.

Cinemas. In 1985 there were 229 cinemas. The National Film Corporation established in 1971 has exclusive rights to import films and arrange distribution of foreign and local films. Films released, 1985, 154.

Newspapers. There are 6 main newspaper groups: Associated Newspapers of Ceylon Ltd (5 daily and 3 weekly papers and other periodicals); Express Newspapers (Ceylon) Ltd (2 daily and 2 weekly papers); Independent Newspapers Ltd. (3 daily and 3 weekly papers and other periodicals); Upali Newspapers Ltd. (2 daily, 2 weekly papers and other periodicals); Wijeya Publications (2 weekly papers and other periodicals); Eelanadu Ltd (1 daily).

There are 6 daily and 4 weekly papers in Sinhala; 6 daily and 4 weekly in Tamil; 4 daily and 4 weekly in English.

JUSTICE, RELIGION, EDUCATION AND WELFARE

Justice. The systems of law which obtain in Sri Lanka are the Roman-Dutch law, the English law, the Tesawalamai, the Moslem law and the Kandyan law.

The Kandyan law applies to the Kandyan Sinhalese in respect of all matters relating to inheritance, matrimonial rights and donations. The law of England is observed in most commercial matters. The law of Tesawalamai is applied to all Tamil inhabitants of Jaffna, in all matters relating to inheritance, marriages, gifts, donations, purchases and sales of land. The Moslem law is applied to all Moslems in respect of succession, donations, marriage, divorce and maintenance. These customary and religious laws have been modified in many respects by local enactments.

The courts of original jurisdiction are the High Court, District Courts, Magistrates' Courts and Primary Courts. The High Court tries major crimes and also exercises admiralty jurisdiction. The District Court has unlimited civil jurisdiction in civil, revenue, trust, insolvency and testamentary matters, over persons and estates of persons of unsound mind, and wards. Family Courts were estabished in 1978; District Courts act as Family Courts. The Magistrates' Courts exercise criminal jurisdiction carrying the power to impose terms of imprisonment not exceeding 2 years and fines not exceeding Rs 1,500. The Primary Courts which were established in 1978 exercise civil jurisdiction where the value of the subject matter does not exceed Rs 1,500 and also have jurisdiction in respect of by-laws of local authorities and matters relating to the recovery of revenue of such local authorities. Primary Courts exercise exclusive criminal jurisdiction in respect of offences which may be prescribed by regulation by the Minister. The Primary Courts have the power to impose sentences of imprisonment not exceeding three months and fines not exceeding Rs 250.

The Constitution of 1978 provided for the establishment of two superior courts, the Supreme Court and the Court of Appeal.

The Supreme Court is the highest and final superior court of record and exercises jurisdiction in respect of constitutional matters, jurisdiction for the protection of fundamental rights, final appellate jurisdiction, consultative jurisdiction, jurisdiction in election petitions and jurisdiction in respect of any breach of the privileges of Parliament. Parliament may provide by law that the Supreme Court exercises the power to grant and issue any of the orders in the nature of Writs of Certiorari, Prohibition, Procedendo, Mandamus or Quo Warranto. The Court of Appeal has appellate jurisdiction to correct all errors in fact or law committed by any court, tribunal or institution; it can grant and issue orders in the nature of the above Writs, and of Writs of Habeas Corpus and injunctions; it can also try election petitions in respect of election of members of Parliament.

Police. The strength of the police service in 1986 was 23,739.

Religion. Buddhism was introduced from India in the 3rd century B.C. and is the religion of 69·3% of the inhabitants. There were (1981) 10,288,325 Buddhists, 2,297,806 Hindus, 1,130,568 Christians, 1,121,717 Moslems and 8,334 others.

Education. Education is free from the kindergarten to the university and is imparted in the medium of the mother tongue. In 1981 about 87% of the population (10 years old and older) was literate.

In 1986 there were 10,099 schools including 9,656 government schools; the rest were private and estate schools, and Pirivenas. The government schools had 142,630 teachers and 3·7m. students from grades kindergarten to XII. Ministry of Education expenditure (1986), Rs 4,117·8m. Education is now administered under 31 regional directors.

The overall control of the education regions is vested in the Ministry of Education.

There are 8 Universities: Peradeniya, Colombo, Jaffna, Sri Jayawardenepura, Moratuwa, Kelaniya, Eastern, and Ruhuna, an Open University. Dumbara Campus comes under Peradeniya University. There are 8 Institutes (4 for postgraduate and 4 for undergraduate studies).

In 1985 there were 18,913 students and 2,051 teachers in the 7 Universities and 1 University College. The Open University had 9,287 students. Postgraduate Institutes had 519 students, the others, 1,214. There were 23 institutions for technical education, 9 of which had grade I status; total enrolment (1985), 20,796.

Health. In 1986 there were 497 hospitals, including 88 maternity homes, and 341 central dispensaries. Hospitals had 46,005 beds and there were 2,222 Department of Health doctors. Total state budget expenditure on health, 1986, Rs 2,095m.

Social Security. The activities of the Department of Social Services include:
(1) Payment of Public Assistance, monthly allowance, tuberculosis assistance and leprosy allowance to all needy persons.
(2) Relief for those affected by widespread distress, such as floods, drought, cyclone.
(3) Custodial care and welfare services to the elderly and infirm.
(4) Vocational training, rehabilitation, aids and appliances for the physically handicapped.
(5) Custodial care, vocational training and rehabilitation for socially handicapped persons.
(6) Distribution of Food Stamps and Kerosene Oil Stamps.
(7) Study of social problems affecting the community with a view to finding appropriate solutions.
(8) Financial assistance to voluntary institutions that provide welfare services.

DIPLOMATIC REPRESENTATIVES

Of Sri Lanka in Great Britain (13 Hyde Park Gdns., London, W2 2LU)
High Commissioner: Chandra Monerawela (accredited 15 May 1984).

Of Great Britain in Sri Lanka (190 Galle Rd., Kollupitiya, Colombo 3)
High Commissioner: D. A. S. Gladstone.

Of Sri Lanka in the USA (2148 Wyoming Ave., NW, Washington, D.C., 20008)
Ambassador: W. S. L. De Alwis.

Of the USA in Sri Lanka (210 Galle Rd., Kollupitiya, Colombo 3)
Ambassador: James Spain.

Of Sri Lanka to the United Nations
Ambassador: Nissanka Wijewardane.

Books of Reference

The Sri Lanka Year Book. Department of Census and Statistics. Colombo, Annual
Census Publications from 1871
Economic Atlas. Department of Census and Statistics. Colombo, 1980
Performance 1985. Ministry of Plan Implementation, Colombo. 1985
Review of the Economy. Central Bank of Ceylon. Annual
Statistical Pocket-Book. Department of Census and Statistics. Colombo, 1984
Statistical Abstract. Department of Census and Statistics, Colombo, 1982

Coomaraswamy, R., *Sri Lanka: The Crisis of the Anglo-American Constitutional Traditions in a Developing Society.* Colombo, 1984
de Silva, K. M. (ed.), *Sri Lanka: A Survey.* London, 1977.—*A History of Sri Lanka.* London, repr. 1982.—*Managing Ethnic Tensions in Multi-Ethnic Societies: Sri Lanka 1880–1985.* New York, 1986
Ferguson's *Ceylon Directory.* Annual (from 1858)
Fernando, T., *Sri Lanka: An Island Republic.* Epping, 1985
International Commission of Jurists, ed., *Sri Lanka: A Mounting Tragedy of Errors.* London, 1984
Johnson, B. L. C., and Scrivenor, M. le M., *Sri Lanka: Land, People and Economy.* London, 1981
Manor, J., *Sri Lanka: In Change and Crisis.* London, 1984
Moore, M., *The State and Peasant Politics in Sri Lanka.* CUP, 1985
Piyadasa, L., *Sri Lanka: The Holocaust and After.* London, 1984
Poonambalam, S., *Dependent Capitalism in Crisis: The Sri Lankan Economy 1948–80.* London, 1981
Ratnasuriya, M. D., and Wijeratne, P. B. F., *Shorter Sinhalese-English Dictionary.* Colombo, 1949
Richards, P., and Gooneratne, W., *Basic Needs, Poverty and Government Policies in Sri Lanka.* Geneva, 1981
Robinson, M. S., *Political Structure in a Changing Sinhalese Village.* CUP, 1975
Samaraweera, V., *Sri Lanka.* [Bibliography] Oxford and Santa Barbara, 1987
Schwarz, W., *The Tamils of Sri Lanka.* London, 1983
Tambiah, S. J., *Sri Lanka: Ethnic Fratricide and the Dismantling of Democracy.* London, 1986
Wilson, A. J., *Politics in Sri Lanka 1947-73.* London, 1974.—*The Gaullist System in Asia: the Constitution of Sri Lanka.* London, 1980

SUDAN

Jamhuryat es-Sudan

Capital: Khartoum
Population: 25·55m. (1987)
GNP per capita: US$400 (1983)

HISTORY. Sudan was proclaimed a sovereign independent republic on 1 Jan. 1956. On 19 Dec. 1955 the Sudanese parliament passed unanimously a declaration that a fully independent state should be set up forthwith, and that a Council of State of 5 should temporarily assume the duties of Head of State. The Codomini, the UK and Egypt, gave their assent on 31 Dec. 1955.

For the history of the Condominium and the steps leading to independence, *see* THE STATESMAN'S YEAR-BOOK, 1955, pp. 340–341.

On 8 July 1965 the Constituent Assembly elected Ismail El-Azhari as President of the Supreme Council. Following a crisis in the coalition Cabinet the Prime Minister, Mohammed Ahmed Mahgoub resigned on 23 April 1969. For political history *see* THE STATESMAN'S YEAR-BOOK, 1973–74, p. 1333. The Government was taken over by a 10-man Revolutionary Council on 25 May 1969 under the Chairmanship of Col. Jaafar M. al Nemery. This Council was dissolved in 1972.

AREA AND POPULATION. Sudan is bounded north by Egypt, north-east by the Red Sea, east by Eritrea and Ethiopia, south by Kenya, Uganda and Zaïre, west by the Central African Republic and Chad, north-west by Libya. Sudan covers an area of 967,500 sq. miles (2,505,813 sq. km) and the population at the census of 14 Feb. 1983 was 20,564,364; latest estimate (1987) 25·55m. The chief cities (census, 1983) are the capital, Khartoum (476,218), its suburbs Omdurman (526,287) and Khartoum North (341,146), Port Sudan (206,727), Wadi Medani (141,065), al-Obeid (140,024), Kassala (98,751 in 1973), Atbara (73,009), al-Qadarif (66,465 in 1973), Kosti (65,257 in 1973) and Juba (56,737 in 1973).

The northern and central thirds of the country are populated by Arab and Nubian peoples, while the southern third is inhabited by Nilotic and Negro peoples; Arabic, the official language, is spoken by 51%, Darfurian by 6% and other northern languages by 12%, while Nilotic languages (chiefly Dinka and Nuer) are spoken by 18%, Nilo-Hamitic by 5%, Sudanic by 5% and others by 3%. In 1987 there were 975,000 refugees in Sudan (337,544 from Ethiopia).

The area and population (census, 1983) of the regions are as follows:

Region	Sq. km	1983	Region	Sq. km	1983
Northern	183,941	1,083,024	Dafur	196,555	3,093,699
Eastern	129,086	2,208,209	Equatoria [1]	76,495	1,406,181
Central	53,716	4,012,543	Bahr al-Ghazal [1]	77,625	2,265,510
Kurdufan	146,932	3,093,294	Upper Nile [1]	92,269	1,599,605
Khartoum (province)	10,883	1,802,299			

[1] Re-united in 1985 as Southern Region.

Local government: Sudan is divided into Khartoum Province (centrally administered) and 6 Regions, each with an elected Regional Assembly and government, and sub-divided into 18 more Provinces.

CLIMATE. Lying wholly within the tropics, the country has a continental climate and only the Red Sea coast experiences maritime influences. Temperatures are generally high throughout the year, with May and June the hottest months. Winters are virtually cloudless and night temperatures are consequently cool. Summer is the rainy season inland, with amounts increasing from north to south, but the northern areas are virtually a desert region. On the Red Sea coast, most rain

1128

falls in winter. Khartoum. Jan. 74°F (23·3°C), July 89°F (31·7°C). Annual rainfall 6″ (157 mm). Juba. Jan. 83°F (28·3°C), July 78°F (25·6°C). Annual rainfall 39″ (968 mm). Port Sudan. Jan. 74°F (23·3°C), July 94°F (34·4°C). Annual rainfall 4″ (94 mm). Wadi Halfa. Jan. 60°F (15·6°C), July 90°F (32·2°C). Annual rainfall 0·1″ (2·5 mm).

CONSTITUTION AND GOVERNMENT. President Nemery was deposed in a military *coup* on 6 April 1985 and the Constitution of 1973 was suspended. A transitional Constitution was approved in Oct. 1985. A Military Council was established to which the Cabinet was responsible prior to elections held in April 1986 for the 301-seat National Assembly. Voting was postponed in some southern constituencies.

The Supreme Council: Ahmad Ali al-Mirghani *(President)*, Idris Albanna, Ali Hasan Taj ad-Din, Muhammad al-Hasan Abdullah Yasin, Pacifico Lado Lolik. All Sworn in 6 May 1986.

Prime Minister and Defence: Sadiq al-Mahdi. *Foreign Affairs:* Mohammed Tawfiq Ahmed.

National flag: Three horizontal stripes of red, white, black, with a green triangle based on the hoist.

DEFENCE.

Army. The Army is organized in 1 Republican Guard brigade, 2 armoured, 1 parachute and 10 infantry brigades, with 3 artillery and 1 engineer regiments, and 3 Air Defence brigades (including 1 surface-to-air missile). Equipment includes 155 T-54 and T-55, 60 Chinese Type-62 and 20 M-60A3 main battle tanks. Strength (1988) 54,000 (including 3,000 in Air Defence brigades). Paramilitary forces are National Guard (500) and Border Guard (2,500).

Navy. The Navy was established in 1962 to operate in the Red Sea and the River Nile, with 4 patrol boats built in Yugoslavia and a training mission from the Yugoslav Navy until 1972. There are also 1 larger *ex*-Yugoslav patrol craft, 3 *ex*-Iranian coastal patrol craft, 4 *ex*-Iranian very small coastguard cutters, 2 *ex*-Yugoslav landing craft, 1 small oiler, 1 small survey vessel and 1 water carrier. The flotilla reportedly has suffered from lack of maintenance and spares. Personnel in 1988 totalled 600 officers and men.

Air Force. The Air Force was built up with Soviet and Chinese assistance, and is now receiving equipment from the USA. Two combat squadrons are equipped with about 10 MiG-21 fighters, 6 Northrop F-5E and 12 F-5 (Chinese-built MiG-17) fighter-bombers. There is 1 transport squadron, with 5 C-130H Hercules, 6 Aviocars and 3 DHC-5D Buffalo turboprop transports; 2 Turbo-Porter light transports; 2 helicopter squadrons have 12 AB.212s and 10 BO 105s, 12 Romanian-built Pumas, 10 Mi-4s and Mi-8s; there are 3 Jet Provost, 3 Strike-master and 1 F-5F jet armed trainers, and some Chinese-built FT-5 (MiG-17) advanced trainers. Personnel totalled (1988) about 3,000.

INTERNATIONAL RELATIONS

Membership. Sudan is a member of UN, OAU, the Arab League and is an ACP state of EEC.

ECONOMY

Planning. The 1984–88, development plan envisaged a total investment of £S2,700m.

Budget. The 1986–87 budget envisages revenue of £S2,683m. and expenditure of £S5,542m.

Currency. The monetary unit is the Sudanese *pound* (£S) divided into 100 *piastres* and 1,000 *milliemes*. Sudanese bank-notes of £S10, £S5, £S1, 50 and 25 *piastres* and Sudanese coins of P. 10, 5, 2; m/ms 10, 5, 2, 1 are in circulation. In March 1988, £1 = £S7·98; US$1 = £S4·50.

Banking. The Bank of Sudan opened in Feb. 1960 with an authorized capital of £S1·5m. as the central bank of the country; it has the sole right to issue currency. All foreign banks were nationalized in 1970.

Weights and Measures. The metric system is in use.

ENERGY AND NATURAL RESOURCES

Electricity. Production (1986) 1,210m. kwh. Supply 240 volts; 50 Hz.

Oil. Two oil wells in the south-west produce 15,000 bbls per day of high quality oil. Production of petrol (1982) 150,000 tonnes.

Minerals. Minerals known to exist include: gold, graphite, sulphur, chromium-ore (estimate, 9,900m. tonnes in 1982), iron-ore, manganese-ore, copper-ore, zinc-ore, fluorspar, natron, gypsum and anhydrite, magnesite, asbestos, talc, halite, kaolin, white mica, coal, diatomite (kieselguhr), limestone and dolomite, pumice, lead-ore, wollastonite, black sands, vermiculite pyrites.

Gold is being exploited on a small scale at Gabeit and at Abirkateib (in Kassala Province); alluvial gold is occasionally exploited in Southern Fung and Equatoria. Iron-ore was discovered in Red Sea area in 1976.

Manganese mining activities started in the 1950s but this industry did not develop well and in 1982 only 200 tonnes was produced. Processed and scrap white mica have been mined since the late fifties; it went out of production for almost a decade, but started again in 1970 when 170 tonnes were produced; 1982, 200 tonnes. A big deposit of vermiculite and a medium-sized deposit of pyrophyllite are known to occur in the Sinkat District. Reserves of metallurgical grade chromite occur in the Ingessana Hills, Blue Nile Province. Huge reserves of chrysotile asbestos are proved in this vicinity and also in Qala El Nahal area, Kassala Province. Deposits of magnesite, with or without talc, are known to occur in the Ingessana Hills and Qala El Nahal areas in addition to other occurrences in the Halaib area, Red Sea Province.

Agriculture. The Sudan is a predominantly agricultural country. Cotton is by far the most important cash crop on which the Sudan depends for earning foreign currency. The two types of cotton grown in the Sudan are: (*a*) long staple sakellaridis and sakel types (derivatives of sakellaridis), grown in Gezira, White Nile, Abdel Magid and private pump schemes; (*b*) short staple, mainly American types, in Equatoria and Nuba Mountains, generally by rain cultivation.

Production (1986) in 1,000 tonnes: Sorghum, 3,605; sugar-cane, 5,200; groundnuts, 454; seed cotton, 440; millet, 544; wheat, 199; sesame, 301; cotton seed, 275.

One of the largest sugar complexes in the world was opened at Kenana in March 1981. It is capable of processing 330,000 tonnes a year.

Livestock (1986): Cattle, 22,389,000; sheep, 15,581,000; goats, 13·5m.; poultry, 30m.

Forestry. Gum arabic, mainly hashab gum from *Acacia senegal*, is the sole forest produce exported on a major scale. Production (1983) 38·16m. cu. metres.

COMMERCE. Total trade for calendar years, in US$1,000:

	1984	1985	1986
Imports	556,000	1,237,000	1,055,000
Exports	519,000	544,000	497,000

In 1983, Saudi Arabia provided 14·3% of imports and the UK 10%, while 17·1% of exports went to Saudi Arabia and 10% to Italy; cotton formed 49% by value of exports and groundnuts 2%, sesame 9% and gum arabic 9%.

Total trade between Sudan and UK (British Department of Trade returns, in £1,000 sterling):

	1983	1984	1985	1986	1987
Imports to UK	18,693	16,858	21,323	12,826	18,850
Exports and re-exports from UK	133,432	95,627	103,635	83,335	75,322

Tourism. There were 42,000 visitors in 1986.

COMMUNICATIONS

Roads. In 1982 there were about 3,000 km of tarmac roads, including the new 1,190 km road from Khartoum to Port Sudan, and 45,000 km of tracks. There were 34,600 passenger cars and 38,000 commercial vehicles in 1980.

Railways. The main railway lines run from Khartoum to El Obeid *via* Wadi Medani, Sennar Junction, Kosti and El Rahad (701 km); El Rahad to Nyala *via* Abu Zabad, Babanousa and Ed-Daein (698 km); Sennar Junction to Kassala *via* Gedaref (455 km) and to Roseires *via* Singa (220 km); Kassala to Port Sudan *via* Haiya Junction and Sinkat (550 km); Khartoum to Wadi Halfa *via* Shendi, El Dammer, Atbara, Berber and Abu Hamad Junction (924 km); Abu Hamad to Karima (248 km); Atbara to Haiya Junction (271 km); Babanousa to Wau (444 km). The main flow of exports and imports is to and from Port Sudan *via* Atbara and Kassala. The total length of line open for traffic (1982) was 4,786 km. The gauge is 1,067 mm. In 1985–86, the railways carried 2·3m. passengers and 837,675 tonnes of freight.

Aviation. Sudan Airways is a government-owned airline, with its headquarters in Khartoum, operating domestic and international services. In 1980 Sudan Airways carried 519,000 passengers and 6·8m. ton-kg of mail and freight.

Shipping. Supplementing the railways are regular river steamer services of the Sudan Railways, between Karima and Dongola, 319 km; from Khartoum to Kosti, 319 km; from Kosti to Juba, 1,436 km, and from Kosti to Gambeila, 1,069 km. Port Sudan is the country's only seaport; it is equipped with 13 berths. A modernization programme began in Feb. 1980.

Post and Broadcasting Number of telephones in 1983 was 68,838 (44,756 in Greater Khartoum). Radio receivers (1982) 5m. The television service broadcasts for 35 hours per week. There were (1982) 1m. TV receivers.

Cinemas. In 1975 there were 58, seating capacity 112,000 and also 43 mobile units.

JUSTICE, RELIGION, EDUCATION AND WELFARE

Justice. The judiciary is a separate and independent department of state directly and solely responsible to the President of the Republic. The general administrative supervision and control of the judiciary is vested in the High Judicial Council.

Civil Justice is administered by the courts constituted under the Civil Justice Ordinance, namely the High Court of Justice—consisting of the Court of Appeal and Judges of the High Court, sitting as courts of original jurisdiction—and Province Courts—consisting of the Courts of Province and District Judges. The law administered is 'justice, equity and good conscience' in all cases where there is no special enactment. Procedure is governed by the Civil Justice Ordinance.

Justice in personal matters for the Moslem population is administered by the Mohammedan law courts, which form the Sharia Divisions of the Court of Appeal, High Courts and Kadis Courts; President of the Sharia Division is the Grand Kadi. The religious law of Islam is administered by these courts in the matters of inheritance, marriage, divorce, family relationship and charitable trusts.

Criminal Justice is administered by the courts constituted under the Code of Criminal Procedure, namely major courts, minor courts and magistrates' courts. Serious crimes are tried by major courts, which are composed of a President and 2 members and have the power to pass the death sentence. Major Courts are, as a rule, presided over by a Judge of the High Court appointed to a Provincial Circuit or a Province Judge. There is a right of appeal to the Chief Justice against any decision or order of a Major Court, and all its findings and sentences are subject to confirmation by him.

Lesser crimes are tried by Minor Courts consisting of 3 Magistrates and presided over by a Second Class Magistrate, and by Magistrates' Courts.

Religion. In 1980 about 73% of the population was Moslem. The population of the 12 northern provinces is almost entirely Moslem (Sunni), while the majority of the 6 southern provinces are animist (18%) or Christian (9%).

Education (1980). 5,729 primary schools had 1·4m. pupils; there were 428,703 pupils in secondary schools and 28,985 in tertiary education. In 1979 Khartoum University with 10 faculties had 8,777 students. The Khartoum branch of Cairo University with 4 faculties had about 5,000 students and the Islamic University of Omdurman with 3 faculties had 1,472 students. Juba University, founded in 1975 with 5 faculties had 425 students.

Health. In 1981 the Ministry of Health maintained 158 hospitals (with 17,205 beds), 887 dispensaries, 1,619 dressing stations and 220 health centres. There were 2,122 doctors and 12,871 nurses.

DIPLOMATIC REPRESENTATIVES

Of Sudan in Great Britain (3 Cleveland Row, London, SW1A 1DD)
Ambassador: Sayed Ibrahim Mohamed Ali (accredited 23 July 1985).

Of Great Britain in Sudan (PO Box No. 801, Khartoum)
Ambassador: John Beaven, CMG, CVO.

Of Sudan in the USA (2210 Massachusetts Ave., NW, Washington, D.C., 20008)
Ambassador: Salah Ahmed.

Of the USA in Sudan (Sharia Ali Abdul Latif, Khartoum)
Ambassador: G. Norman Anderson.

Of Sudan to the United Nations
Ambassador: Amin M. Abdoun.

Books of Reference

Sudan Almanac. Khartoum (annual)
Daly, M. W., *Sudan.* [Bibliography] Oxford and Santa Barbara, 1983
Gurdon, C., *Sudan in Transition: A Political Risk Analysis.* London, 1986
Holt, P. M., *A Modern History of the Sudan.* New York, 3rd ed. 1979
Iten, O., *Le Soudan.* Zurich, 1983

SURINAME

Capital: Paramaribo
Population: 370,000 (1984)
GNP per capita: US$2,980 (1984)

HISTORY. At the peace of Breda (1667) between Great Britain and the United Netherlands, Suriname was assigned to the Netherlands in exchange for the colony of New Netherland in North America, and this was confirmed by the treaty of Westminster of Feb. 1674. Since then Suriname has been twice in British possession, 1799–1802 (when it was restored to the Batavian Republic at the peace of Amiens) and 1804–16, when it was returned to the Kingdom of the Netherlands according to the convention of London of 13 Aug. 1814, confirmed at the peace of Paris of 20 Nov. 1815. On 25 Nov. 1975, Suriname gained full independence and was admitted to the UN on 4 Dec. 1975. On 25 Feb. 1980 the Government was ousted in a *coup*, and a National Military Council (NMC) established. A further *coup* on 13 Aug. replaced several members of the NMC, and the State President. Other attempted coups took place in 1981 and 1982, with the NMC retaining control. Suriname returned to democracy in Jan. 1988 following elections held in Nov. 1987.

AREA AND POPULATION. Suriname is situated on the north coast of South America and bounded on the north by the Atlantic ocean, on the east by the Marowijne River, which separates it from French Guiana, on the west by the Corantijn River, which separates it from Guyana, and on the south by forests and savannas, which separate it from Brazil.

Area, 163,820 sq. km. Census population (1980), 354,860. Estimate (1984) 370,000. The capital, Paramaribo, had (1971 census) 103,738 inhabitants.

Suriname is divided into 9 districts (populations census 1980): Paramaribo (urban district), 67,905; Commewijne,14,351; Coronie, 2,777; Marowijne, 23,402; Nickerie, 34,480; Saramacca, 10,335; Suriname, 166,494; Brokopondo, 20,249 and Para, 14,867.

The official languages are Dutch and English. English is widely spoken next to Hindi, Javanese and Chinese as inter-group communication. A vernacular, called 'Sranan Tongo' or 'Surinamese', is used as a lingua franca. In 1976 it was announced that Spanish would become the nation's principal working language.

CLIMATE. The climate is equatorial, with uniformly high temperatures and rainfall. There is no recognized dry season. Paramaribo. Jan. 80°F (26·7°C), July 81°F (27·2°C). Annual rainfall 89″ (2,225 mm).

CONSTITUTION AND GOVERNMENT. A new Constitution was approved by referendum in Sept. 1980. Elections took place 25 Nov. 1987. The Front for Democracy and Development won (provisional) 40 of the 51 seats in the National Assembly.

President: Ramsewak Shankar (elected for a 5-year term in Jan. 1988).

Flag: Horizontally green, red, green with the red of double width with yellow 5-pointed star in centre of red bar.

DEFENCE

Army. Armed forces of the Republic of Suriname consist of regular local officers and conscripted personnel with a strength of about 2,450 in 1988. Equipment includes 2 PC-7 armed trainers, 4 Defender twin-engined light transports operated alongside and 1 Cessna 206 liaison aircraft. Officers' ranks were abolished in Feb. 1986.

Navy. The flotilla comprises 3 patrol vessels, 3 coastal patrol craft, 3 river patrol launches and 1 coastal cutter all built in the Netherlands. In 1988 personnel totalled 160 officers and men.

INTERNATIONAL RELATIONS

Membership. Suriname is a member of UN, OAS and is an ACP state of the EEC.

ECONOMY

Planning. For 15 years from independence approximately 3,500m. guilders is available from the Netherlands to carry out an extensive social and economic development programme.

Budget. The expenditures and local revenues (derived from import, export and excise duties, taxes on houses and estates, personal imports and some indirect taxes) are as follows (in 1,000 Suriname guilders):

	1978	1979	1980	1981	1982	1983
Revenues	623,100	429,800	480,400	527,000	556,600	509,300
Expenditures	650,500	412,500	454,900	569,700	657,900	711,900

Outstanding loans in 1983: Local, 491·1m.; foreign, 37·3m. Suriname guilders. Public debt in 1980, 100·7m. Suriname guilders.

Currency. Notes ranging from 5 to 1,000 *Suriname guilders* are legal tender. Currency notes of 1·00 and 2·50 guilders are issued by the Government. In March 1988, US$1 = 1·79 *Suriname guilders*; £1 sterling = 3·17 *Suriname guilders*.

Banking. The Central Bank of Suriname is a bankers' bank and also a bank of issue; the Surinaamsche Bank, the Algemene Bank Nederland and the Handels-, Krediet-en Industriebank, are commercial banks; the Suriname People's Credit Bank operates under the auspices of the Government; Surinaamse Postspaarbank (postal savings bank); Surinaamse Hypotheekbank NV (mortgage bank); Surinaamse Investerings Mij. NV (investment bank); Agentschap van de Maatschappij tot financiering van het Nationaal Herstel NV (long-term investments); National Development Bank; The Agrarian Bank.

Weights and Measures. The metric system is in force.

ENERGY AND NATURAL RESOURCES

Electricity. Production (1986) 1,610m. kwh.

Minerals. Bauxite is the most important mineral; it is being mined in the Suriname and Marowijne districts but in 1987 several mines have been closed by attacks by anti-government rebels. Fresh deposits have been found in the western areas. The ore is exported mainly to USA and the Dominican Republic, but partly processed locally into alumina and aluminium. Production (1985 in 1,000 tonnes): Bauxite, 3,738; alumina, (1983) 1,084; aluminium, (1983) 34·5.

Agriculture. Agriculture is restricted to the alluvial coastal zone; cultivated area in 1982, 87,442 hectares. The staple food crop is rice; 72,571 hectares of paddy were planted in 1982, chiefly in the Nickerie, Commewijne, Saramacca and Coronie districts.

Production (1986, in 1,000 tonnes): Sugar-cane, 120; rice, 300; oranges, 10; grapefruit, 1; coconuts, 7; palm oil, 7·2; cassava, 3.

Livestock (1986): 63,000 head of cattle, 3,000 sheep, 5,000 goats, 22,000 pigs, 1m. poultry.

Forestry. Suriname has great timber resources. Production in 1983 included

204,251 cu. metres of logs, 18,420 cu. metres of sleepers (1982), 18,134 cu. metres of plywood and 3,155 cu. metres of particle board.

Fisheries. The fish catch in 1980 amounted to 2,100 tonnes and the shrimp catch, 3,100 tonnes.

INDUSTRY AND TRADE

Industry. In 1981, there were 3 large bauxite plants, 1 alumina and 1 aluminium smelting plants, sugar- and rice-mills, 3 paint factories, 2 fruit-juice plants, 3 shrimp freezing plants, a plywood factory, timber-mills, a milk pasteurization plant, a butter and margarine factory and a number of various medium and small industries. Shortage of skilled personnel inhibits expansion.

Commerce. Imports and exports in calendar years (in 1 m. Suriname guilders):

	1979	1980	1981	1982	1983[1]
Imports	733·5	900·3	1,013·7	921·2	762·5
Exports	792·7	918·2	845·7	765·1	605·4

[1] Estimate.

Principal exports in 1982 (in 1,000 Suriname guilders): Alumina, 411,500; bauxite, 52,400; aluminium, 124,000; rice, 72,100; shrimp, 53,300; wood and wood products, 20,600; bananas, 13,200.

Principal imports in 1982 (in 1,000 Suriname guilders): Raw and auxiliary materials, 356,700; fuels and lubricants, 209,900; investment goods, 117,800; foodstuffs, cars and motorcycles, 73,100; textile yarn and fabrics, 9,600.

Total trade between Suriname and UK (British Department of Trade returns, in £1,000 sterling):

	1983	1984	1985	1986	1987
Imports to UK	11,584	18,316	15,405	15,554	12,488
Exports and re-exports from UK	8,914	9,593	9,398	9,743	7,974

COMMUNICATIONS

Roads. There are 1,335 km of main roads. Two of them lead from Paramaribo to the bauxite centres of Smalkalden (29 km) and Paranam (30 km) and to the airport of Zanderij (49 km). Another main road runs across the districts of Saramacca (71 km) and Coronie (68 km), a fourth across the Commewijne district (41 km) and a fifth in the Marowijne district, from the bauxite centre Moengo to Albina (45 km). The 'East–West connexion' is almost completed, linking the Corantijn and the Marowijne rivers (375 km).

In 1985 there were 31,536 passenger cars, 10,629 trucks, 1,923 buses and 1,034 motor cycles.

Railways. There is a single-track railway, running from Onverwacht to Bronsweg (86 km); part of the track, from Paramaribo to Onverwacht (34 km) has been removed. Another single-track railway runs from Apoera to the Bakhuis Mountains.

Aviation. Regular air services are maintained by KLM, SLM, Aero Cubano and Cruzeiro do Sul. The international airfield at Zanderij is capable of handling all types of planes.

Suriname Airways Ltd provides daily services between all major districts and maintains also a charter service.

In 1975, 1,205 aircraft landed at Zanderij airport with 40,416 passengers and 1,225 tons of incoming mail and freight.

Shipping. The Royal Netherlands Steamship Co. plies between Amsterdam, Rotterdam, Antwerp, Hamburg and Paramaribo, and New York, Baltimore, New Orleans and Paramaribo. Regular sailings are made to Georgetown, Ciudad Bolivar and most Caribbean ports. The Suriname Navigation Co. maintains services from Paramaribo to Georgetown and Cayenne, and once a month to the Caribbean area. A French and an Italian company maintain passenger services to Europe. The Alcoa Steamship Co. has a fortnightly service to New York, Baltimore, Mobile and New Orleans; a Japanese line sails once a month from Hong

Kong and Yokohama to Paramaribo; the Boomerang Line maintains a monthly freight and passenger service between Suriname and Australia. In 1981, 1,021 vessels totalling 4·93m. GRT entered Paramaribo.

Post and Broadcasting. Automatic telephone service links most of the districts in the interior. In 1982 there were 27,495 telephones. Wireless telephone connects Suriname with the Netherlands, USA, Curaçao, Guyana, French Guiana and Trinidad. There are 6 broadcasting and 1 television stations. In 1974 there were 170,000 radios and 36,000 TV sets. Automatic telex was established in 1972.

Cinemas. In 1981 there were 18 cinemas and 1 drive-in cinema.

Newspapers (1983). There is one daily newspaper, *De Ware Tijd*.

JUSTICE, RELIGION, EDUCATION AND WELFARE

Justice. There is a court of justice, whose members are nominated by the President. There are 3 cantonal courts.

Religion. There is entire religious liberty. At the end of 1983 the main religious bodies were: Hindus, 97,170; Roman Catholics, 80,922; Moslems, 69,638; Moravian Brethren, 55,625; Reformed, 6,265; Lutheran, 2,695; Jehovah's Witnesses, 1,626; Seventh Day Adventists, 1,061; others, 24,627.

Education. In 1980–81 there were 285 primary schools with 2,803 teachers and 75,139 pupils, and there were 1,854 teachers and 29,790 pupils at secondary schools. There were 5 technical schools with (1978–79) 249 teachers and 4,394 students, and 5 teacher-training colleges with 148 teachers and 1,275 students. There was also a University with 2,353 students and 155 teaching staff.

Social Security. There were (1980) 13 modern hospitals in the country, 4 of which are operated by missions, 2 by a private company, 1 by the military forces and 6 by the Government.

DIPLOMATIC REPRESENTATIVES

Of Great Britain in Suriname
Ambassador: D. P. Small, MBE (resides in Georgetown).

Of Suriname in the USA (2600 Virginia Ave., NW, Washington, D.C., 20037)
Ambassador: Arnold T. Halfhide.

Of the USA in Suriname (Dr Sophie Redmondstraat 129, Paramaribo)
Ambassador: Robert E. Barbour.

Of Suriname to the United Nations
Ambassador: (Vacant).

Books of Reference

Statistical Information: The General Bureau of Statistics in Paramaribo was established on 1 Jan. 1947. Its publications comprise trade statistics, *Suriname in Figures* (including, from 1953, the former *Handelsstatistiek*) and *Statistische Berichten*.

Economische Voorlichting Suriname. Ministry of Economic Affairs, Paramaribo
Annual Report of the Central Bank of Suriname

SWAZILAND

Capital: Mbabane
Population: 676,049 (1986)
GNP per capita: US$730 (1984)

HISTORY. The Swazi migrated into the country to which they have given their name, in the last half of the 18th century. They settled first in what is now southern Swaziland, but moved northwards under their chief, Sobhuza–known also to the Swazi as Somhlolo. Sobhuza died in 1838 and was succeeded by Mswati. The further order of succession has been Mbandzeni and Bhunu, whose son, Sobhuza II, was installed as King of the Swazi nation in 1921 after a long minority.

The independence of the Swazis was guaranteed in the conventions of 1881 and 1884 between the British Government and the Government of the South African Republic. In 1890, soon after the death of Mbandzeni, a provisional government was established representative of the Swazis, the British and the South African Republic Governments. In 1894 the South African Republic was given powers of protection and administration. In 1902, after the conclusion of the Boer War, a special commissioner took charge, and under an order-in-council in 1903 the Governor of the Transvaal administered the territory, through the Special Commissioner. Swaziland became independent on 6 Sept. 1968.

On 25 April 1967 the British Government gave the country internal self-government. It changed the country's status to that of a protected state with the Ngwenyama, Sobhuza II, recognized as King of Swaziland and head of state. King Sobhuza died on 21 Aug. 1982. On 25 April 1986, King Mswati III was installed as King of Swaziland.

AREA AND POPULATION. Swaziland is bounded on the north, west and south by the Transvaal Province, and on the east by Mozambique and Zululand. The area is 6,705 sq. miles (17,400 sq. km).

The country is divided geographically into 4 longitudinal regions running from north to south; 3 of roughly equal width–Highveld (westernmost), Middleveld, Lowveld–and the Lubombo plateau in the east. The mountainous region on the west rises to an altitude of over 6,000 ft (1,800 metres). The Middleveld is mostly between 1,700 and 3,000 ft, while the Lowveld has an average height of not more than 1,000 ft (300 metres).

Population (census 1986), 676,049. Mbabane, the administrative capital (census 1976, 23,109). The main urban areas with 1983 populations are: Manzini (18,818); Havelock Mine (4,838); Siteki (1,362); Big Bend (2,083); Mhlume (3,921); Nhlangano (2,097) and Pigg's Peak (2,192).

CLIMATE. A temperate climate with two seasons. Nov. to March is the wet season, when temperatures range from mild to hot, with frequent thunderstorms. The cool, dry season from May to Sept. is characterised by clear, bright sunny days. Mbabane. Jan. 68°F (20°C), July 54°F (12·2°C). Annual rainfall 56″ (1,402 mm).

CONSTITUTION AND GOVERNMENT. Britain's protection ended at independence, when a Constitution similar to the 1967 Constitution was brought into force. The general elections (by universal adult franchise) in April 1967 gave the royalist and traditional Imbokodvo National Movement all 24 seats. The Parliament consists of a House of Assembly, with 24 elected and 6 nominated members and the Attorney-General, who has no vote, and a Senate comprising 12 members, 6 of whom are elected by the House of Assembly and 6 appointed by the King. The executive authority is vested in the King and exercised through a Cabinet presided over by the Prime Minister, and consisting of the Prime Minister, the Deputy Prime Minister and up to 8 other ministers. In April 1973 the King assumed supreme power and the Constitution was suspended and in 1976 it was abolished. On 28 Oct. 1983 a general election took place to elect an electoral college of 80 members.

His Majesty the King: Mswati III (crowned 25 April 1986).

In Dec. 1987, the Cabinet was composed as follows:

Prime Minister: Sotja E. Dlamini.

Foreign Affairs: S. J. S. Sibanyoni. *Labour and Public Service:* Prince Phiwokwakhe Dlamini. *Agriculture and Co-operatives:* H. S. Mamba. *Commerce, Industry and Tourism:* D. Von Wissel. *Works and Communications:* K. Mtetwa. *Education:* Prince Khuzulwandle Dlamini. *Finance:* B.S. Dlamini. *Health:* Chief Sipho Shongwe. *Justice:* D. J. Matse. *Interior and Immigration:* P. Mamba. *Defence and Youth:* Brig. F. Dube. *Natural Resources, Land Utilization and Energy:* M. M. Mnisi.

National flag. Horizontally 5 unequal stripes of blue, yellow, crimson, yellow, blue; in the centre of the crimson strip an African shield of black and white, behind which are 2 assegais and a staff, all laid horizontally.

Local Government. The country is divided into the 4 regions of Shiselweni, Lubombo, Manzini and Hhohho. They are administered by Regional Administrators.

DEFENCE

Army Air Wing. First military aircraft acquired by Swaziland, in mid-1979, were 2 Israeli-built Arava light twin-turboprop transports with underwing weapon attachments for light attack duties.

INTERNATIONAL RELATIONS

Membership. Swaziland is a member of UN, OAU, the Commonwealth and is an ACP state of EEC.

ECONOMY

Budget. Revenue and expenditure (in 1,000 emalangeni) for financial years ending 31 March:

	1985–86	1986–87	1987–88
Revenue	218,317	252,416	284,783
Expenditure	225,575	263,294	295,857

Currency. The currency in circulation in Swaziland is the *emalangeni,* but remains in the rand monetary area. In March 1988, £1=3·69 *emalangeni;* US$1=2·11 *emalangeni.*

Banking. Barclays Bank International and the Standard Bank Ltd maintain branches at Mbabane and Manzini; sub-branches and agencies are operated in 17 other places. Bank rates are those in force throughout South Africa and are prescribed by the main South African offices of the 2 banks. The Swaziland Credit and Savings Bank, now known as The Swazi Bank, a statutory body, was opened in 1965. It specializes in credit for agriculture and low-cost housing. Its head office is in Mbabane and it has branches or agencies at 3 other places. A fourth bank, The Bank of Credit and Commerce International opened in Sept. 1978; its head office is in Manzini and it has a branch in Mbabane.

ENERGY AND NATURAL RESOURCES

Electricity. Production (1986) 120m. kwh. Supply 230 volts; 50 Hz.

Minerals. Swaziland produces asbestos from the Havelock Mine (25,130 tonnes in 1985). Coal is mined at Mpaka (166,079 tonnes in 1985). Quarry stone is also mined (83,903 cu. metres in 1985).

A railway has been built from the Ngwenya hæmatite deposits to Goba, in Mozambique, chiefly for the transportation of iron ore. The extensive deposits of low-volatile bituminous coal in the Lowveld are being worked to provide coal for the railway, sugar-mills and export.

Agriculture. In 1983 the cultivated area was 125,350 hectares, the grazing area 1,147,255 hectares and the commercial forest area 100,916 hectares. Production (1986, in 1,000 tonnes): Sugar-cane, 3,526; citrus, 67; rice, 3; seed cotton, 32; maize, 90; sorghum, 2; pineapples, 45; tomatoes, 4; potatoes, 7. Tobacco is also grown. It is usually necessary to import maize from South Africa. Sugar, first produced in 1958, and woodpulp and other forest products are the two main agricultural exports.

Livestock (1986): Cattle, 620,000; goats, 315,000; sheep, 38,000; poultry, 1m.

COMMERCE. By agreement with the Republic of South Africa, Swaziland is united in a customs union with the republic and receives a *pro rata* share of the customs dues collected.

Total exports (1984) amounted to E331,615,400, of which E104,937,300 to the Republic of South Africa. The chief items were (in E1,000): Sugar, 140,565; unbleached woodpulp, 66,771; wood and wood products, 22,706; citrus fruit, 20,987; chrysolite asbestos, 17,937; canned fruit and juices, 17,890; manufactures (including engineering products, clothing and textiles), 14,644.

Total imports (April 1984–March 1985) amounted to E661,546,000, of which E604,752,000 from the Republic of South Africa, and included (in E1,000): Machinery and transport equipment, 177,562; minerals, fuels and lubricants, 107,120; manufactured items, 65,159; food and live animals, 52,765; chemicals and chemical products, 34,593.

Total trade between Swaziland and UK (British Department of Trade returns, in £1,000 sterling):

	1982	1983	1984	1985	1986	1987
Imports to UK	40,049	23,965	41,786	41,281	48,194	36,901
Exports and re-exports from UK	7,654	3,536	2,430	3,122	3,922	2,257

Tourism. There were 256,000 visitors in 1986.

COMMUNICATIONS

Roads. There is daily (except Sundays) communication by railway motor-buses between Manzini, Mbabane and Breyten; Manzini, Mankayana and Piet Retief. There are 631 km of tarred trunk roads. Total length of roads (1983) 2,723 km.

Railways. In 1985 the system comprised 370 km of route, and carried 863,000 tonnes of freight.

Aviation. The country's chief airport is at Matsapa, near Manzini. It is served by Royal Swazi National Airways connecting with Johannesburg, Durban, Lusaka, Nairobi, Harare and Gaborone. Lesotho National Airways flies to Harare and Maputo through Matsapa. In 1986 Zambian Airways inaugurated their weekly flight to Matsapa *via* Gaborone.

Post and Broadcasting. There were (1986) 57 post offices, 2 telephone-telegraph agencies and 10 telephone agencies. There were, 31 Dec. 1985, 18,484 telephones, 8,349 exchange connexions and 309 telex exchange connexions. In 1986 there were over 96,000 radio sets and over 12,000 television receivers.

Cinemas. There were 5 cinemas in 1980 with a total seating capacity of 1,625.

Newspapers. There were in 1986 two dailies, one weekly and one monthly newspaper.

JUSTICE, RELIGION, EDUCATION AND WELFARE

Justice. The judiciary is headed by the Chief Justice. A High Court having full jurisdiction and subordinate courts presided over by Magistrates and District Officers are in existence.

There is a Court of Appeal with a President and 3 Judges. It deals with appeals from the High Court. There are 16 Swazi courts of first instance, 2 Swazi courts of appeal and a Higher Swazi Court of Appeal. The channel of appeal lies from Swazi

Court of first instance to Swazi Court of Appeal, to Higher Swazi Court of Appeal, to the Judicial Commissioner and thence to the High Court of Swaziland.

Religion. In 1984 there were about 120,000 Christians and about 30,000 adults holding traditional beliefs. A large number of churches and missionary societies are established throughout the country and, in addition to evangelism, are doing important work in the fields of education and medicine. In the larger centres there are churches of several denominations—Protestant, Roman Catholics and others.

Education. In 1986 there were 571 schools with 142,206 pupils in primary classes and 30,489 in secondary classes. The Swaziland Agricultural College and University Centre at Luyengo was opened in Oct. 1966. The College is now named the Faculty of Agriculture at the University of Swaziland, which is situated in Matsapa. Technical and vocational training classes are run at the Government's Swaziland College of Technology and the Swaziland Institute of Management and Public Administration. The Government also operates a police college and the Institute of Health Sciences which trains para-medical staff for the hospitals and clinics. There are 3 teacher training colleges with 935 students in 1985–86. There were 540 students enrolled at the Swaziland College of Technology and 1,282 at the University of Swaziland in 1985–86.

Health. In 1984 there were 80 doctors, 13 dentists and 1,608 hospital beds.

DIPLOMATIC REPRESENTATIVES

Of Swaziland in Great Britain (58 Pont St., London SW1X 0AE)
High Commissioner: (Vacant).

Of Great Britain in Swaziland (Allister Miller St., Mbabane)
High Commissioner: J. G. Flynn.

Of Swaziland in the USA (4301 Connecticut Ave., NW, Washington, D.C., 20008)
Ambassador: Peter H. Mtetwa.

Of the USA in Swaziland (PO Box 199, Mbabane)
Ambassador: Harvey F. Nelson, Jr.

Of Swaziland to the United Nations
Ambassador: Dr Timothy L. L. Dlamini.

Books of Reference

Booth, A., *Swaziland: Tradition and Change in a Southern African Kingdom.* Aldershot and Boulder, 1984
Grotpeter, J. J., *Historical Dictionary of Swaziland.* Metuchen, 1975
Jones, D., *Aid and Development in Southern Africa.* London, 1977
Matsebula, J. S. M., *A History of Swaziland.* London, 1972
Nyeko, B., *Swaziland.* [Bibliography] Oxford and Santa Barbara, 1982

SWEDEN

Konungariket Sverige

Capital: Stockholm
Population: 8·4m. (1986)
GNP per capita: US$11,977 (1985)

HISTORY. Organized as an independent unified state in the 10th century, Sweden became a constitutional monarchy in 1809. In 1809 she also ceded Finland to Russia. In 1815 German possessions were ceded to Prussia and Sweden was united with Norway, which union lasted until 1905.

AREA AND POPULATION. Sweden is bounded west and north-west by Norway, east by Finland and the Gulf of Bothnia, south-east by the Baltic Sea and south-west by the Kattegat. The first census took place in 1749, and it was repeated at first every third year, and, after 1775, every fifth year. Since 1860 a general census has been taken every 10 years and, in addition, in 1935, 1945, 1965 and 1975.

Latest census figures: 1940, 6,371,432 (annual increase since 1935: 0·38%); 1950, 7,041,829 (1·1% since 1945); 1960, 7,495,316 (0·64% since 1950); 1965, 7,766,424 (1·04% since 1960); 1970, 8,076,903 (1·04% since 1965); 1975, 8,208,544 (1·02% since 1970); 1980, 8,320,438 (1·01% since 1975); 1985, 8,360,178.

Counties (Län)	Land area: sq. km	Census population 1 Nov. 1985	Estimated population 31 Dec. 1986	Pop. per sq. km 31 Dec. 1986
Stockholm	6,488	1,577,596	1,593,333	246
Uppsala	6,989	251,754	254,938	36
Södermanland	6,061	249,885	249,479	41
Östergötland	10,563	393,668	394,753	37
Jönköping	9,944	300,892	301,413	30
Kronoberg	8,451	174,025	173,853	21
Kalmar	11,166	238,406	237,417	21
Gotland	3,140	56,180	56,174	18
Blekinge	2,941	151,055	150,258	51
Kristianstad	6,089	280,516	280,609	46
Malmöhus	4,939	750,294	753,075	152
Halland	5,454	240,090	242,250	44
Göteborg and Bohus	5,141	715,831	721,553	140
Älvsborg	11,395	426,769	427,638	38
Skaraborg	7,937	270,530	270,111	34
Värmland	17,582	279,503	278,861	16
Örebro	8,520	270,384	269,620	32
Västmanland	6,302	254,858	254,423	40
Kopparberg	28,264	284,029	283,191	10
Gävleborg	18,191	289,452	287,691	16
Västernorrland	21,711	262,555	261,089	12
Jämtland	49,915	134,161	133,543	3
Västerbotten	55,401	245,302	245,204	4
Norrbotten	98,916	262,443	261,039	3
Total	411,503[1]	8,360,178	8,381,515	20

[1] Total area of Sweden, 449,964 sq. km.

On 31 Dec. 1986 there were 4,137,513 males and 4,244,002 females.

On 31 Dec. 1986 aliens in Sweden numbered 390,840. Of these, 134,234 were Finns, 38,406 Yugoslavs, 26,707 Norwegians, 24,790 Danes, 21,879 Turks, 15,608 Poles, 13,270 Iranians, 11,867 West Germans, 10,280 Chileans, 8,816 Britons, 8,045 Greeks, 6,476 Americans, 3,911 Iraqis and 3,895 Italians.

1142   SWEDEN

Vital statistics for calendar years:

	Total living births	To mothers single, divorced or widowed	Stillborn	Marriages	Divorces	Deaths exclusive of still-born
1983	91,780	40,059	340	36,210	20,618	90,791
1984	93,889	41,887	381	36,849	20,377	90,483
1985	98,463	45,640	388	38,297	19,763	94,032
1986	101,950	49,324	423	38,906	19,107	93,295

Immigration: 1982, 30,381; 1983, 27,495; 1984, 31,486; 1985, 33,134; 1986, 39,487. Emigration: 1982, 28,381; 1983, 25,269; 1984, 22,825; 1985, 22,041; 1986, 24,495.

In 1860 the urban population numbered 435,000 (11% of the total population) and on 31 Dec. 1965, 4,177,212 (54%); including other densely populated areas, the urbanized population in 1965 was 77·4%.

On 15 Sept. 1980, population in densely populated areas was 6,910,431 (83·1%).

Population of largest communities, 31 Dec. 1986:

Stockholm	663,217	Halmstad	77,601	Kalmar	54,554
Göteborg	429,339	Karlstad	74,669	Falun	51,900
Malmö	230,056	Skellefteå	74,267	Mölndal	50,164
Uppsala	157,675	Huddinge	71,568	Solna	50,108
Norrköping	118,801	Kristianstad	69,941	Kungsbacka	49,840
Örebro	118,443	Botkyrka	66,957	Trollhättan	49,499
Linköping	117,835	Växjö	66,925	Sollentuna	49,424
Västerås	117,732	Luleå	66,526	Hässleholm	48,390
Jönköping	108,235	Nyköping	64,199	Varberg	46,639
Helsingborg	106,275	Haninge	61,172	Skövde	46,311
Borås	100,054	Nacka	60,315	Uddevalla	45,983
Sundsvall	92,795	Örnsköldsvik	59,631	Borlänge	45,966
Eskilstuna	88,448	Karlskrona	59,007	Norrtälje	42,503
Gävle	87,431	Östersund	56,662	Motala	41,352
Umeå	85,698	Järfälla	56,405	Sandviken	40,096
Lund	83,391	Gotland	56,174	Västervik	39,752
Södertälje	80,003	Täby	55,093		

Befolkningsförändringar (Population Changes). Annual. 3 vols. Statistics Sweden, Stockholm
Folkmängd 31 Dec. (Population). Annual. 2 vols. Statistics Sweden, Stockholm

CLIMATE. North Sweden suffers from severe winters, with snow lying for 4–7 months. Summers are fine but cool, with long daylight hours. Further south, winters are less cold, summers are warm and rainfall generally well-distributed over the year, though with a slight summer maximum. Stockholm. Jan. 24·4°F (−4·1°C), July 59·9°F (17·3°C). Annual rainfall 25″ (622 mm).

REIGNING KING. Carl XVI Gustaf, born 30 April 1946, succeeded on the death of his grandfather Gustaf VI Adolf, 15 Sept. 1973, married 19 June 1976 to *Silvia* Renate Sommerlath, born 23 Dec. 1943 (Queen of Sweden). *Daughter* and *Heir Apparent:* Crown Princess Victoria Ingrid Alice Désirée, Duchess of Västergötland, born 14 July 1977; *son:* Prince Carl Philip Edmund Bertil, Duke of Värmland, born 13 May 1979; *daughter:* Princess Madeleine Thérèse Amelie Josephine, Duchess of Hälsingland and Gästrikland, born 10 June 1982.

Sisters of the King. Princess Margaretha, born 31 Oct. 1934, married 30 June 1964 to Mr John Ambler; Princess Birgitta (Princess of Sweden), born 19 Jan. 1937, married 25 May 1961 (civil marriage) and 30 May 1961 (religious ceremony) to Johann Georg, Prince of Hohenzollern; Princess Désirée, born 2 June 1938, married 5 June 1964 to Baron Niclas Silfverschiöld; Princess Christina, born 3 Aug. 1943, married 15 June 1974 to Tord Magnuson.

Uncles of the King. Sigvard, Count of Wisborg, born on 7 June 1907; Prince Bertil, Duke of Halland, born on 28 Feb. 1912, married 7 Dec. 1976 to Lilian May Davies, born 30 Aug. 1915 (Princess of Sweden, Duchess of Halland); Carl Johan, Count of Wisborg, born on 31 Oct. 1916.

Aunt of the King. Princess Ingrid (Princess of Sweden), born 28 March 1910, married 24 May 1935 to Frederik, Crown Prince of Denmark (King Frederik IX), died 14 Jan. 1972.

The following is a list of the kings and queens of Sweden, with the dates of their accession from the accession of the House of Vasa:

House of Vasa		House of Pfalz-Zwei-		House of Bernadotte	
Gustaf I	1521	brücken (contd.)		Carl XIV Johan	1818
Eric XIV	1560	Carl XII	1697	Oscar I	1844
Johan III	1568	Ulrica Eleonora	1719	Carl XV	1859
Sigismund	1592			Oscar II	1872
Carl IX	1599	House of Hesse		Gustaf V	1907
Gustaf II Adolf	1611	Fredrik I	1720	Gustaf VI Adolf	1950
Christina	1632			Carl XVI Gustaf	1973
		House of Holstein-Gottorp			
House of Pfalz-Zwei-		Adolf Fredrik	1751		
brücken		Gustaf III	1771		
Carl X Gustaf	1654	Gustaf IV Adolf	1792		
Carl XI	1660	Carl XIII	1809		

The royal family of Sweden have a civil list of 12·85m. kronor; this does not include the maintenance of the royal palaces.

CONSTITUTION AND GOVERNMENT. Sweden's present Constitution came into force in 1975 and replaced the 1809 Constitution. Under the present Constitution Sweden is a representative and parliamentary democracy. Parliament (*Riksdag*) is declared to be the central organ of government. The executive power of the country is vested in the Government, which is responsible to Parliament. The King is Head of State, but he does not participate in the government of the country. Since 1971 Parliament has consisted of one chamber. It has 349 members, who are elected for a period of 3 years in direct, general elections.

Every man and woman who has reached the age of 18 years on election-day itself, and who is not under wardship, has the right to vote and to stand for election.

The manner of election to the *Riksdag* is proportional. The country is divided into 28 constituencies. In these constituencies 310 members are elected. The remaining 39 seats constitute a nation-wide pool intended to give absolute proportionality to parties that receive at least 4% of the votes. A party receiving less than 4% of the votes in the country is, however, entitled to participate in the distribution of seats in a constituency, if it has obtained at least 12% of the votes cast there.

The *Riksdag*, elected 1985, has 159 Social Democrats, 76 Conservatives, 44 Centre Party, 51 Liberals and 19 Communists.

The Social Democratic Cabinet was composed as follows in Jan. 1987:

Prime Minister and Minister with special responsibility for Research: Ingvar Carlsson.

Agriculture: Mats Hellström. *Finance:* Kjell-Olof Feldt. *Health and Social Affairs:* Gertrud Sigurdsen. *Housing:* Hans Gustafsson. *Labour:* Anna-Greta Leijon. *Special responsibility for international development co-operation, Ministry of Foreign Affairs:* Lena Hjelm-Wallen. *Industry:* Thage Peterson. *Foreign Affairs:* Sten Andersson. *Justice:* (Vacant). *Transport and Communications:* Sven Hulterström. *Education and Cultural Affairs:* Lennart Bodström. *Education, with special responsibility for cultural affairs, the mass media and comprehensive schools:* Bengt Göransson. *Labour, with special responsibility for immigrant affairs:* Georg Andersson. *Environment and Energy:* Birgitta Dahl. *Defence:* Roine Carlsson. *Public Administration:* Bo Holmberg. *Foreign Trade:* Anita Gradin. *Special responsibility for wages in public administration, Ministry of Finance:* Bengt Johansson. *Special responsibility for family policy, the disabled and elderly, Ministry of Health and Social Affairs:* Bengt Lindquist. *Special responsibility for tourism, recreation and sports, youth, Ministry of Agriculture:* Ulf Lönnquist.

Ministerial decisions are formally made by the Cabinet collectively and not (with some exceptions) by individual ministers.

Public administration in Sweden is characterized by a unique degree of functional decentralization. The Ministries are not really administrative agencies. Their main function is to prepare the decisions of the Cabinet; such decisions may concern bills for the *Riksdag,* general government directives and higher appointments. Only to a small extent does the Cabinet make individual administrative decisions. The routine administrative work is attended to by the central boards (*centrala ämbetsverk*). Each board is in principle subordinate to the government; its sphere of activity depends on the appropriations granted by the *Riksdag.* The Government often asks the boards' opinion on proposed measures.

National flag: Blue with a yellow Scandinavian cross.
National anthem: Du gamla, du fria, du fjällhöga nord (words by R. Dybeck, 1844; folk-tune).
The official language is Swedish. The capital is Stockholm.

Regional and Local Government. For national administrative purposes Sweden is divided into 24 counties (*län*), in each of which the central government is represented by a state county administrative board (*länsstyrelse*). The governor (*landshövding*), appointed by the government, is chairman of the board, which in addition to the governor has 14 members elected by the county council.

Local government and the levying of local taxes are based on the Instrument of Government (the Swedish Constitution) and are regulated by the local government act and special acts. According to the local government act Sweden is divided into municipalities in which all men and women who have reached the age of 18 on election-day itself, and not under wardship, are entitled to elect the municipal council. These councils are named *kommunfullmäktige.* The number of municipalities has, since 1951, been reduced from about 2,500 to 284. The municipalities deal with a great variety of different tasks such as social welfare, education and culture, public health, town planning, housing etc. Each county, except Gotland, which consists of only one municipality, has a county council (*landsting*) elected by men and women who enjoy local suffrage. The county councils chiefly administer the health services and medical care. The municipalities of Gothenburg and Malmö do not belong to county councils. Ecclesiastical affairs in all parishes with more than 500 inhabitants entitled to vote are dealt with by church councils (*kyrkofullmäktige*); smaller parishes may make the same arrangement. All elections are conducted on a proportional basis.

Boalt, G., *The Political Process.* Stockholm, 1984
Gustafsson, A., *Local Government in Sweden.* Stockholm, 1983
Hadenius, S., *Swedish Politics During the 20th Century.* Stockholm, 1985
Lewin, L., Jansson, B., and Sorbom, D., *The Swedish Electorate 1887–1968.* Stockholm, 1972
Strömberg, L., and Westerstahl, J., *The New Swedish Communes.* Gothenburg, 1984
Vinde, P., *Swedish Government Administration.* 2nd rev. ed. Stockholm, 1978
Wahlbäck, K., *The Roots of Swedish Neutrality.* Stockholm, 1986

DEFENCE. A Supreme Commander is, under the Government, in command of the three services. He is assisted by the Defence Staff under a chief of staff.

The military forces are recruited on the principle of national service, supplemented by voluntarily enlisted personnel who form the permanent cadres for training purposes, staff duties, etc.

Liability to service commences at the age of 18, and lasts till the end of the 47th year. The period of training for the Army and Navy is 7½-12 months and for the Airforce 8-12 months.

The territorial organization consists of 6 military commands each one under a general officer commanding.

Army. The C.-in-C. of the Swedish Army has at his disposal the Army Staff under a chief of staff. The peace-time Army consists for training purposes of 16 infantry, 2 cavalry, 7 armour, 6 artillery, 5 AA, 3 engineer, 2 signal and 3 Army Service Corps units, most of which are called 'regiments' (*regementen*). The Army Aviation Corps comprises 2 Battalions operating 20 Bulldog aircraft and 20 JetRanger helicopters for observation, 15 AB.204B transport helicopters, and 10 Hughes 300C helicopters and 2 DO 27 aircraft for transport.

The Army is organized and equipped with regard to the varying geographical and climatic conditions of the country. The voluntary Home Guard (*Hemvärnet*) with a total strength of more than 100,000 men ready for action within 2 hours, raised during the War continues to be in force.

Sweden's ground forces, total 850,000 men (including the voluntary Home Guard), can be said to consist of an Army which for the most part is on indefinite leave, but which on short notice can be ready for action. One of the basic principles of the Swedish system of mobilization is the local recruitment of as many units as possible. The storage of equipment and supplies is decentralized on more than 3,000 places.

The active personnel of the Army comprises (1988) about 47,000, including 37,700 conscripts doing basic training.

Navy. The C.-in-C. of the Swedish Navy is assisted by the Chief of Naval Staff, the Chief of Naval Material and the Commander-in-Chief of Coastal Fleet. The Navy is divided into two branches, the Navy and the Royal Coast Artillery. There are 4 Naval Command Areas: those of the southern, eastern, western and northern coasts. The coast artillery defence areas are those of the Stockholm archipelago, Blekinge, Gothenburg, Gotland and Norrland. There are 5 coastal artillery regiments.

There are 12 diesel-powered patrol submarines, 2 missile-armed small corvettes (leaders for fast attack craft), 28 fast missile craft, 4 fast torpedo boats, 5 patrol craft, 3 minelayers, 1 mine countermeasures support ship, 13 coastal minelayers, 6 new minehunters, 9 coastal minesweepers, 18 inshore minesweepers, 32 coastal patrol craft, 2 mine transports, 1 electronic surveillance ship, 3 torpedo recovery vessels, 10 tenders, 5 surveying vessels, 7 icebreakers, 3 oilers, 1 salvage vessel, 10 artillery landing craft, 83 utility landing craft, 30 minor landing craft, 2 sail training ships, 1 supply ship, 2 water carriers and 17 tugs.

Four submarines, 4 missile armed fast attack craft leaders (officially classed as corvettes), 6 coastal minelayers and 2 more minehunters are under construction. Five submarines are projected.

The Naval Air Arm comprises 10 Boeing Vertol 107 helicopters and 10 Jet-Ranger helicopters. Three Aviocars and 4 Boeing Vertol 107 helicopters acquired for anti-submarine warfare and electronic surveillance.

The personnel of the navy and coast artillery in 1988 totalled 9,350 officers and men, comprising 3,250 regulars and 6,100 national servicemen.

The Coast Guard operates 150 cutters, patrol boats and service craft and lists 5 aircraft. Personnel in 1988 numbered 570.

Air Force. The C-in-C. of the Swedish Air Force has at his disposal the Air Staff under a chief of staff.

The combat force consists of 3 fighter-interceptor, 3 ground-attack and 3 mixed interceptor/reconnaissance wings (*flottiljer*), each with 2-3 squadrons of 12-15 aircraft, including 6 reconnaissance squadrons (*divisioner*). Total peace-time strength of the combat units is 16 squadrons with nearly 400 first-line aircraft.

Night and all-weather fighters are the Swedish-built Saab J35 Draken, equipping 3 squadrons, and JA37 Viggen, equipping 8 squadrons. The ground-attack wings have 5 squadrons of Saab AJ37 Viggens, and there is provision for 4 light ground-attack squadrons of twin-jet Saab-105s (Sk60s), which could be withdrawn in war-time from training units. The 6 reconnaissance squadrons have SF37 (photo) and SH37 (maritime, radar) Viggen reconnaissance aircraft; and there are transport, helicopter and other support units. The Sk60A is the Air Force's standard advanced trainer, to which pupils progress after initial training on piston-engined Bulldogs. Other trainers in service include the Sk61 Bulldog, Sk35C Draken and Sk37 Viggen.

Active strength (1988) 8,000 personnel, including 5,000 conscripts.

INTERNATIONAL RELATIONS

Membership. Sweden is a member of UN and EFTA.

ECONOMY

Budget. Revenue and expenditure of the total budget (Current and Capital) for financial years ending 30 June (in 1 m. kr.):

	Revenue	Expenditure		Revenue	Expenditure
1981–82	167,131	235,164	1984–85	260,596	330,281
1982–83	191,280	277,031	1985–86	275,099	322,241
1983–84	221,165	297,881	1986–87 [1]	318,561	335,667

[1] Preliminary.

The preliminary revenue and expenditure for the financial year 1 July 1986 to 30 June 1987 was as follows (in 1 m. kr.):

Revenue		Expenditure	
Taxes:		Royal Household and residences	36
Taxes on income,		Justice	10,919
capital gains and		Foreign Affairs	9,536
profits	75,802	Defence	26,746
Statutory social		Health and Social Affairs	86,702
security fees	58,581	Transport and Communications	12,661
Taxes on property	13,360	Ministry of Finance	18,436
Value-added tax	72,292	Education and Cultural Affairs	42,560
Other taxes on goods		Agriculture	7,806
and services	52,526	Labour	23,194
Total revenue		Housing and Physical Planning	17,754
from taxes	272,561	Industry	10,822
Non-tax revenue	31,547	Civil Service Affairs	4,024
Capital revenue	1,244	Parliament and agencies	454
Loan repayment	8,795	Interest on National Debt, etc.	63,812
Computed revenue	4,413	Unforeseen expenditure	5
Total revenue	318,561	Changed appropriation of	
		short-term credits	200
		Total expenditure	335,667

On 31 Dec. 1986 the national debt amounted to 630,784m. kr.

Riksgäldskontoret (National Debt Office), *årsbok.* Annual. Stockholm, from 1920
Riksskatteverket (National Tax Board), *årsbok.* Annual. Stockholm, from 1971
The Swedish Budget. Ministry of Economic Affairs and Ministry of the Budget, from 1962/63

Currency. The monetary unit is the Swedish *krona,* of 100 *öre.* In March 1988, £1 = 10·62 *krona*; US$1 = 5·99 *krona.*

Gold coins do not exist as a currency. Central banknotes for 5, 10, 50, 100, 500, 1,000 and 10,000 kr. are legal means of payment.

Banking. The Riksbank, or Central Bank of Sweden, belongs entirely to the State and is managed by directors elected for 3 years by the Parliament, except the chairman, who is designated by the Government. The bank is under the guarantee of the Parliament, its capital and reserve capital are fixed by its constitution. Since 1904, only the Riksbank has the right to issue notes. On 31 Dec. 1986 its note circulation amounted to 55,869m. kr.; its gold and foreign-exchange reserves totalled 45,648m. kr. There are 26 commercial banks. On 31 Dec. 1986 their total deposits amounted to 292,246m. kr.; advances to the public amounted to 298,462m. kr.

On 31 Dec. 1986 there were 119 savings banks; their total deposits amounted to 128,047m. kr.; advances to the public were 94,614m. kr. Co-operative banks had total deposits of 33,879m. kr.; advances to the public were 20,850m. kr.

Sveriges Riksbank, årsbok. Annual. Stockholm, from 1908
Skandinaviska Enskilda Banken, Kvartalskrift. Quarterly Review (in English). Stockholm, from 1920

Weights and Measures. The metric system is obligatory.

ENERGY AND NATURAL RESOURCES

Electricity. Sweden is rich in hydro-power resources. The total electric energy net production in 1986 was 133,700m. kwh. About 45% of this energy was produced in hydro-electric plants and 50% in nuclear power plants. The remaining 5% was produced in conventional thermal power plants. Supply 220 volts; 50 Hz.

Minerals. Sweden is one of the leading exporters of iron ore. The largest deposits are found north of the polar circle in the area of Kiruna and Gällivare-Malmberget. The ore is exported *via* the Norwegian port of Narvik and the Swedish port of Luleå. There are also important resources of iron ore in southern Sweden (Bergslagen). The most important fields are Grängesberg and Stråssa and the ores are shipped *via* the port of Oxelösund. Some of the southern deposits have, in contrast to the fields in North Sweden, a low phosphorus content.

There are also some deposits of copper, lead and zinc ores especially in the Boliden area in the north of Sweden. These ores are often found together with pyrites. Non-ferrous ores, except zinc ores, are used in the Swedish metal industry and barely satisfy domestic needs.

The total production of iron ores amounted to 20·5m. tons in 1985 and exports to 18·3m. tons. The production of copper ore was 375,217 tons, of lead ore 112,572 tons, of zinc ore 387,546 tons.

There are also deposits of raw materials for aluminium not worked at present. In southern Sweden there are big resources of alum shale, containing oil and uranium.

Agriculture. According to the farm register which is revised annually the following data was provided for 1986. The number of farms in cultivation of more than 2 hectares of arable land, was 106,279; of these there were 62,305 of 2-20 hectares; 40,353 of 20-100 hectares; 3,621 of above 100 hectares. Of the total land area of Sweden (41,161,500 hectares), 2,907,706 [1] hectares were arable land, 339,776[1] hectares cultivated pastures and (1981) 22,742,235 hectares forests.

Chief crops	Area (1,000 hectares) [1]			Production (1,000 tonnes)		
	1984	1985	1986	1984	1985	1986
Wheat	325·8	286·7	321·4	1,776	1,338	1,731
Rye	64·9	48·3	40·4	246	157	159
Barley	686·6	710·7	680·9	2,732	2,309	2,327
Oats	458·1	474·7	486·8	1,904	1,668	1,486
Mixed grain	68·6	56·1	50·0	...	...	...
Peas and vetches	49·8	45·5	41·0	...	...	...
Potatoes	39·3	37·7	37·5	1,307	1,266	1,209
Sugarbeet	52·6	51·9	51·3	2,508	2,156	2,187
Tame hay	691·9	676·1	671·0	3,185	4,121	3,981
Oil seed	169·9	172·5	175·8	382	371	379

Area of rotation meadows for pasture was (in 1,000 hectares[1]): 1981, 192; 1982, 193; 1983, 184; 1984, 182; 1985, 181; 1986, 180.

Total production of milk (in 1,000 tonnes): 1981, 3,514; 1982, 3,652; 1983, 3,715; 1984, 3,821; 1985, 3,724; 1986, 3,566. Butter production in the same years was (in 1,000 tonnes): 64, 69, 72, 78, 75, 68; and cheese 108, 114, 115, 116, 115, 113.

Livestock (1986): Cattle, 1·7m.; sheep, 407,000; pigs, 2·4m.; poultry, 11·4m.

Number of farm tractors in 1986, 183,828; combines in 1986, 47,089.

The number of pelts produced in 1984–85 was as follows: Fox, 34,044; mink, 1·52m.; others, 17,525.

[1] Figures refer to holdings of more than 2 hectares of arable land.

Forestry. In 1980–84 the forests covered an area of 23·6m. hectares, *i.e.* roughly 57% of the country's land area. Municipal and State ownership accounts for one-fourth of the forests, companies own another fourth, and the remaining half is in private hands. In the felling seasons, 1983–84 and 1984–85 respectively, 51·8m. and 50·3m. cu. metres (solid volume excluding bark) of wood were removed from the forests in Sweden. The sawmill, wood pulp and paper industries are all of great importance. The number of sawmills in 1984 was about 2,500, 370 of which were commercial sawmills, with more than 90% of the total production of sawn hard- and soft-wood. In 1985 the total production was about 11·5m. cu. metres. The wood pulp factories total output amounted to 9·1m. tons (including dissolving pulp) (dry weight).

Fisheries. In 1986 the total catch of the sea fisheries was 201,025 tons, landed weight, value 722m. kr.

INDUSTRY AND TRADE

Manufacturing. The most important sector of Swedish manufacturing is the production of metals, metal products, machinery and transport equipment, covering almost half of the total value added by manufacturing. Production of high-quality steel is an old Swedish speciality. A large part of this production is exported. The production of ordinary steel is slightly decreasing and is still short of domestic demand. The total production of steel amounted to 4·1m. tons in 1983. There is also a large production of other metals (aluminium, lead, copper) and rolled semi-manufactured goods of these metals.

These basic metal industries are an important basis for the production of more developed metal products, machinery and equipment, which are to a large extent sold on the world market, *i.e.*, hand tools, mining drills, ball-bearings, turbines, pneumatic machinery, refrigerating equipment, machinery for pulp and paper industries, etc., sewing machines, machine tools, office machinery, high-voltage electric machinery, telephone equipment, cars and trucks, ships and aeroplanes.

Another important manufacturing sector is based on Sweden's forest resources. This sector includes saw-mills, plywood factories, joinery industries, pulp- and paper-mills, wallboard and particle board factories, accounting for about 20% of the total value of manufacturing. A fast increasing sector is the chemical industry, especially the petro-chemical branch. Minerals industries include production of building materials, decorative arts products of glass and china.

	No. of establishments		Average no. of wage-earners		Sales value of production (gross) in 1m. kr.	
Industry groups	1984	1985	1984	1985	1984	1985
Mining and quarrying	*110*	*111*	*8,506*	*8,471*	*5,667*	*6,425*
Metal-ore mining	34	35	7,412	7,397	4,966	5,694
Other mining	76	76	1,094	1,074	901	731
Manufacturing	*9,223*	*9,095*	*533,028*	*535,140*	*475,963*	*510,994*
Manufacture of food, beverages and tobacco	849	837	50,225	50,579	65,568	70,801
Textile, wearing apparel and leather industries	650	626	25,297	24,417	10,052	10,780
Manufacture of wood products including furniture	1,462	1,413	47,270	45,577	39,980	32,876
Manufacture of paper and paper products, printing and publishing	1,076	1,079	66,063	65,925	68,913	71,163
Manufacture of chemicals and chemical, petroleum, coal, rubber and plastic products	696	703	40,983	41,324	75,336	79,105
Manufacture of non-metallic mineral products, except products of petroleum and coal	399	391	16,309	16,123	10,076	10,793
Basic metal industries	161	160	36,961	36,359	38,297	40,191
Manufacture of fabricated metal products, machinery and equipment	3,826	3,786	247,170	252,022	173,371	193,828
Other manufacturing industries	104	100	2,750	2,814	1,369	1,456
Electricity, gas and water	*817*	*825*	*11,386*	*10,968*	*62,928*	*77,325*
Electricity, gas and steam	691	699	10,791	10,368	61,418	75,715
Water works and supply	126	126	595	600	1,510	1,610

Arbetsmarknadsstatistik (Labour Market Statistics). Monthly. National Labour Market Board, Stockholm, from 1963

Arbetsmarknadsstatistisk Årsbok (Year Book of Labour Statistics). Statistics Sweden, Stockholm, from 1973

Historisk statistik för Sverige, II (Climate, land surveying, agriculture, forestry, fisheries). Statistics Sweden, Stockholm, 1959

Johansson, Ö., *The Gross Domestic Product of Sweden and its Composition 1861–1955.* Stockholm, 1967

Jörberg, L., *A History of Prices in Sweden 1732–1914.* 2 vols. Stockholm, 1972

Thalberg, B., and Marno, N., eds., *Economic Growth, Welfare and Industrial Relations: A Comparative Study of Japan and Sweden.* Tokyo, 1984

Jordbruksekonomiska meddelanden (Journal of Agricultural Economics, published monthly by the National Agricultural Market Board). Stockholm, from 1939

Jordbruksstatistisk årsbok (Yearbook of Agricultural Statistics). Statistics Sweden, Stockholm, from 1965

The Swedish Economy. Ministry of Economic Affairs and National Institute of Economic Research. Stockholm, from 1960

Trade Unions. The Swedish Federation of Trade Unions (LO) had 24 member unions with a total membership of 2,277,062 in 1986; the Swedish Central Organization of Salaried Employees (TCO) had 21, with 1,233,234; the Swedish Confederation of Professional Associations (SACO-SR) had 25, with 292,118.

Commerce. The imports and exports of Sweden, unwrought gold and coin not included, have been as follows (in 1 m. kr.):

	1980	1981	1982	1983	1984	1985	1986
Imports	141,641	146,040	173,932	200,368	218,569	244,654	231,445
Exports	131,002	144,876	168,134	210,516	242,811	260,481	265,040

Imports and exports by products (in 1 m. kr.):

	Imports 1985	Imports 1986	Exports 1985	Exports 1986
Food and live animals chiefly for food	13,124	14,389	6,148	4,966
Cereals and cereal preparations	812	810	2,171	1,321
Vegetables and fruit	4,147	4,305	346	404
Coffee, tea, cocoa, spices and manufactures thereof	3,517	4,220	533	602
Feeding stuff for animals (not including unmilled cereals)	1,114	985	96	148
Beverages and tobacco	1,851	1,948	331	355
Crude materials, inedible, except fuels	10,759	10,191	26,142	24,287
Hides, skins and furskins, raw	505	550	840	927
Crude rubber (including synthetic and reclaimed)	537	498	147	156
Cork and wood	1,886	2,614	9,569	9,516
Pulp and waste paper	587	570	9,628	8,795
Textile fibres (other than wool tops) and their wastes (not manufactured into yarn or fabric)	404	366	363	258
Crude fertilizers and crude minerals (excluding coal, petroleum and precious stones)	1,454	1,315	437	443
Metalliferous ores and metal scrap	3,760	2,644	4,684	3,837
Mineral fuels, lubricants and related materials	46,285	24,955	12,738	7,610
Coal, coke and briquettes	2,527	1,875	164	192
Petroleum, petroleum products and related materials	42,201	22,366	11,601	6,590
Chemicals and related products, n.e.s.	23,156	22,553	16,280	17,780
Artificial resins and plastic materials, and cellulose esters and ethers	6,223	6,606	4,446	4,975
Manufactured goods classified chiefly by material	36,812	38,348	67,764	69,794
Paper, paperboard, and articles of paper pulp, of paper or of paperboard	2,711	3,056	25,326	27,453
Textile yarn, fabrics, made-up articles, n.e.s., and related products	6,339	6,476	3,294	3,480
Non-metallic mineral manufactures, n.e.s.	3,360	3,725	2,802	2,858
Iron and steel	8,169	8,400	17,138	16,356
Non-ferrous metals	5,317	4,859	4,921	4,601
Machinery and transport equipment	80,429	83,628	108,977	116,110
Power generating machinery and equipment	5,558	5,825	6,643	7,393
Machinery specialized for particular industries	8,152	7,286	12,234	13,113
Metal working machinery	2,189	2,543	2,522	2,637
General industrial machinery and equipment, n.e.s. and machine parts, n.e.s.	11,954	12,409	17,366	18,355
Office machines and automatic data processing equipment	10,433	10,049	7,974	7,897

	Imports		Exports	
	1985	1986	1985	1986
Telecommunications and sound recording and reproducing apparatus and equipment	5,782	6,175	11,437	10,149
Electrical machinery apparatus and appliances, n.e.s., and electrical parts thereof (including non-electrical counterparts, n.e.s., of electrical household type equipment)	14,913	14,101	9,471	10,669
Road vehicles (including air cushion vehicles)	17,631	20,444	35,845	39,401
Other transport equipment	3,817	4,795	5,485	6,496
Miscellaneous manufactured articles	30,309	33,574	19,133	20,506

Principal import and export countries (in 1 m. kr.):

	Imports from		Exports to	
	1985	1986	1985	1986
Belgium-Luxembourg	6,665	7,243	10,285	10,736
Denmark	16,572	15,828	21,489	21,142
Federal Republic of Germany	43,861	47,420	29,901	30,666
Finland	15,991	15,804	14,674	16,219
France	11,353	12,071	12,553	13,586
Italy	7,990	8,943	8,686	9,117
Netherlands	9,532	9,862	11,460	12,276
Norway	15,968	13,034	27,255	29,665
Switzerland	4,670	5,089	4,642	5,359
USSR	5,616	3,518	2,688	2,134
UK	33,161	24,117	25,768	27,666
USA	20,506	18,110	30,228	29,903

Total trade between Sweden and UK (British Department of Trade returns, in £1,000 sterling):

	1983	1984	1985	1986	1987
Imports to UK	2,051,931	2,416,383	2,465,582	2,756,536	2,952,453
Exports and re-exports from UK	2,937,464	2,888,625	3,006,890	2,307,900	2,322,235

Historisk Statistik för Sverige, 3: Utrikeshandel [Foreign Trade], *1732–1970*. Statistics Sweden, Stockholm, 1972

Utrikeshandel, årsstatistik [Foreign Trade, Annual Bulletin]. Statistics Sweden, Stockholm. 5 vols. Statistical Reports, Series H

Utrikeshandel, månadsstatistik [Foreign Trade, Monthly Bulletin]. Statistics Sweden, Stockholm.

Utrikeshandel, kvartalsstatistik [Foreign Trade, Quarterly Bulletin]. Statistics Sweden, Stockholm. January – December. Exports respectively imports. Statistical Reports, Series H

Utrikeshandel, års statistik [Foreign Trade, Annual]. Official Statistics of Sweden, Statistics Sweden, Stockholm. Imports and exports. Distribution by country and commodity according to the SITC

Utrikeshandel, årsstatistik [Foreign Trade, Annual]. Official Statistics of Sweden, Statistics Sweden, Stockholm. Imports and exports. Commodities according to the CCCN.

COMMUNICATIONS

Roads. On 1 Jan. 1987 there were 200,000 km of public roads comprising State-administered roads, 98,337 km, municipal, 32,000 km, private roads with subsidies, 76,876 km, of which 68,762 km were surfaced. Motor vehicles on 31 Dec. 1986 included 3,253,601 passenger cars, 243,696 buses and lorries and 29,007 motor cycles (all in use).

Railways. At the end of 1986 the total length of railways was 11,715 km; 7,464 km were electrified which carried 86m. passengers and 56m. tonnes of freight.

Aviation. Commercial air traffic is maintained in (1) Sweden and other parts of the world by Scandinavian Airlines System (SAS), of which AB Aerotransport (ABA = Swedish Air Lines) is the Swedish partner (DDL = Danish Air Lines and DNL = Norwegian Air Lines being the other two); (2) only within Sweden by Linjeflyg AB. Scandinavian Airlines System have a joint paid-up capital of about Sw. kronor 3,771m. Capitalization of ABA, Sw. kronor 976m., of which 50% is owned by the Government and 50% by private enterprises. Capitalization of Linjeflyg, Sw. kronor 557m., of which 50% is owned by SAS and 50% by ABA.

In scheduled air traffic during 1986 the total number of km flown was 90·7m.; passenger-km, 6,810·2m.; goods, 173·7m. ton-km; mail, 22m. ton-km. These figures represent the Swedish share of the SAS traffic (Swedish domestic and three-sevenths of international traffic) and the Linjeflyg traffic.

Shipping. The Swedish mercantile marine consisted on 30 June 1987 of 424 vessels of 2·2m. gross tons (only vessels of at least 100 gross tons, and excluding fishing vessels and tugs). Stockholm and Göteborg, with together 182 vessels of 1·6m. gross tons in Dec. 1986, are the two major home ports for the Swedish mercantile marine.

Vessels entered from and cleared for foreign countries, exclusive of passenger liners and ferries, with cargoes and in ballast, in 1985, are as follows (only vessels of at least a gross tonnage of 75): With cargoes, 26,551 with a gross tonnage of 96·5m.; in ballast, 13,576 with a gross tonnage of 51·2m.

Post and Broadcasting. On 1 Jan. 1987 there were 5,372,000 main telephone lines.

Number of combined radio and television reception fees paid at the end of 1986 was 3,278,000, of which 3m. included extra fees for colour television. As from 1 April 1978, special sound broadcasting licences were discontinued.

Sveriges Radio AB is a non-commercial semi-governmental corporation, transmitting 3 programmes on long-, medium-, and short-waves and on FM. There are also regional programmes. It also broadcasts 2 TV programmes. Colour programmes are broadcast by PAL system.

The overseas radio-telegraph and radio-telephone services are conducted by the Swedish Telecommunications Administration.

The number of post offices at the end of 1985 was 1,836. For receipts of the post and telecommunication services *see* the section on Economy.

Cinemas (1986). There were 1,129 cinemas.

Newspapers (1986). There were 186 daily newspapers with a total circulation of 4·9m.

JUSTICE, RELIGION, EDUCATION AND WELFARE

Justice. The administration of justice is entirely independent of the Government. The *Justitiekansler*, or Attorney General (a royal appointment) and the *Justitieombudsmän* (Parliamentary Commissioners appointed by the Diet), exercise a check on the administration. In 1968 a reform was carried through which meant that the offices of the former *Justitieombudsman* (Ombudsman for civil affairs) and the *Militieombudsman* (Ombudsman for military affairs) were turned into one sole institution with 3 Ombudsmen, each styled *Justitieombudsman*. They exert a general supervision over all courts of law, the civil service, military laws and the military services. In 1986–87 they received altogether 3,021 cases; of these, 84 were instituted on their own initiative and 2,889 on complaints.

The *Riksåklagaren* (a royal appointment) is the chief public prosecutor.

The kingdom has a Supreme Court of Judicature and is divided into 6 Courts of Appeal districts (*hovrätter*) and 97 district-court divisions (*tingsrätter*). There is also a Housing Appeal Court and 12 rent and tenancy tribunals.

Of the district courts 27 also serve as real estate courts and 6 as water rights courts.

These district courts (or courts of first instance) deal with both civil and criminal cases. Each member of the court has an individual vote and is legally responsible for the decision. In the voting, the majority rules. When the votes are evenly divided in a criminal case, the opinion implying the least severe sentence applies, and in cases where there is no opinion that could be considered the mildest, the Chair has the casting vote, as is also the case in family civil cases and matters; petty cases are tried by the judge alone. Civil cases are tried as a rule by 3 to 4 judges or in minor cases by 1 judge. Disputes of greater consequence relating to the Marriage Code or the Code relating to Parenthood and Guardianship are tried by a judge and a *nämnd* of 3-4 lay assessors. When cases concerning real estate are being tried the court consists of 2 qualified lawyers, 1 specialist on technical matters and 2 lay assessors.

Criminal cases are tried by a judge and a jury of 5 members (lay assessors) in felony cases, and of 3 members in misdemeanour cases. The cases in Courts of Appeal are generally tried by 4 or 5 judges, but the same cases, which are tried with a judge and a *nämnd* in the first instance, are tried by 3 or 4 judges and a *nämnd* of 2-3 members. In cases concerning real estate the court consists of a specialist on technical matters in place of one of the judges and in water-right cases of 3 or 4 judges and 1 or 2 specialists on technical water matters.

Those with low incomes can receive free legal aid out of public funds. In criminal cases a suspected person has the right to a defence counsel, paid out of public funds.

The Attorney-General (*Justitiekanslern*) and the Parliamentary Commissioner (*Justitieombudsmannen*) for the Judiciary and Civil Administration supervise the application in the public sector of acts of parliament and regulations. The Attorney-General is the Government's legal adviser and also the Public Prosecutor.

The holders of the office of Parliamentary Commissioner are 4 in number.

There were 76 penal and correctional institutions for offenders in 1986 with an average population of 4,161 male and 122 female inmates (including offenders in remand prison). Besides, there were 560 children or young people registered for care in treatment and/or residential homes on 31 Dec. 1986, admitted under the 'Care of Young Persons' Act.

Anderman, S., ed., *Law and the Weaker Party: An Anglo-Swedish Comparative Study*. Abingdon, 1981–83

Bruzelius, A., and Ginsburg, R. B., *The Swedish Code of Judicial Procedure*. South Hackensack, Rev. ed., 1979

Strömholm, S., *An Introduction to Swedish Law*. Stockholm, 1981

al-Wahab, I., *The Swedish Institution of Ombudsmen*. Stockholm, 1979

Justitieombudsmännens ämbetsberättelse avgiven till Riksdagen. Annual. Stockholm

The Penal Code of Sweden: As Amended 1 Jan. 1972. South Hackensack, 1972

Rättsstatistisk årsbok (Year Book of Legal Statistics). Statistics Sweden, Stockholm, from 1975

Religion. The overwhelming majority of the population belong to the Evangelical Lutheran Church, which is the established national church. In 1987 there were 13 bishoprics (Uppsala being the metropolitan see) and 2,565 parishes. The clergy are chiefly supported from the parishes and the proceeds of the church lands. The non-conformists mostly still adhere to the national church. The largest denominations, on 1 Jan. 1986, were: Pentecost Movement, 100,679; The Mission Covenant Church of Sweden, 79,178; Salvation Army, 29,910; Swedish Evangelical Mission, 23,404; Swedish Baptist Church, 20,996; Orebro Missionary Society, 22,252; Swedish Alliance Missionary Society, 13,471; Holiness Mission, 6,125.

There were also 120,185 Roman Catholics (under a Bishop resident at Stockholm).

Parliament and Convocation (*Kyrkomötet*) decided in 1958 to admit women to ordination as priests.

Education. By the Swedish Higher Educational Act of 1977 a unified educational system was created by integrating institutions which had previously been administered separately. This new *högskola* includes not only traditional university studies but also those of various former professional colleges as well as a number of study programmes earlier offered by the secondary school system. One of the goals of the 1977 university reform was to introduce an increased element of vocational training into part of Swedish higher education and to widen admission. A Certificate of Education (B.Sc., M.Sc., U.C. etc.) is awarded on completion of a general study programme. This certificate states the number of courses taken as well as the points and grades obtained on each course in the study programme.

In autumn 1986 there were, in these new integrated institutions for higher education, *högskola*, about 161,400 enrolled for undergraduate studies of whom 110,500 were distributed by sector as follows: Education for technical professions, 30,300; education for social work, economic and administrative professions, 33,100; education for medical and paramedical professions, 21,300; education for the teaching professions, 19,700; and education for information, communication and cultural professions, 6,100. The number of students enrolled for post-graduate studies was 12,000.

In autumn term in the school year 1986–87 there were 600,000 pupils in primary education (grades 1–6 in compulsory comprehensive schools). Secondary education at the lower stage (grades 7–9 in compulsory comprehensive schools) comprised 334,200 pupils. In secondary education at the higher stage (the integrated upper secondary school), there were 248,900 pupils (excluding about 10,000 pupils in the fourth year of the technical line regarded as third-level education). The folk high schools, 'people's colleges', had 15,100 pupils in courses of more than 15 weeks.

In municipal adult education there were 143,000 pupils (corresponding to a gross number of 335,000 participants). Basic education for adults had 20,100 pupils.

There are also special schools for pupils with visual and hearing handicaps (about 650 in 1986–87) and for those who are mentally retarded (about 12,200 pupils).

Education Policy for Planning: Goals for Educational Policy in Sweden. OECD, Paris, 1980
Educational Reforms in Sweden. OECD, Paris, 1981
Science and Technology Policies in Sweden. Ministry of Education and Cultural Affairs, Stockholm, 1986
The Swedish Folk High School. Swedish National Board of Education, Stockholm, 1986
Yearbook of Educational Statistics 1986, Statistics Sweden, Stockholm, 1986
Boucher, L., *Tradition and Change in Swedish education.* OUP, 1982
Düring, A., *Swedish Research.* Stockholm, 1985
Götberg, B., and Svärd, S., *The Swedish 'Folk High School': Its Background and its Present Situation.*
Kim, L., *Widened Admission to Higher Education in Sweden.* Stockholm, 1982
Marklund, S., *Educational Administration and Educational Development.* Univ. of Stockholm, 1979.—*The Democratization of Education in Sweden.* Univ. of Stockholm, 1980
Paulston, C. B., *Swedish Research and Debate about Bilingualism.* Stockholm, 1983
Stenholm, B., *The Swedish School System.* Stockholm, 1984
Sundgvist, A., *New Rules for Swedish Study Circles.* Stockholm, 1983
Ueberschlag, G., *La Folkhögskola.* Paris, 1981

Social Welfare. The social security schemes are greatly expanding. Supported by a referendum, the Diet in 1958 and 1959 decided that the national pensions should be increased successively until 1968 and supplementary pensions paid from 1963. These pensions are of invariable value. In 1969 the Diet decided that as from 1 July 1969 an increment to the basic pension was to be paid to persons without supplementary pensions, and this amount is to be successively increased in a 10-year period. The basic and supplementary pensions consist of old-age and family pensions, as well as pensions paid to the disabled. The financing of the supplementary system is based on the current-cost method.

The most important social welfare schemes are described in the conspectus below.

Type of scheme	Intro-duced	Scope	Principal benefits
Sickness insurance (compulsory—current law, 1962)	1955	All residents	Hospital fees, most private doctors charge the insured person normally 55 kr., district physicians and doctors in hospitals charge the insured person only 50 kr. for full medical treatment, some reimbursement of cost of transportation as well as costs of physiotherapy, convalescent care, etc., medicines at reduced prices or free of charge. During sickness daily allowance 90% of the yearly income in between 6,000 and 180,750 kr. There is generally no maximum benefit period. Dental care is available to all residents from 20 years of age, the maximum payable by the patient being 60% up to 2,500 kr. and 25% thereafter. Before 20 years of age dental care is given free through the national dental service.

Type of scheme	Intro-duced	Scope	Principal benefits
Employment injury insurance (compulsory–current law, 1976)	1901	All employed persons	Medical treatment, medicine and medical appliances, hospital care, sickness benefit 100% of the yearly income in between 6,000 and 180,750 kr. (first 90 days covered by sickness insurance), disability annuities, funeral benefit and survivor's pensions.
Unemployment insurance (current law, 1973)	1935	Members of recognized unemployment insurance societies (about 70% of all employees)	130-360 kr. per day subject to tax.
Basic pensions (current law, 1962)			
Old-age	1914	All citizens	Payable from the age of 65 or, at a reduced rate, from the age of 60. 61,986 kr. per annum for married couples, 35,280 kr. for others (including the special increment of 23,520 kr. and 11,760 kr. respectively for those without supplementary pension); about half of them receive municipal housing supplement.
Disability	1914	All citizens	Payable before the age of 65. Full pension 47,040 kr. per annum (including the special increment of 23,520 kr.).
Survivors	1948	All citizens	Widow's pension is payable before the age of 65. The pension is 35,280 kr. (including the special increment of 11,760 kr.) but less for those who have become widows before the age of 50 and have no child below 16. Many of them receive municipal housing supplements. Child pension is payable before the age of 18. The pension amounts to 10,045 kr. (fatherless or motherless) and 15,190 kr. (orphans).
Supplementary pensions (current law, 1962)			
Old-age	1960	All gainfully occupied persons	Payable from the same age as the basic pension (see above). The pension is in principle 60% of the insured person's average annual earnings during the best 15 years except an amount corresponding to the basic pension and subject to a ceiling.
Disability	1960	All gainfully occupied persons	Payable before the age of 65. Full pension corresponds in principle to supplementary old-age pension.

Type of scheme	Intro-duced	Scope	Principal benefits
Survivors	1960	All gainfully occupied persons	Payable to widow and children, before the age of 19, of a deceased person as a certain percentage of the deceased's supplementary pension.
Partial pensions (current law, 1979)	1976	All employees between 60–65 years of age	The pension is payable between 60-65 years of age. The insured must have reduced his working time by 5 hours on an average a week and the part-time work must thereafter comprise at least 17 hours per week. Furthermore the insured must have worked during at least 5 of the last 12 months and achieved a right to supplementary pension for 10 years after the age of 45. The partial pension is paid out by 65% of the loss of income in connection with the change-over to part-time work.
Parents benefit	1974	All resident parents in connection with confinement	Parents cash benefit of 60 kr. a day during 360 days until the child reaches 4 years of age. Employed parents entitled to daily parents cash benefit of 90% of the daily income (in between 6,000–180,750 kr. yearly) for 270 days. Maximum daily parents cash benefit 486 kr. and for the last 90 days 60 kr. a day will be paid.
Temporary parents benefit	1974	All resident parents	Temporary parents cash benefit with the same amount as for parents cash benefit for care of each child which is ill during 60 days for the parents together until the child reaches 12 years of age.
Children's allowances	1948	All children below 16	From 1 Jan. 1987 5,820 kr. per annum. An additional allowance is paid out for the third child with one-half of an allowance and a full allowance for each additional child.
		Children at school 16–18	485 kr. per month during school-courses.

Total social expenditure, including also hygiene, care of the sick and social assistance, amounted to 269,107m. kr. in 1985, representing 31% of the GDP.

The Cost and Financing of the Social Services in Sweden, 1981. Stockholm, 1983
Ministry of Health and Social Affairs, *The Evolution of the Swedish Health Insurance.* Stockholm, 1978
Socialnytt (Official Journal of the National Board of Health and Welfare). Stockholm, from 1968
Social Insurance Statistics. Facts 1986. National Social Insurance Board, Stockholm, 1986
The Swedish Health Services in the 1990s. The National Board of Health and Welfare, Stockholm, 1985
Forsberg, M., *The Evolution of Social Welfare Policy in Sweden.* Stockholm, 1984
Heclo, H., *Modern Social Politics in Britain and Sweden: From Relief to Income Maintenance.* New Haven, 1974
Lagerström, L., *Pension Systems in Sweden.* Stockholm, 1976.—*Social Security in Sweden.* Stockholm, 1976

DIPLOMATIC REPRESENTATIVES

Of Sweden in Great Britain (11 Montagu Pl., London, W1H 2AL)
Ambassador: Leif Leifland, GCVO (accredited on 10 Nov. 1982).

Of Great Britain in Sweden (Skarpögatan 6-8, 115 27 Stockholm)
Ambassador: Sir John Ure, KCMG, LVO.

Of Sweden in the USA (600 New Hampshire Ave., NW, Washington, D.C., 20037)
Ambassador: Count Wilhelm H. F. Wachtmeister.

Of the USA in Sweden (Strandvägen 101, 115 27 Stockholm)
Ambassador: Gregory J. Newell.

Of Sweden to the United Nations
Ambassador: Anders Ferm.

Books of Reference

Statistical Information: Statistics Sweden, (Statistiska, Centralbyrån, S-11581 Stockholm) was founded in 1858, in succession to the Kungl. Tabellkommissionen, which had been set up in 1756. *Director-General:* Sten Johansson. Its Publications include:
  Levnadsförhållanden, årsbok (Living Conditions). Annual. From 1975.—*Rapport.* From 1976
  Statistisk årsbok för Sverige (Statistical Abstract of Sweden). From 1914
  Siffror om Sverige (Sweden). From 1971. Also in English as *Sweden*
  Historisk statistik för Sverige (Historical Statistics of Sweden). 1955 ff. (4 vols. to date)
  Allmän månadsstatistik (Monthly Digest of Swedish Statistics). From 1963
  Statistiska meddelanden (Statistical Reports). From 1963
Andersson, L., *A History of Sweden.* Stockholm, 1962
Atlas över Sverige. Stockholm, 1953–71. [Publ. in separate parts dealing with population, economics, etc.]
Publications on Sweden. Stockholm, 1985
Documents on Swedish Foreign Policy, 1981. Stockholm, 1983
Grosskopf, G., *The Swedish Tax System.* Stockholm, 1986
Gullberg, I. E., *Swedish–English Dictionary of Technical Terms.—Svensk-Engelsk Fackordbok.* Stockholm, 2nd ed. 1977
Hadenius, S., *Swedish Politics during the Twentieth Century.* Stockholm, 1985
Hansson, I., Jonung, L., Myhrman, J. and Söderström, H. T., *Sweden – the Road to Stability.* Stockholm, 1985
Hellberg, T. and Jansson, L. M., *Alfred Nobel.* Stockholm, 1984
Linton, M., *The Swedish Road to Socialism.* London, 1985
Meyerson, P-M., *Eurosclerosis, The Case of Sweden.* Stockholm, 1985
Nordic Council, *Yearbook of Nordic Statistics.* From 1962 (in English and one Nordic Language)
Sather, L. B., and Swanson, A., *Sweden.* [Bibliography] Oxford and Santa Barbara, 1987
Scott, F. D., *Sweden: The Nation's History.* Univ. of Minnesota Press, 1983
Söderström, H. T., *Getting Sweden Back to Work.* Stockholm, 1986
Turner, B., *Sweden.* London, 1976
Sveriges statskalender. Published by Vetenskapsakademien. Annual, from 1813

National Library: Kungliga Biblioteket, Stockholm. *Director:* Lars Tynell.

SWITZERLAND

Schweiz—Suisse—Svizzera

Capital: Bern
Population: 6·5m. (1986)
GNP per capita: US$14,030 (1985)

HISTORY. On 1 Aug. 1291 the men of Uri, Schwyz and Unterwalden entered into a defensive league. In 1353 the league included 8 members and in 1513, 13. Various territories were acquired either by single cantons or by several in common, and in 1648 the league became formally independent of the Holy Roman Empire, but no addition was made to the number of cantons till 1798. In that year, under the influence of France, the unified Helvetic Republic was formed. This failed to satisfy the Swiss, and in 1803 Napoleon Bonaparte, in the Act of Mediation, gave a new Constitution, and out of the lands formerly allied or subject increased the number of cantons to 19. In 1815 the perpetual neutrality of Switzerland and the inviolability of her territory were guaranteed by Austria, France, Great Britain, Portugal, Prussia, Russia, Spain and Sweden, and the Federal Pact, which included 3 new cantons, was accepted by the Congress of Vienna. In 1848 a new Constitution was passed. The 22 cantons set up a Federal Government (consisting of a Federal Parliament and a Federal Council) and a Federal Tribunal. This Constitution, in turn, was on 29 May 1874 superseded by the present Constitution. In a national referendum held in Sept. 1978, 69·9% voted in favour of the establishment of a new canton, Jura, which was established on 1 Jan. 1979.

AREA AND POPULATION. Switzerland is bounded west and north-west by France, north by the Federal Republic of Germany, east by Austria and south by Italy. Area and population, according to the census held on 1 Dec. 1980 and estimate 31 Dec. 1986.

Canton	Area (sq. km)	Census 1 Dec. 1980	Estimate 31 Dec. 1986	Pop. per sq. km, 1980
Zürich (Zurich) (1351)	1,729	1,122,839	1,131,600	650
Bern (Berne) (1553)	6,049	912,022	925,600	151
Luzern (Lucerne) (1332)	1,492	296,159	306,100	198
Uri (1291)	1,076	33,883	33,500	31
Schwyz (1291)	908	97,354	103,400	107
Obwalden (Obwald) (1291)	491	25,865	27,600	53
Nidwalden (Nidwald) (1291)	276	28,617	31,000	104
Glarus (Glaris) (1352)	685	36,718	36,600	54
Zug (Zoug) (1352)	239	75,930	81,600	318
Fribourg (Freiburg) (1481)	1,670	185,246	194,600	111
Solothurn (Soleure) (1481)	791	218,102	219,500	276
Basel-Stadt (Bâle-V.) (1501)	37	203,915	194,300	5,485
Basel-Land (Bâle-C.) (1501)	428	219,822	225,800	513
Schaffhausen (Schaffhouse) (1501)	298	69,413	69,800	233
Appenzell A.-Rh. (Rh.-Ext.) (1513)	243	47,611	49,300	196
Appenzell I.-Rh. (Rh.-Int.) (1513)	172	12,844	13,100	75
St Gallen (St Gall) (1803)	2,014	391,995	403,900	195
Graubünden (Grisons) (1803)	7,106	164,641	166,500	23
Aargau (Argovie) (1803)	1,405	453,442	472,700	323
Thurgau (Thurgovie) (1803)	1,013	183,795	192,400	181
Ticino (Tessin) (1803)	2,811	265,899	277,200	95
Vaud (Waadt) (1803)	3,218	528,747	550,300	164
Valais (Wallis) (1815)	5,226	218,707	232,600	42
Neuchâtel (Neuenburg) (1815)	797	158,368	156,200	199
Genève (Genf) (1815)	282	349,040	363,500	1,237
Jura (1979)	837	64,986	64,700	78
Total	41,293[1]	6,365,960	6,523,400	154

[1] 15,943 sq. miles.

1157

The German language is spoken by the majority of inhabitants in 19 of the 26 cantons above (French names given in brackets), the French in 6 (Fribourg, Vaud, Valais, Neuchâtel, Jura and Genève, for which the German names are given in brackets), the Italian in 1 (Ticino). In 1980, 65% spoke German, 18·4% French, 9·8% Italian, 0·8% Romansch and 6% other languages; counting only Swiss nationals, the percentages were 73·5, 20·1, 4·5, 0·9 and 1. On 8 July 1937 Romansch was made the fourth national language; it is spoken mostly in Graubünden.

At the end of 1985 the 5 largest cities were Zürich (351,500); Basel (174,600); Geneva (159,900); Berne (138,600); Lausanne (125,000). At the end of 1985 the population figures of the *'agglomérations'* or conurbations were as follows: Zürich, 840,000; Basel, 363,600; Geneva, 382,000; Bern, 301,100; Lausanne, 260,200; other towns (and their conurbations) were Winterthur, 84,400 (107,400); St Gallen, 73,200 (125,400); Luzern, 60,600 (160,000); Biel, 52,000 (83,000).

The number of foreigners resident in Switzerland in Jan. 1985 was 960,700. Of these, 186,600 were in Zürich canton, 109,100 in Vaud and 122,900 in Geneva.

Vital statistics for calendar years:

| | Live births | | | | | |
	Total	Illegitimate	Marriages	Divorces	Still births	Deaths
1984	74,700	4,300	38,600	11,200	350	58,600
1985	74,700	4,200	38,800	11,400	340	59,600
1986	76,300	4,300	40,200	11,400	330	60,100

In 1983 there were 91,300 emigrants and 88,000 immigrants; in 1984, 85,000 and 97,000; in 1985, 85,000 and 99,000.

CLIMATE. The climate is largely dictated by relief and altitude and includes continental and mountain types. Summers are generally warm, with quite considerable rainfall; winters are fine, with clear, cold air. Bern. Jan. 32°F (0°C), July, 65°F (18·5°C). Annual rainfall 39·4″ (986 mm).

CONSTITUTION AND GOVERNMENT. Switzerland is a republic. The highest authority is vested in the electorate, *i.e.*, all Swiss citizens of over 20. This electorate—besides electing its representatives to the Parliament—has the voting power on amendments to, or on the revision of, the Constitution. It also takes decisions on laws and international treaties if requested by 50,000 voters or 8 cantons (facultative referendum), and it has the right of initiating constitutional amendments, the support required for such demands being 100,000 voters (popular initiative).

The Federal Government is supreme in matters of peace, war and treaties; it regulates the army, the railway, telecommunication systems, the coining of money, the issue and repayment of bank-notes and the weights and measures of the republic. It also legislates on matters of copyright, bankruptcy, patents, sanitary policy in dangerous epidemics, and it may create and subsidize, besides the Polytechnic School at Zürich and that at Lausanne, 2 federal universities and other educational institutions. There has also been entrusted to it the authority to decide concerning public works for the whole or great part of Switzerland, such as those relating to rivers, forests and the construction of national highways and railways. By referendum of 13 Nov. 1898 it is also the authority in the entire spheres of common law. In 1957 the Federation was empowered to legislate on atomic energy matters and in 1961 on the construction of pipelines of petroleum and gas.

National flag: Red with a white couped cross.

National anthem: Trittst im Morgenrot daher (words by Leonard Widmer, 1808–68; tune by Alberik Zwyssig, 1808–54); adopted by the Federal Council in 1962.

The legislative authority is vested in a parliament of 2 chambers, a *Ständerat*, or Council of States, and a *Nationalrat*, or National Council.

The *Ständerat* is composed of 46 members, chosen and paid by the 23 cantons of the Confederation, 2 for each canton. The mode of their election and the term of membership depend entirely on the canton. Three of the cantons are politically divided—Basel into Stadt and Land, Appenzell into Ausser-Rhoden and Inner-Rhoden, and Unterwalden into Obwalden and Nidwalden. Each of these 'half-cantons' sends 1 member to the State Council.

The *Nationalrat*—after the referendum taken on 4 Nov. 1962—consists of 200 National Councillors, directly elected for 4 years, in proportion to the population of the cantons, with the proviso that each canton or half-canton is represented by at least 1 member. The members are paid from federal funds at the rate of 150 francs for each day during the session and a nominal sum of 10,000 francs per annum.

In 1983 the 200 members were distributed among the cantons[1] as follows:

Zürich (Zurich)	35	Appenzell—Outer- and Inner-Rhoden	3
Bern (Berne)	29	St Gallen (St Gall)	12
Luzern (Lucerne)	9	Graubünden (Grisons)	5
Uri	1	Aargau (Argovie)	14
Schwyz	3	Thurgau (Thurgovie)	6
Unterwalden–Upper and Lower	2	Ticino (Tessin)	8
Glarus (Glaris)	1	Vaud (Waadt)	17
Zug (Zoug)	2	Valais (Wallis)	7
Fribourg (Freiburg)	6	Neuchâtel (Neuenburg)	5
Solothurn (Soleure)	7	Geneve (Genf)	11
Basel (Bâle)—town and country	13	Jura	2
Schaffhausen (Schaffhouse)	2		

[1] The name of the canton is given in German, French or Italian, according to the language most spoken in it, and alternative names are given in brackets.

Composition of the National Council in 1983: Social Democrats, 47; Radicals, 54; Christian-Democratic People's Party, 42; Swiss People's Party, 23; Liberals, 8; Independents, 8; National Campaign/Vigilance, 5; Evangelical Party, 3; Progressive Organizations, 3; Environmentalists, 3; Others, 4.

Council of States (1983): Christian Democrats, 18; Radicals, 14; Social Democrats, 6; Swiss People's Party, 5.

A general election takes place by ballot every 4 years. Every citizen of the republic who has entered on his 20th year is entitled to a vote, and any voter, not a clergyman, may be elected a deputy. Laws passed by both chambers may be submitted to direct popular vote, when 50,000 citizens or 8 cantons demand it; the vote can be only 'Yes' or 'No'. This principle, called the *referendum*, is frequently acted on.

Women's suffrage, although advocated by the Federal Council and the Federal Assembly, was on 1 Feb. 1959 rejected, but in a subsequent referendum, held on 7 Feb. 1971, women's suffrage was carried.

The chief executive authority is deputed to the *Bundesrat*, or Federal Council, consisting of 7 members, elected from 7 different cantons for 4 years by the *Vereinigte Bundesversammlung, i.e.*, joint sessions of both chambers. The members of this council must not hold any other office in the Confederation or cantons, nor engage in any calling or business. In the Federal Parliament legislation may be introduced either by a member, or by either House, or by the Federal Council (but not by the people). Every citizen who has a vote for the National Council is eligible for becoming a member of the executive.

The President of the Federal Council (called President of the Confederation) and the Vice-President are the first magistrates of the Confederation. Both are elected by the Federal Assembly for 1 calendar year and are not immediately re-eligible to the same offices. The Vice-President, however, may be, and usually is, elected to succeed the outgoing President.

President of the Confederation. (1988): Otto Stich.

The 7 members of the Federal Council—each of whom has a salary of 203,000 francs per annum, while the President has 215,000 francs—act as ministers, or chiefs of the 7 administrative departments of the republic. The city of Berne is the seat of the Federal Council and the central administrative authorities.

The Federal Council was composed as follows in 1988.

Foreign Affairs: René Felber.

Interior: Flavio Cotti.
Justice and Police: Elisabeth Kopp.
Military: Arnold Koller.
Finance: Otto Stich.
Public Economy: Jean-Pascal Delamuraz.
Transport, Communications and Energy: Adolf Ogi.

Local Government. Each of the cantons and demi-cantons is sovereign, so far as its independence and legislative powers are not restricted by the federal constitution; all cantonal governments, though different in organization (membership varies from 5 to 11, and terms of office from 1 to 5 years), are based on the principle of sovereignty of the people.

In all cantons a body chosen by universal suffrage, usually called *der Grosse Rat*, or *Kantonsrat*, exercises the functions of a parliament. In all the cantonal constitutions, however, except those of the cantons which have a *Landsgemeinde*, the referendum has a place. By this principle, where it is most fully developed, as in Zürich, all laws and concordats, or agreements with other cantons, and the chief matters of finance, as well as all revisions of the Constitution, must be submitted to the popular vote. In Appenzell, Glarus and Unterwalden the people exercise their powers direct in the *Landsgemeinde, i.e.*, the assembly in the open air of all male citizens of full age. In all the cantons the *popular initiative* for constitutional affairs, as well as for legislation, has been introduced, except in Lucerne, where the *initiative* exists only for constitutional affairs. In most cantons there are districts (*Amtsbezirke*) consisting of a number of communes grouped together, each district having a Prefect (*Regierungsstatthalter*) representing the cantonal government. In the larger communes, for local affairs, there is an Assembly (legislative) and a Council (executive) with a president, maire or syndic, and not less than 4 other members. In the smaller communes there is a council only, with its proper officials.

DEFENCE. There are fortifications in all entrances to the Alps and on the important passes crossing the Alps and the Jura. Large-scale destructions of bridges, tunnels and defiles are prepared for an emergency.

Army. Switzerland depends for defence upon a *national militia*. Service in this force is compulsory and universal, with few exemptions except for physical disability. Those excused or rejected pay certain taxes in lieu. Liability extends from the 20th to the end of the 50th year for soldiers and of the 55th year for officers. The first 12 years are spent in the first line, called the *Auszug*, or *Élite*, the next 10 in the *Landwehr* and 8 in the *Landsturm*. The unarmed *Hilfsdienst* comprises all other males between 20 and 50 whose services can be made available for non-combatant duties of any description.

The initial training of the Swiss militia soldier is carried out in recruits' schools, and the periods are 118 days for infantry, engineers, artillery, etc. The subsequent trainings, called 'repetition courses', are 20 days annually; but after going through 8 courses further attendance is excused for all under the rank of sergeant. The *Landwehr* men are called up for training courses of 13 days every 2 years, and the *Landsturm* men have to undergo a refresher course of 13 days.

The Army is divided into 3 field corps each of 1 armoured and 2 infantry divisions, 11 independent frontier brigades, 3 mountain divisions, and independent redoubt-, fortress- and territorial-brigades, organized in 4 army corps. Strength on mobilization (1988): 580,000, and 400,000 reserves.

The administration of the Swiss Army is partly in the hands of the Cantonal authorities, who can promote officers up to the rank of captain. But the Federal Government is concerned with all general questions and makes all the higher appointments.

In peace-time the Swiss Army has no general; only in time of war the Federal Assembly in joint session of both Houses appoints a general.

The Swiss infantry are armed with the Swiss automatic rifle and with machine-guns, bazookas and mortars. The field artillery is armed with a Q.F. shielded 10·5 Bofors and field howitzers of 10·5 cm calibre. The heavy artillery is armed with guns of 10·5 cm and howitzers of 15 cm calibre. Equipment includes Leopard, Centurian and P3-61/-68 tanks and 600 M-63/-73/-64 armoured personnel carriers.

Air Force. The Air Force has 3 flying regiments, with about 270 combat aircraft. The fighter squadrons are equipped with Swiss-built F-5E Tiger IIs (7 squadrons), Mirage IIIS supersonic interceptor/ground-attack (2 squadrons), Mirage IIIRS fighter/reconnaissance (1 squadron), and Hunter interceptor/ground-attack (9 squadrons) aircraft. Bloodhound surface-to-air missile batteries are operational.

Training aircraft are Pilatus P-3 and PC-7 Turbo-Trainer and Vampire; there are also communications and transport aircraft and helicopters. The Vampires will be replaced by Hawk trainers in 1989–90. Personnel (1988), 45,000 on mobilization.

INTERNATIONAL RELATIONS

Membership. Switzerland is a member of OECD, EFTA and the Council of Europe. In a referendum in 1986 the electorate voted against joining the UN.

ECONOMY

Budget. Revenue and expenditure of the Confederation, in 1m. francs, for calendar years:

	1980	1981	1982	1983	1984	1985	1986
Revenue	16,460	17,400	18,900	19,400	20,770	22,200	23,700
Expenditure	17,532	17,570	19,300	20,300	21,400	22,900	23,600

The public debt, including internal debt, of the Confederation in 1980 amounted to 24,409m. francs; 1981, 24,677m.; 1982, 24,968m.; 1983, 25,249m.; 1984, 27,700m.; 1985, 29,200m.

Schweizerisches Finanz-Jahrbuch. Bern. Annual. From 1899

Currency. The *franc* of 100 *Rappen* or *centimes* is the monetary unit. On 10 May 1971 there was a revaluation to 0·21759 gramme of fine gold.

The legal gold coins are 20- and 10-franc pieces; cupro-nickel coins are 5, 2, 1 and ½ franc, 20, 10 and 5 centimes; bronze, 2 and 1 centime. Notes are of 1,000, 500, 100, 50, 20, 10 and 5 francs.

On 10 July 1981 the notes in circulation (of francs of nominal value) was as follows: In 1,000 franc notes, 8,685·1m. francs; in 500, 4,201·9m. francs; in 100, 6,687·3m. francs; in 50, 1,058·3m. francs, and in lower denominations 1,195·8m.

In March 1988, £1 = 2·47 *francs*; US$1 = 1·39 *francs*.

Banking. The National Bank, with headquarters divided between Bern and Zürich, opened on 20 June 1907. It has the exclusive right to issue bank-notes. In 1984 the condition of the bank was as follows (in 1m. francs): Gold, 11,904, foreign exchange (currency), 38,800; currency in circulation, 26,500.

In 1986 there were 1,689 banking institutions with total assets of 805,000m. Swiss francs. They included 29 cantonal banks (154,600m. francs), 5 big banks (436,800m.), 215 regional banks (69,600m.), 1,243 loan and *Raiffeisen* banks (23,000m.), 197 other banks (121,000m.).

On 31 Dec. 1986 the total amount of savings deposits, deposit and investment accounts in Swiss banks was 167,100m. francs.

National Bank: Bulletin mensuel.—Das schweizerische Bankwesen. Yearly. From 1920

Weights and Measures. The metric system of weights and measures was made compulsory by the federal law on 3 July 1875 and since 1 Jan. 1887 only metric units have been legal. By the federal law of 24 June 1909 the international electric units were also adopted.

ENERGY AND NATURAL RESOURCES

Electricity. The total production of energy amounted to 57,330m. kwh. in 1986 of which 33,589m. kwh. were generated by hydro-electric plants. Supply 220 volts; 50 Hz.

Gas. The production of gas in 1986 was 54·52m. cu. metres.

Minerals. There are 2 salt-mining districts; that in Bex (Vaud) belongs to the canton, but is worked by a private company, and those at Schweizerhalle, Rheinfelden and Ryburg are worked by a joint-stock company formed by the cantons interested. The output of salt of all kinds in 1982 was 361,964 tonnes.

Agriculture. Of the total area of the country of 4,129,315 hectares, about 1,057,794 hectares (25·6%) are unproductive. Of the productive area of 3,071,521 hectares, 1,051,991 hectares are wooded. The agricultural area, in 1985, totalled 1,076,339 hectares, of which 287,049 hectares arable land, 13,450 hectares vineyards, 7,229 hectares intensive fruit growing and 642,194 hectares permanent meadow and pasture land. In 1985 there were 119,731 farms. The gross value of agricultural products was estimated at 7,243·1m. francs in 1980 and 8,325m. francs in 1983.

In 1985, 100,806 hectares were planted with bread grains; 83,113 hectares fodder cereals; 20,063 hectares potatoes; 14,247 hectares sugar-beet; 42,218 hectares silo and green maize. Production, 1986 (in 1,000 tonnes): Potatoes, 789; sugar-beet, 790; wheat, 530; barley, 270; maize, 157; tobacco, 1·5. Milk production (in 1,000 tonnes): 1960, 3,112; 1970, 3,204; 1980, 3,679; 1986, 3,867.

The fruit production (in 1,000 tonnes) in 1986 was: Apples, 280; pears, 130; plums, 38; cherries, 37; nuts, 5.

Wine is produced in 18 of the cantons. In 1986 Swiss vineyards yielded 1,344,492 hectolitres of wine.

Livestock (1986): 48,000 horses, 365,000 sheep, 1,902,000 cattle (including about 815,000 milch cows), 1,973,000 pigs, (1985) 6m. poultry.

Forestry. Of the forest area of 999,795 hectares, 56,876 were owned by the Federation or the cantons, 636,069 by communes and 306,850 by private persons or companies in 1982. Production (1985) 3,488 cu. metres of softwood and 1,073 cu. metres of hardwood.

INDUSTRY AND TRADE

Industry. The chief food producing industries, based on Swiss agriculture, are the manufacture of cheese, butter, sugar and meat. The production in 1985 was (in tonnes): Cheese, 126,400; butter, 37,800; sugar, 147,000; meat, 3,239,000. There are 46 breweries, producing in 1978, 4·05m. hectolitres of beer. Tobacco products in 1982: Cigars, 373·08m.; cigarettes, 26,497m.

Among the other industries, the manufacture of textiles, wearing apparel and footwear, chemicals and pharmaceutical products, bricks, glass and cement, the manufacture of basic iron and steel and of other metal products, the production of machinery (including electrical machinery and scientific and optical instruments) and watch and clock making are the most important. In 1981 there were 8,738 factories with 693,243 workers. In 1982, 41,200 were working in textile industries, 45,000 in the manufacture of clothing and footwear, 70,200 in chemical works, 194,700 in the construction industry, 168,600 in manufacture of metal products, 252,000 in the manufacture of machinery and 55,300 in watch and clock making and in the manufacture of jewellery.

Production in 1982 was: Woollen and blended yarn, 15,467 tonnes; woollen and blended cloth, 7,534 metres; footwear (1981), 5·87m. pairs; cement, 4,099,874 tonnes; raw aluminium, 75,256 tonnes; chocolate, 76,605 tonnes, 25·38m. watches and clocks were exported (1981).

Labour. In 1986, the total working population was 3,218,700, of which 209,200 were active in agriculture and forestry, 1,222,000 in manufacture and construction and 1,787,500 in services.

The foreign labour force with permit of temporary residence was 756,000 in Aug. 1985. Of the number recorded 281,800 were Italians, 89,400 Spaniards, 79,700 Frenchmen, 67,600 Germans and 28,700 Austrians.

The Swiss Federal Union of Administrative and Public Service Workers had, in 1985, a membership of 123,300. The Federation of Trade Unions had about 443,000 members.

Commerce. The special commerce, excluding gold (bullion and coins) and silver (coins), was (in 1m. Swiss francs) as follows:

	1978	1979	1980	1981	1982	1983	1984	1985	1986
Imports	42,299	48,730	60,859	60,094	58,060	61,064	69,024	74,750	73,513
Exports	41,779	44,024	49,608	52,822	52,659	53,724	60,654	66,624	67,004

The following table, in 1m. francs, shows the distribution of the special trade of Switzerland among the principal countries:

Countries	Imports from				Exports to			
	1983	1984	1985	1986	1983	1984	1985	1986
Federal Rep. of Germany	17,413·2	20,128·0	22,912·7	24,267·1	10,697·6	11,853·3	13,103·2	14,146·2
France	7,131·1	7,565·2	8,344·2	8,423·6	4,640·8	5,022·7	5,552·5	6,065·0
Italy	6,140·7	6,808·2	7,243·0	7,487·4	3,803·7	4,461·0	4,956·4	5,161·3
Netherlands	2,691·3	3,031·9	3,412·6	3,069·9	1,420·4	1,602·3	1,767·4	1,829·8
Belgium–Luxembourg	2,490·9	2,910·4	3,009·4	2,593·1	1,252·3	1,461·7	1,344·5	1,450·8
UK	3,303·2	4,974·7	5,425·2	5,375·0	3,481·5	4,834·6	5,298·9	5,182·1
Denmark	556·1	612·6	677·6	713·0	662·9	730·2	889·8	904·3
Portugal	–	–	–	271·6	–	–	–	413·2
Ireland	240·9	309·2	354·2	402·9	162·6	175·1	153·1	150·2
Spain	–	–	–	944·5	–	–	–	1,098·7
Greece	79·1	107·8	135·1	127·4	302·2	380·1	406·0	348·4
EEC Total	40,046·5	46,448·0	51,514·0	53,675·5	26,424·2	30,521·0	33,471·7	36,750·0
Austria	2,166·8	2,430·9	2,666·1	2,896·9	2,211·1	2,359·5	2,582·6	2,605·2
Norway	222·2	238·9	302·5	285·0	419·1	491·7	560·0	586·0
Sweden	1,030·1	1,199·1	1,377·2	1,330·6	1,067·2	1,204·5	1,317·3	1,300·2
Portugal	183·3	228·2	244·1	–	390·8	372·2	377·8	–
Finland	350·0	419·4	418·5	454·0	453·9	477·1	530·0	562·9
Iceland	90·2	74·4	66·9	64·5	17·1	18·4	20·3	19·6
EFTA	4,042·7	4,509·9	5,075·4	5,031·0	4,559·2	4,923·4	5,388·0	5,073·8
Spain	883·1	978·7	1,089·8	–	1,264·7	1,176·4	1,186·4	–
Gibraltar, Malta	1·6	2·3	4·1	...	23·8	23·3	25·0	...
German Dem. Republic	91·6	111·3	133·3	129·4	145·6	148·7	189·8	243·0
Poland	75·1	143·1	134·2	101·3	191·2	257·6	300·2	264·3
Czechoslovakia	199·0	189·8	194·6	163·4	244·9	261·7	310·2	324·4
Hungary	229·0	378·3	351·2	271·1	305·9	307·0	335·1	321·7
Yugoslavia	199·6	181·4	197·7	167·9	421·7	465·3	462·3	512·4
Bulgaria	25·0	49·8	33·4	23·2	225·2	287·8	233·3	279·2
Romania	32·5	38·4	48·9	38·9	48·5	59·4	84·8	52·3
USSR	1,412·6	1,217·1	1,196·4	722·0	463·0	466·1	636·5	535·2
Turkey	118·3	140·3	200·1	228·6	408·0	427·9	590·1	667·9
Other European countries	18·3	12·6	23·2	19·8	33·1	38·6	45·1	63·1
Europe Total	47,374·9	54,482·0	60,196·3	60,572·1	34,759·0	39,364·2	43,258·5	45,087·3
Egypt	61·6	82·8	58·2	27·0	414·5	437·9	395·9	291·3
Sudan	4·2	10·1	2·9	1·7	67·2	50·4	44·9	36·5
Libya	868·2	1,038·1	949·1	410·7	209·1	242·7	170·4	117·4
Tunisia	159·6	150·0	21·6	33·5	52·1	50·4	52·0	50·2
Algeria	523·3	447·3	417·6	166·3	162·6	203·3	242·3	200·7
Morocco	18·4	24·9	23·6	25·2	82·6	75·3	90·2	81·1
Côte d'Ivoire	33·6	51·0	67·3	56·5	39·8	42·9	46·2	55·3
Guinea	3·1	1·4	1·8	0·2	9·7	10·9	11·4	8·2
Ghana	32·6	23·9	30·3	30·1	20·6	20·6	21·5	32·8
Nigeria	155·8	160·1	439·0	147·8	340·3	242·4	344·6	279·7
Zaire	5·9	5·1	6·2	10·0	28·7	34·4	38·0	41·2
Angola	13·3	16·6	6·4	5·6	15·1	17·4	37·3	23·0
S Africa, Rep. of	193·5	203·7	171·4	154·3	489·3	549·5	482·9	430·9

Countries	Imports from				Exports to			
	1983	1984	1985	1986	1983	1984	1985	1986
Zambia	13·9	9·7	5·7	10·6	12·3	17·8	19·2	8·0
Zimbabwe	43·5	49·4	34·3	19·4	24·8	30·6	32·8	37·1
Tanzania	5·0	6·9	3·9	1·7	26·5	26·5	26·6	22·9
Kenya	26·9	37·1	35·0	40·7	31·1	30·7	35·6	43·7
Other African countries	94·6	89·3	117·5	101·2	399·9	199·5	216·4	223·4
Africa Total	2,257·0	2,407·4	2,391·8	1,242·5	2,426·2	2,283·2	2,308·2	1,983·4
Syria	5·4	1·8	3·1	6·5	129·1	79·2	95·3	59·1
Lebanon	78·3	76·9	55·4	93·2	138·1	144·5	81·4	75·5
Israel	215·8	255·5	260·3	233·6	549·6	597·7	843·0	749·3
Iraq	5·2	3·7	1·2	1·1	419·9	241·6	256·5	169·0
Kuwait	6·3	5·3	2·4	1·2	202·9	195·6	189·1	111·3
Iran	89·2	124·2	66·7	87·4	642·8	662·1	475·6	420·0
Saudi Arabia	349·2	387·1	307·7	188·7	1,717·1	1,571·7	1,410·7	981·6
UAE	52·2	7·0	96·3	7·1	275·3	408·4	342·0	224·3
Pakistan	51·7	47·7	46·9	54·0	136·6	158·8	197·8	259·2
India	140·6	149·9	173·8	173·3	301·6	368·7	381·4	549·9
Thailand	118·8	163·1	155·7	200·7	175·2	224·9	248·5	201·8
Malaysia	47·2	54·6	72·2	54·9	186·1	128·3	142·2	144·0
Singapore	85·3	242·4	93·8	87·1	422·7	586·5	457·7	415·6
China	157·4	194·5	218·0	185·3	262·6	291·0	589·1	738·3
Hong Kong	688·6	776·3	802·7	722·1	875·2	932·0	1,086·4	1,305·7
Taiwan	181·9	231·6	233·7	277·1	240·9	260·9	265·6	260·7
Korea, Rep. of	165·4	210·1	227·9	244·7	174·7	205·7	252·8	280·5
Japan	2,342·4	2,631·3	2,960·2	3,418·6	1,508·2	1,998·0	1,122·2	2,171·5
Philippines	33·4	44·8	41·0	31·7	93·4	87·9	101·2	104·6
Indonesia	43·4	52·7	70·2	64·4	152·4	186·4	155·9	193·6
Other Asian countries	57·3	83·0	73·6	97·4	409·3	448·2	543·4	464·6
Asia Total	4,915·0	5,743·5	5,962·8	6,230·1	9,013·7	9,778·1	10,237·8	9,880·1
Canada	270·9	262·2	274·7	240·9	575·2	554·4	759·8	719·5
USA	4,993·3	4,562·6	4,390·9	3,970·1	4,594·1	5,943·2	6,870·8	6,343·0
Mexico	36·3	52·4	43·6	40·4	180·8	258·5	358·5	341·3
Guatemala	48·4	41·3	47·3	55·3	21·5	30·7	28·1	17·2
Honduras	34·1	38·6	50·5	43·6	26·7	29·4	20·2	15·5
Costa Rica	46·3	49·4	68·4	63·3	10·4	15·7	15·2	17·6
Panama	270·9	428·8	217·8	161·6	268·9	307·8	233·6	176·9
Cuba	11·7	13·9	14·5	14·4	56·0	56·1	65·8	40·7
Colombia	84·7	119·3	140·6	145·2	120·0	107·1	160·9	127·1
Venezuela	16·0	10·3	17·3	9·2	166·8	205·2	190·0	215·2
Brazil	271·7	352·2	421·9	304·6	383·1	358·3	473·5	557·1
Uruguay	28·2	26·1	24·0	29·3	27·5	29·6	29·3	27·3
Argentina	113·0	109·2	132·0	83·5	228·2	228·4	293·1	223·7
Chile	17·4	18·0	18·1	21·2	72·7	80·6	83·0	95·0
Bolivia	3·1	5·1	2·5	0·7	6·3	12·2	9·4	11·9
Peru	28·8	19·9	35·7	34·8	69·9	74·2	86·0	126·4
Ecuador	9·2	15·4	23·5	20·0	48·0	52·3	68·4	67·4
Other American countries	104·8	132·0	126·7	89·1	185·3	238·3	338·5	230·9
Australia and Oceania	128·5	134·8	149·5	140·6	483·1	646·6	735·1	699·5

Custom receipts (in 1,000 francs): 1980, 3,170,700; 1981, 3,243,631; 1982, 3,243,000; 1983, 3,382,000; 1984, 3,393,000; 1985, 3,449,000.

Total trade between Switzerland (including Liechtenstein) and UK for calendar years (British Department of Trade, in £1,000 sterling):

	1983	1984	1985	1986	1987
Imports to UK	2,154,085	2,490,593	2,371,090	2,989,112	3,298,009
Exports and re-exports from UK	1,385,694	1,549,469	1,306,757	1,575,247	1,835,851

Federal Customs Office, *Statistique mensuelle du commerce extérieur de la Suisse.* From 1925.—*Statistique annuelle du commerce extérieur de la Suisse.* 2 vols. From 1840. —*Rapport annuel de la statistique du commerce Suisse.* From 1889

Tourism. Tourism is an important industry. In 1986, overnight stays in hotels and sanatoria were 35,461,000 and in other accommodation 39,427,000 (34,929,000 by foreign visitors).

COMMUNICATIONS

Roads. There were (1983) 70,848 km of main roads, including 1,300 km of 'national roads' for motor cars only. There is a postal autobus service, which, in 1976, carried 53·7m. passengers. Motor vehicles, as at 30 Sept. 1986, numbered 3,306,000, including 2,679,000 private cars, 207,000 trucks, 226,000 motor cycles, 11,000 buses and 184,000 commercial and agricultural vehicles.

Railways. Railway history in Switzerland begins in 1847. In 1986 the length of the general traffic railways was 5,034 km, and of special lines (funiculars etc.), 814 km. The operating receipts of general traffic lines amounted to (1984) 2,763,400,000 francs; operating expenses, 5,073,000,000 francs. Traffic (1986) was 45·1m. tonnes and 228·5m. passengers.

There are many privately-owned lines, the most important of which are the Bern–Lotschberg–Simplon (115 km) and Rhaetian (363 km) networks.

Aviation. In 1985 Swiss aviation on domestic and international routes carried 7,498,000 passengers.

The air transport organization Swissair (founded in 1931) in 1982 carried 189,139 tonnes of freight and 7,168,567 passengers. Swissair had a capital of 422m. francs on 15 May 1977. Its fleet consisted of 53 aircraft in Jan. 1983.

Shipping. A merchant marine was created by a decree of the Swiss Government dated 9 April 1941, the place of registry of its vessels being Basel. In 1985 it consisted of 39 vessels with a total of 225,434 GRT. In 1981, 8,277,359 tonnes of goods were handled in the port of Basel.

Post and Broadcasting. In 1985 there were 3,880 post offices. On 1 Jan. 1985 there were 5,435,800 telephones, all integrated in one dial system.

Wireless communication is furnished by 3 main medium-wave stations and 1 short-wave station. There are 3 television studios and more than 100 transmitters. TV programmes are financed by licence fees and advertisements. Advertisements are limited to 15 minutes each day. All stations are operated by the Federal Post, Telephone and Telegraph (PTT) services. Radio-telegraph circuits are operated by Radio Suisse SA, radio-telephone circuits by the PTT. Radio licences, 1985, 2,467,200; television licences, 2,186,500.

The total expenditure of the PTT in 1985 was 7,812·4m. francs, the total gross receipts 8,098·3m. francs.

Cinemas (1985). There were 437 cinemas with a seating capacity of 128,000.

Newspapers (1985). The number of daily newspapers was estimated to be 399.

JUSTICE, RELIGION, EDUCATION AND WELFARE

Justice. The Federal Tribunal (*Bundes-Gericht*), which sits at Lausanne, consists of 26-28 members, with 11-13 supplementary judges, appointed by the Federal Assembly for 6 years and eligible for re-election; the President and Vice-President serve for 2 years and cannot be re-elected. The President has a salary of 170,000 francs a year, and the other members 158,000 francs. The Tribunal has original and final jurisdiction in suits between the Confederation and cantons; between cantons and cantons; between the Confederation or cantons and corporations or individuals, the value in dispute being not less than 8,000 francs; between parties who refer their case to it, the value in dispute being at least 20,000 francs; in such suits as the constitution or legislation of cantons places within its authority; and in many classes of railway suits. It is a court of appeal against decisions of other federal authorities, and of cantonal authorities applying federal laws. The Tribunal also tries persons accused of treason or other offences against the Confederation. For this purpose it is divided into 4 chambers: Chamber of Accusation, Criminal Chamber (*Cour d'Assises*), Federal Penal Court and Court of Cassation. The jurors who serve in the Assize Courts are elected by the people, and are paid 100 francs a day when serving.

On 3 July 1938 the Swiss electorate accepted a new federal penal code, to take the place of the separate cantonal penal codes. The new code, which abolished capital punishment, came into force on 1 Jan. 1942.

Religion. There is complete and absolute liberty of conscience and of creed. No one is bound to pay taxes specially appropriated to defraying the expenses of a creed to which he does not belong. No bishoprics can be created on Swiss territory without the approbation of the Confederation.

According to the census of 1 Dec. 1980 Roman Catholics numbered 3,030,069 (47·6%) of the population; Protestants, 2,822,266 (44·3%) and others, 513,625 (8·1%). In 1960 Protestants were in a majority in 10 of the cantons and Catholics in 12. Of the more populous cantons, Zürich, Bern, Vaud, Neuchâtel and Basel (town and land) were mainly Protestant, while Luzern, Fribourg, Ticino, Valais and the Forest Cantons are mainly Catholic. The Roman Catholics are under 6 Bishops, viz., of Basel (resident at Solothurn), Chur, St Gallen, Lugano, Lausanne–Geneva–Fribourg (resident at Fribourg) and Sitten (Sion), all of them immediately subject to the Holy See. The Old Catholics have a theological faculty at the university of Bern.

Education. Education is administered by the cantons and is compulsory. Before the year 1848 most of the cantons had organized a system of primary schools, and since that year elementary education has steadily advanced. In 1874 it was made obligatory for the whole country (the school age varying in the different cantons) and placed under the civil authority. In some cantons the cost falls almost entirely on the communes, in others it is divided between the canton and communes. In all the cantons primary instruction is free. In 1986–87 there were 127,428 pupils in nursery schools and 373,245 in primary schools.

In most cantons there are also secondary schools for youths of from 12 to 15, gymnasia, higher schools for girls, teachers' seminaries, commercial and administrative schools, trade schools, art schools, technical schools, schools for the instruction of girls in domestic economy and other subjects, agricultural schools, schools for horticulture, for viticulture, for arboriculture and for dairy management. There are also institutions for the blind, the deaf and dumb and feeble-minded. In 1986–87 there were 316,370 pupils in secondary schools.

There are 7 universities in Switzerland. These universities are organized on the model of those of Germany, governed by a rector and a senate, and divided into faculties (theology, jurisprudence, philosophy, medicine, etc.). In 1986–87 the Federal Institute of Technology at Zürich (founded in 1855) had 632 teachers and 10,263 matriculated students; the Federal Institute of Technology at Lausanne, independent of the university since 1946, had 149 teachers and 3,170 students; the St Gall School of Economics and Social Sciences, founded in 1899, had 215 teachers and 3,198 matriculated students.

University statistics in the winter of 1986–87:

	The-ology	Humanities etc	Law	Eco-nomics	Medi-cine	Science	Teach-ing staff (1985–86)
Basel (1460)	223	1,687	881	848	1,761	1,275	625
Zürich (1523 & 1833)	358	7,463	3,138	2,239	3,354	2,101	1,661
Bern (1528 & 1834)	374	2,696	1,657	848	1,798	1,628	723
Genève (1559[1] & 1873[1])	130	4,578	995	2,411	1,506	1,645	913
Lausanne (1537[1] & 1890[2])	85	1,678	889	1,405	1,503	875	476
Fribourg (1889)	504	1,999	995	1,129	225	506	548
Neuchâtel (1866 & 1909)	52	870	310	444	57	524	240

[1] Founded as an academy. [2] Reorganized as a university.

These numbers are exclusive of 'visitors', but inclusive of women students. In 1985–86 there were 74,806 students attending universities.

Health. In 1985 there were 17,667 doctors, 37,360 (1980) nurses, 4,700 dentists and 9,900 physiotherapists. There were (1985) 456 hospitals and 1,366 pharmacies.

Social Security. The Federal Insurance Law against illness and accident, of 13 June 1911, entitles all Swiss citizens to insurance against illness; foreigners may be admitted to the benefits. Compulsory insurance against illness does not exist as yet, but cantons and communities are entitled to declare insurance obligatory for certain classes or to establish public benefit (sick fund) associations, and to make employers responsible for the payment of the premiums of their employees.

Unemployment insurance is based since 13 June 1976 upon a Constitution amendment which stipulates unemployment insurance as compulsory for all wage-earners.

Insurance against accident is compulsory for all officials, employees and workmen of all the factories, trades, etc., which are under the federal liability law.

On 6 July 1947 a federal law was accepted by a referendum, providing compulsory old age and widows and widowers insurance for the whole population, as from 1 Jan. 1948. In March 1985 the number of normal pensioners was 1,033,000.

DIPLOMATIC REPRESENTATIVES

Of Switzerland in Great Britain (16–18 Montagu Pl., London, W1H 2BQ)
Ambassador: François-Charles Pictet (accredited 9 Feb. 1984).

Of Great Britain in Switzerland (Thunstrasse 50, 3005 Bern)
Ambassador: Christopher Long.

Of Switzerland in the USA (2900 Cathedral Ave., NW, Washington, D.C., 20008)
Ambassador: Klaus Jacobi.

Of the USA in Switzerland (Jubilaeumstrasse 93, 3005, Bern)
Ambassador: Faith R. Whittlesey.

Books of Reference

Statistical Information: Bureau fédéral de statistique (Hallwylstr. 15, 3003 Bern) was established in 1860. *Director:* Carlo Malaguerra. Its principal publications are:

Annuaire statistique de la Suisse. Bâle. From 1891
Bibliographie Suisse de statistique et d'économie politique. Annual, from 1937
Reflêts de l'économie (monthly)

Swiss Confederation
Annuaire; Budget; Message du Budget; Compte d'Etat (annual) *Feuille Fédérale; Recueil des Lois fédérales* (weekly)
Recueil systématique des lois et ordonnances, 1848–1947 (in German, French and Italian). Bern, 1951
Sammlung der Bundes- und Kantonsverfassungen (in German, French and Italian). Bern, 1937

Federal Department of Economics
La vie économique (and supplements). Monthly. From 1928
Législation sociale de la Suisse. Annual, from 1928

McPhee, J., *The Swiss Army.* London, 1985
Riklin, A., *et al, Handbuch der schweizerischen Aussenpolitik.* Bern, 1975
Schwarz, U., *The Eye of the Hurricane: Switzerland in World War Two.* Boulder, 1980

National Library: Bibliothèque Nationale Suisse, Hallwylstr.15, 3003, Bern. *Director:* F. G. Maier.

SYRIA

Capital: Damascus
Population: 10·96m. (1986)
GNP per capita: US$2,000 (1984)

al-Jumhuriya al-Arabya as-Suriya

HISTORY. For the history of Syria from 1920 to 1946 *see* THE STATESMAN'S YEAR-BOOK, 1957, pp. 1408 f. Complete independence was achieved on 12 Apr. 1946. Syria merged with Egypt to form the United Arab Republic from 2 Feb. 1958 until 29 Sept. 1961, when independence was resumed following a *coup* the previous day. Lieut.-Gen. Hafez al-Assad became Prime Minister following the fifth *coup* of that decade on 13 Nov. 1970, and assumed the Presidency on 22 Feb. 1971.

AREA AND POPULATION. Syria is bounded by the Mediterranean and the Lebanese Republic on the west, by Israel and Jordan on the south, by Iraq on the east and by Turkey on the north. The frontier between Syria and Turkey (Nisibim-Jeziret ibn Omar) was settled by the Franco-Turkish agreement of 22 June 1929.

The area of Syria is 185,180 sq. km (71,498 sq. miles), of which 35,000 sq. km have been surveyed. The census of 1981 gave a total population of 9,050,204. Estimate (1986) 10·96m. of whom 49% were urban.

The areas and populations (1981 Census) of the 14 *mohafaza* (districts) are:

	Sq. km	1981 Census		Sq. km	1981 Census
City of Damascus	105	1,112,214	Idlib	6,097	579,581
Dimashq (Damascus)	18,032	917,364	Hasakah	23,334	669,887
Aleppo	18,500	1,878,701	Raqqah	19,616	348,383
Homs	42,223	812,517	Suwaydá	5,550	199,114
Hama	8,883	736,412	Dará	3,730	362,969
Lattakia	2,297	554,384	Tartous	1,892	443,290
Dayr az-Zawr	33,060	409,130	Qunaytirah	1,861	26,258

Principal towns (census 1981), Damascus, 1,251,028; Aleppo, 976,727; Homs, 354,508; Lattakia, 196,791; Hama, 176,640.

Arabic is the official language, spoken by 89% of the population, while 6% speak Kurdish (chiefly Hasakah governorate), 3% Armenian and 2% other languages.

CLIMATE. The climate is Mediterranean in type, with mild wet winters and dry, hot summers, though there are variations in temperatures and rainfall between the coastal regions and the interior, which even includes desert conditions. The more mountainous parts are subject to snowfall. Damascus. Jan. 45°F (7°C), July 81°F (27°C). Annual rainfall 9" (225 mm). Aleppo. Jan. 43°F (6·1°C), July 83°F (28·3°C). Annual rainfall 16" (401 mm). Homs. Jan. 45°F (7·2°C), July 83°F (28·3°C). Annual rainfall 12" (300 mm).

CONSTITUTION AND GOVERNMENT. A new Constitution was approved by plebiscite on 12 March 1973 and promulgated on 14 March. It confirmed the Arab Socialist Renaissance *(Ba'ath)* Party, in power since 1963, as the 'leading party in the State and society'. Legislative power is held by a 195-member People's Council, elected for a 4-year term. At the latest elections on 10 Nov. 1981, all seats were won by the National Progressive Front, a coalition of the Ba'ath Party and 4 smaller ones.

President: Lieut.-Gen. Hafez al-Assad (re-elected for further 7-year terms in 1978 and 1985).
First Vice-President: Abdul Halim Khaddam *(Political and Foreign Affairs).* *Second Vice-President:* Rifaat al-Assad *(Defence and Security). Third Vice-President:* Mohammed Zuhair Mashrqa *(Party Affairs).*

Prime Minister: Mahmoud Zubi.

National flag: Three horizontal stripes of red, white, black, with 2 green stars on the white stripe.

DEFENCE. Military service is compulsory for a period of 30 months.

Army. The Army is organized into 5 armoured and 4 mechanized divisions, 1 special forces division, 7 independent special forces regiments, 3 artillery, 3 surface-to-surface missile brigades and 9 surface-to-air missile battalions. Strength (1988) about 300,000 (including 130,000 conscripts) and reserves 50,000. There are a further 25,000 men in paramilitary forces. Equipment includes 1,800 T-54/-55, 1,100 T-62 and 1,100 T-72/-72M main battle tanks.

Navy. The Navy includes 3 old *ex*-Soviet diesel-powered patrol submarines (and another used as a battery changing platform), 2 small frigates, 12 fast missile boats, 3 minesweepers, 2 coastal minesweepers, 4 inshore minesweepers, 6 coastal patrol craft and 1 diving ship (all *ex*-Soviet). Personnel in 1988 totalled 2,500 officers and men.

Air Force. The Air Force, including Air Defence Command, was believed (1988) to have about 70,000 personnel and over 500 first-line jet combat aircraft, made up of about 200 MiG-21, 60 MiG-23 and 24 MiG-25 supersonic interceptors, 60 MiG-23, 40 Su-7, 60 Su-22 and 50 MiG-17 fighter-bombers, plus some MiG-25 reconnaissance aircraft. Additional aircraft are being purchased from the USSR. Training units have Spanish-built Flamingo piston-engined primary trainers and Czechoslovakian L-29 Delfin and L-39 jet basic trainers. There are also transport units with Il-76, An-12, An-24/26, Il-14 and other types, and helicopter units with Soviet-built Ka-25s, Mi-6s, Mi-8s and Mi-24 gunships, and French-built Gazelles. 'Guideline', 'Goa', 'Gainful' and 'Gaskin' surface-to-air missiles are widely deployed in Syria by Air Defence Command, and 'Gammon' long-range surface-to-air missiles in Lebanon.

INTERNATIONAL RELATIONS

Membership. Syria is a member of UN and the Arab League.

ECONOMY

Planning. The total investment envisaged in the fifth 5-year plan (1981–85) £Syr.101,493m.

Budget. The ordinary budget for the calendar year 1986 provides for expenditure of £Syr.43,841m.

Currency. The monetary unit is the Syrian *pound*, divided into 100 *piastres*. In March 1988, £1 = £Syr.53·21; US$1 = £Syr.30·00.

Banking. The Central Bank has the sole right of issuing currency. Other banks were nationalized in March 1963, namely, the Omaya Bank and its subsidiary, the Popular Mortgage Bank; the Orient Arab Bank; the Bank of Syria and Overseas; the Agricultural Bank; the Arab World Bank. Number of branches, 1973: Central Bank of Syria, 9; Commercial Bank of Syria, 22; Industrial Bank, 3; Agricultural Co-operative Bank, 50; Real Estate Bank, 3; Bank of Popular Discount, 27.

Weights and Measures. A decree dated 22 Aug. 1935 makes the use of the metric system legal and obligatory throughout the whole of the country. In outlying districts the former weights and measures may still be in use. They are: 1 *okiya* = 0·47 lb.; 6 *okiyas* = 1 *oke* = 2·82 lb.; 2 *okes* = 1 *rottol* = 5·64 lb.; 200 *okes* = 1 *kantar.*

ENERGY AND NATURAL RESOURCES

Electricity. Production (1986) 8,050m. kwh.

Oil. A branch of the Iraq Petroleum Co.'s oil pipeline from Kirkuk crosses Syria between Makaleb in the east and Nahr el Kebir valley in the west. The Iraq Petroleum Co. has constructed a new pipeline from Kirkuk to the small fishing port of Banias (south of Lattakia), which came into use in April 1952; the Trans-Arabian Pipeline Co.'s line to Sidon crosses southern Syria. Crude oil production (1987) 12m. tonnes. Reserves (1983) 1,521m. bbls.

Gas. Gas reserves (1982) 700,000m. cubic ft. Production (1983) 75·86m. cu. metres.

Minerals. Phosphate deposits have been discovered at two places near al-Shargiya and at Khneifis. Production, 1983, 1·23m. tonnes; other minerals were salt, 87,000 tonnes and gypsum 350,000 tonnes. There are indications of lead, copper, antimony, nickel, chrome and other minerals widely distributed. Sodium chloride and bitumen deposits are being worked.

Agriculture. In 1986, 162,000 hectares were under cotton, 1,098,000 hectares under wheat and 1,548,000 hectares under barley. The total cultivable area in 1983 was 14,592,000 hectares, including 500,000 hectares of forest and 8,444,000 hectares of steppe and pasture.

Production of principal crops, 1986 (in 1,000 tonnes): Wheat, 1,969; barley, 1,116; seed cotton, 419; olives, 399; lentils, 63; millet, 10; sugar-beet, 508.

Livestock (1986): Cattle, 750,000; asses, 198,000; sheep, 12·5m.; goats, 1,075,000; poultry, 15m.

Fisheries. The total catch in 1983 was 3,777 tonnes.

INDUSTRY AND TRADE

Industry. The most important industries are flour, oils, soap, cement, tanning, tobacco, textiles, knitwear, glassware, spinning, sugar, margarine, hosiery, footwear and brassware. Industrial production in 1980 included (in 1,000 tonnes): Woollen fabrics, 1,200; cement, 2,310; sugar, 141; salt, 111; cotton yarn, 25·2; manufactured tobacco, 9·9.

Commerce. Trade in calendar years in £Syr.1m. was as follows:

	1981	1982	1983	1984
Imports	19,781	15,727	17,829	16,155
Exports	8,254	7,954	7,548	7,275

In 1984 imports came from Iran (22·7%), Libya (7·7%), Federal Germany (5·9%), France (5·1%), Italy (4·6%) and included crude oil and power generating machinery. Exports went to Romania (28·2%), Italy (19·8%), USSR (11·5%) and France (12·2%) and included petroleum products (63·1%).

Total trade between Syria and UK (British Department of Trade returns, in £1,000 sterling):

	1983	1984	1985	1986	1987
Imports to UK	18,859	59,245	78,575	31,298	24,937
Exports and re-exports from UK	72,320	91,909	80,901	55,511	34,053

Tourism. In 1986, there were 1·16m. visitors.

COMMUNICATIONS

Roads. In 1980 there were 13,000 km of asphalted roads, 1,300 km of macadam non-asphalted road and 6,000 km of earth roads. The first-class roads are capable of carrying all types of modern motor transport and are usable all the year round, while the second-class roads are usable during the dry season only, *i.e.*, for about 9 months. The motor vehicles registered in 1981 were 93,000 motor cycles, 9,935 buses, 75,200 cars and 93,300 goods vehicles.

Railways. Network totals 1,686 km of 1,435 mm gauge (Syrian Railways) and 246 km of 1,050 mm gauge (Hedjaz-Syrian Railway). In 1985 the Syrian Railways network carried 3·4m. passengers and 4·6m. tonnes of freight.

Aviation. In 1980, 12,557 aircraft arrived at Damascus and Aleppo airports, disembarking 559,430 passengers.

Shipping. The amount of cargo discharged in 1980 was 2·6m. tons and the amount loaded 430,000 tons.

Post and Broadcasting. Number of telephones (1983), 468,922; of these, 152,203 were in Damascus and 71,135 in Aleppo. There were 2m. radio sets in 1985 and 400,000 television receivers.

Newspapers. There were (1984) 3 national daily newspapers in Damascus; other dailies and periodicals appear in Hama, Homs, Aleppo and Lattakia.

JUSTICE, RELIGION, EDUCATION AND WELFARE

Justice. Syrian law is based on both Islamic and French jurisprudence. There are 2 courts of first instance in each district, one for civil and 1 for criminal cases. There is also a Summary Court in each sub-district, under Justices of the Peace. There is a Court of Appeal in the capital of each governorate, with a Court of Cassation in Damascus.

Religion. The population is composed 90% of Sunni Moslems and there are also Shiites and Ismailis. There are also Druzes and Alawites. Christians include Greek Orthodox, Greek Catholics, Armenian Orthodox, Syrian Orthodox, Armenian Catholics, Protestants, Maronites, Syrian Catholics, Latins, Nestorians and Assyrians. There are also Jews and Yezides.

Education. The Syrian University was founded in 1924, although the faculties of law and of medicine had existed previously. In 1975 there were 3 universities with 94,794 students.

In 1983–84 there were 8,489 primary schools with 67,086 teachers and 1,823,684 pupils; secondary and intermediate schools, with 26,366 teachers and 701,330 pupils; vocational and teacher-training schools had 5,447 teachers and 64,596 pupils; 41 higher education establishments had 123,735 students.

Health. In 1984 there were 11,595 hospital beds (1 per 875 persons) in 182 hospitals; there were also 5,543 doctors, 2,045 dentists, 2,367 pharmacists, 2,071 midwives and 7,923 nursing personnel.

DIPLOMATIC REPRESENTATIVES

Of Syria in the USA (2215 Wyoming Ave., NW, Washington, D.C., 20008)
Chargé d'Affaires: Bushra Kanafani.

Of the USA in Syria (Abu Rumaneh, Al Mansur St., Damascus)
Ambassador: William L. Eagleton, Jr.

Of Syria to the United Nations
Ambassador: (Vacant).

Diplomatic relations with Syria were broken off by the UK on 31 Oct. 1986.

Books of Reference

Statistical Information: There is a Central Statistics Bureau affiliated to the Council of Ministers, Damascus. It publishes a monthly summary and an annual Statistical Abstract (in Arabic and English).

Abd-Allah, U. F., *The Islamic Struggle in Syria.* Berkeley, 1983
Barthélemy, A., *Dictionnaire arabe-français. Dialectes de Syrie.* 4 vols. Paris, 1935–50
Devlin, J. F., *Syria: Modern State in an Ancient Land.* Boulder, 1983
Maoz, M., and Yaniv, A., *Syria under Assad.* New York, 1986
Seale, P., *The Struggle for Syria.* London, 1986
Seccombe, I. J., *Syria.* [Bibliography] Oxford and Santa Barbara, 1987

TANZANIA

Jamhuri ya Muungano wa Tanzania

Capital: Dodoma
Population: 23·2m. (1987)
GNP per capita: US$210 (1984)

HISTORY. German East Africa was occupied by German colonialists from 1884 and placed under the protection of the German Empire in 1891. It was conquered in the First World War and subsequently divided between the British and Belgians. The latter received the territories of Ruanda and Urundi and the British the remainder, except for the Kionga triangle, which went to Portugal. The country was administered as a League of Nations mandate until 1946 and then as a UN trusteeship territory until 9 Dec. 1961.

Tanganyika achieved responsible government in Sept. 1960 and full self-government on 1 May 1961. On 9 Dec. 1961 Tanganyika became a sovereign independent member state of the Commonwealth of Nations. It adopted a republican form of government on 9 Dec. 1962. For history from the end of the 17th century until 1884 *see* THE STATESMAN'S YEAR-BOOK 1982–83, p. 1170.

On 24 June 1963 Zanzibar became an internal self-governing state and on 9 Dec. 1963 she became independent. On 24 June 1963 the Legislative Council was replaced by a National Assembly.

On 12 Jan. 1964 the sultanate was overthrown and the sultan sent into exile by a revolt of the Afro-Shirazi Party leaders who established the People's Republic of Zanzibar.

On 26 April 1964 Tanganyika, Zanzibar and Pemba combined to form the United Republic of Tanganyika and Zanzibar (named Tanzania on 29 Oct.).

AREA AND POPULATION. Tanzania is bounded north-east by Kenya, north by Lake Victoria and Uganda, north-west by Rwanda and Burundi, west by Lake Tanganyika, south-west by Zambia and Malaŵi and south by Mozambique. Total area 945,050 sq. km (364,886 sq. miles). The census of Aug. 1978 gave 17,551,925 for the United Republic, of which 17,076,270 were counted in mainland Tanzania and 475,655 in Zanzibar and Pemba. Estimate (1987) 23·2m. There were also (1986) about 209,000 refugees living in Tanzania.

The chief towns (1978 census populations) are Dar es Salaam, the chief port and former capital (757,346), Zanzibar Town (110,669), Mwanza (110,611), Dodoma, the capital (45,703), Tanga (103,409), Arusha (55,281), Mbeya (76,606), Morogoro (61,890), Mtwara (48,510), Tabora (67,392), Iringa (57,182), and Kigoma (50,044).

The United Republic is divided into 25 administrative regions of which 20 are in mainland Tanzania, 3 in Zanzibar and 2 in Pemba. The 1985 estimated population of the islands was 571,000, of which 45% (256,950) were in Pemba and 55% (314,050) in Zanzibar.

The estimated populations of the 20 mainland regions were as follows in 1985:

Arusha	1,183,000	Lindi	604,000	Rukwa	603,000
Dar es Salaam	1,394,000	Mara	862,000	Ruvuma	691,000
Dodoma	1,171,000	Mbeya	1,335,000	Shinyanga	1,662,000
Iringa	1,100,000	Morogoro	1,134,000	Singida	730,000
Kagera	1,298,000	Mtwara	878,000	Tabora	1,089,000
Kigoma	782,000	Mwanza	1,736,000	Tanga	1,236,000
Kilimanjaro	1,093,000	Pwani	578,000		

Kiswahili is the national language and English is the official language.

CLIMATE. The climate is very varied and is controlled very largely by altitude and distance from the sea. There are three climatic zones: the hot and humid coast, the drier central plateau with seasonal variations of temperature, and the semi-temperate mountains. Dodoma. Jan. 75°F (23·9°C), July 67°F (19·4°C). Annual

1172

rainfall 23″ (572 mm). Dar es Salaam. Jan. 82°F (27·8°C), July 74°F (23·3°C). Annual rainfall 43″ (1,064 mm).

CONSTITUTION AND GOVERNMENT. A permanent Constitution was approved in April 1977. The country is a one-party state. The Tanganyika African National Union and the Afro-Shirazi Party in Zanzibar merged into one revolutionary party, *Chama cha Mapinduzi*, in Feb. 1977.

The President of the United Republic is head of state, chairman of the party and commander-in-chief of the armed forces. The second vice-president is head of the executive in Zanzibar.The Prime Minister and first vice-president is also the leader of government business in the National Assembly.

According to the Constitution of 1977, as amended in Oct. 1984, the National Assembly is composed of a total of 244 members: 169 Members of Parliament elected from the Constituencies (119 from the mainland and 50 from Zanzibar); 15 National Members elected by the National Assembly; 15 women members elected by the National Assembly, 5 from Zanzibar; 5 members elected by the House of Representatives in Zanzibar; 25 ex-officio Members (20 Regional Commissioners from the mainland and 5 from Zanzibar) and 15 Nominated Members (by the President), 5 from Zanzibar.

In Dec. 1979 a separate Constitution for Zanzibar was approved. Although at present (1981) under the same Constitution as Tanzania, Zanzibar has, in fact, been ruled by decree since 1964.

The Government was in Jan. 1988 composed as follows:

President of the United Republic: Ndugu Ali Hassan Mwinyi (sworn in 5 Nov. 1985 for 5-year term).

Prime Minister and First Vice President: Joseph S. Warioba.

President of Zanzibar and Second Vice President: Idris A. Wakil. *Without Portfolio:* Rashidi Kawawa. *Deputy Prime Minister, Defence and National Service:* Salim Ahmed Salim. *Finance, Economic Affairs and Planning:* Cleopa D. Msuya. *Foreign Affairs:* Benjamin Mkapa. *Agriculture and Livestock Development:* Jackson Makwetta. *Local Government and Co-operatives:* K. Ngombale Mwiru. *Communications and Works:* Mustafa Nyang'anyi. *Labour and Manpower Development:* Paul Bomani. *Home Affairs:* Muhiddin Kimario. *Education:* Kighoma Malima. *Mineral Resources and Energy:* Al Noor Kassum. *Lands, Natural Resources and Tourism:* Getrude Mongella. *Industries and Trade:* Daudi Mwallawago. *Health and Social Welfare:* Dr Aaron Chiduo. *Attorney General and Justice:* Damian Lubuva. *Water:* Dr Pius Ng'wandu. *Community Development, Culture, Youth and Sports:* Fatma Saidi Ali. There are 6 Ministers of State and 10 Deputy Ministers.

National flag: Divided diagonally green, black, blue, with the black strip edged in yellow.

DEFENCE

Army. The Army consists of 8 infantry, 1 tank brigade; 2 artillery, 2 anti-aircraft, 2 mortar, 1 surface-to-air missile, 2 anti-tank and 2 signals battalions. Equipment includes 30 Chinese Type-59 main battle tanks. Strength (1988) 38,350. There is also a Citizen's Militia of 100,000 men.

Navy. There are 6 *ex*-Chinese fast gunboats, 4 *ex*-GDR gunboats, 4 *ex*-Chinese fast torpedo hydrofoil boats, 4 *ex*-North Korean patrol craft, 4 *ex*-Chinese coastal patrol boats, 1 survey launch, 1 research vessel and 2 *ex*-Chinese minor landing craft. Personnel in 1988 totalled some 700.

Air Force. The Tanzanian People's Defence Force Air Wing was built up initially with the help of Canada, but combat equipment is now being acquired from China. Personnel totalled about 1,000 in 1988, with about 10 F-7 (MiG-21), 10 F-6 (MiG-19) and 3 F-5 (MiG-17) jet fighters; 1 F28 Fellowship VIP transport; 5 Buffalo twin-engined STOL transports; 3 HS 748 turboprop transports; 2 Cessna 404 liaison aircraft; 2 Agusta-built Chinook helicopters; 4 Agusta-Bell AB.205 transport helicopters, and 4 JetRanger and 2 Bell 47G light helicopters; and Piper Cherokee, Cessna 310 and FT-2 (Chinese-built MiG-15 UTI) trainers.

INTERNATIONAL RELATIONS

Membership. Tanzania is a member of UN, OAU, the Commonwealth, Non-Aligned Movement and is an ACP state of EEC.

ECONOMY

Planning. The fourth 5-year development (1981–86) plan envisaged investment of Sh. 40,200m. and a growth rate of 6%.

Budget. Revenue and expenditure (in Tanzanian Sh. 1m.) for financial years ending 30 June:

	1980–81	1981–82	1982–83[1]	1983–84[1]	1984–85[1]
Revenue	12,296·1	10,460	10,700	12,500	18,000
Expenditure	14,802·4	13,687	14,144	15,620	20,674

[1]Estimate.

Currency. The monetary unit is the *Tanzanian shilling* divided into 100 *cents*. The Tanzanian coinage has denominations of 5, 10, 20, 50 cents, 1 Sh., 5 Sh., 20 Sh. and 1,500 Sh.; notes, 10 Sh., 20 Sh., 50 Sh., 100 Sh. and 200 Sh. In March 1988, £1 = Sh. 163·10; US$ = Sh. 92·82.

Banking. On 14 June 1966 the central bank called the Bank of Tanzania, with a government-owned capital of Sh. 20m., began operations.

On 6 Feb. 1967 all commercial banks with the exception of National Co-operative Banks were nationalized and their interests vested in the National Bank of Commerce on the mainland and the Peoples' Bank in Zanzibar.

Weights. The metric system is in force.

ENERGY AND NATURAL RESOURCES

Electricity. A 21 mw hydro-electric power-station on the Pangani River was commissioned in 1964. The first phase of the Kidatu power-station in Morogoro region with an installed capacity of 100 mw was commissioned in 1975. The second phase with an additional 100 mw was commissioned in 1981. The third phase (Mtera power-station) with a capacity of 80 mw is scheduled for completion in 1988. Production (1986) 830m. kwh. Supply 230 volts; 50 Hz.

Minerals. Production (1984): Diamonds, 53,195 grammes; gold, 96,530 grammes; salt, 29,907 tonnes; gemstones, 38,884 kg. Large deposits of coal and tin exist but mining is on a small scale. Exploration is going on to establish economic deposits of copper, cobalt and nickel, and feasibility studies to exploit iron ore deposits in south-western Tanzania. Work is under way to utilize natural gas deposits at Songo Songo off the coast south of Dar es Salaam.

Agriculture. Production of main agricultural crops in 1985 (in 1,000 tonnes) was: Sisal, 40; seed cotton, 136; sugar-cane, 1,310; coffee, 56; tobacco, 17; maize, 2,093; wheat, 83; cashew nuts, 45; citrus, 30. Production of sisal has been declining since 1967. The Tanganyika Sisal Corporation has embarked on a diversification programme by introducing various new crops. Crops already planned are cardamom, beans, cashew nuts, citrus, cocoa, coconuts, cotton, maize and timber. Cattle ranching, dairying and twine spinning have also been introduced.

Zanzibar provides the greater part of the world's supply of cloves, which account for over 90% of foreign earnings. There are about 40,000 hectares under cloves with about 1·5m. trees; five-sixths of the clove output is produced on Pemba. The clove industry is undergoing a rehabilitation programme to increase production, which in 1980–81 was 7,497 tons; 1984–85, over 8,700 tons.

A 10-year programme to rehabilitate the coconut industry started in 1980. By 1985 over 23m. trees were under plantation on the mainland and Zanzibar. Chillies, cocoa, limes, other tropical fruits and coil tobacco are also cultivated. The chief food crops are rice, bananas, cassava, pulses, maize and sorghum.

Livestock (1986, including Zanzibar): 14·3m. cattle, 4·3m. sheep, 6·5m. goats, 31m. poultry.

Forestry. Total forested land 43m. hectares. Total production (1983) 114,900 cu. metres.

Fisheries. A Fisheries Development Co. is catching sardines and tuna for export. Catch (1983) 237,148 tonnes of which, inland waters, 202,662 tonnes.

INDUSTRY AND TRADE

Industry. Industry is limited and is mainly textiles, petroleum and chemical products, food processing, tobacco, brewing and paper manufacturing.

Commerce. Total trade (in Sh. 1m.):

	1979	1980	1981	1982	1983	1984
Imports	8,941	10,047	10,065	7,781	8,877	11,953
Exports	4,296	4,165	5,248	4,117	4,138	5,661

Imports and exports (in Tanzanian Sh. 1m.), by country, 1984:

Country	Imports	Exports	Country	Imports	Exports
Bahrain	207·3	–	Iran	795·3	–
Belgium	510·1	79·2	Italy	990·8	320·7
China	250·8	40·0	Japan	1,167·5	306·1
Denmark	273·4	29·7	Netherlands	560·0	399·1
Federal Republic			Sweden	476·6	12·5
of Germany	1,294·2	1,206·8	Switzerland	207·7	217·1
India	180·0	361·5	Thailand	338·0	5·6

Major export items 1984 (in Sh. 1m.): Coffee, 2,216; cotton, 713; sisal, 146; cloves, 136; tea, 330; tobacco, 110; cashew nuts, 439; diamonds, 327.

Total trade between Tanzania and UK (British Department of Trade returns, in £1,000 sterling):

	1984	1985	1986	1987
Imports to UK	43,179	46,640	40,268	26,400
Exports and re-exports from UK	60,440	88,622	62,869	91,874

Tourism. In 1985 about 59,000 visitors.

COMMUNICATIONS

Roads. In 1984 there were 45,202 km of roads and (1983) 43,248 cars and 12,579 licensed commercial vehicles of which 11,290 were trucks and 1,289 buses.

Railways. On 23 Sept. 1977 the independent Tanzanian Railway Corporation was formed following the break-up of the East African Railways administration. The network totals 2,600 km (metre-gauge), excluding the Tan-Zam Railway 969 km in Tanzania (1,067 mm gauge) operated by a separate administration. In 1986, the state railway carried 3m. passengers and 989,000 tonnes of freight while in 1983–84 the Tan-Zam Railway carried 950,000 tonnes of freight and 1m. passengers.

Aviation. There are 53 aerodromes and landing strips maintained or licensed by Government; of these, 2 are of international standards category (Dar es Salaam and Kilimanjaro) and 18 are suitable for Dakotas. Air Tanzania Corporation provide regular and frequent services to all the more important towns within the territory and to Mozambique, Zambia, Seychelles, Comoro, Rwanda, Burundi and Madagascar.

There is an all-weather landing-ground in Zanzibar and a smaller all-weather landing-ground in Pemba.

Shipping. In 1980 there were 1,296 ships of 3,176,000 NRT.

Post and Broadcasting. In 1983 there were 99,885 telephones. There are 2 broadcasting stations (1 for mainland Tanzania and 1 for Zanzibar) and colour television operates in Zanzibar. In 1984 there were 9,000 television receivers (on Zanzibar only) and 2m. radio receivers.

Newspapers (1985). There were 3 dailies, 2 weeklies and several monthly magazines.

JUSTICE, RELIGION, EDUCATION AND WELFARE

Justice. The Judiciary is independent in both judicial and administrative matters and is composed of a 4-tier system of Courts: Primary Courts; District and Resident Magistrates' Courts; the High Court and the Court of Appeal. The Chief Justice is head of the Court of Appeal and the Judiciary Department. The Court's main registry is at Dar es Salaam; its jurisdiction includes Zanzibar. The Principal Judge is head of the High Court, also headquartered at Dar es Salaam, which has resident judges at 7 regional centres.

Religion. In 1984 some 40% were Christian, including Roman Catholics under the Archbishops of Dar es Salaam and Tabora, Anglicans under the Archbishop of Tanzania, and Lutherans. Moslems amount to 33%, but reach 66% in the coastal towns; Zanzibar is 96% Moslem and 4% Hindu. Some 23% follow traditional religions.

Education. In 1984 there were 10,110 primary schools with 3,493,469 pupils, and 170 secondary schools (85 private) with 74,208 students.

Technical and vocational education is provided at several secondary and technical schools and at the Dar es Salaam Technical College.

There were, in 1984, 63 teachers' colleges, including the college at Chang'ombe for secondary-school teachers, with 14,270 students.

The University of Dar es Salaam, independent since 1970, has faculties of law, arts, social sciences, medicine, engineering, commerce and management. Sokoine University of Agriculture, established in 1984, has faculties of agriculture, forestry and veterinary medicine. The total number of students in both universities was 3,320 in 1984.

Health. In 1984 there were 1,065 doctors and 152 hospitals with 22,800 beds.

DIPLOMATIC REPRESENTATIVES

Of Tanzania in Great Britain (43 Hertford St., London, W1)
High Commissioner: Anthony Balthazar Nyakyi.

Of Great Britain in Tanzania (Hifadhi Hse., Samora Ave., Dar es Salaam)
High Commissioner: Colin H. Imray, CMG.

Of Tanzania in the USA (2139 R. St., NW, Washington, D.C., 20008)
Ambassador: Asterius M. Hyera.

Of the USA in Tanzania (36 Laibon Rd., Dar es Salaam)
Ambassador: Donald Petterson.

Of Tanzania to the United Nations
Ambassador: Dr Wilbert K. Chagula.

Books of Reference

Atlas of Tanganyika. 3rd ed. Dar es Salaam, 1956
Tanganyika Notes and Records. Tanganyika Society, Dar es Salaam. (Twice yearly, from 1936) *The Economic Development of Tanganyika. Report . . . by the International Bank.* Johns Hopkins Univ. Press and OUP, 1961
Ayany, S. G., *A History of Zanzibar.* Nairobi, 1970
Coulson, A., *Tanzania: A Political Economy.* OUP, 1982
Nyerere, J., *Freedom and Development.* New York, 1976
Resnick, I. N., *The Long Transition: Building Socialism in Tanzania.* New York and London, 1981
Samoff, J., *Tanzania: Local Politics and the Structure of Power.* Univ. of Wisconsin Press, 1975
Yeager, R., *Tanzania: An African Experiment.* Aldershot, 1982

THAILAND

Capital: Bangkok
Population: 52·5m. (1986)
GNP per capita: US$720 (1985)

Prathes Thai, or Muang-Thai

HISTORY. Until 24 June 1932 Siam was an absolute monarchy. On that date a *coup d'état* was effected and a Provisional Constitution Act was promulgated on 27 June. This was replaced by the constitution of 10 Dec. 1932, which in turn was superseded by new constitutions.

AREA AND POPULATION. Thailand is bounded west by Burma, north and east by Laos and south-east by Cambodia. In the south it becomes a peninsula bounded west by the Indian Ocean, south by Malaysia and east by the Gulf of Thailand. Area is 513,115 sq. km (198,456 sq. miles).

At the census taken in 1980 the registration gave a population of 46,961,338, of whom 30·4% lived in the Central region, 35·2% in the North-East region, 12·5% in the South region, 21·9% in the North region. Estimate (1986) 52,545,529 (26,114,610 females).

Vital statistics, 1983: Births, 1,055,802 (520,728 females); deaths, 252,592 (107,776 females).

Thailand is divided into 73 provinces. Provinces with over 1m. population 1986 were Nakhon Ratchasima (2,243,845), Ubon Ratchathani (1,758,868), Udon Thani (1,690,356), Khon Kaen (1,600,732), Nakhon Si Thamarat (1,359,740), Buri Ram (1,316,393), Chiang Mai (1,285,662), Si Saket (1,222,743), Surin (1,203,943), Roi Ed (1,157,174), Nakhon Sawan (1,047,163) and Songkhla (1,008,198).

Bangkok Metropolis is the capital (population 1986, 5,446,708). Other towns (1980 census) are Chiang Mai (101,595), Hat Yai (93,519), Khon Kaen, (85,863), Phitsanulok (79,942), Nakhon Ratchasima (78,246), Udon Thani (71,142), Songkhla (67,945), Nakhon Sawan (63,935), Nakhon Si Thammarat (63,162), Ubon Ratchathani (50,788), Ayutthaya (47,189), Nakhon Pathom (45,242), Lampang (42,301) and Ratchaburi (40,404).

Thai is the national language. Several Chinese dialects are also spoken in Bangkok and the north and some Malay in the south. English is increasingly used in tourist areas.

CLIMATE. The climate is tropical, with high temperatures and humidity. Over most of the country, 3 seasons may be recognized. The rainy season is June to Oct., the cool season from Nov. to Feb. and the hot season is March to May. Rainfall is generally heaviest in the south and lightest in the north east.

Bangkok. Jan. 78°F (25·6°C), July 83°F (28·3°C). Annual rainfall 56″ (1,400 mm).

REIGNING KING. Bhumibol Adulyadej, born 5 Dec. 1927, younger brother of King Ananda Mahidol, who died on 9 June 1946. King Bhumibol married on 28 April 1950 Princess Sirikit, and was crowned 5 May 1950. Children: Princess Ubol Ratana (born 5 April 1951, married Aug. 1972 Peter Ladd Jensen), Crown-Prince Vajiralongkorn (born 28 July 1952, married 3 Jan. 1977 Soamsawali Kitiyakra), Princess Maha Chakri Sirindhorn (born 2 April 1955), Princess Chulabhorn (born 4 July 1957, married 7 Jan. 1982 Virayudth Didyasarin).

CONSTITUTION AND GOVERNMENT. The military government resigned on 14 Oct. 1973 and a new government was formed. A new Constitution designed to restore democracy was promulgated in Dec. 1978. A general election was held on 27 July 1986. Of the 347 seats in Parliament, the Democrat Party won 100, the Chart Thai Party 63.

The cabinet in Dec. 1987 was composed as follows:

Prime Minister: Gen. Prem Tinasulanonda.

Deputy Prime Ministers: Bhichai Rattakul, Maj.-Gen. Chatichai Choonhavan, Pong Sarasin, Adm. Sonthi Boonyachai, Gen. Tienchai Sirisumpun. *Ministers of the Prime Minister's Office:* Meechai Ruchupan, Arun Bhanupong, Flight-Lieut. Sulee Mahasanthana, Chaisiri Ruangkanchanases, Amnuay Suwankiri, Vichit Saengthong. *Interior:* Gen. Prachuab Soontarangkun. *Industry:* Pramuan Sapavasu. *Communications:* Banharn Silpa-acha. *Commerce:* Montree Pongpanit. *Education:* Marut Bunnag. *Agriculture and Cooperatives:* Gen. Han Leenanond. *Finance:* Suthee Singsaneh. *Public Health:* Therdpong Chaiyanand. *Defence:* Air Chief Marshal Panieng Kantarat. *Science, Technology and Energy:* Banyat Banthadthan. *University Affairs:* Subin Pinkhayan. *Foreign Affairs:* Air Chief Marshal Siddhi Savetsila. *Justice:* Sa-ad Piyawan.

National flag: Five horizontal stripes of red, white, blue, white, red, with the blue of double width.

Local Government. For purposes of administration Thailand is divided into 73 provinces *(changwads)*, each under the control of a *changwad* governor. The *changwads* are subdivided into 640 districts *(amphurs)* and 83 sub-districts *(king amphurs)*, 6,331 communes *(tambons)* and 56,608 villages *(moobans)*. Local legislative and executive bodies with limited powers are being established with functions, procedure and method of election modelled on those of central Assembly.

DEFENCE. Under the Ministry of Defence Organization Act of 1960 the Ministry of Defence has assumed the Supreme Command and the control of the Army, Navy and Air Force with the advice of the Defence Council headed by the Ministry of Defence. The National Defence College, the Armed Forces Staff College and the Military Preparatory School serve the education of officers. Each service has its own C.-in-C., service council, schools of arms and Command and General Staff College.

Under the Military Service Act of 1954 every able-bodied man between the ages of 21 and 30 is liable to serve 2 years with the colours; 7 years in the first reserve; 10 years in the second reserve; 6 years in the third reserve.

Army. The Army is organized in 4 Regions and consists of 1 cavalry, 1 armoured, 7 infantry, 2 special forces, 1 artillery and 1 anti-aircraft divisions; 11 engineer and 8 independent infantry battalions; and 4 reconnaissance companies. Equipment includes 190 M-48A5 and 200 M-41 main battle tanks. There is also an Army Aviation force including over 100 transport helicopters (mostly UH-1 Iroquois), 12 U-17 Skywagon and 75 O-1 Bird Dog observation aircraft and 4 C-47 and 2 Shorts 330 twin-turboprop transports. Strength (1988) 166,000, with 500,000 reserves.

Navy. The Fleet includes 4 frigates (1 built 1973 in Britain, 2 *ex*-US, and 1 *ex*-US destroyer escort all 3 built in 1943), 4 corvettes (small frigates) – 2 new missile-armed and 2 modernised – all US-built, 3 fast large attack gunboats, 6 fast missile craft, 4 coastal minesweepers, 10 patrol vessels, 1 mine counter-measures support ship, 20 gunboats, 26 coastal patrol boats, 9 landing ships, 13 landing craft, 42 minor landing craft, 5 minesweeping boats, 3 surveying ships, 3 surveying boats, 40 river patrol craft, 2 transports, 5 oilers, 3 training ships (old frigate, old corvette, old escort minesweeper), 2 transports, 2 water carriers and 4 tugs. The air element includes 10 S-2 Trackers, 6 F27 Maritimes, 8 N24A Nomads and 2 CL-215s for maritime patrol, 5 C-47s and 2 F27s for transport duties, 9 Cessna 337 armed light transports, and 11 UH-1H Iroquois helicopters.

A third missile-armed corvette similar to the two built by Tacoma is planned to be built in Thailand.

Naval personnel in 1988 totalled 18,300 officers and ratings, 900 in the Naval

Air Arm and 20,000 in the Marine Corps. The Royal Naval Academy is at Paknam.

At the mouth of the Chao Praya River are the Paknam forts. The naval dockyard was reconstructed.

The coast guard force operates 4 patrol vessels, 3 coastal patrol craft, 8 river patrol boats and a considerable number of service craft.

Air Force. The Royal Thai Air Force was reorganized with the assistance of a US Military Air Advisory Group. It had a strength (1988) 48,000 personnel, and is made up of a headquarters and Combat, Logistics Support, Training and Special Services Groups. Combat units comprise 2 squadrons of F-5E/F interceptors, 1 squadron of F-5A/B fighter-bombers and RF-5A reconnaissance aircraft, 1 squadron with A-37B light jet attack aircraft, 2 with OV-10 Bronco light reconnaissance/attack aircraft, 1 squadron with T-33A/AT-33 armed jet trainers, 1 with AT-28A armed piston-engined trainers, and 2 with AU-23A Peacemakers and 1 squadron with C-47s for security duties. Three Aravas are used for electronic intelligence gathering. There are transport units equipped with a total of about 70 C-130H/H-30 Hercules, DC-8-62F, HS 748, C-123B Provider, C-47 and smaller aircraft, including 20 Australian-built Missionmasters; there are 25 UH-1H and 18 S-58T helicopters; 20 O-1 Bird Dog observation aircraft; training units with Air trainer CT/4 primary trainers built in New Zealand, Italian-built SF.260MTs, T-37 intermediate and T-33A advanced trainers. In 1984, delivery began of 31 Model 400 and 16 Model 600 Fantrainers, of which the first 6 were built in the Federal Republic of Germany, the remainder are being partially manufactured and assembled in Thailand. Twenty T-33As were received from Singapore in 1986 and 18 F-16 Fighting Falcons and 3 Learjets are on order for delivery from 1988.

INTERNATIONAL RELATIONS

Membership. Thailand is a member of UN, ASEAN and the Colombo Plan.

ECONOMY

Planning. The Sixth National Economic and Social Development Plan (1987–91) envisages emphasis on the less capital-intensive industries and on export growth.

Budget. Expenditure (1986, 1m. baht) 218,000: Economy, 34,088 (of which 17,202 for agriculture); education, 39,978; defence, 41,257; internal security, 10,829; public health, 23,792; administration, 5,823; debt, 50,719. Revenue, 185,000 (1m. baht).

Currency. The unit of currency is the *baht*, formerly called in English the *tical*, which is divided into 100 *satang*. Only nickel, copper, tin and bronze coins are now minted, in denominations of 1, 2, 5 *baht*, 25, 50 *satang*. Currency notes, first issued in 1902, now comprise, 5, 10, 20, 50, 100, 500 *baht* notes.

On 31 March 1976 the total amount of notes and coins in circulation was 30,280m. baht.

In March 1988, £1 = 44·30 *baht*; US$1 = 25·26 *baht*.

Banking. In 1942 the Bank of Thailand was established under the Bank of Thailand Act, B.E. 2485 (1942) and began operations on 10 Dec. 1942, with the functions of a central bank. The Bank has its banking activities entirely separate from the management of the note issue. The Bank also took over the note issue previously performed by the Treasury Department of the Ministry of Finance. Although the entire capital is owned by the Government, the Bank is an independent body.

Banks incorporated under Thai law include the Bangkok Bank Ltd, the Bangkok Bank of Commerce Ltd, the Bank of Asia for Industry & Commerce Ltd, the Bank of Ayudhya Ltd, Bangkok Metropolitan Bank Ltd, the Laem Thong Bank Ltd, the Siam City Bank Ltd, the Siam Commercial Bank Ltd, First Bangkok City Bank Ltd, Union Bank of Bangkok Ltd, the Bank of Agriculture and Agricultural Co-operatives, the Government Housing Bank, the Sayam Bank and the Wang Lee Chan Bank Ltd. Foreign banks include the Chartered Bank, the Hongkong and Shanghai Banking Corporation, the Citibank, Banque de l'Indochine, Bank of

Canton Ltd, Bank of China Ltd, Bank of America, N.T. & S.A., the Mitsui Bank Ltd, The Asia Trust Bank Ltd, Bharat Overseas Bank Ltd, The Chase Manhattan Bank, United Malayan Banking Corporation and the Bank of Tokyo Ltd.

The commercial Thai banks had, in 1983, 1,709 branches in Thailand and 19 abroad. The deposits held by commercial banks in Oct. 1985 amounted to 539,325m. baht and had reserves of 21,700m. baht.

Government-owned banks include Government Savings Bank, which was established as an independent organization in 1947, and the Government Housing Bank.

Weights and Measures. The metric system was made compulsory by a law promulgated on 17 Dec. 1923. The actual weights and measures prescribed by law are: Units of weight: 1 *standard picul* = 60 kg; 1 *standard catty* (¹⁄₁₀₀ picul) = 600 grammes; 1 *standard carat* = 20 centigrammes. Units of length: 1 *sen* = 40 metres; 1 *wah* (¹⁄₂₀ sen) = 2 metres; 1 *sauk* (¹⁄₂ wah) = 0·50 metre; 1 *keup* (¹⁄₂ sauk) = 0·25 metre. Units of square measure: 1 *rai* (1 sq. sen) = 1,600 sq. metres; 1 *ngan* (¹⁄₄ rai) = 400 sq. metres; 1 *sq. wah* (¹⁄₁₀₀ ngan) = 4 sq. metres. Units of capacity: 1 *standard kwien* = 2,000 litres; 1 *standard ban* (¹⁄₂ kwien) = 1,000 litres; 1 *standard sat* (¹⁄₅₀ ban) = 20 litres; 1 *standard tannan* (¹⁄₂₀ sat) = 1 litre.

Legislation passed in 1940 provided that the calendar year shall coincide with the Christian Year, and that the year of the Buddhist era 2484 shall begin on 1 Jan. 1941. (The New Year's Day was previously 1 April.) The years B.E. 2517–2518 therefore correspond to A.D. 1974 and 1975.

ENERGY AND NATURAL RESOURCES

Electricity. In 1981, steam power accounted for 52% of production (81% of the fuel being imported) and hydro-electric power for 34%. A lignite-fuelled plant at Mae-Moh had 7 generators producing 825,000 km in 1985. A natural gas-fuelled plant (1·82m. kw) opened at Bang Pakong in 1985. Production (1986) 24,060m. kwh. Supply 220 volts; 50 Hz.

Oil. Thailand is heavily dependent on oil. There is extensive oil and gas exploration in the Gulf of Thailand. In 1987 the Sirikit oil field, which came on stream in 1983, remained Thailand's only significant find. Proven oil reserves in 1987 were less than 160m. bbls. Production of crude oil (1987) 1·8m. tonnes providing 15% of needs.

Gas. Production of natural gas (1985) 132,272m. cu. ft.

Minerals. The mineral resources are extensive and varied, including cassiterite (tin ore), wolfram, scheelite, antimony, coal, copper, gold, iron, lead, manganese, molybdenum, rubies, sapphires, silver, zinc and zircons. Ore output in 1986 (in tonnes): Iron, 37,330; manganese, 4,888; tin, 23,299; lead, 61,885; antimony, 2,397; zinc, 373,833; lignite, 5,542,247; gypsum, 1,665,557; tungsten, 963; fluorite, 189,712.

Agriculture. The chief produce of the country is rice, which forms the national food and the staple article of export. The area under paddy is about 18m. acres. In 1987 40% of the total land area was cultivated.

Output of the major crops in 1986 was (in 1,000 tonnes): Paddy, 19,100; coffee, 26; maize, 4,197; sugar-cane, 24,093; jute and kenaf, 254; tobacco, 85; tapioca-root (1985), 19,263; soybeans, 331; coconut, 1,278; mung beans (1985), 323; cotton, 93; groundnuts, 178.

Livestock, 1986 (in 1,000): horses, 21; buffaloes, 6,302; cattle, 4,835; pigs, 4,215; poultry, 99,000.

Forestry. About 25% of the land area of Thailand was under forest in 1984. In the north, mixed deciduous forests with teak *(Tectona grandis, Linn.)*, growing in mixture with several other species, predominate. In the north-eastern section hardwood of the *Dipterocarpus* species, especially *Shorea obtusa* and *Pentacme Siamensis, Kurz* exist in most parts. In all other regions of the country tropical evergreen forests are found, with the well-known timber of commerce, Yang

(*Dipterocarpus alatus, Roxb* and *Dipterocarpus* spp.) as the outstanding crops. Most of the teak timber exploited in northern Thailand is floated down to Bangkok.

About one-third of the teak-forest area is being exploited by the Forest Industry Organization, and the remaining two-thirds is to be worked by timber company lessees and other private enterprises.

Output of main forestry products in 1985: Teak, 39,200 cu. metres; yang and other woods, 1,843,500 cu. metres. By-products in 1985: firewood, 690,600 cu. metres; charcoal, 363,900 cu. metres; 16m. bamboo and 139,711 decalitres of yang oil (1984).

Rubber production (in 1,000 tonnes), 1955, 133·3; 1960, 170·8; 1969, 281·8; 1973, 384; 1978, 467; 1979, 531; 1980, 501; 1981, 510; 1982, 540; 1983, 587; 1984, 629; 1985, 722.

Fisheries. In 1984 the catch of sea fish was 1,973,000 tonnes including marine prawns, shrimps and crabs, 117,400 tonnes; of freshwater fish, 161,800 tonnes.

INDUSTRY AND TRADE

Industry. Production of manufactured goods in 1984 included 8,239,970 tonnes of cement, 60,927 tonnes of white cement, 2,431,054 tonnes of sugar, 82,073 tonnes of sweetened condensed milk, 15,495 tonnes of evaporated milk, 163·9m. litres of beer, and in 1983 included 975m. sq. yd of cotton textiles, 1,226·9m. sq. yd of man-made textiles, 3,990,000 sheets of plywood, 65,500 tonnes of paper, 36,127 passenger cars and 74,910 commercial vehicles.

Labour. In 1986, 26,013,000 persons out of a labour force of 27,910,000 were employed: 17,065,000 in agriculture and 2,321,000 in manufacturing.

Trade Unions. The Thai National Trade Union Congress is a member of the International Confederation of Free Trade Unions.

Commerce. The foreign trade (in 1m. baht) was as follows:

	1981	1982	1983	1984	1985	1986
Imports (c.i.f.)	216,746	196,616	236,609	245,155	251,169	241,358
Exports (f.o.b.)	153,001	159,728	146,472	175,237	193,366	233,383

In 1986 the main items of export were (in 1m. baht, provisional): Textiles, 29,986; rice, 20,317; tapioca products, 19,111; canned and frozen seafood, 19,080; rubber, 15,115; precious stones, 13,186; integrated circuits, 11,617; maize, 9,326; sugar, 7,293; tin, 3,084.

In 1985 imports from Japan (26%), USA (11·2%), Singapore (7·3%), Malaysia (5·8%), Federal Republic of Germany (5·2%), France (4·5%), Oman (3·6%) and Saudi Arabia (2·8%). Exports to USA (19·6%), Japan (13·3%), Singapore (8%), Netherlands (7·1%), Malaysia (4·9%), Hong Kong (4%), China (3·8%) and Federal Republic of Germany (3·7%).

Total trade between Thailand and UK (British Department of Trade returns, in £1,000 sterling):

	1983	1984	1985	1986	1987
Imports to UK	87,823	112,353	131,806	182,756	239,430
Exports and re-exports from UK	131,833	149,742	157,723	158,195	206,571

Tourism. In 1986 2,818,092 foreigners visited Thailand. Earnings (1985) 31·768m. baht.

COMMUNICATIONS

Roads. In 1985 the total length of roads was 156,776 km, of which 44,534 km (29%) were national highways and 112,242 km (71%) provincial roads. Motor vehicles registered in 1982 included 492,742 passenger cars, 32,114 buses (1979), 419,143 lorries (1979) and 1,401,918 motor cycles.

Railways. In 1986 the State Railway totalled 3,735 km (metre gauge) and carried 76m. passengers and 5·2m. tonnes of freight.

Aviation. There are international airports at Bangkok, Chiang Mai in the north and

Phuket and Hat Yai in the south. Thai Airways Co. Ltd (TAC), established in 1947, is the sole Thai air transport enterprise, with authorized capital of 300m. baht. The Company operates 11 domestic routes and 3 international routes and carried more than 1m. passengers in 1984. On 24 Aug. 1959 Thai Airways and the Scandinavian Airlines System set up a new company, Thai Airways International, to operate the international air services from Thailand. In 1984, more than 2·7m. passengers were carried.

Shipping. In 1983, 3,137 vessels of 14,174,828 NRT entered and 2,648 of 11,663,452 NRT cleared the port of Bangkok.

The port of Bangkok, about 30 km from the mouth of the Chao Phya River, is capable of berthing ocean-going vessels of 10,000 gross tons and 28 ft draught. Bangkok is now a port of entry for Laos, and goods arriving in transit are sent up by rail to Nong Khai and ferried across the river Mekhong to Vientiane.

Post and Broadcasting. In 1974 there were 555 post offices proper, 341 licensed and Amphur post offices and 545 railway-station post offices. In 1985 there were 576,082 telephones, of which 389,096 were in Bangkok.

In 1985, there were 275 radio stations and 9 television stations,7,629,998 radios and 4,122,000 televisions.

Cinemas (1983). There were 651 cinemas with a seating capacity of 438,787.

Newspapers (1986). There are 23 daily newspapers in Bangkok, including 3 in English and 7 in Chinese, with a combined circulation of about 2m.

JUSTICE, RELIGION, EDUCATION AND WELFARE

Justice. The judicial power is exercised in the name of the King, by *(a)* courts of first instance, *(b)* the court of appeal *(Uthorn)* and *(c)* the Supreme Court *(Dika)*. The King appoints, transfers and dismisses judges, who are independent in conducting trials and giving judgment in accordance with the law.

Courts of first instance are subdivided into 20 magistrates' courts *(Kwaeng)* with limited civil and minor criminal jurisdiction; 85 provincial courts *(Changwad)* with unlimited civil and criminal jurisdiction; the criminal and civil courts with exclusive jurisdiction in Bangkok; the central juvenile courts for persons under 18 years of age in Bangkok.

The court of appeal exercises appellate jurisdiction in civil and criminal cases from all courts of first instance. From it appeals lie to Dika Court on any point of law and, in certain cases, on questions of fact.

The Supreme Court is the supreme tribunal of the land. Besides its normal appellate jurisdiction in civil and criminal matters, it has semi-original jurisdiction over general election petitions. The decisions of Dika Court are final. Every person has the right to present a petition to the Government who will deal with all matters of grievance.

Religion. In 1983 there were 47,049,223 Buddhists, 1,869,427 Moslems, 267,381 Christians and 64,369 Hindus, Sikhs and others.

Education. Primary education is compulsory for children between the ages of 7–14 and free in local municipal schools. In 1984 there were 532,097 students enrolled at pre-primary level, 7,229,064 at primary level, 1,304,520 at lower secondary level, 945,260 at upper secondary level and 361,819 in higher education. In 1980 there were 36 teachers' training colleges with 5,317 teachers and 63,983 students and about 180 government vocational schools and colleges with 11,240 teachers and 208,088 students. There are 8 schools for deaf children, 2 for the blind, 1 for multiple-handicapped and 2 for the mentally retarded. In 1984 the 36 teacher training colleges were regionally consolidated into 8 United Colleges also offering 4-year programmes in science and technology, management, social development, agriculture, arts and journalism. In 1986 there were 14 universities 3 of which were private: Chulalongkorn University (1916), Thammasat University (1934), Universities of Medical Science, Agriculture and Fine Arts; Ramkamhaeng University (1971)—all in Bangkok; Chiengmai University (1964), the Khon Kaen University (1966) in the north-east and Prince of Songkhla University (1968) in the south.

Health. The Primary Health Care Programme had provided health services in 95% of villages in 1986. In 1982 there were 434 hospitals and 6,496 health centres. In 1982 there were 6,550 physicians, 1,122 dentists and (1981) 2,680 pharmacists.

DIPLOMATIC REPRESENTATIVES

Of Thailand in Great Britain (30 Queen's Gate, London, SW7 5JB)
Ambassador: Sudhee Prasasvinitchai (accredited 4 Nov. 1986).

Of Great Britain in Thailand (Wireless Rd., Bangkok)
Ambassador: Derek Tonkin, CMG.

Of Thailand in the USA (2300 Kalorama Rd., NW, Washington, D.C., 20008)
Ambassador: Asa Sarasin.

Of the USA in Thailand (95 Wireless Rd., Bangkok)
Ambassador: William A. Brown.

Of Thailand to the United Nations
Ambassador: M. L. Birabhongse Kasemsri.

Books of Reference

Thailand into the 80's. Office of the Prime Minister, Bangkok, Rev. ed., 1984
Thailand Statistical Yearbook. National Statistical Office, Bangkok
Thailand in Brief. 7th ed. Bangkok, 1985
Bibliography of Materials About Thailand in Western Languages. Chulalongkorn University, Bangkok, 1960
Douner, W., *The Five Faces of Thailand.* Hamburg and London, 1978
Girling, J. I. S., *Thailand: Society and Politics.* Cornell Univ. Press, 1981
Haas, M. R., *Thai–English Student's Dictionary.* OUP, 1966
Morrell, D. and Samudavanija, C., *Political Conflict in Thailand.* Cambridge, Mass., 1981
Watts, M., *Thailand.* [Bibliography] Oxford and Santa Barbara, 1986

TOGO

Capital: Lomé
Population: 3·16m. (1987)
GNP per capita: US$280 (1983)

République Togolaise

HISTORY. A German protectorate from July 1884, Togo was occupied by British and French forces in Aug. 1914 and subsequently partitioned between the two countries on 20 July 1922 under a League of Nations mandate. British Togo subsequently joined Ghana. The French mandate was renewed by the UN as a trusteeship on 14 Dec. 1946.

On 28 Oct. 1956 a plebiscite was held to determine the status of the territory. Out of 438,175 registered voters, 313,458 voted for an autonomous republic within the French Union and the end of the trusteeship system. The trusteeship was abolished on the achievement of independence on 27 April 1960.

On 13 Jan. 1963 the first President Sylvanus Olympio was murdered by n.c.o.s. of the army. Nicolas Grunitzky, a former prime minister and Olympio's brother-in-law, was appointed President. On 13 Jan. 1967 in a bloodless *coup* the army under Lieut.-Col. Etienne Eyadéma made President Grunitzky 'voluntarily withdraw'. On 14 April 1967 Col. Eyadéma assumed the Presidency. There was a return to constitutional government on 13 Jan. 1980.

AREA AND POPULATION. Togo is bounded west by Ghana, north by Burkina Faso, east by Benin and south by the Gulf of Guinea. The area is 56,785 sq. km. The population of Togo in 1981 (census) was 2,700,982; 1987 (estimate) 3,158,000. The capital is Lomé (population, 1983, 366,476), other towns (1981, population) being Sokodé (48,098), Kpalimé (31,800), Atakpamé (27,100), Bassar (21,800), Tsévié (17,000) and Aného (14,000).

The areas, populations and chief towns of the 5 regions are:

Region	Sq. km	Census 1981	Chief town
Des Savanes	8,602	326,826	Dapaong
De La Kara	11,630	432,626	Kara
Centrale	13,182	269,174	Sokodé
Des Plateaux	16,975	561,656	Atakpamé
Maritime	6,396	1,039,700	Lomé

The south is largely populated by Ewe-speaking peoples (forming 47% of the population) and related groups, while the north is mainly inhabited by Hamitic groups speaking Voltaic (Gur) languages such as Kabyè (22%), Gurma (14%) and Tem (4%). The official language is French but Ewe and Kabre are also taught in schools. In 1984, 27% lived in urban areas and (1981) 48% were male.

Vital statistics, 1979: Births, 102,398; deaths, 7,691.

CLIMATE. The tropical climate produces wet seasons from March to July and from Oct. to Nov. in the south. The north has one wet season, from April to July. The heaviest rainfall occurs in the mountains of the west, south-west and centre. Lomé. Jan. 81°F (27·2°C), July 76°F (24·4°C). Annual rainfall 35″ (875 mm).

CONSTITUTION AND GOVERNMENT. Following approval in a referendum on 30 Dec. 1979, a new Constitution came into force on 13 Jan. 1980, when the Third Togolese Republic was proclaimed. It provides for an Executive President, directly elected for a 7-year term, and for a National Assembly of 77 deputies, elected on a regional list system for a 5-year term. Elections to the Assembly were held on 24 March 1985.

All candidates are approved by the *Rassemblement du peuple togolais*, the sole legal Party since 1969; it is administered by a 46-member Central Committee and a 13-member Political Bureau elected at its fourth Party Congress in Dec. 1986.

The government in Oct. 1987 was composed as follows:

President, Minister of Defence: Gen. Gnassingbé Eyadéma (re-elected for a further 7-year term in Dec. 1986).

Foreign Affairs and Co-operation: Yaovi Adada. *Rural Development:* Koffi Walla. *Justice, Keeper of the Seals:* Kpotivi Têvî-Djidjogbé Laclé. *Economy and Finance:* Komlan Alipui. *Planning and Mines:* Barry Moussa Barque. *Posts and Telecommunications:* Ayeva Nassirou. *Public Works, Labour and Civil Service:* Bitokotipou Yagninim. *Minister-Delegate to Presidency in charge of Information:* Gbegnon Amegboh. *Youth, Sports and Culture:* Komlavi Gnemegna. *National Education and Scientific Research:* Tchalim Tcha Koza. *Interior:* Komlan Agbétiafa. *Commerce and Transport:* W'souwodji Kawo Ehe. *Public Health, Social and Women's Affairs:* Dr Ayissah Agbetra. *Industry and State Enterprises:* Koffi Djondo. *Technical and Professional Training:* Koffi Edoh. *Environment and Tourism:* Yao Komlavi.

National flag: Five horizontal stripes of green and yellow, a red quarter with a white star.

Local Government: There are 5 regions, each under an inspector appointed by the President; they are divided into 21 *prefectures,* each administered by a district chief assisted by an elected district council.

DEFENCE. Armed forces numbered (1988) about 5,910, all forming part of the Army.

Army. The Army consists of 2 infantry, 1 Presidential Guard commando and 1 para-commando regiments, with artillery and logistic support units. Equipment includes 9 Scorpion and 2 T-54/-55 main battle tanks. Strength (1988) 4,000, with a further 1,550 men in a paramilitary force.

Navy. In 1988 there were 2 coastal patrol craft, 2 defence launches and a naval base at Lomé. Naval personnel, 105 officers and men.

Air Force. An Air Force, established with French assistance, has 6 Brazilian-built EMB-326 Xavante (Aermacchi MB.326) armed jet trainers; 4 Alpha Jet advanced trainers, with strike capability, 1 DC-8 and 1 twin-turbofan F28 Fellowship for VIP use, 2 turboprop Buffalo transports; 2 Beech Barons and 2 Cessna 337s for liaison; 3 Epsilon basic trainers; 1 Puma and 2 Lama helicopters. Personnel (1988) 260.

INTERNATIONAL RELATIONS

Membership. Togo is a member of UN, OAU and ECOWAS, and is an ACP state of EEC.

ECONOMY

Planning. The fourth 5-year development plan (1981–85) provided for investment of 368,490m. francs CFA, of which 116,397m. were for rural development, 98,625m. for industrial development and 100,690m. for infrastructure.

Budget. The ordinary budget for 1987 balanced at 89,690m. francs CFA.

Currency. The unit of currency is the *franc* CFA with a parity rate of 50 *francs* CFA to 1 French *franc.* The rate of exchange (March 1988) was 507 francs CFA to £1; US$1 = 285·56.

Banking. The bank of issue is the *Banque Centrale des Etats de l'Afrique de l'Ouest.* Seven commercial and 3 development banks are based in Lomé.

ENERGY AND NATURAL RESOURCES

Electricity. Production (1986) 203m. kwh. There is a hydro-electric plant at Kpalimé. Supply 127 and 220 volts; 50 Hz.

Minerals. A Mines Department was set up in 1953 after the discovery of very rich deposits of phosphate and bauxite; mining began in 1961. Output of phosphate rock (1984) 2·8m. tonnes. Other mineral deposits are limestone, estimated at 200m. tons; iron ore, estimated at 550m. tons with iron content varying between 40% and 55%, and marble estimated at 20m. tonnes. Salt production (1982) 600,000 tonnes.

Agriculture. Inland the country is hilly, rising to 3,600 ft, with streams and water-falls. There are long stretches of forest and brushwood, while dry plains alternate with arable land. Maize, yams, cassava, plantains, groundnuts, etc., are cultivated; oil palms and dye-woods grow in the forests; but the main commerce is based on coffee, cocoa, palm-oil, palm-kernels, copra, groundnuts, cotton, manioc. There are considerable plantations of oil and cocoa palms, coffee, cacao, kola, cassava and cotton. Production, 1986 (in 1,000 tonnes): Cassava, 442; tomatoes, 6; yams 336; maize, 133; sorghum, 90; millet, 70; seed cotton, 70; rice, 15; groundnuts, 22; coffee 10.

Livestock (1986): Cattle, 276,000; sheep, 850,000; swine, 288,000; horses, 1,000; asses, 1,000; goats, 744,000.

Forestry. Forests cover 28% of the land surface. Roundwood production (1983) 735,000 cu. metres.

Fisheries. Catch (1984) 14,547 tonnes.

INDUSTRY AND TRADE

Industry. There is a cement works (production, 1982; 279,000 tonnes); a second is being built in co-operation with Ghana and Côte d'Ivoire with a capacity of 1·2m. tonnes per annum. An oil refinery of 1m. tonne capacity opened in Lomé in 1978 and a steel mill (20,000 tonne capacity) in 1979. Industry, though small, is developing and there are about 40 medium sized enterprises in the public and private sectors, including textile and food processing plants.

Commerce (in 1m. francs CFA):

	1980	1981	1982	1983	1984
Imports	116,357	117,769	128,354	108,141	118,460
Exports	71,285	56,241	58,173	61,921	83,588

In 1985, of the exports, phosphates amounted to 38%, cotton 11%, coffee 11% and cocoa beans 6% by value; 22% of exports went to France and 18% to the Netherlands. Of the imports, France supplied 27%, the Netherlands, 11% and UK, 10%.

Total trade between Togo and UK (British Department of Trade returns, in £1,000 sterling):

	1983	1984	1985	1986	1987
Imports to UK	2,161	3,224	4,597	5,008	2,579
Exports and re-exports from UK	12,212	12,166	17,034	17,488	15,431

Tourism. There were about 99,000 tourists in 1986.

COMMUNICATIONS

Roads. There were, in 1986, 7,850 km of roads, of which 1,500 km were paved. In Dec. 1984 there were 36,372 passenger cars and 17,963 commercial vehicles.

Railways. There are 4 metre-gauge railways connecting Lomé, with Aného (continuing to Cotonou in Benin), Kpalimé, Tabligbo and (via Atakpamé) Blitta; total length 525 km. In 1982 the railways carried 16m. tonne-km and 105m. passenger-km.

Aviation: Air services connect Tokoin airport, near Lomé, with Paris, Dakar, Abidjan, Douala, Accra, Lagos, Cotonou and Niamey and by internal services with Sokodé, Mango, Dapaong, Atakpamé and Niamtougou.

Shipping. In 1983, vessels landed 654,000 tonnes and cleared 683,000 tonnes at Lomé; 31,058 containers passed through the port in 1981. The merchant marine comprised (1985) 11 vessels of 77,989 DWT. In 1981 some 2·2m. tonnes of phosphate were loaded at the port of Kpémé.

Post and Broadcasting. There were (1983) 388 post offices and 11,105 telephones. Togo is connected by telegraph and telephone with Ghana, Benin, Côte d'Ivoire and Senegal, and by wireless telegraphy with Europe and America. There were 14,000 television receivers and 250,000 radio receivers in 1985.

Newspapers. There was (1984) 1 daily newspaper (circulation 10,000).

JUSTICE, RELIGION, EDUCATION AND WELFARE

Justice. The Supreme Court and two Appeal Courts are in Lomé, one for criminal cases and one for civil and commercial cases. Each receives appeal from a series of local tribunals.

Religion. In 1980, 28% of the population were Catholics, 17% Moslem (chiefly in the north) and 9% Protestant; while 46% follow animist religions.

Education. In 1984 there were 454,209 pupils and 10,225 teachers in 2,329 primary schools in 1982, 122,925 pupils and 3,982 teachers in 248 secondary schools, 6,932 (1981) students and (1978) 326 teachers in technical schools and 374 students and 22 teachers at the teacher-training college. The University of Benin at Lomé (founded in 1970) had 4,190 students and 283 teaching staff in 1984.

Health. In 1979 there were 69 hospitals with (1982) 3,655 beds; and in 1985, 168 doctors, 7 dentists, 51 pharmacists, 586 midwives (1979) and 1,763 nursing staff (1979).

DIPLOMATIC REPRESENTATIVES

Of Togo in Great Britain (30 Sloane St., London, SW1)
Ambassador: Assiongbon Agbenou (accredited 10 Oct. 1986).

Of Great Britain in Togo
Ambassador: A. H. Wyatt, CMG (resides in Accra).

Of Togo in the USA (2208 Massachusetts Ave., NW, Washington, D.C., 20008)
Ambassador: Ellom-Kodjo Schuppius.

Of the USA in Togo (Rue Pelletier Caventou, Lomé)
Ambassador: David A. Korn.

Of Togo to the United Nations
Ambassador: Dr Kwam Kouassi.

Books of Reference

Cornevin, R., *Histoire du Togo.* 3rd ed., Paris, 1969
Feuillet, C., *Le Togo en general.* Paris, 1976
Piraux, M., *Le Togo aujourd'hui.* Paris, 1977

TONGA

Capital: Nuku'alofa
Population: 94,535 (1986)
GNP per capita: US$580 (1986)

Friendly Islands

HISTORY. The Kingdom of Tonga attained unity under Taufa'ahau Tupou (George I) who became ruler of his native Ha'apai in 1820, of Vava'u in 1833 and of Tongatapu in 1845. By 1860 the kingdom had become converted to Christianity (George himself having been baptized in 1831). In 1862 the king granted freedom to the people from arbitrary rule of minor chiefs and gave them the right to the allocation of land for their own needs. These institutional changes, together with the establishment of a parliament of chiefs, paved the way towards the democratic constitution under which the kingdom is now governed, and provided a background of stability against which Tonga was able to develop her agricultural economy.

The kingdom continued up to 1899 to be a neutral region in accordance with the Declaration of Berlin, 6 April 1886. By the Anglo-German Agreement of 14 Nov. 1899 subsequently accepted by the USA, the Tonga Islands were left under the Protectorate of Great Britain. A protectorate was proclaimed on 18 May 1900, and a British Agent and Consul appointed. On 4 June 1970 the UK Government ceased to have any responsibility for the external relations of Tonga.

The Tongatapu group was discovered by Tasman in 1643.

AREA AND POPULATION. The kingdom consists of some 169 islands and islets with a total area of 289 sq. miles (748 sq. km; including inland waters), and lies between 15° and 23° 30′ S. lat and 173° and 177° W. long., its western boundary being the eastern boundary of Fiji. The islands are split up into the following groups reading from north to south: The Niuas, Vava'u, Ha'apai, Kotu, Nomuka, Otu Tolu and Tongatapu. The 3 main groups, both from historical and administrative significance, are Tongatapu in the south, Ha'apai in the centre and Vava'u in the north.

The capital is Nuku'alofa on Tongatapu, population (1986) 28,899.

The islands to the east, being mostly of limestone formation, are low lying and with but a few exceptions seldom exceed 100 ft above sea-level. The islands to the west are of a volcanic nature, approximately 11, average between 350 and 3,433 ft in height. After a violent volcanic eruption in Sept. 1946 on the island of Niuafo'ou (Tin Can Island to philatelists, so named because of the method that was used of collecting and delivering mail) the 1,300 inhabitants were evacuated, most of them to Tongatapu and 'Eua, but more than 600 have returned since 1958.

Census population (provisional, 1986) 94,535 (males, 47,589).

CLIMATE. Generally a healthy climate, though Jan. to March is hot and humid, with temperatures of 90°F (32·2°C). Rainfall amounts are comparatively high, being greatest from Dec. to March. Nuku'alofa. Jan. 78°F (25·6°C), July 70°F (21·1°C). Annual rainfall 63″ (1,576 mm). Vava'u. Jan. 80°F (26·7°C), July 73°F (22·8°C). Annual rainfall 110″ (2,750 mm).

CONSTITUTION AND GOVERNMENT. The present Constitution is almost identical with that granted in 1875 by King George Tupou I. There is a Privy Council, Cabinet, Legislative Assembly and Judiciary. The legislative assembly, which meets annually, is composed of 9 nobles elected by their peers, 9 elected representatives of the people and the Privy Councillors (numbering 11); the King appoints one of the 9 nobles to be the Speaker. The elections are held triennially. In 1960, women voted for the first time.

King: HM King Taufa'ahau Tupou IV, GCVO, GCMG, KBE, born 4 July 1918,

1188

succeeded on 16 Dec. 1965 on the death of his mother, Queen Salote Tupou III; his coronation took place on 4 July 1967.

Prime Minister: HRH Prince Fatafehi Tu'pelehake, KCMG, KBE, younger brother of the King.

Deputy Prime Minister: Hon. Baron Tuita, CBE.

Foreign Affairs and Defence: HRH Crown Prince Tupouto'a.

National flag: Red with a white quarter bearing a red couped cross.

INTERNATIONAL RELATIONS

Membership. Tonga is a member of the Commonwealth and is an ACP state of EEC.

ECONOMY

Budget. Recurrent revenue and expenditure in T$1,000:

	1985–86	*1986–87* [1]	*1987–88* [1]
Revenue	26,940	26,113	29,846
Expenditure	26,940	26,113	29,846

[1] Estimate.

The principal sources of revenue are import dues, income tax, sales tax, port and service tax, wharfage and philatelic revenue.

Public debt at 30 June 1986, T$42·7m.

Currency. There is a government note issue of *pa'anga* (T$) 20, 10, 5, 2 and 1 and coin issue of T$2, T$1 and *seniti* 50, 20, 10, 5, 2 and 1. In March 1988, £1 = 2·46 *pa'anga*; US$1 = 1·39 *pa'anga*.

Banking. The Bank of Tonga and the Tonga Development Bank are both situated in Nuku'alofa (Tongatapu) with branches in the main islands 'Eua, Ha'apai, Vava'u and the Niuas.

ENERGY AND NATURAL RESOURCES

Electricity. Production (1986) 8m. kwh. Supply 230 volts; 50 Hz.

Agriculture. Production (1986, in 1,000 tonnes) consisted of coconuts (52), fruit and vegetables (19), copra (6) and cassava (17).

Livestock (1986): Cattle, 8,000; horses, 9,000; pigs, 65,000; goats, 11,000; poultry (1982), 175,000.

Fisheries. Catch (1982) 2,500 tonnes.

INDUSTRY AND TRADE

Commerce. In 1986, imports were valued at T$56,575,200 while exports and re-exports were T$8,186,600 and T$677,500.

Main imports (1986, in T$): Food 13,904,500, beverages and tobacco 3,375,300, crude materials 2,181,300, fuel and lubricants 7,019,100, oils and fats 131,300, chemicals 4,598,300, manufactured goods 10,839,700, machinery and transport equipment 9,487,200, miscellaneous manufactured articles 4,906,200.

Main exports (1986, in T$): Coconut oil 1,762,200, vanilla 1,201,700, bananas 1,270,700, dessicated coconut 691,600, water melons 4,900, knitted clothes 420,500, tarotaruas 8,500, manufactured machinery, 358,000.

Principal destinations for Tongan exports/re-exports in 1986 were: New Zealand (T$3,623,100), Australia (T$2,286,100), USA (T$1,517,500), UK (T$4,500). Of 1986 imports (in T$), New Zealand furnished 22,248,000; Australia, 16,938,300; Japan, 5,186,200; Singapore, 1,211,800; Fiji, 3,305,700; China (Mainland), 850,000; UK, 1,751,100.

Total trade between Tonga and UK (British Department of Trade returns, in £1,000 sterling):

	1984	*1985*	*1986*	*1987*
Imports to UK	328	70	86	100
Exports and re-exports from UK	842	699	936	2,013

Tourism. There were 44,677 visitors in 1986–87.

COMMUNICATIONS

Roads. In 1986–87 there were over 4,000 registered motor vehicles and (1987) 1,242 km of roads (263 km paved).

Aviation. International air service connexions to Tongatapu are now provided by Air New Zealand, Polynesian Airlines, Air Pacific and Hawaiian Air with 4 flights per week to Auckland, 3 to Apia, 4 to Suva and 2 to Nadi. Hawaiian Air provides a twice weekly service to Hawaii via Pagopago. Internal air service flights are operated during the week to 'Eua, Ha'apai, Vava'u and Niuatoputapu by Friendly Island Airways.

Shipping. Pacific Forum Line maintains a four weekly service New Zealand–Fiji–Samoas–Tonga from Sydney, Australia–Noumea–Fiji–Samoas–Tonga. Warner Pacific Line maintains a monthly service New Zealand–Tonga–Samoas–Tonga–New Zealand and a monthly service Tonga–New Zealand–Australia–Funufuti–Tarawa–Samoas–Tonga.

Post and Broadcasting. The kingdom has its own issue of postage stamps. Telephones numbered 3,500 in 1986 and there were 65,000 radio receivers.

JUSTICE, RELIGION, EDUCATION AND WELFARE

Justice. Since the lapse of British extra-territorial jurisdiction British and foreign nationals charged with an offence against the laws of Tonga (the enforcement of which is a responsibility of the Minister of Police) are fully subject to the jurisdiction of the Tongan courts to which they are already subject in all civil matters.

Religion. The Tongans are Christian, over 30,000 being adherents of the Wesleyan Church.

Education. In 1986 there were 101 government and 10 denominational primary schools, with a total of 16,912 pupils. There were 5 government and 45 mission schools and 1 private school offering secondary education, with a total roll of 14,321. There was one government teacher-training college with 113 students; 3 government technical and vocational schools with 117 trainees and 8 non-government technical and vocational schools with 323 trainees. 201 students were undertaking tertiary training overseas under an official scholarship in 1985.

Health. In 1986–87 there were 47 doctors, 11 dentists, 2 pharmacists, 27 midwives, 216 nursing personnel and 4 hospitals with 307 beds.

DIPLOMATIC REPRESENTATIVES

Of Tonga in Great Britain (New Zealand Hse., Haymarket, London, SW1Y 4TE) *High Commissioner:* S. T. 'Aho (accredited 17 Feb. 1986). Also Ambassador to the USA.

Of Great Britain in Tonga (Nuku'alofa) *High Commissioner:* A. P. Fabian.

Books of Reference

Churchward, C. M., *Tongan Dictionary.* London, 1959
Luke, Sir Harry, *Queen Salote and Her Kingdom.* London, 1954
Packett, C. N., *Travel and Holiday Guide to Tongatapu Island.* Bradford, 1984

TRINIDAD AND TOBAGO

Capital: Port-of-Spain
Population: 1·22m. (1987)
GNP per capita: US$6,360 (1985)

HISTORY. Trinidad was discovered by Columbus in 1498 and colonized by the Spaniards in the 16th century. During the French Revolution a large number of French families settled in the island. In 1797, Great Britain being at war with Spain, Trinidad was occupied by the British and ceded to Great Britain by the Treaty of Amiens in 1802. Trinidad and Tobago were joined in 1889.

Under the Bases Agreement concluded between the governments of the UK and the USA on 27 March 1941, and the concomitant Trinidad–US Bases Lease of 22 April 1941, defence bases were leased to the US Government for 99 years. On 8 Dec. 1960 the US agreed to abandon 21,000 acres of leased land and the US has since given up the remaining territory, except for a small tracking station.

On 31 Aug. 1962 Trinidad and Tobago became an independent member state of the British Commonwealth. A Republican Constitution was adopted on 1 Aug. 1976.

AREA AND POPULATION. The island of Trinidad is situated in the Caribbean Sea, about 12 km off the north-east coast of Venezuela; several islets, the largest being Chacachacare, Huevos, Monos and Gaspar Grande, lie in the Gulf of Paria which separates Trinidad from Venezuela. The smaller island of Tobago lies about 31 km further to the north-east. Altogether, the islands cover 5,124 sq. km (1,978 sq. miles) of which Trinidad (including the islets) has 4,821 sq. km (1,861 sq. miles) and Tobago 303 sq. km (117 sq. miles). Population (census 1980): 1,079,800. (Trinidad, 1,039,100; Tobago, 40,700). Capital, Port-of-Spain, 58,400; other important towns, San Fernando (34,200) and Arima (24,600). Those of African descent are 40·8% of the population, Indians, 40·7%, mixed races, 16·3%, European, Chinese and others, 2·2%. English is spoken generally. Estimated population in 1987, 1·22m.

Vital statistics (rate per 1,000), 1983: Births, 29·2; deaths, 6·6; infant deaths, 12·6. Proportion of population under 15 years (1984) 39·2%.

Tobago is situated about 30·7 km north-east of Trinidad. Main town is Scarborough.

Principal goods shipped from Tobago to Trinidad are copra, cocoa, livestock and poultry, fresh vegetables, coconut oil and coconut fibre.

CLIMATE. A tropical climate whose dry season runs from Jan. to June, with a wet season for the rest of the year. Temperatures are uniformly high the year round. Port-of-Spain. Jan. 78°F (25·6°C), July 79°F (26·1°C). Annual rainfall 65″ (1,631 mm).

CONSTITUTION AND GOVERNMENT. The 1976 Constitution provides for a bicameral legislature of a Senate and a House of Representatives. The Senate consists of 31 members, 16 being appointed by the President on the advice of the Prime Minister, 6 on the advice of the Leader of the Opposition and 9 at the discretion of the President.

Tobago has a 15-man House of Assembly (with limited powers).

The House of Representatives consists of 36 (34 for Trinidad and 2 for Tobago) elected members and a Speaker elected from within or outside the House.

The Cabinet consists of the Prime Minister, appointed by the President, and other Ministers, including the Attorney-General.

At the general elections in Dec. 1986 the National Alliance for Reconstruction won 33 seats; the People's National Movement won 3 seats.

President: Noor Hassanali.
Prime Minister and Minister of Finance and Economy: A. N. R. Robinson.

Local Government: Trinidad is divided into a city (the capital), 3 boroughs and 6 counties; Tobago has since 1980 had a 15-member elected House of Assembly with limited powers of self-government.

National flag: Red with a diagonal black strip edged in white.

DEFENCE. The Defence Force has a regular and a reserve infantry battalion and a support battalion equipped with 81mm mortars, and there is also a small air element, equipped with 2 Cessna 402 light transports. Personnel in 1988 totalled 2,075.

In 1988 there were 2 Swedish (Karlskrona)-built patrol vessels, 2 British (Vosper, Portsmouth)-built patrol craft, 7 minor patrol boats, 1 survey vessel, 2 research craft and 1 sail training ship. A Commodore is Chief of Defence Staff while a Commander directs the Coast Guard. Of total defence personnel (1988) 640 were coastguard. The Police operate 6 coastal patrol cutters.

INTERNATIONAL RELATIONS

Membership. Trinidad and Tobago is a member of UN, the Commonwealth, OAS, Caricom and is an ACP state of EEC.

ECONOMY

Budget. The 1987 budget envisaged revenue (in TT$) as 5,845·5m. and expenditure as 5,545·6m.

Total external debt at 31 Dec. 1986, TT$5,600m.

Currency. The currency is the *Trinidad and Tobago dollar* of 100 *cents.* £1 = TT$6·38; US$1 = TT$3·60 (March 1988).

Banking. Banks operating: Republic Bank of Trinidad and Tobago Ltd; Royal Bank of Trinidad and Tobago Ltd; Bank of Commerce, Trinidad and Tobago Ltd; Bank of Nova Scotia; United Bank of Trinidad and Tobago Ltd; National Commercial Bank of Trinidad and Tobago; Workers' Bank of Trinidad and Tobago; Trinidad Co-operative Bank Ltd. A Central Bank began operations in Dec. 1964.

Government savings banks are established in 69 offices, with a head office in Port-of-Spain.

ENERGY AND NATURAL RESOURCES

Electricity. In 1986, 3,182m. kwh was generated. Supply 115 and 230 volts; 60 Hz.

Oil. Oil production is one of Trinidad's leading industries and an important source of revenue. Commercial production began in 1909; production of crude oil in 1987 was 8·3m. tonnes. Trinidad also possesses 2 refineries, with rated distillation capacity of 305,000 bbls annually; crude oil is imported from Venezuela, Indonesia, Ecuador, Nigeria, Brazil, and Saudi Arabia and refined in Trinidad. The 'Pitch Lake' is an important source of asphalt; production, 1986, 5,360,700 cu. metres.

Gas. In 1985 production was 7,413m. cu. ft., of which 1,601m. cu. ft. was flared and lost.

Agriculture. Hectares under cultivation and care include (1984): Cocoa, 21,000; sugar, 18,000. Sugar production in 1986 was 92,300 (1985: 80,900) tonnes. The territory is still largely dependent on imported food supplies, especially flour, dairy products, meat and rice. Areas have been irrigated for rice, and soil and forest conservation is practised.

Livestock (1986): Cattle, 77,000; sheep, 11,000; goats, 50,000; pigs, 83,000; poultry, 8m.

INDUSTRY AND TRADE

Industry. In 1985, 474,300 tonnes of iron and steel were produced at the first integrated steelworks to be constructed in the Caribbean which was opened in 1981. Other manufacturing includes ammonia (production, 1985, 1,323,500 tonnes), fertilizers (1986 production, 1,888,000 tonnes), cement (338,000 tonnes, 1986), rum (2,307,000 proof gallons, 1986), beer (20,716 litres, 1986), cigarettes (920,000 kg, 1986).

Labour. The working population in 1986 was 471,300 and unemployment was about 17%; about 30% of the labour force belong to unions.

Commerce. Exports in 1986 were TT$4,962·2m. of which TT$3,504·4m. was mineral fuels and products and chemicals, TT$766·8m. USA took 61·5% of exports. Imports totalled TT$4,902·8m. of which TT$1,792·9m. was for machinery and transport of which the USA supplied 41·8%.

Total trade of Trinidad and Tobago with UK (British Department of Trade returns, in £1,000 sterling):

	1983	1984	1985	1986	1987
Imports to UK	52,748	164,715	81,719	41,662	38,600
Exports and re-exports from UK	148,811	113,312	93,897	79,029	57,016

Tourism. In 1986, 182,640 foreigners visited Trinidad and Tobago spending (estimate) TT$293·9m.

COMMUNICATIONS

Roads. There were (1985) about 6,435 km of main and local roads. Motor vehicles registered in 1985 totalled 336,769, including 127,716 private cars, 26,392 hired and rented cars, and 33,846 goods vehicles.

Aviation. The following airlines operate scheduled passenger, mail and freight services. British West Indian Airways, Ltd, Air Canada, PANAM, KLM, Linea Aeropostal Venezolana, Leeward Islands Air Transport, Caribair, British Airways, American Airlines, Guyana Airways, ALM Antillean Airline, Cruzeiro (Brazil), Eastern Airlines, Caribbean Airways and Viasa.

Shipping. In 1983 19·2m. tons of cargo were handled.

Post and Broadcasting. International communications to all parts of the world are provided by Trinidad and Tobago External Telecommunications Co. Ltd (TEXTEL) by means of a satellite earth station and various high quality radio circuits. The marine radio service is also maintained by TEXTEL. Number of post offices (1984), 69; postal agencies, 166; number of telephones (1986), 182,325. Four wireless stations are maintained by the Trinidad Government and 3 by airline companies. There were 500,000 radio and 300,000 television receivers in 1985. A meteorological station is maintained at Piarco airport.

Cinemas (1986). There are 57 cinemas and 3 drive-in cinemas.

Newspapers (1986). There are 4 daily newspapers with a total daily circulation (1984) of 166,380, 2 Sunday newspapers with a total circulation (1984) of 161,832, and 3 weekly newspapers.

JUSTICE, RELIGION, EDUCATION AND WELFARE

Justice. The High Court consists of the Chief Justice and 11 puisne judges. In criminal cases a judge of the High Court sits with a jury of 12 in cases of treason and murder, and with 9 jurors in other cases. The Court of Appeal consists of the Chief Justice and 3 Justices of Appeal; there is a limited right of appeal from it to the Privy Council. There are 3 High Courts and 12 magistrates' courts.

Religion. In 1980, 15% of the population were Anglicans (under the Bishop of Trinidad and Tobago), 33·6% Roman Catholics (under the Archbishop of Port-of-Spain), 25% Hindus and 5·9% Moslems.

Education. In 1985–86 there were 172,424 pupils enrolled in primary schools,

12,622 in government secondary schools, 17,576 in assisted secondary schools, 39,188 in junior secondary schools, 21,614 in senior comprehensive schools, 3,564 in composite schools and 4,419 in technical and vocational schools. The University of the West Indies campus in St Augustine had 2,684 full- and part-time students in 1984–85.

Health. In 1985 there were 1,103 physicians, 129 dentists, 496 pharmacists and 31 hospitals and nursing homes with 4,087 beds. There were 3,344 nurses and midwives and 980 nursing assistants in government institutions.

DIPLOMATIC REPRESENTATIVES

Of Trinidad and Tobago in Great Britain (42 Belgrave Sq., London, SW1X 8NT)
High Commissioner: Mervyn Assam.

Of Great Britain in Trinidad and Tobago (Furness Hse., 90 Independence Sq., Port-of-Spain)
High Commissioner: Sir Martin Berthoud, KCVO, CMG.

Of Trinidad and Tobago in the USA (1708 Massachusetts Ave., NW, Washington, D.C., 20036)
Ambassador: J. P. Dumas.

Of the USA in Trinidad and Tobago (15 Queen's Park West, Port-of-Spain)
Ambassador: Sheldon J. Krys.

Of Trinidad and Tobago to the United Nations
Ambassador: D. H. N. Alleyne.

Books of Reference

Statistical Information: The Central Statistical Office, Government of Trinidad and Tobago, 2 Edward St., Port-of-Spain. *Director:* J. Harewood. Publications include *Annual Statistical Digest, Quarterly Economic Report, Annual Overseas Trade Report, Population and Vital Statistics Annual Report, Report on Education Statistics.*

Facts on Trinidad and Tobago. Ministry of Information, Port-of-Spain, 1983
Immigration Guidelines. Government Printer, Port-of-Spain, 1980
Oil and Energy, Trinidad and Tobago. Government Printer, Port-of-Spain, 1980
Trinidad and Tobago Year Book. Port-of-Spain. Annual (from 1865)
Chambers, F., *Trinidad and Tobago.* [Bibliography] Oxford and Santa Barbara, 1987
Cooper, St G. C. and Bacon, P. R. (eds.), *The Natural Resources of Trinidad and Tobago.* London, 1981

Central Library: The Central Library of Trinidad and Tobago, Queen's Park East, Port-of-Spain. *Acting Librarian:* Mrs L. Hutchinson.

TUNISIA

Capital: Tunis
Population: 7·32m. (1986)
GNP per capita: US$1,250 (1985)

al-Jumhuriya
at-Tunisiya

HISTORY. Tunisia was a French protectorate from 1883 and achieved independence on 20 March 1956. The Constituent Assembly, elected on 25 March 1956, abolished the monarchy (of the Bey of Tunis) on 25 July 1957 and proclaimed a republic.

AREA AND POPULATION. The boundaries are on the north and east the Mediterranean Sea, on the west Algeria and on the south Libya. The area is about 154,530 sq. km (59,664 sq. miles), including that portion of the Sahara which is to the east of the Djerid (salt marsh), extending towards Ghadamès.

At the census of 30 March 1984 there were 6,966,173 inhabitants (3,547,487 males and 3,419,026 females) of whom 52·8% were urban. Estimate (1986) 7,317,000.

The census populations of the 23 *gouvernorats* were as follows as at 30 March 1984:

	Sq. km	1984		Sq. km	1984
Aryanah	1,558	374,192	Qasrayn (Kassérine)	8,066	297,959
Bajah (Béja)	3,558	274,706	Qayrawan (Kairouan)	6,712	421,607
Banzart (Bizerta)	3,685	394,670	Qibili (Kebili)	22,084	95,371
Bin Arus	761	246,193	Safaqis (Sfax)	7,545	577,992
Jundubah (Jendouba)	3,102	359,429	Sidi Bu Zayd		
Kaf (Le Kef)	4,965	247,672	(Sidi Bouzid)	6,994	288,528
Madaniyin (Médénine)	8,588	295,889	Silyanah (Siliana)	4,631	222,038
Mahdiyah (Mahdia)	2,966	270,435	Susah (Sousse)	2,621	322,491
Munastir (Monastir)	1,019	278,478	Tatawin (Tataouine)	38,889	100,329
Nabul (Nabeul)	2,788	461,405	Tawzar (Tozeur)	4,719	67,943
Qabis (Gabès)	7,175	240,016	Tunis	346	774,364
Qafsah (Gafsa)	8,990	235,723	Zaghwan (Zaghouan)	2,768	118,743

Tunis, the capital, had (census, 1984) 596,654 inhabitants: Sfax, 231,911; Aryanah, 98,655; Bizerta, 94,509; Djerba, 92,269; Gabès, 92,259; Sousse, 83,509; Kairouan, a holy city of the Moslems, 72,254; Bardo, 65,669; La Goulette, 61,609; Gafsa, 60,870; Béja, 46,708.

Vital statistics (1982). Births, 221,027; deaths, 49,200; marriages, 50,177.

The official language is Arabic but the use of French is widespread.

CLIMATE. The climate ranges from warm temperate in the north, where winters are mild and wet and the summers hot and dry, to desert in the south. Tunis. Jan. 48°F (8·9°C), July 78°F (25·6°C). Annual rainfall 16″ (400 mm). Bizerta. Jan. 52°F (11·1°C), July 77°F (25°C). Annual rainfall 25″ (622 mm). Sfax. Jan. 52°F (11·1°C), July 78°F (25·6°C). Annual rainfall 8″ (196 mm).

CONSTITUTION AND GOVERNMENT. The Constitution of the republic was promulgated on 1 June 1959. The President and the National Assembly are elected simultaneously by direct universal suffrage for a period of 5 years. The President cannot be re-elected more than 3 times consecutively, however on 18 March 1975 the National Assembly proclaimed Bourguiba 'President for Life'. An amendment to the Constitution in 1969 gives the Prime Minister power to act as President in case of a sudden vacancy of the Presidency.

Elections were held on 2 Nov. 1986, when all 125 seats in the National Assembly were won by the *Front National*, an alliance of the ruling *Parti Socialiste Destour-*

ien, renamed Rassemblement Democratique Constitutionelle, and the *Union générale des travailleurs tunisiens*. The elections were boycotted by opposition parties.

President of the Republic: Zine El Abidine Ben Ali (appointed 7 Nov. 1987).

The Cabinet in Jan. 1988 was composed as follows:

Prime Minister: Hedi Baccouche.
Justice: Mohamed Salah Ayari. *National Defence:* Salaheddine Bali. *Foreign Affairs:* Mahmoud Mestiri. *Interior:* Habib Ammar. *Information:* Abdelwahab Abdallah. *National Economy:* Salaheddine Ben M'Barek. *Finance:* Nouri Zorgati. *Education, Higher Education and Scientific Research:* Tijani Chelly. *Supplies and Housing:* Sadok Ben Jemma. *Transport and Tourism:* Abderrazak Kefi. *Social Affairs:* Taoufik Cheikhrouhou. *Public Health:* Souad Lyacoubi. *Agriculture:* Lassaad Ben Osman. *Agricultural Production and Agri-Business Industries:* Mohamed Ghedira. *Cultural Affairs:* Zakaria Ben Mustapha. *Youth and Sports:* Fouad Mebazza. *Communications:* Brahim Khouaja. *Governor of the Central Bank:* Ismail Khelil. *Ministers-Delegate to the Prime Minister:* Hamed Karoui *(Director of the Socialist Destourien Party)*, Mohamed Ghannouchi *(Planning)*, Houssine Cherif *(Public Service and Administrative Reform)*.

There were 9 Secretaries of State.

Local Government. The country is divided into 23 *gouvernorats*, sub-divided into 199 districts and then into *communes and imadas*.

Flag: Red with a white circle in the middle, on which is a 5-pointed red star encircled by a red crescent.

DEFENCE. Selective military service is 1 year. Officer-cadets are being trained in France.

Army. The Army consists of 2 combined arms, 1 Sahara and 1 para-commando brigades; 1 armoured reconnaissance, 1 field, 2 anti-aircraft, 1 anti-tank and 1 engineer regiments. Equipment includes 14 M-48 and 54 M-60A3 main battle, and 45 AMX-13 and 10 M-41 light tanks. Strength (1988) 31,000. There are also the paramilitary gendarmerie (2,000 men) and National Guard (7,000 men).

Navy. The flotilla consists of 1 frigate (*ex*-US 45-year-old destroyer-escort), 3 fast missile craft, 2 fast gunboats (*ex*-Chinese), 2 fast attack craft (British-built in 1977), 2 *ex*-US-coastal minesweepers used as patrol ships, 4 patrol vessels (French built), 10 coastal patrol boats, 4 protection launches and 1 large tug. In 1988 naval personnel totalled 4,500 officers and ratings.

Air Force. Equipment of the Air Force, acquired from various Western sources, includes 1 squadron of Aermacchi M.B.326K/L jet light attack aircraft; 1 squadron of F-5E/F Tiger II fighters; 12 SF.260W piston-engined light trainer/attack aircraft; 2 C-130H Hercules transports, 2 S.208 liaison aircraft, 6 SF.260M trainers, 7 M.B.326B jet trainers, 6 UH-1H, 18 AB.205, 6 Ecureuil and about 12 Alouette II and III helicopters. Personnel (1988) about 4,100.

INTERNATIONAL RELATIONS
Membership. Tunisia is a member of UN, OAU, the Islamic Conference and the Arab League.

ECONOMY
Planning. A seventh development plan (1987–91) envisaged investment of 8,000m. dinars.

Budget (in dinars). Budget estimates, 1984, revenue, 2,613m.; expenditure, 2,575m.

Currency. On 1 Nov. 1958 a new currency, the *dinar*, divided into 1,000 *millimes*, was established. Note circulation, Aug. 1980, was 910m. *dinars*.

Currency consists of coins of 1, 2, 5, 10, 20, 50, 100 and 500 *millimes*, and notes of 500 *millimes*, 1 *dinar*, 5 and 10 *dinars*. £1 = 1·45 *dinar*; US$1 = 0·82 *dinar* (March 1988).

Banking. The Central Bank of Tunisia is the bank of issue. In 1983 there were 39 banks operating in Tunisia, including 7 off-shore banks. In 1984 there were 8 development banks. Bank deposits amounted to 2,115m. dinars at 31 Dec. 1982.

Weights and Measures. The metric system of weights and measures has almost entirely taken the place of those of Tunisia, but corn is still sold in *kaffis* and *wibas*. The *kfiz* (of 16 *wiba*, each of 12 *sa'*) = 16 bushels. The *ounce* = 31·487 grammes.
The principal measure of length is the metre.

ENERGY AND NATURAL RESOURCES

Electricity. Electrical energy generated was 3,820m. kwh. in 1986. Supply 127 and 220 volts; 50 Hz.

Oil. Crude oil production (1987) 5m. tonnes.

Gas. Natural gas production (1984) 430m. cu. metres.

Minerals. Mineral production (in 1,000 tonnes) in 1984 (and 1981): Phosphate, 5,385 (4,978); iron ore, 309 (400); lead ore, 6·5 (14); zinc ore, 12·1 (15).
Processed minerals (in 1,000 tonnes) in 1982: Pig iron, 97; crude steel, 105.

Agriculture. Tunisia may be divided into 5 districts—the north, characterized by its mountainous formation, having large and fertile valleys (*e.g.*, the valley of the Medjerdah and the plains of Mornag, Mateur and Béja); the north-east, with the peninsula of Cap Bon, the soil being specially suited for the cultivation of oranges, lemons and tangerines; the Sahel, where olive trees abound; the centre, the region of high table lands and pastures, and the desert of the south, famous for its oases and gardens, where dates grow in profusion.
Agriculture is the chief industry, and large estates predominate. Of the total area of 15,583,000 hectares, about 9m. hectares are productive, including 2m. under cereals, 3·6m. used as pasturage, 900,000 forests and 1·3m. uncultivated. Production, 1985 (in 1,000 tonnes) wheat, 1,400; barley, 686; olive oil, 115; citrus fruits, 225; dates, 60. Wine (1985) 67,000 tonnes.
Other products are apricots, pears, apples, peaches, plums, figs, pomegranates, almonds, shaddocks, pistachios, esparto grass, henna and cork.
Livestock (1986): Horses, 55,000; asses, 217,000; mules, 75,000; cattle, 643,000; sheep, 5·3m.; goats, 1·1m.; camels, 181,000; pigs, 4,000.

Fisheries. In 1980, 6,209 boats with 22,555 men were engaged in fishing. In 1984 the catch amounted to 73,500 tonnes; 1981, 57,500.

INDUSTRY AND TRADE

Industry. Major modern plants include a sugar refinery in Béja (57,700 tonnes in 1975), a cellulose plant in Kassérine (22,000 tonnes in 1976), a petroleum refinery in Bizerta and a steel plant at Menzel Bourguiba. There is a marble work plant and a tyre factory at Mégrine.
Production, 1984 (in 1,000 tonnes): Crude steel, 166; cement, 2,742; lime, 484; phosphoric acid, 550; petrol, 215.

Trade Unions. The Union Générale des Travailleurs Tunisiens won 27 seats in the parliamentary elections (1 Nov. 1981). There are also the Union Tunisienne de l'Industrie, du Commerce et de l'Artisanat (UTICA, the employers' union) and the Union National des Agriculteurs (UNA, farmers' union).

Commerce. The imports and exports for calendar years (in 1,000 dinars) were as follows:

	1980	1981	1982	1983	1984	1985
Imports	1,428,400	1,866,000	2,008,000	2,116,100	2,472,500	2,287,000
Exports	904,100	1,234,000	1,188,000	1,263,900	1,396,800	1,443,000

Exports to France in 1985 totalled 384m. dinars, and imports from France, 632m. dinars and exports to USA were valued at 107m. dinars and imports from USA were valued at 133m. dinars.

Total trade between Tunisia and UK (British Department of Trade returns, in £1,000 sterling):

	1983	1984	1985	1986	1987
Imports to UK	18,125	21,086	39,826	17,292	14,714
Exports and re-exports from UK	44,559	47,077	43,209	39,824	24,943

Tourism. In 1986, there were 1·5m. tourists and 40,000 cruise passengers.

COMMUNICATIONS

Roads. In 1984 there were 26,200 km of roads, of which 11,000 km were main roads. Number of motor vehicles, 1982, included 141,185 private cars, 141,426 commercial vehicles and 11,669 motor cycles.

Railways. In 1986 there were 2,175 km of railways (465 km of 1,435 mm gauge and 1,689 km of 1,000 mm gauge), of which 21 km electrified and ran 1,877m. tonne-km and 750m. passenger-km. A suburban railway links Tunis and La Marsa, and a light rail network opened in Tunis in 1985.

Aviation. The national airline is Tunis-Air. There are 5 international airports, the main one is at Tunis-Carthage. In 1983, 3,420,600 passengers were carried.

Shipping. The main port is Tunis, and its outer port is Tunis-Goulette. These two ports and Sfax, Sousse and Bizerta are directly accessible to ocean going vessels. The port of La Skhirra, in the south, is used for the shipping of Algerian and Tunisian oil.

In 1983, 5,370 ships of 19,224,000 tons entered Tunisian ports.

Post and Broadcasting. There were, in 1983, 218,808 telephones. There were, in 1978, 403 post offices, and 6 wireless transmitting stations. Wireless sets in use in 1985 were 1·15m. Television began in 1966 and in 1985 there were 400,000 sets.

Cinemas (1976). There were 175 cinemas with a seating capacity of 44,000.

Newspapers. There were (1985) 2 Arabic and 4 French daily newspapers.

JUSTICE, RELIGION, EDUCATION AND WELFARE

Justice. There are 51 magistrates' courts, 13 courts of first instance, 3 courts of appeal (in Tunis, Sfax and Sousse) and the High Court in Tunis.

A Personal Status Code was promulgated on 13 Aug. 1956 and applied to Tunisians from 1 Jan. 1957. This raised the status of women, made divorce subject to a court decision, abolished polygamy and decreed a minimum marriage age.

Religion. The constitution recognizes Islam as the state religion. There are about 20,000 Roman Catholics, under the Prelate of Tunis. The Greek Church, the French Protestants and the English Church are also represented.

Education. All education was in 1956 made dependent on the Ministry of National Education. The 208 independent koranic schools have been nationalized and the distinction between religious and public schools has been abolished. All education is free from primary schools to university. A teachers' training college (*école normale supérieure*) was established in 1955. There are also a high school of law, 2 centres of economic studies, 2 schools of engineering, 2 medical schools, a faculty of agriculture, 2 institutes of business administration and one school of dentistry.

In 1983–84 there were 3,074 primary schools with 33,546 teachers and 1,201,645 pupils; 326 secondary schools with 17,500 teachers and 378,349 pupils. In 1980–81 there were 60,137 students at technical and vocational schools and 4,101 students in teacher-training. The University of Tunis had 38,829 students and 5,019 teaching staff in 1984–85.

Health. In 1980 there were 98 hospitals (13,571 beds). The registered medical personnel in Tunisia comprised 1,800 doctors, 313 pharmacists, 176 dentists and 60 veterinaries.

Social Security. A system of social security was set up in 1950 (amended 1963, 1964 and 1970).

DIPLOMATIC REPRESENTATIVES

Of Tunisia in Great Britain (29 Prince's Gate, London, SW7 1QG)
Ambassador: Hamadi Khouini, CBE (accredited 12 March 1987).

Of Great Britain in Tunisia (5 Place de la Victoire, Tunis)
Ambassador and Consul-General: S. P. Day.

Of Tunisia in the USA (1515 Massachusetts Ave., NW, Washington, D.C., 20005)
Ambassador: Habib Ben Yahia.

Of the USA in Tunisia (144 Ave. de la Liberté, Tunis)
Ambassador: Robert H. Pelletreau, Jr.

Of Tunisia to the United Nations
Ambassador: Ahmed Ghezal.

Books of Reference

Statistical Information: Institut National de la Statistique (27 Rue de Liban, Tunis) was set up in 1947. Its main publications are: *Annuaire statistique de la Tunisie* (latest issue, 1975).
Findlay, Allan M., Findlay, Anne M., and Lawless, R. I., *Tunisia.* [Bibliography] Oxford and Santa Barbara, 1982
Ling, D. L., *Tunisia: From Protectorate to Republic.* Indiana Univ. Press, 1967
Rudebeck, L., *The Tunisian Experience: Party and People.* London, 1970
Salem, N., *Habib Bourguiba, Islam and the Creation of Tunisia.* London, 1984
Tomkinson, M., *Tunisia: A Holiday Guide.* London and Hammamet, 1984

TURKEY

Türkiye Cumhuriyeti

Capital: Ankara
Population: 50·67m. (1985)
GNP per capita: US$1,020 (1986)

HISTORY. The Turkish War of Independence (1919–22), following the disintegration of the Ottoman Empire, was led and won by Mustafa Kemal (Atatürk) on behalf of the Grand National Assembly which first met in Ankara on 23 April 1920. On 20 Jan. 1921 the Grand National Assembly voted a constitution which declared that all sovereignty belonged to the people and vested all power, both executive and legislative, in the Grand National Assembly. The name 'Ottoman Empire' was later replaced by 'Turkey'. On 1 Nov. 1922 the Grand National Assembly abolished the office of Sultan and Turkey became a republic on 29 Oct. 1923.

Religious courts were abolished in 1924, Islam ceased to be the official state religion in 1928, women were given the franchise and western-style surnames were adopted in 1934.

On 27 May 1960 the Turkish Army, directed by a National Unity Committee under the leadership of Gen. Cemal Gürsel, overthrew the government of the Democratic Party. The Grand National Assembly was dissolved and party activities were suspended. Party activities were legally resumed on 12 Jan. 1961. A new constitution was approved in a referendum held on 9 July 1961 and general elections were held the same year.

On 12 Sept. 1980, the Turkish armed forces overthrew the Demirel Government (Justice Party). Parliament was dissolved and all activities of political parties were suspended. The Constituent Assembly was convened in Oct. 1981, and prepared a new Constitution which was enforced after a national referendum on 7 Nov. 1982.

AREA AND POPULATION. Turkey is bounded west by the Aegean Sea and by Greece, north by Bulgaria and the Black Sea, east by the USSR and Iran, and south by Iraq, Syria and the Mediterranean.

The area (including lakes) is 779,452 sq. km (300,947 sq. miles). Area in Europe (Trakya), 23,764 sq. km. Area in Asia (Anadolu), 755,688 sq. km; population (census 1985), 50,664,458.

The census population is given as follows:

	Total		Total		Total
1927	13,648,270	1950	20,947,188	1970	35,605,176
1935	16,158,018	1955	24,064,763	1975	40,347,719
1940	17,820,950	1960	27,754,820	1980	44,736,957
1945	18,790,174	1965	31,391,421	1985	50,664,458

The population of the provinces, at the census in 1985, was as follows:

Adana	1,725,940	Çankırı	263,964	İzmir	2,317,829
Adıyaman	430,728	Çorum	599,204	Kahramanmaraş	840,472
Afyonkarahisar	666,978	Denizli	667,478	Kars	722,431
Ağrı	421,131	Diyarbakir	934,505	Kastamonu	450,353
Amasya	358,289	Edirne	389,638	Kayseri	864,060
Ankara	3,306,327	Elâzığ	483,715	Kırklareli	297,098
Antalya	891,149	Erzincan	299,985	Kırşehir	260,156
Artvin	226,338	Erzurum	856,175	Kocaeli	742,245
Aydın	743,419	Eskişehir	597,397	Konya	1,769,050
Balıkesir	910,282	Gaziantep	966,490	Kütahya	543,384
Bilecik	160,909	Gireşun	502,151	Malatya	665,809
Bingöl	241,548	Gümüşhane	283,753	Manisa	1,050,130
Bitlis	300,843	Hakkari	182,645	Mardin	652,069
Bolu	504,778	Hatay	1,002,252	Muğla	486,290
Burdur	248,002	Isparta	382,844	Muş	339,492
Bursa	1,324,015	İçel	1,034,085	Nevşehir	278,129
Çanakkale	417,121	İstanbul	5,842,985	Niğde	560,386

Ordu	763,857	Sinop	280,140	Tunceli	151,906
Rize	374,206	Sivas	772,209	Uşak	271,261
Sakarya	610,500	Tekirdağ	402,721	Van	547,216
Samsun	1,108,710	Tokat	679,071	Yozgat	545,301
Şanliurfa	795,034	Trabzon	786,194	Zonguldak	1,044,945
Siirt	524,741				

The population of towns of over 100,000 inhabitants, at the census of Oct. 1985, was as follows:

İstanbul	5,494,916	Diyarbakir	305,259	Denizli	171,360
Ankara	2,251,533	Samsun	280,068	Trabzon	155,960
İzmir	1,489,817	Antalya	258,139	Sakarya	155,041
Adana	776,000	Erzurum	252,648	Balikesir	152,402
Bursa	614,133	Malatya	251,257	Manisa	126,319
Gaziantep	466,302	Kocaeli	236,144	Van	121,306
Konya	438,859	K. Maraş	212,206	Kütahya	120,354
Kayseri	378,458	Şanliurfa	206,385	Zonguldak	119,125
Eskişehir	367,328	Sivas	197,266	Hatay	109,233
İçel	314,105	Elaziğ	181,253	Isparta	101,784

CLIMATE. Coastal regions have a Mediterranean climate, with mild, moist winters and hot, dry summers. The interior plateau has more extreme conditions, with low and irregular rainfall, cold and snowy winters and hot, almost rainless summers. Ankara. Jan. 32·5°F (0·3°C), July 73°F (23°C). Annual rainfall 14·7″ (367 mm). Istanbul. Jan. 41°F (5°C), July 73°F (23°C). Annual rainfall 28·9″ (723 mm). Izmir. Jan. 46°F (8°C), July 81°F (27°C). Annual rainfall 28″ (700 mm).

CONSTITUTION AND GOVERNMENT. The Turkish Grand National Assembly was dissolved on 12 Sept. 1980. The National Security Council took over its functions and powers. On 23 Oct. 1981 a Consultative Assembly was inaugurated, to prepare a new Constitution to replace that of 1961. The Assembly began its work in Oct. 1981 under the presidency of Sadi Irmak and on 7 Nov. 1982 a national referendum established that 98% of the electorate were in favour of the new Constitution.

Turkish men and women are entitled to vote at the age of 21 to elect members of a single-chamber parliament.

Elections were held on 29 Nov. 1987. Of the 450 seats in the Grand National Assembly the Motherland Party won 292; The Social Democratic Populist Party, 99; The True Path Party, 59.

Past Presidents of the Republic: Mustafa Kemal Atatürk (29 Oct. 1923–10 Nov. 1938), İsmet İnönü (11 Nov. 1938–21 May 1950), Celâl Bayar (22 May 1950–27 May 1960), Cemal Gürsel (26 Oct. 1961–27 March 1966), Cevdet Sunay (29 March 1966–28 March 1973), Fahri S. Korutürk (6 April 1973–6 April 1980).

President: Kenan Evren.

The Cabinet in Jan. 1988 was composed as follows:

Prime Minister: Turgut Özal.

Deputy Prime Minister and Minister of State: Kaya Erdem. *Justice:* Oltan Sungurlu. *Defence:* Ercan Vuralhan. *Interior:* Mustafa Kalemli. *Foreign Affairs:* Mesut Yilmaz. *Finance and Customs:* Kurtcebe Alptemuçin. *Education, Youth and Sports:* Hasan Celal Güzel. *Health and Social Welfare:* Bülent Akarcali. *Agriculture, Forestry and Rural Affairs:* Hüsnü Doğan. *Transportation and Communications:* Ekrem Pakdemirli. *Labour:* İmren Aykut. *Industry and Commerce:* Sükrü Yürür. *Energy and Natural Resources:* Fahrettin Kurt. *Culture and Tourism:* Mustafa Tinaz Titiz. *Public Works and Housing:* Safa Giray.

There are 9 Ministers of State.

National flag: A white crescent and star on red.

National anthem: Korkma! Sönmez bu şafaklarda yüzen al sancak (words by Mehmed Akif Ersoy; tune by Zeki Güngör; adopted 12 March 1921).

Local Government. The Constitution of 1921 provided for the administrative division of the country into *İl*, (province, now 67 in number), divided into *İlçe* (district), subdivided in their turn into *Bucak* (township or commune). At the head of each Il is a Vali representing the Government. Each Il has its own elective council.

The Ilçe is regarded as a mere grouping of Bucaks for certain purposes of general administration. The Bucak or commune is an autonomous entity and possesses an elective council charged with the administration of such matters as are not reserved to the State.

According to the municipal law passed in 1930, Turkish women have the right to be electors and to be elected at local and national elections.

DEFENCE. Several bills for the reorganization of the armed forces were passed in June 1961 by the Grand National Assembly. One of these placed all organizations connected with national defence under the authority of the Minister of National Defence. Another created a Supreme Council of National Security, under the chairmanship of the Prime Minister, with the object of co-ordinating the resources of the country in case of war. Besides the Minister of National Defence and the Chief of the General Staff, the heads of economic Ministries are members of this council.

Military service in Army, Air Force and Navy is 18 months. Men are called up when they reach the age of 20.

Army. The Army consists of 16 infantry divisions (2 mechanized), 6 armoured, 4 mechanized, 11 infantry, 1 parachute and 2 commando brigades; 5 coastal defence, 20 artillery battalions. Equipment includes 1,085 M-48, 900 M-47 and 77 Leopard main battle tanks. Army Aviation has over 300 aircraft and helicopters, including Cessna light observation aircraft. Strength (1988) 542,000 (including 497,000 conscripts), and reserves number 808,000. There is also a paramilitary gendarmerie of 125,000 men.

Navy. The fleet includes 16 diesel-powered submarines (6 new designed in Federal Republic of Germany and 10 very old *ex*-US patrol submarines), 14 very old *ex*-US (1943–46 built) destroyers, 6 frigates (2 new FRG-built, 2 Turkish-built and 2 old *ex*-German Navy), 1 large minelayer, 6 coastal minelayers, 1 fast attack gunboat (light corvette type), 14 fast missile craft, 5 fast torpedo boats, 22 coastal minesweepers, 6 patrol vessels, 4 inshore minesweepers, 7 minehunting boats, 20 patrol craft, 3 repair ships, 2 submarine support ships, 1 large training ship, 1 training ship (*ex*-German support frigate), 7 landing ships, 47 landing craft, 20 minor landing craft, 3 submarine rescue ships, 9 oilers, 10 transports, 1 survey ship, 1 survey boat, 4 boom defence vessels, 3 depot ships, 4 training craft, 7 gate vessels, 30 auxiliary vessels, 14 tugs, 2 tenders, 9 water carriers, and 7 floating docks.

Future construction includes 6 diesel-electric patrol submarines designed in the Federal Republic of Germany, but to be built in Turkey; and 2 frigates, of German design but built in Gölcük.

The naval bases are at Gölcük in the Gulf of İzmit, at İskenderun, at Taskizak (İstanbul) and at İzmir.

The air component has 20 Tracker aircraft and 15 helicopters for anti-submarine and patrol duties.

Personnel strength in 1988 totalled 49,000 naval officers and ratings, 900 in the Naval Air Arm and 4,000 marines.

The Coast Guard, formed in July 1982 from the naval wing of the Jandarma, with a rear-admiral as Commander-in-Chief, has 28 patrol vessels, 8 medium patrol craft, 9 coastal patrol cutters, 4 transports, 4 service craft; and an establishment of 1,000 officers and men.

Air Force. The Air Force is under the control of the General Staff and, operationally, under 6 ATAF. It is organized as 2 tactical air forces, with headquarters at Eskisehir and Diyarbakir, each having a flight of C-47s, UH-1H helicopters, AT-11s and T-33s. Combat aircraft comprise F-104G and F-104S Starfighters in 8 squadrons; F-5As in 1 squadron; RF-5As in 1 squadron; F-4E and RF-4E Phantoms in 7 squadrons; plus Nike-Hercules surface-to-air missile batteries. The 6 transport squadrons are equipped with Transall C-160, C-130 Hercules, Citation,

Viscount and C-47 aircraft, and UH-IH helicopters. Training types include T-33A, T-37 and T-38 advanced trainers, T-34 basic and T-41 primary trainers and F-100s for weapons training. Personnel strength (1988) 57,400, with over 320 combat aircraft. Delivery of 160 F16 Fighting Falcons began late in 1987.

INTERNATIONAL RELATIONS

Membership. Turkey is a member of UN, OECD, NATO and Council of Europe and an Associate of EEC.

ECONOMY

Planning. The development plan 1985–90 envisaged an investment of TL14,412,900m.

Budget. Estimates of revenue and expenditure (in TLm.) for financial years 1 March–28/29 Feb.:

	1982–83	1983–84	1984–85	1985–86
Revenue	1,591,043	2,558,903	3,211,982	4,173,510
Expenditure	1,654,709	2,783,141	5,412,082	5,766,727

Currency. The Turkish *Lira* (TL) is divided into 100 *kuruş (piastres)*. Coins in general circulation are of the following values: 25 and 50 *kuruş,;* 1, 2½, 5, 10 and 100 *Lira.* Bank-notes in circulation are as follows: 5, 10, 20, 50, 100, 500, 1,000, 5,000 and 10,000 *Lira.* In March 1988, US$1 = 1,183 *Lira*; £1 = 2,076.

Banking. The Turkish banking system is composed of the Central Bank of the Republic of Turkey (Merkez Bankası) and 61 other banks. The assets and liabilities of deposit money banks in 1986 were TL22,085,868m.

Weights and Measures. The metric system came into force on 1 Jan. 1934. On 24 May 1928 the Grand National Assembly made European numerals obligatory as from 1 June 1929.

On 1 March 1917 the Gregorian calendar was introduced into Turkey, to be used side by side with the Hegira calendar, while as from 26 Dec. 1925 it was decided finally to adopt the Gregorian calendar alone.

ENERGY AND NATURAL RESOURCES

Electricity. The potential hydro-electric power in Turkey is estimated at 56,000m. kwh. In 1986 the electrical power plants (hydro-electric or thermal) produced 38,490m. kwh. Supply 220 volts; 50 Hz.

Oil. Oil is being produced in Garzan and Raman by the Turkish Petroleum Co. Under the oil law of 14 Oct. 1954 private companies can explore and produce oil. Crude oil production (1987) was 2·3m. tonnes. The 3 refineries refined 12m. tons of crude oil in 1975. With a fourth refinery, introduced in 1973, total refining capacity now reaches 24m. tons a year. The oil pipeline Batman–Iskenderun (494 km) was opened on 4 Jan. 1967. Imports (refined locally) in 1983 were 14·3m. tonnes.

Minerals. The Turkish provinces, especially those in Asia, are reported rich in minerals. Turkey is one of the four principal producers of chrome in the world.
Production of principal minerals (in 1,000 tonnes) was:

	1984	1985	1986
Coal	3,632	3,605	3,526
Lignite	17,832	22,828	20,797
Chromite	217	222	...
Copper concentrate	140	136	...
Refined sulphur	4	43	40

Of the Government organizations producing these ores, Zonguldak coal mines operate under the Turkish State Coal Exploitation; while the copper mines at Murgul and Ergani, the Eastern chromite mines, Keçiborlu sulphur, Emet cole-manite, Küre pyrite and cupriferous pyrite, Keban argentiferous lead mines operate under the Etibank.

Agriculture. The number of people aged 15 and over engaged in agriculture in 1980 was 10,482,856.

In 1986, 23,939,000 hectares were crop land, 18,168,000 hectares of it sown and 5,771,000 hectares fallow; vineyards, fruit orchards and olive groves occupied 2,925,000 hectares; forest occupied 20,199,000 hectares.

The soil for the most part is very fertile; the principal products are cotton, tobacco, cereals (especially wheat), figs, silk, olives and olive oil, dried fruits, liquorice root, nuts, almonds, mohair, skins and hides, furs, wool, gums, canary seed, linseed and sesame. The principal tobacco districts are Samsun, Bafra, Çarsamba, İzmit and İzmir. Two-thirds of the exports of leaf tobacco goes to the USA. The principal centre for silk production is Bursa. The production of olives for olive oil, mainly confined to the Ils of Aydın and Balıkesir, is very important (808,000 tonnes in 1986). Sugar production (refined) in 1985 was 1,429,586 tonnes. Agricultural production (in tonnes) in 1986 included 3m. grapes, 750,000 oranges and 310,000 lemons, 300,000 hazelnuts, 1,865,000 apples, 600,000 olives, 4m. potatoes. Tea production (fresh leaves, 1986) was 689,202 tonnes.

Turkey produced 600 tonnes of flax fibre and 4,500 tonnes of hemp fibre in 1986. Cotton production was 518,000 tonnes in 1986. Agricultural tractors numbered 612,731 in 1986.

Production (in 1,000 tonnes) of principal crops:

	1982	1983	1984	1985	1986
Wheat	17,500	16,400	17,200	17,000	19,000
Barley	6,400	5,425	6,500	6,500	7,000
Maize	1,360	1,480	1,500	1,900	2,300
Rye	430	380	360	360	350
Tobacco	208	234	178	170	170
Oats	330	320	316	314	350
Rice	210	189	168	162	165

Livestock (1986): 40·4m. sheep, 13·1m. goats, 16·2m. cattle, 1·2m. asses, 620,000 horses, 540,000 buffaloes.

In 1985 Turkey produced 62,000 tonnes of wool, 230,000 tonnes of cattle meat and 315,000 tonnes of sheep meat and (1981) 256,000 tonnes of poultry.

Forestry. The most wooded Ils are Kastamonu, Aydın, Bursa, Bolu, Trabzon, Konya and Balıkesir. In 1986 total forest land was 20,199,000 hectares. Produce (1,000 cu. metres) in 1986: Logs, 3,746; pit props, 608; industrial wood, 392; poles, 244. Also 4,895,000 tonnes of firewood.

Fisheries. Catch (1986): Sea fish, 525,381 tonnes; crustaceans and molluscs, 14,183,812 kg; fresh water fish, 40,279,930 kg. There were 8,661 fishing boats.

INDUSTRY AND TRADE

Industry. In 1986 Turkey produced (in tonnes) 6,742,160 of fuel oil; 5,683,949 of motor oil; 3,578,722 of crude iron; 347,406 of pig iron; 3,596,153 of steel ingots; 2,130,195 of super phosphate; 2,888,655 of coke; 20,003,548 of cement and 474,571 of paper. In 1986, 83,032 passenger cars were produced and in 1987, 33,635 tractors. There are steel works at Karabük, Ereğli and Iskenderun.

Trade Unions. The trade-union movement began in 1947. There are 4 national confederations (including Türk-İş and Disk) and 6 federations. There are 35 unions affiliated to Türk-İş and 17 employers' federations affiliated to Disk, whose activities were banned on 12 Sept. 1980. In 1986, labour unions totalled 97 and employers' unions, 46.

Employment, 1980: Manufacturing, 2,036,843; construction, 813,838; transport, communications and warehousing, 545,686; mining, 179,127; services, 41,923. There were 157,466 manufacturing firms, 236,995 trading establishments and 580,635 service establishments in 1975.

Commerce. Imports and exports (in US$1m.) for calendar years:

	1983	1984	1985	1986
Imports	9,235	10,757	11,343	11,105
Exports	5,728	7,134	7,958	7,457

Exports (1986) in US$1m.: Clothing, 1,245; fruits and vegetables, 1,232; textile yarn, fabrics and products, 936; iron and steel, 747; machinery and transport equipment, 415; chemicals, 410; beverages and tobacco, 278; petroleum and products, 183.

Imports (1986) in US$1m.: Machinery and transport equipment, 4,035; petroleum and products, 1,944; chemicals, 1,585; iron and steel, 743; metalliferous ores and metal scrap, 283; instruments, photographic and optical goods, watches and clocks, 228; non-ferrous metals, 221; textile fibres, 192; textile yarn, fabrics and products, 159; cereals and preparations, 153; beverages and tobacco, 125.

In 1986 imports (in US$1m.) were: From USA, 1,177; Iraq, 769; Japan, 684; EEC, 4,574, of which Federal Republic of Germany, 1,772; Italy, 866; France, 545; UK, 519. Exports: Iran, 564; Iraq, 553; USA, 549; EEC, 3,263, of which Federal Republic of Germany, 1,444; Italy, 580.

Total trade between Turkey and UK (British Department of Trade returns, in £1,000 sterling):

	1983	1984	1985	1986	1987
Imports to UK	184,976	204,131	538,462	406,605	579,366
Exports and re-exports from UK	244,024	331,360	460,220	433,753	513,479

Tourism. The number of foreign tourists was 2,395,790 in 1986; earnings from tourism in 1986, US$637m.

COMMUNICATIONS

Roads. In 1986 there were 30,986 km of state highways and 28,153 km of provincial roads; 55,753 km were surfaced. In 1986 there were 1,087,234 cars, 441,866 trucks and pick-ups, 148,715 buses and minibuses and 327,326 motorcycles.

Railways. Total length of railway lines in 1986 was 8,401 km (1,435 mm gauge) of which 479 km electrified; 129·3m. passengers and 13·7m. tonnes of freight were carried.

Aviation. In 1986 Turkish Airlines fleet of 31 planes flew 2,746,000 passengers and carried 37,952 tons of freight.

Shipping. In 1985 the gross tonnage of cargo ships totalled 690,784; passenger ships 131,325 and tankers 186,267. The main ports are: İstanbul, İzmir, Samsun, Mersin, İskenderun and Trabzon.

Coastal shipping, 1986: 25,543 vessels handled; 632,004 passengers entered, 626,602 cleared; 23·3m. tons of goods entered, 20·6m. cleared. International shipping: 12,383 vessels handled; 385,628 passengers entered, 380,440 cleared; 3,717m. tons of goods entered, 58·5m. cleared.

Post and Broadcasting. Number of telephones in 1983 was 2·39m.; İstanbul, 656,908; Ankara, 385,819.

In 1984 there were 6,023,000 licensed radio sets. There were 6,933,285 television receivers.

Newspapers. In 1985, 13 dailies were published in Ankara, 29 dailies in İstanbul, 5 dailies in İzmir, 4 dailies in Bursa and 3 dailies in Konya.

JUSTICE, RELIGION, EDUCATION AND WELFARE

Justice. The unified legal system consists of: (1) justices of the peace (single judges with limited but summary penal and civil jurisdiction); (2) courts of first instance (single judges, dealing with cases outside the jurisdiction of (3) and (4)); (3) central criminal courts (a president and 2 judges, dealing with cases where the crime is punishable by imprisonment over 5 years); (4) commercial courts (3 judges); (5) state security courts, to prosecute offences against the integrity of the state (a president and 4 judges, 2 of the latter being military).

The civil and military Courts of Cassation sit at Ankara.

The Council of State is the highest administration tribunal; it consists of 5 chambers. Its 31 judges are nominated from among high-ranking personalities in politics, economy, law, the army, etc.

The Military Court of Cassation in Ankara is the highest military tribunal. The Military Administrative Court deals with the judicial control of administrative acts and deeds concerning military personnel.

The Constitutional Court, set up under the Constitution, can review and annul legislation and try the President of the Republic, Ministers and senior judges. It consists of 15 regular and 5 alternate members.

The Civil Code and the Code of Obligations have been adapted from the corresponding Swiss codes. The Penal Code is largely based upon the Italian Penal Code, and the Code of Civil Procedure closely resembles that of the Canton of Neuchâtel. The Commercial Code is based on the German.

Religion. Freedom of religion is guaranteed by the Constitution. Although Islam is not the official state religion of Turkey, Moslems form 98.2% of the population. The administration of the Moslem religious organizations is in charge of the Presidency of Religious Affairs, attached to the Prime Minister's office. The Turkish Republic is a secular state.

İstanbul is the seat of the Œcumenical Patriarch, who is the head of the Orthodox Church in Turkey. The Armenian Church (Gregorian) is ruled by a Patriarch in İstanbul who is subordinate to the Katholikos of Etchmiadzin, the spiritual head of all Armenians. The Armenian Apostolic Church is ruled by the Patriarch of Cilicia. The Chaldeans (Nestorian Uniats) have a Bishop at Mardin. The Syrian Uniats have a See of Mardin and Amida, but it is united with their Patriarchate of Antioch (residence, Damascus). Greek Uniats (Byzantine Rite) have as their Ordinary in İstanbul, the Titular Bishop of Gratianopolis. The Latins have an Apostolic Delegate in İstanbul and an Archbishop in İzmir, but their Patriarch of İstanbul is titular and non-resident. There is a Grand Rabbi (Hahambaşı) in Istanbul for the Jews, who are nearly all Sephardim.

A law passed in Dec. 1934 forbids the wearing of clerical garb for those other than religious leaders except in places of worship and during divine service. The constitution forbids the political exploitation of religion or any impairment of the secular character of the republic.

Education. Elementary education is compulsory and co-educational and, in state schools, free. All children from 7 to 12 are to receive primary instruction, which may be given in state schools, schools maintained by communities, or private schools, or, subject to certain tests, at home. The state schools are under the direct control of the Ministry of Education. They include primary schools, secondary or middle schools, and *lycées* or secondary schools of a superior kind. There are also training schools for male and female teachers, and technical schools. In 1985 there were 27 universities and over 100 other institutes of higher education. The important non-Moslem communities in İstanbul maintain their own schools, which, like all 'private' schools, are subject to the supervision of the Ministry of Education.

Literacy of the population of 6 years and over was 10.6% in 1927, 19.2% in 1935, 29% in 1945, 40.9% in 1955, 48.7% in 1965, 49% in 1970, 61.7% in 1975, 67.5% in 1980.

Religious instruction in schools, hitherto prohibited, was made optional in elementary and middle schools in May 1948. There are many training schools for Moslem clergy as well as a Faculty of Theology in Ankara.

Statistics for 1985–86	*Number*	*Teachers*	*Students*
Primary schools (state and private)	49,096	212,717	6,636,000
Secondary schools (state and private)	4,501	42,514	1,674,000
High schools (state and private)	1,283	52,892	628,000
Vocational and technical schools	2,025	43,276	617,000
Faculties (university and higher education)	310	22,968	449,000

Health. Public health is the responsibility of the Ministry of Health and Social Welfare, established in 1920; social insurance for workers comes under the Workers' Insurance Institution attached to the Ministry of Labour. A law promulgated in 1961 and implemented from 1963 provided for the nationalization of the health services within 15 years. In 1986, 2.8m. workers and employees were covered by social insurance, including free medical care.

In 1986 there were 37,142 doctors, 8,410 dentists and 107,152 beds in 642 hospitals and 94 health centres.

DIPLOMATIC REPRESENTATIVES

Of Turkey in Great Britain (43 Belgrave Sq., London, SW1X 8PA)
Ambassador: Rahmi Gümrükçüoğlu (accredited 4 Aug. 1981).

Of Great Britain in Turkey (Sehit Ersan Caddesi 46/A, Cankaya, Ankara)
Ambassador: T. L. A. Daunt, CMG.

Of Turkey in the USA (1606 23rd St., NW, Washington, D.C., 20008)
Ambassador: Dr Şükrü Elekdağ.

Of the USA in Turkey (110 Ataturk Blvd., Ankara)
Ambassador: Robert Strausz-Hupé.

Of Turkey to the United Nations
Ambassador: Ilter Türkmen.

Books of Reference

Statistical Information: The State Institute of Statistics in Ankara consists of a research bureau and 10 sections dealing with agriculture, education, foreign trade, etc. It published an *Annuaire Statistique/Istatistik Yıllığı* (1928–53) and *Aylık Istatistik Bülteni,* Monthly Bulletin of Statistics.

Almanac: Turkey 1983. 1983
The Turkish Constitution, 1971. Ankara, 1972
Resmî Gazete, Official Gazette. Ankara
Konjonktür. Ministry of Commerce (three times a year, from 1940)
Banque Centrale de la République de Turquie. *Bulletin Mensuel* (from Jan. 1953)
Bulletins of the Chambers of Commerce of Istanbul and Izmir
Barchard, D., *Turkey and the West.* London, 1985
Dodd, C. H., *The Crisis of Turkish Democracy.* Beverley, 1983
Goodwin, G., *A History of Ottoman Architecture.* London, 1971
Guclu, M., *Turkey.* [Bibliography] Oxford and Santa Barbara, 1981
Hale, W., *The Political and Economic Development of Modern Turkey.* London, 1981
Hesper, M., *The State Tradition in Turkey.* Beverley, 1985
Kazancigil, A. and Ozbudun, E., (eds.) *Atatürk: Founder of a Modern State.* London, 1981
Kinross, Lord, *Atatürk.* London, 1964
Lewis, B., *The Emergence of Modern Turkey.* OUP, 1968
Mackenzie, K., *Turkey in Transition: The West's Neglected Ally.* London, 1984
Sezer, D. B., *Turkey's Security Policies.* London, 1981
Tachau, F., *Turkey: The Politics of Authority, Democracy and Development.* New York, 1984
Weiker W., *The Modernization of Turkey.* New York, 1981

State Library: MilliKütüphane Müdürlüğü, Ankara.

THE TURKS
AND CAICOS
ISLANDS

Capital: Grand Turk
Population: 7,436 (1980)

HISTORY. After a long period of rival French and Spanish claims the islands were eventually secured to the British Crown by the appointment in 1766 of a Resident British Agent, and became a separate colony in 1973 after association at various times with the colonies of the Bahamas and Jamaica.

AREA AND POPULATION. The Turks and Caicos Islands are geographically part of the Bahamas extremity, of which they form the south-eastern archipelago. There are upwards of 30 small cays; area 192 sq. miles (430 sq. km). Only 6 are inhabited; the largest, Grand Caicos, is 30 miles long by 2 to 3 miles broad. The seat of government is at Grand Turk, 7 miles long by 1·25 broad; 3,146 inhabitants. Population, 1980 census, 7,436; South Caicos, 1,392; Middle Caicos, 371; North Caicos, 1,266; Providenciales, 979; Salt Cay, 282.

Vital statistics (1985): Births, 217; marriages, 49; deaths, 72.

CLIMATE. An equable and healthy climate as a result of regular trade winds, though hurricanes are sometimes experienced. Grand Turk. Jan. 76°F (24·4°C), July 83°F (28·3°C). Annual rainfall 29″ (725 mm).

CONSTITUTION AND GOVERNMENT. A new Constitution was introduced in Aug. 1976, providing for an Executive Council and a Legislative Council. The Governor retains responsibility for external affairs, internal security, defence and certain other matters. The Executive Council comprises 3 official members: the Chief Secretary, the Financial Secretary and the Attorney-General; a Chief Minister and 3 other ministers from among the elected members of the Legislative Council; and is presided over by the Governor. The Legislative Council consists of a Speaker, the 3 official members of the Executive Council, 13 elected members and 2 appointed members. At general elections held on 3 March 1988 for the 13 elective seats on the Legislative Council, 11 seats were won by the People's Democratic Movement.

Governor: M. J. Bradley.
Chief Minister: Oswald Skipping
Flag: British Blue Ensign with the shield of the Colony in the fly.

ECONOMY
Budget. 1985–86 revenue US$10,559,954; budgetary aid, US$1,776,798; expenditure, US$12,842,752.

Currency. The currency in circulation is US$.

Banking. In 1984 there were 4 commercial banks. Barclays Bank, Bank of Nova Scotia and Turks and Caicos Banking Company have offices in Grand Turk.

COMMERCE (1984–85). Exports, US$3,535,497, and imports (1983–84), US$26,318,927. Principal imports, food, drink, tobacco and clothing. Origin of imports (1983–84 in US$1): USA, 19,648,143; UK, 1,536,724. The main exports are crawfish (US$1·08m. in 1985–86), dried and fresh conch (US$2·4m. in 1985–86), and conch shells. Nearly all crawfish, conch and other fish exports go to the USA. The catch is processed in three plants operating in South Caicos.

Total trade between Turks and Caicos Islands and UK (British Department of Trade returns, in £1,000 sterling):

	1983	1984	1985	1986	1987
Imports to UK	18	12	6	86	31
Exports and re-exports from UK	902	1,533	1,063	1,025	496

TOURISM. Number of hotels and guest houses, 34 (620 rooms/units) including 492 room Club Mediterranée. Number of visitors, 1985, 29,220.

COMMUNICATIONS

Aviation. There is a 6,335 ft paved airfield on Grand Turk. On South Caicos there is a 6,000 ft paved airstrip and on Providenciales a 7,000 ft paved airstrip. There are small paved and unpaved airstrips on the other 3 inhabited islands. Atlantic Gulf Airlines and Pan Am operate passenger services to Miami. Turks and Caicos National Airlines operates daily service to the islands and a number of flights a week to Cap Haitien (Haiti), the Dominican Republic and the Bahamas. Turks Air Ltd operates a regular weekly cargo service to Miami.

Shipping. Registered shipping (1985), 168 sailing vessels of 2,445 tons and 49 motor vessels of 5,517 tons.

Post and Broadcasting. Air-mail is received and dispatched by Miami twice or thrice weekly. Surface mail from all parts of the world is routed *via* the US arriving at 3 weekly intervals from Miami, Florida. There is no regular outgoing surface mail. Cable & Wireless (West Indies) provide internal and international cable, telephone, telex and telegraph services. There were (1985) 1,446 telephones. North Caicos and Salt Cay are linked with the Providenciales and Grand Turk exchanges respectively. The Government operates a radio broadcasting service from the Islands to Grand Turk, call sign VSI radio Turks and Caicos, for a total of 106 hours a week on 1,460 KHZ medium wave. Number of receivers, approximately 6,000.

Newspapers. The *Turks and Caicos News* is published weekly.

JUSTICE, RELIGION, EDUCATION AND WELFARE

Justice. Laws are a mixture of Statute and Common Law. There is a Magistrates Court and a Supreme Court. Appeals lie from the Supreme Court to the Court of Appeal which sits in Nassau, Bahamas. There is a further appeal in certain cases to the Privy Council in London.

Religion. The Christian faith predominates with Anglican, Methodist, Baptist. Church of God of Prophecy and New Testament Church of God being the largest group.

Education. Education is free and compulsory up to 15 years of age in the 14 government primary and 3 government secondary schools. There are also 3 private primary schools. Pupils at Turks and Caicos High School, 372; South Caicos and Providenciales, 208; North Caicos Junior High, 91. Expenditure on education 1984–85 was US$1,390,575.

Health. In 1987 there were 5 doctors and 30 hospital beds.

TUVALU

Capital: Funafuti
Population: 8,229 (1985)
GNP per capita: US$500 (1984)

HISTORY. Formerly the Ellice Islands, a British Protectorate since 1892. On the recommendation of a Commissioner, appointed by the British Government, to consider requests that the island group be separated from the Gilbert Islands, a referendum was held in 1974. There was a large majority in favour of separation and this took place in Oct. 1975. Independence was achieved on 1 Oct. 1978.

AREA AND POPULATION. Tuvalu (formerly the Ellice Islands) lies between 5° 30′ and 11° S. lat. and 176° and 180° E. long. and comprise Nanumea, Nanumanga, Niutao, Nui, Vaitupu, Nukufetau, Funafuti (administrative centre), Nukulaelae and Niulakita. Population (census 1985) 8,229 and 1,500 work abroad, mainly in Nauru. Area approximately 9½ sq. miles (24 sq. km). The population is of a Polynesian race.

CLIMATE. A pleasant but monotonous climate with temperatures averaging 86°F (30°C), though trade winds from the east moderate conditions for much of the year. Rainfall ranges from 120″ (3,000 mm) to over 160″ (4,000 mm). Funafuti. Jan. 84°F (28·9°C), July 81°F (27·2°C). Annual rainfall 160″ (4,003 mm).

CONSTITUTION AND GOVERNMENT. The Constitution provides for a Prime Minister and 4 other Ministers to be elected from among the 12 elected members of the House of Parliament, for which general elections took place in Sept. 1985. The Cabinet, chaired by the Prime Minister, consists of the 4 ministers and 2 *ex officio* members, the Attorney-General and the Secretary to Government, who are also *ex officio* members of the House of Assembly.

Governor-General: Tupua Leupena, GCVO, MBE.
Prime Minister: Rt. Hon. Dr Tomasi Puapua.
Finance: Kitiseni Lopati. *Social Services:* Telava Tevasa. *Commerce and Natural Resources:* Lale Seluka. *Works and Communications:* Solomona M. Tealof.

National flag: Light blue with the Union Jack in the canton, and 9 gold stars in the fly arranged in the same pattern as the 9 islands.

Local Government. There is a town council on Funafuti and island councils on the 7 other atolls, each consisting of 6 elected members including a president. Since 1966 Members of Parliament have been *ex-officio* members of Island Councils. The island of Niulakita is administered as part of Niutao.

INTERNATIONAL RELATIONS

Membership. Tuvalu is a member of the Commonwealth and is an ACP state of EEC.

ECONOMY

Budget. In 1987 the budget envisaged expenditure of $A4,194,830.

Currency. The unit of currency is the Australian *dollar* although Tuvaluan coins up to $A1 are in local circulation.

Banking. The Tuvalu National Bank was established at Funafuti in 1980 and is a joint venture between the Tuvalu Government and Wespac International.

ENERGY AND NATURAL RESOURCES

Electricity. Production (1986) 3m. kwh.

Agriculture. Coconut palms are the main crop. Production of copra (1984), 860 tonnes. Fruit and vegetables are grown for local consumption.

Fisheries. Sea fishing is excellent but is largely unexploited.

INDUSTRY AND TRADE

Industry. The main sources of income are from overseas remittances from Tuvaluans working abroad, philatelic and copra sales, and handicrafts.

Employment. A significant number of the population are employed in the phosphate industry on Nauru. The remainder are engaged in harvesting coconuts and fishing.

Commerce. Commerce is dominated by co-operative societies, the Tuvalu Co-operative Wholesale Society being the main importer. Imports (1984) $A3·96m.

Total trade between Tuvalu and UK (British Department of Trade returns, in £1,000 sterling):

	1984	1985	1986	1987
Imports to UK	11	—	88	2
Exports and re-exports from UK	82	87	78	106

Tourism. In 1979 there were 474 visitors.

COMMUNICATIONS

Aviation. Tuvalu is linked to the outside world by Fiji Air which operates three times a week, on Monday, Wednesday and Friday, and Air Marshal once a week on Saturdays from Kiribati and Sundays from Fiji.

Shipping. Funafuti is the only port and a deep-water wharf was opened in 1980. Inter-island communication is by ship.

Post and Broadcasting. The Tuvalu Broadcasting Service transmits daily in Tuvaluan and English and all islands have daily radio communication with Funafuti. There were 120 telephones and 2,000 radio receivers in 1984.

JUSTICE, RELIGION, EDUCATION AND WELFARE

Justice. There is a High Court presided over by the Chief Justice of Fiji. Appeals lie to the Fiji Court of Appeal.

Religion. The majority of the population are Christians mainly Protestant but with small groups of Roman Catholics, Seventh Day Adventists, Jehovah's Witnesses, Mormons and Bahai's. There are some Moslems.

Education. In 1985 there was 1 secondary school jointly administered by the Government and the Church with 250 pupils. In addition there were 9 primary schools with (1985, inclusive of 326 pupils in community training centres) 924 pupils run by Island Councils and subsidized by the central government. In 1979, a maritime school was opened on Amatuku islet. Tuvaluans requiring further education must seek it abroad.

Health. In 1984 there was 1 central hospital with 36 beds situated at Funafuti. There were 4 doctors.

DIPLOMATIC REPRESENTATIVES

Of Great Britain in Tuvalu
High Commissioner: R. A. R. Barltrop CVO (resides in Suva).

Of Tuvalu in the USA
Ambassador: Gregory Polson (resides in Tuvalu).

UGANDA

Capital: Kampala
Population: 16·79m. (1987)
GNP per capita: US$230 (1984)

HISTORY. Uganda became a British Protectorate in 1894, the province of Buganda being recognized as a native kingdom under its Kabaka. In 1961 Uganda was granted internal self-government with federal status for Buganda.

Uganda became a fully independent member of the Commonwealth on 9 Oct. 1962 after nearly 70 years of British rule. Full sovereign status was granted by the Uganda Independence Act, 1962, and the Constitution is embodied in the Uganda (Independence) Order in Council, 1962. The post of Governor-General was on 9 Oct. 1963 replaced by that of President as head of state, elected by the National Assembly for a 5-year term. Uganda became a republic on 8 Sept. 1967.

In 1971, Dr A. Milton Obote was overthrown by troops led by Gen. Idi Amin.

In April 1979 a force of the Tanzanian Army and Ugandan exiles advanced into Uganda taking Kampala on 11 April. On 14 April Dr Yusuf Lule was sworn in as President and the country was administered, initially, by the Uganda National Liberation Front.

The former Attorney-General, Godfrey Lukongwa Binaisa, QC, was appointed President by the National Consultative Council on 20 June 1979. Dr Lule subsequently left the country. Dr Binaisa was subsequently overthrown in May 1980 by the Military Commission, the military arm of Uganda National Liberation Front.

At the elections held on 10–11 Dec. 1980, the Uganda People's Congress, led by Dr A. Milton Obote, was declared to have held 72 of the 124 elective seats in the new Parliament, the Democratic Party 51 seats, and the Uganda Patriotic Movement 1 seat. There were 17 specially elected members.

On 27 July 1985 President Obote was overthrown, the Constitution suspended and the borders closed. Lieut.-Gen. Tito Okello became head of State on 29 July but on the following day the National Resistance Army stated that it was not prepared to co-operate with the new regime. A ceasefire between the NRA, under Yoweri Museveni, and government forces was agreed on 17 Dec. 1985.

AREA AND POPULATION. Uganda is bounded on the north by Sudan, on the east by Kenya, on the south by Tanzania and Rwanda, and the west by Zaïre. Total area 91,343 sq. miles (236,860 sq. km), including 15,217 sq. miles (39,459 sq. km) of swamp and water.

The population was (census 1980) 12,630,076; (estimate 1987) 16,789,000. In 1980, 12% lived in urban areas, the largest towns (1980 Census) being Kampala, the capital (458,423), Jinja (45,060), Masaka (29,123), Mbale (28,039), Mbarara (23,155), Entebbe (20,472) and Gulu (14,958). The areas, populations and capitals of the 10 provinces are:

Province	Sq. km	Census 1980	Capital
Busoga	13,340	1,221,872	Jinja
Central	6,270	1,117,648	Kampala
Eastern	22,260	2,015,530	Mbale
Karamoja	26,960	350,908	Moroto
Nile	15,730	811,755	Arua
North Buganda	27,010	1,554,371	Bombo
Northern	41,520	1,261,364	Gulu
South Buganda	15,970	905,754	Masaka
Southern	21,280	1,963,428	Mbarara
Western	30,980	1,427,446	Butebe

About 70% of the population (10·7m. inhabitants in 1986) speak Bantu languages, the major groups being the Baganda (18%), Banyoro (14%), Banyankole (8%), Bagisu (10%), Basoga (8%) and Bachiga (7%). About 16% were Nilotic groups

1212

in the north, chiefly the Lango (6·5%) and Acholi (4%), and the rest mainly Nilo-Hamitic, predominantly Turkana (8%) and Karamojong (3%) in the northeast. The official language is English, but Kiswahili is also widely used as a lingua franca.

CLIMATE. Although in equatorial latitudes, the climate is more tropical, because of its elevation, and is characterized the year round by hot sunshine, cool breezes and showers of rain. The wettest months are March to June and there is no dry season. Temperatures vary little over the year. Kampala. Jan. 74°F (23·3°C), July 70°F (21·1°C). Annual rainfall 46″ (1,150 mm). Entebbe. Jan. 72°F (22·2°C), July 69°F (20·6°C). Annual rainfall 60″ (1,506 mm).

CONSTITUTION AND GOVERNMENT. Following the seizure of control by the National Resistance Army on 26 Jan. 1986, a 24-member National Resistance Council was formed as the principal political body. In Sept. 1987 the government was composed as follows (also *see* Addenda):

President, Minister of Defence: Yoweri Museveni (sworn in 29 Jan. 1986).
Prime Minister: Dr Samson Kisekka.
Foreign Affairs: Ibrahim Mukiibi. *Finance:* Dr Crispas Kiyonga. *Co-operatives and Marketing:* John Ssebana Kizito. *Animal Husbandry:* Dr Shebe Musaba. *Health:* Dr Ruhukanu Rugunda. *Public Service and Cabinet Affairs:* D. Kibirango. *Industry and Technology:* Prof. Stanley Tumwine. *Works:* Daniel Kigozi Serwano. *Internal Affairs:* Paul Ssemogerere. *Information and Broadcasting:* Abubakar Mayanja. *Planning and Economic Development:* Joseph Okune. *Commerce:* Dr George Kanyeihamba. *Rehabilitation:* Dr Alex Ofumbi. *Lands and Surveys:* James Oboi Ochola. *Water and Mineral Development:* Chango Macho. *Justice and Attorney-General:* Joseph Mulenga. *Tourism and Wildlife:* Anthony Butele. *Education:* Joshua Mayanja Nkangi. *Agriculture and Forestry:* Robert Kitariko. *Transport and Communications:* Ali Kirunda Kivenjinjya. *Energy:* Jaberi Badandi-Saali. *Youth, Culture and Sports:* Stanley Okurut. *Without Portfolio:* Tom Rubale.

National flag: Six horizontal stripes of black, yellow, red, black, yellow, red, in the centre a small white disc bearing a representation of a Balearic Crested Crane.

Local government: There are 10 provinces divided into 33 districts.

DEFENCE

Army. The National Resistance Army had a strength of about 20,000 in 1988 and is loosely organized in brigades and battalions. Equipment includes 10 T-34/-54/-55 and 3 M-4 tanks.

Navy. A small lake patrol was initiated in 1977.

Air Force. Since 1979, the service has been in a period of decline. As far as is known in early 1988, the equipment received from the East Bloc (MiG-17 and MiG-21 combat aircraft and L-29 jet trainers) is in storage. It is understood that some aircraft of Western European origin are still serviceable, including a small number of AS.202 Bravo and SF.260 trainers and about 6 Agusta-Bell helicopters. The Police Air Wing still operates 2 fixed-wing aircraft and 7 Bell helicopters.

INTERNATIONAL RELATIONS

Membership. Uganda is a member of UN, OAU, the Non-Aligned Movement, the Commonwealth and is an ACP state of EEC.

ECONOMY

Budget. The revenue and expenditure for fiscal years (1 July–30 June) in Uganda Sh. 1m.:

	1980–81	1981–82	1982–83	1983–84
Revenue	2,835	25,292	40,653	90,258
Expenditure	7,568	21,422	47,400	99,300

Currency. The monetary unit is the *Uganda shilling* divided into 100 *cents*. In May 1987 a new 'heavy' shilling was introduced worth 100 old shillings. In March 1988, £1 = 106·08 Uganda shillings; US$1 = 60·10 Uganda shillings.

Banking. The Bank of Uganda was set up on 16 May 1966; its external assets as at 31 Aug. 1967 were £9m. The Uganda Credit and Savings Bank, set up in 1950, was on 9 Oct. 1965 reconstituted as the Uganda Commercial Bank, with its capital fully owned by the Government.

Barclays Bank of Uganda Ltd. has 4 branches, Standard Bank Uganda Ltd. has 1 branch, Bank of Baroda Uganda Ltd. has 3 branches and the Libyan Arab Uganda Bank for Foreign Trade and Development has 3 branches, the Uganda Commercial Bank has 56 branches. The Co-operative Bank which is owned by the Co-operative Movement. There are 2 Development Banks; the East African Development Bank and the Uganda Development Bank.

ENERGY AND NATURAL RESOURCES

Electricity. Industrial expansion is based on hydro-electric power provided by the Owen Falls scheme, which has a capacity of 150,000 kwh. Production (1986) 287m. kwh.

Minerals. The Kilembe Mines, which used to produce both copper for export and phosphate rock, ceased production in 1979.

Agriculture. In 1987, agriculture was still recovering from the administration of 1971–79. Cotton and coffee are the principal exports, the former being grown entirely and the latter very largely by African farmers. Production (1986) in 1,000 tonnes: Tobacco, 4; coffee, 195; cotton lint, 8; tea, 3; sugar-cane, 550.

Livestock (1986): Cattle, 5·1m.; sheep, 1·7m.; goats, 3·3m.; pigs, 250,000; poultry, 19m.

Forestry. Exploitable forests consist almost entirely of hardwoods. About 50% of the timber exported goes to the UK and another 25% to Kenya and Tanzania, from which the bulk of the softwood imports are obtained.

Fisheries. With its 13,600 sq. miles of lakes and many rivers, Uganda possesses one of the largest fresh-water fisheries in the world. In 1983 fish production was 172,000 tonnes. Fish farming (especially carp and tilapia) is a growing industry.

COMMERCE. Trade (in US$1m.):

	1982	1983[1]	1984[1]
Imports	458	510	509
Exports	335	330	380

[1] Estimate.

Total trade between Uganda and UK (British Department of Trade returns, in £1,000 sterling):

	1983	1984	1985	1986	1987
Imports to UK	29,645	46,750	48,571	50,870	37,076
Exports and re-exports from UK	21,092	29,294	39,925	26,046	38,545

Tourism. There were 35,000 tourists in 1986.

COMMUNICATIONS

Roads. There were (1985) 7,582 km of all-weather roads maintained by the Ministry of Works, of which 1,934 km are two-lane bitumenized highways, and some 19,640 km of other roads, maintained by district governments.

Railways. On 26 Aug. 1977 Uganda Railways was formed following break-up of the East African Railways administration. The network totals 1,286 km (metre gauge). In 1986 railways carried 1·5m. passengers and 315,819 tonnes of freight.

Aviation. Dr Obote International Airport, formerly Entebbe, has direct flights to Europe, Zimbabwe, Sudan, Kenya, Burundi, Ghana, Ethiopia, Zaïre, Nigeria, USSR, and Rwanda by Sudan Airways, Air Congo, SABENA, Air France, Ethiopian

Airlines, Air Zaïre and Aeroflot. Eleven other government airfields are used for internal communications.

Posts and Broadcasting. There were 48,884 telephones in use at 1 Jan. 1978. There were 275,000 radio receivers and about 75,000 television sets in 1982

Cinemas. In 1971 there were 16 cinemas with a seating capacity of 8,000.

JUSTICE, RELIGION, EDUCATION AND WELFARE

Justice. The High Court of Uganda, presided over by the Chief Justice and 15 puisne judges, exercises original and appellate jurisdiction throughout Uganda. Subordinate courts, presided over by Chief Magistrates and Magistrates of the first, second and third grade, are established in all areas: jurisdiction varies with the grade of Magistrate. Chief and first-grade Magistrates are professionally qualified; second-and third-grade Magistrates are trained to diploma level at the Law School, Entebbe. Chief Magistrates exercise supervision over and hear appeals from second- and third-grade courts.

The Court of Appeal of Uganda hears appeals from the High Court.

Religion. About 62% of the population are Christian and 6% Moslem.

Education. In 1982 there were 1,616,791 pupils in 5,300 primary schools, 132,051 pupils in 257 secondary schools, 13,338 students in 23 technical schools and primary teacher-training colleges, and 7,312 students in the 4 higher education establishments.

Health. In 1983 there were 76 hospitals and 20,343 hospital beds. The medical department has 8 such schools for training nurses, midwives, medical assistants, health inspectors, and other medical staff.

DIPLOMATIC REPRESENTATIVES

Of Uganda in Great Britain (Uganda Hse., Trafalgar Sq., London, WC2N 5DX)
High Commissioner: Ernest Rusita (accredited 16 July 1986).

Of Great Britain in Uganda (10/12 Parliament Ave., Kampala)
High Commissioner: D. M. March, CBE.

Of Uganda in the USA (5909 16th St., NW, Washington, D.C., 20011)
Ambassador: Princess Elizabeth Bagaaya-Nyabongo.

Of the USA in Uganda (British High Commission Bldg., Obote Ave., Kampala)
Ambassador: Robert G. Houdek.

Of Uganda to the United Nations
Ambassador: Wanume Kibedi.

Books of Reference

Atlas of Uganda. Dept. of Lands and Surveys. Kampala, 1962
Collison, R. L., *Uganda.* [Bibliography] Oxford and Santa Barbara, 1981
Jørgensen, J. J., *Uganda: A Modern History.* London, 1981
Kitching, A. L., and Blackledge, G. R., *A Luganda–English and English–Luganda Dictionary.* Kampala, 1925
Larimore, A. E., *The Alien Town: Patterns of Settlement in Uganda.* Chicago, 1959
Listowel, J., *Amin.* Irish Univ. Press, 1973
Mamdani, M., *Imperialism and Fascism in Uganda.* London, 1983

UNION OF
SOVIET SOCIALIST
REPUBLICS

Capital: Moscow
Population: 284·5m. (1988)

Soyuz Sovyetskikh
Sotsialisticheskikh
Respublik

POST-REVOLUTION HISTORY. Up to 12 March 1917 the territory now forming the USSR, together with that of Finland, Poland and certain tracts ceded in 1918 to Turkey, but less the territories then forming part of the German, Austro-Hungarian and Japanese empires–East Prussia, Eastern Galicia, Transcarpathia, Bukovina, South Sakhalin and Kurile Islands–which were acquired during and after the Second World War, was constituted as the Russian Empire. It was governed as an autocracy under the Tsar, with the aid of Ministers responsible to himself and a State Duma with limited legislative powers, elected by provincial assemblies chosen by indirect elections on a restricted franchise.

On 8 March 1917 a revolution broke out. The Duma parties, on 12 March, set up a Provisional Committee of the State Duma, while the factory workmen and the insurgent garrison of Petrograd elected a Council (Soviet) of Workers' and Soldiers' Deputies. Soviets were also elected by the workmen in other towns, in the Army and Navy and, as time went on, by the peasantry. On 15 March 1917 the Tsar abdicated, and the Provisional Committee, by agreement with the Petrograd Soviet, appointed a Provisional Government and, on 14 Sept., proclaimed a republic. However, a political struggle went on between the supporters of the Provisional Government–the Mensheviks and the Socialist Revolutionaries–and the Bolsheviks, who advocated the assumption of power by the Soviets. When they had won majorities in the Soviets of the principal cities and of the armed forces on several fronts, the Bolsheviks organized an insurrection through a Military-Revolutionary Committee of the Petrograd Soviet. On 7 Nov. 1917 the Committee arrested the Provisional Government and transferred power to the second All-Russian Congress of Soviets. This elected a new government, the Council of People's Commissars, headed by Lenin.

On 25 Jan. 1918 the third All-Russian Congress of Soviets issued a Declaration of Rights of the Toiling and Exploited People, which proclaimed Russia a Republic of Soviets of Workers', Soldiers' and Peasants' Deputies; and on 10 July 1918 the fifth Congress adopted a Constitution for the Russian Soviet Federal Socialist Republic. In the course of the civil war other Soviet Republics were set up in the Ukraine, Belorussia and Transcaucasia. These first entered into treaty relations with the RSFSR and then, in 1922, joined with it in a closely integrated Union.

AREA AND POPULATION. The total area of the Soviet Union in April 1987 was 22·4m. sq. km (8·65m. sq. miles). The census population on 15 Jan. 1970 was 241·7m. (111·4m. males, 130·3m. females; 136m. urban, 105·7m. rural). The census population on 17 Jan. 1979 was 262·4m. (122·3m. males, 140·1m. females, 163·6m. urban, 98·9m. rural). The increase of 27·6m. in urban population between 1970 and 1979 was due to natural increase and 15·6m. rural dwellers becoming part of the urban population resulting from migration because of the development of industry and transport, and increased farm mechanization, and from the urbanization of large rural centres. Consequently, despite a natural increase of 8·7m. in rural areas, there was a net decrease of 6·9m. over this period. Population at 1 Jan. 1987, 281·7m. (132·5m. males, 149·2m. females; 186m. urban; 95·7m. rural).

The Soviet social structure is officially described as consisting of two friendly social classes–workers and collective farm peasantry–and a social stratum, the intelligentsia, who are engaged in mental rather than manual labour. In 1987 workers (in industry and agriculture) accounted for 61·8% of total population, collective farmers for 12% and intelligentsia for 26·2%.

The areas (in 1,000 sq. km) and population (in 1m., in Jan. 1987) of the constituent republics are as follows (capitals in brackets):

Constituent Republics	Area	Population	Constituent Republics	Area	Population
RSFSR (Moscow)	17,075	145·3	Tadzhikistan (Dushanbe)	143	4·8
Ukraine (Kiev)	604	51·2	Kirgizia (Frunze)	199	4·1
Uzbekistan (Tashkent)	447	19·0	Lithuania (Vilnius)	65	3·6
Kazakhstan (Alma-Ata)	2,717	16·2	Armenia (Yerevan)	30	3·4
Belorussia (Minsk)	208	10·1	Turkmenistan (Ashkhabad)	488	3·4
Azerbaijan (Baku)	87	6·8	Latvia (Riga)	64	2·6
Georgia (Tbilisi)	70	5·3	Estonia (Tallinn)	45	1·6
Moldavia (Kishinev)	34	4·2			

Nationalities. The most numerous nationalities at the 1979 census were: 137·4m. Russians, 42·3m. Ukrainians, 12·5m. Uzbeks, 9·5m. Belorussians, 6·6m. Kazakhs, 6·3m. Tatars, 5·5m. Azerbaijanians, 4·1m. Armenians, 3·6m. Georgians, 3m. Moldavians, 2·9m. Tadzhiks, 2·9m. Lithuanians, 2m. Turkmenians, 1·9m. Germans, 1·9m. Kirgiz, 1·8m. Jews, 1·8m. Chuvashes, 1·4m. Latvians, 1·4m. Bashkirs, 1·2m. Mordovians, 1·2m. Poles, 1m. Estonians. The great majority (in each case 73-99%) indicated the language of their nationality as their native tongue; exceptions were the Bashkirs (67%), Germans (57%), Poles (29%) and Jews (14%).

Estimated losses of population in the Second World War, 20m., of which 7m. were military losses.

The following tables show the growth of the population in Russia:

1897 (Russian Empire)	126,900,000	1959 (census)	208,826,650
1913 (Russian Empire)	170,900,000	1970 (census)	241,720,134
1913 (present frontiers)	159,153,000	1979 (census)	262,436,227
1939 (census)	170,557,093		

The following was the population on 1 Jan. 1987 of the larger towns (in 1,000):

Aktyubinsk	248	Dzerzhinsk (Gorky		Komsomolsk-on-	
Alma-Ata	1,108	region)	281	Amur	316
Andizhan	288	Engels	182	Kostroma	276
Andropov	254	Ferghana	203	Kramatorsk	198
Angarsk	262	Frunze	632	Krasnodar	623
Arkhangelsk	416	Gomel	488	Krasnoyarsk	899
Armavir	172	Gorlovka	345	Kremenchug	230
Ashkhabad	382	Gorky	1,425	Krivoi Rog	698
Astrakhan	509	Grodno	263	Kuibyshev	1,280
Baku	1,741	Grozny	404	Kurgan	354
Barnaul	596	Irkutsk	609	Kursk	434
Belaya Tserkov	194	Ivano-Frankovsk	225	Kustanai	212
Belgorod	293	Ivanovo	479	Kutaisi	220
Berezniki	200	Izhevsk	631	Kzyl-Orda	189
Biisk	231	Kalinin	447	Leninakan	228
Blagoveshchensk	202	Kaliningrad	394	Leningrad	4,948
Bobruisk	232	Kaluga	307	Lipetsk	465
Bratsk	249	Kamensk-		Lvov	767
Brest	238	Uralskii	204	Lyubertsy	162
Bryansk	445	Karaganda	633	Magnitogorsk	430
Bukhara	220	Kaunas	417	Makeyevka	455
Cheboksary	414	Kazan	1,068	Makhachkala	320
Chelyabinsk	1,119	Kemerovo	520	Melitopol	174
Cherepovetz	315	Kerch	173	Minsk	1,543
Cherkassy	287	Khabarovsk	591	Mogilev	359
Chernigov	291	Kharkov	1,587	Moscow	8,815
Chernovtzy	254	Kherson	358	Murmansk	432
Chimkent	389	Kiev	2,554	Naberezhnye Chelny	480
Chita	349	Kirov	421	Nalchik	236
Djambul	315	Kirovabad		Namangan	291
Dneprodzerzhinsk	279	(Azerbaijan)	270	Nikolayev	501
Dnepropetrovsk	1,182	Kirovograd	269	Nizhnii Tagil	427
Donetsk	1,090	Kishinev	663	Norilsk	181
Dushanbe	582	Klaipeda	201	Novgorod	228

Novocherkassk	188	Rubtsovsk	168	Tomsk	489
Novokuznetsk	589	Ryazan	508	Tselinograd	276
Novorossiisk	179	Samarkand	388	Tula	538
Novosibirsk	1,423	Saransk	323	Tyumen	456
Odessa	1,141	Saratov	918	Ufa	1,092
Omsk	1,134	Semipalatinsk	330	Ulan-Ude	351
Ordzhonikidze		Sevastopol	350	Ulyanovsk	589
(Vladikavkaz)	313	Severodvinsk	239	Uralsk	201
Orel	335	Shakhty	225	Ust-Kamenogorsk	321
Orenburg	537	Simferopol	338	Vilnius	566
Orsk	273	Smolensk	338	Vinnitsa	383
Osh	209	Sochi	317	Vitebsk	347
Pavlodar	331	Stavropol	306	Vladimir	343
Penza	540	Sterlitamak	251	Vladivostok	615
Perm	1,075	Sumgait	234	Volgograd	988
Petropavlovsk-		Sumy	268	Vologda	278
Kamchatskii	252	Sverdlovsk	1,331	Volzhsky	257
Petropavlovsk (North		Syktyvkar	224	Voronezh	872
Kazakhstan)	233	Syzran	174	Voroshilovgrad	509
Petrozavodsk	264	Taganrog	295	Yaroslavl	634
Podolsk	209	Tallinn	478	Yerevan	1,168
Poltava	309	Tambov	305	Yoshkar-Ola	243
Prokopyevsk	278	Tashkent	2,124	Zaporozhye	875
Pskov	202	Tbilisi	1,194	Zhdanov	529
Riga	900	Temirtau	228	Zhitomir	287
Rostov-on-Don	1,004	Togliatti	627	Zlatoust	206
Rovno	233				

Narodnoe khozyaistvo SSSR. Moscow, annual
Ezhegodnik Bol'shoi Sovetskoi Entsiklopedii. Moscow, annual
Itogi Vsesoyuznoi perepisi naseleniya 1959 goda. SSSR (svodnyi tom). Moscow, 1962
Itogi Vsesoyuznoi perepisi naseleniya 1970 goda, 7 vols. Moscow, 1972–74
Chislennost' i sostav naseleniya SSSR po dannym Vsesoyuznoi perepisi 1979 goda. Moscow, 1984
Sovetskii Soyuz. Geograficheskoe opisanie, 22 vols. Moscow, 1966–72
Cole, J. P., *Geography of the Soviet Union.* London, 1984
Howe, G. Melvyn, *The Soviet Union: a Geographical Survey* (2nd ed.). London, 1983
Symons, L., (ed.), *The Soviet Union: a Systematic Geography.* London, 1983
Wixman, R., *The Peoples of Russia and the USSR.* London, 1984

CLIMATE. The USSR comprises several different climatic regions, ranging from polar conditions in the north, through sub-arctic and humid continental, to subtropical and semi-arid conditions in the south. Rainfall amounts are greatest in areas bordering the Baltic, Black Sea, Caspian Sea and eastern coasts of Asiatic Russia. In most cases, there is a summer maximum.

Moscow. Jan. 15°F (–9·4°C), July 65°F (18·3°C). Annual rainfall 25·2" (630 mm). Arkhangelsk. Jan. 5°F (–15°C), July 57°F (13·9°C). Annual rainfall 20·1" (503 mm). Kiev. Jan. 21°F (–6·1°C), July 68°F (20°C). Annual rainfall 22" (554 mm). Leningrad. Jan. 17°F (–8·3°C), July 64°F (17·8°C). Annual rainfall 19·5" (488 mm). Vladivostok. Jan. 6°F (–14·4°C), July 65°F (18·3°C). Annual rainfall 24" (599 mm).

CONSTITUTION

Constituent Republics. The Union of Soviet Socialist Republics was formed by the union of the RSFSR, the Ukrainian Soviet Socialist Republic, the Belorussian Soviet Socialist Republic and the Transcaucasian Soviet Socialist Republic; the Treaty of Union was adopted by the first Soviet Congress of the USSR on 30 Dec. 1922. In Oct. 1924 the Uzbek and Turkmen Autonomous Soviet Socialist Republics and in Dec. 1929 the Tadzhik Autonomous Soviet Socialist Republic were declared constituent members of the USSR, becoming Union Republics.

At the 8th Congress of the Soviets, on 5 Dec. 1936, a new constitution of the USSR was adopted. The Transcaucasian Republic was split up into the Armenian Soviet Socialist Republic, the Azerbaijan Soviet Socialist Republic and the Georgian Soviet Socialist Republic, each of which became constituent republics of the Union. At the same time the Kazakh Soviet Socialist Republic and the Kirghiz Soviet Socialist Republic, previously autonomous republics within the RSFSR, were proclaimed constituent republics of the USSR.

In Sept. 1939 Soviet troops occupied eastern Poland as far as the 'Curzon line', which in 1919 had been drawn on ethnographical grounds as the eastern frontier of Poland, and incorporated it into the Ukrainian and Belorussian Soviet Socialist Republics. In Feb. 1951 some districts of the Drogobych Region of the Ukraine and the Lublin Voivodship of Poland were exchanged.

On 31 March 1940 territory ceded by Finland was joined to that of the Autonomous Soviet Socialist Republic of Karelia to form the Karelo-Finnish Soviet Socialist Republic, which was admitted into the Union as the 12th Union Republic. On 16 July 1956 the Supreme Soviet of the USSR adopted a law altering the status of the Karelo-Finnish Republic from that of a Union (constituent) Republic of the USSR to that of an Autonomous (Karelian) Republic within the RSFSR.

On 2 Aug. 1940 the Moldavian Soviet Socialist Republic was constituted as the 13th Union Republic. It comprised the former Moldavian Autonomous Soviet Socialist Republic and Bessarabia (44,290 sq. km, ceded by Romania on 28 June 1940), except for the districts of Khotin, Akerman and Ismail, which, together with Northern Bukovina (10,440 sq. km), were incorporated in the Ukrainian Soviet Republic. The Soviet-Romanian frontier thus constituted was confirmed by the peace treaty with Romania, signed on 10 Feb. 1947. On 29 June 1945 Ruthenia (Sub-Carpathian Russia, 12,742 sq. km) was by treaty with Czechoslovakia incorporated into the Ukrainian Soviet Socialist Republic.

On 3, 5 and 6 Aug. 1940 Lithuania, Latvia and Estonia were incorporated in the Soviet Union as the 14th, 15th and 16th Union Republics respectively. The change in the status of the Karelo-Finnish Republic reduced the number of Union Republics to 15.

After the defeat of Germany it was agreed by the governments of the UK, the USA and the USSR (by the Potsdam declaration) that part of East Prussia should be embodied in the USSR. The area (11,655 sq. km), which includes the towns of Konigsberg (renamed Kaliningrad), Tilsit (renamed Sovyetsk) and Insterburg (renamed Chernyakhovsk), was joined to the RSFSR by decree of 7 April 1946.

By the peace treaty with Finland, signed on 10 Feb. 1947, the province of Petsamo (Pechenga), ceded to Finland on 14 Oct. 1920 and 12 March 1946, was returned to the Soviet Union. On 19 Sept. 1955 the Soviet Union renounced its treaty rights to the naval base of Porkkala-Udd and on 26 Jan. 1956 completed the withdrawal of the forces from Finnish territory.

In 1945, after the defeat of Japan, the southern half of Sakhalin (36,000 sq. km) and the Kurile Islands (10,200 sq. km) were, by agreement with the Allies, incorporated in the USSR. [1]

[1] However, Japan asks for the return of the Etorofu and Kunashiri Islands as not belonging to the Kurile Islands proper. The Soviet Government informed Japan on 27 Jan. 1960 that the Habomai Islands and Shikotan would be handed back to Japan on the withdrawal of the American troops from Japan.

GOVERNMENT. The Soviet Union is a socialist state of the whole people (1977 constitution), the political units of which are the Soviets of People's Deputies. All central and local authority is vested in these Soviets.

The economic foundation of the USSR is the socialist system of economy and the socialist ownership of the means of production. There are two forms of socialist property: (1) state property (property of the whole people); (2) co-operative and collective farm (*kolkhoz*) property (property of individual collective farms and property of co-operative associations). The land, mineral deposits, waters, forests, mills, factories, mines, railways, water and air transport, banks, means of communication, state farms (*sovkhozy*), as well as municipal enterprises and the principal dwelling-house properties in the cities and industrial localities, are state property, but the land occupied by collective farmers is secured to them in perpetuity so long as they use it in accordance with the laws of the country. The members of the *kolkhozy* may have small plots of land attached to their dwellings for their own use. Peasants unwilling to enter a kolkhoz may retain their individual farms, but they are not allowed to employ hired labour. The right of personal property of citizens in their income from work and in their savings, in their dwelling houses and auxiliary household economy, their domestic furniture and utensils and objects of personal use and comfort, as well as the right of inheritance of personal property of citizens, are protected by law. The constitution recognizes the right of all citizens to work, rest, leisure, education, health protection, housing, maintenance in old age, sickness or incapacity, without distinction of sex, race or nationality, and lays down that any direct or indirect restriction of the rights of, or conversely, the establishment of direct or indirect privileges for, citizens on account of their race, or nationality, as well as the advocacy of racial or national exclusiveness, or hatred or contempt, is punishable by law. The franchise is enjoyed by all citizens of the USSR, including members of the Armed Forces, who have reached the age of 18, irrespective of sex, with the exception of the legally certified insane. Candidates for election to the Supreme Soviet of the USSR must be 21 years of age; for all other authorities the minimum age for candidates is 18. A member of any Soviet may be recalled by a decision of a majority of his or her electors if he or she fails to give satisfaction (law on procedure for this, 30 Oct. 1959).

The USSR consists of 15 Union Republics, each inhabited by a major nationality which gives its name to the republic. These are divided into 129 territories and regions, and these again into 3,225 districts, 2,176 towns, 662 urban districts and 3,992 urban settlements (1 Jan. 1987). Within the districts there are 42,411 rural Soviets (usually each including a number of villages). The territories and regions also include a number of smaller nationalities, forming their own self-governing units–20 Autonomous Soviet Socialist Republics, 8 Autonomous Regions and 10 Autonomous Areas.

The highest legislative organ is the Supreme Soviet of the USSR. It consists of two chambers with equal legislative rights, elected for a term of 5 years: the Council of the Union and the Council of Nationalities. Each has 750 members. The present Supreme Soviet, the 'Eleventh Convocation', was elected on 4 March 1984.

The Council of the Union is elected by the citizens of the USSR on the basis of constituencies with equal populations (approximately 1 deputy for every 360,000 population). Its Chairman (elected 1984) is L. N. Tolkunov. The Council of Nationalities is elected by the citizens of the USSR on the basis of national-territorial areas (32 deputies from each Union Republic, 11 from each Autonomous Republic, 5 from each Autonomous Region and 1 from each Autonomous Area). Its Chairman (elected 1984) is A. E. Voss. Plenary sessions of the Supreme Soviet are normally held twice a year for two or three days at a time.

Each chamber elects 17 standing commissions: mandates; legislative proposals; foreign affairs; planning and budget; industry; power engineering; transport and communications; construction and the building materials industry; agro-industrial complex; science and technology; consumer goods and services; housing and municipal services; health and social security; education and culture; women's work and social conditions and the protection of motherhood and childhood; youth affairs; and conservation and the rational use of natural resources. Membership of the commissions presently embraces 1,210 deputies (80.7% of the total).

Deputies are elected by the voters on the basis of universal, equal and direct suffrage by secret ballot. The only legal political party is the Communist Party of the Soviet Union; non-members are classed as non-party citizens. Candidates are selected at preliminary 'constituency electoral consultation' meetings (selection conferences), to which organizations which have put forward nominations send delegates, who discuss the various nominees. As a consequence, to date, a single candidate has been agreed upon in each constituency, whose name appears on the ballot paper to be endorsed (by non-deletion) or struck out as the voter desires. These procedures are governed by the Law on Elections to the Supreme Soviet of the USSR, adopted in April 1978. At the election on 4 March 1984, 184,006,373 electors voted (99.99% of the total); the vote in favour of the single list of candidates was 99.94% and 99.95% in each of the two chambers. The Supreme Soviet elected on that day consists of 1,071 Communist and 428 non-party deputies; 492 are women, 527 manual workers in industry and state farms, and 242 collective farmers.

The highest executive and administrative body of state authority in the USSR is the Council of Ministers of the USSR, which is appointed by the USSR Supreme Soviet at a joint sitting of the two chambers. It consists of a Chairman (in effect the Soviet Prime Minister), First Vice-Chairmen and Vice-Chairmen, Ministers of the USSR, and Chairmen of State Committees of the USSR. Chairmen of the Councils of Ministers of the Union Republics are *ex officio* members of the USSR Council of Ministers. The Council of Ministers of the USSR had more than 100 members in 1988, and day-to-day co-ordination of governmental matters is accordingly delegated to a smaller body, the Presidium of the Council of Ministers, which meets approximately every week. The Council of Ministers is responsible and accountable to the Supreme Soviet and is required to report regularly to the Supreme Soviet upon its work. Between sessions of the Supreme Soviet the Council of Ministers is responsible to the Presidium of the USSR Supreme Soviet.

The Presidium of the Supreme Soviet of the USSR is elected from among the deputies at a joint session of both chambers of the Supreme Soviet. It consists of a chairman (in effect the President of the USSR), a first vice-chairman, 15 vice-chairmen (1 from each Union Republic), 21 members and a secretary (39 members in all). The Presidium acts as the supreme state authority between sessions of the Supreme Soviet and is accountable to it for all its actions. The Presidium convenes sessions of the Supreme Soviet and co-ordinates the work of its standing commissions; it interprets the law of the USSR and ratifies and denounces international treaties; it confers medals, orders and other distinctions; it decides matters such as citizenship, amnesties, pardons, martial law and states of emergency; and it appoints the high command of the Soviet Armed forces and Soviet diplomatic representatives. It is empowered to adopt decrees *(ukazy)* and resolutions *(postanovleniya)*.

Soon after the adoption of the 1936 Constitution all the constituent republics of the Union held their Soviet congresses, at which they adopted their own constitutions based in all essentials upon the Constitution of the Union but adapted where necessary to local requirements. In April 1978 the Supreme Soviets of the Union Republics similarly adopted new republican constitutions based upon the new Constitution of the USSR approved by the Supreme Soviet in Oct. 1977. Article 73 of the 1977 Constitution of the USSR reserves to the central government the spheres of war and peace, diplomatic relations, defence, foreign trade, state security, economic planning, education, the basic principles of legislation, and other matters of 'all-Union significance'. The right of the constituent republics to withdraw from the Union is, however, formally recognized in Article 72. Union Republics have their own Supreme Soviets, Presidiums and Councils of Ministers, and exercise a wide range of devolved powers in local matters.

There are 20 Autonomous Republics in the USSR, which are similarly governed by their own Supreme Soviets, Presidiums and Councils of Ministers exercising devolved powers over local matters. Most (16) are in the RSFSR; 2 are in Georgia and 1 each in Azerbaijan and Uzbekistan. Five Autonomous Regions are in the RSFSR, 1 each in Azerbaijan, Georgia, and Tadzhikistan. All 10 Autonomous Areas are in the RSFSR. Elections are held every five years to the Supreme Soviets of Union and Autonomous Republics. At the most recent elections (Feb. 1985), 10,190 deputies were elected; 3,830 (37·6%) were women, 3,495 (34·3%) were non-Party, 3,605 (35·4%) were industrial workers and 1,557 (15·3%) were collective farmers.

Regions and territories, districts, towns and rural areas are similarly governed by their own Soviets, elected for a term of 2½ years. At the most recent elections (June 1987), 2,321,766 deputies were elected to these Soviets; 1,146,329 (49·4%) were women, 1,317,009 (56·7%) were non-Party, 976,552 (42·1%) were industrial workers and 562,052 (24·2%) were collective farmers. In 162 districts elections were conducted, as an experiment, with more candidates nominated than seats available. On 1 Jan. 1988 there were 52,602 rural and urban Soviets in the USSR with 2·3m. deputies and over 30m. voluntary co-opted members participating in the work of their standing committees.

State flag: Red, with sickle and hammer in gold in the upper corner near the staff, and above them a 5-pointed star bordered in gold.

National anthem: Soyuz nerushimy respublik svobodnykh (words by S. Mikhalkov and G. El-Registan; music by A. V. Alexandrov; 1944, revised 1977).

Chairman of the Presidium of the Supreme Soviet of the USSR: A. A. Gromyko.
First Vice-Chairman: P. N. Demichev.
Secretary of the Presidium: Tengiz Menteshashvili.
Chairman of the Council of Ministers of the USSR: N. I. Ryzhkov.
First Vice-Chairmen: N. V. Talyzin; V. S. Murakhovsky.
Minister of Defence: Marshal D. T. Yazov. *Minister of Foreign Economic Relations:* K. F. Katushev. *Minister for Foreign Affairs:* E. A. Shevardnadze. *Minister of Internal Affairs:* A. V. Vlasov. *Minister of Finance:* B. I. Gostev. *Chairman, State Security Committee (KGB):* V. M. Chebrikov. *Chairman, State Planning Committee (Gosplan):* Yu. D. Maslyukov.

Constitution (Fundamental Law) of the USSR. Moscow, 1977
Konstitutsiya SSSR. Konstitutsii Soyuznykh Sovetskikh Respublik. Moscow, 1978
Feldbrugge, F. J. M. (ed.), *The Constitution of the USSR and the Union Republics.* Alphen aan den Rijn, 1979
Unger, A. L., *Constitutional Development in the USSR.* London, 1981

Communist Party of the Soviet Union. According to the revised rules adopted by the 27th Congress of the Party in March 1986, the Communist Party of the Soviet Union 'unites, on a voluntary basis, the more advanced, politically more conscious section of the working class, collective-farm peasantry and intelligentsia of the USSR', and represents the 'highest form of socio-political organization, the nucleus of the political system and the leading and guiding force of Soviet society'. According to the Party Programme, adopted in a revised version in 1986, the party aims to achieve the 'planned and all-round perfection of socialism', 'further advance to communism through the country's accelerated socio-economic development', and 'peace and social progress'.

The Party is organized on the territorial-industrial principle. The supreme organ is the Party Congress. Ordinary congresses are convened not less than every 5 years. The Congress elects a Central Committee which meets at least every 6 months, carries on the work of the Party between congresses, and guides the work of central Soviet and public organizations through Party groups within them.

The Central Committee forms a Political Bureau *(Politburo)* to direct the work of the Central Committee between plenary meetings, a Secretariat to direct current work and a Party Control Committee to deal with disciplinary matters; it also elects the General Secretary. Similar rules hold for the regional, territorial and republican levels of the party organization. The 'basis of the Party', the primary Party organization, exists in factories, state and collective farms, units of the Soviet Army and Navy, in villages, offices, educational establishments etc. where there are at least 3 Party members. There were over 441,851 primary Party organizations in 1987.

The Central Committee elected by the 27th Congress in March 1986 consisted of 307 members and 170 candidate (non-voting) members. Of these 42·3% were drawn from the central and regional party apparatus, and 5·9% were workers or peasants.

In March 1988 the Politburo of the Central Committee consisted of the following members: M. S. Gorbachev, V. M. Chebrikov, A. A. Gromyko, E. K. Ligachev, V. P. Nikonov, N. I. Ryzhkov, V. V. Shcherbitsky, E. A. Shevardnadze, N. N. Slyunkov, M. S. Solomentsev, V. I. Vorotnikov, A. N. Yakovlev and L. N. Zaikov and the following candidate (non-voting) members: P. N. Demichev, V. I. Dolgikh, Yu. D. Maslyukov, G. P. Razumovsky, Yu. F. Solov'ev, N. V. Talyzin, D. T. Yazov.

Secretariat: M. S. Gorbachev *(General Secretary);* O. D. Baklanov; A. P. Biryukova; A. F. Dobrynin; V. I. Dolgikh; E. K. Ligachev; A. I. Lukyanov; V. A. Medvedev; V. P. Nikonov; G. P. Razumovsky; N. N. Slyunkov; A. N. Yakovlev and L. N. Zaikov.
Chairman of the Party Control Committee: M. S. Solomentsev.
Chairman of the Central Auditing Commission: G. F. Sizov.

In July 1987 the Communist Party had 19,412,153 members (about 9·3% of the adult population). Of these, 45·3% were classified as workers, 11·6% as collective farmers and 43·1% as office workers; 29·3% were women, and 59% were Russians. The party's youth wing, the Komsomol (All-Union Leninist Communist Union of Youth), had 41·9m. members in 1986. V. I. Mironenko was re-elected First Secretary of its Central Committee at its 20th Congress in April 1987.

Istoriya Kommunisticheskoi partii Sovetskogo Soyuza, 7th ed. Moscow, 1985
Rules of the Communist Party of the Soviet Union. Moscow, 1986
KPSS v rezolyutsiyakh i resheniyakh s''ezdov, konferentsii i plenumov TsK, 9th ed., vol. 1ff. Moscow, 1983ff.
Resolutions and Decisions of the Communist Party of the Soviet Union, ed. R. H. McNeal, 5 vols. Toronto, 1974–82
Spravochnik partiinogo rabotnika. Moscow, annual
Hill, R. and Frank, P., *The Soviet Communist Party.* 3rd ed., London, 1987
Schapiro, L. B., *The Communist Party of the Soviet Union.* 2nd ed., London, 1970

DEFENCE. On 25 Feb. 1946 the control of the Soviet Armed Forces was unified under a single Ministry of the Armed Forces. On 25 Feb. 1950 the Defence Ministry was divided into a War Ministry and a Navy Ministry; on 15 March 1953 a single Ministry of Defence was reconstituted. In 1955 the Air Defence Command and in 1960 the Strategic Rocket Forces were established as the 4th and 5th 'branches' of the armed forces beside the army, navy and air force. Overall supervision of defence and security matters is exercised by the Defence Council of the USSR, headed by the General Secretary of the CPSU.

The direction of Party and political work in the Armed Forces is exercised by the Central Committee of the Communist Party of the Soviet Union through the chief political directorate of the Ministry of Defence. The chiefs of the political departments of military commands, fleets and armies must be Party members of 5 years' standing and the chiefs of political departments of divisions and regiments Party members of 3 years' standing. About 90% of the officers are members of the Communist Party or Young Communist League, and 50% have had an engineering and technical education.

Military service begins at the age of 19 (or 18 for graduates of secondary schools). Active service lasts 2 years for privates in the Army and M.V.D. troops, 3 years for n.c.o.s in the Army and M.V.D. troops and for privates and n.c.o.s in the Air Force, 4 years for privates and n.c.o.s in the Coastal Defence, 5 years for ratings in the Navy. Reserve service lasts up to the ages of 35, 45 or 50 years according to fitness, family status and other considerations. Conscientious objection is treated as a criminal offence. Students in places of higher education are freed from military service, but receive military instruction. About half the service personnel have had higher, or 10-year, education and over 80% are members of the Communist Party.

Total strength of the armed forces was over 5·25m. in 1988, with a probable 55m. reserves and a further 570,000 in paramilitary forces.

Declared budgetary expenditure on defence (in 1m. rubles) for 1960 was 9,300; 1970, 17,900; 1980, 17,100; 1987, 20,600.

Army. The Army is thought to consist of 52 tank, 150 motor rifle, 7 airborne and 18 artillery divisions; 10 air assault brigades; and various independent tank, artillery, missile and engineer units. Equipment includes some 33,200 T-54/-55/-62, 9,300 T-64 and 10,800 T-72/-80 main battle tanks. Strength (1988) 2m. (including 1·4m. conscripts).

There are 6 operational rocket armies deploying 1,418 intercontinental ballistic missiles (SS-11,-13,-17,-18,-19), capable of delivering over 5,000 nuclear warheads yielding over 4,000 megatons. Intermediate range ballistic missiles (SS-20) number 441. There are a further 112 medium range ballistic missiles, but these are being phased out. Personnel number 300,000, with reserves of 520,000.

Navy. The Soviet Fleet is steadily expanding and progressively modernizing under a continuity of policy and technology. The overall picture is of an unprecedentedly powerful and well-balanced navy, the capacity of which is increasing annually by scientific application and numerical strength.

The principal surface ships of the Soviet Navy are as follows:

Completed	Name	Standard displacement Tons	Aircraft	Principal armament	Shaft horsepower	Speed Knots

Aircraft Carriers [1]

Completed	Name	Standard displacement Tons	Aircraft	Principal armament	Shaft horsepower	Speed Knots
1986 Baku 1982 Novorossiisk 1978 Minsk 1976 Kiev		34,000	13 fixed wing aircraft 20 helicopters	4 twin SS missile launchers; 4 twin SA missile launchers; 1 twin AS missile launcher; 2 twin 76-mm AA guns	200,000	32

[1] See Aircraft carriers under construction and projected, successors of *Kiev* class, page 1226.

Battle Cruisers [1]

Completed	Name	Standard displacement Tons	Aircraft	Principal armament	Shaft horsepower	Speed Knots
1984 Frunze 1980 Kirov		22,000	3 helicopters	20 single SS missile launchers; 32 SA missile launchers; 2 AS missile launchers; 2 100-mm guns *(Kirov)* 1 twin 130-mm guns *(Frunze)*	150,000 (nuclear power)	33

[1] The first battle cruisers, and the largest combatant warships, apart from aircraft carriers, to be built for any navy since the Second World War. Main engines comprise 2 nuclear reactors and oil-fired superheat boilers for steam turbines.

Helicopter Carriers

Completed	Name	Standard displacement Tons	Aircraft	Principal armament	Shaft horsepower	Speed Knots
1968 Leningrad 1967 Moskva		16,500	14 helicopters	2 twin SA missile launchers; 1 twin AS missile launcher; 2 twin 57-mm guns	100,000	31

Cruisers

Completed	Name	Standard displacement Tons	Aircraft	Principal armament	Shaft horsepower	Speed Knots
1987 Marshal Shaposhnikov 1986 Admiral Tributs 1985 Admiral Spiridonov 1984 Admiral Zakorov 1984 Marshal Vasilevsky 1982 Vize Admiral Kulakov 1982 Udaloy [1]		8,500 (loaded)	2 helicopters and 2 hangars	2 quadruple SS missile launchers; 8 SA single vertical missile launchers; 2 single 100-mm guns	110,000	32

[1] Three more light cruisers of the *Udaloy* class rated as large anti-submarine ships are being completed.

Completed	Name	Standard displacement Tons	Aircraft	Principal armament	Shaft horsepower	Speed Knots
1988 Stoyky 1987 Boyevoy 1986 Bezuprechuy 1985 Osmotritelmy 1984 Otlichnny 1983 Otchyanny 1982 Sovremenny [1]		8,000 (loaded)	1 helicopter (telescopic hangar)	2 quadruple SS missile launchers; 2 single SA missile launchers; 2 twin 130-mm guns	110,000	32

[1] Four more light cruisers or large destroyers of the Sovremenny class are under construction.

Completed	Name	Standard displacement Tons	Aircraft	Principal armament	Shaft horsepower	Speed Knots
1983 Slava		10,500	1 helicopter (carrying AS torpedoes and depth bombs)	16 SS launchers; 8 SA vertical launchers; 2 AS launchers; 2 130-mm guns	120,000	34

Two more heavy cruisers of this class are reportedly scheduled for completion or commissioning.

Completed	Name	Standard displacement Tons	Aircraft	Principal armament	Shaft horsepower	Speed Knots

Cruisers

Completed	Name	Standard displacement Tons	Aircraft	Principal armament	Shaft horsepower	Speed Knots
1979	Tallin					
1978	Tashkent			2 quadruple SS		
1977	Petropavlovsk			missile launchers;		
1976	Azov[3]	8,200	1 helicopter (hangar aft)	4 twin SA	122,000	34
1975	Kerch			missile launchers;		
1974	Ochakov			2 twin 76-mm guns		
1973	Nikolaiev					

[3] *Azov*, nominally of this Kara class, is of a modified design, with a different guided missiles system (6 launchers), as trials ship for the armament of subsequent classes of cruisers.

Of 18 other missile-armed major vessels, 10 of the Kresta II class, displacing 6,000 tons standard, completed in 1964–77, are officially rated as large anti-submarine ships; 4 of the Kresta I class, 6,140 tons, completed in 1967–69 were originally rated as large anti-submarine ships; and the 4 of the Kynda class, completed in 1962–65, although only of 4,400 tons were rated as rocket cruisers.

Completed	Name	Standard displacement Tons	Aircraft	Principal armament	Shaft horsepower	Speed Knots
1958	Admiral Senyavin[1]					
1957	Mikhail Kutuzov					
1956	Dimitri Pojarski					
1956	Oktyabrskaya Revolutsiya [3]					
1956	Admiral Lazarev					
1955	Alexandr Suvorov	16,000		12 6-in.; 12 3·9-in.	110,000	32
1954	Admiral Ushakov					
1954	Dzerzhinski [2]					
1953	Alexandr Nevski					
1953	Murmansk					
1953	Zhdanov [1]					
1953	Sverdlov [4]					

[1] *Admiral Senyavin* now has a helicopter pad and hangar ('X' and 'Y' turrets removed), leaving her with only six 6-mm guns, while *Zhdanov* has high deckhouse ('X' turret removed). Each carries twin surface-air missile launchers. Both latterly employed as command and communications ships.

[2] *Dzerzhinski* has only nine 6-in. guns in 3 triple turrets, 'X' turret having been replaced by a twin surface-air missile launcher.

[3] This ship, first named *Molotovsk*, was renamed in 1957.

[4] Of 24 vessels of the Sverdlov class originally projected only 14 were completed; *Ordzhonikidze* transferred 1962 to Indonesia (scrapped 1972) and *Admiral Nakhimov* deleted 1969. Of the older cruisers, *Kirov* and *Slava* (ex-*Molotov*) were deleted from the effective list in 1976-77 and *Zheleznyakov* in 1978. *Komsomolets* was latterly used as a training ship.

Capital Support Ship

Completed	Name	Standard displacement Tons	Aircraft	Principal armament	Shaft horsepower	Speed Knots
1977	Berezina [1]	36,000 (loaded)	2 helicopters	Twin SA missile launcher; 4 57-mm guns	60,000	22

[1] Very impressive militarised replenishment ship designed to support the new Soviet aircraft carriers.

Submarines

77(15)[3]	SSBN	Nuclear powered	Ballistic missile armed [1] *q.v.*
15	SSB	Diesel-electric powered	Ballistic missile armed
53	SSGN	Nuclear powered	Cruise (guided) missile armed
17	SSG	Diesel-electric powered	Cruise missile armed
78	SSN	Nuclear powered	Torpedo (only) armed
215[2]	SS	Diesel powered	Torpedo (only) armed

[1] See table. All missile-carrying submarines are also armed with torpedoes.
[2] Including 65 patrol submarines in reserve or used for training only and 13 auxiliary (special purpose) submarines.
[3] Fifteen had missile tubes removed on conversion to fleet submarines, SSN (nuclear propelled).

Capital (Strategic) Submarines (SSBN)

Class	No.	Displace-ment (dived) Tons	Missile Tubes (vertical)	Nuclear Reactors	Shaft horse-power [4]	Speed (dived) Knots
Typhoon [1]	4	25,000	20 SS–N–20	2	100,000	30
D4	4	13,600	16 SS–NX–23	2	60,000	24
D3	14	13,250	16 SS–N–18	2	50,000	24
D2	4	12,750	16 SS–N–8	2	50,000	25
D1	18	11,000	12 SS–N–8	2	50,000	26
Y	18 (15) [3]	9,600	16 SS–N–6	1	50,000	28
H3	1	6,500	6 SS–N–8	1	30,000	22

[1] These vessels, of battleship dimensions, are the largest submarines ever built. Launched from Sept. 1980 onwards. The vertical missile cylinders are mounted forward of the fin.
Note: All these classes also carry six 21-inch torpedo tubes.
[4] Shaft horsepower for all these classes reportedly uprated in 1987

There are also 40 missile-armed destroyers, 30 gun-armed destroyers, (including 13 in reserve), 32 missile-armed frigates, 50 gun-armed frigates, 3 ocean mine-layers, 120 missile-armed corvettes, 60 gun-armed corvettes, 28 patrol ships, 125 fleet minesweepers, 90 coastal minesweepers, 50 minehunters, 60 inshore mine-sweepers, 50 minesweeping boats, 80 fast missile craft, 10 fast torpedo boats, 80 fast anti-submarine boats, 110 fast attack craft, 15 multi-purpose patrol vessels, 17 hydrofoil missile boats, 30 hydrofoil torpedo boats, 15 hydrofoil gunboats, 30 coastal patrol launches, 110 river patrol boats, 100 major amphibious and auxiliary roll-on roll-off ships, 2 dock landing ships, 35 tank landing ships, 50 medium landing ships, 30 utility landing craft, 50 minor landing craft, 65 intelligence collecting ships, 85 major support ships, 11 space associated ships, 150 survey ships, 115 oceanographic research ships, 7 missile range ships, 4 nuclear powered icebreakers, 70 icebreakers, 20 training ships, 190 fishery protection ships, 28 fleet replenishment ships, 75 oilers, 13 special tankers, 45 salvage vessels, 90 transports, 21 submarine rescue ships, 135 tenders, 10 lifting ships, 12 cable ships, 35 degaussing ships, 100 fleet tugs, 80 hovercraft and thousands of auxiliaries, para-military ships and service craft.

The new construction programme includes 2 aircraft carriers, considerably larger and reportedly nuclear-powered, more very large nuclear powered ballistic missile submarines, 2 nuclear powered cruise missile submarines, 6 nuclear powered torpedo-armed submarines, 3 diesel-electric propelled patrol submarines, 2 more nuclear powered guided missile armed battle cruisers, 8 guided missile cruisers and large anti-submarine leaders, 4 frigates and 4 corvettes.

In the progressive forward procurement programme more conventionally propelled aircraft carriers of improved 'follow-on' class are envisaged, together with nuclear powered surface ships, conventionally propelled submarines and specialized support ships, to fit into the Soviet global and strategic maritime scenario.

There are 5 shipyards in and near Leningrad; Black Sea yards are at Nikolaiev and Sevastopol, new shipyards are at Molotovsk in the White Sea region and at Komsomolsk on the Amur.

The completion of a through canal system between the Baltic and White Seas, allowing regular traffic *via* the North-East Passage (during the ice-free season), facilitates the navigation of suitable ships between the Baltic and Far East.

Estimated number of personnel in 1988 totalled over 495,000, including naval aviation, naval infantry, coastal defence, cadets and apprentices (but excluding some 75,000 civilians in administration and new construction). About 25% of naval personnel are volunteers, *i.e.*, officers and petty officers, the remainder comprising national service men serving 3 years at sea and 2 if ashore.

Air Force. The Soviet Air Force (excluding the strategic bomber force and Voyska PVO air defence force) was believed to have a personnel strength, in 1987, of over 454,000 officers and men. To supplement long-range rocket missiles (estimated at 1,398 emplaced ICBM, 600 MRBM/IRBM), the strategic bomber force has still about 125 Tupolev Tu-95 ('Bear')[1] 4-turboprop bombers, 50 Myasishchev M-4 4-jet bombers and flight-refuelling tankers ('Bison'), 300 twin-jet Tupolev Tu-16 ('Badger'), and 135 supersonic Tupolev Tu-22 ('Blinder') bombers, ECM and reconnaissance aircraft, and at least 150 Tupolev ('Backfire') swing-wing bombers. All types are used also by the Naval Air Force for long-range maritime reconnaissance; the Tu-16, Tu-95, Tu-22 and 'Backfire' can carry air-to-surface guided self-propelled cruise missiles and all 5 types have provision for flight refuelling. A new swing-wing strategic bomber ('Blackjack'), larger and faster than the American B-1, is being flight tested.

The tactical air forces, under local army command in the field, have an estimated total of 6,000 ground attack, air combat, ECM and reconnaissance aircraft, including 2,600 MiG-23/27 ('Flogger') and 500 two-seat Sukhoi Su-24 ('Fencer') supersonic swing-wing aircraft, 150 twin-jet Yakovlev Yak-28 ('Brewer') reconnaissance aircraft, 1,000 swing-wing Su-17 ('Fitter-C/D/G/H/J'), and 600 MiG-21 ('Fishbed') fighter-bombers, 600 Su-15 ('Flagon'), 200 MiG-25 ('Foxbat') and some MiG-31 ('Foxhound') interceptors, and an increasing number of new Su-25 ('Frogfoot') twin-engined ground attack aircraft supported by 60 MiG-21 and 170 MiG-25 ('Foxbat') reconnaissance aircraft, and over 3,500 helicopters, including very large Mi-26 ('Halo') transports and over 1,000 heavily-armed Mi-24 ('Hind') assault helicopters, in gunship/transport versions. Electronic warfare duties are performed by a variety of aircraft, including Yak-28s and Mi-8 and Mi-17 helicopters. The Voyska PVO defence forces, organized as a separate service, have an estimated total of 1,300 jet interceptors. A high proportion of the squadrons are equipped with MiG-23 ('Flogger'), Su-15 ('Flagon'), MiG-25 ('Foxbat') and improved MiG-31 ('Foxhound') all-weather interceptors, armed with air-to-air missiles plus the MiG-29 and Su-27 new-generation aircraft now entering service. The twin-jet Yak-28P ('Firebar') and Tu-28P ('Fiddler') make up the balance of the force. Early warning and fighter-control duties are performed by about 10 radar-carrying adaptations of the Tu-114 turboprop transport, redesignated Tu-126 ('Moss'); which are being replaced by a more effective radar-equipped AWACS version ('Mainstay') of the Il-76 transport. Very large numbers of surface-to-air guided missiles are operational, on some 10,000 launchers, including the new high-performance SA-10 (low-altitude) and SA-12 (high-altitude) with capability against cruise and submarine-launched missiles respectively, the older 'Guild', 'Guideline', 'Goa', 'Gainful' and 'Ganef', the long-range 'Gammon' and the 'Galosh' which is deployed around Moscow on 32 launchers and has anti-missile capability.

[1] For convenience Soviet aircraft and missiles are usually referred to by invented English names in non-Soviet military writings.

Soviet Air Force transport squadrons have 200 An-12 ('Cub') 4-turboprop transports and 100 An-24s ('Coke') and An-26s ('Curl'), with 50 An-22s ('Cock'), and 350 Il-76 ('Candid') heavy four-jet freighters. The very large four-jet An-124 ('Condor') is entering service to replace the An-22. Training aircraft include the piston-engined Yak-18 primary trainer and its Yak-52 successor, the Czech-built L-29 Delfin and L-39 jet basic trainers and versions of operational types such as MiG-21, MiG-23, MiG-25, MiG-15, Su-7, Su-15, Su-17, Yak-28 and Tu-22.

Naval Air Force. With 1,100 fixed-wing aircraft and helicopters, the Soviet Navy has the world's second largest naval air arm. Under the control of the various naval commands, *i.e.*, Baltic, Black Sea and Pacific, the Naval Air Arm has an estimated 220 Tu-16 ('Badger') twin-jet bombers, and 130 'Backfire' swing-wing bombers, able to carry air-to-surface missiles, 40 supersonic twin-jet Tu-22 ('Blinder') maritime reconnaissance aircraft, about 70 Su-17 ('Fitter') shore-based fighters, and 90 Beriev M-12 ('Mail') maritime patrol amphibians. For reconnaissance, anti-submarine and electronic warfare there are about 100 Tu-95 and Tu-142 ('Bear') 4-engined bombers, 90 Tu-16s, and a few Tu-22s, plus a small number of Il-20s ('Coot-A') and 60 Il-38s ('May'). The Tu-142 also has an important targeting rôle for ships fitted with anti-shipping missile launchers. Over 250 anti-submarine and missile targeting/guidance helicopters, notably the Ka-27 ('Helix') and Ka-25 ('Hormone'), are carried in naval vessels, including 3 aircraft carriers (which also operate Yak-36 ('Forger') VTOL attack/reconnaissance aircraft) and 2 helicopter carriers. Several hundred transport, flight refuelling tanker ('Badger'), utility and training fixed-wing aircraft and Mi-14 ('Haze') shore-based ASW helicopters are also under Navy control.

Berman, H. J., and Kerner, M. (ed.), *Soviet Military Law and Administration.* 2 vols. Harvard Univ. Press, 1955
Scott, H. F., and Scott, W. F., *The Armed Forces of the USSR.* 2nd ed. Boulder, 1981
Smith, M. J., *The Soviet Navy, 1941–1978: A Guide to Sources in English.* Oxford and Santa Barbara, 1981
Suvorov, V., *The Liberators: The Soviet Army.* London, 1981
Watson, B. W., *Red Navy at Sea.* Boulder, 1982

INTERNATIONAL RELATIONS

Membership. USSR is a member of UN, Comecon and the Warsaw Pact.

ECONOMY

Planning. Planning is based on public ownership in industry and trade, and on mixed public and collective (co-operative) ownership in agriculture. The first plan drawn up by Gosplan (the State Planning Commission) was the 'Goelro' drawn up in 1920. This was to be the basis for the economic development of the country and for the construction of a system of electrical power plants with an aggregate capacity of 1·75m. kw. in the course of 15 years.

For details of Planning 1925–1942 *see* THE STATESMAN'S YEAR-BOOK, 1981–82, p. 1226.

For details of the fourth 5-year plan, 1946–50, *see* THE STATESMAN'S YEAR-BOOK, 1952, pp. 1424 f. The 1950 target of the gross output of industry was exceeded by 2%.

On 10 Oct. 1952 the 19th Congress of the Communist Party issued directives for the fifth 5-year plan, 1951–55; for details, *see* THE STATESMAN'S YEAR-BOOK, 1953, pp. 1435-36. During Sept. and Oct. 1953 the Government issued a number of decrees to stimulate the development of agriculture, the output of consumer goods and the expansion of the home trade. For details of these decrees, *see* THE STATESMAN'S YEAR-BOOK, 1955, pp. 1448-50.

The directives for the sixth 5-year plan, 1956-60, were adopted by the 20th Congress of the Communist Party on 25 Feb. 1956; for details *see* THE STATESMAN'S YEAR-BOOK, 1958, p. 1472.

In May 1955 Gosplan was reorganized to consist of 2 state commissions for long-term planning (Gosplan) and for current planning (Gosekonomkomissiya); at the same time a committee was set up to improve the application to industry of advanced science and technology (Gostekhnika).

Between 1954 and 1956 considerable changes were made in planning methods. In March 1954 collective farms were given greater authority over planning their own output, only the quantities required by the State in fixed deliveries being determined beforehand, and voluntary sales by contract. In 1955 they were authorized to make changes in their statutes, which had followed a fixed model since 1935. In 1955-57 over 15,000 industrial establishments in various basic industries, previously controlled by the Union Government, and later a number of entire light industries were turned over to the constituent (Union) Republics. By 1962 they controlled from 95 to 100% of all industrial output.

In 1957 a comprehensive plan for decentralization of management of industry was initiated. Industrial establishments responsible for about 71% of all Soviet industrial output were turned over to Economic Councils set up in 104 (in 1963: 47) economic administrative areas. These in 1962 controlled 73% of all industrial production. The Ministries previously responsible for the industries concerned were either abolished or transformed into purely planning and supervisory bodies. The State Committee for current planning was abolished, and Gosplan was given wider powers.

In consequence of this change a 7-year plan for 1959-65 was adopted by the 21st Congress of the Communist Party in Feb. 1959. Industrial output was to increase by 80%; it was in fact, in 1965, 84% above that of 1959. Capital investments would roughly equal the total for 1917-58: special attention was to be given to mechanization of agriculture and arduous industrial labour, automation and new technological processes, and housing. Diesel or electric traction of railway freight was to rise to 85%. Real incomes were to rise 40%, the 7-hour day (6 hours for miners) became general in 1960 and the 40-hour week in 1961, and introduction of the 35-hour week (30 hours for miners) began in 1964.

In Oct. 1965 the regional and Republic Economic Councils were abolished and also 28 Ministries for various branches of industry (17 Union-Republican, *i.e.*, corresponding to similar Ministries in the Union Republics, and 11 All-Union).

A 20-year plan was adopted by the 22nd Congress of the Communist Party on 31 Oct. 1961, which envisaged a ninefold growth in electricity output and big increases in production of steel, oil, coal, machinery and cement, and also in grain, milk and meat. Two new iron and steel centres were to be developed in Kazakhstan and in Kursk region. A single deepwater system was to link the main inland waterways in the European USSR. Some rivers in northern Asia were to be diverted south for irrigation purposes. A 6-hour day for a 6-day week or 35 hours for a 5-day week were to be achieved by 1970. Housing, water, gas, heating, public urban transport and school meals were to be free by 1980. These and cognate measures were to provide 'the material and technical basis of communism'.

The 23rd Congress of the Communist Party in April 1966 adopted directives for a 5-year plan for 1966-70. Under these, power output was to reach 830,000-850,000m. kwh.; oil, 345-355m. tons; coal, 665-675m. tons; steel, 124-129m. tons; mineral fertilizers, 62-65m. tons; machine-tools, 220,000-230,000; cars, 700,000-800,000; tractors, 600,000-625,000; paper, 5-5·3m. tons; cement, 100-105m. tons; fabrics, 9·5-9·8m. sq. metres; leather footwear, 610-630m. pairs; meat, 5·9-6·2m. tons; butter, 1·2m. tons; sugar, 9·8-10m. tons. The average annual output of grain was to increase by 30%; 7,000 km of new railway line, 63,000 km of new motor roads and 35-40 new airports were to be built; and marine tonnage was to be increased by 50%.

The 9th Five-Year Plan adopted in 1971 provided for an increase in electric power output to 1,065,000m. kwh.; oil to 496m. tons; gas, 320,000m. cu. metres; steel, 146m. tons; coal, 695m. tons; mineral fertilizers, 90m. tons; tractors, 575,000; passenger cars, 1·26m., and lorries, 750,000. Grain output was to rise to 195m. tons in 1975; meat, approximately 16m. tons; milk, 100m. tons; textiles, 11,000m. sq. metres; leather footwear, 830m. pairs. Average wages were to increase by 22%, incomes of collective farmers 30-35%, and the average of real incomes by 31%. 3,400 miles of new railway tracks were to be built and 3,700 miles electrified, with 17,000 miles of new oil pipelines, and 40% more cargo carried by sea. Over 16m. flats and houses were to be built.

By July 1972, 43,000 industrial plants had been transferred to the new system of decentralized cost-accounting; they produced 94% of total output of Soviet industry and 95% of its total profit. All public establishments in trade and catering and all the state farms have gone over to the new system.

On 29 Oct. 1976, the Supreme Soviet adopted the 10th Five-Year Plan (1976–80). This provided for an increase of industrial output from 104·3% of the 1975 level to 136%, an average annual increase of agricultural output by 16%, freight traffic (all forms) from 105·7% to 132%, state capital investments from 105·1% of the 1975 level in 1976 to 114·6% in 1980, real income per head from 103·7% to 121%, retail commodity turnover from 103·6% to 128·7%. 550m. sq. metres of new housing were to be built. Children in pre-school establishments would increase by 104·4% in 1976 and 125·5% in 1980, pupils in day schools from 108·9% to 148·8%, and students in higher education from 100·4% to 105·4%. Hospital beds were to increase from 102·2% in the first year to 109·7% in the final year.

The 11th Five-Year Plan, adopted in 1981, aimed to raise living standards. The focus was Siberia and the Soviet Far East, with their large resources of energy and raw materials, and also Central Asia, with its favourable combination of labour resources and raw materials. Virtually no industries were to be developed in the European part of the USSR and the plan envisages speeding up the development of labour-intensive branches of agriculture, consumer goods and engineering industries in Central Asia. National income (in the Soviet definition) was to increase by 18% between 1981 and 1985; industrial production was to increase by 26%, capital investment by 5·4%, freight traffic by 19·4%, real incomes by 16·5%, agricultural production by 13%, and retail trade in the state and co-operative sectors by 23% over the same period. Pensions were to be raised and the minimum wage was to be increased to 80 rubles a month, and efforts were to be made to increase state assistance to families with young children and to improve the food and care given to them in schools and pre-school institutions.

The 12th Five-Year Plan, adopted in 1986, also places its main emphasis upon raising popular living and cultural standards. This in turn is held to require an acceleration of socio-economic development and an intensification and increase in the effectiveness of production on the basis of scientific-technical progress. The plan covers the period 1986–90 and up to the year 2,000, by which time real living standards are planned to increase by 1·6 to 1·8 times; manual labour should account for no more than 15–20% of all productive work; state and co-operative retail trade should increase by 1·8 times; and health, educational and other social expenditure should double. Over the same period the national income should approximately double and industrial production more than double, entirely as a result of increased productivity, which is planned to increase by 2·3 to 2·5 times. Greater economy is to be achieved in the use of energy and natural resources; investment is to be concentrated in priority areas; and scientific-technical progress is to be accelerated and related more closely to production. Continued emphasis is placed upon the Energy Programme, the Food Programme and the Complex Programme for the Development of Consumer Goods and Services, which were adopted between 1982 and 1985. In the 5-year period 1986–90 national income is to increase by 22%, industrial production by 25%, labour productivity by 12–25%, and real incomes by 14%.

In 1987 national income produced increased by 2·3% (1981–85 average, 2·9%), gross industrial production by 3·8% (1981–85 average, 3·7%) and labour productivity by 2·4% (1981–85 average, 3·1%).

Narodnoe khozyaistvo SSSR. Moscow, annual
Resheniya partii i pravitel'stva po khozyaistvennym voprosam. Vol. 1ff. Moscow, 1967ff
Istoriya sotsialisticheskoi ekonomiki SSSR. 7 vols. Moscow, 1976–80
Nove, A., *An Economic History of the USSR.* Rev. ed., Harmondsworth, 1982.—*The Soviet Economic System.* 3rd ed., London, 1986
US Congress, Joint Economic Committee, *The Soviet Economy in the 1980s,* 2 vols. Washington D.C., 1983
Gregory, P. R. and Stuart, R. C., *Soviet Economic Structure and Performance.* 3rd ed., New York, 1986

Budget. Revenue and expenditure in 1m. rubles for calendar years:

	1980	1985	1986	1987[1]	1988[1]
Revenue	302,700	390,603	419,500	435,683	443,645
Expenditure	294,600	386,469	417,400	435,510	443,645

[1] Estimate.

The 1988 budget allotted 241,035m. rubles to the national economy, 20,244m. to defence and 153,550m. to social and cultural services.

The social insurance budget, which is controlled by the Central Council for Trade Unions and its affiliated bodies, was 29,476m. rubles in 1977, 31,179m. in 1978, 33,089m. in 1979, 35,296 in 1980 and 58,708m. (plan) in 1988.

The national income was assessed (in 1,000m. rubles) at 145·0 in 1960, 289·9 in 1970, 462·2 in 1980 and 587·4 in 1986.

Income tax was abolished on 1 Oct. 1961 for earnings up to 60 rubles per month and reduced for earnings between 61 and 70 rubles; in Dec. 1967 further cuts of 25% were made for earnings from 61 to 80 rubles; in 1972 earnings up to 70 rubles were freed of income tax, and taxes on incomes up to 90 rubles were cut by about 33⅓%. Capital investment (1986) was 194,400m. rubles, including 176,100m. by State and co-operative enterprises, 15,500m. by collective farms and 2,800m. by individuals (on housing).

Currency. As from 1 Jan. 1961 the gold content of the *ruble* was raised from 0·222 168 to 0·987 412 gramme. The official exchange rates (March 1988) 1·06 *rubles* = £1; 0·60 *rubles* = US$1.

The gold holdings of the USSR were, in Dec. 1955, estimated at about 200m. fine oz. (US$7,000m.), or about 20% of the world total of monetary gold.

The currency in circulation is: (1) State Bank notes in denominations of 10, 25, 50 and 100 *rubles;* (2) Treasury notes in denominations of 1, 3 and 5 *rubles;* (3) cupro-nickel coins in denominations of 10, 15, 20 and 50 *kopeks* and 1 *ruble*; (4) cupro-zinc coins in denominations of 1, 2, 3 and 5 *kopeks.*

Banking. The State Bank began operations on 16 Nov. 1921. By an edict of 7 April 1959 a number of specialized banks for planned long-term investments, which had existed since 1932, were abolished. The State Bank, in addition to short-term credits, effects long-term investments in agriculture and in individual rural house building. The Bank for Financing Capital Investments (*Stroibank*) covers industry, transport, urban housing schemes and public utilities and individual house-building in towns.

Deposits in 77,900 savings banks were over 242,800m. rubles to the credit of 178·4m. depositors at 1 Jan. 1987.

Weights and Measures. The metric system has been in use since 1 Jan. 1927.

The Gregorian Calendar was adopted as from 14 Feb. 1918.

ENERGY AND NATURAL RESOURCES

Electricity. There were (1983) 57 fuel-burning power stations of over 1m. kw. capacity, and these account for over 80% of the country's electricity.

Hydro-electric stations have been constructed on major rivers. Among them are the Bratsk (4·5m. kw.), completed in 1967, Ust-Ilimsk, Central Siberia (3·6m. kw.), Krasnoyarsk (6m. kw.) and a 1·26m. kw. station on the River Pechora (Far North). The Sayano-Shushenskaya hydro-power station, part of the Yenisei chain has a capacity of 6·4m. kw. A 245m. high dam has to be built before completion, in a gorge in the Sayan Range. Another large hydro-electric station is under construction on the River Kureika, Siberia, to provide energy for the mining and metallurgical centre at Norilsk in the Arctic.

Total installed capacity of power stations in 1938 was 8·7m. kw. and 338m. kw. in 1987. Industry consumes about 70% of the total electricity. Over 35,000 small rural power stations have been closed in recent years owing to supply from State stations becoming available, but there are still many operating in the countryside. 800 towns and urban settlements were heated by central thermal plants.

The world's first commercial nuclear power station in Obninsk, built in 1954, was followed by the Beloyarsk, Novo-Voronezh, Leningrad, Kursk, Chernobyl, Armenian and Shevchenko nuclear stations. Soviet nuclear power plants so far have standard slow 1m. kw. reactors, but a 1·5m. kw. reactor has now been designed. A fast reactor is functioning at Shevchenko.

The general design for a nuclear thermal station has been developed, and practical experience in this field has been obtained at the Bilibino nuclear power station in the Arctic, which supplies electricity and heat to the inhabitants on the Chukchi Peninsula.

In 1979 a 500,000 kw. MHD pilot project was started in Ryazan. This first-generation MHD station will have an efficiency of 50% as against 40% in the best thermal power stations and will consume about 20% less fuel. An experimental tidal energy station is working at Kislaya Guba (Murman coast).

Total electricity output in 1987 was 1,665,000m. kwh.

The country's integrated power grid is now in operation, covering over 900 power stations, which are handled by a central control panel in Moscow through (in 1986) 939,400 km. of cable of 35 kw. or greater capacity. A unified power grid ('Mir') with all the Socialist countries of eastern Europe was built up between 1962 and 1967. Supply 127 and 220 volts; 50 Hz.

Oil. In the 1930s practically all Soviet oil came from the Caucasian fields, of which the Baku fields yielded 75-80% and the Grozny and Maikop fields between them 15%. Since then, the distribution has considerably changed. The Ural-Volga area, the 'Second Baku', has 4 large centres in operation, at Samarska Luka (Kuibyshev), Tuimazy (Bashkiria), Ishimbaev (Bashkiria) and Perm, producing nearly 100m. tonnes annually.

A large new oilfield has been developed in the Trans-Volga area of the Saratov region. The Tyumen (West Siberian) complex now accounts for over 50% of the USSR's oil output. In 1987 the USSR extracted 624m. tonnes of oil.

The total length of pipeline on 1 Jan. 1939 was 4,212 km, divided as follows: Baku-Batumi, 1,717 km; Grozny-Makhachkala, 150 km; Grozny-Armavir-Tuapse, 618 km; Armavir-Trudovaya, 488 km; Guriev-Orsk, 845 km, and other, 394 km. One pipeline (1,700 km) was completed in 1955, connecting Tuimazy in Bashkiria with the refineries of Omsk. In 1957 the Almetyevsk-Gorky pipeline (580 km) and 479 km of the Stavropol-Moscow pipeline were completed. At the end of 1981 there were 70,800 km of pipeline, through which (in 1981) were conveyed 637·7m. tonnes of oil.

The construction of the 'Druzhba' pipeline of about 5,327 km from the oilfields near Kuibyshev to Poland and the German Democratic Republic (northern branch) and to Czechoslovakia and Hungary (southern branch)–separating in Belorussia–begun in 1960, was completed in 1965. Now a double line, it has an annual throughput of 50m. tonnes.

In 1986 the USSR exported 186·8m. tonnes of crude oil and oil products.

Meyerhoff, A. A., *The Oil and Gas Potential of the Soviet Far East*. Beaconsfield, 1981

Gas. A natural-gas pipeline from Gazli, near Khiva, to Voskresensk, near Moscow (2,750 km), with a planned capacity of 100m. cu. metres per day, began operating in Oct. 1967. Since then it has been extended to Czechoslovakia, where a 1,000 km extension, for transmission of Soviet gas to Austria, Italy and German Democratic Republic and Federal Republic of Germany, is under construction and another to Bulgaria. Another natural-gas pipeline, over 3,000 km from Medvezhye (Tyumen Region) to Moscow, began operating in Oct. 1974. A second pipeline from this region, linking the Urengoi deposit with Petrovsky in the Central European area of the USSR, became operational in 1980, and is to be continued to the southern Ukraine, to a total length of 3,000 km. A gas pipeline starting from Orenburg (Urals), passing across the Volga at Kamyshin, and continuing across the Ukraine *via* Kremenchug and Vinnitsa to Czechoslovakia (2,750 km), supplies Czechoslovakia, Poland, Bulgaria and Hungary with 14,000m. cu. metres annually and Romania with 1,500m. A unified gas-grid exceeding 124,000 km now exists.

By Dec. 1981 construction work had begun on the 5,000 km Urengoi (West Siberia)-Uzhgorod-West Europe gas pipeline.

In 1987, 727,000m. cu. metres of gas were produced (in 1940, 3,200 m., in 1970, 197,900m.).

Minerals. Mining experts are trained in 6 mining, 3 oil and 1 peat institutes, the mining faculties of 17 higher educational establishments, oil faculties of 2 industrial institutes and a peat faculty at the Belorussian Polytechnical Institute.

The Soviet Union is rich in minerals. Soviet scientists claim that it contains 58% of the world's coal deposits, 58·7% of its oil, 41% of its iron ore, 76·7% of its apatite, 25% of all timber land, 88% of its manganese, 54% of its potassium salts and nearly one-third of its phosphates.

Estimated output (in tonnes) in 1962: Copper, 634,900; zinc, 399,000; lead, 363,000; tungsten, 10,500; antimony, 5,980; silver, 27m. fine oz. Output in 1963: Baryte, 199,500; magnesium, 31,745; aluminium, 961,400; manganese ore (1977), 8·6m.; graphite, 54,000; bauxite, 4·3m.; asbestos, 1·3m.; phosphate rock, 3·7m. (plus 7·4m. apatite); chromite, 1·23m.; gold, 12·5m. fine oz.; molybdenum, 12·5m. lb.; cadmium (1956), 160.

Output of iron and steel in the USSR (in 1 m. tonnes):

	Pig-iron	Ingot steel	Rolled steel		Pig-iron	Ingot steel	Rolled steel
1913	4·2	4·2	3·5	1960	46·8	65·3	50·9
1928–29	4·0	4·8	3·9	1965	66·2	91·0	61·7
1932	6·2	5·9	4·4	1970	85·9	115·9	80·6
1940	14·9	18·3	13·1	1980	107·3	147·9	118·3
1946	10·0	13·4	9·6	1985	110·0	155·0	128·4
1950	19·2	27·3	20·9	1986	114·0	161·0	133·5

Coal production (in 1m. tonnes) was 29·1 in 1913, 165·9 in 1940, 261·1 in 1950, 509·6 in 1960, 624·1 in 1970, 716·4 in 1980, 751 in 1986.

The main centre of the atomic ore industry is at Ust-Kamenogorsk in the Altai Mountains. Uranium deposits are being worked near Taboshar (south-east of Tashkent), Andizhan (in the Tynya-Muyan Mountains), Slyudianka (near Lake Baikal), on the Kolyma River and in Southern Armenia.

Agriculture. The Soviet Union, up to about 1928 predominantly agricultural in character, has become an industrial-agricultural country. Of produced national income in 1986, industry accounted for 43·9%, agriculture for 20·6%, trade etc. for 17·3%, construction for 12% and transport and communications for 6·2%. Of the total state land fund of 2,227·6m. hectares, agricultural land in use in 1986 amounted to 1,048·5m., state forests and state reserves to 1,108·5m. hectares. 19% of all gainfully employed in 1986 were engaged in agriculture and forestry (1913, 75%; 1940, 54%).

The total area under cultivation (including single-owner peasant farms, state farms and collective farms) was (in the same territory) 118·2m. hectares in 1913, 150·6m. in 1940, 146·3m. in 1950, 203m. in 1960, 206·7m. in 1970, 217·3 in 1980, and 210·3m. in 1986.

Collective farms in 1986 possessed 92·2m. hectares of cultivated land, of which 50m. were under crops of various kinds; state farms and other state agricultural undertakings possessed 112·4m. hectares, of which 65·5m. were under crops; personal subsidiary holdings (private plots and allotments) accounted for 5·7m. hectares.

State procurements (after consumption by farms) were, in 1m. tonnes, for the present area of the USSR:

	1950	1960	1970	1986		1950	1960	1970	1986
Grain	32·3	46·7	73·3	78·8	Meat[2] and fats	1·3	4·8	8·1	20·0
Raw Cotton[1]	3·5	4·3	6·9	8·2	Milk and milk				
Sugar-beet	19·7	52·2	71·4	70·7	products	11·4	29·1	48·0	71·8
Potatoes	14·0	13·7	18·1	19·0	Sunflower seed	1·1	2·3	4·6	4·3
Other vegetables	4·3	8·0	13·8	20·9	Eggs (1,000m.)	3·5	10·5	22·1	53·6

[1] Seed-cotton unginned.   [2] Slaughter weight.

Since 1954 grain crops have been measured in 'barn crop' (*i.e.*, net quantities delivered to barns) and not in 'gross harvest' or 'biological yield' (*i.e.*, calculated as growing crops) as previously. Average annual crops (in 1m. tonnes): 1909–13, 72·5; 1946–50, 64·8; 1951–55, 88·5; 1956–60, 121·5; 1961–65, 130·3; 1966–70, 167·5; 1971–75, 181·6; 1976–80, 205; 1981–85, 180·3; 1986, 210·1; 1987, 211·3.

Other produce (in 1m. tonnes) in 1987: Milk, 103·4; sugar-beet, 90; potatoes, 75·9; vegetables, 29·1; meat (slaughter weight), 18·6; raw cotton, 8·1; sunflower seed, 4·8; wool, 0·5; eggs, 82,100m.

In 1987 there were 26,300 collective farms employing 12·6m. collective farmers. Total value of output, 77,800m. rubles. In 1985 they produced 89% of all sugar-beet, cotton 66%, milk 37%, meat 30%, potatoes 21%, other vegetables 24%, eggs 7%, sunflower seeds 74%, wool 30%. In Nov. 1969 the Third Congress of collective farmers adopted a new model constitution, considerably enlarging the planning powers of collective farms and making payments to their members a priority.

In 1987 there were 22,929 state farms employing 12m. workers (10m. engaged in agriculture) and producing an output valued at 81,000m. rubles.

By 1983 the main field work on state and collective farms and joint inter-farm enterprises (ploughing, sowing of grain, cotton and sugar-beet, and the harvesting of grain and silage crops) was fully mechanized; in 1984, 45% of potato harvesting was mechanized, 94% of sugar-beet pulling, and 66% of vegetable planting.

Rural power stations in 1940 had a capacity of 47·5 h.p.; in 1985, 719m. h.p. Energy consumption in 1985 was 30·7 h.p. per employee. In 1984 agriculture consumed 138,814m. kwh. of electric power.

Investments in agriculture in 1986 were 31,300m. rubles by the state and 14,700m. by collective farms. Total agricultural output in 1986 was valued at 121,200m. rubles.

In 1913 the total of irrigated land was 4m. hectares; in 1953, 11m.; in 1986, 20·2m. The total of land drained was 8·4m. hectares in 1956 and 14·9m. in 1986. In 1986, 2,615m. rubles were spent on conservation measures (1,798m. on water resources and 263m. on the atmosphere).

In 1913, 188,000 tonnes of mineral fertilizers were used; in 1950, 5·3m. tonnes, and in 1981, 84m. On 1 Jan. 1987 there were 2·8m. tractors, 826,800 grain combine harvesters and 1·1m. motorized ploughs in the countryside.

An All-Union Academy of Agricultural Sciences, founded in 1929, has regional branches in Siberia and Central Asia and 310 research institutes.

Livestock (1 Jan. 1988), in 1m. head: Cattle, 120·5 (including 42 milch cows); pigs, 77·3; sheep, 142·2; goats, 6·5. Since 1957 the enumeration of livestock has been made on 1 Jan. instead of 1 Oct., *i.e.*, after the winter sales and slaughter for the market. Percentage of farm production in 1985:

	Grain	Cotton	Sugar-beet	Pota-toes	Other vegetables	Meat	Milk	Eggs	Wool
State	48	35	12	18	46	42	32	66	44
Collective	51	65	88	22	25	30	39	6	30
Private [1]	1	0	0	60	29	28	29	28	26

[1] *i.e.*, household plots of collective farmers.

Forestry. Of the 810·9m. hectares of forest land of the USSR, 792·1m. hectares is administered and worked by the State; the remainder, 18·8m. hectares in extent, is granted for use to the peasantry free of charge.

The largest forest areas are 515m. hectares in the Asiatic part of USSR, 51·4m. along the northern seaboard, 25·4m. in the Urals and 17·95m. in the north-west.

On 24 Oct. 1948 a plan was published for planting crop-protecting forest belts, introducing crop rotation with grasses and building of ponds and water reservoirs in the steppe and forest-steppe areas of the European part of the USSR. By the middle of 1952 some 2·6m. hectares had been planted with shelter-belt trees and 13,500 ponds and reservoirs had been built. The planting of the shelter belts in the Kamyshin-Volgograd and Byelgorod-Don areas has in the main been completed. A Volga forest belt has been planted along 1,200 km of railway. Re-afforestation was carried out on 2·2m. hectares of state land in 1986.

Fisheries. The fishing catch including whaling (in 1,000 tons): 1913, 1,051; 1940, 1,422; 1960, 3,541; 1985, 12,400. There were 422 fishing co-operatives in 1985 with a total output valued at 772m. rubles.

Blandon, P., *Soviet Forest Industries.* Boulder, 1983
Johnson, D. G., and Brooks, K. M., *The Prospects for Soviet Agriculture in the 1980s.* Bloomington, 1983
Shaffer, H. G., *Soviet Agriculture.* New York, 1977
Symons, L., *Russian Agriculture: A Geographic Survey.* London, 1972

INDUSTRY AND TRADE

Industry. The organization of industry in the USSR is based on state ownership and control, administered by a separate ministry for each large industry.

Under the successive 5-year plans, large-scale modern industrial works have been constructed, namely: 1st, over 1,500; 2nd, 4,500; 3rd (up to June 1941), 3,000; wartime, 3,500 (apart from reconstruction of destroyed plants); 4th, 6,200; 5th, 3,200; 6th, 2,700; 7th (1959–65), 5,470; 8th (1966–70), 1,870; 9th (1971–75), 2,000; 10th (1976–80), 1,200.

Output of some heavy industries was as follows:

Industry	1913	1950	1960	1970	1980	1987
Iron ore (1m. tonnes)	9·2	39·7	106·2	197·3	244·7	251·0
Oil (1m. tonnes)	9·2	37·9	148·0	353·0	603·2	624·0
Electric power (1,000m. kwh.)	1·9	91·2	292·0	740·9	1,295·0	1,665·0
Coal (1m. tonnes)	29·2	261·1	509·6	624·1	716·4	760·0
Steel (1m. tonnes)	4·2	27·3	65·3	115·9	147·9	162·0
Rolled steel (finished, 1m. tonnes)	3·3	18·0	43·7	80·6	102·9	114·0
Steam and gas turbines (1,000 kw.)	5·9	2,381·0	9,200·0	16,191·0	20,300·0	22,500·0
Steel pipe (1m. tonnes)	–	2·0	5·8	12·4	18·2	20·3
Chemical fibres (1m. tonnes)	–	0·0	0·2	0·6	1·2	1·5
Mineral fertilizer [2] (1m. tonnes)	0·0	1·3	3·3	13·1	24·8	36·3
Automobiles (1,000)	–	64·6	138·8	344·2	1,327·0	1,300·0
Tractors (1m. h.p.)	–	5·5	11·4	29·4	47·0	52·1
Sulphuric acid (1m. tonnes)	0·1	2·1	5·4	12·1	23·0	28·5
Excavators (no.)	–	3,540·0	12,290·0	30,800·0	42,000·0	41,500·0
Timber (commercial, 1m. cu. metres) [1]	27·2	161·0	261·5	298·5	277·7	295·0
Cement (1m. tonnes)	1·8	10·2	45·5	95·2	125·0	137·0

[1] Excluding collective farm production.   [2] Recalculated base.

The process of industrial mechanization and the installation of automatic remote control is being pushed ahead. About 93% of Soviet pig-iron and 87% of the steel is produced in fully automatic furnaces. All hydro-electric plants (in terms of capacity) are fully automatic. Coal production in open-cast mines has been completely mechanized; hydraulic mining is coming into general use. Coal-cutting and underground haulage was over 99% mechanized by the end of 1962 (loading on inclined seams 56%); peat-cutting, 100%, and loading, nearly 80%; timber-cutting, 98%; haulage to loading centres, 93%, and despatch, 97%.

Output in some consumer industries was as follows:

Industry	1913	1950	1960	1970	1980	1987
Cotton fabrics (1m. linear metres)	2,672	3,899	6,387	7,482	8,063	
Woollen fabrics (1m. linear metres)	108	156	342	496	564	12,700
Silk fabrics (1m. linear metres)	43	130	810	1,241	1,632	
Leather footwear (1m. pairs)	60	203	419	679	744	805
Clocks and watches (1m.)	1	8	26	40	67	71
Radio receivers (1m.)	–	1	4	8	9	8
Television sets (1m.)	–	–	2	7	8	9
Refrigerators (1,000)	–	1	530	4,140	5,925	6,000
Paper (1,000 tonnes)	269	1,193	2,334	4,185	5,288	6,200
Meat (slaughter weight, 1m. tonnes)	5	5	9	12	15	19
Butter (1,000 tonnes)	104	336	737	963	1,278	1,700
Granulated sugar (1,000 tonnes)	1,363	2,523	6,360	10,221	10,127	13,700
Canned foods (1m. tins)	116	1,113	4,864	10,678	15,268	20,500

Since 1945 the cotton industry has expanded, especially in the Urals, Central Asia and Siberia. Large mills have been built at Kamyshin, Kherson, Barnaul, Engels, Alma-Ata, Chernigov and Frunze.

Trade Unions and Labour. Trade unions are organized on an industrial basis, all workers, whether manual or brain, in every branch of a given industry being eligible for membership of the same union. Collective farmers may join trade unions.

Since 1933 the trade unions have carried out the functions of the former Labour Commissariat; they control and supervise the application of labour laws, introduce new labour laws for approval by the Government and administer social insurance and factory inspection. Social insurance is non-contributory. The All-Union Congress has met at irregular intervals; the 17th Congress met in 1982 and the 18th in 1987.

In 1944 there were 176 unions. This number was reduced by amalgamation of unions to 22 in 1958, but increased to 31 by 1987. Contributions range from 0·5 to 6% of wages. There are 173 regional and Republican Trades Councils. Membership (1987) 140m.

Chairman, Central Council of Trade Unions: S. A. Shalayev.

Industrial and clerical workers engaged (1986) in the whole national economy were 118·5m., 51% of them women; a further 12·4m. were engaged in collective-farm agriculture. The 7-hour day (6 hours for miners underground and other heavy trades) was generally in operation by the end of 1960. The average working week since 1970 has been 39 hours and in industry 39·6 hours. The 5-day week (without reduction of total working hours) was introduced in 1967.

New 'Fundamentals of Labour Legislation', intended to codify and extend labour laws adopted in the last 40 years, were adopted by the Supreme Soviet in July 1970. They lay down, *inter alia,* the right to receive wages irrespective of the income of the enterprise concerned, the right to free vocational and advanced technical training; the right to form trade unions without state registration; the right of trade unions to participate in and supervise management and planning, labour legislation, safety regulation and housing, fixing of working conditions and wages, etc. Pensioners in Jan. 1987 numbered 56·8m., including 40·5m. old age. Average monthly wages in the state sector were 201 rubles in 1987.

Profsoyuzy SSSR. Dokumenty i materialy. 5 vols., Moscow, 1963–74
Sbornik postanovlenii VTsSPS. Moscow, 1960ff, quarterly
Ruble, B. A., *Soviet Trade Unions. Their Development in the 1970s.* CUP, 1981

Commerce. Retail home trade takes three forms–state, co-operative and the free market, *i.e.,* sales by individual collective-farm members and by the collective farms of their surplus products, after having fulfilled their statutory deliveries and made their regular allocations to their members.

In 1986 retail trade by the State, co-operatives and collective farms totalled 340,800m. rubles; of this state and co-operative trade amounted to 332,100m. rubles (in 1970, 159,400m. and 155,200m. rubles respectively). Employees in retail trade were 7·7m. in 1986 (annual average); there were 716,300 retail trade outlets with a total floor area of 53·6m. sq. metres. The state retail price index (1970 = 100) was 110 in 1986. Trade by collective farm markets amounted to 8,700m. rubles in 1986; this was 2·6% by value of all retail trade and 4·9% by value of all food sales.

Foreign trade is organized as a state monopoly. Importation and exportation of goods are effected under licences issued by the Ministry for Foreign Economic Relations and its respective departments in pursuance of a plan annually sanctioned by the Government. The right of purchasing goods for importation, and that of selling Soviet exports abroad, is vested in trade delegations and representatives of the appropriate state corporations in foreign countries.

There are 29 state import and export organizations, including chartering and tourist corporations (one, Vostokintorg, dealing with Mongolia, Sinkiang and Afghánistán). The Central Union of Consumers' Societies (Tsentrosoyuz) is also authorized to conduct foreign trade operations.

Foreign trade in 1986 was conducted with 145 foreign countries (in 1950, 45), and had by 1986 increased 45 times by value since 1950. Exports in 1986 were valued at 68,347m. rubles (45,661m. to the socialist countries), and imports at 62,587m. rubles (41,840m. from the socialist countries).

Soviet imports of machinery and equipment, between 1940 and 1986, rose from 32·4 to 40·7%, ores and concentrates fell from 26·6 to 8·3%, foodstuffs rose from 14·9 to 17·1% and manufactured consumer goods rose from 1·4 to 13·4% by value; exports of fuel and electricity increased from 13·2 to 47·3% and of machinery and equipment from 2 to 15% by value over the same period.

Main items of exports in 1986:

Crude oil (1m. tonnes)	130·0	Gas (1m. cu. metres)	79,200·0
Iron ore (1m. tonnes)	36·0	Tractors (1,000)	39·1
Rolled metal (1m. tonnes)	8·9	Motor cars (1,000)	306·0
Paper (1,000 tonnes)	717·0	Clocks and watches (1m.)	17·6
Cotton cloth (1,000 tonnes)	713·0	Grain (1m. tonnes)	1·5

Total trade between the USSR and UK for calendar years (British Department of Trade returns, in £1,000 sterling):

	1984	1985	1986	1987
Imports to UK	854,307	724,453	694,624	875,431
Exports and re-exports from UK	735,173	536,555	539,368	491,615

Tourism. Pre-revolutionary Russia was never a country for any but the most hardy and better-off tourists, as the introductory pages of Baedeker's guide made clear. For her subjects, too, touring was no more inviting. Acute shortage of hotels and boarding-houses, poor roads, lack of ordinary services for visitors were among the least of their difficulties. These have not by any means been fully overcome: but very great efforts to meet them have been made. The first tourist organizations came into existence in 1885–90 in St Petersburg, Tiflis and Odessa; and in 1901 the Russian Society of Tourists was formed (about 5,000 members in 1914). Organized tourism in the Soviet period began in the early 1920s; the Russian Society of Tourists was revived, and other tourist organizations, notably 'Intourist' (founded 1929), were established. The development of tourism on a massive scale is however a development of the post-Second World War period.

Tourist facilities for Soviet and foreign citizens are presently made available under state, trade union and other auspices, all of which come ultimately under the supervision of the State Committee on Tourism which is attached to the USSR Council of Ministers. The number of hotels available to such tourists increased from 222 in 1960 to 971 in 1986, with a total accommodation of 416,300 (in 1960, 36,000); the number of tourist bases, for the hire of equipment and shorter stays, increased to 8,057, with a total accommodation of 791,900. In 1986 these facilities were used by 34·4m. and 9m. tourists respectively (in 1970, 5m. and 1·7m.). A total of 50·3m. citizens in 1986 made use of all forms of tourist accommodation, including sanatoria and boarding houses (in 1960, 6·7m.; in 1970, 16·8m.). In 1986 a further 219m. citizens took part in tourist excursions.

Visitors to the USSR from foreign countries are catered for by 'Intourist' and its offices in foreign countries. In 1970, the USSR had 2,059,338 foreign visitors (43,490 from the UK, and 66,365 from the USA); in 1980 there were 5,590,000 foreign visitors. Intourist also arranges the visits of Soviet citizens to foreign countries, and in the 1970s assisted about 2m. annually.

COMMUNICATIONS

Roads. By 1940 there were over 1·5m. km of constructed roads, of which 143,000 km were suitable for motor traffic. The total length of motor roads in 1987 was 827,000 km. Road freights by lorry amounted to 859m. tonnes in 1940 and 27,000m. tonnes in 1986. Passengers carried were 590m. in 1940 and 48,800m. in 1986. In 1986, 23,300 inter-urban bus routes had a total length of 3,497,000 km.

Railways. The length of railways in Jan. 1987 was 145,600 km (1913: 58,500 km), of which 50,600 km was electrified. Diesel and electric traction now account for almost 100% of all movements, with the electrified network handling 56% of the traffic. In 1986, 47% of all domestic tonne-km of freight and 37% of all passenger-km of traffic went by rail. In 1986 railways carried 4,078m. tonnes of freight (representing 3,834,500 tonne-km) and carried 4,345m. passengers (representing 390,000m. passenger-km).

Operations are centred on 32 regions with headquarters at: Baku, Alma-Ata, Tyndin, Minsk, Irkutsk, Gorki, Khabarovsk, Donetsk, Chita, Tbilisi, Aktyubinsk, Novosibirsk, Kemerovo, Krasnoyarsk, Kuibyshev, Lvov, Kishinev, Moscow, Odessa, Leningrad, Riga, Saratov, Dnepropetrovsk, Sverdlovsk, Yaroslavl, Rostov-on-Don, Tashkent, Tselinograd, Voronezh, Kharkov and Chelyabinsk.

Extensive railway construction is in progress, including routes northwards from Surgut to Urengoi and Nizhe-Vartovskoye, while the great Baikal-Amur Magistral (BAM) project was completed in 1985. This is a new main line to the east, sited well to the north of the existing Trans-Siberian route to the Pacific ports of Nakhodka and Vladivostok. It runs from Lena, on the Lena river, to Komsomolsk-on-Amur, 3,145 km distant. BAM is intended to become the principal route for export traffic to the eastern ports, easing the very heavy pressure on the Trans-Siberian line, which is only partially electrified and not double-track throughout.

BAM was the most arduous railway building project ever tackled by Soviet engineers, and the greatest drawback to development of the region has been its severe geological and climatic conditions. There is permafrost throughout the area, and winter temperatures fall to –60°C. Construction work occupied nearly a decade, and has required over 3,200 bridges, tunnels and culverts.

Underground railways have been built in Moscow, Leningrad, Kiev, Tbilisi, Kharkov, Tashkent, Baku, Gorky, Minsk, Yerevan and Novosibirsk. Others are under construction at Omsk, Dnepropetrovsk, Kuibyshev and Sverdlovsk.

Aviation. In 1986 total length of internal airlines in the USSR was approximately 971,000 km; 116·1m. passengers were carried internally and externally, and 3·2m. tonnes of freight. The Central Asian Airways in some instances provide the only means of communication across the desert and mountainous regions of the local republics. An 8,500-km air service was opened in Feb. 1941 between Moscow and Anadyr (Eastern Siberia), through Archangel, Igarka, Khatanga, Tiksi Bay and Cape Schmidt, *i.e.*, along the entire course of the Northern Sea Route. There are also other Arctic airlines, *e.g.*, Igarka-Gulf of Kozhevnikov; Igarka-Dickson Island; Yakutsk-Tiksi Bay; Yakutsk-Viluisk; Yakutsk-Verkhoiansk.

Direct air services are maintained throughout the year between Moscow and the capitals of all Soviet republics as well as London, New York, Montreal, Tōkyō, Delhi, Rangoon, Belgrade, Peking, Pyongyang, Ulan Bator, Kábul, Tirana, Paris, Warsaw, Prague, Budapest, Bucharest, Sofia, Vienna, Berlin, Helsinki, Stockholm,

Copenhagen, Jakarta, Dakar and Gander. Soviet air services reached 87 countries in 1981, and 20 foreign lines have regular services to the USSR, including British Airways, KLM, SAS, Air France, Sabena, Air India, PANAM. The first Soviet airbus, the 350-seater IL-86, began flights on civil aviation routes in 1981. The 120-seater YAK-42 will gradually replace the TU-134 and AN-24 on major shorter routes.

MacDonald, H., *Aeroflot: Soviet Air Transport Since 1923*. London, 1975

Shipping. In 1977 the Soviet mercantile marine comprised 7,000 self-propelled vessels, of which 80% were built between 1957 and 1966. By May 1977 the gross cargo capacity was (including fishing vessels) 20·8m. registered tonnes (16m. tonnes dead-weight).

Freights carried on domestic waterways were: In 1913 (present frontiers), 35·1m. tonnes; in 1940, 73·9m. tonnes; and in 1986, 639m. tonnes; 136m. passengers were carried. The Soviet share in world marine tonnage was 2% in 1960 and 6% in 1977. Deep-sea ports are under construction at Vostochny (Far East) and Grigorevsky (Black Sea) with new deep-sea wharves at Ventspils (Latvia), Murmansk and Archangel (for Arctic traffic). Archangel is kept open by icebreakers all the year round from 1979. Foreign freights in 1977 totalled 14% of all Soviet seaborne trade.

The North Sea route affords convenient communication between the European USSR and the Far East along the Soviet coast, for the produce of the basins of the Ob, Yenissei, Lena and Kolyma rivers.

The length of navigable rivers and canals in exploitation was (1986) 123,200 km, of which the length of floatable rivers is 85,000 km. There are several thousand miles of canals and other artificial waterways; among them the Baltic and White Sea Canal (235 km), the Moscow-Volga Canal (130 km). Goods turnover on inland waterways was 28,900m. tonne-km in 1913, 35,900m. in 1940, 45,900m. in 1950 and 261,600m. in 1985.

The Volga-Don Shipping Canal was opened for traffic in 1952. The Volga-Don waterway from Volgograd to Rostov is 540 km long, of which the Volga-Don canal comprises 101 km. The canal has transformed the section of the river from Kalach, where the Don is joined by the Volga-Don canal, to Rostov into a deep-water highway suitable for big Volga shipping. The canal links the White, Baltic, Caspian, Azov and Black Seas into a single water transport system. In Oct. 1964 the 2,430-km Baltic-Volga waterway, linking Klaipeda on the Baltic to Kakhovka at the mouth of the Dnieper and suitable for 5,000-tonne vessels, was begun. Reconstruction of the 18th-century Mariinsky canal system in north-west Russia was completed, providing a through waterway from Leningrad to Rybinsk (on the Upper Volga) and cutting the passage of freight from 18 to 2½ days.

At the end of 1977 the longest train ferry route in the world was opened between the Soviet Union and Bulgaria (Ilyichovsk-Varna).

The first section of Vostochny port, in Wrangel Bay on the Pacific coast, is completed. It will be the country's largest deep-sea port.

In 1962 a canal was completed across the Kara-Kum desert in southern Turkmenistan (replacing an earlier project for a more costly scheme across the north of the republic). The canal, from Bussag on the river Amu-Darya to Archnan, northwest of Ashkhabad, through the Murgab oasis, 900 km long, supplies water to an area exceeding 200,000 hectares, suitable for cotton, fruit, vineyards and livestock. An extension to the Caspian (500 km) is under construction: the complete system will irrigate 1m. hectares.

An irrigation canal system (250 miles), bringing water from Kakhovka on the Dnieper to the North Crimea, is nearing completion. Work to divert water from the Pechora and Vychegda rivers (flowing into the White Sea) south to the Volga is in progress. Work has begun on a 300-mile canal which will supply water from the Irtysh to Karaganda in Central Kazakhstan, irrigating over 150,000 acres; the first 37 miles were opened in 1965 and another 45 miles in Dec. 1967. Most of the 11 reservoirs required had been completed by 1 Jan. 1972. Other irrigation canals under construction are Kuibyshev (279 km long, to supply over 100,000 hectares) and Stavropol (481 km, irrigating 200,000 hectares); the second section of the latter went into commission in Nov. 1974, 14 months ahead of schedule. In Sept. 1972 the Saratov Canal (irrigating 1 m. hectares) went into commission.

Post and Broadcasting. In Jan. 1987 the number of post, telegraph and telephone offices was 92,000 and of general telephones 33m.

The international radio-telecommunications services are operated by the Ministry of Communications of the USSR. The Great Northern Telegraph Co., Ltd, of Denmark, operates cables connecting Denmark with Leningrad, whence connexion is made by means of a trans-Siberian landline with Vladivostok. From the latter place the Great Northern Telegraph Co. owns cables connecting with Japan, China and Hong Kong. Direct radio and telephone communication with India is provided for in an agreement concluded in 1955.

The State Committee for Broadcasting and Television produces 3 programmes in Moscow, broadcasting throughout the Union. In addition the regional radio stations produce 1, 2 or 3 programmes for the republics as well as local programmes for a town or region. The foreign service from Moscow is beamed to all parts of the world, in 64 languages. Chinese has 28½ hours programme time a day. Several republics have their own foreign services. English is broadcast from Moscow, Kiev, Tashkent, Vilnius and Yerevan. There are 120 TV centres in the USSR, several of them producing more than 1 programme. In Moscow there are 4 programmes. Colour programmes are broadcast by the SECAM system. A nationwide system of space telecommunications, consisting of satellites and ground stations, takes TV broadcasts to distant parts of the country.

Number of receivers, Jan. 1987: radio, 83m. (1960, 28m); television, 85m. (1960, 5m.).

Cinemas and theatres (Jan. 1987). There were 152,700 cinemas to which 3,882m. visits were made annually. In Jan. 1987 there were 640 theatres, to which 126m. visits were made.

Newspapers. In 1986, 8,515 newspapers with a total daily circulation of 198·1m. copies were published in 57 languages of the USSR.

JUSTICE, RELIGION, EDUCATION AND WELFARE

Justice. The basis of the judicial system is the same throughout the Soviet Union, but the constituent republics have the right to introduce modifications and to make their own rules for the application of the codes of laws. The Supreme Court of the USSR is the chief court and supervising organ for all constituent republics and is elected by the Supreme Soviet of the USSR for 5 years. Chairman (elected 1984) V. I. Terebilov. Supreme Courts of the Union and Autonomous Republics are elected by the Supreme Soviets of these republics, and Territorial, Regional and Area Courts by the respective Soviets, each for a term of 5 years. At the lowest level are the People's Courts, which are elected directly by the population.

Court proceedings are conducted in the local language with full interpreting facilities as required. All cases are heard in public, unless otherwise provided for by law, and the accused is guaranteed the right of defence.

Laws establishing common principles of legislation in various fields are adopted by the Supreme Soviet and are then enacted in more specific form and implemented by subordinate levels of state and judicial authority.

The Law Courts are divided into People's Courts and higher courts. The People's Courts consist of the People's Judge and 2 Assessors, and their function is to examine, as the first instance, most of the civil and criminal cases, except the more important ones, some of which are tried at the Regional Court, and those of the highest importance at the Supreme Court. The Regional Courts supervise the activities of the People's Courts and also act as Courts of Appeal from the decisions of the People's Court. Special chambers of the higher courts deal with offences committed in the Army and the public transport services.

People's Judges and Assessors, who serve on a rota basis, are elected directly by the citizens of each constituency: judges for 5 years, assessors for 2½. Should a judge be found not to perform his duties conscientiously and in accordance with the mandate of the people, he may be recalled by his electors.

The People's Assessors are called upon for duty for 2 weeks in a year. The People's Assessors for the Regional Court must have had at least 2 years' experience in public or trade-union work. The list of Assessors for the Supreme Court is drawn up by the Supreme Soviet of the republic.

The Labour Session of the People's Court supervises the regulations relating to the working conditions and the protection of labour and gives decisions on conflicts arising between managements and employees, or the violation of regulations.

Disputes between State institutions must be referred to an arbitration commission. Disputes between Soviet State institutions and foreign business firms may be referred by agreement to a Foreign Trade Arbitration Commission of the All-Union Chamber of Commerce.

The Procurator-General of the USSR (since 1984, A. M. Rekunkov) is appointed for 5 years by the Supreme Soviet. All procurators of the republics, autonomous republics and autonomous regions are appointed by the Procurator-General of the USSR for a term of 5 years. The procurators supervise the correct application of the law by all state organs, and have special responsibility for the observance of the law in places of detention. The procurators of the Union republics are subordinate to the Procurator-General of the USSR, whose duty it is to see that acts of all institutions of the USSR are legal, that the law is correctly interpreted and uniformly applied; he has to participate in important cases in the capacity of State Prosecutor.

Capital punishment was abolished on 26 May 1947, but was restored on 12 Jan. 1950 for treason, espionage and sabotage, on 7 May 1954 for certain categories of murder, in Dec. 1958 for terrorism and banditry, on 7 May 1961 for embezzlement of public property, counterfeiting and attack on prison warders and, in particular circumstances, for attacks on the police and public order volunteers and for rape (15 Feb. 1962) and for accepting bribes (20 Feb. 1962).

In view of criminal abuses, extending over many years, discovered in the security system, the powers of administrative trial and exile previously vested in the security authorities (MVD) were abolished in 1953; accelerated procedures for trial on charges of high treason, espionage, wrecking, etc., by the Supreme Court were abolished in 1955; and extensive powers of protection of persons under arrest or serving prison terms were vested in the Procurator-General's Office (1955). Supervisory commissions, composed of representatives of trade unions, youth organizations and local authorities, were set up in 1956 to inspect places of detention.

Further reforms of the civil and criminal codes were decreed on 25 Dec. 1958. Thereby the age of criminal responsibility has been raised from 14 to 16 years; deportation and banishment have been abolished; a presumption of innocence is not accepted, but the burden of proof of guilt has been placed upon the prosecutor. Secret trials and the charge of 'enemy of the people' have been abolished. Articles 70 and 190 of the Criminal Code, which deal with 'anti-Soviet agitation and propaganda' and 'crimes against the system of administration' respectively, have however been widely used against political dissidents in more recent years.

Butler, W. E., *The Soviet Legal System. Selected Contemporary Legislation and Documents.* New York, 1978.—*Soviet Law.* London, 1983
Feldbrugge, F. J. M. (ed.), *Encyclopedia of Soviet Law.* 2nd ed. Dordrecht, 1985
Hazard, J., Butler, W. E. and Maggs, P., *The Soviet Legal System.* 3rd ed., New York, 1977
Simons, W. B. (ed.), *The Soviet Codes of Law.* Alphen aan den Rijn, 1980

Religion. With the Revolution the Orthodox Church lost its position as the dominant religion and all religions were placed on an equal footing. Article 52 of the 1977 Soviet Constitution reads as follows: 'Citizens of the USSR are guaranteed freedom of conscience, that is, the right to profess or not to profess any religion, and to conduct religious worship or atheistic propaganda. Incitement of hostility or hatred on religious grounds is prohibited. In the USSR the church is separated from the state, and school from the church.'

By decree of 2 Feb. 1918 the Orthodox Church was disestablished; its property, together with that of all other denominations, was nationalized. The congregations themselves have to maintain their churches and clergy, regardless of confession or denomination. A minimum of 20 persons may request and receive the use of a church building, free of charge, except for maintenance, insurance, land taxes, etc. About two-thirds of all the churches have been closed since 1917, but about 20,000 churches and 18 religious seminaries were reported to be in operation in 1986. Religious instruction may be given in private, but otherwise only in church classes. The income of religious communities is not subject to taxation. Religious instruction in classes for persons under 18 is forbidden. The state supplies paper and printing facilities to all denominations for producing the Bible, the Koran, prayer books, missals, etc.

Relations between the religious communities of all creeds and the Government are maintained through a Council for Religious Affairs which is attached to the Council of Ministers of the USSR. (*Chairman*, K. M. Kharchev).

The Russian Orthodox Church, represented by the Patriarchate of Moscow, had, in 1987, about 50m. regular worshippers. There are still many Old Believers, whose schism from the Orthodox Church dates from the 17th century. The Russian Church is headed by the Patriarch of Moscow and All Russia, assisted by the Holy Synod, which has 7 members–the Patriarch himself and the Metropolitans of Krutitsy and Kolomna (Moscow), Leningrad and Kiev *ex officio*, and 3 bishops alternating for 6 months in order of seniority from the 3 regions forming the Moscow Patriarchate. The Patriarchate of Moscow maintains jurisdiction over a few parishes of Russian Orthodox abroad, at Tehrán, Jerusalem, German Democratic Republic, France (1 archbishop), England, North and South America (2 bishops). There are 19 monasteries and nunneries, and 6 Orthodox academies and seminaries with 10 journals.

After the Russian Orthodox Church the next Christian community in importance are the Armenians; their Catholicos (Patriarch), whose seat is at Etchmiadzin, is head of all the Armenian (Gregorian) communities throughout the world. There is an Armenian Orthodox academy and a seminary.

The Georgian Orthodox Church has its own organization under a Catholicos (Patriarch) who is resident in Tbilisi and who directs the church's seminary in Mtskheta.

Protestantism is represented chiefly by the Evangelical Christian Baptists, with over 512,000 baptized adult members and some 5,000 churches; the Lutherans are concentrated mainly in the Baltic States (350,000 in Estonia, 600,000 in Latvia), the Reformed in the Transcarpathian Region of the Ukraine (70,000). Both Baptists and Lutherans conduct theological courses. The Methodist Church functions in Estonia.

The Roman Catholics are most numerous in Lithuania and the western Ukraine. There are 2 Roman Catholic arch-episcopates and 4 episcopates in Lithuania with 630 churches and a seminary at Kaunas providing a 5-year course. In 1946 some 3·5m. Uniates in the USSR were compelled to withdraw their allegiance to Rome and came under the jurisdiction of the Orthodox Patriarchate in Moscow. In Latvia there are an arch-episcopate and 1 episcopate (Riga and Liepaja) of the Roman Catholic Church.

The Moslems (estimate 30m. members, mainly Sunnis), are divided into 4 administrative regions, 3 of them (Central Asia and Kazakhstan, European Russia and Siberia, Northern Caucasus) headed by a Mufti; the largest (Transcaucasia, with its centre at Baku) by a Sheikh-ul-Islam.

There is a Moslem academy and a madrasah in Central Asia. Several editions of the Koran have appeared in recent years.

There are various Jewish communities, the chief being in Moscow and Kiev. Large synagogues maintain bakeries for producing unleavened bread. There is a Jewish Yeshiva in Moscow (established 1956) and 180 synagogues as well as several dozen minyans. The Central Buddhist Council of the USSR is headed by a Lama with communities in Buryatia, Tuva, Kalmykia and in the national (minority) areas of the Chita and Irkutsk regions.

O religii i tserkvi: sbornik vazhneishikh vyskazivanii klassikov Marksizma-Leninizma, dokumentov KPSS i sovetskogo gosudarstva. 2nd ed., Moscow, 1981
Bordeaux, M., *Opium of the People. The Christian Religion in the USSR.* London, 1965.—*Religious Ferment in Russia.* London, 1968

Curtiss, J. S., *The Russian Church and the Soviet State, 1917–50*. New York, 1953
Ellis, J., *The Russian Orthodox Church*. London, 1986
Kochan, L., (ed.), *Jews in Soviet Russia since 1917*. 3rd ed., Oxford, 1977
Lane, C., *Christian Religion in the Soviet Union*. London, 1978

Education. Education is free and compulsory from 7 to 16/17. There are 2 types of general schools, with an 8-year or a 10-year curriculum; the minimum school-leaving age is now 17. Pupils who leave an 8-year school continue their education at either a 10-year school or a vocational training school. A 10-year school pupil may also transfer to vocational school after the 8th year. Under directives adopted in 1984, there will be a gradual transition towards an 11-year school system, starting at 6, from 1986 onwards; efforts are also being made to improve pupils' preparation for employment and the status and working conditions of teachers.

In 1986–87 there were 138,000 primary and secondary schools. Pupils in general educational schools numbered 43·9m. (6·5m. of them in the ninth and tenth forms) and the teachers 3m. Those at vocational and specialized technical secondary schools numbered 9·8m.

At the end of 1940 labour reserve schools (both vocational and industrial) were organized, admitting applicants from 14 to 17 years of age. From 1959 onwards these and other technical schools were reorganized as town and rural vocational and technical schools, at which pupils stay for a year longer than at general schools, combining completion of general secondary education with vocational training. From 1940 to 1977 inclusive they trained 35m. skilled workers. In 1978, 2·3m. graduated from such schools, including 628,000 for agriculture; 600,000 agricultural mechanics were trained in state and collective farms. Over 4,300 vocational training schools existed in 1981, training 2·17m. boys and girls, all of whom receive a full secondary education. In 1986, 16·5m. children of from 3 to 7 years of age attended kindergartens. Children in boarding schools numbered over 800,000 in 1972–73.

In 1986–87 there were 4,506 technical colleges with 4·5m. students, and 896 universities, institutes and other places of higher education, with 5·1m. students (including 1·8m. taking correspondence or evening courses). Among the 65 university towns are: Moscow, Leningrad, Kharkov, Odessa, Tartu, Kazan, Saratov, Tomsk, Kiev, Sverdlovsk, Tbilisi, Alma-Ata, Tashkent, Minsk, Gorky and Vladivostok.

On 1 Jan. 1987 there were 1·5m. scientific workers in 5,070 places of higher education, research institutes and Academies of Sciences. There are 33,000 foreign students from 130 countries.

The Academy of Sciences of the USSR had 785 members and corresponding members. Total learned institutions under the USSR Academy of Sciences number 244, with 58,492 scientific staff. Each Union Republic (other than the RSFSR) has its own Academy of Sciences, with scientific staff numbering 49,988. There are also Siberian, Far Eastern and other branches of the USSR Academy. On 1 Jan. 1987 there were 96,125 post-graduate students in Academy and other higher educational institutions, 52% studying on a part-time basis.

The Academy of Pedagogical Sciences had 14 research institutes with 1,668 staff.

In 1987 over 110m. people were studying at schools, colleges and training or correspondence courses. 125 per 1,000 of the employed population had a higher education (1939, 13; 1970, 65).

Grant, N., *Soviet Education*. 4th ed., Harmondsworth, 1979
Matthews, M., *Education in the Soviet Union*. London, 1982

Health and Social Security. All health services are free of charge although payment is required for medicines; but private practice exists. The health service is administered by the Ministry of Health of the USSR, which supervises the work of the Health Ministries of the Union Republics and the Autonomous Republics.

In 1944 an Academy of Medical Sciences was formed; in 1987 it had 472 members and corresponding members working in 64 research institutes in which 7,106 staff were employed. Smallpox, trachoma and malaria have been virtually eliminated.

In Jan. 1987 there were 23,500 civil hospitals with 3·7m. beds. There were 837,000 infants in day nurseries. 1,202,000 doctors (including dentists) were in the health service. All confinements in towns and 75% in the country were in hospital.

There were 40,100 outpatients' clinics, apart from the 28,400 women's consultation centres and children's clinics.

The death-rate in the USSR in 1986 was 9·8 per 1,000, and the birth rate 20 per 1,000. Infant death rate was 25·4 (per 1,000 live births) in 1986, compared with 273 in 1913, 184 in 1940 and 81 in 1950. Average expectation of life, 69·6 (1913, 32).

Social insurance is administered by the trade unions, through social insurance councils elected in places of work and social insurance sub-committees of factory committees: about 5m. volunteers are engaged in this work. 50·3m. people went to holiday sanatoria or rest homes in 1986. 56·8m. people, including 10m. collective farmers, were receiving state pensions in Jan. 1987; of these, 40·5m. (8·9m. collective farmers) were old-age pensioners.

Total number of holiday sanatoria providing toning-up treatment at resorts in 1986 was 2,414, with accommodation for 605,000; in addition, there were 3,175 overnight sanatoria at large plants for treatment of mild disorders without absence from work, accommodating 269,000. There were also 1,239 trade union-managed holiday hotels with a capacity of 384,000, holidays being partly or wholly at trade unions' expense. In 1986, 92m. citizens were systematically engaged in physical culture and sport; there were 3,481 stadiums seating 1,500 or more, 2,601 swimming pools and 103,000 football pitches.

State expenditure (in 1m. rubles) on health services and physical education: 1940, 0·9; 1970, 9,300; 1980, 14,800; 1986, 18,000.

Between 1950 and 1980 62,766,000 apartments (in towns) and houses (in rural areas) were built. In 1986, 2·1m. apartments and houses were built. Rents in the USSR have not been increased since 1928 and in 1987 accounted for about 3% of the expenditure of an average worker's family. By the end of 1986, 78% of all urban housing had a gas supply installed, 92% had running water, 89% had central heating and 84% had bathrooms. 60% of total housing space is publicly and 40% is privately owned.

DIPLOMATIC REPRESENTATIVES

Of the USSR in Great Britain (13 Kensington Palace Gdns., London, W8 4QX)
Ambassador: Leonid M. Zamyatin.

Of Great Britain in the USSR (Naberezhnaya Morisa Toreza 14, Moscow 72)
Ambassador: Sir Bryan Cartledge, KCMG.

Of the USSR in the USA (1125 16th St., NW, Washington, D.C., 20036)
Ambassador: Yuri V. Dubinin.

Of the USA in the USSR (Ulitsa Chaikovskogo 19, Moscow)
Ambassador: Jack F. Matlock, Jr.

Of the USSR to the United Nations
Ambassador: Alexander Belonogov.

Books of Reference

Narodnoe Khozvaistvo SSSR za 70 let (National Economy of the USSR for 70 years). Jubilee Statistical Yearbook. Moscow, 1987
Pravda (Truth). Daily organ of the Central Committee of the Communist Party
Izvestiya (News). Daily organ of the Presidium of the Supreme Soviet of the USSR
Vedomosti Verkhovnovo Soveta. Bulletin of the Supreme Soviet of the USSR in the languages of the 15 republics; published weekly
Sovetskaya Torgovlya. Monthly publication of the Ministry of Trade of the USSR

Planovoye Khozyaistvo. Monthly. Moscow
Vestnik Statistiki. Monthly publication of the USSR Statistical Committee
Vneshnyaya Torgovlya. Published by the Ministry for Foreign Trade. Monthly. Moscow
Trud. The daily organ of the All-Union Central Council of Trade Unions
Professionalnye Soyuzy. A trade union fortnightly. Moscow
Kommunist. A fortnightly organ of the Communist Party of the Soviet Union
Finansy SSSR. A monthly publication of the Ministry for Finance
Bolshaya Sovetskaya Entsiklopedia. 65 vols. Moscow, 1926–47; 2nd ed., 51 vols. Moscow,
     1949–58; 3rd ed., Moscow, 1959–78; annual supplement (*Yezhegodnik*)
Soviet Union. A monthly pictorial. Moscow. (In English)
Soviet Import-Export Dictionary (in Russian, with English, etc., terms). Moscow, 1952
Soviet Studies; A Quarterly Review. Ed. R. A. Clarke. Glasgow, quarterly.
The Current Digest of the Soviet Press. Published by Joint Committee on Slavic Studies.
     Columbus, Ohio, weekly.
Baylis, J., and Segal, G., (eds.) *Soviet Strategy.* London, 1981
Beloff, M., *The Foreign Policy of Soviet Russia, 1929–41.* 2 vols. 1947–49.—*Soviet Policy in the
     Far East.* Oxford, 1953.—*Soviet Policy in Asia, 1944–52.* Oxford, 1953
Bialer, S., *The Soviet Paradox: External Expansion, Internal Decline.* London, 1987
Brown, A., and Kaser, M., *The Soviet Union Since the Fall of Khrushchev.* London, 2nd ed.
     1978.—*Soviet Policy for the 1980s.* London, 1982
Byrnes, J. F. (ed.), *After Brezhnev. Sources of Soviet Conduct in the 1980s.* London, 1983
Cambridge Encyclopedia of Russia and the Soviet Union. CUP, 1982
Carr, E. H., *A History of Soviet Russia.* 14 vols. London, 1951–78
Clarke, R. A., and Matko, D. J. I., (eds.), *Soviet Economic Facts 1917–80.* London, 1983
Cracraft, J., *The Soviet Union Today.* Chicago, 1983
Degras, J. (compiler), *Soviet Documents on Foreign Policy, 1917–41.* 3 vols. London, 1948–52
Deutscher, I., *Trotsky.* 3 vols. OUP, 1954 ff.
Edmonds, R., *Soviet Foreign Policy: the Brezhnev Years.* Oxford, 1983
Falla, P. S., *The Oxford English-Russian Dictionary.* OUP, 1984
Fitzsimmons, T., and others, *USSR; Its People, Its Society, Its Culture.* New Haven, 1960
Galperin, I. R., *New English-Russian Dictionary.* 2 vols. Moscow, 1972
Gruzinov, V. F., *The USSR's Management of Foreign Trade.* London, 1980
Hammond, T. T. (ed.), *Soviet Foreign Relations and World Communism: A Selected Biblio-
     graphy.* Princeton, 1965
Hill, R. J., *The Soviet Union. Politics, Economics and Society.* London, 1985
Hosking, G., *A History of the Soviet Union.* London, 1985
Hough, J. F. and Fainsod, M., *How the Soviet Union is Governed.* Rev. ed. Harvard Univ.
     Press, 1979
Hutchings, R., *The Soviet Budget.* London, 1983
Jensen, R. G. et al (eds.) *Soviet National Resources in the World Economy.* Univ. of Chicago
     Press, 1983
Jones, D. L., *Books in English in the Soviet Union 1917–73: A Bibliography.* London and New
     York, 1975
Kaiser, R. G., *Russia: The People and the Power.* London, 1976
Kelley, D. R., (ed.), *Soviet Politics in the Brezhnev Era.* London, 1980
McCauley, M., *The Soviet Union since 1917.* London, 1981
Nove, A., *The Soviet Economic System.* London, 1977
Pares, Sir B., *A History of Russia.* London, 1962
Paxton, J., *Companion to Russian History.* London and New York, 1984
Preobrazhensky, A. G., *Etymological Dictionary of the Russian Language.* Columbia Univ.
     Press, 1951
Riasanovsky, N. V., *A History of Russia.* 4th ed. OUP, 1984
Shabad, T., and Mote, V.L., *Gateway to Siberian Resources (The BAM).* New York and
     London, 1977
Schapiro, L., and Godson, J., *The Soviet Worker.* London, 1981
Schmidt-Häuer, C., *Gorbachov: The Path to Power.* London, 1986
Slusser, R. M., and Triska, J. F., *A Calendar of Soviet Treaties, 1917–57.* Stanford Univ. Press,
     1959—and Ginsburgs, G., *A Calendar of Soviet Treaties, 1958–1973,* Alphen aan den Rijn,
     1981
Smirnitsky, A. I. (ed.), *Russko-angliiskii slovar.* 4th ed. Moscow 1959
Thompson, A., *Russia/USSR: A Selective Annotated Bibliography of Books in English.*
     Oxford and Santa Barbara, 1979
Treadgold, D. W., *Twentieth Century Russia.* 6th ed. Boston, 1987
Utechin, S. V. (ed.), *Everyman's Concise Encyclopaedia of Russia.* London, 1961
Vernadsky, G., *A History of Russia.* 5th ed. Yale Univ. Press, 1961
Walker, M., *The Waking Giant: Gorbachev's Russia.* New York, 1987
Wheeler, M., *The Oxford Russian-English Dictionary.* OUP, 2nd ed., 1984

RUSSIAN SOVIET FEDERAL SOCIALIST REPUBLIC (RSFSR)

Rossiiskaya Sovyetskaya Federativnaya Sotsialisticheskaya Respublika

AREA AND POPULATION. The RSFSR occupies over 76% of the total area of the USSR stretching from the Far North to the Black Sea in the south and from the Far East to Kaliningrad in the west. 82·6% of its population in Jan. 1979 were Russians, the rest being 38 national minorities such as the Tatars, Ukrainians, Jews, Mordovians, Chuvashis, Bashkirs, Poles, Germans, Udmurts, Buryats, Mari, Yakuts and Ossetians. The 2 principal cities are Moscow, the capital, with a population (Jan. 1986) of 8·7m. (without suburbs, 8,533,000) and Leningrad, the second capital, 4,901,000 (without suburbs, 4,359,000). Among other important large towns are Gorky, Rostov-on-Don, Volgograd, Sverdlovsk, Novosibirsk, Chelyabinsk, Kazan, Omsk and Kuibyshev. Population, 1987, 145,311,000.

The RSFSR contains great mineral resources: iron ore in the Urals, the Kerch Peninsula and Siberia; coal in the Kuznets Basin, Eastern Siberia, Urals and the sub-Moscow Basin; oil in the Urals, Azov-Black Sea area, Bashkiria, and West Siberia. It also has abundant deposits of gold, platinum, copper, zinc, lead, tin and rare metals.

The RSFSR produces about 70% of the total industrial and agricultural output of the Soviet Union. Industrial and office workers averaged 67·6m. in 1985.

CONSTITUTION AND GOVERNMENT. The RSFSR adopted its present constitution at a meeting of the Supreme Soviet in April 1978, following 330,000 town and country meetings in which 25m. citizens took part.

Chairman, Presidium of the Supreme Soviet: V. P. Orlov.
Chairman, Council of Ministers: V. I. Vorotnikov.
Foreign Minister: V. M. Vinogradov.

The RSFSR consists of:

(1) *Territories:* Altai, Khabarovsk, Krasnodar, Krasnoyarsk, Primorye, Stavropol.

(2) *Regions:* Amur, Archangel, Astrakhan, Belgorod, Briansk, Chelyabinsk, Chita, Gorky, Irkutsk, Ivanovo, Kaluga, Kalinin, Kaliningrad, Kamchatka, Kemerovo, Kirov, Kostroma, Kuibyshev, Kurgan, Kursk, Leningrad, Lipetsk, Magadan, Moscow, Murmansk, Novgorod, Novosibirsk, Omsk, Orel, Orenburg, Penza, Perm, Pskov, Rostov, Ryazan, Sakhalin, Saratov, Smolensk, Sverdlovsk, Tambov, Tomsk, Tula, Tyumen, Ulyanovsk, Vladimir, Volgograd, Vologda, Voronezh, Yaroslavl.

(3) *Autonomous Soviet Republics:* Bashkir, Buryat, Chechen-Ingush, Chuvash, Daghestan, Kabardin-Balkar, Kalmyk, Karelian, Komi, Mari, Mordovian, North Ossetia, Tartar, Tuva, Udmurt, Yakut.

Subordinate to and within Territories and Regions are the following:

(4) *Autonomous Regions:* Adygei, Gorno-Altai, Jewish, Karachayevo-Cherkess, Khakass.

(5) *Autonomous Areas:* Agin-Buryat, Chukot, Evenki, Khanty-Mansi, Komi-Permyak, Koryak, Nenets, Taimyr (Dolgano-Nenets), Ust-Ordyn-Buryat, Yamalo-Nenets.

The Supreme Soviet, elected in Feb. 1985, consisted of 975 deputies (1 per 150,000 population); 649 were Communists, 344 women, 492 workers and collective farmers.

In June 1987, 1,159,264 deputies were elected to local authorities; 576,523 (49·7%) were women, 663,357 (57·2%) non-Party and 737,588 (63·6%) industrial workers and collective farmers.

FINANCE. Revenue and expenditure balanced as follows (in 1m. rubles): 1987,

105,353; 1988 (plan), 110,102. These figures, and those for the other 14 Union Republics, include grants from the Union Budget.

COMMUNICATIONS. Length of railways on 1 Jan. 1986 was 84,920 km, hard-surface motor roads, 521,000 km. In 1985, 242,692m. tonne-km of freight was carried on inland waterways.

Newspapers. In 1985 there were 4,567 newspapers, 4,260 of them in Russian. Daily circulation of Russian-language newspapers, 129.4m., other languages, 2.7m.

EDUCATION. In 1985–86 there were 20.2m. pupils in primary and secondary schools; 2,966,100 students in 502 higher educational establishments (including correspondence students) and 2,478,300 students in 2,566 technical colleges of all kinds (including correspondence students). There were 9.2m. children attending pre-school institutions. There were, on 1 Jan. 1986, 1,019,100 scientific staff in over 3,000 learned and scientific institutions.

In 1957 a Siberian branch of the Academy of Sciences was organized, in charge of all scientific research institutions from the Urals to the Pacific.

There is an Academy of Municipal Economy (with 5 research institutions and a staff of 502).

HEALTH. Doctors in 1985 numbered 646,800, and hospital beds 1.9m. (133,400 in 1913 and 482,000 in 1940).

BASHKIR AUTONOMOUS SOVIET SOCIALIST REPUBLIC

Area 143,600 sq. km (55,430 sq. miles), population (Jan. 1986) 3.87m. Capital, Ufa. Bashkiria was annexed to Russia in 1557. It was constituted as an Autonomous Soviet Republic on 23 March 1919. Population, census 1979, included 24.3% Bashkirians, 40.3% Russians, 24.5% Tatars, and 3.2% Chuvashes.

280 deputies were elected to the republican Supreme Soviet on 24 Feb. 1985, 108 of them women.

In 1985–86 there were 547,000 pupils in 3,195 secondary schools. There is a state university and a branch of the USSR Academy of Sciences with 8 learned institutions (511 research workers). There were 126,000 students in technical colleges and higher schools.

In Jan. 1986 there were 13,108 doctors and 52,100 hospital beds.

There are expanding chemical, coal, steel, electrical engineering, timber and paper industries. There were 629 collective farms and 159 state farms in 1980. Crop area was 4,587,000 hectares. Bashkiria is a major oil producer in USSR.

BURIAT AUTONOMOUS SOVIET SOCIALIST REPUBLIC

Area is 351,300 sq. km (135,650 sq. miles). The Buriat Republic, situated to the south of the Yakut Republic, adopted the Soviet system 1 March 1920. This area was penetrated by the Russians in the 17th century and finally annexed from China by the treaties of Nerchinsk (1689) and Kyakhta (1727). The population (Jan. 1986) was 1,014,000. Capital, Ulan-Ude. The name of the republic was changed from 'Buriat-Mongol' on 7 July 1958. The population (1979 census) includes 23% Buriats and 72% Russians.

170 deputies were elected to the republican Supreme Soviet on 24 Feb. 1985, 60 of them women.

The main industries are coal, timber, building materials, fisheries, sheep and cattle farming. In 1980 there were 105 state and 61 collective farms. Crop area was 827,100 hectares. Gold, molybdenum and wolfram are mined.

In 1985–86 there were 549 schools with 162,000 pupils, 21 technical colleges with 17,700 students and 4 higher educational institutions with 22,200 students. A branch of the Siberian Department of the Academy of Sciences had 4 learned institutions with 281 research workers.

In 1986 there were 3,628 doctors and 13,600 hospital beds.

CHECHENO-INGUSH AUTONOMOUS SOVIET SOCIALIST REPUBLIC

Area, 19,300 sq. km (7,350 sq. miles); population (Jan. 1986), 1·23m. Capital, Grozny. After 70 years of almost continuous fighting, the Chechens and Ingushes were conquered by Russia in the late 1850s. In 1918 each nationality separately established its 'National Soviet' within the Terek Autonomous Republic, and in 1920 (after the Civil War) were constituted areas within the Mountain Republic. The Chechens separated out as an Autonomous Region on 30 Nov. 1922 and the Ingushes on 7 July 1924. In Jan. 1934 the two regions were united, and on 5 Dec. 1936 constituted as an Autonomous Republic. This was dissolved in 1944, but reconstituted on 9 Jan. 1957: 232,000 Chechens and Ingushes returned to their homes in the next 2 years. The population (1979 census) includes 52·9% Chechens, 11·7% Ingushes, and 29·1% Russians.

175 deputies were elected to the republican Supreme Soviet on 24 Feb. 1985, 78 of them women.

The republic has one of the major Soviet oilfields: also a number of large engineering works, chemical factories, building materials works and food canneries. There is an expanding timber, woodworking and furniture industry. In 1984 there were 122 state and 39 collective farms. Crop area was 453,900 hectares.

There were, in 1985–86, 532 schools with 249,000 pupils, 12 technical colleges with 13,400 students and 3 places of higher education with 13,600 students.

In 1986 there were 3,426 doctors and 12,800 hospital beds.

CHUVASH AUTONOMOUS SOVIET SOCIALIST REPUBLIC

Area, 18,300 sq. km (7,064 sq. miles); population (Jan. 1986), 1,320,000. Capital, Cheboksary. The territory was annexed by Russia in the middle of the 16th century. On 24 June 1920 it was constituted as an Autonomous Region, and on 21 April 1925 as an Autonomous Republic. The population (1979 census) includes Chuvashes (68·4%), Russians (26%), Tatars (2·9%) and Mordovians (1·6%).

200 deputies were elected to the republican Supreme Soviet on 24 Feb. 1985, 79 of them women.

Like most of the Autonomous Republics, Chuvashia before 1914 was a region of primitive agriculture with a certain development of the timber industry. Today it has several big railway repair works, an expanding electrical and other engineering industries, building materials, chemicals, textiles and food industries; timber felling and haulage are largely mechanized. In 1985 there were 179 collective farms and 104 state farms. Grain crops account for nearly two-thirds of all sowings and fodder crops for nearly a quarter. Fruit and wine-growing are a developing branch of agriculture. Crop area was 732,400 hectares.

In 1985–86 there were 209,000 pupils at 695 schools, 24,200 students at technical colleges and 17,900 students undertaking higher education.

In 1986 there were 4,366 doctors and 17,400 hospital beds.

DAGESTAN AUTONOMOUS SOVIET SOCIALIST REPUBLIC

Area, 50,300 sq. km (19,416 sq. miles); population (Jan. 1986), 1·8m. Capital, Makhachkala. Over 30 nationalities inhabit this republic apart from Russians

(11·6% at 1979 census); the most numerous are the Avartsy (25·7%), Dargintsy (15·2%), Lezginy (11·6%), Kumyki (12·4%), Laki (5·1%), Tabasarany (4·4%) and Azerbaijanis (4%). Annexed from Persia in 1723, Dagestan was constituted an Autonomous Republic on 20 Jan. 1921.

210 deputies were elected to the republican Supreme Soviet on 24 Feb. 1985, 84 of them women.

There are large engineering, oil, chemical, woodworking, textile, food and other light industries. Agriculture is very varied, ranging from wheat to grapes, with sheep farming and cattle breeding; in 1983 there were 249 collective farms and 262 state farms. Crop area was 427,800 hectares. A chain of power stations is under construction in the Sulak River (total capacity 2·5m. kw.).

In 1985–86 there were 1,516 schools with 397,000 pupils, 24,300 technical students and 5 higher education establishments with 24,800 students; and a branch of the USSR Academy of Sciences with 4 learned institutions (373 research workers). In Jan. 1986 there were 6,923 doctors and 21,300 hospital beds.

KABARDINO-BALKAR AUTONOMOUS SOVIET SOCIALIST REPUBLIC

Area, 12,500 sq. km (4,825 sq. miles); population (Jan. 1986) 724,000. Capital, Nalchik. Kabarda was annexed to Russia in 1557. The republic was constituted on 5 Dec. 1936. Population (1979 census) includes Kabardinians (45·6%), Balkars (9%), Russians (35·1%).

160 deputies were elected to the republican Supreme Soviet on 24 Feb. 1985, 69 of them women.

Main industries are ore-mining, timber, engineering, coal, food processing, timber and light industries, building materials. Grain, livestock breeding, dairy farming and wine-growing are the principal branches of agriculture. There were, in 1983, 59 state and 66 collective farms.

In 1985–86 there were 238 schools with 118,000 pupils, 9,700 students in 11 technical colleges and 9,800 students receiving higher education. In Jan. 1986 there were 3,241 doctors and 8,700 hospital beds.

KALMYK AUTONOMOUS SOVIET SOCIALIST REPUBLIC

Area, 75,900 sq. km (29,300 sq. miles); population (Jan. 1986), 325,000. Capital, Elista (64,000). The population (1979 census) includes 41·5% Kalmyks, 42·6% Russians, 6·6% Kazakhs, Chechens and Dagestanis.

The Kalmyks migrated from western China to Russia (Nogai Steppe) in the early 17th century. The territory was constituted an Autonomous Region on 4 Nov. 1920, and an Autonomous Republic on 22 Oct. 1935; this was dissolved in 1943. On 9 Jan. 1957 it was reconstituted as an Autonomous Region and on 29 July 1958 as an Autonomous Republic once more.

130 deputies were elected to the republican Supreme Soviet on 24 Feb. 1985, 54 of them women.

Main industries are fishing, canning and building materials. Cattle breeding and irrigated farming (mainly fodder crops) are the principal branches of agriculture. In 1983 there were 79 state and 23 collective farms. Crop area was 859,000 hectares.

In 1985–86 there were 50,000 pupils in 251 schools, 6,600 students in technical colleges and 4,500 in higher education. There were 1,257 doctors and 4,900 hospital beds.

KARELIAN AUTONOMOUS SOVIET SOCIALIST REPUBLIC

HISTORY. Before 1917, Karelia (then known as the Olonets Province) was noted chiefly as a place of exile for political and other prisoners.

After the November Revolution of 1917, Karelia formed part of the RSFSR. In June 1920 a Karelian Labour Commune was formed and in July 1923 this was transformed into the Karelian Autonomous Soviet Socialist Republic (one of the autonomous republics of the RSFSR). On 31 March 1940, after the Soviet–Finnish war, practically all the territory (with the exception of a small section in the neighbourhood of the Leningrad area) which had been ceded by Finland to the USSR was added to Karelia and the Karelian Autonomous Republic was transformed into the Karelo-Finnish Soviet Socialist Republic as the 12th republic of the USSR. In 1946, however, the southern part of the republic, including its whole seaboard and the town of Viipuri (Vyborg) and Keksholm, was attached to the RSFSR and in 1956 the republic reverted to ASSR status with the RSFSR.

AREA AND POPULATION. The Karelian Autonomous Republic, capital Petrozavodsk, covers an area of 172,400 sq. km, with a population of 787,000 (Jan. 1986). Karelians represent 11·1% of the population, Russians, 71·3%, Belorussians 8·1%, Ukrainians 3·2%, Finns 2·7% (1979 census).

150 deputies were elected to the republican Supreme Soviet on 24 Feb. 1985, 57 of them women.

NATURAL RESOURCES. Karelia is chiefly noted for its wealth of timber, some 70% of its territory being forest land. It is also rich in other natural resources, having large deposits of diabase, spar, quartz, marble, granite, zinc, lead, silver, copper, molybdenum, tin, baryta, iron ore, etc. Karelia takes first place in the USSR for the production of mica. It has 43,643 lakes, which, as well as its rivers, are rich in fish.

Agriculture. There were 9 collective farms and 59 state farms in 1983. The crop area was 78,900 hectares (over 85% under fodder crops).

INDUSTRY. The republic has 25 large-scale enterprises, such as timber-mills, paper-cellulose works, mica, chemical plants, power stations and furniture factories. Output, 1984: Timber, 10·9m. cu. metres; paper, 1·2m. tonnes; cellulose, 786,000 tonnes; power, 3,799m. kwh.; confectionery, 5,900 tonnes.

The construction of the White Sea–Baltic Canal had a powerful influence on the economic development of Karelia. New refrigerating plants, cellulose factories and timber industry equipment began working in 1970.

COMMUNICATIONS. A railway between Petrozavodsk and Suoyarvi connects the capital and the Murmansk Railway with the main railway line Sortavala–Vyborg. A railway line was also laid between Kandalaksha and Kuolayarvi. Length of track, 1,600 km.

EDUCATION. In 1985–86 there were 106,000 pupils in 315 schools. There were 9,600 students in 2 places of higher education and 14,300 in 16 technical colleges.

HEALTH. In Jan. 1986 there were 3,742 doctors, and 11,800 hospital beds.

KOMI AUTONOMOUS SOVIET SOCIALIST REPUBLIC

Area, 415,900 sq. km (160,540 sq. miles); population (Jan. 1986), 1·2m. Capital, Syktyvkar (218,000). Annexed by the princes of Moscow in the 14th century and occupied by British and American forces in 1918–19, the territory was constituted as an Autonomous Region on 22 Aug. 1921 and as an Autonomous Republic on 5 Dec. 1936. The population (1979 census) includes Komi (25·3%), Russians (56·7%), Ukrainians and Belorussians (10·7%).

180 deputies were elected to the republican Supreme Soviet on 24 Feb. 1985, 59 of them women.

There are large coal, oil, timber, gas, asphalt and building materials industries; light industry is expanding. Livestock breeding (including dairy farming) is the main branch of agriculture. There were 56 state farms in 1983. Crop area, 92,000 hectares.

In 1985–86 there were 179,000 pupils in 540 schools, 12,000 students receiving higher education, 16,400 students in 18 technical colleges; and a branch of the Academy of Sciences with 4 learned institutions (297 research workers).

In Jan. 1986 there were 4,753 doctors and 16,900 hospital beds.

MARI AUTONOMOUS SOVIET SOCIALIST REPUBLIC

Area, 23,200 sq. km (8,955 sq. miles); population (Jan. 1986), 731,000. Capital, Yoshkar-Ola. The Mari people were annexed to Russia, with other peoples of the Kazan Tatar Khanate, when the latter was overthrown in 1552. On 4 Nov. 1920 the territory was constituted as an Autonomous Region, and on 5 Dec. 1936 as an Autonomous Republic. The population (1979 census) includes Mari (43·5%), Tatars (5·8%), Chuvashes (1·1%), Russians (47·5%).

150 deputies were elected to the republican Supreme Soviet on 24 Feb. 1985, 60 of them women.

There are over 300 modern factories. The main industries are metalworking, timber, paper, woodworking and food processing. In 1983 there were 89 collective farms and 82 state farms. Over 69% of cultivated land is grain, but flax, potatoes, fruit and vegetables are also expanding branches of agriculture, as is also livestock farming. 638,000 hectares were under crops.

Estimated reserves of the Pechora coalfield are 262,000m. tons.

In 1985–86 there were 427 schools with 100,000 pupils. Technical colleges and higher education establishments had 10,500 and 15,700 students respectively.

In Jan. 1986 there were 2,335 doctors and 9,900 hospital beds.

MORDOVIAN AUTONOMOUS SOVIET SOCIALIST REPUBLIC

Area, 26,200 sq. km (10,110 sq. miles); population (Jan. 1986), 964,000. Capital, Saransk. By the 13th century the Mordovian tribes had been subjugated by the Russian princes of Ryazan and Nizhni-Novgorod. In 1928 the territory was constituted as a Mordovian Area within the Middle-Volga Territory, on 10 Jan. 1930 as an Autonomous Region and on 20 Dec. 1934 as an Autonomous Republic. The population (1979 census) includes Mordovians (34·2%), Russians (59·7%), Tatars (4·6%)

175 deputies were elected to the republican Supreme Soviet on 24 Feb. 1985, 74 of them women.

The republic has a wide range of industries: electrical, timber, cable, building materials, furniture, textile, leather and other light industries. Agriculture is devoted chiefly to grain, sugar-beet, sheep and dairy farming. In 1983 there were 78 state and 273 collective farms.

In 1985–86 there were 131,000 pupils at school, 16,300 students in technical colleges and 20,000 attending higher educational institutions. In Jan. 1986 there were 3,446 doctors and 14,100 hospital beds.

NORTH OSSETIAN AUTONOMOUS SOVIET SOCIALIST REPUBLIC

Area, 8,000 sq. km (3,088 sq. miles); population (Jan. 1986), 616,000. Capital, Ordzhonikidze (formerly Vladikavkaz). The Ossetians, known to antiquity as Alani (who were also called by their immediate neighbours 'Ossi' or 'Yassi'), were annexed to Russia after the latter's treaty of Kuchuk-Kainardji with Turkey, and in 1784 the key fortress of Vladikavkaz was founded on their territory (given the name of Terek region in 1861). On 4 March 1918 the latter was proclaimed an Autonomous Soviet Republic, and after the Civil War this territory with others was set up as the Mountain Autonomous Republic (20 Jan. 1921), with North Ossetia as the Ossetian (Vladikavkaz) Area within it. On 7 July 1924 the latter was constituted as an Autonomous Region and on 5 Dec. 1936 as an Autonomous Republic. The population (1979 census) comprises chiefly Ossetians (50·5%), Russians (33·9%), Ingushi and other Caucasian nationalities (8·1%).

150 deputies were elected to the republican Supreme Soviet on 24 Feb. 1985, 68 of them women.

The main industries are non-ferrous metals (mining and metallurgy), maize-processing (at the Beslan Works, the largest in Europe), timber and woodworking, textiles, building materials, distilleries and food processing. There is also a prosperous and varied agriculture. In 1983 there were 38 state and 45 collective farms.

There were in 1985–86, 94,000 children in 208 schools, 13,700 students in technical colleges and 17,700 students in 4 higher educational establishments (pedagogical, agriculture, medical and mining-metallurgical institutes). In Jan. 1986 there were 4,006 doctors and 7,600 hospital beds.

TATAR AUTONOMOUS SOVIET SOCIALIST REPUBLIC

Area, 68,000 sq. km (26,250 sq. miles); population (Jan. 1986), 3,537,000. Capital, Kazan. From the 10th to the 13th centuries this was the territory of the flourishing Volga-Kama Bulgar State; conquered by the Mongols, it became the seat of the Kazan (Tatar) Khans when the Mongol Empire broke up in the 15th century, and in 1552 was conquered again by Russia. On 27 May 1920 it was constituted as an Autonomous Republic. The population (1979 census) includes Tatars (47·7%), Chuvashes, Mordovians and Udmurts (5·9%), Russians (44%).

250 deputies were elected to the republican Supreme Soviet on 24 Feb. 1985, 97 of them women.

The republic has highly developed engineering, oil and chemical industries, while timber, building materials, textiles, clothing and food industries are also expanding. The Kama works at Brezhnev plan to produce 400,000 vehicles annually. In 1983, 557 collective and 250 state farms served a total area under crops of 3·4m. hectares.

In 1985–86 there were 2,279 schools with 482,000 pupils, 62 technical colleges with 61,000 students and 13 higher educational establishments with 70,000 students (including a state university). There is a branch of the USSR Academy of Sciences with 5 learned institutions (512 research workers).

Doctors in Jan. 1986 numbered 13,104 and hospital beds 44,300.

TUVA AUTONOMOUS SOVIET SOCIALIST REPUBLIC

Area, 170,500 sq. km (65,810 sq. miles); population (Jan. 1986), 284,000. Capital, Kyzyl (77,000). Tuva was incorporated in the USSR as an autonomous region on 13 Oct. 1944 and elevated to an Autonomous Republic on 10 Oct. 1961. It is situated to the north-west of Mongolia, between 50° and 53°N. lat. and between 90°

and 100°E. long. It is bounded to the east, west and north by Siberia, and to the south by Mongolia. The Tuvans are a Turkic people, formerly ruled by hereditary or elective tribal chiefs. (For the earlier history of the former Tannu-Tuva Republic, *see* THE STATESMAN'S YEAR-BOOK, 1946, p. 798.) The population (1979 census) includes Tuvans (60·5%) and Russians (36·2%).

130 deputies were elected to the republican Supreme Soviet on 24 Feb. 1985, 53 of them women.

Tuva is well-watered and has much good pastoral land; 47 hydro-electric stations have been set into operation. The Tuvans are mainly herdsmen and cattle farmers, but, in 1983, 371,000 hectares were under crops. There are deposits of gold, cobalt and asbestos. The main exports are hair, hides and wool, and the imports manufactured goods and iron. There are 60 state farms. Mining, wood-working, garment, leather, food and other industries are rapidly developing.

In 1985–86 there were 154 schools with 66,000 pupils; 6 technical colleges with 4,000 students, and 1 higher education institution with 3,000 students.

In Jan. 1986 there were 1,000 doctors and 5,300 hospital beds.

UDMURT AUTONOMOUS SOVIET SOCIALIST REPUBLIC

Area, 42,100 sq. km (16,250 sq. miles); population (Jan. 1986), 1,571,000. Capital, Izhevsk. The Udmurts (formerly known as 'Votyaks') were annexed by the Russians in the 15th and 16th centuries. On 4 Nov. 1920 the Votyak Autonomous Region was constituted (the name was changed to Udmurt—used by the people themselves—in 1932), and on 28 Dec. 1934 was raised to the status of an Autonomous Republic. The population (1979 census) includes Udmurts (32·2%), Tatars (6·6%), Russians (58·3%).

200 deputies were elected to the republican Supreme Soviet on 24 Feb. 1985, 79 of them women.

Heavy industry includes the manufacture of locomotives, machine tools and other engineering products, timber and building materials. There are also light industries—clothing, leather, furniture, food, etc.

There were 96 state and 244 collective farms in 1983; crop area 1·4m. hectares.

In 1985–86 there were 848 schools with 226,000 pupils; there were 22,300 students at technical colleges and 25,600 at 5 higher educational institutions.

In Jan. 1986 there were 6,375 doctors and 20,000 hospital beds.

YAKUT AUTONOMOUS SOVIET SOCIALIST REPUBLIC

The area is 3,103,200 sq. km (1,197,760 sq. miles); population (Jan. 1986), 1,009,000. Capital, Yakutsk (184,000). The Yakuts were subjugated by the Russians in the 17th century. The territory was constituted an Autonomous Republic on 27 April 1922. The population (1979 census) includes Yakuts (36·9%), other northern peoples (2·2%), Russians (50·4%).

205 deputies were elected to the republican Supreme Soviet on 24 Feb. 1985, 92 of them women.

The principal industries are mining (gold, tin, mica, coal) and livestock-breeding. The Soviet Soyuz-Zoloto Trust and a number of individual prospectors are working the fields. Silver- and lead-bearing ores and coal are worked; large diamond fields have been opened up. Timber and food industries are developing. There was 1 collective farm in 1985 and 88 state farms, with an area under crops of 107,100 hectares. Trapping and breeding of fur-bearing animals (sable, squirrel, silver fox, etc.) are an important source of income. A severe climate and lack of railways are serious obstacles to the economic development of the republic. There are, however, 10,000 km of roads and internal air lines totalling 10,000 km including an air service between Irkutsk and Yakutsk.

In 1985–86 there were 180,000 secondary school pupils, 9,800 technical college students and 8,400 attending a single higher education institution.
In Jan. 1986 there were 4,260 doctors and 15,100 hospital beds.

ADYGEI AUTONOMOUS REGION

Part of Krasnodar Territory. Area, 7,600 sq. km (2,934 sq. miles); population (Jan. 1986), 423,000. Capital, Maikop (128,000). Established 27 July 1922.

Chief industries are timber, woodworking, food processing; but engineering is rapidly expanding. Cattle breeding predominates in agriculture. There were 38 collective and 33 state farms in 1983.

In 1985–86 there were 163 schools with 58,000 pupils, 6 technical colleges with 7,300 students and a pedagogical institute with 4,900 students. Regional newspapers are in Adygei and Russian. In Jan. 1986 there were 1,637 doctors and 6,000 hospital beds.

GORNO-ALTAI AUTONOMOUS REGION

Part of Altai Territory. Area, 92,600 sq. km (35,740 sq. miles); population (Jan. 1986), 179,000. Capital, Gorno-Altaisk (39,000). Established 1 June 1922 as Oirot Autonomous Region; renamed 7 Jan. 1948.

Chief industries are gold, mercury and brown-coal mining, timber, chemicals and dairying. Cattle breeding predominates; pasturages and hay meadows cover over 1m. hectares, but 142,000 hectares are under crops. There were 20 collective and 37 state farms in 1983.

In 1985–86 there were 32,000 school pupils; technical colleges had 4,100 students and 3,100 students were attending a pedagogical institute. There were 708 doctors and 2,700 hospital beds.

JEWISH AUTONOMOUS REGION

Part of Khabarovsk Territory. Area, 36,000 sq. km (13,895 sq. miles); population (Jan. 1986), 211,000 (1979 census, Russians, 84·1%; Ukrainians, 6·3%; Jews, 5·4%). Capital, Birobijan (80,000). Established as Jewish National District in 1928, became an Autonomous Region 7 May 1934.

Chief industries are non-ferrous metallurgy, building materials, timber, engineering, textiles, paper and food processing. There were 161,000 hectares under cultivation in 1983; main crops are wheat, soya, oats, barley. There were 36 state farms and 2 collective farms in 1983.

In 1985–86 there were 33,000 schoolchildren; students in technical colleges numbered 5,200. There are a Yiddish national theatre, a Yiddish newspaper and a Yiddish broadcasting service. Doctors numbered 718 and hospital beds 3,200.

KARACHAYEVO-CHERKESS AUTONOMOUS REGION

Part of Stavropol Territory. Area, 14,100 sq. km (5,442 sq. miles); population (Jan. 1986), 396,000. Capital, Cherkessk (105,000). A Karachai Autonomous Region was established on 26 April 1926 (out of a previously united Karachayevo-Cherkess Autonomous Region created in 1922), and dissolved in 1943. A Cherkess Autonomous Region was established on 30 April 1928. The present Autonomous Region was re-established on 9 Jan. 1957.

Ore-mining, engineering, chemical and woodworking industries have been built up since 1917. There are 70 large factories, and a copper works and sugar factory are under construction. A large irrigation scheme, Kuban-Kalaussi, is being developed, to irrigate 200,000 hectares. Livestock breeding and grain growing predominate in agriculture; crop area in 1983 was 196,000 hectares. There were 15 collective farms and 37 state farms in 1983.

In 1985–86 there were 65,000 pupils in secondary schools, 6 technical colleges with 6,000 students and 1 institute with 3,900 students. In Jan. 1986 there were 1,298 doctors and 4,500 hospital beds.

KHAKASS AUTONOMOUS REGION

Part of Krasnoyarsk Territory. Area, 61,900 sq. km (23,855 sq. miles); population (Jan. 1986), 547,000. Capital, Abakan (148,000). Established 20 Oct. 1930.

Coal- and ore-mining, timber and woodworking industries have been highly developed since 1917. The region is linked by rail with the Trans-Siberian line. Large textile and sugar factories are being built.

In 1985, 1·8m. hectares were under crops. Livestock breeding, dairy and vegetable farming are developed. There are 56 state farms.

In 1985–86 there were 81,000 pupils in secondary schools, 8,600 students in technical colleges and 5,200 students in higher educational institutions. In Jan. 1986 there were 2,022 doctors and 8,200 hospital beds. A Khakass alphabet was created after the Revolution.

AUTONOMOUS AREAS

Agin-Buryat Situated in Chita region (Eastern Siberia); area, 26,000 sq. km, population (1986), 77,000. Capital, Aginskoe. Formed 1937, its economy is basically pastoral.

Chukot Situated in Magadan region (Far East), its area of 737,700 sq. km in the far northeast. Population (1986), 155,000. Capital, Anadyr. Formed 1930. Population chiefly Russian, also Chukchi, Koryak, Yakut, Even. Minerals are extracted in the north, including gold, tin, mercury and tungsten.

Evenki Situated in Krasnoyarsk territory (Eastern Siberia); area, 745,000 sq. km, population (1986) 21,000, chiefly Evenks. Capital, Tura.

Khanty-Mansi Situated in Tyumen region (Western Siberia); area, 523,100 sq. km, population (1986) 1,047,000, chiefly Russians but also Khants and Mansi. Capital, Khanti-Mansiisk. Formed 1930.

Komi-Permyak Situated in Perm region (Northern Russia); area, 32,900 sq. km, population (1986) 162,000, chiefly Komi-Permyaks. Formed 1925. Capital, Kudymkar. Forestry is the main occupation.

Koryak Situated in Kamchatka region (Far East); area, 301,500 sq. km, population (1986) 39,000. Capital, Palana. Formed 1930.

Nenets Situated in Archangel region (Northern Russia); area, 176,700 sq. km, population (1986) 53,000. Capital, Naryan-Mar.

Taimyr Situated in Krasnoyarsk territory, this most northerly part of Siberia comprises the Taimyr peninsula and the Arctic islands of Severnaya Zemlya. Area, 862,100 sq. km, population (1986) 54,000, excluding the mining city of Norilsk which is separately administered. Capital, Dudinka.

Ust-Ordyn-Buryat Situated in Irkutsk region (Eastern Siberia); area, 22,100 sq. km, population (1986) 129,000. Capital, Ust-Ordynsk. Formed 1937.

Yamalo-Nenets Situated in Tyumen region (Western Siberia); area, 750,300 sq. km, population (1986) 383,000. Capital, Salekhard. Formed 1930.

Books of Reference

Armstrong, T., *Russian Settlement in the North.* CUP, 1965
Conolly, V., *Beyond the Urals. Economic Developments in Soviet Asia.* London, 1967
Dallin, D. J., *The Rise of Russia in Asia.* New York, 1949.—*Soviet Russia and the Far East.* London, 1949

Kolarz, W., *The Peoples of the Soviet Far East*. London, 1954
Istoriya Sibiri s drevneishikh vremen do nashikh dnei. 5 vols., Leningrad, 1968–69

UKRAINE
Ukrainska Radyanska Sotsialistichna Respublika

HISTORY. The Ukrainian Soviet Socialist Republic was proclaimed on 25 Dec. 1917 and was finally established in Dec. 1919. In Dec. 1920 it concluded a military and economic alliance with the RSFSR and on 30 Dec. 1922 formed, together with the other Soviet Socialist Republics, the Union of Soviet Socialist Republics. On 1 Nov. 1939 Western Ukraine (about 88,000 sq. km) was incorporated in the Ukrainian SSR. On 2 Aug. 1940 Northern Bukovina (about 6,000 sq. km) ceded to the USSR by Romania 28 June 1940, and the Khotin, Akkerman and Izmail provinces of Bessarabia were included in the Ukrainian SSR, and on 29 June 1945 Ruthenia (Sub-Carpathian Russia), about 7,000 sq. km, was also incorporated. From the new territories 2 new regions were formed, Chernovits and Izmail.

AREA AND POPULATION. The Ukraine is in south-west USSR; it has a Black Sea coast and western frontiers with Romania, Hungary, Poland and Czechoslovakia. It is bounded north by Belorussia and otherwise by the RSFSR. In 1938 the Ukrainian SSR covered an area of 445,000 sq. km (171,770 sq. miles); it now covers 603,700 sq. km (231,990 sq. miles).

Population, Jan. 1987, 51,201,000 (in 1979 census, 73·6% Ukrainians, 21·1% Russians, 1·3% Jews, 0·8% Belorussians).

The principal towns are the capital Kiev, Kharkov, Donetsk, Odessa, Dnepropetrovsk, Lvov, Zaporozhye and Krivoi Rog.

The Ukrainian Soviet Socialist Republic consists of the following regions: Cherkassy, Chernigov, Chernovtsy, Crimea (transferred from the RSFSR on 19 Feb. 1954), Dnepropetrovsk, Donetsk, Ivan Franko, Khmelnitsky (formerly Kamenets-Podolsk), Kharkov, Kherson, Kiev, Kirovograd, Lvov, Nikolayev, Odessa, Poltava, Rovno, Sumy, Ternopol, Vinnitsa, Volhynia, Voroshilovgrad, Zakarpatskaya (Transcarpathia), Zaporozhye, Zhitomir.

CONSTITUTION AND GOVERNMENT. The Supreme Soviet, elected on 24 Feb. 1985, consists of 650 deputies (1 per 90,000 population); 444 are Communists and 234 women. A new Constitution, based on that of the USSR, was adopted in April 1978.

At elections to regional, district, urban and rural Soviets (21 June 1987), out of 527,799 deputies returned, 259,795 (49·2%) were women, 297,136 (56·3%) non-Party and 378,000 (72·1%) industrial workers and collective farmers.

Chairman, Presidium of the Supreme Soviet: V. S. Shevchenko.
Chairman, Council of Ministers: V. A. Masol.
Foreign Minister: V. A. Kravtsev.
First Secretary, Communist Party: V. V. Shcherbitsky.

FINANCE. Budget estimates (in 1m. rubles), 1987, 34,247; 1988 (plan), 33,164.

AGRICULTURE. The Ukraine contains some of the richest land in the USSR. It raises wheat, buckwheat, beet, sunflower, cotton, flax, tobacco, soya, hops, the rubber plant kok-sagyz, fruit and vegetables, and in 1985 produced 46% by value of the USSR's total agricultural output. The area under cultivation was 27·9m. hectares in 1913, 27m. in 1939 before the new territories were added, and 48·7m. in Nov. 1985.

Output (in 1m. tonnes) in 1985 (1913 figures in tons in brackets): Grain, 40·5; sugar-beet, 43·6 (9·3); vegetables, 7·4; sunflower seed, 2·3 (0·07); potatoes, 20·3 (8·5); meat and fats, 3·9 (1·1); milk, 23 (4·7); wool, 0·029 (0·015); 16,600m. eggs (3,005m.).

On 1 Jan. 1986 there were 26·6m. cattle, 20·1m. pigs, 9·2m. sheep and goats. In 1949 silver-fox breeding farms were started.

On 1 Jan. 1986 there were 2,273 state farms and 7,363 collective farms.

Irrigation networks supplied 1·82m. hectares of land; 2·2m. hectares were drained.

Tractors numbered 445,800 at 1 Jan. 1986 and combine harvesters, 111,700.

INDUSTRY. Coal in the Donets field (25,900 sq. km stretching from Donetsk to Rostov), estimated to contain 60% of the bituminous and anthracite coal reserves of the USSR, yielded, in 1980, 197·1m. tonnes—about 28% of the USSR production. Large new seams have been found near Novo-Moskovsk (Dnepropetrovsk region), Kharkov, Lugansk (beyond the Don) and on the left bank of the Dnieper. Within the present frontiers of the Ukraine, coal output was 22·8m. tons in 1913, 83·8m. tons in 1940, 78m. tons in 1950 and 217m. tons in 1977.

Combining coal from the Donets field with the iron-ore from the mines in Krivoi Rog has made possible the development of a large ferrous metallurgical industry in the Ukraine. Output of iron ore was 123m. tons in 1984. Manganese is obtained at Nikopol; output in 1984, 7·2m. tons. Output of finished rolled metal products, 37·7m. tonnes in 1985 (36m. in 1980); of steel pipe, 6·7m. (6·3m.).

The Ukraine also contains oil, rich deposits of salt and various important chemicals. Oil output was 1m. tons in 1913 (in present frontiers), 353,000 tons in 1940 and 10·5m. tons in 1977; with 68·7m. cu. metres of natural gas.

The Ukraine has highly developed chemical and machine-construction industries producing one-fifth of the total output of machinery and chemicals in the USSR. Output in 1985 of paper, 299,000 tonnes; of chemical fibre, 165,000 tonnes; of sulphuric acid, 4·1m. tonnes; of caustic soda, 500,000 tonnes; of televisions, 3·1m.; of refrigerators, 741,000.

In Northern Bukovina there are deposits of gypsum, oil, alabaster, brown coal and timber. Output in 1985 of paper, 299,000 tonnes; of mineral fertilizers (recalculated base), 5·1m. tonnes.

Consumer goods and food industries are important. Output in 1985 of knitwear, 319·6m. items; of hosiery, 387·8m. pairs; of granulated sugar, 6·2m. tonnes; of leather footwear, 185·7m. pairs; of preserves, 4,000m. standard jars.

The number of industrial and office workers at the end of 1950 was 6·9m., and the average in 1985, 20·7m. There were 3·9m. collective farmers in 1985.

During the first 5-year plan (1929–32) the Dnieper power-station was built; destroyed during the War, it was restored during the fourth plan (1946–50). Another large hydro-electric station at Kakhovka began operations during the fifth plan (1951–55). Power output (in 1,000m. kwh.) increased as follows: 1913, 0·5; 1940, 12·4; 1950, 14·7; 1985, 272.

COMMUNICATIONS. The total length of railways of the Ukrainian SSR in Jan. 1986 was 22,700 km, of hard-surface motor roads 201,900 km. In 1985 12,245 tonne-km of freight was carried on inland waterways.

Airlines connect Kiev, Lvov, Chernovtsy and Odessa with Crimean and Caucasian spas, Kiev with Tbilisi, Odessa with Riga and Donetsk.

Newspapers (1985). Out of 1,799 newspapers, 1,283 were in Ukrainian. Daily circulation of Ukrainian-language newspapers, 15·3m., other languages, 7·7m.

RELIGION. Several Christian Churches have their adherents in the Ukraine, the chief being the Orthodox Greek Church and the Catholic Church. The Western Ukraine Uniate Church, which in 1596 had been forced by the Poles to establish unity with the Roman Church, severed this connexion in March 1946 and joined the Orthodox Church. There are also some Protestants as well as Jews and others.

EDUCATION. In 1985–86 the number of pupils in 21,900 primary and secondary schools was 7·2m.; 146 higher educational establishments had 853,100 students, and 731 technical colleges 808,900 students; 2·6m. children were attending pre-school institutions.

The Ukrainian Academy of Sciences was established in 1919; in 1986 it had 78 institutions with 15,097 scientific staff. There is an academy of building and architecture. Total scientific staff in all institutions was 210,300 in Jan. 1986.

HEALTH. Doctors numbered 210,600 in 1985, and hospital beds, 668,800.

Books of Reference

Allen, W. E. D., *The Ukraine: A History.* 2nd ed. Cambridge, 1963
Andrusyshen, C. H. (ed.), *Ukrainian-English Dictionary.* Toronto, 1955
Bazham, M. P. (ed.), *Soviet Ukraine.* Kiev, 1970
Chirovsky, N. L., *The Ukrainian Economy.* New York, Paris, Toronto, 1965
Hrushevsky, M., *A History of the Ukraine.* New Haven, 1941
Koropecky, I. S. (ed.), *The Ukraine within the USSR: An Economic Balance Sheet.* New York, 1977
Kubiojovyc, V. (ed.), *Encyclopedia of Ukraine,* 4 vols. Toronto, 1984ff
Magoci, P. R., and Matthews, G. J., *Ukraine: A Historical Atlas.* Univ. of Toronto Press, 1985
Manning, C. A., *Twentieth-century Ukraine.* New York, 1951

BELORUSSIA
Belaruskaya Sovietskaya Sotsialistychnaya Respublika

HISTORY. The Belorussian Soviet Socialist Republic was set up on 1 Jan. 1919. It forms one of the constituent republics of the USSR.

AREA AND POPULATION. Belorussia is situated along the Western Dvina and Dnieper. It is bounded west by Poland, north by Latvia and Lithuania, east by the RSFSR and south by the Ukraine. The area is 207,600 sq. km (80,134 sq. miles). The capital is Minsk. Other important towns are Gomel, Vitebsk, Mogilev, Bobruisk, Grodno and Brest. On 2 Nov. 1939 western Belorussia was incorporated with an area of over 108,000 sq. km and a population of 4·8m. The population (Jan. 1987) was 10,078,000; 79·4% of this population in 1979 (census) were Belorussians, 4·2% Poles, 11·9% Russians, 2·4% Ukrainians and 1·4% Jews.

Belorussia now comprises the following regions: Brest, Gomel, Grodno, Mogilev, Minsk, Vitebsk.

CONSTITUTION AND GOVERNMENT. The Supreme Soviet, elected in 1985, consists of 485 deputies (1 per 20,000 population); 328 are Communists and 180 women. A new Constitution was adopted in April 1978.

At elections to regional, district, urban and rural Soviets (21 June 1987), of 85,375 deputies returned, 41,518 (48·6%) were women, 47,377 (55·5%) non-Party and 56,932 (66·7%) industrial workers and collective farmers.

Chairman, Presidium of the Supreme Soviet: G. S. Tarazevich.
Chairman, Council of Ministers: M. V. Kovalev.
Foreign Minister: A. E. Gurinovich
First Secretary, Communist Party: E. E. Sokolov.

FINANCE. Budget estimates (in 1m. rubles), 1987, 8,217; 1988 (plan), 8,893.

NATURAL RESOURCES. Belorussia is hilly, with a general slope towards the south. It contains large tracts of marsh land, particularly to the south-west, and valuable forest land wooded with oak, elm, maple and white beech: there are over 6,500 peat deposits.

AGRICULTURE. Agriculturally, Belorussia may be divided into three main sections—Northern: growing flax, fodder, grasses and breeding cattle for meat and dairy produce; Central: potato growing and pig breeding; Southern: good natural pasture land, hemp cultivation and cattle breeding for meat and dairy produce. The area under cultivation (in hectares) was 4·5m. in 1913, 5·2m. in 1940 and 12·3m. in Nov. 1986. There were 7·5m. cattle, 5m. pigs and 700,000 sheep and goats on 1 Jan. 1986.

Output of main agricultural products (in 1,000 tonnes) in 1985: Grain, 6,800; wool, 1·2; meat, 1,032; milk, 6,800; eggs, 3,363m.; potatoes, 10,600; vegetables, 828; sugar-beet, 1,600.

On 1 Jan. 1986 there were 1,715 collective farms and 918 state farms. About 2·5m. hectares of marsh land had been drained for agricultural use, 828,200 of these for crops. This land has been found to be as rich as the soil of the Black Earth Zone, and yields good harvests of grain, fodder, potatoes, kok-sagyz and other crops. In Jan. 1986 there were 131,200 tractors and 34,900 grain combine harvesters.

INDUSTRY. Industry in this republic was almost completely destroyed during the years 1941–45. By 1956, aggregate industrial output was three times what it had been in 1940. Plants producing tip-lorries, machine-tools and agricultural machinery are prominent.

The republic also contains timber works; a match factory in Borisov; building materials, machine, prefabricated house construction, glass-blowing and other factories; canneries, creameries and other food industries; chemical, textiles, artificial-silk, flax-spinning and leather works and an automobile and tractor industry.

In 1985 output was as follows: Electric light bulbs, 293m.; potato harvesting machines, 24,400; paper, 189,000 tonnes; building bricks, 2,012m.; window glass, 15m. cu. metres; carpets, 17·8m. sq. metres; knitwear, 136·5m. garments; leather footwear, 44·2m. pairs.

Particular attention has been paid to the development of the peat industry with a view to making Belorussia as far as possible self-supporting in fuel, and in 1939 local peat provided 67·5% of her total requirements of fuel. The average annual output is about 18m. tonnes. There are also rich deposits of rock salt.

Output of electricity in 1985, 33,200m. kwh. (508m. in 1940). New power-plants have been built in Baranovichi, Grodno, Molodechno and Lida.

The number of industrial and office workers in 1985 was 4,271,000.

COMMUNICATIONS. In Jan. 1986 there were 5,540 km of railways, 55,000 km of motor roads (45,500 km hard-surface) and 2,242m. tonne-km of freight was carried on inland waterways.

Newspapers (1985). Of 212 newspapers published 130 were in Belorussian. Daily circulation of Belorussian-language newspapers, 1·6m., other languages, 3m.

EDUCATION. In 1985–86 there were 181,900 students in 33 places of higher education and 160,500 students in 139 technical colleges. There were (Jan. 1986) 42,400 scientific personnel in 178 institutions, and 562,300 specialists with a higher education employed in the national economy. The Belorussian Academy of Sciences controlled 32 learned institutions with 5,761 scientific staff. The number of children in 6,200 primary and secondary schools was 1·5m. in 1985–86. 595,000 children were attending pre-school institutions in Jan. 1986.

HEALTH. In 1985 there were 37,800 doctors and 130,200 hospital beds.

Books of Reference

Belaruskaya Sovietskaya Entsyklapediya. Minsk, 1960–76
Lubachko, I. S., *Belorussia under Soviet Rule, 1917–57*. Lexington, 1972
Vakar, N. P., *Belorussia*. Harvard Univ. Press, 1956.—*A Bibliographical Guide to Belorussia*. Harvard Univ. Press, 1956

AZERBAIJAN
Azarbaijchan Soviet Sotsialistik Respublikasy

HISTORY. The 'Mussavat' (Nationalist) party, which dominated the National Council or Constituent Assembly of the Tatars, declared the independence of Azerbaijan on 28 May 1918, with a capital, first at Ganja (Elizavetpol) and later at Baku. On 28 April 1920 Azerbaijan was proclaimed a Soviet Socialist Republic. From 1922, with Georgia and Armenia it formed the Transcaucasian Soviet

Federal Socialist Republic. In 1936 it assumed the status of one of the Union Republics of the USSR.

AREA AND POPULATION. Azerbaijan covers an area of 86,600 sq. km (33,430 sq. miles) and has a population (Jan. 1987) of 6,811,000. Its capital is Baku. Other important towns are Kirovabad and Sumgait. Nakhichevan is the capital of the Autonomous Republic of the same name.

Azerbaijan includes the Nakhichevan Autonomous Republic and the Nagorno-Karabakh Autonomous Region. Situated in the eastern area of Transcaucasia, it is protected by mountains in the west and north, washed by the Caspian Sea in the east and bounded by Iran in the south. Its climate is inclined to drought.

In 1979 (census) 78·1% of the population were Azerbaijanis, who are mainly Shi'a Moslems. Other nationalities were Russians (7·9%), Armenians (7·9%) and Daghestanis (3·4%).

CONSTITUTION AND GOVERNMENT. The Supreme Soviet, elected in 1985, consists of 450 deputies (1 per 10,000 population); 311 are Communists and 179 women. A new Constitution was adopted in April 1978.

At elections to the Nagorno-Karabakh regional Soviet and the district, urban and rural Soviets (21 June 1987), of 51,681 deputies returned, 24,859 (48·1%) were women, 28,484 (55·1%) non-Party and 35,047 (67·8%) industrial workers and collective farmers.

Chairman, Presidium of the Supreme Soviet: S. B. Tatliev.
Chairman, Council of Ministers: G. N. Seidov.
First Secretary, Communist Party: K. M. Bagirov.

FINANCE (in 1m. rubles). Budget estimates, 1987, 3,100; 1988 (plan), 3,361.

AGRICULTURE. The chief agricultural products are grain, cotton, rice, grapes, fruit, vegetables, tobacco and silk. The Mexican rubber plant *grayule* has been acclimatized. A new kind of high-yielding winter wheat has been produced for use in mountainous parts of the republic.

Livestock on 1 Jan. 1986: Cattle, 2m.; pigs, 200,000; sheep and goats, 5·6m.

Output of main agricultural products (in 1,000 tonnes) in 1985: Grain, 1,299; cotton, 788; grapes, 1,790; vegetables, 871; tobacco, 61; potatoes, 220; tea, 32·1; meat, 168; milk, 951; eggs, 948m.; wool, 11·2.

Azerbaijan has become an important cotton-growing and sub-tropical base. About 70% of cultivated land is irrigated. On the irrigated land crops of Egyptian and Sea-Island cotton are obtained. Here, too, rice and lucerne are cultivated, and in the mountain valleys there are also orchards, vineyards and silk cultures.

In the south along the coast of the Caspian, where the climate is more moist, there are tea plantations, and citrus fruits and other sub-tropical plants are grown.

In 1941 a scientific research institute for sub-tropical research was opened to develop the culture of sub-tropical plants in Azerbaijan and other parts of Transcaucasia. A forestry research institute was opened in 1949.

There were on 1 Jan. 1986, 608 collective farms, 808 state farms, 38,400 tractors and 4,500 grain combine harvesters.

INDUSTRY. The republic is rich in natural resources: oil, iron, aluminium, copper, lead, zinc, precious metals, sulphur pyrites, limestone and salt. Iron and steel and aluminium works have been built at Sumgait.

The most important industry is the oil industry, especially in the Baku region. The output of oil was 7·7m. tonnes in 1913, 22·2m. tonnes in 1940 and 16·5m. tonnes in 1976. The largest producing area lies along the western shore of the Caspian Sea, north and south of Baku, where the largest refineries are located. Other wells lie west of Baku, and some have been drilled in the Caspian itself, off the Apsheron Peninsula. Baku is connected by a double pipeline with Batum on the Black Sea. All the oilfields have been electrified and are connected with Baku.

Azerbaijan has also copper, chemical, cement and building material, food, timber, salt, textiles and fishing industries. In 1985, 582,000 tonnes of steel pipe were produced, 40·8m. items of knitwear, 227,000 tonnes of caustic soda, 22·9m. pairs leather footwear, 4·3m. sq. metres of linoleum and 42·2m. pairs of hosiery.

In addition to Baku, other important industrial centres are Kirovabad, Nukha, Stepanakert, Nakhichevan, Lenkoran.

In 1985 electric power output was 20,700m. kwh. Output of gas, which began in 1928 with 176m. cu. metres, was 10,989m. in 1976. Pipelines from Karadag to Baku and Sumgait supply gas fuel for all oil-cracking factories and most engineering works.

Synthetic rubber works (Sumgait), tyre works and a worsted combine (Baku) and a large textile combine (Mingechaur) have been built.

The number of industrial and office workers in 1985 was 2,058,000.

COMMUNICATIONS. Total length of railways in 1986, 2,070 km, of motor roads 30,200 km (25,500 km hard surface).

Newspapers (1985). There were 144 newspapers, 115 in the Azerbaijani language (circulation 2·2m.), other languages, 471,000.

EDUCATION. In 1985–86 there were 1·5m. pupils in 4,500 primary and secondary schools and 165,000 children attending pre-school institutions. There were 77 technical colleges with 76,200 students, 18 higher educational institutions, including a state university at Baku, with 105,900 students (including correspondence students). The Azerbaijan Academy of Sciences, founded in 1945, has 30 research institutions with 4,493 research workers. There were 23,200 research workers in the republic as a whole in Jan. 1986.

HEALTH. In 1985 there were 25,300 doctors and 65,900 hospital beds.

NAKHICHEVAN AUTONOMOUS SOVIET SOCIALIST REPUBLIC

Area, 5,500 sq. km (2,120 sq. miles), population (Jan. 1986), 272,000. Capital, Nakhichevan (37,000). This territory, on the borders of Turkey and Iran, forms part of the Azerbaijan SSR although separated from it by the territory of Soviet Armenia. Its population, mainly Azerbaijanis, had a chequered history for 1,500 years under the ancient Persians, Arabs, Seljuk Turks, Mongols, Ottoman Turks and modern Persians before being annexed by Russia in 1828. On 9 Feb. 1924 it was constituted as an Autonomous Republic within Azerbaijan. Its Supreme Soviet, elected 24 Feb. 1985, has 110 members including 52 women.

The republic has silk, clothing, cotton, canning, meat-packing and other factories. Nearly 70% of the people are engaged in agriculture, of which the main branches are cotton and tobacco growing. Fruit and grapes are also produced in increasing quantity. There are 35 collective and 37 state farms. Crop area 37,400 hectares.

In 1984–85 there were 219 primary and secondary schools with 66,000 pupils, and 2,100 were studying in higher educational institutions.

In Jan. 1983 there were 599 doctors and 2,500 hospital beds.

NAGORNO-KARABAKH AUTONOMOUS REGION

Area, 4,400 sq. km (1,700 sq. miles); population (Jan. 1986), 177,000. Capital, Stepanakert (33,000). Populated by Armenians (75·9%) and Azerbaijanis (23%), a separate khanate in the 18th century, it was established on 7 July 1923 as an Autonomous Region within Azerbaijan.

Main industries are silk, wine, dairying and building materials. Crop area is 67,200 hectares; cotton, grapes and winter wheat are grown. There are 33 collective and 38 state farms.

In 1984–85 34,000 pupils were studying in primary and secondary schools, 2,400 in colleges and 2,100 in higher educational institutions. In Jan. 1983 there were 523 doctors and 1,800 hospital beds.

Books of Reference

Baddeley, J. F., *The Rugged Flanks of Caucasus*. 2 vols. Oxford, 1941
Guseinov, I. A., et al, *Istoriya Azerbaidzhana*. 8 vols. Baku, 1958–63

GEORGIA

Sakartvelos Sabchota Sotsialisturi Respublica

HISTORY. The independence of the Georgian Social Democratic Republic was declared at Tiflis on 26 May 1918 by the National Council, elected by the National Assembly of Georgia on 22 Nov. 1917. The independence of Georgia was recognized by the USSR on 7 May 1920. On 12 Feb. 1921 a rising broke out in Mingrelia, Abkhazia and Adjaria, and Soviet troops invaded the country, which, on 25 Feb. 1921, was proclaimed the Georgian Soviet Socialist Republic. At the first Transcaucasian Soviet Congress, 15 Dec. 1922, Georgia, together with Armenia and Azerbaijan, united to form the Transcaucasian Soviet Federal Socialist Republic, and a federal constitution was adopted and published 10 Jan. 1923. In 1936 the Georgian Soviet Socialist Republic became one of the constituent republics of the USSR.

AREA AND POPULATION. Georgia is bounded west by the Black Sea and south by Turkey, Armenia and Azerbaijan. It occupies the whole of the western part of Transcaucasia and covers an area of 69,700 sq. km (26,900 sq. miles). Its population on 1 Jan. 1987 was 5,266,000. The capital is Tbilisi (Tiflis). Other important towns are Kutaisi (207,000), Rustavi (139,000), Batumi (129,000), Sukhumi (122,000), Poti (54,000), Gori (59,000).

Protected from the north by the Caucasian mountains and receiving in the west the warm, moist winds from the Black Sea into which most of its rivers flow, Georgia is outstanding for its fine, warm climate and its natural wealth, variety and beauty. It has the highest snow-capped peaks of the Caucasian mountains. Georgia contains valuable sulphur and other medicinal springs. Georgians, an ancient people, were (1979 census) 68·8% of the population; Armenians 9%; Russians, 7·4%; Azerbaijanis, 5·1%; Ossetians, 3·2%; Abkhazians, 1·7%.

CONSTITUTION AND GOVERNMENT. The Georgian Soviet Socialist Republic includes the Abkhazian ASSR, the Adjarian ASSR and the South Ossetian Autonomous Region.

The Supreme Soviet, elected in 1985, consists of 440 deputies; 160 are women, 290 Communists. A new Constitution was adopted in April 1978.

At elections to the district, rural and urban Soviets, and that of the South Ossetian region (21 June 1987), of 50,982 deputies returned 25,826 (50·7%) were women, 28,974 (56·8%) non-Party and 34,930 (68·5%) industrial workers and collective farmers.

Chairman, Presidium of the Supreme Soviet: P. G. Gilashvili.
Chairman, Council of Ministers: O. E. Cherkeziya.
First Secretary, Communist Party: D. I. Patiashvili.

FINANCE (in 1m. rubles). Budget estimates, 1987, 3,154; 1988 (plan), 3,360.

AGRICULTURE. There are 3 main agricultural areas: (1) The moist subtropical area along the Black Sea Coast, where are cultivated tea, citrus fruits (lemons, oranges, mandarins, etc.), the tung tree (which yields special industrial oils), eucalyptus, bamboo, high-quality tobacco; (2) Imeretia (the Kutais region) where the chief cultures are grapes and silk, and (3) Kakhetia, along the Alazani (a tributary of the Kura river), famed for its orchards and wines. Land (in hectares) under cultivation was 748,000 in 1913, 896,000 in 1940, 778,000 in 1961, 730,000 in 1985.

Output of main agricultural products (in 1,000 tonnes) in 1985: Grain, 640; tea leaf, 581·7; fruit, 724; sugar-beet, 66; potatoes, 394; vegetables, 604; grapes, 915; sunflower seeds, 9; meat, 167; milk, 684; eggs, 823m.; wool, 6·3.

On 1 Jan. 1986 there were 719 collective farms working over 66% of all agricultural land, 594 state farms working nearly 34% of such land. In the Colchis area 115,000 hectares of extremely rich land have been reclaimed. There are 389,000 hectares of irrigated land. 151,400 hectares of marsh land have been drained. Tractors numbered 28,800 on 1 Jan. 1986; grain combines, 1,300.

Livestock on 1 Jan. 1986: Cattle, 1·7m.; pigs, 1·2m.; sheep and goats, 2m.

Georgia is rich in forest lands where fine varieties of timber are grown. Area covered by forests, 2·4m. hectares.

INDUSTRY. The most important mining industry of Georgia is the exploitation of the manganese deposits, the richest of which lie in the Chiatura region. Manganese deposits are calculated at 250m. tonnes, distributed over an area of 140 sq. km. The most important coal seams are at Tkvarcheli (deposits estimated at 250m. tonnes) and Tkibuli (deposits of 80m. tonnes). Other important minerals are baryta, the best in the USSR, fire-resisting and other clays, diatomite shale, oil, agate, marble, cement, alabaster, iron and other ores, building stone, arsenic, molybdenum, tungsten and mercury. In 1941 a goldfield was discovered. Output of coal in 1976 was 1·9m. tonnes (625,000 in 1940).

Since the Second World War the Transcaucasian Metallurgical Plant has been built at Rustavi (near Tbilisi) and a motor works at Kutaisi. There are modern factories for processing green tea-leaves, creameries and breweries; Georgia has also textile and silk industries.

In 1985, 2·7m. tonnes of manganese ore were produced, 524,000 tonnes of steel pipe, 114,000 tonnes (recalculated base) of mineral fertilizer, 40,000 tonnes of paper, 17·1m. pairs leather footwear, 55·7m. knitwear garments, 27,000 colour televisions and 49,700 tonnes of granulated sugar.

Georgia's fast flowing rivers form an abundant source of energy. One of the most powerful stations completed in recent years is Tbilisi (1m. kw.). Power output in 1985 was 14,400m. kwh. (742m. in 1940).

There were 2,178,000 industrial and office workers in 1985.

COMMUNICATIONS. Length of railways in 1986, 1,470 km, of motor roads 36,800 (with hard surface 32,600).

Newspapers (1984). Out of 144 newspapers, 126 were in Georgian. Daily circulation of Georgian-language newspapers, 2·8m., other languages, 474,000.

EDUCATION. In 1985–86 there were 900,000 pupils in 3,800 primary and secondary schools, 54,100 in 91 technical colleges and 88,500 students in 19 higher educational institutions. Tbilisi University has 16,300 students. In towns, 11 years' education is usual. In Abastuman there is an astro-physical observatory. In 1936 a branch of the Academy of Sciences of the USSR was formed in Tbilisi, and in Feb. 1941 a Georgian Academy of Sciences was opened, which in Jan. 1986 had 42 institutions with scientific staff totalling 5,657. There were in all 194 research institutions with 27,600 scientific staff.

In Jan. 1986, 189,000 children were attending pre-school institutions.

HEALTH. There were 28,200 doctors and 55,400 hospital beds in 1985.

ABKHAZIAN AUTONOMOUS SOVIET SOCIALIST REPUBLIC

Area, 8,600 sq. km (3,320 sq. miles); population (Jan. 1986), 530,000. Capital Sukhumi. This area, the ancient Colchis, included Greek colonies from the 6th century B.C. onwards. From the 2nd century B.C. onwards, it was a prey to many invaders—Romans, Byzantines, Arabs, Ottoman Turks—before accepting a Russian protectorate in 1810. However, from the 4th century A.D. a West Georgian kingdom was established by the Lazi princes in the territory (known to the Romans as 'Lazica') and by the 8th century the prevailing language was Georgian and the name Abkhazia. In March 1921 a congress of local Soviets proclaimed it a Soviet Republic, and its status as an Autonomous Republic, within Georgia, was confirmed on 17 April 1930.

Population (1979 census) Abkhazians, 17·1%, Georgians, 43·9% and Russians, 16·4%.

140 deputies were elected to the republican Supreme Soviet on 24 Feb. 1980, 57 of them women.

The Abkhazian coast (along the Black Sea) possesses a famous chain of health resorts—Gagra, Sukhumi, Akhali-Antoni, Gulripsha and Gudauta—sheltered by thickly forested mountains.

The republic has coal, electric power, building materials and light industries. In 1985 there were 89 collective farms and 56 state farms; main crops are tobacco, tea, grapes, oranges, tangerines and lemons. Crop area 43,900 hectares.

Livestock, 1 Jan. 1985: 144,100 cattle, 120,200 pigs, 25,200 sheep and goats.

In 1984–85 about 107,700 pupils were engaged in study at all levels. A university has been opened in Sukhumi.

In Jan. 1985 there were 2,300 doctors and 6,000 hospital beds.

ADJARIAN AUTONOMOUS SOVIET SOCIALIST REPUBLIC

Area, 3,000 sq. km (1,160 sq. miles); population (Jan. 1986), 382,000. Capital, Batumi. After a history similar to that of Abkhazia, it fell under Turkish rule in the 17th century, and was annexed to Russia (rejoining Georgia) after the Berlin Treaty of 1878. On 16 July 1921 the territory was constituted as an Autonomous Republic within the Georgian SSR.

Population (1979 census) Georgians, 80·1%, Russians, 9·8% and Armenians 4·6%.

110 deputies were elected to the republican Supreme Soviet on 24 Feb. 1980, 45 of them women.

The republic specializes in sub-tropical agricultural products. These include tea, mandarines and lemons, grapes, bamboo, eucalyptus, etc. Livestock (Jan. 1985): 132,900 cattle, 8,600 pigs, 11,600 sheep and goats. In 1980 there were 69 collective farms and 21 state farms.

There are shipyards at Batumi, modern oil-refining plant (the pipeline from the Baku oilfields ends at Batumi), food-processing and canning factories, clothing, building materials, drug factories, etc.

Health resorts are Kobuleti, Tsikhisdziri, Batumi on the coast and Beshumi in the hills. The sub-tropical climate and flora, and the combination of mountains and sea, make this republic (like Abkhazia) a favourite holiday area.

In 1984–85 there were 77,300 pupils at school, 8 technical colleges with 3,500 students, a pedagogical institute and several research institutions. 2,200 students were receiving a higher education.

In Jan. 1985 there were 1,430 doctors and 3,900 hospital beds.

SOUTH OSSETIAN AUTONOMOUS REGION

This area was populated by Ossetians from across the Caucasus (North Ossetia), driven out by the Mongols in the 13th century. The region was set up within the Georgian SSR on 20 April 1922. Area, 3,900 sq. km (1,505 sq. miles); population (Jan. 1986), 99,000 (1979 census, Ossetians, 66·4% and Georgians, 28·8%). Capital, Tskhinvali (34,000).

Main industries are mining, timber, electrical engineering and building materials. Crop area, chiefly grains, was 21,600 hectares in 1985; other pursuits are sheep-farming (160,300 sheep and goats) and vine-growing. There were 14 collective farms and 18 state farms.

In 1984–85 there were 19,540 pupils in elementary and secondary schools, 1,019 in college and 1,908 in higher education.

In Jan. 1985 there were 500 doctors and 1,400 hospital beds.

Books of Reference

Lang, D. M., *A Modern History of Georgia*. London, 1962. — *The Georgians*. London, 1966
Gvarjaladze, T. and I., (eds.), *English-Georgian and Georgian-English Dictionary*. Tbilisi, 1974
Istoriya Gruzii. 3 vols. Tbilisi, 1962–73

ARMENIA
Haikakan Sovetakan Sotsialistakan Hanrapetoutioun

HISTORY. On 29 Nov. 1920 Armenia was proclaimed a Soviet Socialist Republic. The Armenian Soviet Government, with the Russian Soviet Government, was a party to the Treaty of Kars (March 1921), which confirmed the Turkish possession of the former Government of Kars and of the Surmali District of the Government of Yerevan. From 1922 to 1936 it formed part of the Transcaucasian Soviet Federal Socialist Republic. In 1936 Armenia was proclaimed a constituent republic of the USSR.

AREA AND POPULATION. Armenia covers an area of 29,800 sq. km (11,490 sq. miles). It is bounded in the north by Georgia, in the east by Azerbaijan and in the south and west by Turkey and Iran. It is a very mountainous country with but little forest land, has many turbulent rivers and a highly fertile soil, but is subject to drought. In Jan. 1986 the population was 3,362,000. Census (1979) 89·7% of the population were Armenians, the rest are Russians (2·3%), Kurds (1·7%), Azerbaijanians (5·3%). The capital is Yerevan. Other large towns are Leninakan (218,000) and Kirovakan (159,000).

CONSTITUTION AND GOVERNMENT. The Supreme Soviet, elected in 1985, consists of 338 deputies; 121 are women, 216 Communists. A new Constitution was adopted in April 1978.

At elections to the district, urban and rural Soviets (21 June 1987), of 27,776 deputies returned 13,758 (49·5%) were women, 15,681 (56·5%) non-Party and 19,149 (68·9%) industrial workers and collective farmers.

Chairman, Presidium of the Supreme Soviet: G. M. Voskanyan.
Chairman, Council of Ministers: F. T. Sarkisian.
First Secretary, Communist Party: K. S. Demirchian.

FINANCE. Budget estimates (in 1m. rubles), 1987, 2,065; 1988 (plan), 2,243.

AGRICULTURE. The chief agricultural area is the valley of the Arax and the area round Yerevan. Here there are considerable cotton plantations as well as orchards and vineyards. Sub-tropical plants, such as almonds and figs, are also grown. Olive groves and pomegranate plantations occupy large areas; experiments are being made to naturalize cork oak. In the mountainous areas the chief pursuit is livestock raising. In 1913 the total cultivated area of Armenia amounted to 346,000 hectares; in 1940, 434,000; in 1965, 400,000; in 1970, 409,000; in 1985, 446,000.

Output of main agricultural products (in 1,000 tonnes) in 1985: Grain, 284; potatoes, 306; vegetables, 620; sugar-beet, 129; fruit, 165; grapes, 252; meat, 107; milk, 546; eggs, 573m.; wool, 4·4.

Area of irrigated land in Armenia in 1982 was 284,000 hectares.

There were, on 1 Jan. 1986, 280 collective farms, and these together with the 513 state farms tilled 99·9% of the total cultivated area. Livestock included 300,000 pigs, 900,000 cattle and 1·9m. sheep and goats. All the state farms and collective farms had been electrified by the end of 1960. There were 13,900 tractors and 1,500 grain and cotton combines in Jan. 1986.

INDUSTRY. Armenia contains large deposits of copper, zinc, aluminium, molybdenum and other metals. It is also rich in marble, granite, cement and other building materials. The mining of these minerals is becoming more and more important. Among other industries are the chemical, producing chiefly synthetic rubber and fertilizers, and the extraction and processing of building materials such as cement, pumice-stone, tuffs, marble, volcanic basalt and fire-proof clay, ginning- and textile-mills, carpet weaving, food, including wine-making, fruit, meat-canning and creameries. Machine-tool and electrical engineering works have also been established. Among the industrial centres are Yerevan, Leninakan, Alaverdi, Kafan, Kirovakan, Daval, Megri and Oktemberyan. Output of electricity in 1985 was 14,900m. kwh. A chain ('cascade') of 8 hydro-electric stations on the river Razdan, as it falls about 3,300 ft from the mountain lake Sevan to its junction with the Arax, has been completed.

In 1985 output included 15,000 tonnes of paper, 185·9m. electric light bulbs, 1·4m. cu. metres ferroconcrete, 168,000 tonnes caustic soda, 4·8m. watches and clocks, 18·4m. pairs leather footwear, 90·4m. pairs hosiery, 96·5m. items knitwear, 443·3m. cans of preserves, and 317·3m. decalitres of mineral water.

There were 1,355,000 industrial and office workers employed in the national economy in 1985.

COMMUNICATIONS. Length of railways in Jan. 1986, 760 km; motor roads, 12,200 km (hard surface, 10,400).

Newspapers (1985). Out of 92 newspapers 81 appeared in Armenian. Daily circulation of Armenian-language newspapers, 1·4m., other languages, 124,000.

EDUCATION. In 1985–86 there were 600,000 pupils in 1,500 primary and secondary schools; 66 technical colleges with 47,900 students; 13 higher educational institutions with 54,800 students (including correspondence students). Yerevan houses the Armenian Academy of Sciences, 43 scientific institutes, a medical institute and other technical colleges, and a state university. In Jan. 1986, 33 learned institutions with 3,304 scientific staff are under the Academy of Sciences; scientific workers in 101 institutions totalled 21,500.

In Jan. 1986 there were 150,000 children in pre-school institutions.

HEALTH. In 1985 there were 12,800 doctors and 28,100 hospital beds.

Books of Reference

Kurkjian, V., *A History of Armenia.* New York, 1958
Lang, D.M., *Armenia: Cradle of Civilization.* London, 1978.—*The Armenians. A People in Exile.* London, 1981
Missakian, J., *A Searchlight on the Armenian Question, 1878–1950.* Boston, Mass., 1950
Shaginyan, M., *A Journey Through Soviet Armenia.* (English ed.) Moscow, 1954

MOLDAVIAN SOVIET SOCIALIST REPUBLIC

Respublika Sovietike Sochialiste Moldovenyaske

HISTORY. The Moldavian Soviet Socialist Republic, capital Kishinev, was formed by the union of part of the former Moldavian Autonomous Soviet Socialist Republic (organized 12 Oct. 1924), formerly included in the Ukrainian Soviet Socialist Republic, and the areas of Bessarabia (ceded by Romania to the USSR, 28 June 1940) with a mainly Moldavian population. As from 2 Aug. 1940 the MSSR includes the following regions of the former Moldavian Autonomous Soviet Socialist Republic: Grigoriopol, Dubossarsk, Kamensk, Rybnits, Slobodzeisk and Tiraspol, and the following districts of Bessarabia: Beltsk, Bendery, Kagulsk, Kishinev, Orgeev and Sorok. The republic, however, is divided not into regions but into 36 rural districts, 21 towns and 45 urban settlements.

AREA AND POPULATION. Moldavia is bounded in the east and south by the Ukraine and on the west by Romania. The area is 33,700 sq. km (13,000 sq. miles). In Jan. 1987 the population was 4,185,000, of whom (1979 census) 63·9% are Moldavians. Others include Ukrainians (14·2%), Russians (12·8%), Gagauzi (3·5%), Jews (2%). Apart from Kishinev, larger towns are Tiraspol (154,000), Beltsy (139,000) and Bendery (114,000).

CONSTITUTION AND GOVERNMENT. The Supreme Soviet, elected in 1985, consists of 380 deputies; 138 are women, 253 Communists. A new Constitution was adopted in April 1978.

At elections to the district, urban and rural Soviets (21 June 1987), of 38,808 deputies returned, 19,060 (49·1%) were women, 21,951 (56·6%) non-Party and 25,930 (66·9%) industrial workers and collective farmers.

Chairman, Presidium of the Supreme Soviet: A. A. Mokanu.
Chairman, Council of Ministers: I. P. Kalin.
First Secretary, Communist Party: S. K. Grossu.

FINANCE. Budget estimates (in 1m. rubles), 1987, 2,724; 1988 (plan), 3,000.

AGRICULTURE. On 1 Jan. 1986 there were 368 collective farms and 473 state farms. All ploughing and sowing is mechanized. Livestock included (1 Jan. 1986) 1·3m. cattle, 2m. pigs and 1·2m. sheep and goats. There were 54,700 tractors and 4,500 combine harvesters in Jan. 1986.

Output of main agricultural products (in 1,000 tonnes) in 1985: Grain, 2,373; sugar-beet, 2,361; sunflower seeds, 244; potatoes, 408; vegetables, 1,245; fruit, 999; grapes, 654; meat, 303; milk, 1,402; eggs, 1,075m.; wool, 2·7.

Bessarabia has an equable climate and very fertile soil. It contains nearly one quarter of the vineyards of the USSR. Bessarabia is also rich in fish in the south: sturgeon, mackerel, brill.

INDUSTRY. There are canning plants, wine-making plants, woodworking and metallurgical factories, a factory of ferro-concrete building materials, and footwear and textile plants. Moldavia takes third place in the USSR in the production of wine, tobacco and food-canning. Production in 1985 included 107,400 centrifugal pumps, 5·4 cu. metres carpet, 18·2m. pairs leather footwear, 218·6m. bricks, 39·7m. pairs hosiery, 63·6m. items knitwear, 459,000 tonnes granulated sugar, 1,587m. cans of preserves and 1·7m. cu. metres ferroconcrete. Meat and dairy produce are rapidly expanding food industries.

There are lignite, phosphorites, gypsum and valuable building materials.

In 1985 there were 1,619,000 industrial and office workers working in the national economy. Electricity generated (1985) 16,800m. kwh.

COMMUNICATIONS. Length of railways in Jan. 1986, 1,150 km. There are

17,700 km of motor roads (12,400 hard surface), and 308m. tonne-km of freight was carried on inland waterways.

Newspapers (1985). There were 191 newspapers, 80 in Moldavian. Daily circulation of Moldavian-language newspapers, 1,169,000, other languages, 1,032,000.

EDUCATION. In 1985–86 there were 700,000 pupils in 1,700 primary, secondary and special schools, 60,600 students in 53 technical colleges and 53,200 students in 9 higher educational institutions including the state university. A Moldavian Academy of Sciences was established in 1961: it had 17 research institutions and a scientific staff of 1,177 in Jan. 1986. In all, there are 68 learned institutions with 10,300 scientific staff. In Jan. 1986 there were 310,000 children attending pre-school institutions.

HEALTH. Doctors in 1985 numbered 15,600; hospital beds, 51,500.

Books of Reference

Zlatova, Y., and Kotelnikov, V., *Across Moldavia* (English ed.). Moscow, 1959
Istoriya Moldavskoi SSR. 2nd ed. 2 vols. Kishinev, 1965–68

ESTONIA
Eesti Nõukogude Sotsialistlik Vabariik

HISTORY. The workers' and soldiers' Soviets in Estonia took over power on 8 Nov. 1917, were overthrown by the German occupying forces in March 1918, and were restored to power as the Germans withdrew in Nov. 1918, establishing the 'Estland Labour Commune'. It was overthrown with the assistance of British naval forces in May 1919, and a democratic republic proclaimed. In March 1934 this regime was, in turn, overthrown by a fascist *coup*.

The secret protocol of the Soviet-German agreement of 23 Aug. 1939 assigned Estonia to the Soviet sphere of interest. An ultimatum (16 June 1940) led to the formation of a government acceptable to the USSR; on 21 July the State Duma proclaimed the establishment of an Estonian Soviet Socialist Republic and applied to join the USSR: on 6 Aug. the Supreme Soviet accepted the application. The incorporation has been accorded *de facto* recognition by the British Government, but not by the US Government, which continues to recognize an Estonian consul-general in New York.

AREA AND POPULATION. Estonia is bounded west and north by the Baltic, east by the RSFSR and south by Latvia. Area, 45,100 sq. km (17,413 sq. miles); population, 1,556,000 (Jan. 1987). Census (1979) 64·7% were Estonians, 27·9% Russians, 2·5% Ukrainians and 1·6% Belorussians. The capital is Tallinn. Other large towns are Tartu, Narva, Kohtla-Järve and Pärnu. There are 15 districts, 33 towns and 26 urban settlements.

CONSTITUTION AND GOVERNMENT. The Supreme Soviet, elected in 1985, consists of 285 deputies (1 per 10,000 population); 102 are women, 192 Communists. A new Constitution was adopted in April 1978.

At elections to district, urban and rural Soviets (21 June 1987), out of 11,164 deputies returned 5,472 (49%) were women, 6,140 (55%) non-Party and 7,325 (65·6%) industrial workers and collective farmers.

Chairman, Presidium of the Supreme Soviet: A. F. Riutel.
Chairman, Council of Ministers: B. E. Saul.
First Secretary, Communist Party: K. G. Vaino.

FINANCE. Budget estimates (in 1m. rubles), 1987, 1,665; 1988 (plan), 1,797.

AGRICULTURE. Agriculture and dairy farming are the chief occupations. Area under cultivation was 697,000 hectares in 1913, 918,000 hectares in 1940 and 931,000 hectares in 1985. There were 142 agricultural and 8 fishery collectives and 152 state farms in 1986 using 20,600 tractors and 3,400 grain combines. 97% of state farms and 70% of collective farms were receiving electric power.

On 1 Jan. 1986 there were 800,000 head of cattle, 158,000 sheep and goats, and 1·1m. pigs.

Output of main agricultural products (in 1,000 tonnes) in 1985: Grain, 929; potatoes, 833; vegetables, 124; meat, 216; milk, 1,260; eggs, 528m.

INDUSTRY. Some 22% of the territory is covered by forests which provide good material for its sawmills, furniture, match and pulp industries, as well as wood fuel. Since the end of the war, 80,000 hectares have been afforested. 966,700 hectares of marsh land had been reclaimed by 1977.

Estonia has rich high-quality shale deposits (particularly in the north-east) which are estimated at 3,700m. tons. Shale output was 1·9m. tons in 1940 and 27·4m. in 1984. A factory for the production of gas from shale and a pipeline (208 km long) from Kohtla-Järve supplies shale gas to Leningrad and Tallinn. Estonian factories are now turning out agricultural and peat-digging machines, complex control and measuring instruments. The 'Volta' factory in Tallinn produces electric motors.

In the neighbourhood of Tallinn, phosphorites have been found, and in 1947 a plant for refining and for the production of super-phosphates was started. Estonia also contains valuable peat deposits, and some of her electrical stations work on peat. There are 350 rural electric stations. Electricity generated (1985) 17,800m. kwh. Output of paper in 1985 was 90,000 tonnes; leather footwear, 5·8m. pairs; knitwear, 22·2m. garments; hosiery, 15·5m. pairs.

In 1985 there were 718,000 industrial and office workers engaged in the national economy.

COMMUNICATIONS. Length of railways in 1986, 1,010 km. Estonia has 20 ports, but Tallinn handles four-fifths of the total sea-going transport. Length of motor roads, 28,100 km (hard surface, 26,400 km). Airlines link Tallinn with Moscow, Leningrad, Riga and the Estonian islands.

Newspapers (1985). There were 49 newspapers, 35 of them in Estonian. Daily circulation of Estonian-language newspapers, 1,109,000, other languages, 200,000.

EDUCATION. Estonia has retained an 11-year school curriculum, when it was reduced to 10 years elsewhere in the USSR. In 1985–86 pupils in 600 primary, secondary and special schools numbered 200,000. There were 23,500 students in 6 higher educational establishments, including Tartu (Dorpat) University, founded in 1632, and 22,200 students in 37 technical colleges.

The Estonian Academy of Sciences, founded in 1946, had 24 institutions with 1,151 scientific staff in Jan. 1986; in all, 7,000 scientific staff were working in 72 institutions.

In Jan. 1986 there were 90,000 children attending pre-school institutions.

HEALTH. In 1985 there were 7,100 doctors and 19,100 hospital beds.

Books of Reference

Istoriya Estonskoi SSR. 3 vols. Tallin, 1961–74
Küng, A., *A Dream of Freedom.* Cardiff, 1980
Misiuras, R.-J., and Taagepera, R., *The Baltic States: Years of Dependence 1940–1980.* Farnborough, 1983
Parming, T., and Jarvesro, E., (eds.) *A Case Study of a Soviet Republic.* Boulder, 1978
Rank, M., *Inglise—eesti Sõnaraamat.* Toronto, 1965
Saagpakk, P. F., *Estonian-English Dictionary.* New Haven, 1982

LATVIA

Latvijas Padomju Socialistiska Republika

HISTORY. In the part of Latvia unoccupied by the Germans, the Bolsheviks won 72% of the votes in the Constituent Assembly elections (Nov. 1917). Soviet power was proclaimed in Dec. 1917, but was overthrown when the Germans occupied all Latvia (Feb. 1918). Restored when they withdrew (Dec. 1918), it was overthrown once more by combined British naval and German military forces (May–Dec. 1919), and a democratic government set up. This régime was in turn replaced when a fascist *coup* took place in May 1934.

The secret protocol of the Soviet–German agreement of 23 Aug. 1939 assigned Latvia to the Soviet sphere of interest. An ultimatum (16 June 1940) led to the formation of a government acceptable to the USSR. On 21 July a People's Diet proclaimed the establishment of the Latvian Soviet Socialist Republic and applied to join the USSR, whose Supreme Soviet accepted the application on 5 Aug. The incorporation has been accorded *de facto* recognition by the British Government, but not by the US Government, which continues to recognize the Chargé d'Affaires in Washington, D.C.

AREA AND POPULATION. Latvia is bounded north by Estonia and the Baltic Sea, west by the Baltic, south by Lithuania and Belorussia and east by the RSFSR. Latvia has a total area of 63,700 sq. km (24,595 sq. miles). Population, Jan. 1987, 2,647,000, of whom (1979 census) 53·7% are Latvians and 32·8% Russians. There are 26 districts, 56 towns and 37 urban settlements.

The chief town is Riga (the capital); other principal towns are Daugavpils (Dvinsk), Liepāja, Jurmala, Jelgava (Mitau) and Ventspils (Windau).

CONSTITUTION AND GOVERNMENT. The Supreme Soviet, elected in 1985, consists of 325 deputies (1 per 10,000 population); 115 are women, 219 Communists. A new Constitution was adopted in April 1978.

At elections to district, urban and rural Soviets (21 June 1987), of 23,398 deputies returned, 11,392 (48·7%) were women, 12,715 (54·3%) non-Party and 14,133 (60·4%) industrial workers and collective farmers.

Chairman, Presidium of the Supreme Soviet: J. J. Vagris.
Chairman, Council of Ministers: Y. Y. Ruben.
First Secretary, Communist Party: B. K. Pugo.

FINANCE. Budget estimates (in 1m. rubles), 1987, 2,595; 1988 (plan), 2,733.

AGRICULTURE. Latvia is now no longer mainly an agricultural country. The urban population, 35% of the total in 1939, was 71% in Jan. 1986.

Latvian forest lands, state and private (2·4m. hectares), produced in 1937–38, 3·4m. cu. metres of timber; 1983 output, 4·2m. cu. metres.

Area under cultivation was 1·4m. hectares in 1913, 2m. in 1940, 1·7m. in 1985. 1·8m. hectares of marsh land have been drained (1983).

Cattle breeding and dairy farming are the chief agricultural occupations. Oats, barley, rye, potatoes and flax are the main crops.

After the establishment of the Soviet regime about 960,000 hectares were distributed among the landless peasants or those with very small holdings. On 1 Jan. 1986 there were 248 state farms and 331 (including 11 fishery) collective farms. There were 36,700 tractors and 7,700 grain combine harvesters. By 1 Jan. 1964, all state farms and collective farms were using electric power.

Livestock (1 Jan. 1986): Cattle, 1·5m. (1939: 1·3m.); sheep and goats, 200,000 (1939: 1·5m.); pigs, 1·7m. (1939: 891,500).

Output of main agricultural products (in 1,000 tonnes) in 1985: Grain, 1,610; sugar-beet, 347; flax fibre, 4; potatoes, 1,272; vegetables, 217; meat, 324; milk, 1,957; eggs, 880m.

INDUSTRY. Latvia is the main producer of electric railway passenger cars and long-distance telephone exchanges in the USSR, fourth in output of paper and woollen goods, fifth of sawn timber, sixth of mineral fertilizers.

Industrial output in 1985 (in 1,000 tonnes) included: Paper, 167; hosiery, 76m. pairs; knitwear, 45m. garments; leather footwear, 10·5m. pairs; radios, 1·6m.; washing machines, 647,000; ferroconcrete, 1·3m. cu. metres; granulated sugar, 249; cans of preserves, 415m. Electricity generated (1985) 5,000m. kwh.

Peat deposits extend over 645,000 hectares or about 10% of the total area, and it is estimated that total deposits are 3,000–4,000m. tons; output, 1971, 2·3m. tons. There are also gypsum deposits; amber is frequently found in the coastal districts.

In 1985 industrial and office workers numbered 1,231,000.

COMMUNICATIONS. In Jan. 1986 the length of railways was 2,380 km, and motor roads, 27,900 km (hard surface, 19,500 km). Riga is the largest port in the Baltic after Leningrad. In 1986, 211m. tonne-km of freight was carried on inland waterways.

Newspapers (1985). There were 108 newspapers (64 in Lettish). Daily circulation of Lettish-language newspapers, 1·3m., other languages 518,000.

RELIGION. The Latvian Lutheran Church numbered 600,000 members in 1956.

EDUCATION. In 1985–86 there were 900 primary and secondary schools, with a total of 400,000 pupils: 131,000 children attended pre-school institutions. Ten places of higher education had 43,900 students, 55 technical colleges had 40,800 students; there were also 21 music and art schools, 3 teachers' training colleges and an agricultural academy. In 1946 an Academy of Sciences was opened which in Jan. 1986 had 15 research institutes with a staff of 1,621 scientific workers; there were over 13,500 scientific workers in 101 research institutions.

HEALTH. There were 12,600 doctors and 36,500 hospital beds in 1985.

Books of Reference

Latvian Academy of Sciences, *Istoriya Latviiskoi SSR.* Riga. 3 vols. 1952–58
Bilmanis, A., *A History of Latvia.* Princeton Univ. Press, 1951
Roze, B. and K., *Latviska–Angliska Vārdnīcā.* Göppingen, 1948
Spekke, A., *History of Latvia.* Stockholm, 1951
Turkina, E., *Angliski–Latviska Vārdnīca.*Riga, 1948.—*Latviešu-Anglu Vārdnīca.* Riga, 1962

LITHUANIA
Lietuvos Tarybu Socialistine Respublika

HISTORY. In 1914–15 the German army occupied the whole of Lithuania. On its withdrawal (Dec. 1918) Soviets were elected in all towns and a Soviet republic was proclaimed. In the summer of 1919 it was overthrown by Polish, German and nationalist Lithuanian forces, and a democratic republic established. In Dec. 1926 this regime was in turn overthrown by a fascist *coup.*

The secret protocol of the Soviet–German frontier treaty of 28 Sept. 1939 assigned the greater part of Lithuania to the Soviet sphere of influence. In Oct. 1939 the province and city of Vilnius (in Polish occupation 1920–39) were ceded by the USSR. An ultimatum (16 June 1940) led to the formation of a government acceptable to the USSR. A people's Diet, elected on 14–15 July, proclaimed the establishment of the Lithuanian Soviet Socialist Republic on 21 July and applied for admission to the USSR, which was effected by decree of the USSR Supreme Soviet on 3 Aug. and included also those parts of Lithuania which had been reserved for inclusion in Germany. This incorporation has been accorded *de facto* recognition by the British Government, but not by the US Government, which continues to recognize a Lithuanian Chargé d'Affaires in Washington, D.C.

AREA AND POPULATION. Lithuania is bounded north by Latvia, east and south by Belorussia, west by Poland, the Kaliningrad area of the RSFSR and the Baltic Sea. The total area of Lithuania is 65,200 sq. km (25,170 sq. miles) and the population (Jan. 1986) 3,603,000, of whom 80% were Lithuanians, 8·6% Russians and 7·7% Poles (1979 census).

The capital is Vilnius (Vilna). Other large towns are Kaunas (Kovno), Klaipeda (Memel), Šiauliai (130,000) and Panévežys (112,000). There are 44 rural districts, 92 towns and 22 urban settlements.

CONSTITUTION AND GOVERNMENT. The Supreme Soviet, elected in 1985, consists of 350 deputies (1 per 15,000 population); 125 are women, 235 Communists. A new Constitution was adopted in April 1978.

At elections to district, urban and rural Soviets (21 June 1987), of 28,354 deputies returned, 13,680 (48·2%) were women, 15,321 (54%) non-Party and 18,197 (64·1%) industrial workers and collective farmers.

Chairman, Presidium of the Supreme Soviet: V. S. Astrauskas.
Chairman, Council of Ministers: V. V. Sakalauskas.
First Secretary, Communist Party: R.-B. I. Songaila.

FINANCE. Budget estimates (in 1m. rubles), 1987, 3,784; 1988 (plan), 3,962.

AGRICULTURE. Lithuania before 1940 was a mainly agricultural country, but has since been considerably industrialized. The urban population was 23% of the total in 1937 and 66% in Jan. 1986. The resources of the country consist of timber and agricultural produce. Of the total area, 49·1% is arable land, 22·2% meadow and pasture land, 16·3% forests and 12·4% unproductive lands.

Area under cultivation in 1913 was 1·9m.; in 1938, 2·7m.; in 1986, 2·4m. hectares. By 1981 over 2·7m. hectares of swamps had been drained.

Output of main agricultural products (in 1,000 tonnes) in 1985: Grain, 2,867; potatoes, 1,851; sugar-beet, 933; vegetables, 331; flax fibre, 14; meat, 504; milk, 2,973; eggs, 1,116m.

On 1 Jan. 1986 there were 2·5m. cattle, 2·7m. pigs, 100,000 sheep and goats.

Forests cover 1,554,000 hectares; 70% of the forests consist of conifers, mostly pines. Peat reserves total 4,000m. cu. metres.

Between 1940 and 1947 about 575,500 hectares (about 1·4m. acres) were distributed among the landless and poor peasant farmers. In 1986 there were 51,000 tractors and 12,500 grain combines serving 737 collective farms and 311 state farms.

INDUSTRY. Heavy engineering, shipbuilding and building material industries are developing. Industrial output included, in 1985, 20,200 metal-cutting lathes; fuel pumps, 331,000; sulphuric acid, 440,000 tonnes; paper, 120,000 tonnes; carpet, 6·7m. sq. metres; tape recorders, 238,000; televisions, 609,000; leather footwear, 10·7m. pairs; granulated sugar, 221,800 tonnes; felled timber, 2m. cu. metres; knitwear, 61·3m. garments; hosiery, 99·3m. pairs; electric power, 21,000m. kwh.

In 1985 there were 1,563,000 industrial and office workers employed in the national economy.

COMMUNICATIONS. Length of railways in Jan. 1986, 2,010 km. Vilnius has one of the largest airports of the USSR. There are 39,000 km of motor roads (26,600 km hard surface) and 157m. tonne-km of freight was carried on inland waterways in 1985. Klaipeda, as a non-freezing harbour and fishery base, is of national importance.

Newspapers (1985). Of 134 newspapers, 105 were in Lithuanian. Daily circulation of Lithuanian-language newspapers, 2·1m., other languages, 276,000.

RELIGION. In 1956, the Lithuanian Lutheran Church had 215,000 members; Roman Catholics, including those in Estonia and Latvia, numbered 2·5m.

EDUCATION. In 1985–86 there were 600,000 pupils in 2,200 primary and secondary schools. The University of Vytautas the Great, at Kaunas, was opened on 16 Feb. 1922. On 15 Jan. 1940 certain faculties were transferred to Vilnius to join the ancient University of Vilnius (founded 1570). In 1985–86 there were 12 higher educational institutions with 65,300 students: in 66 technical colleges of all kinds there were 61,100 students. The Lithuanian Academy of Sciences, founded in 1941, had 12 institutions with a total scientific staff of 1,817 in Jan. 1986; there were 88 scientific institutions with 14,800 research personnel. 189,000 children in Jan. 1986 were attending pre-school institutions.

HEALTH. In 1985 there were 15,400 doctors and 45,300 hospital beds.

Books of Reference

Jurgėla, C. R., *History of the Lithuanian Nation.* New York, 1948
Kantantas, A. and F., *A Lithuanian Bibliography.* Univ. of Alberta Press, 1975
Peteraitis, V., *Lithuanian–English Dictionary.* 2 vols. Chicago, 1960
Suziedlis, S., (ed.), *Encyclopedia Lituanica.* 6 vols. Boston, 1970–78
Vardys, S., (ed.), *Lithuania under the Soviets: Portrait of a Nation, 1940–45.* New York, 1965

SOVIET CENTRAL ASIA

Soviet Central Asia embraces the Kazakh Soviet Socialist Republic, the Uzbek Soviet Socialist Republic, the Turkmen Soviet Socialist Republic, the Tadzhik Soviet Socialist Republic and the Kirghiz Soviet Socialist Republic.

Turkestan (by which name part of this territory was then known) was conquered by the Russians in the 1860s. In 1866 Tashkent was occupied and in 1868 Samarkand, and subsequently further territory was conquered and united with Russian Turkestan. In the 1870s Bokhara was subjugated, the emir, by the agreement of 1873, recognizing the suzerainty of Russia. In the same year Khiva became a vassal state to Russia. Until 1917 Russian Central Asia was divided politically into the Khanate of Khiva, the Emirate of Bokhara and the Governor-Generalship of Turkestan.

In the summer of 1919 the authority of the Soviet Government became definitely established in these regions. The Khan of Khiva was deposed in Feb. 1920, and a People's Soviet Republic was set up, the medieval name of Khorezm being revived. In Aug. 1920 the Emir of Bokhara suffered the same fate, and a similar regime was set up in Bokhara. The former Governor-Generalship of Turkestan was constituted an Autonomous Soviet Socialist Republic within the RSFSR on 11 April 1921.

In the autumn of 1924 the Soviets of the Turkestan, Bokhara and Khiva Republics decided to redistribute the territories of these republics on a nationality basis; at the same time Bokhara and Khiva became Socialist Republics. The redistribution was completed in May 1925, when the new states of Uzbekistan, Turkmenistan and Tadzhikistan were accepted into the USSR as Union Republics. The remaining districts of Turkestan populated by Kazakhs were united with Kazakhstan which was established as an ASSR in 1925 and became a Union Republic in 1936. Kirghizia, until then part of the RSFSR, was established as a Union Republic in 1936.

Books of Reference

Akiner, S., *The Islamic Peoples of the Soviet Union.* Rev. ed. London, 1986
Bennigsen, A., and Broxup, M., *The Islamic Threat to the Soviet State.* London, 1983
Nove, A. and Newth, J. A., *The Soviet Middle East.* London, 1967
Rwykin, M., *Moscow's Muslim Challenge.* New York, 1982
Wheeler, G., *The Modern History of Soviet Central Asia.* London, 1964.—*The Peoples of Soviet Central Asia.* London, 1966

KAZAKHSTAN
Kazak Soviettik Sotzialistik Respublikasy

HISTORY. On 26 Aug. 1920 Uralsk, Turgai, Akmolinsk and Semipalatinsk provinces formed the Kirgiz (in 1925 renamed Kazakh) Autonomous Soviet Socialist Republic within the RSFSR. It was made a constituent republic of the USSR on 5 Dec. 1936. To this republic were added the parts of the former Governorship of Turkestan inhabited by a majority of Kazakhs. It consists of the following regions: Aktyubinsk, Alma-Ata, Chimkent, Dzhambul, Dzhezkazgan, East Kazakhstan, Guryev, Karaganda, Kokchetav, Kustanai, Kzyl-Orda, Mangyshlak, North Kazakhstan, Pavlodar, Semipalatinsk, Taldy-Kurgan, Tselinograd, Turgai, Uralsk.

AREA AND POPULATION. Kazakhstan is bounded on the west by the Caspian Sea and the RSFSR, on the east by China, on the north by the RSFSR and on the south by Uzbekistan and Kirghizia. The area of the republic is 2,717,300 sq. km (1,049,155 sq. miles). It is the next in size to the RSFSR, is far larger than all the other Central Asian Soviet Republics combined and stretches nearly 3,000 km from west to east and over 1,500 km from north to south. Population (Jan. 1986) 16,028,000, of whom 55% live in urban areas. The Kazakhs form 36%, Russians 40·8% and Ukrainians 6·1% of the population (1979 census), as a result of the industrialization of the country since 1941 and the opening of virgin lands since 1945. The population includes over 100 nationalities.

The capital is Alma-Ata, formerly Verny; other large towns are Karaganda, Semipalatinsk, Chimkent and Petropavlovsk. In all there are 82 towns, 197 urban settlements and 221 rural districts.

CONSTITUTION AND GOVERNMENT. The Supreme Soviet, elected in 1985, consists of 510 deputies (1 per 20,000 population); 183 are women, 336 Communists. A new Constitution was adopted in April 1978.

At elections to the regional, district, urban and rural Soviets (21 June 1987), out of 131,074 deputies returned, 64,717 (49·4%) were women, 75,748 (57·8%) non-Party and 89,350 (68·2%) industrial workers and collective farmers.

President, Presidium of the Supreme Soviet: Z. Kamalidenov.
Chairman, Council of Ministers: N. A. Nazarbaev.
First Secretary, Communist Party: G. V. Kolbin.

FINANCE. The budget (in 1m. rubles) balanced as follows: 1987, 12,250; 1988 (plan), 12,697.

AGRICULTURE. Kazakh agriculture has changed from primarily nomad cattle breeding to production of grain, cotton and other industrial crops. In 1985 the crop area was 35·8m. hectares—over 16% of the total cultivated area of the USSR (1913, 4·2m.; 1940, 6·8m.).

2,047,000 hectares of land have an irrigation network.

The 'Ukrainka' winter wheat has been transformed into a spring wheat suitable for cultivation in Kazakhstan. Tobacco, rubber plants and mustard are also cultivated. Kazakhstan has rich orchards and vineyards, which accounted for 95,000 hectares of cultivated land in 1985. Between 1954 and 1959, over 23m. hectares of virgin and long fallow land were opened up, 544 new state grain farms being organized for the purpose. State purchases of grain were 1·3m. tonnes in 1940, 12·3m. in 1971–75 (average), 12·6m. in 1981–85 (average) and 13·8m. in 1985.

Kazakhstan is noted for its livestock, particularly its sheep, from which excellent quality wool is obtained. The Akharomerino is a newly developed crossbreed of merino sheep and the wild Akhar mountain ram. Livestock on 1 Jan. 1986 included 9·2m. cattle, 35·5m. sheep and goats and 3m. pigs.

There were, on 1 Jan. 1986, 388 collective farms and 2,140 state farms with

248,700 tractors and 118,700 grain combine harvesters. There were 5,293 rural power stations of 307,800 kwh. capacity.

Output of main agricultural products (in 1m. tonnes) in 1985: Grain, 24·2; sugar-beet, 1·9; sunflower seeds, 0·9; potatoes, 2·2; vegetables, 1·1; fruit, 0·1; grapes, 0·1; meat, 1·1; milk, 4·8; eggs, 3,803m.; wool, 0·1.

INDUSTRY. Kazakhstan is extremely rich in mineral resources. Coal and tungsten in Karaganda (in the centre), oil along the river Emba (in the west), copper, lead and zinc—Kazakhstan contains about one-half of the total deposits of these three metals contained in the USSR—Iceland spar (in the south), nickel and chromium in the Kustanai and Semipalatinsk regions, molybdenum and other minerals.

In 1943 big deposits of manganese were found in Eastern Kazakhstan; new coal seams were also discovered there. In South Kazakhstan new copper and bauxite deposits have been found.

Coal, oil, non-ferrous metallurgy, heavy engineering and chemical industries have brought Kazakhstan to the third place among the industrial republics of the USSR. Production (1m. tonnes) in 1985 included iron ore, 25; sulphuric acid, 1·7; ferroconcrete, 6·5m. cu. metres; leather footwear, 32·3m. pairs; rolled metal, 4·2; cans of preserves, 392·4; coal, 130·8; oil, 22·8; cotton cloth, 91,900 tonnes; knitwear, 100·3; hosiery, 76·7m. pairs. The Leninogorsk and Chimkent lead plants, the Balkhash, Irtysh and Karaskpai copper-smelting works and others supply the country with non-ferrous metals. A meat-packing plant has been built in Semipalatinsk, a fish cannery in Guryev, a chemical plant in Aktyubinsk, a tractor works at Pavlodar, and a superphosphate plant in Dzhambul. The oil industry in Emba and Aktyubinsk yields high-quality aviation oil.

Aviation plays an important part in agriculture. About 14m. hectares were in 1984 treated from the air (destruction of pests, surface feeding of sugar-beet plantations, pollination of orchards, etc.).

Among recent enterprises are a large textile combine at Kustanai, hosiery factories at Djezkazgan, Leninogorsk and Aktyubinsk, a sugar factory at Aksu, meat canneries at Djetygar and Kzyl-Orda.

Electric power output in 1985 was 81,300m. kwh.

There were, in 1985, 6,500,000 industrial and office workers in the national economy.

COMMUNICATIONS

Roads. In 1986 there were 112,900 km of motor roads (89,300 km hard surface).

Railways. In 1986 the total length of railways in operation was 14,490 km. Over 600 km of narrow-gauge line and 700 km of broad-gauge line were built in the virgin lands area in 1951-57.

Inland waterways. In 1985 3,437m. tonne-km of freight was carried on inland waterways.

Newspapers (1985). Of 449 newspapers, 169 were in the Kazakh language. Daily circulation of Kazakh-language newspapers, 1·9m., in all languages, 5·8m.

EDUCATION. In 1985–86 there were 3·3m. pupils at 8,700 elementary and secondary schools; 246 technical colleges with 277,600 students, 55 higher educational institutions with 273,400 students, and 207 research institutes with 40,400 scientific personnel. The Kazakh Academy of Sciences, founded in 1945, had, in 1986, 31 institutions, the scientific staff of which numbered 4,410. 986,000 children were attending pre-school institutions in Jan. 1986.

HEALTH. In 1985 there were 59,700 doctors and 214,400 hospital beds.

Books of Reference

Istoriya Kazakhskoi SSR. 2 vols. Alma-Ata, 1957–59

Alampiev, P., *Soviet Kazakhstan.* Moscow, 1958.—*Where Economic Inequality is No More.* Moscow, 1959

TURKMENISTAN
Tiurkmenostan Soviet Sotsialistik Respublikasy

HISTORY. The Turkmen Soviet Socialist Republic was formed on 27 Oct. 1924 and covers the territory of the former Trans-Caspian Region of Turkestan, the Charjiui vilayet of Bokhara and a part of Khiva situated on the right bank of the Oxus. In May 1925 the Turkmen Republic entered the Soviet Union as one of its constituent republics.

AREA AND POPULATION. Turkmenistan is bounded on the north by the Autonomous Kara-Kalpak Republic, a constituent of Uzbekistan, by Iran and Afghánistán on the south, by the Uzbek Republic on the east and the Caspian Sea on the west. The principal Turkmen tribes are the Tekkés of Merv and the Tekkés of the Attok, the Ersaris, Yomuds and Goklans. All speak closely related varieties of a Turkic language (of the south-western group); many are Sunni Moslems.

The country passed under Russian control in 1881, after the fall of the Turkoman stronghold of GökTépé. Census (1979) 68·4% of the population were Turkmenians, most of whom were nomads before the First World War. 12·6% are Russians living mostly in urban areas, and 8·5% Uzbeks. There are also Kazakhs (2·9%), Tatars, Ukrainians, Armenians and others.

The area of Turkmenistan is 488,100 sq. km (186,400 sq. miles), and its population in Jan. 1986 was 3,270,000.

There are 5 regions: Chardzhou, Mary, Ashkhabad, Tashauz and Krasnovodsk, comprising 42 rural districts, 15 towns and 74 urban settlements.

The capital is Ashkhabad (Poltoratsk); other large towns are Chardzhou (162,000), Mary (Merv) (87,000), Nebit-Dag (83,000) and Krasnovodsk (58,000).

CONSTITUTION AND GOVERNMENT. The Supreme Soviet, elected in 1985, consists of 330 deputies (1 per 5,000 population); 118 are women, 222 Communists. A new Constitution was adopted in April 1978.

At elections to regional, district, urban and rural Soviets (21 June 1987), of 23,743 deputies returned, 11,501 (48·4%) were women, 13,420 (56·5%) non-party and 16,044 (67·5%) industrial workers and collective farmers.

Chairman, Presidium of the Supreme Soviet: B. Yazkuliev.
Chairman, Council of Ministers: A. Kh. Khodzhamuradov.
First Secretary, Communist Party: S. A. Niyazov.

FINANCE. Budget estimates (in 1m. rubles), 1987, 1,639; 1988 (plan), 1,683.

AGRICULTURE. The main occupation of the people is agriculture, based on irrigation. Turkmenistan produces cotton, wool, Astrakhan fur, etc. It is also famous for its carpets, and produces a special breed of Turkoman horses and the famous Karakul sheep.

There were 350 collective farms and 134 state farms in 1986, with 41,200 tractors and 1,400 grain combines. There were 608 rural power stations.

A considerable area is under Egyptian cotton, and from it has been evolved an original Soviet long-fibred cotton.

The main grain grown is maize. Sericulture, fruit and vegetable growing are also important; dates, olives, figs, sesame and other southern plants are grown. There is fishing in the Caspian. 1,028,000 hectares were under cultivation in 1985 (1913, 318,000; 1940, 411,000).

Between 1958 and 1970 the Kara-Kum Canal was extended to 860 km. In 1971 the fourth section, to reach the Caspian, was begun to reach 1,000 km. By 1982 over 1,011,000 hectares had been irrigated.

Livestock on 1 Jan. 1986: Cattle, 700,000; pigs, 200,000; sheep and goats, 4·7m.

Output of main agricultural products (in 1,000 tonnes) in 1985: Grain, 322; cotton, 1,287; vegetables, 312; fruit, 39; grapes, 105; meat, 86; milk, 348; eggs, 275m.; wool, 15·4.

INDUSTRY. Turkmenistan is rich in minerals, such as ozocerite, oil, coal, sulphur and salt. Industry is being developed, and there are now chemical, tailoring, textile, light, food, agricultural implements, cement and other factories, oil refineries, as well as ore-mining.

In the Kara-Kum Desert deposits of magnesium, minerals and coal have been discovered, as well as some 50 new saltmines. Here a new oil town, Nebit-Dag, has sprung up. On the Kara-Bogaz bay a sulphate industry has been developed. Industrial output in 1985 included 348,000 tonnes cotton fibre, 5·4m. pairs hosiery, 4·6m. pairs leather footwear, 147m. bricks. Electric power output was 11,000m. kwh. in 1985.

In 1985 there were 811,000 industrial and office workers in the national economy.

COMMUNICATIONS. Length of motor roads in 1986, 20,800 km (16,100 km hard surface). Motor communication exists between Ashkhabad and Meshed (Iran).

Length of railways, 2,120 km. The line Chardzhou–Kungrad crosses the Chardzhou and Tashauz regions of Turkmenia and runs across Uzbekistan. Another line connects Chardzhou and Urgench. Inland waterways, 1,300 km.

Airlines connect Leninsk and Tashauz, and Ashkhabad and remote areas in the west, north and east.

Newspapers (1985). Of 69 newspapers, 56 were in the Turkmen language. Daily circulation of Turkmenian-language newspapers, 827,000; in all languages, 1,031,000.

EDUCATION. In 1985–86 there were 1,900 primary and secondary schools with 800,000 pupils, 9 higher educational institutions with 38,800 students, 35 technical colleges with 37,000 students, and 11 music and art schools. The Turkmen Academy of Sciences, founded in 1951, directs the work of 15 learned institutions with a staff of 1,069 scientific staff; there were 58 research institutions in all, with 5,600 research workers, in Jan. 1986.

In Jan. 1986, 153,000 children were attending pre-school institutions.

HEALTH. In 1985 there were 10,700 doctors and 34,400 hospital beds.

Book of Reference

Istoriya Turkmenskoi SSR. 2 vols. Ashkhabad, 1957

UZBEKISTAN
Ozbekiston Soviet Sotsialistik Respublikasy

HISTORY. In Oct. 1917 the Tashkent Soviet assumed authority, and in the following years established its power throughout Turkestan. The semi-independent Khanates of Khiva and Bokhara were first (1920) transformed into People's Republics, then (1923–24) into Soviet Socialist Republics and finally merged in the Uzbek SSR and other republics.

The Uzbek Soviet Socialist Republic was formed on 27 Oct. 1924 from lands formerly included in Turkestan. It includes a large part of the Samarkand region, the southern part of the Syr Darya, Western Ferghana, the western plains of Bukhara, the Kara-Kalpak ASSR and the Uzbek regions of Khorezm. In May 1925

Uzbekistan, by the decision of the Congress of Soviets of the USSR, was accepted as one of the constituent republics of the Soviet Union.

AREA AND POPULATION. Uzbekistan is bordered on the north by the Kazakh Soviet Socialist Republic, on the east by the Kirghiz Soviet Socialist Republic and the Tadzhik Soviet Socialist Republic, on the south by Afghánistán and on the west by the Turkmen Soviet Socialist Republic. The Uzbeks, who form 68·7% (1979 census) of the population, were the ruling race in Central Asia until the arrival of the Russians during the third quarter of the 19th century. The several native states over which Uzbek dynasties formerly ruled were founded in the 15th century upon the ruins of Tamerlane's empire. The Uzbek speak Jagatai Turkish, which is related to Osmanli and Azerbaijan Turkish; many are Sunni Moslems. Russians numbered (census 1979) 10·8%, Tadzhiks, 3·9%, Tatars 4·2%.

The area of Uzbekistan is 447,400 sq. km (172,741 sq. miles). The population in Jan. 1986 was 18,487,000 (42% urban). The country comprises the following regions: Andizhan, Bukhara, Dzhizak, Ferghana, Kashkadar, Khorezm, Namangan, Navoi, Samarkand, Surkhan-Darya, Syr-Darya, Tashkent and the Autonomous Soviet Socialist Republic of Kara Kalpakia. The capital of the Republic is Tashkent; other large towns are Samarkand, Andizhan, Namangan. There are 109 towns, 93 urban settlements and 156 rural districts.

On 19 Sept. 1963 the Supreme Soviet of the USSR confirmed decisions of the Supreme Soviets of Kazakhstan and Uzbekistan, transferring over 40,000 sq. km from the former to the latter to ensure more efficient use of the 'Hungry Steppe'.

CONSTITUTION AND GOVERNMENT. The Supreme Soviet, elected in 1985, consists of 510 deputies (1 per 15,000 population); 183 are women, 346 Communists. A new Constitution was adopted in April 1978.

At elections to the regional, district, urban and rural Soviets (21 June 1987), of 105,484 deputies returned, 50,460 (47·8%) were women, 58,448 (55·4%) non-Party and 66,918 (63·4%) industrial workers and collective farmers.

President, Presidium of the Supreme Soviet: A. Salimov.
Chairman, Council of Ministers: G. Kh. Kadyrov.
First Secretary, Communist Party: R. N. Nishanov.

FINANCE. Budget estimates (in 1m. rubles), 1987, 8,902; 1988 (plan), 9,012.

AGRICULTURE. Uzbekistan is a land of intensive farming, based on artificial irrigation. It is the chief cotton-growing area in the USSR and the third in the world. About 3·7m. hectares of collective and state farmland have irrigation networks, totalling over 150,000 km in length, and all are in full use.

In 1939 the Ferghana Canal (270 km) was built. During 1940, among the irrigation canals completed were: the North Ferghana Canal (165 km), and Andreyev South Ferghana Canal (108 km) and the first section of the Tashkent Canal (63 km). A canal from the Amu-Darya to Bokhara across the Kzyl-Kum and Ust-Urt deserts (180 km) was completed in 1965. A 200-km canal joining the river Zeravshan with the Kashka Darya at the village of Paruz was completed in Aug. 1955; it is part of the Iski–Angara Canal. The first section (93 km) of a canal irrigating the southern 'Hungry Steppe' was opened in 1960; 500,000 hectares of this desert were under cultivation in 1967.

Agriculture flourishes, particularly in the well-watered, warm, rich oases areas, such as the Ferghana valley, Zeravshan, Tashkent and Khorezm, where cotton, fruit, silk and rice are cultivated. In the higher-lying plains grain is grown; the wide desert and semi-desert area of Western Uzbekistan is mainly given to pasture land and the breeding of the Karakul sheep; there is a Karakul institute at Samarkand.

Orchards occupied 206,000 hectares and the vineyards 133,000 hectares in 1985. The Central Asian Branch of the Scientific Research Institute of Viticulture in Tashkent has produced new frost resistant grapes by crossing the wild Amur grape with Central Asian and European types. In 1985 there were 856 collective farms and 1,085 state farms, with 188,900 tractors and 11,400 cotton picking and grain combines. Ploughing, cotton-sowing and cultivation are completely mechanized; cotton picking over 46%.

Uzbekistan provides 65% of the total cotton, 50% of the total rice and 60% of the total lucerne grown in the USSR. The area under crops was 2,189,000 hectares in 1913, 3,036,000 hectares in 1940 and 4,400,000 hectares in 1986.

Livestock on 1 Jan. 1986: 4·1m. cattle, 9·3m. sheep and goats and 700,000 pigs.

Output of main agricultural products (in 1,000 tonnes) in 1985: Grain, 1,541; cotton, 5,382; potatoes, 241; vegetables, 2,386; fruit, 631; grapes, 635; meat, 386; milk, 2,439; eggs, 1,948m.; wool, 23·5.

Afforestation over an area of 50,000 hectares has been carried out to protect the Bokhara and Karakul oases from the advancing Kzyl-Kum sands and to stop the sand-drifts in a number of districts of Central Ferghana.

INDUSTRY. Of its mineral resources, in addition to oil and coal, copper and building materials and ozocerite deposits are now also exploited. New very rich coal deposits were discovered in 1944 and 1947 near Tashkent.

There are over 1,600 factories and mills. They include a factory of agricultural machinery (in Tashkent), a cement factory, a sulphur-mine, an oxygen factory, a paper-mill, a leather factory, textile-mills, clothing factories, iron and steel works, the Chirchik electro-chemical plant, a superphosphate plant in Kokand and oil refineries, coalmines, etc. Output in 1985 included 26,400 tractors, 1,868m. bricks, 1·6m. tonnes cotton fibre, 2,007 tonnes silk fabrics, 35·2m. pairs leather footwear, 881m. cans of preserves, 63·9m. pairs hosiery. Gold is being worked at Muruntau, Chadak and Kochbulak.

The Tashkent power station (2m. kw.) was completed in 1971. Power output in 1985 was 47,900m. kwh. (481m. kwh. in 1940). Two natural-gas pipelines (Djai-kak–Tashkent, Ferghana–Kokand) and a third from Bokhara to the Urals are operating. Natural gas output (1976) was 36,100m. cu. metres.

In 1985 there were 4,834,000 industrial and office workers in the national economy.

COMMUNICATIONS. The total length of railway in 1986 was 3,480 km. Branches lead to Karshe-Kitab, Kerki-Termez, Jalal-Abad, Namangan, Andijan and other centres. In 1947–55 a new line was built from Chardzhou to Kungrad.

The Great Uzbek Highway was completed in April 1941. Total length of motor roads in 1986 was 80,300 km (hard surface, 66,700 km). Inland waterways, 1,100 km.

An airline, serving all of Central Asia, is most developed in Uzbekistan.

Newspapers (1985). There were 195 newspapers in the Uzbek language out of a total of 286. Daily circulation of Uzbek-language newspapers, 4·1m.; in all languages, 5·5m.

EDUCATION. In 1985–86 there were 9,200 elementary and secondary schools with 4·4m. pupils, 42 higher educational establishments with 285,500 students and 249 technical colleges with 281,700 students. Uzbekistan has an Academy of Sciences, founded in 1943, with 37 institutions and 4,149 academic staff; there were 188 research institutes with a scientific staff of 38,100 in Jan. 1986. There are universities and medical schools in Tashkent and Samarkand. In Jan. 1986, 1,096,000 children were attending pre-school institutions.

The Uzbek Arabic script was in 1929 replaced by the Latin alphabet which in 1940 was superseded by one based on the Cyrillic alphabet.

HEALTH. In 1985 there were 61,900 doctors and 223,500 hospital beds.

Book of Reference

Istoriya Uzbekskoi SSR. 4 vols. Tashkent, 1967–68
Waterson, N., (ed.), *Uzbek-English Dictionary.* London, 1980

KARAKALPAK AUTONOMOUS SOVIET SOCIALIST REPUBLIC

Area, 164,900 sq. km (63,920 sq. miles); population (Jan. 1986), 1,108,000. Capital, Nukus (146,000). The Karakalpaks are first mentioned in written records in the 16th century as tributary to Bokhara, and later to the Kazakh Khanate. In the second half of the 19th century, as a result of the Russian conquest of Central Asia, they came under Russian rule. On 11 May 1925 the territory was constituted within the then Kazakh Autonomous Republic (of the Russian Federation) as an Autonomous Region. On 20 March 1932 it became an Autonomous Republic within the Russian Federation, and on 5 Dec. 1936 it became part of the Uzbek SSR. Census (1979) Karakalpaks were 31·1% of population, Uzbeks, 31·5% and Kazakhs, 26·9%.

185 deputies were elected to its Supreme Soviet on 24 Feb. 1985, of whom 69 were women and 118 Communists.

Its manufactures are in the field of light industry—bricks, leather goods, furniture, canning, wine. In Jan. 1985 cattle numbered 332,200 and sheep and goats, 594,500. There were 38 collective and 124 state farms. The total cultivated area in 1985 was 350,400 hectares.

In 1984–85 there were 287,600 pupils at schools, 19,700 at technical colleges, and 6,169 at university. There is a branch of the Uzbek Academy of Sciences with 190 scientific staff.

There were 2,600 doctors and 12,800 hospital beds.

TADZHIKISTAN
Respublikai Sovieth Sotsialistii Tojikiston

HISTORY. The Tadzhik Soviet Socialist Republic was formed from those regions of Bokhara and Turkestan where the population consisted mainly of Tadzhiks. It was admitted as a constituent republic of the Soviet Union on 5 Dec. 1929.

AREA AND POPULATION. Tadzhikistan is situated between 39° 40′ and 36° 40′ N. lat. and 67° 20′ and 75° E. long., north of the Oxus (Amu-Darya). On the west and north it is bordered by Uzbekistan and by the Kirghiz Soviet Socialist Republic; on the east by Chinese Turkestan and on the south by Afghánistán. It includes three regions (Leninabad, Kurgan-Tyube and Kulyab) and 43 rural districts, 18 towns and 49 urban settlements, together with the Gorno-Badakhshan Autonomous Region. Its highest mountains are Communism Peak (7,495 metres) and Lenin Peak (7,127 metres). Even the lowest valleys in the Pamirs are not below 3,500 metres above sea-level. The huge mountain glaciers are the source of many rapid rivers—the tributaries of the Amu-Darya, which flows from east to west along the southern border of Tadzhikistan. About 58·8% of the population are Tadzhiks. They speak an Iranian dialect, little different from Persian, and they are considered to be the descendants of the original Aryan population of Turkestan. Unlike the Persians, the Tadzhiks are mostly Sunnis. Of the rest, 22·9% are Uzbeks living in the north-west of the republic. Russians and Ukrainians number 10·4% (1979 census).

The area of the territory is 143,100 sq. km (55,240 sq. miles). Population (Jan. 1987), 4,807,000. The capital is Dushanbe. Other large towns are Leninabad (153,000), Kurgan-Tyube, Kulyab.

CONSTITUTION AND GOVERNMENT. The Supreme Soviet, elected in 1985, consists of 350 deputies (1 per 5,000 population); 126 are women and 238 Communists. A new Constitution was adopted in April 1978.

At elections to the district, urban and rural Soviets and the regional Soviet of

Gorno-Badakhshan (21 June 1987), out of 28,801 deputies returned 14,116 (49%) were women, 16,440 (57·1%) non-Party and 20,398 (70·8%) industrial workers and collective farmers.

Chairman, Presidium of the Supreme Soviet: G. Pallaev.
Chairman, Council of Ministers: I. Kh. Khaeev.
First Secretary, Communist Party: K. M. Makhkamov.

FINANCE. Budget estimates (in 1 m. rubles), 1987, 1,977; 1988 (plan), 2,109.

AGRICULTURE. The occupations of the population are mainly farming, horticulture and cattle breeding. Area under crops in 1986 was 803,000 hectares (1913, 494,000; 1940, 807,000). There are 43,000 km of irrigation canals: the irrigation networks cover about 634,000 hectares of land.

Tadzhikistan grows many varieties of fruit, including apricots, figs, olives, pomegranates, a local variety of lemons and oranges, and in the south sugar-cane has been grown. Even on the highest mountain plateaux of the Pamirs, 'the roof of the world', the biological station of Tadzhikistan (3,860 metres above sea-level) has succeeded in raising crops of 60 varieties of barley, 10 varieties of oats, 4 of wheat, as well as vegetables. Eucalyptus and geranium are grown for the perfumery industry. Jute, rice and millet are also grown.

Tadzhikistan contains rich pasture lands, and cattle breeding is a very important branch of its agriculture. Livestock on 1 Jan. 1986: 1·4m. cattle, 3·2m. sheep and goats and 183,600 pigs.

The Gissar sheep is famous in the south for its meat and fat; the Karakul sheep is widely bred for its wool.

There were 157 collective farms (all with electric power) and 299 state farms in 1986, with 35,200 tractors and 1,600 cotton and grain combine harvesters.

Output of main agricultural products (in 1,000 tonnes) in 1985: Grain, 326; cotton, 935; potatoes, 185; vegetables, 473; fruit, 240; grapes, 171; meat, 105; milk, 547; eggs, 469m.; wool, 5.

INDUSTRY. The original small-scale handicraft industries have been replaced by big industrial enterprises, including mining, engineering, food, textile, clothing and silk factories.

There are rich deposits of brown coal, lead, zinc and oil (in the north of the republic), rare elements, such as uranium, radium, arsenic and bismuth. Asbestos, mica, corundum and emery, lapis lazuli, potassium salts, sulphur and other minerals have been found in other parts of the republic.

Industrial output in 1985 included 1,066,000 cu. metres ferroconcrete, 303·4m. bricks, 282,700 tonnes cotton fibre, 12·6m. items knitwear, 33·1m. pairs hosiery, 9·8m. pairs leather footwear.

There are 80 big electrical stations. The hydro-electric Varzob station began to operate in 1954, that at Kairak-Kum on the Syr Darya River was completed in 1957 and 2 more at Murgab in 1964. Output in 1985 was 15,700m. kwh. (in 1940, 62m. kwh.).

Construction of an electro-chemical combine, the largest in the USSR, has begun in the Yavan steppe in south Tadzhikistan, and the 3·2m. kw. power station in the upper reaches of the Vakhsh River was near completion in 1979.

In 1985 there were 1,101,000 industrial and office workers in the national economy.

COMMUNICATIONS

Roads. In Jan. 1986 there were 19,200 km of motor roads. Of these, 15,800 km are hard surface, including the Osh–Khorog (700 km), Yasui–Bazar–Charm (107 km) and Dushanbe–Khorog in the Pamirs (557 km) roads.

Railways. A railway line between Termez and Dushanbe (258 km) connects the republic with the railway system of the USSR. The mountainous nature of the republic makes ordinary railway construction difficult; accordingly 345 km of narrow gauge railways have been constructed (Kurgan–Tyube–Piandzh and Dushanbe–Kurgan–Tyube, connecting Dushanbe with the cotton-growing Vakhsh valley are particularly important). Length of railways, 1986, 470 km.

Aviation. Dushanbe is connected by air with Moscow, Tashkent, Baku and the regional and district centres of the republic.

Shipping. A steamship line on the Amu-Darya runs between Termez, Sarava and Jilikulam on the river Vakhsh (200 km).

Newspapers (1985). There were 71 newspapers, 60 in Tadzhik. Daily circulation of Tadzhik-language newspapers, 1,087,000; in all languages, 1,437,000.

EDUCATION. In 1985–86 there were 3,100 primary and secondary schools with 1.2m. pupils, 10 higher educational institutions with 55,100 students and 39 technical colleges with 40,200 students; the Tadzhik state university had 12,467 students. In Jan. 1986, 131,000 children were attending pre-school institutions. In 1951 an Academy of Sciences was established; it has 16 institutions, the scientific staff of which numbers 1,514; there are 61 research institutions in all, with 8,400 scientific personnel in Jan. 1986. The Pamir research station is the highest altitude meteorological observatory in the world.

In 1940 a new alphabet based on Cyrillic was introduced.

HEALTH. There are 277 hospitals as well as maternity homes, clinics and special institutes to combat tropical diseases. There were 12,400 doctors in 1985 and 48,500 hospital beds.

GORNO-BADAKHSHAN AUTONOMOUS REGION

Comprising the Pamir massif along the borders of Afghánistán and China, the region was set up on 2 Jan. 1925. Area, 63,700 sq. km (24,590 sq. miles); population (Jan. 1986), 149,000 (83% Tadjiks, 11% Kirghiz). Capital, Khorog (14,800). The inhabitants are predominantly Ismaili Moslems.

Mining industries are developed (gold, rock-crystal, mica, coal, salt). Wheat, fruit and fodder crops are grown and cattle and sheep are bred in the western parts. In 1985 there were 73,400 cattle, 345,500 sheep and goats. Total area under cultivation, 18,400 hectares.

In 1984–85 44,800 pupils were attending 266 schools.

Books of Reference

Academy of Science of Tadzhikistan, *Istoriya Tadzhikskogo Naroda.* 3 vols. Moscow, 1963–65
Luknitsky, P., *Soviet Tajikistan* [In English]. Moscow, 1954

KIRGHIZIA
Kyrgyz Sovietik Sotsialistik Respublikasy

HISTORY. After the establishment of the Soviet regime in Russia, Kirghizia became part of Soviet Turkestan, which itself became an Autonomous Soviet Socialist Republic within the RSFSR in April 1921. In 1924, when Central Asia was reorganized territorially on a national basis, Kirghizia was separated from Turkestan and formed into an autonomous region within the RSFSR. On 1 Feb. 1926 the Government of the RSFSR transformed Kirghizia into an Autonomous Soviet Socialist Republic within the RSFSR, and finally in Dec. 1936 Kirghizia was proclaimed one of the constituent Soviet Socialist Republics of the USSR.

AREA AND POPULATION. The territory of Kirghizia covers 198,500 sq. km (76,460 sq. miles), and its population in Jan. 1987 was 4,143,000. The republic comprises 3 regions: Issyk-Kul, Naryn and Osh. There are 18 towns, 31 urban settlements and 40 rural districts. Its capital is Frunze (formerly Pishpek). Other large towns are Osh (188,000), Przhevalsk (56,000), Kyzyl-Kiya, Tokmak.

Kirghizia is situated on the Tien-Shan mountains and bordered on the east by China, on the west by Kazakhstan and Uzbekistan, on the north by Kazakhstan and in the south by Tadzhikistan. The Kirghizians are of Turkic origin and form 47·9% (1979 census) of the population; the rest are Russians (25·9%), Ukrainians (3·1%), Uzbeks (12·1%) and Tatars (2%).

CONSTITUTION AND GOVERNMENT. The Supreme Soviet, elected in 1985, consists of 350 deputies (1 per 5,000 population); 127 are women, 235 Communists. A new Constitution was adopted in April 1978.

At elections to the regional, district, urban and rural Soviets (21 June 1987), of the 28,063 deputies returned, 13,652 (48·6%) were women, 15,817 (56·4%) non-Party and 18,663 (66·5%) industrial workers and collective farmers.

Chairman, Presidium of the Supreme Soviet: T. Akmatov.
Chairman, Council of Ministers: A. D. Dzhumagulov.
First Secretary, Communist Party: A. M. Masaliev.

FINANCE. Budget estimates (in 1m. rubles), 1987, 2,266; 1988 (plan), 2,388.

AGRICULTURE. Kirghizia is famed for its livestock breeding. On 1 Jan. 1986 there were 1·1m. cattle, 400,000 pigs, 10·2m. sheep and goats. Yaks are bred as meat and dairy cattle, and graze on high altitudes unsuitable for other cattle. Crossed with domestic cattle, hybrids are produced much heavier than ordinary Kirghiz cattle and giving twice the yield of milk. The Kirghizian horse is famed for its endurance, but it is of small stature; it has in recent years been crossed with Don, Arab and other breeds.

On 1 Jan. 1986 there were 176 collective and 290 state farms. Area under crops (1985), 1·3m. hectares (1913, 640,000; 1940, 1,056,000). There were 29,100 tractors and 5,100 grain combine harvesters in 1986; nearly all collective and state farms received electric power.

Kirghizia raises wheat sufficient for its own use and other grains and fodder, particularly lucerne; also sugar-beet, hemp, kenaf, kendyr, tobacco, medicinal plants and rice. Sericulture, fruit, grapes and vegetables and bee-keeping are major branches of Kirghiz agriculture. Agriculture is highly mechanized; nearly all the area under crops is worked by tractors. In 1983 irrigation networks in collective and state farms covered 974,000 hectares; practically all were in use. A canal in the western Tien-Shan ranges and a reservoir in the Urto-Tokoi mountains are being constructed.

The health resorts of Jety-Oguz (7,200 ft) and Jalal-Abad are famous for their mild alpine climate and mineral springs.

Output of main agricultural products (in 1,000 tonnes) in 1985: Grain, 1,477; sunflower seeds, 58; potatoes, 306; vegetables, 445; fruit, 76; grapes, 27; meat, 169; milk, 771; eggs, 532m.; wool, 32·5.

INDUSTRY. Kirghizia contains over 500 large modern industrial enterprises including sugar refineries, tanneries, cotton and wool-cleansing works, flour-mills, a tobacco factory, food, timber, textile, engineering, metallurgical, oil and mining enterprises.

Production in 1985 included 378m. electric lamps, 18·4m. items knitwear, 221,000 washing machines, 905,400 cu. metres ferroconcrete, 23·5m. pairs hosiery, 11·4m. pairs leather footwear, 106·3m. cans conserves.

Hydro-electric power stations are being built in the Central Tien-Shans and the cotton-growing districts in the Osh Region, the Chui valley and on the shore of Lake Issyk-Kul. Power output (1985) was 10,500m. kwh.

There were, in 1985, 1,239,000 industrial and office workers in the national economy.

COMMUNICATIONS. In the north a railway runs from Lugovaya through Frunze to Rybachi on Lake Issyk-Kul. Towns in the southern valleys are linked by short lines with the Ursatyevskaya–Andizhan railway in Uzbekistan. Total length of railway (Jan. 1986) is 370 km. Most of the traffic is by road; there were 32,100 km of motor roads (23,100 hard surface) in 1986. A road tunnel through the Tien-Shan mountains at an altitude of 9,600 ft, connecting Frunze and Osh, is being constructed. Inland waterways, 600 km. Airlines link Frunze with Moscow and Tashkent.

Newspapers (1985). Of 111 newspapers with a daily 1.4m. circulation, 61 with 792,000 circulation are in the Kirghiz language.

EDUCATION. Kirghizia had 1,800 primary and secondary schools with 900,000 pupils in 1985–86; 176,000 children were attending pre-school institutions. There were also 10 higher educational institutions with 58,200 students, 45 technical and teachers' training colleges with 50,900 students, as well as music and art schools. The Kirghizian Academy of Sciences was established in 1954. In 1986 there were 18 research institutes, with 1,571 scientific staff, operating under its auspices; altogether there were 9,100 scientific staff in 1986. A university was opened in 1951. In Sept. 1940 a new alphabet, based on Cyrillic, was introduced.

HEALTH. In 1985 there were 13,500 doctors and 48,200 hospital beds.

Books of Reference

Istoriya Kirgizskoi SSR. 5 vols. Frunze, 1984 ff.
Ryazantsev, S. N., *Kirghizia.* Moscow, 1951

UNITED ARAB EMIRATES

Federal Capital: Abu Dhabi
Population: 1·77m. (1986)
GNP per capita: US$19,270 (1985)

HISTORY. From Sha'am, 35 miles south-west of Ras Musam dam, for nearly 400 miles to Khor al Odeid at the south-eastern end of the peninsula of Qatar, the coast, formerly known as the Trucial Coast, of the Gulf (together with 50 miles of the coast of the Gulf of Oman) belongs to the rulers of the 7 Trucial States. In 1820 these rulers signed a treaty prescribing peace with the British Government. This treaty was followed by further agreements providing for the suppression of the slave trade and by a series of other engagements, of which the most important are the Perpetual Maritime Truce (May 1853) and the Exclusive Agreement (March 1892). Under the latter, the sheikhs, on behalf of themselves, their heirs and successors, undertook that they would on no account enter into any agreement or correspondence with any power other than the British Government, receive foreign agents, cede, sell or give for occupation any part of their territory save to the British Government.

British forces withdrew from the Gulf at the end of 1971 and the treaties whereby Britain had been responsible for the defence and foreign relations of the Trucial States were terminated, being replaced on 2 Dec. 1971 by a treaty of friendship between Britain and the United Arab Emirates. The United Arab Emirates (formed 2 Dec. 1971) consists of the former Trucial States: Abu Dhabi, Dubai, Sharjah, Ajman, Umm al Qaiwain, Ras al Khaimah (joined in Feb. 1972) and Fujairah. The small state of Kalba was merged with Sharjah in 1952.

AREA AND POPULATION. The Emirates are bounded north by the Gulf and Oman, east by the Gulf of Oman and Oman, south and west by Saudi Arabia, north-west by Qatar. The area of these states is approximately 32,300 sq. miles (83,657 sq. km). The total population at census (1985), 1,622,393. Estimate (1986) 1·77m. In 1980, 69% were male and 72% lived in urban areas. About one-tenth are nomads.

Population of the 7 Emirates, 1985 census: Abu Dhabi, 670,125; Ajman, 64,318; Dubai, 419,104; Fujairah, 54,425; Ras al-Khaimah, 116,470; Sharjah, 268,722; Umm al Qaiwain, 29,229.

The chief cities (1980 census) are Dubai (265,702), Abu Dhabi, the provisional federal capital (242,975), Sharjah (125,149) and Ras al-Khaimah (42,000).

CLIMATE. The country experiences desert conditions, with rainfall both limited and erratic. The period May to Nov. is generally rainless, while the wettest months are Feb. and March. Temperatures are very high in the summer months. Dubai. Jan. 74°F (23·4°C), July 108°F (42·3°C). Annual rainfall 2·4" (60 mm). Sharjah. Jan. 64°F (17·8°C), July 91°F (32°C). Annual rainfall 4·2" (105 mm).

GOVERNMENT. The Emirates is a federation, headed by a Supreme Council which is composed of the 7 rulers and which in turn appoints a Council of Ministers. The Council of Ministers drafts legislation and a federal budget; its proposals are submitted to a federal National Council of 40 elected members which may propose amendments but has no executive power.

President: HH Sheikh Zayed bin Sultan al Nahyan, Ruler of Abu Dhabi.

Members of the Supreme Council of Rulers:

HH Sheikh Rashid bin Said al-Maktoum, Vice-President and Ruler of Dubai.
HH Sheikh Sultan bin Mohammed al-Qasimi, Ruler of Sharjah.
HH Sheikh Saqr bin Mohammed al-Qasimi, Ruler of Ras al-Khaimah.
HH Sheikh Rashid bin Ahmed al-Mualla, Ruler of Umm al Qaiwain.
HH Sheikh Hamad bin Mohammed al Sharqi, Ruler of Fujairah.
HH Sheikh Humaid bin Rashid al-Nuaimi, Ruler of Ajman.

The Council of Ministers in Nov. 1987 was:

Prime Minister: H.H. Sheikh Rashid bin Said al-Maktoum.

Deputy Prime Ministers: Sheikh Maktoum bin Rashid al-Maktoum; Sheikh Hamdan bin Mohammed al-Nahyan.

Interior: Sheikh Mubarak bin Mohammed al-Nahyan. *Finance and Industry:* Sheikh Hamdan bin Rashid al-Maktoum. *Defence:* Sheikh Mohammed bin Rashid al-Maktoum. *Economy and Trade:* Saif al-Jarwan. *Information and Culture:* Sheikh Ahmed bin Hamed. *Communications:* Mohammed Saeed al-Mualla. *Public Works and Housing:* Mohammed Khalifa al-Kindi. *Education and Youth:* Faraj al-Mazroui. *Petroleum and Mineral Resources:* Dr Mana Said al-Oteiba. *Electricity and Water:* Hamaid Nasser al-Owais. *Justice:* Abdullah Hamid al-Mazroui. *Health:* Hamad al-Madfa. *Labour and Social Affairs:* Khalfan Mohammed al-Roumi. *Planning:* Sheikh Humaid al-Mualla. *Agriculture and Fisheries:* Saeed al-Raghbani. *Minister of State for Internal Affairs:* Hamouda bin Ali Dhahiri. *Minister of State for Foreign Affairs:* Rashid Abdulla Al Nuaimi. *Minister of State for Cabinet Affairs:* Said al-Ghaith. *Minister of State for Supreme Council Affairs:* Sheikh Abdel Aziz al-Qasimi. *Islamic Affairs and AWQAF:* Sheikh Mohammed al-Khazraji. *Minister of State for Finance and Industry:* Ahmad Hamid al-Tayer. *Without Portfolio:* Sheikh Ahmad bin Sultan al-Qasimi.

National flag: Three horizontal stripes of green, white, black, with a vertical red strip in the hoist.

DEFENCE

Army. The Army consists of 1 Royal Guard, 1 armoured, 1 mechanized infantry, 2 infantry, 1 artillery and 1 air defence brigades. Equipment includes 100 AMX-30 and 36 Lion OF-40 Mk 2 main battle tanks. The strength was (1988) 40,000.

Navy. The naval flotilla includes 6 new German-built missile armed fast attack craft, 9 British-built patrol craft, 1 maintenance craft and 2 tenders. Personnel in 1988 numbered 1,200 officers and ratings.

The Coast Guard flotilla comprises 11 armed coastal patrol craft, 20 armed small patrol cutters, 26 light launches, 1 amphibious craft, 2 diving tenders, 1 water carrier and 5 tugs.

Air Force. Formation of an air wing in Abu Dhabi, to support land forces, began in 1968 with the purchase of some light STOL transports and helicopters. Expansion has been rapid. Current equipment includes 24 Mirage 5 supersonic fighter-bombers, 3 Mirage 5R tactical reconnaissance aircraft and 3 Mirage 5D 2-seat trainers (to be replaced by Mirage 2000s, with delivery of first 18 beginning early in 1988); 4 C-130 Hercules and 4 Buffalo turboprop transports; 4 CASA C-212 Avio-car ECM/elint aircraft; about 40 Gazelle, Alouette III, Puma, Super Puma and Ecureuil helicopters; 23 PC-7 Turbo-Trainers and 15 Hawk light attack/trainers. Initial personnel were mostly British but considerable assistance is now being received from Arab countries and from Pakistan. The air wing became the Air Force of Abu Dhabi in 1972, in which year 3 JetRanger helicopters were transferred to the air wing of the Union Defence Force, since combined with the Dubai Police Air Wing to form a single component of the United Emirates Air Force. Current equipment of the Dubai Air Wing of the UEAF, bought mainly in Italy, comprises 4 Aermacchi MB 326K jet light attack aircraft, 1 Aeritalia G222 twin-turboprop transport, 1 piston-engined SF.260W armed basic trainer, 5 SF.260TP turboprop trainers, and 2 MB 326L, 6 MB 339 and 8 Hawk jet trainers, 4 Bell 205A-1, 3 Bell 212, 4 Bell 214 and 6 JetRanger helicopters and 1 Cessna 182 liaison aircraft, plus 2 L-100-30 Hercules transports and a variety of other types for VIP use. Sharjah formed a small aviation force, the Amiri Guard Air Wing, at the end of 1984. The service is essentially an internal security and transport force operating 1 Short 330 and 1 Skyvan for transport duties and 3 JetRanger helicopters. Personnel (1988) 1,500.

INTERNATIONAL RELATIONS

Membership. The UAE is a member of UN, GCC and of the Arab League.

ECONOMY

Budget. Revenue is principally derived from oil-concession payments. The federal budget (1986) was expenditure DH 14,023m. and revenue 12,837m.

Currency. The UAE issued its own currency in 1972 based on the *dirham*. 1 UAE *dirham* = 100 *fils*. There are notes of 5, 10, 50, 100 and 500 *dirham* and coins of 1 and 5 *dirham* and 1, 5, 10, 25 and 50 *fils*. Rate of exchange, March 1988: £1 = 6·50 *dirham*; US$1 = 3·67 *dirham*.

Banking. The UAE Central Bank was established in 1980. The Union Bank of the Middle East took over the Emirates National Bank in Jan. 1985 and the Dubai Bank in April 1985. Three of Abu Dhabi's largest local banks (Khaleej Commercial Bank, Emirates Commercial Bank and Federal Commercial Bank) merged in May 1985 to form Abu Dhabi Commercial Bank, with authorized capital of 1,500m. dirhams and paid-up capital of 1,250m. dirhams. 60% of its shares are owned by the Abu Dhabi government and the balance by private investors. The National Bank of Abu Dhabi had a paid-up capital of 880m. dirhams at the end of 1984. By Nov. 1986, the foreign assets of commercial banks were DH 45,800m. The government-funded Emirates Industrial Bank was established in 1983.

In 1987 there were 53 commercial banks, 19 of which were local and 34 foreign-owned with over 284 branches.

ENERGY AND NATURAL RESOURCES

Electricity. Production (1986) 16,440m. kwh. Supply in Abu Dhabi 230 volts; Dubai 220 volts and in the remaining Emirates 240 volts; all 50 Hz.

Oil. Total production of crude oil (1985) 442·3m. bbls. Reserves (1986) 33,000m. bbls.

Abu Dhabi. Ownership in 1976 was as follows: *ADPC*, 60% Government; 9·5% BP; 9·5% Shell; 9·5% CFP; 4·75% Mobil; 2% Partex. *ADMA*, 60% Government; 26·7% BP/Japan Oil Development Co.; 13·3% CFP. A Japanese company, Abu Dhabi Oil Co. (ADOCO) began production from its Mubarraz field in 1973. There are other companies which have concessions in the State: Japan's Middle East Oil; a US consortium led by Pan Ocean Oil and Sunningdale Oils of Canada. A State Petroleum Co., the Abu Dhabi National Oil Co. (ADNOC), was formed in 1971 and began to set up its own tanker fleet known as the Abu Dhabi National Tankers Co. (ADNATCO). At the end of 1972 Abu Dhabi signed a participation agreement which would have given it an immediate 25% interest in the companies, rising to 51% by 1982. Oil production, 1987, 51·1m. tonnes.

Dubai. In July 1975 Dubai decided to take full control of all foreign oil and gas operations in the State. The companies were to remain however. A Dubai producing group was set up to comprise the foreign interests–US and continental companies. Dubai Petroleum Co. (DPC–a subsidiary of Continental Oil) has a 30% interest in this group; the other members are Dubai Marine Areas (*Compagnie Française des Pétroles*) with 50%; Deutsche Texaco with 10%; Dubai Sun Oil 5%; and Delfzee Dubai Petroleum (Wintershall) 5%. Oil production (1987) 18·2m. tonnes.

Sharjah. In Sharjah the concession is given to Crescent Oil, its shareholders are: Ashland Oil, Skelly Oil, Kerr-McGee, Cities Services and Juniper. Other oil concessions have recently been given to the Crystal Oil Co. of USA and the Reserves Oil and Gas Co. Oil production, 1987, 3·1m. tonnes.

Ajman. An oil concession was awarded to United Refining in 1974.

Umm al Qawain. The concession here was given to US Occidental Petroleum; another was awarded to a consortium led by the US company United Refinery.

Ras al-Khaimah. The Dutch oil firm Vitol took over Union's concession in 1973. Shell began prospecting in 1969 but pulled out in 1971. A concession in the same area was awarded to Peninsula Petroleum, a subsidiary of the US California Time Group, in 1973.

Gas. Abu Dhabi has reserves of natural gas, nationalized in 1976. The Abu Dhabi

Gas Liquefaction Plant at Das Island (51% ADNOC) has a capacity of 2m. tons LNG, 1m. tons LPG, 220,000 tons of light distillate and 230,000 tons of pelletized sulphur. Gas exports (1986) DH4,500m.

Water. Production of drinking water (1986) 11,600m. gallons. In 1986 the solar-powered Umm al Nar station produced 15,000 gallons a day. The first phase of the biggest solar-operated water production plant in the Gulf region (with an estimated daily capacity of 21m. gallons and 265 mw of electricity) was scheduled to be completed at Al Taweela in 1987, the second phase (40m. gallons and 400 mw) in 1990.

Agriculture. The fertile Buraimi Oasis, known as Al Ain, is largely in Abu Dhabi territory, but owing to lack of water and good soil there is little agriculture in the rest of UAE. Cultivated area (1985) 320,000 hectares. Production (1985): Red meat, 12,000 tonnes; poultry, 6,000 tonnes; dates, 60,000 tonnes; vegetables, 216; wheat, 1.

Livestock (1986): Cattle, 46,000; camels, 115,000; sheep, 382,000; goats, 778,000.

Fisheries. Sharjah exports shrimps and prawns; a fishmeal plant is operating in Ras al-Khaimah and plants are planned for Ajman and Sharjah. Catch (1984) 74,000 tonnes.

INDUSTRY AND TRADE

Industry. A fertilizer plant at Ruwais in Abu Dhabi, opened in 1984, produced 343,000 tonnes of ammonia and 353,000 tonnes of urea in 1985. Umm al-Nar has a plant producing salt, hydrochloric acid, chlorine, caustic soda and distilled water.

There were about 100 industrial and commercial companies in the Jebel Ali industrial zone in Dubai by 1987, including an aluminium smelter and power and desalination plant, opened in 1979. Production of aluminium in 1986, 155,605 tonnes, nearly all of which was exported.

There were 8 cement plants in 1987 (3 of them in Ras al-Khaimah), with a total annual capacity of 8m. tonnes. The home market for cement amounted to 25% of the total installed capacity of 6m. tonnes in 1986.

The 2 main steel rolling mills are in Dubai and Sharjah. Plastics are produced at factories in Dubai and Sharjah and mechanical dies and tools in Dubai. Fujairah has rockwool and ceramics factories. Ship repairs and steel fabrication are carried on in Ajman.

Commerce. Imports in 1985 for UAE were DH23,500m. Exports and re-exports (non-oil) totalled DH5,562m. Oil exports accounted for DH40,000m. and gas. DH5,200m.

Total trade between the UAE (excluding Abu Dhabi) and UK (British Department of Trade returns, in £1,000 sterling):

	1983	1984	1985	1986	1987
Imports to UK	107,574	60,550	71,688	59,428	81,218
Exports and re-exports from UK	254,862	296,948	374,616	413,651	329,008

Total trade between Abu Dhabi and UK (British Department of Trade returns, in £1,000 sterling):

	1983	1984	1985	1986	1987
Imports to UK	202,232	21,981	24,866	14,584	13,771
Exports and re-exports from UK	312,902	215,947	246,732	168,111	149,989

Tourism. In 1987 there were 85 hotels.

COMMUNICATIONS

Roads. In 1984 there were 2,200 km of roads and 230,000 vehicles.

Aviation. In 1987 there were 4 international airports. A number of cargo airlines also fly regularly to the country's major airports. An air-taxi service, Emirates Air Services, flying between Abu Dhabi and Dubai, began in June 1976. Dubai set up the airline, Emirates, in 1985.

Shipping. In 1987 there were 7 commercial sea ports. Jebel Ali is the largest. Abu

Dhabi has dry docks and there are smaller ports at Sharjah, Ras al-Khaimah and Fujairah. Jebel Ali is a port and industrial estate 35 km south-west of Dubai city and had (1982) 66 berths.

Post and Broadcasting. In 1983 there were 319,246 telephones, of which 113,629 were in Abu Dhabi and 98,010 in Dubai. In Sharjah a new telephone company has been formed and the other Northern States are now linked by telephone. The new Cable and Wireless Station at Jebel Ali in the State of Dubai links the system with the international communication network.

Television stations are at Abu Dhabi and Dubai, with extension of the service well advanced to the rest of the Emirates. Stations for The Voice of the Gulf Co-operation Council, a 6-state radio station, began broadcasting from Abu Dhabi in Aug. 1985. Estimated radios (1984) 190,000 and television sets over 110,000.

Newspapers (1987). There are a number of daily and weekly publications mostly in Arabic, but some in English, notably *The Emirates News* of Abu Dhabi, *The Gulf News*, a daily, published in Dubai and the *Khaleej Times* (daily), also published in Dubai.

JUSTICE, RELIGION, EDUCATION AND WELFARE

Justice. UAE subjects and citizens of all Arab and Moslem states are subject to the jurisdiction of the local courts. In the local courts the rules of Islamic law prevail. A new code of law is being produced for Abu Dhabi. In Dubai there is a court run by a *qadi*, while in some of the other States all legal cases are referred immediately to the Ruler or a member of his family, who will refer to a *qadi* only if he cannot settle the matter himself. In Abu Dhabi a professional Jordanian judge presides over the Ruler's Court.

Religion. Nearly all the inhabitants are Moslem of the Sunni, and a small minority of the Shi'ite sects.

Education In 1986–87 there were 122,543 in primary schools, 36,810 in preparatory schools and 20,753 in secondary schools. There were 1,712 students in religious schools, 597 in technical schools and (1987–88) 2,075 at university. There were 17,088 teachers and 551 schools in 1984–85.

Health. In 1984 there were 28 hospitals (4,853 beds) and 119 clinics. There were 1,840 physicians.

DIPLOMATIC REPRESENTATIVES

Of the UAE in Great Britain (30 Prince's Gate, London, SW7 1PT)
Chargé d'Affaires: Ali Mubarak Al Mansoori.

Of Great Britain in the UAE
Ambassador: M. L. Tait, CMG, LVO (at the British Embassy, Abu Dhabi).

Of the UAE in the USA (600 New Hampshire Ave., NW, Washington, D.C., 20037)
Ambassador: Ahmed S. Al-Mokarrab.

Of the USA in the UAE (Al-Sudan St., Abu Dhabi)
Ambassador: David Lyle Mack.

Of the UAE to the United Nations
Ambassador: Mohammed Hussain Al-Shaali.

Books of Reference

Middle East Annual Review. London
Bey, F. H., *From Trucial States to United Arab Emirates.* London, 1982
Heard-Bey, F., *From Trucial States to United Arab Emirates.* London, 1982
Khalifa, A. M., *The U.A.E.: Energy Development.* London, 1980
Mallakh, R.S., *The Economic Development of the United Arab Emirates,* London, 1981
Mostyn, T., *UAE-A MEED Practical Guide.* 2nd ed. London, 1986
Soffan, L. U., *Women of the United Arab Emirates.* London, 1980
Zahlan, R. S., *The Origins of the United Arab Emirates.* London, 1978

UNITED KINGDOM OF GREAT BRITAIN AND NORTHERN IRELAND

Capital: London
Population: 55·78m. (1981)
GNP per capita: US$7,860 (1985)

'Great Britain' is a geographical term describing the main island of the British Isles which comprises England, Scotland and Wales (so called to distinguish it from 'Little Britain' or Brittany). By the Act of Union, 1801, Great Britain and Ireland formed a legislative union as the United Kingdom of Great Britain and Ireland. Since the separation of Great Britain and Ireland in 1921 Northern Ireland remained within the Union which is now the United Kingdom of Great Britain and Northern Ireland. The United Kingdom does not include the Channel Islands or the Isle of Man which are direct dependencies of the Crown with their own legislative and taxation systems.

GREAT BRITAIN

AREA AND POPULATION. Area (in sq. km) and population (present on census night) at the census taken 5 April 1981:

Divisions	Area	Total
England	130,357	46,362,836
Wales	20,761	2,791,851
Scotland	78,762	5,130,735
	229,880	54,285,422

Population at the 4 previous decennial censuses:

Divisions	1931	1951	1961	1971
England [1]	37,359,045	41,159,213	43,460,525	46,019,000
Wales	2,158,374	2,598,675	2,644,023	2,731,000
Scotland	4,842,980	5,096,415	5,178,490	5,228,963
Army, Navy and Merchant Seamen abroad	434,532	—	—	—
Total	44,794,931	48,854,303	51,283,038	53,978,963

[1] Areas now recognised as part of Gwent, Wales, formed the English county of Monmouthshire until 1974.

Population (usually resident) at the census of 1981:

Divisions	Males	Females	Total
England	22,288,395	23,483,561	45,771,956
Wales	1,336,323	1,413,317	2,749,640
Scotland	2,428,472	2,606,843	5,035,315
Great Britain	26,053,190	27,503,721	53,556,911

In 1981 in Wales 21,283 persons 3 years of age and upwards were able to speak Welsh only, and 482,276 able to speak Welsh and English (preliminary figures): these totals represent 19% of the total population. In Scotland in 1981, 79,307 of the usually resident population could speak Gaelic (1·3%); 3,113 could read or write Gaelic, but could not speak it.

At the census of 1981, in England and Wales, there were 17,706,492 private households; in Great Britain, 19,500,113.

The age distribution in 1981 of the 'usually resident' population of England and Wales and Scotland was as follows (in 1,000):

Age-group		England and Wales	Scotland	Great Britain
Under	5	2,910	308	3,219
5 and under	10	3,207	344	3,551
10 ,,	15	3,846	425	4,271
15 ,,	20	4,020	447	4,467
20 ,,	25	3,564	394	3,959
25 ,,	35	6,931	701	7,632
35 ,,	45	5,885	588	6,473
45 ,,	55	5,474	575	6,049
55 ,,	65	5,410	541	5,951
65 ,,	70	2,426	241	2,667
70 ,,	75	2,062	204	2,265
75 ,,	85	2,280	221	2,501
85 and upwards		507	46	552
Total		48,522	5,035	53,557

At 30 June 1986 the estimated population of Great Britain was 55,196,400. Age and sex distribution: between 0 and 15, 5,339,700 males, 5,061,500 females; 15 and under 65, 18,185,700 males; 15 and under 60, 16,555,000 females; aged 65 and over, 3,353,200 males; 60 and over, 6,701,300 females.

England and Wales: The census population, (present on census night) of England and Wales 1801 to 1981:

Date of enumeration	Population	Pop. per sq. mile	Date of enumeration	Population	Pop. per sq. mile[1]
1801	8,892,536	152	1891	29,002,525	497
1811	10,164,256	174	1901	32,527,843	558
1821	12,000,236	206	1911	36,070,492	618
1831	13,896,797	238	1921	37,886,699	649
1841	15,914,148	273	1931	39,952,377	685
1851	17,927,609	307	1951	43,757,888	750
1861	20,066,224	344	1961	46,104,548	791
1871	22,712,266	389	1971	48,749,575	323
1881	25,974,439	445	1981	49,154,687	325

[1] Per sq. km from 1971

There is only one other major country in Europe, Netherlands (population density 421 persons per sq. km), more crowded than England and Wales.

The birth places of the 1981 'usually resident' population were: England, 41,552,500; Wales, 2,758,026; Scotland, 752,188; Northern Ireland, 209,042; Ireland, 579,833; Commonwealth, 1,429,407; foreign countries, 1,209,091.

Local authority areas in being from April 1974. Area in sq. km and population estimate 30 June 1986:

ENGLAND Metropolitan counties	Area sq. km	Population	Non-Metropolitan counties—contd.	Area sq. km	Population
Greater London	1,580	6,775,200	Derbyshire	2,631	916,800
Greater Manchester	1,286	2,579,500	Devon	6,715	999,000
Merseyside	652	1,467,600	Dorset	2,554	638,200
South Yorkshire	1,560	1,297,900	Durham	2,436	599,600
Tyne and Wear	540	1,135,500	East Sussex	1,795	689,700
West Midlands	899	2,632,300	Essex	3,674	1,512,100
West Yorkshire	2,039	2,053,100	Gloucestershire	2,638	517,100
			Hampshire	3,772	1,527,700
Non-metropolitan counties			Hereford and Worcester	3,927	654,500
Avon	1,338	946,600	Hertfordshire	1,634	985,700
Bedfordshire	1,235	521,000	Humberside	3,512	848,500
Berkshire	1,256	734,100	Isle of Wight	381	124,600
Buckinghamshire	1,883	612,900	Kent	3,732	1,500,900
Cambridgeshire	3,409	635,200	Lancashire	3,043	1,380,700
Cheshire	2,322	946,500	Leicestershire	2,553	875,000
Cleveland	583	557,600	Lincolnshire	5,885	567,300
Cornwall and Isles of			Norfolk	5,355	727,800
Scilly	3,546	448,200	Northamptonshire	2,367	554,400
Cumbria	6,809	486,600	Northumberland	5,033	301,000
			North Yorkshire	8,317	699,800

Non-Metropolitan counties—contd.	Area sq. km	Population	WALES	Area sq. km	Population
Nottinghamshire	2,164	1,006,400	Clwyd	2,425	399,600
Oxfordshire	2,611	574,700	Dyfed	5,765	339,000
Shropshire	3,490	392,700	Gwent	1,376	441,800
Somerset	3,458	448,900	Gwynedd	3,868	234,600
Staffordshire	2,716	1,021,000	Mid-Glamorgan	1,019	534,500
Suffolk	3,800	628,600	Powys	5,077	112,400
Surrey	1,655	1,011,400	South Glamorgan	416	395,700
Warwickshire	1,981	480,700	West Glamorgan	815	363,400
West Sussex	2,016	694,700			
Wiltshire	3,481	545,200			
			Total Wales		2,821,000
Total England		47,254,500			
			Total—England and Wales		50,075,400

County districts with populations of over 90,000 (estimate, 30 June 1986):

ENGLAND			
Allerdale	95,800	East Lindsey	110,500
Amber Valley	109,700	East Staffordshire	93,900
Arun	126,900	Elmbridge	110,300
Ashfield	106,700	Epping Forest	114,100
Ashford	92,400	Erewash	106,200
Aylesbury Vale	142,500	Exeter	99,300
Barnsley	222,200	Fareham	95,700
Basildon	156,900	Gateshead	207,300
Basingstoke and Deane	137,900	Gedling	107,100
Bassetlaw	104,900	Gillingham	95,900
Beverley	109,700	Gloucester	90,900
Birmingham	1,004,100	Gravesham	93,800
Blackburn	139,100	Grimsby	90,400
Blackpool	145,400	Guildford	125,000
Bolton	261,600	Halton	123,200
Bournemouth	152,200	Harrogate	145,200
Bracknell	93,200	Hartlepool	90,700
Bradford	463,100	Havant	118,900
Braintree	115,800	Hinckley and Bosworth	94,100
Breckland	101,900	Horsham	105,800
Brighton	141,900	Huntingdon	141,700
Bristol	391,500	Ipswich	118,300
Broadland	100,800	King's Lynn and West Norfolk	128,300
Broxtowe	106,100	Kingston upon Hull	258,000
Bury	172,600	Kirklees	376,600
Calderdale	193,100	Knowsley	163,800
Cambridge	99,800	Lancaster	130,000
Canterbury	127,700	Langbaurgh	146,800
Carlisle	101,400	Leeds	710,900
Charnwood	144,900	Leicester	281,100
Chelmsford	149,800	Lichfield	91,700
Cherwell	121,500	Liverpool	483,000
Chester	116,600	Luton	166,300
Chesterfield	96,700	Macclesfield	151,800
Chichester	104,400	Maidstone	133,700
Chiltern	90,800	Manchester	451,400
Chorley	94,500	Mansfield	100,300
Colchester	145,100	Mendip	93,500
Coventry	310,400	Mid-Bedfordshire	110,800
Crewe and Nantwich	96,500	Middlesbrough	144,300
Dacorum	132,600	Mid-Sussex	119,900
Darlington	99,200	Milton Keynes	161,800
Derby	216,200	Newark and Sherwood	106,600
Doncaster	289,300	Newbury	134,100
Dover	103,800	Newcastle under Lyme	117,800
Dudley	300,900	Newcastle upon Tyne	281,400
Easington	96,500	New Forest	159,000
East Devon	113,200	Northampton	172,500
East Hampshire	97,800	Northavon	126,200
East Hertfordshire [1]	118,100	North Bedfordshire	134,900
Eastleigh	99,500	North-East Derbyshire	97,600
		North Hertfordshire	111,600

ENGLAND—contd.

North Norfolk	90,200	Suffolk Coastal	106,000
North Tyneside	192,300	Sunderland	297,700
North Wiltshire	109,400	Swale	110,900
Norwich	121,600	Tameside	215,200
Nottingham	277,800	Taunton Deane	91,300
Nuneaton and Bedworth	113,100	Teignbridge	105,400
Oldham	220,000	Tendring	122,800
Oxford	116,200	Test Valley	99,300
Peterborough	148,200	Thamesdown	162,800
Plymouth	256,000	Thanet	123,600
Poole	126,400	Thurrock	124,100
Portsmouth	186,900	Tonbridge and Malling	99,700
Preston	125,000	Torbay	117,300
Reading	135,000	Trafford	216,300
Reigate and Banstead	115,800	Tunbridge Wells	98,400
Rochdale	206,600	Vale of White Horse	110,400
Rochester upon Medway	146,200	Vale Royal	113,500
Rotherham	252,100	Wakefield	309,300
Rushcliffe	96,900	Walsall	261,800
St Albans	128,700	Warrington	180,000
St Edmundsbury	91,500	Warwick	117,300
St Helens	187,900	Waveney	104,600
Salford	239,300	Waverley	112,500
Salisbury	103,400	Wealden	127,600
Sandwell	301,100	Welwyn Hatfield	93,300
Scarborough	103,700	West Lancashire	106,800
Sedgemoor	94,100	West Oxfordshire	93,600
Sefton	298,000	West Wiltshire	102,200
Sevenoaks	110,100	Wigan	306,600
Sheffield	534,300	Winchester	94,200
Shrewsbury and Atcham	91,300	Windsor and Maidenhead	132,400
Slough	98,500	Wirral	334,800
Solihull	202,200	Wokingham	140,900
Southampton	200,500	Wolverhampton	251,900
South Bedfordshire	109,000	Woodspring	177,800
South Cambridgeshire	117,200	Worthing	95,900
Southend on Sea	159,900	Wrekin	130,200
South Kesteven	101,600	Wychavon	98,800
South Lakeland	98,500	Wycombe	156,700
South Norfolk	99,400	Wyre	100,100
South Oxfordshire	133,000	Wyre Forest	93,000
South Ribble	98,300	York	101,600
South Somerset	139,000	WALES	
South Staffordshire	104,900	Cardiff	279,500
South Tyneside	156,900	Newport	129,800
Stafford	118,000	Ogwr	134,400
Staffordshire Moorlands	96,000	Rhymney Valley	104,100
Stockport	289,900	Swansea	187,000
Stockton on Tees	175,800	Taff Ely	94,800
Stoke on Trent	246,900	Torfaen	90,900
Stratford on Avon	105,700	Vale of Glamorgan	116,100
Stroud	106,700	Wrexham Maelor	114,700

The following table shows the distribution of the urban and rural population of England and Wales in 1951, 1961, 1971, and 1981.

		Population		Percentage	
	England and Wales	Urban districts [1]	Rural districts [1]	Urban [1]	Rural
1951	43,757,888	35,335,721	8,422,167	80·8	19·2
1961	46,071,604	36,838,442	9,233,162	80·0	20·0
1971	48,755,000	38,151,000	10,598,000	78·2	21·5
1981	49,011,417	37,686,863	11,324,554	76·9	23·1

[1] As existing at each census.

Conurbations. These are aggregates of local-authority areas with high population densities. In April 1981 there were 6 in England and Wales, with a population of 14·7m. (30% of total population): Greater London, 6·7m.; Tyneside, 0·7m.; W. Yorks., 1·67m.; S.E. Lancs., 2·24m.; Merseyside, 1·13m.; W. Midlands, 2·24m.

Greater London Boroughs. Estimated population on 30 June 1986.

Barking and Dagenham	148,100	Hammersmith and Fulham	150,800	Lambeth	245,000
Barnet	304,600	Haringey	196,100	Lewisham	232,000
Bexley	220,100	Harrow	201,900	Merton	164,800
Brent	255,700	Havering	238,100	Newham	205,200
Bromley	297,000	Hillingdon	232,000	Redbridge	227,900
Camden	183,300	Hounslow	194,900	Richmond-on-	
Croydon	319,300	Islington	168,000	Thames	162,000
Ealing	295,500	Kensington and		Southwark	216,000
Enfield	265,400	Chelsea	137,400	Sutton	168,700
Greenwich	217,800	Kingston upon		Tower Hamlets	152,800
Hackney	187,100	Thames	133,800	Waltham Forest	215,800
				Wandsworth	257,100
				Westminster	176,100

The City of London (677 acres) is part of the County of Greater London but retains some independent powers. Resident population (1986 estimate) 4,800.

Census of England and Wales, 1961. HMSO. 1961–65
Royal Commission on Local Government in Greater London, Report. HMSO, 1960 (Cmnd. 1164)
Census 1971, England and Wales. HMSO, 1971–75
Census 1971, Great Britain; Advance Analysis. HMSO, 1972
Census 1981, Great Britain. HMSO, 1981–83
Census 1981, England and Wales. HMSO, 1981–83

Scotland: Area 78,762 sq. km, including its islands, 186 in number, and inland water 1,580 sq. km.

Population (including military in the barracks and seamen on board vessels in the harbours) at the dates of each census:

Date of enumeration	Population	Pop. per sq. mile	Date of enumeration	Population	Pop. per sq. mile [1]
1811	1,805,864	60	1901	4,472,103	150
1821	2,091,521	70	1911	4,760,904	160
1831	2,364,386	79	1921	4,882,497	164
1841	2,620,184	88	1931	4,842,980	163
1851	2,888,742	97	1951	5,096,415	171
1861	3,062,294	100	1961	5,179,344	174
1871	3,360,018	113	1971	5,229,963	68
1881	3,735,573	125	1981	5,130,735	66
1891	4,025,647	135			

[1] per sq. km from 1971.

The 1981 population present on census night included 2,466,000 males, 2,664,000 females.

Population of the local authority areas:

Regions	Districts	Area sq.km	Estimated population 1986
Borders		4,662	101,804
	Berwickshire		18,748
	Ettrick and Lauderdale		33,223
	Roxburgh		35,225
	Tweeddale		14,608
Central		2,590	271,819
	Clackmannan		47,586
	Falkirk		143,063
	Stirling		81,170
Dumfries and Galloway		6,475	146,770
	Annandale and Eskdale		35,911
	Nithsdale		57,339
	Stewartry		23,136
	Wigtown		30,384
Fife		1,308	343,825
	Dunfermline		129,099
	Kirkcaldy		148,193
	N.E. Fife		66,533

Regions	Districts	Area sq. km	Estimated population 1986
Grampian		8,550	502,850
	Aberdeen City		216,273
	Banff and Buchan		83,174
	Gordon		70,788
	Kincardine and Deeside		47,822
	Moray		84,793
Highland		26,136	200,764
	Badenoch and Strathspey		10,605
	Caithness		27,134
	Inverness		60,773
	Lochaber		19,369
	Nairn		10,239
	Ross and Cromarty		47,906
	Skye and Lochalsh		11,526
	Sutherland		13,212
Lothian		1,756	741,910
	E. Lothian		81,872
	Edinburgh City		438,232
	Midlothian		81,261
	W. Lothian		140,545
Strathclyde		13,856	2,344,585
	Argyll and Bute		65,586
	Bearsden and Milngavie		40,171
	Clydebank		49,204
	Clydesdale		58,293
	Cumbernauld and Kilsyth		62,503
	Cumnock and Doon Valley		43,528
	Cunninghame		137,147
	Dumbarton		79,295
	E. Kilbride		81,837
	Eastwood		56,060
	Glasgow City		725,130
	Hamilton		106,945
	Inverclyde		97,227
	Kilmarnock and Loudoun		81,058
	Kyle and Carrick		113,081
	Monklands		107,010
	Motherwell		148,016
	Renfrew		203,220
	Strathkelvin		89,274
Tayside		7,668	392,346
	Angus		93,150
	Dundee		176,208
	Perth and Kinross		122,988
Island Authority Areas			
Orkney Islands		974	19,266
Shetland Islands		1,427	23,580
Western Isles		2,901	31,494

Population of cities and large towns:

Census population

	1971	1981	Estimate 1985
Glasgow	893,790	762,288	733,794
Edinburgh	453,025	419,187	439,672
Dundee	182,930	174,746	177,674
Aberdeen	181,785	190,200	215,246
Paisley	95,067	84,789	...
Greenock	69,171	57,324	...

Census population

	1971	1981
Kilmarnock	48,992	52,080
Dunfermline	51,738	52,057
Clydebank	48,170	51,656
Hamilton	46,376	51,529
Coatbridge	51,985	50,866

New Towns (1985, estimate): East Kilbride, 69,900; Irvine, 56,300; Cumbernauld, 49,500; Livingstone, 39,200; Glenrothes, 37,400.

The birthplaces of the 1981 "usually resident" population were: Scotland, 4,548,708; England, 297,784; Wales, 12,733; Northern Ireland, 33,927; Ireland 27,018; Commonwealth, 48,515; foreign countries, 65,384.

The population of the Central Clydeside conurbation in 1985 was 1,682,079.

At 30 June 1986 the estimated sex distribution of the population in Scotland was: between 0 and 15, 502,300 males, 477,600 females; 15 and 65, 1,689,900 males, 15 and 60, 1,563,200 females; 65 and over, 282,700 males, 60 and over, 605,100 females.

Isle of Man and Channel Islands:

Islands	Area in sq. km	Population 1961	Population 1971	Population 1986
Isle of Man	572	48,151	56,289	55,482
Jersey	116	57,200	69,329	80,212 [1]
Guernsey, Herm and Jethou	64			
Alderney	8	47,178	53,734	64,282
Sark, Brechou and Lihou	6			

[1] 1985.

Vital statistics for England and Wales:

	Estimated home population at 30 June [1]	Total live births	Illegitimate live births	Deaths	Marriages	Divorces, annulments and dissolutions
1981	49,634,300	634,492	80,983	577,890	351,973	145,713
1982	49,601,400	625,931	89,857	581,861	342,166	146,698
1983	49,653,700	629,134	99,211	579,608	344,334	147,479
1984	49,763,600	636,818	110,465	566,881	349,186	144,501
1985	49,923,500	656,417	126,250	590,734	346,389	160,300
1986	50,075,400	661,018	141,345	...	347,924	153,903

[1] The population actually in England and Wales.

In 1985 the proportion of male to female births was 1,054 male to 1,000 female; the live birth rate was 13·1 and the death rate 11·8 per 1,000 of the population; infant mortality rate 9·4 per 1,000 of live births. The average age at marriage in 1986 was 30·5 years for males and 27·8 years for females.

Vital statistics for Scotland:

	Estimated home population at 30 June [1]	Total births	Illegitimate births	Deaths	Marriages	Divorces, annulments and dissolutions
1981	5,149,500	69,054	8,447	63,828	36,237	9,895
1982	5,166,557	66,196	9,395	65,022	34,942	11,288
1983	5,150,405	65,078	9,581	63,454	34,962	13,238
1984	5,145,722	65,106	10,640	62,345	36,253	11,915
1985	5,136,509	66,676	12,362	63,967	36,385	13,373
1986	5,121,013	65,812	13,547	63,467	35,790	13,063

[1] Includes merchant navy at home and forces stationed in Scotland.

In 1986 the proportion of male to female births was 1,061 male to 1,000 female; the live birth rate was 12·9 and the death rate 12·4 per 1,000 of the population; infant mortality rate, 8·2 per 1,000 live births. The average age of marriage was 29 years for males and 26 years for females.

Emigration and Immigration. During the last hundred years the UK has most often been a net exporter of population. Throughout the period 1881–1931 there was a consistent net loss from migration, though the fifteen years 1931–46 brought a reversal of the trend as a result of immigration from Europe. Since the Second World War the loss has largely continued. However, during the five years 1956–1961, increased immigration particularly from the new Commonwealth and Pakistan, resulted in a net gain. There were also net gains in 1979, 1983 and 1984 but these were due to decreased emigration. The latest year, 1984, shows a net gain of 59,000 due to continuing low in emigration and increased immigration.

Since 1964 migration figures have been available from the International Passenger Survey. This is a sample survey conducted by the Office of Population Censuses and Surveys, covering all the principal air and sea routes between the UK and overseas, except those to and from the Republic of Ireland. For the years 1964–73 the survey shows an average annual net loss for the UK of 63,000. During the decade 1974–1983 the annual net outflow has been an average of 37,000.

The table below, derived from the International Passenger survey, summarizes migration statistics for 1986 (in 1,000):

By country of last or future intended residence	Into UK	Out from UK	Balance
All Countries	250	213	+37
Australia, Canada, New Zealand	30	50	−20
India, Bangladesh, Sri Lanka	16	4	+11
Other Commonwealth	34	21	+13
EEC	69	58	+11
USA	26	34	−8
Republic of South Africa	18	2	+16
Rest of World	57	43	+15

By sex/age in 1985				
Males	0–14	24·7	14·1	+10·5
	15–24	24·2	24·1	+0·1
	25–44	36·6	40·6	−4·0
	45 and over	13·5	12·3	+1·1
	All ages	98·9	91·1	+7·8
Females	0–14	24·0	17·5	+6·5
	15–24	46·6	21·1	+25·5
	25–44	52·9	34·4	+18·5
	45 and over	9·9	9·6	+0·3
	All ages	133·3	82·6	+50·8

Walvin, J., *Passage to Britain: Immigration in British History and Politics.* London, 1984

CLIMATE. The climate is cool temperate oceanic, with mild conditions and rainfall evenly distributed over the year, though the weather is very changeable because of cyclonic influences. In general, temperatures are higher in the west and lower in the east in winter and rather the reverse in summer. Rainfall amounts are greatest in the west, where most of the high ground occurs.

London. Jan. 40°F (4·5°C), July 64°F (18°C). Annual rainfall 24″ (600 mm).
Aberdeen. Jan. 39°F (4°C), July 57°F (14°C). Annual rainfall 33″ (823 mm).
Belfast. Jan. 40°F (4·5°C), July 61°F (16·1°C). Annual rainfall 34·6″ (865 mm).
Birmingham. Jan. 38°F (3·3°C), July 61°F (16·1°C). Annual rainfall 30″ (749 mm).
Cardiff. Jan. 40°F (4·4°C), July 61°F (16·1°C). Annual rainfall 42·6″ (1,065 mm).
Edinburgh. Jan. 38°F (3·5°C), July 58°F (14·5°C). Annual rainfall 28″ (708 mm).
Glasgow. Jan. 39°F (4°C), July 60°F (15·5°C). Annual rainfall 37·2″ (930 mm).
Manchester. Jan. 41°F (5°C), July 62°F (16·5°C). Annual rainfall 34·1″ (853 mm).

QUEEN, HEAD OF THE COMMONWEALTH. Elizabeth II Alexandra Mary, born 21 April 1926 daughter of King George VI and Queen Elizabeth; married on 20 Nov. 1947 Lieut. Philip Mountbatten (formerly Prince Philip of Greece), created Duke of Edinburgh, Earl of Merioneth and Baron Greenwich on the same day and created Prince Philip, Duke of Edinburgh, 22 Feb. 1957; succeeded to the crown on the death of her father, on 6 Feb. 1952. Offspring: *Charles* Philip Arthur George, Prince of Wales (Heir Apparent), born 14 Nov. 1948, married Lady Diana Spencer on 29 July 1981. Offspring: *William* Arthur Philip Louis, born 21 June 1982; *Henry* Charles Albert David, born 15 Sept. 1984. Princess *Anne* Elizabeth Alice Louise, the Princess Royal, born 15 Aug. 1950, married Mark Anthony Peter Phillips on 14 Nov. 1973. Offspring: *Peter* Mark Andrew, born 15 Nov. 1977; *Zara* Anne Elizabeth, born 15 May 1981. Prince *Andrew*, Albert Christian Edward, created Duke of York, 23 July 1986, born 19 Feb. 1960, married Sarah Margaret Ferguson on 23 July 1986; Prince *Edward* Antony Richard Louis, born 10 March 1964.

The Queen Mother: Queen Elizabeth, born 4 Aug. 1900, daughter of the 14th Earl of Strathmore and Kinghorne; married the Duke of York, afterwards King George VI, on 26 April 1923.

Sister of the Queen: Princess Margaret Rose, born 12 Aug. 1930; married Antony Armstrong-Jones (created Earl of Snowdon, 3 Oct. 1961) on 6 May 1960; divorced, 1978. Offspring: *David* Albert Charles (Viscount Linley), born 3 Nov. 1961; Lady *Sarah* Frances Elizabeth Armstrong-Jones, born 1964.

Children of the late Duke of Gloucester (died 10 June 1974): William Henry Andrew Frederick, born 18 Dec. 1941, died 28 Aug. 1972; Richard Alexander Walter George, Duke of Gloucester, born 26 Aug. 1944, married Birgitte van Deurs on 8 July 1972 (offspring: Alexander Patrick Gregers Richard Windsor, Earl of Ulster, born 24 Oct. 1974; Davina Elizabeth Alice Benedikte Windsor, born 19 Nov. 1977; Rose Victoria Birgitte Louise Windsor, born 1 March 1980).

Children of the late Duke of Kent (died 25 Aug. 1942): Edward George Nicholas Patrick, Duke of Kent, born 9 Oct. 1935; married Katharine Worsley on 8 June 1961 (offspring: George Philip Nicholas, Earl of St Andrews, born 26 June 1962, married Sylvania Tomaselli on 9 Jan. 1988; Lady Helen Windsor, born 28 April 1964; Lord Nicholas Charles Edward Jonathan Windsor, born 25 July 1970). Alexandra Helen Elizabeth Olga Christabel, born 25 Dec. 1936; married 24 April 1963, Angus Ogilvy (offspring: James Robert Bruce, born 29 Feb. 1964; Marina Victoria Alexandra, born 31 July 1966). Michael George Charles Franklin, born 4 July 1942; married Marie-Christine von Reibnitz on 30 June 1978 (offspring: Lord *Frederick* Michael George David Louis Windsor, born 6 April 1979; Lady *Gabriela* Marina Alexander Ophelia Windsor, born 23 April 1981).

The Queen's legal title rests on the statute of 12 and 13 Will. III, ch. 3, by which the succession to the Crown of Great Britain and Ireland was settled on the Princess Sophia of Hanover and the 'heirs of her body being Protestants'. By proclamation of 17 July 1917 the royal family became known as the House and Family of Windsor. On 8 Feb. 1960 the Queen issued a declaration varying her confirmatory declaration of 9 April 1952 to the effect that while the Queen and her children should continue to be known as the House of Windsor, her descendants, other than descendants entitled to the style of Royal Highness and the title of Prince or Princess, and female descendants who marry and their descendants should bear the name of Mountbatten-Windsor. For the Royal Style and Titles of Queen Elizabeth *see* Commonwealth section.

By letters patent of 30 Nov. 1917 the titles of Royal Highness and Prince or Princess are restricted to the Sovereign's children, the children of the Sovereign's sons and the eldest living son of the eldest son of the Prince of Wales.

Provision is made for the support of the royal household by the settlement of the Civil List soon after the beginning of each reign. (For historical details, *see* THE STATESMAN'S YEAR-BOOK, 1908, p. 5, and 1935, p. 4). According to the Civil List Act of 1 Jan. 1972 and the Civil List (Increase of Financial Provision) Order 1975, the Civil List of the Queen, after the usual surrender of hereditary revenues, was (1988) £4,500,000.

The Civil List of 1988 provides for an annuity of £135,600 to the Princess Royal; £217,700 to Prince Philip; £390,300 to Queen Elizabeth (the Queen Mother); £132,100 to the Princess Margaret; £86,500 to the Duke of York; £20,000 to Prince Edward.

Sovereigns of Great Britain, from the Restoration (with dates of accession):

House of Stewart		George III	25 Oct. 1760
Charles II	29 May 1660	George IV	29 Jan. 1820
James II	6 Feb. 1685	William IV	26 June 1830
		Victoria	20 June 1837
House of Stewart-Orange			
William and Mary	13 Feb. 1689	*House of Saxe-Coburg and Gotha*	
William III	28 Dec. 1694	Edward VII	22 Jan. 1901
House of Stewart			
Anne	19 March 1702	*House of Windsor*	
		George V	6 May 1910
House of Hanover		Edward VIII	20 Jan. 1936
George I	1 Aug. 1714	George VI	11 Dec. 1936
George II	11 June 1727	Elizabeth II	6 Feb. 1952

CONSTITUTION AND GOVERNMENT. The supreme legislative power is vested in Parliament, which in its present form, as divided into two Houses of

Legislature, the Lords and the Commons, dates from the middle of the 14th century.

Parliament is summoned by the writ of the sovereign issued out of Chancery, by advice of the Privy Council, at least 20 days previous to its assembling. A Parliament may last up to 5 years, normally divided into annual sessions. A session is ended by prorogation, and all public Bills which have not been passed by both Houses then lapse. A Parliament ends by dissolution, either by will of the sovereign (that is, on the advice of the Prime Minister) or by lapse of the 5-year period. A dissolution is commonly followed by a general election.

Under the Parliament Acts 1911 (1 and 2 Geo. V, ch. 13) and 1949 (12, 13 and 14 Geo. VI, ch. 103), all Money Bills (so certified by the Speaker of the House of Commons), if not passed by the House of Lords without amendment, may become law without their concurrence on the Royal Assent being signified within 1 month. Public Bills, other than Money Bills or a Bill extending the maximum duration of Parliament, if passed by the House of Commons in 2 successive sessions, whether of the same Parliament or not, and rejected each time, or not passed, by the House of Lords, may become law without their concurrence on the Royal Assent being signified, provided that 1 year has elapsed between the second reading in the first session of the House of Commons and the third reading in the second session. All Bills coming under this Act must reach the House of Lords at least 1 month before the end of the session.

The House of Lords consists of: (1) 789 hereditary peers and peeresses sitting by virtue of creation or descent, other than those who have disclaimed their titles for life under the provisions of the Peerage Act, 1963; (2) life peers being *(a)* 21 Lords of Appeal (active and retired), under the Appellate Jurisdiction Act, 1876, as amended; *(b)* (30 Dec. 1987) 359 life peers (including 47 women peers) under the Life Peerages Act, 1958: (3) 2 archbishops and 24 bishops of the Church of England (as long as they hold their sees).

The full House thus consists of 1,195, and the average attendance is about 320; at the end of Dec. 1987 187 peers were on leave of absence and 86 peers (including 3 minors) were without writs of summons.

The House of Commons consists of members (of both sexes) representing constituencies determined by the Boundary Commissions. Persons under 21 years of age, Clergy of the Church of England and of the Scottish Episcopal Church, Ministers of the Church of Scotland, Roman Catholic clergymen, civil servants, members of the regular armed forces, policemen, most judicial officers and other office-holders named in the House of Commons (Disqualification) Act are disqualified from sitting in the House of Commons. No English or Scottish peer can be elected to the House of Commons unless he has disclaimed his title for life under the Peerage Act, 1963, but Irish peers and holders of courtesy titles, who are not members of the House of Lords, are eligible.

In Aug. 1911 provision was first made for the payment of a salary of £400 per annum to members, other than those already in receipt of salaries as officers of the House, as Ministers or as officers of Her Majesty's household. As from 1 Jan. 1988 the salaries of members are £22,548 per annum, with income-tax relief on expenses incurred in the course of parliamentary duties. There is a secretarial allowance of up to £20,140 per annum and a living allowance, for an additional home, of up to £8,107 per annum. Members of the House of Lords are unsalaried but may recover expenses incurred in attending sittings of the House within maxima for each day's attendance of £21 for day subsistence, £57 for night subsistence and £22 for secretarial and research assistance or general office expenses. Additionally, Members of the House who are disabled may recover the extra cost of attending the House incurred by reason of their disablement. In connection with their attendance at the House and for parliamentary duties within the UK Lords may also recover the cost of travelling to and from their main place of residence.

Select Committees consisting of 10–15 Members of all parties exist in order to investigate most areas of public policy.

The Representation of the People Act 1948, abolished the business premises and

University franchises, and the only persons entitled to vote at Parliamentary elections are those registered as residents or as service voters. No person may vote in more than one constituency at a general election. Persons may apply on certain grounds to vote by post or by proxy.

All persons over 18 years old and not subject to any legal incapacity to vote and who are either British subjects or citizens of Ireland are entitled to be included in the register of electors for the constituency containing the address at which they were residing on the qualifying date for the register and are entitled to vote at elections held during the period for which the register remains in force.

Members of the armed forces, Crown servants employed abroad, and the wives accompanying their husbands, are entitled, if otherwise qualified, to be registered as 'service voters' provided they make a 'service declaration'. To be effective for a particular register, the declaration must be made on or before the qualifying date for that register.

The Representation of the People Act 1969, abolished the occupier's qualification for voting in Local Government elections.

The House of Commons (Redistribution of Seats) Acts 1944, 1949 and 1958, provided for the setting up of Boundary Commissions for England, Wales, Scotland and Northern Ireland. The Commissions are required to make general reports at intervals of not less than 10 and not more than 15 years and to submit reports from time to time with respect to the area comprised in any particular constituency or constituencies where some change appears necessary. Any changes giving effect to reports of the Commissions are to be made by Orders in Council laid before Parliament for approval by resolution of each House. The electorate of the United Kingdom and Northern Ireland in the register in 1986 numbered 43,391,831, of whom 36,158,417 were in England, 2,159,361 in Wales, 3,986,654 in Scotland and 1,087,399 in Northern Ireland.

At the general election held in 1987, 650 members were returned, 523 from England, 72 from Scotland, 38 from Wales and 17 from Northern Ireland. Every constituency returns a single member.

The following is a table of the duration of Parliaments called since Nov. 1935.

Reign	When met	When dissolved	Duration (years and days)	
George V, Edward VIII and George VI	26 Nov. 1935	15 June 1945	9	205
George VI	1 Aug. 1945	3 Feb. 1950	4	188
,,	1 Mar. 1950	5 Oct. 1951	1	219
George VI and Elizabeth II	31 Oct. 1951	6 May 1955	3	188
Elizabeth II	7 June 1955	18 Sept. 1959	4	105
,,	20 Oct. 1959	25 Sept. 1964	4	341
,,	27 Oct. 1964	10 Mar. 1966	1	134
,,	18 Apr. 1966	29 May 1970	4	81
,,	29 June 1970	8 Feb. 1974	3	225
,,	12 Mar. 1974	20 Sept. 1974	0	224
,,	22 Oct. 1974	7 April 1979	4	167
,,	9 May 1979	13 May 1983	4	4
,,	15 June 1983	18 May 1987	3	338
,,	25 June 1988	—	—	—

The executive government is vested nominally in the Crown, but practically in a committee of Ministers, called the Cabinet, which is dependent on the support of a majority in the House of Commons.

The head of the Ministry is the Prime Minister, a position first constitutionally recognized, and special precedence accorded to the holder, in 1905. His colleagues in the Ministry are appointed on his recommendation, and he dispenses the greater portion of the patronage of the Crown.

Heads of the Administrations since 1935 (C. = Conservative, L. = Liberal, Lab. = Labour, Nat. = National, Coal. = Coalition, Care. = Caretaker):

S. Baldwin (Nat.)	7 June 1935	H. Macmillan (C.)	10 Jan. 1957
N. Chamberlain (Nat.)	28 May 1937	Sir Alec Douglas-Home (C.)	18 Oct. 1963
W. S. Churchill (Coal.)	10 May 1940	H. Wilson (Lab.)	16 Oct. 1964
W. S. Churchill (Care.)	23 May 1945	E. Heath (C.)	19 June 1970
C. R. Attlee (Lab.)	26 July 1945	H. Wilson (Lab.)	12 Mar. 1974
W. S. Churchill (C.)	26 Oct. 1951	J. Callaghan (Lab.)	5 Apr. 1976
Sir Anthony Eden (C.)	6 Apr. 1955	M. Thatcher (C.)	4 May 1979

In March 1988 the Government consisted of the following members:

(a) MEMBERS OF THE CABINET

1. *Prime Minister and First Lord of the Treasury and Minister for Civil Service:* Rt Hon. Margaret Thatcher, MP, born 1925. (Salary £34,157 per annum.)

2. *Secretary of State for Foreign and Commonwealth Affairs:* Rt Hon. Sir Geoffrey Howe, QC, MP, born 1926. (£34,157.)

3. *Chancellor of the Exchequer:* Rt Hon. Nigel Lawson, MP, born 1932. (£34,157.)

4. *Lord Chancellor:* Rt Hon. The Lord Mackay of Clashfern, QC, born 1927. (£83,000.)

5. *Secretary of State for the Home Department:* Rt Hon. Douglas Hurd, CBE, MP, born 1930. (£34,157.)

6. *Secretary of State for Wales:* Rt Hon. Peter Walker, MBE, MP, born 1932. (£34,157.)

7. *Secretary of State for Defence:* Rt Hon. George Younger, TD, MP, born 1931. (£34,157.)

8. *Secretary of State for Employment:* Rt Hon. Norman Fowler, MP, born 1938. (£34,157.)

9. *Secretary of State for Northern Ireland:* Rt Hon. Tom King, MP, born 1933. (£34,157.)

10. *Secretary of State for the Environment:* Rt Hon. Nicholas Ridley, MP, born 1929. (£34,157.)

11. *Secretary of State for Trade and Industry:* Rt Hon. The Lord Young of Graffham, born 1932. (£40,438.)

12. *Secretary of State for Education and Science:* Rt Hon. Kenneth Baker, MP, born 1934. (£34,157.)

13. *Chancellor of the Duchy of Lancaster:* Rt Hon. Kenneth Clarke, QC, MP, born 1940. (£34,157.)

14. *Minister of Agriculture, Fisheries and Food:* Rt Hon. John MacGregor, OBE, MP, born 1937. (£34,157.)

15. *Secretary of State for Scotland:* Rt Hon. Malcolm Rifkind, QC, MP, born 1946. (£34,157.)

16. *Secretary of State for Transport:* Rt Hon. Paul Channon, MP, born 1935. (£34,157.)

17. *Secretary of State for Social Services:* Rt Hon. John Moore, MP, born 1937. (£34,157.)

18. *Lord President of the Council and Leader of the House of Commons:* Rt Hon. John Wakeham, MP, born 1932. (£34,157.)

19. *Lord Privy Seal and Leader of the House of Lords:* Rt Hon. The Lord Belstead, JP, born 1932. (£40,438.)

20. *Secretary of State for Energy:* Rt Hon. Cecil Parkinson, MP, born 1931. (£34,157.)

21. *Chief Secretary to the Treasury:* Rt Hon. John Major, MP, born 1943. (£34,157.)

(b) Law Officers

22. *Attorney-General:* Rt Hon. Sir Patrick Mayhew, QC, MP, born 1929. (£36,357.)

23. *Lord Advocate:* Rt Hon. The Lord Cameron of Lochbroom, QC, born 1931. (£40,508.)

24. *Solicitor-General:* Sir Nicholas Lyell, QC, MP, born 1938. (£29,637.)

25. *Solicitor-General for Scotland:* Peter Lovat Fraser, QC, MP, born 1945. (£34,956.)

(c) Ministers not in the Cabinet

26. *Parliamentary Secretary, Treasury (Chief Whip):* Rt Hon. David Waddington, QC, MP, born 1929. (£28,267.)

27. *Minister of State, Privy Council Office, Minister for the Arts:* Rt Hon. Richard Luce, MP, born 1936. (£23,887.)

28. *Minister of State, Foreign and Commonwealth Office:* Rt Hon. The Lord Glenarthur, born 1944. (£34,688.)

29. *Minister of State, Foreign and Commonwealth Office:* Rt Hon. Lynda Chalker, MP, born 1942. (£23,887.)

30. *Minister of State, Foreign and Commonwealth Office, Minister for Overseas Development:* Christopher Patten, MP, born 1944. (£23,887.)

31. *Minister of State, Foreign and Commonwealth Office:* David Mellor, QC, MP, born 1949. (£23,887.)

32. *Financial Secretary, Treasury:* Rt Hon. Norman Lamont, MP, born 1942. (£23,887.)

33. *Paymaster General (Treasury):* Rt Hon. Peter Brooke, MP, born 1934. (£23,887.)

34. *Minister of State, Home Office:* John Patten, MP, born 1945. (£23,887.)

35. *Minister of State, Home Office:* Timothy Renton, MP, born 1932. (£23,887.)

36. *Minister of State, Home Office:* The Earl Ferrers, born 1929. (£34,688.)

37. *Minister of State, Department of Energy:* Rt Hon. Peter Morrison, MP, born 1944. (£23,887.)

38. *Minister of State, Ministry of Defence, Armed Forces:* Ian Stewart, MP, born 1935. (£23,887.)

39. *Minister of State, Ministry of Defence, Defence Procurement:* The Lord Trefgarne, born 1941. (£34,688.)

40. *Minister of State, Department of Health and Social Security, Minister for Health:* Rt Hon. Antony Newton, OBE, MP, born 1937. (£23,887.)

41. *Minister of State, Department of Health and Social Security, Minister for Social Security and the Disabled:* Nicholas Scott, MP, born 1933. (£23,887.)

42. *Minister of State, Northern Ireland Office:* Rt Hon. John Stanley, MP, born 1942. (£23,887.)

43. *Minister of State, Ministry of Agriculture, Fisheries and Food:* Rt Hon. John Selwyn Gummer, MP, born 1939. (£23,887.)

44. *Minister of State, Department of the Environment, Minister for Local Government:* Michael Howard, QC, MP, born 1941. (£23,887.)

45. *Minister of State, Department of the Environment, Minister for Water, Environmental Protection, Countryside and Heritage:* The Earl of Caithness, MP, born 1948. (£34,688.)

46. *Minister of State, Department of the Environment, Minister for Housing and Planning:* Hon. William Waldegrave, MP, born 1946. (£23,887.)

47. *Minister of State, Department of Education and Science:* Angela Rumbold, CBE, MP, born 1932. (£23,887.)

48. *Minister of State, Scottish Office:* The Lord Sanderson of Bowden, born 1933. (£34,688.)

49. *Minister of State, Department of Trade and Industry:* Hon. Alan Clark, MP, born 1928. (£23,887.)

50. *Minister of State, Department of Transport:* David Mitchell, MP, born 1928. (£23,887.)

Leader of the Opposition in the House of Commons: Rt Hon. Neil Kinnock, MP, born 1942. (£31,237.)

Leader of the Opposition in the House of Lords: Rt Hon. The Lord Cledwyn of Penrhos, born 1916. (£28,688.)

The Constitution of the House of Commons after the 1987 general election was as follows: Conservative, 375; Labour, 229; Liberals, 17, SDP, 5; Others, 24.

Ball, A., *British Political Parties: The Emergence of a Modern Party System.* 1981
Butler, D., and Butler, G., *British Political Facts, 1900–85.* London, 1986
Butler, D., and Kavanagh, D., *The British General Election of 1983.* 1984
Drewry, G. (ed.), *The New Select Committees.* OUP, 1985
Jennings, Sir I., *Cabinet Government.* 3rd. ed. CUP, 1959.—*The British Constitution.* 5th ed. CUP, 1966.—*Parliament.* 2nd ed. CUP, 1957.—*Party Politics.* 3 vols. CUP, 1960–62
King, A. (ed.), *The British Prime Minister.* Rev. ed. London, 1985.—*British Members of Parliament.* London, 1974
Mackintosh, J. P., *The British Cabinet.* 3rd ed. London, 1977.—*The Government and Politics of Britain.* 4th ed. London, 1977
May, Sir T. E., *Treatise on the Law, Privileges, Proceedings and Usage of Parliament.* 20th ed., London, 1983
Norton, P., *Parliament in the 1980s.* Oxford, 1985
Parker, F. K., *Conduct of Parliamentary Elections.* London, 1983
Pelling, H., *A Short History of the Labour Party.* London, 1976
Silk, E. P., *How Parliament Works.* London, 1987
Taylor, E., *The House of Commons at Work.* 9th ed. London, 1979
The Times Guide to the House of Commons, June 1987. London, 1987

European Parliament: On 14 June 1984 Great Britain elected 81 representatives to the European Parliament, of which 66 came from England, 8 from Scotland and 4 from Wales, each constituency returning a single member by a first past the post system. Northern Ireland returned 3 members by single transferable vote. The seats were won as follows: Conservative 45, Labour 32, Scottish Nationalists 1, Ulster Unionists 1, Democratic Unionists 1, Social, Democratic and Labour Party 1.

Local Government. Local Administration is carried out by four different types of bodies, namely: (i) local branches of some central ministries, such as the Department of Health and Social Security; (ii) local sub-managements of nationalized industries; (iii) specialist authorities such as water authorities; and (iv) the system of local government described below. The phrase 'local government' has come to mean that part of the local administration conducted by elected councils.

There are two separate systems: one for England and Wales and one for Scotland, but both systems are financed by a species of tax on property, levied locally, supplemented by government grants. This local tax is called 'the rate'. The system of financing local government was the subject of a major review in 1975 and a further review in 1985 led to the publication of the Green Paper *Paying for Local Government*. The key proposals were: Abolition of domestic rates and introduction of a community charge to be paid at a flat rate by each adult; setting of a uniform, national non-domestic rate; and a streamlined grant system. The new system will start to come into effect in 1989 in Scotland and 1990 in England and Wales.

Local Government: England and Wales—*Outside London.* England and Wales have slightly differing systems. Each country has three types of councils namely, county, district and English parish or Welsh Community Councils. In addition, England has some metropolitan district councils.

Councillors are elected by their local electors for 4 years. The chairman of the council is one of the councillors elected by the rest. In a district with the status of city or borough his title is mayor, or in a few famous places Lord Mayor. Any parish or community council can by simple resolution adopt the style 'town council' and the status of town for the parish or community. The chairman of the council will be known as the town mayor.

Counties and Districts: There are 47 non-metropolitan counties (of which 8 are in Wales). The 6 metropolitan counties (Greater Manchester, Merseyside, South Yorkshire, Tyne and Wear, West Yorkshire and West Midlands) have no councils, the metropolitan districts having most of the county functions. Within the counties there are 369 districts (36 metropolitan and 333 non-metropolitan, of which 37 are in Wales).

Parishes and Communities: There are some 10,000 parishes within the English districts, of which 8,000 or so have councils. About 300 are former small boroughs or urban districts which became successor parishes.

In Wales, parishes are known as communities. Unlike England, where some urban areas are not in any parish, communities have been established for the whole of Wales. There is one for each former parish, county borough, borough or urban district (or part thereof where the former area is divided by a new boundary). There are about 1,000 communities altogether, of which 800 or so have councils.

The Local Government Act 1972 laid down the boundaries for all the counties and districts in England and Wales except the English non-metropolitan districts.

Permanent Local Government Boundary Commissions for England and for Wales advise the Secretaries of State on boundaries and electoral arrangements.

A council has only those powers which have been conferred upon it expressly by Act of Parliament, and no more. The relationship between the different types of council is one of specialization, not of hierarchy. The larger do not supervise the smaller; each being, within its own sphere, entitled to make its own decisions. Government sanction, however, is required to borrow money and to sell land below its market value, and certain types of land use are subject to planning control.

Councils are kept within the law by a system of publicly regulated audit, and in the last resort they can be restrained from exceeding their powers by the courts.

Local government functions may be classified into county, district and parish or community functions, but whereas county and district functions are distinct, the parish and community functions are mostly concurrent with those of the districts. Arrangements may, however, be made so that any council may discharge functions of any other as its agent.

The following is the classification of powers given above: *Parish and Community Functions.* Allotments, burial and cremation, halls, meeting places and entertainments, facilities for exercise and recreation, public lavatories, street lighting, off-street vehicle parking, footpaths, the support of local arts and crafts, the encouragement of tourism and the right to be consulted by the district council on planning applications and certain byelaws. *District Functions.* In addition to the Parish and Community functions, aerodromes, civic restaurants, housing, markets, refuse collection, the administration of planning control, the formulation of local plans, sewerage on behalf of the water authority, museums, the licensing of places of entertainment and refreshment, and the constitutional oversight of parishes and communities. *County Functions.* The formulation of structure plans, traffic, transportation and roads, education, public libraries and museums, youth employment and social services.

There are, in addition, a number of special arrangements. Four district councils in Wales are designated as library authorities and Welsh district councils have powers in relation to allotments currently with community councils. The county councils in England and Wales separately or jointly appoint the fire and police authorities, and the bodies responsible for national parks. In Metropolitan counties, there are no county councils and all functions are performed by the districts (in some cases jointly). The total number of local government electors in England and Wales was 38,557,738 in 1987.

Greater London. From 1965–86 London was governed by the Greater London Council, covering the whole metropolitan area, and by 32 London boroughs and the Corporation of the City of London, each with responsibilities in its own area. The GLC was abolished on 1 April 1986. In the City and the 12 boroughs covering the inner part of Greater London, education is now the responsibility of the directly elected Inner London Education Authority, while in the 20 outer boroughs the individual borough councils are the education authorities. Fire services in Greater London are the responsibility of the London Fire and Civil Defence Authority, whose members are appointed by the boroughs and the City. Flood prevention is the responsibility of the Thames Water Authority. Waste regulation for the whole of Greater London is the function of the London Waste Regulation Authority. Waste collection is the responsibility of the boroughs. Waste disposal is the responsibility of the boroughs acting individually or in groups. Except in the City, the police authority is the Metropolitan Police, which is responsible to central government. London Regional Transport is likewise responsible to central government for passenger transport. Other local government functions are the responsibility of the boroughs, acting either individually or jointly, and the City.

Estimated population of Greater London in June 1986 was 6,775,190, and rateable value at 1 April 1987 was £2,093,517,545. Net current expenditure for all London authorities in 1987–88 was estimated at £4,704m. (including £994m. for ILEA but excluding Metropolitan Police). Gross capital expenditure (excluding leasing) for all London authorities and the London Residuary Body was estimated at £1,100m. in 1986–87.

Scotland. Under the system, which came into effect in 1975, the Scots mainland is divided into 9 regions, and in addition there are the 3 islands areas of Orkney, Shetland and the Western Isles. The regions are divided into districts which total 53. All these units have a council consisting of councillors elected for 4 years and a chairman elected by the councillors for 4 years. Community councils have been established under schemes submitted by district and islands councils. These community councils cannot claim public funds as of right, nor do they have powers directly conferred by Statute: consequently they are not local authorities in the sense that Welsh Community Councils are.

As in England and Wales a permanent Local Government Boundary Commission advises the Secretary of State on Local Authority Boundaries and electoral arrangements.

On the mainland, functions are allocated between regional and district authorities, in the same way (with minor exceptions) as they are allocated between English counties on the one hand and English districts and parishes on the other, but the councils of the islands areas, which have no districts, perform both sets of functions.

Despite differences of nomenclature the effect of the reforms of 1972 (England) and 1973 (Scotland) is to assimilate the systems of mainland Scotland and of England and Wales more closely than has been the case in the past.

The total number of local government electors in Scotland was 3,957,390 in 1985.

Complaints. Under both systems, complaints, by members of the public, of maladministration may be investigated by a Commissioner for Local Administration. Initially a complaint must be referred to him through a councillor, but a direct approach to him is possible if this fails. He can deal only with matters for which there is no other remedy; he reports to the council concerned and may publish his report.

Our Changing Democracy: Devolution to Scotland and Wales. HMSO, 1975
Arnold-Baker, C., *The Local Government Act 1972.* London, 1973

DEFENCE. The Defence Council was established on 1 April 1964 under the chairmanship of the Secretary of State for Defence, who is responsible to the Sovereign and Parliament for the defence of the realm. Vested in the Defence Council are the functions of commanding and administering the Armed Forces. The Secretary of State heads the Ministry of Defence as a Department of State. There are 4 subordinate Ministers; 2 Ministers of State and 2 Parliamentary Under-Secretaries of State.

Defence Council membership comprises the Secretary of State, 3 Ministers of State, the 2 Parliamentary Under-Secretaries, the Chief of the Defence Staff, the 2 single Service Chiefs of Staff, the Vice-Chief of Defence Staff, the Chief of Defence Procurement, the Chief Scientific Adviser, the Permanent Under-Secretary of State and the Second Permanent Under Secretary of State.

There are 3 Service Boards, each of which enjoys delegated powers for the administration of matters relating to the naval, military and air forces respectively.

Defence policy decision making is a collective Governmental responsibility. Important matters of policy are considered by the full Cabinet or, more frequently, by the Defence and Oversea Policy Committee under the chairmanship of the Prime Minister. Other members of this Committee include the Secretary of State for Defence, the Foreign and Commonwealth Secretary and the Home Secretary.

Logistics Services. Since the inception of a unified Ministry of Defence in 1964, progress has been made in the rationalization of the logistics services of the Royal Navy, the Army and the Royal Air Force. The Air Force Department is responsible for accommodation stores for maintenance and for the initial furnishing of new buildings; the Army Department is the single management authority for the design, development, procurement and inspection of clothing other than certain specialized clothing; the Navy Department has for some time been responsible for ration policy provisioning, procurement, storing and distribution of food to main depots and to Army forward supply depots in BAOR and is responsible for water transport to its tri-service responsibilities. The supply of Naval air stores has been integrated with those of the RAF.

The Procurement Executive. An important development in 1971 was the creation of a Procurement Executive to combine the Defence Procurement responsibilities of the Ministry of Defence and the former Ministry of Aviation Supply.

Service Strengths at 30 Nov. 1987, all ranks, males and females, UK personnel only: Royal Navy and Royal Marines, 66,118; Army, 159,846; Royal Air Force, 93,394; total, 319,358. The Ministry of Defence employed 145,499 civilians in Dec. 1987.

Defence Budget Estimates: 1988–89, £19,208m.; 1989–90, £19,950m; 1990–91, £20,560m.

Army. Control of the British Army is vested in the Defence Council and is exercised through the Army Board. The Secretary of State for Defence is Chairman of the Army Board. The other civilian members are the 4 subordinate Ministers; the Controller Establishments, Research and Nuclear Programmes and the Second Permanent Under Secretary of State.

The Military members of the Army Board are the Chief of the General Staff, the Adjutant General, the Quartermaster General and the Master General of the Ordnance. The Chief of the General Staff is the professional head of his Service and the professional adviser to Ministers on the Army aspects of military matters. He is responsible for the fighting efficiency of his Service; for Army advice on the conduct of operations; and for the issuing of such single Service operational orders as may be appropriate resulting from defence policy decisions. He is also responsible for the Territorial Army. The Chief of the General Staff is a member of the Chiefs of Staff Committee which is collectively responsible to HM Government for professional advice on strategy and military operations and on the military implication of defence policy. This advice is tendered to the Secretary of State for Defence by the Chief of the Defence Staff. The Adjutant-General is responsible for Army manpower within the policy set by the General Staff; for recruiting and selection; for the administration and individual training of military personnel; for the discipline of the Army; for pay and allowances and pensions; for legal services; for the veterinary and remount services; for the Army Cadet Forces; for questions of Army welfare and education including school children overseas; and for resettlement and sports. The Quartermaster-General is responsible for logistic planning for the Army; for the storage, distribution, maintenance, repair and inspection of equipment, stores and ammunition; for development of stores; for supply, transport and accommodation; for the development, production and inspection of clothing; for military movements and transportation; for the Army postal, catering, salvage and fire services; and for questions connected with canteens, institutes and military labour. The Master General of the Ordnance is a member of both the Army Board and of the Procurement Executive Management Board. He is responsible to the Chief of Defence Procurement for the financial and technical management of the approved programme for the procurement of land service equipment for the Armed Services, and to the Army Board for the co-ordination of the Army's total equipment programme.

Headquarters United Kingdom Land Forces at Wilton commands all Army units in UK except Ministry of Defence controlled units. The Ministry of Defence retains direct operational control of units in Northern Ireland. Command by HQ United Kingdom Land Forces is exercised through 9 district headquarters. There are 3 major overseas Commands: Land Forces Cyprus, Hong Kong and the British Army of the Rhine. There are also garrisons in Berlin, Gibraltar, Falkland Islands, Brunei and Belize.

The strength of the Regular Army (less the Brigade of Gurkhas and locally enlisted personnel) on 1 Jan. 1987 was 153,800 men and 6,500 women. Strength of reserve forces were: Regular reserves, 151,700; territorial army, 76,100.

The Territorial Army role is to provide a national reserve for employment on specific tasks at home and overseas and to meet the unexpected when required; and, in particular, to complete the Army Order of Battle of NATO committed forces and to provide certain units for the support of NATO Headquarters, to assist in maintaining a secure UK base in support of forces deployed on the Continent of Europe and to provide a framework for any future expansion of the Reserves. In addition, men who have completed service in the Regular Army normally have some liability to serve in the Regular Reserve. All members of the TA and Regular Reserve may be called out by a Queen's Order in time of emergency of imminent national danger and most of the TA and a large proportion of the Regular Reserve may be called out by a Queen's Order when warlike operations are in preparation or in progress. There is a special reserve force in Northern Ireland, the Ulster Defence Regiment, 6,600 strong, which gives support to the regular army.

Men, women and juniors enlist in the Army for 22 years' active and reserve service. However, under a scheme introduced in May 1981 they are entitled to give 12 months' notice (18 months' for women) to leave active service provided they serve for a minimum of 3 years. Alternatively, they can agree to serve for 6 or 9 years to receive the benefit of higher rates of pay. Those enlisting in certain technical trades must agree to serve for a minimum of 6 years. Recruits under the age of

17½ on reaching the age of 18 are entitled either to confirm their original engagement or to reduce their period of service to 3 years.

Women serve in both the Regular Army and the TA in the Queen Alexandra's Royal Army Nursing Corps, the Ulster Defence Regiment and the Women's Royal Army Corps, the latter's employments including communications, motor transport, clerical and catering duties. Some officers of the Women's Royal Army Corps are employed on the staffs of military headquarters.

Blaxford, G., *The Regiments Depart: A History of the British Army 1945–70.* London, 1971
Brereton, J. M., *The British Soldier.* London, 1985
Johnson, F. A., *Defence by Ministry: The British Ministry of Defence 1944–1974.* London, 1980
Stanhope, H., *The Soldiers: An Anatomy of the British Army.* London, 1979

Navy. Control of the Royal Navy is vested in the Defence Council and is exercised through the Admiralty Board, which consists of 7 civilian and 4 service members. The Secretary of State for Defence is chairman of the Admiralty Board. The other civilian members are the Ministers and Under Secretaries of State for the Armed Forces and for Defence Procurement; the Second Permanent Under Secretary of State; the Controller, Research and Development Establishments, Research and Nuclear.

The naval members are the Chief of the Naval Staff and First Sea Lord (professional head of the Royal Navy) responsible for fighting efficiency, planning and operations advice (aided by the Assistant Chief of the Naval Staff); the Chief of Naval Personnel and Second Sea Lord, responsible for the manning of the Fleet, service conditions, training, discipline and welfare; the Controller of the Navy, responsible for research and development, design, production, inspection, repair and maintenance of ships, their weapons and equipment; and the Chief of Fleet Support, responsible for the provision of naval armament, victualling and medical stores and fuels, and for the movement of material, transport of personnel, and head of the naval dockyard organization and servicing the Fleet and of the Royal Fleet Auxiliary.

The Commander in Chief Fleet at Northwood exercises command of the Fleet. All Naval Air Stations and units at non-naval Air Stations and establishments in the United Kingdom are commanded by the Flag Officer Naval Air Command. The command of all other naval establishments in the UK, except Ministry of Defence-controlled units including Royal dockyards and the Naval Air Repair Organization, and those under the full command of the Commandant General Royal Marines, is exercised by the C.-in-C. Naval Home Command at Portsmouth through Area Flag Officers.

The Royal Naval Reserve (RNR) and the Royal Marines Reserve (RMR) currently have provision for 5,500 and 1,500 personnel respectively. The role of the RNR is to provide a reserve of trained personnel who will be available in times of war to undertake such duties as Naval Control of Shipping, Mine Counter-Measures (manning minesweepers, etc); HQ Command and Communications, and Rotary Wing Aircrew. The main roles of the RMR are to provide reinforcements and to carry out other specialist tasks with the UK-Netherlands Amphibious Force. In addition, men who have completed service in the Royal Navy and the Royal Marines have a liability to serve in the Royal Fleet Reserve. All members of the RNR, the RMR and the Royal Fleet Reserve have a liability to be called out under the provisions of the Reserve Forces Act 1980. Officers of the Retired and Emergency Lists and Pensioners also have a Reserve liability.

Royal Navy ratings enlist to complete 22 years' active service (at the end of which there is selective re-engagement open to senior, chief and charge specialists for a further 5 or 10 years) with the option to leave at 18 months notice on completion of a minimum of 2½ years' productive service. Those who leave before completing 22 years have a liability for up to 3 years' service in the Royal Fleet Reserve. Royal Marine ranks, WRNS ratings and QARNNS ratings enlist to complete an initial 9 year engagement but they may apply to re-engage to complete 14 years and 22 years. Servicewomen have no reserve liability.

Women serve in both the WRNS and the QARNNS, and their reserves. In the former, they are employed on a wide range of duties including secretarial, communications, stores accounting, catering, education and training support.

The following is a summary of the more important units:

Category	1980	1981	1982	1983	1984	1985	1986	1987	1988
Aircraft carriers	3	3	3	3	3	3	3	3	3
Submarines	31	32	33	31	32	32	32	30	28
Destroyers	14	15	13	14	15	14	13	13	13
Frigates	55	47	47	46	48	42	39	36	34

There are also 2 assault ships, 2 aviation training (helicopter support) ships, 1 forward repair ship, 2 maintenance ships, 2 ice patrol ships, 15 patrol vessels of corvette size, 9 surveying vessels, 26 minehunters, 5 coastal minesweepers, 12 deep (fleet) minesweepers, 1 mine countermeasures support ship, 4 trials ships, 1 large seabed operations vessel, 2 diving support ships, 6 patrol craft, 19 coastal training craft, 11 mooring, salvage and boom vessels, 4 fleet replenishment ships, 14 fleet oilers, 35 other auxiliaries, 7 logistic landing ships, 50 minor landing craft, 14 fleet tugs, 46 other tugs, and 60 tenders.

In the following table the principal surface warships are listed, in descending order of modernity.

Com-pleted	Name	Standard displacement Tons	Aircraft	Armament	Shaft horse-power	Speed knots

Light Aircraft Carriers [3]

Com-pleted	Name	Standard displacement Tons	Aircraft	Armament	Shaft horse-power	Speed knots
1985	Ark Royal	20,000	8 Sea Harriers; 9 ASW Sea Kings; 3 AEW Sea Kings;	Twin 'Sea Dart' surface-to-air missile launchers; 2 Phalanx guns; (3 in *Ark Royal*);	94,000 (gas)	28·0
1982	Illustrious [1]	16,250	5 Sea Harriers; 9 Sea King helicopters (original aircraft complement – see notes below)	2 20 mm guns (being replaced by 3 'Goalkeeper' systems		
1980	Invincible [2]					

[1] Two AEW (airborne early warning) Sea Kings added to complement – to be increased to three in each ship.

[2] Originally designed as 'Command Cruiser', subsequently re-rated as 'Through-deck Cruiser' (meaning long underdeck hangar with flat-top or near full-length flight deck) and later designated 'Anti-Submarine Cruiser'. Officially listed as anti-submarine warfare carrier in 1980. Slightly angled deck and 7 degree ski-jump ramp, like *Illustrious*, but *Ark Royal* has 12 degree ski-jump for Harriers. During the Falklands campaign *Invincible* embarked ten Harriers and nine Sea Kings. In 1986 she paid off for refit at Devonport to include a higher, 12-degree, ski-jump ramp, greater capacity for 22 aircraft and improved armament and sensors. When she becomes operational in early 1989 *Illustrious* will be reduced to maintenance reserve until refit scheduled for 1991 to 1994.

[3] The aircraft carrier *Hermes*, 24,000 tons, was sold to India in 1986 and renamed *Viraat*; she was refitted at Devonport, completed in mid-1987, before becoming operational in the Indian Navy.

Note: For disposals of the *Ark Royal* and *Eagle*, large fixed-wing aircraft carriers; the original sister carriers of *Hermes* (*Bulwark*, *Albion* and *Centaur*) and the rebuilt carrier *Victorious*; the helicopter cruisers *Blake* and *Tiger*, original sister ship *Lion*, and the other orthodox cruisers *Belfast* (museum ship on the *Thames*), *Ceylon*, *Newfoundland*, *Birmingham*, *Jamaica*, *Superb*, *Kenya*, *Swiftsure*, *Bermuda*, *Mauritius*, *Sheffield* and *Gambia*, see 1983–84 and earlier editions. (*Tiger* was towed to Spain in Sept. 1986 for breaking up).

Capital (Strategic) Submarines

Class	No.	Displacement (submerged) tons	Missile Tubes (vertical)	Nuclear Reactors	Shaft horse- power	Speed Knots
"R"	4 [1]	8,500	16 Polaris A3	1	15,000	25 dived 20 surface

[1] *Renown, Repulse, Resolution* and *Revenge* (former battleship names) completed in 1967–69. All also have six 21-in. torpedo tubes.

Other submarines are of the following classes: 'Upholder' (diesel electric-propelled) for completion in 1988, 1; 'Trafalgar' (nuclear propelled), 5; 'Swiftsure' (nuclear propelled), 6; 'Churchill' (nuclear propelled), 3; 'Valiant' (nuclear propelled), 2; 'Oberon' (completed 1960–67), 11.

The destroyers of the Royal Navy are of the following classes: Type 42 (completed 1976–85), twelve; Type 82 (completed 1973), one.

Frigates are of the following classes; Type 22 (1979–88), twelve; Type 21 (1974–78), six; 'Leander' (completed 1963–73), 16.

Ships under construction or on order include 4 nuclear armed ('Trident') and nuclear powered submarines displacing 15,000 tons dived, *Vanguard, Vengeance, Victorious* and *Venerable*; 2 nuclear propelled fleet submarines, 3 diesel driven patrol submarines, 6 frigates, and 7 mine counter-measures vessels.

The Fleet Air Arm has 320 aircraft of which 280 are active, in 14 operational squadrons, 3 with Sea Harrier fighter/reconnaissance aircraft, 5 with Sea King, 1 with Gazelle, 1 with Lynx and 1 with Wasp anti-submarine helicopters, 2 with Sea King helicopters for commando transport, and 1 with Sea King helicopters converted for airborne early warning. There are 7 training and second-line squadrons, all equipped with helicopters except for 1 with Jetstream aircraft.

The total number of male and female personnel (including Royal Marines) was (in 1,000) 1985–86, 68·2; 1986–87, 67·4; 1987–88, 65·7.

Blackman, R. V. B., *The World's Warships.* London, annual
Blackman, R. V. B., *Ships of the Royal Navy.* London, annual
Sharpe, R. G. (ed.), *Jane's Fighting Ships.* London, annual

Air Force. In May 1912 the Royal Flying Corps first came into existence with military and naval wings, of which the latter became the independent Royal Naval Air Service in July 1914. On 2 Jan. 1918 an Air Ministry was formed, and on 1 April 1918 the Royal Flying Corps and the Royal Naval Air Service were amalgamated, under the Air Ministry, as the Royal Air Force.

In 1937 the units based on aircraft carriers and naval shore stations again passed to the operational and administrative control of the Admiralty, as the Fleet Air Arm. In 1964 control of the RAF became a responsibility of the Ministry of Defence.

The Royal Air Force is administered by the Air Force Board, of which the Secretary of State for Defence is Chairman. The Minister of State for the Armed Forces is Vice-Chairman, and normally acts as Chairman on behalf of the Secretary of State. Other members of the Board are the Minister of State for Defence Procurement, the Under-Secretary of State for the Armed Forces, the Under-Secretary of State for Defence Procurement, the Chief of the Air Staff, Air Member for Personnel, Air Member for Supply and Organization, Controller of Aircraft, Second Permanent Under-Secretary of State and Controller R & D Establishments, Research and Nuclear. The RAF is organized into commands:

Home Commands. Strike and Support Commands. The Air Training Corps and the Air Sections of the Combined Cadet Force are under the administrative control of Support Command and functionally controlled by the Ministry of Defence.

The RAF College, which trains general-duties, engineering, and supply and secretarial graduates for permanent commissions, is at Cranwell. The RAF Staff College is at Bracknell. The Department of Air Warfare is at Cranwell. The RAF Central Flying School is at Scampton. Estimated strength in Nov. 1987, including WRAF and boys, was 93,334.

Strike Command is made up of 3 Groups. Nos 1 and 38 Groups merged in late 1983 to form a new No 1 Group, responsible for the strike/attack, reconnaissance, tanker, battlefield support and transport forces. The Tornado GR1 and Jaguar provide the strike/attack and reconnaissance. Victor, VC10, TriStar and Hercules tanker aircraft are used for air refuelling. Battlefield support forces comprise Harrier GR3s, plus Harrier GR5s now entering service, and Chinook, Puma and Wessex support helicopters. The strategic and tactical transport force comprises VC10s and Hercules, and communications aircraft. No 11 Group controls the air defence forces: Tornado F3 and Phantom supersonic all-weather intercepters, Bloodhound surface-to-air missiles, and ground environment radars, the associated communication systems, and the Ballistic Missile Early Warning System at Fylingdales. No 11 Group also controls the Hawks of the Tactical Weapons Units which, in war, would supplement air defence fighters at bases throughout the UK. UK air defence is undergoing major improvements. The Boeing E-3 will enter service in 1990–91, replacing the Shackleton, and in the ground environment, there are new radars and communications systems entering service. No 18 Group is responsible for maritime air operations. ASW is the duty of the Nimrod Mk 2, which also has a capability against surface ships, although Buccaneers provide the main offensive force against a maritime surface threat. No 18 Group also operates Canberras in a multitude of roles, including photo-reconnaissance, target towing and ECM training, as well as Nimrod special-purpose aircraft. Search and rescue units are equipped with Sea King and Wessex helicopters. RAF Regiment short-range air defence squadrons, armed with Rapier, and the field squadrons form part of 1 Group, as does The Queen's Flight, which has 2 BAe 146s and 2 Wessex helicopters. The Military Air Traffic Operations organization also has the status of a Group. Strike Command has NATO commitments, but is available for overseas reinforcement. The training element of RAF Support Command utilizes Bulldog and Chipmunk primary trainers, Jet Provost basic trainers (to be replaced by turboprop Tucanos), Hawk advanced trainers, Jetstreams for multi-engine pilot training, twin-jet Dominies for training navigators and other non-pilot aircrew, and Gazelle and Wessex helicopters.

Overseas Commands. Royal Air Force Germany. Small units in Gibraltar, the Falkland Islands, Belize, Cyprus and Hong Kong.

Squadrons of RAF Germany, which form part of NATO's 2nd Allied Tactical Air Force under SACEUR, have Tornado GR1, Harrier GR3 and Jaguar attack and reconnaissance aircraft, Phantom fighters, Chinook and Puma Helicopters, Andover communications aircraft, and Rapier surface-to-air missile squadrons of the RAF Regiment.

A squadron of Phantom aircraft, a squadron of Chinook and Sea King helicopters for transport and search and rescue, and a flight of Harriers and a flight of Hercules tankers are based in the Falkland Islands; a squadron of Wessex helicopters is based in Hong Kong and Cyprus.

The Royal Air Force, 1939–45. Vols. I, II, III. HMSO, 1953–54
Taylor J. W. R. (ed.), *Jane's All the World's Aircraft.* London. Annual from 1909

INTERNATIONAL RELATIONS

Membership. The UK is a member of UN, Commonwealth, the European Communities, OECD, the Council of Europe, NATO and the Colombo Plan.

ECONOMY

Budget. Revenue and expenditure for years ending 31 March, in £ sterling:

Revenue	Estimated in the Budgets	Actual receipts into the Exchequer	More than estimates
1985	98,000,000,000	98,400,000,000	400,000,000
1986	106,500,000,000	105,800,000,000	– 700,000,000
1987	108,600,000,000	111,100,000,000	2,500,000,000
1988	168,800,000,000	173,700,000,000	4,900,000,000

The Budget estimate of ordinary revenue for 1988–89 is £184,900m.

Expenditure	Budget and supplementary estimates	Actual payments out of the Exchequer	More than estimates
1985	103,400,000,000	105,800,000,000	2,400,000,000
1986	159,500,000,000	157,700,000,000	– 1,800,000,000
1987	163,900,000,000	164,900,000,000	– 1,000,000,000
1988	173,500,000,000	171,800,000,000	– 1,700,000,000

The Budget estimate of ordinary expenditure for 1988–89 is £182,900m.

The imperial revenue in detail for 1987–88 and the expenditure, are given below, as is the budget estimate for 1988–89 (in £1m.):

Sources of revenue	Net receipts 1987–88	Budget estimate 1988–89
Inland Revenue:		
Income	41,400	42,100
Corporation tax	15,600	19,800
Petroleum revenue tax	2,330	1,180
Capital Gains tax	1,350	1,950
Development land tax	25	10
Inheritance tax	1,070	1,000
Stamp duties	2,440	1,950
Total Inland Revenue	64,200	68,000
Customs and Excise:		
Value Added Tax	24,100	26,200
Oil	7,800	8,400
Tobacco	4,800	5,000
Spirits, beer, wine, cider and perry	4,400	4,500
Betting and gaming	810	890
Car tax	1,150	1,260
Other excise duties	20	20
Customs duties	1,490	1,550
Agricultural levies	190	120
Total Customs and Excise	44,700	47,900
Vehicle Excise duties	2,700	2,770
Miscellaneous receipts:		
Broadcasting receiving licences	1,030	1,140
Interest and dividends	1,080	680
Gas levy	500	420
Other, including oil royalties	9,100	7,300
Total Consolidated Fund Revenue	123,200	128,200

The following are the branches of expenditure for year ended 31 March 1988 and the estimates for the year 1988–89 (in £1m.):

	Estimates 1987–88	Estimates 1988–89
Social Security	46,300	48,500
Defence	18,600	19,200
Health and Personal Social Services	19,700	20,700
Educational and Science	17,100	18,000
Other	49,300	52,000
Privatization proceeds	– 5,000	– 5,000
	146,000	156,800
Interest Payments	17,500	17,500
Other Adjustments	8,300	8,600
Total	171,800	182,900

A single graduated income tax came into operation on 6 April 1973, replacing the existing income tax and surtax.

Rates of Personal Tax from 6 April 1988	%
Income between	
£0–£19,300	25
Over £19,300	40

Under the tax system, the amounts of the personal allowances are adjusted so that they retain their equivalent in relation to earned income.

Personal Allowances	1988–89 £
Single person } Wife's earned income }	2,605
Married man	4,095
Additional allowance	1,490
Age allowance (age 65 or over):	
Single	3,180
Married	5,035
Age allowance (age 80 or over):	
Single	3,310
Married	5,205

Deductions of tax under PAYE extend over the full range of unified tax rates and not merely the basic rate. Similarly, assessment on business profits and on other income which was directly assessed to tax, such as rents and interest on bank deposits, are made by reference to the full scale of rates, including where appropriate the investment income surcharge.

The standard rate of 25% is the rate at which tax is deducted from payments of interest, etc., and corresponds under the corporation tax system, to the tax credit on dividends. Where an individual's total income is such that he is liable on this taxed investment income at rates exceeding 25%, or if his investment income is high enough to make him liable to the surcharge, the higher rate or surcharge liability on this taxed investment income will in general be assessed separately after the end of the tax year.

Corporation Tax. Corporation Tax applies, with certain exceptions, to trades or businesses carried on by bodies corporate or by unincorporated societies or other bodies and this tax came into force from April 1966 replacing Profits Tax. Corporation Tax for companies was 35% for 1988–89. Small companies rates, 1988–89, 25%.

Capital Gains Tax. Gains resulting from the disposal of capital assets (other than British Government and Government guaranteed securities and certain exempted forms of property such as a private car and personal residences) are taxed under the Finance Act 1965. In 1988–89 exemption was granted for all gains made in a financial year which in total did not exceed £5,000 and most trusts on the first £2,500 but the base was brought forward from 1965 to 1982.

Inheritance Tax. Formerly Capital Transfer Tax. From 18 March 1986 there is no lifetime charge on gifts between individuals. From 1988 a flat rate of 40% was introduced with a threshold of £110,000.

Value Added Tax. Value Added Tax was introduced from 1 April 1973 at the rate of 10% on the supply of goods (with certain exceptions) and services. From 18 June 1979 the rate of tax was fixed at 15%. From 16 March 1988 the registration limits became £22,100 per annum and £7,500 a quarter.

Kay, J. A. and King, M. A., *The British Tax System.* OUP, 1980

Local Taxation. The rateable value on which rates were leviable in England and

Wales on 1 April 1987 was £8,025m. In England and Wales, the average amount of rates collected per £ of rateable value was £0·34 in 1913–14 and estimated to be 226·8p for 1987–88. In Scotland the rateable value on which rates are leviable on 1 April 1986 was £3,190m. and the average amount per £ of rateable value of the rates was 67·2p.

Under the Local Government Planning and Land Act 1980, the Government gives general financial assistance to local authorities by means of rate support grants. The Rate Support Grant Supplementary Report (England) 1987–88 deals with the distribution of these grants to local authorities in England only. The grants for 1987–88 contain (i) Block Grant £8,739m., the object of which is to give authorities sufficient grant to put them in a position where they can provide similar standards of service for a similar rate in the £, and (ii) Domestic Grant £717m., which will provide a relief of 18½p for domestic ratepayers except for those in the Cities of London and Westminster where the relief provided is 38p and 28p respectively. There is also provision in the 1980 Act for payment of National Parks Supplementary Grant (£7·3m.) to county councils with all or part of a national park in their area, and Transport Supplementary Grant (£180m.) payable to county councils and the Greater London Council. Grants are also payable on revenue expenditure for specific services, including police and housing, and capital expenditure on certain services also attracts grant.

In Scotland, rate support grants are paid under the Local Government (Scotland) Act 1966 as amended. The total rate support grant and the amounts of the component parts for the local authority financial year 1988–89, as prescribed in the Rate Support Grant (Scotland) (No 3) Order 1987 are as follows: total £2,037·93m. comprising needs element £1,730·23m.; resources element £215·8m.; domestic element £91·9m. The needs element is designed to provide varying levels of support to take account of variations in the demand for services and the cost of providing them with a similar degree of efficiency per head of population in different areas. The resources element, by compensating for deficiencies in local rating resources, enables local authorities receiving it to raise the same amount in rates per head of population for the same rate poundage. The domestic element is paid to rating authorities to offset the cost of reducing by 7p in the £ rates payable on domestic properties. As in England and Wales capital and revenue grants are also payable on expenditure for certain specified services.

Rates and Rateable Values, 1974–75. HMSO
Rates and Rateable Values in Scotland, 1977–78. HMSO
Estimates, 1982–83. GLC
Analysis of Rateable Values List. GLC, 1977
Report on Rate Support Grant Order 1979. HMSO

Gross National Product:	1946	1960	1970	1980	1986
Expenditure (£1m.)					
Consumers' expenditure	7,273	16,939	31,773	135,738	234,167
Central government final consumption	2,282	4,206	8,961	48,424	79,423
Gross domestic fixed capital formation	925	4,190	9,462	39,411	64,227
Value of physical increase in stocks and work in progress	−126	562	425	−2,706	551
Total domestic expenditure at market prices	10,354	25,897	50,581	220,867	378,368
Exports of goods and services	1,775	5,153	11,533	63,158	97,835
Less Imports of goods and services	−2,083	−5,549	−11,122	−57,913	−101,308
Less Taxes on expenditure	−1,573	−3,378	−8,416	−36,882	−62,273
Subsidies	384	493	884	5,308	6,467
Gross domestic product at factor cost	8,855	22,616	43,460	194,538	319,089

Factor incomes (£1m.)	1946	1960	1970	1980	1986
Income from employment	5,758	15,174	30,404	136,050	209,445
Income from self-employment[1]	1,126	2,008	3,735	17,581	34,340
Gross trading profits of companies[1]	1,476	3,730	5,935	27,708	50,785
Gross trading surplus of public corporations[1]	20	534	1,447	6,222	8,126
Gross trading surplus of other public enterprises[1]	86	189	151	242	161
Rent[2]	429	1,086	2,833	13,390	22,497
Total domestic income before providing for depreciation and stock appreciation	8,895	22,863	44,837	203,304	328,380
Less Stock appreciation	−125	−122	−1,090	−6,456	−2,331
Residual error	…	−125	−287	−2,310	−6,960
Gross domestic product at factor cost	8,770	22,616	43,460	194,538	319,089
Net property income from abroad	85	233	559	−273	4,686
Gross national product	8,855	22,849	44,019	194,265	323,775
Less Capital consumption	…	−2,047	−4,420	−27,223	−46,004
National income	…	20,802	39,599	167,042	277,771

[1] Before providing for depreciation and stock appreciation.
[2] Before providing for depreciation.

National Economic Development Council. The NEDC, which first met in 1962, is the national forum for economic consultation between government, management and unions. It includes leading representatives of the Government, CBI and TUC, chairmen of nationalized industries and independent members. It meets usually under the chairmanship of the Chancellor of the Exchequer, other Secretaries of State and occasionally, the Prime Minister. Discussions at the monthly council meetings are normally based on papers, presented by the participating parties, which deal primarily with questions of quarterly economic performance and growth prospects, besides seeking to agree on ways of improving industrial efficiency. Council meetings are held in private to encourage the frank exchange of views between members, and discussions are summarized at a press conference taken by the Director-General of the National Economic Development Office (NEDO) following each meeting. The Sector Groups and Working Parties, like the NEDC, bring together representatives of management and unions, officials from Government and others, who use this multi-party meeting place to study the efficiency and prospects of individual industries and sectors and to suggest ways in which these could be improved. The National Economic Development Office (NEDO) provides the professional staff for the NEDC and the Sector Groups and Working Parties.

Currency. The monetary unit of Great Britain is the *pound sterling*. A gold standard was adopted in 1816, the sovereign or twenty-shilling piece weighing 7·98805 grammes 0·916⅔ fine. Currency notes for £1 and 10s. were first issued by the Treasury in 1914, replacing the circulation of sovereigns. The issue of £1 and 10s. notes was taken over by the Bank of England in 1928. The issue of 10s. notes ceased on the issue of the 50p coin in 1969.

In March 1988, £1 = US$ 1·77.

When the pound was floated in June 1972 measures were also introduced to control payments between the 'Scheduled Territories' (*i.e.*, the UK including the Channel Islands, the Isle of Man and Ireland), and the rest of the Sterling Area as well as the rest of the world. Exchange control restrictions were lifted in Oct. 1979 except for Zimbabwe and these were lifted in Dec. 1979.

Coinage. The sovereign (£1) weighs 123·27447 grains, or 7·98805 grammes, 0·916⅔ (or eleven-twelfths) fine, and consequently it contains 113·00159 grains or 7·32238 grammes of fine gold. On 15 Feb. 1971 (Decimalization Day) a decimal currency system was introduced retaining the *pound sterling* as the major unit but now divided into 100 *new pence* instead of 240 old pence. The decimal coins are the £1 (22·5 mm diameter, 9·5 grammes weight); 50p (equilateral curve heptagon, 30 mm diameter, 13·5 grammes); 20p (equilateral curved heptagon 21·4 mm diameter, 5 grammes); 10p (28·5 mm, 11·31 grammes); 5p (23·6 mm, 5·65 grammes); 2p (25·9 mm, 7·12 grammes) and 1p (20·3 mm, 3·56 grammes). The Decimal Currency Act, 1967 and the Proclamation of 27 Dec. 1968 required that the 50p, 10p and 5p be made of cupro-nickel and the 2p, 1p and ½p of mixed metal; copper, tin and zinc (bronze). The Decimal Currency Act, 1969, provided that the coins of the Queen's Maundy Money should continue to be made in silver to a millesimal fineness of 925.

By Proclamation dated 28 July 1971, which came into force on 30 Aug. 1971, the crown, double-florin, the florin, the shilling and the sixpence are to be treated as coins of the new currency and as being of the denominations respectively of 25, 20, 10, 5 and 2½ new pence. The sixpence was demonetised on 30 June 1980 and the ½p on 31 Dec. 1984.

The Coinage Act, 1971, specified that the legal tender limits for coins were: Gold coins, for payment of any amount; coins of cupro-nickel and silver of denominations of more than 10p, for payment of any amount not exceeding £10; coins of cupro-nickel and silver of not more than 10p, for payment of any amount not exceeding £5; coins of bronze, for payment of any amount not exceeding 20p. The £1 coin is legal tender to any amount.

UK coins issued in the 12 months up to March 1987 totalled £31m.

It is estimated that the following coins were in circulation in the UK at 31 March 1987, in millions: £1 783, 50p 744, 20p 1,005, 10p 1,510, 5p 1,860, 2p 2,700, 1p 4,200, ½p 1,400.

Bank-notes. The Bank of England issues notes in denominations of £5, £10, £20 and £50 for the amount of the fiduciary note issue. Under the provisions of the Currency and Bank Notes Act, 1954, which came into force on 22 Feb. 1954, the amount of the fiduciary note issue was fixed at £1,575m., but this figure might be altered by direction of HM Treasury after representations made by the Bank of England.

All Bank of England notes are legal tender in England and Wales. The banks in Scotland and Northern Ireland have certain note-issuing powers.

The total amount of Bank of England notes issued at 31 Dec. 1987 was £14,550m., of which £14,542m. were in the hands of other banks and the public and £8m. in the Banking Department of the Bank of England.

Banking. The Bank of England, Threadneedle Street, London, is the Government's banker and the 'banker's bank'. It has the sole right of note issue in England and Wales and manages the National Debt. The Bank operates under royal charters of 1694 and 1946 and the Bank of England Act, 1946. The capital stock has, since 1 March 1946, been held by the Treasury.

The statutory return is published weekly. End-Dec. figures for the past 4 years are as follows (in £1m.):

	Notes in circulation	Notes and coin in Banking Department	Public deposits (government)	Other deposits[1]
1984	13,477	13	106	2,082
1985	12,863	7	104	2,006
1986	13,482	8	163	2,499
1987	14,542	8	100	3,144

[1] Including Special Deposits.

The fiduciary note issue was £14,550m. at 31 Dec. 1987. All the profits of the note issue are passed on to the National Loans Fund.

Official reserves of gold and convertible currencies, SDR and reserve position in the IMF at the end of Dec. 1987 were US$44,326m.

The value of paper debit bank clearings for 1987, £8,324,927m. Paper credit clearings for 1987, £91,980m. Automatic direct debits, 1987, £126,835m.; automatic credit transfers, 1987, £229,509m.

The following statistics relate to the London and Scottish banks' groups at 31 Dec. 1987. Total deposits (sterling and currency), £250,410m.; sterling market loans £45,168m.; advances (sterling and currency), £154,842m.; sterling investments £11,402m.

Total net profits/losses from the operations of the main London clearing bank groups in 1987 amounted to £45m. following substantial provisions for sovereign debt, of which £549m. in gross dividends, £542m. transferred from reserves.

The clearing banks cover all aspects of banking business in UK including corporate business, and are also actively involved in international banking.

Trustee Savings Banks (TSB). Trustee Savings Banks started in Scotland in 1810 and incorporated in Scotland on 21 Oct. 1985 as TSB Group plc. An offer was made to the public to purchase shares on 12 Sept. 1986; the offer was successful and in 1988 there were about 1·9m. shareholders.

On 31 Oct. 1987 the total assets of TSB totalled £17,194m., the total number of accounts exceeded 11m.

National Savings Bank. Statistics for 1985 and 1986:

	Ordinary accounts		Investment accounts	
	1985	1986	1985	1986
Accounts open at 31 Dec.	15,193,626[1]	15,353,745[1]	3,197,212	3,485,775
Amounts—	£1,000	£1,000	£1,000	£1,000
Received	655,913	641,485	1,264,662	1,370,004
Interest credited	78,589[2]	78,630[2]	595,875	616,495
Paid	780,475	747,552	1,310,196	1,332,386
Due to depositors at 31 Dec.	1,694,123	1,666,686	5,506,531	6,160,644
Average amount due to each depositor in active accounts	£111·45	£108·55	£1,722·29	£1,767·36

[1] Excluding non-computerized accounts, amounting to £104m. in 1985 and £101·7m. in 1986.

[2] The interest credited to depositors for the Ordinary account for 1986 has been calculated on the same basis as 1985. (6% per annum payable on accounts with a minimum balance of £500, 3% on accounts with a minimum balance of less than £500).

The amount due to depositors in Ordinary Accounts on 1 Jan. 1988 was approximately £1,677,844,572 and in Investment Accounts £6,946,153,534.

The National Girobank (founded 1968) had (1986) 1·95m. customers with balances of £1,019m.

Bank of England Quarterly Bulletin. Bank of England
Bank of England Annual Report. Bank of England
British Banking and other Financial Institutions. HMSO, 1977
Central Statistical Office, Financial Statistics. HMSO (monthly)
Report of the Committee on the Working of the Monetary System. HMSO, 1959
Report of the Select Committee on Nationalised Industries—The Bank of England. HMSO, 1970
The Royal Mint. 6th ed. HMSO, 1977
Sayers, R. H., *The Bank of England 1891–1944.* CUP, 1976

Weights and Measures. Conversion to the metric system was in progress (1987) which will replace the imperial system at present in force.

ENERGY AND NATURAL RESOURCES

Electricity. The electricity industry was vested in the British Electricity Authority on 1 April 1948. Following the re-organization of the electricity supply industry after the passing of the Electricity Act, 1957, the statutory bodies comprising the electricity service in England and Wales are the Electricity Council, the Central Electricity Generating Board and the 12 Area Electricity Boards.

The Electricity Council has functioned from Jan. 1958 as the central council for the supply industry in England and Wales for consultation on, and formulation of, general policy; its main functions are to advise the Secretary of State for Energy on all matters affecting the supply industry, and to promote and assist the maintenance and development by the Central Electricity Generating Board and the Area Boards (known collectively as Electricity Boards) of an efficient, co-ordinated and economical system of electricity supply. The Council can also perform services for the Boards, and, in addition, has certain specific functions, particularly in matters of finance, research and industrial relations.

The Central Electricity Generating Board is responsible for the generation and bulk supply of electricity to the 12 Area Boards in England and Wales. It therefore plans the provision of new generating and transmission capacity, including the siting and construction of new generating stations, both conventional and nuclear, and is responsible for the operation and maintenance of generating stations and the main transmission system.

Area Electricity Boards. Each of the 12 Area Electricity Boards acquires bulk supplies of electricity from the Generating Board and is responsible for distribution networks and sales of electricity to its Area consumers. Thus distribution and utilization of electricity, and also the contracting and sale of appliances side of the industry, are their responsibilities.

The number of power stations owned by the Generating Board in England and Wales on 31 March 1987 was 78 with a total output capacity, of 52,363 mw. Total number of customers in England and Wales on 31 March 1987 was 21,715,000 (on 31 March 1986, 21,487,941).

Electricity sold in England and Wales in 1986–87 amounted to 219,551m. units. Operating profit before MWCA in 1986–87 was £1,150m. Coal used for electricity generation in 1986–87 amounted to 77m. tonnes (79m. tonnes in 1985–86). Total fuel (coal equivalent) used in 1985–86 amounted to 100·8m. tonnes and in 1986–87 to 100m. tonnes. Ten nuclear stations of total output capacity 5,029 mw provided 16·4% of total units supplied in 1986–87. Eight of these are gas cooled graphite-moderated stations using natural uranium fuel canned in magnesium alloy (Magnox) and 2 are advanced gas-cooled stations (AGR).

The number of persons employed by the Generating Board, the Electricity Council and Area Boards at the end of March 1987 was 131,067.

The North of Scotland Hydro-Electric Board, established under the Hydro-Electric Development (Scotland) Act 1943, is a nationalized authority responsible for the generation, transmission, distribution and sale of electricity to its (1987) 584,577 consumers.

The Board's district covers a quarter of the land mass of Great Britain and lies generally north and west of a line joining the firths of Clyde and Tay as well as all the island groups extending to the Outer Hebrides, Orkney and Shetland. Over 99% of potential consumers have now been provided with supply.

On the mainland the Board operates generating stations with a total installed generating capacity of 3,216 mw consisting of 1,762 mw of hydro power and pumped storage, together with 1,320 mw of steam. Diesel stations with a total installed capacity of 102 mw supply the principal island groups together with 32 mw gas turbine. A 1,320 mw of oil/gas fired thermal plant is now operating at Peterhead.

The main transmission system consists of 5,097 circuit km of 275 kv and 132 kv lines linking the power stations and the bulk supply points serving the distribution networks. The system control centre at Pitlochry co-ordinates the operation of the transmission system and power stations together with the continuous interchange of power with the South of Scotland Electricity Board. The number of staff in Dec. 1987 was 3,795.

The South of Scotland Electricity Board was established in April 1955 by the Electricity Reorganisation (Scotland) Act 1954, replacing in South Scotland 2 Electricity Boards and 2 Divisions of the British Electricity Authority. The area of Scotland served by the Board lies south of a line from the Firth of Clyde to the Firth of Tay and extends to about 8,000 sq. miles (21,000 sq. km), including the industrial belt of Scotland, with a population of 4m. By special arrangement a small part of North-East England is also supplied. The remainder of Scotland is served by the North of Scotland Hydro-Electric Board.

The Board differs from those established in England and Wales in that its responsibilities cover not only the distribution of electricity and retail sale of electrical appliances but also the generation and transmission of bulk power within South Scotland.

In 1988 the Board operated 15 generating stations (3 nuclear, 8 hydro-electric stations and 1 gas) with a total output capacity of 6,918 mw including 1,400 mw from Tornes Power Station.. In 1986–87 the Board sold 18,874m. units to more than 1·6m. consumers and had a total revenue of £906m. The number of staff employed at the end of the year was 12,066.

Oil. Production 1985, in 1,000 tonnes (1986 in brackets): Throughput of crude and process oils, 78,341 (80,155); refinery use, 5,179 (5,404); gases, 1,496 (1,421); naphtha, 2,883 (2,652); motor spirit, 22,254 (23,360); kerosene, 7,564 (7,960); diesel oil, 21,701 (22,408); fuel oil, 12,896 (12,523); lubricating oils, 1,188 (909); bitumen, 1,764 (1,887). Total output of refined products, 72,904 (74,089).

Gas. Following the Gas Act of 1986, British Gas plc became the successor company to the British Gas Corporation. Its primary activities are the purchase, distribution and sale of gas, supported by a broad range of services to customers. It also explores for and produces hydrocarbons. It is organized into a headquarters and twelve Regions.

British Gas explores for gas through 3 wholly owned subsidiary companies: Gas Council (Exploration) Limited (UK onshore and Denmark offshore); Hydrocarbons Great Britain Limited (Irish Sea and Cardigan Bay); Hydrocarbons Ireland Limited, (offshore Eire). British Gas owns and operates two gas fields, Morecambe and Rough field. The latter is used as a gas store and both have been developed to help meet peak winter demand.

In 1986–87, British Gas sold 18,894m. therms of gas to over 17m. customers. Just over 50% of the gas went to domestic customers, the rest to industrial and commercial enterprizes. The industry won 269,000 new customers in the period and made a before-tax profit of £1,062m. with a turnover of £7,610m.

In March 1986, there were 89,000 people employed directly by the industry. British Gas spends £74m. each year on its research and development programme and its international consultancy service works in about 20 countries.

Minerals. Coal. The number of British Coal Corporation producing collieries on 31 March 1987 was 110. Statistics of the coalmining industry for recent years are as follows:

Output, 1m. tonnes:	1983–84 [1]	1984–85 [2]	1985–86	1986–87
BCC mines (inc. tip and capital coal)	90·1	27·6	88·4	88·0
Opencast	13·8	13·6	14·1	13·3
Licensed	1·4	1·5	2·0	2·0
Total	105·3	42·7	104·5	103·3

Manpower and Productivity:

Men on colliery books (in 1,000) average	191·5	175·4	154·6	125·4
Overall output per man shift (tonnes)	2·43	2·08	2·72	3·29

[1] 53 week year. [2] Strike year.

Total stocks of coal on 31 March 1987 amounted to 34·5m. tonnes (24·7m. tonnes distributed, 9·8m. tonnes undistributed). Operating profit made by British Coal for the year ended March 1987 amounted to £369m. Interest payable was £386m. There was a deficit grant of £288m. from the Government for the year ended March 1987.

Production of coke (including coke breeze), 1986–87, 1·4m. tonnes.

In 1986–87 inland consumption of coal (in 1m. tonnes) was power stations, 82·4; coke ovens, 10·9; domestic, 8·1; other inland, 11; exports, 2·2. Coal imports (1986–87) 9·9m. tonnes.

The UK is among the 10 largest steel producing countries in the world. Output in recent years was as follows (in 1,000 tonnes):

			Home consumption	
	Pig-iron	Crude steel	Finished steel products	Crude steel equivalent
1984	9,562	15,120	11,451	14,290
1985	10,458	15,722	11,855	14,240
1986	9,785	14,730	12,143	14,740
1987	12,110	17,425	...	...

Exports of finished steel products were 6·2m. tonnes in 1987 and imports 4·3m. tonnes.

The industry is divided between the 'public sector' and the 'private sector'.

The British Steel Corporation, which was established by the Iron and Steel Act 1967, took over the 14 largest UK iron and steel making concerns (and their subsidiaries) in July 1967 and merged them into a single publicly owned business. With a turnover of more than £3,461m. in 1986–87, the British Steel Corporation ranks as one of Britain's major manufacturing industries and is one of the world's largest steel makers. The number of employees at the end of 1987 was 52,000. A substantial part of the British steel industry remains in private ownership and there were in 1988 a number of significant producers in mixed public/private ownership. Companies other than the British Steel Corporation are now responsible for about 22% of total UK liquid steel production, and 33% of finished steel production. These independent producers are represented by BISPA (British Independent Steel Producers Association) and for some products such as wire rod, reinforcement steel, bright bars, wire, open-die forgings and high speed tool and engineering steels, they cover nearly all UK production.

Pig iron produced in blast furnaces was 12·11m. tonnes in 1987 (9·78m. in 1986). Consumption of pig iron in steelworks, 11·93m. tonnes in 1987 (9·61m. in 1986); in iron foundries, 141,000 tonnes (160,000).

Production of non-ferrous metals in 1985 (in 1,000 tonnes): Refined copper, 125·5 (136·9 in 1984); refined lead, 307·7 (338·4); tin metal, 13·8 in 1984; virgin aluminium, 275·4 (287·9); slab zinc, 74·3 (85·6).

Agriculture. The total land area of the UK is 24m. hectares, of which 17·46m. (1986) is agricultural.

Distribution of the cultivated area in the UK (in 1,000 hectares):

	1985	1986
Corn crops[1]	4,015	4,024
Green crops[2]	1,150	1,154
Hops	5	4
Fruit	54	53
Bare fallow	41	48
Rotation grasses including lucerne	1,796	1,723
Permanent pasture	5,019	5,077

[1] Includes wheat, barley, rye and oats.
[2] Green crops include beans, potatoes, turnips and swedes, mangolds, sugar-beet, cabbage, etc., for fodder, vegetables, and all other crops.

The number of workers employed in agriculture, forestry and fishing in the UK was, in June 1986, 329,000; 311,000 were solely engaged in agriculture; there were also (June 1985) 291,700 farmers, partners and directors.

Principal crops in the UK as at June in each year:

	Wheat	Barley	Oats	Beans	Potatoes	Fodder crops	Sugar-beet	Rape for oilseed
				Area (1,000 hectares)				
1982	1,663	2,222	129	52	192	166	204	174
1983	1,695	2,143	108	45	195	180	199	222
1984	1,939	1,978	106	42	198	191	199	205
1985	1,902	1,965	133	56	191	229	269	296
1986	1,997	1,916	97	70	178	239	205	299
				Total product (1,000 tonnes)				
1982	10,310	10,960	575	229	6,875	7,565	10,005	581
1983	10,880	10,080	465	188	4,780	6,160	7,494	563
1984	14,970	11,070	515	223	7,395	7,085	9,015	925
1985	12,050	9,740	615	243	6,895	6,655	7,715	895
1986	13,910	10,010	505	311	6,446	7,325	8,120	965

Livestock in the UK as at June in each year (in 1,000):

	1982	1983	1984	1985	1986
Cattle	13,242	13,290	13,213	12,865	12,533
Sheep	33,053	34,069	34,802	35,628	37,016
Pigs	8,023	8,174	7,689	7,865	7,937
Poultry	135,363	128,260	127,507	128,968	...

Forestry. On 31 March 1985 the area of productive woodland in Britain was 2,037,000 hectares of which the Forestry Commission managed 892,000 hectares and the private sector 1,145,000 hectares.

The Forestry Commission employed 6,275 staff in 1985. In addition a further 10,900 were employed in private forestry with an estimated 8,100 engaged in the wood processing industry.

In 1984–85 a total of 4·77m. cu. metres of timber was thinned and felled.

New Planting (1984–85) 21,200 hectares (5,200, Forestry Commission; 16,000, private woodlands).

James, N. D. G., *A History of English Forestry*. London, 1981

Fisheries. Quantity (in 1,000 tonnes) and value (in £1,000) of fish of British taking landed in Great Britain (excluding salmon and sea-trout):

Quantity	1982	1983	1984	1985	1986
Wet fish	709·7	676·2	661·0	687·2	629·3
Shell fish	64·9	72·2	72·0	74·8	87·6
	774·6	748·4	733·7	762·1	716·9
Value					
Wet fish	218,129	229,233	240,587	258,904	284,161
Shell fish	42,495	51,030	57,274	64,920	77,519
	260,624	280,263	297,863	323,825	361,680

The fishing fleet of England and Wales comprised (1986) 5,284 vessels including 1,561 trawlers and 687 line fishing vessels; the Scottish fleet (1986) 2,183 vessels including 758 trawlers and 982 shell fishing vessels other than nephrops (Norway lobster) trawlers.

INDUSTRY AND TRADE

Industry. Statistics of a cross-section of industrial production are as follows (in 1,000 tonnes):

	1984	1985	1986
Sulphuric acid	2,654	2,525	2,330
Synthetic resins	1,442	1,402	1,083
Cotton single yarn	38	39	40
Wool tops	43	45	44
Woollen yarn	61	64	73
Man-made fibres (rayon, nylon, etc.)	383	330	288
Newsprint	236	349	458
Other paper and board	3,352	3,335	3,465
Cement	13,481	13,339	13,413
Fabricated aluminium (to consumers)	474	466	...

Engineering. Manufacturers' sales (in £1m.) for 1986 (1985 in brackets): Motor vehicles and engines, 7,255 (6,746); motor vehicle bodies and parts, 3,921 (3,716); boilers and process plant, 1,511 (1,577); mechanical lifting and handling equipment, 1,602 (1,573); refrigerating, space-heating, ventilating and air conditioning equipment, 1,264 (1,210); construction and earth-moving equipment, 1,007 (1,011), wheeled tractors, 896 (982); industrial (including marine) engines, 781 (880).

Electrical Goods. Manufacturers' sales (in £1m.) for 1986 (1985 in brackets): Radio and electronic capital goods, 2,829 (2,683); basic electrical equipment, 2,633 (2,367); electronic data processing equipment, 3,195 (3,459); telephone and telegraph apparatus and equipment, 1,742 (1,668); domestic electrical appliances, 1,315 (1,208).

Textile Manufacturers. Production of woven cloth for 1986 (1985 in brackets): cotton (1m. metres), 275 (274); man-made fibres (1m. metres), 217·7 (206·6); woven woollen and worsted fabrics (1m. sq. metres), deliveries, 93·1 (90·9).

Construction. Total value (in £1m.) of constructional work by all agencies in 1986 was 30,123 (27,850 in 1985), including new work, 16,286 (14,921) of which new housing, 5,539 (4,766). Houses for private developers, 4,697 (3,848). New work (other than housing) for private developers, 6,859 (6,368), for public authorities, 3,888 (3,786).

Annual Abstract of Statistics. HMSO
Statistical Summary of the Mineral Industry. HMSO, annual

Labour. The distribution of total manpower in Great Britain was in June 1986 (in 1,000): Total working population, 27,096 (16,009 males, 11,087 females). Total employed in armed forces and women's services, 322. Total in civil employment, 21,011, including agriculture, 292; energy and water supply, 530 (of which coal-mining, 183); manufacture, 5,137; public administration and defence, 1,561; transport and communications, 1,323; construction, 968; distributive trades, 2,970; insurance, banking, business services, 2,175; education, 1,597; medicine, 1,271. The average monthly numbers (based on claimants in 1,000) of registered unemployed in Great Britain were: 1981, 2,422 (1,773 males; 649 females); 1982, 2,809 (2,056; 753); 1983, 2,988 (2,134; 854); 1984, 3,038 (2,110; 929); 1985, 3,149 (2,164; 986); 1986, 3,055.

Trade Unions. In Jan. 1987 there were 86 unions affiliated to the Trades Union Congress with a total membership of 9,243,297 (including about 3m. women). The unions affiliated to the TUC in 1987 ranged in size from the Transport and General Workers' Union, with 1,377,944 members, to the Sheffield Wool Shear Workers' Society with 17 members. Non-manual workers accounted for nearly a third of the total TUC membership.

The TUC's executive body, the General Council, is elected at the annual Congress. It is composed of 48 members made up of 31 members nominated by unions with a membership of over 100,000, entitled to automatic representation in proportion to their size, 11 members elected by and from unions smaller than 100,000 and 6 members elected by Congress as a whole to represent women workers.

The General Secretary is elected by the Congress but is not subject to annual re-election.

The TUC General Council appoints committees, which draw upon the services of specialist departments in preparing policies on economic, education, international, employment, industrial organization, and social questions.

The TUC is affiliated to the International Confederation of Free Trade Unions, the Trade Union Advisory Committee of OECD, the Commonwealth Trade Union Council and the European Trade Union Confederation. The TUC provides a service of trade union education. It provides members to serve, with representatives of employers, on joint committees advising the Government on issues of national importance (e.g., National Economic Development Council and various Royal Commissions) and on the managing boards of such bodies as the Health and Safety Commission; Advisory, Conciliation and Arbitration Service; and Manpower Services Commission.

The following table relates to trade disputes for recent years:

	No. of workers involved	Working days lost through stoppages
1982	2,103,000	5,313,000
1983	571,000	3,754,000
1984	1,391,000	27,135,000
1985	791,000	6,402,000
1986	720,000	1,920,000

Commerce. Value of the imports and exports of merchandise (excluding bullion and specie and foreign merchandise transhipped under bond) of the UK for 6 recent years (in £1,000):

	Total imports	Total exports		Total imports	Total exports
1982	56,940,267	55,538,408	1985	84,789,605	78,331,360
1983	65,993,096	60,533,692	1986	86,066,650	73,009,049
1984	78,705,170	70,511,345	1987	94,015,696	79,851,395

The value of goods imported is generally taken to be that at the port and time of entry, including all incidental expenses (cost, insurance and freight) up to the landing on the quay. For goods consigned for sale, the market value in this country is required and recorded in the returns. For exports, the value at the port of shipment (including the charges of delivering the goods on board) is taken. Imports are entered as from the country whence the goods were consigned to the UK, which may, or may not, be the country whence they were last shipped. Exports are credited to the country of ultimate destination as declared by the exporters.

For details of imports and exports for 1986 and 1987, see pp. 1323–27.

Trade according to countries for 1986 and 1987 (in £1,000):

Countries	Imports of merchandise from 1986[1]	1987[1]	Exports of merchandise to 1986[1]	1987[1]
Foreign countries				
Europe and Overseas Possessions—				
Albania	129	91	2,887	2,565
Austria	705,732	781,986	403,000	463,187
Belgium and Luxembourg	4,083,883	4,362,463	3,832,605	3,857,717
Bulgaria	32,459	24,249	80,504	88,761
Czechoslovakia	125,399	141,472	108,841	114,101
Denmark and Faroe Islands	1,773,554	1,892,734	1,217,346	1,238,262
Finland	1,346,058	1,539,011	664,461	797,236
France	7,348,574	8,381,984	6,210,216	7,781,546
German Dem. Rep.	195,513	180,299	81,276	81,489
Germany (Fed. Rep. of)	14,139,097	15,783,904	8,542,196	9,404,257
Greece	308,644	355,320	356,020	444,500
Hungary	77,228	83,267	101,557	101,300
Iceland	173,140	178,314	73,640	84,866
Italy	4,658,036	5,216,751	3,472,364	4,145,659
Netherlands	6,615,851	7,148,036	5,442,503	5,856,164
Netherlands Antilles	79,085	5,429	24,232	25,287
Norway	3,265,157	3,290,339	1,147,790	1,220,844
Poland	309,746	303,418	182,841	181,451
Portugal, Azores and Madeira	768,470	847,980	472,078	699,915
Romania	86,730	92,526	82,011	55,688
Spain	1,777,385	2,099,139	1,908,241	2,164,221
Canary Islands	63,529	77,191	66,949	86,185
Sweden	2,756,536	2,952,453	2,307,900	2,322,235
Switzerland and Liechtenstein	2,989,112	3,298,009	1,575,247	1,835,851
Turkey	406,605	579,366	433,753	513,479
USSR	694,624	875,431	539,368	491,615
Yugoslavia	145,127	175,301	188,390	206,932
European Communities	44,505,878	79,778,131	35,003,469	63,008,930
EFTA	11,235,735	12,040,111	6,172,036	6,724,219
Africa—				
Algeria	140,860	172,927	129,624	73,115
Angola	43,147	2,312	30,896	29,573
Burundi	3,074	1,330	2,324	2,867
Cameroon	7,634	14,201	34,368	28,057
Côte d'Ivoire	117,058	90,246	34,266	26,834
Egypt	328,053	127,261	371,007	342,195
Ethiopia	22,343	12,875	50,049	46,146
Liberia	7,574	7,284	22,056	13,538
Libya	136,390	133,649	260,529	220,626
Mali	8,282	6,937	4,121	5,573
Mauritania	2,184	8,724	2,496	3,862
Morocco	65,419	61,108	84,510	94,487
Mozambique	1,335	6,580	13,175	21,168
Rwanda	7,487	4,291	1,681	2,526
Senegal	13,881	11,307	12,328	11,878
South Africa, Republic of	829,305	658,162	849,557	948,584
S.W. Africa/Namibia	6,826	7,681	2,915	3,909
Sudan	12,826	18,850	83,335	75,322
Tunisia	17,292	14,714	39,824	24,943
Zaïre	17,192	8,544	34,217	26,142
Asia—				
Afghánistán	11,913	11,289	11,444	10,735
Bahrain	19,732	60,687	130,991	125,189
Burma	6,092	3,826	10,835	24,715
China	327,032	391,766	535,943	416,012
Indonesia	141,242	144,819	196,629	236,027
Iran	100,303	187,572	399,373	307,853
Iraq	66,129	33,871	443,890	271,655
Israel	385,164	437,014	462,407	523,591
Japan	4,932,497	5,463,116	1,193,933	1,495,111
Jordan	49,766	29,285	130,385	188,998
Korea (South)	661,975	936,038	288,421	427,229
Kuwait	58,517	81,530	300,586	225,168

[1] Provisional figures.

Countries	Imports of merchandise from 1986[1]	1987[1]	Exports of merchandise to 1986[1]	1987[1]
Asia—(contd.)				
Lebanon	9,845	9,528	55,867	40,707
Pakistan	131,296	167,315	227,064	252,978
Philippines	182,852	202,707	79,809	113,784
Qatar	29,587	13,765	112,143	105,087
Saudi Arabia	435,930	383,143	1,507,062	1,978,440
Syria	31,298	24,937	55,511	34,053
Thailand	182,756	239,430	158,195	206,571
America—				
Argentina	28,635	64,595	10,115	10,267
Bolivia	10,225	14,799	3,663	3,658
Brazil	552,559	636,675	295,152	347,916
Chile	128,007	112,843	67,459	105,838
Colombia	94,112	66,531	58,084	61,385
Costa Rica	30,318	16,752	12,007	14,407
Cuba	8,555	12,776	58,760	41,510
Dominican Republic	7,599	8,637	15,178	23,887
Ecuador	11,339	14,002	46,673	37,934
El Salvador	1,323	1,890	6,917	9,595
Guatemala	8,098	7,536	9,288	13,926
Haiti	899	621	5,147	5,327
Honduras	5,280	4,703	9,213	10,449
Mexico	116,078	244,719	162,328	198,992
Nicaragua	1,307	717	7,349	7,883
Panama	4,950	4,919	44,975	40,020
Paraguay	1,455	1,409	31,010	25,409
Peru	82,141	91,689	48,275	49,324
Puerto Rico	81,131	76,347	49,620	39,405
Uruguay	41,366	40,474	24,465	26,484
USA	8,468,160	9,136,016	10,379,585	11,014,242
Venezuela	96,339	91,749	170,101	157,760
Total (including those not specified above)	75,731,040	83,236,022	61,296,656	67,311,740
Commonwealth countries:				
In Europe—				
Cyprus	124,198	118,250	140,387	141,129
Gibraltar	6,021	3,367	46,200	49,986
Malta	49,197	52,105	101,877	107,941
In Africa				
West Africa:				
Gambia	2,273	3,038	16,707	19,765
Ghana	103,480	113,859	113,218	138,081
Nigeria, Federation of	329,036	159,386	566,176	481,568
Sierra Leone	11,599	12,679	17,403	16,221
South Africa:				
Botswana	16,652	11,836	8,629	10,275
Lesotho	277	486	2,128	1,112
Malawi	56,983	44,223	28,557	18,069
Swaziland	48,194	36,901	3,922	2,257
Zambia	27,260	30,310	77,840	75,178
Zimbabwe	80,702	79,771	61,937	63,181
East Africa:				
Kenya	163,745	129,236	170,671	199,059
Mauritius	153,271	163,271	32,087	44,395
Tanzania	40,268	26,400	62,869	91,874
Uganda	50,870	37,076	26,046	38,545
Seychelles	938	884	9,639	10,770
St Helena	380	189	8,196	8,065
In Asia—				
Bangladesh	34,117	35,454	48,218	54,382
Hong Kong	1,530,786	1,531,681	960,956	1,013,038
India	440,681	536,704	941,169	1,090,146
Malaysia	350,058	397,122	226,912	257,970
Singapore	462,878	473,814	547,419	602,627
Sri Lanka	51,860	53,817	83,316	84,680

[1] Provisional figures.

Countries	Imports of merchandise from		Exports of merchandise to	
	1986[1]	1987[1]	1986[1]	1987[1]
In Oceania—				
Australia	643,238	673,837	1,227,647	1,223,613
Fiji Islands	66,500	53,062	8,775	7,381
Nauru	148	674	1,239	394
New Zealand	455,694	487,332	343,145	378,368
Papua New Guinea	38,474	46,045	12,084	16,693
Western Samoa	622	531	433	1,650
In America—				
Bahamas	10,266	15,943	95,816	27,063
Barbados	11,661	23,320	38,338	33,067
Belize	17,954	22,757	8,232	7,543
Bermuda	1,262	1,208	26,180	25,383
Canada	1,499,600	1,568,305	1,698,372	1,938,237
Falkland Islands	14,286	8,148	11,135	7,353
Guyana	55,535	58,502	13,737	15,371
Jamaica	87,416	85,655	43,378	54,644
Leeward Islands (Anguilla; St. Kitts-Nevis; Antigua and Barbuda; Montserrat)	6,916	9,275	28,844	27,703
Trinidad and Tobago	41,622	38,600	79,029	57,016
Windward Islands (Dominica; St. Lucia; St. Vincent and the Grenadines)	107,628	98,199	29,509	32,156
Total, Commonwealth countries (including those not specified above)	7,281,803	7,291,268	8,154,021	8,707,918
Ireland	3,053,807	3,488,406	3,558,372	3,831,737
Grand Total	86,066,650	94,015,696	73,009,049	79,851,395

[1] Provisional figures.

Imports and exports for 1986 and 1987 (Great Britain and Northern Ireland) (in £1,000):

Import values c.i.f. Export values f.o.b.	Total imports		Domestic exports	
	1986[1]	1987[1]	1986[1]	1987[1]
0. Food and Live Animals				
Live animals (excluding zoo animals, dogs and cats)	293,411	236,452	299,907	325,819
Meat and meat preparations	1,465,501	1,562,249	521,928	625,964
Dairy products and eggs	653,335	617,780	331,530	314,129
Fish and fish preparations	748,667	759,194	323,568	407,164
Cereals and cereal preparations	769,332	741,168	1,177,089	831,201
Fruit and vegetables	2,184,378	2,394,045	251,738	300,289
Sugar, sugar preparations, honey	530,321	521,183	170,374	218,563
Coffee, tea, cocoa, spices	1,220,802	997,188	363,992	377,512
Feeding stuff for animals	527,311	506,492	139,285	155,835
Miscellaneous food preparations	326,888	389,032	160,639	173,895
Total of Section 0	8,719,946	8,724,783	3,740,050	3,730,370
1. Beverages and Tobacco				
Beverages	1,008,272	1,105,383	1,331,668	1,411,631
Tobacco and tobacco manufactures	338,764	327,860	406,271	449,774
Total of Section 1	1,347,036	1,433,243	1,737,939	1,861,405
2. Crude Materials, Inedible, except Fuels				
Hides, skins and furskins, undressed	216,377	264,149	260,183	311,455
Oil seeds, oil nuts and oil kernels	271,253	254,962	155,505	86,244
Crude rubber (including synthetic and reclaimed)	203,581	227,116	183,040	179,995
Wood and cork	1,000,399	1,198,452	22,913	25,950
Pulp and waste paper	523,309	657,198	25,015	33,864
Textile fibres and their waste	546,891	633,534	373,020	396,996
Crude fertilizers and crude minerals (excluding fuels)	316,955	286,632	272,281	340,572

[1] Provisional figures.

| _Import values c.i.f._ | Total imports | | Domestic exports | |
Export values f.o.b.	1986[1]	1987[1]	1986[1]	1987[1]
2. _Crude Materials, Inedible, except Fuels_—Contd.				
Metalliferous ores and metal scrap	1,139,774	1,222,885	538,593	451,063
Crude animal and vegetable materials, not elsewhere specified	404,164	438,588	110,390	99,767
Total of Section 2	4,622,702	5,183,516	1,940,940	1,925,905
3. _Mineral Fuels, Lubricants and Related Materials_				
Coal, coke and briquettes	479,523	412,697	190,888	111,062
Petroleum and petroleum products	4,393,537	4,493,299	8,221,244	8,465,823
Gas, natural and manufactured	1,380,102	968,805	271,244	192,070
Total[2] of Section 3	6,294,083	6,116,960	8,683,376	8,768,955
4. _Animal and Vegetable Oils and Fats_	365,132	426,967	105,279	263,525
5. _Chemicals_				
Chemical elements and compounds	2,783,337	3,013,235	3,708,712	3,931,190
Dyeing, tanning and colouring materials	396,544	448,173	763,295	878,979
Medicinal and pharmaceutical products	679,664	786,335	1,532,790	1,620,747
Essential oils and perfume; toilet and cleansing preparations	480,276	554,482	807,770	886,404
Fertilizers, manufactured	212,666	210,584	67,394	85,389
Plastic materials	1,985,787	2,415,867	1,401,435	1,553,091
Total[2] of Section 5	7,345,713	8,330,391	9,691,770	10,519,696
6. _Manufactured Goods Classified Chiefly by Material_				
Leather and dressed furs	247,931	299,409	321,610	372,941
Rubber	589,750	682,549	611,899	677,930
Wood and cork (excluding furniture)	686,571	784,623	77,239	85,627
Paper, paperboard	2,702,999	3,238,154	824,334	971,085
Textile yarn, fabrics	3,162,566	3,497,575	1,711,509	1,886,174
Non-metallic mineral manufactures	2,661,661	2,747,628	2,549,241	2,654,082
Iron and steel	1,796,339	1,890,118	1,866,690	2,185,983
Non-ferrous metals	1,836,184	1,942,504	1,551,482	1,502,187
Manufactures of metal, not elsewhere specified	1,643,853	1,887,784	1,464,989	1,541,310
Total of Section 6	15,327,853	16,970,343	10,978,993	11,877,320
7. _Machinery and Transport Equipment_				
Boilers, engines, motors and power-units	2,238,013	2,513,251	3,248,615	3,241,405
Agricultural and Industrial machinery	5,763,271	6,436,664	6,718,008	8,189,085
Office machinery	4,545,107	5,431,207	3,561,693	4,483,163
Electrical machinery, apparatus, not elsewhere specified	6,848,681	7,853,254	4,785,367	5,353,760
Transport equipment	9,374,129	10,560,803	7,035,243	8,635,717
Total of Section 7	28,769,201	32,795,189	25,348,927	28,803,130

[1] Provisional figures.
[2] Includes items not specified here.

Import values c.i.f.	Total imports		Domestic exports	
Export values f.o.b.	1986[1]	1987[1]	1986[1]	1987[1]
8. *Miscellaneous Manufactured Articles*				
Sanitary, plumbing, heating and lighting fixtures	216,700	254,514	126,275	133,080
Furniture	776,027	878,085	356,359	394,689
Travel goods, handbags and similar articles	199,865	230,878	30,576	34,831
Clothing	2,386,678	2,778,406	1,228,286	1,428,803
Footwear	735,020	799,275	167,209	186,564
Scientific instruments; cameras, watches and clocks	3,077,792	3,261,544	3,127,684	3,304,710
Miscellaneous manufactured articles, not elsewhere specified	3,998,874	4,685,362	3,539,146	4,357,078
Total of Section 8	11,390,957	12,888,063	8,575,536	9,839,755
9. *Commodities and Transactions not Classified According to Kind*				
Total of Section 9	1,884,027	1,146,242	2,205,241	2,261,332
Total[2] of all classes	86,066,650	94,015,696	73,009,049	79,851,395

[1] Provisional figures. [2] Includes items not specified here.

Tourism. There were an estimated 15·6m. overseas visitors in 1987. Foreign exchange from tourism was approximately £7,600m. including fares paid to British air and shipping lines.

COMMUNICATIONS

Roads. Central government responsibility for highways in England rests with the Secretary of State for Transport. His responsibilities are administered by the Department of Transport through a number of Directorates at Headquarters together with 9 Regional Offices. For Welsh and Scottish roads central government responsibility rests with the Secretaries of State for Wales and Scotland respectively.

The Secretary of State is the highway authority responsible for all trunk roads. The Shire County Councils, the Metropolitan District Councils, the London Borough Councils and the Common Council of the City of London are the highway authorities responsible for local roads in their own areas.

The Secretary of State has powers to provide roads designed for limited classes of motor traffic, and to confirm schemes for the provision of such special roads by local authorities. The former have the status of trunk roads; the latter principal roads. 2,980 km of motorway were open to traffic in Great Britain in 1987 (2,540 km of trunk motorway in England, 340 km in Scotland and Wales and 101 km of principal motorway).

The design and supervision of the construction of major trunk road schemes is carried out by firms of consulting engineers and by local authorities which act as the Secretary of State's agents. The Regional Offices ensure that schemes progress in accordance with the Secretary of State's statutory and financial responsibilities. Directors (Transport) are responsible for smaller trunk road schemes and for the maintenance of all trunk roads, including motorways. Local authorities can act as the Secretary of State's agents for construction and maintenance. The work is carried out by them or by contractors on their behalf and the cost borne by Central Government.

Aid to local authorities' transport expenditure is now given through Rate Support Grant and through Transport Supplementary Grant; the latter is paid to all local highway authorities on capital expenditure on roads and traffic regulation accepted by the Secretary of State as being of more than local importance.

Public highways in Great Britain in 1987, excluding lengths of unsurfaced roads (green lanes), totalled 352,292 km (England, 268,456 km; Wales, 32,711 km; Scotland, 51,125 km). There were 12,425 km of all-purpose trunk roads, 2,980 km of trunk and principal motorways, 34,899 km of principal roads (excluding motorways) and 301,988 km of other roads.

Motor vehicles for which licences were current under the Vehicle (Excise) Act, 1971, at 31 Dec. 1986, numbered 21·7m., including 16·98m. private cars. 1·1m. mopeds, scooters and motor cycles, 125,000 public transport vehicles and 2·25m. goods vehicles.

New vehicle registrations in 1986 numbered 2·33m.

Road casualties in Great Britain numbered in 1986, 321,000 including 5,382 killed; in 1985, 318,000 including 5,165 killed.

Railways. The British Railways Board as a public authority owns and manages British Rail: The national rail network, British Rail Engineering Ltd, British Rail Maintenance Ltd, British Rail Property Board, Freightliners Ltd, Transportation Systems and Market Research Ltd. (Transmark) and Travellers-Fare. The role of the Board is to determine policies, establish the organization to carry them out, monitor performance and take major decisions to meet objectives set by the Secretary of State for Transport.

The Group turnover 1986–87 was £3,183·5m. and 166,989 staff were employed, of whom 140,069 were involved in the railway business.

The management of the railways is the responsibility of the Vice-Chairman. He establishes plans and budgets for the achievement of objectives set by the Board, monitors and achieves results against the plans and budgets, and directs the organization and deployment of manpower resources. He is assisted by other Board members with responsibility for functions such as Engineering, Research, Finance and Planning, Marketing, Operating, Productivity and Personnel.

In the year ending 31 March 1987, British Rail carried 138·4m. tonnes of freight and parcels and 689·4m. passenger journeys were made.

The rail business is split into 5 sectors and directors act on behalf of the Vice-Chairman to control policy. The sectors are InterCity, Network South East, Provincial, Freight and Parcels. A director is responsible for efficient operation and budgeting within his sector, each of which bears its fair share of the fixed costs of operation, such as signalling and track maintenance. The day-to-day running of the rail network is the responsibility of 6 geographical regional general managers to whom local area and station managers report.

		1985–86	1986–87
Passenger Receipts and Traffic			
1 Receipts	£m.	1,319·6	1,427·5
Passenger journeys	m.	685·9	689·4
Passenger miles (estimated)	m.	18,800·0	19,150·0
Freight Train Traffic			
Receipts	£m.	528·5	534·6
Traffic	m. tonnes	139·7	138·4
Net tonne miles (trainload and			
wagonload)	m.	9,971·0	10,293·0
Locomotives			
Diesel		2,338	2,201
Electric		243	240
High Speed Tains			
Power cars		197	197
Passenger carriages		722	712
Coaching vehicles		14,062	13,677
Freight vehicles (excluding			
brake vans)		39,007	33,649
Stations		2,526	2,530
Route open for traffic	miles	10,395	10,358

The London Regional Transport (formerly London Transport Executive) is the authority responsible for the operation of the capital's Underground and bus services. Overall policy and financial control is exercised by the Secretary of State for Transport. In Dec. 1987, London Underground had 244 route miles of railway open for traffic and also operated over 10 route miles owned by British Rail. Rolling stock owned: Underground, 3,875 (2,475 motor cars, 1,400 trailer cars); buses, 4,825. In the financial year 1986–87, the number of train miles run in passenger service was 30·6m.; number of bus miles run in passenger service was 162m. The number of passenger journeys was: Underground 769m.; buses 1,165m.

Aviation. Pursuant to the Civil Aviation Act 1980, the business and undertaking of British Airways Board was transferred to and vested in a limited liability company, British Airways Plc, with effect from 1 April 1984. Although HM Government initially held all the shares in the new company, the company was privatized in Feb. 1987.

British Airways is engaged in the provision of air transport services for passengers, cargo and mail worldwide, both on scheduled and charter services. It operates long and short haul international services, as well as an extensive domestic network. In 1986–87, it carried 20m. passengers, and at 31 March 1987 it had a fleet of 164 aircraft and employed 39,498 personnel.

In addition to British Airways, there were in 1986 about 50 independent air transport operators, the principal ones being Britannia Airway and British Midland Airways. In recent years there has been a significant expansion of the independent operators.

Following the Civil Aviation Act 1971, the Civil Aviation Authority was established as an independent public body responsible for the economic and safety regulation of British civil aviation. It took over the responsibilities of the former Air Transport Licensing Board and Air Registration Board, and also runs the National Air Traffic Services in conjunction with the Ministry of Defence.

In addition to the public transport operators there are a number of companies engaged in miscellaneous aviation activities such as crop-spraying, aerial survey and photography, and flying instruction.

The operating and traffic statistics of the UK airlines on scheduled services during the calendar year 1985 (and 1986) are as follows: Aircraft km flown, 371m. (385m.); revenue passengers carried, 24·8m. (25m.); cargo (freight and mail) carried 358,927 (376,927) tonnes.

Traffic between the UK airports and places abroad in 1985 (and 1984) on all services included 579,303 (566,319) air transport aircraft movements.

There were 11,932 and 11,237 civil aircraft registered in the UK at 31 Dec. 1987 and 1986 respectively.

Shipping. The UK flag merchant fleet in July 1987 totalled 10·8m. DWT (dry cargo, 5·3m. DWT; tankers 5·5m. DWT) representing 1·7% of the world fleet. The total number of UK flag ships was 846.

Capital investment in new tonnage and facilities by British shipping companies 1982–86 (inclusive) was over £2,200m. In 1986 capital expenditure was an estimated £150m. The average age of UK owned and registered tonnage in mid-1987 was 11 years.

Total gross earnings by UK owned and registered ships in 1986 amounted to £2,619m. The net contribution to UK balance of payments was £979m. and, in addition, there were gross import savings of £673m.

On 30 Nov. 1987, 29 UK flag ships (351,000 DWT) were laid up out of a world total of 683 ships (17·2m. DWT).

Inland Waterways. There are approximately 2,500 miles of navigable canals and locked river navigations in Great Britain. Of these, the British Waterways Board is responsible for some 350 miles of commercial waterways (maintained for freight traffic) and some 1,200 miles of cruising waterways (maintained for pleasure cruising, fishing and amenity). The Board is also responsible for a further 600 miles of canals, some of which are no longer navigable and whose future is being considered in conjunction with local authorities; a number of these lengths have been restored for cruising or as local amenities. The Board's turnover for the 12 months to 31 March 1987 was £19·16m. The total freight traffic on the Board's waterways for the same period was 3·89m. tonnes.

The most important of the river navigations and canals under other authorities include the rivers Thames, Great Ouse, Nene and Yorkshire Ouse, the Norfolk Broads and the Manchester Ship Canal.

The Port of Manchester was opened to maritime traffic in 1894 by the construction of the Manchester Ship Canal, which is 35¼ miles in length and owned and operated by the Manchester Ship Canal Company. The entrance lock is 80 ft (24·38 metres) wide and the maximum width of other locks within the canal is 65 ft (19·81 metres). Ships up to 28 ft 10 in. (8·78 metres) freshwater draught can navigate to Ince Oil Berth; ships up to 24 ft (7·31 metres) draught can navigate to Manchester docks but within these docks draught is limited to 22 ft (6·70 metres).

The Port of Manchester includes the Queen Elizabeth II Oil Dock at Eastham (separate entrance lock 100 ft wide), the oil docks at Stanlow and a considerable number of public and private wharves and installations along the canal, as well as the container terminal at Ellesmere Port. Total sea-borne and barge traffic in 1985 amounted to 9·75m. tonnes; operating revenue, £21·2m.; loss after tax, £1·85m. The total issued share capital at 31 Dec. 1985 was £8m.

Farnie, D. A., *The Manchester Ship Canal and the Rise of the Port of Manchester.* Manchester Univ. Press, 1980
Hadfield, C., *British Canals.* 6th ed. Newton Abbot, 1979

Posts and Telecommunications. In Oct. 1981 the Post Office ceased to control telecommunications services, which became the responsibility of a separate corporation, British Telecom. The Post Office operates as 4 distinct but interdependent businesses. Every area of the country has separate district offices for each of the letters, parcels and counters businesses. Girobank also has a regional network for account holders. The Post Office provides: Royal Mail general collection and delivery services, handling 50m. letters and parcels a day; Premium Services including guaranteed delivery to UK addresses on the same day and overnight (Datapost), and by facsimile transmission to many UK and overseas centres; International Datapost offering guaranteed swift delivery to over 100 countries; postal, National Girobank and many agency services on behalf of government departments and other public sector organizations at 21,000 post office counters; full banking facilities through National Girobank. Number of post offices at 31 March 1987 was 21,211; number of posting boxes including those at post offices, over 100,000; staff employed, 188,732 (excluding 19,719 sub-postmasters employed on an agency basis).

	1983–84 (1m.)	1984–85 (1m.)	1985–86 (1m.)	1986–87 (1m.)
Correspondence (incl. registered items) posted	10,700	11,200	11,700	12,500
Parcels handled	195	203	194	192

Income (1986–87) £3,473·3m. Profit retained, £130·8m.

At 31 Oct. 1987 there were 6,776 local exchanges, 491 trunk exchanges and 6 international exchanges operated by British Telecom. At 30 Sept. 1987 there were 4,814,000 business and 17,821,000 residential telephone connexions and 115,000 telex connexions. In 1988 British Telecom's modernization programme was in full progress and there were over 1,300 digital installations.

At 31 Dec. 1987 over 100,000 customers were connected to Cellnet, the cellular mobile radio network launched in 1985 and run jointly by BT and Securicor and about 60,000 customers are connected to cable TV systems. At 31 Oct. 1987 BT employed a total staff of 224,164.

Daunton, M. J., *Royal Mail: The Post Office since 1840.* London, 1985

Broadcasting. Radio and television services are provided by the BBC and by the Independent Broadcasting Authority and its programme contractors. The BBC, constituted by Royal Charter until 31 Dec. 1996, has responsibility for providing domestic and external broadcast services, the former financed from the television licence revenue, the latter by Government grant. The domestic services include 2 national television services, 4 national radio network services and an expanding local radio service.

The IBA constituted until 31 Dec. 2005 provides an independent television service on a regional basis, with programmes provided by its programme contractors. The 1981 Act provided for the establishment of the fourth television channel and of the Welsh Fourth Channel Authority (WFCA) which provides a Welsh service on that channel in Wales; they started broadcasting in Nov. 1982. The IBA also provides independent local radio services. All these services are financed by the sale of broadcast advertising time.

The BBC's domestic radio services are available on LF, MF and VHF; those of the IBA on MF and VHF. The television services of the 2 authorities BBC1, BBC2, ITV, and Channel 4 are broadcast at UHF in 625-line definition and in colour.

The broadcasting authorities, whose governing bodies are appointed (by HM the Queen in the case of the BBC and by the Home Secretary in the case of the IBA and WFCA) as trustees for the public interest in broadcasting, are independent of government in matters of programme content and are publicly accountable to Parliament for the discharge of their responsibilities.

In 1981 the Broadcasting Complaints Commission was set up to consider and adjudicate upon complaints of unfair or unjust treatment in broadcast programmes or of unwarranted infringement of privacy in or in the making of programmes. The number of broadcast receiving licences in force on 31 March 1987 was 18·9m., including 16·5m. for colour.

Cinemas. In 1984 there were 1,200 screens in 70 cinemas and there were 55m. admissions.

Newspapers. In 1987 there were 14 national dailies.

Benn's Press Directory. Tunbridge Wells, Annual

JUSTICE, RELIGION, EDUCATION AND WELFARE

Justice. *England and Wales.* The legal system of England and Wales, divided into civil and criminal courts has at the head of the superior courts, as the ultimate court of appeal, the House of Lords, which hears each year a number of appeals in civil matters, including a certain number from Scotland and Northern Ireland, as well as some appeals in criminal cases. In order that civil cases may go from the Court of Appeal to the House of Lords, it is necessary to obtain the leave of either the Court of Appeal or the House itself, although in certain cases an appeal may lie direct to the House of Lords from the decision of the High Court. An appeal can be brought from a decision of the Court of Appeal or the Divisional Court of the Queen's Bench Division of the High Court in a criminal case provided that the Court is satisfied that a point of law 'of general public importance' is involved, and either the Court or the House of Lords is of the opinion that it is desirable in the public interest that a further appeal should be brought. As a judicial body, the House of Lords consists of the Lord Chancellor, the Lords of Appeal in Ordinary, commonly called Law Lords, and such other members of the House as hold or have held high judicial office. The final court of appeal for certain of the Commonwealth countries is the Judicial Committee of the Privy Council which, in addition to Privy Counsellors who are or have held high judicial office in the UK, includes others who are or have been Chief Justices or Judges of the Superior Courts of Commonwealth countries.

Civil Law. The main courts of original civil jurisdiction are the county courts for less important cases, and the High Court for the more important ones.

There are about 300 county courts located throughout the country, grouped in districts, and each presided over by a circuit judge. They have a general jurisdiction to determine all actions founded on contract or tort involving sums of not more than £5,000 and can also deal with other classes of case, such as landlord and tenant, probate, equity and admiralty, up to certain limits. Certain matters, such as actions of libel and slander, are entirely reserved for the High Court. In addition, certain designated county courts have jurisdiction in matrimonial proceedings. Divorce proceedings must now commence in these courts and, subject to being transferred to the High Court upon becoming defended, are determined in the county court.

The High Court has both appellate and original jurisdiction, covering virtually all civil causes not determined in the county court. The judges of the High Court are attached to one of its 3 divisions: Chancery; Queen's Bench; and Family; each with its separate field of jurisdiction. The presiding judges of the 3 divisions are the Lord Chief Justice (Queen's Bench), the Vice Chancellor (Chancery), and the President of the Family Division. In addition there are 77 High Court judges, called puisne judges. For the hearing of cases at first instance, the High Court judges sit singly. Appellate jurisdiction is usually exercised by Divisional Courts consisting of 2 (sometimes 3) judges, though in certain circumstances a judge sitting alone may hear the appeal.

The Restrictive Practices Court was set up in 1956 under the Restrictive Trade Practices Act, and is responsible for deciding whether a restrictive trade agreement is in the public interest. It is presided over by a High Court judge, but laymen sit on the bench also. Another specialist court is the Employment Appeal Tribunal, with similar composition, which hears appeals in employment cases from lower tribunals.

The Court of Appeal (Civil Division) hears appeals in civil actions from the High Court and county courts and certain special courts such as the Restrictive Practices Court and the Employment Appeal Tribunal. Its President is the Master of the Rolls, aided by 27 Lords Justices of Appeal sitting in 6 or 7 divisions of 2 or 3 judges each.

Civil proceedings are instituted by the aggrieved person, but, as they are a private matter, they are frequently settled by the parties to a dispute through their lawyers before the matter actually comes to court. In some cases, at the instance of either party, a jury may sit to decide questions of fact and award of damages.

Criminal Law. At the base of the system of criminal courts in England and Wales are the magistrates' courts which try over 97% of criminal cases. In general, in exercising their summary jurisdiction, they have power to pass a sentence of up to six months imprisonment and to impose a fine of up to £2,000 on any one offence. They also deal with the preliminary hearing of cases triable only at the Crown Court. In addition to dealing summarily with over 2m. cases, which include thefts, assaults, road traffic infringements, drug abuse, etc, they also have a limited civil jurisdiction.

Magistrates' courts normally comprise three lay justices. Although unpaid they are entitled to loss of earnings and travel and subsistence allowance. They undergo training after appointment and they are advised by a professional justices' clerk. In central London and in some provincial areas full-time stipendiary magistrates have been appointed. Generally they possess the same powers as the lay bench, but they sit alone. On 1 Jan. 1986 the total strength of the lay magistracy was 27,687 including 11,264 women. Justices are appointed on behalf of the Queen by the Lord Chancellor, except in Greater Manchester, Merseyside and Lancashire where they are appointed by the Chancellor of the Duchy of Lancaster.

Specially qualified justices sit in juvenile courts to deal with cases involving persons under 17 years of age charged with criminal offences (other than homicide and other grave offences) or brought before the court as being in need of care or control. These courts normally sit with three justices, including at least one man or one woman, and are accommodated separately from other courts.

Domestic Proceedings courts deal with matrimonial applications, custody, guardianship and maintenance of children, affiliation and adoption. These courts normally sit with three justices including at least one man or one woman.

Above the magistrates' courts is the Crown Court. This was set up by the Courts Act 1971 to replace quarter sessions and assizes. Unlike quarter sessions and assizes, which were individual courts, the Crown Court is a single court which is capable of sitting anywhere in England and Wales. It has power to deal with all trials on indictment and has inherited the jurisdiction of quarter sessions to hear appeals, proceedings on committal of persons for sentence, and certain original proceedings on civil matters under individual statutes.

The jurisdiction of the Crown Court is exercisable by a High Court judge, a Circuit judge or a Recorder (who is a part-time judge) sitting alone, or, in specified circumstances, with justices of the peace. The Lord Chief Justice has given directions as to the types of case to be allocated to High Court judges (the more serious cases) and to Circuit judges or Recorders respectively.

Appeals from magistrates' courts go either to a Divisional Court of the High Court (when a point of law alone is involved) or to the Crown Court where there is a complete re-hearing. Appeals from the Crown Court in cases tried on indictment lie to the Court of Appeal (Criminal Division). Appeals on questions of law go by right, and appeals on other matters by leave. The Lord Chief Justice or a Lord Justice sits with judges of the High Court to constitute this court.

There remains as a last resort the invocation of the royal prerogative exercised on the advice of the Home Secretary. In 1965 the death penalty was abolished for murder.

All contested criminal trials, except those which come before the magistrates' courts, are tried by a judge and a jury consisting of 12 members. Each defendant is entitled to object, without showing cause, to up to 3 jurors. The prosecution may ask that any number may 'stand by' until the jury panel is exhausted, and only then need to show cause. When these peremptory challenges have been exhausted further challenges may only be made for cause and this rarely happens. The jury decides whether the accused is guilty or not. The judge is responsible for summing up on the facts and explaining the law; he sentences convicted offenders. If, after at least 2 hours of deliberation, a jury is unable to reach a unanimous verdict it may, provided that in a full jury of 12 at least 10 of its members are agreed, bring in a majority verdict. The failure of a jury to agree on a unanimous verdict or to bring in a majority verdict involves the retrial of the case before a new jury.

The Employment Appeal Tribunal. The Employment Appeal Tribunal which is a superior Court of Record with the like powers, rights, privileges and authority of the High Court, was set up in 1976 to hear appeals on questions of fact and law against decisions of industrial tribunals and of the Certification Officer. The appeals are heard by a High Court Judge sitting with 2 members (in exceptional cases 4) appointed for their special knowledge or experience of industrial relations either on the employer or the trade union side, with always an equal number on each side. The great bulk of their work is concerned with the problems which can arise between employees and their employers.

Military Courts. Offences by persons subject to service law against the system of military law created under the powers of the Army Act, Air Force Act or Naval Discipline Act are dealt with either summarily or by courts-martial.

The Personnel of the Law. All judicial officers except the Lord Chancellor (who is a member of the Cabinet) are independent of Parliament and the Executive. They are all appointed by the Crown on the advice of the Prime Minister or the Lord Chancellor and hold office until retiring age. The legal profession is divided; barristers, who advise on legal problems and conduct cases in court, usually act for the public only through solicitors, who deal directly with the legal business brought to them by the public. Barristers of 10 years standing are eligible for appointment as High Court Judges, while only solicitors (of 7 years standing) may apply for appointment as County Court and District Registrars. Long-standing members of both professions are eligible for appointment to most other judicial offices, solicitors having first to serve for at least 3 years as Recorders before qualifying for appointment as Circuit Judges.

Legal Aid. Broadly there are 3 kinds of legal aid. Firstly there is legal advice and assistance, otherwise known as the 'Green Form' scheme. This includes advice and help on any question of English law, both civil and criminal, but does not normally cover any form of representation before a court or tribunal. As an extension of the scheme, however, assistance by way of representation has been available for certain proceedings, chiefly civil, in magistrates' courts. Under the Legal Aid Acts 1974 and 1982 legal advice and assistance also provides for duty solicitor schemes at magistrates' courts and police stations. Under the magistrates' courts schemes, initial advice, and representation where necessary, is available to unrepresented defendants at court, from duty solicitors either in attendance at courts or on call. The scheme covers advice to a defendant in custody, making a bail application, representing a defendant in custody on a guilty plea, and certain other cases. The advice and assistance at police stations scheme enables any person who has been arrested and taken to a police station, or who is assisting the police with their enquiries, to receive advice and assistance, from either a duty solicitor or the person's own solicitor. Secondly, under Part I of the Legal Aid Act 1974, there is legal aid for civil court proceedings. Under the provisions of the Act, aid is available to those of low or moderate means either free or subject to a contribution, depending on means. In 1986–87 there were over 980,000 payments for advice and assistance under the Legal Advice and Assistance Scheme and over 250,000 civil legal aid certificates were issued. The cost of legal aid in civil cases is met from (a) contributions from assisted persons; (b) the operation of the statutory charge which gives the Law Society a first charge on money or property recovered or preserved for an assisted person to the extent of that person's liability for his own costs; (c) costs recovered from opposing parties and (d) a grant from the Exchequer. The net cost of civil legal aid to the state (excluding administration costs of the scheme) in the year 1985–86 amounted to £95·1m. and the cost of the legal advice and assistance scheme was £62·8m. of which £11·1m. was accounted for by assistance by way of representation. Thirdly under Part II of the Legal Aid Act 1974 a court dealing with criminal proceedings may order legal aid to be given if it considers it is desirable in the interests of justice and if it also considers that the defendant (or appellant) requires financial assistance in meeting the costs he may incur. The interests of justice are not statutorily defined but may include, for example, situations where the defendant is in real danger of going to prison or losing his job, where substantial questions of law are to be argued or where the defendant is unable to follow the proceedings and explain his case due to inadequate knowledge of English, mental illness or other mental or physical disability. Legal aid must be granted, subject to means, in the following circumstances: where a person is committed for trial on a charge of murder, where the prosecutor appeals or applies for leave to appeal from the criminal division of the Court of Appeal or the Courts-Martial Appeal Court to the House of Lords, and in certain circumstances where the court is considering depriving a defendant of his liberty.

The costs of legal aid in criminal proceedings are paid by the central government, but courts have power to require legally aided persons to contribute towards the cost of legal aid given to them. The net cost of legal aid in criminal proceedings in the year 1986–87 was £176·9m., £91·1m. of this was for legal aid in the higher courts which is paid for out of the Lord Chancellor's vote and £85·8m. for legal aid in the magistrates' courts which is paid from the legal aid fund.

Police. The authorized establishment of the police force in England and Wales in Dec. 1987 was 124,370: the actual strength was 111,489 men and 12,613 women. In addition there were 16,209 special constables (including 5,282 women). The estimated total expenditure on the police service in England and Wales for 1986–87 was £3,166,000,000.

SCOTLAND. The High Court of Justiciary is the supreme criminal court in Scotland and has jurisdiction in all cases of crime committed in any part of Scotland, unless expressly excluded by statute. It consists of the Lord Justice-General, the Lord Justice-Clerk and 22 other judges, who are the same judges as of the Court of Session, the Scottish supreme civil court. One judge is seconded to the Scottish Law Commission. The Court, which is presided over by the Lord Justice-General, whom failing, the Lord Justice-Clerk, exercises an appellate jurisdiction as well as one of first instance, sits as business requires in Edinburgh both as a Court of Appeal (the *quorum* being 3 judges) and as a court of first instance and on circuit as a court of first instance. The decisions of the Court in either case are not subject to review by the House of Lords. One judge sitting with a jury of 15 persons can, and usually does, try cases, but 2 or more (with a jury) may do so in important or complex cases. It has a privative jurisdiction over cases of treason, murder, rape, deforcement of messengers and breach of duty by magistrates. It also, in practice, is the only court which tries serious crimes against person or property and generally those cases in which a sentence greater than imprisonment for 3 years may be imposed either under statute or common law. Moreover, the Court has inherent power to try and to punish all acts which are plainly criminal though previously unknown and not dealt with by any statute.

The appellate jurisdiction of the High Court of Justiciary extends to all cases tried on indictment, whether in the High Court or the Sheriff Court, and persons so convicted may appeal to the Court against conviction or sentence or both except that there is no appeal against any sentence fixed by law. The Lord Advocate may refer a point of law which has arisen during a trial on indictment in which accused has been acquitted for the opinion of the Court. By such appeal, a person may bring under review of the High Court of Justiciary any alleged miscarriage of justice including any alleged miscarriage of justice on the basis of the existence and significance of additional evidence which was not heard at the trial and which was not available and could not reasonably have been made available at the trial. It is also a court of review from courts of summary criminal jurisdiction, and on the final determination of any summary prosecution a convicted person may appeal to the Court by way of stated case on questions of law, etc., but not on questions of fact, except in relation to a miscarriage of justice alleged by the person accused on the basis of the existence and significance of additional evidence which was not heard at the trial and which was not available and could not reasonably have been made available at the trial. A prosecutor may appeal only on a point of law. A further or complementary form of process of review which can be resorted to by convicted persons in these courts is by Bill of Suspension (and Liberation), but it is of strictly limited application. A prosecutor in cases tried on indictment or under summary criminal procedure may also bring under review a decision in law, prior to final judgment of the case, by way of Bill of Advocation. The Court also hears appeals under the Courts-Martial (Appeals) Act 1951.

The Sheriff Court has an inherent universal criminal jurisdiction (as well as an extensive civil one) limited in general to crimes and offences committed within a sheriffdom (a specifically defined region), which has, however, been curtailed by statute or practice under which the High Court of Justiciary has exclusive jurisdiction in relation to the crimes above-mentioned. This Court is presided over by a Sheriff-Principal or Sheriff, and when trying cases on indictment sits with a jury of 15 persons. His power of awarding punishment involving imprisonment is restricted to 3 years in the maximum, but he may under certain statutory powers remit the prisoner to the High Court for sentence. The Sheriff also exercises a wide summary criminal jurisdiction and when doing so sits without a jury; and he has concurrent jurisdiction with every other court within his Sheriff Court District in regard to all offences competent for trial in summary courts. The great majority of offences which come before the courts are of a minor nature and, as such, are disposed of in the Sheriff Summary Courts or in the District Courts (see below). In cases to be tried on indictment either in the High Court of Justiciary or in the Sheriff Court, the judge may, and in some cases must, before the trial, hold a Preliminary Diet to decide questions of a preliminary nature, whether to the competency or relevancy or otherwise. Any decision at a preliminary diet can be the subject of an appeal to the High Court of Justiciary prior to the trial.

District Courts in each local authority district have jurisdiction in minor offences occurring within the district. These courts are presided over by lay magistrates, known as justices, and have limited powers of fine and imprisonment.

The Court of Session, presided over by the Lord President (the Lord Justice-General in criminal cases), is divided into an Inner House comprising 2 divisions of 4 judges each with mainly appellate function, and an Outer House comprising 15 single judges, sitting individually at first instance; it exercises the highest civil jurisdiction in Scotland, with the House of Lords as a court of appeal.

Police. The police forces in Scotland at the end of 1986 had an authorized establishment of 13,575; the strength was 12,587 men and 841 women. There were 3,425 part-time special constables. The total police net expenditure in Scotland was £279m. for 1985–86.

CIVIL JUDICIAL STATISTICS

ENGLAND AND WALES	1984	1985	1986
Appellate Courts			
Judicial Committee of the Privy Council	77	59	71
House of Lords	72	79	61
Court of Appeal	1,491	1,545	1,565
High Court of Justice (appeals and special cases from inferior courts)	2,053	1,910	1,565
Courts of First Instance (excluding Magistrates' Courts and Tribunals)			
High Court of Justice:			
Chancery Division[1]	19,478	21,176	26,156
Queen's Bench Division[2]	191,336	209,967	235,536
Family Division: Principal Registry matters[3]	1,266	1,279	1,528
District Registry wardships	1,456	1,850	2,250
Official Referee's	965	1,150	1,183
County courts: Matrimonial suits[4]	186,074	194,534	183,826
Other[5]	2,204,905	2,224,667	2,356,922
Restrictive Practices Court	8	17	3
SCOTLAND			
House of Lords (Appeals from Court of Session)	6	6	...
Court of Session—General Department	27,158	16,853	...
Sheriff's Ordinary Cause	46,540	61,332	...
Sheriff's Summary Cause	142,718	139,583	...

[1] Including Companies Court, Bankruptcy petitions and Patents Court.
[2] Including Admiralty Court.
[3] Adoption, guardianship and wardship.
[4] Including petitions filed at Principal Registry.
[5] Plaint, Admiralty, Bankruptcy and Companies, Adoption, Guardianship and miscellaneous.

CRIMINAL STATISTICS

ENGLAND AND WALES

	Total number of offenders		Indictable offences[1]	
	1985	1986	1985	1986
Aged 10 and over				
Proceeded against in magistrates' courts[2]	2,147,167	2,170,618	519,833	463,006
Found guilty at magistrates' courts	1,828,870	1,814,719	361,889	304,719
Found guilty at the Crown Court	82,047	79,490	82,047	79,490
Cautioned[3]	218,717	213,429	145,381	136,863
Aged 10 and under 17				
Proceeded against in magistrates' courts[2]	93,899	74,632	71,468	57,008
Found guilty at magistrates' courts	80,991	61,095	61,517	46,471
Found guilty at the Crown Court	1,640	1,535	1,640	1,535
Cautioned[3]	134,567	113,496	112,460	93,508

[1] Includes offences which can be tried either at the Crown Court or at magistrates' courts.
[2] Almost all defendants are initially proceeded against at magistrates' courts.
[3] Offenders who, on admission of guilt, are given an oral caution by or on the instruction of a senior police officer as an alternative to court proceedings. Such cautions are not given for motoring offences.

CRIMINAL STATISTICS

SCOTLAND

	All Crimes and Offences		Crimes[1]	
	1985	1986	1985	1986
All persons and companies				
Proceeded against in all courts	210,748	204,933	71,766	70,138
Charge proved	190,240	184,276	62,302	60,760
Children (aged 8–15)				
Proceeded against in all courts	604	471	401	310
Given formal police warning/ referred to reporter	23,335	22,073	18,102	16,915

[1] Crimes are generally the more serious criminal acts and offences the less serious. 'Crimes' are not equivalent in coverage to 'indictable/triable either way offences'.

Average population in prisons, youth custody centres and detention centres (1986) in England and Wales was 46,770 (convicted 38,003; untried 8,530, and 238 non-criminal prisoners); in Scotland (1986), 5,588 (sentenced, 4,570; remanded, 1,017 and 1 other).

Criminal statistics, England and Wales, 1986. HMSO, 1986
Prison statistics, England and Wales, 1986. HMSO, 1986
Paterson, A., *The Law Lords.* London, 1982

Religion. The Anglican Communion has originated from the Church of England and parallels in its fellowship of autonomous churches the evolution of British influence beyond the seas from colonies to dominions and independent nations. There is no terrestrial head of the Anglican Communion; the Archbishop of Canterbury presides as *primus inter pares* at the decennial meetings of the bishops of the Anglican Communion at the Lambeth Conference. The next Conference will be held in Canterbury in 1988.

The Anglican churches, in addition to the Church of England, comprise the churches, councils, and provinces in communion with the see of Canterbury; which are situated in Wales; Ireland; Scotland; United States of America; Canada; Australia; New Zealand; West Indies; Brazil; Southern Africa; Central Africa; West Africa; Jerusalem and the Middle East; South East Asia; Burma; Sri Lanka; Japan; South America; China; Indian Ocean; Papua New Guinea; Melanesia; Nigeria; Uganda; Kenya; Tanzania; Burundi, Rwanda and Zaïre; Sudan.

In addition to the dioceses included within the Provinces of Canterbury and York, there are several dioceses overseas over which the Archbishop of Canterbury exercises metropolitical jurisdiction, while Church of England chaplaincies in North and Central Europe formerly under the jurisdiction of the Bishop of London now form the diocese of Europe. There are also two small Iberian churches which have been accepted into membership.

England and Wales. The established Church of England, which baptizes about 30% of the children born in England (*i.e.* excluding Wales but including the Isle of Man and the Channel Islands), is Protestant Episcopal. Civil disabilities on account of religion do not attach to any class of British subject. Under the Welsh Church Acts, 1914 and 1919, the Church in Wales and Monmouthshire was disestablished as from 1 April 1920, and Wales was formed into a separate Province.

The Queen is, under God, the supreme governor of the Church of England, with the right, regulated by statute, to nominate to the vacant archbishoprics and bishoprics. The Queen, on the advice of the First Lord of the Treasury, also appoints to such deaneries, prebendaries and canonries as are in the gift of the Crown, while a large number of livings and also some canonries are in the gift of the Lord Chancellor.

There are 2 archbishops (at the head of the 2 Provinces of Canterbury and York), and 42 diocesan bishops including the bishop of the diocese of Europe, which is part of the Province of Canterbury. Each archbishop has also his own particular diocese, wherein he exercises episcopal, as in his Province he exercises metropolitan, jurisdiction. In Dec. 1987 there were 67 suffragan and assistant bishops, 38 deans and provosts of cathedrals and 108 archdeacons. The General Synod, in

England, consists of a House of Bishops, a House of Clergy and a House of Laity, and has power to frame legislation regarding Church matters. The first two Houses consist of the members of the Convocations of Canterbury and York, each of which consists of the diocesan bishops and elected representatives of the suffragan bishops, 6 for Canterbury province and 3 for York (forming an Upper House), deans, provosts, and archdeacons, and a certain number of proctors elected as the representatives of the inferior clergy, together with, in the case of Canterbury Convocation, 4 representatives of the Universities of Oxford, Cambridge, London and the Southern Universities and in the case of York 2 representatives for the Universities of Durham and Newcastle and the other Northern Universities; the chaplains in the Forces and 2 representatives of the Religious Communities (forming the Lower House). The House of Laity is elected by the lay members of the Deanery Synods but also includes 3 representatives of the Religious Communities and *ex-officio* Church Commissioners and Ecclesiastical Judges. Parochial affairs are managed by annual parochial church meetings and parochial church councils. Every Measure passed by the General Synod must be submitted to the Ecclesiastical Committee, consisting of 15 members of the House of Lords nominated by the Lord Chancellor and 15 members of the House of Commons nominated by the Speaker. This committee reports on each Measure to Parliament, and the Measure receives the Royal Assent and becomes law if each House of Parliament resolves that the Measure be presented to the Queen.

At 31 Dec. 1986 there were 13,287 ecclesiastical parishes, inclusive of the Isle of Man and the Channel Islands. These parishes do not, in many cases, coincide with civil parishes. Although most parishes have their own churches, not every parish nowadays can have its own incumbent or minister. In Dec. 1987 there were 6,870 beneficed clergymen excluding dignitaries, 1,329 other clergymen of incumbent status and 1,746 assistant curates working in the parishes.

During 1987 women were admitted to Holy Orders for the first time in the Church of England. 439 women were ordained as full-time stipendiary deacons.

Private persons possess the right of presentation to over 2,000 benefices; the patronage of the others belongs mainly to the Queen, the bishops and cathedrals, the Lord Chancellor, and the universities of Oxford and Cambridge. In addition to the 9,961 parochial incumbents and assistant curates, there were (1986) 374 dignitaries, 306 non-parochial clergymen working within the diocesan framework and approximately 2,000 non-parochial clergymen outside the framework.

In 1985 there were estimated to be 1·6m. Easter and 1·7m. Christmas Communicants.

Of the 40,431 churches and chapels registered for the solemnization of marriages at 30 June 1986, 16,607 belonged to the Established Church and the Church in Wales and 23,824 to other religious denominations. Of the 347,924 marriages celebrated in 1986 (346,389 in 1985), 34% were in the Established Church and the Church in Wales, 18% in churches or chapels of other denominations and 48% were civil marriages in a Register Office.

Roman Catholics in England and Wales were 4,164,040 in 1987. There were 5 archdioceses and 19 dioceses, 6,224 clergy and 2,766 parish churches and 1,201 other churches open to the public. Convents, 1,250.

The Unitarians have about 250 places of worship and 8,000 members. The Salvation Army, had, in British Territory, 1986, over 1,800 officers. They operate 40 eventide homes, 52 centres for the homeless, 12 homes for children and adolescents and 9 alcoholic rehabilitation centres.

The following is a summary of recent statistics of certain churches:

Denomination	Full members	Ministers in charge	Local and lay preachers
Methodist	458,592	3,457	13,984
Independent Methodist	4,108	138	—
Wesleyan Reform Union	3,224	20	153
United Reform	136,000	1,000	—
Baptist	170,318	1,485	—
Calvinistic Methodist Church of Wales	68,585	152	—
Moravian	4,000	40	—
Society of Friends	18,076	—	—

There were (1987) about 410,000 Jews in the UK with about 295 synagogues; Moslems (900,000); Sikhs (175,000); Hindus (140,000).

Scotland. The Church of Scotland (established in 1560 at the Reformation and re-established in 1688 as part of the Revolution Settlement) is Presbyterian, the ministers all being of equal rank. There is in each parish a kirk session consisting of the minister and a number of laymen called elders. There are presbyteries (formed by groups of parishes), meeting frequently throughout the year, and these are again grouped in synods, which meet half-yearly and can be appealed to against the decisions of the presbyteries.

The supreme court is the General Assembly, which now consists of some 1,250 members, half clerical and half lay, chosen by the different presbyteries. It meets annually in May (under the presidency of a Moderator appointed by the Assembly, the Sovereign being present or represented by a Lord High Commissioner, appointed by the Queen on the nomination of the Government of the day), and sits for 7 days. Any matters not decided during this period may be left to a Commission which will sit if required.

On 2 Oct. 1929 the Church of Scotland and the United Free Church of Scotland were reunited under the name of The Church of Scotland, and the two bodies met in General Assembly in Edinburgh as one. The united Church had, in Scotland, on 31 Dec. 1986, 1,745 congregations, 854,311 members; 18,633 teachers and 104,552 scholars in attendance in Sunday schools. The Church courts are the General Assembly, 12 synods, 46 presbyteries in Scotland, 1 in England and 2 on the Continent. Income in 1981 was £41,740,070. There are divinity faculties in 4 Scottish universities of Edinburgh, Glasgow, Aberdeen and St Andrews, with 60 professors and lecturers who are mostly ministers of the Church of Scotland.

The Episcopal Church of Scotland is a province of the Anglican Church and is one of the historic Scottish churches. It consists of 7 dioceses. As at 31 Dec. 1987 it had 265 churches and missions, 283 clergy and 61,231 members, of whom 36,418 were communicants.

There are in Scotland some small outstanding Presbyterian bodies and also Baptists, Congregationalists, Methodists and Unitarians.

The Roman Catholic Church which celebrated the centenary of the restoration of the Hierarchy in 1978, had in Scotland (1987) 1 cardinal, 2 archbishops and 9 bishops, 1,066 clergy, 472 parishes, and 798,150 adherents.

The proportion of marriages in Scotland according to the rites of the various Churches in 1986 was: Church of Scotland, 39·4%; Roman Catholic, 13·1%; Episcopal, 1·4%; United Free, 0·4%; others, 4·4%; civil, 41·3%.

Education. *The Publicly Maintained System of Education England and Wales:* Compulsory schooling begins at the age of 5 and the minimum leaving age for all pupils is 16. No tuition fees are payable in any publicly maintained school (but it is open to parents, if they choose, to pay for their children to attend other schools). The post-school stage, which is voluntary, includes universities, polytechnics and other further education establishments (including those which provide courses for the training of teachers), as well as adult education and the youth service. Financial assistance is generally available to students on higher education courses in the university and non-university sectors and to some students on other courses in further education.

Nursery Education. Provision for children under 5 is made in either nursery schools or in nursery or infant classes in primary schools. In the public sector no fees are payable. In Jan. 1987 there were 558 maintained nursery schools and 4,295 primary schools with nursery classes. There were 49,502 pupils under 5 attending nursery schools and 467,262 pupils under 5 in nursery and infant classes. About 49% of all these children were attending part-time.

Primary Schools. These provide for pupils from the age of 5 up to the age of 11. In January 1987 there were 18,829 primary schools in England of which 2,902 were infant schools providing for pupils up to the age of about 7, the remainder mainly taking pupils from age 5 through to 11. Nearly all primary schools take both boys and girls. Just over 13% of primary schools had 100 full time pupils or less.

There are 1,774 primary schools in Wales. In those primary schools (and some secondary schools) which are in the predominantly Welsh-speaking areas, the main language of instruction is Welsh. There are also 'Welsh', or, more accurately, bilingual schools in mainly English-speaking parts of Wales. Generally children transfer from primary to secondary schools at 11.

¹ As a result of the Education (School Leaving Dates) Act 1976, one of the two former leaving dates was amended. This means that pupils whose dates of birth fall between 1 Feb. and 31 Aug. (inclusive) cease to be of compulsory school age on the Friday before the last Monday in May. Some of these pupils will leave school before their 16th birthdays. Pupils whose dates of birth fall between 1 Sept. and 31 Jan. (inclusive) remain of compulsory school age until the end of the Easter term following their 16th birthdays.

Middle Schools. A number of local education authorities operate a middle school system. These provide for pupils from the age of 8, 9 or 10 up to the age of 12, 13 or 14. In Jan. 1987 there were 1,213 middle schools in England deemed either primary or secondary according principally to the age range of the school concerned. This number is 31 fewer than in 1986.

Secondary Schools. These usually provide for pupils from the age of 11 upwards. In Jan. 1987 there were 3,611 secondary schools in England. Some local education authorities have retained selection at age 11 for entry to grammar schools of which there were 152 such schools in 1987. There were a small number of technical schools in 1987 which specialise to a greater or lesser extent in technical studies. There were 234 secondary modern schools in 1987 providing a general education up to the minimum school leaving age of 16, although exceptionally some pupils may be allowed to stay on beyond that age in these schools.

All local education authorities operate a system of comprehensive schools to which pupils are admitted without reference to ability or aptitude. In Jan. 1987 there were 3,206 such schools in England with just under 2·8m. pupils. With the development of comprehensive education various patterns of secondary schools have come into operation. Principally these are: 1. all through schools with pupils aged 11 to 18 or 11 to 16; pupils over 16 being able to transfer to an 11 to 18 school or a sixth form college providing for pupils aged 16 to 19. (There were 106 sixth form colleges in England in 1987). 2. local education authorities operating a three-tier system involving middle schools where transfer to secondary school is at ages 12, 13 or 14. These correspond to 12 to 18, 13 to 18 and 14 to 18 comprehensive schools respectively; or 3. in areas where there are no middle schools a two-tier system of junior and senior comprehensive schools for pupils aged 11 to 18 with optional transfer to these schools at age 13 or 14.

There were a number of other secondary schools of various combinations of grammar, technical or modern in Wales in 1988. There were 41 secondary using Welsh as a teaching medium, of these 16 are designated bilingual schools.

Direct Grant Grammar Schools. These were schools which were independent of local education authorities and which received grants direct from the Department of Education and Science for pupils in their secondary departments (upper schools). The system began to be phased out in 1976 and in Jan. 1987 only one grammar school was in receipt of the grant. It is expected that direct grant payments to grammar schools will cease in 1988.

Assisted Places Scheme. In order to give able children a wider range of educational opportunity the government set up, in 1981, the assisted places scheme to give help with tuition fees at independent schools to parents who could not otherwise afford them. In the school year 1987–88, the 226 participating schools offered a total of 5,516 assisted places, 4,488 for entry at age 11, 12 or 13, and 1,020 for entry at sixth form level.

Special Education. Since 1971, when the education of severely mentally handicapped children became the responsibility of the education service, the right to education of all handicapped children has been recognised.

The Education Act 1981, which came into force in April 1983, switched the focus of attention from a child's disability to his or her special educational needs.

The Act restated the Government's policy that no child should be placed in a special school if his or her needs can be met in an ordinary school and many children with special educational needs are being educated in ordinary schools. The Act provided that local education authorities should maintain 'statements' on children whom they had assessed as having special educational needs and for whom they were of the opinion that they should determine the special educational provision which should be made to meet these needs – that is, the more severely affected children.

The majority of children with statements of special educational needs attend special schools, of which there are at present around 1,493, including hospital special schools. Some 100,000 pupils with statements are educated in special schools, of whom around 1,300 are in hospital special schools. Additionally, around 5,700 pupils with statements are educated in independent schools under arrangements made by local education authorities.

Of maintained special schools, 1,126 are day schools, 194 are mainly boarding schools and there are 85 hospital special schools. Attendance is compulsory from 5–16. In addition, the Act's definition of special educational needs applies to children under 5 who are likely to have a learning difficulty when over this age, or whose learning difficulty would be likely to persist if special educational provision were not made for them. Authorities also have a duty to make special educational provision either in a school or in a college of further education for children aged 16–18 who have been assessed as being in need of, and who want, such provision. In addition to the provision in ordinary and special schools, authorities can make special arrangements for educating children at home, in small groups or in hospitals. There are also some establishments which provide further education, P.E. vocational training and for assessment for employment purely for handicapped school leavers.

The statistics in the preceding paragraphs on special education are for England only and were valid at Jan. 1985. The figures are not comparable with those given for 1984 (when transitional arrangements were in force) or previous years because of changes in the way statistics are collected as a result of the 1981 Act.

Ancillary Services. Local education authorities may provide registered pupils at any school maintained by them with milk, meals and refreshment and they may make such charges as they think fit for anything they provide. For pupils whose parents are in receipt of supplementary benefit or family income supplement, however, authorities are required to ensure that such provision is made for the pupil at mid-day as appears to them to be requisite and anything which is provided must be free of charge. Authorities are also required to remit the whole or part of any charge for anything they provide for other pupils if having regard to their circumstances, they consider it appropriate to do so. Facilities must also be provided, free of charge, for consuming any meals or other refreshments which pupils bring to school themselves.

Local education authorities also have power to provide milk, meals and refreshment for pupils in non-maintained schools, if they wish to do so, under such terms as may be agreed with the proprietors as long as the cost does not exceed what it would have been if the pupils had been at a school maintained by an authority.

Further and Higher Education (Non-University). In Nov. 1986 there were about 480 institutions in England providing courses of further education, ranging from shorthand instruction to degree-level, postgraduate work and courses of teacher-training. Course enrolments numbered 594,820 full-time (including 74,847 sandwich students) and 1·6m. part-time and evening (including 480,321 students released by their employers). There were in addition 2,718 Adult Education Centres (formerly known as Evening Institutes), which provided mainly part-time courses of non-advanced general education and were attended by 1,454,966 students. The major providers of higher education, outside the university sector, are the 29 polytechnics. These are engaged mainly in higher education, offering CNAA degrees of a standard comparable to those of universities, professional qualifications and courses in a wide range of disciplines leading to awards of the

Business and Technician Education Council. Many other colleges of further education are however involved to a greater or lesser extent in the higher education sector of further education. Most polytechnics and further education colleges cater for a mixture of full and part-time students, and also sandwich students whose periods of study at college alternate with periods of practical training in industry or other employment. The Secretary of State receives advice on the funding and management of advanced further education from the National Advisory Body for Public Sector Higher Education (NAB) whose remit covers almost all non-university provision at this level, most of which is maintained by local education authorities.

Courses were also provided by the Workers' Educational Association, the University extramural departments and the Welsh National Council of YMCAs.

Education at institutions of further education is not free, but fees are generally low, and are remitted for most students under the age of 18 by the local authority.

The Youth Service. A wide range of facilities for the leisure-time recreation and informal social education of young people primarily of post-school age is provided by local education authorities and voluntary youth organizations. A duty is laid upon local education authorities by the provisions of the 1944 Education Act to secure the adequacy of such facilities for young people in their area; to this end they either provide, maintain and staff youth clubs, centres and other facilities themselves or assist voluntary agencies to do so.

Grants to voluntary agencies to help meet the cost of regional and national capital projects and to national voluntary bodies towards their headquarters and training expenses are made by the Government.

Awards to Students. Local education authorities are responsible for making mandatory awards to suitably qualified students taking first-degree and comparable courses, courses of initial teacher-training and certain other advanced level courses. These awards cover fees and maintenance but the maintenance grants are subject to the income of the student and his parents or spouse. In addition scholarships may be available both from universities and other sources. The authorities may also give discretionary awards to students who do not qualify for mandatory awards including those taking non-degree level courses.

In 1985–86 there were 437,721 full value awards current, 44% at universities and 33,618 mandatory awards for initial teacher-training courses. Lesser value awards, which are paid below the full rate of the student's fees and maintenance, were also made by the authorities. There were 111,941 such awards taken up in the academic year 1985–86.

The Research Council gave over 6,800 new awards in 1986–87 and there were more than 14,000 current awards in that academic year. In 1987–88 the British Academy gave 870 new awards and the Department 618 state bursaries and 70 state scholarships.

Teachers. In order to qualify for work in maintained schools in England and Wales, most teachers take a course of professional training. Graduates and holders of some specialist qualifications obtained before 1 Jan. 1970 are regarded as qualified to teach without training, but anyone obtaining these qualifications after that date is obliged to take a training course before being appointed for the first time to a primary or special school, and since 1 Jan. 1974 before first appointment to a secondary school.

In 1987 there were some 58 non-university institutions (including 20 polytechnics) and 31 university departments of education providing recognized courses of initial teacher-training in England and Wales.

In Nov. 1987 there were about 38,300 students on initial teacher-training courses.

On 30 Sept. 1985, 409,000 full-time teachers were employed by local education authorities in maintained nursery, primary and secondary schools in England and Wales.

Finance. Total current and capital expenditure on education in England (including Universities GB, and Mandatory Awards England and Wales) from public funds is estimated at £16,512m. for 1987–88 as compared with £15,083m. for 1986–87.

Scotland. The statistics on schools relate to education authority and grant-aided schools. From 1974–75 all teachers employed in these schools require to be qualified; figures given are full-time equivalents.

Nursery Education. In Sept. 1985 there were 560 nursery schools and departments, with a total enrolment of 38,120 pupils in 1984.

Primary Education. In Sept. 1985 there were 2,426 primary schools and departments and the number on the registers was 435,916. In Sept. 1985, 21,877 teachers were employed in primary schools and departments.

Secondary Education. In Sept. 1985 there were 441 secondary schools with 361,210 pupils. Of these schools in 1984, 382 were all-through comprehensive establishments providing the full range of Scottish Certificate of Education courses and also non-certificate courses. A further 59 schools were comprehensive in intake and provided both non-certificate and certificate courses, the latter however only up to Ordinary grade. The remaining 18 schools, these were selective in intake providing certificate courses only (Ordinary grade and Higher grade). Pupils who start their secondary education in schools which do not cater for courses beyond Ordinary grade may in the light of their performance, or for other reasons, be transferred at the end of their second or fourth year to schools providing Higher grade courses. There were 26,719 teachers in secondary schools at Sept. 1985.

Special Schools. In Sept. 1985 there were 339 special schools and departments. The total number of handicapped children under instruction was 9,892, 339 had general learning difficulties, 2,262 had social and emotional handicaps, 1,966 were physically handicapped, 704 had visual handicap and 750 had hearing difficulties, and 827 were otherwise handicapped. Children can have more than one handicap.

Further Education. Centres and colleges for formal further education numbered 181 in 1985–86.

The student population was 238,314, of whom 58,344 attended full-time (advanced courses, 30,003; non-advanced, 28,341) and 179,970 part-time (advanced courses, 32,272; non-advanced, 147,698).

Teacher-Training. In Nov. 1985 there were 3,027 students in 7 colleges of education on pre-service courses of teacher-training.

Finance. Total expenditure on education met from revenue in 1985–86 was £1,593m. (excluding university education and loan charges).

Independent Schools. Outside the state system of education there were in England 2,276 independent schools in Jan. 1987, ranging from large 'public' schools to small local ones. There were (Jan. 1987) 514,855 full-time and 16,182 part-time pupils in these schools. In Wales 11,013 full-time pupils attended 67 independent schools. Fees are charged by all these schools, which receive no grant from central government sources. All independent schools in England are required to be registered by the Department and are liable to the inspection by HM Inspector. The term 'public schools' refers to independent schools in membership of the Headmasters' Conference, Governing Bodies Association or the Governing Bodies of Girls' Schools Association. Qualifications under which a school may be represented at the Headmasters' Conference include the measure of independence enjoyed by the governing body and the amount of advanced courses undertaken. Some of these schools are for boarders only, but the majority include non-resident 'day-pupils'. In Scotland there were 103 independent schools, with a total of 31,899 pupils in Sept. 1985. A small number of the Scottish independent schools are of the 'public school' type but they are not known as 'public schools' since in Scotland this term is used to denote education authority (*i.e.*, state) schools.

The earliest of the schools were founded by, and attached to, the medieval churches. Many were founded as 'grammar' (classical) schools in the 16th century, receiving charters from the reigning sovereign. Reformed mainly in the middle of the 19th century, these schools now provide the highest form of English pre-university education. Among the most well-known independent schools are Eton College, founded in 1440 by Henry VI, with 1,259 pupils; Winchester College, 1394, founded by William of Wykeham, Bishop of Winchester, 649 pupils; Harrow School, founded in 1560 as a grammar school by John Lyon, a yeoman, 760 pupils; Charterhouse, 1611, 704 pupils. Among the earliest foundations are King's School, Canterbury, founded 600 (with 716 pupils); King's School, Rochester, 604 (569); St Peter's, York, 627 (666).

Universities. In *England* there are 34 traditional degree-giving universities. In addition there are the London and Manchester Business Schools and the Open University. Eight new universities have been established since 1961 and 8 former Colleges of Advanced Technology gained university status in the 1960's.

In *Wales* there is 1 university, the University of Wales, with colleges at Aberystwyth, Bangor, Cardiff, Lampeter and Swansea. The University of Wales School of Medicine is a school of the University, and the University of Wales Institute of Science and Technology became a constituent college in Nov. 1967.

In *Scotland* there are 8 universities, St Andrew's, Glasgow, Aberdeen and Edinburgh Universities date from the 15th and 16th centuries while the others, Strathclyde, Heriot-Watt, Stirling and Dundee have been formally established since the early 1960s.

All these universities and colleges are independent, self-governing institutions, although they receive substantial aid from the State (in the case of the Open University by direct grant from the Department of Education and Science, and the traditional universities through the University Grants Committee). The UGC is a committee appointed by the Secretary of State for Education and Science designed to advise the Government on the needs of the universities, to prepare plans for their future development and to distribute grants between the universities. The members are drawn from education and industry. The Government receives advice on the universities' requirements for central computing facilities from the Computer Board for the Universities and Research Councils whose members are also drawn from the universities and industry.

The Royal College of Art and the Cranfield Institute of Technology are primarily postgraduate institutions which award higher degrees under charters granted in 1967 and 1969 respectively. They receive grants direct from the Department of Education and Science.

The local education authorities have no responsibility for universities.

The Open University received its Royal Charter on 1 June 1969 and is an independent, self-governing institution, awarding its own degrees. It is financed by the Government through the Department of Education and Science and by the receipt of students' fees.

Tuition is by means of correspondence textbooks, audio and video cassettes, radio and television broadcasts, summer and residential schools. Students can also attend one of 260 local study centres. No formal qualifications are required for entry to undergraduate or associate student courses.

Anyone resident in the UK aged 18 or over may apply. There are 140 undergraduate courses; many are available on a one-off basis to associate students.

In 1987 it had 68,037 undergraduates, about 74,000 continuing education students and clients and over 2,100 postgraduate students. The university has 2,600 full-time staff working at its Milton Keynes headquarters and in 13 regional centres throughout the country. There are 5,000 tutors and counsellors.

The University of Buckingham offers two-year degree courses. The academic year commencing in Jan. and consisting of four ten-week terms. There are four Schools of Studies: Accounting, Business, and Economics; Humanities; Law; and Sciences. A number of postgraduate courses are also offered. In 1987, there were 680 full-time students. Opened in 1976, the University of Buckingham received its Royal Charter in March 1983.

All universities charge fees, but financial help is available to students from several sources. The universities themselves provide scholarships of various kinds and local education authorities make awards to help suitable students to attend university. The amount of aid given generally depends upon the parents' means. The majority of the students at the English and Welsh universities are in receipt of some form of financial assistance.

Awards known as state studentships are offered on a competitive basis by the Department from among candidates considered by the universities and other higher education institutions to be qualified for postgraduate studies in the humanities; similar awards, tenable at universities or other higher education institutions, are offered by the Research Councils to students studying topics within the broad spectrum of agriculture and food; the biological sciences; man's natural environment; science and engineering and the social sciences at post-graduate level.

The following table gives the number of professors, lecturers, etc., and students (full-time and sandwich courses) for 1986–87:

University or college	Students	Staff	University or college	Students	Staff
Aston	3,605	349	Reading	5,834	775
Bath	3,661	500	Salford	3,747	458
Birmingham	9,300	1,520	Sheffield	8,218	1,064
Bradford	4,395	507	Southampton	6,537	1,068
Bristol	7,089	1,196	Surrey	3,391	585
Brunel	2,913	382	Sussex	4,533	617
Cambridge	12,219	1,838	Warwick	5,857	768
City	3,204	386	York	3,709	481
Durham	5,093	608			
East Anglia	4,232	513	*Wales—*		
Essex	3,110	371	Aberystwyth U.C.	3,150	372
Exeter	5,045	553	Bangor U.C.	2,846	377
Hull	4,766	516	Cardiff U.C.	5,675	650
Keele	2,847	311	St David's, Lampeter	743	70
Kent	4,201	472	Swansea U.C.	4,492	482
Lancaster	4,558	606	Univ. of Wales Institute of		
Leeds	10,340	1,488	Science and Technology	2,855	350
Leicester	4,886	717	Univ. of Wales		
Liverpool	7,748	1,137	College of Medicine	795	337
London Business School	261	78			
London	40,063	8,449	*Scotland—*		
Loughborough	5,210	729	Aberdeen	5,629	795
Manchester Business School	233	50	Dundee	3,300	513
Manchester	11,333	1,778	Edinburgh	10,127	1,728
Univ. of Manchester Inst. of			Glasgow	10,521	1,466
Science and Technology	4,119	710	Heriot-Watt	3,487	415
Newcastle	7,808	1,205	St Andrews	3,627	420
Nottingham	7,300	1,114	Stirling	2,897	356
Oxford	12,173	2,037	Strathclyde	7,642	976

Women students are admitted on equal terms with men. Number of women students: England, 93,213; Wales, 8,865; Scotland, 19,716. There are, however, colleges exclusively for female students at Oxford and Cambridge. Total number of full-time or sandwich students at universities listed above: England, 233,538; Wales, 20,556; Scotland, 47,230; total, 301,324.

McIntosh, N. E., Calder, J.A. and Swift, B., *A Degree of Difference.* London, 1976
Perry, W., *Open University: A Personal Account.* Open Univ. Press, 1976

The British Council. The British Council was established in Nov. 1934 and incorporated by Royal Charter in 1940. Its aims are the promotion of an enduring understanding and appreciation of Britain in other countries through cultural, educational and technical co-operation.

The Council's total budget in 1986–87 amounted to £242·1m. Funds included a grant-in-aid of £52·7m. from the Foreign and Commonwealth Office (Diplomatic Wing) and contributions of £21·2m. from the Overseas Development Administration (ODA) of the Foreign and Commonwealth Office. The ODA provided a further £101·8m. representing reimbursement of sums expended by the British Council on technical co-operation schemes, including the costs of their administration. The Foreign and Commonwealth Office provided a further £9m. The balance of £57·4m. was derived from Council earnings and from international agencies, overseas governments, etc. for educational services.

The Council is governed by a board consisting of up to 30 members, 2 of whom are nominated by Ministers. There are advisory committees for Scotland and Wales and also advisory committees for the main branches of the Council's work. In Feb. 1988 the Council had staff in 84 countries.

The Council is designated by the British Government to carry out over 30 bilateral cultural agreements, including that with the Soviet Union. The Council's work broadly divides into English language teaching; education and training; the development of university links and interchange; the promotion of wider use and availability of British books and periodicals; the development of personal contacts and the provision of information abroad on British experience and resources in the fields of education, medicine, science, technology and the arts.

The general policy in the field of English language teaching is to advise and assist education authorities overseas, particularly in curriculum and materials development and the training of local teachers of English; courses are provided in Britain and abroad for the further training of English language teaching experts from overseas. In many countries the Council runs its own English teaching centres. The Council acts as a centre for the dissemination of information about British educational thought and practice at all levels and, through its complement of education specialists working overseas, it has become closely involved with the administration of aid on behalf of the Overseas Development Administration. It assists in producing English teaching and other educational television and radio programmes overseas and arranges overseas consultancies and training in TV, radio and the application of media to development both in Britain and overseas. A prominent aspect of its education work is the assistance given in developing countries to the adoption of modern and locally relevant methods of science and mathematics teaching in schools. Following the merger with TETOC in 1982, the Council is responsible for advising ODA on its policies in the fields of technical education, industrial training, agricultural education, public administration and management development. Over 1,500 teachers of English or advisers, recruited by the British Council are working overseas. The Council is concerned to promote closer international academic collaboration through a variety of interchange and linking schemes, and through the provision of information and advice on educational institutions; it also administers the British Government's Technical Co-operation Training Programme and scholarship programmes on behalf of a large number of international organizations, notably UN and EEC. It administers examinations on behalf of a number of British examining boards.

During recent years the Council has collaborated with British educational institutions and firms in designing and implementing a wide range of education projects, for which overseas authorities or multilateral agencies pay the full cost.

The sciences, including medicine, technology and agriculture, form an increasingly important part of Council work. Contacts are built up and information collected and distributed through the specialist departments in London and the qualified scientists serving overseas, who also advise on training in Britain and the provision of experts abroad.

The importance of the arts as a medium for fostering cultural relations is reflected in the Council's encouragement of the appreciation of British achievements in the performing and the visual arts, both by supporting local activity and by sending theatre and ballet companies, orchestras and chamber groups, and exhibitions both of fine arts, crafts and photographs, from Britain on tours overseas. The Council also produces booklets, records and tapes on a wide range of literary and artistic subjects and in addition makes extensive use of films and video cassettes in support of its arts and educational work.

The Council runs, or is associated with, over 100 libraries in the countries in which it is represented. It arranges touring exhibitions of new British books and periodicals. Additional publicity for British books is provided by the publication *British Book News*, and the distribution of specialized book lists. The Council also administers ODA funds for the presentation of books to educational institutions in developing countries and the subsidized publication of low-priced books for students under the imprint of the English Language Book Society.

The Council arranges short advisory tours overseas by British experts. In a number of countries it is also the overseas administrative arm of the British Volunteer Programme. It awards scholarships and bursaries and arranges study programmes for some 25,000 visitors a year in Britain. It administers central government funds for youth exchanges with other countries.

In Britain the Council administers the programmes of award schemes for overseas students, meets many students on arrival from overseas, and provides an accommodation service for students from overseas for whom it has a special responsibility. The Council runs offices in Britain, mainly in university cities, for these purposes.

The Council is increasingly called on to administer training schemes and educational services financed by overseas authorities, or by multilateral agencies, on a contractual basis. The Council's specialist courses and summer schools provide advanced study in a number of fields, notably medicine, science, literature and the arts, English language and education. Payment is made by the student, or their parent organization, or by some other sponsor.

The Council produces the following periodicals: *Studying in Britain, Media in Education and Development, British Book News* and *Britain Abroad*. Other publications include the series *Writers and their Work, Notes on Literature, British Education, British Books and Libraries* and a number of booklets including *Scholarships Abroad, Introducing Wales, How to Live in Britain* and *Statistics of Overseas Students in the United Kingdom*. The Council has sponsored two major series of literature recordings, *The Complete Works of Shakespeare* and *The English Poets from Chaucer to Yeats*.

Chairman: Sir David Orr, MC.
Director-General: Richard Francis.
Headquarters: 10 Spring Gdns., London, SW1A 2BN.

Arts Council of Great Britain. The Arts Council is an independent organization established by Royal Charter in 1946, and is the principal channel for British Government aid to the arts. The Council's objects are to develop and improve the knowledge, understanding and practice of the arts, to increase their accessibility to the public, and to advise and co-operate with government departments, local authorities and other organizations.

The Council consists of a Chairman and not more than 19 other members who are appointed by the Minister for the Arts, after consultation with the Secretaries of State for Scotland and Wales.

The Council receives a grant-in-aid from the Government voted annually by Parliament.

As well as giving financial help and advice to several hundred artistic organizations from the major opera, dance, drama companies, orchestras and festivals, to the smallest touring theatre and experimental group, the Council encourages such diverse interests as contemporary dance, photography, art films, and helps professional creative writers, dramatists, poets, musicians, composers, artists and photographers by means of bursary and award schemes.

The Council is responsible for the administration of the South Bank Arts complex including the Hayward Gallery, the Wigmore Hall and Serpentine Gallery. The Council mounts art exhibitions at the Hayward and Serpentine and other galleries throughout the regions. Other direct promotions include tours of opera and drama companies, of the Council's own films on the arts and of music groups under the Contemporary Music Network scheme. The Council has a library of contemporary British poetry at its headquarters and library and information service covering cultural policy, also administration and funding.

National Insurance. The National Insurance Act, 1946, came into operation on 5 July 1948, repealing the existing schemes of health, pensions and unemployment insurance. This Act, along with later legislation, was consolidated as the National Insurance Act, 1965.

The Social Security Act 1975 introduced, from 6 April 1975, a new system of national insurance contributions to replace the previous system of flat-rate and graduated contributions. Since 6 April 1975, Class 1 contributions have been related to the employee's earnings and are collected with PAYE income tax, instead of by affixing stamps to a card. Class 2 and Class 3 contributions remain flat-rate, but, in addition to Class 2 contributions, those who are self-employed may be liable to pay Class 4 contributions, which for the year 1988–89 will be at the rate of 6·3% on profits or gains between £4,750 and £15,860, which are assessable for income tax under Schedule D. The non-employed and others whose contribution record is not sufficient to give entitlement to benefits are able to pay a Class 3 contribution voluntarily to qualify for a limited range of benefits. Class 2 weekly contributions for 1988–89 for men and women are £4·05. Class 3 contributions are £3·95 a week.

From 6 April 1978 the Social Security Pensions Act 1975 introduced earnings-related retirement, invalidity and widows' pensions. Employee's national insurance contribution liability depends on whether he is in contracted-out or not contracted-out employment.

For non contracted-out employment in 1988–89: On earnings between £41 and £69.99 a week, employee and employer both pay 5%; on earnings between £70 and £104.99 a week, employee and employer both pay 7%; on earnings between £105 and £154.99 a week, employee and employer both pay 9%; on earnings between £155 and £305 a week the employee pays 9% and the employer pays 10·45%; on earnings of over £305 a week the employee pays 9% of £305 but the employer pays 10·45% on all earnings. For contracted-out employment in 1988–89: On earnings between £41 and £69.99 a week the employee pays 5% on the first £41 and 2·85% on the remainder and the employer pays 5% on the first £41 and 0·9% on the remainder; on earnings between £70 and £104.99 a week the employee pays 7% on the first £41 and 4·85% on the remainder and the employer pays 7% on the first £41 and 2·9% on the remainder; on earnings between £105 and £154.99 a week the employee pays 9% on the first £41 and 6·85% on the remainder and the employer pays 9% on the first £41 and 4·9% on the remainder; on earnings between £155 and £305 a week the employee pays 9% on the first £39 and 6·85% on the remainder and the employer pays 10·45% on the first £41 and 6·35% on the remainder; on earnings exceeding £305 a week the employee pays 9% on the first £41 and 6·85% on earnings between £41 and £305 and the employer pays 10·45% on the first £41, 6·35% on earnings between £41 and £305 and 10·45% on the remainder.

The State supplements the contributions paid by contributors and employers, from general taxation. Contributions and supplement together with interest on investments form the income of the National Insurance Fund from which benefits are paid.

Statutory Sick Pay (SSP). Employers are now responsible for paying statutory sick pay (SSP) to their employees for up to 28 weeks in any period of incapacity for work. Basically, all employees aged 16 years and over are covered by the scheme whenever they are sick for 4 or more days consecutively. For most employees SSP completely replaces their entitlement to State sickness benefit which is not payable as long as any employer's responsibility for SSP remains.

Benefits. Qualification for any benefit depends upon fulfilment of the appropriate contribution conditions. Persons who are incapable of work as the result of an industrial accident may get sickness benefit followed by invalidity benefit without having to satisfy the contributions conditions. Employed persons may qualify for all the benefits; self-employed may not qualify for unemployment benefit.

Sickness Benefit. From 11 April 1988 the rate is £31·30 a week plus £19·40 a week for an adult dependant.

Unemployment Benefit is paid through the local unemployment benefit offices of the Department of Employment. The rate is £32·75 a week plus £20·20 a week for an adult dependant.

Invalidity Benefit replaces sickness benefit after 168 days of entitlement. It comprises a basic invalidity pension of £41·15 weekly and an invalidity allowance of £8·65 if incapacity began before age 40: £5·50 if incapacity began between 40 and

50 or £2·75 if it began between 50 and 60 (55 for women). Increases are: £24·75 for an adult dependant plus £8·40 for each child for whom child benefit is payable. Invalidity allowance is reduced or extinguished by the amount of any additional invalidity pension and/or guaranteed minimum pension to which there is title.

Maternity Benefit. Statutory maternity pay may be payable to a woman from her employer if she has been employed by him for 6 months and her earnings were above the lower earnings limit. If she has been employed by the same employer for at least 2 years, payment for the first 6 weeks of maternity absence may be at 90% of her average earnings. Payment for the remainder of the period is at a standard rate of £34·25. Women who do not qualify for statutory maternity pay may be entitled to maternity allowance from DHSS if they satisfy a test of recent work and contributions paid. From April 1988, the weekly rate is £31·30. Both statutory maternity pay and maternity allowance can be paid for up to 18 weeks. Payment can start at the earliest 11 weeks before the expected week of confinement but the woman has some choice in deciding when to give up work and still retain title to the full 18 weeks.

Widow's Benefits. From 11 April 1988 the three main widow's benefits, will be: Widow's payment, widowed mother's allowance, widow's pension.

A widow cannot get any widow's benefits based on her husband's NI if: She had been divorced from the man who has died; or she was living with the man as if she were married to him, but without being legally married to him; or she is living with another man as if she is married to him. A widow can only get widow's benefits if her husband has paid enough NI contributions. The rules about the number of NI contributions that are needed for these benefits can be complicated.

Widow's Payment: A widow may be able to get this benefit if her husband has paid enough NI contributions and: She was under 60 when her husband died; or her husband was under 65 when he died; or if her husband was 65 or over when he died, and he was not getting a State Retirement Pension.

A widow who is entitled to a widow's payment will get a single payment of £1,000. This will be tax-free.

Widowed Mothers Allowance: A widow may be able to get a widowed mother's allowance if her husband has paid enough NI contributions and: She is receiving child benefit for one of her children; or her husband was receiving child benefit, or she is expecting her husband's baby.

A widow who is entitled to a widowed mother's allowance will get an amount that is based on her husband's NI contributions. The maximum will be £41·15 a week. She will also get £8·40 a week for each of her children and she may also get an additional pension based on her husband's earnings since 1978. Widowed mother's allowance is usually paid as long as the widow is getting child benefit. Widowed Mother's Allowance is taxable.

Widow's Pension: A widow may be able to get a widow's pension if her husband has paid enough NI contributions. She must be 45 or over when her husband died or when her widowed mother's allowance ends. A widow cannot get a widow's pension at the same time as a widowed mother's allowance. A widow who is entitled to a widow's pension will get an amount that depends on her age when her husband died or when her widowed mother's allowance ends. If she was 55 or over she will get the full rate of widow's pension. The maximum amount of widow's pension will be £41·15 a week. She may also get an additional pension based on her husband's earnings since 1978. Widow's pension is usually paid until the widow is entitled to state retirement pension, when she is 60 or older. Widow's pension is taxable.

Guardian's Allowance. A person who is responsible for an orphan child may be entitled to a guardian's allowance of £8·40 a week in addition to the amount of child benefit payable in respect of that child. Normally both the child's parents must be dead but when the child is illegitimate, or the parents were divorced, or one parent is missing, or serving a long sentence of imprisonment, the allowance may, in certain circumstances, be paid on the death of one parent only.

Retirement Pension. In order to receive a retirement pension, men between 65 and 70, and women between 60 and 65 must have retired from regular employment. From 6 April 1979 a woman divorced over the age of 60 must satisfy the retirement conditions before a pension is payable. The standard rates of basic pensions are £39·50 a week for a man or woman on his or her own contributions and £24·75 for a married woman through her husband's contributions. Proportionately reduced pensions are payable where contribution records are deficient. For a person who reaches pension age on or after 6 April 1979, additional pension may also be payable. This is based on the earnings on which he or she has paid Class 1 contributions in each complete tax year between April 1978 and pension age. If the person has been a member of a contracted-out occupational pension scheme, that scheme will be responsible for paying the whole or part of the additional pension. An increase of £24·75 a week may be payable for a dependent wife. If she resides with the beneficiary the increase is gradually reduced for earnings over £45·09 a week. This tapered earnings rule does not apply to new claims from 16 Sept. 1985. From that date the following earnings rule will apply in these circumstances. When the spouse/woman looking after the claimant's child is living with the claimant an adult dependant's allowance will only be payable if the dependant's earnings do not exceed the standard rate of unemployment benefit for a person under pensionable age (currently £32·75). If she does not reside with the beneficiary an increase is not payable if she earns more than £24·75 a week. In addition £8·40 a week may be payable for each child for whom child benefit is payable. In certain circumstances an increase of £24·75 a week may be payable for a woman having care of the pensioner's children. In addition, a man who had paid graduated contributions receives 5p per week for every £7·50 of graduated contributions paid, and a woman 5p per week for every £9 paid. Although no further graduated contributions have been paid after April 1975, pension already earned will be paid along with the basic pension in the normal way. If, after being awarded a retirement pension, a man under 70 or a woman under 65 earns more than £75 in a calendar week the pension for the next pension week, including any increase for dependants, will be reduced by 5p for every 10p earned between £75 and £79 and by 5p for every 5p earned over £79. If retirement is postponed after minimum pension age increments of all components of the pension can be earned for periods of deferred retirement. From 6 April 1979 increments are earned at the rate of one-seventh penny per £1 of basic pension for every 6 days (excluding Sundays) for which pension has been foregone. Any days for which another benefit has been paid will not count. These increments must be at least 1% of the pension rate unless the minimum was earned under the arrangements which applied before 6 April 1979. For periods between 6 April 1975 and that date, the rate was one-eighth penny per £1 of the basic pension rate for every 6 days and for periods of deferred retirement before 6 April 1975 increments were based on the number of contributions paid as an employed or self-employed person. At age 70 for a man (65 for a woman) the pension for which a person has qualified may be paid in full whether a person continues in work or not irrespective of the amount of earnings. At the age of 80 an age addition of £0·25 a week is payable. In addition non-contributory pensions are now payable, subject to residence conditions, to persons aged 80 and over who do not qualify for a retirement pension or qualify for one at a low rate. The rates of these pensions, which are financed by Exchequer funds, are £24·75 a week for a single person and £14·80 for a married woman. These amounts do not include the £0·25 age addition. From 22 Dec. 1984 the lower rate of category D retirement pension payable to married women was abolished.

The Industrial Injuries Provisions of the Social Security Act, 1975. The Industrial Injuries Act, which also came into operation on 5 July 1948, with its later amending Acts, was consolidated as the National Insurance (Industrial Injuries) Act, 1965. This legislation was incorporated in the Social Security Act, 1975. The scheme provides a system of insurance against 'personal injury by accident arising out of and in the course of employment' and against certain prescribed diseases and injuries due to the nature of the employment. It takes the place of the Workmen's Compensation Acts and covers persons who are employed earners under the Social Security Act. There are no contribution conditions for the payment of benefit. Three types of benefit are provided:

(1) Disablement benefit. This is payable where, as the result of an industrial accident or prescribed disease, there is a loss of physical or mental faculty. The loss of faculty will be assessed as a percentage by comparison with a person of the same age and sex whose condition is normal. If the assessment is between 14-100% benefit will be paid as weekly pension; 14-19% are payable at the 20% rate. The rates vary from £13·44 (20% disabled) to £67·60 (100% disablement). Assessments of less than 14% do not normally attract basic benefit except for certain progressive chest diseases. The following increases can be paid with disablement benefit: Reduced earnings allowance (previously known as special hardship allowance) is now a seperate benefit which can be paid in addition to disablement benefit. This applies where as a result of the injury or disease the claimant is unable to return to his regular job and cannot do work of a similar standard. Disablement must be assessed at 1% or more, but it is not essential to be receiving disablement benefit (*e.g.* where disablement is assessed at less than 14%); there is a need for constant attendance; there is exceptionally severe disablement and the need for constant attendance is likely to be permanent. Pensions for persons under 18 are at a reduced rate. When injury benefit was abolished for industrial accidents occurring and prescribed diseases commencing on or after 6 April 1983, a common start date was introduced for the payment of disablement benefit 90 days (excluding Sundays) after the date of the relevant accident or onset of the disease.

(2) Death Benefit. On the death of a person occuring before 11 April 1988 as the result of an industrial accident or a prescribed disease, certain dependants may qualify for benefit. Benefit for a widow is a pension normally of £57·65 weekly for the first 26 weeks and thereafter £41·15, depending on such factors as age, entitlement to a child's allowance and permanent incapacity for self-support. If the conditions for pension at the higher rate are not satisfied the widow may receive a pension of £12·35 a week. Child allowances may be payable to the widow, or other person, entitled to child benefit for children of the deceased. For widows, these allowances are usually at the rate of £8·40 a week for each child; other persons do not normally qualify for these allowances. An allowance of £1 is payable to a woman having care of a child of the deceased. Benefit for widowers, parents and certain other relatives takes the form of pensions, allowances or gratuities according to the relationship to, and degree of maintenance by, the deceased. Deaths which occur on or after 11 April 1988: A widow is entitled to full widow's benefits even if her late husband did not satisfy the contribution condition, if he died as a result of an industrial accident or a prescribed disease.

War Pensions. The number of beneficiaries in receipt of war (1914–18) pensions or allowances as at 31 Dec. 1986 was 11,328. The number of beneficiaries in receipt of war (1939–45 and later) pensions or allowances in payment as at 31 Dec. 1986 was 263,532. The expenditure for both wars for 1985–86 was £581m..

National Insurance Fund. At 1 April 1986 the balance of the National Insurance Fund amounted to £5,293,024,000. Income during the period 1 April 1986 to 31 March 1987, consisting of contributions from insured persons and employers, payments from the Exchequer and interest on investments, etc., was £25,339,886,000. Payments of benefit in respect of unemployment were £1,733,537,000; injury and sickness, £178,954,000; invalidity, £2,647,129,000; maternity, £168,842,000; widows, £827,620,000; guardian's allowance and child's special allowance, £1,181,000; retirement pension, £17,817,145,000; death grants, £18,439,000; disablement benefits, £439,618,000; death benefit, £61,214,000. Included in these figures are the following estimated amounts of additional component, £219,092,000; earnings related supplement having ceased. Administrative and other payments cost approximately £1,032,265,000. The balance at 31 March 1987 was £5,706,966,000.

From 1 April 1975 the National Insurance Reserve Fund and the Industrial Injuries Fund were merged with the National Insurance Fund. All basic scheme contributions payable under the 1975 Social Security Act are paid into the single fund out of which the existing range of benefits will continue to be financed. The new national insurance fund will continue to receive a Treasury Supplement; for 1986–87 this was set at a level of 9% of total contribution income.

Child Benefit. Child benefit is a tax-free cash allowance for all children. The weekly rate for each child is £7·25 from 6 April 1987. Child benefit is payable for all children under age 16 and for those under age 19 receiving full-time non-advanced education at a college or school. One Parent Benefit. This is a tax-free cash allowance for certain people bringing up children alone. It is payable for the first or only child in the family in addition to child benefit. The weekly rate from 11 April 1988 is £4·90.

Family Credit. Family Credit is a tax-free benefit for working families with children. To be able to get Family Credit there must be at least one child under 16 in the family (or under 19 if in full-time education up to, and including, A level OND Standard). The claimant or partner (husband, wife or someone the claimant lives with as if they were married) must be working at least 24 hours a week to qualify. They may be employed or self-employed. The claim may be from a couple or a lone parent bringing up a child alone. The amount of family credit payable depends on the income of the claimant and partner, how many children there are in the family and their ages. A family will usually get Family Credit if the net weekly income of the claimant and partner (not including child benefit and one parent benefit) is less than £96·50 plus £8·50, £16·00, £21·00 or £30·50 for each child, depending on his or her age Family Credit is normally paid for 26 weeks at a time. The amount of the award will usually stay the same even if earnings, or other circumstances, change during that period.

Attendance allowance. This is a tax-free non-contributory allowance for severely disabled people, including children aged 2 or over, who require a lot of help from another person. There are 2 rates, the higher rate of £32·95 a week for those who require attention or supervision by day and night, and the lower rate of £22 a week for those who need the attendance either by day or night. In addition to the medical requirements a simple test of residence and presence in Great Britain must also be satisfied.

Invalid Care Allowance. This is a non-contributory taxable benefit which may be paid to those under pensionable age who stay at home to care for a person who is receiving attendance allowance or constant attendance allowance. Current rate £24·75 a week, with increases for dependants.

Supplementary Benefit. Under the Supplementary Benefits Act, 1976, as amended by the Social Security Act 1980, benefit is payable to any persons in Great Britain aged 16 years or over (excluding persons at school or college or anyone directly involved in a trade dispute) who are not in full-time remunerative work and who are without resources, or whose resources (including national insurance benefits) need to be supplemented in order to meet their requirements. A person who is excluded from benefit under the normal rules may, nevertheless, receive payments to meet urgent need. The general standards by reference to which supplementary benefit is granted are determined by statutory regulations approved by Parliament. Persons who are dissatisfied with the amount of benefit granted to them may appeal to an independent Appeal Tribunal established under the Act.

During the financial year 1986–87 net payments on supplementary benefit amounted to £7,967m.

Newman, T. S., *Digest of British Social Insurance*. London, 1947 (and supplements, to date)

National Health. The National Health Service in England and Wales started on 5 July 1948 under the National Health Service Act, 1946. There is a separate Act for Scotland and also one for Northern Ireland, where the Health Services are run on similar lines to those in England and Wales.

The National Health Service, which is available to every man, woman and child, is a charge on the national income in the same way as the armed forces and other facilities.

Every person normally resident in this country is entitled to use any complete part of the services, and no insurance qualification is necessary. Most of the cost of running the service is met from the national exchequer, *i.e.*, from taxes.

Since Sept. 1957 a small weekly National Health Service contribution has been payable by contributors and where applicable by their employers. For convenience this contribution is collected with the National Insurance contribution and for 1986–87 is estimated to be £2,233m. for Great Britain.

Organization. Under the provisions of the NHS Act 1977 and the Health Service Act 1980, the administration of the National Health Service in England and Wales is organized under a system of regional and district health authorities accountable to the Secretary of State for the Social Services and the Secretary of State for Wales. In Scotland the National Health Service is administered under the National Health Service (Scotland) Act 1978, by 15 Health Boards and a Common Services Agency all accountable to the Secretary of State for Scotland.

There are 191 district health authorities in England responsible for the administration and development of health services in their district. Fourteen regional health authorities, each consisting of a number of health districts, are responsible for allocating resources between the district health authorities in their regions and for monitoring their performance. The regional authorities are responsible for developing strategic plans and priorities and for carrying out certain executive functions.

Services. The National Health Service broadly consists of hospital and specialist services, general medical, dental and ophthalmic services, pharmaceutical services, community health services and school health services. All these services are free of charge except for such things as prescriptions, spectacles, dentures and dental treatment, amenity beds in hospitals and for some of the community services, for which charges are made with certain exemptions.

The total cost of the Health and Personal Social Services (Great Britain) is estimated at £22,600m. for 1986–87 and the estimated net expenditure by the Exchequer (except for the Local Authority Personal Social Services, where the rates and the Exchequer grants are estimated at about £3,270m.) in 1986–87 is £18,200m.

The number of abortions performed in 1986 under the provisions of the Abortion Act, 1967, was 172,286, of which 147,619 related to England and Wales residents. Of these 147,619 abortions, 93,041 (63%) were to single women, 38,203 (26%) were to married women, and 16,375 (11%) were to widowed, divorced or separated women and to women who did not state their marital status.

The number of abortion notifications received in Scotland in 1986 under the provisions of the Abortion Act 1967, was 9,549, of which 9,533 related to Scottish residents. Of these 9,533 notifications, 6,019 (63·1%) were to single women, 2,364 (24·8%) were to married women, and 1,150 (12·1%) were to widowed, divorced or separated women and to women who did not state their marital status.

In Great Britain in 1986 there were 31,854 general medical practitioners, 16,744 general dental practitioners and 287,700 qualified nurses and midwives. There were (1986) 408,700 average daily available hospital beds in the UK.

Personal Social Services. Under the Local Authority Social Services Act 1970 and in Scotland the Social Work (Scotland) Act 1968 the welfare and social work services provided by local authorities were made the responsibility of a new local authority department—the Social Services Department in England and Wales, and

Social Work Departments in Scotland headed by a Director of Social Work. The social services thus administered include: the fostering, care and adoption of children, welfare services and social workers for the mentally disordered, the disabled and the aged, and accommodation for those needing residential care services. In Scotland the social work departments' functions also include the supervision of persons on probation, of adult offenders and of persons released from penal institutions or subject to fine supervision orders.

The number of supported residents in residential accommodation for the elderly and younger disabled was as follows:

England and Wales (31 March)	Residential accommodation Adults and Children	Scotland (31 March)	Residential accommodation Adults and Children
1984	129,093	1984	15,200
1985	126,147	1985	14,787
1986	121,793	1986	14,637

England and Wales. Expenditure and income relating to the personal social services administered by local authorities (in £1,000 sterling):

Year ended 31 March	Gross current expenditure	Income from sales, fees and charges	Net current expenditure
1984	2,625,060	378,520	2,246,540
1985	2,781,541	390,122	2,391,419
1986	2,952,048	456,825	2,798,099
1987 [1]	3,286,262	488,163	2,798,099

Capital Spending

Year ended 31 March	Gross expenditure	Income from sales of fixed assets	Net expenditure
1984	95,903	17,940	77,963
1985	106,708	23,041	83,667
1986	107,913	27,366	80,547
1987 [1]	103,871	23,662	80,209

[1] Provisional.

Scotland. The total local authority expenditure for 1985–86 in respect of residential accommodation and welfare services under the Social Work (Scotland) Act, 1968, was £330·1m. Central Government expenditure on social work totalled £11·1m.

Klein, R., *The Politics of the National Health Service.* London, 1983
Watkin, B., *The National Health Service.* London, 1978

DIPLOMATIC REPRESENTATIVES

Of the USA in Great Britain (Grosvenor Sq., London, W1A 1AE)
Ambassador: Charles H. Price II.

Of Great Britain in the USA (3100 Massachusetts Ave., NW, Washington, D.C., 20008)
Ambassador: Sir Antony Acland, GCMG, KCVO.

Of Great Britain to the United Nations
Ambassador: Sir Crispin Tickell, KCVO.

Books of Reference

The annual and other publications of the various Public Departments and the Reports, etc. of Royal Commissions and Parliamentary Committees. (These may be obtained from HM Stationery Office.)
Bickmore, D. P., and Shaw, M. A. (ed.), *The Atlas of Great Britain and Northern Ireland.* OUP, 1963

Central Statistical Office. *Annual Abstract of Statistics.* HMSO.—*Monthly Digest of Statistics.* HMSO
Central Office of Information. *Britain: An Official Handbook.* HMSO, annual.
Directory of British Associations. Beckenham, annual
Government Statistical Service. *Social Trends.* HMSO.—*Regional Statistics.* HMSO
Government Statistics: A Brief Guide to Sources. HMSO, 1984
Halsey, A. H., *Trends in British Society Since 1900.* London, 1972
Hornsby-Smith, M.P., *Roman Catholics in England.* CUP, 1987
Jenkin, M., *British Industry and the North Sea.* London, 1981
Kendall, M. G. (ed.), *The Source and Nature of the Statistics of the United Kingdom.* 2 vols. London, 1952–1957
Mitchell, B. R., *Abstract of British Historical Statistics.* OUP, 1962
Oxford History of England. 15 vols. OUP, 1936–75
Waller, R. (ed.), *The Almanack of British Politics.* London, 1987

Scotland

Scottish Council (Development and Industry). *Inquiry into the Scottish Economy, 1900–61.* Edinburgh, 1961
Scottish Office. *Scottish Economic Bulletin.* HMSO (quarterly).—*Scottish Abstract of Statistics.* HMSO (annual)
The New Scottish Local Authorities: Organisation and Management Structures. HMSO, 1973
Brand, J., *The National Movement in Scotland.* London, 1978
Campbell, R. H., *The Rise and Fall of Scottish Industry, 1707–1939.* Edinburgh, 1981
Donaldson, G. (ed.), *The Edinburgh History of Scotland.* 4 vols. Edinburgh, 1965–75
Drucker, N. and H. M., *The Scottish Government Year Book.* London, 1980
Grant, E., *Scotland.* [Bibliography] Oxford and Santa Barbara, 1982
Hogg, A., and Hutcheson, A. MacG., *Scotland and Oil.* 2nd ed. Edinburgh, 1975
Johnston, T. L., *Structure and Growth in the Scottish Economy.* London, 1971
Kellas, J. G., *The Scottish Political System.* 3rd ed. CUP, 1984
Meikle, H. W. (ed.), *Scotland: A Description of Scotland and Scottish Life.* London, 1947
Monies, G., *Local Government in Scotland.* Edinburgh, 1985

Wales

Wales: The Way Ahead (Cmnd 3334.) HMSO, 1971
Wales: Employment and the Economy. Cardiff, 1972
Digest of Welsh Statistics. HMSO (annual)
Jenkins, G. H., *The Foundations of Modern Wales 1642–1780.* Oxford, 1988
Williams, D., *A History of Modern Wales.* New ed. London, 1977
Williams, G., (ed.) *Social and Cultural Change in Contemporary Wales.* London, 1978

NORTHERN IRELAND

AREA AND POPULATION. Area (revised by the Ordnance Survey Department) and population were as follows:

District	Population (usually resident) 1981 Census [1]	Population estimate 30 June 1986	Area (Hectares)
Antrim	45,016	45,900	41,510
Ards	57,792	63,000	36,789
Armagh	49,223	51,200	66,733
Ballymena	54,813	55,800	63,384
Ballymoney	22,946	23,800	41,687
Banbridge	30,110	31,700	44,174
Belfast	314,270	303,600	11,140
Carrickfergus	28,625	29,000	8,484
Castlereagh	60,785	58,000	8,426
Coleraine	46,739	47,600	47,763
Cookstown	28,257	27,800	51,207

District	Population (usually resident) 1981 Census [1]	Population estimate 30 June 1986	Area (Hectares)
Craigavon	73,260	76,100	27,945
Down	53,193	55,800	63,835
Dungannon	43,883	43,800	76,266
Fermanagh	51,594	51,000	169,952
Larne	29,076	28,600	33,744
Limavady	26,964	29,100	58,523
Lisburn	83,998	91,900	43,595
Derry (Londonderry)	89,101	95,700	37,258
Magherafelt	32,494	33,200	56,186
Moyle	14,396	15,100	49,378
Newry and Mourne	76,574	86,100	88,589
Newtownabbey	72,246	72,200	15,956
North Down	66,264	69,800	7,329
Omagh	44,288	45,100	112,354
Strabane	36,279	35,900	86,090
Northern Ireland	1,532,186	1,566,800	1,348,297

[1] Arising from difficulties during the Census taking, a number of households were not enumerated. The population effect of this non-enumeration is estimated at about 50,000 and is included in this column.

Chief towns (population, estimate 1983): Belfast, 322,600; Londonderry, 96,100.
Vital statistics for calendar years:

	Marriages	Divorces	Births	Deaths
1982	9,913	1,383	27,028	15,918
1983	9,990	1,678	27,255	16,039
1984 [1]	10,361	1,547	27,693	15,692
1985 [1]	10,343	1,602	27,635	15,955
1986 [1]	10,227	1,427	28,152	16,065

[1] Provisional.

CONSTITUTION AND GOVERNMENT. Northern Ireland is part of the United Kingdom. As such it shares in the written and unwritten constitution of the United Kingdom and is subjected to the fundamental constitutional provisions which apply to the rest of the United Kingdom. However, in the Northern Ireland Constitution Act 1973 and the Northern Ireland Act 1982, Parliament provides for a measure of devolved government in Northern Ireland. This can only be introduced if both Houses of Parliament agree that the arrangements for devolution are likely to command widespread acceptance throughout the community in Northern Ireland.

Such matters as the Crown, Parliament, international relations, the armed forces and the raising of taxes cannot be devolved in any circumstances and remain the responsibility of the UK Parliament and Government. In the event of agreement on widely-acceptable arrangements for devolution, powers over a range of social and economic matters would be devolved first. The Northern Ireland Assembly would have power to make laws on these subjects and Members of the Assembly would be appointed as heads of the relevant Northern Ireland government departments. Such powers were devolved on 1 Jan. 1974, following an agreement among the Northern Ireland political parties to form a power-sharing Executive. This collapsed on 28 May 1974 and there had been no devolution by 31 Dec. 1985.

In the interim and in the absence of devolved arrangements which command widespread acceptance, Northern Ireland is governed by 'direct rule' under the provisions of the Northern Ireland Act 1974. This provides for Parliament to approve all laws for Northern Ireland and places the Northern Ireland departments under the direction and control of a UK Cabinet Minister, the Secretary of State for Northern Ireland.

A 78-member Assembly was elected by proportional representation in 1982. In May 1984 the Assembly set up a Committee on Devolution to consider and report on how the Assembly might be strengthened and progress made towards legislative and executive devolution. The Committee's third report was published in Oct. 1985. The Assembly was dissolved on 23 June 1986.

In Nov. 1985 the governments of the UK and the Republic of Ireland entered into a formal Agreement which is designed to promote peace and stability in Northern Ireland, help to reconcile the two major traditions in Ireland, create a new climate of friendship and co-operation between the people of the two countries and improve co-operation in combating terrorism. Under the Agreement an Intergovernmental Conference was established in which the Irish Government will put forward views and proposals concerning stated aspects of Northern Ireland affairs; in which the promotion of cross-border co-operation will be discussed; and in which determined efforts will be made to resolve any differences between the two governments. A Secretariat was also established by the two governments to service the Conference.

What began ostensibly as a Civil Rights campaign in 1968 escalated into a full-scale offensive designed to overthrow the State. This offensive was originally mounted by an illegal organization, the Irish Republican Army (not to be confused with the legitimate Army of the Republic of Ireland). At times counter-measures have required the services of over 20,000 regular troops, in addition to the Royal Ulster Constabulary, the RUC Reserve and the part-time Ulster Defence Regiment.

Secretary of State for Northern Ireland: Rt Hon. Tom King, MP.

Local Government. Northern Ireland has a single-tier system of 26 district councils based on main centres of population.

The district councils are responsible for the provision of a wide range of local services including refuse collection and disposal, street cleansing, litter prevention, consumer protection, environmental health, miscellaneous licensing including dog control, the provision and management of recreational and cultural facilities, the promotion of tourist development schemes, the enforcement of building regulations and gas supply. They have in addition both a representative role in which they send forward representatives to sit as members of statutory bodies including the Northern Ireland Housing Council, the Fire Authority and the Area Boards for health and personal social services and education and libraries; and a consultative role under which the Department of Environment (NI) and the Northern Ireland Housing Executive, among others, have an obligation to consult them regarding the provision of the regional services for which these bodies are responsible.

The Government's policy for the future development of the Province is contained in the *Regional Physical Development Strategy 1975–95* which was published in May 1977. Basically the policy advocates that the main town in each District Council area should be developed to fulfil its function as the prime centre in the district and for any other specialized rôles it may have such as an industrial centre, port or tourist resort. The Strategy also recognizes that the smaller towns and villages have an important rôle to play, depending on the availability of services, as locations for smaller scale industries service centres and as dormitory centres for people not wishing to live in the towns where they find employment.

The Regional Strategy provides a framework within which development plans can be prepared for all the districts. Since its adoption of the Strategy the Department has been engaged in formulating the detailed policies and proposals for future communications, the location of industry, housing and major services in the light of anticipated population growth and distribution.

A development plan sets down the broad policies and proposals for the development or other use of land in the area covered by the plan over a period of up to 15 years ahead. Development plans covering almost all of Northern Ireland have been published and work is progressing on the remaining areas, together with review of some earlier plans.

FINANCE. There exists a separate Northern Ireland Consolidated Fund from which is met the expenditure of Northern Ireland Departments. Its main sources of revenue are: *(i)* The Northern Ireland attributed share of UK taxes; *(ii)* A non-specific grant in aid of Northern Ireland's revenue, payable by the Secretary of State for Northern Ireland; *(iii)* Rates and other receipts of Northern Ireland Departments.

The general principle underlying the financial arrangements is that Northern Ireland should have parity of taxation and services with Great Britain.

Since the financial year 1985–86 the income of the Northern Ireland Consolidated Fund has been as follows (in £ sterling):

	1985–86	1986–87	1987–88
Attributed share of UK taxes	1,808,174,974[1]	2,030,834,826[2]	2,140,080,000[3]
Payments by UK Government:			
Grant in Aid	955,000,000	845,000,000	874,244,953
Refund of value added tax	26,804,048	33,302,021	35,000,000
Regional and district rates	208,000,000	243,250,000	253,900,000
Other receipts	336,783,368	348,366,285	360,000,000
Total	3,334,762,390	3,500,753,132	3,663,224,953

[1] Including final adjustment for 1984–85.
[2] Including final adjustment for 1985–86.
[3] Provisional.

The public debt at 31 March 1987 was as follows: Ulster Savings Certificates, £162,751,000; Ulster Development Bonds, £30,175; borrowing from UK Government, £1,091,392,487; borrowing from Northern Ireland Government Funds, £105,382,599; European Investment Bank Loan, £16,217,269; assets from abolished funds, £347,440,052; total, £1,723,213,582.

The above amount of public debt is offset by equal assets in the form of loans from Government to public and local bodies and of cash balances.

ENERGY AND NATURAL RESOURCES

Electricity. The planning, generation and distribution of electricity supplies are the responsibility of the Northern Ireland Electricity Service.

With Kilroot power station out of action for conversion to coal/oil burning, the installed capacity of the system is 1,800 mw largely provided from 3 thermal power-stations.

The total sales of electricity in Northern Ireland in the year ended 31 March 1987 amounted to 5,161m. units supplied to a total of 570,387 consumers.

Water Supplies and Sewerage. The Department of the Environment Water Service is responsible for water supply and sewerage. Some 691 megalitres of water are supplied throughout Northern Ireland per day to approximately 97% of the population. Approximately 92% of the population live in property which is connected to sewers or modern septic tanks.

The Department is also responsible for the conservation and planned development of the water resources of Northern Ireland.

Minerals. The output of minerals (in 1,000 tonnes) during 1986 was approximately: Basalt and igneous rock (other than granite), 6,731; grit and conglomerate, 2,693; limestone, 3,436; sand and gravel, 4,228; and other minerals (rocksalt, flint, sandstone, diatomite, granite, chalk, clay and shale), 1,017. Lignite has been discovered near Crumlin in County Antrim and in some other areas.

Agriculture. Estimated gross output in 1986:

		Quantity (1,000)	Value (£m.)			Quantity (1,000)	Value (£m.)
Fat cattle		523	259·0	Grass seed		—	—
Calves		11	1·8	Hay and straw		10	0·8
Store cattle		7	2·6	Fruit	tonnes	25	3·7
Exports of breeding	head			Vegetables		18	3·5
livestock		9	2·1	Mushrooms		8	9·0
Fat sheep and lambs		911	31·4	Flowers		—	6·0
Fat pigs		1,217	76·1	Other items		—	61·0
Poultry (tonnes)		60	43·7				
Eggs: for human							
consumption (dozen)		69	25·4				
Wool (tonnes)		2,379	2·1	Total receipts			748·1
Milk (litres)		1,324	194·7	Value of changes in			
Potatoes		222	18·1	stocks due to volume			+3·0
Oats		4	0·5				
Barley	tonnes	56	6·3	Gross output			751·1
Wheat		2	0·3				

Area (in 1,000 hectares) of crops at June census (1985 and 1986):

	1985	1986		1985	1986
Oats	2·6	2·4	Crop silage	4·3	5·9
Wheat	5·0	3·8	Other crops	1·4	0·8
Barley	46·2	47·4	Fruit	2·1	2·0
Other cereals and pulses	0·4	0·3	Grass for mowing	265·4	263·8
Potatoes	13·0	11·8	Grass for grazing	500·7	500·8
Turnips, swedes, kale			Rough grazing (excluding		
and cabbage[1]	0·7	0·8	common land)	185·4	183·5
Vegetables	1·1	1·3			

[1] Stock feeding only.

Livestock (1,000) at June census (1985 and 1986):

	1985	1986		1985	1986
Dairy cows	294	292	Total sheep	1,590	1,701
Beef cows	201	198	Breeding sows	64	62
Total cattle	1,514	1,471	Total pigs	617	617
Breeding ewes	769	819	Total poultry	10,061	9,924

INDUSTRY AND TRADE

Industry. In 1987 (March) employment in manufacturing and construction amounted to 123,630, just under 25·5% of the total workforce. Of this number, 29,760 (24·1%) were engaged in the engineering and allied industries, which include shipbuilding and aircraft manufacture. The former predominance of shipbuilding has diminished, and the engineering sector now produces an impressive variety of goods; from textile machinery, air-conditioning plant and oilfield equipment to automobile and aero-engine components, data-processing equipment, and electronic components. The textile and man-made fibre industries, with a workforce of 11,930 includes longer established sectors such as spinning and weaving as well as more recently established activities such as the production of carpets, man-made fibres and hosiery. The related clothing and footwear sector employs 16,430 people. Taken together, food, drink and tobacco account for 18,550 jobs, the remainder of the manufacturing sector comprising a multiplicity of activities, such as chemicals, rubber and plastic goods, and furniture accounting for 22,720. The construction industry employs 24,430 people.

In Aug. 1987 the average number of unemployed claimants was 127,285, this represents 18·6% of the working population. The Department of Economic Development provides an all-age guidance and placement service through a network of jobmarkets situated in the principal towns of Northern Ireland. They maintain registers of persons voluntarily seeking employment (either full- or part-time) and those already in employment who wish to change their job. In the financial year 1986–87, 35,180 persons (adult and young people) were placed into employment in Northern Ireland by the Employment Service. A further 16,128 persons were placed into training.

The Government offers a comprehensive range of incentives to encourage the establishment of new and the expansion of existing industry. At June 1987 there were 202 new projects and 244 expansions of existing projects giving employment to 72,013 workers.

Through the Department of Economic Development, there are various employment and training grants available to assist employers with recruitment and training of workers. These grants cover a wide spectrum of industry, age groups, and types of training.

Assistance is available to employers who transfer key workers temporarily or permanently to Northern Ireland from other countries or within Northern Ireland in connection with the establishment or expansion of an industrial undertaking.

The Department of Economic Development maintains a register of disabled persons who are in the employment field and under the provisions of the Disabled Persons (Employment) Acts (NI) 1945 and 1960, makes efforts to find suitable work for those who are unemployed. Employment rehabilitation courses are provided at the Employment Rehabilitation Unit at Felden House, Newtownabbey and training courses at various locations are available to assist unemployed disabled persons to readjust themselves to working conditions and to enhance their prospects of obtaining suitable employment. Allowances are paid to persons attending these courses.

The Youth Training Programme is a two year vocational training programme administered by the Department of Economic Development in partnership with the Department of Education for Northern Ireland. The programme provides:

(a) full-time training places for 16 and 17 year old school leavers not yet in employment;

(b) employment with training opportunities for 17 year olds (YTP Workscheme);

(c) increased vocational preparation for young people remaining in full-time education.

In 1987–88 the Programme provided some 9,400 training places in a variety of schemes. Provision was also made for up to 5,000 entrants to YTP Workscheme, a scheme which encourages employers to recruit and train 17 year old employees.

Enterprise Ulster is an independent statutory body whose objective as a direct labour organization is to give employment to the long term and less skilled unemployed. Employment is provided through a structured industrial approach with an emphasis on: (a) rehabilitation into the disciplines of work; (b) training in semi-skilled and traditional trades; (c) placement in more conventional employment. Work that is carried out mainly for public bodies and projects, which might not otherwise be done, is of community and amenity value. In Sept. 1987, 180 projects were providing employment for 1,400 employees.

The Action for Community Employment Scheme, which came into operation in April 1981, provides temporary employment for long-term unemployed adults on projects which are of benefit to the community. In Sept. 1987 some 400 such projects were operational, providing employment for some 6,200 people.

There are 12 Training Centres in Northern Ireland which provide over 3,000 training places and an annual output of over 5,000 trainees.

Training Centres contribute to the Youth Training Programme having up to 2,200 places available for 16–17 year olds who have been unable to find employment. A special six-month broad-based modular course provides basic training in a wide variety of skills and the six-month craft skill courses provide initial apprentice training. Advanced vocational training is available to young people who have completed the basic training course and have been unable to obtain a place in an apprentice course. The remaining places are for adult trainees.

To supplement the Training Centres facilities, arrangements have been made for the use of spare training capacity in industry and commerce to attach people to firms for training courses. By this means a wide variety of training is made available and this has been further supplemented by use of spare capacity in other training agencies and in Colleges of Further Education.

The Department of Economic Development administers an Entry to Management Programme for unemployed trainees and a Management Development Programme for private sector firms. The former Programme contains training opportunities schemes for those wishing to enter or re-enter management or to set up new businesses – at the peak time of the training year up to 220 people can be in training. The latter Programme is designed to encourage companies to develop management structures and to train individual managers to a high level of competence. Each year about 2,000 grants are awarded to support training courses or training places in companies. Also, up to 2,800 places were available in the financial year 1987–88 under the Enterprise Allowance Scheme, to encourage unemployed people to set up in business, by paying them £40 a week for up to 52 weeks as a business receipt to compensate for loss of unemployment or supplementary benefit.

Labour. The main sources of statistics in Northern Ireland are the census of employment which was last conducted in 1984 and the quarterly employment enquiry. In March 1987 there were 485,290 jobs for employees in Northern Ireland; of which 257,190 were taken up by males.

TOURISM. Tourism earns a substantial amount of revenue for Northern Ireland and total spending by some 824,000 visitors in 1986 was £82m. Altogether tourism provides over 9,000 full-time jobs. The Northern Ireland Tourist Board has the main responsibility for promoting tourist traffic to and within Northern Ireland.

Scenic beauty, scientific and nature interest, and wildlife are protected by the Department of the Environment under the Access to the Countryside (NI) Order 1983, the Nature Conservation and Amenity Lands (NI) Order 1985 and the Wildlife (NI) Order 1985. The Department is advised by the Ulster Countryside Committee and the Committee for Nature Conservation. Eight Areas of Outstanding Natural Beauty and 48 Areas of Scientific Interest have been designated, where special attention is given respectively to the amenity and scientific aspects of planning applications. Country Parks have been established at Crawfordsburn, Redburn and Scrabo, Co. Down, at the Roe Valley and Ness Wood, Co. Derry, and at Castle Archdale, Co. Fermanagh. At The Birches in N. Armagh a Peatlands Park is being developed. The Lagan Valley between Belfast and Lisburn is Northern Ireland's first Regional Park. Forty-one National Nature Reserves have been declared, and more are being acquired.

The Department is advised by the Historic Monuments Council on the exercise of its powers under the Historic Monuments Act (NI) 1971 in respect of the conservation of historic monuments and the preservation of objects of archaeological or historic interest. At present there are some 163 monuments in State care and approximately 744 are scheduled. The Department, advised by the Historic Buildings Council, is also responsible for listing buildings of special architectural or historic interest and for designating areas of similar interest the character or appearance of which it is desirable to preserve or enhance. To date some 7,000 buildings have been listed and 25 conservation areas have been designated. Grants are payable by the Department to assist in the repair or maintenance of listed buildings and for schemes of enhancement in conservation areas.

COMMUNICATIONS

Road and Rail. All train services are operated by the Northern Ireland Railways Co. Ltd which is a subsidiary of the Northern Ireland Transport Holding Co. The number of track km operated is 357; passenger route miles, 210. In 1986–87 railways carried 5·5m. passengers. Most bus services are operated by two other subsidiaries, Ulsterbus Ltd and Citybus Ltd. Ulsterbus runs services outside the Belfast area while all the services within the Belfast area are run by Citybus.

The Department of the Environment (NI) administers a licensing system for professional hauliers with the objective of maintaining standards and conditions necessary for the safe operation of vehicles and fair competition between hauliers. The level of services provided and the rates charged by the industry are determined by the normal economic forces of supply and demand. At 31 March 1987 there were 1,444 professional hauliers and 2,670 vehicles licensed to engage in road haulage.

The number of motor vehicles licensed at 31 Dec. 1986 was 459,120, comprising private cars, 422,880; motor cycles, 10,820; hackney vehicles, 2,450; goods vehicles, 15,660; agricultural tractors, 7,310. In addition, there were 13,445 vehicles which were not subject to licence duty.

At 1 April 1987 the total mileage of roads was 14,778, graded for administrative purposes as follows: Motorway 69 miles; Class I dual carriageway, 81 miles; Class I single carriageway, 1,283 miles; Class II, 1,774 miles; Class III, 2,937 miles; unclassified, 8,634 miles.

Aviation. Northern Ireland Airports Ltd is responsible for the operation of Belfast International Airport. A major 4-stage development programme was started in 1977; 3 stages have been completed. The completion of the programme will leave the airport better equipped to handle traffic growth in the foreseeable future. Passenger and freight services operate between Belfast International Airport and airports throughout the UK. In 1986, 1·9m. passengers and 30,000 tonnes of freight and mail were handled.

Scheduled air services are available from Belfast (Harbour) Airport to 7 destinations in the UK.

There are 3 other licensed airfields in Northern Ireland and apart from some scheduled services during the summer months, these airfields are used principally by flying clubs, by private owners and by expanding air taxi businesses flying to destinations in Ireland, the UK and continental Europe.

Shipping. Passenger services operate between Belfast and Liverpool and between Larne and (i) Cairnryan and (ii) Stranraer. Conventional cargo services have given way in many cases to container, unit load and drive on/drive off services. The latter type of service now operates between Belfast, Larne and Warrenpoint to various ports in UK.

JUSTICE, RELIGION, EDUCATION AND WELFARE

Justice. The Lord Chancellor has responsibility for the administration of all courts in Northern Ireland through the Northern Ireland Court Service, and is responsible for the appointment of judges and resident magistrates.

The court structure in Northern Ireland has 3 tiers–the Supreme Court of Judicature of Northern Ireland (comprising the Court of Appeal, the High Court and the Crown Court), the County Courts and the Magistrates' Courts. There are 25 Petty Sessions districts which when grouped together for administration purposes form 7 County Court Divisions and 4 Circuits.

The County Court has general civil jurisdiction subject to an upper monetary limit of £5,000. Appeals from the Magistrates' Courts lie to the County Court, while appeals from the County Court lie to the High Court or, on a point of law, to the Court of Appeal by way of case stated. Circuit Registrars have jurisdiction to deal with most defended actions up to £500 and most undefended actions up to £5,000. They also deal, by an informal arbitration procedure, with small claims whose value does not exceed £300. An appeal from the decision of a Circuit Registrar lies to the High Court other than in small claims cases.

Police. The police force consists of the Royal Ulster Constabulary, supported by the Royal Ulster Constabulary Reserve, a mainly part-time force.

Religion. According to the census of 1981 of the total enumerated population of 1,481,959 there were: Roman Catholics, 414,532; Presbyterians, 339,818; Church of Ireland, 281,472; Methodists, 58,731. Those belonging to other Churches and of no stated denomination numbered 387,406. 18·5% of the enumerated population failed to answer the voluntary question on religion.

Education. Education in Northern Ireland is administered centrally by the Department of Education and locally by 5 education and library boards. The Department is concerned with the whole range of education from nursery education through to higher education and continuing education; for sport and recreation; for youth services; for the arts and culture (including libraries) and for community relations and community development. District councils are the main providers of sport, recreation and community facilities and the education and library boards have a responsibility where the facilities are intended primarily for education and youth service activities. The Department assists with grants as far as the district councils are concerned and meets the full cost in relation to education and library boards.

The 5 education and library boards which took over responsibility for the local administration of the education and library services on 1 Oct. 1973 are required to ensure that there are sufficient schools of all kinds to meet the needs of their area. They provide primary and secondary schools, special schools for handicapped pupils and institutions of further education. The boards also make contributions towards the cost of maintaining voluntary schools; award university and other scholarships; meet the tuition fees of the great majority of pupils attending grammar schools; provide milk and meals; free books and transport for pupils; enforce school attendance; regulate the employment of children and young people and secure the provision of recreational and youth service facilities. They are also required to develop a comprehensive and efficient library service for their areas. The following are the statistics for the 1985–86 academic year:

Universities. Northern Ireland now has 2 Universities of Higher Education, the Queen's University of Belfast (QUB) and the University of Ulster (UU). The Queen's University of Belfast (founded in 1849 as a college of the Queen's University of Ireland and reconstituted as a separate university in 1908) had 105 professors, 235 readers and senior lecturers, 609 lecturers and tutors and 7,164 full-time students in 1985–86. The University of Ulster, formed on 1 Oct. 1984, has campuses in Belfast, Coleraine, Jordanstown and Londonderry. In 1985–86 the University had 40 professors, 183 readers and senior lecturers, 554 lecturers and demonstrators and 7,458 full-time students.

Secondary Education. 77 grammar schools with 57,627 pupils and 3,635 full-time teachers; 177 secondary (intermediate) schools with 99,245 pupils and 6,714 full-time teachers.

Primary Education. 1,001 primary schools with 181,087 pupils and 7,740 teachers; 84 nursery schools with 4,681 pupils and 156 teachers.

Further Education. 26 institutions of further education with 2,181 full-time and 2,135 part-time teachers and an enrolment of 15,139 full-time, 22,895 part-time day and 17,036 evening students on vocational courses; and 46,141 students on non-vocational (mostly evening) courses.

Special Educational Treatment. 33 special schools, including hospital schools with 2,832 pupils and 355 teachers.

Teachers. There were 20,743 full-time teachers (8,447 men and 12,296 women) in grant-aided schools and institutions of further education. The principal initial teacher-training courses are the Bachelor of Education (3 year and 4 year honours), general or honours BA and BSc. degrees with education (3, 4 and 5 year) and the one year Certificate of Education for graduates. There were 1,626 students (344 men and 1,282 women) in training at the 2 Colleges of Education and the 2 Universities during 1985–86.

Expenditure by the Department of Education (1985–86) £604·1m.

Health and Personal Social Services. Under the provisions of the Health and Personal Social Services (NI) Order 1972, the Department of Health and Social Services is responsible for the provision of integrated health and personal social services in Northern Ireland, designed to promote the physical and mental health of the people of Northern Ireland through the prevention, diagnosis and treatment of illness, and also to promote their social welfare. Four Health and Social Services Boards, Eastern, Northern, Southern and Western, established under the above Order, administer health and personal social services, as the Department directs, within their designated areas.

Social Security. The social security schemes in Northern Ireland are similar to those in force in Great Britain.

National Insurance. During the year ended 31 March 1987, £11·7m. sickness benefit was paid to an average of 8,180 persons and £54·4m. unemployment benefit was paid to an average of 32,613 persons. Widows' benefits amounting to £29·7m. were paid to 13,000 persons and retirement pensions totalling £391·1m. were paid to an average of 210,894 persons. Invalidity pensions and allowances totalling £117·2m. were paid to approximately 40,481 persons. Industrial disablement benefit amounting to £13m. was paid to an average of 5,424 persons. Maternity benefit totalling £5·8m. was paid to approximately 12,570 persons. Receipts, of the Northern Ireland Insurance Fund in the year ended 31 March 1987 were £698·8m. and payments were £655·7m.

Child Benefit. During the year ended 31 March 1987, £173m. was paid to an average of 216,186 families.

Supplementary Benefits. In 1986–87, £339·7m. was paid to an average of 190,029 persons.

Family Income Supplement. In 1986–87, £13·7m. was paid to an average of 14,940 persons.

Books of Reference

The annual and other publications of the various Departments and the Reports, etc., of Parliamentary Committees may be obtained from HM Stationery Office, Belfast.

Northern Ireland Social Security Statistics

Ulster Year Book, 1985. (Bi-annual). Belfast, HMSO, 1985

Census of Population Reports, Northern Ireland. Belfast, HMSO, 1981

Annual Abstract of Statistics. Belfast, HMSO

Northern Ireland: A Trade Directory. Belfast, HMSO, 1st ed. 1985

Reports on the Census of Production of Northern Ireland. Belfast, HMSO

The Statutes Revised: Northern Ireland. HMSO, 1982

Bell, G., *The Protestants of Ulster.* London, 1976

Biggs-Davison, J., *The Hand is Red.* London, 1974

Flackes, W. D., *Northern Ireland: Political Directory 1968–83.* London, 1983

Kelly, K., *The Longest War: Northern Ireland and the IRA.* Dingle, Westport and London, 1982

Kenny, A., *The Road to Hillsborough.* London, 1986

Wallace, M., *British Government in Northern Ireland: From Devolution to Direct Rule.* Newton Abbot, 1982

Watt, D. (ed.), *The Constitution of Northern Ireland.* London, 1981

ISLE OF MAN

AREA AND POPULATION. Area, 221 sq. miles (572 sq. km); resident population census April 1986, 64,282. The principal towns are Douglas (population, 20,368), Ramsey (5,778), Peel (3,660), Castletown (3,019). Vital statistics, 1986: Births, 709; deaths, 951; marriages, 355.

CONSTITUTION AND GOVERNMENT. The Isle of Man is administered in accordance with its own laws by the Court of Tynwald, consisting of the Governor, appointed by the Crown; the Legislative Council, composed of the Lord Bishop of Sodor and Man, the Attorney-General (who does not vote) and 8 members selected by the House of Keys, total 10 members; and the House of Keys, a representative assembly of 24 members chosen on adult suffrage. The Island is not bound by Acts of the Imperial Parliament unless specially mentioned in them.

A special relationship exists between the Isle of Man and the European Economic Community providing for free trade and adoption by the Isle of Man of the EEC's external trade policies with third countries. The Island remains free to levy its own system of taxes.

An Executive Council to advise the Governor on all matters of government was set up under the Isle of Man Constitution Act, 1961. It consists at present of the Chief Minister and the ministers of the 9 major departments of Government.

Lieut.-Governor: Maj.-Gen. Laurence New, CB, CBE.
Government Secretary: P. J. Hulme.

Flag: Red, with 3 steel-coloured legs armoured and spurred (knees and spurs, yellow) in the centre.

ECONOMY

Budget. Revenue is derived from customs duties, value added tax and from income tax. In 1987–88 the budget allowed for expenditure of £161·5m. Income tax was 20p in the £. There are no inheritance or capital gains taxes. A non-resident company duty of £450 was introduced on 6 April 1987 on every company incorporated in the Isle of Man which trades and is controlled outside the island.

The Island currently makes an annual contribution to the UK Government towards the cost of defence and other common services provided by the UK Government. That contribution currently amounts to about £1·2m.

Currency. The Isle of Man Government issues its own notes and coin on a par with

£ sterling. £50, £20, £10, £5, £1 and 50p notes and £5, £2, £1, 50p, 20p, 10p, 5p, 2p and 1p coins are issued. Various commemorative coins have been minted together with legal tender gold coins and a platinum bullion coin.

Banking. Government regulation of the banking sector is exercised through the Financial Supervision Commission. The Commission was established in 1982 and is responsible for the licensing and supervision of banks, deposit-takers and certain financial intermediaries giving financial advice and receiving client monies for investment and management. In 1986 there were 45 licensed banking institutions and 10 deposit-taking licence holders. In March 1987 the deposit base was £3,302m.

AGRICULTURE. The area farmed is about 120,000 acres out of a total land area of around 140,000 acres. About 66,000 acres is devoted to grass whilst a further 37,000 acres are accounted for by rough grazing. Barley accounts for most of the remaining land under cultivation and some barley is exported. There are approximately 147,000 sheep, 32,000 cattle, 71,000 poultry and 8,000 pigs on farms in the Island. Agriculture contributes less than 3% of the Island's GNP.

TOURISM. In 1985–86 tourism contributed around 12% of national income; there were about 330,000 visitors during the 1987 summer season.

COMMUNICATIONS

Roads. There are 500 miles of good roads. The International TT Motor Cycle Races and cycle races take place annually. Omnibus services operate to all parts of the island.

On 31 March 1987 there were about 33,000 licensed vehicles on the roads, including 2,600 motorcycles.

Railways. Several novel transport systems operate on the Island during the summer season, including 100-year-old horse-drawn trams, and the Manx Electric Railway, linking Douglas, Ramsey and Snaefell Mountain (2,036 ft). The Isle of Man Steam Railway also operates between Douglas and Port Erin.

Aviation. Ronaldsway Airport handles scheduled services operated by Manx Airlines, Aer Lingus, Jersey European and Loganair to and from London, Manchester, Belfast, Dublin, Glasgow, Liverpool, Blackpool, etc. Air taxi services also operate.

Shipping. Car ferries of the Isle of Man Steam Packet Co. link the Island with Heysham throughout the year and similar services operate to Liverpool, Fleetwood, Stranraer, Dublin and Belfast during the summer season.

Broadcasting. The first constitutionally licensed commercial radio station in the British Isles, Manx Radio, is operated by Government on medium and VHF wavelengths from Douglas.

Newspapers. In 1987 there were 3 weekly newspapers and 1 twice weekly newspaper.

JUSTICE AND EDUCATION

Police. The police force numbered 191 all ranks in 1987.

Education. Education is compulsory between the ages of 5 and 16. In 1987 there were 33 primary schools with 5,057 pupils in attendance. The net expenditure on education for 1987–88 amounted to £20·7m. There are 7 secondary schools, 5 provided by the Board of Education (4,531 registered pupils), 1 direct grant school for girls (119 senior and 110 junior registered pupils), 1 independent co-educational public school (235 senior and 112 junior registered pupils), 1 college of further education (383 full-time pupils in 1987).

Books of Reference

Isle of Man Digest of Economic and Social Statistics, 1985. Isle of Man Government, 1985
Isle of Man Family Expenditure Survey 1981–82. Isle of Man Government, 1983

Tynwald Companion 1985. Isle of Man Government, 1985
Kinvig, R. H., *History of the Isle of Man.* Oxford, 1945.—*The Isle of Man: A Social, Cultural and Political History.* Liverpool Univ. Press, 1975
Mais, S. P. B., *Isle of Man.* London, 1954
Solly, M., *The Isle of Man: A Low Tax Area.* London, 1984
Stenning, E. H., *Portrait of the Isle of Man.* London, 1984

CHANNEL ISLANDS

AREA. The Channel Islands are situated off the north-west coast of France and are the only portions of the 'Duchy of Normandy' now belonging to the Crown of England, to which they have been attached since the Conquest. They consist of Jersey (28,717 acres), Guernsey (15,654 acres) and the following dependencies of Guernsey–Alderney (1,962), Brechou (74), Great Sark (1,035), Little Sark (239), Herm (320), Jethou (44) and Lihou (38), a total of 48,083 acres, or 75 sq. miles (194 sq. km).

CLIMATE. The climate is mild, with an average temperature for the year of 11.5°C. Average yearly rainfall totals: Jersey, 862.9mm; Guernsey, 858.9mm. The wettest months are in the winter. Highest temperatures recorded: Jersey, 34.8°C.; Guernsey, 31.7°C. Maximum temperatures usually occur in July and Aug. (daily maximum 20.8°C. in Jersey, slightly lower in Guernsey). Lowest temperatures recorded: Jersey, 10.3°C.; Guernsey, 7.8°C. Jan. and Feb. are the coldest months (mean temperature approximately 6°C.).

CONSTITUTION. The Lieut.-Governors and Cs.-in-C. of Jersey and Guernsey are the personal representatives of the Sovereign, the Commanders of the Armed Forces of the Crown and the channel of communication between the Crown and the insular governments. They are appointed by the Crown and have a voice but no vote in the Assemblies of the States (the insular legislatures). The Secretaries to the Lieut.-Governors are their staff officers.

The Bailiffs are appointed by the Crown and are Presidents both of the Assembly of the States and of the Royal Courts of Jersey and Guernsey. They have in the States a casting vote.

LANGUAGE. The official languages are French and English, but English is the main language. In the country districts of Jersey and Guernsey and throughout Sark some people also speak a Norman-French dialect; that of Alderney has died out.

TRADE. From 1958 the trade of the Channel Islands with the UK has been regarded as internal trade.

COMMUNICATIONS

Road. Omnibus services operate in all parts of Jersey and Guernsey.

Aviation. Scheduled air services are maintained by British Airways, British Caledonian, Aer Lingus, Air UK, Jersey European, British Midland, Aurigny Air Services, Dan-Air, Brymon Airways, Guernsey Airlines, NLM City Hopper and other companies between the islands and airports in the UK, Ireland, the Netherlands and France. During the summer months these services are greatly increased, both in the number of airports served and in the frequency of flights.

Shipping. Passenger and cargo services between Jersey, Guernsey and England are maintained by British Channel Island Ferries; between Guernsey, Jersey and England and St Malo by the Commodore Shipping Co.; between Guernsey, Jersey, Alderney, England and France by Condor Ltd (hydrofoil), and between Guernsey and Alderney and England and Guernsey and Sark by local companies.

Post and Broadcasting. Postal and overseas telephone and telegraph services are maintained by the respective Postal Administrations of each bailiwick. The local telephone services are maintained by the insular authorities. There were, in 1986, 39,835 working telephones in Jersey and 51,259 stations in Guernsey.

There is an independent television station in Jersey and local radio stations, BBC Radio Jersey and Guernsey, opened in 1982.

JUSTICE AND RELIGION

Justice. Justice is administered by the Royal Courts of Jersey and Guernsey, each of which consists of the Bailiff and 12 Jurats, the latter being elected by an electoral college. There is an appeal from the Royal Courts to the Courts of Appeal of Jersey and of Guernsey. A final appeal lies to the Privy Council in certain cases. A stipendiary magistrate in each, Jersey and Guernsey, deals with minor civil and criminal cases.

Church. Jersey and Guernsey each constitutes a deanery under the jurisdiction of the Bishop of Winchester. The rectories (12 in Jersey; 10 in Guernsey) are in the gift of the Crown. The Roman Catholic and various Nonconformist Churches are represented.

Books of Reference

Ambrière, F., *Les Iles Anglo-Normandes.* Paris, 1971
Coysh, V., *The Channel Islands: A New Study.* Newton Abbot, 1977
Cruickshank, C., *The German Occupation of the Channel Islands.* London, 1975
Jee, N., *The Landscape of the Channel Islands.* Chichester, 1982
Lemprière, R., *Portrait of the Channel Islands.* London, 1970.—*History of the Channel Islands.* Rev. ed. London, 1980
Myhill, H., *Introducing the Channel Islands.* London, 1964
Uttley, J., *The Story of the Channel Islands.* London, 1966

JERSEY

POPULATION (census 1986), 80,212. In the year ended 31 Dec. 1985 there were 907 births and 875 deaths. The town is St Helier on the south coast.

CONSTITUTION. The States consist of 12 senators (elected for 6 years, 6 retiring every third year), 12 Constables (triennial) and 29 Deputies (triennial), all elected on universal suffrage by the people.

The island legislature is 'The States of Jersey'. The States comprises the Bailiff, the Lieut.-Governor, 12 Senators, the Constables of the 12 parishes of the island, 29 Deputies, the Dean of Jersey, the Attorney-General and the Solicitor-General. They all have the right to speak in the Assembly, but only the 53 elected members (the Senators, Constables and Deputies) have the right to vote; the Bailiff has a casting vote. General elections for Senators and Deputies are held every third year. Except in specific instances, enactments passed by the States require the sanction of The Queen-in-Council. The Lieut.-Governor has the power of veto on certain forms of legislation.

Flag: White with a red diagonal cross. In the top centre of the flag a shield of the arms of Jersey ensigned with the Plantagenet Crown.

Lieut.-Governor and C.-in-C. of Jersey: Adm. Sir William Pillar, GBE, KCB.
Secretary and ADC to the Lieut.-Governor: Cdr D. M. L. Braybrooke, LVO, RN (Retd).

Bailiff of Jersey and President of the States: Sir Peter Crill, OBE.
Deputy Bailiff: V. A. Tomes.

ECONOMY

Budget (year ending 31 Dec. 1986). Revenue, £200,477,716; expenditure, £181,366,144; public debt, £1,065,055. The standard rate of income tax is 20p in the pound. No super-tax or death duties are levied. Parochial rates of moderate amount are payable by owners and occupiers.

Currency. The States issue bank-notes in denominations of £20, £10, £5 and £1.

INDUSTRY AND TRADE

Industry. Principal activities: Tourism; total number of hotel and guesthouse bedrooms (1986), 11,483; expenditure of tourists (1985), £190m. Agriculture, total output (1986), £38,213,000; total exports (1986), £24,365,000. Light industry, mainly electrical goods, textiles and clothing. Total exports (1980), £29m. Banking and finance, total bank deposits and balances due to parent companies by deposit-taking institutions (1986), £22,800m.

Commerce (1980). Principal imports: Machinery and transport equipment, £57·3m.; manufactured goods, £43·4m.; food, £40m.; mineral fuels, £21·5m.; chemicals, £15·1m., and miscellaneous, £53·6m. Principal exports (1980): Machinery and transport equipment, £28m.; food, £22·2m; manufactured goods, £15·6m., and miscellaneous, £24·1m.

COMMUNICATIONS

Aviation. The Jersey airport is situated at St Peter. It covers approximately 375 acres. Number of aircraft movements (1986) in 33,986, out 33,847; number of passenger arrivals, 785,262.

Shipping (1986). All vessels arriving in Jersey from outside Jersey waters report at St Helier or Gorey on first arrival. There is a harbour of minor importance at St Aubin. Number of vessels entering St Helier, 11,792; number of registered craft (of 8 ft and over, excluding speedboats), 3,873. Passengers arrived in 1986, 453,649.

EDUCATION (1986). There were 5 States secondary schools and 1 high school, and 22 States primary schools; 4,400 pupils attended the primary schools, 3,750 the secondary schools. There were 8 private primary schools with 1,240 pupils and 4 private secondary schools with 831 pupils. Highlands College offers full- and part-time courses to Ordinary and National Certificate and Diploma levels or similar standards and, together with Les Quennevais Adult Community Centre, evening classes in technical and recreational subjects.

Books of Reference

Balleine, G. R., *Biographical Dictionary of Jersey.* London, 1948.—*A History of the Island of Jersey.* Rev. ed. Chichester, 1981.—*The Bailiwick of Jersey.* 3rd ed. London, 1970
Bois, F. de L., *The Constitutional History of Jersey.* Jersey, 1970
Carre, A. L., *English–Jersey Language Vocabulary.* Jersey, 1972
Le Maistre, F., *Dictionnaire Jersiais-Français.* Jersey, 1966
Powell, G. C., *Economic Survey of Jersey.* Jersey, 1971

States of Jersey Library: Royal Square, St Helier. *Librarian:* J. K. Antill, FLA.

GUERNSEY

POPULATION. Census population (1986) 55,482. Births during 1986 were 680; deaths, 630. The town is St Peter Port.

CONSTITUTION. The government of the island is conducted by committees appointed by the States.

The States of Deliberation, the Parliament of Guernsey, is composed of the following members: The Bailiff, who is President *ex officio;* 12 Conseillers; H.M. Procureur and H.M. Comptroller (Law Officers of the Crown), who have a voice but no vote; 33 People's Deputies elected by popular franchise; 10 Douzaine Representatives elected by their Parochial Douzaines; 2 representatives of the States of Alderney.

The States of Election, an electoral college, elects the Jurats and Conseillers. It is composed of the following members: The Bailiff (President *ex officio*); the 12 Jurats or 'Jurés-Justiciers'; the 12 Conseillers; H.M. Procureur and H.M. Comptroller; the 33 People's Deputies; 34 Douzaine Representatives; and (for the election of Conseillers) 4 representatives of the States of Alderney.

Since Jan. 1949 all legislative powers and functions (with minor exceptions) formerly exercised by the Royal Court have been vested in the States of Deliberation. Projets de Loi (Bills) require the sanction of The Queen-in-Council.

Flag: White bearing a red cross of St George, with an argent with a cross gules superimposed on the cross.

Lieut.-Governor and C.-in-C. of Guernsey and its Dependencies: Lieut.-Gen. Sir Alexander Boswell, KCB, CBE.

Secretary and ADC to the Lieut.-Governor: Capt. D. P. L. Hodgetts.

Bailiff of Guernsey and President of the States: Sir Charles Frossard.
Deputy Bailiff of Guernsey: G. M. Dorey.

FINANCE (year ending 31 Dec. 1986). Revenue, including Alderney, £90,633,226; expenditure, including Alderney, £73,068,154. The standard rate of income tax is 20p in the pound. States and parochial rates are very moderate. No super-tax or death duties are levied.

COMMERCE (1986). Principal imports: Coal, 16,912 tonnes; petrol and oils, 138,251,163 litres. Principal exports: Tomatoes (1986), £6,504,747; flowers and fern, £19,866,207; sweet peppers, £91,647; aubergines, £5,583; other vegetables, £1,305,137; plants, £1,449,421.

COMMUNICATIONS

Aviation. The airport in Guernsey, situated at La Villiaze, has a landing area of approximately 124 acres and a tarmac runway of 4,800 ft. In 1986, passenger arrivals totalled 673,521.

Shipping. The principal harbour is that of St Peter Port, and there is a harbour at St Sampson's (used mainly for commercial shipping). In 1986 passenger arrivals totalled 360,308. Ships registered in Guernsey at 31 Dec. 1986 numbered 1,012 and 490 fishing vessels. In 1986, 10,480 yachts visited Guernsey.

EDUCATION. There are 2 public schools in the island: Elizabeth College, founded by Queen Elizabeth in 1563, for boys, and the Ladies' College, for girls. The States grammar school provides for education up to University entrance requirements, and there are numerous modern secondary and primary schools and a College of Further Education. The total number of school children was (1986) 8,309. Facilities are available for the study of art, domestic science and many other subjects of a technical nature. There is also a convent school with boarding facilities for girls.

ALDERNEY. Population (1986 census, 2,130). The island has an airport. The Constitution of the island (reformed 1987) provides for its own popularly elected President and States (12 members), and its own Court. The town is St Anne's.

Flag: White with a red cross with the island badge in the centre.

President of the States: J. Kay-Mouat.
Clerk of the States: D. V. Jenkins.
Clerk of the Court: P. J. Beer.

SARK. Population (1986 estimate, 550). The Constitution is a mixture of feudal and popular government with its Chief Pleas (parliament), consisting of 40 tenants and 12 popularly elected deputies, presided over by the Seneschal. The head of the island is the Seigneur. Sark has no income tax. Motor vehicles, except tractors, are not allowed.

Flag: White with a red cross and a red first quarter bearing two gold lions.

The Seigneur: J. M. Beaumont.
Seneschal: L. P. de Carteret.

Books of Reference

Carteret, A. R. de, *The Story of Sark.* London, 1956
Clark, L., *Sark Discovered.* London, 1956
Coysh, V., *Alderney.* Newton Abbot, 1974
Durand, R., *Guernsey, Present and Past.* Guernsey, 1933.—*Guernsey under German Rule.* London, 1946
Hathaway, Sybil, *Dame of Sark: An Autobiography.* London, 1961
Le Huray, C. P., *The Bailiwick of Guernsey.* London, 1952
Marr, L. J., *A History of Guernsey.* Chichester, 1982
Robinson, G. W. S., *Guernsey.* Newton Abbot, 1977
Wood, A. and M. S., *Islands in Danger.* 2nd ed. London, 1957
Wood, J., *Herm, Our Island Home.* London, 1973

UNITED
STATES OF
AMERICA

Capital: Washington, D.C.
Population: 238·7m. (1985)
GNP per capita: US$16,710 (1985)

HISTORY. The Declaration of Independence of the 13 states of which the American Union then consisted was adopted by Congress on 4 July 1776. On 30 Nov. 1782 Great Britain acknowledged the independence of the USA, and on 3 Sept. 1783 the treaty of peace was concluded and was ratified by the USA on 14 Jan. 1784.

AREA AND POPULATION. Population of USA at each census from 1790 to 1980, and for USA including Alaska and Hawaii, from 1960. Residents of Puerto Rico, Guam, American Samoa, the Virgin Islands of the USA, Northern Mariana Islands, the remainder of the Trust Territory of the Pacific Islands, Midway, Wake, Johnston and US population abroad are excluded from the figures of this table. Residents of Indian reservations are excluded prior to 1890.

	White	Negroes [1]	Other races [2]	Total	Decennial increase %
1790	3,172,464 [3]	757,208	—	3,929,672	—
1800	4,306,446	1,002,037	—	5,308,483	35·1
1810	5,862,073	1,377,808	—	7,239,881	36·4
1820	7,866,797	1,771,562	—	9,638,359	33·1
1830	10,537,378	2,328,642	—	12,866,020	33·5
1840	14,195,805	2,873,648	—	17,069,453	32·7
1850	19,553,068	3,638,808	—	23,191,876	35·9
1860	26,922,537	4,441,830	78,954 [4]	31,443,321	35·6
1870 [5]	33,589,377	4,880,009	88,985	38,558,371	22·6
1870 [5]	*34,337,292*	*5,392,172*	*88,985*	*39,818,449*	*26·6*
1880	43,402,970	6,580,793	172,020	50,155,783	30·1
1890	55,101,258	7,488,676	357,780	62,947,714	25·5
1900	66,868,508	8,834,395	509,265	76,212,168	21·0
1910	81,812,405	9,828,667	587,459	92,228,531	21·0
1920	94,903,540	10,463,607	654,421	106,021,568	14·9 [6]
1930	110,395,753 [7]	11,891,842	915,065	123,202,660	16·1 [6]
1940	118,357,831	12,865,914	941,384	132,165,129	7·3
1950	135,149,629	15,044,937	1,131,232	151,325,798	14·5
1960 [8]	158,831,732	18,871,831	1,619,612	179,323,175	18·5
1970	177,748,975	22,580,289	2,882,662	203,211,926	13·3
1980	188,371,622	26,495,025	11,679,158	226,545,805	11·4

[1] Seventeen southern states (including D.C.) in 1900 had 7,922,969 Negroes (89·7% of the total Negro population); in 1920, 8,912,231 (85·2%); in 1940, 9,904,619 (77%); in 1950, 10,225,407 (68%); in 1960, 11,311,607 (59·9%); in 1970, 11,969,961 (53%); in 1980, 14,048,000 (53%).

[2] 1870: 63,199 Chinese, 55 Japanese and 25,731 Indians; 1880, 105,465 Chinese, 148 Japanese and 66,407 Indians; 1890, 107,488 Chinese, 2,039 Japanese and 248,253 Indians; 1900, 118,746 Chinese, 85,716 Japanese, 237,196 Indians, 67,607 other races; 1910, 94,414 Chinese, 152,745 Japanese, 276,927 Indians, 2,767 Filipino, 60,606 other races; 1920, 85,202 Chinese, 220,596 Japanese, 244,437 Indians, 26,634 Filipino, 77,552 other races; 1930, 343,352 Indians, 102,159 Chinese, 278,743 Japanese, 108,424 Filipino, 82,387 other races; 1940, 345,252 Indians, 106,334 Chinese, 285,115 Japanese, 98,535 Filipino, 106,148 other races; 1950, 357,499 Indians, 326,379 Japanese, 150,005 Chinese, 122,707 Filipino, 174,642 other races; 1960, 523,591 Indians, 464,332 Japanese, 237,292 Chinese, 176,310 Filipino, 218,087 other races; 1970, 792,730 Indians, 591,290 Japanese, 435,062 Chinese, 343,060 Filipino, 720,520 other races; 1980, 1,364,033 Indians, 700,974 Japanese, 806,040 Chinese, 774,652 Filipino, 8,033,459 other races.

[3] Made up of Anglo-Scottish, 89·1%; German, 5·6%; Dutch, 2·5%; Irish, 1·9%; French, 0·6%.

[4] 34,933 Chinese and 44,021 Indians.

[5] Enumeration in 1870 incomplete. Figures in italics represent estimated corrected population.

[*Footnotes continued on p. 1372.*]

Total population in 1980 at 226,545,805 comprised 110,053,161 males and 116,492,644 females; 167,054,638 were urban and 59,491,167 were rural. Negroes, 12,519,189 males and 13,975,836 females.

Estimated population, including Alaska and Hawaii, and armed forces overseas, on 1 July 1950, 152,271,000; 1955, 165,931,000; 1960, 180,671,000; 1965, 194,303,000; 1970, 204,878,000; 1975, 215,973,000; 1980, 227,658,000; 1982, 232,100,000; 1983, 234,200,000; 1984, 236,600,000; 1985, 238,740,000.

The age distribution by sex of the total population of the US (excluding armed forces overseas, US population abroad and outlying areas) at the 1980 census was as follows:

Age-group	Male	Female	Total
Under 5	8,362,009	7,986,245	16,348,254
5–9	8,539,080	8,160,876	16,699,956
10–14	9,316,221	8,925,908	18,242,129
15–19	10,755,409	10,412,715	21,168,124
20–24	10,663,231	10,655,473	21,318,704
25–34	18,381,903	18,699,936	37,081,839
35–44	12,569,719	13,064,991	25,634,710
45–54	11,008,919	11,790,868	22,799,787
55–59	5,481,863	6,133,391	11,615,254
60–64	4,669,892	5,417,729	10,087,621
65–74	6,756,502	8,824,103	15,580,605
75 and over	3,548,413	6,420,409	9,968,822
Total	110,053,161	116,492,644	226,545,805

The following table includes population statistics, the year in which each of the original 13 states ratified the constitution, and the year when each of the other states was admitted into the Union. Postal abbreviations for the names of the states are shown in brackets. Land area includes land temporarily or partially covered by water, and lakes, etc., of less than 40 acres. (For census population by states and regions in 1940 and 1950 see THE STATESMAN'S YEAR-BOOK, 1952, pp. 552 and 553.)

Geographic divisions and states		Land area: sq. miles 1980	Census population 1 April 1970	Census population 1 April 1980	Pop. per sq. mile, 1980
United States		3,539,289	203,302,031	226,545,805	64·0
New England		63,012	11,847,186	12,348,493	196·0
Maine (1820)	(Me.)	30,995	993,663	1,124,660	36·3
New Hampshire (1788)	(N.H.)	8,993	737,681	920,610	102·4
Vermont (1791)	(Vt.)	9,273	444,732	511,456	55·2
Massachusetts (1788)	(Mass.)	7,824	5,689,170	5,737,037	733·3
Rhode Island (1790)	(R.I.)	1,055	949,723	947,154	897·8
Connecticut (1788)	(Conn.)	4,872	3,032,217	3,107,576	637·8
Middle Atlantic		99,733	37,283,339	36,786,790	368·9
New York (1788)	(N.Y.)	47,377	18,241,266	17,558,072	370·6
New Jersey (1787)	(N.J.)	7,468	7,168,164	7,364,823	986·2
Pennsylvania (1787)	(Pa.)	44,888	11,793,909	11,863,895	264·3

[6] Between the 1910 census (15 April 1910) and the 1920 census (1 Jan. 1920), the period covered was 116 months (less than a full decade). Adjusting for this, the exact rate of increase for the decade was 15·4%. Similarly correcting for the 123 months between the 1920 and 1930 censuses, the true rate of increase was 15·7%.

[7] Figures for 1930 have been revised to include Mexicans (1,422,533), who were classified with 'Other Races' in the 1930 census reports.

[8] Figures for 1960 strictly comparable with those given for other years (i.e., excluding Alaska and Hawaii) are: White, 158,454,956; Negroes, 18,860,117; other races, 1,149,163; total, 178,464,236; decennial increase, 18·4%.

Geographic divisions and states		Land area: sq. miles 1980	Census population 1 April 1970	Census population 1 April 1980	Pop. per sq. mile, 1980
East North Central		243,961	40,252,678	41,682,217	170·9
Ohio (1803)	(Oh.)	41,004	10,652,017	10,797,630	263·3
Indiana (1816)	(Ind.)	35,932	5,193,669	5,490,224	152·8
Illinois (1818)	(Ill.)	55,645	11,113,976	11,426,518	205·3
Michigan (1837)	(Mich.)	56,954	8,875,083	9,262,078	162·6
Wisconsin (1848)	(Wis.)	54,426	4,417,933	4,705,767	86·5
West North Central		508,132	16,344,389	17,183,453	33·8
Minnesota (1858)	(Minn.)	79,548	3,805,069	4,075,970	51·2
Iowa (1846)	(Ia.)	55,965	2,825,041	2,913,808	52·1
Missouri (1821)	(Mo.)	68,945	4,677,399	4,916,686	71·3
North Dakota (1889)	(N.D.)	69,300	617,761	652,717	9·4
South Dakota (1889)	(S.D.)	75,952	666,257	690,768	9·1
Nebraska (1867)	(Nebr.)	76,644	1,483,791	1,569,825	20·5
Kansas (1861)	(Kans.)	81,778	2,249,071	2,363,679	28·9
South Atlantic		266,910	30,671,337	36,959,123	138·5
Delaware (1787)	(Del.)	1,932	548,104	594,338	307·6
Maryland (1788)	(Md.)	9,837	3,922,399	4,216,975	428·7
Dist. of Columbia (1791)	(D.C.)	63	756,510	638,333	10,132·3
Virginia (1788)	(Va.)	39,704	4,648,494	5,346,818	134·7
West Virginia (1863)	(W. Va.)	24,119	1,744,237	1,949,644	80·8
North Carolina (1789)	(N.C.)	48,843	5,082,059	5,881,766	120·4
South Carolina (1788)	(S.C.)	30,203	2,590,516	3,121,820	103·4
Georgia (1788)	(Ga.)	58,056	4,589,575	5,463,105	94·1
Florida (1845)	(Fla.)	54,153	6,789,443	9,746,324	180·0
East South Central		178,824	12,804,552	14,666,423	82·0
Kentucky (1792)	(Ky.)	39,669	3,219,311	3,660,777	92·3
Tennessee (1796)	(Tenn.)	41,155	3,924,164	4,591,120	111·6
Alabama (1819)	(Al.)	50,767	3,444,165	3,893,888	76·7
Mississippi (1817)	(Miss.)	47,233	2,216,912	2,520,638	53·4
West South Central		427,271	19,322,458	23,746,816	55·6
Arkansas (1836)	(Ark.)	52,078	1,923,295	2,286,435	43·9
Louisiana (1812)	(La.)	44,521	3,643,180	4,205,900	94·5
Oklahoma (1907)	(Okla.)	68,655	2,559,253	3,025,290	44·1
Texas (1845)	(Tex.)	262,017	11,196,730	14,229,191	54·3
Mountain		855,193	8,283,585	11,372,785	13·3
Montana (1889)	(Mont.)	145,388	694,409	786,690	5·4
Idaho (1890)	(Id.)	82,412	713,008	943,935	11·5
Wyoming (1890)	(Wyo.)	96,989	332,416	469,557	4·8
Colorado (1876)	(Colo.)	103,595	2,207,259	2,889,964	27·9
New Mexico (1912)	(N. Mex.)	121,335	1,016,000	1,302,894	10·7
Arizona (1912)	(Ariz.)	113,508	1,772,482	2,718,215	23·9
Utah (1896)	(Ut.)	82,073	1,059,273	1,461,037	17·8
Nevada (1864)	(Nev.)	109,894	488,738	800,493	7·3
Pacific		896,253	26,525,774	31,799,705	35·5
Washington (1889)	(Wash.)	66,511	3,409,169	4,132,156	62·1
Oregon (1859)	(Oreg.)	96,184	2,091,385	2,633,105	27·4
California (1850)	(Calif.)	156,299	19,953,134	23,667,902	151·4
Alaska (1959)	(Ak.)	570,833	302,173	401,851	0·7
Hawaii (1960)	(Hi.)	6,425	769,913	964,691	150·1

Geographic divisions and states	Land area: sq. miles 1980	Census population 1 April 1970	Census population 1 April 1980	Pop. per sq. mile, 1980
Outlying Territories, total	4,691	4,720,306	3,565,376	760
Puerto Rico (1898)	3,515	2,712,033	3,196,520	909
Virgin Islands (1917)	132	62,438	96,569	731
American Samoa (1900)	77	27,159	32,297	419
Guam (1898)	209	84,996	105,979	507
Northern Marianas (1947)	184	9,640	16,780	91
Marshall Islands (1947)	70	22,888	30,873	441
Micronesia, Fed. States (1947)	271	47,202	73,160	270
Palau (1947)	192	11,210	12,116	63
Midway Islands (1867)	2	2,220	453	226
Wake Island (1898)	3	1,647	302	100
Johnston and Sand Islands (1858)	...	1,007	327	...

The 1980 census showed 9,323,946 foreign-born Whites. The 9 countries contributing the largest numbers who were foreign-born were Mexico, 2,199,221; Germany, 849,384; Canada, 842,859; Italy, 831,922; UK, 669,149; Cuba, 607,814; Philippines, 501,440; Poland, 418,128; USSR, 406,022.

Increase or decrease of native White, and foreign-born White, population from 1860 to 1980, by decades:

	Native White			Foreign-born White		
	Total	Increase	Per cent increase	Total	Increase or decrease (−)	Per cent. change
1860	22,825,784	5,513,251	31·8	4,096,753	1,856,218	82·8
1870	28,095,665	5,269,881	23·1	5,493,712	1,396,959	34·1
1880	36,843,291	8,747,626	31·1	6,559,679	1,065,967	19·4
1890	45,979,391	9,018,732 [1]	24·5	9,121,867	2,562,188	39·1
1900	56,595,379	10,615,988	23·1	10,213,817	1,091,950	12·0
1910	68,386,412	11,791,033	20·8	13,345,545	3,131,728	30·7
1920	81,108,161	12,721,749	18·6	13,712,754	367,209	2·8
1930	96,303,335	15,195,174	18·7	13,983,405	270,651	2·0
1940	106,795,732	10,492,397	10·9	11,419,138	−2,564,267	−18·3
1950	124,780,860	17,985,128	16·8	10,161,168	−1,257,970	−11·0
1960	149,543,638	24,762,778	19·8	9,293,992	− 867,176	− 8·5
1970	169,385,451	19,841,813	13·3	8,733,770	− 560,222	− 6·0
1980	179,711,066	10,325,615	6·0	9,323,946	590,176	6·7

[1] Exclusive of population specially enumerated in 1890 in Indian Territory and on Indian reservations.

The population of leading cities (with over 100,000 inhabitants) at the censuses of 1970 and 1980 were as follows:

Cities	1 April 1970	1 April 1980	Cities	1 April 1970	1 April 1980
New York, N.Y.	7,895,563	7,071,639	Boston, Mass.	641,071	562,994
Chicago, Ill.	3,369,357	3,005,072	New Orleans, La.	593,471	557,515
Los Angeles, Calif.	2,811,801	2,966,850	Jacksonville, Fla.	504,265	540,920
Philadelphia, Pa.	1,949,996	1,688,210	Seattle, Wash.	530,831	493,846
Houston, Tex.	1,233,535	1,595,138	Denver, Colo.	514,678	492,365
Detroit, Mich.	1,514,063	1,203,339	Nashville-Davidson,		
Dallas, Tex.	844,401	904,078	Tenn.	426,029	455,651
San Diego, Calif.	697,471	875,538	St Louis, Mo.	622,236	453,085
Phoenix, Ariz.	584,303	789,704	Kansas City, Mo.	507,330	448,159
Baltimore, Md.	905,787	786,775	El Paso, Tex.	322,261	425,259
San Antonio, Tex.	645,153	785,880	Atlanta, Ga.	495,039	425,022
Indianapolis, Ind.	736,856	700,807	Pittsburgh, Pa.	520,089	423,938
San Francisco, Calif.	715,674	678,974	Oklahoma City, Okla.	368,164	403,213
Memphis, Tenn.	623,988	646,356	Cincinnati, Ohio	453,514	385,457
Washington, D.C.	756,668	638,333	Fort Worth, Tex.	393,455	385,164
Milwaukee, Wisc.	717,372	636,212	Minneapolis, Minn.	434,400	370,951
San José, Calif.	459,913	629,442	Portland, Oregon	379,967	366,383
Cleveland, Ohio	750,879	573,822	Honolulu, Hawaii	324,871	365,048
Columbus, Ohio	540,025	564,871	Long Beach, Calif.	358,879	361,334

Cities	1 April 1970	1 April 1980	Cities	1 April 1970	1 April 1980
Tulsa, Okla.	330,350	360,919	Springfield, Mass.	163,905	152,319
Buffalo, N.Y.	462,768	357,870	Gary, Ind.	175,415	151,953
Toledo, Ohio	383,062	354,635	Raleigh, N.C.	122,830	150,255
Miami, Fla.	334,859	346,865	Stockton, Calif.	109,963	149,779
Austin, Tex.	253,539	345,496	Amarillo, Tex.	127,010	149,230
Oakland, Calif.	361,561	339,337	Hialeah, Fla.	102,452	145,254
Albuquerque, N. Mex.	244,501	331,767	Newport News, Va.	138,177	144,903
Tucson, Ariz.	262,933	330,537	Bridgeport, Conn.	156,542	142,546
Newark, N.J.	381,930	329,248	Huntsville, Ala.	139,282	142,513
Charlotte, N.C.	241,420	314,447	Savannah, Ga.	118,349	141,390
Omaha, Nebr.	346,929	314,255	Rockford, Ill.	147,370	139,712
Louisville, Ky.	361,706	298,451	Glendale, Calif.	132,664	139,060
Birmingham, Ala.	300,910	284,413	Garland, Tex.	81,437	138,857
Wichita, Kans.	276,554	279,272	Paterson, N.J.	144,824	137,970
Sacramento, Calif.	257,105	275,741	Hartford, Conn.	158,017	136,392
Tampa, Fla.	277,714	271,523	Springfield, Mo.	120,096	133,116
St Paul, Minn.	309,866	270,230	Fremont, Calif.	100,869	131,945
Norfolk, Va.	307,951	266,979	Winston-Salem, N.C.	133,683	131,885
Virginia Beach, Va.	172,106	262,199	Evansville, Ind.	138,764	130,496
Rochester, N.Y.	295,011	241,741	Lansing, Mich.	131,403	130,414
St Petersburg, Fla.	216,159	238,647	Torrance, Calif.	134,968	129,881
Akron, Ohio	275,425	237,177	Orlando, Fla.	99,006	128,291
Corpus Christi, Tex.	204,525	231,999	New Haven, Conn.	137,707	126,109
Jersey City, N.J.	260,350	223,532	Peoria, Ill.	126,963	124,160
Baton Rouge, La.	165,921	219,419	Garden Grove, Calif.	121,155	123,307
Anaheim, Calif.	166,408	219,311	Hampton, Va.	120,779	122,617
Richmond, Va.	249,332	219,214	Hollywood, Fla.	106,873	121,323
Fresno, Calif.	165,655	218,202	Erie, Pa.	129,265	119,123
Colorado Springs, Colo.	135,517	215,150	Pasadena, Calif.	112,951	118,550
Shreveport, La.	182,064	205,820	Beaumont, Tex.	117,548	118,102
Lexington-Fayette, Ky.	108,137	204,165	San Bernardino, Calif.	106,869	117,490
Santa Ana, Calif.	155,710	203,713	Macon, Ga.	122,423	116,896
Dayton, Ohio	243,023	203,371	Youngstown, Ohio	140,909	115,436
Jackson, Miss.	153,968	202,895	Topeka, Kans.	125,011	115,266
Mobile, Ala.	190,026	200,452	Chesapeake, Va.	89,580	114,486
Yonkers, N.Y.	204,297	195,351	Lakewood, Colo.	92,743	112,860
Des Moines, Iowa	201,404	191,003	Pasadena, Tex.	89,957	112,560
Grand Rapids, Mich.	197,649	181,843	Independence, Mo.	111,630	111,806
Montgomery, Ala.	133,386	177,857	Cedar Rapids, Iowa	110,642	110,243
Knoxville, Tenn.	174,587	175,030	Irving, Tex.	97,260	109,943
Anchorage, Alaska	48,081	174,431	South Bend, Ind.	125,580	109,727
Lubbock, Tex.	149,101	173,979	Sterling Heights, Mich.	61,365	108,999
Fort Wayne, Ind.	178,269	172,196	Oxnard, Calif.	71,225	108,195
Lincoln, Nebr.	149,518	171,932	Ann Arbor, Mich.	100,035	107,966
Spokane, Wash.	170,516	171,300	Tempe, Ariz.	63,550	106,743
Riverside, Calif.	140,089	170,876	Sunnyvale, Calif.	95,976	106,618
Madison, Wisc.	171,809	170,616	Modesto, Calif.	61,712	106,602
Huntington Beach, Calif.	115,960	170,505	Elizabeth, N.J.	112,654	106,201
Syracuse, N.Y.	197,297	170,105	Eugene, Oregon	79,028	105,624
Chattanooga, Tenn.	119,923	169,565	Bakersfield, Calif.	69,515	105,611
Columbus, Ga.	155,028	169,441	Livonia, Mich.	110,109	104,814
Las Vegas, Nev.	125,787	164,674	Portsmouth, Va.	110,963	104,577
Salt Lake City, Utah	175,885	163,033	Allentown, Pa.	109,871	103,758
Worcester, Mass.	176,572	161,799	Berkeley, Calif.	114,091	103,328
Warren, Mich.	179,260	161,134	Concord, Calif.	85,164	103,255
Kansas City, Kans.	168,213	161,087	Waterbury, Conn.	108,033	103,266
Arlington, Tex.	90,229	160,113	Davenport, Iowa	98,469	103,264
Flint, Mich.	193,317	159,611	Alexandria, Va.	110,927	103,217
Aurora, Colo.	74,974	158,588	Stamford, Conn.	108,798	102,453
Little Rock, Ark.	132,483	158,461	Boise City, Idaho	74,990	102,451
Tacoma, Wash.	154,407	158,501	Albany, N.Y.	115,781	101,727
Providence, R.I.	179,116	156,804	Pueblo, Colo.	97,774	101,686
Greensboro, N.C.	144,076	155,642	Waco, Tex.	95,326	101,261
Fort Lauderdale, Fla.	139,590	153,279	Columbia, S.C.	113,542	101,208
Mesa, Ariz.	63,049	152,453	Durham, N.C.	72,863	100,831
			Reno, Nev.	92,115	100,756
			Roanoke, Va.	95,438	100,220

Vital Statistics: Vital statistics are based on records of births, deaths, fœtal deaths, marriages and divorces filed with registration officials of states and cities. Figures for the US include Alaska beginning with 1959 and Hawaii beginning with 1960.

Annual collection of mortality records from a national death-registration area was inaugurated in 1900. A national birth-registration area was established in 1915. These areas, which at their inception comprised 10 states and the District of Columbia, expanded gradually until 1933, when both the birth- and death-registration areas covered the entire continental US. Marriage and divorce statistics are compiled from reports furnished by state and local officials. Data on annulments are included in the divorce statistics. The marriage-registration area was established in 1957 with 30 states and 3 other areas. The divorce-registration area was established in 1958 with 14 states and 2 other areas. In Jan. 1980 the marriage-registration area included 42 states and D.C., and the divorce-registration area included 30 states.

	Live births [1]	Deaths [2]	Marriages [3]	Divorces [4]	Maternal deaths [5]	Deaths under 1 year [6]
1900	—	343,217	709,000	56,000	—	—
1910	2,777,000	696,856	948,000	83,000	—	—
1920	2,950,000	1,118,070	1,274,476	170,505	16,320	170,911
1930	2,618,000	1,327,240	1,126,856	195,961	14,915	143,201
1940	2,559,000	1,417,269	1,595,874	264,000	8,876	110,984
1950	3,632,000	1,452,454	1,667,231	385,144	2,960	103,825
1960	4,257,850 [7]	1,711,982	1,523,000	393,000	1,579	110,873
1970	3,731,386 [7]	1,921,031	2,158,802	708,000	803	74,667
1980	3,612,258	1,989,841	2,390,252	1,189,000	334	45,526
1984	3,699,141	2,039,369	2,487,000 [8]	1,155,000 [8]	220 [8]	39,200 [8]
1985	3,760,561	2,086,440	2,425,000 [8]	1,187,000 [8]	295	40,030
1986 [8]	3,731,000	2,099,000	2,400,000	1,159,000	250	38,600

[1] Figures through 1959 include adjustment for under-registration (the 1959 registered count was 4,244,796); beginning 1960 figures represent number registered.
[2] Excluding fœtal deaths and deaths among the armed forces overseas.
[3] Estimates for all years except 1970.
[4] Includes reported annulments. Estimated for all years.
[5] Deaths for 1979–81 (Ninth Revision, International Classification of Diseases, 1975). Deaths from complications of pregnancy, childbirth and the puerperium. Deaths for 1968–78 were classified according to the Eighth Revision, International Classification of Diseases, adopted, 1965. Deaths for 1958–67 were classified according to the Seventh Revision of the International Lists of Diseases and Causes of Death, those for 1949–57 according to the Sixth Revision and those for 1939–48, according to the Fifth Revision.
[6] Excluding fœtal deaths. [7] Based on a 50% sample. [8] Provisional.

The crude birth rate, based on total live-birth estimates per 1,000 total population, fell from 29·5 in 1915 to 18·4 in 1933; it rose to a peak of 26·6 in 1947—its highest for 25 years. This peak reflects demobilization (1945–46), the record marriage rate that followed, and the high levels of employment and income. The decrease in the following 3 years was moderate. In 1951 the rate moved upward and levelled off in 1957 at about 25 per 1,000 population. Since 1957 the crude birth rate declined every year to 18·4 live births per 1,000 population in 1966. The crude birth rate for 1986 was 15·5. Estimated number of illegitimate births in 1983 was 737,893, a ratio of 202·8 illegitimate births per 1,000 registered live births.

Deaths, excluding fœtal deaths (per 1,000 population), declined from 17·2 in 1900 to 10 in 1946. The death rate has been below 10 per 1,000 since 1947, fluctuating slightly from year to year, mainly under the impact of occurrences of outbreaks of severe respiratory diseases. The rate for 1970, 9·5; 1980, 8·8; 1981, 8·6; 1982, 8·6; 1983, 8·6; 1984, 8·7; 1985, 8·7; 1986, 8·7.

Leading causes of death, 1986, per 100,000 population: Diseases of heart, 318·7; malignant neoplasms, 193·3; cerebrovascular diseases, 61·3; accidents, 39·7; suicides, 13·1; homicides, 8·9.

The marriage rate per 1,000 population for selected years are: 1920, 12; 1932, 7·9; 1946, 16·4; 1951, 10·4; 1961, 8·5; 1970, 10·6; 1975, 10; 1980, 10·6; 1981, 10·6; 1982, 10·8; 1983, 10·5; 1984, 10·5; 1985, 10·2; 1986, 10. The divorce rates per 1,000 population for selected years are: 1920, 1·6; 1946, 4·3; 1951, 2·5; 1961, 2·3; 1971, 3·7; 1979, 5·3; 1980, 5·2; 1981, 5·3; 1982, 5·1; 1983, 5; 1984, 4·9; 1985, 5; 1986, 4·8.

Maternal mortality rates (deaths of mothers from conditions associated with deliveries and complications of pregnancy, childbirth and the puerperium) per 100,000 live births, were 1915–19, 727·9 and thereafter declined: 493·9 for 1935–39; 376 for 1940; 207·2 for 1945; 83·3 for 1950; 47 for 1955; 37·1 for 1960; 31·6 for 1965; 21·5 for 1970; 12·8 for 1975; 9·2 for 1980; 8·5 for 1981; 8·9 for 1982; 8 for 1983. The 1983 rate for white women was 5·9 and for all other women 16·3.

The infant mortality rates, per 1,000 live births were: 1915–19, 95·7; 1920–24, 76·7; 1925–29, 69; 1930–34, 60·4; 38·3 in 1945; 29·2 in 1950; 26·4 in 1955; 26 in 1960; 20 in 1970; 16·1 in 1975; 12·6 in 1980; 11·9 in 1981; 11·5 in 1982; 11·2 in 1983; 10·8 in 1984; 10·6 in 1985; 10·4 in 1986. In 1984 the rate for whites was 9·4; for all other, 16·1.

Immigration: The Immigration and Nationality Act, as amended, provides for the numerical limitation of most immigration. Public Law 96–212, the Refugee Act of 1980, reduced the worldwide numerical limitation to 280,000 for 1980 and 270,000 thereafter, with a maximum of 20,000 visas available for one country. The colonies and dependencies of a foreign state are limited to 600 per year, chargeable to the country limitation of the mother country. Visas are allocated under a system of 6 preference categories, 4 of which are designed to reunite close relatives of US citizens and resident aliens of the US, and 2 for skilled and professional workers. Visa numbers not used in the preference categories are made available to qualified non-preference immigrants. The non-preference category has not been available since 1978 due to high demand in other categories. Immigrants not subject to any numerical limitation are spouses, children, and parents of US citizens, who are 21 years of age or older; certain former US citizens; ministers of religion; certain long-term US government employees; and refugees adjusting to immigrant status.

Immigrant aliens admitted to US for permanent residence, by country or region of birth.

Country or region of birth	Immigrants admitted			
	1979	1980	1984	1985
All countries	460,348	530,639	543,903	570,009
Europe	60,845	72,121	64,076	63,043
Germany (GDR and FRG)	6,314	6,595	6,875	7,235
Greece	5,090	4,699	2,865	2,579
Italy	6,174	5,467	3,130	3,214
Poland	4,413	4,725	9,466	9,464
Portugal	7,085	8,408	3,779	3,781
Spain	1,933	1,879	1,393	1,413
UK	13,907	15,485	13,949	13,408
Yugoslavia	2,171	2,099	1,569	1,662
Other Europe	13,758	22,764	21,050	19,987
Asia	189,293	236,097	256,273	264,691
China and Taiwan	24,264	27,651	35,841	39,682
Hong Kong	4,119	3,860	5,465	5,171
India	19,708	22,607	24,964	26,026
Japan	4,048	4,225	4,043	4,086
Korea (North and South)	29,248	32,320	33,042	35,253
Philippines	41,300	42,316	42,768	47,978
Thailand	3,194	4,115	4,885	5,239
Other Asia	63,412	99,003	105,265	101,256
North America	157,579	164,772	166,706	182,045
Canada	13,772	13,609	10,791	11,385
Mexico	52,096	56,680	57,557	61,077
Cuba	15,585	15,054	10,599	26,334
Dominican Republic	17,519	17,245	23,147	23,787
Haiti	6,433	6,540	9,839	10,165
Jamaica	19,714	18,970	19,822	18,923
Trinidad and Tobago	5,225	5,154	2,900	2,831
Other Caribbean	9,598	10,333	7,958	7,241
Central America	17,547	20,968	24,088	26,302
Other North America	90	219	5	—

Country or region of birth	Immigrants admitted			
	1979	1980	1984	1985
South America	35,344	39,717	37,460	39,058
Colombia	10,637	11,289	11,020	11,982
Ecuador	4,383	6,133	4,164	4,482
Other South America	20,324	22,295	22,276	22,594
Africa	12,838	13,981	15,540	17,117
Australia and New Zealand	1,999	2,209	1,903	2,041
Other countries	2,450	1,742	1,945	2,014

The total number of immigrants admitted from 1820 up to 30 Sept. 1985 was 52,520,358; this included 7,031,370 from Germany (GDR and FRG), and from Italy 5,330,064.

Aliens coming to the US for temporary periods of time are classified as non-immigrants. During fiscal year 1985, a total of 9,675,650 non-immigrants were admitted. This is inclusive of multiple entry documents and excludes border crossers, crewmen and insular travellers. Tourists, primarily from Mexico, Japan, the UK, the Caribbean, Germany (GDR and FRG) and Canada numbered 3,600,947 (total tourists, 6,608,590). There were 1,066,862 aliens expelled during fiscal year 1985. Of this number, 20,560 were deported and 1,046,302 were required to depart without formal orders of deportation.

In accordance with the Immigration and Nationality Act, 5,381,106 aliens reported their address in Jan. 1980. Of this total, 4,532,647 were permanent residents and 848,459 were aliens here temporarily. Of the permanent resident aliens who reported the best represented nationalities were the following: Mexico, 992,765; Canada, 301,085; Cuba, 279,100; UK, 273,521; Philippines, 223,743; Italy, 163,700; Germany (GDR and FRG), 147,647. Over 76% of the permanent resident aliens reported their states of residence as: California, 1,261,069; New York, 690,383; Texas, 411,163; Florida, 335,457; Illinois, 256,091; New Jersey, 238,883; Massachusetts, 152,916, and Michigan, 118,588.

In the year ended 30 Sept. 1985, 244,717 persons became US citizens through naturalization; this includes, 214,831 naturalized under the general provisions of 5-year residence in the US, 23,520 spouses and children of US citizens, 3,266 military and 43 who were naturalized under other provisions. Of the total, there were 10,487 former nationals of Cuba, 28,954 of the Philippines, 15,150 of China and Taiwan, 16,824 of Korea, 8,833 of UK, 3,816 of Italy, 23,042 of Mexico and 4,809 of Jamaica.

CLIMATE. For temperature and rainfall figures, see entries on individual states as indicated by regions, below, of mainland USA.

Pacific Coast. The climate varies with latitude, distance from the sea and the effect of relief, ranging from polar conditions in North Alaska through cool to warm temperate climates further south. The extreme south is temperate desert. Rainfall everywhere is moderate. *See* Alaska, California, Oregon, Washington.

Mountain States. Very varied, with relief exerting the main control; very cold in the north in winter, with considerable snowfall. In the south, much higher temperatures and aridity produce desert conditions. Rainfall everywhere is very variable as a result of rain-shadow influences. *See* Arizona, Colorado, Idaho, Montana, Nevada, New Mexico, Utah, Wyoming.

High Plains. A continental climate with a large annual range of temperature and moderate rainfall, mainly in summer, although unreliable. Dust storms are common in summer and blizzards in winter. *See* Nebraska, North Dakota, South Dakota.

Central Plains. A temperate continental climate, with hot summers and cold winters, except in the extreme south. Rainfall is plentiful and comes at all seasons, but there is a summer maximum in western parts. *See* Mississippi, Missouri, Oklahoma, Texas.

Mid-West. Continental, with hot summers and cold winters. Rainfall is moderate, with a summer maximum in most parts. *See* Indiana, Iowa, Kansas.

Great Lakes. Continental, resembling that of the Central Plains, with hot summers but very cold winters because of the freezing of the lakes. Rainfall is moderate with a slight summer maximum. *See* Illinois, Michigan, Minnesota, Ohio, Wisconsin.

Appalachian Mountains. The north is cool temperate with cold winters, the south warm temperate with milder winters. Precipitation is heavy, increasing to the south but evenly distributed over the year. *See* Kentucky, Pennsylvania, Tennessee, West Virginia.

Gulf Coast. Conditions vary from warm temperate to sub-tropical, with plentiful rainfall, decreasing towards the west but evenly distributed over the year. *See* Alabama, Arkansas, Florida, Louisiana.

Atlantic Coast. Temperate maritime climate but with great differences in temperature according to latitude. Rainfall is ample at all seasons; snowfall in the north can be heavy. *See* Delaware, District of Columbia, Georgia, Maryland, New Jersey, New York, North Carolina, South Carolina, Virginia.

New England. Cool temperate, with severe winters and warm summers. Precipitation is well distributed with a slight winter maximum. Snowfall is heavy in winter. *See* Connecticut, Maine, Massachusetts, New Hampshire, Rhode Island, Vermont. *See* also Hawaii and Outlying Territories.

CONSTITUTION AND GOVERNMENT. The form of government of the USA is based on the constitution of 17 Sept. 1787.

By the constitution the government of the nation is composed of three co-ordinate branches, the executive, the legislative and the judicial.

The National Government has authority in matters of general taxation, treaties and other dealings with foreign Powers, foreign and inter-state commerce, bankruptcy, postal service, coinage, weights and measures, patents and copyright, the armed forces (including, to a certain extent, the militia), and crimes against the USA; it has sole legislative authority over the District of Columbia and the possessions of the US.

The 5th article of the constitution provides that Congress may, on a two-thirds vote of both houses, propose amendments to the constitution, or, on the application of the legislatures of two-thirds of all the states, call a convention for proposing amendments, which in either case shall be valid as part of the constitution when ratified by the legislatures of three-fourths of the several states, or by conventions in three-fourths thereof, whichever mode of ratification may be proposed by Congress. Ten amendments (called collectively 'the Bill of Rights') to the constitution were added 15 Dec. 1791; two in 1795 and 1804; a 13th amendment, 6 Dec. 1865, abolishing slavery; a 14th in 1868, including the important 'due process' clause; a 15th, 3 Feb. 1870, establishing equal voting rights for white and coloured; a 16th, 3 Feb. 1913, authorizing the income tax; a 17th, 8 April 1913, providing for popular election of senators; an 18th, 16 Jan. 1919, prohibiting alcoholic liquors; a 19th, 18 Aug. 1920, establishing woman suffrage; a 20th, 23 Jan. 1933, advancing the date of the President's and Vice-President's inauguration and abolishing the 'lame-duck' sessions of Congress; a 21st, 5 Dec. 1933, repealing the 18th amendment; a 22nd, 26 Feb. 1951, limiting a President's tenure of office to 2 terms, or to 2 terms plus 2 years in the case of a Vice-President who has succeeded to the office of a President; a 23rd, 30 March 1961, granting citizens of the District of Columbia the right to vote in national elections; a 24th, 4 Feb. 1964, banning the use of the poll-tax in federal elections; a 25th, 10 Feb. 1967, dealing with Presidential disability and succession; a 26th, 22 June 1970, establishing the right of citizens who are 18 years of age and older to vote.

National flag: Seven red and 6 white alternating stripes, horizontal; with a blue canton, extending down to the lower edge of the 4th red stripe from the top, and displaying 50 white 5-pointed stars, one for each state. The stars have one point directed vertically upward, and they are arranged in 6 rows of 5 each, alternating with 5 rows of 4 each. On the admission of additional states, stars are added, effective on 4 July following the date of admission. Congress, by law of 22 Dec. 1942, has codified 'existing rules and customs' pertaining to the display of the flag, for civilians.

National anthem: The Star-spangled Banner, 'Oh say, can you see by the dawn's early light' (words by F. S. Key, 1814; tune by J. S. Smith; formally adopted by Congress 3 March 1931).

National motto: 'In God we trust'; formally adopted by Congress 30 July 1956.

Presidency. The executive power is vested in a president, who holds office for 4 years, and is elected, together with a vice-president chosen for the same term, by electors from each state, equal to the whole number of senators and representatives to which the state may be entitled in the Congress. The President must be a natural-born citizen, resident in the country for 14 years, and at least 35 years old.

The presidential election is held every fourth (leap) year on the Tuesday after the first Monday in November. Technically, this is an election of presidential electors, not of a president directly; the electors thus chosen meet and give their votes (for the candidate to whom they are pledged, in some states by law, but in most states by custom and prudent politics) at their respective state capitals on the first Monday after the second Wednesday in December next following their election; and the votes of the electors of all the states are opened and counted in the presence of both Houses of Congress on the sixth day of January. The total electorate vote is one for each senator and representative.

If the successful candidate for President dies before taking office the Vice-President-elect becomes President; if no candidate has a majority or if the successful candidate fails to qualify, then, by the 20th amendment, the Vice-President acts as President until a president qualifies. The duties of the Presidency, in absence of the President and Vice-President by reason of death, resignation, removal, inability or failure to qualify, devolve upon the Speaker of the House under legislation enacted 18 July 1947. And in case of absence of a Speaker for like reason, the presidential duties devolve upon the President *pro tem.* of the Senate and successively upon those members of the Cabinet in order of precedence, who have the constitutional qualifications for President.

The presidential term, by the 20th amendment to the constitution, begins at noon on 20 Jan. of the inaugural year. This amendment also installs the newly elected Congress in office on 3 Jan. instead of—as formerly—in the following December. The President's salary is $200,000 per year, plus $50,000 to assist in defraying expenses resulting from official duties. Also he may spend up to $100,000 non-taxable for travel and $20,000 for official entertainment. The office of Vice-President carries a salary of $91,000, plus $10,000 allowance for travel, all taxable.

The President is C.-in-C. of the Army, Navy and Air Force, and of the militia when in the service of the Union. The Vice-President is *ex-officio* President of the Senate, and in the case of 'the removal of the President, or of his death, resignation, or inability to discharge the powers and duties of his office', he becomes the President for the remainder of the term.

President of the United States: Ronald Reagan, of California, born at Tampico, Illinois, in 1911; Governor of California, 1967–75.

At the Presidential election on 6 Nov. 1984 total vote cast, including men and women in the armed services, was 92,267,879, of which Ronald Reagan (R.) received 54,455,075 (59%), Walter Mondale (D.) 37,577,185 (41%) and David Bergland (Libertarian Party) 235,619. Electoral college votes: Reagan 525; Mondale 13; Bergland 0.

PRESIDENTS OF THE USA

Name	From state	Term of service	Born	Died
George Washington	Virginia	1789–97	1732	1799
John Adams	Massachusetts	1797–1801	1735	1826
Thomas Jefferson	Virginia	1801–09	1743	1826
James Madison	Virginia	1809–17	1751	1836
James Monroe	Virginia	1817–25	1759	1831
John Quincy Adams	Massachusetts	1825–29	1767	1848

Name	From state	Term of service	Born	Died
Andrew Jackson	Tennessee	1829–37	1767	1845
Martin Van Buren	New York	1837–41	1782	1862
William H. Harrison	Ohio	Mar.–Apr. 1841	1773	1841
John Tyler	Virginia	1841–45	1790	1862
James K. Polk	Tennessee	1845–49	1795	1849
Zachary Taylor	Louisiana	1849–July 1850	1784	1850
Millard Fillmore	New York	1850–53	1800	1874
Franklin Pierce	New Hampshire	1853–57	1804	1869
James Buchanan	Pennsylvania	1857–61	1791	1868
Abraham Lincoln	Illinois	1861–Apr. 1865	1809	1865
Andrew Johnson	Tennessee	1865–69	1808	1875
Ulysses S. Grant	Illinois	1869–77	1822	1885
Rutherford B. Hayes	Ohio	1877–81	1822	1893
James A. Garfield	Ohio	Mar.–Sept. 1881	1831	1881
Chester A. Arthur	New York	1881–85	1830	1886
Grover Cleveland	New York	1885–89	1837	1908
Benjamin Harrison	Indiana	1889–93	1833	1901
Grover Cleveland	New York	1893–97	1837	1908
William McKinley	Ohio	1897–Sept. 1901	1843	1901
Theodore Roosevelt	New York	1901–09	1858	1919
William H. Taft	Ohio	1909–13	1857	1930
Woodrow Wilson	New Jersey	1913–21	1856	1924
Warren Gamaliel Harding	Ohio	1921–Aug. 1923	1865	1923
Calvin Coolidge	Massachusetts	1923–29	1872	1933
Herbert C. Hoover	California	1929–33	1874	1964
Franklin D. Roosevelt	New York	1933–Apr. 1945	1882	1945
Harry S. Truman	Missouri	1945–53	1884	1972
Dwight D. Eisenhower	New York	1953–61	1890	1969
John F. Kennedy	Massachusetts	1961–Nov. 1963	1917	1963
Lyndon B. Johnson	Texas	1963–69	1908	1973
Richard M. Nixon	California	1969–74	1913	—
Gerald R. Ford	Michigan	1974–77	1913	—
James Earl Carter	Georgia	1977–81	1924	—
Ronald Reagan	California	1981–	1911	—

VICE-PRESIDENTS OF THE USA

Name	From state	Term of service	Born	Died
John Adams	Massachusetts	1789–97	1735	1826
Thomas Jefferson	Virginia	1797–1801	1743	1826
Aaron Burr	New York	1801–05	1756	1836
George Clinton	New York	1805–12 [1]	1739	1812
Elbridge Gerry	Massachusetts	1813–14 [1]	1744	1814
Daniel D. Tompkins	New York	1817–25	1774	1825
John C. Calhoun	South Carolina	1825–32 [1]	1782	1850
Martin Van Buren	New York	1833–37	1782	1862
Richard M. Johnson	Kentucky	1837–41	1780	1850
John Tyler	Virginia	Mar.–Apr. 1841 [1]	1790	1862
George M. Dallas	Pennsylvania	1845–49	1792	1864
Millard Fillmore	New York	1849–50 [1]	1800	1874
William R. King	Alabama	Mar.–Apr. 1853 [1]	1786	1853
John C. Breckinridge	Kentucky	1857–61	1821	1875
Hannibal Hamlin	Maine	1861–65	1809	1891
Andrew Johnson	Tennessee	Mar.–Apr. 1865 [1]	1808	1875
Schuyler Colfax	Indiana	1869–73	1823	1885
Henry Wilson	Massachusetts	1873–75 [1]	1812	1875
William A. Wheeler	New York	1877–81	1819	1887
Chester A. Arthur	New York	Mar.–Sept. 1881 [1]	1830	1886
Thomas A. Hendricks	Indiana	Mar.–Nov. 1885 [1]	1819	1885
Levi P. Morton	New York	1889–93	1824	1920

[1] Position vacant thereafter until commencement of the next presidential term.

Name	From state	Term of service	Born	Died
Adlai Stevenson	Illinois	1893–97	1835	1914
Garret A. Hobart	New Jersey	1897–99 [1]	1844	1899
Theodore Roosevelt	New York	Mar.–Sept. 1901 [1]	1858	1919
Charles W. Fairbanks	Indiana	1905–09	1855	1920
James S. Sherman	New York	1909–12 [1]	1855	1912
Thomas R. Marshall	Indiana	1913–21	1854	1925
Calvin Coolidge	Massachusetts	1921–Aug. 1923 [1]	1872	1933
Charles G. Dawes	Illinois	1925–29	1865	1951
Charles Curtis	Kansas	1929–33	1860	1935
John N. Garner	Texas	1933–41	1868	1967
Henry A. Wallace	Iowa	1941–45	1888	1965
Harry S. Truman	Missouri	1945–Apr. 1945 [1]	1884	1972
Alben W. Barkley	Kentucky	1949–53	1877	1956
Richard M. Nixon	California	1953–61	1913	—
Lyndon B. Johnson	Texas	1961–Nov. 1963 [1]	1908	1973
Hubert H. Humphrey	Minnesota	1965–69	1911	1978
Spiro T. Agnew	Maryland	1969–73	1918	—
Gerald R. Ford	Michigan	1973–74	1913	—
Nelson Rockefeller	New York	1974–77	1908	1979
Walter Mondale	Minnesota	1977–81	1928	—
George Bush	Texas	1981–	1924	—

[1] Position vacant thereafter until commencement of the next presidential term.

Cabinet. The administrative business of the nation has been traditionally vested in several executive departments, the heads of which, unofficially and *ex officio*, formed the President's Cabinet. Beginning with the Interstate Commerce Commission in 1887, however, an increasing amount of executive business has been entrusted to some 60 so-called independent agencies, such as the Veterans Administration, Housing and Home Finance Agency, Tariff Commission, etc.

All heads of departments and of the 60 or more administrative agencies are appointed by the President, but must be confirmed by the Senate.

The Cabinet consisted of the following (Feb. 1987):

1. *Secretary of State* (created 1789). George P. Shultz; businessman, Secretary of Labor, 1969–70, Secretary of the Treasury, 1972–74; born 1920.

2. *Secretary of the Treasury* (1789). James Addison Baker III, of Texas, lawyer; Presidential Chief of Staff 1981–85; born 1930.

3. *Secretary of Defense* (1947). Frank Carlucci, Foreign Service officer and government official, National Security Adviser 1986–87; born 1930.

4. *Attorney-General* (Department of Justice, 1870). Edwin Meese, of California; lawyer and special counsellor to the President; born 1931.

5. *Secretary of the Interior* (1849). Donald P. Hodel, of Oregon, lawyer; former Secretary of Energy; born 1935.

6. *Secretary of Agriculture* (1889). Richard E. Lyng, of California, farming consultant, Deputy Secretary of Agriculture 1981–85; born 1918.

7. *Secretary of Commerce* (1903). C. William Verity Jr., of Ohio, businessman, Board of Advisers, Private Sector Initiatives, 1985–87.

8. *Secretary of Labor* (1913). Anne Dore McLaughlin, of New Jersey, public relations consultant, Under Secretary, Department of the Interior, 1984–87; born 1941.

9. *Secretary of Health and Human Services* (1953). Otis R. Bowen, of Indiana, physician, Governor of Indiana 1973–81; born 1918.

10. *Secretary of Housing and Urban Development* (1966). Samuel J. Pierce, of New York; lawyer; born 1922.

11. *Secretary of Transportation* (1967). James H. Burnley IV, lawyer and government official, Deputy Secretary, Department of Transportation, 1983–87; born 1948.

12. *Secretary of Energy* (1977). John Herrington, of California, lawyer; formerly special assistant to the President; born 1939.

13. *Secretary of Education* (1979). William Bennett; chairman of National Endowment of the Humanities 1981–85; born 1943.

Each of the above Cabinet officers receives an annual salary of $80,100 and holds office during the pleasure of the President.

Congress: The legislative power is vested by the Constitution in a Congress, consisting of a Senate and House of Representatives.

Electorate: By amendments of the constitution, disqualification of voters on the ground of race, colour or sex is forbidden. Accordingly, the electorate consists theoretically of all citizens of both sexes over 18 years of age, but the franchise is not universal. There are requirements of residence varying in the several states as to length from 6 months to 2 years and differing requirements as to registration. In 20 states the ability to read (usually an extract from the constitution) is required—in Alaska the ability to read English; in Hawaii, English or Hawaiian; in Louisiana, English or one's native tongue. In Alabama the voter must take an 'anti-Communist oath' and fill out a questionnaire to the satisfaction of the registrars. In some southern states voters are required to give a reasonable explanation of what they read. In most states convicts are excluded from the franchise, in some states duellists and fraudulent voters.

Legislation designed to discourage the rise of third parties has been adopted in a few states. In Illinois a new party must present a petition signed by at least 25,000 voters, including at least 200 in each of 50 of the 102 counties.

The method of balloting varies greatly. Seventeen states use different ballots for federal, state and local elections. In Delaware and South Carolina the various political parties furnish their own ballot-papers to the voters as he or she enters the polling-booth.

Senate: The Senate consists of 2 members from each state, chosen by popular vote for 6 years, one-third retiring or seeking re-election every 2 years. Senators must be no less than 30 years of age; must have been citizens of the USA for 9 years, and be residents in the states for which they are chosen. The Senate has complete freedom to initiate legislation, except revenue bills (which must originate in the House of Representatives); it may, however, amend or reject any legislation originating in the lower house. The Senate is also entrusted with the power of giving or withholding its 'advice and consent' to the ratification of all treaties initiated by the President with foreign Powers, a two-thirds majority of senators present being required for approval. (However, it has no control over 'international executive agreements' made by the President with foreign governments; such 'agreements', representing an important but very recent development, cover a wide range and are actually more numerous than formal treaties.) It also has the power of confirming or rejecting major appointments to office made by the President, but it has no direct control over the appointment by the President of 'personal representatives' or 'personal envoys' on missions abroad. Members of the Senate constitute a High Court of Impeachment, with power, by a two-thirds vote, to remove from office and disqualify any civil officer of the USA impeached by the House of Representatives, which has the sole power of impeachment.

The Senate has 16 Standing Committees to which all bills are referred for study, revision or rejection. The House of Representatives has 22 such committees. In both Houses each Standing Committee has a chairman and a majority representing the majority party of the whole House; each has numerous sub-committees. The jurisdictions of these Committees correspond largely to those of the appropriate executive departments and agencies. Both Houses also have a few special Committees with limited duration; there were (1987) 4 Joint Committees.

House of Representatives: The House of Representatives consists of 435 members elected every second year. The number of each state's representatives is determined by the decennial census, in the absence of specific Congressional legislation affecting the basis. The states, in 1987, had the following representatives:

Alabama	7	Indiana	10	Nebraska	3	South Carolina	6
Alaska	1	Iowa	6	Nevada	2	South Dakota	1
Arizona	5	Kansas	5	New Hampshire	2	Tennessee	9
Arkansas	4	Kentucky	7	New Jersey	14	Texas	27
California	45	Louisiana	8	New Mexico	3	Utah	3
Colorado	6	Maine	2	New York	34	Vermont	1
Connecticut	6	Maryland	8	North Carolina	11	Virginia	10
Delaware	1	Massachusetts	11	North Dakota	1	Washington	8
Florida	19	Michigan	18	Ohio	21	West Virginia	4
Georgia	10	Minnesota	8	Oklahoma	6	Wisconsin	9
Hawaii	2	Mississippi	5	Oregon	5	Wyoming	1
Idaho	2	Missouri	9	Pennsylvania	23		
Illinois	22	Montana	2	Rhode Island	2		

The Supreme Court decided on 17 Feb. 1964, that the federal constitution requires congressional districts within each state to be substantially equal in population. By almost invariable custom the representative lives in the district from which he is elected.

Representatives must be not less than 25 years of age, citizens of the USA for 7 years and residents in the state from which they are chosen. The District of Columbia, Guam, American Samoa and the Virgin Islands have one non-voting delegate each. The House also admits a 'resident commissioner' from Puerto Rico, who has the right to speak on any subject and to make motions, but not to vote; he is elected in the same manner as the representatives but for a 4-year term. Each of the two Houses of Congress is sole 'judge of the elections, returns and qualifications of its own members'; and each of the Houses may, with the concurrence of two-thirds, expel a member. The period usually termed 'a Congress' in legislative language continues for 2-years, terminating at noon on 3 Jan.

The salary of a senator is $75,100 per annum, with tax-free expense allowance and allowances for travelling expenses and for clerical hire. The salary of the Speaker of the House of Representatives is $97,900 per annum, with a taxable allowance. The salary of a Member of the House is $75,100.

No senator or representative can, during the time for which he is elected, be appointed to any *civil* office under authority of the USA which shall have been created or the emoluments of which shall have been increased during such time; and no person holding *any* office under the USA can be a member of either House during his continuance in office. No religious text may be required as a qualification to any office or public trust under the USA or in any state.

The 100th Congress (1987–89) was constituted (Jan 1987) as follows: Senate, 45 Republicans, 55 Democrats; House of Representatives, 259 Democrats, 176 Republicans.

Indians: By an Act passed on 2 June 1924 full citizenship was granted to all Indians born in the USA, though those remaining in tribal units were still under special federal jurisdiction. Those remaining in tribal units constitute from one-half to three-fourths of the Indian population. The Indian Reorganization Act of 1934 gave the tribal Indians, at their own option, substantial opportunities to self-government and of self-controlled corporate enterprises empowered to borrow money, buy land, machinery and equipment; these corporations are controlled by democratically elected tribal councils; by 1945 roughly a third of the Indians had taken advantage of this Act. Recently a trend towards releasing Indians from federal supervision has resulted in legislation terminating supervision over specific tribes. Indian lands (1981) amounted to 52,473,000 acres, of which 41,062,000 was tribally owned and 10·96m. in trust allotments. Indian lands are held free of taxes. Total Indian population at the 1980 census was 1,418,195, of which Oklahoma, Arizona, California and New Mexico accounted for 628,400.

State and Local Government: The Union comprises 13 original states, 7 states which were admitted without having been previously organized as territories, and

30 states which had been territories—50 states in all. Each state has its own constitution (which the USA guarantees shall be republican in form), deriving its authority, not from Congress, but from the people of the state. Admission of states into the Union has been granted by special Acts of Congress, either (1) in the form of 'enabling Acts' providing for the drafting and ratification of a state constitution by the people, in which case the territory becomes a state as soon as the conditions are fulfilled, or (2) accepting a constitution already framed, and at once granting admission.

Each state is provided with a legislature of two Houses (except Nebraska, which since 1937 has had a single-chamber legislature), a governor and other executive officials, and a judicial system. Both Houses of the legislature are elective, but the senators (having larger electoral districts usually covering 2 or 3 counties compared with the single county or, in some states, the town, which sends 1 representative to the Lower House) are less numerous than the representatives, while in 38 states their terms are 4 years; in 12 states the term is 2 years. Of the 4-year senates, Illinois, Montana and New Jersey provide for two 4-year terms and one 2-year term in each decade. Terms of the lower houses are usually shorter; in 45 states, 2 years.

Members of both Houses are paid at the same rate, which varies from $200 per biennium (New Hampshire) to $46,800 per year (Alaska). The trend is towards annual sessions of state legislatures; in 1987, 36 were constitutionally required to meet annually (in 1939, only 4), the other 14 holding biennial sessions, 12 in the odd-numbered and 2 in the even-numbered years. Of these 14, 6 met annually in practice by invoking flexible constitutional powers to reconvene at intervals during the biennium.

The Governor has power to summon an extraordinary session, but not to dissolve or adjourn. The duties of the two Houses are similar, but in many states money bills must be introduced first in the Lower House. The Senate sits as a court for the trial of officials impeached by the other House, and often has power to confirm or reject appointments made by the Governor.

State legislatures are competent to deal with all matters not reserved for the federal government by the federal constitution nor specifically prohibited by the federal or state constitutions. Among their powers are the determination of the qualifications for the right of suffrage, and the control of all elections to public office, including elections of members of Congress and electors of President and Vice-President; the criminal law, both in its enactment and in its execution, with unimportant exceptions, and the administration of prisons; the civil law, including all matters pertaining to the possession and transfer of, and succession to, property; marriage and divorce, and all other civil relations; the chartering and control of all manufacturing, trading, transportation and other corporations, subject only to the right of Congress to regulate commerce passing from one state to another; labour; education; charities; licensing; fisheries within state waters, and game laws (apart from the hunting of migratory birds, which is a federal concern under treaties with Canada and Mexico). Taxes on income were left to the states until 1913, when the 16th amendment authorized the imposition of federal taxes on income without regard to apportionment.

The Governor is chosen by direct vote of the people over the whole state. His term of office varies in the several states from 2 to 4 years, and his salary from $35,000 (Arkansas, Maine) to $100,000 (New York). His duty is to see to the faithful administration of the law, and he has command of the military forces of the state. He may recommend measures but does not present bills to the legislature. In some states he presents estimates. In all but one of the states (North Carolina) the Governor has a veto upon legislation, which may, however, be overridden by the two Houses, in some states by a simple majority, in others by a three-fifths or two-thirds majority. In some states the Governor, on his death or resignation, is succeeded by a Lieut.-Governor who was elected at the same time and has been presiding over the state Senate. In several states the Speaker of the Lower House succeeds the Governor.

The chief officials by whom the administration of state affairs is carried on (secretaries, treasurers, members of boards of commissioners, etc.) are usually chosen by the people at the general state elections for terms similar to those for which governors hold office.

Local Government. The chief unit of local government is the county, of which there were (1986) 2,992 with definite functions; in addition, Rhode Island has 5 'counties' which have no functions; Alaska does not have 'counties' as such and, since Oct. 1960, there has been no active county government in Connecticut. Louisiana has 64 'parishes'. The counties maintain public order through the sheriff and his deputies, who may, in a crisis, be drawn temporarily from willing citizens; in many states the counties maintain the smaller local highways; other functions are the granting of licences and the apportionment and collection of taxes. In a few states they also manage the schools.

The unit of local government in New England is the rural township, governed directly by the voters, who assemble annually or oftener if necessary, and legislate in local affairs, levy taxes, make appropriations and appoint and instruct the local officials (selectmen, clerk, school-committee, etc.). Townships are grouped to form counties. Where cities exist, the township government is superseded by the city government.

The **District of Columbia,** ceded by the State of Maryland for the purposes of government in 1791, is the seat of the US Government. It includes the city of Washington, and embraces a land area of 61 sq. miles. The Reorganization Plan No. 3 of 1967 instituted a Mayor Council form of government with appointed officers. In 1973 an elected Mayor and elected councillors were introduced; in 1974 they received power to legislate in local matters. Congress retains power to enact legislation and to veto or supersede the Council's acts. Since 1961 citizens have had the right to vote in national elections. On 23 Aug. 1978 the Senate approved a constitutional amendment giving the District full voting representation in Congress. This has still to be ratified.

The **Commonwealth of Puerto Rico, American Samoa, Guam and the Virgin Islands** each have a local legislature, whose acts may be modified or annulled by Congress, though in practice this has seldom been done. Puerto Rico since its attainment of commonwealth status on 25 July 1952, enjoys practically complete self-government, including the election of its governor and other officials. The conduct of foreign relations, however, is still a federal function and federal bureaux and agencies still operate in the island.

General supervision of territorial administration is exercised by the Office of Territories in the Department of Interior.

Congress and the Nation, 4 vols., Congressional Quarterly, Washington, from 1965.—*Congressional Ethics,* Rev. ed., 1980.—*Congressional Quarterly Almanac,* annual
Constitution of the US, National and State. 2 vols. [with subsequent amendments]. Dobbs Ferry, 1962
Political profiles. 5 vols. New York, from 1978
Adrian, C. R., *State and Local Government.* 4th ed. New York, 1977
Barone, M. (ed.), *The Almanac of American Politics.* New York and London, Annual
Bone, H. A., *American Politics and the Party System.* 4th ed. New York, 1971
Brenner, P., *The Limits and Possibilities of Congress.* New York, 1983
Corwin, E. S., *Presidential Power and the Constitution.* Cornell Univ. Press, 1976
Egger, R. A., *The President of the United States.* 2nd ed. New York, 1972
Ferguson, J. H., and McHenry, D. E., *Elements of American Government.* 6th ed. New York, 1963.—*The American Federal Government.* 12th ed. New York, 1973.—*The American System of Government.* 12th ed. New York, 1973
Fisher, L., *Presidential Spending Power.* Princeton Univ. Press, 1975
Hardin, C. M., *Presidential Power and Accountability: Towards a New Constitution.* Univ. of Chicago Press, 1974
Kelly, A. H., and Harbison, W. A., *The American Constitution, Its Origin and Development.* 4th ed. New York, 1970
Koenig, L. W., *The Chief Executive.* 3rd ed. New York, 1975
Levine, E. L., *An Introduction to American Government.* 2nd ed. New York, 1974
Maddox, R. W., and Fuquay, R. F., *State and Local Government.* 3rd ed. New York, 1975
Pritchett, C. H., *The American Constitution.* 2nd ed. New York, 1968.—*The American Constitutional System.* New York, 1977
Ripley, R. B., *American National Government and Public Policy.* New York, 1974

Robinson, J. A., *State Legislative Innovation.* New York, 1973
Scheer, R., *America after Nixon: The Politics of the New World Order.* New York, 1975
Seymour – Ure, C., *The American President: Power and Communication.* London, 1982
Tugwell, R. G., *The Emerging Constitution.* New York, 1974
White, T. H., *The Making of the President.* New York, 1960.—*The Making of the President, 1964.* New York, 1965.—*The Making of the President, 1968.* New York, 1969

DEFENCE. The President is C.-in-C. of the Army, Navy and Air Force.

The National Security Act of 1947 provides for the unification of the Army, Navy and Air Forces under a single Secretary of Defense with cabinet rank. The President is also advised by a National Security Council and the Office of Civil and Defense Mobilization.

The major components of the Department of Defense are the Office of the Secretary of Defense and the Joint Chiefs of Staff, who provide immediate staff assistance and advice to the Secretary; the departments of the Army, Navy and Air Force, each separately organized under a civilian head (not of cabinet rank); and the unified and specified commands.

Army. *Secretary of the Army:* John O. Marsh Jr.

Central Administration. The Secretary of the Army is the head of the Department of the Army. Subject to the authority of the President as C.-in-C. and of the Secretary of Defense, he is responsible for all affairs of the Department.

The Secretary of the Army is assisted by the Under Secretary of the Army, 5 Assistant Secretaries of the Army (Civil Works, Financial Management, Installations and Logistics, Manpower and Reserve Affairs, Research, Development and Acquisition), Chief of Public Affairs, Chief of Legislative Liaison, General Counsel, Administrative Assistant, and the Army Staff headed by the Chief of Staff, US Army. The Office of the Under Secretary of the Army includes a Deputy Under Secretary (Operations Research).

The Chief of Staff is the principal military adviser to the Secretary of the Army, and performs his duties under the direction of the Secretary of the Army, except as otherwise prescribed by law, by the President or by the Secretary of Defense. He has supervision of all members and organizations of the Army. The Vice Chief of Staff assists and advises the Chief of Staff.

The Army General Staff is the principal element of the Army Staff and includes the Offices of the Chief of Staff, Deputy Chief of Staff for Operations and Plans, Deputy Chief of Staff for Personnel, Deputy Chief of Staff for Logistics, Deputy Chief of Staff for Research, Development and Acquisition, the Comptroller of the Army, the Assistant Chief of Staff for Intelligence, and Assistant Chief of Staff for Information Management. Other elements of the Army Staff are the offices of the Judge Advocate General, Surgeon General, Adjutant General, Inspector General and the Auditor General, Chief of Chaplains, Chief, Army Reserve, Chief, National Guard Bureau, and Chief of Engineers.

The Army consists of the volunteer Army, the Army National Guard of the US, the Army Reserve and civilian workforce; and all persons appointed to or enlisted into the Army without component; and all persons serving under call or conscription, including members of the National Guard of the States, etc., when in the service of the US.

The strength of the Army was (1987) 770,904 (including some 76,000 women).

The US Army Forces Command, with headquarters at Fort McPherson, Georgia, commands the Third US Army and the continental US Armies and all assigned Active Army and US Army Reserve troop units in the continental US, Alaska, Hawaii, Panama, Guam, Johnston Island, the Commonwealth of Puerto Rico, and the Virgin Islands of the USA. The headquarters of the continental US Armies are: First US Army, Fort George G. Meade, Maryland; Second US Army, Fort Gillem, Georgia; Fourth US Army, Fort Sheridan, Illinois; Fifth US Army, Fort Sam Houston, Texas; Sixth US Army, Presidio of San Francisco, California. The US Army Training and Doctrine Command, with headquarters at Fort Monroe, Virginia, co-ordinates and integrates the total combat development effort of the Army as well as developing, managing and supervising the training of individuals of the US Army and authorized foreign nationals. The US Army Health Services Command, with headquarters at Fort Sam Houston, Texas, provides health services in the continental US for the US Army and provides professional education and training for medical personnel of the US Army and authorized foreign national personnel. The US Army Materiel Command, with headquarters in Alexandria, Virginia, is responsible for all US Army operations dealing with equipment development, procurement, delivery, supply and maintenance. The US Army Communications Command, with headquarters at Fort Huachuca, Arizona, provides worldwide communication to the Department of the Army and supports the Defense Communications Systems. The US Army Military District of Washington, with headquarters at Fort McNair, Washington, D.C. provides support to the Department of the Army and the Department of Defense at the seat of Government.

Some 40% of the Army is deployed overseas. Two divisions, two-thirds of which are located in the USA, keep equipment in the Federal Republic of Germany and can be flown there in 48–72 hours. Headquarters of US Seventh and Eighth Armies are in Europe and Korea respectively.

Operational Commands and Weapons. The larger commands are the theater army and the corps. The typical theater army may consist of a variable number of corps; combat forces of armour and infantry; air defense artillery and Pershing missile battalions; combat support forces of aviation, engineer and signal elements; and combat service support forces. A typical corps consists of a variable number and mixture of infantry, mechanized infantry, armoured, air assault, and airborne divisions; one or more separate infantry, mechanized infantry or armoured brigades; one or more armoured cavalry regiments; corps artillery (155-mm howitzer, 203-mm howitzer, multiple launch rocket system (MLRS), *Lance* missile battalions); an air defense element of a size commensurate with the hostile air threat (*Patriot, Hawk* and *Chaparral/Vulcan* battalions), and a target acquisition unit; combat support and combat service support forces.

US Army Divisions have a common base (containing command, aviation, divisional artillery, combat support units and combat service support units) and a varying mixture of combat manoeuvre battalions (usually 10 in number in 3 brigades) to make up airborne, infantry, armoured, mechanized infantry and airborne divisions. Divisions can in this way be 'tailored' to fit a variety of strategic or tactical situations. An infantry division, with about 18,600 soldiers, may have 8 infantry battalions, an armoured battalion and a mechanized infantry battalion; a mechanized infantry division, with about 17,100 soldiers, may have 5 mechanized infantry battalions and 5 armoured battalions; an armoured division, with about 16,800 soldiers, may have 4 mechanized infantry battalions and 6 armoured battalions; an airborne division, with 13,100 soldiers, may have 9 infantry (airborne) battalions.

The newly created 10,800-man light divisions consist of infantry, airborne or air assault forces. All offer rapid strategic force projection, especially the airborne division. Infantry divisions can operate in all environments and are general purpose forces. The air assault division is a highly specialized force capable of battlefield helicopter operations for infantry, artillery and necessary support forces.

Small arms include the M-16 and the M-249 Squad Automatic Weapon both of which fire a 5·56-mm cartridge. The standard general-purpose machine-gun is the M-60 (23 lb.; 550 rounds of 7·62-mm per minute). Infantry weapons also include M-203 grenade launcher attachment for the M-16A1 rifle, which fire a 40-mm grenade up to 400 metres; the *Tow* and *Dragon* anti-tank missile system, and the M-72 rocket, a light anti-tank weapon.

Combat vehicles of the US Army are the tank, armoured personnel carrier, infantry fighting vehicle, and the armoured command vehicle. The first-line tanks are the M1 Abrams tank, and the M60A3 with 105-mm main armament. The standard armoured infantry personnel carrier is the M2 Bradley Fighting Vehicle (BFV); it carries a mechanized infantry squad, a 25-mm Bushmaster gun and *Tow* missile launchers. The BFV is also being utilized as the ground scout vehicle in armoured cavalry regiments, squadrons and in scout platoons of armoured and mechanized infantry battalions.

The approved calibres of artillery are: light, 105-mm howitzer, medium 155-mm howitzer; the heavy, 203-mm howitzer. The 107-mm mortars and the 81-mm mortar are used by the combat manoeuvre elements. The *Tow* is the primary anti-tank weapon. *Chaparral, Vulcan* and *Stinger*, forward-area air-defence weapons, provide the capability of low-altitude defence against high-performance aircraft.

The Army has two categories of missiles—surface-to-surface (field artillery) and surface-to-air (air defence artillery). Surface-to-surface missiles are: *Pershing II*, terminally-guided, nuclear warhead, range about 1,000 miles (1,800 km) operational; *Lance*, guided, nuclear warhead, storable, liquid propellant, operational. Surface-to-air missiles, for air defence, are: *Patriot*, guided, field or fixed installation, conventional warhead, operational; *Hawk*, homing type, low-to-mid-altitude, field operational (an improved system has replaced the basic *Hawk*); *Chaparral*, infra-red homing, low-altitude, forward area, operational (improvements to the basic system are under development); *Stinger*, hand-held, infra-red homing, low-altitude, forward area, operational. Anti-tank missiles are: *Tow*, tube launched, optically tracked, wire guided, anti-armour, forward area, operational; *Hellfire*, terminal homing under development and *Dragon*, light wire-guided, anti-armour, forward area, operational.

The Army employs rotary- and fixed-wing aircraft as organic elements of its ground formations where their use is required on a full-time basis and their immediate and constant availability is essential. The front line commander exploits the benefits of aviation technology to perform traditional land battle tasks in the third dimension. This concept of airmobility for ground formation utilizes aerial vehicles as a highly integrated team to perform all five functions of land combat: reconnaissance, command and control, logistics and that inseparable combination, firepower and manoeuvre.

The Army has nearly 9,000 aircraft, all but about 500 of them helicopters. The principal types are 3,500 UH-1 Iroquois and 900 UH-60 Black Hawk transport helicopters, 1,900 OH-58 Kiowa observation helicopters, 1,200 AH-1 Huey Cobra anti-armour helicopters, and 450 Chinook medium-lift helicopters.

Enlistment, Terms of Service. Since 1974 the Army has operated a 'zero draft' system making it, in effect, an all-regular force both regular and reserve components. Terms of service may be 2, 3, 4, 5 or 6 years. Men and women who enlist incur an 8-year obligation and must serve in the reserve any part of the period not served on active duty.

The Army National Guard is the only reserve military component with a dual mission: a state and federal rôle. Enlistment is voluntary. The members are recruited by each state, but are equipped and paid by the federal government (except when performing state missions). Training is supervised by the active Army (FORSCOM), and unit organization parallels that for the active army; training facilities are made available by the USA and each state. As the organized militia of the several states, the District of Columbia, Puerto Rico and the Territories of the Virgin Islands and Guam, the Guard may be called into service for local emergencies by the chief executives in those jurisdictions; and may be called into federal service by the President to thwart invasion or rebellion or to enforce federal law. In its role as a reserve component of the Army, the Guard is subject to the order of the President in the event of national emergency.

The Army Reserve is designed to supply qualified and experienced units and individuals in an emergency. US Army Forces Command is charged with the command, support and training supervision of US Army Reserve units. Members of units are assigned to one category, the Ready Reserve. The Ready Reservist is subject to call by the President in case of national emergency without declaration of war by Congress. The Standby Reserve and the Retired Reserve may be called only after declaration of war or national emergency by Congress.

The Army Almanac. Dept. of the Army, Washington, D.C.
Coker, C., *US Military Power in the 1980s.* London, 1984
Kinnell, S., *Military History of the United States: An Annotated Bibliography.* Oxford and Santa Barbara, 1986

Navy. *Secretary of the Navy:* William Ball.

The Department of the Navy is administered under the Secretary of Defense by the Secretary of the Navy, assisted by the Under Secretary; 4 Assistant Secretaries, for Financial Management; for Shipbuilding and Logistics; for Manpower and Reserve Affairs; and for Research, Engineering and Systems, as well as by the Chief of Naval Operations and the Commandant of the Marine Corps. The 3 divisions of the Department of the Navy are:

Navy Department, comprised of staff offices of the Secretary for Legislative Affairs, Information, the Judge Advocate General, Auditor General, Program Appraisal, General Counsel, Naval Research and Comptroller; offices of the Chief of Naval Operations which include the Vice Chief, the Assistant Vice Chief/Director of Naval Administration, 6 Deputy Chiefs and 8 Directors; Naval Inspector General; the Surgeon General; Bureau of Naval Personnel; and Headquarters U.S. Marine Corps.

The Shore Establishment comprises commands dealing with air, naval acquisition support, space and warfare systems, facilities engineering, sea (including ordnance) and supply systems; and other commands: Space, Medical, Education and Training, Data Automation, Telecommunications, Intelligence, Oceanography, Legal Service, Security Group, and Investigative Service; as well as supporting establishment of the Marine Corps and Marine Corps Reserve.

The Operating Forces are the Military Sealift Command, U. S. Naval Forces Europe, the Atlantic and Pacific Fleet including Fleet Marine Forces; operating forces of the Marine Corps, the Mine Warfare Command, Operational Test and Evaluation Force, Naval Forces Southern and Central Commands, and the Naval Reserve Forces.

Major shore activities include 8 shipyards, 27 air stations and facilities, 2 amphibious bases, 5 submarine bases and 13 naval stations and bases. By agreement dated 2 Sept. 1940, Britain granted leases for naval and air bases in Newfoundland, Bermuda, Bahamas, Jamaica, St Lucia, Trinidad, Antigua and Guyana; but these are not all now active.

Naval appropriations in recent fiscal years: 1980, $47,084m.; 1981, $57,834m.; 1982, $68,792m.; 1983, $81,936m.; 1984, $81,999m.; 1985, $95,549m.; 1986, $100,207m.; 1987, $95,849m.; 1988, $101,707m. (planned).

The active personnel on duty in 1988 was 587,000 Navy officers and enlisted men, plus 199,600 Marine Corps officers and men.

The following is a tabulated statement of US vessels listed on 31 Dec.:

Category	1980	1981	1982	1983	1984	1985	1986	1987
Multi-purpose aircraft carriers	15	15	15	14	14	14	15	15
ASW and other carriers	5[1]	4[1]	5[1]	5[1]	5[1]	5[1]	5[1]	3[2]
Helicopter carriers	12	12	25[2]	25[2]	25[2]	25[2]	25[2]	25[2]
Command ships	3[3]	3[3]	3[3]	3[3]	3[3]	3[3]	3[3]	3[3]
Nuclear powered submarines	118	124	129	135[7]	139[7]	140[7]	140[7]	141[7]
Submarines (conventional)	10	8	6	6	5	5	5	5
Battleships	4	4	4	4	4	4	4	4
Cruisers	29[4]	31[4]	32[4]	33[4]	32[4]	34[4]	38[4]	40[4]
Destroyers	98[5]	93[5]	88[5]	86[5]	84[5]	83[5]	82[5]	82[5]
Frigates	67[6]	77[6]	82[6]	102[6]	105[6]	112[6]	115[6]	116[6]

[1] Comprises 1 training carrier and 2 other Essex class aircraft carriers laid up in reserve.

[2] Comprises 5 flat-top hangar/dock heavy amphibious assault ships and 7 lighter flat-top hangar ships and 13 lighter semi-flat-top amphibious transports dock.

[3] Includes 1 Middle East Flagship (converted amphibious transport dock).

[4] Includes 24 frigates (destroyer leaders, DLG) reclassified as cruisers in 1975 and 1980.

[5] Includes 10 frigates (destroyer leaders, DLG) reclassified as destroyers in 1975. Of the 82 destroyers 40 are classified as DDG.

[6] Includes 65 escort ships reclassified as frigates on 1 July 1975.

[7] Includes 9 Trident (Ohio class) ballistic missile armed very large (see Table) vessels, 29 other ballistic missile submarines and 103 attack submarines.

The table below shows principal surface ships, guns under 3-in. calibre not given:

Completed	Name	Standard displacement Tons	Aircraft	Principal armament	Shaft horsepower	Speed Knots

Multi-Purpose (Former Attack) Aircraft Carriers

Completed	Name	Standard displacement Tons	Aircraft	Principal armament	Shaft horsepower	Speed Knots
1987	Theodore Roosevelt	81,600				
1982	Carl Vinson	81,600	90	3 BPDMS[3] launchers with Sea Sparrow missiles	260,000 (nuclear power)	33
1977	Eisenhower	81,600				
1975	Nimitz	81,600				
1968	John F. Kennedy	61,000	85	3 BPDMS launchers with NATO Sea Sparrow missiles	280,000	34
1965	America	60,300				
1962	Enterprise	75,700	84	3 NATO Sea Sparrow missile launchers	300,000 (nuclear power)	35
1962	Constellation	61,000	85	3 Sea Sparrow missile launchers	280,000	34
1961	Kitty Hawk	61,000	85	3 BPDMS launchers with NATO Sea Sparrow missiles	280,000	34
1959	Independence	60,000	80 to 75	3 BPDMS launchers with Sea Sparrow missiles	280,000	34
1957	Ranger	60,000				
1956	Saratoga	59,100	80 to 75	3 BPDMS launchers with Sea Sparrow missiles	260,000	33
1955	Forrestal	59,100	70			
1950	*Oriskany [1]	33,250	70	2 5-in. guns	150,000	33
1947	Coral Sea [2]	52,500	75	2 Sea Sparrow missile launchers	212,000	33
1945	Midway [2]	51,000	75	2 Sea Sparrow missile launchers	212,000	33
1944	*Bon Homme Richard [1]	33,100	70	4 5-in. guns	150,000	33

[1] In reserve, *Bon Homme Richard* still as CVA, and *Oriskany* still as CV.
[2] Sister ship *Franklin D. Roosevelt* was stricken from the Navy List in 1977.
[3] Basic Point Defence Missile System.

*Of sister ships *Intrepid* was stricken in 1982 to become a memorial ship at New York City, *Shangri La* was scrapped in 1983 and the anti-submarine support aircraft carriers *Bennington* and *Hornet* were deleted from the list in 1987.

Training Carrier

Completed	Name	Standard displacement Tons	Aircraft	Principal armament	Shaft horsepower	Speed Knots
1943	Lexington	32,800	—	Removed	150,000	33

The 'Essex' class originally comprised 24 ships, the *Essex, Yorktown, Intrepid, Hornet, Franklin, Lexington, Bunker Hill, Wasp, Ticonderoga, Hancock, Randolph, Bennington, Bon Homme Richard, Shangri-La, Tarawa, Antietam, Boxer, Kearsarge, Lake Champlain, Leyte, Philippine Sea, Princeton, Valley Forge, Oriskany*. For dates and other details of the 18 stricken during 1964–81, and of the 'Bogue' class, 'Commencement Bay' class, and other former aircraft carriers, see 1981–82 and earlier editions.

Helicopter Carriers [1] (Amphibious Assault Ships)

Completed	Name	Standard displacement Tons	Aircraft	Principal armament	Shaft horsepower	Speed Knots
1981	Pelileu					
1980	Nassau		26 to 42 helicopters (or V/STOL aircraft)	2 Sea Sparrow missile launchers (BPDMS); 3 5-in. guns	70,000	24
1978	Belleau Wood	39,300 (full load)				
1977	Saipan					
1976	Tarawa [2]					

[1] According to official statistics eleven of the 12 amphibious transports dock (the other is a command ship) of the Austin class; of 12,000 tons, and the two of the Raleigh class, each with a capacity of six helicopters, are now listed under the generic heading of helicopter carriers.
[2] In many ways these five heavy through deck hangar ships are equivalent to orthodox large aircraft carriers in other principal navies.

Com-pleted	Name	Standard displace-ment Tons	Aircraft	Principal armament	Shaft horse-power	Speed Knots

Helicopter Carriers [1] (Amphibious Assault Ships)

1970	Inchon		20 to 26			
1968	New Orleans		helicopters	2 Sea Sparrow		
1966	Tripoli	18,800	(or 4 V/STOL	missile launchers	23,000	23
1965	Guam [1]	(full load)	aircraft	(BPDMS);		
1963	Guadalcanal		instead of	4 3-in. guns		
1962	Okinawa		helos)			
1961	Iwojima					

[1] *Guam* was modified in 1971–72 as 'interim' sea control ship and operated Harrier fixed wing aircraft but reverted to the amphibious role in 1974.

Command Ships [1]

1971	Mount Whitney	19,100	1	2 Sea Sparrow missile launchers;	22,000	23
1970	Blue Ridge	(full load)	helicopter	4 3-in. guns (twin)		

[1] *Northampton*, originally heavy cruiser; and: *Wright*, originally light fleet aircraft carrier, converted into Command Ships were stricken from the Navy List in 1977–78.

The amphibious transport dock *Coronado* was converted to a command ship to relieve *La Salle* as flagship of the Middle East Force.

Battleships

1944	Missouri [1] Wisconsin [1]			9 16-in.; 20 5-in. (*Missouri* has been and *Wisconsin* is being refitted with guided missiles like sister ships below		
		45,000			212,000	33
1943	Iowa [1] New Jersey [2]			9 16-in.; 12 5m.; 8 quadruple Tomahawk cruise missile launchers; 4 quadruple Harpoon launch cannisters		

[1] All laid up in reserve since 1955–58 but reactivation scheduled for recommissioning and modernisation and conversion to cruise missile carrier in 1984 (*Iowa*) followed by *Missouri* deployed at sea in 1986 and *Wisconsin* to be completed by Dec. 1988 (scheduled).
[2] Reactivated in 1967 and commissioned 1968–69, reserve 1969 to July 1981. Reactivated Oct. 1981 and recommissioned Dec. 1982 on modernisation and conversion to cruise missile carrier. Began first operational deployment in March 1983.

Cruisers

1988	Princeton			2 vertical missile		
1988	Philippine Sea			launchers and 8		
1988	Lake Champlain			quadruple Tomahawk		
1987	San Jacinto			launchers in earliest 5		
1987	Leyte Gulf			ships, later 8 ships		
1987	Antietam			8 quadruple 'Harpoon'		
1987	Mobile Bay	9,000	2	and 2 twin Standard/	80,000	30
1986	Bunker Hill		helicopters	ASROC launchers	(gas)	
1986	Thomas S. Gates			(but will be equipped		
1986	Valley Forge			as earlier ships);		
1985	Vincennes			2 5-in.		
1984	Yorktown					
1983	Ticonderoga [1]					
			deck	2 quadruple Harpoon, 2 quadruple 'Tomahawk'	80,000	
1961	Long Beach	15,540	for helicopter	and 2 twin Terrier/ Standard; guided mis-sile launchers; 2 5-in.	(nuclear power)	30

[1] Originally rated as guided missile destroyer. *Ticonderoga*, DDG 47, was redesignated CG47 in 1980 when the new type were reclassified as guided missile cruisers.

Of the heavy cruisers of the 'Des Moines' class *Salem* and *Des Moines* (17,000 tons, 8-inch guns) were deleted from the list in 1987. Sister ship *Newport News* was stricken from the Navy List on 31 July 1978.

Albany and *Chicago* were to have been disposed of in 1980 but in 1981 it was planned to retain these ships in reserve for a minimum of three years and *Oklahoma City* retained for logistic support but she was again listed for disposal in 1983. *Chicago* was again listed for disposal in 1984 (possible naval memorial) and *Albany* was deleted from the list in 1986.

For conversions and disposals of other cruisers of the 'Oregon City', 'Baltimore', 'Cleveland' and 'Juneau' classes see 1981–82 and earlier editions.

Completed	Name	Standard displacement Tons	Aircraft	Principal armament	Shaft horsepower	Speed Knots

Cruisers, Former Frigates (Destroyer Leaders)

Completed	Name	Standard displacement Tons	Aircraft	Principal armament	Shaft horsepower	Speed Knots
1980 1978 1977 1976	Arkansas Mississippi Texas Virginia	9,600	2 helicopters	2 quadruple Harpoon; 2 quadruple Tomahawk; 2 twin Standard/ ASROC'; 2 5-in.	100,000 (nuclear power)	33
1974 1973	South Carolina California	9,560	—	2 quadruple Harpoon; 2 single Standard; 2 5-in.	60,000 (nuclear power)	30
1967	Truxtun	8,400	1 helicopter	2 quadruple Harpoon; 1 twin 'Standard'; 1 5-in.;	60,000 (nuclear power)	30
1962	Bainbridge	7,800	—	2 quadruple Harpoon; 2 twin 'Standard'		
1964–67	9 Belknap Class [1]	6,570	1 helicopter	2 quadruple Harpoon; 'Tomahawk' being fitted; 1 twin Standard; 1 5-in.	85,000	34
1962–64	9 Leahy Class [2]	5,670	—	2 quadruple Harpoon; 2 twin Standard	85,000	34

[1] The 'Belknap' class comprises *Belknap, Biddle, Fox, Horne, Josephus Daniels, Jouett, Sterett, Wainwright* and *William H. Standley.*

[2] The 'Leahy' class comprises *Dale, England, Gridley, Halsey, Harry E. Yarnell, Leahy, Reeves, Richmond K. Turner* and *Worden.*

The 10 'Coontz' class comprises *Coontz, Dahlgren, Dewey, Farragut, King, Luce, Macdonough, Mahan, Preble* and *William V. Pratt.* They were reclassified from frigates (DLG) to destroyers (DDG) on 1 July 1975 when the later frigates above were reclassified as cruisers. See 1981–82 edition for earlier destroyer leader/frigates.

Capital (Strategic) Submarines [1]

Class	No.	Displacement (submerged) Tons	Ballistic Missile Tubes (Vertical)	Nuclear Reactors	Shaft Horsepower	Speed Knots
'726'	9	18,700	24 Trident	1	60,000	30 dived 20 surface
'640'	12 [2]	8,500	16 Poseidon (or Trident)	1	15,000	30 dived 20 surface
'616'	17 [2]	8,250	16 Poseidon (or Trident)	1	15,000	30 dived 21 surface

Completion:- '726' or 'Ohio' class in 1981–86 (five more to follow in 1988–91); '640' or 'Benjamin Franklin' class 1965–67; '616' or 'Lafayette' class in 1963–64; '608' or 'Ethan Allen' class (formerly Polaris armed) in 1961–63; '598' or 'George Washington' class (formerly Polaris armed) in 1959–61. All ballistic missile armed submarines also have four 21-inch torpedo tubes.

[1] Of the '608' or *Ethan Allen* class reclassified as fleet submarines. *Ethan Allen* (608) stricken in 1983 (target), *Thomas A. Edison* and *Thomas Jefferson* deleted in 1985.

Three of '598' or *George Washington* class converted to fleet submarines (of which *George Washington* and *Patrick Henry* have been stricken) and two scrapped, *Theodore Roosevelt* (600) and *Abraham Lincoln* (602) both targets.

[2] Six converted to Trident missile system.

In addition to the above named principal surface ships there are 141 nuclear-powered submarines (including the ballistic missile armed vessels in the table), 5 conventionally propelled submarines, 82 destroyers, 116 frigates, 4 mine countermeasures vessels, 21 ocean minesweepers (reserve training), 4 patrol vessels, 6 hydrofoil missile patrol craft, 70 amphibious warfare ships, 150 landing craft, 40 replenishment ships, 100 sealift ships, 130 fleet support ships and auxiliaries, 60 oilers, 100 minor landing craft and 1,000 service craft.

Ships under construction include 5 submarines of 18,700 tons submerged with nuclear propulsion and ballistic missiles, 17 nuclear propelled attack (fleet) submarines of 6,900 tons submerged; the giant nuclear propelled aircraft carriers *Abraham Lincoln* and *George Washington* each of 93,500 tons full load; 9 guided missile cruisers, 3 guided missile destroyers and 4 mine countermeasures vessels.

Projected new construction includes 10 more 'Ohio' class nuclear propelled deterrent or 'strategic' submarines; 5 more nuclear propelled fleet or 'attack' submarines; 5 guided missile cruisers, 26 guided missile destroyers, 6 mine countermeasures vessels and 17 coastal minehunters.

Naval Aviation. The official figures for the total aircraft inventory are (1988) 6,000 in the Navy and Marine Corps, of which 5,100 are active and 4,500 are operating. The main fighters are the F-14 Tomcat and F/A-18 Hornet; the A-6 Intruder, A-7 Corsair, F/A-18 Hornet, A-4 Skyhawk and AV-8 Harrier are assigned to strike missions; the E-2C Hawkeye is used for airborne early warning; the EA-6B Prowler is used for electronic countermeasures support; the P-3 Orion and S-3 Viking for anti-submarine warfare and maritime patrol; the SH-2 Seasprite, SH-3 Sea King and SH-60 Sea Hawk helicopters for ASW and anti-shipping; transports include the C-130 Hercules, C-2 Greyhound and C-9 Skytrain II aircraft plus UH-1 Iroquois, CH-46 Sea Knight and CH-53 Sea Stallion helicopters; the T-34C Turbo-Mentor, T-2 Buckeye, T-44 King Air, F-5E/F Tiger II, F-2 Kfir and TH-57 Sea Ranger helicopters are used for primary and advanced training.

The US Coast Guard operates under the Department of Transportation in time of peace and as a part of the Navy in time of war or when directed by the President. The act of establishment stated the Coast Guard 'shall be a military service and branch of the armed forces of the United States at all times'. The Coast Guard did operate as part of the Navy during the First and Second World Wars. It also had some units serving in Vietnam. It comprises 250 ships including cutters of destroyer, frigate, corvette and patrol vessel types, powerful icebreakers, and paramilitary auxiliaries and tenders, plus over 2,000 rescue and utility craft. It also maintains 70 fixed-wing aircraft and 130 helicopters. The Coast Guard missions include maintenance of aids to navigation, enforcement of maritime laws, enforcement of international treaties, environmental protection (especially waterway pollution), commercial vessel safety programmes, recreational boating safety, and search and rescue efforts. In the new construction programme are 2 cutters of frigate size and utility each capable of carrying a helicopter. The strength of personnel in 1988 was 5,000 officers, 1,240 warrant officers and 30,500 enlisted personnel and 700 cadets.

Air Force. *Secretary of the Air Force:* Edward C. Aldridge, Jr.

The Department of the Air Force was activated within the Department of Defense on 18 Sept. 1947, under the terms of the National Security Act of 1947. It is administered by a Secretary of the Air Force, assisted by an Under Secretary and 3 Assistant Secretaries (Research, Development and Logistics; Financial Management; and Manpower, Reserve Affairs and Installations). The USAF, under the administration of the Department of the Air Force, is supervised by a Chief of Staff, who is a member of the Joint Chiefs of Staff. He is assisted by a Vice Chief of Staff, Assistant Vice Chief of Staff, and 5 Deputy Chiefs of Staff (Manpower and Personnel; Programs and Resources; Research, Development and Acquisition; Plans and Operations; and Logistics and Engineering).

The USAF consists of active duty Air Force officers and enlisted personnel, civilian employees, the Air National Guard and the Air Force Reserve. For operational purposes the service is organized into 13 major commands, 16 separate operating agencies and 6 direct reporting units. The Strategic Air Command, equipped with long-range bombers based both in the USA and overseas, and with intercontinental ballistic missiles, is maintained primarily for strategic air operations anywhere on the globe. Tactical Air Command is the Air Force's mobile strike force, able to deploy US general-purpose air forces anywhere in the world for tactical air combat operations. The Military Airlift Command provides air transportation of personnel and cargo for all military services on a worldwide basis; and is also responsible for Air Force audio-visual products, weather service, and aerospace rescue and recovery operations.

The other major commands are the Air Force Systems Command, Air Force Logistics Command, Air Force Communications Command, Electronic Security Command, Air Training Command, Alaskan Air Command, Pacific Air Forces, Air Force Space Command, United States Air Forces in Europe, and Air University. The Alaskan, Pacific and European commands conduct, control and coordinate offensive and defensive air operations according to tasks assigned by their respective theatre commanders.

The separate operating agencies are the Air Force Accounting and Finance Center, Air Force Audit Agency, Air Force Commissary Service, Air Force Engineering and Services Center, Air Force Inspection and Safety Center, Air Force Intelligence Service, Air Force Office of Security Police, Air Force Military and Personnel Center, Air Force Office of Medical Support, Air Force Management Engineering Agency, Air Force Service Information and News Center, Air Force Legal Services Center, Air Force Office of Special Investigations, Air Force Operational Test and Evaluation Center, Air Force Reserve, and Air Reserve Personnel Center. Air Force direct reporting units are the Air Force Academy, Air National Guard, Air Force Technical Applications Center, Air Force District of Washington, D.C., Air Force Civilian Personnel Management Center and USAF Historical Research Center.

Of the fighter and interceptor aircraft in service, the F-15 Eagle, F-5 Tiger II, F-16 Fighting Falcon, F-106 Delta Dart, F-111 and F-4 Phantom II fly faster than the speed of sound in level flight and can carry a variety of armament. The E-3 Sentry (AWACS) is a large long-range airborne warning and control aircraft; the EF-111A Raven is a tactical electronics jamming aircraft produced by conversion of the F-111A fighter. The subsonic A-7 Corsair II, the A-10 Thunderbolt and the AC-130H are close air support aircraft. The OA-37 and the OV-10 are observation aircraft. Strategic bombers are the B-52 Stratofortress and the B-1B heavy bombers and the 'swing-wing' FB-111A. The Strategic Air Command also operates the KC-10A Extender and the KC-135 Stratotanker for aerial refuelling and the SR-71 Blackbird and the U-2 and TR-1 for reconnaissance. Primary transports include the C-141 Starlifter the C-5 Galaxy, KC-10A Extender and the turboprop-powered C-130 Hercules. Intercontinental ballistic missiles in USAF service are the Minuteman II and III and Peace Keeper (M-x) now being deployed. United States Air Forces in Europe operates the Ground Launched Cruise Missiles.

In 1988, the Air Force had about 606,800 military personnel. The service operates approximately 9,500 aircraft in the active Air Force, the Air National Guard and the Air Force Reserve.

INTERNATIONAL RELATIONS

Membership. USA is a member of UN, OAS, NATO, OECD and the Colombo Plan.

ECONOMY

Budget. The budget covers virtually all the programmes of federal government, including those financed through trust funds, such as for social security, Medicare and highway construction. Receipts of the Government include all income from its sovereign or compulsory powers; income from business-type or market-orientated activities of the Government is offset against outlays. Budget receipts and outlays (in $1m.):

Year ending 30 June	Receipts [2]	Outlays [2]	Surplus (+) or deficit (−)
1945	45,159	92,712	−47,553
1950	39,443	42,562	− 3,119
1955	65,451	68,444	− 2,993
1960	92,492	92,191	+ 301
1970	192,807	195,649	− 2,842
1982 [1]	617,766	745,706	−127,940
1983	600,562	808,327	−207,764
1984	666,457	851,781	−185,324
1985	734,057	946,316	−212,260
1986	769,091	989,815	−220,725
1987 [3]	858,494	1,016,893	−158,399
1988 [3]	909,029	1,032,294	−123,266

[1] From 1977 the fiscal year changed from a 1 July–30 June basis to a 1 Oct.–30 Sept. basis.
[2] From 1970, revised to include Medicare premiums and collections.
[3] Aug. 1987 estimates.

Budget receipts, by source, for fiscal years (in $1m.):

Source	1986	1987 [1]	1988 [1]
Individual income taxes	348,959	392,804	396,121
Corporation income taxes	63,143	89,620	105,413
Social insurance taxes and contributions	283,901	301,872	331,846
Excise taxes	32,919	31,947	32,733
Estate and gift taxes	6,958	8,144	7,917
Customs	13,327	14,753	15,814
Miscellaneous	19,884	19,354	19,185
Total	769,091	858,494	909,029

[1] Aug. 1987 estimates and includes off-budget receipts.

Budget outlays, by function, for fiscal years (in $1m.):

Source	1986	1987	1988
National defence [1]	273,375	282,176	297,536
International affairs	14,152	13,560	14,821
General science, space, and technology	8,976	9,551	11,556
Energy	4,735	3,678	3,406
Natural resources and environment	13,639	14,342	14,816
Agriculture	31,449	28,969	21,179
Commerce and housing credit	4,448	8,471	7,477
Transportation	28,117	27,602	26,264
Community and regional development	7,233	6,039	5,424
Education, training, employment and social services	30,585	30,741	33,307
Health	35,936	40,344	40,876
Medicare	70,164	73,652	73,161
Income security	119,796	123,985	124,833
Social Security	198,757	207,558	220,102
Veterans' benefits and services	26,356	26,992	28,600
Administration of justice	6,603	8,172	9,265
General government	6,102	7,043	7,005
General purpose fiscal assistance	6,431	1,629	1,484
Central federal credit activities	...	...	−7,557
Net interest	135,969	139,634	144,737
Allowances [2]	...	−18	−686
Undistributed offsetting receipts	−33,007	−37,226	−45,311
Total budget outlays	989,815	1,016,893	1,032,294

[1] Includes allowances for civilian and military pay raises for the Department of Defense.
[2] Includes allowances for civilian agency pay raises and contingencies.

Budget outlays, by agency, for fiscal years (in $1m.):

Agency	1986	1987	1988
Legislative branch	1,665	2,112	2,215
The Judiciary	1,069	1,234	1,431
Executive Office of the President	107	117	122
Funds appropriated to the President	11,377	12,197	10,656
Agriculture	58,679	53,291	46,215
Commerce	2,083	2,460	2,427
Defence—Military [1]	265,636	274,200	289,277

Agency	1986	1987	1988
Defence—Civil [1]	20,254	20,818	22,270
Education [2]	17,673	17,506	19,223
Energy [2]	11,026	10,548	10,864
Health and Human Services, except Social Security	143,253	148,227	148,952
Health and Human Services, Social Security	190,684	202,634	215,299
Housing and Urban Development	14,139	15,573	19,783
Interior	4,789	5,397	4,598
Justice	3,768	4,578	5,827
Labor	24,141	23,952	24,508
State	2,865	2,969	3,664
Transportation	27,378	26,805	25,371
Treasury	179,242	182,875	186,414
Environmental Protection Agency	4,867	4,874	4,752
General Services Administration	223	101	-385
National Aeronautics and Space Administration	7,403	7,888	9,639
Office of Personnel Management	23,955	27,443	27,115
Small Business Administration	557	247	-393
Veterans Administration	26,536	27,147	28,486
Other Independent Agencies	11,423	14,880	10,552
Allowances [3]	...	-18	-686
Undistributed offsetting receipts	-64,978	73,160	-85,903
Total budget outlays	989,815	1,016,893	1,032,294

[1] Includes allowances for civilian and military pay raises for the Department of Defense.
[2] The Administration proposed in the 1983 Budget that the Departments of Education and Energy be eliminated and that their programmes be transferred to other agencies. Many of the Education programmes went to the proposed Foundation for Education Assistance.
[3] Includes allowances for civilian agency pay raises and contingencies.

National Debt: Gross federal debt outstanding (in $1m.), and *per capita* debt (in $1) on 30 June to 1970 and then on 30 Sept.:

	Public debt	Per capita [2]		Public debt	Per capita [2]
1919 [1]	25,485	243	1970	382,603	1,866
1920	24,299	228	1980	914,317	4,014
1930 [1]	16,185	132	1984	1,576,748	6,652
1940	50,696	382	1985	1,827,470	7,637
1950	256,853	1,687	1986	2,130,060	8,821
1960	290,862	1,610	1987 [3]	2,377,116	9,759

[1] On 31 Aug. 1919 gross debt reached its First World War (1914–18) peak of $26,596,702,000, which was the highest ever reached up to 1934; on 31 Dec. 1930 it had declined to $16,026m., the lowest it has been since the First World War. On the 30 Nov. 1941, just preceding Pearl Harbor, debt stood at $61,363,867,932. The highest Second World War debt was $279,764,369,348 on 28 Feb. 1946.
[2] *Per capita* figures, beginning with 1960, have been revised; they are based on the Census Bureau's estimates of the total population of the US, including Alaska and Hawaii.
[3] Estimate.

State and Local Finance: Revenue of the 50 states and all local governments (82,340 in 1985) from their own sources amounted to $613,904m. in fiscal year 1984–85; in addition they received $106,158m. in revenue from fiscal aid, shared revenues and reimbursements from the federal government, bringing total revenue from all sources to $720,062m. Of the revenue from state and local sources, taxes provided $350,367m., of which property taxes (mainly imposed by local governments) yielded $103,757m. or 30% of all tax revenue; and sales taxes, both general sales taxes and selective excises, provided $126,376m. (36%).

State tax revenue totalled $215,893m. in fiscal year 1985. Largest sources of state tax revenue are general sales taxes (imposed during 1985 by 45 states), motor fuel sales taxes (all states), individual income (44 states), motor vehicle and operators' licences (all states), corporation income (46 states), tobacco products (all states) and alcoholic beverage sales taxes (all states).

General revenue of local units from own sources in fiscal year 1984–85 totalled $216,014m. In addition they received $138,104m. from state and federal aids. Property taxes provided 28% of total general revenue.

Total expenditures of state and local governments were $657,986m. in 1984–85, of which approximately 72% was for current operation. Education took $192,686m. in current and capital expenditure; highways, $44,989m.; welfare (chiefly public assistance), $69,523m., and health and hospitals, $49,678m. Capital outlays (construction, equipment and land purchases) totalled $79,901m.

Gross debt of state and local governments totalled $568,633m. or $2,382 *per capita* at the close of their 1984–85 fiscal year. Total cash and investment assets of state and local governments were $786,913m., about 21% being in cash and deposits, and the remainder in investments, mainly non-governmental securities.

US Bureau of the Census, *Governmental Finances in 1984–85*. Washington, 1986
American Economic Association, *Readings in Fiscal Policy*. Homewood, Ill., 1985
Brookings Institute and National Bureau of Economic Research, *Role of Direct and Indirect Taxes in the Federal Revenue System*. Washington, D.C., 1964

National Income. The Bureau of Economic Analysis of the Department of Commerce prepares detailed estimates on the national income and product of the United States. The principal tables are published monthly in *Survey of Current Business;* the complete set of national income and product tables are published in the *Survey* regularly each July, showing data for recent years. *The National Income and Product Accounts of the United States, 1929–1982: Statistical Tables* (1986) and the July 1987 *Survey* contain complete sets of tables from 1929 through 1986. The conceptual framework and statistical methods underlying the US accounts were described in *National Income, 1954*. Subsequent limited changes were described in *US Income and Output* (1958), and in *Survey of Current Business* (Aug. 1965, Jan. 1976, Dec. 1980, Oct. 1985 and Dec. 1985).

These latest figures [1] in $1,000m. for various years are as follows:

	1929[2]	1933[3]	1950	1960	1970	1980	1986
I. Gross National Product	103·9	56·0	288·3	515·3	1,015·5	2,732·0	4,235·0
(a) Personal consumption expenditures	77·3	45·8	192·1	330·7	640·0	1,732·6	2,799·8
(b) Gross private domestic investment	16·7	1·6	55·1	78·2	148·8	437·0	671·0
(c) Net exports of goods and services	1·1	0·4	2·2	5·9	8·5	32·1	−105·5
(d) Government purchases of goods and services	8·9	8·3	38·8	100·6	218·2	530·3	869·7
1. GNP *less* capital consumption allowances with capital consumption adjustment, indirect business tax and non-tax liability, business transfer payments, statistical discrepancy, *plus* subsidies less current surplus of government enterprises, equals:							
2. National Income	84·7	39·4	239·8	424·9	832·6	2,203·5	3,422·0
which, *less* corporate profits with inventory valuation and capital consumption adjustments, contributions for social insurance, wage accruals less disbursements, *plus* government transfer payments to persons, interest paid by government to persons and business less interest received by government, interest paid by consumers, personal dividend income, business transfer payments, equals:							
3. Personal income whereof	84·3	46·3	228·1	409·4	831·8	2,258·5	3,534·3
4. Personal tax and non-tax payments take leaving	2·6	1·4	20·6	50·5	116·2	340·5	512·2
5. Disposal personal income divided into	81·7	44·9	207·5	358·9	715·6	1,918·0	3,022·1
(e) Personal outlays [4]	79·2	46·5	194·8	338·1	657·9	1,781·1	2,891·5
(f) Personal saving	2·6	−1·6	12·6	20·8	57·7	136·9	130·6

	1929[2]	1933[3]	1950	1960	1970	1980	1986
IA. GNP in constant (1982) $s	709·6	498·5	1,203·7	1,665·3	2,416·2	3,187·1	3,713·3
(a) Personal consumption expenditures	471·4	378·7	733·2	1,005·1	1,492·0	2,000·4	2,450·5
(b) Gross private domestic investment	139·2	22·7	234·9	260·5	381·5	509·3	654·0
(c) Net exports of goods and services	4·7	-1·4	4·7	-4·0	-30·0	57·0	-145·8
(d) Government purchases of goods and services	94·2	98·5	230·8	403·7	572·6	620·5	754·5
II. National Income composed of	84·7	39·4	239·8	424·9	832·6	2,203·5	3,422·0
Compensation of employees	51·1	29·6	155·4	296·7	618·3	1,638·2	2,504·9
(g) Salaries and wages	50·5	29·0	147·2	272·8	551·5	1,372·0	2,089·1
(h) Supplements to wages and salaries	0·7	0·6	8·2	23·8	66·8	266·3	415·8
Proprietors' income [5]	14·4	5·4	38·8	52·2	80·2	180·7	289·8
(i) Farm [5]	6·1	2·5	13·6	11·6	14·7	20·5	37·2
(j) Business and professional [5]	8·3	2·9	25·2	40·5	65·4	160·1	252·6
Personal income from rents [6]	4·9	2·0	7·7	15·3	18·2	6·6	16·7
Net interest	4·7	4·1	3·0	11·3	41·2	200·9	326·1
Corporate profits with inventory valuation and capital consumption adjustments	9·6	-1·5	34·9	49·5	74·7	177·2	284·4
(k) Tax liabilities	1·4	0·5	17·9	22·7	34·4	84·8	105·0
(l) Inventory valuation adjustment	0·5	-2·1	-5·0	-0·2	-6·6	-43·1	6·5
(m) Capital consumption adjustment	-0·9	-0·3	-3·0	-0·3	5·2	-16·8	46·0
(n) Dividends	5·8	2·0	8·8	12·9	22·5	54·7	86·8
(o) Undistributed profits	2·8	-1·6	16·2	14·3	19·2	97·6	40·0

[1] The inclusion of statistics for Alaska and Hawaii beginning in 1960 does not significantly affect the comparability of the data.

[2] Peak year between First and Second World Wars.   [3] Low point of the depression.

[4] Includes personal consumption expenditures, interest paid by consumers and personal transfer payments to foreigners (net).

[5] With inventory valuation and capital consumption adjustment.

[6] With capital consumption adjustment.

Currency. Prior to the banking crisis that occurred early in 1933, the monetary system had been on the gold standard for more than 50 years. An Act of 14 March 1900 required the Secretary of the Treasury to maintain at a parity with gold all forms of money issued by the USA. For a description of these, *see* THE STATESMAN'S YEAR-BOOK, 1934, p. 491.

The old gold dollar had a par value of 49·32*d*., or $4·8666 to the £ sterling; it contained 25·8 grains (or 1·6718 grammes) of gold 0·900 fine. By the act of 12 May 1933 the President of the USA was given authority to reduce the gold content of the dollar by not more than 50% and by the Gold Reserve Act of 30 Jan. 1934 the minimum reduction which he could make was fixed at 40%; on 31 Jan. 1934 he fixed its value at 59·06%, or 15⁵/₂₁ grains of gold 0·900 fine. This was equal to a price for gold of $35 a fine oz. (old price, $20·67183). The President's power to alter the gold content of the dollar to 50% of its value, which was extended by Congress in 1937, 1939 and 1941, was not yet again extended in 1943.

The Par Value Modification Act (Public Law 92–268), enacted on 31 March 1972, authorized and directed the Secretary of the Treasury to take the steps necessary to establish a new par value of the dollar of $1 = 0·818513 gramme of fine gold or $38 per fine troy oz. of gold. The Secretary of the Treasury, pursuant to the statutory directive, proposed the new par value for the US dollar to the International Monetary Fund, which par value became effective on 8 May 1972.

In Public Law 93–110, enacted on 21 Sept. 1973, Congress amended the Par Value Modification Act of 1972, and authorized and directed the Secretary of the Treasury to take the steps necessary to establish a new par value of $1 equals 0·828948 Special Drawing Right or 1/42⅔ of a fine troy ounce of gold. Pursuant to the statutory directive, the Secretary of the Treasury notified the International Monetary Fund that, effective 18 Oct. 1973, the par value of the dollar would be changed from 1/38 to 1/42⅔ a fine troy ounce of gold. Expressed in terms of gold, the new par value of the dollar was 0·736662 gramme of gold per dollar, or $42.2222 per fine troy ounce of gold. Expressed in percentage, the change in the par value of the dollar amounted to a reduction of 10% in the former gold content of the dollar. This is the equivalent to an 11·1% increase in the former dollar price of gold.

The USA, on 1 April 1978, accepted the second amendment to the Articles of Agreement of the International Monetary Fund. The par value of the dollar is no longer defined in terms of the Special Drawing Right and gold, and the USA is not obliged to establish and maintain a par value for the dollar.

At the time of the banking crisis in March 1933 gold payments by banks and the Treasury were suspended by the Government, and an embargo was placed on gold exports. Steps were taken to withdraw from circulation all gold coin and gold certificates and to prohibit the private ownership of all gold certificates, gold bullion and gold coin except for numismatic purposes. Public Law 93–373, 14 Aug. 1974, amended the Par Value Modification Act so as to provide for the termination of all governmental restrictions on private ownership of gold, including gold coins, no later than 31 Dec. 1974.

Currency in the USA for many years has comprised several varieties. Prior to May 1933 the legal tender qualities of the classes varied, but in that month all types of currency were made equally legal tender. Under the Coinage Act of 1965, all coins and currencies of the USA, regardless of when coined or issued, are legal tender for all debts, public and private.

Only one of the eight kinds of notes outstanding is now significant: Federal Reserve notes in denominations of $1, $2, $5, $10, $20, $50 and $100. The issue of (a) $500, $1,000, $5,000 and $10,000 Federal Reserve notes; of (b) silver certificates, and of (c) $100, $5 and $2 US notes have been discontinued, although they are still outstanding. The following issues were stopped many years ago and have been in process of retirement: (1) Federal Reserve Bank notes; (2) National Bank notes; (3) Treasury notes of 1890; (4) fractional currency.

Federal Reserve notes are obligations of the USA and a first lien on the assets of the Federal Reserve Banks, through which they are issued. Each of the 12 banks issues them against the security of an equal volume of collateral.

Banking. On 30 June 1985 there were 14,579 insured commercial banks and insured mutual savings banks with deposits of $1,777,076m. filing report of condition and income statements with the Federal Reserve Board.

The Federal Reserve System, established under an Act of 1913, comprises the Board of 7 Governors, the 12 regional Federal Reserve Banks with their 25 branches, the Federal Open Market Committee and the Federal Advisory Council. The 7 members of the Board of Governors are appointed by the President with the consent of the Senate. Each Governor is appointed to a full term of 14 years or an unexpired portion of a term, one term expiring every 2 years. No two may come from the same Federal Reserve District. The Board supervises the Reserve Banks which bear the likeness of the late President Eisenhower, are sold at premium price and the issue and retirement of Federal Reserve notes; it designates 3 of the 9 directors of each Reserve Bank and designates the Chairman and Deputy Chairman; it passes on the admission of state banks to the System and has power to correct unsound conditions in State member banks or violations of banking law by them, including, if necessary, disciplinary action to remove officers and directors for unsafe or unsound banking practices or for continuous violations of banking laws; it also authorizes State member bank branches and approves mergers and consolidations if the acquiring, assuming or resulting bank is to be a State member; and it has power to control the expansion of bank holding companies and to require divestment of certain non-banking interests. The 12 members of the Federal Open Market Committee include the 7 members of the Board of Governors and 5 of the 12 Federal Reserve Bank presidents. The latter serve 1-year terms on the Committee in rotation except for the President of the Federal Reserve Bank of New York, who is a permanent member. The Federal Open Market Committee influences credit market conditions, money and bank credit, by buying or selling US Government securities; and it also supervises System operations in foreign currencies for the purpose of helping to safeguard the value of the dollar in international exchange markets and facilitating co-operation and efficiency in the international monetary system. The Board also influences credit conditions through powers to set reserve requirements, to approve discount rates at Federal Reserve Banks, and to fix margin requirements on stock-market credit.

The Reserve Banks advance funds to depository institutions, issue Federal Reserve notes, which are the principal form of currency in the US, act as fiscal agent for the Government, and afford nation-wide cheque-clearing and fund transfer arrangements. They may discount paper for depository institutions and increase or reduce the country's supply of reserve funds by buying or selling Government securities and other obligations at the direction of the Federal Open Market Committee. The purchase and sale of securities in the open market is conducted by the Federal Reserve Bank of New York. Their capital stock is held by the member banks, but it carries no voting rights except in the election of directors.

Every member bank is required to subscribe to stock in the Reserve Bank of its district in an amount equal to 6% of its paid-up capital and surplus. Only one-half of the par value of the stock is paid in, the other half remaining subject to call by the Board of Governors. However, no call has been made for the second half of the subscription. All depository institutions with certain transaction accounts and time deposits are required to hold reserves with the Federal Reserve.

From 1968, the Congress passed a number of consumer financial protection acts, the first of which was the Truth in Lending Act, for which it has directed the Board to write implementing regulations and assume partial enforcement responsibility. Others include the Equal Credit Opportunity Act, Home Mortgage Disclosure Act, Consumer Leasing Act, Fair Credit Billing Act, and Electronic Fund Transfer Act. To manage these responsibilities the Board has established a Division of Consumer and Community Affairs. To assist it, the Board consults with a Consumer Advisory Council, established by the Congress as a statutory part of the Federal Reserve System.

The Consumer Advisory Council was established by Congress in 1976 at the suggestion of the Board of Governors. Representing both consumer/community and financial industry interests, the Council meets several times a year to advise the Board on its implementation of consumer regulations and other consumer related matters.

Another statutory body, the Federal Advisory Council, consists of 12 members (one from each district); it meets in Washington at least four times a year to advise the Board of Governors on general business and financial conditions.

Following the passage of the Monetary Control Act of 1980, the Board of Governors established the Thrift Institutions Advisory Council to provide information and views on the special needs and problems of thrift institutions. The group is comprised of representatives of mutual savings banks, savings and loan associations, and credit unions.

Banks which participate in the federal deposit insurance fund have their deposits insured against loss up to $100,000 for each depositor. The fund is administered by the Federal Deposit Insurance Corporation established in 1933; it obtains resources through annual assessments on participating banks.

All members of the Federal Reserve System are required to insure their deposits through the Corporation, and non-member banks may apply and qualify for insurance. On 31 Dec. 1984, 14,506 commercial banks and 267 mutual savings banks with insured deposits of $1,400,000m. were members of the insurance fund. There are also 37 co-operative Farm Credit Banks, supervised by the Farm Credit Administration, that make agricultural and rural housing loans as well as loans to farmer co-operatives and to businesses providing on-farm services. In this system, farm mortgage loans are originated by local federal land bank associations, while farm production loans are made by local production credit associations. Moreover, the Federal Home Loan Bank System, which includes 12 district banks, is one of several government-sponsored agencies established for the public purpose of assisting home ownership. The Federal Home Loan Banks borrow in the financial markets and lend these funds to savings and loan associations and savings banks, which hold most of their assets in home mortgages. The Federal Home Loan Bank System is privately owned and does not receive any direct federal funding, although it seems to carry an implicit promise of financial support from the federal government because of its public purpose.

Board of Governors of the Federal Reserve System. *The Federal Reserve System: Purposes and Functions.* 7th ed., 1984.—*Federal Reserve Bulletin.* Monthly.—*Annual Report.*— *Annual Statistical Digest.*—*The Federal Reserve Act, As Amended Through 1984*
Chandler, L. V., *Economics of Money and Banking.* 7th ed. New York, 1977
Horovitz, P. M., *Monetary Policy and the Financial System.* 4th ed. Englewood Cliffs, 1979
Meek, P., *U.S. Monetary Policy and Financial Markets.* New York, 1982
Timberlake, R. H., *The Origins of Central Banking in the United States.* Cambridge, Massachusetts, 1978

Weights and Measures. British weights and measures are usually employed, but the old Winchester bushel and wine gallon are used instead of the new or Imperial standards: *Wine gallon* = 0·83268 Imperial gallon; *Bushel* = 0·9690 Imperial bushel. Instead of the British cwt of 112 lb., one of 100 lb. is used; the *short* or *net ton* contains 2,000 lb.; the *long* or *gross ton*, 2,240 lb.

ENERGY AND NATURAL RESOURCES

Electricity. Production (public utilities only, 1985) 2,679,857,000m. kwh.

Minerals. Total value of non-fuel minerals produced in US (including Alaska and Hawaii) in 1984 was estimated at $23,150m. ($21,100m. in 1983). Details are given in the following tables.

Production of metallic minerals (long tons, 2,240 lb.; short tons, 2,000 lb.):

	1984		1985	
		Value		*Value*
Metallic minerals	*Quantity*	*($1,000)*	*Quantity*	*($1,000)*
Bauxite (dried equiv.) tonnes	856	15,643	674	12,855
Copper (recoverable content), tonnes	1,102,613	1,625,116	1,105,758	1,632,483
Gold (recoverable content), troy oz.	2,084,615	751,833	2,475,436	786,345
Lead (recoverable content), tonnes	322,677	181,745	413,955	174,008
Molybdenum (content of concentrate), 1,000 lb.	102,405	326,780	111,936	347,812
Silver (recoverable content), 1,000 troy oz.	44,592	363,006	39,357	241,740
Zinc (recoverable content), tonnes	252,768	270,833	226,545	201,607
Other metals	—	2,469,044	—	2,224,150
Total metals	—	6,004,000	—	5,621,000

The US is wholly or almost wholly dependent upon imports for industrial diamonds, bauxite, tin, chromite, nickel, strategic-grade mica and long-fibre asbestos; it imports the bulk of its tantalum, platinum, manganese, mercury, tungsten, cobalt and flake graphite, and substantial quantities of antimony, cadmium, arsenic, fluorspar, zinc and bismuth.

In 1984 precious metals were mined mainly in Idaho, Nevada, Montana, Utah and Arizona (in order of combined output of gold and silver).

Statistics of important non-metallic minerals and mineral fuels are:

	1984		1985	
		Value		*Value*
Non-metallic minerals	*Quantity*	*($1,000)*	*Quantity*	*($1,000)*
Boron minerals, short tons	1,367,000	456,687	1,269,000	404,775
Cement:				
Portland, 1,000 short tons	74,376	3,810,446	74,250	3,817,335
Masonry, 1,000 short tons	3,281	219,877	3,187	213,096
Clays, 1,000 short tons	43,702	1,032,127	44,974	1,011,377
Gypsum, 1,000 short tons	14,319	113,671	14,726	114,229
Lime, 1,000 short tons	15,922	811,183	15,690	809,000
Phosphate rock, 1,000 tonnes	49,197	1,182,244	50,835	1,203,265
Potassium salts, 1,000 tonnes (K_2O equivalent)	1,639	241,800	1,266	178,400
Salt (common), 1,000 short tons	39,225	675,099	39,484	741,799
Sand and gravel, 1,000 short tons	803,280	2,621,200	829,530	2,812,070

| | 1984 | | 1985 | |
| | | Value | | Value |
Non-metallic minerals	Quantity	($1,000)	Quantity	($1,000)
Stone, 1,000 short tons	957,157	3,910,549	1,001,921	4,224,667
Sulphur (Frasch-process), 1,000 tonnes	5,001	546,106	4,678	573,570
Other non-metallic minerals	—	1,536,011	—	1,508,417
Total non-metallic minerals	—	17,157,000	—	17,612,000

Mineral fuels	1985		1986	
Coal: Bitum. and lignite, 1,000 short tons	879,000	22,062,900	884,400	21,667,800
Pennsylv. anthracite,[1] 1,000 short tons	4,700	215,260	3,800	171,000
Gas: Natural gas,[2] 1m. cu. ft	16,380,000	41,113,800	15,970,000	29,863,900
Petroleum (crude), 1,000 bbls of 42 gallons	3,274,400	78,880,657	3,163,800	40,053,961

[1] Includes a small quantity of anthracite mined in states other than Pennsylvania.
[2] Value at wells.

Minerals Yearbook. Bureau of Mines. Washington, D.C. Annual from 1932–33; continuing the *Mineral Resources of the United States* series (1866–1931); from 1977 in 3 vols. *(Metals and Minerals; Area Reports, Domestic; and Area Reports, International)*

Agriculture. Agriculture in the USA is characterized by its ability to adapt to widely varying conditions, and still produce an abundance and variety of agricultural products. From colonial times to about 1920 the major increases in farm production were brought about by adding to the number of farms and the amount of land under cultivation. During this period nearly 320m. acres of virgin forest were converted to crop land or pasture, and extensive areas of grass lands were ploughed. Improvident use of soil and water resources was evident in many areas.

During the next 20 years the number of farms reached a plateau of about 6·5m., and the acreage planted to crops held relatively stable around 330m. acres. The major source of increase in farm output arose from the substitution of power-driven machines for horses and mules. Greater emphasis was placed on development and improvement of land, and the need for conservation of basic agricultural resources was recognized. A successful conservation programme, highly co-ordinated and on a national scale—to prevent further erosion, to restore the native fertility of damaged land and to adjust land uses to production capabilities and needs—has been in operation since early in the 1930s.

Following the Second World War the uptrend in farm output has been greatly accelerated by increased production per acre and per farm animal. These increases are associated with a higher degree of mechanization; greater use of lime and fertilizer; improved varieties, including hybrid maize and grain sorghums; more effective control of insects and disease; improved strains of livestock and poultry; and wider use of good husbandry practices, such as nutritionally balanced feeds, use of superior sites and better housing. During this period land included in farms decreased slowly, crop land harvested declined somewhat more rapidly, but the number of farms declined sharply.

Some significant changes during these transitions are:

All land in farms totalled less than 500m. acres in 1870, rose to a peak of over 1,200m. acres in the 1950s and declined to 1,232m. acres in 1982, even with the addition of the new States of Alaska and Hawaii in 1960. The number of farms declined from 6·35m. in 1940 to 2·37m. in 1983, as the average size of farms doubled. The average size of farms in 1983 was 437 acres, but ranged from a few acres to many thousand acres. In 1978, 215,088 farms (128,254 in 1974) were less than 10 acres; 475,241 (379,543), 10–49 acres; 814,689 (827,884), 50–179 acres; 596,356 (616,098), 180–499 acres; 215,112 (207,297), 500–999 acres; 98,521 (92,712), 1,000–1,999 acres; 63,635 (62,225) 2,000 acres or more.

Farms operated by owners or part-owners, 1978, were 2,165,000 (87% of all farms), by all tenants, 314,000 (13%). The average size of farms in 1978 was 235 acres for full-owners, 792 acres for part-owners and 396 acres for tenants. Farms with white operators numbered 2,398,726, and those with operators who were black or of other races were 79,916. A higher proportion of blacks and operators of other races were tenants and operated a significantly smaller acreage than white operators.

In 1983 (with 1960 figures in parentheses) large-scale, highly mechanized farms with sales of agricultural products totalling $20,000 and over per farm made up 39·5% (8·6%) of all farms and accounted for 93·2% (48·3%) of the value of farm products sold. Farms selling between $19,999 and $2,500 worth of products per farm were 39·1% (44·8%) of all farms and sold 6·2% (43·3%) of all sales. The remaining 21·4% (46·6%) of all farms sold less than $2,500 worth of products per farm, 0·6% (8·4%) of total sales. Operators in every sales category received off-farm income, but operators selling less than $20,000 per year received more of their average income from non-farm sources than from farming in 1983. Total income per operator: farms with sales of $500,000 and over, $444,808 (of which $416,205 is from farm sources); sales $200,000–$499,999, income $50,007 ($35,397); sales $20,000–$39,999, income $13,850 ($303); sales under $5,000, income $20,407 (farm losing $687).

A century ago three-quarters of the total US population was rural, and practically all rural people lived on farms. In April 1980 26% of the population was rural. Farm residents accounted for 3% of the total population.

During the week of July 12–18, 1987, there were 3·47m. people working on farms and ranches. The workforce comprised 1·35m. self-employed farm operators, 587,000 unpaid workers, 1·27m. workers hired directly by farm operators and 258,000 Agricultural Service employees.

Cash receipts from farm marketings and government payments (in $1m.):

	Crops	Livestock and livestock products	Government payments	Total
1932	1,996	2,752	—	4,748
1945	9,655	12,008	742	22,405
1950	12,356	16,105	283	28,744
1960	15,259	18,989	702	34,950
1970	20,976	29,563	3,717	54,256
1979	63,394	68,522	1,375	133,291
1980	69,026	67,405	1,286	137,717
1981	74,920	68,478	1,930	145,328
1982	74,353	70,199	3,492	148,043
1983	69,516	69,203	9,294	148,014

Realized gross farm income (including government payments), in $1m., was 160,000 in 1981, 164,400 in 1982 and 163,200 in 1983; net income of farm operators (only from farm sources), 30,966 in 1981, 22,339 in 1982 and 16,100 in 1983. Farm real estate debt including farm households, in 1982, was $105,539m.; 1983, $109,507m.; in 1984 $111,600m.

US agricultural exports, fiscal year, totalled: 1978–79, $31,979m.; 1979–80, $40,481m.; 1980–81, $43,780m.; 1981–82, $39,095m.; 1982–83, $34,769m.; 1983–84, $38,027m.; 1984–85, $31,201m.; 1985–86, $26,325m.

Total area of farm land under irrigation in 1982 was 49,002,000 acres.

Federal income taxes paid by farm people: $15m. in 1941, $1,365m. in 1948, $1,182m. in 1967, $3,434m. in 1971, $5,309m. in 1972, $8,364m. in 1973 and $8,277m. in 1974. Total taxes levied on farm real estate were $3,039m. in 1977, $3,021m. in 1978, $3,215m. in 1979, $3,450·9m. in 1980, $3,695·5m. in 1981; $3,907·1m. in 1982.

According to census returns and estimates of the Economic Research Service, the acreage and specified values of farms has been as follows (area in 1,000 acres; value in $1,000):

	Farm area [1]	Crop land available for crops	Value, land, bldgs, machinery, livestock	Value of products sold in preceding year
1910	878,798	432,000	41,089,000	...
1930	986,771	480,000	57,815,000	9,609,924
1940	1,060,852	467,000	41,829,000	6,681,581
1950	1,158,566	478,000	99,366,000	22,051,129
1959	1,125,508	448,100	164,200,000	30,492,721
1969	1,063,346	459,048	206,751,000	44,519,658
1978	1,029,695	461,341	5,653,400,000	108,113,519

[1] Acreages are for the preceding year except for 1959.

The areas and production of the principal crops for 3 years were:

	1984			1985			1986		
	Har-vested 1,000 acres	Produc-tion 1,000	Yield per acre	Har-vested 1,000 acres	Produc-tion 1,000	Yield per acre	Har-vested 1,000 acres	Produc-tion 1,000	Yield per acre
Corn for grain (bu.)	71,915	7,674,020	106·7	75,224	8,876,706	118·0	69,189	8,252,834	119·3
Oats (bu.)	8,163	473,661	58·0	8,177	520,800	63·7	6,870	384,546	56·0
Barley (bu.)	11,231	599,204	53·4	11,603	591,383	51·0	12,007	610,497	50·8
All wheat (bu.)	66,928	2,594,777	38·8	64,734	2,425,105	37·5	60,688	2,086,780	34·4
Rice (cwt.) [1]	2,802	138,810	4,954	2,492	134,913	5,414	2,380	134,416	5,648
Soybeans for beans (bu.)	66,113	1,860,863	28·2	61,584	2,098,531	34·1	59,427	2,007,033	33·8
Flaxseed (bu.)	538	7,022	13·1	584	8,293	14·2	683	11,538	16·9
All Cotton [1] (bales)	10,379	12,981·8	600	10,229	13,432·2	630	8,492	9,784·6	553
Potatoes (cwt.)	1,301	362,612	279	1,361	407,109	299	1,215	354,468	292
Tobacco (lb.)	792	1,727,962	2,183	688	1,511,638	2,197	597	1,198,264	2,006

[1] Yield in lb.

Corn (Maize). The chief corn-growing states (1986) were (estimated production, corn for grain in 1,000 bu.): Iowa, 1,626,750; Illinois, 1,404,000; Nebraska, 896,000; Minnesota, 707,600; Indiana, 695,400; Ohio, 476,160; Wisconsin, 365,800; Missouri, 280,720; South Dakota, 233,700.

Wheat. The chief wheat-growing states (1986) were (estimated production in 1,000 bu.): Kansas, 336,600; N. Dakota, 289,820; Oklahoma, 150,800; Montana, 138,520; Texas, 120,000; Washington, 116,850; S. Dakota, 108,660; Minnesota, 103,666; Colorado, 96,430; Idaho, 81,750; Nebraska, 76,000.

Cotton. Leading production, 1986, by state (in 1,000 bales, 480 lb. net weight) was: Texas, 2,576; California, 2,245; Mississippi, 1,190; Arizona, 823; Louisiana, 673; Arkansas, 602; Tennessee, 396; Alabama, 330; Oklahoma, 210; Missouri, 196; Georgia, 185; N. Carolina, 109.

Tobacco. Production (1,000 lb.) of the chief tobacco-growing states was, in 1986: N. Carolina, 444,790; Kentucky, 314,940; Tennessee, 82,707; S. Carolina, 75,480; Virginia, 73,524; Georgia, 67,890.

Fruit. Production, in tonnes:

	1984	1985	1986
Apples	3,779,770	3,593,110	3,589,940
Citrus Fruit	9,790,320	9,514,550	10,012,610
Grapes	4,711,830	5,127,140	5,076,520

Dairy produce. In 1984, production of milk was 135,400m. lb.; cheese solid, 4,673·78m. lb.; butter, 1,103·3m. lb.; ice-cream, 883·5m. gallons; non-fat dry milk for human consumption, 1,158·9m. lb.; cottage cheese, 961·6m. lb.

Livestock (1 Jan. 1987): Cattle and calves, 102,031,000; sheep and lambs, 10,328,000; hogs and pigs (1 Dec. 1986), 50,960,000.

On 1 Dec. 1984 there were 373·95m. chickens, excluding broilers. In 1984 171·3m. turkeys were raised; 4,282m. broilers were produced, 1 Dec. 1983–30 Nov. 1984. Eggs produced, same period, 68,193m. (value $4,108·9m.).

Value of production (in $1m.) was:

	1985	1986
Cattle and calves	21,196,786	20,924,859
Sheep and lambs	427,805	443,565
Hogs and pigs	8,871,310	9,531,589

Total value of livestock, excluding poultry and goats and, from 1961, horses and mules (in $1m.) on farms in the USA on 1 Jan. was: 1930, 6,061; 1933 (low point of the agricultural depression), 2,733; 1970, 22,886; 1978, 31,952; 1979, 50,612; 1980, 60,598; 1981, 60,016; 1982, 53,601; 1983 (preliminary), 52,148.

In 1982 the production of shorn wool was 105m. lb. from 13·1m. sheep (average

1970–74, 320m. lb. from 18·2m. sheep); of pulled wool, 1·15m. lb. (1970–74, 10·1m. lb.).

Forestry. In 1977 the US forest lands, including Alaska and Hawaii, capable of producing timber for commercial use, covered 482,485,900 acres (more than one-fifth of the land area), classified as follows: Saw-timber stands, 215,435,700 acres; pole timber stands, 135,609,900 acres, seedling and sapling stands, 115,032,100 acres; non-stocked and other areas, 16,408,200 acres. Ownership of commercial forest land is distributed as follows: Federal government, 99,410,400 acres; state, county, municipal and Indian, 36,311,200 acres; privately owned, 346,764,300 acres, including 115,777,100 acres on farms. Of the saw-timber stand (2,578,940m. bd ft) Douglas fir constitutes 514,317; Southern pine, 321,563; Western yellow (ponderosa and jeffrey) pine, 192,070; other softwoods, 957,458; hardwoods, 255,189. In 1976 growing stock timber removals amounted to 14,229,023,000 cu. ft compared to net annual growth of about 21,664,316,000 cu. ft. Saw-timber removals amounted to 65,176,618,000 bd ft against an annual growth of 74,620,832,000 bd ft. The net area of the 156 national forests and other areas in USA and Puerto Rico administered by the US Department of Agriculture's Forest Service, including commercial and non-commercial forest land, was in Oct. 1986, 191m. acres.

Fire takes a heavy annual toll in the forest; total area burned over in 1986 was 3,191,125 acres; 1,500m. acres of land are now under organized fire-protection service. Federal land that was planted or seeded in forest and wind barrier nursery stock in the year ending 30 Sept. 1986 was 300,640 acres.

Land Areas of National Forest System. Forest Service, US Dept. of Agriculture, 1985
Report of the Forest Service, 1985

Fisheries. Total US catch (edible and industrial), 1985, 2·8m. tonnes valued at $2,300m.; harvest outside the US (mostly tuna) and joint venture operations (mostly Alaskan pollock), 1·1m. tonnes valued at $277m.; foreign catch in the 200 mile wide US fishery zone (mostly Alaskan pollock, 73%; Pacific flounders, 13% and Pacific cod, 6%), 1·2m. tonnes.

Major species caught, 1985: Menhaden, 2,700m. lb, value $101m. (44% of total US catch); salmon, 727m. lb, $440m.; crabs, 338m. lb, $390m.; shrimp, 473m. lb, $306m.; cod, 303m. lb, $54m.; sea herring, 199m. lb, $50m.; tuna, 516m. lb, $212m. Major landing areas, 1985: By value (in $1m.): Alaska, 591; Massachusetts, 232; Louisiana, 229; Texas, 177; Florida, 171. By volume (in 1m. lb): Louisiana, 1,700; Alaska, 1,200; Virginia, 723; Mississippi, 471; California, 363.

Exports, 1985, totalled $1,100m.; imports, $6,700m. *Per capita* consumption, 1985, 14·5 lb edible meat; estimated live weight equivalent about 43 lb *per capita*.

Tennessee Valley Authority. Established by Act of Congress, 1933, the TVA is a multiple-purpose federal agency which carries out its duties in an area embracing some 41,000 sq. miles, in 125 counties (aggregate population, about 4·7m.) in the 7 Tennessee River Valley states: Tennessee, Kentucky, Mississippi, Alabama, North Carolina, Georgia and Virginia. In addition, 76 counties outside the Valley are served by TVA power distributors. Its 3 directors are appointed by the President, with the consent of the Senate; headquarters are in Knoxville, Tenn. There were 32,000 employees in Aug. 1987.

In the 1930s and 1940s, the Tennessee Valley offered the world a model of the first effort to develop all resources of a major river valley under one comprehensive programme, the Tennessee Valley Authority. The multipurpose development of the Tennessee River for flood control, navigation, and electric power production was the first big task for TVA. But there were other needs; controlling erosion on the land, introducing better fertilizers and new farming practices, eradicating malaria, demonstrating ways electricity could lighten the burdens in the home and increase production on the farm, and a multitude of potential job-producing enterprises.

In the depression year, 1933, the *per capita* income in the Valley was $168, compared with the national average of $375. Through the years, TVA has placed a strong emphasis on the economic development of the Valley. In recent years average income levels in the region have been nearly 80% of the national level.

Taming the Tennessee River has had two positive effects on the Valley: flood damages averted by river control now total more than $3,000m., and a navigable channel system 650 miles long, connecting with the American system of inland waterways, provides a readily accessible transportation system for industry. In 1984, 33·2m. (estimate) tons of barge-traffic travelled the TVA river system.

Another activity is experimentation in the development and manufacture of chemical fertilizers, accompanied by programmes designed to encourage proper fertilizer use in all parts of the United States and the world. TVA's National Fertilizer Development Center is recognized world-wide for its expertise in fertilizer technology. TVA also works closely with other federal agencies, and with state and local authorities in combating soil erosion, improving forest resources, improving agriculture, and in the development of local industries based on natural resources.

In recent years, attention has focused mainly on TVA's power programme. TVA supplies electric power to 160 local distribution systems serving 2·9m. customers. The power system originated with the water-power development of the Tennessee River, but has become predominantly a coal-fired system as power requirements have outgrown the region's hydro-electric potential. In fiscal year 1986, the TVA system generated 94,600m. kwh. Installed capacity in 1986 was 32·1m. kw, with another 5·2m. kw under construction at TVA's nuclear plants.

Power operations are financially self-supporting from revenues. In fiscal year 1986 power revenues were $4,639m. Power facilities are financed from revenues and the sale of revenue bonds and notes, and TVA is repaying appropriations previously invested in power facilities. Other TVA resource development programmes continue to be financed from congressional appropriations.

Annual Report of the TVA. Knoxville, 1934 to date

Clapp, G.R., *The TVA; An Approach to the Development of a Region.* Univ. of Chicago Press, 1955

Lilienthal, D. E., *TVA; Democracy on the March.* 20th Anniversary ed. New York and London, 1953

Owen, M., *The Tennessee Valley Authority.* New York, 1973

Tennessee Valley Authority. *A History of the Tennessee Valley Authority.* Knoxville, Tennessee, 1982.—*TVA: The First Twenty Years* (ed. R. C. Martin), Univ. of Tennessee Press, 1956

INDUSTRY AND TRADE

Industry. The following table presents industry statistics of manufactures as reported at various censuses from 1909 to 1982 and from the Annual Survey of Manufactures for years in which no census was taken. The figures for 1958 to 1982 include data for some establishments previously classified as non-manufacturing. The figures for 1939, but not for earlier years, have been revised to exclude data for establishments classified as non-manufacturing in 1954. The figures for 1909–33 were previously revised by the deduction of data for industries excluded from manufacturing during that period.

The statistics for 1958, 1963, 1967, 1972, 1977 and 1982 relate to all establishments employing 1 or more persons anytime during the year; for 1950, 1956–57, 1959–62, 1966 and 1968–74 on a representative sample of manufacturing establishments of 1 or more employees; for 1929 through 1939, those reporting products valued at $5,000 or more; and for 1909 and 1919, those reporting products valued at $500 or more. These differences in the minimum size of establishments included in the census affect only very slightly the year-to-year comparability of the figures.

The annual Surveys of Manufactures carry forward the key measures of manufacturing activity which are covered in detail by the Census of Manufactures. The estimate for 1950 is based on reports for approximately 45,000 plants out of a total of more than 260,000 operating manufacturing establishments; those for 1956–57 on about 50,000, and those for 1959–62, 1966 and 1968–74 on about 60,000 out of about 300,000. Included are all large plants and representative samples of the much more numerous small plants. The large plants in the surveys account for approximately two-thirds of the total employment in operating manufacturing establishments in the US.

	Number of establish-ments	Production workers (average for year)	Production workers' wages total ($1,000)	Value added by manufacture [1] ($1,000)
1909	264,810	6,261,736	3,205,213	8,160,075
1919	270,231	8,464,916	9,664,009	23,841,624
1929	206,663	8,369,705	10,884,919	30,591,435
1933	139,325	5,787,611	4,940,146	14,007,540
1939	173,802	7,808,205	8,997,515	24,487,304
1950	260,000	11,778,803	34,600,025	89,749,765
1960	...	12,209,514	55,555,452	163,998,531
1963	306,317	12,232,041	62,093,601	192,082,900
1967	305,680	13,955,300	81,393,600	261,983,800
1969	...	14,357,800	93,459,600	304,440,700
1970	...	13,528,000	91,609,000	300,227,600
1971	...	12,874,900	93,231,700	314,138,400
1972	312,662	13,526,500	105,494,700	353,974,200
1973	...	14,233,100	118,332,300	405,623,500
1974	...	13,970,900	124,983,200	452,468,400
1975	...	12,567,900	121,427,200	442,485,800
1976	...	13,051,200	137,564,000	511,470,900
1977	350,757	13,691,000	157,163,700	585,165,600
1978	...	14,228,700	176,416,800	657,412,000
1979	...	14,537,800	192,881,500	747,480,500
1980	...	13,900,100	198,164,000	773,831,300
1982	348,385	12,400,600	204,787,200	824,117,700
1983	...	12,203,000	212,416,400	882,014,500
1984	...	12,572,800	231,783,900	983,227,700
1985	...	12,171,100	235,731,700	999,065,800

[1] For the period 1954–67 value added represents adjusted value added and for earlier years unadjusted value added. Unadjusted is obtained by subtracting cost of materials, supplies and containers, fuel, electricity and contract work from the value of shipments for products manufactured plus receipts for services rendered. Adjusted value added also takes into account value added by merchandizing operations plus net change in finished goods and work-in-process inventories between the beginning and end of the year.

For comparison of broad types of manufacturing, the industries covered by the Census of Manufactures have been divided into 20 general groups according to the *Standard Industrial Classification.*

Code No.	Industry group	Year	Production workers (average for year)	Production workers' wages, total ($1,000)	Value added by manu-facture [1] ($1,000)
20. Food and kindred products		1983	1,012,700	16,637,000	93,437,800
		1984	1,009,500	17,061,400	98,037,400
		1985	993,600	17,427,700	104,140,000
21. Tobacco products		1983	41,900	958,100	9,692,100
		1984	38,600	933,200	10,786,600
		1985	36,900	440,900	11,893,700
22. Textile mill products		1983	624,000	7,803,100	21,333,400
		1984	610,500	7,852,300	22,110,400
		1985	565,300	7,609,200	20,193,300
23. Apparel and other textile products		1983	995,900	9,193,400	27,339,400
		1984	977,100	9,280,300	28,858,800
		1985	904,000	9,003,000	27,728,400
24. Lumber and wood products		1983	531,400	7,507,800	19,530,500
		1984	541,500	7,860,000	21,035,100
		1985	514,200	7,835,800	21,065,500
25. Furniture and fixtures		1983	359,300	4,564,000	14,282,200
		1984	383,700	5,148,700	15,905,600
		1985	380,000	5,345,500	16,478,800
26. Paper and allied products		1983	460,800	9,736,700	35,611,600
		1984	468,100	10,515,800	40,884,700
		1985	462,100	10,783,400	40,387,200
27. Printing and publishing		1983	722,600	12,052,500	60,062,000
		1984	733,400	12,916,200	67,021,600
		1985	742,100	13,554,400	73,054,300

[1] Figures represent adjusted value added. For definitions see footnote to previous table.

Code No.	Industry group	Year	Production workers (average for year)	Production workers' wages, total ($1,000)	Value added by manu- facture [1] ($1,000)
28. Chemical and allied products		1983	496,000	10,867,600	86,472,400
		1984	490,700	11,444,400	94,728,200
		1985	476,000	11,602,000	95,257,500
29. Petroleum and coal products		1983	95,100	2,723,300	21,043,500
		1984	89,800	2,648,600	16,163,400
		1985	83,500	2,533,900	17,111,600
30. Rubber and miscellaneous plastics products		1983	527,200	8,229,100	29,804,700
		1984	573,800	9,439,400	34,183,400
		1985	578,400	9,799,200	35,708,300
31. Leather and leather products		1983	161,900	1,613,000	4,852,600
		1984	145,200	1,482,600	4,510,700
		1985	124,800	1,342,200	4,107,500
32. Stone, clay and glass products		1983	408,300	7,508,800	25,326,200
		1984	416,400	8,039,000	27,706,600
		1985	403,800	8,196,200	28,841,800
33. Primary metal industries		1983	585,100	13,642,400	35,996,600
		1984	616,000	14,915,700	42,290,900
		1985	571,000	14,277,900	38,081,900
34. Fabricated metal products [2]		1983	1,050,400	18,979,300	61,326,800
		1984	1,112,200	21,158,500	67,644,800
		1985	1,103,500	21,976,800	69,161,500
35. Machinery (except electrical)		1983	1,234,200	23,588,400	94,752,800
		1984	1,297,600	26,749,100	112,346,300
		1985	1,236,600	26,510,500	110,234,100
36. Electric and electronic equipment		1983	1,187,700	20,370,100	92,519,800
		1984	1,287,400	23,493,100	109,904,200
		1985	1,233,100	23,658,800	109,861,500
37. Transportation equipment [2]		1983	1,072,100	26,917,400	99,642,900
		1984	1,159,800	30,768,000	114,498,700
		1985	1,179,600	33,171,400	120,953,100
38. Instruments and related products [2]		1983	348,300	6,001,100	35,258,100
		1984	358,100	6,533,600	39,869,900
		1985	348,000	6,192,600	40,278,300
39. Miscellaneous manufacturing		1983	280,000	3,415,800	13,702,400
		1984	263,400	3,544,000	14,740,400
		1985	234,600	3,415,300	14,031,600

[1] Figures represent adjusted value added. For definitions see footnote to previous table, p. 1408.

[2] Figures for 1967 are not comparable to 1972 due to revisions in the Standard Industrial Classification System.

Iron and Steel: Output of the iron and steel industries (in net tons of 2,000 lb.), according to figures supplied by the American Iron and Steel Institute, was:

	Fur- naces in blast 31 Dec.	Pig-iron (including ferro- alloys)	Raw steel	Steel by method of production [1]			
				Open hearth	Bessemer	Electric [2]	Basic Oxygen
1932 [3]	44	9,835,227	15,322,901	13,336,210	1,715,925	270,044	...
1939	195	35,677,097	52,798,714	48,409,800	3,358,916	1,029,067	...
1944 [4]	218	62,866,198	89,641,600	80,363,953	5,039,923	4,237,699	...
1950	234	66,400,311	96,336,075	86,262,509	4,534,558	6,039,008	...
1960	114	68,566,384	99,281,601	86,367,506	1,189,196	8,378,743	3,346,156
1970	152	87,933,000	131,514,000	48,022,000	—	20,162,000	63,330,000
1980	...	70,329,000	111,835,000	13,054,000	—	31,166,000	67,617,000
1985	...	50,446,000	88,259,000	6,428,000	—	29,946,000	51,885,000
1986	...	43,952,000	81,606,000	3,330,000	—	30,390,000	47,885,000

[1] The sum of these 4 items should equal the total in the preceding column; any difference appearing is due to the very small production of crucible steel, omitted prior to 1950.

[2] Includes crucible production beginning 1950.   [3] Low point of the depression.

[4] Peak year of war production.

Wholesale price index of iron and steel mill products (1967 = 100) was: 1950, 59·4; 1960, 96·4; 1970, 114·3; 1980, 302·7; 1982, 349·7; 1983, 352·5; 1984, 366·1; 1985, 366·2.

The iron and steel industry in 1986 employed 128,418 wage-earners (compared with 449,888 in 1960), who worked an average of 38 hours per week and earned an average of $16.22 per hour: total wages were $4,203m. and total salaries for 46,365 employees were $1,736m.

Annual Statistics Report. American Iron and Steel Institute

Labour. The American labour movement comprises about 190 national and international labour organizations plus a large number of small independent local or single-firm labour organizations. In 1985 total membership was approximately 20·1m. The American Federation of Labor (founded 1881 and taking its name in 1886) and the Congress of Industrial Organizations merged into one organization, named the AFL–CIO, in Dec. 1955, representing 16·8m. workers in 1980.

Unaffiliated or independent labour organizations, inter-state in scope, including those organizing coalminers, teamsters and government employees and railroad workers, had an estimated total membership excluding all foreign members (1980) of about 6·8m.

Labour organizations represented 19·9% (19·3m.) of the labour force in 1986; 17·5% (17m.) were actual members of unions.

The Labor–Management Relations (Taft–Hartley) Act, 1947, applicable to industries affecting inter-state commerce, prohibits the closed shop, but permits union shop arrangements except where forbidden by state laws. Statutes regulating, restricting or prohibiting union shop or other types of union security agreements are in effect in 21 states (Alabama, Arizona, Arkansas, Florida, Georgia, Idaho, Iowa, Kansas, Louisiana, Mississippi, Nebraska, Nevada, North Carolina, North Dakota, South Carolina, South Dakota, Tennessee, Texas, Utah, Virginia and Wyoming). Colorado and Wisconsin ban all-union agreements unless a certain percentage of employees have voted for them; in Hawaii an all-union agreement may be entered into unless a majority of employees votes against it. Thirteen states have acts to prevent industrial disputes between public utilities and their employees by means of compulsory arbitration or seizure; however, a number of these laws have been declared unconstitutional in so far as industries in inter-state commerce are concerned. Laws to restrict or regulate picketing or other strike activities have been enacted in over half the states. About one-half of the states also prohibit certain types of strikes, as 'sit down', jurisdictional or sympathy strikes.

The Employee Retirement Income Security Act of 1974 protects the interests of workers and their beneficiaries who are entitled to benefits from employee pension and welfare plans. The law requires disclosure of plan provisions and financial information and establishes standards of conduct for trustees and administrators of welfare and pension plans. It provides funding, participation and vesting requirements for pension plans and makes termination insurance available for most pension plans. The law does not require a company to establish a welfare or pension plan.

Minimum wage laws governing private employers are in operation in 45 jurisdictions: 41 states, the District of Columbia, Guam, Puerto Rico and the Virgin Islands have minimum wage laws and minimum wage rates. As of 1 Aug. 1978, all but one of the laws cover men, women and, usually, minors. The exception covers only women and minors. The minimum wage rate under federal law is $3.35 per hour for employees who are engaged in commerce, in the production of goods for commerce or in certain enterprises which are engaged in commerce as well as federal employees.

A total of 69 strikes and lockouts of 1,000 workers or more occurred in 1986, involving 533,000 workers and 11·9m. idle days; the number of idle days was 0·05% of the year's total working time of all workers.

There are 3 federal agencies which provide formal machinery for the adjustment of labour disputes: (1) The Federal Mediation and Conciliation Service, now an independent agency, whose mediation services are available 'in any labor dispute in any industry affecting commerce'; under Executive Order 11491, as amended, to federal agencies and organizations of federal employees involved in negotiation disputes; and in state and local government collective bargaining disputes when adequate dispute resolution machinery is not available to the parties. Its aim is to prevent and minimize work stoppages. (2) The National Mediation Board (1934) provides much the same facilities for the railroad and air-transport industries pursuant to the Railway Labor Act. (3) The National Railroad Adjustment Board (1934) acts as a board of final appeal for grievances arising over the interpretation of existing collective agreements under the Railway Labor Act; its decisions are binding upon both sides and enforceable by the courts.

The National Labor Relations Act, as amended by the Labor–Management Relations (Taft–Hartley) Act, 1947 (*see* THE STATESMAN'S YEAR-BOOK, 1955, p. 617), was amended by the Labor–Management Reporting and Disclosure Act, 1959, and again amended in 1974. The 1959 Act requires extensive reporting and disclosure of certain financial and administrative practices of labour organizations, employers and labour relations consultants. In addition, certain powers are vested in the Secretary of Labor to prevent abuses in the administration of trusteeships by labour organizations, to provide minimum standards and procedures for the election of union officers and to establish rules prescribing minimum standards for determining the adequacy of union procedures for the removal of officers. Other provisions impose a fiduciary responsibility upon union officers and provide for the exclusion of those convicted of certain named felonies from office for specified periods; more stringently regulate secondary boycotts and banning of 'hot' cargo agreements; put limitations upon organizational and recognition picketing and permit States to assert jurisdiction over labour disputes where the National Labor Relations Board declines to act. The Act also contains a 'Bill of Rights' for union members (enforceable directly by them) dealing with such things as equal rights in the nomination and election of union officers, freedom of speech and assembly subject to reasonable union rules, and safeguards against improper disciplinary action.

The Bureau of Labor Statistics estimated that in 1986 the labour force was 119,540,000 (65·6% of those 16 years and over); the resident armed forces accounted for 1,706,000 and the civilian labour force for 117,834,000, of whom 109,597,000 were employed and 8,237,000—or 7%—were unemployed. The following table shows civilian employment by industry and sex and percentage distribution of the total:

Industry Group	Male	Female	Total	Percentage distribution
Employed (1,000 persons):	60,892	48,706	109,597	100·0
Agriculture, forestry and fisheries	2,511	652	3,163	2·9
Mining	736	143	880	0·8
Construction	6,663	625	7,288	6·6
Manufacturing:				
Durable goods	9,289	3,315	12,605	11·5
Non-durable (including not specified)	4,936	3,421	8,357	7·6
Transportation, communication and other				
public utilities	5,553	2,097	7,650	7·0
Wholesale and retail trade	11,990	10,823	22,813	20·8
Finance, insurance and real estate	3,021	4,380	7,401	6·8
Services	13,199	21,137	34,337	31·3
Private households	184	1,057	1,241	1·1
Other services	13,015	20,080	33,096	30·2
Professional services	7,229	14,945	22,174	20·2
Public administration	2,992	2,112	5,104	4·7

A Guide to Basic Law and Procedures under the National Labor Relations Act, National Labor Relations Board, Washington, D.C., 1976

Brody, D., *Workers in Industrial America: Essays on the Twentieth-century Struggle.* New York, 1980

Commerce. The subjoined table gives the total value of the imports and exports of merchandise by yearly average or by year (in $1m.):

	Exports Total	Exports US mdse.[1]	General imports		Exports[2] Total	Exports[2] US mdse.[1]	General imports[2]
1946–50	11,829	11,673	6,659	1982	212,275	207,158	243,952
1951–55	15,333	15,196	10,832	1983	200,538	195,969	258,048
1956–60	19,204	19,029	13,650	1984	217,888	212,057	325,726
1961–65	24,006	24,707	17,659	1985	213,146	206,925	345,276
1970	43,224	42,590	39,952	1986	217,304	206,376	369,961

[1] Excludes re-exports.   [2] Includes US Virgin Islands trade with foreign countries.

For a description of how imports and exports are valued, see *Explanation of Statistics of Report FT990, Highlights of US Export and Import Trade,* Bureau of the Census, US Department of Commerce, Washington, D.C., 1946.

The 'most favoured nation' treatment in commerce between Great Britain and US was agreed to for 4 years by the treaty of 1815, was extended for 10 years by the treaty of 1818, and indefinitely (subject to 12 months' notice) by that of 1827.

Imports and exports of gold and silver bullion and specie in calendar years (in $1,000):

	Gold Exports	Gold Imports	Silver Exports	Silver Imports
1932	809,528	363,315	13,850	19,650
1940	4,995	4,749,467	3,674	58,434
1944	959,228	113,836	126,915	23,373
1955	7,257	104,592	8,331	72,932
1960	1,647	335,032	25,789	57,438
1965	1,285,097	101,669	54,061	64,769
1970	36,887	227,472	53,003	58,838
1975	429,278	406,583	104,086	274,106
1980	2,787,431	2,508,520	1,326,878	1,336,009
1985	919,400	2,109,500	81,746	855,528
1986	1,207,783	5,016,558	56,785	688,296

The domestic exports of US produce, including military, and the imports for consumption by economic classes for 3 calendar years were (in $m.):

	Exports (US merchandise) 1984	1985	1986	Imports for consumption 1984	1985	1986
Food and live animals	24,463	19,268	17,303	17,973	18,668	20,644
Crude materials	20,249	16,939	17,324	11,082	10,295	10,347
Machinery and transport equipment	89,973	94,278	95,290	119,192	136,613	161,999
Chemicals	22,336	21,759	22,766	13,697	14,420	14,851
Total of the above main groups	157,021	152,244	152,683	163,928	179,996	207,841

Leading exports of US merchandise are listed below for the calendar year 1986: Special category merchandise is included. Data for major subdivisions of certain classes are also given:

Commodity	$1m.	Commodity	$1m.
Machinery, total	60,809	Chemicals	22,766
Power generating machinery	9,165	Chemical elements and compounds	1,771
Metalworking machinery	1,467	Plastic materials and resins	4,301
Agricultural machines and tractors	1,688	Soybeans	4,334
Office machinery and computers	15,456	Cotton	773
Telecommunications apparatus	4,407	Textiles and apparel	3,469
Electrical machinery and apparatus	13,630	Tobacco and cigarettes	2,732
Electrical power apparatus and switchgear	3,496	Iron and steel-mill products	1,020
Road motor vehicles (and parts)	17,709	Non-ferrous base metals and alloys	1,195
Aircraft and spacecraft		Pulp, paper and products	4,265
(and parts)	15,106	Coal	3,928
Grains and preparations	7,368	Fruits and vegetables	2,657
Wheat (and flour)	3,217	Petroleum and products	3,639
		Firearms of war and ammunition	2,282

Chief imports for 27 commodity classes for consumption for the calendar year 1986:

Commodity	$1m.	Commodity	$1m.
Petroleum products,		Wool and other hair	188
crude and refined	33,746	Metal manufactures n.e.s.	7,031
Petroleum	22,608	Diamonds (excl. industrial)	3,459
Petroleum products	10,819	Rubber	920
Non-ferrous metals	5,745	Textile yarn, fabrics and products	1,597
Copper	1,365	Clothing	17,207
Aluminium	2,747	Cotton fabrics, woven	989
Nickel	515	Machinery, total	86,078
Lead	62	Agricultural machinery and tractors	1,826
Tin	242	Office machinery	14,691
Paper, paperboard and		Coffee	4,288
products	6,357	Chemicals and related products	14,851
Newsprint	3,682	Chemicals	7,955
Wood pulp	1,581	Oils and fats	502
Fertilizers	865	Cocoa beans	418
Sugar	624	Glass, pottery and china	2,465
Iron and steel-mill products	8,054	Footwear	6,461
Cattle, meat and preparations	2,779	Toys and sports goods	4,516
Automobiles and parts	68,614	Furs, undressed	145
Fish (and shellfish)	4,689	Telecommunications apparatus	20,142
Fruit and vegetables	4,101	Artworks and antiques	2,092
Alcoholic beverages	2,973	Natural and manufactured gas	2,994

Total trade beween the USA and the UK for 5 years (British Department of Trade returns, in £1,000 sterling):

	1983	1984	1985	1986	1987
Imports to UK	7,442,671	9,356,029	9,919,689	8,468,160	9,136,015
Exports and re-exports from UK	8,336,979	10,149,479	11,498,802	10,379,585	11,014,242

Imports and exports by continents, areas and selected countries for calendar years (in $1m.):

	General imports		Exports incl. re-exports [1]	
Area and country	1985	1986	1985	1986
Western Hemisphere	115,916	110,701	78,271	76,410
Canada	69,006	68,253	47,251	45,333
20 Latin American Republics	43,448	39,541	27,850	27,968
Central American Common Market	1,722	2,061	1,622	1,767
Costa Rica	501	641	422	483
El Salvador	396	385	445	518
Guatemala	409	601	405	400
Honduras	375	433	308	363
Nicaragua	41	8	42	3
Panama	410	366	675	711
Latin American FTA	39,943	35,655	24,414	24,180
Argentina	1,069	856	721	944
Bolivia	99	124	120	112
Brazil	7,526	6,813	3,140	3,885
Chile	745	820	682	823
Colombia	1,331	1,874	1,468	1,318
Ecuador	1,837	1,465	591	601
Mexico	19,132	17,302	13,635	12,392
Paraguay	24	30	99	171
Peru	1,087	803	496	693
Uruguay	557	473	64	100
Venezuela	6,537	5,097	3,399	3,141
Dominican Republic	982	1,085	742	921
Haiti	390	375	396	387
Bahamas	626	442	786	761
Netherlands Antilles	808	471	427	398
Jamaica	273	299	404	457
Trinidad and Tobago	1,258	793	504	532

Area and country	General imports		Exports incl. re-exports [1]	
	1985	1986	1985	1986
Europe				
Western Europe	79,756	89,825	56,763	61,642
OECD Countries	79,165	89,130	56,084	61,003
European Economic Community	64,761	75,736	45,776	53,154
Belgium and Luxembourg	3,387	4,006	4,918	5,399
Denmark	1,665	1,757	706	758
France	9,482	10,129	6,096	2,615
Germany (Fed. Rep.)	20,239	25,124	9,050	10,561
Greece	395	394	498	430
Ireland	901	1,003	1,342	1,434
Italy	9,674	10,607	4,625	4,838
Netherlands	4,081	4,066	7,269	...
UK	14,937	15,396	11,273	11,418
Turkey	602	633	1,295	1,160
EFTA countries				
Austria	834	864	441	464
Norway	1,164	1,079	666	937
Portugal	546	552	695	638
Sweden	4,124	4,420	1,925	1,871
Switzerland	3,476	5,253	2,288	2,977
Finland	895	908	438	381
Iceland	248	238	38	60
Spain	2,515	2,702	2,524	2,615
Yugoslavia	542	646	595	528
Soviet bloc.	1,936	532	3,215	590
Poland	220	233	238	151
USSR	409	558	2,423	1,248
Asia [2]	131,884	153,869	60,745	64,532
Near East	6,267	7,890	9,709	8,415
Bahrain	84	77	107	195
Iran	725	569	74	34
Iraq	474	440	427	528
Israel	2,123	2,418	2,580	2,239
Kuwait	184	267	551	7
Lebanon	19	30	141	106
Saudi Arabia	1,907	3,612	4,474	657
Japan	68,783	81,911	22,631	26,882
Other Asia	59,236	67,186	34,239	34,514
Bangladesh	196	230	219	165
Hong Kong	8,396	8,891	2,786	3,030
India	2,295	2,283	1,642	1,536
Indonesia	4,569	3,312	795	946
Korea, Republic of	10,013	12,729	5,956	6,355
Malaysia	2,300	2,421	1,539	1,730
Singapore	4,260	4,725	3,476	3,380
Pakistan	274	325	1,042	830
Philippines	2,145	1,972	1,379	1,363
Sri Lanka	282	337	73	66
Thailand	1,428	1,748	849	936
Taiwan (Formosa)	16,396	19,791	4,700	5,524
Vietnam [3]	...	2	...	30
China	3,862	4,771	3,856	3,106
Oceania	3,819	3,717	6,399	6,659
Australia	2,837	2,632	5,441	5,551
New Zealand and W. Samoa	883	984	729	883

[1] 'Special category' exports are included in these totals.
[2] Excludes Yemen (Aden) (formerly Southern Yemen).
[3] Included in China from 1984.

Area and country	General imports		Exports incl. re-exports [1]	
	1985	1986	1985	1986
Africa	11,964	10,348	7,388	5,978
Algeria	2,333	1,831	430	453
Egypt	79	112	2,323	1,982
Ethiopia	43	75	203	104
Libya	44	2	311	46
Morocco	39	43	279	487
Ghana	90	191	54	84
Liberia	83	82	73	65
Nigeria	3,002	2,530	676	409
Kenya	92	141	97	70
Zaïre	401	221	105	105
South Africa, Republic of [4]	2,071	2,365	1,205	1,158

[1] See note on previous page.
[4] Includes also South-West Africa (Namibia).

US Department of Commerce, Bureau of Census. Report FT 990, Highlights of US Export and Import Trade

Tourism. In 1986, 25·4m. visitors travelled to the USA and spent over US$12,913m. (excluding transportation paid to US international carriers). They came mainly from Canada (10·9m.), Europe (8·9m.) and Mexico (5·6m.).[1] Approximately 37·6m. US visitors travelled abroad, mainly to Canada (14·1m.), Mexico (11·4m.), Europe (5·2m.), and the Caribbean (3·5m.).

[1] Changed method of counting for Mexico.

COMMUNICATIONS

Roads. On 31 Dec. 1986 the total US public road[1] mileage, including rural and urban roads, amounted to 3,879,538 miles, of which 3,504,394 miles were surfaced roads. The total mileage cited includes 703,900 miles of rural roads under control of the states, 2,188,664 miles of local rural roads, 232,120 miles of federal park and forest roads, and 701,414 miles of urban roads and streets. Expenditures for construction and maintenance amounted to $43,163m. in 1985.

By the end of 1986, toll roads administered by state and local toll authorities, totalled 4,692 miles (including some under construction) compared with 344 miles in 1940.

Motor vehicles registered in the calendar year 1986 were (Federal Highways Administration) 176,191.339, including 135,431,112 automobiles, 593,728 buses and 40,166,499 trucks.

Inter-city trucks (private and for hire) averaged 605,000m. revenue net ton-miles in 1984. Of the 593,728 buses in service in 1986, 479,076 were school buses. Inter-city service operated a total of 1,137m. bus-miles and carried a total of 362m. revenue passengers in 1984.

There were 46,056 deaths in road accidents in 1986.

[1] Public road mileage excludes that mileage not open to public travel, not maintained by public authority, or not passable by standard four-wheel vehicles. This excluded mileage was reported to the US Federal Highway Administration prior to 1981.

Railways. Railway history in the USA commences in 1828, but the first railway to convey both freight and passengers in regular service (between Baltimore and Ellicott's Mills, Md., 13 miles) dates from 24 May 1830. Mileage rose to 52,922 miles in 1870; to 167,191 miles in 1890, and to a peak of 266,381 miles in 1916, falling thereafter to 261,871 in 1925; 246,739 in 1940 and 222,164 in 1969 (these include some duplication under trackage rights and some mileage operated in Canada by US companies). The ordinary gauge is 4 ft 8½ in. (about 99·6% of total mileage). The USA has about 29% of the world's railway mileage.

In addition to the independent railroad companies, railway service is provided by two federally-assisted organizations, the National Railroad Passenger Corporation (Amtrak), and the Consolidated Rail Corporation (Conrail).

Amtrak was set up on 1 May 1971 to maintain a basic network of inter-city passenger trains with government assistance, and is responsible for almost all non-commuter services with 40,000 miles of route including 1,256 km owned (555 electrified) and carried 21m. passengers in 1985. From 1 Jan. 1983, an Amtrak commuter division took over from Conrail all commuter services not acquired by State or regional agencies.

Conrail was established on 1 April 1976 to run freight services in the industrial north-east formerly operated by the bankrupt Penn Central, Reading, Lehigh Valley, Central of New Jersey, Erie Lackawanna, Lehigh & Hudson railroads, and Pennyslvania-Reading Seashore Lines which was returned to the private sector in 1985.

The following table, based on the figures of the Interstate Commerce Commission, shows some railway statistics for 4 calendar years:

	1960	1970	1980 [2]	1986 [1] [2]
Classes I and II Railroads				
Mileage owned (first main tracks)	223,779	204,621	157,078	135,782
Revenue freight originated (1m. short tons)	1,421	1,572	1,537	1,306
Freight ton-mileage (1m. ton-miles)	591,550	771,012	932,748	867,722
Passengers carried (1,000)	488,019	289,469	281,503	[3]
Passenger-miles (1m.)	31,790	10,786	6,557	[3]
Operating revenues ($1m.)	9,587	12,209	28,708	26,204
Operating expenses ($1m.)	7,135	9,806	26,761	24,896
Net railway operating income ($1m.)	1,055	506	1,364	507
Net income after fixed charges ($1m.)	855	126	2,029	1,579
Class I Railroads:				
Locomotives in service	40,949	27,086	28,240	21,045
Steam locomotives	25,640	—	—	—
Freight-train cars (excluding caboose cars)	1,721,269	1,423,921	1,101,343	713,954
Passenger-train cars	57,146	11,177	2,219	672
Average number of employees	1,220,784	566,282	458,996	275,817
Average wage per week ($1)	72.59	188.71	474.21	690.27

[1] Class I railroads only. From 1981, Class II railroads were no longer required to file annual reports.
[2] Data for National Railroad Passenger Corporation excluded.
[3] This data has been discontinued.

Aviation. In civil aviation there were, on 31 Dec. 1985, 709,540 certified pilots (including 146,652 student pilots) and 273,979 registered civil aircraft.

Airports on 31 Dec. 1985: Air carrier, 700; general aviation, 15,379. Of these airports, 12,648 were conventional land-based, while 384 were seaplane bases, 2,982 were heliports and 65 stolports (Stol—Short Take-Off and Landing).

Statistics from the Department of Transportation indicate that for 12 months ended June 1986 on US flag carriers in scheduled international service there were 24·8m. enplanements with 365·4m. aircraft miles (excluding all-cargo) for a total of 64,933m. revenue passenger-miles. The non-scheduled airlines had a total of 13,788m. revenue passenger-miles internationally and domestically. Domestically US scheduled airlines in 1986 had 370·9m. enplanements with a total of 3,084·7m. aircraft miles for 282,744m. revenue passenger-miles. (A revenue passenger-mile is one paying passenger carried per mile.).

Shipping. On 1 Sept. 1986 the US merchant marine included 735 sea-going vessels of 1,000 gross tons or over, with aggregate dead-weight tonnage of 24m. This included 255 tankers of 15·4m. DWT.

On 1 Sept. 1986 US merchant ocean-going vessels were employed as follows: Active, 385 of 16·3m. DWT, of which 149 of 5·2m. tons were foreign trade, 169 of 9·5m. tons in domestic trade and 67 of 1·6m. tons in other US agency operations. Inactive vessels totalled 8m. DWT; 89 of 4·4m. DWT privately owned were laid up and 261 of 3·6m. tons were Government-owned National Defense reserve fleet. Of the total vessels in the US fleet, 464 of 21m. DWT were privately owned.

US exports and imports carried on dry cargo and tanker vessels in the year 1985 totalled 643·1m. long tons, of which 27·4m. long tons or 4·3% were carried in US flag vessels.

Post and Broadcasting. Until the beginning of 1984 the telephone business was largely in the hands of the American Telephone and Telegraph Company (AT & T) and its telephone operating subsidiaries, which together were known as the Bell System. Pursuant to a government anti-trust suit, the Bell System was broken up, with the telephone operating companies being divested from AT & T to create seven regional companies for providing local service. There are also many hundreds of smaller telephone companies having no common ownership affiliation with the Bell companies, but which connect with them for universal service, countrywide and worldwide. In addition, several new entrants have begun to compete with AT & T in the long-distance telephone market. The message telegraph and telex services are in the hands of The Western Union Telegraph Company, and the international record carriers, which compete with the telephone industry in providing leased private lines. Western Union also provides an inter-city telephone service.

The number of telephones in service in the USA has increased in the period since 1945 at a much faster rate than has the population. Among principal reasons are the significant increase in the percentage of households with telephone service and the enormous growth in the number of extension telephones.

In marked contrast, the number of public telegrams has decreased by a substantial amount. Telegrams have lost favour due to shifts in user preference to the air-mail and to the telephone. The telex services of the telegraph company have also found broad acceptance in place of telegrams for business purposes. The following table contains key data items on a comparative basis for the domestic telephone and message telegraph services:

	1960	1970	1980	1986
All telephone systems:				
Total telephones	74,342,000	120,218,000	180,425,000	122,203,000
Bell System:				
Total telephones	60,735,100	96,561,000	141,674,000	97,007,000
Average daily telephone calls	219,093,000	368,363,000	580,230,000	1,083,567,802
Local	209,373,000	346,505,000	527,543,000	995,544,339
Long distance	9,720,000	21,858,000	52,687,000	88,023,463
Total plant in service ($1,000)	24,072,499	54,813,202	132,831,794	168,008,759
Total operating revenues ($1,000)	7,958,125	17,094,846	51,203,404	63,896,509
Employees, number	580,405	772,980	847,768	506,643
Western Union Telegraph Co.:				
Public telegrams for year	102,931,000	46,084,000	40,801,398	20,040,189
Total plant ($1,000)	398,023	1,029,149	2,101,007	1,991,343
Revenue from public telegrams ($1,000)	160,746	126,739	115,612	85,724
Total operating revenues ($1,000)	262,365	402,456	696,972	573,109
Employees, number	32,655	24,293	12,649	...

International communication services, providing overseas connexions with all parts of the world, are furnished principally by the American Telephone and Telegraph Company and three telegraph companies. The old submarine cable telegraph systems have all been abandoned in favour of using telegraph circuits derived from voice channels in the newer telephone ocean cables, which have also made inroads on the use of high-frequency radio. More recently, satellite communications facilities have been utilized not only for telephone and telegraph services but for television and data transmission as well.

International overseas telegrams, inbound to and outbound from the continental US, numbered 9·2m. in 1982 (11·7m. in 1980). This service has tended to decline in volume in recent years. It first lost ground to the air-mail and then to the telex and telephone services. For the US and its possessions the volume of international overseas telephone calls has grown enormously with the availability of the excellent voice-transmission qualities provided in the telephone ocean cables and in the satellite radio relays. Whereas international telephone calls were 990,000 in 1955, the last year in which there was no cable service available, there were 149·6m. such calls in 1980.

Postal business for the years ended 30 Sept. included the following items:

	1983	1984	1985	1986
Number of post offices, on 30 June [1]	39,445	39,386	39,327	39,270
Postal operating revenue ($1,000)	23,581,667	25,313,554	27,736,071	30,716,595
Postal expenses ($1,000)	24,083,073	26,357,353	29,207,201	29,411,987

[1] The US Postal Service was established 1 July 1971. Financial statements prior to that date are those of the Post Office Department. Such statements for 1968–71 have been restated to be in a format and on an accounting principle basis generally consistent with 1972.

On 1 Jan. 1975 there were in the USA and Territories, 7,068 authorized commercial radio stations, 711 commercial television stations: of non-commercial stations 717 were for radio, 241 for television.

Cinemas. Cinemas increased from 17,003 in 1940 to 20,239 in 1950 and decreased to 20,200 in 1984, of which 2,832 were drive-ins.

Newspapers. Of the daily newspapers being published in the USA in 1971, 339 were morning papers with a circulation of 26,116,000, and 1,425 were evening papers with a circulation of 36,115,000. The 590 Sunday papers had a total circulation of 49·7m.

JUSTICE, RELIGION, EDUCATION AND WELFARE

Justice. Legal controversies may be decided in two systems of courts: the federal courts, with jurisdiction confined to certain matters enumerated in Article III of the Constitution, and the state courts, with jurisdiction in all other proceedings. The federal courts have jurisdiction exclusive of the state courts in criminal prosecutions for the violation of federal statutes, in civil cases involving the government, in bankruptcy cases and in admiralty proceedings, and have jurisdiction concurrent with the state courts over suits between parties from different states, and certain suits involving questions of federal law.

The highest court is the Supreme Court of the US, which reviews cases from the lower federal courts and certain cases originating in state courts involving questions of federal law. It is the final arbiter of all questions involving federal statutes and the Constitution; and it has the power to invalidate any federal or state law or executive action which it finds repugnant to the Constitution. This court, consisting of 9 justices who receive salaries of $104,100 a year (the Chief Justice, $108,400), meets from Oct. until June every year and disposes of about 4,450 cases, deciding about 380 on their merits. In the remainder of cases it either summarily affirms lower court decisions or declines to review. A few suits, usually brought by state governments, originate in the Supreme Court, but issues of fact are mostly referred to a master.

The US courts of appeals number 13 (in 11 circuits composed of 3 or more states and 1 circuit for the District of Columbia and 1 Court of Appeals for the Federal Circuit); the 168 circuit judges receive salaries of $83,200 a year. Any party to a suit in a lower federal court usually has a right of appeal to one of these courts. In addition, there are direct appeals to these courts from many federal administrative agencies. In the year ending 30 June 1986, 35,455 appeals were filed in the courts of appeals.

The trial courts in the federal system are the US district courts, of which there are 89 in the 50 states, 1 in the District of Columbia and 1 each in the territories of Puerto Rico, Virgin Islands, Guam and the Northern Marianas. Each state has at least 1 US district court, and 3 states have 4 apiece. Each district court has from 1 to 27 judgeships. There are 575 US district judges ($78,700 a year), who handle about 254,800 civil cases and 57,000 criminal defendants every year.

In addition to these courts of general jurisdiction, there are special federal courts of limited jurisdiction. US Claims Court (16 judges at $70,200 a year) decides claims for money damages against the federal government in a wide variety of matters; the Court of International Trade (9 judges at $78,700) determines controversies concerning the classification and valuation of imported merchandise.

The judges of all these courts are appointed by the President with the approval of the Senate; to assure their independence, they hold office during good behaviour and cannot have their salaries reduced. This does not apply to the territorial judges, who hold their offices for a term of years or to judges of the US Claims Court. The judges may retire with full pay at the age of 70 years if they have served a period of 10 years, or at 65 if they have 15 years of service, but they are subject to call for such judicial duties as they are willing to undertake. Only 9 US judges up to 1986 have been involved in impeachment proceedings, of whom 4 district judges and 1 commerce judge were convicted and removed from office.

Of the 254,828 civil cases filed in the district courts in the year ending 30 June 1986, about 113,392 arose under various federal statutes (such as labour, social security, tax, patent, securities, antitrust and civil rights laws); 42,326 involved personal injury or property damage claims; 88,352 dealt with contracts; and 10,674 were actions concerning real property.

Of the 41,490 criminal cases filed in the district courts in the year ending 30 June 1986, about 2,010 were charged with alleged infractions of the immigration laws; 340, the transport of stolen motor vehicles; about 3,540 larceny and theft; 8,570, embezzlement and fraud; and 7,890 narcotics laws.

Persons convicted of federal crimes are either fined, released on probation under the supervision of the probation officers of the federal courts, confined in prison for a period of up to 6 months and then put on probation (known as split sentencing) or confined in one of the following institutions: 3 for juvenile and youths; 7 for young adults; 7 for intermediate term adults; 7 for short-term adults; 2 for females; 1 hospital and 15 community service centres. In addition, prisoners are confined in centres operated by the National Institutes of Mental Health. In addition, prisoner drug addicts may be committed to US Public Health Service hospitals for treatment. Prisoners confined in institutions operated by the US Bureau of Prisons for the year ending 30 Sept. 1982, numbered 28,133.

The state courts have jurisdiction over all civil and criminal cases arising under state laws, but decisions of the state courts of last resort as to the validity of treaties or of laws of the US, or on other questions arising under the Constitution, are subject to review by the Supreme Court of the US. The state court systems are generally similar to the federal system, to the extent that they generally have a number of trial courts and intermediate appellate courts, and a single court of last resort. The highest court in each state is usually called the Supreme Court or Court of Appeals with a Chief Justice and Associate Justices, usually elected but sometimes appointed by the Governor with the advice and consent of the State Senate or other advisory body; they usually hold office for a term of years, but in some instances for life or during good behaviour. Their salaries range from $24,000 to $84,584 a year. The lowest tribunals are usually those of Justices of the Peace; many towns and cities have municipal and police courts, with power to commit for trial in criminal matters and to determine misdemeanours for violation of the municipal ordinances; they frequently try civil cases involving limited amounts.

The death penalty is illegal in Alaska, Hawaii, Iowa, Maine, Minnesota, Oregon, West Virginia, Wisconsin and Michigan; in North Dakota it is legal only for treason and first-degree murder committed by a prisoner serving a life sentence for first-degree murder, in Rhode Island only for murder committed by a prisoner serving a life sentence and in Vermont and New York for the murder of a peace officer in the line of duty and for first-degree murder by those who kill while serving a life sentence for murder. The death penalty is legal in 37 states. Until 1982 it had fallen into disuse and had been abolished *de facto* in many states. The US Supreme Court had held the death penalty, as applied in general criminal statutes, to contravene the eighth and fourteenth amendments of the US constitution, as a cruel and unusual punishment when used so irregularly and rarely as to destroy its deterrent value.

In 1967 only 2 persons were executed under civil authority; both for murder. There were no executions 1968–76. In 1977 a convicted murderer requested that he should be executed and after a lengthy legal dispute the sentence was carried out at Utah state prison. Six persons were executed between 1977 and 1982. In Jan. 1983, 1,050 prisoners in 31 states were reported under sentence of death.

The total number of civilian executions carried out in the US from 1930 to 1982 was 3,866.

Federal 'Political' Crimes. Prosecutions for what may be loosely described as 'political' offences, or crimes directed towards the overthrow by violence of the federal government, which were somewhat numerous in the early 1950s, have declined sharply over the last 20 years and are now exceedingly rare.

A Guide to Court Systems. Institute of Judicial Administration. New York, 1960
The United States Courts. Administrative Office of the US Courts, Washington, D.C., 20544
Blumberg, A. S., *Criminal Justice: Issues and Ironies.* 2nd ed. New York, 1973
Huston, L. A., *The Department of Justice.* New York, 1967
Huston, L. A., and others, *Roles of the Attorney General of the United States.* New York, 1968
McCloskey, R. G., *The Modern Supreme Court.* Harvard Univ. Press, 1972
McLauchlan, W. P., *American Legal Processes.* New York, 1977
Walker, S. E., *Popular Justice.* New York, 1980

Religion. *The Yearbook of American and Canadian Churches for 1987,* published by the National Council of the Churches of Christ in the USA, New York, presents the latest figures available from official statisticians of church bodies. The large majority of reports are for the calendar year 1985, or a fiscal year ending 1985. The 1985 reports indicated that there were 142,926,363 (142,172,000 in 1984) members with 345,961 local churches. There were 325,411 clergymen serving in local congregations in 1985. The principal religious bodies (numerically or historically) or groups of religious bodies are shown below:

Denominations	Local churches	Total membership
Summary:		
Protestant bodies	314,713	79,095,746
Roman Catholic Church	24,251	52,654,908
Jews [1]	3,416	5,834,635
Eastern Churches	1,659	4,025,698
Old Catholic, Polish National Catholic and Armenian	428	1,024,330
Buddhists	100	100,000
Miscellaneous [2]	1,124	191,046
1985 totals	345,961	142,926,363 [3]

[1] Includes Orthodox, Conservative and Reformed bodies.
[2] Includes non-Christian bodies such as Spiritualists, Ethical Culture, Unitarian-Universalists.
[3] Care should be taken in interpreting membership statistics for the US Churches. Some statistics are accurately compiled and others are estimates. Also statistics are not always comparable.

Protestant Church Membership	Total membership
Baptist bodies	
Southern Baptist Convention	14,477,364
National Baptist Convention, USA	5,500,000 [1]
National Baptist Convention of America, Inc.	2,668,799 [1]
National Primitive Baptist Convention	250,000 [1]
American Baptist Churches in the USA	1,559,683
American Baptist Association	225,000
Conservative Baptist Association of America	225,000
Regular Baptist Churches	300,839
Free Will Baptists	217,838
Baptist Missionary Association of America	227,720
Christian Church (Disciples of Christ)	1,116,326
Christian Churches and Churches of Christ	1,051,469
Church of the Nazarene	552,082
Churches of Christ	1,604,000
The Episcopal Church	2,739,422
Latter-Day Saints:	
Church of Jesus Christ of Latter-Day Saints	3,860,000
Reorganized Church of Jesus Christ of Latter-Day Saints	192,082
Lutheran Bodies:	
Lutheran Church in America	2,898,202
The Lutheran Church-Missouri Synod	2,638,164
The American Lutheran Church	2,332,316
Wisconsin Evangelical Lutheran Synod	415,389

Protestant Church Membership	*Total membership*
Methodist Bodies:	
United Methodist Church	9,192,172
African Methodist Episcopal Church	2,210,000
African Methodist Episcopal Zion Church	1,202,229
Christian Methodist Episcopal Church	718,922
Pentecostal Bodies:	
Assemblies of God	2,082,878
Church of God (Cleveland, Tenn.)	500,000
United Pentecostal Church, International, Inc.	475,000
Presbyterian Bodies: [1]	
Presbyterian Church (USA)	3,048,235
Others	351,446
Reformed Churches:	
Reformed Church in America	342,275
Christian Reformed Church	219,988
The Salvation Army	427,825
Seventh-day Adventists	651,954
United Church of Christ	1,683,777

[1] Figures date from 1976 or earlier.

Yearbook of American and Canadian Churches. Annual, from 1951. New York

Education. Under the system of government in the USA, elementary and secondary education is committed in the main to the several states. Each of the 50 states and the District of Columbia has a system of free public schools, established by law, with courses covering 12 years plus kindergarten. There are 3 structural patterns in common use; the K8–4 plan, meaning kindergarten plus 8 elementary grades followed by 4 high school grades; the K6–3–3 plan, or kindergarten plus 6 elementary grades followed by a 3-year junior high school and a 3-year senior high school; and the K6–6 plan, kindergarten plus 6 elementary grades followed by a 6-year high school. All plans lead to high-school graduation, usually at age 17 or 18. Vocational education is an integral part of secondary education. In addition, some states have, as part of the free public school system, 2-year colleges in which education is provided at a nominal cost. Each state has delegated a large degree of control of the educational programme to local school districts (numbering 15,734 in autumn 1986), each with a board of education (usually 3 to 9 members) selected locally and serving mostly without pay. The school policies of the local school districts must be in accord with the laws and the regulations of their state Departments of Education. While regulations differ from one jurisdiction to another, in general it may be said that school attendance is compulsory from age 7 to 16.

The Census Bureau estimates that in Nov. 1979 only 1m. or 0·6% of the 170m. persons who were 14 years of age or older were unable to read and write; in 1930 the percentage was 4·8. In 1940 a new category was established—the 'functionally illiterate', meaning those who had completed fewer than 5 years of elementary schooling; for persons 25 years of age or over this percentage was 2·7 in March 1985 (for the non-white population alone it was 6%); it was 0·8% for white and 0·5% for non-whites in the 25–29-year-old group. The Bureau reported that in March 1985 the median years of school completed by all persons 25 years old and over was 12·6, and that 19·4% had completed 4 or more years of college. For the 25–29-year-old group, the median school years completed was 12·9 and 22·2% had completed 4 or more years of college.

In the autumn of 1985, 12,247,000 students (5,818,000 men and 6,429,000 women) were enrolled in 3,340 colleges and universities; 2,292,000 were first-time students. About 27·8% of the population between the ages of 18 and 24 were enrolled in colleges and universities.

Public elementary and secondary school revenue is supplied from the county and other local sources (43·8% in 1985–86), state sources (49·8%) and federal sources (6·5%). In 1985–86 expenditure for public elementary and secondary education totalled about $150,900m., including $137,600m. for regular day school programmes, $2,200m. for other programmes, $8,600m. for capital outlay and $2,600m. for interest on school debt. The current expenditure per pupil in average daily attendance was about $3,755. The total cost per pupil, also including capital outlay and interest, amounted to about $4,060. Estimated total expenditures, for private elementary and secondary schools in 1985–86 were about $13,200m. In 1985–86 the 3,340 universities and colleges expended $100,101m. from current funds, of which $65,067m. was spent by institutions under public control. The federal government contributed 12·7% of total current-fund revenue; state governments, 29%; student tuition and fees, 22·4%; and all other sources, 35·9%.

Vocational education below college grade, including the training of teachers to conduct such education, has been federally aided since 1918. Federal support for vocational education in 1985–86 amounted to about $813m. Many public high schools offer vocational courses in addition to their usual academic programmes. In 1981–82 enrolments in the vocational classes were: Agriculture, 420,000; business, 5,874,000; home economics, 3,024,000; industrial arts, 2,980,000; trade and industry, 1,874,000.

Summary of statistics of regular schools (public and private), teachers and pupils in autumn 1985 (compiled by the US National Center for Education Statistics):

Schools by level	Number of schools 1985–86	Teachers autumn 1985	Enrolment autumn 1985
Elementary schools:			
Public	58,827 [1]	1,230,000	24,275,000
Private	22,000	246,000 [2]	4,300,000 [2]
Secondary schools:			
Public	23,916 [1]	981,000	15,238,000
Private	8,200	97,000 [2]	1,300,000 [2]
Higher education:			
Public	1,498	499,000 [2]	9,479,000
Private	1,842	211,000 [2]	2,768,000
Total	116,283	3,264,000	57,360,000

[1] Data for 1984–85. [2] Estimated.

Most of the private elementary and secondary schools are affiliated with religious denominations. Of the children attending private elementary and secondary schools in 1985, nearly 3·1m. or 55·4% were enrolled in Roman Catholic schools.

During the school year 1985–86 high-school graduates numbered about 2,644,000 (about 49·5% boys and 50·5% girls). Institutions of higher education conferred 987,823 bachelor's degrees during the year 1985–86, 485,923 to men and 501,900 to women; 288,567 master's degrees, 143,508 to men and 145,059 to women; 33,653 doctorates, 21,819 to men and 11,834 to women; and 73,910 first professional degrees, 49,621 to men and 24,649 to women.

During the academic year, 1985–86, 343,780 foreign students were enrolled in American colleges and universities. The percentages of students coming from various areas in 1985–86 were: South and East Asia, 45·6; Middle East, 15·3; Latin America, 13·2; Africa, 9·9; Europe, 10; North America, 4·7; Oceania, 1·2.

School enrolment, Oct. 1985, embraced 96% of the children who were 5 and 6 years old; 99% of the children aged 7–13 years; 95% of those aged 14–17, 52% of those aged 18 and 19, 35% of those aged 20 and 21, and 17% of those aged 22–24 years.

The US Center for Education Statistics estimates the total enrolment in the autumn of 1987 at all of the country's elementary, secondary and higher educational institutions (public and private) at 58m. (57·8m. in the autumn of 1986); this was 23·8% of the total population of the USA as of 1 Sept. 1987.

Enrolment at the elementary and secondary school level was expected to rise by 0·7% in autumn 1987 and total enrolment in the colleges and universities to decline by about 0·8%.

The number of teachers in regular public and private elementary and secondary schools in the autumn of 1987 was expected to increase slightly to 2,645,000. The average annual salary of the public school teachers was about $26,700 in 1986–87.

Digest of Education Statistics. Annual. Dept. of Education, Washington 20202, D.C. (from 1962)

American Community, Technical and Junior Colleges. 9th ed. American Council on Education. Washington, 1984

American Universities and Colleges. 12th ed. American Council on Education. Washington, 1983

Ayer's Directory of Newspapers and Periodicals. Annual, from 1880. Philadelphia

Health and Welfare. Admission to the practice of medicine (for both doctors of medicine and doctors of osteopathic medicine) is controlled in each state by examining boards directly representing the profession and acting with authority conferred by state law. Although there are a number of variations, the usual time now required to complete training is 8 years beyond the secondary school with up to 3 or more years of additional graduate training. Certification as a specialist may require between 3 and 5 more years of graduate training plus experience in practice. In academic year 1984–85 the 142 US schools (15 osteopathic and 127 allopathic) graduated 17,697 physicians. About 32% of first-year students were women. In Dec. 1985 the estimated number of active physicians (MD and DO—in all forms of practice) in the US, Puerto Rico and outlying US areas was 520,700 (1 active physician to 459 population). The distribution of physicians throughout the country is uneven, both by state and by urban–rural areas.

In 1984–85 the 60 dental schools graduated 5,410 dentists. Active dentists in Dec. 1985 numbered 140,800 (1 active dentist to 1,704 population).

In academic year 1983–84, there were 1,477 registered nursing programmes in the US and 80,312 graduates. In Dec. 1985 registered nurses employed full- or part-time were 1 to 159 population.

Number of hospitals listed by the American Hospital Association in 1984 was 6,872, with 1,339,000 beds and 37,938,000 admissions during the year; average daily census was 970,000. Of the total, 341 hospitals with 112,000 beds were operated by the federal government; 1,662 with 203,000 beds by state and local government; 3,366 with 717,000 beds by non-profit organizations (including church groups); 786 with 100,000 beds are proprietary. The categories of non-federal hospitals are 5,814 short-term general and special hospitals with 1,020,000 beds; 131 non-federal long-term general and special hospitals with 30,000 beds; 579 psychiatric hospitals with 175,000 beds; 7 tuberculosis hospitals with 1,000 beds.

Social welfare legislation was chiefly the province of the various states until the adoption of the Social Security Act of 14 Aug. 1935. This as amended provides for a federal system of old-age, survivors and disability insurance; health insurance for the aged and disabled; supplemental security income for the aged, blind and disabled; federal state unemployment insurance; and federal grants to states for public assistance (medical assistance for the aged and aid to families with dependent children generally) and for maternal and child-health and child-welfare services. The Social Security Administration of the Department of Health and Human Services has responsibility for the programmes—old-age, survivors and disability insurance and supplemental security income. The Family Support Administration has federal responsibility for the programmes—aid to families with dependent children, low income energy assistance, child support enforcement, refugee and entry assistance and community services block grant. The Health Care Financing Administration, an agency of the same Department, has federal responsibility for health insurance for the aged and disabled (Medicare) and medical assistance (Medicaid). The Department's Office of Human Development administers human service programmes for such groups as the elderly, children, youth, native Americans and persons with developmental disabilities, and its Public Health Service supports maternal and child-health services. Unemployment insurance is the responsibility of the Department of Labor.

The Social Security Act provides for protection against the cost of medical care through the two-part programme of health insurance for people 65 and over and for certain disabled people under 65, who receive disability insurance payments or who have permanent kidney failure (Medicare). During fiscal year 1985, payments totalling $47,710m. were made under the hospital part of Medicare on behalf of

30·1m. people. During the same period, $21,808m. was paid under the voluntary medical insurance part of Medicare on behalf of 29·5m. people.

In 1986 about 123m. persons worked in employment covered by old-age, survivors and disability insurance.

In June 1986 over 37·3m. beneficiaries were on the rolls, and the average benefit paid to a retired worker (not counting any paid to his dependants) was about $480 per month.

Benefits paid during calendar year 1985 totalled $185,988m., including $18,836m. paid to disabled workers and their dependants.

In Dec. 1985, 10·9m. persons (adults and children) were receiving payments under aid to families with dependent children (average monthly payment, $339 per family). Total payments under aid to families with dependent children were $15,200m. for the calendar year 1985.

In June 1986, about 4·2m. persons were receiving supplementary security income payments, including 1·5m. persons aged 65 or over; 82,000 blind persons, and over 2·6m. disabled persons. Payments, including supplemental amounts from various states, totalled $10,750m. in 1985.

In 1986, federal appropriations for the social services block grant amounted to $2,584m. In addition, 1986 federal appropriations for human development and family social services to selected target groups totalled $2,790m. Included in this amount were $1,955m. for children and youth; $671m. for the elderly; $77m. for persons with developmental disabilities; and $28m. for native Americans. During 1986, the Public Health Services awarded a total of $457·4m. for maternal and child health services, $388·8m. as block grants to the states and the remaining $68·6m. for special projects of regional and national significance. In addition, approximately $195·5m. was spent for research and $11·5m. for training in the fields of maternal and child health. Other block grants awarded by the Public Health Service in 1986 included $88m. for preventive health; $469m. for alcohol, drug abuse and mental health; and $580·6m. for the primary care block grant. The latter amount included $396m. for community health centres; $3·3m. for black lung clinics; $44·9m. for migrant health; and $136·4m. for family planning.

Burns, E. M., *Social Security and Public Policy.* New York, 1956 (Repr. 1976).—*Health Services for Tomorrow.* New York, 1973

DIPLOMATIC REPRESENTATIVES

Of the United States in Great Britain (Grosvenor Sq., London, W1A 1AE)
Ambassador: Charles H. Price II (accredited 20 Dec. 1983).

Of Great Britain in the USA (3100 Massachusetts Ave., Washington, D.C., 20008)
Ambassador: Sir Antony Acland, KCMG, KCVO.

Of the United States to the United Nations
Ambassador: Gen. Vernon A. Walters.

Books of Reference

I. STATISTICAL INFORMATION

The Office of Management and Budget, Washington, D.C. 20503 is part of the Executive Office of the President; it is responsible for co-ordinating all the statistical work of the different Federal Government agencies. The Office does not collect or publish data itself. The main statistical agencies are as follows:

(1) Data User Services Division, Bureau of the Census, Department of Commerce, Washington, D.C. 20233. Responsible for decennial censuses of population and housing, quinquennial census of agriculture, manufactures and business; current statistics on population and the labour force, manufacturing activity and commodity production, trade and services, foreign trade, state and local government finances and operations. (*Statistical Abstract of the United States*, annual, and others).

(2) Bureau of Labor Statistics, Department of Labor, 441 G Street NW, Washington, D.C. 20212. (*Monthly Labor Review* and others).

(3) Information Division, Economic Research Service, Department of Agriculture, Washington, D.C. 20250. (*Agricultural Statistics*, annual, and others).

(4) National Center for Health Statistics, Department of Health and Human Services, 3700 East-West Highway, Hyattsville Md. 20782. (*Vital Statistics of the United States*, monthly and annual, and others).

(5) Bureau of Mines Office of Technical Information, Department of the Interior, Washington, D.C. 20241. (*Minerals Yearbook*, annual, and others).

(6) Office of Energy Information Services, Energy Information Administration, Department of Energy, Washington, D.C. 20461.

(7) Statistical Publications, Department of Commerce, Room 5062 Main Commerce, 14th St and Constitution Avenue NW, Washington, D.C. 20230; the Department's Bureau of Economic Analysis and its Office of Industry and Trade Information are the main collectors of data.

(8) Center for Education Statistics, Department of Education, 555 New Jersey Avenue NW, Washington, D.C. 20208.

(9) Public Correspondence Division, Office of the Assistant Secretary of Defense (Public Affairs P.C.), The Pentagon, Washington, D.C. 20301-1400.

(10) Bureau of Justice Statistics, Department of Justice, 633 Indiana Avenue NW, Washington, D.C. 20531.

(11) Public Inquiry, APA 200, Federal Aviation Administration, Department of Transportation, 800 Independence Avenue SW, Washington, D.C. 20591.

(12) Office of Public Affairs, Federal Highway Administration, Department of Transportation, 400 7th St. SW, Washington, D.C. 20590.

(13) Statistics Division, Internal Revenue Service, Department of the Treasury, 1201 E St. NW, Washington, D.C. 20224.

Statistics on the economy are also published by the Division of Research and Statistics, Federal Reserve Board, Washington, D.C. 20551; the Congressional Joint Committee on the Economy, Capitol; the Office of the Secretary, Department of the Treasury, 1500 Pennsylvania Avenue NW, Washington, D.C. 20220.

The Office of Management and Budget (*see* above) issues a pamphlet: *Statistical Services of the United States Government* describes the organization of the system and the principal types of economic statistics; it also includes an annotated bibliography of about 100 publications.

II. OTHER OFFICIAL PUBLICATIONS

Guide to the Study of the United States of America. General Reference and Bibliography Division, Library of Congress. 1960.

Historical Statistics of the United States, Colonial Times to 1957: A Statistical Abstract Supplement. Washington, 1960.—*Continuation to 1962 and Revisions,* 1965.

United States Government Manual. Washington. Annual.

The official publications of the USA are issued by the US Government Printing Office and are distributed by the Superintendent of Documents, who issued in 1940 a cumulative *Catalog of the Public Documents of the . . . Congress and of All the Departments of the Government of the United States.* This *Catalog* is kept up to date by *United States Government Publications, Monthly Catalog* with annual index and supplemented by *Price Lists.* Each *Price List* is devoted to a special subject or type of material, *e.g., American History* or *Census.* Useful guides are Schmeckebier, L. F., and Eastin, R. B. (eds.), *Government Publications and Their Use.* 2nd ed., Washington, D.C., 1961; Boyd, A. M., *United States Government Publications.* 3rd ed. New York, 1949, and Leidy, W. P., *Popular Guide to Government Publications.* 2nd ed. New York and London, 1963.

Treaties and other International Acts of the United States of America (Edited by Hunter Miller), 8 vols. Washington, 1929–48. This edition stops in 1863. It may be supplemented by *Treaties, Conventions . . . Between the US and Other Powers, 1776–1937* (Edited by William M. Malloy and others). 4 vols. 1909–38. A new Treaty Series, *US Treaties and Other International Agreements* was started in 1950.

Writings on American History. Washington, annual from 1902 (except 1904–5 and 1941–47).

III. NON-OFFICIAL PUBLICATIONS

A. Handbooks

National Historical Publications Commission. *Guide to Archives and Manuscripts in the United States,* ed. P. M. Hamer. Yale Univ. Press, 1961

Adams, J. T. (ed.), *Dictionary of American History.* 2nd ed. 7 vols. New York, 1942

Dictionary of American Biography, ed. A. Johnson and D. Malone. 23 vols. New York, 1929–64.—*Concise Dictionary of American Biography.* New York, 1964

Current Biography. New York, annual from 1940; monthly supplements

Handlin, O., and others. *Harvard Guide to American History.* Cambridge, Mass., 1954

Herstein, S. R. and Robbins, N., *United States of America.* [Bibliography] Oxford and Santa Barbara, 1982
Lord, C. L. and E. H., *Historical Atlas of the US.* Rev. ed. New York, 1969
Who's Who in America. Chicago, 1899–1900 to date; monthly Supplement. 1940 to date

B. General History
Barck, Jr, O. T., and Blake, N. M., *Since 1900: A History of the United States.* 5th ed. New York, 1974
Bellot, H. H., *American History and American Historians.* London, 1952, repr. 1974
Brogan, H., *The Longman History of the United States of America.* London, 1985
Carman, H. J., and others, *A History of the American People.* 3rd ed. 2 vols. New York, 1967
Commager, H. S. (ed.), *Documents of American History.* 8th ed. New York, 1966
Divine, R. A., *Since 1945: Politics and Diplomacy in Recent American History.* New York, 1975
Hicks, J. D., *The American Nation, A History of the United States from 1865.* 5th ed. Boston, 1971
Link, A. S., and Catton, W. B., *American Epoch: A History of the United States Since the 1890s.* 4th ed. New York, 1967
Morison, S. E., *The Oxford History of the American People.* OUP, 1968
Morison, S. E., with Commager, H. S., *The Growth of the American Republic.* 2 vols. 5th ed. OUP, 1962–63
Nicholas, H. G., *The Nature of American Politics.* OUP, 1980
Parkes, H. B., *The United States of America, A History.* 3rd ed. New York, 1968
Scammon, R. N. (ed.), *American Votes: A Handbook of Contemporary American Election Statistics.* Washington, D.C., 1956 to date (biennial)
Schlesinger, A. M., *The Rise of Modern America, 1865–1951.* 4th ed. New York, 1951.—*The Age of Roosevelt.* 4 vols. New York and London, 1957–62.—*A Thousand Days: John F. Kennedy in the White House.* New York and London, 1965
Snowman, D., *America Since 1920.* London, 1978
Watson, R. A., *The Promise and Performance of American Democracy.* 2nd ed. New York, 1975

C. Minorities
Bennett, M. T., *American Immigration Policies: A History.* Washington, D.C., 1963
Burma, J. J., *Spanish-speaking Groups in the US.* Duke University Press, 1954, repr. 1974
Frazier, E. F., *The Negro Family in the United States.* Chicago Univ. Press, 1966
McNickle, D., *The Indian Tribes of the United States.* OUP, 1962.—*Native American Tribalism.* OUP, 1973
Sklare, M., *The Jew in American Society.* New York, 1974
Wissler, Clark, *Indians of the United States.* Rev. ed. New York, 1966

D. Economic History
The Economic History of the United States. 9 vols. New York, 1946 ff.
Bining, A. C., and Cochran, T. C., *The Rise of American Economic Life.* 4th ed. New York, 1963
Dorfman, J., *The Economic Mind in American Civilization.* 5 vols. New York, 1946–59
Faulkner, H. U., *American Economic History.* 8th ed. New York, 1960
Friedman, M., and Schwartz, A. J., *A Monetary History of the United States, 1867–1960.* New York, 1963
Mund, V. A., *Government and Business.* 4th ed. New York, 1965

E. Foreign Relations
Documents on American Foreign Relations. Princeton, from 1948. Annual
The United States in World Affairs. 1931 ff. Council on Foreign Relations. New York, from 1932. Annual
Allison, G., and Szanton, P., *Remaking Foreign Policy: The Organizations Connection.* New York, 1976
Bartlett, R. (ed.), *The Record of American Diplomacy; Documents and Readings in the History of American Foreign Relations.* 4th ed. New York, 1964
Beloff, M., *The United States and the Unity of Europe.* London, 1963, repr. 1976
Connell-Smith, G., *The United States and Latin America.* London, 1975
DeConde, A., *The American Secretary of State.* London, 1963, repr. 1976
Morgan, R., *The United States and West Germany, 1945–73.* OUP, 1975
Schwab, G., (ed.), *United States Foreign Policy at the Crossroads.* Westport, 1982
Smith, R. F., *The United States and Cuba: Business and Diplomacy, 1917–1960.* New York, 1962
Stebbins, R. P., and Adam, E. A., *Documents of American Foreign Relations, 1968–69.* New York, 1972
Vance, C., *Hard Choices: Critical Years in America's Foreign Policy.* New York, 1983

Wilcox, F. O., and Frank, R. A., *The Constitution and the Conduct of Foreign Policy.* New York, 1976

F. National Character
Coan, O. W., *America in Fiction, An Annotated List of Novels.* 5th ed. Stanford Univ. Press, 1967

Curti, M. B., *The Growth of American Thought.* 3rd ed. New York, 1964

Degler, C. N., *Out of Our Past: The Forces That Shaped Modern America.* Rev. ed. New York, 1970

Duigan, P., and Rabushka, A., (eds.), *The United States in the 1980s.* Stanford, 1980

Fawcett, E., and Thomas, T., *America and the Americans.* London, 1983

National Library: The Library of Congress. Washington 25, D.C. *Librarian:* Lawrence Quincy Mumford, AB, MA, BS.

STATES AND TERRITORIES

For information as to State and Local Government, see under UNITED STATES, *pp.* 1384–86.

Against the names of the Governors and the Secretaries of State, (D.) stands for Democrat and (R.) for Republican.

Figures for the revenues and expenditures of the various states are those of the Federal Bureau of the Census unless otherwise stated, which takes the original state figures and arranges them on a common pattern so that those of one state can be compared with those of any other.

Official publications of the various states and insular possessions are listed in the *Monthly Check-List of State Publications,* issued by the Library of Congress since 1910. Their character and contents are discussed in J. K. Wilcox's *Manual on the Use of State Publications* (1940). Of great importance bibliographically are the publications of the Historical Records Survey and the American Imprints Inventory, which record local archives, official publications and state imprints. These publications supplement those of state historical societies which usually publish journals and monographs on state and local history. An outstanding source of statistical data is the material issued by the various state planning boards and commissions, to which should be added the annual *Governmental Finances* issued by the US Bureau of the Census.

The Book of the States. Biennial. Council of State Governments, Lexington, 1953 ff.

State Government Finances. Annual. Dept. of Commerce, 1966 ff.

Regionalism
Odum, H. W., *American Regionalism, A Cultural–Historical Approach to National Integration.* New York, 1938

Visher, S. X., *Climatic Atlas of the USA.* Harvard Univ. Press, 1954

A. North-East
Gottman, J., *Megalopolis, the Urbanized North-eastern Seaboard of the US.* New York, 1964

B. The South
Clement, E., *A History of the Old South.* New York, 1949

Ezell, J. S., *The South Since 1865.* New York and London, 1963

Heseltine, W. B., and Smiley, D. L., *The South in American History.* 2nd ed. Englewood Cliffs, 1960

Stephenson, W. H., and Coulter, E. M. (ed.), *A History of the South.* 10 vols. Louisiana State Univ. Press, 1947–67

C. The Middle West
Lynd, R. S. and H. M., *Middletown: A Study in Contemporary American Culture.* New York and London, 1929.—*Middletown in Transition: A Study in Cultural Conflicts.* New York and London, 1937

Nye, R. B., *Midwestern Progressive Politics, 1870–1938.* Michigan State Univ. Press, 1959

D. The West
Fogelson, R. U., *The Fragmented Metropolis: Los Angeles, 1850–1930.* Harvard Univ. Press, 1967

Fuller, G. W., *History of the Pacific Northwest.* 2nd ed. New York, 1938

Johansen, D. O., and Gates, C. M., *Empire of the Columbia: A History of the Pacific North-West,* New York, 1957

Parrish, P. H., *Before the Covered Wagon.* Portland, Oreg., 1931

Quiett, G. C., *They Built the West: An Epic of Rails and Cities.* New York and London, 1934

Scott, H. W., *History of the Oregon Country.* 6 vols. Cambridge, Mass., 1924

Winther, O. O., *The Great Northwest: A History.* 2nd ed., rev. New York, 1950

ALABAMA

HISTORY. Alabama, settled in 1702 as part of the French Province of Louisiana, and ceded to the British in 1763, was organized as a Territory, 1817, and admitted into the Union on 14 Dec. 1819.

AREA AND POPULATION. Alabama is bounded north by Tennessee, east by Georgia, south by Florida and the Gulf of Mexico and west by Mississippi. Area, 51,998 sq. miles, including 1,562 sq. miles of inland water. Census population, 1 April 1980, 3,893,888, an increase of 13·06% over that of 1970. Estimate (1985) 4,021,500. Births, 1986, 59,441 (14·5 per 1,000 population); deaths, 37,690 (9·2); infant deaths (under 1 year), 788 (13·3 per 1,000 live births); marriages, 45,778 (11·2); divorces, 25,356 (6·2).

Population in 5 census years was:

	White	Negro	Indian	Asiatic	Total	Per sq. mile
1910	1,228,832	908,282	909	70	2,138,093	41·4
1930	1,700,844	944,834	465	105	2,646,248	51·3
1960	2,283,609	980,271	1,726	915	3,266,521	64·0
			All others			
1970	2,533,831	903,467	6,867		3,444,165	66·7
1980	2,872,621	996,335	24,932		3,893,888	74·9

Of the total population in 1980, 49% were male, 61% were urban and 65% were 21 years or older.

The large cities (1980 census) were: Birmingham, 284,413 (metropolitan area, 847,487); Mobile, 200,452 (443,536); Huntsville, 142,513 (308,593); Montgomery (capital), 177,857 (272,687); Tuscaloosa, 75,211 (137,541).

CLIMATE. Birmingham. Jan. 46°F (7·8°C), July 80°F (26·7°C). Annual rainfall 54″ (1,346 mm). Mobile. Jan. 52°F (11·1°C), July 82°F (27·8°C). Annual rainfall 63″ (1,577 mm). Montgomery. Jan. 49°F (9·4°C), July 81°F (27·2°C). Annual rainfall 53″ (1,321 mm). *See* Gulf Coast, p. 1379. The growing season ranges from 190 days (north) to 270 days (south).

CONSTITUTION AND GOVERNMENT. The present constitution dates from 1901; it has had 471 amendments (at 20 Oct. 1987). The legislature consists of a Senate of 35 members and a House of Representatives of 105 members, all elected for 4 years. The Governor and Lieut.-Governor are elected for 4 years.

The state is represented in Congress by 2 senators and 7 representatives. Applicants for registration must take an oath of allegiance to the United States and fill out a questionnaire to the satisfaction of the registrars. In the 1984 presidential election Reagan polled 872,849 votes, Mondale, 551,899.

Montgomery is the capital.

Governor: Guy Hunt (R.), 1987–91 ($70,223).
Lieut.-Governor: Jim Folsom, Jr. (D.) ($2,100 a month plus allowances).
Secretary of State: Glen Browder (D.) ($36,234 plus $14,400 allowances).

BUDGET. The total net revenue for the fiscal year ending 30 Sept. 1986 was $14,974m. ($3,073m. from tax, $1,330m. from federal payments); total net expenditure was $15,143m. ($2,290m. on education, $529m. on highways, $503m. on public welfare, $555m. on health).

The outstanding debt on 30 Sept. 1986 amounted to $2,952m.
Per capita income (1986) was $11,601.

ENERGY AND NATURAL RESOURCES

Minerals. Principal minerals (1986): Coal, limestone, sand and gravel, petroleum (21·1m. bbl.) and natural gas (146,606m. cu. ft.). Total mineral output (1986) was valued at $2,001m. of which fuels, $1,440m.

Agriculture. The number of farms in 1987 was 49,000, covering 11·0m. acres; average farm had 224 acres and was valued at about $164,000.

Cash receipts from farm marketings, 1986: Crops, $645m.; livestock and poultry products, $1,431m.; and total, $2,076m. Principal crops: peanuts, soybeans, cotton, corn, wheat and potatoes; hay, sorghum, pecans, peaches and vegetables are also important. In 1986, poultry accounted for the largest percentage of cash receipts from farm marketings; cattle and calves were second, peanuts third, horticulture fourth.

Forestry. Area of national forest lands, Oct. 1983, 644,432 acres; state-owned forest, 147,400; industrial forest, 4,458,000; private non-industrial forest, 16m.; other government-owned forest, 324,200.

INDUSTRY. Alabama is predominantly industrial. In 1986 manufacturing establishments employed 357,500 workers; government, 297,000; trade, 320,400; services, 258,200; transport and public utilities, 71,500 (total non-agricultural workforce 1·5m.).

TOURISM. In 1986 about 28·6m. travelled to or through Alabama from other states. Total income from tourism (including receipts from Alabama holiday-makers) was about $4,000m.

COMMUNICATIONS

Roads. Paved roads of all classes at 5 Jan. 1987 totalled 60,254 miles; total highways, 87,798 miles.

Railways. At 5 Jan. 1987 the railways had a length of 6,377 miles including side and yard tracks.

Aviation. In 1987 the state had 103 public-use airports; 91 were publicly owned and 12 privately owned.

Shipping. There are 1,200 miles of navigable inland water and 50 miles of Gulf Coast. The only deep-water port is Mobile, with a large ocean-going trade; total tonnage (1983), 34·9m. tons. The docks can handle 33 ocean-going vessels at once. The 9-ft channel of the Tennessee River traverses North Alabama for 200 miles; the Tennessee-Tombigbee waterway (232 miles), open Feb. 1985, connects the Tennessee River with the Tombigbee River for access to the Gulf of Mexico. The Warrier–Tombigbee system (476 miles) connects the Birmingham industrial area to the Gulf. The Coosa-Alabama River system reaches central Alabama as far north as Montgomery from Mobile and the Gulf Intracoastal Waterway. The Alabama State Docks also operates a system of 11 inland docks; there are several privately-run inland docks.

JUSTICE, RELIGION, EDUCATION AND WELFARE

Justice. The prison population on 30 Sept. 1986 was 11,471.

From 1 Jan. 1927 to 28 Aug. 1987 there were 156 executions (electrocution): 124 for murder, 25 for rape, 5 for armed robbery, 1 for burglary and 1 for carnal knowledge. Before 1 Jan. 1927, persons executed in Alabama were hanged locally by the sheriffs in the counties of their conviction.

In 41 counties the sale of alcoholic beverage is permitted, and in 26 counties it is prohibited; but it is permitted in 7 cities within those 26 counties.

Religion. Chief religious bodies (in 1980) are: Southern Baptist Convention (about 1,182,018), Churches of Christ (113,919), United Methodist (about 344,790), Roman Catholic (106,123), African Methodist Episcopal Zion (139,714), Christian Methodist Episcopal (about 53,493) and Assemblies of God (48,610).

Education. In the school year 1986–87 the 1,326 public elementary and high schools required 36,695 teachers to teach 719,715 pupils enrolled in grades K-12. In 1987 there were 16 senior public institutions with 106,343 students and 5,625 faculty members. In 1986 the 14 junior colleges had 38,169 students and 838 teachers, 20 technical schools had 22,191 students and 1,118 teachers.

Health. In 1986 there were 112 hospitals (20,144 beds) licensed by the State Board of Health. In 1986 hospitals for mental diseases had 2,236 beds. Facilities for the mentally retarded (1 Oct. 1987) had 1,320 certified beds.

Pensions and Security. In March 1987 Alabama paid supplements (to federal welfare payments) to 11,681 recipients of old-age assistance, receiving an average of \$53.34 each; 5,952 permanently and totally disabled, \$57.49; 129 blind, \$54.73. Combined state–federal aid to dependent children was paid to 47,874 families, average \$114.36 per family.

Books of Reference

Alabama Official and Statistical Register. Montgomery. Quadrennial
Alabama Encyclopædia. Vol. I. Northport, 1965
Economic Abstract of Alabama. Center for Business and Economic Research, Univ. of Alabama, 1987
McCurley, R. L., Jr., ed., *The Legislative Process.* Alabama Law Institute, 3rd ed., 1984
Thigpen, R. A., and Coleman, B. R., Jr., *Alabama Government Manual.* Alabama Law Institute, 6th ed., 1982
Wiggins, S. W., (ed.) From Civil War to Civil Rights, 1860–1960. Univ. of Alabama Press, 1987

ALASKA

HISTORY. Discovered in 1741 by Vitus Bering, its first settlement, on Kodiak Island, was in 1784. The area known as Russian America with its capital (1806) at Sitka was ruled by a Russo-American fur company and vaguely claimed as a Russian colony. Alaska was purchased by the United States from Russia under the treaty of 30 March 1867 for \$7·2m. It was not organized until 1884, when it became a 'district' governed by the code of the state of Oregon. By Act of Congress approved 24 Aug. 1912 Alaska became an incorporated Territory; its first legislature in 1913 granted votes to women, 7 years in advance of the Constitutional Amendment.

Alaska officially became the 49th state of the Union on 3 Jan. 1959.

AREA AND POPULATION. Alaska is bounded north by the Beaufort Sea, west and south by the Pacific and east by Canada. It has the largest area of any state, being more than twice the size of Texas. The gross area (land and water) is 591,004 sq. miles; the land area is 586,412 sq. miles of which 85% was in federal ownership in 1984. Census population, 1 April 1980, was 401,851, including military personnel, an increase of 33·5% over 1970. Estimate (1985), 521,000. Births, 1984, were 12,247 (24·5 per 1,000 population); deaths, 1,993 (4); infant deaths, 147 (12 per 1,000 live births); marriages, 6,519 (13); divorces, 3,904 (7·8).

Population in 5 census years was:

	White	Negro	All Others	Total	Per sq. mile
1940	39,170	...	33,354	72,524	0·13
1950	92,808	...	35,835	128,643	0·23
1960	174,649	...	51,518	226,167	0·40
1970	236,767	8,911	54,704	300,382	0·53
1980	309,728	13,643	78,480	401,851	0·70

Of the total population in 1980, 53·01% were male, 64·34% were urban and 68·57% were aged 21 years or over.

The largest city is Anchorage, which had a 1980 census area population of 174,430 (1983 estimate, 227,100). Other census area populations, 1980 (and 1983 estimate), Fairbanks North Star, 53,983 (64,800); Juneau, 19,528 (26,000); Kenai Peninsula, 25,282 (34,900); Ketchikan Gateway, 11,316 (12,700); Kodiak Island, 9,939 (12,900); Matanuska-Susitna 17,816 (29,800). There are 11 boroughs and 142 incorporated cities.

CLIMATE. Anchorage. Jan. 12°F (−11·1°C), July 57°F (13·9°C). Annual rainfall 15″ (371 mm). Fairbanks. Jan. −11°F (−23·9°C), July 60°F (15·6°C). Annual rainfall 12″ (300 mm). Sitka. Jan. 33°F (0·6°C), July 55°F (12·8°C). Annual rainfall 87″ (2,175 mm). *See* Pacific Coast, p. 1378.

CONSTITUTION AND GOVERNMENT. An important provision of the Enabling Act is that the state has the right to select 103·55m. acres of vacant and unappropriated public lands in order to establish 'a tax basis'; it can open these lands to prospectors for minerals, and the state is to derive the principal advantage in all gains resulting from the discovery of minerals. In addition, certain federally administered lands reserved for conservation of fisheries and wild life have been transferred to the state. Special provision is made for federal control of land for defence in areas of high strategic importance.

The constitution of Alaska was adopted by public vote, 24 April 1956. The state legislature consists of a Senate of 20 members (elected for 4 years) and a House of Representatives of 40 members (elected for 2 years). The state sends 2 senators and 1 representative to Congress. The franchise may be exercised by all citizens over 18.

The capital is Juneau. A new capital site near Anchorage was chosen in 1976.

In the 1984 presidential election Reagan polled 138,392 votes, Mondale, 62,018.

Governor: Stephen Cowper (D.), 1986–90 ($81,648).
Lieut.-Governor: Steve McAlpine (D.) 1986–90 ($76,188).

ECONOMY

Budget. Total state government revenue for the year ended 30 June 1984 (Annual Financial Report figures) was $3,935·8m. ($2,914m. from petroleum revenue, $109·4m. from taxation). Total expenditure was $3,931·3m.

In 1976 a Permanent Fund was set up for the deposit of at least 25% of all mineral-related revenue; total assets at 30 June, 1984, $5,530·8m.

General obligation bonds at 30 June 1984, $169·5m.

Per capita income (1985) was $18,187.

ENERGY AND NATURAL RESOURCES

Oil and Gas. Commercial production of crude petroleum began in 1959 and by 1961 had become the most important mineral by value. Production: 1961, 6·3m. bbls (of 42 gallons); 1976, 67m. bbls; 1977, 169m. bbls; 1981, 587m. bbls; 1985, 666m. bbls. Oil comes mainly from Prudhoe Bay, the Kuparuk River field and several Cook Inlet fields. Natural gas marketed production, 1985, 324,000m. cu. ft. Alaska receives 84% of its total revenue from petroleum. Revenue to the state from oil production in 1984 was $2,861·6m. from corporate petroleum tax $265·1m. and from royalties $1,047·5m., severance tax, $1,393·1m., property tax, $131m., bonus sale, $10·1m., rents, $3·8m., intergovernmental receipts, $11·1m.

Oil from the Prudhoe Bay arctic field is now carried by the Trans-Alaska pipeline to Prince William Sound on the south coast, where a tanker terminal has been built at Valdez.

Minerals. Value of production, 1983: gold (169,000 troy oz.) $67·6m.; antimony (22,400 lb.) $25,000; platinum $100,000; silver (33,200 troy oz.) $332,000; tin (215,000 lb.) $1·1m.; jade and soapstone (2·3 tons) $42,000; sand and gravel (50m. short tons) $120m.; building stone (5·27m. short tons) $25m.; coal (803,000m. short tons) $18m. Total value, $232,399,000.

Agriculture. In some parts of the state the climate during the brief spring and summer (about 100 days in major areas and 152 days in the south-eastern coastal area) is suitable for agricultural operations, thanks to the long hours of sunlight, but Alaska is a food-importing area. In 1985 about 2m. acres was farmland; 90% of this was unimproved pasture primarily government leases for grazing of sheep and beef cattle in south-west Alaska. In 1980 (preliminary) there were 8,400 cattle, 1,100 milch cows, 1,800 hogs and 4,300 sheep stock.

Farm income in 1985: $26m. of which $18m. was from crops (mainly hay and potatoes) and $8m. from livestock and dairy products.

There were about 25,000 reindeer in western Alaska in 1980, owned by individual Eskimo herders except for 750 at Nome owned by the Government.

Forestry. In south-eastern Alaska timber fringes the shore of the mainland and all the islands extending inland to a depth of 5 miles. The state's enormous forests could produce an estimated annual sustained yield of 1,500m. bd ft of lumber, nearly twice Alaska's record 1973 cut. Alaska has 2 national forests: the Tongass of 16·9m. acres and the Chugach of 5·9m. acres. An estimated total of 446m. bd ft was cut in 1981, of which 387·5m. came from national forests and 53,687,000 from state forests, 4,275,000 from land held by the Bureau of Indian Affairs and 362,000 from the Bureau of Land Management. Alaska has 2 large pulp-mills at Ketchikan and Sitka.

Fisheries. The catch for 1985 was 1,185m. lb. of fish and shellfish having a value to fishermen of $591m. The most important fish are salmon, crab, herring and shrimp.

INDUSTRY. Main industries with employment, 1985: Government, 68,000; trade, 46,000; services, 45,000; contract construction, 19,000; manufacturing, 12,000; mining including oil and gas, (1984) 7,900; transport, communication and utilities, 19,000; finance, insurance and property, 13,000.

The major manufacturing industry was food processing, followed by timber industries. Total non-agricultural employment, 1984, 224,100. Total wages and salaries, 1983, $6,075·7m.

TOURISM. About 691,200 tourists visited the state in 1984.

COMMUNICATIONS

Roads. Alaska's highway and road system, 1984, totalled 15,315 miles, including marine highway systems, local service roads, borough and city streets, national park, forest and reservation roads and military roads. Registered motor vehicles, 1985, 382,000.

The Alaska Highway extends 1,523 miles from Dawson Creek, British Columbia, to Fairbanks, Alaska. It was built by the US Army in 1942, at a cost of $138m. The greater portion of it, because it lies in Canada, is maintained by Canada.

Railways. There is a railway of 111 miles from Skagway to the town of Whitehorse, the White Pass and Yukon route, in the Canadian Yukon region (this service was suspended in 1982 but may reopen). The government-owned Alaska Railroad runs from Seward to Fairbanks, a distance of 471 miles. This is a freight service with only occasional passenger use. A passenger service operates from Anchorage to Fairbanks via Denali National Park in the tourist season.

Aviation. In 1982 the state had about 1,070 airports, of which about half were publicly owned. Commercial passengers by air from Alaska's largest international airports Anchorage and Fairbanks numbered 1·1m. at Anchorage and 273,512 at Fairbanks. General aviation aircraft in the state per 1,000 population was about ten times the US average.

Shipping. Regular shipping services to and from the US are furnished by 2 steamship and several barge lines operating out of Seattle and other Pacific coast ports. A Canadian company also furnishes a regular service from Vancouver, B.C. Anchorage is the main port.

A 1,435 nautical-mile ferry system for motor cars and passengers (the 'Alaska Marine Highway') operates from Seattle, Washington and Prince Rupert (British Columbia) to Juneau, Haines (for access to the Alaska Highway) and Skagway. A second system extends throughout the south-central region of Alaska linking the Cook Inlet area with Kodiak Island and Prince William Sound.

JUSTICE, RELIGION, EDUCATION AND WELFARE

Justice. There is no death penalty in Alaska. At 31 Dec. 1985 there were 2,311 prisoners in state and federal institutions.

Religion. Many religions are represented, including the Russian Orthodox, Roman Catholic, Episcopalian, Presbyterian, Methodist and other denominations.

Education. Total expenditure on public schools in 1986 was $806m. or $1,548 per capita. There were 19,100 elementary and 17,900 secondary school teachers, salary, $17,900. During 1984 there were 100,000 pupils at public schools, 3,868 at private schools. The Bureau of Indian Affairs schools had 1,005 pupils. The University of Alaska (founded in 1922) had (Spring 1984) 11,808 students in Fairbanks, Anchorage and Juneau and 19,296 in community colleges. Other colleges had 1,775 students in 1984.

Health. In 1983 there were 26 acute care hospitals with 1,800 beds, of which 7 were federal public health hospitals; 1 mental hospital; 24 mental health clinics.

Welfare. Old-age assistance was established under the Federal Social Security Act; in 1985 aid to dependent children covered a monthly average of 6,400 households; payments, an average of $501 per month; aid to the disabled was given to a monthly average of 2,300 persons receiving on average $251 per month. An average of 1,100 aged per month received $166.

Books of Reference

Statistical Information: Department of Commerce and Economic Development, Economic Analysis Section, Juneau.

Alaska Blue Book, Department of Education, Juneau. Biennial
Alaska Economic Outlook, Department of Labor, Juneau.
Alaska Economy, The. Division of Economic Enterprise, Juneau. Annual
Alaska Statistical Review. Office of the Governor, Juneau. Biennial
Annual Financial Report, Department of Administration, Juneau.
Gardey, J., *Alaska: The Sophisticated Wilderness.* London, 1976
Hulley, Clarence C., *Alaska Past and Present.* Portland, Oregon, 1970
Hunt, W. R., *Alaska, a Bicentennial History.* New York, 1976
Pearson, R. W., and Lynch, D. F., *Alaska, a Geography.* Boulder, 1984
Thomas, L., Jr., *Alaska and the Yukon.* New York, 1983
Tourville, M., *Alaska, a Bibliography, 1570–1970.* 1971

State Library: Pouch G, Juneau. *Librarian:* Richard Engen.—Alaska Historical Library, Pouch G, Juneau. *Librarian:* Phyllis de Muth.

ARIZONA

HISTORY. Arizona was settled in 1752, organized as a Territory in 1863 and became a state on 14 Feb. 1912.

AREA AND POPULATION. Arizona is bounded north by Utah, east by New Mexico, south by Mexico, west by California and Nevada. Area, 113,417 sq. miles, including 347 sq. miles of inland water. Of the total area in 1985, 28% was Indian Reservation, 18% was in individual or corporate ownership, 16% was held by the US Bureau of Land Management, 15% by the US Forest Service, 13% by the State and 10% by others. Census population on 1 April 1980 was 2,718,425, an increase of 53·4% over 1970. Estimate (1986) 3,296,000. Births, 1985, 59,344; deaths, 24,577; infant deaths (1983), 509; marriages, 35,723; divorces, 21,157.

Population in 5 census years:

	White	Negro	Indian	Chinese	Japanese	Total	Per sq. mile
1910	171,468	2,009	29,201	1,305	371	204,354	1·8
1930	378,551	10,749	43,726	1,110	879	435,573	3·8
1960	1,169,517	43,403	83,387	2,937	1,501	1,302,161	11·3
				All others			
1970	1,604,498	53,344		117,557		1,775,399	15·6
1980	2,260,288	74,159		383,768		2,718,215 ¹	23·9

¹ Preliminary.

Of the population in 1980, 1,375,214 were male, 2,278,728 were urban and 1,872,447 were aged 20 and over.

The 1980 census population of Phoenix was 789,704 (1986 estimate, 881,640); Tucson, 330,537 (384,385); Scottsdale, 88,412 (108,447); Tempe, 106,743 (132,942); Mesa, 152,453 (239,587); Glendale, 97,172 (122,392).

CLIMATE. Phoenix. Jan. 52°F (11·1°C), July 90°F (32·2°C). Annual rainfall 8″ (191 mm). Yuma. Jan. 55°F (12·8°C), July 91°F (32·8°C). Annual rainfall 3″ (75 mm). *See* Mountain States, p. 1378.

CONSTITUTION AND GOVERNMENT. The state constitution (1910, with 103 amendments) placed the government under direct control of the people through the Initiative, Referendum and the Recall. The state Senate consists of 30 members, and the House of Representatives of 60, all elected for 2 years. Arizona sends to Congress 2 senators and 5 representatives. In the 1984 presidential election Reagan polled 669,353 votes, Mondale, 325,924.

The state capital is Phoenix. The state is divided into 15 counties.

Governor: Evan Mecham (R.), 1987–91 ($75,000).

Secretary of State: Rose Mofford (D.) ($50,000).

BUDGET. General revenues, year ending 30 June 1985 (US Census Bureau figures), were $2,197m. (taxation, $2,049·4m.); general expenditures, $3,133m. (education, $1,329·7m.; transport $438m., and public health and welfare, $769·4m.).

Per capita income (1985) was $12,454.

NATURAL RESOURCES

Minerals. The mining industries of the state are important, but less so than agriculture and manufacturing. By value the most important mineral produced is copper. Production (1985) 887,052 short tons; gold and silver are both largely recovered from copper ore. Other minerals include sand and gravel and lead. Total value of minerals mined in 1985 was $1,532·6m.

Agriculture. Arizona, despite its dry climate, is well suited for agriculture along the water-courses and where irrigation is practised on a large scale from great reservoirs constructed by the US as well as by the state government and private interests. Irrigated area, 1984, 1·07m. acres. The wide pasture lands are favourable for the rearing of cattle and sheep, but numbers are either stationary or declining compared with 1920.

In 1986 Arizona contained 9,000 farms and ranches with 1·05m. acres of crop land, out of a total farm and pastoral area of 38m. acres. The average farm was estimated at 4,222 acres. Farming is highly commercialized and mechanized and concentrated largely on cotton picked by machines and by Indian, Mexican and migratory workers.

Area under cotton (1985), 415,300 acres; 1,037,000m. bales (of 480 lb.) of cotton were harvested.

Cash income, 1985, from crops, $896·3m.; from livestock, $686·3m. Most important cereals are wheat, corn and barley; other crops include oranges, grapefruit and lettuce. On 1 Jan. 1985 there were 1,050,000 all cattle, 82,000 milch cows, 306,000 sheep.

Forestry. The national forests in the state had an area (1983) of 11·22m. acres.

INDUSTRY. In 1985 there were 3,482 manufacturing establishments with 163,445 production workers, earning $3,792m.

TOURISM. In 1982 15·7m. tourists visited Arizona; direct employment, 71,700; indirect, 114,600; state tax revenue, $204m.

COMMUNICATIONS

Roads. In 1982 there were 76,290 miles of public roads and streets; in 1985 2,119,000 motor vehicles were registered in the state.

Aviation. Airports, 1984, numbered 251, of which 82 were for public use; 6,079 aircraft were registered.

JUSTICE, RELIGION, EDUCATION AND WELFARE

Justice. A 'right-to-work' amendment to the constitution, adopted 5 Nov. 1946, makes illegal any concessions to trade-union demands for a 'closed shop'.

The Arizona state and federal prisons 31 Dec. 1985 held 8,518. There have been no executions since 1963; from 1930 to 1963 there were 38 executions (lethal gas) all for murder, and all men (28 whites, 10 Negro).

Religion. The leading religious bodies are Roman Catholics and Mormons (Latter Day Saints); others include Methodists, Presbyterians, Baptists and Episcopalians.

Education. School attendance is compulsory to grade 9 (from 1985–86) and to grade 10 (from 1986–87). In autumn 1985 there were 513,498 pupils enrolled in grades K-12. In 1986 spending on public schools was $1,589m. or $499 per capita. The state maintains 3 universities: the University of Arizona (Tucson) with an enrollment of 32,318 in autumn 1985; Arizona State University (Tempe) with 38,029; Northern Arizona University (Flagstaff) with 11,935.

Health. In 1985 there were 88 hospitals reported by the State Department of Health; capacity 13,890 beds; the hospitals had 1,522 physicians and dentists, 8,437 registered nurses and 1,503 licensed practical nurses.

Social Security. Old-age assistance (maximum depending on the programme) is given, with federal aid, to needy citizens 65 years of age or older. In June 1985, federal Social Security Insurance payments went to 10,500 aged ($158 each), and 22,000 disabled ($251); 71,900 people in 25,200 families received aid for families with dependent children.

Books of Reference

Arizona Statistical Review. 42nd ed. Valley National Bank, Phoenix, 1986
Federal Writers' Project. *Arizona: The Grand Canyon State.* 4th ed. New York, 1966
Comeaux, M. L., *Arizona: a Geography.* Boulder, 1981
Faulk, O. B., *Arizona: A Short History.* Univ. Oklahoma Press, 1970
Goff, J. S., *Arizona Civilization.* 2nd ed. Cave Creek, 1970
Mason, B. B., and Hink, H., *Constitutional Government of Arizona.* 7th ed. Tempe, 1982

State Library: Department of Library, Archives and Public Records, Capitol, Phoenix 85007. *Director:* Sharon G. Turgeon.

ARKANSAS

HISTORY. Arkansas was settled in 1686, made a territory in 1819 and admitted into the Union on 15 June 1836. The name originated with the Quapaw Indian tribe. The constitution, which dates from 1874, has been amended 59 times.

AREA AND POPULATION. Arkansas is bounded north by Missouri, east by Tennessee and Mississippi, south by Louisiana, south-west by Texas and west by Oklahoma. Area, 53,187 sq. miles (1,109 sq. miles being inland water). Census population on 1 April 1980 was 2,286,435, an increase of 18·9% from that of 1970. Estimate (1984) 2,349,000. Births, 1983, were 34,904 (15·3 per 1,000 population); deaths, 23,086 (10·1); infant deaths, 373 (10·6 per 1,000 live births); marriages, 30,066 (13·1); divorces 15,681 (6·9).

Population in 5 census years was:

	White	Negro	Indian	Asiatic	Total	Per sq. mile
1910	1,131,026	442,891	460	72	1,574,449	30·0
1930	1,375,315	478,463	408	296	1,854,482	35·2
1960	1,395,703	388,787	580	1,202	1,786,272	34·0
			All others			
1970	1,565,915	352,445	4,935		1,923,295	37·0
1980	1,890,332	373,768	22,335		2,286,435	43·9

Of the total population in 1980, 48·3% were male, 51·6% were urban, 60·2% were 21 years of age or older.

Little Rock (capital) had a population of 158,461 in 1980; Fort Smith, 71,626; North Little Rock, 64,288; Pine Bluff, 56,636; Fayetteville, 36,608; Hot Springs, 35,781; Jonesboro, 31,530; West Memphis, 28,138. The population of the largest standard metropolitan statistical areas: Little Rock–North Little Rock, 393,774; Fayetteville–Springdale, 178,609; Fort Smith (Arkansas portion), 132,064; Pine Bluff, 90,718; Memphis (Arkansas portion), 49,499; Texarkana (Arkansas portion), 37,766.

CLIMATE. Little Rock. Jan. 42°F (5·6°C), July 81°F (27·2°C). Annual rainfall 49″ (1,222 mm). *See* Gulf Coast, p. 1379.

GOVERNMENT. The General Assembly consists of a Senate of 35 members elected for 4 years, partially renewed every 2 years, and a House of Representatives of 100 members elected for 2 years. The sessions are biennial and usually limited to 60 days. The Governor and Lieut.-Governor are elected for 2 years. The state is represented in Congress by 2 senators and 4 representatives.

In the 1984 presidential election Reagan polled 533,624 votes, Mondale, 338,829.

The state is divided into 75 counties; the capital is Little Rock.

Governor: Bill Clinton (D.), 1987–91 ($35,000).
Lieut.-Governor: Winston Bryant (D.) ($14,000).
Secretary of State: W. J. McCuen (D.) ($22,500).

FINANCE

Budget. The state's general revenue for the fiscal year 1985 was $1,745m., of which taxation furnished $690·6m. and federal aid, $818·1m. General expenditure was $2,797·2m., of which education took $1,232·7m.; highways, $363·4m., and public welfare, $461·5m.

Net long-term debt for the financial year 1985 was $135·2m.
Per capita income (1986) was $11,073.

Banking. In 1986 total bank deposits were $14,844·7m.

ENERGY AND NATURAL RESOURCES

Minerals. In 1987 crude petroleum amounted to 38·1m. bbls; natural gas, 418·4m. cu. ft; the state is an important source of bauxite, bromine, special abrasive silica stone and barite; it is one of four states producing tripoli and vanadium and one of two shipping gallium.

Agriculture. In 1986 50,525 farms had a total area of 14m. acres; average farm was of 291 acres; 7,484,316 acres were harvested cropland; 2,022,695 acres were irrigated.

The largest sources of income in 1985 were chickens including broilers

($1,993·2m.); soybeans ($558·7m.); cattle and calves ($250·1m.); rice ($421·9m.); wheat ($58·4m.). Cash farm income (1985) was $3,280m.; from crops, $1,454·9m., and from livestock, $1,825·3m.

Livestock on 1 Jan. 1987 included 1·8m. all cattle, 62,000 milch cows and 460,000 swine.

INDUSTRY. In July 1987 total employment averaged 1,003,200 (53,200 agricultural, 219,900 manufacturing, 193,500 wholesale and retail trade, 131,800 government). The Arkansas Department of Labor estimated that 179,900 factory production workers earned an average $325.56 per week (40·09 hours). The most important manufacturing group was food and kindred products employing 46,300, followed by electric and electronic equipment (23,000) and lumber and wood products (19,200). Construction employed 37,400.

COMMUNICATIONS

Roads. Total road mileage, 82,648 miles. State-maintained highways (1 Jan. 1987) total 16,126 miles; local county highways, 49,664 miles; city streets, 9,627 miles; federal roads, 1,639 miles; roads not publicly maintained, 5,598 miles. In 1986 there were 1,870,767 registered motor vehicles.

Railways. In 1987 there were in the state 3,282 miles of commercial railway.

Aviation. Six air carrier and 1 commuter airlines serve the state; there were, in 1986, 167 airports (92 public-use and 75 private).

Waterways. There are about 1,000 miles of navigable streams, including the Mississippi, Arkansas, Red, White and Ouachita Rivers. The Arkansas River/ Kerr-McClellan Channel flows diagonally eastward across the state and gives access to the sea *via* the Mississippi River.

RELIGION, EDUCATION AND WELFARE

Religion. Main protestant churches in 1980: Baptist (603,844), Methodist (214,925), Church of Christ (90,671), Assembly of God (53,555). Roman Catholics (1980), 56,911.

Education. In the school year 1985–86 public elementary and secondary schools had 433,410 enrolled pupils and 21,242 classroom teachers. Average salaries of teachers in elementary schools was $19,021, secondary $20,075. Expenditure on elementary and secondary education was $1,201m.

An educational TV network provides a full 12-hour-day telecasting; it had 5 stations in 1984.

Higher education is provided at 32 institutions: 12 state universities, 1 medical college, 12 private or church colleges, 10 community or junior colleges. Total enrolment in institutions of higher education, 1986–87, was 81,810.

There were (1986–87) 24 vocational-technical schools with 34,876 students, including extension class students. Total expenditure, $28·5m.

Health. There were 106 licensed hospitals (12,858 beds) in 1987, and 230 licensed nursing homes (21,443 beds).

Social Welfare. In 1985 440,000 persons drew social security payments; retired workers, $246,000; disabled workers, $40,000; widows and widowers, $64,000.

State prisons in Oct. 1985 had 4,620 inmates (197 per 100,000 population).

Books of Reference

Current Employment Developments. Arkansas Employment Security Division, Little Rock
Arkansas State and County Economic Data. Regional Economic Analysis, Univ. Arkansas, Little Rock
State Government Finances. U.S. Dept. of Commerce, Bureau of the Census.
Agricultural Statistics for Arkansas. U.S. Dept. of Agriculture, Crop Reporting Service, Little Rock, 1985
Ferguson and Atkinson, *Historic Arkansas.* Little Rock, 1966
Fletcher, J. G., *Arkansas.* Univ. N. Carolina, Chapel Hill, 1947

CALIFORNIA

HISTORY. California, first settled in July 1769, was from its discovery until 1846 politically associated with Mexico. On 7 July 1846 the American flag was hoisted at Monterey, and a proclamation was issued declaring California to be a portion of the US. On 2 Feb. 1848, by the treaty of Guadalupe–Hidalgo, the territory was formally ceded by Mexico to the US, and was admitted to the Union 9 Sept. 1850 as the thirty-first state, with boundaries as at present.

AREA AND POPULATION. Area, 158,693 sq. miles (2,120 sq. miles being inland water). In 1985 the federal government owned 48m. acres (48% of the land area); in 1984, 570,000 acres were under jurisdiction of the Bureau of Indian Affairs, of which 501,000 acres were tribal. Public lands, vacant in 1975, totalled 15,607,125 acres, practically all either mountains or deserts.

Census population, 1 April 1980, 23,667,902, an increase of 18·5% over 1970, making California the most populous state of the USA (New York: 17,557,288). Estimate (1987) 27,662,900. Births in 1984, 455,075 (17·8 per 1,000 population); deaths, 195,430 (7·6); infant deaths, 4,245 (9·3 per 1,000 live births); marriages, 226,560 (8·8); divorces, dissolutions and nullities, 129,131 in 1983 (5·1).

Population in 5 census years was:

	White	Negro	Japanese	Chinese	Total (incl. all others)	Per sq. mile
1910	2,259,672	21,645	41,356	36,248	2,377,549	15·0
1930	5,408,260	81,048	97,456	37,361	5,677,251	35·8
1960	14,455,230	883,861	157,317	95,600	15,717,204	99·0
1970	17,761,032	1,400,143	213,280	170,131	19,953,134	125·7
1980	18,030,893	1,819,281	All other 3,817,728		23,667,902	149·1

Of the 1980 population 49·3% were male, 91·3% were urban and 67·2% were 21 years old or older.

The largest cities with 1980 census population are:

Los Angeles	2,966,850	Anaheim	219,494	Fremont	131,945
San Diego	875,538	Fresno	217,289	Torrance	129,881
San Francisco	678,974	Santa Ana	204,023	Garden Grove	123,307
San José	629,546	Riverside	170,591	San Bernardino	118,794
Long Beach	361,334	Huntington Beach	170,505	Pasadena	118,550
Oakland	339,337	Stockton	149,779	Oxnard	108,195
Sacramento	275,741	Glendale	139,060		

Urbanized areas (1980 census): Los Angeles–Long Beach, 9,477,926; San Francisco–Oakland, 3,191,913; San Diego, 1,704,352; San José, 1,243,900; Sacramento, 796,266; San Bernardino–Riverside, 703,316; Oxnard–Ventura–Thousand Oaks, 378,420; Fresno, 331,551.

CLIMATE. Los Angeles. Jan. 55°F (12·8°C), July 70°F (21·1°C). Annual rainfall 15″ (381 mm). Sacramento. Jan. 45°F (7·2°C), July 74°F (23·3°C). Annual rainfall 19″ (472 mm). San Diego. Jan. 55°F (12·8°C), July 69°F (20·6°C). Annual rainfall 10″ (259 mm). San Francisco. Jan. 50°F (10°C), July 59°F (15°C). Annual rainfall 22″ (561 mm). Death Valley. Jan. 52°F (11°C), July 100°F (38°C). Annual rainfall 1·6″ (40 mm). *See* Pacific Coast, p. 1378.

CONSTITUTION AND GOVERNMENT. The present constitution became effective from 4 July 1879; it has had numerous amendments since 1962. The Senate is composed of 40 members elected for 4 years—half being elected each 2 years—and the Assembly, of 80 members, elected for 2 years. Two-year regular sessions convene in Dec. of each even-numbered year. The Governor and Lieut.-Governor are elected for 4 years.

California is represented in Congress by 2 senators and 45 representatives.

In the 1984 presidential election Reagan polled 5,291,747 votes, Mondale, 3,803,913.

The capital is Sacramento. The state is divided into 58 counties.

Governor: George Deukmejian (R.), 1987–91 ($49,100).
Lieut.-Governor: Leo McCarthy (D.), 1987–91 ($42,500).
Secretary of State: March Fong Eu (D.) ($42,500).

BUDGET. For the year ending 30 June 1987 total General Fund revenues were $31,469m.; total General Fund expenditures were $36,840m. ($17,030m. for education, $9,556m. for health and welfare).

The long-term state debt (general obligation bonds outstanding) was $8,029m. on 30 June 1987.

Per capita personal income (1986) was $16,904.

ENERGY AND NATURAL RESOURCES

Minerals. California is one of the three most important petroleum-producing states of the US (Texas and Louisiana being the other two); crude oil output was estimated at 378,537m. bbls in 1986. Output of natural gas was 416,413m. cu. ft; of natural gas liquids, (1985) 340m. bbls. Gold output was 223,097 troy oz. (1985); asbestos, boron minerals, diatomite, tungsten, sand and gravel, salt, magnesium compounds, lead, zinc, copper and iron ore are also produced. The estimated value of all the minerals produced was $2,218m. in 1985.

Agriculture. Extending 700 miles from north to south, and intersected by several ranges of mountains, California has almost every variety of climate, from the very wet to the very dry, and from the temperate to the semi-tropical.

In 1985 there were 82,468 farms, comprising 32m. acres; average farm, 390 acres. Cotton, fruit, poultry and vegetables are important. Cash receipts, 1985, from crops, $13,976m.; from livestock and poultry, $4,165m. Dairy produce, cattle, grapes, nursery products, cotton, hay, flowers and foliage, and lettuce (in that order) are the main sources of farm income.

Production of cotton lint, 1986, was 538,800 short tons; other field crops included sugar-beet (4·8m. short tons). Principal crops include wine, table and raisin grapes (4·8m. short tons); peaches (714,000 short tons); pears (294,000 short tons); apricots (55,200 short tons); prunes (99,000 short tons); plums, nectarines, avocados, olives and cherries. Citrus fruit crops were: oranges, 2·1m. short tons; lemons, 573,800 short tons; grapefruit, 276,000 short tons.

On 1 Jan. 1986 the farm animals were: 1m. milch cows, 5m. all cattle, 860,000 sheep and 145,000 swine.

Forestry. Total forest area in 1985 was 20,578,000 acres, of which 8,286,000 acres were commercial forest. California ranks third to Oregon and Washington in volume of standing timber; total annual cut is about 4,099m. bd ft (1986). National forest service land in 1986 was 20·6m. acres.

Fishery. California ranks sixth as a fishing state (by value of fishery products). The catch in 1986 was 422·5m. lb.; leading species were mackerel, tuna and squid.

INDUSTRY. In 1986, manufacturing employed about 2·1m. The fastest-growing industries were transport equipment, printing and publishing and textile mill products. The aerospace industry is important, as is food-processing.

COMMUNICATIONS

Roads. In 1986 California had 56,534 miles of roads inside cities and 118,558 miles outside. In 1986 there were about 15·2m. registered cars and over 4·5m. commercial vehicles, leading all states in all items by a wide margin.

Railways. Total mileage of railways in 1986, was 8,044 miles. There are 2 systems: Amtrak and Southern Pacific Railroad commuter trains. Amtrak carries about 1·7m. passengers per year on the intra-state routes. Southern Pacific carries about 5·4m. on a commuter route. Amtrak services run from San Francisco and Los Angeles. Southern Pacific runs the Caltrains commuter route from San Francisco to San Jose. There is a metro (BART) and light rail (Muni) system in San Francisco. There is a light rail line in San Diego and Sacramento and another under construction in San Jose.

Aviation. In 1986 there were 283 public airports and 739 private airstrips.

Shipping. The chief ports are San Francisco and Los Angeles.

JUSTICE, RELIGION, EDUCATION AND WELFARE

Justice. State prisons, 1 Jan. 1987, had 55,920 male and 3,564 female inmates. From 1893 to 1942, 307 inmates were executed by hanging. From 1938 to 1976, 194 inmates were executed by lethal gas. No further death sentences were passed until 1980.

Religion. The Roman Catholic Church is much stronger than any other single church; next are the Jewish congregations, then Methodists, Presbyterians, Baptists and Episcopalians.

Education. Full-time attendance at school is compulsory for children from 6 to 16 years of age for a minimum of 175 days per annum, and part-time attendance is required from 16 to 18 years. In autumn 1986 there were 4·4m. pupils enrolled in elementary and secondary schools. Estimated expenditure on public schools, 1986–87, was $17,297m.

Community Colleges had 1,046,099 students in autumn 1986.

California has two publicly supported higher education systems: the University of California (1868) and the California State University and Colleges. In autumn 1985, the University of California with campuses for resident instruction and research at Berkeley, Los Angeles, San Francisco and 6 other centres, had 152,065 full-time students. California State University and Colleges with campuses at Sacramento, Long Beach, Los Angeles, San Francisco and 15 other cities had 333,424 full-time students. In addition to the 28 publicly supported institutions for higher education there are 117 private colleges and universities which had a total estimated enrolment of 178,286 in the autumn of 1986.

Health. In 1987 there were 512 general hospitals; capacity, 105,353 beds. On 30 June 1987 state hospitals for the mentally disabled had 4,812 patients.

Social Security. On 1 Jan. 1974 the federal government (Social Security Administration) assumed responsibility for the Supplemental Security Income/State Supplemental Program which replaced the State Old-Age Security. The SSI/SSP provides financial assistance for needy aged (65 years or older), blind or disabled persons. An individual recipient may own assets up to $1,900; a couple up to $2,850, subject to specific exclusions. There are federal, state and county programmes assisting the aged, the blind, the disabled and needy children. In 1986 4,935 families per month were receiving an average of $345 per family.

Books of Reference

California Almanac, 1984–85. Fay, J. S., (ed.) Oxford, 1984
California Government and Politics. Hoeber, T. R., et al, (eds.) Sacramento, Annual
California Handbook. California Institute, 1981
California Statistical Abstract. 27th ed. Dept. of Finance, Sacramento, 1987
Economic Report of the Governor. Dept. of Finance, Sacramento, Annual
Lavender, D. S., *California.* New York, 1976

State Library: The California State Library, Library-Courts Bldg, Sacramento 95814.

COLORADO

HISTORY. Colorado was first settled in 1858, made a Territory in 1861 and admitted into the Union on 1 Aug. 1876.

AREA AND POPULATION. Colorado is bounded north by Wyoming, north-east by Nebraska, east by Kansas, south-east by Oklahoma, south by New Mexico and west by Utah. Area, 104,090 sq. miles (496 sq. miles being inland water). Federal lands, 1974, 23,974,000 acres (36% of the land area).

Census population, 1 April 1980, was 2,889,964, an increase of 680,368 or 30·8% since 1970. Estimated (1986), 3,267,118. Births, 1985, were 55,115 (17·1 per 1,000 population); deaths, 20,234 (6·4); infant deaths, 519 (9 per 1,000 live births); marriages, 33,616 (12·5); dissolutions, 19,193 (6·6).

Population in 5 census years was:

	White	Negro	Indian	Asiatic	Total	Per sq. mile
1910	783,415	11,453	1,482	2,674	799,024	7·7
1930	1,018,793	11,828	1,395	3,775	1,035,791	10·0
1950	1,296,653	20,177	1,567	5,870	1,325,089	12·7
1970	2,112,352	66,411	8,836	10,388	2,207,259	21·3
			All others			
1980	2,571,498	101,703	216,763		2,889,964	27·7

Of the total population in 1980, 49·6% were male, 80·6% were urban; 68% were aged 20 years or older. Large cities with 1980 census population (and 1986 estimate): Denver, 492,365 (514,950); Colorado Springs, 215,150 (270,724); Aurora, 158,588 (220,066); Lakewood, 112,860 (121,729); Pueblo, 101,686 (102,852); Arvada, 84,576 (90,698); Boulder, 76,685 (80,002); Fort Collins, 65,092 (78,038); Wheat Ridge, 30,293 (29,864); Greeley, 53,006 (59,036); Westminster, 50,211 (69,335).

Main metropolitan areas (1986): Denver–Boulder, 1,843,757; Fort Collins, 174,636; Colorado Springs, 380,025; Greeley, 137,271; Pueblo, 128,671; Front Range Urban Area, 2,692,304.

CLIMATE. Denver. Jan. 31°F (–0·6°C), July 73°F (22·8°C). Annual rainfall 14″ (358 mm). Pueblo. Jan. 30°F (–1·1°C), July 83°F (28·3°C). Annual rainfall 12″ (312 mm). *See* Mountain States, p. 1378.

CONSTITUTION AND GOVERNMENT. The constitution adopted in 1876 is still in effect with (1983) 78 amendments. The General Assembly consists of a Senate of 35 members elected for 4 years, one-half retiring every 2 years, and of a House of Representatives of 65 members elected for 2 years. Sessions are annual, beginning 1951. The Governor, Lieut.-Governor, Attorney-General, Secretary of State and Treasurer are elected for 4 years. Qualified as electors are all citizens, male and female (except convicted, incarcerated criminals), 18 years of age, who have resided in the state and the precinct for 32 days immediately preceding the election. The state is divided into 63 counties. The state sends to Congress 2 senators and 6 representatives.

In the 1984 presidential election Reagan polled 768,711 votes, Mondale, 434,560.

The capital is Denver.

Governor: Roy Romer (D.), 1987–91 ($60,000).
Lieut.-Governor: Nancy Dick (D.), 1987–91 ($32,500).
Secretary of State: Natalie Meyer (R.), 1987–91 ($32,500).

BUDGET. The state's total budget, 1985–86, is $3,497m., of which taxation and other revenue furnish $2,859m. and federal grants $637m. Education takes $1,708m.; health, welfare and rehabilitation, $1,037m., and highways, $440m. Total state and local taxes *per capita* (1985) were $2,167.

The state has no general obligation debt. The net long-term debt (in revenue bond) on 30 June 1985 was $139m.

Per capita personal income (1986) was $15,113.

ENERGY AND NATURAL RESOURCES

Minerals. Colorado has a variety of mineral resources. Among the most important are crude oil, metals and coal. Mineral production in 1986 (estimate) $1,000m. in value. An estimated 23,700 people were employed in extracting petroleum and natural gas in 1986; 5,000 in metals and 4,300 in coal and non-metals.

Agriculture. In May 1985 farms numbered 26,700, with a total area of 34·4m. acres. (66·7% of the land area); 7,375,000 acres were harvested crop land; average farm (1984), 1,282 acres. Cash income, 1985, from crops $1,085m.; from livestock, $1,950m. In 1984 there were 3,200,000 acres under irrigation.

Production of principal crops in 1984: Maize for grain, 134m. bu. (from 680,000 acres); wheat, 115·3m. bu. (3·0m.); hay, 3·3m. tons (1·4m.); dry beans, 2·26m. cwt (170,000); potatoes, 19·2m. cwt (51,400); sugar-beet, 920,600 tons (46,000); oats, barley and sorghums are grown, as well as fruit.

On 1 Jan. 1984 the number of farm animals was: 75,000 milch cows, 3·1m. all cattle, 690,000 sheep, 210,000 swine. The wool clip in 1984 yielded 7m. lb. of wool.

INDUSTRY. In 1986 1,448,300 were employed in non-agricultural sectors, of which 367,800 were in trade; 328,800 in services; 247,800 in government; 196,500 in manufacturing; 87,900 in construction; 88,500 in transport and public utilities; 33,000 in mining; 98,000 in finance, insurance and property. In manufacturing the biggest employers were non-electrical machinery, foods and kindred products, and printing.

TOURISM. In 1985 about 20m. people spent holidays in Colorado, of whom about 3% were Colorado residents. Overall expenditure, $4,500m.

COMMUNICATIONS

Roads. The state highway system (1983) included 9,232 miles of highway. County roads totalled 56,898, and city streets, 9,352 miles. Total road mileage, 80,483, of which 5,001 miles are unmaintained county and city roads.

Railways. In 1982 there were in the state 4,500 miles of main-track and branch railway.

Aviation. There were (1984) 233 airports in the state. Of these, 68 are publicly owned and open to the public; 16 are privately owned and open to the public; 149 are private and not open to the public.

JUSTICE, RELIGION, EDUCATION AND WELFARE

Justice. At 30 Sept. 1984 there were 3,050 people committed to the State Department of Corrections, inmates of the State Penitentiary, the State Reformatory and other institutions. In 1967 there was 1 execution; since 1930 executions (by lethal gas) numbered 47, including 41 whites, 5 Negroes and 1 other; all were for murder.

Colorado has a Civil Rights Act (1935) forbidding places of public accommodation to discriminate against any persons on the grounds of race, religion, sex, colour or nationality. No religious test may be applied to teachers or students in the public schools, 'nor shall any distinction or classification of pupils be made on account of race or colour'. In 1957 the General Assembly prohibited discrimination in employment of persons in private industry and in 1959 adopted the Fair Housing Act to discourage discrimination in housing. A 1957 Act permits marriages between white persons and Negroes or mulattoes.

Religion. In 1984 the Roman Catholic Church had 550,300 members; the ten main Protestant denominations had 350,900 members; the Jewish community had 45,000 members. Buddhism is among other religions represented.

Education. In autumn 1984 the public elementary and secondary schools had 526,336 pupils and 34,500 teachers and administrators; total instructional salaries averaged $25,000. Enrolments in universities and larger colleges, autumn 1983, were: US Air Force Academy (Colorado Springs), 6,000 students; University of Colorado (Boulder), 25,500; University of Colorado (Denver), 10,560; University of Colorado (Colorado Springs), 5,500; University of Colorado (Medical Center), 1,585; Colorado State University (Fort Collins), 17,500; University of Denver

(Denver), 9,300; Colorado School of Mines (Golden), 3,200; University of Northern Colorado (Greeley), 10,700; University of Southern Colorado (Pueblo), 5,000; Western State College (Gunnison), 1,700; Adams State College (Alamosa), 2,000; Metropolitan State College (Denver), 17,690; Colorado College (Colorado Springs), 1,950; Fort Lewis College (Durango), 3,650; Mesa College (Grand Junction), 3,400.

Health. Approved hospitals, 1983, numbered 98. In 1983, there were 25 public mental health centres and clinics.

Social Security. A constitutional amendment, adopted 1956, provides for minimum old age pensions of $100 per month, which may be raised on a cost-of-living basis; for a $5m. stabilization fund and for a $10m. medical and health fund for pensioners. In 1984 the maximum monthly retirement pension (for citizens of 65 and older) was $703; maximum monthly benefit for a disabled worker, $854.

Books of Reference

Directory of Colorado Manufacturers, 1986. Business Research Division, School of Business, Univ. of Colorado, Boulder, 1987
State of Colorado Business Development Manual. Office of Business Development, Denver, 1986
Economic Outlook Forum, 1986. Colorado Division of Commerce and Development, and the College of Business, Univ. of Colorado, Denver, 1987
Griffiths, M., and Rubright, L., *Colorado: a Geography.* Boulder, 1983
Sprague, M., *Colorado: A History.* New York, 1976

State Library: Colorado State Library, State Capitol, Denver, 80203.

CONNECTICUT

HISTORY. Connecticut was first settled in 1634 and has been an organized commonwealth since 1637. In 1629 a written constitution was adopted which, it is claimed, was the first in the history of the world formed under the concept of a social compact. This constitution was confirmed by a charter from Charles II in 1662, and replaced in 1818 by a state constitution, framed that year by a constitutional convention.

AREA AND POPULATION. Connecticut is bounded north by Massachusetts, east by Rhode Island, south by the Atlantic and west by New York. Area, 5,018 sq. miles (147 sq. miles being inland water).

Census population, 1 April 1980, 3,107,576, an increase of 2·5% since 1970. Estimate (1983) 3,138,000. Births (1984) were 39,237 (12·4 per 1,000 population); deaths, 27,633 (8·8); infant deaths, 320 (8·2 per 1,000 live births); marriages, 25,080 (8); divorces, 11,226 (3·6).

Population in 5 census years was:

	White	Negro	Indian	Asiatic	Total	Per sq. mile
1910	1,098,897	15,174	152	533	1,114,756	231·3
1930	1,576,700	29,354	162	687	1,606,903	328·0
1960	2,423,816	107,449	923	3,046	2,535,234	517·5
			All others			
1970	2,835,458	181,177	15,074		3,031,709	629·0
1980	2,799,420	217,433	4,533	18,970	3,107,576	634·3

Of the total population in 1980, 1,498,005 persons were male, 2,449,774 persons were urban. Those 19 years old or older numbered 2,228,805.

The chief cities and towns, with census population 1 April 1980, are:

Bridgeport	142,546	New Britain	73,840
Hartford	136,392	West Hartford	61,301
New Haven	126,109	Danbury	60,470
Waterbury	103,266	Greenwich	59,578
Stamford	102,453	Bristol	57,370
Norwalk	77,767	Meriden	57,118

Larger urbanized areas, 1980 census: Hartford, 726,114; Bridgeport, 395,455; New Haven, 417,592; Waterbury, 228,178; Stamford, 198,854.

CLIMATE. New Haven: Jan. 28°F (–2·2°C), July 72°F (22·2°C). Annual rainfall 46″ (1,151 mm). *See* New England, p. 1379.

CONSTITUTION AND GOVERNMENT. The 1818 Constitution was revised in June 1953 effective 1 Jan. 1955. On 30 Dec. 1965 a new constitution went into effect, having been framed by a constitutional convention in the summer of 1965 and approved by the voters in Dec. 1965.

The 1965 Constitution provides for 30 to 50 members of the Senate (instead of 24 to 36) and for 125 to 225 members of the House of Representatives, to be elected from assembly districts, rather than 2 or 1 from each town, as in the former constitution. The convention has added a new provision for a 3-day session following each regular or special session, solely to reconsider bills vetoed by the Governor.

The General Assembly consists of a Senate of 36 members and a House of Representatives of 151 members. Members of each House are elected for the term of 2 years (annual salary $9,500 first year, $7,500 second year; expenses $2,000 and mileage allowance). Legislative sessions are annual. The Governor and Lieut.-Governor are elected for 4 years. All citizens (with necessary exceptions and the usual residential requirements) have the right of suffrage.

Connecticut is one of the original 13 states of the Union. The state is represented in Congress by 2 senators and 6 representatives.

In the 1984 presidential election Reagan polled 883,486 votes, Mondale, 560,712. The state capital is Hartford.

Governor: William A. O'Neill (D.), 1987–91 ($65,000).
Lieut.-Governor: Joseph J. Fauliso (D.), ($40,000).
Secretary of State: Julia Tashjian (D.) ($35,000).

BUDGET. For the year ending 30 June 1982 (state government figures) general revenues were $5,588m. (taxation, $3,723m., and federal aid, $998m.); general expenditures were $5,330m. (education, $1,843m., highways, $376m., and public welfare, $737m.).

The total long-term debt on 30 June 1982 was $4,452m.

Per capita income, 1985, was $18,089.

NATURAL RESOURCES

Minerals. The state has some mineral resources: sheet mica, sand, gravel, clays and stone; total production in 1982 was valued at $56m.

Agriculture. In 1985 the state had 4,000 farms with a total area of about 500,000 acres; average farm was of 118 acres, valued at $3,208 per acre. Total cash income, 1985, was $316m., including $110m. from crops and $206m. from livestock and products (mainly from dairy products and poultry). Principal crops are hay, silage, forest, greenhouse and nursery products, tobacco, potatoes, sweet corn, tomatoes, apples, peaches, pears, vegetables and small fruit.

Livestock (1 Jan. 1980): 108,000 all cattle (value $70·7m.), 5,200 sheep ($387,000), 11,000 swine ($699,000) and 5·8m. poultry ($12m.).

Forestry. The state had (1980) 137,782 acres of state forest land, which is about 4·2% of the total land area.

INDUSTRY. Total non-agricultural labour force in 1985 was 1,569,000. The main employers are manufacturers (411,000 workers mainly in transport equipment, non-electrical machinery and fabricated metals); trade (350,000 workers); services (353,000) and government (189,000).

COMMUNICATIONS

Roads. The state (1 Jan. 1981) maintains 4,035 miles of highways, all surfaced. Motor vehicles registered in 1985 numbered 2,422,000.

Railways. In 1981 there were 950 miles of railway track.

Aviation. In 1981 there were 61 airports (27 commercial including 5 state-owned, and 34 heliports).

JUSTICE, RELIGION, EDUCATION AND WELFARE

Justice. In 1981 there were no executions; since 1930 there have been 22 executions (19 by electrocution, 3 by hanging), including 19 whites and 3 Negroes, all for murder. In 1984 there were 5,718 inmates of the state and federal prisons.

The Civil Rights Act makes it a punishable offence to discriminate against any person or persons 'on account of alienage, colour or race' and to hold up to ridicule any persons 'on account of creed, religion, colour, denomination, nationality or race'. Places of public resort are forbidden to discriminate. Insurance companies are forbidden to charge higher premiums to persons 'wholly or partially of African descent'. Schools must be open to all 'without discrimination on account of race or colour'.

Religion. The leading religious denominations (1980) in the state are the Roman Catholic (1·4m. members), United Churches of Christ, Protestant Episcopal, Jewish, Greek Orthodox, Methodist, Baptist, Presbyterian.

Education. Elementary instruction is free for all children between the ages of 4 and 16 years, and compulsory for all children between the ages of 7 and 16 years. In 1983 there were 719 public elementary schools, 237 secondary schools and 25 combined. In 1983 there were 478,000 pupils and 32,500 elementary and secondary teachers. Expenditure of the state on public schools, 1986, $2,321m. or $731 per capita. Average salary of teachers in public schools, 1986, $26,750.

Connecticut has 47 colleges, of which one state university, 4 state colleges, 5 state technical colleges and 12 regional community colleges are state funded. The University of Connecticut at Storrs, founded 1881, had 1,253 faculty and 22,407 students in 1980–81. Yale University, New Haven, founded in 1701, had 2,088 faculty and 9,626 students. Wesleyan University, Middletown, founded 1831, had 297 faculty and 2,775 students. Trinity College, Hartford, founded 1823, had 145 faculty and 2,007 students. Connecticut College, New London, founded 1915, had 203 faculty and 1,974 students. The University of Hartford, founded 1877, had 305 faculty and 9,836 students. The regional community colleges (2-year course) had 514 faculty and 34,082 students.

Health. Hospitals listed by the American Hospital Association, 1983, numbered 65, with 18,200 beds. The state operated one general hospital, one veterans' hospital, 8 hospitals for the mentally ill (2,450 patients in Jan. 1981), 2 training schools for the mentally retarded (and 12 regional centres), one chronic disease hospital (56 in-patients in Jan. 1981) and a state-aided institution for the blind.

Social Security. Disbursements during the year ending 30 June 1986 amounted to $66·1m. in aid to the aged (6,500 persons per month receiving an average of $153) and disabled (19,400, receiving $239). In other areas of welfare, there was an average of 40,700 cases for aid to families with dependent children comprising 118,800 recipients.

Books of Reference

The Register and Manual of Connecticut. Secretary of State. Hartford. Annual
The Structure of Connecticut's State Government. Connecticut Public Expenditure Council. Hartford, 1973
Adams, V. Q., *Connecticut: The Story of Your State Government.* Chester, 1973
Halliburton, W. J., *The People of Connecticut.* Norwalk, 1985
Roth, David M., ed., *Series in Connecticut History.* 5 vols., Chester, 1975
Smith, Allen R., *Connecticut, a Thematic Atlas.* Newington, 1974

Van Dusen, Albert E., *Connecticut*. New York, 1961

State Library: Connecticut State Library, Capitol Avenue, Hartford, 06015. *State Librarian:* Clarence R. Walters.

DELAWARE

HISTORY. Delaware, permanently settled in 1638, is one of the original 13 states of the Union, and the first one to ratify the Federal Constitution.

AREA AND POPULATION. Delaware is bounded north by Pennsylvania, north-east by New Jersey, east by Delaware Bay, south and west by Maryland. Area 2,044 sq. miles (112 sq. miles being inland water). Census population, 1 April 1980 was 594,338, an increase of 46,234 or 8·4% since 1970. Estimate (1986), 633,000. Births in 1985, 8,980; deaths, 5,001; infant deaths, 138; marriages, 5,613; divorces, 2,991.

Population in 5 census years was:

	White	Negro	Indian	Asiatic	Total	Per sq. mile
1910	171,102	31,181	5	34	202,322	103·0
1930	205,718	32,602	5	55	238,380	120·5
1960	384,327	60,688	597	410	446,292	224·0
			All others			
1970	466,459	78,276	3,369		548,104	276·5
1980	488,002	96,157	10,179		594,338	290·8

Of the total population in 1980, 48·4% were male, 70·7% were urban and 65·7% were 21 years old or older.

The 1980 census figures show Wilmington with population of 70,195; Newark, 25,241; Dover, 23,512; Elsmere Town, 6,493; Milford City, 5,356; Seaford City, 5,256.

CLIMATE. Wilmington. Jan. 32°F (0°C), July 75°F (23·9°C). Annual rainfall 43″ (1,076 mm). *See* Atlantic Coast, p. 1379.

CONSTITUTION AND GOVERNMENT. The present constitution (the fourth) dates from 1897, and has had 51 amendments; it was not ratified by the electorate but promulgated by the Constitutional Convention. The General Assembly consists of a Senate of 21 members elected for 4 years and a House of Representatives of 41 members elected for 2 years. The Governor and Lieut.-Governor are elected for 4 years.

With necessary exceptions, all adult citizens, registered as voters, who are *bona fide* residents, and have complied with local residential requirements, have the right to vote.

Delaware is represented in Congress by 2 senators and 1 representative, elected by the voters of the whole state.

In the 1984 presidential election Reagan polled 151,494 votes, Mondale, 100,632.

The state capital is Dover. Delaware is divided into 3 counties.

Governor: Michael N. Castle (R.), 1984–88 ($70,000).
Lieut.-Governor: S. B. Woo (D.), ($19,200).
Secretary of State: Michael Harkins (R.) ($49,300) (appointed by the Governor).

FINANCE. For the year ending 30 June 1986 total revenue was $1,987m., of which federal grants were $297·7m. Total expenditure was $799m.

On 30 June 1986 the total debt was $603·1m.

Per capita income (1985) was $14,272.

ENERGY AND NATURAL RESOURCES

Minerals. The mineral resources of Delaware are not extensive, consisting chiefly of clay products, stone, sand and gravel and magnesium compounds. Value of mineral production in 1980 was $2m.

Agriculture. Delaware is mainly an industrial state, but 650,000 acres is in farms, which in 1985 numbered 3,500; average farm was of 186 acres. The average farm was valued (land and buildings) at $323,500 in 1984.

Cash income, 1985, from crops and livestock, $491·2m., of which $383·5m. was from livestock and products. The chief crops are corn and soybeans.

INDUSTRY. In 1985 manufacturing establishments employed 72,100 people; value added by manufacture (1982), $2,466m., mainly from chemicals, transport equipment and food.

COMMUNICATIONS

Roads. The state in 1986 maintained 4,702 miles of roads and streets and 1,387 miles of federally-aided highways. There were also 601 miles of municipal maintained streets. Vehicles registered in year ended 30 June 1986, 503,828.

Railways. In 1986 the state had 285 miles of railway.

Aviation. Delaware had 12 airports, all of which were for general use in 1986.

JUSTICE, RELIGION, EDUCATION AND WELFARE

Justice. State prisons, 1 July 1985–30 June 1986, had daily average of 2,621 inmates. The death penalty was illegal from 2 April 1958 to 18 Dec. 1961. Executions since 1930 (by hanging) have totalled 12 (none since 1946).

Religion. Membership, 1979–80: Methodists, 60,489; Roman Catholics, 103,060; Episcopalians, 18,696; Lutherans, 10,000.

Education. The state has free public schools and compulsory school attendance. In Sept. 1986 the elementary and secondary public schools had 94,410 enrolled pupils and 5,883 full-time equivalent classroom teachers. Another 21,800 children were enrolled in private and parochial schools. Appropriation for public schools (financial year 1985–86) was about $359·5m. Average salary of classroom teachers (financial year 1985–86), $24,624. The state supports the University of Delaware at Newark (1834) which had 783 full-time faculty members and 18,631 students in Sept. 1986, Delaware State College, Dover (1892), with 157 full-time faculty members and 2,327 students, and the 4 campuses of Delaware Technical and Community College (Wilmington, Stanton, Dover and Georgetown) with 124 full-time faculty members and 6,000 students.

Health. In 1986 there were 7 short-term general hospitals. During financial year 1982 patients in mental hospitals numbered 1,963.

Social Security. In 1974 the federal Supplemental Security Income (SSI) programme lessened state responsibility for the aged, blind and disabled. SSI payments in Delaware (1984), $13·1m. Provisions are also made for the care of dependent children; in 1983 there were 26,000 recipients in 9,500 families (average monthly payment per family, $246). The total state programme for the year ending 30 June 1984 was $27m. for the care of dependent children.

Books of Reference

Information: Division of Historical and Cultural Affairs, Hall of Records, Dover.
Delaware Data Book. Delaware Development Office. Dover, 1985
State Manual, Containing Official List of Officers, Commissions and County Officers. Secretary of State, Dover. Annual

Hoffecker, C. E., *Delaware: a Bicentennial History.* New York, 1977
Smeal, L., *Delaware Historical and Biographical Index.* New York, 1984
Weslager, C. A., *Delaware Indians, a History.* Rutgers Univ. Press, 1972
Topical History of Delaware. Division of Historical and Cultural Affairs. Dover, 1977

DISTRICT OF COLUMBIA

HISTORY. The District of Columbia, organized in 1790, is the seat of the Government of the US, for which the land was ceded by the states of Maryland and Virginia to the US as a site for the national capital. It was established under Acts of Congress in 1790 and 1791. Congress first met in it in 1800 and federal authority over it became vested in 1801. In 1846 the land ceded by Virginia (about 33 sq. miles) was given back.

AREA AND POPULATION. The District forms an enclave on the Potomac River, where the river forms the south-west boundary of Maryland. The area of the District of Columbia is 68·68 sq. miles, 6 sq. miles being inland water.

Census population, 1 April 1980, was 638,333, a decrease of 16% from that of 1970. Estimate (1983) 623,000. Metropolitan statistical area of Washington, D.C.–Md–Va. (1980), 3m. Density of population in the District, 1980, 10,453 per sq. mile. Births, 1984, in the District were 19,123 (30·7 per 1,000 population); resident deaths, 8,302 (13·3); infant deaths, 393 (20·6 per 1,000 live births); marriages, 5,488 (8·8); divorces, 2,874 (4·6).

Population in 5 census years was:

	White	Negro	Indian	Chinese and Japanese	Total	Per sq. mile
1910	236,128	94,446	68	427	331,069	5,517·8
1930	353,981	132,068	40	780	486,869	7,981·5
1960	345,263	411,737	587	3,532	763,956	12,523·9

	White	Negro	All others	Total	Per sq. mile
1970	209,272	537,712	9,526	756,510	12,321·0
1980	171,768	448,906	17,659	638,333	10,184·0

CLIMATE. Washington. Jan. 34°F (1·1°C), July 77°F (25°C). Annual rainfall 43″ (1,064 mm). *See* Atlantic Coast, p. 1379.

GOVERNMENT. Local government, from 1 July 1878 until Aug. 1967, was that of a municipal corporation administered by a board of 3 commissioners, of whom 2 were appointed from civil life by the President, and confirmed by the Senate, for a term of 3 years each. The other commissioner was detailed by the President from the Engineer Corps of the Army. Reorganization Plan No. 3 of 1967 submitted by the President to Congress on 1 June 1967 abolished the Commission form of government and instituted a new Mayor Council form of government with officers appointed by the President with the advice and consent of the Senate. On 24 Dec. 1973 the appointed officers were replaced by an elected Mayor and councillors, with full legislative powers in local matters as from 1974. Congress retains the right to legislate, to veto or supersede the Council's acts. The 23rd amendment to the federal constitution (1961) conferred the right to vote in national elections; in the 1984 presidential election Mondale polled 172,459 votes, Reagan, 26,805. Since 1971 the District has had a delegate (two, by 1987) in Congress who may vote in Committees but not on the House floor.

BUDGET. The District's revenues are derived from a tax on real and personal property, sales taxes, taxes on corporations and companies, licences for conducting various businesses and from federal payments.

The District of Columbia has no bonded debt not covered by its accumulated sinking fund. *Per capita* personal income, 1985, $18,186.

INDUSTRY. The District's main industries (1985) are government service (263,000 workers); services (214,000); wholesale and retail trade (64,000); finance, real estate, insurance (35,000), communications, transport and utilities (26,000); total workforce, 1985, 629,000.

TOURISM. About 17m. visitors stay in the District every year and spend about $1,000m.

COMMUNICATIONS

Roads. Within the District are 340 miles of bus routes. There are 1,101 miles of streets maintained by the District; of these, 673 miles are local streets, 262 miles are major arterial roads. In 1985 233,000 vehicles were registered.

Railways. There is a rapid rail transit system including a town subway system. This coordinates with the bus system and connects with Union railway station and the National Airport. Nine rail lines serve the District.

Aviation. The District is served by 3 general airports; across the Potomac River in Arlington, Va., is National Airport, in Chantilly, Va., is Dulles International Airport and in Maryland is Baltimore—Washington International Airport.

JUSTICE, RELIGION, EDUCATION AND WELFARE

Justice. Since 1958 there have been no executions; from 1930 to 1957 there were 40 executions (electrocution) including 3 whites for murder and 35 Negroes for murder and 2 for rape. The death penalty was declared unconstitutional in the District of Columbia on November 16, 1973. At 31 Dec. 1985 there were 6,404 prisoners in state and federal institutions.

The District's Court system is the Judicial Branch of the District of Columbia. It is the only completely unified court system in the United States, possibly because of the District's unique city-state jurisdiction. Until the District of Columbia Court Reform and Criminal Procedure Act of 1970, the judicial system was almost entirely in the hands of Federal Government. Since that time, the system has been similar in most respects to the autonomous systems of the states.

Religion. The largest churches are the Protestant and Roman Catholic Christian churches; there are also Jewish, Eastern Orthodox and Islamic congregations.

Education. In 1983–84 there were about 89,000 pupils in secondary and elementary schools. Expenditure on public schools, 1986, $404m. or $645 per capita; public school teachers' average salary was $34,000. Higher education is given through the Consortium of Universities of the Metropolitan Washington Area, which consists of six universities and three colleges: Georgetown University, founded in 1795 by the Jesuit Order (11,688 students in 1985–86); George Washington University, non-sectarian founded in 1821 (17,948); Howard University, founded in 1867 (11,184); Catholic University of America, founded in 1887 (6,805); American University (Methodist) founded in 1893 (8,032); University of D.C., founded 1976 (12,080); Gallaudet College, founded 1864 (2,128); Trinity College, founded 1897 (926). There are altogether 18 institutes of higher education.

All benefit from such facilities as the 12 museums of the Smithsonian Institution, the Library of Congress, National Archives, and the Legal Libraries of the US Supreme Court and Department of Justice.

Social Security The District government provides primary health care for residents, mainly through its Department of Human Services. In 1983 there were 17 hospitals with 8,700 beds. The welfare programme of aid to families with dependent children gave money to 55,900 recipients in 21,600 families in 1985; 4,100 aged and 11,600 disabled also received aid, total payments $43·8m.

Books of Reference

Statistical Information: The Metropolitan Washington Board of Trade publications.
Reports of the Commissioners of the District of Columbia. Annual. Washington
Federal Writers' Project. *Washington, D.C.: A Guide to the Nation's Capital.* New York

FLORIDA

HISTORY. White men, probably Spaniards but possibly English, saw Florida for the first time in the period 1497–1512. Juan Ponce de Leon sighted Florida on 27 March 1513. Going ashore between 2 and 8 April in the vicinity of what is now St Augustine, he named the land 'Pasqua de Flores' because his landing was 'in the time of the Feast of Flowers'. The first permanent settlement in the entire US was made at St Augustine, 8 Sept. 1565. It was claimed by Spain until 1763, then ceded to England; back to Spain in 1783, and to the US in 1821. Florida became a Territory in 1821 and was admitted into the Union on 3 March 1845.

AREA AND POPULATION. Florida is a peninsula bounded west by the Gulf of Mexico, south by the Straits of Florida, east by the Atlantic, north by Georgia and north-west by Alabama. Area, 58,664 sq. miles, including 4,510 sq. miles of inland water. Census population, 1 April 1980, was 9,746,324, an increase of 43·4% since 1970. Estimate (1 July 1987) 12,036,806. Births in 1986 were 167,628; deaths, 123,540; infant deaths, 1,837; marriages, 129,363; divorces and other dissolutions, 78,114.

Population in 5 federal census years was:

	White	Negro	All Others	Total	Per Sq. Mile
1940	1,381,986	514,198	1,230	1,897,414	35·0
1950	2,166,051	603,101	2,153	2,771,305	51·1
1960	4,063,881	880,168	7,493	4,952,788	91·5
1970	5,719,343	1,041,651	28,449	6,789,443	125·6
1980	8,319,448	1,342,478	84,398	9,746,324	180·1

Of the population in 1980, 48% of the total were male; 84·3% were urban and 72·4% were 20 years of age or over.

The largest cities in the state, 1980 census (and 1986 estimates) are: Jacksonville, 540,898 (609,614); Miami, 346,931 (371,975); Tampa, 271,523 (278,755); St Petersburg, 236,893 (243,090); Fort Lauderdale, 153,256 (151,048); Hialeah, 145,254 (161,119); Orlando, 128,394 (148,104); Hollywood, 117,188 (124,448); Miami Beach, 96,298 (96,962); Clearwater, 85,450 (97,882); Tallahassee, 81,548 (120,023); Gainesville, 81,371 (83,060); West Palm Beach, 62,530 (67,991); Largo, 58,977 (62,624); Pensacola, 57,619 (61,422); Pompano Beach, 52,618 (68,759).

CLIMATE. Jacksonville. Jan. 55°F (12·8°C), July 81°F (27·2°C). Annual rainfall 54″ (1,353 mm). Key West. Jan. 70°F (21·1°C), July 83°F (28·3°C). Annual rainfall 39″ (968 mm). Miami. Jan. 67°F (19·4°C), July 82°F (27·8°C). Annual rainfall 60″ (1,516 mm). Tampa. Jan. 61°F (16·1°C), July 81°F (27·2°C). Annual rainfall 51″ (1,285 mm). See Gulf Coast, p. 1379.

CONSTITUTION AND GOVERNMENT. The 1968 Legislature revised the constitution of 1885. The state legislature consists of a Senate of 40 members, elected for 4 years, and House of Representatives with 120 members elected for 2 years. Sessions are held annually, and are limited to 60 days. The Governor is elected for 4 years, and can hold two terms in office. Two senators and 19 representatives are elected to Congress.

In the 1984 presidential election Reagan polled 2,512,318 votes and Mondale, 1,373,137.

The state capital is Tallahassee. The state is divided into 67 counties.

Governor: Bob Martinez (R.), 1987–91 ($69,550).
Lieut.-Governor: Bobby Brantley (R.), 1987–91 ($60,455).
Secretary of State: Jim Smith (R.), 1987–91 ($59,385).

FINANCE. There is no state income tax on individuals. For the year ending 30 June 1987 the state had a total revenue of $29,246m. and total expenditure of $28,723m. General revenue fund expenditure was $7,793m.

Net long-term debt, 30 June 1987, amounted to $3,450m.

Per capita personal income (1986) was $14,646.

NATURAL RESOURCES

Minerals. Chief mineral is phosphate rock, of which marketable production in 1986 was 29·7m. tonnes.

Agriculture. In 1985, there were 40,000 farms; net income per farm was $45,000. Total value of all farm land and buildings, $20,500m. There were 624,492 acres in citrus groves in 1986 and 12·4m. acres of other farms and ranches. Total cash receipts from crops and livestock (1986), $4,680m., of which crops provided $3,680m. Oranges, grapefruit, melons and vegetables are important. Other crops are soybeans, sugar-cane, tobacco and peanuts. On 1 Jan. 1986 the state had 1·89m. cattle, including 185,152 milch cows, and 158,000 swine.

The national forests area in Sept. 1986 was 1,146,675 acres. There were 15·66m. acres of commercial forest.

Fisheries. Florida has extensive fisheries for oysters, shrimp, red snapper, crabs, mackerel and mullet. Catch (1986), 169m. lb. valued at $171m.

INDUSTRY. In 1986 there were 15,262 manufacturers. They employed 516,580 persons. The metal-working, lumber, chemical, woodpulp, food-processing and instruments industries are important.

TOURISM. During 1986 35·7m. tourists visited Florida. They spent $22,800m. making tourism one of the biggest industries in the state. There were (1985) 136 state parks, 4 state forests, 2 national parks and 2 national forests. The state parks were visited by 13·6m. people in 1985–86, 1·2m. of them campers.

COMMUNICATIONS

Roads. The state (1987) had 122,810·7 miles of road and streets of which 102,966·5 miles were in the state and local system (63,917·1 miles being county roads), and 19,844·2 miles were federally-aided roads.

In 1982–83, 11·4m. vehicle licence plates were issued.

Railways. In 1987 there were 3,379 miles of railway.

Aviation. In 1986 Florida had 135 public use airports of which 22 have scheduled commercial service.

JUSTICE, RELIGION, EDUCATION AND WELFARE

Justice. Since 1968 there have been 13 executions, by electrocution, for murder; from 1930 to 1968 there were 168 executions (electrocution), including 130 for murder, 37 for rape and 1 for kidnapping. State prisons, 30 June 1985, had 28,281 in-mates.

Religion. The main Christian churches are Roman Catholic, Baptist, Methodist, Presbyterian and Episcopalian.

Education. Attendance at school is compulsory between 7 and 16.

In 1985–86 the public elementary and secondary schools had 1,558,918 enrolled pupils. Total expenditure on public schools was $7,611·9m. The state maintains 28 community colleges with 698,718 enrolments in 1983–84.

There are 9 universities in the state system, namely the University of Florida at Gainesville (founded 1853) with 35,692 students in 1986; the Florida State University (founded at Tallahassee in 1857) with 22,912; the University of South Florida at Tampa (founded 1960) with 28,806; Florida A. & M. University at Tallahassee (founded 1887) with 5,240; Florida Atlantic University (founded 1964) at Boca Raton with 10,705; the University of West Florida at Pensacola with 6,107; the University of Central Florida at Orlando with 16,530; the University of North Florida at Jacksonville with 6,546; Florida International University at Miami with 16,403.

Health. Hospitals, 1987, numbered 306 with 70,132 beds; there were 228 general, 77 special and 1 tuberculosis hospitals.

Social Security. From 1974 aid to the aged, blind and disabled became a federal responsibility. The state continued to give aid to families with dependent children and general assistance. Monthly payments 1986–87: aid to 3,064 blind averaged

$234.91; aid to 201,867 dependent children averaged $79.11; aid to 107,186 disabled averaged $234.78; aid to 77,201 aged averaged $186.76.

Books of Reference

Florida Population: Summary of the 1980 Census. Univ. of Florida Press, 1981
Report. Florida Secretary of State. Tallahassee. Biennial
Report of the Comptroller. Tallahassee. Biennial
Morris, Allen. *The Florida Handbook.* Tallahassee. Biennial
Fernald, E. A., (ed.) *Atlas of Florida.* Florida State Univ., 1981
Tebeau, C. W., *A History of Florida.* Univ. Miami Press, rev. ed., 1980

State Library: Gray Building, Tallahassee. *Librarian:* Barratt Wilkins.

GEORGIA

HISTORY. Georgia (so named from George II) was founded in 1733 as the 13th original colony; she became the 4th original state.

AREA AND POPULATION. Georgia is bounded north by Tennessee and North Carolina, north-east by South Carolina, east by the Atlantic, south by Florida and west by Alabama. Area, 58,910 sq. miles, of which 854 sq. miles are inland water. Census population, 1 April 1980, was 5,464,265. Estimate (1983), 5,732,000. Births, 1984, were 91,761 (15·7 per 1,000 population); deaths, 47,303 (8·1); infant deaths, 1,221 (13·3 per 1,000 live births); marriages, 75,817 (13); divorces and annulments, 34,084 (5·8).

Population in 5 census years was:

	White	Negro	Indian	Asiatic	Total	Per sq. mile
1910	1,431,802	1,176,987	95	237	2,609,121	44·4
1930	1,837,021	1,071,125	43	317	2,908,506	49·7
1960	2,817,223	1,122,596	749	2,004	3,943,116	67·7

	White	Negro	All others	Total	Per sq. mile
1970	3,391,242	1,187,149	11,184	4,589,575	79·0
1980	3,948,007	1,465,457	50,801	5,464,265	92·7

Of the 1980 population, 2,641,030 were male, 3,406,171 were urban and those 20 years of age and over numbered 3,601,895.

The largest cities are: Atlanta (capital), with population, 1980 census, of 422,293 (urbanized area, 2,010,368); Columbus, 168,598 (238,593); Savannah, 133,672 (225,581); Macon, 116,044 (251,736); Albany, 74,471 (112,257).

CLIMATE. Atlanta. Jan. 43°F (6·1°C), July 78°F (25·6°C). Annual rainfall 49″ (1,234 mm). *See* Atlantic Coast, p. 1379.

CONSTITUTION AND GOVERNMENT. A new constitution was ratified in the general election of 2 Nov. 1976, proclaimed on 22 Dec. 1976 and became effective 1 Jan. 1977. The General Assembly consists of a Senate of 56 members and a House of Representatives of 180 members, both elected for 2 years. The Governor and Lieut.-Governor are elected for 4 years. Legislative sessions are annual, beginning the 2nd Monday in Jan. and lasting for 40 days.

Georgia was the first state to extend the franchise to all citizens 18 years old and above. The state is represented in Congress by 2 senators and 10 representatives.

Registered voters, 1976, numbered 2,178,623. At the 1984 presidential election Reagan polled 1,050,852 votes, Mondale, 696,181.

The state capital is Atlanta. Georgia is divided into 159 counties.

Governor: Joe F. Harris (D.), 1987–91 ($79,358).
Lieut.-Governor: Zell Miller (D.), ($41,496).
Secretary of State: Max Cleland (D.), ($51,896).

BUDGET. For the fiscal year ending 30 June 1982 general revenue was

$9,009m. (taxes, $4,666m.; federal aid, $2,158m.); general expenditure was $8,401m. (education, $2,900m.; public welfare, $895m.; hospitals, $1,384m.).

On 30 June 1982 total liability was $6,877m.

Estimated *per capita* personal income (1985), was $12,543.

NATURAL RESOURCES

Minerals. Georgia is the leading producer of kaolin. The state ranks first in production of crushed and dimensional granite, second in production of fuller's earth and marble (crushed and dimensional).

Mineral products, 1982, had a value of $718m.

Agriculture. In 1986, 49,000 farms covered 13m. acres; average farm was of 265 acres; total value, land and buildings, $11,094m. For 1985 cotton output was 370,000 bales (of 480 lb.). Other crops include tobacco, corn, wheat, soybeans, peanuts and pecans. Cash income, 1985, $3,327m: from crops, $1,600m.; from livestock, $1,727m.

On 1 Jan. 1986 farm animals included 1·7m. all cattle, including 119,000 milch cows, and 1·2m. swine.

Forestry. The forested area in 1980 was 25m. acres.

INDUSTRY. In 1985 the state's manufacturing establishments had 554,000 workers; the main groups were textiles, transport equipment, food, wood products and paper, chemicals. Trade employed 648,000, services 463,000, government, 447,000.

TOURISM. In 1982 tourists spent $6,380m.

COMMUNICATIONS

Roads. Total road mileage (Dec. 1980) was 134,500 including 88,900 rural and 11,850 primary federal-aided. Motor vehicles registered, 1985, numbered 4,606,000.

Railways. In 1976 there were 5,417 miles of railways. A metro opened in Atlanta in 1979.

Aviation. In 1981 there were 125 public and 168 private airports.

Shipping. The principal port is Savannah.

JUSTICE, RELIGION, EDUCATION AND WELFARE

Justice. State and federal prisons, 31 Dec. 1985, had 16,118 inmates. Since 1964 there have been two executions (for murder). From 1924 to 1964 there were 415 executions (electrocution), including 75 whites and 268 Negroes for murder, 3 whites and 63 Negroes for rape and 6 Negroes for armed robbery.

Under a Local Option Act, the sale of alcoholic beverages (not including malt beverages and light wines) is prohibited in more than half the counties.

Religion. An estimated 78% of the population are church members. Of the total population, 74·3% are Protestant, 3·2% are Roman Catholic and 1·5% Jewish.

Education. Since 1945 education has been compulsory; tuition is free for pupils between the ages of 6 and 18 years. In 1983 there were 1,303 public elementary schools and 438 public secondary schools; in autumn 1983 they had 1m. pupils and (1985) 56,310 teachers. Teachers' salaries averaged $21,700 for elementary and $22,500 for secondary schools in 1986. Expenditure on public schools (1986), $3,295m. or $551 per capita. Integration in public schools is now an accepted practice.

The University of Georgia (Athens) was founded in 1785 and was the first chartered State University in the US (25,408 students in 1985–86). Other institutions of higher learning include Georgia Institute of Technology, Atlanta (11,078), Emory University, Atlanta (8,421), Georgia College, Milledgeville (3,940), Georgia State

University, Atlanta (21,612) and Mercer University, Macon (2,332). The Atlanta University Center, devoted primarily to Negro education, includes Clark College (1,860) and Morris Brown College (1,257, co-educational, Morehouse (2,160), a liberal arts college for men, Interdenominational Theological Center, a co-educational theological school, and Spelman College, the first liberal arts college for Negro women in the US. Atlanta University serves as the graduate school centre for the complex. Wesleyan College near Macon is the oldest chartered women's college in the US.

Health. Hospitals licensed by the Department of Human Resources, 1983, numbered 191 with 33,500 beds. State facilities for the mentally retarded had 1,363 resident patients in 1980; there were 4,527 in mental care hospitals.

Social Security. In Dec. 1985, 60,300 persons were receiving SSI old-age assistance of an average $128 per month; 82,500 families were receiving as aid to dependent children an average $186 per family; aid to 89,500 disabled persons was $217 monthly.

Books of Reference

Georgia History in Outline. Univ. of Georgia Press, Athens, 1978

Bonner, J. C., and Roberts, L. E., eds., *Studies in Georgia History and Government.* Reprint Company, Spartanburg, 1940 Repr.

Pound, M. B., and Saye, A. B., *Handbook on the Constitution of the U.S. and Georgia.* Univ. of Georgia Press, Athens, 1978

Rowland, A. R., *A Bibliography of the Writings on Georgia History.* Hamden, Conn., 1978

Saye, A. B., *A Constitutional History of Georgia, 1732–1968.* Univ. of Georgia, Athens, Rev. ed., 1970

State Library: Judicial Building, Capital Sq., Atlanta. *State Librarian:* John D. M. Folger.

HAWAII

HISTORY. The Hawaiian Islands, formerly known as the Sandwich Islands, were discovered by Capt. James Cook in Jan. 1778. During the greater part of the 19th century the islands formed an independent kingdom, but in 1893 the reigning Queen, Liliuokalani (died 11 Nov. 1917), was deposed and a provisional government formed; in 1894 a Republic was proclaimed, and in accordance with the request of the Legislature of the Republic, and a resolution of the US Congress of 6 July 1898 (signed 7 July by President McKinley), the islands were on 12 Aug. 1898 formally annexed to the US. On 14 June 1900 the islands were constituted as a Territory of Hawaii.

Statehood was granted to Hawaii on 18 March 1959.

AREA AND POPULATION. The Hawaiian Islands lie in the North Pacific Ocean, between 18° 50′ and 28° 15′ N. lat. and 154° 40′ and 178° 15′ W. long., about 2,090 nautical miles south-west of San Francisco. There are more than 136 islands and islets in the group, of which 7 are inhabited. The land and inland water area of the state is 6,471 sq. miles, with census population, 1 April 1980, of 964,691, an increase of 194,778 or 25·4% since 1970; density was 163·8 per sq. mile.

The principal islands are Hawaii, 4,035 sq. miles and population, 1980, 92,053 (estimate, 1986, 111,800); Maui, 735 and 62,823 (78,700); Oahu, 618 and 762,534 (816,700); Kauai, 558 and 38,856 (46,100); Molokai, 264 and 6,049 (6,700); Lanai, 141 and 2,119 (2,200); Niihau, 71 and 226 (200); Kahoolawe, 46 (uninhabited). The capital Honolulu, on the island of Oahu, had a population in 1980 of 365,048 and Hilo on the island of Hawaii, 35,269.

Figures for racial groups, 1980, are: 331,925 White, 239,734 Japanese, 132,075 Filipinos, 118,251 Hawaiian, 55,916 Chinese, 17,453 Korean, 17,687 Negroes, 51,650 all others. Of the total, approximately 93% were citizens of the US.

Inter-marriage between the races is popular. Of the 16,219 persons married in the calendar year 1986, 31·4% married a wife or husband of a different race. Births, 1984, were 18,756; deaths, 5,942; infant deaths, 205; marriages, 14,982; divorces and annulments, 4,769.

CLIMATE. All the islands have a tropical climate, with an abrupt change in conditions between windward and leeward sides, most marked in rainfall. Temperatures vary little. Honolulu. Jan. 71°F (21·7°C), July 78°F (25·6°C). Annual rainfall 31″ (775 mm).

CONSTITUTION AND GOVERNMENT. The constitution took effect on 21 Aug. 1959.

The Legislature consists of a Senate of 25 members elected for 4 years, and a House of Representatives of 51 members elected for 2 years. The constitution provides for annual meetings of the legislature with 60-day regular sessions. The Governor and Lieut.-Governor are elected for 4 years. The registered voters, 1986, numbered 419,794.

The state sends to Congress 2 senators and 2 representatives.

In the 1984 presidential election Reagan polled 185,050 votes, Mondale, 147,154.

Governor: John Waihee (D.), 1986–90 ($80,000).

BUDGET. Revenue is derived mainly from taxation of sales and gross receipts, real property, corporate and personal income, and inheritance taxes, licences, public land sales and leases. For the year ending 30 June 1986 state general fund receipts amounted to $1,406·6m.; special fund receipts, $140·9m., and federal grants, $394m. (included as $10·3m. of general funds and $383·7m. of special funds). State expenditures were $2,456·12m. (education, $773·2m.; highways, $104·5m.; public welfare, $322·5m.; figures include both special and general funds).

Net long-term debt, 31 Dec. 1986, amounted to $2,720·4m.

Estimated *per capita* personal income (1986) was $14,886.

NATURAL RESOURCES

Minerals. Total value of mineral production, 1986, amounted to $68,422,000. Cement shipped from plants amounted to 310,000 short tons; stone, 7,100,000 short tons.

Agriculture. Farming is highly commercialized, aiming at export to the American market, and highly mechanized. In 1985 there were 4,600 farms with an acreage of 1·95m.

Sugar and pineapples are the staple crops. Income from crop sales, 1986, was $481·2m., and from livestock, $83·4m. The sugar crop was valued at $233·8m.; pineapples, $99·7m.; other crops, $147·7m.

Forestry. Forest and wildlife lands held by the federal government totalled 255,620 acres in 1985.

INDUSTRY AND TRADE

Industry. In 1985 manufacturing establishments employed 15,800 production workers who earned an estimated $228·5m.

Commerce. In 1986 imports were $1,556·9m.; exports, $231·1m.

Tourism. Tourism is an outstanding factor in Hawaii's economy. Tourist arrivals numbered 109,798 in 1955, and reached 7·06m. in 1986. Tourist expenditures, $55m. in 1955, contributed $5,500m. to the state's economy in 1986.

COMMUNICATIONS

Roads. In 1986 there were 790,855 motor vehicles, and a total of 4,040 miles of highways (including 94 miles of freeways).

Aviation. There were 8 commercial airports in 1986; passengers arriving from overseas numbered 6·04m., and there were 8·3m. passengers between the islands.

Shipping. Several lines of steamers connect the islands with the mainland USA, Canada, Australia, the Philippines, China and Japan. In 1986, 1,825 overseas and 2,697 inter-island vessels entered the port of Honolulu.

Post. There were 493,079 telephones access lines at 31 Dec. 1986.

JUSTICE, RELIGION, EDUCATION AND WELFARE

Justice. There is no capital punishment in Hawaii.

Religion. The residents of Hawaii are mainly Christians, though there are many Buddhists. A sample survey in 1979 showed that 31% were Roman Catholic, 34% Protestant, 12% Buddhist, 2·5% Latter Day Saints.

Education. Education is free, and compulsory for children between the ages of 6 and 18. The language in the schools is English. In 1986–87 there were 232 public schools (164,640 pupils with 8,244 teachers) and 145 private schools (36,548 pupils and 2,544 teachers) ranging from kindergarten through the 12th grade. The University of Hawaii-Manoa, founded in 1907, had 18,965 day students in 1986; total attendance at all campuses of the University of Hawaii system, 42,825; 9,082 at private colleges.

Social Security. During 1986 4,820 people were receiving SSI old-age assistance of an average $204 per month; 74,915 families, $404 in aid to dependent children; 20,583 disabled people, $273.

Books of Reference

Government in Hawaii. Tax Foundation of Hawaii. Honolulu, 1987
Guide to Government in Hawaii. 8th ed. Legislative Reference Bureau. State of Hawaii, Honolulu, 1984
All About Hawaii: Thrum's Hawaiian Annual and Standard Guide. Honolulu, 1875 to 1974
State of Hawaii Data Book. Hawaii Dept. of Business and Economic Development, 1987
Allen, G. E., *Hawaii's War Years.* 2 vols. Hawaii Univ. Press, 1950–52
Bell, R. J., *Last Among Equals: Hawaiian Statehood and American Politics.* Honolulu, 1984
Kuykendall, R. S., and Day, A. G., *Hawaii, A History.* Rev. ed. New Jersey, 1961
Morgan, J. R., *Hawaii.* Boulder, 1982
Pukui, M. K., and Elbert, S. H., *Hawaiian–English Dictionary.* Rev. ed. Honolulu, 1986

IDAHO

HISTORY. Idaho was first permanently settled in 1860, although there was a mission for Indians in 1836 and a Mormon settlement in 1855. It was organized as a Territory in 1863 and admitted into the Union as a state on 3 July 1890.

AREA AND POPULATION. Idaho is bounded north by Canada, east by the Rocky Mountains of Montana and Wyoming, south by Nevada and Utah, west by Oregon and Washington. Area, 83,564 sq. miles, of which 1,153 sq. miles are inland water. In 1983 the federal government owned 34,282,000 acres (65% of the state area). Census population, 1 April 1980, 943,935, an increase of 32·4% since 1970. Estimate (1984) 1,001,000.

Births, 1984, 17,996 (18 per 1,000 population); deaths, 7,229 (7·2); infant deaths, 174 (9·7 per 1,000 live births); marriages, 13,264 (13·3); divorces, 6,210 (6·2).

Population in 5 census years was:

	White	Negro	Indian	Asiatic	Total	Per sq. mile
1910	319,221	651	3,488	2,234	325,594	3·9
1930	438,840	668	3,638	1,886	445,032	5·4
1960	657,383	1,502	5,231	2,958	667,191	8·1
1970	693,375	3,655	5,413	2,526	713,008	8·5
			All others			
1980	901,641	2,716	39,578		943,935	11·3

Of the total 1980 population, 471,155 were male, 509,702 were urban and those 20 years of age or older 600,242.

The largest cities are Boise (capital) with 1980 census population of 102,160 (1984 estimate, 107,188); Pocatello, 46,340 (45,334); Idaho Falls, 39,734 (41,774); Lewiston, 27,986 (28,050); Twin Falls, 26,209 (28,168); Nampa, 25,112 (27,347).

CLIMATE. Boise. Jan. 29°F (–1·7°C), July 74°F (23·3°C). Annual rainfall 12″ (303 mm). *See* Mountain States, p. 1378.

CONSTITUTION AND GOVERNMENT. The constitution adopted in 1890 is still in force; it has had 104 amendments. The Legislature consists of a Senate of 42 members and a House of Representatives of 84 members, all the legislators being elected for 2 years. The Governor, Lieut.-Governor and Secretary of State are elected for 4 years. Voters are citizens, over the age of 18 years. The state is represented in Congress by 2 senators and 2 representatives.

In the 1984 presidential election Reagan polled 279,523 votes, Mondale, 108,510.

The state is divided into 44 counties. The capital is Boise.

Governor: Cecil Andrus (D.), 1987–91 ($50,000).
Lieut.-Governor: C. L. Otter (R.), 1987–91 ($14,000).
Secretary of State: Pete Cenarrusa (R.), 1987–91 ($37,500).

BUDGET. For the year ending 30 June 1985 (State Auditor's Office) general revenues were $551·1m. and general expenditures, $555·5m. (which includes $3·4m. outstanding obligations).

Per capita personal income (1985) was $11,120.

NATURAL RESOURCES

Minerals. Production of the most important minerals (1984): Silver, 18·87m. troy oz.; copper, 3,701 tonnes; antimony, 557 short tons. There is some gold, lead, zinc and vanadium. Non-metallic minerals include phosphate rock (4·7m. tonnes), lime (87,000 short tons), garnet, gypsum, perlite, pumice, tungsten, molybdenum, crushed stone (1·8m. short tons), sand and gravel and dimension stone. Value of total mineral output was $412m. in 1984.

Agriculture. Agriculture is the leading industry, although a great part of the state is naturally arid. Extensive irrigation works have been carried out, bringing an estimated 4m. acres under irrigation; 83 reservoirs have a total capacity of 10·4m. acre-ft, 7·3m. acre-ft of which is primarily used for irrigation.

In 1985 there were 24,600 farms with a total area of 14·7m. acres (27% of the land area); average farm had 598 acres with land and buildings valued at approximately $749 per acre.

In 1984 there were 51 soil conservation districts, managed by local farmers and ranchers, covering most of the state.

Cash receipts from marketings, 1985, was $2,063m. ($1,200m. from crops and $862m. from livestock). The most important crops are potatoes and wheat—potatoes leading all states; in 1985 the production amounted to 103m. cwt, cash receipts $323m.; wheat, 72m. bu., $235m. Other crops are sugar-beet, alfalfa, barley, field peas and beans, onions and apples. On 1 Jan. 1985 the number of sheep was 313,000; milch cows, 165,000; all cattle, 1·78m.; swine, 112,000.

Forestry. In 1983 a total of 20,635,700 acres (37·6% of the state's area) was in forests; 13,540,600 acres of this was commercial (non-reserved) forest. The volume of sawtimber in commercial forests was 139,600m. bd ft. The stumpage value of forest products was about $124m., and about $531m. was added by processing. Ownership of commercial forests is 70% federal, 6·5% state and local government, 0·5% Indian, 22·3% private. Some 16,100 workers are involved in forestry.

INDUSTRY. In 1985 85,000 were employed in trade, 70,000 in government, 66,000 in services, 55,000 in manufacturing.

TOURISM. Money spent by travellers in 1984 was about $1,200m. Estimated state and local tax receipts from tourism, $48m. Jobs generated, 25,000 (pay-roll over $300m.).

COMMUNICATIONS

Roads. The state maintained in 1985, 4,954 miles of the total of 68,808 miles of public roads; 745,462 passenger vehicles were registered in 1985.

Railways. The state had (1985) 1,910 miles of railways (including 2 AMTRAK routes).

Aviation. There were 68 municipally owned airports in 1985.

Shipping. Water transport is provided from the Pacific to the Port of Lewiston, by way of the Columbia and Snake rivers, a distance of 464 miles.

JUSTICE, RELIGION, EDUCATION AND WELFARE

Justice. The death penalty may be imposed for first degree murder, but the judge must consider mitigating circumstances before imposing a sentence of death. Since 1926 only 4 men (white) have been executed, by hanging (1 in 1926, 2 in 1951 and 1 in 1957). At 1 Oct. 1985 14 prison inmates (13 men and 1 woman) were under sentence of death. Execution is now by lethal injection. The state prison system, 1 Oct. 1985, had 1,260 inmates.

Religion. The leading religious denominations are the Church of Jesus Christ of Latter Day Saints (Mormon Church), Roman Catholics, Methodists, Presbyterians, Episcopalians and Lutherans.

Education. In 1984–85 public elementary schools (grades K to 6) had 118,647 pupils and 5,481 classroom teachers; secondary schools had 92,053 pupils and 4,980 classroom teachers.

Average salary, 1984–85, of elementary and secondary classroom teachers, $20,032. The University of Idaho, founded at Moscow in 1889, had 459 professors and 8,970 students in 1984–85. There are 9 other institutions of higher education; 5 of them are public institutions with a total enrolment (1984–85) of 21,914 (excluding vocational-technical colleges).

Social Welfare. Old-age assistance is granted to persons 65 years of age and older. In Aug. 1985, 1,014 persons were drawing an average of $105.86 per month; 6,023 families with 10,858 children were drawing an average of $243.85 per case (or $90.10 per eligible person); 28 blind persons, $73.21; 569 children were receiving $248.88 per child for foster care; 1,827 permanently and totally disabled persons, $133.69.

Health. In Sept. 1985 skilled nursing covered 4,761 beds; intermediate care, 107; intermediate care for the mentally retarded 528. Hospitals had 3,547 beds and home health agencies totalled 36.

Books of Reference

Idaho Blue Book. Secretary of State. Boise, 1983–84
Idaho. Idaho First National Bank
Idaho Almanac. Division of Economic and Community Affairs, 1977
Idaho's Yesterdays. State Historical Society. Quarterly

ILLINOIS

HISTORY. Illinois was first discovered by Joliet and Marquette, two French explorers, in 1673. In 1763 the country was ceded by the French to the British. In 1783 Great Britain recognized the United States' title to the land that became Illinois; it was organized as a Territory in 1809 and admitted into the Union on 3 Dec. 1818.

AREA AND POPULATION. Illinois is bounded north by Wisconsin, north-east by Lake Michigan, east by Indiana, south-east by the Ohio River (forming the boundary with Kentucky), west by the Mississippi River (forming the boundary with Missouri and Iowa). Area, 56,400 sq. miles, of which 652 sq. miles are inland water. Census population, 1980, 11,426,518, an increase of 2·71% since 1970. Estimate (1985), 11,535,000. Births in 1984 were 175,907 (15·3 per 1,000 population); deaths, 98,151 (8·5); infant deaths, 2,073 (11·8 per 1,000 live births); marriages 102,504 (8·9); divorces, 48,914 (4·2).

Population in 5 census years was:

	White	Negro	Indian	All others	Total	Per sq. mile
1910	5,526,962	109,049	188	2,392	5,638,591	100·6
1930	7,295,267	328,972	469	5,946	7,630,654	136·4
1960	9,010,252	1,037,470	4,704	28,732	10,081,158	180·3
				All others		
1970	9,600,381	1,425,674		87,921	11,113,976	199·4
1980	9,233,327	1,675,398		517,793	11,426,518	203·0

Of the total population in 1980, 5,537,737 were male, 9,518,039 persons were urban and 5,597,360 were 18 years of age or older.

The most populous cities with population (1980 census), are:

Chicago	3,005,072
Rockford	139,712
Peoria	124,160
Springfield (cap.)	99,637
Decatur	94,081
Joliet	77,956
Aurora	81,293
Evanston	73,706
Waukegan	67,653
Arlington Heights	66,116

Standard Metropolitan Statistical Area population, 1980 census (and 1985 estimate): Chicago, 7,102,378 (7,580,800); East St Louis, 565,874 (570,400); Peoria, 365,864 (347,700); Rockford, 279,514 (279,800); Springfield, 176,089 (189,600); Decatur, 131,375 (128,200).

CLIMATE. Chicago. Jan. 25°F (−3·9°C), July 73°F (22·8°C). Annual rainfall 33″ (836 mm). *See* Great Lakes, p. 1379.

CONSTITUTION AND GOVERNMENT. The present constitution became effective 1 July 1971. The General Assembly consists of a House of Representatives of 118 members, elected for 2 years and a Senate of 59 members who are divided into three groups; in one, they are elected for terms of four years, four years, and two years; in the next, for terms of four years, two years, and four years; and in the last, for terms of two years, four years, and four years. Sessions are annual. The Governor and Lieut.-Governor are elected as a team for 4 years; the Comptroller and Secretary of State are elected for 4 years. Electors are citizens 18 years of age, having the usual residential qualifications.

The state is divided into legislative districts, in each of which 1 senator is chosen; each district is divided into 2 representative districts, in each of which 1 representative is chosen.

Illinois is represented in Congress by 2 senators and 22 representatives.

In the 1984 presidential election Reagan polled 2,667,721 votes, Mondale, 2,036,337.

The capital is Springfield. The state has 102 counties.

Governor: James R. Thompson (R.), 1987–91 ($88,825).
Lieut.-Governor: George Ryan (R.), 1987–91 ($62,700).
Secretary of State: Jim Edgar, 1987–91 ($78,375).

BUDGET. For the year ending 30 June 1985 general revenues were $18,312m. and general expenditures were $17,991m.

Total net long-term debt, 30 June 1985, was $9,861m.
Per capita personal income (1985) was $14,738.

ENERGY AND NATURAL RESOURCES

Minerals. Chief mineral product is coal; 52 operative mines had an output (1985) of 60·5m. tons. Mineral production also included: Crude petroleum, fluorspar tripoli and lime. Total value of mineral products, 1984, was $3,616·9m.

Agriculture. In 1986, 87,000 farms had an area of 28·7m. acres; the average farm was 330 acres.

Cash receipts, 1985, from crops, $5,379m.; from livestock and livestock products, $2,176m. Illinois is a large producer of maize and soybeans, the state's leading cash commodities. Output, 1985: soybeans, 382·5m. bu; wheat, 36·7m. bu; maize, 1,534·9m. bu. In Jan. 1986 there were 230,000 milch cows, 2·47m. all cattle; 109,000 sheep and (Dec. 1985) 5·4m. swine. The wool clip in 1985 was 1m. lb.

Forestry. National forest area under the US Forest Service administration, Sept. 1985, was 262,291 acres. Total forest land, 5·2m. acres.

INDUSTRY AND TRADE

Industry. In 1983, manufacturing establishments employed 1,024,300 workers; annual payroll, $22,908·9m. Largest industry was food and kindred products. Gross state product, 1985, $192,749,000.

Labour. In 1985 there were 4·76m. employees, of whom 981,000 were in manufacturing, 1·2m. in trade, 1·1m. in services, 693,000 in government.

COMMUNICATIONS

Roads. In 1985 there were 6·5m. passenger cars, 1·26m. trucks and buses, 16,384 taxis, liveries and ambulances, 502,316 trailers and semi-trailers, 222,448 motor cycles and 26,258 other vehicles registered in the state. At 31 Dec. 1985 there were 13,168·78 miles of state primary roads of which 1,621·9 miles were interstate; 3,864·02 miles of state supplementary roads and 269·18 miles of toll roads and toll bridges.

Railways. There were, 1984, 8,841 miles of Class I railway. Chicago is served by Amtrak long-distance trains on several routes, and by a metro (CTA) system, and by 7 groups of commuter railways controlled by the Northeast Illinois Railroad Corporation (now called Metra).

Shipping. In 1983 the seaport of Chicago handled 24,454,287 short tons of cargo.

Aviation. There were (1986) 127 public airports and 722 restricted landing areas.

JUSTICE, RELIGION, EDUCATION AND WELFARE

Justice. In 1985 there were no executions; since 1930 there have been 90 executions (electrocution), including 58 white men, 1 white woman and 31 Negro men, all for murder. In June 1986 the total average daily prison population was 18,513.

A Civil Rights Act (1941), as amended, bans all forms of discrimination by places of public accommodation, including inns, restaurants, retail stores, railroads, aeroplanes, buses, etc., against persons on account of 'race, religion, colour, national ancestry or physical or mental handicap'; another section similarly mentions 'race or colour.'

The Fair Employment Practices Act of 1961, as amended, prohibits discrimination in employment based on race, colour, sex, religion, national origin or ancestry, by employers, employment agencies, labour organizations and others. These principles are embodied in the 1971 constitution.

The Illinois Human Rights Act (1979), prevents unlawful discrimination in employment, real property transactions, access to financial credit, and public accommodations, by authorizing the creation of a Department of Human Rights to enforce, and a Human Rights Commission to adjudicate, allegations of unlawful discrimination.

Religion. Among the larger religious denominations are: Roman Catholic (3·6m.), Jewish (50,000), Presbyterian Church, USA (200,000), Lutheran Church in America (200,000), Lutheran Church Missouri Synod (325,000), American Baptist (105,000), Disciples of Christ (75,000), and United Methodist (505,000), Southern Baptist (265,000), United Church of Christ (192,000), Church of Nazarene (50,000), Assembly of God (63,000).

Education. Education is free and compulsory for children between 7 and 16 years of age. In autumn 1985 public school elementary enrolments were 1,246,496 pupils and 57,279 teachers; secondary enrolments, 597,982 pupils and 29,848 teachers. Enrolment (1985–86) in non-public schools was 261,950 elementary and 84,233 secondary. Teachers' salaries, 1985–86, averaged $25,812. Total enrolment in 179 institutions of higher education (autumn 1985) was 698,521.

Colleges and universities with over 3,000 students:

Founded	Name	Place	Control	Autumn 1985 Enrolment
1851	Northwestern University	Evanston	Methodist	15,861
1857	Illinois State University	Normal	Public	21,178
1867	University of Illinois	Urbana	Public	65,169
1867	Chicago State University [1]	Chicago	Public	7,327
1869	Southern Illinois University	Carbondale	Public	33,614
1870	Loyola University	Chicago	Roman Catholic	14,406
1890	University of Chicago	Chicago	Non-Sect.	9,636
1895	Eastern Illinois University	Charleston	Public	10,491
1895	Northern Illinois University	DeKalb	Public	24,311
1897	Bradley University	Peoria	Non-Sect.	4,950
1898	DePaul University	Chicago	Roman Catholic	12,836
1899	Western Illinois University	Macomb	Public	11,845
1940	Illinois Institute of Technology [2]	Chicago	Non-Sect.	6,227
1945	Roosevelt University	Chicago	Non-Sect.	6,385
1961	Northeastern Illinois University [3]	Chicago	Public	10,081

[1] Formerly Illinois Teachers College (South).
[2] Illinois Institute of Technology formed in 1940 by merger of two older technical schools.
[3] Formerly Illinois Teachers' College (North).

Health. In 1984 hospitals listed by the American Hospital Association numbered 277, with 69,403 beds. At June 1985 state institutions had 4,637 developmentally disabled and 3,488 mentally ill residents.

Social Security. State-administered Supplemental Security Income (SSI) was paid to 45,830 recipients in financial year 1986; gross payments (no adjustments) totalled $53·2m.; medical payments, $130m. Aid to families with dependent children was paid to 243,868 families, average monthly payment per family, $308·23; total payments, $902m.; medical payments, $484·8m.

Books of Reference

Blue Book of the State of Illinois. Edited by Secretary of State. Springfield. Biennial

Angle, P. M., and Beyer, R. L., *A Handbook of Illinois History.* Illinois State Historical Society, Springfield, 1943

Clayton, J., *The Illinois Fact Book and Historical Almanac 1673–1968.* Southern Illinois Univ., 1970

Howard, R. P., *Illinois: A History of the Prairie State.* Grand Rapids, 1972

Pease, T. C., *The Story of Illinois.* 3rd ed. Chicago, 1965

The Illinois State Library: Springfield, Il.62756. *State Librarian:* Jim Edgar.

INDIANA

HISTORY. Indiana, first settled in 1732–33, was made a Territory in 1800 and admitted into the Union on 11 Dec. 1816.

AREA AND POPULATION. Indiana is bounded west by Illinois, north by Michigan and Lake Michigan, east by Ohio and south by Kentucky across the Ohio River. Area, 36,185 sq. miles, of which 253 sq. miles are inland water. Census population, 1 April 1980, was 5,490,224, an increase of 294,832 or 5·7% since 1970. Estimate (1986) 5,503,000. In 1985 births were 80,928 (14·7 per 1,000 population); deaths 48,173 (8·8); infant deaths, 886 (10·9 per 1,000 live births); marriages 51,063 (9·3).

Population in 5 census years was:

	White	Negro	Indian	Asiatic	Total	Per sq. mile
1910	2,639,961	60,320	279	316	2,700,876	74·9
1930	3,125,778	111,982	285	458	3,238,503	89·4
1960	4,388,554	269,275	948	2,447	4,662,498	128·9
			All others			
1970	4,820,324	357,464	15,881		5,193,669	143·9
1980	5,004,394	414,785	71,045		5,490,224	152·8

Of the total in 1980, 2,665,805 were male, 3,525,298 were urban and 3,545,431 were 21 years of age or older.

The largest cities with census population, 1980 (and 1986 estimates), are: Indianapolis (capital), 711,539 (719,820); Fort Wayne, 172,196 (172,900); Gary, 151,953 (136,790); Evansville, 130,496 (129,480); South Bend, 109,727 (107,190); Hammond, 93,714 (86,380); Muncie, 77,216 (72,600); Anderson, 64,695 (61,020); Terre Haute, 61,125 (57,920).

CLIMATE. Indianapolis. Jan. 29°F (–1·7°C), July 76°F (24·4°C). Annual rainfall 41″ (1,034 mm). *See* The Mid-West, p. 1378.

CONSTITUTION AND GOVERNMENT. The present constitution (the second) dates from 1851; it has had (as of Nov. 1983) 34 amendments. The General Assembly consists of a Senate of 50 members elected for 4 years, and a House of Representatives of 100 members elected for 2 years.

A constitutional amendment of 1970 allows the legislators to set the length and frequency of sessions, which are currently held annually. The Governor and Lieut.-Governor are elected for 4 years. The state is represented in Congress by 2 senators and 10 representatives.

In the 1984 presidential election Reagan polled 1,332,679 votes, Mondale, 814,659.

The state capital is Indianapolis. The state is divided into 92 counties and 1,008 townships.

Governor: Robert D. Orr (R.), 1984–88 ($66,000 plus expenses).
Lieut.-Governor: John Mutz (R.), 1984–88 ($51,000 plus expenses).
Secretary of State: Evan Bayh (D.), 1986–90 ($46,000).

BUDGET. In the fiscal year 1984–85 (US Census Bureau figures) total revenues were $7,916·9m. ($1,616·8m. from federal government, $4,336·1m. from taxes), total expenditures were $7,084·1m. ($2,908m. for education, $1,009·4m. for public welfare and $769m. for highways).

Total long-term debt, on 30 June 1985, was $1,624·0m.
Per capita personal income (1986) was $13,136.

ENERGY AND NATURAL RESOURCES

Minerals. The state produced 26·7m. short tons of crushed stone and 159,000 short tons of dimension stone in 1984; the output of coal was 30·9m. short tons; petroleum, 5m. bbls (of 42 gallons).

Agriculture. Indiana is largely agricultural, about 75% of its total area being in farms. In 1986, 78,000 farms had 16·2m. acres (average, 208 acres). Cash income, 1985, from crops, $2,869·3m.; from livestock and products, $1,727·6m.

The chief crops (1982) were maize (815m. bu.), winter wheat (46·4m. bu.), oats (6·1m. bu.), soybeans (183·2m. bu.), popcorn, rye, barley, hay (alfalfa, clover, timothy), lespedeza seed, mint, clover seed, apples, strawberries, tomatoes, water-melons and tobacco.

The livestock on 1 Jan. 1982 included 1·75m. all cattle, 207,000 milch cows, 138,000 sheep and lambs, 4·1m. swine, 21·9m. chickens. In 1982 the wool clip yielded 852,000 lb. of wool from 124,000 sheep.

Forestry. The national forests area, 9 Sept. 1983, was 188,252 acres; 13 state forests and 2 state nurseries totalled 142,336 acres in July 1983.

INDUSTRY. Manufacturing establishments employed, in 1984, 587,400 workers, earning $14,580·5m. The steel industry is the largest in the country.

COMMUNICATIONS

Roads. In 1982 there were 91,654 miles of highways, roads and streets, of which 66,412 miles were county highways and 11,148 miles state highways. Motor vehicles registered, 1986, 4,533,362.

Railways. In 1980 there were 5,252 miles of mainline railway, 921 miles of secondary track and 3,295 miles of side and yard track.

Aviation. Of airports, 1984, 127 were for public use, 401 were private and 3 were military.

JUSTICE, RELIGION, EDUCATION AND WELFARE

Justice. In 1963–80 there were no executions; there have since been 4, for murder. State correctional institutions, 31 Aug. 1986, had 10,873 inmates.

The Civil Rights Act of 1885 forbids places of public accommodation to bar any persons on grounds not applicable to all citizens alike; no citizen may be disqualified for jury service 'on account of race or colour'. An Act of 1947 makes it an offence to spread religious or racial hatred.

A 1961 Act provided 'all . . . citizens equal opportunity for education, employment and access to public conveniences and accommodations' and created a Civil Rights Commission.

Religion. Religious denominations include Methodists, Roman Catholic, Disciples of Christ, Baptists, Lutheran, Presbyterian churches, Society of Friends.

Education. School attendance is compulsory from 7 to 16 years. In 1986–87 public and parochial schools, had 929,654 pupils and 51,972 teachers. Teachers' salaries, grades 1–12, averaged $24,397 (1986–87). Total expenditure for public schools, $2,566·6m.

The principal institutions for higher education are (1985–86):

Founded	Institution	Control	Students (full-time)
1801	Vincennes University	State	6,863
1824	Indiana University, Bloomington	State	32,417
1837	De Pauw University, Greencastle	Methodist	2,372
1842	University of Notre Dame	R.C.	9,628
1850	Butler University, Indianapolis	Independent	3,645
1859	Valparaiso University, Valparaiso	Evangelical Lutheran Church	3,749
1870	Indiana State University, Terre Haute	State	11,208
1874	Purdue University, Lafayette	State	32,984
1898	Ball State University, Muncie	State	18,766
1963	Indiana Vocational Technical College, Indianapolis	State	4,410

Health. Hospitals listed by the Indiana State Board of Health (1981) numbered 120 (23,929 beds). On 30 June 1983, 11 state mental hospitals had 6,273 patients enrolled (4,472 present).

Social Security. Old-age assistance, assistance to the blind and to the disabled were transferred from state to federal programmes in June 1974. In Jan.–July 1987, state supplemental assistance and/or Federal Supplemental Security assistance was paid to an average of 11,609 elderly persons per month (total $8·5m.), 1,217 blind ($1·7m.) and 37,452 disabled ($49·3m.).

Books of Reference

Indiana State Chamber of Commerce. *Here is Your Indiana Government*. 22nd ed. Indianapolis, 1985

State Library: Indiana State Library, 140 North Senate, Indianapolis 46204. *Director:* C. Ray Ewick.

IOWA

HISTORY. Iowa, first settled in 1788, was made a Territory in 1838 and admitted into the Union on 28 Dec. 1846.

AREA AND POPULATION. Iowa is bounded east by the Mississippi River (forming the boundary with Wisconsin and Illinois), south by Missouri, west by the Missouri River (forming the boundary with Nebraska), north-west by the Big Sioux River (forming the boundary with South Dakota) and north by Minnesota. Area, 56,275 sq. miles, including 310 sq. miles of inland water. Census population, 1 April 1980, 2,913,387, an increase of 3·17% since 1970. Estimate, 1984, 2,836,890. Births, 1984, were 42,340; deaths, 26,972; infant deaths, 376; marriages, 26,366; dissolutions of marriages, 10,509.

Population in 5 census years was:

	White	Negro	Indian	Asiatic	Total	Per sq. mile
1870	1,188,207	5,762	48	3	1,194,020	21·5
1930	2,452,677	17,380	660	222	2,470,939	44·1
1960	2,729,286	25,354	1,708	1,022	2,757,537	49·2
			All others			
1970	2,782,762	32,596	10,010		2,825,368	50·5
1980	2,838,805	41,700	32,882		2,913,387	51·7

At the census of 1980, 1,416,195 were male, 1,624,547 were urban and 1,971,502 were 20 years of age or older.

The largest cities in the state, with their census population in 1980 are: Des Moines (capital), 191,003; Cedar Rapids, 110,243; Davenport, 103,243; Sioux City, 82,003; Waterloo, 75,985; Dubuque, 62,321; Council Bluffs, 56,449; Iowa City, 50,508; Ames, 45,775; Cedar Falls, 36,322; Clinton, 32,828; Mason City, 30,144; Burlington, 29,529; Fort Dodge, 29,423; Ottumwa, 27,381.

CLIMATE. Cedar Rapids. Jan. 18·5°F (–7·5°C), July 74·3°F (23·5°C). Annual rainfall 36" (903 mm). Des Moines. Jan. 18·6°F (–7·5°C), July 76·3°F (29·6°C). Annual rainfall 31" (773 mm). *See* The Mid-West, p. 1378.

CONSTITUTION AND GOVERNMENT. The constitution of 1857 still exists; it has had 37 amendments. The General Assembly comprises a Senate of 50 and a House of Representatives of 100 members, meeting annually for an unlimited session. Senators are elected for 4 years, half retiring every second year: representatives for 2 years. The Governor and Lieut.-Governor are elected for 4 years. The state is represented in Congress by 2 senators and 6 representatives. Iowa is divided into 99 counties; the capital is Des Moines.

In the 1984 presidential election Reagan polled 698,239 votes, Mondale, 601,946.

Governor: Terry Branstad (R.), 1987–91 ($64,000).
Lieut.-Governor: Joann Zimmerman (D.), 1987–91 ($21,900).
Secretary of State: Elaine Baxter (D.) ($41,000).

BUDGET. For fiscal year 1984 state tax revenue was $1,977·8m. General expenditures were $1,120m. for education, $448·5m. for public welfare, and $41·3m. for transport.

On 30 June 1982 the net long-term debt was $857·3m.

Per capita personal income (1985) was $12,594.

ENERGY AND NATURAL RESOURCES

Minerals. The leading products by value are crushed stone (28·4m. tons in 1983) and cement (1·68m. short tons in 1983). Coalfields produced 526,929 tons in 1982. The value of mineral products, 1983, was $247·4m.

Agriculture. Iowa is the wealthiest of the agriculture states, partly because nearly the whole area (95·5%) is arable and included in farms. It has escaped large-scale commercial farming. The average farm (in 1985) was 306 acres.

Cash farm income (1985 estimate) was $9,201m.; from livestock, $4,811m., and from crops, $4,390m. Production of corn was 1,707m. bu., value $3,927m. and soybeans, 310m. bu., value $1,595m. On 1 Dec. 1986 livestock included swine, 13·5m. (leading all states); milch cows, 360,000; all cattle, 4·9m., and sheep and lambs, 350,000. The wool clip (1984) yielded 3·3m. lb. of wool.

INDUSTRY. In 1985 manufacturing establishments employed 205,000 people: Trade, 277,000; services, 231,000.

COMMUNICATIONS

Roads. On 1 Jan. 1984 number of miles of streets and highways was 112,484; there were 2·6m. licensed drivers and 2·96m. registered vehicles.

Railways. The state, 1984, had 4,695 miles of track, and 6 Class I railways.

Aviation. Airports (1983), numbered 350, including 138 lighted airports and 93 all-weather runways. There were almost 3,100 private aircraft.

JUSTICE, RELIGION, EDUCATION AND WELFARE

Justice. There is now no capital punishment in Iowa. State prisons, 31 Dec. 1985, had 2,607 inmates.

Religion. Chief religious bodies in 1980 were: Roman Catholic (542,698 members); United Methodists, 258,252; American Lutheran, 200,712 baptised members; United Presbyterians, 85,000; United Church of Christ, 50,679.

Education. School attendance is compulsory for 24 consecutive weeks annually during school age (7–16). In 1983–84 545,387 were attending primary and secondary schools; 50,422 pupils attending non-public schools. Classroom teachers numbered 30,900 in 1986 with average salary of $21,650; total expenditure on public schools was $1,748m. or $606 per capita. Leading institutions for higher education (1985–86) were:

Founded	Institution	Control	Full-time Professors	Students
1843	Clarke College, Dubuque	Independent	65	857
1847	University of Iowa, Iowa City	State	1,800	29,651
1847	Grinnell College, Grinnell	Independent	118	1,250
1852	Wartburg College, Waverly	American Lutheran	94	1,323
1853	Cornell College, Mount Vernon	Independent	96	1,101
1858	Iowa State University, Ames	State	2,137	26,529
1876	Univ. of Northern Iowa, Cedar Falls	State	735	11,514
1881	Drake University, Des Moines	Independent	306	5,502
1881	Coe College, Cedar Rapids	Independent	121	1,184
1894	Morningside College, Sioux City	Methodist	99	1,217

Health. In 1985, the state had 136 hospitals (18,615 beds). In Oct. 1984 hospitals for mental diseases had 1,372 resident patients.

Social Security. Iowa has a Civil Rights Act (1939) which makes it a misdemeanour for any place of public accommodation to deprive any person of 'full and equal enjoyment' of the facilities it offers the public.

Supplemental security income (SSI) assistance is available for the aged (65 or older), the blind and the disabled. In Aug. 1985, 8,593 elderly persons were drawing an average of $102 per month, 878 blind persons $192 per month, and 16,831 disabled persons $194 per month. Aid to dependent children, established in 1974, was received by 39,813 families representing 123,762 persons at a monthly average of $335 per family.

Books of Reference

Statistical Information: State Departments of Health, Public Instruction and Social Services; State Aeronautics, Commerce and Development Commissions; Crop and Livestock Reporting Services, Des Moines; Iowa Dept. of Transportation, Ames; Geological Survey, Iowa City; Iowa College Aid Commission.
Annual Survey of Manufactures. US Department of Commerce
Government Finance. US Department of Commerce
Official Register. Secretary of State. Des Moines. Biennial
Petersen, W. J., *Iowa History Reference Guide.* Iowa City, 1952
Smeal, L., *Iowa Historical and Biographical Index.* New York, 1984
Vexler, R. I., *Iowa Chronology and Factbook.* Oceana, 1978

Iowa State Library: Des Moines 50319.

KANSAS

HISTORY. Kansas, settled in 1727, was made a Territory (along with part of Colorado) in 1854, and was admitted into the Union with its present area on 29 Jan. 1861.

AREA AND POPULATION. Kansas is bounded north by Nebraska, east by Missouri, with the Missouri River as boundary in the north-east, south by Oklahoma and west by Colorado. Area, 82,277 sq. miles, including 499 sq. miles of inland water. Census population, 1 April 1980, 2,364,236, an increase of 5·1% since 1970. Estimate (1985) 2,450,000. Vital statistics, 1984: Births, 38,570 (15·8 per 1,000 population); deaths, 21,742 (8·9); infant deaths, 336 (8·7 per 1,000 live births); marriages, 24,795 (10·2); divorces 12,915 (5·3).

Population in 5 federal census years was:

	White	Negro	Indian	Asiatic	Total	Per sq. mile
1870	346,377	17,108	914	—	364,399	4·5
1930	1,811,997	66,344	2,454	204	1,880,999	22·9
1960	2,078,666	91,445	5,069	2,271	2,178,611	26·3
			All others			
1970	2,122,068	106,977	17,533		2,249,071	27·5
1980	2,168,221	126,127	69,888		2,364,236	28·8

Of the total population in 1980, 1,156,941 were male, 1,575,899 were urban and those 20 years of age or older numbered 1,620,368.

Cities, with 1980 census population, are Wichita, 279,835; Kansas City, 161,148; Topeka (capital), 115,266; Overland Park, 81,784; Lawrence, 52,738.

CLIMATE. Dodge City. Jan. 29°F (–1·7°C), July 78°F (25·6°C). Annual rainfall 21″ (518 mm). Kansas City. Jan. 30°F (–1·1°C), July 79°F (26·1°C). Annual rainfall 38″ (947 mm). Topeka. Jan. 28°F (–2·2°C), July 78°F (25·6°C). Annual rainfall 35″ (875 mm). Wichita. Jan. 31°F (–0·6°C), July 81°F (27·2°C). Annual rainfall 31″ (777 mm). *See* Mid-West, p. 1378.

CONSTITUTION AND GOVERNMENT. The year 1861 saw the adoption of the present constitution; it has had 78 amendments. The Legislature includes a Senate of 40 members, elected for 4 years, and a House of Representatives of 125 members, elected for 2 years. Sessions are annual. The Governor and Lieut.-Governor are elected for 4 years. The right to vote (with the usual exceptions) is possessed by all citizens. The state is represented in Congress by 2 senators and 5 representatives.

The state was the first (of 42 states) to establish in 1933 a Legislative Council; this is now called the Legislative Coordinating Council and has 7 members.

In the 1984 presidential election Reagan polled 649,423 votes, Mondale, 321,010.

The capital is Topeka. The state is divided into 105 counties.

Governor: Mike Hayden (R.), 1987–91 ($65,000).
Lieut.-Governor: Thomas Docking (D.), 1987–91 ($18,207).
Secretary of State: Bill Graves (R.) ($50,000).

BUDGET. For the year ending 30 June 1986 (Governor's Budget Report) general revenue fund was $1,863m. General expenditures were $1,738m.

Bonded debt outstanding for 1982 amounted to $316·9m.

Per capita personal income (1985) was $13,775.

ENERGY AND NATURAL RESOURCES

Minerals. Important minerals are coal, petroleum (75m. bbl. in 1985), natural gas (513,000m. cu. ft.), lead and zinc.

Agriculture. Kansas is pre-eminently agricultural, but sometimes suffers from lack of rainfall in the west. In 1985, 72,000 farms covered 48m. acres; average farm, 667 acres.

Cash income, 1985, from crops was $2,478m.; from livestock and products, $3,264m.

Kansas is a great wheat-producing state. Its output in 1985 was 433·2m. bu. valued at $1,321m. Other crops in 1985 (in bushels) were maize, 140m. ($351m.); sorghum, 207m.; soybeans, 44m.; oats and barley. The state has an extensive livestock industry, comprising, on 1 Jan. 1986, 115,000 milch cows, 5·8m. all cattle, 210,000 sheep and lambs 1·5m. swine.

INDUSTRY. Employment distribution (1985): total workforce 975,000, of which 245,000 were in trade; 191,000 in government; 187,000 in services; 174,000 in manufacturing; 65,000 in transport and utilities; 53,000 in finance, insurance and real estate; 44,000 in construction. The slaughtering industry, other food processing, aircraft, the manufacture of transport equipment and petroleum refining are important.

COMMUNICATIONS

Roads. The state in Dec. 1982 had 135,087 miles of roads and streets including 8,916 miles of interstate and other primary and federally-aided highways. In 1985 2,157 vehicles were registered.

Railways. There were 7,273 miles of railway in Jan. 1982.

Aviation. There were 384 airports and landing strips in 1983, of which 168 were public.

JUSTICE, RELIGION, EDUCATION AND WELFARE

Justice. There were 4,748 prisoners in state institutions, 31 Dec. 1985. The death penalty (by hanging) for murder was abolished in 1907 and restored in 1935; there have been no executions since 1968; executions 1934 to 1968 have been 15 (all for murder).

For the various Civil Rights Acts forbidding racial or political discrimination, *see* THE STATESMAN'S YEAR-BOOK, 1955, p. 666. The 1965 Kansas Act against Discrimination declared that it is the policy of the state to eliminate and prevent discrimination in all employment relations, and to eliminate and prevent discrimination, segregation or separation in all places of public accommodations covered by the Act.

Religion. The most numerous religious bodies are Roman Catholic, Methodists and Disciples of Christ.

Education. In 1982–83 organized school districts had 1,519 elementary and secondary schools which had 407,074 pupils and 26,053 teachers. Average salary of public school teachers, 1986, $22,800 (elementary and secondary). There were 20 independent colleges, 20 community colleges, 2 Bible colleges, 1 municipal university.

Kansas has 6 state-supported institutions of higher education: the University of Kansas, Lawrence, founded in 1865, had 24,774 students in 1985–86; Kansas State University, Manhattan (1863), had 17,570; Emporia State University, Emporia, had 5,344; Pittsburg State University, Pittsburg, had 5,096; Fort Hays State University, Hays, had 5,657 and Wichita State University, Wichita, had 16,902. The state also supports a two-year technical school, Kansas Technical Institute, at Salina.

Health. In 1983 the state had 165 hospitals (18,300 beds) listed by the American Hospital Association; hospitals had an average daily occupancy rate of 70·3%.

Social Security. In Dec. 1985, 20,900 persons received state and federal aid under programmes of aid to the aged or disabled, and 66,800 in 22,700 families received aid to dependent children. Average monthly payment to the aged, $121; the disabled, $206, per family with dependent children, $303 (1984).

Books of Reference

Annual Economic Report of the Governor. Topeka
Directory of State Officers, Boards and Commissioners and Interesting Facts Concerning Kansas. Topeka, Biennial
Drury, J. W., *The Government of Kansas.* Lawrence, Univ. of Kansas, 1970
Zornow, W. F., *Kansas: A History of the Jayhawk State.* Norman, Okla., 1957

State Library: Kansas State Library, Topeka.

KENTUCKY

HISTORY. Kentucky, first settled in 1765, was originally part of Virginia; it was admitted into the Union on 1 June 1792 and its first legislature met on 4 June.

AREA AND POPULATION. Kentucky is bounded north by the Ohio River (forming the boundary with Illinois, Indiana and Ohio), north-east by the Big Sandy River (forming the boundary with West Virginia), east by Virginia, south by Tennessee and west by the Mississippi River (forming the boundary with Missouri). Area, 40,409 sq. miles, of which 740 sq. miles are water. Census population, 1980 3,660,777, an increase of 13·6% since 1970. Estimate (1986) 3,728,000. Births in 1985, 52,681 (14·2 per 1,000 population); deaths, 34,807 (9·3); infant deaths, 592 (11·2 per 1,000 live births); marriages, 45,975 (12·3); divorces, 18,254 (4·9).

Population in 5 census years was:

	White	Negro	All others	Total	Per sq.mile
1930	2,388,364	226,040	185	2,614,589	65·1
1950	2,742,090	201,921	795	2,944,806	73·9
1960	2,820,083	215,949	2,124	3,038,156	76·2
1970	2,981,766	230,793	6,147	3,218,706	81·2
1980	3,379,006	259,477	22,294	3,660,777	92·3

Of the total population in 1980, 1,789,039 were male, 1,862,183 were urban and 2,359,614 were 21 years old or older.

The principal cities with census population in 1980 are: Louisville, 298,694 (urbanized area, 654,938); Lexington-Fayette, 204,165; Owensboro, 54,450; Covington, 49,585; Bowling Green, 40,450; Paducah, 29,315; Hopkinsville, 27,318; Ashland, 27,064; Frankfort (capital), 25,973.

CLIMATE. Kentucky has a temperate climate. Temperatures are moderate during both winter and summer, precipitation is ample without a pronounced dry season, and there is little snow during the winter. Lexington. Jan. 33°F (0·6°C), July 76°F (24·4°C). Annual rainfall 45" (1,126 mm). Louisville. Jan. 33°F (0·6°C), July 77°F (25°C). Annual rainfall 43" (1,077 mm). *See* Appalachian Mountains, p.1379.

CONSTITUTION AND GOVERNMENT.

The constitution dates from 1891; there had been 3 preceding it. The 1891 constitution was promulgated by convention and provides that amendments be submitted to the electorate for ratification. The General Assembly consists of a Senate of 38 members elected for 4 years, one half retiring every 2 years, and a House of Representatives of 100 members elected for 2 years. A constitutional amendment approved by the voters in Nov. 1979, changes the year in which legislators are elected from odd to even numbered years and establishes an organizational session of the legislature, limited to ten legislative days, in odd-numbered years. The amendment provides for regular sessions limited to 60 legislative days between the first Tuesday after the first Monday of Jan. and 15 April of even numbered years. The Governor and Lieut.-Governor are elected for 4 years. All citizens are (with necessary exceptions) qualified as electors; the voting age was in 1955 reduced from 21 to 18 years. Registered voters, May 1986: 1,994,473. In the 1984 presidential election Reagan polled 822,782 votes, Mondale, 539,589.

The state is represented in Congress by 2 senators and 7 representatives.

The capital is Frankfort. The state is divided into 120 counties.

Governor: Martha Layne Collins (D.), 1983–87 ($65,483).[1]
Lieut.-Governor: Stephen L. Beshear (D.) ($55,647).[1]
Secretary of State: Drexell R. Davis (D.) ($55,647).[1]

[1] 1987. Salaries are revised annually by the percentage change in the Consumer Price Index.

BUDGET.

For the fiscal year ending 30 June 1986 revenues received within the five major operating funds amounted to $5,223·8m. Included in this figure are $2,736·8m. General Fund revenues and $1,373·7m. Federal Fund revenues. Total expenditures amounted to $4,857·7m. including education and humanities, $1,310·8m.; human resources benefits payments, $543·9m.; and transport, $467·8m.

The general obligation bonded indebtedness on 30 June 1986 was $164·7m.

Per capita personal income (1986) was $11,238.

ENERGY AND NATURAL RESOURCES

Minerals. The principal mineral product of Kentucky is coal, 149·9m. short tons mined in 1985, value $4,234m. Output of petroleum, 7·8m. bbls (of 42 gallons); natural gas, 73,126m. cu. ft; stone, 38·2m. short tons, value $139m.; clay 787,000 short tons, value $7·1m.; sand and gravel, 7·6m. short tons, value $19m. Total value of non-fuel mineral products in 1985 was $262,267,000. Other minerals include fluorspar, ball clay, lead, zinc, silver, cement, lime, industrial sand and gravel, oil shale and tar sands.

Agriculture. In 1987, 99,000 farms had an area of 14·5m. acres. The average farm was 146 acres.

Cash income, 1986, from crops, $1,078m., and from livestock, $1,310m. The chief crop is tobacco: production, in 1986, 315m. lb., ranking second to N. Carolina in US. Other principal crops include corn, soybeans, wheat, barley, sorghum grain, hay, oats and rye.

Stock-raising is important in Kentucky, which has long been famous for its horses. The livestock in 1986 included 223,000 milch cows, 2·5m. cattle and calves, 32,000 sheep, 880,000 swine.

Forestry. Total forests area, 1978, 12,160,800 acres. Total commercial forest land, 1978, 11,901,900 acres; 92% is privately owned.

INDUSTRY.

In 1986 the state's 3,632 manufacturing plants had 187,800

production workers; value added by manufacture in 1985 was $15,514.5m. The leading manufacturing industries (by employment) are non-electrical machinery, electrical equipment, apparel and other fabric products and foods. Direct foreign investment in manufacturing was $2,300m. in 1986.

TOURISM. In 1986 tourist expenditure was $3,581m., producing over $252m. in tax revenues and generating 112,353 jobs. The state had (1986) 807 hotels and motels, 233 campgrounds and 45 state parks.

COMMUNICATIONS

Roads. In 1987 the state had over 70,194 miles of federal, state and local roads. There were over 2.7m. motor vehicle registrations in 1986.

Railways. In 1987 there were about 3,100 miles of railway.

Aviation. There are (1987) 74 publicly-used airports and 2,070 registered aircraft in Kentucky.

Shipping. There is an increasing amount of barge traffic on 1,090 miles of navigable rivers. There are 5 river ports, 2 under construction and 2 planned.

JUSTICE, RELIGION, EDUCATION AND WELFARE

Justice. There are 10 prisons within the Department of Adult Institutions and one privately-run adult institution; average daily population (1986–87), 6,119, including 4,745 in prison, 201 in a private prison, 862 in jails awaiting incarceration, 311 in local community centers.

There has been no execution since 1962. A session of Congress in 1976 limited the death penalty to cases of kidnap and murder.

Total executions, 1911–62, were 162, including 76 whites and 86 Negroes; 144 were for murder, 7 for rape, 6 for criminal offences, 5 for armed robbery. There are (1987) 32 people under death sentences.

Religion. The chief religious denominations in 1980 were: Southern Baptists, with 883,096 members, Roman Catholic (365,277), United Methodists (234,536), Christian Churches and Church of Christ (81,222) and Christian (Disciples of Christ) (78,275).

Education. Attendance at school between the ages of 5 and 15 years (inclusive) is compulsory, the normal term being 175 days. In 1986–87, 23,129 teachers were employed in public elementary and 11,338 in secondary schools, in which 429,085 and 213,693 pupils enrolled respectively. Expenditure on elementary and secondary day schools in 1986–87 was $1,918.8m.; public school classroom teachers' salaries (1986–87) averaged $22,470.

There were also 4,020 teachers working in private elementary and secondary schools with 66,951 students.

The state has 25 universities and senior colleges, 4 junior colleges and 14 community colleges, with a total (autumn 1986) of 136,204 students. Of these universities and colleges, 23 are state-supported, and the remainder are supported privately. The largest of the institutions of higher learning are (autumn 1986): University of Kentucky, with 21,240 students; University of Louisville, 20,710 students; Western Kentucky University, 12,257 students; Eastern Kentucky University, 12,737 students; Murray State University, 7,073 students; Morehead State University, 5,894 students; Northern Kentucky University, 8,661 students. Five of the several privately endowed colleges of standing are Berea College, Berea; Centre College, Danville; Transylvania University, Lexington; Georgetown College, Georgetown; and Bellarmine College, Louisville.

Health. In 1987 the state had 126 licensed hospitals (19,225 beds). There were 518 licensed long-term care facilities (29,034) and 517 licensed family care homes (1,447).

Welfare. In April 1987 there were 270,914 persons receiving financial assistance;

101,961 of these persons received the Federal Supplemental Security Income (SSI); 32,567 of them were aged, 2,078 blind, 67,316 disabled. Also, in the all state funded Supplementation programme, payments were made in April 1987 to 7,040 persons, of which 3,597 were aged, 91 blind and 3,352 disabled. The average State Supplementation payment was $118.70 to aged, $64.51 to blind and $121.46 to disabled.

In the Aid to Families with Dependent Children Programme as of April 1987, aid was given to 161,913 persons in 60,492 families. The average payment per person was $72.00, per family $192.71.

In addition to money payments, medical assistance, food stamps and social services are available.

Books of Reference

Kentucky Economic Statistics. Department of Economic Development, Frankfort
Lee, L. G., *A Brief History of Kentucky and its Counties.* Berea, 1981

LOUISIANA

HISTORY. Louisiana was first settled in 1699. That part lying east of the Mississippi River was organized in 1804 as the Territory of New Orleans, and admitted into the Union on 30 April 1812. The section west of the river was added very shortly thereafter.

AREA AND POPULATION. Louisiana is bounded north by Arkansas, east by Mississippi, with the Mississippi River forming the boundary in the north-east, south by the Gulf of Mexico and west by Texas, with the Sabine River forming most of the boundary. Area, 52,453 sq. miles, including lakes, rivers and coastal waters inside 3-mile limit; land area, 44,873 sq. miles. Census population, 1 April 1980, 4,205,900, an increase of 15·5% since 1970. Estimate (1985) 4,481,000. Births, 1984, 83,195 (18·6 per 1,000 population); deaths, 36,549 (8·2); infant deaths, 1,037 (12·5 per 1,000 live births); marriages, 41,295 (9·3); divorces, 17,377 (1982).

Population in 5 census years was:

	White	Negro	Indian	Asiatic	Total	Per sq. mile
1910	941,086	713,874	780	648	1,656,388	36·5
1930	1,322,712	776,326	1,536	1,019	2,101,593	46·5
1960	2,211,715	1,039,207	3,587	2,004	3,257,022	72·2
			All others			
1970	2,541,498	1,086,832	12,976		3,641,306	81·1
1980	2,911,243	1,237,263	55,466		4,203,972 [1]	93·5

[1] Preliminary.

Of the 1980 total, 2,039,894 were male, 2,885,535 were urban; those 20 years of age or older numbered 2,699,100.

The largest cities with their 1980 census population are: New Orleans, 557,482; Baton Rouge (capital), 219,486; Shreveport, 205,815; Lafayette, 81,961; Lake Charles, 75,051; Kenner, 66,382.

CLIMATE. New Orleans. Jan. 54°F (12·2°C), July 83°F (28·3°C). Annual rainfall 58″ (1,458 mm). *See* Gulf Coast, p. 1379.

CONSTITUTION AND GOVERNMENT. The present constitution dates from 1974.

The Legislature consists of a Senate of 39 members and a House of Representatives of 105 members, both chosen for 4 years. Sessions are annual; a fiscal session is held in odd years. The Governor and Lieut.-Governor are elected for 4 years.

A Governor may serve a second consecutive term. Qualified electors are (with the usual exceptions) all registered citizens with the usual residential qualifications.

In the 1984 presidential election Reagan polled 1,030,091 votes, Mondale, 648,040.

The state sends to Congress 2 senators and 8 representatives. Louisiana is divided into 64 parishes (corresponding with the counties of other states).

Governor: Edwin W. Edwards (D.), 1984–88 ($73,440).
Lieut.-Governor: Robert Freeman (D.), 1984–88 ($63,367).
Secretary of State: James Brown (D.), 1984–88 ($60,169).

BUDGET. For the fiscal year ending 30 June 1982 (Louisiana State Budget Office figures) general revenues were $6,091,714,373, of which $1,236,983,444 were federal funds; total expenditures were $6,067,203,315 (education, $2,077,432,518; transport and development, $416,170,800; health, hospitals and public welfare, $1,578,334,592).

Per capita personal income (1985) was $11,274.

ENERGY AND NATURAL RESOURCES

Minerals. The yield in 1985 of crude petroleum was 508m. bbls; marketed production of natural gas, 5,146,000m. cu. ft. Rich sulphur mines are found in the state, and wells for the extraction of sulphur by means of hot water and compressed air are in operation; output, 1980, 2·6m. tonnes.

Louisiana is the USA's main salt producer. Output of salt (1980) was 12·6m. short tons valued at $132·2m. Total output of minerals in 1982 was valued at $31,364m., of which $30,946m. was from fuel minerals.

Agriculture. The state is divided into two parts, the uplands and the alluvial and swamp regions of the coast. A delta occupies about one-third of the total area. Manufacturing is the leading industry, but agriculture is important. In 1985 there were about 36,000 farms with annual average sales of at least $1,000; average farm, 278 acres; average value per acre $1,256.

Cash income, 1985, from crops $968m.; from livestock, $491m. Production of crops (1985): Corn for grain, 23m. bu. (value $61m.); cotton lint, 742,000 bales ($194m.); soybeans, 44m. bu. ($223m.); wheat, hay, rice and sugar are also important.

In 1983 the state contained 102,000 milch cows, 1·4m. all cattle, 9,000 sheep and 135,000 swine.

Fisheries. The catch in 1985 was 1,693m. lb., value $225m.

Forestry. Forests, 14·5m. acres, represent 47% of the state's area. Income from manufactured products exceeds $2,500m. annually. In 1982 pulpwood cut, 3,867,994·3 cords; sawtimber cut, 927·4m. bd ft.

INDUSTRY. The manufacturing industries are chiefly those associated with petroleum, chemicals, lumber, food, paper. In 1985 178,000 were employed in manufacturing, 387,000 in trade and 320,000 in service industries.

TOURISM. Travellers spent an estimated $3,300m. in 1982. State tax revenue, $99·3m. (3% of state tax revenue).

COMMUNICATIONS

Roads. The state has more than 16,326 miles of public roads. In June 1985, over 3m. vehicles were registered in the state.

Railways. In 1980 the railways in the state had a length of about 3,700 miles.

Aviation. There were, 1981, about 240 commercial and private airports.

Shipping. In 1981 New Orleans handled 188·9m. tons of cargo. The Mississippi and other waterways provide 7,500 miles of navigable water.

JUSTICE, RELIGION, EDUCATION AND WELFARE

Justice. State and federal prisons, Oct. 1984, had 13,919 inmates. Execution is by electrocution; there were 135 between 1930 and 1961, 6 between 1977 and 1985.

Religion. The Roman Catholic Church is the largest denomination in Louisiana. The leading Protestant Churches are Southern Baptist and Methodist.

Education. School attendance is compulsory between the ages of 7 and 15, both inclusive. In 1983 there were 782,000 pupils in public elementary and secondary schools. In 1986 the 42,900 instructional staff had an average salary of $20,600. There are 16 four-year public colleges and universities and 12 non-public four-year institutions of higher learning. There are 53 state trade and vocational-technical schools. Superior instruction is given in the Louisiana State University with 36,128 students (1985–86). Tulane University in New Orleans had 10,106; The Roman Catholic Loyola University in New Orleans had 4,809; Dillard University in New Orleans had 1,189; and the Southern University, 3,000.

Health. In 1983 the state had 158 licensed hospitals (26,400 beds); there were 3 mental hospitals.

Social Security. In Dec. 1985, assistance was being given to 49,400 elderly persons; 78,800 families with dependent children; 74,700 disabled people. Aid was from state and federal sources.

Books of Reference

Louisiana Almanac. New Orleans, 1979–80

The History and Government of Louisiana. Legislative Council, Baton Rouge, 1975

Louisiana State Agencies Handbook. Public Affairs Research Council of Louisiana. Baton Rouge, 1979

The State of the State: an Economic and Social Report to the Governor. Louisiana State Planning Office, New Orleans, 1978

Statistical Abstract of Louisiana. Division of Business and Economic Research, Univ. of New Orleans, 1977

Davis, E. A., *Louisiana, the Pelican State.* Louisiana State Univ. Press, Baton Rouge, 1975

Hansen, H., (ed.), *Louisiana, a Guide to the State.* Rev. ed. New York, 1971

Kniffen, F. B., *Louisiana, its Land and People.* Louisiana State Univ. Press, Baton Rouge, 1968

State Library: The Louisiana State Library, Baton Rouge, Louisiana. *State Librarian:* Thomas F. Jaques.

MAINE

HISTORY. After a first attempt in 1607, Maine was settled in 1623. From 1652 to 1820 it was part of Massachusetts and was admitted into the Union on 15 March 1820.

AREA AND POPULATION. Maine is bounded west, north and east by Canada, south-east by the Atlantic, south and south-west by New Hampshire. Area, 33,265 sq. miles, of which 2,269 are inland water. Of the state's total area, about 17·2m. acres (87%) are in timber and wood lots. Census population, 1 April 1980 1,125,027, an increase of 13·29% since 1970. Estimate (1986) 1,174,000. In 1984 live births numbered 16,513 (14·3 per 1,000 population); deaths, 10,796 (9·3); infant deaths, 119 (7·2 per 1,000 live births); marriages, 12,430 (10·8); divorces 5,864 (5·1).

Population for 5 census years was:

	White	Negro	Indian	Asiatic	Total	Per sq. mile
1910	739,995	1,363	892	121	742,371	24·8
1930	795,185	1,096	1,012	130	797,423	25·7
1950	910,846	1,221	1,522	185	913,774	29·4
			All others			
1970	985,276	2,800	3,972		992,048	31·0
1980	1,109,850	3,128	12,049		1,125,027	36·3

Of the total population in 1980, 48·5% were male, 40·7% were urban and 60·5% were 21 years or older.

The largest city in the state is Portland with a census population of 61,572 in 1980. Other cities (with population in 1980) are: Lewiston, 40,481; Bangor, 31,643; Auburn, 23,128; South Portland, 22,712; Augusta (capital), 21,819; Biddeford, 19,638; Waterville, 17,779.

CLIMATE. Average maximum temperatures range from 56·3°F in Waterville to 48·3°F in Caribou, but record high (since *c.* 1950) is 103°F. Average minimum ranges from 36·9°F in Rockland to 28·3°F in Greenville, but record low (also in Greenville) is –42°F. Average annual rainfall ranges from 48·85″ in Machias to 36·09″ in Houlton. Average annual snowfall ranges from 118·7″ in Greenville to 59·7″ in Rockland. *See* New England, p. 1379.

CONSTITUTION AND GOVERNMENT. The constitution of 1820 is still in force, but it has been amended 153 times. In 1951, 1965 and 1973 the Legislature approved recodifications of the constitution as arranged by the Chief Justice under special authority.

The Legislature consists of the Senate with 35 members and the House of Representatives with 151 members, both Houses being elected simultaneously for 2 years. Apart from these legislators and the Governor (elected for 4 years), no other state officers are elected. The Justices of the Supreme Judicial Court give their opinion upon important questions of law and upon solemn occasions when required by the Governor, Senate or House of Representatives. The suffrage is possessed by all citizens, 18 years of age; persons under guardianship for reasons of mental illness have no vote. Indians residing on tribal reservations and otherwise qualified have the vote in all county, state and national elections but retain the right to elect their own tribal representative to the legislature.

In the 1984 presidential election Reagan polled 336,500 votes, Mondale, 214,515.

The state sends to Congress 2 senators and 2 representatives.

The capital is Augusta. The state is divided into 16 counties.

Governor: John McKernan (R.), 1987–91 ($35,000).
Secretary of State: Rodney S. Quinn (D.), 1987–91 ($30,000).

BUDGET. For the financial year ending 30 June 1986 general revenue was $932m. and expenditure was $927m.

Total net long-term debt on 30 June 1984 was $294·5m.

Per capita personal income (1986) was $12,709.

NATURAL RESOURCES

Minerals. Minerals include sand and gravel, stone, lead, clay, copper, peat, silver and zinc. Mineral output, 1986, was valued at $46m.

Agriculture. In 1985, 8,000 farms occupied 2m. acres; the average farm was 250 acres.

Cash receipts, 1985, $378m., of which $80m. came from potatoes; Maine is the third largest producer of potatoes (about 7% of the country's total of 325·7m. cwt). Other important items include eggs ($94m.), dairy products ($107·5m.) and poultry ($29·7m.); these with potatoes provide 78% of receipts. Sweet corn, peas and beans, oats, hay, apples and blueberries are also grown. On 1 Jan. 1983 the farm animals included 57,000 milch cows, 146,000 all other cattle, and 14,000 sheep.

Forestry. Lumber, wood turnings and pulp are important. In 1982 the cut of softwood was 769,195m. bd ft; hardwood, 150,878m. bd ft, and pulpwood, 3,417,586 cords. Spruce and fir, white pine, hemlock, white and yellow birch, sugar maple, northern white cedar, beech and red oak are the most important species cut. There were (1982) 17,600,000 acres of commercial forest (98% in private ownership). National forests comprise 37,500 acres; other federal, 35,800;

state forests, 163,000 acres; municipal, 75,200 acres. Wood products industries are of great economic importance; in 1982 the lumber, wood and paper industries' production was valued at $3,355,731. There were (1982) 342 primary manufacturers and over 1,400 secondary.

Fisheries. In 1983, 202,657,000 lb. of fish and shellfish (valued at $107,889,000 were landed; the catch included 21,976,000 lb. of lobsters (valued at $51,234,000). 1·97m. lb. of scallops ($10·8m.); 4·14m. lb. of soft clams ($7·24m.); 12·31m. lb of dabs ($6·0m.); 42·4m. lb. of menhaden ($846,000); 40m. lb. of herring ($2·14m.).

INDUSTRY. Total non-agricultural workforce, 1985, 459,000. Manufacturing employed 106,000; trade, 108,000; services, 95,000; government, 86,000; the main manufacture is paper at 47 plants, producing about 34% of manufacturing value added.

LABOUR. The four largest employers are government, education, health and tourism.

TOURISM. In 1983 there were about 4m. tourists (including state residents on holiday), generating about $655·5m. in business. Eating, drinking and accommodation produce 12·4% of sales tax.

COMMUNICATIONS

Roads. In 1983 there were 22,098 miles of roads, of which 3,973 miles were state highways and 4,359 miles were state-aided; town streets and miscellaneous, 13,766 miles. In July 1984, 847,922 motor vehicles were registered, including 669,240 passenger vehicles, 87,267 commercial vehicles and 40,361 motorcycles.

Railways. In 1984 there were 1,516 miles of mainline railway tracks.

Aviation. Licensed airports, 1984, numbered 76, including 37 commercial public airports, 12 non-commercial and 4 commuter airports, 15 commercial and 4 non-commercial seaplane bases, and 4 air-carrier airports. There were also 2 military airports and 23 private landing strips.

JUSTICE, RELIGION, EDUCATION AND WELFARE

Justice. The state's penal system in Sept. 1984 held 435 adults in the State Prison, 237 in the Correctional Center and 332 juveniles in the Youth Center. There is no capital punishment. Inmates serving life sentences are eligible for parole consideration after 15 years, less remission for good conduct, provided they were imprisoned before the passage of a new Criminal Code by the 107th Maine Legislature, which abolished the parole system.

Religion. The largest religious bodies are: Roman Catholic (270,283 members), Baptists (36,808 members) and Congregationalists (40,750 members), and other Christian Churches (34,066 members).

Education. Education is free for pupils from 5 to 21 years of age, and compulsory from 7 to 17. In 1983–84 the 756 public schools (610 elementary, 105 secondary and 41 combined elementary and secondary) had 12,283 staff and 209,753 enrolled pupils. In 1983–84 there were 126 private schools with 1,035 teachers and 15,461 pupils. Public school teachers' salaries, 1983–84, averaged $17,328. Total public expenditure on public elementary and secondary education in 1982–83, $461,252,847.

The state University of Maine, founded in 1865, had (1983–84) 1,003 teaching staff and 28,591 students at 7 locations; Bowdoin College, founded in 1794 at Brunswick, (107 and 1,371); Bates College at Lewiston, (104 and 1,424); Colby College at Waterville, (125 and 1,733); Husson College, Bangor, (31 and 1,465); Westbrook College at Westbrook, (56 and 1,120); Unity College at Unity, (23 and 325), and the University of New England (formerly St Francis College) at Biddeford, (55 and 848).

Health. In 1984 the state had 42 general hospitals (4,571 beds for acute care); 3 hospitals for mental diseases, acute and psychiatric care (541 beds); 144 nursing homes (10,220 beds).

Social Security. Supplemental Security Income (SSI) (maximum payment for single person, $324·30 per month) is administered by the Social Security Administration. It became effective on 1 Jan. 1974 and replaces former aid to the aged, blind and disabled, administered by the state with state and federal funds. SSI is supplemented by Medicaid for nursing home patients or hospital patients. State payments for SSI recipients for 1985 totalled $42·3m., covering 22,000 cases. Aid to families with dependent children is granted where one or both parents are disabled or absent and income is insufficient; aid was being granted in Aug. 1985 to 20,100 families (58,300 children) with an average payment per family of $321 per month. Payments under Maine Medicaid Assistance programme totalled $217m. for the financial year 1983–84. There is a programme of assistance for catastrophic illness. Child welfare services include basic child protective services, enforcing child support, establishing paternity and finding missing parents, foster home placements, adoptions; services in divorce cases and licensing of foster homes, day care and residential treatment services, and public guardianship. There are also protective services for adults.

Books of Reference

Maine Register, State Year-Book and Legislative Manual. Tower Publishing, Portland. Annual
Banks, R., *Maine Becomes A State.* Wesleyan U.P., 1970
Caldwell, B., *Rivers of Fortune.* Gannett, 1983
Calvert, M. R., *Dawn over the Kennebec.* Private Pr., 1983
Clark, C., *Maine.* New York, 1977

MARYLAND

HISTORY. Maryland, first settled in 1634, was one of the 13 original states.

AREA AND POPULATION. Maryland is bounded north by Pennsylvania, east by Delaware and the Atlantic, south by Virginia and West Virginia, with the Potomac River forming most of the boundary, and west by West Virginia. Chesapeake Bay almost cuts off the eastern end of the state from the rest. Area, 10,460 sq. miles, of which 623 sq. miles are inland water; in addition, water area under Maryland jurisdiction in Chesapeake Bay amounts to 1,726 sq. miles. Census population, 1 April 1980, 4,216,975, an increase since 1970 of 293,078 or 7·5%. Estimate (1986) 4,463,000. In 1985 births were 67,985 (15·5 per 1,000 population); deaths, 36,607 (8·3); infant deaths, 811 (11·9 per 1,000 live births); marriages, 46,063 (10·5); divorces, 16,187 (3·7).

Population for 5 federal censuses was:

	White	Negro	Indian	Asiatic	Total	Per sq. mile
1920	1,204,737	244,479	32	413	1,449,661	145·8
1930	1,354,226	276,379	50	871	1,631,526	165·0
1960	2,573,919	518,410	1,538	5,700	3,100,689	314·0
			All others			
1970	3,194,888	499,479	28,032		3,922,399	396·6
1980	3,158,838	958,150	99,987		4,216,975	428·7

Of the total population in 1980, 2,042,810 were male, 3,386,555 persons were urban and those 20 years old or older numbered 2,890,196.

The largest city in the state (containing 16·9% of the population) is Baltimore, with 786,741 in 1980 (and 752,800 in 1986); Baltimore metropolitan area, 2·3m. Maryland residents in the Washington, D.C., metropolitan area total more than 1·6m. Other cities (1980) are Dundalk (71,293); Towson (51,083); Silver Spring

(72,893); Bethesda (62,736). Incorporated places, estimate 1984: Rockville, 45,065; Bowie, 34,461; Hagerstown, 33,036; Frederick, 31,943; Annapolis, 31,898; Gaithersburg, 29,548; Cumberland, 24,090; Cambridge, 11,207.

CLIMATE. Baltimore. Jan. 36°F (2·2°C), July 79°F (26·1°C). Annual rainfall 41″ (1,026 mm). *See* Atlantic Coast, p. 1379.

CONSTITUTION AND GOVERNMENT. The present constitution dates from 1867; it has had 125 amendments. The General Assembly consists of a Senate of 47, and a House of Delegates of 141 members, both elected for 4 years, as are the Governor and Lieut.-Governor. Voters are citizens who have the usual residential qualifications. At the 1984 presidential election Reagan polled 836,295 votes, Mondale, 757,635.

Maryland sends to Congress 2 senators and 8 representatives.

The state capital is Annapolis. The state is divided into 23 counties and Baltimore City.

Governor: William D. Schaefer (D.), 1987–97 ($75,000).
Lieut.-Governor: J. Joseph Curran (D.), 1987–91 ($62,500).
Secretary of State: Patricia Holtz ($45,000).

BUDGET. For the fiscal year ending 30 June 1986 general revenues were $6,751,471,000 ($4,713,904,000 from taxation). General expenditures, $6,659,000,000, including $1,516,492,000 for education and $2,080,925,000 for public welfare and health; $1,229,520,000 for transport.

Total authorized long-term state debt, 30 June 1986 was $2,986,127,000. (Issued and outstanding, $2,110,075,000; authorized but not issued, $876,052,000.)

Per capita personal income (1986) was $16,588.

ENERGY AND NATURAL RESOURCES

Minerals. Value of non-fuel mineral production, 1986, was $294m. Sand and gravel (16·7m. short tons) and stone (26·2m. short tons) account for over 65% of the total value. Coal is the leading mineral commodity by value followed by Portland cement, stone, sand and gravel. Output of coal was 4·1m. short tons, valued at about $109m. Natural gas is produced from 1 field in Garrett County; 39m. cu. ft in 1985. A second gas field in the same county is used for natural gas storage.

Agriculture. Agriculture is an important industry in the state. In 1986 there were approximately 17,000 farms with an area of 2·5m. acres (40% of the land area).

Farm animals, 1 Jan. 1987, were: Milch cows, 125,000; all cattle, 330,000; swine, 190,000; sheep, 25,000; chickens (not broilers), 5·1m.. The most important crops, 1986, were: corn for grain, 42·3m. bu.; soybeans, 10·9m. bu.; tobacco, 24·3m. lb., and hay, 509,000 tons.

Cash receipts from farm marketings, 1986, were $1,203m.; from livestock and livestock products, $814m., and crops, $389m. Dairy products and broilers are important.

INDUSTRY. In 1985 manufactories had 141,500 production workers earning $2,867·4m.; value added by manufacture, $11,906·6m. Chief industries are electrical and electronic equipment, food and kindred products, chemicals and products, printing and publishing.

TOURISM. Tourism is one of the state's leading industries. In 1986 tourists spent over $4,707m.

COMMUNICATIONS

Roads. The state highway department maintained, 1 Jan. 1987, 5,238 miles of highways, of which 84 miles were toll roads. The 23 counties maintained 17,873 miles of highways, and the 159 municipalities (including the city of Baltimore) maintained 4,010 miles of streets and alleys. Total mileage, 1 Jan. 1987, of public highways, streets and alleys, 27,121 miles. In 1986, about 3·5m. automobiles were registered.

Railways. Railways, in 1987, had 1,150 miles of line.

Aviation. There were, 1987, 38 commercially licensed airports.

Shipping. In 1986 Baltimore was the sixth largest US seaport in value of trade, seventh in tonnage handled.

JUSTICE, RELIGION, EDUCATION AND WELFARE

Justice. Prisons on 1 Oct. 1987 had about 12,381 men and 443 women; the total equalled 285 per 100,000 population, a high rate, which may be explained by the fact that Maryland incarcerates domestic relations law violators in state prisons; state prisons also receive a considerable number of persons committed for misdemeanours by magistrates' courts of the counties as well as from Baltimore's court system.

Since 1930 there have been 68 executions (by lethal gas since 1957; earlier by hanging)—7 whites and 37 Negroes for murder, and 6 whites and 18 Negroes for rape. Last execution was June 1961.

Maryland's prison system has conducted a work-release programme for selected prisoners since 1963. All institutions have academic and vocational training programmes.

In accordance with the 1950 Supreme Court decisions declaring segregation unconstitutional, the University of Maryland and other public and private colleges began admitting Black students in Sept. 1956; elementary and secondary schools followed.

Religion. Maryland was the first US state to give religious freedom to all who came within its borders. Present religious affiliations of the population are approximately: Protestant, 32%; Roman Catholic, 24%; Jewish, 10%; remaining 34% is non-related and other faiths.

Education. Education is compulsory from 6 to 16 years of age. In Sept. 1986 the public elementary schools (including kindergartens and secondary schools) had 675,747 pupils. Teachers and principals in the elementary and secondary schools numbered 41,836. Average salary, teachers and principals (Oct. 1985) was $27,806. Current expenditure by local school boards on education, 1985–86, was $2,682·3m., of which the state's contribution was $1,076m.

In 1986 there were 30 degree-granting 4-year institutions and 23 2-year colleges. The largest two were the University of Maryland system, with 66,331 students (Sept. 1986) and Towson State College with 15,411 students (Sept. 1986).

Health. In April 1987, 84 hospitals (21,414 beds) were licensed by the State Department of Health and Mental Hygiene.

The Maryland State Department of Health, organized in 1874, was in 1969 made part of the Department of Health and Mental Hygiene which performs its functions through its central office, 23 county health departments and the Baltimore City Health Department. For the financial year 1986 the department's budget was $1,411·9m., of which $995·8m. were general funds and $30·5m. special funds appropriated by the General Assembly. The balance of the budget, $385·7m., derives from federal funds.

During financial year 1986 Maryland's programme of medical care for indigent and medically indigent patients covered 398,721 persons. The programme, which covers in-patient and out-patient hospital services, laboratory services, skilled nursing home care, physician services, pharmacy services, dental services and home health services, cost approximately $759m.

Social Security. Under the supervision of the Department of Human Resources, local social service departments administer public assistance for needy persons. In May 1987 families with dependent children received $20,759,308 (182,686 recipients, average actual monthly payment $113.55); general public assistance payments were $2,670,578 (18,443 recipients, average actual monthly payments $144.88).

Books of Reference

Statistical Information: Maryland Department of Economic and Employment Development, Baltimore City, 21202.

Maryland Manual: A Compendium of Legal, Historical and Statistical Information Relating to the State of Maryland. Annapolis. Biennial

DiLisio, J. E., *Maryland.* Boulder, 1982

Papenfuse, E. C., et al., *Maryland, a New Guide to the Old Line State.* Johns Hopkins Univ. Press, 1976

Rollo, V. F., *Maryland's Constitution and Government.* Maryland Hist. Press, Rev. ed., 1982

State Library: Maryland State Library, Annapolis. *Director:* Michael S. Miller.

MASSACHUSETTS

HISTORY. The first permanent settlement within the borders of the present state was made at Plymouth in Dec. 1620, by the Pilgrims from Holland, who were separatists from the English Church, and formed the nucleus of the Plymouth Colony. In 1628 another company of Puritans settled at Salem, forming eventually the Massachusetts Bay Colony. In 1630 Boston was settled. In the struggle which ended in the separation of the American colonies from the mother country, Massachusetts took the foremost part, and on 6 Feb. 1788 became the sixth state to ratify the US constitution.

AREA AND POPULATION. Massachusetts is bounded north by Vermont and New Hampshire, east by the Atlantic, south by Connecticut and Rhode Island and west by New York. Area, 8,284 sq. miles, 460 sq. miles being inland water. The census population 1 April 1980, was 5,737,037, an increase of 47,867 or 0·8% since 1970. Estimate (1984) 5,741,000. Births, 1984 were 79,386 (13·7 per 1,000 population); deaths, 59,104 (10·2 per 1,000); infant deaths, 739 (9·3 per 1,000 live births); marriages, 53,198 (9·2); divorces, 16,957 (2·9).

Population at 4 federal census years was:

	White	Negro	Other	Total	Per sq. mile
1950	4,611,503	73,171	5,840	4,690,514	598·4
1960	5,023,144	111,842	13,592	5,148,578	656·8
1970	5,477,624	175,817	35,729	5,689,170	725·8
1980	5,362,836	221,279	152,922	5,737,037	732·0

Of the total population in 1980, 47·6% were male, 83·8% were urban and 32% were 21 years old or older.

In 1980 the population of the principal towns and cities was:

Boston	562,994	Fall River	92,574	Framingham	65,113
Worcester	161,799	Lowell	92,418	Lawrence	63,175
Springfield	153,319	Quincy	84,743	Waltham	58,200
New Bedford	98,478	Newton	83,622	Medford	58,076
Cambridge	95,322	Lynn	78,471	Weymouth	55,601
Brockton	95,172	Somerville	77,372	Chicopee	55,112

The largest of 10 standard metropolitan statistical areas, 1980 census were: Boston, 2,763,357; Springfield–Chicopee–Holyoke, 530,668; Worcester, 372,940.

CLIMATE. Boston. Jan. 28°F (−2·2°C), July 71°F (21·7°C). Annual rainfall 41" (1,036 mm). *See* New England, p. 1379.

CONSTITUTION AND GOVERNMENT. The constitution dates from 1780 and has had 116 amendments. The legislative body, styled the General Court of the Commonwealth of Massachusetts, meets annually, and consists of the Senate with 40 members, elected biennially, and the House of Representatives of 160 members, elected for 2 years. The Governor and Lieut.-Governor are elected for 4 years. The state sends 2 senators and 11 representatives to Congress.

At the 1984 presidential election Reagan polled 1,293,367 votes, Mondale, 1,219,513.

Electors are all citizens 18 years of age or older.

The capital is Boston. The state has 14 counties, 39 cities and 312 towns.

Governor: Michael S. Dukakis (D.), 1987–91 ($75,000).
Lieut.-Governor: Evelyn Murphy (D.), 1987–91 ($60,000).
Secretary of the Commonwealth: Michael J. Connolly (D.) ($60,000).

BUDGET. For the fiscal year ending 30 June 1984 the total revenue of the state was $8,763,776,497 ($5,659·5m. from taxes and $1,800·3m. from federal aid); general expenditures, $8,649,394,825 ($603·4m. for education, $330·5m. for highway and transport construction and $2,097m. for public welfare).

The net long-term debt on 30 June 1984 amounted to $3,346m.

Per capita personal income (1985) was $16,380.

NATURAL RESOURCES

Minerals. There is little mining within the state. Total mineral output in 1983 was valued at $95·7m., of which most came from sand, gravel and stone.

Agriculture. On 1 Jan. 1986 there were approximately 6,000 farms (11,179 in 1959) with an area of 598,900 acres.

Cash income, 1986, totalled $425·2m.; dairy, $76·3m.; greenhouse and nursery, $118m.; poultry, $30·8m.; vegetables, $38·8m.; tobacco, $7m.; cranberries, $98·6m.; other fruit, $23·2m.; potatoes, $2·6m. Total from crops, $295·2m., from livestock, $130m.

Principal 1986 crops include cranberries, 1·69m. bbls; apples, 2·1m. bu. in 1985; potatoes, 825,000 cwt in 1985. On 1 Jan. 1982 farms in the state had 48,000 milch cows, 98,000 all cattle, 49,000 swine. In 1982 farms produced 145,000 turkeys and 0·8m. chickens.

Forestry. About 68% of the state is forest. State forests cover about 256,000 acres. Total forest land covers about 3m. acres. Commercially important hardwoods are sugar maple, northern red oak and white ash; softwoods are white pine and hemlock. About 240m. bd ft of timber are cut annually.

Fisheries. The 1985 catch amounted to 296m. lb. of fish and shellfish valued at $232m.

INDUSTRY. In 1985, manufacturing establishments employed an average of 661,000 workers. The 3 most important manufacturing groups, based on employment, were electric and electronic equipment, machinery (except electrical), instruments and related products. Service industries employed 779,000 and trade, 680,000. Total non-agricultural workforce, 2,926,000.

COMMUNICATIONS

Roads. In Oct. 1984 the state had 33,800 miles of roads and streets and in 1985 registered 3·8m. motor vehicles.

Railways. In 1984 there were 1,310 miles of mainline railway.

Aviation. There were, in 1983, 52 aircraft landing areas for commercial operation, of which 27 were publicly owned.

Shipping. The state has 3 deep-water harbours, the largest of which is Boston (port trade (1983), 16,767,585 short tons). Other ports are Fall River and New Bedford.

JUSTICE, RELIGION, EDUCATION AND WELFARE

Justice. On 31 Dec. 1985 state penal institutions held 5,447 inmates. There have been no executions since 1947.

Religion. The principal religious bodies are the Roman Catholics, Jewish Congregations, Methodists, Episcopalians and Unitarians.

Education. A regulation effective from 1 Sept. 1972 makes school attendance compulsory for ages 6–16. In 1985–86 expenditure by cities and towns on public schools was $3,521m. or $605 per capita, including debt retirement and service payments. In 1985–86 there were 56,400 classroom teachers and approximately 900,000 pupils.

Within the state there were (1982) 126 degree-granting institutions of higher learning (including 89 colleges and universities). Some leading institutions are:

Year opened	Name and location of universities and colleges	Students 1985
1636	Harvard University, Cambridge [1]	16,217
1793	Williams College, Williamstown [1]	1,983
1821	Amherst College, Amherst [1]	1,540
1837	Mount Holyoke College, South Hadley [2]	1,950
1843	College of the Holy Cross, Worcester [1]	2,684
1852	Tufts University, Medford [1,3]	7,415
1861	Mass. Institute of Technology, Cambridge [1]	9,626
1863	University of Massachusetts, Amherst [1]	27,852
1863	Boston College (RC), Chestnut Hill [1]	14,476
1865	Worcester Polytechnic Institute, Worcester [1]	4,449
1869	Boston University, Boston [1]	27,181
1870	Wellesley College, Wellesley [2]	2,230
1875	Smith College, Northampton [1]	2,637
1885	Springfield College, Springfield [1]	2,280
1887	Clark University, Worcester [1]	2,799
1894	University of Lowell [1]	15,262
1898	Northeastern University, Boston [1,4]	35,271
1899	Simmons College, Boston [2]	3,958
1948	Brandeis University, Waltham [1]	3,403

[1] Co-educational.   [3] Includes Jackson College for women.
[2] For women only.   [4] Includes Forsyth Dental Center School.

Health. In 1984 the state had 177 hospitals (with 41,200 beds); average daily census, 1982, 32,736, including patients in public and private mental hospitals and institutions for the mentally retarded.

Social Security. The Department of Public Welfare had an appropriation of $1,828m. in financial year 1984 and paid $388m. in aid to families with dependent children (average 95,798 families per month); other main items were general relief (average 27,242 cases), Supplemental Security Income (average 105,402 cases) and Medical Assistance only (average 65,841 cases).

Books of Reference

Annual Reports. Massachusetts and US Boards, Commissions, Departments and Divisions, Boston, annual
Business Climate Studies (1983). Alexander Grant, Boston 1983
Manual for the General Court. By Clerk of the Senate and Clerk of the House of Representatives, Boston, Mass. Biennial
Hart, Albert B., (ed.), *Commonwealth History of Massachusetts, Colony, Province and State.* 5 vols., New York, 1966
Levitan, D., with Mariner, E. C., *Your Massachusetts Government.* Newton, Mass., 1984
Higher Education Publications, Washington, D.C., 1983

MICHIGAN

HISTORY. Michigan, first settled by Marquette at Sault Ste Marie in 1668, became the Territory of Michigan in 1805, with its boundaries greatly enlarged in 1818 and 1834; it was admitted into the Union with its present boundaries on 26 Jan. 1837.

AREA AND POPULATION. Michigan is divided into two by Lake Michigan. The northern part is bounded south by the lake and by Wisconsin, west and north by Lake Superior, east by the North Channel of Lake Huron; between the two latter lakes the Canadian border runs through straits at Sault Ste Marie. The southern part is bounded west and north by Lake Michigan, east by Lake Huron, Ontario and Lake Erie, south by Ohio and Indiana. Area, 58,527 sq. miles, of which 56,954 sq. miles are land area, 1,573 sq. miles are inland water. Census population, 1 April 1980, 9,262,078, an increase of 380,252 or 4·3% since 1970. Estimate (1986) 9,145,000. In 1985 births were 138,902 (15·2 per 1,000 population); deaths, 78,515 (8·7); infant deaths, 1,575 (11·4 per 1,000 live births); marriages, 79,022 (17·4); divorces, 38,775 (8·5).

Population of 5 federal census years was:

	White	Negro	Indian	Asiatic	Total	Per sq. mile
1910	2,785,247	17,115	7,519	292	2,810,173	48·9
1930	4,663,507	169,453	7,080	2,285	4,842,325	84·9
1960	7,085,865	717,581	9,701	10,047	7,823,194	137·2

			All others			
1970	7,833,474	991,066	50,543		8,875,083	156·2
1980	7,872,241	1,199,023	190,814		9,262,078	162·6

Of the total population in 1980, 4,516,189 were male, 6,551,551 persons were urban and those 20 years old or older numbered 6,146,694. 162,440 were of Spanish origin.

Population of the chief cities (census of 1 April 1980) was:

Detroit	1,203,339	Dearborn	90,660	Royal Oak	70,893
Grand Rapids	181,843	Westland	84,603	Dearborn Heights	67,706
Warren	161,134	Kalamazoo	79,722	Troy	67,102
Flint	159,611	Taylor	77,568	Wyoming	59,616
Lansing (capital)	130,414	Saginaw	77,508	Farmington Hills	58,056
Sterling Heights	108,999	Pontiac	76,715	Roseville	54,311
Ann Arbor	107,316	St Clair Shores	76,210		
Livonia	104,814	Southfield	75,568		

Larger standard metropolitan areas, 1980 census: Detroit, 4,353,413; Grand Rapids, 601,680; Flint, 521,589; Lansing, 471,565.

CLIMATE. Detroit. Jan. 22·1°F (−5·5°C), July 72°F (22·2°C). Annual rainfall 32″ (813 mm). Grand Rapids. Jan. 23·8°F (−4·6°C), July 72·6°F (22·5°C). Annual rainfall 33·6″ (833 mm). Lansing. Jan. 21·7°F (−5·7°C), July 71°F (21·7°C). Annual rainfall 30·8″ (782 mm). See Great Lakes, p. 1379.

CONSTITUTION AND GOVERNMENT. The present constitution was adopted in April 1963 and became effective on 1 Jan. 1964. The Senate consists of 38 members, elected for 4 years, and the House of Representatives of 110 members, elected for 2 years. The Governor and Lieut.-Governor are elected for 4 years. Electors are all citizens over 18 years of age meeting the usual residential requirements. The state sends to Congress 2 senators and 18 representatives.

At the 1984 presidential election Reagan polled 2,251,571 votes, Mondale, 1,529,638.

The capital is Lansing. The state is organized in 83 counties.

Governor: James J. Blanchard (D.), 1987–91 ($100,077).
Lieut.-Governor: Martha Griffiths (D.), 1987–91 ($67,377).
Secretary of State: Richard H. Austin (D.), 1987–91 ($89,000).

BUDGET. For the financial year ending 30 Sept. 1986, the general fund revenue was $12,769,500,000 (taxation, $9,270,600,000, and federal aid, $3,298,600,000); total revenue, $13,607,400,000; special revenue funds, $837,900,000; general expenditures, $12,235,600,000.

Per capita personal income (1985 estimate) was $13,608.

ENERGY AND NATURAL RESOURCES

Minerals. Most important minerals by value of production are iron ore, petroleum and cement. Output (1985): Iron ore, 12·69m. long tons; Portland cement, 4·75m. short tons; petroleum, 31·5m. bbls; sand and gravel, 41·35m. short tons; lime, 534,000 short tons; natural gas, 153,484,651m. cu. ft; Salt, 991,000 short tons. Mineral output in 1984 was valued at $2,695·2m.

Agriculture. The state, formerly agricultural, is now chiefly industrial. In 1985 it contained 63,000 farms with a total area of 11m. acres; the average farm was 175 acres. Cash income, 1985, from crops, $1,729·6m.; from livestock and products, $1,237m. Principal crops are maize (production, 1985, 287·6m. bu. of grain), oats (26·1m. bu.), wheat (45m. bu.), sugar-beet (2·33m. tons); soybeans (34·6m. bu.), hay (5·7m. tons). On 1 Jan. 1986 there were in the state 108,000 sheep, 397,000 milch cows, 1·41m. all cattle and 1·19m. swine; 8·9m. chickens and 38,000 (1985) turkey breeder hens. In 1985 the wool clip yielded 902,000 lb. of wool.

Forestry. The forests of Michigan consist of 18·4m. acres, about 51% of total state land area. About 17·5m. acres of this total is commercial forest, 64% of which is privately owned, 20% state forest, 14% federal forest and 1·5% in various public ownerships. Three-fourths of the timber volume is hardwoods, principally hard and soft maples, aspen, oak and birch. Christmas trees are another important forest crop.

Michigan leads in the number of state parks and public campsites. There are 83 state parks and recreation areas, 6 state forests, 3 national forests and 3 national parks. There are 169 state forest campgrounds and 64 state game areas.

INDUSTRY. Transport equipment and non-electrical machinery are the most important manufactures. The state ranks first in 19 manufacturing categories; among principal products are motor vehicles and trucks, cement, chemicals, furniture, paper, cereal, baby food and pharmaceuticals. Total non-agricultural labour force, 1986, 4,386,000, of which 975,000 are in manufacturing.

COMMUNICATIONS

Roads. State trunk-line mileage (31 July 1980) totalled, 9,500, all hard surfaced. Passenger car registrations, 1986, 5,501,421.

Railways. On 1 Jan. 1986 there were 4,770 miles of railway and 67 miles of active car-ferry routes.

Aviation. Airports (1986) numbered 245 licensed airports and 22 air carrier airports.

JUSTICE, RELIGION, EDUCATION AND WELFARE

Justice. The 1963 Constitution provides that no person shall be denied the equal protection of the law; nor shall any person be denied the enjoyment of his civil or political rights or be discriminated against in the exercise thereof because of religion, colour or national origin. A Civil Rights Commission was established, and its powers and duties were implemented by legislation in the extra session of 1963. Earlier statutory enactments guaranteeing civil rights in specific areas are as follows. An Act of 1885, last amended in 1956, orders all places of public accommodation and resort, etc., to furnish equal accommodations without discrimination. An Act of 1941, as last amended, forbids the Civil Service in counties with population exceeding 1m. to discriminate against employees or applicants on the ground of political, racial or religious opinions or affiliations. An Act of 1881 incorporated into the school code of 1955 forbids any discrimination in school facilities. An Act of 1893 incorporated in the insurance code of 1956 prohibits insurance companies from discriminating between white and coloured persons.

In 1951 the legislature restored the unique one-man grand jury system abandoned in 1949.

Religion. Roman Catholics make up the largest body; largest Protestant denominations, Lutherans, United Methodists, United Presbyterians, Episcopalians.

Education. Education is compulsory for children from 6 to 16 years of age. The operating expenditure for graded and ungraded public schools for the fiscal year 1985, was $5,704m. In 1984–85 there were 567 school districts (elementary and secondary schools) with 1,678,458 pupils and 75,193 teachers. Teachers' salaries in 1985 averaged $28,440.

In 1985 there were 98 institutes of higher education with 508,000 students.

Universities and students (autumn 1986):

Founded	Name	Students
1817	University of Michigan	34,947
1849	Eastern Michigan University	21,349
1855	Michigan State University	44,088
1884	Ferris State College	11,274
1885	Michigan Technological University	6,326
1868	Wayne State University	34,764
1892	Central Michigan University	17,993
1889	Northern Michigan University	7,852
1903	Western Michigan University	21,747
1946	Lake Superior State College	2,660
1959	Oakland University	12,707
1960	Grand Valley State College	8,321
1965	Saginaw Valley College	5,377

Social Welfare. Old-age assistance is provided for persons 65 years of age or older who have resided in Michigan for one year before application; assets must not exceed various limits. In 1974 federal Supplementary Security Income (SSI) replaced the adults' programme. In Jan. 1987 aid was supplied to a monthly average of 418,572 dependent children in 188,972 families at $463.86 per family.

Health. In 1983 the state had 231 hospitals (47,812 beds) licensed by the state and 12 psychiatric hospitals, 7 centres for developmental disabilities, 5 centres for emotionally disturbed children.

In 1986 the Medicaid programme disbursed (with federal support) $1,642·9m. to 469,226 persons.

Books of Reference

Michigan Manual. Dept of *Management and Budget.* Lansing. Biennial
Bureau of Business Research, Wayne State University. *Michigan Statistical Abstract.* Detroit, 1983
Bald, F. C., *Michigan in Four Centuries.* 2nd ed. New York, 1961
Blanchard, J. J., *Economic Report of the Governor 1985.* Lansing, 1985
Catton. B., *Michigan—a Bicentennial History.* Norton, New York, 1976
Lewis, F. E., *State and Local Government in Michigan.* Lansing, 1979
Dunbar, W. F., and May, G. S., *Michigan: A History of the Wolverine State.* Grand Rapids, 1980
Sommers, L. (ed.), *Atlas of Michigan.* East Lansing, 1977

State Library Services: Library of Michigan, Lansing 48909. *State Librarian:* James W. Fry.

MINNESOTA

HISTORY. Minnesota, first explored in the 17th century and first settled in the 20 years following the establishment of Fort Snelling (1819), was made a Territory in 1849 (with parts of North and South Dakota), and was admitted into the Union, with its present boundaries, on 11 May 1858.

AREA AND POPULATION. Minnesota is bounded north by Canada, east by Lake Superior and Wisconsin, with the Mississippi River forming the boundary in the south-east, south by Iowa, west by South and North Dakota, with the Red River forming the boundary in the north-west. Area, 84,402 sq. miles, of which 4,854 sq. miles are inland water. Census population, 1 April 1980, 4,075,970, an increase of 7·1% since 1970. Estimate (1986), 4,214,013. Births in 1986, 65,766

(15·6 per 1,000 population); deaths, 35,064 (8·3); infant deaths, 600 (9·1 per 1,000 live births); marriages, 34,199 (8·1); divorces, 14,426 (3·4).

Population in 5 census years was:

	White	Negro	Indian	Asiatic	Total	Per sq. mile
1910	2,059,227	7,084	9,053	344	2,075,708	25·7
1930	2,542,599	9,445	11,077	832	2,563,953	32·0
1960	3,371,603	22,263	15,496	3,642	3,413,864	42·7
			All others			
1970	3,736,038	34,868	34,163		3,805,069	47·6
1980	3,935,770	53,344	86,856		4,075,970	51·4

Of the 1980 population, 1,997,826 were male; 2,725,270 were urban; those 21 years of age or older numbered 2,656,947.

The largest cities are Minneapolis, 370,951; St Paul (capital), 270,230 (Minneapolis–St Paul standard metropolitan statistical area, 2,113,533 in 1980); Duluth, 92,811; Bloomington, 81,831; Rochester, 57,890.

CLIMATE. Duluth. Jan. 8°F (–13·3°C), July 63°F (17·2°C). Annual rainfall 29″ (719 mm). Minneapolis-St. Paul. Jan. 12°F (–11·1°C), July 71°F (21·7°C). Annual rainfall 26″ (656 mm). *See* Great Lakes, p. 1379.

CONSTITUTION AND GOVERNMENT. The present constitution dates from 1858; it has had 94 amendments. The Legislature consists of a Senate of 67 members, elected for 4 years, and a House of Representatives of 134 members, elected for 2 years. The Governor and Lieut.-Governor are elected for 4 years. The state sends to Congress 2 senators and 8 representatives.

In the 1984 presidential election Mondale polled 971,648 votes, Reagan 941,609.

The capital is St Paul. There are 87 counties, four containing less than 400 sq. miles, the largest being 6,092 sq. miles.

Governor: Rudy Perpich (DFL.), 1987–91 ($91,460).
Lieut.-Governor: Marlene Johnson (DFL.), 1987–91 ($50,305).
Secretary of State: Joan Anderson Growe (DFL.), 1987–91 ($50,305).

BUDGET. The general fund budget for the 1987–89 2-year period was $11,351m.; tax relief $2,293m., education $5,827m., public welfare $1,605m., transport $62m.

Net long-term debt, 1 Oct. 1987, was $1,294m.

Per capita personal income (1986) was $14,737.

NATURAL RESOURCES

Minerals. The iron ore and taconite industry is the most important in the USA. Production of usable iron ore in 1985 was 35m. tons, value $1,430m. Other important minerals are sand and gravel, crushed and dimension stone, lime and manganiferous ore. Total value of mineral production, 1985, $1,548m.

Agriculture. In 1987 there were 92,000 farms with a total area of 30m. acres (60% of the land area); the average farm was of 323 acres. Average value of land and buildings (1985) $247,800. Commercial farms in 1982 numbered 94,385; 12% of the farms were operated by tenant-farmers. Cash income, 1986, from crops, $2,680m.; from livestock, $3,395m. In 1986 Minnesota ranked first in sugarbeet and processing sweet corn, and second in spring wheat, hay, dry milk, cheese, mink and turkeys. Other important products are wild rice, butter, eggs, flaxseed, milch cows, milk, corn, barley, swine, cattle for market, soybeans, honey, potatoes, rye, chickens, sunflower seed and dry edible beans. Of livestock, cattle represents 14% of total farm income, swine 11% and milk 20%. Of crops, corn represents 17% and soybeans 14%. On 1 Jan. 1987 the farm animals included 3·15m. all cattle, 855,000 milch cows, 237,000 sheep and lambs, 4·26m. swine and 12·8m. chickens. Turkey production, 1986, 34m. In 1986 the wool clip amounted to 1·63m. lb. of wool from 250,000 sheep.

Most US commercial wild rice paddies are in Minnesota. Production from 25,000 acres (1986), 5·1m. lb. of processed wild rice.

Forestry. Forests of commercial timber cover 14m. acres, of which 53% is government-owned. The value of forest products in 1985 was $3,771m.; $881m. of this was from pulp and paper and $2,529m. from secondary manufacturing. Logging, pulping, saw-mills and associated industries employed 51,600 in 1985.

INDUSTRY. In 1985 manufacturing establishments employed 367,800 workers; value added by manufacture was $19,400m. Largest manufacturing industry is non-electrical machinery (73,000 employees); then food products (39,000), printing and publishing (38,000).

TOURISM. In 1985, travellers spent about $5,209·4m. The industry employed about 106,100.

COMMUNICATIONS

Roads. The state highway system (interstate and state trunk highways) covered 12,100 miles in 1987; total highway, road and street mileage, 132,000. In 1986, 3,250,000 passenger automobiles were registered.

Railways. There are 3 Class I and 14 Class II and smaller railroads operating, with total mileage of 5,091.

Aviation. In 1987 there were 141 airports for public use and 15 public seaplane bases.

JUSTICE, RELIGION, EDUCATION AND WELFARE

Justice. A Civil Rights Act (1927) forbids places of public resort to exclude persons 'on account of race or colour' and another section forbids insurance companies to discriminate 'between persons of the same class on account of race'. Contractors on public works may have their contracts cancelled if 'in the hiring of common or skilled labour' they are found to have discriminated on the grounds of 'race, creed or colour'. The state's penal reformatory system on 30 June 1986 held 2,403 men and women. There is no death penalty in Minnesota.

Religion. The chief religious bodies are: Lutheran with 1,088,304 members in 1980; Roman Catholic, 1,041,781; Methodist, 146,422. Total membership of all denominations, 2,653,161.

Education. In 1986, there were 60,844 kindergarten students, 312,907 elementary students, and 332,045 secondary students enrolled in 1,511 public schools. There were 90,530 kindergarten, elementary, and secondary students enrolled in 628 private schools. The University of Minnesota, chartered in 1851 and opened in 1869, had a total enrolment in 1986 of 56,426 students on all campuses. The 18 public community colleges (2-year) had a total enrolment of 41,542. There are seven state universities (4-year) at Bemidji, Mankato, Marshall, Moorhead, St Cloud, Winona, Minneapolis and St Paul. Enrollment in all institutions of higher education, 1986, 233,610.

Health. In 1986 the state had 173 general acute hospitals with 19,969 beds. Patients resident in institutions under the Department of Human Services in Aug. 1986 included 1,067 mentally ill, 1,604 mentally retarded, 432 chemically dependent and 520 in state nursing homes.

Social Security. Programmes of old age assistance, aid to the disabled, and aid to the blind are administered under the federal Supplemental Security Income (SSI) Programme. Minnesota has a supplementary programme, Minnesota Supplemental Aid (MSA) to cover individuals not eligible for SSI, to supplement SSI benefits for others whose income is below state standards, and to provide one-time payments for emergency needs such as major home repair, essential furniture or appliances, moving expenses, fuel, food and shelter.

Books of Reference

Statistical Information: Current information is obtainable from the State Planning Agency (300 Centennial Office Building, 658 Cedar Street, St Paul 55155); non-current material from the Reference Library, Minnesota Historical Society, St Paul 55101.

Legislative Manual. Secretary of State. St Paul. Biennial
Manufacturers' Directory. Nelson Name Service, Minneapolis, Biennial
Minnesota Agriculture Statistics. Dept. of Agric., St Paul. Annual
Minnesota Pocket Data Book 1985–86, St Paul, 1985

MISSISSIPPI

HISTORY. Mississippi, settled in 1716, was organized as a Territory in 1798 and admitted into the Union on 10 Dec. 1817. In 1804 and in 1812 its boundaries were extended, but in March 1817 a part was taken to form the new Territory of Alabama, leaving the boundaries substantially as at present.

AREA AND POPULATION. Mississippi is bounded north by Tennessee, east by Alabama, south by the Gulf of Mexico and Louisiana, west by the Mississippi River forming the boundary with Louisiana and Arkansas. Area, 47,689 sq. miles, 457 sq. miles being inland water. Census population, 1 April 1980, 2,520,638, an increase of 13·6% since 1970. Estimate (1985), 2,656,600. Births, occurring in the state, 1986, were 41,242; deaths, 23,584; infant deaths, 472; marriages, 24,283; divorces, 12,871.

Population of 6 federal census years was:

	White	Negro	Indian	Asiatic	Total	Per sq. mile
1910	786,111	1,009,487	1,253	263	1,797,114	38·8
1930	998,077	1,009,718	1,458	568	2,009,821	42·4
1950	1,188,632	986,494	2,502	1,286	2,178,914	46·1
1960	1,257,546	915,743	3,119	1,481	2,178,141	46·1
			All others			
1970	1,393,283	815,770	7,859		2,216,912	46·9
1980	1,615,190	887,206	18,242		2,520,638	53·0

Of the population in 1980, 1,213,878 were male, 1,192,805 were urban and 1,601,157 were 20 years old or older.

The largest city (1980) is Jackson, 202,895. Others are: Biloxi, 49,311; Meridian, 46,577; Hattiesburg, 40,829; Greenville, 40,613; Gulfport, 39,676; Pascagoula, 29,318; Columbus, 27,383; Vicksburg, 25,434; Tupelo, 23,905.

CLIMATE. Jackson.Jan. 47°F (8·3°C), July 82°F (27·8°C). Annual rainfall 49″ (1,221 mm). Vicksburg. Jan. 48°F (8·9°C), July 81°F (27·2°C). Annual rainfall 52″ (1,311 mm). *See* Central Plains, p. 1378.

CONSTITUTION AND GOVERNMENT. The present constitution was adopted in 1890 without ratification by the electorate; 94 amendments by 1988.

The Legislature consists of a Senate (52 members) and a House of Representatives (122 members), both elected for 4 years, as are also the Governor and Lieut.-Governor. Electors are all citizens who have resided in the state 1 year, in the county 1 year, in the election district 6 months next before the election and have been registered according to law. In the 1984 presidential election Reagan polled 577,378 votes, Mondale, 351,195.

The state is represented in Congress by 2 senators and 5 representatives.

The capital is Jackson; there are 82 counties.

Governor: Ray Mabus (D.), 1988–92 ($63,000).
Lieut.-Governor: Bradford Johnson Dye (D.) ($34,000).
Secretary of State: Dick Molpus (D.) ($45,000).

BUDGET. For the fiscal year ending 30 June 1987 the general revenues were

$3,404,824,819 (taxation, $2,048,698,474; federal aid, $1,051,441,229; other state resources, $304,685,116), and general expenditures were $4,555,373,423 ($1,174,353,643 for education, $339,753,275 for highways and $837,746,902 for public welfare).

On 30 June 1987 the total net long-term debt was $427,222,908.

Per capita personal income (1986) was $9,716 (lowest in US).

ENERGY AND NATURAL RESOURCES

Minerals. Petroleum and natural gas account for about 90% (by value) of mineral production. Output of petroleum, 1986, was 29,996,554 bbls and of natural gas 207,870,866m. cu. ft. There are 6 oil refineries. Value of oil and gas products sold 1987 was $838,036,151.

Agriculture. Agriculture is the leading industry of the state because of the semitropical climate and a rich productive soil. In 1987 there were 82 soil conservation districts covering 30m. acres. In 1984 farms with annual sales of $1,000 or more numbered 50,000 with an area of 14·2m. acres. Average size of farm was 284 acres. This compares with an average farm size of 138 acres in 1960.

Cash income from all crops and livestock during 1983, including government payments, was $2,334·4m. Cash income from crops was $1,185·9m. and from livestock and products, $926·7m. The chief product is cotton, cash income $426·7m. from 1m. acres producing 1·65m. bales of 480 lb. Soybeans, rice, corn, hay, wheat, oats, sorghum, peanuts, pecans, sweet potatoes, peaches, other vegetables, nursery and forest products continue to contribute.

On 1 Jan. 1984 there were 1·7m. head of cattle and calves on Mississippi farms. Milch cows and heifers which had calved totalled 95,000, beef cows and heifers that had calved, 831,000; hogs and pigs, 300,000. Of cash income from livestock and products, 1983, $218·6m. was credited to cattle and calves. Cash income from poultry and eggs totalled $457·3m.; dairy products, $124·3m.; swine, $42·2m.

Forestry. In 1986 income from forestry amounted to $447m.; output of logs, lumber, etc., was 1,498,159 bd ft; pulpwood, 5,118,003 cords; distillate wood, 12,749 tons. There are about 16·9m. acres of forest (56% of the state's area). National forests area, 1987, 1·21m. acres.

INDUSTRY. In 1986 the 3,267 manufacturing establishments employed 224,020 workers, earning $3,895,224,854.

TOURISM. Total receipts, 1986, $97·7m. from about 1·5m. tourists.

COMMUNICATIONS

Roads. The state in July 1987 maintained 10,352 miles of highways, of which 10,286 miles were paved. In 1986, 1,739,556 cars were registered.

Railways. The state in 1987 had 2,794 miles of railway.

Aviation. There were 76 public airports in 1987, 69 of them general. There were also 4 privately owned airports.

JUSTICE, RELIGION, EDUCATION AND WELFARE

Justice. In 1987 there were no executions; from 1955 to 1987 executions (by gaschamber) totalled 32 (8 whites and 14 Negroes for murder, 9 Negroes for rape and 1 Negro for armed robbery). On 31 Dec. 1986 the state prisons had 6,914 inmates.

Religion. Southern Baptists in Mississippi (1986), 654,735 members; United Methodists (1987) 198,000; Roman Catholics (1987), 96,916 in Biloxi and Jackson dioceses; Negro Baptists about 477,000.

The number of churches relative to the population is the highest in the US (one church per 289 persons; national average, 814).

Education. Attendance at school is compulsory as laid down in the Education

Reform Act of 1982. The public elementary and secondary schools in 1986–87 had 473,544 pupils and 26,217 classroom teachers.

In 1986–87, teachers' average salary was $19,448. The expenditure per pupil in average daily attendance, 1986–87, was $2,204.

There are 16 universities and senior colleges, of which 8 are state-supported. The University of Mississippi, at Oxford (1844), had, 1987–88, 391 instructors and 9,542 students; Mississippi State University, Starkville, 755 instructors and 12,801 students; Mississippi University for Women, at Columbus, 106 instructors and 2,043 students; University of Southern Mississippi, Hattiesburg, 557 instructors and 11,937 students; Jackson State University, Jackson, 265 instructors and 6,045 students; Delta State University, Cleveland, 171 instructors and 3,513 students; Alcorn State University, Lorman, 136 instructors and 2,604 students; Mississippi Valley State University, Itta Bena, 102 instructors and 1,859 students. State support for the 8 universities (1987–88) was $155·5m.

Junior colleges had (1986–87) 52,371 students and 2,189 instructors. The state appropriation for junior colleges, 1986–87, was $50m.

Health. In 1987 the state had 127 acute general hospitals (15,846 beds) listed by the State Department of Health. The 14 hospitals with facilities for care of the mentally ill had 2,310 beds.

Social Security. The state Medicaid commission paid (1986–87) $372·1m. for medical services, including $46·5m. for drugs, $51·3m. for skilled nursing home care, $102·6m. for hospital services. There were 63,580 persons eligible for Aged Medicaid and 69,363 persons eligible for Disabled Medicaid benefits at 30 June 1987. In June 1986 53,685 families with 115,124 dependent children received $6,120,199 in the Aid to Dependent Children programme. The average monthly payment was $114 per family or $53.16 per child.

Books of Reference

1980 Census of Population and Housing: Mississippi.
Mississippi Official and Statistical Register. Secretary of State. Jackson. Biennial
Bettersworth, J. K., *Mississippi: A History.* Rev. ed. Austin, Tex., 1964

Mississippi Library Commission: PO Box 10700 Jackson, MS. 39209–0700. *Director:* David M. Woodburn.

MISSOURI

HISTORY. Missouri, first settled in 1735 at Ste Genevieve, was made a Territory on 1 Oct. 1812, and admitted to the Union on 10 Aug. 1821. In 1837 its boundaries were extended to their present limits.

AREA AND POPULATION. Missouri is bounded north by Iowa, east by the Mississippi River forming the boundary with Illinois and Kentucky, south by Arkansas, south-west by Oklahoma, west by Kansas and Nebraska, with the Missouri River forming the boundary in the north-west. Area, 69,697 sq. miles, 752 sq. miles being water.

Census population, 1 April 1980, 4,916,766, an increase since 1970 of 5·1%. Estimate (1986), 5,066,000. Births, 1985, were 78,760 (15·7 per 1,000 population); deaths, 51,635 (10·3); infant deaths, 784 (10·2 per 1,000 live births); marriages, 49,484 (9·8); divorces, 24,990 (5).

Population of 5 federal census years was:

	White	Negro	Indian	Asiatic	Total	Per sq. mile
1910	3,134,932	157,452	313	638	3,293,335	47·9
1930	3,403,876	223,840	578	1,073	3,629,367	52·4
1960	3,922,967	390,853	1,723	3,146	4,319,813	62·5
			All others			
1970	4,177,495	480,172	19,732		4,677,399	67·0
1980	4,345,521	514,276	56,889		4,916,686	71·3

Of the total population in 1980, 2,365,487 were male, 3,350,746 persons were urban and those 18 years of age or older numbered 3,554,203.

The principal cities at the 1980 census (and estimates, 1984) are:

St Louis	453,085 (429,296)	Columbia	62,061 (63,294)
Kansas City	448,159 (443,095)	Florissant	55,372 (55,949)
Springfield	133,116 (136,628)	University City	42,738 (42,929)
Independence	111,806 (112,121)	Joplin	38,893 (39,650)
St Joseph	76,691 (74,860)	St Charles	37,379 (47,216)

Metropolitan areas, 1980: St Louis, 2,356,000; Kansas City, 1,327,000.

CLIMATE. Kansas City. Jan. 30°F (−1·1°C), July 79°F (26·1°C). Annual rainfall 38″ (947 mm). St. Louis. Jan. 32°F (0°C), July 79°F (26·1°C). Annual rainfall 40″ (1,004 mm). *See* Central Plains, p. 1378.

CONSTITUTION AND GOVERNMENT. A new constitution, the fourth, was adopted on 27 Feb. 1945; it has been amended 27 times. The General Assembly consists of a Senate of 34 members elected for 4 years (half for re-election every 2 years), and a House of Representatives of 163 members elected for 2 years. The Governor and Lieut.-Governor are elected for 4 years. Missouri sends to Congress 2 senators and 9 representatives.

Voters (with the usual exceptions) are all citizens and those adult aliens who, within a prescribed period, have applied for citizenship. In the 1984 presidential election Reagan polled 1,242,678, Mondale, 808,601.

Jefferson City is the state capital. The state is divided into 114 counties and the city of St Louis.

Governor: John D. Ashcroft (R.), 1985–88 ($81,000).
Lieut.-Governor: Harriett Woods (D.), 1985–88 ($48,600).
Secretary of State: Roy D. Blunt (R.), 1985–88 ($64,800).

BUDGET. For the year 1985 the total revenues from all funds were $6,682m. (federal revenue, $1,500·7m., general revenue, $5,786m.).

Total outstanding debt, 1985, was $3,319m.

Per capita personal income (1986) was $13,724.

NATURAL RESOURCES

Minerals. Principal minerals are lead (ranks first in USA), zinc (ranks second), clays, coal, iron ore, and stone for cement and lime manufacture. Value of production (1984) $731·9m.

Agriculture. In 1986 there were 115,000 farms in Missouri covering 30·7m. acres. Production of principal crops, 1986: Corn, 280·7m. bu.; soybeans, 177·5m. bu.; wheat, 18·8m. bu.; sorghum grain, 92·3m. bu.; oats, 5m. bu.; cotton, 196,000 bales (of 480 lb.). Cash receipts from farming, 1986, $3,507·7m. Export value of farm produce, 1986, $910·4m., to which soybeans contributed $479·2m.

Forestry. Forest land area, 1986, 12·9m. acres.

INDUSTRY. The largest employer in 1985 was manufacturing, in which the transport equipment industry employed 67,191 workers. Other large industries are food and kindred products, electrical equipment and supplies, apparel and related products and non-electrical machinery, leather products, chemicals, paper, metal industries, stone, clay and glass. Retail trade employed 354,141 in 1985; wholesale trade employed 136,411.

LABOUR. The State Board of Mediation has jurisdiction in labour disputes involving only public utilities. The Prevailing Wage Law (1959) provides that no less than the local hourly rate of wages for work of a similar character shall be paid to any workmen engaged in public works. The Industrial Commission has authority to inspect records and to institute actions for penalties described in the Act. There is a state programme for industrial safety in hand, under the Federal Occupational and Health Act. In 1986 the annual average number of employed was 2,318,238, and 165,175 were unemployed; the unemployment rate was 6·7%.

COMMUNICATIONS

Roads. Federal and state highways, Sept. 1986, totalled 119,155 miles. In 1985 there were 3·6m. vehicles licensed in the state, of which 3,318 were private and commercial buses.

Railways. The state has 10 Class I railways; approximate total mileage, 8,081. There are 7 other railways (switching, terminal or short-line), total mileage 229.

Aviation. In 1987 there were 129 public airports and 282 private airports.

Shipping. Ten carrier barge lines (1984) operated on about 1,000 miles of navigable waterways including the Missouri and Mississippi Rivers. Boat shipping seasons: Missouri River, April–end Nov.; Mississippi River, all seasons.

Post and Broadcasting. There were 262 commercial radio stations and 35 TV stations in 1987.

Newspapers. There were (1986) 45 daily and 213 weekly newspapers.

JUSTICE, RELIGION, EDUCATION AND WELFARE

Justice. State prisons in 1986 had an average of 10,239 inmates including 406 females. The median age was 27·8, 52·3% were between age 15 and 25. There have been no executions since 1965 although the death penalty was reinstated in 1978; since 1930 executions (by lethal gas) have totalled 40, including 31 for murder, 6 for rape and 3 for kidnapping. The Missouri Law Enforcement Assistance Council was created in 1969 for law reform.

Religion. Chief religious bodies (1980) are Catholic, with 800,228 members, Southern Baptists (700,053), United Methodists (270,469), Christian Churches (175,101), Lutheran (157,928), Presbyterian (38,254). Total membership, all denominations, about 2·6m. in 1980.

Education. School attendance is compulsory for children from 7 to 16 years for the full term. In the 1986–87 school year, public schools (kindergarten through grade 12) had 800,606 pupils. Total expenditure for public schools in 1985–86, $2,202m. Salaries for teachers (kindergarten through grade 12), 1985–86, averaged $21,945. Institutions for higher education include the University of Missouri, founded in 1839 with campuses at Columbia, Rolla, St Louis and Kansas City, with 4,389 accredited teachers and 51,935 students in 1986–87. Washington University at St Louis, founded in 1857, is an independent co-ed university with 8,311 students in 1986–87. St Louis University (1818), is an independent Roman Catholic co-ed university with 9,869 students in 1986–87. Sixteen state colleges had 234,250 students in 1986–87. Private colleges had (1986–87) 35,545 students. Church-affiliated colleges (1986–87) had 33,042 students. Public junior colleges had 52,838 students. There are about 82 secondary and post-secondary institutions offering vocational courses, and about 290 private career schools. There were 240,719 students in higher education in autumn 1986.

Health. There were 9 state mental health hospitals and centres and 2 children's hospitals in 1986–87, admitting 23,661 patients.

Social Security. In 1985 the number of recipients of medicaid was 356,000. The number of recipients of Aid to Dependent Children was 198,500 with an average monthly payment per family of $239.

Books of Reference

Missouri Area Labor Trends, Department of Labour and Industrial Relations, monthly
Missouri Farm Facts, Department of Agriculture, annual
Report of the Public Schools of Missouri. State Board of Education, annual
Statistical Abstract for Missouri. State and Regional Fiscal Studies Unit, College of Business and Public Administration, Columbia 1985

MONTANA

HISTORY. Montana, first settled in 1809, was made a Territory (out of portions of Idaho and Dakota Territories) in 1864 and was admitted into the Union on 8 Nov. 1889.

AREA AND POPULATION. Montana is bounded north by Canada, east by North and South Dakota, south by Wyoming and west by Idaho and the Bitterroot Range of the Rocky Mountains. Area, 147,138 sq. miles, including 1,551 sq. miles of water, of which the federal government, 1983, owned 27,409,000 acres or 29·4%. US Bureau of Indian Affairs (1982) administered 5·03m. acres, of which 2,820,000 were allotted to tribes. Census population, 1 April 1980, 786,690, an increase of 13·3% since 1970. Estimate (1986), 819,000. Births, 1985, were 13,846 (16·8 per 1,000 population); deaths, 6,644 (8·1); infant deaths, 103 (7·4 per 1,000 live births); marriages, 7,677 (9·3); divorces 4,407 (5·3).

Population in 5 census years was:

	White	Negro	Indian	Asiatic	Total	Per sq. mile
1910	360,580	1,834	10,745	2,870	376,053	2·6
1930	519,898	1,256	14,798	1,239	537,606	3·7
1950	572,038	1,232	16,606	—	591,024	4·1
1970	663,043	1,995	27,130	1,099	694,409	4·7
1980	740,148	1,786	37,270	2,503	786,690	5·3

Of the total population in 1980, 392,625 were male, 416,402 persons (52·9%) were urban. Persons 20 years of age or older numbered 524,836. Median age, 29 years. Households, 283,742.

The largest cities, 1980 (and 1982 estimate) are Billings, 66,798 (68,787); Great Falls, 56,725 (57,143). Others: Butte-Silver Bow, 37,205 (35,753); Missoula, 33,388 (33,078); Helena (capital), 23,938 (24,289); Bozeman, 21,645 (22,532); Anaconda-Deer Lodge County, 12,518 (11,583); Havre, 10,891 (11,290); Kalispell, 10,648 (10,558).

CLIMATE. Helena. Jan. 18°F (−7·8°C), July 69°F (20·6°C). Annual rainfall 13″ (325 mm). *See* Mountain States, p. 1378.

CONSTITUTION AND GOVERNMENT. A new constitution was ratified by the voters on 6 June 1972, and fully implemented on 1 July 1973; the Senate to consist of 50 senators, elected for 4 years, one half at each biennial election. The 100 members of the House of Representatives are elected for 2 years.

The Governor and Lieut.-Governor are elected for 4 years. Montana sends to Congress 2 senators and 2 representatives.

In the 1984 presidential election Reagan polled 207,163 votes, Mondale, 131,975.

The capital is Helena. The state is divided into 56 counties.

Governor: Ted Schwinden (D.), 1985–89 ($50,452).
Lieut.-Governor: George Turman (D.), 1985–89 ($36,141).
Secretary of State: Jim Waltermire (R.), 1985–89 ($33,342).

BUDGET. Total state revenues for the year ending 30 June 1983 were $1,376,038,000 ($513·6m. taxes); total expenditures were $1,263,305,000 ($384m. for education, $168·3m. for highways and $151·5m. for public welfare).

Total net long-term debt on 30 June 1983 was $127,157,000.
Per capita personal income (1986) was $11,904.

ENERGY AND NATURAL RESOURCES

Electricity. Electric power generated in March 1985 was 1,662 gwh., of which 695 gwh. was hydro-electric and 953 gwh. from coal-fired plants; 2 from oil-fired, 5 from gas-fired plants and 6 gwh. from other sources.

Minerals (1983). Output of crude petroleum, 29·2m. bbls; copper, 33,337 tonnes; sand and gravel, 5·3m. short tons; phosphate rock, undisclosed; silver, 5·7m. troy oz.; gold, 161,436 troy oz.; zinc, undisclosed; natural gas, 35,647m. cu. ft; coal, 28·9m. short tons. Value of total mineral production (1983), $1,339·5m., with petroleum ($765·4m.) the first, coal ($411·3m.) the second, natural gas ($106·6m.) the third and copper ($56·25m.) the fourth most important commodity.

Agriculture. In 1985 there were 24,000 farms and ranches (50,564 in 1935) with an area of 61·1m. acres (47,511,868 acres in 1935). Large-scale farming predominates; in 1985 the average size per farm was 2,542 acres. Income from all farm marketings was $1,659m. in 1984 (crops, $647m.; livestock, $772m.). Irrigated area harvested in 1983 was 1·54m. acres; non-irrigated, 7·16m. acres.

The chief crops are wheat, amounting in 1983 to 136·9m. bu.; barley, 77·7m. bu.; oats, 5·28m. bu.; sugar-beet, hay, potatoes, alfalfa, dry beans, flax and cherries. In 1985 there were 27,000 milch cows, 2·96m. all cattle; 155,000 swine and 423,000 sheep.

Forestry. Total forest area (1986), 22·6m. acres. In 1983 there were 16·8m. acres within 11 national forests.

INDUSTRY. In 1981 manufacturing establishments numbering 612 had 17,264 production workers; value added by manufacture was (1982) $722·7m.

LABOUR (June 1985). Work force, 426,600; total employed, 397,600; total non-agricultural workers, 362,900; agricultural workers, 34,700. Workers employed by major industry group: Mining, 7,100 (average net weekly earnings, $543.15); contract construction, 13,900 ($529.58); manufacturing, 22,100 ($432.22); transport and public utilities, 19,800 ($479.46; wholesale/retail trade, 77,800 ($207.21); finance/insurance/real estate, 13,600 ($243.21); services, 62,200 ($236.49); government, 71,600 (no income figures available). Average weekly earnings for all workers in private non-agricultural industries $292.58. Total unemployed 29,000 (6·8% of the work force in June 1985 as compared to 7·3% nationally for that month).

There were 14 work stoppages in 1981 involving 9,200 workers, with a total of 42,200 man days idle during the year.

COMMUNICATIONS

Roads. In 1983 the state had 58,331 miles of maintained public roads and streets including 11,746 miles of the federal-aid system. At 30 Sept. 1985 there were 517,804 passenger vehicles, 326,625 trucks and 45,929 motor cycles registered.

Railways. In Nov. 1985 there were 3,418 route miles of railway in the state.

Aviation. There were 121 airports open for public use in Dec. 1985, of which 120 were publicly owned.

JUSTICE, RELIGION, EDUCATION AND WELFARE

Justice. In Dec. 1985 the Montana state prison held 895 inmates and the Women's Correctional Center, 27. Since 1943 there have been no executions; total since 1930 (all by hanging) was 6; 4 whites and 2 Negroes, for murder.

Religion. The leading religious bodies are (1984): Roman Catholic with 132,600 active members; Lutheran, 77,000; Methodist, 19,500 (church estimates).

Education. In Oct. 1983 public elementary and secondary schools had 154,000 pupils. Public elementary and secondary school teachers (9,700 in 1985) had an average salary of $21,900. Expenditure on public school education (1984–85) was $626m.

The Montana University system consists of the Montana State University, at Bozeman (autumn 1985 enrolment: 10,710 students), the University of Montana, at Missoula, founded in 1895 (8,989), the Montana College of Mineral Science and Technology, at Butte (1,932), Northern Montana College, at Havre (1,729),

Eastern Montana College, at Billings (4,173) and Western Montana College, at Dillon (970).

Social Security. In Aug. 1985, 4,416 persons over age 65 were receiving in medical assistance an average of $758.85 per month; 51 blind persons, $450.08; 4,427 totally disabled, $544.15; 8,196 families (15,242 dependent children) receiving in aid-to-dependent children assistance an average of $325 per month. Aid was from state and federal sources.

Health. In Aug. 1985 the state had 62 hospitals (3,426 beds) listed by the Montana Board of Health. Four centres for mental disease and development disorders had 733 beds and 620 patients.

Books of Reference

Montana Agricultural Statistics. U.S. Dept. of Agriculture, Montana Crop and Livestock Reporting Service. Biennial from 1946

Montana Employment and Labor Force. Montana Dept. of Labor and Industry. Monthly from 1971

Montana Federal-Aid Road Log. Montana Dept. of Highways and US Dept. of Transportation, Federal Highway Administration. Annual from 1938

Montana Vital Statistics. Montana Dept. of Health and Environmental Sciences. Annually from 1954

Statistical Report. Montana Dept. of Social and Rehabilitation Services. Monthly from 1947

Lang, W, L., and Myers, R. C., *Montana, Our Land and People.* Pruett, 1979

Malone, M. P., and Roeder, R. B., *Montana, A History of Two Centuries.* Univ. of Washington Press, 1976

Spence, C. C., *Montana, a History.* New York, 1978

NEBRASKA

HISTORY. The Nebraska region was first reached by white men from Mexico under the Spanish general Coronado in 1541. It was ceded by France to Spain in 1763, retroceded to France in 1801, and sold by Napoleon to the US as part of the Louisiana Purchase in 1803. Its first settlement was in 1847, and on 30 May 1854 it became a Territory and on 1 March 1867 a state. In 1882 it annexed a small part of Dakota Territory, and in 1908 it received another small tract from South Dakota.

AREA AND POPULATION. Nebraska is bounded north by South Dakota, with the Missouri River forming the boundary in the north-east and the boundary with Iowa and Missouri to the east; south by Kansas, south-west by Colorado and west by Wyoming. Area, 77,355 sq. miles, of which 711 sq. miles are water. Census population, 1980: 1,569,825, an increase of 5·7% since 1970. Estimate (1985), 1,605,574. Births, 1986, were 24,425 (15·3 per 1,000 population); deaths, 14,662 (9·2); infant deaths, 246 (10·1 per 1,000 live births); marriages, 12,107 (7·6): divorces, 6,127 (3·8).

Population in 5 census years was:

	White	Negro	Indian	Asiatic	Total	Per sq. mile
1910	1,180,293	7,689	3,502	730	1,192,214	15·5
1920	1,279,219	13,242	2,888	1,023	1,296,372	16·9
1960	1,374,764	29,262	5,545	1,195	1,411,330	18·3
			All others			
1970	1,432,867	39,911	10,715		1,483,791	19·4
1980	1,490,381	48,390	31,054		1,569,825	20·5

Of the total population in 1980, 48·8% were male, 62·9% were urban 65·6% were 21 years of age or older. The largest cities in the state are: Omaha, with a census population, 1980, of 313,911; Lincoln (capital), 171,932; Grand Island, 33,180; North Platte, 24,509; Fremont, 23,979; Hastings, 23,045; Bellevue, 21,813; Kearney, 21,158; Norfolk, 19,449.

The Bureau of Indian Affairs, as of 30 June 1984, administered 65,000 acres, of which 23,000 acres were allotted to tribal control.

CLIMATE. Omaha. Jan. 22°F (–5·6°C), July 77°F (25°C). Annual rainfall 29″ (721 mm). *See* High Plains, p. 1378.

CONSTITUTION AND GOVERNMENT. The present constitution was adopted in 1875; it has been amended 188 times. By an amendment adopted in Nov. 1934 Nebraska has a single-chambered legislature (elected for 4 years) of 49 members—the only state in the Union to have one. The Governor and Lieut.-Governor are elected for 4 years. Amendments adopted in 1912 and 1920 provide for legislation through the initiative and referendum and permit cities of more than 5,000 inhabitants to frame their own charters. A 'right-to-work' amendment adopted 5 Nov. 1946 makes illegal the 'closed shop' demands of trade unions. Nebraska is represented in Congress by 2 senators and 3 representatives.

In the 1984 presidential election Reagan polled 446,938 votes, Mondale, 183,838.

The capital is Lincoln. The state has 93 counties.

Governor: Kay Orr (R.), 1987–90 ($58,000).
Lieut.-Governor: William E. Nichol (R.) ($40,000).
Secretary of State: Allen Beerman (R.) ($32,000).

BUDGET. For the fiscal year ending 30 June 1985 (US Census Bureau figures) the state's revenues were $2,144m. (taxation, $1,040m. and federal aid, $525m.); general expenditures were $2,067m. ($693m. for education, $369m. for highways and $329m. for public welfare).

The state has a bonded indebtedness limit of $100,000.

Per capita personal income (1986) was $13,777.

ENERGY AND NATURAL RESOURCES

Minerals. The total output of minerals, 1985, was valued at $212·2m., petroleum (7·1m. bbls) and sand and gravel (11·1m. tons) being the most important.

Agriculture. Nebraska is one of the most important agricultural states. In 1986 it contained approximately 56,000 farms, with a total area of 47·2m. acres. The average farm was 843 acres.

In 1986, 7·9m. acres were irrigated and 71,338 irrigation wells were registered.

Cash income from crops (1986), $2,669m., and from livestock, $4,260m. Principal crops, with estimated 1986 yield: Maize, 896m. bu. (ranking third in US); wheat, 76m. bu.; sorghums for grain, 139·7m. bu.; oats, 21·2m. bu.; soybeans, 95·6m. bu. About 750 farms grow sugar-beet for 3 factories; output, 1986, 1·4m. short tons. On 1 Jan. 1987 the state contained 5·5m. all cattle (ranking third in US), 167,000 milch cows, 173,000 sheep and 3·9m. swine.

Forestry. The area of national forest, 1985, was 352,000 acres.

INDUSTRY. In 1984 there were 1,830 manufacturing establishments; 66,000 production workers earned $1,160m. and value added by manufacturing was $5,147m. The chief industry is meat-packing.

COMMUNICATIONS

Roads. The state-maintained highway system embraced 9,961 miles in 1986; local roads, 86,207 miles. In 1986, 860,882 automobiles were registered.

Railways. In 1983 there were 7,185 miles of railway.

Aviation. Airports (1984) numbered 324, of which 111 were publicly owned.

JUSTICE, RELIGION, EDUCATION AND WELFARE

Justice. A 'Civil Rights Act' revised in 1969 provides that all people are entitled to a 'full and equal enjoyment of the accommodations, advantages, facilities and privileges' of hotels, restaurants, public conveyances, amusement places and other places. The state university is forbidden to discriminate between students 'because of age, sex, color or nationality'. An Act of 1941 declares it to be 'the policy of this state' that no trade union should discriminate, in collective bargaining, 'against any person because of his race or color'.

The state's prisons had, 9 Sept. 1986, 1,931 inmates (120 per 100,000 population). From 1930 to 1962 there were 4 executions (electrocution), 3 white men and 1 American Indian, all for murder, and none since.

Religion. The Roman Catholics had 337,855 members in 1985; Protestant Churches, 737,361; Jews, 7,865 members. Total, all denominations, 1,083,081.

Education. School attendance is compulsory for children from 7 to 16 years of age. Public elementary schools, autumn 1985, had 144,949 enrolled pupils. Teachers' salaries, 1985–86, averaged $21,163. Estimated public school expenditure for year ending 30 Aug. 1985 was $788·4m. Total enrolment in 27 institutions of higher education, autumn 1985, was 97,283 students. The largest institutions were (1985):

Opened	Institution	Students
1867	Peru State College, Peru (State)	1,312
1869	Univ. of Nebraska, Lincoln (State)	26,374
1878	Creighton Univ., Omaha (RC)	5,927
1882	Hastings College (Presbyterian)	825
1883	Midland Lutheran College, Fremont (Lutheran)	801
1887	Nebraska Wesleyan Univ. (Methodist)	1,285
1891	Union College, Lincoln (Seventh Day Adventist)	700
1894	Concordia Teachers' College, Seward (Lutheran)	858
1905	Kearney State College, Kearney (State)	8,725
1908	Univ. of Nebraska, Omaha (State)	13,789
1910	Wayne State College, Wayne (State)	2,669
1911	Chadron State College, Chadron (State)	2,169
1923	College of St. Mary	1,009
1966	Bellevue College, Bellevue (Private)	2,407

The state holds 1·52m. acres of land as a permanent endowment of her schools; permanent public school endowment fund in Aug. 1986 was $86·3m.

Health. In 1986 the state had 112 hospitals and 584 patients in mental hospitals.

Social Security. The administration of public welfare is the responsibility of the County Divisions of Welfare with policy-forming, regulatory, advisory and supervisory functions performed by the State Department of Public Welfare. In 1985 public welfare provided financial aid and/or services as follows: for 7,785 individuals who were aged, blind or disabled, with an average state supplement of $55.29; for 15,244 families with dependent children, with an average payment of $320.36 per family; for 90,000 individuals who had medical needs, $1,738.43, per individual; for 3,010 children in need of child welfare services; for 3,469 children who were in need of crippled children's services and medical care. The amount of aid is based on need in accordance with State assistance standards; the programme of aid to families with dependent children is limited to a maximum maintenance payment of $293 for 1 child plus $71 for each additional child.

Books of Reference

Agricultural Atlas of Nebraska. Univ. of Nebraska Press, 1977
Climatic Atlas of Nebraska. Univ. of Nebraska Press, 1977
Economic Atlas of Nebraska. Univ. of Nebraska Press, 1977
Nebraska. A Guide to the Cornhusker State. Univ. of Nebraska Press, 1979
Nebraska Statistical Handbook, 1988–89. Nebraska Dept. of Econ. Development, Lincoln
Nebraska Blue-Book. Legislative Council. Lincoln. Biennial
Olson, J. C., *History of Nebraska.* Univ. of Nebraska Press, 1955

State Library: State Law Library, State House, Lincoln. *Librarian:* Reta Johnson.

NEVADA

HISTORY. Nevada, first settled in 1851, when it was a part of the Territory of Utah (created 1850), was made a Territory in 1861, enlarged in 1862 by an addition from Utah Territory and admitted into the Union on 31 Oct. 1864 as the 36th state. In 1866 and 1867 the area of the state was significantly enlarged at the expense of the Territories of Utah and Arizona.

AREA AND POPULATION. Nevada is bounded north by Oregon and Idaho, east by Utah, south-east by Arizona, with the Colorado River forming most of the boundary, south and west by California. Area 110,561 sq. miles, 667 sq. miles being water. The federal government in 1982 owned 60,275,632 acres, or 85% of the land area. Vacant public lands, 47,977,331 acres. The Bureau of Indian Affairs controlled 1·06m. acres.

Census population on 1 April 1980, 799,184, an increase of 310,446 or 63·5% since 1970. Estimate (1986) 1,007,850. Births, 1985, were 15,293 (16·1 per 1,000 population); deaths, 7,221 (7·5); infant deaths (1984), 154 (10·1 per 1,000 live births); marriages, 106,500 (109·2 per 1,000 population); divorces, 13,300 (13·7).

Population in 5 census years was:

	White	Negro	Indian	Asiatic and all others	Total	Per sq. mile
1910	74,276	513	5,240	1,846	81,875	0·7
1930	84,515	516	4,871	1,156	91,058	0·8
1960	263,443	13,484	6,681	1,670	285,278	2·6
1970	449,850	27,579	7,329	3,980	488,738	4·4
			All others			
1980	699,377	50,791	49,016		799,184	7·2

Of the total population in 1980, 404,372 were male, 681,682 were urban and 556,021 were 20 years of age or older.

The largest cities are Las Vegas, with population at the 1980 census of 164,674 (1986 estimate, 201,500); Reno, 100,756 (115,210); North Las Vegas, 39,196 (47,250); Sparks, 38,114 (50,400); Carson City, 30,807 (36,040); and Henderson, 20,905 (42,180). Clark County (Las Vegas, North Las Vegas and Henderson) and Washoe County (Reno and Sparks) together had 81% of the total state population in 1980 (82% in 1982).

CLIMATE. Las Vegas. Jan. 44°F (6·7°C), July 85°F (29·4°C). Annual rainfall 4″ (112 mm). Reno. Jan. 32°F (0°C), July 69°F (20·6°C). Annual rainfall 7″ (178 mm). *See* Mountain States, p. 1378.

CONSTITUTION AND GOVERNMENT. The constitution adopted in 1864 is still in force, with over 60 amendments. The Legislature meets biennially (and in special sessions) and consists of a Senate of 20 members elected for 4 years, half their number retiring every 2 years, and an Assembly of 40 members elected for 2 years. The Governor, Lieut.-Governor and Attorney-General are elected for 4 years. Qualified electors are all citizens with the usual residential qualification. Nevada is represented in Congress by 2 senators and 2 representatives. A Supreme Court of 5 members is elected for 4 years on a non-partisan ballot.

In the 1984 presidential election Reagan polled 188,794 votes, Mondale, 91,654.

The state capital is Carson City. There are 16 counties, 17 incorporated cities and towns, 44 unincorporated towns and 1 city-county (Carson City).

Governor: Richard Bryan (D.), 1987–91 ($65,000).
Lieut.-Governor: Bob Miller (D.) ($10,500).
Secretary of State: F. S. Del Papa (D.) ($42,500).

BUDGET. For the fiscal year ending 30 June 1986, state general fund revenues were $482·2m., including federal receipts; budget expenditures were $461·9m.

Education, followed by human resources and public safety, received the largest appropriations.

State bonded indebtedness on 30 June 1986, was $25·3m. The state has no franchise tax, capital stock tax, special intangibles tax, chain stores tax, stock transfer tax, admissions tax, gift tax, income taxes or inheritance tax. The sales and use tax and gaming taxes are the largest revenue producers.

Per capita personal income (1986) was $15,074.

ENERGY AND NATURAL RESOURCES

Electricity. Electricity power stations in 1986 supplied about 352,174 residential customers, 51,078 commercial, and 477 industrial customers.

Minerals. Production, 1985, in order of value was gold ($364·4m.), petroleum ($56·6m.), silver ($38·7m.), sand and gravel ($24·8m.), barite ($14·4m.), gypsum ($9·9m.). Other minerals are iron ore, mercury, lime, lithium, gemstones, lead, molybdenum, fluorspar, perlite, pumice, clays, talc, salt, tungsten, magnesite, diatonite and zinc.

Agriculture. In 1986, an estimated 2,400 farms had a farm area of 8·8m. acres (9·2m. in 1960). Farms averaged 3,667 acres. Area under irrigation (1986) was 829,761 acres compared with 542,976 acres in 1959.

Gross income, 1986, from crops, livestock and government payments, $262·3m. Cattle, hay, dairy products, potatoes and sheep are the principal commodities in order of cash receipts. Total value of crops produced, $134·1m. On 1 Jan. 1986 there were 27,000 milch cows, 523,000 beef cattle, 86,000 sheep and lambs.

Forestry. The area of national forests (1983) under US Forest Service administration was 5,150,088 acres. National forests: Toiyabe (2,561,441 acres); Humboldt (2,527,938), Inyo (60,656); Eldorado (53).

INDUSTRY. The main industry is the service industry (32% of employment), especially tourism and legalized gambling; others include, mining and smelting, livestock and irrigated agriculture, chemical manufacturing, and lumber processing. In 1986 there were 999 manufacturing establishments with 22,254 employees, earning $483m.

Gaming industry gross revenue for financial year 1986, $3,532m. There were at the same time 1,952 gaming licences in force and 4,269 licensed games.

LABOUR. The annual average unemployment for 1986 was 6% of the work force. All industries employed 509,000 workers. Main industries and employees, 1986: Service industries, 207,300; retail trade, 78,100; government, 61,500; finance, insurance and real estate, 10,100; transport, 15,200; public works and utilities, 11,400; mining, 6,300.

COMMUNICATIONS

Roads. Highway mileage (federal, state and local) totalled 51,118 in 1984, of which 16,798 miles were surfaced; motor vehicle registrations at 31 Dec. 1985 numbered 825,727.

Railways. In 1987 there were 1,465 miles of main-line railway. Nevada is served by Southern Pacific, Union Pacific and Western Pacific railways, and Amtrak passenger service for Las Vegas, Elko, Reno and Sparks.

Aviation. There were 124 civil airports and heliports in 1984. During 1986 McCarren International Airport (Las Vegas) handled 12·4m. passengers and Reno-Cannon International Airport handled 3·2m. passengers.

Post. In 1986 there were 84 telephone exchanges, 11 local exchange carriers with 566,846 telephones in service.

JUSTICE, RELIGION, EDUCATION AND WELFARE

Justice. Prohibition of marriage between persons of different race was repealed by statute in 1959.

A 1965 Civil Rights Act makes it illegal for persons operating public accommodations, employers of 15 or more employees, labour unions, and employment agencies to discriminate on the basis of race, colour, religion or national origin; a 1971 law makes racial discrimination in the sale or renting of houses illegal. A Commission on Equal Rights of Citizens is charged with enforcing these laws.

Between 1924 and 1967 executions (by lethal gas—the first state to adopt this method, in 1921), numbered 31. Capital punishment was abolished in 1972 and later re-introduced; there was 1 execution (by lethal gas) in 1979.

Religion. Roman Catholics were the most numerous religious group at the 1980 census, followed by members of the Church of Jesus Christ of Latter-day Saints (Mormons) and various Protestant churches.

Education. School attendance is compulsory for children from 7 to 17 years of age. In 1986 the 195 public elementary schools had 88,831 pupils; there were 95 secondary public schools with 72,408. There were 3,683 elementary teachers (average salary $26,569), 3,022 secondary teachers with an average salary of $27,914. There were 70 private schools. The University of Nevada, Reno, had, in 1985–86, 330 full-time instructors and 9,718 students (regular, non-degree and correspondent), and University of Nevada, Las Vegas, 349 instructors and 12,279 students. Two-year community colleges operate as part of the University of Nevada system in Reno, Carson City, Elko and Las Vegas. There were (1985–86) 199 instructors and 24,803 students.

Health. In 1986 the state had 35 hospitals (4,125 beds); there were 30 skilled nursing units (2,957 beds).

Social Security. In 1986 benefits were paid to 130,000 persons: 86 retired (aged 62 and over) workers (average payment $491 per month); 14,000 widows and widowers ($453); 10,000 disabled workers ($514), their wives and husbands (9,000 at $247), 11,000 children ($251). Social Security beneficiaries represented 13·5% of the population.

Books of Reference

Information: Bureau of Business and Economic Research (Univ. of Nevada).

Bushnell, E., and Driggs, D. W., *The Nevada Constitution: Origin and Growth.* Univ. of Nevada Press, 5th ed., 1980
Hulse, James W., *The Nevada Adventure, A History.* Univ. of Nevada Press, 2nd ed., 1969
Laxalt, R., *Nevada: A History.* New York, 1977
Mack, E. M., and Sawyer, B. W., *Here is Nevada: A History of the State.* Sparks, Nevada, 1965
Paher, S. W., *Nevada, an Annotated Bibliography.* Nevada, 1980

State Library: Nevada State Library, Carson City. *State Librarian:* Mildred J. Heyer.

NEW HAMPSHIRE

HISTORY. New Hampshire, first settled in 1623, is one of the 13 original states of the Union.

AREA AND POPULATION. New Hampshire is bounded north by Canada, east by Maine and the Atlantic, south by Massachusetts and west by Vermont. Area, 9,279 sq. miles, of which 286 sq. miles are inland water. Census population, 1 April 1980, 920,610, an increase of 24·8% since 1970. Estimate (1985), 998,000. Births, 1984, were 12,656 (13 per 1,000 population); deaths, 7,749 (7·9); infant deaths, 106 (8·4 per 1,000 live births); marriages, 11,363 (11·6); divorces, 4,808 (4·9).

Population at 5 federal censuses was:

	White	Negro	Indian	Asiatic	Total	Per sq. mile
1910	429,906	564	34	68	430,572	47·7
1930	464,351	790	64	88	465,293	51·6
1960	604,334	1,903	135	549	606,921	65·2
			All others			
1970	733,106	2,505	2,070		737,681	81·7
1980	910,099	3,990	6,521		920,610	101·9

Of the total population in 1980, 448,462 were male, 480,325 were urban; those 20 years of age or older numbered 625,562.

The largest city of the state is Manchester, with a 1980 census population of 90,757. Other cities are: Nashua, 67,817; Concord (capital), 30, 400; Portsmouth, 26,214; Dover, 22,265; Keene, 21,385; Rochester, 21,579; Berlin, 13,090; Laconia, 15,579; Claremont, 14,575; Lebanon, 11,052; Somersworth, 10,313.

CLIMATE. Manchester. Jan. 22°F (−5·6°C), July 70°F (21·1°C). Annual rainfall 40″ (1,003 mm). *See* New England, p. 1379.

CONSTITUTION AND GOVERNMENT. While the present constitution dates from 1784, it was extensively revised in 1792 when the state joined the Union. Since 1775 there have been 16 state conventions with 49 amendments adopted to amend the constitution.

The Legislature consists of a Senate of 30 members, elected for 2 years, and a House of Representatives, restricted to between 375 and 400 members, elected for 2 years. The Governor and 5 administrative officers called 'Councillors' are also elected for 2 years.

Electors must be adult citizens, able to read and write, duly registered and not paupers or under sentence for crime. New Hampshire sends to the Federal Congress 2 senators and 2 representatives.

In the 1984 presidential election Reagan polled 244,790 votes, Mondale, 110,268.

The capital is Concord. The state is divided into 10 counties.

Governor: John Sununu (R.), 1985–88 ($44,520).
Secretary of State: William M. Gardner (D.) ($31,270).

BUDGET. The state government's general revenue for the fiscal year ending 30 June 1982 (US Census Bureau figures) was $1,306m. ($732m. from taxes, $320m. from federal aid); general expenditures, $1,392m. ($504m. on education, $188m. on public welfare, $174m. on highways).

Net long-term debt, 30 June 1982, was $1,480m.

Per capita personal income (1985) was $14,964.

NATURAL RESOURCES

Minerals. Minerals are little worked; they consist mainly of sand and gravel, stone, and clay for building and highway construction.

Agriculture. In 1985, there were 3,000 farms occupying 1m. acres; average farm was 333 acres. Average value per acre, $1,419. The US Soil Survey estimates that the state has 164,167 acres of excellent soil, 486,615 acres of fair soil, 530,630 of poor soil and 3,843,798 of non-arable soil. Only 636,195 acres (11% of the total area) show moderate erosion.

Cash income, 1986, from crops, $42·7m., and livestock, $71·6m. The chief field crops are hay and vegetables; the chief fruit crop is apples.

Forestry. In 1979 forest land totalled 5m. acres; national forest, 705,000 acres.

Fisheries. The 1985 catch was 8m. lb., worth $5m.

INDUSTRY. Total non-agricultural employment (1985), 466,000, of which 123,000 are in manufacturing, 113,000 in trade, 99,000 in services.

Principal manufactures: electrical machinery, non-electrical machinery, metal products, textiles and shoes.

COMMUNICATIONS

Roads. On 1 Jan. 1982 the state's highway mileage was 12,400 miles of rural roads, 2,100 miles of urban roads; there were 1,352 miles of federal-aid highways (primary), of which 202 miles were interstate. Motor vehicles registered, 1985, numbered 905,000.

Railways. In 1975 the length of railway in the state was 826 miles.

Aviation. In 1981 there were 15 public and 37 private airports.

JUSTICE, RELIGION, EDUCATION AND WELFARE

Justice. The state prison held 683 persons on 31 Dec. 1985. Since 1930 there has been only one execution (by hanging)—a white man, for murder, in 1939.

Religion. The Roman Catholic Church is the largest single body. The largest Protestant churches are Congregational, Episcopal, Methodist and United Baptist Convention of N.H.

Education. School attendance is compulsory for children from 6 to 14 years of age during the whole school term, or to 16 if their district provides a high school. Employed illiterate minors between 16 and 21 years of age must attend evening or special classes, if provided by the district.

In 1983–84 the public elementary and secondary schools had 159,000 pupils and (1986) 10,500 classroom teachers. Public school salaries, 1986, averaged $20,150. Total expenditure on public schools in 1986 was estimated at $482m. or $483 per capita.

Of the 4-year colleges, the University of New Hampshire (1866) had 10,609 students in 1985–86; New Hampshire College (1932) had 3,373; Keene State College (1909) had 2,981; River College (1933) had 2,285. Dartmouth College, at Hanover was founded in 1769 (4,604 students in 1985–86).

Health. In 1983 the state had 34 hospitals (4,600 beds). On 1 Jan. 1980 mental hospitals had 608 patients, and there were 679 persons in state institutions for the mentally retarded.

Social Security. The Division of Welfare handles public assistance for (1) aged citizens 65 years or over, (2) needy aged aliens, (3) needy blind persons, (4) needy citizens between 18 and 64 years inclusive, who are permanently and totally disabled, (5) needy children under 21 years, (6) Medicaid and the medically needy not eligible for a monthly grant.

In Dec. 1985, 1,800 persons were receiving SSI old-age assistance of an average $109 per month; 4,300 permanently and totally disabled, $220 per month; 5,000 families with dependent children, $300 per month.

Books of Reference

Delorme, D. (ed.), *New Hampshire Atlas and Gazetteer.* Freeport, 1983
Morison, E. E., and E. F., *New Hampshire.* New York, 1976
Squires, J. D., *The Granite State of the United States: A History of New Hampshire from 1623 to the present.* 4 vols., New York, 1956

NEW JERSEY

HISTORY. New Jersey, first settled in the early 1600s, is one of the 13 original states in the Union.

AREA AND POPULATION. New Jersey is bounded north by New York, east by the Atlantic with Long Island and New York City to the north-east, south by Delaware Bay and west by Pennsylvania. Area (US Bureau of Census), 7,787 sq. miles (319 sq. miles being inland water). Census population, 1 April 1980, 7,364,823, an increase of 2·7% since 1970. Estimate (1985) 7,562,000. Births, 1984, were 97,488 (13 per 1,000 population); deaths, 66,477 (8·8); infant deaths, 908 (9·3 per 1,000 live births); marriages, 62,192 (8·3); divorces, 28,469 (3·8).

Population at 5 federal censuses was:

	White	Negro	Indian	Asiatic	All others	Total	Per sq. mile
1910	2,445,894	89,760	168	1,345	—	2,537,167	337·7
1930	3,829,663	208,828	213	2,630	122	4,041,334	537·3
1960	5,539,003	514,875	1,699	8,778	2,427	6,066,782	739·5
1970	6,349,908	770,292	4,706	20,537	22,721	7,168,164	953·1
1980	6,127,467	925,066	8,394	103,847	200,048	7,364,823	986·2

Of the population in 1980, 3,533,012 were male, 6,557,377 persons were urban, 5,116,581 were 20 years of age or older.

Census population of the larger cities and towns in 1980 was:

Newark	329,248	Irvington	61,493	Parsippany-	
Jersey City	223,532	Union City	55,593	Troy Hills	49,868
Paterson	137,970	Vineland	53,753	Middletown	62,574
Elizabeth	106,201	Passaic	52,463	Union Township	50,184
Trenton (capital)	92,124	Woodbridge	90,074	Bloomfield	47,792
Camden	84,910	Hamilton	82,801	Atlantic City	40,199
Clifton	74,388	Edison	70,193	Plainfield	45,555
East Orange	77,025	Cherry Hill	68,785	Hoboken	42,460
Bayonne	65,047			Montclair	38,321

Largest urbanized areas (1980) were: Newark, 1,963,000; Jersey City, 555,483; Paterson-Clifton-Passaic, 447,785; Trenton (NJ–Pa.), 305,678.

CLIMATE. Jersey City. Jan. 31°F (–0·6°C), July 75°F (23·9°C). Annual rainfall 41″ (1,025 mm). Trenton. Jan. 32°F (0°C), July 76°F (24·4°C). Annual rainfall 40″ (1,003 mm). *See* Atlantic Coast, p. 1379.

CONSTITUTION AND GOVERNMENT. The legislative power is vested in a Senate and a General Assembly, the members of which are chosen by the people, all citizens (with necessary exceptions) 18 years of age, with the usual residential qualifications, having the right of suffrage. The present constitution, ratified by the registered voters on 4 Nov. 1947, has been amended 27 times. In 1966 the Constitutional Convention proposed, and the people adopted, a new plan providing for a 40-member Senate and an 80-member General Assembly. This plan, as certified by the Apportionment Commission and modified by the courts, provides for 40 legislative districts, with 1 senator and 2 assemblymen elected for each. Assemblymen serve 2 years, senators 4 years, except those elected at the election following each census, who serve for 2 years. The Governor is elected for 4 years.

The state sends to Congress 2 senators and 14 representatives.

In the 1984 presidential election Reagan polled 1,861,774 votes, Mondale, 1,229,206.

The capital is Trenton. The state is divided into 21 counties, which are subdivided into 567 municipalities—cities, towns, boroughs, villages and townships.

Governor: Thomas H. Kean (R.), 1986–90 ($85,000).
Secretary of State: Jane Burgio ($66,000).

BUDGET. For the year ending 30 June 1985 (budget figures) general revenues were $9,080·2m. (taxation $4,921m. and federal aid, $2,419·6m.); general expenditures were $8,824m. (education, $2,663m.; highways, $117·5m., and public welfare, $912·7m.).

Total net long-term debt, 31 Dec. 1984, was $2,381·2m.
Per capita personal income (1984) was $15,282.

NATURAL RESOURCES

Minerals. The chief minerals are stone ($15m., 1984) and sand and gravel ($34·3m.); others are zinc ($3m.), clay products ($986,000), peat and gemstones. New Jersey is a leading producer of greensand marl, magnesium compounds and peat. Total value of mineral products, 1984, was $149m.

Agriculture. Livestock raising, market-gardening, fruit-growing, horticulture and forestry are pursued. In 1984, 9,400 farms had a total area of 970,000 acres; average farm in 1984 had 103 acres valued at $3,056 per acre.

Cash income, 1984, from crops and livestock, $513m.

Leading crops are tomatoes (value, $18·2m., 1984), all corn ($29·6m.), peaches ($29·8m.), hay ($11·7m.), blueberries ($18·2m.), soybeans ($22·8m.).

Farm animals on 1 Jan. 1984 included 40,000 milch cows, 100,000 all cattle, (1982) 8,000 sheep and lambs and 41,000 swine.

INDUSTRY. In 1984 manufacturing establishments employed 731,200 workers, receiving (preliminary) $19,700m. in wages. The principal industries by value are: Chemicals and allied products, construction, electrical and electronic equipment, machinery (except electrical).

COMMUNICATIONS

Roads. In 1983 there were 33,879 miles of roads (municipal, 24,043 miles; state, 2,246 miles; county, 6,680 miles; others, 910 miles).

Railways. In Sept. 1985, the state had 1,882·05 route miles of railway.

Aviation. There were (1985) 95 airports (31 restricted), of which 14 (3) were publicly owned and 50 (28) privately owned.

JUSTICE, RELIGION, EDUCATION AND WELFARE

Justice. State prisons in Aug. 1985 had 12,814 adult and 587 juvenile inmates. The last execution (by electrocution) was in 1963; it was the 160th, all for murder. Future executions would be by lethal injection.

The constitution of New Jersey forbids discrimination against any person on account of 'religious principles, race, color, ancestry or national origin'. The state has had, since 1945, a 'fair employment act', *i.e.*, a Civil Rights statute forbidding any employer, public or private (with 6 or more employees), to discriminate against any applicant for work (or to discharge any employee) on the grounds of 'race, creed, color, national origin or ancestry'. Trade unions may not bar Negroes from membership.

Religion. The Roman Catholic population of New Jersey in 1984 was 3·1m. The five largest Protestant sects were United Methodists, 150,000; United Presbyterians, 174,000; Episcopalians, 147,000; Lutherans, 89,000; American Baptists, 74,000. There were 40,000 African Methodists and 4,000 Christian Methodist Episcopalians. The main Jewish sects were Reform (38,000) and Conservative (27,000).

Education. Elementary instruction is compulsory for all from 6 to 16 years of age and free to all from 5 to 20 years of age. In autumn 1984 public elementary schools had 725,700 and secondary schools had 422,138 enrolled pupils; public colleges in autumn 1984 had 313,985 students, including 117,212 in community colleges, and independent colleges had 63,607. The total cost of public schools, 1984–85, $5,507m. Average salary of all elementary and secondary classroom teachers in public schools 1984–85 was $25,000.

Rutgers, the State University (founded as Queen's College in 1766) had, in 1984, an opening autumn enrolment of 47,200 full- and part-time students. Princeton (founded in 1746) had 4,500 undergraduate and 1,500 graduate students. Fairleigh Dickinson (1941) had 9,770 undergraduate and 5,658 graduate students; Kean College, 12,930 students in 1983; Montclair State College, 14,949 in 1983; Glassboro State College, 8,960 in 1983; Trenton State College, 9,268 in 1983.

Health. In 1984 the state had 136 hospitals (34,445 beds), listed by the American Hospital Association.

Social Security. In the financial year 1982 gross expenditure for all public assistance programmes was $563,000,000. Average monthly total of cases was $358,000 with an average grant per case of $350.

Books of Reference

Legislative District Data Book. Bureau of Government Research. Annual

Manual of the Legislature of New Jersey. Trenton. Annual

Boyd, J. P. (ed.), *Fundamentals and Constitutions of New Jersey, 1664–1954.* Princeton, 1964

Cunningham, J. T., *New Jersey: America's Main Road.* Rev. ed. New York, 1976

Kull, I. Stoddard, (ed.), *New Jersey, a History.* New York, 1930

League of Women Voters of New Jersey. *New Jersey: Spotlight on Government.* Rutgers Univ. Press, 3rd ed., 1978

Lehne, R., and Rosenthal, A. (eds.), *Politics in New Jersey.* Rev. ed., Rutgers Univ. Press, 1979

State Library: 185 W. State Street, Trenton, N.J. 08625. *State Librarian:* Barbara F. Weaver.

NEW MEXICO

HISTORY. The first European settlement was established in 1598. Until 1771 New Mexico was the Spanish kings' 'Kingdom of New Mexico'. In 1771 it was annexed to the northern province of New Spain. When New Spain won its independence in 1821, it took the name of Republic of Mexico and established New Mexico as its northernmost department. When the war between the US and Mexico was concluded on 2 Feb. 1848 New Mexico was recognized as belonging to the US, and on 9 Sept. 1850 it was made a Territory. Part of the Territory was assigned to Texas; later Utah was formed into a separate Territory; in 1861 another part was transferred to Colorado, and in 1863 Arizona was disjoined, leaving to New Mexico its present area. New Mexico became a state in Jan. 1912.

AREA AND POPULATION. New Mexico is bounded north by Colorado, north-east by Oklahoma, east by Texas, south by Texas and Mexico and west by Arizona. Land area 121,335 sq. miles (258 sq. miles water). Public lands, administered by federal agencies (1975) amounted to 26·7m. acres or 34% of the total area. The Bureau of Indian Affairs held 7·3m. acres; the State of New Mexico held 9·4m. acres; 34·4m. acres were privately owned.

Census population, 1 April 1980, 1,302,894, an increase of 285,839 or 28% since 1970. Estimate (1987) 1,500,000. Vital statistics, 1986: Births, 27,281 (18·4 per 1,000 population); deaths, 10,007 (6·8); infant deaths, 254 (9·3 per 1,000 live births); marriages, 14,142 (9·6); divorces, 8,872 (6·0).

The population in 5 census years was:

	White	Negro	Indian	Asian and Pacific Islander	Other	Total	Per sq. mile
1910	304,594	1,628	20,573	506		327,301	2·7
1940	492,312	4,672	34,510	324		531,818	4·4
1960	875,763	17,063	56,255	1,942		951,023	7·8
1970	915,815	19,555	72,788	7,842 [1]		1,016,000	8·4
1980	1,164,053	24,406	106,119	6,825	1,491	1,302,894	10·7

[1] Includes unspecified races, 1970.

Of the 1980 total, 642,157 were male, 939,963 persons were urban; 884,987 were 18 years of age or older.

Before 1930 New Mexico was largely a Spanish-speaking state, but since 1945 an influx of population from other states has reduced the percentage of persons of Spanish origin or descent to 36·6%.

The largest cities are Albuquerque, with census population, 1980, 332,336 (and 1986 estimate, 366,750); Santa Fé (capital), 48,953 (55,980); Las Cruces, 45,086 (54,090); Roswell, 39,676 (44,110); Farmington, 31,222 (39,050).

CLIMATE. Santa Fé. Jan. 29°F (–1·7°C), July 68°F (20°C). Annual rainfall 15" (366 mm). *See* Mountain States, p. 1378.

CONSTITUTION AND GOVERNMENT. The constitution of 1912 is still in force with 105 amendments. The state Legislature, which meets annually, consists of 42 members of the Senate, elected for 4 years, and 70 members of the House of Representatives, elected for 2 years. The Governor and Lieut.-Governor are elected for 4 years. The state sends to Congress 2 senators and 3 representatives.

In the 1984 presidential election Reagan polled 304,950 votes, Mondale 200,953.

The state capital is Santa Fé. For local government the state is divided into 33 counties.

Governor: Garrey Carruthers (R.), 1987–91 ($63,000).
Lieut.-Governor: Jack Stahl (R.), 1987–91 ($40,425).
Secretary of State: Rebecca Vigil (D.), 1987–91 ($40,425).

BUDGET. For the year ending 30 June 1985 (US Census Bureau figures) the states general revenues were $3,124m. ($1,439m. from taxation and $527m. from federal government); general expenditures, $2,816m. (education, $159m.; highways, $100m., and public welfare, $190m.).

Long-term debt on 30 June 1985 was $289m.
Per capita personal income (1986) was $11,422.

ENERGY AND NATURAL RESOURCES

Minerals. New Mexico is the country's largest domestic source of uranium, perlite and potassium salts. Production of recoverable U_3O_8 was 1·3m. lb. in 1986; perlite, 386,000 short tons; potassium salts, 1·1m. short tons; petroleum, 75m. bbls (of 42 gallons); natural gas, 710m. cu. ft; natural gas liquids, 34·1m. bbls (of 42 gallons); copper, 294,265 short tons (1985); coal, 21m. short tons marketed. The value of the total mineral output (1985) was $5,658m. An average of 16,300 persons were employed monthly in the mining industry in 1986.

Agriculture. New Mexico produces cereals, vegetables, fruit, livestock and cotton. Dry farming and irrigation have proved profitable in periods of high prices. There were 13,600 farms and ranches covering 44·6m. acres in 1986; in the 1982 US Census of Agriculture average farm (or ranch) was valued (land and buildings) at $618,708; 3,732 farms and ranches were of 1,000 acres and over.

Cash income, 1986 (preliminary), from crops, $306·5m., and from livestock products, $712·1m. Principal crops are wheat (10·1m. bu. from 460,000 acres), hay (1·3m. tons from 310,000 acres) and sorghum/grains (10·4m. bu. from 250,000 acres). Farm animals on 1 Jan. 1987 included 61,000 milch cows, 1·4m. all cattle, 480,000 sheep and 36,000 swine (1986). National forest area (1982) covered 9·3m. acres.

INDUSTRY. Average monthly non-agricultural employment during 1987 was 529,500: 38,400 were employed in manufacturing, 138,200 in government. Value of manufactures shipments, 1985, $4,073·7m.; leading commodities, food and kindred products, transport and equipment, lumber and wood.

COMMUNICATIONS

Roads. On 13 March 1987 the state had 79,735 miles of road, of which the state maintained 11,722 miles. Motor vehicle registrations, 1986, 1,315,745.

Railways. On 31 Dec. 1986 there were 2,062 miles of railway.

Aviation. There were 72 public-use airports in Sept. 1987.

JUSTICE, RELIGION, EDUCATION AND WELFARE

Justice. The number of state prison inmates in Sept. 1987 was 2,620, including

442 in juvenile centres; there were also 71 New Mexico prisoners held outside the state. The death penalty (by electrocution formerly, and now by lethal injection) has been imposed on 8 persons since 1933, 6 whites and 2 Negroes, all for murder. The last execution was in 1961.

Since 1949 the denial of employment by reason of race, colour, religion, national origin or ancestry has been forbidden. A law of 1955 prohibits discrimination in public places because of race or colour. An 'equal rights' amendment was added to the constitution in 1972.

Religion. There were (1975) approximately 356,530 Protestant Church members and 315,470 Roman Catholics.

Education. Elementary education is free, and compulsory between 6 and 17 years or high-school graduation age. In 1985–86 the 88 school districts had an estimated enrolment of 291,185 students in elementary and secondary schools of which private and parochial schools had 24,983. There were 14,693 teachers receiving an average salary of $21,982. Public expenditure for elementary and secondary schools was $993m.

The state-supported 4-year institutes of higher education are (1985–86 [1]):

	Full-time Faculty	Students
University of New Mexico, Albuquerque	1,228	27,479
New Mexico State University, Las Cruces	684	17,402
Eastern New Mexico University, Portales	286	7,358
New Mexico Highlands University, Las Vegas	122	2,063
Western New Mexico University, Silver City	83	1,565
New Mexico Institute of Mining and Technology, Socorro	86	1,220

[1] Figures include branches outside main campus in cities listed.

Health. In 1987 the state had 49 short-term hospitals (4,284 beds).

Social Security. In Dec. 1985, 16,483 persons were receiving federal supplemental security income for the disabled (average $235.25 per month); 9,329 persons were receiving old-age assistance (average $135.91 per month); 513 persons were receiving aid to the blind (average $229.70 per month). In 1985 a monthly average of 50,831 people received aid to families with dependent children (average $83.64 per month).

Books of Reference

New Mexico Business (monthly; annual review in Jan.–Feb. issue). Bureau of Business and Economic Research, Univ. of N.M., Albuquerque
New Mexico Progress Economic Review (annual). Sunwest, Albuquerque
New Mexico Statistical Abstract: 1984. Bureau of Business and Economic Research, Univ. of N.M., Albuquerque, 1984
Beck, W., *New Mexico: a History of Four Centuries.* Univ. of Oklahoma, 1979
Garcia, C., Haine, P., and Rhodes, H., *State and Local Government in New Mexico.* Albuquerque, 1979
Jenkins, M., and Schroeder, A., *A Brief History of New Mexico.* Univ. of New Mexico, 1974
Muench, D., and Hillerman, T., *New Mexico.* Belding, Portland, Oregon, 1974

NEW YORK STATE

HISTORY. From 1609 to 1664 the region now called New York was claimed by the Dutch; then it came under the rule of the English, who governed the country until the outbreak of the War of Independence. On 20 April 1777 New York adopted a constitution which transformed the colony into an independent state; on 26 July 1788 it ratified the constitution of the US, becoming one of the 13 original states. New York dropped its claim to Vermont after the latter was admitted to the Union in 1791. With the annexation of a small area from Massachusetts in 1853, New York assumed its present boundaries.

AREA AND POPULATION. New York is bounded west and north by

Canada with Lake Erie, Lake Ontario and the St Lawrence River forming the boundary; east by Vermont, Massachusetts and Connecticut, south-east by the Atlantic, south by New Jersey and Pennsylvania. Area, 49,108 sq. miles (1,731 sq. miles being water). Census population, 1 April 1980, 17,557,288, a decrease of 3·7% since 1970. Estimate (1985) 17,783,000. Births in 1984 were 251,062 (14·2 per 1,000 population); deaths, 168,852 (9·5); infant deaths, 2,789 (11·1 per 1,000 live births); marriages, 168,860 (9·5); divorces, 61,075 (3·4, includes all dissolutions).

Population in 5 census years was:

	White	Negro	Indian	Asiatic	Total	Per sq. mile
1910	8,966,845	134,191	6,046	6,532	9,113,614	191·2
1930	12,143,191	412,814	6,973	15,088	12,588,066	262·6
1960	15,287,071	1,417,511	16,491	51,678	16,782,304	350·2

	White	Negro	All others	Total	Per sq. mile
1970	15,834,090	2,168,949	233,828	18,236,967	380·3
1980	13,961,106	2,401,842	1,194,340	17,557,288	367·0

Of the 1980 population, 8,338,961 were male, 14,857,202 were urban; those 20 years of age or older numbered 12,232,284. Aliens registered in Jan. 1980 numbered 801,411.

The population of New York City, by boroughs, census of 1 April 1980 was: Manhattan, 1,427,533; Bronx, 1,169,115; Brooklyn, 2,230,936; Queens, 1,891,325; Staten Island, 352,121; total, 7,071,030. The New York metropolitan statistical area had, in 1980, 9,080,777.

Population of other large cities and incorporated places census, April 1980, was:

Buffalo	357,002	Albany (capital)	101,767	Schenectady	67,877
Rochester	241,509	Utica	75,435	Mount Vernon	66,023
Yonkers	194,557	Niagara Falls	71,344	Troy	56,614
Syracuse	170,292	New Rochelle	70,345	Binghamton	55,745
White Plains	46,999	N. Tonawanda	35,760	Lindenhurst	26,919
Rome	43,826	Elmira	35,327	Rockville Center	25,405
Hempstead	40,404	Auburn	32,548	Newburgh	23,438
Freeport	38,272	Poughkeepsie	29,757	Garden City	22,927
Jamestown	35,775	Watertown	27,861	Massapequa Park	19,779
Valley Stream	35,769				

Other large urbanized areas, census 1980; Buffalo, 1·2m.; Rochester, 970,313; Albany–Schenectady–Troy, 794,298.

CLIMATE. Albany. Jan. 24°F (−4·4°C), July 73°F (22·8°C). Annual rainfall 34″ (855 mm). Buffalo. Jan. 24°F (−4·4°C), July 70°F (21·1°C). Annual rainfall 36″ (905 mm). New York. Jan. 30°F (−1·1°C), July 74°F (23·3°C). Annual rainfall 43″ (1,087 mm). See Atlantic Coast, p. 1379.

CONSTITUTION AND GOVERNMENT. The present constitution dates from 1894; a later constitutional convention, 1938, is now legally considered merely to have amended the 1894 constitution, which has now had 93 amendments. The Constitutional Convention of 1967 (4 April through 26 Sept.) was composed of 186 delegates who proposed a new state constitution; however this was rejected by the registered voters on 7 Nov. 1967. The Senate consists of 60 members, and the Assembly of 150 members, both elected every 2 years. The Governor and Lieut.-Governor are elected for 4 years. The right of suffrage resides in every adult who has been a citizen for 90 days, and has the residential qualifications; new voters must establish, by certificates or test, that they have had at least an elementary education.

The state is represented in Congress by 2 senators and 34 representatives.

In the 1984 presidential election Reagan polled 3,525,266 votes, Mondale, 3,013,521.

The state capital is Albany. For local government the state is divided into 62 counties, 5 of which constitute the city of New York. New York leads in state parks and recreation areas, covering 252,984 acres in 1979.

Cities are in 3 classes, the first class having each 175,000 or more inhabitants and the third under 50,000. Each is incorporated by charter, under special legislation. The government of New York City is vested in the mayor (Edward Koch), elected for 4 years, and a city council, whose president and members are elected for 4 years. The council has a President and 37 members, each elected from a state senatorial district wholly within the city. The mayor appoints all the heads of departments, except the comptroller, who is elected. Each of the 5 city boroughs (Manhattan, Bronx, Brooklyn, Queens and Richmond) has a president, elected for 4 years. Each borough is also a county bearing the same name except Manhattan borough, which, as a county, is called New York, and Brooklyn, which is Kings County.

Governor: Mario Cuomo (D.), 1987–91 ($130,000).
Lieut.-Governor: Stan Lundine (D.), 1987–91 ($110,000).
Secretary of State: Gail Schaefer (D.), 1987–91 ($79,218).

BUDGET. The state's general revenues for the financial year ending 31 March 1982 were $16,142m. ($14,959m. from taxes); general expenditures were $16,126m. ($5,298m. for education, $8,049m. for social services, $1,893m. for transport).

Per capita personal income was $14,121 in 1984.

The assessed valuation in 1980 of taxable real property in New York City was $38,056m. The assessed valuation of the state was $86,741m.

ENERGY AND NATURAL RESOURCES

Minerals. Production of principal minerals in 1980: Sand and gravel (22,000 short tons), salt (5,500 short tons), zinc (33,629 tonnes), petroleum (824,296 bbls), natural gas (15,680m. cu. ft). The state is a leading producer of titanium concentrate, talc, abrasive garnet, wollastonite and emery. Quarry products include trap rock, slate, marble, limestone and sandstone. Value of mineral output in 1980 $497·9m.

Agriculture. New York has large agricultural interests. In 1985 it had 45,000 farms, with a total area of 9m. acres; average farm was 200 acres; average value per acre, $808.

Cash income, 1985, from crops $719m. and livestock, $1,845m. Dairying, with 18,500 farms, 1981, is an important type of farming with produce at a market value of $1,383m. Field crops comprise maize, winter wheat, oats and hay. New York ranks second in US in the production of apples, and maple syrup. Other products are grapes, tart cherries, peaches, pears, plums, strawberries, raspberries, cabbages, onions, potatoes, maple sugar. Estimated farm animals, 1986, included 2m. all cattle, 968,000 milch cows, 55,000 sheep, 130,000 swine and 8m. chickens.

INDUSTRY. The main employers (1982 census) are service industries (997,800), trade (1,381,000) and manufacture (1,418,800). Leading industries were clothing, non-electrical machinery, printing and publishing, electrical equipment, instruments, food and allied products and fabricated metals.

COMMUNICATIONS

Roads. There were (1981) 109,485 miles of municipal and rural roads. The New York State Thruway extends 559 miles from New York City to Buffalo; in 1985 receipts from tolls amounted to $189,273,009. The Northway, a 176-mile toll-free highway, is a connecting road from the Thruway at Albany to the Canadian border at Champlain, Quebec.

Motor vehicle registrations in 1985 were 9·6m., most of which (7·7m.) were private passenger vehicles.

Railways. There were in 1981, 3,891 miles of Class I railways. New York City has NYCTA and PATH metro systems, and commuter railways run by Metro-North, New Jersey Rail and Long Island Rail Road.

Aviation. There were 472 airports and landing areas in 1986.

Shipping. The canals of the state, combined in 1918 in what is called the Improved Canal System, have a length of 524 miles, of which the Erie or Barge canal has 340 miles. In 1981 the canals carried 807,925 tons of freight.

JUSTICE, RELIGION, EDUCATION AND WELFARE

Justice. The State Human Rights Law was approved 12 March 1945, effective 1 July, 1945. The State Division of Human Rights is charged with the responsibility of enforcing this law. The division may request and utilize the services of all governmental departments and agencies; adopt and promulgate suitable rules and regulations; test, investigate and pass judgment upon complaints alleging discrimination in employment, in places of public accommodation, resort or amusement, education, and in housing, land and commercial space; hold hearings, subpoena witnesses and require the production for examination of papers relating to matters under investigation; grant compensatory damages and require repayment of profits in certain housing cases among other provisions; apply for court injunctions to prevent frustration of orders of the Commissioner.

On 30 Dec. 1984, 33,155 persons were in state prisons.

In 1963–81 there were no executions. Total executions (by electrocution) from 1930 to 1962 were 329 (234 whites, 90 Negroes, 5 other races; all for murder except 2 for kidnapping).

In 1985 murders reported in New York were 1,688; total violent crimes, 165,145. Police strength (sworn officers) in 1985 was 61,009 (39,193 New York City).

Religion. The churches are Roman Catholic, with 6,367,576 members in 1981, Jewish congregations (about 2m. in 1981) and Protestant Episcopal (299,929 in 1980).

Education. Education is compulsory between the ages of 7 and 16. In 1985 the public elementary and secondary schools had 2,605,363 pupils; classroom teachers numbered 175,256 in public schools. Total expenditure on public schools in 1985 was $13,244m. Teachers' salaries, 1985, averaged $29,200.

The state's educational system, including public and private schools and secondary institutions, universities, colleges, libraries, museums, etc., constitutes (by legislative act) the 'University of the State of New York', which is governed by a Board of Regents consisting of 15 members appointed by the Legislature. Within the framework of this 'University' was established in 1948 a 'State University' which controls 64 colleges and educational centres, 30 of which are locally operated community colleges. The 'State University' is governed by a board of 16 Trustees, appointed by the Governor with the consent and advice of the Senate.

Higher education in the state is conducted in 296 institutions (642,000 full-time and 371,000 part-time students in autumn 1982); 573,000 students are in public-control colleges and 439,000 in private.

In autumn 1980 the institutions of higher education in the state included:

Founded	Name and place	Teachers	Students
1754	Columbia University, New York	3,965	17,410
1795	Union University, Schenectady and Albany	178	2,071
1824	Rensselaer Polytechnic Institute, Troy	442	6,145
1831	New York University, New York	2,615	45,000
1846	Colgate University, New York	205	2,550
1846	Fordham University, New York	958	14,653
1847	University of the City of New York, New York	12,426	172,683
1848	University of Rochester, Rochester	1,549	11,159
1854	Polytechnic Institute of New York	242	4,583
1856	St Lawrence University, Canton	173	2,375
1857	Cooper Union Institute of Technology, New York	161	872
1861	Vassar College, Poughkeepsie	230	2,364
1863	Manhattan College, New York	291	3,498
1865	Cornell University, Ithaca	1,863	17,866
1870	Syracuse University, Syracuse	1,100	11,819
1948	State University of New York	13,228	372,415

The Saratoga Performing Arts Centre (5,100 seats), a non-profit, tax-exempt organization, which opened in 1966, is the summer residence of the New York City Ballet and the Philadelphia Orchestra—two groups which present special educational programmes for students and teachers.

Health. In 1981 the state had 278 hospitals (67,798 beds), 585 skilled nursing homes (62,435 beds) and 241 other institutions (24,302 beds). In 1986 mental health facilities had 21,836 patients and institutions for the mentally retarded had 10,581 patients.

Social Security. The federal Supplemental Security Income programme covered aid to the needy aged, blind and disabled from 1 Jan. 1975. In the state programme for 1980, $4,543m. was paid in Medicaid to 2,288,000 people; aid to dependent children in 1985 went to 1,109,610 recipients, average benefits $371 per family per month.

Books of Reference

New York Red Book. Albany, 1979–80
Legislative Manual. Department of State, 1980–81
Managing Modern New York: the Carey Era. Rockefeller Institute, Albany, 1985
New York State Statistical Yearbook, 1986–87. Rockefeller Institute, Albany
Connery, R. and G. B., *Governing New York State: The Rockefeller Years.* Academy of Political Science, New York, 1974
Ellis, D. M., *History of New York State.* Cornell Univ. Press, 1967
Flick, A. (ed.), *History of the State of New York.* Columbia Univ. Press, 1933–37
Lincoln, C., *Constitutional History of New York 1809–1877.* Rochester, 1906
Wolfe, G. R., *New York: A Guide to the Metropolis.* New York Univ. Press, 1975

State Library: The New York State Library, Albany 12230. *State Librarian and Assistant Commissioner for Libraries:* Joseph Shubert.

NORTH CAROLINA

HISTORY. North Carolina, first settled in 1585 by Sir Walter Raleigh and permanently settled in 1663, was one of the 13 original states of the Union.

AREA AND POPULATION. North Carolina is bounded north by Virginia, east by the Atlantic, south by South Carolina, south-west by Georgia and west by Tennessee. Area, 52,669 sq. miles, of which 3,826 sq. miles are inland water. Census population, 1 April 1980, 5,874,429, an increase of 15·5% since 1970. Estimated population (1986), 6,331,000.

Births, 1984, were 86,705 (14·1 per 1,000 population); marriages, 52,123 (8·5); deaths, 51,496 (8·4); infant deaths, 1,099 (12·7 per 1,000 live births); divorces and annulments, 29,125 (4·7).

Population in 6 census years was:

	White	Negro	Indian	Asiatic	Total	Per sq. mile
1910	1,500,511	697,843	7,851	82	2,206,287	45·3
1930	2,234,958	918,647	16,579	92	3,170,276	64·5
1950	2,983,121	1,047,353	3,742	—	4,061,929	82·7
1960	3,399,285	1,116,021	38,129	2,012	4,556,155	92·2
			All others			
1970	3,901,767	1,126,478	53,814		5,082,059	104·1
1980	4,453,010	1,316,050	105,369		5,874,429	111·5

Of the total population in 1980, 2,852,012 were male, 2,818,794 were urban and 3,976,359 were 20 years old or older; 14·8% were non-white.

Cities (with census population in 1980) are: Charlotte, 314,447; Greensboro, 155,642; Winston-Salem, 131,885; Raleigh (capital), 149,771; Durham, 100,831; High Point, 64,107; Asheville, 53,281; Fayetteville, 59,507.

CLIMATE. Climate varies sharply with altitude; the warmest area is in the south east near Southport and Wilmington; the coldest is Mount Mitchell (6,684 ft). Raleigh. Jan. 42°F (5·6°C), July 79°F (26·1°C). Annual rainfall 46″ (1,158 mm). *See* Atlantic Coast, p. 1379.

CONSTITUTION AND GOVERNMENT. The present constitution dates from 1971 (previous constitution, 1776 and 1868/76); it has had 19 amendments. The General Assembly consists of a Senate of 50 members and a House of Representatives of 120 members; all are elected by districts for 2 years. The Governor and Lieut.-Governor are elected for 4 years. The Governor may succeed himself but has no veto. There are 19 other executive heads of department, 8 elected by the people and 9 appointed by the Governor. All registered citizens with the usual residential qualifications have a vote.

The state is represented in Congress by 2 senators and 11 representatives.

In the presidential election of 1984 Reagan polled 1,314,802 votes, Mondale, 809,876.

The capital is Raleigh, established in 1792.

Governor: James G. Martin, (R.), 1985–89 ($100,000, plus $11,500 annual expenses).

Lieut.-Governor: Robert B. Jordan, III (D.) ($61,044, plus $11,500 annual expenses).

Secretary of State: Thad Eure (D.) ($61,044).

BUDGET. General revenue for the year ending 30 June 1986 was $4,910·9m. General expenditure was $4,971·9m.

On 30 June 1986 the net total long-term debt amounted to $757m.

Per capita personal income (1985–86) was $11,903.

NATURAL RESOURCES

Minerals. Mining production in 1985 was valued at $474·7m. Principal minerals were stone, sand and gravel, phosphate rock, feldspar, lithium minerals, olivine, kaolin and talc. North Carolina ranked first in the production of scrap mica, feldspar, lithium minerals, olivine and phrophyllite. It is also the leading producer of bricks, making more than 1,000m. bricks a year.

Agriculture. In 1985 there were 76,000 farms in North Carolina covering 10·8m. acres; average size of farms was 142 acres and total estimated value $18,500m.

Cash receipts from farming (1984), $4,125m., of which $2,198m. was from crops and $1,927m. from livestock, dairy and poultry products. Main crop production: flue-cured tobacco, maize, soybeans, peanuts, wheat, sweet potatoes and apples. On 1 Jan. 1985 farms had 1·17m. all cattle, 2·3m. swine and 20·2m. chickens.

Forestry. Commercial forest covered 18·5m. acres (60% of land area), in 1984. Main products are hardwood veneer and hardwood plywood, furniture woods, pulp, paper and lumber.

Fisheries. Commercial fish catch, 1985, amounted to 215m. lb.; value approximately $65m. The catch is mainly of menhaden, crabmeat, bay scallops, flounder, croaker, shrimps, sea trout, spots and clams.

INDUSTRY. North Carolina's manufacturing establishments in 1985 had 827,400 workers. The leading industries by employment are textiles, clothing, furniture, electrical machinery and equipment, non-electrical machinery, and food processing. In 1985 investment in new and expanded industry was $2,758m. About 576,200 are employed in trade, 422,800 in government and 427,600 in services.

TOURISM. Total receipts of the travel industry, $4,500m. in 1985.

COMMUNICATIONS

Roads. The state maintained, 1985, 76,459 miles of highways, comprising all rural roads and 5,088 miles of urban streets which are major thoroughfares. In Oct. 1986, 3,499,178 automobiles, 1,152,156 trucks and 1,274,137 other vehicles were registered.

Railways. The state in 1986 contained 3,682 miles of railway operating in 91 of the 100 counties. There are 22 Class I, II and III rail companies.

Aviation. In 1986 there were 82 public airports of which 14 are served by major airlines.

Shipping. There are 2 ocean ports, Wilmington and Morehead City.

JUSTICE, RELIGION, EDUCATION AND WELFARE

Justice. Total executions 1910–86, 365. There was one execution (by lethal injection) in 1986. Prison population at 31 Oct. 1986, 17,700.

Religion. Leading denominations are the Baptists (48·9% of church membership), Methodists (20·7%), Presbyterians (7·7%), Lutherans (3%) and Roman Catholics (2·7%). Total estimate of all denominations in 1983 was 2·6m.

Education. School attendance is compulsory between 6 and 16.

Public school enrolment, 1985–86, was 1,080,887; elementary and secondary schools numbered 1,968. Instructional staff (1986) consisted of 57,630 classroom teachers; average salary $22,476. Expenditure for public schools was $2,770m., 65·5% from state, 25·2% from local and 9·3% from federal sources.

In autumn 1985–86 state-supported colleges and universities included 58 community and technical colleges with 654,000 full and part time students. The 16 senior universities are all part of the University of North Carolina system, the largest campus being North Carolina State University and Raleigh, with 23,400 students. The university system was founded in 1789 at Chapel Hill and first opened in 1792. Its 1986 autumn enrolment was 130,000 students.

In addition to the state-supported institutions there were 7 private junior colleges with an enrolment of 2,585 and 31 private senior institutions with a total enrolment of 19,009. The total undergraduate enrolment in private institutions for 1985 was 21,594.

Health. In Oct. 1986 the state had 160 hospitals (34,438 beds).

Social Security. In June 1982 there were 900,070 persons receiving $300·4m. in social security benefits. Of that number 496,020 were retired, receiving $186·67m.; 85,640 were disabled ($34·7m.); 318,410 others received $79m.

Books of Reference

North Carolina Manual. Secretary of State. Raleigh. Biennial

Clay, J. W., *et al*, (eds.), *North Carolina Atlas: Portrait of a Changing Southern State.* Univ. of North Carolina Press, 1975

Corbitt, D. L., *The Formation of the North Carolina Counties.* Raleigh, 1969

Lefler, H. T., and Newsome, A. R., *North Carolina: The History of a Southern State.* Univ. of N.C., Chapel Hill, 1973

NORTH DAKOTA

HISTORY. North Dakota was admitted into the Union, with boundaries as at present, on 2 Nov. 1889; previously it had formed part of the Dakota Territory, established 2 March 1861.

AREA AND POPULATION. North Dakota is bounded north by Canada, east by the Red River (forming a boundary with Minnesota), south by South Dakota and west by Montana. Land area, 69,262 sq. miles, and 1,403 sq. miles of water. The Federal Bureau of Indian Affairs administered (1971) 850,000 acres, of which 153,000 acres were assigned to tribes. Census population, 1 April 1980,

652,717, an increase of 34,956 or 5·7% since 1970. Estimate (1984), 686,000. Births in 1984 were 11,833 (17 per 1,000 population); deaths, 5,538 (8·0); infant deaths, 97; marriages, 5,786; divorces, 2,249.

Population at 5 census years was:

	White	Negro	Indian	Asiatic	Total	Per sq. mile
1910	569,855	617	6,486	98	577,056	8·2
1930	671,851	377	8,617	194	680,845	9·7
1960	619,538	777	11,736	274	632,446	9·1
			All others			
1970	599,485	2,494	15,782		617,761	8·9
1980	625,557	2,568	24,692		652,717	9·4

Of the total population in 1980, 328,126 were male, 317,821 were urban and 419,234 were 21 years old or older. Estimated outward migration, 1970–80, 16,983.

The largest cities are Fargo with population (census), 1980, of 61,383; Grand Forks, 43,765; Bismarck (capital), 44,485, and Minot, 32,843.

CLIMATE. Bismarck. Jan. 8°F (–13·3°C), July 71°F (21·1°C). Annual rainfall 16″ (402 mm). Fargo. Jan. 6°F (–14·4°C), July 71°F (21·1°C). Annual rainfall 20″ (503 mm). *See* High Plains and Mid-West (SW North Dakota is in the Plains, the rest in the mid-west lowlands), p. 1378.

CONSTITUTION AND GOVERNMENT. The present constitution dates from 1889; it has had 95 amendments. The Legislative Assembly consists of a Senate of 53 members elected for 4 years, and a House of Representatives of 106 members elected for 2 years. The Governor and Lieut.-Governor are elected for 4 years. Qualified electors are (with necessary exceptions) all citizens and civilized Indians. The state sends to Congress 2 senators elected by the voters of the entire state and 1 representative.

In the 1984 presidential election Reagan polled 155,856 votes, Mondale, 80,839.

The capital is Bismarck. The state has 53 organized counties.

Governor: George A. Sinner (D.), 1985–89 ($60,862 plus expenses).
Lieut.-Governor: Ruth Meiers (D.), 1985–89 ($12,500 plus expenses).
Secretary of State: Ben Meier (R.), 1985–89 ($43,380 plus expenses).

FINANCE. General revenue of state and local government year ending 30 June 1982, was $1,286m.; general expenditures, $1,191m., taxation provided $533m. and federal aid, $252m.; education took $449m.; highways, $148m., and public welfare, $104m.

Total net long-term debt (local government) on 30 June 1982, $325m.
Per capita personal income (1985) was $12,052.

ENERGY AND NATURAL RESOURCES

Minerals. The mineral resources of North Dakota consist chiefly of oil which was discovered in 1951. Production of crude petroleum in 1984 was 52·6m. bbls; of natural gas, 76,800m. cu. ft. Output of lignite coal was 21·7m. short tons. Total value of mineral output, 1984, $1,724m.

Agriculture. Agriculture is the chief pursuit of the North Dakota population. In 1985 there were 33,000 farms (61,963 in 1954) with an area of 41m. acres (41,876,924 in 1954); the average farm was of 1,242 acres. The greater number of farms are cash-grain or livestock farms with annual sales of $20,000–$39,999.

Cash income, 1985, from crops, $2,060m., and from livestock, $686m. North Dakota leads in the production of barley, sunflowers, flaxseed and durum. Other important products are wheat, pinto beans, sugar-beet, potatoes, hay, oats, rye and maize.

The state has also an active livestock industry, chiefly cattle raising. On 1 Jan.

1985 the farm animals were: 97,000 milch cows, 2m. all cattle, 215,000 sheep and 250,000 swine. The wool clip yielded (1984), 1·6m. lb. of wool from 180,000 sheep.

Forestry. National forest area, 1977, 422,000 acres, of which 115,000 acres are federally owned or managed.

INDUSTRY. From 1970 to 1984 agricultural employment fell from 51,920 to 51,480; non-agricultural jobs rose from 148,910 to 268,300. In 1985, 68,000 were employed in trade, 63,000 in government, 58,000 in services, 16,000 in transport and utilities, 15,000 in manufacturing.

COMMUNICATIONS

Roads. The state highway department maintained, in 1985, 7,237 miles of highway; local authorities, 95,750 miles, and municipal, 3,243 miles.
    Car and truck registrations in 1985 numbered 712,000.

Railways. In 1984 there were 5,262 miles of railway.

Aviation. Airports in 1984 numbered 262, of which 107 were publicly owned.

JUSTICE, RELIGION, EDUCATION AND WELFARE

Justice. The state penitentiary, on 31 Dec. 1985, held 407 inmates. There is no death penalty.

Religion. The leading religious denominations are the Roman Catholics, with 171,185 members in 1975; Combined Lutherans, 216,579; Methodists, 28,880; Presbyterians, 18,636.

Education. School attendance is compulsory between the ages of 7 and 16, or until the 17th birthday if the eighth grade has not been completed. In Oct. 1983 the public elementary schools had 81,797 pupils; secondary schools, 34,892 pupils. State expenditure on public schools, 1986, $379m. or $553 per capita. Teachers (4,900 in elementary and 2,900 in secondary schools) earned an average $20,850 in 1986.
    The university at Grand Forks, founded in 1883, had 11,068 students in 1984; the state university of agriculture and applied science, at Fargo, 9,453 students. Total enrolment in the 8 public institutions of higher education, 1984, 33,748.

Health. In 1985 the state had 59 hospitals (6,000 beds), and 81 nursing homes (6,400).

Social Security. In 1985 6,500 received SSI payments, including 2,400 aged (average $116 per month). 4,000 disabled ($209); total paid, $12·7m.; 13,100 recipients in 4,700 families received Aid to Families with Dependent Children.

Books of Reference

North Dakota Growth Indicators, 1984. 20th ed. Economic Development Commission, Bismarck, 1985
North Dakota Blue Book. Secretary of State, Bismarck, 1981
Statistical Abstract of North Dakota, 1983. Bureau of Business and Economic Research, Univ. of North Dakota, 1983
Glaab, C. L., et al, *The North Dakota Political Tradition.* Iowa State Univ. Press, 1981
Jelliff, T. B., *North Dakota: A Living Legacy.* Fargo, 1983
Robinson, E. B., *History of North Dakota.* Univ. of Nebraska Press, 1966

OHIO

HISTORY. The first organized white settlement was in 1788; Ohio unofficially entered the Union on 19 Feb. 1803; entrance was made official, retroactive to 1 March 1803, on 8 Aug. 1953.

AREA AND POPULATION. Ohio is bounded north by Michigan and Lake Erie, east by Pennsylvania, south-east and south by the Ohio River (forming a boundary with West Virginia and Kentucky) and west by Indiana. Area, 41,330 sq. miles, of which 325 sq. miles are inland water. Census population, 1 April 1980 10,797,630, an increase of 145,402 or 1·4% since 1970. Estimate (1985) 10,744,000. In 1984 births numbered 159,939 (14·9 per 1,000 population); deaths, 96,937 (9); infant deaths, 1,598 (10 per 1,000 live births); marriages, 98,708 (9·2); divorces and annulments, 53,492 (5).

Population at 5 census years was:

	White	Negro	Indian	Asiatic	Total	Per sq. mile
1910	4,654,897	111,452	127	645	4,767,121	117·0
1930	6,335,173	309,304	435	1,785	6,646,697	161·6
1960	8,909,698	786,097	1,910	8,692	9,706,397	236·9

			All others		
1970	9,646,997	970,477	34,543	10,652,017	260·0
1980	9,597,458	1,076,748	123,424	10,797,630	263·2

Of the total population in 1980, 5,217,027 were male, 7,918,259 persons were urban. Those 20 years old or older numbered 7,294,471.

Census population of chief cities on 1 April 1980 was:

Cleveland	573,822	Hamilton	63,189	Cuyahoga Falls	43,890
Columbus	565,032	Lakewood	61,963	Mentor	42,065
Cincinnati	385,457	Kettering	61,186	Newark	41,200
Toledo	354,635	Euclid	59,999	Marion	37,040
Akron	237,177	Elyria	57,538	East Cleveland	36,957
Dayton	193,444	Cleveland Heights	56,438	North Olmsted	36,486
Youngstown	115,436	Warren	47,381	Upper Arlington	35,648
Canton	93,077	Mansfield	53,927	Lancaster	34,953
Parma	92,548	Lima	47,381	Garfield Heights	34,938
Lorain	75,416	Middletown	43,719	Zanesville	28,655
Springfield	72,563				

Urbanized areas, 1980 census: Cleveland, 1,898,825; Cincinnati, 1,401,491; Columbus (the capital), 1,093,316; Dayton, 830,070; Akron, 660,328; Toledo, 791,599; Youngstown-Warren, 531,350; Canton, 404,421.

CLIMATE. Cincinnati. Jan. 33°F (0·6°C), July 78°F (25·6°C). Annual rainfall 39″ (978 mm). Cleveland. Jan. 27°F (–2·8°C), July 71°F (21·1°C). Annual rainfall 35″ (879 mm). Columbus. Jan. 29°F (–1·7°C), July 75°F (23·9°C). Annual rainfall 34″ (850 mm). See Great Lakes, p. 1379.

CONSTITUTION AND GOVERNMENT. The question of a general revision of the constitution drafted by an elected convention is submitted to the people every 20 years. The constitution of 1851 had 141 amendments by 1983.

In the 117th General Assembly the Senate consisted of 33 members and the House of Representatives of 99 members. The Senate is elected for 4 years, half each 2 years; the House is elected for 2 years; the Governor, Lieut.-Governor and Secretary of State for 4 years. Qualified as electors are (with necessary exceptions) all citizens 18 years of age who have the usual residential qualifications. Ohio sends 2 senators and 21 representatives to Congress.

In the 1984 presidential election Reagan polled 2,678,559 votes, Mondale, 1,825,440.

The capital (since 1816) is Columbus. Ohio is divided into 88 counties.

Governor: Richard Celeste (D.), 1987–90 ($65,000).
Lieut.-Governor: Paul Leonard (D.), 1987–90 ($42,543).
Secretary of State: Sherrod Brown (D.), 1987–90 ($60,775).

BUDGET. For the year ending 30 June 1987 general revenue fund income was 11,183·9m. and expenditure, $10,550·7m.

The bonded debt on 30 June 1986 was $3,378m.

Per capita personal income (1985) was $13,226 (current dollars).

ENERGY AND NATURAL RESOURCES

Minerals. Ohio has extensive mineral resources, of which coal is the most important by value: output (1984) 39m. short tons; value at the mine, $1,269m. Production of crude petroleum, 1984, 15m. bbls ($420m.); natural gas, 186,479·6m. cu. ft ($588·4m.). Other minerals include stone, clay, sand and gravel. Value of non-fuel minerals, 1984, $283·9m.

Agriculture. Ohio is extensively devoted to agriculture. In 1985, 89,000 farms covered 16m. acres; average farm value per acre, $1,126.

Cash income 1984, from crop and livestock and products, $3,843m. The most important crops in 1983 were: Maize (232m. bu.), wheat (58·6m. bu.), oats (15·4m. bu.), soybeans (101·7m. bu.). On 1 Jan. 1985 there were 1·97m. swine 1·8m. all cattle and 265,000 sheep.

Forestry. State forest area, 1982, 195,000 acres; total forest, 6,147,000 acres.

INDUSTRY. In May 1987, manufacturing employed 1,091,000 workers; nonmanufacturing, 3,315,000. The largest industry was manufacturing of nonelectrical machinery, then transport equipment and fabricated metals.

COMMUNICATIONS

Roads. In 1985 the state had 30,466 miles of urban and 82,518 miles of rural highway. The federal-aid highway system included 8,194 miles of primary roads, of which 1,549 miles were interstate. In 1985 there were (estimate) 8·1m. cars, trucks and buses, and 277,501 motorcycles.

Railways. Class I railroads operated 6,238 miles in 1985.

Aviation. Ohio had (1985) 194 commercial airports including one seaplane base; 597 non-commercial airports; 31 commercial heliports and 222 non-commercial. There were 5,825 licensed aeroplanes at 31 Dec. 1984.

JUSTICE, RELIGION, EDUCATION AND WELFARE

Justice. A Civil Rights Act (1933) forbids inns, restaurants, theatres, retail stores and all other places of public resort to discriminate against citizens on grounds of 'colour or race'; none may be denied the right to serve on juries on the grounds of 'colour or race'; insurance companies are forbidden to discriminate between 'white persons and coloured, wholly or partially of African descent'.

A state Civil Rights Commission (created 1959) has general administrative powers to prevent discrimination because of race, colour, religion, national origin or ancestry in employment, labour organization membership, use of public accommodations and in obtaining 'commercial housing' or 'personal residence'. Ohio has no *de jure* segregation in the public schools.

The state's adult correctional institutions, Sept. 1985, held 20,000 inmates (average daily count). Total executions (by electrocution) since 1930 were 170, all for murder. There have been no executions since 1963. The Department of Rehabilitation and Correction was created in July 1972, and has established probation services in counties where services would otherwise be inadequate or nonexistent.

Religion. Many religious faiths are represented, including (but not limited to) the Baptist, Jewish, Lutheran, Methodist, Presbyterian and Roman Catholic.

Education. School attendance during full term is compulsory for children from 6 to 18 years of age. In autumn 1985 public schools had 1,793,775 enrolled pupils and 98,264 full-time equivalent classroom teachers. Teachers' salaries (1985–86) averaged (estimate) $24,500. Operating expenditure on elementary and secondary schools for 1984–85 was $5,500m.: state average per pupil, $3,257. Universities and colleges had a total enrolment (autumn 1985) of 514,745 students of whom 135,481 were in private colleges. State appropriation to state universities 1984–85, $1,100m. Average annual charge (undergraduate) at 4-year institutions: $4,081 (state); $7,432 (private).

Main bodies, 1986: (figures are for main campus in named city):

Founded	Institutions	Enrolments
1804	Ohio University, Athens (State)	14,684
1809	Miami University, Oxford (State)	15,430
1819	University of Cincinnati (State)	30,830
1826	Case Western Reserve University, Cleveland (Indep.)	8,352
1850	University of Dayton (R.C.)	10,693
1870	University of Akron (State)	26,644
1870	Ohio State University, Columbus (State)	53,446
1872	University of Toledo (State)	21,039
1887	Sinclair Community College, Dayton	16,247
1908	Youngstown University (State)	15,252
1910	Bowling Green State University (State)	17,104
1910	Kent State University (State)	20,324
1962	Cuyahoga Community College District (State/local)	24,972
1964	Cleveland State University (State)	18,032
1964	Wright State University (State)	14,580

Health. In 1983 the state had 236 hospitals (62,405 beds) listed by the American Hospital Association. State facilities for the severely mentally retarded had 2,862 resident in 1984.

Mentally retarded who do not need constant supervision occupy 1,024 group homes (7,993 beds) in residential areas (1983). In 1986 17 psychiatric hospitals had a daily average of 4,012 residents. In 1984, general hospitals had 74 units (3,080 beds) for the mentally ill and 56 beds for mentally retarded. There were 384 community mental health agencies in 1986.

Social Security. Public assistance is administered through 6 basic programmes: aid to dependent children, emergency assistance, Medicaid, general relief, food stamps and social services; 49% of the costs (except general relief and adult emergency assistance) are met by the federal government.

In 1985 Medicaid cost $1,767·3m. and served an average 1·5m. people. Aid to dependent children cost $759·5m., to 672,414 people per month at $290 maximum grant for a family of three. Food stamps cost $57·3m. General relief cost $206·8m., receipts varying from county to county. Optional State Supplement is paid to aged, blind or disabled adults. Free social services are available to those eligible by income or circumstances.

Books of Reference

Official Roster: Federal State, County Officers and Department Information. Secretary of State, Columbus. Biennial

Rosebloom, E. H., and Weisenburger, F. P., *A History of Ohio.* State Arch. and Hist. Soc., Columbus, 1953

OKLAHOMA

HISTORY. An unorganized area in the centre of the present state was thrown open to white settlers on 22 April 1889. The Territory of Oklahoma, organized in 1890 to include this area and other sections, was opened to white settlements by runs or lotteries during the next decade. In 1893 the Territory was enlarged by the addition of the Cherokee Outlet, which fixed part of the present northern boundary. On 16 Nov. 1907 Oklahoma was combined with the remaining part of the Indian Territory and admitted as a state with boundaries substantially as now.

AREA AND POPULATION. Oklahoma is bounded north by Kansas, north-east by Missouri, east by Arkansas, south by Texas (the Red River forming part of the boundary) and, at the western extremity of the 'panhandle', by New Mexico and Colorado. Area 69,919 sq. miles, of which 1,137 sq. miles are water. Census population, 1 April 1980, 3,025,290, an increase of 465,827 or 18% since 1970. Estimate (1986), 3,305,000. Births, 1986, were 50,536; deaths, 29,708; infant deaths 517; marriages, 33,805; divorces, including annulments, 24,747.

The population at 5 federal censuses was:

	White	Negro	Indian	Other	Total	Per sq. mile
1910	1,444,531	137,612	74,825	187	1,657,155	23·9
1930	2,130,778	172,198	92,725	339	2,396,040	34·6
1960	2,107,900	153,084	68,689	1,414	2,328,284	33·8
1970	2,280,362	171,892	97,179	10,030	2,559,253	37·2
1980	2,597,783	204,658	169,292	53,557	3,025,290	43·2

In 1980, 1,476,719 were male, 2,035,082 were urban and those 20 years of age or older numbered 2,052,729. The US Bureau of Indian Affairs is responsible for 37 Indian tribes, 201,456 Indians on 1,229,341 acres (1984).

The most important cities with population, 1980 (and estimate 1986) are Oklahoma City (capital), 403,213 (445,300), Tulsa, 360,919 (373,000); Lawton, 80,054 (82,700); Norman, 68,020 (78,300); Enid, 50,363 (50,300); Midwest City, 49,559 (53,700); Broken Arrow, 35,761 (52,000); Edmond, 34,637 (51,200).

CLIMATE. 1985: Oklahoma City. Jan. 30·6°F (–0·8°C), July 80·9°F (27·2°C). Annual rainfall 44·2″ (1,123 mm). Tulsa. Jan. 30·2°F (1·0°C), July 82·9°F (28·3°C). Annual rainfall 51·31″ (1,303 mm). *See* Central Plains, p. 1378.

CONSTITUTION AND GOVERNMENT. The present constitution, dating from 1907, provides for amendment by initiative petition and legislative referendum; it has had 114 amendments.

The Legislature consists of a Senate of 48 members, who are elected for 4 years, and a House of Representatives elected for 2 years and consisting of 101 members. The Governor and Lieut.-Governor are elected for 4-year terms; the Governor can only be elected for two terms in succession. Electors are (with necessary exceptions) all citizens 18 years or older, with the usual qualifications.

The state is represented in Congress by 2 senators and 6 representatives.

In the 1984 presidential election Reagan polled 793,258 votes, Mondale, 362,771.

The capital is Oklahoma City. The state has 77 counties.

Governor: Henry Bellmon (R.), 1987–91 ($70,000).
Lieut.-Governor: Robert S. Kerr (R.), 1987–91 ($40,000).
Secretary of State: Hannah Atkins (D.), 1988–91 ($37,500).

BUDGET. Total revenue for the year ending 30 June 1987 (State Budget Office figures) was $5,018·3m. Total expenditure, $5,052·9m.

Bonded indebtedness for the year ending 30 June 1985, $1,599·6m.

Per capita personal income (1985) was $10,270.

ENERGY AND NATURAL RESOURCES

Minerals. Production of mineral fuels, 1986: Petroleum, 149m. bbls; natural gas (wet), 1,927,964,000,000m. cu. ft.; coal, 2·9m. short tons. In 1986 there were 93,997 oilwells and 25,762 natural gaswells in production. Non-fuel mineral production (short tons), 1985: Cement, 1·6m.; gypsum, 1·6m.; sand and gravel (construction), 12·6m.; stone, 31·2m.; clays, 997,000; other important minerals are iodine, tripoli, barite, cadmium, feldspar, refined germanum, helium, lime, nitrogen, pumice and zinc. Value of non-fuel production, 1985, $251·6m.

Agriculture. In 1985 the state had 71,000 farms with a total area of 33m. acres; average farm was 465 acres. In 1982, 2·2% of the population were engaged in farming or ranching. Of these, 58% were full-time farmers or ranchers, 32% part-owners and 10·78% tenants.

Cash income from crops and livestock products 1985, $2,664m. The most valuable crop is wheat (production, 1985, 165m. bu.). Other crops included hay, cotton, lint and grain sorghums. Livestock on farms, 1985: Cattle and calves, 5·2m. head (valued at $1,050·1m.); milch cows, 113,000; sheep and lambs, 90,000; chickens, 3·4m.; hogs and pigs, 200,000.

The Oklahoma Conservation Commission works with 91 conservation districts, universities, state and federal government agencies. The early work of the conservation districts, beginning in 1937, was limited to flood and erosion control: since 1970, they include urban areas also.

Irrigated production has increased in the Oklahoma 'panhandle'. The Ogalala aquifer is the primary source of irrigation water there and in western Oklahoma, a finite source because of its isolation from major sources of recharge. Declining groundwater levels necessitate the most effective irrigation practices.

Forestry. There are 8·5m. acres of forest, one half considered commercial. The forest products industry is concentrated in the 18 eastern counties. There are 3 forest regions: Ozark (oak, hickory); Ouachita highlands (pine, oak); Cross-Timbers (post oak, black jack oak). Southern pine is the chief commercial species, at almost 80% of saw-timber harvested annually.

Replanting is essential and encouraged by a federal investment tax credit (10%) to non-industrial forest land owners; the federal Forestry Incentives Program is also available in 7 counties, for planting on non-industrial private land.

INDUSTRY. Total civilian labour force, 1985, 1·6m.; wholesale and retail trade employed 288,000; government and government enterprises, 252,400; services, 225,700; manufacturing, 172,400; mining, 66,300; finance, insurance and real estate, 64,000; transport and public utilities, 64,400; construction, 46,700. Unemployment, 1985, 7·1%.

COMMUNICATIONS

Roads. In 1985–86 there were 668·8 miles of inter-state (non-toll) highways, and 11,565·71 miles of other state highway open; there were 485·83 miles of toll roads (including inter-state), 317·46 miles of state park roads and 86,475·79 miles of county roads; 11,275·68 miles of local city streets; total roads and streets, 1986, 110,787·27 miles.

Railways. In 1987 Oklahoma had 4,352 miles of railway operated by 19 companies.

Aviation. Airports, 1987, numbered 320, of which 125 were publicly owned. Six cities were served by commercial airlines.

Shipping. The McClellan-Kerr Arkansas Navigation System provides access from east central Oklahoma to New Orleans through the Verdigris, Arkansas and Mississippi rivers. The Tulsa port of Catoosa handled 1·41m. tons inward and outward on 11,997 barges in 1986; about 30% arose from international trade. Muskogee handled 119,630 tons inward and outward, 30% international. Total tonnage, 3·1m. tons, mainly chemical fertilizer, farm produce, petroleum products, iron and steel, coal, sand and gravel.

Broadcasting. In 1987 there were 179 radio and 16 television broadcasting stations, and 7 cable-TV companies.

Newspapers. In 1987 there were 51 daily and 183 weekly newspapers.

JUSTICE, RELIGION, EDUCATION AND WELFARE

Justice. Penal institutions, 15 Sept. 1987, held 8,281 inmates (7,743 of them male). There were 13 correction centres, 8 community treatment centres and 7 probation and parole centres.

The death penalty was suspended in 1966 and re-imposed in 1976. Since 1915 there have been 83 (52 whites, 27 Negroes, 4 other races) executions. Electrocution was replaced (1977) by lethal injection.

Religion. The chief religious bodies in 1980 were Baptists, 674,766; United Methodists, 248,635; Roman Catholics, 122,820; Churches of Christ, about 80,000; Assembly of God, 63,992; Disciples of Christ, 45,070; Presbyterian, 38,605; Lutheran, 33,664; Nazarene, 22,090; Episcopal, 21,500.

Education. In 1984–85 there were 617,931 pupils enrolled in grades K–12. There were 40,889 teachers at elementary and secondary schools on average salaries of $22,458. Total expenditure on public schools, $1,631·67m. In 1985–86 total expenditure for vocational-technical education was $78,060,127; there were 28,028 students enrolled.

Institutions of higher education with over 4,000 students:

Founded	Name	Place	1985–86 Enrollment
1891	Oklahoma State University	Stillwater, Okla.	34,400
		City, Okmulgee	18,833
1891	Central State University	Edmond	27,435
1892	University of Oklahoma	Norman	6,019
1894	University of Tulsa	Tulsa	6,744
1903	Southwestern Oklahoma State University	Weatherford	5,644
1909	East Central Oklahoma State University	Ada	10,737
1909	Northeastern Oklahoma State University	Tahlequah	5,820
1909	Southeastern Oklahoma State University	Durant	7,519
1909	Cameron University	Lawton	4,307
1965	Oral Roberts University	Tulsa	5,064
1968	Rose State College	Midwest City	16,232
1969	Tulsa Junior College	Tulsa	25,748
1970	Oklahoma City Community College	Oklahoma City	15,887

Total enrolment in institutions of higher education, 1985–86, 239,389; total expenditure, $5,172·39m.

Health. In 1986 there were 142 hospitals (17,700 beds).

Welfare. In 1985–86 the Oklahoma Department of Human Services provided for field operations, $72·7m., for payments and services, $184·4m.; children and youth services, $72·2m.; developmental disability, $64·3m., medical services, $490m.; rehabilitation, $41·9m.; the ageing, $23·2m.; teaching hospitals, $148·9m.; administration, management information, and construction, $54·2m.

In 1985 social security payments were being drawn by 497,000 persons; average monthly payments were: Retired workers, $452; disabled workers, $470; and widows and widowers, $407. There were 402,000 military veterans; 420,000 enrolled in medicare (payment $853m.); 270,000 receiving medicaid ($460m.); 1m. workers (taxable wages $6,432m.) per month covered by state unemployment insurance; average weekly insured unemployment, 27,000 people.

Books of Reference

Directory of Oklahoma. Dept. of Libraries, Oklahoma City (irregular), 1985–86
Chronicles of Oklahoma. State Historical Society, Oklahoma City (from 1921, quarterly)
Statistical Abstract of Oklahoma, 1984. Centers for Economic and Management Research, Univ. of Oklahoma, Norman, 1984
Dale, E. E., and Aldrich, G., *History of Oklahoma.* New York, 1969
Gibson, A. M., *The History of Oklahoma.* Rev. ed., Univ. of Oklahoma, Norman, 1984
McReynolds, Edwin C., *Oklahoma: A History of the Sooner State.* Rev. ed. Univ. of Oklahoma, Norman, 1964
Ruth, K., *et al.,* (eds.), *Oklahoma: A Guide to the Sooner State.* Rev. ed. Univ. of Oklahoma, Norman, 1957
Strain, J. W., *Outline of Oklahoma Government.* Rev. ed., Central State Univ., Edmond, 1983

State Library: Oklahoma Dept. of Libraries, 200 N.E. 18th Street, Oklahoma City 73105.
State Librarian and State Archivist: Robert L. Clark, Jr.

OREGON

HISTORY. Oregon was first settled in 1811 by the Pacific Fur Co. at Astoria, a provisional government was formed on 5 July 1834; a Territorial government was organized, 14 Aug. 1848, and on 14 Feb. 1859 Oregon was admitted to the Union.

AREA AND POPULATION. Oregon is bounded north by Washington, with the Columbia River forming most of the boundary, east by Idaho, with the Snake River forming most of the boundary, south by Nevada and California and west by the Pacific. Area, 97,073 sq. miles, 889 sq. miles being inland water. The federal government owned (1976) 32,370,216 acres (52·55% of the state area). Census population, 1 April 1980, 2,633,105, an increase of 541,720 or 26% since 1970. Estimated population (1986), 2,698,000. In 1984 births numbered 39,536 (14·8 per 1,000 population). In 1984 deaths 23,229 (8·7); infant deaths 415 (10·5 per 1,000 live births); marriages, 22,594 (8·4), and divorces, 15,463 (5·8).

Population at 5 federal censuses was:

	White	Negro	Indian	Asiatic	Total	Per sq. mile
1910	655,090	1,492	5,090	11,093	672,765	7·0
1930	938,598	2,234	4,776	8,179	953,786	9·9
1960	1,732,037	18,133	8,026	9,120	1,768,687	18·4
1970	2,032,079	26,308	13,510	13,290	2,091,385	21·7
1980	2,490,610	37,060	27,314	34,775	2,633,105	27·3

Of the total population in 1980, 1,296,566 were male, 1,788,354 persons were urban. Those 18 years and older numbered 1,910,048.

The US Bureau of Indian Affairs (area headquarters in Portland) administers (1976) 742,151·74 acres, of which 597,222·94 acres are held by the US in trust for Indian tribes, and 144,928·8 acres for individual Indians.

The largest towns, according to 1980 census figures, are: Portland, 366,383; Eugene, 105,664; Salem (the capital), 89,233; Corvallis, 40,960; Medford, 39,603; Springfield, 41,621; Beaverton, 31,926; Albany, 26,678. Metropolitan areas (1980): Portland, 1,236,294; Eugene-Springfield, 273,114; Salem, 249,655.

CLIMATE. Portland. Jan. 39°F (3·9°C), July 67°F (19·4°C). Annual rainfall 44" (1,100 mm). See Pacific Coast, p. 1378.

CONSTITUTION AND GOVERNMENT. The present constitution dates from 1859; some 80 items in it have been amended. The Legislative Assembly consists of a Senate of 30 members, elected for 4 years (half their number retiring every 2 years), and a House of 60 representatives, elected for 2 years. The Governor is elected for 4 years. The constitution reserves to the voters the rights of initiative and referendum and recall. In Nov. 1912 suffrage was extended to women.

The state sends to Congress 2 senators and 5 representatives.

In the 1984 presidential election Reagan polled 618,824 votes, Mondale, 496,237.

The capital is Salem. There are 36 counties in the state.

Governor: Neil Goldschmidt (D.), 1987–91 ($72,050).
Secretary of State: Barbara Roberts (D.) ($45,619).

BUDGET. Oregon has 2-year financial periods. Total resources for the biennium 1983–85 were $17,192,893,776 (federal funds, $1,267m.; taxes, $4,355·9m.); total expenditures, $10,525,619,308 (education, $2,660·2m.; economic development and consumer services, $2,958·3m.; human resources, $2,377·3m.).

In Feb. 1983 the outstanding bonded debt was $6,000m.

Per capita personal income (1985) was $12,622.

ENERGY AND NATURAL RESOURCES

Electricity. On 1 Jan. 1984 four privately owned utilities, 11 municipally owned utilities, 18 co-operatives and 5 utility districts provided electricity in the state. The privately owned companies provided 77% of the electricity. Hydroelectricity plants (102 in 1985) have an installed capacity of 5·1m. kw., of which multi-purpose federal projects like the Bonneville Power Administration accounted for 3·5m. kw. The Trojan Nuclear plant has a capacity of 1,080mw., and Boardman coal-fired plant, 530mw.

Minerals. Oregon's mineral resources include gold, silver, nickel copper, lead, mercury, chromite, sand and gravel, stone, clays, lime, silica, diatomite, expansible shale, scoria, pumice and uranium. There is geothermal potential. Value of mineral products, 1986, was $131m.

Agriculture. Oregon, which has an area of 61,557,184 acres, is divided by the Cascade Range into two distinct zones as to climate. West of the Cascade Range there is a good rainfall and almost every variety of crop common to the temperate zone is grown; east of the Range stock-raising and wheat-growing are the principal industries and irrigation is needed for row crops and fruits.

There were, in 1985, 37,000 farms with an acreage of 18·3m. (29·7% of the land area); average farm size was 486 acres; most are family-owned corporate farms. Average value per acre, $579.

Cash receipts from crops in 1985 amounted to $1,156m., and from livestock and livestock products, $622m., of which cattle and calves made most. Principal crops are hay (1·3m. tons), wheat (56m. bu.), potatoes, peppermint, ryegrass seed, pears, onions, snap beans, sweet corn and barley.

Livestock, 1 Jan. 1985: Milch cows, 96,000; cattle and calves, 1·65m.; sheep and lambs, 430,000; swine, 110,000.

Forestry. About 29·8m. acres is forested, almost half of the state. Of this amount, 24·2m. is commercial forest land suitable for timber production; ownership is as follows (acres): US Forestry service, 11·6m. (48%); Forest Industry, 5·5m. (22·8%); Small non-industrial landowners, 3·6m. (14·7%); US Bureau of Land Management, 2·2m. (9%); State of Oregon, 820,000 acres (3·4%) and other owners (city, county, Indian), 496,000 acres (2·1%). Oregon's commercial forest lands provided an estimated 1982 harvest of 5,200m. bd ft of logs, as well as the benefits of recreation, water, grazing, wildlife and fish. Trees vary from the coastal forest of hemlock and spruce to the state's primary species, Douglas-fir, throughout much of western Oregon. In eastern Oregon, ponderosa pine, lodgepole pine and true firs are found. Here, forestry is often combined with livestock grazing to provide an economic operation. Along the Cascade summit and in the mountains of northeast Oregon, alpine species are found.

Production, 1981: plywood, 5,561m. sq. ft (value $991·5m.); Douglas Fir lumber, 3,842m. bd. ft ($948·3m.); Ponderosa Pine lumber, 1,273m. bd. ft ($386m.); pulp and paper, 4·8m. tons ($8·5m.).

Fisheries. All food and shellfish landings in the calendar year 1985 amounted to a value of $46m. The most important are: tuna, crabs, bottom fish, shrimp.

INDUSTRY. Forest products manufacturing is Oregon's leading industry, and provides for 20% of the country's softwood lumber needs, 40% of its plywood and more than 25% of the hardboard. More than one-third of the economy depends directly or indirectly on timber industries; about 78,130 (1981) people are employed. The payroll was $1,600m. and value of production, $3,490m. During 1985, manufacturing employed 200,000; trade, 259,000; services, 215,000; government, 197,000.

TOURISM. In 1983, 15·5m. out-of-state tourists visited Oregon; the total income from tourism was estimated to be $2,030m.

COMMUNICATIONS

Roads. The state maintains (1985) 7,555 miles of primary and secondary highways, almost all surfaced; counties maintain 27,823 miles, and cities 7,077 miles; there were 79,167 miles in national parks and federal reservations. Registered motor vehicles, 31 Dec. 1985, totalled 2·22m.

Railways. The state had (1980) 19 common carrier railways with a total mileage of 4,428.

Aviation. In Oct. 1984 there were 4 public-use and 85 personal-use heliports; 3 public-use seaplane bases; 203 personal-use airports; 111 public-use airports including 37 state-owned airports.

Shipping. Portland is a major seaport for large ocean-going vessels and is 101 miles inland from the mouth of the Columbia River. In 1983 the port handled 7·1m.

short tons of cargo; main commodities for this and other Columbia River ports are grain and petroleum.

Post and Broadcasting. In Dec. 1984 there were 137 commercial radio stations and 13 educational radio stations. There were 16 commercial television stations and 6 educational television stations. There were also 5 campus limited radio stations and 1 subscription radio station.

Newspapers. In 1985 there were 22 daily newspapers with a circulation of more than 650,000 and 92 non-daily newspapers.

JUSTICE, RELIGION, EDUCATION AND WELFARE

Justice. There are 3 correctional institutions in Oregon, all in Salem. The Oregon State Penitentiary, on 30 June 1982, held 1,779 males; the Women's Correctional Center had a resident population of 73; and the Oregon Correctional Institution, which is for first offenders, had a population of 926. The Oregon Correctional Division's Release Center in Salem held 323 inmates, 110 inmates were held in Oregon State Hospital wards and 16,174 offenders were on parole or probation.

The sterilization law, originally passed in 1917, was amended in 1967. The amendments changed the number of persons on the Board of Social Protection from 15 to 7 and provided that the Public Defender would automatically represent all persons examined. The basis on which a person would be subject to examination by the Board are: *(a)* if such person would be likely to procreate children having an inherited tendency to mental retardation or mental illness, or *(b)* if such person would be likely to procreate children who would become neglected or dependent because of the person's inability by reason of mental illness or mental retardation to provide adequate care.

Religion. The chief religious bodies are Catholic, Baptist, Lutheran, Methodists, Presbyterian and Mormon.

Education. School attendance is compulsory from 7 to 18 years of age if the twelfth year of school has not been completed; those between the ages of 16 and 18 years, if legally employed, may attend part-time or evening schools. Others may be excused under certain circumstances. In 1983–84 the public elementary schools had 321,087 students and the secondary schools, 146,389. Total expenditure on elementary and secondary education (1986) was $1,802m.; teachers' average salary (1986), $26,000.

Leading state-supported institutions of higher education (autumn 1986) included:

	Students
University of Oregon, Eugene	17,142
Oregon Health Sciences University:	1,263
Oregon State University, Corvallis	15,199
Portland State University, Portland	15,640
Western Oregon State College, Monmouth	3,394
Southern Oregon State College, Ashland	4,552
Eastern Oregon State College, La Grande	1,604
Oregon Institute of Technology, Klamath Falls	2,995

Largest of the privately endowed universities are Lewis and Clark College, Portland, with (1986) 2,846 students; University of Portland, 2,610 students; Willamette University, Salem, 1,948 students; Reed College, Portland, 1,243 students, and Linfield College, McMinnville, 1,098 students. There are 13 community colleges and 1 area education district with an estimated enrolment of 237,564 students in 1983–84.

Health. In Oct. 1982 there were 91 licensed hospitals. In Oct. 1979 there were 4 state hospitals for mentally ill and mentally retarded (2 for mentally ill, 1 for mentally retarded and 1 with both programmes). On 30 June 1982 there were 931 mentally ill patients and 1,629 mentally retarded.

Social Security. The State Adult and Family Services Division provides cash payments, medical care, food stamps, day care and help in finding jobs: In 1984–85 there were about 70,000 people on low incomes, many of them children in single-parent families, benefiting from the Aid to Families with Dependent Children Programme; about 225,000 people received food stamps.

There is also a Children's Services Division.

A system of unemployment benefit payments, financed by employers, with administrative allotments made through a federal agency, started 2 Jan. 1938.

Books of Reference

Oregon Blue Book. Issued by the Secretary of State. Salem. Biennial

Federal Writers' Project. *Oregon: End of the Trail.* Rev. ed. Portland, 1972

Baldwin, E. M., *Geology of Oregon.* Rev. ed. Dubuque, Iowa, 1976

Carey, C. H., *General History of Oregon, prior to 1861.* 2 vol. (1 vol. reprint, 1971) Portland, 1935

Corning, H. M. (ed.), *Dictionary of Oregon History.* New York, 1956

Dicken, S. N., *Oregon Geography.* 5th ed. Eugene, 1973.—with Dicken, E. F., *Making of Oregon: a Study in Historical Geography.* Portland, 1979.—with Dicken, E. F., *Oregon Divided: A Regional Geography.* Portland, 1982

Dodds, G. B., *Oregon: A Bicentennial History.* New York, 1977

Friedman, R., *Oregon for the Curious.* 3rd ed. Portland, 1972

Highsmith, R. M. Jr. (ed.), *Atlas of the Pacific Northwest.* Corvallis, 1973

McArthur, L. A., *Oregon Geographic Names.* 4th ed., rev. and enlarged. Portland, 1974

Patton, Clyde P., *Atlas of Oregon.* Univ. Oregon Press, Eugene, 1976

State Library: The Oregon State Library, Salem. *Librarian:* Marcia Lowell.

PENNSYLVANIA

HISTORY. Pennsylvania, first settled in 1682, is one of the 13 original states in the Union.

AREA AND POPULATION. Pennsylvania is bounded north by New York, east by New Jersey, south by Delaware and Maryland, south-west by West Virginia, west by Ohio and north-west by Lake Erie. Area, 45,308 sq. miles, of which 420 sq. miles are inland water. Census population, 1 April 1980, 11,863,895, an increase of 63,129 or 0·5% since 1970. Estimate (1986) 11,889,000. Births, 1984, 156,799; deaths, 121,358; infant deaths, 1,908; marriages, 91,610; reported divorces, 40,375.

Population at 5 census years was:

	White	Negro	Indian	All others	Total	Per sq. mile
1910	7,467,713	193,919	1,503	1,976	7,665,111	171·0
1930	9,196,007	431,257	523	3,563	9,631,350	213·8
1960	10,454,004	852,750	2,122	10,490	11,319,366	251·5
			All others			
1970	10,745,219	1,015,884	39,663		11,800,766	262·9
1980	10,652,320	1,046,810	164,765		11,863,895	264·3

Of the total population in 1980, 47·9% were male, 69·3% were urban and 68·1% were 21 years of age or older.

The population of the larger cities and townships, 1980 census, was:

Philadelphia	1,688,210	Scranton	88,117	Lancaster	54,725
Pittsburgh	423,938	Reading	78,686	Harrisburg	53,264
Erie	119,123	Bethlehem	70,419	Wilkes-Barre	51,551
Allentown	103,758	Altoona	57,078	York	44,619

Larger urbanized areas, 1980 census: Philadelphia (in Pennsylvania), 3,682,709; Pittsburgh, 2,263,894; Northeast, 640,396, Allentown–Bethlehem–Easton (in Pennsylvania), 551,052; Harrisburg, 446,576.

CLIMATE. Philadelphia. Jan. 32°F (0°C), July 77°F (25°C). Annual rainfall 40″

(1,006 mm). Pittsburgh. Jan. 31°F (–0.6°C), July 74°F (23.3°C). Annual rainfall 37" (914 mm). *See* Appalachian Mountains, p. 1379.

CONSTITUTION AND GOVERNMENT. The present constitution dates from 1968. The General Assembly consists of a Senate of 50 members chosen for 4 years, one-half being elected biennially, and a House of Representatives of 203 members chosen for 2 years. The Governor and Lieut.-Governor are elected for 4 years. Every citizen 18 years of age, with the usual residential qualifications, may vote. The state sends to Congress 2 senators and 23 representatives. Registered voters in Nov. 1985, 6,029,390.

In the 1984 presidential election Reagan polled 2,564,273 votes, Mondale, 2,209,137.

The state capital is Harrisburg. The state is organized in counties (numbering 67), cities, boroughs, townships and school districts.

Governor: Robert Casey (D.), 1987–91 ($85,000).
Lieut.-Governor: William W. Scranton (R.) ($54,500).

BUDGET. Total revenues for the year ending 30 June 1985 were $24,577·4m.; general fund expenditure, $11,225·5m.; transport, $1,293·9m.; public welfare, $3,417m.).

On 30 June 1985 outstanding long-term debt (excluding highway bonds) amounted to $4,987·7m.

Per capita personal income (1985) was $13,437.

ENERGY AND NATURAL RESOURCES

Minerals. Pennsylvania is almost the sole producer of anthracite coal; its output reached a peak of 100,445,299 short tons in 1917 with a labour-force of 156,148 men. Production in 1985: Anthracite, 5·23m. tons, with about 3,225 employees; bituminous coal, 65·5m. tons, with about 19,661 men; crude petroleum (1985), 4·26m. bbls; natural gas (1983), 360,076m. cu. ft. Total value of minerals produced (1983), $3,456m., of which $2,821m. was for fuel minerals.

Agriculture. Agriculture, market-gardening, fruit-growing, horticulture and forestry are pursued within the state. In 1984 there were 58,000 farms with a total farm area of 8·7m. acres (4·5m. acres in crops). Cash income, 1985, from crops, $966m., and from livestock and products, $2,184m.

Pennsylvania ranks first in the production of mushrooms (279·7m. lb., value $205·2m. in 1984). Other crops are (1984) tobacco (22·4m. lb., $20·98m.), wheat (8·4m. bu.), oats (15·96m. bu.), maize (148·5m. bu.), barley (3·6m. bu.) and potatoes (5·2m. cwt). On 1 Jan. 1985 there were on farms: 1·96m. cattle and calves, including 792,000 milch cows, 88,000 sheep, 800,000 swine. Milk production, 1984, was 9,423m. lb. valued at $1,329·96m., and eggs numbered 4,282m. valued at $256·9m. Pennsylvania is also a major fruit producing state; in 1984 apples totalled 575m. lb.; peaches, 85m. lb.; tart cherries, 9m. lb.; sweet cherries, 900 tons; and grapes, 60,000 tons. Other important items are soybeans (5·95m. bu.), vegetables for processing (93,000 tons), fresh vegetables (1·16m. cwt) and broiler-chickens (121m.).

Forestry. In 1982 national forest lands totalled 510,517 acres; state forests, 2,064,533 acres; state parks, 278,930 acres; state game land, 1,250,980 acres; game land leased but not owned by the state, 3,957,438 acres (co-operative and safety-zone programmes).

INDUSTRY. Pennsylvania is third in national production of iron and steel. Output of steel, 1985, 12·1m. net tons.

In 1985, manufacturing employed 1,090,000 workers; services, 1,171,000; trade, 1,069,000; government, 679,000.

COMMUNICATIONS

Roads. Highways and roads in the state (federal, local and state combined) totalled

(1985) 114,865 miles. Registered motor vehicles for 1985 numbered 7,860,497 (including 5,854,497 passenger cars, 1,682,411 trucks, truck-tractors and trailers).

Railways. In 1983, 41 railways operated within the state with a line mileage of about 6,300.

Aviation. There were (1982) 161 commercial airports, 3 public landing strips, 242 heliports, 391 airports for personal use and 16 seaplane bases.

Shipping. Trade at the ports of Philadelphia (1985), imports 56·1m. short tons, exports 7·4m.

Post and Broadcasting. Broadcasting stations comprised (1982) 41 television stations and 378 radio stations.

Newspapers. There were (1983) 111 daily and 219 weekly newspapers.

JUSTICE, RELIGION, EDUCATION AND WELFARE

Justice. No executions took place in 1963–85; since 1930 there have been 149 executions (electrocution), all for murder.

State prison population, on 31 Dec. 1985, was 14,260.

Religion. The chief religious bodies in 1977 were the Roman Catholic, with 3,717,667 members; Protestant, 3,150,920 (1971); and Jewish, 469,078. The 5 largest Protestant denominations (by communicants) were: Lutheran Church in America, 766,276; United Methodist, 728,915 (1971), United Presbyterian Church in the USA, 573,905 (1971); United Church of Christ, 257,138; Episcopal, 193,399 (1971).

Education. School attendance is compulsory for children 8–17 years of age. In 1985–86 the public kindergartens and elementary schools had 841,419 pupils; public secondary schools had 841,802 pupils. Non-public schools had 270,541 elementary pupils and 103,857 secondary pupils. Average salary, public school professional personnel, men $29,155; women $24,967; for classroom teachers, men $25,292, women $23,412.

Leading senior academic institutions included:

Founded	Institutions	Faculty (Autumn 1986)	Students (Autumn 1986)
1740	University of Pennsylvania (non-sect.)	3,364	21,742
1787	University of Pittsburgh	2,827	28,449
1832	Lafayette College, Easton (Presbyterian)	205	2,032
1833	Haverford College	114	1,112
1842	Villanova University (R.C.)	824	12,261
1846	Bucknell University (Baptist)	243	3,453
1851	St Joseph's University, Philadelphia (R.C.)	336	5,715
1852	California University of Pennsylvania	310	5,179
1855	Pennsylvania State University	1,846	35,261
1855	Millersville University of Pennsylvania	338	7,166
1863	LaSalle University, Philadelphia (R.C.)	242	6,136
1864	Swarthmore College	150	1,327
1866	Lehigh University, Bethlehem (non-sect.)	440	6,334
1871	West Chester University of Pennsylvania	541	10,385
1875	Indiana University of Pennsylvania	792	13,248
1878	Duquesne University, Pittsburgh (R.C.)	492	6,580
1884	Temple University, Philadelphia	2,564	26,447
1885	Bryn Mawr College	197	1,794
1888	University of Scranton (R.C.)	296	4,789
1891	Drexel University, Philadelphia	858	12,500
1900	Carnegie-Mellon University, Pittsburgh	607	6,579

Health. In 1985 the state had 300 hospitals (51,216 beds) listed by the State Health Department, excluding federal hospitals and mental institutions.

Social Security. During the year ending 30 June 1985 the monthly average number of cases receiving public assistance was: aid to families with dependent children, 553,003; blind pension, 3,649; general assistance, 146,194.

Payments for medical assistance for the year ending 30 June 1985 totalled $2,246m. Under the medical assistance programme payments are made for inpatient hospital care ($195m.); care in public institutions (nursing homes, mental institutions and geriatric centres) ($444·5m.); private nursing home care ($317·2m.); other medical care ($76·7m.).

Books of Reference

Encyclopaedia of Pennsylvania, New York, 1984
Pennsylvania Manual. General Services, Bureau of Publications, Harrisburg. Biennial
Pennsylvania's Regions, A Survey of the Commonwealth. State Planning Board. Harrisburg, 1967
Pennsylvania Statistical Abstract. Dept. of Commerce, Harrisburg. Annual
Pennsylvania State Industrial Directory. Harris, Ohio. Annual
Cochran, T. C., *Pennsylvania,* New York, 1978
Klein, P. S., and Hoogenboom, A., *A History of Pennsylvania.* New York, 1973
League of Women Voters of Pennsylvania, *Key to the Keystone State.* Philadelphia, 1972
Majumdar, S. K., and Miller, E. W., *Pennsylvania Coal: Resources, Technology and Utilisation.* Pennsylvania Science, 1983
Pennsylvania Chamber of Commerce, *Pennsylvania Government Today.* State College, Pa., 1973
Weigley, R. F., (ed.) *Philadelphia: A 300-year History.* New York, 1984
Wilkinson, N. B., *Bibliography of Pennsylvania History.* Pa. Historical & Museum Commission. Harrisburg, 1957

RHODE ISLAND

HISTORY The earliest settlers in the region which now forms the state of Rhode Island were colonists from Massachusetts who had been driven forth on account of their non-acceptance of the prevailing religious beliefs. The first of the settlements was made in 1636, settlers of every creed being welcomed. In 1647 a patent was executed for the government of the settlements, and on 8 July 1663 a charter was executed recognizing the settlers as forming a body corporate and politic by the name of the 'English Colony of Rhode Island and Providence Plantations, in New England, in America'. On 29 May 1790 the state accepted the federal constitution and entered the Union as the last of the 13 original states.

AREA AND POPULATION. Rhode Island is bounded north and east by Massachusetts, south by the Atlantic and west by Connecticut. Area, 1,214 sq. miles, of which 165 sq. miles are inland water. Census population, 1 April 1980, 947,154 a decrease of 0·3% since 1970. Estimate (1986), 975,000.

Births, 1986, were 13,324; deaths (excluding foetal deaths), 9,587; infant deaths, 125; marriages, 8,103; divorces, 3,683.

Population of 5 census years was:

	White	Negro	Indian	Asiatic	Total	Per sq. mile
1910	532,492	9,529	284	305	542,610	508·5
1930	677,026	9,913	318	240	687,497	649·3
1960	838,712	18,332	932	1,190	859,488	812·4
1970	914,757	25,338	1,390	5,240	949,723 [1]	905·0
			All other			
1980	896,692	27,584	22,878		947,154	903·0

[1] Through tabulation errors there were 2,998 people unaccounted for, as to race and sex, in 1970.

Of the total population in 1980, 451,251 were male, 824,004 were urban and 665,054 were 20 years of age or older.

The chief cities and their population (census, 1980) are Providence, 156,804; Warwick, 87,123; Cranston, 71,992; Pawtucket, 71,204; East Providence, 50,980; Woonsocket, 45,914; Newport, 29,259; North Providence (town), 29,188; Cumberland (town), 27,069. The Providence–Pawtucket–Warwick Standard Metropolitan Statistical Area had a population of 919,216 in 1980.

CLIMATE. Providence. Jan. 28°F (–2·2°C), July 72°F (22·2°C). Annual rainfall 43" (1,079 mm). *See* New England, p. 1379.

CONSTITUTION AND GOVERNMENT. The present constitution dates from 1843; it has had 42 amendments. The General Assembly consists of a Senate of 50 members and a House of Representatives of 100 members, both elected for 2 years, as are also the Governor and Lieut.-Governor. Every citizen, 18 years of age, who has resided in the state for 30 days, and is duly registered, is qualified to vote.

Rhode Island sends to Congress 2 senators and 2 representatives.

At the 1984 presidential election Reagan polled 212,080 votes, Mondale, 197,106.

The capital is Providence. The state has 5 counties (unique in having no political functions) and 39 cities and towns.

Governor: Edward DiPrete (R.), 1987–89 ($69,900).
Lieut.-Governor: Richard Licht (D.), 1987–89 ($52,000).
Secretary of State: Kathleen Connell (D.), 1987–89 ($52,000).

BUDGET. For the fiscal year ending 30 June 1987 (Office of the State Controller) total revenues were $1,585·7m. (taxation, $1,032·8m., and federal aid, $361·1m.); general expenditures were $1,529·1m. (education, $442·6m.; and public welfare, $453·1m.).

Total net long-term debt on 30 June 1986 was $261·8m.

Per capita personal income (1986) was $14,670.

NATURAL RESOURCES

Minerals. The small mineral output, mostly stone, sand and gravel, was valued (1986) at an estimated $14m.

Agriculture. While Rhode Island is predominantly a manufacturing state, agriculture contributed $105m. to the general cash income in 1986; it had 697 farms with an area of 73,000 acres (11% of the total land area), of which 31,000 acres were crop land; the average farm was 86 acres.

Fisheries. In 1986 the catch was 94m. lb (live weight) valued at $73·5m.

INDUSTRY. Total non-agricultural employment in 1987 was 451,400, of which 116,500 were manufacturing, 334,900 non-manufacturing. Manufacturing firms totalled 3,170; average weekly earnings for production workers in manufacturing, $327.60; value added by manufacture (1984), $4,241m. Principal industries are metals and machinery, jewellery–silverware and transport equipment.

COMMUNICATIONS

Roads. The state had (1 Jan. 1987) 5,860 miles of road, of which 1,857 were state-owned. In 1987, 754,294 motor vehicles were registered.

Railways. In 1987, 5 railways operated 135 line-miles.

Aviation. In 1987 there were 6 state-owned airports. Theodore Francis Green airport at Warwick, near Providence, is served by 12 airlines, and handled over 2m. passengers and 22m. lb. of freight in 1987.

Shipping. Waterborne freight through the port of Providence (1985) totalled 1·9m. tons.

Broadcasting. There are 24 radio stations and 5 television stations; there are 8 cable television companies.

JUSTICE, RELIGION, EDUCATION AND WELFARE

Justice. The state's penal institutions, June 1986, had 1,349 inmates (138 per 100,000 population).

The death penalty is illegal, except that it is mandatory in the case of murder committed by a prisoner serving a life sentence.

Religion. Chief religious bodies are (estimated figures Sept. 1987): Roman Catholic with 550,000 members; Protestant Episcopal (baptized persons), 50,000; Baptist, 22,500; Congregational, 12,000; Methodist, 10,000; Jewish, 24,000.

Education. In 1986–87 the 231 public elementary schools had 3,854 teachers and total enrolment of 68,698 pupils; about 28,000 pupils were enrolled in private and parochial schools. The 61 senior and vocational high schools had 3,702 teachers and 65,451 pupils. Teachers' salaries (1987) averaged $23,400. Local expenditure, for schools (including evening schools) in 1986–87 totalled $547·7m.

There are 11 institutions of higher learning in the state, including 1 junior college. The state maintains Rhode Island College, at Providence, with 600 faculty members, and 5,300 full-time students (1986), and the University of Rhode Island, at South Kingstown, with over 900 faculty members and over 13,000 students (including graduate students). Brown University, at Providence, founded in 1764, is now non-sectarian; in 1986 it had over 600 full-time faculty members and 7,000 full-time students. Providence College, at Providence, founded in 1917 by the Order of Preachers (Dominican), had (1986) 210 professors and 5,200 students. The largest of the other colleges are Bryant College, at Smithfield, with 160 faculty and 4,400 students, and the Rhode Island School of Design, in Providence, with about 155 faculty and 1,800 students.

Health. In 1987 the state had 22 hospitals (over 7,000 beds), including 4 mental hospitals.

Social Security. In 1986 aid to dependent children was granted to 44,200 children in 15,900 families at an average payment per family of $361 per month, and the state also had a general assistance programme. (All other aid programmes were taken over by the federal government.)

Books of Reference

Rhode Island Manual. Prepared by the Secretary of State. Providence
Providence Journal Almanac: A Reference Book for Rhode Islanders. Providence. Annual
Rhode Island Basic Economic Statistics. Rhode Island Dept. of Economic Development. Providence, 1987
McLoughlin, W. G., *Rhode Island: a History.* Norton, 1978
Wright, M. I., and Sullivan, R. J., *Rhode Island Atlas.* Rhode Island Pubs., 1983

State Library: Rhode Island State Library, State House, Providence 02908. State Librarian: Elliott E. Andrews.

SOUTH CAROLINA

HISTORY. South Carolina, first settled permanently in 1670, was one of the 13 original states of the Union.

AREA AND POPULATION. South Carolina is bounded in the north by North Carolina, east and south-east by the Atlantic, south-west and west by Georgia. Area, 31,113 sq. miles, of which 909 sq. miles are inland water. Census population, 1 April 1980, 3,121,833, an increase of 20·5 since 1970. Estimate July 1986 3,376,000. Births, 1985, were 51,846 (15·5 per 1,000 population); deaths, 27,072 (8·1); marriages, 52,805 (15·8); divorces and annulments, 13,456 (4); infant deaths, 735 (14·2 per 1,000 live births).

The population in 5 census years was:

	White	Negro	Indian	Asiatic	Total	Per sq. mile
1910	679,161	835,843	331	65	1,515,400	49·7
1930	944,049	793,681	959	76	1,738,765	56·8
1960	1,551,022	829,291	1,098	946	2,382,594	78·7
			All others			
1970	1,794,432	789,040	3,588		2,587,060	83·2
1980	2,150,507	948,623	22,703		3,121,833	100·3

Of the total population in 1980, 49% were male, 54·1% were urban and 55% were 25 years old or older. Median age, 28.

Populations of large towns in 1986 (with those of associated metropolitan areas): Columbia (capital), 93,020 (444,700); Charleston, 68,900 (485,600); Greenville, 58,370; Spartanburg, 44,210 (Greenville–Spartanburg, 606,400).

CLIMATE. Columbia. Jan. 47°F (8·3°C), July 81°F (27·2°C). Annual rainfall 45″ (1,125 mm). See Atlantic Coast, p. 1379.

CONSTITUTION AND GOVERNMENT. The present constitution dates from 1895, when it went into force without ratification by the electorate. The General Assembly consists of a Senate of 46 members, elected for 4 years, and a House of Representatives of 124 members, elected for 2 years. The Governor and Lieut.-Governor are elected for 4 years. Only registered citizens have the right to vote. South Carolina sends to Congress 2 senators and 6 representatives.

At the 1984 presidential election Reagan polled 615,539 votes, Mondale 344,459 and Bergland 4,359.

The capital is Columbia.

Governor: Carroll Campbell (R.), 1987–91 ($60,000).
Lieut.-Governor: N. A. Theodore (D.), 1987–91 ($35,000).
Secretary of State: John Tucker Campbell (D.), 1987–91 ($55,000).

BUDGET. For the fiscal year ending 30 June 1986 general revenues were $2,509·3m.; general expenditures were $2,592·3m.

On 30 June 1985 the total bonded debt was $626·6m.

Per capita personal income (1986) was $11,096.

NATURAL RESOURCES

Minerals. Non-metallic minerals are of chief importance: value of mineral output in 1985 was $159·4m., chiefly from limestone for cement, clay, stone, sand and gravel. Production of kaolin, vermiculite, scrap mica and fuller's earth is also important.

Agriculture. In 1986 there were 27,500 farms covering a farm area of 5·5m. acres. The average farm was of 200 acres. Of the 24,929 farms of the 1982 Census of Agriculture, there were 1,031 of 1,000 acres or more, average farm 224 acres; owners operated 14,756 farms; tenants 2,160. There were 2,331 farms with $100,000 or more in value of sales.

Cash receipts from farm marketing in 1985 amounted to $646·1m. for crops and $414·9m. for livestock, including poultry. Chief crops are tobacco ($167·5m.), soybeans ($129·6m.), and corn ($85·9m.). Production, 1985: Cotton 180,000 bales; peaches, 230m. lb.; soybeans, 24·6m. bu.; tobacco, 98·9m. lb.; eggs, 1,573m. Livestock on farms, 1986: 635,000 all cattle, 400,000 swine.

Forestry. The forest industry is important; total forest land (1986), 12·3m. acres. National forests amounted to 576,518 acres.

INDUSTRY. A monthly average of 364,944 workers were employed in manufacturing in 1986, earning $7,726m. Major sectors are textiles (28·6%), apparel (12·4%) and chemicals (8·8%).

Tourism is important; tourists spent an estimated $3,750m. in 1986, and tourism employed 85,000.

COMMUNICATIONS

Roads. Total highway mileage in the combined highway system in June 1987 was 40,562 miles. Motor vehicle registrations numbered 2·4m. in 1986.

Railways. In 1986 the length of railway in the state was about 2,300 miles.

Aviation. In 1985 there were 139 aircraft facilities (63 public, 76 private) including 126 airports, 12 heliports and 1 seaplane base. Registered aircraft numbered 2,259 in 1986.

Shipping. The state has 3 deep-water ports.

JUSTICE, RELIGION, EDUCATION AND WELFARE

Justice. At 31 Dec. 1985 penal institutions held 10,538 prisoners under State and federal jurisdiction.

Education. In 1985–86 the total public-school enrolment (K-12) was 619,369; there were 358,580 white pupils and 260,789 non-white pupils. The total number of teachers was 34,834; average salary was $21,595.

For higher education the state operates the University of South Carolina, founded at Columbia in 1801, with, (autumn 1986), 22,965 enrolled students; Clemson University, founded in 1889, with 13,062 students; The Citadel, at Charleston, with 3,339 students; Winthrop College, Rock Hill, with 5,323 students; Medical University of S. Carolina, at Charleston 2,468 students; S. Carolina State College, at Orangeburg, with 3,869 students, and Francis Marion College, at Florence, with 3,673 students; the College of Charleston has 5,531 students and Lander College, Greenwood, 2,276. There are 16 technical institutions (34,306).

There are also 493 private kindergartens, elementary and high schools with total enrolment (1985–86) of 50,150 pupils, and 31 private and denominational colleges and junior colleges with (autumn 1986) enrolment of 50,150 students.

Health. In 1985 the state had 289 non-federal health facilities with 29,246 beds licensed by the South Carolina Department of Health and Environmental Control.

Social Security. In 1985 there were 483,000 recipients of social security benefits. The average monthly expenditure in benefits was $183m.

Books of Reference

South Carolina Legislative Manual. Columbia. Annual
South Carolina Statistical Abstract. South Carolina Budget and Control Board, Columbia. Annual

Jones, L., *South Carolina: A Synoptic History for Laymen.* Lexington, 1978
State Library: South Carolina State Library, Columbia.

SOUTH DAKOTA

HISTORY. South Dakota was first visited by Europeans in 1743 when Verendrye planted a lead plate (discovered in 1913) on the site of Fort Pierre, claiming the region for the French crown. Beginning with a trading post in 1794, it was settled from 1857 to 1861 when Dakota Territory was organized. It was admitted into the Union on 2 Nov. 1889.

AREA AND POPULATION. South Dakota is bounded north by North Dakota, east by Minnesota, south-east by the Big Sioux River (forming the boundary with Iowa), south by Nebraska (with the Missouri River forming part of the boundary) and west by Wyoming and Montana. Area, 77,116 sq. miles, of which 1,164 sq. miles are water. Area administered by the Bureau of Indian Affairs, 1985, covered 5m. acres (10% of the state), of which 2·6m. acres were held by tribes. The federal government, 1985, owned 3,148,000 acres or 6·4% of the total.

Census population, 1 April 1980, 690,178, an increase of 3·5% since 1970. Estimate (1986) 708,000. Births, 1984, were 12,431 (17·8 per 1,000 population); deaths, 6,512 (9·3); infant deaths, 124 (10 per 1,000 live births); marriages, 8,057 (11·5); divorces, 2,498 (3·6).

Population in 5 federal censuses was:

	White	Negro	Indian	Asiatic	Total	Per sq. mile
1910	563,771	817	19,137	163	583,888	7·6
1930	669,453	646	21,833	101	692,849	9·0
1960	653,098	1,114	25,794	336	680,514	8·9
			All others			
1970	630,333	1,627	34,297		666,257	8·8
1980	638,955	2,144	49,079		690,178	9·0

Of the total population in 1980, 340,370 were male, 320,223 were urban and 441,851 were 21 years of age or older.

Population of the chief cities (census of 1980) was: Sioux Falls, 81,071; Rapid City, 46,340; Aberdeen, 25,973; Watertown, 15,632, Mitchell, 13,917; Brookings, 14,915; Huron, 13,000.

CLIMATE. Rapid City. Jan. 25°F (–3·9°C), July 73°F (22·8°C). Annual rainfall 19″ (474 mm). Sioux Falls. Jan. 14°F (–10°C), July 73°F (22·8°C). Annual rainfall 25″ (625 mm). *See* High Plains, p. 1378.

CONSTITUTION AND GOVERNMENT. Voters are all citizens 18 years of age or older who have complied with certain residential qualifications. The people reserve the right of the initiative and referendum. The Senate has 35 members, and the House of Representatives 70 members, all elected for 2 years; the Governor and Lieut.-Governor are elected for 4 years. The state sends 2 senators and 1 representative to Congress.

In the 1984 presidential election Reagan polled 198,119 votes, Mondale, 114,967.

The capital is Pierre (population, 1980, 11,973). The state is divided into 66 organized counties.

Governor: George Mickelson, Jr. (R.), 1987–89 ($57,325).

Lieut.-Governor: Walter D. Miller, 1987–89 ($7,980, and $75 daily expense allowance).

Secretary of State: Joyce Hazeltine, 1987–89 ($38,940).

BUDGET. For the fiscal year ending 30 June 1986 the estimated general fund revenues were $349·93m. ($191·5m. from sales and use tax); expenditure was also $349·93m. ($78·6m. on education).

Per capita personal income (1986) was $11,850.

NATURAL RESOURCES

Minerals. The mineral products include gold (310,527 troy oz. in 1984, second largest yield of all states), silver (50,000 troy oz.). Mineral products, 1984, were valued at $193·4m., of which gold accounts for $111·9m. and silver, $707,000.

Agriculture. In 1985, 37,000 farms had an acreage of 45m.; the average farm had 1,203 acres. Farm units are large; in 1982 there were only 4,024 farms of 50 acres or less, compared with 10,165 exceeding 1,000 acres. 17,371 farms sold produce valued at $40,000 or over.

South Dakota ranks first in the US as producer of oats (79·5m. bu. in 1985) and rye (4·4m. bu.) and second in sunflower seed (609·9m. lb.). The other important crops are flaxseed (1·3m. bu.), hay (3·2m. tons), durum wheat (2·6m. bushels), barley (32·4m. bu.), corn for grain (252m. bu.), soybeans (40·6m. bu.) and potatoes

(1·9m. cwt.). The farm livestock on 1 Jan. 1986 included 3·6m. cattle, 540,000 sheep, 1·6m. swine.

Forestry. National forest area, 1985, 1,997,000 acres.

INDUSTRY. In 1985, manufacturing establishments had 23,531 workers who earned $416·7m. Food processing is by far the largest industry with 96 plants employing 7,678 workers. Contract construction has 1,712 establishments employing 6,878. There are 179 printing and publishing plants employing 2,432 workers. Also significant are mining (59 establishments employing 2,381), dairy, lumber and wood products, machinery, transport equipment, electronics, stone, glass and clay products.

COMMUNICATIONS

Roads. Total highway mileage was 17,056 in 1981; hard surface (1985), 8,324. Registered passenger cars numbered 637,000 in 1981.

Railways. In 1986 there were 1,983·7 miles of railway in operation. The state owns 847·9 miles of track which is operating and 302·7 which is not.

Aviation. In 1985 there were 61 general aviation airports and 9 commercial airports.

JUSTICE, RELIGION, EDUCATION AND WELFARE

Justice. The State prisons had, in 1986, 316 inmates. The death penalty was illegal from 1915 to 1938; since 1938, one person has been executed, in 1949 (by electrocution), for murder.

Religion. The chief religious bodies are: Lutherans, Roman Catholics, Methodist, Disciples of Christ, Presbyterian, Baptist and Episcopal.

Education. Elementary and secondary education are free from 6 to 21 years of age. Between the ages of 8 and 16, attendance is compulsory. In 1984–85 137,764 pupils were attending elementary and high (including parochial) schools (8,324 full-time equivalent classroom teachers).

Teachers' salaries (1985–86) averaged an estimated $17,356. Total expenditure on public schools, $316m.

Higher education (1985–86): The School of Mines at Rapid City, established 1885, had 2,260 students; the State University at Brookings, 6,837 students; the University of South Dakota, founded at Vermillion in 1882, 5,520; Northern State College, had 2,818; Black Hills State College, 2,117; Dakota State College, 867. The 11 private colleges had 8,442 students. The federal Government maintains Indian schools on its reservations and 1 outside at Flandreau.

Health. In 1986 there were 70 licensed hospitals (5,157 beds).

Social Security. In financial year 1985–86, 3,144 aged persons received $348,270; 135 blind persons received $28,610; 4,713 disabled persons received $908,370. Aid to dependent children was $1,469,308, to 11,339 children.

Books of Reference

Governor's Budget Report. South Dakota Bureau of Finance and Management. Annual
South Dakota Historical Collections. 1902–82
South Dakota Legislative Manual. Secretary of State, Pierre, S.D. Biennial
Berg, F. M., *South Dakota: Land of Shining Gold.* Hettinger, 1982
Karolevitz, Robert F., *Challenge: the South Dakota Story.* Sioux Falls, 1975
Milton, John R., *South Dakota; a Bicentennial History.* New York, W. W. Norton, 1977
Schell, H. S., *History of South Dakota.* 3rd ed. Lincoln, Neb., 1975
Vexler, R. I., *South Dakota Chronology and Factbook.* New York, 1978

State Library: South Dakota State Library, 800 Governor's Drive, Pierre, S.D., 57501–2294.
State Librarian: Dr Jane Kolbe.

TENNESSEE

HISTORY. Tennessee, first settled in 1757, was admitted into the Union on 1 June 1796.

AREA AND POPULATION. Tennessee is bounded north by Kentucky and Virginia, east by North Carolina, south by Georgia, Alabama and Mississippi and west by the Mississippi River (forming the boundary with Arkansas and Missouri). Area, 42,144 sq. miles (989 sq. miles water). Census population, 1 April 1980, 4,591,120, an increase of 665,102 or 16·9% since 1970. Estimate (1986), 4,803,000. Vital statistics, 1986: Births, 66,246 (13·9 per 1,000 population); deaths, 44,236 (9·1); infant deaths 726 (11 per 1,000 live births); marriages, 59,730 (24·6); divorces, 30,031 (12·4).

Population in 6 census years was:

	White	Negro	Indian	Asiatic	Total	Per sq. mile
1910	1,711,432	473,088	216	53	2,184,789	52·4
1930	2,138,644	477,646	161	105	2,616,556	62·4
1950	2,760,257	530,603	339	334	3,291,718	78·8
1960	2,977,753	586,876	638	1,243	3,567,089	85·4
			All others			
1970	3,293,930	621,261	8,496		3,923,687	95·3
1980	3,835,452	725,942	29,726		4,591,120	111·6

Of the population in 1980, 2,216,600 were male, 2,773,573 were urban and those 21 years of age or older numbered 3,026,398.

The cities, with population, 1980 (and estimates 1986), are Memphis, 646,356 (652,640); Nashville (capital), 455,651 (473,670); Knoxville, 175,030 (173,210); Chattanooga, 169,565 (162,170); Clarksville, 54,777 (60,730); Jackson, 49,131 (52,810); Johnson City, 39,753 (44,700); Murfreesboro, 32,845 (40,960); Kingsport, 32,027 (31,470); Oak Ridge, 27,662 (26,920). Standard metropolitan areas 1980 (1986): Memphis, 810,043 (959,500); Nashville, 850,505 (930,700); Knoxville, 476,517 (591,100); Chattanooga, 320,761 (425,500); Johnson City–Bristol–Kingsport, 343,041 (443,400); Clarksville, 83,342 (154,400); Jackson, 74,546 (78,000).

CLIMATE. Memphis. Jan. 41°F (5°C), July 82°F (27·8°C). Annual rainfall 49" (1,221 mm). Nashville. Jan. 39°F (3·9°C), July 79°F (26·1°C). Annual rainfall 48" (1,196 mm). *See* Appalachian Mountains, p. 1379.

CONSTITUTION AND GOVERNMENT. The state has operated under 3 constitutions, the last of which was adopted in 1870 and has been since amended 22 times (first in 1953). Voters at an election may authorize the calling of a convention limited to altering or abolishing one or more specified sections of the constitution. The General Assembly consists of a Senate of 33 members and a House of Representatives of 99 members, senators elected for 4 years and representatives for 2 years. Qualified as electors are all citizens (usual residential and age (18) qualifications). Tennessee sends to Congress 2 senators and 9 representatives.

In the 1984 presidential election Reagan polled 990,212 votes, Mondale, 711,714.

For the Tennessee Valley Authority *see* pp. 1406–07.

The capital is Nashville. The state is divided into 95 counties.

Governor: Ned McWherter (D.), 1987–91 ($85,000).
Lieut.-Governor: John S. Wilder (D.), 1987–91 ($12,500).
Secretary of State: Gentry Crowell (D.), ($62,500).

BUDGET. For 1985–86 total revenue was $5,354m.; general expenditure, $4,652m.

Total net long-term debt on 30 June 1986 amounted to $696·1m.

Per capita personal income (1986) was $12,002.

ENERGY AND NATURAL RESOURCES

Minerals. Total value added by mining 1982: fuel minerals (mainly coal), $217·1m.; non-fuel (mainly stone and zinc), $154·4m.

Agriculture. In 1986, 96,000 farms covered 13m. acres. The average farm was of 135 acres (only a few states had a smaller average) valued, land and buildings, at $992.

Cash income (1985) from crops was $1,057m.; from livestock, $1,000m. Main crops were cotton, tobacco and soybeans.

On 1 Jan. 1986 the domestic animals included 210,000 milch cows, 2·5m. all cattle, 10,000 sheep, 950,000 swine.

Forestry. Forests occupy 13·16m. acres (50% of total land area). The forest industry and industries dependent on it employ about 40,000 workers, earning $150m. per year. Wood products are valued at over $500m. per year. National forest system land (1985) 627,000 acres.

INDUSTRY. The manufacturing industries include iron and steel working, but the most important products are chemicals, including synthetic fibres and allied products, electrical equipment and food. In 1983, manufacturing establishments employed 457,400 workers; value added by manufactures was $19,868·3m.

TOURISM. In 1986 39·1m. out-of-state tourists spent $4,124m.

COMMUNICATIONS

Roads. In 1985 there were 68,768 miles of municipal and rural roads. The state is served by 115 intrastate bus companies and 31 privately owned internal bus services.

Motor-vehicle registrations, 1986, totalled 4,289,592, of which 3,639,848 were cars.

Railways. The state had (1985) 2,857 miles of track.

Aviation. The state is served by 11 major airlines. In 1985 there were 74 public airports and 78 private; there were 71 heliports and 2 military air bases.

JUSTICE, RELIGION, EDUCATION AND WELFARE

Justice. There has been no execution since 1960; since 1930 there have been 22 whites and 44 Negroes executed (by electrocution) for murder and 5 whites and 22 Negroes for rape. A US Supreme Court ruling prohibits the use of capital punishment under present Tennessee law, except for first degree murder.

Prison population, 30 June 1987, 7,239.

The law prohibiting the inter-marriage of white and Negro was declared unconstitutional by the US Supreme Court in June 1967.

Religion. The leading religious bodies are the Southern Baptists, Methodists and Negro Baptists.

Education. School attendance has been compulsory since 1925 and the employment of children under 16 years of age in workshops, factories or mines is illegal.

In 1985–86 there were 1,645 public schools with a net enrolment of 846,823 pupils; 41,103 teachers earned an average salary of $21,874. Total expenditure for operating public schools (kindergarten to Grade 12) was $2,016m. Tennessee has 49 accredited colleges and universities, 18 2-year colleges and 28 vocational schools. The universities include the University of Tennessee, Knoxville (founded 1794), with 25,463 students in 1986–87; Vanderbilt University, Nashville (1873) with 8,968, Tennessee State University (1912) with 6,734, the University of Tennessee at Chattanooga (1886) with 7,484, Memphis State University (1912), 20,046 and Fisk University (1866) with 538.

Health. In 1985 the state had 155 hospitals with 28,434 beds. State facilities for the mentally retarded had 2,109 resident patients and mental hospitals had 1,723 in 1984.

Social Security. In 1985 Tennessee paid $3,483m. to retired workers and their survivors and to disabled workers. Total beneficiaries: 500,000 retired; 162,000 survivors and 100,000 disabled. 362,000 people received $578m. in Medicaid. 58,000 families received aid to dependent children ($84m.). Supplemental Security Income ($278m.) was paid to 127,994.

Books of Reference

Tennessee Dept. of Finance and Administration, Annual Report, Annual
Dept. of Education Annual Report for Tennessee, Annual
Tennessee Blue Book. Secretary of State, Nashville
Tennessee Statistical Abstract, Center for Business and Economic Research, Univ. of Tennessee. Annual

Corlew, R. E., *Tennessee: A Short History.* Univ. Tennessee, 2nd ed., 1981
Davidson, D., *Tennessee: Vol. I, The Old River Frontier to Secession,* Univ. Tennessee, 1979
Dykeman, W., *Tennessee,* Rev. Ed., New York, 1984

State Library: State Library and Archives, Nashville. *Librarian:* Edwin Gleaves. *State Historian:* Wilma Dykeman.

TEXAS

HISTORY. In 1836 Texas declared its independence of Mexico, and after maintaining an independent existence, as the Republic of Texas, for 10 years, it was on 29 Dec. 1845 received as a state into the American Union. The state's first settlement dates from 1686.

AREA AND POPULATION. Texas is bounded north by Oklahoma, northeast by Arkansas, east by Louisiana, south-east by the Gulf of Mexico, south by Mexico and west by New Mexico. Area, 266,807 sq. miles (including 4,790 sq. miles of inland water). Census population, 1 April 1980 (provisional), 14,228,383, an increase of 27% since 1970. Estimate (1985), 16,370,000. Vital statistics for 1984: Births, 306,192 (19·2 per 1,000 population); deaths, 119,531 (7·5); infant deaths, 3,178 (10·4 per 1,000 live births); marriages, 207,631 (13); divorces, 98,074 (6·1).

Population for 5 census years was:

	White	Negro	Indian	Asiatic	Total	Per sq. mile
1910	3,204,848	690,049	702	943	3,896,542	14·8
1930	4,967,172	854,964	1,001	1,578	5,824,715	22·1
1960	8,374,831	1,187,125	5,750	9,848	9,579,677	36·5

	White	Negro	All others	Total	Per sq. mile
1970	9,717,128	1,399,005	80,597	11,196,730	42·7
1980	11,197,663	1,710,250	1,320,470	14,228,383	54·2

Of the population in 1980, 6,998,301 were male, 11,327,159 persons were urban. Those 20 years old and older numbered 9,357,309. A census report, 1980, showed, 2,985,643 persons of Spanish origin.

The largest cities, with census population in 1980, are:

Houston	1,595,138	Amarillo	149,230	Odessa	90,027
Dallas	904,078	Beaumont	118,102	Garland	138,857
San Antonio	785,882	Wichita Falls	94,201	Laredo	91,449
Fort Worth	385,164	Irving	109,943	San Angelo	73,240
El Paso	425,259	Waco	101,261	Galveston	61,902
Austin (capital)	345,496	Arlington	160,113	Midland	70,525
Corpus Christi	231,999	Abilene	98,315	Tyler	70,508
Lubbock	173,979	Pasadena	112,560	Port Arthur	61,195

Larger urbanized areas, 1980: Houston, 2,891,146; Dallas-Fort Worth, 2,964,342; San Antonio, 1,070,245.

CLIMATE. Dallas. Jan. 45°F (7·2°C), July 84°F (28·9°C). Annual rainfall 38″ (945 mm). El Paso. Jan. 44°F (6·7°C), July 81°F (27·2°C). Annual rainfall 9″ (221 mm). Galveston. Jan. 54°F (12·2°C), July 84°F (28·9°C). Annual rainfall 46″ (1,159 mm). Houston. Jan. 52°F (11·1°C), July 83°F (28·3°C). Annual rainfall 48″ (1,200 mm). *See* Central Plains, p. 1378.

CONSTITUTION AND GOVERNMENT. The present constitution dates from 1876; it has been amended 233 times. The Legislature consists of a Senate of 31 members elected for 4 years (half their number retire every 2 years), and a House of Representatives of 150 members elected for 2 years.

The Governor and Lieut.-Governor are elected for 4 years. Qualified electors are all citizens with the usual residential qualifications. Texas sends to Congress 2 senators and 27 representatives.

In the 1984 presidential election Reagan polled 3,301,024 votes, Mondale, 1,873,499.

The capital is Austin. The state has 254 counties.

Governor: Bill Clements (R.), 1987–91 ($90,700).
Lieut.-Governor: William P. Hobby (D.), 1987–91 ($7,200).
Secretary of State: John W. Fainter, Jr. (D.), ($61,200).

BUDGET. In the fiscal year ending 31 Aug. 1982 general revenues were $23,617m. ($13,671m. from taxes, $4,154m. federal aid); general expenditures, $21,334m. ($8,743m. on education, $2,506m. on highways, $2,067m. on hospitals, $1,741m. on public welfare). Texas has a large revenue derived from the severance tax (*i.e.*, tax on the removal of oil, natural gas and sulphur from the soil or waters of the state).

Net long-term debt, 31 Aug. 1985, was $4,009m.
Per capita personal income (1985) was $13,483.

ENERGY AND NATURAL RESOURCES

Minerals. Production, 1985: Crude petroleum, 889m. bbls, natural gas 6,012,000 m.c.f.; other minerals include natural gasoline, butane and propane gases, helium, crude gypsum, granite and sandstone, salt and cement. Total value of mineral products in 1982, $45,388m., of which $43,834 was for fuels.

Agriculture. Texas is one of the most important agricultural states of the Union. In 1985 it had 184,000 farms covering 136m. acres; average farm was of 739 acres valued, land and buildings, at $652 per acre. Large-scale commercial farms, highly mechanized, dominate in Texas; farms of 1,000 acres or more in number far exceed that of any other state. But small-scale farming persists.

Soil erosion is serious in some parts. For some 97,297,000 acres drastic curative treatment has been indicated and for 51,164,000 acres, preventive treatment.

Production, 1985: Cotton, 3,945,000 bales (of 480 lb., value $981m.); maize (157m. bu., value $422m.), wheat (187·2m. bu., value $580m.), oats, barley, soybeans, peanuts, oranges, grapefruit, peaches, potatoes, sweet potatoes.

Cash income, 1985, from crops was $3,857m.; from livestock, $5,441m.

The state has a very great livestock industry, leading in the number of all cattle, 13·6m. on 1 Jan. 1986, and sheep, 1·8m.; it also had 322,000 milch cows, and 435,000 swine.

Forestry. There were (1980) 23·3m. acres of forested land.

INDUSTRY. In 1985 manufacturing establishments employed 1m. workers; trade employed 1·7m.; government, 1m.; services, 1·3m.; construction, 448,000; finance, insurance and real estate, 442,000; transport and public utilities, 383,000. Chemical industries along the Gulf Coast, such as the production of synthetic rubber and of primary magnesium (from sea-water), are increasingly important.

COMMUNICATIONS

Roads. In 1979 there were 264,900 miles of roads including 199,500 miles of rural roads. Motor registration in 1985, 12·6m.

Railways. The railways (1974) had a total mileage of 19,134 miles, of which 13,303 miles were main lines.

Aviation. In 1981 there were 322 public and 1,109 private airports.

Shipping. The port of Houston, connected by the Houston Ship Channel (50 miles long) with the Gulf of Mexico, is the largest inland cotton market in the world. Cargo handled 1981, 100·9m. tonnes.

JUSTICE, RELIGION, EDUCATION AND WELFARE

Justice. In Dec. 1985 the state prison held 37,532 men and women. Execution is by lethal injection; there were 300 between 1930 and 1968; between 1977 and 1986 there were 8.

Texas has adopted 11 laws governing the activities of trade unions. An Act of 1955 forbids the state's payment of unemployment compensation to workers engaged in certain types of strikes.

Religion. The largest religious bodies are Roman Catholics, Baptists, Methodists, Churches of Christ, Lutherans, Presbyterians and Episcopalians.

Education. School attendance is compulsory from 7 to 17 years of age.

In autumn 1983 public elementary and secondary schools had 2,990,000 enrolled pupils; in 1986 there were 175,500 classroom teachers whose salaries averaged $24,500. Total public school expenditure, 1986, $11,943m. or $750 per capita.

The largest institutions of higher education, with faculty numbers and student enrolment, 1985–86, were:

Founded	Institutions	Control	Faculty	Students
1845	Baylor University, Waco	Baptist	636	11,481
1852	St Mary's University, San Antonio	R.C.	209	3,298
1869	Trinity University, San Antonio	Presb.	255	2,759
1873	Texas Christian University, Fort Worth	Christian	519	6,925
1876	Texas A. and M. Univ., College Station	State	2,240	35,675
1876	Prairie View Agr. and Mech. Coll., Prairie View	State	297	4,627
1879	Sam Houston State University	State	365	10,345
1883	University of Texas System (every campus)	State	6,328	105,810
1890	North Texas State University, Denton	State	884	21,210
1891	Hardin-Simmons University, Abilene	Baptist	124	1,817
1889	East Texas State University, Commerce	State	363	6,867
1899	South West Texas State University, San Marcos	State	833	19,267
1903	Texas Woman's University, Denton	State	520	8,197
1906	Abilene Christian University, Abilene	Church of Christ	275	4,505
1911	Southern Methodist University, Dallas	Methodist	650	9,048
1923	Stephen F. Austin State University	State	517	12,500
1923	Texas Technical University, Lubbock	State	1,444	23,589
1925	Texas Arts and Industries University, Kingsville	State	234	5,117
1934	University of Houston, Houston	State	2,100	30,000
1947	Texas Southern University, Houston	State	544	14,230
1951	Lamar University, Beaumont	State	545	14,094

Health. In 1983, the state had 562 hospitals (84,900 beds) listed by the American Hospital Association; on 1 Jan. 1980 mental hospitals had 6,559 resident patients and state institutions for the mentally retarded, 11,178 resident patients (1980).

Social Security. Aid is from state and federal sources. Old-age assistance (SSI) was being granted in Dec. 1985 to 123,400 persons, who received an average of $133 per month; aid was given to 127,100 disabled ($217) and 398,900 dependent children (average payment per family, $142 per month).

Books of Reference

Texas Almanac. Dallas. Biennial
Texas Factbook. Univ. of Texas, 1983
Benton, W. E., *Texas, its Government and Politics.* 4th ed., Englewood Cliffs, 1977
Cruz, G. R. and Irby, J. A. (eds.), *Texas Bibliography.* Austin, 1982
Fehrenbach, T. R., *Lone Star: A History of Texas and the Texans.* London, 1986
Jordan, T. G., and Bean, J. L., Jr., *Texas.* Boulder, 1983
MacCorkle, S. A., and Smith, D., *Texas Government.* 7th ed. New York, 1974
Richardson, R. N., *Texas, the Lone Star State.* 3rd ed. New York, 1970

Legislative Reference Library: Box 12488, Capitol Station, Austin, Texas 78811. *Director:* James R. Sanders.

UTAH

HISTORY. Utah, which had been acquired by the US during the Mexican war, was settled by Mormons in 1847, and organized as a Territory on 9 Sept. 1850. It was admitted as a state into the Union on 4 Jan. 1896 with boundaries as at present.

AREA AND POPULATION. Utah is bounded north by Idaho and Wyoming, east by Colorado, south by Arizona and west by Nevada. Area, 84,899 sq. miles, of which 2,826 sq. miles are water. The federal government (1967) owned 35,397,274 acres or 67·1% of the area of the state. The area of unappropriated and unreserved lands was 23,268,250 acres in 1974. The Bureau of Indian Affairs in 1974 administered 3,035,190 acres, all of which were allotted to Indian tribes.

Census population, 1 April 1980, 1,461,037, an increase of 38% since 1970. Estimate (1985), 1,645,000. Births in 1984 were 39,677 (24 per 1,000 population); deaths, 9,295 (5·6); infant deaths, 407 (10·3 per 1,000 live births); marriages, 17,579 (10·6); divorces, 8,134 (4·9).

Population at 5 federal censuses was:

	White	Negro	Indian	Asiatic	Total	Per sq. mile
1910	366,583	1,144	3,123	2,501	373,851	4·5
1930	499,967	1,108	2,869	3,903	507,847	6·2
1960	873,828	4,148	6,961	5,207	890,627	10·8
1970	1,031,926	6,617	11,273	6,230	1,059,273	12·9
1980	1,382,550	9,225	19,256	15,076	1,461,037	17·7

Of the total in 1980, 724,501 were male, 1,232,908 persons were urban; 860,304 were 20 years of age or older.

The largest cities are Salt Lake City (capital), with a population (census, 1980) of 162,960; Provo, 74,007; Ogden, 64,444; Bountiful, 32,877; Orem, 52,399; Sandy City, 51,022 and Logan, 26,844.

CLIMATE. Salt Lake City. Jan. 29°F (−1·7°C), July 77°F (25°C). Annual rainfall 16″ (401 mm). *See* Mountain States, p. 1378.

CONSTITUTION AND GOVERNMENT. Utah adopted its present constitution in 1896 (now with 61 amendments). It sends to Congress 2 senators and 3 representatives.

The Legislature consists of a Senate (in part renewed every 2 years) of 30 members, elected for 4 years, and of a House of Representatives of 75 members elected for 2 years. The Governor is elected for 4 years. The constitution provides for the initiative and referendum. Electors are all citizens, who, not being insane or criminal, have the usual residential qualifications.

The capital is Salt Lake City. There are 29 counties in the state.

In the 1984 presidential election Reagan polled 464,535 votes, Mondale, 154,239.

Governor: Norman Bangerter (R.), 1985–88 ($52,000).
Lieut.-Governor: W. Val Oveson (R.), 1985–88 ($35,500).

BUDGET. For the year ending 30 June 1982 general revenue was $2,490m. ($1,332m. from taxes, $612m. from federal aid) while general expenditures were $2,490m. ($1,104m. on education, $279m. on highways, $234m. on public welfare).

The net long-term debt on 30 June 1982 was about $2,171m.

Per capita personal income (1985) was $10,493.

ENERGY AND NATURAL RESOURCES

Minerals The principal minerals are: copper, gold, petroleum, lead, silver and zinc. The state also has natural gas, clays, tungsten, molybdenum, uranium and phosphate rock.

Agriculture. In 1985 Utah had 14,000 farms covering 12m. acres, of which about 2m. acres were crop land and about 300,000 acres pasture. About 1m. acres had irrigation; the average farm was of 857 acres.

Of the total surface area, 9% is severely eroded and only 9·4% is free from erosion; the balance is moderately eroded.

Cash income, 1985, from crops, $138m. and from livestock, $409m. The principal crops are: Barley, wheat (spring and winter), oats, potatoes, hay (alfalfa, sweet clover and lespedeza), maize. In 1985 there were 515,000 sheep; 80,000 milch cows; 800,000 all cattle; 28,000 swine.

Forestry. Area of national forests, 1981, was 9,129,000 acres, of which 8·05m. acres were under forest service administration.

INDUSTRY. In 1985 manufacturing establishments had 94,000 workers. Leading manufactures by value added are primary metals, ordinances and transport, food, fabricated metals and machinery, petroleum products. Service industries employed 132,000; trade, 148,000; government, 138,000.

COMMUNICATIONS

Roads. The state has about 50,000 miles of highway. In 1985 there were 1,103,000 motor vehicles registered.

Railways. On 1 July 1974 the state had 1,734 miles of railways.

Aviation. In 1981 there were 57 public and 45 private airports.

JUSTICE, RELIGION, EDUCATION AND WELFARE

Justice. The number of inmates of the state prison in Dec. 1985 was 1,570. Since 1930 total executions have been 14 (13 by shooting, 1 by hanging—the condemned man has choice), all whites, and all for murder.

Religion. Latter-day Saints (Mormons) form about 73% of the church membership of the state; their church is a substantial property-owner. The Roman Catholic church and most Protestant denominations are represented.

Education. School attendance is compulsory for children from 6 to 18 years of age. There are 40 school districts. Teachers' salaries, 1985, averaged $21,500. There were (autumn 1983) 379,000 pupils in public elementary and secondary schools, and (1986) 16,700 classroom teachers, average salary, $22,550; estimated public school expenditure was $1,092m. or $664 per capita.

The University of Utah (1850) (24,770 students in 1985–86) is in Salt Lake City; the Utah State University (1890) (11,804) is in Logan. The Mormon Church maintains the Brigham Young University at Provo (1875) with 26,894 students. Other colleges include: Westminster College, Salt Lake City (1,302); Weber State College, Ogden (11,117); Southern Utah State College, Cedar City (2,587); College of Eastern Utah, Price (1,132); Snow College, Ephraim (1,328); Dixie College, St George (2,234).

Health. In 1983, the state had 44 hospitals (5,400 beds) listed by the Utah Department of Social Services. Mental hospitals had 317 resident patients on 1 Jan. 1980; state facilities for the mentally retarded had 763.

Social Security. In Dec. 1985 the state department of public welfare provided assistance to 37,800 persons receiving aid to dependent children at an average $322 per family per month; aid to the aged, the blind and disabled is provided from federal funds; there were 1,900 aged recipients in 1985 (average $150 per month), 6,600 disabled ($224).

Books of Reference

Compiled Digest of Administrative Reports. Secretary of State, Salt Lake City. Annual
Statistical Abstract of Government in Utah. Utah Foundation, Salt Lake City. Annual
Utah Agricultural Statistics. Dept. of Agriculture, Salt Lake City. Annual
Utah: Facts. Bureau of Economic and Business Research, Univ. of Utah, 1975
Arrington, L., *Great Basin Kingdom: An Economic History of the Latter-Day Saints, 1830–1900.* Cambridge, Mass., 1958
Petersen, C. S., *Utah, a History.* New York, 1977

VERMONT

HISTORY. Vermont, first settled in 1724, was admitted into the Union as the fourteenth state on 4 March 1791. The first constitution was adopted by convention at Windsor, 2 July 1777, and established an independent state government.

AREA AND POPULATION. Vermont is bounded north by Canada, east by New Hampshire, south by Massachusetts and west by New York. Area, 9,614 sq. miles, of which 341 sq. miles are inland water. Census population, 1 April 1980, 511,456, an increase of 15% since 1970. Estimate (1986) 541,000. Births, 1985, were 8,027 (15 per 1,000 population); deaths, 4,657 (8·7); infant deaths, 68 (8·5 per 1,000 live births); marriages, 5,375 (10·1); divorces, 2,173 (4·1).

Population at 5 census years was:

	White	Negro	Indian	Asiatic	Total	Per sq. mile
1910	354,298	1,621	26	11	355,956	39·0
1930	358,966	568	36	41	359,611	38·8
1960	389,092	519	57	172	389,881	42·0
1970	442,553	761	229	787	444,732	48·0
1980	506,736	1,135	984	1,355	511,456	55·1

Of the population in 1980, 249,080 were male, 172,735 persons were urban; those 20 years of age or older numbered 343,666. The largest cities are Burlington, with a population in 1980 of 37,712; Rutland, 18,436; Barre, 9,824.

CLIMATE. Burlington. Jan. 17°F (−8·3°C), July 70°F (21·1°C). Annual rainfall 33″ (820 mm). *See* New England, p. 1379.

CONSTITUTION AND GOVERNMENT. The constitution was adopted in 1793 and has since been amended. Amendments are proposed by two-thirds vote of the Senate every 4 years, and must be accepted by two sessions of the legislature; they are then submitted to popular vote. The state Legislature, consisting of a Senate of 30 members and a House of Representatives of 150 members (both elected for 2 years), meets in Jan. in odd-numbered years. The Governor and Lieut.-Governor are elected for 2 years. Electors are all citizens who possess certain residential qualifications and have taken the freeman's oath set forth in the constitution.

The state is divided into 14 counties; there are 251 towns and cities and other minor civil divisions. The state sends to Congress 2 senators and 1 representative, who are elected by the voters of the entire state.

In the 1984 presidential election Reagan polled 134,252 votes, Mondale, 94,518.

The capital is Montpelier (8,241, census of 1980).

Governor: Madeleine Kunin (D.), 1987–89 ($50,003).
Lieut.-Governor: Howard Dean (D.) ($22,006).
Secretary of State: James Douglas (R.) ($29,993).

BUDGET. The total revenue for the year ending 30 June 1986 was $866m.; total disbursements, $865·6m.

Total net long-term debt, 30 June 1986, was $254·7.

Per capita personal income (1984) was $10,692.

NATURAL RESOURCES

Minerals. Stone, chiefly granite, marble and slate, is the leading mineral produced in Vermont, contributing about 60% of the total value of mineral products. Other products include asbestos, talc, peat, sand and gravel. Total value of mineral products, 1982, $50m.

Agriculture. Agriculture is the most important industry. In 1985 the state had 7,000 farms covering 2m. acres; the average farm was of 286 acres. Cash income, 1984, from livestock and products, $369m.; from crops, $31m. The dairy farms produce about 2,300m. lb. of milk annually. The chief agricultural crops are hay, apples and maple syrup. In 1981 Vermont had 355,000 cattle, 11,000 sheep, 9,000 swine, 425,000 poultry.

Forestry. In 1982 the harvest was 82m. bd ft hardwood and 93m. bd ft softwood saw-logs, and 267,000 cords of pulpwood and boltwood. About 600,000 cords was cut for firewood.

The state is nearly 80% forest, with 12% in public ownership. National forests area (1983), 285,000 acres. State-owned forests, parks, fish and game areas, 250,000 acres; municipally-owned, 38,500 acres.

INDUSTRY. In 1984, manufacturing establishments employed an average 49,000 workers; main manufactures include machine tools and electronic components. Service industries employed 52,000 and trade, 47,000.

COMMUNICATIONS

Roads. The state had 14,000 miles of roads in 1984, including 12,900 miles of rural roads. Motor vehicle registrations, 1984, 510,267.

Railways. There were, in 1983, 756 miles of main line railway, 300 of which was leased by the state to private operators.

Aviation. There were 22 airports in 1983, of which 10 were state operated, 2 municipally owned and 10 privately owned but open to public use.

JUSTICE, RELIGION, EDUCATION AND WELFARE

Justice. In financial year 1984 6 prisons and centres had an average of 524 inmates; average total inmates, 576; there were an average of 4,350 people on probation and 313 on parole.

Religion. The principal denominations are Roman Catholic, United Church of Christ, United Methodist, Protestant Episcopal, Baptist and Unitarian–Universalist.

Education. School attendance during the full school term is compulsory for children from 7 to 16 years of age, unless they have completed the 10th grade or undergo approved home instruction. In 1982–83 the public elementary schools had 48,166 enrolled pupils; the public secondary schools had 43,344 pupils; the 82 private schools had 8,580 pupils. Full-time teachers for public elementary schools numbered 2,941, secondary schools 3,310. Teachers' salaries for 1983 averaged

$15,794 (elementary) and $16,747 (secondary). Total expenditure on public schools, 1984, $301m.

The University of Vermont (1791) had 9,218 full-time students in 1981–82, of whom 7,833 were undergraduates; Middlebury College (1800), 1,932 students; Norwich University (1834 but founded as an academy 1819), 2,308 students (including Vermont College); St Michael's College, 1,721 students; the 5 state colleges, 3,796 students; all other colleges, 3,120.

Health. In Sept. 1983 the state had 16 general hospitals (898 beds), 2 mental hospitals and 1 T.B. hospital. There was 1 federal general hospital with 224 beds.

Social Security. Old-age assistance (SSI) was being granted in 1980 to 2,400 persons, drawing an average of $108 per month; aid to dependent children was being granted to 24,300 persons, drawing an average of $340 per family per month; and aid to the permanently and totally disabled was being granted to 5,200 persons, drawing an average of $192.

Books of Reference

Legislative Directory. Secretary of State, Montpelier. Biennial
Vermont Annual Financial Report. Auditor of Accounts, Montpelier. Annual
Vermont Facts and Figures. Office of Statistical Co-ordination, Montpelier
Vermont Year-Book, formerly *Walton's Register.* Chester. Annual
Bassett T., and Seymour D. (eds.), *Vermont: A Bibliography of its History,* Boston, 1981
Delorme, D. (ed.), *Vermont Atlas and Gazetteer,* Rev. ed., Freeport, 1983
Morrissey, C. T., *Vermont,* New York, 1981

State Library: Vermont Dept. of Libraries, Montpelier. *State Librarian:* Patricia Klinck.

VIRGINIA

HISTORY. The first English Charter for settlements in America was that granted by James I in 1606 for the planting of colonies in Virginia. The state was one of the 13 original states in the Union. Virginia lost just over one-third of its area when West Virginia was admitted into the Union (1863).

AREA AND POPULATION. Virginia is bounded north-west by West Virginia, north-east by Maryland, east by the Atlantic, south by North Carolina and Tennessee and west by Kentucky. Area, 40,767 sq. miles including 1,063 sq. miles of inland water. Census population, 1 April 1980, 5,346,818, an increase of 695,370 or 14.9% since 1970. Estimate 1986 5,787,000. In 1985 there were 85,984 births (15 per 1,000 population); 45,236 deaths (7.9); 990 infant deaths (11.5 per 1,000 live births); 66,541 marriages and 24,131 divorces.

Population for 5 federal census years was:

	White	Negro	Indian	Asiatic	Total	Per sq. mile
1910	1,389,809	671,096	539	168	2,061,612	51.2
1930	1,770,441	650,165	779	466	2,421,851	60.7
1960	3,142,443	816,258	2,155	4,725	3,966,949	99.3
			All others			
1970	3,761,514	861,368	25,612		4,648,494	116.9
1980	4,230,000	1,008,311	108,517		5,346,818	134.7

Of the total population in 1980, 49% were male, 66% were urban and 59% were 21 years of age or older.

The population (census of 1980) of the principal cities was: Norfolk, 266,979; Virginia Beach, 262,199; Richmond, 219,214; Newport News, 144,903; Hampton, 122,617; Chesapeake, 114,226; Portsmouth, 104,577; Alexandria, 103,219; Roanoke, 100,427; Lynchburg, 66,743.

CLIMATE. Average temperatures in Jan. are 41°F in the Tidewater coastal area and 32°F in the Blue Ridge mountains; July averages, 78°F and 68°F respectively. Precipitation averages 36″ in the Shenandoah valley and 44″ in the south. Snowfall is 5-10″ in the Tidewater and 25-30″ in the western mountains. Norfolk. Jan.

41°F (5°C), July 79°F (26·1°C). Annual rainfall 46″ (1,145 mm). *See* Atlantic Coast, p. 1379.

CONSTITUTION AND GOVERNMENT. The present constitution dates from 1971.

The General Assembly consists of a Senate of 40 members, elected for 4 years, and a House of Delegates of 100 members, elected for 2 years. The Governor and Lieut.-Governor are elected for 4 years. Qualified as electors are (with few exceptions) all citizens 18 years of age, fulfilling certain residential qualifications, who have registered. The state sends to Congress 2 senators and 10 representatives.

In the 1984 presidential election Reagan polled 1,325,516 votes, Mondale, 793,711.

The state capital is Richmond; the state contains 95 counties and 41 independent cities.

Governor: Gerald L. Baliles (D.), 1986–90 ($75,000).
Lieut.-Governor: L. Douglas Wilder (D.) $20,000.
Secretary of the Commonwealth: Sandra D. Bowen (D.) ($45,959).

BUDGET. General revenue for the year ending 30 June 1985 was $6,652,678,000 (taxation, $4,489,878,000, and federal aid, $1,298,159,000); general expenditures, $5,844,421,000 ($1,644,836,000 for education, $1,079,596,000 for transport and $1,950,440,000 for public welfare).

Total net long-term debt, 30 June 1984, amounted to $521,032,000.
Per capita personal income (1986) was $15,374.

ENERGY AND NATURAL RESOURCES

Minerals. Coal is the most important mineral, with output (1984) of 35,500,000 short tons. Lead and zinc ores, stone, sand and gravel, lime and titanium ore are also produced. Total mineral output was $382m. in 1986.

Agriculture. In 1985 there were 55,000 farms with an area of 10m. acres; average farm had 182 acres and was valued at $106,220.

Income, 1985, from crops, $623m., and from livestock and livestock products, $1,004m. The chief crops are corn, hay, peanuts and tobacco.

Animals on farms on 1 Jan. 1985 included 162,000 milch cows, 1·76m. all cattle, 125,000 sheep and 370,000 swine (Dec. 1984).

Forestry. National forests, 1984, covered 1,634,000 acres.

INDUSTRY. The manufacture of cigars and cigarettes and of rayon and allied products and the building of ships lead in value of products.

TOURISM. Tourists spend about $4,100m. a year in Virginia, attracted mainly by the state's outstanding scenery, coastline and historical interest.

COMMUNICATIONS

Roads. The state highways system, 31 Dec. 1983, had 61,977 miles of highways, of which 8,958 miles were primary roads. Motor registrations, 1985, 4·1m.

Railways. In 1985 there were 3,693 miles of railways.

Aviation. There were, in 1985, 81 airports, of which 58 were publicly owned.

JUSTICE, RELIGION, EDUCATION AND WELFARE

Justice. Executions (by electrocution) since 1930 totalled 100. Prison population, 31 Dec. 1985, 12,073 in federal and state prisons.

Religion. The principal churches are the Baptist, Methodist, Protestant-Episcopal, Roman Catholic and Presbyterian.

Education. Elementary and secondary instruction is free, and for ages 6–17 attendance is compulsory. No child under 12 may be employed in any mining or manufacturing work.

In 1984 the 135 school districts had, in primary schools, 578,305 pupils and 34,167 teachers and in public high schools, 369,956 pupils and 26,286 teachers. Teachers' salaries (1986) averaged $23,450. Total expenditure on education, 1986, was $3,233m. The more important institutions for higher education (1986) were:

Founded	Name and place of college	Staff	Students
1693	College of William and Mary, Williamsburg (State)	526	6,616
1749	Washington and Lee University, Lexington	194	1,804
1776	Hampden-Sydney College, Hampden-Sydney (Pres.)	74	825
1819	University of Virginia, Charlottesville (State)	1,772	17,149
1832	Randolph-Macon College, Ashland (Methodist)	102	1,013
1832	University of Richmond, Richmond (Baptist)	349	4,705
1838	Virginia Commonwealth University, Richmond	1,885	19,641
1839	Virginia Military Institute Lexington (State)	100	1,350
1865	Virginia Union University, Richmond	98	1,311
1868	Hampton University	297	4,483
1872	Virginia Polytechnic Institute and State University	2,209	22,345
1882	Virginia State University, Petersburg	263	3,583
1908	James Madison University, Harrisonburg	600	9,757
1910	Radford University (State)	365	7,500
1930	Old Dominion University, Norfolk	713	15,463
1956	George Mason University (State)	715	17,652

Health. In 1983 the state had 135 hospitals (31,300 beds) listed by the American Hospital Association.

Social Security. In 1938 Virginia established a system of old-age assistance under the Federal Security Act; in March 1983 persons in 2,034 cases were drawing an average grant of $202.79; aid to permanently and totally disabled, 1,766 cases, average grant $218.96; aid to dependent children, 164,383 persons, average grant $85.77; general relief, 6,642 persons, average grant $146.62.

Books of Reference

Virginia Facts and Figures. Virginia Division of Industrial Development, Richmond. Annual
Dabney, V., *Virginia, the New Dominion.* 1971
Friddell, G., *The Virginia Way.* Burda, 1973
Gottmann, J., *Virginia in our Century.* Charlottesville, 1969
Morton, R. L., *Colonial Virginia.* 2 vols. Univ. Press of Virginia, 1960
Rouse, P. *Virginia: a Pictorial History.* Scribner, 1975
Rubin, L. D., Jr., *Virginia: a Bicentennial History.* Norris, 1977

State Library: Virginia State Library, Richmond 23219. *State Librarian:* Ella Gaines Yates.

WASHINGTON

HISTORY. Washington, formerly part of Oregon, was created a Territory in 1853, and was admitted into the Union as a state on 11 Nov. 1889. Its settlement dates from 1811.

AREA AND POPULATION. Washington is bounded north by Canada, east by Idaho, south by Oregon with the Columbia River forming most of the boundary, and west by the Pacific. Area, 68,139 sq. miles, of which 1,627 sq. miles are inland water. Lands owned by the federal government, 1977, were 12·4m. acres or 29·1% of the total area. Census population, 1 April 1980 (preliminary), 4,130,163, an increase of 730,994 or 21·4% since 1970. Estimated population (1985), 4,409,000. Births, 1984 were 73,605 (16·9 per 1,000 population); deaths, 35,212 (8·1); infant deaths, 690 (9·4 per 1,000 live births); marriages, 44,730 (10·3); divorces and annulments, 27,313 (6·3).

Population in 5 federal census years was:

	White	Negro	Indian	Asiatic and others	Total	Per sq. mile
1910	1,109,111	6,058	10,997	15,824	1,141,990	17·1
1930	1,521,661	6,840	11,253	23,642	1,563,396	23·3
1960	2,751,675	48,738	21,076	31,725	2,853,214	42·8
1970	2,351,055	71,308	33,386	53,420	3,409,169	51·2
1980	3,777,296	105,544	60,771	186,552	4,130,163	62·0

Of the total population in 1980, 2,051,369 were male, 3,037,765 persons were urban; 2,837,607 were 20 years of age or older.

There are 24 Indian reservations, the largest being held by the Yakima tribe. Indian reservations in Sept. 1979 covered 2,496,423 acres, of which 1,996,018 acres were tribal lands and 497,218 acres were held by individuals. Total Indian population, 1980, 60,771.

Leading cities are Seattle, with a population (1980 census) of 491,897; Spokane, 170,993; Tacoma, 158,101; Bellevue, 73,711. Others : Yakima, 49,826; Everett, 54,413; Vancouver, 42,834; Bellingham, 45,794; Bremerton, 36,208; Richland, 33,578; Longview, 31,052; Renton, 30,612; Edmonds, 27,526; Walla Walla, 25,618. Urbanized areas (1980 census): Seattle–Everett, 1,600,944; Tacoma, 482,692; Spokane, 341,058.

CLIMATE. Seattle. Jan. 40°F (4·4°C), July 63°F (17·2°C). Annual rainfall 34″ (848 mm). Spokane. Jan. 27°F (–2·8°C), July 70°F (21·1°C). Annual rainfall 14″ (350 mm). *See* Pacific Coast, p. 1378.

CONSTITUTION AND GOVERNMENT. The constitution, adopted in 1889, has had 63 amendments. The Legislature consists of a Senate of 49 members elected for 4 years, half their number retiring every 2 years, and a House of Representatives of 98 members, elected for 2 years. The Governor and Lieut.-Governor are elected for 4 years. The state sends 2 senators and 7 representatives to Congress.

Qualified as voters are (with some exceptions) all citizens 18 years of age, having the usual residential qualifications.

In the 1984 presidential election Reagan polled 939,124 votes, Mondale, 731,440.

The capital is Olympia (population, 1980 census, 27,447). The state contains 39 counties.

Governor: Booth Gardner (D.), 1985–89 ($63,000).
Lieut.-Governor: John A. Cherberg (D.), 1985–89 ($28,600).
Secretary of State: Ralph Munro (R.), 1985–89 ($31,000).

BUDGET. For the 2-year budget period 1981–83 the state's total revenue is (projected) $13,545·2m.; general expenditure is (projected) $13,873·5m. (education, $6,150·7m.; transportation, $706·6m., and human resources, $3,636m.).

Total outstanding debt in 1982 was $2,492m.

Per capita personal income (1985) was $13,876.

ENERGY AND NATURAL RESOURCES

Electricity. With about 20% of potential water-power resources of US, the state has ample developed and potential hydro-electricity.

Minerals. Mining and quarrying are not as important as forestry, agriculture or manufacturing. Uranium is mined but figures are not disclosed; other minerals include sand and gravel, stone, coal and clays.

Agriculture. Agriculture is constantly growing in value because of more intensive and diversified farming and because of the 1m.-acre Columbia Basin Irrigation Project.

In 1985 there were 38,000 farms with an acreage of 16m.; average farm was of 421 acres. Average value per acre, $923.

Cash return from farm marketing, 1985, was $2,797m. (from crops, $1,865m.; from livestock and dairy products, $932m.). Wheat, cattle and calves, milk and apples are important.

On 1 Jan. 1985 animals on farms included 211,000 milch cows, 1·47m. all cattle, 53,000 sheep and 45,000 swine.

Forestry. Forests cover about 23m. acres, of which 9m. acres are national forest. In 1982, lumber production was 3,014m. bd ft; plywood, 1,200m. bd ft, and pulp wood (1981) 3,494,000 short tons.

Fisheries. Salmon and halibut are important; total catch, 1985, 167m. lb.; value, $93m.

INDUSTRY. In 1985 manufacturing employed 294,000 workers, of whom about half were in aerospace and the forest products industry.

Abundance of electric power has made Washington the leading producer of primary aluminium.

In 1985 trade employed 422,000, service industries, 373,000; government, 343,000.

COMMUNICATIONS

Roads. The state (1979) maintained 6,920 miles of highway; the counties, 40,767 miles; municipalities, 9,888 miles. Motor vehicle registrations (1985), 3,576,000.

Railways. The railways had, in 1980, 6,057 miles.

Aviation. There were in 1979, 365 airports, 120 publicly owned. In 1978 Seattle–Tacoma Airport traffic was 8·3m. passengers, 48,000 tons of mail and 185,000 tons of freight and express.

JUSTICE, RELIGION, EDUCATION AND WELFARE

Justice. The adult population in state prisons in Dec. 1985 was 6,909. Since 1963 there have been no executions; total 1930–63 (by hanging) was 47, including 40 whites, 5 Negroes and 2 other races, all for murder, except 1 white for kidnapping.

Religion. Chief religious bodies are the Roman Catholic, United Methodist, Lutheran, Presbyterian, Latter-day Saints and Episcopalian.

Education. Education is given free to all children between the ages of 5 and 21 years, and is compulsory for children from 8 to 15 years of age. In autumn 1983 there were 736,000 pupils in public elementary and secondary schools. In 1986 there were 36,200 classroom teachers, average salary, $26,100. The total expenditure on public elementary and secondary schools for the school year 1986 was $3,124m. or $708 per capita.

The University of Washington, founded 1861, at Seattle, had, 1985–86, 34,086 students, and Washington State University at Pullman, founded 1890, for science and agriculture, had 16,139 students. Twenty-seven community colleges had (1981) a total enrolment of 161,244 students (89,263 full-time equivalent).

Health. In 1981 the 2 state hospitals for mental illness had a daily average of 1,204 patients; schools for handicapped children, 1,999 residents in Sept. 1981.

In 1982 the state had 121 general hospitals (15,700 beds); in 1981, 3 licensed psychiatric hospitals (181 beds) and 3 alcoholism hospitals (174 beds).

Social Security. Old-age assistance is provided for persons 65 years of age or older without adequate resources (and not in need of continuing home care) who are residents of the state. In Dec. 1985, 12,100 people were drawing an average of $157 per month; aid to 189,000 children in 67,900 families averaged $419 per family monthly; to 35,000 totally disabled, $266 monthly.

Books of Reference

Washington State Research Council. *Handbook: A Compendium of Statistical and Explanatory Information about State and Local Government in Washington.* 4th ed. Olympia, 1973.—*The Book of Numbers: A Statistical Handbook on Washington State Government.* Olympia, 1977

Avery, M. W., *Washington, a History of the Evergreen State.* Univ. of Wash. Press, 1965.— *Government of Washington State.* Univ. of Wash. Press, revised ed. 1973

State Library: Washington State Library, Olympia. *State Librarian:* Roderick Swartz.

WEST VIRGINIA

HISTORY. In 1862, after the state of Virginia had seceded from the Union, the electors of the western portion ratified an ordinance providing for the formation of a new state, which was admitted into the Union by presidential proclamation on 20 June 1863, under the name of West Virginia. Its constitution was adopted by the voters almost unanimously on 26 March 1863.

AREA AND POPULATION. West Virginia is bounded north by Pennsylvania and Maryland, east and south by Virginia, south-west by the Sandy River (forming the boundary with Kentucky) and west by the Ohio River (forming the boundary with Ohio). Area, 24,282 sq. miles, of which 102 sq. miles are water. Census population, 1 April 1980, 1,949,644, an increase of 11·8% since 1970. Estimate (1985), 1,936,000. Births, 1986, 23,066 (11·9 per 1,000 population); deaths, 19,659 (10·2); infant deaths, 234 (10·1 per 1,000 live births); marriages, 13,900 (7·2); divorces, 9,797 (5·1).

Population in 5 federal census years was:

	White	Negro	Indian	Asiatic	Total	Per sq. mile
1910	1,156,817	64,173	36	93	1,221,119	50·8
1940	1,614,191	114,893	18	103	1,729,205	71·8
1960	1,770,133	89,378	181	419	1,860,421	77·3
1970	1,673,480	67,342	751	1,463	1,744,237	71·8
1980	1,874,751	65,051	1,610	5,194	1,949,644	80·3

Of the total population in 1980, 945,408 were male, 705,319 were urban; those 20 years of age or older numbered 1,319,566.

The 1980 census (and 1985 estimate) population of the principal cities was: Huntington, 63,684 (61,086); Charleston, 63,968 (59,371). Others: Wheeling, 43,070 (42,082); Parkersburg, 39,967 (39,399); Morgantown, 27,605 (27,786); Weirton, 24,736 (23,878); Fairmont, 23,863 (22,822); Clarksburg, 22,371 (21,379).

CLIMATE. Charleston. Jan. 34°F (1·1°C), July 76°F (24·4°C). Annual rainfall 40″ (1,010 mm). *See* Appalachian Mountains, p. 1379.

CONSTITUTION AND GOVERNMENT. The present constitution was adopted in 1872; it has had 60 amendments.

The Legislature consists of the Senate of 34 members elected for a term of 4 years, one-half being elected biennially, and the House of Delegates of 100 members, elected biennially. The Governor is elected for 4 years and may succeed himself once. Voters are all citizens (with the usual exceptions) 18 years of age and meeting certain residential requirements. The state sends to Congress 2 senators and 4 representatives.

In the 1984 presidential election Reagan polled 396,332 votes, Mondale, 322,142.

The state capital is Charleston. There are 55 counties.

Governor: Arch Moore Jr. (R.), 1985–89 ($72,000).
Secretary of State: Ken Hechler (D.), ($43,200).

FINANCE. General revenues for the year ending 30 June 1986 were $3,130m.

($1,547m. from taxes, $846m. from federal funds); general expenditures were $3,291m. (education, $1,333m.; highways, $629m.; public welfare, $673m.).

Debts outstanding were $1,026·7m. on 30 June 1986.

Estimated *per capita* personal income (1987) was $10,576.

ENERGY AND NATURAL RESOURCES

Minerals. 38% of the state is underlain with mineable coal; 127·5m. short tons of coal were produced in 1985. Petroleum output, 3·3m. bbls; natural gas production was 144,883m. cu. ft. Salt, sand and gravel, sandstone and limestone are also produced. The total value of mineral output in 1985 was $5,198m.

Agriculture. In 1987 the state had 21,000 farms with an area of 3·7m. acres; average size of farm was 176 acres and valued at $527 per acre. Livestock farming predominates.

Cash income, 1986, from crops was $71·3m.; from government payments, $8·4m., and from livestock and products, $156·1m. Main crops harvested, 1985: hay (1·2m. tons); all corn (7·7m. bu.); tobacco (3·4m. lb.). Area of main crops, 1986: hay, 570,000 acres; corn, 95,000 acres. Apples (230m. lb. in 1986) and peaches (23m. lb.) are important fruit crops. Livestock on farms, 1 Jan. 1987, included 560,000 cattle, of which 32,000 were milch cows; sheep, 78,000; hogs, 37,000; chickens, 670,000 excluding broilers. Production, 1986, included 29m. broilers, 109m. eggs; 2·2m. turkeys.

Forestry. State forests, 1985, covered 79,365 acres; national forests, 1,673,000 gross acres; 75% of the state is woodland.

INDUSTRY. In 1986, 1,613 manufactories had 86,892 production workers who earned $2,154m. Leading manufactures are primary and fabricated metals, glass, chemicals, wood products, textiles and apparel, and machinery.

In 1986 non-agricultural employment was 596,800 of whom 136,700 were in trade, 128,700 in government and 120,900 in service industries.

The first commercial coal liquefaction plant in the USA is being built near Morgantown with the co-operation of the governments of Federal Republic of Germany and Japan and the Gulf Oil Co.

COMMUNICATIONS

Roads. Total highways on 30 June 1986, 37,739 miles (state maintained, 33,835 miles; inter-state, 393 miles; national parks and other roads, 3,904 miles). Registered motor vehicles, financial year ending 30 June 1986, numbered 1,479,937.

Railways. In 1986 the state had 3,430 miles of railway, all operated by diesel or electric trains.

Aviation. There were 42 licensed airports in 1986.

Post and Broadcasting. There are 64 AM radio stations, 64 FM radio stations. Television stations number 9 VHF and 5 UHF.

Newspapers. Daily newspapers number 27; weekly newspapers 65.

JUSTICE, RELIGION, EDUCATION AND WELFARE

Justice. The state court system consists of a Supreme Court and 31 circuit courts. The Supreme Court of Appeals, exercising original and appellate jurisdiction, has 5 members elected by the people for 12-year terms. Each circuit court has from 1 to 7 judges (as determined by the Legislature on the basis of population and case-load) chosen by the voters within each circuit for 8-year terms.

Effective on 1 July 1967, the West Virginia Human Rights Act prohibits discrimination in employment and places of public accommodations based on race, religion, colour, national origin or ancestry.

There are 5 penal and correctional institutions which had, on 30 June 1985, 1,574 inmates. In 1965 the state legislature abolished capital punishment.

Religion. Chief denominations in 1987 were United Methodist (159,000 members, estimate), Baptists (116,000) and Roman Catholics (109,000).

Education. Public school education is free for all from 5 to 21 years of age, and school attendance is compulsory for all between the ages of 7 and 16 (school term, 200 days—180–185 days of actual teaching). The public schools are non-sectarian. In autumn 1986 public elementary and secondary schools had 352,397 pupils and 25,532 classroom teachers. Average salary of teachers in 1986, $21,396. Total 1986 expenditures for public schools, $1,196m.

Leading institutions of higher education in 1985:

Founded		Full-time students
1837	Marshall University, Huntington	11,229
	School of Medicine	196
1837	West Liberty State College, West Liberty	2,552
1867	Fairmont State College, Fairmont	5,230
1868	West Virginia University, Morgantown	15,828
	School of Medicine	1,346
1872	Concord College, Athens	2,356
1872	Glenville State College, Glenville	2,061
1872	Shepherd College, Shepherdstown	3,853
1891	West Virginia State College	4,383
1895	West Virginia Institute of Technology, Montgomery	2,833
1895	Bluefield State College, Bluefield	2,593
1901	Potomac State College of West Virginia Univ., Keyser	1,040
1972	West Virginia College of Graduate Studies	2,835
1976	School of Osteopathic Medicine, Lewisburg	234

In addition to the universities and state-supported schools, there are 3 community colleges (8,510 students in 1986), 10 denominational and private institutions of higher education (9,074 students in 1986) and 18 business colleges.

Health. In 1986 the state had 76 hospitals and 50 licensed personal care homes, 81 skilled-nursing homes and 3 mental hospitals.

Social Security. The Department of Human Services, originating in the 1930s as the Department of Public Assistance, is both state and federally financed. In the year ending 30 June 1987 day care for 4,592 children per month was provided; aid was given to 28,399 families with dependent children (average award, $248.63 per month); handicapped children's services conducted 9,777 examinations; 94,307 families per month received food stamps.

On 1 Jan. 1974 all blind, aged and disabled services were converted to the Federal Supplemental Security Income programme.

Books of Reference

West Virginia Blue Book. Legislature, Charleston. Annual, since 1916
West Virginia Statistical Handbook, 1974. Bureau of Business Research, W. Va. Univ., Morgantown, 1974
Bibliography of West Virginia. 2 parts. Dept. of Archives and History, Charleston, 1939
West Virginia History. Dept. of Archives and History. Charleston. Quarterly, from 1939
Conley, P., and Doherty, W. T., *West Virginia History.* Charleston, 1974
Davis, C. J., and others, *West Virginia State and Local Government.* West Virginia Univ. Bureau for Government Research, 1963
Rice, O. K., *West Virginia: A History.* Univ. Press of Kentucky, Lexington, 1985
Williams, J. A., *West Virginia: A Bicentennial History.* New York, 1976

State Library: Division of Archives and History, Dept. of Culture and History, Charleston.

WISCONSIN

HISTORY. Wisconsin was settled in 1670 by French traders and missionaries. Originally a part of New France, it was surrendered to the British in 1763 and in 1783, when ceded to the US, became part of the North-west Territory. It was then contained successively in the Territories of Indiana, Illinois and Michigan. In 1836 it became part of the Territory of Wisconsin, which also included the present states of Iowa, Minnesota and parts of the Dakotas. It was admitted into the Union with its present boundaries on 29 May 1848.

AREA AND POPULATION. Wisconsin is bounded north by Lake Superior and the Upper Peninsula of Michigan, east by Lake Michigan, south by Illinois, west by Iowa and Minnesota, with the Mississippi River forming most of the boundary. Area, 56,154 sq. miles, including 1,439 sq. miles of inland water, but excluding any part of the Great Lakes. Census population, 1 April 1980 4,705,642, an increase of 6·5% since 1970. Estimated population (1987), 4,794,792. Births in 1986 were 72,229 (15·1 per 1,000 population); deaths, 41,027 (8·8); infant deaths, 663 (9·2 per 1,000 live births); marriages, 38,373 (8·0); divorces and annulments, 16,395 (3·4).

Population in 5 census years was:

	White	Negro	All others	Total	Per sq. mile
1910	2,320,555	2,900	10,405	2,333,860	42·2
1930	2,916,255	10,739	12,012	2,939,006	53·7
1960	3,858,903	74,546	18,328	3,951,777	72·2
1970	4,258,959	128,224	30,750	4,417,933	80·8
1980	4,443,035	182,592	80,015	4,705,642	86·4

Of the total population in 1980, 49% were male, 64·2% were urban and 67% were 20 years old or older.

Population of the larger cities, 1980 census, was as follows:

Milwaukee	636,297	Appleton	58,913	Beloit	35,207
Madison	170,616	Oshkosh	49,620	Fond du Lac	35,863
Racine	85,725	La Crosse	48,347	Manitowoc	32,547
Green Bay	87,889	Sheboygan	48,085	Wausau	32,426
Kenosha	77,685	Janesville	51,071	Superior	29,571
West Allis	63,982	Eau Claire	51,509	Brookfield	34,035
Wauwatosa	51,308	Waukesha	50,365		

Population of larger urbanized areas, 1980 census: Milwaukee, 1,207,008; Madison, 213,678; Duluth–Superior (Minn.–Wis.), 132,585; Racine, 118,987; Green Bay, 142,747.

CLIMATE. Milwaukee. Jan. 19°F (–7·2°C), July 70°F (21·1°C). Annual rainfall 29" (727 mm). *See* Great Lakes, p. 1379.

CONSTITUTION AND GOVERNMENT. The constitution, which dates from 1848, has 125 amendments. The legislative power is vested in a Senate of 33 members (1987 term: 19 Democrats, 14 Republicans) elected for 4 years, one-half elected alternately, and an Assembly of 99 members (1987 term: 55 Democrats, 43 Republicans, one vacancy) all elected simultaneously for 2 years. The Governor and Lieut.-Governor are elected for 4 years. All 6 constitutional officers serve 4-year terms.

Wisconsin has universal suffrage for all citizens 18 years of age or over; but, as there is no official list of voters, the size of the electorate is unknown; 2,211,689 voted for President in 1984.

Wisconsin is represented in Congress by 2 senators and 9 representatives.

In the 1984 presidential election Reagan polled 1,198,584 votes, Mondale, 995,740.

The capital is Madison. The state has 72 counties.

Governor: Tommy G. Thompson (R.), 1987–91 ($86,149).
Lieut.-Governor: Scott McCallum (R.), 1987–91 ($46,360).
Secretary of State: Douglas La Follette (D.), 1987–91 ($42,089).

BUDGET. For the year ending 30 June 1987 (Wisconsin Bureau of Financial Operations figures) total revenue for all funds was $13,194,862,901 ($5,414,384,761 from taxation and $2,105,167,430 from federal aid). General expenditure from all funds was $10,898,836,365 ($3,092,150,212 for education, $3,312,484,638 for human resources).

Per capita personal income (1986) was $14,249.

ENERGY AND NATURAL RESOURCES

Electricity. There were, Dec. 1986, 87 hydro-electric power plants (15 of them municipal, 57 private in Wisconsin; 15 private outside the state) operated by public utilities with a total installed capacity of 454,332 kw.; output, 1986, was 2,283,713mwh. The 15 outside plants are in Michigan; installed capacity 99,990 kw., output 436,351mwh.

Fossil fuel and nuclear plants numbered 23 (4 municipal); the former had a total installed capacity of 7,052,828 kw.; total output, (1986), 25,905,900mwh; the 2 nuclear plants had an installed capacity of 1,540,682 kw. and a total output (1986) of 11,093,856mwh.

There were also 32 internal combustion reciprocating plants (one in Michigan), with a total installed capacity of 116,042 kw. and a total output of (1985) 4,962mwh., and 17 internal combustion turbine plants with a total installed capacity of 1,285,950 kw.; total output was (1985) 15,212mwh.

There was a total of 155 plants, with a total installed capacity of 10,408,449 kw. and a total output of (1986) 39,279,826mwh.

Minerals. Sand and gravel, crushed stone and lime are the chief mineral products. Mineral production in 1985 was valued at $125·1m. This value included $51m. for sand and gravel, $42m. for crushed stone and about $19m. for lime. Value of all other minerals including natural abrasives, peat, cement and gemstones, $13m.

The large Forest County sulphide deposit (5,000 ft long, about 200 ft wide and over 2,000 ft deep and almost vertical) south of Crandon is estimated at over 77m. tons, averaging 5% zinc, 1% copper and lesser amounts of lead, silver and gold.

Agriculture. The total number of farms has declined in the last 50 years, but farms have become larger and more productive. On 1 Jan. 1987 there were 82,000 farms with a total acreage of 17·6m. acres and an average size of 214·6 acres, compared with 142,000 farms with a total acreage of 22·4m. acres and an average of 158 acres in 1959.

Cash income from products sold by Wisconsin farms in 1986, $5,001m.; $4,112m. from livestock and livestock products and $889m. from crops.

Wisconsin ranked first among the states in 1986 in the number of milch cows, milk and butter production, output of American, Brick, Muenster, Italian and Blue Mold Cheese. Production of all cheese accounted for 34·8% of the nation's total. The state also ranked first in bulk whole condensed milk, bulk skim condensed milk lactose for human use, whey solids in wet blends, whey protein concentrate and dry whey. The state also ranked first in mink pelts. In crops the state ranked first for snap beans and green peas for processing, all hay and corn for silage. Production of the principal field crops in 1986 included: Corn for grain, 365·8m. bu.; corn for silage, 10·64m. tons; oats, 52·7m. bu.; all hay, 10·8m. tons. Other crops of importance 20·2m. cwt of potatoes, 10·8m. lb. of tobacco, 1·2m. bbls of cranberries, 1·5m. cwt of carrots and the processing crops of 656,200 tons of sweet corn, 114,200 tons of green peas and 247,400 tons of snap beans.

Forestry. Wisconsin has an estimated 14·8m. acres of forest land (about 41·5% of land area). Of more than 14m. acres of commercial forest (June 1986) national forests covered 1·4m. acres; state forests, 0·7m.; county and municipal forests, 2·2m.; forest industry, 1·2m.; private land, 8·6m.

Growing stock (1985), 15,500m. cu. ft, of which 11,900m. cu. ft is hardwood and 3,600m. cu. ft, softwood. Largest timber stands: maple and birch, 4m. acres; aspen, 3·3m.; conifers, 2·8m.

INDUSTRY. Wisconsin has much heavy industry, particularly in the Milwaukee area. Non-electrical machinery is the major industrial group (19% of all manufacturing employment). Wood-using industries come second in value of product (over $9,000m. in 1986). Also important are food processing, fabricated metals, electrical machinery, paper and products, transport equipment, primary metals and printing. Manufacturing establishments in 1986 provided 26% of all employment, 31% of all earnings. The total number of establishments was 8,923 in 1986; the biggest concentration is in the south-east.

TOURISM. The tourist-vacation industry ranks among the first three in economic importance. The decline of lumbering and mining in the northern section of the state has increased dependency on the recreation industry. The Division of Tourism of the Department of Development spent $4,607,790 to promote tourism in financial year 1986–87.

COMMUNICATIONS

Roads. The state had on 1 Jan. 1987, 108,535 miles of highway. 75% of all roads in the state have a bituminous (or similar) surface. There are 11,869 miles of state trunk roads and 19,552 miles of county trunk roads.

In the year ending 1 Jan. 1986 Wisconsin registered 3,418,789 motor vehicles.

Railways. On 1 Aug. 1985 the state had 4,675 road-miles of railway.

Aviation. There were, in 1986, 97 publicly operated airports. Twelve scheduled air carrier airports were served by 8 regional and national air carriers.

Shipping. With the opening of the St Lawrence Seaway in 1959, 14 Wisconsin ports became accessible to ocean-going vessels. Green Bay, Kenosha, Manitowoc, Marinette, Milwaukee, Sheboygan and Superior (one of the world's largest iron-ore and grain ports) have developed foreign waterborne commerce. Cargo is also carried by barge on the river Mississippi. Other ports handle mainly Great Lakes traffic.

JUSTICE, RELIGION, EDUCATION AND WELFARE

Justice. The state's penal, reformatory and correctional system on 31 July 1987 held 5,580 men, 311 women and 526 juveniles in 15 state-owned and other institutions for adult and juvenile offenders; the probation and parole system was supervising 21,604 men and 4,593 women. Wisconsin does not impose the death penalty.

Religion. Wisconsin church affiliation, as a percentage of the 1980 population, was estimated at 32·2% Catholic, 20·06% Lutheran, 3·74% Methodist, 10·41% other churches and 32·6% un-affiliated.

Education. All children between the ages of 7 and 16 are required to attend school full-time to the end of the school term in which they become 16 years of age. Children living in a district with a vocational school must attend until 18. In 1986–87 the public school grades kindergarten–8 had 499,892 pupils and 30,116 (full-time equivalent) teachers; school grades 9–12 had 267,927 pupils and 16,926 teachers. Grade kindergarten–8 teachers' salaries, 1986–87, averaged $25,950; grade 9–12 teachers, $27,133.

In 1986–87 vocational, technical and adult schools had an enrolment of 438,082, and there were 6,719 faculty members (full-time equivalent). There is a school for the visually handicapped and a school for the deaf.

The University of Wisconsin, established in 1848, was joined by law in 1971 with the Wisconsin State Universities System to become the University of Wisconsin System with 13 degree granting campuses, 13 two-year campuses in the Center System, and the University Extension. The 26 campuses had, in 1986–87, 7,164 full-time professors and instructors and 1,896 (full-time equivalent) teaching assistants. In autumn 1986, 164,518 students enrolled (11,103 at Eau Claire, 4,978 at Green Bay, 9,659 at La Crosse, 44,384 at Madison, 25,930 at Milwaukee, 11,800 at Oshkosh, 5,195 at Parkside, 5,321 at Platteville, 5,612 at River Falls, 9,555 at Stevens Point, 7,686 at Stout, 2,307 at Superior, 10,897 at Whitewater and 10,091 in the Center System freshman-sophomore centres). There are also several independent institutions of higher education. These (with 1985–86 enrolment) include 2 universities (12,469), 18 liberal arts colleges (18,205), 5 technical and professional schools (4,067), and 4 theological seminaries (466).

The total expenditure, 1985–86, for all public education (except capital outlay and debt service) was \$4,479m.

The state maintains an educational broadcasting and television service.

Health. In Oct. 1986 the state had 141 general and allied special hospitals (20,156 beds), 18 mental hospitals (1,876 beds), 10 treatment centres for alcoholism and 1 rehabilitation centre. Patients in state mental hospitals and institutions for the mentally retarded in June 1986 averaged 2,632.

Social Security. On 1 Jan. 1974 the US Social Security administration assumed responsibility for financial aid (Supplemental Security Income) to persons 65 years old and over, blind persons and totally disabled persons, who satisfy requirements as to need. Recipients receive a federal payment plus a federally administered state supplementary payment, except for those who reside in a medical institution. In Oct. 1987, there were 77,941 SSI recipients in the state; payments were \$443 for a single individual, \$494 for an eligible individual with an ineligible spouse, and \$676 for an eligible couple. A special payment level of \$543 for an individual and \$1,029 for a couple may be paid with special approval for SSI recipients who are developmentally disabled or chronically mentally ill, living in a non-medical living arrangement not his or her own home. All SSI recipients receive state medical assistance coverage.

Under the Aid to Families with Dependent Children programme, 94,802 families constituting 287,488 persons received an average of \$498.81 per family in Aug. 1987; there were 3,892 county foster care cases (average cost per case of \$256.06) and 157 state cases (\$385.54). There were 537 group-home cases.

Books of Reference

Wisconsin Statistical Abstract. Wis. Dept. of Administration, State Bureau of Planning and Budget, Madison, 1979
Dictionary of Wisconsin Biography. Wis. Historical Society, Madison, 1960
Wisconsin Blue Book. Wis. Legislative Reference Bureau, Madison. Biennial
Current, R. N., *The History of Wisconsin,* Vol. II. State Historical Society of Wisconsin, Madison, 1976.—*Wisconsin, a History.* New York, 1977
Nesbit, R. C., *Wisconsin, A History.* State Historical Society of Wisconsin, Madison, 1973
Smith, Alice E., *The History of Wisconsin,* Vol. 1. State Historical Society of Wisconsin, Madison, 1973
Vexler, R. I., *Wisconsin Chronology and Factbook.* New York, 1978

State Information Agency: Legislative Reference Bureau, State Capitol, Madison, Wis. 53702. *Chief:* Dr H. Rupert Theobald.

WYOMING

HISTORY. Wyoming, first settled in 1834, was admitted into the Union on 10 July 1890. The name originated with the Delaware Indians.

AREA AND POPULATION. Wyoming is bounded north by Montana, east by South Dakota and Nebraska, south by Colorado, south-west by Utah and west by Idaho. Area 97,809 sq. miles, of which 820 sq. miles are water. The Yellowstone National Park occupies about 2,221,733 acres; the Grand Teton National Park has 310,350 acres. The federal government in 1979 owned 28,888,546 acres (46·1% of the total area of the state). The Federal Bureau of Land Management administers 17,546,188 acres.

Census population, 1 April 1980, 469,557, an increase of 41·25% since 1970. Estimate (1986) 485,111. Births in 1984 were 9,741 (20 per 1,000 population); deaths, 3,172 (6·4); infant deaths, 104 (10 per 1,000 live births); marriages, 5,783; divorces, 3,705.

Population in 5 census years was:

	White	Negro	Indian	Asiatic	Total	Per sq. mile
1910	140,318	2,235	1,486	1,926	145,965	1·5
1930	221,241	1,250	1,845	1,229	225,565	2·3
1960	322,922	2,183	4,020	805	330,066	3·4
			All others			
1970	323,619	2,568	6,229		332,416	3·4
1980	446,488	3,364	19,705		469,557	4·8

Of the total population in 1980, 240,560 were male, 295,898 were urban and those over 21 years of age numbered 295,908.

The largest towns are Cheyenne (capital), with census population in 1980 of 58,429; Casper, 59,287; Laramie, 24,410; Rock Springs, 19,458.

CLIMATE. Cheyenne. Jan. 25°F (−3·9°C), July 66°F (18·9°C). Annual rainfall 15″ (376 mm). Yellowstone Park. Jan. 18°F (−7·8°C), July 61°F (16·1°C). Annual rainfall 18″ (444 mm). *See* Mountain States, p. 1378.

CONSTITUTION AND GOVERNMENT. The constitution, drafted in 1890, has since had 43 amendments. The Legislature consists of a Senate of 30 members elected for 4 years, and a House of Representatives of 64 members elected for 2 years. The Governor is elected for 4 years.

The state sends to Congress 2 senators and 1 representative, elected by the voters of the entire state. The suffrage extends to all citizens, male and female, who have the usual residential qualifications.

In the 1984 presidential election Reagan polled 131,998 votes, Mondale, 53,154.

The capital is Cheyenne. The state contains 23 counties.

Governor: Mike Sullivan (D.), 1987–90 ($70,000).
Secretary of State: Kathy Karpan (D.), 1987–90 ($52,500).

BUDGET. In the fiscal year ending 1 July 1987 (State Treasurer's figures) cash receipts were $1,681,314,115; general expenditures were $1,504,570,195.

Per capita personal income (1984) was $12,238.

ENERGY AND NATURAL RESOURCES

Minerals. Wyoming is largely an oil-producing state. In 1986 the output of petroleum was valued at $2,889m.; natural gas, $1,238m. Other mining: Coal, $1,256m.; trona, $97m.; uranium, $17m.; other minerals mined include iron ore, feldspar, gypsum, limestone, phosphate, sand, gravel and marble, taconite, bentonite and hematite.

Agriculture. Wyoming is semi-arid, and agriculture is carried on by irrigation and by dry farming. In 1986 there were 8,800 farms and ranches; total land area 34·8m. acres.

Cash receipts, 1986, from crops, $236·4m.; from livestock and products, $314m. Principal commodities are wheat, cattle and calves, lambs and sheep, sugar-beet, barley, hay and wool. Animals on farms on 1 Jan. 1987 included 10,000 milch cows, 1·3m. all cattle, 775,000 sheep and lambs and 35,000 swine.

INDUSTRY AND TRADE

Industry. In 1987 there were 531 manufacturing establishments. There were 964 mining companies or producers. A large portion of the manufacturing in the state is based on natural resources, mainly oil and farm products. Leading industries are food, wood products (except furniture) and machinery (except electrical). There were 931 new business incorporations in 1986. The Wyoming Industrial Development Corporation assists in the development of small industries by providing credit.

Labour. The mining industry employed an average of 17,700 workers in June 1987. The total civilian labour force for June 1987 was 253,682; non-agricultural, 198,800. The average unemployment rate (Jan.-July 1987) was 8·3% and average weekly earnings $611 for mining (production workers).

Tourism. There are over 5m. tourists annually, mainly sportsmen. The state has the largest elk and pronghorn antelope herds in the world, 11 fish hatcheries and numerous wild game. Receipts from hunters and fishermen in 1986, $14,628,081.

COMMUNICATIONS

Roads. The roads in 1986 comprised 5,240 miles of federal highways, 349 miles of state highways and 914 miles of inter-state highway. There were (1986) 616,718 registered motor vehicles and 12 bus companies.

Railways. The railways, 1986, had a length of 2,615 mainline miles and 550 branch miles.

Aviation. There were 11 towns with commuter air services and 2 towns on jet routes in 1987.

JUSTICE, RELIGION, EDUCATION AND WELFARE

Justice. The state penitentiary in Oct. 1987 held 684 inmates and 16 on work release, the Womens' Center, 50. There are 2 other state correctional institutions. There have been 14 executions in Wyoming, 8 by hanging and 6 by lethal gas.

Religion. Chief religious bodies are the Roman Catholic (with 45,917 members in 1974), Mormon (28,954 in 1971) and Protestant churches (83,327 in 1974). There were 5,000 members of the Eastern Orthodox Church in 1972.

Education. In 1986–87 public elementary and secondary schools had 98,455 pupils. Enrolment in the parochial elementary and secondary schools was about 4,000. Approximately 6,273 public school teachers earned an average of $28,230. The average total expenditure per pupil for 1985–86 was $4,970.

The University of Wyoming, founded at Laramie in 1887, had in academic year 1986–87 9,980 students. There are 2-year colleges at Casper, Riverton, Torrington, Cheyenne, Powell, Rock Springs and Sheridan with credit course enrolment of 16,780 students in 1985–86.

Social Welfare. In Jan. 1974 the federal government assumed many of the previous state programmes including old age assistance, aid to the blind and disabled. In 1987 financial year, $16·2m. was distributed in food stamps; $17·6m. in aid to families with dependent children; $626,314 in general assistance; $1,189,902 in emergency assistance; $41m. in Medicaid. Total state expenditure on public assistance and social services programmes, financial year 1987, $123·5m.

Health. In 1986 the state had 30 hospitals. There are 29 registered nursing homes.

Books of Reference

News of Big Wyoming. Cheyenne, 1975
Official Directory. Secretary of State. Cheyenne. Biennial
1987 Wyoming Data Handbook. Dept. of Administration and Fiscal Control. Division of Research and Statistics, Cheyenne, 1987
Brown, R. H., *Wyoming: A Geography.* Boulder, 1980
Larsen, T. A., *History of Wyoming.* Rev. ed. Univ. of Nebraska, 1979
Treadway, T., *Wyoming.* New York, 1982
Vexler, R. I., *Wyoming Chronology and Factbook.* New York, 1978

OUTLYING TERRITORIES

Non-Self-Governing Territories: Summaries of Information Transmitted to the Secretary-General of the United Nations. Annual
Perkins, W. T., *The United States and its Dependencies.* Leiden, 1962
Wiens, H. J., *Pacific Island Bastions of the US.* New York and London, 1962

GUAM

HISTORY. Magellan is said to have discovered the island in 1521; it was ceded by Spain to the US by the Treaty of Paris (10 Dec. 1898). The island was captured by the Japanese on 10 Dec. 1941, and retaken by American forces from 21 July 1944. Guam is of great strategic importance; substantial numbers of naval and air force personnel occupy about one-third of the usable land.

AREA AND POPULATION. Guam is the largest and most southern island of the Marianas Archipelago, in 13° 26′ N. lat., 144° 43′ E. long. The length is 30 miles, the breadth from 4 to 10 miles, and there are about 209 sq. miles (541 sq. km). Agaña, the seat of government is about 8 miles from the anchorage in Apra Harbour. The census on 1 April 1980 showed a population of 105,979, an increase of 20,983 or 24·7% since 1970; those of Guamanian ancestry numbered about 50,794; foreign-born, 28,572; density was 507 per sq. mile. Estimated population (1984), 115,756. On 1 July 1980 transient residents connected with the military were estimated at 20,000. The Malay strain is predominant. The native language is Chamorro; English is the official language and is taught in all schools.

CLIMATE. Tropical maritime, with little difference in temperatures over the year. Rainfall is copious at all seasons, but is greatest from July to Oct. Agaña. Jan. 81°F (27·2°C), July 81°F (27·2°C). Annual rainfall 93″ (2,325 mm).

CONSTITUTION AND GOVERNMENT. Guam's constitutional status is that of an 'unincorporated territory' of the US. Entry of US citizens is unrestricted; foreign nationals are subject to normal regulations. In 1949–50 the President transferred the administration of the island from the Navy Department (who held it from 1899) to the Interior Department. The transfer conferred full citizenship on the Guamanians, who had previously been 'nationals' of the US. There was a referendum on status, 30 Jan. 1982. 38% of eligible voters voted; 48·5% of those favoured Commonwealth status.

The Governor and his staff constitute the executive arm of the government. The Legislature is unicameral; its powers are similar to those of an American state legislature. At the general election of Nov. 1982, the Democratic Party won 14 seats and the Republicans 7. All adults 18 years of age or over are enfranchised. Guam returns one non-voting delegate to the House of Representatives.

Governor: Ricardo Bordallo (D.), 1982–85. ($50,000).
Lieut.-Governor: Edward D. Reyes (D.), 1982–85.

ECONOMY

Budget. At 30 Sept. 1983 total assets were $65·1m.; federal grants $35·2m., taxes, $26·7m.: total liabilities were $149·3m.

Banking. Recent changes in banking law make it possible for foreign banks to operate in Guam.

NATURAL RESOURCES

Water. Supplies are from springs, reservoirs and groundwater; 65% comes from water-bearing limestone in the north. The Navy and Air Force conserve water in reservoirs. The Water Resources Research Centre is at Guam University.

Agriculture. The major products of the island are sweet potatoes, cucumbers, water melons and beans. In 1982 there were 140 full-time and 1,904 part-time farmers. Livestock (1985) included 2,000 cattle, 8,000 pigs, and (1984) 36,430 poultry. Commercial productions (1983) amounted to 6·6m. lb. of fruit and vegetables ($3·4m.), 567,000 doz. eggs ($811,093). There is an agricultural experimental station at Inarajan.

Fisheries. Fresh fish caught in 1982, 319,300 lb. Offshore fishing produced 100,687 lb., including 6,080 lb. of shrimps.

INDUSTRY AND TRADE

Industry. Guam Economic Development Authority controls three industrial estates: Cabras Island (32 acres); Calvo estate at Tamuning (26 acres); Harmon estate (16 acres). Industries include textile manufacture, cement and petroleum distribution, warehousing, printing, plastics and ship-repair. Other main sources of income are construction and tourism.

Labour. In 1983 51% of employment was in government, 18% in trade, 5% in construction, 13% in services, 4% in manufacturing, 5% in transport and 4% in finance.

Trade. Guam is the only American territory which has complete 'free trade'; excise duties are levied only upon imports of tobacco, liquid fuel and liquor. In the year ending 31 Dec. 1980 imports were valued at $544·1m. and accounted for 90% of trade.

Tourism. Tourism is developing; there were 1,900 visitors in 1964 and 407,100 in 1986.

COMMUNICATIONS

Roads. There are 419 miles of all-weather roads.

Aviation. Seven commercial airlines serve Guam.

Post and Broadcasting. Overseas telephone and radio dispatch facilities are available. In 1983 there were 23,442 telephones.

There are 4 commercial stations, a commercial television station, a public broadcasting station and a cable television station with 24 channels.

Newspapers. There is 1 daily newspaper, a twice-weekly paper, and 4 weekly publications (all of which are of military or religious interest only).

JUSTICE, RELIGION, EDUCATION AND WELFARE

Justice. The Organic Act established a District Court with jurisdiction in matters arising under both federal and territorial law; the judge is appointed by the President subject to Senate approval. There is also a Supreme Court and a Superior Court; all judges are locally appointed except the Federal District judge. Misdemeanours are under the jurisdiction of the police court. The Spanish law was superseded in 1933 by 5 civil codes based upon California law.

Religion. About 98% of the Guamanians are Roman Catholics; others are Baptists, Episcopalians, Bahais, Lutherans, Mormons, Presbyterians, Jehovah's Witnesses and members of the Church of Christ and Seventh Day Adventists.

Education. Elementary education is compulsory. There are Chamorro Studies courses and bi-lingual teaching programmes to integrate the Chamorro language and culture into elementary and secondary school courses. There were, Dec. 1983, 24 elementary schools, 6 junior high schools, 5 senior high schools, one vocational-technical school for high school students and adults and 1 school for handicapped children. There were 17,725 elementary school pupils, 7,418 junior high and 5,776 senior high school pupils. Department of Education staff included 1,258 teachers. The Catholic schools system also operates 3 senior high schools, 3 junior high and 5 elementary schools. The Seventh Day Adventist Guam Mission Academy operates a school from grades 1 through 12, serving over 100 students. St John's Episcopal Preparatory School provides education for 530 students between kindergarten and the 9th grade. The University of Guam (an accredited institution) had 2,774 students, 1983–84.

Health. There is a hospital, 8 nutrition centres, a school health programme and an extensive immunization programme. Emphasis is on disease prevention, health education and nutrition.

Books of Reference

*Report (Annual) of the Governor of Guam to the US Department of Interior
Guam Annual Economic Review.* Economic Research Center, Agaña

Carano, P., and Sanchez, P. C., *Complete History of Guam.* Rutland, Vt., 1964

FREELY-ASSOCIATED STATES

HISTORY. Under the Treaty of Versailles (1919) Japan was appointed mandatory to the former German possessions north of the Equator. In 1946 the US agreed to administer the former Japanese-mandated islands of the Caroline, Marshall and Mariana groups (except Guam) as a Trusteeship for the United Nations; the trusteeship agreement was approved by the Security Council 27 April 1947 and came into effect on 18 July 1947. The Trust Territory was administered by the US Navy until 1951, when all the islands except Tinian and Saipan in the Marianas were transferred to the Secretary of the Interior. In 1962 the Interior Department assumed responsibility for them also. In April 1976 the US government separated the administration of the Northern Marianas (*see* below) from that of the rest of the Trust Territory. The rest was 3 entities, each with its own constitution: the Marshall Islands, the Federated States of Micronesia (Yap, Kosrae, Truk and Pohnpei) and the Republic of Palau. The US Congress agreed compacts of free association with all except Palau (*see* below) in 1985–86; free association gives the USA the authority to control military and defence activities in return for federal government assistance and budget supports to the autonomous constitutional governments.

AREA AND POPULATION. The territories extend from 1° to 22° N. lat. and from 137° to 172° E. long. The area is generally known as Micronesia, or 'land of the small islands' (Guam, Kiribati and Nauru, not part of the territories, are also ethnically and geographically Micronesian).

Areas, populations and headquarters:

	Sq. miles	1980 Census	Estimate 1984	Headquarters
Kosrae	42	5,491	6,262	Lelu
Pohnpei	134	22,081	26,922	Kolonia
Truk	49	37,488	44,596	Moen
Yap	46	8,100	10,595	Colonia
Federated States of Micronesia	271	73,160	88,375	Kolonia
Marshall Islands	70	30,873	34,923	Majuro
Total	341	104,033	123,298	

Nine different languages are spoken, each with variations; English is used in the schools and is the official language.

CLIMATE. Marked by high temperatures throughout the year and high rainfall. Marshall Islands, Jaluit. Jan. 81°F (27·2°C), July 82°F (27·8°C). Annual rainfall 161″ (4,034 mm). Caroline Islands, Ponape. Jan. 80°F (26·7°C), July 79°F (26·1°C). Annual rainfall 194″ (4,859 mm).

CONSTITUTION AND GOVERNMENT. The Federated States of Micronesia has a congress, a Federal President and Vice-President, both elected for four-year terms; each state has an elected governor (four years) and a unicameral assembly. The congress consists of 1 four-year Senator from each state, and 10 two-year Senators elected on a population basis. The Marshall Islands form a republic with an elected assembly and an elected president, both serving four-year terms. The assembly has 33 members, and a presidential candidate must be a member.

INDUSTRY. Tourism is the main source of income from overseas; industrial development is limited. There is some commercial fishing and agriculture, a coconut-processing plant and a tuna-freezing plant. Small scale manufacturing has begun, mainly of garments, buttons (from trochus shell) and handicraft goods.

COMMUNICATIONS

Aviation. The island groups are served by Continental Air Micronesia, Japan Airlines and Air Nauru providing connexions to the South Pacific, Taiwan, the Philippines, Japan, Hawaii and Guam. Several small commuter airlines connect Guam with Yap and Ulithi, Pohnpei and Kosrae, Pingelap and Mokil. Air Marshall Islands serves the Marshall Islands, Kosrae and Pohnpei. There are connexions to international routes in Guam.

JUSTICE, RELIGION, EDUCATION AND WELFARE

Justice. Local constitutions and government statutes are the basis for law. Local customs are recognized and protected in legal practice, when not in conflict with higher law.

Religion. Freedom of religion is guaranteed in all constitutions.

Education. Education is free and compulsory through elementary school (grades 1–8). There are public and private elementary and secondary schools and government post-secondary education at the 2-year College of Micronesia.

Health. The public health system, which includes 7 main hospitals as well as other hospitals in population centres and dispensaries on outlying islands, is carried on by a staff consisting chiefly of trained Micronesian medical and dental officers and assistants, US doctors, UN volunteers and local support staff.

Books of Reference

Report to the United Nations Trusteeship Council, 1979. Dept. of State, Washington, D.C., 1984
Basic Information. Office of Freely Associated States' Affairs, Department of State, Washington D.C. 20520; Office of the President, Republic of the Marshall Islands, Majuro; Office of the President, Federated States of Micronesia, Ponape, Caroline Islands.

REPUBLIC OF PALAU

The Republic lies west of the Federated States of Micronesia, and has a land area of 192 sq. miles, divided between 26 larger islands and more than 300 islets. The largest island is Babelthuap (143 sq. miles). Population (1980 census) 12,116; 1987 estimate, 15,000. The language is Palauan.

The headquarters is Koror. The Republic has a bicameral parliament with an 18-member Senate, and 16-member House of Delegates, both elected for four years as are the president and vice-president. The Constitution, adopted in July 1980, provided for ultimate free-association status, but it also defines Palau as a nuclear-free zone; this is in conflict with the United States' intention of basing nuclear weapons on the islands, as part of the defence responsibility included in the Free Association Compact. To cancel the anti-nuclear clause and accept the Compact required a 75% vote at referendum. When this was not achieved by successive referenda, the constitution was amended to allow a simple majority to suffice. Palau voted in favour of the Compact (67%) in Aug. 1987; the decision was to be ratified by the US Congress early in 1988.

THE NORTHERN MARIANAS

The islands form a chain, extending 560 km north from Guam; there are 16 islands, all mountainous, with a combined land area of 477 sq. km (184 sq. miles). On 17

June 1975 the voters of the Northern Mariana Islands, in a plebiscite observed by the UN, adopted the covenant to establish a Commonwealth of the Northern Mariana Islands in Union with the USA. In April 1976 the US government approved the convenant and separated the administration of the Northern Marianas from that of the rest of the Pacific Islands Trust Territory.

The Northern Marianas form a Commonwealth with an elected governor and lieutenant-governor, both serving 4-year terms; the bicameral parliament has a 9-member Senate, elected for four years, and a 15-member House of Representatives (elected for two).

The population, 1980 census, 16,780 (1984 estimate, 19,635). Saipan is the seat of government. The official language is English, 55% (1980) speak Chamorro.

Books of Reference

Basic Information. Office of the Governor, Commonwealth of the Northern Mariana Islands, Saipan.

AMERICAN SAMOA

HISTORY. The Samoan Islands were first visited by Europeans in the 18th century; the first recorded visit was in 1722. On 14 July 1889 a treaty between the USA, Germany and Great Britain proclaimed the Samoan islands neutral territory, under a 4-power government consisting of the 3 treaty powers and the local native government. By the Tripartite Treaty of 7 Nov. 1899, ratified 19 Feb. 1900, Great Britain and Germany renounced in favour of the US all rights over the islands of the Samoan group east of 171° long. west of Greenwich, the islands to the west of that meridian being assigned to Germany (now the Independent State of Western Samoa, *see* p. 1592). The islands of Tutuila and Aunu'u were ceded to the US by their High Chiefs on 17 April 1900, and the islands of the Manu'a group on 16 July 1904. Congress accepted the islands under a Joint Resolution approved 20 Feb. 1929. Swain's Island, 210 miles north of the Samoan Islands, was annexed in 1925 and is administered as an integral part of American Samoa.

AREA AND POPULATION. The islands (Tutuila, Aunu'u, Ta'u, Olosega, Ofu and Rose) are approximately 650 miles east-north-east of Fiji. The total area of American Samoa is 76·1 sq. miles (197 sq. km); population, 1980, 32,297, nearly all Polynesians or part-Polynesians. The island's 3 Districts are Eastern (population, 1980, 17,311), Western (13,227) and Manu'a (1,732). There is also Swain's Island, with an area of 1·9 sq. miles and 29 inhabitants (1980), which lies 210 miles to the north west. Rose Island (uninhabited) is 0·4 sq. mile in area. In 1981 there were 1,158 births and 153 deaths.

CLIMATE. A tropical maritime climate with a small annual range of temperature and plentiful rainfall. Pago-Pago. Jan. 83°F (28·3°C), July 80°F (26·7°C). Annual rainfall 194″ (4,850 mm).

CONSTITUTION AND GOVERNMENT. American Samoa is constitutionally an unorganized unincorporated territory of the US administered under the Department of the Interior. Its indigenous inhabitants are US nationals and are classified locally as citizens of American Samoa with certain privileges under local laws not granted to non-indigenous persons. Polynesian customs (not inconsistent with US laws) are respected.

Fagatogo is the seat of the Government.

The islands are organized in 15 counties grouped in 3 districts; these counties and districts correspond to the traditional political units. On 25 Feb. 1948 a bicameral legislature was established, at the request of the Samoans, to have advisory legislative functions. With the adoption of the Constitution of 22 April 1960, and the revised Constitution of 1967, the legislature was vested with limited law-making authority. The lower house, or House of Representatives, is composed of

20 members elected by universal adult suffrage and 1 non-voting member for Swain's Island. The upper house, or Senate, is comprised of 18 members elected, in the traditional Samoan manner, in meetings of the chiefs.

Governor: A. P. Lutali.
Lieut.-Governor: Eni F. Hunkin, Jr.

ECONOMY

Planning. The first formal Economic Development and Planning Office completed its first year in 1971. Much has been done to promote economic expansion within the Territory and a large amount of outside investment interest has been stimulated.

The Office initiated the first Territorial Comprehensive Plan. This plan when completed will, with periodic updating, provide a guideline to territorial development for the next 20 years. The planning programme was made possible under a Housing and Urban Development '701' grant programme, and Economic Development Administration '302' planning programmes.

The focus will be on physical development and the problems of a rapidly increasing population with severely limited labour resources.

Budget. The chief sources of revenue are annual federal grants from the US, and local revenues from taxes, and duties, and receipts from commercial operations (enterprise and special revenue funds), utilities, rents and leases and liquor sales. During the financial year 1983–84 the Government had a revenue of $76·6m. including local appropriations of $9·5m., federal appropriations of $39·6m. and enterprise funds of $17·5m.

Banking. The American Samoa branch of the Bank of Hawaii and the American Samoa Bank offer all commercial banking services. The Development Bank of American Samoa, government owned, is concerned primarily through loans and guarantees with the economic advancement of the Territory.

ENERGY AND NATURAL RESOURCES

Electricity. Net power generated (financial year 1981) was 72·2m. kwh., of which 23·1m. kwh. was supplied to large power users and 20·2m. kwh. to householders. All the Manu'a islands have electricity.

Agriculture. Of the 48,640 acres of land area, 11,000 acres are suitable for tropical crops; most commercial farms are in the Tafuna plains and west Tutuila. Principal crops are taro, bread-fruit, yams, bananas and coconuts. Local sales (1982): taro, 770,315 lb.; bananas, 1m. lb.; vegetables, 584,143 lb.

Livestock (1986): Pigs, 11,000; (1984) goats, 8,000; poultry, 45,000.

INDUSTRY AND TRADE

Industry. Fish canning is important, employing the second largest number of people (after government). Attempts are being made to provide a variety of light industries. Tuna fishing and local inshore fishing are both expanding.

Commerce. In 1982 American Samoa exported goods valued at $186,782,060 and imported goods valued at $119,416,918. Chief exports are canned tuna, watches, pet foods and handicrafts. Chief imports are building materials, fuel oil, food, jewellery, machines and parts, alcoholic beverages and cigarettes.

COMMUNICATIONS

Roads. There are (1983) about 76 miles of paved roads and 16 miles of unpaved within the Federal Aid highway system. There are 21 miles of other unpaved roads. Motor vehicles registered, 1983, 3,657.

Aviation. South Pacific Island Airways and Polynesian Airlines operate daily services between American Samoa and Western Samoa. South Pacific Island Airways also operates between Pago Pago and Honolulu, and between Pago Pago and Tonga. The islands are also served by Air Nauru which operates between Pago Pago, Tahiti and Auckland, and Air Pacific (Fiji and westward). South Pacific and Manu'a Air Transport run local services.

Shipping. The harbour at Pago Pago, which nearly bisects the island of Tutuila, is the only good harbour for large vessels in Samoa. By sea, there is a twice-monthly service between Fiji, New Zealand and Australia and regular service between US, South Pacific ports, Honolulu and Japan.

Post and Broadcasting. A commercial radiogram service is available to all parts of the world through 2 principal trunks, United States and Western Samoa. Commercial phone and telex services are operated to all parts of the world on a 24-hour service. Number of telephones (Sept. 1983), 6,029; telex subscribers, 78.

JUSTICE, EDUCATION AND WELFARE

Justice. Judicial power is vested firstly in a High Court. The trial division has original jurisdiction of all criminal and civil cases. The probate division has jurisdiction of estates, guardianships, trusts and other matters. The land and title division decides cases relating to disputes involving communal land and Matai title court rules on questions and controversy over family titles. The appellate division hears appeals from trial, land and title and probate divisions as well as having original jurisdiction in selected matters. The appellate court is the court of last resort. Two American judges sit with 5 Samoan judges permanently. In addition there are temporary judges or assessors who sit occasionally on cases involving Samoan customs. There is also a District Court with limited jurisdiction and there are 69 village courts.

Education. Education is compulsory between the ages of 6 and 18. The Government (1983) maintains 24 consolidated elementary schools, 5 senior high schools with technical departments, 1 community college, special education classes for the handicapped and 92 Early Childhood Education Centres for pre-school children. Total elementary and secondary enrolment (1983), 8,300; in ECE schools, 1,611; classes for the handicapped, 68; total elementary and secondary classroom teachers, 480. Ten private schools had 2,108 students. Learning is by a variety of media including television.

Health. The Department of Health provides the only curative and preventive medical and dental care in American Samoa. It operates a general hospital (173 beds including 49 bassinets), 3 dispensaries on Tutuila, 4 dispensaries in the Manu'a group, 1 on Aunu'u and 1 on Swain's Island. A $3·5m. tropical medical centre was completed and placed in service in 1968. This now embraces the general hospital as well as preventive health services and out-patient clinics for surgery, obstetrics, gynaecology, emergencies, family practice, internal medicine, paediatrics; there are clinics for treatment of the eye, ear, nose and throat, dental and public health departments.

In 1983 there were 27 doctors, 7 dentists, 2 optometrists, 3 nurse anaesthetists, and 3 physician assistants. Total number of health service employees, 397.

OTHER PACIFIC TERRITORIES

Johnston Atoll. Two small islands 1,150 km south-west of Hawaii, administered by the US Air Force. Area, under 1 sq. mile; population (1980 census) 327, with Sand Island.

Midway Islands. Two small islands at the western end of the Hawaiian chain, administered by the US Navy. Area, 2 sq. miles; population (1980 census) 453.

Wake Island. Three small islands 3,700 km west of Hawaii, administered by the US Air Force. Area, 3 sq. miles; population (1980 census) 302.

COMMONWEALTH OF PUERTO RICO

HISTORY. Puerto Rico, by the treaty of 10 Dec. 1898 (ratified 11 April 1899), was ceded by Spain to the US. The name was changed from Porto Rico to Puerto Rico by an Act of Congress approved 17 May 1932. Its territorial constitution was determined by the 'Organic Act' of Congress (2 March 1917) known as the 'Jones Act', which ruled until 25 July 1952, when the present constitution of the Commonwealth of Puerto Rico was proclaimed.

AREA AND POPULATION. Puerto Rico is the most easterly of the Greater Antilles and lies between the Dominican Republic and the US Virgin Islands. The island has a land area of 3,459 sq. miles and a population, according to the census of 1980, of 3,196,520, an increase of 484,487 or 17·9% over 1970. Of the population in 1970 about 529,000 were bilingual, Spanish being the mother tongue and (with English) one of the two official languages. Urban population (1980) 2,134,365 (66·8%).

Vital statistics (1984–85): Births, 63,629 (19·4 per 1,000 population); deaths, 23,194 (7·1); deaths under 1 year, 947 (14·9 per 1,000 live births).

Chief towns (1980) are: San Juan, 434,849; Bayamón, 196,207; Ponce, 189,046; Carolina, 165,954; Caguas, 117,759; Mayaguez, 96,193; Arecibo, 86,766.

The Puerto Rican island of Vieques, 10 miles to the east, has an area of 51·7 sq. miles and 7,662 inhabitants. The island of Culebra, with 1,265 inhabitants, between Puerto Rico and St Thomas, has a good harbour.

CONSTITUTION AND GOVERNMENT. Puerto Rico has representative government, the franchise being restricted to citizens 18 years of age or over, residence (1 year) and such additional qualifications as may be prescribed by the Legislature of Puerto Rico, but no property qualification may be imposed. Women were enfranchised in 1932 (with a literacy test) and fully in 1936. Puerto Ricans do not vote in the US presidential elections, though individuals living on the mainland are free to do so subject to the local electoral laws. The executive power resides in a Governor, elected directly by the people every 4 years. Fourteen heads of departments form the Governor's advisory council, also designated as his Council of Secretaries. The legislative functions are vested in a Senate, composed of 27 members (2 from each of the 8 senatorial districts and 11 senators at large), and the House of Representatives, composed of 51 members (1 from each of the 40 representative districts and 11 elected at large). Puerto Rico sends to Congress a Resident Commissioner to the US, elected by the people for a term of 4 years, but he has no vote in Congress. Puerto Rican men are subject to conscription in US services.

On 27 Nov. 1953 President Eisenhower sent a message to the General Assembly of the UN stating 'if at any time the Legislative Assembly of Puerto Rico adopts a resolution in favour of more complete or even absolute independence' he 'will immediately thereafter recommend to Congress that such independence be granted'.

For an account of the constitutional developments prior to 1952, see THE STATESMAN'S YEAR-BOOK, 1952, p. 742. The new constitution was drafted by a Puerto Rican Constituent Assembly and approved by the electorate at a referendum on 3 March 1952. It was then submitted to Congress, which struck out Section 20 of Article 11 covering the 'right to work' and the 'right to an adequate standard of living'; the remainder was passed and proclaimed by the Governor on 25 July 1952.

At the election on 4 Nov. 1984 the Popular Democratic Party, headed by Rafael Hernández Colon, polled 822,783 votes (47·8% of the total); the New Progressive Party, headed by Carlos Romero Barceló, polled 768,742 votes (44·6% of the total); the Independence Party (full independence by constitutional means), 61,316 (3·6% of the total); Renewal Puerto Rican Party, 69,865 votes (3·6% of the total).

Governor: Rafael Hernández Colon (Popular Democratic Party), 1984–88 ($35,000).

ECONOMY

Budget. Central Government budget, year ending 30 June 1986: Balance at 1 July 1985, $63,752,000; receipts, $6,079,319,000; disbursements, $5,863,929,000.

Assessed value of property, 30 June 1985, was $9,544·6m., and bonded indebtedness (30 June 1987), $2,551m.

The US administers and finances the postal service and maintains air and naval bases. US payments in Puerto Rico, including direct expenditures (mainly military), grants-in-aid and other payments to individuals and to business totalled: 1983–84, $3,699·6m; 1984–85, $3,882·9m.; 1985–86, $4,180·2m.; $4,221·6m.

Banking. Banks on 30 June 1987 had total deposits of $21,990·9m. Bank loans were $9,980m. This includes 18 commercial banks, 2 government banks and 3 trust companies.

NATURAL RESOURCES

Minerals. Production: Cement (1984–85), 1m. short tons; stone (1984), 5·8m. short tons, value $27·7m. Total value of mineral production in 1984 (estimate) was $120m.

Agriculture. In 1974 there were 47 'proportional profit' farms of 22,051 cords (about 22,704 acres) (mostly sugar-cane). The land had been bought from the big corporations by the Land Authority.

Production of raw sugar, 96 degrees basis, 1987 crop year, was 96,416 tons.

Livestock (1987): Cattle, 579,129; pigs, 197,962; poultry, 9·3m.

COMMERCE. In 1986–87 imports amounted to $10,723·8m., of which $6,977·4m. came from US; exports were valued at $12,067·8m., of which $10,515·6m. went to US.

In financial year 1987 the US took: Sugar, 11,692 short tons; cigarettes, cigars and cheroots, 1,049,930,000 units; other tobacco and products, 2,475,470 lb.; rum, 20,474,669 proof gallons.

Puerto Rico is not permitted to levy taxes on imports.

Total trade between Puerto Rico and UK (British Department of Trade returns, in £1,000 sterling):

	1983	1984	1985	1986	1987
Imports to UK	58,804	76,854	126,971	81,131	76,347
Exports and re-exports from UK	35,936	72,695	117,861	49,620	39,405

COMMUNICATIONS

Roads. The Department of Public Works had under maintenance in June 1985, 6,876·1 km of paved road. Motor vehicles registered 30 June 1987, 1,569,309.

Shipping. In financial year 1986–87, 9,338 American and foreign vessels of 53,378,302 gross tons entered and cleared Puerto Rico.

Post and Broadcasting. In 1987 there were 104 broadcasting stations and 14 television companies. There were (1987) 871,311 telephones (excluding Puerto Rico Communication Authority).

Cinemas (1983–84). Cinemas had an annual attendance of 5·6m.

Newspapers. In 1987 there were 5 main newspapers, *El Nuevo Día* had a daily circulation of about 194,605 (Aug. 1987); *El Vocero*, 212,470 (Oct. 1986); *San Juan Star*, 47,000 (May 1986); *El Mundo*, 120,000 (Aug. 1987) and *El Reportero*, 35,000 (1987).

JUSTICE AND EDUCATION

Justice. The Commonwealth judiciary system is headed by a Supreme Court of 7 members, appointed by the Governor, and consists of a Superior Tribunal with 11 sections and 92 superior judges, a District Tribunal with 38 sections and 99 district judges, and 60 municipal judges all appointed by the Governor. The police force (1984) consisted of 10,052 men and women.

Education. Education was made compulsory in 1899, but in 1981, 3·6% of the children still had no access to schooling. The percentage of illiteracy in 1980 was 10·3% of those 10 years of age or older. Total enrolment in public schools, 1986–87, was 679,489. Accredited private schools had 99,488 pupils (1985–86). All instruction below senior high school standard is given in Spanish only.

The University of Puerto Rico, in Río Piedras, 7 miles from San Juan, had 56,549 students in 1986–87 of which 3,713 were in 5 Regional Colleges. Higher education is also available in the Inter-American University of Puerto Rico (41,690 students in 1986–87), the Catholic University of Puerto Rico (11,762), the Sacred Heart College (8,274) and the Fundacion Educativa Ana G. Méndez (17,530). These and other private colleges and universities had 98,486 students.

Books of Reference

Statistical Information: The area of Economic Research and Evaluation of the Puerto Rico Planning Board publishes: *(a)* annual *Economic Report to the Governor; (b) External Trade Statistics* (annual report); *(c) Reports on national income and balance of payments; (d) Socio-Economic Statistics* (since 1940); *(e) Puerto Rico Monthly Economic Indicators.* In addition there are annual reports by various Departments.

Annual Reports. Governor of Puerto Rico. Washington
Bloomfield, R. J., *Puerto Rico: The Search for a National Policy.* Boulder, 1985
Carr, R., *Puerto Rico: A Colonial Experiment.* New York Univ. Press, 1984
Cevallos, E., *Puerto Rico.* [Bibliography], Oxford and Santa Barbara, 1985
Crampsey, R. A., *Puerto Rico.* Newton Abbot, 1973
Dietz, J. L., *Economic History of Puerto Rico: Institutional Change and Capital Development.* Princeton Univ. Press, 1987
Falk, P. S., (ed.) *The Political Status of Puerto Rico.* Lexington, Mass., 1986

Commonwealth Library: Univ. of Puerto Rico Library, Rio Piedras. *Librarian:* José Lázaro.

VIRGIN ISLANDS OF THE UNITED STATES

HISTORY. The Virgin Islands of the United States, formerly known as the Danish West Indies, were named and claimed for Spain by Columbus in 1493. They were later settled by Dutch and English planters, invaded by France in the mid-17th century and abandoned by the French *c.* 1700, by which time Danish influence had been established. St Croix was held by the Knights of Malta between two periods of French rule.

They were purchased by the United States from Denmark for $25m. in a treaty ratified by both nations and proclaimed 31 March 1917. Their value was wholly strategic, inasmuch as they commanded the Anegada Passage from the Atlantic Ocean to the Caribbean Sea and the approach to the Panama Canal. Although the inhabitants were made US citizens in 1927, the islands are, constitutionally, an 'unincorporated territory'.

AREA AND POPULATION. The Virgin Islands group, lying about 40 miles due east of Puerto Rico, comprises the islands of St Thomas (28 sq. miles), St Croix (84 sq. miles), St John (20 sq. miles) and about 50 small islets or cays, mostly un-inhabited. The total area of the 3 principal islands is 136 sq. miles, of which the US Government owns 9,599 acres as National Park.

The population, according to the census of 1 April 1985, was 110,800, an increase of 15,209 or 16% since 1980. Population had slowly declined since 1835, when it stood at 43,000, but began to recover in the 1940s, and increased greatly after 1960. Population of St Croix, 55,300; St Thomas, 52,660; St John, 2,800. About 20–25% (1980) are native-born, 35–40% from other Caribbean islands, 10% from mainland USA and 5% from Europe. St Croix has over 40% of Puerto Rican origin or extraction, Spanish speaking. In financial year 1986, live births were 2,266 and deaths, 507.

The capital and only city, Charlotte Amalie, on St Thomas, had a population

(1985) of 52,660; there are two towns on St Croix. Christiansted with (1980) 2,856 and Frederiksted with 1,054.

CLIMATE. Average temperatures vary from 77°F to 82°F throughout the year; humidity is low. Average annual rainfall, about 45 inches. The islands lie in the hurricane belt; tropical storms with heavy rainfall can occur in late summer, but hurricanes rarely.

CONSTITUTION AND GOVERNMENT. The Organic Act of 22 July 1954 gives the US Department of the Interior full jurisdiction; some limited legislative powers are given to a single-chambered legislature, composed of 15 senators elected for 2 years representing the two legislative districts of St Croix and St Thomas-St John.

The Governor is elected by the residents. Since 1954 there have been four attempts to redraft the Constitution, to provide for greater autonomy. Each has been rejected by the electorate. The latest was defeated in a referendum in Nov. 1981, 50% of the electorate participating.

For administration, there are 15 executive departments, 14 of which are under commissioners and the other, the Department of Justice, under an Attorney-General. The US Department of the Interior appoints a Federal Comptroller of government revenue and expenditure.

The franchise is vested in residents who are citizens of the United States, 18 years of age or over. In 1986 there were 34,183 voters, of whom 26,377 participated in the local elections that year.

They do not participate in the US presidential election but they have a non-voting representative in Congress.

The capital is Charlotte Amalie, on St Thomas Island.

Governor: Alexander A. Farrelly ($62,400).
Lieut.-Governor: Derek N. Hodge ($57,000).

ECONOMY

Budget. Under the 1954 Organic Act finances are provided partly from local revenues—customs, federal income tax, real and personal property tax, trade tax, excise tax, pilotage fees, etc.—and partly from Federal Matching Funds, being the excise taxes collected by the federal government on such Virgin Islands products transported to the mainland as are liable.

Budget for financial year 1987, $255·5m.

Currency and Banking. United States currency became legal tender on 1 July 1934. Banks are the Chase Manhattan Bank; the Bank of Nova Scotia; the First Federal Savings and Loan Association of Puerto Rico; Barclays Bank International; Citibank; First Pennsylvania Bank; Banco Popular de Puerto Rico, and the First Virgin Islands Federal Savings Bank.

ENERGY AND NATURAL RESOURCES

Electricity. The Virgin Islands Water and Power Authority provides electric power from generating plants on St Croix and St Thomas; St John is served by power cable and emergency generator.

Water. There are 6 de-salinization plants with maximum daily capacity of 8·7m. gallons of fresh water. Rain-water remains the most reliable source. Every building must have a cistern to provide rain-water for drinking, even in areas served by mains (10 gallons capacity per sq. ft of roof for a single-storey house).

Agriculture. Land for fruit, vegetables and animal feed is available on St Croix, and there are tax incentives for development. Sugar has been terminated as a commercial crop and over 4,000 acres of prime land could be utilized for food crops.

Livestock (1986): Cattle, 5,802; goats, 4,556; pigs, 2,300; sheep, 2,879, poultry, 18,360.

Fisheries. There is a fishermen's co-operative with a market at Christiansted. There is a shellfish-farming project at Rust-op-Twist, St Croix.

INDUSTRY AND TRADE

Industry. The main occupations on St Thomas are tourism and government service; on St Croix manufacturing is more important. Manufactures include rum (the most valuable product), watches, pharmaceuticals and fragrances. Industries in order of revenue: tourism, refining oil, watch assembly, rum distilling, construction.

Commerce. Exports, calendar year 1986, totalled $2,119m. (of which $2,052m. to USA) and imports $2,643m. ($1,453m.).

Total trade between the US Virgin Islands and UK (financial years, British Department of Trade returns, in £1,000 sterling):

	1984	1985	1986	1987
Imports to UK	56,871	514	5,455	2,674
Exports and re-exports from UK	3,657	4,060	5,955	6,503

Tourism. Tourism is the most important business. There were about 1·52m. visitors in 1986 spending $509·8m.; 728,700 came by air and 827,151 on cruise ships, mainly to St Thomas which has a good, natural deepwater harbour.

COMMUNICATIONS

Roads. The Virgin Islands have (1986) 660 miles of roads, and 48,800 motor vehicles registered.

Aviation. There is a daily cargo and passenger service between St Thomas and St Croix. Alexander Hamilton Airport on St Croix can take all aircraft except Concorde. Cyril E. King Airport on St Thomas takes 727-class aircraft. There are air connexions to mainland USA, other Caribbean islands, Latin America and Europe.

Shipping. The whole territory has free port status. There is an hourly boat service between St Thomas and St John.

Post and Broadcasting. All three Virgin Islands have a dial telephone system. In Dec. 1986 there were 39,232 telephones. Direct dialling to Puerto Rico and the mainland, and internationally, is now possible. Worldwide radio telegraph service is also available.

The islands are served by 10 radio stations, 4 television stations 3 newspapers, 2 of them daily, and several monthlies.

RELIGION AND EDUCATION

Religion. There are churches of the Protestant, Roman Catholic and Jewish faiths in St Thomas and St Croix and Protestant and Roman Catholic churches in St John.

Education. Education is compulsory between the ages of 4½ and 16 years, inclusive. In 1987–88 there were 34 public schools (ranging from kindergarten to high schools); enrolment was 24,000; 36 private schools had 6,460 pupils. In 1985–86 revenues to school district were $103·2m., of which $85·83m. was from local, and $17·4m. from federal sources. Public school expenditure was $76·75m., of which $52·2m. was for instruction. In autumn 1987 the University of the Virgin Islands had 2,545 registered students; 2,361 undergraduates and 184 graduate students. The College is part of the United States land-grant network of higher education.

Books of Reference

Boyer, W. W., *America's Virgin Islands.* Durham, N.C., 1983
Dookhan, I., *A History of the Virgin Islands of the United States.* Caribbean Univ. Press, 1974
Lewis, G. K., *The Virgin Islands: A Caribbean Lilliput.* Northwestern University Press, Evanston, 1972

URUGUAY

Capital: Montevideo
Population: 2·95m. (1986)
GNP per capita: US$1,800 (1984)

República Oriental del Uruguay

HISTORY. The Republic of Uruguay, formerly a part of the Spanish Viceroyalty of Río de la Plata and subsequently a province of Brazil, declared its independence 25 Aug. 1825 which was recognized by the treaty between Argentina and Brazil signed at Rio de Janeiro 27 Aug. 1828. The first constitution was adopted 18 July 1830.

AREA AND POPULATION. Uruguay is bounded on the north-east by Brazil, on the south-east by the Atlantic, on the south by the Río de la Plata and on the west by Argentina. The area is 186,926 sq. km (72,172 sq. miles). The following table shows the area and the population of the 19 departments at census 1975:

Departments	Sq. km	Census 1975	Capital	Census 1975
Artigas	11,928	58,404	Artigas	29,256
Canelones	4,536	325,594	Canelones	15,938
Cerro-Largo	13,648	74,027	Melo	38,260
Colonia	6,106	111,832	Colonia	16,895
Durazno	11,643	55,699	Durazno	25,811
Flores	5,144	24,745	Trinidad	17,598
Florida	10,417	67,129	Florida	25,030
Lavalleja	10,016	65,180	Minas	35,433
Maldonado	4,793	76,211	Maldonado	22,159
Montevideo	530	1,237,227	Montevideo	1,237,227
Paysandú	13,922	98,508	Paysandú	62,412
Río Negro	9,282	50,123	Fray Bentos	19,569
Rivera	9,370	82,043	Rivera	49,013
Rocha	10,551	60,258	Rocha	21,672
Salto	14,163	103,074	Salto	71,881
San José	4,992	88,000	San José	28,427
Soriano	9,008	80,614	Mercedes	34,667
Tacuarembó	15,438	84,535	Tacuarembó	34,152
Treinta y Tres	9,529	45,683	Treinta y Tres	25,757

Total population, census (1975) 2,788,429 and estimate 1986 was 2,947,000. In 1980 Montevideo (the capital) had an estimated population of 1,362,000.

CLIMATE. A warm temperate climate, with mild winters and warm summers. The wettest months are March to June, but there is really no dry season. Montevideo. Jan. 72°F (22·2°C), July 50°F (10°C). Annual rainfall 38″ (950 mm).

CONSTITUTION AND GOVERNMENT. Since 1900 Uruguay has been unique in her constitutional innovations, all designed to protect her from the emergence of a dictatorship. The favourite device of the group known as the 'Batllistas' (a *Colorado* faction) which, until defeated at the 1958 elections, held the majority for over 90 years, has been the collegiate system of government, in which the two largest political parties were represented.

One such pattern lasted from 1917 to 1933, when it was abolished by a dictator who re-established the system of an individual President. Until 1951 Presidents were elected every 4 years and they selected their own Cabinet Ministers (*see* list of Presidents in THE STATESMAN'S YEAR-BOOK, 1956, p. 1493).

Presidential elections were held on 25 Nov. 1984 and Julio Maria Sanguinetta of the Colorado Party was elected. The first-choice candidates of the National (Blanco) Party and the Broad Front Party were vetoed by the military government.

Gen. Gregorio Alvarez resigned on 12 Feb. 1985 and a return to civilian rule took place on 1 March 1985.

President: Julio Maria Sanguinetta (sworn in on 1 March 1985).

The Cabinet in Dec. 1986 was as follows:

Vice-President: Enrique Tarigo.
Defence: Juan Vicente Chiarino. *Foreign Affairs:* Enrique Iglesias. *Interior:* Antonio Marchesano. *Economy:* Ricardo Zerbino. *Public Health:* Dr Raul Ugarte. *Industry and Energy:* Jorge Presno. *Transport and Public Works:* Jorge Sanguinetti. *Labour:* Hugo Fernandez. *Agriculture:* Pedro Bonino. *Justice, Education and Culture:* Dr Adela Reta. *Tourism:* Alfredo Silvera

National flag: Nine horizontal stripes of white and blue, a white canton with the 'Sun of May' in gold.

National anthem: Orientales, la patria ó la tumba (words by Francisco Acuña de Figueroa; music by Francisco José Deballi).

DEFENCE

Army. The Army consists of volunteers who enlist for 1-2 years service. There are 3 cavalry brigades and a Presidential Escort regiment; 1 infantry, 1 engineering and 1 signals brigade; 4 infantry divisions including mechanized, motorized, airborne, artillery and engineer units. Equipment includes 17 M-24, 28 M-3A1 and 22 M-41 light tanks. Strength (1988) 18,800, with 120,000 former regulars as reserve.

Navy. The Navy consists of 3 small frigates (*ex*-US old destroyer escorts, 2 of 1943 vintage, 1 of 1954), 1 corvette (*ex*-1942 US fleet minesweeper), 1 patrol vessel (*ex*-coastal minesweeper), 4 other patrol vessels, 3 coastal patrol craft, 1 transport, 1 training ship, 1 salvage vessel, 7 minor amphibious craft, 2 oilers and 1 tender. Personnel in 1988: totalled 4,500 officers and ratings including 550 naval infantry (marines) and Coastguard, and the small US-equipped naval air service of 390 with 18 aircraft and 3 helicopters.

Air Force. Organized with US aid, the Air Force had (1988) about 3,000 personnel and 110 aircraft, including 1 counter-insurgency squadron with 6 IA 58 Pucara, 4 AT-33 armed jet trainers and 6 A-37B light strike aircraft, a reconnaissance and training squadron with 10 T-6Gs, 3 transport squadrons with 2 turboprop F.27 Friendships, 5 Brazilian-built EMB-110 Bandeirantes (1 equipped for photographic duties), 5 CASA C-212 Aviocars and 6 Queen Airs, a search and rescue squadron with Cessna U-17A aircraft and Bell helicopters, and a number of Cessna 182 light aircraft for liaison duties. Basic training types are the T-41 and T-34.

INTERNATIONAL RELATIONS

Membership. Uruguay is a member of UN, OAS and LAIA (formerly LAFTA).

ECONOMY

Budget. The receipts and expenditure of the national accounts as approved by the National Council of Government (UR$1m.):

	1981	1982	1983	1984
Revenue	21,260,000	19,551,900	29,486,400	55,513,000
Expenditure	21,368,600	30,761,400	36,897,300	69,373,000

Currency. The unit of currency is the *Nuevo Peso* (1,000 old pesos) of 100 *centésimos.* The actual circulating medium consists of paper notes issued by the Central Bank in *Nuevo Peso* denominations of 50, 100, 500 and 1,000 *Nuevo Peso,* and 1, 2, 5 and 10 coins. In March 1988, US$1 = 304 *pesos;* £1 = 534·69 *pesos.*

Banking. The Bank of the Republic (founded 1896), whose president and directors are appointed by the Government has a paid-up capital of N$1,852m. The Banco Central was inaugurated on 16 May 1967. Note circulation in Dec. 1983 was N$10,538·7m.

A state-owned National Insurance Bank *(Banco de Seguros del Estado)* has a monopoly of new insurance business of all kinds.

Weights and Measures. The metric system was adopted in 1862.

ENERGY AND NATURAL RESOURCES

Electricity. Power output in 1986 was 3,730m kwh.

Oil. Petroleum production (1981) 185,000 tonnes.

Agriculture. Uruguay is primarily a pastoral country. Of the total land area of 46m. acres some 41m. are devoted to farming, of which 90% to livestock and 10% to crops. Some large *estancias* have been divided up into family farms; rural land-lordism is much less than elsewhere. Animals and animal products constituted 34·9% of the exports in 1983.

There were (1986) 9,961,000 cattle, 24,526,000 sheep, 500,000 horses, 195,000 pigs, 12,000 goats and 6m. poultry.

The wool clip in 1984 was 91,000 tonnes.

Agricultural products are raised chiefly in the departments of Paysandú, Río Negro, Colonia, San José, Soriano and Florida. The average farm is about 250 acres. The principal crops and their estimated yield (in tonnes) in 2 crop years were as follows:

	1985	1986		1985	1986
Wheat	440,000	234,000	Barley	140,000	77,000
Linseed	8,000	7,000	Maize	108,000	92,000
Oats	48,000	34,000	Rice	423,000	421,000

Uruguay is self-sufficient in rice, with a surplus for export. Three sugar refineries handle cane and (mainly) beet, their total production being approximately 92,000 tonnes, and approaching self-sufficiency.

Wine is produced chiefly in the departments of Montevideo, Canelones and Colonia, about enough for domestic consumption. The country has some 6m. fruit trees, principally peaches, oranges, tangerines and pears.

Forestry. In 1983 roundwood removals were 2,975,000 cu. metres.

Fisheries. In 1984, the total catch was 134,000 tonnes.

INDUSTRY AND TRADE

Industry. Industries include meat packing, oil refining, cement manufacture, food-stuffs, beverages, leather and textile maufacture, chemicals, light engineering and transport equipment. There are about 100 textile mills, but with the exception of half a dozen large plants, these are on the whole small.

Trade Unions. Trade unions number about 150,000 members. About 1·05m. (35%) population are classed as gainfully occupied.

Commerce. The foreign trade (officially stated in US$, with the figure for imports based on the clearance permits granted and that for exports on export licences utilized) was as follows (in US$1,000):

	1981	1982	1983	1984
Imports	1,598·9	1,057·9	705·0	732·0
Exports	1,215·4	975·8	1,044·5	925·0

Of the imports in 1984 (in US$1m.) USA, 65·9; Nigeria, 113·3; Brazil, 135; Argentina, 88·4; Federal Republic of Germany, 48·6; UK, 18·2. Of the exports in 1984 Brazil took 144·8; Argentina, 88·3; Federal Republic of Germany, 79·3; USSR, 45·7; USA, 123·9; Iran, 49·2; UK, 37·7.

Principal imports (1984) (in US$1,000): Mineral products, 262,500; chemical products, 113,252; machinery and appliances, 94,219. Exports: Textiles and textile products, 281,703; live animals and animal products, 229,079; skins and hides, 146,508; vegetable products, 129,110.

Total trade between Uruguay and UK (British Department of Trade returns, in £1,000 sterling):

	1983	1984	1985	1986	1987
Imports to UK	33,361	33,292	28,824	41,366	40,474
Exports and re-exports from UK	10,763	13,980	15,513	24,465	26,484

Tourism. There were 1,168,000 tourists in 1986.

COMMUNICATIONS

Roads. There were (1984) about 52,000 km of roads including 12,000 km of motorways.

Registered motor vehicles, 31 Dec. 1981, are estimated at 281,275 passenger cars and 47,102 trucks and buses.

Railways. The total railway system open for traffic was (1986) 2,991 km of 1,435 mm gauge. In 1986 it carried 3·3m. passengers and 867,000 tonnes of freight.

Aviation. Carrasco, 22·5 km from Montevideo, is the most important airport. US, Argentine, Brazilian, Chilean, Dutch, French, Fed. German, Scandinavian and Paraguayan airlines fly to and from Uruguay. The state-operated civil airline PLUNA runs services in the interior of the country and to Brazil, Paraguay and Argentina, and Spain.

Shipping. In 1983 there were 13 merchant vessels and 3 tankers. In 1982, 1,115 vessels cleared Montevideo. River transport (1,270 km) is extensive, its main importance being to link Montevideo with Paysandú and Salto.

Post and Broadcasting. The telephone system in Montevideo is controlled by the State; small companies operate in the interior. Telephone instruments, 1986, numbered 337,000. There are 1,277 post offices. Uruguay has 85 long-wave and 17 short-wave broadcasting stations. There were (1984) about 1·6m. wireless sets and 440,000 television receivers. There are 4 television stations in Montevideo and 11 in the interior. The State itself operates one of the most powerful sound broadcasting stations in South America.

Cinemas (1980). Cinemas numbered 85 with seating capacity of 47,000.

Newspapers (1984). There were 5 daily newspapers in Montevideo with aggregate daily circulation of about 210,000; most of the 25–30 provincial newspapers appear bi-weekly.

JUSTICE, RELIGION, EDUCATION AND WELFARE

Justice. The Ministry of Justice was created in 1977 to be responsible for relations between the Executive Power and the Judiciary and other jurisdictional entities. The Court of Justice is made up by 5 members appointed by the Council of the Nation at the suggestion of the Executive Power, for a period of 5 years. This court has original jurisdiction in constitutional, international and admiralty cases and hears appeals from the appellate courts, of which there are 4, each with 3 judges.

In Montevideo there are also 8 courts for ordinary civil cases, 3 for government *(Juzgado de Hacienda)*, as well as criminal and correctional courts. Each departmental capital has a departmental court; each of the 224 judicial divisions has a justice of peace court.

Religion. State and Church are separated, and there is complete religious liberty. The faith professed by 66% of the inhabitants is Roman Catholic although only 50% attend church.

Education. Primary education is obligatory; both primary and superior education are free.

In 1983 there were 350,178 primary school pupils, and 1983, 197,890 secondary school pupils.

The University of the Republic at Montevideo, inaugurated in 1849, has about 16,200 students; tuition is free to both native-born and foreign students; there are 10 faculties. There are 43 normal schools for males and females, and a college of arts and trades with about 33,000 students. There are also many religious seminaries throughout the Republic with a considerable number of pupils, a school for the blind, 2 for deaf and dumb and a school of domestic science.

Health. Hospital beds, 1981, numbered (estimate) 23,000; physicians numbered 5,600.

DIPLOMATIC REPRESENTATIVES

Of Uruguay in Great Britain (48 Lennox Gdns., London, SW1X 0DL)
Ambassador: Dr Luis Alberto Solé-Romeo.

Of Great Britain in Uruguay (Calle Marco Bruto 1073, Montevideo)
Ambassador: Eric Vines, CMG, OBE.

Of Uruguay in the USA (1918 F. St., NW, Washington, D.C., 20006)
Ambassador: Dr Hector Luisi.

Of the USA in Uruguay (Lauro Muller 1776, Montevideo)
Ambassador: Malcolm R. Wilkey.

Of Uruguay to the United Nations
Ambassador: Felipe Héctor Paolillo.

Books of Reference

The official gazette is the *Diario Oficial*
Statistical Reports of the Government. Montevideo. Annual and biennial
Anales de Instruccion Primaria. Montevideo. Quarterly

Finch, M.H.J., *A Political Economy of Uruguay Since 1870.* London, 1981
Salgado, José, *Historia de la Republica O. del Uruguay.* 8 vols. Montevideo, 1943

National Library: Biblioteca Nacional del Uruguay, Guayabo 1793, Montevideo. It publishes *Anuario Bibliográfico Uruguayo.*

VANUATU

Capital: Vila
Population: 141,400 (1987)
GNP per capita: US$350 (1981)

Republic of Vanuatu

HISTORY. The group was administered for some purposes jointly, for others unilaterally, as provided for by Anglo-French Convention of 27 Feb. 1906, ratified 20 Oct. 1906, and a protocol signed at London on 6 Aug. 1911 and ratified on 18 March 1922. On 30 July 1980 the Condominium of the New Hebrides achieved independence and became the Republic of Vanuatu.

AREA AND POPULATION. The Vanuatu group lies roughly 500 miles west of Fiji and 250 miles north-east of New Caledonia. The estimated land area is 5,700 sq. miles (14,760 sq. km). The larger islands of the group are: (Espiritu) Santo, Malekula, Epi, Pentecost, Aoba, Maewo, Paama, Ambrym, Efate, Erromanga, Tanna and Aneityum. They also claim Matthew and Hunter islands. Population at the census (1979) 112,596. Estimate (1987) 141,400. Vila (the capital) 15,000. There are 3 active volcanoes, on Tanna, Ambrym and Lopevi, respectively. Earth tremors are of common occurrence.

Language: The national language is Bislama (spoken by 82% of the population); English and French are also official languages.

CLIMATE. The climate is tropical, but moderated by oceanic influences and by trade winds from May to Oct. High humidity occasionally occurs and cyclones are possible. Rainfall ranges from 90″ (2,250 mm) in the south to 155″ (3,875 mm) in the north. Vila. Jan. 80°F (26·7°C), July 72°F (22·2°C). Annual rainfall 84″ (2,103 mm). A cyclone hit Vila in Feb. 1987.

CONSTITUTION AND GOVERNMENT. General elections took place in Nov. 1975 to elect a 42-member Representative Assembly, replacing the former advisory council. Further general elections took place in 1979 and 1983. A committee system was instituted and the Assembly chose its own President from its own members. Legislative power resides in a 39-member unicameral Parliament elected for a term of 4 years. Executive power is vested in the Council of Ministers.

President: Ati George Sokomanu, MBE (re-elected in 1984).

The cabinet in Jan. 1984 was composed as follows:

Prime Minister: Walter Hadye Lini, CBE.
Home Affairs and Deputy Prime Minister: S. Regenvanu. *Foreign Affairs and Trade:* S. Molisa. *Education:* O. Tahi. *Finance:* K. Kalsakau. *Health:* W. Korisa. *Transport, Communications and Public Works:* A. Sande. *Agriculture, Forestry, Fisheries:* J. Hopa. *Lands:* D. Kalpokas.

Flag: Red over green, with a black triangle in the hoist, the three parts being divided by fimbriations of black and yellow, and in the centre of the black triangle a boar's tusk overlaid by two crossed fern leaves.

INTERNATIONAL RELATIONS

Membership. Vanuatu is a member of the UN and the Commonwealth and is an ACP state of EEC.

ECONOMY

Planning. A Development Plan (1982-86) envisaged expenditure of US$12m.

Budget. The budget for 1986 envisages expenditure of 5,298m. Vatu and revenue of

6,130m. Vatu. The main sources of revenue were import and taxes on goods and services.

Currency. The currency is the *Vatu.* March 1988: £1 = 183 *Vatu*; US$1 = 103.

Banking (1986). The Finance Centre, established in 1970–71 and based primarily in Vila, consists of 4 international banks (including the Hongkong and Shanghai Banking Corporation) and 6 trust companies (including Melanesia International Trust Company Ltd, a Hongkong Bank group associate). In Aug. 1984 the Asian Development Bank opened a regional office in Vila.

Weights and Measures. The metric system is in force.

ENERGY AND NATURAL RESOURCES

Electricity. Production (1986) 20m. kwh.

Minerals. The manganese mine, established at Forari on Efate closed in 1978 and the extraction of pozzolana to supply the local cement industry ceased in 1985. Preliminary prospecting for gold began in 1985 and prospects have been identified on Efate, Malekula and Santo.

Agriculture. The main commercial crops are copra, cocoa and coffee. In 1984 almost 47,000 tonnes of copra were exported, accounting for 62% of total exports by value. Production, 1985: Copra, 38,319 tonnes; cocoa, 967 tonnes; coffee, 65. In 1985 about 80% of the population were engaged in subsistence agriculture. Yams, taro, manioc, sweet potatoes and bananas are grown for local consumption. A large number of cattle are reared on plantations, and an up-grading programme using pure-bred Charolais, Limousins and Illawarras has begun. A beef industry is developing.

Livestock (1985): Cattle, 130,000; goats, 8,000; pigs, 71,000.

Forestry. In 1987 some 1,900 hectares of plantation had been established. Production (1985) 37,900 cu. metres of logs and sawn timber.

Fisheries. The principal catch is tuna (1985, 3,962 tonnes) mainly exported to USA. Small-scale commercial fishing (1985) over 200 tonnes.

INDUSTRY AND TRADE

Industry. Industries in 1987 included copra processing, meat canning and fish freezing, a saw-mill, soft drinks factories and a print works. Building materials, furniture and aluminium were also produced, and in 1984 a cement plant opened.

Commerce. Imports and exports were (in 1m. Vatu):

	1982	1983	1984	1985
Imports	5,794	5,287	5,801	7,529
Exports	2,199	2,940	4,300	3,263

In 1985 the main exports (in 1m. Vatu) were: Copra, 1,392; fish, 761; beef and veal, 198; logs and sawn timber, 136; cocoa, 133. 48% of exports went to the Netherlands, 17% to Japan, 14% to Belgium and 12% to France. Australia (36%), Japan (12%), New Zealand (10%) and France (8%) were the major sources of imports and principal imports (in 1m. Vatu) were machinery and transport equipment (1,413), food and live animals (1,234), basic manufactures (1,084), fuels and lubricants (667) and chemicals (397).

Total trade between Vanuatu and UK (British Department of Trade returns, in £1,000 sterling):

	1985	1986	1987
Imports to UK	174	62	15
Exports and re-exports from UK	768	1,037	1,058

Tourism. In 1986 there were 18,000 visitors to Vanuatu. In addition there were over 56,000 tourists from cruise ships. Earnings from tourism 2,000m. Vatu.

COMMUNICATIONS

Roads. In 1984 there were 1,062 km of roads in Vanuatu, of these about 250 km are paved, mostly on Efate Island and Espiritu Santo. There were 3,087 registered cars in Vanuatu (1984).

Aviation (1986). Air Vanuatu provides services to Australia; Air Nauru, Air Pacific, Air Caledonie, Solair and UTA serve Pacific routes; Air Melanisia provides regular services to 16 domestic airfields, and charter services. There are international airfields at Vila and Santo.

Shipping. Several international shipping lines serve Vanuatu, linking the country with Australia, New Zealand, other Pacific territories notably Hong Kong, Japan, North America and Europe. The chief ports are Vila and Santo. In 1977, 394 vessels arrived including 48 cruise ships carrying 40,412 visitors. 92,340 tons of cargo were exported and 102,867 tons discharged. Small vessels provide frequent interisland services.

Telecommunications. Internal telephone and telegram services are provided by the Posts and Telecommunications and Radio Departments. There are automatic telephone exchanges at Vila and Santo; rural areas are served by a network of tele-radio stations. In 1983 there were 6 post offices and 3,000 telephones.

External telephone, telegram and telex services are provided by VANITEL, through their satellite earth station at Vila. There are direct circuits to Noumea, Sydney, Hong Kong and Paris and high quality communications are available on a 24-hour basis to most countries in the world. Air radio facilities are provided. Marine coast station facilities are available at Vila and Santo. Radio Vanuatu operates a service 7 days a week in, French, English and Bislama.

JUSTICE, RELIGION, EDUCATION AND WELFARE

Justice. A study was being made in 1980 which could lead to unification of the judicial system.

Religion. Over 80% of the population are Christians, but animist beliefs are still prevalent.

Education. There were (1987) 224 English primary schools with 13,000 pupils, 105 French primary schools with 10,000 pupils, 11 government and denominational secondary schools with 2,000 pupils and Matevulu College. Tertiary education is provided at the Vanuatu Technical Institute and the Teachers College, while other technical and commercial training is through regional institutions in the Solomon Islands, Fiji and Papua New Guinea. Eleven new secondary institutions are planned to open in 1987.

Health. In 1987 there were 10 government-run hospitals throughout the islands (2 in Vila) and a number of clinics and dispensaries. In 1984 there were 19 doctors and, in 1982, 2 dentists, 3 pharmacists, 5 midwives and 266 nursing personnel.

DIPLOMATIC REPRESENTATIVES

Of Vanuatu in Great Britain
High Commissioner: (Vacant).

Of Great Britain in Vanuatu (Melitco Hse., Rue Pasteur, Vila)
High Commissioner: Malcolm Creek, LVO, OBE.

Of Vanuatu to the United Nations
Ambassador: Nikenike Vurobaravu.

VATICAN CITY STATE

Stato della Città del Vaticano

HISTORY. For many centuries the Popes bore temporal sway over a territory stretching across mid-Italy from sea to sea and comprising some 17,000 sq. miles, with a population finally of over 3m. In 1859–60 and 1870 the Papal States were incorporated into the Italian Kingdom. The consequent dispute between Italy and successive Popes was only settled on 11 Feb. 1929 by three treaties between the Italian Government and the Vatican: (1) A Political Treaty, which recognized the full and independent sovereignty of the Holy See in the city of the Vatican; (2) a Concordat, to regulate the condition of religion and of the Church in Italy; and (3) a Financial Convention, in accordance with which the Holy See received 750m. lire in cash and 1,000m. lire in Italian 5% state bonds. This sum was to be a definitive settlement of all the financial claims of the Holy See against Italy in consequence of the loss of its temporal power in 1870. The treaty and concordat were ratified on 7 June 1929. The treaty has been embodied in the Constitution of the Italian Republic of 1947. A revised Concordat between the Italian Republic and the Holy See was subsequently negotiated and came into force on 3 June 1985.

The Vatican City State is governed by a Commission appointed by the Pope. The reason for its existence is to provide an extra-territorial, independent base for the Holy See, the government of the Roman Catholic Church.

AREA AND POPULATION. The area of the Vatican City is 44 hectares (108·7 acres). It includes the Piazza di San Pietro (St Peter's Square), which is to remain normally open to the public and subject to the powers of the Italian police. It has its own railway station (for freight only), postal facilities, coins and radio. Twelve buildings in and outside Rome enjoy extra-territorial rights, including the Basilicas of St John Lateran, St Mary Major and St Paul without the Walls, the Pope's summer villa at Castel Gandolfo and a further Vatican radio station on Italian soil. *Radio Vaticana* broadcasts an extensive service in 34 languages from the transmitters in the Vatican City and in Italy.

The Vatican City has about 1,000 inhabitants.

CONSTITUTION. The Pope exercises sovereignty and has absolute legislative, executive and judicial powers. The judicial power is delegated to a tribunal in the first instance, to the Sacred Roman Rota in appeal and to the Supreme Tribunal of the Signature in final appeal.

The Pope is elected by the College of Cardinals, meeting in secret conclave. The election is by scrutiny and requires a two-thirds majority.

Name and family	Election	Name and family	Election
Benedict XIV *(Lambertini)*	1740	Leo XIII *(Pecci)*	1878
Clement XIII *(Rezzonico)*	1758	Pius X *(Sarto)*	1903
Clement XIV *(Ganganelli)*	1769	Benedict XV *(della Chiesa)*	1914
Pius VI *(Braschi)*	1775	Pius XI *(Ratti)*	1922
Pius VII *(Chiaramonti)*	1800	Pius XII *(Pacelli)*	1939
Leo XII *(della Genga)*	1823	John XXIII *(Roncalli)*	1958
Pius VIII *(Castiglioni)*	1829	Paul VI *(Montini)*	1963
Gregory XVI *(Cappellari)*	1831	John Paul I *(Luciani)*	1978
Pius IX *(Mastai-Ferretti)*	1846	John Paul II *(Wojtyla)*	1978

Supreme Pontiff: **John Paul II** (Karol Wojtyla), born at Wadowice near Cracow,

Poland, 18 May 1920. Archbishop of Cracow 1964–78, created Cardinal in 1967, elected Pope 16 Oct. 1978, inaugurated 22 Oct. 1978.

Pope John Paul II was the first non-Italian to be elected since Pope Adrian VI (a Dutchman) in 1522.

Secretary of State: Cardinal Agostino Casaroli (appointed May 1979).

Flag: Vertically yellow and white, with on the white the crossed keys and tiara of the Papacy.

ROMAN CATHOLIC CHURCH. The Roman Pontiff (in orders a Bishop, but in jurisdiction held to be by divine right the centre of all Catholic unity, and consequently Pastor and Teacher of all Christians) has for advisers and coadjutors the Sacred College of Cardinals, consisting in Sept. 1987 of 140 Cardinals appointed by him from senior ecclesiastics who are either the bishops of important Sees or the heads of departments at the Holy See. In addition to the College of Cardinals, the Pope has created a ' Synod of Bishops'. This consists of the Patriarchs and certain Metropolitans of the Catholic Church of Oriental Rite, of elected representatives of the national episcopal conferences and religious orders of the world, of the Cardinals in charge of the Roman Congregations and of other persons nominated by the Pope. The Synod meets as and when decided by the Pope. The last Synod (on the laity) met in Oct. 1987.

The central administration of the Roman Catholic Church is carried on by a number of permanent committees called Sacred Congregations, each composed of a number of Cardinals and diocesan bishops (both appointed for 5-year periods), with Consultors and Officials. Besides the Secretariat of State and the Council for Public Affairs of the Church (which deals with external relations) there are now 10 Sacred Congregations, viz.: Doctrine, Oriental Churches, Bishops, the Sacraments, Divine Worship, Clergy, Religious, Catholic Education, Evangelization of the Peoples and Causes of the Saints. There are also 3 Secretariats: for Christian Unity, Non-Christians and Non-Believers; a Prefecture of Economic Affairs, a Prefecture of the Pontifical Household and a Statistical Office. Furthermore, the Roman Curia contains 3 tribunals, the Apostolic Penitentiary, the Supreme Tribunal of the Apostolic Signature and the Sacred Roman Rota; and, lastly, various other councils and commissions dealing with the Laity, Justice and Peace, Women, the Family, the Information and Revision of Canon Law, Social Communications, Migration and Tourism and Culture. The Pontifical Academy of Sciences was revived by Pius XI in 1936 with 70 members.

DIPLOMATIC REPRESENTATIVES

In its diplomatic relations with foreign countries the Holy See is represented by the Secretariat of State and the Council for Public Affairs of the Church. It maintains permanent observers to the UN in New York and Geneva and to UNESCO and FAO. The Holy See is a member of IAEA and the Vatican City State is a member of UPU and ITU. It therefore attends as a member those international conferences open to State members of the UN and specialized agencies.

Of the Holy See in Great Britain (54 Parkside, London, SW19 5NF)
Apostolic Pro-Nuncio in Great Britain: Archbishop Luigi Barbarito (accredited 7 April 1986).

Of Great Britain at the Holy See (91 Via Condotti, 00187, Rome).
Ambassador: J. K. E. Broadley. *First Secretary:* P. J. McCormick.

Of the Holy See in the USA (3339 Massachusetts Ave., NW, Washington, D.C., 20008).
Apostolic Pro Nuncio: Most Rev. Pio Laghi.

Of the USA at the Holy See (Villino Pacelli, Via Aurelia 294, 00165, Rome).
Ambassador: Frank Shakespeare.

Books of Reference

Acta Apostolicæ Sedis Romanæ. Rome
Annuario Pontificio. Rome. Annual
L'Attivita della Santa Sede. Rome. Annual
The Catholic Directory. London. Annual
Code of Canon Law. London, 1983
The Catholic Directory for Scotland. Glasgow. Annual
The New Catholic Encyclopædia. New York
The Catholic Almanac. Huntingdon, Annual
Bull, G., *Inside the Vatican.* London, 1982
Cardinale, Mgr. Igino, *Le Saint-Siège et la diplomatie.* Paris and Rome, 1962.—*The Holy See and the International Order.* Gerrards Cross, 1976
Hales, E. E., *The Catholic Church and the Modern World.* London, 1958
Hebblethwaite, P., *In the Vatican.* London, 1986
Mayer, F. *et al, The Vatican: Portrait of a State and a Community.* Dublin, 1980
Nichols, P., *The Pope's Divisions.* London, 1981
Walsh, M. J., *Vatican City State.* [Bibliography] Oxford and Santa Barbara, 1983

VENEZUELA

República de Venezuela

Capital: Caracas
Population: 17·32m. (1985)
GNP per capita: US$2,680 (1985)

HISTORY. Venezuela formed part of the Spanish colony of New Granada until 1821 when it became independent in union with Colombia. A separate, independent republic was formed in 1830.

AREA AND POPULATION. Venezuela is bounded north by the Caribbean, east by Guyana, south by Brazil, south-west and west by Colombia. The official estimate of the area is 912,050 sq. km (352,143 sq. miles); the frontiers with Colombia, Brazil and Guyana extend for 4,782 km and its Caribbean coastline stretches for some 3,200 km. Population (1981) census, 14,516,735. Estimate (1985) 17,316,740. The 1981 census excluded tribal Indians estimated at 53,350 (chiefly in Amazonas Territory) and illegal immigrants, estimated (1979) at about 3m. The official language is Spanish, spoken by all but 2·5% of the population.

The areas, populations and capitals of the 20 states and 4 federally-controlled areas are:

State	Sq. km	Census 1981	Capital	Census 1981
Anzoátegui	43,300	683,717	Barcelona	156,519
Apure	76,500	188,187	San Fernando	54,000 [1]
Aragua	7,014	891,623	Maracay	440,048
Barinas	35,200	326,166	Barinas	109,906
Bolívar	238,000	668,340	Ciudad Bolívar	181,864
Carabobo	4,650	1,062,268	Valencia	616,037
Cojedes	14,800	133,991	San Carlos	30,000 [1]
Falcón	24,800	503,896	Coro	71,000 [1]
Guárico	64,986	393,467	San Juan	53,000 [1]
Lara	19,800	945,064	Barquisimeto	496,684
Mérida	11,300	459,361	Mérida	142,752
Miranda	7,950	1,421,442	Los Teques	112,206
Monagas	28,900	388,536	Maturin	154,957
Nueva Esparta	1,150	197,198	La Asunción	9,000 [1]
Portuguesa	15,200	424,984	Guanare	47,000 [1]
Sucre	11,800	585,698	Cumaná	191,941
Táchira	11,100	660,234	San Cristóbal	198,578
Trujillo	7,400	433,735	Trujillo	42,000 [1]
Yaracuy	7,100	300,597	San Felipe	56,000 [1]
Zulia	63,100	1,674,252	Maracaibo	888,824
Ter. Amazonas	175,750	45,667	Puerto Ayacucho	15,000 [1]
Ter. Delta Amacuro	40,200	56,720	Tucupita	29,000 [1]
Federal District	1,930	2,070,742	Caracas	1,816,901
Federal Dependencies	120	850	—	—

[1] Estimate, 1980.

Other large towns (1980) are Petare (334,800), Ciudad Guyana (314,041, census 1981), Baruta (180,100), Cabimas (138,529, census 1981), Acarigua (126,000), Maiquetiá (120,200), Valera (101,981, census 1981), Chacao (101,900), Puerto Cabello (94,000), Carúpano (82,000) and Puerto La Cruz (81,800).

Venezuela is the most urbanised Latin American nation; in 1985, 86% of the population lived in urban areas. Over half the population live in the valleys of Carabobo and Valencia (once the capital). At the 1981 census, 69% were of mixed ethnic origin (*mestizo*), 20% white, 9% black and 2% amerindian.

Vital statistics (1981 estimates): 510,000 births, 102,000 marriages, 81,000 deaths. Life expectancy (1981) 68 years with 40·5% of population under 15 years.

CLIMATE. The climate ranges from warm temperate to tropical. Temperatures vary little throughout the year and rainfall is plentiful. The dry season is from Dec. to April. Caracas. Jan. 65°F (18·3°C), July 69°F (20·6°C). Annual rainfall 32" (833 mm). Ciudad Bolivar. Jan. 79°F (26·1°C), July 81°F (27·2°C). Annual rainfall 41" (1,016 mm). Maracaibo. Jan. 81°F (27·2°C), July 85°F (29·4°C). Annual rainfall 23" (577 mm).

CONSTITUTION AND GOVERNMENT. The constitution of 1961 provides for popular election for a term of 5 years of a President, a National Congress, and State and Municipal legislative assemblies, and guarantees the freedom of labour, industry and commerce. Aliens are assured of treatment equal to that extended to nationals.

Congress consists of a Senate and a Chamber of Deputies. At least 2 Senators are elected for each State and for the Federal District. Senators must be Venezuelans by birth and over 30 years of age. Deputies must be native Venezuelans over 21 years of age; there is 1 for every 50,000 inhabitants. The territories, on reaching the population fixed by law, also elect deputies. Voting (by proportional representation) is compulsory for men and women over 18. Owing to the high rate of illiteracy, voting is by coloured ballot cards.

The President must be a Venezuelan by birth and over 30 years of age; he has a qualified power of veto.

The following is a list of presidents since 1941:

	Took Office		Took Office
Gen. Isaias Medina Angarita	6 May 1941	Dr Edgard Sanabria	14 Nov. 1958[3]
Rómulo Betancourt	20 Oct. 1945	Rómulo Betancourt	13 Feb. 1959
Rómulo Gallegos	15 Feb. 1948	Raul Leoni	11 March 1964
Lieut.-Col. Carlos Delgado		Rafael Caldera	11 March 1969
Chalbaud	24 Nov. 1948 [4]	Carlos Andrés Pérez	
Dr G. Suárez Flamerich	27 Nov. 1950 [2]	Rodríguez	12 March 1974
Col. Marcos Pérez Jiménez.	3 Dec. 1952 [1]	Dr Luis Herrera Campíns	12 March 1979
Rear-Adm. Wolfgang		Dr Jaime Lusinchi	2 Feb. 1984
Larrazábal Ugueto	23 Jan. 1958 [2] [3]		

[1] Deposed.　　[2] Resigned.　　[3] Provisional.　　[4] Assassinated 13 Nov. 1950.

President: Dr Jaime Lusinchi, elected 4 Dec. 1983 with 57% of the votes, assumed office on 2 Feb. 1984.

Foreign Minister: Germán Nava Carrillo. *Finance Minister:* Héctor Hurtado Navarro.

At the Congressional elections held 4 Dec. 1983, 112 of the 200 seats in the Chamber of Deputies were won by Acción Democrática, 61 by COPEI (the Social Christians) and 27 by other parties.

The city of Caracas is the capital. The 20 states, autonomous and politically equal, have each a legislative assembly and a governor. The states are divided into 156 districts and 613 municipalities. There are also 2 federal territories with 7 departments, and a federal district with 2 departments and 2 parishes. Each district has a municipal council, and each municipio a communal junta. The federal district and the 2 territories are administered by the President of the Republic.

National flag: Three horizontal stripes of yellow, blue, red, with an arc of 7 white stars in the centre, and the national arms in the canton.

National anthem: Gloria al bravo pueblo (1811; words by Vicente Salias, tune by Juan Landaeta).

DEFENCE. All Venezuelans on reaching 18 years of age are liable for 2 years in the Armed Forces.

Army. The Army consists of 1 cavalry and 3 infantry divisions; 1 Ranger brigade, supporting regiments and groups. Equipment includes 81 AMX-30 main battle and 36 AMX-13 light tanks. Army aviation comprises 16 helicopters and 15 aircraft. Strength (1988) 34,000.

Navy. Strength includes 3 diesel-powered patrol submarines (2 modern built in Federal Republic of Germany and 1 very old *ex*-US submarine), 6 modern frigates built in Italy, 5 tank landing ships, 2 transports, 1 logistic support ship, 2 utility landing craft, 12 minor landing craft, 1 survey ship, 2 survey launches, 12 river patrol craft, 1 training ship and 3 tugs.

The Coastguard, under Naval control (commanded by a Rear-Admiral) comprises 2 old Italian-built frigates, 6 British-built fast attack craft and 2 large armed tugs. Coastal patrol boats operated by the National Guard *(Fuerzas Armadas de Cooperacion)* now number 40, and there are 25 service craft.

New construction (delayed) planned includes 4 corvettes, 2 more submarines, several mine countermeasures vessels, 2 landing ships and 1 survey ship.

There is a naval academy and sail training ship for the training of officer cadets and a school of staff studies and various technical training schools.

Personnel in 1988 totalled: 10,000 officers and men including the Marine Corps, the Coastguard, the National Guard and the Naval Air Arm comprising 6 S-2E Trackers, 8 Aviocars and 1 Dash-7, 6 Agusta AB-212 shipborne helicopters and 2 Bell 47 helicopters for search and rescue and training and 6 light twin aircraft for various and coastguard duties.

Air Force. Formed in 1920, the Air Force of some 5,000 officers and men is a small, but well-equipped service with a total of about 200 aircraft. There are 7 combat squadrons. Two are equipped with 18 F-16A and 6 F-16B Fighting Falcons. Another has 14 Canadair CF-5A fighter-bombers and 6 two-seat CF-5Ds, and one has 10 Mirage III/5s respectively. Two bomber squadrons are equipped with 19 modernized Canberra jet-bombers and a single reconnaissance Canberra. Another operational squadron has 14 OV-10E Bronco twin-turboprop counter-insurgency aircraft. A helicopter force consists of more than 40 Bell JetRangers, 212s, 214STs and 412s, UH-1B/D/H Iroquois and Alouette IIIs. Transport units are equipped with 12 C-123 Providers, 5 C-130H Hercules, 5 C-47s and 6 Aeritalia G222s. Communications aircraft are Queen Airs and other types. T-34 Mentors are used for training, together with 20 T-2D Buckeye advanced jet trainers, which have a secondary attack role along with 30 Tucanos now being delivered from Brazil. A battalion of paratroops comes within Air Force responsibility. There is a staff college and a cadet academy.

National Guard, a volunteer force of some 22,000 under the Ministry of Defence, is broadly responsible for internal security. It includes customs and forestry duties among its tasks.

INTERNATIONAL RELATIONS

Membership. Venezuela is a member of UN, OAS, LAIA (formerly LAFTA), OPEC and the Andean Group.

ECONOMY

Planning. The seventh 5-year plan (1984–88) aimed to achieve economic growth but with a reorientation of priorities towards production of tradeable goods and services, agriculture, industry and tourism. There are 8 major projects: Caracas underground, Guri hydro-electric scheme, INOS water supply, major housing schemes, the Eastern Motorway, the Carbozulia coal mines, the Bauxiven bauxite mines and the upgrading of aluminium plants. Total planned investment, Bs. 170,000m. for the period 1986–88.

Budget. The revenue and expenditure for calendar years were, in Bs.1m., as follows:

	1984	1985	1986	1987	1988
Revenue	102,808	118,039	...	165,000	180,000
Expenditure	103,539	113,307	...	165,000	180,000

Currency. The *bolívar* (Bs.) is divided into 100 *céntimos*. Gold coins, 100 (*pachanos*), 20 and 10 *bolívars* have been minted but are no longer in circulation; silver coins are 5 (*fuerte*), 2, 1 *bolívars*; nickel, 50 (*real*), 25 (*medio*) and 12·5 *céntimos* (*locha*), coppernickel, 5 *céntimos* (*puya*).

The bank-notes in circulation are 500, 100, 50, 20 and 10 bolívars. The circulation of foreign bank-notes is forbidden.

In March 1988, £1 = Bs.51·08; US$1 = 29·40 on the free market.

Banking. The major banks include: Banco Provincial SAICA, Banco de Venezuela, Banco Consolidado, Banco Unión, Banco Mercantil, Banco Latino, Banco de Maracaibo, Banco Industrial de Venezuela, Bank of America.

ENERGY AND NATURAL RESOURCES

Electricity. Production (1986) 50,240m. kwh. The Guri dam hydroelectric project was opened in Nov. 1986. It will supply 70% of the country's needs.

Oil. The oil-producing region around Maracaibo, covering some 30,000 sq. miles, produces about three-quarters of Venezuelan petroleum. Deposits in the Orinoco region are likely to prove one of the largest heavy oil reserves in the world. Nationalization of the privately owned oil sector in 1976 has proved successful. New distribution channels have been established, with the result that the major transnational companies which took 80% of Venezuela's oil in 1976 handled only 50% in 1980. Crude oil production (1987) 90·2m. tonnes.

Proven crude oil reserves in Dec. 1986 stood at 55,521m. bbls. However, these are considered conservative estimates and new fields off-shore have estimated reserves of 6,000–40,000m. bbls. The Orinoco tar sands belt has reserves variously estimated at between 700,000m. bbls. and 3,000,000m. bbls.

Gas. Production (1985) 33,059m. cu. metres.

Minerals. Bauxite is being exploited in the Guayana region by Bauxien, a state agency. There are important goldmines in the region south-east of Bolívar State, and new deposits have been discovered near El Callao (1959) and Sosa Méndez (1961) in the Guayana region. Output, 1982, amounted to 902 kg. Diamond output, from Amazonas territory, was 687,000 carats in 1977. Manganese deposits, estimated at several million tons, were discovered in 1954. Phosphate-rock deposits (yielding from 64 to 82% tricalcium phosphate) are found in the state of Falcón; reserves of 15m. tons of high-quality rock have been established. The state of Sucre has large sulphur deposits. Coal is worked in the states of Táchira, Aragua and Anzoátegui. Coal proven reserves in Zulia (160m. tons) are to be developed to service a new thermal power station in the Maracaibo area. An important nickel deposit (at Loma de Hierro near Tejerías) is estimated to equal 600,000 tons of pure nickel. Saltmines are now worked by the Government on the Araya peninsula. Asbestos and copper pyrite are being exploited. There were proven reserves (1984) of bauxite totalling 200m. tonnes and production of about 3m. per annum are scheduled from 1986.

Iron ore is exploited in Bolívar State by the Orinoco Mining Co. and Iron Mines of Venezuela, subsidiaries respectively of the US Steel Corp. and the Bethlehem Steel Co. Proven reserves at the end of 1980 were 1,800m. tonnes. National output of iron ore, 1985, 14·9m. tonnes of which 9m. was exported.

Agriculture. Venezuela is divided into 3 distinct zones—the agricultural, the pastoral and the forest zone. In the first are grown coffee, cocoa, sugar-cane, maize, rice, wheat (grown in the Andes), tobacco, cotton, beans, sisal, etc.; the second affords grazing for more than 6m. cattle and numerous horses; and in the third, which covers a very large portion of the country, tropical products, such as caoutchouc, balatá (a gum resembling rubber), tonka beans, dividivi, copaiba, vanilla, growing wild, are worked by the inhabitants. The 1986 livestock estimate showed cattle, 12,371,000; pigs, 2,852,000; goats, 1·34m.; sheep, 422,000; poultry, 51m. Area under cultivation is 5,530,898 acres. Over 50% of all farmers are engaged in subsistence agriculture and growth rates in agricultural production have not kept pace with the high population increase. Government has introduced a programme of price support, tax incentives and price increases.

Production (1986, in 1,000 tonnes) rice, 322; maize, 1,300; cassava, 312; sugarcane, 6,535; bananas, 1,002; oranges, 382; potatoes, 250; tomatoes, 107; coffee, 69; sesame seed, 65; tobacco, 14; cocoa, 12.

The coffee plantations number 62,673, covering 543,400 acres with 135m. bushes. The Venezuelan cocoa, from 13,000 plantations, is considered to be of high quality; it is grown chiefly in the states of Sucre and Miranda. The sugar industry has 6 government and 20 privately owned mills.

Forestry. Resources have been barely tapped; 600 species of wood have been identified.

Fisheries. Total catch (1985) was 263,840 tonnes.

INDUSTRY AND TRADE

Industry. Production (1985): Steel, 2·72m. tonnes; aluminium, 407,000; ammonia, 490,000; fertilizers, 650,000; cement, 5·12m.; paper, 550,000; vehicles (units) 116,000.

Industrial development is concentrated in capital intensive areas where it can have a competitive advantage within the Andean Group, whereas in more labour intensive industries, the low labour costs of other member countries gives them an advantage. However, Venezuela currently produces 90% of its requirements of processed food, beverages, tobacco, clothing and textiles.

Labour. The labour force in 1985 was 6m., 16·3% were in agriculture, 15·3% in manufacturing and 7% in construction.

Wages are the highest in Latin America, there is a high turnover of labour and a corresponding rate of absenteeism.

45% of the labour force is unionized. The most powerful confederation is the CTV (*Confederacion de Trabajadores de Venezuela*, formed 1947), which is dominated by the Accion Democratica party. Estimated membership, 1·1m., claims 2m. Comprises 68 regional and industrial federations with over 6,000 unions, including: FCV (peasants), 700,000; FETRACONS (construction workers), 1m.; FETRASALUD (health workers), 45,000; FETRAMETAL (metal workers and miners), 32,000; the very important FEDEPETROL (oil workers), 6,000; Federacion Venezolana de Maestros (teachers).

Other confederations are CUTV (*Confederacion Unitaria de Trabajadores Venezolanos*, formed 1963). Estimated membership, 40,000, claims 100,000. Comprises 8 regional and 5 industrial federations in 185 local unions; and, CODESA (*Confederacion de Sindicatos Autonomos de Venezuela*, formed 1964). Estimated membership, 10,000, claims 35,000. Dominated by COPEI party. Comprises 120 local unions, including textile, petrol distribution, public health and education workers' federations.

Commerce. Venezuela's exports and imports (in US$1m.):

	1983	1984	1985	1986
Exports	14,759	15,967	14,178	8,880
Imports	6,409	7,262	7,388	7,600

Main export markets in 1982 were USA, Netherlands Antilles because of its oil refining and transhipment facilities, Canada, Puerto Rico, Italy and Spain.

Principal imports are machinery and equipment, manufactured goods, chemical products, foodstuffs.

The USA supplied 47% of all imports in 1982, followed by Federal Republic of Germany, Japan, Italy and the UK.

Total trade between UK and Venezuela (British Department of Trade returns, in £1,000 sterling):

	1983	1984	1985	1986	1987
Imports to UK	183,731	253,770	238,879	96,339	91,749
Exports and re-exports from UK	87,937	102,400	165,268	170,101	157,760

Tourism. 317,300 tourists visited Venezuela in 1986.

COMMUNICATIONS

Roads. There were, 1985, 62,601 km of road fit for traffic the year round; of these 24,036 km are paved. There are 10,097 km of high-speed 4-lane motorway type. The motorway system runs from Caracas to Puerto Cabello *via* Valencia and will shortly be linked direct with one from La Guaira to Caracas.

Railways. Plans have existed since 1950 for large-scale railway construction but only the Puerto Cabello to Barquisimeto and Acarigua lines (336 km–1,435 mm gauge) has been completed. In 1986 it carried 17·1m. passenger-km and 11·5m. tonne-km. A metro is under construction in Caracas the first section of which was opened in March 1983.

Aviation. In 1985 there were 7 international airports, 51 national and over 200 private airports. The chief Venezuelan airlines are LAV (Líneas Aéreas Venezolanas), a government-owned concern, and AVENSA (Aerovías Venezolanas). Both operate numerous internal services. VIASA operates international routes in conjunction with KLM. There are also 3 specialist air freight companies. In all there are over 100 commercial aircraft in operation. In addition to Venezuelan international services, a number of US and Latin American and European lines operate services to Venezuela. British Airways operates twice-weekly flights between London and Caracas.

Shipping. Foreign vessels are not permitted to engage in the coasting trade, except by special concessions or by contract with the Government. La Guaira, Maracaibo, Puerto Cabello, Puerto Ordaz and Guanta are the chief ports. In Dec. 1978 the merchant fleet had an aggregate gross tonnage of 824,000; this included tankers of 368,000 gross tons.

The principal navigable rivers are the Orinoco and its tributaries Apure and Arauca, from San Fernando to Tucupita through Ciudad Bolívar, Puerto Ordaz and San Félix; San Juan from Carípito to the Gulf of Paria; and Escalante in Lake Maracaibo.

Post and Broadcasting. There were 1,165,699 telephones in 1985. An international telex service operates in the Caracas metropolitan zone. There is a submarine telephone link with USA.

In 1983 there were 5m. radio receivers and 77 radio stations at Caracas, Maracaibo, Maracay and other towns. There were 3 television stations in Caracas (two privately owned), of which 2 cover, with relays, most of the country. In 1986 there were about 2·75m. homes with TV receivers and 6·75m. radio receivers.

Cinemas (1977). There were 563 cinemas and 25 drive-ins.

Newspapers (1983). There were 25 leading daily newspapers with a circulation of over 1·7m.

JUSTICE, RELIGION, EDUCATION AND HEALTH

Justice. The Supreme Court, which operates in Divisions, each with 5 members, is elected by Congress for 5 years. The country is divided into 20 legal districts. They select their own President and Vice-President. The Federal Procurator-General is appointed for 5 years. There are lower federal courts.

Each state has a Supreme Court with 3 members, a superior court, or superior tribunal, courts of first instance, district courts and municipal courts. In the territories there are civil and military judges of first instance, and also judges in the municipios. Finally, there is an income-tax claims tribunal.

Religion. The Roman Catholic is the prevailing religion, but there is toleration of all others. There are 4 archbishops, 1 at Caracas, who is Primate of Venezuela, 2 at Mérida and 1 at Ciudad Bolívar. There are 19 bishops. In the state primary schools instruction is given only to those children whose parents expressly request it. Protestants number about 20,000.

Education. In 1982–83 there were 12,816 primary and secondary schools with 130,505 teachers and 2,998,803 pupils. The number of students in higher education was 282,274 with 25,268 teaching staff in the 106 establishments, including 17 universities.

Health. In 1976 there were 14,211 doctors and 386 hospitals and dispensaries with 36,126 beds.

DIPLOMATIC REPRESENTATIVES

Of Venezuela in Great Britain (1 Cromwell Rd., London, SW7)
Ambassador: Dr Francisco Kerdel-Vegas, CBE (accredited 5 Nov. 1987).

Of Great Britain in Venezuela (Torre Las Mercedes, Avenida La Estancia, Chuao, Caracas 1060)
Ambassador: Giles Fitzherbert.

Of Venezuela in the USA (2445 Massachusetts Ave., NW, Washington, D.C., 20008)
Ambassador: Valentin Hernandez.

Of the USA in Venezuela (Avenida Francisco de Miranda and Avenida Principal de la Floresta, Caracas)
Ambassador: Otto J. Reich.

Of Venezuela to the United Nations
Ambassador: Dr Andrés Aguilar.

Books of Reference

Statistical Information: The following are some of the principal publications:
   Dirección General de Estadística, Ministerio de Fomento, *Boletín Mensual de Estadística.—Anuario Estadístico de Venezuela.* Caracas, Annual
   Banco Central, *Memoria Annual* and *Boletín Mensual*
   Ministerio de Sanidad y Asistencia Social, Dirección de Salud Pública, *Anuario de Epidemiología y Asistencia Social*

Bigler, G. E., *Politics and State Capitalism in Venezuela.* Madrid, 1981
Braveboy-Wagner, J. A., *The Venezuela-Guyana Border Dispute: Britain's Colonial Legacy in Latin America.* Boulder and Epping, 1984
Buitrón, A., *Causas y Efectos del Éxodo Rural en Venezuela.—Efectos Económicos y Sociales de las Inmigraciones en Venezuela.—Las Inmigraciones en Venezuela.* Pan American Union, Washington, D.C., 1956
Ewell, J., *Venezuela: A Century of Change.* London, 1984
Lombard, J., *Venezuelan History: A Comprehensive Working Bibliography.* Boston, 1977.—*Venezuela: The Search for Order, the Dream of Progress.* OUP, 1982
Martz, J. D., and Myers, D. J., *Venezuela: The Democratic Experience.* New York, 1986

VIETNAM

Capital: Hanoi
Population: 61·95m. (1986)
GNP per capita: US$300 (1984)

Công Hòa Xã Hôi Chu Nghĩa Viêt Nam—The Socialist Republic of Vietnam

HISTORY. The history of Vietnam can be traced to the beginning of the Christian era. Conquered by the Chinese in B.C. 111, it broke free of Chinese domination in 939, though at many subsequent periods it was a nominal Chinese vassal. (For subsequent history until the cessation of hostilities with France at the Geneva Conference of July 1954 *see* THE STATESMAN'S YEAR-BOOK, 1985–86).

The Geneva conference stipulated that elections should take place in 1956. Ngo Dinh Diem became Prime Minister of South Vietnam (Republic of Vietnam) in 1954 and President in 1955. Elections were never held. In 1963 Diem was overthrown. In 1965 Nguyen Van Thieu took power as chairman of a National Leadership Committee, becoming President in 1967. From 1959 the North promoted insurgency in the South; US involvement began in 1961.

In Paris on 27 Jan. 1973 an agreement was signed ending the war in Vietnam. After the US withdrawal, however, hostilities continued between the North and the South until the latter's defeat in 1975. 150,000–200,000 South Vietnamese fled the country, including the former President Thieu.

For details of the former Republic of Vietnam, *see* THE STATESMAN'S YEAR-BOOK, 1975–76. After the collapse of Thieu's regime the Provisional Revolutionary Government established an administration in Saigon. A general election was held on 25 April 1976 for a National Assembly representing the whole country. Voting was by universal suffrage of all citizens of 18 or over, except former functionaries of South Vietnam undergoing 're-education', the last of whom (approximately 7,000) were released in Sept. 1987 and Feb. 1988. The unification of North and South Vietnam into the Socialist Republic of Vietnam took place formally on 2 July 1976. In 1978 Vietnam signed a 25-year treaty of friendship and co-operation with the USSR. Relations with China correspondingly deteriorated, an exacerbating factor being the Vietnamese military intervention in Cambodia. Occasional skirmishing along the China–Vietnam border continued into 1987.

AREA AND POPULATION. The country has a total area of 329,566 sq. km and is divided administratively into 40 provinces. Areas and populations (in 1,000) at the census of Oct. 1979 were as follows:

Province	Sq. km	1979	Province	Sq. km	1979
Lai Chau	17,408	322,077	Thai Binh	1,344	1,506,235
Son La	14,656	487,793	Hai Phong (city) [1]	1,515	1,279,067
Hoang Lien Son	14,125	778,217	Ha Nam Ninh	3,522	2,781,409
Ha Tuyen	13,519	782,453	Thanh Hoa	11,138	2,532,261
Cao Bang	} 13,731	{ 479,823	Nghe Tinh	22,380	3,111,989
Lang Son		{ 484,657	Binh Tri Thien	19,048	1,901,713
Bac Thai	8,615	815,105	Quang Nam – Da Nang	11,376	1,529,520
Quang Ninh	7,076	750,055	Nghia Binh	14,700	2,095,354
Vinh Phu	5,187	1,488,348	Gia Lai – Kon Tum	18,480	595,906
Ha Bac	4,708	1,662,671	Dac Lac	18,300	490,198
Ha Son Binh	6,860	1,537,190	Phu Khanh	9,620	1,188,637
Hanoi (city) [1]	597	2,570,905	Lam Dong	10,000	396,657
Hai Hung	2,526	2,145,662	Thuan Hai	11,000	938,255

[1] Autonomous city.

1587

Province	Sq. km	1979	Province	Sq. km	1979
Dong Nai	12,130	1,304,799	Ben Tre	2,400	1,041,838
Song Be	9,500	659,093	Cuu Long	4,200	1,504,215
Tay Ninh	4,100	684,006	An Giang	4,140	1,532,362
Long An	5,100	957,264	Hau Giang	5,100	2,232,891
Dong Thap	3,120	1,182,787	Kien Giang	6,000	994,673
Thanh Pho–			Minh Hai	8,000	1,219,595
Ho Chi Minh [1]	1,845	3,419,978	Vung Tau – Con Dao [2]	—	91,160
Tien Giang	2,350	1,264,498			
				329,466	52,741,766

[1] Autonomous city.   [2] Special area.

At the census of Oct. 1979 the population was 52,741,766 (25,580,582 male; 19.7% urban).

Population (1986), 61.95m. (Ho Chi Minh 4m.; Hanoi, 2m. (1979); growth rate (1986) 2.8% per annum. Density, 181 per sq. km. Women are urged to confine their families to two children, one not before 22 and one 5 years later.

84% of the population are Vietnamese (Kinh). There are also over 60 minority groups thinly spread in the extensive mountainous regions. The largest minorities are (1976 figures in 1,000): Tay (742); Khmer (651); Thai (631); Muong (618); Nung (472); Meo (349); Dao (294). In 1987 1m. Vietnamese were living abroad, mainly in USA. There is a plan to resettle 12m. inhabitants of the congested Red River Delta in the less populated highland and central districts.

From 1979 to July 1984 59,730 persons emigrated legally. Between Apr. 1975 and Aug. 1984 a further 554,000 illegal emigrants ('boat people') succeeded in finding refuge abroad. In 1985 it was estimated that 'boat people' were still leaving Vietnam at the rate of about 1,000 a month, putting some strain on the resources of the UN High Commission for Refugees and countries such as Indonesia. In 1986 1,400 people a month were leaving legally under the UN's orderly departure scheme. (For previous details *see* THE STATESMAN'S YEAR-BOOK, 1981–82). In Jan. 1988 the USA announced a plan to accept all Asian-American children in Vietnam as refugees. An airlift of 30,000 persons over 2 years is envisaged.

CLIMATE. The humid monsoon climate gives tropical conditions in the south and sub-tropical conditions in the north, though real winter conditions can affect the north when polar air blows south over Asia. In general, there is little variation in temperatures over the year. Hanoi. Jan. 62°F (16.7°C), July 84°F (28.9°C). Annual rainfall 72″ (1,830 mm).

CONSTITUTION AND GOVERNMENT. A new Constitution was adopted in Dec. 1980. It states that Vietnam is a state of proletarian dictatorship and is developing according to Marxism–Leninism.

At the elections for the National Assembly held on 19 April 1987, 829 candidates stood and 496 were elected. Turn-out of voters was said to be 99.32%.

Local government authorities are the people's councils, which appoint executive committees. Local elections were held with the National Assembly elections in 1987.

'The standing organ of the National Assembly and presidium of the Republic' is the State Council:

Chairman: Vo Chi Cong. *Vice-Chairmen:* Nguyen Huu Tho, Le Quang Do, Nguyen Quyet, Dam Quang Trung, Huynh Tan Phat, Mrs Nguyen Thi Dinh.

Chairman of the National Assembly: Le Quang Do.

8 ministers were dismissed in June 1986 and 12 in Feb. 1987.

All political power stems from the Communist Party of Vietnam (until Dec. 1976 known as the Workers' Party of Vietnam), founded in 1930; it had 1.7m. members in 1986. In Dec. 1986 Truong Chinh *(First Secretary)* and other senior veteran leaders left its Politburo, which in April 1988 consisted of Nguyen Van Linh *(First Secretary)*; Vo Chi Cong *(Chairman, State Council)*; Do Muoi *(Deputy Prime Minister)*; Vo Van Kiet *(Acting Prime Minister and Chairman, State Planning Commission)*; Le Duc Anh *(Minister of Defence)*; Nguyen Duc Tam; Nguyen Co Thach *(Deputy Prime Minister and Foreign Minister)*; Dong Si Nguyen

(Deputy Prime Minister); Tran Xuan Bach; Nguyen Thanh Binh; Doan Khue; Mai Chi Tho *(Minister of the Interior)*. Candidate: Dao Duy Tung. Ministers not in the Politburo include: Vo Nguyen Giap; Tran Quynh; Vu Dinh Lieu; Nguyen Ngoc Triu *(Deputy Prime Ministers)*; Doan Duy Than *(Deputy Prime Minister and Foreign Trade)*; Hoang Quy *(Finance)*; Tran Hoan *(Information)*.

There are 2 puppet parties, the Democratic (founded 1944) and the Socialist (1946), which are unified with the trade and youth unions in the Fatherland Front.

National flag: Red, with a yellow 5-pointed star in the centre.
National anthem: 'Tien quan ca' ('The troops are advancing').

DEFENCE. Vietnam has the world's largest armed forces after USSR, China and USA. Men between 18 and 35 and women between 18 and 25 are liable for conscription of 3 years, specialists 4 years.

Army. The Army consists of 1 armoured division, 65 infantry divisions (of varying strengths), 8 engineer and 16 economic construction divisions, and 10 field artillery brigades, 8 engineer divisions. Equipment includes some 1,600 main battle and 450 light tanks. Strength was (1988) about 1m. Paramilitary forces are Border Defence (60,000) and Peoples' Defence Force (1m.). In 1988 some 50,000 troops were stationed in Laos and 140,000 in Cambodia.

Navy. Before the North Vietnamese victory in 1975 the Navy comprised 3 old coastal escorts, 2 fast missile boats, 28 fast torpedo boats, 22 fast motor gunboats, 34 small patrol boats, 24 landing craft, 4 minesweeping boats, 10 tenders, 100 auxiliaries and 200 armed junks. It also had 10 Mi-4 SAR helicopters.

At least 1 frigate, several other major warships and a considerable number of auxiliaries were captured after the South Vietnamese surrender.

The fleet reportedly includes 5 *ex*-Soviet escorts, 2 old frigates, 2 old corvettes, 1 fleet minesweeper, 8 old patrol vessels, 8 fast missile boats, 16 fast torpedo boats, 5 fast hydrofoil torpedo craft, 15 fast gunboats, 9 fast patrol craft, 6 coastal patrol cutters, 9 landing ships, 12 landing craft, 1 torpedo recovery vessel, 1 fleet minesweeper, 2 coastal minesweepers, 1 inshore minehunter, 1 survey ship, 15 auxiliaries and 100 armed junks; but due to the lack of maintenance, spares and trials it is difficult to accurately assess the operational availability, fitness for sea or steaming capacity of this heterogeneous collection or the availability of trained personnel.

It is estimated that 4 missile craft, 6 torpedo boats, 22 gunboats, 3 minesweepers, 24 patrol craft, 25 coastguard cutters and 100 motor launches are non-operational together with 580 riverine craft, 100 landing craft, 30 monitors, 100 converted amphibious craft, 26 vedettes, 36 auxiliaries and 75 service craft.

In 1988 there were an estimated 6,000 naval personnel but there had been up to 34,000 additional conscripts.

Air Force. The Air Force, built up with Soviet and Chinese assistance, has about 20,000 personnel and 350 combat aircraft (plus many stored), including modern US types captured in war. There are reported to be 3 squadrons of variable-geometry MiG-23s, 6 squadrons of MiG-17s and Su-20s, over 150 MiG-21 interceptors; An-2, Li-2, C-47, An-24, An-26 and Il-14 transports; and a strong helicopter force with UH-1 Iroquois, Mi-6, Mi-8 and Mi-24 helicopters. 'Guideline', 'Goa' and 'Gainful' missiles are operational in large numbers.

INTERNATIONAL RELATIONS

Membership. Vietnam is a member of UN, Comecon and IMF.

ECONOMY

Planning. Long-term forward planning gives priority to self-sufficiency in agriculture and stimulating regional industry. The fourth 5-year plan covers 1986–90. (For previous plans *see* THE STATESMAN'S YEAR-BOOK, 1985–86.).

Curtailment of Western aid, and resistance to Government measures have contributed to a shortage of consumer goods and widespread malnutrition. Small family businesses were legalized in 1986.

Since assuming Party leadership in Dec. 1986 Nguyen Van Linh has denounced the inefficiency and bureaucracy of the past and announced major economic reforms injecting free enterprise principles and reducing central control.

Currency. The monetary unit is the *dong*. A currency reform of 14 Sept. 1985 substituted a new *dong* at a rate of 1 new *dong* = 10 (old) *dong*. Notes are issued for 1, 2, 5, 10, 20, 50, 100 and 500 new *dong*. (For former currency *see* THE STATESMAN'S YEAR-BOOK, 1985–86). In March 1988 £1 = 653 *dong*; US$1 = 368 *dong*. Inflation was 700% in 1986.

Banking. The bank of issue is the National Bank of Vietnam (founded in 1951). There is also a Bank for Foreign Trade (Vietcombank).

ENERGY AND NATURAL RESOURCES

Electricity. In 1986, 5,400m. kwh. of electricity were produced. A hydro-electric power station with a capacity of 2m. kw. is being built at Hoa-Binh with Soviet assistance.

Minerals. North Vietnam is rich in anthracite, lignite and hard coal: total reserves are estimated at 20,000m. tonnes. Anthracite production in 1975 was 5m. tonnes. Coal production was 5·3m. tonnes in 1980. There are deposits of iron ore, manganese, titanium, chromite, bauxite and a little gold. Reserves of apatite are some of the biggest in the world. A Soviet-Vietnamese enterprise claimed to have struck oil in May 1984.

Agriculture. In 1985, 62% of the population was engaged in agriculture. In 1977 there were 15,200 co-operatives in the North averaging 300–500 hectares (less than 100 hectares in mountain regions) and a workforce of 1,000–2,000. The intemperate collectivization of agriculture in the South after 1977 had disastrous effects which the Government is now trying to rectify by a system of incentives to peasants which allows them small private plots and the right to market some of their own produce. There were 105 state farms employing in all 70,000 workers and with 55,000 hectares arable and 50,000 hectares of pasture. Other crops include maize, sugar-cane, sweet potatoes and cotton. The cultivated area in 1980 was 6·97m. hectares (5·54m. hectares for rice).

In 1984 there were some 23,000 production collectives and 268 agricultural co-operatives in the South accounting for 47% of the cultivated area. There were about 300 state farms.

Production in 1,000 tonnes in 1986: Rice (16,179), soybeans (120), tea (29), rubber (60), maize (600), tobacco (38), potatoes (235), sweet potatoes (2,000) from 400,000 hectares, sorghum (53) from 33,000 hectares, dry beans (76) from 63,000 hectares, coffee (8). Cereals production was 16·85m. tonnes in 1986.

Livestock (1986): Cattle 2·5m.; pigs, 13m.; goats, 273,000; poultry, 100m.

Animal products, 1985: Eggs, 147,100 tonnes, meat, 948,000 tonnes.

Forestry. 1,626,000 cu. metres of timber were produced in 1980.

Fisheries. Fishing is important, especially in Halong Bay. In 1976, 6m. tonnes of sea fish and 180,000 tonnes of freshwater fish were caught.

INDUSTRY AND TRADE

Industry. Next to mining, food processing and textiles are the most important industries; there is also some machine building. Older industries include cement, cotton and silk manufacture.

Private businesses were taken over in 1978. Foreign firms, principally French, are continuing to function, but all US property has been nationalized. There is little heavy industry. Most industry is concentrated in the Ho-Chi-Minh area.

Production (1980, in 1,000 tonnes) iron, 125; steel, 106; sulphuric acid, 6,700;

caustic soda, 4,500; mineral fertilizer, 260; pesticides, 18,400; paper, 54,000; sugar, 94,000, cement, 705. 1,500 tractors were built in 1980, and 621 railway coaches. Footwear production, 200,000 pairs. Beer, 942,000 hectolitres.

Labour. Average wage (1984) 200 dong per month. Workforce (1985) 28·76m., of whom 17·91m. were in agriculture.

Commerce. 65% of exports are to, and 85% of imports from, Communist countries. USSR and Japan are Vietnam's main trading partners; others are Singapore and Hong Kong. Main exports are coal, farm produce, sea produce and livestock. Imports: Oil, steel, artificial fertilizers. There is an aid agreement with the USSR for 1986–90 amounting to about 9,000m. roubles. In 1987 Vietnam's total indebtedness was estimated at US$6,000m. In 1978 the IMF approved a virtually interest-free loan of US$90m. repayable over 50 years, but in April 1985 suspended all further credits to Vietnam. Sweden gives annual aid of US$47m. A law of June 1987 regulates foreign firms established in Vietnam; concessions include light taxation and authorization to export all profits.

Trade between Vietnam and UK (British Department of Trade returns, in £1,000 sterling):

	1984	1985	1986	1987
Imports to UK	1,154	1,758	1,200	357
Exports and re-exports from UK	1,787	2,077	1,288	2,598

COMMUNICATIONS

Roads. In 1986 there were about 65,000 km of roads described as 'main roads'.

Railways. Route length was 4,200 km in 1986. The Hanoi–Ho Chi Minh City line is being rebuilt in a programme of reconstruction and extension. About 50m. passengers and 10m. tonnes of freight are carried annually.

Aviation. Air Vietnam operates internal services from Hanoi to Ho Chi Minh City, Cao Bang, Na Son and Dien Bien, Vinh and Hue, and from Ho Chi Minh City to Ban Me Thuot and Da Nang, Can Tho, Con Son Island and Quan Long and from Hanoi to Bangkok in conjunction with Thai Airways. Aeroflot (USSR) operate regular services from Ho Chi Min City to Moscow and from Hanoi to Moscow, Rangoon and Vientiane, Interflug (German Dem. Rep.) to Berlin, Moscow and Dacca, Philippine Airlines to Manila, and Air France to Paris.

Shipping. In 1986 there were 150 ships totalling 338,668 GRT. The major ports are Haiphong, which can handle ships of 10,000 tons, Ho Chi Minh City and Da Nang, and there are ports at Hong Gai and Haiphong Ben Thuy. There are regular services to Hong Kong, Singapore, Kampuchea and Japan. In 1987 there were some 6,000 km of navigable waterways.

Cargo is handled by the Vietnam Ocean Shipping Agency; other matters by the Vietnam Foreign Trade Transport Corporation.

Post and Broadcasting. In 1984 there were 6m. radios. There were 106,100 telephones in 1984. There were 2·25m. TV sets in 1984.

Cinemas and theatres. 116 films were produced in 1980 (including 10 full-length). There were 145 theatres.

Newspapers and books. The Party daily is *Nhan Dan* ('The People') circulation, 1985: 500,000. The official daily in the South is *Giai Phong.* Two unofficial dailies, *Cong Giao Va Dan Toc* (Catholic) and *Tin Sang* (independent) are also published. 2,564 books were published in 1980 totalling 90·9m. copies.

JUSTICE, RELIGION, EDUCATION AND WELFARE

Justice. A new penal code came into force 1 Jan. 1986 'to complete the work of the 1980 Constitution'. Penalties (including death) are prescribed for opposition to the people's power, and for economic crimes. There are the Supreme People's Court, local people's courts and military courts. The president of the Supreme Court is responsible to the National Assembly, as is the Procurator-General, who heads the Supreme People's Office of Supervision and Control.

Religion. Taoism is the traditional religion but Buddhism is widespread. At a Conference for Buddhist Reunification in Nov. 1981, 9 sects adopted a charter for a new Buddhist church under the Council of Sangha. The Hoa Hao sect, associated with Buddhism, claimed 1·5m. adherents in 1976. Caodaism, a synthesis of Christianity, Buddhism and Confucianism founded in 1926, has some 2m. followers. There are some 500,000 Roman Catholics (mainly in the south) headed by Cardinal Trinh Van Can, Archbishop of Hanoi and 13 bishops. There were 2 seminaries in 1988. In 1983 the Government set up a Solidarity Committee of Catholic Patriots.

Education. Primary education consists of a 10-year course divided into 3 levels of 4, 3 and 3 years respectively. There were 500,000 teachers in 1988. Numbers of pupils and students in 1980–81: nurseries, 2·66m.; primary schools, 12·1m.; complementary education, 2·19m.; vocational secondary education, 130,000. In 1980–81 there were 92,913 nurseries. There were 11,400 schools and 280 vocational secondary schools, with 357,000 and 13,000 teachers respectively.

In 1980–81 there were 83 institutions of higher education (including 3 universities: (Hanoi, Ho Chi Minh City, Central Highlands University at Ban Me Thuot), 13 industrial colleges, 7 agricultural colleges, 5 economics colleges, 9 teacher-training colleges, 7 medical schools and 3 art schools, in all with 16,000 teachers and 159,000 students. In 1981 there were 5,000 Vietnamese studying in the USSR.

Health. In 1975 there were 1,996 hospitals and dispensaries and 93 sanatoria. There were some 13,517 doctors and dentists in 1981 and 197,000 hospital beds.

DIPLOMATIC REPRESENTATIVES

Of Vietnam in Great Britain (12–14 Victoria Rd., London, W8)
Ambassador: Tran Van Hung (accredited 29 Oct. 1986).

Of Great Britain in Vietnam (16 Pho Ly Thuong Kiet, Hanoi)
Ambassador: Emrys T. Davies, CMG.

Of Vietnam to the United Nations
Ambassador: (Vacant).

Books of Reference

Bui Phung, *Vietnamese-English Dictionary.* Hanoi, 1987
Chen, J. H.-M., *Vietnam: A Comprehensive Bibliography.* London, 1973
Dellinger, D., *Vietnam Revisited.* Boston (Mass.), 1986
Duiker, W. J., *The Communist Road to Power in Vietnam.* Boulder, 1981.—*Vietnam: Nation in Revolution,* Boulder, 1983
Fforde, A., *The Limits of National Liberation: Problems of Economic Management in the Democratic Republic of Vietnam.* London, 1987
Harrison, J. P., *The Endless War: Fifty Years of Struggle in Vietnam.* New York, 1982
Higgins, H., *Vietnam.* 2nd ed. London, 1982
Ho Chi Minh, *Selected Writings, 1920–1969.* Hanoi, 1977
Hodgkin, T., *Vietnam: The Revolutionary Path:* London, 1981
Houtart, F., *Hai Van: Life in a Vietnamese Commune.* London, 1984
Karnow, S., *Vietnam: A History.* New York, 1983
Lawson, E. K., *The Sino-Vietnamese Conflict.* New York, 1984
Lewy, G., *America in Vietnam.* OUP, 1979
Leitenberg, M., and Burns, R. D., *War in Vietnam.* 2nd ed. Oxford and Santa Barbara, 1982
Nguyen Tien Hung, C., *Economic Developments of Socialist Vietnam, 1955–80.* New York, 1977
Nguyen Van Canh, *Vietnam under Communism, 1975–1982.* Stanford Univ. Press, 1983
Popkin, S. L., *The Rational Peasant: The Political Economy of Rural Society in Vietnam.* Berkeley, 1979
Smith, R. B., *An International History of the Vietnam War.* London, 1983
Truong Chinh, *Selected Writings.* Hanoi, 1977
Truong Nhu Tang, *Journal of a Vietcong.* London, 1986

BRITISH VIRGIN ISLANDS

Capital: Road Town
Population: 12,034 (1980)
GNP per capita: US$4,500 (1982)

HISTORY. The Virgin Islands were discovered by Columbus on his second voyage in 1493. The British Virgin Islands were first settled by the Dutch in 1648 and taken over in 1666 by a group of English planters. In 1774 constitutional government was granted and in 1834 slavery was abolished.

AREA AND POPULATION. The British Virgin Islands form the eastern extremity of the Greater Antilles and, exclusive of small rocks and reefs, number 40, of which 15 are inhabited. The largest are Tortola (1980 population, 9,322), Virgin Gorda (1,443), Anegada (169) and Jost Van Dyke (136). Other islands in the group have a total population of 82; Marine population, 220; Institutional population, 662. Total area about 59 sq. miles (130 sq. km); population (1980), 12,034. Road Town, on the south-east of Tortola, is a port of entry; population, approximately 3,976.

CLIMATE. A pleasantly healthy sub-tropical climate with summer temperatures lowered by sea breezes. Nights are cool and rainfall averages 50" (1,250 mm).

CONSTITUTION AND GOVERNMENT. In 1950 representative government was introduced and in 1967 a new Constitution was granted (amended 1977). The Governor is responsible for defence and internal security, external affairs, the public service, and the courts. The Executive Council consists of the Governor, 1 *ex-officio* member who is the Attorney-General and 4 ministers in the Legislature. The Legislative Council consists of 1 *ex-officio* member who is the Attorney-General and 9 elected members, one of whom is the Chief Minister and Minister of Finance; the Speaker is elected from outside the Council.

Governor: J. Mark Herdman, LVO.
Chief Minister: H. Lavity Stoutt.
Flag: The British Blue Ensign with the arms of the Territory in the fly.

ECONOMY

Budget. In 1987 revenue (estimate) was US$24,401,000; expenditure, US$23,511,100.

Currency. The unit of currency is the US dollar.

Banking. Bank of Nova Scotia, Barclays Bank PLC, Chase Manhattan Bank NA, Craigmuir Trust Company Ltd and First Pennsylvania Bank NA hold General Banking Licences and had total deposits of US$191m. at 31 Dec. 1985. Five institutions hold restricted banking licences and there are also a large number of trust companies.

ENERGY AND NATURAL RESOURCES

Electricity. Production, 1986, 31m. kwh.

Agriculture. Agricultural production is limited, with the chief products being livestock (including poultry), fish, fruit and vegetables. Fruit production, 1986, 1,000 tonnes. In 1985 the Agriculture Department was extended to include an abattoir.

Livestock (1986): Cattle, 2,000; pigs, 3,000; sheep, 8,000; goats, 12,000.

INDUSTRY AND TRADE

Industry. The entire economy is based on tourism, from which is derived directly or indirectly some 75% of GDP. The construction industry is a significant employer.

Commerce. There is a very small export trade almost entirely with the Virgin Islands of the USA. In 1983 imports were US$67·2m. and exports US$3·1m.

Total trade between the British Virgin Islands and UK (British Department of Trade returns, in £1,000 sterling):

	1985	1986	1987
Imports to UK	698	267	752
Exports and re-exports from UK	3,522	3,491	3,310

Tourism. There were 176,451 visitors in 1986. In 1985 visitors spent (estimate) US$97,291,000.

COMMUNICATIONS

Roads. There were (1985) over 70 miles of roads and (1986) 4,706 licensed vehicles.

Aviation. Beef Island Airport, about 16 km from Road Town, is capable of receiving 80-seat short-take-off-and-landing jet aircraft. Air BVI operates internal flights and external flights to San Juan (main route), Puerto Rico; the USVI and St Kitts. Other services to the BVI are Eastern Metro Express, LIAT and American Eagle.

Shipping. There are services to Europe, the USA and other Caribbean islands, and daily services by motor launches to the US Virgin Islands.

Post and Broadcasting. There were (1986) nearly 3,000 telephones and 83 telex subscribers, and an external telephone service links Tortola with Bermuda and the rest of the world, and cable communications also exist to all parts of the world. Radio ZBVI transmits 10,000 watts and has stand-by transmitting facilities of 1,000 watts. British Virgin Islands operates Cable TV of approximately 12 television channels plus a number of FM stereo broadcasting stations.

RELIGION, EDUCATION AND WELFARE

Religion. There are Anglican, Methodist, Seventh-Day Adventist, Roman Catholic and Baptist Churches in the Territory. The Church of God is also represented.

Education. Primary education is provided in 16 government schools, two with secondary divisions, and 9 private schools. Total number of pupils (Dec. 1986) 2,415.

Secondary education to the GCE level and Caribbean Examination Council level is provided by 3 local High Schools. Total number of secondary level pupils (Dec. 1986) 1,444 including those attending Literacy and Skills Programme at post-primary level.

Government expenditure, 1987 (estimate), US$3·2m. In 1987 the total number of teachers in all Government schools was 182. In 1986 a branch of the Hull University (England) School of Education was established.

Health. In 1987 there were 7 doctors, 42 nurses, 50 public hospital beds and 1 private hospital with 8 beds. Expenditure, 1987 (estimate) was US$2·4m.

Books of Reference

Dookhan, I., *A History of the British Virgin Islands.* Epping, 1975
Harrigan, N., and Varlack, P., *British Virgin Islands: A Chronology.* London, 1971.
Pickering, V. W., *Early History of the British Virgin Islands.* London, 1983.

Library: Public Library, Road Town. *Librarian:* Mr Peter Moll.

WESTERN SAMOA

Capital: Apia
Population: 163,000 (1986)
GNP per capita: US$770 (1984)

Samoa i Sisifo

HISTORY. Western Samoa, a former German protectorate (1899–1914), was administered by New Zealand from 1920 to 1961, at first under a League of Nations Mandate and from 1946 under a United Nations Trusteeship Agreement. In May 1961 a plebiscite held under the supervision of the United Nations on the basis of universal adult suffrage voted overwhelmingly in favour of independence as from 1 Jan. 1962, on the basis of the Constitution, which a Constitutional Convention had adopted in Aug. 1960. In Oct. 1961 the General Assembly of the United Nations passed a resolution to terminate the trusteeship agreement as from 1 Jan. 1962, on which date Western Samoa became an independent sovereign state.

Under a treaty of friendship signed on 1 Aug. 1962 New Zealand acts, at the request of Western Samoa, as the official channel of communication between the Samoan Government and other governments and international organizations outside the Pacific islands area. Liaison is maintained by the New Zealand High Commissioner in Apia.

AREA AND POPULATION. Western Samoa lies between 13° and 15° S. lat. and 171° and 173° W. long. It comprises the two large islands of Savai'i and Upolu, the small islands of Manono and Apolima, and several uninhabited islets lying off the coast. The total land area is 1,093 sq. miles (2,830·8 sq. km), of which 659·4 sq. miles (1,707·8 sq. km) are in Savai'i, and 431·5 sq. miles (1,117·6 sq. km) in Upolu; other islands, 2·1 sq. miles (5·4 sq. km). The islands are of volcanic origin, and the coasts are surrounded by coral reefs. Rugged mountain ranges form the core of both main islands and rise to 3,608 ft in Upolu and 6,094 ft in Savai'i. The large area laid waste by lava-flows in Savai'i is a primary cause of that island supporting less than one-third of the population of the islands despite its greater size than Upolu.

The population at the 1981 census was 158,130, of whom 114,980 were in Upolu (including Manono and Apolima) and 43,150 in Savai'i. The capital and chief port is Apia in Upolu (population 33,170 in 1981). Estimate (1986) 163,000.

CLIMATE. A tropical marine climate, with cooler conditions from May to Nov. and a rainy season from Dec. to April. The rainfall is unevenly distributed, with south and east coasts having the greater quantities. Average annual rainfall is about 100″ (2,500 mm) in the drier areas. Apia. Jan. 80°F (26·7°C), July 78°F (25·6°C). Annual rainfall 112″ (2,800 mm).

CONSTITUTION AND GOVERNMENT. The Constitution provides for a Head of State known as 'Ao o le Malo', which position from 1 Jan. 1962 was held jointly by the representatives of the two royal lines of Tuiaana/Tuiatua and Malietoa. On the death of HH Tupua Tamasese Mea'ole, CBE, on 5 April 1963, HH Malietoa Tanumafili II, CBE, became, as provided by the constitution, the sole Head of State for life. Future Heads of State will be elected by the Legislative Assembly and hold office for 5-year terms.

The executive power is vested in the Head of State, who appoints the Prime Minister and, on the Prime Minister's advice, the 8 Ministers to form the Cabinet which has general direction and control of the executive Government.

The Legislative Assembly has 45 members elected from territorial constituencies on a franchise confined to matais or chiefs (of whom there are about 11,000) and 2 members elected on universal adult suffrage from the individual voters roll, which has replaced the old European roll (approximately 1,350 in 1971). One Member is elected as Speaker. The Constitution also provides for a Council of Deputies of 3 members. In the elections held Feb. 1985, the Human Rights Protection Party won 31 seats.

The official languages are Samoan and English.

Head of State and O le Ao o le Malo: HH Malietoa Tanumafili II, GCMG, CBE.

The cabinet in Feb. 1987 was composed as follows:

Prime Minister, Minister of Foreign Affairs, Internal Affairs, Immigration, Police and Prisons, Attorney General: Va'ai Kolone.
Works: Tupuola Efi. *Finance:* Faasootauloa Semu Saili. *Agriculture:* Fuimaono Mimio. *Economic Affairs:* Le Tagaloa Pita. *Education:* Le Mamea Ropati Mualia. *Health:* Toeolesulusulu Siueva. *Justice:* George Michael Lober. *Lands:* Faumuina Anapapa.
National flag: Red with a blue quarter bearing 5 white stars of the Southern Cross.

INTERNATIONAL RELATIONS

Membership. Western Samoa is a member of UN, the Commonwealth, the South Pacific Forum and is an ACP state of EEC.

ECONOMY

Budget. In 1987 budgeted revenue was $WS82·2m.; expenditure, $WS118m.

Currency. The Western Samoa currency is the *talà* (dollar). In March 1988, £1 = 3·53; US$1 = 1·00.

Banking. A Central Bank was established in 1984. In 1959 the Bank of Western Samoa was established with a capital of $WS500,000, of which $WS275,000 was subscribed by the Bank of New Zealand and $WS225,000 by the Government of Western Samoa. In 1977 the Pacific Commercial Bank was established jointly by Australia's Bank of New South Wales and the Bank of Hawaii.

ENERGY AND NATURAL RESOURCES

Electricity. Production (1986) 79m. kwh.

Agriculture. The main products (1986, in 1,000 tonnes) are coconuts (200), taro (39), copra (24), bananas (23), papayas (12), mangoes (6), pineapples (6) and cocoa beans (2).
Livestock (1986): Horses, 3,000; cattle, 27,000; pigs, 64,000; poultry 1m.

Fisheries. The total catch (1983) was 3,150 tonnes, valued at $WS5·1m.

INDUSTRY AND TRADE

Industry. Some industrial activity is being developed associated with agricultural products and forestry.

Commerce. In 1985, imports were valued at $WS115,074,000 and exports at $WS36,195,000. Principal exports were coconut oil (10,926 tonnes; $WS15,622,000), cocoa (581 tons; $WS2,356,000), taro (22,000 cases, $WS5,113,000), coconut cream ($WS2,833,000); fruit juice ($WS1,002,000); beer ($WS385,000) and cigarettes ($WS5,558,000). Chief imports in 1983 included food and live animals ($WS15,195,000), beverages and tobacco ($WS1,913,000), machinery and transport equipment ($WS14,968,000), mineral fuels, lubricants and other materials ($WS13,133,000), chemicals ($WS4,221,000) and miscellaneous manufactured articles ($WS5,279,000).

Total trade between Western Samoa and UK (British Department of Trade returns, in £1,000 sterling):

	1983	1984	1985	1986	1987
Imports to UK	156	421	292	622	531
Exports and re-exports from UK	468	1,183	619	433	1,650

Tourism. There were 49,710 visitors in 1986.

COMMUNICATIONS

Roads (1987). Western Samoa has 2,085 km of roads, 400 km of which are surfaced and 1,200 km plantation roads fit for light traffic.

In 1984 there were 1,498 private cars, 1,909 pick-up trucks, 398 trucks, 187 buses, 297 taxis and 144 motor cycles.

Aviation. Western Samoa is linked by daily air service with American Samoa, which is on the route of the weekly New Zealand–Tahiti and New Zealand–Honolulu air services, with connexions to Fiji, Australia, USA and Europe. There are also services throughout the week to and from Tonga, Fiji, Nauru, the Cook Islands and New Zealand. Internal services link Upolu and Savai'i.

Shipping. Western Samoa is linked to Japan, USA, Europe, Fiji, Australia and New Zealand by regular shipping services.

Post and Broadcasting. There is a radio communication station at Apia. Radio telephone service connects Western Samoa with American Samoa, Fiji, New Zealand, Australia, Canada, USA and UK. Telephone subscribers numbered 3,641 in 1984. In 1982 there were 70,000 radio receivers and about 2,500 television sets.

Cinemas. In 1987 there were 4 cinemas.

Newspapers. In 1985, there were 4 weeklies, circulation 12,000 and 2 monthlies (8,000); all were in Samoan and English.

RELIGION, EDUCATION AND WELFARE

Religion. In 1981, 47% of the population are Congregationalists, 22% Roman Catholic and 16% Methodist.

Education. In 1983 there were 162 primary schools with 31,447 pupils, 38 secondary schools with 20,404 pupils, and 8 vocational schools and 2 teacher-training colleges with a total of 1,213 students.

Health. In 1987 there were 16 hospitals and 16 subcentres (with a total of 682 beds) and 44 doctors.

DIPLOMATIC REPRESENTATIVES

Of Western Samoa in Great Britain
High Commissioner: Feesago George Fepulea'i (resides in Brussels).

Of Great Britain in Western Samoa
High Commissioner: R. A. C. Byatt, CMG (resides in Wellington, New Zealand).

Of Western Samoa in the USA and to the United Nations
Ambassador: Maiava Iulai Toma.

Books of Reference

Statistical Year-Book. Annual
Fox, J. W. (ed.), *Western Samoa.* Univ. of Auckland, 1963
Milner, G. B., *Samoan–English, English–Samoan Dictionary.* OUP, 1965

YEMEN ARAB REPUBLIC

Capital: San'a
Population: 6·53m. (1987)
GNP per capita: US$510 (1983)

al Jamhuriya al Arabiya al Yamaniya

HISTORY. On the death of the Iman Ahmad on 18 Sept. 1962, army officers seized power on 26–27 Sept., declared his son, Saif Al-Islam Al-Badr (Iman Mansur Billah Muhammad), deposed and proclaimed a republic. The republican régime was supported by Egyptian troops, whereas the royalist tribes received aid from Saudi Arabia. On 24 Aug. 1965 President Nasser and King Faisal signed an agreement according to which the two powers are to support a plebiscite to determine the future of the Yemen; a conference of republican and royalist delegates met at Haradh on 23 Nov. 1965, but no plebiscite was agreed upon. At a meeting of the Arab heads of state in Aug. 1967 the President and the King agreed upon disengaging themselves from the civil war in Yemen. At the time there were still about 50,000 Egyptian troops in the country, holding San'a, Ta'iz, Hodeida and the plains, whereas the mountains were in the hands of the royalist tribes. By the end of 1967 the Egyptians had withdrawn.

AREA AND POPULATION. In the north the boundary between the Yemen and Saudi Arabia has been defined by the Treaty of Taif concluded in June 1934. This frontier starts from the sea at a point some 5 or 10 miles north of Maidi and runs due east inland until it reaches the hills some 30 miles from the coast, whence it runs northwards for approximately 50 miles so as to leave the Sa'da Basin within the Yemen. Thence it runs in an easterly and south-easterly direction until it reaches the desert area near Nejran. The area is about 73,300 sq. miles (195,000 sq. km) with a population of 7,160,851, census 1981; estimate (1987) 6,533,265. There were 1,395,123 citizens working abroad mainly in Saudi Arabia and the United Arab Emirates not included in the census total. The capital is San'a with a population of (1981) 277,817. Other important towns are the port of Hodeida (population, 126,386), and Ta'iz (119,572); other towns are Ibb, Yerim, Dhamar and the ports of Mokha and Loheiya.

CLIMATE. A desert climate, modified by relief. San'a. Jan. 57°F (13·9°C), July 71°F (21·7°C). Annual rainfall 20″ (508 mm).

CONSTITUTION AND GOVERNMENT. A provisional Constitution was promulgated on 19 June 1974 by the Command Council, which later established a 99-member People's Constituent Assembly on 6 Feb. 1978 (membership raised to 159 on 8 May 1979) before dissolving itself on 22 April 1978. The Assembly elects the President of the Republic, who appoints a Prime Minister and other members of the Cabinet. A General People's Congress met in 1982 composed of 1,000 members (700 elected).

President of the Republic: Col. Ali Abdullah Saleh (elected 17 July 1978; re-elected 22 May 1983).
The Council of Ministers in Dec. 1987 was composed of:
Chairman (Prime Minister), Vice-President: Maj. Abdel Aziz Abdel Ghani.
Vice-President: Abd al-Karim al Arishi.
Deputy Prime Ministers: Col. Mujahid Abu Shawrib; Dr Abdul Karim al-Iryani *(Foreign Affairs)*; Dr Hassan Mohammed Makki.
Agriculture and Fisheries: Dr Husayn Abdallah al-Amri. *Waafs and Guidance:* Qadi Ali ibn Ali Samman. *Civil Service:* Ismail Ahmad al Wazir. *Transport:*

Ahmad Muhammad al Ansi. *Development:* Dr Muhammad Said al Attar. *Economy:* Muhammad al-Khadim al-Wajih. *Education:* Abdallah al Jayfi. *Finance:* Alwi Salah as-Salami. *Health:* Dr Muhammad Ahmad al Kabab. *Justice:* Qadi Ahmad Muhammad al Jubi. There are also 2 Ministers of State.

National flag: Three horizontal stripes of red, white, black, with a green star in the centre.

Local government: There are 8 provinces *(Liwa'):* Sa'dah, al-Bayda, San'a, al-Hudaydah (Hodeida), Hajjah, Rida, Ibb and Ta'iz.

DEFENCE. Military service for 3 years is compulsory.

Army. The Army consists of 6 armoured, 3 mechanized, 9 infantry, 1 para-commando, 1 Special Forces brigade, 3 artillery brigades, 1 central guard force and 3 anti-aircraft artillery and 2 air defence battalions. Equipment includes 125 T-34, 460 T-54/-55, 34 T-62 and 64 M-60A1 main battle tanks. Strength (1988) 35,000.

Navy. The flotilla consists of 3 patrol craft, 2 fast attack craft, 2 inshore mine-hunters, 4 landing craft (all 11 *ex*-Soviet) and 12 small coastal patrol boats. Person-nel in 1988 numbered 600 regular officers and men.

Air Force. Built up with aid from both the USA and USSR, as well as Saudi Arabia, the Air Force is believed to be receiving many new Soviet aircraft. Current equip-ment includes 15 Su-22 fighter-bombers, 25 MiG-21 and 14 F-5 fighters, a total of 14 Il-14, An-24/26, C-130 Hercules and Skyvan transports, and over 30 Mi-8 and Agusta-Bell JetRanger and 212 helicopters. Personnel (1988) about 1,000.

INTERNATIONAL RELATIONS

Membership. The Yemen Arab Republic is a member of UN and the Arab League.

ECONOMY

Planning. The second development plan (1982–86) envisaged expenditure of 29,300m. riyals.

Budget. The budget for 1986 provided for expenditure of 9,944,396,000 riyal and revenue of 7,179,029,000 riyal.

Currency. The currency is the *riyal* of 100 *fils.* In March 1988, 18·20 *riyal*=£1 and 9·88 *riyal*=US$1.

ENERGY AND NATURAL RESOURCES

Electricity. Production (1986) 556m. kwh.

Oil. The first large-scale oilfield and pipeline was inaugurated in 1987, following the discovery in 1984.

Minerals. The only commercial mineral being exploited is salt and (1981) production was 64,000 tons. Reserves (estimate) 25m. tonnes.

Agriculture. Of the total area of 19·5m. hectares, 1·3m. are arable or permanent crops. Cotton is grown in the Tihama, the coastal belt, round Bait al Faqih and Zabid. Fruit is plentiful, especially fine grapes from the San'a district. Production (1986, in 1,000 tonnes): Sorghum, 391; potatoes, 208; grapes, 85; dates, 7; wheat, 85; barley, 41; maize, 49.

Livestock (1986): Cattle, 952,000; camels, 57,000; sheep, 1·85m.; goats, 2·26m.; poultry, 16m.

Fisheries. Total catch (1984) 18,300 tonnes.

INDUSTRY AND TRADE

Industry. There is very little industry. The largest is a textile factory at San'a. Production of cement (1982) 85,000 tonnes.

Commerce. Imports totalled US$1·2m. riyals in 1985, the largest items being food and live animals. Exports totalled US$1·2m. in 1985.

Total trade between Yemen Arab Republic and UK (British Department of Trade returns, in £1,000 sterling):

	1983	1984	1985	1986	1987
Imports to UK	1,857	2,536	2,312	2,106	2,306
Exports and re-exports from UK	56,315	58,761	94,382	58,149	55,334

Tourism. There were about 44,000 tourists in 1986.

COMMUNICATIONS

Roads. There were (1984) 36,000 km of roads.

Aviation. There are 3 international airports: San'a, Ta'iz and Hodeida.

Shipping. Hodeida, Mokha, Salif and Loheiya are the 4 main ports.

Post and Broadcasting. There were about 35,000 telephones in 1984. In 1984 there were 37,000 television and 110,000 radio receivers.

RELIGION, EDUCATION AND WELFARE

Religion. The population is almost entirely Moslem, comprising 39% Sunni (Shafi'i) and 59% Shi'a (Zaidi).

Education. There were (1983) 731,989 pupils at primary schools, 78,700 in secondary schools, and 4,489 at teacher-training establishments. In 1982 the University of San'a (founded in 1974) had 6,719 students.

Health. In 1983 there were 60 hospitals and health centres with 4,000 beds.

DIPLOMATIC REPRESENTATIVES

Of Yemen Arab Republic in Great Britain (41 South St., London, W1Y 5PD)
Ambassador: Ahmed Daifellah Al-Azeib (accredited 16 Oct. 1982).

Of Great Britain in Yemen Arab Republic (129 Haddah Rd., San'a)
Ambassador: M. A. Marshall.

Of Yemen Arab Republic in the USA (600 New Hampshire Ave., NW, Washington, D.C., 20037)
Ambassador: Mohsin A. Alaini.

Of the USA in Yemen Arab Republic (P.O. Box 1088, San'a)
Ambassador: William A. Rugh.

Of Yemen Arab Republic to the United Nations
Ambassador: Mohamed Salem Basendwah.

Books of Reference

Bidwell, R., *The Two Yemens.* Boulder and London, 1983
El Mallakh, R., *The Economic Development of the Yemen Arab Republic.* London, 1986
Peterson, J. E., *Yemen: The Search for a Modern State.* London, 1982
Smith, G. R., *The Yemens.* [Bibliography] Oxford and Santa Barbara, 1984
Stookey, R. W., *Yemen: The Politics of the Yemen Arab Republic.* Boulder, 1978

THE PEOPLE'S DEMOCRATIC REPUBLIC OF YEMEN

Capital: Aden
Population: 2·3m. (1987)
GNP per capita: US$500 (1985)

Jumhuriyah al-Yemen al Dimuqratiyah al Sha'abiyah— Southern Yemen

HISTORY. Between Aug. and Oct. 1967 the 17 sultanates of the Federation of South Arabia (*see* map in the STATESMAN'S YEAR-BOOK, 1965–66) were overrun by the forces of the National Liberation Front (NLF). The rulers were deposed, resigned or fled. At the same time the rival organization of FLOSY (Front for the Liberation of Occupied South Yemen) fought a civil war against NLF and harassed the British forces and civilians in Aden. In Nov. the UAR withdrew its support from FLOSY, and with the backing of the Army the NLF took over throughout the country.

The last British troops left Aden on 29 Nov. 1967, and on 30 Nov. the Southern Yemen People's Republic was proclaimed and the name was subsequently changed to the People's Democratic Republic of Yemen in 1970.

AREA AND POPULATION. The People's Democratic Republic of Yemen is bounded north by the Yemen Arab Republic and Saudi Arabia, east by Oman, south by the Gulf of Aden and west by the Yemen Arab Republic and Bab Al-Mandab Strait. The Republic covers an area of approximately 130,065 sq. miles (336,869 sq. km). Land area can be divided into 4 areas: (*i*) the coastal lands in the south, nearly 1,200 km long and 12·25 km wide; (*ii*) the inner lands and plateaus; (*iii*) the northern desert to the north of Hadhramaut; (*iv*) the green valleys scattered between the high lands. Population (estimate, 1987) 2,278,000; urban, 33%; rural, 57% and nomads, 10%. The main towns are (1984) Aden (capital) (population, 318,000), and Mukalla (158,000).

The island of **Kamaran** in the Red Sea (area 181 sq. km) was in British occupation from 1915 to 1967, when the inhabitants opted in favour of remaining with the Republic but Yemen Arab Republic occupied it in 1972.

The island of **Perim** (300 sq. km) was first occupied by the French in 1738. In 1799 the British took formal possession but evacuated the island the same year. It was re-occupied by the British in Jan. 1851 and was later used as a coaling station. In Nov. 1967 the inhabitants opted in favour of remaining with the Republic.

The island of **Socotra** lying to the east of the Horn of Africa in the Arabian sea (area 3,500 sq. km) was formerly part of the Sultanate of Qishn and Socotra and became part of the Republic in 1967.

CLIMATE. A desert climate prevails, modified in parts by altitude, which affects temperatures by up to 12°C, as well as rainfall, which is very low in coastal areas. Aden. Jan. 75°F (24°C), July 90°F (32°C). Annual rainfall 1·8″ (46 mm).

CONSTITUTION AND GOVERNMENT

An amended Constitution was approved by the Supreme People's Council on 31 Oct. 1978.

Meetings took place during 1984–85 between President Mohammed and the President Saleh of the Yemen Arabic Republic, to discuss further steps towards unification.

On 13 Jan. 1986 there was a *coup* attempt against President Ali Nasser Mohammed which developed into virtual civil war. By 24 Jan. the rebel forces had taken control of the capital, Aden, and at a meeting of the Socialist Party Central Committee the presidium of the Supreme People's Council announced that the Acting President was Haidar al-Attas. He was elected President on 6 Feb. 1986.

National flag. Three horizontal stripes of red, white, black, with a blue triangle based on the hoist bearing a red star.

Local Government. There are 6 governorates (Aden, Lahej, Abyan, Shabwa, Hadhramaut and Al-Mahra), sub-divided into 30 provinces.

DEFENCE. Military service for 2 years is compulsory.

Army. The Army comprises 1 armoured, 3 mechanized, 8 infantry, 3 artillery, 2 rocket and 2 surface-to-surface missile brigades and 10 artillery battalions. Equipment includes 470 T-34/-54/-55/-62 main battle tanks. Strength (1988) about 24,000.

Navy. The Navy comprises 8 fast missile craft, 2 fast torpedo-boats, 2 fast attack craft, 1 tank landing ship, 3 medium landing ships and 5 minor landing craft, all transferred from the Soviet Navy and 10 very small British-built launches. Personnel in 1988 totalled 1,000 officers and men.

Air Force. Formed in 1967, the Air Force is now equipped mainly with aircraft of Soviet design. It has received about 50 MiG-21 fighters, 35 MiG-17 and 25 MiG-23 fighter-bombers, 30 Su-22 attack aircraft, 15 Mi-24 gunship helicopters, 4 An-24 and 2 An-26 twin-turboprop transports and about 30 Mi-8 and 6 Mi-4 helicopters. Personnel (1988) about 2,500.

INTERNATIONAL RELATIONS

Membership. The People's Democratic Republic of Yemen is a member of UN and the Arab League.

ECONOMY

Planning. The development plan (1986–91) envisaged expenditure of 998·2m. dinars.

Budget. The budget (in 1m. Yemeni dinars) for 1986 envisaged general revenue at 214·4 and general expenditure at 341·4.

Currency. The currency is the South Yemen *dinar* and is divided into 1,000 *fils*. Coins: 50, 25, 5 *fils*; notes: 10, 5 and 1 *dinar*, 500 and 250 *fils*. In March 1988, £1 = 0·608 *dinars*; US$1 = 0·343 *dinars*.

Banking. The only commercial bank is the National Bank of Yemen with the Bank of Yemen carrying on the functions of the Central Bank. All foreign banks have been nationalized.

ENERGY AND NATURAL RESOURCES

Electricity. Production (1986) 556m. kwh.

Agriculture. Agriculture is the main occupation of the people. This is largely of a subsistence nature, sorghum, sesame and millet being the chief crops, and wheat and barley widely grown at the higher elevations. Of increasing importance, however, are the cash crops which have been developed since the Second World

War, by far the most important of which is the Abyan long-staple cotton, now the country's major export.

Owing to paucity of rainfall, cultivation is largely confined to fertile valleys and flood plains on silt, built up and irrigated in the traditional manner. These traditional methods are being augmented and replaced by the use of modern earth moving machinery and pumps. Irrigation schemes with permanent installations are in progress. Production (1985 in 1,000 tonnes): Millet, 80; wheat, 15; cotton lint, 5; cotton seed, 10; sesame, 3; barley, 2.

Livestock (1986): Cattle, 96,000; sheep, 930,000; goats, 1·38m.; poultry, 2m.

Fisheries. There is a thriving fisheries industry, fish being the Republic's major export after cotton. Catch (1985) 80,000 tonnes.

INDUSTRY AND TRADE

Industry. Light industry is being established and paint, match and textile factories are in production.

Commerce. Trade is mainly transhipment and entrepôt, Aden serving as a centre of distribution to and from neighbouring territories. Transit trade is mainly in cotton piece-goods, grains, coffee, hides and skins, and cheap consumer goods. Importation of all commodities specified for local consumption is subject to a prior import licence from the Ministry of Trade, Industry and Supply. Importation of any commodities is completely forbidden except by virtue of a valid import licence.

In 1985 imports totalled 241m. dinar; exports and re-exports, 10m. dinar.

Total trade between Republic of Yemen and UK (British Department of Trade returns, in £1,000 sterling):

	1983	1984	1985	1986	1987
Imports to UK	10,627	18,238	7,938	4,848	1,056
Exports and re-exports from UK	36,673	45,221	34,827	23,928	28,271

COMMUNICATIONS

Roads. There were (1986) 1,929 km of roads. Registered motor vehicles in 1984 numbered 51,884.

Aviation. There are airports at Khormaksar (Aden) and Mukalla. Nine airlines operate scheduled services: Alyemda, Air-France, Ethiopian Airlines, Middle East Airlines, Yemen Airlines, Aeroflot, Saudi Airlines, Kuwait Airways, and Air Djibouti.

Shipping. Because of its favourable geographical position and its efficient service to ships, Aden used to be one of the busiest oil-bunkering ports in the world, handling some 550 ships a month. In 1983, 4·8m. tonnes of cargo were unloaded and 3·6m. tonnes loaded. Five alongside berths were under construction in 1988.

Post and Broadcasting. The automatic telephone system provided service to about 31,000 subscribers in 1985.

In 1985 there were 180,000 radio and 30,000 television receivers.

Cinemas (1971). There were 19 cinemas with a seating capacity of about 20,000.

JUSTICE, RELIGION, EDUCATION AND WELFARE

Justice. There is a Supreme Court and Magistrates' Courts. In some areas Moslem and local Common Law are administered.

Religion. The majority of the population is Moslem. There are small numbers of Christians and Hindus.

Education. There were (1984, estimate) 238,004 primary school pupils and 27,908 secondary school pupils. A state university was founded in 1975 and the number of students is increasing. In 1985, 400,000 students were studying at schools at various levels. Efforts are being made to eradicate illiteracy among adults.

Welfare. There were (1986) 54 hospitals with 4,499 beds and about 652 doctors.

DIPLOMATIC REPRESENTATIVES

Of the People's Democratic Republic of Yemen in Great Britain (57 Cromwell Rd., London, SW7 2ED)
Ambassador: Ahmed Abdo Rageh (accredited 18 Feb. 1987).

Of Great Britain in the People's Democratic Republic of Yemen (28 Shara Ho Chi Minh, Khormaksar, Aden)
Ambassador: Arthur S.-M. Marshall, CBE.

Of the People's Democratic Republic of Yemen to the United Nations
Ambassador: Abdalla Saleh Al-Ashtal.

The US Embassy in Aden was closed on 26 Oct. 1969 and UK acts as the protective power.

Books of Reference

Bidwell, R., *The Two Yemens*. London, 1984
Ismael, T. Y., and Ismael, J. S., *The People's Democratic Republic of Yemen: Politics, Economics and Society*. London, 1986
Kostiner, J., *The Struggle for South Yemen*. London and New York, 1984
Lackner, H., *P.D.R. Yemen: Outpost of Socialist Development in Arabia*. London, 1985
Smith, G. R., *The Yemens*. [Bibliography] Oxford and Santa Barbara, 1984
Stookey, R. W., *South Yemen: A Marxist Republic in Arabia*. Boulder and London, 1982
Thesiger, W., *Arabian Sands*. London, 1959

YUGOSLAVIA

Capital: Belgrade
Population: 23·27m. (1986)
GNP per capita: US$5,600 (1985)

Socijalistička Federativna
Republika Jugoslavija—
Socialist Federal
Republic of Yugoslavia

HISTORY. In 1917 the Yugoslav Committee in London drew up the Pact of Corfu, which proclaimed that all Yugoslavs would unite after the first world war to form a kingdom under the Serbian royal house. The Kingdom of Serbs, Croats and Slovenes was proclaimed on 1 Dec. 1918. In 1929 the name was changed to Yugoslavia. During the Second World War Tito's partisans set up a provisional government (AVNOJ) which was the basis of a Constituent Assembly after the war. On 29 Nov. 1945 Yugoslavia was proclaimed a republic.

The peace treaty with Italy, signed in Paris on 10 Feb. 1947, stipulated the cession to Yugoslavia of the greater part of the Italian province of Venezia Giulia, the commune of Zara and the island of Pelagosa and the adjacent islets.

By an agreement of 10 Nov. 1975 the city of Trieste ('Zone A') was recognized as Italian and the Adriatic coastal portion of the former Free Territory of Trieste ('Zone B') as Yugoslav. A free industrial zone was set up in the Fernetici–Sezana region on both sides of the frontier.

AREA AND POPULATION. Yugoslavia is bounded in the north by Austria and Hungary, north-east by Romania, east by Bulgaria, south by Greece and west by Albania, the Adriatic Sea and Italy. The area is 255,804 sq. km. Population at the 1981 census: 22,424,771. Population by sex at the 1981 census: females, 11,340,933. Estimate (1986) 23,271,000.

The federal capital is Belgrade (Beograd). Population (census, 1981) 1,470,073 and of other principal towns (B = Bosnia and Herzegovina; C = Croatia; K = Kosovo; Ma = Macedonia; Mo = Montenegro; Se = Serbia; Sl = Slovenia; V = Vojvodina):

Banja Luka (B)	183,618	Priština (K)	216,040
Bitolj (Ma)	137,835	Prizren (K)	134,526
Čačak (Se)	110,676	Rijeka (C)	193,044
Čakovec (C)	116,825	Šabac (Se)	119,669
Gostivar (Ma)	101,188	Sarajevo (B)	448,500
Kragujevac (Se)	164,823	Skopje (Ma)	506,547
Kraljevo (Se)	121,622	Slavonski Brod (C)	106,400
Kruševac (Se)	132,972	Smederevo (Se)	107,366
Kumanovo (Ma)	126,368	Split (C)	235,922
Leskovac (Se)	159,001	Subotica (V)	154,611
Ljubljana (Sl)	305,211	Tetovo (Ma)	162,414
Maribor (Sl)	185,699	Titograd (Mo)	132,290
Mostar (B)	110,377	Titova Mitrovica (K)	105,323
Niš (Se)	230,711	Tuzla (B)	121,717
Novi Sad (V)	257,685	Uroševac (K)	113,680
Osijek (C)	158,790	Zadar (C)	116,174
Pančevo (V)	123,791	Zagreb (C)	1,174,512
Peć (K)	111,071	Zenica (B)	132,733
Prijedor (B)	108,868	Zrenjanin (V)	139,300

Population (1981 census) by ethnic group was *(i)* the 6 'leading nations': Serbs, 8,140,452; Croats, 4,428,005; Moslems, 1,999,957; Slovenes, 1,753,554; Macedonians, 1,339,729; Montenegrins, 579,023; *(ii)* of the 18 other 'nationalities': Albanians, 1,730,364; Hungarians, 426,866. 1,219,045 persons declared themselves 'Yugoslavs' (i.e. not wanting to be listed with any minority). In 1986 about 460,000 nationals worked abroad. There were 181,000 Gypsies in 1986.

Vital statistics, 1986 (per 1,000 population): Live births, 15·4; deaths, 9; marriages, 6·9; infant mortality, 27·1; natural increase, 6·4. Divorces per 1,000 marriages: 132·1. Expectation of life in 1981: males, 67·2; females, 73·6.

The Yugoslav (*i.e.*, South Slav) languages proper are Slovene, Macedonian and Serbo-Croat, the latter having 2 variants (Serbian and Croatian) which are regarded as constituting one language. There are claims, largely politically-motivated, that Croatian is a separate language and Macedonian a dialect of Bulgarian. Macedonian and Serbian may be written in the Cyrillic alphabet. There are also substantial Albanian and Hungarian-speaking minorities. Art. 246 of the Constitution lays down that 'The languages of the nations and nationalities and their alphabets shall be equal throughout the territory of Yugoslavia'. In practice Serbo-Croat serves as a *lingua franca* throughout the country.

CLIMATE. Most parts have a central European type of climate, with cold winters and hot summers, but the whole coast experiences a Mediterranean climate with mild, moist winters and hot, brilliantly sunny summers with less than average rainfall. Belgrade. Jan. 32°F (0°C), July 72°F (22°C). Annual rainfall 24·4" (610 mm). Sarajevo. Jan. 31°F (–0·5°C), July 67°F (19·6°C). Annual rainfall 34" (856 mm). Šibenik. Jan. 45°F (7°C), July 78°F (25·5°C). Annual rainfall 32·5" (813 mm). Split. Jan. 47°F (8·5°C), July 78°F (25·6°C). Annual rainfall 35" (870 mm). Zagreb. Jan. 32°F (0°C), July 72°F (22°C). Annual rainfall 34·6" (865 mm).

CONSTITUTION AND GOVERNMENT. The Constitution passed on 31 Jan. 1946 declared the Federal Republic to be composed of 6 republics: Serbia, Croatia, Slovenia, Bosnia and Herzegovina, Macedonia and Montenegro.

On 13 Jan. 1953 a new Constitution confirmed the management of all public affairs by the workers and their representatives.

The Constitution promulgated 7 April 1963 set up the 2 socialist autonomous provinces of Kosovo and Vojvodina within the framework of Serbia.

Under this Constitution, social self-government was exercised by the representative bodies of communes, districts, autonomous provinces, republics and the Federation and the rights to self-government and distribution of income proclaimed in 1953 were extended to those employed in public services. The former Council of Producers was replaced by Councils of Working Communities representing employees in every field of social activity.

All the means of production and all natural resources are social property. Exceptions are peasants' holdings (up to 10 hectares of arable land) and handicrafts. Citizens may be owners of dwellings for personal and family needs.

A new Constitution was proclaimed on 21 Feb. 1974. This directly transfers economic and political decision making to the working people through the 'assembly system'. An assembly is defined (Art. 132) as 'a body of social self-management and the supreme organ of power within the framework of the rights and duties of its socio-political community'. Assemblies are based upon the workplace or community and take various forms depending upon the nature of employment. Art. 133 states, 'working people in basic self-managing organizations and communities and in socio-political organizations shall form delegations for the purpose of the direct exercise of their rights, duties and responsibilities and of organized participation in the performance of the functions of the assemblies of the socio-political communities', and Art. 135, 'Candidates for members of delegations of basic self-managing organizations and communities shall be proposed and determined by the working people in these organizations and communities in the Socialist Alliance of the Working People ... or in trade union organizations'. At the apex of the assembly system is the federal legislature, the Assembly of the Socialist Federal Republic of Yugoslavia which has 2 Chambers: the Federal Chamber and the Chamber of Republics and Autonomous Provinces.

The Federal Chamber consists of 30 delegates of self-managing organizations, communities and socio-political organizations from each Republic, and 20 delegates from each Autonomous Province. The Chamber of Republics and Autonomous Provinces consists of 12 delegates from each Republican Assembly and of 8 delegates from each Autonomous Province's Assembly. Delegates are elected for 4 years. They retain their normal employment.

A parliamentary commission was set up in 1987 to study a radical series of proposed constitutional amendments.

President of the Federal Assembly: Marjan Rožič.

Every citizen over the age of 18 has the suffrage (16 if employed). The last elections were held from Jan. to April 1986.

The State Presidency is elected by the Federal Assembly every 5 years. It has 9 members: 8 representatives of the Republics and Autonomous Provinces, and the President of the Presidium of the League of Communists *ex officio*. The annual President is head of state. The President-elect, Hamdija Pozderac, resigned in Sept. 1987 following a financial scandal.

Membership of the state Presidency:

Bosnia and Herzegovina: Raif Dizdarević *(President, 1988–89)*; *Croatia:* Josip Vrhovec; *Macedonia:* Lazar Mojsov; *Montenegro:* Veselin Djuranović; *Serbia:* Gen. Nikola Ljubičić; *Slovenia:* Stane Dolanc; *Kosovo:* Sinan Hasani; *Vojvodina:* Radovan Vlajković.

The Government is the Federal Executive Council of President (i.e. Prime Minister), Vice-Presidents, Ministers without Portfolio and Federal Secretaries, who are elected by the Federal Assembly every 4 years in conformity with equality of representation of the Republics and Autonomous Provinces. The present Government consists of Branko Mikulić *(Prime Minister)*, Miloš Milosavljević and Janez Zemljarič *(Deputy Prime Ministers)*, the following Federal Secretaries: Sava Vujkov *(Agriculture)*, Aleksandar Donev *(Economy)*, Svetozar Rikanović *(Finance)*, Vacant *(Foreign Affairs)*, Nenad Krekić *(Foreign Trade)*, Andrej Ocvirk *(Industry)*, Svetozar Durutović *(Information)*, Dobroslav Čulafić *(Internal Affairs)*, Petar Vajović *(Justice)*, Janko Obocki *(Labour)*, Lojze Ude *(Law)*, Admiral Branko Mamula *(Defence)*, Božidar Matić *(Science)*, Miodrag Mirović *(Tourism)*, Mustafa Pljakić *(Transport)*, Ilija Vakić *(Veterans)*, and 12 Ministers without Portfolio.

The only political party is the League of Communists, which had 2,167,860 members in 1985 (30·3% workers; 25% under 27 years). The Presidium of its Central Committee in March 1988 consisted of Boško Krunić *(President)*; Ivan Brigić, Dušan Ckrebić, Radiša Gačić, Štefan Korošec, Marko Orlandić, Milan Pančevski, Ivica Račan, Milenko Renovica, Franc Setinc, Kol Shiroka, Stipe Šuvar, Vasile Tupurkovski, Vidoje Žarković. There are also 9 *ex-officio* members.

National flag: Three horizontal stripes of blue, white, red, with a large red, yellow-bordered star in the centre.

National anthem: Hej, Slaveni, jošte živi reč naših dedova—O Slavs, our ancestors' words still live.

Local Government. Within the federal framework of republics Yugoslavia is administratively divided into 527 communes *(opština)*.

DEFENCE. Military service for 12 months is compulsory. The General People's Defence Law of 1969 bases Yugoslavia's defence on the principle of a nation in arms ready to wage partisan war against any invader. The partisan Territorial Defence Force number about 3m.

Army. The Army is divided into 7 Military Regions and comprises 12 infantry divisions; 8 independent tank, 9 independent infantry, 3 mountain and 1 airborne brigades; 6 field artillery, 11 anti-aircraft, 6 anti-tank and 4 surface-to-air missile regiments. Equipment includes 760 T-54/-55, 200 M-84 and 60 M-47 main battle tanks. Strength (1988) 165,000 (including 110,500 conscripts), with a reserve of 500,000.

Navy. The Navy comprises 5 diesel powered patrol submarines, 8 midget (four 5-man and four 2-man) submarines, 3 new *ex*-Soviet frigates, 16 fast missile boats, 15 fast torpedo boats, 3 small corvette-style patrol vessels, 10 fast attack craft, 4 minehunters, 17 patrol boats, 10 inshore minesweepers, 21 river minesweepers, 3 tank landing ships, 12 minelaying landing craft, 1 survey ship, 1 salvage vessel, 2 headquarters ships, 6 transports, 2 training ships, 22 minor landing craft, 2 oilers and 12 tugs. The Naval Air Arm operates 4 fixed-wing amphibians and 20 'Hip', Mi-8 and 10 'Holmone' Ka-25 helicopters. Personnel in 1988 totalled: 1,500 officers and 11,600 ratings.

Air Force. The Air Force has about 250 combat aircraft and is organized in 2 Air Corps, with HQ at Zagreb and Zemun. There are 2 fighter divisions equipped primarily with about 125 Russian-built MiG-21s, 2 ground-attack divisions of locally-built Jastreb and Orao jet attack aircraft, and 2 squadrons of Jastreb jet reconnaissance aircraft. Transport units fly Il-14 and An-26 twin-engined aircraft, 4-turboprop An-12s, and a few other types in small numbers, notably CL-215 amphibians, C-47s, Turbo-Porters and Yak-40s, Mystère 50s and Learjets for VIP duties. Training types are the nationally-designed UTVA-75 armed primary trainer, Galeb jet basic trainer and the Super Galeb jet advanced trainer. A large number of Gazelle, Agusta-Bell 205, Mi-4 and Mi-8 helicopters are in service. 'Guideline' and 'Goa' surface-to-air missiles have been supplied by the USSR. Personnel (1988) 36,000.

INTERNATIONAL RELATIONS

Membership. Yugoslavia is a member of UN and has special relationships with Comecon and OECD.

ECONOMY

Planning. A 5-year plan of economic development for 1981–85 envisaged that industrial production should increase by 4·5–5%, and that of agriculture by 4·5%. A Long-Term Economic Stabilisation Programme was introduced in 1983 to deal with the economic crisis, and laws were passed to ensure the prompt repayment of foreign debts. By a law of Aug. 1985 planning at Federal level was introduced into the activities of railways, the post office, energy suppliers and large enterprises. Foreign indebtedness was US$20,000m. in 1987. Control of some consumer goods prices and sharp increases in others were introduced in Nov. 1987 in an attempt to control inflation, which was officially put at 136%. Balance of payments (in US$1m.) in 1984: receipts, 17,356; expenditure, 16,852.

Budget. Revenue and expenditure for 1987, 1,971,600m. dinars. 459,609m. dinars were allotted to defence in 1985.

Currency. On 26 July 1965 the value of 1 *dinar*, divided into 100 *para*, was fixed at 0·710937 milligrammes of fine gold instead of 2·96224 milligrammes. A new *dinar*, equivalent of 100 old dinars, was introduced on 1 Jan. 1966. There are coins of 1, 2, 5, 10, 20, 50 and 100 *dinars*, and notes of 5, 10, 20, 50, 100, 500 and 1,000 *dinars*. Currency in circulation in 1985 was 551,300m. *dinars*. There have been several devaluations since 1980. In March 1988, £1 = 2,387 *dinars*; US$1 = 1,353 *dinars*. International reserves, 1987: US$1,539m.

Banking. The National Bank is the bank of issue. There are also republican National Banks, 115 (in 1980) 'internal banks', 160 'basic banks' and 9 'associated banks'. In 1985 credits amounted to 590,900m. dinars. Savings deposits totalled 1,070,400m. dinars in 1985, foreign exchange savings 2,494,200m.

Weights and Measures. The metric weights and measures have been in use since 1883. The *wagon* of 10 tonnes is used as a unit of measure for coal, roots and corn. The Gregorian calendar was adopted in 1919.

ENERGY AND NATURAL RESOURCES

Electricity. Output in 1985, 74,802m. kwh, of which 24,270m. was hydro-electric. There is a 664-mw nuclear power plant at Krško (opened 1981). This was closed for investigation in Feb. 1987. Plans for 4 more have been shelved.

Oil. Crude oil production (1987) 10·5m. tonnes.

Minerals. Yugoslavia has considerable mineral resources, including coal (chiefly brown coal), iron, copper ore, gold, lead, chrome, antimony and cement. The most important iron mines are at Vareš and Ljubija in Bosnia, and there are also considerable siderite and limonite iron ores between Prijedor, Sanski Most and Topusko. Copper ore is exploited chiefly at Bor (Serbia). The principal lead mines are at Trepča and Mežice. Chrome mines are in southern Serbia (Kosovo) and Macedonia (Skopje, Kumanovo). There are 2 antimony mines in western Serbia (Podrinje).

Mining output, in 1,000 tonnes, in 1985 (and 1984): Coal, 400 (388); lignite, 56,635 (53,293); bauxite, 3,250 (3,347); salt, 410 (379); manganese ore, 32 (21); iron ore, 5,478 (5,321); copper ore, 26,166 (25,279); lead and zinc ore, 4,590 (4,634); antimony ore, 71 (51); pyrite concentrates, 507 (609); magnesite, 417 (326). In 1983, gold output was 4,238 kg; silver (1984), 128,000 kg.

Agriculture. The economically active agricultural population was 2,488,000 in 1981 (47·5% female). The cultivated area was 8·41m. hectares in 1985 of which 8·32m. were in private farms and 1·52m. in agricultural organizations, of which there were 3,593 in 1985. In 1984 only 6·5% of the 2·6m. private farms were more than 10 hectares of land.

Area (in hectares) and yield (in 1,000 tonnes) in 1985: Maize, 2·4m. (9,896); wheat, 1·4m. (4,859); sugar beet, 150,000 (6,268); rye, 45,000 (77); tobacco, 68,272 (79); sunflower, 112,000 (233); potatoes, 274,000 (2,431).

Livestock, 1986: cattle, 5,034,000; pigs, 7,821,000; sheep, 7,693,000; poultry, 78,281,000.

1985 yield of fruit (in 1,000 tonnes): Apples, 368; grapes, 962; plums, 484. 6·3m. hectolitres of wine were produced.

There were 881,693 tractors in 1985, of which 850,000 were in private hands.

Forestry. The forest areas consist largely of beech, oak and fir. Forest area in 1985: 9,405,000 hectares (3,025,000 in private hands). Gross timber cut: 22,428,000 cu. metres.

Fisheries. In 1985 the landings of fish were (in tonnes): salt-water, 49,373; freshwater, 25,684. The number of fishing craft was 285 motor vessels (11,536 GRT) and 1,363 sailing and rowing vessels.

INDUSTRY AND TRADE

Employment. In 1984 there were 9,666 large industrial enterprises and 1,492 small businesses in the social sector, and 151,690 small businesses in the private sector. In Dec. 1985 (women in brackets) there were 138,000 (51,000) employed in the private sector and 6·5m. (2·45m.) in the social sector (excluding armed forces) of whom 2·52m. (0·92m.) were in manufacturing and mining, and 1·08m. (0·66m.) in the social services. There were 1,091,000 unemployed in 1986. Average monthly income per worker in 1986: 60,000 dinars. There were (1982) 5,485,000 trade union members. A wage freeze was imposed in Feb. 1987.

Industry. The majority of industries are situated in the north-west part of the country.

Industrial output (in 1,000 tonnes) in 1985 (and 1984): Pig-iron, 3,120 (2,845); steel, 4,480 (4,236); cement, 9,027 (9,315); sulphuric acid, 1,489 (1,471); fertilizers, 2,445 (2,486); plastics, 586 (551). Fabrics (in 1m. sq. metres): Cotton, 344 (318); woollen, 101 (99). Sugar (1,000 tonnes), 933 (891). Motor cars (in 1,000s), 228 (244).

Commerce. Foreign trade, in 1m. dinars, for calendar years (Before 1984 official figures were given at a parity of US$1 = 63·40 dinars, in 1984 at US$1 = 124·80 and since 1985 at US$1 = 185·70. Figures for 1983 and 1984 are given at both parities to facilitate comparison):

	1982	1983	1984	1985
Imports	557,353	789,330 (1,475,783)	1,498,285 (2,162,300)	2,262,138
Exports	428,071	637,170 (1,209,709)	1,279,978 (1,855,622)	1,977,957

Structure of exports (and imports) in 1985 (%): investment goods, 19·2 (13·8); intermediate goods, 49·7 (82); consumer goods, 31·1 (4·2). Largest suppliers in 1985 (goods in 1m. dinars): USSR, 376,329; Federal Republic of Germany, 290,662; Iraq, 159,662; Italy, 186,875; Czechoslovakia, 108,967; USA, 137,493; Libya, 109,058. Largest export markets: USSR, 623,056; Italy, 175,168; Federal Germany, 167,592; Czechoslovakia, 102,264; USA, 85,745; Iraq, 50,359.

Main exports as % share in 1985: Machinery and transport equipment, 32·7; other manufactures, 17·5; food and tobacco, 9; chemicals, 11·2; raw materials, 4·1; fuel, 3·1. Imports: Fuel, 28·3; machinery and transport equipment, 23·8; chemicals, 13·6; raw materials, 12·2.

Joint ventures with Western firms are permitted, and since 1984 the Western partner has been able to own 98% of the capital. There were 186 joint ventures in 1984.

In April 1983 a five-year trade and co-operation agreement with the EEC was signed. A trade pact was signed with the USSR in March 1983.

Total trade between Yugoslavia and UK (British Department of Trade returns, in £1,000 sterling):

	1983	1984	1985	1986	1987
Imports to UK	83,951	108,479	122,132	145,127	175,301
Exports and re-exports from UK	148,645	163,871	177,530	188,390	206,932

Tourism. In 1985, 8,436,000 (1986: 8,431,000) tourists visited Yugoslavia.

COMMUNICATIONS

Roads (1985). There were 66,999 km of asphalted roads and 33,227 km of macadamized roads. There were 2,824,267 passenger motor cars and 218,551 trucks and buses in 1985. In 1985, 1,045m. passengers and 221m. tonnes of freight were carried by public road transport. The north–south highway is being converted to 6-lane motorway. There were 60,135 road traffic casualties in 1985 (4,142 deaths).

Railways. In 1985 Yugoslavia had 9,283 km of railway, of which 3,534 km are electrified, and ran 11,999m. passenger-km and 28,719m. tonne-km of freight.

Aviation. The national airline, Jugoslovenski Aero Transport (Inex Adria-aviopromet, Panadria and Aviogenex) in 1985 flew on its home and international services, 60·7m. km and carried 5·3m. passengers and 93m. ton-km of freight; international services (without Panadria), 5·9m. passengers and 61·2m. ton-km of freight. The chief airfields are Belgrade, Zagreb, Ljubljana, Sarajevo, Skopje, Dubrovnik, Split, Titograd, Tivat, Pula and Zadar.

Shipping. In 1985 Yugoslavia possessed a total of 472 vessels of 2·8m. gross tons.

In 1985 vessels of 51m. net tons entered the ports of Yugoslavia.

In 1985 Yugoslavia had 1,179 river craft with 1,991 passenger capacity. The length of the navigable rivers amounted to 1,673 km, that of canals to 664 km. There are 2 navigable lakes: Skadar (391 sq. km, of which 243 in Yugoslavia) and Ohrid (348 sq. km, of which 230 in Yugoslavia). A Tisza-Danube canal system is under construction.

Pipeline. An oil pipeline runs from Krk to Pančevo.

Post and Broadcasting. There were 3,956 post offices and 3,322,000 telephone subscribers in 1985. *Jugoslovenska Radiotelevizija* consists of almost 250 main, relay and local stations operating on medium-waves and FM. In 1986 23 broadcasts a week were made in 10 foreign languages. *Radio Koper* also broadcasts commercial programmes in Italian for northern parts of Italy. National and regional TV programmes are broadcast. Advertisements are broadcast for maximum 170 minutes each week. Number of receivers in 1985: radio, 4·7m.; television, 4·1m.

Cinemas (1985). 1,298, seating 437,000. 24 full-length films were made in 1985.

Theatres (1984–85). 70, seating 27,885.

Newspapers and Books (1985). There were 27 dailies and 4,721 other newspapers and periodicals. There are no party newspapers but *Borba* and *Politika* (circulation in 1985: 47,000 and 256,000) enjoy semi-official status. 11,175 book titles (960 by foreign authors) were published in 1985.

JUSTICE, RELIGION, EDUCATION AND WELFARE

Justice. There are county tribunals, district courts, supreme courts of the constituent republics and a Supreme Court. There are also self-management courts, including courts of associated labour. In county tribunals and district courts the judicial functions are exercised by professional judges and by lay assessors constituted into collegia. There are no assessors at the supreme courts.

All judges are elected by the socio-political communities in their jurisdiction. The judges exercise their functions in accordance with the legal provisions enacted since the liberation of the country.

The constituent republics enact their own criminal legislation, but offences concerning state security and the administration are dealt with at federal level.

In 1985 262,000 crimes were reported, 164,000 charges made and 108,000 convictions obtained (excluding juveniles).

Religion. Religious communities are separate from the State and are free to perform religious affairs. All religious communities recognized by law enjoy the same rights.

Serbia has been traditionally Orthodox and Croatia Roman Catholic. Moslems are found in the south as a result of the Turkish occupation. The 1953 percentage of the denominations was: Orthodox, 41·2%; Roman Catholic, 31·7%; Moslems, 12·3%; Protestants, 0·9%; without religion, 12·6%. 1984 estimates of believers: Orthodox, 9m.; Roman Catholic, 7m.; Moslems, 4m.

The Serbian Orthodox Church with its seat in Belgrade has 20 bishoprics within the country and 4 abroad, 3 in US and Canada and 1 in Hungary. The Serbian Orthodox Church numbers about 2,000 priests.

The Macedonian Orthodox Church with the Archbishop of Ohrid and Macedonia as its head in Skopje, has 4 bishoprics in the country and 1 abroad (American–Canadian–Australian). The Macedonian Orthodox Church numbers about 300 priests.

The Roman Catholic Church is divided into two provinces: Zagreb with 4 suffragan sees, and Sarajevo with 2 suffragan sees. In addition, the Roman Catholic Church has 4 archbishoprics, 10 independent bishoprics directly connected with the Vatican and 3 Apostolic Administrators. There is a National Conference of Bishops with the Archbishop of Zagreb, Cardinal Franjo Kuharič, at its head. The Roman Catholic Church has about 4,000 priests, 2 theological faculties and 15 seminaries. Relations with the Vatican are regulated by a 'Protocol' of 1966.

The Moslem Religious Union has 4 republic Superiorates in Sarajevo, Skopje, Titograd and Priština. The highest authority is the supreme synod of the Islamic Religious Community, which elects the Reis-ul-Ulema and the Supreme Islamic Superiorate. The Moslem religious community has about 2,000 priests.

The Protestant churches covering 4 independent Lutheran Churches, numbering about 150,000 believers, the Reformed Christian Church, numbering about 60,000 believers, include also several much smaller churches of Baptists, Methodists, Adventists, Nazarenes, etc., numbering together about 100,000 believers. The Protestant churches have about 450 priests.

Also there are independent Old Catholic Churches with Synodal Council at Zagreb.

The Jewish religion has about 35 communities making up a common league of Jewish Communities with its seat in Belgrade.

Education. Compulsory general education lasts 8 years, secondary 3–4 years. In 1985–86 there were 12,148 primary schools with 134,884 teachers and 2,846,845 pupils, 1,212 secondary schools with 62,643 teachers and 952,904 pupils, 126 primary schools for adults with 8,908 pupils, and 138 secondary schools for adults with 33,304 pupils. 88·6% of primary school leavers entered secondary school.

Primary (and secondary) schools of ethnic minorities: Albanian, 1,198 (180); Hungarian, 153 (68); Bulgarian, 50 (nil); Czech, 13 (1); Slovak, 20 (8); Italian, 28 (15); Romanian, 31 (7); Turkish, 64 (16); Ukrainian, 4 (2).

In 1984–85 there were 340 institutes of higher education with 359,175 students and 15,701 teachers.

Health. In 1985 there were 49,341 doctors and dentists, and 141,039 hospital beds (10,192 psychiatric).

Health insurance benefits totalled 281,773m. dinars and pensions 395,458m. dinars in 1984. 25,042m. dinars were paid in child allowances in 1983. Consumption of food per capita in 1985: meat, 54·6 kg.; cereals, 151·4 kg.; milk, 113·6 litres; vegetables and fruit, 184·5. Daily consumption: 14,897 kilojoules.

DIPLOMATIC REPRESENTATIVES

Of Yugoslavia in Great Britain (5 Lexham Gdns., London, W8 5JJ)
Ambassador: Mitko Čalovski.

Of Great Britain in Yugoslavia (46 Generala Ždanova, Belgrade)
Ambassador: Andrew Wood, CMG.

Of Yugoslavia in the USA (2410 California St., NW, Washington, D.C., 20008)
Chargé d'Affaires: Vladimir Matic.

Of the USA in Yugoslavia (50 Kneza Miloša, Belgrade)
Ambassador: John D. Scanlan.

Of Yugoslavia to the United Nations
Ambassador: Dragoslav Pejić.

Books of Reference

Statistical Information: The Federal Statistical Office (Savezni Zavod za Statistiku; Kneza Miloša 20, Belgrade) was founded in Dec. 1944. *Director:* Dr D. Grupković. It publishes: *Indeks* (from April 1952, with English and French translations); *Statistički bilten* (1950 ff., with English or French translations); *Statistical Yearbook* (from 1954, with English, Russian and French translations); *Statistics of Foreign Trade of the SFR Yugoslavia* (annual, from 1946; half-yearly, from 1951); *Statistical Pocket-book* (from 1955; in 5 eds.: Yugoslav, English, French, Russian, German).

The Assembly of the SFR of Yugoslavia. Belgrade, 1974
The Constitution of the Socialist Federal Republic of Yugoslavia. Belgrade, 1974
Alexander, S., *Church and State in Yugoslavia since 1945.* CUP, 1979
Artesien, P. F. R., *Joint Ventures in Yugoslav Industry.* Aldershot, 1985
Banac, I., *The National Question in Yugoslavia.* Cornell Univ. Press, 1985
Burg, S. L., *Conflict and Cohesion in Socialist Yugoslavia: Political Decision-Making since 1966.* Princeton Univ. Press, 1983
Čičin-Šain, A. and Ellis, M. (eds.), *Doing Business with Yugoslavia: Economic and Legal Aspects.* Belgrade, 1986
Cohen, L. J., *Political Cohesion in a Fragile Mosaic: The Yugoslav Experience.* Boulder, 1983
Dedijer, V., *et al., History of Yugoslavia.* New York, 1974
Djilas, M., *Memoir of a Revolutionary.* New York, 1973.—*Rise and Fall.* London, 1985
Doder, D. *The Yugoslavs.* New York, 1978
Drvodelić, M., *Croatian or Serbian-English Dictionary.* 4th ed. Zagreb, 1978
Filipović, R., *English-Croatian or Serbian Dictionary.* Zagreb, 1980.—*The New Foreign Exchange and Foreign Trade Regime of Yugoslavia.* Belgrade, 1986
Horton, J. J., *Yugoslavia.* [Bibliography] Oxford and Santa Barbara, 1978
Horvat, B., *The Yugoslav Economic System.* White Plains, 1976
Kotnik, J., *Slovensko–angleski slovar.* 4th ed. Ljubljana, 1959
Milošević, D., *Investing in Yugoslavia and Other Forms of Long-Term Economic Co-operation with Yugoslav Enterprises.* 2nd ed. Belgrade, 1986
Minić, M., *The Foreign Policy of Yugoslavia, 1973–1980.* Belgrade, 1982
Prout, C., *Market Socialism in Yugoslavia.* OUP, 1985
Ramet, P., *Nationalism and Federalism in Yugoslavia, 1963–1983.* Indiana Univ. Press, 1984. —*Yugoslavia in the 1980s.* Boulder, 1985
Singleton, F., *Twentieth Century Yugoslavia.* London, 1976.—(with B. Carter) *The Economy of Yugoslavia.* London, 1982.—*A Short History of the Yugoslav Peoples.* CUP, 1985
Sirc, L., *The Yugoslav Economy under Self-Management.* London, 1979
Stojanović, R., (ed.) *The Functioning of the Yugoslav Economy.* New York, 1982
Tito, J. B., *The Essential Tito.* New York, 1970

REPUBLICS AND AUTONOMOUS PROVINCES

The Federal Republic of Yugoslavia comprises the 6 republics of Bosnia and Herzegovina, Croatia, Macedonia, Montenegro, Serbia and Slovenia, and the 2 autonomous provinces of Kosovo and Vojvodina within the Republic of Serbia.

Each has its own Constitution, Assembly of 3 Chambers (of Associated Labour; of Communes; Socio-Political) and League of Communists within the League of Communists of Yugoslavia, though the latter is not formally a federal institution. State Presidents and League of Communist Secretaries in 1988: *Bosnia and Herzegovina:* Mato Andrić, Živko Grubor; *Croatia:* Mika Špiljak, Stanko Stojčević; *Kosovo:* Svetislav Dolašević, Bajram Seljani; *Macedonia:* Milan Pančevski, Jakov Lazarovski; *Montenegro:* Vidoje Žarković, Velisav Vuksanović; *Serbia:* Petar Gračanin, Radiša Gačić; *Slovenia:* Andrej Marinc, Miha Ravnik; *Vojvodina:* Boško Krunić, Katalin Hajnal.

Indicators (in %) for 1985:

	Population	Workers	Social product[1]	Investments[1]
Yugoslavia	*100*	*100*	*100*	*100*
Bosnia and Herzegovina	18·7	15·5	13·5	15·8
Croatia	20·1	23·8	25·5	22·5
Macedonia	8·7	7·7	5·8	5·1
Montenegro	2·7	2·4	2·1	3·6
Serbia	41·5	37·7	37·7	38·6
Slovenia	8·3	12·9	15·4	14·4

[1] 1984.

BOSNIA AND HERZEGOVINA

HISTORY. The country was settled by Slavs in the 7th century, the original clan system evolving between the 12th and 14th centuries into a principality under a *Ban,* during which time the Bogomil Christian heresy became entrenched. Bosnia was conquered by the Turks in 1463, and the majority of the Bogomils were converted to Islam. At the Congress of Berlin (1878) the territory was assigned to Austro-Hungarian administration under nominal Turkish suzerainty. Austria-Hungary's outright annexation in 1908 generated tensions which contributed to the outbreak of the first world war.

AREA AND POPULATION. The republic is bounded in the north and west by Croatia, in the east by Serbia and in the south-east by Montenegro. It is virtually land-locked, having a coastline of only 20 km with no harbours. Its area is 51,129 sq. km. The capital is Sarajevo.

Population at the 1981 census: 4,124,256 (2,073,343 females), of whom the predominating ethnic groups were Moslems (1,630,033), Serbs (1,320,738) and Croats (758,140). Population density per sq. km: 80·7. Population, 1985, 4·31m.

Vital statistics:

	Live births	Marriages	Deaths	Growth rate per 1,000
1984	72,056	35,190	28,968	10·6
1985	69,913	34,446	26,892	10·0

ECONOMY

Agriculture. In 1984 the agricultural area was 2·53m. hectares. Yields (in 1,000 tonnes) and areas sown (in 1,000 hectares) of principal crops were: Wheat, 420 (147); barley, 73 (36); maize, 873 (248); soya, 8,829 (5,354); potatoes, 357 (51). Livestock in 1985 (1,000 head): Horses, 130; cattle, 984; sheep, 1,508; pigs, 793. Timber cut in 1984: 7·1m. cu. metres.

Industry. Production (1985): Electricity, 11,990m. kwh; lignite, 7·39m. tonnes; iron ore, 4·61m. tonnes; pig iron, 1·31m. tonnes; bauxite, 1·38m. tonnes; cement, 674,000 tonnes; cotton fabrics, 20m. sq. metres; cars, 26,000.

Employment. Population of working age, 1985, 2·84m.; non-agricultural workforce, 1m., of whom 0·84m. worked in production.

CROATIA

HISTORY. The Croats migrated to their present territory in the 6th century and were converted to Roman Catholicism. Croatia was conquered by Hungary in 1091 and remained under Hungarian domination until after the first world war. During the second world war an independent fascist state was set up.

AREA AND POPULATION. Croatia is bounded in the north by Slovenia and Hungary and in the east by Serbia. It has an extensive Adriatic coastline well provided with ports, and includes the historical areas of Dalmatia, Istria and Slavonia, which no longer have administrative status. The capital is Zagreb. Its area is 56,538 sq. km. Population at the 1981 census was 4,601,469 (2,374,579 females), of whom the predominating ethnic groups were Croats (3,454,661) and Serbs (531,502). Population density per sq. km: 81·4. Population, 1985, 4·66m.

Vital statistics:

	Live births	Marriages	Deaths	Growth rate per 1,000
1984	65,532	32,763	54,822	2·3
1985	63,170	31,717	52,673	2·3

ECONOMY

Agriculture. In 1985 the agricultural area was 3·24m. hectares. Yields (in 1,000 tonnes) and areas sown (in 1,000 hectares) of principal crops were: Wheat, 1,131 (284); barley, 212 (65); maize, 2,564 (523); sugar beet, 1,295 (29); soya, 37,520 (16,270); potatoes, 677 (80). Livestock in 1985 (1,000 head): Horses, 57; cattle, 914; sheep, 717; pigs, 1,963. Timber cut in 1983: 5·26m. cu. metres.

Industry. Production (1984): Electricity, 8,059m. kwh; coal, 254,000 tonnes; bauxite, 375; crude petroleum, 2·85m. tonnes; steel, 423,000 tonnes; plastics, 154,000 tonnes; cement, 3·2m. tonnes; cotton fabrics, 66m. sq. metres; sugar, 211,000 tonnes.

Employment. Population of working age, 1985: 3·05m.; non-agricultural workforce, 1·55m., of whom 1·26m. worked in production.

MACEDONIA

HISTORY. The Slavs settled in Macedonia since the 6th century, who had been Christianized by Byzantium, were conquered by the non-Slav Bulgars in the 7th century and in the 9th century formed a Macedo-Bulgarian empire, the western part of which survived until Byzantine conquest in 1014. In the 14th century it fell to Serbia, and in 1355 to the Turks. After the Balkan Wars of 1912-13 Turkey was ousted, and Serbia received the greater part of the territory, the rest going to Bulgaria and Greece. In 1918 Yugoslav Macedonia was incorporated into Serbia as 'South Serbia'. Possession of this territory has long been a source of contention between Bulgaria and Yugoslavia.

AREA AND POPULATION. Macedonia is land-locked, and is bounded in the north by Serbia and Kosovo, in the east by Bulgaria, in the south by Greece and in the west by Albania. The capital is Skopje. Its area is 25,713 sq. km. Population at the 1981 census was 1,909,136 (940,993 females), of whom the predominating ethnic groups were Macedonians (1,279,323), Albanians (377,208) and Turks (86,591). Population density per sq. km, 74·2. Population, 1985, 2·02m.

Vital statistics:

	Live births	Marriages	Deaths	Growth rate per 1,000
1984	39,811	16,492	14,464	12·7
1985	39,133	16,507	14,844	12·0

ECONOMY

Agriculture. In 1985 the agricultural area was 1·33m. hectares. Yields (in 1,000 tonnes) and areas sown (in 1,000 hectares) of principal crops were: Wheat, 288 (112); barley, 113 (54); maize, 80 (42); cotton, 888 (1,531); tobacco, 30 (28). Livestock in 1985 (1,000 head): Horses, 82; cattle, 286; sheep, 2,315; pigs, 202. Timber cut in 1984: 1,086,000 cu. metres.

Industry. Production (1985): Electricity, 3,575m. kwh; lignite, 3,327,000 tonnes; iron ore, 786,000 tonnes; pig-iron, 232,000 tonnes; steel, 397,000 tonnes; copper ore, 2,851,000 tonnes; sulphuric acid, 84,000 tonnes; cement, 684,000 tonnes; cotton fabrics, 53m. sq. metres.

Employment. Population of working age, 1985: 1·27m.; non-agricultural workforce, 0·45m., of whom 0·4m. worked in production.

MONTENEGRO

HISTORY. Montenegro emerged as a separate entity on the break-up of the Serbian Empire in 1355. It was never effectively subdued by Turkey. It was ruled by Bishop Princes until 1851, when a royal house was founded.

AREA AND POPULATION. Montenegro is a mountainous region which opens to the Adriatic in the south-west. It is bounded in the north-west by Bosnia and Herzegovina, in the north-east by Serbia and in the south-east by Albania. The capital is Titograd. Its area is 13,812, sq. km. Population at the 1981 census was 584,310 (294,571 females), of whom the predominating ethnic groups were Montenegrins (400,488), Moslems (78,080) and Albanians (37,735). Population density per sq. km: 42·3. Population, 1985, 0·61m.

Vital statistics:

	Live births	Marriages	Deaths	Growth rate per 1,000
1984	10,473	4,181	3,706	11·2
1985	10,268	4,198	3,751	10·6

ECONOMY

Agriculture. In 1985 the agricultural area was 517,000 hectares. Yields (in 1,000 tonnes) and areas sown (in 1,000 hectares) of principal crops were: Wheat, 11 (4); barley, 12 (6); maize, 10 (8); potatoes, 30 (7). Livestock in 1985 (1,000 head): Horses, 23; cattle, 189; sheep, 481; pigs, 30. Timber cut in 1984: 885,000 cu. metres.

Industry. Production (1985): Electricity, 2,878m. kwh; lignite, 2·73m. tonnes; bauxite, 735,000 tonnes; cement, 168,000 tonnes.

Employment. Population of working age, 1985: 0·39m.; non-agricultural workforce, 0·15m., of whom 0·13m. worked in production.

SERBIA

HISTORY. The Serbs received Orthodox Christianity from the Byzantines. They threw off the latter's suzerainty to become a large prosperous medieval state, which was destroyed by the Turks at the Battle of Kosovo in 1389. After revolutions in 1804 and 1815 Serbia won increasing degrees of autonomy from Turkey; complete independence came with the Treaty of Berlin in 1878. Its prince took the title of king in 1881.

AREA AND POPULATION. Serbia is land-locked and is bounded in the north-west by Croatia, in the north by Hungary, in the north-east by Romania, in the east by Bulgaria, in the south by Macedonia and in the west by Albania, Montenegro and Bosnia and Herzegovina. It includes the Autonomous Provinces of Kosovo in the south and Vojvodina in the north, which have substantial Albanian and Hungarian populations respectively. Without these its area is 55,968 sq. km. The capital is Belgrade. Population at the 1981 census was 9,313,676 (4,684,349 females), of whom the predominating ethnic group was Serbs (6,182,155). Population density per sq. km: 105·4. Population, 1985, 9·6m.

Vital statistics:

	Live births	Marriages	Deaths	Growth rate per 1,000
1984	160,288	67,783	92,187	7·1
1985	156,524	64,313	92,180	6·7

ECONOMY

Agriculture. In 1985 the agricultural area was 5·74m. hectares. Yields (in 1,000 tonnes) and areas sown (in 1,000 hectares) of principal crops were: Wheat, 2,900 (765); barley, 262 (91); maize, 6,227 (1,502); sugar-beet, 4,597 (110); soya, 128,798 (79,115); potatoes, 873 (92). Livestock in 1986: (in 1,000 head): Horses, 130; cattle, 2,249; sheep, 2,633; pigs, 5,064. Timber cut in 1984: 3·94m. cu. metres.

Industry. (1985): Electricity, 35,805m. kwh; coal, 38·45m. tonnes; lignite, 37,848,000 tonnes; pig-iron, 531,000 tonnes; steel, 669,000 tonnes; copper ore, 23,315,000 tonnes; lorries, 11,672; cars, 158,000; sulphuric acid, 988,000 tonnes; plastics, (1984) 79,000 tonnes; cement, 2,742,000 tonnes; sugar, 650,000 tonnes; cotton fabrics, 73m. sq. metres; woollens, 42m. sq. metres.

Employment. Population of working age, 1985: 6·21m.; non-agricultural workforce, 2·46m., of whom 1·98m. were in production.

KOSOVO

AREA AND POPULATION. Area: 10,887 sq. km. The capital is Priština. Population at the 1981 census, 1,584,441 (766,048 females), of whom the predominating ethnic groups were Albanians (1,226,736), and Serbs (209,498). Albanian-Serb tensions have led to outbreaks of violence since 1987. Population density per sq. km: 145·5. Population, 1985, 1·76m.

Vital statistics:

	Live births	Marriages	Deaths	Growth rate per 1,000
1984	53,324	12,617	9,949	25·2
1985	54,436	12,569	9,947	25·3

ECONOMY

Agriculture. The agricultural area in 1985 was 585,000 hectares. Yields (in 1,000 tonnes) and sown areas (in 1,000 hectares) of principal crops were: Wheat, 275 (97); maize, 115 (96); sugar-beet, 61 (3); potatoes, 53 (8). Livestock in 1985 (1,000 head): Horses, 35; cattle, 404; sheep, 396; pigs, 64. Timber cut in 1984, 420,000 cu. metres.

Industry. Production (1985): Electricity, 5,393m. kwh; lignite, 9·78m. tonnes; sulphuric acid, 78,000 tonnes; cement, 290,000 tonnes.

Employment. Population of working age, 1985: 0·95m.; non-agricultural workforce, 201,905, of whom 157,044 worked in production.

VOJVODINA

AREA AND POPULATION. Area: 21,506 sq. km. The capital is Novi Sad. Population at the 1981 census, 2,034,772 (1,041,392 females), of whom the predominating ethnic groups were Serbs (1,107,378) and Hungarians (385,356). Population density per sq. km: 94·6. Population, 1985, 2·05m.

Vital statistics:

	Live births	Marriages	Deaths	Growth rate per 1,000
1984	26,250	14,922	23,931	1·1
1985	25,005	14,248	23,584	1·0

ECONOMY

Agriculture. The agricultural area in 1984 was 1·78m. hectares. Yields (in 1,000 tonnes) and sown areas (in 1,000 hectares) of principal crops were: Wheat, 1,737 (325); barley, 219 (50); maize, 4,821 (743); sugar-beet, 4,342 (88); soya, 164,006 (82,722); potatoes, 315 (23). Livestock in 1985 (1,000 head): Horses, 35; cattle, 297; sheep, 345; pigs, 2,239. Timber cut in 1984: 754,000 cu. metres.

Industry. Production (1985): Electricity, 1,395m. kwh; crude petroleum, 1·13m. tonnes; sulphuric acid, 55,000 tonnes; plastics, (1984) 53,000 tonnes; cement, 1·28m. tonnes.

Employment. Population of working age, 1985: 1·36m.; non-agricultural workforce, 0·53m., of whom 0·5m. worked in production.

SLOVENIA

HISTORY. The lands originally settled by Slovenes in the 6th century were steadily encroached upon by Germans. Slovenia developed as part of Austria-Hungary and only gained independence in 1918.

AREA AND POPULATION. Slovenia is bounded in the north by Austria, in the north-east by Hungary, in the south-east by Croatia and in the west by Italy. There is a small strip of coast south of Trieste. Its area is 20,251 sq. km. The capital is Ljubljana. Population at the 1981 census: 1,891,864 (973,098 females), of whom the predominating ethnic group were Slovene (1,712,445). Population density per sq. km: 93·4. Population, 1985, 1·93m.

Vital statistics:

	Live births	Marriages	Deaths	Growth rate per 1,000
1984	28,276	11,541	20,960	3·8
1985	27,925	10,658	20,297	4·0

ECONOMY

Agriculture. In 1985 the agricultural area was 877,000 hectares. Yields (in 1,000 tonnes) and sown areas (in 1,000 hectares) of principal crops were: Wheat, 162 (44); maize, 299 (63); sugar-beet, 159 (5); potatoes, 422 (32). Livestock in 1985 (1,000 head): Horses, 16; cattle, 577; sheep, 26; pigs, 620. Timber cut in 1984: 3·54m. cu. metres.

Industry. Production (1985): Electricity, 12,205m. kwh; lignite, 5m. tonnes; steel, 814,000 tonnes; lorries, 4,100; cars, 43,000; sulphuric acid, 232,000 tonnes; sugar, 36,000 tonnes; cement, 1·31m. tonnes; cotton fabrics, 121m. sq. metres; woollens, 24m. sq. metres.

Employment. Population of working age, 1985: 1·24m.; non-agricultural workforce, 0·80m., of whom 0·7m. worked in production.

ZAÏRE

République du Zaïre

Capital: Kinshasa
Population: 31·78m. (1987)
GNP per capita: US$160 (1983)

HISTORY. Until the middle of the 19th century the territory drained by the Congo River was practically unknown. When Stanley reached the mouth of the Congo in 1877, King Leopold II of the Belgians recognized the immense possibilities of the Congo Basin and took the lead in exploring and exploiting it. The Berlin Conference of 1884–85 recognized King Leopold II as the sovereign head of the Congo Free State.

The annexation of the state to Belgium was provided for by treaty of 28 Nov. 1907, which was approved by the chambers of the Belgian Legislature in Aug. and Sept. and by the King on 18 Oct. 1908. The law of 18 Oct. 1908, called the Colonial Charter (last amended in 1959), provided for the government of the Belgian Congo, until the country became independent on 30 June 1960. The country's name was changed from Congo to Zaïre in Oct. 1971. For subsequent history to 1977 see THE STATESMAN'S YEAR-BOOK, 1980–81, p. 1613.

AREA AND POPULATION. Zaïre is bounded north by the Central African Republic, north-east by Sudan, east by Uganda, Rwanda, Burundi and Lake Tanganyika, south by Zambia, south-west by Angola, north-west by Congo. There is a 40-km Atlantic coastline separating Angola's province of Cabinda from the rest of that country.

The area of the republic is estimated at 2,344,885 sq. km (905,365 sq. miles). The population is composed almost entirely of Bantu groups, with minorities of Sudanese (in the north), Nilotes (northeast), Pygmies and Hamites (in the east). In the 1984 census the population was 29,671,407 (44%, urban). Estimate (1987) 31·78m. In Dec. 1986 there were about 301,000 refugees in Zaïre including 261,000 from Angola.

The area (in sq. km) and populations (census) 1984 of the regions were as follows, together with their chief towns:

Region	Sq. km	Population Census 1984	Chief town	Population Census 1984
Bandundu	295,658	3,682,845	Bandundu (Banningville)	96,841 [1]
Bas-Zaïre	53,920	1,971,520	Matadi	144,742
Equateur	403,293	3,405,512	Mbandaka (Coquilhatville)	125,263
Haut-Zaïre	503,239	4,206,069	Kisangani (Stanleyville)	282,650
Kasai Occidental	156,967	2,287,416	Kananga (Luluabourg)	290,898
Kasai Oriental	168,216	2,402,603	Mbuji-Mayi (Bakwanga)	423,363
Kinshasa City	9,965	2,653,558	Kinshasa (Leopoldville)	2,653,558
Kivu	256,662	5,187,865	Bukavu (Costermansville)	171,064
Shaba	496,965	3,874,019	Lubumbashi (Elizabethville)	543,268

[1] 1976.

Other large towns (1976): Likasi (194,465 in 1984); Kikwit (146,784 in 1984); Kalémié (172,297); Kamina (160,020); Ilebo (142,036); Boma (93,965) and Kolwezi (77,277).

French is the only official language, but of more than 200 languages spoken, 4 are recognized as national languages. Of these, Kiswahili is used in the east, Tshiluba in the south, Kikongo in the area between Kinshasa and the coast, while Lingala is spoken widely in and around Kinshasa and along the river; Lingala has become the *lingua franca* after French.

CLIMATE. Because of the size and the relief of the country, the climate is very varied, the central region having an equatorial climate, with year-long high tem-

1618

peratures and rain at all seasons. Elsewhere, depending on position north or south of the Equator, there are well-marked wet and dry seasons. The mountains of the east and south have a temperate mountain climate, with the highest summits having considerable snowfall. Kinshasa. Jan. 79°F (26·1°C), July 73°F (22·8°C). Annual rainfall 45″ (1,125 mm). Kananga. Jan. 76°F (24·4°C), July 74°F (23·3°C). Annual rainfall 62″ (1,584 mm). Kisangani. Jan. 78°F (25·6°C), July 75°F (23·9°C). Annual rainfall 68″ (1,704 mm). Lubumbashi. Jan. 72°F (22·2°C), July 61°F (16·1°C). Annual rainfall 50″ (1,237 mm).

CONSTITUTION AND GOVERNMENT. A new Constitution was promulgated on 15 Feb. 1978 and amended in Nov. 1980. The supreme institution is the sole political party, the *Mouvement Populaire de la Révolution* (MPR), whose leader and President is automatically Head of State, of the National Executive Council and of the National Legislative Council. His nomination by the Political Bureau of the MPR (whose 38 members are all nominated by him) is confirmed for a 7-year term (renewable once) by election by universal adult suffrage (all Zaïreans acquire automatic membership of the MPR at birth).

Former President: Joseph Kasavubu, 1 July 1960–25 Nov. 1965 (deposed in *coup*).

President: Marshal Mobutu Sésé Séko Kuku Ngbendu wa Zabanga (took office 25 Nov. 1965, elected 1 Nov. 1970 and re-elected Dec. 1977 and July 1984).

The National Executive Council is composed of State Commissioners appointed by the President. In July 1987 it was composed as follows:

Prime Minister: Mabi Mulumba.

Vice-Prime Minister: Sambwa Pida Nbangui. *Planning:* Mulumba Lukoji. *Finance:* Kinzonzi Mvutukidi Ngi. *Economy and Industry:* Nyembo Shabani. *Budget:* Kamitatu Masamba. *Portfolio:* Tambwe Masamba. *Justice:* N'Singa Udjuu Ongwakebi Untumbe. *Territorial Administration and Decentralization:* Duga Kugbe Toro. *Foreign Affairs and International Co-operation:* Ekila Liyonda. *Citizens' Rights:* Nimy Mayidika Ngimbi. *Information and Press:* Mandungu Bula Nyati. *Foreign Trade:* Kasereka Kasai. *Agriculture:* Kayinga Onsi Ndal. *Rural Development:* D'Zbo Kalogi. *Mines and Energy:* Ileo Itambala. *Public Works and Regional Development:* Mokolo Wa Mpombo. *Transport and Communications:* Sampassa Kaweta Milombe. *Land Affairs, Environment and Conservation:* Pendje Demodetdo. *Higher Education, Universities and Scientific Research:* Mokondo Bonza. *Primary and Secondary Education:* Nzege Aliazimbana. *Youth, Sports and Leisure:* Tshimbombo Mukuna. *Women's and Family Affairs:* Mayuma Kala. *Public Health and Social Affairs:* Dr Ngandu Kabeya. *Civil Service:* Mwando Nsimba. *Labour and Social Security:* Kisolokele Wamba. *Posts and Telecommunications:* Tokwaulu Bolamba. *Culture, Arts and Tourism:* Beyeye Djema.

There are 16 Secretaries of State.

Parliament consists of a unicameral National Legislative Council comprising People's Commissioners (one per 100,000 inhabitants) elected by universal suffrage for a 5-year term. At the latest elections (Sept. 1982) 310 People's Commissioners were elected from a list of 1,409 candidates presented by the MPR.

National flag: Green, with a yellow disc bearing an arm holding a flaming torch.

Local government: Zaïre is composed of the *ville neutre* of Kinshasa (administered by a Governor) and 8 regions, each under a Regional Commissioner and 6 Councillors; all are appointed by the President. The regions are divided into 13 urban and 24 rural sub-regions.

DEFENCE

Army. The Army is divided into 3 Military Regions and comprises 1 infantry division (3 infantry brigades), and 1 Special Forces division (1 parachute, 1 commando and 1 Presidential Guard brigades). Equipment includes 50 Chinese Type-62 light tanks, and 95 AML-60 and 60 AML-90 armoured cars. Strength (1988) 22,000. There is a paramilitary gendarmerie which is responsible for security and also numbered (1988) about 25,000, organized in 40 battalions.

Navy. The Navy consists of 3 flotillas, 1 coastal, 1 river and 1 lake, comprising 35 coastal patrol boats including 6 US-built and 29 French-built. Personnel in 1988 numbered 1,500 officers and men including 600 marines.

Air Force. The Air Force has been built up with training assistance from Italy. In 1987 it operated 7 Mirage 5 supersonic fighters, 12 Aermacchi MB.326GB and 3 MB.326K armed jet trainers, 5 C-130 Hercules and 3 DHC-5 Buffalo turboprop transports, 8 C-47, 13 Bell 47, Puma and Super Puma helicopters, 9 SIAI-Marchetti SF.260MC basic trainers and a variety of other transport and training aircraft. Personnel (1988) 2,500.

INTERNATIONAL RELATIONS

Membership. Zaïre is a member of UN, OAU and is an ACP state of EEC.

ECONOMY

Planning. The 5-year Development Plan, 1986–90 envisages expenditure of US$5,000m. emphasis is being placed on promoting food production and increasing agricultural exports.

Budget. Revenue was envisaged at 67·9m. zaïres in 1986, and expenditure, 70·6m.

Currency. The currency unit, is the *zaïre*, divided into 100 *makuta*. Each *likuta* (plural *makuta*) is divided into 100 *sengi*. Bank-notes are issued in the following denominations: 50, 10, 5 and 1 *zaïre* and 50 *makuta*; there are coins of 20, 10 and 5 *makuta*, 1 *likuta* and 10 *sengi*. In March 1988, £1 sterling = 246·20 *zaïre*; US$1 = 143·55 *zaïre*.

Banking. The central bank is Banque du Zaïre. A development bank with state backing is the Société Financière de Développement (SOFIDE). Commercial banks operating in Zaïre are Banque de Paris et des Pays-Bas, Banque de Kinshasa, National & Grindlays Bank, Barclays Bank SZPRL, First National City Bank, Union Zaïroise de Banques, Banque Commerciale Zaïroise, Banque du Peuple, Caisse Nationale d'Epargne et de Crédit Immobilier and Banque Internationale pour L'Afrique au Zaïre.

Weights and Measures. The metric system was introduced by law on 17 Aug. 1910.

ENERGY AND NATURAL RESOURCES

Electricity. Production (1986) 5,280m. kwh. A huge new dam at Inga, on the Zaïre River near Matadi, has a potential capacity of 39,600 mw.

Oil. Offshore oil production began in Nov. 1975; crude production (1987) was 1·4m. tonnes.

Minerals. In 1984 33% of Zaïre's foreign exchange was derived from mining of copper (502,600 tonnes), zinc (197,700 tonnes), cobalt (19,600 in 1985), as well as manganese, tin, gold and silver. The most important mining area is in the region of Shaba (formerly Katanga). The principal mining companies are the State-owned Gécamines; the Zaïre-Japanese Sodimiza; the international Société Minière du Tenke-Fungurume which started production in 1976; and 2 diamond companies, MIBA and British Zaïre Diamond Distributors. Production (1985) 19·6m. metric carats.

Agriculture. There were (1984) 5·65m. hectares of arable land and 24·8m. hectares of pastures and meadows. The main food crops (1986 production in 1,000 tonnes) are: Cassava, 15,570; plantains, 1,500; sugar-cane, 1,050; maize, 730; groundnuts, 400; bananas, 335; yams, 220; rice, 300. Cash crops (1986) include palm oil, 160; coffee, 90; palm kernels, 70; rubber, 26; seed cotton 77. There are also (1986) pineapples, 170; mangoes, 150; oranges, 147.
    Livestock (1986): Cattle, 1·4m.; sheep, 770,000; goats, 2·93m.; pigs, 780,000; poultry, 18m.

Forestry. Equatorial rain forests cover 55% of Zaïre's land surface, and 32·6m. cu. metres of timber were produced in 1984.

Fisheries. The catch for 1984 was 101,000 tonnes, almost entirely from inland waters.

INDUSTRY AND TRADE

Industry. The main manufactures are foodstuffs, beverages, tobacco, textiles, leather, wood products, cement and building materials, metallurgy and metal extraction, small river craft, and bicycles.

Commerce. Imports in 1982 totalled 2,759·7m. zaïres, exports totalled 9,924·9m. zaïres. In 1982, 40% of the exports (by value) consisted of copper, 19% of coffee, 12% of diamonds and 7% of cobalt. 36% of all exports went to USA, 31% to Belgium and 6% to France, while 22% of imports came from Belgium, 13% from France, 10% from USA and 10% from Federal Republic of Germany.

Total trade between Zaïre and UK (British Department of Trade returns, in £1,000 sterling):

	1983	1984	1985	1986	1987
Imports to UK	11,192	7,720	35,198	17,192	8,544
Exports and re-exports from UK	21,129	36,254	34,975	34,217	26,142

Tourism. There were 51,000 visitors in 1986 spending US$16·3m.

COMMUNICATIONS

Roads. In 1984 of 160,000 km of roads only 20,600 km are of national importance and all roads are earth-surfaced. In 1982 there were 89,471 passenger cars and 16,807 commercial vehicles.

Railways. There are two railway operators, the Zaïre National Railways (SNCZ) and the National Office of Transport and Communications (Onatra), which leases two lines from SNCZ. Length in 1985 was 5,116 km on 3 gauges, of which 858 km is electrified. In 1985 SNCZ carried 292m. passenger-km and 1,955m. tonne-km of freight.

Aviation. There are 4 international airports at Kinshasa (Ndjili), Lubumbashi (Luano), Kisangani and Bukavu. There are another 40 airports with regular scheduled internal services, and over 150 other landing strips.

More than twelve international airlines, including British Caledonian Airways, operate in and out of Kinshasa from Europe, Africa and the USA. The national airline Air Zaïre, operates on all the main internal routes as well as on international routes to Europe and other African cities.

Shipping. The Zaïre River and its tributaries are navigable for about 13,700 km. Regular traffic has been established between Kinshasa and Kisangani as well as Ilebo, on the Lualaba (*i.e.*, the river above Kisangani), on some tributaries and on the lakes. Zaïre has only 40 km of sea coast. The merchant marine in 1981 comprised 34 vessels with a total tonnage of 92,044 GRT. Kinshasa, Matadi and Boma are the main seaports; in 1978, 629,422 tonnes of freight were unloaded and 498,380 loaded.

Post and Broadcasting. In 1978 there were 351 post offices. Length of telegraph lines, 2,459 km. There were 15 broadcasting stations, 161 stations of wireless telegraphy and 206 telegraph offices; telephones numbered 31,200 in 1985. There is a ground satellite communications station outside Kinshasa. In 1986 there were 525,000 radio and 15,000 television receivers.

Cinemas (1974): 91 cinemas had a seating capacity of 23,300.

Newspapers. There were (1984) 4 dailies: *Salongo* (mornings) and *Elima* (evenings) in Kinshasa; *Njumbe* in Lubumbashi and *Boyoma* in Kisangani.

JUSTICE, RELIGION, EDUCATION AND WELFARE

Justice. A Justice Department was established in Jan. 1980 to replace the Judicial

Council. There is a Supreme Court at Kinshasa, 9 Courts of Appeal and 32 courts of first instance.

Religion. In 1985 there were about 15m. Roman Catholics, 9m. Protestants and 5m. Kimbanguistes, as well as some 400,000 Moslems and 2,000 Jews. The remaining inhabitants (about 1m.) adhere to animist beliefs.

Education. In 1983 there were 4,654,613 pupils and 112,077 teachers in 10,065 primary schools; and in 1978–79 there were 611,349 pupils in 2,511 secondary schools; 70,342 students in technical schools and 138,170 in teacher-training colleges. In 1971 all Institutes of Higher Education combined to form the National University of Zaïre, but in 1981 this was divided to form 3 Universities at Kinshasa, Kisangani and Lubumbashi; in 1978–79 in all there were 28,430 students and 2,782 teaching staff at 36 higher education establishments.

Health. In 1979 there were 1,900 doctors, 58 dentists, 414 pharmacists, 3,043 mid-wives, 14,661 nursing personnel and 942 hospitals and medical centres with 79,244 beds.

DIPLOMATIC REPRESENTATIVES

Of Zaïre in Great Britain (26 Chesham Pl., London, SW1X 8HH)
Ambassador: Nkikele Kitshode (accredited 17 Feb. 1988).

Of Great Britain in Zaïre (Ave. de l'Equateur, Kinshasa)
Ambassador: R. L. B. Cormack.

Of Zaïre in the USA (1800 New Hampshire Ave., NW, Washington, D.C., 20009)
Ambassador: Nguza Karl-I.-Bond.

Of the USA in Zaïre (310 Ave. des Aviateurs, Kinshasa)
Ambassador: (Vacant).

Of Zaïre to the United Nations
Ambassador: Bagbeni Adeito Nzengeya.

Books of Reference

Area Handbook for the Democratic Republic of the Congo (Kinshasa). US Government Printing Office, Washington, 1971
Atlas Général du Congo. Académie Royale, Brussels
Gran, G., *Zaire: The Political Economy of Underdevelopment.* New York, 1979
Slade, R. M., *King Leopold's Congo: Aspects of the Development of Race Relations in the Congo's Independent State.* OUP, 1962
Young, C., and Turner, T., *The Rise and Decline of the Zaïrian State.* Univ. of Wisconsin Press, 1985

ZAMBIA

Capital: Lusaka
Population: 7·12m. (1987)
GNP per capita: US$410 (1984)

HISTORY. The independent Republic of Zambia (formerly Northern Rhodesia) came into being on 24 Oct. 1964 after 9 months of internal self-government following the dissolution of the Federation of Rhodesia and Nyasaland on 31 Dec. 1963.

AREA AND POPULATION. Zambia is bounded by Tanzania in the north, Malaŵi in the east, Mozambique in the south-east and by Zimbabwe and South West Africa (Namibia) in the south. The area is 290,586 sq. miles (752,614 sq. km). Population (1980 census) 5,679,808 of which 43% urban; estimate (1987) 7·12m.

The republic is divided into 9 provinces. Their names, headquarters, area (in sq. km) and census population in 1980 were as follows:

Province	Headquarters	Area	Population	Province	Headquarters	Area	Population
Copperbelt	Ndola	31,328	1,248,888	Eastern	Chipata	69,106	656,381
Luapula	Mansa	50,567	412,798	Southern	Livingstone	85,283	686,469
Northern	Kasama	147,826	677,894	N.-Western	Solwezi	125,827	301,677
Central	Kabwe	94,395	513,835	Western	Mongu	126,386	487,988
Lusaka	Lusaka	21,898	693,878				

The seat of Government is at Lusaka (population, 1980, 538,469); other large towns are Kitwe (314,794), Ndola (282,439), Mufulira (149,778), Chingola (145,869), Luanshya (132,164), Chililabombwe (61,928) and Kalulushi (59,213) on the Copperbelt; Kabwe, the oldest mining township (143,635); Livingstone, the old capital (71,987); and other provincial capitals at Kasama (38,093), Mansa (34,801), Chipata (32,291) and Mongu (24,919).

The official language is English and the main ethnic groups are the Bemba (34%), Tonga (16%), Malawi (14%) and Lozi (9%).

CLIMATE. The climate is tropical, but has three seasons. The cool, dry one is from May to Aug., a hot dry one follows until Nov., when the wet season commences. Frosts may occur in some areas in the cool season. Lusaka. Jan. 70°F (21·1°C), July 61°F (16·1°C). Annual rainfall 33″ (836 mm). Livingstone. Jan. 75°F (23·9°C), July 61°F (16·1°C). Annual rainfall 27″ (673 mm). Ndola. Jan. 70°F (21·1°C), July 59°F (15°C). Annual rainfall 52″ (1,293 mm).

CONSTITUTION AND GOVERNMENT. The Constitution provides for a President, elected in the first instance by the General Conference of the ruling party, the United National Independence Party, and thereafter he is elected by the electorate. On 13 Dec. 1972 President Kaunda signed a new Constitution based on one-party rule.

The single political party is the United National Independence Party. Its full-time executive organ (headed by a Secretary-General) is the Central Committee, whose 24 members are elected by the General Conference of the Party. The Central Committee has precedence over the legislative body, the National Assembly, which is led by the Prime Minister and consists of 125 elected members and up to 10 nominated members, including a cabinet of 18 ministers.

Presidential elections were held in Oct. 1983 and on 30 Oct. President Kaunda was sworn in for a fifth 5-year term.

The Cabinet, as in Jan. 1988, was composed as follows:

President and Commander-in-Chief: Dr Kenneth David Kaunda.
Secretary General of the Party: A. G. Zulu.
Prime Minister: K. S. K. Musokotwane.
Defence: M. Masheke. *Foreign Affairs:* L. Mwananshiku. *Finance and Planning:* G. Chigaga. *Attorney-General:* F. M. Chomba. *Higher Education:* L. Goma.

Health: R. Sakuhuka. *Industry:* J. K. M. Kalaluka. *Home Affairs:* P. Malukutila. *Mines:* P. S. Chitambala. *Agriculture:* F. Chuula. *Power:* Gen. G. K. Chinkuli. *Works:* H. Mwale. *Labour and Social Services:* U. G. Mwila. *Tourism:* L. S. Subulwa. *Information:* J. C. M. Punabantu. *Youth:* F. Hapunda. *Education and Culture:* B. R. Kabwe. *Co-operatives:* J. Mukando.

National flag: Green, with in the fly a panel of 3 vertical strips of dark red, black and orange, and above these a soaring eagle in gold.

National anthem: Stand and Sing of Zambia, Proud and Free.

The 9 provinces (sub-divided into 53 districts) are administered by Central Committee Members for the provinces who are responsible for the overall government and Party administration of their respective areas.

DEFENCE

Army. The Army consists of 1 armoured regiment and 6 infantry battalions, with supporting artillery, engineer and signals units. Equipment includes some 30 main battle tanks and 78 armoured cars. Strength (1988) 15,000. There are also paramilitary police units numbering 1,200 men.

Air Force. Creation of the Zambian Air Force was assisted initially by an RAF mission. Training and expansion of the Air Force was next taken over by Italy, with the purchase of 23 Aermacchi M.B.326G armed jet basic trainers (of which 18 remain in service), 8 SIAI-Marchetti SF.260M piston-engined trainers and the 15 Agusta-Bell 47G, 10 AB.205 and 2 AB.212 helicopters. Twelve F-6 (MiG-19) jet fighter-bombers and some BT-6 primary trainers have since been acquired from China, a squadron of 14 MiG-21 fighters, 3 Yak-40 light jet transports, 4 An-26 twin-turboprop transports and 6 Mi-8 helicopters from the Soviet Union, 5 DHC-5 Buffalo twin-turboprop transports from Canada, 6 C-47s built in the USA, 10 Do 28D Skyservant light transports from Germany, 15 Supporter armed light trainers from Sweden. Serviceability of most types is reported to be low. The survivors of 6 Jastreb light attack aircraft and 2 Galeb trainers supplied by Yugoslavia are thought to be in storage. Personnel (1988) 1,200.

INTERNATIONAL RELATIONS

Membership. Zambia is a member of UN, the Commonwealth, SADCC, OAU and is an ACP state of EEC.

ECONOMY

Budget. Revenue and expenditure for 1986 (in K1m.): envisaged expenditure of 4,556 and revenue of 3,472.

Currency. The *Kwacha* (K) is divided into 100 *ngwee* (n). There are coins of 50, 20, 10, 5, 2 and 1 *ngwee* and banknotes of K20, K10, K5, K2 and K1 are in use. In March 1988, £1 = 13·80 *Kwacha*; US$1 = 8·05 *Kwacha*.

Banking. Barclays Bank has 25 branches, 6 sub-branches and 17 agencies; Standard Bank has 18 branches and 17 agencies; National & Grindlays, 10 branches and 1 sub-branch; Zambia National Commercial Bank, 10 branches and 1 in London; the post office saving bank has branches throughout the republic.

The Finance Development Corporation (FINDECO) controls the building societies, all insurance companies, one commercial bank and has shares in a second one. The Agricultural Finance Corporation provides loans to farmers, co-operatives, farmers' associations and agricultural societies.

ENERGY AND NATURAL RESOURCES

Electricity. The total installed capacity of hydro and thermal power stations, excluding Zambia's share of Kariba South, amounts to 1,924,700 kw and the energy production during 1986 amounted to some 11,100m. kwh. Zambia exports electricity to Zaïre, Zimbabwe and Angola.

The hydro stations are located at Mbala, Mansa, Kasama, Mulungushi, Lunsemfwa and Victoria Falls, Lusiwasi and Kafue Gorge. Work has started on the Kariba North Project. The thermal stations are located on the Copperbelt. A number of diesel power stations have been installed, mostly in the North-Western and Northern Provinces.

Minerals. The total value of minerals produced in 1982 was:

	Output (1,000 tonnes)	Value (K1,000)		Output (1,000 tonnes)	Value (K1,000)
Copper	584·2	710,636	Coal	603·9	22,346
Zinc	38·9	27,648	Cobalt	2·4	45,257
Lead	14·5	6,050	Other	–	43,227

Agriculture. Although 70% of the population is dependent on agriculture only 10% of GDP is provided by the industry. Principal agricultural products (1986) were maize, 1,112,000 tonnes; sugar-cane, 1·18m. tonnes; seed cotton, 31,000 tonnes; tobacco, 4,000 tonnes; groundnuts, 15,000 tonnes.

Livestock (1986): 2·77m. cattle; 214,000 pigs; 46,000 sheep; 240,000 goats, and 14m. poultry.

Fisheries. Total catch (1983) 67,000 tonnes.

INDUSTRY AND TRADE

Industry. In Dec. 1982 there were 34,020 persons employed in agriculture, forestry and fisheries; 60,270 in mining and quarrying; 48,070 in manufacturing; 8,060 in electricity and water; 42,150 in construction and 25,350 in transport and communications.

Commerce. Trade in 1m. kwacha for 3 years:

	1983	1984	1985
Imports	893·2	1,107·9	2,089·5
Exports	1,047·5	1,188·1	1,486·1

In 1983, copper provided 89% of all exports (by value), cobalt 4%, zinc 2%.

Total trade between Zambia and UK (British Department of Trade returns, in £1,000 sterling):

	1984	1985	1986	1987
Imports to UK	48,069	27,879	27,260	30,310
Exports and re-exports from UK	66,746	85,949	77,840	75,178

Tourism. There were 100,000 visitors in 1985.

COMMUNICATIONS

Roads. There were (1984) 37,279 km of roads including over 5,592 km of tarred roads. In 1982 there were 33,000 commercial vehicles and 68,000 cars.

Railways. In 1985 the total route-km was 1,266 km (1,067 mm gauge). In 1985 the Zambian railways (excluding Tan-Zam) carried 1·8m. passengers and 4·9m. tonnes of freight. The Tan–Zam railway, giving Zambia access to Dar es Salaam, comprises 892 km of route in Zambia.

Aviation. There were (1982) 130 airports in Zambia (46 government owned). Lusaka is the principal international airport. Seven foreign airlines use Lusaka.

Post and Broadcasting. There were (1982) 13 head post offices and 236 other post offices. In 1984 there were 72,000 telephones, 1m. radio and 240,000 television receivers.

Cinemas. In 1971 there were 28 cinemas with a seating capacity of 13,400.

Newspapers. There were (1984) 2 national daily papers: *The Times of Zambia* (circulation, 65,000) and *Zambia Daily Mail* (45,000) and *The Sunday Times* (74,000).

JUSTICE, RELIGION, EDUCATION AND WELFARE

Justice. The Judiciary consists of the Supreme Court, the High Court and 4 classes of magistrates' courts; all have civil and criminal jurisdiction.

The Supreme Court hears and determines appeals from the High Court. Its seat is at Lusaka.

The High Court exercises the powers vested in the High Court in England, subject to the High Court ordinance of Zambia. Its sessions are held where occasion requires, mostly at Lusaka and Ndola.

All criminal cases tried by subordinate courts are subject to revision by the High Court.

Religion. Freedom of worship is one of the constitutional rights of Zambian citizens. The Christian faith with 66% of the population has largely replaced traditional African religions. There are 20,000 Moslems.

Education. In 1982 there were 1,121,769 pupils in 2,894 primary schools, secondary schools, 104,859 in 142 schools. In 1984 there were 4,910 students in technical colleges and 4,653 students were enrolled for teacher-training. In 1984 the University of Zambia had 3,621 full-time students.

Health. In 1981 there were 821 doctors, 52 dentists, 36 pharmacists, 866 midwives and 871 nursing personnel. There were also 636 hospitals and clinics with 20,638 beds.

DIPLOMATIC REPRESENTATIVES

Of Zambia in Great Britain (2 Palace Gate, London, W8 5LS)
High Commissioner: W. J. Phiri (accredited 9 Oct. 1986).

Of Great Britain in Zambia (Independence Ave., Lusaka)
High Commissioner: J. M. Willson, CMG.

Of Zambia in the USA (2419 Massachusetts Ave., NW, Washington, D.C., 20008)
Ambassador: Nalumino Mundia.

Of the USA in Zambia (PO Box 31617, Lusaka)
Ambassador: Paul J. Hare.

Of Zambia to the United Nations
Ambassador: Peter Dingi Zuze.

Books of Reference

General Information: The Director, Zambia Information Services, PO Box 50020, Lusaka.

Laws of Zambia. 13 vols. Govt. Printer, Lusaka
Beveridge, A. A., and Oberschall, A. R., *African Businessmen and Development in Zambia.* Princeton Univ. Press, 1980
Bliss, A. M. and Riggs, J. A., *Zambia.* [Bibliography] Oxford and Santa Barbara, 1984
Gertzel, C. (ed.), *The Dynamics of a One-Party State in Zambia.* Manchester Univ. Press, 1984
Kaunda, Kenneth D., *Zambia Shall be Free.* London, 1962.—*Humanism in Zambia.* Lusaka. 2 vols. 1967 and 1974.—*Zambia's Economic Revolution.* Lusaka, 1968.—*Zambia's Guidelines for the Next Decade.* Lusaka, 1968.—*Letter to my Children.* Lusaka, 1973
Roberts, A., *A History of Zambia.* London, 1977

ZIMBABWE

Capital: Harare
Population: 8·64m. (1987)
GNP per capita: US$780 (1984)

HISTORY. Prior to Oct. 1923 Southern Rhodesia, like Northern Rhodesia, was under the administration of the British South Africa Co. In Oct. 1922 Southern Rhodesia voted in favour of responsible government. On 12 Sept. 1923 the country was formally annexed to His Majesty's Dominions, and on 1 Oct. 1923 government was established under a governor, assisted by an executive council, and a legislature, with the status of a self-governing colony. For the history of the period 1961–1979 including the period of unilateral declaration of independence *see* THE STATESMAN'S YEAR-BOOK, 1980–81, pp. 1623–25. Rhodesia (Southern Rhodesia) became the Republic of Zimbabwe on 18 April 1980.

AREA AND POPULATION. Zimbabwe is bounded north by Zambia, east by Mozambique, south by the Republic of South Africa and west by Botswana. The area is 150,699 sq. miles (390,308 sq. km). The capital is Harare (Salisbury). The total population was (1982 census) 7,539,300; 1987 estimate, 8·64m.

There are 8 provinces:

Province	Sq. km	Census 1982	Province	Sq. km	Census 1982
Manicaland	35,219	1,099,202	Masvingo	55,777	1,031,697
Mashonaland Central	29,482	563,407	Matabeleland North	76,813	885,339
Mashonaland East	26,813	1,495,984	Matebeleland South	54,941	519,606
Mashonaland West	55,737	858,962	Midlands	55,977	1,091,844

Population of main urban areas (1982 census): Bindura, 18,243; Bulawayo, 414,800; Masvingo (Fort Victoria) 31,000; Kadoma (Gatooma) 45,000; Gweru (Gwelo) 79,000; Chegutu (Hartley) 26,617; Marondera (Marandellas) 37,092; Kwekwe (Que Que) 48,000; Redcliffe, 22,000; Harare (Salisbury) 656,100; Zvishavane (Shabani) 27,000; Chinhoyi (Sinoia) 24,322; Mutare (Umtali) 70,000; Hwange (Wankie) 39,000; Chitungwiza, 175,000.

In 1982 23% were urban and 51% under 15.

Vital statistics (1986): Birth rate was 37·2 per 1,000 population, the death rate 10·8 per 1,000.

The official language is English. Shona and Sindebele are the main spoken languages.

CLIMATE. Though situated in the tropics, conditions are remarkably temperate throughout the year because of altitude, and an inland position keeps humidity low. The warmest weather occurs in the three months before the main rainy season, which starts in Nov. and lasts till March. The cool season is from mid-May to mid-Aug. and, though days are mild and sunny, nights are chilly. Harare. Jan. 69°F (20·6°C), July 57°F (13·9°C). Annual rainfall 33″ (828 mm). Bulawayo. Jan. 71°F (21·7°C), July 57°F (13·9°C). Annual rainfall 24″ (594 mm). Victoria Falls. Jan. 78°F (25·6°C), July 61°F (16·1°C). Annual rainfall 28″ (710 mm).

CONSTITUTION AND GOVERNMENT. At the Commonwealth Conference held in Lusaka in Aug. 1979 agreement was reached for a new Constitutional Conference to be held in London and this took place between 10 Sept. and 15 Dec. 1979 at Lancaster House. This was attended by the various factions in Zimbabwe-Rhodesia, including Abel Muzorewa, Robert Mugabe and Joshua Nkomo, and was chaired by Lord Carrington. It achieved 3 objectives: (*i*) the terms of the Constitution for an independent Zimbabwe; (*ii*) terms for a return to legality: and (*iii*) a ceasefire. Lord Soames became Governor of Southern Rhodesia in Dec. 1979 and elections took place in March 1980, resulting in victory for the Zimbabwe African National Union (ZANU, PF).

The Constitution provides for a bicameral Parliament. Parliament consists of a 40-member Senate elected by the common roll; 10 chiefs elected by all the country's tribal chiefs; 6 nominated by the Prime Minister and a 100-member House of Assembly; Universal suffrage for citizens over the age of 18; A President (elected for a 6-year term of office by Parliament) who heads the Executive; An independent judiciary enjoying security of tenure; A justiciable Declaration of Rights, derogation from certain of the provisions being permitted, within specified limits, during a state of emergency; Independent Service Commissions exercising powers in respect of staffing and conditions of service in the Public Service, the uniformed forces and the judiciary; Special entrenchment of certain provisions of the Constitution until April 1990 (the protective provisions of the Declaration of Rights).

In 1987 there were 2 constitutional changes: Racial representation was abolished and an executive presidency established.

Under the Constitution no Parliament may continue in existence for more than 5 years.

In March 1988 the composition of the House of Assembly was, ZANU, PF 78 members, the Zimbabwe African People's Party (ZAPU) 14, ZANU, 1 and Independents, 6.

Executive President: Robert G. Mugabe (sworn in on 30 Dec. 1987).

The Cabinet in March 1988 was composed as follows:

Ministers in the Office of the President: Joshua Nkomo, Maurice Nyagumbo, Dr Bernard Chidzero. *Foreign Affairs:* Dr Nathan Shamuyarira. *Telecommunications:* Dr Witness Mangwende. *Higher Education:* Dr Dzingai Mutumbuka. *Primary and Secondary Education:* Fay Chung. *Industry and Technology:* Dr Callistus Ndlovu. *Trade and Commerce:* Oliver Munyaradzi. *Transport:* Simbarashe Mumbengegwi. *Construction and National Housing:* Joseph Msika. *Mines:* Richard Hove. *Defence:* Enos Nkala. *Lands, Agriculture and Rural Settlement:* David Karimanzira. *Youth, Sports and Culture:* Dr Kewdini. *Community Development, Co-operatives and Women's Affairs:* Joyce Wachuru. *Justice, Legal and Parliamentary Affairs:* Emmerson Munangagwa. *National Supplies:* Simbi Mubako. *Health:* Brig. Felix Muchemwa. *Energy, Water Resources and Development:* Kumbirai Kangai. *Labour, Manpower Planning and Social Welfare:* John Nkomo. *Home Affairs:* Moven Mahachi. *Natural Resources and Tourism:* Victoria Chitepo. *Local Government, Rural and Urban Development:* Enos Chikowore. There are 3 Ministers of State.

National flag: Seven horizontal stripes of green, yellow, red, black, red, yellow and green; on a white black-edged triangle in the hoist a red star surmounted by the Zimbabwe Bird in yellow.

The first municipal elections were held in Nov. 1980.

DEFENCE

Army. The Army consists of 1 armoured, 1 air-defence and 1 artillery regiments; 20 infantry, 1 commando and 2 parachute battalions; and 7 engineer and 7 signals squadrons. Equipment includes 8 T-54 and 35 Ch T-59 main battle tanks. Strength was (1988) 46,000, and there are a further 15,000 paramilitary police.

Air Force. The Zimbabwe Air Force (regular) has a strength of (1987) about 1,000 personnel and 130 aircraft in 8 squadrons, of which 2 are intended primarily for a training role. Headquarters ZAF and the main ZAF stations are in Harare; the second main base is at Gweru, with many secondary airfields throughout the country. Equipment includes 1 squadron of Hunter FGA.9 fighter-bombers, 1 squadron of Hawk training and light attack aircraft, a transport squadron with 6 turboprop CASA Aviocars, 6 twin-engined Islanders and 12 C-47s; a squadron with 9 Reims/Cessna 337 Lynx attack aircraft; a squadron with 14 SIAI-Marchetti SF.260W Genet and 17 SF.260C Genet trainers; a helicopter liaison/transport squadron with 40 Alouette II/IIIs, a helicopter casualty evacuation/transport squadron with 10 Agusta-Bell 205s and 12 Bell 412s. Nine Canberra bombers are in storage. Reports of the supply of Chinese-built MiG-21 fighters had not been confirmed in early 1988.

INTERNATIONAL RELATIONS

Membership. Zimbabwe is a member of UN, the Commonwealth, OAU, SADCC, the Non-Aligned Movement and is an ACP state of the EEC.

ECONOMY

Planning. The 5-year development plan (1986–90) emphasizes greater public-sector involvement in all parts of the economy.

Budget. Revenue and expenditure (in Z$1,000):

	1983–84	1984–85	1985–86	1986–87
Revenue	2,000,417	2,212,839	2,616,185	2,997,000
Expenditure	2,431,978	2,641,260	3,136,738	3,828,528

Receipts during the year ended 30 June 1985 were (in Z$1,000): Income and profits tax, 1,066,584; taxes on goods and services, 1,137,808; miscellaneous taxes and other income, 311,757.

The gross amount of the public debt outstanding in June 1986 was Z$5,192,729,612.

Currency. On 17 Feb. 1970 decimal currency was adopted. The unit of currency is the Zimbabwe *dollar* divided into 100 *cents*. In March 1988, £1 = Z$3·08; US$1 = Z$1·74.

Banking. The Reserve Bank of Zimbabwe is the country's central bank; it became operative when the Bank of Rhodesia and Nyasaland ceased operations on 1 June 1965. It acts as banker to the Government and to the commercial banks and as agent of the Government for important financial operations. It is also the central note-issuing authority and co-ordinates the application of the Government's monetary policy. The Zimbabwe Development Bank, established in 1983 as a development finance institution, is 51% Government-owned.

The post office savings bank had Z$652,787,470 deposits at 30 June 1985.

The 5 commercial banks are Barclays Bank of Zimbabwe Ltd, Grindlays Bank Ltd, Zimbabwe Banking Corporation Ltd, Standard Chartered Bank Zimbabwe Ltd, Bank of Credit and Commerce Zimbabwe (Pvt) Ltd. In 1986 they had 119 branches and 75 agencies. The 4 merchant banks are Standard Chartered Merchant Bank, Merchant Bank of Central Africa, RAL Merchant Bank and Syfrets Merchant Bank. There are 5 registered finance houses, 3 of which are subsidiaries of commercial banks.

Weights and Measures. The metric system is in use but the US short ton is also used.

ENERGY AND NATURAL RESOURCES

Electricity. Production (1986) 4,670m. kwh.

Minerals. The total value of all minerals produced in 1986 was Z$699,386,000. Output (in 1,000 tonnes) and value (in Z$1,000):

	Output			Value		
	1984	1985	1986	1984	1985	1986
Asbestos	165·3	173·5	163·6	80,778	84,544	85,789
Gold (1,000 oz.)	478·0	472·0	478·0	214,120	241,312	292,770
Chrome ore	476·4	526·5	553·1	29,719	33,676	39,698
Coal	3,109·0	3,114·0	4,047·0	58,264	66,844	89,144
Copper	22·6	20·7	20·6	33,764	43,339	43,272
Nickel	10·3	9·9	9·7	59,704	73,429	60,672
Iron Ore	925·0	1,098·0	1,115·0	14,532	18,930	21,144
Silver (1,000 oz.)	895·0	799·0	840·0	9,031	7,869	10,612

Agriculture. The most important single food crop in Zimbabwe is maize, the staple food of a large proportion of the population; deliveries to the Grain Marketing Board in 1985 were 1·7m. tonnes. The export potential for the livestock industry has increased with the possibility of new markets in EEC countries. Milk production by the Dairy Marketing Board in 1985 was 202,119,075 litres.

The country is suitable for the production of both citrus and deciduous fruits and fruit production is now well established. In 1985–86 seed cotton production was 297,538 tonnes and irrigated wheat production was 205,528 tonnes. Tea is grown in the Inyanga and Chipinge districts and production in 1985–86 was 14,000 tonnes. Coffee growing is of increasing importance (production, 1985–86, 11,354 tonnes) as is sugar (production, 1985, 430,000 tonnes). Other crops grown in substantial quantities include small grains (sorghums and millet), soya-beans and groundnuts. A wide variety of vegetable crops are also produced.

Tobacco is the most important single product, accounting for over 40% of the value of earnings from agricultural exports. In 1984 tobacco exports were valued at Z$282m. In 1985 tobacco production was 294,905 tonnes and exports accounted for 17% of all Zimbabwean foreign exchange earnings.

Production, 1986 in 1,000 tonnes, of maize, 2,546; wheat, 248; sorghum, 131; barley, 29; millet, 141; soyabeans, 108; seed cotton, 203; fruit, 129.

Livestock (1986): Cattle, 4·8m.; pigs, 170,000; sheep, 550,000; goats, 1·55m.

Fisheries. Trout is farmed in Nyanga, prawns at Lake Kariba and bream at Mount Hampden near Harare to supplement supplies of fish caught in dams and lakes. In 1986 trout were caught at the rate of 200,000 a year, and the planned production of bream was 400–500 tonnes a year.

INDUSTRY AND TRADE

Industry. Metal products account for over 20% of industrial output. Important agro-industries include food processing, textiles, furniture and other wood products.

Labour. The labour force (1985) was 2·8m. In 1984, 1,036,400 were employed; of whom 271,200 were in agriculture, forestry and fishing and 166,300 in manufacturing.

Commerce. The Customs Agreement with the Republic of South Africa was extended in March, 1982 pending further discussion. Zimbabwe has also entered into Trade Agreements with Zambia, Mozambique, Tanzania, Angola and Swaziland and with countries outside Africa. Imports and exports (in Z$1,000):

	1982	1983	1984	1985	1986
Imports	999,000	1,061,600	1,200,700	543,700	...
Exports	1,118,000	1,150,200	1,453,000	1,545,343	1,699,764

Principal imports in 1984 (in Z$1,000): Machinery and transport equipment, 373,550; petroleum products, 256,924; chemicals, 178,111; manufactured goods, 177,851; miscellaneous manufactured goods, 78,615.

Principal exports in 1986 (in Z$1,000): Unmanufactured tobacco, 238,213; ferro-alloys, 210,079; asbestos, 82,741; cotton lint, 130,548.

In 1985, 13% of exports (excluding gold) went to UK, 10·8% to the Republic of South Africa, 9·9% to Federal Republic of Germany, 8·1% to USA, 5·9% to Italy and 4·6% to Japan, while the Republic of South Africa provided 18·9% of imports, UK 10·4%, USA 10·1%, Federal Republic of Germany 6·9%, Japan 3·9% and Italy 3%.

Total trade between Zimbabwe and UK (British Department of Trade returns, in £1,000 sterling):

	1983	1984	1985	1986	1987
Imports to UK	68,445	74,090	90,398	80,702	79,771
Exports and re-exports from UK	64,734	66,636	73,571	61,937	63,181

Tourism. In 1987, 454,779 tourists visited Zimbabwe. The main tourist areas are Victoria Falls, Kariba, Hwange, the Eastern Highlands and Great Zimbabwe. The Zimbabwe Tourist Development Corporation is in Harare and Victoria Falls.

COMMUNICATIONS

Roads. The Ministry of Transport is responsible for the construction and maintenance of all State roads and bridges, and all road bridges outside municipal areas. The Ministry offers advice and help on roads and bridges, through Provincial Road Engineers, to district councils. State roads are those connecting all the main centres of population, international routes, major links in the system and main roads serving rural communities. The total length of roads is approximately 85,237 km including surfaced, 12,000; gravel, 46,187; earth, 27,000.

Number of motor vehicles, 1984: Passenger cars, 237,128; commercial vehicles, 17,058; motor cycles, 24,347; trailers, 33,227; tractors, 5,695.

Railways. Zimbabwe is served by the National Railways of Zimbabwe, which connect with the South African Railways to give access to the South African ports; with the Mozambique Railways to give access to the ports of Beira and Maputo; and with the Zambia railway system. In 1985 there were 3,394 km (1,067 mm gauge) of railways including 311 km electrified. In the year ending 30 June 1986 National Railways of Zimbabwe carried 14m. tonnes of freight and 2·7m. passengers.

Aviation. Air Zimbabwe operates domestic services and also regular flights to Zambia, Kenya, Malawi, Botswana and South Africa, and to London, Frankfurt and Athens in Europe and also to Perth and Sydney in Australia in association with Qantas. The country is also served by British Airways, Kenya Airways, Ethiopian Airlines, Air Tanzania, Air Malawi, Zambian Airways, Balkan Bulgarian Airlines, Mozambique Airlines, South African Airways, Air Botswana, the Royal Swazi Airlines, TAP Air Portugal, Qantas, Lesotho Airways and Air India. Services by KLM, Swissair and UTA were temporarily suspended in 1986. In 1985, 660,858,000 passenger-km were flown by Air Zimbabwe.

Shipping. Zimbabwe outlets to the sea are Maputo and Beira in Mozambique, Dar-es-Salaam, Tanzania and the South African ports.

Post and Broadcasting. At 31 Aug. 1986 there were 170 full post offices, 47 postal telegraph agencies and 86 postal agencies. At 30 June 1986 there were 251,344 telephones in Zimbabwe served by 96 exchanges; 2,102 telex connexions, served by 2 telex exchanges. Zimbabwe Broadcasting Corporation is an independent statutory body broadcasting a general service in English, Shona, N'debele, Nyanja, Tonga and Kalanga. There are 3 national semi-commercial services, Radio 1, 2 and 3, in English, Shona and N'debele. Radio 4 transmits formal and informal educational programmes. Zimbabwe Television broadcasts 2 channels 95 hours a week *via* 11 transmitters. In June 1986 there were 130,500 television and 450,000 radio licences.

JUSTICE, RELIGION, EDUCATION AND WELFARE

Justice. The general common law of Zimbabwe is the Roman Dutch law as it applied in the Colony of the Cape of Good Hope on 10 June, 1891, as subsequently modified by statute. Provision is made by statute for the application of African customary law by all courts in appropriate cases.

The Supreme Court consists of the Chief Justice and at least two (in 1985 there were three) permanent Supreme Court judges. It is Zimbabwe's final court of appeal. It exercises appellate jurisdiction in appeals from the High Court and other courts and tribunals; its only original jurisdiction is that conferred on it by the Constitution to enforce the protective provisions of the Declaration of Rights. The Court's permanent seat is in Harare but it sits regularly in Bulawayo also.

The High Court is also headed by the Chief Justice, supported by the Judge President and an appropriate number of High Court judges. It has full original jurisdiction, in both Civil and Criminal cases, over all persons and all matters in Zimbabwe. The Judge President is in charge of the Court, subject to the directions of the

Chief Justice. The Court has permanent seats in both Harare and Bulawayo and sittings are held three times a year in three other principal towns.

Regional courts, established in Harare and Bulawayo but also holding sittings in other centres, exercise a solely criminal jurisdiction that is intermediate between that of the High Court and the Magistrates' courts.

Magistrates' courts, established in twenty centres throughout the country, and staffed by full-time professional magistrates, exercise both civil and criminal jurisdiction.

The tribal courts and district commissioners' courts of colonial days were abolished in 1981, to be replaced by a system of primary courts, consisting of village courts and community courts. By 1982 1,100 village and 50 community courts had been established. Village courts are presided over by officers selected for the purpose from the local population, sitting with two assessors. They deal with certain classes of civil cases only and have jurisdiction only where African customary law is applicable. Community courts are presided over by presiding officers in full-time public service who may be assisted by assessors. They have jurisdiction in all civil cases determinable by African customary law and also deal with appeals from village courts. They also have limited criminal jurisdiction in respect of petty offences against the general law.

Religion. The largest religious groups are the Anglicans and Roman Catholics. Other denominations include Presbyterians, the Methodist Church in Zimbabwe and the United Methodist Church. Islam, Hinduism and traditional indigenous religions are represented.

Education. Education is non-racial at all levels and is compulsory.

All primary schools offer free tuition; government secondary schools charge from Z$8–Z$25 per term. All instruction is given in English. There are also over 3,800 private primary schools and over 950 private secondary schools, all of which must be registered by the Ministry of Education. In 1986 there were 2,260,367 pupils at primary schools and 545,841 pupils at secondary schools.

There are 10 teachers' training colleges, 8 of which are in association with the University of Zimbabwe. In addition, there are 4 special training centres for teacher trainees in the Zimbabwe Integrated National Teacher Education Course. In 1986 there were 12,029 students enrolled at teachers' training colleges, 875 students at agricultural colleges and 11,261 students at technical colleges.

The University of Zimbabwe provides facilities for higher education. In 1986 the total enrolment of students in the 9 Faculties of Agriculture, Arts, Commerce and Law, Education, Engineering, Medicine, Science, Social Studies and Veterinary Science, was 5,886.

Health. In 1985 there were 162 hospitals, 1,062 static rural clinics and health centres and 32 mobile rural clinics operated by the Ministry of Health. All mission health institutions get 100% government grants-in-aid for recurrent expenditure. There is a medical school attached to the University of Zimbabwe in Harare, four government training schools attached to the 4 central hospitals for training state registered nurses, 14 training schools for medical assistants out of which 11 are administered by missions, and two for training maternity assistants, health assistants/health inspectors.

Social Services. It is a statutory responsibility of the government in many areas to provide: Processing and administration of war pensions and old age pensions; protection of children; administration of remand, probation and correctional institutions; registration and supervision of welfare organisations.

DIPLOMATIC REPRESENTATIVES

Of Zimbabwe in Great Britain (Zimbabwe Hse., 429 Strand, London, WC2R 0SA)
High Commissioner: Dr Herbert M. Murerwa (accredited 1 March 1984).

Of Great Britain in Zimbabwe (Stanley Hse., Stanley Ave., Harare)
High Commissioner: Michael Ramsay Melhuish, CMG.

Of Zimbabwe in the USA (2852 McGill Terr., NW, Washington, D.C., 20008)
Ambassador: Edmund Richard Mashoko Garwe.

Of the USA in Zimbabwe (172 Rhodes Ave., Harare)
Ambassador: James Wilson Rawlings.

Of Zimbabwe to the United Nations
Ambassador: Dr Stanley Mudenge.

Books of Reference

Statistical Information: The Central Statistical Office, PO Box 8063, Causeway, Harare, Zimbabwe, originated in 1927 as the Southern Rhodesian Government Statistical Bureau. Ten years later its name was changed to Department of Statistics, and in 1948 it assumed its present title when it took over responsibility for certain Northern Rhodesian and Nyasaland statistics (which it relinquished in Dec. 1963 on the dissolution of the Federation). It publishes *Monthly Digest of Statistics*.

Akers, M., *Encyclopaedia Rhodesia*. Harare, 1973

Caute, D., *Under the Skin: The Death of White Rhodesia*. London, 1983

Davies, D. K., *Race Relations in Rhodesia*. London, 1975

Keppel-Jones, A., *Rhodes and Rhodesia: The White Conquest of Zimbabwe, 1884–1902*. Univ. of Natal Press, 1983

Linden, I., *The Catholic Church and the Struggle for Zimbabwe*. London, 1980

Martin, D., and Johnson, P., *The Struggle for Zimbabwe*. London, 1981.—*Destructive Engagement*. Harare, 1986

Meredith, M., *The Past is Another Century: Rhodesia 1890–1979*. London, 1979

Morris-Jones, W. H., (ed.) *From Rhodesia to Zimbabwe*. London, 1980

Nkomo, J., *Nkomo: The Story of My Life*. London, 1984

O'Meara, P., *Rhodesia: Racial Conflict or Co-Existence*. Cornell Univ. Press, 1975

Pollak, K. and Pollak, O. B., *Rhodesia/Zimbabwe* [Bibliography] Oxford and Santa Barbara, 1979

Schatzberg, M. G., *The Political Economy of Zimbabwe*. New York, 1984

Stoneham, C., *Zimbabwe's Inheritance*. London, 1982

Thornycroft, P., *A Field for Investment*. Harare, annual

Verrier, A., *The Road to Zimbabwe, 1890–1980*. London, 1986

Wiseman, H. and Taylor, A. M., *From Rhodesia to Zimbabwe: The Politics of Transition*. Elmsford, N.Y., 1981

Reference Library: National Archives of Zimbabwe, PO Box 8043, Causeway, Harare.

PLACE AND INTERNATIONAL ORGANIZATIONS INDEX

Somerville (Mass.), 1479
Somogy (Hungary), 609
Sonamura (India), 682
Sønderjyllands (Denmark), 413
Sondre Sromfiord (Greenland), 426
Song Be (Vietnam), 1588
Songkhla (Thail.), 1177
Songo Songo (Tanzania), 1174
Son La (Vietnam), 1587
Sonora (Mex.), 853, 857
Sonsonate (El Salv.), 451, 453, 454
Sopore (India), 658
Soria (Spain), 1108
Soriano (Urug.), 1569, 1571
Sørkapp, see Spitsbergen
Soroçaba (Brazil), 228
Sorok (USSR), 1266
Sortavala (USSR), 1249
Sør-Trøndelag (Norway), 936
Sosa Méndez (Venez.), 1583
Sosnowiez (Poland), 998
Sotavento (Cape Verde Is.), 335–36
Soubré (Côte d'Ivoire), 388
Soum (Burkina Faso), 248
Sourou (Burkina Faso), 248
Sousse (Tunisia), 1195, 1198
South Africa, Republic of, 1077–1105, see also under provinces
Southampton (UK), 1292, 1345
South Australia, 95–96, 99
109–11, 114, 142–47
—agriculture, 144
—area and pop., 142
—education, 146
—govt. and representation, 142–43
South Bedfordshire (UK), 1292
South Bend (Ind.), 1375, 1462
South Buganda (Uganda), 1212
South Caicos, 1208–09
South Cambridgeshire (UK), 1292
South Carolina (USA), 1373, 1379, 1383–84, 1405, 1410, 1526–28
South Cholla (Korea), 771
South Chungchong (Korea), 771
South Dakota (USA), 1373, 1378, 1384, 1405, 1410, 1531–32
South-East Lancs (UK), 1292
Southend-on-Sea (UK), 1292
Southern Dist. (Israel), 724
Southern Dist. (Sikkim), 677
Southern Fung (Sudan), 1130
Southern Highlands (Papua New Guinea), 972–73
Southern Prov. (Saudi Arabia), 1045
Southern Prov. (Sri Lanka), 1120
Southern Prov. (Uganda), 1212
Southern Prov. (Zambia), 1623
Southern Region (Malawi), 817–18
Southern Region (Sierra Leone) 1059
Southern Tagalog (Philipp.), 990
Southfield (Mich.), 1482
South Georgia, 1106
South Georgias, 89
South Glamorgan (UK), 1291
South Hadley (Mass.), 1481
South Hamgyong (N. Korea), 777
South Hwanghai (N. Korea), 777
South Is. (Coco Is.), 125
South Is. (NZ), 908–09

South Kesteven (UK), 1292
South Kingstown (R.I.), 1529
South Kyongsang (Korea), 771
South Lakeland (UK), 1292
Southland (NZ), 904
South Norfolk (UK), 1292
South Orcados, 89
South Orkney Is., 236
South Ossetia (USSR), 1264
South Oxfordshire (UK), 1292
South Pacific Forum, 55
Southport (N.G.), 1511
South Portland (Maine), 1473
South Pyongan (N. Korea), 777
South Region (Iceland), 617
South Region (Thail.), 1177
South Ribble (UK), 1292
South Sandwich Is., 89, 1106
South Shetlands, 236
South Somerset (UK), 1292
South Staffordshire (UK), 1292
South Tyneside (UK), 1292
Southwark (UK), 1293
South-West Africa, 1094–98
South West Peninsula (Iceland), 617
South Yorkshire (UK), 1290, 1303
Soviet Central Asia (USSR), 1272
Soviet Union; see Union of Soviet Socialist Republics
Sovyetsk (USSR), 1218
Spain, 1107–19
Spanish Africa, 1119
Spanish Town (Jamaica), 744
Sparks (Nev.), 1497, 1499
Spartanburg (S.C.), 1530
Sparte (Greece), 566
Spelthorne (UK), 1292
Speyer (FRG), 554
Spijkenisse (Neth.), 888
Spiti (India), 655
Spitsbergen (Svalbard), 948
Split (Yug.), 1605–06, 1610
Spokane (Wash.), 1375, 1546
Springdale (Ark.), 1436
Springfield (Ill.), 1459
Springfield (Mass.), 1375, 1479, 1481
Springfield (Mo.), 1375, 1490
Springfield (Ohio), 1515
Springfield (Ore.), 1521
Springlands (Guyana), 590
Springs (Transvaal), 1078
Spruce Grove (Alb.), 298
Sri Jayawardenepura (Sri Lanka), 1126
Sri Lanka, 1120–27
—agriculture, 1123
—area and pop., 1120
—education, 1126
—govt. and representation, 1121
Srinagar (India), 625, 646, 658–59, 684
Stadskanaal (Neth.), 888
Stafford (UK), 1292
Staffordshire (UK), 1291
Staffordshire Moorlands (UK), 1292
Stalingrad, see Volgograd
Stalinogrod, see Katowice
Stamford (Conn.), 1375, 1443
STANAVFORCHAN, 38
STANAVFORLANT, 38
Stanley (Falkland Is.), 464–66
Stanleyville, see Kisangani

Stanlow (UK), 1330
Stann Creek (Belize), 203
Stanton (Dela.), 1448
Stara Zagora (Bulg.), 241, 245
Starbuck (Kiribati), 768
Starkenburg (FRG), 548
Starkville (Miss.), 1489
Staten Is. (N.Y.), 1507
Stavanger (Norway), 937
Stavropol (USSR), 1218, 1232, 1239, 1245
Steenwijk (Neth.), 888
Steiermark, see Styria
Stein (Neth.), 888
Steinkjer (Norway), 937
Stellenbosch (Cape), 1087
Stepanakert (USSR), 1260
Stephenville (Nfndlnd.), 311
Sterling Heights (Mich.), 1375, 1482
Sterlitamak (USSR), 1218
Stettin, see Szczecin
Stevens Point (Wisc.), 1553
Stewart Is. (NZ), 903
Stewartry (UK), 1293
Steyr (Austria), 168
Stillwater (Okla.), 1517
Stirling (UK), 1291, 1344–45
Stockholm (Sweden), 1141–42, 1145, 1151, 1156
Stockport (UK), 1292
Stockton (Calif.), 1375, 1438
Stockton-on-Tees (UK), 1292
Stoke-on-Trent (UK), 1292
Stoney Creek (New Bruns.), 309
Storrs (Conn.), 1445
Storstrøms (Denmark), 413
Stout (Wisc.), 1553
Strabane (N. Ireland), 1356
Straits Settlements, see Singapore
Strasbourg (France), 481–83
Strässa (Sweden), 1147
Stratford on Avon (UK), 1292
Strathclyde Region (UK), 1294, 1344–45
Strathkelvin (UK), 1294
Stredoçeský (Czech.), 406
Stredoslovenský (Czech.), 406
Stromo Is., 424
Stroud (UK), 1292
Stuttgart (FRG), 530, 538, 541–42
Styria (Austria), 168–69
Suakoko (Liberia), 797
Suao (Taiwan), 368
Subansiri (India), 649
Subotica (Yug.), 1605
Suceava (Romania), 1021
Suchitepéquez (Guat.), 576
Sucre (Bolivia), 217–18, 221–22
Sucre (Colom.), 370
Sucre (Venez.), 1580, 1583–84
Sud Dept. (Haiti), 592
Sudan, Republic of the, 1128–32
Sudan, French, see Mali
Sudbury (Ont.), 271, 319
Sudero Is., 424
Sud Prov. (Cameroon), 264
Sud-Est Dept. (Haiti), 592
Sud-Ouest Prov. (Cameroon), 264
Suez (Egypt), 444
Suez Canal, 449
Suez City (Egypt), 449
Suffolk, Coastal (UK), 1292
Suffolk, East and West (UK), 1291

Suhl (GDR), 523
Sui (Pak.), 960
Suita (Japan), 749
Sukabumi (Indon.), 693
Sukarnapura, see Jayapura
Sukhumi (USSR), 1261, 1263
Sukkur (Pak.), 957
Sukuta (Gambia), 519
Sulawesi (Indon.), 692–93, 697
Sulawesi Selatan (Indon.), 693
Sulawesi Tengah (Indon.), 693
Sulawesi Tenggala (Indon.), 693
Sulawesi Utara (Indon.), 693
Sumatera Barat (Indon.), 692
Sumatera Selatan (Indon.), 692
Sumatera Utara (Indon.), 692
Sumatra (Indon.), 692–93, 696–97
Sumgait (USSR), 1218, 1259–60
Summerside (P.E.I.), 322
Sumy (USSR), 1218, 1255
Sunday Is. (NZ), 917
Sunderland (UK), 1292
Sundsvall (Sweden), 1142
Sunel Tappa (India), 674–75
Sungei Golok (Pen. Malaysia), 827
Sunnyvale (Calif.), 1375
Sunshine Coast (Aust.), 137
Sunyani (Ghana), 558, 561
Suoyarvi (USSR), 1249
Superior (Wisc.), 1551, 1553
Sur (Oman), 951
Surabaya (Indon.), 693, 696
Surakarta (Indon.), 693
Surat (India), 625, 652, 655, 687
Surendranagar (India), 652
Surgut (USSR.), 1237
Surin (Thail.), 1177
Suriname, 1133–36
Suriname Dist., 1133–34
Surkhan-Darya (USSR), 1277
Surrey (B.C.), 304
Surrey (UK), 1291, 1345
Surt (Libya), 801
Surtsey Is. (Iceland), 617
Sussex (New Bruns.), 309
Sussex (East and West) (UK), 1345
Sutherland (UK), 1294
Sutton (UK), 1293
Suva (Fiji), 467–70
Suwaiq (Oman), 951
Suwalki (Poland), 998
Suwarrow (Cook Is.), 919
Suwayda (Syria), 1168
Suweon (Korea), 772
Svalbard (Norway), 940, 948–49
Sverdlovsk (USSR), 1218, 1237, 1242, 1245
Swain's Is. (Samoa, USA), 1561
Swale (UK), 1292
Swan Hill (Vic.), 152
Swansea (UK), 1292, 1344–45
Swaziland, 1137–40
Sweden, 1141–56
Swedru (Ghana), 558
Swift Current (Sask.), 327
Switzerland, 1157–67
Sydney (N.S.), 315
Sydney (NSW), 95–96, 100–101, 111, 128, 132–35
Sydney Mines (N.S.), 315
Syktyvkar (USSR), 1218, 1249
Sylhet (Bangladesh), 184
Syra (Greece), 571

Syracuse (N.Y.), 1375, 1507, 1509
Syr Darya (USSR), 1277
Syria, 1168–71
Syzran (USSR), 1218
Szabolcs-Szatmár (Hungary), 609
Szczecin (Poland), 998
Szechwan, see Sichuan
Szeged (Hungary), 609, 615
Székesfehérvar (Hungary), 609
Szekszard (Hungary), 609
Szolnok (Hungary), 609
Szombathely (Hungary), 609

Taabo (Côte d'Ivoire), 390
Tabasco (Mex.), 853, 857
Tabiteuea (Kiribati), 768
Tabligbo (Togo), 1186
Tabora (Tanz.), 1172, 1176
Taboshar (USSR), 1233
Tabouk (Saudi Arabia), 1045
Tabriz (Iran), 699–700
Tabuaeran (Kiribati), 768
Täby (Sweden), 1142
Táchira (Venez.), 1580, 1583
Tacloban (Philipp.), 990
Tacna (Peru), 984
Tacoma (Wash.), 1375, 1546–47
Tacuarembo (Urug.), 1569
Tadjoura (Djibouti), 428
Tadzhikistan (USSR), 1217–18, 1221, 1272, 1279–81
Taegu (Korea), 771–72
Taejon (Korea), 772
Taff Ely (UK), 1272
Taganrog (USSR), 1218
Tagant (Mauritania), 846
Tahaa (Fr. Polyn.), 511
Tahiti (Fr. Polyn.), 511, 513
Tahlequah (Okla.), 1520
Tahoua (Niger), 927
Tahuata (Fr. Polyn.), 512
Taibei (Taiwan), 353
Taichung (Taiwan), 365, 368
Taif (Saudi Arabia), 1049
Taimyr (USSR), 1245, 1254
Tainan (Taiwan), 365
Taiohae (Fr. Polyn.), 512
Taipa (Maçao), 1014
Taipei (Taiwan), 365
Taiping (Malaysia), 821
Tai Po (Hong Kong), 602
Taitung (Taiwan), 365
Tai Wai (Hong Kong), 606
Taiwan (China), 352, 367–69
Taiyuan (China), 353
Ta'iz (Yemen), 1598–600
Takamatsu (Japan), 750
Takatsuki (Japan), 750
Takeo (Cambodia), 263
Takoradi (Ghana), 561
Takutea (N.Z.), 919
Talara (Peru), 986
Talca (Chile), 346
Talcahuano (Chile), 346
Taldy-Kurgan (USSR), 1272
Tallahassee (Fla.), 1450–51
Tallinn (Estonia, USSR), 1217–18, 1267–68
Talwara (India), 656
Tamale (Ghana), 558–59, 561
Tamana (Kiribati), 768
Tamanrasset (Algeria), 72
Tamatave (see Toamasina)
Tamaulipas (Mex.), 853
Tambacounda (Senegal), 1052, 1054
Tambao (Burkina Faso), 249–50

Tambov (USSR), 1218, 1245
Tameside (UK), 1292
Tamil Nadu (India), 625, 628, 636–37, 646, 679–81
Ta'mim (Iraq), 705
Tammerfors, see Tampere
Tampa (Fla.), 1375, 1450–51
Tampere (Finland), 472, 478
Tampico (Mex.), 854, 858
Tamuning (Guam), 1558
Tamworth (NSW), 128
Tananarive, see Antananarivo
Tandil (Argen.), 93
Tandjile (Chad), 343
Tanga (Tanz.), 1172
Tangail (Bangladesh), 184
Tangier (Morocco), 870–71
Tangshan (China), 353
Tanjungkarang (Indon.), 692
Tanjung Priok (Indon.), 697
Tanna (Vanuatu), 1574
Tânta (Egypt), 444
Tan-Tan (Morocco), 870
Tanzania, 1172–74
Taoudenni (Mali), 838
Taounate (Morocco), 870
Taoyuan (Taiwan), 365, 368
Tapoa (Burkina Faso), 248
Tappita (Liberia), 797
Tarapaca (Chile), 346, 349
Taranaki (NZ), 903, 908
Taranto (Italy), 733, 736–37
Tarawa (Kiribati), 764, 770
Tarcoola (Aust.), 109, 122
Taree Greater (NSW), 128
Tarhuna (Libya), 801
Tarija (Bolivia), 217–18, 221–22
Tarkwa (Ghana), 558
Tarnobrzeg (Poland), 998
Tarnow (Poland), 998
Taroudant (Morocco), 870
Tarrafal (Cape Verde Is.), 336
Tarragona (Spain), 1108–09
Tarrasa (Spain), 1109
Tartar (USSR), 1245
Tartous (Syria), 1168
Tartu (Estonia, USSR), 1242, 1267–68
Tashauz (USSR), 1275–77
Tashguzar (Afghán.), 64
Tashkent (USSR), 1217–18, 1237, 1239, 1242, 1277–78
Taskizak (Turkey), 1202
Tasmania (Aust.), 95–96, 99, 109–11, 113–14, 147–52
—agriculture, 149–50
—area and pop., 147
—education, 151
—govt. and representation, 147–48
Ta-Ta (Morocco), 870
Tatabánya (Hungary), 609
Tatar Rep. (USSR), 1251
Tatawin (Tunisia), 1195
Tatung, see Dadong
Ta'u Is. (Samoa, USA), 1561
Taunggye (Burma), 252, 256
Taunton Deane (UK), 1292
Taupo (NZ), 903
Tauranga (NZ), 903–04
Tavastehus (Finland), 471–72
Tawau (Sabah), 830–31
Tawzar (Tunisia), 1195
Tayeh, see Daye
Taylor (Mich.), 1482
Tayninp (Vietnam), 1588
Tayside Region (UK), 1294
Taza (Morocco), 870–71

PRODUCT INDEX

References are to production data

NAMES INDEX